Collins

FRENCH
DICTIONARY
& GRAMMAR

HarperCollins Publishers
Westerhill Road
Bishopbriggs
Glasgow
G64 2QT

Eighth Edition 2018

10 9 8 7 6 5 4

© HarperCollins Publishers 1997, 2000,
2004, 2006, 2007, 2010, 2014, 2018

ISBN 978-0-00-824138-4

Collins® is a registered trademark of
HarperCollins Publishers Limited

www.collinsdictionary.com
www.collins.co.uk

A catalogue record for this book is
available from the British Library

Typeset by Davidson Publishing Solutions

Printed in Italy by Grafica Veneta S.p.A.

Acknowledgements
We would like to thank those authors
and publishers who kindly gave
permission for copyright material to be
used in the Collins Corpus. We would also
like to thank Times Newspapers Ltd for
providing valuable data.

EDITOR
Susie Beattie

CONTRIBUTORS
Laurence Larroche
Persephone Lock
Sinda Lopez
Anna Stevenson

FOR THE PUBLISHER
Gerry Breslin
Janice McNeillie
Sheena Shanks

TECHNICAL SUPPORT
Claire Dimeo
Ross Taggart
Agnieszka Urbanowicz

MIX
Paper from
responsible sources
FSC™ C007454

FSC
www.fsc.org

This book is produced from independently certified FSC™ paper
to ensure responsible forest management.

For more information visit: www.harpercollins.co.uk/green

Table des matières

Contents

Abréviations

Abbreviations

masculin	*m*	masculine
mathématiques, algèbre	*Math*	mathematics, calculus
médecine	*Méd, Med*	medical term, medicine
masculin *ou* féminin	*m/f*	masculine *or* feminine
domaine militaire	*Mil*	military matters
musique	*Mus*	music
nom	N	noun
navigation, nautisme	*Navig, Naut*	sailing, navigation
nom *ou* adjectif numéral	NUM	numeral noun *or* adjective
	o.s.	oneself
péjoratif	*péj, pej*	derogatory, pejorative
photographie	*Phot(o)*	photography
physiologie	*Physiol*	physiology
pluriel	*pl*	plural
politique	*Pol*	politics
participe passé	*pp*	past participle
préposition	PRÉP, PREP	preposition
pronom	PRON	pronoun
psychologie, psychiatrie	*Psych*	psychology, psychiatry
temps du passé	*pt*	past tense
quelque chose	*qch*	
quelqu'un	*qn*	
religion, domaine ecclésiastique	*Rel*	religion
	sb	somebody
enseignement, système scolaire et universitaire	*Scol*	schooling, schools and universities
(verbe anglais) dont la particule est séparable	*sep*	(phrasal verb) where the particle is separable
singulier	*sg*	singular
	sth	something
subjonctif	*sub*	subjunctive
sujet (grammatical)	*su(b)j*	(grammatical) subject
superlatif	*superl*	superlative
techniques, technologie	*Tech*	technical term, technology
télécommunications	*Tél, Tel*	telecommunications
théâtre	*Théât, Theat*	theatre
télévision	TV	television
typographie	*Typ(o)*	typography, printing
anglais des USA	US	American English
verbe auxiliaire	VB (AUX)	(auxiliary) verb
verbe intransitif	VI	intransitive verb
verbe pronominal	*vpr*	pronominal verb
verbe transitif	VT	transitive verb
zoologie	*Zool*	zoology
marque déposée	®	registered trademark
vulgaire ou injurieux	(!)	offensive
indique une équivalence culturelle	≈	introduces a cultural equivalent

Transcription phonétique

Consonnes		Consonants
poupée	p	*puppy*
bombe	b	*baby*
tente thermal	t	*tent*
dinde	d	*daddy*
coq qui képi	k	*cork kiss chord*
gag bague	g	*gag guess*
sale ce nation	s	*so rice kiss*
zéro rose	z	*cousin buzz*
tache chat	ʃ	*sheep sugar*
gilet juge	ʒ	*pleasure beige*
	tʃ	*church*
	dʒ	*judge general*
fer phare	f	*farm raffle*
valve	v	*very rev*
	θ	*thin maths*
	ð	*that other*
lent salle	l	*little ball*
rare rentrer	ʀ	
	r	*rat rare*
maman femme	m	*mummy comb*
non nonne	n	*no ran*
agneau vigne	ɲ	
	ŋ	*singing bank*
hop!	h	*hat reheat*
yaourt paille	j	*yet*
nouer oui	w	*wall bewail*
huile lui	ɥ	
	x	*loch*

Divers		Miscellaneous
pour l'anglais : le **r** final se prononce en liaison devant une voyelle	ʳ	in English transcription: final **r** can be pronounced before a vowel
pour l'anglais : précède la syllabe accentuée	'	in French wordlist: no liaison before aspirate **h**

NB : p, b, t, d, k, g sont suivis d'une aspiration en anglais.
p, b, t, d, k, g are not aspirated in French.

En règle générale, la prononciation est donnée entre crochets après chaque entrée. Toutefois, du côté anglais-français et dans le cas des expressions composées de deux ou plusieurs mots non réunis par un trait d'union et faisant l'objet d'une entrée séparée, la prononciation doit être cherchée sous chacun des mots constitutifs de l'expression en question.

Phonetic transcription

Voyelles

ici vie lyrique	i i:
	ɪ
jouer été	e
lait jouet merci	ɛ
plat amour	a æ
bas pâte	ɑ ɑ:
	ʌ
le premier	ə
beurre peur	œ
peu deux	ø ə:
or homme	ɔ
mot eau gauche	o ɔ:
genou roue	u
	u:
rue urne	y

Vowels

heel bead	i i:
hit pity	ɪ
set tent	ɛ
bat apple	a æ
after car calm	ɑ ɑ:
fun cousin	ʌ
over above	ə
urgent fern work	ø ə:
wash pot	ɔ
born cork	o ɔ:
full hook	u
boom shoe	u:

Diphtongues

Diphthongs

	ɪə	beer tier
	ɛə	tear fair there
	eɪ	date plaice day
	aɪ	life buy cry
	au	owl foul now
	əu	low no
	ɔɪ	boil boy oily
	uə	poor tour

Voyelles nasales

Nasal vowels

matin plein	ɛ̃
brun	œ̃
sang an dans	ɑ̃
non pont	ɔ̃

NB : La mise en équivalence de certains sons n'indique qu'une ressemblance approximative.
The pairing of some vowel sounds only indicates approximate equivalence.

In general, we give the pronunciation of each entry in square brackets after the word in question. However, on the English–French side, where the entry is composed of two or more unhyphenated words, each of which is given elsewhere in this dictionary, you will find the pronunciation of each word in its alphabetical position.

French verb tables

a Present participle b Past participle c Present d Imperfect e Future f Conditional g Present subjunctive h Imperative

1 ARRIVER a arrivant b arrivé c arrive, arrives, arrive, arrivons, arrivez, arrivent d arrivais e arriverai f arriverais g arrive

2 FINIR a finissant b fini c finis, finis, finit, finissons, finissez, finissent d finissais e finirai f finirais g finisse

3 PLACER a plaçant b placé c place, places, place, plaçons, placez, placent d plaçais, plaçais, plaçait, placions, placiez, plaçaient e placerai, placeras, placera, placerons, placerez, placeront f placerais, placerais, placerait, placerions, placeriez, placeraient g place

3 BOUGER a bougeant b bougé c bouge, bougeons d bougeais, bougions e bougerai f bougerais g bouge

4 appeler a appelant b appelé c appelle, appelons d appelais e appellerai f appellerais g appelle

4 jeter a jetant b jeté c jette, jetons d jetais e jetterai f jetterais g jette

5 geler a gelant b gelé c gèle, gelons d gelais e gèlerai f gèlerais g gèle

6 CÉDER a cédant b cédé c cède, cèdes, cède, cédons, cédez, cèdent d cédais, cédais, cédait, cédions, cédiez, cédaient e céderai, céderas, cédera, céderons, céderez, céderont f céderais, céderais, céderait, céderions, céderiez, céderaient g cède

7 épier a épiant b épié c épie, épions d épiais e épierai f épierais g épie

8 noyer a noyant b noyé c noie, noyons d noyais e noierai f noierais g noie

9 ALLER a allant b allé c vais, vas, va, allons, allez, vont d allais e irai f irais g aille

10 HAÏR a haïssant b haï c hais, hais, hait, haïssons, haïssez, haïssent d haïssais, haïssais, haïssait, haïssions, haïssiez, haïssaient e haïrai, haïras, haïra, haïrons, haïrez, haïront f haïrais, haïrais, haïrait, haïrions, haïriez, haïraient g haïsse

11 courir a courant b couru c cours, courons d courais e courrai f courrais g coure

12 cueillir a cueillant b cueilli c cueille, cueillons d cueillais e cueillerai f cueillerais g cueille

13 assaillir a assaillant b assailli c assaille, assaillons d assaillais e assaillirai f assaillirais g assaille

14 servir a servant b servi c sers, servons d servais e servirai f servirais g serve

15 bouillir a bouillant b bouilli c bous, bouillons d bouillais e bouillirai f bouillirais g bouille

16 partir a partant b parti c pars, partons d partais e partirai f partirais g parte

17 fuir a fuyant b fui c fuis, fuyons, fuient d fuyais e fuirai f fuirais g fuie

18 couvrir a couvrant b couvert c couvre, couvrons d couvrais e couvrirai f couvrirais g couvre

19 mourir a mourant b mort c meurs, mourons, meurent d mourais e mourrai f mourrais g meure

20 vêtir a vêtant b vêtu c vêts, vêtons d vêtais e vêtirai f vêtirais g vête

21 acquérir a acquérant b acquis c acquiers, acquérons, acquièrent d acquérais e acquerrai f acquerrais g acquière

22 venir a venant b venu c viens, venons, viennent d venais e viendrai f viendrais g vienne

23 pleuvoir a pleuvant b plu c pleut, pleuvent d pleuvait e pleuvra f pleuvrait g pleuve

24 prévoir like voir e prévoirai f prévoirais

25 pourvoir like voir e pourvoirai f pourvoirais

26 asseoir a asseyant b assis c assieds, asseyons, asseyez, asseyent d asseyais e assiérai f assiérais g asseye

27 MOUVOIR a mouvant b mû c meus, meus, meut, mouvons, mouvez, meuvent d mouvais e mouvrai f mouvrais g meuve, meuves, meuve, mouvions, mouviez, meuvent

28 RECEVOIR a recevant b reçu c reçois, reçois, reçoit, recevons, recevez, reçoivent d recevais e recevrai f recevrais g reçoive

29 valoir a valant b valu c vaux, vaut, valons d valais e vaudrai f vaudrais g vaille

30 voir a voyant **b** vu **c** vois, voyons, voient **d** voyais **e** verrai **f** verrais **g** voie

31 vouloir a voulant **b** voulu **c** veux, veut, voulons, veulent **d** voulais **e** voudrai **f** voudrais **g** veuille **h** veuillez !

32 savoir a sachant **b** su **c** sais, savons, savent **d** savais **e** saurai **f** saurais **g** sache **h** sache ! sachons ! sachez !

33 pouvoir a pouvant **b** pu **c** peux, peut, pouvons, peuvent **d** pouvais **e** pourrai **f** pourrais **g** puisse

34 AVOIR a ayant **b** eu **c** ai, as, a, avons, avez, ont **d** avais **e** aurai **f** aurais **g** aie, aies, ait, ayons, ayez, aient

35 conclure a concluant **b** conclu **c** conclus, concluons **d** concluais **e** conclurai **f** conclurais **g** conclue

36 rire a riant **b** ri **c** ris, rions **d** riais **e** rirai **f** rirais **g** rie

37 dire a disant **b** dit **c** dis, disons, dites, disent **d** disais **e** dirai **f** dirais **g** dise

38 nuire a nuisant **b** nui **c** nuis, nuisons **d** nuisais **e** nuirai **f** nuirais **g** nuise

39 écrire a écrivant **b** écrit **c** écris, écrivons **d** écrivais **e** écrirai **f** écrirais **g** écrive

40 suivre a suivant **b** suivi **c** suis, suivons **d** suivais **e** suivrai **f** suivrais **g** suive

41 RENDRE a rendant **b** rendu **c** rends, rends, rend, rendons, rendez, rendent **d** rendais **e** rendrai **f** rendrais **g** rende

42 vaincre a vainquant **b** vaincu **c** vaincs, vainc, vainquons **d** vainquais **e** vaincrai **f** vaincrais **g** vainque

43 lire a lisant **b** lu **c** lis, lisons **d** lisais **e** lirai **f** lirais **g** lise

44 croire a croyant **b** cru **c** crois, croyons, croient **d** croyais **e** croirai **f** croirais **g** croie

45 CLORE a closant **b** clos **c** clos, clos, clôt, closent **e** clorai, cloras, clora, clorons, clorez, cloront **f** clorais, clorais, clorait, clorions, cloriez, cloraient

46 vivre a vivant **b** vécu **c** vis, vivons **d** vivais **e** vivrai **f** vivrais **g** vive

47 MOUDRE a moulant **b** moulu **c** mouds, mouds, moud, moulons, moulez, moulent **d** moulais, moulais, moulait, moulions, mouliez, moulaient **e** moudrai, moudras, moudra, moudrons, moudrez, moudront **f** moudrais, moudrais, moudrait, moudrions, moudriez, moudraient **g** moule

48 coudre a cousant **b** cousu **c** couds, cousons, cousez, cousent **d** cousais **e** cousai **f** coudrais **g** couse

49 joindre a joignant **b** joint **c** joins, joignons **d** joignais **e** joigdrai **f** joindrais **g** joigne

50 TRAIRE a trayant **b** trait **c** trais, trais, trait, trayons, trayez, traient **d** trayais, trayais, trayait, trayions, trayiez, trayaient **e** trai rai, trairas, traira, trairons, trairez, trairont **f** trairais, trairais, trairait, trairions, trairiez, trairiaent **g** traie

51 ABSOUDRE a absolvant **b** absous **c** absous, absous, absout, absolvons, absolvez, absolvent **d** absolvais, absolvais, absolvait, absolvions, absolviez, absolvaient **e** absoudrai, absoudras, absoudra, absoudrons, absoudrez, absoudront **f** absoudrais, absoudrais, absoudrait, absoudrions, absoudriez, absoudraient **g** absolve

52 craindre a craignant **b** craint **c** crains, craignons **d** craignais **e** craindrai **f** craindrais **g** craigne

53 boire a buvant **b** bu **c** bois, buvons, boivent **d** buvais **e** boirai **f** boirais **g** boive

54 plaire a plaisant **b** plu **c** plais, plaît, plaisons **d** plaisais **e** plairai **f** plairais **g** plaise

55 croître a croissant **b** crû, crue, crus, crues **c** croîs, croissons **d** croissais **e** croîtrai **f** croîtrais **g** croisse

56 mettre a mettant **b** mis **c** mets, mettons **d** mettais **e** mettrais **f** mettrais **g** mette

57 connaître a connaissant **b** connu **c** connais, connaît, connaissons **d** connaissais **e** connaîtrai **f** connaîtrais **g** connaisse

58 prendre a prenant **b** pris **c** prends, prenons, prennent **d** prenais **e** prendrai **f** prendrais **g** prenne

59 naître a naissant **b** né **c** nais, naît, naissons **d** naissais **e** naîtrai **f** naîtrais **g** naisse

60 FAIRE a faisant **b** fait **c** fais, fais, fait, faisons, faites, font **d** faisais **e** ferai **f** ferais **g** fasse

61 ÊTRE a étant **b** été **c** suis, es, est, sommes, êtes, sont **d** étais **e** serai **f** serais **g** sois, sois, soit, soyons, soyez, soient

Les nombres

un (une)	1
deux	2
trois	3
quatre	4
cinq	5
six	6
sept	7
huit	8
neuf	9
dix	10
onze	11
douze	12
treize	13
quatorze	14
quinze	15
seize	16
dix-sept	17
dix-huit	18
dix-neuf	19
vingt	20
vingt et un (une)	21
vingt-deux	22
trente	30
quarante	40
cinquante	50
soixante	60
soixante-dix	70
soixante et onze	71
soixante-douze	72
quatre-vingts	80
quatre-vingt-un (-une)	81
quatre-vingt-dix	90
cent	100
cent un (une)	101
deux cents	200
deux cent un (une)	201
quatre cents	400
mille	1000
cinq mille	5000
un million	1000000

Numbers

one
two
three
four
five
six
seven
eight
nine
ten
eleven
twelve
thirteen
fourteen
fifteen
sixteen
seventeen
eighteen
nineteen
twenty
twenty-one
twenty-two
thirty
forty
fifty
sixty
seventy
seventy-one
seventy-two
eighty
eighty-one
ninety
a hundred, one hundred
a hundred and one
two hundred
two hundred and one
four hundred
a thousand
five thousand
a million

Les nombres

Numbers

premier (première), 1er (1ère)	first, 1st
deuxième, 2e *or* 2ème	second, 2nd
troisième, 3e *or* 3ème	third, 3rd
quatrième, 4e *or* 4ème	fourth, 4th
cinquième, 5e *or* 5ème	fifth, 5th
sixième, 6e *or* 6ème	sixth, 6th
septième	seventh
huitième	eighth
neuvième	ninth
dixième	tenth
onzième	eleventh
douzième	twelfth
treizième	thirteenth
quatorzième	fourteenth
quinzième	fifteenth
seizième	sixteenth
dix-septième	seventeenth
dix-huitième	eighteenth
dix-neuvième	nineteenth
vingtième	twentieth
vingt et unième	twenty-first
vingt-deuxième	twenty-second
trentième	thirtieth
centième	hundredth
cent unième	hundred-and-first
millième	thousandth

L'heure

The time

quelle heure est-il?
il est ...
minuit
une heure (du matin)
une heure cinq
une heure dix
une heure et quart
une heure vingt-cinq
une heure et demie,
  une heure trente
deux heures moins vingt-cinq,
  une heure trente-cinq
deux heures moins vingt,
  une heure quarante
deux heures moins le quart,
  une heure quarante-cinq
deux heures moins dix,
  une heure cinquante
midi
deux heures (de l'après-midi),
  quatorze heures
sept heures (du soir),
  dix-neuf heures

what time is it?
it's ...
midnight, twelve a.m.
one o'clock (in the morning), one (a.m.)
five past one
ten past one
a quarter past one, one fifteen
twenty-five past one, one twenty-five
half past one,
  one thirty
twenty-five to two,
  one thirty-five
twenty to two,
  one forty
a quarter to two,
  one forty-five
ten to two,
  one fifty
twelve o'clock, midday, noon
two o'clock (in the afternoon),
  two (p.m.)
seven o'clock (in the evening),
  seven (p.m.)

à quelle heure?
à minuit
à sept heures

(at) what time?
at midnight
at seven o'clock

dans vingt minutes
il y a un quart d'heure

in twenty minutes
fifteen minutes ago

La date

The date

aujourd'hui	today
demain	tomorrow
après-demain	the day after tomorrow
hier	yesterday
avant-hier	the day before yesterday
la veille	the day before, the previous day
le lendemain	the next or following day
le matin	morning
le soir	evening
ce matin	this morning
ce soir	this evening
cet après-midi	this afternoon
hier matin	yesterday morning
hier soir	yesterday evening
demain matin	tomorrow morning
demain soir	tomorrow evening
dans la nuit du samedi au dimanche	during Saturday night, during the night of Saturday to Sunday
il viendra samedi	he's coming on Saturday
le samedi	on Saturdays
tous les samedis	every Saturday
samedi passé ou dernier	last Saturday
samedi prochain	next Saturday
samedi en huit	a week on Saturday
samedi en quinze	a fortnight or two weeks on Saturday
du lundi au samedi	from Monday to Saturday
tous les jours	every day
une fois par semaine	once a week
une fois par mois	once a month
deux fois par semaine	twice a week
il y a une semaine ou huit jours	a week ago
il y a quinze jours	a fortnight or two weeks ago
l'année dernière	last year
dans deux jours	in two days
dans huit jours ou une semaine	in a week
dans quinze jours	in a fortnight or two weeks
le mois prochain	next month
l'année prochaine	next year

quel jour sommes-nous?
le 1er/24 octobre 2018

en 2018
mille neuf cent quatre-vingt seize
deux mille dix-huit

44 av. J.-C.
14 apr. J.-C.
au XIXe (siècle)
dans les années trente

what day is it?
the 1st/24th of October 2018,
  October 1st/24th 2018
in 2018
nineteen ninety-six
two thousand (and) eighteen,
  twenty eighteen

44 BC
14 AD
in the nineteenth century
in the thirties

Aa

A, a [a] NM INV A, a; **A comme Anatole** A for Andrew (BRIT) *ou* Able (US); **de a à z** from a to z; **prouver qch par a + b** to prove sth conclusively ▶ ABR = **anticyclone**; **are**; (*ampère*) amp; (*autoroute*) ≈ M (BRIT)

★**a** [a] VB *voir* **avoir**

à [a]

(*à + le* = **au**, *à + les* = **aux**) PRÉP **1** (*endroit, situation*) at, in; **être à Paris/au Portugal** to be in Paris/Portugal; **être à la maison/à l'école** to be at home/at school; **à la campagne** in the country; **c'est à 10 m/km/à 20 minutes (d'ici)** it's 10 m/km/20 minutes away

2 (*direction*) to; **aller à Paris/au Portugal** to go to Paris/Portugal; **aller à la maison/à l'école** to go home/to school; **à la campagne** to the country

3 (*temps*): **à 3 heures/minuit** at 3 o'clock/midnight; **au printemps** in the spring; **au mois de juin** in June; **à Noël/Pâques** at Christmas/Easter; **au départ** at the start, at the outset; **à demain/la semaine prochaine !** see you tomorrow/next week!; **visites de 5 heures à 6 heures** visiting from 5 to *ou* till 6 o'clock

4 (*attribution, appartenance*) to; **le livre est à Paul/à lui/à nous** this book is Paul's/his/ours; **donner qch à qn** to give sth to sb; **un ami à moi** a friend of mine; **c'est à moi de le faire** it's up to me to do it

5 (*moyen*) with; **se chauffer au gaz** to have gas heating; **à bicyclette** on a *ou* by bicycle; **à pied** on foot; **à la main/machine** by hand/machine; **à la télévision/la radio** on television/the radio

6 (*provenance*) from; **boire à la bouteille** to drink from the bottle

7 (*caractérisation, manière*): **l'homme aux yeux bleus** the man with the blue eyes; **à la russe** the Russian way; **glace à la framboise** raspberry ice cream

8 (*but, destination*): **tasse à café** coffee cup; **maison à vendre** house for sale; **je n'ai rien à lire** I don't have anything to read; **à bien réfléchir ...** thinking about it ..., on reflection ...; **problème à régler** problem to sort out

9 (*rapport, évaluation, distribution*): **100 km/unités à l'heure** 100 km/units per *ou* an hour; **payé à l'heure** paid by the hour; **cinq à six** five to six

10 (*conséquence, résultat*): **à ce qu'il prétend** according to him; **à leur grande surprise** much to their surprise; **à nous trois nous n'avons pas su le faire** we couldn't do it even between the three of us; **ils sont arrivés à quatre** four of them arrived (together)

AB ABR = **assez bien**

abaissement [abɛsmɑ̃] NM lowering; pulling down

abaisser [abese] /1/ VT to lower, bring down; (*manette*) to pull down; (*fig*) to debase; to humiliate ■ **s'abaisser** VPR to go down; (*fig*) to demean o.s.; **s'~ à faire/à qch** to stoop *ou* descend to doing/to sth

abandon [abɑ̃dɔ̃] NM abandoning; deserting; giving up; withdrawal; surrender, relinquishing; (*fig*) lack of constraint; relaxed pose *ou* mood; **être à l'~** to be in a state of neglect; **laisser à l'~** to abandon

abandonné, e [abɑ̃dɔne] ADJ (*solitaire*) deserted; (*route, usine*) disused; (*jardin*) abandoned

abandonner [abɑ̃dɔne] /1/ VT (*personne*) to leave, abandon, desert; (*projet, activité*) to abandon, give up; (*Sport*) to retire *ou* withdraw from; (*Inform*) to abort; (*céder*) to surrender, relinquish; **~ qch à qn** to give sth up to sb ■ **s'abandonner** VPR to let o.s. go; **s'~ à** (*paresse, plaisirs*) to give o.s. up to

abasourdi, e [abazuʀdi] ADJ stunned, dumbfounded

abasourdir [abazuʀdiʀ] /2/ VT to stun, stagger

abat *etc* [aba] VB *voir* **abattre**

abâtardi, e [abɑtaʀdi] ADJ (*style, langue*) bastardized, watered-down

abat-jour [abaʒuʀ] NM INV lampshade

abats [aba] VB *voir* **abattre** ▶ NMPL (*de bœuf, porc*) offal *sg* (BRIT), entrails (US); (*de volaille*) giblets

abattage [abataʒ] NM cutting down, felling

abattant [abatɑ̃] VB *voir* **abattre** ▶ NM leaf, flap

abattement [abatmɑ̃] NM (*physique*) enfeeblement; (*moral*) dejection, despondency; (*déduction*) reduction; **~ fiscal** ≈ tax allowance

abattis [abati] VB *voir* **abattre** ▶ NMPL giblets

abattoir [abatwaʀ] NM abattoir (BRIT), slaughterhouse

abattre [abatʀ] /41/ VT (*arbre*) to cut down, fell; (*mur, maison*) to pull down; (*avion, personne*) to shoot down; (*animal*) to shoot, kill; (*fig: physiquement*) to wear out, tire out; (: *moralement*) to demoralize; **~ ses cartes** (*aussi fig*) to lay one's cards on the table; **~ du travail** *ou* **de la besogne** to get through a lot of work; **ne pas se laisser ~** to keep one's spirits up, not to let things get one down ■ **s'abattre** VPR to crash down; **s'~ sur** (*pluie*) to beat down on; (*coups, injures*) to rain down on

abattu, e [abaty] PP de **abattre** ▶ADJ (*déprimé*) downcast

abbatiale [abasjal] NF abbey (*church*)

abbaye [abei] NF abbey

abbé [abe] NM priest; (*d'abbaye*) abbot; **M l'~** Father

abbesse [abɛs] NF abbess

abc, ABC [abese] NM alphabet primer; (*fig*) rudiments *pl*

abcès [apsɛ] NM abscess

abdication [abdikasjɔ̃] NF abdication

abdiquer [abdike] /1/ VI to abdicate ▶VT to renounce, give up

abdomen [abdɔmɛn] NM abdomen

abdominal, e, -aux [abdɔminal, -o] ADJ abdominal **abdominaux** NMPL: **faire des abdominaux** to do sit-ups

abdos [abdo] NMPL (*fam: muscles*) abs (*fam*); (: *exercices*) abdominal exercises, ab exercises (*fam*)

abécédaire [abesedɛr] NM alphabet primer

★**abeille** [abɛj] NF bee

aberrant, e [aberɑ̃, -ɑ̃t] ADJ absurd

aberration [aberasjɔ̃] NF aberration

abêtir [abetir] /2/ VT to make idiots (*ou* an idiot) of

abêtissant, e [abetisɑ̃, -ɑ̃t] ADJ stultifying

abhorrer [abɔre] /1/ VT to abhor, loathe

abîme [abim] NM abyss, gulf

abîmé, e [abime] ADJ (*objet*) damaged; **~ dans la prière** deep in prayer, lost in prayer

abîmer [abime] /1/ VT to spoil, damage ▪ **s'abîmer** VPR to get spoilt *ou* damaged; (*fruits*) to spoil; (*tomber*) to sink, founder; **s'~ les yeux** to ruin one's eyes *ou* eyesight

abject, e [abʒɛkt] ADJ abject, despicable

abjection [abʒɛksjɔ̃] NF abjectness

abjurer [abʒyre] /1/ VT to abjure, renounce

ablatif [ablatif] NM ablative

ablation [ablasjɔ̃] NF removal

ablutions [ablysjɔ̃] NFPL: **faire ses ~** to perform one's ablutions

abnégation [abnegasjɔ̃] NF (self-)abnegation

aboie *etc* [abwa] VB *voir* **aboyer**

aboiement [abwamɑ̃] NM bark, barking *no pl*

aboierai *etc* [abware] VB *voir* **aboyer**

abois [abwa] NMPL: **aux ~** at bay

abolir [abɔlir] /2/ VT to abolish

abolition [abɔlisjɔ̃] NF abolition

abolitionniste [abɔlisjɔnist] ADJ, NMF abolitionist

abominable [abɔminabl] ADJ abominable

abomination [abɔminasjɔ̃] NF abomination

abondamment [abɔ̃damɑ̃] ADV abundantly

abondance [abɔ̃dɑ̃s] NF abundance; (*richesse*) affluence; **en ~** in abundance

abondant, e [abɔ̃dɑ̃, -ɑ̃t] ADJ plentiful, abundant, copious

abonder [abɔ̃de] /1/ VI to abound, be plentiful; **~ en** to be full of, abound in; **~ dans le sens de qn** to concur with sb

abonné, e [abɔne] NM/F subscriber; season ticket holder ▶ADJ: **être ~ à un journal** to subscribe to *ou*

have a subscription to a periodical; **être ~ au téléphone** to be on the (tele)phone

abonnement [abɔnmɑ̃] NM subscription; (*pour transports en commun, concerts*) season ticket

abonner [abɔne] /1/: **s'abonner** VPR: **s'~ à** to subscribe to, take out a subscription to; **s'~ aux tweets de qn** to follow sb on Twitter

★**abord** [abɔr] NM: **être d'un ~ facile** to be approachable; **être d'un ~ difficile** (*personne*) to be unapproachable; (*lieu*) to be hard to reach *ou* difficult to get to; **de prime ~, au premier ~** at first sight, initially; **d'~** adv first; **tout d'~** first of all ▪ **abords** NMPL (*environs*) surroundings

abordable [abɔrdabl] ADJ (*personne*) approachable; (*marchandise*) reasonably priced; (*prix*) affordable, reasonable

abordage [abɔrdaʒ] NM boarding

aborder [abɔrde] /1/ VI to land ▶VT (*sujet, difficulté*) to tackle; (*personne*) to approach; (*rivage etc*) to reach; (*Navig: attaquer*) to board; (: *heurter*) to collide with

aborigène [abɔriʒɛn] NMF aborigine, native

Abou Dhabî, Abu Dhabî [abudabi] N Abu Dhabi

abouler [abule] VT (*fam: payer*) to fork out (*fam*); **~ le fric** to fork out (*fam*)

abouti, e [abuti] ADJ accomplished

aboutir [abutir] /2/ VI (*négociations*) to succeed; **~ à/dans/sur** to end up at/in/on; **n'~ à rien** to come to nothing

aboutissants [abutisɑ̃] NMPL *voir* **tenant**

aboutissement [abutismɑ̃] NM success; (*de concept, projet*) successful realization; (*d'années de travail*) successful conclusion

aboyer [abwaje] /8/ VI to bark

abracadabrant, e [abrakadabrɑ̃, -ɑ̃t] ADJ incredible, preposterous

abrasif, -ive [abrazif, -iv] ADJ, NM abrasive

abrasion [abrazjɔ̃] NF abrasion

abrégé [abreʒe] NM summary; **en ~** in a shortened *ou* abbreviated form

abréger [abreʒe] /3, 6/ VT (*texte*) to shorten, abridge; (*mot*) to shorten, abbreviate; (*réunion, voyage*) to cut short, shorten

abreuver [abrœve] /1/ VT to water; (*fig*): **~ qn de** to shower *ou* swamp sb with; (*injures etc*) to shower sb with ▪ **s'abreuver** VPR to drink

abreuvoir [abrœvwar] NM watering place

abréviation [abrevjasjɔ̃] NF abbreviation

★**abri** [abri] NM shelter; **être à l'~** to be under cover; **se mettre à l'~** to shelter; **à l'~ de** sheltered from; (*danger*) safe from

Abribus® [abribys] NM bus shelter

★**abricot** [abriko] NM apricot

abricotier [abrikɔtje] NM apricot tree

abrité, e [abrite] ADJ sheltered

abriter [abrite] /1/ VT to shelter; (*loger*) to accommodate ▪ **s'abriter** VPR to shelter, take cover

abrogation [abrɔgasjɔ̃] NF (*Jur*) repeal, abrogation

abroger [abrɔʒe] /3/ VT to repeal, abrogate

abrupt, e [abrypt] ADJ sheer, steep; (*ton*) abrupt

abruti, e [abʀyti] ADJ stunned, dazed; **~ de travail** overworked ▸ NM/F (*fam*) idiot

abrutir [abʀytiʀ] /**2**/ VT to daze; (*fatiguer*) to exhaust; (*abêtir*) to stupefy ▸ **s'abrutir** VPR (*s'abêtir*) to vegetate; **s'~ de travail** to work o.s. stupid; **s'~ devant la télé** to vegetate in front of the TV

abrutissant, e [abʀytisã, -ãt] ADJ (*bruit, travail*) stupefying

abscisse [apsis] NF X axis, abscissa

abscons, e [apskɔ̃, -ɔ̃s] ADJ abstruse

★**absence** [apsɑ̃s] NF absence; (*Méd*) blackout; **en l'~ de** in the absence of; **avoir des absences** to have mental blanks

★**absent, e** [apsã, -ãt] ADJ absent; (*chose*) missing, lacking; (*distrait: air*) vacant, faraway ▸ NM/F absentee

absentéisme [apsãteism] NM absenteeism

absenter [apsãte] /**1**/: **s'absenter** VPR to take time off work; (*sortir*) to leave, go out

abside [apsid] NF (*Archit*) apse

absinthe [apsɛ̃t] NF (*boisson*) absinth(e); (*Bot*) wormwood, absinth(e)

absolu, e [apsɔly] ADJ absolute; (*caractère*) rigid, uncompromising ▸ NM (*Philosophie*): **l'~** the Absolute; **dans l'~** in the absolute, in a vacuum

★**absolument** [apsɔlymã] ADV absolutely

absolution [apsɔlysjɔ̃] NF absolution; (*Jur*) dismissal (*of case*)

absolutisme [apsɔlytism] NM absolutism

absolvais *etc* [apsɔlvɛ] VB *voir* **absoudre**

absorbant, e [apsɔʀbã, -ãt] ADJ absorbent; (*tâche*) absorbing, engrossing

absorbé, e [apsɔʀbe] ADJ absorbed, engrossed

absorber [apsɔʀbe] /**1**/ VT to absorb; (*Méd: manger, boire*) to take; (*Écon: firme*) to take over, absorb ▸ **s'absorber** VPR: **s'~ dans** (*dans un travail, une activité*) to be absorbed in

absorption [apsɔʀpsjɔ̃] NF absorption

absoudre [apsudʀ] /**51**/ VT to absolve; (*Jur*) to dismiss

absous, -oute [apsu, -ut] PP *de* **absoudre**

abstenir [apstəniʀ] /**22**/: **s'abstenir** VPR (*Pol*) to abstain; **s'~ de qch/de faire** to refrain from sth/ from doing

abstention [apstãsjɔ̃] NF abstention

abstentionnisme [apstãsjɔnism] NM abstaining

abstentionniste [apstãsjɔnist] NMF abstentionist

abstenu, e [apstəny] PP *de* **abstenir**

abstiendrai [apstjɛ̃dʀe], **abstiens** *etc* [apstjɛ̃] VB *voir* **abstenir**

abstinence [apstinãs] NF abstinence; **faire ~** to abstain (*from meat on Fridays*)

abstint *etc* [apstɛ̃] VB *voir* **abstenir**

abstraction [apstʀaksjɔ̃] NF abstraction; **faire ~ de** to set *ou* leave aside; **~ faite de …** leaving aside …

abstraire [apstʀɛʀ] /**50**/ VT to abstract ▸ **s'abstraire** VPR: **s'~ (de)** (*s'isoler*) to cut o.s. off (from)

abstrait, e [apstʀɛ, -ɛt] PP *de* **abstraire** ▸ ADJ abstract ▸ NM: **dans l'~** in the abstract

abstraitement [apstʀɛtmã] ADV abstractly

abstrayais *etc* [apstʀɛje] VB *voir* **abstraire**

absurde [apsyʀd] ADJ absurd ▸ NM absurdity; (*Philosophie*): **l'~** absurd; **par l'~** ad absurdum

absurdité [apsyʀdite] NF absurdity

abus [aby] NM (*excès*) abuse, misuse; (*injustice*) abuse; **~ de biens sociaux** misuse of company assets; (*détournement de fonds*) embezzlement; **~ de confiance** breach of trust; **~ de pouvoir** abuse of power; **~ sexuels** sexual abuse *no pl*; **il y a de l'~ !** (*fam*) that's a bit much!

abuser [abyze] /**1**/ VI to go too far, overstep the mark ▸ VT to deceive, mislead; **~ de** (*force, droit*) to misuse; (*alcool*) to take to excess; (*violer, duper*) to take advantage of ■ **s'abuser** VPR (*se méprendre*) to be mistaken

abusif, -ive [abyzif, -iv] ADJ exorbitant; (*punition*) excessive; (*pratique*) improper

abusivement [abyzivmã] ADV exorbitantly; excessively; improperly

abyssal, e [abisal] ADJ (*Géo: faune*) abyssal; (*fig: déficit, décalage*) huge; **fosse abyssale** deep-sea trench

abysse [abis] NM (*fonds marins*) abyssal zone ■ **abysses** NMPL: **les abysses** the abyss

AC SIGLE F = **appellation contrôlée**

acabit [akabi] NM: **du même ~** of the same type

acacia [akasja] NM (*Bot*) acacia

académicien, ne [akademisjɛ̃, -ɛn] NM/F academician

académie [akademi] NF (*société*) learned society; (*école: d'art, de danse*) academy; (*Art: nu*) nude; (*Scol: circonscription*) ≈ regional education authority; **l'A~ (française)** the French Academy

> The **Académie française** was founded by Cardinal Richelieu in 1635, during the reign of Louis XIII. It is made up of forty elected scholars and writers who are known as *les Quarante* or *les Immortels*. One of the *Académie*'s functions is to keep an eye on the development of the French language, and its recommendations are frequently the subject of lively public debate. It has produced several editions of its famous dictionary and also awards various literary prizes.

académique [akademik] ADJ academic

Acadie [akadi] NF: **l'~** the Maritime Provinces

acadien, ne [akadjɛ̃, -ɛn] ADJ Acadian, of *ou* from the Maritime Provinces

acajou [akaʒu] NM mahogany

acariâtre [akaʀjɑtʀ] ADJ sour(-tempered) (*BRIT*), cantankerous

acarien [akaʀjɛ̃] NM dust mite

accablant, e [akablɑ̃, -ãt] ADJ (*chaleur*) oppressive; (*témoignage, preuve*) overwhelming

accablé, e [akable] ADJ (*effondré*) overwhelmed; **l'air ~** looking overwhelmed; **~ de** (*dettes, soucis*) weighed down with; **~ de chagrin** grief-stricken

accablement [akabləmã] NM deep despondency

accabler [akable] /**1**/ VT (*suj: témoignage*) to condemn, damn; **~ qn d'injures** to heap *ou* shower abuse on sb; **~ qn de travail** to overwork sb

accalmie [akalmi] NF lull

accaparant, e [akaparᾶ, -āt] ADJ that takes up all one's time ou attention

accaparer [akapaʀe] /**1**/ VT to monopolize; (*travail etc*) to take up (all) the time ou attention of

accéder [aksede] /**6**/: ~ **à** vt (*lieu*) to reach; (*fig: pouvoir*) to accede to (:*poste*) to attain; (*accorder: requête*) to grant, accede to

accélérateur [akseleʀatœʀ] NM accelerator

accélération [akseleʀasjɔ̃] NF speeding up; acceleration

accéléré [akseleʀe] NM: **en ~** (*Ciné*) speeded up

accélérer [akseleʀe] /**6**/ VT (*mouvement, travaux*) to speed up ▶ VI (*Auto*) to accelerate ■ **s'accélérer** VPR (*processus, rythme*) to speed up

★**accent** [aksᾶ] NM accent; (*inflexions expressives*) tone (of voice); (*Phonétique, fig*) stress; **aux accents de** (*musique*) to the strains of; **mettre l'~ sur** (*fig*) to stress; **~ aigu/grave/circonflexe** acute/grave/circumflex accent

accentuation [aksᾶtɥasjɔ̃] NF accenting; stressing

accentué, e [aksᾶtɥe] ADJ marked, pronounced

accentuer [aksᾶtɥe] /**1**/ VT (*Ling: orthographe*) to accent; (: *phonétique*) to stress, accent; (*fig*) to accentuate, emphasize; (*effort, pression*) to increase ■ **s'accentuer** VPR to become more marked ou pronounced

acceptable [akseptabl] ADJ satisfactory, acceptable

acceptation [akseptasjɔ̃] NF acceptance

★**accepter** [aksepte] /**1**/ VT to accept; (*tolérer*): **~ que qn fasse** to agree to sb doing; **~ de faire** to agree to do

acception [aksepsjɔ̃] NF meaning, sense; **dans toute l'~ du terme** in the full sense ou meaning of the word

accès [akse] NM (*à un lieu, Inform*) access; (*Méd*) attack; (: *de toux*) fit; (: *de fièvre*) bout; **d'~ facile/malaisé** easily/not easily accessible; **facile d'~** easy to get to; **donner ~ à** (*lieu*) to give access to; (*carrière*) to open the door to; **avoir ~ auprès de qn** to have access to sb; **l'~ aux quais est interdit aux personnes non munies d'un billet** ticket-holders only on platforms, no access to platforms without a ticket; **~ de colère** fit of anger; **~ de joie** burst of joy ▶ NMPL (*routes etc*) means of access, approaches

accessible [aksesibl] ADJ accessible; (*personne*) approachable; (*livre, sujet*): **~ à qn** within the reach of sb; (*sensible*): **~ à la pitié/l'amour** open to pity/love

accession [aksesjɔ̃] NF: **~ à** accession to; (*à un poste*) attainment of; **~ à la propriété** home-ownership

accessit [aksesit] NM (*Scol*) ≈ certificate of merit

accessoire [akseswaʀ] ADJ secondary, of secondary importance; (*frais*) incidental ▶ NM accessory; (*Théât*) prop

accessoirement [akseswaʀmᾶ] ADV secondarily; incidentally

accessoiriste [akseswaʀist] NMF (*TV, Ciné*) property man/woman

★**accident** [aksidᾶ] NM accident; **par ~** by chance; **~ de parcours** mishap; **~ de la route** road accident;

~ du travail accident at work; industrial injury ou accident; **accidents de terrain** unevenness of the ground

accidenté, e [aksidᾶte] ADJ damaged ou injured (in an accident); (*relief, terrain*) uneven; hilly

accidentel, le [aksidᾶtel] ADJ accidental

accidentellement [aksidᾶtelmᾶ] ADV (*par hasard*) accidentally; (*mourir*) in an accident

accise [aksiz] NF: **droit d'~(s)** excise duty

acclamation [aklamasjɔ̃] NF: **par ~** (*vote*) by acclamation ■ **acclamations** NFPL cheers, cheering sg

acclamer [aklame] /**1**/ VT to cheer, acclaim

acclimatation [aklimatasjɔ̃] NF acclimatization

acclimater [aklimate] /**1**/ VT to acclimatize ■ **s'acclimater** VPR to become acclimatized

accointances [akwɛ̃tᾶs] NFPL: **avoir des ~ avec** to have contacts with

accolade [akɔlad] NF (*amicale*) embrace; (*signe*) brace; **donner l'~ à qn** to embrace sb

accoler [akɔle] /**1**/ VT to place side by side

accommodant, e [akɔmɔdᾶ, -āt] ADJ accommodating, easy-going

accommodement [akɔmɔdmᾶ] NM compromise

accommoder [akɔmɔde] /**1**/ VT (*Culin*) to prepare; (*points de vue*) to reconcile; **~ qch à** (*adapter*) to adapt sth to ■ **s'accommoder** VPR: **s'~ de** to put up with; (*se contenter de*) to make do with; **s'~ à** (*s'adapter*) to adapt to

accompagnateur, -trice [akɔ̃paɲatœʀ, -tʀis] NM/F (*Mus*) accompanist; (*de voyage*) guide; (*de voyage organisé*) courier; (*d'enfants*) accompanying adult

accompagnement [akɔ̃paɲmᾶ] NM (*Mus*) accompaniment; (*Mil*) support

★**accompagner** [akɔ̃paɲe] /**1**/ VT to accompany, be ou go ou come with; (*Mus*) to accompany ■ **s'accompagner** VPR: **s'~ de** to bring, be accompanied by

accompli, e [akɔ̃pli] ADJ accomplished

accomplir [akɔ̃pliʀ] /**2**/ VT (*tâche, projet*) to carry out; (*souhait*) to fulfil ■ **s'accomplir** VPR to be fulfilled

accomplissement [akɔ̃plismᾶ] NM carrying out; fulfilment (BʀIT), fulfillment (US)

★**accord** [akɔʀ] NM (*entente, convention, Ling*) agreement; (*entre des styles, tons etc*) harmony; (*consentement*) agreement, consent; (*Mus*) chord; **donner son ~** to give one's agreement; **mettre deux personnes d'~** to make two people come to an agreement, reconcile two people; **se mettre d'~** to come to an agreement (with each other); **être d'~** to agree; **être d'~ avec qn** to agree with sb; **d'~!** OK!, right!; **d'un commun ~** of one accord; **~ parfait** (*Mus*) tonic chord

accord-cadre [akɔʀkadʀ] (*pl* **accords-cadres**) NM framework ou outline agreement

accordéon [akɔʀdeɔ̃] NM (*Mus*) accordion

accordéoniste [akɔʀdeɔnist] NMF accordionist

accorder [akɔʀde] /**1**/ VT (*faveur, délai*) to grant; (*attribuer*): **~ de l'importance/de la valeur à qch** to attach importance/value to sth; (*harmoniser*) to match; (*Mus*) to tune; **je vous accorde que ...** I grant you that ... ■ **s'accorder** VPR to get on together; (*être d'accord*) to agree; (*couleurs, caractères*) to go together, match; (*Ling*) to agree

accordeur [akɔʀdœʀ] NM (*Mus*) tuner

accoster [akɔste] /1/ VT (*Navig*) to draw alongside; (*personne*) to accost ▶ VI (*Navig*) to berth

accotement [akɔtmɑ̃] NM (*de route*) verge (BRIT), shoulder; **~ stabilisé/non stabilisé** hard shoulder/soft verge *ou* shoulder

accoter [akɔte] /1/ VT: **~ qch contre/à** to lean *ou* rest sth against/on ■ **s'accoter** VPR: **s'~ contre/à** to lean against/on

accouchement [akuʃmɑ̃] NM delivery, (child) birth; (*travail*) labour (BRIT), labor (US); **~ à terme** delivery at (full) term; **~ sans douleur** natural childbirth

accoucher [akuʃe] /1/ VI to give birth, have a baby; (*être en travail*) to be in labour (BRIT) *ou* labor (US); **~ d'un garçon** to give birth to a boy ▶ VT to deliver

accoucheur [akuʃœʀ] NM: **(médecin) ~** obstetrician

accoucheuse [akuʃøz] NF midwife

accouder [akude] /1/: **s'accouder** VPR: **s'~ à/ contre/sur** to rest one's elbows on/against/on; **accoudé à la fenêtre** leaning on the windowsill

accoudoir [akudwaʀ] NM armrest

accouplement [akupləmɑ̃] NM coupling; mating

accoupler [akuple] /1/ VT to couple; (*pour la reproduction*) to mate ■ **s'accoupler** VPR to mate

accourir [akuʀiʀ] /11/ VI to rush *ou* run up

accoutrement [akutʀəmɑ̃] NM (*péj*) getup (BRIT), outfit

accoutrer [akutʀe] /1/ VT (*péj*) to do *ou* get up ■ **s'accoutrer** VPR to do *ou* get o.s. up

accoutumance [akutymɑ̃s] NF (*gén*) adaptation; (*Méd*) addiction

accoutumé, e [akutyme] ADJ (*habituel*) customary, usual; **comme à l'accoutumée** as is customary *ou* usual

accoutumer [akutyme] /1/ VT: **~ qn à qch/faire** to accustom sb to sth/to doing ■ **s'accoutumer** VPR: **s'~ à** to get accustomed *ou* used to

accréditer [akʀedite] /1/ VT (*nouvelle*) to substantiate; **~ qn (auprès de)** to accredit sb (to)

accro [akʀo] NMF (*fam*: = *accroché(e)*) addict

accroc [akʀo] NM (*déchirure*) tear; (*fig*) hitch, snag; **sans ~** without a hitch; **faire un ~ à** (*vêtement*) to make a tear in, tear; (*fig*: *règle etc*) to infringe

accrochage [akʀɔʃaʒ] NM hanging (up); hitching (up); (*Auto*) (minor) collision; (*Mil*) encounter, engagement; (*dispute*) clash, brush

accroche-cœur [akʀɔʃkœʀ] NM kiss-curl

★**accrocher** [akʀɔʃe] /1/ VT (*suspendre*) to hang; (*fig*) to catch, attract; **~ qch à** (*suspendre*) to hang sth (up) on; (*attacher*: *remorque*) to hitch sth (up) to; (*déchirer*) to catch sth (on); **il a accroché ma voiture** he bumped into my car ▶ VI to stick, get stuck; (*fig*: *pourparlers etc*) to hit a snag; (*plaire*: *disque etc*) to catch on ■ **s'accrocher** VPR (*se disputer*) to have a clash *ou* brush; (*ne pas céder*) to hold one's own, hang on in (*fam*); **s'~ à** (*rester pris à*) to catch on; (*agripper*, *fig*) to hang on *ou* cling to

accrocheur, -euse [akʀɔʃœʀ, -øz] ADJ (*vendeur, concurrent*) tenacious; (*publicité*) eye-catching; (*titre*) catchy, eye-catching

accroire [akʀwaʀ] /44/ VT: **faire** *ou* **laisser ~ à qn qch/que** to give sb to believe sth/that

accrois [akʀwa], **accroissais** *etc* [akʀwasɛ] VB *voir* **accroître**

accroissement [akʀwasmɑ̃] NM increase

accroître [akʀwatʀ] /55/ VT to increase ■ **s'accroître** VPR to increase

accroupi, e [akʀupi] ADJ squatting, crouching (down)

accroupir [akʀupiʀ] /2/: **s'accroupir** VPR to squat, crouch (down)

accru, e [akʀy] PP *de* **accroître**

accu [aky] NM (*fam*: = *accumulateur*) accumulator, battery

★**accueil** [akœj] NM welcome; (*endroit*) reception (desk); (*dans une gare*) information kiosk; **comité/ centre d'~** reception committee/centre

★**accueillant, e** [akœjɑ̃, -ɑ̃t] ADJ welcoming, friendly

★**accueillir** [akœjiʀ] /12/ VT to welcome; (*aller chercher*) to meet, collect; (*loger*) to accommodate

acculer [akyle] /1/ VT: **~ qn à** *ou* **contre** to drive sb back against; **~ qn dans** to corner sb in; **~ qn à** (*faillite*) to drive sb to the brink of

acculturation [akyltyʀasjɔ̃] NF acculturation

accumulateur [akymylatœʀ] NM accumulator, battery

accumulation [akymylasjɔ̃] NF accumulation; **chauffage/radiateur à ~** (night-)storage heating/heater

accumuler [akymyle] /1/ VT to accumulate, amass ■ **s'accumuler** VPR to accumulate; to pile up

accusateur, -trice [akyzatœʀ, -tʀis] NM/F accuser ▶ ADJ accusing; (*document, preuve*) incriminating

accusatif [akyzatif] NM (*Ling*) accusative

accusation [akyzasjɔ̃] NF (*gén*) accusation; (*Jur*) charge; (*partie*): **l'~** the prosecution; **mettre en ~** to indict; **acte d'~** bill of indictment

accusé, e [akyze] NM/F accused; (*prévenu(e)*) defendant ▶ NM: **~ de réception** acknowledgement of receipt

★**accuser** [akyze] /1/ VT to accuse; (*fig*) to emphasize, bring out; (: *montrer*) to show; **~ qn de** to accuse sb of; (*Jur*) to charge sb with; **~ qn/qch de qch** (*rendre responsable*) to blame sb/sth for sth; **~ réception de** to acknowledge receipt of; **~ le coup** (*fig*) to be visibly affected ■ **s'accuser** VPR (*s'accentuer*) to become more marked; **s'~ de qch/d'avoir fait qch** to admit sth/having done sth; to blame o.s. for sth/for having done sth

acerbe [asɛʀb] ADJ caustic, acid

acéré, e [aseʀe] ADJ sharp

acétate [asetat] NM acetate

acétique [asetik] ADJ: **acide ~** acetic acid

acétone [asetɔn] NF acetone

acétylène [asetilɛn] NM acetylene

ach. ABR = **achète**

achalandé, e [aʃalɑ̃de] ADJ: **bien ~** (*magasin*: *en marchandises*) well-stocked; (: *en clients*) with a large clientele

acharné, e [aʃaʀne] ADJ (*lutte, adversaire*) fierce, bitter; (*travail*) relentless, unremitting

acharnement [aʃaʀnəmɑ̃] NM fierceness; relentlessness

acharner [aʃaʀne] /1/: **s'acharner** VPR: **s'~ sur** to go at fiercely, hound; (ennemi) to set o.s. against; to dog, pursue; (malchance) to hound; **s'~ à faire** to try doggedly to do; to persist in doing

★**achat** [aʃa] NM buying no pl; (article acheté) purchase; **faire l'~ de** to buy, purchase; **faire des achats** to do some shopping, buy a few things

acheminement [aʃ(ə)minmɑ̃] NM conveyance

acheminer [aʃ(ə)mine] /1/ VT (courrier) to forward, dispatch; (troupes) to convey, transport; (train) to route ▪ **s'acheminer vers** VPR to head for

★**acheter** [aʃ(ə)te] /5/ VT to buy, purchase; (soudoyer) to buy, bribe; **~ qch à** (marchand) to buy ou purchase sth from; (ami etc: offrir) to buy sth for; **~ à crédit** to buy on credit

acheteur, -euse [aʃ(ə)tœʀ, -øz] NM/F buyer; shopper; (Comm) buyer; (Jur) vendee, purchaser

achevé, e [aʃ(ə)ve] ADJ: **d'un ridicule ~** thoroughly ou absolutely ridiculous; **d'un comique ~** absolutely hilarious

achèvement [aʃɛvmɑ̃] NM completion, finishing

achever [aʃ(ə)ve] /5/ VT to complete, finish; (blessé) to finish off ▪ **s'achever** VPR to end

achoppement [aʃɔpmɑ̃] NM: **pierre d'~** stumbling block

achopper [aʃɔpe] VI to stumble; **~ sur** (problème) to come up against

★**acide** [asid] ADJ sour, sharp; (ton) acid, biting; (Chimie) acid(ic) ▶ NM acid

acidifiant [asidifjɑ̃] NM acidifier

acidifier [asidifje] /7/ VT to acidify ▪ **s'acidifier** VPR to acidify

acidité [asidite] NF sharpness; acidity

acidulé, e [asidyle] ADJ slightly acid; **bonbons acidulés** acid drops (BRIT), ≈ lemon drops (US)

acier [asje] NM steel; **~ inoxydable** stainless steel

aciérie [asjeʀi] NF steelworks sg

acné [akne] NF acne

acolyte [akɔlit] NM (péj) associate

acompte [akɔ̃t] NM deposit; (versement régulier) instalment; (sur somme due) payment on account; (sur salaire) advance; **un ~ de 10 euros** 10 euros on account

acoquiner [akɔkine] /1/: **s'acoquiner avec** VPR (péj) to team up with

Açores [asɔʀ] NFPL: **les ~** the Azores

à-côté [akote] NM side-issue; (argent) extra

à-coup [aku] NM (du moteur) (hic)cough; (fig) jolt; **sans à-coups** smoothly; **par à-coups** by fits and starts

acouphène [akufɛn] NM (Méd) tinnitus; **souffrir d'acouphènes** to have tinnitus

acoustique [akustik] NF (d'une salle) acoustics pl; (science) acoustics sg ▶ ADJ acoustic

acquéreur [akeʀœʀ] NM buyer, purchaser; **se porter/se rendre ~ de qch** to announce one's intention to purchase/to purchase sth

acquérir [akeʀiʀ] /21/ VT to acquire; (par achat) to purchase, acquire; (valeur) to gain; (résultats) to achieve; **ce que ses efforts lui ont acquis** what his efforts have won ou gained (for) him

acquiers etc [akjɛʀ] VB voir **acquérir**

acquiescement [akjɛsmɑ̃] NM acquiescence, agreement

acquiescer [akjese] /3/ VI (opiner) to agree; (consentir): **~ (à qch)** to acquiesce ou assent (to sth)

acquis, e [aki, -iz] PP de **acquérir** ▶ NM (accumulated) experience; (avantage) gain ▶ ADJ (achat) acquired; (valeur) gained; (résultats) achieved; **être ~ à** (plan, idée) to be in full agreement with; **son aide nous est acquise** we can count on ou be sure of his help; **tenir qch pour ~** to take sth for granted

acquisition [akizisjɔ̃] NF acquisition; (achat) purchase; **faire l'~ de** to acquire; to purchase

acquit [aki] VB voir **acquérir** ▶ NM (quittance) receipt; **pour ~** received; **par ~ de conscience** to set one's mind at rest

acquittement [akitmɑ̃] NM acquittal; payment, settlement

acquitter [akite] /1/ VT (Jur) to acquit; (facture) to pay, settle ▪ **s'acquitter de** VPR to discharge; (promesse, tâche) to fulfil (BRIT), fulfill (US), carry out

âcre [akʀ] ADJ acrid, pungent

âcreté [akʀəte] NF acridness, pungency

acrimonie [akʀimɔni] NF acrimony

acrimonieux, -euse [akʀimɔnjø, -jøz] ADJ (ton, débat) acrimonious

acrobate [akʀɔbat] NMF acrobat

acrobatie [akʀɔbasi] NF (art) acrobatics sg; (exercice) acrobatic feat; **~ aérienne** aerobatics sg

acrobatique [akʀɔbatik] ADJ acrobatic

acronyme [akʀɔnim] NM acronym

Acropole [akʀɔpɔl] NF: **l'~** the Acropolis

acrosport [akʀɔspɔʀ] NM acrosport

acrostiche [akʀɔstiʃ] NM (poème) acrostic

acrylique [akʀilik] ADJ, NM acrylic

acte [akt] NM act, action; (Théât) act; **prendre ~ de** to note, take note of; **faire ~ de présence** to put in an appearance; **faire ~ de candidature** to submit an application; **~ d'accusation** charge (BRIT), bill of indictment; **~ de baptême** baptismal certificate; **~ de mariage/naissance** marriage/birth certificate; **~ de vente** bill of sale ▪ **actes** NMPL (compte-rendu) proceedings

★**acteur** [aktœʀ] NM actor

★**actif, -ive** [aktif, -iv] ADJ active; **prendre une part active à qch** to take an active part in sth; **population active** working population ▶ NM (Comm) assets pl; (Ling) active (voice); (fig): **avoir à son ~** to have to one's credit; **mettre à son ~** to add to one's list of achievements; **~ toxique** toxic asset; **l'~ et le passif** assets and liabilities ▪ **actifs** NMPL people in employment

action [aksjɔ̃] NF (gén) action; (Comm) share; **une bonne/mauvaise ~** a good/an unkind deed; **mettre en ~** to put into action; **passer à l'~** to take action; **sous l'~ de** under the effect of; **l'~ syndicale** (the) union action; **un film d'~** an action film ou movie; **~ en diffamation** libel action; **~ de grâce(s)** (Rel) thanksgiving

actionnaire [aksjɔnɛʀ] NMF shareholder

actionnariat [aksjɔnaʀja] NM (statut) shareholding; (actionnaires) shareholders pl

actionner [aksjɔne] /1/ VT to work; (mécanisme) to activate; (machine) to operate

activation [aktivasjɔ̃] NF (de dispositif, logiciel) activation; (Bio, Chimie: de gène, cellule) activation

active [aktiv] ADJ F voir **actif**

activement [aktivmɑ̃] ADV actively

activer [aktive] /1/ VT (dispositif, logiciel) to activate; (Bio, Chimie) to activate ◼ **s'activer** VPR (s'affairer) to bustle about; (se hâter) to hurry up

activisme [aktivism] NM activism

activiste [aktivist] NMF activist

activité [aktivite] NF activity; **en ~** (volcan) active; (fonctionnaire) in active life; (militaire) on active service

★**actrice** [aktʀis] NF actress

actualisation [aktɥalizasjɔ̃] NF (de connaissances, réglementation, base de données) updating; (Finance: de valeur, coûts) conversion to current value

actualiser [aktɥalize] /1/ VT (connaissances) to bring up to date; (base de données) to update

actualité [aktɥalite] NF (d'un problème) topicality; (événements): **les actualités** current events; **l'~** (Ciné, TV) the news; **l'~ politique/sportive** the political/sports ou sporting news; **les actualités télévisées** the television news; **d'~** topical

actuel, le [aktɥɛl] ADJ (présent) present; (d'actualité) topical; **à l'heure actuelle** at this moment in time, at the moment

---
actuel is not usually translated by actual.

★**actuellement** [aktɥɛlmɑ̃] ADV at present, at the present time

acuité [akɥite] NF acuteness

acuponcteur, acupuncteur [akypɔ̃ktœʀ] NM acupuncturist

acuponcture, acupuncture [akypɔ̃ktyʀ] NF acupuncture

adage [adaʒ] NM adage

adagio [ada(d)ʒjo] ADV, NM adagio

adaptable [adaptabl] ADJ adaptable

adaptateur, -trice [adaptatœʀ, -tʀis] NM/F adapter

adaptation [adaptasjɔ̃] NF adaptation

adapter [adapte] /1/ VT to adapt; **~ qch à** (approprier) to adapt sth to (fit); **~ qch sur/dans/à** (fixer) to fit sth on/into/to ◼ **s'adapter** VPR: **s'~ (à)** (personne) to adapt (to); (objet, prise etc) to apply (to)

addenda [adɛda] NM INV addenda

addictologie [adiktɔlɔʒi] NF addiction studies pl

Addis-Ababa [adisababa], **Addis-Abeba** [adisababa] N Addis Ababa

additif [aditif] NM additional clause; (substance) additive; **~ alimentaire** food additive

★**addition** [adisjɔ̃] NF addition; (au café) bill

additionnel, le [adisjɔnɛl] ADJ additional

additionner [adisjɔne] /1/ VT to add (up); **~ un produit d'eau** to add water to a product ◼ **s'additionner** VPR to add up

adduction [adyksjɔ̃] NF (de gaz, d'eau) conveyance

adepte [adɛpt] NMF follower

adéquat, e [adekwa(t), -at] ADJ appropriate, suitable

adéquation [adekwasjɔ̃] NF appropriateness; (Ling) adequacy

adhérence [adeʀɑ̃s] NF adhesion

adhérent, e [adeʀɑ̃, -ɑ̃t] NM/F (de club) member

adhérer [adeʀe] /6/ VI (coller) to adhere, stick; **~ à** (coller) to adhere ou stick to; (se rallier à: parti, club) to join, be a member of; (: opinion, mouvement) to support

adhésif, -ive [adezif, -iv] ADJ adhesive, sticky; **ruban ~** sticky ou adhesive tape ▶ NM adhesive

adhésion [adezjɔ̃] NF (à un club) joining; membership; (à une opinion) support

ad hoc [adɔk] ADJ INV ad hoc

adieu, x [adjø] EXCL goodbye ▶ NM farewell; **dire ~ à qn** to say goodbye ou farewell to sb; **dire ~ à qch** (renoncer) to say ou wave goodbye to sth

adipeux, -euse [adipø, -øz] ADJ bloated, fat; (Anat) adipose

adiposité [adipozite] NF adiposity

adjacent, e [adʒasɑ̃, -ɑ̃t] ADJ: **~ (à)** adjacent (to)

adjectif [adʒɛktif] NM adjective; **~ attribut** adjectival complement; **~ épithète** attributive adjective

adjectival, e, -aux [adʒɛktival, -o] ADJ adjectival

adjoignais etc [adʒwaɲɛ] VB voir **adjoindre**

adjoindre [adʒwɛ̃dʀ] /49/ VT: **~ qch à** to attach sth to; (ajouter) to add sth to; **~ qn à** (personne) to appoint sb as an assistant to; (comité) to appoint sb to, attach sb to ◼ **s'adjoindre** VPR (collaborateur etc) to take on, appoint

adjoint, e [adʒwɛ̃, -wɛ̃t] PP de **adjoindre** ▶ NM/F assistant; **~ au maire** deputy mayor; **directeur ~** assistant manager

adjonction [adʒɔ̃ksjɔ̃] NF attaching; addition; appointment

adjudant [adʒydɑ̃] NM (Mil) warrant officer; **adjudant-chef** ≈ warrant officer 1st class (BRIT), ≈ chief warrant officer (US)

adjudicataire [adʒydikatɛʀ] NMF successful bidder, purchaser; (pour travaux) successful tenderer (BRIT) ou bidder (US)

adjudicateur, -trice [adʒydikatœʀ, -tʀis] NM/F (aux enchères) seller

adjudication [adʒydikasjɔ̃] NF sale by auction; (pour travaux) invitation to tender (BRIT) ou bid (US)

adjuger [adʒyʒe] /3/ VT (prix, récompense) to award; (lors d'une vente) to auction (off); **adjugé!** (vendu) gone!, sold! ◼ **s'adjuger** VPR to take for o.s.

adjurer [adʒyʀe] /1/ VT: **~ qn de faire** to implore ou beg sb to do

adjuvant [adʒyvɑ̃] NM (médicament) adjuvant; (additif) additive; (stimulant) stimulant

admettre [admɛtʀ] /56/ VT (visiteur) to admit, let in; (candidat: Scol) to pass; (Tech: gaz, eau, air) to admit; (tolérer) to allow, accept; (reconnaître) to admit, acknowledge; (supposer) to suppose; **j'admets que ...** I admit that ...; **je n'admets pas que tu fasses cela** I won't allow you to do that; **admettons que ...** let's suppose that ...; **admettons** let's suppose so

administrateur, -trice [administʀatœʀ, -tʀis] NM/F (Comm) director; (Admin) administrator; **~ délégué** managing director; **~ judiciaire** receiver

administratif, -ive [administʀatif, -iv] ADJ administrative

7

administration [administRasjɔ̃] NF administration; **l'A~** ≈ the Civil Service

administrativement [administRativmɑ̃] ADV (rattaché, dépendre) for administrative purposes

administré, e [administRe] NM/F ≈ citizen

administrer [administRe] /1/ VT (firme) to manage, run; (biens, remède, sacrement etc) to administer

admirable [admiRabl] ADJ admirable, wonderful

admirablement [admiRabləmɑ̃] ADV admirably

admirateur, -trice [admiRatœR, -tRis] NM/F admirer

admiratif, -ive [admiRatif, -iv] ADJ admiring

admiration [admiRasjɔ̃] NF admiration; **être en ~ devant** to be lost in admiration before

admirativement [admiRativmɑ̃] ADV admiringly

★**admirer** [admiRe] /1/ VT to admire

admis, e [admi, -iz] PP de **admettre**

admissibilité [admisibilite] NF eligibility; admissibility, acceptability

admissible [admisibl] ADJ (candidat) eligible; (comportement) admissible, acceptable; (Jur) receivable

admission [admisjɔ̃] NF admission; **tuyau d'~** intake pipe; **demande d'~** application for membership; **service des admissions** admissions

admonester [admɔnɛste] /1/ VT to admonish

ADN SIGLE M (= acide désoxyribonucléique) DNA

ado [ado] NMF (fam: = adolescent(e)) ado, teenager, adolescent

adolescence [adɔlesɑ̃s] NF adolescence

★**adolescent, e** [adɔlesɑ̃, -ɑ̃t] NM/F adolescent, teenager

adonner [adɔne] /1/: **s'adonner à** VPR (sport) to devote o.s. to; (boisson) to give o.s. over to

adopter [adɔpte] /1/ VT to adopt; (projet de loi etc) to pass

adoptif, -ive [adɔptif, -iv] ADJ (parents) adoptive; (fils, patrie) adopted

adoption [adɔpsjɔ̃] NF adoption; **son pays/sa ville d'~** his adopted country/town

adorable [adɔRabl] ADJ adorable

adoration [adɔRasjɔ̃] NF adoration; (Rel) worship; **être en ~ devant** to be lost in adoration before

★**adorer** [adɔRe] /1/ VT to adore; (Rel) to worship

adossé, e [adose] ADJ: **~ à** (mur, contreforts: personne) leaning against; (: maison) built right up against

adosser [adose] /1/ VT: **~ qch à** ou **contre** to stand sth against ■ **s'adosser** VPR: **s'~ à** ou **contre** to lean with one's back against

adouber [adube] VT (Hist: vassal) to dub; (nommer: successeur, ministre) to name

adoucir [adusiR] /2/ VT (goût, température) to make milder; (avec du sucre) to sweeten; (peau, voix, eau) to soften; (caractère, personne) to mellow; (peine) to soothe, allay ■ **s'adoucir** VPR to become milder; to soften; (caractère) to mellow

adoucissant [adusisɑ̃] NM (pour le linge) fabric softener

adoucissement [adusismɑ̃] NM becoming milder; sweetening; softening; mellowing; soothing

adoucisseur [adusisœR] NM: **~ (d'eau)** water softener

adr. ABR = **adresse; adresser**

adrénaline [adRenalin] NF adrenaline

★**adresse** [adRɛs] NF skill, dexterity; (domicile, Inform) address; **à l'~ de** (pour) for the benefit of; **~ électronique** email address; **~ Web** web address

adresser [adRese] /1/ VT (lettre: expédier) to send; (: écrire l'adresse sur) to address; (injure, compliments) to address; **~ qn à un docteur/bureau** to refer ou send sb to a doctor/an office; **~ la parole à qn** to speak to ou address sb ■ **s'adresser** VPR: **s'~ à** (parler à) to speak to, address; (s'informer auprès de) to go and see, go and speak to; (: bureau) to enquire at; (livre, conseil) to be aimed at

Adriatique [adRijatik] NF: **l'~** the Adriatic

adroit, e [adRwa, -wat] ADJ (joueur, mécanicien) skilful (BRIT), skillful (US), dext(e)rous; (politicien etc) shrewd, skilled

adroitement [adRwatmɑ̃] ADV skilfully (BRIT), skillfully (US), dext(e)rously; shrewdly

AdS SIGLE F = **Académie des Sciences**

ADSL SIGLE M (= asymmetrical digital subscriber line) ADSL, broadband; **avoir l'~** to have broadband

adulation [adylasjɔ̃] NF adulation

aduler [adyle] /1/ VT to adulate

★**adulte** [adylt] NMF adult, grown-up; **formation/ film pour adultes** adult training/film ▶ ADJ (personne, attitude) adult, grown-up; (chien, arbre) fully-grown, mature; **l'âge ~** adulthood

adultère [adyltɛR] ADJ adulterous ▶ NMF adulterer/adulteress ▶ NM (acte) adultery

adultérin, e [adylteRɛ̃, -in] ADJ born of adultery

advenir [advəniR] /22/ VI to happen; **qu'est-il advenu de …?** what has become of …?; **quoi qu'il advienne** whatever befalls ou happens

adventiste [advɑ̃tist] NMF (Rel) Adventist

adverbe [advɛRb] NM adverb; **~ de manière** adverb of manner

adverbial, e, -aux [advɛRbjal, -o] ADJ adverbial

adversaire [advɛRsɛR] NMF (Sport, gén) opponent, adversary; (Mil) adversary, enemy

adverse [advɛRs] ADJ opposing

adversité [advɛRsite] NF adversity

AELE SIGLE F (= Association européenne de libre-échange) EFTA (= European Free Trade Association)

AEN SIGLE F (= Agence pour l'énergie nucléaire) ≈ AEA (= Atomic Energy Authority)

aérateur [aeRatœR] NM ventilator

aération [aeRasjɔ̃] NF airing; (circulation de l'air) ventilation; **conduit d'~** ventilation shaft; **bouche d'~** air vent

aéré, e [aeRe] ADJ (pièce, local) airy, well-ventilated; (tissu) loose-woven; **centre ~** outdoor centre

aérer [aeRe] /6/ VT to air; (fig) to lighten ■ **s'aérer** VPR to get some (fresh) air

aérien, ne [aeRjɛ̃, -ɛn] ADJ (Aviat) air cpd, aerial; (câble, métro) overhead; (fig) light; **compagnie aérienne** airline (company); **ligne aérienne** airline

aérobic [aeRɔbik] NF aerobics sg

aérobie [aeRɔbi] ADJ aerobic

aéro-club [aeRɔklœb] NM flying club

a

aérodrome [aeʀɔdʀɔm] NM airfield, aerodrome

aérodynamique [aeʀɔdinamik] ADJ aerodynamic, streamlined ▸ NF aerodynamics *sg*

aérofrein [aeʀɔfʀɛ̃] NM air brake

aérogare [aeʀɔgaʀ] NF airport (buildings); *(en ville)* air terminal

aéroglisseur [aeʀɔglisœʀ] NM hovercraft

aérogramme [aeʀɔgʀam] NM air letter, aerogram(me)

aéromodélisme [aeʀɔmɔdelism] NM model aircraft making

aéronaute [aeʀɔnot] NMF aeronaut

aéronautique [aeʀɔnotik] ADJ aeronautical ▸ NF aeronautics *sg*

aéronaval, e [aeʀɔnaval] ADJ air and sea *cpd*

Aéronavale [aeʀɔnaval] NF ≈ Fleet Air Arm (BRIT), ≈ Naval Air Force (US)

aéronef [aeʀɔnɛf] NM aircraft

aérophagie [aeʀɔfaʒi] NF wind; *(Méd)* aerophagia; **il fait de l'~** he suffers from abdominal wind

aéroport [aeʀɔpɔʀ] NM airport; **~ d'embarquement** departure airport

aéroporté, e [aeʀɔpɔʀte] ADJ airborne, airlifted

aéroportuaire [aeʀɔpɔʀtɥɛʀ] ADJ of an *ou* the airport, airport *cpd*

aéropostal, e, -aux [aeʀɔpɔstal, -o] ADJ airmail *cpd*

aérosol [aeʀɔsɔl] NM aerosol

aérospatial, e, -aux [aeʀɔspasjal, -o] ADJ aerospace ▸ NF the aerospace industry

aérostat [aeʀɔsta] NM aerostat

aérotrain [aeʀɔtʀɛ̃] NM hovertrain

AF SIGLE FPL = **allocations familiales** ▸ SIGLE F *(SUISSE)* = **Assemblée fédérale**

affabilité [afabilite] NF affability

affable [afabl] ADJ affable

affabulateur, -trice [afabylatœʀ, -tʀis] NM/F storyteller

affabulation [afabylasjɔ̃] NF invention, fantasy

affabuler [afabyle] /1/ VI to make up stories

affacturage [afaktyʀaʒ] NM factoring

affadir [afadiʀ] /2/ VT to make insipid *ou* tasteless ▪ **s'affadir** to become insipid *ou* tasteless

affaibli, e [afebli] ADJ *(parti, autorité)* weakened; *(personne, voix)* weak

affaiblir [afebliʀ] /2/ VT *(parti, autorité)* to weaken ▪ **s'affaiblir** VPR to weaken, grow weaker; *(vue)* to grow dim

affaiblissement [afeblismɑ̃] NM weakening

★**affaire** [afeʀ] NF *(problème, question)* matter; *(criminelle, judiciaire)* case; *(scandaleuse etc)* affair; *(entreprise)* business; *(marché, transaction)* (business) deal, *(piece of)* business *no pl*; *(occasion intéressante)* good deal; **tirer qn/se tirer d'~** to get sb/o.s. out of trouble; **ceci fera l'~** this will do (nicely); **avoir ~ à** *(comme adversaire)* to be faced with; *(en contact)* to be dealing with; **tu auras ~ à moi !** *(menace)* you'll have me to contend with!; **c'est une ~ de goût/d'argent** it's a question *ou* matter of taste/money; **c'est l'~ d'une minute/heure** it'll only take a minute/an hour ▪ **affaires** NFPL affairs; *(activité commerciale)* business *sg*; *(effets personnels)* things, belongings; **affaires de sport** sports gear; **ce sont mes affaires** *(cela me concerne)* that's my business; **occupe-toi de tes affaires !** mind your own business!; **toutes affaires cessantes** forthwith; **les affaires étrangères** *(Pol)* foreign affairs

affairé, e [afeʀe] ADJ busy

affairer [afeʀe] /1/: **s'affairer** VPR to busy o.s., bustle about

affairisme [afeʀism] NM wheeling and dealing

affairiste [afeʀist] NMF wheeler-dealer

affaissé, e [afese] ADJ *(sol, épaules)* sagging

affaissement [afɛsmɑ̃] NM subsidence; collapse

affaisser [afese] /1/: **s'affaisser** VPR *(terrain, immeuble)* to subside, sink; *(personne)* to collapse; *(dos, épaules)* to sag

affalé, e [afale] ADJ: **~ dans un fauteuil** slumped in an armchair; **~ sur un banc** slumped on a bench

affaler [afale] /1/: **s'affaler** VPR: **s'~ dans/sur** to collapse *ou* slump into/onto

affamé, e [afame] ADJ starving, famished

affamer [afame] /1/ VT to starve

affectation [afɛktasjɔ̃] NF allotment; appointment; posting; affectedness

affecté, e [afɛkte] ADJ affected

affecter [afɛkte] /1/ VT *(émouvoir)* to affect, move; *(feindre)* to affect, feign; *(telle ou telle forme etc)* to take on, assume; **~ qch à** to allocate *ou* allot sth to; **~ qn à** to appoint sb to; *(diplomate)* to post sb to; **~ qch de** *(de coefficient)* to modify sth by

affectif, -ive [afɛktif, -iv] ADJ emotional, affective

affection [afɛksjɔ̃] NF affection; *(mal)* ailment; **avoir de l'~ pour** to feel affection for; **prendre en ~** to become fond of

affectionner [afɛksjɔne] /1/ VT to be fond of

affectueusement [afɛktɥøzmɑ̃] ADV affectionately

affectueux, -euse [afɛktɥø, -øz] ADJ affectionate

afférent, e [afeʀɑ̃, -ɑ̃t] ADJ: **~ à** pertaining *ou* relating to

affermir [afɛʀmiʀ] /2/ VT to consolidate, strengthen ▪ **s'affermir** VPR *(tendance, position)* to become stronger; *(peau, muscles)* to become firmer

affichage [afiʃaʒ] NM billposting, billsticking; *(électronique)* display; « **~ interdit** » "stick no bills", "billsticking prohibited"; **~ à cristaux liquides** liquid crystal display, LCD; **~ numérique** *ou* **digital** digital display

★**affiche** [afiʃ] NF poster; *(officielle)* (public) notice; *(Théât)* bill; **être à l'~** *(Théât)* to be on; **tenir l'~** to run

affiché, e [afiʃe] ADJ *(ambition, volonté, optimisme)* declared

afficher [afiʃe] /1/ VT *(affiche)* to put up, post up; *(réunion)* to put up a notice about; *(électroniquement)* to display; *(fig)* to exhibit, display; « **défense d'~** » "no bill posters" ▪ **s'afficher** VPR *(péj)* to flaunt o.s.; *(électroniquement)* to be displayed

affichette [afiʃɛt] NF small poster *ou* notice

affilé, e [afile] ADJ sharp

affilée [afile]: **d'~** *adv* at a stretch

affiler [afile] /**1**/ VT to sharpen

affiliation [afiljasjɔ̃] NF affiliation

affilié, e [afilje] ADJ: **être ~ à** to be affiliated to ▶ NM/F affiliated party *ou* member

affilier [afilje] /**7**/: **s'affilier à** VPR to become affiliated to

affinage [afinaʒ] NM (*de fromages, des huîtres*) maturing; (*de métaux*) refining

affiner [afine] /**1**/ VT (*métaux, concept*) to refine; (*fromages*) to mature; (*huîtres*) to allow to mature ▪ **s'affiner** VPR to become (more) refined

affinité [afinite] NF affinity

affirmatif, -ive [afiʀmatif, -iv] ADJ affirmative ▶ NF: **répondre par l'affirmative** to reply in the affirmative; **dans l'affirmative** (*si oui*) if (the answer is) yes ..., if he does (*ou* you do *etc*) ...

affirmation [afiʀmasjɔ̃] NF assertion

affirmativement [afiʀmativmɑ̃] ADV affirmatively, in the affirmative

affirmé, e [afiʀme] ADJ (*volonté*) declared; (*personnalité*) assertive

affirmer [afiʀme] /**1**/ VT (*prétendre*) to maintain, assert; (*autorité*) to assert ▪ **s'affirmer** VPR to assert o.s.; to assert itself

affleurer [aflœʀe] /**1**/ VI to show on the surface

affliction [afliksjɔ̃] NF affliction

affligé, e [afliʒe] ADJ distressed, grieved; **~ de** (*maladie, tare*) afflicted with

affligeant, e [afliʒɑ̃, -ɑ̃t] ADJ distressing

affliger [afliʒe] /**3**/ VT (*peiner*) to distress, grieve ▪ **s'affliger** VPR (*être attristé*): **s'~ de** to be distressed about

affluence [aflyɑ̃s] NF crowds *pl*; **heures d'~** rush hour *sg*; **jours d'~** busiest days

affluent [aflyɑ̃] NM tributary

affluer [aflye] /**1**/ VI (*secours, biens*) to flood in, pour in; (*sang*) to rush, flow

afflux [afly] NM flood, influx; rush

affolant, e [afɔlɑ̃, -ɑ̃t] ADJ terrifying

affolé, e [afɔle] ADJ panic-stricken, panicky

affolement [afɔlmɑ̃] NM panic

affoler [afɔle] /**1**/ VT to throw into a panic ▪ **s'affoler** VPR to panic

affranchi, e [afʀɑ̃ʃi] ADJ (*lettre*) stamped; **~ de qch** (*conventions, entraves*) liberated from sth; **esprit ~** free spirit

affranchir [afʀɑ̃ʃiʀ] /**2**/ VT (*lettre*) to put a stamp *ou* stamps on; (*à la machine*) to frank (BRIT), meter (US); (*esclave*) to enfranchise, emancipate; (*fig*) to free, liberate; **machine à ~** franking machine, postage meter ▪ **s'affranchir de** VPR to free o.s. from

affranchissement [afʀɑ̃ʃismɑ̃] NM (*Postes*) franking (BRIT), metering (US); (*prix payé*) postage; (*des esclaves*) freeing; **tarifs d'~** postage rates

affres [afʀ] NFPL: **dans les ~ de** in the throes of

affréter [afʀete] /**6**/ VT to charter

affreusement [afʀøzmɑ̃] ADV dreadfully, awfully

★**affreux, -euse** [afʀø, -øz] ADJ dreadful, awful

affriolant, e [afʀijɔlɑ̃, -ɑ̃t] ADJ tempting, enticing

affront [afʀɔ̃] NM affront

affrontement [afʀɔ̃tmɑ̃] NM (*Mil, Pol*) clash, confrontation

affronter [afʀɔ̃te] /**1**/ VT to confront, face ▪ **s'affronter** VPR to confront each other

affubler [afyble] /**1**/ VT (*péj*): **~ qn de** to rig *ou* deck sb out in; (*surnom*) to attach to sb

affût [afy] NM (*de canon*) gun carriage; **à l'~ (de)** (*gibier*) lying in wait (for); (*fig*) on the look-out (for)

affûter [afyte] /**1**/ VT to sharpen, grind

afghan, e [afgɑ̃, -an] ADJ Afghan

Afghanistan [afganistɑ̃] NM: **l'~** Afghanistan

afin [afɛ̃]: **~ que** *conj* so that, in order that; **~ de faire** in order to do, so as to do

AFNOR [afnɔʀ] SIGLE F (= *Association française de normalisation*) industrial standards authority

a fortiori [afɔʀsjɔʀi] ADV all the more, a fortiori

AFP SIGLE F = **Agence France-Presse**

AFPA SIGLE F = **Association pour la formation professionnelle des adultes**

★**africain, e** [afʀikɛ̃, -ɛn] ADJ African ▶ NM/F: **Africain, e** African

afrikaans [afʀikɑ̃] NM, ADJ INV Afrikaans

afrikaner [afʀikanɛʀ] ADJ Afrikaner ▶ NM/F: **Afrikaner** Afrikaner

★**Afrique** [afʀik] NF: **l'~** Africa; **l'~ australe/du Nord/du Sud** southern/North/South Africa

afro [afʀo] ADJ INV: **coupe ~** afro hairstyle ▶ NMF: **Afro** Afro

afro-américain, e [afʀoamerikɛ̃, -ɛn] ADJ Afro-American

AG SIGLE F = **assemblée générale**

ag. ABR = **agence**

agaçant, e [agasɑ̃, -ɑ̃t] ADJ irritating, aggravating

agacement [agasmɑ̃] NM irritation, aggravation

★**agacer** [agase] /**3**/ VT to pester, tease; (*involontairement*) to irritate, aggravate ▪ **s'agacer** VPR to get annoyed; **s'~ de qch** to get annoyed about sth

agapes [agap] NFPL (*humoristique: festin*) feast

agate [agat] NF agate

agave [agav] NM agave

AGE SIGLE F = **assemblée générale extraordinaire**

★**âge** [ɑʒ] NM age; **quel ~ as-tu?** how old are you? **une femme d'un certain ~** a middle-aged woman, a woman who is getting on (in years); **bien porter son ~** to wear well; **prendre de l'~** to be getting on (in years), grow older; **limite d'~** age limit; **dispense d'~** special exemption from age limit; **le troisième ~** (*personnes âgées*) senior citizens; (*période*) retirement; **l'~ ingrat** the awkward *ou* difficult age; **~ légal** legal age; **~ mental** mental age; **l'~ mûr** maturity, middle age; **~ de raison** age of reason

★**âgé, e** [ɑʒe] ADJ old, elderly; **~ de 10 ans** 10 years old

★**agence** [aʒɑ̃s] NF agency, office; (*succursale*) branch; **~ immobilière** estate agent's (office) (BRIT), real estate office (US); **~ matrimoniale** marriage bureau; **~ de placement** employment agency; **~ de publicité** advertising agency; **~ de voyages** travel agency

agencé, e [aʒɑ̃se] ADJ: **bien/mal ~** well/badly put together; well/badly laid out ou arranged

agencement [aʒɑ̃smɑ̃] NM putting together; arrangement, laying out

agencer [aʒɑ̃se] /3/ VT to put together; (local) to arrange, lay out

agenda [aʒɛ̃da] NM diary; **~ électronique** PDA

agenouillé, e [aʒ(ə)nuje] ADJ kneeling, kneeling down

agenouiller [aʒ(ə)nuje] /1/: **s'agenouiller** VPR to kneel (down)

agent, e [aʒɑ̃, -ɑ̃t] NM/F (aussi: **agent(e) de police**) policeman (policewoman); (Admin) official, officer; (fig: élément, facteur) agent; **~ d'assurances** insurance broker; **~ de change** stockbroker; **~ commercial** sales representative; **~ immobilier** estate agent (BRIT), realtor (US); **~ (secret)** (secret) agent

agglo [aglo] NM (fam) = **aggloméré**

agglomérat [aglɔmeʀa] NM (Géo) agglomerate

agglomération [aglɔmeʀasjɔ̃] NF town; (Auto) built-up area; **l'~ parisienne** the urban area of Paris

aggloméré [aglɔmeʀe] NM (bois) chipboard; (pierre) conglomerate

agglomérer [aglɔmeʀe] /6/ VT to pile up; (Tech: bois, pierre) to compress ■ **s'agglomérer** VPR to pile up

agglutiner [aglytine] /1/ VT to stick together ■ **s'agglutiner** VPR to congregate

aggravant, e [agʀavɑ̃, -ɑ̃t] ADJ: **circonstances aggravantes** aggravating circumstances

aggravation [agʀavasjɔ̃] NF worsening, aggravation; increase

aggraver [agʀave] /1/ VT to worsen, aggravate; (Jur: peine) to increase; **~ son cas** to make one's case worse ■ **s'aggraver** VPR to worsen

agile [aʒil] ADJ agile, nimble

agilement [aʒilmɑ̃] ADV nimbly

agilité [aʒilite] NF agility, nimbleness

agios [aʒjo] NMPL bank charges, charges

★**agir** [aʒiʀ] /2/ VI (se comporter) to behave, act; (faire quelque chose) to act, take action; (avoir de l'effet) to act; **il s'agit de** it's a matter ou question of; (ça traite de) it is about; (il importe que): **il s'agit de faire** we (ou you etc) must do; **de quoi s'agit-il?** what is it about?

agissements [aʒismɑ̃] NMPL (péj) schemes, intrigues

agitateur, -trice [aʒitatœʀ, -tʀis] NM/F agitator

agitation [aʒitasjɔ̃] NF (hustle and) bustle; (trouble) agitation, excitement; (politique) unrest, agitation

agité, e [aʒite] ADJ (remuant) fidgety, restless; (troublé) agitated, perturbed; (journée) hectic; (mer) rough; (sommeil) disturbed, broken

★**agiter** [aʒite] /1/ VT (bouteille, chiffon) to shake; (bras, mains) to wave; (préoccuper, exciter) to trouble, perturb; **«~ avant l'emploi»** "shake before use" ■ **s'agiter** VPR to bustle about; (dormeur) to toss and turn; (enfant) to fidget; (Pol) to grow restless

★**agneau, x** [aɲo] NM lamb; (toison) lambswool

agnelet [aɲ(ə)lɛ] NM little lamb

agnostique [agnɔstik] ADJ, NMF agnostic

agonie [agɔni] NF mortal agony, death pangs pl; (fig) death throes pl

agonir [agɔniʀ] /2/ VT: **~ qn d'injures** to hurl abuse at sb

agoniser [agɔnize] /1/ VI to be dying; (fig) to be in its death throes

agoraphobe [agɔʀafɔb] ADJ agoraphobic

agoraphobie [agɔʀafɔbi] NF agoraphobia

agrafe [agʀaf] NF (de vêtement) hook, fastener; (de bureau) staple; (Méd) clip

agrafer [agʀafe] /1/ VT to fasten; to staple

agrafeuse [agʀaføz] NF stapler

agraire [agʀɛʀ] ADJ agrarian; (mesure, surface) land cpd

★**agrandir** [agʀɑ̃diʀ] /2/ VT (magasin, domaine) to extend, enlarge; (trou) to enlarge, make bigger; (Photo) to enlarge, blow up ■ **s'agrandir** VPR (ville, famille) to grow, expand; (trou, écart) to get bigger

agrandissement [agʀɑ̃dismɑ̃] NM extension; enlargement; (photographie) enlargement

agrandisseur [agʀɑ̃disœʀ] NM (Photo) enlarger

agréable [agʀeabl] ADJ pleasant, nice

agréablement [agʀeabləmɑ̃] ADV pleasantly

agréé, e [agʀee] ADJ: **concessionnaire ~** registered dealer; **magasin ~** registered dealer('s)

agréer [agʀee] /1/ VT (requête) to accept; **~ à** vt to please, suit; **veuillez ~, Monsieur/Madame, mes salutations distinguées** (personne nommée) yours sincerely; (personne non nommée) yours faithfully

agrég [agʀɛg] NF (fam) = **agrégation**

agrégat [agʀega] NM aggregate

agrégateur [agʀegatœʀ] NM (Inform) aggregator

agrégation [agʀegasjɔ̃] NF highest teaching diploma in France

agrégé, e [agʀeʒe] NM/F holder of the agrégation

agréger [agʀeʒe] /3/: **s'agréger** VPR to aggregate

agrément [agʀemɑ̃] NM (accord) consent, approval; (attraits) charm, attractiveness; (plaisir) pleasure; **voyage d'~** pleasure trip

agrémenter [agʀemɑ̃te] /1/ VT: **~ (de)** to embellish (with), adorn (with)

agrès [agʀɛ] NMPL (gymnastics) apparatus sg

agresser [agʀese] /1/ VT to attack

agresseur [agʀesœʀ] NM aggressor, attacker; (Pol, Mil) aggressor

agressif, -ive [agʀesif, -iv] ADJ aggressive

agression [agʀesjɔ̃] NF attack; (Pol, Mil, Psych) aggression

agressivement [agʀesivmɑ̃] ADV aggressively

agressivité [agʀesivite] NF aggressiveness

agreste [agʀɛst] ADJ rustic

★**agricole** [agʀikɔl] ADJ agricultural, farm cpd

★**agriculteur, -trice** [agʀikyltœʀ, -tʀis] NM/F farmer

★**agriculture** [agʀikyltyʀ] NF agriculture; farming

agripper [agʀipe] /1/ VT to grab, clutch; (pour arracher) to snatch, grab ■ **s'agripper à** VPR to cling (on) to, clutch, grip

agritourisme [agʀituʀism] NM agritourism

agroalimentaire [agroalimãtɛr] ADJ farming *cpd* ▶ NM farm-produce industry; **l'~** agribusiness

agrocarburant [agrokarbyrã] NM agrofuel

agro-industrie [agroɛ̃dystri] NF: **l'~** agribusiness; **les agro-industries** agribusiness

agronome [agrɔnɔm] NMF agronomist

agronomie [agrɔnɔmi] NF agronomy

agronomique [agrɔnɔmik] ADJ agronomic(al)

agrume [agrym] NM citrus fruit

aguerri, e [ageri] ADJ (*soldat, sportif, homme politique*) battle-hardened

aguerrir [agerir] /2/ VT to harden ■ **s'aguerrir** VPR: **s'~ (contre)** to become hardened (to)

aguets [agɛ]: **aux ~** *adv*: **être aux ~** to be on the look-out

aguichant, e [agiʃã, -ãt] ADJ enticing

aguicher [agiʃe] /1/ VT to entice

aguicheur, -euse [agiʃœr, -øz] ADJ enticing

ah [ɑ] EXCL ah!; **ah bon?** really?, is that so?; **ah mais …** yes, but …; **ah non!** oh no!

ahuri, e [ayri] ADJ (*stupéfait*) flabbergasted; (*idiot*) dim-witted

ahurir [ayrir] /2/ VT to stupefy, stagger

ahurissant, e [ayrisã, -ãt] ADJ stupefying, staggering, mind-boggling

ai [ɛ] VB *voir* **avoir**

★**aide** [ɛd] NMF assistant; **~ de camp** *nmf* aide-de-camp; **~ comptable** *nmf* accountant's assistant; **~ électricien** *nmf* electrician's mate; **~ de laboratoire** *nmf* laboratory assistant ▶ NF assistance, help; (*secours financier*) aid; **à l'~ de** with the help ou aid of; **aller à l'~ de qn** to go to sb's aid, go to help sb; **venir en ~ à qn** to help sb, come to sb's assistance; **appeler (qn) à l'~** to call for help (from sb); **à l'~!** help!; **~ familiale** *nf* mother's help, ≈ home help; **~ judiciaire** *nf* legal aid; **~ ménagère** *nf* ≈ home help (Brit) ou helper (US); **~ technique** *nf* ≈ VSO (Brit) ≈ Peace Corps (US); **~ sociale** *nf* (*assistance*) state aid

aide-éducateur, -trice [ɛdedykatœr, -tris] NM/F classroom assistant

aide-mémoire [ɛdmemwar] NM INV memoranda pages *pl*; (*key facts*) handbook

★**aider** [ede] /1/ VT to help; **~ à qch** to help (towards) sth; **~ qn à faire qch** to help sb to do sth ■ **s'aider de** VPR (*se servir de*) to use, make use of

aide-soignant, e [ɛdswaɲã, -ãt] NM/F auxiliary nurse

aie *etc* [ɛ] VB *voir* **avoir**

aïe [aj] EXCL ouch!

AIEA SIGLE F (= *Agence internationale de l'énergie atomique*) IAEA (= *International Atomic Energy Agency*)

aïeul, e [ajœl] NM/F grandparent, grandfather/grandmother; (*ancêtre*) forebear

aïeux [ajø] NMPL grandparents; forebears, forefathers

aigle [ɛgl] NM eagle

aiglefin [ɛgləfɛ̃] NM = **églefin**

aigre [ɛgr] ADJ sour, sharp; (*fig*) sharp, cutting; **tourner à l'~** to turn sour

aigre-doux, -douce [ɛgrədu, -dus] ADJ (*fruit*) bitter-sweet; (*sauce*) sweet and sour

aigrefin [ɛgrəfɛ̃] NM swindler

aigrelet, te [ɛgrəlɛ, -ɛt] ADJ (*goût*) sourish; (*voix, son*) sharpish

aigrette [ɛgrɛt] NF (*plume*) feather

aigreur [ɛgrœr] NF sourness; sharpness; **aigreurs d'estomac** heartburn *sg*

aigri, e [egri] ADJ embittered

aigrir [egrir] /2/ VT (*personne*) to embitter; (*caractère*) to sour ■ **s'aigrir** VPR to become embittered; to sour; (*lait etc*) to turn sour

★**aigu, ë** [egy] ADJ (*objet, arête*) sharp, pointed; (*son, voix*) high-pitched, shrill; (*note*) high(-pitched); (*douleur, intelligence*) acute, sharp

aigue-marine [ɛgmarin] (*pl* **aigues-marines**) NF aquamarine

aiguillage [eguijaʒ] NM (Rail) points *pl*

aiguille [eguij] NF needle; (*de montre*) hand; **~ à tricoter** knitting needle

aiguiller [eguije] /1/ VT (*orienter*) to direct; (Rail) to shunt

aiguillette [eguijɛt] NF (Culin) aiguillette

aiguilleur [eguijœr] NM: **~ du ciel** air traffic controller

aiguillon [eguijɔ̃] NM (*d'abeille*) sting; (*fig*) spur, stimulus

aiguillonner [eguijɔne] /1/ VT to spur ou goad on

aiguiser [egize] /1/ VT to sharpen, grind; (*fig*) to stimulate; (*: esprit*) to sharpen; (*: sens*) to excite

aiguisoir [egizwar] NM sharpener

aïkido [ajkido] NM aikido

★**ail** [aj] NM garlic

aile [ɛl] NF wing; (*de voiture*) wing (Brit), fender (US); **battre de l'~** (*fig*) to be in a sorry state; **voler de ses propres ailes** to stand on one's own two feet; **~ libre** hang-glider

ailé, e [ele] ADJ winged

aileron [ɛlrɔ̃] NM (*de requin*) fin; (*d'avion*) aileron

ailette [ɛlɛt] NF (Tech) fin; (*: de turbine*) blade

ailier [elje] NM (Sport) winger

aille *etc* [aj] VB *voir* **aller**

aillé, e [aje] ADJ (*pain, sauce*) garlic *cpd*

★**ailleurs** [ajœr] ADV elsewhere, somewhere else; **partout/nulle part ~** everywhere/nowhere else; **d'~** *adv* (*du reste*) moreover, besides; **par ~** *adv* (*d'autre part*) moreover, furthermore

ailloli [ajɔli] NM garlic mayonnaise

★**aimable** [ɛmabl] ADJ kind, nice; **vous êtes bien ~** that's very nice ou kind of you, how kind (of you)!

aimablement [ɛmabləmã] ADV kindly

aimant¹ [ɛmã] NM magnet

aimant², e [ɛmã, -ãt] ADJ loving, affectionate

aimanté, e [ɛmãte] ADJ magnetic

aimanter [ɛmãte] /1/ VT to magnetize

★**aimer** [eme] /1/ VT to love; (*d'amitié, affection, par goût*) to like; (*souhait*): **j'aimerais …** I would like …; **je n'aime pas beaucoup Paul** I don't like Paul much, I don't care much for Paul; **~ faire qch** to like doing sth, to like to do sth; **j'aime faire du ski** I like skiing; **je t'aime** I love you; **aimeriez-vous que je vous accompagne?** would you like me to come with you?; **j'aimerais (bien) m'en aller** I should (really) like to go; **bien ~ qn/qch** to like

a

sb/sth; **j'aime mieux Paul (que Pierre)** I prefer Paul (to Pierre); **j'aime mieux ou autant vous dire que** I may as well tell you that; **j'aimerais autant ou mieux y aller maintenant** I'd sooner ou rather go now; **j'aime assez aller au cinéma** I quite like going to the cinema ■ **s'aimer** VPR to love each other; to like each other

aine [ɛn] NF groin

★**aîné, e** [ene] ADJ elder, older; (le plus âgé) eldest, oldest ▶ NM/F oldest child ou one, oldest boy ou son/girl ou daughter; **il est mon ~ (de 2 ans)** he's (2 years) older than me, he's (2 years) my senior ■ **aînés** NMPL (fig: anciens) elders

aînesse [ɛnɛs] NF: **droit d'~** birthright

★**ainsi** [ɛ̃si] ADV (de cette façon) like this, in this way, thus; (ce faisant) thus ▶ CONJ thus, so; **~ que** (comme) (just) as; (et aussi) as well as; **pour ~ dire** so to speak, as it were; **~ soit-il** (Rel) so be it; **et ~ de suite** and so on (and so forth)

aïoli [ajɔli] NM = **ailloli**

★**air** [ɛr] NM air; (mélodie) tune; (expression) look, air; (atmosphère, ambiance) **dans l'~** in the air (fig); **prendre de grands airs (avec qn)** to give o.s. airs (with sb); **en l'~** (up) into the air; **tirer en l'~** to fire shots in the air; **paroles/menaces en l'~** empty words/threats; **prendre l'~** to get some (fresh) air; (avion) to take off; **avoir l'~** (sembler) to look, appear; **avoir l'~ triste** to look ou seem sad; **avoir l'~ de qch** to look like sth; **avoir l'~ de faire** to look as though one is doing, appear to be doing; **courant d'~** draught (BRIT), draft (US); **le grand ~** the open air; **mal de l'~** air-sickness; **tête en l'~** scatterbrain; **~ comprimé** compressed air; **~ conditionné** air-conditioning

airbag [ɛrbag] NM airbag

aire [ɛr] NF (zone, fig, Math) area; (nid) eyrie (BRIT), aerie (US); **~ d'atterrissage** landing strip; landing patch; **~ de jeu** play area; **~ de lancement** launching site; **~ de stationnement** parking area

airelle [ɛrɛl] NF bilberry

aisance [ɛzɑ̃s] NF ease; (Couture) easing, freedom of movement; (richesse) affluence; **être dans l'~** to be well-off ou affluent

aise [ɛz] NF comfort; **frémir d'~** to shudder with pleasure; **être à l'~ ou à son ~** to be comfortable; (pas embarrassé) to be at ease; (financièrement) to be comfortably off; **se mettre à l'~** to make o.s. comfortable; **être mal à l'~ ou à son ~** to be uncomfortable; (gêné) to be ill at ease; **mettre qn à l'~** to put sb at his (ou her) ease; **mettre qn mal à l'~** to make sb feel ill at ease; **à votre ~** please yourself, just as you like; **en faire à son ~** to do as one likes; **en prendre à son ~ avec qch** to be free and easy with sth, do as one likes with sth ▶ ADJ: **être bien ~ de/que** to be delighted to/that ■ **aises** NFPL: **aimer ses aises** to like one's (one's creature) comforts; **prendre ses aises** to make o.s. comfortable

aisé, e [eze] ADJ easy; (assez riche) well-to-do, well-off

aisément [ezemã] ADV easily

aisselle [ɛsɛl] NF armpit

ait [ɛ] VB voir **avoir**

ajonc [aʒɔ̃] NM gorse no pl

ajouré, e [aʒure] ADJ openwork cpd

ajournement [aʒurnəmã] NM adjournment; deferment, postponement

ajourner [aʒurne] /1/ VT (réunion) to adjourn; (décision) to defer, postpone; (candidat) to refer; (conscrit) to defer

ajout [aʒu] NM addition; **merci pour l'~** (Internet) thanks for the add

★**ajouter** [aʒute] /1/ VT to add; **~ à** (accroître) to add to; **~ que** to add that; **~ foi à** to lend ou give credence to ■ **s'ajouter à** VPR to add to

ajustage [aʒystaʒ] NM fitting

ajusté, e [aʒyste] ADJ: **bien ~** (robe etc) close-fitting

ajustement [aʒystəmã] NM adjustment

ajuster [aʒyste] /1/ VT (régler) to adjust; (vêtement) to alter; (coup de fusil) to aim; (cible) to aim at; (adapter): **~ qch à** to fit sth to; **~ sa cravate** to adjust one's tie

ajusteur [aʒystœr] NM metal worker

alaise [alɛz] NF = **alèse**

alambic [alãbik] NM still

alambiqué, e [alãbike] ADJ convoluted, overcomplicated

alangui, e [alãgi] ADJ languid

alanguir [alãgir] /2/: **s'alanguir** VPR to grow languid

alarmant, e [alarmã, -ãt] ADJ alarming

alarme [alarm] NF alarm; **donner l'~** to give ou raise the alarm; **jeter l'~** to cause alarm

alarmer [alarme] /1/ VT to alarm ■ **s'alarmer** VPR to become alarmed

alarmiste [alarmist] ADJ alarmist

Alaska [alaska] NM: **l'~** Alaska

albanais, e [albanɛ, -ɛz] ADJ Albanian ▶ NM (Ling) Albanian ▶ NM/F: **Albanais, e** Albanian

Albanie [albani] NF: **l'~** Albania

albâtre [albɑtr] NM alabaster

albatros [albatros] NM albatross

albigeois, e [albiʒwa, -waz] ADJ of ou from Albi

albinos [albinos] NMF albino

album [albɔm] NM album; **~ à colorier** colouring book; **~ de timbres** stamp album

albumen [albymɛn] NM albumen

albumine [albymin] NF albumin; **avoir ou faire de l'~** to suffer from albuminuria

alcalin, e [alkalɛ̃, -in] ADJ alkaline

alchimie [alʃimi] NF alchemy

alchimiste [alʃimist] NMF alchemist

alco(o)lo [alkɔlo] (fam) ADJ alcoholic ▶ NMF alcoholic, alkie (fam)

★**alcool** [alkɔl] NM: **l'~** alcohol; **un ~** a spirit, a brandy; **bière sans ~** non-alcoholic ou alcohol-free beer; **~ à brûler** methylated spirits (BRIT), wood alcohol (US); **~ à 90°** surgical spirit; **~ camphré** camphorated alcohol; **~ de prune** etc plum etc brandy

alcoolémie [alkɔlemi] NF blood alcohol level

alcoolique [alkɔlik] ADJ, NMF alcoholic

alcoolisé, e [alkɔlize] ADJ alcoholic; **une boisson non alcoolisée** a soft drink

alcoolisme [alkɔlism] NM alcoholism

alcootest® [alkɔtɛst] NM (objet) Breathalyser®;

(test) breath-test; **faire subir l'~ à qn** to Breathalyse® sb

alcopop [alkɔpɔp] NM alcopop

alcôve [alkov] NF alcove, recess

aléas [alea] NMPL hazards

aléatoire [aleatwaʀ] ADJ uncertain; *(Inform, Statistique)* random

alémanique [alemanik] ADJ: **la Suisse ~** German-speaking Switzerland

ALENA [alena] SIGLE M (= *Accord de libre-échange nord-américain*) NAFTA (= *North American Free Trade Agreement*)

alentour [alɑ̃tuʀ] ADV around (about) ▪ **alentours** NMPL surroundings; **aux alentours de** in the vicinity *ou* neighbourhood of, around about; *(temps)* around about

alerte [alɛʀt] ADJ agile, nimble; *(style)* brisk, lively ▶ NF alert; warning; **donner l'~** to give the alert; **à la première ~** at the first sign of trouble *ou* danger; **~ à la bombe** bomb scare

alerter [alɛʀte] /1/ VT to alert

alèse [alɛz] NF *(drap)* undersheet, draw-sheet

aléser [aleze] /6/ VT to ream

alevin [alvɛ̃] NM alevin, young fish

alevinage [alvinaʒ] NM fish farming

Alexandrie [alɛksɑ̃dʀi] N Alexandria

alexandrin [alɛksɑ̃dʀɛ̃] NM alexandrine

alezan, e [alzɑ̃, -an] ADJ chestnut

algarade [algaʀad] NF row, dispute

algèbre [alʒɛbʀ] NF algebra

algébrique [alʒebʀik] ADJ algebraic

Alger [alʒe] N Algiers

Algérie [alʒeʀi] NF: **l'~** Algeria

algérien, ne [alʒeʀjɛ̃, -ɛn] ADJ Algerian ▶ NM/F: **Algérien, ne** Algerian

algérois, e [alʒeʀwa, -waz] ADJ of *ou* from Algiers ▶ NM: **l'A~** *(région)* the Algiers region

algorithme [algɔʀitm] NM algorithm

algue [alg] NF seaweed *no pl*; *(Bot)* alga

alias [aljas] ADV alias

alibi [alibi] NM alibi

aliénation [aljenasjɔ̃] NF alienation

aliéné, e [aljene] NM/F insane person, lunatic *(péj)*

aliéner [aljene] /6/ VT to alienate; *(bien, liberté)* to give up ▪ **s'aliéner** VPR to alienate

aligné, e [aliɲe] ADJ *(politiquement)* aligned; *(en rang)* in a line, lined up; **~ sur** aligned with; **pays non alignés** non-aligned countries

alignement [aliɲ(ə)mɑ̃] NM alignment, lining up; **à l'~** in line

aligner [aliɲe] /1/ VT to align, line up; *(idées, chiffres)* to string together; *(adapter)*: **~ qch sur** to bring sth into alignment with ▪ **s'aligner** VPR *(soldats etc)* to line up; **s'~ sur** *(Pol)* to align o.s. with

aliment [alimɑ̃] NM food; **~ complet** whole food

alimentaire [alimɑ̃tɛʀ] ADJ food *cpd*; *(péj: besogne)* done merely to earn a living; **produits alimentaires** foodstuffs, foods

★**alimentation** [alimɑ̃tasjɔ̃] NF feeding; *(en eau etc, de moteur)* supplying, supply; *(commerce)* food trade; *(régime)* groceries *pl*; *(régime)* diet; *(Inform)* feed;

~ (générale) (general) grocer's; **~ de base** staple diet; **~ en feuilles/en continu/en papier** form/stream/sheet feed

alimenter [alimɑ̃te] /1/ VT to feed; *(Tech)*: **~ (en)** to supply (with), feed (with); *(fig)* to sustain, keep going

alinéa [alinea] NM paragraph; **«nouvel ~»** "new line"

alité, e [alite] ADJ *(malade)* confined to bed; **infirme ~** bedridden person *ou* invalid

aliter [alite] /1/: **s'aliter** VPR to take to one's bed

alizé [alize] ADJ, NM: **(vent) ~** trade wind

allaitement [alɛtmɑ̃] NM feeding; **~ maternel/au biberon** breast-/bottle-feeding; **~ mixte** mixed feeding

allaiter [alete] /1/ VT *(femme)* to (breast-)feed, nurse; *(animal)* to suckle; **~ au biberon** to bottle-feed

allant [alɑ̃] NM drive, go

alléchant, e [aleʃɑ̃, -ɑ̃t] ADJ tempting, enticing

allécher [aleʃe] /6/ VT: **~ qn** to make sb's mouth water; to tempt sb, entice sb

allée [ale] NF *(de jardin)* path; *(en ville)* avenue, drive; **allées et venues** comings and goings

allégation [alegasjɔ̃] NF allegation

allégé, e [aleʒe] ADJ *(yaourt etc)* low-fat

allègement [alɛʒmɑ̃] NM *(de charges)* lightening

alléger [aleʒe] /3, 6/ VT *(voiture)* to make lighter; *(chargement)* to lighten; *(souffrance)* to alleviate, soothe

allégorie [alegɔʀi] NF allegory

allégorique [alegɔʀik] ADJ allegorical

allègre [alɛgʀ] ADJ lively, jaunty *(BRIT)*; *(personne)* gay, cheerful

allègrement [alɛgʀəmɑ̃] ADV cheerfully; *(péj)* blithely

allégresse [alegʀɛs] NF elation, gaiety

allegretto [al(l)egʀet(t)o] ADV, NM allegretto

allegro [al(l)egʀo] ADV, NM allegro

alléguer [alege] /6/ VT to put forward (as proof *ou* an excuse)

★**Allemagne** [almaɲ] NF: **l'~** Germany; **l'~ de l'Est/Ouest** East/West Germany; **l'~ fédérale (RFA)** the Federal Republic of Germany (FRG)

★**allemand, e** [almɑ̃, -ɑ̃d] ADJ German ▶ NM *(Ling)* German ▶ NM/F: **Allemand, e** German; **A~ de l'Est/l'Ouest** East/West German

★**aller** [ale] /9/ NM *(trajet)* outward journey; *(billet)* single *(BRIT)* *ou* one-way ticket *(US)*; **~ simple** *(billet)* single *(BRIT)* *ou* one-way ticket; **~ (et) retour** *(trajet)* return trip *ou* journey *(BRIT)*, round trip *(US)*; *(billet)* return *(BRIT)* *ou* round-trip *(US)* ticket ▶ VI *(gén)* to go; **~ à** *(convenir)* to suit; *(forme, pointure etc)* to fit; **cela me va** *(couleur)* that suits me; *(vêtement)* that suits me; that fits me; *(projet, disposition)* that suits me, that's fine *ou* OK by me; **~ à la chasse/pêche** to go hunting/fishing; **~ avec** *(couleurs, style etc)* to go (well) with; **je vais le faire/me fâcher** I'm going to do it/to get angry; **~ voir/chercher qn** to go and see/look for sb; **comment allez-vous?** how are you?; **comment ça va?** how are you?; *(affaires etc)* how are things?; **ça va? — oui (ça va)!** how are things? — fine!; **pour ~ à** how do I get to; **ça va (comme**

ça) that's fine (as it is); **il va bien/mal** he's well/ not well, he's fine/ill; **ça va bien/mal** (affaires etc) it's going well/not going well; **tout va bien** everything's fine; **ça ne va pas !** (mauvaise humeur etc) that's not on!, hey, come on!; **ça va pas sans difficultés** it's not without difficulties; **~ mieux** to be better; **il y va de leur vie** their lives are at stake; **se laisser ~** to let o.s. go; **~ jusqu'à** to go as far as; **ça va de soi, ça va sans dire** that goes without saying; **tu y vas un peu fort** you're going a bit (too) far; **allez !** go on!; come on!; **allons !** come now!; **allons-y !** let's go!; **allez, au revoir !** right ou OK then, bye-bye!

allergène [alɛʀʒɛn] NM allergen

allergie [alɛʀʒi] NF allergy

allergique [alɛʀʒik] ADJ allergic; **~ à** allergic to

allergologue [alɛʀɡɔlɔɡ] NMF allergist, allergy specialist

allez [ale] VB voir **aller**

alliage [aljaʒ] NM alloy

alliance [aljɑ̃s] NF (Mil, Pol) alliance; (mariage) marriage; (bague) wedding ring; **neveu par ~** nephew by marriage

allié, e [alje] NM/F ally; **parents et alliés** relatives and relatives by marriage

allier [alje] /7/ VT (métaux) to alloy; (Pol, gén) to ally; (fig) to combine ■ **s'allier** VPR to become allies; (éléments, caractéristiques) to combine; **s'~ à** to become allied to ou with

alligator [aligatɔʀ] NM alligator

allitération [aliteʀasjɔ̃] NF alliteration

allô [alo] EXCL hullo, hallo

allocataire [alɔkatɛʀ] NMF beneficiary

allocation [alɔkasjɔ̃] NF allowance; **~ (de) chômage** unemployment benefit; **~ (de) logement** rent allowance; **allocations familiales** ≈ child benefit no pl; **allocations de maternité** maternity allowance

allocs [alɔk] NFPL (fam: allocations familiales) ≈ child benefit no pl

allocution [alɔkysjɔ̃] NF short speech

allongé, e [alɔ̃ʒe] ADJ (étendu): **être ~** to be stretched out ou lying down; (long) long; (étiré) elongated; (oblong) oblong; **rester ~** to be lying down; **mine allongée** long face

allongement [alɔ̃ʒmɑ̃] NM (de jours) lengthening; (de durée de travail) extension

allonger [alɔ̃ʒe] /3/ VT to lengthen, make longer; (étendre: bras, jambe) to stretch (out); (sauce) to spin out, make go further; **~ le pas** to hasten one's step(s) ■ **s'allonger** VPR to get longer; (se coucher) to lie down, stretch out

allouer [alwe] /1/ VT: **~ qch à** to allocate sth to, allot sth to

allumage [alymaʒ] NM (Auto) ignition

allume-cigare [alymsigaʀ] NM INV cigar lighter

allume-gaz [alymgɑz] NM INV gas lighter

★**allumer** [alyme] /1/ VT (lampe, phare, radio) to put ou switch on; (pièce) to put ou switch the light(s) on in; (feu, bougie, cigare, pipe, gaz) to light; (chauffage) to put on; **~ (la lumière ou l'électricité)** to put on the light ■ **s'allumer** VPR (lumière, lampe) to come ou go on

★**allumette** [alymɛt] NF match; (morceau de bois) matchstick; (Culin): **~ au fromage** cheese straw; **~ de sûreté** safety match

allumeuse [alymøz] NF (péj) tease (woman)

allure [alyʀ] NF (vitesse) speed; (: à pied) pace; (démarche) walk; (maintien) bearing; (aspect, air) look; **avoir de l'~** to have style; **à toute ~** at full speed

allusion [a(l)lyzjɔ̃] NF allusion; (sous-entendu) hint; **faire ~ à** to allude ou refer to; to hint at

alluvions [alyvjɔ̃] NFPL alluvial deposits, alluvium sg

almanach [almana] NM almanac

aloès [alɔɛs] NM (Bot) aloe

aloi [alwa] NM: **de bon/mauvais ~** of genuine/ doubtful worth ou quality

---

alors [alɔʀ]

ADV **1** (à ce moment-là) then, at that time; **il habitait alors à Paris** he lived in Paris at that time; **jusqu'alors** up till ou until then

2 (par conséquent): **tu as fini ? alors je m'en vais** have you finished? I'm going then

3 (expressions): **alors ? quoi de neuf ?** well ou so? what's new?; **et alors ?** so (what)?; **ça alors !** (well) really!

▶ CONJ **1**: **alors que** (au moment où) when, as; **il est arrivé alors que je partais** he arrived as I was leaving

2: **alors que** (tandis que) whereas, while; **alors que son frère travaillait dur, lui se reposait** while his brother was working hard, HE would rest

3: **alors que** (bien que) even though; **il a été puni alors qu'il n'a rien fait** he was punished, even though he had done nothing

4: **alors que** (pendant que) while, when; **alors qu'il était à Paris, il a visité ...** while ou when he was in Paris, he visited ...

---

alouette [alwɛt] NF (sky)lark

alourdir [aluʀdiʀ] /2/ VT to weigh down, make heavy ■ **s'alourdir** VPR to grow heavy ou heavier

aloyau [alwajo] NM sirloin

alpaga [alpaga] NM (tissu) alpaca

alpage [alpaʒ] NM high mountain pasture

★**Alpes** [alp] NFPL: **les ~** the Alps

alpestre [alpɛstʀ] ADJ alpine

alphabet [alfabɛ] NM alphabet; (livre) ABC (book), primer

alphabétique [alfabetik] ADJ alphabetic(al); **par ordre ~** in alphabetical order

alphabétisation [alfabetizasjɔ̃] NF literacy teaching

alphabétiser [alfabetize] /1/ VT to teach to read and write; (pays) to eliminate illiteracy in

alphanumérique [alfanymeʀik] ADJ alphanumeric

alpin, e [alpɛ̃, -in] ADJ (plante etc) alpine; (club) climbing

★**alpinisme** [alpinism] NM mountaineering, climbing

alpiniste [alpinist] NMF mountaineer, climber

Alsace [alzas] NF Alsace; **l'~** Alsace

alsacien, ne [alzasjɛ̃, -ɛn] ADJ Alsatian ▶ NM/F: **Alsacien, ne** Alsatian

altercation [altɛʀkasjɔ̃] NF altercation

alter ego [altɛʀego] NM alter ego

altérer [alteʀe] /6/ VT (faits, vérité) to falsify, distort; (qualité) to debase, impair; (données) to corrupt; (donner soif à) to make thirsty ■ **s'altérer** VPR to deteriorate; to spoil

altermondialisation [altɛʀmɔ̃djalizasjɔ̃] NF anti-globalization

altermondialisme [altɛʀmɔ̃djalism] NM anti-globalism

altermondialiste [altɛʀmɔ̃djalist] ADJ, NMF anti-globalist

alternance [altɛʀnɑ̃s] NF alternation; **en ~** alternately; **formation en ~** sandwich course

alternateur [altɛʀnatœʀ] NM alternator

alternatif, -ive [altɛʀnatif, -iv] ADJ alternating

alternative NF (choix) alternative

alternativement [altɛʀnativmɑ̃] ADV alternately

alterner [altɛʀne] /1/ VT to alternate; **(faire) ~ qch avec qch** to alternate sth with sth ▶ VI: **~ (avec)** to alternate (with)

Altesse [altɛs] NF Highness

altier, -ière [altje, -jɛʀ] ADJ haughty

altimètre [altimɛtʀ] NM altimeter

altiport [altipɔʀ] NM mountain airfield

altiste [altist] NMF viola player, violist

altitude [altityd] NF altitude, height; **à 1000 m d'~** at a height ou an altitude of 1000 m; **en ~** at high altitudes; **perdre/prendre de l'~** to lose/gain height; **voler à haute/basse ~** to fly at a high/low altitude

alto [alto] NM (instrument) viola ▶ NF (contr)alto

altruisme [altʀɥism] NM altruism

altruiste [altʀɥist] ADJ altruistic

alu [aly] NM (fam: aluminium) foil; **en ~** foil

aluminium [alyminjɔm] NM aluminium (BRIT), aluminum (US)

alun [alœ̃] NM alum

alunir [alyniʀ] /2/ VI to land on the moon

alunissage [alynisaʒ] NM (moon) landing

alvéole [alveɔl] NM ou F (de ruche) alveolus

alvéolé, e [alveɔle] ADJ honeycombed

AM SIGLE F = **assurance maladie**

amabilité [amabilite] NF kindness; **il a eu l'~ de** he was kind ou good enough to

amadou [amadu] NM touchwood, amadou

amadouer [amadwe] /1/ VT to coax, cajole; (adoucir) to mollify, soothe

amaigri, e [amegʀi] ADJ (visage, personne): **je l'ai trouvée très amaigrie depuis ma dernière visite** I thought she was a lot thinner than the last time I visited her, I thought she'd lost a lot of weight since I last visited her

amaigrir [amegʀiʀ] /2/ VT to make thin ou thinner ■ **s'amaigrir** VPR to get thinner

amaigrissant, e [amegʀisɑ̃, -ɑ̃t] ADJ: **régime ~** slimming (BRIT) ou weight-reduction (US) diet

amalgame [amalgam] NM amalgam; (fig: de gens, d'idées) hotch-potch, mixture

amalgamer [amalgame] /1/ VT to amalgamate

amande [amɑ̃d] NF (de l'amandier) almond; (de noyau de fruit) kernel; **en ~** (yeux) almond cpd, almond-shaped

amandier [amɑ̃dje] NM almond (tree)

amanite [amanit] NF (Bot) mushroom of the genus Amanita; **~ tue-mouches** fly agaric

amant [amɑ̃] NM lover

amarre [amaʀ] NF (Navig) (mooring) rope ou line ■ **amarres** NFPL moorings

amarrer [amaʀe] /1/ VT (Navig) to moor; (gén) to make fast

amaryllis [amaʀilis] NF amaryllis

amas [amɑ] NM heap, pile

amasser [amɑse] /1/ VT to amass ■ **s'amasser** VPR to pile up, accumulate; (foule) to gather

★**amateur** [amatœʀ] NM amateur; **en ~** (péj) amateurishly; **musicien/sportif ~** amateur musician/sportsman; **~ de musique/sport** etc music/sport etc lover

amateurisme [amatœʀism] NM amateurism; (péj) amateurishness

Amazone [amazɔn] NF: **l'~** the Amazon

amazone [amazɔn] NF horsewoman; **en ~** side-saddle

Amazonie [amazɔni] NF: **l'~** Amazonia

ambages [ɑ̃baʒ]: **sans ~** adv without beating about the bush, plainly

ambassade [ɑ̃basad] NF embassy; (mission): **en ~** on a mission; **l'~ de France** the French Embassy

ambassadeur, -drice [ɑ̃basadœʀ, -dʀis] NM/F ambassador/ambassadress

★**ambiance** [ɑ̃bjɑ̃s] NF atmosphere; **il y a de l'~** everyone's having a good time

ambiant, e [ɑ̃bjɑ̃, -ɑ̃t] ADJ (air, milieu) surrounding; (température) ambient

ambidextre [ɑ̃bidɛkstʀ] ADJ ambidextrous

ambigu, ë [ɑ̃bigy] ADJ ambiguous

ambiguïté [ɑ̃bigɥite] NF ambiguousness no pl, ambiguity

ambitieux, -euse [ɑ̃bisjø, -jøz] ADJ ambitious

★**ambition** [ɑ̃bisjɔ̃] NF ambition

ambitionner [ɑ̃bisjɔne] /1/ VT to have as one's aim ou ambition

ambivalence [ɑ̃bivalɑ̃s] NF ambivalence

ambivalent, e [ɑ̃bivalɑ̃, -ɑ̃t] ADJ ambivalent

amble [ɑ̃bl] NM: **aller l'~** to amble

ambre [ɑ̃bʀ] NM: **~ (jaune)** amber; **~ gris** amber-gris

ambré, e [ɑ̃bʀe] ADJ (couleur) amber; (parfum) ambergris-scented

★**ambulance** [ɑ̃bylɑ̃s] NF ambulance

ambulancier, -ière [ɑ̃bylɑ̃sje, -jɛʀ] NM/F ambulanceman/-woman (BRIT), paramedic (US)

ambulant, e [ɑ̃bylɑ̃, -ɑ̃t] ADJ travelling, itinerant

âme [ɑm] NF soul; **rendre l'~** to give up the ghost; **bonne ~** (aussi ironique) kind soul; **un joueur/tricheur dans l'~** a gambler/cheat through and through; **~ sœur** kindred spirit

amélioration [ameljɔʀasjɔ̃] NF improvement

améliorer [ameljɔʀe] /1/ VT to improve ■ **s'améliorer** VPR to improve, get better

aménagé, e [amenaʒe] ADJ (*cave, grenier*) converted; **ferme aménagée** converted farmhouse

aménagement [amenaʒmɑ̃] NM fitting out; laying out; development; **w aménagements** NMPL developments; **aménagements fiscaux** tax adjustments

aménager [amenaʒe] /**3**/ VT (*agencer: espace, local*) to fit out; (*: terrain*) to lay out; (*: quartier, territoire*) to develop; (*installer*) to fix up, put in

★**amende** [amɑ̃d] NF fine; **mettre à l'~** to penalize; **faire ~ honorable** to make amends

amendement [amɑ̃dmɑ̃] NM (*Jur*) amendment

amender [amɑ̃de] /**1**/ VT (*loi*) to amend; (*terre*) to enrich **w s'amender** VPR to mend one's ways

amène [amɛn] ADJ affable; **peu ~** unkind

★**amener** [am(ə)ne] /**5**/ VT to bring; (*causer*) to bring about; (*baisser: drapeau, voiles*) to strike; **~ qn à qch/à faire** to lead sb to sth/to do **w s'amener** VPR (*fam*) to show up, turn up

amenuiser [amənɥize] /**1**/: **s'amenuiser** VPR to dwindle; (*chances*) to grow slimmer, lessen

★**amer, amère** [amɛʀ] ADJ bitter

amèrement [amɛʀmɑ̃] ADV bitterly

américain, e [ameʀikɛ̃, -ɛn] ADJ American; **en vedette américaine** as a special guest (star) ▶ NM (*Ling*) American (English) ▶ NM/F: **Américain, e** American

américaniser [ameʀikanize] /**1**/ VT to Americanize

américanisme [ameʀikanism] NM Americanism

amérindien, ne [ameʀɛ̃djɛ̃, -ɛn] ADJ Amerindian, American Indian

Amérique [ameʀik] NF America; **l'~ centrale** Central America; **l'~ latine** Latin America; **l'~ du Nord** North America; **l'~ du Sud** South America

Amerloque [amɛʀlɔk] NMF (*fam*) Yank, Yankee

amerrir [ameʀiʀ] /**2**/ VI to land (on the sea); (*capsule spatiale*) to splash down

amerrissage [ameʀisaʒ] NM landing (on the sea); splash-down

amertume [amɛʀtym] NF bitterness

améthyste [ametist] NF amethyst

ameublement [amœbləmɑ̃] NM furnishing; (*meubles*) furniture; **articles d'~** furnishings; **tissus d'~** soft furnishings, furnishing fabrics

ameuter [amøte] /**1**/ VT (*badauds*) to draw a crowd of; (*peuple*) to rouse, stir up

★**ami, e** [ami] NM/F friend; (*amant/maîtresse*) boyfriend/girlfriend; **un ~ des arts** a patron of the arts; **un ~ des chiens** a dog lover; **petit ~/petite amie** boyfriend/girlfriend; **ajouter qn à sa liste d'amis** (*réseaux sociaux*) to friend sb; **supprimer qn de sa liste d'amis** (*réseaux sociaux*) to unfriend sb ▶ ADJ: **pays/groupe ~** friendly country/group; **être (très) ~ avec qn** to be (very) friendly with sb; **être ~ de l'ordre** to be a lover of order

amiable [amjabl]: **à l'~** adv (*Jur*) out of court; (*gén*) amicably

amiante [amjɑ̃t] NM asbestos

amibe [amib] NF amoeba

★**amical, e, -aux** [amikal, -o] ADJ friendly ▶ NF (*club*) association

★**amicalement** [amikalmɑ̃] ADV in a friendly way; (*formule épistolaire*) regards

amidon [amidɔ̃] NM starch

amidonner [amidɔne] /**1**/ VT to starch

amincir [amɛ̃siʀ] /**2**/ VT (*objet*) to thin (down); **~ qn** to make sb thinner *ou* slimmer; (*vêtement*) to make sb look slimmer **w s'amincir** VPR to get thinner *ou* slimmer

amincissant, e [amɛ̃sisɑ̃, -ɑ̃t] ADJ slimming; **régime ~** diet; **crème amincissante** slimming cream

aminé, e [amine] ADJ: **acide ~** amino acid

amiral, -aux [amiʀal, -o] NM admiral

amirauté [amiʀote] NF admiralty

amitié [amitje] NF friendship; **prendre en ~ to** take a liking to; **faire** *ou* **présenter ses amitiés à qn** to send sb one's best wishes; **amitiés** (*formule épistolaire*) (with) best wishes

ammoniac [amɔnjak] NM: **(gaz) ~** ammonia

ammoniaque [amɔnjak] NF ammonia (water)

amnésie [amnezi] NF amnesia

amnésique [amnezik] ADJ amnesic

Amnesty International [amnɛsti-] N Amnesty International

amniocentèse [amnjosɛ̃tɛz] NF amniocentesis

amnistie [amnisti] NF amnesty

amnistier [amnistje] /**7**/ VT to amnesty

amocher [amɔʃe] /**1**/ VT (*fam*) to mess up

amoindrir [amwɛ̃dʀiʀ] /**2**/ VT to reduce

amollir [amɔliʀ] /**2**/ VT to soften

amonceler [amɔ̃s(ə)le] /**4**/ VT to pile *ou* heap up **w s'amonceler** VPR to pile *ou* heap up; (*fig*) to accumulate

amoncellement [amɔ̃sɛlmɑ̃] NM piling *ou* heaping up; accumulation; (*tas*) pile, heap; accumulation

amont [amɔ̃]: **en ~** adv upstream; (*sur une pente*) uphill; **en ~ de** prép upstream from; uphill from, above

amoral, e, -aux [amɔral, -o] ADJ amoral

amorce [amɔʀs] NF (*sur un hameçon*) bait; (*explosif*) cap; (*tube*) primer; (*: contenu*) priming; (*fig: début*) beginning(s), start

amorcer [amɔʀse] /**3**/ VT to bait; to prime; (*commencer*) to begin, start

amorphe [amɔʀf] ADJ passive, lifeless

amortir [amɔʀtiʀ] /**2**/ VT (*atténuer: choc*) to absorb, cushion; (*: bruit, douleur*) to deaden; (*Comm: dette*) to pay off, amortize; (*: mise de fonds, matériel*) to write off; **~ un abonnement** to make a season ticket pay (for itself)

amortissable [amɔʀtisabl] ADJ (*Comm*) that can be paid off

amortissement [amɔʀtismɑ̃] NM (*de matériel*) writing off; (*d'une dette*) paying off

amortisseur [amɔʀtisœʀ] NM shock absorber

★**amour** [amuʀ] NM love; (*liaison*) love affair, love; (*statuette etc*) cupid; **un ~ de** a lovely little; **faire l'~** to make love

amouracher [amuʀaʃe] /**1**/: **s'amouracher de** VPR (*péj*) to become infatuated with

amourette [amuʀɛt] NF passing fancy

amoureusement [amuʀøzmã] ADV lovingly

amoureux, -euse [amuʀø, -øz] ADJ (regard, tempérament) amorous; (vie, problèmes) love cpd; (personne): **être ~ (de qn)** to be in love (with sb); **tomber ~ de qn** to fall in love with sb; **être ~ de qch** to be passionately fond of sth ▸ NM/F lover; **un ~ de la nature** a nature lover

amour-propre [amuʀpʀɔpʀ] (pl **amours-propres**) NM self-esteem, pride

amovible [amɔvibl] ADJ removable, detachable

ampère [ãpɛʀ] NM amp(ere)

ampèremètre [ãpɛʀmɛtʀ] NM ammeter

amphétamine [ãfetamin] NF amphetamine

amphi [ãfi] NM (Scol: fam: = amphithéâtre) lecture hall ou theatre

amphibie [ãfibi] ADJ amphibious

amphibien [ãfibjɛ̃] NM (Zool) amphibian

amphithéâtre [ãfiteatʀ] NM amphitheatre; (d'université) lecture hall ou theatre

amphore [ãfɔʀ] NF amphora

ample [ãpl] ADJ (vêtement) roomy, ample; (gestes, mouvement) broad; (ressources) ample; **jusqu'à plus ~ informé** (Admin) until further details are available

amplement [ãpləmã] ADV amply; **~ suffisant** ample, more than enough

ampleur [ãplœʀ] NF scale, size; (de dégâts, problème) extent, magnitude

ampli [ãpli] NM (fam: = amplificateur) amplifier, amp

amplificateur [ãplifikatœʀ] NM amplifier

amplification [ãplifikasjɔ̃] NF amplification; expansion, increase

amplifier [ãplifje] **/7/** VT (son, oscillation) to amplify; (fig) to expand, increase ■ **s'amplifier** VPR (oscillations) to become amplified; (contestation) to intensify

ampliforme [ãplifɔʀm] ADJ (soutien-gorge) maximizer cpd

amplitude [ãplityd] NF amplitude; (des températures) range

★**ampoule** [ãpul] NF (électrique) bulb; (de médicament) phial; (aux mains, pieds) blister

ampoulé, e [ãpule] ADJ (péj) pompous, bombastic

amputation [ãpytasjɔ̃] NF amputation

amputer [ãpyte] **/1/** VT (Méd) to amputate; (fig) to cut ou reduce drastically; **~ qn d'un bras/pied** to amputate sb's arm/foot

Amsterdam [amstɛʀdam] N Amsterdam

amulette [amylɛt] NF amulet

★**amusant, e** [amyzã, -ãt] ADJ (divertissant, spirituel) entertaining, amusing; (comique) funny, amusing

amusé, e [amyze] ADJ amused

amuse-gueule [amyzgœl] NM INV appetizer, snack

amusement [amyzmã] NM (voir amusé) amusement; (voir amuser) entertaining, amusing; (jeu etc) pastime, diversion

★**amuser** [amyze] **/1/** VT (divertir) to entertain, amuse; (égayer, faire rire) to amuse; (détourner l'attention de) to distract ■ **s'amuser** VPR (jouer) to

amuse o.s., play; (se divertir) to enjoy o.s., have fun; (fig) to mess around; **s'~ de qch** (trouver comique) to find sth amusing; **s'~ avec** ou **de qn** (duper) to make a fool of sb

amusette [amyzɛt] NF idle pleasure, trivial pastime

amuseur [amyzœʀ] NM entertainer; (péj) clown

amygdale [amidal] NF tonsil; **opérer qn des amygdales** to take sb's tonsils out

amygdalite [amidalit] NF tonsillitis

AN SIGLE F = **Assemblée nationale**

★**an** [ã] NM year; **être âgé de** ou **avoir 3 ans** to be 3 (years old); **en l'an 1980** in the year 1980; **le jour de l'an, le premier de l'an, le nouvel an** New Year's Day

anabolisant [anabɔlizã] NM anabolic steroid

anachronique [anakʀɔnik] ADJ anachronistic

anachronisme [anakʀɔnism] NM anachronism

anaconda [anakɔ̃da] NM (Zool) anaconda

anaérobie [anaeʀɔbi] ADJ anaerobic

anagramme [anagʀam] NF anagram

ANAH SIGLE F = **Agence nationale de l'habitat**

anal, e, -aux [anal, -o] ADJ anal

analgésique [analʒezik] NM analgesic

anallergique [analɛʀʒik] ADJ hypoallergenic

analogie [analɔʒi] NF analogy

analogique [analɔʒik] ADJ (Logique: raisonnement) analogical; (calculateur, montre etc) analogue; (Inform) analog

analogue [analɔg] ADJ: **~ (à)** analogous (to), similar (to)

analphabète [analfabɛt] NMF illiterate

analphabétisme [analfabetism] NM illiteracy

analyse [analiz] NF analysis; (Méd) test; **faire l'~ de** to analyse; **une ~ approfondie** an in-depth analysis; **en dernière ~** in the last analysis; **avoir l'esprit d'~** to have an analytical turn of mind; **~ grammaticale** grammatical analysis, parsing (Scol)

analyser [analize] **/1/** VT to analyse; (Méd) to test

analyste [analist] NMF analyst; (psychanalyste) (psycho)analyst

analyste-programmeur, -euse [analist-] (pl **analystes-programmeurs, analystes-programmeuses**) NM/F systems analyst

analytique [analitik] ADJ analytical

analytiquement [analitikmã] ADV analytically

★**ananas** [anana(s)] NM pineapple

anarchie [anaʀʃi] NF anarchy

anarchique [anaʀʃik] ADJ anarchic

anarchisme [anaʀʃism] NM anarchism

anarchiste [anaʀʃist] ADJ anarchistic ▸ NMF anarchist

anathème [anatɛm] NM: **jeter l'~ sur, lancer l'~ contre** to anathematize, curs

anatomie [anatɔmi] NF anatomy

anatomique [anatɔmik] ADJ anatomical

ancestral, e, -aux [ãsɛstʀal, -o] ADJ ancestral

ancêtre [ãsɛtʀ] NMF ancestor; (fig): **l'~ de** the forerunner of

anche [ãʃ] NF reed

anchois [ɑ̃ʃwa] NM anchovy

★**ancien, ne** [ɑ̃sjɛ̃, -jɛn] ADJ old; (*de jadis, de l'antiquité*) ancient; (*précédent, ex-*) former, old; (*par l'expérience*) senior; **un ~ ministre** a former minister; **mon ancienne voiture** my previous car; **être plus ~ que qn dans une maison** to have been in a firm longer than sb; (*dans la hiérarchie*) to be senior to sb in a firm; **~ combattant** ex-serviceman; **~ (élève)** (*Scol*) ex-pupil (BRIT), alumnus (US) ▶ NM (*mobilier ancien*): **l'~** antiques pl ▶ NM/F (*dans une tribu etc*) elder

anciennement [ɑ̃sjɛnmɑ̃] ADV formerly

ancienneté [ɑ̃sjɛnte] NF oldness; antiquity; (*Admin*) (length of) service; (*privilèges obtenus*) seniority

ancrage [ɑ̃kʀaʒ] NM anchoring; (*Navig*) anchorage; (*Constr*) anchor

ancre [ɑ̃kʀ] NF anchor; **jeter/lever l'~** to cast/weigh anchor; **à l'~** at anchor

ancrer [ɑ̃kʀe] /1/ VT (*Constr: câble etc*) to anchor; (*fig*) to fix firmly ■ **s'ancrer** VPR (*Navig*) to (cast) anchor

andalou, -ouse [ɑ̃dalu, -uz] ADJ Andalusian

Andalousie [ɑ̃daluzi] NF: **l'~** Andalusia

andante [ɑ̃dɑ̃t] ADV, NM andante

Andes [ɑ̃d] NFPL: **les ~** the Andes

andin, e [ɑ̃dɛ̃, -in] ADJ Andean

Andorre [ɑ̃dɔʀ] NF Andorra

andouille [ɑ̃duj] NF (*Culin*) sausage made of chitterlings; (*fam*) clot, nit

andouillette [ɑ̃dujɛt] NF small andouille

androgyne [ɑ̃dʀɔʒin] ADJ (*allure, visage*) androgynous

âne [ɑn] NM donkey, ass; (*péj*) dunce, fool

anéantir [aneɑ̃tiʀ] /2/ VT (*ville, armée*) to annihilate, wipe out; (*fig: espoirs*) to dash, destroy; (*déprimer*) to overwhelm

anéantissement [aneɑ̃tismɑ̃] NM (*d'armée, ville*) annihilation; (*d'espoirs*) dashing

anecdote [anɛkdɔt] NF anecdote

anecdotique [anɛkdɔtik] ADJ anecdotal

anémie [anemi] NF anaemia

anémié, e [anemje] ADJ anaemic; (*fig*) enfeebled

anémique [anemik] ADJ anaemic

anémone [anemɔn] NF anemone; **~ de mer** sea anemone

ânerie [ɑnʀi] NF stupidity; (*parole etc*) stupid ou idiotic comment etc

anéroïde [anerɔid] ADJ voir **baromètre**

ânesse [ɑnɛs] NF she-ass

anesthésiant, e [anɛstezjɑ̃, -ɑ̃t] ADJ, NM anaesthetic

anesthésie [anɛstezi] NF anaesthesia; **sous ~** under anaesthetic; **~ générale/locale** general/local anaesthetic; **faire une ~ locale à qn** to give sb a local anaesthetic

anesthésier [anɛstezje] /7/ VT to anaesthetize

anesthésique [anɛstezik] ADJ, NM anaesthetic

anesthésiste [anɛstezist] NMF anaesthetist

aneth [anɛt] NM dill; **du saumon à l'~** salmon in dill

anfractuosité [ɑ̃fʀaktɥozite] NF crevice

ange [ɑ̃ʒ] NM angel; **être aux anges** to be over the moon; **~ gardien** guardian angel

angélique [ɑ̃ʒelik] ADJ angelic(al) ▶ NF angelica

angelot [ɑ̃ʒ(ə)lo] NM cherub

angélus [ɑ̃ʒelys] NM angelus; (*cloches*) evening bells pl

angevin, e [ɑ̃ʒ(ə)vɛ̃, -in] ADJ of ou from Anjou; of ou from Angers

angine [ɑ̃ʒin] NF sore throat, throat infection; **~ de poitrine** angina (pectoris)

angiome [ɑ̃ʒjom] NM angioma

★**anglais, e** [ɑ̃glɛ, -ɛz] ADJ English; **filer à l'anglaise** to take French leave; **à l'anglaise** (*Culin*) boiled ▶ NM (*Ling*) English ▶ NM/F: **Anglais, e** Englishman/-woman; **les A~** the English

anglaises [ɑ̃glɛz] NFPL (*cheveux*) ringlets

angle [ɑ̃gl] NM angle; (*coin*) corner; **~ droit/obtus/aigu/mort** right/obtuse/acute/dead angle

★**Angleterre** [ɑ̃glətɛʀ] NF: **l'~** England

anglican, e [ɑ̃glikɑ̃, -an] ADJ, NM/F Anglican

anglicanisme [ɑ̃glikanism] NM Anglicanism

anglicisme [ɑ̃glisism] NM anglicism

angliciste [ɑ̃glisist] NMF English scholar; (*étudiant*) student of English

anglo... [ɑ̃glɔ] PRÉFIXE Anglo(-)

anglo-américain, e [ɑ̃glɔamerikɛ̃, -ɛn] ADJ Anglo-American ▶ NM (*Ling*) American English

anglo-arabe [ɑ̃glɔaʀab] ADJ Anglo-Arab

anglo-canadien, ne [ɑ̃glɔkanadjɛ̃, -ɛn] ADJ Anglo-Canadian ▶ NM (*Ling*) Canadian English

anglo-normand, e [ɑ̃glɔnɔʀmɑ̃, -ɑ̃d] ADJ Anglo-Norman; **les îles anglo-normandes** the Channel Islands

anglophile [ɑ̃glɔfil] ADJ Anglophilic

anglophobe [ɑ̃glɔfɔb] ADJ Anglophobic

anglophone [ɑ̃glɔfɔn] ADJ English-speaking

anglo-saxon, ne [ɑ̃glɔsaksɔ̃, -ɔn] ADJ Anglo-Saxon

angoissant, e [ɑ̃gwasɑ̃, -ɑ̃t] ADJ harrowing

angoisse [ɑ̃gwas] NF: **l'~** anguish no pl

angoissé, e [ɑ̃gwase] ADJ anguished; (*personne*) distressed

angoisser [ɑ̃gwase] /1/ VT to harrow, cause anguish to ▶ VI to worry, fret

Angola [ɑ̃gɔla] NM: **l'~** Angola

angolais, e [ɑ̃gɔlɛ, -ɛz] ADJ Angolan

angora [ɑ̃gɔʀa] ADJ, NM angora

anguille [ɑ̃gij] NF eel; **~ de mer** conger (eel); **il y a ~ sous roche** (*fig*) there's something going on, there's something beneath all this

angulaire [ɑ̃gylɛʀ] ADJ angular

anguleux, -euse [ɑ̃gylø, -øz] ADJ angular

anhydride [anidʀid] NM anhydride

anicroche [anikʀɔʃ] NF hitch, snag

★**animal, e, -aux** [animal, -o] ADJ, NM animal; **~ domestique/sauvage** domestic/wild animal

animalerie [animalʀi] NF (*magasin*) pet shop

animalier, -ière [animalje, -jɛʀ] ADJ: **peintre ~** animal painter

animalité [animalite] NF animality

★**animateur, -trice** [animatœʀ, -tʀis] NM/F (*de télévision*) host; (*de music-hall*) compère; (*de groupe*) leader, organizer; (*Ciné: technicien*) animator

animation [animasjɔ̃] NF (*voir animé*) busyness; liveliness; (*Ciné: technique*) animation; **centre d'~** ≈ community centre ▪ **animations** NFPL (*activité*) activities

animé, e [anime] ADJ (*rue, lieu*) busy, lively; (*conversation, réunion*) lively, animated; (*opposé à inanimé, aussi Ling*) animate

animer [anime] /1/ VT (*ville, soirée*) to liven up, enliven; (*mettre en mouvement*) to drive; (*stimuler*) to drive, impel ▪ **s'animer** VPR to liven up, come to life

animisme [animism] NM animism

animiste [animist] ADJ (*tribu, peuple*) animist

animosité [animozite] NF animosity

anis [ani(s)] NM (*Culin*) aniseed; (*Bot*) anise

anisé, e [anize] ADJ (*apéritif, goût*) aniseed

anisette [anizɛt] NF anisette

Ankara [ɑ̃kaʀa] N Ankara

ankyloser [ɑ̃kiloze] /1/: **s'ankyloser** VPR to get stiff

annales [anal] NFPL annals

anneau, x [ano] NM (*de rideau, bague*) ring; (*de chaîne*) link; (*Sport*): **exercices aux anneaux** ring exercises; **~ gastrique** (*Méd*) gastric band

année [ane] NF year; **souhaiter la bonne ~ à qn** to wish sb a Happy New Year; **tout au long de l'~** all year long; **d'une ~ à l'autre** from one year to the next; **d'~ en ~** from year to year; **l'~ scolaire/fiscale** the school/tax year

année-lumière [anelymjɛʀ] (*pl* **années-lumières**) NF light year

annexe [anɛks] ADJ (*problème*) related; (*document*) appended; (*salle*) adjoining ▸ NF (*bâtiment*) annex(e); (*de document, ouvrage*) annex, appendix; (*jointe à une lettre, un dossier*) enclosure

annexer [anɛkse] /1/ VT to annex; **~ qch à** (*joindre*) to append sth to ▪ **s'annexer** VPR (*pays*) to annex

annexion [anɛksjɔ̃] NF annexation

annihiler [aniile] /1/ VT to annihilate

★**anniversaire** [anivɛʀsɛʀ] NM birthday; (*d'un événement, bâtiment*) anniversary ▸ ADJ: **jour ~** anniversary

★**annonce** [anɔ̃s] NF announcement; (*signe, indice*) sign; (*aussi*: **annonce publicitaire**) advertisement; (*Cartes*) declaration; **~ personnelle** personal message; **les petites annonces** the small *ou* classified ads

★**annoncer** [anɔ̃se] /3/ VT to announce; (*être le signe de*) to herald; (*Cartes*) to declare; **je vous annonce que ...** I wish to tell you that ...; **~ la couleur** (*fig*) to lay one's cards on the table ▪ **s'annoncer** VPR: **s'~ bien/difficile** to look promising/difficult

annonceur, -euse [anɔ̃sœʀ, -øz] NM/F (*TV, Radio: speaker*) announcer; (*publicitaire*) advertiser

annonciateur, -trice [anɔ̃sjatœʀ, -tʀis] ADJ: **~ d'un événement** presaging an event

Annonciation [anɔ̃sjasjɔ̃] NF: **l'~** (*Rel*) the Annunciation; (*jour*) Annunciation Day

annotation [anɔtasjɔ̃] NF annotation

annoter [anɔte] /1/ VT to annotate

★**annuaire** [anɥɛʀ] NM yearbook, annual; **~ téléphonique** (telephone) directory, phone book

annuel, le [anɥɛl] ADJ annual, yearly

annuellement [anɥɛlmɑ̃] ADV annually, yearly

annuité [anɥite] NF annual instalment

annulaire [anylɛʀ] NM ring *ou* third finger

annulation [anylasjɔ̃] NF cancellation; annulment; quashing, repeal

★**annuler** [anyle] /1/ VT (*rendez-vous, voyage*) to cancel, call off; (*mariage*) to annul; (*jugement*) to quash (BRIT), repeal (US); (*résultats*) to declare void; (*Math, Physique*) to cancel out ▪ **s'annuler** VPR to cancel each other out

anoblir [anɔbliʀ] /2/ VT to ennoble

anoblissement [anɔblismɑ̃] NM ennoblement

anode [anɔd] NF anode

anodin, e [anɔdɛ̃, -in] ADJ harmless; (*sans importance*) insignificant, trivial

anomalie [anɔmali] NF anomaly

ânon [anɔ̃] NM baby donkey; (*petit âne*) little donkey

ânonner [anɔne] /1/ VI, VT to read in a drone; (*hésiter*) to read in a fumbling manner

anonymat [anɔnima] NM anonymity; **garder l'~** to remain anonymous

★**anonyme** [anɔnim] ADJ anonymous; (*fig*) impersonal

anonymement [anɔnimmɑ̃] ADV anonymously

★**anorak** [anɔʀak] NM anorak

anorexie [anɔʀɛksi] NF anorexia

anorexique [anɔʀɛksik] ADJ, NMF anorexic

anormal, e, -aux [anɔʀmal, -o] ADJ abnormal; (*insolite*) unusual, abnormal

anormalement [anɔʀmalmɑ̃] ADV abnormally; unusually

anse [ɑ̃s] NF handle; (*Géo*) cove

antagonisme [ɑ̃tagɔnism] NM antagonism

antagoniste [ɑ̃tagɔnist] ADJ antagonistic ▸ NM antagonist

antalgique [ɑ̃talʒik] ADJ, NM analgesic

antan [ɑ̃tɑ̃]: **d'~** *adj* of yesteryear, of long ago

antarctique [ɑ̃taʀktik] ADJ Antarctic; **le cercle A~** the Antarctic Circle; **l'océan A~** the Antarctic Ocean ▸ NM: **l'A~** the Antarctic

antécédent [ɑ̃tesedɑ̃] NM (*Ling*) antecedent ▪ **antécédents** NMPL (*Méd etc*) past history *sg*; **antécédents professionnels** record, career to date

antédiluvien, ne [ɑ̃tedilyvjɛ̃, -ɛn] ADJ (*fig*) ancient, antediluvian

anténatal, e, -aux [ɑ̃tenatal, -o] ADJ antenatal

★**antenne** [ɑ̃ten] NF (*de radio, télévision*) aerial; (*d'insecte*) antenna, feeler; (*poste avancé*) outpost; (*petite succursale*) sub-branch; **sur l'~** on the air; **passer à/avoir l'~** to go/be on the air; **deux heures d'~** two hours' broadcasting time; **hors ~** off the air; **~ chirurgicale** (*Mil*) advance surgical unit; **~ parabolique** satellite dish; **antenne-relais** mobile phone mast (BRIT), cell tower (US)

antépénultième [ɑ̃tepenyltjem] ADJ antepenultimate

antérieur, e [ɑ̃teʀjœʀ] ADJ (*d'avant*) previous, earlier; (*de devant*) front; ~ **à** prior ou previous to; **passé/futur** ~ (Ling) past/future anterior

antérieurement [ɑ̃teʀjœʀmɑ̃] ADV earlier; (*précédemment*) previously; ~ **à** prior ou previous to

antériorité [ɑ̃teʀjɔʀite] NF precedence (*in time*)

anthologie [ɑ̃tɔlɔʒi] NF anthology

anthracite [ɑ̃tʀasit] NM anthracite ▸ ADJ: **(gris)** ~ charcoal (grey)

anthropocentrisme [ɑ̃tʀɔposɑ̃tʀism] NM anthropocentrism

anthropologie [ɑ̃tʀɔpɔlɔʒi] NF anthropology

anthropologique [ɑ̃tʀɔpɔlɔʒik] ADJ anthropological

anthropologue [ɑ̃tʀɔpɔlɔg] NMF anthropologist

anthropomorphisme [ɑ̃tʀɔpɔmɔʀfism] NM anthropomorphism

anthropophage [ɑ̃tʀɔpɔfaʒ] ADJ cannibalistic

anthropophagie [ɑ̃tʀɔpɔfaʒi] NF cannibalism, anthropophagy

anti... [ɑ̃ti] PRÉFIXE anti...

antiaérien, ne [ɑ̃tiaeʀjɛ̃, -ɛn] ADJ anti-aircraft; **abri** ~ air-raid shelter

antialcoolique [ɑ̃tialkɔlik] ADJ anti-alcohol; **ligue** ~ temperance league

antiatomique [ɑ̃tiatɔmik] ADJ: **abri** ~ fallout shelter

antibactérien, ne [ɑ̃tibakteʀjɛ̃, -jɛn] ADJ antibacterial

antibiotique [ɑ̃tibjɔtik] NM antibiotic

antibrouillard [ɑ̃tibʀujaʀ] ADJ: **phare** ~ fog lamp

antibruit [ɑ̃tibʀɥi] ADJ INV: **mur** ~ (*sur autoroute*) sound-muffling wall

antibuée [ɑ̃tibɥe] ADJ INV: **dispositif** ~ demister; **bombe** ~ demister spray

anticalcaire [ɑ̃tikalkɛʀ] ADJ INV anti-liming, anti-scale

anticancéreux, -euse [ɑ̃tikɑ̃seʀø, -øz] ADJ cancer *cpd*

anticapitaliste [ɑ̃tikapitalist] ADJ (*parti, mouvement*) anticapitalist

anticasseur, anticasseurs [ɑ̃tikɑsœʀ] ADJ: **loi/mesure** ~**(s)** law/measure against damage done by demonstrators

antichambre [ɑ̃tiʃɑ̃bʀ] NF antechamber, anteroom; **faire** ~ to wait (for an audience)

antichar [ɑ̃tiʃaʀ] ADJ antitank

antichoc [ɑ̃tiʃɔk] ADJ shockproof

anticipation [ɑ̃tisipasjɔ̃] NF anticipation; (*Comm*) payment in advance; **par** ~ in anticipation, in advance; **livre/film d'**~ science fiction book/film

anticipé, e [ɑ̃tisipe] ADJ (*règlement, paiement*) early, in advance; (*joie etc*) anticipated, early; **avec mes remerciements anticipés** thanking you in advance ou anticipation

anticiper [ɑ̃tisipe] /1/ VT (*événement, coup*) to anticipate, foresee; (*paiement*) to pay ou make in advance ▸ VI to look ou think ahead; (*en racontant*) to jump ahead; (*prévoir*) to anticipate; ~ **sur** to anticipate

anticlérical, e, -aux [ɑ̃tikleʀikal, -o] ADJ anticlerical

anticoagulant, e [ɑ̃tikɔagylɑ̃, -ɑ̃t] ADJ, NM anticoagulant

anticolonialisme [ɑ̃tikɔlɔnjalism] NM anticolonialism

anticonceptionnel, le [ɑ̃tikɔ̃sɛpsjɔnɛl] ADJ contraceptive

anticonformisme [ɑ̃tikɔ̃fɔʀmism] NM nonconformism

anticonformiste [ɑ̃tikɔ̃fɔʀmist] ADJ, NMF nonconformist

anticonstitutionnel, le [ɑ̃tikɔ̃stitysjɔnɛl] ADJ unconstitutional

anticorps [ɑ̃tikɔʀ] NM antibody

anticyclone [ɑ̃tisiklon] NM anticyclone

antidater [ɑ̃tidate] /1/ VT to backdate, predate

antidémocratique [ɑ̃tidemɔkratik] ADJ antidemocratic; (*peu démocratique*) undemocratic

antidépresseur [ɑ̃tidepʀɛsœʀ] NM antidepressant

antidérapant, e [ɑ̃tideʀapɑ̃, -ɑ̃t] ADJ nonskid

antidopage [ɑ̃tidɔpaʒ], **antidoping** [ɑ̃tidɔpiŋ] ADJ (*lutte*) antidoping; (*contrôle*) dope *cpd*

antidote [ɑ̃tidɔt] NM antidote

anti-émeute, antiémeute [ɑ̃tiemøt] ADJ (*police*) riot; (*lutte*) against rioting

antienne [ɑ̃tjɛn] NF (*fig*) chant, refrain

antieuropéen, ne [ɑ̃tiøʀɔpeɛ̃, -ɛn] ADJ, NM/F anti-European

antigang [ɑ̃tigɑ̃g] ADJ INV: **brigade** ~ commando unit

antigel [ɑ̃tiʒɛl] NM antifreeze

antigène [ɑ̃tiʒɛn] NM antigen

antigouvernemental, e, -aux [ɑ̃tiguvɛʀnəmɑ̃tal, -o] ADJ antigovernment

Antigua et Barbude [ɑ̃tigaeba̞ʀbyd] NF Antigua and Barbuda

antihéros [ɑ̃tieʀo] NM antihero

antihistaminique [ɑ̃tiistaminik] NM antihistamine

anti-inflammatoire [ɑ̃tiɛ̃flamatwaʀ] ADJ anti-inflammatory

anti-inflationniste [ɑ̃tiɛ̃flasjɔnist] ADJ anti-inflationary

antillais, e [ɑ̃tijɛ, -ɛz] ADJ West Indian, Caribbean ▸ NM/F: **Antillais, e** West Indian, Caribbean

Antilles [ɑ̃tij] NFPL: **les** ~ the West Indies; **les Grandes/Petites** ~ the Greater/Lesser Antilles

antilope [ɑ̃tilɔp] NF antelope

antimatière [ɑ̃timatjɛʀ] NF antimatter

antimilitarisme [ɑ̃timilitaʀism] NM antimilitarism

antimilitariste [ɑ̃timilitaʀist] ADJ antimilitarist

antimissile [ɑ̃timisil] ADJ antimissile

antimite, antimites [ɑ̃timit] ADJ, NM: **(produit)** ~**(s)** moth proofer, moth repellent

antimondialisation [ɑ̃timɔ̃djalizasjɔ̃] NF antiglobalization

antinucléaire [ɑ̃tinykleɛʀ] ADJ antinuclear

antioxydant [ɑ̃tiɔksidɑ̃] NM antioxidant

antiparasite [ɑ̃tipaʀazit] ADJ (*Radio, TV*) anti-interference; **dispositif** ~ suppressor

antipathie [ɑ̃tipati] NF antipathy

antipathique [ɑ̃tipatik] ADJ unpleasant, disagreeable

antipelliculaire [ɑ̃tipelikylɛʀ] ADJ anti-dandruff

antipersonnel [ɑ̃tipɛʀsɔnɛl] ADJ INV (*mines*) antipersonnel

antiphrase [ɑ̃tifʀɑz] NF: **par ~** ironically

antipodes [ɑ̃tipɔd] NMPL (*Géo*): **les ~** the antipodes; (*fig*) **être aux ~ de** to be the opposite extreme of

antipoison [ɑ̃tipwazɔ̃] ADJ INV: **centre ~** poison centre

antipoliomyélitique [ɑ̃tipɔljɔmjelitik] ADJ polio *cpd*

antipollution [ɑ̃tipɔlysjɔ̃] ADJ environmentally friendly, eco-friendly

antiquaire [ɑ̃tikɛʀ] NMF antique dealer

antique [ɑ̃tik] ADJ antique; (*très vieux*) ancient, antiquated

antiquité [ɑ̃tikite] NF (*objet*) antique; **l'A~** Antiquity; **magasin/marchand d'antiquités** antique shop/dealer

antirabique [ɑ̃tiʀabik] ADJ rabies *cpd*

antiracisme [ɑ̃tiʀasism] NM anti-racism

antiraciste [ɑ̃tiʀasist] ADJ antiracist

antireflet [ɑ̃tiʀəflɛ] ADJ INV (*verres*) antireflective

antirépublicain, e [ɑ̃tiʀepyblikɛ̃, -ɛn] ADJ antirepublican

antirides [ɑ̃tiʀid] ADJ INV (*crème*) anti wrinkle

antirouille [ɑ̃tiʀuj] ADJ INV anti-rust *cpd*; **peinture ~** antirust paint; **traitement ~** rustproofing

antisémite [ɑ̃tisemit] ADJ anti-Semitic

antisémitisme [ɑ̃tisemitism] NM anti-Semitism

antiseptique [ɑ̃tisɛptik] ADJ, NM antiseptic

antisismique [ɑ̃tisismik] ADJ (*dispositif, protection*) earthquake *cpd*; (*construction*) earthquake-safe; **normes antisismiques** earthquake safety standards

antisocial, e, -aux [ɑ̃tisɔsjal, -o] ADJ antisocial

antispasmodique [ɑ̃tispasmɔdik] ADJ, NM antispasmodic

antisportif, -ive [ɑ̃tispɔʀtif, -iv] ADJ unsporting; (*hostile au sport*) antisport

antisystème [ɑ̃tisistɛm] ADJ INV anti-establishment

antitabac [ɑ̃titaba] ADJ INV (*lutte, campagne*) anti-smoking

antiterroriste [ɑ̃titeʀɔʀist] ADJ (*mesures, loi*) anti-terrorist

antitétanique [ɑ̃titetanik] ADJ tetanus *cpd*

antithèse [ɑ̃titɛz] NF antithesis

antitrust [ɑ̃titʀœst] ADJ INV (*loi, mesures*) antimonopoly

antituberculeux, -euse [ɑ̃titybɛʀkylø, -øz] ADJ tuberculosis *cpd*

antitussif, -ive [ɑ̃titysif, -iv] ADJ antitussive, cough *cpd*

antivariolique [ɑ̃tivaʀjɔlik] ADJ smallpox *cpd*

antiviral, e, -aux [ɑ̃tiviʀal, -o] ADJ (*Méd*) antiviral ▶ NM (*Méd*): **un ~** an antiviral

antivirus [ɑ̃tiviʀys] (*Inform*) ADJ INV (*protection, logiciel*) antivirus ▶ NM antivirus program

antivol [ɑ̃tivɔl] ADJ, NM: (*dispositif*) ~ antitheft device; (*pour vélo*) padlock

antonyme [ɑ̃tɔnim] NM antonym

antre [ɑ̃tʀ] NM den, lair

anus [anys] NM anus

Anvers [ɑ̃vɛʀ] N Antwerp

anxiété [ɑ̃ksjete] NF anxiety

anxieusement [ɑ̃ksjøzmɑ̃] ADV anxiously

anxieux, -euse [ɑ̃ksjø, -jøz] ADJ anxious, worried; **être ~ de faire** to be anxious to do

anxiogène [ɑ̃ksjɔʒɛn] ADJ (*situation, climat*) stressful

anxiolytique [ɑ̃ksjɔlitik] NM anxiolytic

AOC SIGLE F (= *Appellation d'origine contrôlée*) guarantee of quality of wine

aorte [aɔʀt] NF aorta

août [u(t)] NM August; *voir aussi* **Assomption**; **juillet**

aoûtien, ne [ausjɛ̃, -ɛn] NM/F August holiday-maker

AP SIGLE F = **Assistance publique**

apaisant, e [apɛzɑ̃, -ɑ̃t] ADJ soothing

apaisement [apɛzmɑ̃] NM calming; soothing; (*aussi Pol*) appeasement ■ **apaisements** NMPL soothing reassurances; (*pour calmer*) pacifying words

apaiser [apeze] /**1**/ VT (*colère*) to calm, quell, soothe; (*faim*) to appease, assuage; (*douleur*) to soothe; (*personne*) to calm (down), pacify ■ **s'apaiser** VPR (*tempête, bruit*) to die down, subside; (*personne*) to calm down

apanage [apanaʒ] NM: **être l'~ de** to be the privilege *ou* prerogative of

aparté [apaʀte] NM (*Théât*) aside; (*entretien*) private conversation; **en ~** *adv* in an aside (*BRIT*); (*entretien*) in private

apartheid [apaʀtɛd] NM apartheid

apathie [apati] NF apathy

apathique [apatik] ADJ apathetic

apatride [apatʀid] NMF stateless person

APCE SIGLE F (= *Agence pour la création d'entreprises*) business start-up agency

★**apercevoir** [apɛʀsəvwaʀ] /**28**/ VT to see ■ **s'apercevoir de** VPR to notice; **s'~ que** to notice that; **sans s'en ~** without realizing *ou* noticing

aperçu, e [apɛʀsy] PP *de* **apercevoir** ▶ NM (*vue d'ensemble*) general survey; (*intuition*) insight

apéritif, -ive [apeʀitif, -iv] ADJ which stimulates the appetite ▶ NM (*boisson*) aperitif; (*réunion*) (pre-lunch *ou* -dinner) drinks pl; **prendre l'~** to have drinks (before lunch *ou* dinner) *ou* an aperitif

apéro [apeʀo] NM (*fam: apéritif*) aperitif, drink (*before lunch or dinner*); **prendre l'~** to have an aperitif

apesanteur [apəzɑ̃tœʀ] NF weightlessness

à-peu-près [apøpʀɛ] NM INV (*péj*) vague approximation

apeuré, e [apœʀe] ADJ frightened, scared

aphasie [afazi] NF aphasia

aphone [afɔn] ADJ voiceless

aphorisme [afɔʀism] NM aphorism

aphrodisiaque [afʀɔdizjak] ADJ, NM aphrodisiac

aphte [aft] NM mouth ulcer

aphteuse [aftøz] ADJ F: **fièvre ~** foot-and-mouth disease

à-pic [apik] NM cliff, drop

apicole [apikɔl] ADJ beekeeping cpd

apiculteur, -trice [apikyltœr, -tʀis] NM/F bee-keeper

apiculture [apikyltyʀ] NF beekeeping, apiculture

apitoiement [apitwamã] NM pity, compassion

apitoyer [apitwaje] /8/ VT to move to pity; ~ qn sur qn/qch to move sb to pity for sb/over sth ▪ **s'apitoyer** VPR to feel pity ou compassion; **s'~ (sur qn/qch)** to feel pity ou compassion (for sb/over sth)

ap.J.-C. ABR (= après Jésus-Christ) AD

APL SIGLE F (= aide personnalisée au logement) housing benefit

aplanir [aplaniʀ] /2/ VT to level; (fig) to smooth away, iron out

aplati, e [aplati] ADJ flat, flattened

aplatir [aplatiʀ] /2/ VT to flatten ▪ **s'aplatir** VPR to become flatter; (écrasé) to be flattened; (fig) to lie flat on the ground; (: fam) to fall flat on one's face; (: péj) to grovel

aplomb [aplɔ̃] NM (équilibre) balance, equilibrium; (fig) self-assurance; (: péj) nerve; **d'~** adv steady; (Constr) plumb

APN SIGLE M (= appareil photo(graphique) numérique) digital camera

apnée [apne] NF: **apnées du sommeil** sleep apnoea; **la plongée en ~** free-diving

apocalypse [apɔkalips] NF apocalypse

apocalyptique [apɔkaliptik] ADJ (fig) apocalyptic

apocryphe [apɔkʀif] ADJ apocryphal

apogée [apɔʒe] NM (fig) peak, apogee

apolitique [apɔlitik] ADJ (indifférent) apolitical; (indépendant) unpolitical, non-political

apologie [apɔlɔʒi] NF praise; (Jur) vindication

apoplexie [apɔplɛksi] NF apoplexy

a posteriori [apɔsteʀjɔʀi] ADV after the event, with hindsight, a posteriori

apostolat [apɔstɔla] NM (Rel) apostolate, discipleship; (gén) evangelism

apostolique [apɔstɔlik] ADJ apostolic

apostrophe [apɔstʀɔf] NF (signe) apostrophe; (appel) interpellation

apostropher [apɔstʀɔfe] /1/ VT (interpeller) to shout at, address sharply

apothéose [apɔteoz] NF pinnacle (of achievement); (Mus etc) grand finale

apothicaire [apɔtikɛʀ] NM apothecary

apôtre [apotʀ] NM apostle, disciple

apparaître [apaʀɛtʀ] /57/ VI to appear ▸ VB COPULE to appear, seem

apparat [apaʀa] NM: **tenue/dîner d'~** ceremonial dress/dinner

★**appareil** [apaʀɛj] NM (outil, machine) piece of apparatus, device; (électrique etc) appliance; (politique, syndical) machinery; (avion) (aero)plane (BRIT), (air)plane (US), aircraft inv; (téléphonique) telephone; (dentier) brace (BRIT), braces (US); **~ digestif/reproducteur** digestive/reproductive system ou apparatus; **l'~ productif** the means of production; **qui est à l'~?** who's speaking?; **dans le plus simple ~** in one's birthday suit; **~ (photo)** camera; **~ numérique** digital camera

appareillage [apaʀɛjaʒ] NM (appareils) equipment; (Navig) casting off, getting under way

appareiller [apaʀeje] /1/ VI (Navig) to cast off, get under way ▸ VT (assortir) to match up; (Méd: prothèse) to fit with a prosthesis; (: appareil acoustique) to fit with a hearing aid

appareil photo [apaʀɛjfɔto] (pl **appareils photos**) NM camera

apparemment [apaʀamã] ADV apparently

apparence [apaʀɑ̃s] NF appearance; **malgré les apparences** despite appearances; **en ~** apparently, seemingly

apparent, e [apaʀɑ̃, -ãt] ADJ visible; (évident) obvious; (superficiel) apparent; **coutures apparentes** topstitched seams; **poutres apparentes** exposed beams

apparenté, e [apaʀɑ̃te] ADJ: **~ à** related to; (fig) similar to

apparenter [apaʀɑ̃te] /1/: **s'apparenter à** VPR to be similar to

apparier [apaʀje] /7/ VT (gants) to pair, match

appariteur [apaʀitœʀ] NM attendant, porter (in French universities)

apparition [apaʀisjɔ̃] NF appearance; (surnaturelle) apparition; **faire son ~** to appear

★**appartement** [apaʀtəmã] NM flat (BRIT), apartment (US)

appartenance [apaʀtənɑ̃s] NF: **~ à** belonging to, membership of

★**appartenir** [apaʀtəniʀ] /22/: **~ à** vt to belong to; (faire partie de) to belong to, be a member of; **il lui appartient de** it is up to him to

appartiendrai [apaʀtjɛ̃dʀe], **appartiens** etc [apaʀtjɛ̃] VB voir **appartenir**

apparu, e [apaʀy] PP de **apparaître**

appas [apɑ] NMPL (d'une femme) charms

appât [apɑ] NM (Pêche) bait; (fig) lure, bait

appâter [apɑte] /1/ VT (hameçon) to bait; (poisson, fig) to lure, entice

appauvrir [apovʀiʀ] /2/ VT to impoverish ▪ **s'appauvrir** VPR to grow poorer, become impoverished

appauvrissement [apovʀismã] NM impoverishment

★**appel** [apɛl] NM call; (nominal) roll call; (: Scol) register; (Mil: recrutement) call-up; (Jur) appeal; **faire ~ à** (invoquer) to appeal to; (avoir recours à) to call on; (nécessiter) to call for, require; **faire ou interjeter ~** (Jur) to appeal, lodge an appeal; **faire l'~** to call the roll; (Scol) to call the register; **indicatif d'~** call sign; **numéro d'~** (Tél) number; **produit d'~** (Comm) loss leader; **sans ~** (fig) final, irrevocable; **~ d'air** in-draught; **~ d'offres** (Comm) invitation to tender; **faire un ~ de phares** to flash one's headlights; **~ (téléphonique)** (tele)phone call; **~ vidéo** video call

appelé [ap(ə)le] NM (Mil) conscript

★**appeler** [ap(ə)le] /4/ VT to call; (Tél) to call, ring; (faire venir: médecin etc) to call, send for; (fig: nécessiter) to call for, demand; **~ au secours** to call for help; **~ qn à l'aide** ou **au secours** to call to sb to help; **~ qn à un poste/des fonctions** to appoint sb to a post/assign duties to sb; **être appelé à** (fig) to be destined to; **~ qn à comparaître** (Jur) to summon sb to appear; **en ~ à** to appeal to

■ **s'appeler** VPR: **elle s'appelle Gabrielle** her name is Gabrielle, she's called Gabrielle; **comment vous appelez-vous?** what's your name?; **comment ça s'appelle?** what is it *ou* that called?

appellation [apelasjɔ̃] NF designation, appellation; **vin d'~ contrôlée** "appellation contrôlée" wine, *wine guaranteed of a certain quality*

appelle *etc* [apɛl] VB *voir* **appeler**

appendice [apɛ̃dis] NM appendix

appendicectomie [apɛ̃disɛktɔmi] NF appendicectomy, appendectomy (US)

appendicite [apɛ̃disit] NF appendicitis

appentis [apɑ̃ti] NM lean-to

appert [apɛR] VB: **il ~ que** it appears that, it is evident that

appesantir [apəzɑ̃tiR] /2/: **s'appesantir** VPR to grow heavier; **s'~ sur** *(fig)* to dwell at length on

appétissant, e [apetisɑ̃, -ɑ̃t] ADJ appetizing, mouth-watering

appétit [apeti] NM appetite; **couper l'~ à qn** to take away sb's appetite; **bon ~!** enjoy your meal!

applaudimètre [aplodimɛtR] NM applause meter

applaudir [aplodiR] /2/ VT to applaud ▶ VI to applaud, clap; **~ à** vt *(décision)* to applaud, commend

applaudissements [aplodismɑ̃] NMPL applause *sg*, clapping *sg*

appli [apli] NF app

applicable [aplikabl] ADJ applicable

applicateur [aplikatœR] NM applicator

application [aplikasjɔ̃] NF application; *(d'une loi)* enforcement; **mettre en ~** to implement

applique [aplik] NF wall lamp

appliqué, e [aplike] ADJ *(élève etc)* industrious, assiduous; *(science)* applied

appliquer [aplike] /1/ VT to apply; *(loi)* to enforce; *(donner: gifle, châtiment)* to give ■ **s'appliquer** VPR *(élève etc)* to apply o.s.; **s'~ à** *(loi, remarque)* to apply to; **s'~ à faire qch** to apply o.s. to doing sth, take pains to do sth; **s'~ sur** *(coïncider avec)* to fit over

appoint [apwɛ̃] NM (extra) contribution *ou* help; **avoir/faire l'~** *(en payant)* to have/give the right change *ou* money; **chauffage d'~** extra heating

appointements [apwɛ̃tmɑ̃] NMPL salary *sg*, stipend

appointer [apwɛ̃te] /1/ VT: **être appointé à l'année/au mois** to be paid yearly/monthly

appontage [apɔ̃taʒ] NM landing *(on an aircraft carrier)*

appontement [apɔ̃tmɑ̃] NM landing stage, wharf

apponter [apɔ̃te] /1/ VI *(avion, hélicoptère)* to land

apport [apɔR] NM supply; *(argent, biens etc)* contribution

★**apporter** [apɔRte] /1/ VT to bring; *(preuve)* to give, provide; *(modification)* to make; *(remarque)* to contribute, add

apposer [apoze] /1/ VT to append; *(sceau etc)* to affix

apposition [apozisjɔ̃] NF appending; affixing; *(Ling)*: **en ~** in apposition

appréciable [apResjabl] ADJ *(important)* appreciable, significant

appréciation [apResjasjɔ̃] NF appreciation; estimation, assessment ■ **appréciations** NFPL *(avis)* assessment *sg*, appraisal *sg*

apprécier [apResje] /7/ VT to appreciate; *(évaluer)* to estimate, assess ■ **s'apprécier** VPR *(monnaie)* to rise; **l'euro s'est apprécié de 8,4% par rapport au dollar** the euro has risen 8.4% against the dollar

appréhender [apReɑ̃de] /1/ VT *(craindre)* to dread; *(arrêter)* to apprehend; **~ que** to fear that; **~ de faire** to dread doing

appréhensif, -ive [apReɑ̃sif, -iv] ADJ apprehensive

appréhension [apReɑ̃sjɔ̃] NF apprehension

★**apprendre** [apRɑ̃dR] /58/ VT to learn; *(événement, résultats)* to learn of, hear of; **~ qch à qn** *(informer)* to tell sb (of) sth; *(enseigner)* to teach sb sth; **tu me l'apprends!** that's news to me!; **~ à faire qch** to learn to do sth; **~ à qn à faire qch** to teach sb to do sth

apprenti, e [apRɑ̃ti] NM/F apprentice; *(fig)* novice, beginner

★**apprentissage** [apRɑ̃tisaʒ] NM learning; *(Comm, Scol: période)* apprenticeship; **école** *ou* **centre d'~** training school *ou* centre; **faire l'~ de qch** *(fig)* to be initiated into sth

apprêt [apRɛ] NM *(sur un cuir, une étoffe)* dressing; *(sur un mur)* size; *(sur un papier)* finish; **sans ~** *(fig)* without artifice, unaffectedly

apprêté, e [apRɛte] ADJ *(fig)* affected

apprêter [apRɛte] /1/ VT to dress, finish ■ **s'apprêter** VPR: **s'~ à qch/à faire qch** to prepare for sth/for doing sth

appris, e [apRi, -iz] PP *de* **apprendre**

apprivoisé, e [apRivwaze] ADJ tame, tamed

apprivoiser [apRivwaze] /1/ VT to tame

approbateur, -trice [apRɔbatœR, -tRis] ADJ approving

approbatif, -ive [apRɔbatif, -iv] ADJ approving

approbation [apRɔbasjɔ̃] NF approval; **digne d'~** *(conduite, travail)* praiseworthy, commendable

approchant, e [apRɔʃɑ̃, -ɑ̃t] ADJ similar, close; **quelque chose d'~** something similar

approche [apRɔʃ] NF approaching; *(arrivée, attitude)* approach; **à l'~ du bateau/de l'ennemi** as the ship/enemy approached *ou* drew near; **l'~ d'un problème** the approach to a problem; **travaux d'~** *(fig)* manoeuvrings ■ **approches** NFPL *(abords)* surroundings

approché, e [apRɔʃe] ADJ approximate

★**approcher** [apRɔʃe] /1/ VI to approach, come near ▶ VT *(vedette, artiste)* to approach, come close to; *(rapprocher)*: **~ qch (de qch)** to bring *ou* put *ou* move sth near (to sth); **~ de** vt *(lieu, but)* to draw near to; *(quantité, moment)* to approach ■ **s'approcher de** VPR to approach, go *ou* come *ou* move near to; **approchez-vous** come *ou* go nearer

approfondi, e [apRɔfɔ̃di] ADJ thorough, detailed

approfondir [apRɔfɔ̃diR] /2/ VT to deepen; *(question)* to go further into; **sans ~** without going too deeply into it

approfondissement [apRɔfɔ̃dismɑ̃] NM *(de connaissances)* deepening

appropriation [apRɔpRijasjɔ̃] NF appropriation

approprié, e [apRɔpRije] ADJ: ~ **(à)** appropriate (to), suited (to)

approprier [apRɔpRije] /7/ VT (adapter) adapt ■ **s'approprier** VPR to appropriate, take over

approuver [apRuve] /1/ VT to agree with; (autoriser: loi, projet) to approve, pass; (trouver louable) to approve of; **je vous approuve entièrement/ne vous approuve pas** I agree with you entirely/don't agree with you; **lu et approuvé** (read and) approved

approvisionnement [apRɔvizjɔnmɑ̃] NM supplying; (provisions) supply, stock

approvisionner [apRɔvizjɔne] /1/ VT to supply; (compte bancaire) to pay funds into; ~ **qn en** to supply sb with ■ **s'approvisionner** VPR: **s'~ dans un certain magasin/au marché** to shop in a certain shop/at the market; **s'~ en** to stock up with

approximatif, -ive [apRɔksimatif, -iv] ADJ approximate, rough; (imprécis) vague

approximation [apRɔksimasjɔ̃] NF approximation

approximativement [apRɔksimativmɑ̃] ADV approximately, roughly; vaguely

appt ABR = **appartement**

appui [apɥi] NM support; **prendre ~ sur** to lean on; (objet) to rest on; **point d'~** fulcrum; (fig) something to lean on; **à l'~ de** (pour prouver) in support of; **à l'~** adv to support one's argument; **l'~ de la fenêtre** the windowsill, the window ledge

appuie etc [apɥi] VB voir **appuyer**

appui-tête, appuie-tête [apɥitɛt] NM INV headrest

appuyé, e [apɥije] ADJ (regard) meaningful; (: insistant) intent, insistent; (excessif: politesse, compliment) exaggerated, overdone

★**appuyer** [apɥije] /8/ VT (poser, soutenir: personne, demande) to support, back (up); ~ **qch sur/contre/à** to lean ou rest sth on/against ▸ VI: ~ **sur** (bouton) to press, push; (mot, détail) to stress, emphasize; ~ **sur le frein** to brake, apply the brakes; ~ **sur le champignon** to put one's foot down; ~ **contre** (toucher: mur, porte) to lean ou rest against; ~ **à droite** ou **sur sa droite** to bear (to the) right ■ **s'appuyer** VPR (chose: peser sur) to lean on, rest (heavily) on, press against; (compter sur) to rely on; **s'~ sur qn** to lean on sb

apr. ABR = **après**

âpre [ɑpR] ADJ acrid, pungent; (fig) harsh; (lutte) bitter; ~ **au gain** grasping, greedy

après [apRɛ] PRÉP after; **d'~** prép (selon) according to; **d'~ lui** according to him; **d'~ moi** in my opinion; ~ **quoi** after which; **et (puis) ~?** so what? ▸ ADV afterwards; **deux heures ~** two hours later; ~ **qu'il est parti/avoir fait** after he left/having done; **courir ~ qn** to run after sb; **crier ~ qn** to shout at sb; ~ **coup** adv after the event, afterwards; **être toujours ~ qn** (critiquer etc) to be always on at sb; ~ **tout** adv (au fond) after all

après-demain [apRɛdmɛ̃] ADV the day after tomorrow

après-guerre [apRɛgɛR] NM post-war years pl; **d'~** adj post-war

après-midi [apRɛmidi] NM OU F INV afternoon

après-rasage [apRɛRazaʒ] NM INV after-shave

après-shampo(o)ing [apRɛʃɑ̃pwɛ̃] NM INV conditioner

après-ski [apRɛski] NM INV (chaussure) snow boot; (moment) après-ski

après-soleil [apRɛsɔlɛj] ADJ INV after-sun cpd ▸ NM after-sun cream ou lotion

après-vente [apRɛvɑ̃t] ADJ INV after-sales cpd

âpreté [ɑpRəte] NF (voir âpre) pungency; harshness; bitterness

à-propos [apRɔpo] NM (d'une remarque) aptness; **faire preuve d'~** to show presence of mind, do the right thing; **avec ~** suitably, aptly

apte [apt] ADJ: ~ **à qch/faire qch** capable of sth/doing sth; ~ **(au service)** (Mil) fit (for service)

aptitude [aptityd] NF ability, aptitude

apurer [apyRe] /1/ VT (Comm) to clear

aquabike [akwabajk] NM aquabike

aquaculture [akwakyltyR] NF fish farming

aquagym® [akwaʒim] NF aquaerobics sg

aquaplanage [akwaplanaʒ] NM (Auto) aquaplaning

aquaplane [akwaplan] NM (planche) aquaplane; (sport) aquaplaning

aquaplaning [akwaplaniŋ] NM aquaplaning

aquarelle [akwaRɛl] NF (tableau) watercolour (BRIT), watercolor (US); (genre) watercolo(u)rs pl, aquarelle

aquarelliste [akwaRelist] NMF painter in watercolo(u)rs

aquarium [akwaRjɔm] NM aquarium

aquatique [akwatik] ADJ aquatic, water cpd

aqueduc [ak(ə)dyk] NM aqueduct

aqueux, -euse [akø, -øz] ADJ aqueous

aquilin [akilɛ̃] ADJ M: **nez ~** aquiline nose

AR SIGLE M = **accusé de réception**; (Aviat, Rail etc) = **aller (et) retour; lettre/paquet avec AR** recorded delivery letter/parcel ▸ ABR (Auto) = **arrière**

arabe [aRab] ADJ Arabic; (désert, cheval) Arabian; (nation, peuple) Arab ▸ NM (Ling) Arabic ▸ NMF: **Arabe** Arab

arabesque [aRabɛsk] NF arabesque

Arabie [aRabi] NF: **l'~** Arabia; **l'~ Saoudite** ou **Séoudite** Saudi Arabia

arable [aRabl] ADJ arable

arachide [aRaʃid] NF groundnut (plant); (graine) peanut, groundnut

araignée [aRɛɲe] NF spider; ~ **de mer** spider crab

araser [aRaze] /1/ VT to level; (en rabotant) to plane (down)

aratoire [aRatwaR] ADJ: **instrument ~** ploughing implement

arbalète [aRbalɛt] NF crossbow

arbitrage [aRbitRaʒ] NM refereeing; umpiring; arbitration

arbitraire [aRbitRɛR] ADJ arbitrary

arbitrairement [aRbitRɛRmɑ̃] ADV arbitrarily

★**arbitre** [aRbitR] NMF (Sport) referee; (: Tennis, Cricket) umpire; (fig) arbiter, judge; (Jur) arbitrator

arbitrer [aRbitRe] /1/ VT to referee; to umpire; to arbitrate

arboré, e [aRbɔRe] ADJ (jardin) planted with trees

arborer [aʀbɔʀe] /1/ vt to bear, display; (avec ostentation) to sport

arborescence [aʀbɔʀesɑ̃s] nf tree structure

arboricole [aʀbɔʀikɔl] adj (animal) arboreal; (technique) arboricultural

arboriculture [aʀbɔʀikyltyʀ] nf arboriculture; ~ **fruitière** fruit (tree) growing

★ **arbre** [aʀbʀ] nm tree; (Tech) shaft; ~ **à cames** (Auto) camshaft; ~ **fruitier** fruit tree; ~ **généalogique** family tree; ~ **de Noël** Christmas tree; ~ **de transmission** (Auto) drive shaft

arbrisseau, x [aʀbʀiso] nm shrub

arbuste [aʀbyst] nm small shrub, bush

arc [aʀk] nm (arme) bow; (Géom) arc; (Archit) arch; ~ **de cercle** arc of a circle; **en ~ de cercle** adj semicircular

arcade [aʀkad] nf arch(way); ~ **sourcilière** arch of the eyebrows ∎ **arcades** nfpl arcade sg, arches

arcanes [aʀkan] nmpl mysteries

arc-boutant [aʀkbutɑ̃] (pl **arcs-boutants**) nm flying buttress

arc-bouter [aʀkbute] /1/: **s'arc-bouter** vpr: **s'~ contre qch** to lean ou press against sth; (fig) to resist sth

arceau, x [aʀso] nm (métallique etc) hoop

arc-en-ciel [aʀkɑ̃sjɛl] (pl **arcs-en-ciel**) nm rainbow

archaïque [aʀkaik] adj archaic

archaïsme [aʀkaism] nm archaism

archange [aʀkɑ̃ʒ] nm archangel

arche [aʀʃ] nf arch; ~ **de Noé** Noah's Ark

archéologie [aʀkeɔlɔʒi] nf arch(a)eology

archéologique [aʀkeɔlɔʒik] adj arch(a)eological

archéologue [aʀkeɔlɔg] nmf arch(a)eologist

archer [aʀʃe] nm archer

archet [aʀʃɛ] nm bow

archétype [aʀketip] nm (modèle) archetype; **être l'~ de qch** to epitomize sth

archevêché [aʀʃəveʃe] nm archbishopric; (palais) archbishop's palace

archevêque [aʀʃəvɛk] nm archbishop

archi... [aʀʃi] préfixe (très) dead, extra

archibondé, e [aʀʃibɔ̃de] adj chock-a-block (Brit), packed solid

archiduc [aʀʃidyk] nm archduke

archiduchesse [aʀʃidyʃɛs] nf archduchess

archipel [aʀʃipɛl] nm archipelago

archisimple [aʀʃisɛpl] adj dead easy ou simple

★ **architecte** [aʀʃitɛkt] nmf architect

architectural, e, -aux [aʀʃitɛktyʀal, -o] adj architectural

architecture [aʀʃitɛktyʀ] nf architecture

architrave [aʀʃitʀav] nf (Archit) architrave

archivage [aʀʃivaʒ] nm filing

archive [aʀʃiv] nf file ∎ **archives** nfpl (collection) archives

archiver [aʀʃive] /1/ vt to file

archiviste [aʀʃivist] nmf archivist

arçon [aʀsɔ̃] nm voir **cheval**

arctique [aʀktik] adj Arctic; **le cercle A~** the Arctic Circle; **l'océan A~** the Arctic Ocean ▸ nm: **l'A~** the Arctic

ardemment [aʀdamɑ̃] adv ardently, fervently

ardent, e [aʀdɑ̃, -ɑ̃t] adj (soleil) blazing; (fièvre) raging; (amour) ardent, passionate; (prière) fervent

ardeur [aʀdœʀ] nf blazing heat; (fig) fervour, ardour

ardoise [aʀdwaz] nf slate

ardu, e [aʀdy] adj (travail) arduous; (problème) difficult; (pente) steep, abrupt

are [aʀ] nm are, 100 square metres

arène [aʀɛn] nf arena; (fig): **l'~ politique** the political arena ∎ **arènes** nfpl bull-ring sg

arête [aʀɛt] nf (de poisson) bone; (d'une montagne) ridge; (Géom etc) edge (where two faces meet)

arg. abr = **argus**

★ **argent** [aʀʒɑ̃] nm (métal) silver; (monnaie) money; (couleur) silver; **en avoir pour son ~** to get value for money; **gagner beaucoup d'~** to earn a lot of money; ~ **comptant** (hard) cash; ~ **de poche** pocket money; ~ **liquide** ready money, (ready) cash

argenté, e [aʀʒɑ̃te] adj silver(y); (métal) silver-plated

argenter [aʀʒɑ̃te] /1/ vt to silver(-plate)

argenterie [aʀʒɑ̃tʀi] nf silverware; (en métal argenté) silver plate

argentin, e [aʀʒɑ̃tɛ̃, -in] adj Argentinian, Argentine ▸ nm/f: **Argentin, e** Argentinian, Argentine

Argentine [aʀʒɑ̃tin] nf: **l'~** Argentina, the Argentine

argentique [aʀʒɑ̃tik] adj (appareil photo) film cpd

argile [aʀʒil] nf clay

argileux, -euse [aʀʒilø, -øz] adj clayey

argot [aʀgo] nm slang

> **Argot** was the term originally used to describe the jargon of the criminal underworld, characterized by colourful images and distinctive intonation and designed to confuse the outsider. Some French authors wrote in argot and so have helped it spread and grow. More generally, the special vocabulary used by any social or professional group is also known as argot.

argotique [aʀgɔtik] adj slang cpd; (très familier) slangy

arguer [aʀgɥe] /1/: ~ **de** vt to put forward as a pretext ou reason; ~ **que** to argue that

argument [aʀgymɑ̃] nm argument

argumentaire [aʀgymɑ̃tɛʀ] nm list of sales points; (brochure) sales leaflet

argumentation [aʀgymɑ̃tasjɔ̃] nf (fait d'argumenter) arguing; (ensemble des arguments) argument

argumenter [aʀgymɑ̃te] /1/ vi to argue

argus [aʀgys] nm guide to second-hand car etc prices

arguties [aʀgysi] nfpl pettifoggery sg (Brit), quibbles

aride [aʀid] adj arid

aridité [aʀidite] nf aridity

arien, ne [aʀjɛ̃, -ɛn] adj Arian

aristocrate [aʀistɔkʀat] nmf aristocrat

aristocratie [aʀistɔkʀasi] nf aristocracy

aristocratique [aʀistɔkʀatik] adj aristocratic

arithmétique [aʀitmetik] adj arithmetic(al) ▸ nf arithmetic

armada [aRmada] NF *(fig)* army

armagnac [aRmaɲak] NM Armagnac

armateur [aRmatœR] NM shipowner

armature [aRmatyR] NF framework; *(de tente etc)* frame; *(de corset)* bone; *(de soutien-gorge)* wiring

★**arme** [aRm] NF weapon; **se battre à l'~ blanche** to fight with blades; **~ à feu** firearm; *(section de l'armée)* arm ■ **armes** NFPL weapons, arms; *(blason)* (coat of) arms; **les armes** *(profession)* soldiering *sg*; **à armes égales** on equal terms; **en armes** up in arms; **passer par les armes** to execute (by firing squad); **prendre/présenter les armes** to take up/present arms; **armes de destruction massive** weapons of mass destruction

armé, e [aRme] ADJ armed; **~ de** armed with

armée [aRme] NF army; **~ de l'air** Air Force; **l'~ du Salut** the Salvation Army; **~ de terre** Army

armement [aRməmã] NM *(matériel)* arms *pl*, weapons *pl*; *(: d'un pays)* arms *pl*, armament; *(action d'équiper: d'un navire)* fitting out; **armements nucléaires** nuclear armaments; **course aux armements** arms race

Arménie [aRmeni] NF: **l'~** Armenia

arménien, ne [aRmenjɛ̃, -ɛn] ADJ Armenian ▶ NM *(Ling)* Armenian ▶ NM/F: **Arménien, ne** Armenian

armer [aRme] /1/ VT to arm; *(arme à feu)* to cock; *(appareil photo)* to wind on; **~ qch de** to fit sth with; *(renforcer)* to reinforce sth with; **~ qn de** to arm *ou* equip sb with ■ **s'armer** VPR: **s'~ de** to arm o.s. with

armistice [aRmistis] NM armistice; **l'A~** = Remembrance *(BRIT)* *ou* Veterans *(US)* Day

★**armoire** [aRmwaR] NF *(tall)* cupboard; *(penderie)* wardrobe *(BRIT)*, closet *(US)*; **~ à pharmacie** medicine chest

armoiries [aRmwaRi] NFPL coat of arms *sg*

armure [aRmyR] NF armour *no pl*, suit of armour

armurerie [aRmyRRi] NF arms factory; *(magasin)* gunsmith's (shop)

armurier [aRmyRje] NM gunsmith; *(Mil, d'armes blanches)* armourer

ARN SIGLE M *(= acide ribonucléique)* RNA

arnaque [aRnak] NF *(fam)* swindling; **c'est de l'~** it's daylight robbery

arnaquer [aRnake] /1/ VT *(fam)* to do *(fam)*, swindle; **se faire ~** to be had *(fam)* ou done

arnaqueur [aRnakœR] NM swindler

arnica [aRnika] NM: **(teinture d')arnica** arnica

arobase [aRobaz] NF *(Inform)* "at" symbol, @; **« paul ~ société point fr »** "paul at société dot fr"

aromates [aRɔmat] NMPL seasoning *sg*, herbs (and spices)

aromathérapie [aRɔmateRapi] NF aromatherapy

aromatique [aRɔmatik] ADJ aromatic

aromatisé, e [aRɔmatize] ADJ flavoured

arôme [aRom] NM aroma; *(d'une fleur etc)* fragrance

arpège [aRpɛʒ] NM arpeggio

arpentage [aRpãtaʒ] NM *(land)* surveying

arpenter [aRpãte] /1/ VT to pace up and down

arpenteur [aRpãtœR] NM land surveyor

ARPP SIGLE M *(= Autorité de régulation professionnelle de la publicité)* advertising standards authority

arqué, e [aRke] ADJ arched; *(jambes)* bow *cpd*, bandy

arr. ABR = **arrondissement**

arrachage [aRaʃaʒ] NM: **~ des mauvaises herbes** weeding

arraché [aRaʃe] NM *(Sport)* snatch; **obtenir à l'~** *(fig)* to snatch

arrache-pied [aRaʃpje]: **d'~** adv relentlessly

arracher [aRaʃe] /1/ VT to pull out; *(page etc)* to tear off, tear out; *(déplanter: légume, herbe, souche)* to pull up; *(bras etc: par explosion)* to blow off; *(: par accident)* to tear off; **~ qch à qn** to snatch sth from sb; *(fig)* to wring sth out of sb, wrest sth from sb; **~ qn à** *(solitude, rêverie)* to drag sb out of; *(famille etc)* to tear *ou* wrench sb away from; **se faire ~ une dent** to have a tooth out *ou* pulled *(US)* ■ **s'arracher** VPR *(article très recherché)* to fight over; **s'~ de** *(lieu)* to tear o.s. away from; *(habitude)* to force o.s. out of

arraisonner [aRɛzɔne] /1/ VT to board and search

arrangeant, e [aRãʒã, -ãt] ADJ accommodating, obliging

arrangement [aRãʒmã] NM arrangement

★**arranger** [aRãʒe] /3/ VT to arrange; *(réparer)* to fix, put right; *(régler)* to settle, sort out; *(convenir à)* to suit, be convenient for; **cela m'arrange** that suits me (fine) ■ **s'arranger** VPR *(se mettre d'accord)* to come to an agreement *ou* arrangement; *(s'améliorer: querelle, situation)* to be sorted out; *(se débrouiller)*: **s'~ pour que ...** to arrange things so that ...; **je vais m'~** I'll manage; **ça va s'~** it'll sort itself out; **s'~ pour faire** to make sure that *ou* see to it that one can do

arrangeur [aRãʒœR] NM *(Mus)* arranger

arrestation [aRɛstasjɔ̃] NF arrest

arrêt [aRɛ] NM stopping; *(de bus etc)* stop; *(Jur)* judgment, decision; *(Football)* save; **être à l'~** to be stopped, have come to a halt; **rester** *ou* **tomber en ~ devant** to stop short in front of; **sans ~** without stopping, non-stop; *(fréquemment)* continually; **~ d'autobus** bus stop; **~ facultatif** request stop; **~ de mort** capital sentence; **~ de travail** stoppage (of work) ■ **arrêts** NMPL *(Mil)* arrest *sg*

arrêté, e [aRete] ADJ *(idées)* firm, fixed ▶ NM order, decree; **~ municipal** = bylaw, bye-law

arrêter [aRete] /1/ VT to stop; *(chauffage etc)* to turn off, switch off; *(Comm: compte)* to settle; *(Couture: point)* to fasten off; *(fixer: date etc)* to appoint, decide on; *(criminel, suspect)* to arrest; **~ de faire** to stop doing; **arrête de te plaindre** stop complaining; **ne pas ~ de faire** to keep on doing ■ **s'arrêter** VPR to stop; *(s'interrompre)* to stop o.s.; **s'~ de faire** to stop doing; **s'~ sur** *(choix, regard)* to fall on

arrhes [aR] NFPL deposit *sg*

arrière [aRjɛR] NM back; *(Sport)* fullback; **à l'~** adv behind, at the back; **en ~** adv behind; *(regarder)* back, behind; *(tomber, aller)* backwards; **en ~ de** prép behind ▶ ADJ INV: **siège/roue ~** back *ou* rear seat/wheel ■ **arrières** NMPL *(fig)*: **protéger ses arrières** to protect the rear

arriéré, e [aRjeRe] ADJ *(péj)* backward ▶ NM *(d'argent)* arrears *pl*

arrière-boutique [aRjɛRbutik] NF back shop

arrière-cour [aRjɛRkuR] NF backyard

arrière-cuisine [aRjɛRkɥizin] NF scullery

arrière-garde [aʀjɛʀɡaʀd] NF rearguard

arrière-goût [aʀjɛʀɡu] NM aftertaste

★**arrière-grand-mère** [aʀjɛʀɡʀɑ̃mɛʀ] (*pl* **arrière-grands-mères**) NF great-grandmother

arrière-grand-père [aʀjɛʀɡʀɑ̃pɛʀ] (*pl* **arrière-grands-pères**) NM great-grandfather

arrière-grands-parents [aʀjɛʀɡʀɑ̃paʀɑ̃] NMPL great-grandparents

arrière-pays [aʀjɛʀpei] NM INV hinterland

arrière-pensée [aʀjɛʀpɑ̃se] NF ulterior motive; (*doute*) mental reservation

arrière-petite-fille [aʀjɛʀpətitfij] (*pl* **arrière-petites-filles**) NF great-granddaughter

arrière-petit-fils [aʀjɛʀpətifis] (*pl* **arrière-petits-fils**) NM great-grandson

arrière-petits-enfants [aʀjɛʀpətizɑ̃fɑ̃] NMPL great-grandchildren

arrière-plan [aʀjɛʀplɑ̃] NM background; **à l'~** in the background; **d'~** *adj* (*Inform*) background *cpd*

arrière-saison [aʀjɛʀsɛzɔ̃] NF late autumn

arrière-salle [aʀjɛʀsal] NF back room

arrière-train [aʀjɛʀtʀɛ̃] NM hindquarters *pl*

arrimer [aʀime] /1/ VT (*cargaison*) to stow; (*fixer*) to secure, fasten securely

arrivage [aʀivaʒ] NM consignment

arrivant, e [aʀivɑ̃, -ɑ̃t] NM/F newcomer

arrivée [aʀive] NF arrival; (*ligne d'arrivée*) finish; **~ d'air/de gaz** air/gas inlet; **courrier à l'~** incoming mail; **à mon ~** when I arrived

★**arriver** [aʀive] /1/ VI to arrive; (*survenir*) to happen, occur; **j'arrive!** (I'm) just coming!; **il arrive à Paris à 8 h** he gets to *ou* arrives in Paris at 8; **~ à destination** to arrive at one's destination; **~ à** (*atteindre*) to reach; **~ à (faire) qch** (*réussir*) to manage (to do) sth; **~ à échéance** to fall due; **en ~ à faire ...** to end up doing ..., get to the point of doing ...; **il arrive que ...** it happens that ...; **il lui arrive de faire ...** he sometimes does ...

arrivisme [aʀivism] NM ambition, ambitiousness

arriviste [aʀivist] NMF go-getter

arrobase [aʀɔbaz] NF (*Inform*) "at" symbol, @

arrogance [aʀɔɡɑ̃s] NF arrogance

arrogant, e [aʀɔɡɑ̃, -ɑ̃t] ADJ arrogant

arroger [aʀɔʒe] /3/: **s'arroger** VPR to assume (without right); **s'~ le droit de ...** to assume the right to ...

arrondi, e [aʀɔ̃di] ADJ round ▶ NM roundness

arrondir [aʀɔ̃diʀ] /2/ VT (*forme, objet*) to round; (*somme*) to round off; **~ ses fins de mois** to supplement one's pay ▪ **s'arrondir** VPR to become round(ed)

★**arrondissement** [aʀɔ̃dismɑ̃] NM (*Admin*) ≈ district

An **arrondissement municipal** is an administrative subdivision of the cities of Paris, Lyon and Marseille, which have 20, 9 and 16 *arrondissements* respectively. Each *arrondissement* has an elected *conseil* which, in turn, chooses a mayor. It is not to be confused with the *arrondissement départemental*, which is a subdivision of a *département* made up of several *cantons*.

arrosage [aʀozaʒ] NM watering; **tuyau d'~** hose(pipe)

★**arroser** [aʀoze] /1/ VT to water; (*victoire etc*) to celebrate (over a drink); (*Culin*) to baste

arroseur [aʀozœʀ] NM (*tourniquet*) sprinkler

arroseuse [aʀozøz] NF water cart

arrosoir [aʀozwaʀ] NM watering can

arrt ABR = **arrondissement**

arsenal, -aux [aʀsənal, -o] NM (*Navig*) naval dockyard; (*Mil*) arsenal; (*fig*) gear, paraphernalia

arsenic [aʀsənik] NM arsenic

art [aʀ] NM art; **avoir l'~ de faire** (*fig: personne*) to have a talent for doing; **les arts** the arts; **livre/critique d'~** art book/ critic; **objet d'~** objet d'art; **~ dramatique** dramatic art; **arts martiaux** martial arts; **arts et métiers** applied arts and crafts; **arts ménagers** home economics *sg*; **arts plastiques** plastic arts

art. ABR = **article**

artère [aʀtɛʀ] NF (*Anat*) artery; (*rue*) main road

artériel, le [aʀteʀjɛl] ADJ arterial

artériosclérose [aʀteʀjoskleʀoz] NF arteriosclerosis

arthrite [aʀtʀit] NF arthritis

arthropode [aʀtʀɔpɔd] NM arthropod

arthroscopie [aʀtʀɔskɔpi] NF arthroscopy

arthrose [aʀtʀoz] NF (degenerative) osteoarthritis

artichaut [aʀtiʃo] NM artichoke

★**article** [aʀtikl] NM article; (*Comm*) item, article; **faire l'~** (*Comm*) to do one's sales spiel; **faire l'~ de** (*fig*) to sing the praises of; **à l'~ de la mort** at the point of death; **~ défini/indéfini** definite/indefinite article; **~ de fond** (*Presse*) feature article; **articles de bureau** office equipment; **articles de voyage** travel goods *ou* items

articulaire [aʀtikylɛʀ] ADJ of the joints, articular

articulation [aʀtikylasjɔ̃] NF articulation; (*Anat*) joint

articulé, e [aʀtikyle] ADJ (*membre*) jointed; (*poupée*) with moving joints

articuler [aʀtikyle] /1/ VT to articulate ▪ **s'articuler sur** VPR (*Anat, Tech*) to articulate (with); **s'~ autour de** (*fig*) to centre around *ou* on, turn on

artifice [aʀtifis] NM device, trick

artificiel, le [aʀtifisjɛl] ADJ artificial

artificiellement [aʀtifisjɛlmɑ̃] ADV artificially

artificier [aʀtifisje] NM pyrotechnist

artificieux, -euse [aʀtifisjø, -øz] ADJ guileful, deceitful

artillerie [aʀtijʀi] NF artillery, ordnance

artilleur [aʀtijœʀ] NM artilleryman, gunner

artisan [aʀtizɑ̃] NM artisan, (self-employed) craftsman; **l'~ de la victoire/du malheur** the architect of victory/of the disaster

artisanal, e, -aux [aʀtizanal, -o] ADJ of *ou* made by craftsmen; (*péj*) cottage industry *cpd*, unsophisticated; **de fabrication artisanale** home-made

artisanalement [aʀtizanalmɑ̃] ADV by craftsmen

artisanat [aʀtizana] NM arts and crafts *pl*

★**artiste** [aʀtist] NMF artist; (*Théât, Mus*) artist, performer; (*de variétés*) entertainer

artistique [aʀtistik] ADJ artistic

artistiquement [aʀtistikmɑ̃] ADV artistically

arum [aʀɔm] NM arum lily

aryen, ne [aʀjɛ̃, -ɛn] ADJ Aryan

AS SIGLE F (*Sport*: = *Association sportive*) ≈ FC (= *Football Club*)

as VB [a] *voir* **avoir** ▸ NM [ɑs] ace

a/s ABR (= *aux soins de*) c/o

ASBL SIGLE F (= *association sans but lucratif*) non-profit-making organization

asc. ABR = **ascenseur**

ascendance [asɑ̃dɑ̃s] NF (*origine*) ancestry; (*Astrologie*) ascendant

ascendant, e [asɑ̃dɑ̃, -ɑ̃t] ADJ upward ▸ NM influence ◾ **ascendants** NMPL ascendants

★**ascenseur** [asɑ̃sœʀ] NM lift (BRIT), elevator (US)

ascension [asɑ̃sjɔ̃] NF ascent; (*de montagne*) climb; **l'A~** (*Rel*) the Ascension (: *jour férié*) Ascension (Day); *see note*; **(île de) l'A~** Ascension Island

> The **fête de l'Ascension** is a public holiday in France. It always falls on a Thursday, usually in May. Many French people take the following Friday off work too and enjoy a long weekend, a practice known as *faire le pont* (see note at entry *pont*).

ascète [asɛt] NMF ascetic

ascétique [asetik] ADJ ascetic

ascétisme [asetism] NM asceticism

ascorbique [askɔʀbik] ADJ: **acide ~** ascorbic acid

ASE SIGLE F (= *Agence spatiale européenne*) ESA (= European Space Agency)

asepsie [asɛpsi] NF asepsis

aseptique [asɛptik] ADJ aseptic

aseptisé, e [asɛptize] ADJ (*péj*) sanitized

aseptiser [asɛptize] VT (*stériliser*: *pièce, instruments*) to sterilize; (*fig, péj*) to sanitize

asexué, e [asɛksɥe] ADJ asexual

ashkénaze [aʃkenɑz] ADJ, NMF Ashkenazi

asiatique [azjatik] ADJ Asian, Asiatic ▸ NMF: **Asiatique** Asian

★**Asie** [azi] NF: **l'~** Asia

asile [azil] NM (*refuge*) refuge, sanctuary; (*pour malades, vieillards etc*) home; **droit d'~** (*Pol*: political) asylum; **accorder l'~ politique à qn** to grant *ou* give sb political asylum; **chercher/trouver ~ quelque part** to seek/find refuge somewhere

asocial, e, -aux [asɔsjal, -o] ADJ antisocial

aspartame [aspaʀtam] NM aspartame

aspect [aspɛ] NM appearance, look; (*fig*) aspect, side; (*Ling*) aspect; **à l'~ de** at the sight of

asperge [aspɛʀʒ] NF asparagus *no pl*

asperger [aspɛʀʒe] /3/ VT to spray, sprinkle

aspérité [aspeʀite] NF excrescence, protruding bit (of rock *etc*)

aspersion [aspɛʀsjɔ̃] NF spraying, sprinkling

asphalte [asfalt] NM asphalt

asphyxiant, e [asfiksjɑ̃, -ɑ̃t] ADJ suffocating; **gaz ~** poison gas

asphyxie [asfiksi] NF suffocation, asphyxia, asphyxiation

asphyxier [asfiksje] /7/ VT to suffocate, asphyxiate; (*fig*) to stifle; **mourir asphyxié** to die of suffocation *ou* asphyxiation

aspic [aspik] NM (*Zool*) asp; (*Culin*) aspic

aspirant, e [aspiʀɑ̃, -ɑ̃t] ADJ: **pompe aspirante** suction pump ▸ NM (*Navig*) midshipman

★**aspirateur** [aspiʀatœʀ] NM vacuum cleaner, hoover®; **passer l'~** to vacuum

aspiration [aspiʀasjɔ̃] NF inhalation, sucking (up); drawing up ◾ **aspirations** NFPL (*ambitions*) aspirations

aspirer [aspiʀe] /1/ VT (*air*) to inhale; (*liquide*) to suck (up); (*appareil*) to suck *ou* draw up; **~ à** VT to aspire to

★**aspirine** [aspiʀin] NF aspirin

assagir [asaʒiʀ] /2/ VT to quieten down, settle down ◾ **s'assagir** VPR to quieten down, settle down

assaillant, e [asajɑ̃, -ɑ̃t] NM/F assailant, attacker

assaillir [asajiʀ] /13/ VT to assail, attack; **~ qn de** (*questions*) to assail *ou* bombard sb with

assainir [aseniʀ] /2/ VT to clean up; (*eau, air*) to purify

assainissement [asenismɑ̃] NM cleaning up; purifying

assaisonnement [asɛzɔnmɑ̃] NM seasoning

assaisonner [asɛzɔne] /1/ VT to season; **bien assaisonné** highly seasoned

assassin [asasɛ̃] NM murderer; assassin

assassinat [asasina] NM murder; assassination

assassiner [asasine] /1/ VT to murder; (*Pol*) to assassinate

assaut [aso] NM assault, attack; **prendre d'~** (take by) storm, assault; **donner l'~ (à)** to attack; **faire ~ de** (*rivaliser*) to vie with *ou* rival each other in

assèchement [asɛʃmɑ̃] NM draining, drainage

assécher [aseʃe] /6/ VT to drain

assemblage [asɑ̃blaʒ] NM (*action*) assembling; (*Menuiserie*) joint; **un ~ de** (*fig*) a collection of; **langage d'~** (*Inform*) assembly language

assemblée [asɑ̃ble] NF (*réunion*) meeting; (*public, assistance*) gathering; assembled people; (*Pol*) assembly; (*Rel*): **l'~ des fidèles** the congregation; **l'A~ nationale (AN)** the (French) National Assembly; *see note*

> The **Assemblée nationale** is the lower house of the French Parliament, the upper house being the *Sénat*. It is housed in the Palais Bourbon in Paris. Its members, or *députés*, are elected every five years.

assembler [asɑ̃ble] /1/ VT (*joindre, monter*) to assemble, put together; (*amasser*) to gather (together), collect (together) ◾ **s'assembler** VPR to gather, collect

assembleur [asɑ̃blœʀ] NM assembler, fitter; (*Inform*) assembler

assener, asséner [asene] /**5**/ VT: ~ **un coup à qn** to deal sb a blow

assentiment [asɑ̃timɑ̃] NM assent, consent; (*approbation*) approval

★**asseoir** [aswaʀ] /**26**/ VT (*malade, bébé*) to sit up; (*personne debout*) to sit down; (*autorité, réputation*) to establish; **faire ~ qn** to ask sb to sit down; **~ qch sur** to build sth on; (*appuyer*) to base sth on ■ **s'asseoir** VPR to sit (o.s.) up; to sit (o.s.) down; **asseyez-vous !, assieds-toi !** sit down!

assermenté, e [asɛʀmɑ̃te] ADJ sworn, on oath

assertion [asɛʀsjɔ̃] NF assertion

asservir [asɛʀviʀ] /**2**/ VT to subjugate, enslave

asservissement [asɛʀvismɑ̃] NM (*action*) enslavement; (*état*) slavery

assesseur [asescœʀ] NM (*Jur*) assessor

asseyais *etc* [asejɛ] VB *voir* **asseoir**

★**assez** [ase] ADV (*suffisamment*) enough, sufficiently; (*passablement*) rather, quite, fairly; **~ !** enough!, that'll do!; **~/pas ~ cuit** well enough done/underdone; **est-il ~ fort/rapide ?** is he strong/fast enough?; **il est passé ~ vite** he went past rather *ou* quite *ou* fairly fast; **~ de pain/livres** enough *ou* sufficient bread/books; **vous en avez ~ ?** have you got enough?; **en avoir ~ de qch** (*en être fatigué*) to have had enough of sth; **j'en ai ~ !** I've had enough!; **travailler ~** to work (hard) enough

assidu, e [asidy] ADJ assiduous, painstaking; (*régulier*) regular; **~ auprès de qn** attentive towards sb

assiduité [asidɥite] NF assiduousness, painstaking regularity; attentiveness ■ **assiduités** NFPL assiduous attentions

assidûment [asidymɑ̃] ADV assiduously, painstakingly; attentively

assied *etc* [asje] VB *voir* **asseoir**

assiégé, e [asjeʒe] ADJ under siege, besieged

assiéger [asjeʒe] /**3, 6**/ VT to besiege, lay siege to; (*foule, touristes*) to mob, besiege

assiérai *etc* [asjeʀe] VB *voir* **asseoir**

★**assiette** [asjɛt] NF plate; (*contenu*) plate(ful); (*équilibre*) seat; (*de colonne*) seating; (*de navire*) trim; **il n'est pas dans son ~** he's not feeling quite himself; **~ à dessert** dessert *ou* side plate; **~ anglaise** assorted cold meats; **~ creuse** (soup) dish, soup plate; **~ de l'impôt** basis of (tax) assessment; **~ plate** (dinner) plate

assiettée [asjete] NF plateful

assignation [asiɲasjɔ̃] NF assignation; (*Jur*) summons; (*: de témoin*) subpoena; **~ à résidence** compulsory order of residence

assigner [asiɲe] /**1**/ VT: **~ qch à** to assign *ou* allot sth to; (*valeur, importance*) to attach sth to; (*somme*) to allocate sth to; (*limites*) to set *ou* fix sth to; (*cause, effet*) to ascribe *ou* attribute sth to; **~ qn à**

(*affecter*) to assign sb to; **~ qn à résidence** (*Jur*) to give sb a compulsory order of residence

assimilable [asimilabl] ADJ easily assimilated *ou* absorbed

assimilation [asimilasjɔ̃] NF assimilation, absorption

assimilé, e [asimile] ADJ (*semblable*) similar; **ils sont assimilés aux infirmières** (*Admin*) they are classed as nurses ▶ NM: **cadres et assimilés** managers and those of equivalent grade

assimiler [asimile] /**1**/ VT to assimilate, absorb; (*comparer*): **~ qch/qn à** to liken *ou* compare sth/sb to ■ **s'assimiler** VPR (*s'intégrer*) to be assimilated *ou* absorbed

★**assis, e** [asi, -iz] PP *de* **asseoir** ▶ ADJ sitting (down), seated; **~ en tailleur** sitting cross-legged ▶ NF (*Constr*) course; (*Géo*) stratum (*pl* -a); (*fig*) basis (*pl* bases), foundation

assises [asiz] NFPL (*Jur*) assizes; (*congrès*) (annual) conference

assistanat [asistana] NM assistantship; (*à l'université*) probationary lectureship

assistance [asistɑ̃s] NF (*public*) audience; (*aide*) assistance; **porter** *ou* **prêter ~ à qn** to give sb assistance; **A~ publique** public health service; **enfant de l'A~ (publique)** child in care; **~ technique** technical aid

assistant, e [asistɑ̃, -ɑ̃t] NM/F assistant; (*d'université*) probationary lecturer; **assistante sociale** social worker ■ **assistants** NMPL (*auditeurs etc*) those present

assisté, e [asiste] ADJ (*Auto*) power-assisted; **~ par ordinateur** computer-assisted; **direction assistée** power steering ▶ NM/F (*péj*) person receiving aid from the State

★**assister** [asiste] /**1**/ VT to assist; **~ à** VT (*scène, événement*) to witness; (*conférence*) to attend, be (present) at; (*spectacle, match*) to be at, see

associatif, -ive [asɔsjatif, -iv] ADJ: **mouvement ~** community movement; **vie/radio associative** community life/radio; **tissu ~** fabric of community life

association [asɔsjasjɔ̃] NF association; (*Comm*) partnership; **~ d'idées/images** association of ideas/images

associé, e [asɔsje] NM/F associate; (*Comm*) partner

associer [asɔsje] /**7**/ VT to associate; **~ qn à** (*profits*) to give sb a share of; (*affaire*) to make sb a partner in; (*joie, triomphe*) to include sb in; **~ qch à** (*joindre, allier*) to combine sth with ■ **s'associer** VPR to join together; (*Comm*) to form a partnership; (*collaborateur*) to take on (as a partner); **s'~ à** (*couleurs, qualités*) to be combined with; (*opinions, joie de qn*) to share in; **s'~ à** *ou* **avec qn pour faire** to join (forces) *ou* join together with sb to do

assoie *etc* [aswa] VB *voir* **asseoir**

assoiffé, e [aswafe] ADJ thirsty; **~ de** (*sang*) thirsting for; (*gloire*) thirsting after

assoirai [aswaʀe], **assois** *etc* [aswa] VB *voir* **asseoir**

assolement [asɔlmɑ̃] NM (systematic) rotation of crops

assombrir [asɔ̃bʀiʀ] /**2**/ VT to darken; (*fig*) to fill with gloom ■ **s'assombrir** VPR to darken; (*devenir*

> Fairly, **quite** et **rather** servent tous à modifier un adjectif ou un adverbe, mais avec des nuances : **rather** est moins neutre que **quite** et **fairly**. Par exemple, **it's rather expensive** suggère que la personne qui parle trouve la chose en question un peu trop chère, alors que **it's quite** ou **fairly expensive** est plus neutre.

nuageux, fig: visage) to cloud over; (fig) to become gloomy

assommant, e [asɔmɑ̃, -ɑ̃t] ADJ (ennuyeux) deadly boring, deadly dull; **c'est ~** it's a real bore

assommer [asɔme] /1/ VT to knock out, stun; (fam: ennuyer) to bore stiff

Assomption [asɔ̃psjɔ̃] NF: **l'~** the Assumption

> The **fête de l'Assomption**, more commonly known as le 15 août, is a national holiday in France. Traditionally, large numbers of people either set off on or return from their holidays on 15 August, frequently causing chaos on the roads.

assorti, e [asɔrti] ADJ matched, matching; **fromages/légumes assortis** assorted cheeses/vegetables; **~ à** matching; **~ de** accompanied with; (conditions, conseils) coupled with; **bien/mal ~** well/ill-matched

assortiment [asɔrtimɑ̃] NM (choix) assortment, selection; (harmonie de couleurs, formes) arrangement; (Comm: lot, stock) selection

assortir [asɔrtir] /2/ VT to match; **~ qch à** to match sth with; **~ qch de** to accompany sth with ▪ **s'assortir** VPR to go well together, match; **s'~ de** to be accompanied by

assoupi, e [asupi] ADJ dozing, sleeping; (fig) (be) numbed; (sens) dulled

assoupir [asupir] /2/: **s'assoupir** VPR (personne) to doze off; (sens) to go numb

assoupissement [asupismɑ̃] NM (sommeil) dozing; (fig: somnolence) drowsiness

assouplir [asuplir] /2/ VT to make supple, soften; (membres, corps) to limber up, make supple; (fig) to relax; (: caractère) to soften, make more flexible ▪ **s'assouplir** VPR to soften; to limber up; to relax; to become more flexible

assouplissant [asuplisɑ̃] NM (fabric) softener

assouplissement [asuplismɑ̃] NM softening; limbering up; relaxation; **exercices d'~** limbering up exercises

assourdir [asurdir] /2/ VT (étouffer) to deaden, muffle; (bruit) to deafen

assourdissant, e [asurdisɑ̃, -ɑ̃t] ADJ (bruit) deafening

assouvir [asuvir] /2/ VT to satisfy, appease

assouvissement [asuvismɑ̃] NM (action, résultat) satisfaction

assoyais etc [aswajɛ] VB voir **asseoir**

assujetti, e [asyʒeti] ADJ: **~ (à)** subject (to); (Admin) **~ à l'impôt** subject to tax(ation)

assujettir [asyʒetir] /2/ VT to subject, subjugate; (fixer: planches, tableau) to fix securely; **~ qn à** (règle, impôt) to subject sb to

assujettissement [asyʒetismɑ̃] NM subjection, subjugation

assumer [asyme] /1/ VT (fonction, emploi) to assume, take on; (accepter: conséquence, situation) to accept

★**assurance** [asyrɑ̃s] NF (certitude) assurance; (confiance en soi) (self-)confidence; (contrat) insurance (policy); (secteur commercial) insurance; **prendre une ~ contre** to take out insurance ou an insurance policy against; **~ contre l'incendie** fire insurance; **~ contre le vol** insurance against

theft; **société d'~, compagnie d'assurances** insurance company; **~ au tiers** third party insurance; **~ maladie** health insurance; **~ tous risques** (Auto) comprehensive insurance; **assurances sociales** ≈ National Insurance (BRIT), ≈ Social Security (US)

assurance-vie [asyrɑ̃svi] (pl **assurances-vie**) NF life assurance ou insurance

assurance-vol [asyrɑ̃svɔl] (pl **assurances-vol**) NF insurance against theft

assuré, e [asyre] ADJ (réussite, échec, victoire etc) certain, sure; (démarche, voix) assured; (pas) steady, (self-)confident; (certain): **~ de** confident of; (Assurances) insured ▸ NM/F insured (person); **~ social** ≈ member of the National Insurance (BRIT) ou Social Security (US) scheme

assurément [asyremɑ̃] ADV assuredly, most certainly

★**assurer** [asyre] /1/ VT (Comm) to insure; (stabiliser) to steady, stabilize; (victoire etc) to ensure, make certain; (frontières, pouvoir) to make secure; (service, garde) to provide, operate; **~ qch à qn** (garantir) to secure ou guarantee sth for sb; (certifier) to assure sb of sth; **~ à qn que** to assure sb that; **je vous assure que non/si** I assure you that that is not the case/is the case; **~ qn de** to assure sb of; **~ ses arrières** (fig) to be sure one has something to fall back on ▪ **s'assurer** VPR (Comm): **s'~ (contre)** to insure o.s. (against); **s'~ de/que** (vérifier) to make sure of/that; **s'~ (de)** (aide de qn) to secure; **s'~ sur la vie** to take out life insurance; **s'~ le concours/la collaboration de qn** to secure sb's aid/collaboration

assureur [asyrœr] NM insurance agent; (société) insurers pl

Assyrie [asiri] NF: **l'~** Assyria

assyrien, ne [asirjɛ̃, -jɛn] ADJ Assyrian ▸ NM/F: **Assyrien, ne** Assyrian

astérisque [asterisk] NM asterisk

astéroïde [asterɔid] NM asteroid

asthénie [asteni] NF asthenia

asthmatique [asmatik] ADJ, NMF asthmatic

asthme [asm] NM asthma

asticot [astiko] NM maggot

asticoter [astikɔte] /1/ VT (fam) to needle, get at

astigmate [astigmat] ADJ (Méd: personne) astigmatic, having an astigmatism

astiquer [astike] /1/ VT to polish, shine

astrakan [astrakɑ̃] NM astrakhan

astral, e, -aux [astral, -o] ADJ astral

astre [astr] NM star

astreignant, e [astrɛɲɑ̃, -ɑ̃t] ADJ demanding

astreindre [astrɛ̃dr] /49/ VT: **~ qn à qch** to force sth upon sb; **~ qn à faire** to compel ou force sb to do ▪ **s'astreindre à** VPR to compel ou force o.s. to

astreinte [astrɛ̃t] NF on-call duty; **être d'~** to be on call

astringent, e [astrɛ̃ʒɑ̃, -ɑ̃t] ADJ astringent

astrologie [astrɔlɔʒi] NF astrology

astrologique [astrɔlɔʒik] ADJ astrological

astrologue [astrɔlɔg] NMF astrologer

astronaute [astrɔnot] NMF astronaut

astronautique [astrɔnotik] NF astronautics sg

astronef [astʀɔnɛf] NM spacecraft, spaceship

astronome [astʀɔnɔm] NMF astronomer

astronomie [astʀɔnɔmi] NF astronomy

astronomique [astʀɔnɔmik] ADJ astronomic(al)

astrophysicien, ne [astʀɔfizisjɛ̃, -ɛn] NM/F astrophysicist

astrophysique [astʀɔfizik] NF astrophysics *sg*

astuce [astys] NF shrewdness, astuteness; *(truc)* trick, clever way; *(plaisanterie)* wisecrack

astucieusement [astysjøzmɑ̃] ADV shrewdly, cleverly, astutely

astucieux, -euse [astysjø, -øz] ADJ shrewd, clever, astute

asymétrie [asimetʀi] NF asymmetry

asymétrique [asimetʀik] ADJ asymmetric(al)

asymptomatique [asɛ̃ptɔmatik] ADJ *(maladie, sujet)* asymptomatic

AT SIGLE M (= *Ancien Testament*) OT

atavique [atavik] ADJ atavistic

atavisme [atavism] NM atavism, heredity

ataxie [ataksi] NF ataxia

★**atelier** [atəlje] NM workshop; *(de peintre)* studio

atermoiements [atɛʀmwamɑ̃] NMPL procrastination *sg*

atermoyer [atɛʀmwaje] /**8**/ VI to temporize, procrastinate

athée [ate] ADJ atheistic ▶ NMF atheist

athéisme [ateism] NM atheism

Athènes [atɛn] N Athens

athénien, ne [atenjɛ̃, -ɛn] ADJ Athenian

athlète [atlɛt] NMF *(Sport)* athlete; *(costaud)* muscleman

athlétique [atletik] ADJ athletic

athlétisme [atletism] NM athletics *sg*; **faire de l'~** to do athletics; **tournoi d'~** athletics meeting

Atlantide [atlɑ̃tid] NF: **l'~** Atlantis

★**atlantique** [atlɑ̃tik] ADJ Atlantic ▶ NM: **l'(océan) A~** the Atlantic (Ocean)

atlantiste [atlɑ̃tist] ADJ, NMF Atlanticist

Atlas [atlɑs] NM: **l'~** the Atlas Mountains

atlas [atlɑs] NM atlas

atmosphère [atmɔsfɛʀ] NF atmosphere

atmosphérique [atmɔsfeʀik] ADJ atmospheric

atoll [atɔl] NM atoll

atome [atom] NM atom

atomique [atɔmik] ADJ atomic, nuclear; *(usine)* nuclear; *(nombre, masse)* atomic

atomiser [atɔmize] VT *(vaporiser)* to spray

atomiseur [atɔmizœʀ] NM atomizer

atomiste [atɔmist] NMF *(aussi:* **savant atomiste***)* atomic scientist

atone [atɔn] ADJ lifeless; *(Ling)* unstressed, unaccented

atours [atuʀ] NMPL attire *sg*, finery *sg*

atout [atu] NM trump; *(fig)* asset; *(: plus fort)* trump card; **«~ pique/trèfle »** "spades/clubs are trumps"

ATP SIGLE F (= *Association des joueurs de tennis professionnels*) ATP (= *Association of Tennis Professionals*) ▶ SIGLE MPL = **arts et traditions populaires**; **musée des ~** ≈ folk museum

âtre [ɑtʀ] NM hearth

atroce [atʀɔs] ADJ atrocious, horrible

atrocement [atʀɔsmɑ̃] ADV atrociously, horribly

atrocité [atʀɔsite] NF atrocity

atrophie [atʀɔfi] NF atrophy

atrophier [atʀɔfje] /**7**/: **s'atrophier** VPR to atrophy

atropine [atʀɔpin] NF *(Chimie)* atropine

attablé, e [atable] ADJ: **être ~** to be sitting at the table

attabler [atable] /**1**/: **s'attabler** VPR to sit down at (the) table; **s'~ à la terrasse** to sit down (at a table) on the terrace

ATTAC SIGLE F (= *Association pour la taxation des transactions financières et pour l'action citoyenne*) ATTAC, *organization critical of globalization originally set up to demand a tax on foreign currency speculation*

attachant, e [ataʃɑ̃, -ɑ̃t] ADJ engaging, likeable

attache [ataʃ] NF clip, fastener; *(fig)* tie; **à l'~** *(chien)* tied up ■ **attaches** NFPL *(relations)* connections

attaché, e [ataʃe] ADJ: **être ~ à** *(aimer)* to be attached to ▶ NM/F *(Admin)* attaché; **~ de presse/ d'ambassade** press/embassy attaché; **~ commercial** commercial attaché

attaché-case [ataʃekɛz] NM INV attaché case *(BRIT)*, briefcase

attachement [ataʃmɑ̃] NM attachment

★**attacher** [ataʃe] /**1**/ VT to tie up; *(étiquette)* to attach, tie on; *(ceinture)* to fasten; *(souliers)* to do up; **~ qch à** to tie ou fasten ou attach sth to; **~ qn à** *(fig: lier)* to attach sb to; **~ du prix/de l'importance à** to attach great value/attach importance to ▶ VI *(poêle, riz)* to stick ■ **s'attacher** VPR *(robe etc)* to do up; **s'~ à** *(par affection)* to become attached to; **s'~ à faire qch** to endeavour to do sth

attaquant [atakɑ̃] NM *(Mil)* attacker; *(Sport)* striker, forward

attaque [atak] NF attack; *(cérébrale)* stroke; *(d'épilepsie)* fit; **être/se sentir d'~** to be/feel on form; **~ à main armée** armed attack

★**attaquer** [atake] /**1**/ VT to attack; *(en justice)* to sue, bring an action against; *(travail)* to tackle, set about ▶ VI to attack ■ **s'attaquer** VPR *(personne)* to attack; *(épidémie, misère)* to tackle, attack

attardé, e [ataʀde] ADJ *(passants)* late; *(enfant)* backward; *(conceptions)* old-fashioned

attarder [ataʀde] /**1**/: **s'attarder** VPR *(sur qch, en chemin)* to linger; *(chez qn)* to stay on

atteignais *etc* [atɛɲɛ] VB *voir* **atteindre**

atteindre [atɛ̃dʀ] /**49**/ VT to reach; *(blesser)* to hit; *(contacter)* to reach, contact, get in touch with; *(émouvoir)* to affect

atteint, e [atɛ̃, -ɛ̃t] PP *de* **atteindre** ▶ ADJ *(Méd)*: **être ~ de** to be suffering from ▶ NF attack; **hors d'atteinte** out of reach; **porter atteinte à** to strike a blow at, undermine

attelage [at(ə)laʒ] NM *(de remorque etc)* coupling *(BRIT)*, *(trailer)* hitch *(US)*; *(animaux)* team; *(harnachement)* harness; *(: de bœufs)* yoke

atteler [at(ə)le] /**4**/ VT *(cheval, bœufs)* to hitch up; *(wagons)* to couple ■ **s'atteler à** VPR *(travail)* to buckle down to

attelle [atɛl] NF splint

attenant, e [at(ə)nɑ̃, -ɑ̃t] ADJ: **~ (à)** adjoining

★**attendant** [atɑ̃dɑ̃]: **en ~** adv (*dans l'intervalle*) meanwhile, in the meantime

★**attendre** [atɑ̃dʀ] **/41/** VT to wait for; (*être destiné ou réservé à*) to await, be in store for; **je n'attends plus rien (de la vie)** I expect nothing more (from life); **attendez-moi, s'il vous plaît** wait for me, please; **~ un enfant** to be expecting a baby; **~ qch de** to expect sth of; **~ de pied ferme** to wait determinedly; **~ de faire/d'être** to wait until one does/is; **~ que** to wait until; **attendez qu'il vienne** wait until he comes; **faire ~ qn** to keep sb waiting; **se faire ~** to keep people (*ou us etc*) waiting; **en attendant** adv voir **attendant ▶** I didn't expect (that); **attendez que je réfléchisse** wait while I think ■ **s'attendre** VPR: **s'~ à (ce que)** (*escompter*) to expect (that); **je ne m'y attendais pas** I didn't expect that; **ce n'est pas ce à quoi je m'attendais** that's not what I expected

attendri, e [atɑ̃dʀi] ADJ tender

attendrir [atɑ̃dʀiʀ] **/2/** VT to move (to pity); (*viande*) to tenderize ■ **s'attendrir** VPR: **s'~ (sur)** to be moved ou touched (by)

attendrissant, e [atɑ̃dʀisɑ̃, -ɑ̃t] ADJ moving, touching

attendrissement [atɑ̃dʀismɑ̃] NM (*tendre*) emotion; (*apitoyé*) pity

attendrisseur [atɑ̃dʀisœʀ] NM tenderizer

attendu, e [atɑ̃dy] PP de **attendre ▶** ADJ (*événement*) long-awaited; (*prévu*) expected ▶ NM: **attendus** reasons adduced for a judgment; **~ que** conj considering that, since

attentat [atɑ̃ta] NM (*contre une personne*) assassination attempt; (*contre un bâtiment*) attack; **~ à la bombe** bomb attack; **~ à la pudeur** (*exhibitionnisme*) indecent exposure no pl; (*agression*) indecent assault no pl; **~ suicide** suicide bombing

attente [atɑ̃t] NF wait; (*espérance*) expectation; **contre toute ~** contrary to (all) expectations

attenter [atɑ̃te] **/1/**: **~ à** vt (*liberté*) to violate; **~ à la vie de qn** to make an attempt on sb's life; **~ à ses jours** to make an attempt on one's life

attentif, -ive [atɑ̃tif, -iv] ADJ (*auditeur*) attentive; (*soin*) scrupulous; (*travail*) careful; **~ à** paying attention to; (*devoir*) mindful of; **~ à faire** careful to do

★**attention** [atɑ̃sjɔ̃] NF attention; (*prévenance*) attention, thoughtfulness no pl; **mériter ~** to be worthy of attention; **à l'~ de** for the attention of; **porter qch à l'~ de qn** to bring sth to sb's attention; **attirer l'~ de qn sur qch** to draw sb's attention to sth; **faire ~ (à)** to be careful (of); **faire ~ (à ce) que** to be ou make sure that; **~ !** careful!, watch!, watch out!; **~ à la voiture !** watch out for that car!; **~, si vous ouvrez cette lettre** (*sanction*) just watch out, if you open that letter; **~, respectez les consignes de sécurité** be sure to observe the safety instructions

attentionné, e [atɑ̃sjɔne] ADJ thoughtful, considerate

attentisme [atɑ̃tism] NM wait-and-see policy

attentiste [atɑ̃tist] ADJ (*politique*) wait-and-see ▶ NMF believer in a wait-and-see policy

attentivement [atɑ̃tivmɑ̃] ADV attentively

atténuant, e [atenɥɑ̃, -ɑ̃t] ADJ: **circonstances atténuantes** extenuating circumstances

atténuer [atenɥe] **/1/** VT (*douleur*) to alleviate, ease; (*couleurs*) to soften; (*diminuer*) to lessen; (*amoindrir*) to mitigate the effects of ■ **s'atténuer** VPR to ease; (*violence etc*) to abate

atterrant, e [ateʀɑ̃, -ɑ̃t] ADJ appalling

atterrer [ateʀe] **/1/** VT to dismay, appal

★**atterrir** [ateʀiʀ] **/2/** VI to land

atterrissage [ateʀisaʒ] NM landing; **~ sur le ventre/sans visibilité/forcé** belly/blind/forced landing

attestation [atɛstasjɔ̃] NF certificate, testimonial; **~ médicale** doctor's certificate

attesté, e [atɛste] ADJ (*mot, emploi*) attested

attester [atɛste] **/1/** VT to testify to, vouch for; (*démontrer*) to attest, testify to; **~ que** to testify that

attiédir [atjediʀ] **/2/**: **s'attiédir** VPR to become lukewarm; (*fig*) to cool down

attifé, e [atife] ADJ (*fam*) got up (BRIT), decked out

attifer [atife] **/1/** VT to get (BRIT) ou do up, deck out

attique [atik] NM: **appartement en ~** penthouse (flat (BRIT) ou apartment (US))

attirail [atiraj] NM gear; (*péj*) paraphernalia

attirance [atiʀɑ̃s] NF attraction; (*séduction*) lure

attirant, e [atiʀɑ̃, -ɑ̃t] ADJ attractive, appealing

attirer [atiʀe] **/1/** VT to attract; (*appâter*) to lure, entice; **~ qn dans un coin/vers soi** to draw sb into a corner/towards one; **~ l'attention de qn** to attract sb's attention; **~ l'attention de qn sur qch** to draw sb's attention to sth; **~ des ennuis à qn** to make trouble for sb ■ **s'attirer** VPR: **s'~ des ennuis** to bring trouble upon o.s., get into trouble

attiser [atize] **/1/** VT (*feu*) to poke (up), stir up; (*fig*) to fan the flame of, stir up

attitré, e [atitʀe] ADJ qualified; (*agréé*) accredited, appointed

attitude [atityd] NF attitude; (*position du corps*) bearing

attouchements [atuʃmɑ̃] NMPL touching sg; (*sexuels*) fondling sg, stroking sg

attractif, -ive [atʀaktif, -iv] ADJ attractive

attraction [atʀaksjɔ̃] NF attraction; (*de cabaret, cirque*) number

attrait [atʀɛ] NM appeal, attraction; (*plus fort*) lure; **éprouver de l'~ pour** to be attracted to ■ **attraits** NMPL attractions

attrape [atʀap] NF voir **farce**

attrape-nigaud [atʀapnigo] NM con

★**attraper** [atʀape] **/1/** VT to catch; (*habitude, amende*) to get, pick up; (*fam: duper*) to con, take in (BRIT); **se faire ~** (*fam*) to be told off

attrayant, e [atʀɛjɑ̃, -ɑ̃t] ADJ attractive

attribuer [atʀibɥe] **/1/** VT (*prix*) to award; (*rôle, tâche*) to allocate, assign; (*imputer*): **~ qch à** to attribute sth to, ascribe sth to, put sth down to ■ **s'attribuer** VPR (*s'approprier*) to claim for o.s.

attribut [atʀiby] NM attribute; (*Ling*) complement

attribution [atʀibysjɔ̃] NF (*voir attribuer*) awarding; allocation; assignment; attribution; **complément d'~** (*Ling*) indirect object ■ **attributions** NFPL (*compétence*) attributions

attristant, e [atʀistɑ̃, -ɑ̃t] ADJ saddening

attrister [atʀiste] /1/ VT to sadden ■ **s'attrister** VPR: **s'~ de qch** to be saddened by sth

attroupement [atʀupmɑ̃] NM crowd, mob

attrouper [atʀupe] /1/: **s'attrouper** VPR to gather

atypique [atipik] ADJ (*aussi Méd*) atypical

★**au** [o] PRÉP *voir* **à**

aubade [obad] NF dawn serenade

aubaine [obɛn] NF godsend; (*financière*) windfall; (*Comm*) bonanza

aube [ob] NF dawn, daybreak; (*Rel*) alb; **à l'~** at dawn *ou* daybreak; **à l'~ de** (*fig*) at the dawn of

aubépine [obepin] NF hawthorn

★**auberge** [obɛʀʒ] NF inn; **~ de jeunesse** youth hostel

aubergine [obɛʀʒin] NF aubergine (*BRIT*), eggplant (*US*)

aubergiste [obɛʀʒist] NMF inn-keeper, hotelkeeper

auburn [obœʀn] ADJ INV auburn

★**aucun, e** [okœ̃, -yn] ADJ, PRON no; (*positif*) any; **il n'y a ~ livre** there isn't any book, there is no book; **~ homme** no man; **sans ~ doute** without any doubt; **sans aucune hésitation** without any hesitation; **en aucune façon** in no way at all ▶ PRON none; (*positif*) any(one); **je n'en vois ~ qui ...** I can't see any which ..., I (can) see none which ...; **plus qu'~ autre** more than any other; **il le fera mieux qu'~ de nous** he'll do it better than any of us; **plus qu'~ de ceux qui ...** more than any of those who ...; **~ des deux** neither of the two; **~ d'entre eux** none of them; **d'aucuns** (*certains*) some

aucunement [okynmɑ̃] ADV in no way, not in the least

audace [odas] NF daring, boldness; (*péj*) audacity; **il a eu l'~ de ...** he had the audacity to ...; **vous ne manquez pas d'~ !** you're not lacking in nerve *ou* cheek!

audacieusement [odasjøzmɑ̃] ADV daringly

audacieux, -euse [odasjø, -øz] ADJ daring, bold

au-dedans [odədɑ̃] ADV, PRÉP inside

au-dehors [odəɔʀ] ADV, PRÉP outside

au-delà [od(ə)la] ADV beyond; **~ de** *prép* beyond ▶ NM: **l'~** the hereafter

★**au-dessous** [odsu] ADV underneath; below; **~ de** *prép* under(neath), below; (*limite, somme etc*) below, under; (*dignité, condition*) below; **~ de tout** the (absolute) limit

★**au-dessus** [odsy] ADV above; **~ de** *prép* above

au-devant [od(ə)vɑ̃]: **~ de** *prép*: **aller ~ de** (*personne, danger*) to go (out) and meet; (*souhaits, désirs de qn*) to anticipate; **aller ~ de qn** to go out to meet sb; **aller ~ des ennuis** *ou* **difficultés** to be asking for trouble

audible [odibl] ADJ audible

audience [odjɑ̃s] NF audience; (*Jur: séance*) hearing; **trouver ~ auprès de** to arouse much interest among, get the (interested) attention of

audimat® [odimat] NM (*taux d'écoute*) ratings *pl*

audio [odjo] ADJ INV (*fichier, matériel*) audio

audiodescription [odjodɛskʀipsjɔ̃] NF audio-description

audioguide [odjogid] NM audio guide

audiovisuel, le, audio-visuel, le [odjovizɥɛl] ADJ audio-visual ▶ NM (*équipement*) audio-visual aids *pl*; (*méthodes*) audio-visual methods *pl*; (*média, secteur*): **l'~** radio and television

audit [odit] NM audit

auditeur, -trice [oditœʀ, -tʀis] NM/F (*à la radio*) listener; (*à une conférence*) member of the audience, listener; **~ libre** unregistered student (*attending lectures*), auditor (*US*)

auditif, -ive [oditif, -iv] ADJ (*mémoire*) auditory; **appareil ~** hearing aid

audition [odisjɔ̃] NF (*ouïe, écoute*) hearing; (*Jur: de témoins*) examination; (*Mus, Théât: épreuve*) audition

auditionner [odisjɔne] /1/ VT, VI to audition

auditoire [oditwaʀ] NM audience

auditorium [oditɔʀjɔm] NM (public) studio

auge [oʒ] NF trough

★**augmentation** [ɔgmɑ̃tasjɔ̃] NF (*action*) increasing; raising; (*résultat*) increase; **~ (de salaire)** rise (in salary) (*BRIT*), (pay) raise (*US*)

★**augmenter** [ɔgmɑ̃te] /1/ VT to increase; (*salaire, prix*) to increase, raise, put up; (*employé*) to increase the salary of, give a (salary) rise (*BRIT*) *ou* (pay) raise (*US*) to ▶ VI to increase; **~ de poids/volume** to gain (in) weight/volume

augure [ogyʀ] NM soothsayer, oracle; **de bon/mauvais ~** of good/ill omen

augurer [ɔgyʀe] /1/ VT: **~ qch de** to foresee sth (coming) from *ou* out of; **~ bien de** to augur well for

auguste [ogyst] ADJ august, noble, majestic

★**aujourd'hui** [oʒuʀdɥi] ADV today; **aujourd'hui en huit/quinze** a week/two weeks today, a week/two weeks from now; **à dater** *ou* **partir d'aujourd'hui** from today('s date)

aulne [o(l)n] NM alder

aumône [omon] NF alms *sg* (*pl inv*); **faire l'~ (à qn)** to give alms (to sb); **faire l'~ de qch à qn** (*fig*) to favour sb with sth

aumônerie [omonʀi] NF chaplaincy

aumônier [omonje] NM chaplain

★**auparavant** [opaʀavɑ̃] ADV before(hand)

auprès [opʀɛ]: **~ de** *prép* next to, close to; (*recourir, s'adresser*) to; (*en comparaison de*) compared with, next to; (*dans l'opinion de*) in the opinion of

auquel [okɛl] PRON *voir* **lequel**

aura *etc* [ɔʀa] VB *voir* **avoir**

aurai *etc* [ɔʀe] VB *voir* **avoir**

auréole [ɔʀeɔl] NF halo; (*tache*) ring

auréolé, e [ɔʀeɔle] ADJ (*fig*): **~ de gloire** crowned with *ou* in glory

auriculaire [ɔʀikylɛʀ] NM little finger

aurifère [ɔʀifɛʀ] ADJ gold-bearing

aurons *etc* [ɔʀɔ̃] VB *voir* **avoir**

aurore [ɔʀɔʀ] NF dawn, daybreak; **~ boréale** northern lights *pl*

auscultation [ɔskyltasjɔ̃] NF auscultation

ausculter [ɔskylte] /1/ VT to sound; **~ un patient** to listen to a patient's chest

auspices [ɔspis] NMPL: **sous les ~ de** under the patronage ou auspices of; **sous de bons/mauvais ~** under favourable/unfavourable auspices

★**aussi** [osi] ADV (également) also, too; (de comparaison) as; **~ fort que** as strong as; **moi ~** me too; **lui ~** (sujet) he too; (objet) him too; **~ bien que** (de même que) as well as ▸ CONJ therefore, consequently

> **Also** est rarement placé en fin de phrase, contrairement à **too**.
> Il était aussi artiste. **He was also an artist**.
> Elle est chanteuse et aussi actrice. **She's a singer and an actress too**.

aussitôt [osito] ADV straight away, immediately; **~ que** as soon as; **~ envoyé** as soon as it is (ou was) sent; **~ fait** no sooner done

austère [ɔstɛʀ] ADJ austere; (sévère) stern

austérité [ɔsterite] NF austerity; **plan/budget d'~** austerity plan/budget

austral, e [ɔstral] ADJ southern; **l'océan A~** the Antarctic Ocean; **les Terres Australes** Antarctica

★**Australie** [ɔstrali] NF: **l'~** Australia

★**australien, ne** [ɔstraljɛ̃, -ɛn] ADJ Australian ▸ NM/F: **Australien, ne** Australian

★**autant** [otɑ̃] ADV so much; **je ne savais pas que tu la détestais ~** I didn't know you hated her so much; (comparatif): **~ (que)** as much (as); (nombre) as many (as); **~ (de)** so much (ou many); as much (ou many); **n'importe qui aurait pu en faire ~** anyone could have done the same ou as much; **~ partir** we (ou you etc) may as well leave; **~ ne rien dire** best not say anything; **~ dire que ...** one might as well say that ...; **fort ~ que courageux** as strong as he is brave; **pour ~** for all that; **il n'est pas découragé pour ~** he isn't discouraged for all that; **pour ~ que** conj assuming, as long as; **d'~** adv accordingly, in proportion; **d'~ plus/ mieux (que)** all the more/the better (since)

autarcie [otarsi] NF autarky, self-sufficiency

autel [otɛl] NM altar

★**auteur** [otœʀ] NM author; **l'~ de cette remarque** the person who said that; **droit d'~** copyright

auteur-compositeur [otœʀkɔ̃pozitœʀ] (pl **auteurs-compositeurs**) NMF composer-songwriter

authenticité [otɑ̃tisite] NF authenticity

authentification [otɑ̃tifikasjɔ̃] NF authentication

authentifier [otɑ̃tifje] /7/ VT to authenticate

authentique [otɑ̃tik] ADJ authentic, genuine

autisme [otism] NM autism

autiste [otist] ADJ autistic ▸ NMF autistic person

★**auto** [oto] NF car; **autos tamponneuses** bumper cars, Dodgems®

auto... [oto] PRÉFIXE auto..., self-

autobiographie [otobjɔgrafi] NF autobiography

autobiographique [otobjɔgrafik] ADJ autobiographical

autobronzant [otobʀɔ̃zɑ̃] NM self-tanning cream (ou lotion etc)

★**autobus** [otɔbys] NM bus

★**autocar** [otɔkaʀ] NM coach

autochtone [otɔktɔn] NMF native

★**autocollant, e** [otokɔlɑ̃, -ɑ̃t] ADJ self-adhesive; (enveloppe) self-seal ▸ NM sticker

auto-couchettes [otokuʃɛt] ADJ INV: **train ~** car sleeper train, motorail® train (BRIT)

autocratie [otokrasi] NF autocracy

autocratique [otokratik] ADJ autocratic

autocritique [otokritik] NF self-criticism

autocuiseur [otokwizœʀ] NM (Culin) pressure cooker

autodéfense [otodefɑ̃s] NF self-defence; **groupe d'~** vigilante committee

autodérision [otoderizjɔ̃] NF self-mockery

autodestruction [otodɛstryksjɔ̃] NF self-destruction

autodétermination [otodetɛrminasjɔ̃] NF self-determination

autodidacte [otodidakt] NMF self-taught person

autodiscipline [otodisiplin] NF self-discipline

autodrome [otodrom] NM motor-racing stadium

auto-école [otoekɔl] NF driving school

autoentrepreneur, -euse [otoɑ̃trəprənœr, øz] NM/F self-employed businessman/-woman

autofinancement [otofinɑ̃smɑ̃] NM self-financing

autogéré, e [otoʒere] ADJ self-managed, managed internally

autogestion [otoʒɛstjɔ̃] NF joint worker-management control

autographe [otograf] NM autograph

autoguidé, e [otogide] ADJ self-guided

automate [ɔtɔmat] NM (robot) automaton; (machine) (automatic) machine

automatique [ɔtɔmatik] ADJ automatic

automatiquement [ɔtɔmatikmɑ̃] ADV automatically

automatisation [ɔtɔmatizasjɔ̃] NF automation

automatiser [ɔtɔmatize] /1/ VT to automate

automatisme [ɔtɔmatism] NM (Tech: mécanisme) automatic device; (activité) automatic reflex; **devenir un ~** to become an automatic reflex

automédication [otomedikasjɔ̃] NF self-medication

automitrailleuse [otomitrajøz] NF armoured car

automnal, e, -aux [ɔtɔnal, -o] ADJ autumnal

★**automne** [ɔtɔn] NM autumn (BRIT), fall (US)

★**automobile** [ɔtɔmɔbil] ADJ motor cpd ▸ NF (motor) car; **l'~** motoring; (industrie) the car ou automobile (US) industry

★**automobiliste** [ɔtɔmɔbilist] NMF motorist

automutilation [otomytilasjɔ̃] NF self-harm

automutiler [otomytile] /1/: **s'automutiler** VPR to self-harm

autonettoyant, e [otonɛtwajɑ̃, -ɑ̃t] ADJ: **four ~** self-cleaning oven

autonome [ɔtɔnɔm] ADJ autonomous

autonomie [ɔtɔnɔmi] NF autonomy; (Pol) self-government, autonomy; **~ de vol** range

autonomiste [ɔtɔnɔmist] NMF separatist

autoportrait [otopɔrtrɛ] NM self-portrait

autoproclamé, e [otoprɔklame] ADJ (*leader, vainqueur*) self-proclaimed; **le président ~** the self-proclaimed president

autoproclamer [otoprɔklame]: **s'autoproclamer** VPR to declare o.s.

autopsie [ɔtɔpsi] NF post-mortem (examination), autopsy

autopsier [ɔtɔpsje] /7/ VT to carry out a post-mortem *ou* an autopsy on

autoradio [otoradjo] NF car radio

autorail [otoraj] NM railcar

autorisation [ɔtɔrizasjɔ̃] NF permission, authorization; (*papiers*) permit; **donner à qn l'~ de** to give sb permission to, authorize sb to; **avoir l'~ de faire** to be allowed *ou* have permission to do, be authorized to do

autorisé, e [ɔtɔrize] ADJ (*opinion, sources*) authoritative; (*permis*): **~ à faire** authorized *ou* permitted to do; **dans les milieux autorisés** in official circles

autoriser [ɔtɔrize] /1/ VT to give permission for, authorize; (*fig*) to allow (of), sanction; **~ qn à faire** to give permission to sb to do, authorize sb to do ■ **s'autoriser** VPR (*audace, dépenses*) to allow o.s.; **s'~ à faire** to permit o.s. to do; **il s'est autorisé à faire des commentaires** he permitted himself to make some remarks; **elle ne s'autorise que trois morceaux de chocolat par semaine** she only allows herself three pieces of chocolate a week

autoritaire [ɔtɔritɛr] ADJ authoritarian

autoritarisme [ɔtɔritarism] NM authoritarianism

autorité [ɔtɔrite] NF authority; **faire ~** to be authoritative; **autorités constituées** constitutional authorities

★**autoroute** [otorut] NF motorway (BRIT), expressway (US); **~ de l'information** (*Inform*) information superhighway; *see note*

French **autoroutes**, indicated by blue road signs with the letter A followed by a number, are toll roads. The speed limit is 130 km/h (110 km/h when it is raining). At the tollgate, the lanes marked with an orange T are reserved for people who subscribe to *télépéage*, an electronic payment system.

autoroutier, -ière [otorutje, -jɛr] ADJ motorway *cpd* (BRIT), expressway *cpd* (US)

autosatisfaction [otosatisfaksjɔ̃] NF self-satisfaction

auto-stop [otostɔp] (*pl* **autos-stops**) NM: **l'~** hitch-hiking; **faire de l'~** to hitch-hike; **prendre qn en ~** to give sb a lift

auto-stoppeur, -euse [otostɔpœr, -øz] NM/F hitch-hiker, hitcher (BRIT)

autosuffisance [otosyfizɑ̃s] NF self-sufficiency

autosuffisant, e [otosyfizɑ̃, -ɑ̃t] ADJ self-sufficient

autosuggestion [otosygʒɛstjɔ̃] NF autosuggestion

★**autour** [otur] ADV around; **~ de** *prép* around; (*environ*) around, about; **tout ~** *adv* all around

---

autre [otr]

ADJ **1** (*différent*) other, different; **je préférerais un autre verre** I'd prefer another *ou* a different glass; **d'autres verres** different glasses; **se sentir autre** to feel different; **la difficulté est autre** the difficulty is *ou* lies elsewhere

2 (*supplémentaire*) other; **je voudrais un autre verre d'eau** I'd like another glass of water

3: **autre chose** something else; **autre part** somewhere else; **d'autre part** on the other hand

▶ PRON **1**: **un autre** another (one); **nous/vous autres** us/you; **d'autres** others; **l'autre** the other (one); **les autres** the others; (*autrui*) others; **l'un et l'autre** both of them; **ni l'un ni l'autre** neither of them; **se détester l'un l'autre/les uns les autres** to hate each other *ou* one another; **d'une semaine/minute à l'autre** from one week/minute *ou* moment to the next; (*incessamment*) any week/minute *ou* moment now; **de temps à autre** from time to time; **entre autres** (*personnes*) among others; (*choses*) among other things

2 (*expressions*): **j'en ai vu d'autres** I've seen worse; **à d'autres !** pull the other one!

★**autrefois** [otrəfwa] ADV in the past

★**autrement** [otrəmɑ̃] ADV differently; (*d'une manière différente*) in another way; (*sinon*) otherwise; **je n'ai pas pu faire ~** I couldn't do anything else, I couldn't do otherwise; **~ dit** in other words; (*c'est-à-dire*) that is to say

★**Autriche** [otriʃ] NF: **l'~** Austria

★**autrichien, ne** [otriʃjɛ̃, -ɛn] ADJ Austrian ▶ NM/F: **Autrichien, ne** Austrian

autruche [otryʃ] NF ostrich; **faire l'~** (*fig*) to bury one's head in the sand

autrui [otrɥi] PRON others

auvent [ovɑ̃] NM canopy

auvergnat, e [ɔvɛrɲa, -at] ADJ of *ou* from the Auvergne

Auvergne [ɔvɛrɲ] NF: **l'~** the Auvergne

★**aux** [o] PRÉP *voir* **à**

auxiliaire [ɔksiljɛr] ADJ, NMF auxiliary

auxquels, auxquelles [okɛl] PRON *voir* **lequel**

AV SIGLE M (*Banque*: = *avis de virement*) advice of bank transfer ▶ ABR (*Auto*) = **avant**

av. ABR (= *avenue*) Av(e)

avachi, e [avaʃi] ADJ limp, flabby; (*chaussure, vêtement*) out-of-shape; (*personne*): **~ sur qch** slumped on *ou* across sth

avais *etc* [avɛ] VB *voir* **avoir**

aval [aval] NM (*accord*) endorsement, backing; (*Géo*): **en ~** downstream, downriver; (*sur une pente*) downhill; **en ~ de** downstream *ou* downriver from; downhill from

avalanche [avalɑ̃ʃ] NF avalanche; **~ poudreuse** powder snow avalanche

★**avaler** [avale] /1/ VT to swallow

avaliser [avalize] /1/ VT (*plan, entreprise*) to back, support; (*Comm, Jur*) to guarantee

★**avance** [avɑ̃s] NF (*de troupes etc*) advance; (*progrès*) progress; (*d'argent*) advance; (*opposé à retard*) lead; being ahead of schedule; **une ~ de 300 m/4 h** (*Sport*)

a 300 m/4 hour lead; **(être) en ~** (to be) early; *(sur un programme)* (to be) ahead of schedule; **on n'est pas en ~ !** we're kind of late!; **être en ~ sur qn** to be ahead of sb; **d'~, à l'~, par ~** in advance; **~ (du) papier** (*Inform*) paper advance ■ **avances** NFPL overtures; *(amoureuses)* advances

★**avancé, e** [avɑ̃se] ADJ advanced; *(travail etc)* well on, well under way; *(fruit, fromage)* overripe; **il est ~ pour son âge** he is advanced for his age ▶ NF projection; overhang; *(progrès)* advance; **une avancée majeure** a major advance

avancement [avɑ̃smɑ̃] NM *(professionnel)* promotion; *(de travaux)* progress

avancer [avɑ̃se] /3/ VI to move forward, advance; *(projet, travail)* to make progress; *(être en saillie)* to overhang; to project; *(montre, réveil)* to be fast; (: *d'habitude*) to gain; **j'avance (d'une heure)** I'm (an hour) fast ▶ VT to move forward, advance; *(argent)* to advance; *(montre, pendule)* to put forward; *(faire progresser: travail etc)* to advance, move on ■ **s'avancer** VPR to move forward, advance; *(fig)* to commit o.s.; *(faire saillie)* to overhang; to project

avanies [avani] NFPL snubs (BRIT), insults

★**avant** [avɑ̃] PRÉP before; **~ tout** *(surtout)* above all; **en ~ de** in front of; **à l'~** *(dans un véhicule)* in (the) front; **~ qu'il parte/de partir** before he leaves/leaving; **~ qu'il (ne) pleuve** before it rains (*ou* rained) ▶ ADV: **trop/plus ~** too far/further forward; **en ~** *(se pencher, tomber)* forward(s); **partir en ~** to go on ahead ▶ ADJ INV: **siège/roue ~** front seat/wheel ▶ NM *(d'un véhicule, bâtiment)* front; *(Sport: joueur)* forward; **aller de l'~** to steam ahead *(fig)*, make good progress

★**avantage** [avɑ̃taʒ] NM advantage; *(Tennis)*: **~ service/dehors** advantage *ou* van (BRIT) *ou* ad (US) in/out; **tirer ~ de** to take advantage of; **vous auriez ~ à faire** you would be well-advised to do, it would be to your advantage to do; **à l'~ de qn** to sb's advantage; **être à son ~** to be at one's best; **avantages en nature** benefits in kind; **avantages sociaux** fringe benefits

avantager [avɑ̃taʒe] /3/ VT *(favoriser)* to favour; *(embellir)* to flatter

avantageusement [avɑ̃taʒøzmɑ̃] ADV: **remplacer ~ qch** to be a good replacement for sth

avantageux, -euse [avɑ̃taʒø, -øz] ADJ *(prix)* attractive; *(intéressant)* attractively priced; *(portrait, coiffure)* flattering; **conditions avantageuses** favourable terms

avant-bras [avɑ̃bʀa] NM INV forearm

avant-centre [avɑ̃sɑ̃tʀ] NM centre-forward

avant-coureur [avɑ̃kuʀœʀ] ADJ INV *(bruit etc)* precursory; **signe ~** advance indication *ou* sign

avant-dernier, -ière [avɑ̃dɛʀnje, -jɛʀ] ADJ, NM/F next to last, last but one

avant-garde [avɑ̃gaʀd] NF *(Mil)* vanguard; *(fig)* avant-garde; **d'~** avant-garde

avant-goût [avɑ̃gu] NM foretaste

★**avant-hier** [avɑ̃tjɛʀ] ADV the day before yesterday

avant-poste [avɑ̃pɔst] NM outpost

avant-première [avɑ̃pʀəmjɛʀ] NF *(de film)* preview; **en ~** as a preview, in a preview showing

avant-projet [avɑ̃pʀɔʒɛ] NM preliminary draft

avant-propos [avɑ̃pʀɔpo] NM foreword

avant-veille [avɑ̃vɛj] NF: **l'~** two days before

★**avare** [avaʀ] ADJ miserly, avaricious; **~ de compliments** stingy *ou* sparing with your compliments ▶ NMF miser

avarice [avaʀis] NF avarice, miserliness

avarie [avaʀi] NF *(Navig)* damage *sg*; **en cas d'~** in the event of damage

avarié, e [avaʀje] ADJ *(viande, fruits)* rotting, going off (BRIT); *(Navig: navire)* damaged

avaries [avaʀi] NFPL *(Navig)* damage *sg*

avatar [avataʀ] NM misadventure; *(transformation)* metamorphosis

★**avec** [avɛk] PRÉP with; *(à l'égard de)* to(wards), with; **~ habileté/lenteur** skilfully/slowly; **~ eux/ces maladies** with them/these diseases; **~ ça** *(malgré ça)* for all that; **et ~ ça ?** *(dans un magasin)* anything *ou* something else? ▶ ADV *(fam)* with it *(ou him etc)*

avenant, e [av(ə)nɑ̃, -ɑ̃t] ADJ pleasant ▶ NM *(Assurances)* additional clause; **à l'~** *adv* in keeping

avènement [avɛnmɑ̃] NM *(d'un roi)* accession, succession; *(d'un changement)* advent; *(d'une politique, idée)* coming

★**avenir** [avniʀ] NM: **l'~** the future; **à l'~** in future; **sans ~** no future, without a future; **carrière/politicien d'~** career/politician with prospects *ou* a future

Avent [avɑ̃] NM: **l'~** Advent

★**aventure** [avɑ̃tyʀ] NF: **l'~** adventure; **une ~** an adventure; *(amoureuse)* an affair; **partir à l'~** to go off in search of adventure; *(au hasard)* to go where one's fancy takes one; **roman/film d'~** adventure story/film

aventurer [avɑ̃tyʀe] /1/ VT *(somme, réputation, vie)* to stake; *(remarque, opinion)* to venture ■ **s'aventurer** VPR to venture; **s'~ à faire qch** to venture into sth

aventureux, -euse [avɑ̃tyʀø, -øz] ADJ adventurous, venturesome; *(projet)* risky, chancy

aventurier, -ière [avɑ̃tyʀje, -jɛʀ] NM/F adventurer ▶ NF *(péj)* adventuress

avenu, e [av(ə)ny] ADJ: **nul et non ~** null and void

★**avenue** [avny] NF avenue

avéré, e [aveʀe] ADJ recognized, acknowledged

avérer [aveʀe] /6/: **s'avérer** VPR: **s'~ faux/coûteux** to prove (to be) wrong/expensive

★**averse** [avɛʀs] NF shower

aversion [avɛʀsjɔ̃] NF aversion, loathing

averti, e [avɛʀti] ADJ (well-)informed

★**avertir** [avɛʀtiʀ] /2/ VT: **~ qn (de qch/que)** to warn sb (of sth/that); *(renseigner)* to inform sb (of sth/that); **~ qn de ne pas faire qch** to warn sb not to do sth

★**avertissement** [avɛʀtismɑ̃] NM warning

avertisseur [avɛʀtisœʀ] NM horn, siren; **~ (d'incendie)** (fire) alarm

aveu, x [avø] NM confession; **passer aux aveux** to make a confession; **de l'~ de** according to

aveuglant, e [avœglɑ̃, -ɑ̃t] ADJ blinding

★**aveugle** [avœgl] ADJ blind ▶ NMF blind person; **les aveugles** blind people; **test en (double) ~** (double) blind test

aveuglement [avœɡləmɑ̃] NM blindness

aveuglément [avœɡlemɑ̃] ADV blindly

aveugler [avœɡle] /1/ VT to blind

aveuglette [avœɡlɛt]: **à l'~** adv groping one's way along; (fig) in the dark, blindly

avez [ave] VB voir **avoir**

aviaire [avjɛʀ] ADJ avian

aviateur, -trice [avjatœʀ, -tʀis] NM/F aviator, pilot

aviation [avjasjɔ̃] NF (secteur commercial) aviation; (sport, métier de pilote) flying; (Mil) air force; **terrain d'~** airfield; **~ de chasse** fighter force

aviculteur, -trice [avikyltœʀ, -tʀis] NM/F poultry farmer; bird breeder

aviculture [avikyltyʀ] NF (de volailles) poultry farming

avide [avid] ADJ eager; (péj) greedy, grasping; **~ de** (sang etc) thirsting for; **~ d'honneurs/d'argent** greedy for honours/money; **~ de connaître/d'apprendre** eager to know/learn

avidement [avidmɑ̃] ADV avidly

avidité [avidite] NF (péj) greed; eagerness

avilir [aviliʀ] /2/ VT to debase

avilissant, e [avilisɑ̃, -ɑ̃t] ADJ degrading

avilissement [avilismɑ̃] NM (abjection) abasement

aviné, e [avine] ADJ drunken

★**avion** [avjɔ̃] NM (aero)plane (BRIT), (air)plane (US); **aller (quelque part) en ~** to go (somewhere) by plane, fly (somewhere); **par ~** by airmail; **~ de chasse** fighter; **~ de ligne** airliner; **~ à réaction** jet (plane)

avion-cargo [avjɔ̃kaʀɡo] (pl **avions-cargos**) NM air freighter

avion-citerne [avjɔ̃sitɛʀn] (pl **avions-citernes**) NM air tanker

aviron [aviʀɔ̃] NM oar; (sport): **l'~** rowing

★**avis** [avi] NM opinion; (notification) notice; (Comm): **~ de crédit/débit** credit/debit advice; **à mon ~** in my opinion; **je suis de votre ~** I share your opinion, I am of your opinion; **être d'~ que** to be of the opinion that; **changer d'~** to change one's mind; **sauf ~ contraire** unless you hear to the contrary; **sans ~ préalable** without notice; **jusqu'à nouvel ~** until further notice; **~ de décès** death announcement

avisé, e [avize] ADJ sensible, wise; **être bien/mal ~ de faire** to be well-/ill-advised to do

aviser [avize] /1/ VT (voir) to notice, catch sight of; (informer): **~ qn de/que** to advise ou inform ou notify sb of/that ▶ VI to think about things, assess the situation; **nous aviserons sur place** we'll work something out once we're there ■ **s'aviser** VPR: **s'~ de qch/que** to become suddenly aware of sth/that; **s'~ de faire** to take it into one's head to do

aviver [avive] /1/ VT (douleur, chagrin) to intensify; (intérêt, désir) to sharpen; (colère, querelle) to stir up; (couleur) to brighten up

av. J.-C. ABR (= avant Jésus-Christ) BC

★**avocat, e** [avɔka, -at] NM/F (Jur) ≈ barrister (BRIT), lawyer; (fig) advocate, champion; **se faire l'~ du diable** to be the devil's advocate; **l'~ de la défense/partie civile** the counsel for the defence/

plaintiff; **~ d'affaires** business lawyer; **~ général** assistant public prosecutor ▶ NM (Culin) avocado (pear)

avocat-conseil [avɔkakɔ̃sɛj] (pl **avocats-conseils**) NM ≈ barrister (BRIT)

avocat-stagiaire [avɔkastaʒjɛʀ] (pl **avocats-stagiaires**) NM ≈ barrister doing his articles (BRIT)

avoine [avwan] NF oats pl

---

avoir [avwaʀ]

/34/ VT **1** (posséder) to have; **elle a deux enfants/une belle maison** she has (got) two children/a lovely house; **il a les yeux bleus** he has (got) blue eyes; **vous avez du sel?** do you have any salt?; **avoir du courage/de la patience** to be brave/patient

2 (éprouver): **qu'est-ce que tu as?, qu'as-tu?** what's wrong?, what's the matter?; **avoir de la peine** to be ou feel sad; voir aussi **faim**; **peur** etc

3 (âge, dimensions) to be; **il a 3 ans** he is 3 (years old); **le mur a 3 mètres de haut** the wall is 3 metres high

4 (fam: duper) to do, have; **on vous a eu!** you've been done ou had!; (fait une plaisanterie) we ou they had you there!

5: **en avoir contre qn** to have a grudge against sb; **en avoir assez** to be fed up; **j'en ai pour une demi-heure** it'll take me half an hour; **n'avoir que faire de qch** to have no use for sth

6 (obtenir, attraper) to get; **j'ai réussi à avoir mon train** I managed to get ou catch my train; **j'ai réussi à avoir le renseignement qu'il me fallait** I managed to get (hold of) the information I needed

▶ VB AUX **1** to have; **avoir mangé/dormi** to have eaten/slept; **hier je n'ai pas mangé** I didn't eat yesterday

2 (avoir+à +infinitif): **avoir à faire qch** to have to do sth; **vous n'avez qu'à lui demander** you only have to ask him; **tu n'as pas à me poser des questions** it's not for you to ask me questions

▶ VB IMPERS **1**: **il y a** (+ singulier) there is; (+ pluriel) there are; **il y avait du café/des gâteaux** there was coffee/there were cakes; **qu'y a-t-il?, qu'est-ce qu'il y a?** what's the matter?, what is it?; **il doit y avoir une explication** there must be an explanation; **il n'y a qu'à ... we** (ou you etc) will just have to ...; **il ne peut y en avoir qu'un** there can only be one

2: **il y a** (temporel): **il y a 10 ans** 10 years ago; **il y a 10 ans/longtemps que je le connais** I've known him for 10 years/a long time; **il y a 10 ans qu'il est arrivé** it's 10 years since he arrived

▶ NM assets pl, resources pl; (Comm) credit; **avoir fiscal** tax credit

---

avoisinant, e [avwazinɑ̃, -ɑ̃t] ADJ neighbouring

avoisiner [avwazine] /1/ VT to be near ou close to; (fig) to border ou verge on

avons [avɔ̃] VB voir **avoir**

avorté, e [avɔʀte] ADJ (tentative, révolution) abortive

avortement [avɔʀtəmɑ̃] NM abortion

avorter [avɔʀte] /1/ VI (Méd) to have an abortion; (fig) to fail; **faire ~** to abort; **se faire ~** to have an abortion

avorton [avɔʀtɔ̃] NM (*péj*) little runt

avouable [avwabl] ADJ respectable; **des pensées non avouables** unrepeatable thoughts

avoué, e [avwe] ADJ avowed ▶ NM (*Jur*) ≈ solicitor (BRIT), lawyer

avouer [avwe] /1/ VT (*crime, défaut*) to confess (to); **~ avoir fait/que** to admit *ou* confess to having done/that; **~ que oui/non** to admit that that is so/not so ▶ VI (*se confesser*) to confess; (*admettre*) to admit

★**avril** [avʀil] NM April; *voir aussi* **juillet**

axe [aks] NM axis (*pl* axes); (*de roue etc*) axle; (*fig*) main line; **dans l'~ de** directly in line with; **~ routier** trunk road (BRIT), main road, highway (US)

axer [akse] /1/ VT: **~ qch sur** to centre sth on

axial, e, -aux [aksjal, -o] ADJ axial

axiome [aksjom] NM axiom

ayant [εjɑ̃] VB *voir* **avoir** ▶ NM: **~ droit** assignee; **~ droit à** (*pension etc*) person eligible for *ou* entitled to

ayatollah [ajatɔla] NM ayatollah

ayons *etc* [εjɔ̃] VB *voir* **avoir**

azalée [azale] NF azalea

Azerbaïdjan [azɛʀbaidʒɑ̃] NM Azerbaijan

azerbaïdjanais, e [azɛʀbajdʒanɛ, -ɛz] ADJ Azerbaijani ▶ NM/F: **Azerbaïdjanais, e** Azerbaijani

azimut [azimyt] NM azimuth; **tous azimuts** adj (*fig*) omnidirectional

azote [azɔt] NM nitrogen

azoté, e [azɔte] ADJ nitrogenous

AZT SIGLE M (= *azidothymidine*) AZT

aztèque [aztɛk] ADJ Aztec

azur [azyʀ] NM (*couleur*) azure, sky blue; (*ciel*) sky, skies *pl*

azyme [azim] ADJ: **pain ~** unleavened bread

Bb

B, b [be] NM INV B, b; **B comme Bertha** B for Benjamin (BRIT) ou Baker (US) ▶ ABR = **bien**

BA SIGLE F (= *bonne action*) good deed

baba [baba] ADJ INV: **en être ~** (*fam*) to be flabbergasted ▶ NM: **~ au rhum** rum baba

B.A.-BA [beaba] NMSG ABC; **le ~ de qch** the basics of sth

babil [babi] NM prattle

babillage [babijaʒ] NM chatter

babiller [babije] /1/ VI to prattle, chatter; (*bébé*) to babble

babines [babin] NFPL chops

babiole [babjɔl] NF (*bibelot*) trinket; (*vétille*) trifle

bâbord [babɔʀ] NM: **à** ou **par ~** to port, on the port side

babouin [babwɛ̃] NM baboon

baby-foot [babifut] NM INV table football

Babylone [babilɔn] N Babylon

babylonien, ne [babilɔnjɛ̃, -ɛn] ADJ Babylonian

baby-sitter [babisitœʀ] NMF baby-sitter

★**baby-sitting** [babisitiŋ] NM baby-sitting; **faire du ~** to baby-sit

★**bac** [bak] NM (*Scol*) = **baccalauréat**; (*bateau*) ferry; (*récipient*) tub; (: *Photo etc*) tray; (: *Industrie*) tank; **~ à glace** ice-tray; **~ à légumes** vegetable compartment ou rack

baccalauréat [bakalɔʀea] NM ≈ A-levels pl (BRIT), ≈ high school diploma (US); *see note*

> The **baccalauréat**, more commonly known as the *bac*, is the school-leaving examination taken by final-year pupils at French *lycées*, when they are around 18 years old. It marks the end of seven years' secondary education. Several subject combinations are available, although in all cases a broad range is studied. Successful candidates can go on to study at university.

bâche [baʃ] NF tarpaulin, canvas sheet

bachelier, -ière [baʃəlje, -jɛʀ] NM/F holder of the *baccalauréat*

bâcher [baʃe] /1/ VT to cover (with a canvas sheet ou a tarpaulin)

bachot [baʃo] NM = **baccalauréat**

bachotage [baʃɔtaʒ] NM (*Scol*) cramming

bachoter [baʃɔte] /1/ VI (*Scol*) to cram (for an exam)

bacille [basil] NM bacillus

bâcler [bakle] /1/ VT to botch (up)

bacon [bekɔn] NM bacon

bactéricide [bakteʀisid] NM (*Méd*) bactericide

bactérie [bakteʀi] NF bacterium

bactérien, ne [bakteʀjɛ̃, -ɛn] ADJ bacterial

bactériologie [bakteʀjɔlɔʒi] NF bacteriology

bactériologique [bakteʀjɔlɔʒik] ADJ bacteriological

bactériologiste [bakteʀjɔlɔʒist] NMF bacteriologist

badaud, e [bado, -od] NM/F idle onlooker

baderne [badɛʀn] NF (*péj*): **(vieille) ~** old fossil

badge [badʒ] NM badge

badger [badʒe] VI to swipe one's card

badigeon [badiʒɔ̃] NM distemper; colourwash

badigeonner [badiʒɔne] /1/ VT to distemper; to colourwash; (*péj: barbouiller*) to daub; (*Méd*) to paint

badin, e [badɛ̃, -in] ADJ light-hearted, playful

badinage [badinaʒ] NM banter

badine [badin] NF switch (*stick*)

badiner [badine] /1/ VI: **~ avec qch** to treat sth lightly; **ne pas ~ avec qch** not to trifle with sth

badminton [badmintɔn] NM badminton

BAFA [bafa] SIGLE M (= *Brevet d'aptitude aux fonctions d'animation*) *diploma for youth leaders and workers*

baffe [baf] NF (*fam*) slap, clout

Baffin [bafin] NF: **terre de ~** Baffin Island

baffle [bafl] NM baffle (board)

bafouer [bafwe] /1/ VT to deride, ridicule

bafouillage [bafujaʒ] NM (*fam: propos incohérents*) jumble of words

bafouiller [bafuje] /1/ VI, VT to stammer

bâfrer [bafʀe] /1/ VI, VT (*fam*) to guzzle, gobble

bagage [bagaʒ] NM: **bagages** luggage sg, baggage sg; (*connaissances*) background, knowledge; **faire ses bagages** to pack (one's bags); **~ littéraire** (stock of) literary knowledge; **bagages à main** hand luggage

> **Luggage** est indénombrable : il ne peut pas désigner un seul sac ou une seule valise. Pour traduire *un bagage*, il faut dire **a piece of luggage**. Notez que **luggage** ne prend jamais de **-s** et s'emploie avec un verbe au singulier.
> *Vos bagages sont trop lourds.* **Your luggage is too heavy**
> *Vous avez droit à un seul bagage à main.* **You are only allowed one piece of hand luggage.**

bagagiste [bagaʒist] NMF baggage handler

bagarre [bagaʀ] NF fight, brawl; **il aime la ~** he loves a fight, he likes fighting

bagarrer [bagaʀe] /1/ VI to fight ■ **se bagarrer** VPR to (have a) fight

bagarreur, -euse [bagaʀœʀ, -øz] ADJ pugnacious ▸ NM/F: **c'est un ~** he loves a fight

bagatelle [bagatɛl] NF trifle, trifling sum (ou matter)

Bagdad, Baghdâd [bagdad] N Baghdad

bagnard [baɲaʀ] NM convict

bagne [baɲ] NM penal colony; **c'est le ~** (fig) it's forced labour

★**bagnole** [baɲɔl] NF (fam) car, wheels pl (BRIT)

bagout [bagu] NM glibness; **avoir du ~** to have the gift of the gab

★**bague** [bag] NF ring; **~ de fiançailles** engagement ring; **~ de serrage** clip

baguenauder [bagnode] /1/: **se baguenauder** VPR to trail around, loaf around

baguer [bage] /1/ VT to ring

★**baguette** [bagɛt] NF stick; (cuisine chinoise) chopstick; (de chef d'orchestre) baton; (pain) French stick, baguette; (Constr: moulure) beading; **mener qn à la ~** to rule sb with a rod of iron; **~ magique** magic wand; **~ de sourcier** divining rod; **~ de tambour** drumstick

Bahamas [baamas] NFPL: **les (îles) ~** the Bahamas

Bahreïn [baʀɛn] NM Bahrain ou Bahrein

bahut [bay] NM chest

bai, e [bɛ] ADJ (cheval) bay

baie [bɛ] NF (Géo) bay; (fruit) berry; **~ (vitrée)** picture window

baignade [bɛɲad] NF (action) bathing; (bain) bathe; (endroit) bathing place; **« ~ interdite »** "no bathing"

baigné, e [beɲe] ADJ: **~ de** bathed in; (trempé) soaked with; (inondé) flooded with

baigner [beɲe] /1/ VT (bébé) to bath ▸ VI: **~ dans son sang** to lie in a pool of blood; **~ dans la brume** to be shrouded in mist; **ça baigne!** (fam) everything's great! ■ **se baigner** VPR to go swimming ou bathing; (dans une baignoire) to have a bath

baigneur, -euse [beɲœʀ, -øz] NM/F bather ▸ NM (poupée) baby doll

★**baignoire** [beɲwaʀ] NF bath(tub); (Théât) ground-floor box

bail [baj] (pl **baux** [bo]) NM lease; **donner** ou **prendre qch à ~** to lease sth

bâillement [bajmɑ̃] NM yawn

bâiller [baje] /1/ VI to yawn; (être ouvert) to gape

bailleur [bajœʀ] NM: **~ de fonds** sponsor, backer; (Comm) sleeping ou silent partner

bâillon [bajɔ̃] NM gag

bâillonner [bajɔne] /1/ VT to gag

★**bain** [bɛ̃] NM (dans une baignoire, Photo, Tech) bath; (dans la mer, une piscine) swim; **costume de ~** bathing costume (BRIT), swimsuit; **prendre un ~** to have a bath; **se mettre dans le ~** (fig) to get into (the way of) it ou things; **~ de bouche** mouthwash; **~ de foule** walkabout; **~ moussant** bubble bath; **~ de pieds** footbath; (au bord de la mer)

paddle; **~ de siège** hip bath; **~ de soleil** sunbathing no pl; **prendre un ~ de soleil** to sunbathe; **bains de mer** sea bathing sg; **bains(-douches) municipaux** public baths

bain-marie [bɛ̃maʀi] (pl **bains-marie**) NM double boiler; **faire chauffer au ~** (boîte etc) to immerse in boiling water

baïonnette [bajɔnɛt] NF bayonet; (Élec): **douille à ~** bayonet socket; **ampoule à ~** bulb with a bayonet fitting

baisemain [bɛzmɛ̃] NM kissing a lady's hand

★**baiser** [beze] /1/ NM kiss ▸ VT (main, front) to kiss; (!) to screw (!)

baisse [bɛs] NF fall, drop; (Comm): **« ~ sur la viande »** "meat prices down"; **en ~** (cours, action) falling; **à la ~** downwards

★**baisser** [bese] /1/ VT to lower; (radio, chauffage) to turn down; (Auto: phares) to dip (BRIT), lower (US) ▸ VI to fall, drop, go down; (vue, santé) to fail, dwindle ■ **se baisser** VPR to bend down

baissier, -ière [besje, -jɛʀ] ADJ (Finance: à la baisse: marché, cycle) bearish; **une spirale baissière** a downward spiral; **la tendance baissière** the downward trend

bajoues [baʒu] NFPL chaps, chops

★**bal** [bal] NM dance; (grande soirée) ball; **~ costumé/masqué** fancy-dress/masked ball; **~ musette** dance (with accordion accompaniment)

balade [balad] (fam) NF (à pied) walk, stroll; (en voiture) drive; **faire une ~** to go for a walk ou stroll; to go for a drive

balader [balade] /1/ VT (fam: traîner) to trail around ■ **se balader** VPR to go for a walk ou stroll; to go for a drive

★**baladeur** [baladœʀ] NM personal stereo, Walkman®; **~ numérique** MP3 player

baladeuse [baladøz] NF inspection lamp

baladin [baladɛ̃] NM wandering entertainer

baladodiffusion [baladodifyzjɔ̃] NF podcasting

balafre [balafʀ] NF gash, slash; (cicatrice) scar

balafrer [balafʀe] /1/ VT to gash, slash

balai [balɛ] NM broom, brush; (Auto: d'essuie-glace) blade; (Mus: de batterie etc) brush; **donner un coup de ~** to give the floor a sweep; **~ mécanique** carpet sweeper

balai-brosse [balɛbʀɔs] (pl **balais-brosses**) NM (long-handled) scrubbing brush

balance [balɑ̃s] NF (à plateaux) scales pl; (de précision) balance; (Comm, Pol): **~ des comptes** ou **paiements** balance of payments; (signe): **la B~** Libra, the Scales; **être de la B~** to be Libra; **~ commerciale** balance of trade; **~ des forces** balance of power; **~ romaine** steelyard

balancelle [balɑ̃sɛl] NF garden hammock-seat

balancer [balɑ̃se] /3/ VT to swing; (lancer) to fling, chuck; (renvoyer, jeter) to chuck out ▸ VI to swing ■ **se balancer** VPR to swing; (bateau) to rock; (branche) to sway; **se ~ de qch** (fam) not to give a toss about sth

balancier [balɑ̃sje] NM (de pendule) pendulum; (de montre) balance wheel; (perche) (balancing) pole

balançoire [balɑ̃swaʀ] NF swing; (sur pivot) seesaw

balayage [balɛjaʒ] NM sweeping; scanning

balayer [baleje] **/8/** VT (*feuilles etc*) to sweep up, brush up; (*pièce, cour*) to sweep; (*chasser*) to sweep away *ou* aside; (*radar*) to scan; (*phares*) to sweep across

balayette [balɛjɛt] NF small brush

balayeur, -euse [balɛjœr, -øz] NM/F road sweeper ▶ NF (*engin*) road sweeper

balayures [balɛjyr] NFPL sweepings

balbutiement [balbysimɑ̃] NM (*paroles*) stammering *no pl* ■ **balbutiements** NMPL (*fig: débuts*) first faltering steps

balbutier [balbysje] **/7/** VI, VT to stammer

★**balcon** [balkɔ̃] NM balcony; (*Théât*) dress circle

balconnet [balkɔnɛ] NM half-cup bra (BRIT), demi-cup bra (US)

baldaquin [baldakɛ̃] NM canopy

Bâle [bɑl] N Basle *ou* Basel

Baléares [baleɑr] NFPL: **les ~** the Balearic Islands, the Balearics

baleine [balɛn] NF whale; (*de parapluie*) rib; (*de corset*) bone

baleinier [balenje] NM (*Navig*) whaler

baleinière [balenjɛr] NF whaleboat

balisage [balizaʒ] NM (*signaux*) beacons *pl*; buoys *pl*; runway lights *pl*; signs *pl*, markers *pl*

balise [baliz] NF (*Navig*) beacon, (marker) buoy; (*Aviat*) runway light, beacon; (*Auto, Ski*) sign, marker

baliser [balize] **/1/** VT to mark out (with beacons *ou* lights *etc*)

balistique [balistik] ADJ (*engin*) ballistic ▶ NF ballistics

balivernes [balivern] NFPL twaddle *sg* (BRIT), nonsense *sg*

balkanique [balkanik] ADJ Balkan

Balkans [balkɑ̃] NMPL: **les ~** the Balkans

ballade [balad] NF ballad

ballant, e [balɑ̃, -ɑ̃t] ADJ dangling

ballast [balast] NM ballast

★**balle** [bal] NF (*de fusil*) bullet; (*de sport*) ball; (*du blé*) chaff; (*paquet*) bale; (*fam: franc*) franc; **~ perdue** stray bullet

ballerine [bal(ə)rin] NF (*danseuse*) ballet dancer; (*chaussure*) pump, ballet shoe

ballet [balɛ] NM ballet; (*fig*): **~ diplomatique** diplomatic to-ings and fro-ings

★**ballon** [balɔ̃] NM (*de sport*) ball; (*jouet, Aviat, de bande dessinée*) balloon; (*de vin*) glass; **~ d'essai** (*météorologique*) pilot balloon; (*fig*) feeler(s); **~ de football** football; **~ d'oxygène** oxygen bottle

ballonné, e [balɔne] ADJ bloated; **se sentir ~** to feel bloated; **j'ai le ventre ~** my stomach's bloated

ballon-sonde [balɔ̃sɔ̃d] (*pl* **ballons-sondes**) NM sounding balloon

ballot [balo] NM bundle; (*péj*) nitwit

ballottage [balɔtaʒ] NM (*Pol*) second ballot

ballotter [balɔte] **/1/** VI to roll around; (*bateau etc*) to toss ▶ VT to shake *ou* throw about; to toss; **être ballotté entre** (*fig*) to be shunted between; (: *indécis*) to be torn between

ballottine [balɔtin] NF (*Culin*): **~ de volaille** meat loaf made with poultry

ball-trap [baltrap] NM (*appareil*) trap; (*tir*) clay pigeon shooting

balluchon [balyʃɔ̃] NM bundle (of clothes)

balnéaire [balneɛr] ADJ seaside *cpd*; **station ~** seaside resort

balnéothérapie [balneɔterapi] NF spa bath therapy

BALO SIGLE M (= *Bulletin des annonces légales obligatoires*) ≈ Public Notices (*in newspapers etc*)

balourd, e [balur, -urd] ADJ clumsy ▶ NM/F clodhopper

balourdise [balurdiz] NF clumsiness; (*gaffe*) blunder

balsamique [balsamik] ADJ balsamic; **vinaigre ~** balsamic vinegar

balte [balt] ADJ Baltic ▶ NMF: **Balte** native of the Baltic States

baltique [baltik] ADJ Baltic ▶ NF: **la (mer) B~** the Baltic (Sea)

baluchon [balyʃɔ̃] NM = **balluchon**

balustrade [balystrad] NF railings *pl*, handrail

bambin [bɑ̃bɛ̃] NM little child

bambou [bɑ̃bu] NM bamboo

ban [bɑ̃] NM round of applause, cheer; **être/mettre au ~ de** to be outlawed/to outlaw from; **le ~ et l'arrière-ban de sa famille** every last one of his relatives; **bans (de mariage)** banns, bans

banal, e [banal] ADJ banal, commonplace; (*péj*) trite; **four/moulin ~** village oven/mill

banalisé, e [banalize] ADJ (*voiture de police*) unmarked

banalité [banalite] NF banality; (*remarque*) truism, trite remark

★**banane** [banan] NF banana; (*sac*) waist-bag, bum-bag

bananeraie [bananre] NF banana plantation

bananier [bananje] NM banana tree; (*bateau*) banana boat

★**banc** [bɑ̃] NM seat, bench; (*de poissons*) shoal; **~ des accusés** dock; **~ d'essai** (*fig*) testing ground; **~ de sable** sandbank; **~ des témoins** witness box; **~ de touche** dugout

★**bancaire** [bɑ̃kɛr] ADJ banking; (*chèque, carte*) bank *cpd*

bancal, e [bɑ̃kal] ADJ wobbly; (*personne*) bow-legged; (*fig: projet*) shaky

bandage [bɑ̃daʒ] NM bandaging; (*pansement*) bandage; **~ herniaire** truss

★**bande** [bɑ̃d] NF (*de tissu etc*) strip; (*Méd*) bandage; (*motif, dessin*) stripe; (*Ciné*) film; (*Radio, groupe*) band; (*péj*): **une ~ de** a bunch *ou* crowd of; **par la ~** in a roundabout way; **donner de la ~** to list; **faire ~ à part** to keep to o.s.; **~ dessinée** strip cartoon (BRIT), comic strip; **~ magnétique** magnetic tape; **~ passante** (*Inform*) bandwidth; **~ perforée** punched tape; **~ de roulement** (*de pneu*) tread; **~ sonore** sound track; **~ de terre** strip of land; **~ Velpeau**® (*Méd*) crêpe bandage

bandé, e [bɑ̃de] ADJ bandaged; **les yeux bandés** blindfold

bande-annonce [bɑ̃danɔ̃s] (*pl* **bandes-annonces**) NF (*Ciné*) trailer

bandeau, x [bɑ̃do] NM headband; (*sur les yeux*) blindfold; (*Méd*) head bandage

bandelette [bɑ̃dlɛt] NF strip of cloth, bandage

bander [bɑ̃de] /1/ VT (*blessure*) to bandage; (*muscle*) to tense; (*arc*) to bend; **~ les yeux à qn** to blindfold sb ▶ VI (!) to have a hard on (!)

banderole [bɑ̃dʀɔl] NF banderole; (*dans un défilé etc*) streamer

bande-son [bɑ̃dsɔ̃] (*pl* **bandes-son**) NF (*Ciné*) soundtrack

bandit [bɑ̃di] NM bandit

banditisme [bɑ̃ditism] NM violent crime, armed robberies *pl*

bandoulière [bɑ̃duljɛʀ] NF: **en ~** (slung *ou* worn) across the shoulder

Bangkok [bɑ̃ŋkɔk] N Bangkok

Bangladesh [bɑ̃gladɛʃ] NM: **le ~** Bangladesh

banjo [bɑ̃(d)ʒo] NM banjo

★**banlieue** [bɑ̃ljø] NF suburbs *pl*; **quartiers de ~** suburban areas; **trains de ~** commuter trains

banlieusard, e [bɑ̃ljøzaʀ, -aʀd] NM/F suburbanite

bannière [banjɛʀ] NF banner

bannir [baniʀ] /2/ VT to banish

★**banque** [bɑ̃k] NF bank; (*activités*) banking; **~ des yeux/du sang** eye/blood bank; **~ d'affaires** merchant bank; **~ alimentaire** food bank; **~ de dépôt** deposit bank; **~ de données** (*Inform*) data bank; **~ d'émission** bank of issue; **~ en ligne** online banking

banqueroute [bɑ̃kʀut] NF bankruptcy

banquet [bɑ̃kɛ] NM (*de club*) dinner; (*de noces*) reception; (*d'apparat*) banquet

banquette [bɑ̃kɛt] NF seat

banquier [bɑ̃kje] NM banker

banquise [bɑ̃kiz] NF ice field

bantou, e [bɑ̃tu] ADJ Bantu

baobab [baɔbab] NM (*Bot*) baobab

baptême [batɛm] NM (*sacrement*) baptism; (*cérémonie*) christening; baptism; (*d'un navire*) launching; (*d'une cloche*) consecration, dedication; **~ de l'air** first flight

baptiser [batize] /1/ VT to christen; to baptize; to launch; to consecrate, dedicate

baptiste [batist] ADJ, NM/F Baptist

baquer [bake]: **se baquer** VPR (*fam*) to go for a dip

baquet [bakɛ] NM tub, bucket

★**bar** [baʀ] NM bar; (*poisson*) bass

baragouin [baʀagwɛ̃] NM gibberish

baragouiner [baʀagwine] /1/ VI to gibber, jabber

baraque [baʀak] NF shed; (*fam*) house; **~ foraine** fairground stand

baraqué, e [baʀake] ADJ (*fam*) well-built, hefty

baraquements [baʀakmɑ̃] NMPL huts (*for refugees, workers etc*)

baratin [baʀatɛ̃] NM (*fam*) smooth talk, patter

baratiner [baʀatine] /1/ VT (*fam: fille*) to chat up

baratineur, -euse [baʀatinœʀ, -øz] NM/F (*fam*) smooth talker

baratte [baʀat] NF churn

Barbade [baʀbad] NF: **la ~** Barbados

★**barbant, e** [baʀbɑ̃, -ɑ̃t] ADJ (*fam*) deadly (boring)

barbare [baʀbaʀ] ADJ barbaric ▶ NMF barbarian

Barbarie [baʀbaʀi] NF: **la ~** the Barbary Coast

barbarie [baʀbaʀi] NF barbarism; (*cruauté*) barbarity

barbarisme [baʀbaʀism] NM (*Ling*) barbarism

★**barbe** [baʀb] NF beard; **(au nez et) à la ~ de qn** (*fig*) under sb's very nose; **la ~!** (*fam*) damn it!; **quelle ~!** (*fam*) what a drag *ou* bore!; **~ à papa** candy-floss (BRIT), cotton candy (US)

barbecue [baʀbəkju] NM barbecue

barbelé [baʀbəle] ADJ, NM: **(fil de fer) ~** barbed wire *no pl*

barber [baʀbe] /1/ VT (*fam*) to bore stiff ▪ **se barber** VPR (*fam*) to be bored stiff

barbiche [baʀbiʃ] NF goatee

barbichette [baʀbiʃɛt] NF small goatee

barbiturique [baʀbityʀik] NM barbiturate

barboter [baʀbɔte] /1/ VI to paddle, dabble ▶ VT (*fam*) to filch

barboteuse [baʀbɔtøz] NF rompers *pl*

barbouillé, e [baʀbuje] ADJ: **avoir l'estomac ~** to feel queasy

barbouiller [baʀbuje] /1/ VT to daub; (*péj: écrire, dessiner*) to scribble

barbu, e [baʀby] ADJ bearded

barbue [baʀby] NF (*poisson*) brill

Barcelone [baʀsəlɔn] N Barcelona

barda [baʀda] NM (*fam*) kit, gear

barde [baʀd] NF (*Culin*) piece of fat bacon ▶ NM (*poète*) bard

bardé, e [baʀde] ADJ: **~ de médailles** *etc* bedecked with medals *etc*

bardeaux [baʀdo] NMPL shingle *no pl*

barder [baʀde] /1/ VT (*Culin: rôti, volaille*) to bard ▶ VI (*fam*) **ça va ~** sparks will fly

barème [baʀɛm] NM (*Scol*) scale; (*liste*) table; **~ des salaires** salary scale

barge [baʀʒ] NF barge

barguigner [baʀgiɲe] VI: **sans ~** without any shilly-shallying

baril [baʀi(l)] NM (*tonneau*) barrel; (*de poudre*) keg

barillet [baʀijɛ] NM (*de revolver*) cylinder

bariolé, e [baʀjɔle] ADJ many-coloured, rainbow-coloured

barman [baʀman] NM barman

baromètre [baʀɔmɛtʀ] NM barometer; **~ anéroïde** aneroid barometer

baron [baʀɔ̃] NM baron

baronne [baʀɔn] NF baroness

baroque [baʀɔk] ADJ (*Art*) baroque; (*fig*) weird

baroud [baʀud] NM: **~ d'honneur** gallant last stand

baroudeur [baʀudœʀ] NM (*fam*) fighter

barque [baʀk] NF small boat

barquette [baʀkɛt] NF small boat-shaped tart; (*récipient: en aluminium*) tub; (: *en bois*) basket; (*pour repas*) tray; (*pour fruits*) punnet

barracuda [baʀakyda] NM barracuda

barrage [baʀaʒ] NM dam; (*sur route*) roadblock, barricade; **~ de police** police roadblock

barre [baʀ] NF (*de fer etc*) rod; (*Navig*) helm; (*écrite*) line, stroke; (*Danse*) barre; (*Jur*): **comparaître à la ~** to appear as a witness; (*niveau*): **la livre a franchi la ~ des 1,70 euros** the pound has broken the 1.70 euros barrier; **être à** *ou* **tenir la ~** (*Navig*) to be at the helm; **coup de ~** (*fig*): **c'est le coup de ~ !** it's daylight robbery!; **j'ai le coup de ~ !** I'm all in!; **~ fixe** (*Gym*) horizontal bar; **~ de mesure** (*Mus*) bar line; **~ à mine** crowbar; **barres parallèles/asymétriques** (*Gym*) parallel/asymmetric bars

barreau, x [baʀo] NM bar; (*Jur*): **le ~** the Bar

barrer [baʀe] /1/ VT (*route etc*) to block; (*mot*) to cross out; (*chèque*) to cross (BRIT); (*Navig*) to steer ▪ **se barrer** VPR (*fam*) to clear off

barrette [baʀɛt] NF (*pour cheveux*) (hair) slide (BRIT) *ou* clip (US); (*broche*) brooch

barreur [baʀœʀ] NM helmsman; (*aviron*) coxswain

barricade [baʀikad] NF barricade

barricader [baʀikade] /1/ VT to barricade ▪ **se barricader** VPR: **se ~ chez soi** (*fig*) to lock o.s. in

barrière [baʀjɛʀ] NF fence; (*obstacle*) barrier; (*porte*) gate; **la Grande B~** the Great Barrier Reef; **~ de dégel** (*Admin: on roadsigns*) no heavy vehicles — road liable to subsidence due to thaw; **barrières douanières** trade barriers

barrique [baʀik] NF barrel, cask

barrir [baʀiʀ] /2/ VI to trumpet

bar-tabac [baʀtaba] (*pl* **bars-tabacs**) NM bar (*which sells tobacco and stamps*)

baryton [baʀitɔ̃] NM baritone

★**bas, basse** [ba, bas] ADJ low; (*action*) low, ignoble; **la tête basse** with lowered head; (*fig*) with head hung low; **avoir la vue basse** to be short-sighted; **au ~ mot** at the lowest estimate; **enfant en ~ âge** infant, young child; **~ morceaux** (*viande*) cheap cuts ▶ ADV low; (*parler*) softly; **plus ~** lower down; more softly; (*dans un texte*) further on, below; **mettre ~** VI (*animal*) to give birth; **à ~ la dictature !** down with dictatorship! ▶ NM (*vêtement*) stocking; (*partie inférieure*): **le ~ de** the lower part *ou* foot *ou* bottom of; **de ~ en haut** upwards; from the bottom to the top; **des hauts et des ~** ups and downs; **en ~** down below; (*d'une liste, d'un mur etc*) at (*ou* to) the bottom; (*dans une maison*) downstairs; **en ~ de** at the bottom of; **un ~ de laine** (*fam: économies*) money under the mattress (*fig*) ▶ NF (*Mus*) bass

basalte [bazalt] NM basalt

basané, e [bazane] ADJ (*teint*) tanned, bronzed

bas-côté [bakote] NM (*de route*) verge (BRIT), shoulder (US); (*d'église*) (side) aisle

bascule [baskyl] NF: **(jeu de) ~** seesaw; **(balance à) ~** scales *pl*; **fauteuil à ~** rocking chair; **système à ~** tip-over device; rocker device

basculer [baskyle] /1/ VI to fall over, topple (over); (*benne*) to tip up ▶ VT (*aussi:* **faire basculer**) to topple over; (*contenu*) to tip out; (*: benne*) tip up

base [baz] NF base; (*fondement, principe*) basis (*pl* bases); **la ~** (*Pol*) the rank and file, the grass roots; **jeter les bases de** to lay the foundations of; **à la ~ de** (*fig*) at the root of; **sur la ~ de** (*fig*) on the basis of; **de ~** basic; **à ~ de café** *etc* coffee *etc* -based; **~ de données** (*Inform*) database; **~ de lancement** launching site

base-ball [bɛzbol] NM baseball

baser [baze] /1/ VT: **~ qch sur** to base sth on; **se ~ sur** (*données, preuves*) to base one's argument on; **être basé à/dans** (*Mil*) to be based at/in

bas-fond [bafɔ̃] NM (*Navig*) shallow ▪ **bas-fonds** NMPL (*fig*) dregs

basilic [bazilik] NM (*Culin*) basil

basilique [bazilik] NF basilica

★**basket** [baskɛt], **basket-ball** [baskɛtbol] NM basketball

★**baskets** [baskɛt] NFPL (*chaussures*) trainers (BRIT), sneakers (US)

basketteur, -euse [baskɛtœʀ, -øz] NM/F basketball player

basquaise [baskɛz] ADJ F Basque ▶ NF: **B~** Basque

basque [bask] ADJ, NM (*Ling*) Basque; **le Pays ~** the Basque country ▶ NMF: **Basque** Basque

basques [bask] NFPL skirts; **pendu aux ~ de qn** constantly pestering sb; (*mère etc*) hanging on sb's apron strings

bas-relief [baʀəljɛf] NM bas-relief

basse [bas] ADJ *voir* **bas** ▶ NF (*Mus*) bass

basse-cour [baskuʀ] (*pl* **basses-cours**) NF farmyard; (*animaux*) farmyard animals

bassement [basmɑ̃] ADV basely

bassesse [basɛs] NF baseness; (*acte*) base act

basset [basɛ] NM (*Zool*) basset (hound)

★**bassin** [basɛ̃] NM (*cuvette*) bowl; (*pièce d'eau*) pond, pool; (*de fontaine, Géo*) basin; (*Anat*) pelvis; (*portuaire*) dock; **~ houiller** coalfield

bassine [basin] NF basin; (*contenu*) bowl, bowlful

bassiner [basine] /1/ VT (*plaie*) to bathe; (*lit*) to warm with a warming pan; (*fam: ennuyer*) to bore; (*: importuner*) to bug, pester

bassiste [basist] NMF (double) bass player

basson [basɔ̃] NM bassoon

bastide [bastid] NF (*maison*) country house (in Provence); (*ville*) walled town (in SW France)

bastingage [bastɛ̃gaʒ] NM ship's rail, rail

bastion [bastjɔ̃] NM (*aussi fig, Pol*) bastion

baston [bastɔ̃] NM OU F (*fam*) fistfight, punch-up (BRIT)

bastonner [bastɔne] (*fam*): **se bastonner** VPR to have a punch-up (BRIT), to trade punches

bas-ventre [bavɑ̃tʀ] NM (lower part of the) stomach

bat [ba] VB *voir* **battre**

bât [ba] NM packsaddle

★**bataille** [bataj] NF battle; (*rixe*) fight; **en ~** (*en travers*) at an angle; (*en désordre*) awry; **elle avait les cheveux en ~** her hair was a mess; **~ rangée** pitched battle

bataillon [batajɔ̃] NM battalion

bâtard, e [bɑtaʀ, -aʀd] ADJ (*enfant*) illegitimate; (*fig*) hybrid; **chien ~** mongrel ▶ NM/F illegitimate child, bastard (*péj*) ▶ NM (*Boulangerie*) short French stick *ou* baguette

batavia [batavja] NF ≈ Webb lettuce

★**bateau, x** [bato] NM boat; **~ de pêche/à moteur/à voiles** fishing/motor/sailing boat ▶ ADJ INV (*banal, rebattu*) hackneyed

bateau-citerne [batositɛʀn] (*pl* **bateaux-citernes**) NM tanker

bateau-mouche [batomuʃ] (pl **bateaux-mouches**) NM (passenger) pleasure boat (on the Seine)

bateau-pilote [batopilɔt] (pl **bateaux-pilotes**) NM pilot ship

bateleur, -euse [batlœr, -øz] NM/F street performer

batelier, -ière [batəlje, -jɛr] NM/F ferryman/-woman

bat-flanc [baflã] NM raised boards for sleeping, in cells, army huts etc

bâti, e [bɑti] ADJ (terrain) developed; **bien ~** (personne) well-built ▶ NM (armature) frame; (Couture) tacking

batifoler [batifɔle] /1/ VI to frolic ou lark about

batik [batik] NM batik

bâtiment [bɑtimã] NM building; (Navig) ship, vessel; (industrie): **le ~** the building trade

bâtir [bɑtir] /2/ VT to build; (Couture: jupe, ourlet) to tack; **fil à ~** (Couture) tacking thread

bâtisse [bɑtis] NF building

bâtisseur, -euse [bɑtisœr, -øz] NM/F builder

batiste [batist] NF (Couture) batiste, cambric

bâton [bɑtɔ̃] NM stick; **mettre des bâtons dans les roues à qn** to put a spoke in sb's wheel; **à bâtons rompus** informally; **parler à bâtons rompus** to chat about this and that; **~ de rouge (à lèvres)** lipstick; **~ de ski** ski stick

bâtonnet [bɑtɔnɛ] NM short stick ou rod

bâtonnier [bɑtɔnje] NM (Jur) ≈ President of the Bar

batraciens [batrasjɛ̃] NMPL amphibians

bats [ba] VB voir **battre**

battage [bataʒ] NM (publicité) (hard) plugging

battant, e [batɑ̃, -ɑ̃t] VB voir **battre** ▶ ADJ: **pluie battante** lashing rain; **tambour ~** briskly ▶ NM (de cloche) clapper; (de volets) shutter, flap; (de porte) side; (fig: personne) fighter; **porte à double ~** double door

batte [bat] NF (Sport) bat

battement [batmɑ̃] NM (de cœur) beat; (intervalle) interval (between classes, trains etc); (de paupières) blinking no pl (of eyelids); **un ~ de 10 minutes, 10 minutes de ~** 10 minutes to spare

★**batterie** [batri] NF (Mil, Élec) battery; (Mus) drums pl, drum kit; **~ de cuisine** kitchen utensils pl; (casseroles etc) pots and pans pl; **une ~ de tests** a string of tests

batteur [batœr] NM (Mus) drummer; (appareil) whisk

batteuse [batøz] NF (Agr) threshing machine

battoir [batwar] NM (à linge) beetle (for laundry); (à tapis) (carpet) beater

★**battre** [batr] /41/ VT to beat; (pluie, vagues) to beat ou lash against; (œufs etc) to beat up, whisk; (blé) to thresh; (cartes) to shuffle; (passer au peigne fin) to scour; **~ la mesure** to beat time; **~ en brèche** (Mil: mur) to batter; (fig: théorie) to demolish (: institution etc) to attack; **~ son plein** to be at its height, be going full swing; **~ pavillon britannique** to fly the British flag; **~ la semelle** to stamp one's feet ▶ VI (cœur) to beat; (volets etc) to bang, rattle; **~ des mains** to clap one's hands; **~ des ailes** to flap its wings; **~ de l'aile** (fig) to be in a bad way ou in bad shape; **~ en retraite** to beat a retreat ■ **se battre** VPR to fight

battu, e [baty] PP de **battre** ▶ NF (chasse) beat; (policière etc) search, hunt

baud [bo(d)] NM baud

baudruche [bodryʃ] NF: **ballon en ~** (toy) balloon; (fig) windbag

baume [bom] NM balm; **~ labial** lip balm; (fig): **mettre du ~ au cœur à qn** to hearten sb

bauxite [boksit] NF bauxite

★**bavard, e** [bavar, -ard] ADJ (very) talkative; gossipy

bavardage [bavardaʒ] NM chatter no pl; gossip no pl

★**bavarder** [bavarde] /1/ VI to chatter; (indiscrètement) to gossip; (révéler un secret) to blab

bavarois, e [bavarwa, -waz] ADJ Bavarian ▶ NM (Culin) bavarois ▶ NM/F: **Bavarois, e** Bavarian

bave [bav] NF dribble; (de chien etc) slobber, slaver (BRIT), drool (US); (d'escargot) slime

baver [bave] /1/ VI to dribble; (chien) to slobber, slaver (BRIT), drool (US); (encre, couleur) to run; **en ~** (fam) to have a hard time (of it)

bavette [bavɛt] NF bib

baveux, -euse [bavø, -øz] ADJ dribbling; (omelette) runny

Bavière [bavjɛr] NF: **la ~** Bavaria

bavoir [bavwar] NM (de bébé) bib

bavure [bavyr] NF smudge; (fig) hitch; (policière etc) blunder

bayer [baje] /1/ VI: **~ aux corneilles** to stand gaping

bazar [bazar] NM general store; (fam) jumble

bazarder [bazarde] /1/ VT (fam) to chuck out

BCBG SIGLE ADJ (= bon chic bon genre) smart and trendy, ≈ preppy

BCG SIGLE M (= bacille Calmette-Guérin) BCG

bcp ABR = **beaucoup**

BD SIGLE F (= bande dessinée; (= base de données) DB

bd ABR = **boulevard**

b.d.c. ABR (Typo; = bas de casse) l.c.

beach-volley [bitʃvɔlɛ] NM beach volleyball

béant, e [beɑ̃, -ɑ̃t] ADJ gaping

béarnais, e [bearnɛ, -ɛz] ADJ of ou from the Béarn

béat, e [bea, -at] ADJ showing open-eyed wonder; (sourire etc) blissful

béatitude [beatityd] NF bliss

★**beau, bel, belle, beaux** [bo, bɛl] ADJ beautiful, lovely; (homme) handsome; **un ~ geste** (fig) a fine gesture; **un ~ salaire** a good salary; **un ~ gâchis/rhume** a fine mess/nasty cold; **le ~ monde** high society; **~ parleur** smooth talker; **un ~ jour** (fine) day; **de plus belle** more than ever, even more; **bel et bien** well and truly; (vraiment) really (and truly); **il a ~ jeu de protester** etc it's easy for him to protest etc ▶ NF (Sport): **la belle** the decider; **en faire/dire de belles** to do/say (some) stupid things ▶ ADV: **il fait ~** the weather's fine; **on a ~ essayer** however hard ou no matter how hard we try ▶ NM: **avoir le sens du ~** to have an aesthetic sense; **le temps est au ~** the weather is set fair; **le plus ~ c'est que ...** the best of it is that ...; **c'est le ~ !** that's great, that is!; **faire le ~** (chien) to sit up and beg

beauceron, ne [bos(ə)rɔ̃, -ɔn] ADJ from the Beauce

beaucoup [boku]

ADV **1** a lot; **il boit beaucoup** he drinks a lot; **il ne boit pas beaucoup** he doesn't drink much *ou* a lot

2 (*suivi de plus, trop etc*) much, a lot, far; **il est beaucoup plus grand** he is much *ou* a lot *ou* far taller; **c'est beaucoup plus cher** it's a lot *ou* much more expensive; **il a beaucoup plus de temps que moi** he has much *ou* a lot more time than me; **il y a beaucoup plus de touristes ici** there are a lot *ou* many more tourists here; **beaucoup trop vite** much too fast; **il fume beaucoup trop** he smokes far too much

3: **beaucoup de** (*nombre*) many, a lot of; (*quantité*) a lot of; **pas beaucoup de** (*nombre*) not many, not a lot of; (*quantité*) not much, not a lot of; **beaucoup d'étudiants/de touristes** a lot of *ou* many students/tourists; **beaucoup de courage** a lot of courage; **il n'a pas beaucoup d'argent** he hasn't got much *ou* a lot of money; **il n'y a pas beaucoup de touristes** there aren't many *ou* a lot of tourists

4: **de beaucoup** by far

▶ PRON: **beaucoup le savent** lots of people know that

⋆**beau-fils** [bofis] (*pl* **beaux-fils**) NM son-in-law; (*remariage*) stepson

beau-frère [bofʀɛʀ] (*pl* **beaux-frères**) NM brother-in-law

beau-père [bopɛʀ] (*pl* **beaux-pères**) NM father-in-law; (*remariage*) stepfather

beauté [bote] NF beauty; **de toute ~** beautiful; **en ~** *adv* with a flourish, brilliantly; **finir qch en ~** to complete sth brilliantly

beaux-arts [bozaʀ] NMPL fine arts

beaux-parents [bopaʀɑ̃] NMPL wife's/husband's family, in-laws

bébé [bebe] NM baby

bébé-éprouvette [bebeepʀuvɛt] (*pl* **bébés-éprouvette**) NM test-tube baby

bec [bɛk] NM beak, bill; (*de plume*) nib; (*de cafetière etc*) spout; (*de casserole etc*) lip; (*d'une clarinette etc*) mouthpiece; (*fam*) mouth; **clouer le ~ à qn** (*fam*) to shut sb up; **ouvrir le ~** (*fam*) to open one's mouth; **~ de gaz** (street) gaslamp; **~ verseur** pouring lip

bécane [bekan] NF (*fam*) bike

bécarre [bekaʀ] NM (*Mus*) natural

bécasse [bekas] NF (*Zool*) woodcock; (*fam*) silly goose

bec-de-cane [bɛkdəkan] (*pl* **becs-de-cane**) NM (*poignée*) door handle

bec-de-lièvre [bɛkdəljɛvʀ] (*pl* **becs-de-lièvre**) NM harelip

béchamel [beʃamɛl] NF: **(sauce) ~** white sauce, bechamel sauce

bêche [bɛʃ] NF spade

bêcher [beʃe] /1/ VT (*terre*) to dig; (*personne: critiquer*) to slate; (: *snober*) to look down on

bêcheur, -euse [beʃœʀ, -øz] ADJ (*fam*) stuck-up ▶ NM/F fault-finder; (*snob*) stuck-up person

bécoter [bekɔte] /1/ (*fam*) VT to kiss ▪ **se bécoter** VPR to smooch

becquée [beke] NF: **donner la ~ à** to feed

becqueter [bɛkte] /4/ VT (*fam*) to eat

bedaine [bədɛn] NF paunch

bédé [bede] NF (*fam*) = **bande dessinée**

bedeau, x [bədo] NM beadle

bedonnant, e [bədɔnɑ̃, -ɑ̃t] ADJ paunchy, potbellied

bée [be] ADJ: **bouche ~** gaping

beffroi [befʀwa] NM belfry

bégaiement [begɛmɑ̃] NM stammering, stuttering

bégayer [begeje] /8/ VT, VI to stammer

bégonia [begɔnja] NM (*Bot*) begonia

bègue [bɛg] NMF: **être ~** to have a stammer

bégueule [begœl] ADJ prudish

beige [bɛʒ] ADJ beige

beignet [bɛɲɛ] NM fritter

bel [bɛl] ADJ M *voir* **beau**

bêler [bele] /1/ VI to bleat

belette [bəlɛt] NF weasel

⋆**belge** [bɛlʒ] ADJ Belgian ▶ NMF: **Belge** Belgian

⋆**Belgique** [bɛlʒik] NF: **la ~** Belgium

Belgrade [bɛlgrad] N Belgrade

bélier [belje] NM ram; (*engin*) (battering) ram; (*signe*): **le B~** Aries, the Ram; **être du B~** to be Aries

Bélize [beliz] NM: **le ~** Belize

bellâtre [belɑtʀ] NM dandy

⋆**belle** [bɛl] ADJ, NF *voir* **beau**

belle-famille [bɛlfamij] (*pl* **belles-familles**) NF (*fam*) in-laws *pl*

⋆**belle-fille** [bɛlfij] (*pl* **belles-filles**) NF daughter-in-law; (*remariage*) stepdaughter

belle-mère [bɛlmɛʀ] (*pl* **belles-mères**) NF mother-in-law; (*remariage*) stepmother

belle-sœur [bɛlsœʀ] (*pl* **belles-sœurs**) NF sister-in-law

belliciste [belisist] ADJ warmongering

belligérance [beliʒeʀɑ̃s] NF belligerence

belligérant, e [beliʒeʀɑ̃, -ɑ̃t] ADJ belligerent

belliqueux, -euse [belikø, -øz] ADJ aggressive, warlike

belote [bəlɔt] NF belote (*card game*)

belvédère [bɛlvedɛʀ] NM panoramic viewpoint (*or small building there*)

bémol [bemɔl] NM (*Mus*) flat

ben [bɛ̃] EXCL (*fam*) well

bénédiction [benediksjɔ̃] NF blessing

bénéfice [benefis] NM (*Comm*) profit; (*avantage*) benefit; **au ~ de** in aid of

bénéficiaire [benefisjɛʀ] NMF beneficiary

bénéficier [benefisje] /7/ VI: **~ de** to enjoy; (*profiter*) to benefit by *ou* from; (*obtenir*) to get, be given

bénéfique [benefik] ADJ beneficial

Benelux [benelyks] NM: **le ~** Benelux, the Benelux countries

benêt [bənɛ] NM simpleton

bénévolat [benevɔla] NM voluntary service *ou* work

bénévole [benevɔl] ADJ voluntary, unpaid

bénévolement [benevɔlmɑ̃] ADV voluntarily

Bengale [bɛ̃gal] NM: **le ~** Bengal; **le golfe du ~** the Bay of Bengal

bengali [bɛ̃gali] ADJ Bengali, Bengalese ▶ NM (Ling) Bengali

Bénin [benɛ̃] NM: **le ~** Benin

bénin, -igne [benɛ̃, -iɲ] ADJ minor, mild; (tumeur) benign

bénir [benir] /2/ VT to bless

bénit, e [beni, -it] ADJ consecrated; **eau bénite** holy water

bénitier [benitje] NM stoup, font (for holy water)

benjamin, e [bɛ̃ʒamɛ̃, -in] NM/F youngest child; (Sport) under-13

benne [bɛn] NF skip; (de téléphérique) (cable) car; **~ basculante** tipper (BRIT), dump ou dumper truck; **~ à ordures** (amovible) skip

benzine [bɛ̃zin] NF benzine

béotien, ne [beɔsjɛ̃, -ɛn] NM/F philistine

BEP SIGLE M (= Brevet d'études professionnelles) school-leaving diploma, taken at approx. 18 years

béquille [bekij] NF crutch; (de bicyclette) stand

berbère [bɛrbɛr] ADJ Berber ▶ NM (Ling) Berber ▶ NMF: **Berbère** Berber

bercail [bɛrkaj] NM fold

berceau, x [bɛrso] NM cradle, crib

bercer [bɛrse] /3/ VT to rock, cradle; (musique etc) to lull; **~ qn de** (promesses etc) to delude sb with

berceur, -euse [bɛrsœr, -øz] ADJ soothing ▶ NF (chanson) lullaby

berceuse NF lullaby

Bercy [bɛrsi] N the offices of the French Ministry of Finance and Industry

BERD [bɛrd] SIGLE F (= Banque européenne pour la reconstruction et le développement) EBRD

béret [berɛ] NM (aussi: **béret basque**) beret

bergamote [bɛrgamɔt] NF (Bot) bergamot

berge [bɛrʒ] NF bank

berger, -ère [bɛrʒe, -ɛr] NM/F shepherd/shepherdess; **~ allemand** (chien) alsatian (dog) (BRIT), German shepherd (dog) (US)

bergerie [bɛrʒəri] NF sheep pen

bergeronnette [bɛrʒərɔnɛt] NF wagtail

béribéri [beriberi] NM beriberi

Berlin [bɛrlɛ̃] N Berlin; **Berlin-Est/-Ouest** East/West Berlin

berline [bɛrlin] NF (Auto) saloon (car) (BRIT), sedan (US)

berlingot [bɛrlɛ̃go] NM (emballage) carton (pyramid shaped); (bonbon) lozenge

berlinois, e [bɛrlinwa, -waz] ADJ of ou from Berlin ▶ NM/F: **Berlinois, e** Berliner

berlue [bɛrly] NF: **j'ai la ~** I must be seeing things

bermuda [bɛrmyda] NM (short) Bermuda shorts

Bermudes [bɛrmyd] NFPL: **les (îles) ~** Bermuda

Berne [bɛrn] N Bern

berne [bɛrn] NF: **en ~** at half-mast; **mettre en ~** to fly at half-mast

berner [bɛrne] /1/ VT to fool

bernois, e [bɛrnwa, -waz] ADJ Bernese

berrichon, ne [bɛriʃɔ̃, -ɔn] ADJ of ou from the Berry

besace [bəzas] NF beggar's bag

besogne [bəzɔɲ] NF work no pl, job

besogneux, -euse [bəzɔɲø, -øz] ADJ hard-working

★**besoin** [bəzwɛ̃] NM need; (pauvreté): **le ~** need, want; **le ~ d'argent/de gloire** the need for money/glory; **besoins (naturels)** nature's needs; **faire ses besoins** to relieve o.s.; **avoir ~ de qch/faire qch** to need sth/to do sth; **il n'y a pas de (faire)** there is no need to (do); **au ~, si ~ est** if need be; **pour les besoins de la cause** for the purpose in hand; **être dans le ~** to be in need ou want

bestial, e, -aux [bɛstjal, -o] ADJ bestial, brutish ▶ NMPL cattle

bestiole [bɛstjɔl] NF (tiny) creature

bêta [beta] ADJ, NM INV beta

bétail [betaj] NM livestock, cattle pl

bétaillère [betajɛr] NF livestock truck

bête [bɛt] NF animal; (bestiole) bug, insect; **les bêtes** (the) animals; **chercher la petite ~** to nitpick; **~ noire** pet hate, bugbear (BRIT); **~ sauvage** wild beast; **~ de somme** beast of burden ▶ ADJ stupid, silly

bêtement [bɛtmã] ADV stupidly; **tout ~** quite simply

Bethléem [bɛtleɛm] N Bethlehem

bêtifier [betifje] /7/ VI to talk nonsense

bêtise [betiz] NF stupidity; (action, remarque) stupid thing (to say ou do); (bonbon) type of mint sweet (BRIT) ou candy (US); **faire/dire une ~** to do/say something stupid

bêtisier [betizje] NM collection of howlers

béton [betɔ̃] NM concrete; **(en) ~** (fig: alibi, argument) cast iron; **~ armé** reinforced concrete; **~ précontraint** prestressed concrete

bétonner [betɔne] /1/ VT to concrete (over)

bétonnière [betɔnjɛr] NF cement mixer

bette [bɛt] NF (Bot) (Swiss) chard

betterave [bɛtrav] NF (rouge) beetroot (BRIT), beet (US); **~ fourragère** mangel-wurzel; **~ sucrière** sugar beet

beugler [bøgle] /1/ VI to low; (péj: radio etc) to blare ▶ VT (péj: chanson etc) to bawl out

beur [bœr] ADJ, NMF see note

Beur is a term used to refer to a person born in France of North African immigrant parents. It is not racist and is often used by the media, anti-racist groups and second-generation North Africans themselves. The term itself comes from the reversal of the word arabe. See entry verlan.

★**beurre** [bœr] NM butter; **mettre du ~ dans les épinards** (fig) to add a little to the kitty; **~ de cacao** cocoa butter; **~ noir** brown butter (sauce)

beurré, e [bœre] ADJ (brioche, poêle) buttered; (fam: ivre) plastered (fam); **une tartine beurrée** a piece of bread and butter

beurrer [bœre] /1/ VT to butter

beurrier [bœrje] NM butter dish

beuverie [bœvri] NF drinking session

bévue [bevy] NF blunder

Beyrouth [beʀut] N Beirut

Bhoutan [butɑ̃] NM: **le ~** Bhutan

bi [bi] ADJ, NMF (fam: = bisexuel) bi (fam)

bi... [bi] PRÉFIXE bi..., two-

Biafra [bjafʀa] NM: **le ~** Biafra

biafrais, e [bjafʀɛ, -ɛz] ADJ Biafran

biais [bjɛ] NM (moyen) device, expedient; (aspect) angle; (bande de tissu) piece of cloth cut on the bias; **en ~, de ~** (obliquement) at an angle; (fig) indirectly; **par le ~ de** by means of

biaiser [bjeze] /1/ VI (fig) to sidestep the issue

biathlon [biatlɔ̃] NM biathlon

bibelot [biblo] NM trinket, curio

biberon [bibʀɔ̃] NM (feeding) bottle; **nourrir au ~** to bottle-feed

bible [bibl] NF bible

bibliobus [biblijɔbys] NM mobile library van

bibliographie [biblijɔgʀafi] NF bibliography

bibliophile [biblijɔfil] NMF book-lover

bibliothécaire [biblijɔtekɛʀ] NMF librarian

bibliothèque [biblijɔtɛk] NF library; (meuble) bookcase; **~ municipale** public library

biblique [biblik] ADJ biblical

bibliquement [biblikmɑ̃] ADV: **connaître qn ~** (euphémisme) to know sb in the biblical sense

★**bic®** [bik] NM Biro®

bicarbonate [bikaʀbɔnat] NM: **~ (de soude)** bicarbonate of soda

bicentenaire [bisɑ̃t(ə)nɛʀ] NM bicentenary

biceps [bisɛps] NM biceps

biche [biʃ] NF doe

bichonner [biʃɔne] /1/ VT to groom

bicolore [bikɔlɔʀ] ADJ two-coloured (BRIT), two-colored (US)

bicoque [bikɔk] NF (péj) shack, dump

bicorne [bikɔʀn] NM cocked hat

★**bicyclette** [bisiklɛt] NF bicycle

bidasse [bidas] NM (fam) squaddie (BRIT)

bide [bid] NM (fam: ventre) belly; (Théât) flop

★**bidet** [bidɛ] NM bidet

bidoche [bidɔʃ] NF (fam) meat

bidon [bidɔ̃] NM can ▶ ADJ INV (fam) phoney

bidonnant, e [bidɔnɑ̃, -ɑ̃t] ADJ (fam) hilarious

bidonville [bidɔ̃vil] NM shanty town

bidule [bidyl] NM (fam) thingamajig

bielle [bjɛl] NF connecting rod; (Auto) track rod

biélorusse [bjelɔʀys] ADJ Belarusian ▶ NM (Ling) Belarusian ▶ NMF: **Biélorusse** Belarusian

Biélorussie [bjelɔʀysi] NF Belorussia

---

bien [bjɛ̃]

NM **1** (avantage, profit): **faire le bien** to do good; **faire du bien à qn** to do sb good; **ça fait du bien de faire** it does you good to do; **dire du bien de** to speak well of; **c'est pour son bien** it's for his own good; **changer en bien** to change for the better; **le bien public** the public good; **vouloir du bien à qn** (vouloir aider) to have sb's (best) interests at heart; **je te veux du bien** (pour mettre en confiance) I don't wish you any harm

2 (possession, patrimoine) possession, property; **son bien le plus précieux** his most treasured possession; **avoir du bien** to have property; **biens (de consommation etc)** (consumer etc) goods; **biens durables** (consumer) durables

3 (moral): **le bien** good; **distinguer le bien du mal** to tell good from evil

▶ ADV **1** (de façon satisfaisante) well; **elle travaille/mange bien** she works/eats well; **aller ou se porter bien** to be well; **croyant bien faire, je/il ...** thinking I/he was doing the right thing, I/he ...; **tiens-toi bien!** (assieds-toi correctement) sit up straight!; (debout) stand up straight!; (sois sage) behave yourself!; (prépare-toi) wait for it!

2 (valeur intensive) quite; **bien jeune** quite young; **bien assez** quite enough; **bien mieux** (very) much better; **bien du temps/des gens** quite a time/a number of people; **j'espère bien y aller** I do hope to go; **je veux bien le faire** (concession) I'm quite willing to do it; **il faut bien le faire** it has to be done; **il y a bien deux ans** at least two years ago; **cela fait bien deux ans que je ne l'ai pas vu** I haven't seen him for at least ou a good two years; **il semble bien que** it really seems that; **peut-être bien** it could well be; **aimer bien** to like; **Paul est bien venu, n'est-ce pas?** Paul HAS come, hasn't he?; **où peut-il bien être passé?** where on earth can he have got to?

3 (conséquence, résultat): **si bien que** with the result that; **on verra bien** we'll see; **faire bien de ...** to be right to ...

▶ EXCL right!, OK!, fine!; **eh bien!** well!; **(c'est) bien fait!** it serves you (ou him etc) right!; **bien sûr!, bien entendu!** certainly!, of course!

▶ ADJ INV **1** (en bonne forme, à l'aise): **je me sens bien, je suis bien** I feel fine; **je ne me sens pas bien, je ne suis pas bien** I don't feel well; **on est bien dans ce fauteuil** this chair is very comfortable

2 (joli, beau) good-looking; **tu es bien dans cette robe** you look good in that dress

3 (satisfaisant) good; **elle est bien, cette maison/secrétaire** it's a good house/she's a good secretary; **c'est très bien (comme ça)** it's fine (like that); **ce n'est pas si bien que ça** it's not as good ou great as all that; **c'est bien?** is that all right?

4 (moralement) right; (: personne) good, nice; (respectable) respectable; **ce n'est pas bien de ...** it's not right to ...; **elle est bien, cette femme** she's a nice woman, she's a good sort; **des gens bien** respectable people

5 (en bons termes): **être bien avec qn** to be on good terms with sb

---

bien-aimé, e [bjɛ̃neme] ADJ, NM/F beloved

bien-être [bjɛ̃nɛtʀ] NM well-being

bienfaisance [bjɛ̃fəzɑ̃s] NF charity

bienfaisant, e [bjɛ̃fəzɑ̃, -ɑ̃t] ADJ (chose) beneficial

bienfait [bjɛ̃fɛ] NM act of generosity, benefaction; (de la science etc) benefit

bienfaiteur, -trice [bjɛ̃fɛtœʀ, -tʀis] NM/F benefactor/benefactress

bien-fondé [bjɛ̃fɔ̃de] NM soundness

bien-fonds [bjɛ̃fɔ̃] (pl biens-fonds) NM property

bienheureux, -euse [bjɛ̃nœʀø, -øz] ADJ happy; (Rel) blessed, blest

biennal, e, -aux [bjenal, -o] ADJ biennial

bien-pensant, e [bjɛ̃pɑ̃sɑ̃, -ɑ̃t] ADJ right-thinking ▶ NM/F: **les bien-pensants** right-minded people

bien que [bjɛ̃k] CONJ although

bienséance [bjɛ̃seɑ̃s] NF propriety, decorum *no pl*; **les bienséances** (*convenances*) the proprieties

bienséant, e [bjɛ̃seɑ̃, -ɑ̃t] ADJ proper, seemly

bientôt [bjɛ̃to] ADV soon; **à** – see you soon

bienveillance [bjɛ̃vɛjɑ̃s] NF kindness

bienveillant, e [bjɛ̃vɛjɑ̃, -ɑ̃t] ADJ kindly

★**bienvenu, e** [bjɛ̃vny] ADJ welcome ▶ NM/F: **être le ~/la bienvenue** to be welcome ▶ NF: **souhaiter la bienvenue à** to welcome; **bienvenue à** welcome to

bière [bjɛʀ] NF (*boisson*) beer; (*cercueil*) bier; **~ blonde** lager; **~ brune** brown ale (BRIT), dark beer (US); **~ (à la) pression** draught beer

biffer [bife] /1/ VT to cross out

★**bifteck** [biftɛk] NM steak

bifurcation [bifyʀkasjɔ̃] NF fork (*in road*); (*fig*) new direction

bifurquer [bifyʀke] /1/ VI (*route*) to fork; (*véhicule*) to turn off

bigame [bigam] ADJ bigamous

bigamie [bigami] NF bigamy

bigarré, e [bigaʀe] ADJ multicoloured (BRIT), multicolored (US); (*disparate*) motley

bigarreau, x [bigaʀo] NM *type of cherry*

bigleux, -euse [biglø, -øz] ADJ (*fam: qui louche*) cross-eyed; (: *qui voit mal*) short-sighted; **il est complètement ~** he's as blind as a bat

bigorneau, x [bigɔʀno] NM winkle

bigot, e [bigo, -ɔt] (*péj*) ADJ bigoted ▶ NM/F bigot

bigoterie [bigɔtʀi] NF bigotry

bigoudi [bigudi] NM curler

bigrement [bigʀəmɑ̃] ADV (*fam*) fantastically

★**bijou, x** [biʒu] NM jewel

★**bijouterie** [biʒutʀi] NF (*magasin*) jeweller's (shop) (BRIT), jewelry store (US); (*bijoux*) jewellery, jewelry

bijoutier, -ière [biʒutje, -jɛʀ] NM/F jeweller (BRIT), jeweler (US)

bikini [bikini] NM bikini

bilan [bilɑ̃] NM (*Comm*) balance sheet(s); (*annuel*) end of year statement; (*fig*) (net) outcome; (: *de victimes*) toll; **faire le ~ de** to assess; to review; **déposer son ~** to file a bankruptcy statement; **~ de santé** (*Méd*) check-up; **~ social** statement of a firm's policies towards its employees

bilatéral, e, -aux [bilateʀal, -o] ADJ bilateral

bilboquet [bilbɔkɛ] NM (*jouet*) cup-and-ball game

bile [bil] NF bile; **se faire de la ~** (*fam*) to worry o.s. sick

biler [bile] : **se biler** VPR (*fam*) to get worked up

biliaire [biljɛʀ] ADJ biliary

bilieux, -euse [biljø, -øz] ADJ bilious; (*fig: colérique*) testy

bilingue [bilɛ̃g] ADJ bilingual

bilinguisme [bilɛ̃gɥism] NM bilingualism

billard [bijaʀ] NM billiards *sg*; (*table*) billiard table; **c'est du ~** (*fam*) it's a cinch; **passer sur le ~** (*fam*) to have an (*ou* one's) operation; **~ électrique** pinball

bille [bij] NF ball; (*du jeu de billes*) marble; (*de bois*) log; **jouer aux billes** to play marbles

★**billet** [bijɛ] NM (*aussi*: **billet de banque**) (bank) note; (*de cinéma, de bus etc*) ticket; (*courte lettre*) note; **~ à ordre** *ou* **de commerce** (*Comm*) promissory note, IOU; **~ d'avion/de train** plane/train ticket; **~ circulaire** round-trip ticket; **~ doux** love letter; **~ de faveur** complimentary ticket; **~ de loterie** lottery ticket; **~ de quai** platform ticket; **~ électronique** e-ticket

billetterie [bijɛtʀi] NF ticket office; (*distributeur*) ticket dispenser; (*Banque*) cash dispenser

billion [biljɔ̃] NM billion (BRIT), trillion (US)

billot [bijo] NM block

bimbeloterie [bɛ̃blɔtʀi] NF (*objets*) fancy goods

bimensuel, le [bimɑ̃sɥɛl] ADJ bimonthly, every two months

bimestriel, le [bimɛstʀijɛl] ADJ bimonthly, every two months

bimoteur [bimɔtœʀ] ADJ twin-engined

binaire [binɛʀ] ADJ binary

biner [bine] /1/ VT to hoe

binette [binɛt] NF (*outil*) hoe

binoclard, e [binɔklaʀ, -aʀd] (*fam*) ADJ specky ▶ NM/F four-eyes

binocle [binɔkl] NM pince-nez ■ **binocles** NMPL glasses

binoculaire [binɔkylɛʀ] ADJ binocular

binôme [binom] NM binomial

bio [bjo] ADJ (*fam*) = **biologique**; (*produits, aliments*) organic

bio... [bjo] PRÉFIXE bio...

biocarburant [bjokaʀbyʀɑ̃] NM biofuel

biochimie [bjoʃimi] NF biochemistry

biochimique [bjoʃimik] ADJ biochemical

biochimiste [bjoʃimist] NMF biochemist

biocompatible [bjokɔ̃patibl] ADJ biocompatible

biodégradable [bjodegʀadabl] ADJ biodegradable

biodiesel [bjodjezɛl] NM biodiesel

biodiversité [bjodivɛʀsite] NF biodiversity

bioéthique [bjoetik] NF bioethics *sg*

biogazole NM biodiesel

biographe [bjogʀaf] NMF biographer

biographie [bjogʀafi] NF biography

biographique [bjogʀafik] ADJ biographical

★**biologie** [bjolɔʒi] NF biology

biologique [bjolɔʒik] ADJ biological; (*produits*) organic

biologiste [bjolɔʒist] NMF biologist

biomasse [bjomas] NF biomass

biométrie NF biometrics

biométrique [bjometʀik] ADJ biometric

biopsie [bjɔpsi] NF (*Méd*) biopsy

biosphère [bjosfɛʀ] NF biosphere

biotechnologie [bjotɛknɔlɔʒi] NF biotechnology

bioterrorisme [bjotɛʀɔʀism] NM bioterrorism

bioterroriste [bjotɛʀɔʀist] NMF bioterrorist

biotope [bjɔtɔp] NM biotope

bip [bip] NM: **~ sonore** beep; **laissez votre message après le ~ sonore** leave a message after the beep

bipartisme [bipartism] NM two-party system

bipartite [bipartit] ADJ (*Pol*) two-party, bipartisan

bipède [bipɛd] NM biped, two-footed creature

biphasé, e [bifaze] ADJ (*Élec*) two-phase

biplace [biplas] ADJ, NM (*avion*) two-seater

biplan [biplɑ̃] NM biplane

bipolaire [bipɔlɛʀ] ADJ bipolar

bique [bik] NF nanny goat; (*péj*) old hag

biquet, te [bikɛ, -ɛt] NM/F: **mon ~** (*fam*) my lamb

BIRD [biʀd] SIGLE F (= *Banque internationale pour la reconstruction et le développement*) IBRD

biréacteur [biʀeaktœʀ] NM twin-engined jet

birman, e [biʀmɑ̃, -an] ADJ Burmese

Birmanie [biʀmani] NF Burma; **la ~** Burma

bis¹, e [bi, biz] ADJ (*couleur*) greyish brown ▸ NF (*baiser*) kiss; (*vent*) North wind; **faire une** *ou* **la bise à qn** to kiss sb; **grosses bises (de)** (*sur lettre*) love and kisses (from)

bis² [bis] ADV: **12 ~** 12a *ou* A ▸ EXCL, NM encore

bisaïeul, e [bizajœl] NM/F great-grandfather/great-grandmother

bisannuel, le [bizanɥɛl] ADJ biennial

bisbille [bisbij] NF: **être en ~ avec qn** to be at loggerheads with sb

biscornu, e [biskɔʀny] ADJ crooked; (*bizarre*) weird(-looking)

biscotte [biskɔt] NF toasted bread (*sold in packets*)

★**biscuit** [biskɥi] NM biscuit (*BRIT*), cookie (*US*); (*gâteau*) sponge cake; **~ à la cuiller** sponge finger

biscuiterie [biskɥitʀi] NF biscuit manufacturing

★**bise** [biz] ADJ F, NF *voir* **bis¹**

biseau, x [bizo] NM bevelled edge; **en ~** bevelled

biseauter [bizote] /1/ VT to bevel

bisexué, e [bisɛksɥe] ADJ bisexual

bisexuel, le [bisɛksɥɛl] ADJ, NM/F bisexual

bismuth [bismyt] NM bismuth

bison [bizɔ̃] NM bison

bisou [bizu] NM (*fam*) kiss

Bisounours [bizunuʀs] NMPL: **on n'est pas chez les ~** *ou* **au pays des ~** (*fam*) we're not in la-la land

bisque [bisk] NF: **~ d'écrevisses** shrimp bisque

bissectrice [bisɛktʀis] NF bisector

bisser [bise] /1/ VT (*faire rejouer: artiste, chanson*) to encore; (*rejouer: morceau*) to give an encore of

bissextile [bisɛkstil] ADJ: **année ~** leap year

bistouri [bisturi] NM lancet

bistre [bistʀ] ADJ (*couleur*) bistre; (*peau, teint*) tanned

bistro(t) [bistro] NM bistro, café

bistronomie [bistʀɔnɔmi] NF affordable fine dining served in a bistro setting

BIT SIGLE M (= *Bureau international du travail*) ILO

bit [bit] NM (*Inform*) bit

bite [bit] NF (!: *pénis*) prick (!)

biterrois, e [bitɛʀwa, -waz] ADJ of *ou* from Béziers

bitte [bit] NF: **~ d'amarrage** bollard (*Navig*)

bitume [bitym] NM asphalt

bitumer [bityme] /1/ VT to asphalt

bivalent, e [bivalɑ̃, -ɑ̃t] ADJ bivalent

bivouac [bivwak] NM bivouac

★**bizarre** [bizaʀ] ADJ strange, odd

bizarrement [bizaʀmɑ̃] ADV strangely, oddly

bizarrerie [bizaʀʀi] NF strangeness, oddness

blackbouler [blakbule] /1/ VT (*à une élection*) to blackball

blafard, e [blafaʀ, -aʀd] ADJ wan

blague [blag] NF (*propos*) joke; (*farce*) trick; **sans ~!** no kidding!; **~ à tabac** tobacco pouch

blaguer [blage] /1/ VI to joke ▸ VT to tease

blagueur, -euse [blagœʀ, -øz] ADJ teasing ▸ NM/F joker

blair [blɛʀ] NM (*fam*) conk

blaireau, x [blɛʀo] NM (*Zool*) badger; (*brosse*) shaving brush

blairer [blɛʀe] /1/ VT: **je ne peux pas le ~** I can't bear *ou* stand him

blâmable [blɑmabl] ADJ blameworthy

blâme [blɑm] NM blame; (*sanction*) reprimand

blâmer [blɑme] /1/ VT (*réprouver*) to blame; (*réprimander*) to reprimand

★**blanc, blanche** [blɑ̃, blɑ̃ʃ] ADJ white; (*non imprimé*) blank; (*innocent*) pure; **d'une voix blanche** in a toneless voice; **aux cheveux blancs** white-haired ▸ NM (*couleur*) white; (*linge*): **le ~** whites pl; (*espace non écrit*) blank; (*aussi*: **blanc d'œuf**) (egg-)white; (*aussi*: **blanc de poulet**) breast, white meat; (*aussi*: **vin blanc**) white wine; **le ~ de l'œil** the white of the eye; **laisser en ~** to leave blank; **chèque en ~** blank cheque; **à ~** *adv* (*chauffer*) white hot; (*tirer, charger*) with blanks; **saigner à ~** to bleed white; **~ cassé** off-white ▸ NF (*Mus*) minim (*BRIT*), half-note (*US*); (*fam: drogue*) smack ▸ NM/F: **Blanc, Blanche** white, white man/woman

blanc-bec [blɑ̃bɛk] (*pl* **blancs-becs**) NM greenhorn

blanchâtre [blɑ̃ʃɑtʀ] ADJ (*teint, lumière*) whitish

blancheur [blɑ̃ʃœʀ] NF whiteness

blanchiment [blɑ̃ʃimɑ̃] NM money laundering; **le ~ d'argent sale/de capitaux** money laundering

blanchir [blɑ̃ʃiʀ] /2/ VT (*gén*) to whiten; (*linge, fig: argent*) to launder; (*Culin*) to blanch; (*fig: disculper*) to clear; **blanchi à la chaux** whitewashed ▸ VI to grow white; (*cheveux*) to go white

blanchissage [blɑ̃ʃisaʒ] NM (*du linge*) laundering

blanchisserie [blɑ̃ʃisʀi] NF laundry

blanchisseur, -euse [blɑ̃ʃisœʀ, -øz] NM/F launderer

blanc-seing [blɑ̃sɛ̃] (*pl* **blancs-seings**) NM signed blank paper

blanquette [blɑ̃kɛt] NF (*Culin*): **~ de veau** veal in a white sauce, blanquette de veau

blasé, e [blaze] ADJ blasé

blaser [blaze] /1/ VT to make blasé

blason [blazɔ̃] NM coat of arms

blasphémateur, -trice [blasfematœʀ, -tʀis] NM/F blasphemer

blasphématoire [blasfematwar] ADJ blasphemous

blasphème [blasfɛm] NM blasphemy

blasphémer [blasfeme] /6/ VI to blaspheme ▶ VT to blaspheme against

blatte [blat] NF cockroach

blazer [blazɛʀ] NM blazer

blé [ble] NM wheat; **~ en herbe** wheat on the ear; **~ noir** buckwheat

bled [blɛd] NM (péj) hole; (en Afrique du Nord): **le ~** the interior

blême [blɛm] ADJ pale

blêmir [blemiʀ] /2/ VI (personne) to (turn) pale; (lueur) to grow pale

blennorragie [blenɔʀaʒi] NF blennorrhoea

blessant, e [blɛsɑ̃, -ɑ̃t] ADJ hurtful

blessé, e [blese] ADJ injured ▶ NM/F injured person, casualty; **un ~ grave, un grand ~** a seriously injured ou wounded person

★**blesser** [blese] /1/ VT to injure; (délibérément: Mil etc) to wound; (souliers etc, offenser) to hurt ■ **se blesser** VPR to injure o.s.; **se ~ au pied** etc to injure one's foot etc

★**blessure** [blesyʀ] NF (accidentelle) injury; (intentionnelle) wound

blet, te [blɛ, blɛt] ADJ overripe

blette [blɛt] NF = **bette**

★**bleu, e** [blø] ADJ blue; (bifteck) very rare; **avoir une peur bleue** to be scared stiff; **zone bleue** ≈ restricted parking area; **fromage ~** blue cheese ▶ NM (couleur) blue; (novice) greenhorn; (contusion) bruise; (vêtement: aussi: **bleus**) overalls pl (BRIT), coveralls pl (US); **au ~** (Culin) au bleu; **~ (de lessive)** ≈ blue bag; **~ de méthylène** (Méd) methylene blue; **~ marine/nuit/roi** navy/midnight/royal blue

bleuâtre [bløɑtʀ] ADJ (fumée etc) bluish, blueish

bleuet [bløɛ] NM cornflower

bleuir [bløiʀ] /2/ VT, VI to turn blue

bleuté, e [bløte] ADJ blue-shaded

blindage [blɛ̃daʒ] NM armo(u)r-plating

blinde [blɛ̃d] NF: **ça coûte une ~** (fam) it costs an arm and a leg

blindé, e [blɛ̃de] ADJ armoured (BRIT), armored (US); (fig) hardened ▶ NM armoured ou armored car; (char) tank

blinder [blɛ̃de] /1/ VT to armour (BRIT), armor (US); (fig) to harden

blizzard [blizaʀ] NM blizzard

bloc [blɔk] NM (de pierre etc, Inform) block; (de papier à lettres) pad; (ensemble) group, block; **serré à ~** tightened right down; **en ~** as a whole; wholesale; **faire ~** to unite; **~ opératoire** operating ou theatre block; **~ sanitaire** toilet block; **~ sténo** shorthand notebook

blocage [blɔkaʒ] NM (voir bloquer) blocking; jamming; (des prix) freezing; (Psych) hang-up

bloc-cuisine [blɔkkɥizin] (pl **blocs-cuisines**) NM kitchen unit

bloc-cylindres [blɔksilɛ̃dʀ] (pl **blocs-cylindres**) NM cylinder block

bloc-évier [blɔkevje] (pl **blocs-éviers**) NM sink unit

bloc-moteur [blɔkmɔtœʀ] (pl **blocs-moteurs**) NM engine block

bloc-notes [blɔknɔt] (pl **blocs-notes**) NM note pad

blocus [blɔkys] NM blockade

blog, blogue [blɔg] NM blog; **~ vidéo** vlog

blogging [blɔgiŋ] NM blogging

blogosphère [blɔgɔsfɛʀ] NF (Inform) blogosphere

★**bloguer** [blɔge] /1/ VI to blog

★**blogueur, -euse** [blɔgœʀ, øz] NM/F blogger

★**blond, e** [blɔ̃, -ɔ̃d] ADJ fair; (plus clair) blond; (sable, blés) golden; **~ cendré** ash blond ▶ NM/F fair-haired ou blond man/woman

blondeur [blɔ̃dœʀ] NF fairness; blondness

blondin, e [blɔ̃dɛ̃, -in] NM/F fair-haired ou blond child ou young person

blondinet, te [blɔ̃dinɛ, -ɛt] NM/F blondie

blondir [blɔ̃diʀ] /2/ VI (personne, cheveux) to go fair ou blond

bloquer [blɔke] /1/ VT (passage) to block; (pièce mobile) to jam; (crédits, compte) to freeze; (personne, négociations etc) to hold up; (regrouper) to group; **~ les freins** to jam on the brakes ■ **se bloquer** VPR (pièce mobile) to jam; (tuyau) to get blocked

blottir [blɔtiʀ] /2/: **se blottir** VPR to huddle up

blousant, e [bluzɑ̃, -ɑ̃t] ADJ blousing out

blouse [bluz] NF overall

blouser [bluze] /1/ VI to blouse out

★**blouson** [bluzɔ̃] NM blouson (jacket); **~ noir** (fig) ≈ rocker

blue-jean [bludʒin], **blue-jeans** [bludʒins] NM jeans

blues [bluz] NM blues pl

bluet [blyɛ] NM = **bleuet**

bluff [blœf] NM bluff

bluffer [blœfe] /1/ VI, VT to bluff

BNF SIGLE F = **Bibliothèque nationale de France**

boa [bɔa] NM (Zool): **~ (constricteur)** boa (constrictor); (tour de cou) (feather ou fur) boa

bob [bɔb] NM = **bobsleigh**

bobard [bɔbaʀ] NM (fam) tall story

bobèche [bɔbɛʃ] NF candle-ring

bobine [bɔbin] NF (de fil) reel; (de machine à coudre) spool; (de machine à écrire) ribbon; (Élec) coil; **~ (d'allumage)** (Auto) coil; **~ de pellicule** (Photo) roll of film

bobo [bobo] NMF (= bourgeois bohème) boho ▶ NM (fam) sore spot

boboïser [boboize] /1/: **se boboïser** VPR (quartier, ville) to become more boho

bobonne [bɔbɔn] NF (péj, fam: nom donné à l'épouse légitime) missus (fam)

bobsleigh [bɔbslɛg] NM bob(sleigh)

bocage [bɔkaʒ] NM (Géo) bocage, farmland crisscrossed by hedges and trees; (bois) grove, copse (BRIT)

bocal, -aux [bɔkal, -o] NM jar

bock [bɔk] NM (beer) glass; (contenu) glass of beer

body [bɔdi] NM body(suit); (Sport) leotard

bœuf [bœf] (pl **bœufs** [bø]) NM ox, steer; (Culin) beef; (Mus: fam) jam session

★**bof** [bɔf] EXCL (fam: indifférence) don't care!, meh; (: pas terrible) nothing special

Bogota [bɔgɔta] N Bogotá

bogue [bɔg] NF (Bot) husk ▶ NM (Inform) bug

51

Bohème [bɔɛm] NF: **la ~** Bohemia

bohème [bɔɛm] ADJ happy-go-lucky, unconventional

bohémien, ne [bɔemjɛ̃, -ɛn] ADJ Bohemian ▶ NM/F gipsy

★**boire** [bwaʀ] **/53/** VT to drink; (s'imprégner de) to soak up; **~ un coup** to have a drink

★**bois** [bwa] VB voir **boire** ▶ NM wood; (Zool) antler; (Mus): **les ~** the woodwind; **de ~, en ~** wooden; **~ vert** green wood; **~ mort** deadwood; **~ de lit** bedstead

boisé, e [bwaze] ADJ woody, wooded

boiser [bwaze] **/1/** VT (galerie de mine) to timber; (chambre) to panel; (terrain) to plant with trees

boiseries [bwazri] NFPL panelling sg

★**boisson** [bwasɔ̃] NF drink; **pris de ~** drunk, intoxicated; **boissons alcoolisées** alcoholic beverages ou drinks; **boissons non alcoolisées** soft drinks

boit [bwa] VB voir **boire**

boîte [bwat] NF box; (fam: entreprise) firm, company; **aliments en ~** canned ou tinned (BRIT) foods; **~ à gants** glove compartment; **~ à musique** musical box; **~ à ordures** dustbin (BRIT), trash can (US); **~ aux lettres** letter box, mailbox (US); (Inform) mailbox; **~ crânienne** cranium; **~ d'allumettes** box of matches; (vide) matchbox; **~ de conserves** can ou tin (BRIT) (of food); **~ d'envoi** (pour courriels) outbox; **~ de nuit** night club; **~ de sardines/petits pois** can ou tin (BRIT) of sardines/peas; **mettre qn en ~** (fam) to have a laugh at sb's expense; **~ de vitesses** gear box; **~ noire** (Aviat) black box; **~ postale** PO box; **~ vocale** voice mail

boiter [bwate] **/1/** VI to limp; (fig) to wobble; (: raisonnement) to be shaky

boiteux, -euse [bwatø, -øz] ADJ lame; wobbly; shaky

boîtier [bwatje] NM case; (d'appareil photo) body; **~ de montre** watch case

boitiller [bwatije] **/1/** VI to limp slightly, have a slight limp

boive etc [bwav] VB voir **boire**

★**bol** [bɔl] NM bowl; (contenu): **un ~ de café** etc a bowl of coffee etc; **un ~ d'air** a breath of fresh air; **en avoir ras le ~** (fam) to have had a bellyful; **avoir du ~** (fam) to be lucky

bolée [bɔle] NF bowlful

boléro [bɔleʀo] NM bolero

bolet [bɔlɛ] NM boletus (mushroom)

bolide [bɔlid] NM racing car; **comme un ~** like a rocket

Bolivie [bɔlivi] NF: **la ~** Bolivia

bolivien, ne [bɔlivjɛ̃, -ɛn] ADJ Bolivian ▶ NM/F: **Bolivien, ne** Bolivian

bolognais, e [bɔlɔɲɛ, -ɛz] ADJ Bolognese

Bologne [bɔlɔɲ] N Bologna

boloss, bolosse, bolos [bɔlɔs] (péj, fam) ADJ lame ▶ NMF loser

bombance [bɔ̃bɑ̃s] NF: **faire ~** to have a feast, revel

bombardement [bɔ̃baʀdəmɑ̃] NM bombing

bombarder [bɔ̃baʀde] **/1/** VT to bomb; **~ qn de** (cailloux, lettres) to bombard sb with; **~ qn directeur** to thrust sb into the director's seat

bombardier [bɔ̃baʀdje] NM (avion) bomber; (aviateur) bombardier

bombe [bɔ̃b] NF bomb; (atomiseur) (aerosol) spray; (Équitation) riding cap; **faire la ~** (fam) to go on a binge; **~ atomique** atomic bomb; **~ à retardement** time bomb

bombé, e [bɔ̃be] ADJ rounded; (mur) bulging; (front) domed; (route) steeply cambered

bomber [bɔ̃be] **/1/** VI to bulge; (route) to camber ▶ VT: **~ le torse** to swell out one's chest

---

bon, bonne [bɔ̃, bɔn]

ADJ **1** (agréable, satisfaisant) good; **un bon repas/restaurant** a good meal/restaurant; **être bon en maths** to be good at maths

2 (charitable): **être bon (envers)** to be good (to), be kind (to); **vous êtes trop bon** you're too kind

3 (correct) right; **le bon numéro/moment** the right number/moment

4 (souhaits): **bon anniversaire!** happy birthday!; **bon courage!** good luck!; **bon séjour!** enjoy your stay!; **bon voyage!** have a good trip!; **bon week-end!** have a good weekend!; **bonne année!** happy New Year!; **bonne chance!** good luck!; **bonne fête!** happy holiday!; **bonne nuit!** good night!

5 (approprié): **bon à/pour** fit to/for; **bon à jeter** fit for the bin; **c'est bon à savoir** that's useful to know; **à quoi bon (...)?** what's the point ou use (of ...)?

6 (intensif): **ça m'a pris deux bonnes heures** it took me a good two hours; **un bon nombre de** a good number of

7: **bon enfant** adj inv accommodating, easy-going; **bonne femme** (péj) woman; **de bonne heure** early; **bon marché** cheap; **bon mot** witticism; **pour faire bon poids ...** to make up for it ...; **bon sens** common sense; **bon vivant** jovial chap; **bonnes œuvres** charitable works, charities; **bonne sœur** nun

▶ NM **1** (billet) voucher; (: aussi: **bon cadeau**) gift voucher; **bon de caisse** cash voucher; **bon d'essence** petrol coupon; **bon à tirer** pass for press; **bon du Trésor** Treasury bond

2: **avoir du bon** to have its good points; **il y a du bon dans ce qu'il dit** there's some sense in what he says; **pour de bon** for good

▶ NM/F: **un bon à rien** a good-for-nothing

▶ ADV: **il fait bon** it's ou the weather is fine; **sentir bon** to smell good; **tenir bon** to stand firm; **juger bon de faire ...** to think fit to do ...

▶ EXCL right!, good!; **ah bon?** really?; **bon, je reste** right, I'll stay

voir aussi **bonne**

---

bonasse [bɔnas] ADJ soft, meek

★**bonbon** [bɔ̃bɔ̃] NM (boiled) sweet

bonbonne [bɔ̃bɔn] NF demijohn; carboy

bonbonnière [bɔ̃bɔnjɛʀ] NF sweet (BRIT) ou candy (US) box

bond [bɔ̃] NM leap; (d'une balle) rebound, ricochet; **faire un ~** to leap in the air; **d'un seul ~** in one bound, with one leap; **~ en avant** (fig: progrès) leap forward

bonde [bɔ̃d] NF (d'évier etc) plug; (: trou) plughole; (de tonneau) bung; bunghole

b

bondé, e [bɔ̃de] ADJ packed (full)

bondieuserie [bɔ̃djøzʀi] NF (*péj: objet*) religious knick-knack

bondir [bɔ̃diʀ] /2/ VI to leap; **~ de joie** (*fig*) to jump for joy; **~ de colère** (*fig*) to be hopping mad

★**bonheur** [bɔnœʀ] NM happiness; **avoir le ~ de** to have the good fortune to; **porter ~ (à qn)** to bring (sb) luck; **au petit ~** haphazardly; **par ~** fortunately

bonhomie [bɔnɔmi] NF good-naturedness

★**bonhomme** [bɔnɔm] (*pl* **bonshommes** [bɔ̃zɔm]) NM fellow; **un vieux ~** an old chap; **~ de neige** snowman; **aller son ~ de chemin** to carry on in one's own sweet way ▸ ADJ good-natured

boni [bɔni] NM profit

bonification [bɔnifikasjɔ̃] NF bonus

bonifier [bɔnifje] /7/: **se bonifier** VPR to improve

boniment [bɔnimã] NM patter *no pl*

★**bonjour** [bɔ̃ʒuʀ] EXCL, NM hello; (*selon l'heure*) good morning (*ou* afternoon); **donner** *ou* **souhaiter le ~ à qn** to bid sb good morning *ou* afternoon; **c'est simple comme ~!** it's easy as pie!

Bonn [bɔn] N Bonn

bonne [bɔn] ADJ F *voir* **bon** ▸ NF (*domestique*) maid; **~ à toute faire** general help; **~ d'enfant** nanny

bonne-maman [bɔnmamã] (*pl* **bonnes-mamans**) NF granny, grandma, gran

bonnement [bɔnmã] ADV: **tout ~** quite simply

bonnet [bɔnɛ] NM bonnet, hat; (*de soutien-gorge*) cup; **~ d'âne** dunce's cap; **~ de bain** bathing cap; **~ de nuit** nightcap

bonneterie [bɔnɛtʀi] NF hosiery

bon-papa [bɔ̃papa] (*pl* **bons-papas**) NM grandpa, grandad

★**bonsoir** [bɔ̃swaʀ] EXCL good evening

bonté [bɔ̃te] NF kindness *no pl*; **avoir la ~ de** to be kind *ou* good enough to

bonus [bɔnys] NM (*Assurances*) no-claims bonus; (*de DVD*) extras *pl*

bonze [bɔ̃z] NM (*Rel*) bonze

boomerang [bumʀãg] NM boomerang

booster [buste] VT to boost

boots [buts] NFPL boots

borborygme [bɔʀbɔʀigm] NM rumbling noise

★**bord** [bɔʀ] NM (*de table, verre, falaise*) edge; (*de rivière, lac*) bank; (*de route*) side; (*de vêtement*) edge, border; (*de chapeau*) brim; **(monter) à ~** (to go) on board; **jeter par-dessus ~** to throw overboard; **le commandant de ~/les hommes du ~** the ship's master/crew; **du même ~** (*fig*) of the same opinion; **au ~ de la mer/route** at the seaside/roadside; **être au ~ des larmes** to be on the verge of tears; **virer de ~** (*Navig*) to tack; **sur les bords** (*fig*) slightly; **de tous bords** on all sides; **~ du trottoir** kerb (*Brit*), curb (*US*)

bordeaux [bɔʀdo] NM Bordeaux ▸ ADJ INV maroon

bordée [bɔʀde] NF broadside; **une ~ d'injures** a volley of abuse; **tirer une ~** to go on the town

bordel [bɔʀdɛl] NM brothel; (!) bloody (*Brit*) *ou* goddamn (*US*) mess (!) ▸ EXCL hell!

bordelais, e [bɔʀdəlɛ, -ɛz] ADJ *of ou* from Bordeaux

border [bɔʀde] /1/ VT (*être le long de*) to line, border;

(*qn dans son lit*) to tuck up; **~ qch de** (*garnir*) to line sth with; to trim sth with

bordereau, x [bɔʀdəʀo] NM docket, slip

bordure [bɔʀdyʀ] NF border; (*sur un vêtement*) trim(ming), border; **en ~ de** on the edge of

boréal, e, -aux [bɔʀeal, -o] ADJ boreal, northern

borgne [bɔʀɲ] ADJ one-eyed; **hôtel ~** shady hotel; **fenêtre ~** obstructed window

bornage [bɔʀnaʒ] NM (*d'un terrain*) demarcation

borne [bɔʀn] NF boundary stone; (*aussi*: **borne kilométrique**) kilometre-marker, ≈ milestone; **sans ~(s)** boundless ▸ **bornes** NFPL (*fig*) limits; **dépasser les bornes** to go too far

borné, e [bɔʀne] ADJ narrow; (*obtus: personne*) narrow-minded

Bornéo [bɔʀneo] NM: **le ~** Borneo

borner [bɔʀne] /1/ VT (*délimiter*) to limit; (*limiter*) to confine; **se ~ à faire** (*se contenter de*) to content o.s. with doing; (*se limiter à*) to limit o.s. to doing

bosniaque [bɔznjak] ADJ Bosniak ▸ NMF: **Bosniaque** Bosniak

Bosnie [bɔsni] NF Bosnia

Bosnie-Herzégovine [bɔsniɛʀzegɔvin] NF Bosnia-Herzegovina

bosnien, ne [bɔznjɛ̃, -ɛn] ADJ Bosnian ▸ NM (*Ling*) Bosnian ▸ NM/F: **Bosnien, ne** Bosnian

Bosphore [bɔsfɔʀ] NM: **le ~** the Bosphorus

bosquet [bɔskɛ] NM copse (Brit), grove

bosse [bɔs] NF (*de terrain etc*) bump; (*enflure*) lump; (*du bossu, du chameau*) hump; **avoir la ~ des maths** *etc* (*fam*) to have a gift for maths *etc*; **il a roulé sa ~** (*fam*) he's been around

bosseler [bɔsle] /4/ VT (*ouvrer*) to emboss; (*abîmer*) to dent

bosser [bɔse] /1/ VI (*fam*) to work; (: *dur*) to slave (away), slog (hard) (*Brit*)

bosseur, -euse [bɔsœʀ, -øz] NM/F (hard) worker, slogger (*Brit*)

bossu, e [bɔsy] NM/F hunchback

bot [bo] ADJ M: **pied ~** club foot

botanique [bɔtanik] NF botany ▸ ADJ botanic(al)

botaniste [bɔtanist] NMF botanist

Botswana [bɔtswana] NM: **le ~** Botswana

★**botte** [bɔt] NF (*soulier*) (high) boot; (*Escrime*) thrust; (*gerbe*): **~ de paille** bundle of straw; **~ de radis/d'asperges** bunch of radishes/asparagus; **bottes de caoutchouc** wellington boots

botter [bɔte] /1/ VT to put boots on; (*donner un coup de pied à*) to kick; (*fam*): **ça me botte** I fancy that

bottier [bɔtje] NM bootmaker

bottillon [bɔtijɔ̃] NM bootee

bottin® [bɔtɛ̃] NM directory

bottine [bɔtin] NF ankle boot

botulisme [bɔtylism] NM botulism

bouc [buk] NM goat; (*barbe*) goatee; **~ émissaire** scapegoat

boucan [bukã] NM din, racket

★**bouche** [buʃ] NF mouth; **une ~ à nourrir** a mouth to feed; **les bouches inutiles** the non-productive members of the population; **faire du ~ à ~ à qn** to give sb the kiss of life (*Brit*), give sb mouth-to-mouth resuscitation; **de ~ à oreille** confidentially; **pour la bonne ~** (*pour la fin*) till last; **faire venir l'eau à la ~** to make one's mouth water; **~ cousue!** mum's the word!; **rester ~ bée** to stand open-mouthed; **~ d'aération** air vent; **~ de chaleur** hot air vent; **~ d'égout** manhole; **~ d'incendie** fire hydrant; **~ de métro** métro entrance

★**bouché, e** [buʃe] ADJ (*flacon etc*) stoppered; (*temps, ciel*) overcast; (*carrière*) blocked; (*péj: personne*) thick; (*trompette*) muted; **avoir le nez ~** to have a blocked(-up) nose; **c'est un secteur ~** there's no future in that area; **l'évier est ~** the sink's blocked

bouchée [buʃe] NF mouthful; **ne faire qu'une ~ de** (*fig*) to make short work of; **pour une ~ de pain** (*fig*) for next to nothing; **bouchées à la reine** chicken vol-au-vents

★**boucher** [buʃe] **/1/** NM butcher ► VT (*pour colmater*) to stop up; (*trou*) to fill up; (*obstruer*) to block (up) ■ **se boucher** VPR (*tuyau etc*) to block up, get blocked up; **se ~ le nez** to hold one's nose

bouchère [buʃɛʀ] NF butcher; (*femme du boucher*) butcher's wife

★**boucherie** [buʃʀi] NF butcher's (shop); (*métier*) butchery; (*fig*) slaughter, butchery

bouche-trou [buʃtʀu] NM (*fig*) stop-gap

★**bouchon** [buʃɔ̃] NM (*en liège*) cork; (*autre matière*) stopper; (*de tube*) top; (*fig: embouteillage*) holdup; (*Pêche*) float; **~ doseur** measuring cap

bouchonner [buʃɔne] **/1/** VT to rub down ► VI to form a traffic jam

bouchot [buʃo] NM mussel bed

bouclage [buklaʒ] NM sealing off

★**boucle** [bukl] NF (*forme, figure, aussi Inform*) loop; (*objet*) buckle; **~ (de cheveux)** curl; **~ d'oreille** ear-ring

★**bouclé, e** [bukle] ADJ (*cheveux*) curly; (*tapis*) uncut

boucler [bukle] **/1/** VT (*fermer: ceinture etc*) to fasten; (: *magasin*) to shut; (*terminer*) to finish off; (: *circuit*) to complete; (*budget*) to balance; (*enfermer*) to shut away; (: *condamné*) to lock up; (: *quartier*) to seal off; **~ la boucle** to loop the loop ► VI to curl; **faire ~** (*cheveux*) to curl

bouclette [buklɛt] NF small curl

bouclier [buklije] NM shield

bouddha [buda] NM Buddha

bouddhisme [budism] NM Buddhism

bouddhiste [budist] NMF Buddhist

bouder [bude] **/1/** VI to sulk ► VT (*chose*) to turn one's nose up at; (*personne*) to refuse to have anything to do with

bouderie [budʀi] NF sulking *no pl*

boudeur, -euse [budœʀ, -øz] ADJ sullen, sulky

boudin [budɛ̃] NM (*Tech*) roll; (*Culin*): **~ (noir)** black pudding; **~ blanc** white pudding

boudiné, e [budine] ADJ (*doigt*) podgy; (*serré*): **~ dans** (*vêtement*) bulging out of

boudoir [budwaʀ] NM boudoir; (*biscuit*) sponge finger

boue [bu] NF mud

bouée [bwe] NF buoy; (*de baigneur*) rubber ring; **~ (de sauvetage)** lifebuoy; (*fig*) lifeline

boueux, -euse [bwø, -øz] ADJ muddy ► NM (*fam*) refuse (BRIT) *ou* garbage (US) collector

bouffant, e [bufɑ̃, -ɑ̃t] ADJ puffed out

bouffe [buf] NF (*fam*) grub, food

bouffée [bufe] NF (*de cigarette*) puff; **une ~ d'air pur** a breath of fresh air; **~ de chaleur** (*gén*) blast of hot air; (*Méd*) hot flush (BRIT) *ou* flash (US); **~ de fièvre/de honte** flush of fever/shame; **~ d'orgueil** fit of pride

bouffer [bufe] **/1/** VI (*fam*) to eat; (*Couture*) to puff out ► VT (*fam*) to eat

bouffi, e [bufi] ADJ swollen

bouffon, ne [bufɔ̃, -ɔn] ADJ farcical, comical ► NM jester

bouge [buʒ] NM (*bar louche*) (low) dive; (*taudis*) hovel

bougeoir [buʒwaʀ] NM candlestick

bougeotte [buʒɔt] NF: **avoir la ~** to have the fidgets

★**bouger** [buʒe] **/3/** VI to move; (*dent etc*) to be loose; (*changer*) to alter; (*agir*) to stir; (*s'activer*) to get moving; **les prix/les couleurs n'ont pas bougé** prices/colours haven't changed ► VT to move ■ **se bouger** VPR (*fam*) to move (oneself)

bougie [buʒi] NF candle; (*Auto*) spark(ing) plug

bougon, ne [bugɔ̃, -ɔn] ADJ grumpy

bougonner [bugɔne] **/1/** VI, VT to grumble

bougre [bugʀ] NM chap; (*fam*): **ce ~ de ...** that confounded ...

boui-boui [bwibwi] (*pl* **bouis-bouis**) NM (*fam*) greasy spoon

bouillabaisse [bujabɛs] NF *type of fish soup*

bouillant, e [bujɑ̃, -ɑ̃t] ADJ (*qui bout*) boiling; (*très chaud*) boiling (hot); (*fig: ardent*) hot-headed; **~ de colère** *etc* seething with anger *etc*

bouille [buj] NF (*fam*) mug

bouilleur [bujœʀ] NM: **~ de cru** (home) distiller

bouillie [buji] NF gruel; (*de bébé*) cereal; **en ~** (*fig*) crushed

bouillir [bujiʀ] **/15/** VI to boil; **~ de colère** *etc* to seethe with anger *etc* ► VT (*Culin: aussi:* **faire bouillir**) to boil

bouilloire [bujwaʀ] NF kettle

bouillon [bujɔ̃] NM (*Culin*) stock *no pl*; (*bulles, écume*) bubble; **~ de culture** culture medium

bouillonnement [bujɔnmɑ̃] NM (*d'un liquide*) bubbling; (*des idées*) ferment

bouillonner [bujɔne] **/1/** VI to bubble; (*fig: idées*) to bubble up; (*torrent*) to foam

bouillotte [bujɔt] NF hot-water bottle

★**boulanger, -ère** [bulɑ̃ʒe, -ɛʀ] NM/F baker ► NF (*femme du boulanger*) baker's wife

★**boulangerie** [bulɑ̃ʒʀi] NF bakery, baker's (shop); (*commerce*) bakery; **~ industrielle** bakery

boulangerie-pâtisserie [bulɑ̃ʒʀipatisʀi] (*pl* **boulangeries-pâtisseries**) NF baker's and confectioner's (shop)

★**boule** [bul] NF (*gén*) ball; (*de pétanque*) bowl; (*de machine à écrire*) golf ball; **roulé en ~** curled up in a ball; **se mettre en ~** (*fig*) to fly off the handle, blow one's top; **perdre la ~** (*fig: fam*) to go off one's rocker; **~ de gomme** (*bonbon*) gum(drop), pastille; **~ de neige** snowball; **faire ~ de neige** (*fig*) to snowball

bouleau, x [bulo] NM (silver) birch

bouledogue [buldɔg] NM bulldog

bouler [bule] /1/ VI (*fam*): **envoyer ~ qn** to send sb packing; **je me suis fait ~** (*à un examen*) they flunked me

boulet [bulɛ] NM (*aussi*: **boulet de canon**) cannonball; (*de bagnard*) ball and chain; (*charbon*) (coal) nut

boulette [bulɛt] NF (*de viande*) meatball

★**boulevard** [bulvaʀ] NM boulevard

bouleversant, e [bulvɛʀsɑ̃, -ɑ̃t] ADJ (*récit*) deeply distressing; (*nouvelle*) shattering

bouleversé, e [bulvɛʀse] ADJ (*ému*) deeply distressed; shattered

bouleversement [bulvɛʀsəmɑ̃] NM (*politique, social*) upheaval

bouleverser [bulvɛʀse] /1/ VT (*émouvoir*) to overwhelm; (*causer du chagrin à*) to distress; (*pays, vie*) to disrupt; (*papiers, objets*) to turn upside down, upset

boulier [bulje] NM abacus; (*de jeu*) scoring board

boulimie [bulimi] NF bulimia; compulsive eating

boulimique [bulimik] ADJ bulimic

boulingrin [bulɛ̃gʀɛ̃] NM lawn

bouliste [bulist] NMF bowler

boulocher [bulɔʃe] /1/ VI (*laine etc*) to develop little snarls

boulodrome [bulɔdʀɔm] NM bowling pitch

boulon [bulɔ̃] NM bolt

boulonner [bulɔne] /1/ VT to bolt

★**boulot¹** [bulo] NM (*fam: travail*) work

boulot², te [bulo, -ɔt] ADJ plump, tubby

★**boum** [bum] NM bang ▸ NF (*fam*) party

bouquet [bukɛ] NM (*de fleurs*) bunch (of flowers), bouquet; (*de persil etc*) bunch; (*parfum*) bouquet; (*fig*) crowning piece; **c'est le ~!** that's the last straw!; **~ garni** (*Culin*) bouquet garni

bouquetin [buk(ə)tɛ̃] NM ibex

bouquin [bukɛ̃] NM (*fam*) book

bouquiner [bukine] /1/ VI (*fam*) to read

bouquiniste [bukinist] NMF bookseller

bourbeux, -euse [buʀbø, -øz] ADJ muddy

bourbier [buʀbje] NM (quag)mire

bourde [buʀd] NF (*erreur*) howler; (*gaffe*) blunder

bourdon [buʀdɔ̃] NM bumblebee

bourdonnement [buʀdɔnmɑ̃] NM buzzing *no pl*, buzz; **avoir des bourdonnements d'oreilles** to have a buzzing (noise) in one's ears

bourdonner [buʀdɔne] /1/ VI to buzz; (*moteur*) to hum

bourg [buʀ] NM small market town (*ou* village)

bourgade [buʀgad] NF township

bourgeois, e [buʀʒwa, -waz] ADJ ≈ (upper) middle class; (*péj*) bourgeois; (*maison etc*) very comfortable ▸ NM/F (*autrefois*) burgher

bourgeoisie [buʀʒwazi] NF ≈ upper middle classes *pl*; bourgeoisie; **petite ~** middle classes

bourgeon [buʀʒɔ̃] NM bud

bourgeonner [buʀʒɔne] /1/ VI to bud

bourgogne [buʀgɔɲ] NM Burgundy (wine) ▸ NF: **la B~** Burgundy

bourguignon, ne [buʀgiɲɔ̃, -ɔn] ADJ of *ou* from Burgundy, Burgundian; **bœuf ~** bœuf bourguignon

bourlinguer [buʀlɛ̃ge] /1/ VI to knock about a lot, get around a lot

bourrade [buʀad] NF shove, thump

bourrage [buʀaʒ] NM (*papier*) jamming; **~ de crâne** brainwashing; (*Scol*) cramming

bourrasque [buʀask] NF squall

bourratif, -ive [buʀatif, -iv] ADJ (*fam*) filling, stodgy

bourre [buʀ] NF (*de coussin, matelas etc*) stuffing

bourré, e [buʀe] ADJ (*rempli*): **~ de** crammed full of; (*fam: ivre*) pickled, plastered

bourreau, x [buʀo] NM executioner; (*fig*) torturer; **~ de travail** workaholic, glutton for work

bourrelé, e [buʀ(ə)le] ADJ: **être ~ de remords** to be racked by remorse

bourrelet [buʀlɛ] NM draught (BRIT) *ou* draft (US) excluder; (*de peau*) fold *ou* roll (of flesh)

bourrer [buʀe] /1/ VT (*pipe*) to fill; (*poêle*) to pack; (*valise*) to cram (full); **~ de** to cram (full) with, stuff with; **~ de coups** to hammer blows on, pummel; **~ le crâne à qn** to pull the wool over sb's eyes; (*endoctriner*) to brainwash sb

bourricot [buʀiko] NM small donkey

bourrique [buʀik] NF (*âne*) ass

bourru, e [buʀy] ADJ surly, gruff

★**bourse** [buʀs] NF (*subvention*) grant; (*porte-monnaie*) purse; **sans ~ délier** without spending a penny; **la B~** the Stock Exchange; **~ du travail** ≈ trades union council (regional headquarters)

boursicoter [buʀsikɔte] /1/ VI (*Comm*) to dabble on the Stock Market

boursier, -ière [buʀsje, -jɛʀ] ADJ (*Comm*) Stock Market *cpd* ▸ NM/F (*Scol*) grant-holder

boursouflé, e [buʀsufle] ADJ swollen, puffy; (*fig*) bombastic, turgid

boursoufler [buʀsufle] /1/ VT to puff up, bloat ■ **se boursoufler** VPR (*visage*) to swell *ou* puff up; (*peinture*) to blister

boursouflure [buʀsuflyʀ] NF (*du visage*) swelling, puffiness; (*de la peinture*) blister; (*fig: du style*) pomposity

bous [bu] VB *voir* **bouillir**

bousculade [buskylad] NF (*hâte*) rush; (*poussée*) crush

bousculer [buskyle] /1/ VT to knock over; (*heurter*) to knock into; (*fig*) to push, rush ■ **se bousculer** VPR (*se presser*) to rush

bouse [buz] NF: **~ (de vache)** (cow) dung *no pl* (BRIT), manure *no pl*

bousiller [buzije] /1/ VT (*fam*) to wreck

boussole [busɔl] NF compass

★**bout** [bu] VB *voir* **bouillir** ▸ NM bit; (*extrémité: d'un bâton etc*) tip; (: *d'une ficelle, table, rue, période*) end; **au ~ de** at the end of, after; **au ~ du compte** at the end of the day; **pousser qn à ~** to push sb to the limit (of his patience); **venir à ~ de** to manage to finish (off) *ou* overcome; **à ~** to end; at the end; **à tout ~ de champ** at every turn; **d'un ~ à l'autre, d'un ~ en ~** from one end to the other; **à ~ portant** at point-blank range; **un ~ de chou** (*enfant*) a little tot; **~ d'essai** (*Ciné etc*) screen test; **~ filtre** filter tip

boutade [butad] NF quip, sally

boute-en-train [butɑ̃trɛ̃] NM INV live wire (fig)

★**bouteille** [butɛj] NF bottle; (de gaz butane) cylinder

boutiquaire [butikɛr] ADJ: **niveau ~** shopping level

boutique [butik] NF shop (BRIT), store (US); (de grand couturier, de mode) boutique; **~ en ligne** online store

boutiquier, -ière [butikje, -jɛr] NM/F shopkeeper (BRIT), storekeeper (US)

boutoir [butwar] NM: **coup de ~** (choc) thrust; (fig: propos) barb

★**bouton** [butɔ̃] NM (de vêtement, électrique etc) button; (BOT) bud; (sur la peau) spot; (de porte) knob; **~ de manchette** cuff-link; **~ d'or** buttercup

boutonnage [butɔnaʒ] NM (action) buttoning(-up); **un manteau à double ~** a coat with two rows of buttons

boutonner [butɔne] /1/ VT to button up, do up ■ **se boutonner** VPR to button one's clothes up

boutonneux, -euse [butɔnø, -øz] ADJ spotty

boutonnière [butɔnjɛr] NF buttonhole

bouton-poussoir [butɔ̃puswar] (pl **boutons-poussoirs**) NM pushbutton

bouton-pression [butɔ̃presjɔ̃] (pl **boutons-pression**) NM press stud, snap fastener

bouture [butyr] NF cutting; **faire des boutures** to take cuttings

bouvreuil [buvrœj] NM bullfinch

bovidé [bɔvide] NM bovine

bovin, e [bɔvɛ̃, -in] ADJ bovine ▶ NM: **bovins** cattle pl

★**bowling** [bɔliŋ] NM (tenpin) bowling; (salle) bowling alley

box [bɔks] NM lock-up (garage); (de salle, dortoir) cubicle; (d'écurie) loose-box; (aussi: **box-calf**) box calf; **le ~ des accusés** the dock

boxe [bɔks] NF boxing

boxer [bɔkse] /1/ VI to box ▶ NM [bɔksɛr] (chien) boxer

boxeur [bɔksœr] NM boxer

boyau, x [bwajo] NM (corde de raquette etc) (cat) gut; (galerie) passage(way); (narrow) gallery; (pneu de bicyclette) tubeless tyre ■ **boyaux** NMPL (viscères) entrails, guts

boycottage [bɔjkɔtaʒ] NM (d'un produit) boycotting

boycotter [bɔjkɔte] /1/ VT to boycott

BP SIGLE F = **boîte postale**

brabançon, ne [brabɑ̃sɔ̃, -ɔn] ADJ of ou from Brabant

Brabant [brabɑ̃] NM: **le ~** Brabant

bracelet [braslɛ] NM bracelet

bracelet-montre [braslɛmɔ̃tr] (pl **bracelets-montres**) NM wristwatch

braconnage [brakɔnaʒ] NM poaching

braconner [brakɔne] /1/ VI to poach

braconnier [brakɔnje] NM poacher

brader [brade] /1/ VT to sell off, sell cheaply

braderie [bradri] NF clearance sale; (par des particuliers) ≈ car boot sale (BRIT), ≈ garage sale (US); (magasin) discount store; (sur marché) cut-price (BRIT) ou cut-rate (US) stall

braguette [bragɛt] NF fly, flies pl (BRIT), zipper (US)

braillard, e [brajar, -ard] ADJ (fam) bawling, yelling

braille [braj] NM Braille

braillement [brajmɑ̃] NM (cri) bawling no pl, yelling no pl

brailler [braje] /1/ VI to bawl, yell ▶ VT to bawl out, yell out

braire [brɛr] /50/ VI to bray

braise [brɛz] NF embers pl

braiser [brɛze] /1/ VT to braise; **bœuf braisé** braised steak

bramer [brame] /1/ VI to bell; (fig) to wail

brancard [brɑ̃kar] NM (civière) stretcher; (bras, perche) shaft

brancardier [brɑ̃kardje] NM stretcher-bearer

branchages [brɑ̃ʃaʒ] NMPL branches, boughs

★**branche** [brɑ̃ʃ] NF branch; (de lunettes) side(-piece)

★**branché, e** [brɑ̃ʃe] ADJ (fam) switched-on, trendy ▶ NM/F (fam) trendy

branchement [brɑ̃ʃmɑ̃] NM connection

★**brancher** [brɑ̃ʃe] /1/ VT to connect (up); (en mettant la prise) to plug in; **~ qn/qch sur** (fig) to get sb/sth launched onto

branchies [brɑ̃ʃi] NFPL gills

brandade [brɑ̃dad] NF brandade (cod dish)

brandebourgeois, e [brɑ̃dəburʒwa, -waz] ADJ of ou from Brandenburg

brandir [brɑ̃dir] /2/ VT (arme) to brandish, wield; (document) to flourish, wave

brandon [brɑ̃dɔ̃] NM firebrand

branlant, e [brɑ̃lɑ̃, -ɑ̃t] ADJ (mur, meuble) shaky

branle [brɑ̃l] NM: **mettre en ~** to set swinging; **donner le ~ à** to set in motion

branle-bas [brɑ̃lba] NM INV commotion

branler [brɑ̃le] /1/ VI to be shaky, be loose ▶ VT: **~ la tête** to shake one's head ■ **se branler** VPR (!: se masturber) to jerk off (!), wank (!)

braquage [brakaʒ] NM (fam) stick-up, hold-up; (AUTO): **rayon de ~** turning circle

braque [brak] NM (ZOOL) pointer

braquer [brake] /1/ VI (AUTO) to turn (the wheel) ▶ VT (revolver etc): **~ qch sur** to aim sth at, point sth at; (mettre en colère): **~ qn** to antagonize sb, put sb's back up; **~ son regard sur** to fix one's gaze on ■ **se braquer** VPR: **se ~ (contre)** to take a stand (against)

★**bras** [bra] NM arm; (de fleuve) branch; **~ dessus ~ dessous** arm in arm; **à tour de ~** with all one's might; **~ droit** (fig) right hand man; **~ de fer** arm wrestling; **une partie de ~ de fer** (fig) a trial of strength; **~ de levier** lever arm; **~ de mer** arm of the sea, sound ▶ NMPL (fig: travailleurs) labour sg (BRIT), labor sg (US), hands; **à ~ raccourcis** with fists flying; **baisser les ~** to give up; **se retrouver avec qch sur les ~** (fam) to be landed with sth

brasero [brazero] NM brazier

brasier [brazje] NM blaze, (blazing) inferno; (fig) inferno

Brasilia [brazilja] N Brasilia

bras-le-corps [bralkɔr]: **à ~** adv (a)round the waist

brassage [brasaʒ] NM (de la bière) brewing; (fig) mixing

brassard [bʀasaʀ] NM armband

brasse [bʀas] NF (*nage*) breast-stroke; (*mesure*) fathom; **~ papillon** butterfly(-stroke)

brassée [bʀase] NF armful; **une ~ de** (*fig*) a number of

brasser [bʀase] /1/ VT (*bière*) to brew; (*remuer: salade*) to toss; (: *cartes*) to shuffle; (*fig*) to mix; **~ l'argent/ les affaires** to handle a lot of money/ business

★**brasserie** [bʀasʀi] NF (*restaurant*) bar (*selling food*), brasserie; (*usine*) brewery

brasseur [bʀasœʀ] NM (*de bière*) brewer; **~ d'affaires** big businessman

brassière [bʀasjɛʀ] NF (baby's) vest (BRIT) ou undershirt (US); (*de sauvetage*) life jacket

bravache [bʀavaʃ] NM blusterer, braggart

bravade [bʀavad] NF: **par ~** out of bravado

brave [bʀav] ADJ (*courageux*) brave; (*bon, gentil*) good, kind

bravement [bʀavmɑ̃] ADV bravely; (*résolument*) boldly

braver [bʀave] /1/ VT to defy

★**bravo** [bʀavo] EXCL bravo! ▶ NM cheer

bravoure [bʀavuʀ] NF bravery

BRB SIGLE F (*Police*: = *Brigade de répression du banditisme*) ≈ serious crime squad

break [bʀɛk] NM (*Auto*) estate car (BRIT), station wagon (US)

brebis [bʀəbi] NF ewe; **~ galeuse** black sheep

brèche [bʀɛʃ] NF breach, gap; **être sur la ~** (*fig*) to be on the go

bredouille [bʀəduj] ADJ empty-handed

bredouiller [bʀəduje] /1/ VI, VT to mumble, stammer

★**bref, brève** [bʀɛf, bʀɛv] ADJ short, brief; **d'un ton ~** sharply, curtly; **en ~** in short, in brief; **à ~ délai** shortly ▶ ADV in short ▶ NF (*voyelle*) short vowel; (*information*) brief news item

brelan [bʀəlɑ̃] NM: **un ~** three of a kind; **un ~ d'as** three aces

breloque [bʀələk] NF charm

brème [bʀɛm] NF bream

Brésil [bʀezil] NM: **le ~** Brazil

brésilien, ne [bʀeziljɛ̃, -ɛn] ADJ Brazilian ▶ NM/F: **Brésilien, ne** Brazilian

bressan, e [bʀesɑ̃, -an] ADJ of ou from Bresse

★**Bretagne** [bʀətaɲ] NF: **la ~** Brittany

bretelle [bʀətɛl] NF (*de fusil etc*) sling; (*de vêtement*) strap; (*d'autoroute*) slip road (BRIT), entrance ou exit ramp (US); **~ de contournement** (*Auto*) bypass; **~ de raccordement** (*Auto*) access road ▪ **bretelles** NFPL (*pour pantalon*) braces (BRIT), suspenders (US)

breton, ne [bʀətɔ̃, -ɔn] ADJ Breton ▶ NM (*Ling*) Breton ▶ NM/F: **Breton, ne** Breton

breuvage [bʀœvaʒ] NM beverage, drink

brève [bʀɛv] ADJ F, NF *voir* **bref**

brevet [bʀəvɛ] NM diploma, certificate; **~ d'apprentissage** certificate of apprenticeship; **~ (des collèges)** *school certificate, taken at approx. 16 years*; **~ (d'invention)** patent

breveté, e [bʀəv(ə)te] ADJ patented; (*diplômé*) qualified

breveter [bʀəv(ə)te] /4/ VT to patent

bréviaire [bʀevjɛʀ] NM breviary

BRGM SIGLE M = **Bureau de recherches géologiques et minières**

briard, e [bʀijaʀ, -aʀd] ADJ of ou from Brie ▶ NM (*chien*) briard

bribe [bʀib] NF bit, scrap ▪ **bribes** NFPL (*d'une conversation*) snatches; **par bribes** piecemeal

bric [bʀik] : **de ~ et de broc** ADV with any old thing

bric-à-brac [bʀikabʀak] NM INV bric-a-brac, jumble

★**bricolage** [bʀikɔlaʒ] NM: **le ~** do-it-yourself (jobs); (*péj*) patched-up job

bricole [bʀikɔl] NF (*babiole, chose insignifiante*) trifle; (*petit travail*) small job

★**bricoler** [bʀikɔle] /1/ VI to do odd jobs; (*en amateur*) to do DIY jobs; (*passe-temps*) to potter about ▶ VT (*réparer*) to fix up; (*mal réparer*) to tinker with; (*trafiquer: voiture etc*) to doctor, fix

bricoleur, -euse [bʀikɔlœʀ, -øz] NM/F handyman/-woman, DIY enthusiast

bridage [bʀidaʒ] NM (*Auto*) speed governing

bride [bʀid] NF bridle; (*d'un bonnet*) string, tie; **à ~ abattue** flat out, hell for leather; **tenir en ~** to keep in check; **lâcher la ~ à, laisser ~ sur le cou à** to give free rein to

bridé, e [bʀide] ADJ: **yeux bridés** slit eyes

brider [bʀide] /1/ VT (*réprimer*) to keep in check; (*cheval*) to bridle; (*Culin: volaille*) to truss

bridge [bʀidʒ] NM (*Cartes*) bridge

brie [bʀi] NM Brie (*cheese*)

briefer [bʀife] VT (*fam*) to brief

brièvement [bʀijɛvmɑ̃] ADV briefly

brièveté [bʀijɛvte] NF brevity

brigade [bʀigad] NF (*Police*) squad; (*Mil*) brigade

brigadier [bʀigadje] NM (*Police*) ≈ sergeant; (*Mil*) bombardier; corporal

brigadier-chef [bʀigadjeʃɛf] (*pl* **brigadiers-chefs**) NM ≈ lance-sergeant

brigand [bʀigɑ̃] NM brigand

brigandage [bʀigɑ̃daʒ] NM robbery

briguer [bʀige] /1/ VT to aspire to; (*suffrages*) to canvass

brillamment [bʀijamɑ̃] ADV brilliantly

brillant, e [bʀijɑ̃, -ɑ̃t] ADJ brilliant; (*remarquable*) bright; (*luisant*) shiny, shining ▶ NM (*diamant*) brilliant

★**briller** [bʀije] /1/ VI to shine

brimade [bʀimad] NF vexation, harassment *no pl*; bullying *no pl*

brimbaler [bʀɛ̃bale] /1/ VB = **bringuebaler**

brimer [bʀime] /1/ VT to harass; to bully

brin [bʀɛ̃] NM (*de laine, ficelle etc*) strand; (*fig*): **un ~ de** a bit of; **un ~ mystérieux** *etc* (*fam*) a weeny bit mysterious *etc*; **~ d'herbe** blade of grass; **~ de muguet** sprig of lily of the valley; **~ de paille** wisp of straw

brindille [bʀɛ̃dij] NF twig

bringue [bʀɛ̃g] NF (*fam*): **faire la ~** to go on a binge

bringuebaler [bʀɛ̃g(ə)bale] /1/ VI to shake (about) ▶ VT to cart about

brio [bʀijo] NM brilliance; (*Mus*) brio; **avec ~** brilliantly, with panache

brioche [brijɔʃ] NF brioche (bun); (fam: ventre) paunch

brioché, e [brijɔʃe] ADJ brioche-style

★**brique** [brik] NF brick; (de lait) carton; (fam) 10 000 francs ▸ ADJ INV brick red

briquer [brike] /1/ VT (fam) to polish up

briquet [brikɛ] NM (cigarette) lighter

briqueterie [brik(ə)tri] NF brickyard

bris [bri] NM: ~ de clôture (Jur) breaking in; ~ de glaces (Auto) breaking of windows

brisant [brizɑ̃] NM reef; (vague) breaker

brise [briz] NF breeze

brisé, e [brize] ADJ broken; ~ (de fatigue) exhausted; d'une voix brisée in a voice broken with emotion; pâte brisée shortcrust pastry

brisées [brize] NFPL: aller ou marcher sur les ~ de qn to compete with sb in his own province

brise-glace, brise-glaces [brizglas] NM INV (navire) icebreaker

brise-jet [brizʒɛ] NM tap swirl

brise-lames [brizlam] NM INV breakwater

briser [brize] /1/ VT to break ▪ se briser VPR to break

brise-tout [briztu] NM INV wrecker

briseur, -euse [brizœr, -øz] NM/F: ~ de grève strike-breaker

brise-vent [brizvɑ̃] NM windbreak

bristol [bristɔl] NM (carte de visite) visiting card

★**britannique** [britanik] ADJ British ▸ NMF: Britannique Briton, British person; les Britanniques the British

broc [bro] NM pitcher

brocante [brɔkɑ̃t] NF (objets) secondhand goods pl, junk; (commerce) secondhand trade; junk dealing

brocanteur, -euse [brɔkɑ̃tœr, -øz] NM/F junk shop owner; junk dealer

brocart [brɔkar] NM brocade

broche [brɔʃ] NF brooch; (Culin) spit; (fiche) spike, peg; (Méd) pin; à la ~ spit-roasted, roasted on a spit

broché, e [brɔʃe] ADJ (livre) paper-backed; (tissu) brocaded

brochet [brɔʃɛ] NM pike inv

brochette [brɔʃɛt] NF (ustensile) skewer; (plat) kebab; ~ de décorations row of medals

★**brochure** [brɔʃyr] NF pamphlet, brochure, booklet

brocoli [brɔkɔli] NM broccoli

brodequins [brɔdkɛ̃] NMPL (de marche) (lace-up) boots

broder [brɔde] /1/ VT to embroider ▸ VI: ~ (sur des faits ou une histoire) to embroider the facts

broderie [brɔdri] NF embroidery

bromure [brɔmyr] NM bromide

broncher [brɔ̃ʃe] /1/ VI: sans ~ without flinching, without turning a hair

bronches [brɔ̃ʃ] NFPL bronchial tubes

bronchite [brɔ̃ʃit] NF bronchitis

bronchodilatateur [brɔ̃kodilatatœr] NM bronchodilator

broncho-pneumonie [brɔ̃kɔpnømɔni] NF broncho-pneumonia no pl

bronzage [brɔ̃zaʒ] NM (hâle) (sun)tan

bronze [brɔ̃z] NM bronze

bronzé, e [brɔ̃ze] ADJ tanned

★**bronzer** [brɔ̃ze] /1/ VT to tan ▸ VI to get a tan ▪ se bronzer VPR to sunbathe

★**brosse** [brɔs] NF brush; donner un coup de ~ à qch to give sth a brush; coiffé en ~ with a crewcut; ~ à cheveux hairbrush; ~ à dents toothbrush; ~ à habits clothesbrush

★**brosser** [brɔse] /1/ VT (nettoyer) to brush; (fig: tableau etc) to paint; to draw ▪ se brosser VPR to brush one's clothes; se ~ les dents to brush one's teeth; tu peux te ~ ! (fam) you can sing for it!

brou [bru] NM: ~ de noix (pour bois) walnut stain; (liqueur) walnut liqueur

brouette [bruɛt] NF wheelbarrow

brouhaha [bruaa] NM hubbub

brouillage [brujaʒ] NM (d'une émission) jamming

★**brouillard** [brujar] NM fog; être dans le ~ (fig) to be all at sea

brouille [bruj] NF quarrel

brouillé, e [bruje] ADJ (teint) muddy; (fâché): il est ~ avec ses parents he has fallen out with his parents

brouiller [bruje] /1/ VT (œufs, message) to scramble; (idées) to mix up; to confuse; (Radio) to cause interference to; (: délibérément) to jam; (rendre trouble) to cloud; (désunir: amis) to set at odds; ~ les pistes to cover one's tracks; (fig) to confuse the issue ▪ se brouiller VPR (ciel, vue) to cloud over; (détails) to become confused; se ~ (avec) to fall out (with)

brouillon, ne [brujɔ̃, -ɔn] ADJ (sans soin) untidy; (qui manque d'organisation) disorganized, unmethodical ▸ NM (first) draft; cahier de ~ rough (work) book; (papier) ~ rough paper

broussailles [brusɑj] NFPL undergrowth sg

broussailleux, -euse [brusɑjø, -øz] ADJ bushy

brousse [brus] NF: la ~ the bush

brouter [brute] /1/ VT to graze on ▸ VI to graze; (Auto) to judder

broutille [brutij] NF trifle

broyer [brwaje] /8/ VT to crush; ~ du noir to be down in the dumps

bru [bry] NF daughter-in-law

brucelles [brysɛl] NFPL: (pinces) ~ tweezers

brugnon [brynɔ̃] NM nectarine

bruine [bruin] NF drizzle

bruiner [bruine] /1/ VB IMPERS: il bruine it's drizzling, there's a drizzle

bruire [bruir] /2/ VI (eau) to murmur; (feuilles, étoffe) to rustle

bruissement [bruismɑ̃] NM murmuring; rustling

★**bruit** [brui] NM: un ~ a noise, a sound; (fig: rumeur) a rumour (BRIT), a rumor (US); le ~ noise; pas/trop de ~ no/too much noise; sans ~ without a sound, noiselessly; faire du ~ to make a noise; ~ de fond background noise

bruitage [bruitaʒ] NM sound effects pl

bruiteur, -euse [bruitœr, -øz] NM/F sound-effects engineer

brûlant, e [bʀylɑ̃, -ɑ̃t] ADJ burning (hot); (*liquide*) boiling (hot); (*regard*) fiery; (*sujet*) red-hot

brûlé, e [bʀyle] ADJ burnt; (*fig: démasqué*) blown; (: *homme politique etc*) discredited ▶ NM: **odeur de ~** smell of burning

brûle-pourpoint [bʀylpuʀpwɛ̃]: **à ~** adv point-blank

brûler [bʀyle] /**1**/ VT to burn; (*eau bouillante*) to scald; (*consommer: électricité, essence*) to use; (*feu rouge, signal*) to go through (without stopping); **~ les étapes** to make rapid progress; (*aller trop vite*) to cut corners ▶ VI to burn; **tu brûles** (*jeu*) you're getting warm *ou* hot; **~ (d'impatience) de faire qch** to burn with impatience to do sth, be dying to do sth ■ **se brûler** VPR to burn o.s.; (*s'ébouillan-ter*) to scald o.s.; **se ~ la cervelle** to blow one's brains out

brûleur [bʀylœʀ] NM burner

brûlot [bʀylo] NM (*Culin*) flaming brandy; **un ~ de contestation** (*fig*) a hotbed of dissent

brûlure [bʀylyʀ] NF (*lésion*) burn; (*sensation*) burn-ing *no pl*, burning sensation; **brûlures d'estomac** heartburn *sg*

brume [bʀym] NF mist

brumeux, -euse [bʀymø, -øz] ADJ misty; (*fig*) hazy

brumisateur [bʀymizatœʀ] NM atomizer

★**brun, e** [bʀœ̃, -yn] ADJ (*gén, bière*) brown; (*cheveux, personne, tabac*) dark; **elle est brune** she's got dark hair ▶ NM (*couleur*) brown ▶ NF (*cigarette*) cigarette made of dark tobacco; (*bière*) ≈ brown ale, ≈ stout

brunâtre [bʀynɑtʀ] ADJ brownish

brunch [bʀœntʃ] NM brunch

Brunei [bʀynei] N Brunei; **le sultanat de ~** the Sultanate of Brunei

brunir [bʀyniʀ] /**2**/ VI to get a tan

brushing [bʀœʃiŋ] NM blow-dry

brusque [bʀysk] ADJ (*soudain*) abrupt, sudden; (*rude*) abrupt, brusque

brusquement [bʀyskəmɑ̃] ADV (*soudainement*) abruptly, suddenly

brusquer [bʀyske] /**1**/ VT to rush

brusquerie [bʀyskəʀi] NF abruptness, brusque-ness

brut, e [bʀyt] ADJ raw, crude, rough; (*diamant*) uncut; (*soie, minéral, Inform: données*) raw; (*Comm*) gross; **(champagne) ~** brut champagne; **(pétrole) ~** crude (oil) ▶ NF brute

brutal, e, -aux [bʀytal, -o] ADJ brutal

brutalement [bʀytalmɑ̃] ADV brutally

★**brutaliser** [bʀytalize] /**1**/ VT to handle roughly, manhandle

brutalité [bʀytalite] NF brutality *no pl*

brute [bʀyt] ADJ F, NF *voir* **brut**

★**Bruxelles** [bʀysɛl] N Brussels

bruxellois, e [bʀysɛlwa, -waz] ADJ of *ou* from Brussels ▶ NM/F: **Bruxellois, e** inhabitant *ou* native of Brussels

bruyamment [bʀɥijamɑ̃] ADV noisily

★**bruyant, e** [bʀɥijɑ̃, -ɑ̃t] ADJ noisy

bruyère [bʀyjɛʀ] NF heather

BT SIGLE M (= *Brevet de technicien*) *vocational training certificate, taken at approx. 18 years*

BTA SIGLE M (= *Brevet de technicien agricole*) *agricultural training certificate, taken at approx. 18 years*

BTP SIGLE MPL (= *Bâtiments et travaux publics*) *public buildings and works sector*

BTS SIGLE M (= *Brevet de technicien supérieur*) *vocational training certificate taken at end of two-year higher edu-cation course*

BU SIGLE F = **Bibliothèque universitaire**

bu, e [by] PP *de* **boire**

buanderie [bɥɑ̃dʀi] NF laundry

Bucarest [bykaʀɛst] N Bucharest

buccal, e, -aux [bykal, -o] ADJ: **par voie buccale** orally

bûche [byʃ] NF log; **prendre une ~** (*fig*) to come a cropper (*BRIT*), fall flat on one's face; **~ de Noël** Yule log

bûcher [byʃe] /**1**/ NM (*funéraire*) pyre; bonfire; (*sup-plice*) stake ▶ VI (*fam: étudier*) to swot (*BRIT*), grind (*US*), slave (away) ▶ VT to swot up (*BRIT*), cram, slave away at

bûcheron [byʃʀɔ̃] NM woodcutter

bûchette [byʃɛt] NF (*de bois*) stick, twig; (*pour compter*) rod

bûcheur, -euse [byʃœʀ, -øz] NM/F (*fam: étudiant*) swot (*BRIT*), grind (*US*)

bucolique [bykɔlik] ADJ bucolic, pastoral

Budapest [bydapɛst] N Budapest

★**budget** [bydʒɛ] NM budget

budgétaire [bydʒetɛʀ] ADJ budgetary, budget *cpd*

budgéter [bydʒete], **budgétiser** [bydʒetize] VT to budget (for)

buée [bɥe] NF (*sur une vitre*) mist; (*de l'haleine*) steam

Buenos Aires [bwenɔzɛʀ] N Buenos Aires

★**buffet** [byfɛ] NM (*meuble*) sideboard; (*de réception*) buffet; **~ (de gare)** (station) buffet, snack bar

buffle [byfl] NM buffalo

buis [bɥi] NM box tree; (*bois*) box(wood)

buisson [bɥisɔ̃] NM bush

buissonnière [bɥisɔnjɛʀ] ADJ F: **faire l'école ~** to play truant (*BRIT*), skip school

bulbe [bylb] NM (*Bot, Anat*) bulb; (*coupole*) onion-shaped dome

bulgare [bylgaʀ] ADJ Bulgarian ▶ NM (*Ling*) Bulgarian ▶ NMF: **Bulgare** Bulgarian, Bulgar

Bulgarie [bylgaʀi] NF: **la ~** Bulgaria

bulldozer [buldozɛʀ] NM bulldozer

bulle [byl] ADJ, NM: **(papier) ~** manil(l)a paper ▶ NF bubble; (*de bande dessinée*) balloon; (*papale*) bull; **~ de savon** soap bubble

bulletin [byltɛ̃] NM (*communiqué, journal*) bulletin; (*papier*) form; (: *de bagages*) ticket; (*Scol*) report; **~ d'informations** news bulletin; **~ de naissance** birth certificate; **~ de salaire** pay slip; **~ de santé** medical bulletin; **~ (de vote)** ballot paper; **~ météorologique** weather report

buraliste [byʀalist] NMF (*de bureau de tabac*) tobac-conist; (*de poste*) clerk

bure [byʀ] NF homespun; (*de moine*) frock

★**bureau, x** [byʀo] NM (*meuble*) desk; (*pièce, service*) office; (*Inform*) desktop; **~ de change** (foreign) exchange office *ou* bureau; **~ d'embauche** ≈ job centre; **~ d'études** design office; **~ de location** box office; **~ des objets trouvés** lost property office (BRIT), lost and found (US); **~ de placement** employment agency; **~ de poste** post office; **~ de tabac** tobacconist's (shop), smoke shop (US); **~ de vote** polling station

bureaucrate [byʀokʀat] NMF bureaucrat

bureaucratie [byʀokʀasi] NF bureaucracy

bureaucratique [byʀokʀatik] ADJ bureaucratic

bureautique [byʀɔtik] NF office automation

burette [byʀɛt] NF (de mécanicien) oilcan; (de chimiste) burette

burin [byʀɛ̃] NM cold chisel; (Art) burin

buriné, e [byʀine] ADJ (fig: visage) craggy, seamed

Burkina [byʀkina], **Burkina-Faso** [byʀkinafaso] NM: **le ~(-Faso)** Burkina Faso

burkinabé, e [byʀkinabe] ADJ Burkinabe ▶ NM/F: **Burkinabé, e** Burkinabe

burlesque [byʀlɛsk] ADJ ridiculous; (Littérature) burlesque

burnous [byʀnu(s)] NM burnous

Burundi [buʀundi] NM: **le ~** Burundi

★**bus¹** VB [by] voir **boire**

bus² NM [bys] (véhicule, aussi Inform) bus

busard [byzaʀ] NM harrier

buse [byz] NF buzzard

busqué, e [byske] ADJ: **nez ~** hook(ed) nose

buste [byst] NM (Anat) chest; (: de femme) bust; (sculpture) bust

bustier [bystje] NM (soutien-gorge) long-line bra

★**but** [by] VB voir **boire** ▶ NM (cible) target; (fig) goal, aim; (Football etc) goal; **de ~ en blanc** point-blank; **avoir pour ~ de faire** to aim to do; **dans le ~ de** with the intention of

butane [bytan] NM butane; (domestique) Calor gas® (BRIT), butane

buté, e [byte] ADJ stubborn, obstinate ▶ NF (Archit) abutment; (Tech) stop

buter [byte] /1/ VI: **~ contre** ou **sur** to bump into; (trébucher) to stumble against ▶ VT to antagonize ■ **se buter** VPR to get obstinate, dig in one's heels

buteur [bytœʀ] NM striker

butin [bytɛ̃] NM booty, spoils pl; (d'un vol) loot

butiner [bytine] /1/ VI (abeilles) to gather nectar

butor [bytɔʀ] NM (fig) lout

butte [byt] NF mound, hillock; **être en ~ à** to be exposed to

buvable [byvabl] ADJ (eau, vin) drinkable; (Méd: ampoule etc) to be taken orally; (fig: roman etc) reasonable

buvais etc [byvɛ] VB voir **boire**

buvard [byvaʀ] NM blotter

buvette [byvɛt] NF refreshment room ou stall; (comptoir) bar

buveur, -euse [byvœʀ, -øz] NM/F drinker

buvons etc [byvɔ̃] VB voir **boire**

buzz [bœz] NM (fam) buzz; **faire** ou **créer le ~** to create a buzz

Byzance [bizɑ̃s] N Byzantium

byzantin, e [bizɑ̃tɛ̃, -in] ADJ Byzantine

BZH ABR (= Breizh) Brittany

Cc

C, c [se] NM INV C, c; **C comme Célestin** C for Charlie ▶ ABR (= *centime*) c; (= *Celsius*) C

c' [s] PRON *voir* **ce**

CA SIGLE M = **chiffre d'affaires; conseil d'administration; corps d'armée** ▶ SIGLE F = **chambre d'agriculture**

★**ça** [sa] PRON (*pour désigner*) this; (: *plus loin*) that; (*comme sujet indéfini*) it; **ça m'étonne que** it surprises me that; **ça va?** how are you?; how are things?; (*d'accord?*) OK?, all right?; **où ça?** where's that?; **pourquoi ça?** why's that?; **qui ça?** who's that?; **ça alors!** (*désapprobation*) well!, really!; (*étonnement*) heavens!; **c'est ça** that's right; **ça y est** that's it

çà [sa] ADV: **çà et là** here and there

cabale [kabal] NF (*Théât, Pol*) cabal, clique

caban [kabã] NM reefer jacket, donkey jacket

cabane [kaban] NF hut, cabin

cabanon [kabanɔ̃] NM chalet, (country) cottage

cabaret [kabaʀɛ] NM night club

cabas [kaba] NM shopping bag

cabestan [kabɛstã] NM capstan

cabillaud [kabijo] NM cod *inv*

★**cabine** [kabin] NF (*de bateau*) cabin; (*de plage*) (beach) hut; (*de piscine etc*) cubicle; (*de camion, train*) cab; (*d'avion*) cockpit; **~ (d'ascenseur)** lift cage; **~ d'essayage** fitting room; **~ de projection** projection room; **~ spatiale** space capsule; **~ (téléphonique)** call *ou* (tele)phone box, (tele)phone booth

cabinet [kabinɛ] NM (*petite pièce*) closet; (*de médecin*) surgery (*Brit*), office (*US*); (*de notaire etc*) office; (: *clientèle*) practice; (*Pol*) cabinet; (*d'un ministre*) advisers *pl*; **~ d'affaires** business consultants' (bureau), business partnership; **~ de toilette** toilet; **~ de travail** study ■ **cabinets** NMPL (*w.-c.*) toilet *sg*

câble [kabl] NM cable; **le ~ (TV)** cable television, cablevision (*US*)

câblé, e [kable] ADJ (*fam*) switched on; (*Tech*) linked to cable television

câbler [kable] /1/ VT to cable; **~ un quartier** (TV) to put cable television into an area

câblo-opérateur [kabloɔpeʀatœʀ] NM cable operator

cabossé, e [kabose] ADJ (*voiture, gueule*) battered

cabosser [kabose] /1/ VT to dent

cabot [kabo] NM (*péj: chien*) mutt

cabotage [kabotaʒ] NM coastal navigation

caboteur [kabotœʀ] NM coaster

cabotin, e [kabotɛ̃, -in] NM/F (*péj: personne maniérée*) poseur; (: *acteur*) ham ▶ ADJ dramatic, theatrical

cabotinage [kabotinaʒ] NM playacting; third-rate acting, ham acting

cabrer [kabʀe] /1/: **se cabrer** VPR (*cheval*) to rear up; (*avion*) to nose up; (*fig*) to revolt, rebel; to jib

cabri [kabʀi] NM kid

cabriole [kabʀijɔl] NF caper; (*gymnastique etc*) somersault

cabriolet [kabʀijɔlɛ] NM convertible

CAC [kak] SIGLE F = **Compagnie des agents de change; indice ~** ≈ FT index (*Brit*), ≈ Dow Jones average (*US*)

caca [kaka] NM (*langage enfantin*) poo; (*couleur*): **~ d'oie** greeny-yellow; **faire ~** (*fam*) to do a poo

cacahuète [kakaɥɛt] NF peanut

cacao [kakao] NM cocoa (powder); (*boisson*) cocoa

cachalot [kaʃalo] NM sperm whale

cache [kaʃ] NM mask, card (*for masking*) ▶ NF hiding place

cache-cache [kaʃkaʃ] NM: **jouer à ~** to play hide-and-seek

cache-col [kaʃkɔl] NM scarf

cachemire [kaʃmiʀ] NM cashmere; **le C~** Kashmir ▶ ADJ: **dessin ~** paisley pattern

cache-nez [kaʃne] NM INV scarf, muffler

cache-pot [kaʃpo] NM flower-pot holder

cache-prise [kaʃpʀiz] NM socket cover

★**cacher** [kaʃe] /1/ VT to hide, conceal; **~ qch à qn** to hide *ou* conceal sth from sb ■ **se cacher** VPR (*volontairement*) to hide; (*être caché*) to be hidden *ou* concealed; **il ne s'en cache pas** he makes no secret of it

cache-sexe [kaʃsɛks] NM G-string

★**cachet** [kaʃɛ] NM (*comprimé*) tablet; (*sceau: du roi*) seal; (: *de la poste*) postmark; (*rétribution*) fee; (*fig*) style, character

cacheter [kaʃte] /4/ VT to seal; **vin cacheté** vintage wine

cachette [kaʃɛt] NF hiding place; **en ~** on the sly, secretly

cachot [kaʃo] NM dungeon

cachotterie [kaʃɔtʀi] NF mystery; **faire des cachotteries** to be secretive

cachottier, -ière [kaʃɔtje, -jɛʀ] ADJ secretive
cachou [kaʃu] NM cachou (*sweet*)
cacophonie [kakɔfɔni] NF cacophony, din
cacophonique [kakɔfɔnik] ADJ cacophonous
cactus [kaktys] NM cactus
c.-à-d. ABR (= *c'est-à-dire*) i.e.
cadastre [kadastʀ] NM land register
cadavéreux, -euse [kadaveʀø, -øz] ADJ (*teint, visage*) deathly pale
cadavérique [kadaveʀik] ADJ deathly (pale), deadly pale
cadavre [kadavʀ] NM corpse, (dead) body
Caddie® [kadi] NM (supermarket) trolley (BRIT), (grocery) cart (US)
★**cadeau, x** [kado] NM present, gift; **faire un ~ à qn** to give sb a present *ou* gift; **faire ~ de qch à qn** to make a present of sth to sb, give sb sth as a present
cadenas [kadna] NM padlock
cadenasser [kadnase] /1/ VT to padlock
cadence [kadɑ̃s] NF (*Mus*) cadence; (: *rythme*) rhythm; (*de travail etc*) rate; **en ~** rhythmically; in time ▪ **cadences** NFPL (*en usine*) production rate *sg*
cadencé, e [kadɑ̃se] ADJ rhythmic(al); **au pas ~** (*Mil*) in quick time
cadet, te [kadɛ, -ɛt] ADJ younger; (*le plus jeune*) youngest ▸ NM/F youngest child *ou* one, youngest boy *ou* son/girl *ou* daughter; **il est mon ~ de deux ans** he's two years younger than me, he's two years my junior; **les cadets** (*Sport*) the minors (15-17 years); **le ~ de mes soucis** the least of my worries
cadrage [kadʀaʒ] NM framing (*of shot*)
cadran [kadʀɑ̃] NM dial; **~ solaire** sundial
★**cadre** [kadʀ] NM frame; (*environnement*) surroundings *pl*; (*limites*) scope; **rayer qn des cadres** to discharge sb; to dismiss sb; **dans le ~ de** (*fig*) within the framework *ou* context of ▸ NMF (*Admin*) managerial employee, executive; **~ moyen/supérieur** (*Admin*) middle/senior management employee, junior/senior executive ▸ ADJ: **loi ~** outline *ou* blueprint law
★**cadré, e** [kadʀe] ADJ (*Photo*) centred; (*Inform*): **~ à gauche/à droite** positioned on the left/on the right; **la photo est mal cadrée** the photo is off-centre *ou* (US) off-center
cadrer [kadʀe] /1/ VI: **~ avec** to tally *ou* correspond with ▸ VT (*Ciné, Photo*) to frame
cadreur, -euse [kadʀœʀ, -øz] NM/F (*Ciné*) cameraman/-woman
caduc, -uque [kadyk] ADJ obsolete; (*Bot*) deciduous
CAF SIGLE F (= *Caisse d'allocations familiales*) family allowance office
caf ABR (*coût, assurance, fret*) cif
cafard [kafaʀ] NM cockroach; **avoir le ~** to be down in the dumps, be feeling low
cafardeux, -euse [kafaʀdø, -øz] ADJ (*personne, ambiance*) depressing, melancholy
café [kafe] NM coffee; (*bistro*) café; **~ crème** coffee with cream; **~ au lait** white coffee; **~ noir** black coffee; **~ en grains** coffee beans; **~ en poudre**

instant coffee; **~ liégeois** coffee ice cream with whipped cream ▸ ADJ INV coffee *cpd*
café-concert [kafekɔ̃sɛʀ] (*pl* **cafés-concerts**) NM (*aussi:* **caf'conc'**) café with a cabaret
caféine [kafein] NF caffeine
café-tabac [kafetaba] NM *tobacconist's or newsagent's also serving coffee and spirits*
cafétéria [kafeteʀja] NF cafeteria
café-théâtre [kafeteatʀ] (*pl* **cafés-théâtres**) NM *café used as a venue by (experimental) theatre groups*
cafetière [kaftjɛʀ] NF (*pot*) coffee-pot
cafouillage [kafujaʒ] NM shambles *sg*
cafouiller [kafuje] /1/ VI to get in a shambles; (*machine etc*) to work in fits and starts
★**cage** [kaʒ] NF cage; **~ (des buts)** goal; **en ~** in a cage, caged up *ou* in; **~ d'ascenseur** lift shaft; **~ d'escalier** (stair)well; **~ thoracique** rib cage
cageot [kaʒo] NM crate
cagibi [kaʒibi] NM shed
cagneux, -euse [kaɲø, -øz] ADJ knock-kneed
cagnotte [kaɲɔt] NF kitty
cagoule [kagul] NF cowl; hood; (*Ski etc*) cagoule; (*passe-montagne*) balaclava
★**cahier** [kaje] NM notebook; (*Typo*) signature; (*revue*): **cahiers** journal; **~ de revendications/doléances** list of claims/grievances; **~ de brouillons** rough book, jotter; **~ des charges** specification; **~ d'exercices** exercise book
cahin-caha [kaɛ̃kaa] ADV: **aller ~** to jog along; (*fig*) to be so-so
cahot [kao] NM jolt, bump
cahoter [kaɔte] /1/ VI to bump along, jog along
cahoteux, -euse [kaɔtø, -øz] ADJ bumpy
cahute [kayt] NF shack, hut
caïd [kaid] NM big chief, boss
caillasse [kajas] NF (*pierraille*) loose stones *pl*
caille [kaj] NF quail
caillé, e [kaje] ADJ: **lait ~** curdled milk, curds *pl*
caillebotis [kajbɔti] NM duckboard
cailler [kaje] /1/ VI (*lait*) to curdle; (*sang*) to clot; (*fam*) to be cold
caillot [kajo] NM (blood) clot
caillou, x [kaju] NM (little) stone
caillouter [kajute] /1/ VT (*chemin*) to metal
caillouteux, -euse [kajutø, -øz] ADJ stony; pebbly
cailloutis [kajuti] NM (*petits graviers*) gravel
caïman [kaimɑ̃] NM cayman
Caïmans [kaimɑ̃] NFPL: **les ~** the Cayman Islands
Caire [kɛʀ] NM: **le ~** Cairo
★**caisse** [kɛs] NF box; (*où l'on met la recette*) cashbox; (: *machine*) till; (*où l'on paye*) cash desk (BRIT), checkout counter; (: *au supermarché*) checkout; (*de banque*) cashier's desk; (*Tech*) case, casing; **faire sa ~** (*Comm*) to count the takings; **~ claire** (*Mus*) side *ou* snare drum; **~ éclair** express checkout; **~ enregistreuse** cash register; **~ d'épargne** savings bank; **~ noire** slush fund; **~ de retraite** pension fund; **~ de sortie** checkout; *voir* **grosse**
★**caissier, -ière** [kesje, -jɛʀ] NM/F cashier

caisson [kɛsɔ̃] NM box, case

cajoler [kaʒɔle] /1/ VT to wheedle, coax; to surround with love and care, make a fuss of

cajoleries [kaʒɔlʀi] NFPL coaxing sg, flattery sg

cajou [kaʒu] NM: **noix de ~** cashew nut

cake [kɛk] NM fruit cake

cal [kal] NM callus

cal. ABR = **calorie**

calamar [kalamaʀ] NM = **calmar**

calaminé, e [kalamine] ADJ (Auto) coked up

calamité [kalamite] NF calamity, disaster

calandre [kalɑ̃dʀ] NF radiator grill; (machine) calender, mangle

calanque [kalɑ̃k] NF rocky inlet

calcaire [kalkɛʀ] NM limestone ▶ ADJ (eau) hard; (Géo) limestone cpd

calciné, e [kalsine] ADJ burnt to ashes

calcium [kalsjɔm] NM calcium

★**calcul** [kalkyl] NM calculation; **le ~** (Scol) arithmetic; **~ différentiel/intégral** differential/integral calculus; **~ mental** mental arithmetic; **~ (biliaire)** (gall)stone; **~ (rénal)** (kidney) stone; **d'après mes calculs** by my reckoning

calculateur [kalkylatœʀ] NM, **calculatrice** [kalkylatʀis] NF calculator

calculé, e [kalkyle] ADJ: **risque ~** calculated risk

★**calculer** [kalkyle] /1/ VT to calculate, work out, reckon; (combiner) to calculate; **~ qch de tête** to work sth out in one's head

calculette [kalkylɛt] NF (pocket) calculator

cale [kal] NF (de bateau) hold; (en bois) wedge, chock; **~ sèche** ou **de radoub** dry dock

calé, e [kale] ADJ (fam) clever, bright

calebasse [kalbɑs] NF calabash, gourd

calèche [kalɛʃ] NF horse-drawn carriage

caleçon [kalsɔ̃] NM (d'homme) boxer shorts; (de femme) leggings; **~ de bain** bathing trunks pl

calembour [kalɑ̃buʀ] NM pun

calendes [kalɑ̃d] NFPL: **renvoyer aux ~ grecques** to postpone indefinitely

calendrier [kalɑ̃dʀije] NM calendar; (fig) timetable

cale-pied [kalpje] NM toe clip

calepin [kalpɛ̃] NM notebook

caler [kale] /1/ VT to wedge, chock up; **~ (son moteur/véhicule)** to stall (one's engine/vehicle) ▶ VI (moteur, véhicule) to stall ■ **se caler** VPR: **se ~ dans un fauteuil** to make o.s. comfortable in an armchair

calfater [kalfate] /1/ VT to caulk

calfeutrage [kalføtʀaʒ] NM draughtproofing (BRIT), draughtproofing (US)

calfeutrer [kalføtʀe] /1/ VT to (make) draughtproof (BRIT) ou draughtproof (US) ■ **se calfeutrer** VPR to make o.s. snug and comfortable

calibre [kalibʀ] NM (d'un fruit) grade; (d'une arme) bore, calibre (BRIT), caliber (US); (fig) calibre, caliber

calibrer [kalibʀe] /1/ VT to grade

calice [kalis] NM (Rel) chalice; (Bot) calyx

calicot [kaliko] NM (tissu) calico

calife [kalif] NM caliph

Californie [kalifɔʀni] NF: **la ~** California

californien, ne [kalifɔʀnjɛ̃, -ɛn] ADJ Californian

califourchon [kalifuʀʃɔ̃]: **à ~** adv astride; **à ~ sur** astride, straddling

câlin, e [kɑlɛ̃, -in] ADJ cuddly, cuddlesome; (regard, voix) tender

câliner [kɑline] /1/ VT to fondle, cuddle

câlineries [kɑlinʀi] NFPL cuddles

calisson [kalisɔ̃] NM diamond-shaped sweet or candy made with ground almonds

calleux, -euse [kalø, -øz] ADJ horny, callous

calligraphie [kaligʀafi] NF calligraphy

callosité [kalozite] NF callus

calmant [kalmɑ̃] NM tranquillizer, sedative; (contre la douleur) painkiller

calmar [kalmaʀ] NM squid

★**calme** [kalm] ADJ calm, quiet ▶ NM calm(ness), quietness; **sans perdre son ~** without losing one's cool ou calmness; **~ plat** (Navig) dead calm

calmement [kalmǝmɑ̃] ADV calmly, quietly

calmer [kalme] /1/ VT to calm (down); (douleur, inquiétude) to ease, soothe ■ **se calmer** VPR to calm down

calomniateur, -trice [kalɔmnjatœʀ, -tʀis] NM/F slanderer; libeller

calomnie [kalɔmni] NF slander; (écrite) libel

calomnier [kalɔmnje] /7/ VT to slander; to libel

calomnieux, -euse [kalɔmnjø, -øz] ADJ slanderous; libellous

calorie [kalɔʀi] NF calorie

calorifère [kalɔʀifɛʀ] NM stove

calorifique [kalɔʀifik] ADJ calorific

calorifuge [kalɔʀifyʒ] ADJ (heat-)insulating, heat-retaining

calot [kalo] NM forage cap

calotte [kalɔt] NF (coiffure) skullcap; (gifle) slap; **la ~** (péj: clergé) the cloth, the clergy; **~ glaciaire** icecap

calque [kalk] NM (aussi: **papier calque**) tracing paper; (dessin) tracing; (fig) carbon copy

calquer [kalke] /1/ VT to trace; (fig) to copy exactly

calvados [kalvados] NM Calvados (apple brandy)

calvaire [kalvɛʀ] NM (croix) wayside cross, calvary; (souffrances) suffering, martyrdom

calvitie [kalvisi] NF baldness

camaïeu [kamajø] NM: **(motif en) ~** monochrome motif

★**camarade** [kamaʀad] NMF friend, pal; (Pol) comrade

camaraderie [kamaʀadʀi] NF friendship

camarguais, e [kamaʀgɛ, -ɛz] ADJ of ou from the Camargue

Camargue [kamaʀg] NF: **la ~** the Camargue

cambiste [kɑ̃bist] NM (Comm) foreign exchange dealer, exchange agent

Cambodge [kɑ̃bɔdʒ] NM: **le ~** Cambodia

cambodgien, ne [kɑ̃bɔdʒjɛ̃, -ɛn] ADJ Cambodian ▶ NM/F: **Cambodgien, ne** Cambodian

cambouis [kãbwi] NM dirty oil *ou* grease

cambré, e [kãbʀe] ADJ: **avoir les reins cambrés** to have an arched back; **avoir le pied très ~** to have very high arches *ou* insteps

cambrer [kãbʀe] /1/ VT to arch; **~ la taille** *ou* **les reins** to arch one's back ■ **se cambrer** VPR to arch one's back

cambriolage [kãbʀijɔlaʒ] NM burglary

★**cambrioler** [kãbʀijɔle] /1/ VT to burgle (BRIT), burglarize (US)

cambrioleur, -euse [kãbʀijɔlœʀ, -øz] NM/F burglar

cambrure [kãbʀyʀ] NF (*du pied*) arch; (*de la route*) camber; **~ des reins** small of the back

cambuse [kãbyz] NF storeroom

came [kam] NF: **arbre à cames** camshaft; **arbre à cames en tête** overhead camshaft

camée [kame] NM cameo

caméléon [kameleɔ̃] NM chameleon

camélia [kamelja] NM camellia

camelot [kamlo] NM street pedlar

camelote [kamlɔt] NF (*fam*) rubbish, trash, junk

camembert [kamãbɛʀ] NM Camembert (*cheese*)

caméra [kameʀa] NF (*Ciné, TV*) camera; (*d'amateur*) cine-camera; **~ de vidéosurveillance** CCTV camera

caméraman [kameʀaman] NM cameraman/-woman

Cameroun [kamʀun] NM: **le ~** Cameroon

camerounais, e [kamʀunɛ, -ɛz] ADJ Cameroonian

caméscope® [kameskɔp] NM camcorder

★**camion** [kamjɔ̃] NM lorry (BRIT), truck; (*plus petit, fermé*) van; (*charge*): **~ de sable/cailloux** lorry-load (BRIT) *ou* truck-load of sand/stones; **~ de dépannage** breakdown (BRIT) *ou* tow (US) truck

camion-citerne [kamjɔ̃sitɛʀn] (*pl* **camions-citernes**) NM tanker

camionnage [kamjɔnaʒ] NM haulage (BRIT), trucking (US); **frais/entreprise de ~** haulage costs/business

★**camionnette** [kamjɔnɛt] NF (small) van

camionneur [kamjɔnœʀ] NM (*entrepreneur*) haulage contractor (BRIT), trucker (US); (*chauffeur*) lorry (BRIT) *ou* truck driver; van driver

camisole [kamizɔl] NF: **~ (de force)** straitjacket

camomille [kamɔmij] NF camomile; (*boisson*) camomile tea

camouflage [kamuflaʒ] NM camouflage

camoufler [kamufle] /1/ VT to camouflage; (*fig*) to conceal, cover up

camouflet [kamuflɛ] NM (*fam*) snub

camp [kã] NM camp; (*fig*) side; **~ de nudistes/vacances** nudist/holiday camp; **~ de concentration** concentration camp

campagnard, e [kãpaɲaʀ, -aʀd] ADJ country *cpd* ▶ NM/F countryman/-woman

★**campagne** [kãpaɲ] NF country, countryside; (*Mil, Pol, Comm*) campaign; **en ~** (*Mil*) in the field; **à la ~** in/to the country; **faire ~ pour** to campaign for; **~ électorale** election campaign; **~ de publicité** advertising campaign

> Bien que **country** et **countryside** soient souvent interchangeables, lorsqu'on parle plus précisément des paysages, notamment sous l'angle esthétique, on emploie plutôt **countryside**.
> *La campagne du Dorset est très belle.* **The Dorset countryside is beautiful.**

campanile [kãpanil] NM (*tour*) bell tower

campé, e [kãpe] ADJ: **bien ~** (*personnage, tableau*) well-drawn

campement [kãpmã] NM camp, encampment

★**camper** [kãpe] /1/ VI to camp ▶ VT (*chapeau etc*) to pull *ou* put on firmly; (*dessin*) to sketch ■ **se camper devant** VPR to plant o.s. in front of

campeur, -euse [kãpœʀ, -øz] NM/F camper

camphre [kãfʀ] NM camphor

camphré, e [kãfʀe] ADJ camphorated

★**camping** [kãpiŋ] NM camping; **(terrain de) ~** campsite, camping site; **faire du ~** to go camping; **faire du ~ sauvage** to camp rough

camping-car [kãpiŋkaʀ] NM camper, motor home (US)

camping-gaz® [kãpiŋgaz] NM INV camp(ing) stove

campus [kãpys] NM campus

camus, e [kamy, -yz] ADJ: **nez ~** pug nose

★**Canada** [kanada] NM: **le ~** Canada

canadair® [kanadɛʀ] NM fire-fighting plane

★**canadien, ne** [kanadjɛ̃, -ɛn] ADJ Canadian ▶ NM/F: **Canadien, ne** Canadian ▶ NF (*veste*) fur-lined jacket

canaille [kanaj] NF (*péj*) scoundrel; (*populace*) riff-raff ▶ ADJ raffish, rakish

canal, -aux [kanal, -o] NM canal; (*naturel, TV*) channel; (*Admin*): **par le ~ de** through (the medium of), via; **~ de distribution/télévision** distribution/television channel; **~ de Panama/Suez** Panama/Suez Canal

canalisation [kanalizasjɔ̃] NF (*tuyau*) pipe

canaliser [kanalize] /1/ VT to canalize; (*fig*) to channel

canapé [kanape] NM settee, sofa; (*Culin*) canapé, open sandwich

canapé-lit [kanapeli] (*pl* **canapés-lits**) NM sofa bed

canaque [kanak] ADJ, NMF = **kanak**

★**canard** [kanaʀ] NM duck; (*fam: journal*) rag

canari [kanaʀi] NM canary

Canaries [kanaʀi] NFPL: **les (îles) ~** the Canary Islands, the Canaries

cancaner [kãkane] /1/ VI to gossip (maliciously); (*canard*) to quack

cancanier, -ière [kãkanje, -jɛʀ] ADJ gossiping

cancans [kãkã] NMPL (malicious) gossip *sg*

★**cancer** [kãsɛʀ] NM cancer; (*signe*): **le C~** Cancer, the Crab; **être du C~** to be Cancer; **il a un ~** he has cancer

cancéreux, -euse [kãseʀø, -øz] ADJ cancerous; (*personne*) suffering from cancer

cancérigène [kãseʀiʒɛn] ADJ carcinogenic

cancérologue [kãseʀɔlɔg] NMF cancer specialist

cancre [kãkʀ] NM dunce

cancrelat [kãkʀəla] NM cockroach

candélabre [kãdelɑbʀ] NM candelabrum; (lampadaire) street lamp, lamppost

candeur [kãdœʀ] NF ingenuousness

candi [kãdi] ADJ INV: **sucre ~** (sugar-)candy

★**candidat, e** [kãdida, -at] NM/F candidate; (à un poste) applicant, candidate

candidater [kãdidate] VI to apply

candidature [kãdidatyʀ] NF (Pol) candidature; (à poste) application; **poser sa ~** to submit an application, apply; **poser sa ~ à un poste** to apply for a job; **~ spontanée** unsolicited job application

candide [kãdid] ADJ ingenuous, guileless, naïve

cane [kan] NF (female) duck

caneton [kantɔ̃] NM duckling

canette [kanɛt] NF (de bière) (flip-top) bottle; (de machine à coudre) spool

canevas [kanva] NM (Couture) canvas (for tapestry work); (fig) framework, structure

caniche [kaniʃ] NM poodle

caniculaire [kanikylɛʀ] ADJ (chaleur, jour) scorching

canicule [kanikyl] NF scorching heat; midsummer heat, dog days pl

canif [kanif] NM penknife, pocket knife

canin, e [kanɛ̃, -in] ADJ canine; **exposition canine** dog show ► NF canine (tooth), eye tooth

caniveau, x [kanivo] NM gutter

cannabis [kanabis] NM cannabis

canne [kan] NF (walking) stick; **~ à pêche** fishing rod; **~ à sucre** sugar cane; **les cannes blanches** (les aveugles) blind people

canné, e [kane] ADJ (chaise) cane cpd

cannelé, e [kanle] ADJ fluted

cannelle [kanɛl] NF cinnamon

cannelure [kan(ə)lyʀ] NF fluting no pl

canner [kane] /1/ VT (chaise) to make ou repair with cane

cannibale [kanibal] NMF cannibal

cannibalisme [kanibalism] NM cannibalism

canoë [kanɔe] NM canoe; (sport) canoeing; **~ (kayak)** kayak

canon [kanɔ̃] NM (arme) gun; (Hist) cannon; (d'une arme) barrel; (fig) model; (Mus) canon; **~ rayé** rifled barrel ► ADJ: **droit ~** canon law

cañon [kanɔ̃] NM canyon

canonique [kanɔnik] ADJ: **âge ~** respectable age

canoniser [kanɔnize] /1/ VT to canonize

canonnade [kanɔnad] NF cannonade

canonnier [kanɔnje] NM gunner

canonnière [kanɔnjɛʀ] NF gunboat

canopée [kanɔpe] NF canopy

canot [kano] NM boat, ding(h)y; **~ pneumatique** rubber ou inflatable ding(h)y; **~ de sauvetage** lifeboat

canotage [kanɔtaʒ] NM rowing

canoter [kanɔte] /1/ VI to go rowing

canoteur, -euse [kanɔtœʀ, -øz] NM/F rower

canotier [kanɔtje] NM boater

Cantal [kãtal] NM: **le ~** Cantal

cantate [kãtat] NF cantata

cantatrice [kãtatʀis] NF (opera) singer

cantilène [kãtilɛn] NF (Mus) cantilena

★**cantine** [kãtin] NF canteen; (réfectoire d'école) dining hall

cantique [kãtik] NM hymn

canton [kãtɔ̃] NM district (consisting of several communes); see note; (en Suisse) canton

A French **canton** is the administrative division represented by a councillor in the conseil départemental. It comprises a number of communes and is, in turn, a subdivision of an arrondissement départemental. In Switzerland the cantons are the 23 autonomous political divisions which make up the Swiss confederation.

cantonade [kãtɔnad]: **à la ~** adv to everyone in general; (crier) from the rooftops

cantonais, e [kãtɔnɛ, -ɛz] ADJ Cantonese ► NM (Ling) Cantonese

cantonal, e, -aux [kãtɔnal, -o] ADJ cantonal, = district

cantonnement [kãtɔnmã] NM (lieu) billet; (action) billeting

cantonner [kãtɔne] /1/ VT (Mil) to billet (BRIT), quarter; to station ■ **se cantonner** VPR: **se ~ dans** to confine o.s. to

cantonnier [kãtɔnje] NM roadmender

canular [kanylaʀ] NM hoax

CAO SIGLE F (= conception assistée par ordinateur) CAD

caoutchouc [kautʃu] NM rubber; **~ mousse** foam rubber; **en ~** rubber cpd

caoutchouté, e [kautʃute] ADJ rubberized

caoutchouteux, -euse [kautʃutø, -øz] ADJ rubbery

CAP SIGLE M (= Certificat d'aptitude professionnelle) vocational training certificate taken at secondary school

cap [kap] NM (Géo) cape; (promontoire) headland; (fig) hurdle; (: tournant) watershed; (Navig): **changer de ~** to change course; **mettre le ~ sur** to head for; **doubler** ou **passer le ~** (fig) to get over the worst; **Le C~** Cape Town; **le ~ de Bonne Espérance** the Cape of Good Hope; **le ~ Horn** Cape Horn; **les îles du C~ Vert** (aussi: **le Cap-Vert**) the Cape Verde Islands

capable [kapabl] ADJ able, capable; **~ de qch/faire** capable of sth/doing; **il est ~ d'oublier** he could easily forget; **spectacle ~ d'intéresser** show likely to be of interest

capacité [kapasite] NF (compétence) ability; (Jur, Inform, d'un récipient) capacity; **~ (en droit)** basic legal qualification

caparaçonner [kapaʀasɔne] /1/ VT (fig) to clad

cape [kap] NF cape, cloak; **rire sous ~** to laugh up one's sleeve

capeline [kaplin] NF wide-brimmed hat

CAPES [kapɛs] SIGLE M (= Certificat d'aptitude au professorat de l'enseignement du second degré) secondary teaching diploma

capésien, ne [kapesjɛ̃, -ɛn] NM/F *person who holds the CAPES*

CAPET [kapɛt] SIGLE M (= *Certificat d'aptitude au professorat de l'enseignement technique*) *technical teaching diploma*

capharnaüm [kafaʀnaɔm] NM shambles *sg*

capillaire [kapilɛʀ] ADJ (*soins, lotion*) hair *cpd*; (*vaisseau etc*) capillary; **artiste ~** hair artist *ou* designer

capillarité [kapilaʀite] NF capillary action

capilotade [kapilɔtad]: **en ~** *adv* crushed to a pulp; smashed to pieces

capitaine [kapitɛn] NM captain; **~ des pompiers** fire chief (BRIT), fire marshal (US); **~ au long cours** master mariner

capitainerie [kapitɛnʀi] NF (*du port*) harbour (BRIT) *ou* harbor (US) master's (office)

capital, e, -aux [kapital, -o] ADJ (*œuvre*) major; (*question, rôle*) fundamental; (*Jur*) capital; **d'une importance capitale** of capital importance; **les sept péchés capitaux** the seven deadly sins; **peine capitale** capital punishment ▶ NM capital; (*fig*) stock; asset; **~ (social)** authorized capital; **~ d'exploitation** working capital ▶ NF (*ville*) capital; (*lettre*) capital (letter) ▪ **capitaux** NMPL (*fonds*) capital sg, money *sg*

capitalisation [kapitalizasjɔ̃] NF (*de connaissances, innovations*) capitalizing on; (*de rentes, revenus*) capitalization

capitaliser [kapitalize] /1/ VT to amass, build up; (*Comm*) to capitalize ▶ VI to save

capitalisme [kapitalism] NM capitalism

capitaliste [kapitalist] ADJ, NMF capitalist

capital-risque, **capital risque** (*pl* **capitaux-risques**) NM venture capital

capiteux, -euse [kapitø, -øz] ADJ (*vin, parfum*) heady; (*sensuel*) sensuous, alluring

capitonnage [kapitɔnaʒ] NM padding

capitonné, e [kapitɔne] ADJ padded

capitonner [kapitɔne] /1/ VT to pad

capitulation [kapitylasjɔ̃] NF capitulation

capituler [kapityle] /1/ VI to capitulate

caporal, -aux [kapɔʀal, -o] NM lance corporal

caporal-chef [kapɔʀalʃɛf] (*pl* **caporaux-chefs** [kapɔʀo-]) NM corporal

capot [kapo] NM (*Auto*) bonnet (BRIT), hood (US)

capote [kapɔt] NF (*de voiture*) hood (BRIT), top (US); (*de soldat*) greatcoat; **~ (anglaise)** (*fam*) rubber, condom

capoter [kapɔte] /1/ VI to overturn; (*négociations*) to founder

câpre [kɑpʀ] NF caper

caprice [kapʀis] NM whim, caprice; passing fancy; **faire un ~** to throw a tantrum ▪ **caprices** NMPL (*de la mode etc*) vagaries; **faire des caprices** to be temperamental

capricieux, -euse [kapʀisjø, -øz] ADJ (*fantasque*) capricious; whimsical; (*enfant*) temperamental

Capricorne [kapʀikɔʀn] NM: **le ~** Capricorn, the Goat; **être du ~** to be Capricorn

capsule [kapsyl] NF (*de bouteille*) cap; (*amorce*) primer; cap; (*Bot etc, spatiale*) capsule; **~ de café** coffee capsule

captage [kaptaʒ] NM (*d'une émission de radio*) picking-up; (*d'énergie, d'eau*) harnessing

capter [kapte] /1/ VT (*ondes radio*) to pick up; (*eau*) to harness; (*fig*) to win, capture

capteur [kaptœʀ] NM: **~ solaire** solar collector

captieux, -euse [kapsjø, -øz] ADJ specious

captif, -ive [kaptif, -iv] ADJ, NM/F captive

captivant, e [kaptivɑ̃, -ɑ̃t] ADJ captivating

captiver [kaptive] /1/ VT to captivate

captivité [kaptivite] NF captivity; **en ~** in captivity

capture [kaptyʀ] NF (*action*) capture, catching *no pl*; **~ d'écran** (*Inform*) screenshot; (*prise*) catch

capturer [kaptyʀe] /1/ VT to capture, catch

capuche [kapyʃ] NF hood

capuchon [kapyʃɔ̃] NM hood; (*de stylo*) cap, top

capucin [kapysɛ̃] NM Capuchin monk

capucine [kapysin] NF (*Bot*) nasturtium

capverdien, ne, **cap-verdien, ne** [kapvɛʀdjɛ̃, -jɛn] ADJ (*origine, musique*) Cape Verdean ▶ NM (*créole du Cap-Vert*) Cape Verdean creole

Cap-Vert [kabvɛʀ] NM: **le ~** Cape Verde

caquelon [kaklɔ̃] NM (*ustensile de cuisson*) fondue pot

caquet [kakɛ] NM: **rabattre le ~ à qn** to bring sb down a peg or two

caqueter [kakte] /4/ VI (*poule*) to cackle; (*fig*) to prattle

★**car** [kaʀ] NM coach (BRIT), bus; **~ de police** police van; **~ de reportage** broadcasting *ou* radio van ▶ CONJ because, for

carabine [kaʀabin] NF carbine, rifle; **~ à air comprimé** airgun

carabiné, e [kaʀabine] ADJ violent; (*cocktail, amende*) stiff

Caracas [kaʀakas] N Caracas

caracoler [kaʀakɔle] /1/ VI to caracole, prance

caractère [kaʀaktɛʀ] NM (*gén*) character; **en caractères gras** in bold type; **en petits caractères** in small print; **en caractères d'imprimerie** in block capitals; **avoir du ~** to have character; **avoir bon/mauvais ~** to be good-/ill-natured *ou* tempered; **~ de remplacement** wild card (*Inform*); **caractères/seconde (cps)** characters per second (cps)

caractériel, le [kaʀakteʀjɛl] ADJ (*enfant*) (emotionally) disturbed; **troubles caractériels** emotional problems ▶ NM/F problem child

caractérisé, e [kaʀakteʀize] ADJ: **c'est une grippe/de l'insubordination caractérisée** it is a clear-(cut) case of flu/insubordination

caractériser [kaʀakteʀize] /1/ VT to characterize; **se ~ par** to be characterized *ou* distinguished by

caractéristique [kaʀakteʀistik] ADJ, NF characteristic

★**carafe** [kaʀaf] NF decanter; (*pour eau, vin ordinaire*) carafe

carafon [kaʀafɔ̃] NM small carafe

caraïbe [kaʀaib] ADJ Caribbean ▪ **les Caraïbes** NFPL the Caribbean (Islands); **la mer des Caraïbes** the Caribbean Sea

carambolage [kaʀɑ̃bɔlaʒ] NM multiple crash, pileup

caramel [kaʀamɛl] NM (*bonbon*) caramel, toffee; (*substance*) caramel

caraméliser [kaʀamelize] /1/ VT to caramelize

carapace [kaʀapas] NF shell

carapater [kaʀapate] /1/ (*fam*): **se carapater** VPR to take to one's heels, scram

carat [kaʀa] NM carat; **or à 18 carats** 18-carat gold

★**caravane** [kaʀavan] NF caravan

caravanier [kaʀavanje] NM caravanner

caravaning [kaʀavaniŋ] NM caravanning; (*emplacement*) caravan site

caravelle [kaʀavɛl] NF caravel

carbonate [kaʀbɔnat] NM (*Chimie*): **~ de soude** sodium carbonate

carbone [kaʀbɔn] NM carbon; (*feuille*) carbon, sheet of carbon paper; (*double*) carbon (copy); **compensation ~** carbon offset; **crédit de compensation ~** carbon offset credit

★**carbonique** [kaʀbɔnik] ADJ: **gaz ~** carbon dioxide; **neige ~** dry ice

carbonisé, e [kaʀbɔnize] ADJ charred; **mourir ~** to be burned to death

carboniser [kaʀbɔnize] /1/ VT to carbonize; (*brûler complètement*) to burn down, reduce to ashes

carburant [kaʀbyʀɑ̃] NM (motor) fuel

carburateur [kaʀbyʀatœʀ] NM carburettor

carburation [kaʀbyʀasjɔ̃] NF carburation

carburer [kaʀbyʀe] /1/ VI (*moteur*): **bien/mal ~** to be well/badly tuned

carcan [kaʀkɑ̃] NM (*fig*) yoke, shackles *pl*

carcasse [kaʀkas] NF carcass; (*de véhicule etc*) shell

carcéral, e, -aux [kaʀseʀal, -o] ADJ prison *cpd*

carcinogène [kaʀsinɔʒɛn] ADJ carcinogenic

cardan [kaʀdɑ̃] NM universal joint

carder [kaʀde] /1/ VT to card

cardiaque [kaʀdjak] ADJ cardiac, heart *cpd*; **être ~** to have a heart condition ▶ NMF heart patient

cardigan [kaʀdigɑ̃] NM cardigan

cardinal, e, -aux [kaʀdinal, -o] ADJ cardinal ▶ NM (*Rel*) cardinal

cardiologie [kaʀdjɔlɔʒi] NF cardiology

cardiologue [kaʀdjɔlɔg] NMF cardiologist, heart specialist

cardio-vasculaire [kaʀdjɔvaskylɛʀ] ADJ cardiovascular

cardon [kaʀdɔ̃] NM cardoon

carême [kaʀɛm] NM (*Rel*): **le ~** Lent

carence [kaʀɑ̃s] NF incompetence, inadequacy; (*manque*) deficiency; **~ vitaminique** vitamin deficiency

carène [kaʀɛn] NF hull

caréner [kaʀene] /6/ VT (*Navig*) to careen; (*carrosserie*) to streamline

caressant, e [kaʀɛsɑ̃, -ɑ̃t] ADJ affectionate, caressing, tender

caresse [kaʀɛs] NF caress

caresser [kaʀese] /1/ VT to caress; (*animal*) to stroke, fondle; (*fig: projet, espoir*) to toy with

cargaison [kaʀgɛzɔ̃] NF cargo, freight

cargo [kaʀgo] NM cargo boat, freighter; **~ mixte** cargo and passenger ship

cari [kaʀi] NM = **curry**

caricatural, e, -aux [kaʀikatyʀal, -o] ADJ caricatural, caricature-like

caricature [kaʀikatyʀ] NF caricature; (*politique etc*) (satirical) cartoon

caricaturer [kaʀikatyʀe] /1/ VT (*personne*) to caricature; (*politique etc*) to satirize

caricaturiste [kaʀikatyʀist] NMF caricaturist, (satirical) cartoonist

carie [kaʀi] NF: **la ~ (dentaire)** tooth decay; **une ~** a bad tooth

carié, e [kaʀje] ADJ: **dent cariée** bad *ou* decayed tooth

carillon [kaʀijɔ̃] NM (*d'église*) bells *pl*; (*de pendule*) chimes *pl*; (*de porte*): **~ (électrique)** (electric) door chime *ou* bell

carillonner [kaʀijɔne] /1/ VI to ring, chime, peal

★**caritatif, -ive** [kaʀitatif, -iv] ADJ charitable

carlingue [kaʀlɛ̃g] NF cabin

carmélite [kaʀmelit] NF Carmelite nun

carmin [kaʀmɛ̃] ADJ INV crimson

carnage [kaʀnaʒ] NM carnage, slaughter

carnassier, -ière [kaʀnasje, -jɛʀ] ADJ carnivorous ▶ NM carnivore

carnation [kaʀnasjɔ̃] NF complexion ◼ **carnations** NFPL (*Peinture*) flesh tones

carnaval [kaʀnaval] NM carnival

carné, e [kaʀne] ADJ meat *cpd*, meat-based

★**carnet** [kaʀnɛ] NM (*calepin*) notebook; (*de tickets, timbres etc*) book; (*d'école*) school report; (*journal intime*) diary; **~ d'adresses** address book; **~ de chèques** cheque book (BRIT), checkbook (US); **~ de commandes** order book; **~ de notes** (*Scol*) (school) report; **~ à souches** counterfoil book

carnier [kaʀnje] NM gamebag

carnivore [kaʀnivɔʀ] ADJ carnivorous ▶ NM carnivore

Carolines [kaʀɔlin] NFPL: **les ~** the Caroline Islands

carotide [kaʀɔtid] NF carotid (artery)

★**carotte** [kaʀɔt] NF (*aussi fig*) carrot

Carpates [kaʀpat] NFPL: **les ~** the Carpathians, the Carpathian Mountains

carpe [kaʀp] NF carp

carpette [kaʀpɛt] NF rug

carquois [kaʀkwa] NM quiver

carre [kaʀ] NF (*de ski*) edge

★**carré, e** [kaʀe] ADJ square; (*fig: franc*) straightforward; **mètre/kilomètre ~** square metre/kilometre ▶ NM (*de terrain, jardin*) patch, plot; (*Math*) square; (*Navig: salle*) wardroom; **~ blanc** (*TV*) "adults only" symbol; **~ d'as/de rois** (*Cartes*) four aces/kings; **élever un nombre au ~** to square a number; **~ de soie** silk headsquare *ou* headscarf; **~ d'agneau** loin of lamb

carreau, x [kaʀo] NM (*en faïence etc*) (floor) tile; (*au mur*) (wall) tile; (*de fenêtre*) (window) pane; (*motif*) check, square; (*Cartes: couleur*) diamonds *pl*; (: *carte*) diamond; **tissu à carreaux** checked fabric; **papier à carreaux** squared paper

★**carrefour** [kaʀfuʀ] NM crossroads *sg*

carrelage [kaʀlaʒ] NM tiling; (*sol*) (tiled) floor

carreler [kaʀle] /**4**/ VT to tile

carrelet [kaʀlɛ] NM (*poisson*) plaice

carreleur [kaʀlœʀ] NM (floor) tiler

carrément [kaʀemɑ̃] ADV (*franchement*) straight out, bluntly; (*sans détours, sans hésiter*) straight; (*nettement*) definitely; (*intensif*) completely; **c'est ~ impossible** it's completely impossible; **il l'a ~ mis à la porte** he threw him straight out

carrer [kaʀe] /**1**/: **se carrer** VPR: **se ~ dans un fauteuil** to settle o.s. comfortably *ou* ensconce o.s. in an armchair

carrier [kaʀje] NM: **(ouvrier) ~** quarryman, quarrier

carrière [kaʀjɛʀ] NF (*de roches*) quarry; (*métier*) career; **militaire de ~** professional soldier; **faire ~ dans** to make one's career in

carriériste [kaʀjeʀist] NMF careerist

carriole [kaʀjɔl] NF (*péj*) old cart

carrossable [kaʀɔsabl] ADJ suitable for (motor) vehicles

carrosse [kaʀɔs] NM (horse-drawn) coach

carrosserie [kaʀɔsʀi] NF body, bodywork *no pl* (BRIT); (*activité, commerce*) coachwork (BRIT), (car) body manufacturing; **atelier de ~** (*pour réparations*) body shop, panel beaters' (yard) (BRIT)

carrossier [kaʀɔsje] NM coachbuilder (BRIT), (car) body repairer; (*dessinateur*) car designer

carrousel [kaʀuzɛl] NM (*Équitation*) carousel; (*fig*) merry-go-round

carrure [kaʀyʀ] NF build; (*fig*) stature, calibre

★**cartable** [kaʀtabl] NM (*d'écolier*) satchel, (school) bag

★**carte** [kaʀt] NF (*de géographie*) map; (*marine, du ciel*) chart; (*de fichier, d'abonnement etc, à jouer*) card; (*au restaurant*) menu; (*aussi*: **carte postale**) (post)card; (*aussi*: **carte de visite**) (visiting) card; **avoir/donner ~ blanche** to have/give carte blanche *ou* a free hand; **tirer les cartes à qn** to read sb's cards; **jouer aux cartes** to play cards; **jouer cartes sur table** (*fig*) to put one's cards on the table; **à la ~** (*au restaurant*) à la carte; (*télévision*) on demand; **~ à circuit imprimé** printed circuit; **~ à puce** smartcard, chip and PIN card; **~ bancaire** cash card; **C~ Bleue®** debit card; **~ de crédit** credit card; **~ de fidélité** loyalty card; **la ~ des vins** the wine list; **~ d'état-major** ≈ Ordnance (BRIT) *ou* Geological (US) Survey map; **~ d'identité** identity card; **la ~ grise** (*Auto*) ≈ the (car) registration document; **~ jeune** young person's railcard; **~ mémoire** (*d'appareil photo numérique*) memory card; **~ perforée** punch(ed) card; **~ routière** road map; **~ de séjour** residence permit; **~ SIM** SIM card; **~ téléphonique** phonecard; **la ~ verte** (*Auto*) the green card; **~ vitale** *see note*

The French national healthcare system issues everyone over the age of 16 with a **carte vitale**, a smartcard with a chip containing the medical insurance details of its holder. Doctors and other healthcare services use a card reader to directly submit costs incurred to health insurance providers so that the patient can later be reimbursed.

cartel [kaʀtɛl] NM cartel

carte-lettre [kaʀtəlɛtʀ] (*pl* **cartes-lettres**) NF letter-card

carte-mère [kaʀtəmɛʀ] (*pl* **cartes-mères**) NF (*Inform*) mother board

carter [kaʀtɛʀ] NM (*Auto: d'huile*) sump (BRIT), oil pan (US); (: *de la boîte de vitesses*) casing; (*de bicyclette*) chain guard

carte-réponse [kaʀt(ə)ʀepɔ̃s] (*pl* **cartes-réponses**) NF reply card

cartésien, ne [kaʀtezjɛ̃, -ɛn] ADJ Cartesian

Carthage [kaʀtaʒ] N Carthage

carthaginois, e [kaʀtaʒinwa, -waz] ADJ Carthaginian

cartilage [kaʀtilaʒ] NM (*Anat*) cartilage

cartilagineux, -euse [kaʀtilaʒinø, -øz] ADJ (*viande*) gristly

cartographe [kaʀtɔgʀaf] NMF cartographer

cartographie [kaʀtɔgʀafi] NF cartography, map-making

cartographier [kaʀtɔgʀafje] VT (*faire une carte de: littoral, végétation*) to map; (*représenter: processus, répartition*) to chart

cartomancie [kaʀtɔmɑ̃si] NF fortune-telling, card-reading

cartomancien, ne [kaʀtɔmɑ̃sjɛ̃, -ɛn] NM/F fortune-teller (*with cards*)

★**carton** [kaʀtɔ̃] NM (*matériau*) cardboard; (*boîte*) (cardboard) box; (*d'invitation*) invitation card; (*Art*) sketch; cartoon; **en ~** cardboard *cpd*; **faire un ~** (*au tir*) to have a go at the rifle range; to score a hit; **~ (à dessin)** portfolio

cartonnage [kaʀtɔnaʒ] NM cardboard (packing)

cartonné, e [kaʀtɔne] ADJ (*livre*) hardback, cased

carton-pâte [kaʀtɔ̃pɑt] (*pl* **cartons-pâtes**) NM pasteboard; **de ~** (*fig*) cardboard *cpd*

cartouche [kaʀtuʃ] NF cartridge; (*de cigarettes*) carton

cartouchière [kaʀtuʃjɛʀ] NF cartridge belt

★**cas** [kɑ] NM case; **faire peu de ~/grand ~ de** to attach little/great importance to; **ne faire aucun ~ de** to take no notice of; **le ~ échéant** if need be; **en aucun ~** on no account, under no circumstances (whatsoever); **au ~ où** in case; **dans ce ~** in that case; **en ~ de** in case of, in the event of; **en ~ de besoin** if need be; **en ~ d'urgence** in an emergency; **en ce ~** in that case; **en tout ~** in any case, at any rate; **~ de conscience** matter of conscience; **~ de force majeure** case of absolute necessity; (*Assurances*) act of God; **~ limite** borderline case; **~ social** social problem

Casablanca [kazablɑ̃ka] N Casablanca

casanier, -ière [kazanje, -jɛʀ] ADJ stay-at-home

casaque [kazak] NF (*de jockey*) blouse

cascade [kaskad] NF waterfall, cascade; (*fig*) stream, torrent

cascadeur, -euse [kaskadœʀ, -øz] NM/F stuntman/stuntwoman

★**case** [kɑz] NF (*hutte*) hut; (*compartiment*) compartment; (*pour le courrier*) pigeonhole; (*d'échiquier*) square; (*sur un formulaire, de mots croisés*) box

casemate [kazmat] NF blockhouse

caser [kɑze] /1/ (fam) VT (mettre) to put; (loger) to put up; (péj) to find a job for; to marry off ◼ **se caser** VPR (se marier) to settle down; (trouver un emploi) to find a (steady) job

caserne [kazɛʀn] NF barracks

casernement [kazɛʀnəmɑ̃] NM barrack buildings pl

cash [kaʃ] ADV: **payer ~** to pay cash down

casier [kɑzje] NM (à journaux etc) rack; (de bureau) filing cabinet; (: à cases) set of pigeonholes; (case) compartment; (pour courrier) pigeonhole; (: à clef) locker; (Pêche) lobster pot; **~ à bouteilles** bottle rack; **~ judiciaire** police record

casino [kazino] NM casino

★**casque** [kask] NM helmet; (chez le coiffeur) (hair-)dryer; (pour audition) (head-)phones pl, headset; **les Casques bleus** the UN peacekeeping force

casquer [kaske] /1/ VI (fam) to cough up, stump up (BRIT)

★**casquette** [kaskɛt] NF cap

cassable [kɑsabl] ADJ (fragile) breakable

cassant, e [kɑsɑ̃, -ɑ̃t] ADJ brittle; (fig) brusque, abrupt

cassate [kasat] NF: **(glace) ~** cassata

cassation [kɑsasjɔ̃] NF: **se pourvoir en ~** to lodge an appeal; **recours en ~** appeal to the Supreme Court

casse [kɑs] NF (pour voitures): **mettre à la ~** to scrap, send to the breakers (BRIT); (dégâts): **il y a eu de la ~** there were a lot of breakages; (Typo): **haut/bas de ~** upper/lower case

cassé, e [kɑse] ADJ (voix) cracked; (vieillard) bent

casse-cou [kɑsku] ADJ INV daredevil, reckless; **crier ~ à qn** to warn sb (against a risky undertaking)

casse-croûte [kɑskrut] NM INV snack

casse-noisettes [kɑsnwazɛt], **casse-noix** [kɑsnwa] NM INV nutcrackers pl

★**casse-pieds** [kɑspje] NMF INV (fam): **il est ~, c'est un ~** he's a pain (in the neck)

★**casser** [kɑse] /1/ VT to break; (Admin: gradé) to demote; (Jur) to quash; (Comm): **~ les prix** to slash prices; **~ les pieds à qn** (fam: irriter) to get on sb's nerves; **à tout ~** fantastic, brilliant ◼ **se casser** VPR to break; (fam) to go, leave; **se ~ la jambe/une jambe** to break one's leg/a leg; **se ~ la tête** (fam) to go to a lot of trouble; **se ~ net** to break clean off

★**casserole** [kɑsrɔl] NF saucepan; **à la ~** (Culin) braised

casse-tête [kɑstɛt] NM INV (fig) brain teaser; (difficultés) headache (fig)

cassette [kasɛt] NF (bande magnétique) cassette; (coffret) casket; **~ numérique** digital compact cassette; **~ vidéo** video

casseur [kɑsœr] NM hooligan; rioter

★**cassis** [kasis] NM blackcurrant; (de la route) dip, bump

cassonade [kɑsɔnad] NF brown sugar

cassoulet [kasulɛ] NM sausage and bean hotpot

cassure [kɑsyr] NF break, crack

castagnettes [kastaɲɛt] NFPL castanets

caste [kast] NF caste

castillan, e [kastijɑ̃, -an] ADJ Castilian ▸ NM (Ling) Castilian

Castille [kastij] NF: **la ~** Castile

castor [kastɔr] NM beaver

castrer [kastre] /1/ VT (mâle) to castrate; (femelle) to spay; (cheval) to geld; (chat, chien) to doctor (BRIT), fix (US)

cataclysme [kataklism] NM cataclysm

catacombes [katakɔ̃b] NFPL catacombs

catadioptre [katadjɔptr] NM = **cataphote**

catafalque [katafalk] NM catafalque

catalan, e [katalɑ̃, -an] ADJ Catalan, Catalonian ▸ NM (Ling) Catalan

Catalogne [katalɔɲ] NF: **la ~** Catalonia

catalogue [katalɔg] NM catalogue

cataloguer [katalɔge] /1/ VT to catalogue, list; (péj) to put a label on

catalyse [kataliz] NF catalysis

catalyser [katalize] /1/ VT to catalyze

catalyseur [katalizœr] NM catalyst

catalytique [katalitik] ADJ catalytic; **pot ~** catalytic converter

catamaran [katamarɑ̃] NM (voilier) catamaran

cataphote [katafɔt] NM reflector

cataplasme [kataplasm] NM poultice

catapulte [katapylt] NF catapult

catapulter [katapylte] /1/ VT to catapult

cataracte [katarakt] NF cataract; **opérer qn de la ~** to operate on sb for a cataract

catarrhe [katar] NM catarrh

catarrheux, -euse [katarø, -øz] ADJ catarrhal

★**catastrophe** [katastrɔf] NF catastrophe, disaster; **atterrir en ~** to make an emergency landing; **partir en ~** to rush away

catastropher [katastrɔfe] /1/ VT (personne) to shatter

catastrophique [katastrɔfik] ADJ catastrophic, disastrous

catch [katʃ] NM (all-in) wrestling

catcheur, -euse [katʃœr, -øz] NM/F (all-in) wrestler

catéchiser [kateʃize] /1/ VT to indoctrinate; to lecture

catéchisme [kateʃism] NM catechism

catéchumène [katekymɛn] NMF catechumen, person attending religious instruction prior to baptism

catégorie [kategɔri] NF category; (Boucherie): **morceaux de première/deuxième ~** prime/second cuts

catégorique [kategɔrik] ADJ categorical

catégoriquement [kategɔrikmɑ̃] ADV categorically

catégoriser [kategɔrize] /1/ VT to categorize

caténaire [katenɛr] NF (Rail) catenary

cathédrale [katedral] NF cathedral

cathéter [katetɛr] NM (Méd) catheter

cathode [katɔd] NF cathode

cathodique [katɔdik] ADJ: **rayons cathodiques** cathode rays; **tube/écran ~** cathode-ray tube/screen

catholicisme [katɔlisism] NM (Roman) Catholicism

catholique [katɔlik] ADJ, NMF (Roman) Catholic; **pas très ~** a bit shady *ou* fishy

catimini [katimini]: **en ~** *adv* on the sly, on the quiet

catogan [katɔgɑ̃] NM bow *(tying hair on neck)*

Caucase [kokaz] NM: **le ~** the Caucasus (Mountains)

caucasien, ne [kokazjɛ̃, -ɛn] ADJ Caucasian

★**cauchemar** [koʃmaʀ] NM nightmare

cauchemardesque [koʃmaʀdɛsk] ADJ nightmarish

caudal, e, -aux [kodal, -o] ADJ: **la nageoire caudale** the caudal fin, the tail fin

causal, e [kozal] ADJ causal

causalité [kozalite] NF causality

causant, e [kozɑ̃, -ɑ̃t] ADJ chatty, talkative

★**cause** [koz] NF cause; *(Jur)* lawsuit, case; brief; **faire ~ commune avec qn** to take sides with sb; **être ~ de** to be the cause of; **à ~ de** because of, owing to; **pour ~ de** on account of; owing to; **(et) pour ~** and for (a very) good reason; **être en ~** *(intérêts)* to be at stake; *(personne)* to be involved; *(qualité)* to be in question; **mettre en ~** to implicate; to call into question; **remettre en ~** to challenge, call into question; **c'est hors de ~** it's out of the question; **en tout état de ~** in any case

causer [koze] /1/ VT to cause ▶ VI to chat, talk

causerie [kozʀi] NF talk

causette [kozɛt] NF: **faire la** *ou* **un brin de ~** to have a chat

caustique [kostik] ADJ caustic

cauteleux, -euse [kotlø, -øz] ADJ wily

cautériser [koteʀize] /1/ VT to cauterize

caution [kosjɔ̃] NF guarantee, security; deposit; *(Jur)* bail (bond); *(fig)* backing, support; **payer la ~ de qn** to stand bail for sb; **se porter ~ pour qn** to stand security for sb; **libéré sous ~** released on bail; **sujet à ~** unconfirmed

cautionnement [kosjɔnmɑ̃] NM *(somme)* guarantee, security

cautionner [kosjɔne] /1/ VT to guarantee; *(soutenir)* to support

cavalcade [kavalkad] NF *(fig)* stampede

cavale [kaval] NF: **en ~** on the run

cavalerie [kavalʀi] NF cavalry

cavalier, -ière [kavalje, -jɛʀ] ADJ *(désinvolte)* offhand; **allée** *ou* **piste cavalière** riding path ▶ NM/F rider; *(au bal)* partner ▶ NM *(Échecs)* knight; **faire ~ seul** to go it alone

cavalièrement [kavaljɛʀmɑ̃] ADV offhandedly

★**cave** [kav] NF cellar; *(cabaret)* (cellar) nightclub ▶ ADJ: **yeux caves** sunken eyes; **joues caves** hollow cheeks; **~ à vin** wine cellar

caveau, x [kavo] NM vault

caverne [kavɛʀn] NF cave

caverneux, -euse [kavɛʀnø, -øz] ADJ cavernous

caviar [kavjaʀ] NM caviar(e)

caviste [kavist] NMF wine merchant; *(dans un restaurant)* sommelier

cavité [kavite] NF cavity

Cayenne [kajɛn] N Cayenne

CB [sibi] SIGLE F (= *citizens' band*; *canaux banalisés*) CB; = **carte bancaire**

CC SIGLE M = **le corps consulaire**; **compte courant**

CCI SIGLE F = **chambre de commerce et d'industrie**

CCP SIGLE M = **compte chèque postal**

★**CD** SIGLE M (= *chemin départemental*) secondary road, ≈ B road (BRIT); *(Pol)* = **le corps diplomatique**; (= *compact disc*) CD; (= *comité directeur*) steering committee

CDD SIGLE M (= *contrat à durée déterminée*) fixed-term contract

★**CDI** SIGLE M (= *Centre de documentation et d'information*) school library; (= *contrat à durée indéterminée*) permanent *ou* open-ended contract

CD-ROM [sedeʀɔm] NM INV (= *Compact Disc Read Only Memory*) CD-Rom

CE SIGLE F (= *Communauté européenne*) EC; *(Comm)* = **caisse d'épargne** ▶ SIGLE M *(Industrie)* = **comité d'entreprise**; *(Scol)* = **cours élémentaire**

---

ce, cette [sə, sɛt]

(devant nm **cet** + *voyelle ou h aspiré) (pl* **ces**) ADJ DÉM *(proximité)* this; these *pl*; *(non-proximité)* that; those *pl*; **cette maison-ci/-là** this/that house; **cette nuit** *(qui vient)* tonight; *(passée)* last night

▶ PRON **1**: **c'est** it's, it is; **c'est petit/grand/un livre** it's *ou* it is small/big/a book; **c'est un peintre** he's *ou* he is a painter; **ce sont des peintres** they're *ou* they are painters; **c'est le facteur** *etc (à la porte)* it's the postman *etc*; **qui est-ce?** who is it?; *(en désignant)* who is he/she?; **qu'est-ce?** what is it?; **c'est toi qui lui as parlé** it was you who spoke to him

2: **c'est que**: **c'est qu'il est lent/qu'il n'a pas faim** the fact is, he's slow/he's not hungry

3 *(expressions)*: **c'est ça** *(correct)* that's it, that's right; **c'est toi qui le dis!** that's what YOU say!; *voir aussi* **c'est-à-dire**; *voir* **-ci**; **est-ce que**; **n'est-ce pas**

4: **ce qui, ce que** what; **ce qui me plaît, c'est sa franchise** what I like about him *ou* her is his *ou* her frankness; *(chose qui)*: **il est bête, ce qui me chagrine** he's stupid, which saddens me; **tout ce qui bouge** everything *ou* which moves; **tout ce que je sais** all I know; **ce dont j'ai parlé** what I talked about; **ce que c'est grand!** it's so big!

CEA SIGLE M ≈ AEA (BRIT), ≈ AEC (US)

CECA [seka] SIGLE F (= *Communauté européenne du charbon et de l'acier*) ECSC (= *European Coal and Steel Community*)

ceci [səsi] PRON this

cécité [sesite] NF blindness

céder [sede] /6/ VT to give up ▶ VI *(pont, barrage)* to give way; *(personne)* to give in; **~ à** to yield to, give in to

cédérom [sedeʀɔm] NM CD-ROM

CEDEX [sedɛks] SIGLE M (= *courrier d'entreprise à distribution exceptionnelle*) accelerated postal service for bulk users

cédille [sedij] NF cedilla

cèdre [sɛdʀ] NM cedar

CEE SIGLE F (= *Communauté économique européenne*) EEC

CEI SIGLE F (= *Communauté des États indépendants*) CIS

ceindre [sɛ̃dʀ] /**52**/ VT (*mettre*) to put on; (*entourer*): ~ **qch de qch** to put sth round sth

★**ceinture** [sɛ̃tyʀ] NF belt; (*taille*) waist; (*fig*) ring; belt; circle; ~ **de sauvetage** lifebelt (BRIT), life preserver (US); ~ **de sécurité** safety ou seat belt; ~ **(de sécurité) à enrouleur** inertia reel seat belt; ~ **verte** green belt

ceinturer [sɛ̃tyʀe] /**1**/ VT (*saisir*) to grasp (round the waist); (*entourer*) to surround

ceinturon [sɛ̃tyʀɔ̃] NM belt

cela [s(ə)la] PRON that; (*comme sujet indéfini*) it; ~ **m'étonne que** it surprises me that; **quand/où** ~ **?** when/where (was that?)

célébrant [selebʀɑ̃] NM (*Rel*) celebrant

célébration [selebʀasjɔ̃] NF celebration

célèbre [selɛbʀ] ADJ famous

célébrer [selebʀe] /**6**/ VT to celebrate; (*louer*) to extol

célébrité [selebʀite] NF fame; (*star*) celebrity

céleri [sɛlʀi] NM: ~**(-rave)** celeriac; ~ **(en branche)** celery

célérité [seleʀite] NF speed, swiftness

céleste [selɛst] ADJ celestial; heavenly

célibat [seliba] NM celibacy, bachelor/spinster-hood

célibataire [selibatɛʀ] ADJ single, unmarried; **mère** ~ single mother ▶ NMF bachelor/unmarried ou single woman

celle, celles [sɛl] PRON *voir* **celui**

cellier [selje] NM storeroom

cellophane® [selɔfan] NF cellophane

cellulaire [selylɛʀ] ADJ (*Bio*) cell *cpd*, cellular; **voiture** ou **fourgon** ~ prison ou police van; **régime** ~ confinement

cellule [selyl] NF (*gén*) cell; ~ **(photo-électrique)** electronic eye; ~ **souche** stem cell

cellulite [selylit] NF cellulite

celluloïd® [selylɔid] NM Celluloid

cellulose [selyloz] NF cellulose

celte [sɛlt], **celtique** [sɛltik] ADJ Celt, Celtic

---

celui, celle [səlɥi, sɛl]

(*mpl* **ceux**, *fpl* **celles**) PRON 1: **celui-ci/là**, **celle-ci/là** this one/that one; **ceux-ci, celles-ci** these (ones); **ceux-là, celles-là** those (ones); **celui de mon frère** my brother's; **celui du salon/du dessous** the one in (ou from) the lounge/below 2 (+ *relatif*): **celui qui bouge** the one which ou that moves; (*personne*) the one who moves; **celui que je vois** the one (which ou that) I see; (*personne*) the one (whom) I see; **celui dont je parle** the one I'm talking about 3 (*valeur indéfinie*): **celui qui veut** whoever wants

---

cénacle [senakl] NM (*literary*) coterie ou set

cendre [sɑ̃dʀ] NF ash; **cendres** (*d'un foyer*) ash(es), cinders; (*volcaniques*) ash *sg*; (*d'un défunt*) ashes; **sous la** ~ (*Culin*) in (the) embers

cendré, e [sɑ̃dʀe] ADJ (*couleur*) ashen; (**piste**) **cendrée** cinder track

cendreux, -euse [sɑ̃dʀø, -øz] ADJ (*terrain, substance*) cindery; (*teint*) ashen

★**cendrier** [sɑ̃dʀije] NM ashtray

cène [sɛn] NF: **la** ~ (Holy) Communion; (*Art*) the Last Supper

censé, e [sɑ̃se] ADJ: **être** ~ **faire** to be supposed to do

censément [sɑ̃semɑ̃] ADV supposedly

censeur [sɑ̃sœʀ] NM (*Scol*) deputy head (BRIT), vice-principal (US); (*Ciné, Pol*) censor

censure [sɑ̃syʀ] NF censorship

censurer [sɑ̃syʀe] /**1**/ VT (*Ciné, Presse*) to censor; (*Pol*) to censure

★**cent** [sɑ̃] NUM a hundred, one hundred; **pour** ~ **(%)** per cent (%); **faire les** ~ **pas** to pace up and down ▶ NM (*US, Canada, partie de l'euro etc*) cent

centaine [sɑ̃tɛn] NF: **une** ~ **(de)** about a hundred, a hundred or so; (*Comm*) a hundred; **plusieurs centaines (de)** several hundred; **des centaines (de)** hundreds (of)

centenaire [sɑ̃t(ə)nɛʀ] ADJ hundred-year-old ▶ NMF centenarian ▶ NM (*anniversaire*) centenary; (*monnaie*) cent

centième [sɑ̃tjɛm] NUM hundredth

centigrade [sɑ̃tigʀad] NM centigrade

centigramme [sɑ̃tigʀam] NM centigramme

centilitre [sɑ̃tilitʀ] NM centilitre (BRIT), centiliter (US)

★**centime** [sɑ̃tim] NM centime; ~ **d'euro** euro cent

centimètre [sɑ̃timɛtʀ] NM centimetre (BRIT), centimeter (US); (*ruban*) tape measure, measuring tape

centrafricain, e [sɑ̃tʀafʀikɛ̃, -ɛn] ADJ of ou from the Central African Republic

central, e, -aux [sɑ̃tʀal, -o] ADJ central ▶ NM: ~ **(téléphonique)** (telephone) exchange ▶ NF power station; **centrale d'achat** (*Comm*) central buying service; **centrale électrique/nucléaire** electric/nuclear power station; **centrale syndicale** group of affiliated trade unions

centralisation [sɑ̃tʀalizasjɔ̃] NF centralization

centraliser [sɑ̃tʀalize] /**1**/ VT to centralize

centralisme [sɑ̃tʀalism] NM centralism

centraméricain, e [sɑ̃tʀameʀikɛ̃, -ɛn] ADJ Central American

★**centre** [sɑ̃tʀ] NM centre (BRIT), center (US); ~ **commercial/sportif/culturel** shopping/sports/arts centre; ~ **aéré** outdoor centre; ~ **d'appels** call centre; ~ **d'apprentissage** training college; ~ **d'attraction** centre of attraction; ~ **de gravité** centre of gravity; ~ **de loisirs** leisure centre; ~ **d'enfouissement des déchets** landfill site; ~ **hospitalier** hospital complex; ~ **de tri** (*Postes*) sorting office; **centres nerveux** (*Anat*) nerve centres

centrer [sɑ̃tʀe] /**1**/ VT to centre (BRIT), center (US) ▶ VI (*Football*) to centre the ball

★**centre-ville** [sɑ̃tʀəvil] (*pl* **centres-villes**) NM town centre (BRIT) ou center (US), downtown (area) (US)

centrifuge [sɑ̃tʀify3] ADJ: **force** ~ centrifugal force

centrifuger [sɑ̃tʀify3e] /**3**/ VT to centrifuge

centrifugeuse [sɑ̃tʀify3øz] NF (*pour fruits*) juice extractor

centripète [sɑ̃tʀipɛt] ADJ: **force** ~ centripetal force

centrisme [sātrism] NM centrism

centriste [sātrist] ADJ, NMF centrist

centuple [sātypl] NM: **le ~ de qch** a hundred times sth; **au ~** a hundredfold

centupler [sātyple] /1/ VI, VT to increase a hundredfold

cep [sɛp] NM (vine) stock

cépage [sepaʒ] NM (type of) vine

cèpe [sɛp] NM (edible) boletus

★**cependant** [s(ə)pādā] ADV however, nevertheless

céramique [seramik] ADJ ceramic ▸ NF ceramic; (art) ceramics sg

céramiste [seramist] NMF ceramist

cerbère [sɛrbɛr] NM (fig: péj) bad-tempered doorkeeper

cerceau, x [sɛrso] NM (d'enfant, de tonnelle) hoop

★**cercle** [sɛrkl] NM circle; (objet) band, hoop; **décrire un ~** (avion) to circle; (projectile) to describe a circle; **~ d'amis** circle of friends; **~ de famille** family circle; **~ vicieux** vicious circle

cercler [sɛrkle] /1/ VT: **lunettes cerclées d'or** gold-rimmed glasses

cercueil [sɛrkœj] NM coffin

céréale [sereal] NF cereal

céréalier, -ière [serealje, -jɛr] ADJ (production, cultures) cereal cpd

cérébral, e, -aux [serebral, -o] ADJ (Anat) cerebral, brain cpd; (fig) mental, cerebral

cérémonial [seremɔnjal] NM ceremonial

cérémonie [seremɔni] NF ceremony; **sans ~** (inviter, manger) informally ■ **cérémonies** NFPL (péj) fuss sg, to-do sg

cérémonieux, -euse [seremɔnjø, -øz] ADJ ceremonious, formal

cerf [sɛr] NM stag

cerfeuil [sɛrfœj] NM chervil

cerf-volant [sɛrvɔlā] (pl **cerfs-volants**) NM kite; **jouer au ~** to fly a kite

cerisaie [s(ə)rizɛ] NF cherry orchard

★**cerise** [s(ə)riz] NF cherry

cerisier [s(ə)rizje] NM cherry (tree)

CERN [sɛrn] SIGLE M (= Centre européen de recherche nucléaire) CERN

cerné, e [sɛrne] ADJ: **les yeux cernés** with dark rings ou shadows under the eyes

cerner [sɛrne] /1/ VT (Mil etc) to surround; (fig: problème) to delimit, define

cernes [sɛrn] NFPL (dark) rings, shadows (under the eyes)

★**certain, e** [sɛrtɛ̃, -ɛn] ADJ certain; (sûr): **~ (de/que)** certain ou sure (of/that); **d'un ~ âge** past one's prime, not so young; **un ~ temps** (quite) some time; **sûr et ~** absolutely certain; **un ~ Georges** someone called Georges; **certains** pron, adj some

★**certainement** [sɛrtɛnmā] ADV (probablement) most probably ou likely; (bien sûr) certainly, of course

certes [sɛrt] ADV (sans doute) admittedly; (bien sûr) of course; indeed (yes)

★**certificat** [sɛrtifika] NM certificate; **C~ d'études**

(primaires) former school leaving certificate (taken at the end of primary education); **C~ de fin d'études secondaires** school leaving certificate

certifié, e [sɛrtifje] ADJ: **professeur ~** qualified teacher; (Admin) **copie certifiée conforme (à l'original)** certified copy (of the original)

certifier [sɛrtifje] /7/ VT to certify, guarantee; **~ à qn que** to assure sb that, guarantee to sb that; **~ qch à qn** to guarantee sth to sb

certitude [sɛrtityd] NF certainty

cérumen [serymɛn] NM (ear)wax

cerveau, x [sɛrvo] NM brain; **~ électronique** electronic brain

cervelas [sɛrvəla] NM saveloy

cervelle [sɛrvɛl] NF (Anat) brain; (Culin) brain(s); **se creuser la ~** to rack one's brains

cervical, e, -aux [sɛrvikal, -o] ADJ cervical

cervidé [sɛrvide] NM cervid

★**ces** [se] ADJ DÉM voir **ce**

césarienne [sezarjɛn] NF caesarean (BRIT) ou cesarean (US) (section)

cessantes [sɛsāt] ADJ FPL: **toutes affaires ~** forthwith

cessation [sɛsasjɔ̃] NF: **~ des hostilités** cessation of hostilities; **~ de paiements/commerce** suspension of payments/trading

cesse [sɛs]: **sans ~** adv (tout le temps) continually, constantly; (sans interruption) continuously; **il n'avait de ~ que** he would not rest until

cesser [sese] /1/ VT to stop; **~ de faire** to stop doing ▸ VI to stop, cease; **faire ~** (bruit, scandale) to put a stop to

cessez-le-feu [sesel(ə)fø] NM INV ceasefire

cession [sɛsjɔ̃] NF transfer

c'est [sɛ] = **ce**

c'est-à-dire [sɛtadir] ADV that is (to say); (demander de préciser): **c'est-à-dire?** what does that mean?; **c'est-à-dire que ...** (en conséquence) which means that ...; (manière d'excuse) well, in fact ...

cet [sɛt] ADJ DÉM voir **ce**

cétacé [setase] NM cetacean

★**cette** [sɛt] ADJ DÉM voir **ce**

ceux [sø] PRON voir **celui**

cévenol, e [sevnɔl] ADJ of ou from the Cévennes region

cf. ABR (= confer) cf, cp

CFAO SIGLE F (= conception de fabrication assistée par ordinateur) CAM

CFC SIGLE MPL (= chlorofluorocarbures) CFC

CFDT SIGLE F (= Confédération française démocratique du travail) trade union

CFF SIGLE M (= Chemins de fer fédéraux) Swiss railways

CFL SIGLE M (= Chemins de fer luxembourgeois) Luxembourg railways

CFP SIGLE M = **Centre de formation professionnelle** ▸ SIGLE F = **Compagnie française des pétroles**

CFTC SIGLE F (= Confédération française des travailleurs chrétiens) trade union

CGC SIGLE F (= Confédération générale des cadres) management union

CGT SIGLE F (= *Confédération générale du travail*) trade union

CH ABR (= *Confédération helvétique*) CH

ch. ABR = **charges**; **chauffage**; **cherche**

chacal [ʃakal] NM jackal

★**chacun, e** [ʃakœ̃, -yn] PRON each; (*indéfini*) everyone, everybody

> **Everyone** et **everybody** sont suivis d'un verbe au singulier, mais le possessif qui s'y rapporte doit être au pluriel.
> *Chacun a sa propre opinion à ce sujet.* **Everyone *has their* own view on this**.

chagrin, e [ʃagʀɛ̃, -in] ADJ morose ▶ NM grief, sorrow; **avoir du ~** to be grieved *ou* sorrowful

chagriner [ʃagʀine] /1/ VT to grieve, distress; (*contrarier*) to bother, worry

chahut [ʃay] NM uproar

chahuter [ʃayte] /1/ VT to rag, bait ▶ VI to make an uproar

chahuteur, -euse [ʃaytœʀ, -øz] NM/F rowdy

chai [ʃɛ] NM wine and spirit store(house)

chaîne [ʃɛn] NF chain; (TV) channel; (*Inform*) string; **travail à la ~** production line work; **réactions en ~** chain reactions; **faire la ~** to form a (human) chain; **~ alimentaire** food chain; **~ compacte** music centre; **~ d'entraide** mutual aid association; **~ (haute-fidélité** *ou* **hi-fi)** hi-fi system; **~ (de montage** *ou* **de fabrication)** production *ou* assembly line; **~ (de montagnes)** (mountain) range; **~ de solidarité** solidarity network; **~ (stéréo** *ou* **audio)** stereo (system) ■ **chaînes** NFPL (*liens, asservissement*) fetters, bonds

chaînette [ʃenɛt] NF (small) chain

chaînon [ʃenɔ̃] NM link

chair [ʃɛʀ] NF flesh; **avoir la ~ de poule** to have goose pimples *ou* goose flesh; **bien en ~** plump, well-padded; **en ~ et en os** in the flesh; **~ à saucisse** sausage meat ▶ ADJ INV: **(couleur) ~** flesh-coloured

chaire [ʃɛʀ] NF (*d'église*) pulpit; (*d'université*) chair

★**chaise** [ʃez] NF chair; **~ de bébé** high chair; **~ électrique** electric chair; **~ longue** deckchair

chaland [ʃalɑ̃] NM (*bateau*) barge

châle [ʃal] NM shawl

chalet [ʃalɛ] NM chalet

★**chaleur** [ʃalœʀ] NF heat; (*fig: d'accueil*) warmth; fire, fervour (BRIT), fervor (US); heat; **en ~** (*Zool*) on heat

chaleureusement [ʃalœʀøzmɑ̃] ADV warmly

chaleureux, -euse [ʃalœʀø, -øz] ADJ warm

challenge [ʃalɑ̃ʒ] NM contest, tournament

challenger [ʃalɑ̃ʒœʀ] NM (*Sport*) challenger

chaloupe [ʃalup] NF launch; (*de sauvetage*) lifeboat

chalumeau, x [ʃalymo] NM blowlamp (BRIT), blowtorch

chalut [ʃaly] NM trawl (net); **pêcher au ~** to trawl

chalutier [ʃalytje] NM trawler; (*pêcheur*) trawlerman

chamade [ʃamad] NF: **battre la ~** to beat wildly

chamailler [ʃamaje] /1/: **se chamailler** VPR to squabble, bicker

chamarré, e [ʃamaʀe] ADJ richly brocaded

chambard [ʃɑ̃baʀ] NM rumpus

chambardement [ʃɑ̃baʀdəmɑ̃] NM: **c'est le grand ~** everything has been (*ou* is being) turned upside down

chambarder [ʃɑ̃baʀde] /1/ VT to turn upside down

chamboulé, e [ʃɑ̃bule] ADJ (*fam*) turned upside down; **se trouver ~** to be turned upside down

chamboulement [ʃɑ̃bulmɑ̃] NM (*fam*) disruption

chambouler [ʃɑ̃bule] /1/ VT (*fam*) to turn upside down

chambranle [ʃɑ̃bʀɑ̃l] NM (door) frame

★**chambre** [ʃɑ̃bʀ] NF bedroom; (*Tech*) chamber; (*Pol*) chamber, house; (*Jur*) court; (*Comm*) chamber; federation; **faire ~ à part** to sleep in separate rooms; **stratège/alpiniste en ~** armchair strategist/mountaineer; **~ à un lit/deux lits** single/twin-bedded room; **~ pour une/deux personne(s)** single/double room; **~ d'accusation** court of criminal appeal; **~ d'agriculture** *body responsible for the agricultural interests of a département*; **~ à air** (*de pneu*) (inner) tube; **~ d'amis** spare *ou* guest room; **~ de combustion** combustion chamber; **~ de commerce et d'industrie** chamber of commerce and industry; **~ à coucher** bedroom; **la C~ des députés** the Chamber of Deputies, ≈ the House (of Commons) (BRIT), ≈ the House of Representatives (US); **~ forte** strongroom; **~ froide** *ou* **frigorifique** cold room; **~ à gaz** gas chamber; **~ d'hôte** ≈ bed and breakfast (*in private home*); **~ des machines** engine-room; **~ des métiers** *chamber of commerce for trades*; **~ meublée** bedsit(ter) (BRIT), furnished room; **~ noire** (*Photo*) dark room

chambrée [ʃɑ̃bʀe] NF room

chambrer [ʃɑ̃bʀe] /1/ VT (*vin*) to bring to room temperature

★**chameau, x** [ʃamo] NM camel

chamois [ʃamwa] NM chamois ▶ ADJ INV: **(couleur) ~** fawn, buff

★**champ** [ʃɑ̃] NM (*aussi Inform*) field; (*Photo*): **dans le ~** in the picture; **prendre du ~** to draw back; **laisser le ~ libre à qn** to leave sb a clear field; **~ d'action** sphere of operation(s); **~ de bataille** battlefield; **~ de courses** racecourse; **~ d'honneur** field of honour; **~ de manœuvre** (*Mil*) parade ground; **~ de mines** minefield; **~ de tir** shooting *ou* rifle range; **~ visuel** field of vision

Champagne [ʃɑ̃paɲ] NF: **la ~** Champagne, the Champagne region

champagne [ʃɑ̃paɲ] NM champagne

champenois, e [ʃɑ̃pənwa, -waz] ADJ of *ou* from Champagne; (*vin*): **méthode champenoise** champagne-type

champêtre [ʃɑ̃pɛtʀ] ADJ country *cpd*, rural

★**champignon** [ʃɑ̃piɲɔ̃] NM mushroom; (*terme générique*) fungus; (*fam: accélérateur*) accelerator, gas pedal (US); **~ de couche** *ou* **de Paris** button mushroom; **~ vénéneux** toadstool, poisonous mushroom

★**champion, ne** [ʃɑ̃pjɔ̃, -ɔn] ADJ, NM/F champion

★**championnat** [ʃɑ̃pjɔna] NM championship

★**chance** [ʃɑ̃s] NF: **la ~** luck; **une ~** a stroke *ou* piece of luck *ou* good fortune; (*occasion*) a lucky break;

C

avoir de la ~ to be lucky; **bonne ~!** good luck!; **encore une ~ que tu viennes!** it's lucky you're coming!; **je n'ai pas de ~** I'm out of luck; (*toujours*) I never have any luck; **donner sa ~ à qn** to give sb a chance ■ **chances** NFPL (*probabilités*) chances; **il a des chances de gagner** he has a chance of winning; **il y a de fortes chances pour que Paul soit malade** it's highly probable that Paul is ill

chancelant, e [ʃɑ̃s(ə)lɑ̃, -ɑ̃t] ADJ (*personne*) tottering; (*santé*) failing

chanceler [ʃɑ̃s(ə)le] /4/ VI to totter

chancelier [ʃɑ̃səlje] NM (*allemand*) chancellor; (*d'ambassade*) secretary

chancellerie [ʃɑ̃sɛlʀi] NF (*en France*) ministry of justice; (*en Allemagne*) chancellery; (*d'ambassade*) chancery

chanceux, -euse [ʃɑ̃sø, -øz] ADJ lucky, fortunate

chancre [ʃɑ̃kʀ] NM canker

chandail [ʃɑ̃daj] NM (thick) jumper *ou* sweater

Chandeleur [ʃɑ̃dlœʀ] NF: **la ~** Candlemas

chandelier [ʃɑ̃dəlje] NM candlestick; (*à plusieurs branches*) candelabra

chandelle [ʃɑ̃dɛl] NF (tallow) candle; (*Tennis*): **faire une ~** to lob; (*Aviat*): **monter en ~** to climb vertically; **tenir la ~** to play gooseberry; **dîner aux chandelles** candlelight dinner

change [ʃɑ̃ʒ] NM (*Comm*) exchange; **opérations de ~** (foreign) exchange transactions; **contrôle des changes** exchange control; **gagner/perdre au ~** to be better/worse off (for it); **donner le ~ à qn** (*fig*) to lead sb up the garden path

changeant, e [ʃɑ̃ʒɑ̃, -ɑ̃t] ADJ changeable, fickle

★**changement** [ʃɑ̃ʒmɑ̃] NM change; **~ climatique** climate change; **~ de vitesse** (*dispositif*) gears pl; (*action*) gear change

★**changer** [ʃɑ̃ʒe] /3/ VT (*modifier*) to change, alter; (*remplacer, Comm, rhabiller*) to change; **~ de** (*remplacer: adresse, nom, voiture etc*) to change one's; **~ de train** to change trains; **~ d'air** to get a change of air; **~ de couleur/direction** to change colour/direction; **~ d'avis**, **~ d'idée** to change one's mind; **~ de place avec qn** to change places with sb; **~ de vitesse** (*Auto*) to change gear; **~ qn/qch de place** to move sb/sth to another place; **~ (de bus** *etc*) to change (buses *etc*); **~ qch en** to change sth into ▶ VI to change, alter ■ **se changer** VPR to change (o.s.)

changeur [ʃɑ̃ʒœʀ] NM (*personne*) moneychanger; **~ automatique** change machine; **~ de disques** record changer, autochange

chanoine [ʃanwan] NM canon

★**chanson** [ʃɑ̃sɔ̃] NF song

chansonnette [ʃɑ̃sɔnɛt] NF ditty

chansonnier [ʃɑ̃sɔnje] NM cabaret artist (*specializing in political satire*); (*recueil*) song book

chant [ʃɑ̃] NM song; (*art vocal*) singing; (*d'église*) hymn; (*de poème*) canto; (*Tech*): **posé de** *ou* **sur ~** placed edgeways; **~ de Noël** Christmas carol

chantage [ʃɑ̃taʒ] NM blackmail; **faire du ~** to use blackmail; **soumettre qn à un ~** to blackmail sb

chantant, e [ʃɑ̃tɑ̃, -ɑ̃t] ADJ (*accent, voix*) sing-song

★**chanter** [ʃɑ̃te] /1/ VT, VI to sing; **~ juste/faux** to sing in tune/out of tune; **si cela lui chante** (*fam*) if he feels like it *ou* fancies it

chanterelle [ʃɑ̃tʀɛl] NF chanterelle (*edible mushroom*)

★**chanteur, -euse** [ʃɑ̃tœr, -øz] NM/F singer; **~ de charme** crooner

chantier [ʃɑ̃tje] NM (building) site; (*sur une route*) roadworks pl; **mettre en ~** to start work on; **~ naval** shipyard

chantilly [ʃɑ̃tiji] NF *voir* **crème**

chantonner [ʃɑ̃tɔne] /1/ VI, VT to sing to oneself, hum

chantre [ʃɑ̃tʀ] NM (*fig*) eulogist

chanvre [ʃɑ̃vʀ] NM hemp

chaos [kao] NM chaos

chaotique [kaɔtik] ADJ chaotic

chap. ABR (= *chapitre*) ch

chapardage [ʃapaʀdaʒ] NM pilfering

chaparder [ʃapaʀde] /1/ VT to pinch

★**chapeau, x** [ʃapo] NM hat; (*Presse*) introductory paragraph; **~!** well done!; **~ melon** bowler hat; **~ mou** trilby; **chapeaux de roues** hub caps

chapeauter [ʃapote] /1/ VT (*Admin*) to head, oversee

chapelain [ʃaplɛ̃] NM (*Rel*) chaplain

chapelet [ʃaplɛ] NM (*Rel*) rosary; (*fig*): **un ~ de** a string of; **dire son ~** to tell one's beads

chapelier, -ière [ʃapəlje, -jɛʀ] NM/F hatter; milliner

chapelle [ʃapɛl] NF chapel; **~ ardente** chapel of rest

chapellerie [ʃapɛlʀi] NF (*magasin*) hat shop; (*commerce*) hat trade

chapelure [ʃaplyʀ] NF (dried) breadcrumbs pl

chaperon [ʃapʀɔ̃] NM chaperon

chaperonner [ʃapʀɔne] /1/ VT to chaperon

chapiteau, x [ʃapito] NM (*Archit*) capital; (*de cirque*) marquee, big top

chapitrage [ʃapitʀaʒ] NM (*d'un DVD*) chaptering

chapitre [ʃapitʀ] NM chapter; (*fig*) subject, matter; **avoir voix au ~** to have a say in the matter

chapitrer [ʃapitʀe] /1/ VT to lecture, reprimand

chapon [ʃapɔ̃] NM capon

★**chaque** [ʃak] ADJ each, every; (*indéfini*) every

Each désigne chaque élément (personne ou chose) d'un groupe, pour insister sur son individualité. On utilise **every** pour englober tous les membres d'un groupe de plus de deux éléments, autrement dit pour signifier *tous* les.
Chaque membre du personnel est chargé d'une tâche particulière. **Each member of staff is responsible for a specific task.**
des chances égales pour chaque enfant **an equal chance for every child**

---

char [ʃaʀ] NM (*à foin etc*) cart, waggon; (*de carnaval*) float; **~ (d'assaut)** tank; **~ à voile** sand yacht

charabia [ʃaʀabja] NM (*péj*) gibberish, gobbledygook (BRIT)

charade [ʃaʀad] NF riddle; (*mimée*) charade

★**charbon** [ʃaʀbɔ̃] NM coal; **~ de bois** charcoal

charbonnage [ʃaʀbɔnaʒ] NM: **les charbonnages de France** the (French) Coal Board sg

charbonnier [ʃaʀbɔnje] NM coalman

★**charcuterie** [ʃaʀkytʀi] NF (*magasin*) pork butcher's shop and delicatessen; (*produits*) cooked pork meats *pl*

★**charcutier, -ière** [ʃaʀkytje, -jɛʀ] NM/F pork butcher

chardon [ʃaʀdɔ̃] NM thistle

chardonneret [ʃaʀdɔnʀɛ] NM goldfinch

charentais, e [ʃaʀɑ̃tɛ, -ɛz] ADJ of *ou* from Charente ▸ NF (*pantoufle*) carpet slipper ▸ NM/F: **Charentais, e** person from the Charente region

charge [ʃaʀʒ] NF (*fardeau*) load; (*explosif, Élec, Mil, Jur*) charge; (*rôle, mission*) responsibility; **à la ~ de** (*dépendant de*) dependent upon, supported by; (*aux frais de*) chargeable to, payable by; **j'accepte, à ~ de revanche** I accept, provided I can do the same for you (in return) one day; **prendre en ~** to take charge of; (*véhicule*) to take on; (*dépenses*) to take care of; **~ utile** (*Auto*) live load; (*Comm*) payload ■ **charges** NFPL (*du loyer*) service charges; **charges sociales** social security contributions

chargé, e [ʃaʀʒe] ADJ (*voiture, animal, personne*) laden; (*fusil, batterie, caméra*) loaded; (*occupé: emploi du temps, journée*) busy, full; (*estomac*) heavy, full; (*langue*) furred; (*décoration, style*) heavy, ornate; **~ de** (*responsable de*) responsible for ▸ NM/F: **~ d'affaires** chargé d'affaires; **~ de cours** ≈ lecturer

chargement [ʃaʀʒəmɑ̃] NM (*action*) loading, charging; (*objets*) load

★**charger** [ʃaʀʒe] /3/ VT (*voiture, fusil, caméra*) to load; (*batterie*) to charge; **~ qn de qch/faire qch** to give sb the responsibility for sth/of doing sth; to put sb in charge of sth/doing sth ▸ VI (*Mil etc*) to charge ■ **se charger de** VPR to see to, take care of; **se ~ de faire qch** to take it upon o.s. to do sth

chargeur [ʃaʀʒœʀ] NM (*dispositif: de batterie*) charger; (: *d'arme à feu*) magazine; (: *Photo*) cartridge

★**chariot** [ʃaʀjo] NM trolley; (*charrette*) waggon; (*de machine à écrire*) carriage; **~ élévateur** fork-lift truck

charisme [kaʀism] NM charisma

charitable [ʃaʀitabl] ADJ charitable; kind

charité [ʃaʀite] NF charity; **faire la ~** to give to charity; to do charitable works; **faire la ~ à** to give (something) to; **fête/vente de ~** fête/sale in aid of charity

charivari [ʃaʀivaʀi] NM hullabaloo

charlatan [ʃaʀlatɑ̃] NM charlatan

charlotte [ʃaʀlɔt] NF (*Culin*) charlotte

★**charmant, e** [ʃaʀmɑ̃, -ɑ̃t] ADJ charming

charme [ʃaʀm] NM charm; (*Bot*) hornbeam; **c'est ce qui en fait le ~** that is its attraction; **faire du ~** to be charming, turn on the charm; **aller** *ou* **se porter comme un ~** to be in the pink ■ **charmes** NMPL (*appas*) charms

charmer [ʃaʀme] /1/ VT to charm; **je suis charmé de ...** I'm delighted to ...

charmeur, -euse [ʃaʀmœʀ, -øz] NM/F charmer; **~ de serpents** snake charmer

charnel, le [ʃaʀnɛl] ADJ carnal

charnier [ʃaʀnje] NM mass grave

charnière [ʃaʀnjɛʀ] NF hinge; (*fig*) turning-point

charnu, e [ʃaʀny] ADJ fleshy

charogne [ʃaʀɔɲ] NF carrion *no pl*; (!) bastard (!)

charolais, e [ʃaʀɔlɛ, -ɛz] ADJ of *ou* from the Charolais

charpente [ʃaʀpɑ̃t] NF frame(work); (*fig*) structure, framework; (*carrure*) build, frame

charpenté, e [ʃaʀpɑ̃te] ADJ: **bien** *ou* **solidement ~** (*personne*) well-built; (*texte*) well-constructed

charpenterie [ʃaʀpɑ̃tʀi] NF carpentry

charpentier [ʃaʀpɑ̃tje] NM carpenter

charpie [ʃaʀpi] NF: **en ~** (*fig*) in shreds *ou* ribbons

charretier [ʃaʀtje] NM carter; (*péj: langage, manières*): **de ~** uncouth

charrette [ʃaʀɛt] NF cart

charrier [ʃaʀje] /7/ VT to carry (along); to cart, carry ▸ VI (*fam*) to exaggerate

charrue [ʃaʀy] NF plough (BRIT), plow (US)

charte [ʃaʀt] NF charter

charter [ʃaʀtɛʀ] NM (*vol*) charter flight; (*avion*) charter plane

★**chasse** [ʃas] NF hunting; (*au fusil*) shooting; (*poursuite*) chase; (*aussi:* **chasse d'eau**) flush; **la ~ est ouverte** the hunting season is open; **la ~ est fermée** it is the close (BRIT) *ou* closed (US) season; **aller à la ~** to go hunting; **prendre en ~, donner la ~ à** to give chase to; **tirer la ~ (d'eau)** to flush the toilet, pull the chain; **~ aérienne** aerial pursuit; **~ à courre** hunting; **~ à l'homme** manhunt; **~ gardée** private hunting grounds *pl*; **~ sous-marine** underwater fishing

châsse [ʃas] NF reliquary, shrine

chassé-croisé [ʃasekʀwaze] (*pl* **chassés-croisés**) NM (*Danse*) chassé-croisé; (*fig*) mix-up (*where people miss each other in turn*)

chasse-neige [ʃasnɛʒ] NM INV snowplough (BRIT), snowplow (US)

★**chasser** [ʃase] /1/ VT to hunt; (*expulser*) to chase away *ou* out, drive away *ou* out; (*dissiper*) to chase *ou* sweep away; to dispel, drive away

chasseur, -euse [ʃasœʀ, -øz] NM/F hunter; **~ d'images** roving photographer; **~ de têtes** (*fig*) headhunter ▸ NM (*avion*) fighter; (*domestique*) page (boy), messenger (boy); **chasseurs alpins** mountain infantry

chassieux, -euse [ʃasjø, -øz] ADJ sticky, gummy

châssis [ʃasi] NM (*Auto*) chassis; (*cadre*) frame; (*de jardin*) cold frame

chaste [ʃast] ADJ chaste

chasteté [ʃastəte] NF chastity

chasuble [ʃazybl] NF chasuble; **robe ~** pinafore dress (BRIT), jumper (US)

★**chat**[1] [ʃa] NM cat; **~ sauvage** wildcat

chat[2] [tʃat] NM (*Internet: salon*) chat room; (: *conversation*) chat

châtaigne [ʃatɛɲ] NF chestnut

châtaignier [ʃatɛɲe] NM chestnut (tree)

châtain [ʃatɛ̃] ADJ INV chestnut (brown); (*personne*) chestnut-haired

château, x [ʃato] NM (*forteresse*) castle; (*résidence royale*) palace; (*manoir*) mansion; **~ d'eau** water tower; **~ fort** stronghold, fortified castle; **~ de sable** sand castle

châtelain, e [ʃat(ə)lɛ̃, -ɛn] NM/F lord/lady of the manor ▸ NF (*ceinture*) chatelaine

châtié, e [ʃɑtje] ADJ (langage) refined; (style) polished, refined

châtier [ʃɑtje] /7/ VT to punish, castigate; (fig: style) to polish, refine

chatière [ʃɑtjɛʀ] NF (porte) cat flap

châtiment [ʃɑtimɑ̃] NM punishment, castigation; **~ corporel** corporal punishment

chatoiement [ʃatwamɑ̃] NM shimmer(ing)

chaton [ʃatɔ̃] NM (Zool) kitten; (Bot) catkin; (de bague) bezel; stone

chatouillement [ʃatujmɑ̃] NM (gén) tickling; (dans le nez, la gorge) tickle

chatouiller [ʃatuje] /1/ VT to tickle; (l'odorat, le palais) to titillate

chatouilleux, -euse [ʃatujø, -øz] ADJ ticklish; (fig) touchy, over-sensitive

chatoyant, e [ʃatwajɑ̃, -ɑ̃t] ADJ (reflet, étoffe) shimmering; (couleurs) sparkling

chatoyer [ʃatwaje] /8/ VI to shimmer

châtrer [ʃɑtʀe] /1/ VT (mâle) to castrate; (femelle) to spay; (cheval) to geld; (chat, chien) to doctor (BRIT), fix (US); (fig) to mutilate

★**chatte** [ʃat] NF (she-)cat

chatter [tʃate] /1/ VI (Internet) to chat

chatterton [ʃatɛʀtɔ̃] NM (ruban isolant: Élec) (adhesive) insulating tape

★**chaud, e** [ʃo, -od] ADJ (gén) warm; (très chaud) hot; (fig: félicitations) warm; (discussion) heated ▶ NM: **tenir au ~** to keep in a warm place; **il fait ~** it's warm; it's hot; **manger ~** to have something hot to eat; **avoir ~** to be warm; to be hot; **tenir ~** to keep hot; **ça me tient ~** it keeps me warm; **rester au ~** to stay in the warm

chaudement [ʃodmɑ̃] ADV warmly; (fig) hotly

chaudière [ʃodjɛʀ] NF boiler

chaudron [ʃodrɔ̃] NM cauldron

chaudronnerie [ʃodrɔnri] NF (usine) boiler-works; (activité) boilermaking; (boutique) coppersmith's workshop

★**chauffage** [ʃofaʒ] NM heating; **~ au gaz/à l'électricité/au charbon** gas/electric/solid fuel heating; **~ central** central heating; **~ par le sol** underfloor heating

chauffagiste [ʃofaʒist] NM (installateur) heating engineer

chauffant, e [ʃofɑ̃, -ɑ̃t] ADJ: **couverture chauffante** electric blanket; **plaque chauffante** hotplate

chauffard [ʃofaʀ] NM (péj) reckless driver; road hog; (: après un accident) hit-and-run driver

chauffe-bain [ʃofbɛ̃] NM = **chauffe-eau**

chauffe-biberon [ʃofbibʀɔ̃] NM (baby's) bottle warmer

chauffe-eau [ʃofo] NM INV water heater

chauffe-plats [ʃofpla] NM INV dish warmer

chauffer [ʃofe] /1/ VT to heat ▶ VI to heat up, warm up; (trop chauffer: moteur) to overheat ■ **se chauffer** VPR (se mettre en train) to warm up; (au soleil) to warm o.s.

chaufferie [ʃofʀi] NF boiler room

★**chauffeur** [ʃofœʀ] NM driver; (privé) chauffeur; **voiture avec/sans ~** chauffeur-driven/self-drive car; **~ de taxi** taxi driver

chauffeuse [ʃoføz] NF fireside chair

chauler [ʃole] /1/ VT (mur) to whitewash

chaume [ʃom] NM (du toit) thatch; (tiges) stubble

chaumière [ʃomjɛʀ] NF (thatched) cottage

chaussée [ʃose] NF road(way); (digue) causeway

chausse-pied [ʃospje] NM shoe-horn

chausser [ʃose] /1/ VT (bottes, skis) to put on; (enfant) to put shoes on; **~ du 38/42** to take size 38/42 ▶ VI (souliers): **~ grand/bien** to be big-/well-fitting ■ **se chausser** VPR to put one's shoes on

chausse-trappe [ʃostʀap] NF trap

★**chaussette** [ʃosɛt] NF sock

chausseur [ʃosœʀ] NM (marchand) footwear specialist, shoemaker

★**chausson** [ʃosɔ̃] NM slipper; (de bébé) bootee; **~ (aux pommes)** (apple) turnover

★**chaussure** [ʃosyʀ] NF shoe; (commerce): **la ~** the shoe industry ou trade; **chaussures basses** flat shoes; **chaussures montantes** ankle boots; **chaussures de ski** ski boots

chaut [ʃo] VB: **peu me ~** it matters little to me

★**chauve** [ʃov] ADJ bald

chauve-souris [ʃovsuʀi] (pl **chauves-souris**) NF bat

chauvin, e [ʃovɛ̃, -in] ADJ chauvinistic; jingoistic

chauvinisme [ʃovinism] NM chauvinism; jingoism

chaux [ʃo] NF lime; **blanchi à la ~** whitewashed

chavirer [ʃaviʀe] /1/ VI to capsize, overturn

★**chef** [ʃef] NM head, leader; (patron) boss; (de cuisine) chef; **au premier ~** extremely, to the nth degree; **de son propre ~** on his ou her own initiative; **général/commandant en ~** general-/commander-in-chief; **~ d'accusation** (Jur) charge, count (of indictment); **~ d'atelier** (shop) foreman; **~ de bureau** head clerk; **~ de clinique** senior hospital lecturer; **~ d'entreprise** company head; **~ d'équipe** team leader; **~ d'état** head of state; **~ de famille** head of the family; **~ de file** (de parti etc) leader; **~ de gare** station master; **~ d'orchestre** conductor (BRIT), leader (US); **~ de rayon** department(al) supervisor; **~ de service** departmental head

chef is not the most common translation of the French word **chef**.

chef-d'œuvre [ʃɛdœvʀ] (pl **chefs-d'œuvre**) NM masterpiece

chef-lieu [ʃɛfljø] (pl **chefs-lieux**) NM county town

cheftaine [ʃɛftɛn] NF (guide) captain

cheik, cheikh [ʃɛk] NM sheik

chelou [ʃəlu] ADJ INV (fam) shady, dodgy (BRIT)

★**chemin** [ʃ(ə)mɛ̃] NM path; (itinéraire, direction, trajet) way; **en ~, ~ faisant** on the way; **~ de fer** (BRIT), railroad (US); **par ~ de fer** by rail; **les chemins de fer** the railways (BRIT), the railroad (US); **~ de terre** dirt track

cheminée [ʃ(ə)mine] NF chimney; (à l'intérieur) chimney piece, fireplace; (de bateau) funnel

cheminement [ʃ(ə)minmɑ̃] NM progress; course

cheminer [ʃ(ə)mine] /1/ VI to walk (along)

cheminot [ʃ(ə)mino] NM railwayman (BRIT), railroad worker (US)

★**chemise** [ʃ(ə)miz] NF shirt; (*dossier*) folder; **~ de nuit** nightdress

chemiserie [ʃ(ə)mizri] NF (gentlemen's) outfitters'

chemisette [ʃ(ə)mizɛt] NF short-sleeved shirt

★**chemisier** [ʃ(ə)mizje] NM blouse

chenal, -aux [ʃənal, -o] NM channel

chenapan [ʃ(ə)napã] NM (*garnement*) rascal; (*péj: vaurien*) rogue

chêne [ʃɛn] NM oak (tree); (*bois*) oak

chenet [ʃ(ə)nɛ] NM fire-dog, andiron

chenil [ʃ(ə)nil] NM kennels pl

chenille [ʃ(ə)nij] NF (*Zool*) caterpillar; (*Auto*) caterpillar track; **véhicule à chenilles** tracked vehicle, caterpillar

chenillette [ʃ(ə)nijɛt] NF tracked vehicle

cheptel [ʃɛptɛl] NM livestock

chèque [ʃɛk] NM cheque (BRIT), check (US); **faire/ toucher un ~** to write/cash a cheque; **par ~** by cheque; **~ barré/sans provision** crossed (BRIT)/ bad cheque; **~ en blanc** blank cheque; **~ au porteur** cheque to bearer; **~ postal** post office cheque, ≈ giro cheque (BRIT); **~ de voyage** traveller's cheque

chèque-cadeau [ʃɛkkado] (*pl* **chèques-cadeaux**) NM gift token

chèque-repas [ʃɛkʀəpa] (*pl* **chèques-repas**), **chèque-restaurant** [ʃɛkʀɛstɔʀɑ̃] (*pl* **chèques-restaurant**) NM ≈ luncheon voucher

chéquier [ʃekje] NM cheque book (BRIT), checkbook (US)

★**cher, -ère** [ʃɛʀ] ADJ (*aimé*) dear; (*coûteux*) expensive, dear; **mon ~, ma chère** my dear ▸ ADV: **coûter/ payer ~** to cost/pay a lot; **cela coûte ~** it's expensive, it costs a lot of money ▸ NF: **la bonne chère** good food

★**chercher** [ʃɛʀʃe] /1/ VT to look for; (*gloire etc*) to seek; **~ des ennuis/la bagarre** to be looking for trouble/a fight; **aller ~** to go for, go and fetch; **~ à faire** to try to do

chercheur, -euse [ʃɛʀʃœʀ, -øz] NM/F researcher, research worker; **~ de** seeker of; hunter of; **~ d'or** gold digger

chère [ʃɛʀ] ADJ F, NF *voir* **cher**

chèrement [ʃɛʀmɑ̃] ADV dearly

chéri, e [ʃeʀi] ADJ beloved, dear; **(mon) ~** darling

chérir [ʃeʀiʀ] /2/ VT to cherish

cherté [ʃɛʀte] NF: **la ~ de la vie** the high cost of living

chérubin [ʃeʀybɛ̃] NM cherub

chétif, -ive [ʃetif, -iv] ADJ puny, stunted

★**cheval, -aux** [ʃ(ə)val, -o] NM horse; (*Auto*): **~ (vapeur)** horsepower no pl; **50 chevaux (au frein)** 50 brake horsepower, 50 b.h.p.; **10 chevaux (fiscaux)** 10 horsepower (for tax purposes); **faire du ~** to ride; **à ~** on horseback; **à ~ sur** astride, straddling; (*fig*) overlapping; **~ d'arçons** vaulting horse; **~ à bascule** rocking horse; **~ de bataille** charger; (*fig*) hobby-horse; **~ de course** race horse; **chevaux de bois** (*des manèges*) wooden (fairground) horses; (*manège*) merry-go-round

chevaleresque [ʃ(ə)valʀɛsk] ADJ chivalrous

chevalerie [ʃ(ə)valʀi] NF chivalry; knighthood

chevalet [ʃ(ə)valɛ] NM easel

chevalier [ʃ(ə)valje] NM knight; **~ servant** escort

chevalière [ʃ(ə)valjɛʀ] NF signet ring

chevalin, e [ʃ(ə)valɛ̃, -in] ADJ of horses, equine; (*péj*) horsy; **boucherie chevaline** horse-meat butcher's

cheval-vapeur [ʃəvalvapœʀ] (*pl* **chevaux-vapeur**) NM *voir* **cheval**

chevauchée [ʃ(ə)voʃe] NF ride; cavalcade

chevauchement [ʃ(ə)voʃmɑ̃] NM overlap

chevaucher [ʃ(ə)voʃe] /1/ VI (*aussi:* **se chevaucher**) to overlap (each other) ▸ VT to be astride, straddle

chevaux [ʃəvo] NMPL *voir* **cheval**

chevelu, e [ʃəv(ə)ly] ADJ with a good head of hair, hairy (*péj*)

chevelure [ʃəv(ə)lyʀ] NF hair no pl

chevet [ʃ(ə)vɛ] NM: **au ~ de qn** at sb's bedside; **lampe de ~** bedside lamp

cheveu, x [ʃ(ə)vø] NM hair ▸ NMPL (*chevelure*) hair sg; **avoir les cheveux courts/en brosse** to have short hair/a crew cut; **se faire couper les cheveux** to get ou have one's hair cut; **tiré par les cheveux** (*histoire*) far-fetched

★**cheville** [ʃ(ə)vij] NF (*Anat*) ankle; (*de bois*) peg; (*pour enfoncer une vis*) plug; **être en ~ avec qn** to be in cahoots with sb; **~ ouvrière** (*fig*) kingpin

chèvre [ʃɛvʀ] NF (she-)goat; **ménager la ~ et le chou** to try to please everyone

chevreau, x [ʃəvʀo] NM kid

chèvrefeuille [ʃɛvʀəfœj] NM honeysuckle

chevreuil [ʃəvʀœj] NM roe deer inv; (*Culin*) venison

chevron [ʃəvʀɔ̃] NM (*poutre*) rafter; (*motif*) chevron, v(-shape); **à chevrons** chevron-patterned; (*petits*) herringbone

chevronné, e [ʃəvʀɔne] ADJ seasoned, experienced

chevrotant, e [ʃəvʀɔtɑ̃, -ɑ̃t] ADJ quavering

chevroter [ʃəvʀɔte] /1/ VI (*personne, voix*) to quaver

chevrotine [ʃəvʀɔtin] NF buckshot no pl

chewing-gum [ʃwiŋɡɔm] NM chewing gum

---

chez [ʃe]

PRÉP **1** (*à la demeure de*) at; (: *direction*) to; **chez qn** at/to sb's house ou place; **je suis chez moi** I'm at home; **je rentre chez moi** I'm going home; **allons chez Nathalie** let's go to Nathalie's

2 (*+profession*) at; (: *direction*) to; **chez le boulanger/dentiste** at ou to the baker's/dentist's

3 (*dans le caractère, l'œuvre de*) in; **chez les renards/ Racine** in foxes/Racine; **chez ce poète** in this poet's work; **chez les Français** among the French; **chez lui, c'est un devoir** for him, it's a duty; **c'est ce que je préfère chez lui** that's what I like best about him

4 (*à l'entreprise de*): **il travaille chez Renault** he works for Renault, he works at Renault('s)

▸ NM INV: **mon chez moi/ton chez toi** etc my/ your etc home ou place

---

chez-soi [ʃeswa] NM INV home

Chf. cent. ABR (= *chauffage central*) c.h.

chiadé, e [ʃjade] ADJ (*fam: fignolé, soigné*) wicked

chialer [ʃjale] /1/ VI (*fam*) to blubber; **arrête de ~ !** stop blubbering!

chiant, e [ʃjɑ̃, -ɑ̃t] ADJ (!) bloody annoying (BRIT), damn annoying; **qu'est-ce qu'il est ~ !** he's such a bloody pain! (!)

★**chic** [ʃik] ADJ INV chic, smart; (*généreux*) nice, decent ▶ NM stylishness; **avoir le ~ de** ou **pour** to have the knack of ou for; **de ~** adv off the cuff; **~ !** great!, terrific!

chicane [ʃikan] NF (*obstacle*) zigzag; (*querelle*) squabble

chicaner [ʃikane] /1/ VI (*ergoter*): **~ sur** to quibble about

chiche [ʃiʃ] ADJ (*mesquin*) niggardly, mean; (*pauvre*) meagre (BRIT), meager (US) ▶ EXCL (*en réponse à un défi*) you're on!; **tu n'es pas ~ de lui parler !** you wouldn't (dare) speak to her!

chichement [ʃiʃmɑ̃] ADV (*pauvrement*) meagrely (BRIT), meagerly (US); (*mesquinement*) meanly

chichis [ʃiʃi] NMPL (*fam*) fuss; **faire des ~** to make a fuss

chicorée [ʃikɔʀe] NF (*café*) chicory; (*salade*) endive; **~ frisée** curly endive

chicot [ʃiko] NM stump

★**chien** [ʃjɛ̃] NM dog; (*de pistolet*) hammer; **temps de ~** rotten weather; **vie de ~** dog's life; **couché en ~ de fusil** curled up; **~ d'aveugle** guide dog; **~ de chasse** gun dog; **~ de garde** guard dog; **~ policier** police dog; **~ de race** pedigree dog; **~ de traîneau** husky

chiendent [ʃjɛ̃dɑ̃] NM couch grass

chien-loup [ʃjɛ̃lu] (*pl* **chiens-loups**) NM wolfhound

★**chienne** [ʃjɛn] NF (she-)dog, bitch

chier [ʃje] /7/ VI (!) to crap (!), shit (!); **faire ~ qn** (*importuner*) to bug sb; (*causer des ennuis à*) to piss sb around (!); **se faire ~** (*s'ennuyer*) to be bored rigid

chiffe [ʃif] NF: **il est mou comme une ~, c'est une ~ molle** he's spineless ou wet

chiffon [ʃifɔ̃] NM (*piece of*) rag

chiffonné, e [ʃifɔne] ADJ (*fatigué: visage*) worn-looking

chiffonner [ʃifɔne] /1/ VT to crumple, crease; (*tracasser*) to concern

chiffonnier [ʃifɔnje] NM ragman, rag-and-bone man; (*meuble*) chiffonier

chiffrable [ʃifʀabl] ADJ numerable

★**chiffre** [ʃifʀ] NM (*représentant un nombre*) figure; numeral; (*montant, total*) total, sum; (*d'un code*) code, cipher; **chiffres romains/arabes** Roman/Arabic figures ou numerals; **en chiffres ronds** in round figures; **écrire un nombre en chiffres** to write a number in figures; **~ d'affaires** turnover; **~ de ventes** sales figures

chiffrer [ʃifʀe] /1/ VT (*dépense*) to put a figure to, assess; (*message*) to (en)code, cipher ▶ VI (*fam*) to add up ■ **se chiffrer à** VPR to add up to

chignole [ʃiɲɔl] NF drill

chignon [ʃiɲɔ̃] NM chignon, bun

chiite [ʃiit] ADJ, NMF Shiite

Chili [ʃili] NM: **le ~** Chile

chilien, ne [ʃiljɛ̃, -ɛn] ADJ Chilean ▶ NM/F: **Chilien, ne** Chilean

chimère [ʃimɛʀ] NF (wild) dream, pipe dream, idle fancy

chimérique [ʃimerik] ADJ (*utopique*) fanciful

★**chimie** [ʃimi] NF chemistry

chimio [ʃimjɔ], **chimiothérapie** [ʃimjɔteʀapi] NF chemotherapy

chimiothérapie [ʃimjɔteʀapi] NF chemotherapy

★**chimique** [ʃimik] ADJ chemical; **produits chimiques** chemicals

chimiste [ʃimist] NMF chemist

chimpanzé [ʃɛ̃pɑ̃ze] NM chimpanzee

chinchilla [ʃɛ̃ʃila] NM chinchilla

★**Chine** [ʃin] NF: **la ~** China; **la République de ~** the Republic of China, Nationalist China (*Taiwan*)

chine [ʃin] NM rice paper; (*porcelaine*) china (vase)

chiné, e [ʃine] ADJ flecked

★**chinois, e** [ʃinwa, -waz] ADJ Chinese; (*fig: péj*) pernickety, fussy ▶ NM (*Ling*) Chinese ▶ NM/F: **Chinois, e** Chinese

chinoiserie [ʃinwazʀi] NF, **chinoiseries** NFPL (*péj*) red tape, fuss

chiot [ʃjo] NM pup(py)

chiper [ʃipe] /1/ VT (*fam*) to pinch

chipie [ʃipi] NF shrew

chipolata [ʃipɔlata] NF chipolata

chipoter [ʃipɔte] /1/ VI (*manger*) to nibble; (*ergoter*) to quibble, haggle

★**chips** [ʃips] NFPL (*aussi:* **pommes chips**) crisps (BRIT), (potato) chips (US)

chique [ʃik] NF quid, chew

chiquenaude [ʃiknod] NF flick, flip

chiquer [ʃike] /1/ VI to chew tobacco

chiromancie [kiʀɔmɑ̃si] NF palmistry

chiromancien, ne [kiʀɔmɑ̃sjɛ̃, -ɛn] NM/F palmist

chiropracteur [kiʀɔpʀaktœʀ] NM, **chiropraticien, ne** [kiʀɔpʀatisjɛ̃, -ɛn] NM/F chiropractor

chirurgical, e, -aux [ʃiʀyʀʒikal, -o] ADJ surgical

chirurgie [ʃiʀyʀʒi] NF surgery; **~ esthétique** cosmetic ou plastic surgery

★**chirurgien, ne** [ʃiʀyʀʒjɛ̃, -ɛn] NM/F surgeon; **~ dentiste** dental surgeon

chiure [ʃjyʀ] NF: **chiures de mouche** fly specks

ch.-l. ABR = **chef-lieu**

chlore [klɔʀ] NM chlorine

chloroforme [klɔʀɔfɔʀm] NM chloroform

chlorophylle [klɔʀɔfil] NF chlorophyll

chlorure [klɔʀyʀ] NM chloride

choc [ʃɔk] NM (*heurt*) impact; (*Méd, Psych*) shock; (*collision*) crash; (*affrontement*) clash; **de ~** (*troupe, traitement*) shock cpd; (*patron etc*) high-powered; **~ opératoire/nerveux** post-operative/nervous shock; **~ en retour** return shock; (*fig*) backlash ▶ ADJ (*pl ~* ou **chocs**): **prix ~** amazing ou incredible price/prices

★**chocolat** [ʃɔkɔla] NM chocolate; (*boisson*) (hot) chocolate; **~ chaud** hot chocolate; **~ à cuire** cooking chocolate; **~ au lait** milk chocolate; **~ en poudre** drinking chocolate

chocolaté, e [ʃɔkɔlate] ADJ chocolate cpd, chocolate-flavoured

chocolaterie [ʃɔkɔlatʀi] NF (fabrique) chocolate factory

chocolatier, -ière [ʃɔkɔlatje, -jɛʀ] NM/F chocolate maker

chœur [kœʀ] NM (chorale) choir; (Opéra, Théât) chorus; (Archit) choir, chancel; **en ~** in chorus

choir [ʃwaʀ] VI to fall

choisi, e [ʃwazi] ADJ (de premier choix) carefully chosen; select; **textes choisis** selected writings

★**choisir** [ʃwaziʀ] /2/ VT to choose; (entre plusieurs) to choose, select; **~ de faire qch** to choose ou opt to do sth

★**choix** [ʃwa] NM choice; selection; **avoir le ~ to** have the choice; **je n'avais pas le ~** I had no choice; **de premier ~** (Comm) class ou grade one; **de ~** choice cpd, selected; **au ~** as you wish ou prefer; **de mon/son ~** of my/his ou her choosing

choléra [kɔleʀa] NM cholera

cholestérol [kɔlɛsteʀɔl] NM cholesterol

chômage [ʃomaʒ] NM unemployment; **mettre au ~** to make redundant, put out of work; **être au ~** to be unemployed ou out of work; **~ partiel** short-time working; **~ structurel** structural unemployment; **~ technique** lay-offs pl

chômé [ʃome] ADJ: **jour ~** public holiday

chômer [ʃome] /1/ VI to be unemployed, be idle

chômeur, -euse [ʃomœʀ, -øz] NM/F unemployed person, person out of work

chope [ʃɔp] NF tankard

choper [ʃɔpe] /1/ VT (fam: objet, maladie) to catch

choquant, e [ʃɔkɑ̃, -ɑ̃t] ADJ shocking

choquer [ʃɔke] /1/ VT (offenser) to shock; (commotionner) to shake (up)

choral, e [kɔʀal] ADJ choral ▶ NF choral society, choir

★**chorale** [kɔʀal] NF choir

chorégraphe [kɔʀegʀaf] NMF choreographer

chorégraphie [kɔʀegʀafi] NF choreography

choriste [kɔʀist] NMF choir member; (Opéra) chorus member

chorus [kɔʀys] NM: **faire ~ (avec)** to voice one's agreement (with)

★**chose** [ʃoz] NF thing; **dire bien des choses à qn** to give sb's regards to sb; **parler de ~(s) et d'autre(s)** to talk about one thing and another; **c'est peu de ~** it's nothing much ▶ ADJ INV: **être/se sentir tout ~** (bizarre) to be/feel a bit odd; (malade) to be/feel out of sorts ▶ NM (fam: machin) thingamajig

★**chou, x** [ʃu] NM cabbage; **mon petit ~** (my) sweetheart; **faire ~ blanc** to draw a blank; **feuille de ~** (fig: journal) rag; **~ à la crème** cream bun (made of choux pastry); **~ de Bruxelles** Brussels sprout ▶ ADJ INV cute

choucas [ʃuka] NM jackdaw

chouchou, te [ʃuʃu, -ut] NM/F (Scol) teacher's pet

chouchouter [ʃuʃute] /1/ VT to pet

choucroute [ʃukʀut] NF sauerkraut; **~ garnie** sauerkraut with cooked meats and potatoes

★**chouette** [ʃwɛt] NF owl ▶ ADJ (fam) great, smashing

★**chou-fleur** [ʃuflœʀ] (pl **choux-fleurs**) NM cauliflower

chou-rave [ʃuʀav] (pl **choux-raves**) NM kohlrabi

chouraver [ʃuʀave] VT (fam) to nick (BRIT), to pinch

choyer [ʃwaje] /8/ VT to cherish; to pamper

CHR SIGLE M = **Centre hospitalier régional**

chrétien, ne [kʀetjɛ̃, -ɛn] ADJ, NM/F Christian

chrétiennement [kʀetjɛnmɑ̃] ADV in a Christian way ou spirit

chrétienté [kʀetjɛ̃te] NF Christendom

Christ [kʀist] NM: **le ~** Christ; **christ** (crucifix etc) figure of Christ; **Jésus ~** Jesus Christ

christianiser [kʀistjanize] /1/ VT to convert to Christianity

christianisme [kʀistjanism] NM Christianity

chromatique [kʀɔmatik] ADJ chromatic

chrome [kʀom] NM chromium; (revêtement) chrome, chromium

chromé, e [kʀome] ADJ chrome-plated, chromium-plated

chromosome [kʀɔmozom] NM chromosome

chronique [kʀɔnik] ADJ chronic ▶ NF (de journal) column, page; (historique) chronicle; (Radio, TV): **la ~ sportive/théâtrale** the sports/theatre review; **la ~ locale** local news and gossip

chroniqueur, -euse [kʀɔnikœʀ, -øz] NM, NF columnist; chronicler

chrono [kʀɔno] NM (fam) = **chronomètre**

chronologie [kʀɔnɔlɔʒi] NF chronology

chronologique [kʀɔnɔlɔʒik] ADJ chronological

chronologiquement [kʀɔnɔlɔʒikmɑ̃] ADV chronologically

chronomètre [kʀɔnɔmɛtʀ] NM stopwatch

chronométrer [kʀɔnɔmetʀe] /6/ VT to time

chronométreur [kʀɔnɔmetʀœʀ] NM timekeeper

chrysalide [kʀizalid] NF chrysalis

chrysanthème [kʀizɑ̃tɛm] NM chrysanthemum

Chrysanthèmes are strongly associated with funerals in France and it is customary to lay them on graves on All Saints' Day (1 November). Because of this association they are never given as gifts.

CHU SIGLE M (= Centre hospitalo-universitaire) ≈ (teaching) hospital

chu, e [ʃy] PP de **choir**

chuchotement [ʃyʃɔtmɑ̃] NM whisper

chuchoter [ʃyʃɔte] /1/ VT, VI to whisper

chuintement [ʃɥɛ̃tmɑ̃] NM hiss

chuinter [ʃɥɛ̃te] /1/ VI to hiss

chut [ʃyt] EXCL sh! ▶ VB [ʃy] voir **choir**

chute [ʃyt] NF fall; (de bois, papier: déchet) scrap; **la ~ des cheveux** hair loss; **faire une ~ (de 10 m)** to fall (10 m); **chutes de pluie/neige** rain/snowfalls; **~ (d'eau)** waterfall; **~ du jour** nightfall; **~ libre** free fall; **~ de reins** small of the back

chuter [ʃyte] VI to fall; **~ lourdement** to fall heavily; **~ dans les sondages** (Premier ministre) to slip in the polls; **faire ~** (gouvernement) to bring down, topple; (*champion*) to topple; **faire ~ les cours** to bring prices down

Chypre [ʃipr] NMF Cyprus

chypriote [ʃipriɔt] ADJ, NMF = **cypriote**

-ci, ci- [si] ADV *voir* **par**; **ci-contre**; **ci-joint** *etc* ▶ ADJ DÉM: **ce garçon-ci/-là** this/that boy; **ces femmes-ci/-là** these/those women

CIA SIGLE F CIA

cial ABR = **commercial**

ciao [tʃao] EXCL (*fam*) (bye-)bye

ci-après [siaprɛ] ADV hereafter

cibiste [sibist] NMF CB enthusiast

cible [sibl] NF target

cibler [sible] /1/ VT to target

ciboire [sibwaʀ] NM ciborium (*vessel*)

ciboule [sibul] NF (large) chive

ciboulette [sibulɛt] NF (small) chive

ciboulot [sibulo] NM (*fam*) head, nut; **il n'a rien dans le ~** he's got nothing between his ears

cicatrice [sikatris] NF scar

cicatriser [sikatrize] /1/ VT to heal ▪ **se cicatriser** VPR to heal (up), form a scar

ci-contre [sikɔ̃tr] ADV opposite

CICR SIGLE M (= *Comité international de la Croix-Rouge*) ICRC

ci-dessous [sidəsu] ADV below

ci-dessus [sidəsy] ADV above

ci-devant [sidəvɑ̃] NMF INV aristocrat who lost his/her title in the French Revolution

CIDJ SIGLE M (= *Centre d'information et de documentation de la jeunesse*) careers advisory service

★**cidre** [sidr] NM cider

cidrerie [sidrəri] NF cider factory

Cie ABR (= *compagnie*) Co

★**ciel** [sjɛl] NM sky; (*Rel*) heaven; **à ~ ouvert** open-air; (*mine*) opencast; **tomber du ~** (*arriver à l'improviste*) to appear out of the blue; (*être stupéfait*) to be unable to believe one's eyes; **C~!** good heavens!; **~ de lit** canopy ▪ **ciels** NMPL (*Peinture etc*) skies ▪ **cieux** NMPL sky *sg*, skies; (*Rel*) heaven *sg*

cierge [sjɛʀʒ] NM candle; **~ pascal** Easter candle

cieux [sjø] NMPL *voir* **ciel**

cigale [sigal] NF cicada

cigare [sigaʀ] NM cigar

★**cigarette** [sigaʀɛt] NF cigarette; **~ (à) bout filtre** filter cigarette; **~ électronique** e-cigarette

ci-gît [siʒi] ADV here lies

cigogne [sigɔɲ] NF stork

ciguë [sigy] NF hemlock

ci-inclus, e [siɛ̃kly, -yz] ADJ, ADV enclosed

ci-joint, e [siʒwɛ̃, -ɛ̃t] ADJ, ADV enclosed; (*to email*) attached; **veuillez trouver ~** please find enclosed *ou* attached

cil [sil] NM (eye)lash

ciller [sije] /1/ VI to blink

cimaise [simɛz] NF picture rail

cime [sim] NF top; (*montagne*) peak

ciment [simɑ̃] NM cement; **~ armé** reinforced concrete

cimenter [simɑ̃te] /1/ VT to cement

cimenterie [simɑ̃tri] NF cement works *sg*

cimetière [simtjɛʀ] NM cemetery; (*d'église*) churchyard; **~ de voitures** scrapyard

cinéaste [sineast] NMF film-maker

ciné-club [sineklœb] NM film club; film society

cinéma [sinema] NM cinema; **aller au ~** to go to the cinema *ou* pictures *ou* movies; **~ d'animation** cartoon (film)

cinémascope® [sinemaskɔp] NM Cinemascope®

cinémathèque [sinematɛk] NF film archives *pl ou* library

cinématographie [sinematɔgrafi] NF cinematography

cinématographique [sinematɔgrafik] ADJ film *cpd*, cinema *cpd*

cinéphile [sinefil] NMF film buff

cinérama® [sinerama] NM: **en ~** in Cinerama®

cinétique [sinetik] ADJ kinetic

cingalais, e, cinghalais, e [sɛ̃galɛ, -ɛz] ADJ Sin(g)halese

cinglant, e [sɛ̃glɑ̃, -ɑ̃t] ADJ (*propos, ironie*) scathing, biting; (*échec*) crushing

cinglé, e [sɛ̃gle] ADJ (*fam*) crazy

cingler [sɛ̃gle] /1/ VT to lash; (*fig*) to sting ▶ VI (*Navig*): **~ vers** to make *ou* head for

★**cinq** [sɛ̃k] NUM five

cinquantaine [sɛ̃kɑ̃tɛn] NF: **une ~ (de)** about fifty; **avoir la ~ (*âge*)** to be around fifty

★**cinquante** [sɛ̃kɑ̃t] NUM fifty

cinquantenaire [sɛ̃kɑ̃tnɛʀ] ADJ, NMF fifty-year-old

cinquantième [sɛ̃kɑ̃tjɛm] NUM fiftieth

cinquième [sɛ̃kjɛm] NUM fifth ▶ NF (*Scol*) year 8 (BRIT), seventh grade (US)

cinquièmement [sɛ̃kjɛmmɑ̃] ADV fifthly

cintre [sɛ̃tr] NM coat-hanger; (*Archit*) arch; **plein ~** semicircular arch

cintré, e [sɛ̃tre] ADJ curved; (*chemise*) fitted, slim-fitting

CIO SIGLE M (= *Comité international olympique*) IOC (= *International Olympic Committee*); (= *Centre d'information et d'orientation*) careers advisory centre

circoncis, e [siʀkɔ̃si, -iz] ADJ circumcised

circoncision [siʀkɔ̃sizjɔ̃] NF circumcision

circonférence [siʀkɔ̃ferɑ̃s] NF circumference

circonflexe [siʀkɔ̃flɛks] ADJ: **accent ~** circumflex accent

circonlocution [siʀkɔ̃lɔkysjɔ̃] NF circumlocution

circonscription [siʀkɔ̃skripsjɔ̃] NF district; **~ électorale** (*d'un député*) constituency; **~ militaire** military area

circonscrire [siʀkɔ̃skriʀ] /39/ VT to define, delimit; (*incendie*) to contain; (*propriété*) to mark out; (*sujet*) to define

circonspect, e [siʀkɔ̃spɛkt] ADJ circumspect, cautious

circonspection [siʀkɔ̃spɛksjɔ̃] NF circumspection, caution

circonstance [siʀkɔ̃stɑ̃s] NF circumstance; (*occasion*) occasion; **œuvre de ~** occasional work; **air de ~** fitting air; **tête de ~** appropriate demeanour (BRIT) *ou* demeanor (US); **circonstances atténuantes** mitigating circumstances

circonstancié, e [siʀkɔ̃stɑ̃sje] ADJ detailed

circonstanciel, le [siʀkɔ̃stɑ̃sjɛl] ADJ: **complément/proposition ~(le)** adverbial phrase/clause

circonvenir [siʀkɔ̃v(ə)niʀ] /22/ VT to circumvent

circonvolutions [siʀkɔ̃vɔlysjɔ̃] NFPL twists, convolutions

circuit [siʀkчi] NM (*trajet*) tour, (round) trip; (*Élec, Tech*) circuit; **~ automobile** motor circuit; **~ de distribution** distribution network; **~ fermé** closed circuit; **~ intégré** integrated circuit

circulaire [siʀkylɛʀ] ADJ, NF circular

★**circulation** [siʀkylasjɔ̃] NF circulation; (*Auto*): **la ~** (the) traffic; **bonne/mauvaise ~** good/bad circulation; **mettre en ~** to put into circulation

circulatoire [siʀkylatwaʀ] ADJ: **avoir des troubles circulatoires** to have problems with one's circulation

circuler [siʀkyle] /1/ VI (*véhicules*) to drive (along); (*passants*) to walk along; (*train etc*) to run; (*sang, devises*) to circulate; **faire ~** (*nouvelle*) to spread (about), circulate; (*badauds*) to move on

cire [siʀ] NF wax; **~ à cacheter** sealing wax

ciré [siʀe] NM oilskin

cirer [siʀe] /1/ VT to wax, polish

cireur [siʀœʀ] NM shoeshine boy

cireuse [siʀøz] NF floor polisher

cireux, -euse [siʀø, -øz] ADJ (*fig: teint*) sallow, waxen

★**cirque** [siʀk] NM circus; (*arène*) amphitheatre (BRIT), amphitheater (US); (*Géo*) cirque; (*fig: désordre*) chaos, bedlam; (: *chichis*) carry-on; **quel ~!** what a carry-on!

cirrhose [siʀoz] NF: **~ du foie** cirrhosis of the liver

cisaille [sizaj] NF, **cisailles** NFPL (gardening) shears pl

cisailler [sizaje] /1/ VT to clip

ciseau, x [sizo] NM: **~ (à bois)** chisel; **~ à froid** cold chisel ▶ NMPL (*paire de ciseaux*) (pair of) scissors; **sauter en ciseaux** to do a scissors jump

ciseler [siz(ə)le] /5/ VT to chisel, carve

ciselure [siz(ə)lyʀ] NF engraving; (*bois*) carving

Cisjordanie [sisʒɔʀdani] NF: **la ~** the West Bank (of Jordan)

citadelle [sitadɛl] NF citadel

citadin, e [sitadɛ̃, -in] NM/F city dweller ▶ ADJ town *cpd*, city *cpd*, urban

citation [sitasjɔ̃] NF (*d'auteur*) quotation; (*Jur*) summons *sg*; (*Mil: récompense*) mention

cité [site] NF town; (*plus grande*) city; **~ ouvrière** (workers') housing estate; **~ universitaire** students' residences *pl*

cité-dortoir [sitedɔʀtwaʀ] (*pl* **cités-dortoirs**) NF dormitory town

cité-jardin [siteʒaʀdɛ̃] (*pl* **cités-jardins**) NF garden city

citer [site] /1/ VT (*un auteur*) to quote (from); (*nommer*) to name; (*Jur*) to summon; **~ (en exemple)** (*per-*

sonne) to hold up (as an example); **je ne veux ~ personne** I don't want to name names

citerne [sitɛʀn] NF tank

cithare [sitaʀ] NF zither

citoyen, ne [sitwajɛ̃, -ɛn] NM/F citizen ▶ ADJ (*mouvement, rencontre*) citizens *cpd*; **initiative citoyenne** citizens' initiative

citoyenneté [sitwajɛnte] NF citizenship

citrique [sitʀik] ADJ: **acide ~** citric acid

★**citron** [sitʀɔ̃] NM lemon; **~ pressé** (fresh) lemon juice; **~ vert** lime

citronnade [sitʀɔnad] NF still lemonade

citronné, e [sitʀɔne] ADJ (*boisson*) lemon-flavoured (BRIT) *ou* -flavored (US); (*eau de toilette*) lemon-scented

citronnelle [sitʀɔnɛl] NF citronella

citronnier [sitʀɔnje] NM lemon tree

citrouille [sitʀuj] NF pumpkin

cive [siv] NF chive

civet [sivɛ] NM stew; **~ de lièvre** jugged hare; **~ de lapin** rabbit stew

civette [sivɛt] NF (*Bot*) chives *pl*; (*Zool*) civet (cat)

civière [sivjɛʀ] NF stretcher

civil, e [sivil] ADJ (*Jur, Admin, poli*) civil; (*non militaire*) civilian ▶ NM/F civilian ▶ NM: **en ~** in civilian clothes; **dans le ~** in civilian life

civilement [sivilmɑ̃] ADV (*poliment*) civilly; **se marier ~** to have a civil wedding

civilisation [sivilizasjɔ̃] NF civilization

civilisé, e [sivilize] ADJ civilized

civiliser [sivilize] /1/ VT to civilize

civilité [sivilite] NF civility; **présenter ses civilités** to present one's compliments

civique [sivik] ADJ civic; **instruction ~** (*Scol*) civics *sg*

civisme [sivism] NM public-spiritedness

cl. ABR (= *centilitre*) cl

clafoutis [klafuti] NM batter pudding (*containing fruit*)

claie [klɛ] NF grid, riddle

★**clair, e** [klɛʀ] ADJ light; (*chambre*) light, bright; (*eau, son, fig*) clear; **bleu ~** light blue; **pour être ~** so as to make it plain; **le plus ~ de son temps/argent** the better part of his time/money ▶ ADV: **voir ~** to see clearly; **y voir ~** (*comprendre*) to understand, see ▶ NM: **mettre au ~** (*notes etc*) to tidy up; **tirer qch au ~** to clear sth up, clarify sth; **en ~** (*non codé*) in clear; **~ de lune** moonlight

claire [klɛʀ] NF: **(huître de) ~** fattened oyster

clairement [klɛʀmɑ̃] ADV clearly

claire-voie [klɛʀvwa] NF: **à ~** letting the light through; openwork *cpd*

clairière [klɛʀjɛʀ] NF clearing

clair-obscur [klɛʀɔpskyʀ] (*pl* **clairs-obscurs**) NM half-light; (*fig*) uncertainty

clairon [klɛʀɔ̃] NM bugle

claironner [klɛʀɔne] /1/ VT (*fig*) to trumpet, shout from the rooftops

clairsemé, e [klɛʀsəme] ADJ sparse

clairvoyance [klɛʀvwajɑ̃s] NF clear-sightedness

clairvoyant, e [klɛʀvwajɑ̃, -ɑ̃t] ADJ perceptive, clear-sighted

clam [klam] NM (*Zool*) clam

clamer [klame] /1/ vt to proclaim

clameur [klamœr] nf clamour (Brit), clamor (US)

clan [klɑ̃] nm clan

clandestin, e [klɑ̃dɛstɛ̃, -in] adj clandestine, covert; (Pol) underground, clandestine; (travailleur, immigration) illegal; **passager ~** stowaway

clandestinement [klɑ̃dɛstinmɑ̃] adv secretly; **s'embarquer ~** to stow away

clandestinité [klɑ̃dɛstinite] nf: **dans la ~** (en secret) under cover; (en se cachant: vivre) underground; **entrer dans la ~** to go underground

clapet [klapɛ] nm (Tech) valve

clapier [klapje] nm (rabbit) hutch

clapotement [klapɔtmɑ̃] nm lap(ping)

clapoter [klapɔte] /1/ vi to lap

clapotis [klapɔti] nm lap(ping)

claquage [klakaʒ] nm pulled ou strained muscle

claque [klak] nf (gifle) slap; (Théât) claque ▶ nm (chapeau) opera hat

claqué, e [klake] adj (fam: épuisé) dead beat (fam)

claquement [klakmɑ̃] nm (de porte: bruit répété) banging; (: bruit isolé) slam

claquemurer [klakmyre] /1/: **se claquemurer** vpr to shut o.s. away, closet o.s.

claquer [klake] /1/ vi (drapeau) to flap; (porte) to bang, slam; (fam: mourir) to snuff it; (coup de feu) to ring out; **elle claquait des dents** her teeth were chattering ▶ vt (porte) to slam, bang; (doigts) to snap; (fam: dépenser) to blow ∎ **se claquer** vpr: **se ~ un muscle** to pull ou strain a muscle

claquettes [klakɛt] nfpl tap-dancing sg; (chaussures) flip-flops

clarification [klarifikasjɔ̃] nf (fig) clarification

clarifier [klarifje] /7/ vt (fig) to clarify

clarinette [klarinɛt] nf clarinet

clarinettiste [klarinetist] nmf clarinettist

clarté [klarte] nf lightness; brightness; (d'un son, de l'eau) clearness; (d'une explication) clarity

clash [klaʃ] nm clash

clasher [klaʃe] (fam) vt to slag off (Brit), to badmouth (US) ▶ vi (personnes) to clash; **ça va ~** it's going to kick off

★**classe** [klas] nf class; (Scol: local) class(room); (: leçon, élèves) class, form; **1ère/2ème** ~ 1st/2nd class; **un (soldat de) deuxième ~** (Mil: armée de terre) ≈ private (soldier); (: armée de l'air) ≈ aircraftman (Brit), ≈ airman basic (US); **de ~** luxury cpd; **faire ses classes** (Mil) to do one's (recruit's) training; **faire la ~** (Scol) to be a ou the teacher; to teach; **aller en ~** to go to school; **aller en ~ verte/de neige/de mer** to go to the countryside/skiing/to the seaside with the school; **~ préparatoire** class which prepares students for the Grandes Écoles entry exams; see note; **~ sociale** social class; **~ touriste** economy class

> **Classes préparatoires**, commonly known as prépas, are the two years of intensive study to prepare students for the competitive entry examinations to the grandes écoles (see entry grand). These extremely demanding courses follow the baccalauréat and are usually done at a lycée. Schools which provide such classes are more highly regarded than those which do not.

classement [klasmɑ̃] nm classifying; filing; grading; closing; (rang: Scol) place; (: Sport) placing; (liste: Scol) class list (in order of merit); (: Sport) placings pl; **premier au ~ général** (Sport) first overall

classer [klase] /1/ vt (idées, livres) to classify; (papiers) to file; (candidat, concurrent) to grade; (personne: juger: péj) to rate; (Jur: affaire) to close; **se premier/dernier** to come first/last; (Sport) to finish first/last

★**classeur** [klasœr] nm (cahier) file; (meuble) filing cabinet; **~ à feuillets mobiles** ring binder

classification [klasifikasjɔ̃] nf classification

classifier [klasifje] /7/ vt to classify

★**classique** [klasik] adj (sobre: coupe etc) classic(al), classical; (habituel) standard, classic; **études classiques** classical studies, classics ▶ nm classic; classical author

claudication [klodikasjɔ̃] nf limp

clause [kloz] nf clause

claustrer [klostre] /1/ vt to confine

claustrophobie [klostrɔfɔbi] nf claustrophobia

clavecin [klav(ə)sɛ̃] nm harpsichord

claveciniste [klav(ə)sinist] nmf harpsichordist

clavicule [klavikyl] nf clavicle, collarbone

★**clavier** [klavje] nm keyboard; (de portable) keypad

clé, clef [kle] nf key; (Mus) clef; (de mécanicien) spanner (Brit), wrench (US); **mettre sous ~** to place under lock and key; **prendre la ~ des champs** to run away, make off; **prix clés en main** (d'une voiture) on-the-road price; (d'un appartement) price with immediate entry; **~ de sol/de fa/d'ut** treble/bass/alto clef; **livre/film** etc **à ~** book/film etc in which real people are depicted under fictitious names; **à la ~** (à la fin) at the end of it all; **~ anglaise** ou **~ à molette** adjustable spanner (Brit) ou wrench, monkey wrench; **~ de contact** ignition key; **~ USB** (Inform) USB key, flash drive; **~ de voûte** keystone ▶ adj inv: **problème/position ~** key problem/position

clématite [klematit] nf clematis

clémence [klemɑ̃s] nf mildness; leniency

clément, e [klemɑ̃, -ɑ̃t] adj (temps) mild; (indulgent) lenient

clémentine [klemɑ̃tin] nf (Bot) clementine

clenche [klɑ̃ʃ] nf latch

cleptomane [klɛptɔman] nmf = **kleptomane**

clerc [klɛr] nm: **~ de notaire** ou **d'avoué** lawyer's clerk

clergé [klɛrʒe] nm clergy

clérical, e, -aux [klerikal, -o] adj clerical

clic [klik] nm (Inform) click

cliché [kliʃe] nm (fig) cliché; (Photo) negative; print; (Typo) (printing) plate; (Ling) cliché

★**client, e** [klijɑ̃, -ɑ̃t] nm/f (acheteur) customer, client; (d'hôtel) guest, patron; (du docteur) patient; (de l'avocat) client

clientèle [klijɑ̃tɛl] nf (du magasin) customers pl, clientèle; (du docteur, de l'avocat) practice; **accorder sa ~ à** to give one's custom to; **retirer sa ~ à** to take one's business away from

cligner [kliɲe] /1/ vi: **~ des yeux** to blink (one's eyes); **~ de l'œil** to wink

clignotant [kliɲɔtɑ̃] NM (*Auto*) indicator

clignoter [kliɲɔte] /1/ VI (*étoiles etc*) to twinkle; (*lumière: à intervalles réguliers*) to flash; (: *vaciller*) to flicker; (*yeux*) to blink

★**climat** [klima] NM climate

climatique [klimatik] ADJ climatic

★**climatisation** [klimatizasjɔ̃] NF air conditioning

climatisé, e [klimatize] ADJ air-conditioned

climatiseur [klimatizœʀ] NM air conditioner

clin d'œil [klɛ̃dœj] NM wink; **en un ~** in a flash

★**clinique** [klinik] ADJ clinical ▸ NF nursing home, (private) clinic

clinquant, e [klɛ̃kɑ̃, -ɑ̃t] ADJ flashy

clip [klip] NM (*pince*) clip; (*boucle d'oreille*) clip-on; (**vidéo**) **~** pop (*ou* promotional) video

clique [klik] NF (*péj: bande*) clique, set; **prendre ses cliques et ses claques** to pack one's bags

★**cliquer** [klike] /1/ VI (*Inform*) to click; **~ deux fois** to double-click; **~ sur** to click on ▸ VT to click

cliqueter [klik(ə)te] /4/ VI to clash; (*ferraille, clefs, monnaie*) to jangle, jingle; (*verres*) to chink

cliquetis [klik(ə)ti] NM jangle; jingle; chink

clitoris [klitɔʀis] NM clitoris

clivage [klivaʒ] NM cleavage; (*fig*) rift, split

clivant, e [klivɑ̃, ɑ̃t] ADJ divisive

cloaque [klɔak] NM (*fig*) cesspit

clochard, e [klɔʃaʀ, -aʀd] NM/F tramp

★**cloche** [klɔʃ] NF (*d'église*) bell; (*fam*) clot; (*chapeau*) cloche (hat); **~ à fromage** cheese-cover

cloche-pied [klɔʃpje]: **à ~** adv on one leg, hopping (along)

clocher [klɔʃe] /1/ NM church tower; (*en pointe*) steeple; **de ~** (*péj*) parochial ▸ VI (*fam*) to be *ou* go wrong

clocheton [klɔʃtɔ̃] NM pinnacle

clochette [klɔʃet] NF bell

clodo [klɔdo] NM (*fam: = clochard*) tramp

cloison [klwazɔ̃] NF partition (wall); **~ étanche** (*fig*) impenetrable barrier, brick wall (*fig*)

cloisonner [klwazɔne] /1/ VT to partition (off), divide up; (*fig*) to compartmentalize

cloître [klwatʀ] NM cloister

cloîtrer [klwatʀe] /1/: **se cloîtrer** VPR to shut o.s. away; (*Rel*) to enter a convent *ou* monastery

clonage [klonaʒ] NM cloning

clone [klon] NM clone

cloner [klone] /1/ VT to clone

clope [klɔp] NM OU F (*fam*) fag (BRIT), cigarette

clopin-clopant [klɔpɛ̃klɔpɑ̃] ADV hobbling along; (*fig*) so-so

clopiner [klɔpine] /1/ VI to hobble along

cloporte [klɔpɔʀt] NM woodlouse

cloque [klɔk] NF blister

cloqué, e [klɔke] ADJ: **étoffe cloquée** seersucker

cloquer [klɔke] /1/ VI (*peau, peinture*) to blister

clore [klɔʀ] /45/ VT to close; **~ une session** (*Inform*) to log out

clos, e [klo, -oz] PP de **clore** ▸ ADJ *voir* **maison**; **huis**; **vase** ▸ NM (enclosed) field

clôt [klo] VB *voir* **clore**

clôture [klotyʀ] NF closure, closing; (*barrière*) enclosure, fence

clôturer [klotyʀe] /1/ VT (*terrain*) to enclose, close off; (*festival, débats*) to close

★**clou** [klu] NM nail; (*Méd*) boil; **le ~ du spectacle** the highlight of the show; **~ de girofle** clove; **pneus à clous** studded tyres ■ **clous** NMPL = **passage clouté**

cloud computing NM cloud computing

clouer [klue] /1/ VT to nail down (*ou* up); (*fig*): **~ sur/contre** to pin to/against

clouté, e [klute] ADJ studded

clown [klun] NM clown; **faire le ~** (*fig*) to clown (about), play the fool

clownerie [klunʀi] NF clowning *no pl*; **faire des clowneries** to clown around

★**club** [klœb] NM club

CM SIGLE F = **chambre des métiers** ▸ SIGLE M = **conseil municipal**; (*Scol*) = **cours moyen**

cm. ABR (= *centimètre*) cm

CMU SIGLE F (= *couverture maladie universelle*) system of free health care for those on low incomes

CNAT SIGLE F (= *Commission nationale d'aménagement du territoire*) national development agency

CNC SIGLE M (= *Conseil national de la consommation*) national consumers' council

CNE SIGLE M (*vieilli: = Contrat nouvelles embauches*) less stringent type of employment contract for use by small companies

CNED SIGLE M (= *Centre national d'enseignement à distance*) ≈ Open University

CNIL SIGLE F (= *Commission nationale de l'informatique et des libertés*) board which enforces law on data protection

CNIT SIGLE M (= *Centre des nouvelles industries et technologies*) exhibition centre in Paris

CNJA SIGLE M (= *Centre national des jeunes agriculteurs*) farmers' union

CNL SIGLE F (= *Confédération nationale du logement*) consumer group for housing

CNRS SIGLE M (= *Centre national de la recherche scientifique*) ≈ SERC (BRIT), ≈ NSF (US)

c/o ABR (= *care of*) c/o

coagulant [kɔagylɑ̃] NM (*Méd*) coagulant

coaguler [kɔagyle] /1/ VI, VT to coagulate ■ **se coaguler** VPR (*sang*) to coagulate

coaliser [kɔalize] /1/: **se coaliser** VPR to unite, join forces

coalition [kɔalisjɔ̃] NF coalition

coasser [kɔase] /1/ VI to croak

coauteur [kɔotœʀ] NM co-author

coaxial, e, -aux [kɔaksjal, -o] ADJ coaxial

cobaye [kɔbaj] NM guinea-pig

COBOL, Cobol [kɔbɔl] NM COBOL, Cobol

cobra [kɔbʀa] NM cobra

★**coca**® [kɔka] NM Coke®

cocagne [kɔkaɲ] NF: **pays de ~** land of plenty; **mât de ~** greasy pole (*fig*)

cocaïne [kɔkain] NF cocaine

cocarde [kɔkaʀd] NF rosette

cocardier, -ière [kɔkaʀdje, -jɛʀ] ADJ jingoistic, chauvinistic; militaristic

83

cocasse [kɔkas] ADJ comical, funny

coccinelle [kɔksinɛl] NF ladybird (BRIT), ladybug (US)

coccyx [kɔksis] NM coccyx

★**cocher** [kɔʃe] /1/ NM coachman ▸ VT to tick off; (*entailler*) to notch

cochère [kɔʃɛR] ADJ F *voir* **porte**

★**cochon, ne** [kɔʃɔ̃, -ɔn] NM pig; ~ **d'Inde** guinea pig; ~ **de lait** (*Culin*) sucking pig ▸ NM/F (*péj: sale*) (filthy) pig; (: *méchant*) swine ▸ ADJ (*fam*) dirty, smutty

cochonnaille [kɔʃɔnaj] NF (*péj: charcuterie*) (cold) pork

cochonnerie [kɔʃɔnRi] NF (*fam: saleté*) filth; (: *marchandises*) rubbish, trash

cochonnet [kɔʃɔnɛ] NM (*Boules*) jack

cocker [kɔkɛR] NM cocker spaniel

cocktail [kɔktɛl] NM cocktail; (*réception*) cocktail party

coco [kɔko] NM *voir* **noix**; (*fam*) bloke (BRIT), dude (US)

cocon [kɔkɔ̃] NM cocoon

cocorico [kɔkɔRiko] EXCL, NM cock-a-doodle-do

cocotier [kɔkɔtje] NM coconut palm

cocotte [kɔkɔt] NF (*en fonte*) casserole; **ma ~** (*fam*) sweetie (pie); ~ **(minute)**® pressure cooker; ~ **en papier** paper shape

cocu [kɔky] NM (*fam*) cuckold

cocufier [kɔkyfje] VT (*fam*) to be unfaithful to

★**code** [kɔd] NM code; ~ **(à) barres** bar code; ~ **de caractère** (*Inform*) character code; ~ **civil** Common Law; ~ **machine** machine code; ~ **pénal** penal code; ~ **postal** (*numéro*) postcode (BRIT), zip code (US); ~ **de la route** highway code; ~ **secret** cipher; **se mettre en ~(s)** to dip (BRIT) *ou* dim (US) one's (head)lights ▸ ADJ: **phares codes** dipped lights

codéine [kɔdein] NF codeine

coder [kɔde] /1/ VT to (en)code

codétenu, e [kɔdet(ə)ny] NM/F fellow prisoner *ou* inmate

codicille [kɔdisil] NM codicil

codifier [kɔdifje] /7/ VT to codify

codirecteur, -trice [kɔdiRɛktœR, -tRis] NM/F co-director

coéditeur, -trice [kɔeditœR, -tRis] NM/F co-publisher; (*rédacteur*) co-editor

coefficient [kɔefisjɑ̃] NM coefficient; ~ **d'erreur** margin of error

coéquipier, -ière [kɔekipje, -jɛR] NM/F teammate, partner

coercitif, -ive [kɔɛRsitif, iv] ADJ (*mesures, moyens*) coercive

coercition [kɔɛRsisjɔ̃] NF coercion

cœur [kœR] NM heart; (*Cartes: couleur*) hearts *pl*; (: *carte*) heart; (*Culin*): ~ **de laitue/d'artichaut** lettuce/artichoke heart; (*fig*): ~ **du débat** heart of the debate; ~ **de l'été** height of summer; ~ **de la forêt** depths *pl* of the forest; **affaire de** ~ love affair; **avoir bon** ~ to be kind-hearted; **avoir mal au** ~ to feel sick; **contre** *ou* **sur son** ~ to one's breast; **opérer qn à** ~ **ouvert** to perform open-heart surgery on sb; **recevoir qn à** ~ **ouvert**

to welcome sb with open arms; **parler à** ~ **ouvert** to open one's heart; **de tout son** ~ with all one's heart; **avoir le** ~ **gros** *ou* **serré** to have a heavy heart; **en avoir le** ~ **net** to be clear in one's own mind (about it); **par** ~ by heart; **de bon** ~ willingly; **avoir à** ~ **de faire** to be very keen to do; **cela lui tient à** ~ that's (very) close to his heart; **prendre les choses à** ~ to take things to heart; **à** ~ **joie** to one's heart's content; **être de tout** ~ **avec qn** to be (completely) in accord with sb

coexistence [kɔɛgzistɑ̃s] NF coexistence

coexister [kɔɛgziste] /1/ VI to coexist

coffrage [kɔfRaʒ] NM (*Constr: dispositif*) form(work)

★**coffre** [kɔfR] NM (*meuble*) chest; (*coffre-fort*) safe; (*d'auto*) boot (BRIT), trunk (US); **avoir du** ~ (*fam*) to have a lot of puff

coffre-fort [kɔfRəfɔR] (*pl* **coffres-forts**) NM safe

coffrer [kɔfRe] /1/ VT (*fam*) to put inside, lock up

coffret [kɔfRɛ] NM casket; ~ **à bijoux** jewel box

cogérant, e [kɔʒeRɑ̃, -ɑ̃t] NM/F joint manager/manageress

cogestion [kɔʒestjɔ̃] NF joint management

cogiter [kɔʒite] /1/ VI to cogitate

cognac [kɔɲak] NM brandy, cognac

cognement [kɔɲmɑ̃] NM knocking

★**cogner** [kɔɲe] /1/ VI to knock, bang ■ **se cogner** VPR to bump o.s.; **se ~ contre** to knock *ou* bump into; **se ~ la tête** to bang one's head

cohabitation [kɔabitasjɔ̃] NF living together; (*Pol, Jur*) cohabitation

cohabiter [kɔabite] /1/ VI to live together

cohérence [kɔeRɑ̃s] NF coherence

cohérent, e [kɔeRɑ̃, -ɑ̃t] ADJ coherent, consistent

cohésion [kɔezjɔ̃] NF cohesion

cohorte [kɔɔRt] NF troop

cohue [kɔy] NF crowd

coi, coite [kwa, kwat] ADJ: **rester** ~ to remain silent

coiffe [kwaf] NF headdress

coiffé, e [kwafe] ADJ: **bien/mal** ~ with tidy/untidy hair; ~ **d'un béret** wearing a beret; ~ **en arrière** with one's hair brushed *ou* combed back; ~ **en brosse** with a crew cut

coiffer [kwafe] /1/ VT (*fig: surmonter*) to cover, top; ~ **qn** to do sb's hair; ~ **qn d'un béret** to put a beret on sb ■ **se coiffer** VPR to do one's hair; to put on a *ou* one's hat

★**coiffeur, -euse** [kwafœR, -øz] NM/F hairdresser ▸ NF (*table*) dressing table

★**coiffure** [kwafyR] NF (*cheveux*) hairstyle, hairdo; (*chapeau*) hat, headgear *no pl*; (*art*): **la** ~ hairdressing

★**coin** [kwɛ̃] NM corner; (*pour graver*) die; (*pour coincer*) wedge; (*poinçon*) hallmark; **l'épicerie du** ~ the local grocer; **dans le** ~ (*aux alentours*) in the area, around about; (*habiter*) locally; **je ne suis pas du** ~ I'm not from here; **au** ~ **du feu** by the fireside; **du** ~ **de l'œil** out of the corner of one's eye; **regard en** ~ side(ways) glance; **sourire en** ~ half-smile

coincé, e [kwɛ̃se] ADJ stuck, jammed; (*fig: inhibé*) inhibited, with hang-ups

coincer [kwɛ̃se] /3/ VT to jam; (*fam*) to catch (out); to nab ■ **se coincer** VPR to get stuck *ou* jammed

coïncidence [kɔɛsidɑ̃s] NF coincidence

coïncider [kɔɛside] /**1**/ VI: **~ (avec)** to coincide (with); (correspondre: témoignage etc) to correspond ou tally (with)

coin-coin [kwɛ̃kwɛ̃] NM INV quack

coing [kwɛ̃] NM quince

coït [kɔit] NM coitus

coite [kwat] ADJ F voir **coi**

coke [kɔk] NM coke

col [kɔl] NM (de chemise) collar; (encolure, cou) neck; (de montagne) pass; **~ roulé** polo-neck; **~ de l'utérus** cervix

coléoptère [kɔleɔptɛʀ] NM beetle

colère [kɔlɛʀ] NF anger; **une ~** a fit of anger; **être en ~ (contre qn)** to be angry (with sb); **mettre qn en ~** to make sb angry; **se mettre en ~ contre qn** to get angry with sb; **se mettre en ~** to get angry

coléreux, -euse [kɔleʀø, -øz], **colérique** [kɔleʀik] ADJ quick-tempered, irascible

colibacille [kɔlibasil] NM colon bacillus

colibacillose [kɔlibasiloz] NF colibacillosis

colifichet [kɔlifiʃɛ] NM trinket

colimaçon [kɔlimasɔ̃] NM: **escalier en ~** spiral staircase

colin [kɔlɛ̃] NM hake

colin-maillard [kɔlɛ̃majaʀ] NM (jeu) blind man's buff

colique [kɔlik] NF diarrhoea (BRIT), diarrhea (US); (douleurs) colic (pains pl); (fam: personne ou chose ennuyeuse) pain

★**colis** [kɔli] NM parcel; **par ~ postal** by parcel post

colistier, -ière [kɔlistje, -jɛʀ] NM/F fellow candidate

colite [kɔlit] NF colitis

coll. ABR = **collection**; **collaborateurs**; **et ~** et al.

collaborateur, -trice [kɔlabɔʀatœʀ, -tʀis] NM/F (aussi Pol) collaborator; (d'une revue) contributor

collaboration [kɔlabɔʀasjɔ̃] NF collaboration

collaboratif, -ive [kɔlabɔʀatif, -iv] ADJ collaborative

collaborer [kɔ(l)labɔʀe] /**1**/ VI to collaborate; **~ à** to collaborate on; (revue) to contribute to

collage [kɔlaʒ] NM (Art) collage

collagène [kɔlaʒɛn] NM collagen

★**collant, e** [kɔlɑ̃, -ɑ̃t] ADJ sticky; (robe etc) clinging, skintight; (péj) clinging ▶ NM (bas) tights pl; (de danseur) leotard

collatéral, e, -aux [kɔlateʀal, -o] NM/F collateral

collation [kɔlasjɔ̃] NF light meal

★**colle** [kɔl] NF glue; (à papiers peints) (wallpaper) paste; (devinette) teaser, riddle; (Scol: fam) detention; **~ forte** superglue®

collecte [kɔlɛkt] NF collection; **faire une ~** to take up a collection

collecter [kɔlɛkte] /**1**/ VT to collect

collecteur [kɔlɛktœʀ] NM (égout) main sewer

collectif, -ive [kɔlɛktif, -iv] ADJ collective; (visite, billet etc) group cpd; **immeuble ~** block of flats ▶ NM: **~ budgétaire** mini-budget (BRIT), mid-term budget

★**collection** [kɔlɛksjɔ̃] NF collection; (Édition) series; **pièce de ~** collector's item; **faire (la) ~ de**

to collect; **(toute) une ~ de ...** (fig) a (complete) set of ...

★**collectionner** [kɔlɛksjɔne] /**1**/ VT (tableaux, timbres) to collect

collectionneur, -euse [kɔlɛksjɔnœʀ, -øz] NM/F collector

collectivement [kɔlɛktivmɑ̃] ADV collectively

collectiviser [kɔlɛktivize] /**1**/ VT to collectivize

collectivisme [kɔlɛktivism] NM collectivism

collectiviste [kɔlɛktivist] ADJ collectivist

collectivité [kɔlɛktivite] NF group; **la ~** the community, the collectivity; **les collectivités locales** local authorities

collège [kɔlɛʒ] NM (école) (secondary) school; see note; (assemblée) body; **~ électoral** electoral college

A **collège** is a secondary school for children between 11 and 15 years of age. Pupils follow a national curriculum consisting of several core subjects, all compulsory, along with several options. Schools are free to arrange their own timetable and choose their own teaching methods. Before leaving this phase of their education, students are assessed by examination and course work for their **brevet des collèges**.

collégial, e, -aux [kɔleʒjal, -o] ADJ collegiate

collégien, ne [kɔleʒjɛ̃, -ɛn] NM/F secondary school pupil (BRIT), high school student (US)

collègue [kɔ(l)lɛg] NMF colleague

★**coller** [kɔle] /**1**/ VT (papier, timbre) to stick (on); (affiche) to stick up; (appuyer, placer contre): **~ son front à la vitre** to press one's face to the window; (enveloppe) to stick down; (morceaux) to stick ou glue together; (Inform) to paste; (fam: mettre, fourrer) to stick, shove; (Scol: fam) to keep in, give detention to; **~ qch sur** to stick (ou paste ou glue) sth on(to); **être collé à un examen** (fam) to fail an exam ▶ VI (être collant) to be sticky; (adhérer) to stick; **~ à** to stick to; (fig) to cling to

collerette [kɔlʀɛt] NF ruff; (Tech) flange

collet [kɔlɛ] NM (piège) snare, noose; (cou): **prendre qn au ~** to grab sb by the throat; **~ monté** adj inv straight-laced

colleter [kɔlte] /**4**/ VT (adversaire) to collar, grab by the throat; **se ~ avec** to wrestle with

colleur, -euse [kɔlœʀ, -øz] NM/F: **~ d'affiches** bill-poster

★**collier** [kɔlje] NM (bijou) necklace; (de chien, Tech) collar; **~ (de barbe), barbe en ~** narrow beard along the line of the jaw; **~ de serrage** choke collar

collimateur [kɔlimatœʀ] NM: **être dans le ~** (fig) to be in the firing line; **avoir qn/qch dans le ~** (fig) to have sb/sth in one's sights

★**colline** [kɔlin] NF hill

collision [kɔlizjɔ̃] NF collision, crash; **entrer en ~ (avec)** to collide (with)

colloque [kɔlɔk] NM colloquium, symposium

collusion [kɔlyzjɔ̃] NF collusion

collutoire [kɔlytwaʀ] NM (Méd) oral medication; (en bombe) throat spray

collyre [kɔliʀ] NM (Méd) eye lotion

colmater [kɔlmate] /**1**/ VT (fuite) to seal off; (brèche) to plug, fill in

coloc [kɔlɔk] NMF (*fam: dans un appartement*) flatmate (BRIT), roommate (US); (: *dans une maison*) housemate (BRIT), roommate (US)

colocation [kɔlɔkasjɔ̃] NF shared flat (BRIT), shared apartment (US); **être en ~** to share a flat (BRIT) *ou* apartment (US)

Cologne [kɔlɔɲ] N Cologne

colombage [kɔlɔ̃baʒ] NM half-timbering; **une maison à colombages** a half-timbered house

colombe [kɔlɔ̃b] NF dove

Colombie [kɔlɔ̃bi] NF: **la ~** Colombia

colombien, ne [kɔlɔ̃bjɛ̃, -ɛn] ADJ Colombian ► NM/F: **Colombien, ne** Colombian

colon [kɔlɔ̃] NM settler; (*enfant*) boarder (*in children's holiday camp*)

côlon [kɔlɔ̃] NM colon (*Méd*)

colonel [kɔlɔnɛl] NM colonel; (*de l'armée de l'air*) group captain

colonial, e, -aux [kɔlɔnjal, -o] ADJ colonial

colonialisme [kɔlɔnjalism] NM colonialism

colonialiste [kɔlɔnjalist] ADJ, NMF colonialist

★**colonie** [kɔlɔni] NF colony; **~ (de vacances)** holiday camp (*for children*)

colonisation [kɔlɔnizasjɔ̃] NF colonization

coloniser [kɔlɔnize] /1/ VT to colonize

colonnade [kɔlɔnad] NF colonnade

colonne [kɔlɔn] NF column; **se mettre en ~ par deux/quatre** to get into twos/fours; **en ~ par deux** in double file; **~ de secours** rescue party; **~ (vertébrale)** spine, spinal column

colonnette [kɔlɔnɛt] NF small column

colophane [kɔlɔfan] NF rosin

colorant [kɔlɔrɑ̃] NM colouring

coloration [kɔlɔrasjɔ̃] NF colour(ing); **se faire faire une ~** (*chez le coiffeur*) to have one's hair dyed

coloré, e [kɔlɔre] ADJ (*fig*) colourful

colorer [kɔlɔre] /1/ VT to colour ■ **se colorer** VPR to turn red; to blush

coloriage [kɔlɔrjaʒ] NM colouring

colorier [kɔlɔrje] /7/ VT to colour (in); **album à ~** colouring book

coloris [kɔlɔri] NM colour, shade

coloriste [kɔlɔrist] NMF colourist

colossal, e, -aux [kɔlɔsal, -o] ADJ colossal, huge

colosse [kɔlɔs] NM giant

colostrum [kɔlɔstrɔm] NM colostrum

colporter [kɔlpɔrte] /1/ VT to peddle

colporteur, -euse [kɔlpɔrtœr, -øz] NM/F hawker, pedlar

colt [kɔlt] NM revolver, Colt®

coltiner [kɔltine] /1/ VT to lug about

colza [kɔlza] NM rape(seed)

COM [kɔm] SIGLE M, SIGLE MPL (= *Collectivité(s) d'outre-mer*) *French overseas departments and regions*; *voir aussi* **DOM-ROM**

coma [kɔma] NM coma; **être dans le ~** to be in a coma

comateux, -euse [kɔmatø, -øz] ADJ comatose

combat [kɔ̃ba] VB *voir* **combattre** ► NM fight; fighting *no pl*; **~ de boxe** boxing match; **~ de rues** street fighting *no pl*; **~ singulier** single combat

combatif, -ive [kɔ̃batif, -iv] ADJ with a lot of fight

combativité [kɔ̃bativite] NF fighting spirit

combattant [kɔ̃batɑ̃] VB *voir* **combattre** ► NM combatant; (*d'une rixe*) brawler; **ancien ~** war veteran

combattre [kɔ̃batr] /41/ VI to fight ► VT to fight; (*épidémie, ignorance*) to combat, fight against

★**combien** [kɔ̃bjɛ̃] ADV (*quantité*) how much; (*nombre*) how many; (*exclamatif*) how; **~ de** how much; (*nombre*) how many; **~ de temps** how long, how much time; **c'est ~ ?, ça fait ~ ?** how much is it?; **~ coûte/pèse ceci ?** how much does this cost/weigh?; **vous mesurez ~ ?** what size are you?; **ça fait ~ en largeur ?** how wide is that?; **on est le ~ aujourd'hui ?** (*fam*) what's the date today?

combinaison [kɔ̃binɛzɔ̃] NF combination; (*astuce*) device, scheme; (*de femme*) slip; (*d'aviateur*) flying suit; (*de plongée*) wetsuit; (*bleu de travail*) boilersuit (BRIT), coveralls *pl* (US)

combine [kɔ̃bin] NF trick; (*péj*) scheme, fiddle (BRIT)

combiné [kɔ̃bine] NM (*aussi:* **combiné téléphonique**) receiver; (*Ski*) combination (event); (*vêtement de femme*) corselet

combiner [kɔ̃bine] /1/ VT to combine; (*plan, horaire*) to work out, devise

comble [kɔ̃bl] ADJ (*salle*) packed (full) ► NM (*du bonheur, plaisir*) height; **de fond en ~** from top to bottom; **pour ~ de malchance** to cap it all; **c'est le ~ !** that beats everything!, that takes the biscuit! (BRIT) ■ **combles** NMPL (*Constr*) attic *sg*, loft *sg*; **sous les combles** in the attic

combler [kɔ̃ble] /1/ VT (*trou*) to fill in; (*besoin, lacune*) to fill; (*déficit*) to make good; (*satisfaire*) to gratify, fulfil (BRIT), fulfill (US); **~ qn de joie** to fill sb with joy; **~ qn d'honneurs** to shower sb with honours

combustible [kɔ̃bystibl] ADJ combustible ► NM fuel

combustion [kɔ̃bystjɔ̃] NF combustion

COMECON [kɔmekɔn] SIGLE M Comecon

comédie [kɔmedi] NF comedy; (*fig*) playacting *no pl*; **jouer la ~** (*fig*) to put on an act; **faire une ~** (*fig*) to make a fuss; **la Comédie-Française** *see note*; **~ musicale** musical

> Founded in 1680 by Louis XIV, the **Comédie-Française** is the French national theatre. The company is subsidized by the state and mainly performs in the *Palais-Royal* in Paris. Its repertoire includes classical French plays as well as more contemporary drama and works from other countries.

comédien, ne [kɔmedjɛ̃, -ɛn] NM/F actor/actress; (*comique*) comedy actor/actress, comedian/comedienne; (*fig*) sham

comestible [kɔmɛstibl] ADJ edible ■ **comestibles** NMPL foods

comète [kɔmɛt] NF comet

comice [kɔmis] NM: **~ agricole** agricultural show

★**comique** [kɔmik] ADJ (*drôle*) comical; (*Théât*) comic ► NMF (*artiste*) comic, comedian ► NM: **le ~ de qch** the funny *ou* comical side of sth

comité [kɔmite] NM committee; **petit ~** select group; **~ directeur** management committee; **~ d'entreprise** works council; **~ des fêtes** festival committee

commandant [kɔmɑ̃dɑ̃] NM (*gén*) commander, commandant; (*Mil: grade*) major; (: *armée de l'air*) squadron leader; (*Navig*) captain; **~ (de bord)** (*Aviat*) captain

★**commande** [kɔmɑ̃d] NF (*Comm*) order; (*Inform*) command; **passer une ~ (de)** to put in an order (for); **sur ~** to order; **à distance** remote control; **à ~ vocale** (*appareil, dispositif*) voice-activated; **véhicule à double ~** vehicle with dual controls ■ **commandes** NFPL (*Aviat etc*) controls

commandement [kɔmɑ̃dmɑ̃] NM command; (*ordre*) command, order; (*Rel*) commandment

★**commander** [kɔmɑ̃de] /1/ VT (*Comm*) to order; (*diriger, ordonner*) to command; ~ **à** (*Mil*) to command; (*contrôler, maîtriser*) to have control over; **~ à qn de faire** to command *ou* order sb to do

commanditaire [kɔmɑ̃ditɛR] NM sleeping (*Brit*) *ou* silent (*US*) partner

commandite [kɔmɑ̃dit] NF: **(société en) ~** limited partnership

commanditer [kɔmɑ̃dite] /1/ VT (*Comm*) to finance, back; to commission

commando [kɔmɑ̃do] NM commando (squad)

---

comme [kɔm]

PRÉP **1** (*comparaison*) like; **tout comme son père** just like his father; **fort comme un bœuf** as strong as an ox; **joli comme tout** ever so pretty **2** (*manière*) like; **faites-le comme ça** do it like this, do it this way; **comme ça** *ou* **cela on n'aura pas d'ennuis** that way we won't have any problems; **comme ci, comme ça** so-so, middling; **comment ça va ? — comme ça** how are things? — OK; **comme on dit** as they say **3** (*en tant que*) as a; **donner comme prix** to give as a prize; **travailler comme secrétaire** to work as a secretary **4**: **comme quoi** (*d'où il s'ensuit que*) which shows that; **il a écrit une lettre comme quoi il ...** he's written a letter saying that ... **5**: **comme il faut** *adv* properly; *adj* (*correct*) proper, correct

▶ CONJ **1** (*ainsi que*) as; **elle écrit comme elle parle** she writes as she talks; **il est malin comme c'est pas permis** he's as smart as anything; **comme si** as if **2** (*au moment où, alors que*) as; **il est parti comme j'arrivais** he left as I arrived **3** (*parce que, puisque*) as, since; **comme il était en retard, il ...** as he was late, he ...

▶ ADV: **comme il est fort/c'est bon!** he's so strong/it's so good!

---

commémoratif, -ive [kɔmemɔRatif, -iv] ADJ commemorative; **un monument ~** a memorial

commémoration [kɔmemɔRasjɔ̃] NF commemoration

commémorer [kɔmemɔRe] /1/ VT to commemorate

★**commencement** [kɔmɑ̃smɑ̃] NM beginning, start, commencement ■ **commencements** NMPL (*débuts*) beginnings

★**commencer** [kɔmɑ̃se] /3/ VT to begin, start, commence; **~ à** *ou* **de faire** to begin *ou* start doing; **~ par qch** to begin with sth; **~ par faire qch** to begin by doing sth ▶ VI to begin, start, commence

commensal, e, -aux [kɔmɑ̃sal, -o] NM/F companion at table

★**comment** [kɔmɑ̃] ADV how; **~?** (*que dites-vous*) (I beg your) pardon?; **~!** what!; **et ~!** and how!; **~ donc!** of course!; **~ faire?** how will we do it?; **~ se fait-il que ...?** how is it that ...? ▶ NM: **le ~ et le pourquoi** the whys and wherefores

commentaire [kɔmɑ̃tɛR] NM comment; remark; **~ (de texte)** (*Scol*) commentary; **~ sur image** voice-over

commentateur, -trice [kɔmɑ̃tatœR, -tRis] NM/F commentator

commenter [kɔmɑ̃te] /1/ VT (*jugement, événement*) to comment (up)on; (*Radio, TV: match, manifestation*) to cover, give a commentary on

commérages [kɔmeRaʒ] NMPL gossip sg

commerçant, e [kɔmɛRsɑ̃, -ɑ̃t] ADJ commercial; trading; (*rue*) shopping cpd; (*personne*) commercially shrewd ▶ NM/F shopkeeper, trader

commerce [kɔmɛRs] NM (*activité*) trade, commerce; (*boutique*) business; **le petit ~** small shop owners pl, small traders pl; **faire ~ de** to trade in; (*fig: péj*) to trade on; **chambre de ~** Chamber of Commerce; **livres de ~** (account) books; **vendu dans le ~** sold in the shops; **vendu hors-commerce** sold directly to the public; **~ en** *ou* **de gros/détail** wholesale/retail trade; **~ électronique** e-commerce; **~ équitable** fair trade; **~ intérieur/extérieur** home/foreign trade; **~ de proximité** local shop

commercer [kɔmɛRse] /3/ VI: **~ avec** to trade with

commercial, e, -aux [kɔmɛRsjal, -o] ADJ commercial, trading; (*péj*) commercial ▶ NM: **les commerciaux** the commercial people

commercialisable [kɔmɛRsjalizabl] ADJ marketable

commercialisation [kɔmɛRsjalizasjɔ̃] NF marketing

commercialiser [kɔmɛRsjalize] /1/ VT to market

commère [kɔmɛR] NF gossip

commettant [kɔmetɑ̃] VB *voir* **commettre** ▶ NM (*Jur*) principal

commettre [kɔmɛtR] /56/ VT to commit ■ **se commettre** VPR to compromise one's good name

commis¹ [kɔmi] NM (*de magasin*) (shop) assistant (*Brit*), sales clerk (*US*); (*de banque*) clerk; **~ voyageur** commercial traveller (*Brit*) *ou* traveler (*US*)

commis², e [kɔmi, -iz] PP *de* **commettre**

commisération [kɔmizeRasjɔ̃] NF commiseration

commissaire [kɔmisɛR] NM (*de police*) ≈ (police) superintendent (*Brit*), ≈ (police) captain (*US*); (*de rencontre sportive etc*) steward; **~ du bord** (*Navig*) purser; **~ aux comptes** (*Admin*) auditor

commissaire-priseur [kɔmisɛRpRizœR] (*pl* **commissaires-priseurs**) NM (official) auctioneer

★**commissariat** [kɔmisaRja] NM (*aussi:* **commissariat de police**) police station; (*Admin*) commissionership

commission [kɔmisjɔ̃] NF *(comité, pourcentage)* commission; *(message)* message; *(course)* errand; **~ d'examen** examining board ▪ **commissions** NFPL *(achats)* shopping *sg*

commissionnaire [kɔmisjɔnɛʀ] NM delivery boy *(ou* man); messenger; *(Transports)* (forwarding) agent

commissure [kɔmisyʀ] NF: **les commissures des lèvres** the corners of the mouth

★**commode** [kɔmɔd] ADJ *(pratique)* convenient, handy; *(facile)* easy; *(air, personne)* easy-going; *(personne)*: **pas ~** awkward (to deal with) ▶ NF chest of drawers

commodité [kɔmɔdite] NF convenience

commotion [kɔmosjɔ̃] NF: **~ (cérébrale)** concussion

commotionné, e [kɔmosjɔne] ADJ shocked, shaken

commuer [kɔmɥe] /**1**/ VT to commute

★**commun, e** [kɔmœ̃, -yn] ADJ common; *(pièce)* communal, shared; *(réunion, effort)* joint; **d'un ~ accord** of one accord; with one accord; **être ~ à** *(chose)* to be shared by; **en ~** *(faire)* jointly; **mettre en ~** to pool, share; **peu ~** unusual; **sans commune mesure** incomparable ▶ NMSG: **le ~ des mortels** the common run of people; **cela sort du ~** it's out of the ordinary ▶ NF *(Admin)* commune, ≈ district; *(: urbaine)* ≈ borough ▪ **communs** NMPL *(bâtiments)* outbuildings

communal, e, -aux [kɔmynal, -o] ADJ *(Admin)* of the commune, ≈ (district *ou* borough) council *cpd*

communard, e [kɔmynaʀ, -aʀd] NM/F *(Hist)* Communard; *(péj: communiste)* commie

communautaire [kɔmynotɛʀ] ADJ community *cpd*

communauté [kɔmynote] NF community; *(Jur)*: **régime de la ~** communal estate settlement

commune [kɔmyn] ADJ F, NF *voir* **commun**

communément [kɔmynemã] ADV commonly

Communes [kɔmyn] NFPL *(en Grande-Bretagne: parlement)* Commons

communiant, e [kɔmynjã, -ãt] NM/F communicant; **premier ~** child taking his first communion

communicant, e [kɔmynikã, -ãt] ADJ communicating

communicatif, -ive [kɔmynikatif, -iv] ADJ *(personne)* communicative; *(rire)* infectious

★**communication** [kɔmynikasjɔ̃] NF communication; **~ (téléphonique)** *(telephone)* call; **avoir la ~ (avec)** to get *ou* be through (to); **vous avez la ~** you're through; **donnez-moi la ~ avec** put me through to; **mettre qn en ~ avec qn** *(en contact)* to put sb in touch with sb; *(au téléphone)* to connect sb with sb; **~ interurbaine** long-distance call; **~ en PCV** reverse charge *(Brit) ou* collect *(US)* call; **~ avec préavis** personal call

communier [kɔmynje] /**7**/ VI *(Rel)* to receive communion; *(fig)* to be united

communion [kɔmynjɔ̃] NF communion

communiqué [kɔmynike] NM communiqué; **~ de presse** press release

communiquer [kɔmynike] /**1**/ VT *(nouvelle, dossier)* to pass on, convey; *(maladie)* to pass on; *(peur etc)* to communicate; *(chaleur, mouvement)* to transmit ▶ VI to communicate; **~ avec** *(salle)* to communicate with ▪ **se communiquer à** VPR *(se propager)* to spread to

communisme [kɔmynism] NM communism

communiste [kɔmynist] ADJ, NMF communist

commutateur [kɔmytatœʀ] NM *(Élec)* (change-over) switch, commutator

commutation [kɔmytasjɔ̃] NF *(Inform)*: **~ de messages** message switching; **~ de paquets** packet switching

Comores [kɔmɔʀ] NFPL: **les (îles) ~** the Comoros (Islands)

comorien, ne [kɔmɔʀjɛ̃, -ɛn] ADJ of *ou* from the Comoros

compact, e [kɔ̃pakt] ADJ *(dense)* dense; *(appareil)* compact

compagne [kɔ̃paɲ] NF companion

compagnie [kɔ̃paɲi] NF *(firme, Mil)* company; *(groupe)* gathering; *(présence)*: **la ~ de** qn sb's company; **homme/femme de ~** escort; **tenir ~ à qn** to keep sb company; **fausser ~ à qn** to give sb the slip, slip *ou* sneak away from sb; **en ~ de** in the company of; **Dupont et ~, Dupont et Cie** Dupont and Company, Dupont and Co; **~ aérienne** airline *(company)*

compagnon [kɔ̃paɲɔ̃] NM companion; *(autrefois: ouvrier)* craftsman; journeyman

comparable [kɔ̃paʀabl] ADJ: **~ (à)** comparable (to)

comparaison [kɔ̃paʀɛzɔ̃] NF comparison; *(métaphore)* simile; **en ~ (de)** in comparison (with); **par ~ (à)** by comparison (with)

comparaître [kɔ̃paʀɛtʀ] /**57**/ VI: **~ (devant)** to appear (before)

comparatif, -ive [kɔ̃paʀatif, -iv] ADJ, NM comparative

comparativement [kɔ̃paʀativmã] ADV comparatively; **~ à** by comparison with

comparé, e [kɔ̃paʀe] ADJ: **littérature** *etc* **comparée** comparative literature *etc*

★**comparer** [kɔ̃paʀe] /**1**/ VT to compare; **~ qch/qn à** *ou* **et** *(pour choisir)* to compare sth/sb with *ou* and; *(pour établir une similitude)* to compare sth/sb to *ou* and

comparse [kɔ̃paʀs] NMF *(péj)* associate, stooge

★**compartiment** [kɔ̃paʀtimã] NM compartment

compartimenté, e [kɔ̃paʀtimãte] ADJ partitioned; *(fig)* compartmentalized

comparu, e [kɔ̃paʀy] PP *de* **comparaître**

comparution [kɔ̃paʀysjɔ̃] NF appearance

compas [kɔ̃pa] NM *(Géom)* (pair of) compasses *pl*; *(Navig)* compass

compassé, e [kɔ̃pase] ADJ starchy, formal

compassion [kɔ̃pasjɔ̃] NF compassion

compatibilité [kɔ̃patibilite] NF compatibility

compatible [kɔ̃patibl] ADJ compatible; **~ (avec)** compatible (with)

compatir [kɔ̃patiʀ] /**2**/ VI: **~ (à)** to sympathize (with)

compatissant, e [kɔ̃patisã, -ãt] ADJ sympathetic

compatriote [kɔ̃patʀijɔt] NMF compatriot, fellow countryman/-woman

compensateur, -trice [kɔ̃pɑ̃satœʀ, -tʀis] ADJ compensatory

compensation [kɔ̃pɑ̃sasjɔ̃] NF compensation; (*Banque*) clearing; **en ~** in *ou* as compensation

compensé, e [kɔ̃pɑ̃se] ADJ: **semelle compensée** platform sole

compenser [kɔ̃pɑ̃se] /1/ VT to compensate for, make up for

compère [kɔ̃pɛʀ] NM accomplice; fellow musician *ou* comedian *etc*

compétence [kɔ̃petɑ̃s] NF competence

compétent, e [kɔ̃petɑ̃, -ɑ̃t] ADJ (*apte*) competent, capable; (*Jur*) competent

compétitif, -ive [kɔ̃petitif, -iv] ADJ competitive

compétition [kɔ̃petisjɔ̃] NF (*gén*) competition; (*Sport: épreuve*) event; **la ~** competitive sport; **être en ~ avec** to be competing with; **la ~ automobile** motor racing

compétitivité [kɔ̃petitivite] NF competitiveness

compilateur [kɔ̃pilatœʀ] NM (*Inform*) compiler

compilation [kɔ̃pilasjɔ̃] NF compilation

compiler [kɔ̃pile] /1/ VT to compile

complainte [kɔ̃plɛ̃t] NF lament

complaire [kɔ̃plɛʀ] /54/: **se complaire** VPR: **se ~ dans/parmi** to take pleasure in/in being among

complaisais *etc* [kɔ̃plɛzɛ] VB *voir* **complaire**

complaisamment [kɔ̃plɛzamɑ̃] ADV kindly; complacently

complaisance [kɔ̃plɛzɑ̃s] NF kindness; (*péj*) indulgence; (: *fatuité*) complacency; **attestation de ~** *certificate produced to oblige a patient etc*; **pavillon de ~** flag of convenience

complaisant, e [kɔ̃plɛzɑ̃, -ɑ̃t] VB *voir* **complaire** ▶ ADJ (*aimable*) kind; obliging; (*péj*) accommodating; (: *fat*) complacent

complaît [kɔ̃plɛ] VB *voir* **complaire**

complément [kɔ̃plemɑ̃] NM complement; (*reste*) remainder; (*Ling*) complement; **~ d'information** (*Admin*) supplementary *ou* further information; **~ d'agent** agent; **~ (d'objet) direct/indirect** direct/indirect object; **~ (circonstanciel) de lieu/temps** adverbial phrase of place/time; **~ de nom** possessive phrase

complémentaire [kɔ̃plemɑ̃tɛʀ] ADJ complementary; (*additionnel*) supplementary

★**complet, -ète** [kɔ̃plɛ, -ɛt] ADJ complete; (*plein: hôtel etc*) full; **pain ~** wholemeal bread ▶ NM (*aussi:* **complet-veston**) suit; **au (grand) ~** all together

complètement [kɔ̃plɛtmɑ̃] ADV (*en entier*) completely; (*absolument: fou, faux etc*) absolutely; (*à fond: étudier etc*) fully, in depth

compléter [kɔ̃plete] /6/ VT (*porter à la quantité voulue*) to complete; (*augmenter: connaissances, études*) to complement, supplement; (: *garde-robe*) to add to ▶ **se compléter** VPR (*personnes*) to complement one another; (*collection etc*) to become complete

complexe [kɔ̃plɛks] ADJ complex ▶ NM (*Psych*) complex, hang-up; (*bâtiments*): **~ hospitalier/industriel** hospital/industrial complex

complexé, e [kɔ̃plɛkse] ADJ mixed-up, hung-up

complexité [kɔ̃plɛksite] NF complexity

complication [kɔ̃plikasjɔ̃] NF complexity, intricacy; (*difficulté, ennui*) complication ■ **complications** NFPL (*Méd*) complications

complice [kɔ̃plis] NMF accomplice

complicité [kɔ̃plisite] NF complicity

★**compliment** [kɔ̃plimɑ̃] NM (*louange*) compliment ■ **compliments** NMPL (*félicitations*) congratulations

complimenter [kɔ̃plimɑ̃te] /1/ VT: **~ qn (sur *ou* de)** to congratulate *ou* compliment sb (on)

compliqué, e [kɔ̃plike] ADJ complicated, complex, intricate; (*personne*) complicated

compliquer [kɔ̃plike] /1/ VT to complicate ■ **se compliquer** VPR (*situation*) to become complicated; **se ~ la vie** to make life difficult *ou* complicated for o.s.

complot [kɔ̃plo] NM plot

comploter [kɔ̃plɔte] /1/ VI, VT to plot

complotiste [kɔ̃plɔtist] ADJ (*théorie, thèse*) conspiracy cpd ▶ NMF conspiracy theorist

complu, e [kɔ̃ply] PP *de* **complaire**

comportement [kɔ̃pɔʀtəmɑ̃] NM behaviour (BRIT), behavior (US); (*Tech: d'une pièce, d'un véhicule*) behavio(u)r, performance

comporter [kɔ̃pɔʀte] /1/ VT (*consister en*) to consist of, be composed of, comprise; (*être équipé de*) to have; (*impliquer*) to entail, involve ■ **se comporter** VPR to behave; (*Tech*) to behave, perform

composant [kɔ̃pozɑ̃] NM component, constituent

composante [kɔ̃pozɑ̃t] NF component

composé, e [kɔ̃poze] ADJ (*visage, air*) studied; (*Bio, Chimie, Ling*) compound; **~ de** made up of ▶ NM (*Chimie, Ling*) compound

★**composer** [kɔ̃poze] /1/ VT (*musique, texte*) to compose; (*mélange, équipe*) to make up; (*faire partie de*) to make up, form; (*Typo*) to (type)set; **~ un numéro** to dial a number ▶ VI (*Scol*) to sit *ou* do a test; (*transiger*) to come to terms ■ **se composer de** VPR to be composed of, be made up of

composite [kɔ̃pozit] ADJ heterogeneous

compositeur, -trice [kɔ̃pozitœʀ, -tʀis] NM/F (*Mus*) composer; (*Typo*) compositor, typesetter

composition [kɔ̃pozisjɔ̃] NF composition; (*Scol*) test; (*Typo*) (type)setting, composition; **de bonne ~** (*accommodant*) easy to deal with; **amener qn à ~** to get sb to come to terms; **~ française** (*Scol*) French essay

compost [kɔ̃pɔst] NM compost

★**composter** [kɔ̃pɔste] /1/ VT to date-stamp; (*billet*) to punch; *see note*

At train stations in France you have to punch (**composter**) your ticket on the platform to validate it before getting on the train. Travellers who fail to do so may be asked to pay a supplementary fare once on board, although tickets bought online and printed out at home are not subject to this rule.

composteur [kɔ̃pɔstœʀ] NM date stamp; punch; (*Typo*) composing stick

compote [kɔ̃pɔt] NF stewed fruit *no pl*; **~ de pommes** stewed apples

compotier [kɔ̃pɔtje] NM fruit dish *ou* bowl

89

compréhensible [kɔ̃pʀeɑ̃sibl] ADJ comprehensible; (attitude) understandable

compréhensif, -ive [kɔ̃pʀeɑ̃sif, -iv] ADJ understanding

compréhension [kɔ̃pʀeɑ̃sjɔ̃] NF understanding; comprehension

★**comprendre** [kɔ̃pʀɑ̃dʀ] /58/ VT to understand; (se composer de) to comprise, consist of; (inclure) to include; **se faire ~** to make o.s. understood; to get one's ideas across; **mal ~** to misunderstand

compresse [kɔ̃pʀɛs] NF compress

compresser [kɔ̃pʀese] /1/ VT to squash in, crush together; (Inform) to zip

compresseur [kɔ̃pʀesœʀ] ADJ M voir **rouleau**

compressible [kɔ̃pʀesibl] ADJ (Physique) compressible; (dépenses) reducible

compression [kɔ̃pʀesjɔ̃] NF compression; (d'un crédit etc) reduction

comprimé, e [kɔ̃pʀime] ADJ: **air ~** compressed air ▶ NM tablet

comprimer [kɔ̃pʀime] /1/ VT to compress; (fig: crédit etc) to reduce, cut down

★**compris, e** [kɔ̃pʀi, -iz] PP de **comprendre** ▶ ADJ (inclus) included; **~ ?** understood?, is that clear?; **~ entre** (situé) contained between; **la maison comprise/non comprise, y/non ~ la maison** including/excluding the house; **service ~** service (charge) included; **100 euros tout ~** 100 euros all inclusive ou all-in

compromettant, e [kɔ̃pʀɔmetɑ̃, -ɑ̃t] ADJ compromising

compromettre [kɔ̃pʀɔmɛtʀ] /56/ VT to compromise

compromis [kɔ̃pʀɔmi] VB voir **compromettre** ▶ NM compromise

compromission [kɔ̃pʀɔmisjɔ̃] NF compromise, deal

comptabiliser [kɔ̃tabilize] /1/ VT (valeur) to post; (fig) to evaluate

comptabilité [kɔ̃tabilite] NF (activité, technique) accounting, accountancy; (d'une société: comptes) accounts pl, books pl; (: service) accounts office ou department; **~ à partie double** double-entry book-keeping

★**comptable** [kɔ̃tabl] NMF accountant ▶ ADJ accounts cpd, accounting

comptant [kɔ̃tɑ̃] ADV: **payer ~** to pay cash; **acheter ~** to buy for cash

★**compte** [kɔ̃t] NM count, counting; (total, montant) count, (right) number; (bancaire, facture) account; **ouvrir un ~** to open an account; **faire le ~ de** to count up, make a count of; **tout ~ fait** on the whole; **à ce compte-là** (dans ce cas) in that case; (à ce train-là) at that rate; **en fin de ~** (fig) all things considered, weighing it all up; **au bout du ~** in the final analysis; **à bon ~** at a favourable price; (fig) lightly; **avoir son ~** (fig: fam) to have had it; **s'en tirer à bon ~** to get off lightly; **pour le ~ de** on behalf of; **pour son propre ~** for one's own benefit; **sur le ~ de qn** (à son sujet) about sb; **travailler à son ~** to work for oneself; **mettre qch sur le ~ de qn** (le rendre responsable) to attribute sth to sb; **prendre qch à son ~** to take responsibility for sth; **trouver son ~ à qch** to do well out of sth; **régler un ~** (s'acquitter de qch) to settle an account; (se venger) to get one's own back; **rendre ~ (à qn) de qch** to give (sb) an account of sth; **tenir ~ de qch** to take sth into account; **~ tenu de** taking into account; **~ en banque** bank account; **~ chèque(s)** current account; **~ chèque postal** Post Office account; **~ client** (sur bilan) accounts receivable; **~ courant** current account; **~ de dépôt** deposit account; **~ d'exploitation** operating account; **~ fournisseur** (sur bilan) accounts payable; **~ à rebours** countdown; **~ rendu** account, report; (de film, livre) review ▪ **comptes** NMPL accounts, books; (fig) explanation sg; **rendre des comptes à qn** (fig) to be answerable to sb

compte-gouttes [kɔ̃tgut] NM INV dropper

★**compter** [kɔ̃te] /1/ VT to count; (facturer) to charge for; (avoir à son actif, comporter) to have; (prévoir) to allow, reckon; (tenir compte de, inclure) to include; (penser, espérer): **~ réussir/revenir** to expect to succeed/return; **sans ~ que** besides which ▶ VI to count; (être économe) to economize; (être non négligeable) to count, matter; (valoir): **~ pour** to count for; (figurer): **~ parmi** to be ou rank among; **~ sur** to count (up)on; **~ avec qch/qn** to reckon with ou take account of sth/sb; **~ sans qch/qn** to reckon without sth/sb; **à ~ du 10 janvier** (Comm) (as) from 10th January

compte-tours [kɔ̃ttuʀ] NM INV rev(olution) counter

compteur [kɔ̃tœʀ] NM meter; **~ de vitesse** speedometer

comptine [kɔ̃tin] NF nursery rhyme

★**comptoir** [kɔ̃twaʀ] NM (de magasin) counter; (de café) counter, bar; (colonial) trading post

compulser [kɔ̃pylse] /1/ VT to consult

comte, comtesse [kɔ̃t, kɔ̃tɛs] NM/F count/countess

con, ne [kɔ̃, kɔn] ADJ (!) bloody (BRIT !) ou damned stupid

concasser [kɔ̃kɑse] /1/ VT (pierre, sucre) to crush; (poivre) to grind

concave [kɔ̃kav] ADJ concave

concéder [kɔ̃sede] /6/ VT to grant; (défaite, point) to concede; **~ que** to concede that

concentration [kɔ̃sɑ̃tʀasjɔ̃] NF concentration

concentrationnaire [kɔ̃sɑ̃tʀasjɔnɛʀ] ADJ of ou in concentration camps

concentré [kɔ̃sɑ̃tʀe] NM concentrate; **~ de tomates** tomato purée

concentrer [kɔ̃sɑ̃tʀe] /1/ VT to concentrate ▪ **se concentrer** VPR to concentrate

concentrique [kɔ̃sɑ̃tʀik] ADJ concentric

concept [kɔ̃sɛpt] NM concept

concepteur, -trice [kɔ̃sɛptœʀ, -tʀis] NM/F designer

conception [kɔ̃sɛpsjɔ̃] NF conception; (d'une machine etc) design

concernant [kɔ̃sɛʀnɑ̃] PRÉP (se rapportant à) concerning; (en ce qui concerne) as regards

concerner [kɔ̃sɛʀne] /1/ VT to concern; **en ce qui me concerne** as far as I am concerned; **en ce qui concerne ceci** as far as this is concerned, with regard to this

★**concert** [kɔ̃sɛʀ] NM concert; **de ~** adv in unison; together; (décider) unanimously

concertation [kɔ̃sɛʁtasjɔ̃] NF (*échange de vues*) dialogue; (*rencontre*) meeting

concerter [kɔ̃sɛʁte] /1/ VT to devise ■ **se concerter** VPR (*collaborateurs etc*) to put our (*ou* their *etc*) heads together, consult (each other)

concertiste [kɔ̃sɛʁtist] NMF concert artist

concerto [kɔ̃sɛʁto] NM concerto

concession [kɔ̃sesjɔ̃] NF concession

concessionnaire [kɔ̃sesjɔnɛʁ] NMF agent, dealer

concevable [kɔ̃s(ə)vabl] ADJ conceivable

concevoir [kɔ̃s(ə)vwaʁ] /28/ VT (*idée, projet*) to conceive (of); (*méthode, plan*) design; (*comprendre*) to understand, conceive; (*enfant*) to conceive ■ **se concevoir** VPR to be conceivable; **ça se conçoit** it's understandable

★**concierge** [kɔ̃sjɛʁʒ] NMF caretaker; (*d'hôtel*) head porter

conciergerie [kɔ̃sjɛʁʒəʁi] NF caretaker's lodge

concile [kɔ̃sil] NM council, synod

conciliable [kɔ̃siljabl] ADJ (*opinions etc*) reconcilable

conciliabules [kɔ̃siljabyl] NMPL (private) discussions, confabulations (BRIT)

conciliant, e [kɔ̃siljɑ̃, -ɑ̃t] ADJ conciliatory

conciliateur, -trice [kɔ̃siljatœʁ, -tʁis] NM/F mediator, go-between

conciliation [kɔ̃siljasjɔ̃] NF conciliation

concilier [kɔ̃silje] /7/ VT to reconcile; **se ~ qn/l'appui de qn** to win sb over/sb's support

concis, e [kɔ̃si, -iz] ADJ concise

concision [kɔ̃sizjɔ̃] NF concision, conciseness

concitoyen, ne [kɔ̃sitwajɛ̃, -ɛn] NM/F fellow citizen

conclave [kɔ̃klav] NM conclave

concluant, e [kɔ̃klyɑ̃, -ɑ̃t] VB *voir* **conclure** ▶ ADJ conclusive

conclure [kɔ̃klyʁ] /35/ VT to conclude; (*signer: accord, pacte*) to enter into; (*déduire*): **~ qch de qch** to deduce sth from sth; **~ à l'acquittement** to decide in favour of an acquittal; **~ au suicide** to come to the conclusion (*ou* (Jur) to pronounce) that it is a case of suicide; **~ un marché** to clinch a deal; **j'en conclus que** from that I conclude that

conclusion [kɔ̃klyzjɔ̃] NF conclusion; **en ~** in conclusion ■ **conclusions** NFPL (Jur) submissions; findings

concocter [kɔ̃kɔkte] /1/ VT to concoct

conçois [kɔ̃swa], **conçoive** etc [kɔ̃swav] VB *voir* **concevoir**

★**concombre** [kɔ̃kɔ̃bʁ] NM cucumber

concomitant, e [kɔ̃kɔmitɑ̃, -ɑ̃t] ADJ concomitant

concordance [kɔ̃kɔʁdɑ̃s] NF concordance; **la ~ des temps** (Ling) the sequence of tenses

concordant, e [kɔ̃kɔʁdɑ̃, -ɑ̃t] ADJ (*témoignages, versions*) corroborating

concorde [kɔ̃kɔʁd] NF concord

concorder [kɔ̃kɔʁde] /1/ VI to tally, agree

concourir [kɔ̃kuʁiʁ] /11/ VI (Sport) to compete; **~ à** vt (*effet etc*) to work towards

★**concours** [kɔ̃kuʁ] VB *voir* **concourir** ▶ NM competition; (Scol) competitive examination; (*assistance*) aid, help; **recrutement par voie de ~** recruitment

by (competitive) examination; **apporter son ~ à** to give one's support to; **~ de circonstances** combination of circumstances; **~ hippique** horse show; *voir* **hors-concours**

concret, -ète [kɔ̃kʁɛ, -ɛt] ADJ concrete

concrètement [kɔ̃kʁɛtmɑ̃] ADV in concrete terms

concrétisation [kɔ̃kʁetizasjɔ̃] NF realization

concrétiser [kɔ̃kʁetize] /1/ VT to realize ■ **se concrétiser** VPR to materialize

conçu, e [kɔ̃sy] PP *de* **concevoir** ▶ ADJ: **maison bien/mal conçue** well-/badly-designed *ou* -planned house

concubin, e [kɔ̃kybɛ̃, -in] NM/F (Jur) cohabitant

concubinage [kɔ̃kybinaʒ] NM (Jur) cohabitation

concupiscence [kɔ̃kypisɑ̃s] NF concupiscence

concurremment [kɔ̃kyʁamɑ̃] ADV concurrently; jointly

concurrence [kɔ̃kyʁɑ̃s] NF competition; **jusqu'à ~ de** up to; **faire ~ à** to be in competition with; **~ déloyale** unfair competition

concurrencer [kɔ̃kyʁɑ̃se] /3/ VT to compete with; **ils nous concurrencent dangereusement** they are a serious threat to us

concurrent, e [kɔ̃kyʁɑ̃, -ɑ̃t] ADJ competing ▶ NM/F (Sport, Écon etc) competitor; (Scol) candidate

concurrentiel, le [kɔ̃kyʁɑ̃sjɛl] ADJ competitive

conçus [kɔ̃sy] VB *voir* **concevoir**

condamnable [kɔ̃danabl] ADJ (*action, opinion*) reprehensible

condamnation [kɔ̃danasjɔ̃] NF (*action*) condemnation; sentencing; (*peine*) sentence; conviction; **~ à mort** death sentence

condamné, e [kɔ̃dane] NM/F (Jur) convict

condamner [kɔ̃dane] /1/ VT (*blâmer*) to condemn; (Jur) to sentence; (*porte, ouverture*) to fill in, block up; (*malade*) to give up (hope for); (*obliger*): **~ qn à qch/à faire** to condemn sb to sth/to do; **~ qn à deux ans de prison** to sentence sb to two years' imprisonment; **~ qn à une amende** to impose a fine on sb

condensateur [kɔ̃dɑ̃satœʁ] NM condenser

condensation [kɔ̃dɑ̃sasjɔ̃] NF condensation

condensé [kɔ̃dɑ̃se] NM digest

condenser [kɔ̃dɑ̃se] /1/: **se condenser** VPR to condense

condescendance [kɔ̃desɑ̃dɑ̃s] NF condescension

condescendant, e [kɔ̃desɑ̃dɑ̃, -ɑ̃t] ADJ (*personne, attitude*) condescending

condescendre [kɔ̃desɑ̃dʁ] /41/ VI: **~ à** to condescend to

condiment [kɔ̃dimɑ̃] NM condiment

condisciple [kɔ̃disipl] NMF school fellow, fellow student

condition [kɔ̃disjɔ̃] NF condition; **sans ~** adj unconditional; adv unconditionally; **sous ~ que** on condition that; **à ~ de** ou **que** provided that; **en bonne ~** in good condition; **mettre en ~** (Sport etc) to get fit; (Psych) to condition (mentally) ■ **conditions** NFPL (*tarif, prix*) terms; (*circonstances*) conditions; **conditions de vie** living conditions

conditionné, e [kɔ̃disjɔne] ADJ: **air ~** air conditioning; **réflexe ~** conditioned reflex

conditionnel, le [kɔ̃disjɔnɛl] ADJ conditional ▸ NM conditional (tense)

conditionnement [kɔ̃disjɔnmɑ̃] NM (*emballage*) packaging; (*fig*) conditioning

conditionner [kɔ̃disjɔne] /1/ VT (*déterminer*) to determine; (*Comm: produit*) to package; (*fig: personne*) to condition

condoléances [kɔ̃dɔleɑ̃s] NFPL condolences

★**conducteur, -trice** [kɔ̃dyktœr, -tris] ADJ (*Élec*) conducting ▸ NM/F (*Auto etc*) driver; (*d'une machine*) operator ▸ NM (*Élec etc*) conductor

> **conducteur** does not usually mean *conductor*.

★**conduire** [kɔ̃dɥir] /38/ VT (*véhicule, passager*) to drive; (*délégation, troupeau*) to lead; **~ qn quelque part** to take sb somewhere; **to drive sb somewhere** ▸ VI: **~ vers/à** to lead towards/to ▪ **se conduire** VPR to behave

conduit, e [kɔ̃dɥi, -it] PP de **conduire** ▸ NM (*Tech*) conduit, pipe; (*Anat*) duct, canal

conduite [kɔ̃dɥit] NF (*en auto*) driving; (*comportement*) behaviour (BRIT), behavior (US); (*d'eau, de gaz*) pipe; **sous la ~ de** led by; **~ forcée** pressure pipe; **~ à gauche** left-hand drive; **~ intérieure** saloon (car); **~ sous l'emprise de stupéfiants** drug-driving

cône [kon] NM cone; **en forme de ~** cone-shaped

conf. ABR = **confort; tt** = all mod cons (BRIT)

confection [kɔ̃fɛksjɔ̃] NF (*fabrication*) making; (*Couture*): **la ~** the clothing industry, the rag trade (*fam*); **vêtement de ~** ready-to-wear *ou* off-the-peg garment

confectionner [kɔ̃fɛksjɔne] /1/ VT to make

confédération [kɔ̃federasjɔ̃] NF confederation

conférence [kɔ̃ferɑ̃s] NF (*exposé*) lecture; (*pourparlers*) conference; **~ de presse** press conference; **~ au sommet** summit (conference)

conférencier, -ière [kɔ̃ferɑ̃sje, -jɛr] NM/F lecturer

conférer [kɔ̃fere] /6/ VT: **~ à qn** (*titre, grade*) to confer on sb; **~ à qch/qn** (*aspect etc*) to endow sth/sb with, give (to) sth/sb

confesser [kɔ̃fese] /1/ VT to confess ▪ **se confesser** VPR (*Rel*) to go to confession

confesseur [kɔ̃fesœr] NM confessor

confession [kɔ̃fesjɔ̃] NF confession; (*culte: catholique etc*) denomination

confessionnal, -aux [kɔ̃fesjɔnal, -o] NM confessional

confessionnel, le [kɔ̃fesjɔnɛl] ADJ denominational

confetti [kɔ̃feti] NM confetti *no pl*

★**confiance** [kɔ̃fjɑ̃s] NF (*en l'honnêteté de qn*) confidence, trust; (*en la valeur de qch*) faith; **avoir ~ en** to have confidence *ou* faith in, trust; **faire ~ à** to trust; **en toute ~** with complete confidence; **de ~** trustworthy, reliable; **mettre qn en ~** to win sb's trust; **vote de ~** (*Pol*) vote of confidence; **inspirer ~ à** to inspire confidence in; **~ en soi** self-confidence; *voir* **question**

confiant, e [kɔ̃fjɑ̃, -ɑ̃t] ADJ confident; trusting

confidence [kɔ̃fidɑ̃s] NF confidence

confident, e [kɔ̃fidɑ̃, -ɑ̃t] NM/F confidant/confidante

confidentiel, le [kɔ̃fidɑ̃sjɛl] ADJ confidential

confidentiellement [kɔ̃fidɑ̃sjɛlmɑ̃] ADV in confidence, confidentially

confier [kɔ̃fje] /7/ VT: **~ à qn** (*objet en dépôt, travail etc*) to entrust to sb; (*secret, pensée*) to confide to sb; **se ~ à qn** to confide in sb

configuration [kɔ̃figyrasjɔ̃] NF configuration, layout; (*Inform*) configuration

configurer [kɔ̃figyre] /1/ VT to configure

confiné, e [kɔ̃fine] ADJ enclosed; (*air*) stale

confiner [kɔ̃fine] /1/ VT: **~ à** to confine to; (*toucher*) to border on; **se ~ dans** *ou* **à** to confine o.s. to

confins [kɔ̃fɛ̃] NMPL: **aux ~ de** on the borders of

confirmation [kɔ̃firmasjɔ̃] NF confirmation

confirmé, e [kɔ̃firme] ADJ (*personne*) experienced

★**confirmer** [kɔ̃firme] /1/ VT to confirm; **~ qn dans une croyance/ses fonctions** to strengthen sb in a belief/his duties

confiscation [kɔ̃fiskasjɔ̃] NF confiscation

★**confiserie** [kɔ̃fizri] NF (*magasin*) confectioner's *ou* sweet shop (BRIT), candy store (US) ▪ **confiseries** NFPL (*bonbons*) confectionery *sg*, sweets, candy *no pl*

confiseur, -euse [kɔ̃fizœr, -øz] NM/F confectioner

confisquer [kɔ̃fiske] /1/ VT to confiscate

confit, e [kɔ̃fi, -it] ADJ: **fruits confits** crystallized fruits ▸ NM: **~ d'oie** potted goose

★**confiture** [kɔ̃fityr] NF jam; **~ d'oranges** (orange) marmalade

conflagration [kɔ̃flagrasjɔ̃] NF cataclysm

conflictuel, le [kɔ̃fliktɥɛl] ADJ full of clashes *ou* conflicts

conflit [kɔ̃fli] NM conflict; **~ d'intérêts** conflict of interests

confluent [kɔ̃flyɑ̃] NM confluence

confondre [kɔ̃fɔ̃dr] /41/ VT (*jumeaux, faits*) to confuse, mix up; (*témoin, menteur*) to confound; **~ qch/qn avec qch/qn d'autre** to mistake sth/sb for sth/sb else ▪ **se confondre** VPR to merge; **se ~ en excuses** to offer profuse apologies, apologize profusely

confondu, e [kɔ̃fɔ̃dy] PP de **confondre** ▸ ADJ (*stupéfait*) speechless, overcome; **toutes catégories confondues** taking all categories together

conformation [kɔ̃fɔrmasjɔ̃] NF conformation

conforme [kɔ̃fɔrm] ADJ: **~ à** (*en accord avec: loi, règle*) in accordance with, in keeping with; (*identique à*) true to; **copie certifiée ~** (*Admin*) certified copy; **~ à la commande** as per order

conformé, e [kɔ̃fɔrme] ADJ: **bien ~** well-formed

conformément [kɔ̃fɔrmemɑ̃] ADV: **~ à** in accordance with

conformer [kɔ̃fɔrme] /1/ VT: **~ qch à** to model sth on; **se ~ à** to conform to

conformisme [kɔ̃fɔrmism] NM conformity

conformiste [kɔ̃fɔrmist] ADJ, NMF conformist

conformité [kɔ̃fɔrmite] NF conformity; agreement; **en ~ avec** in accordance with

C

★**confort** [kɔ̃fɔʀ] NM comfort; **tout ~** (*Comm*) with all mod cons (*Brit*) *ou* modern conveniences

★**confortable** [kɔ̃fɔʀtabl] ADJ comfortable

confortablement [kɔ̃fɔʀtabləmɑ̃] ADV comfortably

conforter [kɔ̃fɔʀte] /1/ VT to reinforce, strengthen

confrère [kɔ̃fʀɛʀ] NM colleague; fellow member

confrérie [kɔ̃fʀeʀi] NF brotherhood

confrontation [kɔ̃fʀɔ̃tasjɔ̃] NF confrontation

confronté, e [kɔ̃fʀɔ̃te] ADJ: **~ à** confronted by, facing

confronter [kɔ̃fʀɔ̃te] /1/ VT to confront; (*textes*) to compare, collate

confus, e [kɔ̃fy, -yz] ADJ (*vague*) confused; (*embarrassé*) embarrassed

confusément [kɔ̃fyzemɑ̃] ADV (*distinguer, ressentir*) vaguely; (*parler*) confusedly

confusion [kɔ̃fyzjɔ̃] NF (*voir confus*) confusion; embarrassment; (*voir confondre*) confusion; mixing up; (*erreur*) confusion; **~ des peines** (*Jur*) concurrency of sentences

congé [kɔ̃ʒe] NM (*vacances*) holiday; (*arrêt de travail*) time off *no pl*, leave *no pl*; (*Mil*) leave *no pl*; (*avis de départ*) notice; **en ~** on holiday; off (work); on leave; **semaine/jour de ~** week/day off; **prendre ~ de qn** to take one's leave of sb; **donner son ~ à** to hand *ou* give in one's notice to; **~ de maladie** sick leave; **~ de maternité** maternity leave; **congés payés** paid holiday *ou* leave

congédier [kɔ̃ʒedje] /7/ VT to dismiss

congélateur [kɔ̃ʒelatœʀ] NM freezer, deep freeze

congélation [kɔ̃ʒelasjɔ̃] NF freezing; (*de l'huile*) congealing

★**congeler** [kɔ̃ʒ(ə)le] /5/ VT to freeze; **les produits congelés** frozen foods ■ **se congeler** VPR to freeze

congénère [kɔ̃ʒenɛʀ] NMF fellow (bear *ou* lion *etc*), fellow creature

congénital, e, -aux [kɔ̃ʒenital, -o] ADJ congenital

congère [kɔ̃ʒɛʀ] NF snowdrift

congestion [kɔ̃ʒɛstjɔ̃] NF congestion; **~ cérébrale** stroke; **~ pulmonaire** congestion of the lungs

congestionner [kɔ̃ʒɛstjɔne] /1/ VT to congest; (*Méd*) to flush

conglomérat [kɔ̃glɔmeʀa] NM conglomerate

Congo [kɔ̃ɡo] NM: **le ~** (*pays, fleuve*) the Congo

congolais, e [kɔ̃ɡɔlɛ, -ɛz] ADJ Congolese ▶ NM/F: **Congolais, e** Congolese

congratuler [kɔ̃gʀatyle] /1/ VT to congratulate

congre [kɔ̃gʀ] NM conger (eel)

congrégation [kɔ̃gʀegasjɔ̃] NF (*Rel*) congregation; (*gén*) assembly; gathering

congrès [kɔ̃gʀɛ] NM congress

congressiste [kɔ̃gʀesist] NMF delegate, participant (at a congress)

congru, e [kɔ̃gʀy] ADJ: **la portion congrue** the smallest *ou* meanest share

conifère [kɔnifɛʀ] NM conifer

conique [kɔnik] ADJ conical

conjecture [kɔ̃ʒɛktyʀ] NF conjecture, speculation *no pl*

conjecturer [kɔ̃ʒɛktyʀe] /1/ VT, VI to conjecture

conjoint, e [kɔ̃ʒwɛ̃, -wɛ̃t] ADJ joint ▶ NM/F spouse

conjointement [kɔ̃ʒwɛ̃tmɑ̃] ADV jointly

conjonctif, -ive [kɔ̃ʒɔ̃ktif, -iv] ADJ: **tissu ~** connective tissue

conjonction [kɔ̃ʒɔ̃ksjɔ̃] NF (*Ling*) conjunction

conjonctivite [kɔ̃ʒɔ̃ktivit] NF conjunctivitis

conjoncture [kɔ̃ʒɔ̃ktyʀ] NF circumstances *pl*; **la ~ (économique)** the economic climate *ou* situation

conjoncturel, le [kɔ̃ʒɔ̃ktyʀɛl] ADJ: **variations/tendances conjoncturelles** economic fluctuations/trends

conjugaison [kɔ̃ʒygɛzɔ̃] NF (*Ling*) conjugation

conjugal, e, -aux [kɔ̃ʒygal, -o] ADJ conjugal; married

conjugué, e [kɔ̃ʒyge] ADJ combined

conjuguer [kɔ̃ʒyge] /1/ VT (*Ling*) to conjugate; (*efforts etc*) to combine

conjuration [kɔ̃ʒyʀasjɔ̃] NF conspiracy

conjuré, e [kɔ̃ʒyʀe] NM/F conspirator

conjurer [kɔ̃ʒyʀe] /1/ VT (*sort, maladie*) to avert; (*implorer*): **~ qn de faire qch** to beseech *ou* entreat sb to do sth

connais [kɔnɛ], **connaissais** *etc* [kɔnɛsɛ] VB *voir* **connaître**

★**connaissance** [kɔnɛsɑ̃s] NF (*savoir*) knowledge *no pl*; (*personne connue*) acquaintance; (*conscience*) consciousness; **être sans ~** to be unconscious; **perdre/reprendre ~** to lose/regain consciousness; **à ma/sa ~** to (the best of) my/his knowledge; **faire ~ avec qn** *ou* **la ~ de qn** (*rencontrer*) to meet sb; (*apprendre à connaître*) to get to know sb; **avoir ~ de** to be aware of; **prendre ~ de** (*document etc*) to peruse; **en ~ de cause** with full knowledge of the facts; **de ~** (*personne, visage*) familiar ■ **connaissances** NFPL knowledge *no pl*

connaissant *etc* [kɔnɛsɑ̃] VB *voir* **connaître**

connaissement [kɔnɛsmɑ̃] NM bill of lading

connaisseur, -euse [kɔnɛsœʀ, -øz] NM/F connoisseur ▶ ADJ expert

connaître [kɔnɛtʀ] /57/ VT to know; (*éprouver*) to experience; (*avoir: succès*) to have; to enjoy; **~ de nom/vue** to know by name/sight ■ **se connaître** VPR to know each other; (*soi-même*) to know o.s.; **ils se sont connus à Genève** they (first) met in Geneva; **s'y ~ en qch** to know about sth

connasse [kɔnas] NF (!) stupid bitch (!) *ou* cow (!)

connecté, e [kɔnɛkte] ADJ (*Inform*) online

connecter [kɔnɛkte] /1/ VT to connect; **se ~ à Internet** to log onto the internet

connectique [kɔnɛktik] NF connectors *pl*

connectivité [kɔnɛktivite] NF (*Inform*) connectivity

connerie [kɔnʀi] NF (*fam*) (bloody) stupid (*Brit*) *ou* damn-fool (*US*) thing to do *ou* say

connexe [kɔnɛks] ADJ closely related

connexion [kɔnɛksjɔ̃] NF connection

connivence [kɔnivɑ̃s] NF connivance

connotation [kɔnɔtasjɔ̃] NF connotation

connu, e [kɔny] PP de **connaître** ▸ ADJ (célèbre) well-known

conque [kɔ̃k] NF (coquille) conch (shell)

conquérant, e [kɔ̃keʀɑ̃, -ɑ̃t] NM/F conqueror

conquérir [kɔ̃keʀiʀ] /21/ VT to conquer, win

conquerrai etc [kɔ̃kɛʀʀe] VB voir **conquérir**

conquête [kɔ̃kɛt] NF conquest

conquière, conquiers etc [kɔ̃kjɛʀ] VB voir **conquérir**

conquis, e [kɔ̃ki, -iz] PP de **conquérir**

★**consacrer** [kɔ̃sakʀe] /1/ VT (Rel) to consecrate; (fig: usage etc) to sanction, establish; **~ qch à** (employer) to devote ou dedicate sth to; (Rel) to consecrate sth to; **se ~ à qch/faire** to dedicate ou devote o.s. to sth/to doing

consanguin, e [kɔ̃sɑ̃gɛ̃, -in] ADJ between blood relations; **frère ~** half-brother (on father's side); **mariage ~** intermarriage

consciemment [kɔ̃sjamɑ̃] ADV consciously

conscience [kɔ̃sjɑ̃s] NF conscience; (perception) consciousness; **avoir/prendre ~ de** to be/become aware of; **perdre/reprendre ~** to lose/regain consciousness; **avoir bonne/mauvaise ~** to have a clear/guilty conscience; **en (toute) ~** in all conscience

consciencieux, -euse [kɔ̃sjɑ̃sjø, -øz] ADJ conscientious

conscient, e [kɔ̃sjɑ̃, -ɑ̃t] ADJ conscious; **~ de** aware ou conscious of

conscription [kɔ̃skʀipsjɔ̃] NF conscription

conscrit [kɔ̃skʀi] NM conscript

consécration [kɔ̃sekʀasjɔ̃] NF consecration

consécutif, -ive [kɔ̃sekytif, -iv] ADJ consecutive; **~ à** following upon

consécutivement [kɔ̃sekytivmɑ̃] ADV consecutively; **~ à** following on

★**conseil** [kɔ̃sɛj] NM (avis) piece of advice, advice no pl; (assemblée) council; (expert): **~ en recrutement** recruitment consultant; **tenir ~** to hold a meeting; to deliberate; **donner un ~ ou des conseils à qn** to give sb (a piece of) advice; **demander ~ à qn** to ask sb's advice; **prendre ~ (auprès de qn)** to take advice (from sb); **~ d'administration** board (of directors); **~ de classe** (Scol) meeting of teachers, parents and class representatives to discuss pupils' progress; **~ départemental** regional council; see note; **~ de discipline** disciplinary committee; **~ de guerre** court-martial; **le ~ des ministres** ≈ the Cabinet; **~ municipal** town council; **~ régional** regional board of elected representatives; **~ de révision** recruitment ou draft (US) board ▸ ADJ: **ingénieur-conseil** engineering consultant

Each *département* of France is run by a **conseil départemental**, whose remit includes maintenance of school buildings, transport and road infrastructure, housing, the fire and rescue service, the environment, tourism and culture. The council is made up of *conseillers généraux* elected for a six-year term under a specific voting system: two *conseillers*, a man and a woman, are jointly elected to represent their *canton*.

Advice est indénombrable, c'est-à-dire qu'il ne peut pas désigner un seul avis. Pour traduire *un conseil*, il faut dire **a piece of advice**. Notez que **advice** ne prend jamais de **-s** et s'emploie avec un verbe au singulier.
Leurs conseils m'ont été précieux. **Their advice was invaluable to me.**
C'est le meilleur conseil qu'on m'ait jamais donné. **This is the best piece of advice I have ever been given.**

★**conseiller¹** [kɔ̃seje] VT (personne) to advise; (méthode, action) to recommend, advise; **~ qch à qn** to recommend sth to sb; **~ à qn de faire qch** to advise sb to do sth

conseiller², -ère [kɔ̃seje, -ɛʀ] NM/F adviser; **~ général** regional councillor; **~ matrimonial** marriage guidance counsellor; **~ municipal** town councillor; **~ d'orientation** (Scol) careers adviser (Brit), (school) counselor (US)

consensuel, le [kɔ̃sɑ̃sɥɛl] ADJ consensual

consensus [kɔ̃sɛ̃sys] NM consensus

consentement [kɔ̃sɑ̃tmɑ̃] NM consent

consentir [kɔ̃sɑ̃tiʀ] /16/ VT: **~ (à qch/faire)** to agree ou consent (to sth/to doing); **~ qch à qn** to grant sb sth

conséquence [kɔ̃sekɑ̃s] NF consequence, outcome; **en ~** (donc) consequently; (de façon appropriée) accordingly; **ne pas tirer à ~** to be unlikely to have any repercussions; **sans ~** unimportant; **de ~** important ■ **conséquences** NFPL consequences, repercussions

conséquent, e [kɔ̃sekɑ̃, -ɑ̃t] ADJ logical, rational; (fam: important) substantial; **par ~** consequently

conservateur, -trice [kɔ̃sɛʀvatœʀ, -tʀis] ADJ conservative ▸ NM/F (Pol) conservative; (de musée) curator ▸ NM (pour aliments) preservative

conservation [kɔ̃sɛʀvasjɔ̃] NF retention; keeping; preserving, preservation

conservatisme [kɔ̃sɛʀvatism] NM conservatism

conservatoire [kɔ̃sɛʀvatwaʀ] NM academy; (Écologie) conservation area

conserve [kɔ̃sɛʀv] NF (gén pl) canned ou tinned (Brit) food; **conserves de poisson** canned ou tinned (Brit) fish; **en ~** canned, tinned (Brit); **de ~** (ensemble) in concert; (naviguer) in convoy

conservé, e [kɔ̃sɛʀve] ADJ: **bien ~** (personne) well-preserved

conserver [kɔ̃sɛʀve] /1/ VT (faculté) to retain, keep; (habitude) to keep up; (amis, livres) to keep; (préserver, Culin) to preserve; **« ~ au frais »** "store in a cool place" ■ **se conserver** VPR (aliments) to keep

conserverie [kɔ̃sɛʀvəʀi] NF canning factory

considérable [kɔ̃sideʀabl] ADJ considerable, significant, extensive

considérablement [kɔ̃sideʀabləmɑ̃] ADV considerably, significantly

considération [kɔ̃sideʀasjɔ̃] NF consideration; (estime) esteem, respect; **prendre en ~** to take into consideration ou account; **ceci mérite ~** this is worth considering; **en ~ de** given, because of ■ **considérations** NFPL (remarques) reflections

considéré, e [kɔ̃sideʀe] ADJ respected; **tout bien ~** all things considered

considérer [kɔ̃sideʀe] /6/ VT to consider; (*regarder*) to consider, study; **~ qch comme** to regard sth as

★**consigne** [kɔ̃siɲ] NF (*Comm*) deposit; (*de gare*) left luggage (office) (BRIT), checkroom (US); (*punition: Scol*) detention; (: *Mil*) confinement to barracks; (*ordre, instruction*) instructions *pl*; **~ automatique** left-luggage locker; **consignes de sécurité** safety instructions

consigné, e [kɔ̃siɲe] ADJ (*Comm: bouteille, emballage*) returnable; **non ~** non-returnable

consigner [kɔ̃siɲe] /1/ VT (*note, pensée*) to record; (*marchandises*) to deposit; (*punir: Mil*) to confine to barracks; (: *élève*) to put in detention; (*Comm*) to put a deposit on

consistance [kɔ̃sistɑ̃s] NF consistency

consistant, e [kɔ̃sistɑ̃, -ɑ̃t] ADJ thick; solid

consister [kɔ̃siste] /1/ VI: **~ en/dans/à faire** to consist of/in/in doing

consœur [kɔ̃sœʀ] NF (lady) colleague; fellow member

consolation [kɔ̃sɔlasjɔ̃] NF consolation *no pl*, comfort *no pl*

console [kɔ̃sɔl] NF console; **~ graphique** *ou* **de visualisation** (*Inform*) visual display unit, VDU; **~ de jeux** games console

consoler [kɔ̃sɔle] /1/ VT to console; **se ~ (de qch)** to console o.s. (for sth)

consolider [kɔ̃sɔlide] /1/ VT to strengthen, reinforce; (*fig*) to consolidate; **bilan consolidé** consolidated balance sheet

consommateur, -trice [kɔ̃sɔmatœʀ, -tʀis] NM/F (*Écon*) consumer; (*dans un café*) customer

consommation [kɔ̃sɔmasjɔ̃] NF (*Écon*) consumption; (*Jur*) consummation; (*boisson*) drink; **~ aux 100 km** (*Auto*) (fuel) consumption per 100 km, ≈ miles per gallon (mpg), ≈ gas mileage (US); **de ~** (*biens, société*) consumer *cpd*

consommé, e [kɔ̃sɔme] ADJ consummate ▶ NM consommé

★**consommer** [kɔ̃sɔme] /1/ VT (*personne*) to eat *ou* drink, consume; (*voiture, usine, poêle*) to use, consume; (*Jur: mariage*) to consummate ▶ VI (*dans un café*) to (have a) drink

consonance [kɔ̃sɔnɑ̃s] NF consonance; **nom à ~ étrangère** foreign-sounding name

consonne [kɔ̃sɔn] NF consonant

consortium [kɔ̃sɔʀsjɔm] NM consortium

consorts [kɔ̃sɔʀ] NMPL: **et ~** (*péj*) and company, and his bunch *ou* like

conspirateur, -trice [kɔ̃spiʀatœʀ, -tʀis] NM/F conspirator, plotter

conspiration [kɔ̃spiʀasjɔ̃] NF conspiracy

conspirationniste [kɔ̃spiʀasjɔnist] NMF conspiracy theorist ▶ ADJ (*théorie*) conspiracy

conspirer [kɔ̃spiʀe] /1/ VI to conspire, plot; **~ à** (*tendre à*) to conspire to

conspuer [kɔ̃spɥe] /1/ VT to boo, shout down

constamment [kɔ̃stamɑ̃] ADV constantly

constance [kɔ̃stɑ̃s] NF permanence, constancy; (*d'une amitié*) steadfastness; **travailler avec ~** to work steadily; **il faut de la ~ pour la supporter** (*fam*) you need a lot of patience to put up with her

constant, e [kɔ̃stɑ̃, -ɑ̃t] ADJ constant; (*personne*) steadfast ▶ NF constant

Constantinople [kɔ̃stɑ̃tinɔpl] N Constantinople

constat [kɔ̃sta] NM (*d'huissier*) certified report (*by bailiff*); (*de police*) report; (*observation*) (observed) fact, observation; (*affirmation*) statement; **~ (à l'amiable)** (*jointly agreed*) statement for insurance purposes; **~ d'échec** acknowledgment of failure

constatation [kɔ̃statasjɔ̃] NF noticing; certifying; (*remarque*) observation

constater [kɔ̃state] /1/ VT (*remarquer*) to note, notice; (*Admin, Jur: attester*) to certify; (*dégâts*) to note; **~ que** (*dire*) to state that

constellation [kɔ̃stelasjɔ̃] NF constellation

constellé, e [kɔ̃stele] ADJ: **~ de** (*étoiles*) studded *ou* spangled with; (*taches*) spotted with

consternant, e [kɔ̃stɛʀnɑ̃, -ɑ̃t] ADJ (*nouvelle*) dismaying; (*attristant, étonnant: bêtise*) appalling

consternation [kɔ̃stɛʀnasjɔ̃] NF consternation, dismay

consterner [kɔ̃stɛʀne] /1/ VT to dismay

constipation [kɔ̃stipasjɔ̃] NF constipation

constipé, e [kɔ̃stipe] ADJ constipated; (*fig*) stiff

constituant, e [kɔ̃stitɥɑ̃, -ɑ̃t] ADJ (*élément*) constituent; **assemblée constituante** (*Pol*) constituent assembly

constitué, e [kɔ̃stitɥe] ADJ: **~ de** made up *ou* composed of; **bien ~** of sound constitution; well-formed

constituer [kɔ̃stitɥe] /1/ VT (*comité, équipe*) to set up, form; (*dossier, collection*) to put together, build up; (*éléments, parties: composer*) to make up, constitute; (: *représenter, être*) to constitute; **se ~ prisonnier** to give o.s. up; **se ~ partie civile** to bring an independent action for damages

constitution [kɔ̃stitysjɔ̃] NF setting up; building up; (*composition*) composition, make-up; (*santé, Pol*) constitution

constitutionnel, le [kɔ̃stitysjɔnɛl] ADJ constitutional

constructeur [kɔ̃stʀyktœʀ] NM manufacturer, builder

constructif, -ive [kɔ̃stʀyktif, -iv] ADJ (*positif*) constructive

construction [kɔ̃stʀyksjɔ̃] NF construction, building

★**construire** [kɔ̃stʀɥiʀ] /38/ VT to build, construct ■ **se construire** VPR: **l'immeuble s'est construit très vite** the building went up *ou* was built very quickly

consul [kɔ̃syl] NM consul

consulaire [kɔ̃sylɛʀ] ADJ consular

consulat [kɔ̃syla] NM consulate

consultant, e [kɔ̃syltɑ̃, -ɑ̃t] ADJ, NM consultant

consultatif, -ive [kɔ̃syltatif, -iv] ADJ advisory

consultation [kɔ̃syltasjɔ̃] NF consultation; **être en ~** (*délibération*) to be in consultation; (*médecin*) to be consulting; **aller à la ~** (*Méd*) to go to the surgery (BRIT) *ou* doctor's office (US); **heures de ~** (*Méd*) surgery (BRIT) *ou* office (US) hours ■ **consultations** NFPL (*Pol*) talks

consulter [kɔ̃sylte] /1/ VT to consult ▶ VI (*médecin*) to hold surgery (BRIT), be in (the office) (US) ■ **se consulter** VPR to confer

consumer [kɔ̃syme] /**1**/ VT to consume ■ **se consumer** VPR to burn; **se ~ de chagrin/douleur** to be consumed with sorrow/grief

consumérisme [kɔ̃symeRism] NM consumerism

contact [kɔ̃takt] NM contact; **au ~ de** (air, peau) on contact with; (gens) through contact with; **mettre/couper le ~** (Auto) to switch on/off the ignition; **entrer en ~** (fils, objets) to come into contact, make contact; **se mettre en ~ avec** (Radio) to make contact with; **prendre ~ avec** (relation d'affaires, connaissance) to get in touch ou contact with

★**contacter** [kɔ̃takte] /**1**/ VT to contact, get in touch with

contagieux, -euse [kɔ̃taʒjø, -øz] ADJ infectious; (par le contact) contagious

contagion [kɔ̃taʒjɔ̃] NF contagion

container [kɔ̃tɛnɛR] NM container

contamination [kɔ̃taminasjɔ̃] NF infection; contamination

contaminer [kɔ̃tamine] /**1**/ VT (par un virus) to infect; (par des radiations) to contaminate

conte [kɔ̃t] NM tale; **~ de fées** fairy tale

contemplatif, -ive [kɔ̃tɑ̃platif, -iv] ADJ contemplative

contemplation [kɔ̃tɑ̃plasjɔ̃] NF contemplation; (Rel, Philosophie) meditation

contempler [kɔ̃tɑ̃ple] /**1**/ VT to contemplate, gaze at

contemporain, e [kɔ̃tɑ̃pɔRɛ̃, -ɛn] ADJ, NM/F contemporary

contenance [kɔ̃t(ə)nɑ̃s] NF (d'un récipient) capacity; (attitude) bearing, attitude; **perdre ~** to lose one's composure; **se donner une ~** to give the impression of composure; **faire bonne ~ (devant)** to put on a bold front (in the face of)

conteneur [kɔ̃t(ə)nœR] NM container; **~ (de bouteilles)** bottle bank

conteneurisation [kɔ̃t(ə)nœRizasjɔ̃] NF containerization

★**contenir** [kɔ̃t(ə)niR] /**22**/ VT to contain; (avoir une capacité de) to hold ■ **se contenir** VPR (se retenir) to control o.s. ou one's emotions, contain o.s.

★**content, e** [kɔ̃tɑ̃, -ɑ̃t] ADJ pleased, glad; **~ de** pleased with; **je serais ~ que tu …** I would be pleased if you …

contentement [kɔ̃tɑ̃tmɑ̃] NM contentment, satisfaction

contenter [kɔ̃tɑ̃te] /**1**/ VT to satisfy, please; (envie) to satisfy ■ **se contenter de** VPR to content o.s. with

contentieux [kɔ̃tɑ̃sjø] NM (Comm) litigation; (: service) litigation department; (Pol etc) contentious issues pl

contenu, e [kɔ̃t(ə)ny] PP de **contenir** ▶ NM (d'un bol) contents pl; (d'un texte) content

conter [kɔ̃te] /**1**/ VT to recount, relate; **en ~ de belles à qn** to tell tall stories to sb

contestable [kɔ̃tɛstabl] ADJ questionable

contestataire [kɔ̃tɛstatɛR] ADJ (journal, étudiant) anti-establishment ▶ NMF (anti-establishment) protester

contestation [kɔ̃tɛstasjɔ̃] NF questioning, contesting; (Pol): **la ~** anti-establishment activity, protest

conteste [kɔ̃tɛst]: **sans ~** adv unquestionably, indisputably

contesté, e [kɔ̃tɛste] ADJ (roman, écrivain) controversial

contester [kɔ̃tɛste] /**1**/ VT to question, contest ▶ VI (Pol: gén) to rebel (against established authority), protest

conteur, -euse [kɔ̃tœR, -øz] NM/F story-teller

contexte [kɔ̃tɛkst] NM context

contiendrai [kɔ̃tjɛ̃dRe], **contiens** etc [kɔ̃tjɛ̃] VB voir **contenir**

contigu, ë [kɔ̃tigy] ADJ: **~ (à)** adjacent (to)

continent [kɔ̃tinɑ̃] NM continent

continental, e, -aux [kɔ̃tinɑ̃tal, -o] ADJ continental

contingences [kɔ̃tɛ̃ʒɑ̃s] NFPL contingencies

contingent [kɔ̃tɛ̃ʒɑ̃] NM (Mil) contingent; (Comm) quota

contingenter [kɔ̃tɛ̃ʒɑ̃te] /**1**/ VT (Comm) to fix a quota on

contins etc [kɔ̃tɛ̃] VB voir **contenir**

continu, e [kɔ̃tiny] ADJ continuous; **faire la journée continue** to work without taking a full lunch break; **(courant) ~** direct current, DC

continuation [kɔ̃tinɥasjɔ̃] NF continuation

continuel, le [kɔ̃tinɥɛl] ADJ (qui se répète) constant, continual; (continu) continuous

continuellement [kɔ̃tinɥɛlmɑ̃] ADV continually; continuously

★**continuer** [kɔ̃tinɥe] /**1**/ VT (travail, voyage etc) to continue (with), carry on (with), go on with; (prolonger: alignement, rue) to continue; **~ à** ou **de faire** to go on ou continue doing ▶ VI (pluie, vie, bruit) to continue, go on; (voyageur) to go on ■ **se continuer** VPR to carry on

continuité [kɔ̃tinɥite] NF continuity; continuation

contondant, e [kɔ̃tɔ̃dɑ̃, -ɑ̃t] ADJ: **arme contondante** blunt instrument

contorsion [kɔ̃tɔRsjɔ̃] NF contortion

contorsionner [kɔ̃tɔRsjɔne] /**1**/: **se contorsionner** VPR to contort o.s., writhe about

contorsionniste [kɔ̃tɔRsjɔnist] NMF contortionist

contour [kɔ̃tuR] NM outline, contour ■ **contours** NMPL (d'une rivière etc) windings

contourner [kɔ̃tuRne] /**1**/ VT to bypass, walk ou drive round; (difficulté) to get round

contraceptif, -ive [kɔ̃tRasɛptif, -iv] ADJ, NM contraceptive

contraception [kɔ̃tRasɛpsjɔ̃] NF contraception

contracté, e [kɔ̃tRakte] ADJ (muscle) tense, contracted; (personne: tendu) tense, tensed up; **article ~** (Ling) contracted article

contracter [kɔ̃tRakte] /**1**/ VT (muscle etc) to tense, contract; (maladie, dette, obligation) to contract; (assurance) to take out ■ **se contracter** VPR (métal, muscles) to contract

contraction [kɔ̃tRaksjɔ̃] NF contraction

contractuel, le [kɔ̃tRaktɥɛl] ADJ contractual ▶ NM/F (agent) traffic warden; (employé) contract employee

contradiction [kɔ̃tRadiksjɔ̃] NF contradiction

contradictoire [kɔ̃tradiktwaʀ] ADJ contradictory, conflicting; **débat ~** (open) debate

contraignant, e [kɔ̃tʀɛɲɑ̃, -ɑ̃t] VB voir **contraindre** ▸ ADJ restricting

contraindre [kɔ̃tʀɛ̃dʀ] /52/ VT: **~ qn à faire** to force ou compel sb to do

contraint, e [kɔ̃tʀɛ̃, -ɛ̃t] PP de **contraindre** ▸ NF constraint; **sans contrainte** unrestrainedly, unconstrainedly

★**contraire** [kɔ̃tʀɛʀ] ADJ, NM opposite; **~ à** contrary to; **au ~** adv on the contrary

contrairement [kɔ̃tʀɛʀmɑ̃] ADV: **~ à** contrary to, unlike

contralto [kɔ̃tʀalto] NM contralto

contrariant, e [kɔ̃tʀaʀjɑ̃, -ɑ̃t] ADJ (personne) contrary, perverse; (incident) annoying

contrarier [kɔ̃tʀaʀje] /7/ VT (personne) to annoy, bother; (fig) to impede; (projets) to thwart, frustrate

contrariété [kɔ̃tʀaʀjete] NF annoyance

contraste [kɔ̃tʀast] NM contrast

contraster [kɔ̃tʀaste] /1/ VT, VI to contrast

★**contrat** [kɔ̃tʀa] NM contract; (fig: accord, pacte) agreement; **~ de travail** employment contract

contravention [kɔ̃tʀavɑ̃sjɔ̃] NF (infraction): **~ à** contravention of; (amende) fine; (PV pour stationnement interdit) parking ticket; **dresser ~ à** (automobiliste) to book; to write out a parking ticket for

★**contre** [kɔ̃tʀ] PRÉP against; (en échange) (in exchange) for; **par ~** on the other hand

contre-amiral, -aux [kɔ̃tʀamiʀal, -o] NM rear admiral

contre-attaque [kɔ̃tʀatak] NF counterattack

contre-attaquer [kɔ̃tʀatake] /1/ VI to counterattack

contrebalancer [kɔ̃tʀəbalɑ̃se] VT to counterbalance; (fig) to offset

contre-balancer [kɔ̃tʀəbalɑ̃se] /3/ VT to counterbalance; (fig) to offset

contrebande [kɔ̃tʀəbɑ̃d] NF (trafic) contraband, smuggling; (marchandise) contraband, smuggled goods pl; **faire la ~ de** to smuggle

contrebandier, -ière [kɔ̃tʀəbɑ̃dje, -jɛʀ] NM/F smuggler

contrebas [kɔ̃tʀəba]: **en ~** adv (down) below

contrebasse [kɔ̃tʀəbas] NF (double) bass

contrebassiste [kɔ̃tʀəbasist] NMF (double) bass player

contre-braquer [kɔ̃tʀəbʀake] /1/ VI to steer into a skid

contrecarrer [kɔ̃tʀəkaʀe] /1/ VT to thwart

contrechamp [kɔ̃tʀəʃɑ̃] NM (Ciné) reverse shot

contrecœur [kɔ̃tʀəkœʀ]: **à ~** adv (be)grudgingly, reluctantly

contrecoup [kɔ̃tʀəku] NM repercussions pl; **par ~** as an indirect consequence

contre-courant [kɔ̃tʀəkuʀɑ̃]: **à ~** adv against the current

contredire [kɔ̃tʀədiʀ] /37/ VT (personne) to contradict; (témoignage, assertion, faits) to refute ▪ **se contredire** VPR to contradict o.s.

contredit, e [kɔ̃tʀədi, -it] PP de **contredire** ▸ NM: **sans ~** without question

contrée [kɔ̃tʀe] NF region; land

contre-écrou [kɔ̃tʀekʀu] NM lock nut

contre-enquête [kɔ̃tʀɑ̃kɛt] NF counter-inquiry

contre-espionnage [kɔ̃tʀɛspjɔnaʒ] NM counter-espionage

contre-exemple [kɔ̃tʀɛgzɑ̃pl(ə)] NF counter-example

contre-expertise [kɔ̃tʀɛkspɛʀtiz] NF second (expert) assessment

contrefaçon [kɔ̃tʀəfasɔ̃] NF forgery; **~ de brevet** patent infringement

contrefaire [kɔ̃tʀəfɛʀ] /60/ VT (document, signature) to forge, counterfeit; (personne, démarche) to mimic; (dénaturer: sa voix etc) to disguise

contrefait, e [kɔ̃tʀəfɛ, -ɛt] PP de **contrefaire** ▸ ADJ misshapen, deformed

contrefasse [kɔ̃tʀəfas], **contreferai** etc [kɔ̃tʀəfʀe] VB voir **contrefaire**

contre-filet [kɔ̃tʀəfilɛ] NM (Culin) sirloin

contreforts [kɔ̃tʀəfɔʀ] NMPL foothills

contre-haut [kɔ̃tʀəo]: **en ~** adv (up) above

contre-indication [kɔ̃tʀɛ̃dikasjɔ̃] (pl **contre-indications**) NF (Méd) contra-indication; **«~ en cas d'eczéma»** "should not be used by people with eczema"

contre-indiqué, e [kɔ̃tʀɛ̃dike] ADJ (Méd) contraindicated; (déconseillé) unadvisable, ill-advised

contre-interrogatoire [kɔ̃tʀɛ̃teʀɔgatwaʀ] NM: **faire subir un ~ à qn** to cross-examine sb

contre-jour [kɔ̃tʀəʒuʀ]: **à ~** adv against the light

contremaître [kɔ̃tʀəmɛtʀ] NM foreman

contre-manifestant, e [kɔ̃tʀəmanifɛstɑ̃, -ɑ̃t] NM/F counter-demonstrator

contre-manifestation [kɔ̃tʀəmanifɛstasjɔ̃] NF counter-demonstration

contremarque [kɔ̃tʀəmaʀk] NF (ticket) pass-out ticket

contre-offensive [kɔ̃tʀɔfɑ̃siv] NF counteroffensive

contre-ordre [kɔ̃tʀɔʀdʀ] NM = **contrordre**

contrepartie [kɔ̃tʀəpaʀti] NF compensation; **en ~** in compensation; in return

contre-performance [kɔ̃tʀəpɛʀfɔʀmɑ̃s] NF below-average performance

contrepèterie [kɔ̃tʀəpɛtʀi] NF spoonerism

contre-pied [kɔ̃tʀəpje] NM (inverse, opposé): **le ~ de ...** the exact opposite of ...; **prendre le ~ de** to take the opposing view of; to take the opposite course to; **prendre qn à ~** (Sport) to wrong-foot sb

contre-plaqué [kɔ̃tʀəplake] NM plywood

contre-plongée [kɔ̃tʀəplɔ̃ʒe] NF low-angle shot

contrepoids [kɔ̃tʀəpwa] NM counterweight, counterbalance; **faire ~** to act as a counterbalance

contre-poil [kɔ̃tʀəpwal]: **à ~** adv the wrong way

contrepoint [kɔ̃tʀəpwɛ̃] NM counterpoint

contrepoison [kɔ̃tʀəpwazɔ̃] NM antidote

contrer [kɔ̃tʀe] /1/ VT to counter

contre-révolution [kɔ̃tʀəʀevɔlysjɔ̃] NF counter-revolution

contre-révolutionnaire [kɔ̃tʀəʀevɔlysjɔnɛʀ] NMF counter-revolutionary

contresens [kɔ̃tʀəsɑ̃s] NM (*erreur*) misinterpretation; (*mauvaise traduction*) mistranslation; (*absurdité*) nonsense *no pl*; **à ~** *adv* the wrong way

contresigner [kɔ̃tʀəsiɲe] /1/ VT to countersign

contretemps [kɔ̃tʀətɑ̃] NM hitch, contretemps; **à ~** *adv* (*Mus*) out of time; (*fig*) at an inopportune moment

contre-terrorisme [kɔ̃tʀətɛʀɔʀism] NM counter-terrorism

contre-terroriste [kɔ̃tʀətɛʀɔʀist(ə)] NMF counter-terrorist

contre-torpilleur [kɔ̃tʀətɔʀpijœʀ] NM destroyer

contrevenant, e [kɔ̃tʀəv(ə)nɑ̃, -ɑ̃t] VB *voir* **contrevenir** ▶ NM/F offender

contrevenir [kɔ̃tʀəv(ə)niʀ] /22/: **~ à** VT to contravene

contre-voie [kɔ̃tʀəvwa]: **à ~** *adv* (*en sens inverse*) on the wrong track; (*du mauvais côté*) on the wrong side

contribuable [kɔ̃tʀibɥabl] NMF taxpayer

★**contribuer** [kɔ̃tʀibɥe] /1/: **~ à** VT to contribute towards

contribution [kɔ̃tʀibysjɔ̃] NF contribution; **les contributions** (*bureaux*) the tax office; **mettre à ~** to call upon; **contributions directes/indirectes** direct/indirect taxation

contrit, e [kɔ̃tʀi, -it] ADJ contrite

contrôlable [kɔ̃tʀolabl] ADJ (*maîtrisable: situation, débit*) controllable; (*alibi, déclarations*) verifiable

contrôle [kɔ̃tʀol] NM checking *no pl*, check; supervision; monitoring; (*test*) test, examination; **perdre le ~ de son véhicule** to lose control of one's vehicle; **~ des changes** (*Comm*) exchange controls; **~ continu** (*Scol*) continuous assessment; **~ d'identité** identity check; **~ des naissances** birth control; **~ des prix** price control

contrôler [kɔ̃tʀole] /1/ VT (*vérifier*) to check; (*surveiller: opérations*) to supervise; (: *prix*) to monitor, control; (*maîtriser, Comm: firme*) to control ■ **se contrôler** VPR to control o.s.

contrôleur, -euse [kɔ̃tʀolœʀ, -øz] NM/F (*de train*) (ticket) inspector; (*de bus*) (bus) conductor/tress; **~ de la navigation aérienne, ~ aérien** air traffic controller; **~ financier** financial controller

contrordre [kɔ̃tʀɔʀdʀ] NM counter-order, countermand; **sauf ~** unless otherwise directed

controverse [kɔ̃tʀɔvɛʀs] NF controversy

controversé, e [kɔ̃tʀɔvɛʀse] ADJ (*personnage, question*) controversial

contumace [kɔ̃tymas]: **par ~** *adv* in absentia

contusion [kɔ̃tyzjɔ̃] NF bruise, contusion

contusionné, e [kɔ̃tyzjɔne] ADJ bruised

conurbation [kɔnyʀbasjɔ̃] NF conurbation

convaincant, e [kɔ̃vɛ̃kɑ̃, -ɑ̃t] VB *voir* **convaincre** ▶ ADJ convincing

convaincre [kɔ̃vɛ̃kʀ] /42/ VT: **~ qn (de qch)** to convince sb (of sth); **~ qn (de faire)** to persuade sb (to do); **~ qn de** (*Jur: délit*) to convict sb of

convaincu, e [kɔ̃vɛ̃ky] PP *de* **convaincre** ▶ ADJ: **d'un ton ~** with conviction

convainquais *etc* [kɔ̃vɛ̃kɛ] VB *voir* **convaincre**

convalescence [kɔ̃valesɑ̃s] NF convalescence; **maison de ~** convalescent home

convalescent, e [kɔ̃valesɑ̃, -ɑ̃t] ADJ, NM/F convalescent

convenable [kɔ̃vnabl] ADJ suitable; (*décent*) acceptable, proper; (*assez bon*) decent, acceptable; adequate, passable

convenablement [kɔ̃vnabləmɑ̃] ADV (*placé, choisi*) suitably; (*s'habiller, s'exprimer*) properly; (*payé, logé*) decently

convenance [kɔ̃vnɑ̃s] NF: **à ma/votre ~** to my/your liking ■ **convenances** NFPL proprieties

convenir [kɔ̃vniʀ] /22/ VI to be suitable; **~ à** to suit; **il convient de** it is advisable to; (*bienséant*) it is right *ou* proper to; **~ de** (*bien-fondé de qch*) to admit (to), acknowledge; (*date, somme etc*) to agree upon; **~ que** (*admettre*) to admit that, acknowledge the fact that; **~ de faire qch** to agree to do sth; **il a été convenu que** it has been agreed that; **comme convenu** as agreed

convention [kɔ̃vɑ̃sjɔ̃] NF convention; **de ~** conventional; **~ collective** (*Écon*) collective agreement ■ **conventions** NFPL (*convenances*) convention *sg*, social conventions

conventionnalisme [kɔ̃vɑ̃sjɔnalism(ə)] NM (*des idées*) conventionality

conventionné, e [kɔ̃vɑ̃sjɔne] ADJ (*Admin*) applying *charges laid down by the state*

conventionnel, le [kɔ̃vɑ̃sjɔnɛl] ADJ conventional

conventionnellement [kɔ̃vɑ̃sjɔnɛlmɑ̃] ADV conventionally

conventuel, le [kɔ̃vɑ̃tɥɛl] ADJ monastic; monastery *cpd*, conventual, convent *cpd*

convenu, e [kɔ̃vny] PP *de* **convenir** ▶ ADJ agreed

convergence [kɔ̃vɛʀʒɑ̃s] NF convergence; **les critères de ~** the convergence criteria

convergent, e [kɔ̃vɛʀʒɑ̃, -ɑ̃t] ADJ convergent

converger [kɔ̃vɛʀʒe] /3/ VI to converge; **~ vers** *ou* **sur** to converge on

★**conversation** [kɔ̃vɛʀsasjɔ̃] NF conversation; **avoir de la ~** to be a good conversationalist

converser [kɔ̃vɛʀse] /1/ VI to converse

conversion [kɔ̃vɛʀsjɔ̃] NF conversion; (*Ski*) kick turn

convertible [kɔ̃vɛʀtibl] ADJ (*Écon*) convertible; (*canapé*) **~** sofa bed

convertir [kɔ̃vɛʀtiʀ] /2/ VT: **~ qn (à)** to convert sb (to); **~ qch en** to convert sth into ■ **se convertir (à)** VPR to be converted (to)

convertisseur [kɔ̃vɛʀtisœʀ] NM (*Élec*) converter

convexe [kɔ̃vɛks] ADJ convex

conviction [kɔ̃viksjɔ̃] NF conviction

conviendrai [kɔ̃vjɛ̃dʀe], **conviens** *etc* [kɔ̃vjɛ̃] VB *voir* **convenir**

convienne *etc* [kɔ̃vjɛn] VB *voir* **convenir**

convier [kɔ̃vje] /7/ VT: **~ qn à** (*dîner etc*) to (cordially) invite sb to; **~ qn à faire** to urge sb to do

convint *etc* [kɔ̃vɛ̃] VB *voir* **convenir**

convive [kɔ̃viv] NMF guest (*at table*)

convivial, e [kɔ̃vivjal] ADJ (ambiance, lieu) convivial; (Inform) user-friendly

convocation [kɔ̃vɔkasjɔ̃] NF (voir convoquer) convening, convoking; summoning; (document) notification to attend; (Jur) summons sg

convoi [kɔ̃vwa] NM (de voitures, prisonniers) convoy; (train) train; **~ (funèbre)** funeral procession

convoité, e [kɔ̃vwate] ADJ (richesses, terres) coveted; **très ~** much coveted ▸ PP de **convoiter**

convoiter [kɔ̃vwate] /1/ VT to covet

convoitise [kɔ̃vwatiz] NF covetousness; (sexuelle) lust, desire

convoler [kɔ̃vɔle] /1/ VI: **~ (en justes noces)** to be wed

convoquer [kɔ̃vɔke] /1/ VT (assemblée) to convene, convoke; (subordonné, témoin) to summon; (candidat) to ask to attend; **~ qn (à)** (réunion) to invite sb (to attend)

convoyer [kɔ̃vwaje] /8/ VT to escort

convoyeur [kɔ̃vwajœʁ] NM (Navig) escort ship; **~ de fonds** security guard

convulsé, e [kɔ̃vylse] ADJ (visage) distorted

convulsif, -ive [kɔ̃vylsif, -iv] ADJ convulsive

convulsions [kɔ̃vylsjɔ̃] NFPL convulsions

cookie [kuki] NM (Inform) cookie

coopérant [kɔɔpeʁɑ̃] NM ≈ person doing Voluntary Service Overseas (BRIT), ≈ member of the Peace Corps (US)

coopératif, -ive [kɔɔpeʁatif, -iv] ADJ, NF co-operative

coopération [kɔɔpeʁasjɔ̃] NF co-operation; (Admin): **la C~** ≈ Voluntary Service Overseas (BRIT) ou the Peace Corps (US: done as alternative to military service)

coopérer [kɔɔpeʁe] /6/ VI: **~ (à)** to co-operate (in)

coordination [kɔɔʁdinasjɔ̃] NF coordination

coordonnateur, -trice [kɔɔʁdɔnatœʁ, -tʁis] ADJ coordinating ▸ NM/F coordinator

coordonné, e [kɔɔʁdɔne] ADJ coordinated ▸ NF (Ling) coordinate clause ■ **coordonnés** NMPL (vêtements) coordinates ■ **coordonnées** NFPL (Math) coordinates; (détails personnels) details; whereabouts; **donnez-moi vos coordonnées** (fam) can I have your details please?

coordonner [kɔɔʁdɔne] /1/ VT to coordinate

★**copain, copine** [kɔpɛ̃, kɔpin] NM/F mate (BRIT), pal; (petit ami/petite amie) boyfriend/girlfriend ▸ ADJ: **être ~ avec** to be pally with

copeau, X [kɔpo] NM shaving; (de métal) turning

Copenhague [kɔpənag] N Copenhagen

★**copie** [kɔpi] NF copy; (Scol) script, paper; exercise; **~ certifiée conforme** certified copy; **~ papier** (Inform) hard copy

★**copier** [kɔpje] /7/ VT, VI to copy; **~ sur** to copy from

copier-coller [kɔpjekɔle] NM INV copy and paste; **faire un ~** to copy and paste

copieur [kɔpjœʁ] NM (photo)copier

copieusement [kɔpjøzmɑ̃] ADV copiously

copieux, -euse [kɔpjø, -øz] ADJ copious, hearty

copilote [kɔpilɔt] NM (Aviat) co-pilot; (Auto) co-driver, navigator

copinage [kɔpinaʒ] NM: **obtenir qch par ~** to get sth through contacts

copinaute [kɔpinot] NMF (fam) online friend

★**copine** [kɔpin] NF voir **copain**

copiste [kɔpist] NMF copyist, transcriber

coproduction [kɔpʁɔdyksjɔ̃] NF coproduction, joint production

copropriétaire [kɔpʁɔpʁijetɛʁ] NMF co-owner

copropriété [kɔpʁɔpʁijete] NF co-ownership, joint ownership; **acheter en ~** to buy on a co-ownership basis

copulation [kɔpylasjɔ̃] NF copulation

copuler [kɔpyle] VI to copulate

copyright [kɔpiʁajt] NM copyright

★**coq** [kɔk] NM cockerel, rooster; **~ de bruyère** grouse; **~ du village** (fig: péj) ladykiller; **~ au vin** coq au vin ▸ ADJ INV (Boxe): **poids ~** bantamweight

coq-à-l'âne [kɔkalɑn] NM INV abrupt change of subject

coque [kɔk] NF (de noix, mollusque) shell; (de bateau) hull; **à la ~** (Culin) (soft-)boiled

coquelet [kɔklɛ] NM (Culin) cockerel

coquelicot [kɔkliko] NM poppy

coqueluche [kɔklyʃ] NF whooping-cough; (fig): **être la ~ de qn** to be sb's flavour of the month

coquet, te [kɔkɛ, -ɛt] ADJ appearance-conscious; (joli) pretty; (logement) smart, charming

coquetier [kɔk(ə)tje] NM egg-cup

coquettement [kɔkɛtmɑ̃] ADV (s'habiller) attractively; (meubler) prettily

coquetterie [kɔkɛtʁi] NF appearance-consciousness

★**coquillage** [kɔkijaʒ] NM (mollusque) shellfish inv; (coquille) shell

coquille [kɔkij] NF shell; (Typo) misprint; **~ de beurre** shell of butter; **~ d'œuf** adj (couleur) eggshell; **~ de noix** nutshell; **~ St Jacques** scallop

coquillettes [kɔkijɛt] NFPL pasta shells

coquin, e [kɔkɛ̃, -in] ADJ mischievous, roguish; (polisson) naughty ▸ NM/F (péj) rascal

cor [kɔʁ] NM (Mus) horn; (Méd): **~ (au pied)** corn; **réclamer à ~ et à cri** to clamour for; **~ anglais** cor anglais; **~ de chasse** hunting horn

corail, -aux [kɔʁaj, -o] NM coral no pl

Coran [kɔʁɑ̃] NM: **le ~** the Koran

coraux [kɔʁo] NMPL de **corail**

corbeau, X [kɔʁbo] NM crow

corbeille [kɔʁbɛj] NF basket; (Inform) recycle bin; (Bourse): **la ~** ≈ the floor (of the Stock Exchange); **~ de mariage** (fig) wedding presents pl; **~ à ouvrage** work-basket; **~ à pain** bread-basket; **~ à papier** waste paper basket ou bin

corbillard [kɔʁbijaʁ] NM hearse

cordage [kɔʁdaʒ] NM rope ■ **cordages** NMPL (de voilure) rigging sg

★**corde** [kɔʁd] NF rope; (de violon, raquette, d'arc) string; (trame): **la ~** the thread; (Athlétisme, Auto): **la ~** the rails pl; **les cordes** (Boxe) the ropes; **les (instruments à) cordes** (Mus) the strings, the stringed instruments; **semelles de ~** rope soles; **tenir la ~** (Athlétisme, Auto) to be in the inside lane; **tomber des cordes** to rain cats and dogs; **tirer sur la ~** to go too far; **la ~ sensible** the right chord; **usé jusqu'à la ~** threadbare; **~ à linge** washing ou clothes line; **~ lisse** (climbing) rope; **~ raide** tightrope; **~ à sauter** skipping rope; **cordes vocales** vocal cords

cordeau, x [kɔrdo] NM string, line; **tracé au ~** as straight as a die

cordée [kɔrde] NF (d'alpinistes) rope, roped party

cordelière [kɔrdəljɛr] NF cord (belt)

cordial, e, -aux [kɔrdjal, -o] ADJ warm, cordial ▶ NM cordial, pick-me-up

cordialement [kɔrdjalmɑ̃] ADV cordially, heartily; (formule épistolaire) (kind) regards

cordialité [kɔrdjalite] NF warmth, cordiality

cordillère [kɔrdijɛr] NF: **la ~ des Andes** the Andes cordillera ou range

cordon [kɔrdɔ̃] NM cord, string; **~ sanitaire/de police** sanitary/police cordon; **~ littoral** sandbank, sandbar; **~ ombilical** umbilical cord

cordon-bleu [kɔrdɔ̃blø] (pl **cordons-bleus**) ADJ, NMF cordon bleu

cordonnerie [kɔrdɔnri] NF shoe repairer's ou mender's (shop)

cordonnier [kɔrdɔnje] NM shoe repairer ou mender, cobbler

cordouan, e [kɔrduã, -an] ADJ Cordovan

Cordoue [kɔrdu] N Cordoba

Corée [kɔre] NF: **la ~** Korea; **la ~ du Sud/du Nord** South/North Korea; **la République (démocratique populaire) de ~** the (Democratic People's) Republic of Korea

coréen, ne [kɔreẽ, -ɛn] ADJ Korean ▶ NM (Ling) Korean ▶ NM/F: **Coréen, ne** Korean

coreligionnaire [kɔr(ə)liʒɔnɛr] NMF fellow Christian/Muslim/Jew etc

Corfou [kɔrfu] N Corfu

coriace [kɔrjas] ADJ tough

coriandre [kɔrjɑ̃dr] NF coriander

Corinthe [kɔrɛ̃t] N Corinth

cormoran [kɔrmɔrɑ̃] NM cormorant

cornac [kɔrnak] NM elephant driver

corne [kɔrn] NF horn; (de cerf) antler; (de la peau) callus; **~ d'abondance** horn of plenty; **~ de brume** (Navig) foghorn

cornée [kɔrne] NF cornea

corneille [kɔrnɛj] NF crow

cornélien, ne [kɔrneljẽ, -ɛn] ADJ (débat etc) where love and duty conflict

cornemuse [kɔrnəmyz] NF bagpipes pl; **joueur de ~** piper

corner¹ [kɔrnɛr] NM (Football) corner (kick)

corner² [kɔrne] VT (pages) to make dog-eared ▶ VI (klaxonner) to blare out

cornet [kɔrne] NM (paper) cone; (de glace) cornet, cone; **~ à pistons** cornet

cornette [kɔrnɛt] NF cornet (headgear)

corniaud [kɔrnjo] NM (chien) mongrel; (péj) twit, clot

corniche [kɔrniʃ] NF (de meuble, neigeuse) cornice; (route) coast road

cornichon [kɔrniʃɔ̃] NM gherkin

Cornouailles [kɔrnwaj] FPL Cornwall

cornue [kɔrny] NF retort

corollaire [kɔrɔlɛr] NM corollary

corolle [kɔrɔl] NF corolla

coron [kɔrɔ̃] NM mining cottage; mining village

coronaire [kɔrɔnɛr] ADJ coronary

corporation [kɔrpɔrasjɔ̃] NF corporate body; (au Moyen-Âge) guild

corporel, le [kɔrpɔrɛl] ADJ bodily; (punition) corporal; **soins corporels** care sg of the body

★**corps** [kɔr] NM (gén) body; (cadavre) (dead) body; **à son ~ défendant** against one's will; **à ~ perdu** headlong; **perdu ~ et biens** lost with all hands; **prendre ~** to take shape; **faire ~ avec** to be joined to; to form one body with; **~ d'armée** army corps; **~ de ballet** corps de ballet; **~ constitués** (Pol) constitutional bodies; **le ~ consulaire** the consular corps; **~ à ~** adv hand-to-hand; nm clinch; **le ~ du délit** (Jur) corpus delicti; **le ~ diplomatique** the diplomatic corps; **le ~ électoral** the electorate; **le ~ enseignant** the teaching profession; **~ étranger** (Méd) foreign body; **~ expéditionnaire** task force; **~ de garde** guardroom; **~ législatif** legislative body; **le ~ médical** the medical profession

corpulence [kɔrpylɑ̃s] NF build; (embonpoint) stoutness (BRIT), corpulence; **de forte ~** of large build

corpulent, e [kɔrpylã, -ɑ̃t] ADJ stout (BRIT), corpulent

corpus [kɔrpys] NM (Ling) corpus

★**correct, e** [kɔrɛkt] ADJ (exact) accurate, correct; (bienséant, honnête) correct; (passable) adequate

correctement [kɔrɛktəmɑ̃] ADV accurately, correctly; adequately

correcteur, -trice [kɔrɛktœr, -tris] NM/F (Scol) examiner, marker; (Typo) proofreader

correctif, -ive [kɔrɛktif, -iv] ADJ corrective ▶ NM (mise au point) rider, qualification

correction [kɔrɛksjɔ̃] NF (voir corriger) correction; marking; (voir correct) correctness; (rature, surcharge) correction, emendation; (coups) thrashing; **~ sur écran** (Inform) screen editing; **~ (des épreuves)** proofreading

correctionnel, le [kɔrɛksjɔnɛl] ADJ (Jur): **tribunal ~** ≈ criminal court

corrélation [kɔrelasjɔ̃] NF correlation

★**correspondance** [kɔrɛspɔ̃dɑ̃s] NF correspondence; (de train, d'avion) connection; **ce train assure la ~ avec l'avion de 10 heures** this train connects with the 10 o'clock plane; **cours par ~** correspondence course; **vente par ~** mail-order business

correspondancier, -ière [kɔrɛspɔ̃dɑ̃sje, -jɛr] NM/F correspondence clerk

★**correspondant, e** [kɔrɛspɔ̃dɑ̃, -ɑ̃t] NM/F correspondent; (Tél) person phoning (ou being phoned)

★**correspondre** [kɔrɛspɔ̃dr] /41/ VI (données, témoignages) to correspond, tally; (chambres) to communicate; **~ à** to correspond to; **~ avec qn** to correspond with sb

Corrèze [kɔrɛz] NF: **la ~** the Corrèze

corrézien, ne [kɔrezjẽ, -ɛn] ADJ of ou from the Corrèze

corrida [kɔrida] NF bullfight

corridor [kɔridɔr] NM corridor, passage

corrigé [kɔriʒe] NM (*Scol: d'exercice*) correct version; fair copy

★**corriger** [kɔriʒe] /3/ VT (*devoir*) to correct, mark; (*texte*) to correct, emend; (*erreur, défaut*) to correct, put right; (*punir*) to thrash; **~ qn de** (*défaut*) to cure sb of; **se ~ de** to cure o.s. of

corroborer [kɔrɔbɔre] /1/ VT to corroborate

corroder [kɔrɔde] /1/ VT to corrode

corrompre [kɔrɔ̃pr] /41/ VT (*dépraver*) to corrupt; (*acheter: témoin etc*) to bribe

corrompu, e [kɔrɔ̃py] ADJ corrupt

corrosif, -ive [kɔrozif, -iv] ADJ corrosive

corrosion [kɔrozjɔ̃] NF corrosion

corruption [kɔrypsjɔ̃] NF corruption; (*de témoins*) bribery

corsage [kɔrsaʒ] NM (*d'une robe*) bodice; (*chemisier*) blouse

corsaire [kɔrsɛr] NM pirate, corsair; privateer

★**corse** [kɔrs] ADJ Corsican ▸ NMF: **Corse** Corsican ▸ NF: **la C~** Corsica

corsé, e [kɔrse] ADJ vigorous; (*café etc*) full-flavoured (BRIT) ou -flavored (US); (*goût*) full; (*sauce*) spicy; (*problème*) tough, tricky

corselet [kɔrsəlɛ] NM corselet

corser [kɔrse] /1/ VT (*difficulté*) to aggravate; (*intrigue*) to liven up; (*sauce*) to add spice to

corset [kɔrsɛ] NM corset; (*d'une robe*) bodice; **~ orthopédique** surgical corset

corso [kɔrso] NM: **~ fleuri** procession of floral floats

cortège [kɔrtɛʒ] NM procession

cortisone [kɔrtizɔn] NF (*Méd*) cortisone

corvée [kɔrve] NF chore, drudgery *no pl*; (*Mil*) fatigue (duty)

cosaque [kɔzak] NM cossack

cosignataire [kɔsiɲatɛr] ADJ, NMF co-signatory

cosinus [kɔsinys] NM (*Math*) cosine

cosmétique [kɔsmetik] NM (*pour les cheveux*) hair oil; (*produit de beauté*) beauty care product

cosmétologie [kɔsmetɔlɔʒi] NF beauty care

cosmique [kɔsmik] ADJ cosmic

cosmonaute [kɔsmɔnot] NMF cosmonaut, astronaut

cosmopolite [kɔsmɔpɔlit] ADJ cosmopolitan

cosmos [kɔsmɔs] NM outer space; cosmos

cosse [kɔs] NF (*Bot*) pod, hull

cossu, e [kɔsy] ADJ opulent-looking, well-to-do

Costa Rica [kɔstarika] NM: **le ~** Costa Rica

costaricien, ne [kɔstarisjɛ̃, -ɛn] ADJ Costa Rican ▸ NM/F: **Costaricien, ne** Costa Rican

costaud, e [kɔsto, -od] ADJ strong, sturdy

★**costume** [kɔstym] NM (*d'homme*) suit; (*de théâtre*) costume

costumé, e [kɔstyme] ADJ dressed up

costumier, -ière [kɔstymje, -jɛr] NM/F (*fabricant, loueur*) costumier; (*Théât*) wardrobe master/mistress

cotangente [kɔtɑ̃ʒɑ̃t] NF (*Math*) cotangent

cotation [kɔtasjɔ̃] NF quoted value

cote [kɔt] NF (*en Bourse etc*) quotation; quoted value; (*d'un candidat etc*) rating; (*mesure: sur une carte*) spot height; (: *sur un croquis*) dimension; (*de classement*) (classification) mark; reference number; **la ~ de** (*d'un cheval*) the odds *pl* on; **avoir la ~** to be very popular; **inscrit à la ~** quoted on the Stock Exchange; **~ d'alerte** danger *ou* flood level; **~ mal taillée** (*fig*) compromise; **~ de popularité** popularity rating

coté, e [kɔte] ADJ: **être ~** to be listed *ou* quoted; **être ~ en Bourse** to be quoted on the Stock Exchange; **être bien/mal ~** to be highly/poorly rated

★**côte** [kot] NF (*rivage*) coast(line); (*pente*) slope; (: *sur une route*) hill; (*Anat*) rib; (*d'un tricot, tissu*) rib, ribbing *no pl*; **~ à ~** *adv* side by side; **la C~ (d'Azur)** the (French) Riviera; **la C~ d'Ivoire** the Ivory Coast; **~ de porc** pork chop

★**côté** [kote] NM (*gén*) side; (*direction*) way, direction; **de chaque ~ (de)** on each side of; **de tous les côtés** from all directions; **de quel ~ est-il parti ?** which way *ou* in which direction did he go?; **de ce/de l'autre ~** this/the other way; **d'un ~ ... de l'autre ~ ...** (*alternative*) on (the) one hand ... on the other (hand) ...; **du ~ de** (*provenance*) from; (*direction*) towards; **du ~ de Lyon** (*proximité*) near Lyons; **du ~ gauche** on the left-hand side; **de ~** *adv* (*regarder*) sideways; on one side; to one side; aside; **laisser de ~** to leave on one side; **mettre de ~** to put aside, put on one side; **mettre de l'argent de ~** to save some money; **de mon ~** (*quant à moi*) for my part; **à ~** *adv* (*right*) nearby; (*voisins*) next door; (*d'autre part*) besides; **à ~ de** beside; next to; (*fig*) in comparison to; **à ~ (de la cible)** off target, wide (of the mark); **être aux côtés de** to be by the side of

coteau, x [kɔto] NM hill

Côte d'Ivoire [kotdivwar] NF: **la ~** Côte d'Ivoire, the Ivory Coast

côtelé, e [kot(ə)le] ADJ ribbed; **pantalon en velours ~** corduroy trousers *pl*

côtelette [kotlɛt] NF chop

coter [kɔte] /1/ VT (*Bourse*) to quote

coterie [kɔtri] NF set

côtier, -ière [kotje, -jɛr] ADJ coastal

cotisation [kɔtizasjɔ̃] NF subscription, dues *pl*; (*pour une pension*) contributions *pl*

cotiser [kɔtize] /1/ VI: **~ (à)** to pay contributions (to); (*à une association*) to subscribe (to) ■ **se cotiser** VPR to club together

★**coton** [kɔtɔ̃] NM cotton; **~ hydrophile** cotton wool (BRIT), absorbent cotton (US)

cotonnade [kɔtɔnad] NF cotton (fabric)

Coton-Tige® [kɔtɔ̃tiʒ] (*pl* **Cotons-Tiges**) NM cotton bud

côtoyer [kotwaje] /8/ VT to be close to; (*rencontrer*) to rub shoulders with; (*longer*) to run alongside; (*fig: friser*) to be bordering *ou* verging on

cotte [kɔt] NF: **~ de mailles** coat of mail

★**cou** [ku] NM neck

couac [kwak] NM (*fam*) bum note

couard, e [kwar, -ard] ADJ cowardly

couchage [kuʃaʒ] NM *voir* **sac**

couchant, e [kuʃɑ̃, ɑ̃t] ADJ: **soleil ~** setting sun

★**couche** [kuʃ] NF (*strate: gén, Géo*) layer, stratum (*pl* -a); (*de peinture, vernis*) coat; (*de poussière, crème*) layer; (de bébé) nappy (BRIT), diaper (US); **~ d'ozone** ozone layer ■ **couches** NFPL (Méd) confinement sg; **couches sociales** social levels ou strata

★**couché, e** [kuʃe] ADJ (étendu) lying down; (au lit) in bed

couche-culotte [kuʃkylɔt] (pl **couches-culottes**) NF (plastic-coated) disposable nappy (BRIT) ou diaper (US)

★**coucher** [kuʃe] /1/ NM (du soleil) setting; **à prendre avant le ~** (Méd) take at night ou before going to bed; **~ de soleil** sunset ▸ VT (personne) to put to bed; (: loger) to put up; (objet) to lay on its side; (écrire) to inscribe, couch ▸ VI (dormir) to sleep, spend the night; **~ avec qn** to sleep with sb, go to bed with sb ■ **se coucher** VPR (pour dormir) to go to bed; (pour se reposer) to lie down; (soleil) to set, go down

★**couchette** [kuʃɛt] NF couchette; (de marin) bunk; (pour voyageur, sur bateau) berth

coucheur [kuʃœr] NM: **mauvais ~** awkward customer

couci-couça [kusikusa] ADV (fam) so-so

coucou [kuku] NM cuckoo ▸ EXCL peek-a-boo

★**coude** [kud] NM (Anat) elbow; (de tuyau, de la route) bend; **~ à ~** adv shoulder to shoulder, side by side

coudée [kude] NF: **avoir ses coudées franches** (fig) to have a free rein

cou-de-pied [kudpje] (pl **cous-de-pied**) NM instep

coudoyer [kudwaje] /8/ VT to brush past ou against; (fig) to rub shoulders with

★**coudre** [kudr] /48/ VT (bouton) to sew on; (robe) to sew (up) ▸ VI to sew

couenne [kwan] NF (de lard) rind

couette [kwɛt] NF duvet ■ **couettes** NFPL (cheveux) bunches

couffin [kufɛ̃] NM Moses basket; (straw) basket

couilles [kuj] NFPL (!) balls (!)

couillu, e [kujy] ADJ (fam: courageux: personne) ballsy (fam)

couiner [kwine] /1/ VI to squeal

coulage [kulaʒ] NM (Comm) loss of stock (due to theft or negligence)

coulant, e [kulɑ̃, -ɑ̃t] ADJ (indulgent) easy-going; (fromage etc) runny

coulée [kule] NF (de lave, métal en fusion) flow; **~ de neige** snowslide

couler [kule] /1/ VI to flow, run; (fuir: stylo, récipient) to leak; (: nez) to run; (sombrer: bateau) to sink; **~ à pic** to sink ou go straight to the bottom; **~ de source** to follow on naturally; **faire ~** (eau) to run; **faire ~ un bain** to run a bath ▸ VT (cloche, sculpture) to cast; (bateau) to sink; (personne) to bring down, ruin; **couler une vie heureuse** to enjoy a happy life; **il a coulé une bielle** (Auto) his big end went ■ **se couler** VPR (se glisser): **se ~ dans** (interstice, ouverture) to slip into; (fig): **se ~ dans le moule** to fit the mould (BRIT) ou mold (US)

★**couleur** [kulœr] NF colour (BRIT), color (US); (Cartes) suit; **de ~** (homme, femme: vieilli) colo(u)red; **sous ~ de** on the pretext of; **de quelle ~** of what colo(u)r ■ **couleurs** NFPL (du teint) colo(u)r sg; **les couleurs** (Mil) the colo(u)rs; **en couleurs** (film) in colo(u)r; **télévision en couleurs** colo(u)r television

couleuvre [kulœvr] NF grass snake

coulissant, e [kulisɑ̃, -ɑ̃t] ADJ (porte, fenêtre) sliding

coulisse [kulis] NF (Tech) runner; **porte à ~** sliding door ■ **coulisses** NFPL (Théât) wings; (fig): **dans les coulisses** behind the scenes

coulisser [kulise] /1/ VI to slide, run

★**couloir** [kulwar] NM corridor, passage; (d'avion) aisle; (de bus) gangway; (: sur la route) bus lane; (Sport: de piste) lane; (Géo) gully; **~ aérien** air corridor ou lane; **~ de navigation** shipping lane

coulpe [kulp] NF: **battre sa ~** to repent openly

★**coup** [ku] NM (heurt, choc) knock; (affectif) blow, shock; (agressif) blow; (avec arme à feu) shot; (de l'horloge) chime, stroke; (Sport: golf) stroke; (: tennis) shot; (Échecs) move; (fam: fois) time; **~ de coude/genou** nudge (with the elbow)/ with the knee; **à coups de hache/marteau** (hitting with an axe/a hammer; **~ de tonnerre** clap of thunder; **~ de sonnette** ring of the bell; **~ de crayon/pinceau** stroke of the pencil/brush; **donner un ~ de balai** to give the floor a sweep, sweep up; **donner un ~ de chiffon** to go round with the duster; **avoir le ~** (fig) to have the knack; **être dans le/hors du ~** to be/not to be in on it; (à la page) to be hip ou trendy; **du ~** as a result; **boire un ~** to have a drink; **d'un seul ~** (subitement) suddenly; (à la fois) at one go in one blow; **du ~** so (you see); **du premier ~** first time ou go, at the first attempt; **du même ~** at the same time; **à ~ sûr** definitely, without fail; **après ~** afterwards; **~ sur ~** in quick succession; **être sur un ~** to be on to something; **sur le ~** outright; **sous le ~ de** (surprise etc) under the influence of; **tomber sous le ~ de la loi** to constitute a statutory offence; **à tous les coups** every time; **tenir le ~** to hold out; **il a raté son ~** he missed his turn; **pour le ~** for once; **~ bas** (fig): **donner un ~ bas à qn** to hit sb below the belt; **~ de chance** stroke of luck; **~ de chapeau** (fig) pat on the back; **~ de couteau** stab (of a knife); **~ dur** hard blow; **~ d'éclat** (great) feat; **~ d'envoi** kick-off; **~ d'essai** first attempt; **~ d'État** coup d'état; **~ de feu** shot; **~ de filet** (Police) haul; **~ de foudre** (fig) love at first sight; **~ fourré** stab in the back; **~ franc** free kick; **~ de frein** (sharp) braking no pl; **~ de fusil** rifle shot; **~ de grâce** coup de grâce; **~ du lapin** (Auto) whiplash; **~ de main: donner un ~ de main à qn** to give sb a (helping) hand; **~ de maître** master stroke; **~ d'œil** glance; **~ de pied** kick; **~ de poing** punch; **~ de soleil** sunburn no pl; **~ de sonnette** ring of the bell; **~ de téléphone** phone call; **~ de tête** (fig) (sudden) impulse; **~ de théâtre** (fig) dramatic turn of events; **~ de tonnerre** clap of thunder; **~ de vent** gust of wind; **en ~ de vent** (rapidement) in a tearing hurry

★**coupable** [kupabl] ADJ guilty; (pensée) guilty, culpable; **~ de** guilty of ▸ NMF (gén) culprit; (Jur) guilty party

coupant, e [kupɑ̃, -ɑ̃t] ADJ (lame) sharp; (fig: voix, ton) cutting

coupe [kup] NF (verre) goblet; (à fruits) dish; (Sport) cup; (de cheveux, de vêtement) cut; (graphique, plan) (cross) section; **être sous la ~ de** to be under the control of; **faire des coupes sombres dans** to make drastic cuts in

coupé, e [kupe] ADJ (communications, route) cut, blocked; (vêtement): **bien/mal ~** well/badly cut ▸ NM (Auto) coupé ▸ NF (Navig) gangway

coupe-circuit [kupsiʀkɥi] NM INV cutout, circuit breaker

coupe-faim [kupfɛ̃] NM INV appetite suppressant

coupe-feu [kupfø] NM INV firebreak

coupe-gorge [kupgɔʀʒ] NM INV cut-throats' den

coupe-ongles [kupɔ̃gl] NM INV (*pince*) nail clippers; (*ciseaux*) nail scissors

coupe-papier [kuppapje] NM INV paper knife

★**couper** [kupe] /1/ VT to cut; (*retrancher*) to cut (out), take out; (*route, courant*) to cut off; (*appétit*) to take away; (*fièvre*) to take down, reduce; (*vin, cidre*) to blend; (: *à table*) to dilute (with water); **~ l'appétit à qn** to spoil sb's appetite; **~ la parole à qn** to cut sb short; **~ les vivres à qn** to cut off sb's vital supplies; **~ le contact** *ou* **l'allumage** (*Auto*) to turn off the ignition; **~ les ponts avec qn** to break with sb; **se faire ~ les cheveux** to have *ou* get one's hair cut; **nous avons été coupés** we've been cut off ▶ VI to cut; (*prendre un raccourci*) to take a short-cut; (*Cartes: diviser le paquet*) to cut; (: *avec l'atout*) to trump ▪ **se couper** VPR (*se blesser*) to cut o.s.; (*en témoignant etc*) to give o.s. away

couper-coller [kupekɔle] NM INV cut and paste; **faire un ~** to cut and paste

couperet [kupʀɛ] NM cleaver, chopper

couperosé, e [kupʀoze] ADJ blotchy

coupe-vent [kupvã] (*pl* **~(s)**) NM windcheater, Windbreaker® (*US*)

couple [kupl] NM couple; **~ de torsion** torque

coupler [kuple] /1/ VT to couple (together)

couplet [kuplɛ] NM verse

coupleur [kuplœʀ] NM: **~ acoustique** acoustic coupler

coupole [kupɔl] NF dome; cupola

coupon [kupɔ̃] NM (*ticket*) coupon; (*de tissu*) remnant; roll

coupon-réponse [kupɔ̃ʀepɔ̃s] (*pl* **coupons-réponses**) NM reply coupon

coupure [kupyʀ] NF cut; (*billet de banque*) note; (*de journal*) cutting; **~ de courant** power cut

★**cour** [kuʀ] NF (*de ferme, jardin*) (court)yard; (*d'immeuble*) back yard; (*Jur, royale*) court; **faire la ~ à qn** to court sb; **~ d'appel** appeal court (*BRIT*), appellate court (*US*); **~ d'assises** court of assizes, ≈ Crown Court (*BRIT*); **~ de cassation** final court of appeal; **~ des comptes** (*Admin*) revenue court; **~ martiale** court-martial; **~ de récréation** (*Scol*) playground, schoolyard

★**courage** [kuʀaʒ] NM courage, bravery

courageusement [kuʀaʒøzmã] ADV bravely, courageously

★**courageux, -euse** [kuʀaʒø, -øz] ADJ brave, courageous

★**couramment** [kuʀamã] ADV commonly; (*parler*) fluently

★**courant, e** [kuʀã, -ãt] ADJ (*fréquent*) common; (*Comm, gén: normal*) standard; (*en cours*) current; **~ octobre** *etc* in the course of October *etc*; **le 10 ~** (*Comm*) the 10th inst. ▶ NM current; (*fig*) movement; (: *d'opinion*) trend; **être au ~ (de)** (*fait, nouvelle*) to know (about); **mettre qn au ~ (de)** (*fait, nouvelle*) to tell sb (about); (*nouveau travail etc*) to teach sb the basics (of), brief sb (about); **se tenir au ~ (de)** (*techniques etc*) to keep o.s.

up-to-date (on); **dans le ~ de** (*pendant*) in the course of; **~ d'air** draught (*BRIT*), draft (*US*); **~ électrique** (electric) current, power

courbature [kuʀbatyʀ] NF ache

courbaturé, e [kuʀbatyʀe] ADJ aching

courbe [kuʀb] ADJ curved ▶ NF curve; **~ de niveau** contour line

courber [kuʀbe] /1/ VT to bend; **~ la tête** to bow one's head ▪ **se courber** VPR (*branche etc*) to bend, curve; (*personne*) to bend (down)

courbette [kuʀbɛt] NF low bow

coure *etc* [kuʀ] VB *voir* **courir**

coureur, -euse [kuʀœʀ, -øz] NM/F (*Sport*) runner (*ou* driver); (*péj*) womanizer/manhunter; **~ cycliste/automobile** racing cyclist/driver

courge [kuʀʒ] NF (*Bot*) gourd; (*Culin*) marrow

courgette [kuʀʒɛt] NF courgette (*BRIT*), zucchini (*US*)

★**courir** [kuʀiʀ] /11/ VI (*gén*) to run; (*se dépêcher*) to rush; (*fig: rumeurs*) to go round; (*Comm: intérêt*) to accrue; **le bruit court que** the rumour is going round that; **par les temps qui courent** at the present time; **~ après qn** to run after sb, chase (after) sb; **laisser ~** to let things alone; **faire ~ qn** to make sb run around (all over the place); **tu peux (toujours) ~!** you've got a hope! ▶ VT (*Sport: épreuve*) to compete in; (*risque*) to run; (*danger*) to face; **~ les cafés/bals** to do the rounds of the cafés/dances

couronne [kuʀɔn] NF crown; (*de fleurs*) wreath, circlet; **~ (funéraire** *ou* **mortuaire)** (funeral) wreath

couronnement [kuʀɔnmã] NM coronation, crowning; (*fig*) crowning achievement

couronner [kuʀɔne] /1/ VT to crown

courons [kuʀɔ̃], **courrai** *etc* [kuʀe] VB *voir* **courir**

courre [kuʀ] VB *voir* **chasse**

courriel [kuʀjɛl] NM email; **envoyer qch par ~** to email sth

★**courrier** [kuʀje] NM mail, post; (*lettres à écrire*) letters *pl*; (*rubrique*) column; **qualité ~** letter quality; **long/moyen ~** *adj* (*Aviat*) long-/medium-haul; **~ du cœur** problem page; **est-ce que j'ai du ~?** are there any letters for me?; **~ électronique** electronic mail, email

courrier does not mean *courier*.

courroie [kuʀwa] NF strap; (*Tech*) belt; **~ de transmission/de ventilateur** driving/fan belt

courrons *etc* [kuʀɔ̃] VB *voir* **courir**

courroucé, e [kuʀuse] ADJ wrathful

★**cours** [kuʀ] VB *voir* **courir** ▶ NM (*leçon*) class; (: *particulier*) lesson; (*série de leçons*) course; (*cheminement*) course; (*écoulement*) flow; (*avenue*) walk; (*Comm: de devises*) rate; (: *de denrées*) price; (*Bourse*) quotation; **donner libre ~ à** to give free expression to; **avoir ~** (*monnaie*) to be legal tender; (*fig*) to be current; (*Scol*) to have a class *ou* lecture; **en ~** (*année*) current; (*travaux*) in progress; **en ~ de route** on the way; **au ~ de** in the course of, during; **le ~ du change** the exchange rate; **~ d'eau** waterway; **~ élémentaire** 2nd and 3rd years of primary school; **~ moyen** 4th and 5th years of primary school; **~ préparatoire** ≈ infants' class (*BRIT*), ≈ 1st grade (*US*); **~ du soir** night school

★**course** [kuʀs] NF running; (*Sport: épreuve*) race; (*trajet: du soleil*) course; (*: d'un projectile*) flight; (*: d'une pièce mécanique*) travel; (*excursion*) outing; (*ascension*) climb; (*d'un taxi, autocar*) journey, trip; (*petite mission*) errand; **à bout de ~** (*épuisé*) exhausted; **~ automobile** car race; **~ de côte** (*Auto*) hill climb; **~ par étapes** *ou* **d'étapes** race in stages; **~ d'obstacles** obstacle race; **~ à pied** walking race; **~ de vitesse** sprint ▪ **courses** NFPL (*achats*) shopping *sg*; (*Hippisme*) races; **faire les** *ou* **ses courses** to go shopping; **jouer aux courses** to bet on the races; **courses de chevaux** horse racing

coursier, -ière [kuʀsje, -jɛʀ] NM/F courier

★**court, e** [kuʀ, kuʀt] ADJ short; **ça fait ~** that's not very long; **tirer à la courte paille** to draw lots; **faire la courte échelle à qn** to give sb a leg up; **~ métrage** (*Ciné*) short (film) ▶ ADV short; **tourner ~** to come to a sudden end; **couper ~ à** to cut short; **à ~ de** short of; **prendre qn de ~** to catch sb unawares; **pour faire ~** briefly, to cut a long story short ▶ NM: **~ (de tennis)** (tennis) court

court-bouillon [kuʀbujɔ̃] (*pl* **courts-bouillons**) NM court-bouillon

court-circuit [kuʀsiʀkɥi] (*pl* **courts-circuits**) NM short-circuit

court-circuiter [kuʀsiʀkɥite] /1/ VT (*fig*) to bypass

courtier, -ière [kuʀtje, -jɛʀ] NM/F broker

courtisan [kuʀtizã] NM courtier

courtisane [kuʀtizan] NF courtesan

courtiser [kuʀtize] /1/ VT to court, woo

courtois, e [kuʀtwa, -waz] ADJ courteous

courtoisement [kuʀtwazmã] ADV courteously

courtoisie [kuʀtwazi] NF courtesy

couru, e [kuʀy] PP *de* **courir** ▶ ADJ (*spectacle etc*) popular; **c'est ~ (d'avance)!** (*fam*) it's a safe bet!

cousais *etc* [kuze] VB *voir* **coudre**

couscous [kuskus] NM couscous

★**cousin, e** [kuzɛ̃, -in] NM/F cousin; **~ germain** first cousin ▶ NM (*Zool*) mosquito

cousons *etc* [kuzɔ̃] VB *voir* **coudre**

★**coussin** [kusɛ̃] NM cushion; **~ d'air** (*Tech*) air cushion

cousu, e [kuzy] PP *de* **coudre** ▶ ADJ: **~ d'or** rolling in riches

coût [ku] NM cost; **le ~ de la vie** the cost of living

coûtant [kutã] ADJ M: **au prix ~** at cost price

★**couteau, x** [kuto] NM knife; **~ à cran d'arrêt** flick-knife; **~ de cuisine** kitchen knife; **~ à pain** bread knife; **~ de poche** pocket knife

couteau-scie [kutosi] (*pl* **couteaux-scies**) NM serrated(-edged) knife

coutelier, -ière [kutəlje, -jɛʀ] ADJ: **l'industrie coutelière** the cutlery industry ▶ NM/F cutler

coutellerie [kutɛlʀi] NF cutlery shop; cutlery

coûter [kute] /1/ VT to cost ▶ VI to cost; **~ à qn** to cost sb a lot; **~ cher** to be expensive; **~ cher à qn** (*fig*) to cost sb dear *ou* dearly; **combien ça coûte?** how much is it?, what does it cost?; **coûte que coûte** at all costs

coûteux, -euse [kutø, -øz] ADJ costly, expensive

coutume [kutym] NF custom; **de ~** usual, customary

coutumier, -ière [kutymje, -jɛʀ] ADJ customary; **elle est coutumière du fait** that's her usual trick

★**couture** [kutyʀ] NF sewing; (*profession*) dressmaking; (*points*) seam

couturier [kutyʀje] NM fashion designer, couturier

couturière [kutyʀjɛʀ] NF dressmaker

couvade [kuvad] NF couvade syndrome, sympathetic pregnancy

couvée [kuve] NF brood, clutch

couvent [kuvã] NM (*de sœurs*) convent; (*de frères*) monastery; (*établissement scolaire*) convent (school)

couver [kuve] /1/ VT to hatch; (*maladie*) to be sickening for; **~ qn/qch des yeux** to look lovingly at sb/sth; (*convoiter*) to look longingly at sb/sth ▶ VI (*feu*) to smoulder (BRIT), smolder (US); (*révolte*) to be brewing

couvercle [kuvɛʀkl] NM lid; (*de bombe aérosol etc, qui se visse*) cap, top

★**couvert, e** [kuvɛʀ, -ɛʀt] PP *de* **couvrir** ▶ ADJ (*ciel*) overcast; (*coiffé d'un chapeau*) wearing a hat; **~ de** covered with *ou* in; **bien ~** (*habillé*) well wrapped up ▶ NM place setting; (*place à table*) place; (*au restaurant*) cover charge; **mettre le ~** to lay the table; **à ~** under cover; **sous le ~ de** under the shelter of; (*fig*) under cover of ▪ **couverts** NMPL place settings; (*ustensiles*) cutlery *sg*

★**couverture** [kuvɛʀtyʀ] NF (*de lit*) blanket; (*de bâtiment*) roofing; (*de livre, fig: d'un espion etc, Assurances*) cover; (*Presse*) coverage; **de ~** (*lettre etc*) covering; **~ chauffante** electric blanket

couveuse [kuvøz] NF (*à poules*) sitter, brooder; (*de maternité*) incubator

couvre *etc* [kuvʀ] VB *voir* **couvrir**

couvre-chef [kuvʀəʃɛf] NM hat

couvre-feu, x [kuvʀəfø] NM curfew

couvre-lit [kuvʀəli] NM bedspread

couvre-pieds [kuvʀəpje] NM INV quilt

couvreur [kuvʀœʀ] NM roofer

★**couvrir** [kuvʀiʀ] /18/ VT to cover; (*dominer, étouffer: voix, pas*) to drown out; (*erreur*) to cover up; (*Zool: s'accoupler à*) to cover ▪ **se couvrir** VPR (*ciel*) to cloud over; (*s'habiller*) to cover up, wrap up; (*se coiffer*) to put on one's hat; (*par une assurance*) to cover o.s.; **se ~ de** (*fleurs, boutons*) to become covered in

cover-girl [kɔvœʀgœʀl] NF model

covoiturage [kɔvwatyʀaʒ] NM car sharing (BRIT), ridesharing (US)

cow-boy [koboj] NM cowboy

coyote [kɔjɔt] NM coyote

CP SIGLE M = **cours préparatoire**

CPAM SIGLE F (= *Caisse primaire d'assurances maladie*) health insurance office

CPME SIGLE F = **Confédération des Petites et Moyennes Entreprises**

cps ABR (= *caractères par seconde*) cps

cpt ABR = **comptant**

CQFD ABR (= *ce qu'il fallait démontrer*) QED (= *quod erat demonstrandum*)

CR SIGLE M = **compte rendu**

★**crabe** [kʀɑb] NM crab

crachat [kʀaʃa] NM spittle *no pl*, spit *no pl*

craché, e [kʀaʃe] ADJ: **son père tout ~** the spitting image of his (*ou* her) father

★**cracher** [kʀaʃe] /**1**/ VI to spit ▶ VT to spit out; (*fig: lave etc*) to belch (out); **~ du sang** to spit blood

crachin [kʀaʃɛ̃] NM drizzle

crachiner [kʀaʃine] /**1**/ VI to drizzle

crachoir [kʀaʃwaʀ] NM spittoon; (*de dentiste*) bowl

crachotement [kʀaʃɔtmã] NM crackling *no pl*

crachoter [kʀaʃɔte] /**1**/ VI (*haut-parleur, radio*) to crackle

crack [kʀak] NM (*intellectuel*) whiz kid; (*sportif*) ace; (*poulain*) hot favourite (BRIT) *ou* favorite (US)

Cracovie [kʀakɔvi] N Cracow

crade [kʀad], **cradingue** [kʀadɛ̃g] ADJ (*fam*) disgustingly dirty, filthy-dirty

craie [kʀɛ] NF chalk

craignais *etc* [kʀɛɲɛ] VB *voir* **craindre**

craindre [kʀɛ̃dʀ] /**52**/ VT to fear, be afraid of; (*être sensible à: chaleur, froid*) to be easily damaged by; **~ de/que** to be afraid of/that; **je crains qu'il (ne) vienne** I am afraid he may come

crainte [kʀɛ̃t] NF fear; **de ~ de/que** for fear of/that

craintif, -ive [kʀɛ̃tif, -iv] ADJ timid

craintivement [kʀɛ̃tivmã] ADV timidly

cramer [kʀame] /**1**/ VI (*fam*) to burn

cramoisi, e [kʀamwazi] ADJ crimson

crampe [kʀãp] NF cramp; **~ d'estomac** stomach cramp; **j'ai une ~ à la jambe** I've got cramp in my leg

crampon [kʀãpɔ̃] NM (*de semelle*) stud; (*Alpinisme*) crampon

cramponner [kʀãpɔne] /**1**/: **se cramponner** VPR: **se ~ (à)** to hang *ou* cling on (to)

cran [kʀã] NM (*entaille*) notch; (*de courroie*) hole; (*courage*) guts *pl*; **~ d'arrêt/de sûreté** safety catch; **~ de mire** bead

crâne [kʀɑn] NM skull

crânement [kʀɑnmã] ADV (*fièrement*) proudly

crâner [kʀɑne] /**1**/ VI (*fam*) to swank, show off

crânien, ne [kʀanjɛ̃, -ɛn] ADJ cranial, skull *cpd*, brain *cpd*

crapaud [kʀapo] NM toad

crapule [kʀapyl] NF villain

crapuleux, -euse [kʀapylø, -øz] ADJ: **crime ~** villainous crime

craquelure [kʀaklyʀ] NF crack; crackle *no pl*

craquement [kʀakmã] NM crack, snap; (*du plancher*) creak, creaking *no pl*

craquer [kʀake] /**1**/ VI (*bois, plancher*) to creak; (*fil, branche*) to snap; (*couture*) to come apart, burst; (*fig: accusé*) to break down, fall apart; (*: être enthousiasmé*) to go wild; **j'ai craqué** (*fam*) I couldn't resist it ▶ VT: **~ une allumette** to strike a match

crash [kʀaʃ] (*pl* **crashs** *ou* **crashes**) NM crash; **~ boursier** stock market crash

crasher [kʀaʃe] (*fam*): **se crasher** VPR to crash

crasse [kʀas] NF grime, filth ▶ ADJ (*fig: ignorance*) crass

crasseux, -euse [kʀasø, -øz] ADJ filthy

crassier [kʀasje] NM slag heap

cratère [kʀatɛʀ] NM crater

cravache [kʀavaʃ] NF (riding) crop

cravacher [kʀavaʃe] /**1**/ VT to use the crop on

★**cravate** [kʀavat] NF tie

cravater [kʀavate] /**1**/ VT to put a tie on; (*fig*) to grab round the neck

crawl [kʀol] NM crawl

crawlé, e [kʀole] ADJ: **dos ~** backstroke

crayeux, -euse [kʀɛjø, -øz] ADJ chalky

★**crayon** [kʀɛjɔ̃] NM pencil; (*de rouge à lèvres etc*) stick, pencil; **écrire au ~** to write in pencil; **~ à bille** ball-point pen; **~ de couleur** crayon; **~ optique** light pen

crayon-feutre [kʀɛjɔ̃føtʀ] (*pl* **crayons-feutres**) NM felt(-tip) pen

crayonner [kʀɛjɔne] /**1**/ VT to scribble, sketch

CRDP SIGLE M (= *Centre régional de documentation pédagogique*) *teachers' resource centre*

créance [kʀeãs] NF (*Comm*) (financial) claim, (recoverable) debt; **donner ~ à qch** to lend credence to sth

créancier, -ière [kʀeãsje, -jɛʀ] NM/F creditor

créateur, -trice [kʀeatœʀ, -tʀis] ADJ creative ▶ NM/F creator ▶ NM: **le C~** (*Rel*) the Creator

créatif, -ive [kʀeatif, -iv] ADJ creative

création [kʀeasjɔ̃] NF creation

créativité [kʀeativite] NF creativity

créature [kʀeatyʀ] NF creature

crécelle [kʀesɛl] NF rattle

crèche [kʀɛʃ] NF (*de Noël*) crib; (*garderie*) crèche, day nursery

crédence [kʀedãs] NF (small) sideboard

crédibilité [kʀedibilite] NF credibility

crédible [kʀedibl] ADJ credible

crédit [kʀedi] NM (*gén*) credit; **acheter à ~** to buy on credit *ou* on easy terms; **faire ~ à qn** to give sb credit; **~ municipal** pawnshop; **~ relais** bridging loan; **~ carbone** carbon credit ▪ **crédits** NMPL funds

crédit-bail [kʀedibaj] (*pl* **crédits-bails**) NM (*Écon*) leasing

créditer [kʀedite] /**1**/ VT: **~ un compte (de)** to credit an account (with)

créditeur, -trice [kʀeditœʀ, -tʀis] ADJ in credit, credit *cpd* ▶ NM/F customer in credit

credo [kʀedo] NM credo, creed

crédule [kʀedyl] ADJ credulous, gullible

crédulité [kʀedylite] NF credulity, gullibility

créer [kʀee] /**1**/ VT to create; (*Théât: pièce*) to produce (for the first time); (*: rôle*) to create

crémaillère [kʀemajɛʀ] NF (*Rail*) rack; (*tige crantée*) trammel; **direction à ~** (*Auto*) rack and pinion steering; **pendre la ~** to have a house-warming party

crémation [kʀemasjɔ̃] NF cremation

crématoire [kʀematwaʀ] ADJ: **four ~** crematorium

crématorium [kʀematɔʀjɔm] NM crematorium

crème [kʀɛm] NF cream; (*entremets*) cream dessert; **~ anglaise** (egg) custard; **~ chantilly** whipped cream, crème Chantilly; **~ fouettée** whipped cream; **~ glacée** ice cream; **~ à raser** shaving cream; **~ solaire** sun cream ▶ ADJ INV cream; **un (café) ~** = a white coffee

crémerie [kʀɛmʀi] NF dairy; (*tearoom*) teashop

crémeux, -euse [kʀemø, -øz] ADJ creamy

crémier, -ière [kʀemje, -jɛʀ] NM/F dairyman/-woman

créneau, x [kʀeno] NM (*de fortification*) crenel(le); (*fig, aussi Comm*) gap, slot; (*Auto*): **faire un ~** to reverse into a parking space (*between cars alongside the kerb*)

créole [kʀeɔl] ADJ, NMF Creole

créosote [kʀeɔzɔt] NF creosote

crêpe [kʀɛp] NF (*galette*) pancake ▶ NM (*tissu*) crêpe; (*de deuil*) black mourning crêpe; (*ruban*) black armband (*ou* hatband *ou* ribbon); **semelle (de) ~** crêpe sole; **~ de Chine** crêpe de Chine

crêpé, e [kʀepe] ADJ (*cheveux*) backcombed

crêperie [kʀɛpʀi] NF pancake shop *ou* restaurant

crépi [kʀepi] NM roughcast

crépir [kʀepiʀ] /2/ VT to roughcast

crépitement [kʀepitmɑ̃] NM (*du feu*) crackling *no pl*; (*d'une arme automatique*) rattle *no pl*

crépiter [kʀepite] /1/ VI to sputter, splutter, crackle

crépon [kʀepɔ̃] NM seersucker

CREPS [kʀɛps] SIGLE M (= *Centres de ressources, d'expertise et de performance sportives*) = sports *ou* leisure centre

crépu, e [kʀepy] ADJ frizzy, fuzzy

crépuscule [kʀepyskyl] NM twilight, dusk

crescendo [kʀeʃɛndo] NM, ADV (*Mus*) crescendo; **aller ~** (*fig*) to rise higher and higher, grow ever greater

cresson [kʀesɔ̃] NM watercress

Crète [kʀɛt] NF: **la ~** Crete

crête [kʀɛt] NF (*de coq*) comb; (*de vague, montagne*) crest

crétin, e [kʀetɛ̃, -in] NM/F cretin

crétois, e [kʀetwa, -waz] ADJ Cretan

cretonne [kʀətɔn] NF cretonne

★**creuser** [kʀøze] /1/ VT (*trou, tunnel*) to dig; (*sol*) to dig a hole in; (*bois*) to hollow out; (*fig*) to go (deeply) into; **ça creuse** that gives you a real appetite; **se ~ (la cervelle)** to rack one's brains

creuset [kʀøzɛ] NM crucible; (*fig*) melting pot, (*severe*) test

creux, -euse [kʀø, -øz] ADJ hollow; **heures creuses** slack periods; (*électricité, téléphone*) off-peak periods ▶ NM hollow; (*fig: sur graphique etc*) trough; **le ~ de l'estomac** the pit of the stomach; **avoir un ~** (*fam*) to be hungry

crevaison [kʀəvɛzɔ̃] NF puncture, flat

crevant, e [kʀəvɑ, -ɑ̃t] ADJ (*fam: fatigant*) knackering; (: *très drôle*) priceless

crevasse [kʀəvas] NF (*dans le sol*) crack, fissure; (*de glacier*) crevasse; (*de la peau*) crack

crevé, e [kʀəve] ADJ (*fam: fatigué*) shattered (BRIT), exhausted

crève-cœur [kʀɛvkœʀ] NM heartbreak

crever [kʀəve] /5/ VT (*papier*) to tear, break; (*tambour, ballon*) to burst; **cela lui a crevé un œil** it blinded him in one eye; **~ l'écran** to have real screen presence ▶ VI (*pneu*) to burst; (*automobiliste*) to have a puncture (BRIT) *ou* a flat (tire) (US); (*abcès, outre, nuage*) to burst (open); (*fam: mourir*) to kick the bucket

★**crevette** [kʀəvɛt] NF: **~ (rose)** prawn; **~ grise** shrimp

CRF SIGLE F (= *Croix-Rouge française*) French Red Cross

★**cri** [kʀi] NM cry, shout; (*d'animal: spécifique*) cry, call; **à grands cris** at the top of one's voice; **c'est le dernier ~** (*fig*) it's the latest fashion

criant, e [kʀijɑ̃, -ɑ̃t] ADJ (*injustice*) glaring

criard, e [kʀijaʀ, -aʀd] ADJ (*couleur*) garish, loud; (*voix*) yelling

crible [kʀibl] NM riddle; (*mécanique*) screen, jig; **passer qch au ~** to put sth through a riddle; (*fig*) to go over sth with a fine-tooth comb

criblé, e [kʀible] ADJ: **~ de** riddled with

cric [kʀik] NM (*Auto*) jack

cricket [kʀikɛt] NM cricket

criée [kʀije] NF: **(vente à la) ~** (sale by) auction

★**crier** [kʀije] /7/ VI (*pour appeler*) to shout, cry (out); (*de peur, de douleur etc*) to scream, yell; (*fig: grincer*) to squeal, screech ▶ VT (*ordre, injure*) to shout (out), yell (out); **sans ~ gare** without warning; **~ grâce** to cry for mercy; **~ au secours** to shout for help

---

crier does not mean *to cry* in the sense of 'weep'.

---

crieur, -euse [kʀijœʀ, -øz] NM/F: **~ de journaux** newspaper seller

★**crime** [kʀim] NM crime; (*meurtre*) murder

Crimée [kʀime] NF: **la ~** the Crimea

criminalité [kʀiminalite] NF criminality, crime

criminel, le [kʀiminɛl] ADJ criminal ▶ NM/F criminal; murderer; **~ de guerre** war criminal

criminologie [kʀiminɔlɔʒi] NF criminology

criminologiste [kʀiminɔlɔʒist] NMF criminologist

criminologue [kʀiminɔlɔg] NMF criminologist

crin [kʀɛ̃] NM (*de cheval*) hair *no pl*; (*fibre*) horsehair; **à tous crins, à tout ~** diehard, out-and-out

crinière [kʀinjɛʀ] NF mane

crique [kʀik] NF creek, inlet

criquet [kʀikɛ] NM grasshopper

★**crise** [kʀiz] NF crisis (*pl* crises); (*Méd*) attack; (: *d'épilepsie*) fit; **~ cardiaque** heart attack; **~ de foi** crisis of belief; **avoir une ~ de foie** to have really bad indigestion; **~ de nerfs** attack of nerves; **piquer une ~ de nerfs** to go hysterical

crispant, e [kʀispɑ̃, -ɑ̃t] ADJ annoying, irritating

crispation [kʀispasjɔ̃] NF (*spasme*) twitch; (*contraction*) contraction; tenseness

crispé, e [kʀispe] ADJ tense, nervous

crisper [kʀispe] /1/ VT to tense; (*poings*) to clench ■ **se crisper** VPR to tense; to clench; (*personne*) to get tense

crissement [kʀismɑ̃] NM crunch; rustle; screech

crisser [kʀise] /1/ VI (*neige*) to crunch; (*tissu*) to rustle; (*pneu*) to screech

cristal, -aux [kʀistal, -o] NM crystal; **~ de plomb** (lead) crystal; **~ de roche** rock-crystal ▪ **cristaux** NMPL (*objets*) crystal(ware) *sg*; **cristaux de soude** washing soda *sg*

cristallin, e [kʀistalɛ̃, -in] ADJ crystal-clear ▶ NM (*Anat*) crystalline lens

cristalliser [kʀistalize] /1/ VI, VT to crystallize ▪ **se cristalliser** VPR to crystallize

critère [kʀitɛʀ] NM criterion (*pl* criteria)

critiquable [kʀitikabl] ADJ open to criticism

critique [kʀitik] ADJ critical ▶ NMF (*de théâtre, musique*) critic ▶ NF criticism; (*Théât etc : article*) review; **la ~** (*activité*) criticism; (*personnes*) the critics *pl*

★**critiquer** [kʀitike] /1/ VT (*dénigrer*) to criticize; (*évaluer, juger*) to assess, examine (critically)

croasser [kʀɔase] /1/ VI to caw

croate [kʀɔat] ADJ Croatian ▶ NM (*Ling*) Croat, Croatian ▶ NMF: **Croate** Croat, Croatian

Croatie [kʀɔasi] NF: **la ~** Croatia

croc [kʀo] NM (*dent*) fang; (*de boucher*) hook

croc-en-jambe [kʀɔkɑ̃ʒɑ̃b] (*pl* **crocs-en-jambe**) NM: **faire un ~ à qn** to trip sb up

croche [kʀɔʃ] NF (*Mus*) quaver (BRIT), eighth note (US); **double ~** semiquaver (BRIT), sixteenth note (US)

croche-pied [kʀɔʃpje] NM = **croc-en-jambe**

crochet [kʀɔʃɛ] NM hook; (*clef*) picklock; (*détour*) detour; (*Boxe*): **~ du gauche** left hook; (*Tricot: aiguille*) crochet hook; (: *technique*) crochet ▪ **crochets** NMPL (*Typo*) square brackets; **vivre aux crochets de qn** to live *ou* sponge off sb

crocheter [kʀɔʃte] /5/ VT (*serrure*) to pick

crochu, e [kʀɔʃy] ADJ hooked; claw-like

crocodile [kʀɔkɔdil] NM crocodile

crocus [kʀɔkys] NM crocus

★**croire** [kʀwaʀ] /44/ VT to believe; **~ qn honnête** to believe sb (to be) honest; **se ~ fort** to think one is strong; **~ que** to believe *ou* think that; **vous croyez ?** do you think so?; **~ être/faire** to think one is/does; **~ à, ~ en** to believe in

croîs *etc* [kʀwa] VB *voir* **croître**

croisade [kʀwazad] NF crusade

croisé, e [kʀwaze] ADJ (*veston*) double-breasted; (*Football: tir, tête*) to the far post; (*Tennis: revers, coup droit*) cross-court ▶ NM (*guerrier*) crusader ▶ NF (*fenêtre*) window, casement; **croisée d'ogives** intersecting ribs; **à la croisée des chemins** at the crossroads

croisement [kʀwazmɑ̃] NM (*carrefour*) crossroads *sg*; (*Bio*) crossing; (: *résultat*) crossbreed

croiser [kʀwaze] /1/ VT (*personne, voiture*) to pass; (*route*) to cross, cut across; (*Bio*) to cross; **~ les jambes/bras** to cross one's legs/ fold one's arms ▶ VI (*Navig*) to cruise ▪ **se croiser** VPR (*personnes, véhicules*) to pass each other; (*routes*) to cross, intersect; (*lettres*) to cross (in the post); (*regards*) to meet; **se ~ les bras** (*fig*) to fold one's arms, twiddle one's thumbs

croiseur [kʀwazœʀ] NM cruiser (*warship*)

croisière [kʀwazjɛʀ] NF cruise; **vitesse de ~** (*Auto etc*) cruising speed

croisillon [kʀwazijɔ̃] NM: **motif/fenêtre à croisillons** lattice pattern/window

croissais *etc* [kʀwasɛ] VB *voir* **croître**

croissance [kʀwasɑ̃s] NF growing, growth; **troubles de la ~** growing pains; **maladie de ~** growth disease; **~ économique** economic growth

★**croissant, e** [kʀwasɑ̃, -ɑ̃t] VB *voir* **croître** ▶ ADJ growing; rising ▶ NM (*à manger*) croissant; (*motif*) crescent; **~ de lune** crescent moon

croître [kʀwatʀ] /55/ VI to grow; (*lune*) to wax

★**croix** [kʀwa] NF cross; **en ~** *adj, adv* in the form of a cross; **la C~ Rouge** the Red Cross

croquant, e [kʀɔkɑ̃, -ɑ̃t] ADJ crisp, crunchy ▶ NM/F (*péj*) yokel, (*country*) bumpkin

★**croque-madame** [kʀɔkmadam] NM INV *toasted cheese sandwich with a fried egg on top*

croque-mitaine [kʀɔkmitɛn] NM bog(e)y-man (*pl* -men)

★**croque-monsieur** [kʀɔkməsjø] NM INV *toasted ham and cheese sandwich*

croque-mort [kʀɔkmɔʀ] NM (*péj*) pallbearer

croquer [kʀɔke] /1/ VT (*manger*) to crunch; (: *fruit*) to munch; (*dessiner*) to sketch; **chocolat à ~** plain dessert chocolate ▶ VI to be crisp *ou* crunchy

croquet [kʀɔkɛ] NM croquet

croquette [kʀɔkɛt] NF croquette

croquis [kʀɔki] NM sketch

cross [kʀɔs], **cross-country** [kʀɔskuntʀi] (*pl* **~(-countries)**) NM cross-country race *ou* run; cross-country racing *ou* running

crosse [kʀɔs] NF (*de fusil*) butt; (*de revolver*) grip; (*d'évêque*) crook, crosier; (*de hockey*) hockey stick

crotale [kʀɔtal] NM rattlesnake

crotte [kʀɔt] NF droppings *pl*; **~ !** (*fam*) damn!

crotté, e [kʀɔte] ADJ muddy, mucky

crottin [kʀɔtɛ̃] NM dung, manure; (*fromage*) (small round) cheese (*made of goat's milk*)

croulant, e [kʀulɑ̃, -ɑ̃t] NM/F (*fam*) old fogey

crouler [kʀule] /1/ VI (*s'effondrer*) to collapse; (*être délabré*) to be crumbling

croupe [kʀup] NF croup, rump; **en ~** pillion

croupi, croupie [kʀupi] ADJ F stagnant; **eau croupie** stagnant water

croupier, ière [kʀupje, -jɛʀ] NM/F croupier ▶ NFPL: **tailler des croupières à qn** (*Écon, Comm*) to steal a march on sb

croupion [kʀupjɔ̃] NM (*d'un oiseau*) rump; (*Culin*) parson's nose

croupir [kʀupiʀ] /2/ VI to stagnate; **~ en prison** to rot in prison

CROUS [kʀus] SIGLE M (= *Centre régional des œuvres universitaires et scolaires*) students' representative body

croustade [kʀustad] NF (*Culin*) croustade

croustillant, e [kʀustijɑ̃, -ɑ̃t] ADJ crisp; (*fig*) spicy

croustiller [kʀustije] /1/ VI to be crisp *ou* crusty

croûte [kʀut] NF crust; (*du fromage*) rind; (*de vol-au-vent*) case; (*Méd*) scab; **en ~** (*Culin*) in pastry, in a pie; **~ aux champignons** mushrooms on toast; **~ au fromage** cheese on toast *no pl*; **~ de pain** (*morceau*) crust (of bread); **~ terrestre** earth's crust

croûton [kʀutɔ̃] NM (*Culin*) crouton; (*bout du pain*) crust, heel

croyable [kʀwajabl] ADJ believable, credible

croyais etc [kʀwajɛ] VB voir **croire**

croyance [kʀwajɑ̃s] NF belief

croyant, e [kʀwajɑ̃, -ɑ̃t] VB voir **croire** ▸ ADJ: **être/ne pas être ~** to be/not to be a believer ▸ NM/F believer

Crozet [kʀɔzɛ] N: **les îles ~** the Crozet Islands

CRS SIGLE FPL (= Compagnies républicaines de sécurité) state security police force ▸ SIGLE M member of the CRS

★**cru, e** [kʀy] PP de **croire** ▸ ADJ (non cuit) raw; (lumière, couleur) harsh; (description) crude; (paroles, langage: franc) blunt; (: grossier) crude; **jambon ~** cured ham; **monter à ~** to ride bareback ▸ NM (vignoble) vineyard; (vin) wine; **un grand ~** a grand cru; **de son (propre) ~** (fig) of his own devising; **du ~** local ▸ NF (d'un cours d'eau) swelling, rising; **en crue** in spate

crû [kʀy] PP de **croître**

cruauté [kʀyote] NF cruelty

cruche [kʀyʃ] NF pitcher, (earthenware) jug

crucial, e, -aux [kʀysjal, -o] ADJ crucial

crucifier [kʀysifje] /7/ VT to crucify

crucifix [kʀysifi] NM crucifix

crucifixion [kʀysifiksjɔ̃] NF crucifixion

cruciforme [kʀysifɔʀm] ADJ cruciform, cross-shaped

cruciverbiste [kʀysivɛʀbist] NMF crossword puzzle enthusiast

crudité [kʀydite] NF crudeness no pl; harshness no pl ■ **crudités** NFPL (Culin) selection of raw vegetables

crue [kʀy] NF (inondation) flood; voir aussi **cru**

cruel, le [kʀyɛl] ADJ cruel

cruellement [kʀyɛlmɑ̃] ADV cruelly

crûment [kʀymɑ̃] ADV (voir cru) harshly; bluntly; crudely

crus, crûs etc [kʀy] VB voir **croire**; **croître**

crustacés [kʀystase] NMPL shellfish

cryptage [kʀiptaʒ] NM (de données) encryption

crypte [kʀipt] NF crypt

crypté, e [kʀipte] ADJ (télévision) encrypted; (chaînes) encrypted, scrambled

crypter [kʀipte] VT (Inform, Tél) to encrypt

cryptogramme [kʀiptɔgʀam] NM (de carte de crédit) security code

CSA SIGLE M (= Conseil supérieur de l'audiovisuel) French broadcasting regulatory body ≈ IBA (BRIT), ≈ FCC (US)

cse ABR = **cause**

CSEN SIGLE F (= Confédération syndicale de l'éducation nationale) group of teachers' unions

CSG SIGLE F (= contribution sociale généralisée) supplementary social security contribution in aid of the underprivileged

CSM SIGLE M (= Conseil supérieur de la magistrature) French magistrates' council

Cte ABR = **Comtesse**

CU SIGLE F = **communauté urbaine**

Cuba [kyba] N Cuba

cubage [kybaʒ] NM cubage, cubic content

cubain, e [kybɛ̃, -ɛn] ADJ Cuban ▸ NM/F: **Cubain, e** Cuban

cube [kyb] NM cube; (jouet) brick, building block; **gros ~** powerful motorbike; **mètre ~** cubic metre; **2 au ~ = 8** 2 cubed is 8; **élever au ~** to cube

cubique [kybik] ADJ cubic

cubisme [kybism] NM cubism

cubiste [kybist] ADJ, NMF cubist

cubitus [kybitys] NM ulna

cueillette [kœjet] NF picking; (quantité) crop, harvest

★**cueillir** [kœjiʀ] /12/ VT (fruits, fleurs) to pick, gather; (fig) to catch

★**cuiller, cuillère** [kɥijɛʀ] NF spoon; **~ à café** coffee spoon; (Culin) ≈ teaspoonful; **~ à soupe** soup spoon; (Culin) ≈ tablespoonful

cuillerée [kɥijʀe] NF spoonful; (Culin): **~ à soupe/café** tablespoonful/teaspoonful

★**cuir** [kɥiʀ] NM leather; (avant tannage) hide; **~ chevelu** scalp

cuirasse [kɥiʀas] NF breastplate

cuirassé [kɥiʀase] NM (Navig) battleship

★**cuire** [kɥiʀ] /38/ VT: **(faire) ~** (aliments) to cook; (au four) to bake; (poterie) to fire ▸ VI to cook; (picoter) to smart, sting, burn

cuisant, e [kɥizɑ̃, -ɑ̃t] VB voir **cuire** ▸ ADJ (douleur) smarting, burning; (fig: souvenir, échec) bitter

★**cuisine** [kɥizin] NF (pièce) kitchen; (art culinaire) cookery, cooking; (nourriture) cooking, food; **faire la ~** to cook

cuisiné, e [kɥizine] ADJ: **plat ~** ready-made meal ou dish

★**cuisiner** [kɥizine] /1/ VT to cook; (fam) to grill ▸ VI to cook

cuisinette [kɥizinet] NF kitchenette

★**cuisinier, -ière** [kɥizinje, -jɛʀ] NM/F cook ▸ NF (poêle) cooker; **cuisinière électrique/à gaz** electric/gas cooker

> Bien qu'en anglais beaucoup de noms de professions se terminent en **-er** (**teacher, bus driver, photographer**, etc.), cuisinier se traduit par **cook**, à ne pas confondre avec **cooker**, qui désigne la cuisinière au sens d'appareil électroménager.

cuisis etc [kɥizi] VB voir **cuire**

cuissardes [kɥisaʀd] NFPL (de pêcheur) waders; (de femme) thigh boots

cuisse [kɥis] NF (Anat) thigh; (Culin) leg

cuisson [kɥisɔ̃] NF cooking; (de poterie) firing

cuissot [kɥiso] NM haunch

cuistre [kɥistʀ] NM prig

cuit, e [kɥi, -it] PP de **cuire** ▸ ADJ (viande): **bien ~** well done; **trop ~** overdone; **pas assez ~** underdone; **~ à point** medium done; **done to a turn** ▸ NF (fam): **prendre une cuite** to get plastered ou smashed

cuiter [kɥite]: **se cuiter** VPR (fam) to get smashed

cuivre [kɥivʀ] NM copper; **les cuivres** (Mus) the brass; **~ rouge** copper; **~ jaune** brass

cuivré, e [kɥivʀe] ADJ coppery; (peau) bronzed

cul [ky] NM (!) arse (BRIT !), ass (US !), bum (BRIT); **~ de bouteille** bottom of a bottle

culasse [kylas] NF (Auto) cylinder-head; (de fusil) breech

culbute [kylbyt] NF somersault; (*accidentelle*) tumble, fall

culbuter [kylbyte] /1/ VI to (take a) tumble, fall (head over heels)

culbuteur [kylbytœR] NM (*Auto*) rocker arm

cul-de-jatte [kydʒat] (*pl* **culs-de-jatte**) NM/F legless cripple (*péj*)

cul-de-sac [kydsak] (*pl* **culs-de-sac**) NM cul-de-sac

culinaire [kylinɛR] ADJ culinary

culminant, e [kylminɑ̃, -ɑ̃t] ADJ: **point ~** highest point; (*fig*) height, climax

culminer [kylmine] /1/ VI to reach its highest point; to tower

culot [kylo] NM (*d'ampoule*) cap; (*fam: effronterie*) cheek, nerve

★**culotte** [kylɔt] NF (*de femme*) panties pl, knickers pl (BRIT); (*d'homme*) underpants pl; (*pantalon*) trousers pl (BRIT), pants pl (US); **~ de cheval** riding breeches pl

culotté, e [kylɔte] ADJ (*pipe*) seasoned; (*cuir*) mellowed; (*effronté*) cheeky

culpabiliser [kylpabilize] /1/ VT: **~ qn** to make sb feel guilty

culpabilité [kylpabilite] NF guilt

culte [kylt] ADJ: **livre/film ~** cult film/book ▶ NM (*religion*) religion; (*hommage, vénération*) worship; (*protestant*) service

cultivable [kyltivabl] ADJ cultivable

cultivateur, -trice [kyltivatœR, -tRis] NM/F farmer

cultivé, e [kyltive] ADJ (*personne*) cultured, cultivated

★**cultiver** [kyltive] /1/ VT to cultivate; (*légumes*) to grow, cultivate ■ **se cultiver** VPR to educate o.s.

★**culture** [kyltyR] NF cultivation; growing; (*connaissances etc*) culture; (*champs de*) cultures land(s) under cultivation; **les cultures intensives** intensive farming; **~ OGM** GM crop; **~ physique** physical training

culturel, le [kyltyRɛl] ADJ cultural

culturisme [kyltyRism] NM body-building

culturiste [kyltyRist] NMF body-builder

cumin [kymɛ̃] NM (*Culin*) cumin

cumul [kymyl] NM (*voir* cumuler) holding (*ou* drawing) concurrently; **~ de peines** sentences to run consecutively

cumulable [kymylabl] ADJ (*fonctions*) which may be held concurrently

cumuler [kymyle] /1/ VT (*emplois, honneurs*) to hold concurrently; (*salaires*) to draw concurrently; (*Jur: droits*) to accumulate

cupide [kypid] ADJ greedy, grasping

cupidité [kypidite] NF greed

curable [kyRabl] ADJ curable

curaçao [kyRaso] NM curaçao ▶ N: **C~** Curaçao

curare [kyRaR] NM curare

curatif, -ive [kyRatif, -iv] ADJ curative

cure [kyR] NF (*Méd*) course of treatment; (*Rel*) cure, ≈ living; presbytery, ≈ vicarage; **faire une ~ de fruits** to go on a fruit cure *ou* diet; **faire une ~ thermale** to take the waters; **n'avoir ~ de** to pay no attention to; **~ d'amaigrissement** slimming course; **~ de repos** rest cure; **~ de sommeil** sleep therapy *no pl*

curé [kyRe] NM parish priest; **M le ~** ≈ Vicar

cure-dent [kyRdɑ̃] NM toothpick

curée [kyRe] NF (*fig*) scramble for the pickings

cure-ongles [kyRɔ̃gl] NM INV nail cleaner

cure-pipe [kyRpip] NM pipe cleaner

curer [kyRe] /1/ VT to clean out; **se ~ les dents** to pick one's teeth

curetage [kyRtaʒ] NM (*Méd*) curettage

curieusement [kyRjøzmɑ̃] ADV oddly

★**curieux, -euse** [kyRjø, -øz] ADJ (*étrange*) strange, curious; (*indiscret*) curious, inquisitive; (*intéressé*) inquiring, curious ▶ NMPL (*badauds*) onlookers, bystanders

curiosité [kyRjozite] NF curiosity, inquisitiveness; (*objet*) curio(sity); (*site*) unusual feature *ou* sight

curiste [kyRist] NMF *person taking the waters at a spa*

curriculum vitae [kyRikylɔmvite] NM INV curriculum vitae

curry [kyRi] NM curry; **poulet au ~** curried chicken, chicken curry

★**curseur** [kyRsœR] NM (*Inform*) cursor; (*de règle*) slide; (*de fermeture-éclair*) slider

cursif, -ive [kyRsif, -iv] ADJ: **écriture cursive** cursive script

cursus [kyRsys] NM degree course

curviligne [kyRviliɲ] ADJ curvilinear

cutané, e [kytane] ADJ cutaneous, skin *cpd*

cuti-réaction [kytiReaksjɔ̃] NF (*Méd*) skin-test

cuve [kyv] NF vat; (*à mazout etc*) tank

cuvée [kyve] NF vintage

cuvette [kyvɛt] NF (*récipient*) bowl, basin; (*du lavabo*) (wash)basin; (*des w.-c.*) pan; (*Géo*) basin

CV SIGLE M (*Auto*) = **cheval (vapeur)**; (*Admin*) = **curriculum vitae**

CVS SIGLE ADJ (= *corrigées des variations saisonnières*) seasonally adjusted

cx ABR (= *coefficient de pénétration dans l'air*) drag coefficient

cyanure [sjanyR] NM cyanide

cyberattaque [sibɛRatak] NF cyberattack

cybercafé [sibɛRkafe] NM internet café

cyberculture [sibɛRkyltyR] NF cyberculture

cyberespace [sibɛRɛspas] NM cyberspace

cyberespionnage [sibɛRɛspjɔnaʒ] NM cyber espionage

cyberfraude [sibɛRfRod] NF cyber fraud

cyberharcèlement [sibɛRaRsɛlmɑ̃] NM, **cyber-intimidation** [sibɛRɛ̃timidasjɔ̃] NF cyberbullying

cybernaute [sibɛRnot] NMF cybernaut

cybernétique [sibɛRnetik] NF cybernetics *sg*

cybersécurité [sibɛRsekyRite] NF cybersecurity

cyclable [siklabl] ADJ: **piste ~** cycle track

cyclamen [siklamɛn] NM cyclamen

cycle [sikl] NM cycle; (*Scol*): **premier/second ~** ≈ middle/upper school (BRIT), ≈ junior/senior high school (US)

cyclique [siklik] ADJ cyclic(al)

★**cyclisme** [siklism] NM cycling

★**cycliste** [siklist] NMF cyclist ▸ ADJ cycle *cpd*; **coureur ~** racing cyclist

cyclo-cross [siklɔkʀɔs] NM (*Sport*) cyclo-cross; (*épreuve*) cyclo-cross race

cyclomoteur [siklɔmɔtœʀ] NM moped

cyclomotoriste [siklɔmɔtɔʀist] NMF moped rider

cyclone [siklon] NM hurricane

cyclotourisme [siklɔtuʀism] NM (bi)cycle touring

cygne [siɲ] NM swan

cylindre [silɛ̃dʀ] NM cylinder; **moteur à 4 cylindres en ligne** straight-4 engine

cylindrée [silɛ̃dʀe] NF (*Auto*) (cubic) capacity;

une (voiture de) grosse ~ a big-engined car

cylindrique [silɛ̃dʀik] ADJ cylindrical

cymbale [sɛ̃bal] NF cymbal

cynique [sinik] ADJ cynical

cyniquement [sinikmɑ̃] ADV cynically

cynisme [sinism] NM cynicism

cyprès [sipʀɛ] NM cypress

cypriote [sipʀijɔt] ADJ Cypriot ▸ NMF: **Cypriote** Cypriot

cyrillique [siʀilik] ADJ Cyrillic

cystite [sistit] NF cystitis

cytise [sitiz] NM laburnum

cytologie [sitɔlɔʒi] NF cytology

Dd

D, d [de] NM INV D, d; **D comme Désiré** D for David (BRIT) *ou* Dog (US) ▶ ABR: **D** (*Météorologie*: = *dépression*) low, depression; *voir* **système**

d' PRÉP, ART *voir* **de**

D1 NF (*Football*: = *première division*) Div 1; **monter en D1** to go up to Div 1

D2 NF (*Football*: = *deuxième division*) Div 2; **la relégation en D2** relegation to Div 2

DAB [dab] NM (= *distributeur automatique de billets*) ATM

Dacca [daka] N Dacca

dactylo [daktilo] NF (*aussi*: **dactylographe**) typist; (*aussi*: **dactylographie**) typing, typewriting

dactylographier [daktilɔgrafje] /7/ VT to type (out)

dada [dada] NM hobby-horse

dadais [dadɛ] NM ninny, lump

dague [dag] NF dagger

dahlia [dalja] NM dahlia

dahoméen, ne [daɔmeɛ̃, -ɛn] ADJ Dahomean

Dahomey [daɔme] NM: **le ~** Dahomey

daigner [dɛɲe] /1/ VT to deign

daim [dɛ̃] NM (*fallow*) deer *inv*; (*peau*) buckskin; (*cuir suédé*) suede

dais [dɛ] NM (*tenture*) canopy

Dakar [dakar] N Dakar

dal. ABR (= *décalitre*) dal.

dallage [dalaʒ] NM paving

dalle [dal] NF slab; (*au sol*) paving stone, flag(stone); **que ~** nothing at all, damn all (BRIT)

daller [dale] /1/ VT to pave

dalmatien, ne [dalmasjɛ̃, -ɛn] NM/F (*chien*) Dalmatian

daltonien, ne [daltɔnjɛ̃, -ɛn] ADJ colour-blind (BRIT), color-blind (US)

daltonisme [daltɔnism] NM colour (BRIT) *ou* color (US) blindness

dam [dam] NM: **au grand ~ de** much to the detriment (*ou* annoyance) of

Damas [dama] N Damascus

damas [dama] NM (*étoffe*) damask

damassé, e [damase] ADJ damask *cpd*

★**dame** [dam] NF lady; (*Cartes, Échecs*) queen; **~ de charité** benefactress; **~ de compagnie** lady's companion ■ **dames** NFPL (*jeu*) draughts *sg* (BRIT), checkers *sg* (US); **les (toilettes des) dames** the ladies' (toilets)

dame-jeanne [damʒɑn] (*pl* **dames-jeannes**) NF demijohn

damer [dame] /1/ VT to ram *ou* pack down; **~ le pion à** (*fig*) to get the better of

damier [damje] NM draughts board (BRIT), checkerboard (US); (*dessin*) check (pattern); **en ~** check

damner [dane] /1/ VT to damn ■ **se damner** VPR to damn o.s.; **être à se ~** (*dessert, beauté*) to be to-die-for; **belle à se ~** stunningly beautiful

dancing [dɑ̃siŋ] NM dance hall

dandiner [dɑ̃dine] /1/: **se dandiner** VPR to sway about; (*en marchant*) to waddle along

★**Danemark** [danmark] NM: **le ~** Denmark

★**danger** [dɑ̃ʒe] NM danger; **mettre en ~** (*personne*) to put in danger; (*projet, carrière*) to jeopardize; **être en ~** (*personne*) to be in danger; **être en ~ de mort** to be in peril of one's life; **être hors de ~** to be out of danger

dangereusement [dɑ̃ʒrøzmɑ̃] ADV dangerously

★**dangereux, -euse** [dɑ̃ʒrø, -øz] ADJ dangerous

★**danois, e** [danwa, -waz] ADJ Danish ▶ NM (*Ling*) Danish ▶ NM/F: **Danois, e** Dane

---

dans [dɑ̃]

PRÉP **1** (*position*) in; (: *à l'intérieur de*) inside; **c'est dans le tiroir/le salon** it's in the drawer/lounge; **dans la boîte** in *ou* inside the box; **marcher dans la ville/la rue** to walk about the town/along the street; **je l'ai lu dans le journal** I read it in the newspaper; **être dans les meilleurs** to be among *ou* one of the best

2 (*direction*) into; **elle a couru dans le salon** she ran into the lounge; **monter dans une voiture/le bus** to get into a car/on to the bus

3 (*provenance*) out of, from; **je l'ai pris dans le tiroir/salon** I took it out of *ou* from the drawer/lounge; **boire dans un verre** to drink out of *ou* from a glass

4 (*temps*) in; **dans deux mois** in two months, in two months' time

5 (*approximation*) about; **dans les 20 euros** about 20 euros

---

dansant, e [dɑ̃sɑ̃, -ɑ̃t] ADJ: **soirée dansante** evening of dancing; (*bal*) dinner dance

danse [dɑ̃s] NF: **la ~** dancing; (*classique*) (ballet) dancing; **une ~** a dance; **~ du ventre** belly dancing

★**danser** [dɑ̃se] /1/ VI, VT to dance

danseur, -euse [dɑ̃sœʀ, -øz] NM/F ballet dancer; (*au bal etc*) dancer; (: *cavalier*) partner; **~ de claquettes** tap-dancer; **en danseuse** (*à vélo*) standing on the pedals

Danube [danyb] NM: **le ~** the Danube

DAO SIGLE M (= *dessin assisté par ordinateur*) CAD

dard [daʀ] NM sting (*organ*)

darder [daʀde] /1/ VT to shoot, send forth

dare-dare [daʀdaʀ] ADV in double quick time

Dar-es-Salaam, Dar-es-Salam [daʀɛsalam] N Dar-es-Salaam

darne [daʀn] NF steak (*of fish*)

darse [daʀs] NF sheltered dock (*in a Mediterranean port*)

dartre [daʀtʀ] NF (*Méd*) sore

datation [datasjɔ̃] NF dating

★**date** [dat] NF date; **faire ~** to mark a milestone; **de longue ~** adj longstanding; **~ de naissance** date of birth; **~ limite** deadline; **~ limite de vente** sell-by date

dater [date] /1/ VT, VI to date; **~ de** to date from, go back to; **à ~ de** (as) from

dateur [datœʀ] NM (*de montre*) date indicator; **timbre ~** date stamp

datif [datif] NM dative

datte [dat] NF date

dattier [datje] NM date palm

daube [dob] NF: **bœuf en ~** beef casserole

dauphin [dofɛ̃] NM (*Zool*) dolphin; (*Hist*) dauphin; (*fig*) heir apparent

★**dauphine** [dofin] NF (*Hist*) dauphine; (*fig*) heir apparent ▶ ADJ INV (*Culin*): **pommes ~** crispy potato balls

Dauphiné [dofine] NM: **le ~** the Dauphiné

dauphinois, e [dofinwa, -waz] ADJ of *ou* from the Dauphiné

daurade [dɔʀad] NF sea bream

davantage [davɑ̃taʒ] ADV more; (*plus longtemps*) longer; **~ de** more; **~ que** more than

DB SIGLE F (*Mil*) = **division blindée**

DCA SIGLE F (= *défense contre avions*) anti-aircraft defence

DCT SIGLE M (= *diphtérie coqueluche tétanos*) DPT

DDASS [dɑs] SIGLE F (*vieilli*) ≈ DWP (*BRIT*), ≈ SSA (*US*)

DDT SIGLE M (= *dichloro-diphénol-trichloréthane*) DDT

---

de, d' [də, d]

(*de + le* = **du**, *de + les* = **des**) PRÉP **1** (*appartenance*) of; **le toit de la maison** the roof of the house; **la voiture d'Elisabeth/de mes parents** Elizabeth's/my parents' car

2 (*provenance*) from; **il vient de Londres** he comes from London; **de Londres à Paris** from London to Paris; **elle est sortie du cinéma** she came out of the cinema

3 (*moyen*) with; **je l'ai fait de mes propres mains** I did it with my own two hands

4 (*caractérisation, mesure*): **un mur de brique/ bureau d'acajou** a brick wall/mahogany desk; **un billet de 10 euros** a 10 euro note; **une pièce de 2 m de large** *ou* **large de 2 m** a room 2 m wide, a 2m-wide room; **un bébé de 10 mois** a 10-month-old baby; **12 mois de crédit/travail** 12 months' credit/work; **elle est payée 20 euros de l'heure** she's paid 20 euros an hour *ou* per hour; **augmenter de 10 euros** to increase by 10 euros; **trois jours de libres** three free days, three days free; **un verre d'eau** a glass of water; **il mange de tout** he'll eat anything

5 (*rapport*) from; **de quatre à six** from four to six

6 (*cause*): **mourir de faim** to die of hunger; **rouge de colère** red with fury

7 (*vb +de +infin*) to; **il m'a dit de rester** he told me to stay

8 (*de la part de*): **estimé de ses collègues** respected by his colleagues

9 (*en apposition*): **cet imbécile de Paul** that idiot Paul; **le terme de «franglais»** the term "franglais"

▶ ART **1** (*phrases affirmatives*) some (*souvent omis*); **du vin, de l'eau, des pommes** (some) wine, (some) water, (some) apples; **des enfants sont venus** some children came; **pendant des mois** for months

2 (*phrases interrogatives et négatives*) any; **a-t-il du vin?** has he got any wine?; **il n'a pas de pommes/d'enfants** he hasn't (got) any apples/ children, he has no apples/children

---

dé [de] NM (*à jouer*) die *ou* dice; (*aussi*: **dé à coudre**) thimble ■ **dés** NMPL (*jeu*) (game of) dice; **un coup de dés** a throw of the dice; **couper en dés** (*Culin*) to dice

DEA SIGLE M (= *Diplôme d'études approfondies*) post-graduate diploma

dealer [dilœʀ] NM (*fam*) (drug) pusher

déambulateur [deɑ̃bylatœʀ] NM Zimmer®

déambuler [deɑ̃byle] /1/ VI to stroll about

déb. ABR = **débutant**; (*Comm*) = **à débattre**

débâcle [debɑkl] NF rout

déballage [debalaʒ] NM (*de marchandises*) display (*of loose goods*); (*fig: fam*) outpourings pl

déballer [debale] /1/ VT to unpack

débandade [debɑ̃dad] NF scattering; (*déroute*) rout

débander [debɑ̃de] /1/ VT to unbandage

débaptiser [debatize] /1/ VT (*rue*) to rename

débarbouiller [debaʀbuje] /1/ VT to wash ■ **se débarbouiller** VPR to wash (one's face)

débarcadère [debaʀkadɛʀ] NM landing stage (*BRIT*), wharf

débardeur [debaʀdœʀ] NM docker, stevedore; (*maillot*) slipover; (*pour femme*) vest top; (*pour homme*) sleeveless top

débarquement [debaʀkəmɑ̃] NM unloading, landing; disembarkation; (*Mil*) landing; **le D~** the Normandy landings

débarquer [debaʀke] /1/ VT to unload, land ▶ VI to disembark; (*fig*) to turn up

débarras [debaʀa] NM (*pièce*) lumber room; (*placard*) junk cupboard; (*remise*) outhouse; **bon ~!** good riddance!

débarrasser [debaʀase] /1/ VT to clear; **~ qn de** (*vêtements, paquets*) to relieve sb of; (*habitude, ennemi*) to rid sb of; **~ qch de** (*fouillis etc*) to clear sth of ▶ VI (*enlever le couvert*) to clear away ■ **se débarrasser de** VPR to get rid of; to rid o.s. of

débat [deba] VB *voir* **débattre** ▸ NM discussion, debate ▪ **débats** NMPL (*Pol*) proceedings, debates

débattre [debatʀ] /**41**/ VT to discuss, debate ▪ **se débattre** VPR to struggle

débauchage [deboʃaʒ] NM (*licenciement*) laying off (of staff); (*par un concurrent*) poaching

débauche [deboʃ] NF debauchery; **une ~ de** (*fig*) a profusion of (: *de couleurs*) a riot of

débauché, e [deboʃe] ADJ debauched ▸ NM/F profligate

débaucher [deboʃe] /**1**/ VT (*licencier*) to lay off, dismiss; (*salarié d'une autre entreprise*) to poach; (*entraîner*) to lead astray, debauch; (*inciter à la grève*) to incite

débile [debil] ADJ weak, feeble; (*fam: idiot*) dim-witted

débilitant, e [debilitã, -ãt] ADJ debilitating

débilité [debilite] NF debility; (*fam: idiotie*) stupidity; **~ mentale** mental debility

débiner [debine] /**1**/: **se débiner** VPR (*fam*) to do a bunk (BRIT *fam*), clear off (*fam*)

débit [debi] NM (*d'un liquide, fleuve*) (rate of) flow; (*d'un magasin*) turnover (of goods); (*élocution*) delivery; (*bancaire*) debit; **avoir un ~ de 10 euros** to be 10 euros in debit; **~ de boissons** drinking establishment; **~ de tabac** tobacconist's (shop) (BRIT), tobacco *ou* smoke shop (US)

débiter [debite] /**1**/ VT (*compte*) to debit; (*liquide, gaz*) to yield, produce, give out; (*couper: bois, viande*) to cut up; (*vendre*) to retail; (*péj: paroles etc*) to come out with, churn out

débiteur, -trice [debitœʀ, -tʀis] NM/F debtor ▸ ADJ in debit; (*compte*) debit *cpd*

déblai [deblɛ] NM (*nettoyage*) clearing ▪ **déblais** NMPL (*terre*) earth; (*décombres*) rubble

déblaiement [deblɛmã] NM clearing; **travaux de ~** earth moving *sg*

déblatérer [deblatere] /**6**/ VI: **~ contre** to go on about

déblayer [debleje] /**8**/ VT to clear; **~ le terrain** (*fig*) to clear the ground

déblocage [deblɔkaʒ] NM (*des prix, cours*) unfreezing

débloquer [deblɔke] /**1**/ VT (*frein, fonds*) to release; (*prix, crédits*) to free ▸ VI (*fam*) to talk rubbish

débobiner [debɔbine] /**1**/ VT to unwind

déboires [debwaʀ] NMPL setbacks

déboisement [debwazmã] NM deforestation

déboiser [debwaze] /**1**/ VT to clear of trees; (*région*) to deforest ▪ **se déboiser** VPR (*colline, montagne*) to become bare of trees

déboîter [debwate] /**1**/ VT (*Auto*) to pull out; **se ~ le genou** *etc* to dislocate one's knee *etc*

débonnaire [debɔnɛʀ] ADJ easy-going, good-natured

débordant, e [debɔʀdã, -ãt] ADJ (*joie*) unbounded; (*activité*) exuberant

débordé, e [debɔʀde] ADJ: **être ~ de** (*travail, demandes*) to be snowed under with

débordement [debɔʀdəmã] NM overflowing

déborder [debɔʀde] /**1**/ VI to overflow; (*lait etc*) to boil over; **~ de qch** (*dépasser*) to extend beyond sth; **~ de** (*joie, zèle*) to be brimming over with *ou* bursting with ▸ VT (*Mil, Sport*) to outflank

débouché [debuʃe] NM (*pour vendre*) outlet; (*perspective d'emploi*) opening; (*sortie*): **au ~ de la vallée** where the valley opens out (onto the plain)

déboucher [debuʃe] /**1**/ VT (*évier, tuyau etc*) to unblock; (*bouteille*) to uncork, open ▸ VI: **~ de** to emerge from, come out of; **~ sur** to come out onto; to open out onto; (*fig*) to arrive at, lead up to; (*études*) to lead on to

débouler [debule] /**1**/ VI to go (*ou* come) tumbling down; (*sans tomber*) to come careering down ▸ VT: **~ l'escalier** to belt down the stairs

déboulonner [debulɔne] /**1**/ VT to dismantle; (*fig: renvoyer*) to dismiss; (: *détruire le prestige de*) to discredit

débours [debuʀ] NMPL outlay

débourser [debuʀse] /**1**/ VT to pay out, lay out

déboussoler [debusɔle] /**1**/ VT to disorientate, disorient

★**debout** [d(ə)bu] ADV: **être ~** (*personne*) to be standing, stand; (*levé, éveillé*) to be up (and about); (*chose*) to be upright; **être encore ~** (*fig: en état*) to be still going; to be still standing; to be still up; **mettre qn ~** to get sb to his feet; **mettre qch ~** to stand sth up; **se mettre ~** to get up (on one's feet); **se tenir ~** to stand; **~ ! stand up!**; (*du lit*) get up!; **cette histoire ne tient pas ~** this story doesn't hold water

débouter [debute] /**1**/ VT (*Jur*) to dismiss; **~ qn de sa demande** to dismiss sb's petition

déboutonner [debutɔne] /**1**/ VT to undo, unbutton ▪ **se déboutonner** VPR to come undone *ou* unbuttoned

débraillé, e [debʀaje] ADJ slovenly, untidy

débrancher [debʀãʃe] /**1**/ VT (*appareil électrique*) to unplug; (*téléphone, courant électrique*) to disconnect, cut off

débrayage [debʀɛjaʒ] NM (*Auto*) clutch; (: *action*) disengaging the clutch; (*grève*) stoppage; **faire un double ~** to double-declutch

débrayer [debʀeje] /**8**/ VI (*Auto*) to declutch, disengage the clutch; (*cesser le travail*) to stop work

débridé, e [debʀide] ADJ unbridled, unrestrained

débrider [debʀide] /**1**/ VT (*cheval*) to unbridle; (*Culin: volaille*) to untruss

débriefer [debʀife] VT to debrief

débris [debʀi] NM (*fragment*) fragment ▸ NMPL (*déchets*) pieces, debris *sg*; rubbish *sg* (BRIT), garbage *sg* (US); **des ~ de verre** bits of glass

débrouillard, e [debʀujaʀ, -aʀd] ADJ smart, resourceful

débrouillardise [debʀujaʀdiz] NF smartness, resourcefulness

débrouiller [debʀuje] /**1**/ VT to disentangle, untangle; (*fig*) to sort out, unravel ▪ **se débrouiller** VPR to manage; **débrouillez-vous** you'll have to sort things out yourself

débroussailler [debʀusaje] /**1**/ VT to clear (of brushwood)

débroussailleuse [debʀusajøz] NF grass trimmer

débusquer [debyske] /**1**/ VT to drive out (from cover)

début [deby] NM beginning, start; **au ~** in *ou* at the beginning, at first; **au ~ de** at the beginning

113

ou start of; **dès le ~** from the start; **~ juin** in early June ∎ **débuts** NMPL beginnings; *(de carrière)* début *sg*; **faire ses débuts** to start out

débutant, e [debytɑ̃, -ɑ̃t] NM/F beginner, novice

débuter [debyte] /**1**/ VI to begin, start; *(faire ses débuts)* to start out

deçà [dəsa]: **en ~ de** *prép* this side of; **en ~** *adv* on this side

décacheter [dekaʃ(ə)te] /**4**/ VT to unseal, open

décade [dekad] NF *(10 jours)* (period of) ten days; *(10 ans)* decade

décadence [dekadɑ̃s] NF decadence; decline

décadent, e [dekadɑ̃, -ɑ̃t] ADJ decadent

décaféiné, e [dekafeine] ADJ decaffeinated, caffeine-free

décalage [dekalaʒ] NM move forward *ou* back; shift forward *ou* back; *(écart)* gap; *(désaccord)* discrepancy; **~ horaire** time difference (between time zones), time-lag

décalaminer [dekalamine] /**1**/ VT to decoke

décalcification [dekalsifikasjɔ̃] NF decalcification

décalcifier [dekalsifje] /**7**/: **se décalcifier** VPR to decalcify

décalcomanie [dekalkɔmani] NF transfer

décalé, e [dekale] ADJ *(humour, style)* offbeat

décaler [dekale] /**1**/ VT *(dans le temps: avancer)* to bring forward; *(: retarder)* to put back; *(changer de position)* to shift forward *ou* back; **~ de 10 cm** to move forward *ou* back by 10 cm; **~ de deux heures** to bring *ou* move forward two hours; to put back two hours

décalitre [dekalitʀ] NM decalitre (BRIT), decaliter (US)

décalogue [dekalɔg] NM Decalogue

décalquer [dekalke] /**1**/ VT to trace; *(par pression)* to transfer

décamètre [dekamɛtʀ] NM decametre (BRIT), decameter (US)

décamper [dekɑ̃pe] /**1**/ VI to clear out *ou* off

décan [dekɑ̃] NM *(Astrologie)* decan

décanter [dekɑ̃te] /**1**/ VT to (allow to) settle (and decant) ∎ **se décanter** VPR to settle

décapage [dekapaʒ] NM stripping; scouring; sanding

décapant [dekapɑ̃] NM acid solution; scouring agent; paint stripper

décaper [dekape] /**1**/ VT to strip; *(avec abrasif)* to scour; *(avec papier de verre)* to sand

décapiter [dekapite] /**1**/ VT to behead; *(par accident)* to decapitate; *(fig)* to cut the top off; *(: organisation)* to remove the top people from

décapotable [dekapɔtabl] ADJ convertible

décapoter [dekapɔte] /**1**/ VT to put down the top of

décapsuler [dekapsyle] /**1**/ VT to take the cap *ou* top off

décapsuleur [dekapsylœʀ] NM bottle-opener

décarcasser [dekaʀkase] /**1**/ VT: **se ~ pour qn/ pour faire qch** *(fam)* to slog one's guts out for sb/ to do sth

décathlon [dekatlɔ̃] NM decathlon

décati, e [dekati] ADJ faded, aged

décédé, e [desede] ADJ deceased

décéder [desede] /**6**/ VI to die

décelable [des(ə)labl] ADJ discernible

déceler [des(ə)le] /**5**/ VT to discover, detect; *(révéler)* to indicate, reveal

décélération [deseleʀasjɔ̃] NF deceleration

décélérer [deseleʀe] /**1**/ VI to decelerate, slow down

décembre [desɑ̃bʀ] NM December; *voir aussi* **juillet**

décemment [desamɑ̃] ADV decently

décence [desɑ̃s] NF decency

décennal, e, -aux [desenal, -o] ADJ *(qui dure dix ans)* having a term of ten years, ten-year; *(qui revient tous les dix ans)* ten-yearly

décennie [deseni] NF decade

décent, e [desɑ̃, -ɑ̃t] ADJ decent

décentralisation [desɑ̃tʀalizasjɔ̃] NF decentralization

décentraliser [desɑ̃tʀalize] /**1**/ VT to decentralize

décentrer [desɑ̃tʀe] /**1**/ VT to throw off centre ∎ **se décentrer** VPR to move off-centre

déception [desɛpsjɔ̃] NF disappointment

décerner [desɛʀne] /**1**/ VT to award

décès [desɛ] NM death, decease; **acte de ~** death certificate

décevant, e [des(ə)vɑ̃, -ɑ̃t] ADJ disappointing

décevoir [des(ə)vwaʀ] /**28**/ VT to disappoint

déchaîné, e [deʃene] ADJ unbridled, raging

déchaînement [deʃɛnmɑ̃] NM *(de haine, violence)* outbreak, outburst

déchaîner [deʃene] /**1**/ VT *(passions, colère)* to unleash; *(rires etc)* to give rise to, arouse ∎ **se déchaîner** VPR to be unleashed; *(rires)* to burst out; *(se mettre en colère)* to fly into a rage; **se ~ contre qn** to unleash one's fury on sb

déchanter [deʃɑ̃te] /**1**/ VI to become disillusioned

décharge [deʃaʀʒ] NF *(dépôt d'ordures)* rubbish tip *ou* dump; *(électrique)* electrical discharge; *(salve)* volley of shots; **à la ~ de** in defence of

déchargement [deʃaʀʒəmɑ̃] NM unloading

décharger [deʃaʀʒe] /**3**/ VT *(marchandise, véhicule)* to unload; *(Élec)* to discharge; *(arme: neutraliser)* to unload; *(: faire feu)* to discharge, fire; **~ qn de** *(responsabilité)* to relieve sb of, release sb from; **~ sa colère (sur)** to vent one's anger (on); **~ sa conscience** to unburden one's conscience; **se ~ dans** *(se déverser)* to flow into; **se ~ d'une affaire sur qn** to hand a matter over to sb

décharné, e [deʃaʀne] ADJ bony, emaciated, fleshless

déchaussé, e [deʃose] ADJ *(dent)* loose

déchausser [deʃose] /**1**/ VT *(personne)* to take the shoes off; *(skis)* to take off ∎ **se déchausser** VPR to take off one's shoes; *(dent)* to come *ou* work loose

dèche [dɛʃ] NF *(fam)*: **être dans la ~** to be flat broke

déchéance [deʃeɑ̃s] NF *(déclin)* degeneration, decay, decline; *(chute)* fall; **~ de nationalité** deprivation of nationality

déchet [deʃɛ] NM *(de bois, tissu etc)* scrap; *(perte gén Comm)* wastage, waste ∎ **déchets** NMPL *(ordures)* refuse *sg*, rubbish *sg* (BRIT), garbage *sg* (US); **déchets nucléaires** nuclear waste; **déchets radioactifs** radioactive waste

déchétarien, ne [deʃetaʀjɛ̃, jɛn] NM/F freegan

déchiffrage [deʃifʀaʒ] NM sight-reading

déchiffrer [deʃifʀe] /1/ VT to decipher

déchiqueté, e [deʃik(ə)te] ADJ jagged(-edged), ragged

déchiqueter [deʃik(ə)te] /4/ VT to tear ou pull to pieces

déchirant, e [deʃiʀɑ̃, -ɑ̃t] ADJ heart-breaking, heart-rending

déchiré, e [deʃiʀe] ADJ torn; (fig) heart-broken

déchirement [deʃiʀmɑ̃] NM (chagrin) wrench, heartbreak; (gén pl: conflit) rift, split

déchirer [deʃiʀe] /1/ VT to tear, rip; (mettre en morceaux) to tear up; (pour ouvrir) to tear off; (arracher) to tear out; (fig) to tear apart ■ **se déchirer** VPR to tear, rip; **se ~ un muscle/tendon** to tear a muscle/ tendon

déchirure [deʃiʀyʀ] NF (accroc) tear, rip; **~ musculaire** torn muscle

déchoir [deʃwaʀ] /25/ VI (personne) to lower o.s., demean o.s.; **~ de** to fall from

déchu, e [deʃy] PP de **déchoir** ▶ ADJ fallen; (roi) deposed

décibel [desibɛl] NM decibel

décidé, e [deside] ADJ (personne, air) determined; **c'est ~** it's decided; **être ~ à faire** to be determined to do

décidément [desidemɑ̃] ADV undoubtedly; really

décider [deside] /1/ VT: **~ qch** to decide on sth; **~ de faire/que** to decide to do/that; **~ qn (à faire qch)** to persuade ou induce sb (to do sth); **~ de qch** to decide upon sth; (chose) to determine sth ■ **se décider** VPR (personne) to decide, make up one's mind; (problème, affaire) to be resolved; **se ~ à qch** to decide on sth; **se ~ à faire** to decide ou make up one's mind to do; **se ~ pour qch** to decide on ou in favour of sth

décideur [desidœʀ] NM decision-maker

décilitre [desilitʀ] NM decilitre (BRIT), deciliter (US)

décimal, e, -aux [desimal, -o] ADJ, NF decimal

décimalisation [desimalizasjɔ̃] NF decimalization

décimaliser [desimalize] /1/ VT to decimalize

décimer [desime] /1/ VT to decimate

décimètre [desimɛtʀ] NM decimetre (BRIT), decimeter (US); **double ~** (20 cm) ruler

décisif, -ive [desizif, -iv] ADJ decisive; (qui l'emporte): **le facteur/l'argument ~** the deciding factor/argument

décision [desizjɔ̃] NF decision; (fermeté) decisiveness, decision; **prendre une ~** to make a decision; **prendre la ~ de faire** to take the decision to do; **emporter ou faire la ~** to be decisive

déclamation [deklamasjɔ̃] NF declamation; (péj) ranting, spouting

déclamatoire [deklamatwaʀ] ADJ declamatory

déclamer [deklame] /1/ VT to declaim; (péj) to spout ▶ VI: **~ contre** to rail against

déclarable [deklaʀabl] ADJ (marchandise) dutiable; (revenus) declarable

déclaration [deklaʀasjɔ̃] NF declaration; registration; (discours: Pol etc) statement; (compte rendu) report; **fausse ~** misrepresentation; **~ (d'amour)** declaration; **~ de décès** registration of death; **~ de guerre** declaration of war; **~ (d'impôts)** statement of income, tax declaration; ≈ tax return; **~ (de sinistre)** (insurance) claim; **~ de revenus** statement of income; **faire une ~ de vol** to report a theft

déclaré, e [deklaʀe] ADJ (juré) avowed

déclarer [deklaʀe] /1/ VT to declare, announce; (revenus, employés, marchandises) to declare; (décès, naissance) to register; (vol etc: à la police) to report; **~ la guerre** to declare war; **rien à ~** nothing to declare ■ **se déclarer** VPR (feu, maladie) to break out

déclassé, e [deklɑse] ADJ relegated, downgraded; (matériel) (to be) sold off

déclassement [deklɑsmɑ̃] NM relegation, downgrading; (Rail etc) change of class

déclasser [deklɑse] /1/ VT to relegate, downgrade; (déranger: fiches, livres) to get out of order

déclenchant, e [deklɑ̃ʃɑ̃, -ɑ̃t] ADJ (situation, cause) trigger cpd; **facteur ~** trigger

déclenchement [deklɑ̃ʃmɑ̃] NM release; setting off

déclencher [deklɑ̃ʃe] /1/ VT (mécanisme) to release; (sonnerie) to set off, activate; (attaque, grève) to launch; (provoquer) to trigger off ■ **se déclencher** VPR to release itself; (sonnerie) to go off

déclencheur [deklɑ̃ʃœʀ] NM release mechanism

déclic [deklik] NM trigger mechanism; (bruit) click

déclin [deklɛ̃] NM decline

déclinable [deklinabl] ADJ: **~ en qch** available in sth; **~ à l'infini** infinitely adaptable

déclinaison [deklinɛzɔ̃] NF declension

décliner [dekline] /1/ VI (santé, jour) to decline ▶ VT (invitation) to decline, refuse; (responsabilité) to refuse to accept; (nom, adresse) to state; (Ling) to decline ■ **se décliner** VPR (Ling) to decline

déclivité [deklivite] NF slope, incline; **en ~** sloping, on the incline

décloisonner [deklwazɔne] /1/ VT to decompartmentalize

déclouer [deklue] /1/ VT to unnail

décocher [dekɔʃe] /1/ VT to hurl; (flèche, regard) to shoot

décoction [dekɔksjɔ̃] NF decoction

décodage [dekɔdaʒ] NM deciphering, decoding

décoder [dekɔde] /1/ VT to decipher, decode

décodeur [dekɔdœʀ] NM decoder

décoiffant, e [dekwafɑ̃, -ɑ̃t] ADJ (fam) mind-blowing

décoiffé, e [dekwafe] ADJ: **elle est toute décoiffée** her hair is in a mess

décoiffer [dekwafe] /1/ VT: **~ qn** to mess up sb's hair ■ **se décoiffer** VPR to take off one's hat

décoincer [dekwɛ̃se] /3/ VT to unjam, loosen ■ **se décoincer** VPR (objet) to come loose; (fig: fam: personne) to let one's hair down; **ça s'est décoincé tout seul** it came loose all by itself; **il s'est décoincé un peu depuis qu'il n'habite plus chez ses parents** he's loosened up a bit since he stopped living with his parents

d

décois *etc* [deswa], **déçoive** *etc* [deswav] VB *voir* **décevoir**

décolérer [dekɔleʀe] /6/ VI: **il ne décolère pas** he's still angry, he hasn't calmed down

décollage [dekɔlaʒ] NM (*Aviat, Écon*) takeoff

décollé, e [dekɔle] ADJ: **oreilles décollées** sticking-out ears

décollement [dekɔlmã] NM (*Méd*): **~ de la rétine** retinal detachment

décoller [dekɔle] /1/ VT to unstick ▶ VI (*avion*) to take off; (*projet, entreprise*) to take off, get off the ground ■ **se décoller** VPR to come unstuck

décolleté, e [dekɔlte] ADJ low-necked, low-cut; (*femme*) wearing a low-cut dress ▶ NM low neck(line); (*épaules*) (bare) neck and shoulders; (*plongeant*) cleavage

décolleter [dekɔlte] /4/ VT (*vêtement*) to give a low neckline to; (*Tech*) to cut

décolonisation [dekɔlɔnizasjɔ̃] NF decolonization

décoloniser [dekɔlɔnize] /1/ VT to decolonize

décolorant [dekɔlɔʀɑ̃] NM decolorant, bleaching agent

décoloration [dekɔlɔʀasjɔ̃] NF: **se faire faire une ~** (*chez le coiffeur*) to have one's hair bleached *ou* lightened

décoloré, e [dekɔlɔʀe] ADJ (*vêtement*) faded; (*cheveux*) bleached

décolorer [dekɔlɔʀe] /1/ VT (*tissu*) to fade; (*cheveux*) to bleach, lighten; **se faire ~ les cheveux** to have one's hair bleached ■ **se décolorer** VPR to fade

décombres [dekɔ̃bʀ] NMPL rubble *sg*, debris *sg*

décommander [dekɔmɑ̃de] /1/ VT to cancel; (*invités*) to put off ■ **se décommander** VPR to cancel, cry off

décomplexé, e [dekɔ̃plɛkse] ADJ self-assured

décomposé, e [dekɔ̃poze] ADJ (*pourri*) decomposed; (*visage*) haggard, distorted

décomposer [dekɔ̃poze] /1/ VT to break up; (*Chimie*) to decompose; (*Math*) to factorize ■ **se décomposer** VPR to decompose

décomposition [dekɔ̃pozisjɔ̃] NF breaking up; decomposition; factorization; **en ~** (*organisme*) in a state of decay, decomposing

décompresser [dekɔ̃pʀese] /1/ VI (*fam: se détendre*) to unwind

décompresseur [dekɔ̃pʀesœʀ] NM decompressor

décompression [dekɔ̃pʀesjɔ̃] NF decompression

décomprimer [dekɔ̃pʀime] /1/ VT to decompress

décompte [dekɔ̃t] NM deduction; (*facture*) breakdown (of an account), detailed account

décompter [dekɔ̃te] /1/ VT to deduct

déconcentration [dekɔ̃sɑ̃tʀasjɔ̃] NF (*des industries etc*) dispersal; **~ des pouvoirs** devolution

déconcentré, e [dekɔ̃sɑ̃tʀe] ADJ (*sportif etc*) who has lost (his/her) concentration

déconcentrer [dekɔ̃sɑ̃tʀe] /1/ VT (*Admin*) to disperse ■ **se déconcentrer** VPR to lose (one's) concentration

déconcertant, e [dekɔ̃sɛʀtɑ̃, -ɑ̃t] ADJ disconcerting

déconcerter [dekɔ̃sɛʀte] /1/ VT to disconcert, confound

déconditionner [dekɔ̃disjɔne] /1/ VT: **~ l'opinion américaine** to change the way the Americans have been forced to think

déconfit, e [dekɔ̃fi, -it] ADJ crestfallen, downcast

déconfiture [dekɔ̃fityʀ] NF collapse, ruin; (*morale*) defeat

décongélation [dekɔ̃ʒelasjɔ̃] NF defrosting, thawing

décongelé, e [dekɔ̃ʒle] ADJ defrosted; « **ne jamais recongeler un produit ~** » "never refreeze a product that has been defrosted"

décongeler [dekɔ̃ʒ(ə)le] /5/ VT to thaw (out)

décongestionner [dekɔ̃ʒɛstjɔne] /1/ VT (*Méd*) to decongest; (*rues*) to relieve congestion in

déconnecté, e [dekɔnɛkte] ADJ: **~ des réalités** out of touch with reality

déconnecter [dekɔnɛkte] /1/ VT to disconnect

déconner [dekɔne] /1/ VI (!: *en parlant*) to talk (a load of) rubbish (BRIT) *ou* garbage (US); (: *faire des bêtises*) to muck about; **sans ~** no kidding

déconnexion [dekɔnɛksjɔ̃] NF disconnection; **droit à la ~** right to disconnect, *the employee's legal right not to reply to work emails outside working hours*

déconseillé, e [dekɔ̃seje] ADJ not recommended; **fortement ~** highly inadvisable; **c'est ~** it's not recommended, it's inadvisable

déconseiller [dekɔ̃seje] /1/ VT: **~ qch (à qn)** to advise (sb) against sth; **~ à qn de faire** to advise sb against doing

déconsidérer [dekɔ̃sideʀe] /6/ VT to discredit

décontamination [dekɔ̃taminasjɔ̃] NF decontamination

décontaminer [dekɔ̃tamine] /1/ VT to decontaminate

décontenancé, e [dekɔ̃tnɑ̃se] ADJ disconcerted

décontenancer [dekɔ̃t(ə)nɑ̃se] /3/ VT to disconcert, discountenance

décontracté, e [dekɔ̃tʀakte] ADJ relaxed, laid-back (*fam*)

décontracter [dekɔ̃tʀakte] /1/ VT to relax ■ **se décontracter** VPR to relax

décontraction [dekɔ̃tʀaksjɔ̃] NF relaxation

déconventionnement [dekɔ̃vɑ̃sjɔnmã] NM (*de médecins*) opting out

déconventionner [dekɔ̃vɑ̃sjɔne] VT (*médecin: pour faute*) to strike off

déconvenue [dekɔ̃v(ə)ny] NF disappointment

décor [dekɔʀ] NM décor; (*paysage*) scenery; **changement de ~** (*fig*) change of scene; **entrer dans le ~** (*fig*) to run off the road; **en ~ naturel** (*Ciné*) on location ■ **décors** NMPL (*Théât*) scenery *sg*, decor *sg*; (*Ciné*) set *sg*

décorateur, -trice [dekɔʀatœʀ, -tʀis] NM/F (interior) decorator; (*Ciné*) set designer

décoratif, -ive [dekɔʀatif, -iv] ADJ decorative

décoration [dekɔʀasjɔ̃] NF decoration

décorer [dekɔʀe] /1/ VT to decorate

décortiqué, e [dekɔʀtike] ADJ shelled; hulled

décortiquer [dekɔʀtike] /1/ VT to shell; (*riz*) to hull; (*fig: texte*) to dissect

décorum [dekɔʀɔm] NM decorum; etiquette

décote [dekɔt] NF tax relief

découcher [dekuʃe] /**1**/ vi to spend the night away

découdre [dekudʀ] /**48**/ vt (vêtement, couture) to unpick, take the stitching out of; (bouton) to take off ▶ vi: **en ~** (fig) to fight, do battle ■ **se découdre** vpr to come unstitched; (bouton) to come off

découler [dekule] /**1**/ vi: **~ de** to ensue ou follow from

découpage [dekupaʒ] nm cutting up; carving; (image) cut-out (figure); **~ électoral** division into constituencies

découpe [dekup] nf (de viande) carving; (Tech: découpage: de pièces, documents) cutting; (forme) shape

découper [dekupe] /**1**/ vt (papier, tissu) to cut up; (volaille, viande) to carve; (détacher: manche, article) to cut out; **se ~ sur** (ciel, fond) to stand out against

découplé, e [dekuple] adj: **bien ~** well-built, well-proportioned

découpures [dekupyʀ] nfpl (morceaux) cut-out bits; (d'une côte, arête) indentations, jagged outline sg

décourageant, e [dekuʀaʒɑ̃, -ɑ̃t] adj discouraging; (personne, attitude) negative

découragement [dekuʀaʒmɑ̃] nm discouragement, despondency

décourager [dekuʀaʒe] /**3**/ vt to discourage, dishearten; (dissuader) to discourage, put off; **~ qn de faire/de qch** to discourage sb from doing/from sth, put sb off doing/sth ■ **se décourager** vpr to lose heart, become discouraged

décousu, e [dekuzy] pp de **découdre** ▶ adj unstitched; (fig) disjointed, disconnected

découvert, e [dekuvɛʀ, -ɛʀt] pp de **découvrir** ▶ adj (tête) bare, uncovered; (lieu) open, exposed; **à visage ~** openly ▶ nm (bancaire) overdraft; **à ~** adv (Mil) exposed, without cover; (fig) openly; (Comm) adj overdrawn

découverte [dekuvɛʀt(ə)] nf discovery; **aller à la ~ de** (lieu) to go off to explore; **partir à la ~ du monde** to go off to explore the world; **faire la ~ de** to discover ▶ adj inv (itinéraire, sentier, séjour) scenic

découvrir [dekuvʀiʀ] /**18**/ vt to discover; (apercevoir) to see; (enlever ce qui couvre ou protège) to uncover; (montrer, dévoiler) to reveal ■ **se découvrir** vpr (chapeau) to take off one's hat; (se déshabiller) to take something off; (au lit) to uncover o.s.; (ciel) to clear; **se ~ des talents** to find hidden talents in o.s.

décrassage [dekʀasaʒ] nm (Sport) warm-down; **une séance de ~** a warm-down session

décrasser [dekʀase] /**1**/ vt to clean

décrêper [dekʀepe] /**1**/ vt (cheveux) to straighten

décrépi, e [dekʀepi] adj peeling; with roughcast rendering removed

décrépit, e [dekʀepi, -it] adj decrepit

décrépitude [dekʀepityd] nf decrepitude; decay

decrescendo [dekʀeʃɛndo] nm (Mus) decrescendo; **aller ~** (fig) to decline, be on the wane

décret [dekʀɛ] nm decree

décréter [dekʀete] /**6**/ vt to decree; (ordonner) to order

décret-loi [dekʀɛlwa] (pl **décrets-lois**) nm statutory order

décrié, e [dekʀije] adj disparaged

décrire [dekʀiʀ] /**39**/ vt to describe; (courbe, cercle) to follow, describe

décrisper [dekʀispe] /**1**/ vt to defuse ■ **se décrisper** vpr (personne, visage) to relax; (relations, situation) to ease; (ambiance) to become more relaxed

décrit, e [dekʀi, -it] pp de **décrire**

décrivais etc [dekʀivɛ] vb voir **décrire**

décrochage [dekʀɔʃaʒ] nm: **~ scolaire** (Scol) ≈ truancy

décrochement [dekʀɔʃmɑ̃] nm (d'un mur etc) recess

décrocher [dekʀɔʃe] /**1**/ vt (dépendre) to take down; (téléphone) to take off the hook; (fig: contrat etc) to get, land; **~ (le téléphone)** (pour répondre) to pick up ou lift the receiver ▶ vi (fam: abandonner) to drop out; (: cesser d'écouter) to switch off ■ **se décrocher** vpr (tableau, rideau) to fall down

décrois etc [dekʀwa] vb voir **décroître**

décroisé, e [dekʀwaze] adj (Football: tir, tête) to the near post; (Tennis: revers, coup droit) down-the-line

décroiser [dekʀwaze] /**1**/ vt (bras) to unfold; (jambes) to uncross

décroissance [dekʀwasɑ̃s] nf (diminution) decline, decrease; (Écon) degrowth

décroissant, e [dekʀwasɑ̃, -ɑ̃t] vb voir **décroître** ▶ adj decreasing, declining, diminishing; **par ordre ~** in descending order

décroître [dekʀwatʀ] /**55**/ vi to decrease, decline, diminish

décrotter [dekʀɔte] /**1**/ vt (chaussures) to clean the mud from; **se ~ le nez** to pick one's nose

décru, e [dekʀy] pp de **décroître**

décrue [dekʀy] nf drop in level (of the waters)

décryptage [dekʀiptaʒ] nm (de génome, médias, information) decoding; (Inform: de fichiers, données, DVD) decryption; **le ~ du génome humain** the decoding of the human genome

décrypter [dekʀipte] /**1**/ vt to decipher; (Inform, Tél) to decrypt

déçu, e [desy] pp de **décevoir** ▶ adj disappointed

déculotter [dekylɔte] /**1**/ vt: **~ qn** to take off ou down sb's trousers ■ **se déculotter** vpr to take off ou down one's trousers

déculpabiliser [dekylpabilize] /**1**/ vt (personne) to relieve of guilt; (chose) to decriminalize ■ **se déculpabiliser** vpr to stop feeling guilty

décuple [dekypl] nm: **le ~ de** ten times; **au ~** tenfold

décupler [dekyple] /**1**/ vt, vi to increase tenfold

déçut etc [desy] vb voir **décevoir**

dédaignable [dedɛɲabl] adj: **pas ~** not to be despised

dédaigner [dedeɲe] /**1**/ vt to despise, scorn; (négliger) to disregard, spurn; **~ de faire** to consider it beneath one to do, not deign to do

dédaigneusement [dedɛɲøzmɑ̃] adv scornfully, disdainfully

dédaigneux, -euse [dedɛɲø, -øz] adj scornful, disdainful

dédain [dedɛ̃] nm scorn, disdain

dédale [dedal] nm maze

★**dedans** [dədɑ̃] ADV inside; (*pas en plein air*) indoors, inside; **en ~** (*vers l'intérieur*) inwards ▸ NM inside; **au ~** on the inside; inside; *voir aussi* **là**

dédicace [dedikas] NF (*imprimée*) dedication; (*manuscrite, sur une photo etc*) inscription

dédicacer [dedikase] /3/ VT: **~ (à qn)** to sign (for sb), autograph (for sb), inscribe (to sb)

dédié, e [dedje] ADJ: **~ à qch** dedicated to sth; **ordinateur ~** dedicated computer

dédier [dedje] /7/ VT to dedicate; **~ à** to dedicate to **■ se dédier** VPR (*se consacrer*): **se ~ à qn/qch** to dedicate o.s. to sb/sth

dédire [dediʀ] /37/: **se dédire** VPR to go back on one's word; (*se rétracter*) to retract, recant

dédit, e [dedi, -it] PP *de* **dédire** ▸ NM (*Comm*) forfeit, penalty

dédommagement [dedɔmaʒmɑ̃] NM compensation

dédommager [dedɔmaʒe] /3/ VT: **~ qn (de)** to compensate sb (for); (*fig*) to repay sb (for)

dédouaner [dedwane] /1/ VT to clear through customs; (*fig*) to clear sb's name **■ se dédouaner** VPR to clear one's name; **se ~ de qch** (*responsabilités, accusation*) to clear o.s. of sth

dédoublement [dedublǝmɑ̃] NM splitting; (*Psych*): **~ de la personnalité** split *ou* dual personality

dédoubler [deduble] /1/ VT (*classe, effectifs*) to split (into two); (*couverture etc*) to unfold; (*manteau*) to remove the lining of; **~ un train/les trains** to run a relief train/additional trains **■ se dédoubler** VPR (*Psych*) to have a split personality

dédramatiser [dedramatize] /1/ VT (*situation*) to defuse; (*événement*) to play down

déductible [dedyktibl] ADJ deductible

déduction [dedyksjɔ̃] NF (*d'argent*) deduction; (*raisonnement*) deduction, inference

déduire [dedɥiʀ] /38/ VT: **~ qch (de)** (*ôter*) to deduct sth (from); (*conclure*) to deduce *ou* infer sth (from)

déesse [dees] NF goddess

DEFA SIGLE M (= *Diplôme d'État relatif aux fonctions d'animation*) diploma for senior youth leaders

défaillance [defajɑ̃s] NF (*syncope*) blackout; (*fatigue*) (sudden) weakness *no pl*; (*technique*) fault, failure; (*morale etc*) weakness; **~ cardiaque** heart failure

défaillant, e [defajɑ̃, -ɑ̃t] ADJ defective; (*Jur: témoin*) defaulting

défaillir [defajiʀ] /13/ VI to faint; to feel faint; (*mémoire etc*) to fail

défaire [defɛʀ] /60/ VT (*installation, échafaudage*) to take down, dismantle; (*paquet etc, nœud, vêtement*) to undo; (*bagages*) to unpack; (*ouvrage*) to undo, unpick; (*cheveux*) to take out; **~ le lit** (*pour changer les draps*) to strip the bed; (*pour se coucher*) to turn back the bedclothes **■ se défaire** VPR to come undone; **se ~ de** (*se débarrasser de*) to get rid of; (*se séparer de*) to part with

défait, e [defɛ, -ɛt] PP *de* **défaire** ▸ ADJ (*visage*) haggard, ravaged ▸ NF defeat; **une défaite annoncée** a predicted defeat; **cinq défaites consécutives** five consecutive defeats

défaites [defɛt] VB *voir* **défaire**

défaitisme [defetism] NM defeatism

défaitiste [defetist] ADJ, NMF defeatist

défalcation [defalkasjɔ̃] NF deduction

défalquer [defalke] /1/ VT to deduct

défasse *etc* [defas] VB *voir* **défaire**

défausser [defose] /1/ VT to get rid of **■ se défausser** VPR (*Cartes*) to discard

défaut [defo] NM (*moral*) fault, failing, defect; (*d'étoffe, métal*) fault, flaw, defect; (*Inform*) bug; (*manque, carence*) lack of; shortage of; **~ de la cuirasse** (*fig*) chink in the armour (BRIT) *ou* armor (US); **en ~** at fault; in the wrong; **prendre qn en ~** to catch sb out; **faire ~** (*manquer*) to be lacking; **à ~** *adv* failing that; **à ~ de** for lack *ou* want of; **par ~** (*Jur*) in his (*ou* her *etc*) absence

défaveur [defavœʀ] NF disfavour (BRIT), disfavor (US)

défavorable [defavɔʀabl] ADJ unfavourable (BRIT), unfavorable (US)

défavoriser [defavɔʀize] /1/ VT to put at a disadvantage

défectif, -ive [defɛktif, -iv] ADJ: **verbe ~** defective verb

défection [defɛksjɔ̃] NF defection, failure to give support *ou* assistance; failure to appear; **faire ~** (*d'un parti etc*) to withdraw one's support, leave

défectueux, -euse [defɛktɥø, -øz] ADJ faulty, defective

défectuosité [defɛktɥozite] NF defectiveness *no pl*; (*défaut*) defect, fault

défendable [defɑ̃dabl] ADJ defensible

défendeur, -eresse [defɑ̃dœʀ, -dʀɛs] NM/F (*Jur*) defendant

défendre [defɑ̃dʀ] /41/ VT to defend; (*interdire*) to forbid; **~ à qn qch/de faire** to forbid sb sth/to do sth **■ se défendre** VPR to defend o.s.; **il se défend** (*fig*) he can hold his own; **ça se défend** (*fig*) it holds together; **se ~ de/contre** (*se protéger*) to protect o.s. from/against; **se ~ de** (*se garder de*) to refrain from; (*nier*) **se ~ de vouloir** to deny wanting

défendu, e [defɑ̃dy] ADJ: **c'est ~** it is forbidden; **le fruit ~** the forbidden fruit

défenestrer [defǝnɛstʀe] /1/ VT to throw out of the window **■ se défenestrer** VPR to defenestrate o.s

défense [defɑ̃s] NF defence (BRIT), defense (US); (*d'éléphant etc*) tusk; **ministre de la ~** Minister of Defence (BRIT), Defence Secretary; **la ~ nationale** defence, the defence of the realm (BRIT); **la ~ contre avions** anti-aircraft defence; **«~ de fumer/cracher»** "no smoking/spitting", "smoking/spitting prohibited"; **prendre la ~ de qn** to stand up for sb; **~ des consommateurs** consumerism

défenseur [defɑ̃sœʀ] NM defender; (*Jur*) counsel for the defence

défensif, -ive [defɑ̃sif, -iv] ADJ, NF defensive; **être sur la défensive** to be on the defensive

déféquer [defeke] /6/ VI to defecate

déferai *etc* [defʀe] VB *voir* **défaire**

déférence [defeʀɑ̃s] NF deference

déférent, e [defeʀɑ̃, -ɑ̃t] ADJ (*poli*) deferential, deferent

déférer [defeʀe] /6/ VT (*Jur*) to refer; **~ à** vt (*requête, décision*) to defer to; **~ qn à la justice** to hand sb over to justice

déferlant, e [defɛʀlɑ̃, -ɑ̃t] ADJ: **vague déferlante** breaker

déferlement [defɛʀləmɑ̃] NM breaking; surge

déferler [defɛʀle] /1/ VI (*vagues*) to break; (*fig*) to surge

défi [defi] NM (*provocation*) challenge; (*bravade*) defiance; **mettre qn au ~ de faire qch** to challenge sb to do sth; **relever un ~** to take up *ou* accept a challenge; **lancer un ~ à qn** to challenge sb; **sur un ton de ~** defiantly

défiance [defjɑ̃s] NF mistrust, distrust

déficeler [defis(ə)le] /4/ VT (*paquet*) to undo, untie

déficience [defisjɑ̃s] NF deficiency

déficient, e [defisjɑ̃, -ɑ̃t] ADJ deficient

déficit [defisit] NM (*Comm*) deficit; (*Psych etc: manque*) defect; **~ budgétaire** budget deficit; **être en ~** to be in deficit

déficitaire [defisitɛʀ] ADJ (*année, récolte*) bad; **entreprise/budget ~** business/budget in deficit

défier [defje] /7/ VT (*provoquer*) to challenge; (*fig*) to defy, brave; **se ~** (*se méfier de*) to distrust, mistrust; **~ qn de faire** to challenge *ou* defy sb to do; **~ qn à** to challenge sb to; **~ toute comparaison/concurrence** to be incomparable/unbeatable

défigurer [defigyʀe] /1/ VT to disfigure; (*boutons etc*) to mar *ou* spoil (the looks of); (*fig: œuvre*) to mutilate, deface

défilé [defile] NM (*Géo*) (narrow) gorge *ou* pass; (*soldats*) parade; (*manifestants*) procession, march; **un ~ de** (*voitures, visiteurs etc*) a stream of

défiler [defile] /1/ VI (*troupes*) to march past; (*sportifs*) to parade; (*manifestants*) to march; (*visiteurs*) to pour, stream; **faire ~** (*bande, film*) to fast forward; (*Inform*) to scroll; **faire ~ un document** to scroll a document ▪ **se défiler** VPR (*se dérober*) to slip away, sneak off; **il s'est défilé** (*fam*) he wriggled out of it

défini, e [defini] ADJ definite

définir [definiʀ] /2/ VT to define

définissable [definisabl] ADJ definable

définitif, -ive [definitif, -iv] ADJ (*final*) final, definitive; (*pour longtemps*) permanent, definitive; (*sans appel*) final, definite ▸ NF: **en définitive** eventually; (*somme toute*) when all is said and done

définition [definisjɔ̃] NF definition; (*de mots croisés*) clue; (*TV*) (picture) resolution

définitivement [definitivmɑ̃] ADV definitively; permanently; definitely

défiscaliser [defiskalize] VT to make tax-exempt

défit *etc* [defi] VB *voir* **défaire**

déflagration [deflagʀasjɔ̃] NF explosion

déflation [deflasjɔ̃] NF deflation

déflationniste [deflasjɔnist] ADJ deflationist, deflationary

déflecteur [deflɛktœʀ] NM (*Auto*) quarterlight (BRIT), deflector (US)

déflorer [deflɔʀe] /1/ VT (*jeune fille*) to deflower; (*fig*) to spoil the charm of

défoncé, e [defɔ̃se] ADJ smashed in; broken down; (*route*) full of potholes ▸ NM/F addict

défoncer [defɔ̃se] /3/ VT (*caisse*) to stave in; (*porte*) to smash in *ou* down; (*lit, fauteuil*) to burst (the springs of); (*terrain, route*) to rip *ou* plough up

▪ **se défoncer** VPR (*se donner à fond*) to give it all one's got

défont [defɔ̃] VB *voir* **défaire**

déforestation [defɔʀɛstasjɔ̃] NF deforestation

déformant, e [defɔʀmɑ̃, -ɑ̃t] ADJ: **glace déformante** *ou* **miroir ~** distorting mirror

déformation [defɔʀmasjɔ̃] NF loss of shape; deformation; distortion; **~ professionnelle** conditioning by one's job

déformer [defɔʀme] /1/ VT to put out of shape; (*corps*) to deform; (*pensée, fait*) to distort ▪ **se déformer** VPR to lose its shape

défoulement [defulmɑ̃] NM release of tension; unwinding

défouler [defule] /1/: **se défouler** VPR (*Psych*) to work off one's tensions, release one's pent-up feelings; (*gén*) to unwind, let off steam

défraîchi, e [defʀeʃi] ADJ faded; (*article à vendre*) shop-soiled

défraîchir [defʀeʃiʀ] /2/: **se défraîchir** VPR to fade; to become shop-soiled

défrayer [defʀeje] /8/ VT: **~ qn** to pay sb's expenses; **~ la chronique** to be in the news; **~ la conversation** to be the main topic of conversation

défrichement [defʀiʃmɑ̃] NM clearance

défricher [defʀiʃe] /1/ VT to clear (for cultivation)

défriser [defʀize] /1/ VT (*cheveux*) to straighten; (*fig*) to annoy

défroisser [defʀwase] /1/ VT to smooth out

défroque [defʀɔk] NF cast-off

défroqué, e [defʀɔke] ADJ (*moine, prêtre, religieuse*) defrocked ▸ NM former monk (*ou* priest)

défroquer [defʀɔke] /1/ VI (*aussi:* **se défroquer**) to give up the cloth, renounce one's vows

défunt, e [defœ̃, -œ̃t] ADJ: **son ~ père** his late father ▸ NM/F deceased

dégagé, e [degaʒe] ADJ (*route, ciel*) clear; (*ton, air*) casual, jaunty; **sur un ton ~** casually

dégagement [degaʒmɑ̃] NM emission; freeing; clearing; (*espace libre*) clearing; passage; clearance; (*Football*) clearance; **voie de ~** slip road; **itinéraire de ~** alternative route (*to relieve traffic congestion*)

dégager [degaʒe] /3/ VT (*exhaler*) to give off, emit; (*délivrer*) to free, extricate; (*Mil: troupes*) to relieve; (*désencombrer*) to clear; (*isoler, mettre en valeur*) to bring out; (*crédits*) to release; **~ qn de** (*engagement, parole*) to release *ou* free sb from ▪ **se dégager** VPR (*odeur*) to emanate, be given off; (*passage, ciel*) to clear; **se ~ de** (*fig: engagement*) to get out of (: *promesse*) to go back on

dégaine [degɛn] NF (*fam*) look

dégainer [degene] /1/ VT to draw

dégarni, e [degaʀni] ADJ bald

dégarnir [degaʀniʀ] /2/ VT (*vider*) to empty, clear ▪ **se dégarnir** VPR to empty; to be cleaned out *ou* cleared; (*tempes, crâne*) to go bald

dégâts [dega] NMPL damage *sg*; **faire des ~** to damage

dégauchir [degoʃiʀ] /2/ VT (*Tech*) to surface

dégazer [degaze] /1/ VI (*pétrolier*) to clean its tanks

dégel [deʒɛl] NM thaw; (*fig: des prix etc*) unfreezing

dégeler [deʒ(ə)le] /5/ VT to thaw (out); (fig) to unfreeze ▶ VI to thaw (out) ■ **se dégeler** VPR (fig) to thaw out

dégénéré, e [deʒeneʀe] ADJ, NM/F degenerate

dégénérer [deʒeneʀe] /6/ VI to degenerate; (empirer) to go from bad to worse; (devenir): **~ en** to degenerate into

dégénérescence [deʒeneʀesɑ̃s] NF degeneration

dégingandé, e [deʒɛ̃gɑ̃de] ADJ gangling, lanky

dégivrage [deʒivʀaʒ] NM defrosting; de-icing

dégivrer [deʒivʀe] /1/ VT (frigo) to defrost; (vitres) to de-ice

dégivreur [deʒivʀœʀ] NM defroster; de-icer

déglinguer [deglɛ̃ge] /1/ VT to bust

déglutir [deglytiʀ] /2/ VT, VI to swallow

déglutition [deglytisjɔ̃] NF swallowing

dégonflé, e [degɔ̃fle] ADJ (pneu) flat; (fam) chicken ▶ NM/F (fam) chicken

dégonfler [degɔ̃fle] /1/ VT (pneu, ballon) to let down, deflate ▶ VI (désenfler) to go down ■ **se dégonfler** VPR (fam) to chicken out

dégorger [degɔʀʒe] /3/ VI (Culin): **faire ~** to leave to sweat; (rivière): **(se) ~ dans** to flow into ▶ VT to disgorge

dégoter [degɔte] /1/ VT (fam) to dig up, find

dégouliner [deguline] /1/ VI to trickle, drip; **~ de** to be dripping with

dégoupiller [degupije] /1/ VT (grenade) to take the pin out of

dégourdi, e [deguʀdi] ADJ smart, resourceful

dégourdir [deguʀdiʀ] /2/ VT to warm (up) ■ **se dégourdir** VPR: **se ~ les jambes** to stretch one's legs

dégoût [degu] NM disgust, distaste

dégoûtant, e [degutɑ̃, -ɑ̃t] ADJ disgusting

dégoûté, e [degute] ADJ disgusted; **~ de** sick of

dégoûter [degute] /1/ VT to disgust; **cela me dégoûte** I find this disgusting ou revolting; **~ qn de qch** to put sb off sth ■ **se dégoûter de** VPR to get ou become sick of

dégoutter [degute] /1/ VI to drip; **~ de** to be dripping with

dégradant, e [degʀadɑ̃, -ɑ̃t] ADJ degrading

dégradation [degʀadasjɔ̃] NF reduction in rank; defacement; degradation, debasement; deterioration; (aussi: **dégradations**: dégâts) damage no pl

dégradé, e [degʀade] ADJ (couleur) shaded off; (teintes) faded; (cheveux) layered ▶ NM (Peinture) gradation

dégrader [degʀade] /1/ VT (Mil: officier) to degrade; (abîmer) to damage, deface; (avilir) to degrade, debase ■ **se dégrader** VPR (relations, situation) to deteriorate

dégrafer [degʀafe] /1/ VT to unclip, unhook, unfasten

dégraissage [degʀesaʒ] NM (Écon) cutbacks pl; **~ et nettoyage à sec** dry cleaning

dégraissant [degʀesɑ̃] NM spot remover

dégraisser [degʀese] /1/ VT (soupe) to skim; (vêtement) to take the grease marks out of; (Écon) to cut back; (: entreprise) to slim down

degré [dəgʀe] NM degree; (d'escalier) step; **brûlure au 1er/2ème ~** 1st/2nd degree burn; **équation du 1er/2ème ~** linear/quadratic equation; **le premier ~** (Scol) primary level; **alcool à 90 degrés** surgical spirit; **vin de 10 degrés** 10° wine (on Gay-Lussac scale); **par degré(s)** adv by degrees, gradually

dégressif, -ive [degʀesif, -iv] ADJ on a decreasing scale, degressive; **tarif ~** decreasing rate of charge

dégrèvement [degʀɛvmɑ̃] NM tax relief

dégrever [degʀəve] /5/ VT to grant tax relief to; to reduce the tax burden on

dégriffé, e [degʀife] ADJ (vêtement) sold without the designer's label; **voyage ~** discount holiday

dégringolade [degʀɛ̃gɔlad] NF tumble; (fig) collapse

dégringoler [degʀɛ̃gɔle] /1/ VI to tumble (down); (fig: prix, monnaie etc) to collapse

dégriser [degʀize] /1/ VT to sober up

dégrossir [degʀosiʀ] /2/ VT (bois) to trim; (fig) to work out roughly; (: personne) to knock the rough edges off

dégroupage [degʀupaʒ] NM (Internet) unbundling

dégroupé, e [degʀupe] ADJ (Internet: zone, ADSL) unbundled

déguenillé, e [deg(ə)nije] ADJ ragged, tattered

déguerpir [degɛʀpiʀ] /2/ VI to clear off

dégueulasse [degœlas] ADJ (fam) disgusting

dégueuler [degœle] /1/ VI (fam) to puke, throw up

déguisé, e [degize] ADJ disguised; dressed up; **~ en** disguised (ou dressed up) as

déguisement [degizmɑ̃] NM disguise; (habits: pour s'amuser) fancy dress; (: pour tromper) disguise

déguiser [degize] /1/ VT to disguise ■ **se déguiser (en)** VPR (se costumer) to dress up (as); (pour tromper) to disguise o.s. (as)

dégustation [degystasjɔ̃] NF tasting; (de fromages etc) sampling, savouring (BRIT), savoring (US); (séance): **~ de vin(s)** wine-tasting

déguster [degyste] /1/ VT (vins) to taste; (fromages etc) to sample; (savourer) to enjoy, savour (BRIT), savor (US)

déhancher [deɑ̃ʃe] /1/: **se déhancher** VPR to sway one's hips; to lean (one's weight) on one hip

★**dehors** [dəɔʀ] ADV outside; (en plein air) outdoors, outside; **mettre** ou **jeter ~** to throw out; **en ~** outside; outwards; **en ~ de** apart from ▶ NM outside; **au ~** outside; (en apparence) outwardly; **au ~ de** outside; **de ~** from outside ▶ NMPL (apparences) appearances, exterior sg

déifier [deifje] /7/ VT to deify

déjà [deʒa] ADV already; (auparavant) before, already; **as-tu ~ été en France ?** have you been to France before?; **c'est ~ pas mal** that's not too bad (at all); **c'est ~ quelque chose** (at least) it's better than nothing; **quel nom, ~ ?** what was the name again?

déjanté, e [deʒɑ̃te] ADJ (fam: personne) nutty; (: spectacle) off-the-wall

déjanter [deʒɑ̃te] /1/: **se déjanter** VPR (pneu) to come off the rim

déjà-vu [deʒavy] NM: **c'est du ~** there's nothing new in that

déjeté, e [deʒ(ə)te] ADJ lop-sided, crooked

déjeuner [deʒœne] /1/ VI to (have) lunch; (le matin) to have breakfast ▶ NM lunch; (petit déjeuner) breakfast; **~ d'affaires** business lunch

déjouer [deʒwe] /1/ VT to elude, foil, thwart

déjuger [deʒyʒe] /3/: **se déjuger** VPR to go back on one's opinion

delà [dəla] ADV: **par ~, en ~ (de), au ~ (de)** beyond

délabré, e [delabʀe] ADJ dilapidated, broken-down

délabrement [delabʀəmɑ̃] NM decay, dilapidation

délabrer [delabʀe] /1/: **se délabrer** VPR to fall into decay, become dilapidated

délacer [delase] /3/ VT (chaussures) to undo, unlace

délai [delɛ] NM (attente) waiting period; (sursis) extension (of time); (temps accordé: aussi: **délais**) time limit; **sans ~** without delay; **à bref ~** shortly, very soon; at short notice; **dans les délais** within the time limit; **un ~ de 30 jours** a period of 30 days; **comptez un ~ de livraison de 10 jours** allow 10 days for delivery

délaissé, e [delese] ADJ abandoned, deserted; neglected

délaisser [delese] /1/ VT (abandonner) to abandon, desert; (négliger) to neglect

délassant, e [delasɑ̃, -ɑ̃t] ADJ relaxing

délassement [delasmɑ̃] NM relaxation

délasser [delase] /1/ VT (reposer) to relax; (divertir) to divert, entertain ■ **se délasser** VPR to relax

délateur, -trice [delatœʀ, -tʀis] NM/F informer

délation [delasjɔ̃] NF denouncement, informing

délavé, e [delave] ADJ faded

délayage [deleʒaʒ] NM mixing; thinning down

délayer [deleje] /8/ VT (Culin) to mix (with water etc); (peinture) to thin down; (fig) to pad out, spin out

delco® [dɛlko] NM (Auto) distributor; **tête de ~** distributor cap

délectation [delɛktasjɔ̃] NF delight

délecter [delɛkte] /1/: **se délecter** VPR: **se ~ de** to revel ou delight in

délégation [delegasjɔ̃] NF delegation; **~ de pouvoir** delegation of power

délégué, e [delege] ADJ delegated; **ministre ~ à** minister with special responsibility for ▶ NM/F delegate; representative

déléguer [delege] /6/ VT to delegate

délestage [delɛstaʒ] NM: **itinéraire de ~** alternative route (to relieve traffic congestion)

délester [delɛste] /1/ VT (navire) to unballast; **~ une route** to relieve traffic congestion on a road by diverting traffic

délétère [deletɛʀ] ADJ (atmosphère, climat) poisonous; (Méd: effet) deleterious; (: rôle) harmful

Delhi [dɛli] N Delhi

délibérant, e [delibeʀɑ̃, -ɑ̃t] ADJ: **assemblée délibérante** deliberative assembly

délibératif, -ive [deliberatif, -iv] ADJ: **avoir voix délibérative** to have voting rights

délibération [deliberasjɔ̃] NF deliberation

délibéré, e [delibeʀe] ADJ (conscient) deliberate; (déterminé) determined, resolute; **de propos ~** (à dessein, exprès) intentionally

délibérément [deliberemɑ̃] ADV deliberately; (résolument) resolutely

délibérer [delibeʀe] /6/ VI to deliberate

délicat, e [delika, -at] ADJ delicate; (plein de tact) tactful; (attentionné) thoughtful; (exigeant) fussy, particular; **procédés peu délicats** unscrupulous methods

délicatement [delikatmɑ̃] ADV delicately; (avec douceur) gently

délicatesse [delikatɛs] NF delicacy; tactfulness; thoughtfulness ■ **délicatesses** NFPL attentions, consideration sg

délice [delis] NM delight

délicieusement [delisjøzmɑ̃] ADV deliciously; delightfully

délicieux, -euse [delisjø, -øz] ADJ (au goût) delicious; (sensation, impression) delightful

délictueux, -euse [deliktɥø, -øz] ADJ criminal

délié, e [delje] ADJ nimble, agile; (mince) slender, fine ▶ NM: **les déliés** the upstrokes (in handwriting)

délier [delje] /7/ VT to untie; **~ qn de** (serment etc) to free ou release sb from

délimitation [delimitasjɔ̃] NF delimitation

délimiter [delimite] /1/ VT (terrain) to delimit, demarcate

délinquance [delɛ̃kɑ̃s] NF criminality; **~ juvénile** juvenile delinquency

délinquant, e [delɛ̃kɑ̃, -ɑ̃t] ADJ, NM/F delinquent

déliquescence [delikesɑ̃s] NF: **en ~** in a state of decay

déliquescent, e [delikesɑ̃, -ɑ̃t] ADJ decaying

délirant, e [deliʀɑ̃, -ɑ̃t] ADJ (Méd: fièvre) delirious; (imagination) frenzied; (fam: déraisonnable) crazy

délire [deliʀ] NM (fièvre) delirium; (fig) frenzy; (: folie) lunacy

délirer [deliʀe] /1/ VI to be delirious; **tu délires!** (fam) you're crazy!

délit [deli] NM (criminal) offence; **~ de droit commun** violation of common law; **~ de fuite** failure to stop after an accident; **~ d'initiés** insider dealing ou trading; **~ de presse** violation of the press laws

délivrance [delivʀɑ̃s] NF freeing, release; (sentiment) relief

délivrer [delivʀe] /1/ VT (prisonnier) to (set) free, release; (passeport, certificat) to issue; **~ qn de** (ennemis) to rid sb of; (fig: poids, tourment) to release sb from; **délivrez-nous du mal** deliver us from evil ■ **se délivrer** VPR: **se ~ de** to free o.s. from; **se ~ de l'emprise de qch** to free o.s. from the clutches of sth

délocalisation [delɔkalizasjɔ̃] NF relocation

délocaliser [delɔkalize] /1/ VT (entreprise, emplois) relocate

déloger [delɔʒe] /3/ VT (locataire) to turn out; (objet coincé, ennemi) to dislodge

déloyal, e, -aux [delwajal, -o] ADJ (personne, conduite) disloyal; (procédé) unfair

Delphes [dɛlf] N Delphi

d

121

delta [dɛlta] NM (*Géo*) delta

deltaplane® [dɛltaplan] NM hang-glider

déluge [delyʒ] NM (*biblique*) Flood, Deluge; (*grosse pluie*) downpour, deluge; (*grand nombre*): ~ **de** flood of

déluré, e [delyʀe] ADJ smart, resourceful; (*péj*) forward, pert

démagnétiser [demaɲetize] /1/ VT to demagnetize

démagogie [demagɔʒi] NF demagogy

démagogique [demagɔʒik] ADJ demagogic, popularity-seeking; (*Pol*) vote-catching

démagogue [demagɔg] ADJ demagogic ▶ NM demagogue

démaillé, e [demaje] ADJ (*bas*) laddered (BRIT), with a run (*ou* runs)

★**demain** [d(ə)mɛ̃] ADV tomorrow; ~ **matin/soir** tomorrow morning/evening; ~ **midi** tomorrow at midday; **à ~!** see you tomorrow!

demande [d(ə)mɑ̃d] NF (*requête*) request; (*revendication*) demand; (*Admin, formulaire*) application; (*Écon*): **la ~** demand; « **demandes d'emploi** » "situations wanted"; **à la ~ générale** by popular request; ~ **en mariage** (marriage) proposal; **faire sa ~ (en mariage)** to propose (marriage); ~ **de naturalisation** application for naturalization; ~ **de poste** job application

demandé, e [d(ə)mɑ̃de] ADJ (*article etc*): **très ~** (very) much in demand

★**demander** [d(ə)mɑ̃de] /1/ VT to ask for; (*question, date, heure, chemin*) to ask; (*requérir, nécessiter*) to require, demand; ~ **qch à qn** to ask sb for sth, ask sb sth; **ils demandent deux secrétaires et un ingénieur** they're looking for two secretaries and an engineer; ~ **la main de qn** to ask for sb's hand (in marriage); ~ **pardon à qn** to apologize to sb; ~ **à** *ou* **de voir/faire** to ask to see/ask if one can do; ~ **à qn de faire** to ask sb to do; ~ **que/pourquoi** to ask that/why; **se ~ si/pourquoi** *etc* to wonder if/why *etc*; (*sens purement réfléchi*) to ask o.s. if/why *etc*; **on vous demande au téléphone** you're wanted on the phone, there's someone for you on the phone; **il ne demande que ça** that's all he wants; **je ne demande pas mieux** I'm asking nothing more; **il ne demande qu'à faire** all he wants is to do

> **demander** is not usually translated by *to demand*.

demandeur, -euse [dəmɑ̃dœʀ, -øz] NM/F: ~ **d'asile** asylum-seeker; ~ **d'emploi** job-seeker

démangeaison [demɑ̃ʒɛzɔ̃] NF itching; **avoir des démangeaisons** to be itching

démanger [demɑ̃ʒe] /3/ VI to itch; **la main me démange** my hand is itching; **l'envie** *ou* **ça me démange de faire** I'm itching to do

démantèlement [demɑ̃tɛlmɑ̃] NM breaking up

démanteler [demɑ̃t(ə)le] /5/ VT to break up; to demolish

démaquillant [demakijɑ̃] NM make-up remover

démaquiller [demakije] /1/: **se démaquiller** VPR to remove one's make-up

démarcage [demaʀkaʒ] NM = **démarquage**

démarcation [demaʀkasjɔ̃] NF demarcation

démarchage [demaʀʃaʒ] NM (*Comm*) door-to-door selling

démarche [demaʀʃ] NF (*allure*) gait, walk; (*intervention*) step; approach; (*fig: intellectuelle*) thought processes *pl*; approach; **faire** *ou* **entreprendre des démarches** to take action; **faire des démarches auprès de qn** to approach sb; **faire les démarches nécessaires (pour obtenir qch)** to take the necessary steps (to obtain sth)

démarcheur, -euse [demaʀʃœʀ, -øz] NM/F (*Comm*) door-to-door salesman/-woman; (*Pol etc*) canvasser

démarquage [demaʀkaʒ] NM marking down

démarque [demaʀk] NF (*Comm: d'un article*) markdown

démarqué, e [demaʀke] ADJ (*Football*) unmarked; (*Comm*) reduced; **prix démarqués** marked-down prices

démarquer [demaʀke] /1/ VT (*prix*) to mark down; (*joueur*) to stop marking ▪ **se démarquer** VPR (*Sport*) to shake off one's marker

démarrage [demaʀaʒ] NM starting *no pl*, start; ~ **en côte** hill start

démarrer [demaʀe] /1/ VT to start up ▶ VI (*conducteur*) to start (up); (*véhicule*) to move off; (*travaux, affaire*) to get moving; (*coureur: accélérer*) to pull away

démarreur [demaʀœʀ] NM (*Auto*) starter

démasquer [demaske] /1/ VT to unmask ▪ **se démasquer** VPR to unmask; (*fig*) to drop one's mask

démâter [demɑte] /1/ VT to dismast ▶ VI to be dismasted

démêlant, e [demelɑ̃, -ɑ̃t] ADJ: **baume ~, crème démêlante** (hair) conditioner ▶ NM conditioner

démêler [demele] /1/ VT to untangle, disentangle

démêlés [demele] NMPL problems

démembrement [demɑ̃bʀəmɑ̃] NM dismemberment

démembrer [demɑ̃bʀe] /1/ VT to dismember

déménagement [demenaʒmɑ̃] NM (*du point de vue du locataire etc*) move; (*: du déménageur*) removal (BRIT), moving (US); **entreprise/camion de ~** removal (BRIT) *ou* moving (US) firm/van

déménager [demenaʒe] /3/ VT (*meubles*) to (re)move ▶ VI to move (house)

déménageur [demenaʒœʀ] NM removal man (BRIT), (*furniture*) mover (US); (*entrepreneur*) furniture remover

démence [demɑ̃s] NF madness, insanity; (*Méd*) dementia

démener [dem(ə)ne] /5/: **se démener** VPR to thrash about; (*fig*) to exert o.s.

dément, e [demɑ̃, -ɑ̃t] VB *voir* **démentir** ▶ ADJ (*fou*) mad (BRIT), crazy; (*fam*) brilliant, fantastic

démenti [demɑ̃ti] NM refutation

démentiel, le [demɑ̃sjɛl] ADJ insane

démentir [demɑ̃tiʀ] /16/ VT (*nouvelle, témoin*) to refute; (*faits etc*) to belie, refute; ~ **que** to deny that; **ne pas se ~** to fail to fail, keep up

démerder [demɛʀde] /1/: **se démerder** VPR (!) to bloody well manage for o.s.

démériter [demeʀite] /1/ VI: ~ **auprès de qn** to come down in sb's esteem

démesure [dem(ə)zyʀ] NF immoderation, immoderateness

démesuré, e [dem(ə)zyʀe] ADJ immoderate, disproportionate

démesurément [dem(ə)zyʀemã] ADV disproportionately

démettre [demɛtʀ] /56/ VT: ~ **qn de** (*fonction, poste*) to dismiss sb from ■ **se démettre** VPR: **se ~ (de ses fonctions)** to resign (from) one's duties; **se ~ l'épaule** *etc* to dislocate one's shoulder *etc*

demeurant [d(ə)mœʀã]: **au ~** *adv* for all that

demeure [d(ə)mœʀ] NF residence; **dernière ~** (*fig*) last resting place; **mettre qn en ~ de faire** to enjoin *ou* order sb to do; **à ~** *adv* permanently

demeuré, e [d(ə)mœʀe] ADJ backward ▸ NM/F backward person

demeurer [d(ə)mœʀe] /1/ VI (*habiter*) to live; (*séjourner*) to stay; (*rester*) to remain; **en ~ là** (*personne*) to leave it at that; (*choses*) to be left at that

★**demi, e** [dəmi] ADJ half; **et ~: trois heures/bouteilles et demie** three and a half hours/bottles; **il est 2 heures et demie** it's half past 2; **il est midi et ~** it's half past 12; **à ~** *adv* half; **ouvrir à ~** to half-open; **faire les choses à ~** to do things by halves ▸ NM (*bière*: = *0.25 litre*) ≈ half-pint; (*Football*) half-back; **~ de mêlée/d'ouverture** (*Rugby*) scrum/fly half ▸ NF: **à la demie** (*heure*) on the half-hour

demi... [dəmi] PRÉFIXE half-, semi..., demi-

demi-bas [dəmiba] NM INV (*chaussette*) knee-sock

demi-bouteille [dəmibutɛj] NF half-bottle

demi-cercle [dəmisɛʀkl] NM semicircle; **en ~** *adj* semicircular; *adv* in a semicircle

demi-douzaine [dəmiduzɛn] NF half-dozen, half a dozen

demi-finale [dəmifinal] NF semifinal

demi-finaliste [dəmifinalist] NM/F semifinalist

demi-fond [dəmifɔ̃] NM (*Sport*) medium-distance running

demi-frère [dəmifʀɛʀ] NM half-brother

demi-gros [dəmigʀo] NM INV wholesale trade

demi-heure [dəmijœʀ] NF: **une ~** a half-hour, half an hour

demi-jour [dəmiʒuʀ] NM half-light

demi-journée [dəmiʒuʀne] NF half-day, half a day

démilitariser [demilitaʀize] /1/ VT to demilitarize

demi-litre [dəmilitʀ] NM half-litre (BRIT), half-liter (US), half a litre *ou* liter

demi-livre [dəmilivʀ] NF half-pound, half a pound

demi-longueur [dəmilɔ̃gœʀ] NF (*Sport*) half-length, half a length

demi-lune [dəmilyn]: **en ~** *adj inv* semicircular

demi-mal [dəmimal] NM: **il n'y a que ~** there's not much harm done

demi-mesure [dəmiməzyʀ] NF half-measure

demi-mot [dəmimo]: **à ~** *adv* without having to spell things out

déminer [demine] /1/ VT to clear of mines

démineur [deminœʀ] NM bomb disposal expert

★**demi-pension** [dəmipɑ̃sjɔ̃] NF half-board; **être en ~** (*Scol*) to take school meals

★**demi-pensionnaire** [dəmipɑ̃sjɔnɛʀ] NM/F: **être ~** to take school lunches

demi-place [dəmiplas] NF half-price; (*Transports*) half-fare

démis, e [demi, -iz] PP *de* **démettre** ▸ ADJ (*épaule etc*) dislocated

demi-saison [dəmisɛzɔ̃] NF: **vêtements de ~** spring *ou* autumn clothing

demi-sel [dəmisɛl] ADJ INV slightly salted

demi-sœur [dəmisœʀ] NF half-sister

demi-sommeil [dəmisɔmɛj] NM doze

demi-soupir [dəmisupiʀ] NM (*Mus*) quaver (BRIT) *ou* eighth note (US) rest

démission [demisjɔ̃] NF resignation; **donner sa ~** to give *ou* hand in one's notice, hand in one's resignation

démissionnaire [demisjɔnɛʀ] ADJ outgoing ▸ NM/F person resigning

démissionner [demisjɔne] /1/ VI (*de son poste*) to resign, give *ou* hand in one's notice

demi-tarif [dəmitaʀif] NM half-price; (*Transports*) half-fare; **voyager à ~** to travel half-fare

demi-teinte [d(ə)mitɛ̃t] NF: **en ~** (*résultats, bilan*) mixed; (*rentrée*) subdued

demi-ton [dəmitɔ̃] NM (*Mus*) semitone

demi-tour [dəmituʀ] NM about-turn; **faire un ~** (*Mil etc*) to make an about-turn; **faire ~** to turn (and go) back; (*Auto*) to do a U-turn

démobilisation [demɔbilizasjɔ̃] NF demobilization; (*fig*) demotivation, demoralization

démobiliser [demɔbilize] /1/ VT to demobilize; (*fig*) to demotivate, demoralize

démocrate [demɔkʀat] ADJ democratic ▸ NM/F democrat

démocrate-chrétien, ne [demɔkʀatkʀetjɛ̃, -ɛn] NM/F Christian Democrat

démocratie [demɔkʀasi] NF democracy; **~ populaire/libérale** people's/liberal democracy

démocratique [demɔkʀatik] ADJ democratic

démocratiquement [demɔkʀatikmã] ADV democratically

démocratisation [demɔkʀatizasjɔ̃] NF democratization

démocratiser [demɔkʀatize] /1/ VT to democratize ■ **se démocratiser** VPR to become more democratic

démodé, e [demɔde] ADJ old-fashioned

démoder [demɔde] /1/: **se démoder** VPR to go out of fashion

démographe [demɔgʀaf] NM/F demographer

démographie [demɔgʀafi] NF demography

démographique [demɔgʀafik] ADJ demographic; **poussée ~** increase in population

demoiselle [d(ə)mwazɛl] NF (*jeune fille*) young lady; (*célibataire*) single lady, maiden lady; **~ d'honneur** bridesmaid

démolir [demɔliʀ] /2/ VT to demolish; (*fig: personne*) to do for

démolisseur [demɔlisœʀ] NM demolition worker

démolition [demɔlisjɔ̃] NF demolition

d

démon [demɔ̃] NM demon, fiend; evil spirit; (*enfant turbulent*) devil, demon; **le ~ du jeu/des femmes** a mania for gambling/women; **le D~** the Devil

démonétiser [demɔnetize] /**1**/ VT to demonetize

démoniaque [demɔnjak] ADJ fiendish

démonstrateur, -trice [demɔ̃stratœʀ, -tʀis] NM/F demonstrator

démonstratif, -ive [demɔ̃stratif, -iv] ADJ, NM (*aussi Ling*) demonstrative

démonstration [demɔ̃strasjɔ̃] NF demonstration; (*aérienne, navale*) display

démontable [demɔ̃tabl] ADJ folding

démontage [demɔ̃taʒ] NM dismantling

démonté, e [demɔ̃te] ADJ (*fig*) raging, wild

démonte-pneu [demɔ̃t(ə)pnø] NM tyre lever (BRIT), tire iron (US)

démonter [demɔ̃te] /**1**/ VT (*machine etc*) to take down, dismantle; (*pneu, porte*) to take off; (*cavalier*) to throw, unseat; (*fig: personne*) to disconcert ■ **se démonter** VPR (*meuble*) to be dismantled, be taken to pieces; (*personne*) to lose countenance

démontrable [demɔ̃trabl] ADJ demonstrable

démontrer [demɔ̃tʀe] /**1**/ VT to demonstrate, show

démoralisant, e [demɔralizɑ̃, -ɑ̃t] ADJ demoralizing

démoralisateur, -trice [demɔralizatœʀ, -tʀis] ADJ demoralizing

démoraliser [demɔralize] /**1**/ VT to demoralize ■ **se démoraliser** VPR to lose heart

démordre [demɔrdʀ] /**41**/ VI: **ne pas ~ de** to refuse to give up, stick to

démotiver [demɔtive] VT to demotivate ■ **se démotiver** VPR to lose one's motivation

démouler [demule] /**1**/ VT (*gâteau*) to turn out

démultiplication [demyltiplikasjɔ̃] NF reduction; reduction ratio

démuni, e [demyni] ADJ (*sans argent*) impoverished; **~ de** without, lacking in

démunir [demyniʀ] /**2**/ VT: **~ qn de** to deprive sb of; **se ~ de** to part with, give up

démuseler [demyzle] /**4**/ VT to unmuzzle

démystifier [demistifje] /**7**/ VT to demystify

démythifier [demitifje] /**7**/ VT to demythologize

dénatalité [denatalite] NF fall in the birth rate

dénationalisation [denasjɔnalizasjɔ̃] NF denationalization

dénationaliser [denasjɔnalize] /**1**/ VT to denationalize

dénaturé, e [denatyʀe] ADJ (*alcool*) denaturized; (*goûts*) unnatural

dénaturer [denatyʀe] /**1**/ VT (*goût*) to alter (completely); (*pensée, fait*) to distort, misrepresent

dénégations [denegasjɔ̃] NFPL denials

déneigement [denɛʒmɑ̃] NM snow clearance

déneiger [deneʒe] /**3**/ VT to clear snow from

dengue [dɛ̃g] NF dengue fever

déni [deni] NM: **~ (de justice)** denial of justice

déniaiser [denjeze] /**1**/ VT: **~ qn** to teach sb about life

dénicher [deniʃe] /**1**/ VT (*fam: objet*) to unearth; (*: restaurant etc*) to discover

dénicotinisé, e [denikɔtinize] ADJ nicotine-free

denier [dənje] NM (*monnaie*) formerly, a coin of small value; (*de bas*) denier; **~ du culte** contribution to parish upkeep; **deniers publics** public money; **de ses (propres) deniers** out of one's own pocket

dénier [denje] /**7**/ VT to deny; **~ qch à qn** to deny sb sth

dénigrement [denigʀəmɑ̃] NM denigration; **campagne de ~** smear campaign

dénigrer [denigʀe] /**1**/ VT to denigrate, run down

dénivelé, e [denivle] ADJ (*chaussée*) on a lower level ▸ NM difference in height

déniveler [deniv(ə)le] /**4**/ VT to make uneven; to put on a lower level

dénivellation [denivelasjɔ̃] NF, **dénivellement** [denivɛlmɑ̃] NM difference in level; (*pente*) ramp; (*creux*) dip

dénombrer [denɔ̃bʀe] /**1**/ VT (*compter*) to count; (*énumérer*) to enumerate, list

dénominateur [denɔminatœʀ] NM denominator; **~ commun** common denominator

dénomination [denɔminasjɔ̃] NF designation, appellation

dénommé, e [denɔme] ADJ: **le ~ Dupont** the man by the name of Dupont

dénommer [denɔme] /**1**/ VT to name

dénoncer [denɔ̃se] /**3**/ VT to denounce ■ **se dénoncer** VPR to give o.s. up, come forward

dénonciation [denɔ̃sjasjɔ̃] NF denunciation

dénoter [denɔte] /**1**/ VT to denote

dénouement [denumɑ̃] NM outcome, conclusion; (*Théât*) dénouement

dénouer [denwe] /**1**/ VT to unknot, undo

dénoyauter [denwajote] /**1**/ VT to stone; **appareil à ~** stoner

dénoyauteur [denwajotœʀ] NM stoner

denrée [dɑ̃ʀe] NF commodity; (*aussi*: **denrée alimentaire**) food(stuff)

dense [dɑ̃s] ADJ dense

densité [dɑ̃site] NF denseness; (*Physique*) density

★**dent** [dɑ̃] NF tooth; **avoir/garder une ~ contre qn** to have/hold a grudge against sb; **se mettre qch sous la ~** to eat sth; **être sur les dents** to be on one's last legs; **faire ses dents** to teethe, cut (one's) teeth; **en dents de scie** serrated; (*irrégulier*) jagged; **avoir les dents longues** (*fig*) to be ruthlessly ambitious; **~ de lait/sagesse** milk/wisdom tooth

dentaire [dɑ̃tɛʀ] ADJ dental; **cabinet ~** dental surgery; **école ~** dental school

denté, e [dɑ̃te] ADJ: **roue dentée** cog wheel

dentelé, e [dɑ̃t(ə)le] ADJ jagged, indented

dentelle [dɑ̃tɛl] NF lace *no pl*

dentelure [dɑ̃t(ə)lyʀ] NF (*aussi*: **dentelures**) jagged outline

dentier [dɑ̃tje] NM denture

★**dentifrice** [dɑ̃tifʀis] ADJ, NM: (**pâte**) **~** toothpaste; **eau ~** mouthwash

★**dentiste** [dɑ̃tist] NMF dentist

dentition [dɑ̃tisjɔ̃] NF teeth *pl*, dentition

dénucléariser [denykleaʀize] /**1**/ VT to make nuclear-free

dénudé, e [denyde] ADJ bare

dénuder [denyde] /**1**/ vt to bare ∎ **se dénuder** vpr (*personne*) to strip

dénué, e [denɥe] adj: ~ **de** lacking in; (*intérêt*) devoid of

dénuement [denymɑ̃] nm destitution

dénutrition [denytʀisjɔ̃] nf undernourishment

déodorant [deɔdɔʀɑ̃] nm deodorant

déodoriser [deɔdɔʀize] /**1**/ vt to deodorize

déontologie [deɔ̃tɔlɔʒi] nf code of ethics; (*professionnelle*) (professional) code of practice

déontologique [deɔ̃tɔlɔʒik] adj (*cadre, charte*) ethical; **les règles déontologiques** rules of professional ethics

dép. abr (= *département*) dept; (= *départ*) dep.

dépannage [depanaʒ] nm: **service/camion de ~** (*Auto*) breakdown service/truck

dépanner [depane] /**1**/ vt (*voiture, télévision*) to fix, repair; (*fig*) to bail out, help out

dépanneur [depanœʀ] nm (*Auto*) breakdown mechanic; (*TV*) television engineer

dépanneuse [depanøz] nf breakdown lorry (Brit), tow truck (US)

dépareillé, e [depaʀeje] adj (*collection, service*) incomplete; (*gant, volume, objet*) odd

déparer [depaʀe] /**1**/ vt to spoil, mar

départ [depaʀ] nm leaving *no pl*, departure; (*Sport*) start; (*sur un horaire*) departure; **à son ~** when he left; **au ~** (*au début*) initially, at the start; **courrier au ~** outgoing mail; **la veille de son ~** the day before he leaves/left

départager [depaʀtaʒe] /**3**/ vt to decide between

département [depaʀtəmɑ̃] nm department; *see note*

France is divided into administrative units called **départements**. There are 96 of these in metropolitan France and a further five overseas. These local government divisions are headed by a state-appointed *préfet* and administered by an elected *conseil départemental*. *Départements* are usually named after prominent geographical features such as rivers or mountain ranges.

départemental, e, -aux [depaʀtəmɑ̃tal, -o] adj departmental

départementaliser [depaʀtəmɑ̃talize] /**1**/ vt to devolve authority (to the département)

départir [depaʀtiʀ] /**16**/: **se ~ de** *vt* to abandon, depart from

dépassé, e [depase] adj superseded, outmoded; (*fig*) out of one's depth

dépassement [depasmɑ̃] nm (*Auto*) overtaking *no pl*

dépasser [depase] /**1**/ vt (*véhicule, concurrent*) to overtake; (*endroit*) to pass, go past; (*somme, limite*) to exceed; (*fig: en beauté etc*) to surpass, outshine; (*être en saillie sur*) to jut out above (*ou* in front of); (*dérouter*): **cela me dépasse** it's beyond me ▶ vi (*Auto*) to overtake; (*jupon*) to show ∎ **se dépasser** vpr to excel o.s.

dépassionner [depasjɔne] /**1**/ vt (*débat etc*) to take the heat out of

dépaver [depave] /**1**/ vt to remove the cobblestones from

dépaysé, e [depeize] adj disoriented

dépaysement [depeizmɑ̃] nm disorientation; change of scenery

dépayser [depeize] /**1**/ vt (*désorienter*) to disorientate; (*changer agréablement*) to provide with a change of scenery.

dépecer [depəse] /**5**/ vt (*boucher*) to joint, cut up; (*animal*) to dismember

dépêche [depɛʃ] nf dispatch; **~ (télégraphique)** telegram, wire

dépêcher [depeʃe] /**1**/ vt to dispatch ∎ **se dépêcher** vpr to hurry; **se ~ de faire qch** to hasten to do sth, hurry (in order) to do sth

dépeindre [depɛ̃dʀ] /**52**/ vt to depict

dépénalisation [depenalizasjɔ̃] nf decriminalization

dépendance [depɑ̃dɑ̃s] nf (*interdépendance*) dependence *no pl*, dependency; (*bâtiment*) outbuilding

dépendant, e [depɑ̃dɑ̃, -ɑ̃t] vb *voir* **dépendre** ▶ adj (*financièrement*) dependent

dépendre [depɑ̃dʀ] /**41**/ vt (*tableau*) to take down; **~ de** vt to depend on, be dependent on; (*appartenir*) to belong to; **ça dépend** it depends

dépens [depɑ̃] nmpl: **aux ~ de** at the expense of

dépense [depɑ̃s] nf spending *no pl*, expense, expenditure *no pl*; (*fig*) consumption; (: *de temps, de forces*) expenditure; **pousser qn à la ~** to make sb incur an expense; **~ physique** (physical) exertion; **dépenses de fonctionnement** revenue expenditure; **dépenses d'investissement** capital expenditure; **dépenses publiques** public expenditure

dépenser [depɑ̃se] /**1**/ vt to spend; (*gaz, eau*) to use; (*fig*) to expend, use up ∎ **se dépenser** vpr (*se fatiguer*) to exert o.s.

dépensier, -ière [depɑ̃sje, -jɛʀ] adj: **il est ~** he's a spendthrift

déperdition [depɛʀdisjɔ̃] nf loss

dépérir [depeʀiʀ] /**2**/ vi (*personne*) to waste away; (*plante*) to wither

dépersonnaliser [depɛʀsɔnalize] /**1**/ vt to depersonalize

dépêtrer [depetʀe] /**1**/ vt: **se ~ de** (*situation*) to extricate o.s. from

dépeuplé, e [depœple] adj depopulated

dépeuplement [depœpləmɑ̃] nm depopulation

dépeupler [depœple] /**1**/ vt to depopulate ∎ **se dépeupler** vpr to become depopulated

déphasage [defazaʒ] nm (*fig*) being out of touch

déphasé, e [defaze] adj (*Élec*) out of phase; (*fig*) out of touch

déphaser [defaze] /**1**/ vt (*fig*) to put out of touch

dépiauter [depjote] vt (*retirer la peau de: lapin, raie*) to skin; (*retirer: emballage*) to take off; (*fig: démonter: appareil*) to take apart

dépilation [depilasjɔ̃] nf hair loss; hair removal

dépilatoire [depilatwaʀ] adj depilatory, hair-removing; **crème ~** depilatory *ou* depilatory cream

dépiler [depile] /**1**/ vt (*épiler*) to depilate, remove hair from

dépistage [depistaʒ] nm (*Méd*) screening

dépister [depiste] /1/ ᴠᴛ to detect; (*Méd*) to screen; (*voleur*) to track down; (*poursuivants*) to throw off the scent

dépit [depi] ɴᴍ vexation, frustration; **en ~ de** *prép* in spite of; **en ~ du bon sens** contrary to all good sense

dépité, e [depite] ᴀᴅᴊ vexed, frustrated

dépiter [depite] /1/ ᴠᴛ to vex, frustrate

déplacé, e [deplase] ᴀᴅᴊ (*propos*) out of place, uncalled-for; **personne déplacée** displaced person

déplacement [deplasmã] ɴᴍ moving; shifting; transfer; (*voyage*) trip, travelling *no pl* (*Bʀɪᴛ*), traveling *no pl* (*US*); **en ~** away (on a trip); **~ d'air** displacement of air; **~ de vertèbre** slipped disc

déplacer [deplase] /3/ ᴠᴛ (*table, voiture*) to move, shift; (*employé*) to transfer, move ▪ **se déplacer** ᴠᴘʀ to move; (*organe*) to become displaced; (*personne: bouger*) to move, walk; (: *voyager*) to travel; **se ~ une vertèbre** to slip a disc

déplafonnement [deplafɔnmã] ɴᴍ (*de dépenses, allocations, loyers*) raising the ceiling, lifting the ceiling; **le ~ des cotisations employeurs** lifting the ceiling on employer contributions

déplafonner [deplafɔne] ᴠᴛ (*allocations, cotisations*) to raise the ceiling on, lift the ceiling on

déplaire [deplɛʀ] /54/ ᴠɪ: **ceci me déplaît** I don't like this, I dislike this; **il cherche à nous ~** he's trying to displease us *ou* be disagreeable to us ▪ **se déplaire** ᴠᴘʀ: **se ~ quelque part** to dislike it *ou* be unhappy somewhere

déplaisant, e [deplɛzã, -ãt] ᴠʙ *voir* **déplaire** ▶ ᴀᴅᴊ disagreeable, unpleasant

déplaisir [depleziʀ] ɴᴍ displeasure, annoyance

déplaît [deplɛ] ᴠʙ *voir* **déplaire**

dépliant [deplijã] ɴᴍ leaflet

déplier [deplije] /7/ ᴠᴛ to unfold ▪ **se déplier** ᴠᴘʀ (*parachute*) to open

déplisser [deplise] /1/ ᴠᴛ to smooth out

déploiement [deplwamã] ɴᴍ (*voir déployer*) deployment; display

déplomber [deplɔbe] /1/ ᴠᴛ (*caisse, compteur*) to break (open) the seal of; (*Inform*) to hack into

déplorable [deplɔrabl] ᴀᴅᴊ deplorable; lamentable

déplorer [deplɔre] /1/ ᴠᴛ (*regretter*) to deplore; (*pleurer sur*) to lament

déployer [deplwaje] /8/ ᴠᴛ to open out, spread; (*Mil*) to deploy; (*montrer*) to display, exhibit ▪ **se déployer** ᴠᴘʀ (*ailes*) to open out; (*tanks*) to be deployed; (*forces, troupes*) to deploy

déplu [deply] ᴘᴘ *de* **déplaire**

déplumé, e [deplyme] ᴀᴅᴊ (*volaille*) plucked; (*au plumage épars ou absent*) featherless; (*fam: dégarni*) balding

déplumer [deplyme]: **se déplumer** ᴠᴘʀ (*fam: perdre ses cheveux*) to go bald; (*oiseau*) to lose its feathers; (*arbre*) to lose its leaves

dépointer [depwɛ̃te] /1/ ᴠɪ to clock out

dépoli, e [depɔli] ᴀᴅᴊ: **verre ~** frosted glass

dépolitiser [depɔlitize] /1/ ᴠᴛ to depoliticize

dépopulation [depɔpylasjɔ̃] ɴꜰ depopulation

déportation [depɔrtasjɔ̃] ɴꜰ deportation

déporté, e [depɔrte] ɴᴍ/ꜰ deportee; (*1939–45*) concentration camp prisoner

déporter [depɔrte] /1/ ᴠᴛ (*Pol*) to deport; (*dévier*) to carry off course ▪ **se déporter** ᴠᴘʀ (*voiture*) to swerve

déposant, e [depozã, -ãt] ɴᴍ/ꜰ (*épargnant*) depositor

dépose [depoz] ɴꜰ taking out; taking down

déposé, e [depoze] ᴀᴅᴊ registered; *voir aussi* **marque**

déposer [depoze] /1/ ᴠᴛ (*gén: mettre, poser*) to lay down, put down, set down; (*à la banque, à la consigne*) to deposit; (*caution*) to put down; (*passager*) to drop (off), set down; (*démonter: serrure, moteur*) to take out; (: *rideau*) to take down; (*roi*) to depose; (*Admin: faire enregistrer*) to file; (*marque*) to register; (*plainte*) to lodge; **~ son bilan** (*Comm*) to go into (voluntary) liquidation ▶ ᴠɪ to form a sediment *ou* deposit; (*Jur*): **~ (contre)** to testify *ou* give evidence (against) ▪ **se déposer** ᴠᴘʀ to settle

dépositaire [depozitɛʀ] ɴᴍꜰ (*Jur*) depository; (*Comm*) agent; **~ agréé** authorized agent

déposition [depozisjɔ̃] ɴꜰ (*Jur*) deposition, statement

déposséder [deposede] /6/ ᴠᴛ to dispossess

dépôt [depo] ɴᴍ (*à la banque, sédiment*) deposit; (*entrepôt, réserve*) warehouse, store; (*gare*) depot; (*prison*) cells *pl*; **~ d'ordures** rubbish (*Bʀɪᴛ*) *ou* garbage (*US*) dump, tip (*Bʀɪᴛ*); **~ de bilan** (voluntary) liquidation; **~ légal** registration of copyright

dépoter [depɔte] /1/ ᴠᴛ (*plante*) to take from the pot, transplant

dépotoir [depɔtwaʀ] ɴᴍ dumping ground, rubbish (*Bʀɪᴛ*) *ou* garbage (*US*) dump; **~ nucléaire** nuclear (waste) dump

dépouille [depuj] ɴꜰ (*d'animal*) skin, hide; (*humaine*): **~ (mortelle)** mortal remains *pl*

dépouillé, e [depuje] ᴀᴅᴊ (*fig*) bare, bald; **~ de** stripped of, lacking in

dépouillement [depujmã] ɴᴍ (*de scrutin*) count, counting *no pl*

dépouiller [depuje] /1/ ᴠᴛ (*animal*) to skin; (*spolier*) to deprive of one's possessions; (*documents*) to go through, peruse; **~ qn/qch de** to strip sb/sth of; **~ le scrutin** to count the votes

dépourvu, e [depurvy] ᴀᴅᴊ: **~ de** lacking in, without; **au ~** *adv*: **prendre qn au ~** to catch sb unawares

dépoussiérer [depusjere] /6/ ᴠᴛ to remove dust from

dépravation [depravasjɔ̃] ɴꜰ depravity

dépravé, e [deprave] ᴀᴅᴊ depraved

dépraver [deprave] /1/ ᴠᴛ to deprave

dépréciation [depresjasjɔ̃] ɴꜰ depreciation

déprécier [depresje] /7/ ᴠᴛ to reduce the value of ▪ **se déprécier** ᴠᴘʀ to depreciate

déprédations [depredasjɔ̃] ɴꜰᴘʟ damage *sg*

dépressif, -ive [depresif, -iv] ᴀᴅᴊ depressive

dépression [depresjɔ̃] ɴꜰ depression; **~ (nerveuse)** (nervous) breakdown

déprimant, e [deprimã, -ãt] ᴀᴅᴊ depressing

déprime [deprim] ɴꜰ (*fam*): **la ~** depression

déprimé, e [deprime] ᴀᴅᴊ (*découragé*) depressed

déprimer [deprime] /1/ ᴠᴛ to depress

déprogrammer [depʀɔgʀame] /1/ VT (*supprimer*) to cancel

DEPS ABR (= *dernier entré premier sorti*) LIFO (= *last in first out*)

dépt ABR (= *département*) dept

dépuceler [depys(ə)le] /4/ VT (*fam*) to take the virginity of

---

depuis [dəpɥi]

PRÉP **1** (*point de départ dans le temps*) since; **il habite Paris depuis 1983/l'an dernier** he has been living in Paris since 1983/last year; **depuis quand?** since when?; **depuis quand le connaissez-vous?** how long have you known him?; **depuis lors** since then

2 (*temps écoulé*) for; **il habite Paris depuis cinq ans** he has been living in Paris for five years; **je le connais depuis trois ans** I've known him for three years; **depuis combien de temps êtes-vous ici?** how long have you been here?

3 (*lieu*): **il a plu depuis Metz** it's been raining since Metz; **elle a téléphoné depuis Valence** she rang from Valence

4 (*quantité, rang*) from; **depuis les plus petits jusqu'aux plus grands** from the youngest to the oldest

▶ ADV (*temps*) since (then); **je ne lui ai pas parlé depuis** I haven't spoken to him since (then); **depuis que** *conj* (ever) since; **depuis qu'il m'a dit ça** (ever) since he said that to me

---

dépuratif, -ive [depyʀatif, -iv] ADJ depurative, purgative

députation [depytasjɔ̃] NF deputation; (*fonction*) position of deputy, ≈ parliamentary seat (BRIT), ≈ seat in Congress (US)

député, e [depyte] NM/F (*Pol*) deputy, ≈ Member of Parliament (BRIT), ≈ Congressman/-woman (US)

députer [depyte] /1/ VT to delegate; **~ qn auprès de** to send sb (as a representative) to

déracinement [deʀasinmɑ̃] NM (*gén*) uprooting; (*d'un préjugé*) eradication

déraciner [deʀasine] /1/ VT to uproot

déradicaliser [deʀadikalize] VT to deradicalize

déraillement [deʀajmɑ̃] NM derailment

dérailler [deʀaje] /1/ VI (*train*) to be derailed, go off *ou* jump the rails; (*fam*) to be completely off the track; **faire ~** to derail

dérailleur [deʀajœʀ] NM (*de vélo*) dérailleur gears *pl*

déraison [deʀɛzɔ̃] NF unreasonableness

déraisonnable [deʀɛzɔnabl] ADJ unreasonable

déraisonner [deʀɛzɔne] /1/ VI to talk nonsense, rave

dérangeant, e [deʀɑ̃ʒɑ̃, -ɑ̃t] ADJ (*question*) troubling; (*scène*) disturbing

dérangement [deʀɑ̃ʒmɑ̃] NM (*gêne, déplacement*) trouble; (*gastrique*) disorder; **en ~** (*téléphone*) out of order

déranger [deʀɑ̃ʒe] /3/ VT (*personne*) to trouble, bother, disturb; (*projets*) to disrupt, upset; (*objets, vêtements*) to disarrange; **est-ce que cela vous dérange si ...?** do you mind if ...?; **ça te dérange-rait de faire ...?** would you mind doing ...? ■ **se déranger** VPR to put o.s. out; **surtout ne vous dérangez pas pour moi** please don't put yourself out on my account; (*se déplacer*) to (take the trouble to) come (*ou* go) out; **ne vous dérangez pas** don't go to any trouble, don't disturb yourself

dérapage [deʀapaʒ] NM skid, skidding *no pl*; going out of control

déraper [deʀape] /1/ VI (*voiture*) to skid; (*personne, semelles, couteau*) to slip; (*fig: économie etc*) to go out of control

dératé, e [deʀate] NM/F: **courir comme un ~** to run like the clappers

dératiser [deʀatize] /1/ VT to rid of rats

déréglé, e [deʀegle] ADJ (*machine, appareil*) not working properly; (*mœurs*) dissolute

dérèglement [deʀɛgləmɑ̃] NM upsetting *no pl*, upset

déréglementation [deʀɛglǝmɑ̃tasjɔ̃] NF deregulation

déréglementer [deʀɛglǝmɑ̃te] VT (*marché, écono-mie*) to deregulate ▶ VI to deregulate

dérégler [deʀegle] /6/ VT (*mécanisme*) to put out of order, cause to break down; (*estomac*) to upset ■ **se dérégler** VPR to break down, go wrong

dérégulation [deʀegylasjɔ̃] NF (*déréglementation: des télécoms, transports*) deregulation; (*du métabo-lisme*) upsetting

déréguler [deʀegyle] VT (*déréglementer: secteur*) to deregulate; (*Bio*) to disturb ▶ VI (*Écon*) to deregu-late

déremboursement [deʀɑ̃buʀs(ǝ)mɑ̃] NM (*de médicaments*) scaling down of system whereby patients claimed the cost of medicines

dérider [deʀide] /1/ VT to cheer up ■ **se dérider** VPR to cheer up

dérision [deʀizjɔ̃] NF derision; **tourner en ~** to deride; **par ~** in mockery

dérisoire [deʀizwaʀ] ADJ derisory

dérivatif [deʀivatif] NM distraction

dérivation [deʀivasjɔ̃] NF derivation; diversion

dérive [deʀiv] NF (*de dériveur*) centre-board; **aller à la ~** (*Navig, fig*) to drift; **~ des continents** (*Géo*) con-tinental drift

dérivé, e [deʀive] ADJ derived ▶ NM (*Ling*) deriva-tive; (*Tech*) by-product ▶ NF (*Math*) derivative

dériver [deʀive] /1/ VT (*Math*) to derive; (*cours d'eau etc*) to divert; **~ de** to derive from ▶ VI (*bateau*) to drift

dériveur [deʀivœʀ] NM sailing dinghy

dermatite [dɛʀmatit] NF dermatitis

dermato [dɛʀmato] NMF (*fam*: = *dermatologue*) der-matologist

dermatologie [dɛʀmatɔlɔʒi] NF dermatology

dermatologue [dɛʀmatɔlɔg] NMF dermatologist

dermatose [dɛʀmatoz] NF dermatosis

dermite [dɛʀmit] NF = **dermatite**

★ **dernier, -ière** [dɛʀnje, -jɛʀ] ADJ (*dans le temps, l'espace*) last; (*le plus récent: gén avant n*) latest, last; (*final, ultime: effort*) final; (: *échelon, grade*) top, highest; **lundi/le mois ~** last Monday/month; **du ~ chic** extremely smart; **le ~ cri** the last word (in fashion); **les der-niers honneurs** the last tribute; **rendre le ~ soupir** to breathe one's last; **en ~** *adv* last ▶ NM (*étage*) top floor ▶ NM/F: **ce ~, cette dernière** the latter

127

dernièrement [dɛʀnjɛʀmɑ̃] ADV recently

dernier-né, **dernière-née** [dɛʀnjene, dɛʀnjɛʀne] NM/F (*enfant*) last-born

dérobade [deʀɔbad] NF side-stepping *no pl*

dérobé, e [deʀɔbe] ADJ (*porte*) secret, hidden; **à la dérobée** surreptitiously

dérober [deʀɔbe] /1/ VT to steal; (*cacher*): ~ **qch à (la vue de) qn** to conceal *ou* hide sth from sb('s view) ■ **se dérober** VPR (*s'esquiver*) to slip away; (*fig*) to shy away; **se ~ sous** (*s'effondrer*) to give way beneath; **se ~ à** (*justice, regards*) to hide from; (*obligation*) to shirk

dérogation [deʀɔgasjɔ̃] NF (special) dispensation

déroger [deʀɔʒe] /3/: ~ **à** VT to go against, depart from

dérouiller [deʀuje] /1/: **se dérouiller** VPR: **se ~ les jambes** to stretch one's legs (*fig*)

déroulant, e [deʀulɑ̃, -ɑ̃t] ADJ (*menus, liste*) drop-down

déroulement [deʀulmɑ̃] NM (*d'une opération*) progress

dérouler [deʀule] /1/ VT (*ficelle*) to unwind; (*papier*) to unroll ■ **se dérouler** VPR to unwind; to unroll, come unrolled; (*avoir lieu*) to take place; (*se passer*) to go; **tout s'est déroulé comme prévu** everything went as planned

déroutant, e [deʀutɑ̃, -ɑ̃t] ADJ disconcerting

déroute [deʀut] NF (*Mil*) rout; (*fig*) total collapse; **mettre en ~** to rout; **en ~** routed

dérouter [deʀute] /1/ VT (*avion, train*) to reroute, divert; (*étonner*) to disconcert, throw (out)

derrick [deʀik] NM derrick (*over oil well*)

derrière [dɛʀjɛʀ] ADV, PRÉP behind; **les pattes de ~** the back legs, the hind legs; **par ~** from behind; (*fig*) in an underhand way, behind one's back ▶ NM (*d'une maison*) back; (*postérieur*) behind, bottom

derviche [dɛʀviʃ] NM dervish

DES SIGLE M (= *diplôme d'études supérieures*) university post-graduate degree

★**des** [de] ART *voir* **de**

★**dès** [dɛ] PRÉP from; ~ **que** *conj* as soon as; ~ **à présent** here and now; ~ **son retour** as soon as he was (*ou* is) back; ~ **réception** upon receipt; ~ **lors** *adv* from then on; ~ **lors que** *conj* from the moment (that)

désabusé, e [dezabyze] ADJ disillusioned

désaccord [dezakɔʀ] NM disagreement

désaccordé, e [dezakɔʀde] ADJ (*Mus*) out of tune

désacraliser [desakʀalize] /1/ VT to deconsecrate; (*fig: profession, institution*) to take the mystique out of

désaffecté, e [dezafɛkte] ADJ disused

désaffection [dezafɛksjɔ̃] NF: ~ **pour** estrangement from

désagréable [dezagʀeabl] ADJ unpleasant, disagreeable

désagréablement [dezagʀeabləmɑ̃] ADV disagreeably, unpleasantly

désagrégation [dezagʀegasjɔ̃] NF disintegration

désagréger [dezagʀeʒe] /3/: **se désagréger** VPR to disintegrate, break up

désagrément [dezagʀemɑ̃] NM annoyance, trouble *no pl*

désaltérant, **e** [dezalteʀɑ̃, -ɑ̃t] ADJ thirst-quenching

désaltérer [dezalteʀe] /6/: **se désaltérer** VPR to quench one's thirst; **ça désaltère** it's thirst-quenching, it quenches your thirst

désamorcer [dezamɔʀse] /3/ VT to remove the primer from; (*fig*) to defuse; (: *prévenir*) to forestall

désappointé, e [dezapwɛ̃te] ADJ disappointed

désapprobateur, -trice [dezapʀɔbatœʀ, -tʀis] ADJ disapproving

désapprobation [dezapʀɔbasjɔ̃] NF disapproval

désapprouver [dezapʀuve] /1/ VT to disapprove of

désarçonner [dezaʀsɔne] /1/ VT to unseat, throw; (*fig*) to throw, nonplus (BRIT), disconcert

désargenté, e [dezaʀʒɑ̃te] ADJ impoverished

désarmant, e [dezaʀmɑ̃, -ɑ̃t] ADJ disarming

désarmé, e [dezaʀme] ADJ (*fig*) disarmed

désarmement [dezaʀməmɑ̃] NM disarmament

désarmer [dezaʀme] /1/ VT (*Mil, aussi fig*) to disarm; (*Navig*) to lay up; (*fusil*) to unload; (: *mettre le cran de sûreté*) to put the safety catch on ▶ VI (*pays*) to disarm; (*haine*) to wane; (*personne*) to give up

désarroi [dezaʀwa] NM helplessness, disarray

désarticulé, e [dezaʀtikyle] ADJ (*pantin, corps*) dislocated

désarticuler [dezaʀtikyle] /1/: **se désarticuler** VPR to contort (o.s.)

désassorti, e [dezasɔʀti] ADJ non-matching, unmatched; (*magasin, marchand*) sold out

désastre [dezastʀ] NM disaster

désastreux, -euse [dezastʀø, -øz] ADJ disastrous

désavantage [dezavɑ̃taʒ] NM disadvantage; (*inconvénient*) drawback, disadvantage

désavantager [dezavɑ̃taʒe] /3/ VT to put at a disadvantage

désavantageux, -euse [dezavɑ̃taʒø, -øz] ADJ unfavourable, disadvantageous

désaveu [dezavø] NM repudiation; (*déni*) disclaimer

désavouer [dezavwe] /1/ VT to disown, repudiate, disclaim

désaxé, e [dezakse] ADJ (*fig*) unbalanced

désaxer [dezakse] /1/ VT (*roue*) to put out of true; (*personne*) to throw off balance

desceller [desele] /1/ VT (*pierre*) to pull free

descendance [desɑ̃dɑ̃s] NF (*famille*) descendants pl, issue; (*origine*) descent

descendant, e [desɑ̃dɑ̃, -ɑ̃t] VB *voir* **descendre** ▶ NM/F descendant

descendeur, -euse [desɑ̃dœʀ, -øz] NM/F (*Sport*) downhiller

★**descendre** [desɑ̃dʀ] /41/ VT (*escalier, montagne*) to go (*ou* come) down; (*valise, paquet*) to take *ou* get down; (*étagère etc*) to lower; (*fam: abattre*) to shoot down; (: *boire*) to knock back ▶ VI to go (*ou* come) down; (*passager: s'arrêter*) to get out, alight; (*niveau, température*) to go *ou* come down, fall, drop; (*marée*) to go out; ~ **à pied/en voiture** to walk/drive down, go down on foot/by car; ~ **de** (*famille*) to be descended from; **~ du train** to get out of *ou* off the train; **~ d'un arbre** to climb down from a tree; **~ de cheval** to dismount, get off one's horse; **~ à l'hôtel** to stay at a hotel; **~ dans la rue** (*manifester*) to take to the streets; **~ en ville** to go into town, go down town

descente [desãt] NF descent, going down; (*chemin*) way down; (Ski) downhill (race); **au milieu de la ~** halfway down; **freinez dans les descentes** use the brakes going downhill; **~ de lit** bedside rug; **~ (de police)** (police) raid

descriptif, -ive [dɛskʀiptif, -iv] ADJ descriptive ▸ NM explanatory leaflet

★**description** [dɛskʀipsjɔ̃] NF description

désembourber [dezãbuʀbe] /1/ VT to pull out of the mud

désembourgeoiser [dezãbuʀʒwaze] /1/ VT: **~ qn** to get sb out of his (*ou* her) middle-class attitudes

désembuer [dezãbɥe] /1/ VT to demist

désemparé, e [dezãpaʀe] ADJ bewildered, distraught; (*bateau, avion*) crippled

désemparer [dezãpaʀe] /1/ VI: **sans ~** without stopping

désemplir [dezãpliʀ] /2/ VI: **ne pas ~** to be always full

désenchanté, e [dezãʃãte] ADJ disenchanted, disillusioned

désenchantement [dezãʃãtmã] NM disenchantment, disillusion

désenclaver [dezãklave] /1/ VT to open up

désencombrer [dezãkɔ̃bʀe] /1/ VT to clear

désenfler [dezãfle] /1/ VI to become less swollen

désengagement [dezãgaʒmã] NM (Pol) disengagement

désensabler [dezãsable] /1/ VT to pull out of the sand

désensibiliser [dezãsibilize] /1/ VT (Méd) to desensitize

désenvenimer [dezãvnime] /1/ VT (*plaie*) to remove the poison from; (*fig*) to take the sting out of

désépaissir [dezepesiʀ] /2/ VT to thin (out)

déséquilibre [dezekilibʀ] NM (*fig: des forces, du budget*) imbalance; (Psych) unbalance; (*position*): **être en ~** to be unsteady

déséquilibré, e [dezekilibʀe] NM/F (Psych) unbalanced person

déséquilibrer [dezekilibʀe] /1/ VT to throw off balance

désert, e [dezɛʀ, -ɛʀt] ADJ deserted ▸ NM desert

déserter [dezɛʀte] /1/ VI, VT to desert

déserteur [dezɛʀtœʀ] NM deserter

désertion [dezɛʀsjɔ̃] NF desertion

désertique [dezɛʀtik] ADJ desert *cpd*; (*inculte*) barren, empty

désescalade [dezɛskalad] NF (Mil) de-escalation

désespérant, e [dezɛspeʀã, -ãt] ADJ hopeless, despairing

désespéré, e [dezɛspeʀe] ADJ desperate; (*regard*) despairing; **état ~** (Méd) hopeless condition

désespérément [dezɛspeʀemã] ADV desperately

désespérer [dezɛspeʀe] /6/ VT to drive to despair ▸ VI: **~ de** to despair of ■ **se désespérer** VPR to despair

désespoir [dezɛspwaʀ] NM despair; **être** *ou* **faire le ~ de qn** to be the despair of sb; **en ~ de cause** in desperation

déshabillé, e [dezabije] ADJ undressed ▸ NM négligée

déshabiller [dezabije] /1/ VT to undress ■ **se déshabiller** VPR to undress (o.s.)

déshabituer [dezabitɥe] /1/ VT: **se ~ de** to get out of the habit of

désherbant [dezɛʀbã] NM weed-killer

désherber [dezɛʀbe] /1/ VT to weed

déshérité, e [dezeʀite] ADJ disinherited ▸ NM/F: **les déshérités** (*pauvres*) the underprivileged, the deprived

déshériter [dezeʀite] /1/ VT to disinherit

déshonneur [dezɔnœʀ] NM dishonour (BRIT), dishonor (US), disgrace

déshonorer [dezɔnɔʀe] /1/ VT to dishonour (BRIT), dishonor (US), bring disgrace upon ■ **se déshonorer** VPR to bring dishono(u)r on o.s.

déshumaniser [dezymanize] /1/ VT to dehumanize

déshydratation [dezidʀatasjɔ̃] NF dehydration

déshydraté, e [dezidʀate] ADJ dehydrated

déshydrater [dezidʀate] /1/ VT to dehydrate

desiderata [deziderata] NMPL requirements

design [dizajn] ADJ (*mobilier*) designer *cpd* ▸ NM (industrial) design

désignation [dezinasjɔ̃] NF naming, appointment; (*signe, mot*) name, designation

designer [dizajnɛʀ] NM designer

désigner [dezine] /1/ VT (*montrer*) to point out, indicate; (*dénommer*) to denote, refer to; (*nommer: candidat etc*) to name, appoint

désillusion [dezilyzjɔ̃] NF disillusion(ment)

désillusionner [dezilyzjɔne] /1/ VT to disillusion

désincarné, e [dezɛ̃kaʀne] ADJ disembodied

désinence [dezinãs] NF ending, inflexion

désinfectant, e [dezɛ̃fɛktã, -ãt] ADJ, NM disinfectant

désinfecter [dezɛ̃fɛkte] /1/ VT to disinfect

désinfection [dezɛ̃fɛksjɔ̃] NF disinfection

désinformation [dezɛ̃fɔʀmasjɔ̃] NF disinformation

désinscrire [dezɛ̃skʀiʀ] /39/ VT to unsubscribe ■ **se désinscrire** VPR to unsubscribe

désinstaller [dezɛ̃stale] /1/ VT to uninstall

désintégration [dezɛ̃tegʀasjɔ̃] NF disintegration

désintégrer [dezɛ̃tegʀe] /6/ VT to break up ■ **se désintégrer** VPR to disintegrate

désintéressé, e [dezɛ̃teʀese] ADJ (*généreux, bénévole*) disinterested, unselfish

désintéressement [dezɛ̃teʀɛsmã] NM (*générosité*) disinterestedness

désintéresser [dezɛ̃teʀese] /1/: **se désintéresser (de)** VPR to lose interest (in)

désintérêt [dezɛ̃teʀɛ] NM (*indifférence*) disinterest

désintoxication [dezɛ̃tɔksikasjɔ̃] NF treatment for alcoholism (*ou* drug addiction); **faire une**

cure de ~ to have *ou* undergo treatment for alcoholism (*ou* drug addiction)

désintoxiquer [dezɛ̃tɔksike] /1/ VT to treat for alcoholism (*ou* drug addiction) ■ **se désintoxiquer** VPR: **se ~ de qch** (*drogue, alcool, tabac*) to get off sth; (*fig: se déshabituer*) to wean o.s. off sth; (*drogué*) to be treated for drug addiction; (*alcoolique*) to be treated for alcoholism

désinvolte [dezɛ̃vɔlt] ADJ casual, off-hand

désinvolture [dezɛ̃vɔltyʀ] NF casualness

désir [deziʀ] NM wish; (*fort, sensuel*) desire

désirable [deziʀabl] ADJ desirable

désirer [deziʀe] /1/ VT to want, wish for; (*sexuellement*) to desire; **je désire ...** (*formule de politesse*) I would like ...; **il désire que tu l'aides** he would like *ou* he wants you to help him; **~ faire** to want *ou* wish to do; **ça laisse à ~** it leaves something to be desired

désireux, -euse [deziʀø, -øz] ADJ: **~ de faire** anxious to do

désistement [dezistəmɑ̃] NM withdrawal

désister [deziste] /1/: **se désister** VPR to stand down, withdraw

désobéir [dezɔbeiʀ] /2/ VI: **~ (à qn/qch)** to disobey (sb/sth)

désobéissance [dezɔbeisɑ̃s] NF disobedience

désobéissant, e [dezɔbeisɑ̃, -ɑ̃t] ADJ disobedient

désobligeant, e [dezɔbliʒɑ̃, -ɑ̃t] ADJ disagreeable, unpleasant

désobliger [dezɔbliʒe] /3/ VT to offend

désodorisant [dezɔdɔʀizɑ̃] NM air freshener, deodorizer

désodoriser [dezɔdɔʀize] /1/ VT to deodorize

désœuvré, e [dezœvʀe] ADJ idle

désœuvrement [dezœvʀəmɑ̃] NM idleness

désolant, e [dezɔlɑ̃, -ɑ̃t] ADJ distressing

désolation [dezɔlasjɔ̃] NF (*affliction*) distress, grief; (*d'un paysage etc*) desolation, devastation

désolé, e [dezɔle] ADJ (*paysage*) desolate; **je suis ~** I'm sorry

désoler [dezɔle] /1/ VT to distress, grieve ■ **se désoler** VPR to be upset

désolidariser [desɔlidaʀize] /1/ VT: **se ~ de** *ou* **d'avec** to dissociate o.s. from

désopilant, e [dezɔpilɑ̃, -ɑ̃t] ADJ screamingly funny, hilarious

désordonné, e [dezɔʀdɔne] ADJ untidy, disorderly

désordre [dezɔʀdʀ] NM disorder(liness), untidiness; (*anarchie*) disorder; **en ~** in a mess, untidy ■ **désordres** NMPL (*Pol*) disturbances, disorder *sg*

désorganisation [dezɔʀganizasjɔ̃] NF (*désordre*) disorganization; **en pleine ~** in complete disarray

désorganisé, e [dezɔʀganize] ADJ (*personne*) disorganized

désorganiser [dezɔʀganize] /1/ VT to disorganize

désorienté, e [dezɔʀjɑ̃te] ADJ disorientated; (*fig*) bewildered

désorienter [dezɔʀjɑ̃te] /1/ VT (*fig*) to confuse

désormais [dezɔʀmɛ] ADV in future, from now on

désosser [dezɔse] /1/ VT to bone

despote [dɛspɔt] NM despot; (*fig*) tyrant

despotique [dɛspɔtik] ADJ despotic

despotisme [dɛspɔtism] NM despotism

desquamer [dɛskwame] /1/: **se desquamer** VPR to flake off

desquels, desquelles [dekɛl] *voir* **lequel**

DESS SIGLE M (= *Diplôme d'études supérieures spécialisées*) post-graduate diploma

dessaisir [deseziʀ] /2/ VT: **~ un tribunal d'une affaire** to remove a case from a court ■ **se dessaisir de** VPR to give up, part with

dessaler [desale] /1/ VT (*eau de mer*) to desalinate; (*Culin: morue etc*) to soak; (*fig: fam: délurer*): **~ qn** to teach sb a thing or two ▶ VI (*voilier*) to capsize

Desse ABR = **duchesse**

desséché, e [deseʃe] ADJ dried up

dessèchement [deseʃmɑ̃] NM drying out; dryness; hardness

dessécher [deseʃe] /6/ VT (*terre, plante*) to dry out, parch; (*peau*) to dry out; (*volontairement: aliments etc*) to dry, dehydrate; (*fig: cœur*) to harden ■ **se dessécher** VPR to dry out; (*peau, lèvres*) to go dry

dessein [desɛ̃] NM design; **dans le ~ de** with the intention of; **à ~** intentionally, deliberately

desseller [desele] /1/ VT to unsaddle

desserrer [deseʀe] /1/ VT to loosen; (*frein*) to release; (*poing, dents*) to unclench; **ne pas ~ les dents** not to open one's mouth ■ **se desserrer** VPR (*liens*) to come loose; (*fig*): **l'étau se desserre** the vice-like grip is relaxing

★**dessert** [desɛʀ] VB *voir* **desservir** ▶ NM dessert, pudding

desserte [desɛʀt] NF (*table*) side table; (*transport*): **la ~ du village est assurée par autocar** there is a coach service to the village; **chemin** *ou* **voie de ~** service road

desservir [desɛʀviʀ] /14/ VT (*ville, quartier*) to serve; (: *voie de communication*) to lead into; (*vicaire, paroisse*) to serve; (*nuire à: personne*) to do a disservice to; (*débarrasser*): **~ (la table)** to clear the table

dessiller [desije] /1/ VT (*fig*): **~ les yeux à qn** to open sb's eyes

★**dessin** [desɛ̃] NM (*œuvre, art*) drawing; (*motif*) pattern, design; (*contour*) (out)line; **le ~ industriel** draughtsmanship (BRIT), draftsmanship (US); **~ animé** cartoon (film); **~ humoristique** cartoon

★**dessinateur, -trice** [desinatœʀ, -tʀis] NM/F drawer; (*de bandes dessinées*) cartoonist; (*industriel*) draughtsman (BRIT), draftsman (US); **dessinatrice de mode** fashion designer

★**dessiner** [desine] /1/ VT to draw; (*concevoir: carrosserie, maison*) to design; (*robe, taille*) to show off ■ **se dessiner** VPR (*forme*) to be outlined; (*fig: solution*) to emerge

dessoûler [desule] /1/ VT, VI to sober up

★**dessous** [d(ə)su] ADV underneath, beneath; **en ~** underneath, below; (*fig: en catimini*) slyly, on the sly; **de ~ le lit** from under the bed; *voir* **ci-dessous**; (*étage inférieur*): **les voisins du ~** the downstairs neighbours; **avoir le ~** to get the worst of it ▶ NMPL (*sous-vêtements*) underwear *sg*; (*fig*) hidden aspects

dessous-de-bouteille [dəsudbutɛj] NM INV bottle mat

dessous-de-plat [dəsudpla] NM INV tablemat

dessous-de-table [dəsudtabl] NM INV (fig) bribe, under-the-counter payment

★**dessus** [d(ə)sy] ADV on top; (collé, écrit) on it; **en ~** above; **bras ~ bras dessous** arm in arm; **sens ~ dessous** upside down ▶ NM top; (étage supérieur): **les voisins/l'appartement du ~** the upstairs neighbours/flat; **avoir/prendre le ~** to have/get the upper hand; **reprendre le ~** to get over it; voir **ci-dessus; là-dessus**

dessus-de-lit [dəsydli] NM INV bedspread

déstabilisation [destabilizasjɔ̃] NF destabilization

déstabiliser [destabilize] /1/ VT (Pol) to destabilize

destin [dɛstɛ̃] NM fate; (avenir) destiny

destinataire [dɛstinatɛʀ] NMF (Postes) addressee; (d'un colis) consignee; (d'un mandat) payee; **aux risques et périls du ~** at owner's risk

★**destination** [dɛstinasjɔ̃] NF (lieu) destination; (usage) purpose; **à ~ de** (avion etc) bound for; (voyageur) bound for, travelling to

destiné, e [dɛstine] ADJ (promis): **être ~ à qch** (carrière, avenir) to be destined for sth; (prévu): **être ~ à** (usage) to be intended for, be meant for; (réservé): **être ~ à** (sort) to be in store for; (remarque) to be intended for; **être ~ à faire qch** to be destined to do sth

destinée [dɛstine] NF fate; (existence, avenir) destiny

destiner [dɛstine] /1/ VT: **~ qn à** (poste, sort) to destine sb for; **~ qch à** (envisager d'affecter) to intend to use sth for; **~ qch à qn** (envisager de donner) to intend sb to have sth, intend to give sth to sb; (adresser) to intend sth for sb; **~ qn/qch à** (prédestiner) to mark sb/sth out for ■ **se destiner à** VPR: **se ~ à l'enseignement** to intend to become a teacher

destituer [dɛstitɥe] /1/ VT to depose; **~ qn de ses fonctions** to relieve sb of his duties

destitution [dɛstitysjɔ̃] NF deposition

déstresser [destʀese] VI to unwind

destructeur, -trice [dɛstʀyktœʀ, -tʀis] ADJ destructive

destructif, -ive [dɛstʀyktif, -iv] ADJ destructive

destruction [dɛstʀyksjɔ̃] NF destruction

déstructuré, e [destʀyktyʀe] ADJ: **vêtements déstructurés** casual clothes

déstructurer [destʀyktyʀe] /1/ VT to break down, take to pieces

désuet, -ète [desɥɛ, -ɛt] ADJ outdated, outmoded

désuétude [desɥetyd] NF: **tomber en ~** to fall into disuse, become obsolete

désuni, e [dezyni] ADJ divided, disunited

désunion [dezynjɔ̃] NF disunity

désunir [dezyniʀ] /2/ VT to disunite ■ **se désunir** VPR (athlète) to get out of one's stride

détachable [detaʃabl] ADJ (coupon etc) tear-off cpd; (capuche etc) detachable

détachant [detaʃɑ̃] NM stain remover

détaché, e [detaʃe] ADJ (fig) detached ▶ NM/F (représentant) person on secondment (BRIT) ou a posting

détachement [detaʃmɑ̃] NM detachment; (fonctionnaire, employé): **être en ~** to be on secondment (BRIT) ou a posting

détacher [detaʃe] /1/ VT (enlever) to detach, remove; (délier) to untie; (Admin): **~ qn (auprès de** ou **à)** to post sb (to), send sb on secondment (to) (BRIT); (Mil) to detail; (vêtement: nettoyer) to remove the stains from ■ **se détacher** VPR (se séparer) to come off; (page) to come out; (se défaire) to come undone; (Sport) to pull ou break away; (se délier: chien, prisonnier) to break loose; **se ~ sur** to stand out against; **se ~ de** (se désintéresser) to grow away from

détail [detaj] NM detail; (Comm): **le ~** retail; **prix de ~** retail price; **au ~** adv (Comm) retail (: individuellement) separately; **donner le ~ de** to give a detailed account of; (compte) to give a breakdown of; **en ~** in detail

détaillant, e [detajɑ̃, -ɑ̃t] NM/F retailer

détaillé, e [detaje] ADJ (récit, plan, explications) detailed; (facture) itemized

détailler [detaje] /1/ VT (Comm) to sell retail; to sell separately; (expliquer) to explain in detail; to detail; (examiner) to look over, examine

détaler [detale] /1/ VI (lapin) to scamper off; (fam: personne) to make off, scarper (fam)

détartrage [detaʀtʀaʒ] NM descaling; (de dents) scaling

détartrant [detaʀtʀɑ̃] NM descaling agent (BRIT), scale remover

détartrer [detaʀtʀe] /1/ VT to descale; (dents) to scale

détaxe [detaks] NF (réduction) reduction in tax; (suppression) removal of tax; (remboursement) tax refund

détaxé, e [detakse] ADJ (produits) tax-free, duty-free

détaxer [detakse] /1/ VT (réduire) to reduce the tax on; (ôter) to remove the tax on

détecter [detɛkte] /1/ VT to detect

détecteur [detɛktœʀ] NM detector, sensor; **~ de fatigue** (de véhicule) (driver) drowsiness detector; **~ de fumée** smoke detector; **~ de mensonges** lie detector; **~ (de mines)** mine detector

détection [detɛksjɔ̃] NF detection

détective [detɛktiv] NM detective; **~ (privé)** private detective ou investigator

déteindre [detɛ̃dʀ] /52/ VI to fade; (au lavage) to run; **~ sur** (vêtement) to run into; (fig) to rub off on

déteint, e [detɛ̃, -ɛ̃t] PP de **déteindre**

dételer [det(ə)le] /4/ VT to unharness; (voiture, wagon) to unhitch ▶ VI (fig: s'arrêter) to leave off (working)

détendeur [detɑ̃dœʀ] NM (de bouteille à gaz) regulator

détendre [detɑ̃dʀ] /41/ VT (fil) to slacken, loosen; (personne, atmosphère, corps, esprit) to relax; (situation) to relieve ■ **se détendre** VPR (ressort) to lose its tension; (personne) to relax

détendu, e [detɑ̃dy] ADJ relaxed

détenir [det(ə)niʀ] /22/ VT (fortune, objet, secret) to be in possession of; (prisonnier) to detain; (record) to hold; **~ le pouvoir** to be in power

détente [detɑ̃t] NF relaxation; (Pol) détente; (d'une arme) trigger; (d'un athlète qui saute) spring

détenteur, -trice [detɑ̃tœʀ, -tʀis] NM/F holder

détention [detɑ̃sjɔ̃] NF *(de fortune, objet, secret)* possession; *(captivité)* detention; *(de record)* holding; **~ préventive** (pre-trial) custody

détenu, e [det(ə)ny] PP *de* **détenir ▸** NM/F prisoner

détergent [detɛʀʒɑ̃] NM detergent

détérioration [deteʀjɔʀasjɔ̃] NF damaging; deterioration

détériorer [deteʀjɔʀe] /1/ VT to damage ■ **se détériorer** VPR to deteriorate

déterminant, e [detɛʀminɑ̃, -ɑ̃t] ADJ: **un facteur ~** a determining factor **▸** NM *(Ling)* determiner

détermination [detɛʀminasjɔ̃] NF determining; *(résolution)* decision; *(fermeté)* determination

déterminé, e [detɛʀmine] ADJ *(résolu)* determined; *(précis)* specific, definite

déterminer [detɛʀmine] /1/ VT *(fixer)* to determine; *(décider)*: **~ qn à faire** to decide sb to do; **se ~ à faire** to make up one's mind to do

déterminisme [detɛʀminism] NM determinism

déterré, e [detere] NM/F: **avoir une mine de ~** to look like death warmed up (BRIT) *ou* warmed over (US)

déterrer [detere] /1/ VT to dig up

détersif, -ive [detɛʀsif, -iv] ADJ, NM detergent

détestable [detɛstabl] ADJ foul, detestable

détester [detɛste] /1/ VT to hate, detest

détiendrai [detjɛ̃dʀe], **détiens** etc [detjɛ̃] VB voir **détenir**

détonant, e [detɔnɑ̃, -ɑ̃t] ADJ: **mélange ~** explosive mixture

détonateur [detɔnatœʀ] NM detonator

détonation [detɔnasjɔ̃] NF detonation, bang, report (of a gun)

détoner [detɔne] /1/ VI to detonate, explode

détonner [detɔne] /1/ VI *(Mus)* to go out of tune; *(fig)* to clash

détordre [detɔʀdʀ] /41/ VT to untwist, unwind

détour [detuʀ] NM detour; *(tournant)* bend, curve; *(fig: subterfuge)* roundabout means; **ça vaut le ~** it's worth the trip; **sans ~** *(fig)* plainly

détourné, e [deturne] ADJ *(sentier, chemin, moyen)* roundabout

détournement [deturnəmɑ̃] NM diversion, rerouting; **~ d'avion** hijacking; **~ (de fonds)** embezzlement *ou* misappropriation (of funds); **~ de mineur** corruption of a minor

détourner [deturne] /1/ VT to divert; *(avion)* to divert, reroute; *(: par la force)* to hijack; *(yeux, tête)* to turn away; *(de l'argent)* to embezzle, misappropriate; **~ la conversation** to change the subject; **~ qn de son devoir** to divert sb from his duty; **~ l'attention (de qn)** to distract *ou* divert (sb's) attention ■ **se détourner** VPR to turn away

détoxifier [detɔksifje] /7/ VT *(organisme, corps)* to detox

détracteur, -trice [detʀaktœʀ, -tʀis] NM/F disparager, critic

détraqué, e [detʀake] ADJ *(machine, santé)* broken-down **▸** NM/F *(fam)*: **c'est un ~** he's unhinged

détraquer [detʀake] /1/ VT to put out of order; *(estomac)* to upset ■ **se détraquer** VPR to go wrong

détrempe [detʀɑ̃p] NF *(Art)* tempera

détrempé, e [detʀɑ̃pe] ADJ *(sol)* sodden, waterlogged

détremper [detʀɑ̃pe] /1/ VT *(peinture)* to water down

détresse [detʀɛs] NF distress; **en ~** *(avion etc)* in distress; **appel/signal de ~** distress call/signal

détriment [detʀimɑ̃] NM: **au ~ de** to the detriment of

détritus [detʀitys] NMPL rubbish *sg*, refuse *sg*, garbage *sg* (US)

détroit [detʀwa] NM strait; **le ~ de Bering** *ou* **Behring** the Bering Strait; **le ~ de Gibraltar** the Straits of Gibraltar; **le ~ du Bosphore** the Bosphorus; **le ~ de Magellan** the Strait of Magellan, the Magellan Strait

détromper [detʀɔ̃pe] /1/ VT to disabuse ■ **se détromper** VPR: **détrompez-vous** don't believe it

détrôner [detʀone] /1/ VT to dethrone, depose; *(fig)* to oust, dethrone

détrousser [detʀuse] /1/ VT to rob

détruire [detʀɥiʀ] /38/ VT to destroy; *(fig: santé, réputation)* to ruin; *(documents)* to shred

détruit, e [detʀɥi, -it] PP *de* **détruire**

★**dette** [dɛt] NF debt; **~ publique** *ou* **de l'État** national debt

DEUG [dœg] SIGLE M = **Diplôme d'études universitaires générales**

deuil [dœj] NM *(perte)* bereavement; *(période)* mourning; *(chagrin)* grief; **porter le ~** to wear mourning; **prendre le/être en ~** to go into/be in mourning

DEUST [dœst] SIGLE M = **Diplôme d'études universitaires scientifiques et techniques**

deutérium [døteʀjɔm] NM deuterium

★**deux** [dø] NUM two; **les ~** both; **ses ~ mains** both his hands, his two hands; **à ~ pas** a short distance away; **tous les ~ mois** every two months, every other month; **~ fois** twice

deuxième [døzjɛm] NUM second

deuxièmement [døzjɛmmɑ̃] ADV secondly, in the second place

deux-pièces [døpjɛs] NM INV *(tailleur)* two-piece (suit); *(de bain)* two-piece (swimsuit); *(appartement)* two-roomed flat (BRIT) *ou* apartment (US)

deux-points [døpwɛ̃] NM INV colon *sg*

deux-roues [døʀu] NM INV two-wheeled vehicle

deux-temps [døtɑ̃] ADJ INV two-stroke

devais etc [dəvɛ] VB voir **devoir**

dévaler [devale] /1/ VT to hurtle down

dévaliser [devalize] /1/ VT to rob, burgle

dévalorisant, e [devalɔʀizɑ̃, -ɑ̃t] ADJ depreciatory

dévalorisation [devalɔʀizasjɔ̃] NF depreciation

dévaloriser [devalɔʀize] /1/ VT to reduce the value of ■ **se dévaloriser** VPR to depreciate

dévaluation [devalɥasjɔ̃] NF depreciation; *(Écon: mesure)* devaluation

dévaluer [devalɥe] /1/ VT to devalue ■ **se dévaluer** VPR to devalue

devancer [d(ə)vɑ̃se] /3/ VT to be ahead of; *(distancer)* to get ahead of; *(arriver avant)* to arrive before; (*prévenir*) to anticipate; **~ l'appel** (*Mil*) to enlist before call-up

devancier, -ière [d(ə)vãsje, -jɛʀ] NM/F precursor

★**devant** [d(ə)vã] VB *voir* **devoir** ▸ ADV in front; (*à distance: en avant*) ahead; (*avec mouvement: passer*) past ▸ PRÉP in front of; (*en avant*) ahead of; (*fig*) before, in front of; (: *face à*) faced with, in the face of; (: *vu*) in view of ▸ NM front; **prendre les devants** to make the first move; **de ~** (*rue, porte*) front; **les pattes de ~** the front legs, the forelegs

devanture [d(ə)vãtyʀ] NF (*façade*) (shop) front; (*étalage*) display; (*vitrine*) (shop) window

dévastateur, -trice [devastatœʀ, -tʀis] ADJ devastating

dévastation [devastasjɔ̃] NF devastation

dévaster [devaste] /**1**/ VT to devastate

déveine [devɛn] NF rotten luck *no pl*

développement [dev(ə)lɔpmã] NM development; **pays en voie de ~** developing countries; **~ durable** sustainable development

développer [dev(ə)lɔpe] /**1**/ VT to develop ▪ **se développer** VPR to develop

développeur, -euse [dev(ə)lɔpœʀ, -øz] NM/F (*de logiciels*) developer

★**devenir** [dəv(ə)niʀ] /**22**/ VI to become; **~ instituteur** to become a teacher; **que sont-ils devenus ?** what has become of them?

devenu, e [dəvny] PP *de* **devenir**

dévergondé, e [devɛʀgɔ̃de] ADJ wild, shameless

dévergonder [devɛʀgɔ̃de] /**1**/ VT to get into bad ways ▪ **se dévergonder** VPR to get into bad ways

déverrouiller [deveʀuje] /**1**/ VT to unbolt

devers [dəvɛʀ] ADV: **par ~ soi** to oneself

déverser [devɛʀse] /**1**/ VT (*liquide*) to pour (out); (*ordures*) to tip (out) ▪ **se déverser dans** VPR (*fleuve, mer*) to flow into

déversoir [devɛʀswaʀ] NM overflow

dévêtir [devetiʀ] /**20**/ VT to undress ▪ **se dévêtir** VPR to undress

devez [dəve] VB *voir* **devoir**

déviation [devjasjɔ̃] NF deviation; (*Auto*) diversion (BRIT), detour (US); **~ de la colonne (vertébrale)** curvature of the spine

dévider [devide] /**1**/ VT to unwind

dévidoir [devidwaʀ] NM reel

deviendrai [dəvjɛ̃dʀe] , **deviens** *etc* [dəvjɛ̃] VB *voir* **devenir**

devienne *etc* [dəvjɛn] VB *voir* **devenir**

dévier [devje] /**7**/ VT (*fleuve, circulation*) to divert; (*coup*) to deflect ▸ VI to deflect; **faire ~** (*projectile*) to deflect; (*véhicule*) to push off course

devin [dəvɛ̃] NM soothsayer, seer

★**deviner** [d(ə)vine] /**1**/ VT to guess; (*prévoir*) to foretell, foresee; (*apercevoir*) to distinguish

devinette [d(ə)vinɛt] NF riddle

devint *etc* [dəvɛ̃] VB *voir* **devenir**

devis [d(ə)vi] NM estimate, quotation; **~ descriptif/estimatif** detailed/preliminary estimate

dévisager [devizaʒe] /**3**/ VT to stare at

devise [dəviz] NF (*formule*) motto, watchword; (*Écon: monnaie*) currency ▪ **devises** NFPL (*argent*) currency *sg*

deviser [dəvize] /**1**/ VI to converse

dévisser [devise] /**1**/ VT to unscrew, undo ▪ **se dévisser** VPR to come unscrewed

de visu [devizy] ADV: **se rendre compte de qch ~** to see sth for o.s.

dévitaliser [devitalize] /**1**/ VT (*dent*) to remove the nerve from

dévoiler [devwale] /**1**/ VT to unveil ▪ **se dévoiler** VPR (*mystère, raisons*) to be revealed

★**devoir** [d(ə)vwaʀ] /**28**/ NM duty; (*Scol*) piece of homework, homework *no pl*; (: *en classe*) exercise; **se faire un ~ de faire qch** to make it one's duty to do sth; **devoirs de vacances** homework set for the holidays ▸ VT (*argent, respect*): **~ qch (à qn)** to owe (sb) sth; **combien est-ce que je vous dois ?** how much do I owe you?; **il doit le faire** (*obligation*) he has to do it, he must do it; **cela devait arriver un jour** (*fatalité*) it was bound to happen; **il doit partir demain** (*intention*) he is due to leave tomorrow; **il doit être tard** (*probabilité*) it must be late; **je devrais faire** I ought to *ou* should do; **tu n'aurais pas dû** you ought not to have *ou* shouldn't have ▪ **se devoir** VPR: **se ~ de faire qch** to be duty bound to do sth; **comme il se doit** (*comme il faut*) as is right and proper

dévolu, e [devɔly] ADJ: **~ à** allotted to ▸ NM: **jeter son ~ sur** to fix one's choice on

devons [dəvɔ̃] VB *voir* **devoir**

dévorant, e [devɔʀã, -ãt] ADJ (*faim, passion*) raging

dévorer [devɔʀe] /**1**/ VT to devour; (*feu, soucis*) to consume; **~ qn/qch des yeux** *ou* **du regard** (*fig*) to eye sb/sth intently; (*convoitise*) to eye sb/sth greedily

dévot, e [devo, -ɔt] ADJ devout, pious ▸ NM/F devout person; **un faux ~** a falsely pious person

dévotion [devosjɔ̃] NF devoutness; **être à la ~ de qn** to be totally devoted to sb; **avoir une ~ pour qn** to worship sb

dévoué, e [devwe] ADJ devoted

dévouement [devumã] NM devotion, dedication

dévouer [devwe] /**1**/: **se dévouer** VPR (*se sacrifier*): **se ~ (pour)** to sacrifice o.s. (for); (*se consacrer*): **se ~ à** to devote *ou* dedicate o.s. to

dévoyé, e [devwaje] ADJ delinquent

dévoyer [devwaje] /**8**/ VT to lead astray; **~ l'opinion publique** to influence public opinion ▪ **se dévoyer** VPR to go off the rails

devrai *etc* [dəvʀe] VB *voir* **devoir**

dextérité [dɛksteʀite] NF skill, dexterity

dextrose [dɛkstʀoz] NM dextrose

dézipper [dezipe] /**1**/ VT (*Inform*) to unzip

dfc ABR (= *désire faire connaissance*) WLTM (= *would like to meet*)

DG SIGLE M = **directeur général**

dg. ABR (= *décigramme*) dg.

DGE SIGLE F (= *Dotation globale d'équipement*) *state contribution to local government budget*

DGSE SIGLE F (= *Direction générale de la sécurité extérieure*) ≈ MI6 (BRIT), ≈ CIA (US)

DGSI SIGLE F (= *Direction Générale de la Sécurité Intérieure*) *internal security service* ≈ MI5 (BRIT)

diabète [djabɛt] NM diabetes *sg*

133

diabétique [djabetik] NMF diabetic

diable [djɑbl] NM devil; **une musique du ~** an unholy racket; **il fait une chaleur du ~** it's fiendishly hot; **avoir le ~ au corps** to be the very devil

diablement [djɑbləmɑ̃] ADV fiendishly

diableries [djɑbləʀi] NFPL (d'enfant) devilment sg, mischief sg

diablesse [djɑblɛs] NF (petite fille) little devil

diablotin [djɑblɔtɛ̃] NM imp; (pétard) cracker

diabolique [djɑbɔlik] ADJ diabolical

diaboliser [djɑbɔlize] VT to demonize

diabolo [djɑbɔlo] NM (jeu) diabolo; (boisson) lemonade and fruit cordial; **~(-menthe)** lemonade and mint cordial

diacre [djɑkʀ] NM deacon

diadème [djɑdɛm] NM diadem

diagnostic [djagnɔstik] NM diagnosis sg

diagnostiquer [djagnɔstike] /1/ VT to diagnose

diagonal, e, -aux [djagɔnal, -o] ADJ, NF diagonal; **en diagonale** diagonally; **lire en diagonale** (fig) to skim through

diagramme [djagʀam] NM chart, graph

dialecte [djalɛkt] NM dialect

dialectique [djalɛktik] ADJ dialectic(al)

dialogue [djalɔg] NM dialogue; **~ de sourds** dialogue of the deaf

dialoguer [djalɔge] /1/ VI to converse; (Pol) to have a dialogue

dialoguiste [djalɔgist] NMF dialogue writer

dialyse [djaliz] NF dialysis

diamant [djamɑ̃] NM diamond

diamantaire [djamɑ̃tɛʀ] NM diamond dealer

diamétralement [djametralmɑ̃] ADV diametrically; **~ opposés** (opinions) diametrically opposed

diamètre [djamɛtʀ] NM diameter

diapason [djapazɔ̃] NM tuning fork; (fig): **être/se mettre au ~ (de)** to be/get in tune (with)

diaphane [djafan] ADJ diaphanous

diaphragme [djafʀagm] NM (Anat, Photo) diaphragm; (contraceptif) diaphragm, cap; **ouverture du ~** (Photo) aperture

diapo [djapo], **diapositive** [djapozitiv] NF transparency, slide

diaporama [djapɔʀama] NM slide show

diapré, e [djapʀe] ADJ many-coloured (BRIT), many-colored (US)

diarrhée [djaʀe] NF diarrhoea (BRIT), diarrhea (US)

diaspora [djaspɔʀa] NF (de Juifs) Diaspora; (de communauté) diaspora

diatribe [djatʀib] NF diatribe

dichotomie [dikɔtɔmi] NF dichotomy

dico [diko] NM (fam) dictionary

dictaphone [diktafɔn] NM Dictaphone®

dictateur [diktatœʀ] NM dictator

dictatorial, e, -aux [diktatɔʀjal, -o] ADJ dictatorial

dictature [diktatyʀ] NF dictatorship

dictée [dikte] NF dictation; **prendre sous ~** to take down (sth dictated)

dicter [dikte] /1/ VT to dictate

diction [diksjɔ̃] NF diction, delivery; **cours de ~** speech production lesson(s)

★**dictionnaire** [diksjɔnɛʀ] NM dictionary; **~ géographique** gazetteer

dicton [diktɔ̃] NM saying, dictum

didacticiel [didaktisjɛl] NM educational software

didactique [didaktik] ADJ didactic

dièse [djɛz] NM (Mus) sharp

diesel [djezɛl] NM, ADJ INV diesel

diète [djɛt] NF (jeûne) starvation diet; (régime) diet; **être à la ~** to be on a diet

diététicien, ne [djetetisjɛ̃, -ɛn] NM/F dietician

diététique [djetetik] NF dietetics sg ▶ ADJ: **magasin ~** health food shop (BRIT) ou store (US)

dieu, x [djø] NM god; **D~** God; **le bon D~** the good Lord; **mon D~!** good heavens!

diffamant, e [difamɑ̃, -ɑ̃t] ADJ slanderous, defamatory; libellous

diffamation [difamasjɔ̃] NF slander; (écrite) libel; **attaquer qn en ~** to sue sb for slander (ou libel)

diffamatoire [difamatwaʀ] ADJ slanderous, defamatory; libellous

diffamer [difame] /1/ VT to slander, defame; to libel

différé [difeʀe] ADJ: **crédit ~** deferred credit; **traitement ~** (Inform) batch processing ▶ NM (TV): **en ~** (pre-)recorded

différemment [difeʀamɑ̃] ADV differently

différence [difeʀɑ̃s] NF difference; **à la ~ de** unlike

différenciation [difeʀɑ̃sjasjɔ̃] NF differentiation

différencier [difeʀɑ̃sje] /7/ VT to differentiate ■ **se différencier** VPR (organisme) to become differentiated; **se ~ de** to differentiate o.s. from; (être différent) to differ from

différend [difeʀɑ̃] NM difference (of opinion), disagreement

différent, e [difeʀɑ̃, -ɑ̃t] ADJ (dissemblable) different; **~ de** different from; **différents objets** different ou various objects; **à différentes reprises** on various occasions

différentiel, le [difeʀɑ̃sjɛl] ADJ, NM differential

différer [difeʀe] /6/ VT to postpone, put off ▶ VI: **~ (de)** to differ (from); **~ de faire** (tarder) to delay doing

★**difficile** [difisil] ADJ difficult; (exigeant) hard to please, difficult (to please); **faire le** ou **la ~** to be hard to please, be difficult

difficilement [difisilmɑ̃] ADV (marcher, s'expliquer etc) with difficulty; **~ lisible/compréhensible** difficult ou hard to read/understand

difficulté [difikylte] NF difficulty; **en ~** (bateau, alpiniste) in trouble ou difficulties; **avoir de la ~ à faire** to have difficulty (in) doing

difforme [difɔʀm] ADJ deformed, misshapen

difformité [difɔʀmite] NF deformity

diffracter [difʀakte] /1/ VT to diffract

diffus, e [dify, -yz] ADJ diffuse

diffuser [difyze] /1/ VT (chaleur, bruit, lumière) to diffuse; (émission, musique) to broadcast; (nouvelle, idée) to circulate; (Comm: livres, journaux) to distribute

diffuseur [difyzœʀ] NM diffuser; distributor

diffusion [difyzjɔ̃] NF diffusion; broadcast(ing); circulation; distribution

digérer [diʒeʀe] /6/ VT (*personne*) to digest; (*machine*) to process; (*fig: accepter*) to stomach, put up with

digeste [diʒɛst] ADJ easily digestible

digestible [diʒɛstibl] ADJ digestible

digestif, -ive [diʒɛstif, -iv] ADJ digestive ▶ NM (*after-dinner*) liqueur

digestion [diʒɛstjɔ̃] NF digestion

Digicode® [diʒikɔd] NM entry system (*using code numbers*)

digit [didʒit] NM: **~ binaire** binary digit

digital, e, -aux [diʒital, -o] ADJ digital

digitale [diʒital] NF digitalis, foxglove

digne [diɲ] ADJ dignified; **~ de** worthy of; **~ de foi** trustworthy

dignement [diɲ(ə)mɑ̃] ADV (*comme il se doit*) fittingly; (*dans la dignité*) with dignity

dignitaire [diɲitɛʀ] NM dignitary

dignité [diɲite] NF dignity

digresser [digʀese] VI to digress

digression [digʀesjɔ̃] NF digression

digue [dig] NF dike, dyke; (*pour protéger la côte*) sea wall

dijonnais, e [diʒɔnɛ, -ɛz] ADJ of ou from Dijon ▶ NM/F: **Dijonnais, e** inhabitant ou native of Dijon

diktat [diktat] NM diktat

dilapidation [dilapidasjɔ̃] NF (*voir vb*) squandering; embezzlement, misappropriation

dilapider [dilapide] /1/ VT to squander, waste; (*détourner: biens, fonds publics*) to embezzle, misappropriate

dilatation [dilatasjɔ̃] NF (*de gaz, métal*) expansion; (*de pupille, vaisseau, orifice*) dilation; (*d'estomac*) distension

dilater [dilate] /1/ VT (*pupilles, orifice*) to dilate; (*gaz, métal*) to cause to expand; (*estomac*) to distend ■ **se dilater** VPR (*gaz, métal*) to expand; (*pupilles*) to dilate

dilemme [dilɛm] NM dilemma

dilettante [diletɑ̃t] NMF dilettante; **en ~** in a dilettantish way

dilettantisme [diletɑ̃tism] NM dilettant(e)ism

diligence [diliʒɑ̃s] NF stagecoach, diligence; (*empressement*) despatch; **faire ~** to make haste

diligent, e [diliʒɑ̃, -ɑ̃t] ADJ prompt and efficient; diligent

diluant [dilɥɑ̃] NM thinner(s)

diluer [dilɥe] /1/ VT to dilute

dilution [dilysjɔ̃] NF dilution

diluvien, ne [dilyvjɛ̃, -ɛn] ADJ: **pluie diluvienne** torrential rain

★**dimanche** [dimɑ̃ʃ] NM Sunday; **le ~ des Rameaux/de Pâques** Palm/Easter Sunday; *voir aussi* **lundi**

dîme [dim] NF tithe

dimension [dimɑ̃sjɔ̃] NF (*grandeur*) size; (*gén pl: cotes, Math: de l'espace*) dimension; (*dimensions*) dimensions

diminué, e [diminɥe] ADJ (*personne: physiquement*) run-down; (: *mentalement*) less alert

★**diminuer** [diminɥe] /1/ VT to reduce, decrease; (*ardeur etc*) to lessen; (*personne: physiquement*) to undermine; (*dénigrer*) to belittle ▶ VI to decrease, diminish

diminutif [diminytif] NM (*Ling*) diminutive; (*surnom*) pet name

diminution [diminysjɔ̃] NF decreasing, diminishing

dînatoire [dinatwaʀ] ADJ: **goûter ~** ≈ high tea (BRIT); **apéritif ~** ≈ evening buffet

★**dinde** [dɛ̃d] NF turkey; (*femme stupide*) goose

dindon [dɛ̃dɔ̃] NM turkey

dindonneau, x [dɛ̃dɔno] NM turkey poult

dîner [dine] /1/ NM dinner; **~ d'affaires/de famille** business/family dinner ▶ VI to have dinner

dînette [dinɛt] NF (*jeu*): **jouer à la ~** to play at tea parties

dingue [dɛ̃g] ADJ (*fam*) crazy

dinosaure [dinɔzɔʀ] NM dinosaur

diocèse [djɔsɛz] NM diocese

diode [djɔd] NF diode

dioxine [diɔksin] NF dioxin

dioxyde [diɔksid] NM dioxide

diphasé, e [difaze] ADJ (*Élec*) two-phase

diphtérie [difteʀi] NF diphtheria

diphtongue [diftɔ̃g] NF diphthong

diplodocus [diplɔdɔkys] NM diplodocus

diplomate [diplɔmat] ADJ diplomatic ▶ NM diplomat; (*fig: personne habile*) diplomatist; (*Culin: gâteau*) dessert made of sponge cake, candied fruit and custard, ≈ trifle (BRIT)

diplomatie [diplɔmasi] NF diplomacy

diplomatique [diplɔmatik] ADJ diplomatic

diplomatiquement [diplɔmatikmɑ̃] ADV diplomatically

diplôme [diplom] NM diploma, certificate; (*examen*) (diploma) examination; **avoir des diplômes** to have qualifications

diplômé, e [diplome] ADJ qualified

diptère [diptɛʀ] ADJ, NM dipteran

diptyque [diptik] NM (*tableau*) diptych; (*film*) two-part film; (*livre*) novel in two parts

★**dire** [diʀ] /37/ VT to say; (*secret, mensonge*) to tell; **~ l'heure/la vérité** to tell the time/the truth; **dis pardon/merci** say sorry/thank you; **~ qch à qn** to tell sb sth; **~ à qn qu'il fasse** ou **de faire** to tell sb to do; **~ que** to say that; **on dit que** they say that; **comme on dit** as they say; **on dirait que** it looks (*ou* sounds *etc*) as though; **on dirait du vin** you'd ou one would think it was wine; **que dites-vous de** (*penser*) what do you think of; **si cela lui dit** if he feels like it, if he fancies it; **cela ne me dit rien** that doesn't appeal to me; **à vrai ~** truth to tell; **pour ainsi ~** so to speak; **cela va sans ~** that goes without saying; **dis donc!, dites donc!** (*pour attirer l'attention*) hey!; (*au fait*) by the way; **et ~ que …** and to think that …; **ceci** ou **cela dit** that being said; (*à ces mots*) whereupon; **c'est dit, voilà qui est dit** so that's settled; **il n'y a pas à ~** there's no getting away from it; **c'est ~ si …** that just shows that …; **c'est beaucoup/peu ~** that's saying a lot/not saying much ▶ NM: **au ~ de** according to; **leurs dires** what they say ■ **se dire**

VPR (*à soi-même*) to say to oneself; **ça ne se dit pas** (*impoli*) you shouldn't say that; (*pas en usage*) you don't say that; **cela ne se dit pas comme ça** you don't say it like that; **se ~ au revoir** to say goodbye (to each other); **ça se dit ... en anglais** that is ... in English

> Seul **say** s'emploie pour citer les paroles de quelqu'un, directement ou indirectement.
> *Il a dit : «Je ne me sens pas bien ».* **He said, "I don't feel well."**
> *Il a dit qu'il ne se sentait pas bien.* **He said (that) he didn't feel well.**
> Lorsque la personne à qui on s'adresse est mentionnée, on peut employer soit **say**, soit **tell**, mais attention à la construction : **say ... to somebody**, mais **tell somebody ...**
> *Elle a dit à sa sœur qu'elle allait partir.* **She said to her sister (that) she was going to leave.** *ou* **She told her sister (that) she was going to leave.**

★**direct, e** [diʀɛkt] ADJ direct; **train/bus ~** express train/bus ▸ NM (*train*) through train; **en ~** (*émission*) live

directement [diʀɛktəmɑ̃] ADV directly

★**directeur, -trice** [diʀɛktœʀ, -tʀis] NM/F (*d'entreprise*) director; (*de service*) manager/eress; (*d'école*) head(teacher) (Bʀɪᴛ), principal (US); **comité ~** management *ou* steering committee; **~ général** general manager; **~ de thèse** ≈ PhD supervisor

★**direction** [diʀɛksjɔ̃] NF (*d'entreprise*) management; conducting; supervision; (*Auto*) steering; (*sens*) direction; **sous la ~ de** (*Mus*) conducted by; **en ~ de** (*avion, train, bateau*) for; **«toutes directions»** (*Auto*) "all routes"

directive [diʀɛktiv] NF directive, instruction; **directives anticipées** (*Méd*) living will

directoire [diʀɛktwaʀ] NM (*de société anonyme*) board of directors

directorial, e, -aux [diʀɛktɔʀjal, -o] ADJ (*bureau*) director's; manager's; head teacher's

★**directrice** [diʀɛktʀis] ADJ F, NF *voir* **directeur**

dirent [diʀ] VB *voir* **dire**

dirigeable [diʀiʒabl] ADJ, NM: **(ballon) ~** dirigible

dirigeant, e [diʀiʒɑ̃, -ɑ̃t] ADJ managerial; (*classes*) ruling ▸ NM/F (*d'un parti etc*) leader; (*d'entreprise*) manager, member of the management

★**diriger** [diʀiʒe] /3/ VT (*entreprise*) to manage, run; (*véhicule*) to steer; (*orchestre*) to conduct; (*recherches, travaux*) to supervise, be in charge of; (*braquer: arme*): **~ sur** to point ou level ou aim at; (*fig: critiques*): **~ contre** to aim at; **~ son regard sur** to look in the direction of ■ **se diriger** VPR (*s'orienter*) to find one's way; **se ~ vers** ou **sur** to make ou head for

dirigisme [diʀiʒism] NM (*Écon*) state intervention, interventionism

dirigiste [diʀiʒist] ADJ interventionist

dirlo [diʀlo] NMF (*fam*) head (Bʀɪᴛ), principal (US)

dis [di], **disais** *etc* [dizɛ] VB *voir* **dire**

discal, e, -aux [diskal, -o] ADJ (*Méd*): **hernie discale** slipped disc

discernement [disɛʀnəmɑ̃] NM discernment, judgment

discerner [disɛʀne] /1/ VT to discern, make out

disciple [disipl] NMF disciple

disciplinaire [disiplinɛʀ] ADJ disciplinary

discipline [disiplin] NF discipline

discipliné, e [disipline] ADJ (well-)disciplined

discipliner [disipline] /1/ VT to discipline; (*cheveux*) to control

disc-jockey [diskʒɔkɛ] (*pl* **disc-jockeys**) NM disc jockey, DJ

disco [disko] ADJ INV, NM disco

discobole [diskɔbɔl] NMF discus thrower

discographie [diskɔgʀafi] NF discography

discontinu, e [diskɔ̃tiny] ADJ intermittent; (*bande: sur la route*) broken

discontinuer [diskɔ̃tinɥe] /1/ VI: **sans ~** without stopping, without a break

disconvenir [diskɔ̃v(ə)niʀ] /22/ VI: **ne pas ~ de qch/que** not to deny sth/that

discophile [diskɔfil] NMF record enthusiast

discordance [diskɔʀdɑ̃s] NF discordance; conflict

discordant, e [diskɔʀdɑ̃, -ɑ̃t] ADJ discordant; conflicting

discorde [diskɔʀd] NF discord, dissension

discothèque [diskɔtɛk] NF (*boîte de nuit*) disco(thèque); (*disques*) record collection; (*dans une bibliothèque*): **~ (de prêt)** record library

discourais *etc* [diskuʀɛ] VB *voir* **discourir**

discourir [diskuʀiʀ] /11/ VI to discourse, hold forth

★**discours** [diskuʀ] VB *voir* **discourir** ▸ NM speech; **~ direct/indirect** (*Ling*) direct/indirect *ou* reported speech

discourtois, e [diskuʀtwa, -waz] ADJ discourteous

discrédit [diskʀedi] NM: **jeter le ~ sur** to discredit

discréditer [diskʀedite] /1/ VT to discredit

discret, -ète [diskʀɛ, -ɛt] ADJ discreet; (*fig: musique, style, maquillage*) unobtrusive; (*: endroit*) quiet

discrètement [diskʀɛtmɑ̃] ADV discreetly

discrétion [diskʀesjɔ̃] NF discretion; **à la ~ de qn** at sb's discretion; in sb's hands; **à ~** (*boisson etc*) unlimited, as much as one wants

discrétionnaire [diskʀesjɔnɛʀ] ADJ discretionary

discrimination [diskʀiminasjɔ̃] NF discrimination; **sans ~** indiscriminately

discriminatoire [diskʀiminatwaʀ] ADJ discriminatory

disculper [diskylpe] /1/ VT to exonerate

discussion [diskysjɔ̃] NF discussion

discutable [diskytabl] ADJ (*contestable*) doubtful; (*à débattre*) debatable

discutailler [diskytaje] VI to quibble

discuté, e [diskyte] ADJ controversial

★**discuter** [diskyte] /1/ VT (*contester*) to question, dispute; (*débattre: prix*) to discuss; **~ de** to discuss ▸ VI to talk; (*protester*) to argue ■ **se discuter** VPR: **ça se discute** that's debatable

dise *etc* [diz] VB *voir* **dire**

disert, e [dizɛʀ, -ɛʀt] ADJ loquacious

disette [dizɛt] NF food shortage

diseuse [dizøz] NF: **~ de bonne aventure** fortune-teller

disgrâce [disgʀɑs] NF disgrace; **être en ~** to be in disgrace

disgracié, e [disgʀasje] ADJ (*en disgrâce*) disgraced

disgracieux, -euse [disgʀasjø, -øz] ADJ ungainly, awkward

disjoindre [disʒwɛ̃dʀ] **/49/** VT to take apart ■ **se disjoindre** VPR to come apart

disjoint, e [disʒwɛ̃, -wɛ̃t] PP *de* **disjoindre** ► ADJ loose

disjoncter [disʒɔ̃kte] VI (*disjoncteur*) to trip; (*fam: personne*) to crack up (*fam*)

disjoncteur [disʒɔ̃ktœʀ] NM (*Élec*) circuit breaker

dislocation [dislɔkasjɔ̃] NF dislocation

disloquer [dislɔke] **/1/** VT (*membre*) to dislocate; (*chaise*) to dismantle; (*troupe*) to disperse ■ **se disloquer** VPR (*parti, empire*) to break up; (*meuble*) to come apart; **se ~ l'épaule** to dislocate one's shoulder

disons *etc* [dizɔ̃] VB *voir* **dire**

disparaître [dispaʀɛtʀ] **/57/** VI to disappear; (*à la vue*) to vanish, disappear; to be hidden *ou* concealed; (*être manquant*) to go missing, disappear; (*se perdre: traditions etc*) to die out; (*personne: mourir*) to die; **faire ~** (*objet, tache, trace*) to remove; (*personne, douleur*) to get rid of

disparate [dispaʀat] ADJ disparate; (*couleurs*) ill-assorted

disparité [dispaʀite] NF disparity

disparition [dispaʀisjɔ̃] NF disappearance; **espèce en voie de ~** endangered species

★**disparu, e** [dispaʀy] PP *de* **disparaître** ► NM/F missing person; (*défunt*) departed; **être porté ~** to be reported missing

dispendieux, -euse [dispɑ̃djø, -øz] ADJ extravagant, expensive

dispensaire [dispɑ̃sɛʀ] NM community clinic

dispense [dispɑ̃s] NF exemption; (*permission*) special permission; **~ d'âge** special exemption from age limit

dispenser [dispɑ̃se] **/1/** VT (*donner*) to lavish, bestow; (*exempter*): **~ qn de** to exempt sb from ■ **se dispenser** VPR: **se ~ de qch** to avoid sth, get out of sth

disperser [dispɛʀse] **/1/** VT to scatter; (*fig: son attention*) to dissipate ■ **se disperser** VPR to scatter; (*fig*) to dissipate one's efforts

dispersion [dispɛʀsjɔ̃] NF scattering; (*des efforts*) dissipation

disponibilité [dispɔnibilite] NF availability; (*Admin*): **être en ~** to be on leave of absence ■ **disponibilités** NFPL (*Comm*) liquid assets

★**disponible** [dispɔnibl] ADJ available

dispos [dispo] ADJ M: **(frais et) ~** fresh (as a daisy)

disposé, e [dispoze] ADJ (*d'une certaine manière*) arranged, laid-out; **bien/mal ~** (*humeur*) in a good/bad mood; **bien/mal ~ pour** *ou* **envers qn** well/badly disposed towards sb; **~ à** (*prêt à*) willing *ou* prepared to

disposer [dispoze] **/1/** VT (*arranger, placer*) to arrange; (*inciter*): **~ qn à qch/faire qch** to dispose *ou* incline sb towards sth/to do sth ► VI: **vous**

pouvez ~ you may leave; **~ de** to have (at one's disposal) ■ **se disposer à faire** VPR to prepare to do, be about to do

dispositif [dispozitif] NM device; (*fig*) system, plan of action; set-up; (*d'un texte de loi*) operative part; **~ de sûreté** safety device

disposition [dispozisjɔ̃] NF (*arrangement*) arrangement, layout; (*humeur*) mood; (*tendance*) tendency; **à la ~ de qn** at sb's disposal; **je suis à votre ~** I am at your service ■ **dispositions** NFPL (*mesures*) steps, measures; (*préparatifs*) arrangements; (*de loi, testament*) provisions; (*aptitudes*) bent *sg*, aptitude *sg*; **prendre ses dispositions** to make arrangements; **avoir des dispositions pour la musique** *etc* to have a special aptitude for music *etc*

disproportion [dispʀɔpɔʀsjɔ̃] NF disproportion

disproportionné, e [dispʀɔpɔʀsjɔne] ADJ disproportionate, out of all proportion

★**dispute** [dispyt] NF quarrel, argument

★**disputer** [dispyte] **/1/** VT (*match*) to play; (*combat*) to fight; (*course*) to run; **~ qch à qn** to fight with sb for *ou* over sth ■ **se disputer** VPR to quarrel, have a quarrel; (*match, combat, course*) to take place

disquaire [diskɛʀ] NMF record dealer

disqualification [diskalifikasjɔ̃] NF disqualification

disqualifier [diskalifje] **/7/** VT to disqualify ■ **se disqualifier** VPR to bring discredit on o.s.

★**disque** [disk] NM (*Mus*) record; (*Inform*) disk, disc; (*forme, pièce*) disc; (*Sport*) discus; **~ compact** compact disc; **~ compact interactif** CD-I®; **~ dur** hard drive; **~ d'embrayage** (*Auto*) clutch plate; **~ laser** compact disc; **~ de stationnement** parking disc; **~ système** system disk

disquette [diskɛt] NF floppy (disk), diskette

dissection [disɛksjɔ̃] NF dissection

dissemblable [disɑ̃blabl] ADJ dissimilar

dissemblance [disɑ̃blɑ̃s] NF dissimilarity, difference

dissémination [diseminasjɔ̃] NF (*voir vb*) scattering; dispersal; (*des armes*) proliferation

disséminer [disemine] **/1/** VT to scatter; (*troupes: sur un territoire*) to disperse

dissension [disɑ̃sjɔ̃] NF dissension ■ **dissensions** NFPL dissension

disséquer [diseke] **/6/** VT to dissect

dissertation [disɛʀtasjɔ̃] NF (*Scol*) essay

disserter [disɛʀte] **/1/** VI: **~ sur** to discourse upon

dissidence [disidɑ̃s] NF (*concept*) dissidence; **rejoindre la ~** to join the dissidents

dissident, e [disidɑ̃, -ɑ̃t] ADJ, NM/F dissident

dissimilitude [disimilityd] NF dissimilarity

dissimulateur, -trice [disimylatœʀ, -tʀis] ADJ dissembling ► NM/F dissembler

dissimulation [disimylasjɔ̃] NF concealing; (*duplicité*) dissimulation; **~ de bénéfices/de revenus** concealment of profits/income

dissimulé, e [disimyle] ADJ (*personne: secret*) secretive; (: *fourbe, hypocrite*) deceitful

dissimuler [disimyle] **/1/** VT to conceal ■ **se dissimuler** VPR to conceal o.s.; to be concealed

dissipation [disipasjɔ̃] NF squandering; unruliness; (*débauche*) dissipation

dissipé, e [disipe] ADJ *(indiscipliné)* unruly

dissiper [disipe] /**1**/ VT to dissipate; *(fortune)* to squander, fritter away ■ **se dissiper** VPR *(brouillard)* to clear, disperse; *(doutes)* to disappear, melt away; *(élève)* to become undisciplined *ou* unruly

dissociable [disɔsjabl] ADJ separable

dissocier [disɔsje] /**7**/ VT to dissociate ■ **se dissocier** VPR *(éléments, groupe)* to break up, split up; **se ~ de** *(groupe, point de vue)* to dissociate o.s. from

dissolu, e [disɔly] ADJ dissolute

dissoluble [disɔlybl] ADJ *(Pol: assemblée)* dissolvable

dissolution [disɔlysjɔ̃] NF dissolving; *(Pol, Jur)* dissolution

dissolvant, e [disɔlvɑ̃, -ɑ̃t] VB *voir* **dissoudre ▶** NM *(Chimie)* solvent; **~ (gras)** nail polish remover

dissonant, e [disɔnɑ̃, -ɑ̃t] ADJ discordant

dissoudre [disudʀ] /**51**/ VT to dissolve ■ **se dissoudre** VPR to dissolve

dissous, -oute [disu, -ut] PP *de* **dissoudre**

dissuader [disɥade] /**1**/ VT: **~ qn de faire/de qch** to dissuade sb from doing/from sth

dissuasif, -ive [disɥazif, -iv] ADJ dissuasive

dissuasion [disɥazjɔ̃] NF dissuasion; **force de ~** deterrent power

★**distance** [distɑ̃s] NF distance; *(fig: écart)* gap; **à ~** at *ou* from a distance; *(mettre en marche, commander)* by remote control; *(situé)* **à ~** *(Inform)* remote; **tenir qn à ~** to keep sb at a distance; **se tenir à ~** to keep one's distance; **à une ~ de 10 km, à 10 km de ~** 10 km away, at a distance of 10 km; **à deux ans de ~** with a gap of two years; **prendre ses distances** to space out; **garder ses distances** to keep one's distance; **tenir la ~** *(Sport)* to cover the distance, last the course; **~ focale** *(Photo)* focal length

distancer [distɑ̃se] /**3**/ VT to outdistance, leave behind

distanciation [distɑ̃sjasjɔ̃] NF detachment

distanciel, le [distɑ̃sjɛl] ADJ *(formation, enseignement)* distance

distancier [distɑ̃sje] /**7**/: **se distancier** VPR to distance o.s.

distant, e [distɑ̃, -ɑ̃t] ADJ *(réservé)* distant, aloof; *(éloigné)* distant, far away; **~ de** *(lieu)* far away *ou* a long way from; **~ de 5 km (d'un lieu)** 5 km away (from a place)

distendre [distɑ̃dʀ] /**41**/ VT to distend ■ **se distendre** VPR to distend

distillation [distilasjɔ̃] NF distillation, distilling

distillé, e [distile] ADJ: **eau distillée** distilled water

distiller [distile] /**1**/ VT to distil; *(fig)* to exude; to elaborate

distillerie [distilʀi] NF distillery

distinct, e [distɛ̃(kt), distɛ̃kt] ADJ distinct

distinctement [distɛ̃ktəmɑ̃] ADV distinctly

distinctif, -ive [distɛ̃ktif, -iv] ADJ distinctive

distinction [distɛ̃ksjɔ̃] NF distinction

distingué, e [distɛ̃ge] ADJ distinguished

distinguer [distɛ̃ge] /**1**/ VT to distinguish ■ **se distinguer** VPR *(s'illustrer)* to distinguish o.s.; *(différer)*: **se ~ (de)** to distinguish o.s. *ou* be distinguished (from)

distinguo [distɛ̃go] NM distinction

distorsion [distɔʀsjɔ̃] NF *(gén)* distortion; *(fig: déséquilibre)* disparity, imbalance

★**distraction** [distʀaksjɔ̃] NF *(manque d'attention)* absent-mindedness; *(oubli)* lapse (in concentration *ou* attention); *(détente)* diversion, recreation; *(passe-temps)* distraction, entertainment

distraire [distʀɛʀ] /**50**/ VT *(déranger)* to distract; *(divertir)* to entertain, divert; *(détourner: somme d'argent)* to divert, misappropriate ■ **se distraire** VPR to amuse *ou* enjoy o.s.

distrait, e [distʀɛ, -ɛt] PP *de* **distraire ▶** ADJ absent-minded

distraitement [distʀɛtmɑ̃] ADV absent-mindedly

distrayant, e [distʀɛjɑ̃, -ɑ̃t] VB *voir* **distraire ▶** ADJ entertaining

★**distribuer** [distʀibɥe] /**1**/ VT to distribute; to hand out; *(Cartes)* to deal (out); *(courrier)* to deliver

★**distributeur** [distʀibytœʀ] NM *(Auto, Comm)* distributor; *(automatique)* *(vending)* machine; **~ de billets** *(Rail)* ticket machine; *(Banque)* cash dispenser

distribution [distʀibysjɔ̃] NF distribution; *(postale)* delivery; *(choix d'acteurs)* casting; **circuits de ~** *(Comm)* distribution network; **~ des prix** *(Scol)* prize giving

district [distʀik(t)] NM district

dit, e [di, dit] PP *de* **dire ▶** ADJ *(fixé)*: **le jour ~** the arranged day; *(surnommé)* **X, ~ Pierrot** X, known as *ou* called Pierrot

dites [dit] VB *voir* **dire**

dithyrambique [ditiʀɑ̃bik] ADJ eulogistic

DIU SIGLE M (= *dispositif intra-utérin*) IUD

diurétique [djyʀetik] ADJ, NM diuretic

diurne [djyʀn] ADJ diurnal, daytime *cpd*

divagations [divagasjɔ̃] NFPL ramblings; ravings

divaguer [divage] /**1**/ VI to ramble; *(malade)* to rave

divan [divɑ̃] NM divan

divan-lit [divɑ̃li] *(pl* **divans-lits***)* NM divan (bed)

divergence [divɛʀʒɑ̃s] NF divergence; **des divergences d'opinion au sein de …** differences of opinion within …

divergent, e [divɛʀʒɑ̃, -ɑ̃t] ADJ divergent

diverger [divɛʀʒe] /**3**/ VI to diverge

divers, e [divɛʀ, -ɛʀs] ADJ *(varié)* diverse, varied; *(différent)* different, various; **(frais) ~** *(Comm)* sundries, miscellaneous (expenses); **« ~ »** *(rubrique)* "miscellaneous"; **diverses personnes** various *ou* several people

diversement [divɛʀsəmɑ̃] ADV in various *ou* diverse ways

diversification [divɛʀsifikasjɔ̃] NF diversification

diversifier [divɛʀsifje] /**7**/ VT to diversify ■ **se diversifier** VPR to diversify

diversion [divɛʀsjɔ̃] NF diversion; **faire ~** to create a diversion

diversité [divɛʀsite] NF diversity, variety

divertir [divɛʀtiʀ] /**2**/ VT to amuse, entertain ■ **se divertir** VPR to amuse *ou* enjoy o.s.

divertissant, e [divɛʀtisɑ̃, -ɑ̃t] ADJ entertaining

divertissement [divɛʀtismɑ̃] NM entertainment; (*Mus*) divertimento, divertissement

dividende [dividɑ̃d] NM (*Math, Comm*) dividend

divin, e [divɛ̃, -in] ADJ divine; (*fig: excellent*) heavenly, divine

divinateur, -trice [divinatœʀ, -tʀis] ADJ perspicacious

divinatoire [divinatwaʀ] ADJ (*art, science*) divinatory; **baguette ~** divining rod

divinement [divinmɑ̃] ADV (*merveilleusement bien*) divinely; **un dessert ~ bon** a heavenly dessert

diviniser [divinize] /**1**/ VT to deify

divinité [divinite] NF divinity

divisé, e [divize] ADJ divided

★**diviser** [divize] /**1**/ VT (*gén, Math*) to divide; (*morceler, subdiviser*) to divide (up), split (up); **~ par** to divide by ▪ **se diviser en** VPR to divide into

diviseur [divizœʀ] NM (*Math*) divisor

divisible [divizibl] ADJ divisible

division [divizjɔ̃] NF (*gén*) division; **~ du travail** (*Écon*) division of labour

divisionnaire [divizjɔnɛʀ] ADJ: **commissaire ~** ≈ chief superintendent (BRIT), ≈ police chief (US)

★**divorce** [divɔʀs] NM divorce

★**divorcé, e** [divɔʀse] NM/F divorcee

★**divorcer** [divɔʀse] /**3**/ VI to get a divorce, get divorced; **~ de** *ou* **d'avec qn** to divorce sb

divulgation [divylgasjɔ̃] NF disclosure

divulguer [divylge] /**1**/ VT to disclose, divulge

★**dix** [di, dis, diz] NUM ten

★**dix-huit** [dizɥit] NUM eighteen

dix-huitième [dizɥitjɛm] NUM eighteenth

dixième [dizjɛm] NUM tenth

★**dix-neuf** [diznœf] NUM nineteen

dix-neuvième [diznœvjɛm] NUM nineteenth

★**dix-sept** [disɛt] NUM seventeen

dix-septième [disɛtjɛm] NUM seventeenth

★**dizaine** [dizɛn] NF (10) ten; (*environ 10*): **une ~ (de)** about ten, ten or so

Djakarta [dʒakaʀta] N Djakarta

Djibouti [dʒibuti] N Djibouti

djihad [dʒi(j)ad] NF jihad

djihadiste [dʒi(j)adist] ADJ, NMF jihadist

dl ABR (= *décilitre*) dl

dm. ABR (= *décimètre*) dm.

DNB SIGLE M (= *Diplôme national du brevet*) school certificate (*taken at approx. 16 years*)

do [do] NM (*note*) C; (*en chantant la gamme*) do(h)

docile [dɔsil] ADJ docile

docilement [dɔsilmɑ̃] ADV docilely

docilité [dɔsilite] NF docility

dock [dɔk] NM dock; (*hangar, bâtiment*) warehouse

docker [dɔkɛʀ] NM docker

docte [dɔkt] ADJ (*péj*) learned

★**docteur, e** [dɔktœʀ] NM/F doctor; **~ en médecine** doctor of medicine

doctoral, e, -aux [dɔktɔʀal, -o] ADJ pompous, bombastic

doctorat [dɔktɔʀa] NM: **~ (d'Université)** ≈ doctorate; **~ d'État** ≈ PhD; **~ de troisième cycle** ≈ doctorate

Students who hold a *master* and wish to go on to do a further postgraduate degree can study for a **doctorat**. This involves three or four years of intensive research and the writing of a thesis. This option often leads to a research job in a state-funded laboratory or private company, or to a lecturing post in various types of higher education institution.

doctoresse [dɔktɔʀɛs] NF lady doctor

doctrinaire [dɔktʀinɛʀ] ADJ doctrinaire; (*sententieux*) pompous, sententious

doctrinal, e, -aux [dɔktʀinal, -o] ADJ doctrinal

doctrine [dɔktʀin] NF doctrine

document [dɔkymɑ̃] NM document

★**documentaire** [dɔkymɑ̃tɛʀ] ADJ, NM documentary

documentaliste [dɔkymɑ̃talist] NMF archivist; (*Presse, TV*) researcher

documentation [dɔkymɑ̃tasjɔ̃] NF documentation, literature; (*Presse, TV: service*) research

documenté, e [dɔkymɑ̃te] ADJ well-informed, well-documented; well-researched

documenter [dɔkymɑ̃te] /**1**/ VT: **se ~ (sur)** to gather information *ou* material (on *ou* about)

Dodécanèse [dɔdekanɛz] NM Dodecanese (Islands)

dodeliner [dɔd(ə)line] /**1**/ VI: **~ de la tête** to nod one's head gently

dodo [dɔdo] NM: **aller faire ~** to go to beddy-byes

dodu, e [dɔdy] ADJ plump

dogmatique [dɔgmatik] ADJ dogmatic

dogmatisme [dɔgmatism] NM dogmatism

dogme [dɔgm] NM dogma

dogue [dɔg] NM mastiff

★**doigt** [dwa] NM finger; **à deux doigts de** within an ace (BRIT) *ou* an inch of; **un ~ de lait/whisky** a drop of milk/whisky; **désigner** *ou* **montrer du ~** to point at; **au ~ et à l'œil** to the letter; **connaître qch sur le bout des doigts** to know sth backwards; **mettre le ~ sur la plaie** (*fig*) to find the sensitive spot; **~ de pied** toe

doigté [dwate] NM (*Mus*) fingering; (*fig: habileté*) diplomacy, tact

doigtier [dwatje] NM fingerstall

dois *etc* [dwa] VB *voir* **devoir**

doit *etc* [dwa] VB *voir* **devoir**

doive *etc* [dwav] VB *voir* **devoir**

doléances [dɔleɑ̃s] NFPL complaints; (*réclamations*) grievances

dolent, e [dɔlɑ̃, -ɑ̃t] ADJ doleful, mournful

dollar [dɔlaʀ] NM dollar

dolmen [dɔlmɛn] NM dolmen

DOM [dɔm] SIGLE M(PL) = **Département(s) d'outre-mer**

domaine [dɔmɛn] NM estate, property; (*fig*) domain, field; **dans le ~ de qch** in the field of sth; **dans tous les domaines** in all areas; **tomber dans le ~ public** (*livre, chanson*) to be out of copyright; **~ skiable** ski slopes *pl*

domanial, e, -aux [dɔmanjal, -o] ADJ national, state *cpd*

dôme [dom] NM dome

domestication [dɔmɛstikasjɔ̃] NF (*voir domestiquer*) domestication; harnessing

domesticité [dɔmɛstisite] NF (domestic) staff

domestique [dɔmɛstik] ADJ domestic ▸ NMF servant, domestic

domestiquer [dɔmɛstike] /1/ VT to domesticate; (*vent, marées*) to harness

domicile [dɔmisil] NM home, place of residence; **à ~** at home; **élire ~ à** to take up residence in; **sans ~ fixe** of no fixed abode; **~ conjugal** marital home; **~ légal** domicile; **livrer à ~** to deliver

domiciliation [dɔmisiljasjɔ̃] NF (*Jur: d'entreprise, société*) domiciliation

domicilié, e [dɔmisilje] ADJ: **être ~ à** to have one's home in *ou* at

dominant, e [dɔminɑ̃, -ɑ̃t] ADJ dominant; (*plus important: opinion*) predominant ▸ NF (*caractéristique*) dominant characteristic; (*couleur*) dominant colour

dominateur, -trice [dɔminatœR, -tRis] ADJ dominating; (*qui aime à dominer*) domineering

domination [dɔminasjɔ̃] NF domination

dominer [dɔmine] /1/ VT to dominate; (*passions etc*) to control, master; (*sujet*) to master; (*surpasser*) to outclass, surpass; (*surplomber*) to tower above, dominate ▸ VI to be in the dominant position ■ **se dominer** VPR to control o.s.

dominicain, e [dɔminikɛ̃, -ɛn] ADJ Dominican

dominical, e, -aux [dɔminikal, -o] ADJ Sunday *cpd*, dominical

Dominique [dɔminik] NF: **la ~** Dominica

domino [dɔmino] NM domino ■ **dominos** NMPL (*jeu*) dominoes *sg*

★**dommage** [dɔmaʒ] NM (*préjudice*) harm, injury; **c'est ~ de faire/que** it's a shame *ou* pity to do/that; **quel ~!, c'est ~!** what a pity *ou* shame! ■ **dommages** (*dégâts, pertes*) damage *no pl*; **dommages corporels** physical injury

dommageable [dɔmaʒabl] ADJ (*conséquences*) detrimental; **~ pour qn/qch** detrimental to sb/sth; **~ pour l'environnement** harmful to the environment

dommages-intérêts [dɔmaʒ(ez)ɛ̃terɛ] NMPL damages

domotique [dɔmɔtik] NF home automation

dompter [dɔ̃(p)te] /1/ VT to tame

dompteur, -euse [dɔ̃tœR, -øz] NM/F trainer; (*de lion*) lion tamer

DOM-ROM [dɔmRɔm], **DOM-TOM** [dɔmtɔm] SIGLE M, SIGLE MPL (= *Département(s) et Région/Territoire(s) d'outre-mer*) French overseas departments and regions; *see note*

> There are five *départements d'outre-mer* or **DOM**s: Guadeloupe, Martinique, La Réunion, French Guyana and Mayotte. They are run in the same way as metropolitan *départements* and their inhabitants are French citizens. In administrative terms they are also *régions*, and in this regard are also referred to as **ROM**s (*régions d'outre-mer*). The term **DOM-TOM** is still commonly used, but the term *territoire d'outre-mer* has been superseded by that of *collectivité d'outre-mer* (**COM**). There are seven **COM**s, each of which is independent but supervised by a representative of the French government.

don [dɔ̃] NM (*cadeau*) gift; (*charité*) donation; (*aptitude*) gift, talent; **avoir des dons pour** to have a gift *ou* talent for; **faire ~ de** to make a gift of; **~ en argent** cash donation; **elle a le ~ de m'énerver** she's got a knack of getting on my nerves

donateur, -trice [dɔnatœR, -tRis] NM/F donor

donation [dɔnasjɔ̃] NF donation

★**donc** [dɔ̃k] CONJ therefore, so; (*après une digression*) so, then; (*intensif*): **voilà ~ la solution** so there's the solution; **je disais ~ que** ... as I was saying, ...; **venez ~ dîner à la maison** do come for dinner; **allons ~!** come now!; **faites ~** go ahead

dongle [dɔ̃gl] NM dongle

donjon [dɔ̃ʒɔ̃] NM keep

don Juan [dɔ̃ʒɥɑ̃] NM Don Juan

donnant, e [dɔnɑ̃, -ɑ̃t] ADJ: **~, ~** fair's fair

donne [dɔn] NF (*Cartes*): **il y a mauvaise** *ou* **fausse ~** there's been a misdeal

donné, e [dɔne] ADJ (*convenu: lieu, heure*) given; (*pas cher*) very cheap; **c'est ~** it's a gift; **étant ~ que** ... given that ... ■ **données** NFPL (*Math, Inform, gén*) data

★**donner** [dɔne] /1/ VT to give; (*vieux habits etc*) to give away; (*spectacle*) to put on; (*film*) to show; **~ qch à qn** to give sb sth, give sth to sb; **~ sur** (*fenêtre, chambre*) to look (out) onto; **~ dans** (*piège etc*) to fall into; **faire ~ l'infanterie** (*Mil*) to send in the infantry; **~ l'heure à qn** to tell sb the time; **~ le ton** (*fig*) to set the tone; **~ à penser/entendre que** ... to make one think/give one to understand that ...; **ça donne soif/faim** it makes you (feel) thirsty/hungry; **se ~ à fond (à son travail)** to give one's all (to one's work); **se ~ du mal** *ou* **de la peine (pour faire qch)** to go to a lot of trouble (to do sth); **s'en ~ à cœur joie** (*fam*) to have a great time (of it)

donneur, -euse [dɔnœR, -øz] NM/F (*Méd*) donor; (*Cartes*) dealer; **~ de sang** blood donor

donneur d'ordres, donneur d'ordre NM (*Jur*) principal

---

dont [dɔ̃]

PRON RELATIF **1** (*appartenance: objets*) whose, of which; (: *êtres animés*) whose; **la maison dont le toit est rouge** the house the roof of which is red, the house whose roof is red; **l'homme dont je connais la sœur** the man whose sister I know **2** (*parmi lesquel(le)s*): **deux livres, dont l'un est** ... two books, one of which is ...; **il y avait plusieurs personnes, dont Gabrielle** there were several people, among them Gabrielle; **10 blessés, dont 2 grièvement** 10 injured, 2 of them seriously **3** (*complément d'adjectif: de verbe*): **le fils dont il est si fier** the son he's so proud of; **le pays dont il est originaire** the country he's from; **ce dont je parle** what I'm talking about; **la façon dont il l'a fait** the way (in which) he did it

---

donzelle [dɔ̃zɛl] NF (*péj*) young madam

dopage [dɔpaʒ] NM (*Sport*) drug use; (*de cheval*) doping

dopant [dɔpɑ̃] NM dope

doper [dɔpe] /1/ VT to dope ■ **se doper** VPR to take dope

doping [dɔpiŋ] NM doping; (*excitant*) dope

dorade [dɔrad] NF = **daurade**

doré, e [dɔʀe] ADJ golden; (*avec dorure*) gilt, gilded

dorénavant [dɔʀenavɑ̃] ADV from now on, henceforth

dorer [dɔʀe] /1/ VT (*cadre*) to gild; **(faire) ~** (*Culin*) to brown (: *gâteau*) to glaze; **~ la pilule à qn** to sugar the pill for sb ■ **se dorer** VPR: **se ~ au soleil** to sunbathe

dorloter [dɔʀlɔte] /1/ VT to pamper, cosset (BRIT); **se faire ~** to be pampered *ou* cosseted

dormant, e [dɔʀmɑ̃, -ɑ̃t] ADJ: **eau dormante** still water

dorme *etc* [dɔʀm] VB *voir* **dormir**

dormeur, -euse [dɔʀmœʀ, -øz] NM/F sleeper

★**dormir** [dɔʀmiʀ] /16/ VI to sleep; (*être endormi*) to be asleep; **~ à poings fermés** to sleep very soundly

dorsal, e, -aux [dɔʀsal, -o] ADJ dorsal

★**dortoir** [dɔʀtwaʀ] NM dormitory

dorure [dɔʀyʀ] NF gilding

doryphore [dɔʀifɔʀ] NM Colorado beetle

★**dos** [do] NM back; (*de livre*) spine; **« voir au ~ »** "see over"; **robe décolletée dans le ~** low-backed dress; **de ~** from the back, from behind; **à ~** back to back; **sur le ~** on one's back; **à ~ de chameau** riding on a camel; **avoir bon ~** to be a good excuse; **se mettre qn à ~** to turn sb against one

dosage [dozaʒ] NM mixture

dos-d'âne [dodɑn] NM humpback; **pont en ~** humpbacked bridge

dose [doz] NF (*Méd*) dose; **forcer la ~** (*fig*) to overstep the mark

doser [doze] /1/ VT to measure out; (*mélanger*) to mix in the correct proportions; (*fig*) to expend in the right amounts *ou* proportions; to strike a balance between; **il faut savoir ~ ses efforts** you have to be able to pace yourself

doseur [dozœʀ] NM measure; **bouchon ~** measuring cap

dossard [dosaʀ] NM number (*worn by competitor*)

dossier [dosje] NM (*renseignements, fichier*) file; (*enveloppe*) folder, file; (*de chaise*) back; (*Presse*) feature; (*Inform*) folder; **un ~ scolaire** a school report; **le ~ social/monétaire** (*fig*) the social/financial question; **~ suspendu** suspension file

dot [dɔt] NF dowry

dotation [dɔtasjɔ̃] NF block grant; endowment

doté, e [dɔte] ADJ: **~ de** equipped with

doter [dɔte] /1/ VT: **~ qn/qch de** to equip sb/sth with

douairière [dwɛʀjɛʀ] NF dowager

★**douane** [dwan] NF (*poste, bureau*) customs *pl*; (*taxes*) (customs) duty; **passer la ~** to go through customs; **en ~** (*marchandises, entrepôt*) bonded

douanier, -ière [dwanje, -jɛʀ] ADJ customs *cpd* ▶ NM/F customs officer

doublage [dublaʒ] NM (*Ciné*) dubbing

★**double** [dubl] ADJ, ADV double; **voir ~** to see double; **en ~ (exemplaire)** in duplicate; **faire ~ emploi** to be redundant; **à ~ sens** with a double meaning; **à ~ tranchant** two-edged; **~ carburateur** twin carburettor; **à doubles commandes** dual-control; **~ toit** (*de tente*) fly sheet; **~ vue** second sight ▶ NM (*autre exemplaire*) duplicate, copy; (*sosie*) double; (*Tennis*) doubles *sg*; (*2 fois plus*): **le ~ (de)** twice as much (*ou* many) (as), double the amount (*ou* number) (of); **~ messieurs/mixte** men's/mixed doubles *sg*

doublé, e [duble] ADJ (*vêtement*): **~ (de)** lined (with)

double-clic [dubl(ə)klik] (*pl* **doubles-clics**) NM double-click

double-cliquer [dubl(ə)klike] /1/ VI (*Inform*) to double-click

doublement [dubləmɑ̃] NM doubling; twofold increase ▶ ADV doubly; (*pour deux raisons*) in two ways, on two counts

★**doubler** [duble] /1/ VT (*multiplier par 2*) to double; (*vêtement*) to line; (*dépasser*) to overtake, pass; (*film*) to dub; (*acteur*) to stand in for; **~ (la classe)** (*Scol*) to repeat a year; **~ un cap** (*Navig*) to round a cape; (*fig*) to get over a hurdle ▶ VI to double, increase twofold ■ **se doubler de** VPR to be coupled with

doublure [dublyʀ] NF lining; (*Ciné*) stand-in

douce [dus] ADJ F *voir* **doux**

douceâtre [dusɑtʀ] ADJ sickly sweet

★**doucement** [dusmɑ̃] ADV gently; (*à voix basse*) softly; (*lentement*) slowly

doucereux, -euse [dus(ə)ʀø, -øz] ADJ (*péj*) sugary

douceur [dusœʀ] NF softness; sweetness; (*de climat*) mildness; (*de quelqu'un*) gentleness; **en ~** gently ■ **douceurs** NFPL (*friandises*) sweets (BRIT), candy *sg* (US)

★**douche** [duʃ] NF shower; **prendre une ~** to have *ou* take a shower; **~ écossaise,** (*fig*) **~ froide** (*fig*) let-down ■ **douches** NFPL shower room *sg*

★**doucher** [duʃe] /1/ VT: **~ qn** to give sb a shower; (*mouiller*) to drench sb; (*fig*) to give sb a telling-off ■ **se doucher** VPR to have *ou* take a shower

doudou [dudu] (*fam*) NM (*morceau de tissu*) comfort blanket; (*peluche*) cuddly toy

doudoune [dudun] NF padded jacket; (*fam*) boob

doué, e [dwe] ADJ gifted, talented; **~ de** endowed with; **être ~ pour** to have a gift for

douille [duj] NF (*Élec*) socket; (*de projectile*) case

douillet, te [dujɛ, -ɛt] ADJ cosy; (*péj*: *à la douleur*) soft

★**douleur** [dulœʀ] NF pain; (*chagrin*) grief, distress; **ressentir des douleurs** to feel pain; **il a eu la ~ de perdre son père** he suffered the grief of losing his father

douloureux, -euse [duluʀø, -øz] ADJ painful

★**doute** [dut] NM doubt; **sans ~** adv no doubt; (*probablement*) probably; **sans nul** *ou* **aucun ~** without (a) doubt; **hors de ~** beyond doubt; **nul ~ que** there's no doubt that; **mettre en ~** to call into question; **mettre en ~ que** to question whether

★**douter** [dute] /1/ VT to doubt; **~ de** vt (*allié, sincérité de qn*) to have (one's) doubts about, doubt; (*résultat, réussite*) to be doubtful of; **~ que** to doubt whether *ou* if; **j'en doute** I have my doubts ■ **se douter** VPR: **se ~ de qch/que** to suspect sth/that; **je m'en doutais** I suspected as much; **il ne se doutait de rien** he didn't suspect a thing

douteux, -euse [dutø, -øz] ADJ (*incertain*) doubtful; (*discutable*) dubious, questionable; (*péj*) dubious-looking

douve [duv] NF (*de château*) moat; (*de tonneau*) stave

★**Douvres** [duvR] N Dover

★**doux, douce** [du, dus] ADJ (*lisse, moelleux, pas vif: couleur, non calcaire: eau*) soft; (*sucré, agréable*) sweet; (*peu fort: moutarde etc, clément: climat*) mild; (*pas brusque*) gentle; **en douce** (*partir etc*) on the quiet

★**douzaine** [duzɛn] NF (12) dozen; (*environ 12*): **une ~ (de)** a dozen or so, twelve or so

douze [duz] NUM twelve

douzième [duzjɛm] NUM twelfth

doyen, ne [dwajɛ̃, -ɛn] NM/F (*en âge, ancienneté*) most senior member; (*de faculté*) dean

DPLG ABR (= *diplômé par le gouvernement*) extra certificate for architects, engineers etc

Dr ABR (= *docteur*) Dr

dr. ABR (= *droit(e)*) R, r

draconien, ne [dRakɔnjɛ̃, -ɛn] ADJ draconian, stringent

dragage [dRagaʒ] NM dredging

dragée [dRaʒe] NF sugared almond; (*Méd*) (sugar-coated) pill

dragéifié, e [dRaʒeifje] ADJ (*Méd*) sugar-coated

dragon [dRagɔ̃] NM dragon

drague [dRag] NF (*filet*) dragnet; (*bateau*) dredger

draguer [dRage] /1/ VT (*rivière: pour nettoyer*) to dredge; (: *pour trouver qch*) to drag; (*fam*) to try and pick up, chat up (BRIT) ▶ VI (*fam*) to try and pick sb up, chat sb up (BRIT)

dragueur [dRagœR] NM (*aussi:* **dragueur de mines**) minesweeper; (*fam*): **quel ~ !** he's a great one for picking up girls!

drain [dRɛ̃] NM (*Méd*) drain

drainage [dRɛnaʒ] NM drainage

drainer [dRene] /1/ VT to drain; (*fig: visiteurs, région*) to drain off

dramatique [dRamatik] ADJ dramatic; (*tragique*) tragic ▶ NF (TV) (television) drama

dramatisation [dRamatizasjɔ̃] NF dramatization

dramatiser [dRamatize] /1/ VT to dramatize

dramaturge [dRamatyRʒ] NM dramatist, playwright

drame [dRam] NM (*Théât*) drama; (*catastrophe*) drama, tragedy; **~ familial** family drama

★**drap** [dRa] NM (*de lit*) sheet; (*tissu*) woollen fabric; **~ de plage** beach towel

drapé [dRape] NM (*d'un vêtement*) hang

★**drapeau, x** [dRapo] NM flag; **sous les drapeaux** with the colours (BRIT) ou colors (US), in the army

draper [dRape] /1/ VT to drape; (*robe, jupe*) to arrange

draperies [dRapRi] NFPL hangings

drap-housse [dRaus] (*pl* **draps-housses**) NM fitted sheet

drapier [dRapje] NM (woollen) cloth manufacturer; (*marchand*) clothier

drastique [dRastik] ADJ drastic

drépanocytose [dRepanositoz] NF sickle-cell anaemia

dressage [dRɛsaʒ] NM training

dresser [dRese] /1/ VT (*mettre vertical, monter: tente*) to put up, erect; (*fig: liste, bilan, contrat*) to draw up; (*animal*) to train; **~ l'oreille** to prick up one's ears; **~ la table** to set ou lay the table; **~ qn contre qn d'autre** to set sb against sb else; **~ un procès-verbal** ou **une contravention à qn** to book sb ■ **se dresser** VPR (*falaise, obstacle*) to stand; (*avec grandeur, menace*) to tower (up); (*personne*) to draw o.s. up

dresseur, -euse [dRɛsœR, -øz] NM/F trainer

dressoir [dRɛswaR] NM dresser

dribbler [dRible] /1/ VT, VI (*Sport*) to dribble

drille [dRij] NM: **joyeux ~** cheerful sort

★**drogue** [dRɔg] NF drug; **la ~** drugs pl; **~ dure/douce** hard/soft drugs pl

drogué, e [dRɔge] NM/F drug addict

★**droguer** [dRɔge] /1/ VT (*victime*) to drug; (*malade*) to give drugs to ■ **se droguer** VPR (*aux stupéfiants*) to take drugs; (*péj: de médicaments*) to dose o.s. up

droguerie [dRɔgRi] NF ≈ hardware shop (BRIT) ou store (US)

droguiste [dRɔgist] NM ≈ keeper (ou owner) of a hardware shop ou store

★**droit, e** [dRwa, dRwat] ADJ (*non courbe*) straight; (*vertical*) upright, straight; (*fig: loyal, franc*) upright, straight(forward); (*opposé à gauche*) right, right-hand ▶ ADV straight; **~ au but** ou **au fait/cœur** straight to the point/heart ▶ NM (*prérogative, Boxe*) right; (*taxe*) duty, tax; (: *d'inscription*) fee; (*lois*): **le ~** law; **avoir le ~ de** to be allowed to; **avoir ~ à** to be entitled to; **être en ~ de** to have a ou the right to; **faire ~ à** to grant, accede to; **être dans son ~** to be within one's rights; **à bon ~** (*justement*) with good reason; **de quel ~ ?** by what right?; **à qui de ~** to whom it may concern; **~ d'auteur** copyright; **avoir ~ de cité (dans)** (*fig*) to belong (to); **~ coutumier** common law; **~ de regard** right of access ou inspection; **~ de réponse** right to reply; **~ de visite** (right of) access; **~ de vote** (right to) vote; **droits d'auteur** (*rémunération*) royalties; **droits de douane** customs duties; **droits de l'homme** human rights; **droits d'inscription** enrolment ou registration fees ▶ NF (*Pol*) right (wing); (*ligne*) straight line; **à droite** on the right; (*direction*) (to the) right; **à droite de** to the right of; **de droite** (*Pol*) right-wing; **sur votre droite** on your right

droitement [dRwatmã] ADV (*agir*) uprightly

droit-fil [dRwafil] (*pl* **droits-fils**) NM: **être dans le ~ de qch** to be wholly in keeping with sth

droitier, -ière [dRwatje, -jɛR] NM/F right-handed person ▶ ADJ right-handed

droiture [dRwatyR] NF uprightness, straightness

drôle [dRol] ADJ (*amusant*) funny, amusing; (*bizarre*) funny, peculiar; **un ~ de ...** (*bizarre*) a strange ou funny ...; (*intensif*) an incredible ..., a terrific ...

drôlement [dRolmã] ADV funnily; peculiarly; (*très*) terribly, awfully; **il fait ~ froid** it's awfully cold

drôlerie [dRolRi] NF funniness; funny thing

dromadaire [dRɔmadɛR] NM dromedary

drone [dRon] NM (*Aviat*) drone

dru, e [dRy] ADJ (*cheveux*) thick, bushy; (*pluie*) heavy ▶ ADV (*pousser*) thickly; (*tomber*) heavily

drugstore [dRœgstɔR] NM drugstore

druide [dRyid] NM Druid

ds ABR = **dans**

DT SIGLE M (= *diphtérie tétanos*) vaccine

DTCP SIGLE M (= *diphtérie tétanos coqueluche polio*) vaccine

DTP SIGLE M (= *diphtérie tétanos polio*) vaccine

DTTAB SIGLE M (= *diphtérie tétanos typhoïde A et B*) vaccine

★**du** [dy] ART *voir* **de**

dû, due [dy] PP *de* **devoir** ▸ ADJ (*somme*) owing, owed; (: *venant à échéance*) due; (*causé par*): **dû à** due to ▸ NM due; (*somme*) dues *pl*

dualisme [dɥalism] NM dualism

Dubaï, Dubay [dybaj] N Dubai

dubitatif, -ive [dybitatif, -iv] ADJ doubtful, dubious

Dublin [dyblɛ̃] N Dublin

duc [dyk] NM duke

duché [dyʃe] NM dukedom, duchy

duchesse [dyʃɛs] NF duchess

duel [dɥɛl] NM duel

duettiste [dɥetist] NMF duettist

duffel-coat [dœfœlkot] NM duffel coat

dûment [dymɑ̃] ADV duly

dumping [dœmpiŋ] NM dumping

dune [dyn] NF dune

Dunkerque [dœ̃kɛʀk] N Dunkirk

duo [dɥo] NM (*Mus*) duet; (*fig: couple*) duo, pair

dupe [dyp] NF dupe ▸ ADJ: (**ne pas**) **être ~ de** (not) to be taken in by

duper [dype] /1/ VT to dupe, deceive

duperie [dypʀi] NF deception, dupery

duplex [dyplɛks] NM (*appartement*) split-level apartment, duplex; (*TV*): **émission en ~** link-up

duplicata [dyplikata] NM duplicate

duplicateur [dyplikatœʀ] NM duplicator; **~ à alcool** spirit duplicator

duplicité [dyplisite] NF duplicity

duquel [dykɛl] *voir* **lequel**

★**dur, e** [dyʀ] ADJ (*pierre, siège, travail, problème*) hard; (*lumière, voix, climat*) harsh; (*sévère*) hard, harsh; (*cruel*) hard(-hearted); (*porte, col*) stiff; (*viande*) tough; **mener la vie dure à qn** to give sb a hard time; **~ d'oreille** hard of hearing ▸ ADV hard ▸ NM (*fam: meneur*) tough nut ▸ NF: **à la dure** rough

durabilité [dyʀabilite] NF durability

durable [dyʀabl] ADJ lasting

durablement [dyʀabləmɑ̃] ADV for the long term

durant [dyʀɑ̃] PRÉP (*au cours de*) during; (*pendant*) for; **~ des mois, des mois ~** for months

durcir [dyʀsiʀ] /2/ VT, VI to harden ▪ **se durcir** VPR to harden

durcissement [dyʀsismɑ̃] NM hardening

durée [dyʀe] NF length; (*d'une pile etc*) life; (*déroulement: des opérations etc*) duration; **pour une ~ illimitée** for an unlimited length of time; **de courte ~** (*séjour, répit*) brief, short-term; **de longue ~** (*effet*) long-term; **pile de longue ~** long-life battery

durement [dyʀmɑ̃] ADV harshly

durent [dyʀ] VB *voir* **devoir**

★**durer** [dyʀe] /1/ VI to last

dureté [dyʀte] NF (*voir dur*) hardness; harshness; stiffness; toughness

durillon [dyʀijɔ̃] NM callus

durit® [dyʀit] NF (car radiator) hose

DUT SIGLE M = **Diplôme universitaire de technologie**

dut *etc* [dy] VB *voir* **devoir**

duvet [dyvɛ] NM down; (**sac de couchage en**) **~** down-filled sleeping bag

duveteux, -euse [dyv(ə)tø, -øz] ADJ downy

DVD SIGLE M (= *digital versatile disc*) DVD

★**dynamique** [dinamik] ADJ dynamic

dynamiser [dinamize] /1/ VT to pep up, enliven; (*équipe, service*) to inject some dynamism into

dynamisme [dinamism] NM dynamism

dynamite [dinamit] NF dynamite

dynamiter [dinamite] /1/ VT to (blow up with) dynamite

dynamo [dinamo] NF dynamo

dynastie [dinasti] NF dynasty

dysenterie [disɑ̃tʀi] NF dysentery

dysfonctionnement [disfɔ̃ksjɔnmɑ̃] NM malfunctioning

dyslexie [dislɛksi] NF dyslexia, word blindness

dyslexique [dislɛksik] ADJ dyslexic

dyspepsie [dispɛpsi] NF dyspepsia

Ee

E, e [ə] NM INV E, e ▶ ABR (= Est) E; **E comme Eugène**
E for Edward (BRIT) ou Easy (US)

EAO SIGLE M (= enseignement assisté par ordinateur)
CAL (= computer-aided learning)

★**EAU** SIGLE MPL (= Émirats arabes unis) UAE (= United
Arab Emirates)

★**eau, x** [o] NF water; **prendre l'~** (chaussure etc) to
leak, let in water; **faire ~** to leak; **tomber à l'~**
(fig) to fall through; **à l'~ de rose** slushy, sentimental; **~ bénite** holy water; **~ de Cologne** eau
de Cologne; **~ courante** running water; **~ distillée** distilled water; **~ douce** fresh water;
~ gazeuse sparkling (mineral) water; **~ de Javel**
bleach; **~ lourde** heavy water; **~ minérale** mineral water; **~ oxygénée** hydrogen peroxide;
~ plate still water; **~ de pluie** rainwater; **~ salée**
salt water; **~ de toilette** toilet water ▶ NFPL (Méd)
waters; **prendre les eaux** to take the waters;
eaux ménagères dirty water (from washing up etc);
eaux territoriales territorial waters; **eaux usées**
liquid waste

eau-de-vie [odvi] (pl **eaux-de-vie**) NF brandy

eau-forte [ofɔʀt] (pl **eaux-fortes**) NF etching

ébahi, e [ebai] ADJ dumbfounded, flabbergasted

ébahir [ebaiʀ] /2/ VT to astonish, astound

ébats [eba] VB voir **ébattre** ▶ NMPL frolics, gam-
bols

ébattre [ebatʀ] /41/: **s'ébattre** VPR to frolic

ébauche [eboʃ] NF (rough) outline, sketch

ébaucher [eboʃe] /1/ VT to sketch out, outline;
(fig): **~ un sourire/geste** to give a hint of a smile/
make a slight gesture ▪ **s'ébaucher** VPR to take
shape

ébène [eben] NF ebony

ébéniste [ebenist] NM cabinetmaker

ébénisterie [ebenist(ə)ʀi] NF cabinetmaking;
(bâti) cabinetwork

éberlué, e [ebɛʀlɥe] ADJ astounded, flabbergasted

éblouir [ebluiʀ] /2/ VT to dazzle

éblouissant, e [ebluisɑ̃, -ɑ̃t] ADJ dazzling

éblouissement [ebluismɑ̃] NM dazzle; (faiblesse)
dizzy turn

ébonite [ebɔnit] NF vulcanite

éborgner [ebɔʀɲe] /1/ VT: **~ qn** to blind sb in one
eye

éboueur [ebwœʀ] NM dustman (BRIT), garbage
man (US)

ébouillanter [ebujɑ̃te] /1/ VT to scald; (Culin) to
blanch ▪ **s'ébouillanter** VPR to scald o.s.

éboulement [ebulmɑ̃] NM falling rocks pl, rock
fall; (amas) heap of boulders etc

ébouler [ebule] /1/: **s'ébouler** VPR to crumble, collapse

éboulis [ebuli] NMPL fallen rocks

ébouriffant, e [ebuʀifɑ̃, -ɑ̃t] ADJ hair-raising

ébouriffé, e [ebuʀife] ADJ tousled, ruffled

ébouriffer [ebuʀife] /1/ VT to tousle, ruffle

ébranlement [ebʀɑ̃lmɑ̃] NM shaking

ébranler [ebʀɑ̃le] /1/ VT to shake; (rendre instable:
mur, santé) to weaken ▪ **s'ébranler** VPR (partir) to
move off

ébrécher [ebʀeʃe] /6/ VT to chip

ébriété [ebʀijete] NF: **en état d'~** in a state of
intoxication

ébrouer [ebʀue] /1/: **s'ébrouer** VPR (souffler) to
snort; (s'agiter) to shake o.s.

ébruiter [ebʀɥite] /1/ VT to spread ▪ **s'ébruiter**
VPR to spread

ébullition [ebylisjɔ̃] NF boiling point; **en ~** boiling; (fig) in an uproar

écaille [ekaj] NF (de poisson) scale; (de coquillage)
shell; (matière) tortoiseshell; (de roc etc) flake

écaillé, e [ekaje] ADJ (peinture) flaking

écailler [ekaje] /1/ VT (poisson) to scale; (huître) to
open ▪ **s'écailler** VPR to flake ou peel (off)

écaler [ekale] VT (œuf dur) to shell, peel

écarlate [ekaʀlat] ADJ scarlet

écarquiller [ekaʀkije] /1/ VT: **~ les yeux** to stare
wide-eyed

écart [ekaʀ] NM gap; (embardée) swerve; (saut) sideways leap; (fig) departure, deviation; **à l'~** adv out
of the way; **à l'~ de** prép away from; (fig) out of;
faire un ~ (voiture) to swerve; **faire le grand ~**
(Danse, Gym) to do the splits; **~ de conduite** misdemeanour

écarté, e [ekaʀte] ADJ (lieu) out-of-the-way,
remote; (ouvert): **les jambes écartées** legs apart;
les bras écartés arms outstretched

écarteler [ekaʀtəle] /5/ VT to quarter; (fig) to tear

écartement [ekaʀtəmɑ̃] NM space, gap; (Rail)
gauge

écarter [ekaʀte] /1/ VT (séparer) to move apart, separate; (éloigner) to push back, move away; (ouvrir:
bras, jambes) to spread, open; (: rideau) to draw
(back); (éliminer: candidat, possibilité) to dismiss;

(*Cartes*) to discard ■ **s'écarter** VPR to part; (*personne*) to move away; **s'~ de** to wander from

ecchymose [ekimoz] NF bruise

ecclésiastique [eklezjastik] ADJ ecclesiastical ▶ NM ecclesiastic

écervelé, e [esɛRvəle] ADJ scatterbrained, feather-brained

ECG SIGLE M (= *électrocardiogramme*) ECG

échafaud [eʃafo] NM scaffold

échafaudage [eʃafodaʒ] NM scaffolding; (*fig*) heap, pile

échafauder [eʃafode] /1/ VT (*plan*) to construct

échalas [eʃala] NM stake, pole; (*personne*) bean-pole

échalote [eʃalɔt] NF shallot

échancré, e [eʃɑ̃kRe] ADJ (*robe, corsage*) low-necked; (*côte*) indented

échancrure [eʃɑ̃kRyR] NF (*de robe*) scoop neckline; (*de côte, arête rocheuse*) indentation

échange [eʃɑ̃ʒ] NM exchange; **en ~** in exchange; **en ~ de** in exchange ou return for; **libre ~** free trade; **~ de lettres/politesses/vues** exchange of letters/civilities/views; **échanges commerciaux** trade; **échanges culturels** cultural exchanges

échangeable [eʃɑ̃ʒabl] ADJ exchangeable

échanger [eʃɑ̃ʒe] /3/ VT: **~ qch (contre)** to exchange sth (for)

échangeur [eʃɑ̃ʒœR] NM (*Auto*) interchange

échangisme [eʃɑ̃ʒism] NM swinging, partner-swapping

échangiste [eʃɑ̃ʒist] ADJ (*club*) swinging, partner-swapping ▶ NMF swinger, partner swapper

échantillon [eʃɑ̃tijɔ̃] NM sample

échantillonnage [eʃɑ̃tijɔnaʒ] NM selection of samples

échantillonner [eʃɑ̃tijɔne] VT (*prélever des échantillons de*) to take samples of; (*Inform*) to digitize; (*Mus*) to sample

échappatoire [eʃapatwaR] NF way out

échappée [eʃape] NF (*vue*) vista; (*Cyclisme*) break-away

échappement [eʃapmɑ̃] NM (*Auto*) exhaust; **~ libre** cutout

échapper [eʃape] /1/: **~ à** vt (*gardien*) to escape (from); (*punition, péril*) to escape; **~ à qn** (*détail, sens*) to escape sb; (*objet qu'on tient: aussi*: **échapper des mains de qn**) to slip out of sb's hands; **laisser ~** to let fall; (*cri etc*) to let out; **l'~ belle** to have a narrow escape

écharde [eʃaRd] NF splinter (of wood)

écharpe [eʃaRp] NF scarf; (*de maire*) sash; (*Méd*) sling; **avoir le bras en ~** to have one's arm in a sling; **prendre en ~** (*dans une collision*) to hit sideways on

écharper [eʃaRpe] /1/ VT to tear to pieces

échasse [eʃas] NF stilt

échassier [eʃasje] NM wader

échauder [eʃode] /1/ VT: **se faire ~** (*fig*) to get one's fingers burnt

échauffement [eʃofmɑ̃] NM overheating; (*Sport*) warm-up

échauffer [eʃofe] /1/ VT (*métal, moteur*) to overheat; (*fig: exciter*) to fire, excite ■ **s'échauffer** VPR (*Sport*) to warm up; (*discussion*) to become heated

échauffourée [eʃofuRe] NF clash, brawl; (*Mil*) skirmish

échéance [eʃeɑ̃s] NF (*d'un paiement: date*) settlement date; (: *somme due*) financial commitment(s); (*fig*) deadline; **à brève/longue ~** adj short-/long-term; adv in the short/long term

échéancier [eʃeɑ̃sje] NM schedule

échéant [eʃeɑ̃]: **le cas ~** adv if the case arises

échec [eʃɛk] NM failure; (*Échecs*): **~ et mat/au roi** checkmate/check; **mettre en ~** to put in check; **tenir en ~** to hold in check; **faire ~ à** to foil, thwart ■ **échecs** NMPL (*jeu*) chess sg

échelle [eʃɛl] NF ladder; (*fig, d'une carte*) scale; **à l'~ de** on the scale of; **sur une grande/petite ~** on a large/small scale; **faire la courte ~ à qn** to give sb a leg up; **~ de corde** rope ladder

échelon [eʃ(ə)lɔ̃] NM (*d'échelle*) rung; (*Admin*) grade

échelonnement [eʃ(ə)lɔnmɑ̃] NM (*de paiements*) spacing out

échelonner [eʃ(ə)lɔne] /1/ VT to space out, spread out; **versements échelonnés** instalments ■ **s'échelonner** VPR (*être compris*): **s'~ entre X et Y** to range between X and Y; **s'~ de X à Y** to range from X to Y

écheveau, x [eʃ(ə)vo] NM skein, hank

échevelé, e [eʃəv(ə)le] ADJ tousled, dishevelled; (*fig*) wild, frenzied

échine [eʃin] NF backbone, spine

échiner [eʃine] /1/: **s'échiner** VPR: **s'~ à faire qch** to break one's back doing sth

échiquier [eʃikje] NM chessboard

écho [eko] NM echo; **rester sans ~** (*suggestion etc*) to come to nothing; **se faire l'~ de** to repeat, spread about ■ **échos** NMPL (*potins*) gossip sg, rumours; (*Presse: rubrique*) "news in brief"

échographie [ekɔgRafi] NF ultrasound (scan); **passer une ~** to have a scan

échoir [eʃwaR] VI (*dette*) to fall due; (*délais*) to expire; **~ à** vt to fall to

échoppe [eʃɔp] NF stall, booth

échouer [eʃwe] /1/ VI to fail; (*débris etc: sur la plage*) to be washed up; (*aboutir: personne dans un café etc*) to arrive ▶ VT (*bateau*) to ground ■ **s'échouer** VPR to run aground

échu, e [eʃy] PP de **échoir** ▶ ADJ due, mature

échut etc [eʃy] VB voir **échoir**

éclabousser [eklabuse] /1/ VT to splash; (*fig*) to tarnish

éclaboussure [eklabusyR] NF splash; (*fig*) stain

éclair [eklɛR] NM (*d'orage*) flash of lightning, lightning no pl; (*Photo: de flash*) flash; (*fig*) flash, spark; (*gâteau*) éclair

éclairage [eklɛRaʒ] NM lighting

éclairagiste [eklɛRaʒist] NMF lighting engineer

éclairant, e [eklɛRɑ̃, -ɑ̃t] ADJ (*loupe*) illuminated; **fusée éclairante** flare

éclaircie [eklɛRsi] NF bright ou sunny interval

éclaircir [eklɛRsiR] /2/ VT to lighten; (*fig: mystère*) to clear up; (*point*) to clarify; (*Culin*) to thin (down) ■ **s'éclaircir** VPR (*ciel*) to brighten up, clear; (*che-*

145

veux) to go thin; (*situation etc*) to become clearer; **s'~ la voix** to clear one's throat

éclaircissement [eklɛʀsismɑ̃] NM clearing up, clarification

éclairé, e [ekleʀe] ADJ (*esprit, amateur*) enlightened

éclairer [eklere] /1/ VT (*lieu*) to light (up); (*personne: avec une lampe de poche etc*) to light the way for; (*fig: instruire*) to enlighten; (: *rendre compréhensible*) to shed light on ▸ VI: ~ **mal/bien** to give a poor/good light ■ **s'éclairer** VPR (*phare, rue*) to light up; (*situation etc*) to become clearer; **s'~ à la bougie/ l'électricité** to use candlelight/have electric lighting

éclaireur, -euse [eklɛʀœʀ, -øz] NM/F (*scout*) (boy) scout/(girl) guide ▸ NM (*Mil*) scout; **partir en ~** to go off to reconnoitre

éclat [ekla] NM (*de bombe, de verre*) fragment; (*du soleil, d'une couleur etc*) brightness, brilliance; (*d'une cérémonie*) splendour; (*scandale*): **faire un ~** to cause a commotion; **action d'~** outstanding action; **voler en éclats** to shatter; **des éclats de verre** broken glass; flying glass; ~ **de rire** burst *ou* roar of laughter; ~ **de voix** shout

éclatant, e [eklatɑ̃, -ɑ̃t] ADJ brilliant, bright; (*succès*) resounding; (*revanche*) devastating

éclatement [eklatmɑ̃] NM (*de groupe, parti*) break-up

éclater [eklate] /1/ VI (*pneu*) to burst; (*bombe*) to explode; (*guerre, épidémie*) to break out; (*groupe, parti*) to break up; ~ **de rire/en sanglots** to burst out laughing/sobbing

éclectique [eklɛktik] ADJ eclectic

éclectisme [eklɛktism] NM eclecticism

éclipse [eklips] NF eclipse

éclipser [eklipse] /1/ VT to eclipse ■ **s'éclipser** VPR to slip away

éclopé, e [eklɔpe] ADJ lame

éclore [eklɔʀ] /45/ VI (*œuf*) to hatch; (*fleur*) to open (out)

éclosion [eklozjɔ̃] NF blossoming

écluse [eklyz] NF lock

écluser [eklyze] (*fam*) VT to down (*fam*), knock back (*fam*) ▸ VI to knock it back (*fam*)

éclusier [eklyzje] NM lock keeper

éco- [eko] PRÉFIXE eco-

écobuage [ekɔbyaʒ] NM swidden, slash-and-burn farming

écocertification [ekosɛʀtifikasjɔ̃] NF eco-labelling, environmental certification

écœurant, e [ekœʀɑ̃, -ɑ̃t] ADJ sickening; (*gâteau etc*) sickly

écœurement [ekœʀmɑ̃] NM disgust

écœurer [ekœʀe] VT: ~ **qn** (*nourriture*) to make sb feel sick; (*fig: conduite, personne*) to disgust sb

école [ekɔl] NF school; **aller à l'~** to go to school; **faire ~** to collect a following; **les grandes écoles** prestige university-level colleges with competitive entrance examinations; ~ **maternelle** nursery school (*Brit*), kindergarten (*US*); *see note*; ~ **primaire** primary (*Brit*) *ou* grade (*US*) school; ~ **secondaire** secondary (*Brit*) *ou* high (*US*) school; ~ **privée/publique/élémentaire** private/ state/elementary school; ~ **de dessin/danse/**

musique art/dancing/music school; ~ **hôtelière** catering college; ~ **normale (d'instituteurs)** *primary school teachers' training college*; ~ **normale supérieure** *grande école for training secondary school teachers*; ~ **de secrétariat** secretarial college

> **L'école maternelle** (nursery school or kindergarten) is publicly funded in France and, though not compulsory, is attended by most children between the ages of three and six. Statutory education begins with primary (grade) school (**l'école primaire**) and is attended by children between the ages of six and 10 or 11.

> Quand le mot **school** désigne l'institution en général, il n'est jamais précédé de l'article défini. Ce n'est pas le cas quand il désigne plus précisément le bâtiment.
> *J'ai appris à jouer du violon quand j'étais à l'école.* **I learned to play the violin when I was at school.**
> *Nous avons dû aller à l'école pour parler à l'instituteur de notre fils.* **We had to go to the school to talk to our son's teacher.**

écolier, -ière [ekɔlje, -jɛʀ] NM/F schoolboy/girl

écolo [ekɔlo] NMF (*fam*) ecological ▸ ADJ ecological

écologie [ekɔlɔʒi] NF ecology; (*sujet scolaire*) environmental studies *pl*

écologique [ekɔlɔʒik] ADJ ecological; environment-friendly

écologiste [ekɔlɔʒist] NMF ecologist; environmentalist

écomusée [ekomyze] NM ecomuseum

éconduire [ekɔ̃dyiʀ] /38/ VT to dismiss

économat [ekɔnɔma] NM (*fonction*) bursarship (*Brit*), treasurership (*US*); (*bureau*) bursar's office (*Brit*), treasury (*US*)

économe [ekɔnɔm] ADJ thrifty ▸ NMF (*de lycée etc*) bursar (*Brit*), treasurer (*US*)

économétrie [ekɔnɔmetri] NF econometrics *sg*

économie [ekɔnɔmi] NF (*vertu*) economy, thrift; (*gain: d'argent, de temps etc*) saving; (*science*) economics *sg*; (*situation économique*) economy; **une ~ de temps/d'argent** a saving in time/of money; ~ **collaborative** sharing economy; ~ **dirigée** planned economy; ~ **de marché** market economy ■ **économies** NFPL (*pécule*) savings; **faire des économies** to save up

économique [ekɔnɔmik] ADJ (*avantageux*) economical; (*Écon*) economic

économiquement [ekɔnɔmikmɑ̃] ADV economically; **les ~ faibles** (*Admin*) the low-paid, people on low incomes

économiser [ekɔnɔmize] /1/ VT, VI to save

économiseur [ekɔnɔmizœʀ] NM: ~ **d'écran** (*Inform*) screen saver

économiste [ekɔnɔmist] NMF economist

écoper [ekɔpe] /1/ VI to bale out; (*fig*) to cop it; ~ **(de)** VT to get

écorce [ekɔʀs] NF bark; (*de fruit*) peel

écorcer [ekɔʀse] /3/ VT to bark

écorché, e [ekɔʀʃe] ADJ: ~ **vif** flayed alive ▸ NM cut-away drawing

écorcher [ekɔrʃe] /1/ vт (*animal*) to skin; (*égratigner*) to graze; **~ une langue** to speak a language brokenly; **s'~ le genou** *etc* to scrape *ou* graze one's knee *etc*

écorchure [ekɔrʃyr] NF graze

écoresponsable [ekɔrɛspɔ̃sabl] ADJ environmentally responsible

écorner [ekɔrne] /1/ vт (*taureau*) to dehorn; (*livre*) to make dog-eared

écossais, e [ekɔsɛ, -ɛz] ADJ Scottish, Scots; (*whisky, confiture*) Scotch; (*écharpe, tissu*) tartan ▶ NM (*Ling*) Scots; (: *gaélique*) Gaelic; (*tissu*) tartan (cloth) ▶ NM/F: **Écossais, e** Scot, Scotsman/-woman; **les É~** the Scots

Écosse [ekɔs] NF: **l'~** Scotland

écosser [ekɔse] /1/ vт to shell

écosystème [ekɔsistɛm] NM ecosystem

écot [eko] NM: **payer son ~** to pay one's share

écotaxe [ekotaks] NF green tax

écotourisme [ekoturism] NM ecotourism

écoulement [ekulmɑ̃] NM (*de faux billets*) circulation; (*de stock*) selling

écouler [ekule] /1/ vт to dispose of ■ **s'écouler** VPR (*eau*) to flow (out); (*foule*) to drift away; (*jours, temps*) to pass (by)

écourter [ekurte] /1/ vт to curtail, cut short

écoute [ekut] NF (*Navig: cordage*) sheet; (*Radio, TV*): **temps d'~** (listening *ou* viewing) time; **heure de grande ~** peak listening *ou* viewing time; **prendre l'~** to tune in; **rester à l'~ (de)** to stay tuned in (to); **écoutes téléphoniques** phone tapping *sg*

écouter [ekute] /1/ vт to listen to ■ **s'écouter** VPR: **si je m'écoutais** if I followed my instincts

écouteur [ekutœr] NM (*Tél*) receiver ■ **écouteurs** NMPL (*casque*) headphones, headset *sg*

écoutille [ekutij] NF hatch

écr. ABR = **écrire**

écrabouiller [ekrabuje] /1/ vт to squash, crush

écran [ekrɑ̃] NM screen; (*Inform*) screen, VDU; **~ de fumée/d'eau** curtain of smoke/water; **porter à l'~** (*Ciné*) to adapt for the screen; **le petit ~** television, the small screen; **~ tactile** touchscreen; **~ total** sunblock

écrasant, e [ekrazɑ̃, -ɑ̃t] ADJ overwhelming

écraser [ekraze] /1/ vт to crush; (*piéton*) to run over; (*Inform*) to overwrite; **se faire ~** to be run over; **écrase(-toi)!** shut up!; **s'~ (au sol)** vi to crash; **s'~ contre** to crash into

écrémage [ekremaʒ] NM (*sélection*) creaming off

écrémé, e [ekreme] ADJ (*lait*) skimmed

écrémer [ekreme] /6/ vт to skim

écrevisse [ekrəvis] NF crayfish *inv*

écrier [ekrije] /7/: **s'écrier** VPR to exclaim

écrin [ekrɛ̃] NM case, box

écrire [ekrir] /39/ vт, vi to write; **~ à qn que** to write and tell sb that ■ **s'écrire** VPR to write to one another; **ça s'écrit comment?** how is it spelt?

écrit, e [ekri, -it] PP *de* **écrire** ▶ ADJ: **bien/mal ~** well/badly written ▶ NM document; (*examen*) written paper; **par ~** in writing

écriteau, x [ekrito] NM notice, sign

écritoire [ekritwar] NF writing case

écriture [ekrityr] NF writing; (*Comm*) entry; **l'É~ (sainte), les Écritures** the Scriptures ■ **écritures** NFPL (*Comm*) accounts, books

écrivaillon, ne [ekrivajɔ̃, -ɔn] NM/F scribbler

écrivain [ekrivɛ̃] NM writer

écrivais *etc* [ekrivɛ] VB *voir* **écrire**

écrou [ekru] NM nut

écrouer [ekrue] /1/ vт to imprison; (*provisoirement*) to remand in custody

écroulé, e [ekrule] ADJ (*de fatigue*) exhausted; (*par un malheur*) overwhelmed; **~ (de rire)** in stitches

écroulement [ekrulmɑ̃] NM collapse

écrouler [ekrule] /1/: **s'écrouler** VPR to collapse

écru, e [ekry] ADJ (*toile*) raw, unbleached; (*couleur*) off-white, écru

écu [eky] NM (*bouclier*) shield; (*monnaie: ancienne*) crown; (: *de la CEE*) ecu

écueil [ekœj] NM reef; (*fig*) pitfall; stumbling block

écuelle [ekɥɛl] NF bowl

éculé, e [ekyle] ADJ (*chaussure*) down-at-heel; (*fig: péj*) hackneyed

écume [ekym] NF foam; (*Culin*) scum; **~ de mer** meerschaum

écumer [ekyme] /1/ vт (*Culin*) to skim; (*fig*) to plunder ▶ vi (*mer*) to foam; (*fig*) to boil with rage

écumoire [ekymwar] NF skimmer

écureuil [ekyrœj] NM squirrel

écurie [ekyri] NF stable

écusson [ekysɔ̃] NM badge

écuyer, -ère [ekɥije, -ɛr] NM/F rider

eczéma [ɛgzema] NM eczema

éd. ABR = **édition**

édam [edam] NM (*fromage*) Edam

edelweiss [edɛlvajs] NM INV edelweiss

éden [edɛn] NM Eden

édenté, e [edɑ̃te] ADJ toothless

EDF SIGLE F (= *Électricité de France*) *national electricity company*

édifiant, e [edifjɑ̃, -ɑ̃t] ADJ edifying

édification [edifikasjɔ̃] NF (*d'un bâtiment*) building, erection

édifice [edifis] NM building, edifice

édifier [edifje] /7/ vт to build, erect; (*fig*) to edify

édiles [edil] NMPL city fathers

Édimbourg [edɛ̃bur] N Edinburgh

édit [edi] NM edict

édit. ABR = **éditeur**

éditer [edite] /1/ vт (*publier*) to publish; (: *disque*) to produce; (*préparer: texte, Inform: annoter*) to edit

éditeur, -trice [editœr, -tris] NM/F publisher; editor; **~ de textes** (*Inform*) text editor

édition [edisjɔ̃] NF editing *no pl*; (*série d'exemplaires*) edition; (*industrie du livre*): **l'~** publishing; **~ sur écran** (*Inform*) screen editing

édito [edito] NM (*fam: éditorial*) editorial, leader

éditorial, -aux [editɔrjal, -o] NM editorial, leader

éditorialiste [editɔrjalist] NMF editorial *ou* leader writer

édredon [edʀədɔ̃] NM eiderdown, comforter (US)

éducateur, -trice [edykatœʀ, -tʀis] NM/F teacher; (en école spécialisée) instructor; **~ spécialisé** specialist teacher

éducatif, -ive [edykatif, -iv] ADJ educational

éducation [edykasjɔ̃] NF education; (familiale) upbringing; (manières) (good) manners pl; **bonne/mauvaise ~** good/bad upbringing; **sans ~** bad-mannered, ill-bred; **l'É~ (nationale)** ≈ the Department for Education; **~ à la citoyenneté** citizenship education; **~ permanente** continuing education; **~ physique** physical education

édulcorant [edylkɔʀɑ̃] NM sweetener

édulcorer [edylkɔʀe] /1/ VT to sweeten; (fig) to tone down

éduquer [edyke] /1/ VT to educate; (élever) to bring up; (faculté) to train; **bien/mal éduqué** well/badly brought up

EEG SIGLE M (= électroencéphalogramme) EEG

effaçable [efasabl] ADJ (feutre, CD) erasable

effacé, e [efase] ADJ (fig) retiring, unassuming

★**effacer** [efase] /3/ VT to erase, rub out; (bande magnétique) to erase; (Inform: fichier, fiche) to delete; **~ le ventre** to pull one's stomach in ■ **s'effacer** VPR (inscription etc) to wear off; (pour laisser passer) to step aside

effaceur [efasœʀ] NM eraser pen

effarant, e [efaʀɑ̃, -ɑ̃t] ADJ alarming

effaré, e [efaʀe] ADJ alarmed

effarement [efaʀmɑ̃] NM alarm

effarer [efaʀe] /1/ VT to alarm

effarouchement [efaʀuʃmɑ̃] NM alarm

effaroucher [efaʀuʃe] /1/ VT to frighten ou scare away; (personne) to alarm

effectif, -ive [efɛktif, -iv] ADJ real; effective ▶ NM (Mil) strength; (Scol) total number of pupils, size; **effectifs** numbers, strength sg; (Comm) manpower sg; **réduire l'~ de** to downsize

★**effectivement** [efɛktivmɑ̃] ADV effectively; (réellement) actually, really; (en effet) indeed

effectuer [efɛktɥe] /1/ VT (opération, mission) to carry out; (déplacement, trajet) to make, complete; (mouvement) to execute, make ■ **s'effectuer** VPR to be carried out

efféminé, e [efemine] ADJ effeminate

effervescence [efɛʀvesɑ̃s] NF (fig): **en ~** in a turmoil

effervescent, e [efɛʀvesɑ̃, -ɑ̃t] ADJ (cachet, boisson) effervescent; (fig) agitated, in a turmoil

★**effet** [efɛ] NM (résultat, artifice) effect; (impression) impression; (Comm) bill; (Jur: d'une loi, d'un jugement): **avec ~ rétroactif** applied retrospectively; **~ de style/couleur/lumière** stylistic/colour/lighting effect; **faire ~** (médicament) to take effect; **faire de l'~** (médicament, menace) to have an effect, be effective; (impressionner) to make an impression; **faire bon/mauvais ~ sur qn** to make a good/bad impression on sb; **sous l'~ de** under the effect of; **donner de l'~ à une balle** (Tennis) to put some spin on a ball; **à cet ~** to that end; **en ~** adv indeed; **~ (de commerce)** bill of exchange; **~ de serre** greenhouse effect ■ **effets** NMPL (vêtements etc) things; **effets de voix** dramatic effects with one's voice; **effets spéciaux** (Ciné) special effects

effeuiller [efœje] /1/ VT to remove the leaves (ou petals) from

★**efficace** [efikas] ADJ (personne) efficient; (action, médicament) effective

efficacement [efikasmɑ̃] ADV effectively; **pour présenter ~ vos idées** so as to present your ideas effectively

efficacité [efikasite] NF (d'une personne) efficiency; (d'un médicament) effectiveness

effigie [efiʒi] NF effigy; **brûler qn en ~** to burn an effigy of sb

effilé, e [efile] ADJ slender; (pointe) sharp; (carrosserie) streamlined

effiler [efile] /1/ VT (cheveux) to thin (out); (tissu) to fray

effilocher [efilɔʃe] /1/: **s'effilocher** VPR to fray

efflanqué, e [eflɑ̃ke] ADJ emaciated

effleurement [eflœʀmɑ̃] NM: **touche à ~** touch-sensitive control ou key

effleurer [eflœʀe] /1/ VT to brush (against); (sujet) to touch upon; (idée, pensée): **~ qn** to cross sb's mind

effluves [eflyv] NMPL exhalation(s)

effondré, e [efɔ̃dʀe] ADJ (abattu) overwhelmed

effondrement [efɔ̃dʀəmɑ̃] NM collapse

effondrer [efɔ̃dʀe] /1/: **s'effondrer** VPR to collapse

efforcer [efɔʀse] /3/: **s'efforcer de** VPR: **s'~ de faire** to try hard to do

effort [efɔʀ] NM effort; **faire un ~** to make an effort; **faire tous ses efforts** to try one's hardest; **faire l'~ de ...** to make the effort to ...; **sans ~** adj effortless; adv effortlessly; **~ de mémoire** attempt to remember; **~ de volonté** effort of will

effraction [efʀaksjɔ̃] NF breaking-in; **s'introduire par ~ dans** to break into

effrangé, e [efʀɑ̃ʒe] ADJ fringed; (effiloché) frayed

★**effrayant, e** [efʀejɑ̃, -ɑ̃t] ADJ frightening, fearsome; (sens affaibli) dreadful

effrayé, e [efʀeje] ADJ frightened, scared

effrayer [efʀeje] /8/ VT to frighten, scare; (rebuter) to put off ■ **s'effrayer (de)** VPR to be frightened ou scared (by)

effréné, e [efʀene] ADJ wild

effritement [efʀitmɑ̃] NM crumbling; erosion; slackening off

effriter [efʀite] /1/: **s'effriter** VPR to crumble; (monnaie) to be eroded; (valeurs) to slacken off

effroi [efʀwa] NM terror, dread no pl

effronté, e [efʀɔ̃te] ADJ insolent

effrontément [efʀɔ̃temɑ̃] ADV insolently

effronterie [efʀɔ̃tʀi] NF insolence

effroyable [efʀwajabl] ADJ horrifying, appalling

effroyablement [efʀwajabləmɑ̃] ADV horribly

effusion [efyzjɔ̃] NF effusion; **sans ~ de sang** without bloodshed

égailler [egaje] /1/: **s'égailler** VPR to scatter, disperse

égal, e, -aux [egal, -o] ADJ (identique, ayant les mêmes droits) equal; (plan: surface) even, level; (constant: vitesse) steady; (équitable) even; **être ~ à** (prix, nombre) to be equal to; **ça m'est ~** it's all the same to me, it doesn't matter to me, I don't mind; **c'est ~, ...** all the same, ... ▶ NM/F equal; **sans ~** matchless, unequalled; **à l'~ de** (comme) just like; **d'~ à ~** as equals

également [egalmã] ADV (aussi) too, as well; (répartir) equally; (étaler) evenly

égaler [egale] /1/ VT to equal

égalisateur, -trice [egalizatœʀ, -tʀis] ADJ (Sport): **but ~** equalizing goal, equalizer

égalisation [egalizasjɔ̃] NF (Sport) equalization

égaliser [egalize] /1/ VT (sol, salaires) to level (out); (chances) to equalize ▶ VI (Sport) to equalize

égalitaire [egalitɛʀ] ADJ egalitarian

égalitarisme [egalitaʀism] NM egalitarianism

égalitariste [egalitaʀist] ADJ (idéologie, mouvement) egalitarian

égalité [egalite] NF (politique, sociale) equality; (Math) identity; **~ de droits** equality of rights; **~ des chances** equal opportunities; **~ d'humeur** evenness of temper; **être à ~ (de points)** to be level

égard [egaʀ] NM, **égards** NMPL consideration sg; **à cet ~** in this respect; **à certains égards/tous égards** in certain respects/all respects; **eu ~ à** in view of; **par ~ pour** out of consideration for; **sans ~ pour** without regard for; **à l'~ de** prép towards; (en ce qui concerne) concerning, as regards

égaré, e [egaʀe] ADJ lost

égarement [egaʀmã] NM distraction; aberration

égarer [egaʀe] /1/ VT (objet) to mislay; (moralement) to lead astray ■ **s'égarer** VPR to get lost, lose one's way; (objet) to go astray; (fig: dans une discussion) to wander

égayer [egeje] /8/ VT (personne) to amuse; (: remonter) to cheer up; (récit, endroit) to brighten up, liven up

Égée [eʒe] ADJ: **la mer ~** the Aegean (Sea)

égéen, ne [eʒeɛ̃, -ɛn] ADJ Aegean

égérie [eʒeʀi] NF: **l'~ de qn/qch** the brains behind sb/sth

égide [eʒid] NF: **sous l'~ de** under the aegis of

églantier [eglãtje] NM wild ou dog rose(-bush)

églantine [eglãtin] NF wild ou dog rose

églefin [egləfɛ̃] NM haddock

église [egliz] NF church; **aller à l'~** to go to church

ego [ego] NM ego

égocentrique [egɔsãtʀik] ADJ egocentric, self-centred

égocentrisme [egɔsãtʀism] NM egocentricity

égoïne [egɔin] NF handsaw

égoïsme [egɔism] NM selfishness, egoism

égoïste [egɔist] ADJ selfish, egoistic ▶ NMF egoist

égoïstement [egɔistəmã] ADV selfishly

égorger [egɔʀʒe] /3/ VT to cut the throat of

égosiller [egozije] /1/: **s'égosiller** VPR to shout o.s. hoarse

égotisme [egɔtism] NM egotism, egoism

égout [egu] NM sewer; **eaux d'~** sewage

égoutier [egutje] NM sewer worker

égoutter [egute] /1/ VT (linge) to wring out; (vaisselle, fromage) to drain ▶ VI to drip ■ **s'égoutter** VPR to drip

égouttoir [egutwaʀ] NM draining board; (mobile) draining rack

égratigner [egʀatiɲe] /1/ VT to scratch ■ **s'égratigner** VPR to scratch o.s.

égratignure [egʀatiɲyʀ] NF scratch

égrener [egʀəne] /5/ VT: **~ une grappe, ~ des raisins** to pick grapes off a bunch ■ **s'égrener** VPR (fig: heures etc) to pass by; (: notes) to chime out

égrillard, e [egʀijaʀ, -aʀd] ADJ ribald, bawdy

Égypte [eʒipt] NF: **l'~** Egypt

égyptien, ne [eʒipsjɛ̃, -ɛn] ADJ Egyptian ▶ NM/F: **Égyptien, ne** Egyptian

égyptologie [eʒiptɔlɔʒi] NF Egyptology

égyptologue [eʒiptɔlɔg] NMF Egyptologist

eh [e] EXCL hey!; **eh bien** well

éhonté, e [eɔ̃te] ADJ shameless, brazen (BRIT)

éjaculation [eʒakylasjɔ̃] NF ejaculation

éjaculer [eʒakyle] /1/ VI to ejaculate

éjectable [eʒɛktabl] ADJ: **siège ~** ejector seat

éjecter [eʒɛkte] /1/ VT (Tech) to eject; (fam) to kick ou chuck out

éjection [eʒɛksjɔ̃] NF ejection

élaboration [elabɔʀasjɔ̃] NF elaboration

élaboré, e [elabɔʀe] ADJ (complexe) elaborate

élaborer [elabɔʀe] /1/ VT to elaborate; (projet, stratégie) to work out; (rapport) to draft

élagage [elagaʒ] NM pruning

élaguer [elage] /1/ VT to prune

élagueur, -euse [elagœʀ, -øz] NM/F (personne) tree surgeon ▶ NF (machine) pruner

élan [elã] NM (Zool) elk, moose; (Sport: avant le saut) run up; (de véhicule) momentum; (fig: de tendresse etc) surge; **prendre son ~/de l'~** to take a run up/gather speed; **perdre son ~** to lose one's momentum

élancé, e [elãse] ADJ slender

élancement [elãsmã] NM shooting pain

élancer [elãse] /3/: **s'élancer** VPR to dash, hurl o.s.; (fig: arbre, clocher) to soar (upwards)

élargir [elaʀʒiʀ] /2/ VT to widen; (vêtement) to let out; (Jur) to release ■ **s'élargir** VPR to widen; (vêtement) to stretch

élargissement [elaʀʒismã] NM widening; letting out

élasticité [elastisite] NF (aussi Écon) elasticity; **~ de l'offre/de la demande** flexibility of supply/demand

élastique [elastik] ADJ elastic ▶ NM (de bureau) rubber band; (pour la couture) elastic no pl

élastomère [elastɔmɛʀ] NM elastomer

Elbe [ɛlb] NF: **l'île d'~** (the Island of) Elba; (fleuve) **l'~** the Elbe

eldorado [ɛldɔʀado] NM Eldorado

électeur, -trice [elɛktœʀ, -tʀis] NM/F elector, voter

électif, -ive [elɛktif, -iv] ADJ elective

élection [elɛksjɔ̃] NF (gén, Pol) election; **sa terre/patrie d'~** the land/country of one's choice;

e

~ partielle ≈ by-election; **élections législatives/présidentielles** general/presidential election *sg*; **élections municipales** local elections

Élections législatives are held in France every five years to elect *députés* to the *Assemblée nationale*. The president is chosen in the **élection présidentielle**, which also takes place every five years. Voting is by direct universal suffrage and is divided into two rounds with the ballots always taking place on a Sunday. Local elections (**élections municipales**) are held every six years to choose *conseillers municipaux*, who in turn then elect the mayor and the deputy mayors.

électoral, e, -aux [elɛktɔral, -o] ADJ electoral, election *cpd*

électoralisme [elɛktɔralism] NM electioneering

électorat [elɛktɔra] NM electorate

électricien, ne [elɛktrisjɛ̃, -ɛn] NM/F electrician

électricité [elɛktrisite] NF electricity; **allumer/éteindre l'~** to put on/off the light; **~ statique** static electricity

électrification [elɛktrifikasjɔ̃] NF (*Rail*) electrification; (*d'un village etc*) laying on of electricity

électrifier [elɛktrifje] /**7**/ VT (*Rail*) to electrify

électrique [elɛktrik] ADJ electric(al)

L'adjectif *électrique* se traduit par **electric** quand il s'agit d'appareils, mais par **electrical** dans les contextes plus techniques ou scientifiques, ou en association avec certains mots précis.
une guitare électrique **an electric guitar**
un ingénieur en génie électrique **an electrical engineer**
un appareil électrique **an electrical appliance**.

électriser [elɛktrize] /**1**/ VT to electrify

électro- [elɛktrɔ] ADJ electro- ▶ NF (*Mus*) electronic (music), electro

électro-aimant [elɛktrɔɛmɑ̃] NM electromagnet

électrocardiogramme [elɛktrɔkardjɔgram] NM electrocardiogram

électrocardiographe [elɛktrɔkardjɔgraf] NM electrocardiograph

électrochoc [elɛktrɔʃɔk] NM electric shock treatment

électrocuter [elɛktrɔkyte] /**1**/ VT to electrocute

électrocution [elɛktrɔkysjɔ̃] NF electrocution

électrode [elɛktrɔd] NF electrode

électro-encéphalogramme [elɛktrɔɑ̃sefalɔgram] NM electroencephalogram

électrogène [elɛktrɔʒɛn] ADJ: **groupe ~** generating set

électroluminescence [elɛktrɔlyminesɑ̃s] NF electroluminescence

électroluminescent, e [elɛktrɔlyminesɑ̃, -ɑ̃t] ADJ electroluminescent

électrolyse [elɛktrɔliz] NF electrolysis *sg*

électromagnétique [elɛktrɔmaɲetik] ADJ electromagnetic

électroménager [elɛktrɔmenaʒe] ADJ M: **appareils électroménagers** domestic (electrical) appliances ▶ NM: **l'~** household appliances

électron [elɛktrɔ̃] NM electron

électronicien, ne [elɛktrɔnisjɛ̃, -ɛn] NM/F electronics (BRIT) *ou* electrical (US) engineer

électronique [elɛktrɔnik] ADJ electronic ▶ NF (*science*) electronics *sg*

électronucléaire [elɛktrɔnykleɛr] ADJ nuclear power *cpd* ▶ NM: **l'~** nuclear power

électrophone [elɛktrɔfɔn] NM record player

électrostatique [elɛktrɔstatik] ADJ electrostatic ▶ NF electrostatics *sg*

électrothérapie [elɛktrɔterapi] NF electrotherapy

élégamment [elegamɑ̃] ADV elegantly

élégance [elegɑ̃s] NF elegance

élégant, e [elegɑ̃, -ɑ̃t] ADJ elegant; (*solution*) neat, elegant; (*attitude, procédé*) courteous, civilized

élégiaque [eleʒjak] ADJ (*style, œuvre*) elegiac

élégie [eleʒi] NF elegy

élément [elemɑ̃] NM element; (*pièce*) component, part ∎ **éléments** NMPL elements

élémentaire [elemɑ̃tɛr] ADJ elementary; (*Chimie*) elemental

éléphant [elefɑ̃] NM elephant; **~ de mer** elephant seal

éléphanteau, x [elefɑ̃to] NM baby elephant

éléphantesque [elefɑ̃tɛsk] ADJ elephantine

élevage [el(ə)vaʒ] NM breeding; (*de bovins*) cattle breeding *ou* rearing; (*ferme*) cattle farm; **truite d'~** farmed trout

élévateur [elevatœr] NM elevator

élévation [elevasjɔ̃] NF (*gén*) elevation; (*voir élever*) raising; (*voir s'élever*) rise

élevé, e [el(ə)ve] ADJ (*prix, sommet*) high; (*fig: noble*) elevated; **bien/mal ~** well-/ill-mannered

élève [elɛv] NMF pupil; **~ infirmière** student nurse

élever [el(ə)ve] /**5**/ VT (*enfant*) to bring up, raise; (*bétail, volaille*) to breed; (*abeilles*) to keep; (*hausser: taux, niveau*) to raise; (*fig: âme, esprit*) to elevate; (*édifier: monument*) to put up, erect; **~ la voix** to raise one's voice; **~ une protestation/critique** to raise a protest/make a criticism; **~ qn au rang de** to raise *ou* elevate sb to the rank of; **~ un nombre au carré/au cube** to square/cube a number ∎ **s'élever** VPR (*avion, alpiniste*) to go up; (*niveau, température, aussi: cri etc*) to rise; (*survenir: difficultés*) to arise; **s'~ à** (*frais, dégâts*) to amount to, add up to; **s'~ contre** to rise up against

éleveur, -euse [el(ə)vœr, -øz] NM/F stock breeder

elfe [ɛlf] NM elf

élidé, e [elide] ADJ elided

élider [elide] /**1**/ VT to elide

éligibilité [eliʒibilite] NF eligibility

éligible [eliʒibl] ADJ eligible

élimé, e [elime] ADJ worn (thin), threadbare

élimer [elime] : **s'élimer** VPR to wear thin, become threadbare

élimination [eliminasjɔ̃] NF elimination

éliminatoire [eliminatwar] ADJ eliminatory; (*Sport*) disqualifying ▶ NF (*Sport*) heat

éliminer [elimine] /**1**/ VT to eliminate

élire [elir] /**43**/ VT to elect; **~ domicile à** to take up residence in *ou* at

élisabéthain, e [elizabetɛ̃, -ɛn] ADJ Elizabethan

élision [elizjɔ̃] NF elision

élite [elit] NF elite; **tireur d'~** crack rifleman; **chercheur d'~** top-notch researcher

élitisme [elitism] NM elitism

élitiste [elitist] ADJ elitist

élixir [eliksiʀ] NM elixir

★**elle** [εl] PRON (sujet) she; (: chose) it; (complément) her; it; **elles** (sujet) they; (complément) them; **elle-même** herself; itself; **elles-mêmes** themselves; voir **il**

ellipse [elips] NF ellipse; (Ling) ellipsis sg

elliptique [eliptik] ADJ elliptical

élocution [elɔkysjɔ̃] NF delivery; **défaut d'~** speech impediment

éloge [elɔʒ] NM praise gén no pl; **faire l'~ de** to praise

élogieusement [elɔʒjøzmã] ADV very favourably

élogieux, -euse [elɔʒjø, -øz] ADJ laudatory, full of praise

éloigné, e [elwaɲe] ADJ distant, far-off; (parent) distant

éloignement [elwaɲmã] NM removal; putting off; estrangement; (fig: distance) distance

éloigner [elwaɲe] /1/ VT (échéance) to put off, postpone; (soupçons, danger) to ward off; **~ qch (de)** to move ou take sth away (from); **~ qn (de)** to take sb away ou remove sb (from) ■ **s'éloigner (de)** VPR (personne) to go away (from); (véhicule) to move away (from); (affectivement) to become estranged (from)

élongation [elɔ̃gasjɔ̃] NF strained muscle

éloquence [elɔkãs] NF eloquence

éloquent, e [elɔkã, -ãt] ADJ eloquent

élu, e [ely] PP de **élire** ▸ NM/F (Pol) elected representative

élucider [elyside] /1/ VT to elucidate

élucubrations [elykybʀasjɔ̃] NFPL wild imaginings

éluder [elyde] /1/ VT to evade

élusif, -ive [elyzif, -iv] ADJ elusive

Élysée [elize] NM: **(le palais de) l'~** the Élysée palace; **les Champs-Élysées** the Champs-Élysées

The **palais de l'Élysée**, situated in the heart of Paris just off the Champs-Élysées, is the official residence of the French President. Built in the eighteenth century, it has performed its present function since 1874. A shorter form of its name, **l'Élysée**, is frequently used to refer to the presidency itself.

émacié, e [emasje] ADJ emaciated

émail, -aux [emaj, -o] NM enamel

e-mail [imεl] NM email; **envoyer qch par ~** to email sth

émaillé, e [emaje] ADJ enamelled; (fig): **~ de** dotted with

émailler [emaje] /1/ VT to enamel

émanation [emanasjɔ̃] NF emanation

émancipation [emãsipasjɔ̃] NF emancipation

émancipé, e [emãsipe] ADJ emancipated

émanciper [emãsipe] /1/ VT to emancipate ■ **s'émanciper** VPR (fig) to become emancipated ou liberated

émaner [emane] /1/: **~ de** VT to emanate from; (Admin) to proceed from

émarger [emaʀʒe] /3/ VT to sign; **~ de 1000 euros à un budget** to receive 1000 euros out of a budget

émasculer [emaskyle] /1/ VT to emasculate

★**emballage** [ãbalaʒ] NM wrapping; packing; (papier) wrapping; (carton) packaging

emballant, e [ãbalã, -ãt] ADJ exciting

★**emballer** [ãbale] /1/ VT to wrap (up); (dans un carton) to pack (up); (fig: fam) to thrill (to bits) ■ **s'emballer** VPR (moteur) to race; (cheval) to bolt; (fig: personne) to get carried away

emballeur, -euse [ãbalœʀ, -øz] NM/F packer

embarcadère [ãbaʀkadεʀ] NM landing stage (Brit), pier

embarcation [ãbaʀkasjɔ̃] NF (small) boat, (small) craft inv

embardée [ãbaʀde] NF swerve; **faire une ~** to swerve

embargo [ãbaʀgo] NM embargo; **mettre l'~ sur** to put an embargo on, embargo

embarqué, e [ãbaʀke] ADJ (électronique, équipement: Auto) in-car cpd; (Aviat, Navig) on-board cpd

★**embarquement** [ãbaʀkəmã] NM embarkation; (de marchandises) loading; (de passagers) boarding

embarquer [ãbaʀke] /1/ VT (personne) to embark; (marchandise) to load; (fam) to cart off; (: arrêter) to nick ▸ VI (passager) to board; (Navig) to ship water ■ **s'embarquer** VPR to board; **s'~ dans** (affaire, aventure) to embark upon

embarras [ãbaʀa] NM (obstacle) hindrance; (confusion) embarrassment; **être dans l'~** (ennuis) to be in a predicament ou an awkward position; (gêne financière) to be in difficulties; **~ gastrique** stomach upset; **vous n'avez que l'~ du choix** the only problem is choosing

embarrassant, e [ãbaʀasã, -ãt] ADJ cumbersome; embarrassing; awkward

embarrassé, e [ãbaʀase] ADJ (encombré) encumbered; (gêné) embarrassed; (explications etc) awkward

embarrasser [ãbaʀase] /1/ VT (encombrer) to clutter (up); (gêner) to hinder, hamper; (fig) to cause embarrassment to; to put in an awkward position ■ **s'embarrasser de** VPR to burden o.s. with

embauche [ãboʃ] NF hiring; **bureau d'~** labour office

embaucher [ãboʃe] /1/ VT to take on, hire ■ **s'embaucher comme** VPR to get (o.s.) a job as

embauchoir [ãboʃwaʀ] NM shoetree

embaumement [ãbommã] NM embalming

embaumer [ãbome] /1/ VT to embalm; (parfumer) to fill with its fragrance; **~ la lavande** to be fragrant with (the scent of) lavender

embellie [ãbeli] NF bright spell, brighter period

embellir [ãbeliʀ] /2/ VT to make more attractive; (une histoire) to embellish ▸ VI to grow lovelier ou more attractive

embellissement [ãbelismã] NM embellishment

emberlificoter [ãbεʀlifikɔte]: **s'emberlificoter** VPR (fam): **s'~ dans qch** to get tangled up in sth

embêtant, e [ãbεtã, -ãt] ADJ annoying

embêté, e [ãbete] ADJ bothered

embêtement [ãbɛtmã] NM problem, difficulty ■ **embêtements** NMPL trouble *sg*

embêter *(fam)* [ãbete] /**1**/ VT to bother; **ça m'embête** it bothers me ■ **s'embêter** VPR *(s'ennuyer)* to be bored; **il ne s'embête pas !** *(ironique)* he does all right for himself!

emblée [ãble]: **d'~** *adv* straightaway

emblématique [ãblematik] ADJ emblematic; **figure ~ de qch** emblem of sth

emblème [ãblɛm] NM emblem

embobiner [ãbɔbine] /**1**/ VT *(enjôler):* **~ qn** to get round sb

emboîtable [ãbwatabl] ADJ interlocking

emboîtement [ãbwatmã] NM: **les lames s'assemblent par ~** the blades interlock *ou* fit together

emboîter [ãbwate] /**1**/ VT to fit together; **~ le pas à qn** to follow in sb's footsteps ■ **s'emboîter dans** VPR to fit into; **s'~ (l'un dans l'autre)** to fit together

embolie [ãbɔli] NF embolism

embonpoint [ãbɔ̃pwɛ̃] NM stoutness (BRIT), corpulence; **prendre de l'~** to grow stout (BRIT) *ou* corpulent

embouché, e [ãbuʃe] ADJ: **mal ~** foul-mouthed

embouchure [ãbuʃyʀ] NF *(Géo)* mouth; *(Mus)* mouthpiece

embourber [ãbuʀbe] /**1**/: **s'embourber** VPR to get stuck in the mud; *(fig):* **s'~ dans** to sink into

embourgeoiser [ãbuʀʒwaze] /**1**/: **s'embourgeoiser** VPR to adopt a middle-class outlook

embout [ãbu] NM *(de canne)* tip; *(de tuyau)* nozzle

★**embouteillage** [ãbuteja3] NM traffic jam, (traffic) holdup (BRIT)

embouteiller [ãbuteje] /**1**/ VT *(véhicules etc)* to block

emboutir [ãbutiʀ] /**2**/ VT *(Tech)* to stamp; *(heurter)* to crash into, ram

embranchement [ãbʀãʃmã] NM *(routier)* junction; *(classification)* branch

embrancher [ãbʀãʃe] /**1**/ VT *(tuyaux)* to join; **~ qch sur** to join sth to

embrasement [ãbʀazmã] NM unrest; **ils craignent un nouvel ~ de la région** they fear more unrest in the region

embraser [ãbʀaze] /**1**/: **s'embraser** VPR to flare up

embrassade [ãbʀasad] NF *(gén pl)* hugging and kissing *no pl*

embrasse [ãbʀas] NF *(de rideau)* tie-back, loop

★**embrasser** [ãbʀase] /**1**/ VT to kiss; *(sujet, période)* to embrace, encompass; *(carrière)* to embark on; *(métier)* to go in for, take up; **~ du regard** to take in (with eyes) ■ **s'embrasser** VPR to kiss (each other)

embrasure [ãbʀazyʀ] NF: **dans l'~ de la porte** in the door(way)

embrayage [ãbʀeja3] NM clutch

embrayer [ãbʀeje] /**8**/ VI *(Auto)* to let in the clutch; **~ sur qch** to begin on sth ▶ VT *(fig: affaire)* to set in motion

embrigadement [ãbʀigadmã] NM *(péj)* recruiting

embrigader [ãbʀigade] /**1**/ VT *(péj)* to recruit

embringuer [ãbʀɛ̃ge] *(fam)* VT to drag in; **~ qn dans qch** to drag sb into sth ■ **s'embringuer** VPR: **s'~ dans qch** to get dragged into sth; **se laisser ~ dans qch** to get dragged into sth

embrocher [ãbʀɔʃe] /**1**/ VT to (put on a) spit *(ou* skewer)

embrouillamini [ãbʀujamini] NM *(fam)* muddle

embrouille [ãbʀuj] NF *(fam: tromperie)* dodgy dealings *(fam)*

embrouillé, e [ãbʀuje] ADJ *(affaire)* confused, muddled

embrouiller [ãbʀuje] /**1**/ VT *(fils)* to tangle (up); *(fiches, idées, personne)* to muddle up ■ **s'embrouiller** VPR to get in a muddle

embroussaillé, e [ãbʀusaje] ADJ overgrown, scrubby; *(cheveux)* bushy, shaggy

embrumé, e [ãbʀyme] ADJ *(paysage, horizon)* misty; *(cerveau, esprit)* befuddled

embruns [ãbʀœ̃] NMPL sea spray *sg*

embryologie [ãbʀijɔlɔʒi] NF embryology

embryon [ãbʀijɔ̃] NM embryo

embryonnaire [ãbʀijɔnɛʀ] ADJ embryonic

embûches [ãbyʃ] NFPL pitfalls, traps

embué, e [ãbɥe] ADJ misted up; **yeux embués de larmes** eyes misty with tears

embuscade [ãbyskad] NF ambush; **tendre une ~ à** to lay an ambush for

embusqué, e [ãbyske] ADJ in ambush ▶ NM *(péj)* shirker, skiver (BRIT)

embusquer [ãbyske] /**1**/: **s'embusquer** VPR to take up position (for an ambush)

éméché, e [emeʃe] ADJ tipsy, merry

émeraude [em(ə)ʀod] NF emerald ▶ ADJ INV emerald-green

émergence [emɛʀʒãs] NF *(fig)* emergence

émergent, e [emɛʀʒã, -ãt] ADJ *(pays, économie)* emerging; *(marché)* emerging, developing

émerger [emɛʀʒe] /**3**/ VI to emerge; *(faire saillie, aussi fig)* to stand out

émeri [em(ə)ʀi] NM: **toile** *ou* **papier ~** emery paper

émérite [emeʀit] ADJ highly skilled

émerveillement [emɛʀvɛjmã] NM wonderment

émerveiller [emɛʀveje] /**1**/ VT to fill with wonder ■ **s'émerveiller de** VPR to marvel at

émet *etc* [emɛ] VB *voir* **émettre**

émétique [emetik] NM emetic

émetteur, -trice [emɛtœʀ, -tʀis] ADJ transmitting; **(poste) ~** transmitter

émetteur-récepteur [emetœʀʀesɛptœʀ] *(pl* **émetteurs-récepteurs**) NM transceiver

émettre [emɛtʀ] /**56**/ VT *(son, lumière)* to give out, emit; *(message etc: Radio)* to transmit; *(billet, timbre, emprunt, chèque)* to issue; *(hypothèse, avis)* to voice, put forward; *(vœu)* to express ▶ VI to broadcast; **~ sur ondes courtes** to broadcast on short wave

émeus *etc* [emø] VB *voir* **émouvoir**

émeute [emøt] NF riot

émeutier, -ière [emøtje, -jɛʀ] NM/F rioter

émeuve *etc* [emœv] VB *voir* **émouvoir**

émietter [emjete] /**1**/ VT *(pain, terre)* to crumble; *(fig)* to split up, disperse ■ **s'émietter** VPR *(pain, terre)* to crumble

émigrant, e [emigʀɑ̃, -ɑ̃t] NM/F emigrant

émigration [emigʀasjɔ̃] NF emigration

émigré, e [emigʀe] NM/F expatriate

émigrer [emigʀe] /1/ VI to emigrate **émincé** [emɛ̃se] ADJ thinly sliced ▸ NM: **un ~ de veau** thin slices of veal

émincer [emɛ̃se] /3/ VT (*Culin*) to slice thinly

éminemment [eminamɑ̃] ADV eminently

éminence [eminɑ̃s] NF distinction; (*colline*) knoll, hill; **Son É~** His Eminence; **~ grise** éminence grise

éminent, e [eminɑ̃, -ɑ̃t] ADJ distinguished

émir [emiʀ] NM emir

émirat [emiʀa] NM emirate; **les Émirats arabes unis (EAU)** the United Arab Emirates (UAE)

émis, e [emi, -iz] PP *de* **émettre**

émissaire [emisɛʀ] NM emissary

émission [emisjɔ̃] NF (*voir émettre*) emission; (*d'un message*) transmission; (*de billet, timbre, emprunt, chèque*) issue; (*Radio, TV*) programme, broadcast

émit *etc* [emi] VB *voir* **émettre**

emmagasinage [ɑ̃magazinaʒ] NM storage; storing away

emmagasiner [ɑ̃magazine] /1/ VT to (put into) store; (*fig*) to store up

emmailloter [ɑ̃majɔte] /1/ VT to wrap up

emmanchure [ɑ̃mɑ̃ʃyʀ] NF armhole

emmêlement [ɑ̃mɛlmɑ̃] NM (*état*) tangle

emmêler [ɑ̃mele] /1/ VT to tangle (up); (*fig*) to muddle up ■ **s'emmêler** VPR to get into a tangle

emménagement [ɑ̃menaʒmɑ̃] NM settling in

emménager [ɑ̃menaʒe] /3/ VI to move in; **~ dans** to move into

★**emmener** [ɑ̃m(ə)ne] /5/ VT to take (with one); (*comme otage, capture*) to take away; **~ qn au cinéma** to take sb to the cinema

emmental, emmenthal [emɛ̃tal] NM (*fromage*) Emmenthal

emmerdement [ɑ̃mɛʀdəmɑ̃] NM (*fam: plus souvent au pluriel: ennui*) trouble *no pl*; **la loi de l'~ maximum** Sod's law (*fam*), Murphy's law

emmerder [ɑ̃mɛʀde] /1/ (*!*) VT to bug, bother; **je t'emmerde !** to hell with you! ■ **s'emmerder** VPR (*s'ennuyer*) to be bored stiff

emmitoufler [ɑ̃mitufle] /1/ VT to wrap up (warmly) ■ **s'emmitoufler** VPR to wrap (o.s.) up (warmly)

emmurer [ɑ̃myʀe] /1/ VT to wall up, immure

émoi [emwa] NM (*agitation, effervescence*) commotion; (*trouble*) agitation; **en ~** (*sens*) excited, stirred

émollient, e [emɔljɑ̃, -ɑ̃t] ADJ (*Méd*) emollient

émoluments [emɔlymɑ̃] NMPL remuneration *sg*, fee *sg*

émonder [emɔ̃de] /1/ VT (*arbre etc*) to prune; (*amande etc*) to blanch

émoticone [emɔtikon] NM (*Inform*) smiley

émotif, -ive [emɔtif, -iv] ADJ emotional

émotion [emɔsjɔ̃] NF emotion; **avoir des émotions** (*fig*) to get a fright; **donner des émotions à** to give a fright to; **sans ~** without emotion, coldly

émotionnel, le [emɔsjɔnɛl] ADJ emotional

émoulu, e [emuly] ADJ: **frais ~ de** fresh from, just out of

émoussé, e [emuse] ADJ blunt

émousser [emuse] /1/ VT to blunt; (*fig*) to dull

émoustiller [emustije] /1/ VT to titillate, arouse

émouvant, e [emuvɑ̃, -ɑ̃t] ADJ moving

émouvoir [emuvwaʀ] /27/ VT (*troubler*) to stir, affect; (*toucher, attendrir*) to move; (*indigner*) to rouse; (*effrayer*) to disturb, worry ■ **s'émouvoir** VPR to be affected; to be moved; to be roused; to be disturbed *ou* worried

empailler [ɑ̃paje] /1/ VT to stuff

empailleur, -euse [ɑ̃pajœʀ, -øz] NM/F (*d'animaux*) taxidermist

empaler [ɑ̃pale] /1/ VT to impale

empaquetage [ɑ̃paktaʒ] NM packing, packaging

empaqueter [ɑ̃pakte] /4/ VT to pack up

emparer [ɑ̃paʀe] /1/: **s'emparer de** VPR (*objet*) to seize, grab; (*comme otage, Mil*) to seize; (*peur etc*) to take hold of

empâter [ɑ̃pate] /1/: **s'empâter** VPR to thicken out

empathie [ɑ̃pati] NF (*Psych*) empathy

empattement [ɑ̃patmɑ̃] NM (*Auto*) wheelbase; (*Typo*) serif

empêché, e [ɑ̃peʃe] ADJ detained

empêchement [ɑ̃peʃmɑ̃] NM (*unexpected*) obstacle, hitch

empêcher [ɑ̃peʃe] /1/ VT to prevent; **~ qn de faire** to prevent *ou* stop sb (from) doing; **~ que qch (n')arrive/qn (ne) fasse** to prevent sth from happening/sb from doing; **il n'empêche que** nevertheless, be that as it may; **il n'a pas pu s'~ de rire** he couldn't help laughing

empêcheur [ɑ̃peʃœʀ] NM: **~ de danser en rond** spoilsport, killjoy (BRIT)

empeigne [ɑ̃peɲ] NF upper (*of shoe*)

empennage [ɑ̃penaʒ] NM (*Aviat*) tailplane

empereur [ɑ̃pʀœʀ] NM emperor

empesé, e [ɑ̃pəze] ADJ (*fig*) stiff, starchy

empeser [ɑ̃pəze] /5/ VT to starch

empester [ɑ̃peste] /1/ VT (*lieu*) to stink out ▸ VI to stink, reek; **~ le tabac/le vin** to stink *ou* reek of tobacco/wine

empêtrer [ɑ̃petʀe] /1/: **s'empêtrer dans** VPR (*fils, contradictions, aussi fig*) to get tangled up in

emphase [ɑ̃faz] NF pomposity, bombast; **avec ~** pompously

emphatique [ɑ̃fatik] ADJ emphatic

empiècement [ɑ̃pjɛsmɑ̃] NM (*Couture*) yoke

empierrer [ɑ̃pjeʀe] /1/ VT (*route*) to metal

empiéter [ɑ̃pjete] /6/: **~ sur** VT to encroach upon

empiler [ɑ̃pile] /1/ VT to pile (up), stack (up) ■ **s'empiler** VPR to pile up

empire [ɑ̃piʀ] NM empire; (*fig*) influence; **style E~** Empire style; **sous l'~ de** in the grip of

empirer [ɑ̃piʀe] /1/ VI to worsen, deteriorate

empirique [ɑ̃piʀik] ADJ empirical

empirisme [ɑ̃piʀism] NM empiricism

153

★**emplacement** [ãplasmã] NM site; **sur l'~ de** on the site of

emplâtre [ãplɑtʀ] NM plaster; (fam) twit

emplette [ãplɛt] NF: **faire l'~ de** to purchase ■ **emplettes** shopping sg; **faire des emplettes** to go shopping

emplir [ãpliʀ] /2/ VT to fill ■ **s'emplir (de)** VPR to fill (with)

★**emploi** [ãplwa] NM use; (poste) job, situation; **l'~** (Comm, Écon) employment; **d'~ facile** easy to use; **le plein ~** full employment; **mode d'~** directions for use; **~ du temps** timetable, schedule

emploie etc [ãplwa] VB voir **employer**

employé, e [ãplwaje] NM/F employee; **~ de bureau/banque** office/bank employee ou clerk; **~ de maison** domestic (servant)

★**employer** [ãplwaje] /8/ VT (outil, moyen, méthode, mot) to use; (ouvrier, main-d'œuvre) to employ; **s'~ à qch/à faire** to apply ou devote o.s. to sth/to doing

employeur, -euse [ãplwajœʀ, -øz] NM/F employer

empocher [ãpɔʃe] /1/ VT to pocket

empoignade [ãpwaɲad] NF row, set-to

empoigne [ãpwaɲ] NF: **foire d'~** free-for-all

empoigner [ãpwaɲe] /1/ VT to grab ■ **s'empoigner** VPR (fig) to have a row ou set-to

empois [ãpwa] NM starch

empoisonné, e [ãpwazɔne] ADJ (nourriture, vin) poisoned; (fig): **un cadeau ~** a poisoned chalice; **des flèches empoisonnées** poisoned arrows

empoisonnement [ãpwazɔnmã] NM poisoning

empoisonner [ãpwazɔne] /1/ VT to poison; (empester: air, pièce) to stink out; (fam): **~ qn** to drive sb mad; **~ l'atmosphère** (aussi fig) to poison the atmosphere; **il nous empoisonne l'existence** he's the bane of our life ■ **s'empoisonner** VPR to poison o.s.

empoissonner [ãpwasɔne] /1/ VT (étang, rivière) to stock with fish

emporté, e [ãpɔʀte] ADJ (personne, caractère) fiery

emportement [ãpɔʀtəmã] NM fit of rage, anger no pl

emporte-pièce [ãpɔʀtəpjɛs] NM INV (Tech) punch; **à l'~** adj (fig) incisive

★**emporter** [ãpɔʀte] /1/ VT to take (with one); (emmener: blessés, voyageurs) to take away; (entraîner) to carry away ou along; (arracher) to tear off; (rivière, vent) to carry away; (Mil: position) to take; (avantage, approbation) to win; **la maladie qui l'a emporté** the illness which caused his death; **l'~** to gain victory; **l'~ (sur)** to get the upper hand (of); (méthode etc) to prevail (over); **boissons à ~** take-away drinks; **plats à ~** take-away meals ■ **s'emporter** VPR to fly into a rage, lose one's temper

empoté, e [ãpɔte] ADJ (maladroit) clumsy

empourpré, e [ãpuʀpʀe] ADJ crimson

empreint, e [ãpʀɛ̃, -ɛ̃t] ADJ: **~ de** marked with; tinged with ▸ NF (marque) print; (: de pied) footprint; (: de main) handprint; (fig) stamp, mark; **des empreintes de pas** footprints; **empreintes digitales** fingerprints; **empreinte écologique** carbon footprint

empressé, e [ãpʀese] ADJ attentive

empressement [ãpʀɛsmã] NM eagerness

empresser [ãpʀese] /1/: **s'empresser** VPR: **s'~ auprès de qn** to surround sb with attentions; **s'~ de faire** to hasten to do

emprise [ãpʀiz] NF hold, ascendancy; **sous l'~ de** under the influence of

emprisonnement [ãpʀizɔnmã] NM imprisonment

emprisonner [ãpʀizɔne] /1/ VT to imprison, jail

emprunt [ãpʀœ̃] NM borrowing no pl, loan (from debtor's point of view); (Ling etc) borrowing; **nom d'~** assumed name; **~ d'État** government ou state loan; **~ public à 5%** 5% public loan

emprunté, e [ãpʀœ̃te] ADJ (fig) ill-at-ease, awkward

★**emprunter** [ãpʀœ̃te] /1/ VT to borrow; (itinéraire) to take, follow; (style, manière) to adopt, assume

emprunteur, -euse [ãpʀœ̃tœʀ, -øz] NM/F borrower

empuantir [ãpɥãtiʀ] /2/ VT to stink out

ému, e [emy] PP de **émouvoir** ▸ ADJ excited; (gratitude) touched; (compassion) moved

émulation [emylasjɔ̃] NF emulation

émule [emyl] NMF imitator

émulsion [emylsjɔ̃] NF emulsion; (cosmétique) (water-based) lotion

émut etc [emy] VB voir **émouvoir**

EN SIGLE F = **l'Éducation (nationale)**; voir **éducation**

---

en [ã]

PRÉP **1** (endroit, pays) in; (: direction) to; **habiter en France/ville** to live in France/town; **aller en France/ville** to go to France/town

2 (moment, temps) in; **en été/juin** in summer/June; **en 3 jours/20 ans** in 3 days/20 years

3 (moyen) by; **en avion/taxi** by plane/taxi

4 (composition) made of; **c'est en verre/coton/laine** it's (made of) glass/cotton/wool; **en métal/plastique** made of metal/plastic; **un collier en argent** a silver necklace; **en deux volumes/une pièce** in two volumes/one piece

5 (description: état): **une femme (habillée) en rouge** a woman (dressed) in red; **peindre qch en rouge** to paint sth red; **en T/étoile** T-/star-shaped; **en chemise/chaussettes** in one's shirt sleeves/socks; **en soldat** as a soldier; **en civil** in civilian clothes; **cassé en plusieurs morceaux** broken into several pieces; **en réparation** being repaired, under repair; **en vacances** on holiday; **en bonne santé** healthy, in good health; **en deuil** in mourning; **le même en plus grand** the same but ou only bigger

6 (avec gérondif) while; on; **en dormant** while sleeping, as one sleeps; **en sortant** on going out, as he etc went out; **sortir en courant** to run out; **en apprenant la nouvelle, il s'est évanoui** he fainted at the news ou when he heard the news

7 (matière): **fort en math** good at maths; **expert en** expert in

8 (conformité): **en tant que** as; **en bon politicien, il ... ** good politician that he is, he ..., like a good ou true politician, he ...; **je te parle en ami** I'm talking to you as a friend

▸ PRON **1** (indéfini): **j'en ai/veux** I have/want

some; **en as-tu?** have you got any?; **il n'y en a pas** there isn't *ou* aren't any; **je n'en veux pas** I don't want any; **j'en ai deux** I've got two; **combien y en a-t-il?** how many (of them) are there?; **j'en ai assez** I've got enough (of it *ou* them); (*j'en ai marre*) I've had enough; **où en étais-je?** where was I?

2 (*provenance*) from there; **j'en viens** I've come from there

3 (*cause*): **il en est malade/perd le sommeil** he is ill/can't sleep because of it

4 (*de la part de*): **elle en est aimée** she is loved by him (*ou* them *etc*)

5 (*complément de nom, d'adjectif, de verbe*): **j'en connais les dangers** I know its *ou* the dangers; **j'en suis fier/ai besoin** I am proud of it/need it; **il en est ainsi** *ou* **de même pour moi** it's the same for me, same here

ENA [ena] SIGLE F (= *École nationale d'administration*) *grande école for training civil servants*

énarque [enaʀk] NMF former ENA student

encablure [ãkablyʀ] NF (*Navig*) cable's length

encadrement [ãkadʀəmã] NM framing; training; (*de porte*) frame; **~ du crédit** credit restrictions

encadrer [ãkadʀe] /1/ VT (*tableau, image*) to frame; (*fig: entourer*) to surround; (*personnel, soldats etc*) to train; (*Comm: crédit*) to restrict

encadreur [ãkadʀœʀ] NM (picture) framer

encaisse [ãkɛs] NF cash in hand; **~ or/métallique** gold/gold and silver reserves

encaissé, e [ãkese] ADJ (*vallée*) steep-sided; (*rivière*) with steep banks

encaisser [ãkese] /1/ VT (*chèque*) to cash; (*argent*) to collect; (*fig: coup, défaite*) to take

encaisseur [ãkesœʀ] NM collector (*of debts etc*)

encan [ãkã]: **à l'~** *adv* by auction

encanailler [ãkanaje] /1/: **s'encanailler** VPR to become vulgar *ou* common; to mix with the riff-raff

encart [ãkaʀ] NM insert; **~ publicitaire** publicity insert

encarter [ãkaʀte] /1/ VT to insert

en-cas [ãka] NM INV snack

encastrable [ãkastʀabl] ADJ (*four, élément*) that can be built in

encastré, e [ãkastʀe] ADJ (*four, baignoire*) built-in

encastrer [ãkastʀe] /1/ VT: **~ qch dans** (*mur*) to embed sth in(to); (*boîtier*) to fit sth into **■ s'encastrer dans** VPR to fit into; (*heurter*) to crash into

encaustique [ãkɔstik] NF polish, wax

encaustiquer [ãkɔstike] /1/ VT to polish, wax

enceinte [ãsɛt] ADJ F: **~ (de six mois)** (six months) pregnant ▶ NF (*mur*) wall; (*espace*) enclosure; **~ (acoustique)** speaker

encens [ãsã] NM incense

encenser [ãsãse] /1/ VT to (in)cense; (*fig*) to praise to the skies

encensoir [ãsãswaʀ] NM thurible (BRIT), censer

encéphalogramme [ãsefalɔgʀam] NM encephalogram

encercler [ãsɛʀkle] /1/ VT to surround

enchaîné [ãʃene] NM (*Ciné*) link shot

enchaînement [ãʃɛnmã] NM (*fig*) linking

enchaîner [ãʃene] /1/ VT to chain up; (*mouvements, séquences*) to link (together) ▶ VI to carry on

enchanté, e [ãʃãte] ADJ (*ravi*) delighted; (*ensorcelé*) enchanted; **~ (de faire votre connaissance)** pleased to meet you, how do you do?

enchantement [ãʃãtmã] NM delight; (*magie*) enchantment; **comme par ~** as if by magic

enchanter [ãʃãte] /1/ VT to delight

enchanteur, -teresse [ãʃãtœʀ, -tʀɛs] ADJ enchanting

enchâsser [ãʃase] /1/ VT: **~ qch (dans)** to set sth (in)

enchère [ãʃɛʀ] NF bid; **faire une ~** to (make a) bid; **mettre/vendre aux enchères** to put up for (sale by)/sell by auction; **les enchères montent** the bids are rising; **faire monter les enchères** (*fig*) to raise the bidding

enchérir [ãʃeʀiʀ] /2/ VI: **~ sur qn** (*aux enchères, aussi fig*) to outbid sb

enchérisseur, -euse [ãʃeʀisœʀ, -øz] NM/F bidder

enchevêtré, e [ãʃ(ə)vetʀe] ADJ tangled, tangled up

enchevêtrement [ãʃ(ə)vetʀəmã] NM tangle

enchevêtrer [ãʃ(ə)vetʀe] /1/ VT to tangle (up)

enclave [ãklav] NF enclave

enclaver [ãklave] /1/ VT to enclose, hem in

enclencher [ãklãʃe] /1/ VT (*mécanisme*) to engage; (*fig: affaire*) to set in motion **■ s'enclencher** VPR to engage

enclin, e [ãklɛ̃, -in] ADJ: **~ à qch/à faire** inclined *ou* prone to sth/to do

enclore [ãklɔʀ] /45/ VT to enclose

enclos [ãklo] NM enclosure; (*clôture*) fence

enclume [ãklym] NF anvil

encoche [ãkɔʃ] NF notch

encoder [ãkɔde] /1/ VT to encode

encodeur [ãkɔdœʀ] NM encoder

encoignure [ãkɔɲyʀ] NF corner

encoller [ãkɔle] /1/ VT to paste

encolure [ãkɔlyʀ] NF (*tour de cou*) collar size; (*col, cou*) neck

encombrant, e [ãkɔ̃bʀã, -ãt] ADJ cumbersome, bulky

encombre [ãkɔ̃bʀ]: **sans ~** *adv* without mishap *ou* incident

encombré, e [ãkɔ̃bʀe] ADJ (*pièce, passage*) cluttered; (*lignes téléphoniques*) engaged; (*marché*) saturated

encombrement [ãkɔ̃bʀəmã] NM (*d'un lieu*) cluttering (up); (*d'un objet: dimensions*) bulk; **être pris dans un ~** to be stuck in a traffic jam

encombrer [ãkɔ̃bʀe] /1/ VT to clutter (up); (*gêner*) to hamper; **~ le passage** to block *ou* obstruct the way **■ s'encombrer de** VPR (*bagages etc*) to load *ou* burden o.s. with

encontre [ãkɔ̃tʀ]: **à l'~ de** *prép* against, counter to

encorbellement [ãkɔʀbɛlmã] NM: **fenêtre en ~** oriel window

encorder [ãkɔʀde] /1/ VT (*Alpinisme*) to rope up **■ s'encorder** VPR (*Alpinisme*) to rope up

155

---

encore [ãkɔʀ]

ADV **1** (*continuation*) still; **il y travaille encore** he's still working on it; **pas encore** not yet

2 (*de nouveau*) again; **j'irai encore demain** I'll go again tomorrow; **encore une fois** (*once*) again

3 (*en plus*) more; **encore un peu de viande?** a little more meat?; **encore un effort** one last effort; **encore deux jours** two more days

4 (*intensif*) even, still; **encore plus fort/mieux** even louder/better, louder/better still; **hier encore** even yesterday; **non seulement ..., mais encore ...** not only ..., but also ...; **encore!** (*insatisfaction*) not again!; **quoi encore?** what now?

5 (*restriction*) even so *ou* then, only; **encore pourrais-je le faire si ...** even so, I might be able to do it if ...; **si encore** if only; **encore que** *conj* although

---

encourageant, e [ãkuʀaʒã, -ãt] ADJ encouraging

encouragement [ãkuʀaʒmã] NM encouragement; (*récompense*) incentive

★**encourager** [ãkuʀaʒe] /**3**/ VT to encourage; **~ qn à faire qch** to encourage sb to do sth

encourir [ãkuʀiʀ] /**11**/ VT to incur

encrasser [ãkʀase] /**1**/ VT to foul up; (*Auto*) to soot up ▪ **s'encrasser** VPR (*tuyau, filtre*) to get fouled up; (*bougies d'allumage*) to get sooted up

encre [ãkʀ] NF ink; **~ de Chine** Indian ink; **~ indélébile** indelible ink; **~ sympathique** invisible ink

encrer [ãkʀe] /**1**/ VT to ink

encreur [ãkʀœʀ] ADJ M: **rouleau ~** inking roller

encrier [ãkʀije] NM inkwell

encroûter [ãkʀute] /**1**/: **s'encroûter** VPR (*fig*) to get into a rut, get set in one's ways

encyclique [ãsiklik] NF encyclical

encyclopédie [ãsiklɔpedi] NF encyclopaedia (*Brit*), encyclopedia (*US*)

encyclopédique [ãsiklɔpedik] ADJ encyclopaedic (*Brit*), encyclopedic (*US*)

endémique [ãdemik] ADJ endemic

endetté, e [ãdete] ADJ in debt; (*fig*): **très ~ envers qn** deeply indebted to sb

endettement [ãdetmã] NM debts *pl*

endetter [ãdete] /**1**/ VT to get into debt ▪ **s'endetter** VPR to get into debt

endeuiller [ãdœje] /**1**/ VT to plunge into mourning; **manifestation endeuillée par** event over which a tragic shadow was cast by

endiablé, e [ãdjable] ADJ furious; (*enfant*) boisterous

endiguer [ãdige] /**1**/ VT to dyke (up); (*fig*) to check, hold back

endimanché, e [ãdimãʃe] ADJ in one's Sunday best; **avoir l'air ~** to be all done up to the nines (*fam*)

endimancher [ãdimãʃe] /**1**/: **s'endimancher** VPR to put on one's Sunday best

endive [ãdiv] NF chicory *no pl*

endocrine [ãdɔkʀin] ADJ F: **glande ~** endocrine (gland)

endoctrinement [ãdɔktʀinmã] NM indoctrination

endoctriner [ãdɔktʀine] /**1**/ VT to indoctrinate

endolori, e [ãdɔlɔʀi] ADJ painful

★**endommager** [ãdɔmaʒe] /**3**/ VT to damage

endormant, e [ãdɔʀmã, -ãt] ADJ dull, boring

endormi, e [ãdɔʀmi] PP *de* **endormir** ▸ ADJ (*personne*) asleep; (*fig: indolent, lent*) sluggish; (*engourdi: main, pied*) numb

endormir [ãdɔʀmiʀ] /**16**/ VT to put to sleep; (*chaleur etc*) to send to sleep; (*Méd: dent, nerf*) to anaesthetize; (*fig: soupçons*) to allay ▪ **s'endormir** VPR to fall asleep, go to sleep

endoscope [ãdɔskɔp] NM (*Méd*) endoscope

endoscopie [ãdɔskɔpi] NF endoscopy

endosser [ãdose] /**1**/ VT (*responsabilité*) to take, shoulder; (*chèque*) to endorse; (*uniforme, tenue*) to put on, don

★**endroit** [ãdʀwa] NM place; (*localité*): **les gens de l'~** the local people; (*opposé à l'envers*) right side; **à cet ~** in this place; **à l'~** right side out; the right way up; (*vêtement*) the right way out; (*objet posé*) the right way round; **à l'~ de** *prép* regarding, with regard to; **par endroits** in places

enduire [ãdɥiʀ] /**38**/ VT to coat; **~ qch de** to coat sth with

enduit, e [ãdɥi, -it] PP *de* **enduire** ▸ NM coating

endurance [ãdyʀãs] NF endurance

endurant, e [ãdyʀã, -ãt] ADJ tough, hardy

endurcir [ãdyʀsiʀ] /**2**/ VT (*physiquement*) to toughen; (*moralement*) to harden ▪ **s'endurcir** VPR (*physiquement*) to become tougher; (*moralement*) to become hardened

endurer [ãdyʀe] /**1**/ VT to endure, bear

énergétique [enɛʀʒetik] ADJ (*ressources etc*) energy *cpd*; (*aliment*) energizing

énergie [enɛʀʒi] NF (*Physique*) energy; (*Tech*) power; (*fig: physique*) energy; (: *morale*) vigour, spirit; **~ éolienne/solaire** wind/solar power

énergique [enɛʀʒik] ADJ energetic; vigorous; (*mesures*) drastic, stringent

énergiquement [enɛʀʒikmã] ADV energetically; drastically

énergisant, e [enɛʀʒizã, -ãt] ADJ energizing

énergumène [enɛʀgymɛn] NM rowdy character *ou* customer

énervant, e [enɛʀvã, -ãt] ADJ irritating, annoying

énervé, e [enɛʀve] ADJ nervy, on edge; (*agacé*) irritated

énervement [enɛʀvəmã] NM nerviness; irritation

énerver [enɛʀve] /**1**/ VT to irritate, annoy ▪ **s'énerver** VPR to get excited, get worked up

enfance [ãfãs] NF (*âge*) childhood; (*fig*) infancy; (*enfants*) children *pl*; **c'est l'~ de l'art** it's child's play; **petite ~** infancy; **souvenir/ami d'~** childhood memory/friend; **retomber en ~** to lapse into one's second childhood

★**enfant** [ãfã] NMF child; **~ adoptif/naturel** adopted/natural child; **bon ~** *adj* good-natured, easy-going; **~ de chœur** *nm* (*Rel*) altar boy; **~ prodige** child prodigy; **~ unique** only child

enfanter [ãfãte] /**1**/ VI to give birth ▸ VT to give birth to

enfantillage [ãfãtijaʒ] NM (*péj*) childish behaviour *no pl*

enfantin, e [ãfãtɛ̃, -in] ADJ childlike; (*péj*) childish; (*langage*) children's *cpd*

enfer [ãfɛʀ] NM hell; **allure/bruit d'~** horrendous speed/noise

★**enfermer** [ãfɛʀme] /**1**/ VT to shut up; (*à clef, interner*) to lock up ■ **s'enfermer** VPR to shut o.s. away; **s'~ à clé** to lock o.s. in; **s'~ dans la solitude/le mutisme** to retreat into solitude/silence

enferrer [ãfeʀe] /**1**/: **s'enferrer** VPR: **s'~ dans** to tangle o.s. up in

enfiévré, e [ãfjevʀe] ADJ (*fig*) feverish

enfilade [ãfilad] NF: **une ~ de** a series *ou* line of; **prendre les rues en ~** to cross directly from one street into the next

enfiler [ãfile] /**1**/ VT (*vêtement*) to slip on; (*rue, couloir*) to take; (*perles*) to string; (*aiguille*) to thread; (*insérer*): **~ qch dans** to stick sth into; **~ un tee-shirt** to slip into a T-shirt ■ **s'enfiler dans** VPR to disappear into

★**enfin** [ãfɛ̃] ADV at last; (*en énumérant*) lastly; (*de restriction, résignation*) still; (*eh bien*) well; (*pour conclure*) in a word; (*somme toute*) after all

enflammé, e [ãflame] ADJ (*torche, allumette*) burning; (*Méd: plaie*) inflamed; (*fig: nature, discours, déclaration*) fiery

enflammer [ãflame] /**1**/ VT to set fire to; (*Méd*) to inflame ■ **s'enflammer** VPR to catch fire; (*Méd*) to become inflamed

enflé, e [ãfle] ADJ swollen; (*péj: style*) bombastic, turgid

enfler [ãfle] /**1**/ VI to swell (up) ■ **s'enfler** VPR to swell

enflure [ãflyʀ] NF swelling

enfoncé, e [ãfɔ̃se] ADJ staved-in, smashed-in; (*yeux*) deep-set

enfoncement [ãfɔ̃smã] NM (*recoin*) nook

enfoncer [ãfɔ̃se] /**3**/ VT (*clou*) to drive in; (*faire pénétrer*): **~ qch dans** to push (*ou* drive) sth into; (*forcer: porte*) to break open; (: *plancher*) to cause to cave in; (*défoncer: côtes etc*) to smash; (*fam: surpasser*) to lick, beat (hollow); **~ un chapeau sur la tête** to cram *ou* jam a hat on one's head; **~ qn dans la dette** to drag sb into debt ■ **s'enfoncer** VPR to sink; (*sol, surface porteuse*) to give way; **s'~ dans** to sink into; (*forêt, ville*) to disappear into

enfouir [ãfwiʀ] /**2**/ VT (*dans le sol*) to bury; (*dans un tiroir etc*) to tuck away ■ **s'enfouir dans/sous** VPR to bury o.s. in/under

enfourcher [ãfuʀʃe] /**1**/ VT to mount; **~ son dada** (*fig*) to get on one's hobby-horse

enfourner [ãfuʀne] /**1**/ VT (*poterie*) to put in the oven, put in the kiln; **~ qch dans** to shove *ou* stuff sth into ■ **s'enfourner dans** VPR (*personne*) to dive into

enfreignais *etc* [ãfʀɛɲɛ] VB *voir* **enfreindre**

enfreindre [ãfʀɛ̃dʀ] /**52**/ VT to infringe, break

enfuir [ãfɥiʀ] /**17**/: **s'enfuir** VPR to run away *ou* off

enfumé, e [ãfyme] ADJ (*salon, bar*) smoky

enfumer [ãfyme] /**1**/ VT to smoke out

enfuyais *etc* [ãfɥijɛ] VB *voir* **enfuir**

engagé, e [ãgaʒe] ADJ (*littérature etc*) engagé, committed

engageant, e [ãgaʒã, -ãt] ADJ attractive, appealing

engagement [ãgaʒmã] NM taking on, engaging; starting; investing; (*promesse*) commitment; (*Mil: combat*) engagement; (: *recrutement*) enlistment; (*Sport*) entry; **prendre l'~ de faire** to undertake to do; **sans ~** (*Comm*) without obligation

engager [ãgaʒe] /**3**/ VT (*embaucher*) to take on; (: *artiste*) to engage; (*commencer*) to start; (*lier*) to bind, commit; (*impliquer, entraîner*) to involve; (*investir*) to invest, lay out; (*faire intervenir*) to engage; (*Sport: concurrents, chevaux*) to enter; (*introduire: clé*) to insert; (*inciter*): **~ qn à faire** to urge sb to do; (*faire pénétrer*): **~ qch dans** to insert sth into; **~ qn à qch** to urge sth on sb ■ **s'engager** VPR to get taken on; (*Mil*) to enlist; (*promettre, politiquement*) to commit o.s.; (*débuter: conversation etc*) to start (up); **s'~ à faire** to undertake to do; **s'~ dans** (*rue, passage*) to turn into, enter; (*s'emboîter*) to engage *ou* fit into; (*fig: affaire, discussion*) to enter into, embark on

engazonner [ãgazɔne] /**1**/ VT to turf

engeance [ãʒãs] NF mob

engelures [ãʒlyʀ] NFPL chilblains

engendrer [ãʒãdʀe] /**1**/ VT to father; (*fig*) to create, breed

engin [ãʒɛ̃] NM machine; (*outil*) instrument; (*Auto*) vehicle; (*péj*) gadget; (*Aviat: avion*) aircraft *inv*; (: *missile*) missile; **~ blindé** armoured vehicle; **~ (explosif)** (explosive) device; **engins (spéciaux)** missiles; **~ explosif improvisé** improvised explosive device

englober [ãglɔbe] /**1**/ VT to include

engloutir [ãglutiʀ] /**2**/ VT to swallow up; (*fig: dépenses*) to devour ■ **s'engloutir** VPR to be engulfed

englué, e [ãglye] ADJ sticky

engoncé, e [ãgɔ̃se] ADJ: **~ dans** cramped in

engorgement [ãgɔʀʒəmã] NM blocking; (*Méd*) engorgement

engorger [ãgɔʀʒe] /**3**/ VT to obstruct, block ■ **s'engorger** VPR to become blocked

engouement [ãgumã] NM (sudden) passion

engouffrer [ãgufʀe] /**1**/ VT to swallow up, devour ■ **s'engouffrer dans** VPR to rush into

engourdi, e [ãguʀdi] ADJ numb

engourdir [ãguʀdiʀ] /**2**/ VT to numb; (*fig*) to dull, blunt ■ **s'engourdir** VPR to go numb

engourdissement [ãguʀdismã] NM numbness

engrais [ãgʀɛ] NM manure; **~ (chimique)** (chemical) fertilizer; **~ organique/inorganique** organic/inorganic fertilizer

engraisser [ãgʀese] /**1**/ VT to fatten (up); (*terre: fertiliser*) to fertilize ► VI (*péj*) to get fat(ter)

engranger [ãgʀãʒe] /**3**/ VT (*foin*) to bring in; (*fig*) to store away

engrenage [ãgʀənaʒ] NM gears *pl*, gearing; (*fig*) chain

engueulade [ãgœlad] NF (*fam*) telling off

engueuler [ãgœle] /**1**/ VT (*fam*) to bawl at *ou* out

enguirlander [ãgiʀlãde] /**1**/ VT (*fam*) to give sb a bawling out, bawl at

enhardir [ãaʀdiʀ] /**2**/: **s'enhardir** VPR to grow bolder

énième [ɑ̃njɛm] ADJ = **nième**

énigmatique [enigmatik] ADJ enigmatic

énigmatiquement [enigmatikmɑ̃] ADV enigmatically

énigme [enigm] NF riddle

enivrant, e [ɑ̃nivrɑ̃, -ɑ̃t] ADJ intoxicating

enivrer [ɑ̃nivre] /**1**/: **s'enivrer** VPR to get drunk; **s'~ de** (fig) to become intoxicated with

enjambée [ɑ̃ʒɑ̃be] NF stride; **d'une ~** with one stride

enjambement [ɑ̃ʒɑ̃bmɑ̃] NM (en poésie) enjambement

enjamber [ɑ̃ʒɑ̃be] /**1**/ VT to stride over; (pont etc) to span, straddle

enjeu, x [ɑ̃ʒø] NM stakes pl

enjoindre [ɑ̃ʒwɛ̃dʀ] /**49**/ VT: **~ à qn de faire** to enjoin ou order sb to do

enjôler [ɑ̃ʒole] /**1**/ VT to coax, wheedle

enjôleur, -euse [ɑ̃ʒolœʀ, -øz] ADJ (sourire, paroles) winning

enjolivement [ɑ̃ʒɔlivmɑ̃] NM embellishment

enjoliver [ɑ̃ʒɔlive] /**1**/ VT to embellish

enjoliveur [ɑ̃ʒɔlivœʀ] NM (Auto) hub cap

enjoué, e [ɑ̃ʒwe] ADJ playful

enlacer [ɑ̃lɑse] /**3**/ VT (étreindre) to embrace, hug; (lianes) to wind round, entwine

enlaidir [ɑ̃ledir] /**2**/ VT to make ugly ▶ VI to become ugly

enlevé, e [ɑ̃l(ə)ve] ADJ (morceau de musique) played brightly

enlèvement [ɑ̃lɛvmɑ̃] NM removal; (rapt) abduction, kidnapping; **l'~ des ordures ménagères** refuse collection

★**enlever** [ɑ̃l(ə)ve] /**5**/ VT (ôter: gén) to remove; (: vêtement, lunettes) to take off; (: Méd: organe) to remove; (emporter: ordures etc) to collect, take away; (kidnapper) to abduct, kidnap; (obtenir: prix, contrat) to win; (Mil: position) to take; (morceau de piano etc) to execute with spirit ou brio; (prendre): **~ qch à qn** to take sth (away) from sb; **la maladie qui nous l'a enlevé** (euphémisme) the illness which took him from us ■ **s'enlever** VPR (tache) to come out ou off

enlisement [ɑ̃lizmɑ̃] NM getting stuck; (fig: de négociations, conflit) stalemate

enliser [ɑ̃lize] /**1**/: **s'enliser** VPR to sink, get stuck; (dialogue etc) to get bogged down

enluminure [ɑ̃lyminyʀ] NF illumination

ENM SIGLE F (= École nationale de la magistrature) grande école for law students

enneigé, e [ɑ̃neʒe] ADJ snowy; (fam) snowed-up; (maison) snowed-in

enneigement [ɑ̃nɛʒmɑ̃] NM depth of snow, snowfall; **bulletin d'~** snow report

★**ennemi, e** [ɛnmi] ADJ hostile; (Mil) enemy cpd; **être ~ de** to be strongly averse ou opposed to ▶ NM/F enemy

ennième [ɛnjɛm] ADJ = **nième**

ennoblir [ɑ̃nɔbliʀ] /**2**/ VT to ennoble

★**ennui** [ɑ̃nɥi] NM (lassitude) boredom; (difficulté) trouble no pl; **avoir des ennuis** to have problems; **s'attirer des ennuis** to cause problems for o.s.

ennuie etc [ɑ̃nɥi] VB voir **ennuyer**

ennuyé, e [ɑ̃nɥije] ADJ (air, personne) preoccupied, worried

★**ennuyer** [ɑ̃nɥije] /**8**/ VT to bother; (lasser) to bore ■ **s'ennuyer** VPR to be bored; (s'ennuyer de: regretter) to miss; **si cela ne vous ennuie pas** if it's no trouble to you

★**ennuyeux, -euse** [ɑ̃nɥijø, -øz] ADJ boring, tedious; (agaçant) annoying

énoncé [enɔ̃se] NM terms pl; wording; (Ling) utterance

énoncer [enɔ̃se] /**3**/ VT to say, express; (conditions) to set out, lay down, state

énonciation [enɔ̃sjasjɔ̃] NF statement

enorgueillir [ɑ̃nɔʀɡœjiʀ] /**2**/: **s'enorgueillir de** VPR to pride o.s. on; to boast

énorme [enɔʀm] ADJ enormous, huge

énormément [enɔʀmemɑ̃] ADV enormously, tremendously; **~ de neige/gens** an enormous amount of snow/number of people

énormité [enɔʀmite] NF enormity, hugeness; (propos) outrageous remark

en part. ABR (= en particulier) esp.

enquérir [ɑ̃keʀiʀ] /**21**/: **s'enquérir de** VPR to inquire about

enquête [ɑ̃kɛt] NF (de journaliste, de police) investigation; (judiciaire, administrative) inquiry; (sondage d'opinion) survey

enquêter [ɑ̃kete] /**1**/ VI to investigate; to hold an inquiry; (faire un sondage): **~ (sur)** to do a survey (on), carry out an opinion poll (on)

enquêteur, -euse, -trice [ɑ̃kɛtœʀ, -øz, -tʀis] NM/F officer in charge of an investigation; person conducting a survey; pollster

enquiers, enquière etc [ɑ̃kjɛʀ, ɑ̃kjɛʀ] VB voir **enquérir**

enquiquiner [ɑ̃kikine] /**1**/ VT to rile, irritate

enquiquineur, -euse [ɑ̃kikinœʀ, -øz] NM/F (fam) pain (fam)

enquis, e [ɑ̃ki, -iz] PP de **enquérir**

enraciné, e [ɑ̃ʀasine] ADJ deep-rooted

enragé, e [ɑ̃ʀaʒe] ADJ (Méd) rabid, with rabies; (furieux) furiously angry; (fig) fanatical; **~ de** wild about

enrageant, e [ɑ̃ʀaʒɑ̃, -ɑ̃t] ADJ infuriating

enrager [ɑ̃ʀaʒe] /**3**/ VI to be furious, be in a rage; **faire ~ qn** to make sb wild with anger

enrayer [ɑ̃ʀeje] /**8**/ VT to check, stop ■ **s'enrayer** VPR (arme à feu) to jam

enrégimenter [ɑ̃ʀeʒimɑ̃te] /**1**/ VT (péj) to enlist

enregistrement [ɑ̃ʀ(ə)ʒistʀəmɑ̃] NM recording; (Admin) registration; **~ des bagages** (à l'aéroport) baggage check-in; **~ magnétique** tape-recording

★**enregistrer** [ɑ̃ʀ(ə)ʒistʀe] /**1**/ VT (Mus) to record; (Inform) to save; (remarquer, noter) to note, record; (Comm: commande) to note, enter; (fig: mémoriser) to make a mental note of; (Admin) to register; (bagages: aussi: **faire enregistrer**: par train) to register; (: à l'aéroport) to check in

enregistreur, -euse [ɑ̃ʀ(ə)ʒistʀœʀ, -øz] ADJ (machine) recording cpd ▶ NM (appareil): **~ de vol** (Aviat) flight recorder

enrhumé, e [ɑ̃ʀyme] ADJ: **il est ~** he has a cold

enrhumer [ɑ̃ʀyme] /1/: **s'enrhumer** VPR to catch a cold

enrichi, e [ɑ̃ʀiʃi] ADJ (*personne*) rich; (*uranium*) enriched

enrichir [ɑ̃ʀiʃiʀ] /2/ VT to make rich(er); (*fig*) to enrich ▪ **s'enrichir** VPR to get rich(er)

enrichissant, e [ɑ̃ʀiʃisɑ̃, -ɑ̃t] ADJ instructive

enrichissement [ɑ̃ʀiʃismɑ̃] NM enrichment

enrobé, e [ɑ̃ʀɔbe] ADJ (*comprimé*) coated

enrober [ɑ̃ʀɔbe] /1/ VT: **~ qch de** to coat sth with; (*fig*) to wrap sth up in

enrôlement [ɑ̃ʀolmɑ̃] NM enlistment

enrôler [ɑ̃ʀole] /1/ VT to enlist ▪ **s'enrôler (dans)** VPR to enlist (in)

enroué, e [ɑ̃ʀwe] ADJ hoarse

enrouer [ɑ̃ʀwe] /1/: **s'enrouer** VPR to go hoarse

enrouler [ɑ̃ʀule] /1/ VT (*fil, corde*) to wind (up); **~ qch autour de** to wind sth (a)round ▪ **s'enrouler** VPR to coil up

enrouleur, -euse [ɑ̃ʀulœʀ, -øz] ADJ (*Tech*) winding ▶ NM *voir* **ceinture**

enrubanné, e [ɑ̃ʀybane] ADJ trimmed with ribbon

ENS SIGLE F = **école normale supérieure**

ensablement [ɑ̃sɑbləmɑ̃] NM (*de port, canal*) silting up; (*d'embarcation*) stranding

ensabler [ɑ̃sɑble] /1/ VT (*port, canal*) to silt up, sand up; (*embarcation*) to strand (on a sandbank) ▪ **s'ensabler** VPR to silt up; to get stranded

ensacher [ɑ̃saʃe] /1/ VT to pack into bags

ensanglanté, e [ɑ̃sɑ̃glɑ̃te] ADJ covered with blood

★**enseignant, e** [ɑ̃sɛɲɑ̃, -ɑ̃t] ADJ teaching ▶ NM/F teacher

enseigne [ɑ̃sɛɲ] NF sign; **à telle ~ que** so much so that; **être logés à la même ~** (*fig*) to be in the same boat; **~ lumineuse** neon sign ▶ NM: **~ de vaisseau** lieutenant

★**enseignement** [ɑ̃sɛɲ(ə)mɑ̃] NM teaching; (*Admin*) education; **~ ménager** home economics; **~ primaire** primary (BRIT) *ou* grade school (US) education; **~ secondaire** secondary (BRIT) *ou* high school (US) education

★**enseigner** [ɑ̃seɲe] /1/ VT, VI to teach; **~ qch à qn/à qn que** to teach sb sth/sb that

★**ensemble** [ɑ̃sɑ̃bl] ADV together; **aller ~** to go together ▶ NM (*assemblage, Math*) set; (*vêtements*) outfit; (*vêtement féminin*) ensemble, suit; (*unité, harmonie*) unity; (*résidentiel*) housing development; **l'~ du/de la** (*totalité*) the whole *ou* entire; **impression/idée d'~** overall *ou* general impression/idea; **dans l'~** (*en gros*) on the whole; **dans son ~** overall, in general; **~ vocal/musical** vocal/musical ensemble

ensemblier [ɑ̃sɑ̃blije] NM interior designer

ensemencement [ɑ̃s(ə)mɑ̃smɑ̃] NM sowing

ensemencer [ɑ̃s(ə)mɑ̃se] /3/ VT to sow

enserrer [ɑ̃seʀe] /1/ VT to hug (tightly)

ensevelir [ɑ̃səv(ə)liʀ] /2/ VT to bury

ensilage [ɑ̃silaʒ] NM (*aliment*) silage

ensoleillé, e [ɑ̃sɔleje] ADJ sunny

ensoleillement [ɑ̃sɔlɛjmɑ̃] NM period *ou* hours pl of sunshine

ensommeillé, e [ɑ̃sɔmeje] ADJ sleepy, drowsy

ensorcelant, e [ɑ̃sɔʀsɑlɑ̃, -ɑ̃t] ADJ (*regard, sourire*) bewitching

ensorceler [ɑ̃sɔʀsəle] /4/ VT to enchant, bewitch

★**ensuite** [ɑ̃sɥit] ADV then, next; (*plus tard*) afterwards, later; **~ de quoi** after which

ensuivre [ɑ̃sɥivʀ] /40/: **s'ensuivre** VPR to follow, ensue; **il s'ensuit que ...** it follows that ...; **et tout ce qui s'ensuit** and all that goes with it

ENT [œnte] SIGLE M (*Scol, Université*: = *espace numérique de travail*) VLE (= virtual learning environment)

entaché, e [ɑ̃taʃe] ADJ: **~ de** marred by; **~ de nullité** null and void

entacher [ɑ̃taʃe] /1/ VT to soil

entaille [ɑ̃taj] NF (*encoche*) notch; (*blessure*) cut; **se faire une ~** to cut o.s.

entailler [ɑ̃taje] /1/ VT to notch; to cut; **s'~ le doigt** to cut one's finger

entamer [ɑ̃tame] /1/ VT (*pain, bouteille*) to start; (*hostilités, pourparlers*) to open; (*fig: altérer*) to make a dent in; to damage

entartrer [ɑ̃taʀtʀe] /1/: **s'entartrer** VPR to fur up; (*dents*) to become covered with plaque

entassement [ɑ̃tɑsmɑ̃] NM (*tas*) pile, heap

entasser [ɑ̃tɑse] /1/ VT (*empiler*) to pile up, heap up; (*tenir à l'étroit*) to cram together ▪ **s'entasser** VPR (*s'amonceler*) to pile up; to cram; **s'~ dans** to cram into

entendant [ɑ̃tɑ̃dɑ̃] NM hearing person

entendement [ɑ̃tɑ̃dmɑ̃] NM understanding

entendeur [ɑ̃tɑ̃dœʀ] NM: **à bon ~, salut !** a word to the wise!

★**entendre** [ɑ̃tɑ̃dʀ] /41/ VT to hear; (*comprendre*) to understand; (*vouloir dire*) to mean; (*vouloir*): **~ être obéi/que** to intend *ou* mean to be obeyed/that; **j'ai entendu dire que** I've heard (it said) that; **je suis heureux de vous l'~ dire** I'm pleased to hear you say it; **~ parler de** to hear of; **laisser ~ que, donner à ~ que** to let it be understood that; **~ raison** to see sense, listen to reason; **qu'est-ce qu'il ne faut pas ~ !** whatever next!; **j'ai mal entendu** I didn't catch what was said; **je vous entends très mal** I can hardly hear you ▪ **s'entendre** VPR (*sympathiser*) to get on; (*se mettre d'accord*) to agree; **s'~ à qch/à faire** (*être compétent*) to be good at sth/doing; **ça s'entend** (*est audible*) it's audible; **je m'entends** I mean; **entendons-nous !** let's be clear what we mean

entendu, e [ɑ̃tɑ̃dy] PP *de* **entendre** ▶ ADJ (*réglé*) agreed; (*au courant: air*) knowing; **étant ~ que** since (it's understood *ou* agreed that); **(c'est)** ~ all right, agreed; **c'est ~** (*concession*) all right, granted; **bien ~** of course

entente [ɑ̃tɑ̃t] NF (*entre amis, pays*) understanding, harmony; (*accord, traité*) agreement, understanding; **à double ~** (*sens*) with a double meaning

entériner [ɑ̃teʀine] /1/ VT to ratify, confirm

entérite [ɑ̃teʀit] NF enteritis *no pl*

enterrement [ɑ̃teʀmɑ̃] NM burying; (*cérémonie*) funeral, burial; (*cortège funèbre*) funeral procession

enterrer [ɑ̃teʀe] /1/ VT to bury

entêtant, e [ɑ̃tɛtɑ̃, -ɑ̃t] ADJ heady

en-tête [ɑ̃tɛt] NM heading; (de papier à lettres) letterhead; **papier à ~** headed notepaper

entêté, e [ɑ̃tete] ADJ stubborn

entêtement [ɑ̃tɛtmɑ̃] NM stubbornness

entêter [ɑ̃tete] /1/: **s'entêter** VPR: **s'~ (à faire)** to persist (in doing)

enthousiasmant, e [ɑ̃tuzjasmɑ̃, -ɑ̃t] ADJ exciting

★**enthousiasme** [ɑ̃tuzjasm] NM enthusiasm; **avec ~** enthusiastically

enthousiasmé, e [ɑ̃tuzjasme] ADJ filled with enthusiasm

enthousiasmer [ɑ̃tuzjasme] /1/ VT to fill with enthusiasm ■ **s'enthousiasmer** VPR: **s'~ (pour qch)** to get enthusiastic (about sth)

enthousiaste [ɑ̃tuzjast] ADJ enthusiastic

enticher [ɑ̃tiʃe] /1/: **s'enticher de** VPR to become infatuated with

★**entier, -ière** [ɑ̃tje, -jɛʀ] ADJ (non entamé, en totalité) whole; (total, complet: satisfaction etc) complete; (fig: caractère) unbending, averse to compromise; **se donner tout ~ à qch** to devote o.s. completely to sth; **lait ~** full-cream milk; **nombre ~** whole number ▶ NM (Math) whole; **en ~** totally; in its entirety

entièrement [ɑ̃tjɛʀmɑ̃] ADV entirely, completely, wholly

entité [ɑ̃tite] NF entity

entomologie [ɑ̃tɔmɔlɔʒi] NF entomology

entomologique [ɑ̃tɔmɔlɔʒik] ADJ entomological

entomologiste [ɑ̃tɔmɔlɔʒist] NMF entomologist

entonner [ɑ̃tɔne] /1/ VT (chanson) to strike up

entonnoir [ɑ̃tɔnwaʀ] NM (ustensile) funnel; (trou) shell-hole, crater

entorse [ɑ̃tɔʀs] NF (Méd) sprain; (fig): **~ à la loi/au règlement** infringement of the law/rule; **se faire une ~ à la cheville/au poignet** to sprain one's ankle/wrist

entortiller [ɑ̃tɔʀtije] /1/ VT: **~ qch dans/avec** (envelopper) to wrap sth in/with ■ **s'entortiller** VPR: **s'~ dans** (draps) to roll o.s. up in; (réponses) to get tangled up in

entourage [ɑ̃tuʀaʒ] NM circle; (famille) family (circle); (d'une vedette etc) entourage; (ce qui enclôt) surround

entouré, e [ɑ̃tuʀe] ADJ (recherché, admiré) popular; **~ de** surrounded by

★**entourer** [ɑ̃tuʀe] /1/ VT to surround; (apporter son soutien à) to rally round; **~ de** to surround with; (trait) to encircle with ■ **s'entourer de** VPR to surround o.s. with; **s'~ de précautions** to take all possible precautions

entourloupe [ɑ̃tuʀlup], **entourloupette** [ɑ̃tuʀlupɛt] NF (fam) mean trick

entournures [ɑ̃tuʀnyʀ] NFPL: **gêné aux ~** in financial difficulties; (fig) a bit awkward

★**entracte** [ɑ̃tʀakt] NM interval

entraide [ɑ̃tʀɛd] NF mutual aid ou assistance

entraider [ɑ̃tʀede] /1/: **s'entraider** VPR to help each other

entrailles [ɑ̃tʀaj] NFPL entrails; (humaines) bowels

entrain [ɑ̃tʀɛ̃] NM spirit; **avec ~** (répondre, travailler) energetically; **faire qch sans ~** to do sth half-heartedly ou without enthusiasm

entraînant, e [ɑ̃tʀɛnɑ̃, -ɑ̃t] ADJ (musique) stirring, rousing

entraînement [ɑ̃tʀɛnmɑ̃] NM training; (Tech): **~ à chaîne/galet** chain/wheel drive; **manquer d'~** to be unfit; **~ par ergots/friction** (Inform) tractor/friction feed

entraîner [ɑ̃tʀene] /1/ VT (tirer: wagons) to pull; (charrier) to carry ou drag along; (Tech) to drive; (emmener: personne) to take (off); (mener à l'assaut, influencer) to lead; (Sport) to train; (impliquer) to entail; (causer) to lead to, bring about; **~ qn à faire** (inciter) to lead sb to do ■ **s'entraîner** VPR (Sport) to train; **s'~ à qch/à faire** to train o.s. for sth/to do

entraîneur [ɑ̃tʀɛnœʀ] NMF (Sport) coach, trainer ▶ NM (Hippisme) trainer

entraîneuse [ɑ̃tʀɛnøz] NF (de bar) hostess

entrapercevoir [ɑ̃tʀapɛʀsəvwaʀ] /28/ VT to catch a glimpse of

entrave [ɑ̃tʀav] NF hindrance

entraver [ɑ̃tʀave] /1/ VT (circulation) to hold up; (action, progrès) to hinder, hamper

★**entre** [ɑ̃tʀ] PRÉP between; (parmi) among(st); **l'un d'~ eux/nous** one of them/us; **le meilleur d'~ eux/nous** the best of them/us; **ils préfèrent rester ~ eux** they prefer to keep to themselves; **~ autres (choses)** among other things; **~ nous, ...** between ourselves ..., between you and me ...; **ils se battent ~ eux** they are fighting among(st) themselves

entrebâillé, e [ɑ̃tʀəbaje] ADJ half-open, ajar

entrebâillement [ɑ̃tʀəbajmɑ̃] NM: **dans l'~ (de la porte)** in the half-open door

entrebâiller [ɑ̃tʀəbaje] /1/ VT to half open

entrechat [ɑ̃tʀəʃa] NM leap

entrechoquer [ɑ̃tʀəʃɔke] /1/: **s'entrechoquer** VPR to knock ou bang together

entrecôte [ɑ̃tʀəkot] NF entrecôte ou rib steak

entrecoupé, e [ɑ̃tʀəkupe] ADJ (paroles, voix) broken

entrecouper [ɑ̃tʀəkupe] /1/ VT: **~ qch de** to intersperse sth with; **~ un récit/voyage de** to interrupt a story/journey with ■ **s'entrecouper** VPR (traits, lignes) to cut across each other

entrecroiser [ɑ̃tʀəkʀwaze] /1/ VT to intertwine ■ **s'entrecroiser** VPR to intertwine

entrée [ɑ̃tʀe] NF entrance; (accès: au cinéma etc) admission; (billet: admission) ticket; (Culin) first course; (Comm: de marchandises) entry; (Inform) entry, input; **d'~** adv from the outset; **erreur d'~** input error; **«~ interdite»** "no admittance ou entry"; **~ des artistes** stage door; **~ en matière** introduction; **~ principale** main entrance; **~ en scène** entrance; **~ de service** service entrance ■ **entrées** NFPL: **avoir ses entrées chez** ou **auprès de** to be a welcome visitor to

entrefaites [ɑ̃tʀəfɛt]: **sur ces ~** adv at this juncture

entrefilet [ɑ̃tʀəfilɛ] NM (article) paragraph, short report

entregent [ɑ̃tʀəʒɑ̃] NM: **avoir de l'~** to have an easy manner

entrejambe [ɑ̃tʀəʒɑ̃b] NM crotch

entrelacement [ɑ̃tʀəlasmɑ̃] NM: **un ~ de ...** a network of ...

entrelacer [ɑ̃tʀəlase] /3/ VT to intertwine ■ **s'entrelacer** VPR to intertwine

entrelacs [ɑ̃tʀəla] NM tracery

entrelarder [ɑ̃tʀəlaʀde] /1/ VT to lard; (fig): **entrelardé de** interspersed with

entremêler [ɑ̃tʀəmele] /1/ VT: ~ **qch de** to (inter)mingle sth with

entremets [ɑ̃tʀəmɛ] NM (cream) dessert

entremetteur, -euse [ɑ̃tʀəmɛtœʀ, -øz] NM/F go-between

entremettre [ɑ̃tʀəmɛtʀ] /56/: **s'entremettre** VPR to intervene

entremise [ɑ̃tʀəmiz] NF intervention; **par l'~ de** through

entrepont [ɑ̃tʀəpɔ̃] NM steerage; **dans l'~** in steerage

entreposer [ɑ̃tʀəpoze] /1/ VT to store, put into storage

entrepôt [ɑ̃tʀəpo] NM warehouse

entreprenant, e [ɑ̃tʀəpʀənɑ̃, -ɑ̃t] VB voir **entreprendre** ▶ ADJ (actif) enterprising; (trop galant) forward

entreprendre [ɑ̃tʀəpʀɑ̃dʀ] /58/ VT (se lancer dans) to undertake; (commencer) to begin ou start (upon); (personne) to buttonhole; ~ **qn sur un sujet** to tackle sb on a subject; ~ **de faire** to undertake to do

entrepreneur, -euse [ɑ̃tʀəpʀənœʀ, -øz] NM/F: ~ **(en bâtiment)** (building) contractor; ~ **de pompes funèbres** funeral director, undertaker

entrepreneuriat [ɑ̃tʀəpʀənœʀja], **entreprenariat** [ɑ̃tʀəpʀənaʀja] NM entrepreneurship

entreprenne etc [ɑ̃tʀəpʀɛn] VB voir **entreprendre**

entrepris, e [ɑ̃tʀəpʀi, -iz] PP de **entreprendre** ▶ NF (société) company, business; (action) undertaking, venture; **en entreprise** in a company, for a company; **entreprise familiale** family business

★**entrer** [ɑ̃tʀe] /1/ VI to go (ou come) in, enter; ~ **dans** (gén) to enter; (pièce) to go (ou come) into, enter; (club) to join; (heurter) to run into; (partager: vues, craintes de qn) to share; (être une composante de) to go into; (faire partie de) to form part of; **faire ~ qch dans** to get sth into; ~ **au couvent** to enter a convent; ~ **à l'hôpital** to go into hospital; ~ **dans le système** (Inform) to log in; ~ **en fureur** to become angry; ~ **en ébullition** (fig) to come to the boil; ~ **en scène** to come on stage; **laisser ~ qn/qch** to let sb/sth in; **faire ~** (visiteur) to show in ▶ VT (Inform) to input, enter

> Entrer dans se traduit le plus souvent par **come into** ou **go into**, selon que le mouvement se rapproche ou s'éloigne de la personne qui parle.
> Le chat est entré dans la chambre où nous dormions.
> **The cat came into the room we were sleeping in**.
> Je les ai vus entrer dans la maison abandonnée. **I saw them go into the abandoned house**.
> En revanche, **come** et **go** peuvent être remplacés par d'autres verbes de mouvement si la formulation française décrit la façon d'entrer avec le gérondif (en …ant).
> Les enfants sont entrés en courant dans la classe. **The children ran into the classroom**.

entresol [ɑ̃tʀəsɔl] NM entresol, mezzanine

entre-temps [ɑ̃tʀətɑ̃] ADV meanwhile, (in the) meantime

entretenir [ɑ̃tʀət(ə)niʀ] /22/ VT to maintain; (amitié) to keep alive; (famille, maîtresse) to support, keep; ~ **qn (de)** to speak to sb (about); ~ **qn dans l'erreur** to let sb remain in ignorance ■ **s'entretenir (de)** VPR to converse (about)

entretenu, e [ɑ̃tʀət(ə)ny] PP de **entretenir** ▶ ADJ (femme) kept; **bien/mal ~** (maison, jardin) well/badly kept

★**entretien** [ɑ̃tʀətjɛ̃] NM maintenance; (discussion) discussion, talk; (pour un emploi) interview; **frais d'~** maintenance charges

entretiendrai [ɑ̃tʀətjɛ̃dʀe], **entretiens** etc [ɑ̃tʀətjɛ̃] VB voir **entretenir**

entretuer [ɑ̃tʀətɥe] /1/: **s'entretuer** VPR to kill one another

entreverrai [ɑ̃tʀ(ə)veʀe], **entrevit** etc [ɑ̃tʀəvi] VB voir **entrevoir**

entrevoir [ɑ̃tʀəvwaʀ] /30/ VT (à peine) to make out; (brièvement) to catch a glimpse of

entrevu, e [ɑ̃tʀəvy] PP de **entrevoir** ▶ NF meeting, (audience) interview

entrouvert, e [ɑ̃tʀuvɛʀ, -ɛʀt] PP de **entrouvrir** ▶ ADJ half-open

entrouvrir [ɑ̃tʀuvʀiʀ] /18/ VT to half open ■ **s'entrouvrir** VPR to half open

entuber [ɑ̃tybe] VT (fam): **se faire ~** to be had (fam)

énucléer [enyklee] VT (cellule) to enucleate

énumération [enymeʀasjɔ̃] NF enumeration

énumérer [enymeʀe] /6/ VT to list, enumerate

énurésie [enyʀezi] NF (Méd) enuresis

★**envahir** [ɑ̃vaiʀ] /2/ VT to invade; (inquiétude, peur) to come over

envahissant, e [ɑ̃vaisɑ̃, -ɑ̃t] ADJ (péj: personne) interfering, intrusive

envahissement [ɑ̃vaismɑ̃] NM invasion

envahisseur [ɑ̃vaisœʀ] NM (Mil) invader

envasement [ɑ̃nvazmɑ̃] NM silting up

envaser [ɑ̃vaze] /1/: **s'envaser** VPR to get bogged down (in the mud)

★**enveloppe** [ɑ̃v(ə)lɔp] NF (de lettre) envelope; (Tech) casing; outer layer; (crédits) budget; **mettre sous ~** to put in an envelope; ~ **autocollante** self-seal envelope; ~ **budgétaire** budget; ~ **à fenêtre** window envelope

enveloppé, e [ɑ̃vlɔpe] ADJ (grassouillet) well-padded, plump

★**envelopper** [ɑ̃v(ə)lɔpe] /1/ VT to wrap; (fig) to envelop, shroud; **s'~ dans un châle/une couverture** to wrap o.s. in a shawl/blanket

envenimer [ɑ̃v(ə)nime] /1/ VT to aggravate ■ **s'envenimer** VPR (plaie) to fester; (situation, relations) to worsen

envergure [ɑ̃vɛʀgyʀ] NF (d'un oiseau, avion) wingspan; (fig: étendue) scope; (: valeur) calibre

enverrai etc [ɑ̃vɛʀe] VB voir **envoyer**

★**envers** [ɑ̃vɛʀ] PRÉP towards; to; ~ **et contre tous** ou **tout** against all opposition ▶ NM other side; (d'une étoffe) wrong side; **à l'~** (verticalement) upside down; (pull) back to front; (vêtement) inside out

enviable [ɑ̃vjabl] ADJ enviable; **peu ~** unenviable

★**envie** [ɑ̃vi] NF (sentiment) envy; (souhait) desire, wish; (tache sur la peau) birthmark; (filet de peau) hangnail; **avoir ~ de** to feel like; (désir plus fort) to want; **avoir ~ de faire** to feel like doing; to want to do; **avoir ~ que** to wish that; **donner à qn l'~ de faire** to make sb want to do; **cette glace me fait ~** I fancy some of that ice cream

envier [ɑ̃vje] /**7**/ VT to envy; **~ qch à qn** to envy sb sth; **n'avoir rien à ~ à** to have no cause to be envious of

envieux, -euse [ɑ̃vjø, -øz] ADJ envious

★**environ** [ɑ̃virɔ̃] ADV: **~ 3 h/2 km, 3 h/2 km ~** (around) about 3 o'clock/2 km, 3 o'clock/2 km or so; voir aussi **environs**

environnant, e [ɑ̃virɔnɑ̃, -ɑ̃t] ADJ surrounding

★**environnement** [ɑ̃virɔnmɑ̃] NM environment

environnemental, e, -aux [ɑ̃virɔnmɑ̃tal, -o] ADJ environmental

environnementaliste [ɑ̃virɔnmɑ̃talist] NMF environmentalist

environner [ɑ̃virɔne] /**1**/ VT to surround

environs [ɑ̃virɔ̃] NMPL surroundings; **aux ~ de** around

envisageable [ɑ̃vizaʒabl] ADJ conceivable

envisager [ɑ̃vizaʒe] /**3**/ VT (examiner, considérer) to contemplate, view; (avoir en vue) to envisage; **~ de faire** to consider doing

envoi [ɑ̃vwa] NM sending; (paquet) parcel, consignment; **~ contre remboursement** (Comm) cash on delivery

envoie etc [ɑ̃vwa] VB voir **envoyer**

envol [ɑ̃vɔl] NM takeoff

envolée [ɑ̃vɔle] NF (fig) flight

envoler [ɑ̃vɔle] /**1**/: **s'envoler** VPR (oiseau) to fly away ou off; (avion) to take off; (papier, feuille) to blow away; (fig) to vanish (into thin air)

envoûtant, e [ɑ̃vutɑ̃, -ɑ̃t] ADJ enchanting

envoûtement [ɑ̃vutmɑ̃] NM bewitchment

envoûter [ɑ̃vute] /**1**/ VT to bewitch

envoyé, e [ɑ̃vwaje] NM/F (Pol) envoy; (Presse) correspondent; **~ spécial** special correspondent ▶ ADJ: **bien ~** (remarque, réponse) well-aimed

★**envoyer** [ɑ̃vwaje] /**8**/ VT to send; (lancer) to hurl, throw; **~ une gifle/un sourire à qn** to aim a blow/flash a smile at sb; **~ les couleurs** to run up the colours; **~ chercher** to send for; **~ par le fond** (bateau) to send to the bottom; **~ promener qn** (fam) to send sb packing; **~ un SMS à qn** to text sb

envoyeur, -euse [ɑ̃vwajœʀ, -øz] NM/F sender

enzyme [ɑ̃zim] NM OU F enzyme

éolien, ne [eɔljɛ̃, -ɛn] ADJ wind cpd; **pompe éolienne** ▶ NF wind turbine

EOR SIGLE M (= élève officier de réserve) ≈ military cadet

éosine [eozin] NF eosin (antiseptic used in France to treat skin ailments)

épagneul, e [epaɲœl] NM/F spaniel

épais, se [epɛ, -ɛs] ADJ thick

épaisseur [epɛsœʀ] NF thickness

épaissir [epesiʀ] /**2**/ VT to thicken ■ **s'épaissir** VPR to thicken

épaississant [epesisɑ̃] NM thickener

épaississement [epesismɑ̃] NM thickening

épanchement [epɑ̃ʃmɑ̃] NM: **un ~ de synovie** water on the knee ■ **épanchements** NMPL (fig) (sentimental) outpourings

épancher [epɑ̃ʃe] /**1**/ VT to give vent to ■ **s'épancher** VPR to open one's heart; (liquide) to pour out

épandage [epɑ̃daʒ] NM manure spreading

épanoui, e [epanwi] ADJ (éclos, ouvert, développé) blooming; (radieux) radiant

épanouir [epanwiʀ] /**2**/: **s'épanouir** VPR (fleur) to bloom, open out; (visage) to light up; (fig: se développer) to blossom (out); (: mentalement) to open up

épanouissement [epanwismɑ̃] NM blossoming; opening up

épargnant, e [epaʀɲɑ̃, -ɑ̃t] NM/F saver, investor

épargne [epaʀɲ] NF saving; **l'épargne-logement** property investment

épargner [epaʀɲe] /**1**/ VT to save; (ne pas tuer ou endommager) to spare; **~ qch à qn** to spare sb sth ▶ VI to save

éparpillement [epaʀpijmɑ̃] NM (de papier) scattering; (des efforts) dissipation

éparpiller [epaʀpije] /**1**/ VT to scatter; (pour répartir) to disperse; (fig: efforts) to dissipate ■ **s'éparpiller** VPR to scatter; (fig) to dissipate one's efforts

épars, e [epaʀ, -aʀs] ADJ (maisons) scattered; (cheveux) sparse

épatant, e [epatɑ̃, -ɑ̃t] ADJ (fam) super, splendid

épaté, e [epate] ADJ: **nez ~** flat nose (with wide nostrils)

épater [epate] /**1**/ VT (fam) to amaze; (: impressionner) to impress

épaule [epol] NF shoulder

épaulé-jeté [epoleʒ(ə)te] (pl **épaulés-jetés**) NM (Sport) clean-and-jerk

épaulement [epolmɑ̃] NM escarpment; (mur) retaining wall

épauler [epole] /**1**/ VT (aider) to back up, support; (arme) to raise (to one's shoulder) ▶ VI to (take) aim

épaulette [epolɛt] NF (Mil, d'un veston) epaulette; (de combinaison) shoulder strap

épave [epav] NF wreck

épeautre [epotʀ] NM spelt

épée [epe] NF sword

épeler [ep(ə)le] /**4**/ VT to spell

épépiner [epepine] VT to take the seeds out of

éperdu, e [epɛʀdy] ADJ (personne) overcome; (sentiment) passionate; (fuite) frantic

éperdument [epɛʀdymɑ̃] ADV (aimer) wildly; **~ amoureux (de)** hopelessly in love (with)

éperlan [epɛʀlɑ̃] NM (Zool) smelt

éperon [epʀɔ̃] NM spur

éperonner [epʀɔne] /**1**/ VT to spur (on); (navire) to ram

épervier [epɛʀvje] NM (Zool) sparrowhawk; (Pêche) casting net

éphèbe [efɛb] NM beautiful young man

éphémère [efemɛʀ] ADJ ephemeral, fleeting

éphéméride [efemeʀid] NF block ou tear-off calendar

épi [epi] NM (de blé, d'orge) ear; (de maïs) cob; **~ de cheveux** tuft of hair; **stationnement/se garer en ~** parking/to park at an angle to the kerb

épice [epis] NF spice

épicé, e [epise] ADJ highly spiced, spicy; (fig) spicy

épicéa [episea] NM spruce

épicentre [episātʀ] NM epicentre

épicer [epise] /3/ VT to spice; (fig) to add spice to

épicerie [episʀi] NF (magasin) grocer's shop; (denrées) groceries pl; **~ fine** delicatessen (shop)

épicier, -ière [episje, -jɛʀ] NM/F grocer

épicurien, ne [epikyʀjɛ̃, -ɛn] ADJ epicurean

épicurisme [epikyʀism] NM (hédonisme) Epicureanism

épidémie [epidemi] NF epidemic

épidémiologie [epidemjɔlɔʒi] NF epidemiology

épidémiologique [epidemjɔlɔʒik] ADJ epidemiological

épidémiologiste [epidemjɔlɔʒist] NMF epidemiologist

épidémique [epidemik] ADJ epidemic

épiderme [epidɛʀm] NM skin, epidermis

épidermique [epidɛʀmik] ADJ skin cpd, epidermic

épier [epje] /7/ VT to spy on, watch closely; (occasion) to look out for

épieu, x [epjø] NM (hunting-)spear

épigramme [epigʀam] NF epigram

épigraphe [epigʀaf] NF epigraph

épilation [epilasjɔ̃] NF removal of unwanted hair

épilatoire [epilatwaʀ] ADJ depilatory, hair-removing

épilepsie [epilɛpsi] NF epilepsy

épileptique [epilɛptik] ADJ, NMF epileptic

épiler [epile] /1/ VT (jambes) to remove the hair from; (sourcils) to pluck; **s'~ les jambes** to remove the hair from one's legs; **s'~ les sourcils** to pluck one's eyebrows; **se faire ~** to get unwanted hair removed; **crème à ~** hair-removing ou depilatory cream; **pince à ~** eyebrow tweezers

épilogue [epilɔg] NM (fig) conclusion, dénouement

épiloguer [epilɔge] /1/ VI: **~ sur** to hold forth on

épinards [epinaʀ] NMPL spinach sg

épine [epin] NF thorn, prickle; (d'oursin etc) spine, prickle; **~ dorsale** backbone

épinette [epinɛt] NF (petit clavecin) spinet

épineux, -euse [epinø, -øz] ADJ thorny, prickly

épinglage [epɛ̃glaʒ] NM pinning

épingle [epɛ̃gl] NF pin; **tirer son ~ du jeu** to play one's game well; **tiré à quatre épingles** well turned-out; **monter qch en ~** to build sth up, make a thing of sth (fam); **~ à chapeau** hatpin; **~ à cheveux** hairpin; **virage en ~ à cheveux** hairpin bend; **~ de cravate** tie pin; **~ de nourrice** ou **de sûreté** ou **double** safety pin, nappy (BRIT) ou diaper (US) pin

épingler [epɛ̃gle] /1/ VT (badge, décoration): **~ qch sur** to pin sth on(to); (Couture: tissu, robe) to pin together; (fam) to catch, nick

épinière [epinjɛʀ] ADJ F voir **moelle**

épinoche [epinɔʃ] NF stickleback

Épiphanie [epifani] NF Epiphany

épiphénomène [epifenɔmɛn] NM epiphenomenon, by-product

épique [epik] ADJ epic

épiscopal, e, -aux [episkɔpal, -o] ADJ episcopal

épiscopat [episkɔpa] NM bishopric, episcopate

épisiotomie [epizjɔtɔmi] NF (Méd) episiotomy

épisode [epizɔd] NM episode; **film/roman à épisodes** serialized film/novel, serial

épisodique [epizɔdik] ADJ occasional; **mémoire ~** (Science) episodic memory

épisodiquement [epizɔdikmã] ADV occasionally

épissure [episyʀ] NF splice

épistémologie [epistemɔlɔʒi] NF epistemology

épistémologique [epistemɔlɔʒik] ADJ epistemological

épistolaire [epistɔlɛʀ] ADJ epistolary; **être en relations épistolaires avec qn** to correspond with sb

épitaphe [epitaf] NF epitaph

épithète [epitɛt] NF (nom, surnom) epithet; **adjectif ~** attributive adjective

épître [epitʀ] NF epistle

épizootie [epizɔɔti, -epizooti] NF epizootic, epizootic disease

éploré, e [eplɔʀe] ADJ in tears, tearful

épluchage [eplyʃaʒ] NM peeling; (de dossier etc) careful reading ou analysis

épluche-légumes [eplyʃlegym] NM INV potato peeler

éplucher [eplyʃe] /1/ VT (fruit, légumes) to peel; (comptes, dossier) to go over with a fine-tooth comb

éplucheur [eplyʃœʀ] NM (automatic) peeler

épluchures [eplyʃyʀ] NFPL peelings

épointer [epwɛ̃te] /1/ VT to blunt

éponge [epɔ̃ʒ] NF sponge; **passer l'~ (sur)** (fig) to let bygones be bygones (with regard to); **jeter l'~** (fig) to throw in the towel; **~ métallique** scourer

éponger [epɔ̃ʒe] /3/ VT (liquide) to mop ou sponge up; (surface) to sponge; (fig: déficit) to soak up, absorb; **s'~ le front** to mop one's brow

éponyme [epɔnim] ADJ (rôle) eponymous

épopée [epɔpe] NF epic

époque [epɔk] NF (de l'histoire) age, era; (de l'année, la vie) time; **d'~** adj (meuble) period cpd; **à cette ~** at this (ou that) time ou period; **faire ~** to make history

épouiller [epuje] /1/ VT to pick lice off; (avec un produit) to delouse

époumoner [epumɔne] /1/: **s'époumoner** VPR to shout (ou sing) o.s. hoarse

épouse [epuz] NF wife

épouser [epuze] /1/ VT to marry; (fig: idées) to espouse; (: forme) to fit

époussetage [epustaʒ] NM dusting

épousseter [epuste] /4/ VT to dust

époustouflant, e [epustuflã, -ãt] ADJ staggering, mind-boggling

époustoufler [epustufle] /1/ VT to flabbergast, astound

épouvantable [epuvɑ̃tabl] ADJ appalling, dreadful

épouvantablement [epuvɑ̃tabləmɑ̃] ADV terribly, dreadfully

épouvantail [epuvɑ̃taj] NM (à moineaux) scarecrow; (fig) bog(e)y; bugbear

épouvante [epuvɑ̃t] NF terror; **film d'~** horror film

épouvanter [epuvɑ̃te] /1/ VT to terrify

époux [epu] NM husband ▶ NMPL: **les ~** the (married) couple, the husband and wife

éprendre [eprɑ̃dr] /58/: **s'éprendre de** VPR to fall in love with

épreuve [eprœv] NF (d'examen) test; (malheur, difficulté) trial, ordeal; (Photo) print; (Typo) proof; (Sport) event; **à l'~ des balles/du feu** (vêtement) bulletproof/fireproof; **à toute ~** unfailing; **mettre à l'~** to put to the test; **~ de force** trial of strength; (fig) showdown; **~ de résistance** test of resistance; **~ de sélection** (Sport) heat

épris, e [epri, -iz] VB voir **éprendre** ▶ ADJ: **~ de** in love with

éprouvant, e [epruvɑ̃, -ɑ̃t] ADJ trying

éprouvé, e [epruve] ADJ tested, proven

éprouver [epruve] /1/ VT (tester) to test; (mettre à l'épreuve) to put to the test; (marquer, faire souffrir) to afflict, distress; (ressentir) to experience

éprouvette [epruvet] NF test tube

★**EPS** SIGLE F (= Éducation physique et sportive) ≈ PE

épuisant, e [epɥizɑ̃, -ɑ̃t] ADJ exhausting

épuisé, e [epɥize] ADJ exhausted; (livre) out of print

épuisement [epɥizmɑ̃] NM exhaustion; **jusqu'à ~ des stocks** while stocks last

épuiser [epɥize] /1/ VT (fatiguer) to exhaust, wear ou tire out; (stock, sujet) to exhaust ■ **s'épuiser** VPR to wear ou tire o.s. out, exhaust o.s.; (stock) to run out

épuisette [epɥizet] NF landing net; shrimping net

épuration [epyrasjɔ̃] NF purification; purging; refinement

épure [epyr] NF working drawing

épurer [epyre] /1/ VT (liquide) to purify; (parti, administration) to purge; (langue, texte) to refine

équarrir [ekarir] /2/ VT (pierre, arbre) to square (off); (animal) to quarter

équarrissage [ekarisaʒ] NM (d'animal) quartering; (de pierre, tronc) squaring off

équateur [ekwatœr] NM equator; **(la république de) l'É~** Ecuador

équation [ekwasjɔ̃] NF equation; **mettre en ~** to equate; **~ du premier/second degré** simple/quadratic equation

équatorial, e, -aux [ekwatɔrjal, -o] ADJ equatorial

équatorien, ne [ekwatɔrjɛ̃, -ɛn] ADJ Ecuadorian ▶ NM/F: **Équatorien, ne** Ecuadorian

équerre [eker] NF (à dessin) (set) square; (pour fixer) brace; **en ~** at right angles; **à l'~, d'~** straight; **double ~** T-square

équestre [ekestr] ADJ equestrian

équeuter [ekøte] /1/ VT (Culin) to remove the stalk(s) from

équidé [ekide] NM (Zool) member of the horse family

équidistance [ekɥidistɑ̃s] NF: **à ~ (de)** equidistant (from)

équidistant, e [ekɥidistɑ̃, -ɑ̃t] ADJ: **~ (de)** equidistant (from)

équilatéral, e, -aux [ekɥilateral, -o] ADJ equilateral

équilibrage [ekilibraʒ] NM (Auto): **~ des roues** wheel balancing

équilibre [ekilibr] NM balance; (d'une balance) equilibrium; **~ budgétaire** balanced budget; **garder/perdre l'~** to keep/lose one's balance; **être en ~** to be balanced; **mettre en ~** to make steady; **avoir le sens de l'~** to be well-balanced

équilibré, e [ekilibre] ADJ (fig) well-balanced, stable

équilibrer [ekilibre] /1/ VT to balance ■ **s'équilibrer** VPR (poids) to balance; (fig: défauts etc) to balance each other out

équilibriste [ekilibrist] NMF tightrope walker

équinoxe [ekinɔks] NM equinox

équipage [ekipaʒ] NM crew; **en grand ~** in great array

équipe [ekip] NF team; (bande: parfois péj) bunch; **travailler par équipes** to work in shifts; **travailler en ~** to work as a team; **faire ~ avec** to team up with; **~ de chercheurs** research team; **~ de secours** ou **de sauvetage** rescue team

équipé, e [ekipe] ADJ (cuisine etc) equipped, fitted(-out); **bien/mal ~** well-/poorly-equipped ▶ NF escapade

équipement [ekipmɑ̃] NM equipment; **biens/dépenses d'~** capital goods/expenditure; **ministère de l'É~** department of public works ■ **équipements** NMPL amenities, facilities; installations; **équipements sportifs/collectifs** sports/community facilities ou resources

équiper [ekipe] /1/ VT to equip; (voiture, cuisine) to equip, fit out; **~ qn/qch de** to equip sb/sth with ■ **s'équiper** VPR (sportif) to equip o.s., kit o.s. out

équipier, -ière [ekipje, -jɛr] NM/F team member

équitable [ekitabl] ADJ fair

équitablement [ekitabləmɑ̃] ADV fairly, equitably

équitation [ekitasjɔ̃] NF (horse-)riding; **faire de l'~** to go (horse-)riding

équité [ekite] NF equity

équivaille etc [ekivaj] VB voir **équivaloir**

équivalence [ekivalɑ̃s] NF equivalence

équivalent, e [ekivalɑ̃, -ɑ̃t] ADJ, NM equivalent

équivaloir [ekivalwar] /29/: **~ à** vt to be equivalent to; (représenter) to amount to

équivaut etc [ekivo] VB voir **équivaloir**

équivoque [ekivɔk] ADJ equivocal, ambiguous; (louche) dubious ▶ NF ambiguity

érable [erabl] NM maple

éradication [eradikasjɔ̃] NF eradication

éradiquer [eradike] /1/ VT to eradicate

érafler [erafle] /1/ VT to scratch; **s'~ la main/les jambes** to scrape ou scratch one's hand/legs

éraflure [eraflyr] NF scratch

éraillé, e [eraje] ADJ (voix) rasping, hoarse

ère [ɛʀ] NF era; **en l'an 1050 de notre ~** in the year 1050 A.D.

érectile [eʀɛktil] ADJ (organe, corps) erectile

érection [eʀɛksjɔ̃] NF erection

éreintant, e [eʀɛ̃tɑ̃, -ɑ̃t] ADJ exhausting

éreinté, e [eʀɛ̃te] ADJ exhausted

éreintement [eʀɛ̃tmɑ̃] NM exhaustion

éreinter [eʀɛ̃te] /1/ VT to exhaust, wear out; (fig: critiquer) to slate; **s'~ (à faire qch/à qch)** to wear o.s. out (doing sth/with sth)

ergonomie [ɛʀɡɔnɔmi] NF ergonomics sg

ergonomique [ɛʀɡɔnɔmik] ADJ ergonomic

ergot [ɛʀɡo] NM (de coq) spur; (Tech) lug

ergoter [ɛʀɡɔte] /1/ VI to split hairs, argue over details

ergoteur, -euse [ɛʀɡɔtœʀ, -øz] NM/F hairsplitter

ergothérapeute [ɛʀɡoteʀapøt] NM/F occupational therapist

ergothérapie [ɛʀɡoteʀapi] NF occupational therapy

ériger [eʀiʒe] /3/ VT (monument) to erect; **~ qch en principe/loi** to make sth a principle/law; **s'~ en critique (de)** to set o.s. up as a critic (of)

ermitage [ɛʀmitaʒ] NM retreat

ermite [ɛʀmit] NM hermit

éroder [eʀɔde] /1/ VT to erode

érogène [eʀɔʒɛn] ADJ erogenous

érosion [eʀozjɔ̃] NF erosion

érotique [eʀɔtik] ADJ erotic

érotiquement [eʀɔtikmɑ̃] ADV erotically

érotisme [eʀɔtism] NM eroticism

érotomane [eʀɔtɔman] NM/F erotomaniac

errance [eʀɑ̃s] NF wandering

errant, e [eʀɑ̃, -ɑ̃t] ADJ: **un chien ~** a stray dog

erratum [eʀatɔm] (pl **errata** [eʀata]) NM erratum

errements [eʀmɑ̃] NMPL misguided ways

errer [eʀe] /1/ VI to wander

★**erreur** [eʀœʀ] NF mistake, error; (Inform) error; **être dans l'~** to be wrong; **induire qn en ~** to mislead sb; **par ~** by mistake; **sauf ~** unless I'm mistaken; **faire ~** to be mistaken; **~ de date** mistake in the date; **~ de fait** error of fact; **~ d'impression** (Typo) misprint; **~ judiciaire** miscarriage of justice; **~ de jugement** error of judgment; **~ matérielle** ou **d'écriture** clerical error; **~ tactique** tactical error ■ **erreurs** NFPL (morale) errors

erroné, e [eʀɔne] ADJ wrong, erroneous

ersatz [ɛʀzats] NM substitute, ersatz; **~ de café** coffee substitute

éructer [eʀykte] /1/ VI to belch

érudit, e [eʀydi, -it] ADJ erudite, learned ▶ NM/F scholar

érudition [eʀydisjɔ̃] NF erudition, scholarship

éruptif, -ive [eʀyptif, -iv] ADJ eruptive

éruption [eʀypsjɔ̃] NF eruption; (cutanée) outbreak; (: boutons) rash; (fig: de joie, colère, folie) outburst

érythème [eʀitɛm] NM rash; **~ fessier** nappy rash

E/S ABR (= entrée/sortie) I/O (= in/out)

es [ɛ] VB voir **être**

ès [ɛs] PRÉP: **licencié ès lettres/sciences** ≈ Bachelor of Arts/Science; **docteur ès lettres** ≈ doctor of philosophy, ≈ PhD

ESB SIGLE F (= encéphalopathie spongiforme bovine) BSE

esbroufe [ɛsbʀuf] NF: **faire de l'~** to have people on

escabeau, x [ɛskabo] NM (tabouret) stool; (échelle) stepladder

escadre [ɛskadʀ] NF (Navig) squadron; (Aviat) wing

escadrille [ɛskadʀij] NF (Aviat) flight

escadron [ɛskadʀɔ̃] NM squadron

★**escalade** [ɛskalad] NF climbing no pl; (Pol etc) escalation

escalader [ɛskalade] /1/ VT to climb, scale

escalator [ɛskalatɔʀ] NM escalator

escale [ɛskal] NF (Navig: durée) call; (: port) port of call; (Aviat) stop(over); **faire ~ à** (Navig) to put in at, call in at; (Aviat) to stop over at; **~ technique** refuelling stop; **vol sans ~** nonstop flight

★**escalier** [ɛskalje] NM stairs pl; **dans l'~** ou **les escaliers** on the stairs; **descendre l'~** ou **les escaliers** to go downstairs; **~ mécanique** ou **roulant** escalator; **~ de secours** fire escape; **~ de service** backstairs; **~ à vis** ou **en colimaçon** spiral staircase

escalope [ɛskalɔp] NF escalope

escamotable [ɛskamɔtabl] ADJ (train d'atterrissage, antenne) retractable; (table, lit) fold-away

escamoter [ɛskamɔte] /1/ VT (esquiver) to get round, evade; (faire disparaître) to conjure away; (dérober: portefeuille etc) to snatch; (train d'atterrissage) to retract; (mots) to miss out

escampette [ɛskɑ̃pɛt] NF: **prendre la poudre d'~** to make off, do a bunk (fam)

escapade [ɛskapad] NF: **faire une ~** to go on a jaunt; (s'enfuir) to run away ou off

escarbille [ɛskaʀbij] NF bit of grit

escarcelle [ɛskaʀsɛl] NF: **faire tomber dans l'~** (argent) to bring in

★**escargot** [ɛskaʀɡo] NM snail

escarmouche [ɛskaʀmuʃ] NF (Mil) skirmish; (fig: propos hostiles) angry exchange

escarpé, e [ɛskaʀpe] ADJ steep

escarpement [ɛskaʀpəmɑ̃] NM steep slope

escarpin [ɛskaʀpɛ̃] NM flat(-heeled) shoe

escarpolette [ɛskaʀpɔlɛt] NF swing

escarre [ɛskaʀ] NF bedsore

Escaut [ɛsko] NM: **l'~** the Scheldt

eschatologique [ɛskatɔlɔʒik] ADJ eschatological

escient [esjɑ̃] NM: **à bon ~** advisedly

esclaffer [ɛsklafe] /1/: **s'esclaffer** VPR to guffaw

esclandre [ɛsklɑ̃dʀ] NM scene, fracas

esclavage [ɛsklavaʒ] NM slavery

esclavagiste [ɛsklavaʒist] ADJ pro-slavery ▶ NMF supporter of slavery

esclave [ɛsklav] NMF slave; **être ~ de** (fig) to be a slave of

escogriffe [ɛskɔɡʀif] NM (péj) beanpole

escompte [ɛskɔ̃t] NM discount

escompter [ɛskɔ̃te] /1/ VT (Comm) to discount; (espérer) to expect, reckon upon; **~ que** to reckon ou expect that

escorte [ɛskɔʀt] NF escort; **faire ~ à** to escort

escorter [ɛskɔʀte] /1/ VT to escort

escorteur [ɛskɔʀtœʀ] NM (Navig) escort (ship)

escouade [ɛskwad] NF squad; (fig: groupe de personnes) group

★**escrime** [ɛskʀim] NF fencing; **faire de l'~** to fence

escrimer [ɛskʀime] /1/: **s'escrimer** VPR: **s'~ à faire** to wear o.s. out doing

escrimeur, -euse [ɛskʀimœʀ, -øz] NM/F fencer

escroc [ɛskʀo] NM swindler, con-man

escroquer [ɛskʀɔke] /1/ VT: **~ qn (de qch)/qch à qn** to swindle sb (out of sth)/sth out of sb

escroquerie [ɛskʀɔkʀi] NF swindle

esgourdes [ɛzguʀd] NFPL (fam) lugs (BRIT fam)

ésotérique [ezɔteʀik] ADJ esoteric

ésotérisme [ezɔteʀism] NM (doctrine) esotericism; (caractère obscur) esoteric nature

★**espace** [ɛspas] NM space; **~ publicitaire** advertising space; **~ vital** living space

espacé, e [ɛspase] ADJ spaced out

espacement [ɛspasmɑ̃] NM: **~ proportionnel** proportional spacing (on printer)

espacer [ɛspase] /3/ VT to space out ■ **s'espacer** VPR (visites etc) to become less frequent

espadon [ɛspadɔ̃] NM swordfish inv

espadrille [ɛspadʀij] NF rope-soled sandal

★**Espagne** [ɛspaɲ] NF: **l'~** Spain

★**espagnol, e** [ɛspaɲɔl] ADJ Spanish ▶ NM (Ling) Spanish ▶ NM/F: **Espagnol, e** Spaniard

espagnolette [ɛspaɲɔlɛt] NF (window) catch; **fermé à l'~** resting on the catch

espalier [ɛspalje] NM (arbre fruitier) espalier

ESPE SIGLE F = **écoles supérieures du professorat et de l'éducation**

espèce [ɛspɛs] NF (Bio, Bot, Zool) species inv; (gén: sorte) sort, kind, type; (péj): **~ de maladroit/de brute !** you clumsy oaf/you brute!; **de toute ~** of all kinds ou sorts; **en l'~** adv in the case in point; **cas d'~** individual case; **l'~ humaine** mankind ■ **espèces** NFPL (Comm) cash sg; (Rel) species; **payer en espèces** to pay (in) cash

espérance [ɛspeʀɑ̃s] NF hope; **~ de vie** life expectancy

espéranto [ɛspeʀɑ̃to] NM Esperanto

espérer [ɛspeʀe] /6/ VT to hope for; **j'espère (bien)** I hope so; **~ que/faire** to hope that/to do; **~ en** to trust in

espiègle [ɛspjɛgl] ADJ mischievous

espièglerie [ɛspjɛgləʀi] NF mischievousness; (tour, farce) piece of mischief, prank

espion, ne [ɛspjɔ̃, -ɔn] NM/F spy; **avion ~** spy plane

espionnage [ɛspjɔnaʒ] NM espionage, spying; **film/roman d'~** spy film/novel

espionner [ɛspjɔne] /1/ VT to spy (up)on

esplanade [ɛsplanad] NF esplanade

★**espoir** [ɛspwaʀ] NM hope; **l'~ de qch/de faire qch** the hope of sth/of doing sth; **avoir bon ~** to have high hopes that ...; **garder l'~ que ...** to remain hopeful that ...; **dans l'~ de/que** in the hope of/that; **reprendre ~** not to lose hope; **un ~ de la boxe/du ski** one of boxing's/skiing's hope-

fuls, one of the hopes of boxing/skiing; **sans ~** adj hopeless

esprit [ɛspʀi] NM (pensée, intellect) mind; (humour, ironie) wit; (mentalité, d'une loi etc, fantôme etc) spirit; **l'~ d'équipe/de compétition** team/competitive spirit; **faire de l'~** to try to be witty; **reprendre ses esprits** to come to; **perdre l'~** to lose one's mind; **avoir bon/mauvais ~** to be of a good/bad disposition; **avoir l'~ à faire qch** to have a mind to do sth; **avoir l'~ critique** to be critical; **~ de contradiction** contrariness; **~ de corps** esprit de corps; **~ de famille** family loyalty; **l'~ malin** (le diable) the Evil One; **esprits chagrins** fault-finders

esquif [ɛskif] NM skiff

esquille [ɛskij] NF (fragment d'os) splinter

esquimau, de, x [ɛskimo, -od] ADJ Eskimo; **chien ~** husky ▶ NM (Ling) Eskimo; (glace): **E~®** ice lolly (BRIT), popsicle (US) ▶ NM/F: **Esquimau, de** Eskimo

esquinter [ɛskɛ̃te] /1/ (fam) VT to mess up ■ **s'esquinter** VPR: **s'~ à faire qch** to knock o.s. out doing sth

esquisse [ɛskis] NF sketch; **l'~ d'un sourire/changement** a hint of a smile/of change

esquisser [ɛskise] /1/ VT to sketch; **~ un sourire** to give a hint of a smile ■ **s'esquisser** VPR (amélioration) to begin to be detectable

esquive [ɛskiv] NF (Boxe) dodging; (fig) sidestepping

esquiver [ɛskive] /1/ VT to dodge ■ **s'esquiver** VPR to slip away

essai [ɛsɛ] NM trying; (tentative) attempt, try; (de produit) testing; (Rugby) try; (Littérature) essay; **à l'~** on a trial basis; **mettre à l'~** to put to the test; **~ gratuit** (Comm) free trial ■ **essais** NMPL (Auto) trials

essaim [ɛsɛ̃] NM swarm

essaimer [eseme] /1/ VI to swarm; (fig) to spread, expand

essayage [esejaʒ] NM (d'un vêtement) trying on, fitting; **salon d'~** fitting room; **cabine d'~** fitting room (cubicle)

★**essayer** [eseje] /8/ VT (gén) to try; (vêtement, chaussures) to try (on); (restaurant, méthode, voiture) to try (out); **~ de faire** to try ou attempt to do ▶ VI to try; **essayez un peu !** (menace) just you try! ■ **s'essayer à faire** VPR to try one's hand at doing

essayeur, -euse [esejœʀ, -øz] NM/F (chez un tailleur etc) fitter

essayiste [esejist] NMF essayist

ESSEC [esɛk] SIGLE F (= École supérieure des sciences économiques et sociales) grande école for management and business studies

★**essence** [esɑ̃s] NF (de voiture) petrol (BRIT), gas(oline) (US); (extrait de plante, Philosophie) essence; (espèce: d'arbre) species inv; **prendre de l'~** to get (some) petrol ou gas; **par ~** (essentiellement) essentially; **~ de citron/rose** lemon/rose oil; **~ sans plomb** unleaded petrol; **~ de térébenthine** turpentine

★**essentiel, le** [esɑ̃sjɛl] ADJ essential ▶ NM: **l'~ d'un discours/d'une œuvre** the essence of a speech/work of art; **emporter l'~** to take the essentials; **c'est l'~** (ce qui importe) that's the main thing; **l'~ de** (la majeure partie) the main part of

essentiellement [esɑ̃sjɛlmɑ̃] ADV essentially

esseulé, e [esœle] ADJ forlorn

essieu, x [esjø] NM axle

essor [esɔʀ] NM (de l'économie etc) rapid expansion; **prendre son ~** (oiseau) to fly off

essorage [esɔʀaʒ] NM wringing out; spin-drying; spinning; shaking

essorer [esɔʀe] /**1**/ VT (en tordant) to wring (out); (par la force centrifuge) to spin-dry; (salade) to spin; (: en secouant) to shake dry

essoreuse [esɔʀøz] NF mangle, wringer; (à tambour) spin-dryer

essoufflé, e [esufle] ADJ out of breath, breathless

essoufflement [esuflǝmɑ̃] NM (de personne) breathlessness; (ralentissement: de croissance, économie, activité) slowing, running out of steam; **l'~ de la croissance** the slowing of economic growth

essouffler [esufle] /**1**/ VT to make breathless ■ **s'essouffler** VPR to get out of breath; (fig: économie) to run out of steam

essuie etc [esɥi] VB voir **essuyer**

essuie-glace [esɥiglas] NM windscreen (BRIT) ou windshield (US) wiper

essuie-mains [esɥimɛ̃] NM hand towel

essuierai etc [esɥiʀe] VB voir **essuyer**

essuie-tout [esɥitu] NM INV kitchen paper

★**essuyer** [esɥije] /**8**/ VT to wipe; (fig: subir) to suffer; **~ la vaisselle** to dry up, dry the dishes ■ **s'essuyer** VPR (après le bain) to dry o.s.

★**est** VB [ɛ] voir **être** ▶ NM [ɛst]: **l'~** the east; **à l'~** in the east; (direction) to the east, east(wards); **à l'~ de** (to the) east of; **les pays de l'E~** the eastern countries ▶ ADJ INV [ɛst] east; (région) east(ern)

estafette [ɛstafɛt] NF (Mil) dispatch rider

estafilade [ɛstafilad] NF gash, slash

est-allemand, e [ɛstalmɑ̃, -ɑ̃d] ADJ East German

estaminet [ɛstaminɛ] NM tavern

estampe [ɛstɑ̃p] NF print, engraving

estamper [ɛstɑ̃pe] /**1**/ VT (monnaies etc) to stamp; (fam: escroquer) to swindle

estampille [ɛstɑ̃pij] NF stamp

★**est-ce que** [ɛskǝ] ADV: **~ c'est cher/c'était bon?** is it expensive/was it good?; **quand est-ce qu'il part?** when does he leave?, when is he leaving?; **où est-ce qu'il va?** where's he going?; voir aussi **que**

este [ɛst] ADJ Estonian ▶ NMF: **Este** Estonian

esthète [ɛstɛt] NMF aesthete

esthéticienne [ɛstetisjɛn] NF beautician

esthétique [ɛstetik] ADJ (sens, jugement) aesthetic; (beau) attractive, aesthetically pleasing ▶ NF aesthetics sg; **l'~ industrielle** industrial design

esthétiquement [ɛstetikmɑ̃] ADV aesthetically

estimable [ɛstimabl] ADJ respected

estimatif, -ive [ɛstimatif, -iv] ADJ estimated

estimation [ɛstimasjɔ̃] NF valuation; assessment; (chiffre) estimate; **d'après mes estimations** according to my calculations

estime [ɛstim] NF esteem, regard; **avoir de l'~ pour qn** to think highly of sb

estimer [ɛstime] /**1**/ VT (respecter) to esteem, hold in high regard; (expertiser: bijou) to value; (évaluer:

coût etc) to assess, estimate; (penser): **~ que/être** to consider that/o.s. to be; **j'estime la distance à 10 km** I reckon the distance to be 10 km ■ **s'estimer** VPR: **s'~ satisfait/heureux** to feel satisfied/ happy

estival, e, -aux [ɛstival, -o] ADJ summer cpd; **station estivale** (summer) holiday resort

estivant, e [ɛstivɑ̃, -ɑ̃t] NM/F (summer) holiday-maker

estoc [ɛstɔk] NM: **frapper d'~ et de taille** to cut and thrust

estocade [ɛstɔkad] NF death-blow

★**estomac** [ɛstɔma] NM stomach; **avoir mal à l'~** to have stomach ache; **avoir l'~ creux** to have an empty stomach

estomaqué, e [ɛstɔmake] ADJ flabbergasted

estomaquer [ɛstɔmake] VT (fam) to flabbergast

estompe [ɛstɔ̃p] NF stump; (dessin) stump drawing

estompé, e [ɛstɔ̃pe] ADJ blurred

estomper [ɛstɔ̃pe] /**1**/ VT (Art) to shade off; (fig) to blur, dim ■ **s'estomper** VPR (sentiments) to soften; (contour) to become blurred

Estonie [ɛstɔni] NF: **l'~** Estonia

estonien, ne [ɛstɔnjɛ̃, -ɛn] ADJ Estonian ▶ NM (Ling) Estonian ▶ NM/F: **Estonien, ne** Estonian

estourbir [ɛsturbir] VT (fam: personne: assommer) to knock out; (: animal: tuer) to knock out

estrade [ɛstrad] NF platform, rostrum

estragon [ɛstragɔ̃] NM tarragon

estropié, e [ɛstrɔpje] NM/F cripple (péj)

estropier [ɛstrɔpje] /**7**/ VT to cripple, maim; (fig) to twist, distort

estuaire [ɛstɥɛr] NM estuary

estudiantin, e [ɛstydjɑ̃tɛ̃, -in] ADJ student cpd

esturgeon [ɛstyrʒɔ̃] NM sturgeon

★**et** [e] CONJ and; **et lui? et alors?**, what about him?; **et alors?**, **et (puis) après?** so what?; (ensuite) and then?

ét. ABR = **étage**

ETA [eta] SIGLE M (Pol) ETA

étable [etabl] NF cowshed

établi, e [etabli] ADJ established ▶ NM (work) bench

établir [etablir] /**2**/ VT (papiers d'identité, facture) to make out; (liste, programme) to draw up; (gouvernement, artisan etc: aider à s'installer) to set up, establish; (entreprise, atelier, camp) to set up; (réputation, usage, fait, culpabilité, relations) to establish; (Sport: record) to set ■ **s'établir** VPR (se faire: entente etc) to be established; **s'~ (à son compte)** to set up in business; **s'~ à/près de** to settle in/near

établissement [etablismɑ̃] NM making out; drawing up; setting up, establishing; (entreprise, institution)' establishment; **~ de crédit** credit institution; **~ hospitalier** hospital complex; **~ industriel** industrial plant, factory; **~ scolaire** school, educational establishment

étage [etaʒ] NM (d'immeuble) storey (BRIT), story (US), floor; (de fusée) stage; (Géo: de culture, végétation) level; **au 2ème ~** on the 2nd (BRIT) ou 3rd (US) floor; **à l'~** upstairs; **maison à deux étages** two-storey house; **c'est à quel ~?** what floor is it on?; **de bas ~** adj low-born; (médiocre) inferior

étager [etaʒe] /3/ vt (cultures) to lay out in tiers
∎ **s'étager** vpr (prix) to range; (zones, cultures) to lie on different levels

étagère [etaʒɛʀ] nf (rayon) shelf; (meuble) shelves pl, set of shelves

étai [etɛ] nm stay, prop

étain [etɛ̃] nm tin; (Bijouterie) pewter no pl

étais etc [etɛ] vb voir **être**

étal [etal] nm stall

étalage [etalaʒ] nm display; (vitrine) display window; **faire ~ de** to show off, parade

étalagiste [etalaʒist] nmf window-dresser

étale [etal] adj (mer) slack

étalement [etalmɑ̃] nm spreading; (échelonnement) staggering

étaler [etale] /1/ vt (carte, nappe) to spread (out); (peinture, liquide) to spread; (échelonner: paiements, dates, vacances) to spread, stagger; (exposer: marchandises) to display; (richesses, connaissances) to parade ∎ **s'étaler** vpr (liquide) to spread out; (fam) to fall flat on one's face, come a cropper (Brit); **s'~ sur** (paiements etc) to be spread over

étalon [etalɔ̃] nm (mesure) standard; (cheval) stallion; **l'étalon-or** the gold standard

étalonnage [etalɔnaʒ] nm calibration

étalonner [etalɔne] /1/ vt to calibrate

étamer [etame] /1/ vt (casserole) to tin(plate); (glace) to silver

étamine [etamin] nf (Bot) stamen; (tissu) butter muslin

étanche [etɑ̃ʃ] adj (récipient, aussi fig) watertight; (montre, vêtement) waterproof; **~ à l'air** airtight

étanchéité [etɑ̃ʃeite] nf watertightness; airtightness

étancher [etɑ̃ʃe] /1/ vt (liquide) to stop (flowing); **~ sa soif** to quench ou slake one's thirst

étançon [etɑ̃sɔ̃] nm (Tech) prop

étançonner [etɑ̃sɔne] /1/ vt to prop up

étang [etɑ̃] nm pond

étant [etɑ̃] vb voir **être**; **donné**

étape [etap] nf stage; (lieu d'arrivée) stopping place; (: Cyclisme) staging point; **faire ~ à** to stop off at; **brûler les étapes** (fig) to cut corners

état [eta] nm (condition) state; (d'un article d'occasion) condition, state; (liste) inventory, statement; (avec une majuscule: Pol) state; **l'É~** the State; **les États du Golfe** the Gulf States; **en bon/mauvais ~** in good/poor condition; **en ~ (de marche)** in (working) order; **remettre en ~** to repair; **hors d'~** out of order; **être en ~/hors d'~ de faire** to be in a state/in no fit state to do; **en tout ~ de cause** in any event; **être dans tous ses états** to be in a state; **faire ~ de** (alléguer) to put forward; **en ~ d'arrestation** under arrest; **~ de grâce** (Rel) state of grace; (fig) honeymoon period; **en ~ de grâce** (fig) inspired; **en ~ d'ivresse** under the influence of drink; **~ de choses** (situation) state of affairs; **~ civil** civil status; (bureau) registry office (Brit); **~ d'esprit** frame of mind; **~ des lieux** inventory of fixtures; **~ de santé** state of health; **~ de siège/d'urgence** state of siege/emergency; **~ de veille** (Psych) waking state; **états d'âme** moods; **états de service** service record sg

étatique [etatik] adj state cpd, State cpd

étatisation [etatizasjɔ̃] nf nationalization

étatiser [etatize] /1/ vt to bring under state control

étatisme [etatism] nm state control

étatiste [etatist] adj (doctrine etc) of state control ▶ nmf partisan of state control

état-major [etamaʒɔʀ] (pl **états-majors**) nm (Mil) staff; (d'un parti etc) top advisers pl; (d'une entreprise) top management

État-providence [etapʀɔvidɑ̃s] (pl **États-providence**) nm welfare state

États-Unis [etazyni] nmpl: **les ~ (d'Amérique)** the United States (of America)

étau, x [eto] nm vice (Brit), vise (US)

étayer [eteje] /8/ vt to prop ou shore up; (fig) to back up

et cætera, et cetera, etc. [ɛtsetera] adv et cetera, and so on, etc

été [ete] pp de **être** ▶ nm summer; **en ~** in summer

éteignais etc [etɛɲɛ] vb voir **éteindre**

éteignoir [etɛɲwaʀ] nm (candle) snuffer; (péj) killjoy, wet blanket

éteindre [etɛ̃dʀ] /52/ vt (lampe, lumière, radio, chauffage) to turn ou switch off; (cigarette, incendie, bougie) to put out, extinguish; (Jur: dette) to extinguish ∎ **s'éteindre** vpr to go off; (feu, lumière) to go out; (mourir) to pass away

éteint, e [etɛ̃, -ɛ̃t] pp de **éteindre** ▶ adj (fig) lacklustre, dull; (volcan) extinct; **tous feux éteints** (Auto: rouler) without lights

étendard [etɑ̃daʀ] nm standard

étendoir [etɑ̃dwaʀ] nm drying rack

étendre [etɑ̃dʀ] /41/ vt (appliquer: pâte, liquide) to spread; (déployer: carte etc) to spread out; (sur un fil: lessive, linge) to hang up ou out; (bras, jambes, par terre: blessé) to stretch out; (diluer) to dilute, thin; (fig: agrandir) to extend; (fam: adversaire) to floor ∎ **s'étendre** vpr (augmenter, se propager) to spread; (terrain, forêt etc): **s'~ jusqu'à/de ... à** to stretch as far as/from ... to; **s'~ (sur)** (s'allonger) to stretch out (upon); (se coucher) to lie down (on); (fig: expliquer) to elaborate ou enlarge (upon)

étendu, e [etɑ̃dy] adj extensive ▶ nf (d'eau, de sable) stretch, expanse; (de problème) extent

éternel, le [etɛʀnɛl] adj eternal; **les neiges éternelles** perpetual snow

éternellement [etɛʀnɛlmɑ̃] adv eternally

éterniser [etɛʀnize] /1/: **s'éterniser** vpr to last for ages; (personne) to stay for ages

éternité [etɛʀnite] nf eternity; **il y a** ou **ça fait une ~ que** it's ages since; **de toute ~** from time immemorial; **ça a duré une ~** it lasted for ages

éternuement [etɛʀnymɑ̃] nm sneeze

éternuer [etɛʀnɥe] /1/ vi to sneeze

êtes [ɛt(z)] vb voir **être**

étêter [etete] /1/ vt (arbre) to poll(ard); (clou, poisson) to cut the head off

éthanol [etanɔl] nm ethanol

éther [etɛʀ] nm ether

éthéré, e [etere] adj ethereal

Éthiopie [etjɔpi] nf: **l'~** Ethiopia

éthiopien, ne [etjɔpjɛ̃, -ɛn] adj Ethiopian

éthique [etik] ADJ ethical ▸ NF ethics *sg*

ethnicité [etnisite] NF ethnicity

ethnie [etni] NF ethnic group

ethnique [ɛtnik] ADJ ethnic

ethnocentrique [ɛtnɔsɑ̃trik] ADJ (*vision, discours*) ethnocentric

ethnocentrisme [ɛtnɔsɑ̃trism] NM ethnocentrism

ethnographe [ɛtnɔgraf] NMF ethnographer

ethnographie [ɛtnɔgrafi] NF ethnography

ethnographique [ɛtnɔgrafik] ADJ ethnographic(al)

ethnologie [ɛtnɔlɔʒi] NF ethnology

ethnologique [ɛtnɔlɔʒik] ADJ ethnological

ethnologue [ɛtnɔlɔg] NMF ethnologist

éthologie [etɔlɔʒi] NF ethology

éthylique [etilik] ADJ alcoholic

éthylisme [etilism] NM alcoholism

éthylomètre [etilɔmɛtr] NM Breathalyser®

éthylotest [etilɔtɛst] NM Breathalyser®

étiage [etjaʒ] NM low water

étiez [etje] VB *voir* **être**

étincelant, e [etɛ̃s(ə)lɑ̃, -ɑ̃t] ADJ sparkling

étinceler [etɛ̃s(ə)le] /4/ VI to sparkle

étincelle [etɛ̃sɛl] NF spark

étioler [etjɔle] /1/: **s'étioler** VPR to wilt

étions [etjɔ̃] VB *voir* **être**

étique [etik] ADJ skinny, bony

étiquetage [etik(ə)taʒ] NM labelling

étiqueter [etik(ə)te] /4/ VT to label

étiquette [etikɛt] NF label; (*protocole*): **l'~** etiquette

étirement [etirmɑ̃] NM (*de muscle*) stretching; **faire des étirements** to do some stretching, to do stretching exercises

étirer [etire] /1/ VT to stretch; (*ressort*) to stretch out ■ **s'étirer** VPR (*personne*) to stretch; (*convoi, route*): **s'~ sur** to stretch out over

étoffe [etɔf] NF material, fabric; **avoir l'~ d'un chef** *etc* to be cut out to be a leader *etc*; **avoir de l'~** to be a forceful personality

étoffer [etɔfe] /1/ VT to flesh out ■ **s'étoffer** VPR to fill out

étoile [etwal] NF star; **la bonne/mauvaise ~ de qn** sb's lucky/unlucky star; **à la belle ~** (out) in the open; **~ filante** shooting star; **~ de mer** starfish; **~ polaire** pole star ▸ ADJ: **danseuse** *ou* **danseur ~** leading dancer

étoilé, e [etwale] ADJ starry

étole [etɔl] NF stole

étonnamment [etɔnamɑ̃] ADV amazingly

étonnant, e [etɔnɑ̃, -ɑ̃t] ADJ surprising

étonné, e [etɔne] ADJ surprised

étonnement [etɔnmɑ̃] NM surprise, amazement; **à mon grand ~ ...** to my great surprise *ou* amazement ...

étonner [etɔne] /1/ VT to surprise, amaze; **cela m'étonnerait (que)** (*j'en doute*) I'd be (very) surprised (if) ■ **s'étonner que/de** VPR to be surprised that/at

étouffant, e [etufɑ̃, -ɑ̃t] ADJ stifling

étouffé, e [etufe] ADJ (*asphyxié*) suffocated; (*assourdi: cris, rires*) smothered ▸ NF: **à l'étouffée** (Culin: *poisson, légumes*) steamed; (: *viande*) braised

étouffement [etufmɑ̃] NM suffocation

étouffer [etufe] /1/ VT to suffocate; (*bruit*) to muffle; (*scandale*) to hush up ▸ VI to suffocate; (*avoir trop chaud, aussi fig*) to feel stifled; **on étouffe** it's stifling ■ **s'étouffer** VPR (*en mangeant etc*) to choke

étouffoir [etufwar] NM (Mus) damper

étoupe [etup] NF tow

étourderie [eturdəri] NF (*caractère*) absent-mindedness *no pl*; (*faute*) thoughtless blunder; **faute d'~** careless mistake

étourdi, e [eturdi] ADJ (*distrait*) scatterbrained, heedless

étourdiment [eturdimɑ̃] ADV rashly

étourdir [eturdir] /2/ VT (*assommer*) to stun, daze; (*griser*) to make dizzy *ou* giddy

étourdissant, e [eturdisɑ̃, -ɑ̃t] ADJ staggering

étourdissement [eturdismɑ̃] NM dizzy spell

étourneau, x [eturno] NM starling

étrange [etrɑ̃ʒ] ADJ strange

étrangement [etrɑ̃ʒmɑ̃] ADV strangely

étranger, -ère [etrɑ̃ʒe, -ɛr] ADJ foreign; (*pas de la famille, non familier*) strange; **~ à** (*mal connu*) unfamiliar to; (*sans rapport*) irrelevant to ▸ NM/F foreigner; stranger ▸ NM: **l'~** foreign countries; **à l'~** abroad; **de l'~** from abroad

étrangeté [etrɑ̃ʒte] NF strangeness

étranglé, e [etrɑ̃gle] ADJ: **d'une voix étranglée** in a strangled voice

étranglement [etrɑ̃gləmɑ̃] NM (*d'une vallée etc*) constriction, narrow passage

étrangler [etrɑ̃gle] /1/ VT to strangle; (*fig: presse, libertés*) to stifle ■ **s'étrangler** VPR (*en mangeant etc*) to choke; (*se resserrer*) to make a bottleneck

étrave [etrav] NF stem

être [ɛtr]

/61/ NM being; **être humain** human being

▸ VB COPULE **1** (*état, description*) to be; **il est instituteur** he is *ou* he's a teacher; **vous êtes grand/intelligent/fatigué** you are *ou* you're tall/clever/tired

2 (*+à: appartenir*) to be; **le livre est à Paul** the book is Paul's *ou* belongs to Paul; **c'est à moi/eux** it is *ou* it's mine/theirs

3 (*+de: provenance*): **il est de Paris** he is from Paris; (: *appartenance*): **il est des nôtres** he is one of us

4 (*date*): **nous sommes le 10 janvier** it's the 10th of January (today)

▸ VI to be; **je ne serai pas ici demain** I won't be here tomorrow

▸ VB AUX **1** to have; to be; **être arrivé/allé** to have arrived/gone; **il est parti** he has left, he has gone

2 (*forme passive*) to be; **être fait par** to be made by; **il a été promu** he has been promoted

3 (*+à +inf: obligation, but*): **c'est à réparer** it needs repairing; **c'est à essayer** it should be tried; **il est à espérer que ...** it is *ou* it's to be hoped that ...

▶ VB IMPERS **1**: **il est** (+ *adj*) it is; **il est impossible de le faire** it's impossible to do it
2: **il est** (*heure, date*): **il est 10 heures** it is *ou* it's 10 o'clock
3 (*emphatique*): **c'est moi** it's me; **c'est à lui de le faire** it's up to him to do it
voir aussi **est-ce que**; **n'est-ce pas**; **c'est-à-dire**; **ce**

étreindre [etʀɛ̃dʀ] /**52**/ VT to clutch, grip; (*amoureusement, amicalement*) to embrace ■ **s'étreindre** VPR to embrace

étreinte [etʀɛ̃t] NF clutch, grip; embrace; **resserrer son ~ autour de** (*fig*) to tighten one's grip on *ou* around

étrenner [etʀene] /**1**/ VT to use (*ou* wear) for the first time

étrennes [etʀɛn] NFPL (*cadeaux*) New Year's present; (*gratifications*) ≈ Christmas box *sg*, ≈ Christmas bonus

étrier [etʀije] NM stirrup

étrille [etʀij] NF (*brosse*) currycomb; (*Zool*) velvet crab

étriller [etʀije] /**1**/ VT (*cheval*) to curry; (*fam: battre*) to slaughter (*fig*)

étriper [etʀipe] /**1**/ VT to gut; (*fam*): **~ qn** to tear sb's guts out

étriqué, e [etʀike] ADJ skimpy

étroit, e [etʀwa, -wat] ADJ narrow; (*vêtement*) tight; (*fig: liens, collaboration*) close, tight; **à l'~** cramped; **~ d'esprit** narrow-minded

étroitement [etʀwatmã] ADV closely

étroitesse [etʀwates] NF narrowness; **~ d'esprit** narrow-mindedness

étron [etʀɔ̃] NM (*fam*) turd (*fam*)

étrusque [etʀysk] ADJ Etruscan

étude [etyd] NF studying; (*ouvrage, rapport, Mus*) study; (*de notaire: bureau*) office; (: *charge*) practice; (*Scol: salle de travail*) study room; **être à l'~** (*projet etc*) to be under consideration; **~ de cas** case study; **~ de faisabilité** feasibility study; **~ de marché** (*Écon*) market research ■ **études** NFPL (*Scol*) studies; **faire des études (de droit/médecine)** to study (law/medicine); **études secondaires/supérieures** secondary/higher education

étudiant, e [etydjã, -ãt] ADJ, NM/F student

étudié, e [etydje] ADJ (*démarche*) studied; (*système*) carefully designed; (*prix*) keen

étudier [etydje] /**7**/ VT, VI to study

étui [etɥi] NM case

étuve [etyv] NF steamroom; (*appareil*) sterilizer

étuvée [etyve] NF: **à l'~** *adv* braised

étymologie [etimɔlɔʒi] NF etymology

étymologique [etimɔlɔʒik] ADJ etymological

EU SIGLE MPL (= *États-Unis*) US

eu, eue [y] PP *de* **avoir**

EUA SIGLE MPL (= *États-Unis d'Amérique*) USA

eucalyptus [økaliptys] NM eucalyptus

Eucharistie [økaʀisti] NF: **l'~** the Eucharist, the Lord's Supper

eucharistique [økaʀistik] ADJ eucharistic

euclidien, ne [øklidjɛ̃, -ɛn] ADJ Euclidian

eugénique [øʒenik] ADJ eugenic ▶ NF eugenics *sg*

eugénisme [øʒenism] NM eugenics *sg*

euh [ø] EXCL er

eunuque [ønyk] NM eunuch

euphémique [øfemik] ADJ euphemistic

euphémisme [øfemism] NM euphemism

euphonie [øfɔni] NF euphony

euphorbe [øfɔʀb] NF (*Bot*) spurge

euphorie [øfɔʀi] NF euphoria

euphorique [øfɔʀik] ADJ euphoric

euphorisant, e [øfɔʀizã, -ãt] ADJ exhilarating

eurafricain, e [øʀafʀikɛ̃, -ɛn] ADJ Eurafrican

eurasiatique [øʀazjatik] ADJ Eurasiatic

Eurasie [øʀazi] NF: **l'~** Eurasia

eurasien, ne [øʀazjɛ̃, -ɛn] ADJ Eurasian

EURATOM [øʀatɔm] SIGLE F (= *European Atomic Energy Community*) Euratom

eurent [yʀ] VB *voir* **avoir**

★**euro** [øʀo] NM euro

euro- [øʀo] PRÉFIXE Euro-

eurocrate [øʀɔkʀat] NMF (*péj*) Eurocrat

eurodevise [øʀɔdəviz] NF Eurocurrency

eurodollar [øʀɔdɔlaʀ] NM Eurodollar

Euroland [øʀɔlãd] NM Euroland

euromonnaie [øʀɔmɔnɛ] NF Eurocurrency

★**Europe** [øʀɔp] NF: **l'~** Europe; **l'~ centrale** Central Europe; **l'~ verte** European agriculture

européanisation [øʀɔpeanizasjɔ̃] NF Europeanization

européaniser [øʀɔpeanize] /**1**/ VT to Europeanize

européen, ne [øʀɔpeɛ̃, -ɛn] ADJ European ▶ NM/F: **Européen, ne** European

europhile [øʀɔfil] ADJ (*homme politique, pays*) Europhile, pro-Europe ▶ NMF Europhile, pro-European

europhobe [øʀɔfɔb] ADJ Europhobic ▶ NMF Europhobe

eurosceptique [øʀɔsɛptik] ADJ, NMF Eurosceptic

Eurovision [øʀɔvizjɔ̃] NF Eurovision; **émission en ~** Eurovision broadcast

eus *etc* [y] VB *voir* **avoir**

euthanasie [øtanazi] NF euthanasia

euthanasier [øtanazje] VT (*animal*) to put down, put to sleep; (*personne*) to euthanize

eux [ø] PRON (*sujet*) they; (*objet*) them; **~, ils ont fait …** THEY did …

évacuation [evakɥasjɔ̃] NF evacuation

évacué, e [evakɥe] NM/F evacuee

évacuer [evakɥe] /**1**/ VT (*salle, région*) to evacuate, clear; (*occupants, population*) to evacuate; (*toxine etc*) to evacuate, discharge

évadé, e [evade] ADJ escaped ▶ NM/F escapee

évader [evade] /**1**/: **s'évader** VPR to escape

évaluation [evalɥasjɔ̃] NF assessment, evaluation

évaluer [evalɥe] /**1**/ VT (*expertiser*) to assess, evaluate; (*juger approximativement*) to estimate

évanescent, e [evanesã, -ãt] ADJ evanescent

évangélique [evãʒelik] ADJ evangelical

évangélisation [evãʒelizasjɔ̃] NF evangelization

évangéliser [evãʒelize] /**1**/ VT to evangelize

évangéliste [evãʒelist] NM evangelist

évangile [evãʒil] NM gospel; *(texte de la Bible)*: **l'É~** the Gospel; **ce n'est pas l'É~** *(fig)* it's not gospel

évanoui, e [evanwi] ADJ in a faint; **tomber ~ to** faint

évanouir [evanwiʀ] **/2/: s'évanouir** VPR to faint, pass out; *(disparaître)* to vanish, disappear

évanouissement [evanwismã] NM *(syncope)* fainting fit; *(Méd)* loss of consciousness

évaporation [evapɔʀasjɔ̃] NF evaporation

évaporé, e [evapɔʀe] ADJ giddy, scatterbrained

évaporer [evapɔʀe] **/1/: s'évaporer** VPR to evaporate

évasé, e [evaze] ADJ *(jupe etc)* flared

évaser [evaze] **/1/** VT *(tuyau)* to widen, open out; *(jupe, pantalon)* to flare **s'évaser** VPR to widen, open out

évasif, -ive [evazif, -iv] ADJ evasive

évasion [evazjɔ̃] NF escape; **littérature d'~** escapist literature; **~ des capitaux** *(Écon)* flight of capital; **~ fiscale** tax avoidance

évasivement [evazivmã] ADV evasively

évêché [eveʃe] NM *(fonction)* bishopric; *(palais)* bishop's palace

éveil [evɛj] NM awakening; **être en ~** to be alert; **mettre qn en ~, donner l'~ à qn** to arouse sb's suspicions; **activités d'~** early-learning activities

éveillé, e [eveje] ADJ awake; *(vif)* alert, sharp

éveiller [eveje] **/1/** VT to (a)waken; *(soupçons etc)* to arouse **s'éveiller** VPR to (a)waken; *(fig)* to be aroused

événement [evɛnmã] NM event

événementiel, le [evɛnmãsjɛl] ADJ *(histoire)* factual; *(agence, animateur, communication)* event cpd, events cpd ▶ NM *(spectacles, grandes manifestations)* events management

éventail [evãtaj] NM fan; *(choix)* range; **en ~** fanned out; fan-shaped

éventaire [evãtɛʀ] NM stall, stand

éventé, e [evãte] ADJ *(parfum, vin)* stale

éventer [evãte] **/1/** VT *(secret, complot)* to uncover; *(avec un éventail)* to fan **s'éventer** VPR *(parfum, vin)* to go stale

éventrer [evãtʀe] **/1/** VT to disembowel; *(fig)* to tear *ou* rip open

éventualité [evãtɥalite] NF eventuality; possibility; **dans l'~ de** in the event of; **parer à toute ~** to guard against all eventualities

éventuel, le [evãtɥɛl] ADJ possible

éventuellement [evãtɥɛlmã] ADV possibly

évêque [evɛk] NM bishop

Everest [ev(ə)ʀɛst] NM: **(mont) ~** (Mount) Everest

évertuer [evɛʀtɥe] **/1/: s'évertuer** VPR: **s'~ à faire** to try very hard to do

éviction [eviksjɔ̃] NF ousting, supplanting; *(de locataire)* eviction

évidemment [evidamã] ADV *(bien sûr)* of course; *(certainement)* obviously

évidence [evidãs] NF obviousness; *(fait)* obvious fact; **se rendre à l'~** to bow before the evidence; **nier l'~** to deny the evidence; **à l'~** evidently; **de toute ~** quite obviously *ou* evidently; **en ~** conspicuous; **être en ~** to be clearly visible; **mettre en ~** *(fait)* to highlight

évident, e [evidã, -ãt] ADJ obvious, evident; **ce n'est pas ~** *(cela pose des problèmes)* it's not (all that) straightforward, it's not as simple as all that

évider [evide] **/1/** VT to scoop out

évier [evje] NM (kitchen) sink

évincer [evɛ̃se] **/3/** VT to oust, supplant

éviscérer [eviseʀe] VT to eviscerate

évitable [evitabl] ADJ avoidable

évitement [evitmã] NM: **place d'~** *(Auto)* passing place

éviter [evite] **/1/** VT to avoid; **~ de faire/que qch ne se passe** to avoid doing/sth happening; **~ qch à qn** to spare sb sth

évocateur, -trice [evɔkatœʀ, -tʀis] ADJ evocative, suggestive

évocation [evɔkasjɔ̃] NF evocation

évolué, e [evɔlɥe] ADJ advanced; *(personne)* broad-minded

évoluer [evɔlɥe] **/1/** VI *(enfant, maladie)* to develop; *(situation, moralement)* to evolve, develop; *(aller et venir: danseur etc)* to move about, circle

évolutif, -ive [evɔlytif, -iv] ADJ evolving

évolution [evɔlysjɔ̃] NF development; evolution **évolutions** NFPL movements

évolutionnisme [evɔlysjɔnism] NM evolutionism

évoquer [evɔke] **/1/** VT to call to mind, evoke; *(mentionner)* to mention

ex. ABR (= *exemple*) ex.

ex- [ɛks] PRÉFIXE ex-; **son ex-mari** her ex-husband; **son ex-femme** his ex-wife

exacerbé, e [ɛɡzasɛʀbe] ADJ *(orgueil, sensibilité)* exaggerated

exacerber [ɛɡzasɛʀbe] **/1/** VT to exacerbate

★**exact, e** [ɛɡza(kt), ɛɡzakt] ADJ *(précis)* exact, accurate, precise; *(correct)* correct; *(ponctuel)* punctual; **l'heure exacte** the right *ou* exact time

★**exactement** [ɛɡzaktəmã] ADV exactly, accurately, precisely; correctly; *(c'est cela même)* exactly

exaction [ɛɡzaksjɔ̃] NF *(d'argent)* exaction; *(gén pl: actes de violence)* abuse(s)

exactitude [ɛɡzaktityd] NF exactitude, accurateness, precision

ex aequo [ɛɡzeko] ADJ INV equally placed; **classé 1er ~** placed equal first; **arriver ~** to finish neck and neck

exagération [ɛɡzaʒeʀasjɔ̃] NF exaggeration

exagéré, e [ɛɡzaʒeʀe] ADJ *(prix etc)* excessive

exagérément [ɛɡzaʒeʀemã] ADV excessively

exagérer [ɛɡzaʒeʀe] **/6/** VT to exaggerate ▶ VI *(abuser)* to go too far; *(dépasser les bornes)* to overstep the mark; *(déformer les faits)* to exaggerate **s'exagérer qch** VPR to exaggerate sth

exaltant, e [ɛɡzaltã, -ãt] ADJ exhilarating

exaltation [ɛɡzaltasjɔ̃] NF exaltation

exalté, e [ɛɡzalte] ADJ *(over)excited* ▶ NM/F *(péj)* fanatic

exalter [ɛɡzalte] **/1/** VT *(enthousiasmer)* to excite, elate; *(glorifier)* to exalt

★**examen** [ɛɡzamɛ̃] NM examination; *(Scol)* exam, examination; **à l'~** *(dossier, projet)* under consideration; *(Comm)* on approval; **~ blanc** mock exam(ination); **~ de la vue** sight test; **~ médical** (medical) examination; (*analyse*) test

examinateur, -trice [ɛgzaminatœr, -tris] NM/F examiner

examiner [ɛgzamine] /1/ VT to examine

exaspérant, e [ɛgzasperɑ̃, -ɑ̃t] ADJ exasperating

exaspération [ɛgzasperasjɔ̃] NF exasperation

exaspéré, e [ɛgzaspere] ADJ exasperated

exaspérer [ɛgzaspere] /6/ VT to exasperate; (*aggraver*) to exacerbate

exaucer [ɛgzose] /3/ VT (*vœu*) to grant, fulfil; **~ qn** to grant sb's wishes

ex cathedra [ɛkskatedra] ADJ INV, ADV ex cathedra

excavateur [ɛkskavatœr] NM excavator, mechanical digger

excavation [ɛkskavasjɔ̃] NF excavation

excavatrice [ɛkskavatris] NF = **excavateur**

excédé, e [ɛksede] ADJ (*à bout*) exasperated; **~ de fatigue** exhausted; **~ de travail** worn out with work

excédent [ɛksedɑ̃] NM surplus; **en ~** surplus; **payer 60 euros d'~** (*de bagages*) to pay 60 euros excess baggage; **~ de bagages** excess baggage; **~ commercial** trade surplus

excédentaire [ɛksedɑ̃tɛr] ADJ surplus, excess

excéder [ɛksede] /6/ VT (*dépasser*) to exceed; (*agacer*) to exasperate

excellence [ɛksɛlɑ̃s] NF excellence; (*titre*) Excellency; **par ~** par excellence

★**excellent, e** [ɛksɛlɑ̃, -ɑ̃t] ADJ excellent

exceller [ɛksele] /1/ VI: **~ (dans)** to excel (in)

excentré, e [ɛksɑ̃tre] ADJ (*quartier*) out of the way

excentricité [ɛksɑ̃trisite] NF eccentricity

excentrique [ɛksɑ̃trik] ADJ eccentric; (*quartier*) outlying ▶ NMF eccentric

excentriquement [ɛksɑ̃trikmɑ̃] ADV eccentrically

excepté, e [ɛksɛpte] ADJ, PRÉP: **les élèves exceptés, ~ les élèves** except for *ou* apart from the pupils; **~ si/quand** except if/when; **~ que** except that

excepter [ɛksɛpte] /1/ VT to except

exception [ɛksɛpsjɔ̃] NF exception; **faire ~** to be an exception; **faire une ~** to make an exception; **sans ~** without exception; **à l'~ de** except for, with the exception of; **d'~** (*mesure, loi*) special, exceptional

★**exceptionnel, le** [ɛksɛpsjɔnɛl] ADJ exceptional; (*prix*) special

exceptionnellement [ɛksɛpsjɔnɛlmɑ̃] ADV exceptionally; (*par exception*) by way of an exception, on this occasion

excès [ɛksɛ] NM excess, surplus; **à l'~** (*méticuleux, généreux*) to excess; **avec ~** to excess; **sans ~** in moderation; **tomber dans l'~ inverse** to go to the opposite extreme; **~ de langage** immoderate language; **~ de pouvoir** abuse of power; **~ de vitesse** speeding *no pl*, exceeding the speed limit; **~ de zèle** overzealousness *no pl* ▶ NMPL excesses; **faire des ~** to overindulge

excessif, -ive [ɛksesif, -iv] ADJ excessive

excessivement [ɛksesivmɑ̃] ADV (*trop: cher*) excessively, inordinately; (*très: riche, laid*) extremely, incredibly; **manger/boire ~** to eat/drink to excess

exciper [ɛksipe] /1/: **~ de** VT to plead

excipient [ɛksipjɑ̃] NM (*Méd*) inert base, excipient

exciser [ɛksize] /1/ VT (*Méd*) to excise

excision [ɛksizjɔ̃] NF (*Méd*) excision; (*rituelle*) circumcision

excitant, e [ɛksitɑ̃, -ɑ̃t] ADJ exciting ▶ NM stimulant

excitation [ɛksitasjɔ̃] NF (*état*) excitement

excité, e [ɛksite] ADJ excited

exciter [ɛksite] /1/ VT to excite; (*café etc*) to stimulate; **~ qn à** (*révolte etc*) to incite sb to ▪ **s'exciter** VPR to get excited

exclamation [ɛksklamasjɔ̃] NF exclamation

exclamer [ɛksklame] /1/: **s'exclamer** VPR to exclaim

exclu, e [ɛkskly] PP *de* **exclure** ▶ ADJ: **il est/n'est pas ~ que ...** it's out of the question/not impossible that ...; **ce n'est pas ~** it's not impossible, I don't rule that out ▪ **exclus** NMPL: **les exclus** the socially excluded, the underclass

exclure [ɛksklyr] /35/ VT (*faire sortir*) to expel; (*ne pas compter*) to exclude, leave out; (*rendre impossible*) to exclude, rule out

exclusif, -ive [ɛksklyzif, -iv] ADJ exclusive; **avec la mission exclusive/dans le but ~ de ...** with the sole mission/aim of ...; **agent ~** sole agent

exclusion [ɛksklyzjɔ̃] NF expulsion; **à l'~ de** with the exclusion *ou* exception of

exclusivement [ɛksklyzivmɑ̃] ADV exclusively

exclusivité [ɛksklyzivite] NF exclusiveness; (*Comm*) exclusive rights *pl*; **film passant en ~ à** film showing only at

excommunication [ɛkskɔmynikasjɔ̃] NF (*Rel*) excommunication

excommunier [ɛkskɔmynje] /7/ VT to excommunicate

excréments [ɛkskremɑ̃] NMPL excrement *sg*, faeces

excréter [ɛkskrete] /6/ VT to excrete

excrétion [ɛkskresjɔ̃] NF excretion

excroissance [ɛkskrwasɑ̃s] NF excrescence, outgrowth

★**excursion** [ɛkskyrsjɔ̃] NF (*en autocar*) excursion, trip; (*à pied*) walk, hike; **faire une ~** to go on an excursion *ou* a trip; to go on a walk *ou* hike

excursionniste [ɛkskyrsjɔnist] NMF tripper; hiker

excusable [ɛkskyzabl] ADJ excusable

★**excuse** [ɛkskyz] NF excuse; **mot d'~** (*Scol*) note from one's parent(s) (*to explain absence etc*) ▪ **excuses** NFPL (*regret*) apology *sg*, apologies; **faire des excuses** to apologize; **faire ses excuses** to offer one's apologies; **lettre d'excuses** letter of apology

★**excuser** [ɛkskyze] /1/ VT to excuse; **~ qn de qch** (*dispenser*) to excuse sb from sth; **« excusez-moi »** "I'm sorry"; (*pour attirer l'attention*) "excuse me"; **se faire ~** to ask to be excused ▪ **s'excuser (de)** VPR to apologize (for)

exécrable [ɛgzekrabl] ADJ atrocious

exécrer [ɛgzekre] /6/ VT to loathe, abhor

exécutable [ɛgzekytabl] (*Inform*) ADJ, NM executable

exécutant, e [ɛgzekytɑ̃, -ɑ̃t] NM/F performer

exécuter [ɛgzekyte] /**1**/ VT (*prisonnier*) to execute; (*tâche etc*) to execute, carry out; (*Mus: jouer*) to perform, execute; (*Inform*) to run ■ **s'exécuter** VPR to comply

exécuteur, -trice [ɛgzekytœʀ, -tʀis] NM/F (*testamentaire*) executor ▶ NM (*bourreau*) executioner

exécutif, -ive [ɛgzekytif, -iv] ADJ, NM (*Pol*) executive

exécution [ɛgzekysjɔ̃] NF execution; carrying out; **mettre à ~** to carry out

exécutoire [ɛgzekytwaʀ] ADJ (*Jur*) (legally) binding

exégèse [ɛgzeʒɛz] NF exegesis

exégète [ɛgzeʒɛt] NM exegete

exemplaire [ɛgzɑ̃plɛʀ] ADJ exemplary ▶ NM copy

★**exemple** [ɛgzɑ̃pl] NM example; **par ~** for instance, for example; (*valeur intensive*) really!; **sans ~** (*bêtise, gourmandise etc*) unparalleled; **donner l'~** to set an example; **prendre ~ sur** to take as a model; **à l'~ de** just like; **pour l'~** (*punir*) as an example

exempt, e [ɛgzɑ̃, -ɑ̃t] ADJ: **~ de** (*dispensé de*) exempt from; (*sans*) free from; **~ de taxes** tax-free

exempter [ɛgzɑ̃te] /**1**/ VT: **~ de** to exempt from

exemption [ɛgzɑ̃psjɔ̃] NF (*de taxes, visa*) exemption

exercé, e [ɛgzɛʀse] ADJ trained

exercer [ɛgzɛʀse] /**3**/ VT (*pratiquer*) to exercise, practise; (*faire usage de: prérogative*) to exercise; (*influence, contrôle, pression*) to exert; (*former*) to exercise, train ▶ VI (*médecin*) to be in practice ■ **s'exercer** VPR (*sportif, musicien*) to practise; (*se faire sentir: pression etc*): **s'~ (sur ou contre)** to be exerted (on); **s'~ à faire qch** to train o.s. to do sth

★**exercice** [ɛgzɛʀsis] NM practice; exercising; (*tâche, travail*) exercise; (*Comm, Admin: période*) accounting period; (*Mil*) drill; **l'~** (*sportif etc*) exercise; **en ~** (*juge*) in office; (*médecin*) practising; **dans l'~ de ses fonctions** in the discharge of his duties; **exercices d'assouplissement** limbering-up (exercises)

exergue [ɛgzɛʀg] NM: **mettre en ~** (*inscription*) to inscribe; **porter en ~** to be inscribed with

exfoliant, e [ɛksfɔljɑ̃, -jɑ̃t] ADJ (*savon, gel*) exfoliating ▶ NM exfoliator, exfoliant

exfoliation [ɛksfɔljasjɔ̃] NF (*gommage*) exfoliation

exfolier [ɛksfɔlje] VT (*peau*) to exfoliate

exhalaison [ɛgzalɛzɔ̃] NF exhalation

exhaler [ɛgzale] /**1**/ VT (*parfum*) to exhale; (*souffle, son, soupir*) to utter, breathe ■ **s'exhaler** VPR to rise (up)

exhausser [ɛgzose] /**1**/ VT to raise (up)

exhausteur [ɛgzostœʀ] NM extractor fan

exhaustif, -ive [ɛgzostif, -iv] ADJ exhaustive

exhiber [ɛgzibe] /**1**/ VT (*montrer: papiers, certificat*) to present, produce; (*péj*) to display, flaunt ■ **s'exhiber** VPR (*personne*) to parade; (*exhibitionniste*) to expose o.s.

exhibition [ɛgzibisjɔ̃] NF (*Sport*) exhibition match

exhibitionnisme [ɛgzibisjɔnism] NM exhibitionism

exhibitionniste [ɛgzibisjɔnist] NMF exhibitionist

exhortation [ɛgzɔʀtasjɔ̃] NF exhortation

exhorter [ɛgzɔʀte] /**1**/ VT: **~ qn à faire** to urge sb to do

exhumation [ɛgzymasjɔ̃] NF (*de corps*) exhumation

exhumer [ɛgzyme] /**1**/ VT to exhume

exigeant, e [ɛgziʒɑ̃, -ɑ̃t] ADJ demanding; (*péj*) hard to please

exigence [ɛgziʒɑ̃s] NF demand, requirement

exiger [ɛgziʒe] /**3**/ VT to demand, require

exigible [ɛgziʒibl] ADJ (*Comm, Jur*) payable

exigu, ë [ɛgzigy] ADJ cramped, tiny

exiguïté [ɛgziguite] NF (*d'un lieu*) cramped nature

exil [ɛgzil] NM exile; **en ~** in exile

exilé, e [ɛgzile] NM/F exile

exiler [ɛgzile] /**1**/ VT to exile ■ **s'exiler** VPR to go into exile

existant, e [ɛgzistɑ̃, -ɑ̃t] ADJ (*actuel, présent*) existing

existence [ɛgzistɑ̃s] NF existence; **dans l'~** in life

existentialisme [ɛgzistɑ̃sjalism] NM existentialism

existentialiste [ɛgzistɑ̃sjalist] ADJ, NMF existentialist

existentiel, le [ɛgzistɑ̃sjɛl] ADJ existential

★**exister** [ɛgziste] /**1**/ VI to exist; **il existe un/des** there is a/are (some)

exocet [ɛgzɔsɛ] NM (*poisson*) flying fish; (*missile*) Exocet®

exode [ɛgzɔd] NM exodus

exogamie [ɛgzɔgami] NF (*Sociol, Bio*) exogamy

exonération [ɛgzɔneʀasjɔ̃] NF exemption

exonéré, e [ɛgzɔneʀe] ADJ: **~ de TVA** zero-rated (for VAT)

exonérer [ɛgzɔneʀe] /**6**/ VT: **~ de** to exempt from

exoplanète [ɛgzɔplanɛt] NF exoplanet

exorbitant, e [ɛgzɔʀbitɑ̃, -ɑ̃t] ADJ exorbitant

exorbité, e [ɛgzɔʀbite] ADJ: **yeux exorbités** bulging eyes

exorciser [ɛgzɔʀsize] /**1**/ VT to exorcize

exorcisme [ɛgzɔʀsism] NM (*Rel*) exorcism

exorciste [ɛgzɔʀsist] NMF exorcist

exorde [ɛgzɔʀd] NM introduction

exotique [ɛgzɔtik] ADJ exotic; **yaourt aux fruits exotiques** tropical fruit yoghurt

exotisme [ɛgzɔtism] NM exoticism

expansif, -ive [ɛkspɑ̃sif, -iv] ADJ expansive, communicative

expansion [ɛkspɑ̃sjɔ̃] NF expansion

expansionnisme [ɛkspɑ̃sjɔnism] NM expansionism

expansionniste [ɛkspɑ̃sjɔnist] ADJ expansionist

expansivité [ɛkspɑ̃sivite] NF expansiveness

expatrié, e [ɛkspatʀije] NM/F expatriate

expatrier [ɛkspatʀije] /**7**/ VT (*argent*) to take ou send out of the country ■ **s'expatrier** VPR to leave one's country

expectative [ɛkspɛktativ] NF: **être dans l'~** to be waiting to see

expectorant, e [ɛkspɛktɔʀɑ̃, -ɑ̃t] ADJ: **sirop ~** expectorant (syrup)

expectorer [ɛkspɛktɔʀe] /1/ vɪ to expectorate

expédient [ɛkspedjɑ̃] NM (parfois péj) expedient; **vivre d'expédients** to live by one's wits

expédier [ɛkspedje] /7/ vᴛ (lettre, paquet) to send; (troupes, renfort) to dispatch; (péj: travail etc) to dispose of, dispatch

expéditeur, -trice [ɛkspeditœʀ, -tʀis] NM/F (Postes) sender

expéditif, -ive [ɛkspeditif, -iv] ADJ quick, expeditious

expédition [ɛkspedisjɔ̃] NF sending; (scientifique, sportive, Mil) expedition; **~ punitive** punitive raid

expéditionnaire [ɛkspedisjɔnɛʀ] ADJ: **corps ~** (Mil) task force

expérience [ɛkspeʀjɑ̃s] NF (de la vie, des choses) experience; (scientifique) experiment; **avoir de l'~** to have experience, be experienced; **avoir l'~ de** to have experience of; **faire l'~ de qch** to experience sth; **~ de chimie/d'électricité** chemical/electrical experiment

expérimental, e, -aux [ɛkspeʀimɑ̃tal, -o] ADJ experimental

expérimentalement [ɛkspeʀimɑ̃talmɑ̃] ADV experimentally

expérimentation [ɛkspeʀimɑ̃tasjɔ̃] NF (fait d'expérimenter) testing; (Science) experimentation

expérimenté, e [ɛkspeʀimɑ̃te] ADJ experienced

expérimenter [ɛkspeʀimɑ̃te] /1/ vᴛ (machine, technique) to test out, experiment with

expert, e [ɛkspɛʀ, -ɛʀt] ADJ: **~ en** expert in ▸ NM/F (spécialiste) expert; **~ en assurances** insurance valuer

expert-comptable [ɛkspɛʀkɔ̃tabl] (pl **experts-comptables**) NM ≈ chartered (BRIT) ou certified public (US) accountant

expertise [ɛkspɛʀtiz] NF valuation; assessment; valuer's (ou assessor's) report; (Jur) (forensic) examination

expertiser [ɛkspɛʀtize] /1/ vᴛ (objet de valeur) to value; (voiture accidentée etc) to assess damage to

expiation [ɛkspjasjɔ̃] NF (Rel) expiation

expiatoire [ɛkspjatwaʀ] ADJ (sacrifice) expiatory

expier [ɛkspje] /7/ vᴛ to expiate, atone for

expiration [ɛkspiʀasjɔ̃] NF expiry (BRIT), expiration; breathing out no pl

expirer [ɛkspiʀe] /1/ vɪ (prendre fin, lit: mourir) to expire; (respirer) to breathe out

explétif, -ive [ɛkspletif, -iv] ADJ (Ling) expletive

explicable [ɛksplikabl] ADJ: **pas ~** inexplicable

explicatif, -ive [ɛksplikatif, -iv] ADJ (mot, texte, note) explanatory

★**explication** [ɛksplikasjɔ̃] NF explanation; (discussion) discussion; (dispute) argument; **~ de texte** (Scol) critical analysis (of a text)

explicite [ɛksplisit] ADJ explicit

explicitement [ɛksplisitmɑ̃] ADV explicitly

expliciter [ɛksplisite] /1/ vᴛ to make explicit

★**expliquer** [ɛksplike] /1/ vᴛ to explain; **~ (à qn) comment/que** to point out ou explain (to sb) how/that ■ **s'expliquer** VPR (se faire comprendre: personne) to explain o.s.; (se disputer) to have it out; (comprendre): **je m'explique son retard/absence** I understand his lateness/absence; **son erreur**

s'explique one can understand his mistake; **s'~ avec qn** (discuter) to explain o.s. to sb

> Lorsque le verbe **explain** est suivi d'un complément d'objet indirect, il faut utiliser la préposition **to** devant ce complément.
> *Explique-moi comment ça fonctionne.* **Explain to me how it works.**

exploit [ɛksplwa] NM exploit, feat

exploitable [ɛksplwatabl] ADJ (gisement etc) that can be exploited; **~ par une machine** machine-readable

exploitant [ɛksplwatɑ̃] NMF: **~ (agricole)** farmer

exploitation [ɛksplwatasjɔ̃] NF exploitation; (d'une entreprise) running; (entreprise): **~ agricole** farming concern

exploiter [ɛksplwate] /1/ vᴛ (personne, don) to exploit; (entreprise, ferme) to run, operate; (mine) to exploit, work

exploiteur, -euse [ɛksplwatœʀ, -øz] NM/F (péj) exploiter

explorateur, -trice [ɛksplɔʀatœʀ, -tʀis] NM/F explorer

exploration [ɛksplɔʀasjɔ̃] NF exploration

explorer [ɛksplɔʀe] /1/ vᴛ to explore

exploser [ɛksploze] /1/ vɪ to explode, blow up; (engin explosif) to go off; (fig: joie, colère) to burst out, explode; (: personne: de colère) to explode, flare up; **faire ~** (bombe) to explode, detonate; (bâtiment, véhicule) to blow up ▸ vᴛ (fam: adversaire) to destroy; (: budget) to blow; **ce n'est pas qu'ils les ont dominés: ils les ont explosés** they didn't just beat them; they absolutely massacred them; **je vais raccrocher sinon je vais ~ mon forfait** I'm going to hang up otherwise I'm going to go way over my limit

explosif, -ive [ɛksplozif, -iv] ADJ, NM explosive

explosion [ɛksplozjɔ̃] NF explosion; **~ de joie/colère** outburst of joy/rage; **~ démographique** population explosion

expo [ɛkspo] NF (fam) exhibition

exponentiel, le [ɛksponɑ̃sjɛl] ADJ exponential

export [ɛkspɔʀ] NM export

exportable [ɛkspɔʀtabl] ADJ exportable

exportateur, -trice [ɛkspɔʀtatœʀ, -tʀis] ADJ export cpd, exporting ▸ NM/F exporter

exportation [ɛkspɔʀtasjɔ̃] NF (action) exportation; (produit) export

exporter [ɛkspɔʀte] /1/ vᴛ to export

exposant [ɛkspozɑ̃] NM exhibitor; (Math) exponent

exposé, e [ɛkspoze] NM (écrit) exposé; (oral) talk ▸ ADJ: **~ au sud** facing south, with a southern aspect; **bien ~** well situated; **très ~** very exposed

exposer [ɛkspoze] /1/ vᴛ (montrer: marchandise) to display; (: peinture) to exhibit, show; (parler de: problème, situation) to explain, expose, set out; (mettre en danger, orienter: Photo) to expose; **~ qn/qch à** to expose sb/sth to; **~ sa vie** to risk one's life ■ **s'exposer à** VPR (soleil, danger) to expose o.s. to; (critiques, punition) to lay o.s. open to

★**exposition** [ɛkspozisjɔ̃] NF (voir exposer) displaying; exhibiting; explanation, exposition; exposure; (voir exposé) aspect, situation; (manifestation)

exhibition; (Photo) exposure; (introduction) exposition

exprès[1] [ɛkspRɛ] ADV (délibérément) on purpose; (spécialement) specially; **faire ~ de faire qch** to do sth on purpose

exprès[2], **-esse** [ɛkspRɛs] ADJ (ordre, défense) express, formal ▸ ADJ INV, ADV (Postes: lettre, colis) express; **envoyer qch en ~** to send sth express

express [ɛkspRɛs] ADJ INV, NM INV: **(café) ~** espresso; **(train) ~** fast train

expressément [ɛkspRɛsemã] ADV expressly, specifically

expressif, -ive [ɛkspRɛsif, -iv] ADJ expressive

★**expression** [ɛkspRɛsjɔ̃] NF expression; **réduit à sa plus simple ~** reduced to its simplest terms; **liberté/moyens d'~** freedom/means of expression; **~ toute faite** set phrase

expressionnisme [ɛkspRɛsjɔnism] NM expressionism

expressivité [ɛkspRɛsivite] NF expressiveness

exprimer [ɛkspRime] /1/ VT (sentiment, idée) to express; (faire sortir: jus, liquide) to press out ▪ **s'exprimer** VPR (personne) to express o.s.

expropriation [ɛkspRɔpRijasjɔ̃] NF expropriation; **frapper d'~** to put a compulsory purchase order on

exproprier [ɛkspRɔpRije] /7/ VT to buy up (ou buy the property of) by compulsory purchase, expropriate

expulser [ɛkspylse] /1/ VT (d'une salle, d'un groupe) to expel; (locataire) to evict; (Football) to send off

expulsion [ɛkspylsjɔ̃] NF expulsion; eviction; sending off

expurger [ɛkspyRʒe] /3/ VT to expurgate, bowdlerize

exquis, e [ɛkski, -iz] ADJ (gâteau, parfum, élégance) exquisite; (personne, temps) delightful

exsangue [ɛksãg] ADJ bloodless, drained of blood

exsuder [ɛksyde] /1/ VT to exude

extase [ɛkstaz] NF ecstasy; **être en ~** to be in raptures

extasier [ɛkstazje] /7/: **s'extasier** VPR: **s'~ sur** to go into raptures over

extatique [ɛkstatik] ADJ ecstatic

extenseur [ɛkstãsœR] NM (Sport) chest expander

extensible [ɛkstãsibl] ADJ extensible

extensif, -ive [ɛkstãsif, -iv] ADJ extensive

extension [ɛkstãsjɔ̃] NF (d'un muscle, ressort) stretching; (fig) extension; expansion; **à l'~** (Méd) in traction

exténuant, e [ɛkstenɥã, -ãt] ADJ exhausting

exténuer [ɛkstenɥe] /1/ VT to exhaust

extérieur, e [ɛksteRjœR] ADJ (de dehors: porte, mur etc) outer, outside; (: commerce, politique) foreign; (: influences, pressions) external; (au dehors: escalier, WC) outside; (apparent: calme, gaieté etc) outer ▸ NM (d'une maison, d'un récipient etc) outside, exterior; (d'une personne: apparence) exterior; (d'un pays, d'un groupe social): **l'~** the outside world; **à l'~** (dehors) outside; (fig: à l'étranger) abroad

extérieurement [ɛksteRjœRmã] ADV (de dehors) on the outside; (en apparence) on the surface

extérioriser [ɛksteRjɔRize] /1/ VT to exteriorize

exterminateur, -trice [ɛkstɛRminatœR, -tRis] ADJ (ange, folie) exterminating

extermination [ɛkstɛRminasjɔ̃] NF extermination, wiping out

exterminer [ɛkstɛRmine] /1/ VT to exterminate, wipe out

externaliser [ɛkstɛRnalize] VT (services, missions) to outsource

externat [ɛkstɛRna] NM day school

externe [ɛkstɛRn] ADJ external, outer ▸ NMF (Méd) non-resident medical student, extern (US); (Scol) day pupil

extincteur [ɛkstɛ̃ktœR] NM (fire) extinguisher

extinction [ɛkstɛ̃ksjɔ̃] NF extinction; (Jur: d'une dette) extinguishment; **~ de voix** (Méd) loss of voice

extirper [ɛkstiRpe] /1/ VT (tumeur) to extirpate; (plante) to root out, pull up; (préjugés) to eradicate

extorquer [ɛkstɔRke] /1/ VT (de l'argent, un renseignement): **~ qch à qn** to extort sth from sb

extorsion [ɛkstɔRsjɔ̃] NF: **~ de fonds** extortion of money

extra [ɛkstRa] ADJ INV first-rate; (fam) fantastic; (marchandises) top-quality ▸ NM INV extra help ▸ PRÉFIXE extra(-)

extracommunautaire [ɛkstRakɔmynotɛR] ADJ (extérieur à la CE: échanges, origine) non-EU, outside the EU

extraconjugal, e, -aux [ɛkstRakɔ̃ʒygal, -o] ADJ (aventure) extramarital

extracteur [ɛkstRaktœR] NM (d'air, chaleur) extractor fan

extraction [ɛkstRaksjɔ̃] NF extraction

extrader [ɛkstRade] /1/ VT to extradite

extradition [ɛkstRadisjɔ̃] NF extradition

extra-fin, e [ɛkstRafɛ̃, -in] ADJ extra-fine

extra-fort, e [ɛkstRafɔR, -ɔRt] ADJ extra strong

extraire [ɛkstRɛR] /50/ VT to extract; **~ qch de** to extract sth from

extrait, e [ɛkstRɛ, -ɛt] PP de **extraire** ▸ NM (de plante) extract; (de film, livre) extract, excerpt; **~ de naissance** birth certificate

extra-lucide [ɛkstRalysid] ADJ: **voyante ~** clairvoyant

★**extraordinaire** [ɛkstRaɔRdinɛR] ADJ extraordinary; (Pol, Admin: mesures etc) special; **ambassadeur ~** ambassador extraordinary; **assemblée ~** extraordinary meeting; **par ~** by some unlikely chance

extraordinairement [ɛkstRaɔRdinɛRmã] ADV extraordinarily

extrapoler [ɛkstRapɔle] /1/ VT, VI to extrapolate

extra-sensoriel, le [ɛkstRasãsɔRjɛl] ADJ extrasensory

extra-terrestre [ɛkstRatɛRɛstR] NMF extraterrestrial

extra-utérin, e [ɛkstRayteRɛ̃, -in] ADJ extrauterine

extravagance [ɛkstRavagãs] NF extravagance no pl; extravagant behaviour no pl

extravagant, e [ɛkstRavagã, -ãt] ADJ (personne, attitude) extravagant; (idée) wild

extraverti, e [ɛkstRavɛRti] ADJ extrovert

extrayais etc [ɛkstʀɛjɛ] vb voir **extraire**

extrême [ɛkstʀɛm] ADJ, NM extreme; (intensif): **d'une ~ simplicité/brutalité** extremely simple/brutal; **d'un ~ à l'autre** from one extreme to another; **à l'~** in the extreme; **à l'~ rigueur** in the absolute extreme

extrêmement [ɛkstʀɛmmɑ̃] ADV extremely

extrême-onction [ɛkstʀɛmɔ̃ksjɔ̃] (pl **extrêmes-onctions**) NF (Rel) last rites pl, Extreme Unction

Extrême-Orient [ɛkstʀɛmɔʀjɑ̃] NM: **l'~** the Far East

extrême-oriental, e, -aux [ɛkstʀɛmɔʀjɑ̃tal, -o] ADJ Far Eastern

extrémisme [ɛkstʀemism] NM extremism

extrémiste [ɛkstʀemist] ADJ, NMF extremist

extrémité [ɛkstʀemite] NF (bout) end; (situation) straits pl, plight; (geste désespéré) extreme action; **à la dernière ~** (à l'agonie) on the point of death ◾ **extrémités** NFPL (pieds et mains) extremities

extroverti, e [ɛkstʀɔvɛʀti] ADJ = **extraverti**

extrusion [ɛkstʀyzjɔ̃] NF (Tech) extrusion

exubérance [ɛgzybeʀɑ̃s] NF exuberance

exubérant, e [ɛgzybeʀɑ̃, -ɑ̃t] ADJ exuberant

exulter [ɛgzylte] /1/ VI to exult

exutoire [ɛgzytwaʀ] NM outlet, release

ex-voto [ɛksvɔto] NM INV ex-voto

eye-liner [ajlajnœʀ] NM eyeliner

Ff

F, f [ɛf] NM INV F, f ▶ ABR = **féminin**; (*appartement*) **un F2/F3** a 2-/3-roomed flat (BRIT) *ou* apartment (US); (= Fahrenheit) F; (= frère) Br(o).; (= femme) W; **F comme François** F for Frederick (BRIT) *ou* Fox (US)

fa [fa] NM INV (*Mus*) F; (*en chantant la gamme*) fa

fable [fabl] NF fable; (*mensonge*) story, tale

fabricant, e [fabʀikɑ̃, -ɑ̃t] NM/F manufacturer, maker

fabrication [fabʀikasjɔ̃] NF manufacture, making

fabrique [fabʀik] NF factory

★**fabriquer** [fabʀike] /1/ VT to make; (*industriellement*) to manufacture, make; (*construire: voiture*) to manufacture, build; (: *maison*) to build; (*fig: inventer: histoire, alibi*) to make up; (*fam*): **qu'est-ce qu'il fabrique?** what is he up to?; **~ en série** to mass-produce

fabulateur, -trice [fabylatœʀ, -tʀis] NM/F: **c'est un ~** he fantasizes, he makes up stories

fabulation [fabylasjɔ̃] NF (*Psych*) fantasizing

fabuleusement [fabyløzmɑ̃] ADV fabulously, fantastically

fabuleux, -euse [fabylø, -øz] ADJ fabulous, fantastic

★**fac** [fak] NF (*fam: Scol: = faculté*) Uni (BRIT *fam*), ≈ college (US)

façade [fasad] NF front, façade; (*fig*) façade

★**face** [fas] NF face; (*fig: aspect*) side; **perdre/sauver la ~** to lose/save face; **regarder qn en ~** to look sb in the face; **la maison/le trottoir d'en ~** the house/pavement opposite; **en ~ de** *prép* opposite; (*fig*) in front of; **de ~** *adv* from the front; face on; **~ à** *prép* facing; (*fig*) faced with, in the face of; **faire ~ à** to face; **faire ~ à la demande** (*Comm*) to meet the demand; **~ à ~** *adv* face to face ▶ ADJ: **le côté ~** heads

face-à-face [fasafas] NM INV encounter

face-à-main [fasamɛ̃] (*pl* **faces-à-main**) NM lorgnette

Facebook® [feisbuk] M Facebook®; **elle m'a envoyé un message sur ~** she facebooked me

facéties [fasesi] NFPL jokes, pranks

facétieux, -euse [fasesjø, -øz] ADJ mischievous

facette [fasɛt] NF facet

fâché, e [fɑʃe] ADJ angry; (*désolé*) sorry

fâcher [fɑʃe] /1/ VT to anger ■ **se fâcher** VPR to get angry; **se ~ avec** (*se brouiller*) to fall out with

fâcherie [fɑʃʀi] NF quarrel

fâcheusement [fɑʃøzmɑ̃] ADV unpleasantly; (*impressionné etc*) badly; **avoir ~ tendance à** to have an irritating tendency to

fâcheux, -euse [fɑʃø, -øz] ADJ unfortunate, regrettable

facho [faʃo] ADJ, NM,F (*fam: = fasciste*) fascist

facial, e, -aux [fasjal, -o] ADJ facial

faciès [fasjɛs] NM (*visage*) features *pl*

★**facile** [fasil] ADJ easy; (*accommodant: caractère*) easy-going

facilement [fasilmɑ̃] ADV easily

facilité [fasilite] NF easiness; (*disposition, don*) aptitude; (*moyen, occasion, possibilité*): **il a la ~ de rencontrer les gens** he has every opportunity to meet people ■ **facilités** NFPL (*possibilités*) facilities; (*Comm*) terms; **facilités de crédit** credit terms; **facilités de paiement** easy terms

faciliter [fasilite] /1/ VT to make easier

façon [fasɔ̃] NF (*manière*) way; (*d'une robe etc*) making-up; cut; (*main-d'œuvre*) labour (BRIT), labor (US); **châle ~ cachemire** (*imitation*) cashmere-style shawl; **de quelle ~?** (in) what way?; **sans ~** *adv* without fuss; *adj* unaffected; **non merci, sans ~** no thanks, honestly; **d'une autre ~** in another way; **en aucune ~** in no way; **de ~ à** so as to; **de ~ à ce que, de (telle) ~ que** so that; **de toute ~** anyway, in any case; **c'est une ~ de parler** it's a way of putting it; **travail à ~** tailoring ■ **façons** NFPL (*péj*) fuss *sg*; **faire des façons** (*péj: être affecté*) to be affected (: *faire des histoires*) to make a fuss

faconde [fakɔ̃d] NF (*liter*) loquacity

façonnage [fasɔnaʒ] NM (*fabrication: de vêtements*) making; (*de verre*) shaping

façonner [fasɔne] /1/ VT (*fabriquer*) to manufacture; (*travailler: matière*) to shape, fashion; (*fig*) to mould, shape

fac-similé [faksimile] NM facsimile

★**facteur, -trice** [faktœʀ, -tʀis] NM/F postman/-woman (BRIT), mailman/-woman (US); **~/factrice d'orgues** organ builder; **~/factrice de pianos** piano maker ▶ NM (*Math, gén: élément*) factor; **~ rhésus** rhesus factor

factice [faktis] ADJ artificial

faction [faksjɔ̃] NF (*groupe*) faction; (*Mil*) guard *ou* sentry (duty); watch; **en ~** on guard; standing watch

factionnaire [faksjɔnɛʀ] NM guard, sentry

factoriel, le [faktɔʀjɛl] ADJ, NF factorial

factotum [faktɔtɔm] NM odd-job man, dogsbody (BRIT)

factuel, le [faktɥɛl] ADJ factual

facturation [faktyʀasjɔ̃] NF invoicing; (bureau) invoicing (office)

facture [faktyʀ] NF (à payer: gén) bill; (: Comm) invoice; (d'un artisan, artiste) technique, workmanship

facturer [faktyʀe] /1/ VT to invoice

facturette [faktyʀɛt] NF credit card slip

facturier, -ière [faktyʀje, -jɛʀ] NM/F invoice clerk

facultatif, -ive [fakyltatif, -iv] ADJ optional; (arrêt de bus) request cpd

faculté [fakylte] NF (intellectuelle, d'université) faculty; (pouvoir, possibilité) power

fada [fada] (fam) ADJ cracked (fam) ▸ NM crackpot (fam)

fadaises [fadɛz] NFPL twaddle sg

fade [fad] ADJ insipid

fadette [fadɛt] NF (Tél) mobile phone records (BRIT); cellphone records (US)

fadeur [fadœʀ] NF (de plat) blandness; (de couleur, style) dullness

fading [fadiŋ] NM (Radio) fading

fagot [fago] NM (de bois) bundle of sticks

fagoté, e [fagɔte] ADJ (fam): **drôlement ~** oddly dressed

FAI SIGLE M (= fournisseur d'accès à Internet) ISP (= internet service provider)

faiblard, e [fɛblaʀ, -aʀd] ADJ (fam, péj: raisonnement, argument, personne) feeble; (: son, lumière) weak

★**faible** [fɛbl] ADJ weak; (voix, lumière, vent) faint; (élève, copie) poor; (rendement, intensité, revenu etc) low ▸ NM weak point; (pour quelqu'un) weakness, soft spot; **~ d'esprit** feeble-minded

faiblement [fɛbləmɑ̃] ADV weakly; (peu: éclairer etc) faintly

faiblesse [fɛblɛs] NF weakness

faiblir [feblir] /2/ VI to weaken; (lumière) to dim; (vent) to drop

faïence [fajɑ̃s] NF earthenware no pl; (objet) piece of earthenware

faignant, e [fɛɲɑ̃, -ɑ̃t] NM/F = **fainéant**

faille [faj] VB voir **falloir** ▸ NF (Géo) fault; (fig) flaw, weakness

failli, e [faji] ADJ, NM/F bankrupt

faillible [fajibl] ADJ fallible

faillir [fajiʀ] /2/ VI: **j'ai failli tomber/lui dire** I almost ou nearly fell/told him; **~ à une promesse/un engagement** to break a promise/an agreement

faillite [fajit] NF bankruptcy; (échec: d'une politique etc) collapse; **être en ~** to be bankrupt; **faire ~** to go bankrupt

★**faim** [fɛ̃] NF hunger; (fig): **~ d'amour/de richesse** hunger ou yearning for love/wealth; **avoir ~** to be hungry; **rester sur sa ~** (aussi fig) to be left wanting more

fainéant, e [fɛneɑ̃, -ɑ̃t] NM/F idler, loafer

fainéanter [fɛneɑ̃te] VI to laze around

fainéantise [fɛneɑ̃tiz] NF idleness, laziness

---

faire [fɛʀ]

/60/ VT **1** (fabriquer, être l'auteur de) to make; (produire) to produce; (construire: maison, bateau) to build; **faire du vin/une offre/un film** to make wine/an offer/a film; **faire du bruit** to make a noise

2 (effectuer: travail, opération) to do; **que faites-vous?** (quel métier etc) what do you do?; (quelle activité: au moment de la question) what are you doing?; **que faire?** what are we going to do?, what can be done (about it)?; **faire la lessive/le ménage** to do the washing/the housework

3 (études) to do; (sport, musique) to play; **faire du droit/du français** to do law/French; **faire du rugby/piano** to play rugby/the piano; **faire du cheval/du ski** to go riding/skiing

4 (visiter): **faire les magasins** to go shopping; **faire l'Europe** to tour ou do Europe

5 (vitesse, distance): **faire du 50 (à l'heure)** to do 50 (km an hour); **nous avons fait 1000 km en 2 jours** we did ou covered 1000 km in 2 days

6 (simuler): **faire le malade/l'ignorant** to act the invalid/the fool

7 (transformer, avoir un effet sur): **faire de qn un frustré/avocat** to make sb frustrated/a lawyer; **ça ne me fait rien** (m'est égal) I don't care ou mind; (me laisse froid) it has no effect on me; **ça ne fait rien** it doesn't matter; **faire que** (impliquer) to mean that

8 (calculs, prix, mesures): **deux et deux font quatre** two and two are ou make four; **ça fait 10 m/15 euros** it's 10 m/15 euros; **je vous le fais 10 euros** I'll let you have it for 10 euros; **je fais du 40** I take a size 40

9 (vb+de): **qu'a-t-il fait de sa valise/de sa sœur?** what has he done with his case/his sister?

10: **ne faire que**: **il ne fait que critiquer** (sans cesse) all he (ever) does is criticize; (seulement) he's only criticizing

11 (dire) to say; **vraiment? fit-il** really? he said

12 (maladie) to have; **faire du diabète/de la tension** to have diabetes sg/high blood pressure

▸ VI **1** (agir, s'y prendre) to act, do; **il faut faire vite** we (ou you etc) must act quickly; **comment a-t-il fait pour?** how did he manage to?; **faites comme chez vous** make yourself at home; **je n'ai pas pu faire autrement** there was nothing else I could do

2 (paraître) to look; **faire vieux/démodé** to look old/old-fashioned; **ça fait bien** it looks good; **tu fais jeune dans cette robe** that dress makes you look young(er)

3 (remplaçant un autre verbe) to do; **ne le casse pas comme je l'ai fait** don't break it as I did; **je peux le voir? — faites!** can I see it? — please do!; **remets-le en place — je viens de le faire** put it back in its place — I just have (done)

▸ VB IMPERS **1**: **il fait beau** etc the weather is fine etc; voir aussi **jour**; **froid** etc

2 (temps écoulé: durée): **ça fait deux ans qu'il est parti** it's two years since he left; **ça fait deux ans qu'il y est** he's been there for two years

▸ VB AUX **1**: **faire** +infinitif (action directe) to make; **faire tomber/bouger qch** to make sth fall/move; **faire démarrer un moteur/chauffer de l'eau** to start up an engine/heat some water; **cela fait dormir** it makes you sleep; **faire travailler les enfants** to make the children work ou get the children to work; **il m'a fait traverser la rue** he helped me to cross the road

2 : **faire** +infinitif (indirectement, par un intermédiaire): **faire réparer qch** to get ou have sth repaired; **faire punir les enfants** to have the children punished; **il m'a fait ouvrir la porte** he got me to open the door

■ **se faire** VPR **1** (vin, fromage) to mature

2 (être convenable): **cela se fait beaucoup/ne se fait pas** it's done a lot/not done

3 +nom ou pron: **se faire une jupe** to make o.s. a skirt; **se faire des amis** to make friends; **se faire du souci** to worry; **se faire des illusions** to delude o.s.; **se faire beaucoup d'argent** to make a lot of money; **il ne s'en fait pas** he doesn't worry

4 +adj (devenir): **se faire vieux** to be getting old; (: délibérément): **se faire beau** to do o.s. up

5 : **se faire à** (s'habituer) to get used to; **je n'arrive pas à me faire à la nourriture/au climat** I can't get used to the food/climate

6 +infinitif: **se faire examiner la vue/opérer** to have one's eyes tested/have an operation; **se faire couper les cheveux** to get one's hair cut; **il va se faire tuer/punir** he's going to get himself killed/get (himself) punished; **il s'est fait aider** he got somebody to help him; **il s'est fait aider par Simon** he got Simon to help him; **se faire faire un vêtement** to get a garment made for o.s.

7 (impersonnel): **comment se fait-il/faisait-il que ?** how is it/was it that?; **il peut se faire que nous utilisions …** it's possible that we could use …

faire-part [fɛʀpaʀ] NM INV announcement (of birth, marriage etc)

fair-play [fɛʀplɛ] ADJ INV fair play

fais [fɛ] VB voir **faire**

faisabilité [fəzabilite] NF feasibility

faisable [fəzabl] ADJ feasible

faisais etc [fəzɛ] VB voir **faire**

faisan, e [fəzɑ̃, -an] NM/F pheasant

faisandé, e [fəzɑ̃de] ADJ high (bad); (fig: péj) corrupt, decadent

faisceau, x [fɛso] NM (de lumière etc) beam; (de branches etc) bundle

faiseur, -euse [fəzœʀ, -øz] NM/F (gén: péj): **~ de** maker of; **~ de projets** schemer ▶ NM (bespoke) tailor

faisons etc [fəzɔ̃] VB voir **faire**

faisselle [fɛsɛl] NF cheese strainer

fait¹ [fɛ] VB voir **faire** ▶ NM (événement) event, occurrence; (réalité, donnée) fact; **le ~ que/de manger** the fact that/of eating; **être le ~ de** (causé par) to be the work of; **être au ~ (de)** to be informed (of); **mettre qn au ~** to inform sb, put sb in the picture; **au ~** (à propos) by the way; **en venir au ~** to get to the point; **de ~** adj (opposé à: de droit) de facto; adv in fact; **du ~ de ceci/qu'il a menti** because of ou on account of this/his having lied; **de ce ~** therefore, for this reason; **en ~** in fact; **en ~ de repas** by way of a meal; **prendre ~ et cause pour qn** to support sb, side with sb; **prendre qn sur le ~** to catch sb in the act; **dire à qn son ~** to give sb a piece of one's mind; **hauts faits** (exploits) exploits;

~ d'armes feat of arms; **~ divers** (short) news item; **les faits et gestes de qn** sb's actions ou doings

fait², e [fɛ, fɛt] PP de **faire** ▶ ADJ (mûr: fromage, melon) ripe; (maquillé: yeux) made-up; (vernis: ongles) painted, polished; **un homme ~** a grown man; **tout(e) ~(e)** (préparé à l'avance) ready-made; **c'en est ~ de notre tranquillité** that's the end of our peace; **c'est bien ~ (pour lui** ou **eux etc)** it serves him (ou them etc) right

faîte [fɛt] NM top; (fig) pinnacle, height

faites [fɛt] VB voir **faire**

faîtière [fɛtjɛʀ] NF (de tente) ridge pole

faitout [fɛtu] NM stewpot

fakir [fakiʀ] NM (Théât) wizard

falaise [falɛz] NF cliff

falbalas [falbala] NMPL fripperies, frills

fallacieux, -euse [fa(l)lasjø, -øz] ADJ (raisonnement) fallacious; (apparences) deceptive; (espoir) illusory

★**falloir** [falwaʀ] **/29/** VB IMPERS: **il faut faire les lits** we (ou you etc) have to ou must make the beds; **il faut que je fasse les lits** I have to ou must make the beds; **il a fallu qu'il parte** he had to leave; **il faudrait qu'elle rentre** she should come ou go back, she ought to come ou go back; **il faut faire attention** you have to be careful; **il me faudrait 100 euros** I would need 100 euros; **il doit ~ du temps** that must take time; **il vous faut tourner à gauche après l'église** you have to turn left past the church; **nous avons ce qu'il (nous) faut** we have what we need; **il faut qu'il ait oublié** he must have forgotten; **il a fallu qu'il l'apprenne** he would have to hear about it; **il ne fallait pas** (pour remercier) you shouldn't have (done); **faut le faire !** (fam) (it) takes some doing!; **comme il faut** adj proper; adv properly ■ **s'en falloir** VPR: **il s'en est fallu de 10 euros/5 minutes** we (ou they etc) were 10 euros short/5 minutes late (ou early); **il s'en faut de beaucoup qu'il soit …** he is far from being …; **il s'en est fallu de peu que cela n'arrive** it very nearly happened; **ou peu s'en faut** or just about, or as good as

fallu [faly] PP de **falloir**

falot, e [falo, -ɔt] ADJ dreary, colourless (BRIT), colorless (US) ▶ NM lantern

falsification [falsifikasjɔ̃] NF falsification

falsifier [falsifje] **/7/** VT to falsify

famé, e [fame] ADJ: **mal ~** disreputable, of ill repute

famélique [famelik] ADJ half-starved

fameux, -euse [famø, -øz] ADJ (illustre parfois péj) famous; (bon: repas, plat etc) first-rate, first-class; (intensif): **un ~ problème** etc a real problem etc; **pas ~** not great, not much good

familial, e, -aux [familjal, -o] ADJ family cpd ▶ NF (Auto) family estate car (BRIT), station wagon (US)

familiariser [familjaʀize] **/1/** VT: **~ qn avec** to familiarize sb with; **se ~ avec** to familiarize o.s. with

familiarité [familjaʀite] NF familiarity; informality; **~ avec** (sujet, science) familiarity with ■ **familiarités** NFPL familiarities

familier, -ière [familje, -jɛʀ] ADJ (connu, impertinent) familiar; (atmosphère) informal, friendly; (Ling) informal, colloquial ▶ NM regular (visitor)

familièrement [familjɛʀmɑ̃] ADV (*sans façon: s'entretenir*) informally; (*cavalièrement*) familiarly

★**famille** [famij] NF family; **il a de la ~ à Paris** he has relatives in Paris

> En anglais britannique, le mot **family** peut fonctionner comme un singulier ou un pluriel selon que l'accent est mis sur le groupe en général ou sur ses membres. Le verbe qui suit peut donc être au singulier ou au pluriel.
> *La famille, c'est très important pour moi.* **Family is very important to me.**
> *Sa famille l'aide beaucoup.* **Her family help her a lot.**

famine [famin] NF famine

fan [fan] NMF fan ▶ NF **~ zone** a space which is temporarily set up for public screenings of major sporting events

fana [fana] ADJ, NMF (*fam*) = **fanatique**

fanal, -aux [fanal, -o] NM beacon; lantern

fanatique [fanatik] ADJ: **~ (de)** fanatical (about) ▶ NMF fanatic

fanatiser [fanatize] VT to make fanatical

fanatisme [fanatism] NM fanaticism

fane [fan] NF (*de carotte, de radis*) top

fané, e [fane] ADJ faded

faner [fane] /1/: **se faner** VPR to fade

fanes [fan] NFPL tops; **des ~ de radis** radish tops

faneur, -euse [fanœʀ, -øz] NM/F haymaker ▶ NF (*Tech*) tedder

fanfare [fɑ̃faʀ] NF (*orchestre*) brass band; (*musique*) fanfare; **en ~** (*avec bruit*) noisily

fanfaron, ne [fɑ̃faʀɔ̃, -ɔn] NM/F braggart

fanfaronnades [fɑ̃faʀɔnad] NFPL bragging *no pl*

fanfaronner [fɑ̃faʀɔne] VI to brag, boast

fanfreluches [fɑ̃fʀəlyʃ] NFPL trimming *no pl*

fange [fɑ̃ʒ] NF mire

fanion [fanjɔ̃] NM pennant

fanon [fanɔ̃] NM (*de baleine*) plate of baleen; (*repli de peau*) dewlap, wattle

fantaisie [fɑ̃tezi] NF (*spontanéité*) fancy, imagination; (*caprice*) whim; extravagance; (*Mus*) fantasia ▶ ADJ: **bijou ~** (piece of) costume jewellery (*Brit*) *ou* jewelry (*US*); **pain ~** fancy bread

fantaisiste [fɑ̃tezist] ADJ (*péj*) unorthodox, eccentric ▶ NMF (*de music-hall*) variety artist *ou* entertainer

fantasmagorique [fɑ̃tasmagɔʀik] ADJ phantasmagorical

fantasmatique [fɑ̃tasmatik] ADJ fantastical

fantasme [fɑ̃tasm] NM fantasy

fantasmer [fɑ̃tasme] /1/ VI to fantasize

fantasque [fɑ̃task] ADJ whimsical, capricious; fantastic

fantassin [fɑ̃tasɛ̃] NM infantryman

★**fantastique** [fɑ̃tastik] ADJ fantastic

fantoche [fɑ̃tɔʃ] NM (*péj*) puppet

fantomatique [fɑ̃tɔmatik] ADJ ghostly

fantôme [fɑ̃tom] NM ghost, phantom

FAO SIGLE F (= *Food and Agricultural Organization*) FAO

faon [fɑ̃] NM fawn (*deer*)

FAQ SIGLE F (= *foire aux questions*) FAQ *pl* (= *frequently asked questions*)

far [faʀ] NM (*aussi:* **far breton**) prune custard flan

faramineux, -euse [faʀaminø, -øz] ADJ (*fam*) fantastic

farandole [faʀɑ̃dɔl] NF farandole

farce [faʀs] NF (*viande*) stuffing; (*blague*) (practical) joke; (*Théât*) farce; **faire une ~ à qn** to play a (practical) joke on sb; **farces et attrapes** jokes and novelties

farceur, -euse [faʀsœʀ, -øz] NM/F practical joker; (*fumiste*) clown

farci, e [faʀsi] ADJ (*Culin*) stuffed

farcir [faʀsiʀ] /2/ VT (*viande*) to stuff; (*fig*) **~ qch de** to stuff sth with ▪ **se farcir** VPR (*fam*): **je me suis farci la vaisselle** I've got stuck *ou* landed with the washing-up

fard [faʀ] NM make-up; **~ à joues** blusher

fardeau, x [faʀdo] NM burden

farder [faʀde] /1/ VT to make up; (*vérité*) to disguise ▪ **se farder** VPR to make o.s. up

farfadet [faʀfadɛ] NM elf

farfelu, e [faʀfəly] ADJ wacky (*fam*), hare-brained

farfouiller [faʀfuje] /1/ VI (*péj*) to rummage around

fariboles [faʀibɔl] NFPL nonsense *no pl*

★**farine** [faʀin] NF flour; **~ de blé** wheatflour; **~ de maïs** cornflour (*Brit*), cornstarch (*US*); **~ lactée** (*pour bouillie*) baby cereal

fariner [faʀine] /1/ VT to flour

farineux, -euse [faʀinø, -øz] ADJ (*sauce, pomme*) floury ▶ NMPL (*aliments*) starchy foods

farniente [faʀnjɛnte] NM idleness

farouche [faʀuʃ] ADJ shy, timid; (*sauvage*) savage, wild; (*violent*) fierce

farouchement [faʀuʃmɑ̃] ADV fiercely

fart [faʀt] NM (ski) wax

farter [faʀte] /1/ VT to wax

fascicule [fasikyl] NM volume

fascinant, e [fasinɑ̃, -ɑ̃t] ADJ fascinating

fascination [fasinasjɔ̃] NF fascination

fasciner [fasine] /1/ VT to fascinate

fascisant, e [faʃizɑ̃, -ɑ̃t] ADJ fascistic

fascisme [faʃism] NM fascism

fasciste [faʃist] ADJ, NMF fascist

fasse *etc* [fas] VB *voir* **faire**

faste [fast] NM splendour (*Brit*), splendor (*US*) ▶ ADJ: **c'est un jour ~** it's his (*ou* our *etc*) lucky day

fast-food [fastfud] (*pl* **fast-foods**) NM fast food; (*restaurant*) snack bar

fastidieux, -euse [fastidjø, -øz] ADJ tedious, tiresome

fastoche [fastɔʃ] ADJ (*fam*) easy-peasy (*fam*)

fastueux, -euse [fastɥø, -øz] ADJ sumptuous, luxurious

fat [fa(t)] ADJ M conceited, smug

fatal, e [fatal] ADJ fatal; (*inévitable*) inevitable

fatalement [fatalmɑ̃] ADV inevitably

fatalisme [fatalism] NM fatalism

fataliste [fatalist] ADJ fatalistic

fatalité [fatalite] NF (*destin*) fate; (*coïncidence*) fateful coincidence; (*caractère inévitable*) inevitability

fatidique [fatidik] ADJ fateful

★**fatigant, e** [fatigɑ̃, -ɑ̃t] ADJ tiring; (agaçant) tiresome

★**fatigue** [fatig] NF tiredness, fatigue; (détérioration) fatigue; **les fatigues du voyage** the wear and tear of the journey

★**fatigué, e** [fatige] ADJ tired

★**fatiguer** [fatige] /1/ VT to tire, make tired; (Tech) to put a strain on, strain; (fig: agacer) to annoy ▶ VI (moteur) to labour (BRIT), labor (US), strain ■ **se fatiguer** VPR to get tired; to tire o.s. (out); **se ~ à faire qch** to tire o.s. out doing sth

fatras [fatrɑ] NM jumble, hotchpotch

fatuité [fatɥite] NF conceitedness, smugness

faubourg [fobuʀ] NM suburb

faubourien, ne [fobuʀjɛ̃, -ɛn] ADJ (accent) working-class

fauche [foʃ] NF (de pré) mowing; (de blé) cutting; (fam: vol) theft

fauché, e [foʃe] ADJ (fam) broke

faucher [foʃe] /1/ VT (herbe) to cut; (champs, blés) to reap; (fig) to cut down; (véhicule) to mow down; (fam: voler) to pinch, nick

faucheur, -euse [foʃœʀ, -øz] NM/F reaper, mower

faucheux [foʃø] NM (araignée) harvestman

faucille [fosij] NF sickle

faucon [fokɔ̃] NM falcon, hawk

fauconnerie [fokɔnʀi] NF (dressage) falconry; (chasse) hawking, falconry

faudra etc [fodʀa] VB voir **falloir**

faufil [fofil] NM (Couture) tacking thread

faufilage [fofilaʒ] NM (Couture) tacking

faufiler [fofile] /1/ VT to tack, baste ■ **se faufiler** VPR: **se ~ dans** to edge one's way into; **se ~ parmi/entre** to thread one's way among/between

faune [fon] NF (Zool) wildlife, fauna; (fig: péj) set, crowd; **~ marine** marine (animal) life ▶ NM faun

faussaire [fosɛʀ] NMF forger

fausse [fos] ADJ F voir **faux²**

faussement [fosmɑ̃] ADV (accuser) wrongly, wrongfully; (croire) falsely, erroneously

fausser [fose] /1/ VT (objet) to bend, buckle; (fig) to distort; **~ compagnie à qn** to give sb the slip

fausset [fosɛ] NM: **voix de ~** falsetto voice

fausseté [foste] NF wrongness; falseness

faut [fo] VB voir **falloir**

★**faute** [fot] NF (erreur) mistake, error; (péché, manquement) misdemeanour; (Football etc) offence; (Tennis) fault; (responsabilité): **par la ~ de** through the fault of, because of; **c'est de sa/ma ~** it's his/my fault; **être en ~** to be in the wrong; **prendre qn en ~** to catch sb out; **~ de** (temps, argent) for ou through lack of; **~ de mieux** for want of anything ou something better; **sans ~** adv without fail; **~ de frappe** typing error; **~ d'inattention** careless mistake; **~ d'orthographe** spelling mistake; **~ professionnelle** professional misconduct no pl

fauter [fote] VI (commettre une faute) to be at fault; (vieilli: femme, fille) to stray

★**fauteuil** [fotœj] NM armchair; **~ à bascule** rocking chair; **~ club** (big) easy chair; **~ d'orchestre** seat in the front stalls (BRIT) ou the orchestra (US); **~ roulant** wheelchair

fauteur [fotœʀ] NM: **~ de troubles** trouble-maker

fautif, -ive [fotif, -iv] ADJ (incorrect) incorrect, inaccurate; (responsable) at fault, in the wrong; **il se sentait ~** he felt he was at fault ▶ NM/F culprit

fauve [fov] NM wildcat; (peintre) Fauve ▶ ADJ (couleur) fawn

fauvette [fovɛt] NF warbler

fauvisme [fovism] NM (Art) Fauvism

★**faux¹** [fo] NF scythe

faux², fausse [fo, fos] ADJ (inexact) wrong; (piano, voix) out of tune; (falsifié: billet) fake, forged; (sournois, postiche) false; **~ ami** (Ling) faux ami; **faire ~ bond à qn** to let sb down; **~ col** detachable collar; **~ départ** (Sport, fig) false start; **faire fausse route** to go the wrong way; **un ~ numéro** a wrong number; **~ frais** nmpl extras, incidental expenses; **~ frère** (fig: péj) false friend; **~ mouvement** awkward movement; **~ nez** false nose; **~ nom** assumed name; **~ pas** tripping no pl; (fig) faux pas; **faire un ~ pas** to trip; (fig) to make a faux pas; **~ témoignage** perjury; **fausse alerte** false alarm; **fausse clé** fake key; **fausse couche** (Méd) miscarriage; **fausse joie** vain joy; **fausse note** wrong note ▶ ADV (chanter, jouer) out of tune ▶ NM (copie) fake, forgery; (opposé au vrai): **le ~** falsehood

faux-filet [fofilɛ] NM sirloin

faux-fuyant [fofɥijɑ̃] NM equivocation

faux-monnayeur [fomɔnɛjœʀ] NM counterfeiter, forger

faux-semblant [fosɑ̃blɑ̃] NM pretence (BRIT), pretense (US)

faux-sens [fosɑ̃s] NM mistranslation

faveur [favœʀ] NF favour (BRIT), favor (US); **traitement de ~** preferential treatment; **à la ~ de** under cover of; (grâce à) thanks to; **en ~ de** in favo(u)r of

favorable [favɔʀabl] ADJ favo(u)rable

favorablement [favɔʀabləmɑ̃] ADV (juger, accueillir) favourably (BRIT), favorably (US)

★**favori, te** [favɔʀi, -it] ADJ, NM/F favo(u)rite

favoris [favɔʀi] NMPL (barbe) sideboards (BRIT), sideburns

favoriser [favɔʀize] /1/ VT to favour (BRIT), favor (US)

favoritisme [favɔʀitism] NM (péj) favo(u)ritism

fax [faks] NM fax

faxer [fakse] /1/ VT to fax

fayot [fajo] NM (fam) crawler

fayoter [fajɔte] VI (fam: élève) to crawl (fam)

FBI SIGLE M FBI

FC SIGLE M (= Football Club) FC

fébrile [febril] ADJ feverish, febrile; **capitaux fébriles** (Écon) hot money

fébrilement [febʀilmɑ̃] ADV feverishly

fécal, e, -aux [fekal, -o] ADJ voir **matière**

fécond, e [fekɔ̃, -ɔ̃d] ADJ fertile

fécondation [fekɔ̃dasjɔ̃] NF fertilization

féconder [fekɔ̃de] /1/ VT to fertilize

fécondité [fekɔ̃dite] NF fertility

fécule [fekyl] NF potato flour

féculent [fekylɑ̃] NM starchy food

fédéral, e, -aux [federal, -o] ADJ federal

fédéralisme [federalism] NM federalism

fédéraliste [federalist] ADJ federalist

fédérateur, -trice [federatœʀ, -tʀis] ADJ (*mouvement, événement*) unifying

fédération [federasjɔ̃] NF federation; **la F~ française de football** the French football association

fédérer [federe] VT (*États*) to federate; (*secteur, membres d'une profession*) to unite ■ **se fédérer** VPR to federate

fée [fe] NF fairy

feeling [filiŋ] NM (*fam: intuition*) feel, instinct; **au ~** by feel, by instinct

féerie [feʀi] NF enchantment

féerique [feʀik] ADJ magical, fairytale *cpd*

feignant, e [fɛɲɑ̃, -ɑ̃t] NM/F = **fainéant**

feindre [fɛ̃dʀ] **/52/** VT to feign; **~ de faire** to pretend to do ▸ VI (*liter*) to dissemble

feint, e [fɛ̃, fɛ̃t] PP *de* **feindre** ▸ ADJ feigned ▸ NF (*Sport: escrime*) feint; (: *Football, Rugby*) dummy (BRIT), fake (US); (*fam: ruse*) sham

feinter [fɛ̃te] **/1/** VI (*Sport: escrime*) to feint; (: *Football, Rugby*) to dummy (BRIT), fake (US) ▸ VT (*fam: tromper*) to fool

fêlé, e [fele] ADJ (*aussi fig*) cracked

fêler [fele] **/1/** VT to crack

félicitations [felisitasjɔ̃] NFPL congratulations

félicité [felisite] NF bliss

féliciter [felisite] **/1/** VT: **~ qn (de)** to congratulate sb (on)

félidé [felide] NM felid

félin, e [felɛ̃, -in] ADJ, NM feline

fellaga, fellagha [fɛlaga] NM North African freedom fighter

fellation [felasjɔ̃] NF fellatio

félon, ne [felɔ̃, -ɔn] ADJ perfidious, treacherous

félonie [feloni] NF treachery

felouque [fəluk] NF felucca

fêlure [felyʀ] NF crack

femelle [fəmɛl] ADJ (*aussi Élec, Tech*) female ▸ NF female

féminin, e [feminɛ̃, -in] ADJ feminine; (*sexe*) female; (*équipe, vêtements etc*) women's; (*parfois péj: homme*) effeminate ▸ NM (*Ling*) feminine

féminisation [feminizasjɔ̃] NF (*de marché du travail, profession, noms de métier*) feminization

féminiser [feminize] **/1/** VT to feminize; (*rendre efféminé*) to make effeminate ■ **se féminiser** VPR: **cette profession se féminise** this profession is attracting more women

féminisme [feminism] NM feminism

féministe [feminist] ADJ, NF feminist

féminité [feminite] NF femininity

★**femme** [fam] NF woman; (*épouse*) wife; **être très ~** to be very much a woman; **devenir ~** to attain womanhood; **~ d'affaires** businesswoman; **~ de chambre** chambermaid; **~ fatale** femme fatale; **~ au foyer** housewife; **~ d'intérieur** (real) homemaker; **~ de ménage** domestic help, cleaning lady; **~ du monde** society woman; **femme-objet** sex object; **~ de tête** determined, intellectual woman

femmelette [famlɛt] NF (*fam, péj*) wimp

fémoral, e, -aux [femoral, -o] ADJ femoral

fémur [femyʀ] NM femur, thighbone

FEN [fɛn] SIGLE F (= *Fédération de l'Éducation nationale*) teachers' trades union

fenaison [fənɛzɔ̃] NF haymaking

fendillé, e [fãdije] ADJ (*terre*) crazed

fendiller [fãdije]: **se fendiller** VPR (*terre*) to crack, craze; (*peau*) to crack

fendre [fãdʀ] VT (*bois*) to split; (*pierre*) to crack; (*fig: air, eau*) to cut through; (*foule*) to push one's way through; **il gèle à pierre ~** it's freezing hard ■ **se fendre** VPR to crack

fendu, e [fãdy] ADJ (*sol, mur*) cracked; (*jupe*) slit

fenêtre [f(ə)nɛtʀ] NF window; **~ à guillotine** sash window

fennec [fenɛk] NM fennec

fenouil [fanuj] NM fennel

fente [fãt] NF (*fissure*) crack; (*de boîte à lettres etc*) slit

féodal, e, -aux [feodal, -o] ADJ feudal

féodalisme [feodalism] NM feudalism

féodalité [feodalite] NF feudalism

★**fer** [fɛʀ] NM iron; (*de cheval*) shoe; **au ~ rouge** with a red-hot iron; **santé/main de ~** iron constitution/ hand; **~ à cheval** horseshoe; **en ~ à cheval** (*fig*) horseshoe-shaped; **~ forgé** wrought iron; **~ à friser** curling tongs; **~ de lance** spearhead; **~ (à repasser)** iron; **~ à souder** soldering iron ■ **fers** NMPL (*Méd*) forceps; **mettre aux fers** (*enchaîner*) to put in chains

ferai *etc* [fəʀe] VB *voir* **faire**

fer-blanc [fɛʀblɑ̃] (*pl* **fers-blancs**) NM tin(plate)

ferblanterie [fɛʀblɑ̃tʀi] NF tinplate making; (*produit*) tinware

ferblantier [fɛʀblɑ̃tje] NM tinsmith

férié, e [feʀje] ADJ: **jour ~** public holiday

ferions *etc* [fəʀjɔ̃] VB *voir* **faire**

férir [feʀiʀ]: **sans coup ~** *adv* without meeting any opposition

fermage [fɛʀmaʒ] NM tenant farming

★**ferme** [fɛʀm] ADJ firm ▸ ADV (*travailler*) hard; (*discuter*) ardently; **tenir ~** to stand firm ▸ NF (*exploitation*) farm; (*maison*) farmhouse

★**fermé, e** [fɛʀme] ADJ closed, shut; (*gaz, eau etc*) off; (*fig: personne*) uncommunicative; (: *milieu*) exclusive

fermement [fɛʀməmɑ̃] ADV firmly

ferment [fɛʀmɑ̃] NM ferment

fermentation [fɛʀmɑ̃tasjɔ̃] NF fermentation

fermenter [fɛʀmɑ̃te] **/1/** VI to ferment

★**fermer** [fɛʀme] **/1/** VT to close, shut; (*cesser l'exploitation de*) to close down, shut down; (*eau, gaz, robinet*) to turn off; (*aéroport, route*) to close; **~ à clef** to lock; **~ au verrou** to bolt; **~ les yeux (sur qch)** (*fig*) to close one's eyes (to sth) ▸ VI to close, shut; (*magasin: définitivement*) to close down, shut down ■ **se fermer** VPR to close, shut; (*fleur, blessure*) to close up; **se ~ à** (*pitié, amour*) to close one's heart *ou* mind to

fermeté [fɛʀmate] NF firmness

fermette [fɛʀmɛt] NF farmhouse

★**fermeture** [fɛʀmətyʀ] NF closing; shutting; closing *ou* shutting down; putting *ou* turning off; (*dispositif*) catch; fastening, fastener; **heure de ~** (*Comm*) closing time; **jour de ~** (*Comm*) day on which the shop (*etc*) is closed; **~ éclair®**, **~ à glissière** zip (fastener) (BRIT), zipper (US); *voir* **fermer**

★**fermier, -ière** [fɛʀmje, -jɛʀ] NM/F farmer ▶ NF (*femme de fermier*) farmer's wife ▶ ADJ: **beurre/ cidre ~** farm butter/cider

fermoir [fɛʀmwaʀ] NM clasp

féroce [feʀɔs] ADJ ferocious, fierce

férocement [feʀɔsmɑ̃] ADV ferociously

férocité [feʀɔsite] NF ferocity, ferociousness

ferons *etc* [fəʀɔ̃] VB *voir* **faire**

ferrage [feʀaʒ] NM (*de cheval*) shoeing

ferraille [feʀaj] NF scrap iron; **mettre à la ~** to scrap; **bruit de ~** clanking

ferrailler [feʀaje] /1/ VI to clank

ferrailleur [feʀajœʀ] NM scrap merchant

ferrant [feʀɑ̃] ADJ M *voir* **maréchal-ferrant**

ferré, e [feʀe] ADJ (*chaussure*) hobnailed; (*canne*) steel-tipped; **~ sur** (*fam: savant*) well up on

ferrer [feʀe] /1/ VT (*cheval*) to shoe; (*chaussure*) to nail; (*canne*) to tip; (*poisson*) to strike

ferreux, -euse [feʀø, -øz] ADJ ferrous

ferronnerie [feʀɔnʀi] NF ironwork; **~ d'art** wrought iron work

ferronnier [feʀɔnje] NM craftsman in wrought iron; (*marchand*) ironware merchant

ferroviaire [feʀɔvjɛʀ] ADJ rail *cpd*, railway *cpd* (BRIT), railroad *cpd* (US)

ferrugineux, -euse [feʀyʒinø, -øz] ADJ ferruginous

ferrure [feʀyʀ] NF (*ornamental*) hinge

ferry(-boat) [feʀe(bot)] NM ferry

fertile [fɛʀtil] ADJ fertile; **~ en incidents** eventful, packed with incidents

fertilisant [fɛʀtilizɑ̃] NM fertilizer

fertilisation [fɛʀtilizasjɔ̃] NF fertilization

fertiliser [fɛʀtilize] /1/ VT to fertilize

fertilité [fɛʀtilite] NF fertility

féru, e [feʀy] ADJ: **~ de** with a keen interest in

férule [feʀyl] NF: **être sous la ~ de qn** to be under sb's (iron) rule

fervent, e [fɛʀvɑ̃, -ɑ̃t] ADJ fervent

ferveur [fɛʀvœʀ] NF fervour (BRIT), fervor (US)

fesse [fɛs] NF buttock; **les fesses** the bottom *sg*, the buttocks

fessée [fese] NF spanking

fesser [fese] VT to spank

fessier [fesje] NM (*fam*) behind

festif, -ive [fɛstif, -iv] ADJ (*ambiance, soirée*) festive, party *cpd*

festin [fɛstɛ̃] NM feast

festival [fɛstival] NM festival

festivalier [fɛstivalje] NM festival-goer

festivités [fɛstivite] NFPL festivities, merrymaking *sg*

feston [fɛstɔ̃] NM (*Archit*) festoon; (*Couture*) scallop

festoyer [fɛstwaje] /8/ VI to feast

fêtard, e [fɛtaʀ, -aʀd] NM/F (*fam, péj*) high liver, merrymaker

fête [fɛt] NF (*religieuse*) feast; (*publique*) holiday; (*en famille etc*) celebration; (*réception*) party; (*kermesse*) fête, fair, festival; (*du nom*) feast day, name day; **faire la ~** to live it up; **faire ~ à qn** to give sb a warm welcome; **se faire une ~ de** to look forward to; to enjoy; **ça va être sa ~ !** (*fam*) he's going to get it!; **jour de ~** holiday; **les fêtes (de fin d'année)** the festive season; **la salle/le comité des fêtes** the village hall/festival committee; **la ~ des Mères/Pères** Mother's/Father's Day; **~ de charité** charity fair *ou* fête; **~ foraine** (fun)fair; **la ~ de la musique** *see note*; **~ mobile** movable feast (day); **la F~ Nationale** the national holiday

> The **Fête de la Musique** is a music festival which has taken place every year since 1981. On 21 June throughout France thousands of musicians, both amateur and professional, perform free of charge in parks, streets and squares.

Fête-Dieu [fɛtdjø] (*pl* **Fêtes-Dieu**) NF: **la ~** Corpus Christi

fêter [fete] /1/ VT to celebrate; (*personne*) to have a celebration for

fétiche [fetiʃ] NM fetish; **animal ~**, **objet ~** mascot

fétichisme [fetiʃism] NM fetishism

fétichiste [fetiʃist] ADJ fetishist

fétide [fetid] ADJ fetid

fétu [fety] NM: **~ de paille** wisp of straw

★**feu¹** [fø] ADJ INV: **~ sa mère** his late mother

feu², x [fø] NM (*gén*) fire; (*signal lumineux*) light; (*de cuisinière*) ring; (*sensation de brûlure*) burning (sensation); **au ~ !** fire!; **à ~ doux/vif** over a slow/brisk heat; **à petit ~** (*Culin*) over a gentle heat; (*fig*) slowly; **faire ~** to fire; **ne pas faire long ~** (*fig*) not to last long; **commander le ~** (*Mil*) to give the order to (open) fire; **tué au ~** (*Mil*) killed in action; **mettre à ~** (*fusée*) to fire off; **pris entre deux feux** caught in the crossfire; **en ~** on fire; **être tout ~ tout flamme** (*passion*) to be aflame with passion; (*enthousiasme*) to be burning with enthusiasm; **prendre ~** to catch fire; **mettre le ~ à** to set fire to, set on fire; **faire du ~** to make a fire; **avez-vous du ~ ?** have you (got) a light?; **~ rouge/vert/orange** (*Auto*) red/green/amber (BRIT) *ou* yellow (US) light; **donner le ~ vert à qch/qn** (*fig*) to give sth/ sb the go-ahead *ou* green light; **~ arrière** (*Auto*) rear light; **~ d'artifice** firework; (*spectacle*) fireworks *pl*; **~ de camp** campfire; **~ de cheminée** chimney fire; **~ de joie** bonfire; **~ de paille** (*fig*) flash in the pan ■ **feux** NMPL fire *sg*; (*Auto*) (traffic) lights; **tous feux éteints** (*Navig, Auto*) without lights; **feux de brouillard** (*Auto*) fog lights *ou* lamps; **feux de croisement** (*Auto*) dipped (BRIT) *ou* dimmed (US) headlights; **feux de position** (*Auto*) sidelights; **feux de route** (*Auto*) headlights (on full (BRIT) *ou* high (US) beam); **feux de stationnement** parking lights

feuillage [fœjaʒ] NM foliage, leaves *pl*

feuillaison [fœjɛzɔ̃] NF foliation

★**feuille** [fœj] NF (*d'arbre*) leaf; **~ (de papier)** sheet (of paper); **rendre ~ blanche** (*Scol*) to give in a blank paper; **~ de calcul** spreadsheet; **~ d'or/de métal** gold/metal leaf; **~ de chou** (*péj: journal*) rag; **~ d'impôts** tax form; **~ de maladie** medical expenses claim form; **~ morte** dead leaf; **~ de paie**, **~ de paye** pay slip; **~ de présence** attendance sheet; **~ de température** temperature chart; **~ de vigne** (*Bot*) vine leaf; (*sur statue*) fig leaf; **~ volante** loose sheet

feuillet [fœjɛ] NM leaf, page

feuilletage [fœjta3] NM (*aspect feuilleté*) flakiness

feuilleté, e [fœjte] ADJ (*Culin*) flaky; (*verre*) laminated; **pâte ~** flaky pastry

★**feuilleter** [fœjte] **/4/** VT (*livre*) to leaf through

★**feuilleton** [fœjtɔ̃] NM serial

feuillette *etc* [fœjɛt] VB *voir* **feuilleter**

feuillu, e [fœjy] ADJ leafy ▶ NM broad-leaved tree

feulement [følmɑ̃] NM growl

★**feutre** [føtʀ] NM felt; (*chapeau*) felt hat; (*stylo*) felt-tip(ped pen)

feutré, e [føtʀe] ADJ feltlike; (*pas, voix, atmosphère*) muffled

feutrer [føtʀe] **/1/** VT to line with felt; (*fig: bruits*) to muffle ▶ VI (*tissu*) to felt ■ **se feutrer** VPR (*tissu*) to felt

feutrine [føtʀin] NF (lightweight) felt

fève [fɛv] NF broad bean; (*dans la galette des Rois*) charm (*hidden in cake eaten on Twelfth Night*)

février [fevʀije] NM February; *voir aussi* **juillet**

fez [fɛz] NM fez

FFF ABR = **Fédération française de football**

FFL SIGLE FPL (= *Forces françaises libres*) Free French Army

Fg ABR = **faubourg**

FGAO SIGLE M (= *Fonds de Garantie des Assurances Obligatoires de dommages*) *fund financed through insurance premiums, to compensate victims of uninsured losses*

FGEN SIGLE F (= *Fédération générale de l'éducation nationale*) *teachers' trade union*

fi [fi] EXCL: **faire fi de** to snap one's fingers at

fiabilité [fjabilite] NF reliability

fiable [fjabl] ADJ reliable

fiacre [fjakʀ] NM (hackney) cab *ou* carriage

fiançailles [fjɑ̃saj] NFPL engagement *sg*

fiancé, e [fjɑ̃se] NM/F fiancé (fiancée) ▶ ADJ: **être ~ (à)** to be engaged (to)

fiancer [fjɑ̃se] **/3/**: **se fiancer** VPR: **se ~ (avec)** to become engaged (to)

fiasco [fjasko] NM fiasco

fibranne [fibran] NF bonded fibre *ou* fiber (*US*)

fibre [fibʀ] NF fibre, fiber (*US*); **avoir la ~ paternelle/militaire** to be a born father/soldier; **~ optique** optical fibre *ou* fiber; **~ de verre** fibreglass (*BRIT*), fiberglass (*US*), glass fibre *ou* fiber

fibreux, -euse [fibʀø, -øz] ADJ fibrous; (*viande*) stringy

fibrillation [fibʀijasjɔ̃] NF (*Méd*) fibrillation

fibrociment [fibʀosimɑ̃] NM fibrocement

fibrome [fibʀom] NM (*Méd*) fibroma

fibroscopie [fibʀɔskɔpi] NF fibrescope (*BRIT*) *ou* fiberscope (*US*) inspection

fibule [fibyl] NF fibula (*brooch*)

ficelage [fis(ə)la3] NM tying (up)

ficelé, e [fis(ə)le] ADJ (*fam*): **être mal ~** (*habillé*) to be badly got up; **bien/mal ~** (*conçu: roman, projet*) well/badly put together

ficeler [fis(ə)le] **/4/** VT to tie up

ficelle [fisɛl] NF string; (*morceau*) piece *ou* length of string; (*pain*) thin stick of French bread; **tirer sur la ~** (*fig*) to go too far ■ **ficelles** NFPL (*fig*) strings

fichage [fiʃa3] NM: **le ~ des salariés** recording information about employees

★**fiche** [fiʃ] NF (*carte*) (index) card; (*formulaire*) form; (*Élec*) plug; **~ de paye** pay slip; **~ signalétique** (*Police*) identification card; **~ technique** data sheet, specification *ou* spec sheet

ficher [fiʃe] **/1/** VT (*dans un fichier*) to file; (: *Police*) to put on file; (*fam: faire*) to do; (: *donner*) to give; (: *mettre*) to stick *ou* shove; (*planter*): **~ qch dans** to stick *ou* drive sth into; **~ qn à la porte** (*fam*) to chuck sb out; **fiche(-moi) le camp** (*fam*) clear off; **fiche-moi la paix** (*fam*) leave me alone; **se ~ dans** (*s'enfoncer*) to get stuck in, embed itself in; **se ~ de** (*fam: rire de*) to make fun of; (*être indifférent à*) not to care about

★**fichier** [fiʃje] NM (*gén, Inform*) file; (*à cartes*) card index; **~ actif** *ou* **en cours d'utilisation** (*Inform*) active file; **~ d'adresses** mailing list; **~ d'archives** (*Inform*) archive file; **~ joint** (*Inform*) attachment

fichtre [fiʃtʀ] EXCL (*vieilli, humoristique*) gosh! (*fam*)

fichtrement [fiʃtʀəmɑ̃] ADV (*vieilli, humoristique*) jolly (*BRIT fam*), darned (*fam*)

fichu, e [fiʃy] PP *de* **ficher** ▶ ADJ (*fam: fini, inutilisable*) bust, done for; (: *intensif*) wretched, darned; **être ~ de** to be capable of; **mal ~** feeling lousy; useless; **bien ~** great ▶ NM (*foulard*) (head)scarf

fictif, -ive [fiktif, -iv] ADJ fictitious

fiction [fiksjɔ̃] NF fiction; (*fait imaginé*) invention

fictivement [fiktivmɑ̃] ADV fictitiously

fidèle [fidɛl] ADJ: **~ (à)** faithful (to) ▶ NMF (*Rel*): **les fidèles** the faithful; (*à l'église*) the congregation

fidèlement [fidɛlmɑ̃] ADV faithfully

fidélisation [fidelizasjɔ̃] NF (*de clientèle*) gaining the loyalty of

fidéliser [fidelize] **/1/** VT (*clientèle*) to gain the loyalty of

fidélité [fidelite] NF (*d'un conjoint*) fidelity, faithfulness; (*d'un ami, client*) loyalty

Fidji [fid3i] NFPL: **(les îles) ~** Fiji

fiduciaire [fidysjɛʀ] ADJ fiduciary; **héritier ~** heir, trustee; **monnaie ~** flat money

fief [fjɛf] NM fief; (*fig*) preserve; stronghold

fieffé, e [fjefe] ADJ (*ivrogne, menteur*) arrant, out-and-out

fiel [fjɛl] NM gall

fiente [fjɑ̃t] NF (*bird*) droppings *pl*

★**fier**[1] [fje]: **se fier à** VPR to trust

fier[2]**, fière** [fjɛʀ] ADJ proud; **~ de** proud of; **avoir fière allure** to cut a fine figure

fièrement [fjɛʀmɑ̃] ADV proudly

fierté [fjɛʀte] NF pride

fièvre [fjɛvʀ] NF fever; **avoir de la ~/39 de ~** to have a high temperature/a temperature of 39°C; **~ typhoïde** typhoid fever

fiévreusement [fjevʀøzmɑ̃] ADV (*fig*) feverishly

fiévreux, -euse [fjevʀø, -øz] ADJ feverish

FIFA [fifa] SIGLE F (= *Fédération internationale de Football association*) FIFA

fifre [fifʀ] NM fife; (*personne*) fife-player

fig ABR (= *figure*) fig

figé, e [fiʒe] ADJ (*manières*) stiff; (*société*) rigid; (*sourire*) set

figer [fiʒe] /**3**/ VT to congeal; (*fig: personne*) to freeze, root to the spot ■ **se figer** VPR to congeal; (*personne*) to freeze; (*institutions etc*) to become set, stop evolving

fignoler [fiɲɔle] /**1**/ VT to put the finishing touches to

figue [fig] NF fig

figuier [figje] NM fig tree

figurant, e [figyʀɑ̃, -ɑ̃t] NM/F (*Théât*) walk-on; (*Ciné*) extra

figuratif, -ive [figyʀatif, -iv] ADJ representational, figurative

figuration [figyʀasjɔ̃] NF walk-on parts *pl*; extras *pl*

★**figure** [figyʀ] NF (*visage*) face; (*image, tracé, forme, personnage*) figure; (*illustration*) picture, diagram; **faire ~ de** to look like; **faire bonne ~** to put up a good show; **faire triste ~** to be a sorry sight; **~ de rhétorique** figure of speech

★**figuré, e** [figyʀe] ADJ (*sens*) figurative

figurer [figyʀe] /**1**/ VI to appear ▶ VT to represent ■ **se figurer que** VPR to imagine that; **figurez-vous que ...** would you believe that ...?

figurine [figyʀin] NF figurine

fil [fil] NM (*brin, fig: d'une histoire*) thread; (*du téléphone*) cable, wire; (*textile de lin*) linen; (*d'un couteau tranchant*) edge; **au ~ des années** with the passing of the years; **au ~ de l'eau** with the stream *ou* current; **de ~ en aiguille** one thing leading to another; **ne tenir qu'à un ~** (*vie, réussite etc*) to hang by a thread; **donner du ~ à retordre à qn** to make life difficult for sb; **coup de ~** (*fam*) phone call; **donner/recevoir un coup de ~** to make/get a phone call; **~ à coudre** (*sewing*) thread *ou* yarn; **~ dentaire** dental floss; **~ électrique** electric wire; **~ de fer** wire; **~ de fer barbelé** barbed wire; **~ à pêche** fishing line; **~ à plomb** plumb line; **~ à souder** soldering wire

filaire [filɛʀ] ADJ (*téléphone*) corded

filament [filamɑ̃] NM (*Élec*) filament; (*de liquide*) trickle, thread

filandreux, -euse [filɑ̃dʀø, -øz] ADJ stringy

filant, e [filɑ̃, -ɑ̃t] ADJ **étoile filante** shooting star

filasse [filas] ADJ INV white blond

filature [filatyʀ] NF (*fabrique*) mill; (*policière*) shadowing *no pl*, tailing *no pl*; **prendre qn en ~** to shadow *ou* tail sb

fil-de-feriste, fildeferiste [fildəfəʀist] NMF high-wire artist

file [fil] NF line; (*Auto*) lane; **~ (d'attente)** queue (BRIT), line (US); **prendre la ~** to join the (end of the) queue *ou* line; **prendre la ~ de droite** (*Auto*) to move into the right-hand lane; **se mettre en ~** to form a line; (*Auto*) to get into lane; **stationner en double ~** (*Auto*) to double-park; **à la ~** adv (*d'affilée*) in succession; (*à la suite*) one after another; **à la** *ou* **en ~ indienne** in single file

filer [file] /**1**/ VT (*tissu, toile, verre*) to spin; (*dérouler: câble etc*) to pay *ou* let out; (*prendre en filature*) to shadow, tail; (*fam: donner*): **~ qch à qn** to slip sb sth; **~ un mauvais coton** to be in a bad way ▶ VI

(*bas, maille, liquide, pâte*) to run; (*aller vite*) to fly past *ou* by; (*fam: partir*) to make off; **~ à l'anglaise** to take French leave; **~ doux** to behave o.s., toe the line

filet [filɛ] NM net; (*Culin*) fillet; (*d'eau, de sang*) trickle; (*piège*) **tendre un ~** (*police*) to set a trap; **~ (à bagages)** (*Rail*) luggage rack; **~ (à provisions)** string bag

filetage [filtaʒ] NM threading; thread

fileter [filte] /**5**/ VT to thread

filial, e, -aux [filjal, -o] ADJ filial ▶ NF (*Comm*) subsidiary; affiliate

filiation [filjasjɔ̃] NF filiation

filière [filjɛʀ] NF (*carrière*) path; **passer par la ~** to go through the (administrative) channels; **suivre la ~** to work one's way up (through the hierarchy)

filiforme [filifɔʀm] ADJ spindly; threadlike

filigrane [filigʀan] NM (*d'un billet, timbre*) watermark; **en ~** (*fig*) showing just beneath the surface

filin [filɛ̃] NM (*Navig*) rope

★**fille** [fij] NF girl; (*opposé à fils*) daughter; **vieille ~** old maid; **~ de joie** prostitute; **~ de salle** waitress

fille-mère [fijmɛʀ] (*pl* **filles-mères**) NF unmarried mother

fillette [fijɛt] NF (little) girl

filleul, e [fijœl] NM/F godchild, godson (goddaughter)

★**film** [film] NM (*pour photo*) (roll of) film; (*œuvre*) film, picture, movie; (*couche*) film; **~ muet/parlant** silent/talking picture *ou* movie; **~ alimentaire** clingfilm; **~ d'amour/d'animation/d'horreur** romantic/animated/horror film; **~ comique** comedy; **~ policier** thriller

filmer [filme] /**1**/ VT to film

filmique [filmik] ADJ (*analyse, langage*) film *cpd*, movie *cpd*

filmographie [filmɔgʀafi] NF (*de réalisateur, acteur*) filmography

filon [filɔ̃] NM vein, lode; (*fig*) lucrative line, money-spinner

filou [filu] NM (*escroc*) swindler

★**fils** [fis] NM son; **~ de famille** moneyed young man; **~ à papa** (*péj*) daddy's boy

filtrage [filtʀaʒ] NM filtering

filtrant, e [filtʀɑ̃, -ɑ̃t] ADJ (*huile solaire etc*) filtering

filtre [filtʀ] NM filter; **« ~ ou sans ~ ?»** (*cigarettes*) "tipped or plain?"; **~ à air** air filter

filtrer [filtʀe] /**1**/ VT to filter; (*fig: candidats, visiteurs*) to screen ▶ VI to filter (through)

★**fin¹** [fɛ̃] NF end; **à (la) ~ mai**, **~ mai** at the end of May; **en ~ de semaine** at the end of the week; **prendre ~** to come to an end; **toucher à sa ~** to be drawing to a close; **mettre ~ à** to put an end to; **mener à bonne ~** to bring to a successful conclusion; **à cette ~** to this end; **à la ~** in the end, eventually; **en ~ de compte** in the end; **sans ~** *adj* endless; *adv* endlessly; **~ de non-recevoir** (*Jur, Admin*) objection; **~ de section** (*de ligne d'autobus*) (fare) stage ■ **fins** NFPL (*but*) ends; **à toutes fins utiles** for your information

fin², e [fɛ̃, fin] ADJ (*papier, couche, fil*) thin; (*cheveux, poudre, pointe, visage*) fine; (*taille*) neat, slim; (*esprit, remarque*) subtle; shrewd; **c'est ~ !** (*ironique*) how clever!; **un ~ gourmet** a gourmet; **un ~ tireur** a crack shot; **avoir la vue/l'ouïe fine** to have keen eyesight/hearing, have sharp eyes/ears; **or/linge/vin** fine gold/linen/wine; **le ~ fond de** the very depths of; **le ~ mot de** the real story behind; **la fine fleur de** the flower of; **une fine mouche** *(fig)* a sly customer; **fines herbes** mixed herbs; **vouloir jouer au plus ~ (avec qn)** to try to outsmart sb ▶ ADV *(moudre, couper)* finely; **~ prêt/ soûl** quite ready/drunk ▶ NF *(alcool)* liqueur brandy

final, e [final] *(mpl* finaux [-o], finals*)* ADJ final ▶ NF finals, final; **parvenir en finale** to get through to the finals *ou* final; **quarts de finale** quarter finals; **8èmes/16èmes de finale** 2nd/1st round *(in 5 round knock-out competition)* ▶ NM *(Mus)* finale

★**finalement** [finalmã] ADV finally, in the end; *(après tout)* after all

finalisation [finalizasjɔ̃] NF *(de vente, commande)* completion

finaliser [finalize] VT *(vente, projet)* to complete

finaliste [finalist] NMF finalist

finalité [finalite] NF *(but)* aim, goal; *(fonction)* purpose

finance [finɑ̃s] NF finance; **moyennant ~** for a fee *ou* consideration ■**finances** NFPL *(situation)* finances; *(activités)* finance *sg*

financement [finɑ̃smã] NM financing; **~ participatif** crowdfunding

financer [finɑ̃se] /3/ VT to finance

financiariser [finɑ̃sjaRize] VT to financialize

financier, -ière [finɑ̃sje, -jɛR] ADJ financial ▶ NM financier

financièrement [finɑ̃sjɛRmã] ADV financially

finasser [finase] /1/ VI *(péj)* to wheel and deal

finaud, e [fino, -od] ADJ wily

fine [fin] ADJ F, NF *voir* **fin²**

finement [finmã] ADV thinly; finely; neatly, slimly; subtly; shrewdly

finesse [finɛs] NF thinness; *(raffinement)* fineness; neatness, slimness; *(subtilité)* subtlety; shrewdness ■**finesses** NFPL *(subtilités)* niceties; finer points

fini, e [fini] ADJ finished; *(Math)* finite; *(intensif)*: **un menteur ~** a liar through and through ▶ NM *(d'un objet manufacturé)* finish

★**finir** [finiR] /2/ VT to finish; **~ de faire** to finish doing; *(cesser)* to stop doing ▶ VI to finish, end; **~ quelque part** to end *ou* finish up somewhere; **~ par faire** to end *ou* finish up doing; **il finit par m'agacer** he's beginning to get on my nerves; **~ en pointe/tragédie** to end in a point/in tragedy; **en ~ avec** to have done with; **à n'en plus ~** *(route, discussions)* never-ending; **il va mal ~** he will come to a bad end; **c'est bientôt fini ?** *(reproche)* have you quite finished?

finish [finiʃ] NM *(Sport)* finish

finissage [finisaʒ] NM finishing

finisseur, -euse [finisœR, -øz] NM/F *(Sport)* strong finisher

finition [finisjɔ̃] NF finishing; *(résultat)* finish

★**finlandais, e** [fɛ̃lɑ̃dɛ, -ɛz] ADJ Finnish ▶ NM/F: **Finlandais, e** Finn

★**Finlande** [fɛ̃lɑ̃d] NF: **la ~** Finland

finnois, e [finwa, -waz] ADJ Finnish ▶ NM *(Ling)* Finnish

fiole [fjɔl] NF phial

fiord [fjɔR(d)] NM = **fjord**

fioriture [fjɔRityR] NF embellishment, flourish

fioul [fjul] NM fuel oil

firent [fiR] VB *voir* **faire**

firmament [fiRmamã] NM firmament, skies *pl*

firme [fiRm] NF firm

fis [fi] VB *voir* **faire**

fisc [fisk] NM tax authorities *pl*, ≈ Inland Revenue *(BRIT)*, ≈ Internal Revenue Service *(US)*

fiscal, e, -aux [fiskal, -o] ADJ tax *cpd*, fiscal

fiscaliser [fiskalize] /1/ VT to subject to tax

fiscaliste [fiskalist] NMF tax specialist

fiscalité [fiskalite] NF tax system; *(charges)* taxation

fissa [fisa] ADV *(fam)* in double-quick time

fissible [fisibl] ADJ fissile

fission [fisjɔ̃] NF fission

fissure [fisyR] NF crack

fissurer [fisyRe] /1/ VT to crack ■**se fissurer** VPR to crack

fiston [fistɔ̃] NM *(fam)* son, lad

fistule [fistyl] NF *(Méd)* fistula

fit [fi] VB *voir* **faire**

FIV SIGLE F *(= fécondation in vitro)* IVF

fixage [fiksaʒ] NM *(Photo)* fixing

fixateur [fiksatœR] NM *(Photo)* fixer; *(pour cheveux)* hair cream

fixatif [fiksatif] NM fixative

fixation [fiksasjɔ̃] NF fixing; *(attache)* fastening; setting; *(de ski)* binding; *(Psych)* fixation

★**fixe** [fiks] ADJ fixed; *(emploi)* steady, regular; **à heure ~** at a set time; **menu à prix ~** set menu ▶ NM *(salaire)* basic salary; *(téléphone)* landline

fixé, e [fikse] ADJ *(heure, jour)* appointed; **être ~ (sur)** *(savoir à quoi s'en tenir)* to have made up one's mind (about); to know for certain (about)

fixement [fiksəmã] ADV fixedly, steadily

fixer [fikse] /1/ VT *(attacher)*: **~ qch (à/sur)** to fix *ou* fasten sth (to/onto); *(déterminer)* to fix, set; *(Chimie, Photo)* to fix; *(poser son regard sur)* to stare at, look hard at; **~ son choix sur qch** to decide on sth ■**se fixer** VPR *(s'établir)* to settle down; **se ~ sur** *(attention)* to focus on

fixité [fiksite] NF fixedness

fjord [fjɔR(d)] NM fjord, fiord

fl. ABR *(= fleuve)* r, R; *(= florin)* fl

★**flacon** [flakɔ̃] NM bottle

flagada [flagada] ADJ INV *(fam: fatigué)* shattered

flagellation [flaʒɛlasjɔ̃] NF flogging

flageller [flaʒele] /1/ VT to flog, scourge

flageolant, e [flaʒɔlɑ̃, -ɑ̃t] ADJ *(personne, jambes)* trembling

flageoler [flaʒɔle] /1/ VI to have knees like jelly

flageolet [flaʒɔlɛ] NM *(Mus)* flageolet; *(Culin)* dwarf kidney bean

flagornerie [flagɔRnəRi] NF toadying, fawning

flagorneur, -euse [flagɔʀnœʀ, -øz] NM/F toady, fawner

flagrant, e [flagʀɑ̃, -ɑ̃t] ADJ flagrant, blatant; **en ~ délit** in the act, in flagrante delicto

flair [flɛʀ] NM sense of smell; (*fig*) intuition

flairer [fleʀe] /1/ VT (*humer*) to sniff (at); (*détecter*) to scent

flamand, e [flamɑ̃, -ɑ̃d] ADJ Flemish ▸ NM (*Ling*) Flemish ▸ NM/F: **Flamand, e** Fleming; **les Flamands** the Flemish

flamant [flamɑ̃] NM flamingo

flambant [flɑ̃bɑ̃] ADV: **~ neuf** brand new

flambé, e [flɑ̃be] ADJ (*Culin*) flambé ▸ NF blaze; (*fig*) flaring-up, explosion

flambeau, x [flɑ̃bo] NM (flaming) torch; **se passer le ~** (*fig*) to hand down the (*ou* a) tradition

flambée [flɑ̃be] NF (*feu*) blaze; (*Comm*): **~ des prix** (sudden) shooting up of prices

flamber [flɑ̃be] /1/ VI to blaze (up) ▸ VT (*poulet*) to singe; (*aiguille*) to sterilize

flambeur, -euse [flɑ̃bœʀ, -øz] NM/F big-time gambler

flamboyant, e [flɑ̃bwajɑ̃, -ɑ̃t] ADJ blazing; flaming

flamboyer [flɑ̃bwaje] /8/ VI to blaze (up); (*fig*) to flame

flamenco [flamɛnko] NM flamenco

flamingant, e [flamɛ̃gɑ̃, -ɑ̃t] ADJ Flemish-speaking ▸ NM/F: **Flamingant, e** Flemish speaker; (*Pol*) Flemish nationalist

flamme [flɑm] NF flame; (*fig*) fire, fervour; **en flammes** on fire, ablaze

flammèche [flamɛʃ] NF (flying) spark

flammerole [flamʀɔl] NF will-o'-the-wisp

flan [flɑ̃] NM (*Culin*) custard tart *ou* pie

flanc [flɑ̃] NM side; (*Mil*) flank; **à ~ de colline** on the hillside; **prêter le ~ à** (*fig*) to lay o.s. open to

flancher [flɑ̃ʃe] /1/ VI (*cesser de fonctionner*) to fail, pack up; (*armée*) to quit

Flandre [flɑ̃dʀ] NF: **la ~** (*aussi:* **les Flandres**) Flanders

flanelle [flanɛl] NF flannel

flâner [flɑne] /1/ VI to stroll

flânerie [flɑnʀi] NF stroll

flâneur, -euse [flɑnœʀ, -øz] ADJ idle ▸ NM/F stroller

flanquer [flɑ̃ke] /1/ VT to flank; (*fam: mettre*) to chuck, shove; **~ par terre/à la porte** (*jeter*) to fling to the ground/chuck out; **~ la frousse à qn** (*donner*) to put the wind up sb, give sb an awful fright

flapi, e [flapi] ADJ dog-tired

flaque [flak] NF (*d'eau*) puddle; (*d'huile, de sang etc*) pool

flash [flaʃ] (*pl* **flashes**) NM (*Photo*) flash; **~ (d'information)** newsflash

flash-back [flaʃbak] NM (*Ciné*) flashback

flasque [flask] ADJ flabby ▸ NF (*flacon*) flask

flatter [flate] /1/ VT to flatter; (*caresser*) to stroke; **se ~ de qch** to pride o.s. on sth

flatterie [flatʀi] NF flattery

flatteur, -euse [flatœʀ, -øz] ADJ flattering ▸ NM/F flatterer

flatulence [flatylɑ̃s], **flatuosité** [flatɥozite] NF (*Méd*) flatulence, wind

FLB ABR (= *franco long du bord*) FAS ▸ SIGLE M (*Pol*) = **Front de libération de la Bretagne**

FLC SIGLE M = **Front de libération de la Corse**

fléau, x [fleo] NM scourge, curse; (*de balance*) beam; (*pour le blé*) flail

fléchage [fleʃaʒ] NM (*d'un itinéraire*) signposting

flèche [flɛʃ] NF arrow; (*de clocher*) spire; (*de grue*) jib; (*trait d'esprit, critique*) shaft; **monter en ~** (*fig*) to soar, rocket; **partir en ~** (*fig*) to be off like a shot; **à ~ variable** (*avion*) swing-wing *cpd*

flécher [fleʃe] /1/ VT to arrow, mark with arrows

fléchette [fleʃɛt] NF dart ▪ **fléchettes** NFPL (*jeu*) darts *sg*

fléchir [fleʃiʀ] /2/ VT (*corps, genou*) to bend; (*fig*) to sway, weaken ▸ VI (*poutre*) to sag, bend; (*fig*) to weaken, flag; (: *baisser: prix*) to fall off

fléchissement [fleʃismɑ̃] NM bending; sagging; flagging; (*de l'économie*) dullness

flegmatique [flɛgmatik] ADJ phlegmatic

flegme [flɛgm] NM composure

flemmard, e [flemaʀ, -aʀd] NM/F lazybones *sg*, loafer

flemmarder [flemaʀde] VI (*fam*) to loaf around (*fam*)

flemme [flɛm] NF (*fam*): **j'ai la ~ de faire** I can't be bothered

flétan [fletɑ̃] NM (*Zool*) halibut

flétri, e [fletʀi] ADJ (*fleur, peau*) withered; (*beauté*) faded

flétrir [fletʀiʀ] /2/ VT to wither; (*stigmatiser*) to condemn (in the most severe terms) ▪ **se flétrir** VPR to wither

flétrissement [fletʀismɑ̃] NM (*de fleur, peau*) withering

★**fleur** [flœʀ] NF flower; (*d'un arbre*) blossom; **être en ~** (*arbre*) to be in blossom; **tissu à fleurs** flowered *ou* flowery fabric; **la (fine) ~ de** (*fig*) the flower of; **être ~ bleue** to be soppy *ou* sentimental; **à ~ de terre** just above the ground; **faire une ~ à qn** to do sb a favour (BRIT) *ou* favor (US); **~ de lis** fleur-de-lis

fleurer [flœʀe] /1/ VT: **~ la lavande** to have the scent of lavender

fleuret [flœʀɛ] NM (*arme*) foil; (*sport*) fencing

fleurette [flœʀɛt] NF: **conter ~ à qn** to whisper sweet nothings to sb

fleurettiste [flœʀetist] NMF foil fencer

fleuri, e [flœʀi] ADJ (*jardin*) in flower *ou* bloom; surrounded by flowers; (*fig: style, tissu, papier*) flowery; (: *teint*) glowing

fleurir [flœʀiʀ] /2/ VI (*rose*) to flower; (*arbre*) to blossom; (*fig*) to flourish ▸ VT (*tombe*) to put flowers on; (*chambre*) to decorate with flowers

★**fleuriste** [flœʀist] NMF florist

fleuron [flœʀɔ̃] NM jewel (*fig*)

★**fleuve** [flœv] NM river; **roman-fleuve** saga; **discours-fleuve** interminable speech

flexibiliser [flɛksibilize] VT (*salaires, horaires de travail*) to make (more) flexible

flexibilité [flɛksibilite] NF flexibility

flexible [flɛksibl] ADJ flexible

flexion [flɛksjɔ̃] NF flexing, bending; (*Ling*) inflection

flibustier [flibystje] NM buccaneer

flic [flik] NM (*fam, péj*) cop

flicage [flikaʒ] NM (*fam, péj*) policing

flicaille [flikɑj] NF (*fam, péj*) cops *pl* (*fam*)

flingue [flɛ̃g] NM (*fam*) shooter

flinguer [flɛ̃ge] VT (*fam: tirer sur*) to blow away (*fam*), shoot; (: *détruire: moteur*) to wreck (*fam*); **se faire ~** to get shot

flippant, e [flipɑ̃, -ɑ̃t] ADJ (*fam: angoissant*) freaky (*fam*), creepy (*fam*); (: *déprimant*): **c'est ~** it gets you down

flipper [flipœʀ] NM pinball (machine) ▸ VI [flipe] /1/ (*fam: être déprimé*) to feel down, be on a downer; (: *être exalté*) to freak out

fliquer [flike] VT (*fam, péj: personnel*) to police

flirt [flœʀt] NM flirting; (*personne*) boyfriend, girlfriend

flirter [flœʀte] /1/ VI to flirt

FLNKS SIGLE M (= *Front de libération nationale kanak et socialiste*) political movement in New Caledonia

flocon [flɔkɔ̃] NM flake; (*de laine etc: boulette*) flock; **flocons d'avoine** oat flakes, porridge oats

floconneux, -euse [flɔkɔnø, -øz] ADJ fluffy, fleecy

flonflons [flɔ̃flɔ̃] NMPL blare *sg*

flop [flɔp] NM (*échec*) flop; **faire un ~** to flop

flopée [flɔpe] NF: **une ~ de** loads of

floraison [flɔʀɛzɔ̃] NF flowering; blossoming; flourishing; *voir* **fleurir**

floral, e, -aux [flɔʀal, -o] ADJ floral, flower *cpd*

floralies [flɔʀali] NFPL flower show *sg*

flore [flɔʀ] NF flora

Florence [flɔʀɑ̃s] N (*ville*) Florence

florentin, e [flɔʀɑ̃tɛ̃, -in] ADJ Florentine

floriculture [flɔʀikyltyʀ] NF flower-growing

florilège [flɔʀilɛʒ] NM (*de textes, poèmes*) anthology; (*de sites web, citations*): **un ~ de ...** a list of the top ...

florissant, e [flɔʀisɑ̃, -ɑ̃t] VB *voir* **fleurir** ▸ ADJ (*économie*) flourishing; (*santé, teint, mine*) blooming

flot [flo] NM flood, stream; (*marée*) flood tide; **être à ~** (*Navig*) to be afloat; (*fig*) to be on an even keel ■ **flots** NMPL (*de la mer*) waves; **à flots** (*couler*) in torrents; **entrer à flots** to stream ou pour in

flottage [flɔtaʒ] NM (*du bois*) floating

flottaison [flɔtɛzɔ̃] NF: **ligne de ~** waterline

flottant, e [flɔtɑ̃, -ɑ̃t] ADJ (*vêtement*) loose(-fitting); (*cours, barème*) floating

flotte [flɔt] NF (*Navig*) fleet; (*fam: eau*) water; (: *pluie*) rain

flottement [flɔtmɑ̃] NM (*fig*) wavering, hesitation; (*Écon*) floating

flotter [flɔte] /1/ VI to float; (*nuage, odeur*) to drift; (*drapeau*) to fly; (*vêtements*) to hang loose; **faire ~** to float ▸ VB IMPERS (*fam: pleuvoir*): **il flotte** it's raining ▸ VT to float

flotteur [flɔtœʀ] NM float

flottille [flɔtij] NF flotilla

flou, e [flu] ADJ fuzzy, blurred; (*fig*) woolly (BRIT), vague; (*non ajusté: robe*) loose(-fitting); **~ artistique** (*Photo*) soft focus

flouer [flue] /1/ VT to swindle

flouze [fluz] NM (*fam*) dough (*fam*)

FLQ ABR (= *franco long du quai*) FAQ

fluctuant, e [flyktɥɑ̃, -ɑ̃t] ADJ (*prix, cours*) fluctuating; (*opinions*) changing

fluctuation [flyktɥasjɔ̃] NF fluctuation

fluctuer [flyktɥe] /1/ VI to fluctuate

fluet, te [flyɛ, -ɛt] ADJ thin, slight; (*voix*) thin

fluide [flɥid] ADJ fluid; (*circulation etc*) flowing freely ▸ NM fluid; (*force*) (mysterious) power

fluidifier [flɥidifje] /7/ VT to make fluid ■ **se fluidifier** VPR (*sang*) to thin; (*circulation*) to move more freely; (*échanges*) to take place more easily

fluidité [flɥidite] NF fluidity; free flow

fluor [flyɔʀ] NM fluorine; **dentifrice au ~** fluoride toothpaste

fluoration [flyɔʀasjɔ̃] NF (*d'eau*) fluoridation

fluoré, e [flyɔʀe] ADJ fluoridated

fluorescence [flyɔʀesɑ̃s] NF fluorescence

fluorescent, e [flyɔʀesɑ̃, -ɑ̃t] ADJ fluorescent

flûte [flyt] NF (*aussi*: **flûte traversière**) flute; (*verre*) flute glass; (*pain*) (thin) baguette; **petite ~** piccolo; **~!** I drat it!; **~ (à bec)** recorder; **~ de Pan** panpipes *pl*

flûté, e [flyte] ADJ (*voix*) reedy, piping

flûtiste [flytist] NMF flautist, flute player

fluvial, e, -aux [flyvjal, -o] ADJ river *cpd*, fluvial

flux [fly] NM incoming tide; (*écoulement*) flow; **le ~ et le reflux** the ebb and flow

fluxion [flyksjɔ̃] NF: **~ de poitrine** pneumonia

FM SIGLE F (= *frequency modulation*) FM

Fme ABR (= *femme*) W

FMI SIGLE M (= *Fonds monétaire international*) IMF

FN SIGLE M (= *Front national*) ≈ NF (= National Front)

FNAC [fnak] SIGLE F (= *Fédération nationale des achats des cadres*) chain of discount shops (hi-fi, photo etc)

FNSEA SIGLE F (= *Fédération nationale des syndicats d'exploitants agricoles*) farmers' union

FO SIGLE F (= *Force ouvrière*) trades union

foc [fɔk] NM jib

focal, e, -aux [fɔkal, -o] ADJ focal ▸ NF focal length

focaliser [fɔkalize] /1/ VT to focus

foehn [føn] NM foehn, föhn

fœtal, e, -aux [fetal, -o] ADJ fetal, foetal (BRIT)

fœtus [fetys] NM fetus, foetus (BRIT)

foi [fwa] NF faith; **sous la ~ du serment** under ou on oath; **ajouter ~ à** to lend credence to; **faire ~** (*prouver*) to be evidence; **digne de ~** reliable; **sur la ~ de** on the word ou strength of; **être de bonne/mauvaise ~** to be in good faith/not to be in good faith; **ma ~!** well!

★**foie** [fwa] NM liver; **~ gras** foie gras; **crise de ~** stomach upset

foin [fwɛ̃] NM hay; **faire les foins** to make hay; **faire du ~** (*fam*) to kick up a row

★**foire** [fwaʀ] NF fair; (*fête foraine*) (fun)fair; (*fig: désordre, confusion*) bear garden; ~ **aux questions** (*Internet*) frequently asked questions; **faire la** ~ to whoop it up; ~ **d'exposition** trade fair

foirer [fwaʀe] VI (*fam: échouer*) to come to nothing; **faire** ~ **qch** to balls sth up (*Brit fam*), cock sth up (*fam*)

foireux, -euse [fwaʀø, -øz] ADJ (*fam: plan, idée*) half-baked (*fam*)

★**fois** [fwa] NF time; **une/deux** ~ once/twice; **trois/vingt** ~ three/twenty times; **deux** ~ **deux** twice two; **deux/quatre** ~ **plus grand (que)** twice/four times as big (as); **une** ~ (*passé*) once; (*futur*) sometime; **une (bonne)** ~ **pour toutes** once and for all; **encore une** ~ again, once more; **il était une** ~ once upon a time; **une** ~ **que c'est fait** once it's done; **une** ~ **parti** once he (*ou I etc*) had left; **des** ~ (*parfois*) sometimes; **si des** ~ ... (*fam*) if ever ...; **non mais des** ~ ! (*fam*) (now) look here!; **à la** ~ (*ensemble*) (all) at once; **à la** ~ **grand et beau** both tall and handsome

foison [fwazɔ̃] NF: **une** ~ **de** an abundance of; **à** ~ *adv* in plenty

foisonnant, e [fwazɔnɑ̃, -ɑ̃t] ADJ teeming

foisonnement [fwazɔnmɑ̃] NM profusion, abundance

foisonner [fwazɔne] /1/ VI to abound; ~ **en** *ou* **de** to abound in

fol [fɔl] ADJ M *voir* **fou**

folâtre [fɔlɑtʀ] ADJ playful

folâtrer [fɔlɑtʀe] /1/ VI to frolic (about)

foldingue [fɔldɛ̃g] ADJ (*fam*) crazy (*fam*)

folichon, ne [fɔliʃɔ̃, -ɔn] ADJ: **ça n'a rien de** ~ it's not a lot of fun

folie [fɔli] NF (*d'une décision, d'un acte*) madness, folly; (*état*) madness, insanity; (*acte*) folly; **la** ~ **des grandeurs** delusions of grandeur; **faire des folies** (*en dépenses*) to be extravagant

folk [fɔlk] NM folk music ▶ ADJ INV folk

folklore [fɔlklɔʀ] NM folklore

folklorique [fɔlklɔʀik] ADJ folk *cpd*; (*fam*) weird

★**folle** [fɔl] ADJ F, NF *voir* **fou**

follement [fɔlmɑ̃] ADV (*très*) madly, wildly

follet [fɔlɛ] ADJ M: **feu** ~ will-o'-the-wisp

fomentateur, -trice [fɔmɑ̃tatœʀ, -tʀis] NM/F agitator

fomenter [fɔmɑ̃te] /1/ VT to stir up, foment

foncé, e [fɔ̃se] ADJ dark; **bleu** ~ dark blue

foncer [fɔ̃se] /3/ VT to make darker; (*Culin: moule etc*) to line ▶ VI to go darker; (*fam: aller vite*) to tear *ou* belt along; ~ **sur** to charge at

fonceur, -euse [fɔ̃sœʀ, -øz] NM/F whizz kid

foncier, -ière [fɔ̃sje, -jɛʀ] ADJ (*honnêteté etc*) basic, fundamental; (*malhonnêteté*) deep-rooted; (*Comm*) real estate *cpd*

foncièrement [fɔ̃sjɛʀmɑ̃] ADV basically; (*absolument*) thoroughly

fonction [fɔ̃ksjɔ̃] NF (*rôle, Math, Ling*) function; (*emploi, poste*) post, position; **entrer en ~(s)** to take up one's post *ou* duties; to take up office; **voiture de** ~ company car; **être** ~ **de** (*dépendre de*) to depend on; **en** ~ **de** (*par rapport à*) according to; **faire** ~ **de** to serve as; **la** ~ **publique** the state *ou*

civil (*Brit*) service ■ **fonctions** NFPL (*professionnelles*) duties

★**fonctionnaire** [fɔ̃ksjɔnɛʀ] NMF state employee *ou* official; (*dans l'administration*) ≈ civil servant (*Brit*)

fonctionnalité [fɔ̃ksjɔnalite] NF (*Inform*) functionality

fonctionnariat [fɔ̃ksjɔnaʀja] NM state employee status

fonctionnariser [fɔ̃ksjɔnaʀize] /1/ VT (*Admin: personne*) to give the status of a state employee to

fonctionnel, le [fɔ̃ksjɔnɛl] ADJ functional

fonctionnellement [fɔ̃ksjɔnɛlmɑ̃] ADV functionally

fonctionnement [fɔ̃ksjɔnmɑ̃] NM working; functioning; operation

★**fonctionner** [fɔ̃ksjɔne] /1/ VI to work, function; (*entreprise*) to operate, function; **faire** ~ to work, operate

★**fond** [fɔ̃] NM *voir aussi* **fonds**; (*d'un récipient, trou*) bottom; (*d'une salle, scène*) back; (*d'un tableau, décor*) background; (*opposé à la forme*) content; (*petite quantité*): **un** ~ **de verre** a drop; (*Sport*): **le** ~ long distance (running); **course/épreuve de** ~ long-distance race/trial; **au** ~ **de** at the bottom of; at the back of; **aller au** ~ **des choses** to get to the root of things; **le** ~ **de sa pensée** his (*ou* her) true thoughts *ou* feelings; **sans** ~ *adj* bottomless; **envoyer par le** ~ (*Navig: couler*) to sink, scuttle; **à** ~ *adv* (*connaître, soutenir*) thoroughly; (*appuyer, visser*) right down *ou* home; **à** ~ **(de train)** *adv* (*fam*) full tilt; **dans le** ~, **au** ~ *adv* (*en somme*) basically, really; **de** ~ **en comble** *adv* from top to bottom; ~ **sonore** background noise; background music; ~ **de teint** foundation

fondamental, e, -aux [fɔ̃damɑ̃tal, -o] ADJ fundamental

fondamentalement [fɔ̃damɑ̃talmɑ̃] ADV fundamentally

fondamentalisme [fɔ̃damɑ̃talism] NM fundamentalism

fondamentaliste [fɔ̃damɑ̃talist] ADJ, NMF fundamentalist

fondant, e [fɔ̃dɑ̃, -ɑ̃t] ADJ (*neige*) melting; (*poire*) that melts in the mouth; (*chocolat*) fondant

fondateur, -trice [fɔ̃datœʀ, -tʀis] NM/F founder; **membre** ~ founder (*Brit*) *ou* founding (*US*) member

fondation [fɔ̃dasjɔ̃] NF founding; (*établissement*) foundation; **travail de** ~ foundation works *pl* ■ **fondations** NFPL (*d'une maison*) foundations

fondé, e [fɔ̃de] ADJ (*accusation etc*) well-founded ▶ NMF: ~ **de pouvoir** authorized representative

fondement [fɔ̃dmɑ̃] NM basis; (*derrière*) behind; **sans** ~ *adj* (*rumeur etc*) groundless, unfounded ■ **fondements** NMPL foundations

fonder [fɔ̃de] /1/ VT to found; (*fig*): ~ **qch sur** to base sth on; **se** ~ **sur** (*personne*) to base o.s. on; ~ **un foyer** (*se marier*) to set up home

fonderie [fɔ̃dʀi] NF smelting works *sg*

fondeur, -euse [fɔ̃dœʀ, -øz] NM/F (*skieur*) cross-country skier ▶ NM: **(ouvrier)** ~ caster

★**fondre** [fɔ̃dʀ] /41/ VT (*aussi*: **faire fondre**) to melt; (: *dans l'eau: sucre, sel*) to dissolve; (*fig: mélanger*) to merge, blend ▶ VI (*à la chaleur*) to melt; to dissolve;

189

(fig) to melt away; *(se précipiter)*: **~ sur** to swoop down on; **~ en larmes** to dissolve into tears ■ **se fondre** VPR *(se combiner, se confondre)* to merge into each other; to dissolve

fondrière [fɔ̃dRijɛR] NF rut

fonds [fɔ̃] NM *(de bibliothèque)* collection; *(Comm)*: **~ (de commerce)** business; *(fig)*: **~ de probité** *etc* fund of integrity *etc*; **F~ monétaire international (FMI)** International Monetary Fund (IMF); **~ de roulement** float ▶ NMPL *(argent)* funds; **à ~ perdus** *adv* with little or no hope of getting the money back; **être en ~** to be in funds; **mise de ~** investment, (capital) outlay

fondu, e [fɔ̃dy] ADJ *(beurre, neige)* melted; *(métal)* molten ▶ NM *(Ciné)*: **~ (enchaîné)** dissolve ▶ NF *(Culin)* fondue

fongicide [fɔ̃ʒisid] NM fungicide

font [fɔ̃] VB *voir* **faire**

★**fontaine** [fɔ̃tɛn] NF fountain; *(source)* spring

fontanelle [fɔ̃tanɛl] NF fontanelle

fonte [fɔ̃t] NF melting; *(métal)* cast iron; **la ~ des neiges** the (spring) thaw

fonts baptismaux [fɔ̃batismo] NMPL (baptismal) font *sg*

★**foot** [fut], **football** [futbol] NM football, soccer

footballeur, -euse [futbolœR, -øz] NM/F footballer (BRIT), football *ou* soccer player

footeux, -euse [futø, -øz] NM/F *(fam)* footie fan *(fam)*

footing [futiŋ] NM jogging; **faire du ~** to go jogging

for [fɔR] NM: **dans** *ou* **en son ~ intérieur** in one's heart of hearts

forage [fɔRaʒ] NM drilling, boring

forain, e [fɔRɛ̃, -ɛn] ADJ fairground *cpd* ▶ NM *(marchand)* stallholder; *(acteur etc)* fairground entertainer

forban [fɔRbɑ̃] NM *(pirate)* pirate; *(escroc)* crook

forçat [fɔRsa] NM convict

force [fɔRs] NF strength; *(puissance: surnaturelle etc)* power; *(Physique, Mécanique)* force; **avoir de la ~** to be strong; **être à bout de ~** to have no strength left; **à la ~ du poignet** *(fig)* by the sweat of one's brow; **à ~ de faire** by dint of doing; **arriver en ~** *(nombreux)* to arrive in force; **cas de ~ majeure** case of absolute necessity; *(Assurances)* act of God; **~ de la nature** natural force; **de ~** *adv* forcibly, by force; **de toutes mes/ses forces** with all my/his strength; **par la ~** using force; **par la ~ des choses/de l'habitude** by force of circumstances/habit; **à toute ~** *(absolument)* at all costs; **faire ~ de rames/voiles** to ply the oars/cram on sail; **être de ~ à faire** to be up to doing; **de première ~** first class; **la ~ armée** *(les troupes)* the army; **~ d'âme** fortitude; **~ de frappe** strike force; **~ d'inertie** force of inertia; **~ publique** the authorities responsible for public order; **dans la ~ de l'âge** in the prime of life ■ **forces** NFPL *(physiques)* strength *sg*; *(Mil)* forces; *(effectifs)*: **d'importantes forces de police** large contingents of police; **forces d'intervention** *(Mil, Police)* peace-keeping force *sg*; **les forces de l'ordre** the police

forcé, e [fɔRse] ADJ forced; *(bain)* unintended; *(inévitable)*: **c'est ~ !** it's inevitable!, it HAS to be!

forcément [fɔRsemɑ̃] ADV necessarily; inevita-

bly; *(bien sûr)* of course; **pas ~** not necessarily

forcené, e [fɔRsəne] ADJ frenzied ▶ NM/F maniac

forceps [fɔRsɛps] NM forceps *pl*

forcer [fɔRse] /3/ VT *(porte, serrure, plante)* to force; *(moteur, voix)* to strain; **~ qn à faire** to force sb to do; **~ la dose/l'allure** to overdo it/increase the pace; **~ l'attention/le respect** to command attention/respect; **~ la consigne** to bypass orders ▶ VI *(Sport)* to overtax o.s. ■ **se forcer** VPR: **se ~ à faire qch** to force o.s. to do sth

forcing [fɔRsiŋ] NM *(Sport)*: **faire le ~** to pile on the pressure

forcir [fɔRsiR] /2/ VI *(grossir)* to broaden out; *(vent)* to freshen

forclore [fɔRklɔR] /45/ VT *(Jur: personne)* to debar

forclusion [fɔRklyziɔ̃] NF *(Jur)* debarment

forer [fɔRe] /1/ VT to drill, bore

forestier, -ière [fɔRɛstje, -jɛR] ADJ forest *cpd*

foret [fɔRɛ] NM drill

★**forêt** [fɔRɛ] NF forest; **Office National des Forêts** *(Admin)* ≈ Forestry Commission (BRIT), ≈ National Forest Service (US); **la F~ Noire** the Black Forest

foreuse [fɔRøz] NF *(electric)* drill

forfait [fɔRfɛ] NM *(Comm: prix fixe)* fixed *ou* set price; *(: prix tout compris)* all-in deal *ou* price; *(crime)* infamy; **~ de (téléphone) portable** phone plan, cell plan; **déclarer ~** to withdraw; **gagner par ~** to win by a walkover; **travailler à ~** to work for a lump sum

forfaitaire [fɔRfɛtɛR] ADJ set; inclusive

forfait-vacances [fɔRfɛvakɑ̃s] *(pl* **forfaits-vacances)** NM package holiday

forfanterie [fɔRfɑ̃tRi] NF boastfulness *no pl*

forge [fɔRʒ] NF forge, smithy

forgé, e [fɔRʒe] ADJ: **~ de toutes pièces** *(histoire)* completely fabricated

forger [fɔRʒe] /3/ VT to forge; *(fig: personnalité)* to form; *(: prétexte)* to contrive, make up

forgeron [fɔRʒəRɔ̃] NM (black)smith

formaliser [fɔRmalize] /1/: **se formaliser** VPR: **se ~ (de)** to take offence (at)

formalisme [fɔRmalism] NM formality

formaliste [fɔRmalist] ADJ *(religion, approche)* formalistic; *(Art)* formalist

formalité [fɔRmalite] NF formality; **simple ~** mere formality

format [fɔRma] NM size; **petit ~** small size; *(Photo)* 35 mm (film)

formatage [fɔRmataʒ] NM *(de disque)* formatting

formater [fɔRmate] /1/ VT *(disque)* to format; *(fig: esprits, élèves)* to brainwash; **non formaté** unformatted

formateur, -trice [fɔRmatœR, -tRis] ADJ formative

formation [fɔRmasjɔ̃] NF forming; *(éducation)* training; *(Mus)* group; *(Mil, Aviat, Géo)* formation; **la ~ permanente** *ou* **continue** continuing education; **la ~ professionnelle** vocational training

★**forme** [fɔRm] NF *(gén)* form; *(d'un objet)* shape, form; **en ~ de poire** pear-shaped, in the shape of a pear; **sous ~ de** in the form of; in the guise of; **sous ~ de cachets** in the form of tablets; **être en (bonne** *ou* **pleine) ~**, **avoir la ~** *(Sport etc)* to be on form; **en bonne et due ~** in due form; **pour la ~** for the sake of form; **sans autre ~ de procès** (*fig*) without further ado; **prendre ~** to take shape ▪ **formes** NFPL (*bonnes manières*) proprieties; (*d'une femme*) figure *sg*

formé, e [fɔʀme] ADJ (*adolescente*) fully developed; (*goût, jugement*) mature

formel, le [fɔʀmɛl] ADJ (*preuve, décision*) definite, positive; (*logique*) formal

formellement [fɔʀmɛlmɑ̃] ADV (*interdit*) strictly; (*absolument*) positively

former [fɔʀme] /**1**/ VT (*gén*) to form; (*éduquer: soldat, ingénieur etc*) to train ▪ **se former** VPR to form; to train

formica® [fɔʀmika] NM Formica®; **en ~** (*mélaminé*) Formica® *cpd*

★**formidable** [fɔʀmidabl] ADJ tremendous

formidablement [fɔʀmidabləmɑ̃] ADV tremendously

formol [fɔʀmɔl] NM formalin, formol

formosan, e [fɔʀmɔzɑ̃, -an] ADJ Formosan

Formose [fɔʀmoz] NM Formosa

★**formulaire** [fɔʀmylɛʀ] NM form

formulation [fɔʀmylasjɔ̃] NF formulation; expression; *voir* **formuler**

formule [fɔʀmyl] NF (*gén*) formula; (*formulaire*) form; (*expression*) phrase; **selon la ~ consacrée** as one says; **~ de politesse** polite phrase; (*en fin de lettre*) letter ending

formuler [fɔʀmyle] /**1**/ VT (*émettre: réponse, vœux*) to formulate; (*expliciter: sa pensée*) to express

fornication [fɔʀnikasjɔ̃] NF fornication

forniquer [fɔʀnike] /**1**/ VI to fornicate

forsythia [fɔʀsisja] NM forsythia

★**fort, e** [fɔʀ, fɔʀt] ADJ strong; (*intensité, rendement*) high, great; (*corpulent*) large; (*doué*): **être ~ (en)** to be good (at); **c'est un peu ~ !** it's a bit much!; **à plus forte raison** even more so, all the more reason; **se faire ~ de faire** to claim one can do; **forte tête** rebel ▶ ADV (*serrer, frapper*) hard; (*sonner*) loud(ly); (*beaucoup*) greatly, very much; (*très*) very; **avoir ~ à faire avec qn** to have a hard job with sb; **~ bien/peu** very well/few ▶ NM (*édifice*) fort; (*point fort*) strong point, forte; (*gén pl: personne, pays*): **le ~, les forts** the strong; **au plus ~ de** (*au milieu de*) in the thick of, at the height of

fortement [fɔʀtəmɑ̃] ADV strongly; (*s'intéresser*) deeply

forteresse [fɔʀtəʀɛs] NF fortress

fortiche [fɔʀtiʃ] ADJ (*fam*) very clever

fortifiant [fɔʀtifjɑ̃] NM tonic

fortifications [fɔʀtifikasjɔ̃] NFPL fortifications

fortifier [fɔʀtifje] /**7**/ VT to strengthen, fortify; (*Mil*) to fortify ▪ **se fortifier** VPR (*personne, santé*) to grow stronger

fortin [fɔʀtɛ̃] NM (small) fort

fortiori [fɔʀtjɔʀi]: **à ~** *adv* all the more so

FORTRAN [fɔʀtʀɑ̃] NM FORTRAN

fortuit, e [fɔʀtɥi, -it] ADJ fortuitous, chance *cpd*

fortuitement [fɔʀtɥitmɑ̃] ADV fortuitously

fortune [fɔʀtyn] NF fortune; **faire ~** to make one's fortune; **de ~** *adj* makeshift; (*compagnon*) chance *cpd*

fortuné, e [fɔʀtyne] ADJ wealthy, well-off

forum [fɔʀɔm] NM forum; **~ de discussion** (*Internet*) message board

fosse [fos] NF (*grand trou*) pit; (*tombe*) grave; **la ~ aux lions/ours** the lions' den/bear pit; **~ commune** common *ou* communal grave; **~ (d'orchestre)** (orchestra) pit; **~ à purin** cesspit; **~ septique** septic tank; **fosses nasales** nasal fossae

fossé [fose] NM ditch; (*fig*) gulf, gap

fossette [fosɛt] NF dimple

fossile [fosil] NM fossil ▶ ADJ fossilized, fossil *cpd*

fossilisé, e [fosilize] ADJ fossilized

fossoyeur [foswajœʀ] NM gravedigger

★**fou, fol, folle** [fu, fɔl] ADJ mad, crazy; (*déréglé etc*) wild, erratic; (*mèche*) stray; (*herbe*) wild; (*fam: extrême, très grand*) terrific, tremendous; **~ à lier, ~ furieux (folle furieuse)** raving mad; **être ~ de** to be mad *ou* crazy about; (*chagrin, joie, colère*) to be wild with; **faire le ~** to play *ou* act the fool; **avoir le ~ rire** to have the giggles ▶ NM/F madman/-woman ▶ NM (*du roi*) jester, fool; (*Échecs*) bishop

foucade [fukad] NF caprice

foudre [fudʀ] NF: **la ~** lightning ▪ **foudres** NFPL (*fig: colère*) wrath *sg*

foudroyant, e [fudʀwajɑ̃, -ɑ̃t] ADJ devastating; (*progrès*) lightning *cpd*; (*succès*) stunning; (*maladie, poison*) violent

foudroyer [fudʀwaje] /**8**/ VT to strike down; **~ qn du regard** to look daggers at sb; **il a été foudroyé** he was struck by lightning

fouet [fwe] NM whip; (*Culin*) whisk; **de plein ~** *adv* (*se heurter*) head on

fouettement [fwetmɑ̃] NM lashing *no pl*

fouetter [fwete] /**1**/ VT to whip; (*crème*) to whisk

fougasse [fugas] NF *type of flat pastry*

fougère [fuʒɛʀ] NF fern

fougue [fug] NF ardour (*BRIT*), ardor (*US*), spirit

fougueusement [fugøzmɑ̃] ADV ardently

fougueux, -euse [fugø, -øz] ADJ fiery, ardent

fouille [fuj] NF search; **passer à la ~** to be searched ▪ **fouilles** NFPL (*archéologiques*) excavations

fouillé, e [fuje] ADJ detailed

fouiller [fuje] /**1**/ VT to search; (*creuser*) to dig; (: *archéologue*) to excavate; (*approfondir: étude etc*) to go into ▶ VI (*archéologue*) to excavate; **~ dans/parmi** to rummage in/among

fouillis [fuji] NM jumble, muddle

fouine [fwin] NF stone marten

fouiner [fwine] /**1**/ VI (*péj*): **~ dans** to nose around *ou* about in

fouineur, -euse [fwinœʀ, -øz] ADJ nosey ▶ NM/F nosey parker, snooper

fouir [fwiʀ] /**2**/ VT to dig

fouisseur, -euse [fwisœʀ, -øz] ADJ burrowing

foulage [fulaʒ] NM pressing

foulante [fulɑ̃t] ADJ F: **pompe ~** force pump

★**foulard** [fulaʀ] NM scarf

★**foule** [ful] NF crowd; **la ~** crowds *pl*; **une ~ de** masses of; **venir en ~** to come in droves

foulée [fule] NF stride; **dans la ~ de** on the heels of

fouler [fule] /**1**/ VT to press; (*sol*) to tread upon; **~ aux pieds** (*fig*) to trample on ▪ **se fouler** VPR (*fam*) to overexert o.s.; **ne pas se ~** not to overexert o.s.; **il ne se foule pas** he doesn't put himself out; **se ~ la cheville** to sprain one's ankle

foultitude [fultityd] NF: **une ~ de qch** (humoristique) oodles of sth

foulure [fulyʀ] NF sprain

★**four** [fuʀ] NM oven; (de potier) kiln; (Théât: échec) flop; **allant au ~** ovenproof

fourbe [fuʀb] ADJ deceitful

fourberie [fuʀbəʀi] NF deceit

fourbi [fuʀbi] NM (fam) gear, junk

fourbir [fuʀbiʀ] /2/ VT: **~ ses armes** (fig) to get ready for the fray

fourbu, e [fuʀby] ADJ exhausted

fourche [fuʀʃ] NF pitchfork; (de bicyclette) fork

fourcher [fuʀʃe] /1/ VI: **ma langue a fourché** it was a slip of the tongue

★**fourchette** [fuʀʃɛt] NF fork; (Statistique) bracket, margin

fourchu, e [fuʀʃy] ADJ split; (arbre etc) forked

fourgon [fuʀgɔ̃] NM van; (Rail) wag(g)on; **~ mortuaire** hearse

fourgonnette [fuʀgɔnɛt] NF (delivery) van

fourguer [fuʀge] VT (fam: vendre) to flog (fam)

fourme [fuʀm] NF blue-veined cow's milk cheese

fourmi [fuʀmi] NF ant; **avoir des fourmis dans les jambes/mains** to have pins and needles in one's legs/hands

fourmilier [fuʀmilje] NM (mammifère) anteater

fourmilière [fuʀmiljɛʀ] NF ant-hill; (fig) hive of activity

fourmillement [fuʀmijmɑ̃] NM (démangeaison) pins and needles pl; (grouillement) swarming no pl

fourmiller [fuʀmije] /1/ VI to swarm; **~ de** to be teeming with, be swarming with

fournaise [fuʀnɛz] NF blaze; (fig) furnace, oven

fourneau, x [fuʀno] NM stove

fournée [fuʀne] NF batch

fourni, e [fuʀni] ADJ (barbe, cheveux) thick; (magasin): **bien ~ (en)** well stocked (with)

fournil [fuʀni] NM bakehouse

fournir [fuʀniʀ] /2/ VT to supply; (preuve, exemple) to provide, supply; (effort) to put in; **~ qch à qn** to supply sth to sb, supply ou provide sb with sth; **~ qn en** (Comm) to supply sb with; **se ~ chez** to shop at

fournisseur, -euse [fuʀnisœʀ, -øz] NM/F supplier; (Internet): **~ d'accès à Internet** (internet) service provider, ISP

fourniture [fuʀnityʀ] NF supply(ing) ■ **fournitures** NFPL supplies; **fournitures de bureau** office supplies, stationery; **fournitures scolaires** school stationery

fourrage [fuʀaʒ] NM fodder

fourrager¹ [fuʀaʒe] VI: **~ dans/parmi** to rummage through/among

fourrager², -ère [fuʀaʒe, -ɛʀ] ADJ fodder cpd ▶ NF (Mil) fourragère

fourré, e [fuʀe] ADJ (bonbon, chocolat) filled; (manteau, botte) fur-lined ▶ NM thicket

fourreau, x [fuʀo] NM sheath; (de parapluie) cover; **robe ~** figure-hugging dress

fourrer [fuʀe] /1/ VT (fam) to stick, shove; **~ qch**

dans to stick ou shove sth into; **se ~ dans/sous** to get into/under; **se ~ dans** (une mauvaise situation) to land o.s. in

fourre-tout [fuʀtu] NM INV (sac) holdall; (péj) junk room (ou cupboard); (fig) rag-bag

fourreur [fuʀœʀ] NM furrier

fourrière [fuʀjɛʀ] NF pound

fourrure [fuʀyʀ] NF fur; (sur l'animal) coat; **manteau/col de ~** fur coat/collar

fourvoyer [fuʀvwaje] /8/: **se fourvoyer** VPR to go astray, stray; **se ~ dans** to stray into

foutaise [futɛz] NF (fam): **c'est de la ~** (bêtises) silly nonsense

foutoir [futwaʀ] NM (fam) bloody shambles (fam); **c'est le ~ ici !** it's a bloody shambles in here!

foutraque [futʀak] ADJ (fam) eccentric

foutre [futʀ] VT (!) = **ficher**

foutrement [futʀəmɑ̃] ADV (fam) bloody (BRIT fam)

foutu, e [futy] ADJ (!) = **fichu**

foyer [fwaje] NM (de cheminée) hearth; (fig) seat, centre; (famille) family; (domicile) home; (local de réunion) (social) club; (résidence) hostel; (salon) foyer; (Optique, Photo) focus; **lunettes à double ~** bi-focal glasses

FP SIGLE F (= franchise postale) exemption from postage

FPA SIGLE F (= Formation professionnelle pour adultes) adult education

FPLP SIGLE M (= Front populaire de libération de la Palestine) PFLP (= Popular Front for the Liberation of Palestine)

frac [fʀak] NM (vieilli) morning coat

fracas [fʀaka] NM din; crash

fracassant, e [fʀakasɑ̃, -ɑ̃t] ADJ (succès) sensational, staggering

fracasser [fʀakase] /1/ VT to smash ■ **se fracasser** VPR: **se ~ contre** ou **sur** to crash against

fraction [fʀaksjɔ̃] NF fraction

fractionnement [fʀaksjɔnmɑ̃] NM division

fractionner [fʀaksjɔne] /1/ VT to divide (up), split (up)

fracturation [fʀaktyʀasjɔ̃] F: **~ hydraulique** fracking

fracture [fʀaktyʀ] NF fracture; **~ du crâne** fractured skull; **~ de la jambe** broken leg; **~ numérique** digital gap; **~ sociale** social divide

fracturer [fʀaktyʀe] /1/ VT (coffre, serrure) to break open; (os, membre) to fracture; **se ~ le crâne** to fracture one's skull

★**fragile** [fʀaʒil] ADJ fragile, delicate; (fig) frail

fragilisation [fʀaʒilizasjɔ̃] NF (de matériau) weakening; (de peau) making more sensitive; (fig) weakening

fragiliser [fʀaʒilize] /1/ VT to weaken, make fragile

fragilité [fʀaʒilite] NF fragility

fragment [fʀagmɑ̃] NM (d'un objet) fragment, piece; (d'un texte) passage, extract

fragmentaire [fʀagmɑ̃tɛʀ] ADJ sketchy

fragmentation [fʀagmɑ̃tasjɔ̃] NF (de molécules, territoire, groupe) fragmentation; **bombes à ~** cluster bombs

fragmenter [fʀagmɑ̃te] /1/ VT to split up

frai [fʀɛ] NM spawn; (*ponte*) spawning

fraîche [fʀɛʃ] ADJ F *voir* **frais**

fraîchement [fʀɛʃmɑ̃] ADV (*sans enthousiasme*) coolly; (*récemment*) freshly, newly

fraîcheur [fʀɛʃœʀ] NF coolness; (*d'un aliment*) freshness

fraîchir [fʀɛʃiʀ] /**2**/ VI (*température*) to get cooler; (*vent*) to freshen

★**frais, fraîche** [fʀɛ, fʀɛʃ] ADJ (*air, eau, accueil*) cool; (*petit pois, œufs, nouvelles, couleur, troupes*) fresh; **le voilà ~!** he's in a (right) mess! ▶ ADV (*récemment*) newly, fresh(ly); **il fait ~** it's cool; **servir ~** chill before serving, serve chilled ▶ NM: **mettre au ~** to put in a cool place; **prendre le ~** to take a breath of cool air ▶ NMPL (*débours*) expenses; (*Comm*) costs; charges; **faire des ~** to spend; to go to a lot of expense; **faire les ~ de** to bear the brunt of; **faire les ~ de la conversation** (*parler*) to do most of the talking; (*en être le sujet*) to be the topic of conversation; **il en a été pour ses ~** he could have spared himself the trouble; **rentrer dans ses ~** to recover one's expenses; **~ de déplacement** travel(ling) expenses; **~ d'entretien** upkeep; **~ généraux** overheads; **~ de scolarité** school fees (BRIT), tuition (US)

★**fraise** [fʀɛz] NF strawberry; (*Tech*) countersink (bit); (*de dentiste*) drill; **~ des bois** wild strawberry

fraiser [fʀeze] /**1**/ VT to countersink; (*Culin: pâte*) to knead

fraiseur, -euse [fʀɛzœʀ, -øz] NM/F (*ouvrier*) cutter

fraiseuse [fʀɛzøz] NF (*Tech*) milling machine

fraisier [fʀezje] NM strawberry plant

★**framboise** [fʀɑ̃bwaz] NF raspberry

framboisier [fʀɑ̃bwazje] NM raspberry bush

★**franc, franche** [fʀɑ̃, fʀɑ̃ʃ] ADJ (*personne*) frank, straightforward; (*visage*) open; (*net: refus, couleur*) clear; (: *coupure*) clean; (*intensif*) downright; (*exempt*): **~ de port** post free, postage paid; (*zone, port*) free; (*boutique*) duty-free ▶ ADV: **parler ~** to be frank *ou* candid ▶ NM franc

français, e [fʀɑ̃sɛ, -ɛz] ADJ French ▶ NM (*Ling*) French ▶ NM/F: **Français, e** Frenchman/-woman; **les F~** the French

franc-comtois, e [fʀɑ̃kɔ̃twa, -waz] ADJ (*mpl* **francs-comtois**) ADJ of *ou* from (the) Franche-Comté

★**France** [fʀɑ̃s] NF: **la ~** France; **en ~** in France

Francfort [fʀɑ̃kfɔʀ] N Frankfurt

franche [fʀɑ̃ʃ] ADJ F *voir* **franc**

Franche-Comté [fʀɑ̃ʃkɔ̃te] NF Franche-Comté

★**franchement** [fʀɑ̃ʃmɑ̃] ADV frankly; clearly; (*nettement*) definitely; (*tout à fait*) downright ▶ EXCL well, really!; *voir* **franc**

franchir [fʀɑ̃ʃiʀ] /**2**/ VT (*obstacle*) to clear, get over; (*seuil, ligne, rivière*) to cross; (*distance*) to cover

franchisage [fʀɑ̃ʃizaʒ] NM (*Comm*) franchising

franchise [fʀɑ̃ʃiz] NF frankness; (*douanière, d'impôt*) exemption; (*Assurances*) excess; (*Comm*) franchise; **~ de bagages** baggage allowance

franchisé, e [fʀɑ̃ʃize] ADJ franchised ▶ NM/F franchisee

franchissable [fʀɑ̃ʃisabl] ADJ (*obstacle*) surmountable

franchissement [fʀɑ̃ʃismɑ̃] NM (*d'obstacle*) clearing; (*de rivière, frontière*) crossing

franchouillard, e [fʀɑ̃ʃujaʀ, -aʀd] ADJ (*péj*) typically French (*in an annoying way*)

francilien, ne [fʀɑ̃siljɛ̃, -ɛn] ADJ of *ou* from the Île-de-France region ▶ NM/F: **Francilien, ne** person from the Île-de-France region

francisation [fʀɑ̃sizasjɔ̃] NF (*de mot, nom*) Gallicization

franciscain, e [fʀɑ̃siskɛ̃, -ɛn] ADJ Franciscan

franciser [fʀɑ̃size] /**1**/ VT to Gallicize, Frenchify

franc-jeu [fʀɑ̃ʒø] (*pl* **francs-jeux**) NM: **jouer ~** to play fair

franc-maçon [fʀɑ̃masɔ̃] (*pl* **francs-maçons**) NM Freemason

franc-maçonnerie [fʀɑ̃masɔnʀi] NF Freemasonry

franco [fʀɑ̃ko] ADV (*Comm*): **~ (de port)** postage paid

franco... [fʀɑ̃ko] PRÉFIXE franco-

franco-canadien [fʀɑ̃kokanadjɛ̃] NM (*Ling*) Canadian French

francophile [fʀɑ̃kofil] ADJ Francophile

francophobe [fʀɑ̃kofɔb] ADJ Francophobe

francophone [fʀɑ̃kofɔn] ADJ French-speaking ▶ NMF French speaker

francophonie [fʀɑ̃kofɔni] NF French-speaking communities *pl*

franco-québécois [fʀɑ̃kokebekwa] NM (*Ling*) Quebec French

franc-parler [fʀɑ̃paʀle] NM INV outspokenness; **avoir son ~** to speak one's mind

franc-tireur [fʀɑ̃tiʀœʀ] NM (*Mil*) irregular; (*fig*) freelance

frange [fʀɑ̃ʒ] NF fringe; (*cheveux*) fringe (BRIT), bangs (US)

frangé, e [fʀɑ̃ʒe] ADJ (*tapis, nappe*): **~ de** trimmed with

frangin [fʀɑ̃ʒɛ̃] NM (*fam*) brother

frangine [fʀɑ̃ʒin] NF (*fam*) sis, sister

frangipane [fʀɑ̃ʒipan] NF almond paste

frangipanier [fʀɑ̃ʒipanje] NM frangipani

franglais [fʀɑ̃glɛ] NM Franglais

franquette [fʀɑ̃kɛt]: **à la bonne ~** *adv* without any fuss

franquisme [fʀɑ̃kism] NM Francoism

franquiste [fʀɑ̃kist] ADJ, NMF Francoist

frappant, e [fʀapɑ̃, -ɑ̃t] ADJ striking

frappe [fʀap] NF (*d'une dactylo, pianiste, machine à écrire*) touch; (*Boxe*) punch; (*péj*) hood, thug

frappé, e [fʀape] ADJ (*Culin*) iced; **~ de panique** panic-stricken; **~ de stupeur** thunderstruck, dumbfounded

★**frapper** [fʀape] /**1**/ VT to hit, strike; (*étonner*) to strike; (*monnaie*) to strike, stamp; **~ à la porte** to knock at the door; **~ dans ses mains** to clap one's hands; **~ du poing sur** to bang one's fist on; **~ un grand coup** (*fig*) to strike a blow ■ **se frapper** VPR (*s'inquiéter*) to get worked up

frasques [fʀask] NFPL escapades; **faire des ~** to get up to mischief

fraternel, le [fʀatɛʀnɛl] ADJ brotherly, fraternal

fraternellement [fʀatɛʀnɛlmɑ̃] ADV in a brotherly way

fraternisation [fʀatɛʀnizasjɔ̃] NF fraternization

fraterniser [fʀatɛʀnize] /**1**/ vi to fraternize

fraternité [fʀatɛʀnite] NF brotherhood

fratricide [fʀatʀisid] ADJ fratricidal

fratrie [fʀatʀi] NF siblings *pl*

fraude [fʀod] NF fraud; (Scol) cheating; **passer qch en ~** to smuggle sth in (*ou* out); **~ fiscale** tax evasion

frauder [fʀode] /**1**/ vi, vt to cheat; **~ le fisc** to evade paying tax(es)

fraudeur, -euse [fʀodœʀ, -øz] NM/F person guilty of fraud; (*candidat*) candidate who cheats; (*au fisc*) tax evader

frauduleusement [fʀodyløzmɑ̃] ADV fraudulently

frauduleux, -euse [fʀodylø, -øz] ADJ fraudulent

frayer [fʀeje] /**8**/ vt to open up, clear ▶ vi to spawn; (*fréquenter*) **~ avec** to mix *ou* associate with ■ **se frayer** VPR: **se ~ un passage dans** to clear o.s. a path through, force one's way through

frayeur [fʀejœʀ] NF fright

fredaines [fʀədɛn] NFPL mischief *sg*, escapades

fredonner [fʀədɔne] /**1**/ vt to hum

freesia [fʀezja] NM freesia

freezer [fʀizœʀ] NM freezing compartment

frégate [fʀegat] NF frigate

★**frein** [fʀɛ̃] NM brake; **mettre un ~ à** (*fig*) to put a brake on, check; **sans ~** (*sans limites*) unchecked; **~ à main** handbrake; **~ moteur** engine braking; **freins à disques** disc brakes; **freins à tambour** drum brakes

freinage [fʀenaʒ] NM braking; **distance de ~** braking distance; **traces de ~** tyre (BRIT) *ou* tire (US) marks

★**freiner** [fʀene] /**1**/ vi to brake ▶ vt (*progrès etc*) to check

frelaté, e [fʀəlate] ADJ adulterated; (*fig*) tainted

frêle [fʀɛl] ADJ frail, fragile

frelon [fʀəlɔ̃] NM hornet

freluquet [fʀəlykɛ] NM (*péj*) whippersnapper

frémir [fʀemiʀ] /**2**/ vi (*de froid, de peur*) to shudder, shiver; (*de colère*) to shake; (*de joie, feuillage*) to quiver; (*eau*) to (begin to) bubble

frémissement [fʀemismɑ̃] NM shiver; quiver; bubbling *no pl*

frêne [fʀɛn] NM ash (tree)

frénésie [fʀenezi] NF frenzy

frénétique [fʀenetik] ADJ frenzied, frenetic

frénétiquement [fʀenetikmɑ̃] ADV frenetically

fréon® [fʀeɔ̃] NM Freon®

fréquemment [fʀekamɑ̃] ADV frequently

fréquence [fʀekɑ̃s] NF frequency

fréquent, e [fʀekɑ̃, -ɑ̃t] ADJ frequent

fréquentable [fʀekɑ̃tabl] ADJ: **il est peu ~** he's not the type one can associate oneself with

fréquentation [fʀekɑ̃tasjɔ̃] NF frequenting; seeing ■ **fréquentations** NFPL (*relations*) company *sg*; **avoir de mauvaises fréquentations** to be in with the wrong crowd, keep bad company

fréquenté, e [fʀekɑ̃te] ADJ: **très ~** (very) busy; **mal ~** patronized by disreputable elements

fréquenter [fʀekɑ̃te] /**1**/ vt (*lieu*) to frequent; (*personne*) to see ■ **se fréquenter** VPR to see a lot of each other

frère [fʀɛʀ] NM brother ▶ ADJ: **partis/pays frères** sister parties/countries

frérot [fʀeʀo] NM (*fam*) bro (*fam*)

fresque [fʀɛsk] NF (Art) fresco

fret [fʀɛ(t)] NM freight

fréter [fʀete] /**6**/ vt to charter

frétillant, e [fʀetijɑ̃, -ɑ̃t] ADJ (*poisson*) wriggling; (*queue*) wagging

frétiller [fʀetije] /**1**/ vi to wriggle; to quiver; **~ de la queue** to wag its tail

fretin [fʀətɛ̃] NM: **le menu ~** the small fry

freudien, ne [fʀødjɛ̃, -ɛn] ADJ Freudian

freux [fʀø] NM (Zool) rook

friable [fʀijabl] ADJ crumbly

friand, e [fʀijɑ̃, -ɑ̃d] ADJ: **~ de** very fond of ▶ NM (Culin) small minced-meat (BRIT) *ou* ground-meat (US) pie; (: *sucré*) small almond cake; **~ au fromage** cheese puff

friandise [fʀijɑ̃diz] NF sweet

fric [fʀik] NM (*fam*) cash, bread

fricassée [fʀikase] NF fricassee

fricative [fʀikativ] NF (Ling) fricative

fric-frac [fʀikfʀak] NM (*fam*) break-in

friche [fʀiʃ]: **en ~** *adj, adv* (lying) fallow

fricoter [fʀikɔte] vi (*fam*): **~ avec qn** to knock about with sb (*fam*)

friction [fʀiksjɔ̃] NF (*massage*) rub, rub-down; (*chez le coiffeur*) scalp massage; (Tech, *fig*) friction

frictionner [fʀiksjɔne] /**1**/ vt to rub (down); to massage

frigidaire® [fʀiʒidɛʀ] NM refrigerator

frigide [fʀiʒid] ADJ frigid

frigidité [fʀiʒidite] NF frigidity

★**frigo** [fʀigo] NM (= *frigidaire*) fridge

frigorifier [fʀigɔʀifje] /**7**/ vt to refrigerate; (*fig: personne*) to freeze

frigorifique [fʀigɔʀifik] ADJ refrigerating

frileusement [fʀiløzmɑ̃] ADV with a shiver

frileux, -euse [fʀilø, -øz] ADJ sensitive to (the) cold; (*fig*) overcautious

frilosité [fʀilozite] NF (*manque d'audace*) overcautiousness

frimas [fʀima] NMPL wintry weather *sg*

frime [fʀim] NF (*fam*): **c'est de la ~** it's all put on; **pour la ~** just for show

frimer [fʀime] /**1**/ vi (*fam*) to show off

frimeur, -euse [fʀimœʀ, -øz] NM/F poser

frimousse [fʀimus] NF (sweet) little face

fringale [fʀɛ̃gal] NF (*fam*): **avoir la ~** to be ravenous

fringant, e [fʀɛ̃gɑ̃, -ɑ̃t] ADJ dashing

fringuer [fʀɛ̃ge] vt (*fam: habiller*) to tog up (*fam*) ■ **se fringuer** VPR to tog o.s. up (*fam*)

fringues [fʀɛ̃g] NFPL (*fam*) clothes, gear *no pl*

fripé, e [fʀipe] ADJ crumpled

friperie [fʀipʀi] NF (*commerce*) secondhand clothes shop; (*vêtements*) secondhand clothes

fripes [fʀip] NFPL secondhand clothes

fripier, -ière [fʀipje, -jɛʀ] NM/F secondhand clothes dealer

fripon, ne [fʀipɔ̃, -ɔn] ADJ roguish, mischievous ▶ NM/F rascal, rogue

fripouille [fʀipuj] NF scoundrel

friqué, e [fʀike] ADJ (fam) loaded (fam)

frire [fʀiʀ] VT to fry ▶ VI to fry

Frisbee® [fʀizbi] NM Frisbee®

frise [fʀiz] NF frieze

★**frisé, e** [fʀize] ADJ (cheveux) curly; (personne) curly-haired ▶ NF: **(chicorée) frisée** curly endive

friser [fʀize] /1/ VT to curl; (fig: surface) to skim, graze; (: mort) to come within a hair's breadth of; (: hérésie) to verge on ▶ VI (cheveux) to curl; (personne) to have curly hair; **se faire ~** to have one's hair curled

frisette [fʀizɛt] NF little curl

frisotter [fʀizɔte] /1/ VI (cheveux) to curl tightly

frisquet [fʀiskɛ] ADJ M chilly

frisson [fʀisɔ̃], **frissonnement** [fʀisɔnmɑ̃] NM (de froid) shiver; (de peur) shudder; quiver

frissonnant, e [fʀisɔnɑ̃, -ɑ̃t] ADJ (de froid, d'épouvante) shuddering; (: feuilles, animal) quivering

frissonner [fʀisɔne] /1/ VI (de fièvre, froid) to shiver; (d'horreur) to shudder; (feuilles) to quiver

frit, e [fʀi, fʀit] PP de **frire** ▶ ADJ fried ▶ NF: **(pommes) frites** chips (BRIT), French fries

friterie [fʀitʀi] NF ≈ chip shop (BRIT), ≈ hamburger stand (US)

friteuse [fʀitøz] NF deep fryer, chip pan (BRIT); **~ électrique** electric fryer

friture [fʀityʀ] NF (huile) (deep) fat; (plat): **~ (de poissons)** fried fish; (Radio) crackle, crackling no pl ▪ **fritures** NFPL (aliments frits) fried food sg

frivole [fʀivɔl] ADJ frivolous

frivolité [fʀivɔlite] NF frivolity

froc [fʀɔk] NM (Rel) habit; (fam: pantalon) trousers pl, pants pl

★**froid, e** [fʀwa, fʀwad] ADJ cold; **battre ~ à qn** to give sb the cold shoulder; **à ~** adv (démarrer) (from) cold ▶ NM cold; (absence de sympathie) coolness no pl; **il fait ~** it's cold; **avoir ~** to be cold; **prendre ~** to catch a chill ou cold; **(pendant) les grands froids** (in) the depths of winter, (during) the cold season; **jeter un ~** (fig) to cast a chill; **être en ~ avec** to be on bad terms with

froidement [fʀwadmɑ̃] ADV (accueillir) coldly; (décider) coolly

froideur [fʀwadœʀ] NF coolness no pl

froissé, e [fʀwase] ADJ (tissu, vêtement) crumpled

froisser [fʀwase] /1/ VT to crumple (up), crease; (fig) to hurt, offend ▪ **se froisser** VPR to crumple, crease; (personne) to take offence (BRIT) ou offense (US); **se ~ un muscle** to strain a muscle

frôlement [fʀolmɑ̃] NM (contact) light touch

frôler [fʀole] /1/ VT to brush against; (projectile) to skim past; (fig) to come very close to, come within a hair's breadth of

★**fromage** [fʀɔmaʒ] NM cheese; **~ blanc** soft white cheese; **~ de tête** pork brawn

fromager, -ère [fʀɔmaʒe, -ɛʀ] NM/F cheese merchant ▶ ADJ (industrie) cheese cpd

fromagerie [fʀɔmaʒʀi] NF cheese dairy

froment [fʀɔmɑ̃] NM wheat

fronce [fʀɔ̃s] NF (de tissu) gather

froncé, e [fʀɔ̃se] ADJ (encolure, jupe) gathered

froncement [fʀɔ̃smɑ̃] NM: **~ de sourcils** frown

froncer [fʀɔ̃se] /3/ VT to gather; **~ les sourcils** to frown

frondaisons [fʀɔ̃dɛzɔ̃] NFPL foliage sg

fronde [fʀɔ̃d] NF sling; (fig) rebellion, rebelliousness

frondeur, -euse [fʀɔ̃dœʀ, -øz] ADJ rebellious

front [fʀɔ̃] NM forehead, brow; (Mil, Météorologie, Pol) front; **avoir le ~ de faire** to have the effrontery to do; **de ~** adv (se heurter) head-on; (rouler) together (2 or 3 abreast); (simultanément) at once; **faire ~ à** to face up to; **~ de mer** (sea) front

frontal, e, -aux [fʀɔ̃tal, -o] ADJ frontal

frontalier, -ière [fʀɔ̃talje, -jɛʀ] ADJ border cpd, frontier cpd ▶ NM/F: **(travailleurs) frontaliers** workers who cross the border to go to work, commuters from across the border

frontière [fʀɔ̃tjɛʀ] NF (Géo, Pol) frontier, border; (fig) frontier, boundary

frontispice [fʀɔ̃tispis] NM frontispiece

frontiste [fʀɔ̃tist] ADJ (électorat) National Front cpd

fronton [fʀɔ̃tɔ̃] NM pediment; (de pelote basque) (front) wall

frottement [fʀɔtmɑ̃] NM rubbing, scraping ▪ **frottements** NMPL (fig: difficultés) friction sg

frotter [fʀɔte] /1/ VI to rub, scrape ▶ VT to rub; (pour nettoyer) to rub (up); (: avec une brosse: pommes de terre, plancher) to scrub; **~ une allumette** to strike a match ▪ **se frotter** VPR: **se ~ à qn** to cross swords with sb; **se ~ à qch** to come up against sth; **se ~ les mains** (fig) to rub one's hands (gleefully)

frottis [fʀɔti] NM (Méd) smear

frottoir [fʀɔtwaʀ] NM (d'allumettes) friction strip; (pour encaustiquer) (long-handled) brush

frou-frou [fʀufʀu] (pl **frous-frous**) NM rustle

froufroutant, e [fʀufʀutɑ̃, -ɑ̃t] ADJ rustling

froussard, e [fʀusaʀ, -aʀd] ADJ (fam): **être ~** to be a chicken (fam) ▶ NM/F chicken (fam)

frousse [fʀus] NF (fam: peur): **avoir la ~** to be in a blue funk

fructifier [fʀyktifje] /7/ VI to yield a profit; **faire ~** to turn to good account

fructose [fʀyktoz] NM fructose

fructueux, -euse [fʀyktɥø, -øz] ADJ fruitful; profitable

frugal, e, -aux [fʀygal, -o] ADJ frugal

frugalement [fʀygalmɑ̃] ADV frugally

frugalité [fʀygalite] NF frugality

★**fruit** [fʀɥi] NM fruit no pl; **fruits de mer** (Culin) seafood sg; **fruits secs** dried fruit sg

fruité, e [fʀɥite] ADJ (vin) fruity

fruiterie [fʀɥitʀi] NF (boutique) greengrocer's (BRIT), fruit (and vegetable) store (US)

fruitier, -ière [fʀɥitje, -jɛʀ] ADJ: **arbre ~** fruit tree ▶ NM/F fruiterer (BRIT), fruit merchant (US)

frusques [fʀysk] NFPL (péj) rags; **de vieilles ~** old rags

fruste [fʀyst] ADJ unpolished, uncultivated

frustrant, e [fʀystʀɑ̃, -ɑ̃t] ADJ frustrating

frustration [fʀystʀasjɔ̃] NF frustration

frustré, e [fʀystʀe] ADJ frustrated

frustrer [fʀystʀe] /1/ VT to frustrate; (*priver*): ~ **qn de qch** to deprive sb of sth

FS ABR (= *franc suisse*) FS, SF

FSE SIGLE M (= *foyer socio-éducatif*) community home

FTP SIGLE MPL (= *Francs-tireurs et partisans*) Communist Resistance in 1940–45

fuchsia [fyʃja] NM fuchsia

fuel(-oil) [fjul(ɔjl)] NM fuel oil; (*pour chauffer*) heating oil

fugace [fygas] ADJ fleeting

fugitif, -ive [fyʒitif, -iv] ADJ (*lueur, amour*) fleeting; (*prisonnier etc*) runaway ▸ NM/F fugitive, runaway

fugue [fyg] NF (*d'un enfant*) running away *no pl*; (*Mus*) fugue; **faire une ~** to run away, abscond

fuguer [fyge] VI to run away

fugueur, -euse [fygœʀ, -øz] ADJ, NM/F runaway

fuir [fɥiʀ] /17/ VT to flee from; (*éviter*) to shun ▸ VI to run away; (*gaz, robinet*) to leak

fuite [fɥit] NF flight; (*écoulement*) leak, leakage; (*divulgation*) leak; **être en ~** to be on the run; **mettre en ~** to put to flight; **prendre la ~** to take flight

fuiter [fɥite] VI to leak out

fulgurant, e [fylgyʀɑ̃, -ɑ̃t] ADJ lightning *cpd*, dazzling

fulminant, e [fylminɑ̃, -ɑ̃t] ADJ (*lettre, regard*) furious; **~ de colère** raging with anger

fulminer [fylmine] /1/ VI: **~ (contre)** to thunder forth (against)

fumant, e [fymɑ̃, -ɑ̃t] ADJ smoking; (*liquide*) steaming; **un coup ~** (*fam*) a master stroke

fumé, e [fyme] ADJ (*Culin*) smoked; (*verre*) tinted ▸ NF smoke; **partir en fumée** to go up in smoke

fume-cigarette [fymsigaʀɛt] NM cigarette holder

★**fumer** [fyme] /1/ VI to smoke; (*liquide*) to steam ▸ VT to smoke; (*terre, champ*) to manure

fumerie [fymʀi] NF: **~ d'opium** opium den

fumerolles [fymʀɔl] NFPL gas and smoke (*from volcano*)

fûmes [fym] VB *voir* **être**

fumet [fymɛ] NM aroma

fumette [fymɛt] NF (*fam: fait de fumer de la drogue*) smoking joints

★**fumeur, -euse** [fymœʀ, -øz] NM/F smoker

fumeux, -euse [fymø, -øz] ADJ (*péj*) woolly (BRIT), hazy

fumier [fymje] NM manure

fumigation [fymigasjɔ̃] NF fumigation

fumigène [fymiʒɛn] ADJ smoke *cpd*

fumiste [fymist] NM (*ramoneur*) chimney sweep ▸ NMF (*péj: paresseux*) shirker; (: *charlatan*) phoney

fumisterie [fymistəʀi] NF (*péj*) fraud, con

fumoir [fymwaʀ] NM smoking room

funambule [fynɑ̃byl] NM tightrope walker

funboard [fœnbɔʀd] NM funboarding

funboarder, funboardeur, -euse [fœnbɔʀdœʀ, -øz] NM/F funboarder

funèbre [fynɛbʀ] ADJ funeral *cpd*; (*fig*) doleful; funereal

funérailles [fyneʀɑj] NFPL funeral *sg*

funéraire [fyneʀɛʀ] ADJ funeral *cpd*, funerary

funérarium [fyneʀaʀjɔm] NM funeral parlour (BRIT), funeral parlor (US)

funeste [fynɛst] ADJ disastrous; deathly

funiculaire [fynikylɛʀ] NM funicular (railway)

funky [fœnki] ADJ (*album, chanson*) funky

FUNU [fyny] SIGLE F (= *Force d'urgence des Nations unies*) UNEF (= *United Nations Emergency Forces*)

fur [fyʀ]: **au ~ et à mesure** *adv* as one goes along; **au ~ et à mesure que** as; **au ~ et à mesure de leur progression** as they advance (*ou* advanced)

furax [fyʀaks] ADJ INV (*fam*) livid

furent [fyʀ] VB *voir* **être**

furet [fyʀɛ] NM ferret

fureter [fyʀ(ə)te] /5/ VI (*péj*) to nose about

fureteur [fyʀ(ə)tœʀ] NM (*Internet*: CANADA: *navigateur*) browser

fureur [fyʀœʀ] NF fury; (*passion*): **~ de** passion for; **être en ~** to be infuriated; **faire ~** to be all the rage

furibard, e [fyʀibaʀ, -aʀd] ADJ (*fam*) livid, absolutely furious

furibond, e [fyʀibɔ̃, -ɔ̃d] ADJ livid, absolutely furious

furie [fyʀi] NF fury; (*femme*) shrew, vixen; **en ~** (*mer*) raging

furieusement [fyʀjøzmɑ̃] ADV furiously

★**furieux, -euse** [fyʀjø, -øz] ADJ furious

furoncle [fyʀɔ̃kl] NM boil

furtif, -ive [fyʀtif, -iv] ADJ furtive

furtivement [fyʀtivmɑ̃] ADV furtively

fus [fy] VB *voir* **être**

fusain [fyzɛ̃] NM (*Bot*) spindle-tree; (*Art*) charcoal

fuseau, x [fyzo] NM (*pantalon*) (ski-)pants *pl*; (*pour filer*) spindle; **en ~** (*jambes*) tapering; (*colonne*) bulging; **~ horaire** time zone

fusée [fyze] NF rocket; **~ éclairante** flare

fuselage [fyz(ə)laʒ] NM fuselage

fuselé, e [fyz(ə)le] ADJ slender; (*galbé*) tapering

fuser [fyze] /1/ VI (*rires etc*) to burst forth

fusible [fyzibl] NM (*Élec: fil*) fuse wire; (: *fiche*) fuse

★**fusil** [fyzi] NM (*de guerre, à canon rayé*) rifle, gun; (*de chasse, à canon lisse*) shotgun, gun; **~ à deux coups** double-barrelled rifle *ou* shotgun; **~ sous-marin** spear-gun

fusilier [fyzilje] NM (*Mil*) rifleman

fusillade [fyzijad] NF gunfire *no pl*, shooting *no pl*; (*combat*) gun battle

fusiller [fyzije] /1/ VT to shoot; **~ qn du regard** to look daggers at sb

fusil-mitrailleur [fyzimitʀajœʀ] (*pl* **fusils-mitrailleurs**) NM machine gun

fusion [fyzjɔ̃] NF fusion, melting; (*fig*) merging; (*Comm*) merger; **en ~** (*métal, roches*) molten

fusionnement [fyzjɔnmɑ̃] NM merger

fusionner [fyzjɔne] /1/ VI to merge

fustiger [fystiʒe] /3/ VT to denounce

fut [fy] VB *voir* **être**

fût [fy] VB *voir* **être** ▶ NM *(tonneau)* barrel, cask; *(de canon)* stock; *(d'arbre)* bole, trunk; *(de colonne)* shaft

futaie [fytɛ] NF forest, plantation

futé, e [fyte] ADJ crafty; **Bison ~®** *TV and radio traffic monitoring service*

fûtes [fyt] VB *voir* **être**

futile [fytil] ADJ *(inutile)* futile; *(frivole)* frivolous

futilement [fytilmã] ADV frivolously

futilité [fytilite] NF futility; frivolousness; *(chose futile)* futile pursuit *(ou thing etc)*

futon [fytɔ̃] NM futon

★futur, e [fytyʀ] ADJ, NM future; **son ~ époux** her husband-to-be; **au ~** *(Ling)* in the future

futurisme [fytyʀism] NM futurism

futuriste [fytyʀist] ADJ futuristic

futurologie [fytyʀɔlɔʒi] NF futurology

fuyant, e [fɥijã, -ãt] VB *voir* **fuir** ▶ ADJ *(regard etc)* evasive; *(lignes etc)* receding; *(perspective)* vanishing

fuyard, e [fɥijaʀ, -aʀd] NM/F runaway

fuyons *etc* [fɥijɔ̃] VB *voir* **fuir**

f

Gg

G, g [ʒe] NM INV G, g ▶ ABR (= *gramme*) g; (= *gauche*) L, l; **G comme Gaston** G for George; **le G8** (*Pol*) the G8 nations, the Group of Eight

gabardine [gabaʀdin] NF gabardine

gabarit [gabaʀi] NM (*fig: dimension, taille*) size; (: *valeur*) calibre; (*Tech*) template; **du même ~** (*fig*) of the same type, of that ilk

gabegie [gabʒi] NF (*péj*) chaos

Gabon [gabɔ̃] NM: **le ~** Gabon

gabonais, e [gabɔnɛ, -ɛz] ADJ Gabonese

gâcher [gɑʃe] /**1**/ VT (*gâter*) to spoil, ruin; (*gaspiller*) to waste; (*plâtre*) to temper; (*mortier*) to mix

gâchette [gɑʃɛt] NF trigger

gâchis [gɑʃi] NM (*désordre*) mess; (*gaspillage*) waste *no pl*

gadget [gadʒɛt] NM thingumajig; (*nouveauté*) gimmick

gadin [gadɛ̃] NM (*fam*): **prendre un ~** to come a cropper (BRIT)

gadoue [gadu] NF sludge

gaélique [gaelik] ADJ Gaelic ▶ NM (*Ling*) Gaelic

gaffe [gaf] NF (*instrument*) boat hook; (*fam: erreur*) blunder; **faire ~** (*fam*) to watch out

gaffer [gafe] /**1**/ VI to blunder

gaffeur, -euse [gafœʀ, -øz] NM/F blunderer

gag [gag] NM gag

gaga [gaga] ADJ (*fam*) gaga

gage [gaʒ] NM (*dans un jeu*) forfeit; (*fig: de fidélité*) token; **mettre en ~** to pawn; **laisser en ~** to leave as security ■ **gages** NMPL (*salaire*) wages; (*garantie*) guarantee *sg*

gager [gaʒe] /**3**/ VT: **~ que** to bet *ou* wager that

gageure [gaʒyʀ] NF: **c'est une ~** it's attempting the impossible

gagnable [gaɲabl] ADJ (*match, circonscription*) winnable

gagnant, e [gaɲɑ̃, -ɑ̃t] ADJ: **billet/numéro ~** winning ticket/number ▶ ADV: **jouer ~** (*aux courses*) to be bound to win ▶ NM/F winner

gagne-pain [gaɲpɛ̃] NM INV job

gagne-petit [gaɲpəti] NM INV low wage earner

★**gagner** [gaɲe] /**1**/ VT (*concours, procès, pari*) to win; (*somme d'argent, revenu*) to earn; (*aller vers, atteindre*) to reach; (*s'emparer de*) to overcome; (*envahir*) to spread to; (*se concilier*): **~ qn** to win sb over; **~ du temps/de la place** to gain time/save space; **~ sa vie** to earn one's living; **~ du terrain** (*aussi fig*) to gain ground; **~ qn de vitesse** to outstrip sb ▶ VI to win; (*fig*) to gain; **~ à faire** (*s'en trouver bien*) to be better off doing; **il y gagne** it's in his interest, it's to his advantage

gagneur [gaɲœʀ] NM winner

gai, e [ge] ADJ cheerful; (*livre, pièce de théâtre*) light-hearted; (*un peu ivre*) merry

gaiement [gemɑ̃] ADV cheerfully

gaieté [gete] NF cheerfulness; **de ~ de cœur** with a light heart ■ **gaietés** NFPL (*souvent ironique*) delights

gaillard, e [gajaʀ, -aʀd] ADJ (*robuste*) sprightly; (*grivois*) bawdy, ribald ▶ NM/F (*strapping*) fellow/wench

gaillardement [gajaʀdəmɑ̃] ADV cheerfully

gain [gɛ̃] NM (*revenu*) earnings *pl*; (*bénéfice: gén pl*) profits *pl*; (*au jeu: gén pl*) winnings *pl*; (*fig: de temps, place*) saving; (: *avantage*) benefit; (: *lucre*) gain; **avoir ~ de cause** to win the case; (*fig*) to be proved right; **obtenir ~ de cause** (*fig*) to win out

gaine [gɛn] NF (*corset*) girdle; (*fourreau*) sheath; (*de fil électrique etc*) outer covering

gaine-culotte [gɛnkylɔt] (*pl* **gaines-culottes**) NF pantie girdle

gainer [gene] /**1**/ VT to cover

gala [gala] NM official reception; **soirée de ~** gala evening

galamment [galamɑ̃] ADV courteously

galant, e [galɑ̃, -ɑ̃t] ADJ (*courtois*) courteous, gentlemanly; (*entreprenant*) flirtatious, gallant; (*aventure, poésie*) amorous; (*scène, rendez-vous*) romantic; **en galante compagnie** (*homme*) with a lady friend; (*femme*) with a gentleman friend

galanterie [galɑ̃tʀi] NF gallantry

galantine [galɑ̃tin] NF galantine

Galapagos [galapagɔs] NFPL: **les (îles) ~** the Galapagos Islands

galaxie [galaksi] NF galaxy

galbe [galb] NM curve(s); shapeliness

galbé, e [galbe] ADJ (*jambes*) (well-)rounded; **bien ~** shapely

gale [gal] NF (*Méd*) scabies *sg*; (*de chien*) mange

galéjade [galeʒad] NF tall story

galère [galɛʀ] NF galley

galérer [galeʀe] /**6**/ VI (*fam*) to work hard, slave (away)

galerie [galʀi] NF gallery; (*Théât*) circle; (*de voiture*) roof rack; (*fig: spectateurs*) audience; **~ marchande** shopping mall; **~ de peinture** (*private*) art gallery

galérien [galeʀjɛ̃] NM galley slave

galeriste [galʀist] NMF gallery owner

galet [galɛ] NM pebble; (*Tech*) wheel ■ **galets** NMPL pebbles, shingle *sg*

galette [galɛt] NF (*gâteau*) flat pastry cake; (*crêpe*) savoury pancake; **la ~ des Rois** *cake traditionally eaten on Twelfth Night*

galeux, -euse [galø, -øz] ADJ: **un chien ~** a mangy dog

Galice [galis] NF: **la ~** Galicia (*in Spain*)

Galicie [galisi] NF: **la ~** Galicia (*in Central Europe*)

galiléen, ne [galileɛ̃, -ɛn] ADJ Galilean

galimatias [galimatja] NM (*péj*) gibberish

galion [galjɔ̃] NM galleon

galipette [galipɛt] NF somersault; **faire des galipettes** to turn somersaults

Galles [gal] NFPL: **le pays de ~** Wales

gallicisme [galisism] NM French idiom; (*tournure fautive*) gallicism

gallinacé [galinase] NM gallinacean

★**gallois, e** [galwa, -waz] ADJ Welsh ▶ NM (*Ling*) Welsh ▶ NM/F: **Gallois, e** Welshman(-woman)

gallo-romain, e [galoʀɔmɛ̃, -ɛn] ADJ Gallo-Roman

galoche [galɔʃ] NF clog

galocher [galɔʃe] VT (*fam*) to French kiss

galon [galɔ̃] NM (*Mil*) stripe; (*décoratif*) piece of braid; **prendre du ~** to be promoted

galop [galo] NM gallop; **au ~** at a gallop; **~ d'essai** (*fig*) trial run

galopade [galɔpad] NF stampede

galopant, e [galɔpɑ̃, -ɑ̃t] ADJ: **inflation galopante** galloping inflation; **démographie galopante** exploding population

galoper [galɔpe] /1/ VI to gallop

galopin [galɔpɛ̃] NM urchin, ragamuffin

galurin [galyʀɛ̃] NM (*fam*) hat, titfer (*fam*)

galvaniser [galvanize] /1/ VT to galvanize

galvaudé, e [galvode] ADJ (*expression*) hackneyed; (*mot*) clichéd

galvauder [galvode] /1/ VT to debase

gambade [gɑ̃bad] NF: **faire des gambades** to skip *ou* frisk about

gambader [gɑ̃bade] /1/ VI (*animal, enfant*) to leap about

gamberger [gɑ̃bɛʀʒe] /3/ (*fam*) VI to (have a) think ▶ VT to dream up

gambette [gɑ̃bɛt] NF (*fam*) leg

Gambie [gɑ̃bi] NF: **la ~** (*pays*) Gambia; (*fleuve*) the Gambia

gambiller [gɑ̃bije] VI (*fam: danser*) to jig about (*fam*)

gamelle [gamɛl] NF mess tin; billy can; (*fam*): **ramasser une ~** to fall flat on one's face

gamète [gamɛt] NM gamete

gamin, e [gamɛ̃, -in] NM/F kid ▶ ADJ mischievous, playful

gaminerie [gaminʀi] NF mischievousness, playfulness

gamme [gam] NF (*Mus*) scale; (*fig*) range

gammé, e [game] ADJ: **croix gammée** swastika

ganache [ganaʃ] NF (*crème*) chocolate cream filling, ganache

Gand [gɑ̃] N Ghent

gang [gɑ̃g] NM (*de criminels*) gang

Gange [gɑ̃ʒ] NM: **le ~** the Ganges

ganglion [gɑ̃glijɔ̃] NM ganglion; (*lymphatique*) gland; **avoir des ganglions** to have swollen glands

gangrène [gɑ̃gʀɛn] NF gangrene; (*fig*) corruption; corrupting influence

gangrener [gɑ̃gʀene] VT (*fig: esprits, relations*) to corrupt ■ **se gangrener** VPR to turn gangrenous

gangster [gɑ̃gstɛʀ] NM gangster

gangstérisme [gɑ̃gsterism] NM gangsterism

gangue [gɑ̃g] NF coating

ganse [gɑ̃s] NF braid

★**gant** [gɑ̃] NM glove; **prendre des gants** (*fig*) to handle the situation with kid gloves; **relever le ~** (*fig*) to take up the gauntlet; **~ de crin** massage glove; **~ de toilette** (face) flannel (*BRIT*), face cloth; **gants de boxe** boxing gloves; **gants de caoutchouc** rubber gloves

ganté, e [gɑ̃te] ADJ: **~ de blanc** wearing white gloves

ganterie [gɑ̃tʀi] NF glove trade; (*magasin*) glove shop

★**garage** [gaʀaʒ] NM garage; **~ à vélos** bicycle shed

★**garagiste** [gaʀaʒist] NMF (*propriétaire*) garage owner; (*mécanicien*) garage mechanic

garant, e [gaʀɑ̃, -ɑ̃t] NM/F guarantor; **se porter ~ de** to vouch for; to be answerable for ▶ NM guarantee

garantie [gaʀɑ̃ti] NF guarantee, warranty; (*gage*) security, surety; **(bon de) ~** guarantee *ou* warranty slip; **~ de bonne exécution** performance bond

garantir [gaʀɑ̃tiʀ] /2/ VT to guarantee; (*protéger*): **~ de** to protect from; **je vous garantis que** I can assure you that; **garanti pure laine/2 ans** guaranteed pure wool/for 2 years

garce [gaʀs] NF (*péj*) bitch (!)

garçon [gaʀsɔ̃] NM boy; (*jeune homme*) boy, lad; (*aussi:* **garçon de café**) waiter; **vieux ~** (*célibataire*) bachelor; **~ boucher/coiffeur** butcher's/hairdresser's assistant; **~ de courses** messenger; **~ d'écurie** stable lad; **~ manqué** tomboy

garçonnet [gaʀsɔnɛ] NM small boy

garçonnière [gaʀsɔnjɛʀ] NF bachelor flat

★**garde** [gaʀd(ə)] NM (*de prisonnier*) guard; (*de domaine etc*) warden; (*soldat, sentinelle*) guardsman; **~ champêtre** rural policeman; **~ du corps** bodyguard; **~ forestier** forest warden; **~ des Sceaux** ≈ Lord Chancellor (*BRIT*), ≈ Attorney General (*US*); **~ mobile** nmf mobile guard ▶ NF guarding; looking after; (*soldats, Boxe, Escrime*) guard; (*faction*) watch; (*d'une arme*) hilt; (*Typo: aussi:* **page** *ou* **feuille de garde**) flyleaf; (: *collée*) endpaper; **de ~** adj, adv on duty; **~ d'enfants** child minder; **~ à vue** (*Jur*) ≈ police custody; **monter la ~** to stand guard; **être sur ses gardes** to be on one's guard; **mettre en ~** to warn; **mise en ~** warning; **prendre ~ (à)** to be careful (of); **avoir la ~ des enfants** (*après divorce*) to have custody of the children

garde-à-vous [gaʀdavu] NM INV: **être/se mettre au ~** to be at/stand to attention; **~ (fixe)!** (*Mil*) attention!

199

garde-barrière [gaʀdəbaʀjɛʀ] (pl **gardes-barrière(s)**) NM/F level-crossing keeper

garde-boue [gaʀdəbu] NM INV mudguard

garde-chasse [gaʀdəʃas] (pl **gardes-chasse(s)**) NM gamekeeper

garde-côte [gaʀdəkot] NM (vaisseau) coastguard boat

garde-feu [gaʀdəfø] NM fender

garde-fou [gaʀdəfu] NM railing, parapet

garde-malade [gaʀdəmalad] (pl **gardes-malade(s)**) NF home nurse

garde-manger [gaʀdmɑ̃ʒe] NM INV (boîte) meat safe; (placard) pantry, larder

garde-meuble [gaʀdəmœbl] NM furniture depository

gardénal [gaʀdenal] NM phenobarbitone

gardénia [gaʀdenja] NM gardenia

garde-pêche [gaʀdəpɛʃ] NM (personne) water bailiff; (navire) fisheries protection ship

★**garder** [gaʀde] /1/ VT (conserver) to keep; (: sur soi: vêtement, chapeau) to keep on; (surveiller: enfants) to look after; (: immeuble, lieu, prisonnier) to guard; ~ **le lit/la chambre** to stay in bed/indoors; ~ **le silence** to keep silent ou quiet; ~ **la ligne** to keep one's figure; ~ **à vue** to keep in custody; **pêche/chasse gardée** private fishing/hunting (ground) ■ **se garder** VPR (aliment: se conserver) to keep; **se ~ de faire** to be careful not to do

garderie [gaʀdəʀi] NF day nursery, crèche

garde-robe [gaʀdəʀɔb] NF wardrobe

gardeur, -euse [gaʀdœʀ, -øz] NM/F (de vaches) cowherd; (de chèvres) goatherd

gardian [gaʀdjɑ̃] NM cowboy (in the Camargue)

★**gardien, ne** [gaʀdjɛ̃, -ɛn] NM/F (garde) guard; (de prison) warder; (de domaine, réserve) warden; (de musée etc) attendant; (de phare, cimetière) keeper; (d'immeuble) caretaker; (fig) guardian; ~ **de but** goalkeeper; ~ **de nuit** night watchman; ~ **de la paix** policeman

gardiennage [gaʀdjɛnaʒ] NM (emploi) caretaking; **société de ~** security firm

gardon [gaʀdɔ̃] NM roach

★**gare** [gaʀ] NF (railway) station, train station (US); ~ **maritime** harbour station; ~ **routière** bus station; (de camions) haulage (BRIT) ou trucking (US) depot; ~ **de triage** marshalling yard ▶ EXCL: ~ **à ...** mind ...!, watch out for ...!; ~ **à ne pas ...** mind you don't ...; ~ **à toi!** watch out!; **sans crier ~** without warning

garenne [gaʀɛn] NF voir **lapin**

★**garer** [gaʀe] /1/ VT to park ■ **se garer** VPR to park; (pour laisser passer) to draw into the side

gargantuesque [gaʀgɑ̃tɥɛsk] ADJ gargantuan

gargariser [gaʀgaʀize] /1/: **se gargariser** VPR to gargle; **se ~ de** (fig) to revel in

gargarisme [gaʀgaʀism] NM gargling no pl; (produit) gargle

gargote [gaʀgɔt] NF cheap restaurant, greasy spoon (fam)

gargouille [gaʀguj] NF gargoyle

gargouillement [gaʀgujmɑ̃] NM = **gargouillis**

gargouiller [gaʀguje] /1/ VI (estomac) to rumble; (eau) to gurgle

gargouillis [gaʀguji] NM (gén pl) rumbling; gurgling

garnement [gaʀnəmɑ̃] NM rascal, scallywag

garni, e [gaʀni] ADJ (plat) served with vegetables (and chips, pasta or rice) ▶ NM (appartement) furnished accommodation no pl (BRIT) ou accommodations pl (US)

garnir [gaʀniʀ] /2/ VT to decorate; (remplir) to fill; (recouvrir) to cover; ~ **qch de** (orner) to decorate sth with; to trim sth with; (approvisionner) to fill ou stock sth with; (protéger) to fit sth with; (Culin) to garnish sth with ■ **se garnir** VPR (pièce, salle) to fill up

garnison [gaʀnizɔ̃] NF garrison

garnissage [gaʀnisaʒ] NM (bourre) stuffing

garniture [gaʀnityʀ] NF (Culin: légumes) vegetables pl; (: persil etc) garnish; (: farce) filling; (décoration) trimming; (protection) fittings pl; ~ **de cheminée** mantelpiece ornaments pl; ~ **de frein** (Auto) brake lining; ~ **intérieure** (Auto) interior trim; ~ **périodique** sanitary towel (BRIT) ou napkin (US)

garrigue [gaʀig] NF scrubland

garrot [gaʀo] NM (Méd) tourniquet; (torture) garrotte

garrotter [gaʀɔte] /1/ VT to tie up; (fig) to muzzle

gars [gɑ] NM lad; (type) guy

Gascogne [gaskɔɲ] NF: **la ~** Gascony; **le golfe de ~** the Bay of Biscay

gascon, ne [gaskɔ̃, -ɔn] ADJ Gascon ▶ NM: **G~** (hâbleur) braggart

gas-oil [gazɔjl] NM diesel oil

gaspillage [gaspijaʒ] NM waste

gaspiller [gaspije] /1/ VT to waste

gaspilleur, -euse [gaspijœʀ, -øz] ADJ wasteful

gastéropode [gasteʀɔpɔd] NM gastropod

gastrique [gastʀik] ADJ gastric, stomach cpd

gastrite [gastʀit] NF gastritis

gastro-entérite [gastʀoɑ̃teʀit] NF (Méd) gastro-enteritis

gastroentérologue [gastʀoɑ̃teʀɔlɔg] NM/F gastroenterologist

gastro-intestinal, e, -aux [gastʀoɛ̃testinal, -o] ADJ gastrointestinal

gastronome [gastʀɔnɔm] NMF gourmet

gastronomie [gastʀɔnɔmi] NF gastronomy

gastronomique [gastʀɔnɔmik] ADJ gastronomic; **menu ~** gourmet menu

gâté, e [gate] ADJ (fruit) bruised; (enfant) spoiled ou spoilt

gâteau, x [gato] NM cake; ~ **d'anniversaire** birthday cake; ~ **de riz** ≈ rice pudding; ~ **sec** biscuit ▶ ADJ INV (fam: trop indulgent): **papa-/maman-gâteau** doting father/mother

gâter [gate] /1/ VT to spoil ■ **se gâter** VPR (dent, fruit) to go bad; (temps, situation) to change for the worse

gâterie [gatʀi] NF little treat

gâteux, -euse [gatø, -øz] ADJ senile

gâtisme [gatism] NM senility

★**gauche** [goʃ] ADJ left, left-hand; (maladroit) awkward, clumsy; **le bras ~** the left arm; **le côté ~** the left-hand side ▶ NF (Pol) left (wing); (Boxe) left; **à ~** on the left; (direction) (to the) left; **à ~ de** (on ou to the) left of; **à la ~ de** to the left of; **sur votre ~** on your left; **de ~** (Pol) left-wing

gauchement [goʃmɑ̃] ADV awkwardly, clumsily

gaucher, -ère [goʃe, -ɛʀ] ADJ left-handed

gaucherie [goʃʀi] NF awkwardness, clumsiness

gauchir [goʃiʀ] /2/ VT (planche, objet) to warp; (fig: fait, idée) to distort

gauchisant, e [goʃizɑ̃, -ɑ̃t] ADJ with left-wing tendencies

gauchisme [goʃism] NM leftism

gauchiste [goʃist] ADJ, NMF leftist

gaudriole [godʀijɔl] NF hanky panky; (fam): **il ne pense qu'à la ~** he has a one-track mind

gaufre [gofʀ] NF (pâtisserie) waffle; (de cire) honeycomb

gaufrer [gofʀe] /1/ VT (papier) to emboss; (tissu) to goffer

gaufrette [gofʀɛt] NF wafer

gaufrier [gofʀije] NM (moule) waffle iron

Gaule [gol] NF: **la ~** Gaul

gaule [gol] NF (perche) (long) pole; (canne à pêche) fishing rod

gauler [gole] /1/ VT (arbre) to beat (using a long pole to bring down fruit); (fruits) to beat down (with a pole)

gaullisme [golism] NM Gaullism

gaulliste [golist] ADJ, NMF Gaullist

gaulois, e [golwa, -waz] ADJ Gallic; (grivois) bawdy ▶ NM/F: **Gaulois, e** Gaul

gauloiserie [golwazʀi] NF bawdiness

gausser [gose] /1/: **se gausser de** VPR to deride

gavage [gavaʒ] NM (d'animaux) force-feeding

gaver [gave] /1/ VT to force-feed; (fig): **~ de** to cram with, fill up with; **se ~ de** to stuff o.s. with

gay [gɛ] ADJ, NM (fam) gay

★**gaz** [gaz] NM INV gas; **mettre les ~** (Auto) to put one's foot down; **chambre/masque à ~** gas chamber/mask; **~ en bouteille** bottled gas; **~ butane** Calor gas® (BRIT), butane gas; **~ carbonique** carbon dioxide; **~ hilarant** laughing gas; **~ lacrymogène** tear gas; **~ naturel** natural gas; **~ de ville** town gas (BRIT), manufactured domestic gas; **ça sent le ~ I** can smell gas, there's a smell of gas

gazage [gazaʒ] NM gassing

gaze [gaz] NF gauze

gazéifié, e [gazeifje] ADJ carbonated, aerated

gazelle [gazɛl] NF gazelle

gazer [gaze] /1/ VT to gas ▶ VI (fam) to be going ou working well

gazette [gazɛt] NF news sheet

gazeux, -euse [gazø, -øz] ADJ gaseous; (eau) sparkling; (boisson) fizzy

gazinière [gazinjɛʀ] NF gas cooker, gas stove

gazoduc [gazodyk] NM gas pipeline

gazole [gazɔl] NM = **gas-oil**

gazomètre [gazɔmɛtʀ] NM gasometer

★**gazon** [gazɔ̃] NM (herbe) turf, grass; (pelouse) lawn

gazonné, e [gazɔne] ADJ grassed

gazonner [gazɔne] /1/ VT (terrain) to grass over

gazouillement [gazujmɑ̃] NM (voir vb) chirping; babbling

gazouiller [gazuje] /1/ VI (oiseau) to chirp; (enfant) to babble

gazouillis [gazuji] NMPL chirp sg

GB SIGLE F (= Grande-Bretagne) GB

gd ABR (= grand) L

GDF SIGLE M (vieilli: = Gaz de France) national gas company

geai [ʒɛ] NM jay

géant, e [ʒeɑ̃, -ɑ̃t] ADJ gigantic, giant; (Comm) giant-size ▶ NM/F giant

gecko [ʒeko] NM gecko

gégène [ʒeʒɛn] NF (torture) electroshock torture

geignard, e [ʒɛɲaʀ, -aʀd] ADJ (fam) moaning

geignement [ʒɛɲmɑ̃] NM groaning, moaning

geindre [ʒɛ̃dʀ] /52/ VI to groan, moan

gel [ʒɛl] NM frost; (de l'eau) freezing; (fig: des salaires, prix) freeze; freezing; (produit de beauté) gel; **~ douche** shower gel

gélatine [ʒelatin] NF gelatine

gélatineux, -euse [ʒelatinø, -øz] ADJ jelly-like, gelatinous

gelé, e [ʒ(ə)le] ADJ frozen ▶ NF (Culin: de fruits) jelly; (gel) frost; **en gelée** in aspic; **gelée blanche** hoarfrost, white frost

★**geler** [ʒ(ə)le] /5/ VT, VI to freeze; **il gèle** it's freezing

gélifiant [ʒelifjɑ̃] NM gelling agent

gélule [ʒelyl] NF (Méd) capsule

gelures [ʒ(ə)lyʀ] NFPL frostbite sg

Gémeaux [ʒemo] NMPL: **les ~** Gemini, the Twins; **être des ~** to be Gemini

gémir [ʒemiʀ] /2/ VI to groan, moan

gémissement [ʒemismɑ̃] NM groan, moan

gemme [ʒɛm] NF gem(stone)

gémonies [ʒemɔni] NFPL: **vouer qn aux ~** to subject sb to public scorn

gén. ABR (= généralement) gen.

gênant, e [ʒɛnɑ̃, -ɑ̃t] ADJ (objet) awkward, in the way; (histoire, personne) embarrassing

gencive [ʒɑ̃siv] NF gum

★**gendarme** [ʒɑ̃daʀm] NM gendarme

gendarmer [ʒɑ̃daʀme] /1/: **se gendarmer** VPR to kick up a fuss

★**gendarmerie** [ʒɑ̃daʀməʀi] NF military police force in countryside and small towns; their police station or barracks

gendre [ʒɑ̃dʀ] NM son-in-law

gène [ʒɛn] NM (Bio) gene

gêne [ʒɛn] NF (à respirer, bouger) discomfort, difficulty; (dérangement) bother, trouble; (manque d'argent) financial difficulties pl ou straits pl; (confusion) embarrassment; **sans ~** adj inconsiderate

gêné, e [ʒene] ADJ embarrassed; (dépourvu d'argent) short (of money)

généalogie [ʒenealɔʒi] NF genealogy

généalogique [ʒenealɔʒik] ADJ genealogical

généalogiste [ʒenealɔʒist] NMF genealogist

gêner [ʒene] /1/ VT (incommoder) to bother; (encombrer) to hamper; (bloquer le passage) to be in the way of; (déranger) to bother; (embarrasser): **~ qn** to make

g

201

sb feel ill-at-ease ■ **se gêner** VPR to put o.s. out; **ne vous gênez pas!** (*ironique*) go right ahead!, don't mind me!; **je vais me ~!** (*ironique*) why should I care?

général, e, -aux [ʒeneral, -o] ADJ, NM general ▶ NF: **(répétition) générale** final dress rehearsal; **en ~** usually, in general; **à la satisfaction générale** to everyone's satisfaction

généralement [ʒeneralmɑ̃] ADV generally

généralisable [ʒeneralizabl] ADJ generally applicable

généralisation [ʒeneralizasjɔ̃] NF generalization

généraliser [ʒeneralize] /1/ VT, VI to generalize ■ **se généraliser** VPR to become widespread

généraliste [ʒeneralist] NMF (*Méd*) general practitioner, GP

généralité [ʒeneralite] NF: **la ~ des ...** the majority of ... ■ **généralités** NFPL generalities; (*introduction*) general points

générateur, -trice [ʒeneratœr, -tris] ADJ: **~ de** which causes *ou* brings about ▶ NF (*Élec*) generator

génération [ʒenerasjɔ̃] NF generation

générer [ʒenere] VT (*emplois, chiffre d'affaires*) to generate

généreusement [ʒenerøzmɑ̃] ADV generously

généreux, -euse [ʒenerø, -øz] ADJ generous

générique [ʒenerik] ADJ generic ▶ NM (*Ciné, TV*) credits *pl*, credit titles *pl*

générosité [ʒenerozite] NF generosity

Gênes [ʒɛn] N Genoa

genèse [ʒənɛz] NF genesis

genêt [ʒ(ə)nɛ] NM (*Bot*) broom *no pl*

généticien, ne [ʒenetisjɛ̃, -ɛn] NM/F geneticist

génétique [ʒenetik] ADJ genetic ▶ NF genetics *sg*

génétiquement [ʒenetikmɑ̃] ADV genetically

gêneur, -euse [ʒɛnœr, -øz] NM/F (*personne qui gêne*) obstacle; (*importun*) intruder

Genève [ʒ(ə)nɛv] N Geneva

genevois, e [ʒən(ə)vwa, -waz] ADJ Genevan

genévrier [ʒənevrije] NM juniper

génial, e, -aux [ʒenjal, -o] ADJ of genius; (*fam: formidable*) fantastic, brilliant

génie [ʒeni] NM genius; (*Mil*): **le ~** ≈ the Engineers *pl*; **avoir du ~** to have genius; **~ civil** civil engineering; **~ génétique** genetic engineering

genièvre [ʒənjɛvr] NM (*Bot*) juniper (tree); (*boisson*) Dutch gin; **grain de ~** juniper berry

génique [ʒenik] ADJ (*Bio*) gene *cpd*

génisse [ʒenis] NF heifer; **foie de ~** ox liver

génital, e, -aux [ʒenital, -o] ADJ genital; **les parties génitales** the genitals

géniteur, -trice [ʒenitœr, -tris] NM/F (*humoristique*) parent

génitif [ʒenitif] NM genitive

génocide [ʒenɔsid] NM genocide

génois, e [ʒenwa, -waz] ADJ Genoese ▶ NF (*gâteau*) ≈ sponge cake

génoise [ʒenwaz] NF (*gâteau*) ≈ sponge cake

génome [ʒenom] NM genome

génotype [ʒenotip] (*Bio*) NM genotype

★**genou, x** [ʒ(ə)nu] NM knee; **à genoux** on one's knees; **se mettre à genoux** to kneel down

genouillère [ʒ(ə)nujɛr] NF (*Sport*) kneepad

★**genre** [ʒɑ̃r] NM (*espèce, sorte*) kind, type, sort; (*allure*) manner; (*Ling*) gender; (*Art*) genre; (*Zool etc*) genus; **se donner du ~** to give o.s. airs; **avoir bon ~** to look a nice sort; **avoir mauvais ~** to be coarse-looking; **ce n'est pas son ~** it's not like him

★**gens** [ʒɑ̃] NMPL (*f in some phrases*) people *pl*; **les ~ d'Église** the clergy; **les ~ du monde** society people; **~ de maison** domestics

gentiane [ʒɑ̃sjan] NF gentian

★**gentil, le** [ʒɑ̃ti, -ij] ADJ kind; (*enfant: sage*) good; (*sympathique: endroit etc*) nice; **c'est très ~ à vous** it's very kind *ou* good *ou* nice of you

gentilhomme [ʒɑ̃tizɔm] NM (*noble*) gentleman

gentilhommière [ʒɑ̃tijɔmjɛr] NF (small) manor house *ou* country seat

gentillesse [ʒɑ̃tijɛs] NF kindness

gentillet, te [ʒɑ̃tijɛ, -ɛt] ADJ nice little

gentiment [ʒɑ̃timɑ̃] ADV kindly

gentleman [dʒɛntləmɛn] NM (*homme courtois*) gentleman

génuflexion [ʒenyflɛksjɔ̃] NF genuflexion

géo ABR (= *géographie*) geography

géodésie [ʒeɔdezi] NF geodesy

géodésique [ʒeɔdezik] ADJ geodesic

géographe [ʒeɔɡraf] NMF geographer

géographie [ʒeɔɡrafi] NF geography

géographique [ʒeɔɡrafik] ADJ geographical

geôlier [ʒolje] NM jailer

géolocalisation [ʒeolokalizasjɔ̃] NF geolocation

géolocaliser [ʒeolokalize] /1/ VT to geolocate

géologie [ʒeɔlɔʒi] NF geology

géologique [ʒeɔlɔʒik] ADJ geological

géologiquement [ʒeɔlɔʒikmɑ̃] ADV geologically

géologue [ʒeɔlɔɡ] NMF geologist

géomancie [ʒeɔmɑ̃si] NF geomancy

géomètre [ʒeɔmɛtr] NM: **(arpenteur-)géomètre** (land) surveyor

géométrie [ʒeɔmetri] NF geometry; **à ~ variable** (*Aviat*) swing-wing

géométrique [ʒeɔmetrik] ADJ geometric

géophysicien, ne [ʒeofizisjɛ̃, -jɛn] NM/F geophysicist

géophysique [ʒeɔfizik] NF geophysics *sg*

géopolitique [ʒeɔpɔlitik] NF geopolitics *sg*

Géorgie [ʒeɔrʒi] NF: **la ~** (*Caucase, USA*) Georgia; **la ~ du Sud** South Georgia

géorgien, ne [ʒeɔrʒjɛ̃, -ɛn] ADJ Georgian

géostationnaire [ʒeɔstasjɔnɛr] ADJ geostationary

géothermie [ʒeɔtɛrmi] NF (*énergie*) geothermal energy

géothermique [ʒeɔtɛrmik] ADJ: **énergie ~** geothermal energy

gérable [ʒerabl] ADJ (*situation, projet*) manageable; (*douleur, désagrément*) bearable

gérance [ʒerɑ̃s] NF management; **mettre en ~** to appoint a manager for; **prendre en ~** to take over (the management of)

géranium [ʒeʁanjɔm] NM geranium

gérant, e [ʒeʁɑ̃, -ɑ̃t] NM/F manager (manageress); **~ d'immeuble** managing agent

gerbe [ʒɛʁb] NF (*de fleurs, d'eau*) spray; (*de blé*) sheaf; (*fig*) shower, burst

gerber [ʒɛʁbe] VI (*fam: vomir*) to puke

gercé, e [ʒɛʁse] ADJ chapped

gercer [ʒɛʁse] /**3**/ VI to chap ■ **se gercer** VPR to chap

gerçure [ʒɛʁsyʁ] NF crack

gérer [ʒeʁe] /**6**/ VT to manage

gerfaut [ʒɛʁfo] NM (*rapace*) gyrfalcon

gériatrie [ʒeʁjatʁi] NF geriatrics *sg*

gériatrique [ʒeʁjatʁik] ADJ geriatric

germain, e [ʒɛʁmɛ̃, -ɛn] ADJ: **cousin ~** first cousin

germanique [ʒɛʁmanik] ADJ Germanic

germaniste [ʒɛʁmanist] NMF German scholar

germanophone [ʒɛʁmanɔfɔn] ADJ German-speaking ▸ NMF German-speaker

germanopratin, e [ʒɛʁmanɔpʁatɛ̃, -in] ADJ from Saint-Germain-des-Prés

germe [ʒɛʁm] NM germ

germer [ʒɛʁme] /**1**/ VI to sprout; (*semence, aussi fig*) to germinate

gérondif [ʒeʁɔ̃dif] NM gerund; (*en latin*) gerundive

gérontocratie [ʒeʁɔ̃tɔkʁasi] NF gerontocracy

gérontologie [ʒeʁɔ̃tɔlɔʒi] NF gerontology

gérontologue [ʒeʁɔ̃tɔlɔg] NMF gerontologist

GES SIGLE M (= *gaz à effet de serre*) GHG (= *greenhouse gas*)

gésier [ʒezje] NM gizzard

gésir [ʒeziʁ] VI to be lying (down); *voir aussi* **ci-gît**

gestation [ʒɛstasjɔ̃] NF gestation

geste [ʒɛst] NM gesture; move; motion; **il fit un ~ de la main pour m'appeler** he signed to me to come over, he waved me over; **ne faites pas un ~** (*ne bougez pas*) don't move

gesticuler [ʒɛstikyle] /**1**/ VI to gesticulate

gestion [ʒɛstjɔ̃] NF management; **~ des disques** (*Inform*) housekeeping; **~ de fichier(s)** (*Inform*) file management

gestionnaire [ʒɛstjɔnɛʁ] NMF administrator; **~ de fichiers** (*Inform*) file manager

gestuelle [ʒɛstɥɛl] NF body movements

geyser [ʒezɛʁ] NM geyser

Ghana [gana] NM: **le ~** Ghana

ghetto [geto] NM ghetto

ghettoïsation [getoizasjɔ̃] NF ghettoization

ghettoïser [getoize] VT to ghettoize

gibbon [ʒibɔ̃] NM gibbon

gibecière [ʒib(ə)sjɛʁ] NF (*de chasseur*) gamebag; (*sac en bandoulière*) shoulder bag

gibelotte [ʒiblɔt] NF *rabbit fricassee in white wine*

gibet [ʒibɛ] NM gallows *pl*

gibier [ʒibje] NM (*animaux*) game; (*fig*) prey

giboulée [ʒibule] NF sudden shower

giboyeux, -euse [ʒibwajø, -øz] ADJ well-stocked with game

Gibraltar [ʒibʁaltaʁ] NM Gibraltar

gibus [ʒibys] NM opera hat

giclée [ʒikle] NF spurt, squirt

gicler [ʒikle] /**1**/ VI to spurt, squirt

gicleur [ʒiklœʁ] NM (*Auto*) jet

GIE SIGLE M = **groupement d'intérêt économique**

gifle [ʒifl] NF slap (in the face)

gifler [ʒifle] /**1**/ VT to slap (in the face)

gigantesque [ʒigɑ̃tɛsk] ADJ gigantic

gigantisme [ʒigɑ̃tism] NM (*Méd*) gigantism; (*des mégalopoles*) vastness

gigaoctet [ʒigaɔktɛ] NM gigabyte

GIGN SIGLE M (= *Groupe d'intervention de la gendarmerie nationale*) *special crack force of the gendarmerie*, ≈ SAS (BRIT)

gigogne [ʒigɔɲ] ADJ: **lits gigognes** truckle (BRIT) *ou* trundle (US) beds; **tables/poupées gigognes** nest of tables/dolls

gigolo [ʒigolo] NM gigolo

gigot [ʒigo] NM leg (of mutton *ou* lamb)

gigoter [ʒigɔte] /**1**/ VI to wriggle (about)

gigue [ʒig] NF (*fam*): **grande ~** beanpole

★**gilet** [ʒilɛ] NM waistcoat; (*pull*) cardigan; (*de corps*) vest; **~ de sauvetage** life jacket; **~ de sécurité** safety vest; **~ pare-balles** bulletproof jacket

gin [dʒin] NM gin; **gin-tonic** gin and tonic

gingembre [ʒɛ̃ʒɑ̃bʁ] NM ginger

gingivite [ʒɛ̃ʒivit] NF inflammation of the gums, gingivitis

ginseng [ʒinsɛŋ] NM ginseng

girafe [ʒiʁaf] NF giraffe

giratoire [ʒiʁatwaʁ] ADJ: **sens ~** roundabout

girofle [ʒiʁɔfl] NM: **clou de ~** clove

giroflée [ʒiʁɔfle] NF wallflower

girolle [ʒiʁɔl] NF chanterelle

giron [ʒiʁɔ̃] NM (*genoux*) lap; (*fig: sein*) bosom

Gironde [ʒiʁɔ̃d] NF: **la ~** the Gironde

gironde [ʒiʁɔ̃d] ADJ F (*fam: bien faite*) well-rounded

Girondin, e [ʒiʁɔ̃dɛ̃, -in] NM/F (*habitant de la Gironde*) person who lives in the Gironde; (*Hist*) Girondin

girophare [ʒiʁofaʁ] NM revolving (flashing) light

girouette [ʒiʁwɛt] NF weather vane *ou* cock

gis [ʒi], **gisais** *etc* [ʒize] VB *voir* **gésir**

gisant [ʒizɑ̃] NM recumbent statue

gisement [ʒizmɑ̃] NM deposit

gît [ʒi] VB *voir* **gésir**

gitan, e [ʒitɑ̃, -an] NM/F gipsy

gîte [ʒit] NM (*maison*) home; (*abri*) shelter; (*du lièvre*) form; **~ (rural)** (*country*) holiday cottage *ou* apartment, gîte (*self-catering accommodation in the country*)

A **gîte rural** is a high-quality holiday rental, usually typical of the region and with access to an outdoor space. *Gîtes ruraux* are mostly detached houses situated, as their name implies, in rural areas. They are classified into 5 categories, from 1 to 5 *épis* (ears of wheat), according to how comfortable and well-equipped they are, how much outdoor space there is, whether they have a swimming pool, and so on.

gîter [ʒite] /**1**/ vi (Navig) to list

givrage [ʒivʀaʒ] NM icing

givrant, e [ʒivʀɑ̃, -ɑ̃t] ADJ: **brouillard ~** freezing fog

givre [ʒivʀ] NM (hoar) frost

givré, e [ʒivʀe] ADJ covered in frost; (fam: fou) nuts; **citron ~/orange givrée** lemon/orange sorbet (served in fruit skin)

glabre [ɡlabʀ] ADJ hairless; (menton) clean-shaven

glaçage [ɡlasaʒ] NM (au sucre) icing; (au blanc d'œuf, de la viande) glazing

★**glace** [ɡlas] NF ice; (crème glacée) ice cream; (verre) sheet of glass; (miroir) mirror; (de voiture) window; **de ~** (fig: accueil, visage) frosty, icy; **rester de ~** to remain unmoved ■ **glaces** NFPL (Géo) ice sheets, ice sg

glacé, e [ɡlase] ADJ (mains, vent, pluie) freezing; (lac) frozen; (boisson) iced

glacer [ɡlase] /**3**/ vt to freeze; (boisson) to chill, ice; (gâteau) to ice (BRIT), frost (US); (papier, tissu) to glaze; (fig): ~ **qn** (intimider) to chill sb; (effrayer) to make sb's blood run cold

glaciaire [ɡlasjɛʀ] ADJ (période) ice cpd; (relief) glacial

glacial, e [ɡlasjal] ADJ icy

glaciation [ɡlasjasjɔ̃] NF (période) glaciation

glacier [ɡlasje] NM (Géo) glacier; (marchand) ice-cream maker

glacière [ɡlasjɛʀ] NF icebox

glaçon [ɡlasɔ̃] NM icicle; (pour boisson) ice cube

gladiateur [ɡladjatœʀ] NM gladiator

glaïeul [ɡlajœl] NM gladiola

glaire [ɡlɛʀ] NF (Méd) phlegm no pl

glaise [ɡlɛz] NF clay

glaive [ɡlɛv] NM two-edged sword

glamour [ɡlamuʀ] ADJ glamorous

gland [ɡlɑ̃] NM (de chêne) acorn; (décoration) tassel; (Anat) glans

glande [ɡlɑ̃d] NF gland

glander [ɡlɑ̃de] /**1**/ vi (fam) to fart around (BRIT !), screw around (US !)

glandeur, -euse [ɡlɑ̃dœʀ, -øz] NM/F (fam) lazy sod (fam)

glandouiller [ɡlɑ̃duje] vi (fam) to bum around (fam)

glaner [ɡlane] /**1**/ vt, vi to glean

glapir [ɡlapiʀ] /**2**/ vi to yelp

glapissement [ɡlapismɑ̃] NM yelping

glas [ɡlɑ] NM knell, toll

glaucome [ɡlokom] NM glaucoma

glauque [ɡlok] ADJ dull blue-green

glissade [ɡlisad] NF (par jeu) slide; (chute) slip; (dérapage) skid; **faire des glissades** to slide

glissant, e [ɡlisɑ̃, -ɑ̃t] ADJ slippery

glisse [ɡlis] NF: **sports de ~** sports involving sliding or gliding (eg skiing, surfing, windsurfing)

glissement [ɡlismɑ̃] NM sliding; (fig) shift; **~ de terrain** landslide

★**glisser** [ɡlise] /**1**/ vi (avancer) to glide ou slide along; (coulisser, tomber) to slide; (déraper) to slip; (être glissant) to be slippery; **~ sur** (fig: détail etc) to skate over ▸ vt to slip; **~ qch sous/dans/à** to slip sth under/into/to ■ **se glisser dans/entre** VPR to slip into/between

glisser-déposer [ɡlisedepoze] NM INV drag-and-drop operation ▸ vt to drag and drop

glissière [ɡlisjɛʀ] NF slide channel; **à ~** (porte, fenêtre) sliding; **~ de sécurité** (Auto) crash barrier

glissoire [ɡliswaʀ] NF slide

global, e, -aux [ɡlɔbal, -o] ADJ overall

globalement [ɡlɔbalmɑ̃] ADV taken as a whole

globalisation [ɡlɔbalizasjɔ̃] NF globalization

globalité [ɡlɔbalite] NF: **dans sa ~** in its entirety

globe [ɡlɔb] NM globe; **sous ~** under glass; **~ oculaire** eyeball; **le ~ terrestre** the globe

globe-trotter [ɡlɔbtʀɔtœʀ] NM globe-trotter

globulaire [ɡlɔbylɛʀ] ADJ (Astronomie: amas) globular; (Méd): **numération ~** blood count; **volume ~** blood volume

globule [ɡlɔbyl] NM (du sang): **~ blanc/rouge** white/red corpuscle

globuleux, -euse [ɡlɔbylø, -øz] ADJ: **yeux ~** protruding eyes

gloire [ɡlwaʀ] NF glory; (mérite) distinction, credit; (personne) celebrity

glorieux, -euse [ɡlɔʀjø, -øz] ADJ glorious

glorifier [ɡlɔʀifje] /**7**/ vt to glorify, extol ■ **se glorifier de** VPR to glory in

gloriole [ɡlɔʀjɔl] NF vainglory

glose [ɡloz] NF gloss

gloser [ɡloze] vi: **~ sur qch** to hold forth on sth

glossaire [ɡlɔsɛʀ] NM glossary

glotte [ɡlɔt] NF (Anat) glottis

glouglouter [ɡluɡlute] /**1**/ vi to gurgle

gloussement [ɡlusmɑ̃] NM (de poule) cluck; (rire) chuckle

glousser [ɡluse] /**1**/ vi to cluck; (rire) to chuckle

glouton, ne [ɡlutɔ̃, -ɔn] ADJ gluttonous, greedy

gloutonnerie [ɡlutɔnʀi] NF gluttony

glu [ɡly] NF birdlime

gluant, e [ɡlyɑ̃, -ɑ̃t] ADJ sticky, gummy

glucide [ɡlysid] NM carbohydrate, (fam) carb; **alimentation** ou **régime pauvre en glucides** low-carb diet

glucose [ɡlykoz] NM glucose

glutamate [ɡlytamat] NM: **~ de sodium** monosodium glutamate

gluten [ɡlytɛn] NM gluten

glycémie [ɡlisemi] NF blood sugar level

glycérine [ɡliseʀin] NF glycerine

glycine [ɡlisin] NF wisteria

GMT SIGLE ADJ (= Greenwich Mean Time) GMT

gnangnan [ɲɑ̃ɲɑ̃] ADJ INV (fam: livre, film) soppy

GNL SIGLE M (= gaz naturel liquéfié) LNG (= liquefied natural gas)

gnognote, gnognotte [ɲɔɲɔt] NF (fam: petite bière): **c'est de la ~ à côté du mien** it's not a patch on mine; **c'est pas de la ~** it's quite something

gnôle [ɲol] NF (fam) booze no pl; **un petit verre de ~** a drop of the hard stuff

gnome [ɡnom] NM gnome

gnon [ɲɔ̃] NM (fam: coup de poing) bash; (: marque) dent

gnou [gnu] NM gnu

GO SIGLE FPL (= *grandes ondes*) LW ▶ SIGLE M (= *gentil organisateur*) title given to leaders on Club Méditerranée holidays; *extended to refer to easy-going leader of any group*

Go ABR (= *gigaoctet*) GB

go [go]: **tout de go** *adv* straight out

goal [gol] NM goalkeeper

gobelet [gɔblɛ] NM (*en métal*) tumbler; (*en plastique*) beaker; (*à dés*) cup

gober [gɔbe] /1/ VT to swallow

goberger [gɔbɛʀʒe] /3/: **se goberger** VPR to cosset o.s.

Gobi [gɔbi] N: **désert de ~** Gobi Desert

godasse [gɔdas] NF (*fam*) shoe

godet [gɔdɛ] NM pot; (*Couture*) unpressed pleat

godiche [gɔdiʃ] (*fam*) NF clumsy oaf ▶ ADJ clumsy

godille [gɔdij] NF (*Navig*) steering oar; (*Ski*) wedeln

godiller [gɔdije] /1/ VI (*Navig*) to scull; (*Ski*) to wedeln

godillot [gɔdijo] NM (*fam*: *gros soulier*) clodhopper (*fam*)

goéland [gɔelɑ̃] NM (sea)gull

goélette [gɔelɛt] NF schooner

goémon [gɔemɔ̃] NM wrack

gogo [gɔgo] NM (*péj*) mug, sucker; **à ~** *adv* galore

goguenard, e [gɔg(ə)naʀ, -aʀd] ADJ mocking

goguette [gɔgɛt] NF: **en ~** on the binge

goinfre [gwɛ̃fʀ] NM glutton

goinfrer [gwɛ̃fʀe] /1/: **se goinfrer** VPR to make a pig of o.s.; **se ~ de** to guzzle

goinfrerie [gwɛ̃fʀəʀi] NF greed

goitre [gwatʀ] NM goitre

★**golf** [gɔlf] NM (*jeu*) golf; (*terrain*) golf course; **~ miniature** crazy *ou* miniature golf

golfe [gɔlf] NM gulf; (*petit*) bay; **le ~ d'Aden** the Gulf of Aden; **le ~ de Gascogne** the Bay of Biscay; **le ~ du Lion** the Gulf of Lions; **le ~ Persique** the Persian Gulf

golfeur, -euse [gɔlfœʀ, -øz] NM/F golfer

gominé, e [gɔmine] ADJ slicked down

gommage [gɔmaʒ] NM (*de peau*) scrub

★**gomme** [gɔm] NF (*à effacer*) rubber (BRIT), eraser; (*résine*) gum; **boule** *ou* **pastille de ~** throat pastille

gommé, e [gɔme] ADJ: **papier ~** gummed paper

gommer [gɔme] /1/ VT (*effacer*) to rub out (BRIT), erase; (*enduire de gomme*) to gum

gond [gɔ̃] NM hinge; **sortir de ses gonds** (*fig*) to fly off the handle

gondole [gɔ̃dɔl] NF gondola; (*pour l'étalage*) shelves *pl*, gondola

gondoler [gɔ̃dɔle] /1/: **se gondoler** VPR to warp, buckle; (*fam*: *rire*) to hoot with laughter; to be in stitches

gondolier [gɔ̃dɔlje] NM gondolier

gonflable [gɔ̃flabl] ADJ inflatable

gonflage [gɔ̃flaʒ] NM inflating, blowing up

gonflant, e [gɔ̃flɑ̃, -ɑ̃t] ADJ (*fam*: *ennuyeux*) boring

gonflé, e [gɔ̃fle] ADJ swollen; (*ventre*) bloated; **il est ~** (*fam*: *courageux*) he's got some nerve (: *impertinent*) he's got a nerve

gonflement [gɔ̃fləmɑ̃] NM inflation; (*Méd*) swelling

★**gonfler** [gɔ̃fle] /1/ VT (*pneu, ballon*) to inflate, blow up; (*nombre, importance*) to inflate ▶ VI (*pied etc*) to swell (up); (*Culin*: *pâte*) to rise

gonflette [gɔ̃flɛt] NF (*fam, péj*): **faire de la ~** to pump iron

gonfleur [gɔ̃flœʀ] NM air pump

gong [gɔ̃g] NM gong

gonzesse [gɔ̃zɛs] NF (*fam*) chick, bird (BRIT)

googler [gugle] /1/ VT to google

goret [gɔʀɛ] NM piglet

★**gorge** [gɔʀʒ] NF (*Anat*) throat; (*poitrine*) breast; (*Géo*) gorge; (*rainure*) groove; **avoir mal à la ~** to have a sore throat; **avoir la ~ serrée** to have a lump in one's throat

gorgé, e [gɔʀʒe] ADJ: **~ de** filled with; (*eau*) saturated with ▶ NF mouthful; (*petite*) sip; (*grande*) gulp; **boire à petites/grandes gorgées** to take little sips/big gulps

gorger [gɔʀʒe] : **se gorger** VPR: **se ~ de qch** to gorge o.s on sth; (*se remplir*) to fill to bursting with sth; **se ~ d'eau** to become saturated; **se ~ de lait** to become engorged

gorgone [gɔʀgɔn] NF (*Mythologie, Art*) gorgon

gorille [gɔʀij] NM gorilla; (*fam*) bodyguard

gosier [gozje] NM throat

gosse [gɔs] NMF kid

gotha [gɔta] NM (*élite*) elite

gothique [gɔtik] ADJ Gothic

gouache [gwaʃ] NF gouache

gouaille [gwaj] NF street wit, cocky humour (BRIT) *ou* humor (US)

goudron [gudʀɔ̃] NM (*asphalte*) tar(mac) (BRIT), asphalt; (*du tabac*) tar

goudronner [gudʀɔne] /1/ VT to tar(mac) (BRIT), asphalt (US)

gouffre [gufʀ] NM abyss, gulf

gougère [guʒɛʀ] NF *choux pastry filled with cheese*

goujat [guʒa] NM boor

goujaterie [guʒatʀi] NF (*comportement*) boorishness

goujon [guʒɔ̃] NM gudgeon

goulée [gule] NF gulp

goulet [gulɛ] NM bottleneck

gouleyant, e [gulejɑ̃, -ɑ̃t] ADJ (*vin*) lively

goulot [gulo] NM (*de bouteille*) (bottle)neck; **boire au ~** to drink from the bottle; **~ d'étranglement** (*fig*) bottleneck

goulu, e [guly] ADJ greedy

goulûment [gulymɑ̃] ADV greedily

goupille [gupij] NF (metal) pin

goupiller [gupije] /1/ VT to pin (together) ▪ **se goupiller** VPR (*fam*): **ça s'est bien goupillé** it's turned out well; **ça s'est mal goupillé** it didn't work out

goupillon [gupijɔ̃] NM (*Rel*) sprinkler; (*brosse*) bottle brush; **le ~** (*fig*) the cloth, the clergy

gourd, e [guʀ, guʀd] ADJ numb (with cold)

gourde [guʀd] NF (*récipient*) flask; (*fam*) (clumsy) clot *ou* oaf ▶ ADJ oafish

g

gourdin [guʀdɛ̃] NM club, bludgeon

gourer [guʀe] /1/ (*fam*): **se gourer** VPR to boob

gourmand, e [guʀmɑ̃, -ɑ̃d] ADJ greedy

gourmandise [guʀmɑ̃diz] NF greed; (*bonbon*) sweet (BRIT), piece of candy (US)

gourmet [guʀme] NM epicure

gourmette [guʀmɛt] NF chain bracelet

gourou [guʀu] NM guru

gousse [gus] NF (*de vanille etc*) pod; **~ d'ail** clove of garlic

gousset [gusɛ] NM (*de gilet*) fob

goût [gu] NM taste; (*fig: appréciation*) taste, liking; **le (bon) ~** good taste; **de bon ~** in good taste, tasteful; **de mauvais ~** in bad taste, tasteless; **avoir bon/mauvais ~** (*aliment*) to taste nice/nasty; (*personne*) to have good/bad taste; **avoir du/manquer de ~** to have/lack taste; **avoir du ~ pour** to have a liking for; **prendre ~ à** to develop a taste *ou* a liking for

goûter [gute] /1/ VT (*essayer*) to taste; (*apprécier*) to enjoy; **~ à** to taste, sample; **~ de** to have a taste of; **je peux ~ ?** can I have a taste? ▸ VI to have (afternoon) tea ▸ NM (afternoon) tea; **~ d'enfants/d'anniversaire** children's tea/birthday party

★**goutte** [gut] NF drop; (*Méd*) gout; (*alcool*) nip (BRIT), tot (BRIT), drop (US); **~ à ~** adv a drop at a time; **tomber ~ à ~** to drip ∎ **gouttes** NFPL (*Méd*) drops

goutte-à-goutte [gutagut] NM INV (*Méd*) drip; **alimenter au ~** to drip-feed

gouttelette [gut(ə)lɛt] NF droplet

goutter [gute] /1/ VI to drip

gouttière [gutjɛʀ] NF gutter

gouvernail [guvɛʀnaj] NM rudder; (*barre*) helm, tiller

gouvernant, e [guvɛʀnɑ̃, -ɑ̃t] ADJ ruling cpd ▸ NF (*de maison*) housekeeper; (*d'un enfant*) governess

gouverne [guvɛʀn] NF: **pour sa ~** for his guidance

★**gouvernement** [guvɛʀnəmɑ̃] NM government

> En anglais britannique, le mot **government** peut fonctionner comme un singulier ou un pluriel selon que l'accent est mis sur l'institution en général ou sur ses membres. Le verbe qui suit peut donc être au singulier ou au pluriel.
> *Le gouvernement a annoncé de nouvelles mesures.*
> **The government *has* announced new measures.**
> *Le gouvernement n'est pas en phase avec l'électorat.*
> **The government *are* out of touch with the electorate.**

gouvernemental, e, -aux [guvɛʀnəmɑ̃tal, -o] ADJ (*politique*) government cpd; (*journal, parti*) pro-government

gouverner [guvɛʀne] /1/ VT to govern; (*diriger*) to steer; (*fig*) to control

gouverneur [guvɛʀnœʀ] NM governor; (*Mil*) commanding officer

goyave [gɔjav] NF guava

GPA SIGLE F (= *gestation pour autrui*) gestational surrogacy

GPL SIGLE M (= *gaz de pétrole liquéfié*) LPG (= *liquefied petroleum gas*)

GPS SIGLE M (= *global positioning system*) GPS

GQG SIGLE M (= *grand quartier général*) GHQ

graal [gʀal] NM (*Rel, aussi fig*) Holy Grail

grabataire [gʀabatɛʀ] ADJ bedridden ▸ NMF bedridden invalid

grabuge [gʀabyʒ] NM (*fam*) scrap

grâce [gʀɑs] NF (*charme, Rel*) grace; (*faveur*) favour; (*Jur*) pardon; **de bonne/mauvaise ~** with (a) good/bad grace; **~ à** prép thanks to; **faire ~ à qn de qch** to spare sb sth; **rendre ~(s) à** to give thanks to; **demander ~** to beg for mercy; **droit de ~** right of reprieve; **recours en ~** plea for pardon ∎ **grâces** NFPL (*Rel*) grace sg; **dans les bonnes grâces de qn** in favour with sb

gracier [gʀasje] /7/ VT to pardon

gracieusement [gʀasjøzmɑ̃] ADV graciously, kindly; (*gratuitement*) freely; (*avec grâce*) gracefully

gracieux, -euse [gʀasjø, -øz] ADJ (*charmant, élégant*) graceful; (*aimable*) gracious, kind; **à titre ~** free of charge

gracile [gʀasil] ADJ slender

gradation [gʀadasjɔ̃] NF gradation

grade [gʀad] NM (*Mil*) rank; (*Scol*) degree; **monter en ~** to be promoted

gradé [gʀade] NM (*Mil*) officer

gradin [gʀadɛ̃] NM (*dans un théâtre*) tier; (*de stade*) step ∎ **gradins** NMPL (*de stade*) terracing *no pl* (BRIT), standing area; **en gradins** terraced

graduation [gʀadyasjɔ̃] NF graduation

gradué, e [gʀadɥe] ADJ (*exercices*) graded (for difficulty); (*thermomètre*) graduated; **verre ~** measuring jug

graduel, le [gʀadɥɛl] ADJ gradual; progressive

graduer [gʀadɥe] /1/ VT (*effort etc*) to increase gradually; (*règle, verre*) to graduate

graff [gʀaf] NM graffiti

graffeur, -euse [gʀafœʀ, øz] NM/F graffiti artist

graffiti [gʀafiti] NMPL graffiti

grailler [gʀaje] VI (*fam: manger*) to nosh; (*corneille*) to caw

grain [gʀɛ̃] NM (*gén*) grain; (*de chapelet*) bead; (*Navig*) squall; (*averse*) heavy shower; (*fig: petite quantité*): **un ~ de** a touch of; **~ de beauté** beauty spot; **~ de café** coffee bean; **~ de poivre** peppercorn; **~ de poussière** speck of dust; **~ de raisin** grape

graine [gʀɛn] NF seed; **mauvaise ~** (*mauvais sujet*) bad lot; **une ~ de voyou** a hooligan in the making

graineterie [gʀɛntʀi] NF seed merchant's (shop)

grainetier, -ière [gʀɛntje, -jɛʀ] NM/F seed merchant

graissage [gʀesaʒ] NM lubrication, greasing

graisse [gʀes] NF fat; (*lubrifiant*) grease; **~ saturée** saturated fat

graisser [gʀese] /1/ VT to lubricate, grease; (*tacher*) to make greasy

graisseux, -euse [gʀesø, -øz] ADJ greasy; (*Anat*) fatty

graminée [gʀamine] NF (*Bot*) grass; **~ ornementale** ornamental grass

grammaire [gʀamɛʀ] NF grammar

grammatical, e, -aux [gʀamatikal, -o] ADJ grammatical

★**gramme** [gʀam] NM gramme

★**grand, e** [gʀɑ̃, gʀɑ̃d] ADJ (*haut*) tall; (*gros, vaste, large*) big, large; (*long*) long; (*plus âgé*) big; (*adulte*) grown-up; (*important, brillant*) great; **un ~ buveur** a heavy drinker; **un ~ homme** a great man; **son ~ frère** his big *ou* older brother; **avoir ~ besoin de** to be in dire *ou* desperate need of; **il est ~ temps de** it's high time to; **il est assez ~ pour** he's big *ou* old enough to; **en ~** on a large scale; **au ~ air** in the open (air); **les grands blessés/brûlés** the severely injured/burned; **de ~ matin** at the crack of dawn; **~ écart** splits *pl*; **~ ensemble** housing scheme; **~ jour** broad daylight; **~ livre** (*Comm*) ledger; **~ magasin** department store; **~ malade** very sick person; **~ public** general public; **grande personne** grown-up; **grande surface** hypermarket, superstore; **grandes écoles** *prestige university-level colleges with competitive entrance examinations; see note*; **grandes lignes** (*Rail*) main lines; **grandes vacances** summer holidays (BRIT) *ou* vacation (US) ► ADV: **~ ouvert** wide open; **voir ~** to think big

The **grandes écoles** are highly respected institutes of higher education which train students for specific careers. Students who have spent two years after the *baccalauréat* in the *classes préparatoires* are recruited by competitive entry examination. The prestigious *grandes écoles* have a strong corporate identity and tend to furnish France with its intellectual, administrative and political élite.

Large et **big** s'emploient pour parler de la taille, mais contrairement à **large**, **big** peut aussi désigner une chose importante ou impressionnante : *les grands clubs de foot* **the big football clubs**.
Large et **great** peuvent caractériser une quantité : *une grande quantité de nourriture* **a large amount of food**.
Ils ont participé en grand nombre. **They took part in great numbers**.

grand-angle [gʀɑ̃tɑ̃gl] (*pl* **grands-angles**) NM (*Photo*) wide-angle lens

grand-angulaire [gʀɑ̃tɑ̃gylɛʀ] (*pl* **grands-angulaires**) NM (*Photo*) wide-angle lens

★**grand-chose** [gʀɑ̃ʃoz] NMF INV: **pas ~** not much

★**Grande-Bretagne** [gʀɑ̃dbʀətaɲ] NF: **la ~** (Great) Britain; **en ~** in (Great) Britain

grandement [gʀɑ̃dmɑ̃] ADV (*tout à fait*) greatly; (*largement*) easily; (*généreusement*) lavishly

grandeur [gʀɑ̃dœʀ] NF (*dimension*) size; (*fig: ampleur, importance*) magnitude; (*: gloire, puissance*) greatness; **~ nature** *adj* life-size

grand-guignolesque [gʀɑ̃giɲɔlɛsk] ADJ gruesome

grandiloquence [gʀɑ̃dilɔkɑ̃s] NF bombast, grandiloquence

grandiloquent, e [gʀɑ̃dilɔkɑ̃, -ɑ̃t] ADJ bombastic, grandiloquent

grandiose [gʀɑ̃djoz] ADJ (*paysage, spectacle*) imposing

grandir [gʀɑ̃diʀ] /2/ VI (*enfant, arbre*) to grow; (*bruit, hostilité*) to increase, grow ► VT: **~ qn** (*vêtement, chaussure*) to make sb look taller; (*fig*) to make sb grow in stature

grandissant, e [gʀɑ̃disɑ̃, -ɑ̃t] ADJ growing

grand-mère [gʀɑ̃mɛʀ] (*pl* **grands-mères**) NF grandmother

grand-messe [gʀɑ̃mɛs] (*pl* **grands-messes**) NF high mass

grand-oncle [gʀɑ̃tɔ̃kl] (*pl* **grands-oncles**) NM great-uncle

grand-peine [gʀɑ̃pɛn]: **à ~** *adv* with (great) difficulty

grand-père [gʀɑ̃pɛʀ] (*pl* **grands-pères**) NM grandfather

grand-route [gʀɑ̃ʀut] NF main road

grand-rue [gʀɑ̃ʀy] NF high street

★**grands-parents** [gʀɑ̃paʀɑ̃] NMPL grandparents

grand-tante [gʀɑ̃tɑ̃t] (*pl* **grands-tantes**) NF great-aunt

grand-voile [gʀɑ̃vwal] (*pl* **grands-voiles**) NF mainsail

grange [gʀɑ̃ʒ] NF barn

granit, granite [gʀanit] NM granite

granité [gʀanite] NM (*sorbet*) granita

granitique [gʀanitik] ADJ granite; (*terrain*) granitic

granulaire [gʀanylɛʀ] ADJ (*Science*) granular

granule [gʀanyl] NM small pill

granulé [gʀanyle] NM granule

granuleux, -euse [gʀanylø, -øz] ADJ granular

graphe [gʀaf] NM graph

graphème [gʀafɛm] NM grapheme

graphie [gʀafi] NF written form

graphique [gʀafik] ADJ graphic ► NM graph

graphisme [gʀafism] NM graphic arts *pl*; graphics *sg*; (*écriture*) handwriting

graphiste [gʀafist] NMF graphic designer

graphite [gʀafit] NM graphite

graphologie [gʀafɔlɔʒi] NF graphology

graphologue [gʀafɔlɔg] NMF graphologist

grappe [gʀap] NF cluster; **~ de raisin** bunch of grapes

grappiller [gʀapije] /1/ VT to glean

grappin [gʀapɛ̃] NM grapnel; **mettre le ~ sur** (*fig*) to get one's claws on

★**gras, se** [gʀa, gʀas] ADJ (*viande, soupe*) fatty; (*personne*) fat; (*surface, main, cheveux*) greasy; (*terre*) sticky; (*toux*) loose, phlegmy; (*rire*) throaty; (*plaisanterie*) coarse; (*crayon*) soft-lead; (*Typo*) bold; **faire la grasse matinée** to have a lie-in (BRIT), sleep late; **matière grasse** fat (content) ► NM (*Culin*) fat

gras-double [gʀadubl] NM (*Culin*) tripe

grassement [gʀasmɑ̃] ADV (*généreusement*): **~ payé** handsomely paid; (*grossièrement: rire*) coarsely

grassouillet, te [gʀasuje, -ɛt] ADJ podgy, plump

gratifiant, e [gʀatifjɑ̃, -ɑ̃t] ADJ gratifying, rewarding

gratification [gʀatifikasjɔ̃] NF bonus

gratifier [gʀatifje] /7/ VT: **~ qn de** to favour (BRIT) *ou* favor (US) sb with; to reward sb with; (*sourire etc*) to favo(u)r sb with

gratin [gʀatɛ̃] NM (*Culin*) cheese- (*ou* crumb-)topped dish; (*: croûte*) topping; **au ~** au gratin; **tout le ~ parisien** all the best people of Paris

gratiné [gʀatine] ADJ (Culin) au gratin; (fam) hellish ▶ NF (soupe) onion soup au gratin

gratiner [gʀatine] VI to bake until golden-brown; **faire ~ qch** to bake sth until golden-brown

gratis [gʀatis] ADV, ADJ INV free

gratitude [gʀatityd] NF gratitude

gratouiller, grattouiller [gʀatuje] VT (fam) to make itch

★**gratte-ciel** [gʀatsjɛl] NM INV skyscraper

grattement [gʀatmɑ̃] NM (bruit) scratching (noise)

gratte-papier [gʀatpapje] NM INV (péj) penpusher

gratter [gʀate] /**1**/ VT (frotter) to scrape; (avec un ongle: bras, bouton) to scratch; (enlever: avec un outil) to scrape off; (: avec un ongle) to scratch off ▶ VI (irriter) to be scratchy; (démanger) to itch ■ **se gratter** VPR to scratch o.s.

grattoir [gʀatwaʀ] NM scraper

★**gratuit, e** [gʀatɥi, -ɥit] ADJ (entrée) free; (billet) free, complimentary; (fig) gratuitous

gratuité [gʀatɥite] NF being free (of charge); gratuitousness

gratuitement [gʀatɥitmɑ̃] ADV (sans payer) free; (sans preuve, motif) gratuitously

gravats [gʀava] NMPL rubble sg

★**grave** [gʀav] ADJ (maladie, accident) serious, bad; (sujet, problème) serious, grave; (personne, air) grave, solemn; (voix, son) deep, low-pitched; **ce n'est pas ~ !** it's all right, don't worry; **blessé ~** seriously injured person ▶ NM (Mus) low register

graveleux, -euse [gʀav(ə)lø, -øz] ADJ (terre) gravelly; (fruit) gritty; (contes, propos) smutty

gravement [gʀavmɑ̃] ADV seriously; badly; (parler, regarder) gravely

graver [gʀave] /**1**/ VT (plaque, nom) to engrave; (CD, DVD) to burn; (fig): **~ qch dans son esprit/sa mémoire** to etch sth in one's mind/memory

graveur [gʀavœʀ] NM engraver; **~ de CD/DVD** CD/DVD burner ou writer

gravier [gʀavje] NM (loose) gravel no pl

gravillons [gʀavijɔ̃] NMPL gravel sg, loose chippings ou gravel

gravir [gʀaviʀ] /**2**/ VT to climb (up)

gravissime [gʀavisim] ADJ very serious

gravitation [gʀavitasjɔ̃] NF gravitation

gravité [gʀavite] NF (de maladie, d'accident) seriousness; (de sujet, problème) gravity; (Physique) gravity

graviter [gʀavite] /**1**/ VI to revolve; **~ autour de** to revolve around

gravure [gʀavyʀ] NF engraving; (reproduction) print; plate

gré [gʀe] NM: **à son ~** adj to his liking; adv as he pleases; **au ~ de** according to, following; **contre le ~ de qn** against sb's will; **de son (plein) ~** of one's own free will; **de ~ ou de force** whether one likes it or not; **de bon ~** willingly; **bon ~ mal ~** like it or not; willy-nilly; **de ~ à ~** (Comm) by mutual agreement; **savoir (bien) ~ à qn de qch** to be (most) grateful to sb for sth

★**grec, grecque** [gʀɛk] ADJ Greek; (classique: vase etc) Grecian ▶ NM (Ling) Greek ▶ NM/F: **Grec, Grecque** Greek

Grèce [gʀɛs] NF: **la ~** Greece

gredin, e [gʀədɛ̃, -in] NM/F rogue, rascal

gréement [gʀemɑ̃] NM rigging

greffe [gʀɛf] NF (Bot, Méd: de tissu) graft; (Méd: d'organe) transplant ▶ NM (Jur) office

greffer [gʀefe] /**1**/ VT (Bot, Méd: tissu) to graft; (Méd: organe) to transplant

greffier [gʀefje] NM clerk of the court

greffon [gʀefɔ̃] NM (Bot, Méd: partie greffée ou transplantée) graft

grégaire [gʀegɛʀ] ADJ gregarious

grège [gʀɛʒ] ADJ: **soie ~** raw silk

grégorien, ne [gʀegɔʀjɛ̃, -jɛn] ADJ (chant) Gregorian

grêle [gʀɛl] ADJ (very) thin ▶ NF hail

grêlé, e [gʀele] ADJ pockmarked; **la région a été grêlée** the region was damaged by hail

grêler [gʀele] /**1**/ VB IMPERS: **il grêle** it's hailing

grêlon [gʀɛlɔ̃] NM hailstone

grelot [gʀəlo] NM little bell

grelottant, e [gʀəlɔtɑ̃, -ɑ̃t] ADJ shivering, shivery

grelotter [gʀəlɔte] /**1**/ VI (trembler) to shiver

Grenade [gʀənad] N Granada ▶ NF (île) Grenada

★**grenade** [gʀənad] NF (explosive) grenade; (Bot) pomegranate; **~ lacrymogène** teargas grenade

grenadier [gʀənadje] NM (Mil) grenadier; (Bot) pomegranate tree

grenadine [gʀənadin] NF grenadine

grenat [gʀəna] ADJ INV dark red

★**grenier** [gʀənje] NM (de maison) attic; (de ferme) loft

★**grenouille** [gʀənuj] NF frog

grenouillère [gʀənujɛʀ] NF (de bébé) leggings; (: combinaison) sleepsuit

grenu, e [gʀəny] ADJ grainy, grained

grès [gʀɛ] NM (roche) sandstone; (poterie) stoneware

grésil [gʀezi] NM (fine) hail

grésillement [gʀezijmɑ̃] NM sizzling; crackling

grésiller [gʀezije] /**1**/ VI to sizzle; (Radio) to crackle

gressin [gʀesɛ̃] NM breadstick

grève [gʀɛv] NF (d'ouvriers) strike; (plage) shore; **se mettre en/faire ~** to go on/be on strike; **~ bouchon** partial strike (in key areas of a company); **~ de la faim** hunger strike; **~ perlée** go-slow (BRIT), slowdown (US); **~ sauvage** wildcat strike; **~ de solidarité** sympathy strike; **~ surprise** lightning strike; **~ sur le tas** sit down strike; **~ tournante** strike by rota; **~ du zèle** work-to-rule (BRIT), slowdown (US)

grever [gʀəve] /**5**/ VT (budget, économie) to put a strain on; **grevé d'impôts** crippled by taxes; **grevé d'hypothèques** heavily mortgaged

gréviste [gʀevist] NMF striker

gribouillage [gʀibujaʒ] NM scribble, scrawl

gribouiller [gʀibuje] /**1**/ VT to scribble, scrawl ▶ VI to doodle

gribouillis [gʀibuji] NM (dessin) doodle; (action) doodling no pl; (écriture) scribble

grief [gʀijɛf] NM grievance; **faire ~ à qn de** to reproach sb for

grièvement [gʀijɛvmɑ̃] ADV seriously

griffe [gʀif] NF claw; (fig) signature; (: d'un couturier, parfumeur) label, signature

griffé, e [gʀife] ADJ designer(-label) cpd

griffer [gʀife] /1/ VT to scratch

griffon [gʀifɔ̃] NM (chien) griffon

griffonnage [gʀifɔnaʒ] NM scribble

griffonner [gʀifɔne] /1/ VT to scribble

griffure [gʀifyʀ] NF scratch

grignotage [gʀiɲɔtaʒ] NM snacking

grignoter [gʀiɲɔte] /1/ VT (personne) to nibble at; (souris) to gnaw at ▸ VI to nibble

grigri [gʀigʀi] NM grigri, gris-gris

gril [gʀil] NM steak ou grill pan

★**grillade** [gʀijad] NF grill

grillage [gʀijaʒ] NM (treillis) wire netting; (clôture) wire fencing

grillager [gʀijaʒe] /3/ VT (objet) to put wire netting on; (périmètre, jardin) to put wire fencing around

★**grille** [gʀij] NF (portail) (metal) gate; (clôture) railings pl; (d'égout) (metal) grate; (fig) grid

grille-pain [gʀijpɛ̃] (pl **grille-pain(s)**) NM toaster

★**griller** [gʀije] /1/ VT (aussi: **faire griller**: pain) to toast; (: viande) to grill (BRIT), broil (US); (: café, châtaignes) to roast; (fig: ampoule etc) to burn out, blow; **~ un feu rouge** to jump the lights (BRIT), run a stoplight (US) ▸ VI (brûler) to be roasting

grillon [gʀijɔ̃] NM (Zool) cricket

grimaçant, e [gʀimasɑ̃, -ɑ̃t] ADJ grimacing

grimace [gʀimas] NF grimace; (pour faire rire): **faire des grimaces** to pull ou make faces

grimacer [gʀimase] /3/ VI to grimace

grimacier, -ière [gʀimasje, -jɛʀ] ADJ: **c'est un enfant ~** that child is always pulling faces

grimer [gʀime] /1/ VT to make up

grimoire [gʀimwaʀ] NM (illisible) unreadable scribble; (livre de magie) book of magic spells

grimpant, e [gʀɛ̃pɑ̃, -ɑ̃t] ADJ: **plante grimpante** climbing plant, climber

★**grimper** [gʀɛ̃pe] /1/ VI, VT to climb; **~ à/sur** to climb (up)/climb onto ▸ NM: **le ~** (Sport) rope-climbing

grimpeur, -euse [gʀɛ̃pœʀ, -øz] NM/F climber

grinçant, e [gʀɛ̃sɑ̃, -ɑ̃t] ADJ grating

grincement [gʀɛ̃smɑ̃] NM grating (noise); creaking (noise)

grincer [gʀɛ̃se] /3/ VI (porte, roue) to grate; (plancher) to creak; **~ des dents** to grind one's teeth

grincheux, -euse [gʀɛ̃ʃø, -øz] ADJ grumpy

gringalet [gʀɛ̃galɛ] ADJ M puny ▸ NM weakling

gringue [gʀɛ̃g] NM (fam): **faire du ~ à qn** to flirt with sb

griotte [gʀijɔt] NF Morello cherry

grippal, e, -aux [gʀipal, -o] ADJ (état) flu-like

★**grippe** [gʀip] NF flu, influenza; **avoir la ~** to have (the) flu; **prendre qn/qch en ~** (fig) to take a sudden dislike to sb/sth; **~ A** swine flu; **~ aviaire** bird flu; **~ porcine** swine flu

grippé, e [gʀipe] ADJ: **être ~** to have (the) flu; (moteur) to have seized up (BRIT) ou jammed

gripper [gʀipe] /1/ VT, VI to jam

grippe-sou [gʀipsu] NMF penny pincher

★**gris, e** [gʀi, gʀiz] ADJ grey (BRIT), gray (US); (ivre) tipsy; **il fait ~** it's a dull ou grey day; **faire grise mine** to look miserable ou morose; **faire grise mine à qn** to give sb a cool reception ▸ NM (couleur) grey (BRIT), gray (US)

grisaille [gʀizɑj] NF greyness (BRIT), grayness (US), dullness

grisant, e [gʀizɑ̃, -ɑ̃t] ADJ intoxicating, exhilarating

grisâtre [gʀizɑtʀ] ADJ greyish (BRIT), grayish (US)

grisé [gʀize] NM (d'un tableau, bandeau) grey

griser [gʀize] /1/ VT to intoxicate; **se ~ de** (fig) to become intoxicated with

griserie [gʀizʀi] NF intoxication

grisonnant, e [gʀizɔnɑ̃, -ɑ̃t] ADJ greying (BRIT), graying (US)

grisonner [gʀizɔne] /1/ VI to be going grey (BRIT) ou gray (US)

Grisons [gʀizɔ̃] NMPL: **les ~** Graubünden

grisou [gʀizu] NM firedamp

gris-vert [gʀivɛʀ] ADJ grey-green

grive [gʀiv] NF (Zool) thrush

grivois, e [gʀivwa, -waz] ADJ saucy

grivoiserie [gʀivwazʀi] NF sauciness

Groenland [gʀɔɛnlɑd] NM: **le ~** Greenland

groenlandais, e [gʀɔɛnlɑdɛ, -ɛz] ADJ Greenlandic ▸ NM (Ling) Greenlandic ▸ NM/F: **Groenlandais, e** Greenlander

grog [gʀɔg] NM grog

groggy [gʀɔgi] ADJ INV dazed

grogne [gʀɔɲ] NF grumble

grognement [gʀɔɲmɑ̃] NM grunt; growl

grogner [gʀɔɲe] /1/ VI to growl; (fig) to grumble

grognon, ne [gʀɔɲɔ̃, -ɔn] ADJ grumpy, grouchy

groin [gʀwɛ̃] NM snout

grolle [gʀɔl] NF (fam: chaussure) shoe

grommeler [gʀɔm(ə)le] /4/ VI to mutter to o.s.

grondement [gʀɔ̃dmɑ̃] NM rumble; growl

gronder [gʀɔ̃de] /1/ VI (canon, moteur, tonnerre) to rumble; (animal) to growl; (fig: révolte) to be brewing ▸ VT to scold; **se faire ~** to get a telling-off

grondin [gʀɔ̃dɛ̃] NM gurnard

groom [gʀum] NM page, bellhop (US)

★**gros, se** [gʀo, gʀos] ADJ big, large; (obèse) fat; (problème, quantité) great; (travaux, dégâts) extensive; (large: trait, fil) thick; (rhume, averse) heavy; **par temps/grosse mer** in rough weather/heavy seas; **~ intestin** large intestine; **~ lot** jackpot; **~ mot** swearword, vulgarity; **~ œuvre** shell (of building); **~ plan** (Photo) close-up; **~ porteur** wide-bodied aircraft, jumbo (jet); **~ sel** cooking salt; **~ titre** headline; **grosse caisse** big drum ▸ ADV: **risquer/gagner ~** to risk/win a lot; **écrire ~** to write in big letters; **en avoir ~ sur le cœur** to be upset ▸ NM/F fat man/woman ▸ NM (Comm): **le ~** the wholesale business; **prix de ~** wholesale price; **le ~ de** the main body of; (du travail etc) the bulk of; **en ~** roughly; (Comm) wholesale

groseille [gʀozɛj] NF: **~ (rouge)/(blanche)** red/white currant; **~ à maquereau** gooseberry

groseillier [gʀozeje] NM red ou white currant bush; gooseberry bush

g

grosse [gʀos] ADJ F *voir* **gros** ▶ NF (*Comm*) gross

grossesse [gʀosɛs] NF pregnancy; **~ nerveuse** phantom pregnancy

grosseur [gʀosœʀ] NF size; fatness; (*tumeur*) lump

grossier, -ière [gʀosje, -jɛʀ] ADJ coarse; (*insolent*) rude; (*dessin*) rough; (*travail*) roughly done; (*imitation, instrument*) crude; (*évident: erreur*) gross

grossièrement [gʀosjɛʀmɑ̃] ADV (*vulgairement*) coarsely; (*sommairement*) roughly; crudely; (*en gros*) roughly

grossièreté [gʀosjɛʀte] NF coarseness; rudeness; (*mot*): **dire des grossièretés** to use coarse language

grossir [gʀosiʀ] /2/ VI (*personne*) to put on weight; (*fig*) to grow, get bigger; (*rivière*) to swell ▶ VT to increase; (*exagérer*) to exaggerate; (*au microscope*) to magnify, enlarge; (*vêtement*): **~ qn** to make sb look fatter

grossissant, e [gʀosisɑ̃, -ɑ̃t] ADJ magnifying, enlarging

grossissement [gʀosismɑ̃] NM (*optique*) magnification

grossiste [gʀosist] NMF wholesaler

grosso modo [gʀosomɔdo] ADV roughly

grotesque [gʀɔtɛsk] ADJ (*extravagant*) grotesque; (*ridicule*) ludicrous

grotte [gʀɔt] NF cave

grouiller [gʀuje] /1/ VI (*foule*) to mill about; (*fourmis*) to swarm about; **~ de** to be swarming with

★**groupe** [gʀup] NM group; **cabinet de ~** group practice; **médecine de ~** group practice; **~ électrogène** generator; **~ de parole** support group; **~ de pression** pressure group; **~ sanguin** blood group; **~ scolaire** school complex

groupement [gʀupmɑ̃] NM grouping; (*groupe*) group; **~ d'intérêt économique** ≈ trade association

grouper [gʀupe] /1/ VT to group; (*ressources, moyens*) to pool ■ **se grouper** VPR to get together

groupie [gʀupi] NF (*de vedette*) groupie

groupuscule [gʀupyskyl] NM clique

gruau [gʀyo] NM: **pain de ~** wheaten bread

grue [gʀy] NF crane; **faire le pied de ~** (*fam*) to hang around (waiting), kick one's heels (BRIT)

gruger [gʀyʒe] /3/ VT to cheat, dupe

grumeaux [gʀymo] NMPL (*Culin*) lumps

grumeleux, -euse [gʀym(ə)lø, -øz] ADJ (*sauce etc*) lumpy; (*peau etc*) bumpy

grutier [gʀytje] NM crane driver

gruyère [gʀyjɛʀ] NM gruyère (BRIT) *ou* Swiss cheese

GSM NM, ADJ (= *Global System for Mobile Communications*) GSM

Guadeloupe [gwadlup] NF: **la ~** Guadeloupe

guadeloupéen, ne [gwadlupeɛ̃, -ɛn] ADJ Guadelupian

Guatémala, Guatemala [gwatemala] NM: **le ~** Guatemala

guatémalien, ne [gwatemaljɛ̃, -ɛn] ADJ Guatemalan

guatémaltèque [gwatemaltɛk] ADJ Guatemalan

gué [ge] NM ford; **passer à ~** to ford

guenilles [gənij] NFPL rags

guenon [gənɔ̃] NF female monkey

guépard [gepaʀ] NM cheetah

guêpe [gɛp] NF wasp

guêpier [gepje] NM (*fig*) trap

guêpière [gepjɛʀ] NF basque

guère [gɛʀ] ADV (*avec adjectif, adverbe*): **ne ... ~** hardly; (*avec verbe: pas beaucoup*) **ne ... ~** (*tournure négative*) much; (*pas souvent*) hardly ever; (*tournure négative*) (very) long; **il n'y a ~ que/de** there's hardly anybody (*ou* anything) but/hardly any; **ce n'est ~ difficile** it's hardly difficult; **nous n'avons ~ de temps** we have hardly any time

guéri, e [geʀi] ADJ (*rétabli*) cured

guéridon [geʀidɔ̃] NM pedestal table

guérilla [geʀija] NF guerrilla warfare

guérillero [geʀijeʀo] NM guerrilla

guérir [geʀiʀ] /2/ VT (*personne, maladie*) to cure; (*membre, plaie*) to heal; **~ de** to be cured of, recover from; **~ qn de** to cure sb of ▶ VI (*personne, malade*) to recover, be cured; (*maladie*) to be cured; (*plaie, chagrin, blessure*) to heal

guérison [geʀizɔ̃] NF (*de maladie*) curing; (*de membre, plaie*) healing; (*de malade*) recovery

guérissable [geʀisabl] ADJ curable

guérisseur, -euse [geʀisœʀ, -øz] NM/F healer

guérite [geʀit] NF (*Mil*) sentry box; (*sur un chantier*) (workman's) hut

Guernesey [gɛʀn(ə)zɛ] NF Guernsey

guernesiais, e [gɛʀnəzjɛ, -ɛz] ADJ of *ou* from Guernsey

★**guerre** [gɛʀ] NF war; (*méthode*): **~ atomique/de tranchées** atomic/trench warfare *no pl*; **en ~** at war; **faire la ~ à** to wage war against; **de ~ lasse** (*fig*) tired of fighting *ou* resisting; **de bonne ~** fair and square; **~ civile/mondiale** civil/world war; **~ froide/sainte** cold/holy war; **~ d'usure** war of attrition

guerrier, -ière [gɛʀje, -jɛʀ] ADJ warlike ▶ NM/F warrior

guerroyer [gɛʀwaje] /8/ VI to wage war

guet [gɛ] NM: **faire le ~** to be on the watch *ou* lookout

guet-apens [gɛtapɑ̃] (*pl* **guets-apens**) NM ambush

guêtre [gɛtʀ(ə)] NF gaiter

guetter [gete] /1/ VT (*épier*) to watch (intently); (*attendre*) to watch (out) for; (: *pour surprendre*) to be lying in wait for

guetteur [gɛtœʀ] NM look-out

gueulante [gœlɑ̃t] NF (*fam*): **pousser une ~ (contre)** to have a good rant (about) (*fam*)

gueulard, e [gœlaʀ, -aʀd] (*fam*) ADJ (*personne, musique*) loud ▶ NM/F loudmouth (*fam*)

gueule [gœl] NF (*d'animal*) mouth; (*fam: visage*) mug; (: *bouche*) gob (!), mouth; **ta ~ !** (*fam*) shut up!; **avoir la ~ de bois** (*fam*) to have a hangover, be hung over

gueule-de-loup [gœldəlu] (*pl* **gueules-de-loup**) NF snapdragon

gueuler [gœle] /1/ VI (*fam*) to bawl

gueuleton [gœltɔ̃] NM (*fam*) blowout (BRIT), big meal

gueux [gø] NM beggar; (*coquin*) rogue

gugusse [gygys] NM (fam) bloke

gui [gi] NM mistletoe

guibole, guibolle [gibɔl] NF (fam: jambe) pin (fam)

★**guichet** [giʃɛ] NM (de bureau, banque) counter, window; (d'une porte) wicket, hatch; **les guichets** (à la gare, au théâtre) the ticket office; **jouer à guichets fermés** to play to a full house

guichetier, -ière [giʃ(ə)tje, -jɛʀ] NM/F counter clerk

★**guide** [gid] NM (personne) guide; (livre) guide(book) ► NF (fille scout) (girl) guide (BRIT), girl scout (US) ■ **guides** NFPL (d'un cheval) reins

guider [gide] /1/ VT to guide

guidon [gidɔ̃] NM handlebars pl

guigne [giɲ] NF (fam): **avoir la ~** to be jinxed

guigner [giɲe] VT (convoiter) to have one's eye on; (regarder à la dérobée) to eye

guignol [giɲɔl] NM ≈ Punch and Judy show; (fig) clown

guili-guili [giligili] NM (fam) tickle tickle; **faire des guili-guilis à qn** to tickle sb

guillemets [gijmɛ] NMPL: **entre ~** in inverted commas ou quotation marks; **~ de répétition** ditto marks

guilleret, te [gijʀɛ, -ɛt] ADJ perky, bright

guillotine [gijɔtin] NF guillotine

guillotiner [gijɔtine] /1/ VT to guillotine

guimauve [gimov] NF (Bot) marshmallow; (fig) sentimentality, sloppiness

guimbarde [gɛ̃baʀd] NF old banger (BRIT), jalopy

guincher [gɛ̃ʃe] VI (fam) to dance

guindé, e [gɛ̃de] ADJ (personne, air) stiff, starchy; (style) stilted

Guinée [gine] NF: **la (République de) ~** (the Republic of) Guinea; **la ~ équatoriale** Equatorial Guinea

Guinée-Bissau [ginebiso] NF: **la ~** Guinea-Bissau

guinéen, ne [gineɛ̃, -ɛn] ADJ Guinean

guingois [gɛ̃gwa]: **de ~** adv askew

guinguette [gɛ̃gɛt] NF open-air café or dance hall

guirlande [giʀlɑ̃d] NF (fleurs) garland; (de papier) paper chain; **~ lumineuse** lights pl, fairy lights pl (BRIT); **~ de Noël** tinsel no pl

guise [giz] NF: **à votre ~** as you wish ou please; **en ~ de** by way of

★**guitare** [gitaʀ] NF guitar

guitariste [gitaʀist] NMF guitarist, guitar player

gustatif, -ive [gystatif, -iv] ADJ gustatory; voir papille

guttural, e, -aux [gytyʀal, -o] ADJ guttural

guyanais, e [gɥijanɛ, -ez] ADJ Guyanese, Guyanan; (français) Guianese, Guianan

Guyane [gɥijan] NF: **la ~** Guyana; **la ~ (française)** (French) Guiana

gvt ABR (= gouvernement) govt

★**gym** [ʒim] NF (exercices) gym

gymkhana [ʒimkana] NM rally; **~ motocycliste** (motorbike) scramble (BRIT), motocross

★**gymnase** [ʒimnɑz] NM gym(nasium)

gymnaste [ʒimnast] NMF gymnast

★**gymnastique** [ʒimnastik] NF gymnastics sg; (au réveil etc) keep-fit exercises pl; **~ corrective** remedial gymnastics

gynéco [ʒineko] NMF (fam: gynécologue) gynaecologist (BRIT), gynecologist (US)

gynécologie [ʒinekɔlɔʒi] NF gynaecology (BRIT), gynecology (US)

gynécologique [ʒinekɔlɔʒik] ADJ gynaecological (BRIT), gynecological (US)

gynécologue [ʒinekɔlɔg] NMF gynaecologist (BRIT), gynecologist (US)

gypse [ʒips] NM gypsum

gyrophare [ʒiʀɔfaʀ] NM (sur une voiture) revolving (flashing) light

H, h [aʃ] NM INV H, h ▶ ABR (= *homme*) M; (= *hydro-gène*) H; = **heure**; **à l'heure H** at zero hour; **bombe H** H bomb; **H comme Henri** H for Harry (BRIT) ou How (US)

'ha¹ ['a] ABR (= *hectare*) ha.

'ha² ['a] EXCL oh ▶ NM INV: **pousser des ho ! et des ha !** (*s'extasier*) to ooh and ah

hab. ABR = **habitant**

★**habile** [abil] ADJ skilful; (*malin*) clever

habilement [abilmã] ADV skilfully; cleverly

habileté [abilte] NF skill, skilfulness; cleverness

habilité, e [abilite] ADJ: ~ **à faire** entitled to do, empowered to do

habiliter [abilite] /1/ VT to empower, entitle

habillage [abijaʒ] NM dressing

habillé, e [abije] ADJ dressed; (*chic*) dressy; ~ **de** (*Tech*) covered with; encased in

habillement [abijmã] NM clothes pl; (*profession*) clothing industry

habiller [abije] /1/ VT to dress; (*fournir en vêtements*) to clothe; (*couvrir*) to cover ■ **s'habiller** VPR to dress (o.s.); (*se déguiser, mettre des vêtements chic*) to dress up; **s'~ de/en** to dress in/dress up as; **s'~ chez/à** to buy one's clothes from/at

habilleuse [abijøz] NF (*Ciné, Théât*) dresser

habit [abi] NM outfit; ~ **(de soirée)** evening dress; (*pour homme*) tails pl; **prendre l'~** (*Rel: entrer en religion*) to enter (holy) orders ■ **habits** NMPL (*vêtements*) clothes

habitabilité [abitabilite] NF (*de logement*) fitness for habitation; (*de voiture*) capacity

habitable [abitabl] ADJ (in)habitable

habitacle [abitakl] NM cockpit; (*Auto*) passenger cell

★**habitant, e** [abitã, -ãt] NM/F inhabitant; (*d'une maison*) occupant, occupier; **loger chez l'~** to stay with the locals

habitat [abita] NM housing conditions pl; (*Bot, Zool*) habitat

habitation [abitasjõ] NF living; (*demeure*) residence, home; (*maison*) house; **habitations à loyer modéré (HLM)** low-rent, state-owned housing, ≈ council flats (BRIT), ≈ public housing units (US)

habité, e [abite] ADJ inhabited; lived in

★**habiter** [abite] /1/ VT to live in; (*sentiment*) to dwell in ▶ VI: ~ **à/dans** to live in ou at/in; ~ **chez** ou **avec qn** to live with sb; ~ **16 rue Montmartre** to live at

number 16 rue Montmartre; ~ **rue Montmartre** to live in rue Montmartre

★**habitude** [abityd] NF habit; **avoir l'~ de faire** to be in the habit of doing; (*expérience*) to be used to doing; **avoir l'~ des enfants** to be used to children; **prendre l'~ de faire qch** to get into the habit of doing sth; **perdre une ~** to get out of a habit; **d'~** usually; **comme d'~** as usual; **par ~** out of habit

habitué, e [abitye] ADJ: **être ~ à** to be used ou accustomed to ▶ NM/F (*de maison*) regular visitor; (*client*) regular (customer)

habituel, le [abityɛl] ADJ usual

habituellement [abityɛlmã] ADV usually

habituer [abitye] /1/ VT: ~ **qn à** to get sb used to ■ **s'habituer à** VPR to get used to

hâbleur, -euse ['ablœr, -øz] ADJ boastful

hache ['aʃ] NF axe

haché, e ['aʃe] ADJ minced (BRIT), ground (US); (*persil*) chopped; (*fig*) jerky

hache-légumes ['aʃlegym] NM INV vegetable chopper

hacher ['aʃe] /1/ VT (*viande*) to mince (BRIT), grind (US); (*persil*) to chop; **hacher menu** to mince ou grind finely; to chop finely

hachette ['aʃet] NF hatchet

hache-viande ['aʃvjãd] NM (*meat*) mincer (BRIT) ou grinder (US); (*couteau*) (meat) cleaver

hachis ['aʃi] NM mince no pl (BRIT), hamburger meat (US); **hachis de viande** minced ou ground (US) meat; **hachis Parmentier** ≈ shepherd's pie

hachisch ['aʃiʃ] NM hashish

hachoir ['aʃwar] NM chopper; (*meat*) mincer (BRIT) ou grinder (US); (*planche*) chopping board

hachurer ['aʃyre] /1/ VT to hatch

hachures ['aʃyr] NFPL hatching sg

hagard, e ['agar, -ard] ADJ wild, distraught

hagiographie [aʒjɔgrafi] NF hagiography

hah ['a] EXCL oh

★**haie** ['ɛ] NF hedge; (*Sport*) hurdle; (*fig: rang*) line, row; **200 m haies** 200 m hurdles; **haie d'honneur** guard of honour

haillons ['ajõ] NMPL rags

haine ['ɛn] NF hatred

haineux, -euse ['ɛnø, -øz] ADJ full of hatred

haïr ['air] /10/ VT to detest, hate ■ **se haïr** VPR to hate each other

'hais ['ɛ], **'haïs** etc ['ai] VB voir **haïr**

'haïssable ['aisabl] ADJ detestable

Haïti [aiti] N Haiti

haïtien, ne [aisjɛ̃, -ɛn] ADJ Haitian

'halage ['alaʒ] NM: **chemin de halage** towpath

'hâle ['ɑl] NM (sun)tan

'hâlé, e ['ɑle] ADJ (sun)tanned, sunburnt

haleine [alɛn] NF breath; **perdre ~** to get out of breath; **à perdre ~** until one is gasping for breath; **avoir mauvaise ~** to have bad breath; **reprendre ~** to get one's breath back; **hors d'~** out of breath; **tenir en ~** (attention) to hold spellbound; (en attente) to keep in suspense; **de longue ~** adj long-term

'haler ['ale] /1/ VT to haul in; (remorquer) to tow

haletant, e ['al(ə)tɑ̃, -ɑ̃t] ADJ (personne, animal) panting; (match, rencontre) gripping

'haleter ['alte] /5/ VI to pant

'hall ['ol] NM hall

hallali [alali] NM kill

'halle ['al] NF (covered) market ■ **halles** NFPL (d'une grande ville) central food market sg

'hallebarde ['albard] NF halberd; **il pleut des hallebardes** (fam) it's bucketing down

hallucinant, e [alysinɑ̃, -ɑ̃t] ADJ staggering

hallucination [alysinasjɔ̃] NF hallucination

hallucinatoire [alysinatwar] ADJ hallucinatory

halluciné, e [alysine] NM/F person suffering from hallucinations; (fou) (raving) lunatic

halluciner [a(l)lysine] /1/ (fam): **j'hallucine!** I can't believe it!; **~ sur qch** to be staggered by sth

hallucinogène [a(l)lysinɔʒɛn] ADJ hallucinogenic ▶ NM hallucinogen

'halo ['alo] NM halo

halogène [alɔʒɛn] NM: **lampe (à) ~** halogen lamp

'halte ['alt] NF stop, break; (escale) stopping place; (Rail) halt ▶ EXCL stop!; **faire halte** to stop

'halte-garderie ['altgardəri] (pl **haltes-garderies**) NF crèche

haltère [altɛr] NM (à boules, disques) dumbbell, barbell; **(poids et) haltères** (activité) weightlifting sg

haltérophile [alterɔfil] NMF weightlifter

haltérophilie [alterɔfili] NF weightlifting

'hamac ['amak] NM hammock

'Hambourg ['ɑ̃bur] N Hamburg

★**'hamburger** ['ɑ̃burɡœr] NM hamburger

'hameau, x ['amo] NM hamlet

hameçon [amsɔ̃] NM (fish) hook

hameçonnage [amsɔnaʒ] NM (Internet) phishing

'hampe ['ɑ̃p] NF (de drapeau etc) pole; (de lance) shaft

★**'hamster** ['amstɛr] NM hamster

'hanche ['ɑ̃ʃ] NF hip

'hand ['ɑ̃d] NM (fam) handball

'hand-ball ['ɑ̃dbal] NM handball

'handballeur, -euse ['ɑ̃dbalœr, -øz] NM/F handball player

'handicap ['ɑ̃dikap] NM (Méd) disability; (fig, Sport) handicap

'handicapé, e ['ɑ̃dikape] ADJ disabled ▶ NM/F person with a disability; **handicapé mental/physique** person with learning difficulties/a

disability; **handicapé moteur** person with a motor disability

'handicaper ['ɑ̃dikape] /1/ VT to handicap

handisport ['ɑ̃dispɔr] ADJ ou ADJ INV (tennis, handball) wheelchair cpd, disabled cpd; **jeux olympiques ~(s)** disabled Olympics

'hangar ['ɑ̃gar] NM shed; (Aviat) hangar

'hanneton ['antɔ̃] NM cockchafer

'Hanovre ['anɔvr] N Hanover

'hanté, e ['ɑ̃te] ADJ (maison, château) haunted

'hanter ['ɑ̃te] /1/ VT to haunt

'hantise ['ɑ̃tiz] NF obsessive fear

'happer ['ape] /1/ VT to snatch; (train etc) to hit

'harangue ['arɑ̃g] NF harangue

'haranguer ['arɑ̃ge] /1/ VT to harangue

'haras ['arɑ] NM stud farm

'harassant, e ['arasɑ̃, -ɑ̃t] ADJ exhausting

'harassé, e ['arase] ADJ (épuisé) exhausted

'harcèlement ['arsɛlmɑ̃] NM harassment; **harcèlement sexuel** sexual harassment

'harceler ['arsəle] /5/ VT (Mil, Chasse) to harass, harry; (importuner) to plague; **harceler qn de questions** to plague sb with questions

'harceleur, euse ['arsəlœr, -øz] NM/F harasser

'hardes ['ard] NFPL rags

'hardi, e ['ardi] ADJ bold, daring

'hardiesse ['ardjɛs] NF audacity

'hardiment ['ardimɑ̃] ADV boldly

'harem ['arɛm] NM harem

'hareng ['arɑ̃] NM herring; **hareng saur** kipper, smoked herring

'hargne ['arɲ] NF aggressivity, aggressiveness

'hargneusement ['arɲøzmɑ̃] ADV belligerently, aggressively

'hargneux, -euse ['arɲø, -øz] ADJ (propos, personne) belligerent, aggressive; (chien) fierce

★**'haricot** ['ariko] NM bean; **haricot blanc/rouge** haricot/kidney bean; **haricot vert** French (BRIT) ou green bean

harissa [arisa] NF harissa

'harki ['arki] NM Algerian soldier who fought on the French side during the War of Independence

harmonica [armɔnika] NM mouth organ

harmonie [armɔni] NF harmony

harmonieusement [armɔnjøzmɑ̃] ADV harmoniously

harmonieux, -euse [armɔnjø, -øz] ADJ harmonious; (couleurs, couple) well-matched

harmonique [armɔnik] ADJ, NM ou F harmonic

harmoniser [armɔnize] /1/ VT to harmonize ■ **s'harmoniser** VPR (couleurs, teintes) to go well together

harmonium [armɔnjɔm] NM harmonium

'harnaché, e ['arnaʃe] ADJ (fig) rigged out

'harnachement ['arnaʃmɑ̃] NM (habillement) rigout; (équipement) harness, equipment

'harnacher ['arnaʃe] /1/ VT to harness

'harnais ['arnɛ] NM harness

'haro ['aro] NM: **crier haro sur qn/qch** to inveigh against sb/sth

'harpe [ˈaʀp] NF harp

'harpie [ˈaʀpi] NF harpy

'harpiste [ˈaʀpist] NMF harpist

'harpon [ˈaʀpɔ̃] NM harpoon

'harponner [ˈaʀpɔne] /1/ VT to harpoon; (fam) to collar

★**'hasard** [ˈazaʀ] NM: **le hasard** chance, fate; **un hasard** a coincidence; (aubaine, chance) a stroke of luck; **au hasard** (sans but) aimlessly; (à l'aveuglette) at random, haphazardly; **par hasard** by chance; **comme par hasard** as if by chance; **à tout hasard** (en espérant trouver ce qu'on cherche) on the off chance; (en cas de besoin) just in case

'hasarder [ˈazaʀde] /1/ VT (mot) to venture; (fortune) to risk; **se hasarder à faire** to risk doing, venture to do

'hasardeux, -euse [ˈazaʀdø, -øz] ADJ hazardous, risky; (hypothèse) rash

'hasch [ˈaʃ] NM (fam) hash (fam)

'haschisch [ˈaʃiʃ] NM hashish

hassidique [asidik] ADJ (chant, tradition) Hassidic

'hâte [ˈɑt] NF haste; **à la hâte** hurriedly, hastily; **en hâte** post-haste, with all possible speed; **avoir hâte de** to be eager ou anxious to

'hâter [ˈɑte] /1/ VT to hasten ■ **se hâter** VPR to hurry; **se hâter de** to hurry ou hasten to

'hâtif, -ive [ˈɑtif, -iv] ADJ (travail) hurried; (décision) hasty; (légume) early

'hâtivement [ˈɑtivmɑ̃] ADV hurriedly; hastily

'hauban [ˈobɑ̃] NM (Navig) shroud

'hausse [ˈos] NF rise, increase; (de fusil) backsight adjuster; **à la hausse** upwards; **en hausse** rising; **être en hausse** to be going up

'haussement [ˈosmɑ̃] NM: **haussement d'épaules** shrug; **haussement de sourcils** raising of eyebrows;

'hausser [ˈose] /1/ VT to raise; **hausser les épaules** to shrug (one's shoulders); **se hausser sur la pointe des pieds** to stand (up) on tiptoe ou tippy-toe (US)

'haussier, -ière [ˈosje, -jɛʀ] ADJ (Finance: marché, scénario) bullish

★**'haut, e** [ˈo, ˈot] ADJ high; (grand) tall; (son, voix) high(-pitched); **haut de 3 m** 3 m high; **haut débit** (Inform) broadband; **haute fidélité** hi-fi, high fidelity; **la haute finance** high finance; **haute trahison** high treason; **haut en couleur** (chose) highly coloured; (personne) **un personnage haut en couleur** a colourful character; **la haute couture/coiffure** haute couture/coiffure; **à haute voix** aloud, out loud; **en haute montagne** in the high mountains; **en haut lieu** in high places ▶ ADV high; **haut les mains!** hands up!, stick 'em up!; **plus haut** higher up, further up; (dans un texte) above; (parler) louder; **en haut** up above; (être/aller) at (ou to) the top; (dans une maison) upstairs; **en haut de** at the top of; **tout haut** aloud, out loud; **tomber de haut** to fall from a height; (fig) to have one's hopes dashed; **dire qch bien haut** to say sth plainly; **prendre qch de (très) haut** to react haughtily to sth; **traiter qn de haut** to treat sb with disdain; **de haut en bas** from top to bottom; downwards ▶ NM top (part); **de 3 m de**
haut 3 m high, 3 m in height; **des hauts et des bas** ups and downs; **du haut de** from the top of

'hautain, e [ˈotɛ̃, -ɛn] ADJ (personne, regard) haughty

'hautbois [ˈobwɑ] NM oboe

'hautboïste [ˈoboist] NMF oboist

'haut-commissaire [ˈokɔmisɛʀ] (pl **hauts-commissaires**) NMF High Commissioner

'haut-commissariat [ˈokɔmisaʀja] (pl **hauts-commissariats**) NM High Commission

'haut débit, 'haut-débit [ˈodebi] ADJ INV (connexion, ligne) high-speed ▶ NM: **le haut débit** the high-speed internet

'haut-de-forme [ˈodfɔʀm] (pl **hauts-de-forme**) NM top hat

'haute-contre [ˈotkɔ̃tʀ] (pl **hautes-contre**) NF counter-tenor

'hautement [ˈotmɑ̃] ADV (ouvertement) openly; (supérieurement): **hautement qualifié** highly qualified

★**'hauteur** [ˈotœʀ] NF height; (Géo) height, hill; (fig) loftiness; haughtiness; **à hauteur de** up to (the level of); **à hauteur des yeux** at eye level; **à la hauteur de** (sur la même ligne) level with; by; (fig: tâche, situation) equal to; **à la hauteur** (fig) up to it, equal to the task

'Haute-Volta [ˈotvɔlta] NF: **la Haute-Volta** Upper Volta

'haut-fond [ˈofɔ̃] (pl **hauts-fonds**) NM shallow

'haut-fourneau [ˈofuʀno] (pl **hauts-fourneaux**) NM blast ou smelting furnace

'haut-le-cœur [ˈolkœʀ] NM INV retch, heave

'haut-le-corps [ˈolkɔʀ] NM INV start, jump

'haut-parleur [ˈopaʀlœʀ] (pl **haut-parleurs**) NM (loud)speaker

'hauturier, -ière [ˈotyʀje, -jɛʀ] ADJ (Navig) deep-sea

'havanais, e [ˈavanɛ, -ɛz] ADJ of ou from Havana

'havane [ˈavan] NM (cigare) Havana (cigar) ▶ NF: **la Havane** Havana

'hâve [ˈav] ADJ gaunt

'havrais, e [ˈavʀɛ, -ɛz] ADJ of ou from Le Havre

'havre [ˈavʀ] NM haven

'havresac [ˈavʀəsak] NM haversack

Hawaï [awai] N Hawaii; **les îles ~** the Hawaiian Islands

hawaïen, ne [awajɛ̃, -ɛn] ADJ Hawaiian ▶ NM (Ling) Hawaiian

'Haye [ˈɛ] N: **la Haye** the Hague

'hayon [ˈɛjɔ̃] NM tailgate

HCR SIGLE M (= Haut-Commissariat des Nations unies pour les réfugiés) UNHCR

hdb. ABR (= heures de bureau) o.h. (= office hours)

'hé [ˈe] EXCL hey!

hebdo [ɛbdo] NM (fam) weekly

hebdomadaire [ɛbdɔmadɛʀ] ADJ, NM weekly

hébergement [ebɛʀʒəmɑ̃] NM accommodation, lodging; taking in

héberger [ebɛʀʒe] /3/ VT (touristes) to accommodate, lodge; (amis) to put up; (réfugiés) to take in

hébergeur [ebɛʀʒœʀ] NM (Internet) host

hébété, e [ebete] ADJ dazed

hébétude [ebetyd] NF stupor

hébraïque [ebʁaik] ADJ Hebrew, Hebraic

hébreu, x [ebʁø] ADJ M, NM Hebrew

Hébrides [ebʁid] NF: **les ~** the Hebrides

HEC SIGLE FPL (= *École des hautes études commerciales*) *grande école for management and business studies*

hécatombe [ekatɔ̃b] NF slaughter

hectare [ɛktaʁ] NM hectare, 10,000 square metres

hecto... [ɛkto] PRÉFIXE hecto...

hectolitre [ɛktolitʁ] NM hectolitre

hectomètre [ɛktomɛtʁ] NM hectometre (*BRIT*), hectometer (*US*)

hédonisme [edɔnism] NM (*Philosophie*) hedonism

hédoniste [edɔnist] ADJ hedonistic

hégémonie [eʒemɔni] NF hegemony

hégémonique [eʒemɔnik] ADJ (*politique*) hegemonic

'hein ['ɛ̃] EXCL eh?; (*sollicitant l'approbation*): **tu m'approuves, hein?** so I did the right thing then?; **Paul est venu, hein?** Paul came, did he?; **que fais-tu, hein?** hey! what are you doing?

'hélas ['elɑs] EXCL alas! ▸ ADV unfortunately

'héler ['ele] /6/ VT to hail

hélice [elis] NF propeller

hélicoïdal, e, -aux [elikɔidal, -o] ADJ helical; helicoid

hélicoptère [elikɔptɛʁ] NM helicopter

héliogravure [eljɔgʁavyʁ] NF heliogravure

héliomarin, e [eljɔmaʁɛ̃, -in] ADJ: **centre ~** *centre offering sea and sun therapy*

héliotrope [eljɔtʁɔp] NM (*Bot*) heliotrope

héliport [elipɔʁ] NM heliport

héliporté, e [elipɔʁte] ADJ transported by helicopter

hélitreuillage [litʁœjaʒ] NM winching up into a helicopter

hélitreuiller [elitʁœje] VT to winch up into a helicopter

hélium [eljɔm] NM helium

hellène [elɛn] ADJ Hellenic ▸ NMF: **H~** Hellene

hellénique [elenik] ADJ Hellenic

helléniste [elenist] NMF Hellenist

Helsinki [ɛlzinki] N Helsinki

helvète [ɛlvɛt] ADJ Helvetian ▸ NMF: **Helvète** Helvetian

Helvétie [ɛlvesi] NF: **la ~** Helvetia

helvétique [ɛlvetik] ADJ Swiss

hématite [ematit] NF (*pierre*) hematite

hématologie [ematɔlɔʒi] NF (*Méd*) haematology.

hématome [ematɔm] NM haematoma

hémicycle [emisikl] NM semicircle; (*Pol*): **l'~** *the benches (in French parliament)*

hémiplégie [emipleʒi] NF paralysis of one side, hemiplegia

hémiplégique [emipleʒik] ADJ, NMF hemiplegic

hémisphère [emisfɛʁ] NM: **~ nord/sud** northern/southern hemisphere

hémisphérique [emisferik] ADJ hemispherical

hémistiche [emistiʃ] NM hemistich

hémodialyse [emodjaliz] NF haemodialysis (*BRIT*), hemodialysis (*US*)

hémoglobine [emɔglɔbin] NF haemoglobin (*BRIT*), hemoglobin (*US*)

hémophile [emɔfil] ADJ haemophiliac (*BRIT*), hemophiliac (*US*)

hémophilie [emɔfili] NF haemophilia (*BRIT*), hemophilia (*US*)

hémorragie [emɔʁaʒi] NF bleeding *no pl*, haemorrhage (*BRIT*), hemorrhage (*US*); **~ cérébrale** cerebral haemorrhage; **~ interne** internal bleeding *ou* haemorrhage

hémorragique [emɔʁaʒik] ADJ haemorrhagic (*BRIT*), hemorrhagic (*US*)

hémorroïdes [emɔʁɔid] NFPL piles, haemorrhoids (*BRIT*), hemorrhoids (*US*)

hémostatique [emɔstatik] ADJ haemostatic (*BRIT*), hemostatic (*US*)

'henné ['ene] NM henna

'hennir ['eniʁ] /2/ VI to neigh, whinny

'hennissement ['enismɑ̃] NM neighing, whinnying

'hep ['ɛp] EXCL hey!

hépatique [epatik] ADJ (*relatif au foie*) hepatic; (*qui souffre du foie*) suffering from a liver complaint

hépatite [epatit] NF hepatitis, liver infection

heptathlon [ɛptatlɔ̃] NM heptathlon

héraldique [eʁaldik] ADJ heraldry

herbacé, e [ɛʁbase] ADJ herbaceous

herbage [ɛʁbaʒ] NM pasture

★**herbe** [ɛʁb] NF grass; (*Culin, Méd*) herb; **herbes de Provence** mixed herbs; **en ~** unripe; (*fig*) budding; **touffe/brin d'~** clump/blade of grass

herbeux, -euse [ɛʁbø, -øz] ADJ grassy

herbicide [ɛʁbisid] NM weed-killer

herbier [ɛʁbje] NM herbarium

herbivore [ɛʁbivɔʁ] NM herbivore

herboriser [ɛʁbɔʁize] /1/ VI to collect plants

herboriste [ɛʁbɔʁist] NMF herbalist

herboristerie [ɛʁbɔʁistʁi] NF (*magasin*) herbalist's shop; (*commerce*) herb trade

hercule [ɛʁkyl] NM (*forain*) strongman; (*Mythologie*): **H~** Hercules

herculéen, ne [ɛʁkyleɛ̃, -ɛn] ADJ (*fig*) herculean

'hère ['ɛʁ] NM: **pauvre hère** poor wretch

héréditaire [eʁeditɛʁ] ADJ hereditary

hérédité [eʁedite] NF heredity

hérésie [eʁezi] NF heresy

hérétique [eʁetik] NMF heretic

'hérissé, e ['eʁise] ADJ bristling; **hérissé de** spiked with; (*fig*) bristling with

'hérisser ['eʁise] /1/ VT: **hérisser qn** (*fig*) to ruffle sb ▪ **se hérisser** VPR to bristle, bristle up

'hérisson ['eʁisɔ̃] NM hedgehog

héritage [eʁitaʒ] NM inheritance; (*fig: coutumes, système*) heritage; (*: legs*) legacy; **faire un (petit) ~** to come into (a little) money

hériter [eʁite] /1/ VI: **~ de qch (de qn)** to inherit sth (from sb); **~ de qn** to inherit sb's property

héritier, -ière [eʁitje, -jɛʁ] NM/F heir/heiress

hermaphrodite [ɛʀmafʀɔdit] ADJ (Bot, Zool) hermaphrodite

hermétique [ɛʀmetik] ADJ (à l'air) airtight; (à l'eau) watertight; (fig: écrivain, style) abstruse; (: visage) impenetrable

hermétiquement [ɛʀmetikmɑ̃] ADV hermetically

hermine [ɛʀmin] NF ermine

'**herniaire** ['ɛʀnjɛʀ] ADJ (sac) hernial; **bandage herniaire** truss

'**hernie** ['ɛʀni] NF hernia

héroïne [eʀɔin] NF heroine; (drogue) heroin

héroïnomane [eʀɔinɔman] NMF heroin addict

héroïque [eʀɔik] ADJ heroic

héroïquement [eʀɔikmɑ̃] ADV heroically

héroïsme [eʀɔism] NM heroism

'**héron** ['eʀɔ̃] NM heron

'**héros** ['eʀo] NM hero

herpès [ɛʀpɛs] NM herpes

'**herse** ['ɛʀs] NF harrow; (de château) portcullis

hertz [ɛʀts] NM (Élec) hertz

hertzien, ne [ɛʀtsjɛ̃, -ɛn] ADJ (Élec) Hertzian

hésitant, e [ezitɑ̃, -ɑ̃t] ADJ hesitant

hésitation [ezitasjɔ̃] NF hesitation

hésiter [ezite] /1/ VI: ~ (à faire) to hesitate (to do); ~ sur qch to hesitate over sth

hétéro [eteʀo] ADJ (hétérosexuel) hetero

hétéroclite [eteʀɔklit] ADJ heterogeneous; (objets) sundry

hétérogène [eteʀɔʒɛn] ADJ heterogeneous

hétérogénéité [eteʀɔʒeneite] NF heterogeneity

hétérosexualité [eteʀosɛksɥalite] NF heterosexuality

hétérosexuel, le [eteʀosɛksɥɛl] ADJ heterosexual

hétérozygote [eteʀozigɔt] ADJ heterozygote

'**hêtre** ['ɛtʀ] NM beech

★**heure** [œʀ] NF hour; (Scol) period; (moment, moment fixé) time; **c'est l'~** it's time; **pourriez-vous me donner l'~, s'il vous plaît?** could you tell me the time, please?; **quelle ~ est-il?** what time is it?; **2 heures (du matin)** 2 o'clock (in the morning); **à la bonne ~!** (parfois ironique) splendid!; **être à l'~** to be on time; (montre) to be right; **le bus passe à l'~** the bus runs on the hour; **mettre à l'~** to set right; **100 km à l'~** = 60 miles an ou per hour; **à toute ~** at any time; **24 heures sur 24** round the clock, 24 hours a day; **à l'~ qu'il est** at this time (of day); (fig) now; **à l'~ actuelle** at the present time; **sur l'~** at once; **pour l'~** for the time being; **d'~ en ~** from one hour to the next; (régulièrement) hourly; **d'une ~ à l'autre** from hour to hour; **à une ~ avancée (de la nuit)** at a late hour (of the night); **de bonne ~** early; **deux heures de marche/travail** two hours' walking/work; **une ~ d'arrêt** an hour's break ou stop; ~ **d'été** summer time (BRIT), daylight saving time (US); ~ **de pointe** rush hour; (téléphone) peak period; **heures de bureau** office hours; **heures supplémentaires** overtime sg

★**heureusement** [œʀøzmɑ̃] ADV (par bonheur) fortunately, luckily; ~ **que** ... it's a good job that ..., fortunately ...

★**heureux, -euse** [œʀø, -øz] ADJ happy; (chanceux) lucky, fortunate; (judicieux) felicitous, fortunate; **être ~ de qch** to be pleased ou happy about sth; **être ~ de faire/que** to be pleased ou happy to do/ that; **s'estimer ~ de qch/que** to consider o.s. fortunate with sth/that; **encore ~ que** ... just as well that ...

'**heurt** ['œʀ] NM (choc) collision ▪ **heurts** NMPL (fig) clashes

'**heurté, e** ['œʀte] ADJ (fig) jerky, uneven; (: couleurs) clashing

'**heurter** ['œʀte] /1/ VT (mur) to strike, hit; (personne) to collide with; (fig) to go against, upset; **heurter qn de front** to clash head-on with sb ▪ **se heurter** VPR (couleurs, tons) to clash; **se heurter à** to collide with; (fig) to come up against

'**heurtoir** ['œʀtwaʀ] NM door knocker

hévéa [evea] NM rubber tree

hexadécimal, e [ɛgzadesimal, -o] ADJ hexadecimal

hexagonal, e, -aux [ɛgzagɔnal, -o] ADJ hexagonal; (français) French (see note at hexagone)

hexagone [ɛgzagɔn] NM hexagon; **l'H~** (la France) France (because of its roughly hexagonal shape)

HF SIGLE F (= haute fréquence) HF

'**hiatal, e** ['jatal, -o] ADJ: **hernie hiatale** hiatus hernia

hiatus [jatys] NM hiatus

hibernation [ibɛʀnasjɔ̃] NF hibernation

hiberner [ibɛʀne] /1/ VI to hibernate

hibiscus [ibiskys] NM hibiscus

'**hibou, x** ['ibu] NM owl

'**hic** ['ik] NM (fam) snag

'**hideusement** ['idøzmɑ̃] ADV hideously

'**hideux, -euse** ['idø, -øz] ADJ hideous

★**hier** [jɛʀ] ADV yesterday; ~ **matin/soir/midi** yesterday morning/evening/lunchtime; **toute la journée d'**~ all day yesterday; **toute la matinée d'**~ all yesterday morning

'**hiérarchie** ['jeʀaʀʃi] NF hierarchy

'**hiérarchique** ['jeʀaʀʃik] ADJ hierarchic

'**hiérarchiquement** ['jeʀaʀʃikmɑ̃] ADV hierarchically

'**hiérarchiser** ['jeʀaʀʃize] /1/ VT to organize into a hierarchy

'**hiérarque** ['jeʀaʀk] NM (de parti, organisme) senior figure

'**hiéroglyphe** ['jeʀɔglif] NM hieroglyphic

'**hiéroglyphique** ['jeʀɔglifik] ADJ hieroglyphic

'**hi-fi** ['ifi] NF INV hi-fi

hilarant, e [ilaʀɑ̃, -ɑ̃t] ADJ hilarious

hilare [ilaʀ] ADJ mirthful

hilarité [ilaʀite] NF hilarity, mirth

Himalaya [imalaja] NM: **l'~** the Himalayas pl

himalayen, ne [imalajɛ̃, -ɛn] ADJ Himalayan

hindou, e [ɛ̃du] ADJ Hindu ▶ NM/F: **Hindou, e** Hindu; (vieilli: Indien) Indian

hindouisme [ɛ̃duism] NM Hinduism

Hindoustan [ɛ̃dustɑ̃] NM: **l'~** Hindustan

'**hippie** ['ipi] NMF hippy

hippique [ipik] ADJ equestrian, horse cpd; **un club ~** a riding centre; **un concours ~** a horse show

hippisme [ipism] NM (horse-)riding

hippocampe [ipɔkɑ̃p] NM sea horse

hippodrome [ipɔdʀom] NM racecourse

hippophagique [ipɔfaʒik] ADJ: **boucherie ~** horse butcher's

hippopotame [ipɔpɔtam] NM hippopotamus

hirondelle [iʀɔ̃dɛl] NF swallow

hirsute [iʀsyt] ADJ (personne) hairy; (barbe) shaggy; (tête) tousled

hispanique [ispanik] ADJ Hispanic

hispanisant, e [ispanizɑ̃, -ɑ̃t] NM/F, **hispaniste** [ispanist] NMF Hispanist

hispano-américain, e [ispanɔameʀikɛ̃, -ɛn] ADJ Spanish-American

hispano-arabe [ispanɔaʀab] ADJ Hispano-Moresque

hispanophone [ispanɔfɔn] ADJ Spanish-speaking ▶ NMF Spanish speaker

'hisser [ˈise] /1/ VT to hoist, haul up ■ **se hisser sur** VPR to haul o.s. up onto

★**histoire** [istwaʀ] NF (science, événements) history; (anecdote, récit, mensonge) story; (affaire) business no pl; (chichis: gén pl) fuss no pl; **l'~ de France** French history, the history of France; **l'~ sainte** biblical history; **~ géo** (fam) history and geography; **une ~ de** (fig) a question of ■ **histoires** NFPL (ennuis) trouble sg

histologie [istɔlɔʒi] NF histology

historien, ne [istɔʀjɛ̃, -ɛn] NM/F historian

★**historique** [istɔʀik] ADJ historical; (important) historic ▶ NM (exposé, récit): **faire l'~ de** to give the background to

historiquement [istɔʀikmɑ̃] ADV historically

hitlérien, ne [itleʀjɛ̃, -ɛn] ADJ (Hist) Hitlerian; **les Jeunesses hitlériennes** (Hist) Hitler Youth

'hit-parade [ˈitpaʀad] NM: **le hit-parade** the charts

'hittite [ˈitit] ADJ Hittite ▶ NMF: **Hittite** Hittite

★**hiver** [iveʀ] NM winter; **en ~** in winter

hivernal, e, -aux [iveʀnal, -o] ADJ (de l'hiver) winter cpd; (comme en hiver) wintry

hivernant, e [iveʀnɑ̃, -ɑ̃t] NM/F winter holiday-maker

hiverner [iveʀne] /1/ VI to winter

★**HLM** SIGLE MF (= habitations à loyer modéré) low-rent, state-owned housing; **un(e) ~** ≈ a council flat (ou house) (BRIT), ≈ a public housing unit (US)

Hme ABR (= homme) M

HO ABR (= hors œuvre) labour not included (on invoices)

'hobby [ˈɔbi] NM hobby

'hochement [ˈɔʃmɑ̃] NM: **hochement de tête** nod; shake of the head

'hocher [ˈɔʃe] /1/ VT: **hocher la tête** to nod; (signe négatif ou dubitatif) to shake one's head

'hochet [ˈɔʃɛ] NM rattle

★**'hockey** [ˈɔkɛ] NM: **hockey (sur glace/gazon)** (ice/field) hockey

'hockeyeur, -euse [ˈɔkɛjœʀ, -øz] NM/F hockey player

'holà [ˈɔla] NM: **mettre le holà à qch** to put a stop to sth

'holding [ˈɔldiŋ] NM holding company

'hold-up [ˈɔldœp] NM INV hold-up

holistique [ɔlistik] ADJ holistic

★**'hollandais, e** [ˈɔlɑ̃dɛ, -ɛz] ADJ Dutch ▶ NM (Ling) Dutch ▶ NM/F: **Hollandais, e** Dutchman/-woman; **les Hollandais** the Dutch

★**'hollande** [ˈɔlɑ̃d] NM (fromage) Dutch cheese ▶ NF: **la Hollande** Holland

hollywoodien, ne [ˈɔliwudjɛ̃, -jɛn] ADJ (cinéma, film) Hollywood cpd

holocauste [ɔlɔkost] NM holocaust

hologramme [ɔlɔgʀam] NM hologram

'homard [ˈɔmaʀ] NM lobster

homélie [ɔmeli] NF homily

homéopathe [ɔmeɔpat] N homoeopath

homéopathie [ɔmeɔpati] NF homoeopathy

homéopathique [ɔmeɔpatik] ADJ homoeopathic

homérique [ɔmeʀik] ADJ Homeric

homicide [ɔmisid] NM murder; **~ involontaire** manslaughter ▶ NMF murderer (murderess)

hominidé [ɔminide] NM hominid

hommage [ɔmaʒ] NM tribute; **rendre ~ à** to pay tribute ou homage to; **en ~ de** as a token of; **faire ~ de qch à qn** to present sb with sth ■ **hommages** NMPL: **présenter ses hommages** to pay one's respects

★**homme** [ɔm] NM man; (espèce humaine): **l'~** man, mankind; **~ d'affaires** businessman; **~ des cavernes** caveman; **~ d'Église** churchman, clergyman; **~ d'État** statesman; **~ de loi** lawyer; **~ de main** hired man; **~ de paille** stooge; **~ politique** politician; **l'~ de la rue** the man in the street; **~ à tout faire** odd-job man

homme-grenouille [ɔmgʀənuj] (pl **hommes-grenouilles**) NM frogman

homme-orchestre [ɔmɔʀkɛstʀ] (pl **hommes-orchestres**) NM one-man band

homme-sandwich [ɔmsɑ̃dwitʃ] (pl **hommes-sandwichs**) NM sandwich (board) man

homo [ɔmo] ADJ, NMF = **homosexuel**

homogène [ɔmɔʒɛn] ADJ homogeneous

homogénéisé, e [ɔmɔʒeneize] ADJ: **lait ~** homogenized milk

homogénéité [ɔmɔʒeneite] NF homogeneity

homographe [ɔmɔgʀaf] NM homograph

homologation [ɔmɔlɔgasjɔ̃] NF ratification; official recognition

homologue [ɔmɔlɔg] NMF counterpart, opposite number

homologué, e [ɔmɔlɔge] ADJ (Sport) officially recognized, ratified; (tarif) authorized

homologuer [ɔmɔlɔge] /1/ VT (Jur) to ratify; (Sport) to recognize officially, ratify

homonyme [ɔmɔnim] NM (Ling) homonym; (d'une personne) namesake

homoparental, e, -aux [ɔmɔpaʀɑ̃tal, -o] ADJ (famille) same-sex

h

homophobe [ɔmɔfɔb] ADJ (*personne, propos*) homophobic ▸ NMF homophobe

homophobie [ɔmɔfɔbi] NF homophobia

homophone [ɔmɔfɔn] NM homophone

homosexualité [ɔmɔsɛksɥalite] NF homosexuality

homosexuel, le [ɔmɔsɛksɥɛl] ADJ homosexual

homozygote [omozigɔt] ADJ homozygote

'Honduras [ɔ̃dyʀas] NM: **le Honduras** Honduras

'hondurien, ne [ɔ̃dyʀjɛ̃, -ɛn] ADJ Honduran

'Hong-Kong [ɔ̃gkɔ̃g] N Hong Kong

'hongre [ɔ̃gʀ] ADJ (*cheval*) gelded ▸ NM gelding

'Hongrie [ɔ̃gʀi] NF: **la Hongrie** Hungary

'hongrois, e [ɔ̃gʀwa, -waz] ADJ Hungarian ▸ NM (*Ling*) Hungarian ▸ NM/F: **Hongrois, e** Hungarian

honnête [ɔnɛt] ADJ (*intègre*) honest; (*juste, satisfaisant*) fair

honnêtement [ɔnɛtmɑ̃] ADV honestly

honnêteté [ɔnɛtte] NF honesty

honneur [ɔnœʀ] NM honour; (*mérite*) **l'~ lui revient** the credit is his; **à qui ai-je l'~ ?** to whom have I the pleasure of speaking?; **« j'ai l'~ de ... »** "I have the honour of ..."; **en l'~ de** (*personne*) in honour of; (*événement*) on the occasion of; **faire ~ à** (*engagements*) to honour; (*famille, professeur*) to be a credit to; (*fig: repas etc*) to do justice to; **être à l'~** to be in the place of honour; **être en ~** to be in favour; **membre d'~** honorary member; **table d'~** top table

Honolulu [ɔnɔlyly] N Honolulu

honorable [ɔnɔʀabl] ADJ worthy, honourable; (*suffisant*) decent

honorablement [ɔnɔʀabləmɑ̃] ADV honourably; decently

honoraire [ɔnɔʀɛʀ] ADJ honorary; **professeur ~** professor emeritus ▪ **honoraires** NMPL fees

honorer [ɔnɔʀe] /1/ VT to honour; (*estimer*) to hold in high regard; (*faire honneur à*) to do credit to; **~ qn de** to honour sb with ▪ **s'honorer de** VPR to pride o.s. upon

honorifique [ɔnɔʀifik] ADJ honorary

★**'honte** [ɔ̃t] NF shame; **avoir honte de** to be ashamed of; **faire honte à qn** to make sb (feel) ashamed

'honteusement [ɔ̃tøzmɑ̃] ADV ashamedly; shamefully

'honteux, -euse [ɔ̃tø, -øz] ADJ ashamed; (*conduite, acte*) shameful, disgraceful

'hop [ɔp] EXCL (*vas-y !*): **« allez hop ! »** "off you go!"; (*et voilà*): **et hop !** bingo!; **un clic de souris et hop ! la commande est enregistrée** one click of the mouse and bingo! the order has gone in

hôpital, -aux [ɔpital, -o] NM hospital; **où est l'~ le plus proche ?** where is the nearest hospital?

> Quand le mot **hospital** désigne l'institution en général, il n'est jamais précédé de l'article défini. Ce n'est pas le cas quand il désigne plus précisément le bâtiment.
> *Ma grand-mère est à l'hôpital depuis une semaine.*
> **My grandmother has been in hospital for a week.**

> *Ce soir, je vais à l'hôpital voir ma grand-mère.*
> **Tonight I'm going to the hospital to visit my grandmother.**

'hoquet [ˈɔkɛ] NM hiccup, hiccough; **avoir le hoquet** to have (the) hiccups *ou* hiccoughs

'hoqueter [ˈɔkte] /4/ VI to hiccough

★**horaire** [ɔʀɛʀ] ADJ hourly ▸ NM timetable, schedule; **~ flexible** *ou* **mobile** *ou* **à la carte** *ou* **souple** flex(i)time ▪ **horaires** NMPL (*heures de travail*) hours

'horde [ˈɔʀd] NF horde

'horions [ˈɔʀjɔ̃] NMPL blows

horizon [ɔʀizɔ̃] NM horizon; (*paysage*) landscape, view; **sur l'~** on the skyline *ou* horizon

horizontal, e, -aux [ɔʀizɔ̃tal, -o] ADJ horizontal ▸ NF: **à l'horizontale** on the horizontal

horizontalement [ɔʀizɔ̃talmɑ̃] ADV horizontally

★**horloge** [ɔʀlɔʒ] NF clock; **l'~ parlante** the speaking clock; **~ normande** grandfather clock; **~ physiologique** biological clock

horloger, -ère [ɔʀlɔʒe, -ɛʀ] NM/F watchmaker; clockmaker

horlogerie [ɔʀlɔʒʀi] NF watchmaking; watchmaker's (shop); clockmaker's (shop); **pièces d'~** watch parts *ou* components

'hormis [ˈɔʀmi] PRÉP save

hormonal, e, -aux [ɔʀmɔnal, -o] ADJ hormonal

hormone [ɔʀmɔn] NF hormone

horodaté, e [ɔʀɔdate] ADJ (*ticket*) time- and date-stamped; (*stationnement*) pay and display

horodateur, -trice [ɔʀɔdatœʀ, -tʀis] ADJ (*appareil*) for stamping the time and date ▸ NM/F (*parking*) ticket machine

horoscope [ɔʀɔskɔp] NM horoscope

★**horreur** [ɔʀœʀ] NF horror; **avoir ~ de** to loathe, detest; **quelle ~ !** how awful!; **avoir ~ de** to loathe *ou* detest

horrible [ɔʀibl] ADJ horrible

horriblement [ɔʀibləmɑ̃] ADV horribly

horrifiant, e [ɔʀifjɑ̃, -ɑ̃t] ADJ horrifying

horrifier [ɔʀifje] /7/ VT to horrify

horrifique [ɔʀifik] ADJ horrific

horripilant, e [ɔʀipilɑ̃, -ɑ̃t] ADJ exasperating

horripiler [ɔʀipile] /1/ VT to exasperate

'hors [ˈɔʀ] PRÉP except (for); **hors de** out of; **hors ligne** (*Inform*) off line; **hors pair** outstanding; **hors de propos** inopportune; **hors série** (*sur mesure*) made-to-order; (*exceptionnel*) exceptional; **hors service (HS), hors d'usage** out of service; **être hors de soi** to be beside o.s.

'hors-bord [ˈɔʀbɔʀ] (*pl* **hors-bord(s)**) NM outboard motor; (*canot*) speedboat (with outboard motor)

'hors-concours [ˈɔʀkɔ̃kuʀ] ADJ INV ineligible to compete; (*fig*) in a class of one's own

'hors-d'œuvre [ˈɔʀdœvʀ] NM INV hors d'œuvre

'hors-jeu [ˈɔʀʒø] (*pl* **hors-jeu(x)**) NM being offside *no pl*

'hors-la-loi [ˈɔʀlalwa] NM INV outlaw

'hors-piste [ˈɔʀpist] (*pl* **hors-pistes**) NM (*Ski*) cross-country

'hors-taxe [ˈɔʀtaks] ADJ (*sur une facture, prix*) excluding VAT; (*boutique, marchandises*) duty-free

'hors-texte ['ɔRtɛkst] (pl **hors-textes**) NM plate

hortensia [ɔRtɑ̃sja] NM hydrangea

horticole [ɔRtikɔl] ADJ horticultural

horticulteur, -trice [ɔRtikyltœR, -tris] NM/F horticulturalist (BRIT), horticulturist (US)

horticulture [ɔRtikyltyR] NF horticulture

hospice [ɔspis] NM (de vieillards) home; (asile) hospice

hospitalier, -ière [ɔspitalje, -jɛR] ADJ (accueillant) hospitable; (Méd: service, centre) hospital cpd

hospitalisation [ɔspitalizasjɔ̃] NF hospitalization

hospitaliser [ɔspitalize] /1/ VT to take (ou send) to hospital, hospitalize

hospitalité [ɔspitalite] NF hospitality

hospitalo-universitaire [ɔspitalɔynivɛRsitɛR] ADJ: **centre ~ (CHU)** ≈ (teaching) hospital

hostie [ɔsti] NF host

hostile [ɔstil] ADJ hostile

hostilité [ɔstilite] NF hostility ∎ **hostilités** NFPL hostilities

hosto [ɔsto] NM (fam) hospital

hôte [ot] NM (maître de maison) host; (client) patron; (fig) inhabitant, occupant ▶ NMF (invité) guest; **~ payant** paying guest

hôtel [otɛl] NM hotel; **aller à l'~** to stay in a hotel; **~ (particulier)** (private) mansion; **~ de ville** town hall; see note

> There are five categories of **hôtel** in France, from 1 star to 5 stars. Prices quoted include VAT but not breakfast. In some towns, guests pay a small additional tourist tax, the taxe de séjour, used to offset tourism-related costs incurred by the town.

hôtelier, -ière [otəlje, -jɛR] ADJ hotel cpd ▶ NM/F hotelier, hotel-keeper

hôtellerie [otɛlRi] NF (profession) hotel business; (auberge) inn

hôtesse [otɛs] NF hostess; **~ de l'air** flight attendant; **~ (d'accueil)** receptionist

'hotte ['ɔt] NF (panier) basket (carried on the back); (de cheminée) hood; **hotte aspirante** cooker hood

'houblon ['ublɔ̃] NM (Bot) hop; (pour la bière) hops pl

'houe ['u] NF hoe

'houille ['uj] NF coal; **houille blanche** hydroelectric power

'houiller, -ère ['uje, -ɛR] ADJ coal cpd; (terrain) coal-bearing ▶ NF coal mine

'houle ['ul] NF swell

'houlette ['ulɛt] NF: **sous la houlette de** under the guidance of

'houleux, -euse ['ulø, -øz] ADJ heavy, swelling; (fig) stormy, turbulent

'houppe ['up], **'houppette** ['upɛt] NF powder puff; (cheveux) tuft

'houppelande ['uplɑ̃d] NF cloak

'hourra ['uRa] NM cheer ▶ EXCL hurrah!

'houspiller ['uspije] /1/ VT to scold

'housse ['us] NF cover; (pour protéger provisoirement) dust cover; (pour recouvrir à neuf) loose ou stretch cover; **housse (penderie)** hanging wardrobe

'houx ['u] NM holly

hovercraft [ovœRkRaft] NM hovercraft

HS ABR = **hors service**

HT ABR = **hors taxe**

'hublot ['yblo] NM porthole

'huche ['yʃ] NF: **huche à pain** bread bin

'huées ['ɥe] NFPL boos

'huer ['ɥe] /1/ VT to boo; (hibou, chouette) to hoot

'huguenot ['yg(ə)no] NM Huguenot

★**huile** [ɥil] NF oil; (Art) oil painting; (fam) bigwig; **mer d'~** (très calme) glassy sea, sea of glass; **faire tache d'~** (fig) to spread; **~ d'arachide** groundnut oil; **~ essentielle** essential oil; **~ de foie de morue** cod-liver oil; **~ de ricin** castor oil; **~ solaire** suntan oil; **~ de table** salad oil

huiler [ɥile] /1/ VT to oil

huilerie [ɥilRi] NF (usine) oil-works

huileux, -euse [ɥilø, -øz] ADJ oily

huilier [ɥilje] NM (oil and vinegar) cruet

huis [ɥi] NM: **à ~ clos** in camera

huissier [ɥisje] NM usher; (Jur) ≈ bailiff

★**huit** ['ɥi(t)] NUM eight; **samedi en huit** a week on Saturday; **dans huit jours** in a week('s time)

'huitaine ['ɥitɛn] NF: **une huitaine de** about eight, eight or so; **une huitaine de jours** a week or so

'huitante ['ɥitɑ̃t] NUM (SUISSE) eighty

'huitième ['ɥitjɛm] NUM eighth

huître [ɥitR] NF oyster

'hululement ['ylylmɑ̃] NM hooting

'hululer ['ylyle] /1/ VI to hoot

humain, e [ymɛ̃, -ɛn] ADJ human; (compatissant) humane ▶ NM human (being)

humainement [ymɛnmã] ADV humanly; humanely

humanisation [ymanizasjã] NF humanization

humaniser [ymanize] /1/ VT to humanize

humanisme [ymanism] NM humanism

humaniste [ymanist] ADJ, NMF humanist

humanitaire [ymanitɛR] ADJ humanitarian

humanitarisme [ymanitaRism] NM humanitarianism

humanité [ymanite] NF humanity

humanoïde [ymanɔid] NMF humanoid

humble [œ̃bl] ADJ humble

humblement [œ̃bləmɑ̃] ADV humbly

humecter [ymɛkte] /1/ VT to dampen; **s'~ les lèvres** to moisten one's lips

'humer ['yme] /1/ VT (parfum) to inhale; (pour sentir) to smell

humérus [ymeRys] NM (Anat) humerus

★**humeur** [ymœR] NF mood; (tempérament) temper; (irritation) bad temper; **de bonne/mauvaise ~** in a good/bad mood; **être d'~ à faire qch** to be in the mood for doing sth

★**humide** [ymid] ADJ (linge) damp; (main, yeux) moist; (climat, chaleur) humid; (saison, route) wet

humidificateur [ymidifikatœR] NM humidifier

humidifier [ymidifje] /7/ VT to humidify

humidité [ymidite] NF humidity; dampness; **traces d'~** traces of moisture ou damp

humiliant, e [ymiljã, -ãt] ADJ humiliating
humiliation [ymiljasjɔ̃] NF humiliation
★**humilier** [ymilje] /7/ VT to humiliate; **s'~ devant qn** to humble o.s. before sb
humilité [ymilite] NF humility, humbleness
humoriste [ymɔʀist] NMF humorist
humoristique [ymɔʀistik] ADJ humorous; humoristic
★**humour** [ymuʀ] NM humour; **avoir de l'~** to have a sense of humour; **~ noir** sick humour
humus [ymys] NM humus
'**huppé, e** ['ype] ADJ crested; (fam) posh
'**hurlement** ['yʀləmã] NM howling no pl, howl; yelling no pl, yell
'**hurler** ['yʀle] /1/ VI to howl, yell; (fig: vent) to howl; (: couleurs etc) to clash; **hurler à la mort** (chien) to bay at the moon
hurluberlu [yʀlybɛʀly] NM (péj) crank ▶ ADJ cranky
'**husky** ['œski] NM (chien) husky
'**hutte** ['yt] NF hut
hybridation [ibʀidasjɔ̃] NF (Bot) hybridization; (Zool) cross-breeding
hybride [ibʀid] ADJ, NM hybrid
hydratant, e [idʀatã, -ãt] ADJ (crème) moisturizing
hydratation [idʀatasjɔ̃] NF (de personne) hydration; (de peau) moisturization
hydrate [idʀat] NM: **hydrates de carbone** carbohydrates
hydrater [idʀate] /1/ VT to hydrate ■ **s'hydrater** VPR (personne) to drink fluids
hydraulique [idʀolik] ADJ hydraulic
hydravion [idʀavjɔ̃] NM seaplane, hydroplane
hydro... [idʀɔ] PRÉFIXE hydro...
hydrocarbure [idʀɔkaʀbyʀ] NM hydrocarbon
hydrocéphale [idʀosefal] ADJ hydrocephalic, hydrocephalous
hydrocution [idʀɔkysjɔ̃] NF immersion syncope
hydroélectricité [idʀoelɛktʀisite] NF hydroelectricity
hydroélectrique, hydro-électrique [idʀɔelɛktʀik] ADJ hydroelectric
hydrogène [idʀɔʒɛn] NM hydrogen
hydrogéné, e [idʀɔʒene] ADJ (huile) hydrogenated
hydroglisseur [idʀɔglisœʀ] NM hydroplane
hydrographie [idʀɔgʀafi] NF (fleuves) hydrography
hydrographique [idʀɔgʀafik] ADJ hydrographic, hydrographical
hydrolyse [idʀɔliz] NF hydrolysis
hydromassage [idʀomasaʒ] NM hydromassage
hydrophile [idʀɔfil] ADJ voir **coton**
hydroponique [idʀopɔnik] ADJ: **culture ~** hydroponics sg
hyène [jɛn] NF hyena
hygiaphone® [iʒjafɔn] NM grill (for speaking through on ticket counters)
hygiène [iʒjɛn] NF hygiene; **~ intime** personal hygiene

hygiénique [iʒjenik] ADJ hygienic
hyménoptère [imenɔptɛʀ] NM hymenopteran
hymne [imn] NM hymn; **~ national** national anthem
hyper... [ipɛʀ] PRÉFIXE hyper...
hyperactif, -ive [ipɛʀaktif, -iv] ADJ hyperactive
hyperactivité [ipɛʀaktivite] NF hyperactivity
hyperappel [ipɛʀapɛl] NM (Inform) hypercall
hyperbole [ipɛʀbɔl] NF (figure de style) hyperbole; (Math) hyperbola
hyperinflation [ipɛʀɛ̃flasjɔ̃] NF hyperinflation
hyperlien [ipɛʀljɛ̃] NM (Inform) hyperlink
hypermarché [ipɛʀmaʀʃe] NM hypermarket
hypermétrope [ipɛʀmetʀɔp] ADJ long-sighted
hypernerveux, -euse [ipɛʀnɛʀvø, -øz] ADJ highly-strung
hyperréalisme [ipɛʀʀealism] NM hyperrealism
hyperréaliste [ipɛʀʀealist] ADJ hyperrealistic
hypersensibilité [ipɛʀsãsibilite] NF hypersensitivity
hypersensible [ipɛʀsãsibl] ADJ hypersensitive
hypertendu, e [ipɛʀtãdy] ADJ having high blood pressure, hypertensive
hypertension [ipɛʀtãsjɔ̃] NF high blood pressure, hypertension
hypertexte [ipɛʀtɛkst] NM (Inform) hypertext
hypertrophie [ipɛʀtʀɔfi] NF (Méd) hypertrophy
hypertrophié, e [ipɛʀtʀɔfje] ADJ hypertrophic
hypnose [ipnoz] NF hypnosis
hypnothérapie [ipnoteʀapi] NF hypnotherapy
hypnotique [ipnɔtik] ADJ hypnotic
hypnotiser [ipnɔtize] /1/ VT to hypnotize
hypnotiseur [ipnɔtizœʀ] NM hypnotist
hypnotisme [ipnɔtism] NM hypnotism
hypoallergénique [ipoalɛʀʒik] ADJ hypoallergenic
hypocalorique [ipokalɔʀik] ADJ low-calorie
hypocondriaque [ipokɔ̃dʀijak] ADJ hypochondriac
hypocrisie [ipɔkʀizi] NF hypocrisy
hypocrite [ipɔkʀit] ADJ hypocritical ▶ NMF hypocrite
hypocritement [ipɔkʀitmã] ADV hypocritically
hypodermique [ipodɛʀmik] ADJ (seringue) hypodermic
hypoglycémie [ipoglisemi] NF hypoglycaemia (BRIT), hypoglycemia (US)
hypokhâgne [ipokaɲ] NF first year of preparatory course for arts section of the École normale supérieure
hypotendu, e [ipotãdy] ADJ having low blood pressure, hypotensive
hypotension [ipotãsjɔ̃] NF low blood pressure, hypotension
hypoténuse [ipotenyz] NF hypotenuse
hypothécaire [ipotekɛʀ] ADJ mortgage; **garantie/prêt ~** mortgage security/loan
hypothèque [ipotɛk] NF mortgage
hypothéquer [ipoteke] /6/ VT to mortgage
hypothermie [ipotɛʀmi] NF hypothermia

hypothèse [ipɔtɛz] NF hypothesis; **dans l'~ où** assuming that

hypothétique [ipɔtetik] ADJ hypothetical

hypothétiquement [ipɔtetikmɑ̃] ADV hypothetically

hystérectomie [isteʀɛktɔmi] NF hysterectomy

hystérie [isteʀi] NF hysteria; **~ collective** mass hysteria

hystérique [isteʀik] ADJ hysterical

Hz ABR (= *Hertz*) Hz

Ii

I, i [i] NM INV I, i; **I comme Irma** I for Isaac (BRIT) *ou* Item (US)

IAC SIGLE F (= *insémination artificielle entre conjoints*) AIH

IAD SIGLE F (= *insémination artificielle par donneur extérieur*) AID

ibère [ibɛʀ] ADJ Iberian ▶ NMF: **Ibère** Iberian

ibérique [iberik] ADJ: **la péninsule ~** the Iberian peninsula

ibid. ABR (= *ibidem*) ibid., ib.

ibis [ibis] NM ibis

iceberg [isbɛʀg] NM iceberg

★**ici** [isi] ADV here; **jusqu'~** as far as this; (*temporel*) until now; **d'~ là** by then; **d'~ demain** by tomorrow; (*en attendant*) in the meantime; **d'~ peu** before long

icône [ikon] NF (*aussi Inform*) icon

iconoclaste [ikɔnɔklast] NMF iconoclast

iconographie [ikɔnɔgrafi] NF iconography; (*illustrations*) (collection of) illustrations

iconographique [ikɔnɔgrafik] ADJ (*sources, ressources*) image *cpd*, picture *cpd*; **fonds ~** image bank

idéal, e, -aux [ideal, -o] ADJ ideal ▶ NM ideal; (*système de valeurs*) ideals *pl*

idéalement [idealmɑ̃] ADV ideally

idéalisation [idealizasjɔ̃] NF idealization

idéaliser [idealize] /1/ VT to idealize

idéalisme [idealism] NM idealism

idéaliste [idealist] ADJ idealistic ▶ NMF idealist

idée [ide] NF idea; (*illusion*): **se faire des idées** to imagine things, get ideas into one's head; **avoir dans l'~ que** to have an idea that; **mon ~, c'est que ...** I suggest that ..., I think that ...; **à l'~ de/que** at the idea of/that, at the thought of/ that; **je n'en ai pas la moindre ~** I haven't the faintest idea; **avoir ~ que** to have an idea that; **avoir des idées larges/étroites** to be broad-/narrow-minded; **venir à l'~ de qn** to occur to sb; **en voilà des idées!** the very idea!; **~ fixe** idée fixe, obsession; **idées noires** black *ou* dark thoughts; **idées reçues** accepted ideas *ou* wisdom

idée-force [idefɔʀs] (*pl* **idées-force(s)**) NF main idea

identifiable [idɑ̃tifjabl] ADJ identifiable

identifiant [idɑ̃tifjɑ̃] NM (*Inform*) login

identification [idɑ̃tifikasjɔ̃] NF identification

identifier [idɑ̃tifje] /7/ VT to identify; **~ qch/qn à** to identify sth/sb with ■ **s'identifier** VPR: **s'~ avec** *ou* **à qn/qch** (*héros etc*) to identify with sb/sth

identique [idɑ̃tik] ADJ: **~ (à)** identical (to)

identitaire [idɑ̃titɛʀ] ADJ: **une crise ~** an identity crisis; **une quête ~** a search for identity

identité [idɑ̃tite] NF identity; **~ judiciaire** (*Police*) ≈ Criminal Records Office

idéogramme [ideɔgram] NM ideogram

idéologie [ideɔlɔʒi] NF ideology

idéologique [ideɔlɔʒik] ADJ ideological

idéologue [ideɔlɔg] NMF ideologue

idiomatique [idjɔmatik] ADJ: **expression ~** idiom, idiomatic expression

idiome [idjom] NM (*Ling*) idiom

★**idiot, e** [idjo, idjɔt] ADJ idiotic ▶ NM/F idiot

idiotie [idjɔsi] NF idiocy; (*propos*) idiotic remark

idiotisme [idjɔtism] NM idiom, idiomatic phrase

idoine [idwan] ADJ fitting

idolâtrer [idɔlatʀe] /1/ VT to idolize

idolâtrie [idɔlatʀi] NF idolatry

idole [idɔl] NF idol

idylle [idil] NF idyll

idyllique [idilik] ADJ idyllic

if [if] NM yew

IFOP [ifɔp] SIGLE M (= *Institut français d'opinion publique*) French market research institute

IGH SIGLE M (= *immeuble de grande hauteur*) high-rise building

igloo [iglu] NM igloo

IGN SIGLE M (= *Institut géographique national*) French national geographical institute

ignare [iɲaʀ] ADJ ignorant

ignifuge [iɲifyʒ] ADJ fireproofing ▶ NM fireproofing (substance)

ignifuger [iɲifyʒe] /3/ VT to fireproof

ignoble [iɲɔbl] ADJ vile

ignominie [iɲɔmini] NF ignominy; (*acte*) ignominious *ou* base act

ignominieux, -euse [iɲɔminjø, -øz] ADJ ignominious

ignorance [iɲɔʀɑ̃s] NF ignorance; **dans l'~ de** in ignorance of, ignorant of

ignorant, e [iɲɔʀɑ̃, -ɑ̃t] ADJ ignorant; **~ de** ignorant of, not aware of; **~ en** ignorant of, knowing nothing of ▶ NM/F: **faire l'~** to pretend one doesn't know

ignoré, e [iɲɔʀe] ADJ unknown

ignorer [iɲɔʀe] /1/ VT (ne pas connaître) not to know, be unaware ou ignorant of; (être sans expérience de: plaisir, guerre etc) not to know about, have no experience of; (bouder: personne) to ignore; **j'ignore comment/si** I do not know how/if; **~ que** to be unaware that, not to know that; **je n'ignore pas que ...** I'm not forgetting that ..., I'm not unaware that ...; **je l'ignore** I don't know

IGPN SIGLE F (= Inspection générale de la police nationale) police disciplinary body

iguane [igwan] NM iguana

★**il** [il] PRON he; (animal, chose, en tournure impersonnelle) it; **ils** they; **il neige** it's snowing; **Pierre est-il arrivé?** has Pierre arrived?; **il a gagné** he won; voir aussi **avoir**

île [il] NF island; **les îles** the West Indies; **l'~ de Beauté** Corsica; **l'~ Maurice** Mauritius; **les îles anglo-normandes** the Channel Islands; **les îles Britanniques** the British Isles; **les îles Cocos** ou **Keeling** the Cocos ou Keeling Islands; **les îles Cook** the Cook Islands; **les îles Scilly** the Scilly Isles, the Scillies; **les îles Shetland** the Shetland Islands, Shetland; **les îles Sorlingues = les îles Scilly**; **les îles Vierges** the Virgin Islands

iliaque [iljak] ADJ (Anat): **os/artère ~** iliac bone/artery

îlien, ne [iljɛ̃, -ɛn] ADJ island cpd ▶ NM/F islander

illégal, e, -aux [ilegal, -o] ADJ illegal, unlawful (Admin)

illégalement [ilegalmɑ̃] ADV illegally

illégalité [ilegalite] NF illegality; unlawfulness; **être dans l'~** to be outside the law

illégitime [ileʒitim] ADJ illegitimate; (optimisme, sévérité) unjustified, unwarranted

illégitimement [ileʒitimmɑ̃] ADV illegitimately

illégitimité [ileʒitimite] NF illegitimacy; **gouverner dans l'~** to rule illegally

illettré, e [iletʀe] ADJ, NM/F illiterate

illettrisme [iletʀism] NM illiteracy

illicite [ilisit] ADJ illicit

illicitement [ilisitmɑ̃] ADV illicitly

illico [iliko] ADV (fam) pronto

illimité, e [ilimite] ADJ (immense) boundless, unlimited; (congé, durée) indefinite, unlimited

illisible [ilizibl] ADJ illegible; (roman) unreadable

illisiblement [iliziblemɑ̃] ADV illegibly

illogique [ilɔʒik] ADJ illogical

illogisme [ilɔʒism] NM illogicality

illumination [ilyminasjɔ̃] NF illumination, floodlighting; (inspiration) flash of inspiration ■ **illuminations** NFPL illuminations, lights

illuminé, e [ilymine] ADJ lit up; illuminated, floodlit ▶ NM/F (fig: péj) crank

illuminer [ilymine] /1/ VT to light up; (monument, rue: pour une fête) to illuminate; (: au moyen de projecteurs) to floodlight ■ **s'illuminer** VPR to light up

illusion [ilyzjɔ̃] NF illusion; **se faire des illusions** to delude o.s.; **faire ~** to delude ou fool people; **~ d'optique** optical illusion

illusionner [ilyzjɔne] /1/ VT to delude ■ **s'illusionner** VPR: **s'~ (sur qn/qch)** to delude o.s. (about sb/sth)

illusionnisme [ilyzjɔnism] NM conjuring

illusionniste [ilyzjɔnist] NMF conjuror

illusoire [ilyzwaʀ] ADJ illusory, illusive

illustrateur, -trice [ilystʀatœʀ, -tʀis] NM/F illustrator

illustratif, -ive [ilystʀatif, -iv] ADJ illustrative

★**illustration** [ilystʀasjɔ̃] NF illustration; (d'un ouvrage: photos) illustrations pl

illustre [ilystʀ] ADJ illustrious, renowned

★**illustré, e** [ilystʀe] ADJ illustrated ▶ NM illustrated magazine; (pour enfants) comic

illustrer [ilystʀe] /1/ VT to illustrate ■ **s'illustrer** VPR to become famous, win fame

îlot [ilo] NM small island, islet; (de maisons) block; (petite zone): **un ~ de verdure** an island of greenery, a patch of green

îlotage [ilɔtaʒ] NM community policing

îlotier, -ière [ilɔtje, -jɛʀ] NM community police officer

★**ils** [il] PRON they

★**image** [imaʒ] NF (gén) picture; (comparaison, ressemblance, Optique) image; **~ de** picture ou image of; **~ d'Épinal** (social) stereotype; **~ de marque** brand image; (d'une personne) (public) image; (d'une entreprise) corporate image; **~ pieuse** holy picture

imagé, e [imaʒe] ADJ (texte) full of imagery; (langage) colourful

imagerie [imaʒʀi] NF (Tech) imagery; **centre d'imagerie médicale** medical imaging centre (BRIT) ou center (US); **~ satellitaire** satellite imaging

imaginable [imaʒinabl] ADJ imaginable; **difficilement ~** hard to imagine

imaginaire [imaʒinɛʀ] ADJ imaginary

imaginatif, -ive [imaʒinatif, -iv] ADJ imaginative

imagination [imaʒinasjɔ̃] NF imagination; (chimère) fancy, imagining; **avoir de l'~** to be imaginative, have a good imagination

★**imaginer** [imaʒine] /1/ VT to imagine; (croire): **qu'allez-vous ~ là?** what on earth are you thinking of?; (inventer: expédient, mesure) to devise, think up; **j'imagine qu'il a voulu plaisanter** I suppose he was joking; **~ de faire** (se mettre dans l'idée de) to dream up the idea of doing ■ **s'imaginer** VPR (se figurer: scène etc) to imagine, picture; **s'~ à 60 ans** to picture ou imagine o.s. at 60; **s'~ que** to imagine that; **s'~ pouvoir faire qch** to think one can do sth

imam [imam] NM imam

imbattable [ɛ̃batabl] ADJ unbeatable

imbécile [ɛ̃besil] ADJ idiotic ▶ NMF idiot; (Méd) imbecile

imbécillité [ɛ̃besilite] NF idiocy; imbecility; idiotic action ou remark etc)

imberbe [ɛ̃bɛʀb] ADJ beardless

imbibé, e [ɛ̃bibe] ADJ: **~ de** (liquide) dipped in; **~ d'eau** (chaussures, étoffe) saturated; (terre) waterlogged

imbiber [ɛ̃bibe] /1/ VT: **~ qch de** to moisten ou wet sth with ■ **s'imbiber de** VPR to become saturated with

imbitable, imbittable [ɛ̃bitabl] ADJ (fam: incompréhensible) meaningless; **c'est ~** it's gibberish

imbriqué, e [ɛ̃bʀike] ADJ overlapping

imbriquer [ɛ̃bʀike] /1/: **s'imbriquer** VPR to overlap (each other); (fig) to become interlinked *ou* interwoven

imbroglio [ɛ̃bʀɔljo] NM imbroglio

imbu, e [ɛ̃by] ADJ: ~ **de** full of; ~ **de soi-même/sa supériorité** full of oneself/one's superiority

imbuvable [ɛ̃byvabl] ADJ undrinkable

imitable [imitabl] ADJ imitable; **facilement ~** easily imitated

imitateur, -trice [imitatœʀ, -tʀis] NM/F (gén) imitator; (Music-Hall: d'une personnalité) impersonator

imitation [imitasjɔ̃] NF imitation; (de personnalité) impersonation; **sac ~ cuir** bag in imitation *ou* simulated leather; **à l'~ de** in imitation of

imiter [imite] /1/ VT to imitate; (personne) to imitate, impersonate; (contrefaire: signature, document) to forge, copy; (ressembler à) to look like; **il se leva et je l'imitai** he got up and I did likewise

imm. ABR = **immeuble**

immaculé, e [imakyle] ADJ spotless, immaculate; **l'Immaculée Conception** (Rel) the Immaculate Conception

immanent, e [imanɑ̃, -ɑ̃t] ADJ immanent

immangeable [ɛ̃mɑ̃ʒabl] ADJ inedible, uneatable

immanquable [ɛ̃mɑ̃kabl] ADJ (cible) impossible to miss; (fatal, inévitable) bound to happen, inevitable

immanquablement [ɛ̃mɑ̃kabləmɑ̃] ADV inevitably

immatériel, le [imateʀjɛl] ADJ ethereal; (Philosophie) immaterial

immatriculation [imatʀikylasjɔ̃] NF registration

> French **plaques d'immatriculation** (licence plates) can bear the number of the *département* the vehicle is registered in, if the owner of the vehicle so wishes. For example, a car registered in Paris can display the number 75 on its licence plate.

immatriculer [imatʀikyle] /1/ VT to register; **faire/se faire ~** to register; **voiture immatriculée dans la Somme** car with a Somme registration (number)

immature [imatyʀ] ADJ immature

immaturité [imatyʀite] NF immaturity

immédiat, e [imedja, -at] ADJ immediate; **dans le voisinage ~ de** in the immediate vicinity of ▶ NM: **dans l'~** for the time being

immédiatement [imedjatmɑ̃] ADV immediately

immémorial, e, -aux [imemɔʀjal, -o] ADJ ancient, age-old

immense [imɑ̃s] ADJ immense

immensément [imɑ̃semɑ̃] ADV immensely

immensité [imɑ̃site] NF immensity

immergé, e [imɛʀʒe] ADJ (terres, partie) submerged

immerger [imɛʀʒe] /3/ VT to immerse, submerge; (câble) to lay under water; (déchets) to dump at sea ■ **s'immerger** VPR (sous-marin) to dive, submerge

immérité, e [imeʀite] ADJ undeserved

immersion [imɛʀsjɔ̃] NF immersion

immettable [ɛ̃metabl] ADJ unwearable

★**immeuble** [imœbl] NM building ▶ ADJ (Jur) immovable, real; ~ **locatif** block of rented flats (Brit), rental building (US); ~ **de rapport** investment property

immigrant, e [imigʀɑ̃, -ɑ̃t] NM/F immigrant

immigration [imigʀasjɔ̃] NF immigration

immigré, e [imigʀe] NM/F immigrant

immigrer [imigʀe] /1/ VI to immigrate

imminence [iminɑ̃s] NF imminence

imminent, e [iminɑ̃, -ɑ̃t] ADJ imminent, impending

immiscer [imise] /3/: **s'immiscer** VPR: **s'~ dans** to interfere in *ou* with

immixtion [imiksjɔ̃] NF interference

immobile [imɔbil] ADJ still, motionless; (pièce de machine) fixed; (fig) unchanging; **rester/se tenir ~** to stay/keep still

immobilier, -ière [imɔbilje, -jɛʀ] ADJ property cpd, real-estate ▶ NM: **l'~** real estate

immobilisation [imɔbilizasjɔ̃] NF immobilization ■ **immobilisations** NFPL (Jur) fixed assets

immobiliser [imɔbilize] /1/ VT (gén) to immobilize; (circulation, véhicule, affaires) to bring to a standstill ■ **s'immobiliser** VPR (personne) to stand still; (machine, véhicule) to come to a halt *ou* a standstill

immobilisme [imɔbilism] NM strong resistance *ou* opposition to change

immobilité [imɔbilite] NF immobility

immodéré, e [imɔdeʀe] ADJ immoderate, inordinate

immodérément [imɔdeʀemɑ̃] ADV immoderately

immolation [imɔlasjɔ̃] NF immolation; ~ **par le feu** immolation

immoler [imɔle] /1/ VT to sacrifice ■ **s'immoler** VPR to sacrifice o.s.; **s'~ par le feu** to set fire to o.s.

immonde [imɔ̃d] ADJ foul; (sale: ruelle, taudis) squalid

immondices [imɔ̃dis] NFPL (ordures) refuse sg; (saletés) filth sg

immoral, e, -aux [imɔʀal, -o] ADJ immoral

immoralisme [imɔʀalism] NM immoralism

immoralité [imɔʀalite] NF immorality

immortaliser [imɔʀtalize] /1/ VT to immortalize

immortalité [imɔʀtalite] NF immortality

immortel, le [imɔʀtɛl] ADJ immortal ▶ NF (Bot) everlasting (flower) ▶ NMPL: **les Immortels** name given to the members of the Académie française

immuable [imɥabl] ADJ (inébranlable) immutable; (qui ne change pas) unchanging; (personne): ~ **dans ses convictions** immoveable (in one's convictions)

immuablement [imɥabləmɑ̃] ADV immutably

immunisation [imynizasjɔ̃] NF immunization

immunisé, e [im(m)ynize] ADJ: ~ **contre** immune to

immuniser [imynize] /1/ VT (Méd) to immunize; ~ **qn contre** to immunize sb against; (fig) to make sb immune to

immunitaire [imynitɛʀ] ADJ immune

immunité [imynite] NF immunity; **~ diplomatique** diplomatic immunity; **~ parlementaire** parliamentary privilege

immunodéficience [imynodefisjɑ̃s] NF immunodeficiency

immunodéprimé, e [imynodeprime] ADJ immunocompromised ▶ NM/F immunocompromised person

immunologie [imynɔlɔʒi] NF immunology

immunosuppresseur [imynosypʀesœʀ] ADJ immunosuppressive, immunosuppressant ▶ NM immunosuppressive, immunosuppressant

immutabilité [imytabilite] NF immutability

impact [ɛ̃pakt] NM impact; **point d'~** point of impact

impacter [ɛ̃pakte] /1/ VT to impact on, have an impact on

impair, e [ɛ̃pɛʀ] ADJ odd; **nombres impairs** odd numbers ▶ NM faux pas, blunder

impalpable [ɛ̃palpabl] ADJ impalpable

impaludation [ɛ̃palydasjɔ̃] NF inoculation against malaria

imparable [ɛ̃paʀabl] ADJ unstoppable

impardonnable [ɛ̃paʀdɔnabl] ADJ unpardonable, unforgivable; **vous êtes ~ d'avoir fait cela** it's unforgivable of you to have done that

imparfait, e [ɛ̃paʀfɛ, -ɛt] ADJ imperfect ▶ NM (Ling) imperfect (tense)

imparfaitement [ɛ̃paʀfɛtmɑ̃] ADV imperfectly

impartial, e, -aux [ɛ̃paʀsjal, -o] ADJ impartial, unbiased

impartialement [ɛ̃paʀsjalmɑ̃] ADV impartially

impartialité [ɛ̃paʀsjalite] NF impartiality

impartir [ɛ̃paʀtiʀ] /2/ VT: **~ qch à qn** to assign sth to sb; (dons) to bestow sth upon sb; **dans les délais impartis** in the time allowed

impasse [ɛ̃pɑs] NF dead-end, cul-de-sac; (fig) deadlock; **être dans l'~** (négociations) to have reached deadlock; **~ budgétaire** budget deficit

impassibilité [ɛ̃pasibilite] NF impassiveness

impassible [ɛ̃pasibl] ADJ impassive

impassiblement [ɛ̃pasibləmɑ̃] ADV impassively

impatiemment [ɛ̃pasjamɑ̃] ADV impatiently

impatience [ɛ̃pasjɑ̃s] NF impatience

impatient, e [ɛ̃pasjɑ̃, -ɑ̃t] ADJ impatient; **~ de faire qch** keen ou impatient to do sth

impatienter [ɛ̃pasjɑ̃te] /1/ VT to irritate, annoy ■ **s'impatienter** VPR to get impatient; **s'~ de/contre** to lose patience at/with, grow impatient at/with

impavide [ɛ̃pavid] ADJ unruffled

impayable [ɛ̃pɛjabl] ADJ (drôle) priceless

impayé, e [ɛ̃peje] ADJ unpaid, outstanding

impeccable [ɛ̃pekabl] ADJ faultless, impeccable; (propre) spotlessly clean; (chic) impeccably dressed; (fam) smashing

impeccablement [ɛ̃pekabləmɑ̃] ADV impeccably

impénétrable [ɛ̃penetrabl] ADJ impenetrable

impénitent, e [ɛ̃penitɑ̃, -ɑ̃t] ADJ unrepentant

impensable [ɛ̃pɑ̃sabl] ADJ (événement hypothétique) unthinkable; (événement qui a eu lieu) unbelievable

imper [ɛ̃pɛʀ] NM (imperméable) mac

impératif, -ive [ɛ̃peratif, -iv] ADJ imperative; (Jur) mandatory ▶ NM (Ling) imperative ■ **impératifs** NMPL (exigences: d'une fonction, d'une charge) requirements; (: de la mode) demands

impérativement [ɛ̃perativmɑ̃] ADV imperatively

impératrice [ɛ̃peratris] NF empress

imperceptible [ɛ̃pɛʀsɛptibl] ADJ imperceptible

imperceptiblement [ɛ̃pɛʀsɛptibləmɑ̃] ADV imperceptibly

imperdable [ɛ̃pɛʀdabl] ADJ that cannot be lost

imperfectible [ɛ̃pɛʀfɛktibl] ADJ which cannot be perfected

imperfection [ɛ̃pɛʀfɛksjɔ̃] NF imperfection

impérial, e, -aux [ɛ̃perjal, -o] ADJ imperial ▶ NF upper deck; **autobus à impériale** double-decker bus

impérialisme [ɛ̃perjalism] NM imperialism

impérialiste [ɛ̃perjalist] ADJ, NMF imperialist

impérieusement [ɛ̃perjøzmɑ̃] ADV: **avoir ~ besoin de qch** to have urgent need of sth

impérieux, -euse [ɛ̃perjø, -øz] ADJ (caractère, ton) imperious; (obligation, besoin) pressing, urgent

impérissable [ɛ̃perisabl] ADJ undying, imperishable

imperméabilisation [ɛ̃pɛʀmeabilizasjɔ̃] NF waterproofing

imperméabiliser [ɛ̃pɛʀmeabilize] /1/ VT to waterproof

imperméabilité [ɛ̃pɛʀmeabilite] NF: **pour assurer l'~ du tissu** to make the material waterproof

imperméable [ɛ̃pɛʀmeabl] ADJ waterproof; (Géo) impermeable; (fig): **~ à** impervious to; **~ à l'air** airtight ▶ NM raincoat

impersonnel, le [ɛ̃pɛʀsɔnɛl] ADJ impersonal

impertinemment [ɛ̃pɛʀtinamɑ̃] ADV impertinently

impertinence [ɛ̃pɛʀtinɑ̃s] NF impertinence

impertinent, e [ɛ̃pɛʀtinɑ̃, -ɑ̃t] ADJ impertinent

imperturbable [ɛ̃pɛʀtyʀbabl] ADJ (personne) imperturbable; (sang-froid) unshakeable; **rester ~** to remain unruffled

imperturbablement [ɛ̃pɛʀtyʀbabləmɑ̃] ADV imperturbably; unshakeably

impétigo [ɛ̃petigo] NM impetigo

impétrant, e [ɛ̃petrɑ̃, -ɑ̃t] NM/F (Jur) applicant

impétueux, -euse [ɛ̃petɥø, -øz] ADJ fiery

impétuosité [ɛ̃petɥozite] NF fieriness

impie [ɛ̃pi] ADJ impious, ungodly

impiété [ɛ̃pjete] NF impiety

impitoyable [ɛ̃pitwajabl] ADJ pitiless, merciless

impitoyablement [ɛ̃pitwajabləmɑ̃] ADV mercilessly

implacable [ɛ̃plakabl] ADJ implacable

implacablement [ɛ̃plakabləmɑ̃] ADV implacably

implant [ɛ̃plɑ̃] NM (Méd) implant

implantation [ɛ̃plɑ̃tasjɔ̃] NF (d'usine, d'usage) establishment; (de colons) settling; (d'idée, de préjugé) implantation

implanter [ɛ̃plɑ̃te] /1/ VT (usine, industrie, usage) to establish; (colons) to settle; (idée, préjugé) to implant ■ **s'implanter dans** VPR to be established in; to settle in; to become implanted in

implémenter [ɛ̃plemɑ̃te] /1/ VT (aussi Inform) to implement

implication [ɛ̃plikasjɔ̃] NF implication

implicite [ɛ̃plisit] ADJ implicit

implicitement [ɛ̃plisitmɑ̃] ADV implicitly

impliquer [ɛ̃plike] /1/ VT to imply; **~ qn (dans)** to implicate sb (in)

implorant, e [ɛ̃plɔrɑ̃, -ɑ̃t] ADJ imploring

implorer [ɛ̃plɔre] /1/ VT to implore

imploser [ɛ̃ploze] /1/ VI to implode

implosion [ɛ̃plozjɔ̃] NF implosion

impoli, e [ɛ̃pɔli] ADJ impolite, rude

impoliment [ɛ̃pɔlimɑ̃] ADV impolitely

impolitesse [ɛ̃pɔlitɛs] NF impoliteness, rudeness; (propos) impolite ou rude remark

impondérable [ɛ̃pɔ̃derabl] NM imponderable

impopulaire [ɛ̃pɔpylɛr] ADJ unpopular

impopularité [ɛ̃pɔpylarite] NF unpopularity

importable [ɛ̃pɔrtabl] ADJ (Comm: marchandise) importable; (vêtement: immettable) unwearable

importance [ɛ̃pɔrtɑ̃s] NF importance; (de somme) size; **avoir de l'~** to be important; **sans ~** unimportant; **d'~** important, considerable; **quelle ~?** what does it matter?

★**important, e** [ɛ̃pɔrtɑ̃, -ɑ̃t] ADJ important; (en quantité: somme, retard) considerable, sizeable; (: gamme, dégâts) extensive; (péj: airs, ton) self-important ▶ NM: **l'~** the important thing

importateur, -trice [ɛ̃pɔrtatœr, -tris] ADJ importing; **pays ~ de blé** wheat-importing country ▶ NM/F importer

importation [ɛ̃pɔrtasjɔ̃] NF import; introduction; (produit) import

importer [ɛ̃pɔrte] /1/ VT (Comm) to import; (maladies, plantes) to introduce ▶ VI (être important) to matter; **~ à qn** to matter to sb; **il importe de** it is important to; **il importe qu'il fasse** he must do, it is important that he should do; **peu m'importe** (je n'ai pas de préférence) I don't mind; (je m'en moque) I don't care; **peu importe (que)** it doesn't matter (if); **peu importe le prix** never mind the price; voir aussi **n'importe**

import-export [ɛ̃pɔrɛkspɔr] (pl **imports-exports**) NM import-export business

importun, e [ɛ̃pɔrtœ̃, -yn] ADJ irksome, importunate; (arrivée, visite) inopportune, ill-timed ▶ NM intruder

importuner [ɛ̃pɔrtyne] /1/ VT to bother

imposable [ɛ̃pozabl] ADJ taxable

imposant, e [ɛ̃pozɑ̃, -ɑ̃t] ADJ imposing

imposé, e [ɛ̃poze] ADJ (soumis à l'impôt) taxed; (Gym etc: figures) set

imposer [ɛ̃poze] /1/ VT (taxer) to tax; (Rel): **~ les mains** to lay on hands; **~ qch à qn** to impose sth on sb; **en ~** to be imposing; **en ~ à** to impress ■ **s'imposer** VPR (être nécessaire) to be imperative; (montrer sa proéminence) to stand out, emerge; (artiste: se faire connaître) to win recognition, come to the fore; **s'~ comme** to emerge as; **s'~ par** to win recognition through; **ça s'impose** it's essential, it's vital

imposition [ɛ̃pozisjɔ̃] NF (Admin) taxation

impossibilité [ɛ̃pɔsibilite] NF impossibility; **être dans l'~ de faire** to be unable to do, find it impossible to do

★**impossible** [ɛ̃pɔsibl] ADJ impossible; **~ à faire** impossible to do; **il m'est ~ de le faire** it is impossible for me to do it, I can't possibly do it ▶ NM: **l'~** the impossible; **faire l'~ (pour que)** to do one's utmost (so that); **si, par ~ …** if, by some miracle …

imposteur [ɛ̃pɔstœr] NM impostor

imposture [ɛ̃pɔstyr] NF imposture, deception

impôt [ɛ̃po] NM tax; (taxes) taxation, taxes pl; **~ direct/indirect** direct/indirect tax; **~ sur le chiffre d'affaires** corporation (BRIT) ou corporate (US) tax; **~ foncier** land tax; **~ sur la fortune** wealth tax; **~ sur les plus-values** capital gains tax; **~ sur le revenu** income tax; **~ sur les sociétés** tax on companies ■ **impôts** NMPL (contributions) (income) tax sg; **payer 1000 euros d'impôts** to pay 1,000 euros in tax; **impôts locaux** rates, local taxes (US), ≈ council tax (BRIT)

impotence [ɛ̃pɔtɑ̃s] NF disability

impotent, e [ɛ̃pɔtɑ̃, -ɑ̃t] ADJ disabled

impraticable [ɛ̃pratikabl] ADJ (projet) impracticable, unworkable; (piste) impassable

imprécation [ɛ̃prekasjɔ̃] NF imprecation

imprécis, e [ɛ̃presi, -iz] ADJ (contours, souvenir) imprecise, vague; (tir) inaccurate, imprecise

imprécision [ɛ̃presizjɔ̃] NF imprecision

imprégnation [ɛ̃preɲasjɔ̃] NF impregnation

imprégner [ɛ̃preɲe] /6/ VT (amertume, ironie) to pervade; **~ (de)** (tissu, tampon) to soak ou impregnate (with); (lieu, air) to fill (with) ■ **s'imprégner de** VPR to become impregnated with; to be filled with; (fig) to absorb

imprenable [ɛ̃prənabl] ADJ (forteresse) impregnable; **vue ~** unimpeded outlook

impresario [ɛ̃presarjo] NM manager, impresario

★**impression** [ɛ̃presjɔ̃] NF impression; (d'un ouvrage, tissu) printing; (Photo) exposure; **faire bonne/mauvaise ~** to make a good/bad impression; **donner une ~ de/l'~ que** to give the impression of/that; **avoir l'~ de/que** to have the impression of/that; **faire ~** to make an impression; **impressions de voyage** impressions of one's journey

impressionnable [ɛ̃presjɔnabl] ADJ impressionable

★**impressionnant, e** [ɛ̃presjɔnɑ̃, -ɑ̃t] ADJ (imposant) impressive; (bouleversant) upsetting

impressionner [ɛ̃presjɔne] /1/ VT (frapper) to impress; (troubler) to upset; (Photo) to expose

impressionnisme [ɛ̃presjɔnism] NM impressionism

impressionniste [ɛ̃presjɔnist] ADJ, NMF impressionist

imprévisible [ɛ̃previzibl] ADJ unforeseeable; (réaction, personne) unpredictable

imprévoyance [ɛ̃prevwajɑ̃s] NF lack of foresight

imprévoyant, e [ɛ̃prevwajɑ̃, -ɑ̃t] ADJ lacking in foresight; (en matière d'argent) improvident

imprévu, e [ɛ̃pʀevy] ADJ unforeseen, unexpected ▸ NM (*incident*) unexpected incident; **l'~** the unexpected; **des vacances pleines d'~** holidays full of surprises; **en cas d'~** if anything unexpected happens; **sauf ~** unless anything unexpected crops up

imprimable [ɛ̃pʀimabl] ADJ (*version, catalogue*) printable

★**imprimante** [ɛ̃pʀimɑ̃t] NF (*Inform*) printer; **~ à bulle d'encre** bubble jet printer; **~ à jet d'encre** ink-jet printer; **~ à laser** laser printer; **~ (ligne par) ligne** line printer; **~ à marguerite** daisy-wheel printer

imprimé [ɛ̃pʀime] NM (*formulaire*) printed form; (*Postes*) printed matter *no pl*; (*tissu*) printed fabric; **un ~ à fleurs/pois** (*tissu*) a floral/polka-dot print

★**imprimer** [ɛ̃pʀime] **/1/** VT to print; (*Inform*) to print (out); (*apposer: visa, cachet*) to stamp; (: *empreinte etc*) to imprint; (*publier*) to publish; (*communiquer: mouvement, impulsion*) to impart, transmit

imprimerie [ɛ̃pʀimʀi] NF printing; (*établissement*) printing works *sg*; (*atelier*) printing house, printery

imprimeur [ɛ̃pʀimœʀ] NM printer; **imprimeur-éditeur/-libraire** printer and publisher/bookseller

improbable [ɛ̃pʀɔbabl] ADJ unlikely, improbable

improductif, -ive [ɛ̃pʀɔdyktif, -iv] ADJ unproductive

impromptu, e [ɛ̃pʀɔ̃pty] ADJ impromptu; (*départ*) sudden

imprononçable [ɛ̃pʀɔnɔ̃sabl] ADJ unpronounceable

impropre [ɛ̃pʀɔpʀ] ADJ inappropriate; **~ à** unsuitable for

improprement [ɛ̃pʀɔpʀəmɑ̃] ADV improperly

impropriété [ɛ̃pʀɔpʀijete] NF: **~ (de langage)** incorrect usage *no pl*

improvisation [ɛ̃pʀɔvizasjɔ̃] NF improvisation

improvisé, e [ɛ̃pʀɔvize] ADJ makeshift, improvised; (*jeu etc*) scratch, improvised; **avec des moyens improvisés** using whatever comes to hand

improviser [ɛ̃pʀɔvize] **/1/** VT, VI to improvise; **~ qn cuisinier** to get sb to act as cook ■ **s'improviser** VPR (*secours, réunion*) to be improvised; **s'~ cuisinier** to (decide to) act as cook

improviste [ɛ̃pʀɔvist]: **à l'~** *adv* unexpectedly, without warning

imprudemment [ɛ̃pʀydamɑ̃] ADV carelessly; unwisely, imprudently

imprudence [ɛ̃pʀydɑ̃s] NF (*d'une personne, d'une action*) carelessness *no pl*; (*d'une remarque*) imprudence *no pl*; act of carelessness; foolish *ou* unwise action; **commettre une ~** to do something foolish

★**imprudent, e** [ɛ̃pʀydɑ̃, -ɑ̃t] ADJ (*conducteur, geste, action*) careless; (*remarque*) unwise, imprudent; (*projet*) foolhardy

impubère [ɛ̃pybɛʀ] ADJ below the age of puberty

impubliable [ɛ̃pyblijabl] ADJ unpublishable

impudemment [ɛ̃pydamɑ̃] ADV impudently

impudence [ɛ̃pydɑ̃s] NF impudence

impudent, e [ɛ̃pydɑ̃, -ɑ̃t] ADJ impudent

impudeur [ɛ̃pydœʀ] NF shamelessness

impudique [ɛ̃pydik] ADJ shameless

impuissance [ɛ̃pɥisɑ̃s] NF helplessness; ineffectualness; impotence

impuissant, e [ɛ̃pɥisɑ̃, -ɑ̃t] ADJ helpless; (*sans effet*) ineffectual; (*sexuellement*) impotent; **~ à faire qch** powerless to do sth ▸ NM impotent man

impulsif, -ive [ɛ̃pylsif, -iv] ADJ impulsive

impulsion [ɛ̃pylsjɔ̃] NF (*Élec, instinct*) impulse; (*élan, influence*) impetus

impulsivement [ɛ̃pylsivmɑ̃] ADV impulsively

impulsivité [ɛ̃pylsivite] NF impulsiveness

impunément [ɛ̃pynemɑ̃] ADV with impunity

impuni, e [ɛ̃pyni] ADJ unpunished

impunité [ɛ̃pynite] NF impunity

impur, e [ɛ̃pyʀ] ADJ impure

impureté [ɛ̃pyʀte] NF impurity

imputable [ɛ̃pytabl] ADJ (*attribuable*): **~ à** imputable to, ascribable to; (*Comm: somme*) **~ sur** chargeable to

imputation [ɛ̃pytasjɔ̃] NF imputation, charge

imputer [ɛ̃pyte] **/1/** VT (*attribuer*): **~ qch à** to ascribe *ou* impute sth to; (*Comm*) **~ qch à** *ou* **sur** to charge sth to

imputrescible [ɛ̃pytʀesibl] ADJ rotproof

in [in] ADJ INV in, trendy

INA [ina] SIGLE M (= *Institut national de l'audiovisuel*) *library of television archives*

inabordable [inabɔʀdabl] ADJ (*lieu*) inaccessible; (*cher*) prohibitive

inaccentué, e [inaksɑ̃tɥe] ADJ (*Ling*) unstressed

inacceptable [inakseptabl] ADJ unacceptable

inaccessible [inaksesibl] ADJ inaccessible; (*objectif*) unattainable; (*insensible*): **~ à** impervious to

inaccoutumé, e [inakutyme] ADJ unaccustomed

inachevé, e [inaʃ(ə)ve] ADJ unfinished

inactif, -ive [inaktif, -iv] ADJ inactive, idle; (*remède*) ineffective; (*Bourse: marché*) slack

inaction [inaksjɔ̃] NF inactivity

inactivité [inaktivite] NF (*Admin*): **en ~** out of active service

inadaptation [inadaptasjɔ̃] NF (*Psych*) maladjustment

inadapté, e [inadapte] ADJ (*Psych: adulte, enfant*) maladjusted; **~ à** not adapted to, unsuited to ▸ NM/F (*péj: adulte: asocial*) misfit

inadéquat, e [inadekwa, -wat] ADJ inadequate

inadéquation [inadekwasjɔ̃] NF inadequacy

inadmissible [inadmisibl] ADJ inadmissible

inadvertance [inadvɛʀtɑ̃s]: **par ~** *adv* inadvertently

inaliénable [inaljenabl] ADJ inalienable

inaltérable [inalteʀabl] ADJ (*matière*) stable; (*fig*) unchanging; **~ à** unaffected by; **couleur ~ (au lavage/à la lumière)** fast colour/fade-resistant colour

inamovible [inamɔvibl] ADJ fixed; (*Jur*) irremovable

inanimé, e [inanime] ADJ (*matière*) inanimate; (*évanoui*) unconscious; (*sans vie*) lifeless

inanité [inanite] NF futility

inanition [inanisjɔ̃] NF: **tomber d'~** to faint with hunger (and exhaustion)

inaperçu, e [inapɛʀsy] ADJ: **passer ~** to go unnoticed

inappétence [inapetɑ̃s] NF lack of appetite

inapplicable [inaplikabl] ADJ inapplicable

inapplication [inaplikasjɔ̃] NF lack of application

inappliqué, e [inaplike] ADJ lacking in application

inappréciable [inapʀesjabl] ADJ (service) invaluable; (différence, nuance) inappreciable

inapproprié, e [inapʀɔpʀije] ADJ inappropriate

inapte [inapt] ADJ: **~ à** incapable of; (Mil) unfit for

inaptitude [inaptityd] NF inaptitude; unfitness

inarticulé, e [inaʀtikyle] ADJ inarticulate

inassimilable [inasimilabl] ADJ that cannot be assimilated

inassouvi, e [inasuvi] ADJ unsatisfied, unfulfilled

inattaquable [inatakabl] ADJ (Mil) unassailable; (texte, preuve) irrefutable

inattendu, e [inatɑ̃dy] ADJ unexpected ▶ NM: **l'~** the unexpected

inattentif, -ive [inatɑ̃tif, -iv] ADJ inattentive; **~ à** (dangers, détails) heedless of

inattention [inatɑ̃sjɔ̃] NF inattention; (inadvertance): **une minute d'~** a minute of inattention, a minute's carelessness; **par ~** inadvertently; **faute d'~** careless mistake

inaudible [inodibl] ADJ inaudible

inaugural, e, -aux [inogyʀal, -o] ADJ (cérémonie) inaugural, opening; (vol, voyage) maiden

inauguration [inogyʀasjɔ̃] NF unveiling; opening; **discours/cérémonie d'~** inaugural speech/ceremony

inaugurer [inogyʀe] /1/ VT (monument) to unveil; (exposition, usine) to open; (fig) to inaugurate

inauthenticité [inotɑ̃tisite] NF inauthenticity

inavouable [inavwabl] ADJ (bénéfices) undisclosable; (honteux) shameful

inavoué, e [inavwe] ADJ unavowed

INC SIGLE M (= Institut national de la consommation) consumer research organization

inca [ɛ̃ka] ADJ Inca ▶ NMF: **Inca** Inca

incalculable [ɛ̃kalkylabl] ADJ incalculable; **un nombre ~ de** countless numbers of

incandescence [ɛ̃kɑ̃desɑ̃s] NF incandescence; **en ~** incandescent, white-hot; **porter à ~** to heat white-hot; **lampe/manchon à ~** incandescent lamp/(gas) mantle

incandescent, e [ɛ̃kɑ̃desɑ̃, -ɑ̃t] ADJ incandescent, white-hot

incantation [ɛ̃kɑ̃tasjɔ̃] NF incantation

incantatoire [ɛ̃kɑ̃tatwaʀ] ADJ: **formule ~** incantation

incapable [ɛ̃kapabl] ADJ incapable; **~ de faire** incapable of doing; (empêché) unable to do

incapacitant, e [ɛ̃kapasitɑ̃, -ɑ̃t] ADJ (Mil) incapacitating

incapacité [ɛ̃kapasite] NF (incompétence) incapability; (Jur: impossibilité) incapacity; **être dans l'~ de faire** to be unable to do; **~ permanente/ de travail** permanent/industrial disablement; **~ électorale** ineligibility to vote

incarcération [ɛ̃kaʀseʀasjɔ̃] NF incarceration

incarcérer [ɛ̃kaʀseʀe] /6/ VT to incarcerate, imprison

incarnat, e [ɛ̃kaʀna, -at] ADJ (rosy) pink

incarnation [ɛ̃kaʀnasjɔ̃] NF incarnation

incarné, e [ɛ̃kaʀne] ADJ incarnate; (ongle) ingrown

incarner [ɛ̃kaʀne] /1/ VT to embody, personify; (Théât) to play; (Rel) to incarnate ▪ **s'incarner dans** VPR (Rel) to be incarnate in

incartade [ɛ̃kaʀtad] NF prank, escapade

incassable [ɛ̃kasabl] ADJ unbreakable

incendiaire [ɛ̃sɑ̃djɛʀ] ADJ incendiary; (fig: discours) inflammatory ▶ NMF fire-raiser, arsonist

★**incendie** [ɛ̃sɑ̃di] NM fire; **~ criminel** arson no pl; **~ de forêt** forest fire

incendier [ɛ̃sɑ̃dje] /7/ VT (mettre le feu à) to set fire to, set alight; (brûler complètement) to burn down

incertain, e [ɛ̃sɛʀtɛ̃, -ɛn] ADJ uncertain; (temps) uncertain, unsettled; (imprécis: contours) indistinct, blurred

incertitude [ɛ̃sɛʀtityd] NF uncertainty

incessamment [ɛ̃sesamɑ̃] ADV very shortly

incessant, e [ɛ̃sesɑ̃, -ɑ̃t] ADJ incessant, unceasing

incessible [ɛ̃sesibl] ADJ (Jur) non-transferable

inceste [ɛ̃sɛst] NM incest

incestueux, -euse [ɛ̃sɛstɥø, -øz] ADJ incestuous

inchangé, e [ɛ̃ʃɑ̃ʒe] ADJ unchanged, unaltered

inchantable [ɛ̃ʃɑ̃tabl] ADJ unsingable

inchauffable [ɛ̃ʃofabl] ADJ impossible to heat

incidemment [ɛ̃sidamɑ̃] ADV in passing

incidence [ɛ̃sidɑ̃s] NF (effet, influence) effect; (Physique) incidence

★**incident** [ɛ̃sidɑ̃] NM incident; **~ de frontière** border incident; **~ de parcours** minor hitch ou setback; **~ technique** technical difficulties pl, technical hitch

incinérateur [ɛ̃sineʀatœʀ] NM incinerator

incinération [ɛ̃sineʀasjɔ̃] NF (d'ordures) incineration; (crémation) cremation

incinérer [ɛ̃sineʀe] /6/ VT (ordures) to incinerate; (mort) to cremate

incise [ɛ̃siz] NF (Ling) interpolated clause

inciser [ɛ̃size] /1/ VT to make an incision in; (abcès) to lance

incisif, -ive [ɛ̃sizif, -iv] ADJ incisive, cutting ▶ NF incisor

incision [ɛ̃sizjɔ̃] NF incision; (d'un abcès) lancing

incitatif, -ive [ɛ̃sitatif, -iv] ADJ: **mesures incitatives** incentives; **mesures fiscales incitatives** tax incentives

incitation [ɛ̃sitasjɔ̃] NF (encouragement) incentive; (provocation) incitement

inciter [ɛ̃site] /1/ VT: **~ qn à (faire) qch** to prompt ou encourage sb to do sth; (à la révolte etc) to incite sb to do sth

incivil, e [ɛ̃sivil] ADJ uncivil

incivilité [ɛ̃sivilite] NF (*grossièreté*) incivility ■ **incivilités** NFPL antisocial behaviour *sg*

inclassable [ɛ̃klɑsabl] ADJ unclassifiable

inclinable [ɛ̃klinabl] ADJ (*dossier etc*) tilting; **siège à dossier ~** reclining seat

inclinaison [ɛ̃klinɛzɔ̃] NF (*déclivité: d'une route etc*) incline; (: *d'un toit*) slope; (*état penché: d'un mur*) lean; (: *de la tête*) tilt; (: *d'un navire*) list

inclination [ɛ̃klinasjɔ̃] NF (*penchant*) inclination, tendency; **montrer de l'~ pour les sciences** *etc* to show an inclination for the sciences *etc*; **inclinations égoïstes/altruistes** egoistic/altruistic tendencies; **~ de (la) tête** nod (of the head); **~ (de buste)** bow

incliné, e [ɛ̃kline] ADJ (*plan*) sloping; (*tête*) to one side

incliner [ɛ̃kline] /1/ VT (*bouteille*) to tilt; (*tête*) to incline; (*inciter*): **~ qn à qch/à faire** to encourage sb towards sth/to do ▸ VI: **~ à qch/à faire** (*tendre à, pencher pour*) to incline towards sth/doing, tend towards sth/to do ■ **s'incliner** VPR (*route*) to slope; (*toit*) to be sloping; **s'~ (devant)** to bow (before)

inclure [ɛ̃klyʀ] /35/ VT to include; (*joindre à un envoi*) to enclose

inclus, e [ɛ̃kly, -yz] PP *de* **inclure** ▸ ADJ included; (*joint à un envoi*) enclosed; (*compris: frais, dépense*) included; (*Math: ensemble*): **~ dans** included in; **jusqu'au troisième chapitre ~** up to and including the third chapter; **jusqu'au 10 mars ~** until 10th March inclusive

inclusion [ɛ̃klyzjɔ̃] NF (*voir* **inclure**) inclusion; enclosing

inclusivement [ɛ̃klyzivmɑ̃] ADV inclusively

inclut [ɛ̃kly] VB *voir* **inclure**

incoercible [ɛ̃kɔɛʀsibl] ADJ uncontrollable

incognito [ɛ̃kɔɲito] ADV incognito ▸ NM: **garder l'~** to remain incognito

incohérence [ɛ̃kɔeʀɑ̃s] NF inconsistency; incoherence

incohérent, e [ɛ̃kɔeʀɑ̃, -ɑ̃t] ADJ (*comportement*) inconsistent; (*geste, langage, texte*) incoherent

incollable [ɛ̃kɔlabl] ADJ (*riz*) that does not stick; (*fam: personne*): **il est ~** he's got all the answers

incolore [ɛ̃kɔlɔʀ] ADJ colourless

incomber [ɛ̃kɔ̃be] /1/: **~ à** VT (*devoirs, responsabilité*) to rest *ou* be incumbent upon (: *frais, travail*) to be the responsibility of

incombustible [ɛ̃kɔ̃bystibl] ADJ incombustible

incommensurable [ɛ̃kɔmɑ̃syʀabl] ADJ immeasurable

incommodant, e [ɛ̃kɔmɔdɑ̃, -ɑ̃t] ADJ (*bruit*) annoying; (*chaleur*) uncomfortable

incommode [ɛ̃kɔmɔd] ADJ inconvenient; (*posture, siège*) uncomfortable

incommodément [ɛ̃kɔmɔdemɑ̃] ADV (*installé, assis*) uncomfortably; (*logé, situé*) inconveniently

incommoder [ɛ̃kɔmɔde] /1/ VT: **~ qn** (*chaleur, odeur*) to bother *ou* inconvenience sb; (*embarrasser*) to make sb feel uncomfortable *ou* ill at ease

incommodité [ɛ̃kɔmɔdite] NF inconvenience

incommunicabilité [ɛ̃kɔmynikabilite] NF (*entre personnes*) absence of communication

incommunicable [ɛ̃kɔmynikabl] ADJ (*Jur: droits, privilèges*) non-transferable; (: *pensée*) incommunicable

incomparable [ɛ̃kɔ̃paʀabl] ADJ not comparable; (*inégalable*) incomparable, matchless

incomparablement [ɛ̃kɔ̃paʀabləmɑ̃] ADV incomparably

incompatibilité [ɛ̃kɔ̃patibilite] NF incompatibility; **~ d'humeur** (mutual) incompatibility

incompatible [ɛ̃kɔ̃patibl] ADJ incompatible

incompétence [ɛ̃kɔ̃petɑ̃s] NF lack of expertise; incompetence

incompétent, e [ɛ̃kɔ̃petɑ̃, -ɑ̃t] ADJ (*ignorant*) inexpert; (*incapable*) incompetent, not competent

incomplet, -ète [ɛ̃kɔ̃plɛ, -ɛt] ADJ incomplete

incomplètement [ɛ̃kɔ̃plɛtmɑ̃] ADV not completely, incompletely

incompréhensible [ɛ̃kɔ̃pʀeɑ̃sibl] ADJ incomprehensible

incompréhensif, -ive [ɛ̃kɔ̃pʀeɑ̃sif, -iv] ADJ lacking in understanding, unsympathetic

incompréhension [ɛ̃kɔ̃pʀeɑ̃sjɔ̃] NF lack of understanding

incompressible [ɛ̃kɔ̃pʀesibl] ADJ (*Physique*) incompressible; (*fig: dépenses*) that cannot be reduced; (*Jur: peine*) irreducible

incompris, e [ɛ̃kɔ̃pʀi, -iz] ADJ misunderstood

inconcevable [ɛ̃kɔ̃s(ə)vabl] ADJ (*conduite etc*) inconceivable; (*mystère*) incredible

inconciliable [ɛ̃kɔ̃siljabl] ADJ irreconcilable

inconditionnel, le [ɛ̃kɔ̃disjɔnɛl] ADJ unconditional; (*partisan*) unquestioning ▸ NM/F (*partisan*) unquestioning supporter

inconditionnellement [ɛ̃kɔ̃disjɔnɛlmɑ̃] ADV unconditionally

inconduite [ɛ̃kɔ̃dɥit] NF bad *ou* unsuitable behaviour *no pl*

inconfort [ɛ̃kɔ̃fɔʀ] NM lack of comfort, discomfort

inconfortable [ɛ̃kɔ̃fɔʀtabl] ADJ uncomfortable

inconfortablement [ɛ̃kɔ̃fɔʀtabləmɑ̃] ADV uncomfortably

incongru, e [ɛ̃kɔ̃gʀy] ADJ unseemly; (*remarque*) ill-chosen, incongruous

incongruité [ɛ̃kɔ̃gʀyite] NF unseemliness; incongruity; (*parole incongrue*) ill-chosen remark

inconnu, e [ɛ̃kɔny] ADJ unknown; (*sentiment, plaisir*) new, strange ▸ NM/F stranger; unknown person (*ou artist etc*) ▸ NM: **l'~** the unknown ▸ NF (*Math*) unknown; (*fig*) unknown factor

inconsciemment [ɛ̃kɔ̃sjamɑ̃] ADV unconsciously

inconscience [ɛ̃kɔ̃sjɑ̃s] NF unconsciousness; recklessness

inconscient, e [ɛ̃kɔ̃sjɑ̃, -ɑ̃t] ADJ unconscious; (*irréfléchi*) thoughtless, reckless; (*sentiment*) subconscious; **~ de** unaware of ▸ NM (*Psych*): **l'~** the unconscious

inconséquence [ɛ̃kɔ̃sekɑ̃s] NF inconsistency; thoughtlessness; (*action, parole*) thoughtless thing to do (*ou* say)

inconséquent, e [ɛ̃kɔ̃sekɑ̃, -ɑ̃t] ADJ (*illogique*) inconsistent; (*irréfléchi*) thoughtless

inconsidéré, e [ɛ̃kɔ̃sidere] ADJ ill-considered

inconsidérément [ɛ̃kɔ̃sideremɑ̃] ADV thoughtlessly

inconsistance [ɛ̃kɔ̃sistɑ̃s] NF (de personne) lack of character; (d'argument) flimsiness

inconsistant, e [ɛ̃kɔ̃sistɑ̃, -ɑ̃t] ADJ flimsy, weak; (crème etc) runny

inconsolable [ɛ̃kɔ̃sɔlabl] ADJ inconsolable

inconstance [ɛ̃kɔ̃stɑ̃s] NF inconstancy, fickleness

inconstant, e [ɛ̃kɔ̃stɑ̃, -ɑ̃t] ADJ inconstant, fickle

inconstitutionnel, le [ɛ̃kɔ̃stitysjɔnɛl] ADJ unconstitutional

incontestable [ɛ̃kɔ̃tɛstabl] ADJ unquestionable, indisputable

incontestablement [ɛ̃kɔ̃tɛstabləmɑ̃] ADV unquestionably, indisputably

incontesté, e [ɛ̃kɔ̃tɛste] ADJ undisputed

incontinence [ɛ̃kɔ̃tinɑ̃s] NF (Méd) incontinence

incontinent, e [ɛ̃kɔ̃tinɑ̃, -ɑ̃t] ADJ (Méd) incontinent ▸ ADV (tout de suite) forthwith

incontournable [ɛ̃kɔ̃turnabl] ADJ unavoidable

incontrôlable [ɛ̃kɔ̃trolabl] ADJ unverifiable; (irrépressible) uncontrollable

incontrôlé, e [ɛ̃kɔ̃trole] ADJ uncontrolled

inconvenance [ɛ̃kɔ̃v(ə)nɑ̃s] NF (parole, action) impropriety

inconvenant, e [ɛ̃kɔ̃v(ə)nɑ̃, -ɑ̃t] ADJ unseemly, improper

inconvénient [ɛ̃kɔ̃venjɑ̃] NM (d'une situation, d'un projet) disadvantage, drawback; (d'un remède, changement etc) risk, inconvenience; **si vous n'y voyez pas d'~** if you have no objections; **y a-t-il un ~ à …?** (risque) is there a risk in …?; (objection) is there any objection to …?

inconvertible [ɛ̃kɔ̃vɛrtibl] ADJ inconvertible

incorporation [ɛ̃kɔrpɔrasjɔ̃] NF (Mil) call-up

incorporé, e [ɛ̃kɔrpɔre] ADJ (micro etc) built-in

incorporel, le [ɛ̃kɔrpɔrɛl] ADJ (Jur): **biens incorporels** intangible property

incorporer [ɛ̃kɔrpɔre] /1/ VT: **~ (à)** to mix in (with); **~ (dans)** (paragraphe etc) to incorporate (in); (territoire, immigrants) to incorporate (into); (Mil: appeler) to recruit (into), call up; (: affecter): **~ qn dans** to enlist sb into ■ **s'incorporer** VPR: **il a très bien su s'~ à notre groupe** he was very easily incorporated into our group

incorrect, e [ɛ̃kɔrɛkt] ADJ (impropre, inconvenant) improper; (défectueux) faulty; (inexact) incorrect; (impoli) impolite; (déloyal) underhand

incorrectement [ɛ̃kɔrɛktəmɑ̃] ADV improperly; faultily; incorrectly; impolitely; in an underhand way

incorrection [ɛ̃kɔrɛksjɔ̃] NF impropriety; incorrectness; underhand nature; (terme impropre) impropriety; (action, remarque) improper behaviour (ou remark)

incorrigible [ɛ̃kɔriʒibl] ADJ incorrigible

incorruptible [ɛ̃kɔryptibl] ADJ incorruptible

incrédibilité [ɛ̃kredibilite] NF incredibility

incrédule [ɛ̃kredyl] ADJ incredulous; (Rel) unbelieving

incrédulité [ɛ̃kredylite] NF incredulity; **avec ~** incredulously

increvable [ɛ̃krəvabl] ADJ (pneu) puncture-proof; (fam) tireless

incriminé, e [ɛ̃krimine] ADJ (article, livre) offending; **l'article ~** the offending article

incriminer [ɛ̃krimine] /1/ VT (personne) to incriminate; (action, conduite) to bring under attack; (bonne foi, honnêteté) to call into question

incrochetable [ɛ̃krɔʃ(ə)tabl] ADJ (serrure) that can't be picked, burglarproof

★**incroyable** [ɛ̃krwajabl] ADJ incredible, unbelievable

incroyablement [ɛ̃krwajabləmɑ̃] ADV incredibly, unbelievably

incroyant, e [ɛ̃krwajɑ̃, -ɑ̃t] NM/F non-believer

incrustation [ɛ̃krystasjɔ̃] NF inlaying no pl; inlay; (dans une chaudière etc) fur no pl, scale no pl

incruster [ɛ̃kryste] /1/ VT (radiateur etc) to coat with scale ou fur; **~ qch dans/qch de** (Art) to inlay sth into/sth with ■ **s'incruster** VPR (invité) to take root; (radiateur etc) to become coated with scale ou fur; **s'~ dans** (corps étranger, caillou) to become embedded in

incubateur [ɛ̃kybatœr] NM incubator

incubation [ɛ̃kybasjɔ̃] NF incubation

inculpation [ɛ̃kylpasjɔ̃] NF charging no pl; charge; **sous l'~ de** on a charge of

inculpé, e [ɛ̃kylpe] NM/F accused

inculper [ɛ̃kylpe] /1/ VT: **~ (de)** to charge (with)

inculquer [ɛ̃kylke] /1/ VT: **~ qch à** to inculcate sth in, instil sth into

inculte [ɛ̃kylt] ADJ uncultivated; (esprit, peuple) uncultured; (barbe) unkempt

incultivable [ɛ̃kyltivabl] ADJ (terrain) unworkable

inculture [ɛ̃kyltyr] NF lack of education

incunable [ɛ̃kynabl] NM incunabulum

incurable [ɛ̃kyrabl] ADJ incurable

incurie [ɛ̃kyri] NF carelessness

incursion [ɛ̃kyrsjɔ̃] NF incursion, foray

incurvé, e [ɛ̃kyrve] ADJ curved

incurver [ɛ̃kyrve] /1/ VT (barre de fer) to bend into a curve ■ **s'incurver** VPR (planche, route) to bend

★**Inde** [ɛ̃d] NF: **l'~** India

indéboulonnable [ɛ̃debulɔnabl] ADJ impossible to budge

indécelable [ɛ̃des(ə)labl] ADJ undetectable

indécemment [ɛ̃desamɑ̃] ADV indecently

indécence [ɛ̃desɑ̃s] NF indecency; (propos, acte) indecent remark (ou act etc)

indécent, e [ɛ̃desɑ̃, -ɑ̃t] ADJ indecent

indéchiffrable [ɛ̃deʃifrabl] ADJ indecipherable

indéchirable [ɛ̃deʃirabl] ADJ tear-proof

indécis, e [ɛ̃desi, -iz] ADJ (par nature) indecisive; (perplexe) undecided

indécision [ɛ̃desizjɔ̃] NF indecision, indecisiveness

indéclinable [ɛ̃deklinabl] ADJ (Ling: mot) indeclinable

indécomposable [ɛ̃dekɔ̃pozabl] ADJ that cannot be broken down

indécrottable [ɛ̃dekʀɔtabl] ADJ *(fam)* hopeless

indéfectible [ɛ̃defɛktibl] ADJ *(attachement)* indestructible

indéfendable [ɛ̃defɑ̃dabl] ADJ indefensible

indéfini, e [ɛ̃defini] ADJ *(imprécis, incertain)* undefined; *(illimité, Ling)* indefinite

indéfiniment [ɛ̃definimɑ̃] ADV indefinitely

indéfinissable [ɛ̃definisabl] ADJ indefinable

indéformable [ɛ̃defɔʀmabl] ADJ that keeps its shape

indélébile [ɛ̃delebil] ADJ indelible

indélicat, e [ɛ̃delika, -at] ADJ tactless; *(malhonnête)* dishonest

indélicatesse [ɛ̃delikatɛs] NF tactlessness; dishonesty

indémaillable [ɛ̃demɑjabl] ADJ run-resist

indemne [ɛ̃dɛmn] ADJ unharmed

indemnisable [ɛ̃dɛmnizabl] ADJ entitled to compensation

indemnisation [ɛ̃dɛmnizasjɔ̃] NF *(somme)* indemnity, compensation

indemniser [ɛ̃dɛmnize] /1/ VT: **~ qn (de)** to compensate sb (for); **se faire ~** to get compensation

indemnité [ɛ̃dɛmnite] NF *(dédommagement)* compensation *no pl; (allocation)* allowance; **~ de licenciement** redundancy payment; **~ de logement** housing allowance; **~ parlementaire** ≈ MP's (BRIT) *ou* Congressman's (US) salary

indémodable [ɛ̃demɔdabl] ADJ *(vêtement, style)* classic, timeless, that won't go out of fashion

indémontable [ɛ̃demɔ̃tabl] ADJ *(meuble etc)* that cannot be dismantled, in one piece

indéniable [ɛ̃denjabl] ADJ undeniable, indisputable

indéniablement [ɛ̃denjabləmɑ̃] ADV undeniably

indépendamment [ɛ̃depɑ̃damɑ̃] ADV independently; **~ de** independently of; *(abstraction faite de)* irrespective of; *(en plus de)* over and above

indépendance [ɛ̃depɑ̃dɑ̃s] NF independence; **~ matérielle** financial independence

indépendant, e [ɛ̃depɑ̃dɑ̃, -ɑ̃t] ADJ independent; **~ de** independent of; **chambre indépendante** room with private entrance; **travailleur ~** self-employed worker

indépendantisme [ɛ̃depɑ̃dɑ̃tism] NM separatism

indépendantiste [ɛ̃depɑ̃dɑ̃tist] ADJ, NMF separatist

indéracinable [ɛ̃deʀasinabl] ADJ *(fig: croyance etc)* ineradicable

indéréglable [ɛ̃deʀeglabl] ADJ which will not break down

indescriptible [ɛ̃dɛskʀiptibl] ADJ indescribable

indésirable [ɛ̃deziʀabl] ADJ undesirable

indestructible [ɛ̃dɛstʀyktibl] ADJ indestructible; *(marque, impression)* indelible

indétectable [ɛ̃detɛktabl] ADJ undetectable

indéterminable [ɛ̃detɛʀminabl] ADJ indeterminable

indétermination [ɛ̃detɛʀminasjɔ̃] NF indecision, indecisiveness

indéterminé, e [ɛ̃detɛʀmine] ADJ *(date, cause, nature)* unspecified; *(forme, longueur, quantité)* indeterminate; indeterminable

index [ɛ̃dɛks] NM *(doigt)* index finger; *(d'un livre etc)* index; **mettre à l'~** to blacklist

indexation [ɛ̃dɛksasjɔ̃] NF indexing

indexé, e [ɛ̃dɛkse] ADJ *(Écon)*: **~ (sur)** index-linked (to)

indexer [ɛ̃dɛkse] /1/ VT *(salaire, emprunt)*: **~ (sur)** to index (on)

indic [ɛ̃dik] NMF *(fam: informateur)* informer, grass (BRIT *fam*)

indicateur, -trice [ɛ̃dikatœʀ, -tʀis] NM/F *(Police)* informer ► NM *(livre)* guide; *(: liste)* directory; *(Tech)* gauge; indicator; *(Écon)* indicator; **~ des chemins de fer** railway timetable; **~ de direction** *(Auto)* indicator; **~ immobilier** property gazette; **~ de niveau** level, gauge; **~ de pression** pressure gauge; **~ de rues** street directory; **~ de vitesse** speedometer ► ADJ: **poteau ~** signpost; **tableau ~** indicator (board)

★**indicatif, -ive** [ɛ̃dikatif, -iv] ADJ: **à titre ~** for (your) information ► NM *(Ling)* indicative; *(d'une émission)* theme *ou* signature tune; *(Tél)* dialling code (BRIT), area code (US); **~ d'appel** *(Radio)* call sign; **quel est l'~ de ...** what's the code for ...?

indication [ɛ̃dikasjɔ̃] NF indication; *(renseignement)* information *no pl*; **~ d'origine** *(Comm)* place of origin ■ **indications** NFPL *(directives)* instructions

indice [ɛ̃dis] NM *(marque, signe)* indication, sign; *(Police: lors d'une enquête)* clue; *(Jur: présomption)* piece of evidence; *(Science, Écon, Tech)* index; *(Admin)* grading; rating; **~ du coût de la vie** cost-of-living index; **~ inférieur** subscript; **~ d'octane** octane rating; **~ des prix** price index; **~ de traitement** salary grading; **~ de protection** (sun protection) factor

indicible [ɛ̃disibl] ADJ inexpressible

★**indien, ne** [ɛ̃djɛ̃, -ɛn] ADJ Indian ► NM/F: **Indien, ne** *(d'Amérique)* Native American; *(d'Inde)* Indian

indifféremment [ɛ̃diferamɑ̃] ADV *(sans distinction)* equally; indiscriminately

indifférence [ɛ̃diferɑ̃s] NF indifference

indifférencié, e [ɛ̃diferɑ̃sje] ADJ undifferentiated

indifférent, e [ɛ̃diferɑ̃, -ɑ̃t] ADJ *(peu intéressé)* indifferent; **~ à** *(insensible à)* indifferent to, unconcerned about; *(peu intéressant pour)* indifferent to; immaterial to; **ça m'est ~ (que ...)** it doesn't matter to me (whether ...); **elle m'est indifférente** I am indifferent to her

indifférer [ɛ̃difere] /6/ VT: **cela m'indiffère** I'm indifferent about it

indigence [ɛ̃diʒɑ̃s] NF poverty; **être dans l'~** to be destitute

indigène [ɛ̃diʒɛn] ADJ native, indigenous; *(de la région)* local ► NMF native

indigent, e [ɛ̃diʒɑ̃, -ɑ̃t] ADJ destitute, poverty-stricken; *(fig)* poor

indigeste [ɛ̃diʒɛst] ADJ indigestible

indigestion [ɛ̃diʒɛstjɔ̃] NF indigestion *no pl*; **avoir une ~** to have indigestion

indignation [ɛ̃diɲasjɔ̃] NF indignation; **avec ~** indignantly

indigne [ɛ̃diɲ] ADJ: **~ (de)** unworthy (of)

indigné, e [ɛ̃diɲe] ADJ indignant

indignement [ɛ̃diɲmɑ̃] ADV shamefully

indigner [ɛ̃diɲe] /1/ VT to make indignant ▪ **s'indigner (de/contre)** VPR to be (ou become) indignant (at)

indignité [ɛ̃diɲite] NF unworthiness no pl; (acte) shameful act

indigo [ɛ̃digo] NM indigo

indiqué, e [ɛ̃dike] ADJ (date, lieu) given, appointed; (adéquat) appropriate, suitable; (conseillé) advisable; (remède, traitement) appropriate

★**indiquer** [ɛ̃dike] /1/ VT: **~ qch/qn à qn** (désigner) to point sth/sb out to sb; (faire connaître: médecin, lieu, restaurant) to tell sb of sth/sb; (suj: pendule, aiguille) to show; (: étiquette, plan) to show, indicate; (renseigner sur) to point out, tell; (déterminer: date, lieu) to give, state; (dénoter) to indicate, point to; **~ du doigt** to point out; **~ de la main** to indicate with one's hand; **~ du regard** to glance towards ou in the direction of; ▶ **pourriez-vous m'~ les toilettes/l'heure ?** could you direct me to the toilets/tell me the time?

indirect, e [ɛ̃diʀɛkt] ADJ indirect

indirectement [ɛ̃diʀɛktəmɑ̃] ADV indirectly; (apprendre) in a roundabout way

indiscernable [ɛ̃disɛʀnabl] ADJ indiscernible

indiscipline [ɛ̃disiplin] NF lack of discipline

indiscipliné, e [ɛ̃disipline] ADJ undisciplined; (fig) unmanageable

indiscret, -ète [ɛ̃diskʀɛ, -ɛt] ADJ indiscreet

indiscrétion [ɛ̃diskʀesjɔ̃] NF indiscretion; **sans ~,** ... without wishing to be indiscreet, ...

indiscutable [ɛ̃diskytabl] ADJ indisputable

indiscutablement [ɛ̃diskytabləmɑ̃] ADV indisputably

indiscuté, e [ɛ̃diskyte] ADJ (incontesté: droit, chef) undisputed

★**indispensable** [ɛ̃dispɑ̃sabl] ADJ indispensable, essential; **~ à qn/pour faire qch** essential for sb/to do sth

indisponibilité [ɛ̃dispɔnibilite] NF unavailability

indisponible [ɛ̃dispɔnibl] ADJ unavailable

indisposé, e [ɛ̃dispoze] ADJ indisposed, unwell

indisposer [ɛ̃dispoze] /1/ VT (incommoder) to upset; (déplaire à) to antagonize

indisposition [ɛ̃dispozisjɔ̃] NF (slight) illness, indisposition

indissociable [ɛ̃disɔsjabl] ADJ indissociable

indissoluble [ɛ̃disɔlybl] ADJ indissoluble

indissolublement [ɛ̃disɔlybləmɑ̃] ADV indissolubly

indistinct, e [ɛ̃distɛ̃, -ɛkt] ADJ indistinct

indistinctement [ɛ̃distɛ̃ktəmɑ̃] ADV (voir, prononcer) indistinctly; (sans distinction) without distinction, indiscriminately

individu [ɛ̃dividy] NM individual

individualiser [ɛ̃dividɥalize] /1/ VT to individualize; (personnaliser) to tailor to individual require-

ments ▪ **s'individualiser** VPR to develop one's own identity

individualisme [ɛ̃dividɥalism] NM individualism

individualiste [ɛ̃dividɥalist] NMF individualist

individualité [ɛ̃dividɥalite] NF individuality

individuel, le [ɛ̃dividɥɛl] ADJ (gén) individual; (opinion, livret, contrôle, avantages) personal; **chambre individuelle** single room; **maison individuelle** detached house; **propriété individuelle** personal ou private property

individuellement [ɛ̃dividɥɛlmɑ̃] ADV individually

indivis, e [ɛ̃divi, -iz] ADJ (Jur: bien, succession) indivisible; (: cohéritiers, propriétaires) joint

indivisible [ɛ̃divizibl] ADJ indivisible

Indochine [ɛ̃dɔʃin] NF: **l'~** Indochina

indochinois, e [ɛ̃dɔʃinwa, -waz] ADJ Indochinese

indocile [ɛ̃dɔsil] ADJ unruly

indo-européen, ne [ɛ̃dɔøʀɔpeɛ̃, -ɛn] ADJ Indo-European ▶ NM (Ling) Indo-European

indolence [ɛ̃dɔlɑ̃s] NF indolence

indolent, e [ɛ̃dɔlɑ̃, -ɑ̃t] ADJ indolent

indolore [ɛ̃dɔlɔʀ] ADJ painless

indomptable [ɛ̃dɔ̃tabl] ADJ untameable; (fig) invincible, indomitable

indompté, e [ɛ̃dɔ̃te] ADJ (cheval) unbroken

Indonésie [ɛ̃dɔnezi] NF: **l'~** Indonesia

indonésien, ne [ɛ̃dɔnezjɛ̃, -ɛn] ADJ Indonesian ▶ NM/F: **Indonésien, ne** Indonesian

indu, e [ɛ̃dy] ADJ: **à une heure indue** at some ungodly hour

indubitable [ɛ̃dybitabl] ADJ indubitable

indubitablement [ɛ̃dybitabləmɑ̃] ADV indubitably

induction [ɛ̃dyksjɔ̃] NF induction

induire [ɛ̃dɥiʀ] /38/ VT: **~ qch de** to induce sth from; **~ qn en erreur** to lead sb astray, mislead sb

indulgence [ɛ̃dylʒɑ̃s] NF indulgence; leniency; **avec ~** indulgently; leniently

indulgent, e [ɛ̃dylʒɑ̃, -ɑ̃t] ADJ (parent, regard) indulgent; (juge, examinateur) lenient

indûment [ɛ̃dymɑ̃] ADV without due cause; (illégitimement) wrongfully

industrialisation [ɛ̃dystʀijalizasjɔ̃] NF industrialization

industrialisé, e [ɛ̃dystʀijalize] ADJ industrialized

industrialiser [ɛ̃dystʀijalize] /1/ VT to industrialize ▪ **s'industrialiser** VPR to become industrialized

★**industrie** [ɛ̃dystʀi] NF industry; **~ automobile/textile** car/textile industry; **~ du spectacle** entertainment business

★**industriel, le** [ɛ̃dystʀijɛl] ADJ industrial; (produit industriellement: pain etc) mass-produced, factory-produced ▶ NM industrialist; (fabricant) manufacturer

industriellement [ɛ̃dystʀijɛlmɑ̃] ADV industrially

industrieux, -euse [ɛ̃dystʀijø, -øz] ADJ industrious

inébranlable [inebʀɑ̃labl] ADJ (*masse, colonne*) solid; (*personne, certitude, foi*) steadfast, unwavering

inédit, e [inedi, -it] ADJ (*correspondance etc*) (hitherto) unpublished; (*spectacle, moyen*) novel, original; (*film*) unreleased

ineffable [inefabl] ADJ inexpressible, ineffable

ineffaçable [inefasabl] ADJ indelible

inefficace [inefikas] ADJ (*remède, moyen*) ineffective; (*machine, employé*) inefficient

inefficacité [inefikasite] NF ineffectiveness; inefficiency

inégal, e, -aux [inegal, -o] ADJ unequal; (*irrégulier*) uneven

inégalable [inegalabl] ADJ matchless

inégalé, e [inegale] ADJ (*record*) unmatched, unequalled; (*beauté*) unrivalled

inégalement [inegalmɑ̃] ADV unequally

inégalitaire [inegalitɛʀ] ADJ (*société, système*) unequal

inégalité [inegalite] NF inequality; unevenness *no pl*; ~ **de deux hauteurs** difference *ou* disparity between two heights; **inégalités de terrain** uneven ground

inélégance [inelegɑ̃s] NF inelegance

inélégant, e [inelegɑ̃, -ɑ̃t] ADJ inelegant; (*indélicat*) discourteous

inéligibilité [ineliʒibilite] NF ineligibility

inéligible [ineliʒibl] ADJ ineligible

inéluctable [inelyktabl] ADJ inescapable

inéluctablement [inelyktabləmɑ̃] ADV inescapably

inemployable [inɑ̃plwajabl] ADJ unusable

inemployé, e [inɑ̃plwaje] ADJ unused

inénarrable [inenaʀabl] ADJ hilarious

inepte [inɛpt] ADJ inept

ineptie [inɛpsi] NF ineptitude; (*propos*) nonsense *no pl*

inépuisable [inepɥizabl] ADJ inexhaustible

inéquitable [inekitabl] ADJ inequitable

inerte [inɛʀt] ADJ (*immobile*) lifeless; (*apathique*) passive, inert; (*Physique, Chimie*) inert

inertie [inɛʀsi] NF inertia

inescompté, e [inɛskɔ̃te] ADJ unexpected, unhoped-for

inespéré, e [inɛspeʀe] ADJ unhoped-for, unexpected

inesthétique [inɛstetik] ADJ unsightly

inestimable [inɛstimabl] ADJ priceless; (*fig: bienfait*) invaluable

inévitable [inevitabl] ADJ unavoidable; (*fatal, habituel*) inevitable

inévitablement [inevitabləmɑ̃] ADV inevitably

inexact, e [inɛgzakt] ADJ inaccurate, inexact; (*non ponctuel*) unpunctual

inexactement [inɛgzaktəmɑ̃] ADV inaccurately

inexactitude [inɛgzaktityd] NF inaccuracy

inexcusable [inɛkskyzabl] ADJ inexcusable, unforgivable

inexécutable [inɛgzekytabl] ADJ impracticable, unworkable; (*Mus*) unplayable

inexistant, e [inɛgzistɑ̃, -ɑ̃t] ADJ non-existent

inexistence [inɛgzistɑ̃s] NF nonexistence

inexorable [inɛgzɔʀabl] ADJ inexorable; (*personne: dur*): ~ **(à)** unmoved (by)

inexorablement [inɛgzɔʀabləmɑ̃] ADV inexorably

inexpérience [inɛkspeʀjɑ̃s] NF inexperience, lack of experience

inexpérimenté, e [inɛkspeʀimɑ̃te] ADJ inexperienced; (*arme, procédé*) untested

inexplicable [inɛksplikabl] ADJ inexplicable

inexplicablement [inɛksplikabləmɑ̃] ADV inexplicably

inexpliqué, e [inɛksplike] ADJ unexplained

inexploitable [inɛksplwatabl] ADJ (*gisement, richesse*) unexploitable; (*données, renseignements*) unusable

inexploité, e [inɛksplwate] ADJ unexploited, untapped

inexploré, e [inɛksplɔʀe] ADJ unexplored

inexpressif, -ive [inɛkspʀesif, -iv] ADJ inexpressive; (*regard etc*) expressionless

inexpressivité [inɛkspʀesivite] NF expressionlessness

inexprimable [inɛkspʀimabl] ADJ inexpressible

inexprimé, e [inɛkspʀime] ADJ unspoken, unexpressed

inexpugnable [inɛkspygnabl] ADJ impregnable

inextensible [inɛkstɑ̃sibl] ADJ (*tissu*) non-stretch

in extenso [inɛkstɛ̃so] ADV in full

inextinguible [inɛkstɛ̃gibl] ADJ (*soif*) unquenchable; (*rire*) uncontrollable

in extremis [inɛkstʀemis] ADV at the last minute ▸ ADJ INV last-minute; (*testament*) death bed *cpd*

inextricable [inɛkstʀikabl] ADJ inextricable

inextricablement [inɛkstʀikabləmɑ̃] ADV inextricably

infaillibilité [ɛ̃fajibilite] NF infallibility

infaillible [ɛ̃fajibl] ADJ infallible; (*instinct*) infallible, unerring

infailliblement [ɛ̃fajibləmɑ̃] ADV (*certainement*) without fail

infaisable [ɛ̃fəzabl] ADJ (*travail etc*) impossible, impractical

infalsifiable [ɛ̃falsifjabl] ADJ impossible to forge, unforgeable

infamant, e [ɛ̃famɑ̃, -ɑ̃t] ADJ libellous, defamatory

infâme [ɛ̃fɑm] ADJ vile

infamie [ɛ̃fami] NF infamy

infanterie [ɛ̃fɑ̃tʀi] NF infantry

infanticide [ɛ̃fɑ̃tisid] NMF child-murderer/ -murderess ▸ NM (*meurtre*) infanticide

infantile [ɛ̃fɑ̃til] ADJ (*Méd*) infantile, child *cpd*; (*péj: ton, réaction*) infantile, childish

infantilisation [ɛ̃fɑ̃tilizasjɔ̃] NF infantilization

infantiliser [ɛ̃fɑ̃tilize] VT to infantilize

infantilisme [ɛ̃fɑ̃tilism] NM infantilism

infarctus [ɛ̃faʀktys] NM: ~ **(du myocarde)** coronary (thrombosis)

infatigable [ɛ̃fatigabl] ADJ tireless, indefatigable

infatigablement [ɛ̃fatigabləmɑ̃] ADV tirelessly, indefatigably

infatué, e [ɛ̃fatɥe] ADJ conceited; **~ de** full of

infécond, e [ɛ̃fekɔ̃, -ɔ̃d] ADJ infertile, barren

infect, e [ɛ̃fɛkt] ADJ revolting; (*repas, vin*) revolting, foul; (*personne*) obnoxious; (*temps*) foul

infecter [ɛ̃fɛkte] /1/ VT (*atmosphère, eau*) to contaminate; (*Méd*) to infect ■ **s'infecter** VPR to become infected ou septic

infectieux, -euse [ɛ̃fɛksjø, -øz] ADJ infectious

infection [ɛ̃fɛksjɔ̃] NF infection; (*puanteur*) stench

inféodé, e [ɛ̃feɔde] ADJ: **être ~ à** to be the vassal of

inféoder [ɛ̃feɔde] /1/: **s'inféoder à** VPR to pledge allegiance to

inférer [ɛ̃feʀe] /6/ VT: **~ qch de** to infer sth from

inférieur, e [ɛ̃feʀjœʀ] ADJ lower; (*en qualité, intelligence*) inferior; **~ à** (*somme, quantité*) less ou smaller than; (*moins bon que*) inferior to; (*tâche: pas à la hauteur de*) unequal to ▶ NM/F inferior

infériorité [ɛ̃feʀjɔʀite] NF inferiority; **~ en nombre** inferiority in numbers

infernal, e, -aux [ɛ̃fɛʀnal, -o] ADJ (*insupportable: chaleur, rythme*) infernal; (: *enfant*) horrid; (*méchanceté, complot*) diabolical

infester [ɛ̃fɛste] /1/ VT to infest; **infesté de moustiques** infested with mosquitoes, mosquito-ridden

infichu, e [ɛ̃fiʃy] ADJ (*fam*): **être ~ de faire qch** to be utterly incapable of doing sth

infidèle [ɛ̃fidɛl] ADJ unfaithful; (*Rel*) infidel

infidélité [ɛ̃fidelite] NF unfaithfulness *no pl*

infiltration [ɛ̃filtʀasjɔ̃] NF infiltration

infiltrer [ɛ̃filtʀe] /1/: **s'infiltrer** VPR: **s'~ dans** to penetrate into; (*liquide*) to seep into; (*fig: noyauter*) to infiltrate

infime [ɛ̃fim] ADJ minute, tiny; (*inférieur*) lowly

infini, e [ɛ̃fini] ADJ infinite ▶ NM infinity; **à l'~** (*Math*) to infinity; (*discourir*) ad infinitum, endlessly; (*agrandir, varier*) infinitely; (*à perte de vue*) endlessly (into the distance)

infiniment [ɛ̃finimɑ̃] ADV infinitely; **~ grand/petit** (*Math*) infinitely great/infinitesimal

infinité [ɛ̃finite] NF: **une ~ de** an infinite number of

infinitésimal, e, -aux [ɛ̃finitezimal, -o] ADJ infinitesimal

infinitif, -ive [ɛ̃finitif, -iv] ADJ, NM infinitive

infirme [ɛ̃fiʀm] ADJ disabled ▶ NMF person with a disability; **~ de guerre** person disabled during the war; **~ du travail** industrially disabled person

infirmer [ɛ̃fiʀme] /1/ VT to invalidate

infirmerie [ɛ̃fiʀməʀi] NF sick bay

★**infirmier, -ière** [ɛ̃fiʀmje, -jɛʀ] NM/F nurse; **infirmière chef** sister; **infirmière diplômée** registered nurse; **infirmière visiteuse** visiting nurse, ≈ district nurse (BRIT) ▶ ADJ: **élève ~** student nurse

infirmité [ɛ̃fiʀmite] NF disability

inflammable [ɛ̃flamabl] ADJ (in)flammable

inflammation [ɛ̃flamasjɔ̃] NF inflammation

inflammatoire [ɛ̃flamatwaʀ] ADJ (*Méd*) inflammatory

inflation [ɛ̃flasjɔ̃] NF inflation; **~ rampante/galopante** creeping/galloping inflation

inflationniste [ɛ̃flasjɔnist] ADJ inflationist

infléchir [ɛ̃fleʃiʀ] /2/ VT (*fig: politique*) to reorientate, redirect ■ **s'infléchir** VPR (*poutre, tringle*) to bend, sag

inflexibilité [ɛ̃flɛksibilite] NF inflexibility

inflexible [ɛ̃flɛksibl] ADJ inflexible

inflexion [ɛ̃flɛksjɔ̃] NF inflexion; **~ de la tête** slight nod (of the head)

infliger [ɛ̃fliʒe] /3/ VT: **~ qch (à qn)** to inflict sth (on sb); (*amende, sanction*) to impose sth (on sb)

influençable [ɛ̃flyɑ̃sabl] ADJ easily influenced

influence [ɛ̃flyɑ̃s] NF influence; (*d'un médicament*) effect

influencer [ɛ̃flyɑ̃se] /3/ VT to influence

influenceur [ɛ̃flyɑ̃sœʀ] NM influencer

influent, e [ɛ̃flyɑ̃, -ɑ̃t] ADJ influential

influer [ɛ̃flye] /1/: **~ sur** VT to have an influence upon

influx [ɛ̃fly] NM: **~ nerveux** (nervous) impulse

info [ɛ̃fo] NF (*renseignement*) piece of information, info *no pl*; (*Presse, TV: nouvelle*) news item; **une ~ de dernière minute** a last-minute news item ■ **infos** NFPL (*TV*) news *sg*; **tu as écouté les infos ?** did you listen to the news?

infobulle [ɛ̃fobyl] NF (*Inform*) help bubble

infographie [ɛ̃fɔgʀafi] NF computer graphics *sg*

infographiste [ɛ̃fɔgʀafist] NMF computer graphics artist, computer graphics designer

infondé, e [ɛ̃fɔ̃de] ADJ (*accusation, critique*) unfounded

informateur, -trice [ɛ̃fɔʀmatœʀ, -tʀis] NM/F informant

★**informaticien, ne** [ɛ̃fɔʀmatisjɛ̃, -ɛn] NM/F computer scientist

informatif, -ive [ɛ̃fɔʀmatif, -iv] ADJ informative

information [ɛ̃fɔʀmasjɔ̃] NF (*renseignement*) piece of information; (*Presse, TV: nouvelle*) item of news; (*diffusion de renseignements, Inform*) information; (*Jur*) inquiry, investigation; **voyage d'~** fact-finding trip; **agence d'~** news agency; **journal d'~** quality (BRIT) ou serious newspaper ■ **informations** NFPL (*TV, Radio*) news *sg*

> **Information** est indénombrable, c'est-à-dire qu'il ne peut pas désigner un seul renseignement. Pour traduire *une information*, il faut dire **a piece of information**. Notez qu'en anglais, **information** ne prend jamais de **-s** et s'emploie avec un verbe au singulier.
> *Ces informations sont très intéressantes.* **This information is very interesting.**
> *Ils m'ont fourni une information précieuse.* **They gave me a valuable piece of information.**

★**informatique** [ɛ̃fɔʀmatik] NF (*technique*) data processing; (*science*) computer science; **~ en nuage** cloud computing ▶ ADJ computer *cpd*

informatisation [ɛ̃fɔʀmatizasjɔ̃] NF computerization

informatiser [ɛ̃fɔʀmatize] /1/ VT to computerize

informe [ɛ̃fɔʀm] ADJ shapeless

informé, e [ɛ̃fɔʀme] ADJ: **jusqu'à plus ample ~** until further information is available

informel, le [ɛ̃fɔʀmɛl] ADJ informal

informer [ɛ̃fɔʀme] /1/ VT: **~ qn (de)** to inform sb (of) ▶ VI (*Jur*): **~ contre qn/sur qch** to initiate inquiries about sb/sth ■ **s'informer (sur)** VPR to inform o.s. (about); **s'~ (de qch/si)** to inquire *ou* find out (about sth/whether *ou* if)

informulé, e [ɛ̃fɔʀmyle] ADJ unformulated

infortune [ɛ̃fɔʀtyn] NF misfortune

infortuné, e [ɛ̃fɔʀtyne] ADJ wretched, unfortunate

infos [ɛ̃fo] NFPL (= *informations*) news

infoutu, e [ɛ̃futy] ADJ (*fam*): **être ~ de faire qch** to be utterly incapable of doing sth

infraction [ɛ̃fʀaksjɔ̃] NF offence; **~ à** violation *ou* breach of; **être en ~** to be in breach of the law

infranchissable [ɛ̃fʀɑ̃ʃisabl] ADJ impassable; (*fig*) insuperable

infrarouge [ɛ̃fʀaʀuʒ] ADJ, NM infrared

infrason [ɛ̃fʀasɔ̃] NM infrasonic vibration

infrastructure [ɛ̃fʀastʀyktyʀ] NF (*d'une route etc*) substructure; (*Aviat, Mil*) ground installations *pl*; (*Écon: touristique etc*) facilities *pl*

infréquentable [ɛ̃fʀekɑ̃tabl] ADJ not to be associated with

infroissable [ɛ̃fʀwasabl] ADJ crease-resistant

infructueux, -euse [ɛ̃fʀyktɥø, -øz] ADJ fruitless, unfruitful

infus, e [ɛ̃fy, -yz] ADJ: **avoir la science infuse** to have innate knowledge

infuser [ɛ̃fyze] /1/ VT (*aussi*: **faire infuser**: *thé*) to brew; (: *tisane*) to infuse ▶ VI to brew; to infuse; **laisser ~** (to leave) to brew

infusion [ɛ̃fyzjɔ̃] NF (*tisane*) infusion, herb tea

ingambe [ɛ̃gɑ̃b] ADJ spry, nimble

ingénier [ɛ̃ʒenje] /7/: **s'ingénier** VPR: **s'~ à faire** to strive to do

ingénierie [ɛ̃ʒeniʀi] NF engineering

ingénieur [ɛ̃ʒenjœʀ] NM engineer; **~ agronome/ chimiste** agricultural/chemical engineer; **~ conseil** consulting engineer; **~ du son** sound engineer

ingénieusement [ɛ̃ʒenjøzmɑ̃] ADV ingeniously

ingénieux, -euse [ɛ̃ʒenjø, -øz] ADJ ingenious, clever

ingéniosité [ɛ̃ʒenjozite] NF ingenuity

ingénu, e [ɛ̃ʒeny] ADJ ingenuous, artless ▶ NF (*Théât*) ingénue

ingénuité [ɛ̃ʒenɥite] NF ingenuousness

ingénument [ɛ̃ʒenymɑ̃] ADV ingenuously

ingérable [ɛ̃ʒeʀabl] ADJ (*situation, crise*) unmanageable

ingérence [ɛ̃ʒeʀɑ̃s] NF interference

ingérer [ɛ̃ʒeʀe] /6/: **s'ingérer** VPR: **s'~ dans** to interfere in ▶ VT to ingest; «**ne pas ingérer**» "do not swallow"

ingestion [ɛ̃ʒestjɔ̃] NF ingestion

ingouvernable [ɛ̃guvɛʀnabl] ADJ ungovernable

ingrat, e [ɛ̃gʀa, -at] ADJ (*personne*) ungrateful; (*sol*) poor; (*travail, sujet*) arid, thankless; (*visage*) unprepossessing

ingratitude [ɛ̃gʀatityd] NF ingratitude

ingrédient [ɛ̃gʀedjɑ̃] NM ingredient

inguérissable [ɛ̃geʀisabl] ADJ incurable

inguinal, e [ɛ̃gɥinal] ADJ inguinal

ingurgiter [ɛ̃gyʀʒite] /1/ VT to swallow; **faire ~ qch à qn** to make sb swallow sth; (*fig: connaissances*) to force sth into sb

inhabile [inabil] ADJ clumsy; (*fig*) inept

inhabitable [inabitabl] ADJ uninhabitable

inhabité, e [inabite] ADJ (*régions*) uninhabited; (*maison*) unoccupied

inhabituel, le [inabitɥɛl] ADJ unusual

inhalateur [inalatœʀ] NM inhaler; **~ d'oxygène** oxygen mask

inhalation [inalasjɔ̃] NF (*Méd*) inhalation; **faire des inhalations** to use an inhalation bath

inhaler [inale] /1/ VT to inhale

inhérent, e [ineʀɑ̃, -ɑ̃t] ADJ: **~ à** inherent in

inhibé, e [inibe] ADJ inhibited

inhiber [inibe] /1/ VT to inhibit

inhibiteur [inibitœʀ] NM inhibitor

inhibition [inibisjɔ̃] NF inhibition

inhospitalier, -ière [inɔspitalje, -jɛʀ] ADJ inhospitable

inhumain, e [inymɛ̃, -ɛn] ADJ inhuman

inhumation [inymasjɔ̃] NF interment, burial

inhumer [inyme] /1/ VT to inter, bury

inimaginable [inimaʒinabl] ADJ unimaginable

inimitable [inimitabl] ADJ inimitable

inimitié [inimitje] NF enmity

ininflammable [inɛ̃flamabl] ADJ non-flammable

inintelligent, e [inɛ̃teliʒɑ̃, -ɑ̃t] ADJ unintelligent

inintelligible [inɛ̃teliʒibl] ADJ unintelligible

inintelligiblement [inɛ̃teliʒibləmɑ̃] ADV unintelligibly

inintéressant, e [inɛ̃teʀesɑ̃, -ɑ̃t] ADJ uninteresting

ininterrompu, e [inɛ̃teʀɔ̃py] ADJ (*file, série*) unbroken; (*flot, vacarme*) uninterrupted, non-stop; (*effort*) unremitting, continuous; (*suite, ligne*) unbroken

inique [inik] ADJ iniquitous

iniquité [inikite] NF iniquity

initial, e, -aux [inisjal, -o] ADJ, NF initial ■ **initiales** NFPL initials

initialement [inisjalmɑ̃] ADV initially

initialisation [inisjalisasjɔ̃] NF initialization

initialiser [inisjalize] /1/ VT to initialize

initiateur, -trice [inisjatœʀ, -tʀis] NM/F initiator; (*d'une mode, technique*) innovator, pioneer

initiation [inisjasjɔ̃] NF initiation; **~ à** introduction to

initiatique [inisjatik] ADJ (*rites, épreuves*) initiatory

initiative [inisjativ] NF initiative; **prendre l'~ de qch/de faire** to take the initiative for sth/of doing; **avoir de l'~** to have initiative, show enterprise; **esprit/qualités d'~** spirit/qualities of initiative; **à** *ou* **sur l'~ de qn** on sb's initiative; **de sa propre ~** on one's own initiative

initié, e [inisje] ADJ initiated ▶ NM/F initiate

initier [inisje] /**7**/ VT to initiate; **~ qn à** to initiate sb into; (faire découvrir: art, jeu) to introduce sb to ∎ **s'initier à** VPR (métier, profession, technique) to become initiated into

injectable [ɛ̃ʒɛktabl] ADJ injectable

injecté, e [ɛ̃ʒɛkte] ADJ: **yeux injectés de sang** bloodshot eyes

injecter [ɛ̃ʒɛkte] /**1**/ VT to inject

injection [ɛ̃ʒɛksjɔ̃] NF injection; **à ~** (Auto) fuel injection cpd

injoignable [ɛ̃ʒwaɲabl] ADJ: **il est ~** he can't be reached, he can't be reached on the phone

injonction [ɛ̃ʒɔ̃ksjɔ̃] NF injunction, order; **~ de payer** (Jur) order to pay

injouable [ɛ̃ʒwabl] ADJ unplayable

injure [ɛ̃ʒyR] NF insult, abuse no pl

injurier [ɛ̃ʒyRje] /**7**/ VT to insult, abuse

injurieux, -euse [ɛ̃ʒyRjø, -øz] ADJ abusive, insulting

injuste [ɛ̃ʒyst] ADJ unjust, unfair

injustement [ɛ̃ʒystəmã] ADV unjustly, unfairly

injustice [ɛ̃ʒystis] NF injustice

injustifiable [ɛ̃ʒystifjabl] ADJ unjustifiable

injustifié, e [ɛ̃ʒystifje] ADJ unjustified, unwarranted

inlassable [ɛ̃lasabl] ADJ tireless, indefatigable

inlassablement [ɛ̃lasabləmã] ADV tirelessly

inné, e [ine] ADJ innate, inborn

innocemment [inɔsamã] ADV innocently

innocence [inɔsãs] NF innocence

innocent, e [inɔsã, -ãt] ADJ innocent ▸ NM/F innocent person; **faire l'~** to play ou come the innocent

innocenter [inɔsãte] /**1**/ VT to clear, prove innocent

innocuité [inɔkɥite] NF innocuousness

innombrable [inɔ̃bRabl] ADJ innumerable

innommable [inɔmabl] ADJ unspeakable

innovant, e [inɔvã, -ãt] ADJ (produit, technologie) innovative

innovateur, -trice [inɔvatœR, -tRis] ADJ innovatory

innovation [inɔvasjɔ̃] NF innovation

innover [inɔve] /**1**/ VI: **~ en matière de** to break new ground in the field of

inobservance [inɔpsɛRvãs] NF non-observance

inobservation [inɔpsɛRvasjɔ̃] NF non-observation, inobservance

inoccupé, e [inɔkype] ADJ unoccupied

inoculation [inɔkylasjɔ̃] NF inoculation

inoculer [inɔkyle] /**1**/ VT: **~ qch à qn** (volontairement) to inoculate sb with sth; (accidentellement) to infect sb with sth; **~ qn contre** to inoculate sb against

inodore [inɔdɔR] ADJ (gaz) odourless; (fleur) scentless

inoffensif, -ive [inɔfãsif, -iv] ADJ harmless, innocuous

inondable [inɔ̃dabl] ADJ (zone) liable to flooding

★**inondation** [inɔ̃dasjɔ̃] NF flooding no pl; (torrent, eau) flood

inondé, e [inɔ̃de] ADJ (terres, zone) flooded

inonder [inɔ̃de] /**1**/ VT to flood; (fig) to inundate, overrun; **~ de** (fig) to flood ou swamp with

inopérable [inɔpeRabl] ADJ inoperable

inopérant, e [inɔpeRã, -ãt] ADJ inoperative, ineffective

inopiné, e [inɔpine] ADJ unexpected, sudden

inopinément [inɔpinemã] ADV unexpectedly

inopportun, e [inɔpɔRtœ̃, -yn] ADJ ill-timed, untimely; inappropriate; (moment) inopportune

inopportunément [inɔpɔRtynemã] ADV at an inopportune moment

inorganisation [inɔRganizasjɔ̃] NF lack of organization

inorganisé, e [inɔRganize] ADJ (travailleurs) non-organized

inoubliable [inublijabl] ADJ unforgettable

inouï, e [inwi] ADJ unheard-of, extraordinary

inox [inɔks] ADJ INV, NM (= inoxydable) stainless (steel)

inoxydable [inɔksidabl] ADJ stainless; (couverts) stainless steel cpd

inqualifiable [ɛ̃kalifjabl] ADJ unspeakable

★**inquiet, -ète** [ɛ̃kjɛ, -ɛt] ADJ (par nature) anxious; (momentanément) worried; **~ de qch/au sujet de qn** worried about sth/sb

inquiétant, e [ɛ̃kjetã, -ãt] ADJ worrying, disturbing

inquiéter [ɛ̃kjete] /**6**/ VT to worry, disturb; (harceler) to harass ∎ **s'inquiéter** VPR to worry, become anxious; **s'~ de** to worry about; (s'enquérir de) to inquire about

inquiétude [ɛ̃kjetyd] NF anxiety; **donner de l'~ ou des inquiétudes à** to worry; **avoir de l'~ ou des inquiétudes au sujet de** to feel anxious ou worried about

inquisiteur, -trice [ɛ̃kizitœR, -tRis] ADJ (regards, questions) inquisitive, prying

inquisition [ɛ̃kizisjɔ̃] NF inquisition

INRA [inRa] SIGLE M = **Institut national de la recherche agronomique**

inracontable [ɛ̃Rakɔ̃tabl] ADJ (trop osé) unrepeatable; (trop compliqué): **l'histoire est ~** the story is too complicated to relate

inrayable [ɛ̃Rejabl] ADJ (CD, DVD) scratch-proof

insaisissable [ɛ̃sezisabl] ADJ (fugitif, ennemi) elusive; (différence, nuance) imperceptible

insalubre [ɛ̃salybR] ADJ unhealthy, insalubrious

insalubrité [ɛ̃salybRite] NF unhealthiness, insalubrity

insanité [ɛ̃sanite] NF madness no pl, insanity no pl

insatiable [ɛ̃sasjabl] ADJ insatiable

insatisfaction [ɛ̃satisfaksjɔ̃] NF dissatisfaction

insatisfait, e [ɛ̃satisfɛ, -ɛt] ADJ (non comblé) unsatisfied; (: passion, envie) unfulfilled; (mécontent) dissatisfied

inscriptible [ɛ̃skRiptibl] ADJ (CD, DVD) writable

inscription [ɛ̃skRipsjɔ̃] NF (sur un mur, écriteau etc) inscription; (à une institution: voir s'inscrire) enrolment; registration

inscrire [ɛ̃skRiR] /**39**/ VT (marquer: sur son calepin etc) to note ou write down; (: sur un mur, une affiche etc) to write; (: *dans la pierre, le métal*) to inscribe; (*mettre sur une liste, un budget etc*) to put down; (*enrôler: soldat*) to enlist; **~ qn à** (*club, école etc*) to enrol sb at ■ **s'inscrire** VPR (*pour une excursion etc*) to put one's name down; **s'~ (à)** (*club, parti*) to join; (*université*) to register *ou* enrol (at); (*examen, concours*) to register *ou* enter (for); **s'~ dans** (*se situer: négociations etc*) to come within the scope of; **s'~ en faux contre** to deny (strongly); (*Jur*) to challenge

inscrit, e [ɛ̃skʀi, -it] PP *de* **inscrire** ▶ ADJ (*étudiant, électeur etc*) registered

insécable [ɛ̃sekabl] ADJ (*Inform*) indivisible; **espace ~** hard space

★**insecte** [ɛ̃sɛkt] NM insect

insecticide [ɛ̃sɛktisid] NM insecticide

insectivore [ɛ̃sɛktivɔʀ] NM insectivore ▶ ADJ insectivorous

insécurité [ɛ̃sekyʀite] NF insecurity, lack of security

INSEE [inse] SIGLE M (= *Institut national de la statistique et des études économiques*) national institute of statistical and economic information

insémination [ɛ̃seminasjɔ̃] NF insemination

insensé, e [ɛ̃sɑ̃se] ADJ insane, mad

insensibiliser [ɛ̃sɑ̃sibilize] /1/ VT to anaesthetize; (*à une allergie*) to desensitize; **~ à qch** (*fig*) to cause to become insensitive to sth

insensibilité [ɛ̃sɑ̃sibilite] NF insensitivity

insensible [ɛ̃sɑ̃sibl] ADJ (*nerf, membre*) numb; (*dur, indifférent*) insensitive; (*imperceptible*) imperceptible

insensiblement [ɛ̃sɑ̃sibləmɑ̃] ADV (*doucement, peu à peu*) imperceptibly

inséparable [ɛ̃sepaʀabl] ADJ: **~ (de)** inseparable (from) ▶ NMPL: **inséparables** (*oiseaux*) lovebirds

insérer [ɛ̃seʀe] /6/ VT to insert ■ **s'insérer dans** VPR to fit into; (*fig*) to come within

INSERM [insɛʀm] SIGLE M (= *Institut national de la santé et de la recherche médicale*) national institute for medical research

insert [ɛ̃sɛʀ] NM enclosed fireplace burning solid fuel

insertion [ɛ̃sɛʀsjɔ̃] NF (*d'une personne*) integration

insidieusement [ɛ̃sidjøzmɑ̃] ADV insidiously

insidieux, -euse [ɛ̃sidjø, -øz] ADJ insidious

insigne [ɛ̃siɲ] NM (*d'un parti, club*) badge ▶ ADJ distinguished ■ **insignes** NMPL (*d'une fonction*) insignia *pl*

insignifiance [ɛ̃siɲifjɑ̃s] NF insignificance

insignifiant, e [ɛ̃siɲifjɑ̃, -ɑ̃t] ADJ insignificant; (*somme, affaire, détail*) trivial, insignificant

insinuant, e [ɛ̃sinɥɑ̃, -ɑ̃t] ADJ ingratiating

insinuation [ɛ̃sinɥasjɔ̃] NF innuendo, insinuation

insinuer [ɛ̃sinɥe] /1/ VT to insinuate, imply ■ **s'insinuer dans** VPR to seep into; (*fig*) to worm one's way into, creep into

insipide [ɛ̃sipid] ADJ insipid

insistance [ɛ̃sistɑ̃s] NF insistence; **avec ~** insistently

insistant, e [ɛ̃sistɑ̃, -ɑ̃t] ADJ insistent

insister [ɛ̃siste] /1/ VI to insist; (*s'obstiner*) to keep on; **~ sur** (*détail, note*) to stress; **~ pour qch/pour faire qch** to be insistent about sth/about doing sth

insociable [ɛ̃sɔsjabl] ADJ unsociable

★**insolation** [ɛ̃sɔlasjɔ̃] NF (*Méd*) sunstroke *no pl*; (*ensoleillement*) period of sunshine

insolence [ɛ̃sɔlɑ̃s] NF insolence *no pl*; **avec ~** insolently

insolent, e [ɛ̃sɔlɑ̃, -ɑ̃t] ADJ insolent

insolite [ɛ̃sɔlit] ADJ strange, unusual

insoluble [ɛ̃sɔlybl] ADJ insoluble

insolvabilité [ɛ̃sɔlvabilite] NF insolvency

insolvable [ɛ̃sɔlvabl] ADJ insolvent

insomniaque [ɛ̃sɔmnjak] ADJ, NMF insomniac

insomnie [ɛ̃sɔmni] NF insomnia *no pl*, sleeplessness *no pl*; **avoir des insomnies** to sleep badly, suffer from insomnia

insondable [ɛ̃sɔ̃dabl] ADJ unfathomable

insonore [ɛ̃sɔnɔʀ] ADJ soundproof

insonorisation [ɛ̃sɔnɔʀizasjɔ̃] NF soundproofing

insonoriser [ɛ̃sɔnɔʀize] /1/ VT to soundproof

insouciance [ɛ̃susjɑ̃s] NF carefree attitude; heedless attitude

insouciant, e [ɛ̃susjɑ̃, -ɑ̃t] ADJ carefree; (*imprévoyant*) heedless; **~ du danger** heedless of (the) danger

insoumis, e [ɛ̃sumi, -iz] ADJ (*caractère, enfant*) rebellious, refractory; (*contrée, tribu*) unsubdued; (*Mil: soldat*) absent without leave ▶ NM (*Mil: soldat*) absentee

insoumission [ɛ̃sumisjɔ̃] NF rebelliousness; (*Mil*) absence without leave

insoupçonnable [ɛ̃supsɔnabl] ADJ unsuspected; (*personne*) above suspicion

insoupçonné, e [ɛ̃supsɔne] ADJ unsuspected

insoutenable [ɛ̃sut(ə)nabl] ADJ (*argument*) untenable; (*chaleur*) unbearable

inspecter [ɛ̃spɛkte] /1/ VT to inspect

inspecteur, -trice [ɛ̃spɛktœʀ, -tʀis] NM/F inspector; (*des assurances*) assessor; **~ d'Académie** (regional) director of education; **~ (de l'enseignement) primaire** primary school inspector; **~ des finances** ≈ tax inspector (BRIT); ≈ Internal Revenue Service agent (US); **~ (de police)** (police) inspector

inspection [ɛ̃spɛksjɔ̃] NF inspection

inspirateur, -trice [ɛ̃spiʀatœʀ, -tʀis] NM/F (*instigateur*) instigator; (*animateur*) inspirer

inspiration [ɛ̃spiʀasjɔ̃] NF inspiration; breathing in *no pl*; (*idée*) flash of inspiration, brainwave; **sous l'~ de** prompted by

inspiré, e [ɛ̃spiʀe] ADJ: **être bien/mal ~ de faire qch** to be well-advised/ill-advised to do sth

inspirer [ɛ̃spiʀe] /1/ VT (*gén*) to inspire; **~ qch à qn** (*œuvre, projet, action*) to inspire sb with sth; (*dégoût, crainte, horreur*) to fill sb with sth; **ça ne m'inspire pas** I'm not keen on the idea ▶ VI (*aspirer*) to breathe in ■ **s'inspirer de** VPR (*artiste*) to draw one's inspiration from; (*tableau*) to be inspired by

instabilité [ɛ̃stabilite] NF instability

instable [ɛ̃stabl] ADJ (*meuble, équilibre*) unsteady; (*population, temps*) unsettled; (*paix, régime, caractère*) unstable

installateur [ɛ̃stalatœʀ] NM fitter

installation [ɛ̃stalasjɔ̃] NF (*mise en place*) installation; putting in *ou* up; fitting out; settling in; (*appareils etc*) fittings *pl*, installations *pl*; **l'~ électrique** the wiring ■ **installations** NFPL installations; (*industrielles*) plant *sg*; (*de sport, dans un camping*) facilities

installé, e [ɛ̃stale] ADJ: **bien/mal ~** well/poorly equipped; (*personne*) well/not very well set up *ou* organized

★**installer** [ɛ̃stale] /1/ VT (*asseoir, coucher*) to settle (down); (*placer*) to put, place; (*meuble*) to put in; (*rideau, étagère, tente*) to put up; (*gaz, électricité etc*) to put in, install; (*appartement*) to fit out; **~ qn** (*loger*) to get sb settled, install sb; **~ une salle de bains dans une pièce** to fit out a room with a bathroom suite ■ **s'installer** VPR (*s'établir: artisan, dentiste etc*) to set o.s. up; (*emménager*) to settle in; (*sur un siège, à un emplacement*) to settle (down); (*fig: maladie, grève*) to take a firm hold *ou* grip; **s'~ à l'hôtel/chez qn** to move into a hotel/in with sb

installeur [ɛ̃stalœʁ] NM (*Inform*) installer

instamment [ɛ̃stamɑ̃] ADV urgently

instance [ɛ̃stɑ̃s] NF (*Jur: procédure*) (legal) proceedings *pl*; (*Admin: autorité*) authority; **affaire en ~** matter pending; **courrier en ~** mail ready for posting; **être en ~ de divorce** to be awaiting a divorce; **train en ~ de départ** train on the point of departure; **tribunal de première instance**; **en seconde ~** on appeal ■ **instances** NFPL (*prières*) entreaties

★**instant** [ɛ̃stɑ̃] NM moment, instant; **dans un ~** in a moment; **à l'~** this instant; **je l'ai vu à l'~** I've just this minute seen him, I saw him a moment ago; **à l'~ (même)** at the (very) moment that *ou* when, (just) as; **à chaque ~**, **à tout ~** at any moment; constantly; **pour l'~** for the moment, for the time being; **par instants** at times; **de tous les instants** perpetual; **dès l'~ où** *ou* **que ...** from the moment when ..., since that moment when ...

instantané, e [ɛ̃stɑ̃tane] ADJ (*lait, café*) instant; (*explosion, mort*) instantaneous ▶ NM snapshot

instantanément [ɛ̃stɑ̃tanemɑ̃] ADV instantaneously

instar [ɛ̃staʁ]: **à l'~ de** *prép* following the example of, like

instauration [ɛ̃stɔʁasjɔ̃] NF (*de régime, démocratie*) establishment

instaurer [ɛ̃stɔʁe] /1/ VT to institute; (*démocratie, régime*) to establish; (*couvre-feu*) to impose ■ **s'instaurer** VPR to set o.s. up; (*collaboration, paix*) to be established; (*doute*) to set in

instigateur, -trice [ɛ̃stigatœʁ, -tʁis] NM/F instigator

instigation [ɛ̃stigasjɔ̃] NF: **à l'~ de qn** at sb's instigation

instiller [ɛ̃stile] /1/ VT to instil, apply

instinct [ɛ̃stɛ̃] NM instinct; **d'~** (*spontanément*) instinctively; **~ grégaire** herd instinct; **~ de conservation** instinct of self-preservation

instinctif, -ive [ɛ̃stɛ̃ktif, -iv] ADJ instinctive

instinctivement [ɛ̃stɛ̃ktivmɑ̃] ADV instinctively

instit [ɛ̃stit] NMF (*fam*) (primary school) teacher

instituer [ɛ̃stitɥe] /1/ VT to establish, institute ■ **s'instituer** VPR: **s'~ défenseur d'une cause** to set o.s. up as defender of a cause

institut [ɛ̃stity] NM institute; **~ de beauté** beauty salon; **~ médico-légal** mortuary; **I~ universitaire de technologie** ≈ Institute of technology

★**instituteur, -trice** [ɛ̃stitytœʁ, -tʁis] NM/F (primary (BRIT) *ou* grade (US) school) teacher

institution [ɛ̃stitysjɔ̃] NF institution; (*collège*) private school ■ **institutions** NFPL (*structures politiques et sociales*) institutions

institutionnaliser [ɛ̃stitysjɔnalize] /1/ VT to institutionalize

institutionnel, le [ɛ̃stitysjɔnɛl] ADJ institutional

instructeur, -trice [ɛ̃stʁyktœʁ, -tʁis] ADJ (*Mil*): **sergent ~** drill sergeant; (*Jur*): **juge ~** examining (BRIT) *ou* committing (US) magistrate ▶ NM/F instructor

instructif, -ive [ɛ̃stʁyktif, -iv] ADJ instructive

instruction [ɛ̃stʁyksjɔ̃] NF (*enseignement, savoir*) education; (*Jur*) (preliminary) investigation and hearing; (*directive*) instruction; (*Admin: document*) directive; **~ civique** civics *sg*; **~ primaire/publique** primary/public education; **~ religieuse** religious instruction; **~ professionnelle** vocational training ■ **instructions** NFPL instructions; (*mode d'emploi*) directions, instructions

instruire [ɛ̃stʁɥiʁ] /38/ VT (*élèves*) to teach; (*recrues*) to train; (*Jur: affaire*) to conduct the investigation for; **~ qn de qch** (*informer*) to inform *ou* advise sb of sth ■ **s'instruire** VPR to educate o.s.; **s'~ auprès de qn de qch** (*s'informer*) to find sth out from sb ▶ VI: **~ contre qn** (*Jur*) to investigate sb

instruit, e [ɛ̃stʁɥi, -it] PP *de* **instruire** ▶ ADJ educated

★**instrument** [ɛ̃stʁymɑ̃] NM instrument; **~ à cordes/vent** stringed/wind instrument; **~ de mesure** measuring instrument; **~ de musique** musical instrument; **~ de travail** (working) tool

instrumental, e, -aux [ɛ̃stʁymɑ̃tal, -o] ADJ instrumental

instrumentation [ɛ̃stʁymɑ̃tasjɔ̃] NF instrumentation

instrumentiste [ɛ̃stʁymɑ̃tist] NMF instrumentalist

insu [ɛ̃sy] NM: **à l'~ de qn** without sb knowing

insubmersible [ɛ̃sybmɛʁsibl] ADJ unsinkable

insubordination [ɛ̃sybɔʁdinasjɔ̃] NF rebelliousness; (*Mil*) insubordination

insubordonné, e [ɛ̃sybɔʁdɔne] ADJ insubordinate

insuccès [ɛ̃syksɛ] NM failure

insuffisamment [ɛ̃syfizamɑ̃] ADV insufficiently

insuffisance [ɛ̃syfizɑ̃s] NF insufficiency; inadequacy; **~ cardiaque** cardiac insufficiency *no pl*; **~ hépatique** liver deficiency ■ **insuffisances** NFPL (*lacunes*) inadequacies

insuffisant, e [ɛ̃syfizɑ̃, -ɑ̃t] ADJ (*en quantité*) insufficient; (*en qualité: élève, travail*) inadequate; (*sur une copie*) poor

insuffler [ɛ̃syfle] /1/ VT: **~ qch dans** to blow sth into; **~ qch à qn** to inspire sb with sth

insulaire [ɛ̃sylɛʁ] ADJ island *cpd*; (*attitude*) insular

insularité [ɛ̃sylaʁite] NF insularity

insuline [ɛ̃sylin] NF insulin

insulinodépendant, e [ɛ̃sylinɔdepɑ̃dɑ̃, -ɑ̃t] ADJ (*diabète, diabétique*) insulin-dependent

insultant, e [ɛ̃syltɑ̃, -ɑ̃t] ADJ insulting

insulte [ɛ̃sylt] NF insult

★**insulter** [ɛ̃sylte] /1/ VT to insult

★**insupportable** [ɛ̃sypɔʀtabl] ADJ unbearable

insupporter [ɛ̃sypɔʀte] VT: **il m'insupporte** I find him intolerable

insurgé, e [ɛ̃syʀʒe] ADJ, NM/F insurgent, rebel

insurger [ɛ̃syʀʒe] /3/: **s'insurger** VPR: **s'~ (contre)** to rise up *ou* rebel (against)

insurmontable [ɛ̃syʀmɔ̃tabl] ADJ (*difficulté*) insuperable; (*aversion*) unconquerable

insurpassable [ɛ̃syʀpasabl] ADJ unsurpassable, unsurpassed

insurrection [ɛ̃syʀɛksjɔ̃] NF insurrection, revolt

insurrectionnel, le [ɛ̃syʀɛksjɔnɛl] ADJ insurrectionary

intact, e [ɛ̃takt] ADJ intact

intangible [ɛ̃tɑ̃ʒibl] ADJ intangible; (*principe*) inviolable

intarissable [ɛ̃taʀisabl] ADJ inexhaustible

intégral, e, -aux [ɛ̃tegʀal, -o] ADJ complete; **texte ~** unabridged version; **bronzage ~** all-over suntan ▶F (*Math*) integral; (*œuvres complètes*) complete works

intégralement [ɛ̃tegʀalmɑ̃] ADV in full, fully

intégralité [ɛ̃tegʀalite] NF (*d'une somme, d'un revenu*) whole (*ou* full) amount; **dans son ~** in its entirety

intégrant, e [ɛ̃tegʀɑ̃, -ɑ̃t] ADJ: **faire partie intégrante de** to be an integral part of, be part and parcel of

intégration [ɛ̃tegʀasjɔ̃] NF integration

intégrationniste [ɛ̃tegʀasjɔnist] ADJ, NMF integrationist

intègre [ɛ̃tegʀ] ADJ perfectly honest, upright

intégré, e [ɛ̃tegʀe] ADJ: **circuit ~** integrated circuit

intégrer [ɛ̃tegʀe] /6/ VT: **~ qch à** *ou* **dans** to integrate sth into ■ **s'intégrer** VPR: **s'~ à** *ou* **dans** to become integrated into; **bien s'~** to fit in

intégrisme [ɛ̃tegʀism] NM fundamentalism

intégriste [ɛ̃tegʀist] ADJ, NMF fundamentalist

intégrité [ɛ̃tegʀite] NF integrity

intellect [ɛ̃telɛkt] NM intellect

intellectualiser [ɛ̃telɛktɥalize] VT, VI to intellectualize

intellectualisme [ɛ̃telɛktɥalism] NM intellectualism

intellectuel, le [ɛ̃telɛktɥɛl] ADJ, NM/F intellectual; (*péj*) highbrow

intellectuellement [ɛ̃telɛktɥɛlmɑ̃] ADV intellectually

intelligemment [ɛ̃teliʒamɑ̃] ADV intelligently

intelligence [ɛ̃teliʒɑ̃s] NF intelligence; (*compréhension*): **l'~ de** the understanding of; (*complicité*): **regard d'~** glance of complicity, meaningful *ou* knowing look; (*accord*): **vivre en bonne ~ avec qn** to be on good terms with sb; **être d'~** to have an understanding; **~ artificielle** artificial intelligence (A.I.) ■ **intelligences** NFPL (*Mil, fig*) secret contacts

★**intelligent, e** [ɛ̃teliʒɑ̃, -ɑ̃t] ADJ intelligent; (*capable*): **~ en affaires** competent in business

intelligentsia [ɛ̃telidʒɛnsja] NF intelligentsia

intelligible [ɛ̃teliʒibl] ADJ intelligible

intello [ɛ̃telo] ADJ, NMF (*fam*) highbrow

intempérance [ɛ̃tɑ̃peʀɑ̃s] NF overindulgence *no pl*; intemperance *no pl*

intempérant, e [ɛ̃tɑ̃peʀɑ̃, -ɑ̃t] ADJ overindulgent; (*moralement*) intemperate

intempéries [ɛ̃tɑ̃peʀi] NFPL bad weather *sg*

intempestif, -ive [ɛ̃tɑ̃pɛstif, -iv] ADJ untimely

intemporel, le [ɛ̃tɑ̃pɔʀɛl] ADJ (*élégance, vêtement*) timeless

intenable [ɛ̃t(ə)nabl] ADJ unbearable

intendance [ɛ̃tɑ̃dɑ̃s] NF (*Mil*) supply corps; (: *bureau*) supplies office; (*Scol*) bursar's office

intendant, e [ɛ̃tɑ̃dɑ̃, -ɑ̃t] NM/F (*Mil*) quartermaster; (*Scol*) bursar; (*d'une propriété*) steward

intense [ɛ̃tɑ̃s] ADJ intense

intensément [ɛ̃tɑ̃semɑ̃] ADV intensely

intensif, -ive [ɛ̃tɑ̃sif, -iv] ADJ intensive; **cours ~** crash course; **~ en main-d'œuvre** labour-intensive; **~ en capital** capital-intensive

intensification [ɛ̃tɑ̃sifikasjɔ̃] NF intensification

intensifier [ɛ̃tɑ̃sifje] /7/: **s'intensifier** VPR to intensify

intensité [ɛ̃tɑ̃site] NF intensity

intensivement [ɛ̃tɑ̃sivmɑ̃] ADV intensively

intenter [ɛ̃tɑ̃te] /1/ VT: **~ un procès contre** *ou* **à qn** to start proceedings against sb

★**intention** [ɛ̃tɑ̃sjɔ̃] NF intention; (*Jur*) intent; **avoir l'~ de faire** to intend to do, have the intention of doing; **dans l'~ de faire qch** with a view to doing sth; **à l'~ de** *prép* for; (*renseignement*) for the benefit *ou* information of; (*film, ouvrage*) aimed at; **à cette ~** with this aim in view; **sans ~** unintentionally; **faire qch sans mauvaise ~** to do sth without ill intent; **agir dans une bonne ~** to act with good intentions

intentionné, e [ɛ̃tɑ̃sjɔne] ADJ: **bien ~** well-meaning *ou* -intentioned; **mal ~** ill-intentioned

intentionnel, le [ɛ̃tɑ̃sjɔnɛl] ADJ intentional, deliberate

intentionnellement [ɛ̃tɑ̃sjɔnɛlmɑ̃] ADV intentionally, deliberately

inter [ɛ̃tɛʀ] NM (*Tél: interurbain*) long-distance call service; (*Sport*): **~ gauche/droit** inside-left/-right

interactif, -ive [ɛ̃teʀaktif, -iv] ADJ (*aussi Inform*) interactive

interaction [ɛ̃teʀaksjɔ̃] NF interaction

interactivité [ɛ̃teʀaktivite] NF interactivity

interagir [ɛ̃teʀaʒiʀ] VI: **~ avec** to interact with

interbancaire [ɛ̃teʀbɑ̃kɛʀ] ADJ interbank

intercalaire [ɛ̃teʀkalɛʀ] ADJ, NM: (**feuillet**) **~** insert; (**fiche**) **~** divider

intercaler [ɛ̃teʀkale] /1/ VT to insert ■ **s'intercaler entre** VPR to come in between; to slip in between

intercéder [ɛ̃teʀsede] /6/ VI: **~ (pour qn)** to intercede (on behalf of sb)

intercepter [ɛ̃teʀsɛpte] /1/ VT to intercept; (*lumière, chaleur*) to cut off

intercepteur [ɛ̃teʀsɛptœʀ] NM (*Aviat*) interceptor

interception [ɛ̃teʀsɛpsjɔ̃] NF interception; **avion d'~** interceptor

239

intercession [ɛ̃tɛʀsesjɔ̃] NF intercession

interchangeable [ɛ̃tɛʀʃɑ̃ʒabl] ADJ interchangeable

interclasse [ɛ̃tɛʀklɑs] NM (Scol) break (between classes)

interclubs [ɛ̃tɛʀklœb] ADJ INV interclub

intercommunal, e, -aux [ɛ̃tɛʀkɔmynal, -o] ADJ intervillage, intercommunity

intercommunautaire [ɛ̃tɛʀkɔmynotɛʀ] ADJ intercommunity

interconnecté, e [ɛ̃tɛʀkɔnɛkte] ADJ (réseaux, zones) interconnected

interconnexion [ɛ̃tɛʀkɔnɛksjɔ̃] NF (Inform) networking

intercontinental, e, -aux [ɛ̃tɛʀkɔ̃tinɑtal, -o] ADJ intercontinental

intercostal, e, -aux [ɛ̃tɛʀkɔstal, -o] ADJ intercostal, between the ribs

interdépartemental, e, -aux [ɛ̃tɛʀdepaʀtəmɑtal, -o] ADJ interdepartmental

interdépendance [ɛ̃tɛʀdepɑdɑs] NF interdependence

interdépendant, e [ɛ̃tɛʀdepɑdɑ, -ɑt] ADJ interdependent

interdiction [ɛ̃tɛʀdiksjɔ̃] NF ban; **~ de faire qch** ban on doing sth; **~ de séjour** (Jur) order banning ex-prisoner from frequenting specified places; **~ de fumer** no smoking

★**interdire** [ɛ̃tɛʀdiʀ] /37/ VT to forbid; (Admin: stationnement, meeting, passage) to ban, prohibit; (: journal, livre) to ban; **~ qch à qn** to forbid sb sth; **~ à qn de faire** to forbid sb to do, prohibit sb from doing; (empêchement) to prevent ou preclude sb from doing ■ **s'interdire** VPR (éviter): **s'~ qch** to refrain ou abstain from sth; (se refuser): **il s'interdit d'y penser** he doesn't allow himself to think about it

interdisciplinaire [ɛ̃tɛʀdisiplinɛʀ] ADJ interdisciplinary

★**interdit, e** [ɛ̃tɛʀdi, -it] PP de **interdire** ▸ ADJ (défendu) forbidden, prohibited; (stupéfait) taken aback; **film ~ aux moins de 18/12 ans** ≈ 18-/12A-rated film; **sens ~** one way; **stationnement ~** no parking; **~ de chéquier** having cheque book facilities suspended; **~ de séjour** subject to an "interdiction de séjour" ▸ NM interdict, prohibition

intéressant, e [ɛ̃teʀesɑ̃, -ɑt] ADJ interesting; (avantageux) attractive; **faire l'~** to draw attention to o.s.

intéressé, e [ɛ̃teʀese] ADJ (parties) involved, concerned; (amitié, motifs) self-interested ▸ NM/F: **l'~** the interested party; **les intéressés** those concerned ou involved

intéressement [ɛ̃teʀesmɑ̃] NM (Comm) profit-sharing

intéresser [ɛ̃teʀese] /1/ VT (captiver) to interest; (toucher) to be of interest ou concern to; (Admin: concerner) to affect, concern; (Comm: travailleur) to give a share in the profits to; (: partenaire) to interest (in the business); **~ qn à qch** to get sb interested in sth ■ **s'intéresser à** VPR to take an interest in, be interested in

intérêt [ɛ̃teʀɛ] NM (aussi Comm) interest; (égoïsme) self-interest; **porter de l'~ à qn** to take an inter-

est in sb; **agir par ~** to act out of self-interest; **avoir des intérêts dans** (Comm) to have a financial interest ou a stake in; **avoir ~ à faire** to do well to do; **tu as ~ à accepter** it's in your interest to accept; **tu as ~ à te dépêcher** you'd better hurry; **il y a ~ à ...** it would be a good thing to ...; **~ composé** compound interest

interface [ɛ̃tɛʀfas] NF (Inform) interface

interférence [ɛ̃tɛʀfeʀɑs] NF interference

interférer [ɛ̃tɛʀfeʀe] /6/ VI: **~ (avec)** to interfere (with)

interféron [ɛ̃tɛʀfeʀɔ̃] NM interferon

intergalactique [ɛ̃tɛʀgalaktik] ADJ intergalactic

intergouvernemental, e, -aux [ɛ̃tɛʀguvɛʀnəmɑtal, -o] ADJ intergovernmental

intérieur, e [ɛ̃teʀjœʀ] ADJ (mur, escalier, poche) inside; (commerce, politique) domestic; (cour, calme, vie) inner; (navigation) inland ▸ NM (d'une maison, d'un récipient etc) inside; (d'un pays: aussi décor, mobilier) interior; (Pol): **l'I~** (the Department of) the Interior, ≈ Home Office (BRIT); **à l'~ (de)** inside; (fig) within; **de l'~** (fig) from the inside; **en ~** (Ciné) in the studio; **vêtement d'~** indoor garment

intérieurement [ɛ̃teʀjœʀmɑ̃] ADV inwardly

intérim [ɛ̃teʀim] NM (période) interim period; (travail) temping; **agence d'~** temping agency; **assurer l'~ (de)** to deputize (for); **président par ~** interim president; **travailler en ~**, **faire de l'~** to temp

intérimaire [ɛ̃teʀimɛʀ] ADJ (directeur, ministre) acting; (secrétaire, personnel) temporary, interim ▸ NMF (secrétaire etc) temporary, temp (BRIT); (suppléant) deputy

intérioriser [ɛ̃teʀjɔʀize] /1/ VT to internalize

interjection [ɛ̃tɛʀʒɛksjɔ̃] NF interjection

interjeter [ɛ̃tɛʀʒəte] /4/ VT (Jur): **~ appel** to lodge an appeal

interligne [ɛ̃tɛʀliɲ] NM inter-line space; **simple/double ~** single/double spacing ▸ NF (Typo) lead, leading

interlocuteur, -trice [ɛ̃tɛʀlɔkytœʀ, -tris] NM/F speaker; (Pol): **~ valable** valid representative; **son ~** the person he ou she was speaking to

interlope [ɛ̃tɛʀlɔp] ADJ illicit; (milieu, bar) shady

interloquer [ɛ̃tɛʀlɔke] /1/ VT to take aback

interlude [ɛ̃tɛʀlyd] NM interlude

intermède [ɛ̃tɛʀmɛd] NM interlude

intermédiaire [ɛ̃tɛʀmedjɛʀ] ADJ intermediate; middle; half-way; (solution) temporary ▸ NMF intermediary; (Comm) middleman; **sans ~** directly; **par l'~ de** through

interminable [ɛ̃tɛʀminabl] ADJ never-ending

interminablement [ɛ̃tɛʀminabləmɑ̃] ADV interminably

interministériel, le [ɛ̃tɛʀministeʀjɛl] ADJ: **comité ~** interdepartmental committee

intermittence [ɛ̃tɛʀmitɑs] NF: **par ~** intermittently, sporadically

intermittent, e [ɛ̃tɛʀmitɑ, -ɑt] ADJ intermittent, sporadic

internat [ɛ̃tɛʀna] NM (Scol) boarding school

★**international, e, -aux** [ɛ̃tɛʀnasjɔnal, -o] ADJ, NM/F international

internationalisation [ɛ̃tɛʀnasjɔnalizasjɔ̃] NF internationalization

internationaliser [ɛ̃tɛʀnasjɔnalize] /1/ VT to internationalize

internationalisme [ɛ̃tɛʀnasjɔnalism] NM internationalism

internaute [ɛ̃tɛʀnot] NMF internet user

★**interne** [ɛ̃tɛʀn] ADJ internal ▶ NMF (Scol) boarder; (Méd) houseman (BRIT), intern (US)

internement [ɛ̃tɛʀnəmɑ̃] NM (Pol) internment; (Méd) confinement

interner [ɛ̃tɛʀne] /1/ VT (Pol) to intern; (Méd) to confine to a psychiatric hospital

Internet [ɛ̃tɛʀnɛt] NM: l'~ the internet

interparlementaire [ɛ̃tɛʀpaʀləmɑ̃tɛʀ] ADJ interparliamentary

interpellation [ɛ̃tɛʀpelasjɔ̃] NF interpellation; (Pol) question

interpeller [ɛ̃tɛʀpele] /1/ VT (appeler) to call out to; (apostropher) to shout at; (Police) to take in for questioning; (Pol) to question; (concerner) to concern ■ **s'interpeller** VPR (s'apostropher) to shout at each other

interphone [ɛ̃tɛʀfɔn] NM intercom; (d'immeuble) entry phone

interplanétaire [ɛ̃tɛʀplanetɛʀ] ADJ interplanetary

Interpol [ɛ̃tɛʀpɔl] SIGLE M Interpol

interpoler [ɛ̃tɛʀpɔle] /1/ VT to interpolate

interposer [ɛ̃tɛʀpoze] /1/ VT to interpose; **par personnes interposées** through a third party ■ **s'interposer** VPR to intervene

interprétariat [ɛ̃tɛʀpʀetaʀja] NM interpreting

interprétation [ɛ̃tɛʀpʀetasjɔ̃] NF interpretation

interprète [ɛ̃tɛʀpʀɛt] NMF interpreter; (porte-parole) spokesman

interpréter [ɛ̃tɛʀpʀete] /6/ VT to interpret; (jouer) to play; (chanter) to sing

interprofessionnel, le [ɛ̃tɛʀpʀɔfesjɔnɛl] ADJ interprofessional

interrègne [ɛ̃tɛʀʀɛɲ] NM interregnum

interrogateur, -trice [ɛ̃teʀɔɡatœʀ, -tʀis] ADJ questioning, inquiring ▶ NM/F (Scol) (oral) examiner

interrogatif, -ive [ɛ̃teʀɔɡatif, -iv] ADJ (Ling) interrogative

interrogation [ɛ̃teʀɔɡasjɔ̃] NF question; (Scol) (written ou oral) test

interrogatoire [ɛ̃teʀɔɡatwaʀ] NM (Police) questioning no pl; (Jur, aussi fig) cross-examination, interrogation

interrogé, e [ɛ̃teʀɔʒe] ADJ: **55% des personnes interrogées** 55% of respondents, 55% of those polled

interroger [ɛ̃teʀɔʒe] /3/ VT to question; (Inform) to search; (Scol: candidat) to test; **~ qn (sur qch)** to question sb (about sth); **~ qn du regard** to look questioningly at sb, give sb a questioning look ■ **s'interroger** VPR to wonder; **s'~ sur qch** to ask o.s. about sth, ponder (about) sth

interrompre [ɛ̃teʀɔ̃pʀ] /41/ VT (gén) to interrupt; (travail, voyage) to break off, interrupt; (négocia-

tions) to break off; (match) to stop ■ **s'interrompre** VPR to break off

interrupteur [ɛ̃teʀyptœʀ] NM switch

interruption [ɛ̃teʀypsjɔ̃] NF interruption; (pause) break; **sans ~** without a break; **~ de grossesse** termination of pregnancy; **~ volontaire de grossesse** voluntary termination of pregnancy, abortion

interscolaire [ɛ̃tɛʀskɔlɛʀ] ADJ interschool(s)

intersection [ɛ̃tɛʀsɛksjɔ̃] NF intersection

intersidéral, e, -aux [ɛ̃tɛʀsideʀal, -o] ADJ interstellar

interstice [ɛ̃tɛʀstis] NM crack, slit

intersyndical, e, -aux [ɛ̃tɛʀsɛ̃dikal, -o] ADJ interunion

intertitre [ɛ̃tɛʀtitʀ] NM (Ciné) caption, subtitle

interurbain, e [ɛ̃tɛʀyʀbɛ̃, -ɛn] (Tél) NM long-distance call service ▶ ADJ long-distance

intervalle [ɛ̃tɛʀval] NM (espace) space; (de temps) interval; **dans l'~** in the meantime; **à deux jours d'~** two days apart; **à intervalles rapprochés** at close intervals; **par intervalles** at intervals

intervenant, e [ɛ̃tɛʀvənɑ̃, -ɑ̃t] VB voir **intervenir** ▶ NM/F speaker (at conference)

intervenir [ɛ̃tɛʀvəniʀ] /22/ VI (gén) to intervene; (survenir) to take place; (faire une conférence) to give a talk ou lecture; **~ auprès de/en faveur de qn** to intervene with/on behalf of sb; **la police a dû ~** police had to step in ou intervene; **les médecins ont dû ~** the doctors had to operate

intervention [ɛ̃tɛʀvɑ̃sjɔ̃] NF intervention; (conférence) talk, paper; (discours) speech; **~ (chirurgicale)** operation

interventionnisme [ɛ̃tɛʀvɑ̃sjɔnism] NM interventionism

interventionniste [ɛ̃tɛʀvɑ̃sjɔnist] ADJ interventionist

intervenu, e [ɛ̃tɛʀv(ə)ny] PP de **intervenir**

intervertible [ɛ̃tɛʀvɛʀtibl] ADJ interchangeable

intervertir [ɛ̃tɛʀvɛʀtiʀ] /2/ VT to invert (the order of), reverse

interviendrai [ɛ̃tɛʀvjɛ̃dʀe], **interviens** etc [ɛ̃tɛʀvjɛ̃] VB voir **intervenir**

★**interview** [ɛ̃tɛʀvju] NF interview

interviewer [ɛ̃tɛʀvjuve] /1/ VT to interview ▶ NM [ɛ̃tɛʀvjuvœʀ] (journaliste) interviewer

intervins etc [ɛ̃tɛʀvɛ̃] VB voir **intervenir**

intestat [ɛ̃tɛsta] ADJ (Jur): **décéder ~** to die intestate

intestin, e [ɛ̃tɛstɛ̃, -in] ADJ internal ▶ NM intestine; **~ grêle** small intestine

intestinal, e, -aux [ɛ̃tɛstinal, -o] ADJ intestinal

intifada [intifada] NF intifada

intime [ɛ̃tim] ADJ intimate; (vie, journal) private; (hygiène, confidences) personal; (convictions) inmost; (dîner, cérémonie) held among friends, quiet; **un journal ~** a private diary/journal ▶ NMF close friend

intimement [ɛ̃timmɑ̃] ADV (profondément) deeply, firmly; (étroitement) intimately

intimer [ɛ̃time] /1/ VT (Jur) to notify; **~ à qn l'ordre de faire** to order sb to do

intimidant, e [ɛ̃timidɑ̃, -ɑ̃t] ADJ intimidating

intimidation [ɛ̃timidasjɔ̃] NF intimidation; **manœuvres d'~** (action) acts of intimidation; (stratégie) intimidatory tactics

intimider [ɛ̃timide] /1/ VT to intimidate

intimiste [ɛ̃timist] ADJ (œuvre, film) intimist

intimité [ɛ̃timite] NF intimacy; (vie privée) privacy; private life; **dans l'~** in private; (sans formalités) with only a few friends, quietly

intitulé [ɛ̃tityle] NM title

intituler [ɛ̃tityle] /1/ VT: **comment a-t-il intitulé son livre?** what title did he give his book? ■ **s'intituler** VPR to be entitled; (personne) to call o.s.

intolérable [ɛ̃tɔlerabl] ADJ intolerable

intolérance [ɛ̃tɔlerɑ̃s] NF intolerance; **~ aux antibiotiques** intolerance to antibiotics

intolérant, e [ɛ̃tɔlerɑ̃, -ɑ̃t] ADJ intolerant

intonation [ɛ̃tɔnasjɔ̃] NF intonation

intouchable [ɛ̃tuʃabl] ADJ (fig) above the law, sacrosanct; (Rel) untouchable

intox [ɛ̃tɔks] NF (fam) brainwashing

intoxication [ɛ̃tɔksikasjɔ̃] NF poisoning no pl; (toxicomanie) drug addiction; (fig) brainwashing; **~ alimentaire** food poisoning

intoxiqué, e [ɛ̃tɔksike] NM/F addict

intoxiquer [ɛ̃tɔksike] /1/ VT to poison; (fig) to brainwash ■ **s'intoxiquer** VPR to poison o.s.

intradermique [ɛ̃tRadɛRmik] ADJ, NF: **(injection) ~** intradermal ou intracutaneous injection

intraduisible [ɛ̃tRadɥizibl] ADJ untranslatable; (fig) inexpressible

intraitable [ɛ̃tRɛtabl] ADJ inflexible, uncompromising

intramusculaire [ɛ̃tRamyskylɛR] ADJ, NF: **(injection) ~** intramuscular injection

intranet [ɛ̃tRanɛt] NM intranet

intransigeance [ɛ̃tRɑ̃ziʒɑ̃s] NF intransigence

intransigeant, e [ɛ̃tRɑ̃ziʒɑ̃, -ɑ̃t] ADJ intransigent; (morale, passion) uncompromising

intransitif, -ive [ɛ̃tRɑ̃zitif, -iv] ADJ (Ling) intransitive

intransportable [ɛ̃tRɑ̃spɔRtabl] ADJ (blessé) unable to travel

intrant [ɛ̃tRɑ̃] NM (Écon, Agr) input

intraveineux, -euse [ɛ̃tRavɛnø, -øz] ADJ intraveneous ▶ NF (aussi: **injection intraveineuse**) intravenous injection

intrépide [ɛ̃tRepid] ADJ dauntless, intrepid

intrépidité [ɛ̃tRepidite] NF dauntlessness

intrigant, e [ɛ̃tRigɑ̃, -ɑ̃t] NM/F schemer

intrigue [ɛ̃tRig] NF intrigue; (scénario) plot

intrigué, e [ɛ̃tRige] ADJ (personne, air) puzzled; **~ par** puzzled by

intriguer [ɛ̃tRige] /1/ VI to scheme ▶ VT to puzzle, intrigue

intrinsèque [ɛ̃tRɛ̃sɛk] ADJ intrinsic

intrinsèquement [ɛ̃tRɛ̃sɛkmɑ̃] ADV intrinsically

intro [ɛ̃tRo] NF (fam: de texte, chanson) intro (fam)

introductif, -ive [ɛ̃tRɔdyktif, -iv] ADJ introductory

introduction [ɛ̃tRɔdyksjɔ̃] NF introduction; **paroles/chapitre d'~** introductory words/chapter; **lettre/mot d'~** letter/note of introduction

introduire [ɛ̃tRɔdɥiR] /38/ VT to introduce; (visiteur) to show in; (aiguille, clef): **~ qch dans** to insert sth into; (personne): **~ à qch** to introduce to sth; (: présenter): **~ qn à qn/dans un club** to introduce sb to sb/to a club ■ **s'introduire** VPR (techniques, usages) to be introduced; **s'~ dans** to gain entry into; (dans un groupe) to get o.s. accepted into; (eau, fumée) to get into

> **introduire** is often translated by a word other than to introduce.

introduit, e [ɛ̃tRɔdɥi, -it] PP de **introduire** ▶ ADJ: **bien ~** (personne) well-received

intronisation [ɛ̃tRɔnizasjɔ̃] NF (de pape, roi) enthronement

introniser [ɛ̃tRɔnize] /1/ VT to enthrone

introspectif, -ive [ɛ̃tRɔspɛktif, -iv] ADJ (personne, œuvre) introspective

introspection [ɛ̃tRɔspɛksjɔ̃] NF introspection

introuvable [ɛ̃tRuvabl] ADJ which cannot be found; (Comm) unobtainable

introverti, e [ɛ̃tRɔvɛRti] NM/F introvert

intrus, e [ɛ̃tRy, -yz] NM/F intruder

intrusion [ɛ̃tRyziɔ̃] NF intrusion; (ingérence) interference

intubation [ɛ̃tybasjɔ̃] NF (Méd) intubation

intuber [ɛ̃tybe] VT (Méd) to intubate

intuitif, -ive [ɛ̃tɥitif, -iv] ADJ intuitive

intuition [ɛ̃tɥisjɔ̃] NF intuition; **avoir une ~** to have a feeling of sth; **avoir l'~ de qch** to have an intuition of sth; **avoir de l'~** to have intuition

intuitivement [ɛ̃tɥitivmɑ̃] ADV intuitively

inuit [inɥit] ADJ Inuit ▶ NMF: **Inuit** Inuit

inusable [inyzabl] ADJ hard-wearing

inusité, e [inyzite] ADJ rarely used

★**inutile** [inytil] ADJ useless; (superflu) unnecessary

inutilement [inytilmɑ̃] ADV needlessly

inutilisable [inytilizabl] ADJ unusable

inutilisé, e [inytilize] ADJ unused

inutilité [inytilite] NF uselessness

invaincu, e [ɛ̃vɛ̃ky] ADJ unbeaten; (armée, peuple) unconquered

invalide [ɛ̃valid] ADJ disabled ▶ NMF: **~ de guerre** disabled ex-serviceman; **~ du travail** industrially disabled person

invalider [ɛ̃valide] /1/ VT to invalidate

invalidité [ɛ̃validite] NF disability

invariable [ɛ̃vaRjabl] ADJ invariable

invariablement [ɛ̃vaRjablamɑ̃] ADV invariably

invasif, -ive [ɛ̃vazif, -iv] ADJ (traitement) invasive

invasion [ɛ̃vazjɔ̃] NF invasion

invective [ɛ̃vɛktiv] NF invective

invectiver [ɛ̃vɛktive] /1/ VT to hurl abuse at ▶ VI: **~ contre** to rail against

invendable [ɛ̃vɑ̃dabl] ADJ unsaleable, unmarketable

invendu, e [ɛ̃vɑ̃dy] ADJ unsold ▶ NM return ■ **invendus** NMPL unsold goods

inventaire [ɛ̃vɑ̃tɛR] NM inventory; (Comm: liste) stocklist; (: opération) stocktaking no pl; (fig) survey; **faire un ~** to make an inventory; (Comm) to take stock; **faire ou procéder à l'~** to take stock

★**inventer** [ɛ̃vɑ̃te] /**1**/ vⴃ to invent; (*subterfuge*) to devise, invent; (*histoire, excuse*) to make up, invent; **~ de faire** to hit on the idea of doing

inventeur, -trice [ɛ̃vɑ̃tœʀ, -tʀis] NM/F inventor

inventif, -ive [ɛ̃vɑ̃tif, -iv] ADJ inventive

invention [ɛ̃vɑ̃sjɔ̃] NF invention; (*imagination, inspiration*) inventiveness

inventivité [ɛ̃vɑ̃tivite] NF inventiveness

inventorier [ɛ̃vɑ̃tɔʀje] /**7**/ vⴃ to make an inventory of

invérifiable [ɛ̃veʀifjabl] ADJ unverifiable

inverse [ɛ̃vɛʀs] ADJ (*ordre*) reverse; (*sens*) opposite; (*rapport*) inverse; **dans l'ordre ~** in the reverse order; **en proportion ~** in inverse proportion; **dans le sens ~ des aiguilles d'une montre** anticlockwise; **en sens ~** in (*ou* from) the opposite direction ▶ NM reverse; inverse; **l'~** the opposite; **à l'~** conversely

inversement [ɛ̃vɛʀsəmɑ̃] ADV conversely

inverser [ɛ̃vɛʀse] /**1**/ vⴃ to reverse, invert; (*Élec*) to reverse

inversion [ɛ̃vɛʀsjɔ̃] NF reversal; inversion

invertébré, e [ɛ̃vɛʀtebʀe] ADJ, NM invertebrate

inverti, e [ɛ̃vɛʀti] NM/F homosexual

investigation [ɛ̃vɛstigasjɔ̃] NF investigation, inquiry

investir [ɛ̃vɛstiʀ] /**2**/ vⴃ to invest; **~ qn de** (*d'une fonction, d'un pouvoir*) to vest *ou* invest sb with ■ **s'investir** VPR (*Psych*) to involve o.s.; **s'~ dans** to put a lot into

investissement [ɛ̃vɛstismɑ̃] NM investment; (*Psych*) involvement

investisseur [ɛ̃vɛstisœʀ] NM investor

investiture [ɛ̃vɛstityʀ] NF investiture; (*à une élection*) nomination

invétéré, e [ɛ̃vetere] ADJ (*habitude*) ingrained; (*bavard, buveur*) inveterate

invincibilité [ɛ̃vɛ̃sibilite] NF invincibility

invincible [ɛ̃vɛ̃sibl] ADJ invincible, unconquerable

invinciblement [ɛ̃vɛ̃sibləmɑ̃] ADV (*fig*) invincibly

inviolabilité [ɛ̃vjɔlabilite] NF: **~ parlementaire** parliamentary immunity

inviolable [ɛ̃vjɔlabl] ADJ inviolable

inviolé, e [ɛ̃vjɔle] ADJ (*nature, région*) inviolate

invisibilité [ɛ̃vizibilite] NF invisibility

invisible [ɛ̃vizibl] ADJ invisible; (*fig: personne*) not available

★**invitation** [ɛ̃vitasjɔ̃] NF invitation; **à/sur l'~ de qn** at/on sb's invitation; **carte/lettre d'~** invitation card/letter

invite [ɛ̃vit] NF invitation

invité, e [ɛ̃vite] NM/F guest

★**inviter** [ɛ̃vite] /**1**/ vⴃ to invite; **~ qn à faire qch** to invite sb to do sth; (*suj: chose*) to induce *ou* tempt sb to do sth

invivable [ɛ̃vivabl] ADJ unbearable, impossible

invocation [ɛ̃vɔkasjɔ̃] NF (*prière*) invocation

involontaire [ɛ̃vɔlɔ̃tɛʀ] ADJ (*mouvement*) involuntary; (*insulte*) unintentional; (*complice*) unwitting

involontairement [ɛ̃vɔlɔ̃tɛʀmɑ̃] ADV involuntarily

invoquer [ɛ̃vɔke] /**1**/ vⴃ (*Dieu, muse*) to call upon, invoke; (*prétexte*) to put forward (as an excuse);

(*témoignage*) to call upon; (*loi, texte*) to refer to; **~ la clémence de qn** to beg sb *ou* appeal to sb for clemency

invraisemblable [ɛ̃vʀɛsɑ̃blabl] ADJ (*fait, nouvelle*) unlikely, improbable; (*bizarre*) incredible

invraisemblance [ɛ̃vʀɛsɑ̃blɑ̃s] NF unlikelihood *no pl*, improbability

invulnérabilité [ɛ̃vylneʀabilite] NF invulnerability

invulnérable [ɛ̃vylneʀabl] ADJ invulnerable

iode [jɔd] NM iodine

iodé, e [jɔde] ADJ iodized

ion [jɔ̃] NM ion

ionique [jɔnik] ADJ (*Archit*) Ionic; (*Science*) ionic

ionisant, e [jɔnizɑ̃, -ɑ̃t] ADJ ionizing

ionisation [jɔnizasjɔ̃] NF ionization

ioniseur [jɔnizœʀ] NM ionizer

iota [jɔta] NM: **sans changer un ~** without changing one iota *ou* the tiniest bit

iPad® [aipad] NM iPad®

IPC SIGLE M (= *Indice des prix à la consommation*) CPI

iPhone® [aifɔn] NM iPhone®

IR ABR = **infrarouge**

IRA [iʀa] SIGLE F (= *Irish Republican Army*) IRA

irai *etc* [iʀe] VB *voir* **aller**

Irak [iʀak] NM: **l'~** Iraq *ou* Irak

irakien, ne [iʀakjɛ̃, -ɛn] ADJ Iraqi ▶ NM/F: **Irakien, ne** Iraqi

Iran [iʀɑ̃] NM: **l'~** Iran

iranien, ne [iʀanjɛ̃, -ɛn] ADJ Iranian ▶ NM/F: **Iranien, ne** Iranian

Iraq [iʀak] NM = **Irak**

iraquien, ne [iʀakjɛ̃, -ɛn] ADJ, NM/F = **irakien**

irascible [iʀasibl] ADJ short-tempered, irascible

iridescent, e [iʀidesɑ̃, -ɑ̃t] ADJ iridescent

irions *etc* [iʀjɔ̃] VB *voir* **aller**

iris [iʀis] NM iris

irisé, e [iʀize] ADJ iridescent

★**irlandais, e** [iʀlɑ̃dɛ, -ɛz] ADJ, NM (*Ling*) Irish ▶ NM/F: **Irlandais, e** Irishman/-woman; **les I~** the Irish

★**Irlande** [iʀlɑ̃d] NF: **l'~** (*pays*) Ireland; **la République d'~** the Irish Republic, the Republic of Ireland, Eire; **~ du Nord** Northern Ireland, Ulster; **~ du Sud** Southern Ireland, Irish Republic, Eire; **la mer d'~** the Irish Sea

IRM SIGLE F (= *imagerie par résonance magnétique*) MRI scan

ironie [iʀɔni] NF irony

ironique [iʀɔnik] ADJ ironical

ironiquement [iʀɔnikmɑ̃] ADV ironically

ironiser [iʀɔnize] /**1**/ vi to be ironical

irons *etc* [iʀɔ̃] VB *voir* **aller**

iroquois, e [iʀɔkwa, -waz] ADJ Iroquois ▶ NM/F: **Iroquois, e** Iroquois

IRPP SIGLE M (= *impôt sur le revenu des personnes physiques*) income tax

irradiation [iʀadjasjɔ̃] NF irradiation

irradier [iʀadje] /**7**/ vi to radiate ▶ vⴃ to irradiate

irraisonné, e [iʀɛzɔne] ADJ irrational, unreasoned

irrationnel, le [iʀasjɔnɛl] ADJ irrational

243

irrattrapable [iʀatʀapabl] ADJ (retard) that cannot be made up; (bévue) that cannot be made good

irréalisable [iʀealizabl] ADJ unrealizable; (projet) impracticable

irréalisme [iʀealism] NM lack of realism

irréaliste [iʀealist] ADJ unrealistic

irréalité [iʀealite] NF unreality

irrecevable [iʀəs(ə)vabl] ADJ unacceptable

irréconciliable [iʀekɔ̃siljabl] ADJ irreconcilable

irrécouvrable [iʀekuvʀabl] ADJ irrecoverable

irrécupérable [iʀekypeʀabl] ADJ unreclaimable, beyond repair; (personne) beyond redemption ou recall

irrécusable [iʀekyzabl] ADJ (témoignage) unimpeachable; (preuve) incontestable, indisputable

irréductible [iʀedyktibl] ADJ indomitable, implacable; (Math: fraction, équation) irreducible

irréductiblement [iʀedyktiblǝmɑ̃] ADV implacably

irréel, le [iʀeɛl] ADJ unreal

irréfléchi, e [iʀefleʃi] ADJ thoughtless

irréfutable [iʀefytabl] ADJ irrefutable

irréfutablement [iʀefytablǝmɑ̃] ADV irrefutably

irrégularité [iʀegylaʀite] NF irregularity; (de travail, d'effort, de qualité) unevenness no pl

irrégulier, -ière [iʀegylje, -jɛʀ] ADJ irregular; (surface, rythme, écriture) uneven, irregular; (travail, effort, qualité) uneven; (élève, athlète) erratic

irrégulièrement [iʀegyljɛʀmɑ̃] ADV irregularly

irrémédiable [iʀemedjabl] ADJ irreparable

irrémédiablement [iʀemedjablǝmɑ̃] ADV irreparably

irremplaçable [iʀɑ̃plasabl] ADJ irreplaceable

irréparable [iʀepaʀabl] ADJ beyond repair, irreparable; (fig) irreparable

irrépréhensible [iʀepreɑ̃sibl] ADJ irreproachable

irrépressible [iʀepʀesibl] ADJ irrepressible

irréprochable [iʀepʀɔʃabl] ADJ irreproachable, beyond reproach; (tenue, toilette) impeccable

irrésistible [iʀezistibl] ADJ irresistible; (preuve, logique) compelling; (amusant) hilarious

irrésistiblement [iʀezistiblǝmɑ̃] ADV irresistibly

irrésolu, e [iʀezɔly] ADJ irresolute

irrésolution [iʀezɔlysjɔ̃] NF irresoluteness

irrespectueux, -euse [iʀɛspɛktɥø, -øz] ADJ disrespectful

irrespirable [iʀɛspiʀabl] ADJ unbreathable; (fig) oppressive, stifling

irresponsabilité [iʀɛspɔ̃sabilite] NF irresponsibility

irresponsable [iʀɛspɔ̃sabl] ADJ irresponsible

irrévérence [iʀeveʀɑ̃s] NF irreverence

irrévérencieux, -euse [iʀeveʀɑ̃sjø, -øz] ADJ irreverent

irréversible [iʀevɛʀsibl] ADJ irreversible

irréversiblement [iʀevɛʀsiblǝmɑ̃] ADV irreversibly

irrévocable [iʀevɔkabl] ADJ irrevocable

irrévocablement [iʀevɔkablǝmɑ̃] ADV irrevocably

irrigation [iʀigasjɔ̃] NF irrigation

irriguer [iʀige] /1/ VT to irrigate

irritabilité [iʀitabilite] NF irritability

irritable [iʀitabl] ADJ irritable

irritant, e [iʀitɑ̃, -ɑ̃t] ADJ irritating; (Méd) irritant

irritation [iʀitasjɔ̃] NF irritation

irrité, e [iʀite] ADJ irritated

irriter [iʀite] /1/ VT (agacer) to irritate, annoy; (Méd: enflammer) to irritate ■ **s'irriter** VPR: **s'~ contre qn/de qch** to get annoyed ou irritated with sb/at sth

irruption [iʀypsjɔ̃] NF irruption no pl; **faire ~ dans** to burst into; **faire ~ chez qn** to burst in on sb

isard [izaʀ] NM izard

ISBN SIGLE M (= International Standard Book Number) ISBN

ISF SIGLE M (= impôt de solidarité sur la fortune) wealth tax

Islam [islam] NM: **l'~** Islam

islamique [islamik] ADJ Islamic

islamisme [islamism] NM Islamism

islamiste [islamist] ADJ, NMF Islamist

islamophobie [islamafɔbi] NF Islamophobia

islandais, e [islɑ̃dɛ, -ɛz] ADJ Icelandic ▶ NM (Ling) Icelandic ▶ NM/F: **Islandais, e** Icelander

Islande [islɑ̃d] NF: **l'~** Iceland

ISMH SIGLE M = **Inventaire supplémentaire des monuments historiques; monument inscrit à l'~** = listed building

isocèle [izɔsɛl] ADJ isoceles

isolant, e [izɔlɑ̃, -ɑ̃t] ADJ insulating; (insonorisant) soundproofing ▶ NM insulator

isolateur [izɔlatœʀ] NM (Élec) insulator

isolation [izɔlasjɔ̃] NF insulation; **~ thermique** thermal insulation; **~ acoustique** soundproofing

isolationnisme [izɔlasjɔnism] NM isolationism

isolationniste [izɔlasjɔnist] ADJ, NMF isolationist

isolé, e [izɔle] ADJ isolated; (Élec: contre le froid) insulated

isolement [izɔlmɑ̃] NM isolation; solitary confinement

isolément [izɔlemɑ̃] ADV in isolation

isoler [izɔle] /1/ VT to isolate; (prisonnier) to put in solitary confinement; (ville) to cut off, isolate; (Élec: contre le froid) to insulate ■ **s'isoler** VPR to isolate o.s.

isoloir [izɔlwaʀ] NM polling booth

isorel® [izɔʀɛl] NM hardboard

isotherme [izɔtɛʀm] ADJ (camion) refrigerated

isotope [izɔtɔp] NM isotope

Israël [israɛl] NM Israel

israélien, ne [israeljɛ̃, -ɛn] ADJ Israeli ▶ NM/F: **Israélien, ne** Israeli

israélite [israelit] ADJ Jewish; (dans l'Ancien Testament) Israelite ▶ NMF: **Israélite** Jew m; Israelite

issu, e [isy] ADJ: **~ de** (né de) descended from; (résultant de) stemming from ▶ NF (ouverture, sortie) exit; (solution) way out, solution; (dénouement) outcome; **à l'issue de** at the conclusion ou close of;

rue sans issue, voie sans issue dead end, no through road (*Brit*), no outlet (*US*); **issue de secours** emergency exit

> The French word **issue** is not translated by the English word *issue*.

Istamboul, Istanbul [istãbul] N Istanbul

isthme [ism] NM isthmus

★**Italie** [itali] NF: **l'~** Italy

★**italien, ne** [italjẽ, -ɛn] ADJ Italian ▸ NM (*Ling*) Italian ▸ NM/F: **Italien, ne** Italian

italique [italik] NM: **en ~(s)** in italics

item [itɛm] NM item; (*question*) question, test

itinéraire [itineRɛR] NM itinerary, route; **~ bis** alternative route

itinérance [itineRãs] NF (*Tél*) roaming

itinérant, e [itineRã, -ãt] ADJ itinerant, travelling

itou [itu] ADV (*fam: aussi*) too; **le sol est crade, les murs ~** the floor is grotty, the walls too

ITP SIGLE M (= *ingénieur des travaux publics*) civil engineer

IUT SIGLE M = **Institut universitaire de technologie**

IVG SIGLE F (= *interruption volontaire de grossesse*) abortion

ivoire [ivwaR] NM ivory

ivoirien, ne [ivwaRjẽ, -ɛn] ADJ of *ou* from the Ivory Coast

ivraie [ivRɛ] NF: **séparer le bon grain de l'~** (*fig*) to separate the wheat from the chaff

★**ivre** [ivR] ADJ drunk; **~ de** (*colère*) wild with; (*bonheur*) drunk *ou* intoxicated with; **~ mort** dead drunk

ivresse [ivRɛs] NF drunkenness; (*euphorie*) intoxication

ivrogne [ivRɔɲ] NMF drunkard

ivrognerie [ivRɔɲRi] NF drunkenness

J j

J, j [ʒi] NM INV J, j ▸ ABR (= *Joule*) J; = **jour**; **jour** J D-day; **J comme Joseph** J for Jack (BRIT) *ou* Jig (US)

★**j'** [ʒ] PRON *voir* **je**

jabot [ʒabo] NM (*Zool*) crop; (*de vêtement*) jabot

jacasser [ʒakase] /1/ VI to chatter

jacasseries [ʒakasʀi] NFPL (*bavardages*) chitter-chatter *sg*

jachère [ʒaʃɛʀ] NF: **(être) en ~** (to lie) fallow

jacinthe [ʒasɛ̃t] NF hyacinth; **~ des bois** bluebell

jack [dʒak] NM jack plug

jackpot [(d)ʒakpɔt] NM jackpot; **toucher le ~** (*fig*) to hit the jackpot

jacquard [ʒakaʀ] ADJ INV Fair Isle

jacquerie [ʒakʀi] NF riot

jacuzzi® [ʒakuzi] NM Jacuzzi®

jade [ʒad] NM jade

jadis [ʒadis] ADV in times past, formerly

jaguar [ʒagwaʀ] NM (*Zool*) jaguar

jaillir [ʒajiʀ] /2/ VI (*liquide*) to spurt out, gush out; (*lumière*) to flood out; (*fig*) to rear up; (*cris, réponses*) to burst out

jaillissement [ʒajismɑ̃] NM spurt, gush

jais [ʒɛ] NM jet; **(d'un noir) de ~** jet-black

jalon [ʒalɔ̃] NM range pole; (*fig*) milestone; **poser des jalons** (*fig*) to pave the way

jalonner [ʒalɔne] /1/ VT to mark out; (*fig*) to mark, punctuate

jalousement [ʒaluzmɑ̃] ADV jealously

jalouser [ʒaluze] /1/ VT to be jealous of

jalousie [ʒaluzi] NF jealousy; (*store*) (venetian) blind

★**jaloux, -ouse** [ʒalu, -uz] ADJ jealous; **être ~ de qn/qch** to be jealous of sb/sth

jamaïquain, e, **jamaïcain, e** [ʒamaikɛ̃, -ɛn] ADJ Jamaican ▸ NM/F: **Jamaïquain, e** Jamaican

Jamaïque [ʒamaik] NF: **la ~** Jamaica

★**jamais** [ʒamɛ] ADV never; (*sans négation*) ever; **ne ... ~** never; **~ de la vie !** never!; **si ~ ...** if ever ...; **à (tout) ~**, **pour ~** for ever and ever; **je ne suis ~ allé en Espagne** I've never been to Spain

> **Never** s'emploie avec un verbe à la forme affirmative ; c'est la traduction de *jamais* dans son sens le plus courant.
> *Elle ne lui pardonnera jamais.* **She will never forgive him.**
> **Ever** s'emploie pour traduire des phrases où *jamais* a un sens positif ou pour donner de la force à une déclaration.

C'est le plus beau tableau que j'aie jamais vu. **It's the most beautiful painting I have ever seen.** *Ne refais jamais ça !* **Don't ever do that again!**

jambage [ʒɑ̃baʒ] NM (*de lettre*) downstroke; (*de porte*) jamb

★**jambe** [ʒɑ̃b] NF leg; **à toutes jambes** as fast as one's legs can carry one

jambières [ʒɑ̃bjɛʀ] NFPL legwarmers; (*Sport*) shin pads

★**jambon** [ʒɑ̃bɔ̃] NM ham; **~ fumé** (*Culin*) smoked ham

jambonneau, x [ʒɑ̃bɔno] NM knuckle of ham

jante [ʒɑ̃t] NF (*wheel*) rim

★**janvier** [ʒɑ̃vje] NM January; *voir aussi* **juillet**

★**Japon** [ʒapɔ̃] NM: **le ~** Japan

★**japonais, e** [ʒapɔnɛ, -ɛz] ADJ Japanese ▸ NM (*Ling*) Japanese ▸ NM/F: **Japonais, e** Japanese

japonaiserie [ʒapɔnɛzʀi] NF (*bibelot*) Japanese curio

japonisant, e [ʒapɔnizɑ̃, -ɑ̃t] ADJ (*style, décor*) Japanese-inspired

jappement [ʒapmɑ̃] NM yap, yelp

japper [ʒape] /1/ VI to yap, yelp

jaquette [ʒakɛt] NF (*de cérémonie*) morning coat; (*de femme*) jacket; (*de livre*) dust cover, (dust) jacket

★**jardin** [ʒaʀdɛ̃] NM garden; **~ d'acclimatation** zoological gardens *pl*; **~ botanique** botanical gardens *pl*; **~ d'enfants** nursery school; **~ potager** vegetable garden; **~ public** (public) park, public gardens *pl*; **jardins suspendus** hanging gardens; **~ zoologique** zoological gardens

jardinage [ʒaʀdinaʒ] NM gardening

jardiner [ʒaʀdine] /1/ VI to garden, do some gardening

jardinerie [ʒaʀdinʀi] NF garden centre (BRIT), garden center (US)

jardinet [ʒaʀdinɛ] NM little garden

★**jardinier, -ière** [ʒaʀdinje, -jɛʀ] NM/F gardener ▸ NF (*de fenêtre*) window box; **jardinière d'enfants** nursery school teacher; **jardinière (de légumes)** (*Culin*) mixed vegetables

jargon [ʒaʀgɔ̃] NM (*charabia*) gibberish; (*publicitaire, scientifique etc*) jargon

jarre [ʒaʀ] NF (earthenware) jar

jarret [ʒaʀɛ] NM back of knee; (*Culin*) knuckle, shin

jarretelle [ʒaʀtɛl] NF suspender (BRIT), garter (US)

jarretière [ʒaʀtjɛʀ] NF garter

jars [ʒaʀ] NM (Zool) gander

jaser [ʒɑze] /1/ VI to chatter, prattle; (indiscrètement) to gossip

jasmin [ʒasmɛ̃] NM jasmine

jaspe [ʒasp] NM jasper

jaspé, e [ʒaspe] ADJ marbled, mottled

jatte [ʒat] NF basin, bowl

jauge [ʒoʒ] NF (capacité) capacity, tonnage; (instrument) gauge; **~ (de niveau) d'huile** (Auto) dipstick

jauger [ʒoʒe] /3/ VT to gauge the capacity of; (fig) to size up; **~ 3 000 tonneaux** to measure 3,000 tons

jaunâtre [ʒonɑtʀ] ADJ (couleur, teint) yellowish

★**jaune** [ʒon] ADJ, NM yellow; **~ d'œuf** (egg) yolk ▶ NMF (briseur de grève) blackleg ▶ ADV (fam): **rire ~** to laugh on the other side of one's face

jaunir [ʒoniʀ] /2/ VI, VT to turn yellow

jaunisse [ʒonis] NF jaundice

Java [ʒava] NF Java

java [ʒava] NF (fam): **faire la ~** to live it up, have a real party

javanais, e [ʒavanɛ, -ɛz] ADJ Javanese

Javel [ʒavɛl] NF: **eau de ~** bleach

javel [ʒavɛl] NF (fam) bleach; voir Javel; **de la ~** some bleach

javelliser [ʒavelize] /1/ VT (eau) to chlorinate

javelot [ʒavlo] NM javelin; (Athlétisme): **faire du ~** to throw the javelin

jazz [dʒaz] NM jazz

jazzy [dʒazi] ADJ INV (morceau, voix) jazzy

J.-C. ABR = **Jésus-Christ**

JDC SIGLE F = **journée défense et citoyenneté**

All 16- and 17-year-olds, both male and female, are required to attend a one-day course, the **JDC** (Journée défense et citoyenneté), which covers basic information on the principles and organization of defence in France, on citizens' rights and duties and on career opportunities in the military and the voluntary sector. There is also an introduction to first aid and a French language test. This course is compulsory – without it, young people cannot take their driving test or any competitive examinations for the public sector.

★**je, j'** [ʒə, ʒ] PRON I

★**jean** [dʒin] NM jeans pl

jeannette [ʒanɛt] NF (planchette) sleeve board; (petite fille scout) Brownie

jeep® [(d)ʒip] NF (Auto) Jeep®

jérémiades [ʒeʀemjad] NFPL moaning sg

jerrycan [ʒeʀikan] NM jerry can

Jersey [ʒɛʀze] NF Jersey

jersey [ʒɛʀzɛ] NM jersey; (Tricot): **point de ~** stocking stitch

jersiais, e [ʒɛʀzjɛ, -ɛz] ADJ Jersey cpd, of ou from Jersey

Jérusalem [ʒeʀyzalɛm] N Jerusalem

jésuite [ʒezɥit] NM Jesuit

Jésus-Christ [ʒezykʀi(st)] N Jesus Christ; **600 avant/après ~** 600 B.C./A.D.

jet¹ [ʒɛ] NM (lancer: action) throwing no pl; (: résultat) throw; (jaillissement: d'eaux) jet; (: de sang) spurt; (de tuyau) nozzle; (fig): **premier ~** (ébauche) rough outline; **arroser au ~** to hose; **d'un (seul) ~** (d'un seul coup) at (ou in) one go; **du premier ~** at the first attempt ou shot; **~ d'eau** spray; (fontaine) fountain

jet² [dʒɛt] NM (avion) jet

jetable [ʒ(ə)tabl] ADJ disposable

jeté [ʒ(ə)te] NM (Tricot): **un ~** make one; **~ de table** (table) runner; **~ de lit** bedspread

jetée [ʒ(ə)te] NF jetty; (grande) pier

★**jeter** [ʒ(ə)te] /4/ VT (gén) to throw; (se défaire de) to throw away ou out; (son, lueur etc) to give out; **~ qch à qn** to throw sth to sb; (de façon agressive) to throw sth at sb; **~ l'ancre** (Navig) to cast anchor; **~ un coup d'œil (à)** to take a look (at); **~ les bras en avant/la tête en arrière** to throw one's arms forward/one's head back(ward); **~ l'effroi parmi** to spread fear among; **~ un sort à qn** to cast a spell on sb; **~ qn dans la misère** to reduce sb to poverty; **~ qn dehors/en prison** to throw sb out/into prison; **~ l'éponge** (fig) to throw in the towel; **~ des fleurs à qn** (fig) to say lovely things to sb; **~ la pierre à qn** (accuser, blâmer) to accuse sb ■ **se jeter** VPR: **se ~ sur** to throw o.s. onto; **se ~ dans** (fleuve) to flow into; **se ~ par la fenêtre** to throw o.s. out of the window; **se ~ à l'eau** (fig) to take the plunge

jeton [ʒ(ə)tɔ̃] NM (au jeu) counter; (de téléphone) token; **jetons de présence** (director's) fees

jette etc [ʒɛt] VB voir **jeter**

★**jeu, x** [ʒø] NM (divertissement, Tech: d'une pièce) play; (défini par des règles, Tennis: partie, Football etc: façon de jouer) game; (Théât etc) acting; (fonctionnement) working, interplay; (série d'objets, jouet) set; (Cartes) hand; (au casino): **le ~** gambling; **cacher son ~** (fig) to keep one's cards hidden, conceal one's hand; **c'est un ~ d'enfant !** (fig) it's child's play!; **en ~** at stake; at work; (Football) in play; **remettre en ~** to throw in; **entrer/mettre en ~** to come/bring into play; **par ~** (pour s'amuser) for fun; **d'entrée de ~** (tout de suite, dès le début) from the outset; **entrer dans le ~/le ~ de qn** (fig) to play the game/sb's game; **jouer gros ~** to play for high stakes; **se piquer/se prendre au ~** to get excited over/get caught up in the game; **~ d'arcade** video game; **~ de boules** game of bowls; (endroit) bowling pitch; (boules) set of bowls; **~ de cartes** card game; (paquet) pack of cards; **~ de construction** building set; **~ d'échecs** chess set; **~ d'écritures** (Comm) paper transaction; **~ électronique** electronic game; **~ de hasard** game of chance; **~ de mots** pun; **le ~ de l'oie** snakes and ladders sg; **~ d'orgue(s)** organ stop; **~ de patience** puzzle; **~ de physionomie** facial expressions pl; **~ de société** board game; **~ télévisé** television quiz; **~ vidéo** video game; **jeux de lumière** lighting effects; **Jeux olympiques** Olympic Games®

jeu-concours [ʒøkɔ̃kuʀ] (pl **jeux-concours**) NM competition

★**jeudi** [ʒødi] NM Thursday; **~ saint** Maundy Thursday; voir aussi **lundi**

jeun [ʒœ̃]: **à ~** adv on an empty stomach; **être à ~** to have eaten nothing; **rester à ~** not to eat anything

★**jeune** [ʒœn] ADJ young; **~ fille** girl; **~ homme** young man; **~ loup** (Pol, Écon) young go-getter; **~ premier** leading man; **jeunes gens** young people; **jeunes** mariés newly weds ▶ADV: **faire/s'habiller ~** to look/dress young ▶NMF: **les jeunes** young people, the young

★**jeûne** [ʒøn] NM fast

jeûner [ʒøne] /1/ VI to fast, go without food

★**jeunesse** [ʒœnɛs] NF youth; (*aspect*) youthfulness; (*jeunes*) young people *pl*, youth

jeunisme [ʒœnism] NM cult of youth, youthism

jeunot, te [ʒœno, -ɔt] (*fam*) ADJ young ▶NM young lad ▶NF young woman

jf SIGLE F = **jeune fille**

jh SIGLE M = **jeune homme**

JI SIGLE M = **juge d'instruction**

jiu-jitsu [ʒyʒitsy] NM (*Sport*) jujitsu

JMF SIGLE F (= *Jeunesses musicales de France*) *association to promote music among the young*

JO SIGLE M = **le Journal officiel (de la République française)** ▶ SIGLE MPL = **Jeux olympiques**

joaillerie [ʒɔajʀi] NF jewel trade; jewellery (BRIT), jewelry (US)

joaillier, -ière [ʒɔaje, -jɛʀ] NM/F jeweller (BRIT), jeweler (US)

job [dʒɔb] NM job

jobard [ʒɔbaʀ] NM (*péj*) sucker, mug

jockey [ʒɔkɛ] NM jockey

jodler [ʒɔdle] /1/ VI to yodel

joggeur, -euse [dʒɔgœʀ, -øz] NM/F jogger

jogging [dʒɔgiŋ] NM jogging; (*survêtement*) tracksuit (BRIT), sweatsuit (US); **faire du ~** to go jogging, jog

joie [ʒwa] NF joy

joignable [ʒwaɲabl] ADJ contactable; **le médecin de garde doit être ~ à tout moment** the duty doctor must be contactable at all times

joignais *etc* [ʒwaɲɛ] VB *voir* **joindre**

joindre [ʒwɛ̃dʀ] /49/ VT to join; (*contacter*) to contact, get in touch with; **~ qch à** (*à une lettre*) to enclose sth with; **~ un fichier à un mail** (*Inform*) to attach a file to an email; **~ les mains/talons** to put one's hands/heels together; **~ les deux bouts** (*fig*) to make ends meet ▪ **se joindre** VPR (*mains etc*) to come together; **se ~ à qn** to join sb; **se ~ à qch** to join in sth

joint, e [ʒwɛ̃, -ɛ̃t] PP *de* **joindre** ▶ADJ: **~ (à)** (*lettre, paquet*) attached (to), enclosed (with) ▶NM joint; (*ligne*) join; (*de ciment etc*) pointing *no pl*; **pièce jointe** (*de lettre*) enclosure; (*de mail*) attachment; **chercher/trouver le ~** (*fig*) to look for/come up with the answer; **~ de cardan** cardan joint; **~ de culasse** cylinder head gasket; **~ de robinet** washer; **~ universel** universal joint

jointure [ʒwɛ̃tyʀ] NF (*Anat: articulation*) joint; (*Tech: assemblage*) joint; (: *ligne*) join

jojo [ʒoʒo] (*fam*) ADJ INV: **pas ~** (*pas joli*) not a pretty sight ▶NM: **un affreux ~** a little rascal

jojoba [ʒɔʒɔba] NM jojoba

joker [ʒɔkɛʀ] NM (*Cartes*) joker; (*Inform*): **(caractère) ~** wild card

★**joli, e** [ʒɔli] ADJ pretty, attractive; **une jolie somme/ situation** a nice little sum/situation; **un ~ gâchis** *etc* a nice mess *etc*; **c'est du ~ !** (*ironique*) that's very nice!; **tout ça, c'est bien ~ mais ...** that's all very well but ...

joliment [ʒɔlimɑ̃] ADV prettily, attractively; (*fam: très*) pretty

jonc [ʒɔ̃] NM (bul)rush; (*bague, bracelet*) band

joncher [ʒɔ̃ʃe] /1/ VT (*choses*) to be strewed on; **jonché de** strewn with

jonction [ʒɔ̃ksjɔ̃] NF junction, joining; **(point de) ~** (*de routes*) junction; (*de fleuves*) confluence; **opérer une ~** (*Mil etc*) to rendez-vous

jongler [ʒɔ̃gle] /1/ VI to juggle; (*fig*): **~ avec** to juggle with, play with

jongleur, -euse [ʒɔ̃glœʀ, -øz] NM/F juggler

jonque [ʒɔ̃k] NF (*bateau*) junk

jonquille [ʒɔ̃kij] NF daffodil

Jordanie [ʒɔʀdani] NF: **la ~** Jordan

jordanien, ne [ʒɔʀdanjɛ̃, -ɛn] ADJ Jordanian ▶NM/F: **Jordanien, ne** Jordanian

jouabilité [ʒuabilite] NF (*d'un jeu*) playability

jouable [ʒwabl] ADJ playable

joual [ʒwal] NM joual (*working-class speech of French-speaking Canadians*)

joue [ʒu] NF cheek; **mettre en ~** to take aim at

★**jouer** [ʒwe] /1/ VT (*partie, carte, coup, Mus: morceau*) to play; (*somme d'argent, réputation*) to stake, wager; (*pièce, rôle*) to perform; (*film*) to show; (*simuler: sentiment*) to affect, feign; **on joue Hamlet au théâtre X** Hamlet is on at the X theatre; **~ un tour à qn** to play a trick on sb; **~ la comédie** (*fig*) to put on an act, put it on ▶ VI to play; (*Théât, Ciné*) to act, perform; (*au casino*) to gamble; (*bois, porte: se voiler*) to warp; (*clef, pièce: avoir du jeu*) to be loose; (*entrer ou être en jeu*) to come into play, come into it; **~ à** (*jeu, sport, roulette*) to play; **~ avec** (*risquer*) to gamble with; **~ de** (*Mus*) to play; **~ sur** (*miser*) to gamble on; **~ au héros** to act ou play the hero; **~ aux courses** to back horses, bet on horses; **~ du couteau/des coudes** to use knives/one's elbows; **~ à la baisse/ hausse** (*Bourse*) to play for a fall/rise; **~ serré** to play a close game; **~ de malchance** to be dogged with ill-luck; **~ sur les mots** to play with words; **à toi/nous de ~** it's your/our go ou turn; **bien joué !** well done! ▪ **se jouer** VPR: **se ~ de** (*difficultés*) to make light of; **se ~ de qn** to deceive ou dupe sb

★**jouet** [ʒwɛ] NM toy; **être le ~ de** (*illusion etc*) to be the victim of

★**joueur, -euse** [ʒwœʀ, -øz] NM/F player; **être beau/ mauvais ~** to be a good/bad loser ▶ADJ (*enfant, chat*) playful

joufflu, e [ʒufly] ADJ chubby(-cheeked)

joug [ʒu] NM yoke

jouir [ʒwiʀ] /2/ VI (*sexe: fam*) to come ▶VT: **~ de** to enjoy

jouissance [ʒwisɑ̃s] NF pleasure; (*Jur*) use

jouisseur, -euse [ʒwisœʀ, -øz] NM/F sensualist

jouissif, -ive [ʒwisif, -iv] ADJ (*fam: génial*) brilliant, brilliant fun (*fam*)

joujou, x [ʒuʒu] NM (*fam*) toy

joule [ʒul] NM joule

★**jour** [ʒuʀ] NM day; (*opposé à la nuit*) day, daytime; (*clarté*) daylight; (*fig: aspect, ouverture*) opening; (*Couture*) openwork *no pl*; **sous un ~ favorable/ nouveau** in a favourable/new light; **de ~** (*crème, service*) day *cpd*; **travailler de ~** to work during the day; **voyager de ~** to travel by day; **au ~ le ~** from day to day; **de nos jours** these days, nowadays;

tous les jours every day; **de ~ en ~** day by day; **d'un ~ à l'autre** from one day to the next; **du ~ au lendemain** overnight; **il fait ~** it's daylight; **en plein ~** in broad daylight; **au ~** in daylight; **au petit ~** at daybreak; **au grand ~** *(fig)* in the open; **mettre au ~** to disclose, uncover; **être à ~** to be up to date; **mettre à ~** to bring up to date, update; **mise à ~** updating; **donner le ~ à** to give birth to; **voir le ~** to be born; **se faire ~** *(fig)* to become clear; **~ férié** public holiday; **le J** D-day; **~ ouvrable** working day

Jourdain [ʒuʀdɛ̃] NM: **le ~** the (River) Jordan

★**journal, -aux** [ʒuʀnal, -o] NM (news)paper; *(personnel)* journal; *(intime)* diary; **~ de bord** log; **~ de mode** fashion magazine; **le J~ officiel (de la République française)** bulletin giving details of laws and official announcements; **~ parlé** radio news *sg*; **~ télévisé** television news *sg*

journalier, -ière [ʒuʀnalje, -jeʀ] ADJ daily; *(banal)* everyday ▶ NM day labourer

journalisme [ʒuʀnalism] NM journalism

★**journaliste** [ʒuʀnalist] NMF journalist

journalistique [ʒuʀnalistik] ADJ journalistic

journée [ʒuʀne] NF day; **la ~ continue** the 9 to 5 working day *(with short lunch break)*

journellement [ʒuʀnɛlmã] ADV *(tous les jours)* daily; *(souvent)* every day

joute [ʒut] NF *(tournoi)* duel; *(verbale)* duel, battle of words

jouvence [ʒuvãs] NF: **bain de ~** rejuvenating experience

jouxter [ʒukste] /1/ VT to adjoin

jovial, e, -aux [ʒɔvjal, -o] ADJ jovial, jolly

jovialité [ʒɔvjalite] NF joviality

joyau, x [ʒwajo] NM gem, jewel

joyeusement [ʒwajøzmã] ADV joyfully, gladly

joyeusetés [ʒwajøzte] NFPL *(ironique)*: **... et autres ~** ... and other joys

★**joyeux, -euse** [ʒwajø, -øz] ADJ joyful, merry; **~ Noël!** Merry *ou* Happy Christmas!; **joyeuses Pâques!** Happy Easter!; **~ anniversaire!** many happy returns!

joystick [dʒɔjstik] NM joystick

JT SIGLE M = **journal télévisé**

jubilation [ʒybilasjɔ̃] NF jubilation

jubilatoire [ʒybilatwaʀ] ADJ exhilarating

jubilé [ʒybile] NM jubilee

jubiler [ʒybile] /1/ VI to be jubilant, exult

jucher [ʒyʃe] /1/ VT: **~ qch sur** to perch sth (up)on ▶ VI *(oiseau)*: **~ sur** to perch (up)on ■ **se jucher sur** VPR to perch o.s. (up)on

judaïque [ʒydaik] ADJ *(loi)* Judaic; *(religion)* Jewish

judaïsme [ʒydaism] NM Judaism

judas [ʒyda] NM *(trou)* spy-hole

Judée [ʒyde] NF: **la ~** Jud(a)ea

judéité [ʒydeite], **judaïté** [ʒydaite] NF Jewishness

judéo- [ʒydeɔ] PRÉFIXE Judeo-

judéo-allemand, e [ʒydeɔalmã, -ãd] ADJ, NM Yiddish

judéo-chrétien, ne [ʒydeɔkʀetjɛ̃, -ɛn] ADJ Judeo-Christian

judiciaire [ʒydisjɛʀ] ADJ judicial

judicieusement [ʒydisjøzmã] ADV judiciously

judicieux, -euse [ʒydisjø, -øz] ADJ judicious

★**judo** [ʒydo] NM judo

judoka [ʒydɔka] NMF judoka

★**juge** [ʒyʒ] NM judge; **~ d'instruction** examining *(BRIT)* ou committing *(US)* magistrate; **~ de paix** justice of the peace; **~ de touche** linesman

jugé [ʒyʒe] : **au ~** *adv* by guesswork

jugement [ʒyʒmã] NM judgment; *(Jur: au pénal)* sentence; *(: au civil)* decision; **~ de valeur** value judgment

jugeote [ʒyʒɔt] NF *(fam)* gumption

juger [ʒyʒe] /3/ VT to judge; *(estimer)* to consider; **~ qn/qch satisfaisant** to consider sb/sth (to be) satisfactory; **~ que** to think ou consider that; **~ bon de faire** to consider it a good idea to do, see fit to do; **~ de** to judge; **jugez de ma surprise** imagine my surprise ▶ NM: **au ~** by guesswork

jugulaire [ʒygylɛʀ] ADJ jugular ▶ NF *(Mil)* chin-strap

juguler [ʒygyle] /1/ VT *(maladie)* to halt; *(révolte)* to suppress; *(inflation etc)* to control, curb

★**juif, -ive** [ʒɥif, -iv] ADJ Jewish ▶ NM/F: **Juif, -ive** Jewish man/woman ou Jew

★**juillet** [ʒɥijɛ] NM July; **le premier ~** the first of July *(BRIT)*, July first *(US)*; **le deux/onze ~** the second/eleventh of July, July second/eleventh; **il est venu le 5 ~** he came on 5th July ou July 5th; **en ~** in July; **début/fin ~** at the beginning/end of July; *see note*

> **Le 14 juillet** is a national holiday in France and commemorates the storming of the Bastille during the French Revolution. Throughout the country there are celebrations, which feature parades, music, dancing and firework displays. In Paris a military parade along the Champs-Élysées is attended by the President.

★**juin** [ʒɥɛ̃] NM June; *voir aussi* **juillet**

juive [ʒɥiv] ADJ, NF *voir* **juif**

jules [ʒyl] NM *(fam: mari)* hubby; *(: petit ami)* boyfriend

julienne [ʒyljɛn] NF *(Culin)* julienne

★**jumeau, -elle, x** [ʒymo, -ɛl] ADJ, NM/F twin; **maisons jumelles** semidetached houses

jumelage [ʒym(ə)laʒ] NM twinning

jumeler [ʒym(ə)le] /4/ VT to twin; **roues jumelées** double wheels; **billets de loterie jumelés** double series lottery tickets; **pari jumelé** double bet

★**jumelle** [ʒymɛl] ADJ F, NF *voir* **jumeau**

jumelles [ʒymɛl] NFPL binoculars

jument [ʒymã] NF mare

jungle [ʒɔ̃gl] NF jungle

junior [ʒynjɔʀ] ADJ junior

junte [ʒœ̃t] NF junta

★**jupe** [ʒyp] NF skirt

jupe-culotte [ʒypkylɔt] *(pl* **jupes-culottes**) NF divided skirt, culotte(s)

jupette [ʒypɛt] NF short skirt

jupon [ʒypɔ̃] NM waist slip ou petticoat

Jura [ʒyʀa] NM: **le ~** the Jura (Mountains)

jurassien, ne [ʒyʀasjɛ̃, -ɛn] ADJ of ou from the Jura Mountains

juré, e [ʒyʀe] NM/F juror ▸ ADJ: **ennemi ~** sworn ou avowed enemy

jurer [ʒyʀe] /1/ VT (obéissance etc) to swear, vow; **~ de faire/que** (s'engager) to swear ou vow to do/that; **~ que** (affirmer) to swear ou vouch that; **~ de qch** (s'en porter garant) to swear to sth; **ils ne jurent que par lui** they swear by him ▸ VI (dire des jurons) to swear, curse; (dissoner): **~ (avec)** to clash (with); **je vous jure!** honestly!

juridiction [ʒyʀidiksjɔ̃] NF jurisdiction; (tribunal, tribunaux) court(s) of law

juridictionnel, le [ʒyʀidiksjɔnel] ADJ jurisdictional

juridique [ʒyʀidik] ADJ legal

juridiquement [ʒyʀidikmɑ̃] ADV (devant la justice) juridically; (du point de vue du droit) legally

jurisconsulte [ʒyʀiskɔ̃sylt] NM jurisconsult

jurisprudence [ʒyʀispʀydɑ̃s] NF (Jur: décisions) (legal) precedents; (: principes juridiques) jurisprudence; **faire ~** (faire autorité) to set a precedent

juriste [ʒyʀist] NMF jurist; lawyer

juron [ʒyʀɔ̃] NM curse, swearword

jury [ʒyʀi] NM (Jur) jury; (Art, Sport) panel of judges; (Scol) board (of examiners), jury

★**jus** [ʒy] NM juice; (de viande) gravy, (meat) juice; **~ de fruits** fruit juice; **~ de raisin/tomates** grape/tomato juice

jusant [ʒyzɑ̃] NM ebb (tide)

jusqu'au-boutiste [ʒyskobutist] NMF extremist, hardliner

★**jusque** [ʒysk]: **jusqu'à** prép (endroit) as far as, (up) to; (moment) until, till; (limite) up to; **~ sur/dans** up to, as far as; (y compris) even on/in; **~ vers** until about; **jusqu'à ce que** conj until; **jusque-là** (temps) until then; (espace) up to there; **jusqu'ici** (temps) until now; (espace) up to here; **jusqu'à présent** ou **maintenant** until now, so far; **jusqu'où?** how far?

justaucorps [ʒystokɔʀ] NM INV (Danse, Sport) leotard

★**juste** [ʒyst] ADJ (équitable) just, fair; (légitime) just, justified; (exact, vrai) right; (pertinent) apt; (étroit) tight; (insuffisant) on the short side; **le ~ milieu** the happy medium; **à ~ titre** rightfully; **c'était ~** it was a close thing ▸ ADV right; tight; (chanter) in tune; (seulement) just; **~ assez/au-dessus** just enough/above; **pouvoir tout ~ faire** to be only just able to do; **au ~** exactly, actually; **comme de ~** of course, naturally

justement [ʒystəmɑ̃] ADV rightly; justly; (précisément) just, precisely; **c'est ~ ce qu'il fallait faire** that's just ou precisely what needed doing

justesse [ʒystɛs] NF (précision) accuracy; (d'une remarque) aptness; (d'une opinion) soundness; **de ~** only just, by a narrow margin

justice [ʒystis] NF (équité) fairness, justice; (Admin) justice; **rendre la ~** to dispense justice; **traduire en ~** to bring before the courts; **obtenir ~** to obtain justice; **rendre ~ à qn** to do sb justice; **se faire ~** to take the law into one's own hands; (se suicider) to take one's life

justiciable [ʒystisjabl] ADJ: **~ de** (Jur) answerable to

justicier, -ière [ʒystisje, -jɛʀ] NM/F judge, righter of wrongs

justifiable [ʒystifjabl] ADJ justifiable

justificatif, -ive [ʒystifikatif, -iv] ADJ (document etc) supporting; **pièce justificative** written proof ▸ NM supporting proof

justification [ʒystifikasjɔ̃] NF justification

justifié, e [ʒystifje] ADJ justified; (Inform): **~ à droite/gauche** right-/left-justified; **non ~** unjustified

justifier [ʒystifje] /7/ VT to justify; **~ de** to prove

jute [ʒyt] NM jute

juteux, -euse [ʒytø, -øz] ADJ juicy

juvénile [ʒyvenil] ADJ young, youthful; voir aussi **délinquance**

juxtaposer [ʒykstapoze] /1/ VT to juxtapose

juxtaposition [ʒykstapozisjɔ̃] NF juxtaposition

Kk

K, k [ka] NM INV K, k ▸ ABR (= *kilo*) kg; **K comme Kléber** K for King

K 7 [kasɛt] NF cassette

Kaboul, Kabul [kabul] N Kabul

kabyle [kabil] ADJ Kabyle ▸ NM (*Ling*) Kabyle ▸ NMF: **Kabyle** Kabyle

Kabylie [kabili] NF: **la ~** Kabylia

kafkaïen, ne [kafkajɛ̃, -ɛn] ADJ Kafkaesque

kaki [kaki] ADJ INV khaki

Kalahari [kalaaʀi] N: **le (désert du) ~** the Kalahari (Desert)

kaléidoscope [kaleidɔskɔp] NM kaleidoscope

Kampala [kãpala] N Kampala

kanak, e, canaque [kanak] ADJ Kanak; **les coutumes kanakes** Kanak customs ▸ NM/F: **Kanak, e** Kanak

kangourou [kãguʀu] NM kangaroo

kaolin [kaɔlɛ̃] NM kaolin

kapok [kapɔk] NM kapok

karaoke [karaoke] NM karaoke

karaoké [karaoke] NM karaoke

karaté [karate] NM karate

karité [karite] NM shea; **beurre de ~** shea butter

kart [kaʀt] NM go-cart

karting [kaʀtiŋ] NM go-carting, karting

kascher [kaʃɛʀ] ADJ INV kosher

kayak [kajak] NM kayak; **faire du ~** to go kayaking

Kazakhstan [kazakstɑ̃] NM Kazakhstan

Kenya [kenja] NM: **le ~** Kenya

kényan, e, kenyan, e [kenjɑ̃, -an] ADJ Kenyan ▸ NM/F: **Kényan, e** Kenyan

képi [kepi] NM kepi

kératine [keʀatin] NF keratin, ceratin

Kerguelen [kɛʀgelɛn] NFPL: **les (îles) ~** Kerguelen

kermesse [kɛʀmɛs] NF bazaar, (charity) fête; village fair

kérosène [keʀozɛn] NM jet fuel; rocket fuel

ketchup [kɛtʃœp] NM ketchup

kg ABR (= *kilogramme*) kg

KGB SIGLE M KGB

khâgne [kaɲ] NF second year of preparatory course for arts section of the École normale supérieure

khmer, -ère [kmɛʀ] ADJ Khmer ▸ NM (*Ling*) Khmer

khôl [kol] NM kohl

kibboutz [kibuts] NM kibbutz

kidnapper [kidnape] /1/ VT to kidnap

kidnappeur, -euse [kidnapœʀ, -øz] NM/F kidnapper

kidnapping [kidnapiŋ] NM kidnapping

kiffer [kife] /1/ (!) VT to like, be into; **je la kiffe trop cette meuf** I'm really into this woman ▸ VI: **ça me fait ~** I like it; **on a kiffé un max** we had a blast

kif-kif [kifkif] ADJ INV (*fam*): **c'est ~** it's all the same

Kilimandjaro [kilimɑ̃dʒaʀo] NM: **le ~** Mount Kilimanjaro

★**kilo** [kilo] NM kilo

★**kilogramme** [kilɔgʀam] NM kilogramme (*BRIT*), kilogram (*US*)

kilométrage [kilɔmetʀaʒ] NM number of kilometres travelled, ≈ mileage

kilomètre [kilɔmɛtʀ] NM kilometre (*BRIT*), kilometer (*US*); **kilomètres-heure** kilometres per hour

kilométrique [kilɔmetʀik] ADJ (*distance*) in kilometres; **compteur ~** ≈ mileage indicator

kilooctet [kilɔɔktɛ] NM kilobyte

kilowatt [kilɔwat] NM kilowatt

kilt [kilt] NM (*traditionnel*) kilt; (*de femme*) kilt, pleated tartan skirt

kimono [kimɔno] NM kimono

Kindle® [kindl] NM Kindle®

kiné [kine] NMF (*fam: kinésithérapeute*) physio (*BRIT*)

kinésithérapeute [kineziteʀapøt] NMF physiotherapist

kinésithérapie [kineziteʀapi] NF physiotherapy

kiosque [kjɔsk] NM kiosk, stall; (*Tél etc*) telephone and/or videotext information service; **~ à journaux** newspaper kiosk

kippa [kipa] NF kippa, skullcap

kir [kiʀ] NM kir (*white wine with blackcurrant liqueur*)

Kirghizistan [kiʀgizistɑ̃] NM Kirghizia

kirsch [kiʀʃ] NM kirsch

kit [kit] NM kit; **~ piéton** *ou* **mains libres** hands-free kit; **en ~** in kit form

kitchenette [kitʃ(ə)nɛt] NF kitchenette

kitsch [kitʃ] ADJ INV (*objet, décor*) kitsch, kitschy ▸ NM (*style, genre*) kitsch

kiwi [kiwi] NM (*Zool*) kiwi; (*Bot*) kiwi (fruit)

klaxon [klaksɔn, klaksɔ̃] NM horn

klaxonner [klaksɔne] /1/ VI, VT to hoot (*BRIT*), honk (one's horn) (*US*)

kleptomane [klɛptɔman] NMF kleptomaniac

km ABR (= *kilomètre*) km

km/h ABR (= *kilomètres/heure*) km/h, kph

knock-out [nɔkawt] NM knock-out

Ko ABR (*Inform*: = *kilooctet*) kB

K.-O. [kao] ADJ INV (*fam*) shattered, knackered

koala [kɔala] NM koala (bear)

kolkhoze [kɔlkoz] NM kolkhoz

Kosovo [kɔsovo] NM: **le ~** Kosovo

Koweït, Koweit [kɔwɛt] NM: **le ~** Kuwait, Koweit

koweïtien, ne, koweitien, ne [kɔwɛtjɛ̃, -ɛn] ADJ Kuwaiti ▶ NM/F: **Koweïtien, ne, Koweitien, ne** Kuwaiti

krach [kʀak] NM (*Écon*) crash

kraft [kʀaft] NM brown *ou* kraft paper

Kremlin [kʀɛmlɛ̃] NM: **le ~** the Kremlin

Kuala Lumpur [kwalalympuʀ] N Kuala Lumpur

kumquat [kɔmkwat] NM kumquat

kurde [kyʀd] ADJ Kurdish ▶ NM (*Ling*) Kurdish ▶ NMF: **Kurde** Kurd

Kurdistan [kyʀdistɑ̃] NM: **le ~** Kurdistan

Kuweit [kɔwɛt] NM = **Koweït**

kW ABR (= *kilowatt*) kW

K-way® [kawɛ] NM (lightweight nylon) cagoule

kW/h ABR (= *kilowatt/heure*) kW/h

kyrielle [kiʀjel] NF: **une ~ de** a stream of

kyste [kist] NM cyst

Ll

L, l [ɛl] NM INV L, l ▸ ABR (= litre) l; **L comme Louis** L for Lucy (BRIT) *ou* Love (US)

★**l'** [l] ART DÉF *voir* **le**

★**la** [la] ART DÉF, PRON *voir* **le** ▸ NM (*Mus*) A; (*en chantant la gamme*) la

★**là** [la] ADV there; (*ici*) here; (*dans le temps*) then; **est-ce que Catherine est là ?** is Catherine there (*ou* here)?; **elle n'est pas là** she isn't here; **c'est là que** this is where; **là où** where; **de là** (*fig*) hence; **par là** (*fig*) by that; **tout est là** (*fig*) that's what it's all about; *voir aussi* **-ci**; **celui**

là-bas [labɑ] ADV there

label [label] NM stamp, seal

labelliser [labelize] VT (*certifier, approuver*) to give one's seal of approval to; **être labellisé** to be approved; **La Bergerie, studio labellisé Gîtes de France** La Bergerie, a Gîtes de France approved flat

labeur [labœʀ] NM toil *no pl*, toiling *no pl*

labial, e, -aux [labjal, -o] ADJ (*Anat, Ling*) labial ▸ NF (*Ling*) labial

labo [labo] NM (= *laboratoire*) lab

laborantin, e [labɔʀɑ̃tɛ̃, -in] NM/F laboratory assistant

★**laboratoire** [labɔʀatwaʀ] NM laboratory; **~ de langues/d'analyses** language/(medical) analysis laboratory

laborieusement [labɔʀjøzmɑ̃] ADV laboriously

laborieux, -euse [labɔʀjø, -øz] ADJ (*tâche*) laborious; **classes laborieuses** working classes

labour [labuʀ] NM ploughing *no pl* (BRIT), plowing *no pl* (US); **cheval de ~** plough- *ou* cart-horse; **bœuf de ~** ox ■ **labours** NMPL (*champs*) ploughed fields

labourage [labuʀaʒ] NM ploughing (BRIT), plowing (US)

labourer [labuʀe] /1/ VT to plough (BRIT), plow (US); (*fig*) to make deep gashes *ou* furrows in

laboureur [labuʀœʀ] NM ploughman (BRIT), plowman (US)

labrador [labʀadɔʀ] NM (*chien*) labrador; (*Géo*) **le L~** Labrador

labyrinthe [labiʀɛ̃t] NM labyrinth, maze

★**lac** [lak] NM lake; **le ~ Léman** Lake Geneva; **les Grands Lacs** the Great Lakes; *voir aussi* **lacs**

lacer [lase] /3/ VT to lace *ou* do up

lacération [laseʀasjɔ̃] NF (*Méd*) laceration

lacérer [laseʀe] /6/ VT to tear to shreds

lacet [lasɛ] NM (*de chaussure*) lace; (*de route*) sharp bend; (*piège*) snare; **chaussures à lacets** lace-up *ou* lacing shoes

lâche [lɑʃ] ADJ (*poltron*) cowardly; (*desserré*) loose, slack; (*morale, mœurs*) lax ▸ NMF coward

lâchement [lɑʃmɑ̃] ADV (*par peur*) like a coward; (*par bassesse*) despicably

lâcher [lɑʃe] /1/ NM (*de ballons, oiseaux*) release ▸ VT (*main*) to let go of; (*verre*) to drop; (*libérer*) to release; (*fig: mot, remarque*) to let slip, come out with; (*Sport: distancer*) to leave behind; **~ prise** to let go ▸ VI (*fil, amarres*) to break, give way; (*freins*) to fail ■ **se lâcher** VPR (*fam*) to let o.s. go

lâcheté [lɑʃte] NF cowardice; (*bassesse*) lowness

lacis [lasi] NM (*de ruelles*) maze

laconique [lakɔnik] ADJ laconic

laconiquement [lakɔnikmɑ̃] ADV laconically

lacrymal, e, -aux [lakʀimal, -o] ADJ (*canal, glande*) tear *cpd*

lacrymogène [lakʀimɔʒɛn] ADJ: **grenade/gaz ~** tear gas grenade/tear gas

lacs [lɑ] NM (*piège*) snare

lactation [laktasjɔ̃] NF lactation

lacté, e [lakte] ADJ milk *cpd*

lactique [laktik] ADJ: **acide/ferment ~** lactic acid/ferment

lactose [laktoz] NM lactose, milk sugar

lactosérum [laktoseʀɔm] NM (*petit lait*) whey

lacune [lakyn] NF gap

lacustre [lakystʀ] ADJ lake *cpd*, lakeside *cpd*

lad [lad] NM stable-lad

là-dedans [ladədɑ̃] ADV inside (there), in it; (*fig*) in that

là-dehors [ladəɔʀ] ADV out there

là-derrière [ladɛʀjɛʀ] ADV behind there; (*fig*) behind that

là-dessous [ladsu] ADV underneath, under there; (*fig*) behind that

là-dessus [ladsy] ADV on there; (*fig: sur ces mots*) at that point; (: *à ce sujet*) about that

là-devant [ladvɑ̃] ADV there (in front)

ladite [ladit] ADJ *voir* **ledit**

ladre [lɑdʀ] ADJ miserly

lagon [lagɔ̃] NM lagoon

lagopède [lagɔpɛd] NM grouse; **~ des Alpes** ptarmigan

Lagos [lagɔs] N Lagos

lagune [lagyn] NF lagoon

là-haut [lao] ADV up there

laïc [laik] ADJ M, NM = **laïque**

laïciser [laisize] /1/ VT to secularize

laïcité [laisite] NF secularity, secularism

Laïcité, or secularism, is one of the main tenets of the French Republic and is enshrined in its constitution. The Revolution gave rise to the idea of a separation between church and state, the main expression of which is in the educational sphere: all French state schools are secular, both in their everyday running and in the national curriculum. In recent years, the concept of *laïcité* has been challenged by the need to accommodate a significant Muslim population whilst banning ostentatious displays of religious belief in state schools, for instance the wearing of the hijab.

★**laid, e** [lɛ, lɛd] ADJ ugly; (*fig: acte*) mean, cheap

laideron [lɛdʀɔ̃] NM ugly girl

laideur [lɛdœʀ] NF ugliness *no pl*; meanness *no pl*

laie [lɛ] NF wild sow

lainage [lɛnaʒ] NM (*vêtement*) woollen garment; (*étoffe*) woollen material

★**laine** [lɛn] NF wool; **~ peignée** worsted (wool); **~ à tricoter** knitting wool; **~ de verre** glass wool; **~ vierge** new wool

laineux, -euse [lɛnø, -øz] ADJ woolly

lainier, -ière [lɛnje, -jɛʀ] ADJ (*industrie etc*) woollen

laïque [laik] ADJ lay, civil; (*Scol*) state *cpd* (*as opposed to Roman Catholic*) ▶ NMF layman(-woman)

laisse [lɛs] NF (*de chien*) lead, leash; **tenir en ~** to keep on a lead *ou* leash

laissé-pour-compte, laissée-pour-compte [lesepuʀkɔ̃t] (*pl* **laissés-pour-compte**) ADJ (*Comm*) unsold; (: *refusé*) returned ▶ NM/F (*fig*) reject; **les laissés-pour-compte de la reprise économique** those who are left out of the economic upturn

★**laisser** [lese] /1/ VT to leave ▶ VB AUX to let; **~ qn faire** to let sb do; **~ qn tranquille** to let *ou* leave sb alone; **laisse-moi faire** let me do it; **rien ne laisse penser que ...** there is no reason to think that ...; **cela ne laisse pas de surprendre** nonetheless it is surprising ■ **se laisser** VPR: **se ~ aller** to let o.s. go; **se ~ exploiter** to let o.s. be exploited

laisser-aller [leseale] NM carelessness, slovenliness

laisser-faire [lesefɛʀ] NM laissez-faire

laissez-passer [lesepase] NM INV pass

★**lait** [lɛ] NM milk; **frère/sœur de ~** foster brother/sister; **~ écrémé/entier/concentré/condensé** skimmed/full-fat/condensed/evaporated milk; **~ en poudre** powdered milk, milk powder; **~ de chèvre/vache** goat's/cow's milk; **~ maternel** mother's milk; **~ démaquillant/de beauté** cleansing/beauty lotion

laitage [lɛtaʒ] NM dairy product

laiterie [lɛtʀi] NF dairy

laiteux, -euse [lɛtø, -øz] ADJ milky

laitier, -ière [letje, -jɛʀ] ADJ dairy *cpd* ▶ NM/F milkman (dairywoman)

laiton [lɛtɔ̃] NM brass

★**laitue** [lety] NF lettuce

laïus [lajys] NM (*péj*) spiel

lama [lama] NM llama

lamantin [lamɑ̃tɛ̃] NM manatee

lamaserie [lamazʀi] NF lamasery

lambda [lɑ̃bda] NM (*lettre grecque*) lambda ▶ ADJ INV (*fam: moyen*) average

lambeau, x [lɑ̃bo] NM scrap; **en lambeaux** in tatters, tattered

lambin, e [lɑ̃bɛ̃, -in] ADJ (*péj*) slow

lambiner [lɑ̃bine] /1/ VI (*péj*) to dawdle

lambris [lɑ̃bʀi] NM panelling *no pl*

lambrissé, e [lɑ̃bʀise] ADJ panelled

lame [lam] NF blade; (*vague*) wave; (*lamelle*) strip; **~ de fond** ground swell *no pl*; **~ de rasoir** razor blade

lamé [lame] NM lamé

lamelle [lamɛl] NF (*lame*) small blade; (*morceau*) sliver; (*de champignon*) gill; **couper en lamelles** to slice thinly

lamellé-collé [lamelekɔle] (*pl* **lamellés-collés**) NM laminated timber

lamellibranche [lamelibʀɑ̃ʃ] NM lamellibranch

lamentable [lamɑ̃tabl] ADJ (*déplorable*) appalling; (*pitoyable*) pitiful

lamentablement [lamɑ̃tabləmɑ̃] ADV (*échouer*) miserably; (*se conduire*) appallingly

lamentation [lamɑ̃tasjɔ̃] NF wailing *no pl*, lamentation; moaning *no pl*

lamenter [lamɑ̃te] /1/: **se lamenter** VPR: **se ~ (sur)** to moan (over)

laminage [laminaʒ] NM lamination

laminer [lamine] /1/ VT to laminate; (*fig: écraser*) to wipe out

laminoir [laminwaʀ] NM rolling mill; **passer au ~** (*fig*) to go (*ou* put) through the mill

lampadaire [lɑ̃padɛʀ] NM (*de salon*) standard lamp; (*dans la rue*) street lamp

★**lampe** [lɑ̃p] NF lamp; (*Tech*) valve; **~ à alcool** spirit lamp; **~ à pétrole** oil lamp; **~ à bronzer** sunlamp; **~ de poche** torch (BRIT), flashlight (US); **~ à souder** blowlamp; **~ témoin** warning light; **~ halogène** halogen lamp

lampée [lɑ̃pe] NF gulp, swig

lampe-tempête [lɑ̃ptɑ̃pɛt] (*pl* **lampes-tempête**) NF storm lantern

lampion [lɑ̃pjɔ̃] NM Chinese lantern

lampiste [lɑ̃pist] NM light (maintenance) man; (*fig*) underling

lamproie [lɑ̃pʀwa] NF lamprey

lance [lɑ̃s] NF spear; **~ d'arrosage** garden hose; **~ à eau** water hose; **~ d'incendie** fire hose

lancée [lɑ̃se] NF: **être/continuer sur sa ~** to be under way/keep going

lance-flammes [lɑ̃sflam] NM INV flamethrower

lance-fusées [lɑ̃sfyze] NM INV rocket launcher

lance-grenades [lɑ̃sɡʀənad] NM INV grenade launcher

lancement [lɑ̃smɑ̃] NM launching *no pl*, launch; **offre de ~** introductory offer

lance-missiles [lɑ̃smisil] NM INV missile launcher

lance-pierres [lɑ̃spjɛʀ] NM INV catapult

★**lancer** [lɑ̃se] /**3**/ NM (*Athlétisme*) throwing *no pl*, throw; **~ du javelot/du disque/du marteau** javelin/discus/hammer throw *ou* throwing; **~ du poids** shot put; (*Pêche*) rod and reel fishing ▶ VT to throw; (*émettre, projeter*) to throw out, send out; (*produit, fusée, bateau, artiste*) to launch; (*injure*) to hurl, fling; (*proclamation, mandat d'arrêt*) to issue; (*emprunt*) to float; (*moteur*) to send roaring away; **~ qch à qn** to throw sth to sb; (*de façon agressive*) to throw sth at sb; **~ un cri** *ou* **un appel** to shout *ou* call out ■ **se lancer** VPR (*prendre de l'élan*) to build up speed; (*se précipiter*): **se ~ sur** *ou* **contre** to rush at; **se ~ dans** (*discussion*) to launch into; (*aventure*) to embark on; (*les affaires, la politique*) to go into

lance-roquettes [lɑ̃sʀɔkɛt] NM INV rocket launcher

lance-torpilles [lɑ̃stɔʀpij] NM INV torpedo tube

lanceur, -euse [lɑ̃sœʀ, -øz] NM/F bowler; (*Baseball*) pitcher; **~ d'alerte** whistleblower ▶ NM (*Espace*) launcher

lancinant, e [lɑ̃sinɑ̃, -ɑ̃t] ADJ (*regrets etc*) haunting; (*douleur*) shooting

lanciner [lɑ̃sine] /**1**/ VI to throb; (*fig*) to nag

landais, e [lɑ̃dɛ, -ɛz] ADJ of *ou* from the Landes

landau [lɑ̃do] NM pram (BRIT), baby carriage (US)

lande [lɑ̃d] NF moor

Landes [lɑ̃d] NFPL: **les ~** the Landes

langage [lɑ̃gaʒ] NM language; **~ d'assemblage** (*Inform*) assembly language; **~ du corps** body language; **~ évolué/machine** (*Inform*) high-level/machine language; **~ de programmation** (*Inform*) programming language

lange [lɑ̃ʒ] NM flannel blanket ■ **langes** NMPL swaddling clothes

langer [lɑ̃ʒe] /**3**/ VT to change (the nappy (BRIT) *ou* diaper (US) of); **table à ~** changing table

langoureusement [lɑ̃guʀøzmɑ̃] ADV languorously

langoureux, -euse [lɑ̃guʀø, -øz] ADJ languorous

langouste [lɑ̃gust] NF crayfish *inv*

langoustine [lɑ̃gustin] NF Dublin Bay prawn

★**langue** [lɑ̃g] NF (*Anat, Culin*) tongue; (*Ling*) language; (*bande*): **~ de terre** spit of land; **tirer la ~ (à)** to stick out one's tongue (at); **donner sa ~ au chat** to give up, give in; **de ~ française** French-speaking; **~ de bois** officialese; **~ maternelle** native language, mother tongue; **~ verte** slang; **langues vivantes** modern languages

For a long time, in the name of national unity, the use of French **langues régionales** was systematically discouraged or banned. As a result, speakers of Breton, Alsatian, Occitan, Catalan, Basque, Corsican and Flemish today represent a very small fraction of the population, despite efforts to teach those languages in special schools. The situation is very different overseas, where regional languages are much more widely spoken.

langue-de-chat [lɑ̃gdəʃa] (*pl* **langues-de-chat**) NF finger biscuit

languedocien, ne [lɑ̃gdɔsjɛ̃, -ɛn] ADJ of *ou* from the Languedoc

languette [lɑ̃gɛt] NF tongue

langueur [lɑ̃gœʀ] NF languidness

languide [lɑ̃gid] ADJ languid

languir [lɑ̃giʀ] /**2**/ VI to languish; (*conversation*) to flag; **faire ~ qn** to keep sb waiting ■ **se languir** VPR to be languishing

languissant, e [lɑ̃gisɑ̃, -ɑ̃t] ADJ languid

lanière [lanjɛʀ] NF (*de fouet*) lash; (*de valise, bretelle*) strap

lanoline [lanɔlin] NF lanolin

lanterne [lɑ̃tɛʀn] NF (*portable*) lantern; (*électrique*) light, lamp; (*de voiture*) (side)light; **~ rouge** (*fig*) tail-ender; **~ vénitienne** Chinese lantern

lanterneau, x [lɑ̃tɛʀno] NM skylight

lanterner [lɑ̃tɛʀne] /**1**/ VI: **faire ~ qn** to keep sb hanging around

Laos [laɔs] NM: **le ~** Laos

laotien, ne [laɔsjɛ̃, -ɛn] ADJ Laotian

lapalissade [lapalisad] NF statement of the obvious

laparotomie [lapaʀɔtɔmi] NF laparotomy

La Paz [lapaz] N La Paz

laper [lape] /**1**/ VT to lap up

lapereau, x [lapʀo] NM young rabbit

lapidaire [lapidɛʀ] ADJ stone *cpd*; (*fig*) terse

lapidation [lapidasjɔ̃] NF stoning

lapider [lapide] /**1**/ VT to stone

★**lapin** [lapɛ̃] NM rabbit; (*peau*) rabbitskin; (*fourrure*) cony; **coup du ~** rabbit punch; **poser un ~ à qn** to stand sb up; **~ de garenne** wild rabbit

lapis [lapis], **lapis-lazuli** [lapislazyli] NM INV lapis lazuli

lapon, e [lapɔ̃, -ɔn] ADJ Lapp, Lappish ▶ NM (*Ling*) Lapp, Lappish ▶ NM/F: **Lapon, e** Lapp, Laplander

Laponie [lapɔni] NF: **la ~** Lapland

laps [laps] NM: **~ de temps** space of time, time *no pl*

lapsus [lapsys] NM slip

laquais [lakɛ] NM lackey

laque [lak] NF (*vernis*) lacquer; (*brute*) shellac; (*pour cheveux*) hair spray ▶ NM lacquer; piece of lacquer ware

laqué, e [lake] ADJ lacquered

laquelle [lakɛl] PRON *voir* **lequel**

larbin [laʀbɛ̃] NM (*péj*) flunkey

larcin [laʀsɛ̃] NM theft

lard [laʀ] NM (*graisse*) fat; (*bacon*) (streaky) bacon

larder [laʀde] /**1**/ VT (*Culin*) to lard

lardon [laʀdɔ̃] NM (*Culin*) piece of chopped bacon; (*fam: enfant*) kid

largage [laʀgaʒ] NM (*de bombe, parachutistes*) dropping; (*de sonde*) release

★**large** [laʀʒ] ADJ wide; broad; (*fig*) generous; **~ d'esprit** broad-minded ▶ ADV: **calculer/voir ~** to allow extra/think big; **ne pas en mener ~** to have one's heart in one's boots ▶ NM (*largeur*): **5 m de ~** 5 m wide *ou* in width; (*mer*) **le ~** the open sea; **en ~** *adv* sideways; **au ~ de** off

largement [laʀʒəmɑ̃] ADV widely; (*de loin*) greatly; (*amplement, au minimum*) easily; (*sans compter: donner etc*) generously; **c'est ~ suffisant** that's ample

largesse [laʀʒɛs] NF generosity ■ **largesses** NFPL (*dons*) liberalities

largeur [laʀʒœʀ] NF (*qu'on mesure*) width; (*impression visuelle*) wideness, width; breadth; (*d'esprit*) broadness

larguer [laʀge] /1/ VT to drop; *(fam: se débarrasser de)* to get rid of; **~ les amarres** to cast off (the moorings)

larme [laʀm] NF tear; *(fig)*: **une ~ de** a drop of; **en larmes** in tears; **pleurer à chaudes larmes** to cry one's eyes out, cry bitterly

larmoyant, e [laʀmwajɑ̃, -ɑ̃t] ADJ tearful

larmoyer [laʀmwaje] /8/ VI *(yeux)* to water; *(se plaindre)* to whimper

larron [laʀɔ̃] NM thief

larvaire [laʀvɛʀ] ADJ *(Bio)* larval; **à l'état ~** in the larval state

larve [laʀv] NF *(Zool)* larva; *(fig)* worm

larvé, e [laʀve] ADJ *(fig)* latent

laryngite [laʀɛ̃ʒit] NF laryngitis

laryngologiste [laʀɛ̃gɔlɔʒist] NMF throat specialist

larynx [laʀɛ̃ks] NM larynx

las, lasse [lɑ, lɑs] ADJ weary

lasagnes [lazaɲ] NFPL lasagne

lascar [laskaʀ] NM character; *(malin)* rogue

lascif, -ive [lasif, -iv] ADJ lascivious

lascivement [lasivmɑ̃] ADV lasciviously

lascivité [lasivite] NF lasciviousness

laser [lazɛʀ] NM: **(rayon) ~** laser (beam); **chaîne ou platine ~** compact disc (player); **disque ~** compact disc

lassant, e [lɑsɑ̃, -ɑ̃t] ADJ tiresome, wearisome

lasse [lɑs] ADJ F *voir* **las**

lasser [lɑse] /1/ VT to weary, tire; **se ~ de** to grow weary *ou* tired of

lassitude [lɑsityd] NF lassitude, weariness

lasso [laso] NM lasso; **prendre au ~** to lasso

latent, e [latɑ̃, -ɑ̃t] ADJ latent

latéral, e, -aux [lateʀal, -o] ADJ side *cpd*, lateral

latéralement [lateʀalmɑ̃] ADV edgeways; *(arriver, souffler)* from the side

latex [latɛks] NM INV latex

★**latin, e** [latɛ̃, -in] ADJ Latin ▶ NM *(Ling)* Latin; **j'y perds mon ~** it's all Greek to me ▶ NM/F: **Latin, e** Latin

latiniste [latinist] NMF Latin scholar *(ou* student)

latino-américain, e [latinɔameʀikɛ̃, -ɛn] ADJ Latin-American

latitude [latityd] NF latitude; *(fig)*: **avoir la ~ de faire** to be left free *ou* be at liberty to do; **à 48° de ~ Nord** at latitude 48° North; **sous toutes les latitudes** *(fig)* world-wide, throughout the world

latrines [latʀin] NFPL latrines

latte [lat] NF lath, slat; *(de plancher)* board

lattis [lati] NM lathwork

laudanum [lodanɔm] NM laudanum

laudatif, -ive [lodatif, -iv] ADJ laudatory

lauréat, e [lɔʀea, -at] NM/F winner

laurier [lɔʀje] NM *(Bot)* laurel; *(Culin)* bay leaves *pl*; ▪ **lauriers** NMPL *(fig)* laurels

laurier-rose [lɔʀjeʀoz] *(pl* **lauriers-roses)** NM oleander

laurier-tin [lɔʀjetɛ̃] *(pl* **lauriers-tins)** NM laurustinus

lavable [lavabl] ADJ washable

★**lavabo** [lavabo] NM washbasin ▪ **lavabos** NMPL toilet *sg*

lavage [lavaʒ] NM washing *no pl*, wash; **~ d'estomac/d'intestin** stomach/intestinal wash; **~ de cerveau** brainwashing *no pl*

lavallière [lavaljɛʀ] NF floppy necktie

lavande [lavɑ̃d] NF lavender

lavandière [lavɑ̃djɛʀ] NF washerwoman

lave [lav] NF lava *no pl*

lave-glace [lavglas] NM *(Auto)* windscreen (BRIT) *ou* windshield (US) washer

lave-linge [lavlɛ̃ʒ] NM INV washing machine

lavement [lavmɑ̃] NM *(Méd)* enema

★**laver** [lave] /1/ VT to wash; *(tache)* to wash off; *(fig: affront)* to avenge; **~ la vaisselle/le linge** to wash the dishes/clothes; **~ qn de** *(accusation)* to clear sb of ▪ **se laver** VPR to have a wash, wash; **se ~ les mains/dents** to wash one's hands/clean one's teeth

laverie [lavʀi] NF: **~ (automatique)** Launderette® (BRIT), Laundromat® (US)

lavette [lavɛt] NF *(chiffon)* dish cloth; *(brosse)* dish mop; *(fam: homme)* wimp, drip

laveur, -euse [lavœʀ, -øz] NM/F cleaner

★**lave-vaisselle** [lavvɛsɛl] NM INV dishwasher

lavis [lavi] NM *(technique)* washing; *(dessin)* wash drawing

lavoir [lavwaʀ] NM wash house; *(bac)* washtub; *(évier)* sink

laxatif, -ive [laksatif, -iv] ADJ, NM laxative

laxisme [laksism] NM laxity

laxiste [laksist] ADJ lax

layette [lɛjɛt] NF layette

layon [lɛjɔ̃] NM trail

lazaret [lazaʀɛ] NM quarantine area

lazzi [ladzi] NM gibe

---

le, la, l' [lə, la, l]

(pl **les)** ART DÉF **1** the; **le livre/la pomme/l'arbre** the book/the apple/the tree; **les étudiants** the students

2 *(noms abstraits)*: **le courage/l'amour/la jeunesse** courage/love/youth

3 *(indiquant la possession)*: **se casser la jambe** *etc* to break one's leg *etc*; **levez la main** put your hand up; **avoir les yeux gris/le nez rouge** to have grey eyes/a red nose

4 *(temps)*: **le matin/soir** in the morning/evening; mornings/evenings; **le jeudi** *etc (d'habitude)* on Thursdays *etc*; *(ce jeudi-là etc)* on (the) Thursday; **nous venons le 3 décembre** *(parlé)* we're coming on the 3rd of December *ou* on December the 3rd; *(écrit)* we're coming (on) 3rd *ou* 3 December

5 *(distribution, évaluation)* a, an; **trois euros le mètre/kilo** three euros a *ou* per metre/kilo; **le tiers/quart de** a third/quarter of

▶ PRON **1** *(personne: mâle)* him; *(: femelle)* her; *(: pluriel)* them; **je le/la/les vois** I can see him/her/them

2 *(animal, chose: singulier)* it; *(: pluriel)* them; **je le** *(ou* **la) vois** I can see it; **je les vois** I can see them

3 *(remplaçant une phrase)*: **je ne le savais pas** I didn't know (about it); **il était riche et ne l'est plus** he was once rich but no longer is

---

lé [le] NM *(de tissu)* width; *(de papier peint)* strip, length

leader [lidœʀ] NM leader
leadership [lidœʀʃip] NM (Pol) leadership
leasing [liziŋ] NM leasing
lèche [lɛʃ] NF (fam): **faire de la ~ à qn** to suck up to sb (fam), lick sb's boots (fam)
lèche-bottes [lɛʃbɔt] NMF INV bootlicker
lèchefrite [lɛʃfʀit] NF dripping pan ou tray
lécher [leʃe] /6/ VT to lick; (laper: lait, eau) to lick ou lap up; (finir, polir) to over-refine; **~ les vitrines** to go window-shopping ■ **se lécher** VPR: **se ~ les doigts/lèvres** to lick one's fingers/lips
lèche-vitrines [lɛʃvitʀin] NM INV: **faire du ~** to go window-shopping
lécithine [lesitin] NF lecithin; **~ de soja** soy lecithin
leçon [l(ə)sɔ̃] NF lesson; **faire la ~** to teach; **faire la ~ à** (fig) to give a lecture to; **leçons de conduite** driving lessons; **leçons particulières** private lessons ou tuition sg (BRIT)
★**lecteur, -trice** [lɛktœʀ, -tʀis] NM/F reader; (d'université) (foreign language) assistant (BRIT), (foreign) teaching assistant (US) ▶ NM (Tech): **~ de cassettes** cassette player; **~ de disquette(s)** disk drive; **~ de CD/DVD** (d'ordinateur) CD/DVD drive; (de salon) CD/DVD player; **~ MP3** MP3 player
lectorat [lɛktɔʀa] NM (foreign language ou teaching) assistantship
★**lecture** [lɛktyʀ] NF reading

> The French word **lecture** is not translated by the English word lecture.

LED [lɛd] SIGLE F (= light emitting diode) LED
ledit, ladite [ləit, ladit] (mpl **lesdits** [ledi], fpl **lesdites** [ledit]) ADJ the aforesaid
légal, e, -aux [legal, -o] ADJ legal
légalement [legalmɑ̃] ADV legally
légalisation [legalizasjɔ̃] NF legalization
légaliser [legalize] /1/ VT to legalize
légaliste [legalist] ADJ (personne, approche) legalistic
légalité [legalite] NF legality, lawfulness; **être dans/sortir de la ~** to be within/step outside the law
légat [lega] NM (Rel) legate
légataire [legatɛʀ] NM legatee
légendaire [leʒɑ̃dɛʀ] ADJ legendary
légende [leʒɑ̃d] NF (mythe) legend; (de carte, plan) key, legend; (de dessin) caption
légender [leʒɑ̃de] VT (carte, plan) to provide with a key; (dessin) to caption, provide with a caption; **une carte légendée** a map with a key; **un dessin légendé** a drawing with a caption
léger, -ère [leʒe, -ɛʀ] ADJ light; (bruit, retard) slight; (boisson, parfum) weak; (couche, étoffe) thin; (superficiel) thoughtless; (volage) free and easy; flighty; (peu sérieux) lightweight; **blessé ~** slightly injured person; **à la légère** adv (parler, agir) rashly, thoughtlessly
légèrement [leʒɛʀmɑ̃] ADV (s'habiller, bouger) lightly; thoughtlessly, rashly; **~ plus grand** slightly bigger; **manger ~** to eat a light meal
légèreté [leʒɛʀte] NF lightness; thoughtlessness; (d'une remarque) flippancy
légiférer [leʒifeʀe] /6/ VI to legislate

légion [leʒjɔ̃] NF legion; **la L~ étrangère** the Foreign Legion; **la L~ d'honneur** the Legion of Honour

> Created by Napoleon in 1802, the **Légion d'honneur** is the highest decoration that can be awarded in France, with recipients admitted to the Ordre national de la Légion d'honneur. The award can be conferred upon anyone (not necessarily a French citizen) the order wishes to reward for bravery or service to the French nation. The French President serves as the Grand Maître (grand master) of the order.

légionellose [leʒjɔneloz] NF legionnaire's disease, legionnaires' disease
légionnaire [leʒjɔnɛʀ] NM (Mil) legionnaire; (de la Légion d'honneur) holder of the Legion of Honour
législateur [leʒislatœʀ] NM legislator, lawmaker
législatif, -ive [leʒislatif, -iv] ADJ legislative ■ **législatives** NFPL general election sg
législation [leʒislasjɔ̃] NF legislation
législature [leʒislatyʀ] NF legislature; (période) term (of office)
légiste [leʒist] NMF jurist ▶ ADJ: **médecin ~** forensic scientist (BRIT), medical examiner (US)
légitimation [leʒitimasjɔ̃] NF (Jur) legitimization
légitime [leʒitim] ADJ (Jur) lawful, legitimate; (enfant) legitimate; (fig) rightful, legitimate; **en état de ~ défense** in self-defence
légitimement [leʒitimmɑ̃] ADV lawfully; legitimately; rightfully
légitimer [leʒitime] /1/ VT (enfant) to legitimize; (justifier: conduite) to justify
légitimité [leʒitimite] NF (Jur) legitimacy
legs [lɛg] NM legacy
léguer [lege] /6/ VT: **~ qch à qn** (Jur) to bequeath sth to sb; (fig) to hand sth down ou pass sth on to sb
légume [legym] NM vegetable; **légumes verts** green vegetables; **légumes secs** pulses
légumier [legymje] NM vegetable dish
leitmotiv [lɛjtmɔtiv] NM leitmotiv, leitmotif
Léman [lemɑ̃] NM voir lac
lémurien [lemyʀjɛ̃] NM lemur
★**lendemain** [lɑ̃dmɛ̃] NM: **le ~** the next ou following day; **le ~ matin/soir** the next ou following morning/evening; **le ~ de** the day after; **au ~ de** in the days following; in the wake of; **penser au ~** to think of the future; **sans ~** short-lived; **de beaux lendemains** bright prospects; **des lendemains qui chantent** a rosy future
lénifiant, e [lenifjɑ̃, -ɑ̃t] ADJ soothing
léniniste [leninist] ADJ, NMF Leninist
★**lent, e** [lɑ̃, lɑ̃t] ADJ slow
lente [lɑ̃t] NF nit
★**lentement** [lɑ̃tmɑ̃] ADV slowly
★**lenteur** [lɑ̃tœʀ] NF slowness no pl ■ **lenteurs** NFPL (actions, décisions lentes) slowness sg
lentille [lɑ̃tij] NF (Optique) lens sg; (Bot) lentil; **~ d'eau** duckweed; **lentilles de contact** contact lenses
léonin, e [leɔnɛ̃, -in] ADJ (fig: contrat etc) one-sided

léopard [leɔpaʀ] NM leopard

LEP [lɛp] SIGLE M (= *lycée d'enseignement professionnel*) secondary school for vocational training, pre-1986

lépidoptère [lepidɔptɛʀ] NM lepidopteran

lèpre [lɛpʀ] NF leprosy

lépreux, -euse [lepʀø, -øz] NM/F leper ▸ ADJ (*fig*) flaking, peeling

léproserie [lepʀozʀi] NF leper hospital

---

lequel, laquelle [ləkɛl, lakɛl]

(*mpl* **lesquels**, *fpl* **lesquelles**) (*à* + *lequel* = **auquel**, *de* + *lequel* = **duquel**) PRON **1** (*interrogatif*) which, which one; **lequel des deux ?** which one? **2** (*relatif: personne: sujet*) who; (: *objet, après préposition*) whom; (: *possessif*) whose; (: *chose*) which; **je l'ai proposé au directeur, lequel est d'accord** I suggested it to the director, who agrees; **la femme à laquelle j'ai acheté mon chien** the woman from whom I bought my dog; **le pont sur lequel nous sommes passés** the bridge (over) which we crossed; **un homme sur la compétence duquel on peut compter** a man whose competence one can count on ▸ ADJ: **auquel cas** in which case

---

les [le] ART DÉF, PRON *voir* **le**

lesbienne [lɛsbjɛn] NF lesbian

lesdits, lesdites [ledi, ledit] ADJ *voir* **ledit**

lèse-majesté [lɛzmaʒɛste] NF INV: **crime de ~** crime of lese-majesty

léser [leze] /6/ VT to wrong; (*Méd*) to injure

lésiner [lezine] /1/ VI: **ne pas ~ sur les moyens** (*pour mariage etc*) to push the boat out

lésion [lezjɔ̃] NF lesion, damage *no pl*; **lésions cérébrales** brain damage

Lesotho [lezɔto] NM: **le ~** Lesotho

lesquels, lesquelles [lekɛl] PRON *voir* **lequel**

lessivable [lesivabl] ADJ washable

lessivage [lesivaʒ] NM (*de murs*) washing

★**lessive** [lesiv] NF (*poudre*) washing powder; (*linge*) washing *no pl*, wash; (*opération*) washing *no pl*; **faire la ~** to do the washing

lessivé, e [lesive] ADJ (*fam*) washed out

lessiver [lesive] /1/ VT to wash; (*fam: fatiguer*) to tire out, exhaust

lessiveuse [lesivøz] NF (*récipient*) washtub

lessiviel, le [lesivjɛl] ADJ detergent

lest [lɛst] NM ballast; **jeter** *ou* **lâcher du ~** (*fig*) to make concessions

leste [lɛst] ADJ (*personne, mouvement*) sprightly, nimble; (*désinvolte: manières*) offhand; (*osé: plaisanterie*) risqué

lestement [lɛstəmɑ̃] ADV nimbly

lester [lɛste] /1/ VT to ballast

letchi [lɛtʃi] NM = **litchi**

léthargie [letaʀʒi] NF lethargy

léthargique [letaʀʒik] ADJ lethargic

letton, ne [letɔ̃, -ɔn] ADJ Latvian, Lett

Lettonie [letɔni] NF: **la ~** Latvia

★**lettre** [letʀ] NF letter; **à la ~** (*au sens propre*) literally; (*ponctuellement*) to the letter; **~ de change** bill of exchange; **~ piégée** letter bomb; **~ de voiture** (**aérienne**) (air) waybill, (air) bill of lading ■ **lettres** NFPL (*étude, culture*) literature *sg*; (*Scol*) arts (subjects); **en lettres majuscules** *ou* **capitales** in capital letters, in capitals; **en toutes lettres** in words, in full; **lettres de noblesse** pedigree

lettré, e [letʀe] ADJ well-read, scholarly

lettre-transfert [letʀətʀɑ̃sfɛʀ] (*pl* **lettres-transferts**) NF (pressure) transfer

lettrine [letʀin] NF dropped initial capital letter

leu [lø] NM *voir* **queue**

leucémie [løsemi] NF leukaemia

leucocyte [løkɔsit] NM leucocyte, leukocyte (*US*)

---

leur [lœʀ]

ADJ POSS their; **leur maison** their house; **leurs amis** their friends; **à leur approche** as they came near; **à leur vue** at the sight of them ▸ PRON **1** (*objet indirect*) (to) them; **je leur ai dit la vérité** I told them the truth; **je le leur ai donné** I gave it to them, I gave them it **2** (*possessif*): **le (la) leur, les leurs** theirs

---

leurre [lœʀ] NM (*appât*) lure; (*fig*) delusion; (: *piège*) snare

leurrer [lœʀe] /1/ VT to delude, deceive

★**leurs** [lœʀ] ADJ *voir* **leur**

levage [ləvaʒ] NM (*de charge*) lifting; **appareil de ~** lifting apparatus

levain [ləvɛ̃] NM leaven; **sans ~** unleavened

levant, e [ləvɑ̃, -ɑ̃t] ADJ: **soleil ~** rising sun; **au soleil ~** at sunrise ▸ NM: **le L~** the Levant

levantin, e [ləvɑ̃tɛ̃, -in] ADJ Levantine ▸ NM/F: **Levantin, e** Levantine

levé, e [ləve] ADJ: **être ~** to be up; **à mains levées** (*vote*) by a show of hands; **au pied ~** at a moment's notice ▸ NM: **~ de terrain** land survey

levée [ləve] NF (*Postes*) collection; (*Cartes*) trick; **~ de boucliers** general outcry; **~ du corps** collection of the body from house of the deceased, before funeral; **~ d'écrou** release from custody; **~ de terre** levee; **~ de troupes** levy

★**lever** [l(ə)ve] /5/ VT (*vitre, bras etc*) to raise; (*soulever de terre, supprimer: interdiction, siège*) to lift; (: *difficulté*) to remove; (*séance*) to close; (*impôts, armée*) to levy; (*Chasse: lièvre*) to start; (: *perdrix*) to flush; (*fam: fille*) to pick up ▸ VI (*Culin*) to rise ▸ NM: **au ~** on getting up; **~ du jour** daybreak; **~ du rideau** (*Théât*) curtain; **~ de rideau** (*pièce*) curtain raiser; **~ de soleil** sunrise ■ **se lever** VPR to get up; (*soleil*) to rise; (*jour*) to break; (*brouillard*) to lift; **levez-vous !**, **lève-toi !** stand up!, get up!; **ça va se ~** (*temps*) it's going to clear up

lève-tard [lɛvtaʀ] NMF INV late riser

lève-tôt [lɛvto] NMF INV early riser, early bird

levier [ləvje] NM lever; **faire ~ sur** to lever up (*ou* off); **~ de changement de vitesse** gear lever

lévitation [levitasjɔ̃] NF levitation

léviter [levite] VI to levitate

levraut [ləvʀo] NM (*Zool*) leveret

lèvre [lɛvʀ] NF lip ■ **lèvres** NFPL (*d'une plaie*) edges; **petites/grandes lèvres** labia minora/majora; **du bout des lèvres** half-heartedly

lévrier [levʀije] NM greyhound

levure [l(ə)vyʀ] NF yeast; **~ chimique** baking powder

lexical, e, -aux [lɛksikal, -o] ADJ lexical

lexicographe [lɛksikɔgʀaf] NMF lexicographer

lexicographie [lɛksikɔgʀafi] NF lexicography, dictionary writing

lexicologie [lɛksikɔlɔʒi] NF lexicology

lexicologue [lɛksikɔlɔg] NMF lexicologist

lexique [lɛksik] NM vocabulary, lexicon; (*glossaire*) vocabulary

lézard [lezaʀ] NM lizard; (*peau*) lizard skin

lézarde [lezaʀd] NF crack

lézarder [lezaʀde] /1/: **se lézarder** VPR to crack

LGBT SIGLE PL (= *lesbiennes, gays, bisexuels et trans-genres*) LGBT (= *lesbian, gay, bisexual and transgender*)

liaison [ljɛzɔ̃] NF (*rapport*) connection, link; (*Rail, Aviat etc*) link; (*relation: d'amitié*) friendship; (: *d'affaires*) relationship; (: *amoureuse*) affair; (*Culin, Phonétique*) liaison; **entrer/être en ~ avec** to get/be in contact with; **~ radio** radio contact; **~ (de transmission de données)** (*Inform*) data link

liane [ljan] NF creeper

liant, e [ljɑ̃, -ɑ̃t] ADJ sociable

liasse [ljas] NF wad, bundle

Liban [libɑ̃] NM: **le ~** (the) Lebanon

libanais, e [libanɛ, -ɛz] ADJ Lebanese ▶ NM/F: **Libanais, e** Lebanese

libations [libasjɔ̃] NFPL libations

libelle [libɛl] NM lampoon

libellé [libele] NM wording

libeller [libele] /1/ VT (*chèque, mandat*): **~ (au nom de)** to make out (to); (*lettre*) to word

libellule [libelyl] NF dragonfly

libéral, e, -aux [liberal, -o] ADJ, NM/F liberal; **les professions libérales** liberal professions

libéralement [liberalmɑ̃] ADV liberally

libéralisation [liberalizasjɔ̃] NF liberalization; **~ du commerce** easing of trade restrictions

libéraliser [liberalize] /1/ VT to liberalize

libéralisme [liberalism] NM liberalism

libéralité [liberalite] NF liberality *no pl*, generosity *no pl*

libérateur, -trice [liberatœʀ, -tʀis] ADJ liberating ▶ NM/F liberator

libération [liberasjɔ̃] NF liberation, freeing; release; discharge; **~ conditionnelle** release on parole

libéré, e [libere] ADJ liberated; **~ de** freed from; **être ~ sous caution/sur parole** to be released on bail/on parole

libérer [libere] /6/ VT (*délivrer*) to free, liberate; (: *moralement, Psych*) to liberate; (*relâcher: prisonnier*) to discharge, release; (: *soldat*) to discharge; (*dégager: gaz, cran d'arrêt*) to release; (*Écon: échanges commerciaux*) to ease restrictions on; **~ qn de** (*liens, dette*) to free sb from; (*promesse*) to release sb from ∎ **se libérer** VPR (*de rendez-vous*) to get out of previous engagements, try and be free

Libéria [libeʀja] NM: **le ~** Liberia

libérien, ne [libeʀjɛ̃, -ɛn] ADJ Liberian ▶ NM/F: **Libérien, ne** Liberian

libéro [libeʀo] NM (*Football*) sweeper

libertaire [libɛʀtɛʀ] ADJ libertarian

liberté [libɛʀte] NF freedom; (*loisir*) free time; **mettre/être en ~** to set/be free; **en ~ provisoire/surveillée/conditionnelle** on bail/probation/parole; **~ d'association** right of association; **~ de conscience** freedom of conscience; **~ du culte** freedom of worship; **~ d'esprit** independence of mind; **~ d'opinion** freedom of thought; **~ de la presse** freedom of the press; **~ de réunion** right to hold meetings; **~ syndicale** union rights *pl* ∎ **libertés** NFPL (*privautés*) liberties; **libertés individuelles** personal freedom *sg*; **libertés publiques** civil rights

liberticide [libɛʀtisid] ADJ (*loi*) that destroys freedom

libertin, e [libɛʀtɛ̃, -in] ADJ libertine, licentious

libertinage [libɛʀtinaʒ] NM licentiousness

libidineux, -euse [libidinø, -øz] ADJ lustful

libido [libido] NF libido

libraire [libʀɛʀ] NMF bookseller

libraire-éditeur [libʀɛʀeditœʀ] (*pl* **libraires-éditeurs**) NM publisher and bookseller

★**librairie** [libʀɛʀi] NF bookshop

librairie-papeterie [libʀɛʀipapetʀi] (*pl* **librairies-papeteries**) NF bookseller's and stationer's

★**libre** [libʀ] ADJ free; (*route*) clear; (*place etc*) vacant, free; (*fig: propos, manières*) open; (*ligne*) not engaged; (*Scol*) non-state, private and Roman Catholic (*as opposed to "laïque"*); **de ~** (*place*) free; **~ de qch/de faire** free from sth/to do; **vente ~** (*Comm*) unrestricted sale; **~ arbitre** free will; **~ concurrence** free-market economy; **~ entreprise** free enterprise

libre-échange [libʀeʃɑ̃ʒ] (*pl* **libres-échanges**) NM free trade

librement [libʀəmɑ̃] ADV freely

libre-penseur, -euse [libʀəpɑ̃sœʀ, -øz] NM/F free thinker

★**libre-service** [libʀəsɛʀvis] NM INV (*magasin*) self-service store; (*restaurant*) self-service restaurant

librettiste [libʀetist] NMF librettist

Libye [libi] NF: **la ~** Libya

libyen, ne [libjɛ̃, -ɛn] ADJ Libyan ▶ NM/F: **Libyen, ne** Libyan

lice [lis] NF: **entrer en ~** (*fig*) to enter the lists

★**licence** [lisɑ̃s] NF (*permis*) permit; (*diplôme*) (first) degree; *see note*; (*liberté*) liberty; (*poétique, orthographique*) licence (BRIT), license (US); (*des mœurs*) licentiousness; **~ ès lettres/en droit** arts/law degree

The **licence générale** is a three-year university course undertaken in a mainstream subject after completing secondary education. The second and third years are more specialized than the first. The course involves at least one period of work experience. The **licence professionnelle** is a one-year course in a vocational subject open to students already in possession of a university-level technical qualification or having completed the first two years of a *licence générale*. Admission to a *licence professionnelle* course is selective and places are usually heavily oversubscribed.

licencié, e [lisãsje] NM/F (Scol): **~ ès lettres/en droit** = Bachelor of Arts/Law, arts/law graduate; (Sport) permit-holder

licenciement [lisãsimã] NM dismissal; redundancy; laying off no pl

★**licencier** [lisãsje] /7/ VT (renvoyer) to dismiss; (débaucher) to make redundant; to lay off

licencieux, -euse [lisãsjø, -øz] ADJ licentious

lichen [likɛn] NM lichen

licite [lisit] ADJ lawful

licorne [likɔRn] NF unicorn

licou [liku] NM halter

lie [li] NF dregs pl, sediment

lié, e [lje] ADJ: **très ~ avec** (fig) very friendly with ou close to; **~ par** (serment, promesse) bound by; **avoir partie liée (avec qn)** to be involved (with sb)

Liechtenstein [liʃtɛnʃtajn] NM: **le ~** Liechtenstein

lie-de-vin [lidvɛ̃] ADJ INV wine(-coloured)

liège [ljɛʒ] NM cork

liégeois, e [ljeʒwa, -waz] ADJ of ou from Liège; **café/chocolat ~** coffee/chocolate ice cream topped with whipped cream ▶ NM/F: **Liégeois, e** inhabitant ou native of Liège

★**lien** [ljɛ̃] NM (corde, fig: affectif, culturel) bond; (rapport) link, connection; (analogie) link; **~ de parenté** family tie; **~ hypertexte** hyperlink

lier [lje] /7/ VT (attacher) to tie up; (joindre) to link up; (fig: unir, engager) to bind; (Culin) to thicken; **~ qch à** (attacher) to tie sth to; (associer) to link sth to; **~ conversation (avec)** to strike up a conversation (with); **se ~ avec** to make friends with; **~ connaissance avec** to get to know

lierre [ljɛR] NM ivy

liesse [ljɛs] NF: **être en ~** to be jubilant

★**lieu, x** [ljø] NM place; **en ~ sûr** in a safe place; **en haut ~** in high places; **en premier ~** in the first place; **en dernier ~** lastly; **avoir ~** to take place; **avoir ~ de faire** to have grounds ou good reason for doing; **tenir ~ de** to take the place of; (servir de) to serve as; **donner ~ à** to give rise to, give cause for; **au ~ de** instead of; **au ~ qu'il y aille** instead of him going; **~ commun** commonplace; **~ géométrique** locus; **~ de naissance** place of birth ■ **lieux** NMPL (locaux) premises; (endroit: d'un accident etc) scene sg; **vider** ou **quitter les lieux** to leave the premises; **arriver/être sur les lieux** to arrive/be on the scene

lieu-dit [ljødi] (pl **lieux-dits**) NM locality

lieue [ljø] NF league

lieutenant [ljøt(ə)nã] NM lieutenant; **~ de vaisseau** (Navig) lieutenant

lieutenant-colonel [ljøtnãkɔlɔnɛl] (pl **lieutenants-colonels**) NM (armée de terre) lieutenant colonel; (armée de l'air) wing commander (BRIT), lieutenant colonel (US)

lièvre [ljɛvR] NM hare; (coureur) pacemaker; **lever un ~** (fig) to bring up a prickly subject

liftier, -ière [liftje, -jɛR] NM/F lift (BRIT) ou elevator (US) attendant

lifting [liftiŋ] NM face lift

ligament [ligamã] NM ligament

ligature [ligatyR] NF ligature

lige [liʒ] ADJ: **homme ~** (péj) henchman

★**ligne** [liɲ] NF (gén) line; (Transports: liaison) service; (: trajet) route; (silhouette) figure; **garder la ~** to keep one's figure; **en ~** (Inform) online; **en ~ droite** as the crow flies; **« à la ~ »** "new paragraph"; **entrer en ~ de compte** to be taken into account; to come into it; **~ de but/médiane** goal/halfway line; **~ d'arrivée/de départ** finishing/starting line; **~ de conduite** course of action; **~ directrice** guiding line; **~ fixe** (Tél) landline; **~ d'horizon** skyline; **~ de mire** line of sight; **~ de touche** touchline

ligné, e [liɲe] ADJ: **papier ~** ruled paper ▶ NF (race, famille) line, lineage; (postérité) descendants pl

ligneux, -euse [liɲø, -øz] ADJ ligneous, woody

lignite [liɲit] NM lignite

ligoter [ligɔte] /1/ VT to tie up

ligue [lig] NF league

liguer [lige] /1/: **se liguer** VPR to form a league; **se ~ contre** (fig) to combine against

lilas [lila] NM lilac

lillois, e [lilwa, -waz] ADJ of ou from Lille

Lima [lima] N Lima

limace [limas] NF slug

limaille [limaj] NF: **~ de fer** iron filings pl

limande [limãd] NF dab

limande-sole [limãdsɔl] (pl **limandes-soles**) NF lemon sole

limbes [lɛ̃b] NMPL limbo sg; **être dans les ~** (fig: projet etc) to be up in the air

lime [lim] NF (Tech) file; (Bot) lime; **~ à ongles** nail file

limer [lime] /1/ VT (bois, métal) to file (down); (ongles) to file; (fig: prix) to pare down

limier [limje] NM (Zool) bloodhound; (détective) sleuth

liminaire [liminɛR] ADJ (propos) introductory

limitatif, -ive [limitatif, -iv] ADJ restrictive

limitation [limitasjɔ̃] NF limitation, restriction; **sans ~ de temps** with no time limit; **~ des naissances** birth control; **~ de vitesse** speed limit

limite [limit] NF (de terrain) boundary; (partie ou point extrême) limit; **dans la ~ de** within the limits of; **à la ~** (au pire) if the worst comes (ou came) to the worst; **sans limites** (bêtise, richesse, pouvoir) limitless, boundless; **vitesse/charge ~** maximum speed/load; **cas ~** borderline case; **date ~** deadline; **date ~ de vente/consommation** sell-by/best-before date; **prix ~** upper price limit; **~ d'âge** maximum age, age limit

limiter [limite] /1/ VT (restreindre) to limit, restrict; (délimiter) to border, form the boundary of ■ **se limiter** VPR: **se ~ (à qch/à faire)** (personne) to limit ou confine o.s. (to sth/to doing sth); (chose) to be limited to

limitrophe [limitRɔf] ADJ border cpd; **~ de** bordering on

limogeage [limɔʒaʒ] NM dismissal

limoger [limɔʒe] /3/ VT to dismiss

limon [limɔ̃] NM silt

★**limonade** [limɔnad] NF lemonade (BRIT), (lemon) soda (US)

limonadier, -ière [limɔnadje, -jɛR] NM/F (commerçant) café owner; (fabricant de limonade) soft drinks manufacturer

limoneux, -euse [limɔnø, -øz] ADJ muddy

limousin, e [limuzɛ̃, -in] ADJ of ou from Limousin ▸ NM (*région*): **le L~** the Limousin ▸ NF limousine

limpide [lɛ̃pid] ADJ limpid

lin [lɛ̃] NM (*Bot*) flax; (*tissu, toile*) linen

linceul [lɛ̃sœl] NM shroud

linéaire [lineɛR] ADJ linear ▸ NM: **~ (de vente)** shelves *pl*

linéament [lineamɑ̃] NM outline

★**linge** [lɛ̃ʒ] NM (*serviettes etc*) linen; (*pièce de tissu*) cloth; (*aussi*: **linge de corps**) underwear; (*aussi*: **linge de toilette**) towel; (*lessive*) washing; **~ sale** dirty linen

lingère [lɛ̃ʒɛR] NF linen maid

lingerie [lɛ̃ʒRi] NF lingerie, underwear

lingette [lɛ̃ʒɛt] NF wipe

lingot [lɛ̃go] NM ingot

linguiste [lɛ̃gɥist] NMF linguist

linguistique [lɛ̃gɥistik] ADJ linguistic ▸ NF linguistics *sg*

lino [lino] NM (*fam*) lino

linoléum [linɔleɔm] NM linoleum

linotte [linɔt] NF: **tête de ~** bird brain

linteau, x [lɛ̃to] NM lintel

★**lion, ne** [ljɔ̃, ljɔn] NM/F lion (lioness); (*signe*): **le L~** Leo, the Lion; **être du L~** to be Leo; **~ de mer** sea lion

lionceau, x [ljɔ̃so] NM lion cub

liposuccion [liposy(k)sjɔ̃] NF liposuction

lippu, e [lipy] ADJ thick-lipped

liquéfier [likefje] /**7**/ VT to liquefy ▪ **se liquéfier** VPR (*gaz etc*) to liquefy; (*fig: personne*) to succumb

liqueur [likœR] NF liqueur

liquidateur, -trice [likidatœR, -tRis] NM/F (*Jur*) receiver; **~ judiciaire** official liquidator

liquidation [likidasjɔ̃] NF (*vente*) sale, liquidation; (*Comm*) clearance (sale); **~ judiciaire** compulsory liquidation

liquide [likid] ADJ liquid ▸ NM liquid; (*Comm*): **en ~** in ready money ou cash; **je n'ai pas de ~** I haven't got any cash

liquider [likide] /**1**/ VT (*société, biens, témoin gênant*) to liquidate; (*compte, problème*) to settle; (*Comm: articles*) to clear, sell off

liquidités [likidite] NFPL (*Comm*) liquid assets

liquoreux, -euse [likɔRø, -øz] ADJ syrupy

★**lire** [liR] /**43**/ NF (*monnaie*) lira ▸ VT, VI to read; **~ qch à qn** to read sth (out) to sb

lis VB [li] *voir* **lire** ▸ NM [lis] = **lys**

lisais *etc* [lize] VB *voir* **lire**

Lisbonne [lizbɔn] N Lisbon

lise *etc* [liz] VB *voir* **lire**

liseré [lizRe] NM border, edging

liseron [lizRɔ̃] NM bindweed

liseuse [lizøz] NF book-cover; (*veste*) bed jacket; (*Inform*) e-reader

lisible [lizibl] ADJ legible; (*digne d'être lu*) readable

lisiblement [liziblǝmɑ̃] ADV legibly

lisière [lizjɛR] NF (*de forêt*) edge; (*de tissu*) selvage

lisons [lizɔ̃] VB *voir* **lire**

lisse [lis] ADJ smooth

lisser [lise] /**1**/ VT to smooth

lisseur [lisøR] NM straighteners *pl*

listage [lista ʒ] NM (*Inform*) listing

★**liste** [list] NF list; (*Inform*) listing; **faire la ~ de** to list, make out a list of; **~ d'attente** waiting list; **~ civile** civil list; **~ électorale** electoral roll; **~ de mariage** wedding (present) list; **~ noire** black list

lister [liste] /**1**/ VT to list

listéria [listeRja] NF listeria

listing [listiŋ] NM (*Inform*) printout; **qualité ~** draft quality

★**lit** [li] NM (*gén*) bed; **petit ~**, **~ à une place** single bed; **grand ~**, **~ à deux places** double bed; **faire son ~** to make one's bed; **aller/se mettre au ~** to go to/get into bed; **chambre avec un grand ~** room with a double bed; **prendre le ~** to take to one's bed; **d'un premier ~** (*Jur*) of a first marriage; **~ de camp** camp bed (BRIT), cot (US); **~ d'enfant** cot (BRIT), crib (US)

litanie [litani] NF litany

lit-cage [likaʒ] (*pl* **lits-cages**) NM folding bed

litchi [litʃi] NM lychee

literie [litRi] NF bedding; (*linge*) bedding, bedclothes *pl*

litho [lito], **lithographie** [litɔgRafi] NF litho(graphy); (*épreuve*) litho(graph)

litière [litjɛR] NF litter

litige [litiʒ] NM dispute; **en ~** in contention

litigieux, -euse [litiʒjø, -øz] ADJ litigious, contentious

litote [litɔt] NF understatement

★**litre** [litR] NM litre; (*récipient*) litre measure

littéraire [liteRɛR] ADJ literary; **elle est très ~** she's very literary ▸ NMF arts student

littéral, e, -aux [literal, -o] ADJ literal

littéralement [literalmɑ̃] ADV literally

littérature [literatyR] NF literature

littoral, e, -aux [litɔral, -o] ADJ coastal ▸ NM coast

Lituanie [litɥani] NF: **la ~** Lithuania

lituanien, ne [litɥanjɛ̃, -ɛn] ADJ Lithuanian ▸ NM (*Ling*) Lithuanian ▸ NM/F: **Lituanien, ne** Lithuanian

liturgie [lityRʒi] NF liturgy

liturgique [lityRʒik] ADJ liturgical

livide [livid] ADJ livid, pallid

living [liviŋ], **living-room** [liviŋRum] NM living room

livrable [livRabl] ADJ (*Comm*) that can be delivered

livraison [livRɛzɔ̃] NF delivery; **~ à domicile** home delivery (service)

★**livre** [livR] NM book; (*secteur*): **le ~** the book industry; **traduire qch à ~ ouvert** to translate sth off the cuff ou at sight; **~ blanc** official report (*on war, natural disaster etc, prepared by independent body*); **~ de bord** (*Navig*) logbook; **~ de comptes** account(s) book; **~ de cuisine** cookery book (BRIT), cookbook; **~ de messe** mass ou prayer book; **~ numérique** e-book; **~ d'or** visitors' book; **~ de poche** paperback ▸ NF (*poids, monnaie*) pound; **~ sterling** pound sterling; **~ verte** green pound

livré, e [livʀe] ADJ: **~ à** (*l'anarchie etc*) given over to; **~ à soi-même** left to oneself *ou* one's own devices ▶ NF livery

★**livrer** [livʀe] /1/ VT (*Comm*) to deliver; (*otage, coupable*) to hand over; (*secret, information*) to give away; **~ bataille** to give battle ■ **se livrer** VPR: **se ~ à** (*se confier*) to confide in; (*se rendre*) to give o.s. up to; (*s'abandonner à: débauche etc*) to give o.s. up *ou* over to; (*faire: pratiques, actes*) to indulge in (: *travail*) to be engaged in, engage in; (: *sport*) to practise; (: *enquête*) to carry out

livresque [livʀesk] ADJ (*péj*) bookish

livret [livʀe] NM booklet; (*d'opéra*) libretto; **~ de caisse d'épargne** (savings) bank-book; **~ de famille** (official) family record book; **~ scolaire** (school) report book

livreur, -euse [livʀœʀ, -øz] NM/F delivery boy *ou* man/girl *ou* woman

LO SIGLE F (= *Lutte ouvrière*) political party

lob [lɔb] NM lob

lobby [lɔbi] (*pl* **lobbys** *ou* **lobbies**) NM lobby

lobe [lɔb] NM: **~ de l'oreille** ear lobe

lobé, e [lɔbe] ADJ (*Archit*) foiled

lober [lɔbe] /1/ VT to lob

local, e, -aux [lɔkal, -o] ADJ local ▶ NM (*salle*) premises *pl* ▶ NMPL premises

localement [lɔkalmɑ̃] ADV locally

localisé, e [lɔkalize] ADJ localized

localiser [lɔkalize] /1/ VT (*repérer*) to locate, place; (*limiter*) to localize, confine

localité [lɔkalite] NF locality

locataire [lɔkatɛʀ] NMF tenant; (*de chambre*) lodger

locatif, -ive [lɔkatif, -iv] ADJ (*charges, réparations*) incumbent upon the tenant; (*valeur*) rental; (*immeuble*) with rented flats, used as a letting *ou* rental (*US*) concern

location [lɔkasjɔ̃] NF (*par le locataire*) renting; (*par l'usager: de voiture etc*) hiring (*Brit*), renting (*US*); (*par le propriétaire*) renting out, letting; hiring out (*Brit*); (*de billets, places*) booking; (*bureau*) booking office; **« ~ de voitures »** "car hire (*Brit*) *ou* rental (*US*)"; **habiter en ~** to live in rented accommodation; **prendre une ~ (pour les vacances)** to rent a house *etc* (for the holidays)

location-vente [lɔkasjɔ̃vɑ̃t] (*pl* **locations-ventes**) NF form of hire purchase (*Brit*) *ou* installment plan (*US*)

lock-out [lɔkawt] NM lockout

locomoteur, -trice [lɔkɔmɔtœʀ, -tʀis] ADJ, NF locomotive

locomotion [lɔkɔmosjɔ̃] NF locomotion

locomotive [lɔkɔmɔtiv] NF locomotive, engine; (*fig*) pacesetter, pacemaker

locuteur, -trice [lɔkytœʀ, -tʀis] NM/F (*Ling*) speaker

locution [lɔkysjɔ̃] NF phrase

loden [lɔdɛn] NM loden

lofer [lɔfe] /1/ VI (*Navig*) to luff

logarithme [lɔgaʀitm] NM logarithm

loge [lɔʒ] NF (*Théât: d'artiste*) dressing room; (: *de spectateurs*) box; (*de concierge, franc-maçon*) lodge

logeable [lɔʒabl] ADJ habitable; (*spacieux*) roomy

★**logement** [lɔʒmɑ̃] NM flat (*Brit*), apartment (*US*); accommodation *no pl* (*Brit*), accommodations *pl* (*US*); (*Pol, Admin*): **le ~** housing; **chercher un ~** to look for a flat *ou* an apartment, look for accommodation(s); **construire des logements bon marché** to build cheap housing; **crise du ~** housing shortage; **~ de fonction** (*Admin*) company flat *ou* apartment, accommodation(s) provided with one's job

★**loger** [lɔʒe] /3/ VT to accommodate; **être logé, nourri** to have board and lodging ▶ VI to live ■ **se loger** VPR: **trouver à se ~** to find accommodation; **se ~ dans** (*balle, flèche*) to lodge itself in

logeur, -euse [lɔʒœʀ, -øz] NM/F landlord (landlady)

loggia [lɔdʒja] NF loggia

★**logiciel** [lɔʒisjɛl] NM (*Inform*) piece of software

logicien, ne [lɔʒisjɛ̃, -ɛn] NM/F logician

★**logique** [lɔʒik] ADJ logical; **c'est ~** it stands to reason ▶ NF logic

logiquement [lɔʒikmɑ̃] ADV logically

logis [lɔʒi] NM home; abode, dwelling

logisticien, ne [lɔʒistisjɛ̃, -ɛn] NM/F logistician

logistique [lɔʒistik] NF logistics *sg* ▶ ADJ logistic

logo [lɔgo], **logotype** [lɔgɔtip] NM logo

★**loi** [lwa] NF law; **faire la ~** to lay down the law; **les lois de la mode** (*fig*) the dictates of fashion; **proposition de ~** (private member's) bill; **projet de ~** (government) bill

loi-cadre [lwakadʀ(ə)] (*pl* **lois-cadres**) NF (*Pol*) blueprint law

★**loin** [lwɛ̃] ADV far; (*dans le temps: futur*) a long way off; (: *passé*) a long time ago; **plus ~** further; **moins ~ (que)** not as far (as); **~ de** far from; **~ d'ici** a long way from here; **pas ~ de 100 euros** not far off 100 euros; **au ~** far off; **de ~** *adv* from a distance; (*fig: de beaucoup*) by far; **il vient de ~** he's come a long way; he comes from a long way away; **de ~ en ~** here and there; (*de temps en temps*) (every) now and then; **~ de là** (*au contraire*) far from it

lointain, e [lwɛ̃tɛ̃, -ɛn] ADJ faraway, distant; (*dans le futur, passé*) distant, far-off; (*cause, parent*) remote, distant ▶ NM: **dans le ~** in the distance

loi-programme [lwapʀɔgʀam] (*pl* **lois-programmes**) NF (*Pol*) act providing framework for government programme

loir [lwaʀ] NM dormouse

Loire [lwaʀ] NF: **la ~** the Loire

loisible [lwazibl] ADJ: **il vous est ~ de ...** you are free to ...

loisir [lwaziʀ] NM: **heures de ~** spare time; **avoir le ~ de faire** to have the time *ou* opportunity to do; **(tout) à ~** (*en prenant son temps*) at leisure; (*autant qu'on le désire*) at one's pleasure ■ **loisirs** NMPL (*temps libre*) leisure *sg*; (*activités*) leisure activities

lombaire [lɔ̃bɛʀ] ADJ lumbar

lombalgie [lɔ̃balʒi] NF back pain

londonien, ne [lɔ̃dɔnjɛ̃, -ɛn] ADJ London *cpd*, of London ▶ NM/F: **Londonien, ne** Londoner

★**Londres** [lɔ̃dʀ] N London

★**long, longue** [lɔ̃, lɔ̃g] ADJ long; **faire ~ feu** to fizzle out; **ne pas faire ~ feu** not to last long; **au ~ cours** (*Navig*) ocean *cpd*, ocean-going; **de longue date** *adj* long-standing; **longue durée** *adj* long-term;

de longue haleine *adj* long-term; **être ~ à faire** to take a long time to do ▶ *ADV*: **en savoir ~** to know a great deal ▶ *NM*: **de 3 m de ~** 3 m long, 3 m in length; **en ~** *adv* lengthwise, lengthways; **(tout) le ~ de** (all) along; **tout au ~ de** (*année, vie*) throughout; **de ~ en large** (*marcher*) to and fro, up and down; **en ~ et en large** (*fig*) in every detail ▶ *NF*: **à la longue** in the end

longanimité [lɔ̃ganimite] *NF* forbearance

long-courrier [lɔ̃kuʀje] *NM* (*Aviat*) long-haul aircraft

longe [lɔ̃ʒ] *NF* (*corde: pour attacher*) tether; (*: pour mener*) lead; (*Culin*) loin

longer [lɔ̃ʒe] /3/ *VT* to go (*ou* walk *ou* drive) along(side); (*mur, route*) to border

longévité [lɔ̃ʒevite] *NF* longevity

longiligne [lɔ̃ʒiliɲ] *ADJ* long-limbed

longitude [lɔ̃ʒityd] *NF* longitude; **à 45° de ~ ouest** at 45° longitude west

longitudinal, e, -aux [lɔ̃ʒitydinal, -o] *ADJ* longitudinal, lengthways; (*entaille, vallée*) running lengthways

★**longtemps** [lɔ̃tɑ̃] *ADV* (for) a long time, (for) long; **ça ne va pas durer ~** it won't last long; **avant ~** before long; **pour/pendant ~** for a long time; **je n'en ai pas pour ~** I shan't be long; **mettre ~ à faire** to take a long time to do; **il en a pour ~** he'll be a long time; **il y a ~ que je travaille** I have been working (for) a long time; **il n'y a pas ~ que je l'ai rencontré** it's not long since I met him

longuement [lɔ̃gmɑ̃] *ADV* (*longtemps: parler, regarder*) for a long time; (*en détail: expliquer, raconter*) at length

longueur [lɔ̃gœʀ] *NF* length; **sur une ~ de 10 km** for *ou* over 10 km; **en ~** *adv* lengthwise, lengthways; **tirer en ~** to drag on; **à ~ de journée** all day long; **d'une ~** (*gagner*) by a length; **~ d'onde** wavelength ▪ **longueurs** *NFPL* (*fig: d'un film etc*) tedious parts

longue-vue [lɔ̃gvy] (*pl* **longues-vues**) *NF* telescope

look [luk] *NM* (*fam*) look, image

looping [lupiŋ] *NM* (*Aviat*): **faire des loopings** to loop the loop

lopin [lɔpɛ̃] *NM*: **~ de terre** patch of land

loquace [lɔkas] *ADJ* talkative, loquacious

loque [lɔk] *NF* (*personne*) wreck ▪ **loques** *NFPL* (*habits*) rags; **être** *ou* **tomber en loques** to be in rags

loquet [lɔkɛ] *NM* latch

lorgner [lɔʀɲe] /1/ *VT* to eye; (*fig: convoiter*) to have one's eye on

lorgnette [lɔʀɲɛt] *NF* opera glasses *pl*

lorgnon [lɔʀɲɔ̃] *NM* (*face-à-main*) lorgnette; (*pince-nez*) pince-nez

loriot [lɔʀjo] *NM* (golden) oriole

lorrain, e [lɔʀɛ̃, -ɛn] *ADJ* of *ou* from Lorraine; **quiche lorraine** quiche

lors [lɔʀ] : **~ de** *prép* (*au moment de*) at the time of; (*pendant*) during; **~ même que** even though

lorsque [lɔʀsk] *CONJ* when, as

losange [lɔzɑ̃ʒ] *NM* diamond; (*Géom*) lozenge; **en ~** diamond-shaped

lot [lo] *NM* (*part*) share; (*de loterie*) prize; (*fig: destin*) fate, lot; (*Comm, Inform*) batch; **le gros ~** the jackpot; **~ de consolation** consolation prize

loterie [lɔtʀi] *NF* lottery; (*tombola*) raffle; **L~ nationale** French national lottery

loti, e [lɔti] *ADJ*: **bien/mal ~** well-/badly off, lucky/unlucky

lotion [losjɔ̃] *NF* lotion; **~ après rasage** aftershave (lotion); **~ capillaire** hair lotion

lotir [lɔtiʀ] /2/ *VT* (*terrain: diviser*) to divide into plots; (*: vendre*) to sell by lots

lotissement [lɔtismɑ̃] *NM* (*groupe de maisons, d'immeubles*) housing development; (*parcelle*) (building) plot, lot

loto [lɔto] *NM* lotto

lotte [lɔt] *NF* (*Zool: de rivière*) burbot; (*: de mer*) monkfish

louable [lwabl] *ADJ* (*appartement, garage*) rentable; (*action, personne*) praiseworthy, commendable

louage [lwaʒ] *NM*: **voiture de ~** hired (BRIT) *ou* rented (US) car; (*à louer*) hire (BRIT) *ou* rental (US) car

louange [lwɑ̃ʒ] *NF*: **à la ~ de** in praise of ▪ **louanges** *NFPL* praise *sg*

loubard, -e [lubaʀ, -aʀd] *NM/F* (*fam*) lout

louche [luʃ] *ADJ* shady, dubious ▶ *NF* ladle

loucher [luʃe] /1/ *VI* to squint; (*fig*): **~ sur** to have one's (beady) eye on

★**louer** [lwe] /1/ *VT* (*maison: propriétaire*) to let, rent (out); (*: locataire*) to rent; (*voiture etc: entreprise*) to hire out (BRIT), rent (out); (*: locataire*) to hire (BRIT), rent; (*réserver*) to book; (*faire l'éloge de*) to praise; **« à ~ »** "to let" (BRIT), "for rent" (US); **~ qn de** to praise sb for ▪ **se louer** *VPR*: **se ~ de** to congratulate o.s. on

loueur, -euse [lwœʀ, -øz] *NM/F* (*compagnie*): **~ de voitures** car hire (BRIT) *ou* rental (US) company; (*personne*) renter

loufoque [lufɔk] *ADJ* (*fam*) crazy, zany

loukoum [lukum] *NM* Turkish delight

loulou [lulu] *NM* (*chien*) spitz; **~ de Poméranie** Pomeranian (dog)

★**loup** [lu] *NM* (*poisson*) bass; (*masque*) (eye) mask; **jeune ~** young go-getter; **~ de mer** (*marin*) old seadog

loupe [lup] *NF* magnifying glass; **~ de noyer** burr walnut; **à la ~** (*fig*) in minute detail

louper [lupe] /1/ *VT* (*fam: manquer*) to miss; (*gâcher*) to mess up, bungle; (*examen*) to flunk

★**lourd, e** [luʀ, luʀd] *ADJ* heavy; (*chaleur, temps*) sultry; (*fig: personne, style*) heavy-handed; **~ de** (*menaces*) charged with; (*conséquences*) fraught with; **artillerie/industrie lourde** heavy artillery/industry ▶ *ADV*: **peser ~** to be heavy

lourdaud, e [luʀdo, -od] *ADJ* clumsy

lourdement [luʀdəmɑ̃] *ADV* heavily; **se tromper ~** to make a big mistake

lourdeur [luʀdœʀ] *NF* heaviness; **~ d'estomac** indigestion *no pl*

loustic [lustik] *NM* (*fam, péj*) joker

loutre [lutʀ] *NF* otter; (*fourrure*) otter skin

louve [luv] *NF* she-wolf

louveteau, x [luv(ə)to] *NM* (*Zool*) wolf-cub; (*scout*) cub (scout)

louvoyer – luxembourgeois

louvoyer [luvwaje] /8/ vi (*Navig*) to tack; (*fig*) to hedge, evade the issue

lover [lɔve] /1/: **se lover** vpr to coil up

loyal, e, -aux [lwajal, -o] ADJ (*fidèle*) loyal, faithful; (*fair-play*) fair

loyalement [lwajalmɑ̃] ADV loyally, faithfully; fairly

loyalisme [lwajalism] NM loyalty

loyauté [lwajote] NF loyalty, faithfulness; fairness

★**loyer** [lwaje] NM rent; **~ de l'argent** interest rate

LP SIGLE M (= *lycée professionnel*) secondary school for vocational training

LPO SIGLE F (= *Ligue pour la protection des oiseaux*) bird protection society

LSD SIGLE M (= *Lyserg Säure Diäthylamid*) LSD

lu, e [ly] PP *de* lire

lubie [lybi] NF whim, craze

lubricité [lybʁisite] NF lust

lubrifiant [lybʁifjɑ̃] NM lubricant

lubrifier [lybʁifje] /7/ vt to lubricate

lubrique [lybʁik] ADJ lecherous

lucarne [lykaʁn] NF skylight

lucide [lysid] ADJ (*conscient*) lucid; (*accidenté*) conscious; (*perspicace*) clear-headed

lucidité [lysidite] NF lucidity

luciole [lysjɔl] NF firefly

lucratif, -ive [lykʁatif, -iv] ADJ lucrative; profitable; **à but non ~** non profit-making

ludique [lydik] ADJ play cpd, playing

ludothèque [lydɔtɛk] NF toy library

luette [lɥɛt] NF uvula

lueur [lɥœʁ] NF (*chatoyante*) glimmer *no pl*; (*métallique, mouillée*) gleam *no pl*; (*rougeoyante*) glow *no pl*; (*pâle*) (faint) light; (*fig*) spark; (: *d'espérance*) glimmer, gleam

luge [lyʒ] NF sledge (*Brit*), sled (*US*); **faire de la ~** to sledge (*Brit*), sled (*US*), toboggan

lugubre [lygybʁ] ADJ gloomy; dismal

---

lui [lɥi]

PP *de* luire

▶ PRON **1** (*objet indirect: mâle*) (to) him; (: *femelle*) (to) her; (: *chose, animal*) (to) it; **je lui ai parlé** I have spoken to him (*ou* to her); **il lui a offert un cadeau** he gave him (*ou* her) a present; **je le lui ai donné** I gave it to him (*ou* her)

2 (*après préposition, comparatif: personne*) him; (: *chose, animal*) it; **elle est contente de lui** she is pleased with him; **je la connais mieux que lui** I know her better than he does; I know her better than him; **cette voiture est à lui** this car belongs to him, this is HIS car; **c'est à lui de jouer** it's his turn *ou* go

3 (*sujet, forme emphatique*) he; **lui, il est à Paris** HE is in Paris; **c'est lui qui l'a fait** HE did it

4 (*objet, forme emphatique*) him; **c'est lui que j'attends** I'm waiting for HIM

5: **lui-même** himself; itself

lui-même [lɥimɛm] PRON (*personne*) himself; (*chose*) itself

luire [lɥiʁ] /38/ vi (*gén*) to shine, gleam; (*surface mouillée*) to glisten; (*reflets chauds, cuivrés*) to glow

luisant, e [lɥizɑ̃, -ɑ̃t] VB *voir* **luire** ▶ ADJ shining, gleaming

lumbago [lɔ̃bago] NM lumbago

lumière [lymjɛʁ] NF light; **à la ~ de** by the light of; (*fig: événements*) in the light of; **faire (toute) la ~ sur** (*fig*) to clarify (completely); **fais de la ~** let's have some light, give us some light; **mettre en ~** (*fig*) to highlight; **~ du jour/soleil** day/sunlight ■ **lumières** NFPL (*d'une personne*) knowledge *sg*, wisdom *sg*

luminaire [lyminɛʁ] NM lamp, light

lumineux, -euse [lyminø, -øz] ADJ (*émettant de la lumière*) luminous; (*éclairé*) illuminated; (*ciel, journée, couleur*) bright; (*relatif à la lumière: rayon etc*) of light, light cpd; (*fig: regard*) radiant

luminosité [lyminɔzite] NF (*Tech*) luminosity

lump [lœp] NM: **œufs de ~** lump-fish roe

lunaire [lynɛʁ] ADJ lunar, moon cpd

lunatique [lynatik] ADJ whimsical, temperamental

lunch [lœ̃tʃ] NM (*réception*) buffet lunch

★**lundi** [lœ̃di] NM Monday; **on est ~** it's Monday; **le ~ 20 août** Monday 20th August; **il est venu ~** he came on Monday; **le(s) ~(s)** on Mondays; **à ~!** see you (on) Monday!; **~ de Pâques** Easter Monday; **~ de Pentecôte** Whit Monday (*Brit*)

★**lune** [lyn] NF moon; **pleine/nouvelle ~** full/new moon; **être dans la ~** (*distrait*) to have one's head in the clouds; **~ de miel** honeymoon

luné, e [lyne] ADJ: **bien/mal ~** in a good/bad mood

lunette [lynɛt] NF: **~ d'approche** telescope; **~ arrière** (*Auto*) rear window ■ **lunettes** NFPL glasses, spectacles; (*protectrices*) goggles; **lunettes noires** dark glasses; **lunettes de soleil** sunglasses

lurent [lyʁ] VB *voir* **lire**

lurette [lyʁɛt] NF: **il y a belle ~** ages ago

luron, ne [lyʁɔ̃, -ɔn] NM/F lad/lass; **joyeux** *ou* **gai ~** gay dog

lus *etc* [ly] VB *voir* **lire**

lustre [lystʁ] NM (*de plafond*) chandelier; (*fig: éclat*) lustre

lustrer [lystʁe] /1/ vt: **~ qch** (*faire briller*) to make sth shine; (*user*) to make sth shiny

lut [ly] VB *voir* **lire**

luth [lyt] NM lute

luthier [lytje] NM (stringed-)instrument maker

lutin [lytɛ̃] NM imp, goblin

lutrin [lytʁɛ̃] NM lectern

lutte [lyt] NF (*conflit*) struggle; (*Sport*): **la ~** wrestling; **de haute ~** after a hard-fought struggle; **~ des classes** class struggle; **~ libre** (*Sport*) all-in wrestling

★**lutter** [lyte] /1/ vi to fight, struggle; (*Sport*) to wrestle

lutteur, -euse [lytœʁ, -øz] NM/F (*Sport*) wrestler; (*fig*) battler, fighter

luxation [lyksasjɔ̃] NF dislocation

luxe [lyks] NM luxury; **un ~ de** (*détails, précautions*) a wealth of; **de ~** adj luxury cpd

Luxembourg [lyksɑ̃buʁ] NM: **le ~** Luxembourg

luxembourgeois, e [lyksɑ̃buʁʒwa, -waz] ADJ of *ou* from Luxembourg ▶ NM/F: **Luxembourgeois, e** inhabitant *ou* native of Luxembourg

luxer [lykse] /**1**/ VT: **se ~ l'épaule** to dislocate one's shoulder

luxueusement [lyksɥøzmɑ̃] ADV luxuriously

★**luxueux, -euse** [lyksɥø, -øz] ADJ luxurious

luxure [lyksyʀ] NF lust

luxuriant, e [lyksyʀjɑ̃, -ɑ̃t] ADJ luxuriant, lush

luzerne [lyzɛʀn] NF lucerne, alfalfa

lycée [lise] NM (state) secondary (BRIT) ou high (US) school; see note

French pupils spend the last three years of their secondary education at a **lycée**, where they sit their *baccalauréat* before leaving school or going on to higher education. There are two types of lycée: *lycée d'enseignement général et technologique*, offering mainstream and technical courses, and *lycée professionnel*, offering vocational courses. Some *lycées*, particularly those with a wide catchment area or those which offer more specialized courses, have facilities for pupils to board.

lycéen, ne [liseɛ̃, -ɛn] NM/F secondary school pupil

Lycra® [likʀa] NM Lycra®

lymphatique [lɛ̃fatik] ADJ (fig) lethargic, sluggish

lymphe [lɛ̃f] NF lymph

lyncher [lɛ̃ʃe] /**1**/ VT to lynch

lynx [lɛ̃ks] NM lynx

Lyon [ljɔ̃] N Lyons

lyonnais, e [ljɔnɛ, -ɛz] ADJ of ou from Lyons; (Culin) Lyonnaise

lyophilisé, e [ljɔfilize] ADJ (café) freeze-dried

lyre [liʀ] NF lyre

lyrique [liʀik] ADJ lyrical; (Opéra) lyric; **artiste ~** opera singer; **comédie ~** comic opera; **théâtre ~** opera house (for light opera)

lyrisme [liʀism] NM lyricism

lys [lis] NM lily

Mm

M, m [ɛm] NM INV M, m ▸ ABR = **masculin; Monsieur; mètre;** (= *million*) M; **M comme Marcel** M for Mike

★**m'** [m] PRON *voir* **me**

★**ma** [ma] ADJ POSS *voir* **mon**

maboul, e [mabul] ADJ (*fam*) loony

macabre [makabʀ] ADJ macabre, gruesome

macadam [makadam] NM tarmac (BRIT), asphalt

Macao [makao] N Macao

macaque [makak] NM (*singe*) macaque

macareux [makaʀø] NM puffin

macaron [makaʀɔ̃] NM (*gâteau*) macaroon; (*insigne*) (round) badge

macaroni [makaʀɔni] NM: **des macaronis au fromage, un gratin de macaronis** macaroni cheese (BRIT), macaroni and cheese (US)

macchabée [makabe] NM (*fam*) stiff (*fam*), corpse

macédoine [masedwan] NF: **~ de fruits** fruit salad; **~ de légumes** mixed vegetables *pl*; **la M~** (*pays, région*) Macedonia

macédonien, ne [masedɔnjɛ̃, -jɛn] ADJ Macedonian ▸ NM/F: **Macédonien, ne** Macedonian

macérer [maseʀe] **/6/** VI, VT to macerate; (*dans du vinaigre*) to pickle

mâche [mɑʃ] NF (*salade*) lamb's lettuce

mâchefer [mɑʃfɛʀ] NM clinker, cinders *pl*

mâcher [mɑʃe] **/1/** VT to chew; **ne pas ~ ses mots** not to mince one's words; **~ le travail à qn** (*fig*) to spoon-feed sb, do half sb's work for him

machette [maʃɛt] NF machete

machiavélique [makjavelik] ADJ Machiavellian

machiavélisme [makjavelism] NM Machiavellianism

★**machin** [maʃɛ̃] NM (*fam*) thingamajig, thing; (*personne*): **M~** what's-his-name

machinal, e, -aux [maʃinal, -o] ADJ mechanical, automatic

machinalement [maʃinalmɑ̃] ADV mechanically, automatically

machination [maʃinasjɔ̃] NF scheming, frame-up

★**machine** [maʃin] NF machine; (*locomotive: de navire etc*) engine; (*fig: rouages*) machinery; (*fam: personne*): **M~** what's-her-name; **faire ~ arrière** (*Navig*) to go astern; (*fig*) to back-pedal; **~ à laver/coudre/tricoter** washing/sewing/knitting machine; **~ à écrire** typewriter; **~ à sous** fruit machine; **~ à vapeur** steam engine

machine-outil [maʃinuti] (*pl* **machines-outils**) NF machine tool

machinerie [maʃinʀi] NF machinery, plant; (*d'un navire*) engine room

machinisme [maʃinism] NM mechanization

machiniste [maʃinist] NM (*Théât*) scene shifter; (*de bus, métro*) driver

machisme [ma(t)ʃism] NM male chauvinism

machiste [ma(t)ʃist] ADJ, NMF male chauvinist

macho [matʃo] (*fam*) ADJ macho (*fam*) ▸ NM male chauvinist

mâchoire [mɑʃwaʀ] NF jaw; **~ de frein** brake shoe

mâchonner [mɑʃɔne] **/1/** VT to chew (at)

mâchouiller [mɑʃuje] VT to chew on

maçon [masɔ̃] NM bricklayer; (*constructeur*) builder

mâcon [makɔ̃] NM Mâcon wine

maçonner [masɔne] **/1/** VT (*revêtir*) to face, render (with cement); (*boucher*) to brick up

maçonnerie [masɔnʀi] NF (*murs: de brique*) brickwork; (: *de pierre*) masonry, stonework; (*activité*) bricklaying; building; **~ de béton** concrete

maçonnique [masɔnik] ADJ masonic

macramé [makʀame] NM macramé

macro [makʀo] NF (*Inform*) macro

macrobiotique [makʀɔbjɔtik] ADJ macrobiotic

macrocéphale [makʀosefal] ADJ macrocephalic

macrocosme [makʀɔkɔsm] NM macrocosm

macroéconomie [makʀoekɔnɔmi] NF macroeconomics *sg*

macrophotographie [makʀofɔtɔgʀafi] NF macrophotography

maculer [makyle] **/1/** VT to stain; (*Typo*) to mackle

Madagascar [madagaskaʀ] NF Madagascar

★**Madame** [madam] (*pl* **Mesdames**) NF: **~ X** Mrs X; **occupez-vous de ~/Monsieur/Mademoiselle** please serve this lady/gentleman/(young) lady; **bonjour ~/Monsieur/Mademoiselle** good morning; (*ton déférent*) good morning Madam/Sir/Madam; (*le nom est connu*) good morning Mrs X/Mr X/Miss X/Ms X; **~/Monsieur/Mademoiselle!** (*pour appeler*) excuse me!; (*ton déférent*) Madam/Sir/Miss!; **~/Monsieur/Mademoiselle** (*sur lettre*) Dear Madam/Sir/Madam; **chère ~/cher Monsieur/chère Mademoiselle** Dear Mrs X/Mr X/Miss X/Ms X; **~ la Directrice** the director; the manageress; the head teacher; **Mesdames** Ladies; **mesdames, mesdemoiselles, messieurs** ladies and gentlemen

Ms est un titre utilisé devant le nom de famille à la place de **Mrs** pour éviter la distinction traditionnelle entre femmes mariées et non mariées.

Madeleine [madlɛn]: **îles de la ~** *nfpl* Magdalen Islands

madeleine [madlɛn] NF madeleine, ≈ sponge finger cake

★**Mademoiselle** [madmwazɛl] (*pl* **Mesdemoiselles** [medmwazɛl]) NF Miss; *voir aussi* **Madame**

madère [madɛʀ] NM Madeira (wine) ▶ NF: **M~** Madeira

madone [madɔn] NF Madonna

madré, e [madʀe] ADJ crafty, wily

Madrid [madʀid] N Madrid

madrier [madʀije] NM beam

madrigal, -aux [madʀigal, -o] NM madrigal

madrilène [madʀilɛn] ADJ of *ou* from Madrid

maestria [maɛstʀija] NF (*masterly*) skill

maestro [maɛstʀo] NM maestro

mafia, maffia [mafja] NF Maf(f)ia

mafieux, -euse [mafjø, -øz] ADJ Mafia ▶ NM/F Mafioso

★**magasin** [magazɛ̃] NM (*boutique*) shop; (*entrepôt*) warehouse; (*d'arme*) magazine; **en ~** (*Comm*) in stock; **faire les magasins** to go (a)round the shops, do the shops; **~ grocer's (shop)** (BRIT), **grocery store** (US); **~ de déstockage** ≈ factory outlet

In France, **magasins** are usually open all day in bigger towns and shopping centres. In smaller towns, they tend to close for lunch, normally between noon and 2pm. Throughout France, most shops are closed on Sundays, with some in smaller towns also closing on Mondays.

magasinier [magazinje] NM warehouseman

★**magazine** [magazin] NM magazine

mage [maʒ] NM: **les Rois Mages** the Magi, the (Three) Wise Men

magenta [maʒɛ̃ta] NM magenta

Maghreb [magʀɛb] NM: **le ~** the Maghreb, North(-West) Africa

maghrébin, e [magʀebɛ̃, -in] ADJ of *ou* from the Maghreb, North African ▶ NM/F: **Maghrébin, e** North African, Maghrebi

magicien, ne [maʒisjɛ̃, -ɛn] NM/F magician

magie [maʒi] NF magic; **~ noire** black magic

magique [maʒik] ADJ (*occulte*) magic; (*fig*) magical

magistral, e, -aux [maʒistʀal, -o] ADJ (*œuvre, adresse*) masterly; (*ton*) authoritative; (*gifle etc*) sound, resounding; (*ex cathedra*): **enseignement ~** lecturing, lectures *pl*; **cours ~** lecture

magistralement [maʒistʀalmɑ̃] ADV brilliantly; **~ interprété par** beautifully acted by

magistrat [maʒistʀa] NM magistrate

magistrature [maʒistʀatyʀ] NF magistracy, magistrature; **~ assise** judges *pl*, bench; **~ debout** state prosecutors *pl*

magma [magma] NM (*Géo*) magma; (*fig*) jumble

magnanerie [maɲanʀi] NF silk farm

magnanime [maɲanim] ADJ magnanimous

magnanimité [maɲanimite] NF magnanimity

magnat [magna] NM tycoon, magnate

magner [maɲe] /1/: **se magner** VPR (*fam*) to get a move on

magnésie [maɲezi] NF magnesia

magnésium [maɲezjɔm] NM magnesium

magnétique [maɲetik] ADJ magnetic

magnétiser [maɲetize] /1/ VT to magnetize; (*fig*) to mesmerize, hypnotize

magnétiseur, -euse [maɲetizœʀ, -øz] NM/F hypnotist

magnétisme [maɲetism] NM magnetism

magnéto [maɲeto] NM (*à cassette*) cassette deck; (*magnétophone*) tape recorder

magnétocassette [maɲetokasɛt] NM cassette deck

magnétophone [maɲetɔfɔn] NM tape recorder; **~ à cassettes** cassette recorder

magnétoscope [maɲetɔskɔp] NM: **~ (à cassette)** video (recorder)

magnificence [maɲifisɑ̃s] NF (*faste*) magnificence, splendour (BRIT), splendor (US); (*générosité*) munificence, lavishness

magnifier [maɲifje] /7/ VT (*glorifier*) to glorify; (*idéaliser*) to idealize

★**magnifique** [maɲifik] ADJ magnificent

magnifiquement [maɲifikmɑ̃] ADV magnificently

magnitude [maɲityd] NF (*de séisme*) magnitude; **un séisme de ~ 4 sur l'échelle de Richter** an earthquake measuring 4 on the Richter scale

magnolia [maɲɔlja] NM magnolia

magnum [magnɔm] NM magnum

magot [mago] NM (*argent*) pile (of money); (*économies*) nest egg

magouille [maguj] NF (*fam*) scheming

magouiller [maguje] VI (*fam*) to scheme

magret [magʀɛ] NM: **~ de canard** duck breast

mahométan, e [maɔmetɑ̃, -an] ADJ Mohammedan, Mahometan

★**mai** [mɛ] NM May; *voir aussi* **juillet**

Le premier mai is a public holiday in France and marks the achievements of workers and the labour movement. Sprigs of lily of the valley are traditionally exchanged. *Le 8 mai* is also a public holiday and commemorates the surrender of the German army to Eisenhower on 7 May 1945. It is marked by parades of ex-servicemen and ex-servicewomen in most towns. The social upheavals of May and June 1968, with their student demonstrations, workers' strikes and general rioting, are usually referred to as *les événements de mai 68*. De Gaulle's government survived, but reforms in education and a move towards decentralization ensued.

★**maigre** [mɛgʀ] ADJ (very) thin, skinny; (*viande*) lean; (*fromage*) low-fat; (*végétation*) thin, sparse; (*fig*) poor; **jours maigres** days of abstinence, fish days ▶ ADV: **faire ~** not to eat meat

maigrelet, te [mɛgʀəlɛ, -ɛt] ADJ skinny, scrawny

maigreur [mɛgRœR] NF thinness

maigrichon, ne [megRiʃɔ̃, -ɔn] ADJ = **maigrelet**

maigrir [megRiR] /2/ VI to get thinner, lose weight; **~ de 2 kilos** to lose 2 kilos ▶ VT: **~ qn** (vêtement) to make sb look slim(mer)

mail [mɛl] NM email; **~ groupé** group email

mailing [mɛliŋ] NM direct mail no pl; **un ~** a mailshot

maille [maj] NF (boucle) stitch; (ouverture) hole (in the mesh); **avoir ~ à partir avec qn** to have a brush with sb; **~ à l'endroit/à l'envers** knit one/ purl one; (boucle) plain/purl stitch

maillechort [majʃɔR] NM nickel silver

maillet [majɛ] NM mallet

maillon [majɔ̃] NM link

maillot [majo] NM (aussi: **maillot de corps**) vest; (de danseur) leotard; (de sportif) jersey; **~ de bain** swimming ou bathing (BRIT) costume, swimsuit; (d'homme) (swimming ou bathing (BRIT)) trunks pl; **~ deux pièces** two-piece swimsuit, bikini; **~ jaune** yellow jersey

★**main** [mɛ̃] NF hand; **la ~ dans la ~** hand in hand; **à deux mains** with both hands; **d'une ~** with one hand; **à la ~** (tenir, avoir) in one's hand; (faire, tricoter etc) by hand; **se donner la ~** to hold hands; **donner** ou **tendre la ~ à qn** to hold out one's hand to sb; **se serrer la ~** to shake hands; **serrer la ~ à qn** to shake hands with sb; **sous la ~** to ou at hand; **haut les mains !** hands up!; **à ~ levée** (Art) freehand; **à mains levées** (voter) with a show of hands; **attaque à ~ armée** armed attack; **à ~ droite/gauche** to the right/left; **à remettre en mains propres** to be delivered personally; **de première ~** (renseignement) first-hand; (Comm: voiture etc) with only one previous owner; **faire ~ basse sur** to help o.s. to; **mettre la dernière ~ à** to put the finishing touches to; **mettre la ~ à la pâte** (fig) to lend a hand; **avoir/passer la ~** (Cartes) to lead/hand over the lead; **s'en laver les mains** (fig) to wash one's hands of it; **se faire/perdre la ~** to get one's hand in/lose one's touch; **avoir qch bien en ~** to have got the hang of sth; **en un tour de ~** (fig) in the twinkling of an eye; **~ courante** handrail

mainate [mɛnat] NM myna(h) bird

main-d'œuvre [mɛ̃dœvʀ] (pl **mains-d'œuvre**) NF manpower, labour (BRIT), labor (US)

main-forte [mɛ̃fɔRt] NF: **prêter ~ à qn** to come to sb's assistance

mainmise [mɛ̃miz] NF seizure; (fig): **avoir la ~ sur** to have a grip ou stranglehold on

mains-libres [mɛ̃libR] ADJ INV (téléphone, kit) hands-free

maint, e [mɛ̃, mɛ̃t] ADJ many a; **maints** many; **à maintes reprises** time and (time) again

maintenance [mɛ̃t(ə)nɑ̃s] NF maintenance, servicing

★**maintenant** [mɛ̃t(ə)nɑ̃] ADV now; (actuellement) nowadays

maintenir [mɛ̃t(ə)niR] /22/ VT (retenir, soutenir) to support; (contenir: foule etc) to keep in check, hold back; (conserver) to maintain, uphold; (affirmer) to maintain ■ **se maintenir** VPR (paix, temps) to hold; (prix) to keep steady; (préjugé) to persist; (malade) to remain stable

maintien [mɛ̃tjɛ̃] NM maintaining, upholding; (attitude) bearing; **~ de l'ordre** maintenance of law and order

maintiendrai [mɛ̃tjɛ̃dRe], **maintiens** etc [mɛ̃tjɛ̃] VB voir **maintenir**

★**maire** [mɛR] NM mayor

★**mairie** [meRi] NF (bâtiment) town hall; (administration) town council

★**mais** [mɛ] CONJ but; **~ non !** of course not!; **~ enfin** but after all; (indignation) look here!; **~ encore ?** is that all?

maïs [mais] NM maize (BRIT), corn (US)

★**maison** [mɛzɔ̃] NF (bâtiment) house; (chez-soi) home; (Comm) firm; (famille): **ami de la ~** friend of the family ▶ ADJ INV (Culin) home-made; (: au restaurant) made by the chef; (Comm) in-house, own; (fam) first-rate; **à la ~** at home; (direction) home; **~ d'arrêt** (short-stay) prison; **~ centrale** prison; **~ close** brothel; **~ de correction** ≈ remand home (BRIT), ≈ reformatory (US); **~ de la culture** ≈ arts centre; **~ des jeunes** ≈ youth club; **~ mère** parent company; **~ de passe** = maison close; **~ de repos** convalescent home; **~ de retraite** old people's home; **~ de santé** psychiatric facility

Maison-Blanche [mɛzɔ̃blɑ̃ʃ] NF: **la ~** the White House

maisonnée [mɛzɔne] NF household, family

maisonnette [mɛzɔnɛt] NF small house

maître, -esse [mɛtR, mɛtRɛs] NM/F master (mistress); (Scol) teacher, schoolmaster(-mistress) ▶ NM (peintre etc) master; (titre): **M~** Maître (term of address for lawyers etc) ▶ NF (amante) mistress ▶ ADJ (principal, essentiel) main; **maison de ~** family seat; **être ~ de** (soi-même, situation) to be in control of; **se rendre ~ de** (pays, ville) to gain control of; (situation, incendie) to bring under control; **être passé ~ dans l'art de** to be a (past) master in the art of; **une maîtresse femme** a forceful woman; **~ d'armes** fencing master; **~ auxiliaire** (Scol) temporary teacher; **~ chanteur** blackmailer; **~ de chapelle** choirmaster; **~ de conférences** ≈ senior lecturer (BRIT), ≈ assistant professor (US); **~/maîtresse d'école** teacher, schoolmaster(-mistress); **~ d'hôtel** (domestique) butler; (d'hôtel) head waiter; **~ de maison** host; **~ nageur** lifeguard; **~ d'œuvre** (Constr) project manager; **~ d'ouvrage** (Constr) client; **~ queux** chef; **maîtresse de maison** hostess; (ménagère) housewife

maître-assistant, e [mɛtRasistɑ̃, -ɑ̃t] (pl **maîtres-assistants, es**) NM/F ≈ lecturer

maître-autel [mɛtRotɛl] (pl **maîtres-autels**) NM high altar

maîtrise [metRiz] NF (aussi: **maîtrise de soi**) self-control, self-possession; (habileté) skill, mastery; (suprématie) mastery, command; (diplôme) ≈ master's degree; (chefs d'équipe) supervisory staff

maîtriser [metRize] /1/ VT (cheval, incendie) to (bring under) control; (sujet) to master; (émotion) to control, master ■ **se maîtriser** VPR to control o.s.

maïzena® [maizena] NF cornflour (BRIT), cornstarch (US)

majesté [maʒɛste] NF majesty

majestueusement [maʒɛstɥøzmɑ̃] ADV majestically

majestueux, -euse [maʒɛstɥø, -øz] ADJ majestic

★**majeur, e** [maʒœʀ] ADJ (*important*) major; (*Jur*) of age; (*fig*) adult; **en majeure partie** for the most part; **la majeure partie de** most of ▶ NM/F (*Jur*) person who has come of age ou attained his (ou her) majority ▶ NM (*doigt*) middle finger

major [maʒɔʀ] NM adjutant; (*Scol*) ~ **de la promotion** first in one's year

majoration [maʒɔʀasjɔ̃] NF increase

majordome [maʒɔʀdɔm] NM major-domo

majorer [maʒɔʀe] /1/ VT to increase

majorette [maʒɔʀɛt] NF majorette

majoritaire [maʒɔʀitɛʀ] ADJ majority *cpd*; **système/scrutin** ~ majority system/ballot

majorité [maʒɔʀite] NF (*gén*) majority; (*parti*) party in power; **en** ~ (*composé etc*) mainly; **avoir la** ~ to have the majority

Majorque [maʒɔʀk] NF Majorca

majorquin, e [maʒɔʀkɛ̃, -in] ADJ Majorcan ▶ NM/F: **Majorquin, e** Majorcan

majuscule [maʒyskyl] ADJ, NF: **(lettre)** ~ capital (letter)

★**mal** (*pl* **maux**) [mal, mo] NM (*opposé au bien*) evil; (*tort, dommage*) harm; (*douleur physique*) pain, ache; (*maladie*) illness, sickness *no pl*; (*difficulté, peine*) trouble; (*souffrance morale*) pain; **dire/penser du** ~ **de** to speak/think ill of; **ne vouloir de** ~ **à personne** to wish nobody any ill; **avoir du** ~ **à faire qch** to have trouble doing sth; **se donner du** ~ **pour faire qch** to go to a lot of trouble to do sth; **ne voir aucun** ~ **à** to see no harm in, see nothing wrong in; **sans penser** ou **songer à** ~ without meaning any harm; **faire du** ~ **à qn** to hurt sb; to harm sb; **se faire** ~ to hurt o.s.; **se faire au pied** to hurt one's foot; **ça fait** ~ it hurts; **j'ai** ~ **(ici)** it hurts (here); **j'ai** ~ **au dos** my back aches, I've got a pain in my back; **avoir** ~ **à la tête/à la gorge** to have a headache/a sore throat; **avoir** ~ **aux dents/à l'oreille** to have toothache/earache; **avoir le** ~ **de l'air** to be airsick; **avoir le** ~ **du pays** to be homesick; ~ **de mer** seasickness; ~ **de la route** carsickness; **maux de ventre** stomach ache *sg*; *voir aussi* **cœur** ▶ ADV badly; **il comprend** ~ he has difficulty in understanding; **il a** ~ **compris** he misunderstood; **se sentir** ou **se trouver** ~ to feel ill ou unwell; ~ **tourner** to go wrong; **être au plus** ~ (*malade*) to be very bad; (*brouillé*) to be at daggers drawn; **craignant** ~ **faire** fearing he *etc* was doing the wrong thing; ~ **en point** in a bad state; **être** ~ **(à l'aise)** to be uncomfortable; **être** ~ **avec qn** to be on bad terms with sb ▶ ADJ: **c'est** ~ **(de faire)** it's bad ou wrong (to do); **il n'a rien fait de** ~ he has done nothing wrong

malabar [malabaʀ] NM (*fam*) muscle man

malachite [malaʃit] NF malachite

★**malade** [malad] ADJ ill, sick; (*poitrine, jambe*) bad; (*plante*) diseased; (*fig: entreprise, monde*) ailing; **tomber** ~ to fall ill; **être** ~ **du cœur** to have heart trouble ou a bad heart ▶ NMF invalid, sick person; (*à l'hôpital etc*) patient; **grand** ~ seriously ill person; ~ **mental** mentally ill person

> Les mots **ill** et **sick** ont souvent un sens et un emploi très comparables, mais en anglais britannique **sick** est surtout employé pour parler d'une personne souffrant de nausées ou de vomissements.

> *Il s'occupe de sa mère, qui est très malade.* **He looks after his mum, who is very sick** ou **ill**.
> *Elle a été malade dans l'avion.* **She was sick on the plane.**

★**maladie** [maladi] NF (*spécifique*) disease, illness; (*mauvaise santé*) illness, sickness; (*fig: manie*) mania; **être rongé par la** ~ to be wasting away (through illness); ~ **d'Alzheimer** Alzheimer's disease; ~ **de peau** skin disease

maladif, -ive [maladif, -iv] ADJ sickly; (*curiosité, besoin*) pathological

maladresse [maladʀɛs] NF clumsiness *no pl*; (*gaffe*) blunder

★**maladroit, e** [maladʀwa, -wat] ADJ clumsy

maladroitement [maladʀwatmɑ̃] ADV clumsily

mal-aimé, e [maleme] NM/F unpopular person; (*de la scène politique, de la société*) persona non grata

malais, e [malɛ, -ɛz] ADJ Malay, Malayan ▶ NM (*Ling*) Malay ▶ NM/F: **Malais, e** Malay, Malayan

malaise [malɛz] NM (*Méd*) feeling of faintness; feeling of discomfort; (*fig*) uneasiness, malaise; **avoir un** ~ to feel faint ou dizzy

malaisé, e [maleze] ADJ difficult

Malaisie [malɛzi] NF: **la** ~ Malaysia; **la péninsule de** ~ the Malay Peninsula

malappris, e [malapʀi, -iz] NM/F ill-mannered ou boorish person

malaria [malaʀja] NF malaria

malavisé, e [malavize] ADJ ill-advised, unwise

Malawi [malawi] NM: **le** ~ Malawi

malaxer [malakse] /1/ VT (*pétrir*) to knead; (*mêler*) to mix

malaxeur [malaksœʀ] NM mixer

malbouffe [malbuf] NF (*fam*): **la** ~ junk food

malchance [malʃɑ̃s] NF misfortune, ill luck *no pl*; **par** ~ unfortunately; **quelle** ~ **!** what bad luck!

malchanceux, -euse [malʃɑ̃sø, -øz] ADJ unlucky

malcommode [malkɔmɔd] ADJ impractical, inconvenient

Maldives [maldiv] NFPL: **les** ~ the Maldive Islands

maldonne [maldɔn] NF (*Cartes*) misdeal; **il y a** ~ (*fig*) there's been a misunderstanding

mâle [mɑl] ADJ (*Élec, Tech*) male; (*viril: voix, traits*) manly ▶ NM male

malédiction [malediksjɔ̃] NF curse

maléfice [malefis] NM evil spell

maléfique [malefik] ADJ evil, baleful

malencontreusement [malɑ̃kɔ̃tʀøzmɑ̃] ADV (*arriver*) at the wrong moment; (*rappeler, mentionner*) inopportunely

malencontreux, -euse [malɑ̃kɔ̃tʀø, -øz] ADJ unfortunate, untoward

malentendant, e [malɑ̃tɑ̃dɑ̃, -ɑ̃t] NM/F: **les malentendants** the hard of hearing

malentendu [malɑ̃tɑ̃dy] NM misunderstanding; **il y a eu un** ~ there's been a misunderstanding

malfaçon [malfasɔ̃] NF fault

malfaisant, e [malfəzɑ̃, -ɑ̃t] ADJ evil, harmful

malfaiteur [malfɛtœʀ] NM lawbreaker, criminal; (*voleur*) burglar, thief

malfamé, e [malfame] ADJ disreputable, of ill repute

malformation [malfɔRmasjɔ̃] NF malformation

malfrat [malfRɑ] NM villain, crook

malgache [malgaʃ] ADJ Malagasy, Madagascan ▶ NM (Ling) Malagasy ▶ NMF: **Malgache** Malagasy, Madagascan

malgré [malgre] PRÉP in spite of, despite; **~ tout** adv in spite of everything

malhabile [malabil] ADJ clumsy

malheur [malœR] NM (situation) adversity, misfortune; (événement) misfortune; (: plus fort) disaster, tragedy; **par ~** unfortunately; **quel ~!** what a shame ou pity!; **faire un ~** (fam: un éclat) to do something desperate; (: avoir du succès) to be a smash hit

★**malheureusement** [malœRøzmɑ̃] ADV unfortunately

★**malheureux, -euse** [malœRø, -øz] ADJ (triste) unhappy, miserable; (infortuné, regrettable) unfortunate; (malchanceux) unlucky; (insignifiant) wretched; **avoir la main malheureuse** (au jeu) to be unlucky; (tout casser) to be ham-fisted ▶ NM/F (infortuné, misérable) poor soul; (indigent, miséreux) unfortunate creature; **les ~** the destitute

malhonnête [malɔnɛt] ADJ dishonest

malhonnêtement [malɔnɛtmɑ̃] ADV dishonestly

malhonnêteté [malɔnɛtte] NF dishonesty; rudeness no pl

Mali [mali] NM: **le ~** Mali

malice [malis] NF mischievousness; (méchanceté): **par ~** out of malice ou spite; **sans ~** guileless

malicieusement [malisjøzmɑ̃] ADV mischievously

malicieux, -euse [malisjø, -øz] ADJ mischievous

malien, ne [maljɛ̃, -ɛn] ADJ Malian

malignité [maliɲite] NF (d'une tumeur, d'un mal) malignancy

malin, -igne [malɛ̃, -iɲ] ADJ (futé: f fam: **maline**) smart, shrewd; (sourire) knowing; (Méd, influence) malignant; **faire le ~** to show off; **éprouver un ~ plaisir à** to take malicious pleasure in

malingre [malɛ̃gR] ADJ puny

malintentionné, e [malɛ̃tɑ̃sjɔne] ADJ ill-intentioned, malicious

malle [mal] NF trunk; (Auto): **~ (arrière)** boot (BRIT), trunk (US)

malléabilité [maleabilite] NF (de matériau) malleability

malléable [maleabl] ADJ malleable

malle-poste [malpɔst] (pl **malles-poste**) NF mail coach

mallette [malɛt] NF (valise) (small) suitcase; (aussi: **mallette de voyage**) overnight case; (pour documents) attaché case

malmener [malməne] /5/ VT to manhandle; (fig) to give a rough ride to

malnutrition [malnytRisjɔ̃] NF malnutrition

malodorant, e [malɔdɔRɑ̃, -ɑ̃t] ADJ foul-smelling

malotru [malɔtRy] NM lout, boor

malouin, e [malwɛ̃, -in] ADJ from Saint Malo

Malouines [malwin] NFPL: **les ~** the Falklands, the Falkland Islands

malpoli, e [malpɔli] NM/F rude individual ▶ ADJ impolite

malpropre [malpRɔpR] ADJ (personne, vêtement) dirty; (travail) slovenly; (histoire, plaisanterie) unsavoury (BRIT), unsavory (US), smutty; (malhonnête) dishonest

malpropreté [malpRɔpRəte] NF dirtiness

malsain, e [malsɛ̃, -ɛn] ADJ unhealthy

malséant, e [malseɑ̃, -ɑ̃t] ADJ unseemly, unbecoming

malsonnant, e [malsɔnɑ̃, -ɑ̃t] ADJ offensive

malt [malt] NM malt; **pur ~** (whisky) malt (whisky)

maltais, e [maltɛ, -ɛz] ADJ Maltese

Malte [malt] NF Malta

malté, e [malte] ADJ (lait etc) malted

maltraitance [maltRɛtɑ̃s] NF ill-treatment; **la ~ à enfants** ill-treatment of children, child abuse

maltraiter [maltRete] /1/ VT (brutaliser) to manhandle, ill-treat; (critiquer, éreinter) to slate (BRIT), roast

malus [malys] NM (Assurances) car insurance weighting, penalty

malveillance [malvɛjɑ̃s] NF (animosité) ill will; (intention de nuire) malevolence; (Jur) malicious intent no pl

malveillant, e [malvɛjɑ̃, -ɑ̃t] ADJ malevolent, malicious

malvenu, e [malvəny] ADJ: **être ~ de** ou **à faire qch** not to be in a position to do sth

malversation [malvɛRsasjɔ̃] NF embezzlement, misappropriation (of funds)

mal-vivre [malvivR] NM INV malaise

malvoyant, e [malvwajɑ̃, -ɑ̃t] NM/F partially sighted person

★**maman** [mamɑ̃] NF mum(my) (BRIT), mom (US)

mamelle [mamɛl] NF teat

mamelon [mam(ə)lɔ̃] NM (Anat) nipple; (colline) knoll, hillock

mamie [mami] NF (fam) granny

mammaire [mamɛR] ADJ mammary

mammectomie [mamɛktɔmi] NF mammectomy

mammifère [mamifɛR] NM mammal

mammographie [mamɔgRafi] NF mammography

mammoplastie [mamɔplasti] NF mammoplasty

mammouth [mamut] NM mammoth

mamours [mamuR] NMPL (fam): **se faire des ~** to bill and coo

management [manadʒmɛnt] NM management

manager [manadʒɛR] NM (Sport) manager; (Comm): **~ commercial** commercial director

managérial, e [manaʒeRjal] ADJ managerial

manant [manɑ̃] NM (vilain) villein

manceau, -elle, -aux [mɑ̃so, -sɛl] ADJ of Le Mans

★**manche** [mɑ̃ʃ] NF (de vêtement) sleeve; (d'un jeu, tournoi) round; (Géo): **la M~** the (English) Channel; **faire la ~** to pass the hat; **~ à air** (Aviat) windsock; **à manches courtes/longues** short-/long-sleeved ▶ NM (d'outil, casserole) handle; (de pelle, pioche etc) shaft; (de violon, guitare) neck; (fam) clumsy oaf; **~ à balai** broomstick; (Aviat) joystick

manchette [mãʃɛt] NF (de chemise) cuff; (coup) forearm blow; (titre) headline

manchon [mãʃɔ̃] NM (de fourrure) muff; **~ à incandescence** incandescent (gas) mantle

manchot [mãʃo] NM one-armed man; armless man; (Zool) penguin

mandale [mãdal] NF (fam) slap, clout (BRIT fam)

mandarin [mãdaRɛ̃] NM (haut fonctionnaire chinois) mandarin; (ponte) mandarin; (langue) Mandarin, Mandarin Chinese

mandarine [mãdaRin] NF mandarin (orange), tangerine

mandarinier [mãdaRinje] NM mandarin tree

mandat [mãda] NM (postal) postal ou money order; (d'un député etc) mandate; (procuration) power of attorney, proxy; (Police) warrant; **~ d'amener** summons sg; **~ d'arrêt** warrant for arrest; **~ de dépôt** committal order; **~ de perquisition** (Police) search warrant

mandataire [mãdatɛR] NMF (représentant, délégué) representative; (Jur) proxy

mandat-carte [mãdakaRt] (pl mandats-cartes) NM money order (in postcard form)

mandater [mãdate] /1/ VT (personne) to appoint; (Pol: député) to elect

mandat-lettre [mãdalɛtR] (pl mandats-lettres) NM money order (with space for correspondence)

mandchou, e [mãtʃu] ADJ Manchu, Manchurian ▶ NM (Ling) Manchu ▶ NM/F: **Mandchou, e** Manchu

Mandchourie [mãtʃuRi] NF: **la ~** Manchuria

mander [mãde] /1/ VT to summon

mandibule [mãdibyl] NF mandible

mandoline [mãdɔlin] NF mandolin(e)

manège [manɛʒ] NM riding school; (à la foire) roundabout (BRIT), merry-go-round; (fig) game, ploy; **faire un tour de ~** to go for a ride on a ou the roundabout (BRIT) etc; **~ (de chevaux de bois)** roundabout (BRIT), merry-go-round

manette [manɛt] NF lever, tap; **~ de jeu** (Inform) joystick

manganèse [mãganɛz] NM manganese

mangeable [mãʒabl] ADJ edible, eatable

mangeaille [mãʒɑj] NF (péj) grub

mangeoire [mãʒwaR] NF trough, manger

★**manger** [mãʒe] /3/ VT to eat; (ronger: rouille etc) to eat into ou away; (utiliser, consommer) to eat up ▶ VI to eat; **donner à ~** (enfant) to feed

mange-tout [mãʒtu] NM INV mange-tout

mangeur, -euse [mãʒœR, -øz] NM/F eater

mangouste [mãgust] NF mongoose

mangrove [mãgRɔv] NF mangrove

mangue [mãg] NF mango

maniabilité [manjabilite] NF (d'un outil) handiness; (d'un véhicule, voilier) manoeuvrability (BRIT), maneuverability (US)

maniable [manjabl] ADJ (outil) handy; (voiture, voilier) easy to handle; manoeuvrable (BRIT), maneuverable (US); (fig: personne) easily influenced, manipulable

maniaque [manjak] ADJ (pointilleux, méticuleux) finicky, fussy; (atteint de manie) suffering from a mania ▶ NMF (méticuleux) fusspot; (fou) maniac

manichéen, ne [manikeɛ̃, -ɛn] ADJ Manichean, Manichaean

manie [mani] NF mania; (tic) odd habit; **avoir la ~ de** to be obsessive about

maniement [manimã] NM handling; **~ d'armes** arms drill

manier [manje] /7/ VT to handle ■ **se manier** VPR (fam) to get a move on

manière [manjɛR] NF (façon) way, manner; (genre, style) style; **de ~ à** so as to; **de telle ~ que** in such a way that; **de cette ~** in this way ou manner; **d'une ~ générale** generally speaking, as a general rule; **de toute ~** in any case; **d'une certaine ~** in a (certain) way; **employer la ~ forte** to use strong-arm tactics ■ **manières** NFPL (attitude) manners; (chichis) fuss sg; **faire des manières** to put on airs

maniéré, e [manjere] ADJ affected

manif [manif] NF (manifestation) demo

manifestant, e [manifɛstã, -ãt] NM/F demonstrator

★**manifestation** [manifɛstasjɔ̃] NF (de joie, mécontentement) expression, demonstration; (symptôme) outward sign; (fête etc) event; (Pol) demonstration

manifeste [manifɛst] ADJ obvious, evident ▶ NM manifesto

manifestement [manifɛstəmã] ADV obviously

manifester [manifɛste] /1/ VT (volonté, intentions) to show, indicate; (joie, peur) to express, show ▶ VI (Pol) to demonstrate ■ **se manifester** VPR (émotion) to show ou express itself; (difficultés) to arise; (symptômes) to appear; (témoin etc) to come forward

manigance [manigãs] NF scheme

manigancer [manigãse] /3/ VT to plot, devise

Manille [manij] N Manila

manioc [manjɔk] NM cassava, manioc

manip [manip] NF (fam: Inform) operation; **quelle est la ~ pour créer un fichier pdf ?** how do you go about creating a PDF file?; **faire une fausse ~** to do sth wrong

manipulateur, -trice [manipylatœR, -tris] NM/F (technicien) technician, operator; (prestidigitateur) conjurer; (péj) manipulator

manipulation [manipylasjɔ̃] NF handling; (Pol, génétique) manipulation

manipuler [manipyle] /1/ VT to handle; (fig) to manipulate

manique [manik] NF (pour saisir les plats chauds) oven glove

manitou [manitu] NM (chez les Indiens d'Amérique) manitou; (fam: chef): **grand ~** big shot (fam)

manivelle [manivɛl] NF crank

manne [man] NF (Rel) manna; (fig) godsend

★**mannequin** [mankɛ̃] NM (Couture) dummy; (Mode) model

manœuvrabilité [manœvRabilite] NF (de bateau, véhicule) handling, manoeuvrability (BRIT), maneuverability (US)

manœuvrable [manœvRabl] ADJ (bateau, véhicule) manoeuvrable (BRIT), maneuverable (US)

manœuvre [manœvR] NF (gén) manoeuvre (BRIT), maneuver (US) ▶ NM (ouvrier) labourer (BRIT), laborer (US)

m

manœuvrer [manœvʀe] /1/ vt to manoeuvre (BRIT), maneuver (US); (levier, machine) to operate; (personne) to manipulate ▶ vi to manoeuvre ou maneuver

manoir [manwaʀ] NM manor ou country house

manomètre [manɔmɛtʀ] NM gauge, manometer

manouche [manuʃ] NMF gipsy

manquant, e [mɑ̃kɑ̃, -ɑ̃t] ADJ missing

manque [mɑ̃k] NM (insuffisance, vide) emptiness, gap; (Méd) withdrawal; ~ **de** lack of; **par ~ de** for want of; ~ **à gagner** loss of profit ou earnings; **être en état de ~** to suffer withdrawal symptoms ▪ **manques** NMPL (lacunes) faults, defects

★**manqué** [mɑ̃ke] ADJ failed; **garçon ~** tomboy

manquement [mɑ̃kmɑ̃] NM: ~ **à** (discipline, règle) breach of

★**manquer** [mɑ̃ke] /1/ vi (faire défaut) to be lacking; (être absent) to be missing; (échouer) to fail; **l'argent qui leur manque** the money they need ou are short of; **la voix lui manqua** his voice failed him; ~ **à qn** (absent etc): **il/cela me manque** I miss him/that ▶ vt to miss; ~ **de** to lack; (Comm) to be out of (stock of); **ne pas ~ de faire: je ne manquerai pas de le lui dire** I'll be sure to tell him; ~ **(de) faire: il a manqué (de) se tuer** he very nearly got killed; ~ **à** (règles etc) to be in breach of, fail to observe; **je n'y manquerai pas** leave it to me, I'll definitely do it ▶ vb IMPERS: **il (nous) manque encore 10 euros** we are still 10 euros short; **il manque des pages (au livre)** there are some pages missing ou some pages are missing (from the book); **il ne manquerait plus qu'il fasse** all we need now is for him to do

mansarde [mɑ̃saʀd] NF attic

mansardé, e [mɑ̃saʀde] ADJ: **chambre mansardée** attic room

mansuétude [mɑ̃sɥetyd] NF leniency

mante [mɑ̃t] NF: ~ **religieuse** praying mantis

★**manteau, x** [mɑ̃to] NM coat; ~ **de cheminée** mantelpiece; **sous le ~** (fig) under cover

mantille [mɑ̃tij] NF mantilla

manucure [manykyʀ] NF manicurist

manucuré, e [manykyʀe] ADJ manicured

★**manuel, le** [manɥɛl] ADJ manual ▶ NM/F manually gifted person ▶ NM (ouvrage) manual, handbook

manuellement [manɥɛlmɑ̃] ADV manually

manufacture [manyfaktyʀ] NF (établissement) factory; (fabrication) manufacture

manufacturé, e [manyfaktyʀe] ADJ manufactured

manufacturier, -ière [manyfaktyʀje, -jɛʀ] NM/F factory owner

manuscrit, e [manyskʀi, -it] ADJ handwritten ▶ NM manuscript

manutention [manytɑ̃sjɔ̃] NF (Comm) handling; (local) storehouse

manutentionnaire [manytɑ̃sjɔnɛʀ] NMF warehouse man(-woman), packer

manutentionner [manytɑ̃sjɔne] /1/ vt to handle

maoïste [maɔist] ADJ Maoist ▶ NMF Maoist

maori, e [maɔʀi] ADJ Maori ▶ NM (Ling) Maori ▶ NM/F: **Maori, e** Maori

maous, se [maus] ADJ (fam) massive

mappemonde [mapmɔ̃d] NF (plan) map of the world; (sphère) globe

maquereau, x [makʀo] NM (Zool) mackerel inv; (fam: proxénète) pimp

maquerelle [makʀɛl] NF (fam) madam

maquette [makɛt] NF (d'un décor, bâtiment, véhicule) (scale) model; (Typo) mockup; (: d'une page illustrée, affiche) paste-up; (: prête à la reproduction) artwork

maquettiste [maketist] NMF (Inform) layout artist; (Archit) model maker

maquignon [makiɲɔ̃] NM horse-dealer

★**maquillage** [makijaʒ] NM making up; faking; (produits) make-up

★**maquiller** [makije] /1/ vt (personne, visage) to make up; (truquer: passeport, statistique) to fake; (: voiture volée) to do over (respray etc) ▪ **se maquiller** VPR to make o.s. up

maquilleur, -euse [makijœʀ, -øz] NM/F make-up artist

maquis [maki] NM (Géo) scrub; (fig) tangle; (Mil) maquis, underground fighting no pl

maquisard, e [makizaʀ, -aʀd] NM/F maquis, member of the Resistance

marabout [maʀabu] NM (Zool) marabou(t)

maraîcher, -ère [maʀeʃe, -ɛʀ] ADJ: **cultures maraîchères** market gardening sg ▶ NM/F market gardener

marais [maʀɛ] NM marsh, swamp; ~ **salant** saltworks

marasme [maʀasm] NM (Pol, Écon) stagnation, sluggishness; (accablement) dejection, depression

marathon [maʀatɔ̃] NM marathon

marathonien, ne [maʀatɔnjɛ̃, -jɛn] NM/F marathon runner

marâtre [maʀatʀ] NF cruel mother

maraude [maʀod] NF pilfering, thieving (of poultry, crops); (dans un verger) scrumping; (vagabondage) prowling; **en ~** on the prowl; (taxi) cruising

maraudeur, -euse [maʀodœʀ, -øz] NM/F marauder; prowler

marbre [maʀbʀ] NM (pierre, statue) marble; (d'une table, commode) marble top; (Typo) stone, bed; **rester de ~** to remain stonily indifferent

marbré, e [maʀbʀe] ADJ (peau) mottled, blotchy; (matériau) marbled; **un gâteau ~** a marble cake ▶ NM (gâteau) marble cake

marbrer [maʀbʀe] /1/ vt to mottle, blotch; (Tech: papier) to marble

marbrerie [maʀbʀəʀi] NF (atelier) marble mason's workshop; (industrie) marble industry

marbrier, -ière [maʀbʀije, -jɛʀ] NM/F monumental mason ▶ NF marble quarry

marbrures [maʀbʀyʀ] NFPL blotches pl; (Tech) marbling sg

marc [maʀ] NM (de raisin, pommes) marc; ~ **de café** coffee grounds pl ou dregs pl

marcassin [maʀkasɛ̃] NM young wild boar

★**marchand, e** [maʀʃɑ̃, -ɑ̃d] NM/F shopkeeper, tradesman(-woman); (au marché) stallholder; (spécifique): ~ **de cycles/tapis** bicycle/carpet dealer; ~ **de charbon/vins** coal/wine merchant; ~ **en gros/ au détail** wholesaler/retailer; ~ **de biens** real estate agent; **~ de canons** (*péj*) arms dealer; **~ de couleurs** ironmonger (BRIT), hardware dealer (US); **~ de fruits** fruiter (BRIT), fruit seller (US); **~ de journaux** newsagent; **~ de légumes** greengrocer (BRIT), produce dealer (US); **~ de poisson** fishmonger (BRIT), fish seller (US); **~ de(s) quatre-saisons** costermonger (BRIT), street vendor (selling fresh fruit and vegetables); **~ de sable** (*fig*) sandman; **~ de tableaux** art dealer ▶ ADJ: **prix/valeur ~(e)** market price/value; **qualité marchande** standard quality

marchandage [maʀʃɑ̃daʒ] NM bargaining; (*péj: électoral*) bargaining, manoeuvring (BRIT), maneuvering (US)

marchander [maʀʃɑ̃de] /1/ VT (*article*) to bargain *ou* haggle over; (*éloges*) to be sparing with ▶ VI to bargain, haggle

marchandisage [maʀʃɑ̃dizaʒ] NM merchandising

marchandise [maʀʃɑ̃diz] NF goods *pl*, merchandise *no pl*

marche [maʀʃ] NF (*d'escalier*) step; (*activité*) walking; (*promenade, trajet, allure*) walk; (*démarche*) walk, gait; (*Mil, Mus*) march; (*fonctionnement*) running; (*progression*) progress; (*des événements*) course; **à une heure de ~** an hour's walk (away); **ouvrir/fermer la ~** to lead the way/bring up the rear; **dans le sens de la ~** (*Rail*) facing the engine; **en ~** (*monter etc*) while the vehicle is moving *ou* in motion; **mettre en ~** to start; **remettre qch en ~** to set *ou* start sth going again; **se mettre en ~** (*personne*) to get moving; (*machine*) to start; **être en état de ~** to be in working order; **~ arrière** (*Auto*) reverse (gear); **faire ~ arrière** (*Auto*) to reverse; (*fig*) to backtrack, back-pedal; **~ à suivre** (correct) procedure; (*sur notice*) (step by step) instructions *pl*

★marché [maʀʃe] NM (*lieu, Comm, Écon*) market; (*ville*) trading centre; (*transaction*) bargain, deal; **par-dessus le ~** into the bargain; **faire son ~** to do one's shopping; **mettre le ~ en main à qn** to tell sb to take it or leave it; **~ au comptant** (*Bourse*) spot market; **~ aux fleurs** flower market; **~ noir** black market; **faire du ~ noir** to buy and sell on the black market; **~ aux puces** flea market; **~ à terme** (*Bourse*) forward market; **~ du travail** labour market

marchepied [maʀʃəpje] NM (*Rail*) step; (*Auto*) running board; (*fig*) stepping stone

★marcher [maʀʃe] /1/ VI to walk; (*Mil*) to march; (*aller: voiture, train, affaires*) to go; (*prospérer*) to go well; (*fonctionner*) to work, run; (*fam: consentir*) to go along, agree; (: *croire naïvement*) to be taken in; **~ sur** to walk on; (*mettre le pied sur*) to step on *ou* in; (*Mil*) to march upon; **~ dans** (*herbe etc*) to walk in *ou* on; (*flaque*) to step in; **faire ~ qn** (*pour rire*) to pull sb's leg; (*pour tromper*) to lead sb up the garden path

marcheur, -euse [maʀʃœʀ, -øz] NM/F walker

marcotter [maʀkɔte] VT (*Jardinage*) to layer

★mardi [maʀdi] NM Tuesday; **M~ gras** Shrove Tuesday; *voir aussi* **lundi**

mare [maʀ] NF pond; (*flaque*) pool; **~ de sang** pool of blood

marécage [maʀekaʒ] NM marsh, swamp

marécageux, -euse [maʀekaʒø, -øz] ADJ marshy, swampy

maréchal, -aux [maʀeʃal, -o] NM marshal; **~ des logis** (*Mil*) sergeant

maréchal-ferrant [maʀeʃalfɛʀɑ̃] (*pl* **maréchaux-ferrants** [maʀeʃo-]) NM blacksmith

maréchaussée [maʀeʃose] NF (*humoristique: gendarmes*) constabulary (BRIT), police

marée [maʀe] NF tide; (*poissons*) fresh (sea) fish; **~ haute/basse** high/low tide; **~ montante/descendante** rising/ebb tide; **~ noire** oil slick

marelle [maʀɛl] NF: **(jouer à) la ~** (to play) hopscotch

marémotrice [maʀemɔtʀis] ADJ F tidal

mareyeur, -euse [maʀejœʀ, -øz] NM/F wholesale (sea) fish merchant

margarine [maʀgaʀin] NF margarine

marge [maʀʒ] NF margin; **en ~** in the margin; **en ~ de** (*fig*) on the fringe of; (*en dehors de*) cut off from; (*qui se rapporte à*) connected with; **~ bénéficiaire** profit margin, mark-up; **~ de sécurité** safety margin

margelle [maʀʒɛl] NF coping

margeur [maʀʒœʀ] NM margin stop

marginal, e, -aux [maʀʒinal, -o] ADJ marginal ▶ NM/F (*original*) eccentric; (*déshérité*) dropout

marginalisation [maʀʒinalizasjɔ̃] NF marginalization

marginaliser [maʀʒinalize] VT to marginalize

marginalité [maʀʒinalite] NF marginality

marguerite [maʀgəʀit] NF marguerite, (oxeye) daisy; (*d'imprimante*) daisy-wheel

marguillier [maʀgije] NM churchwarden

★mari [maʀi] NM husband

★mariage [maʀjaʒ] NM (*union, état, fig*) marriage; (*noce*) wedding; **~ civil/religieux** registry office (BRIT) *ou* civil/church wedding; **un ~ de raison/d'amour** a marriage of convenience/a love match; **~ blanc** marriage of convenience, sham marriage; **~ en blanc** white wedding; *see note*

Since May 2013 same-sex marriage and adoption have been legal in France. The passing of the **Loi sur le mariage pour tous** led to major nationwide protests from conservative, mostly Catholic citizens. Ultimately, however, President François Hollande kept his campaign promise to allow same-sex couples to marry.

marié, e [maʀje] ADJ married ▶ NM/F (bride) groom/bride; **les mariés** the bride and groom; **les (jeunes) mariés** the newly-weds

★marier [maʀje] /7/ VT (*maire, prêtre*) to marry; (*fig*) to blend ■ **se marier** VPR: **se ~ (avec)** to marry, get married (to); (*fig*) to blend (with)

marijuana [maʀiʒwana] NF marijuana

marin, e [maʀɛ̃, -in] ADJ sea *cpd*, marine; **avoir le pied ~** (*garder son équilibre*) to have one's sea legs ▶ NM sailor ▶ NF navy; (*Art*) seascape; (*couleur*) navy (blue); **marine de guerre** navy; **marine marchande** merchant navy; **marine à voiles** sailing ships *pl*

marina [maʀina] NF marina

marinade [maʀinad] NF marinade

marine [maʀin] ADJ F, NF *voir* **marin** ▶ ADJ INV navy (blue) ▶ NM (*Mil*) marine

mariner [maʀine] /1/ VI, VT to marinate, marinade

marinier [maʀinje] NM bargee

marinière [maʀinjɛʀ] NF (blouse) sailor top, Breton (striped) top ▶ ADJ INV: **moules ~** (Culin) mussels in white wine

marionnette [maʀjɔnɛt] NF puppet

marionnettiste [maʀjɔnetist] NMF puppeteer

marital, e, -aux [maʀital, -o] ADJ: **autorisation maritale** husband's permission

maritalement [maʀitalmɑ̃] ADV: **vivre ~** to live together (as husband and wife)

maritime [maʀitim] ADJ sea cpd, maritime; (ville) coastal, seaside; (droit) shipping, maritime

marjolaine [maʀʒɔlɛn] NF marjoram

mark [maʀk] NM mark

marketing [maʀketiŋ] NM (Comm) marketing

marmaille [maʀmɑj] NF (péj) (gang of) brats pl

marmelade [maʀməlad] NF (compote) stewed fruit, compote; **~ d'oranges** (orange) marmalade; **en ~** (fig) crushed (to a pulp)

marmite [maʀmit] NF (cooking-)pot

marmiton [maʀmitɔ̃] NM kitchen boy

marmonner [maʀmɔne] /1/ VT, VI to mumble, mutter

marmot [maʀmo] NM (fam) brat

marmotte [maʀmɔt] NF marmot

marmotter [maʀmɔte] /1/ VT (prière) to mumble, mutter

marne [maʀn] NF (Géo) marl

★**Maroc** [maʀɔk] NM: **le ~** Morocco

★**marocain, e** [maʀɔkɛ̃, -ɛn] ADJ Moroccan ▶ NM/F: **Marocain, e** Moroccan

maronite [maʀɔnit] ADJ Maronite ▶ NMF Maronite

maroquin [maʀɔkɛ̃] NM (peau) morocco (leather); (fig) (minister's) portfolio

maroquinerie [maʀɔkinʀi] NF (industrie) leather craft; (commerce) leather shop; (articles) fine leather goods pl

maroquinier [maʀɔkinje] NM (fabricant) leather craftsman; (marchand) leather dealer

marotte [maʀɔt] NF fad

marquage [maʀkaʒ] NM (Sport) marking; (de bétail) branding; (d'arbre) marking; **une erreur de ~** a defensive error, a marking error; **~ à la culotte** close marking

marquant, e [maʀkɑ̃, -ɑ̃t] ADJ outstanding

★**marque** [maʀk] NF mark; (Sport, Jeu) score; (Comm: de nourriture) brand; (: de voiture, produits manufacturés) make; (insigne: d'une fonction) badge; (fig): **~ d'affection** token of affection; **~ de joie** sign of joy; **à vos marques !** (Sport) on your marks!; **de ~** adj (Comm) brand-name cpd; proprietary; (fig) high-class (: personnage, hôte) distinguished; **produit de ~** quality product; **~ déposée** registered trademark; **~ de fabrique** trademark; **une grande ~ de vin** a well-known brand of wine

marqué, e [maʀke] ADJ marked

★**marquer** [maʀke] /1/ VT to mark; (inscrire) to write down; (bétail) to brand; (Sport: but etc) to score; (: joueur) to mark; (accentuer: taille etc) to emphasize; (manifester: refus, intérêt) to show; **~ qn de son influence/empreinte** to have an influence/leave its impression on sb; **~ un temps d'arrêt** to pause momentarily; **~ le pas** (fig) to mark time; **un jour à ~ d'une pierre blanche** a red-letter day; **~ les points** (tenir la marque) to keep the score ▶ VI (événement, personnalité) to stand out, be outstanding; (Sport) to score

marqueté, e [maʀkəte] ADJ inlaid

marqueterie [maʀketʀi] NF inlaid work, marquetry

marqueur, -euse [maʀkœʀ, -øz] NM/F (Sport: de but) scorer ▶ NM (crayon feutre) marker pen

marquis, e [maʀki, -iz] NM/F marquis ou marquess (marchioness) ▶ NF (auvent) glass canopy ou awning ▶ NFPL: **les (îles) Marquises** the Marquesas Islands

marraine [maʀɛn] NF godmother; (d'un navire, d'une rose etc) namer

Marrakech [maʀakɛʃ] N Marrakech ou Marrakesh

★**marrant, e** [maʀɑ̃, -ɑ̃t] ADJ (fam) funny

★**marre** [maʀ] ADV (fam): **en avoir ~ de** to be fed up with

marrer [maʀe] /1/: **se marrer** VPR (fam) to have a (good) laugh

★**marron, ne** [maʀɔ̃, -ɔn] NM (fruit) chestnut; **marrons glacés** marrons glacés ▶ ADJ INV brown ▶ ADJ (péj) crooked; (: faux) bogus

marronnier [maʀɔnje] NM chestnut (tree)

★**Mars** [maʀs] NF Mars

★**mars** [maʀs] NM March; voir aussi **juillet**

marseillais, e [maʀsɛje, -ɛz] ADJ of ou from Marseille ▶ NF: **la Marseillaise** the French national anthem

---

The **Marseillaise** has been France's national anthem since 1795. The words of the Chant de guerre de l'armée du Rhin, as the song was originally called, were written to an anonymous tune by an army captain called Rouget de Lisle in 1792. Adopted as a marching song by the Marseille battalion, it was finally popularized as the Marseillaise.

Marseille [maʀsɛj] N Marseille

marsouin [maʀswɛ̃] NM porpoise

marsupial, e, -aux [maʀsypjal, -jo] NM marsupial ▶ ADJ: **une souris marsupiale** a marsupial mouse

marteau, x [maʀto] NM hammer; (de porte) knocker; **~ pneumatique** pneumatic drill; **être ~** (fam) to be nuts

marteau-pilon [maʀtopilɔ̃] (pl **marteaux-pilons**) NM power hammer

marteau-piqueur [maʀtopikœʀ] (pl **marteaux-piqueurs**) NM pneumatic drill

martel [maʀtɛl] NM: **se mettre ~ en tête** to worry o.s.

martèlement [maʀtɛlmɑ̃] NM hammering

marteler [maʀtəle] /5/ VT to hammer; (mots, phrases) to rap out

martial, e, -aux [maʀsjal, -o] ADJ martial; **cour martiale** court-martial

martien, ne [maʀsjɛ̃, -ɛn] ADJ Martian, of ou from Mars

martinet [martinɛ] NM (*fouet*) small whip; (*Zool*) swift

martingale [martɛ̃gal] NF (*Couture*) half-belt; (*Jeu*) winning formula

martiniquais, e [martinikɛ, -ɛz] ADJ of *ou* from Martinique

Martinique [martinik] NF: **la ~** Martinique

martin-pêcheur [martɛ̃pɛʃœr] (*pl* **martins-pêcheurs**) NM kingfisher

martre [martr] NF marten; **~ zibeline** sable

martyr, e [martir] NM/F martyr ▶ ADJ martyred; **enfants martyrs** battered children

martyre [martir] NM martyrdom; (*fig: sens affaibli*) agony, torture; **souffrir le ~** to suffer agonies

martyriser [martirize] /1/ VT (*Rel*) to martyr; (*fig*) to bully; (: *enfant*) to batter

marxisme [marksism] NM Marxism

marxiste [marksist] ADJ, NMF Marxist

mas [ma(s)] NM traditional house or farm in Provence

mascara [maskara] NM mascara

mascarade [maskarad] NF masquerade

mascotte [maskɔt] NF mascot

masculin, e [maskylɛ̃, -in] ADJ masculine; (*sexe, population*) male; (*équipe, vêtements*) men's; (*viril*) manly ▶ NM masculine

masculinité [maskylinite] NF masculinity

maso [mazo] (*fam*) ADJ (*masochiste*) masochistic ▶ NMF masochist

masochisme [mazɔʃism] NM masochism

masochiste [mazɔʃist] ADJ masochistic ▶ NMF masochist

masque [mask] NM mask; **~ de beauté** face pack; **~ à gaz** gas mask; **~ de plongée** diving mask

masqué, e [maske] ADJ masked

masquer [maske] /1/ VT (*cacher: porte, goût*) to hide, conceal; (*dissimuler: vérité, projet*) to mask, obscure

massacrant, e [masakrɑ̃, -ɑ̃t] ADJ: **humeur massacrante** foul temper

massacre [masakr] NM massacre, slaughter; **jeu de ~** (*fig*) wholesale slaughter

massacrer [masakre] /1/ VT to massacre, slaughter; (*fig: adversaire*) to slaughter; (: *texte etc*) to murder

massage [masaʒ] NM massage

masse [mas] NF mass; (*Élec*) earth; (*maillet*) sledgehammer; **une ~ de, des masses de** (*fam*) masses *ou* loads of; **la ~** (*péj*) the masses *pl*; **en ~** *adv* (*en bloc*) in bulk; (*en foule*) en masse; *adj* (*exécutions, production*) mass *cpd*; **~ monétaire** (*Écon*) money supply; **~ salariale** (*Comm*) wage(s) bill ■ **masses** NFPL masses

massepain [maspɛ̃] NM marzipan

masser [mase] /1/ VT (*assembler: gens*) to gather; (*pétrir*) to massage ■ **se masser** VPR (*foule*) to gather

masseur, -euse [masœr, -øz] NM/F (*personne*) masseur(-euse) ▶ NM (*appareil*) massager

massicot [masiko] NM (*Typo*) guillotine

massicotier, -ière [masikɔtje, -jɛr] NM/F (*Typo*) guillotine operator

massif, -ive [masif, -iv] ADJ (*porte*) solid, massive; (*visage*) heavy, large; (*bois, or*) solid; (*dose*) massive;

(*déportations etc*) mass *cpd* ▶ NM (*montagneux*) massif; (*de fleurs*) clump, bank; **le M~ Central** the Massif Central

massivement [masivmɑ̃] ADV (*répondre*) en masse; (*administrer, injecter*) in massive doses

massue [masy] NF club, bludgeon ▶ ADJ INV: **argument ~** sledgehammer argument

mastectomie [mastɛktɔmi] NF mastectomy

master [mastɛr] NM (*Scol*) Master's (degree)

> The **master** diploma is awarded to students who have completed two years of study after the *licence*. It includes classes in theoretical and applied topics, an introduction to research and sometimes a period of work experience. A *master* is required to be able to enter some professions, most notably teaching.

mastère [mastɛr] NM ≈ Master's degree (*from a business school or an institute of technology*)

mastic [mastik] NM (*pour vitres*) putty; (*pour fentes*) filler

masticage [mastikaʒ] NM (*d'une fente*) filling; (*d'une vitre*) puttying

mastication [mastikasjɔ̃] NF chewing, mastication

mastiquer [mastike] /1/ VT (*aliment*) to chew, masticate; (*fente*) to fill; (*vitre*) to putty

mastoc [mastɔk] ADJ INV (*fam*) hefty

mastodonte [mastɔdɔ̃t] NM monster (*fig*)

masturbation [mastyrbasjɔ̃] NF masturbation

masturber [mastyrbe] /1/: **se masturber** VPR to masturbate

m'as-tu-vu [matyvy] NMF INV show-off

masure [mazyr] NF tumbledown cottage

mat, e [mat] ADJ (*couleur, métal*) mat(t); (*bruit, son*) dull ▶ ADJ INV (*Échecs*): **être ~** to be checkmate

mât [ma] NM (*Navig*) mast; (*poteau*) pole, post

matamore [matamɔr] NM braggart, blusterer

★**match** [matʃ] NM match; **~ nul** draw (*Brit*), tie (*US*); **faire ~ nul** to draw (*Brit*), tie (*US*); **~ aller** first leg; **~ retour** second leg, return match

★**matelas** [mat(ə)la] NM mattress; **~ pneumatique** air bed *ou* mattress; **~ à ressorts** spring *ou* interior-sprung mattress

matelassé, e [mat(ə)lase] ADJ padded; (*tissu*) quilted

matelasser [mat(ə)lase] /1/ VT to pad

matelot [mat(ə)lo] NM sailor, seaman

mater [mate] /1/ VT (*personne*) to bring to heel, subdue; (*révolte*) to put down; (*fam*) to watch, look at

matérialisation [materjalizasjɔ̃] NF materialization

matérialiser [materjalize] /1/: **se matérialiser** VPR to materialize

matérialisme [materjalism] NM materialism

matérialiste [materjalist] ADJ materialistic ▶ NMF materialist

matériau, x [materjo] NM material ■ **matériaux** NMPL material(s); **matériaux de construction** building materials

matériel, le [materjɛl] ADJ material; (*organisation, aide, obstacle*) practical; (*fig: péj: personne*) materialistic; **il n'a pas le temps ~ de le faire** he doesn't have the time (needed) to do it ▶ NM equipment *no pl*; *(de camping etc)* gear *no pl*; *(Inform)* hardware; **~ d'exploitation** *(Comm)* plant; **~ roulant** rolling stock

matériellement [materjɛlmɑ̃] ADV *(financièrement)* materially; **~ à l'aise** comfortably off; **je n'en ai ~ pas le temps** I simply do not have the time

maternel, le [matɛrnɛl] ADJ *(amour, geste)* motherly, maternal; *(grand-père, oncle)* maternal ▶ NF *(aussi:* **école maternelle**) (state) nursery school

materner [matɛrne] /**1**/ VT *(personne)* to mother

maternisé, e [matɛrnize] ADJ: **lait ~** (infant) formula

maternité [matɛrnite] NF *(établissement)* maternity hospital; *(état de mère)* motherhood, maternity; *(grossesse)* pregnancy; **congé de ~** maternity leave

math [mat] NFPL maths *(Brit)*, math *(US)*

mathématicien, ne [matematisjɛ̃, -ɛn] NM/F mathematician

mathématique [matematik] ADJ mathematical

mathématiques [matematik] NFPL mathematics *sg*

matheux, -euse [matø, -øz] NM/F *(fam)* maths *(Brit)* ou math *(US)* student; *(fort en math)* mathematical genius

★**maths** [mat] NFPL maths *(Brit)*, math *(US)*

matière [matjɛr] NF *(Physique)* matter; *(Comm, Tech)* material; matter *no pl*; *(fig: d'un livre etc)* subject matter, material; *(Scol)* subject; **en ~ de** as regards; **donner ~ à** to give cause to; **~ plastique** plastic; **matières fécales** faeces; **matières grasses** fat (content) *sg*; **matières premières** raw materials

MATIF [matif] SIGLE M (= *Marché à terme des instruments financiers*) body which regulates the activities of the French Stock Exchange

Matignon [matiɲɔ̃] NM: **(l'hôtel) ~** the French Prime Minister's residence

> The **hôtel Matignon** is the Paris office and residence of the French Prime Minister. By extension, the term *Matignon* is often used to refer to the Prime Minister and his or her staff.

★**matin** [matɛ̃] NM, ADV morning; **le ~** *(pendant le matin)* in the morning; **demain/hier/dimanche ~** tomorrow/yesterday/Sunday morning; **tous les matins** every morning; **le lendemain ~** (the) next morning; **du ~ au soir** from morning till night; **une heure du ~** one o'clock in the morning; **de grand** ou **bon ~** early in the morning

matinal, e, -aux [matinal, -o] ADJ *(toilette, gymnastique)* morning *cpd*; *(de bonne heure)* early; **être ~** *(personne)* to be up early; *(: habituellement)* to be an early riser

mâtiné, e [matine] ADJ: **qch ~ de qch** sth mixed with sth, a mixture of sth and sth

matinée [matine] NF morning; *(spectacle)* matinée, afternoon performance

matois, e [matwa, -waz] ADJ wily

matos [matos] NM *(fam)* gear, stuff

matou [matu] NM tom(cat)

matraquage [matrakaʒ] NM beating up; **~ publicitaire** plug, plugging

matraque [matrak] NF *(de malfaiteur)* cosh *(Brit)*, club; *(de policier)* truncheon *(Brit)*, billy *(US)*

matraquer [matrake] /**1**/ VT to beat up (with a truncheon ou billy); to cosh *(Brit)*, club; *(fig: touristes etc)* to rip off; *(: disque)* to plug

matriarcal, e, -aux [matrijarkal, -o] ADJ matriarchal

matrice [matris] NF *(Anat)* womb; *(Tech)* mould; *(Math etc)* matrix

matricule [matrikyl] NF *(aussi:* **registre matricule**) roll, register ▶ NM *(aussi:* **numéro matricule**: *Mil)* regimental number; *(: Admin)* reference number

matrimonial, e, -aux [matrimɔnjal, -o] ADJ marital, marriage *cpd*

matrone [matrɔn] NF matron

mâture [mɑtyr] NF masts *pl*

maturité [matyrite] NF maturity; *(d'un fruit)* ripeness, maturity

maudire [modir] /**2**/ VT to curse

maudit, e [modi, -it] ADJ *(fam: satané)* blasted, confounded

maugréer [mogree] /**1**/ VI to grumble

mauresque [mɔrɛsk] ADJ Moorish

Maurice [mɔris] NF: **(l'île) ~** Mauritius

mauricien, ne [mɔrisjɛ̃, -ɛn] ADJ Mauritian ▶ NM/F: **Mauricien, ne** Mauritian

Mauritanie [mɔritani] NF: **la ~** Mauritania

mauritanien, ne [mɔritanjɛ̃, -ɛn] ADJ Mauritanian ▶ NM/F: **Mauritanien, ne** Mauritanian

mausolée [mozɔle] NM mausoleum

maussade [mosad] ADJ *(air, personne)* sullen; *(ciel, temps)* gloomy

★**mauvais, e** [mɔvɛ, -ɛz] ADJ bad; *(méchant, malveillant)* malicious, spiteful; *(faux)*: **un ~ numéro** a wrong number; **la mer est mauvaise** the sea is rough; **~ coucheur** awkward customer; **~ coup** *(fig)* criminal venture; **~ garçon** tough; **~ pas** tight spot; **~ plaisant** hoaxer; **mauvaise plaisanterie** nasty trick; **~ traitements** ill treatment *sg*; **~ joueur** bad ou sore loser; **mauvaise herbe** weed; **mauvaise langue** gossip, scandalmonger *(Brit)*; **mauvaise passe** difficult situation; *(période)* bad patch; **mauvaise tête** rebellious ou headstrong customer ▶ ADV: **il fait ~** the weather is bad; **sentir ~** to have a nasty smell, smell bad ou nasty

mauve [mov] ADJ *(couleur)* mauve ▶ NF *(Bot)* mallow

mauviette [movjɛt] NF *(péj)* weakling

maux [mo] NMPL *voir* **mal**

max. ABR (= *maximum*) max

maxillaire [maksilɛr] NM jaw; **~ inférieur** lower jaw; **de puissants maxillaires** a strong jaw

maximal, e, -aux [maksimal, -o] ADJ maximal

maxime [maksim] NF maxim

maximiser [maksimize] VT to maximize; **~ ses profits** to maximize profits

maximum [maksimɔm] ADJ, NM maximum; **atteindre un/son ~** to reach a/his peak; **au ~** *adv* *(le plus possible)* to the full; as much as one can; *(: tout au plus)* at the (very) most ou maximum; **faire le ~** to do one's level best

Mayence [majɑ̃s] N Mainz

★**mayonnaise** [majɔnɛz] NF mayonnaise

Mayotte [majɔt] NF Mayotte

mazout [mazut] NM (fuel) oil; **chaudière/poêle à ~** oil-fired boiler/stove

mazouté, e [mazute] ADJ oil-polluted

MDM SIGLE MPL (= Médecins du Monde) medical association for aid to Third-World countries

MDR SIGLE ADJ (= mort de rire) LOL (= laughing out loud)

Mᵉ ABR = **Maître**

★**me, m'** [mə, m] PRON (direct: téléphoner, attendre etc) me; (indirect: parler, donner etc) (to) me; (réfléchi) myself

mea-culpa [meakylpa] NM INV: **faire son ~** to admit one's guilt

méandres [meɑ̃dʀ] NMPL meanderings

mec [mɛk] NM (fam) guy, bloke (BRIT)

mécanicien, ne [mekanisjɛ̃, -ɛn] NM/F mechanic; (Rail) (train ou engine) driver; **~ navigant** ou **de bord** (Aviat) flight engineer

mécanique [mekanik] ADJ mechanical; **ennui ~** engine trouble no pl ▶ NF (science) mechanics sg; (technologie) mechanical engineering; (mécanisme) mechanism; engineering; works pl; **s'y connaître en ~** to be mechanically minded; **~ hydraulique** hydraulics sg; **~ ondulatoire** wave mechanics sg

mécaniquement [mekanikmɑ̃] ADV mechanically

mécanisation [mekanizasjɔ̃] NF mechanization

mécaniser [mekanize] /1/ VT to mechanize

mécanisme [mekanism] NM mechanism; **~ des taux de change** exchange rate mechanism

mécano [mekano] NM (fam) mechanic

mécénat [mesena] NM (appui, promotion) patronage; (soutien financier) sponsorship

mécène [mesɛn] NMF (of the arts) patron

méchamment [meʃamɑ̃] ADV nastily, maliciously; spitefully; viciously

méchanceté [meʃɑ̃ste] NF (d'une personne, d'une parole) nastiness, maliciousness, spitefulness; (parole, action) nasty ou spiteful ou malicious remark (ou action); **dire des méchancetés à qn** to say spiteful things to sb

méchant, e [meʃɑ̃, -ɑ̃t] ADJ nasty, malicious, spiteful; (enfant: pas sage) naughty; (animal) vicious; (avant le nom: péj) nasty

mèche [mɛʃ] NF (de lampe, bougie) wick; (d'un explosif) fuse; (Méd) pack, dressing; (de vilebrequin, perceuse) bit; (de dentiste) drill; (de fouet) lash; (de cheveux) lock; **se faire faire des mèches** (chez le coiffeur) to have highlights put in one's hair, have one's hair streaked; **vendre la ~** to give the game away; **de ~ avec** in league with

méchoui [meʃwi] NM whole sheep barbecue

mécompte [mekɔ̃t] NM (erreur) miscalculation; (déception) disappointment

méconnais etc [mekɔnɛ] VB voir **méconnaître**

méconnaissable [mekɔnɛsabl] ADJ unrecognizable

méconnaissais etc [mekɔnɛsɛ] VB voir **méconnaître**

méconnaissance [mekɔnɛsɑ̃s] NF ignorance

méconnaître [mekɔnɛtʀ] /57/ VT (ignorer) to be unaware of; (mésestimer) to misjudge

méconnu, e [mekɔny] PP de **méconnaître** ▶ ADJ (génie etc) unrecognized

mécontent, e [mekɔ̃tɑ̃, -ɑ̃t] ADJ: **~ (de)** (insatisfait) discontented ou dissatisfied ou displeased (with); (contrarié) annoyed (at) ▶ NM/F malcontent, dissatisfied person

mécontentement [mekɔ̃tɑ̃tmɑ̃] NM dissatisfaction, discontent, displeasure; (irritation) annoyance

mécontenter [mekɔ̃tɑ̃te] /1/ VT to displease

Mecque [mɛk] NF: **la ~** Mecca

mécréant, e [mekʀeɑ̃, -ɑ̃t] ADJ (peuple) infidel; (personne) atheistic

méd. ABR = **médecin**

médaille [medaj] NF medal

médaillé, e [medaje] NM/F (Sport) medal-holder

médaillon [medajɔ̃] NM (portrait) medallion; (bijou) locket; (Culin) médaillon; **en ~** adj (carte etc) inset

médecin [med(ə)sɛ̃] NM doctor; **~ du bord** (Navig) ship's doctor; **~ généraliste** general practitioner, GP; **~ légiste** forensic scientist (BRIT), medical examiner (US); **~ traitant** family doctor, GP

médecine [med(ə)sin] NF medicine; **~ générale** general medicine; **~ infantile** paediatrics sg (BRIT), pediatrics sg (US); **~ légale** forensic medicine; **~ préventive** preventive medicine; **~ du travail** occupational ou industrial medicine; **médecines parallèles** ou **douces** alternative medicine

MEDEF [medɛf] NM (= Mouvement des entreprises de France) national confederation of French employers, ≈ CBI (BRIT)

média [medja] NM media; **les médias** the media; **les médias sociaux** social media

médian, e [medjɑ̃, -an] ADJ median

médiateur, -trice [medjatœʀ, -tʀis] NM/F mediator; arbitrator

médiathèque [medjatɛk] NF media library

médiation [medjasjɔ̃] NF mediation; (dans conflit social etc) arbitration

médiatique [medjatik] ADJ media cpd

médiatisation [medjatizasjɔ̃] NF media coverage

médiatisé, e [medjatize] ADJ reported in the media; **être ~** to get media attention; **ce procès a été très ~** this trial got a great deal of media attention

médiatiser [medjatize] VT to give a lot of media coverage to; **~ un conflit** to turn a conflict into a media event

médiator [medjatɔʀ] NM plectrum

médical, e, -aux [medikal, -o] ADJ medical; **visiteur** ou **délégué ~** medical rep ou representative; **passer une visite médicale** to have a medical

médicalement [medikalmɑ̃] ADV medically

médicalisation [medikalizasjɔ̃] NF (traitement: d'accouchement, vieillesse) management; (recours abusif à la médecine) medicalization

médicament [medikamɑ̃] NM medicine, drug

médicamenteux, -euse [medikamɑ̃tø, -øz] ADJ medicinal

m

médication [medikasjɔ̃] NF medication

médicinal, e, -aux [medisinal, -o] ADJ medicinal

médico-légal, e, -aux [medikɔlegal, -o] ADJ forensic

médico-social, e, -aux [medikɔsɔsjal, -o] ADJ: **assistance médico-sociale** medical and social assistance

médiéval, e, -aux [medjeval, -o] ADJ medieval

médiocre [medjɔkʀ] ADJ mediocre, poor

médiocrité [medjɔkʀite] NF mediocrity

médire [mediʀ] /37/ VI: ~ **de** to speak ill of

médisance [medizɑ̃s] NF scandalmongering *no pl* (BRIT), mud-slinging *no pl*; (*propos*) piece of scandal *ou* malicious gossip

médisant, e [medizɑ̃, -ɑ̃t] VB *voir* **médire** ▶ ADJ slanderous, malicious

médit, e [medi, -it] PP *de* **médire**

méditatif, -ive [meditatif, -iv] ADJ thoughtful

méditation [meditasjɔ̃] NF meditation

méditer [medite] /1/ VT (*approfondir*) to meditate on, ponder (over); (*combiner*) to meditate ▶ VI to meditate; ~ **de faire** to contemplate doing, plan to do

Méditerranée [mediteʀane] NF: **la (mer)** ~ the Mediterranean (Sea)

méditerranéen, ne [mediteʀaneɛ̃, -ɛn] ADJ Mediterranean ▶ NM/F: **Méditerranéen, ne** Mediterranean

médium [medjɔm] NM medium (*spiritualist*)

médius [medjys] NM middle finger

médoc [medɔk] NM (*vin*) Médoc

méduse [medyz] NF jellyfish

méduser [medyze] /1/ VT to dumbfound

meeting [mitiŋ] NM (*Pol, Sport*) rally, meeting; ~ **d'aviation** air show

méfait [mefɛ] NM (*faute*) misdemeanour, wrongdoing ■ **méfaits** NMPL (*ravages*) ravages, damage *sg*

méfiance [mefjɑ̃s] NF mistrust, distrust

méfiant, e [mefjɑ̃, -ɑ̃t] ADJ mistrustful, distrustful

méfier [mefje] /7/: **se méfier** VPR to be wary; (*faire attention*) to be careful; **se ~ de** vt to mistrust, distrust, be wary of; to be careful about

mégabit [megabit] NM (*Inform*) megabit

mégadonnées [megadɔne] NFPL (*Inform*) big data

mégahertz [megaɛʀts] NM megahertz

mégalo [megalo] ADJ, NMF (*fam*) megalomaniac

mégalomane [megalɔman] ADJ, NMF megalomaniac

mégalomanie [megalɔmani] NF megalomania

mégalopole [megalɔpɔl] NF megalopolis

méga-octet [megaɔkte] NM megabyte

mégarde [megaʀd] NF: **par ~** (*accidentellement*) accidentally; (*par erreur*) by mistake

mégatonne [megatɔn] NF megaton

mégawatt [megawat] NM megawatt

mégère [meʒɛʀ] NF (*péj: femme*) shrew

mégot [mego] NM cigarette end *ou* butt

mégoter [megɔte] /1/ VI to nitpick

★**meilleur, e** [mɛjœʀ] ADJ, ADV better; (*valeur superlative*) best; **il fait ~ qu'hier** it's better weather than yesterday; **de meilleure heure** earlier; ~ **marché** cheaper ▶ NM: **le ~** (*celui qui ...*) the best (one); (*ce qui ...*) the best; **le ~ des deux** the better of the two ▶ NF: **la meilleure** the best (one)

méjuger [meʒyʒe] /3/ VT to misjudge

mél [mɛl] NM email

mélancolie [melɑ̃kɔli] NF melancholy, gloom

mélancolique [melɑ̃kɔlik] ADJ melancholy, gloomy

mélanésien, ne [melanezjɛ̃, -jɛn] ADJ Melanesian ▶ NM/F: **Mélanésien, ne** Melanesian

mélange [melɑ̃ʒ] NM (*opération*) mixing; blending; (*résultat*) mixture; blend; **sans ~** unadulterated

mélanger [melɑ̃ʒe] /3/ VT (*substances*) to mix; (*vins, couleurs*) to blend; (*mettre en désordre, confondre*) to mix up, muddle (up) ■ **se mélanger** VPR (*liquides, couleurs*) to blend, mix

mélangeur [melɑ̃ʒœʀ] NM (*robinet*) mixer tap (BRIT), mixer faucet (US); (*machine*) mixer

mélanine [melanin] NF melanin

mélanome [melanom] NM melanoma

mélasse [melas] NF treacle, molasses *sg*

mêlée [mele] NF (*bataille, cohue*) mêlée, scramble; (*lutte, conflit*) tussle, scuffle; (*Rugby*) scrum(mage)

mêler [mele] /1/ VT (*substances, odeurs*) to mix; ~ **à** *ou* **avec** *ou* **de** to mix with; to mingle with; ~ **qn à** (*affaire*) to get sb mixed up *ou* involved in ■ **se mêler** VPR to mix; (*se joindre, s'allier*) to mingle; **se ~ à** (*personne*) to join; (*s'associer à*) to mix with (: *odeurs etc*) to mingle with; **se ~ de** (*personne*) to meddle with, interfere in; **mêle-toi de tes affaires!** mind your own business!

méli-mélo [melimelo] NM INV (*fam*) jumble

mélo [melo] NM, ADJ = **mélodrame; mélodramatique**

mélodie [melɔdi] NF melody

mélodieux, -euse [melɔdjø, -øz] ADJ melodious, tuneful

mélodique [melɔdik] ADJ melodic

mélodramatique [melɔdʀamatik] ADJ melodramatic

mélodrame [melɔdʀam] NM melodrama

mélomane [melɔman] NMF music lover

★**melon** [m(ə)lɔ̃] NM (*Bot*) (honeydew) melon; (*aussi*: **chapeau melon**) bowler (hat); ~ **d'eau** watermelon

mélopée [melɔpe] NF monotonous chant

membrane [mɑ̃bʀan] NF membrane

★**membre** [mɑ̃bʀ] NM (*Anat*) limb; ~ **(viril)** (male) organ ▶ NMF (*personne, pays, élément*) member; **être ~ de** to be a member of ▶ ADJ member *cpd*

mémé [meme] NF (*fam*) granny; (: *vieille femme*) old dear

---

même [mɛm]

ADJ **1** (*avant le nom*) same; **en même temps** at the same time; **ils ont les mêmes goûts** they have the same *ou* similar tastes

2 (*après le nom: renforcement*): **il est la loyauté**

même he is loyalty itself; **ce sont ses paroles mêmes** they are his very words
▸ PRON: **le (la) même** the same one
▸ ADV **1** (*renforcement*): **il n'a même pas pleuré** he didn't even cry; **même lui l'a dit** even HE said it; **ici même** at this very place; **même si** even if
2: **à même**: **à même la bouteille** straight from the bottle; **à même la peau** next to the skin; **être à même de faire** to be in a position to do, be able to do; **mettre qn à même de faire** to enable sb to do
3: **de même** likewise; **faire de même** to do likewise *ou* the same; **lui de même** so does (*ou* did *ou* is) he; **de même que** just as; **il en va de même pour** the same goes for

mémento [memɛto] NM (*agenda*) appointments diary; (*ouvrage*) summary

mémère [memɛʀ] NF (*fam, péj*) old granny

mémo [memo] NM (*fam*) memo

mémoire [memwaʀ] NF memory; **avoir la ~ des visages/chiffres** to have a (good) memory for faces/figures; **n'avoir aucune ~** to have a terrible memory; **avoir de la ~** to have a good memory; **à la ~ de** to the *ou* in memory of; **pour ~** *adv* for the record; **de ~** *adv* from memory; **de ~ d'homme** in living memory; **mettre en ~** (*Inform*) to store; **~ morte** read-only memory, ROM; **~ vive** random access memory, RAM ▸ NM (*Admin, Jur*) memorandum; (*Université*) dissertation, paper ▸ NMPL memoirs

mémorable [memɔʀabl] ADJ memorable

mémorandum [memɔʀɑ̃dɔm] NM memorandum; (*carnet*) notebook

mémorial, -aux [memɔʀjal, -o] NM memorial

mémorisable [memɔʀizabl] ADJ: **facilement ~** easy to remember

mémoriser [memɔʀize] /**1**/ VT to memorize; (*Inform*) to store

menaçant, e [mənasɑ̃, -ɑ̃t] ADJ threatening, menacing

menace [mənas] NF threat; **~ en l'air** empty threat

⋆**menacer** [mənase] /**3**/ VT to threaten; **~ qn de qch/de faire qch** to threaten sb with sth/to do sth

ménage [menaʒ] NM (*travail*) housekeeping, housework; (*couple*) (married) couple; (*famille, Admin*) household; **faire le ~** to do the housework; **faire des ménages** to work as a cleaner (*in private homes*); **monter son ~** to set up house; **se mettre en ~ (avec)** to set up house (with); **heureux en ~** happily married; **faire bon ~ avec** to get on well with; **~ de poupée** doll's kitchen set; **~ à trois** love triangle

ménagement [menaʒmɑ̃] NM care and attention ▪ **ménagements** NMPL (*égards*) consideration *sg*, attention *sg*

ménager¹ [menaʒe] VT (*traiter avec mesure*) to handle with tact; to treat considerately; (*utiliser*) to use with care; (*: économie*) to use sparingly; (*prendre soin de*) to take (great) care of, look after; (*organiser*) to arrange; (*installer*) to put in; to make; **~ qch à qn** (*réserver*) to have sth in store for sb ▪ **se ménager** VPR to look after o.s.

ménager², -ère [menaʒe, -ɛʀ] ADJ household *cpd*, domestic ▸ NF (*femme*) housewife; (*couverts*) canteen (*of cutlery*)

ménagerie [menaʒʀi] NF menagerie

mendiant, e [mɑ̃djɑ̃, -ɑ̃t] NM/F beggar

mendicité [mɑ̃disite] NF begging

mendier [mɑ̃dje] /**7**/ VI to beg ▸ VT to beg (for); (*fig: éloges, compliments*) to fish for

menées [məne] NFPL intrigues, manœuvres (BRIT), maneuvers (US); (*Comm*) activities

⋆**mener** [m(ə)ne] /**5**/ VT to lead; (*enquête*) to conduct; (*affaires*) to manage, conduct, run; **~ qch à bonne fin** *ou* **à terme** *ou* **à bien** to see sth through (to a successful conclusion), complete sth successfully ▸ VI: **~ (à la marque)** to lead, be in the lead; **~ à/dans** (*emmener*) to take to/into

meneur, -euse [mənœʀ, -øz] NM/F leader; (*péj: agitateur*) ringleader; **~ d'hommes** born leader; **~ de jeu** host, quizmaster (BRIT)

menhir [menir] NM standing stone

méninges [menɛ̃ʒ] NFPL (*Anat*) meninges; (*fam*): **se creuser les ~** to rack one's brains

méningite [menɛ̃ʒit] NF meningitis *no pl*

ménisque [menisk] NM (*Anat*) meniscus

ménopause [menopoz] NF menopause

ménopausée [menopoze] ADJ F post-menopausal

menotte [mənɔt] NF (*langage enfantin*) handie ▪ **menottes** NFPL handcuffs; **passer les menottes à** to handcuff

menotter [mənɔte] VT to handcuff

mens [mɑ̃] VB *voir* **mentir**

mensonge [mɑ̃sɔ̃ʒ] NM: **le ~** lying *no pl*; **un ~** a lie

mensonger, -ère [mɑ̃sɔ̃ʒe, -ɛʀ] ADJ false

menstruation [mɑ̃stʀyasjɔ̃] NF menstruation

menstruel, le [mɑ̃stʀɥɛl] ADJ menstrual

mensualisation [mɑ̃sɥalizasjɔ̃] NF (*des salaires*) monthly payment; **les paiements par ~** payment by monthly instalments

mensualiser [mɑ̃sɥalize] /**1**/ VT to pay monthly

mensualité [mɑ̃sɥalite] NF (*somme payée*) monthly payment; (*somme perçue*) monthly salary

mensuel, le [mɑ̃sɥɛl] ADJ monthly ▸ NM/F (*employé*) employee paid monthly ▸ NM (*Presse*) monthly

mensuellement [mɑ̃sɥɛlmɑ̃] ADV monthly

mensurations [mɑ̃syʀasjɔ̃] NFPL measurements

mentais *etc* [mɑ̃tɛ] VB *voir* **mentir**

mental, e, -aux [mɑ̃tal, -o] ADJ mental

mentalement [mɑ̃talmɑ̃] ADV in one's head, mentally

mentalité [mɑ̃talite] NF mentality

menteur, -euse [mɑ̃tœʀ, -øz] NM/F liar

menthe [mɑ̃t] NF mint; **~ (à l'eau)** peppermint cordial

menthol [mɑ̃tɔl] NM menthol

mentholé, e [mɑ̃tɔle] ADJ menthol *cpd*, mentholated

mention [mɑ̃sjɔ̃] NF (*note*) note, comment; (*Scol*): **~ (très) bien/passable** (very) good/satisfactory pass; **faire ~ de** to mention; **« rayer la ~ inutile »** "delete as appropriate"

m

mentionner [mɑ̃sjɔne] /1/ VT to mention

★**mentir** [mɑ̃tiʀ] /16/ VI to lie

★**menton** [mɑ̃tɔ̃] NM chin

mentonnière [mɑ̃tɔnjɛʀ] NF chin strap

★**menu, e** [məny] ADJ (mince) slim, slight; (petit) tiny; (frais, difficulté) minor; **menue monnaie** small change ▶ ADV (couper, hacher) very fine ▶ NM menu; (par le ~) (raconter) in minute detail; **~ touristique** popular ou tourist menu

menuet [mənɥɛ] NM minuet

menuiserie [mənɥizʀi] NF (travail) joinery, carpentry; (d'amateur) woodwork; (local) joiner's workshop; (ouvrages) woodwork no pl

menuisier [mənɥizje] NM joiner, carpenter

méprendre [mepʀɑ̃dʀ] /58/: **se méprendre** VPR: **se ~ sur** to be mistaken about

mépris, e [mepʀi, -iz] PP de **méprendre** ▶ NM (dédain) contempt, scorn; (indifférence): **le ~ de** contempt ou disregard for; **au ~ de** regardless of, in defiance of

méprisable [mepʀizabl] ADJ contemptible, despicable

méprisant, e [mepʀizɑ̃, -ɑ̃t] ADJ contemptuous, scornful

méprise [mepʀiz] NF mistake, error; (malentendu) misunderstanding

mépriser [mepʀize] /1/ VT to scorn, despise; (gloire, danger) to scorn, spurn

★**mer** [mɛʀ] NF sea; (marée) tide; **~ fermée** inland sea; **en ~** at sea; **prendre la ~** to put out to sea; **en haute** ou **pleine ~** off shore, on the open sea; **la ~ Adriatique** the Adriatic (Sea); **la ~ des Antilles** ou **des Caraïbes** the Caribbean (Sea); **la ~ Baltique** the Baltic (Sea); **la ~ Caspienne** the Caspian Sea; **la ~ de Corail** the Coral Sea; **la ~ Égée** the Aegean (Sea); **la ~ Ionienne** the Ionian Sea; **la ~ Morte** the Dead Sea; **la ~ Noire** the Black Sea; **la ~ du Nord** the North Sea; **la ~ Rouge** the Red Sea; **la ~ des Sargasses** the Sargasso Sea; **les mers du Sud** the South Seas; **la ~ Tyrrhénienne** the Tyrrhenian Sea

mercantile [mɛʀkɑ̃til] ADJ (péj) mercenary

mercantilisme [mɛʀkɑ̃tilism] NM (esprit mercantile) mercenary attitude

mercenaire [mɛʀsənɛʀ] NM mercenary, hired soldier

mercerie [mɛʀsəʀi] NF (Couture) haberdashery (BRIT), notions pl (US); (boutique) haberdasher's (shop) (BRIT), notions store (US)

★**merci** [mɛʀsi] EXCL thank you; **~ beaucoup** thank you very much; **~ de** ou **pour** thank you for ▶ NF: **à la ~ de qn/qch** at sb's mercy/the mercy of sth; **sans ~** adj merciless; adv mercilessly

mercier, -ière [mɛʀsje, -jɛʀ] NM/F haberdasher

★**mercredi** [mɛʀkʀadi] NM Wednesday; **~ des Cendres** Ash Wednesday; voir aussi **lundi**

mercure [mɛʀkyʀ] NM mercury

merde [mɛʀd] (!) NF shit (!) ▶ EXCL (bloody) hell (!)

merder [mɛʀde] VI (!: personne) to screw up (fam)

merdeux, -euse [mɛʀdø, -øz] NM/F (!) little bugger (BRIT!), little devil

merdier [mɛʀdje] NM (!: désordre) bloody shambles (!); (: situation) bloody mess (!)

merdique [mɛʀdik] ADJ (!) shitty (!)

mère [mɛʀ] NF mother; **~ célibataire** single mother; **~ de famille** housewife, mother ▶ ADJ INV mother cpd

★**merguez** [mɛʀgɛz] NF spicy North African sausage

méridien [meʀidjɛ̃] NM meridian

méridional, e, -aux [meʀidjɔnal, -o] ADJ southern; (du midi de la France) Southern (French) ▶ NM/F Southerner

meringue [məʀɛ̃g] NF meringue

mérinos [meʀinos] NM merino

merisier [məʀizje] NM wild cherry (tree)

méritant, e [meʀitɑ̃, -ɑ̃t] ADJ deserving

mérite [meʀit] NM merit; **avoir du ~ (à faire qch)** to deserve credit (for doing sth); **le ~ (de ceci) lui revient** the credit (for this) is his

mériter [meʀite] /1/ VT to deserve; **~ de réussir** to deserve to succeed; **il mérite qu'on fasse ...** he deserves people to do ...

méritocratie [meʀitɔkʀasi] NF meritocracy

méritoire [meʀitwaʀ] ADJ praiseworthy, commendable

merlan [mɛʀlɑ̃] NM whiting

merle [mɛʀl] NM blackbird

merlu [mɛʀly] NM hake

mérou [meʀu] NM grouper (fish)

merveille [mɛʀvɛj] NF marvel, wonder; **faire ~** ou **des merveilles** to work wonders; **à ~** perfectly, wonderfully

merveilleusement [mɛʀvɛjøzmɑ̃] ADV beautifully; **~ bien** wonderfully well

★**merveilleux, -euse** [mɛʀvɛjø, -øz] ADJ marvellous, wonderful

★**mes** [me] ADJ POSS voir **mon**

★**mésalliance** [mezaljɑ̃s] NF misalliance, mismatch

mésallier [mezalje] /7/: **se mésallier** VPR to marry beneath (ou above) o.s.

mésange [mezɑ̃ʒ] NF tit(mouse); **~ bleue** bluetit

mésaventure [mezavɑ̃tyʀ] NF misadventure, misfortune

Mesdames [medam] NFPL voir **Madame**

Mesdemoiselles [medmwazɛl] NFPL voir **Mademoiselle**

mésentente [mezɑ̃tɑ̃t] NF dissension, disagreement

mésestimer [mezɛstime] /1/ VT to underestimate, underrate

Mésopotamie [mezɔpɔtami] NF: **la ~** Mesopotamia

mesquin, e [mɛskɛ̃, -in] ADJ mean, petty

mesquinerie [mɛskinʀi] NF meanness no pl, pettiness no pl; (procédé) mean trick

mess [mɛs] NM mess

★**message** [mesaʒ] NM message; **~ d'erreur** (Inform) error message; **~ électronique** (Inform) email; **~ instantané** instant message; **~ publicitaire** ad, advertisement; **~ téléphoné** telegram dictated by telephone; **~ SMS** text message; **elle m'a envoyé un ~ sur Facebook** she messaged me on Facebook

messager, -ère [mesaʒe, -ɛʀ] NM/F messenger

messagerie [mesaʒʀi] NF: **messageries aériennes/maritimes** air freight/shipping service sg; (Internet): **~ électronique** electronic mail, email; **messageries de presse** press distribution service; **~ instantanée** instant messenger, IM; **~ rose** lonely hearts and contact service on videotext; **~ vocale** voice mail

★**messe** [mɛs] NF mass; **aller à la ~** to go to mass; **~ de minuit** midnight mass; **faire des messes basses** (fig, péj) to mutter

messie [mesi] NM: **le M~** the Messiah

Messieurs [mesjø] NMPL voir **Monsieur**

mesurable [məzyʀabl] ADJ measurable; **difficilement ~** difficult to quantify.

mesure [m(ə)zyʀ] NF (évaluation, dimension) measurement; (étalon, récipient, contenu) measure; (Mus: cadence) time, tempo; (: division) bar; (retenue) moderation; (disposition) measure, step; **unité/système de ~** unit/system of measurement; **sur ~** (costume) made-to-measure; (fig) personally adapted; **à la ~ de** (fig: personne) worthy of; (chambre etc) on the same scale as; **dans la ~ où** insofar as, inasmuch as; **dans une certaine ~** to some ou a certain extent; **à ~ que** as; **en ~** (Mus) in time ou tempo; **être en ~ de** to be in a position to; **dépasser la ~** (fig) to overstep the mark

mesuré, e [məzyʀe] ADJ (ton, effort) measured; (personne) restrained

★**mesurer** [məzyʀe] **/1/** VT to measure; (juger) to weigh up, assess; (limiter) to limit, ration; (modérer: ses paroles etc) to moderate; (proportionner): **~ qch à** to match sth to, gear sth to; **il mesure 1 m 80** he's 1 m 80 tall ■ **se mesurer** VPR: **se ~ avec** to have a confrontation with; to tackle

met [mɛ] VB voir **mettre**

métabolisme [metabɔlism] NM metabolism

métairie [meteʀi] NF smallholding

métal, -aux [metal, -o] NM metal

métalangage [metalɑ̃gaʒ] NM metalanguage

métallique [metalik] ADJ metallic

métallisé, e [metalize] ADJ metallic

métallo [metalo] NMF (fam: métallurgiste) metal worker

métallurgie [metalyʀʒi] NF metallurgy

métallurgique [metalyʀʒik] ADJ steel cpd, metal cpd

métallurgiste [metalyʀʒist] NMF (ouvrier) steel ou metal worker; (industriel) metallurgist

métamorphose [metamɔʀfoz] NF metamorphosis

métamorphoser [metamɔʀfoze] **/1/** VT to transform ■ **se métamorphoser** VPR (chenille, larve) to metamorphose; **se ~ en qch** to metamorphose into sth

métaphore [metafɔʀ] NF metaphor

métaphorique [metafɔʀik] ADJ metaphorical, figurative

métaphoriquement [metafɔʀikmɑ̃] ADV metaphorically

métaphysique [metafizik] NF metaphysics sg ▶ ADJ metaphysical

métapsychique [metapsiʃik] ADJ psychic, parapsychological

métastase [metastɑz] NF (Méd) metastasis

métatarse [metataʀs] NM metatarsus

métayer, -ère [meteje, -jɛʀ] NM/F (tenant) farmer

météo [meteo] NF (bulletin) (weather) forecast; (service) ≈ Met Office (BRIT), ≈ National Weather Service (US)

météore [meteɔʀ] NM meteor

météorique [meteɔʀik] ADJ (Astronomie) meteoric; (fig: carrière, parcours) meteoric

météorite [meteɔʀit] NM OU F meteorite

météorologie [meteɔʀɔlɔʒi] NF (étude) meteorology; (service) ≈ Meteorological Office (BRIT), ≈ National Weather Service (US)

météorologique [meteɔʀɔlɔʒik] ADJ meteorological, weather cpd

météorologue [meteɔʀɔlɔg], **météorologiste** [meteɔʀɔlɔʒist] NMF meteorologist, weather forecaster

métèque [metɛk] NM (péj) wop (!)

méthane [metan] NM methane

méthanier [metanje] NM (bateau) (liquefied) gas carrier ou tanker

méthode [metɔd] NF method; (livre, ouvrage) manual, tutor

méthodique [metɔdik] ADJ methodical

méthodiquement [metɔdikmɑ̃] ADV methodically

méthodiste [metɔdist] ADJ, NMF (Rel) Methodist

méthodologie [metɔdɔlɔʒi] NF methodology

méthodologique [metɔdɔlɔʒik] ADJ methodological

méthylène [metilɛn] NM: **bleu de ~** methylene blue

méticuleusement [metikyløzmɑ̃] ADV meticulously

méticuleux, -euse [metikylø, -øz] ADJ meticulous

métier [metje] NM (profession: gén) job; (: manuel) trade; (: artisanal) craft; (technique, expérience) (acquired) skill ou technique; (aussi: **métier à tisser**) (weaving) loom; **être du ~** to be in the trade ou profession

métis, se [metis] ADJ of mixed race ▶ NM/F person of mixed race

métissage [metisaʒ] NM (de cultures, populations) mix; **le ~ de la société** the cultural mix of society

métissé, e [metise] ADJ: **une culture métissée** an ethnically diverse culture

métisser [metise] **/1/** VT (plantes, animaux) to cross(breed)

métonymie [metɔnimi] NF metonymy; **par ~** by metonymy

métrage [metʀaʒ] NM (de tissu) length; (Ciné) footage, length; **long/moyen/court ~** feature ou full-length/medium-length/short film

mètre [mɛtʀ] NM metre (BRIT), meter (US); (règle) metre rule, meter rule; (ruban) tape measure; **~ carré/cube** square/cubic metre ou meter

métrer [metʀe] **/6/** VT (Tech) to measure (in metres ou meters); (Constr) to survey

métreur, -euse [metʀœʀ, -øz] NM/F: **~ (vérificateur)** (quantity) surveyor

métrique [metʀik] ADJ metric ▶ NF metrics sg

m

métro [metʀo] NM underground (BRIT), subway (US)

métronome [metʀɔnɔm] NM metronome

métropole [metʀɔpɔl] NF (capitale) metropolis; (pays) home country

métropolitain, e [metʀɔpolitɛ̃, -ɛn] ADJ metropolitan

mets [mɛ] NM dish ▸ VB voir **mettre**

mettable [mɛtabl] ADJ fit to be worn, decent

metteur, -euse [mɛtœʀ, -øz] NM/F: **~ en scène** (Théât) producer; (Ciné) director; **~ en ondes** (Radio) producer

---

mettre [mɛtʀ]

/56/ VT **1** (placer) to put; **mettre en bouteille/en sac** to bottle/put in bags ou sacks; **mettre qch à la poste** to post sth (BRIT), mail sth (US); **mettre en examen (pour)** to charge (with) (BRIT), indict (for) (US); **mettre une note gaie/amusante** to inject a cheerful/an amusing note; **mettre qn debout/assis** to help sb up ou to their feet/help sb to sit down

2 (vêtements: revêtir) to put on; (: porter) to wear; **mets ton gilet** put your cardigan on; **je ne mets plus mon manteau** I no longer wear my coat

3 (faire fonctionner: chauffage, électricité) to put on; (: réveil, minuteur) to set; **mettre en marche** to start up

4 (installer: gaz, eau) to put in, lay on

5 (consacrer): **mettre du temps/deux heures à faire qch** to take time/two hours to do sth; **y mettre du sien** to pull one's weight

6 (noter, écrire) to say, put (down); **qu'est-ce qu'il a mis sur la carte ?** what did he say ou write on the card?; **mettez au pluriel ...** put ... into the plural

7 (supposer): **mettons que ...** let's suppose ou say that ...

8 (faire + vb): **faire mettre le gaz/l'électricité** to have gas/electricity put in ou installed

■ **se mettre** VPR **1** (se placer): **vous pouvez vous mettre là** you can sit (ou stand) there; **où ça se met?** where does it go?; **se mettre au lit** to get into bed; **se mettre au piano** to sit down at the piano; **se mettre à l'eau** to get into the water; **se mettre de l'encre sur les doigts** to get ink on one's fingers

2 (s'habiller): **se mettre en maillot de bain** to get into ou put on a swimsuit; **n'avoir rien à se mettre** to have nothing to wear

3 (dans rapports): **se mettre bien/mal avec qn** to get on the right/wrong side of sb; **se mettre qn à dos** to get on sb's bad side; **se mettre avec qn** (prendre parti) to side with sb; (faire équipe) to team up with sb; (en ménage) to move in with sb

4: **se mettre à** to begin, start; **se mettre à faire** to begin ou start doing ou to do; **se mettre au piano** to start learning the piano; **se mettre au régime** to go on a diet; **se mettre au travail/à l'étude** to get down to work/one's studies; **il est temps de s'y mettre** it's time we got down to it ou got on with it

---

★**meuble** [mœbl] NM (objet) piece of furniture; (ameublement) furniture no pl ▸ ADJ (terre) loose, friable; (Jur): **biens meubles** movables

---

> **Furniture** est indénombrable : il ne peut pas désigner une seule armoire, un seul canapé, etc. Pour traduire un meuble, il faut dire **a piece of furniture**. Notez que furniture ne prend jamais de **-s** et s'emploie avec un verbe au singulier.
> Tous nos meubles sont d'occasion. **All our furniture is second-hand.**
> un meuble très lourd **a very heavy piece of furniture**

---

meublé [mœble] NM (pièce) furnished room; (appartement) furnished flat (BRIT) ou apartment (US)

meubler [mœble] /1/ VT to furnish; (fig): **~ qch (de)** to fill sth (with) ■ **se meubler** VPR to furnish one's house

meuf [mœf] NF (fam) woman

meuglement [møɡləmɑ̃] NM (de vaches) mooing, lowing

meugler [møɡle] /1/ VI to low, moo

meule [møl] NF (à broyer) millstone; (à aiguiser) grindstone; (à polir) buff wheel; (de foin, blé) stack; (de fromage) round

meunerie [mønʀi] NF (industrie) flour trade; (métier) milling

meunier, -ière [mønje, -jɛʀ] NM miller ▸ NF miller's wife ▸ ADJ F (Culin) meunière

meurs etc [mœʀ] VB voir **mourir**

★**meurtre** [mœʀtʀ] NM murder

meurtrier, -ière [mœʀtʀije, -jɛʀ] ADJ (arme, épidémie, combat) deadly; (accident) fatal; (carrefour, route) lethal; (fureur, instincts) murderous ▸ NM/F murderer(-ess) ▸ NF (ouverture) loophole

meurtrir [mœʀtʀiʀ] /2/ VT to bruise; (fig) to wound

meurtrissure [mœʀtʀisyʀ] NF bruise; (fig) scar

meus etc [mœ] VB voir **mouvoir**

Meuse [møz] NF: **la ~** the Meuse

meute [møt] NF pack

meuve etc [mœv] VB voir **mouvoir**

mévente [mevɑ̃t] NF slump (in sales)

mexicain, e [mɛksikɛ̃, -ɛn] ADJ Mexican ▸ NM/F: **Mexicain, e** Mexican

Mexico [mɛksiko] N Mexico City

Mexique [mɛksik] NM: **le ~** Mexico

mezzanine [mɛdzanin] NF mezzanine (floor)

MF SIGLE MPL = **millions de francs** ▸ SIGLE F (Radio: = modulation de fréquence) FM

Mgr ABR = **monseigneur**

mi [mi] NM (Mus) E; (en chantant la gamme) mi

mi- [mi] PRÉFIXE half, mid-; **à la mi-janvier** in mid-January; **mi-bureau, mi-chambre** half office, half bedroom; **à mi-jambes** to the knees; **à mi-corps** to the waist; **à mi-hauteur** (en montant) halfway up; (en descendant) halfway down; **à mi-pente** (en montant) halfway up the hill; (en descendant) halfway down the hill

miam-miam [mjammjam] EXCL (fam) yum-yum (fam), yummy (fam)

miaou [mjau] NM miaow

miasmes [mjasm] NMPL noxious air

miaulement [mjolmɑ̃] NM (cri) miaow; (continu) miaowing no pl

miauler [mjole] /1/ VI to miaow

mi-bas [miba] NM INV knee-length sock

mica [mika] NM mica

mi-carême [mikarɛm] NF: **la ~** the third Thursday in Lent

miche [miʃ] NF round *ou* cob loaf

mi-chemin [miʃmɛ̃]: **à ~** *adv* halfway, midway

mi-clos, e [miklo, -kloz] ADJ half-closed

micmac [mikmak] NM (*péj*) carry-on

mi-côte [mikot]: **à ~** *adv* halfway up (*ou* down) the hill

mi-course [mikurs]: **à ~** *adv* halfway through the race

micro [mikro] NM mike, microphone; (*Inform*) micro; **~ cravate** lapel mike

microbe [mikrɔb] NM germ, microbe

microbien, ne [mikrɔbjɛ̃, -jɛn] ADJ (*vie, infection*) microbial

microbiologie [mikrɔbjɔlɔʒi] NF microbiology

microchirurgie [mikrɔʃiryrʒi] NF microsurgery

microclimat [mikroklima] NM microclimate

microcosme [mikrɔkɔsm] NM microcosm

micro-édition [mikrɔedisjɔ̃] NF desktop publishing

micro-électronique [mikrɔelɛktrɔnik] NF microelectronics *sg*

microfiche [mikrɔfiʃ] NF microfiche

microfilm [mikrɔfilm] NM microfilm

micro-onde [mikrɔɔ̃d] NF: **four à micro-ondes** microwave oven

micro-ordinateur [mikrɔɔrdinatœr] NM microcomputer

micro-organisme [mikrɔɔrganism] NM micro-organism

microphone [mikrɔfɔn] NM microphone

microplaquette [mikrɔplakɛt] NF microchip

microprocesseur [mikrɔprɔsɛsœr] NM microprocessor

microscope [mikrɔskɔp] NM microscope; **au ~** under *ou* through the microscope

microscopique [mikrɔskɔpik] ADJ microscopic

microsillon [mikrɔsijɔ̃] NM long-playing record

MIDEM [midɛm] SIGLE M (= *Marché international du disque et de l'édition musicale*) music industry trade fair

★**midi** [midi] NM (*milieu du jour*) midday, noon; (*moment du déjeuner*) lunchtime; (*sud*) south; **le M~** (*de la France*) the South (of France), the Midi; **à ~** at 12 (o'clock) *ou* midday *ou* noon; **tous les midis** every lunchtime; **le repas de ~** lunch; **en plein ~** (right) in the middle of the day; (*sud*) facing south

midinette [midinɛt] NF silly young townie

mie [mi] NF inside (of the loaf)

★**miel** [mjɛl] NM honey; **être tout ~** (*fig*) to be all sweetness and light

mielleux, -euse [mjɛlø, -øz] ADJ (*péj: personne*) sugary, syrupy

mien, ne [mjɛ̃, mjɛn] ADJ, PRON: **le (la) ~(ne), les ~(ne)s** mine; **les miens** (*ma famille*) my family

miette [mjɛt] NF (*de pain, gâteau*) crumb; (*fig: de la conversation etc*) scrap; **en miettes** (*fig*) in pieces *ou* bits

---

mieux [mjø]

ADV **1** (*d'une meilleure façon*): **mieux (que)** better (than); **elle travaille/mange mieux** she works/eats better; **aimer mieux** to prefer; **j'attendais mieux de vous** I expected better of you; **elle va mieux** she is better; **de mieux en mieux** better and better

2 (*de la meilleure façon*) best; **ce que je sais le mieux** what I know best; **les livres les mieux faits** the best made books

3 (*intensif*): **vous feriez mieux de faire ...** you would be better to do ...; **crier à qui mieux mieux** to try to shout each other down

▶ ADJ INV **1** (*plus à l'aise, en meilleure forme*) better; **se sentir mieux** to feel better

2 (*plus satisfaisant*) better; **c'est mieux ainsi** it's better like this; **c'est le mieux des deux** it's the better of the two; **le/la mieux, les mieux** the best; **demandez-lui, c'est le mieux** ask him, it's the best thing

3 (*plus joli*) better-looking; (*plus gentil*) nicer; **il est mieux que son frère** (*plus beau*) he's better-looking than his brother; (*plus gentil*) he's nicer than his brother; **il est mieux sans moustache** he looks better without a moustache

4: **au mieux** at best; **au mieux avec** on the best of terms with; **pour le mieux** for the best; **qui mieux est** even better, better still

▶ NM **1** (*progrès*) improvement

2: **de mon/ton mieux** as best I/you can (*ou* could); **faire de son mieux** to do one's best; **du mieux qu'il peut** the best he can; **faute de mieux** for lack *ou* want of anything better, failing anything better

---

mieux-être [mjøzɛtr] NM greater well-being; (*financier*) improved standard of living

mièvre [mjɛvr] ADJ sickly sentimental

mièvrerie [mjɛvrəri] NF soppiness, sickly sentimentality

★**mignon, ne** [miɲɔ̃, -ɔn] ADJ sweet, cute

migraine [migrɛn] NF headache; (*Méd*) migraine

migrant, e [migrɑ̃, -ɑ̃t] ADJ, NM/F migrant

migrateur, -trice [migratœr, -tris] ADJ migratory

migration [migrasjɔ̃] NF migration

migratoire [migratwar] ADJ migratory; **les flux migratoires** flow of migrants

migrer [migre] VI to migrate

mijaurée [miʒɔre] NF pretentious (young) madam

mijoter [miʒɔte] /1/ VT to simmer; (*préparer avec soin*) to cook lovingly; (*affaire, projet*) to plot, cook up ▶ VI to simmer

mil [mil] NUM = **mille**

milan [milɑ̃] NM (*oiseau*) kite; **~ royal** red kite ▶ N: **M~** Milan

milanais, e [milanɛ, -ɛz] ADJ Milanese ▶ NM/F: **Milanais, e** Milanese

mildiou [mildju] NM mildew

mile [majl] NM mile

milice [milis] NF militia

milicien, ne [milisjɛ̃, -ɛn] NM/F militiaman(-woman)

m

★**milieu, x** [miljø] NM (*centre*) middle; (*fig*) middle course *ou* way; (*aussi:* **juste milieu**) happy medium; (*Bio, Géo*) environment; (*entourage social*) milieu; (*familial*) background; circle; (*pègre*): **le ~** the underworld; **au ~ de** in the middle of; **au beau ~** *ou* **en plein ~ (de)** right in the middle (of); **~ de terrain** (*Football: joueur*) midfield player; (*: joueurs*) midfield

★**militaire** [militɛʀ] ADJ military, army *cpd*; **service ~** military service ▶ NM serviceman (servicewoman)

militant, e [militɑ̃, -ɑ̃t] ADJ, NM/F militant

militantisme [militɑ̃tism] NM militancy

militarisation [militaʀizasjɔ̃] NF militarization

militarisé, e [militaʀize] ADJ (*zone*) militarized

militariser [militaʀize] /1/ VT to militarize

militarisme [militaʀism] NM (*péj*) militarism

militer [milite] /1/ VI to be a militant; **~ pour/ contre** to militate in favour of/against

milk-shake [milkʃɛk] NM milk shake

mille [mil] NUM a *ou* one thousand; **mettre dans le ~** to hit the bull's-eye; (*fig*) to be bang on (target) ▶ NM (*mesure*): **~ (marin)** nautical mile

millefeuille [milfœj] NM cream *ou* vanilla slice

millénaire [milenɛʀ] NM millennium ▶ ADJ thousand-year-old; (*fig*) ancient

millénarisme [milenaʀism] NM millenarianism

mille-pattes [milpat] NM INV centipede

millepertuis [milpɛʀtɥi] NM (*plante*) St John's wort

millésime [milezim] NM vintage

millésimé, e [milezime] ADJ vintage *cpd*

millet [mijɛ] NM millet

milliard [miljaʀ] NM milliard, thousand million (BRIT), billion (US)

milliardaire [miljaʀdɛʀ] NMF multimillionaire (BRIT), billionaire (US)

millième [miljɛm] NUM thousandth

millier [milje] NM thousand; **un ~ (de)** a thousand or so, about a thousand; **par milliers** in (their) thousands, by the thousand

milligramme [miligʀam] NM milligramme (BRIT), milligram (US)

millilitre [mililitʀ] NM millilitre (BRIT), milliliter (US)

millimètre [milimɛtʀ] NM millimetre (BRIT), millimeter (US)

millimétré, e [milimetʀe] ADJ: **papier ~** graph paper

millimétrique [milimetʀik] ADJ millimetric; **d'une précision ~** 100% accurate

★**million** [miljɔ̃] NM million; **deux millions de** two million; **riche à millions** worth millions

millionième [miljɔnjɛm] NUM millionth

millionnaire [miljɔnɛʀ] NMF millionaire

mi-lourd [miluʀ] ADJ M, NM light heavyweight

mime [mim] NMF (*acteur*) mime(r); (*imitateur*) mimic ▶ NM (*art*) mime, miming

mimer [mime] /1/ VT to mime; (*singer*) to mimic, take off

mimétisme [mimetism] NM (*Bio*) mimicry

mimi [mimi] ADJ INV (*fam: mignon*) cute ▶ NM (*langage enfantin: baiser*) little kiss

mimique [mimik] NF (*funny*) face; (*signes*) gesticulations *pl*, sign language *no pl*

mimosa [mimoza] NM mimosa

mi-moyen [mimwajɛ̃] ADJ M, NM welterweight

MIN SIGLE M (= *Marché d'intérêt national*) *wholesale market for fruit, vegetables and agricultural produce*

min. ABR (= *minimum*) min

minable [minabl] ADJ (*personne*) shabby(-looking); (*travail*) pathetic

minaret [minaʀɛ] NM minaret

minauder [minode] /1/ VI to mince, simper

minauderies [minodʀi] NFPL simpering *sg*

★**mince** [mɛ̃s] ADJ thin; (*personne, taille*) slim, slender; (*fig: profit, connaissances*) slight, small; (*: prétexte*) weak ▶ EXCL: **~ (alors)!** darn it!

minceur [mɛ̃sœʀ] NF thinness; (*d'une personne*) slimness, slenderness

mincir [mɛ̃siʀ] /2/ VI to get slimmer *ou* thinner

mine [min] NF (*physionomie*) expression, look; (*extérieur*) exterior, appearance; (*de crayon*) lead; (*gisement, exploitation, explosif*) mine; **avoir bonne ~** (*personne*) to look well; (*ironique*) to look an utter idiot; **avoir mauvaise ~** to look unwell; **faire ~ de faire** to make a pretence of doing; **ne pas payer de ~** to be not much to look at; **~ de rien** *adv* with a casual air; although you wouldn't think so; **~ de charbon** coal mine; **~ à ciel ouvert** opencast (BRIT) *ou* open-air (US) mine ▪ **mines** NFPL (*péj*) simpering airs; **les Mines** (*Admin*) *the national mining and geological service, the government vehicle testing department*

miner [mine] /1/ VT (*saper*) to undermine, erode; (*Mil*) to mine

minerai [minʀɛ] NM ore

minéral, e, -aux [mineʀal, -o] ADJ mineral; (*Chimie*) inorganic ▶ NM mineral

minéralier [mineʀalje] NM (*bateau*) ore tanker

minéralisé, e [mineʀalize] ADJ mineralized

minéralogie [mineʀalɔʒi] NF mineralogy

minéralogique [mineʀalɔʒik] ADJ mineralogical; **plaque ~** number (BRIT) *ou* license (US) plate; **numéro ~** registration (BRIT) *ou* license (US) number

minet, te [minɛ, -ɛt] NM/F (*chat*) pussy-cat; (*péj*) young trendy

★**mineur, e** [minœʀ] ADJ minor ▶ NM/F (*Jur*) minor ▶ NM (*travailleur*) miner; (*Mil*) sapper; **~ de fond** face worker

miniature [minjatyʀ] ADJ, NF miniature

miniaturisation [minjatyʀizasjɔ̃] NF miniaturization

miniaturiser [minjatyʀize] /1/ VT to miniaturize

minibus [minibys] NM minibus

minichaîne [miniʃɛn] NF mini system

minier, -ière [minje, -jɛʀ] ADJ mining

minigolf [minigɔlf] NM miniature golf

mini-jupe [miniʒyp] NF mini-skirt

minimal, e, -aux [minimal, -o] ADJ minimum

minimalisme [minimalism] NM minimalism

minimaliste [minimalist] ADJ minimalist

minime [minim] ADJ minor, minimal ▸NMF (*Sport*) junior

minimessage [minimesaʒ] NM text message

minimiser [minimize] /1/ VT to minimize; (*fig*) to play down

minimum [minimɔm] ADJ, NM minimum; **au ~** at the very least; **~ vital** (*salaire*) living wage; (*niveau de vie*) subsistence level

mini-ordinateur [miniɔʀdinatœʀ] NM minicomputer

ministère [ministɛʀ] NM (*cabinet*) government; (*département*) ministry (BRIT), department; (*Rel*) ministry; **~ public** (*Jur*) Prosecution, State Prosecutor

ministériel, le [ministeʀjɛl] ADJ government *cpd*; ministerial, departmental; (*partisan*) progovernment

ministrable [ministʀabl] ADJ (*Pol*): **il est ~** he's a potential minister

★**ministre** [ministʀ] NM minister (BRIT), secretary; (*Rel*) minister; **~ d'État** senior minister *ou* secretary

minium [minjɔm] NM red lead paint

minois [minwa] NM little face

minorer [minɔʀe] /1/ VT to cut, reduce

minoritaire [minɔʀitɛʀ] ADJ minority *cpd*

minorité [minɔʀite] NF minority; **être en ~** to be in the *ou* a minority; **mettre en ~** (*Pol*) to defeat

Minorque [minɔʀk] NF Minorca

minorquin, e [minɔʀkɛ̃, -in] ADJ Minorcan

minoterie [minɔtʀi] NF flour-mill

minou [minu] NM (*langage enfantin: chat*) pussy (*fam*)

★**minuit** [minɥi] NM midnight

minus [minys] NMF (*fam, péj*) loser (*fam*)

minuscule [minyskyl] ADJ minute, tiny ▸NF: (**lettre**) **~** small letter

minutage [minytaʒ] NM timing

★**minute** [minyt] NF minute; (*Jur: original*) minute, draft; **à la ~** (*présent*) (just) this instant; (*passé*) there and then; **entrecôte** *ou* **steak ~** minute steak ▸ EXCL just a minute!, hang on!

minuter [minyte] /1/ VT to time

minuterie [minytʀi] NF time switch

minuteur [minytœʀ] NM timer

minutie [minysi] NF meticulousness; minute detail; **avec ~** meticulously; in minute detail

minutieusement [minysjøzmɑ̃] ADV (*organiser, travailler*) meticulously; (*examiner*) minutely

minutieux, -euse [minysjø, -øz] ADJ (*personne*) meticulous; (*inspection*) minutely detailed; (*travail*) requiring painstaking attention to detail

mioche [mjɔʃ] NM (*fam*) nipper, brat

mirabelle [miʀabɛl] NF (*fruit*) (cherry) plum; (*eau-de-vie*) plum brandy

miracle [miʀakl] NM miracle

miraculé, e [miʀakyle] ADJ who has been miraculously cured (*ou* rescued)

miraculeux, -euse [miʀakylø, -øz] ADJ miraculous

mirador [miʀadɔʀ] NM (*Mil*) watchtower

mirage [miʀaʒ] NM mirage

mire [miʀ] NF (*d'un fusil*) sight; (*TV*) test card; **point de ~** target; (*fig*) focal point; **ligne de ~** line of sight

mirent [miʀ] VB *voir* **mettre**

mirer [miʀe] /1/ VT (*œufs*) to candle ■ **se mirer** VPR: **se ~ dans** (*personne*) to gaze at one's reflection in; (*chose*) to be mirrored in

mirettes [miʀɛt] NFPL (*fam: yeux*) peepers (*fam*); **en prendre plein les ~** to be dazzled

mirifique [miʀifik] ADJ wonderful

mirobolant, e [miʀɔbɔlɑ̃, -ɑ̃t] ADJ fantastic

★**miroir** [miʀwaʀ] NM mirror

miroiter [miʀwate] /1/ VI to sparkle, shimmer; **faire ~ qch à qn** to paint sth in glowing colours for sb, dangle sth in front of sb's eyes

miroiterie [miʀwatʀi] NF (*usine*) mirror factory; (*magasin*) mirror dealer's (shop)

Mis ABR = **marquis**

mis, e [mi, miz] PP *de* **mettre** ▸ ADJ (*couvert, table*) set, laid; (*personne*): **bien ~** well dressed ▸ NF (*argent: au jeu*) stake; (*tenue*) clothing; attire; **être de mise** to be acceptable *ou* in season; **mise en bouteilles** bottling; **mise en examen** charging, indictment; **mise à feu** blast-off; **mise de fonds** capital outlay; **mise à jour** (*Inform*) update; **mise à mort** kill; **mise à pied** (*d'un employé*) suspension; lay-off; **mise sur pied** (*d'une affaire, entreprise*) setting up; **mise en plis** set; **mise au point** (*Photo*) focusing; (*fig*) clarification; **mise à prix** reserve (BRIT) *ou* upset price; **mise en scène** production

misaine [mizɛn] NF: **mât de ~** foremast

misanthrope [mizɑ̃tʀɔp] NMF misanthropist

Mise ABR = **marquise**

mise [miz] ADJ F, NF *voir* **mis**

miser [mize] /1/ VT (*enjeu*) to stake, bet; **~ sur** (*cheval, numéro*) to bet on; (*fig*) to bank *ou* count on

misérable [mizeʀabl] ADJ (*lamentable, malheureux*) pitiful, wretched; (*pauvre*) poverty-stricken; (*insignifiant, mesquin*) miserable ▸ NMF wretch; (*miséreux*) poor wretch

misère [mizɛʀ] NF (*pauvreté*) (extreme) poverty, destitution; **être dans la ~** to be destitute *ou* poverty-stricken; **salaire de ~** starvation wage; **~ noire** utter destitution, abject poverty ■ **misères** NFPL (*malheurs*) woes, miseries; (*ennuis*) little troubles; **faire des misères à qn** to torment sb

miséreux, -euse [mizeʀø, -øz] ADJ poverty-stricken ▸ NM/F down-and-out

miséricorde [mizeʀikɔʀd] NF mercy, forgiveness

miséricordieux, -euse [mizeʀikɔʀdjø, -øz] ADJ merciful, forgiving

misogyne [mizɔʒin] ADJ misogynous ▸ NMF misogynist

misogynie [mizɔʒini] NF misogyny

missel [misɛl] NM missal

missile [misil] NM missile

mission [misjɔ̃] NF mission; **partir en ~** (*Admin, Pol*) to go on an assignment

missionnaire [misjɔnɛʀ] NMF missionary

missive [misiv] NF missive

mistral [mistʀal] NM mistral (wind)

mit [mi] VB *voir* **mettre**

mitaine [mitɛn] NF mitt(en)

m

mitaines [mitɛn] NFPL fingerless gloves; (CANADA: *moufles*) mittens

mitard [mitaʀ] NM (*fam*) cooler (*fam*), solitary

mite [mit] NF clothes moth

mité, e [mite] ADJ moth-eaten

★**mi-temps** [mitɑ̃] NF INV (*Sport*: *période*) half; (: *pause*) half-time; **à ~** adj, adv part-time

miteux, -euse [mitø, -øz] ADJ seedy, shabby

mitigé, e [mitiʒe] ADJ (*conviction, ardeur*) lukewarm; (*sentiments*) mixed

mitochondrie [mitɔkɔ̃dʀi] NF mitochondrion

mitonner [mitɔne] /1/ VT (*préparer*) to cook with loving care; (*fig*) to cook up quietly

mitoyen, ne [mitwajɛ̃, -ɛn] ADJ (*mur*) common, party cpd; **maisons mitoyennes** semi-detached houses; (*plus de deux*) terraced (BRIT) ou row (US) houses

mitraillage [mitʀajaʒ] NM (*avec une mitrailleuse*) machine-gunning; (*fig*: *avec un appareil photo*) clicking, snapping

mitraille [mitʀaj] NF (*balles de fonte*) grapeshot; (*décharge d'obus*) shellfire

mitrailler [mitʀaje] /1/ VT to machine-gun; (*fig*: *photographier*) to snap away at; **~ qn de** to pelt ou bombard sb with

mitraillette [mitʀajɛt] NF submachine gun

mitrailleur [mitʀajœʀ] NM machine gunner ▶ ADJ M: **fusil ~** machine gun

mitrailleuse [mitʀajøz] NF machine gun

mitre [mitʀ] NF mitre

mitron [mitʀɔ̃] NM baker's boy

mi-voix [mivwa]: **à ~** adv in a low ou hushed voice

mix [miks] NM (*aussi Mus*) mix; **~ énergétique** (*Tech*) energy mix

mixage [miksaʒ] NM (*Ciné*) (sound) mixing

mixer, mixeur [miksœʀ] NM (*Culin*) (food) mixer

mixité [miksite] NF (*Scol*) coeducation

★**mixte** [mikst] ADJ (*gén*) mixed; (*Scol*) mixed, coeducational; **à usage ~** dual-purpose; **cuisinière ~** combined gas and electric cooker; **équipe ~** combined team

mixture [mikstyʀ] NF mixture; (*fig*) concoction

MJC SIGLE F (= *maison des jeunes et de la culture*) community arts centre and youth club

ml ABR (= *millilitre*) ml

MLF SIGLE M (= *Mouvement de libération des femmes*) Women's Movement

Mlle (*pl* **Mlles**) ABR = **Mademoiselle**

MM ABR = **Messieurs**; *voir* **Monsieur**

mm ABR (= *millimètre*; *millimètres*) mm

Mme (*pl* **Mmes**) ABR = **Madame**

MMS SIGLE M (= *Multimedia messaging service*) MMS

mn ABR (= *minute*) min

mnémotechnique [mnemɔtɛknik] ADJ mnemonic

MNS SIGLE M (= *maître nageur sauveteur*) ≈ lifeguard

MO SIGLE F (= *main-d'œuvre*) labour costs (on invoices)

Mo ABR = **méga-octet**; **métro**

★**mobile** [mɔbil] ADJ mobile; (*amovible*) loose, removable; (*pièce de machine*) moving; (*élément de meuble etc*) movable ▶ NM (*motif*) motive; (*œuvre d'art*)

mobile; (*Physique*) moving object ou body; (**téléphone**) **~** mobile (phone) (BRIT), cell (phone) (US)

mobilier, -ière [mɔbilje, -jɛʀ] ADJ (*Jur*) personal; **valeurs mobilières** transferable securities; **vente mobilière** sale of personal property ou chattels ▶ NM (*meubles*) furniture

mobilisateur, -trice [mɔbilizatœʀ, -tʀis] ADJ (*projet, thème*) inspiring

mobilisation [mɔbilizasjɔ̃] NF mobilization

mobiliser [mɔbilize] /1/ VT (*Mil, gén*) to mobilize

mobilité [mɔbilite] NF mobility

★**mobylette®** [mɔbilɛt] NF moped

mocassin [mɔkasɛ̃] NM moccasin

★**moche** [mɔʃ] ADJ (*fam*: *laid*) ugly; (*mauvais, méprisable*) rotten

mocheté [mɔʃte] NF (*fam*: *laideur*) ugliness; (: *chose laide*) eyesore; (: *péj*: *femme*) ugly woman

modalité [mɔdalite] NF form, mode ■ **modalités** NFPL (*d'un accord etc*) clauses, terms; **modalités de paiement** methods of payment

★**mode** [mɔd] NF fashion; (*commerce*) fashion trade ou industry; **travailler dans la ~** to be in the fashion business; **à la ~** fashionable, in fashion ▶ NM (*manière*) form, mode, method; (*Ling*) mood; (*Inform, Mus*) mode; **~ dialogué** (*Inform*) interactive ou conversational mode; **~ d'emploi** directions pl (for use); **~ de paiement** method of payment; **~ de vie** way of life

modelage [mɔd(ə)laʒ] NM modelling

modelé [mɔd(ə)le] NM (*Géo*) relief; (*du corps etc*) contours pl

modèle [mɔdɛl] ADJ model ▶ NM model; (*qui pose*: *de peintre*) sitter; (*type*) type; (*gabarit, patron*) pattern; **~ courant** ou **de série** (*Comm*) production model; **~ déposé** registered design; **~ réduit** small-scale model

modeler [mɔd(ə)le] /5/ VT (*Art*) to model, mould; (*vêtement, érosion*) to mould, shape; **~ qch sur/d'après** to model sth on ■ **se modeler** VPR: **se ~ sur** to model o.s. on

modélisation [mɔdelizasjɔ̃] NF (*Math*) modelling

modélisme [mɔdelism] NM model-making

modéliste [mɔdelist] NMF (*Couture*) designer; (*de modèles réduits*) model maker

modem [mɔdɛm] NM (*Inform*) modem

modérateur, -trice [mɔdeʀatœʀ, -tʀis] ADJ moderating ▶ NM/F moderator

modération [mɔdeʀasjɔ̃] NF moderation; **à consommer avec ~** (*sur les bouteilles d'alcool*) please drink responsibly; **~ de peine** reduction of sentence

modéré, e [mɔdeʀe] ADJ, NM/F moderate

modérément [mɔdeʀemɑ̃] ADV moderately, in moderation

modérer [mɔdeʀe] /6/ VT to moderate ■ **se modérer** VPR to restrain o.s.

★**moderne** [mɔdɛʀn] ADJ modern ▶ NM (*Art*) modern style; (*ameublement*) modern furniture

modernisation [mɔdɛʀnizasjɔ̃] NF modernization

moderniser [mɔdɛʀnize] /1/ VT to modernize

modernisme [mɔdɛʀnism] NM modernism

moderniste [mɔdɛʀnist] ADJ, NMF modernist

modernité [mɔdɛʀnite] NF modernity

modeste [mɔdɛst] ADJ modest; (*origine*) humble, lowly

modestement [mɔdɛstəmã] ADV modestly

modestie [mɔdɛsti] NF modesty; **fausse ~** false modesty

modicité [mɔdisite] NF: **la ~ des prix** *etc* the low prices *etc*

modifiable [mɔdifjabl] ADJ modifiable

modificatif, -ive [mɔdifikatif, -iv] ADJ modifying

modification [mɔdifikasjɔ̃] NF modification

modifier [mɔdifje] /7/ VT to modify, alter; (*Ling*) to modify ▪ **se modifier** VPR to alter

modique [mɔdik] ADJ (*salaire, somme*) modest

modiste [mɔdist] NF milliner

modulable [mɔdylabl] ADJ (*mobilier, canapé*) adjustable; (*prêt*) flexible

modulaire [mɔdylɛʀ] ADJ modular

modularité [mɔdylaʀite] NF (*de mobilier, habitacle*) modularity

modulation [mɔdylasjɔ̃] NF modulation; **~ de fréquence (FM** *ou* **MF)** frequency modulation (FM)

module [mɔdyl] NM module

moduler [mɔdyle] /1/ VT to modulate; (*air*) to warble

moelle [mwal] NF marrow; (*fig*) pith, core; **~ épinière** spinal cord

moelleux, -euse [mwalø, -øz] ADJ soft; (*au goût, à l'ouïe*) mellow; (*gracieux, souple*) smooth; (*gâteau*) light and moist

moellon [mwalɔ̃] NM rubble stone

mœurs [mœʀ(s)] NFPL (*conduite*) morals; (*manières*) manners; (*pratiques sociales*) habits; (*mode de vie*) life style *sg*; (*d'une espèce animale*) behaviour *sg* (BRIT), behavior *sg* (US); **femme de mauvaises ~** loose woman; **passer dans les ~** to become the custom; **contraire aux bonnes ~** contrary to proprieties

mohair [mɔɛʀ] NM mohair

★**moi** [mwa] PRON me; (*emphatique*): **~, je ...** for my part, I ..., I myself ...; **c'est ~ qui l'ai fait** I did it, it was me who did it; **apporte-le-moi** bring it to me; **à ~ mine**; (*dans un jeu*) my turn; **à ~!** (*à l'aide*) help (me)! ▪ NM INV (*Psych*) ego, self

moignon [mwaɲɔ̃] NM stump

moi-même [mwamɛm] PRON myself; (*emphatique*) I myself

moindre [mwɛ̃dʀ] ADJ lesser; lower; **le (la) ~, les moindres** the least; the slightest; **le (la) ~ de** the least of; **c'est la ~ des choses** it's nothing at all

moindrement [mwɛ̃dʀəmã] ADV: **pas le ~** not in the least

moine [mwan] NM monk, friar

moineau, x [mwano] NM sparrow

---

moins [mwɛ̃]

ADV **1** *comparatif*: **moins (que)** less (than); **moins grand que** less tall than, not as tall as; **il a trois ans de moins que moi** he's three years younger than me; **il est moins intelligent que moi** he's not as clever as me, he's less clever than me;

moins je travaille, mieux je me porte the less I work, the better I feel
2 *superlatif*: **le moins** (the) least; **c'est ce que j'aime le moins** it's what I like (the) least; **le (la) moins doué(e)** the least gifted; **au moins, du moins** at least; **pour le moins** at the very least
3: **moins de** (*quantité*) less (than); (*nombre*) fewer (than); **moins de sable/d'eau** less sand/water; **moins de livres/gens** fewer books/people; **moins de deux ans** less than two years; **moins de midi** not yet midday
4: **de moins, en moins: 100 euros/3 jours de moins** 100 euros/3 days less; **trois livres en moins** three books fewer; three books too few; **de l'argent en moins** less money; **le soleil en moins** but for the sun, minus the sun; **de moins en moins** less and less; **en moins de deux** in a flash *ou* a trice
5: **à moins de, à moins que** unless; **à moins de faire** unless we do (*ou* he does *etc*); **à moins que tu ne fasses** unless you do; **à moins d'un accident** barring any accident
▪ PRÉP: **quatre moins deux** four minus two; **dix heures moins cinq** five to ten; **il fait moins cinq** it's five (degrees) below (freezing), it's minus five; **il est moins cinq** it's five to
▪ NM (*signe*) minus sign

---

moins-value [mwɛ̃valy] NF (*Écon, Comm*) depreciation

moire [mwaʀ] NF moiré

moiré, e [mwaʀe] ADJ (*tissu, papier*) moiré, watered; (*reflets*) shimmering

★**mois** [mwa] NM month; (*salaire, somme due*) (monthly) pay *ou* salary; **treizième ~, double ~** extra month's salary

moïse [mɔiz] NM Moses basket

moisi, e [mwazi] ADJ mouldy (BRIT), moldy (US), mildewed ▪ NM mould, mold, mildew; **odeur de ~** musty smell

moisir [mwaziʀ] /2/ VI to go mouldy (BRIT) *ou* moldy (US); (*fig*) to rot; (*personne*) to hang about ▪ VT to make mouldy *ou* moldy

moisissure [mwazisyʀ] NF mould *no pl* (BRIT), mold *no pl* (US)

moisson [mwasɔ̃] NF harvest; (*époque*) harvest (time); (*fig*): **faire une ~ de** to gather a wealth of

moissonner [mwasɔne] /1/ VT to harvest, reap; (*fig*) to collect

moissonneur, -euse [mwasɔnœʀ, -øz] NM/F harvester, reaper ▪ NF (*machine*) harvester

moissonneuse-batteuse [mwasɔnøzbatøz] (*pl* **moissonneuses-batteuses**) NF combine harvester

moite [mwat] ADJ (*peau, mains*) sweaty, sticky; (*atmosphère*) muggy

moiteur [mwatœʀ] NF (*d'air*) mugginess; (*de peau*) sweatiness

moitié [mwatje] NF half; (*épouse*): **sa ~** his better half; **la ~** half; **la ~ de** half (of), half the amount (*ou* number) of; **la ~ du temps/des gens** half the time/the people; **à la ~ de** halfway through; **~ moins grand** half as tall; **~ plus long** half as long again, longer by half; **à ~** half (*avant le verbe*), half- (*avant l'adjectif*); **à ~ prix** (at) half price, half-price; **de ~** by half; **~ ~** half-and-half

moka [mɔka] NM (*café*) mocha coffee; (*gâteau*) mocha cake

mol [mɔl] ADJ M *voir* **mou**

molaire [mɔlɛʀ] NF molar

moldave [mɔldav] ADJ Moldavian

Moldavie [mɔldavi] NF: **la ~** Moldavia

môle [mol] NM jetty

moléculaire [mɔlekylɛʀ] ADJ molecular

molécule [mɔlekyl] NF molecule

moleskine [mɔlɛskin] NF imitation leather

molester [mɔlɛste] /1/ VT to manhandle, maul (about)

molette [mɔlɛt] NF toothed *ou* cutting wheel

mollard [mɔlaʀ] NM (!) gob (of spit) (*fam*)

mollasse [mɔlas] ADJ (*péj: sans énergie*) sluggish; (*: flasque*) flabby

mollasson, ne [mɔlasɔ̃, -ɔn] (*fam*) ADJ sluggish ▶ NM/F lazy lump (*fam*)

molle [mɔl] ADJ F *voir* **mou**

mollement [mɔlmɑ̃] ADV softly; (*péj: travailler*) sluggishly; (*protester*) feebly

mollesse [mɔlɛs] NF (*voir* mou) softness; flabbiness; limpness; sluggishness; feebleness

mollet [mɔlɛ] NM calf ▶ ADJ M: **œuf ~** soft-boiled egg

molletière [mɔltjɛʀ] ADJ F: **bande ~** puttee

molleton [mɔltɔ̃] NM (*Textiles*) felt

molletonné, e [mɔltɔne] ADJ (*gants etc*) fleece-lined

mollir [mɔliʀ] /2/ VI (*jambes*) to give way; (*substance*) to go soft; (*Navig: vent*) to drop, die down; (*fig: personne*) to relent; (*: courage*) to fail, flag

mollo [mɔlo] ADV (*fam*): **y aller ~** to take it easy; **vas-y ~!** take it easy!

mollusque [mɔlysk] NM (*Zool*) mollusc; (*fig: personne*) lazy lump

molosse [mɔlɔs] NM big ferocious dog

môme [mom] NMF (*fam: enfant*) brat; (*: fille*) bird (BRIT), chick

★ **moment** [mɔmɑ̃] NM moment; (*occasion*): **profiter du ~** to take (advantage of) the opportunity; **ce n'est pas le ~** this is not the right time; **à un certain ~** at some point; **à un ~ donné** at a certain point; **à quel ~?** when exactly?; **au même ~** at the same time; (*instant*) at the same moment; **pour un bon ~** for a good while; **pour le ~** for the moment, for the time being; **au ~ de** at the time of; **au ~ où** as; at a time when; **à tout ~** at any time *ou* moment; (*continuellement*) constantly, continually; **en ce ~** at the moment; (*aujourd'hui*) at present; **sur le ~** at the time; **par moments** now and then, at times; **d'un ~ à l'autre** any time (now); **du ~ où** *ou* **que** seeing that, since; **n'avoir pas un ~ à soi** not to have a minute to oneself

momentané, e [mɔmɑ̃tane] ADJ temporary, momentary

momentanément [mɔmɑ̃tanemɑ̃] ADV for a moment, for a while

momie [mɔmi] NF mummy

momifier [mɔmifje] VT to mummify

★ **mon, ma** (*pl* **mes**) [mɔ̃, ma, me] ADJ POSS my

monacal, e, -aux [mɔnakal, -o] ADJ monastic

Monaco [mɔnako] N Monaco

monarchie [mɔnaʀʃi] NF monarchy

monarchique [mɔnaʀʃik] ADJ monarchical

monarchisme [mɔnaʀʃism] NM monarchism

monarchiste [mɔnaʀʃist] ADJ, NMF monarchist

monarque [mɔnaʀk] NM monarch

monastère [mɔnastɛʀ] NM monastery

monastique [mɔnastik] ADJ monastic

monceau, x [mɔ̃so] NM heap

mondain, e [mɔ̃dɛ̃, -ɛn] ADJ (*soirée, vie*) society *cpd*; (*obligations*) social; (*peintre, écrivain*) fashionable; (*personne*) society *cpd* ▶ NM/F society man/woman, socialite ▶ NF: **la Mondaine, la police mondaine** ≈ the vice squad

mondanités [mɔ̃danite] NFPL (*vie mondaine*) society life *sg*; (*paroles*) (society) small talk *sg*; (*Presse*) (society) gossip column *sg*

★ **monde** [mɔ̃d] NM world; **le ~** (*personnes mondaines*) (high) society; **être du même ~** (*milieu*) to move in the same circles; **il y a du ~** (*beaucoup de gens*) there are a lot of people; (*quelques personnes*) there are some people; **y a-t-il du ~ dans le salon?** is there anybody in the lounge?; **beaucoup/peu de ~** many/few people; **le meilleur *etc* du ~** the best *etc* in the world; **mettre au ~** to bring into the world; **pas le moins du ~** not in the least; **se faire un ~ de qch** to make a great deal of fuss about sth; **tour du ~** round-the-world trip; **homme/femme du ~** society man/woman

★ **mondial, e, -aux** [mɔ̃djal, -o] ADJ (*population*) world *cpd*; (*influence*) world-wide

mondialement [mɔ̃djalmɑ̃] ADV throughout the world

mondialisation [mɔ̃djalizasjɔ̃] NF globalization; (*d'une technique*) global application; (*d'un conflit*) global spread

mondialiser [mɔ̃djalize]: **se mondialiser** VPR (*économie, marché, politique*) to become globalized

mondialiste [mɔ̃djalist] ADJ internationalist

mondovision [mɔ̃dɔvizjɔ̃] NF (world coverage by) satellite television

monégasque [mɔnegask] ADJ Monegasque, of *ou* from Monaco ▶ NMF: **Monégasque** Monegasque

monétaire [mɔnetɛʀ] ADJ monetary

monétarisme [mɔnetaʀism] NM monetarism

monétariste [mɔnetaʀist] ADJ monetarist

monétique [mɔnetik] NF electronic money

mongol, e [mɔ̃gɔl] ADJ Mongol, Mongolian ▶ NM (*Ling*) Mongolian ▶ NM/F: **Mongol, e** (*de la Mongolie*) Mongolian

Mongolie [mɔ̃gɔli] NF: **la ~** Mongolia

mongolien, ne [mɔ̃gɔljɛ̃, -ɛn] ADJ, NM/F mongol

mongolisme [mɔ̃gɔlism] NM mongolism, Down's syndrome

★ **moniteur, -trice** [mɔnitœʀ, -tʀis] NM/F (*Sport*) instructor (instructress); (*de colonie de vacances*) supervisor; **~ d'auto-école** driving instructor ▶ NM (*écran*) monitor; **~ cardiaque** cardiac monitor

monitorage [mɔnitɔʀaʒ] NM monitoring

monitorat [mɔnitɔʀa] NM (*formation*) instructor's training (course); (*fonction*) instructorship

★ **monnaie** [mɔnɛ] NF (*pièce*) coin; (*Écon: moyen d'échange*) currency; (*petites pièces*): **avoir de la ~** to have (some) change; **faire de la ~** to get (some) change; **avoir/faire la ~ de 20 euros** to have change of/get change for 20 euros; **faire** *ou* **donner à qn la ~ de 20 euros** to give sb change for 20 euros, change 20 euros for sb; **rendre à qn la ~ (sur 20 euros)** to give sb the change (from *ou* out of 20 euros); **servir de ~ d'échange** *(fig)* to be used as a bargaining counter *ou* as bargaining counters; **payer qn en ~ de singe** to fob sb off with empty promises; **c'est ~ courante** it's a common occurrence; **~ légale** legal tender

monnayable [mɔnɛjabl] ADJ *(vendable)* convertible into cash; **mes services sont monnayables** my services are worth money

monnayer [mɔneje] /8/ VT to convert into cash; *(talent)* to capitalize on

monnayeur [mɔnɛjœʀ] NM *voir* **faux-monnayeur**

mono [mɔno] NF *(monophonie)* mono ▶ NM *(monoski)* monoski

monochrome [mɔnɔkʀom] ADJ monochrome

monocle [mɔnɔkl] NM monocle, eyeglass

monocoque [mɔnɔkɔk] ADJ *(voiture)* monocoque ▶ NM *(voilier)* monohull

monocorde [mɔnɔkɔʀd] ADJ monotonous

monoculture [mɔnɔkyltyʀ] NF single-crop farming, monoculture

monogame [mɔnɔgam] ADJ monogamous

monogamie [mɔnɔgami] NF monogamy

monogramme [mɔnɔgʀam] NM monogram

monographie [mɔnɔgʀafi] NF monograph

monokini [mɔnɔkini] NM one-piece bikini, bikini pants *pl*

monolingue [mɔnɔlɛ̃g] ADJ monolingual

monolithe [mɔnɔlit] NM monolith

monolithique [mɔnɔlitik] ADJ *(lit, fig)* monolithic

monolithisme [mɔnɔlitism] NM monolithic nature

monologue [mɔnɔlɔg] NM monologue, soliloquy; **~ intérieur** stream of consciousness

monologuer [mɔnɔlɔge] /1/ VI to soliloquize

monôme [mɔnom] NM *(Math)* monomial; *(d'étudiants)* students' rag procession

mononucléose [mɔnɔnykleoz] NF *(Méd)*: **~ infectieuse** infectious mononucleosis, glandular fever *(BRIT)*

monoparental, e, -aux [mɔnɔpaʀɑ̃tal, -o] ADJ: **famille monoparentale** single-parent *ou* one-parent family

monophasé, e [mɔnɔfaze] ADJ single-phase *cpd*

monophonie [mɔnɔfɔni] NF monophony

monoplace [mɔnɔplas] ADJ, NMF single-seater, one-seater

monoplan [mɔnɔplɑ̃] NM monoplane

monopole [mɔnɔpɔl] NM monopoly

monopolisation [mɔnɔpɔlizasjɔ̃] NF monopolization

monopoliser [mɔnɔpɔlize] /1/ VT to monopolize

monopolistique [mɔnɔpɔlistik] ADJ monopolistic

monorail [mɔnɔʀaj] NM monorail; monorail train

monoski [mɔnɔski] NM monoski

monosyllabe [mɔnɔsilab] NM monosyllable, word of one syllable

monosyllabique [mɔnɔsilabik] ADJ monosyllabic

monothéisme [mɔnɔteism] NM monotheism

monothéiste [mɔnɔteist] ADJ monotheist

monotone [mɔnɔtɔn] ADJ monotonous

monotonie [mɔnɔtɔni] NF monotony

monoxyde [mɔnɔksid] NM monoxide; **~ de carbone** carbon monoxide

monseigneur [mɔ̃sɛɲœʀ] NM *(archevêque, évêque)* Your *(ou* His) Grace; *(cardinal)* Your *(ou* His) Eminence; **M~ Thomas** Bishop Thomas; Cardinal Thomas

★**Monsieur** [məsjø] *(pl* **Messieurs** [mesjø]) NM *(titre)* Mr; **un/le monsieur** *(homme quelconque)* a/the gentleman; **~, ...** *(en tête de lettre)* Dear Sir, ...; *voir aussi* **Madame**

★**monstre** [mɔ̃stʀ] NM monster; **~ sacré** superstar ▶ ADJ *(fam: effet, publicité)* massive; **un travail ~** a fantastic amount of work; an enormous job

monstrueux, -euse [mɔ̃stʀyø, -øz] ADJ monstrous

monstruosité [mɔ̃stʀyozite] NF monstrosity

mont [mɔ̃] NM: **par monts et par vaux** up hill and down dale; **le M~ Blanc** Mont Blanc; **~ de Vénus** mons veneris

montage [mɔ̃taʒ] NM putting up; *(d'un bijou)* mounting, setting; *(d'une machine etc)* assembly; *(Photo)* photomontage; *(Ciné)* editing; **~ sonore** sound editing

montagnard, e [mɔ̃taɲaʀ, -aʀd] ADJ mountain *cpd* ▶ NM/F mountain-dweller

★**montagne** [mɔ̃taɲ] NF *(cime)* mountain; *(région)*: **la ~** the mountains *pl*; **la haute ~** the high mountains; **les montagnes Rocheuses** the Rocky Mountains, the Rockies; **montagnes russes** big dipper *sg*, switchback *sg*

montagneux, -euse [mɔ̃taɲø, -øz] ADJ mountainous; *(basse montagne)* hilly

montant, e [mɔ̃tɑ̃, -ɑ̃t] ADJ *(mouvement, marée)* rising; *(chemin)* uphill; *(robe, corsage)* high-necked ▶ NM *(somme, total)* (sum) total, (total) amount; *(de fenêtre)* upright; *(de lit)* post

mont-de-piété [mɔ̃dpjete] *(pl* **monts-de-piété)** NM pawnshop

monte [mɔ̃t] NF *(accouplement)*: **la ~** stud; *(d'un jockey)* seat

monté, e [mɔ̃te] ADJ: **être ~ contre qn** to be angry with sb; *(fourni, équipé)* **~ en** equipped with

monte-charge [mɔ̃tʃaʀʒ] NM INV goods lift, hoist

montée [mɔ̃te] NF rising, rise; *(escalade)* ascent, climb; *(chemin)* way up; *(côte)* hill; **au milieu de la ~** halfway up; **le moteur chauffe dans les montées** the engine overheats going uphill

Monténégro [mɔ̃tenegʀo] NM: **le ~** Montenegro

monte-plats [mɔ̃tpla] NM INV service lift

★**monter** [mɔ̃te] /1/ VT *(escalier, côte)* to go *(ou* come) up; *(valise, paquet)* to take *(ou* bring) up; *(cheval)* to mount; *(femelle)* to cover, serve; *(étagère)* to raise; *(tente, échafaudage)* to put up; *(machine)* to assemble; *(bijou)* to mount, set; *(Couture)* to sew on; *(: manche)* to set in; *(Ciné)* to edit; *(Théât)* to put on,

m

289

stage; (société, coup etc) to set up; (fournir, équiper) to
equip; ~ qn contre qn to set sb against sb; ~ la
tête à qn to give sb ideas ▶ vi to go (ou come) up;
(avion, voiture) to climb, go up; (chemin, niveau, température, voix, prix) to go up, rise; (brouillard, bruit) to
rise, come up; (passager) to get on; (à cheval):
bien/mal to ride well/badly; ~ à cheval to get on
ou mount a horse; (faire du cheval) to ride (a horse);
~ à bicyclette to get on ou mount a bicycle; (faire
du vélo) to (ride a) bicycle; ~ à pied/en voiture to
walk/ drive up, go up on foot/by car; ~ dans le
train/l'avion to get into the train/plane, board
the train/plane; ~ sur to climb up onto; ~ sur ou à
un arbre/une échelle to climb (up) a tree/ladder;
~ à bord to (get on) board; ~ à la tête de qn to go to
sb's head; ~ sur les planches to go on the stage; ~
en grade to be promoted ■ se monter VPR (s'équiper) to equip o.s., get kitted out (BRIT); se ~ à (frais
etc) to add up to, come to

monteur, -euse [mɔ̃tœʀ, -øz] NM/F (Tech) fitter;
(Ciné) (film) editor

montgolfière [mɔ̃gɔlfjɛʀ] NF hot-air balloon

monticule [mɔ̃tikyl] NM mound

montmartrois, e [mɔ̃maʀtʀwa, -waz] ADJ ou
from Montmartre

★**montre** [mɔ̃tʀ] NF watch; (ostentation): pour la ~
for show; ~ en main exactly, to the minute; faire
~ de to show, display; contre la ~ (Sport) against
the clock; ~ de plongée diver's watch

Montréal [mɔ̃real] N Montreal

montréalais, e [mɔ̃reale, -ɛz] ADJ of ou from
Montreal ▶ NM/F: **Montréalais, e** Montrealer

montre-bracelet [mɔ̃tʀəbʀaslɛ] (pl montres-
bracelets) NF wrist watch

★**montrer** [mɔ̃tʀe] /1/ VT to show; ~ qch à qn to
show sb sth; ~ qch du doigt to point to sth, point
one's finger at sth ■ se montrer VPR to appear; se
~ intelligent to prove (to be) intelligent

montreur, -euse [mɔ̃tʀœʀ,-øz] NM/F: ~ de marion-
nettes puppeteer

monture [mɔ̃tyʀ] NF (bête) mount; (d'une bague)
setting; (de lunettes) frame

★**monument** [mɔnymɑ̃] NM monument; ~ aux
morts war memorial

monumental, e, -aux [mɔnymɑ̃tal, -o] ADJ
monumental

mooc [muk] NM (= massive online open course) MOOC

moquer [mɔke] /1/: se moquer VPR: se ~ de to
make fun of, laugh at; (se désintéresser de) not to
care about; (tromper) se ~ de qn to take sb for a ride

moquerie [mɔkʀi] NF mockery no pl

★**moquette** [mɔkɛt] NF fitted carpet, wall-to-wall
carpeting no pl

moquetter [mɔkete] /1/ VT to carpet

moqueur, -euse [mɔkœʀ, -øz] ADJ mocking

moraine [mɔʀɛn] NF moraine

★**moral, e, -aux** [mɔʀal, -o] ADJ moral; sur le plan ~
morally ▶ NM morale; avoir le ~ (fam) to be in
good spirits; avoir le ~ à zéro to be really down
▶ NF (conduite) morals pl (règles), moral code, ethic;
(valeurs) moral standards pl, morality; (science)
ethics sg, moral philosophy; (conclusion: d'une
fable) moral; contraire à la morale immoral;
faire la morale à to lecture, preach at

moralement [mɔʀalmɑ̃] ADV morally

moralisateur, -trice [mɔʀalizatœʀ, -tʀis] ADJ
moralizing, sanctimonious ▶ NM/F moralizer

moraliser [mɔʀalize] /1/ VT (sermonner) to lecture,
preach at

moraliste [mɔʀalist] NMF moralist ▶ ADJ moralis-
tic

moralité [mɔʀalite] NF (d'une action, attitude)
morality; (conduite) morals pl; (conclusion, enseignement) moral

moratoire [mɔʀatwaʀ] ADJ M: intérêts mora-
toires (Écon) interest on arrears

morbide [mɔʀbid] ADJ morbid

morbidité [mɔʀbidite] NF (Méd) morbidity; taux
de ~ morbidity rate

★**morceau, x** [mɔʀso] NM piece, bit; (d'une œuvre)
passage, extract; (Mus) piece; (Culin: de viande) cut;
(: de sucre) lump; mettre en morceaux to pull
to pieces ou bits; manger un ~ to have a bite (to
eat)

morceler [mɔʀsəle] /4/ VT to break up, divide up

morcellement [mɔʀsɛlmɑ̃] NM breaking up

mordant, e [mɔʀdɑ̃, -ɑ̃t] ADJ (ton, remarque) scathing, cutting; (froid) biting ▶ NM (dynamisme, énergie) spirit; (fougue) bite, punch

mordicus [mɔʀdikys] ADV (fam) obstinately, stubbornly

mordiller [mɔʀdije] /1/ VT to nibble at, chew at

mordoré, e [mɔʀdɔʀe] ADJ lustrous bronze

★**mordre** [mɔʀdʀ] /41/ VT to bite; (lime, vis) to bite
into ▶ vi (poisson) to bite; ~ dans to bite into; ~ sur
(fig) to go over into, overlap into; ~ à qch (comprendre, aimer) to take to; ~ à l'hameçon to bite, rise to
the bait

mordu, e [mɔʀdy] PP de mordre ▶ ADJ (amoureux)
smitten ▶ NM/F enthusiast; un ~ de jazz/de voile
a jazz/sailing fanatic ou buff

morfal, e [mɔʀfal] NM/F (fam) greedy guts (fam)

morfler [mɔʀfle] VI (fam) to get it (fam), catch it
(fam)

morfondre [mɔʀfɔ̃dʀ] /41/: se morfondre VPR to
mope

morgue [mɔʀg] NF (arrogance) haughtiness; (lieu:
de la police) morgue; (: à l'hôpital) mortuary

moribond, e [mɔʀibɔ̃, -ɔ̃d] ADJ dying, moribund

morille [mɔʀij] NF morel (mushroom)

mormon, e [mɔʀmɔ̃, -ɔn] ADJ, NM/F Mormon

morne [mɔʀn] ADJ (personne, visage) glum, gloomy;
(temps, vie) dismal, dreary

morose [mɔʀoz] ADJ sullen, morose; (marché)
sluggish

morosité [mɔʀozite] NF (de personne) sullenness;
(d'économie, marché) sluggishness

morphine [mɔʀfin] NF morphine

morphinomane [mɔʀfinɔman] NMF morphine
addict

morphologie [mɔʀfɔlɔʒi] NF morphology

morphologique [mɔʀfɔlɔʒik] ADJ morphologi-
cal

mors [mɔʀ] NM bit

morse [mɔʀs] NM (Zool) walrus; (Tél) Morse (code)

morsure [mɔʀsyʀ] NF bite

★**mort**[1] [mɔʀ] NF death; **se donner la ~** to take one's own life; **de ~** (*silence, pâleur*) deathly; **blessé à ~** fatally wounded *ou* injured; **à la vie, à la ~** for better, for worse; **~ clinique** brain death; **~ subite du nourrisson, ~ au berceau** cot death

mort[2], **e** [mɔʀ, mɔʀt] PP *de* **mourir** ▶ ADJ dead; **~ ou vif** dead or alive; **~ de peur/fatigue** frightened to death/dead tired ▶ NM/F (*défunt*) dead man/woman; (*victime*): **il y a eu plusieurs morts** several people were killed, there were several killed; **morts et blessés** casualties ▶ NM (*Cartes*) dummy; **faire le ~** to play dead; (*fig*) to lie low

mortadelle [mɔʀtadɛl] NF mortadella

mortaise [mɔʀtɛz] NF mortise

mortalité [mɔʀtalite] NF mortality, death rate

mort-aux-rats [mɔʀ(t)oʀa] NF INV rat poison

mortel, le [mɔʀtɛl] ADJ (*poison etc*) deadly, lethal; (*accident, blessure*) fatal; (*silence, ennemi*) deadly; (*Rel: danger, frayeur, péché*) mortal; (*fig: froid*) deathly; (: *ennui, soirée*) deadly (boring) ▶ NM/F mortal

mortellement [mɔʀtɛlmɑ̃] ADV (*blessé etc*) fatally, mortally; (*pâle etc*) deathly; (*fig: ennuyeux etc*) deadly

morte-saison [mɔʀt(ə)sɛzɔ̃] (*pl* **mortes-saisons**) NF slack *ou* off season

mortier [mɔʀtje] NM (*gén*) mortar

mortifier [mɔʀtifje] /7/ VT to mortify

mort-né, e [mɔʀne] ADJ (*enfant*) stillborn; (*fig*) abortive

mortuaire [mɔʀtɥɛʀ] ADJ funeral *cpd*; **avis mortuaires** death announcements, intimations; **chapelle ~** mortuary chapel; **couronne ~** (funeral) wreath; **domicile ~** house of the deceased; **drap ~** pall

morue [mɔʀy] NF (*Zool*) cod *inv*; (*Culin: salée*) salt-cod

morvandeau, -elle, x [mɔʀvɑ̃do, -ɛl] ADJ of *ou* from the Morvan region

morve [mɔʀv] NF (*fam*) snot (*fam*)

morveux, -euse [mɔʀvø, -øz] ADJ (*fam*) snotty-nosed

mosaïque [mɔzaik] NF (*Art*) mosaic; (*fig*) patchwork

Moscou [mɔsku] N Moscow

moscovite [mɔskɔvit] ADJ *ou* from Moscow, Moscow *cpd* ▶ NMF: **Moscovite** Muscovite

mosquée [mɔske] NF mosque

★**mot** [mo] NM word; (*message*) line, note; (*bon mot etc*) saying; **le ~ de la fin** the last word; **~ à ~** *adj, adv* word for word; **~ pour ~** word for word, verbatim; **sur** *ou* **à ces mots** with these words; **en un ~** in a word; **à mots couverts** in veiled terms; **prendre qn au ~** to take sb at his word; **se donner le ~** to send the word round; **avoir son ~ à dire** to have a say; **~ d'ordre** watchword; **~ de passe** password; **mots croisés** crossword (puzzle) *sg*

motard, e [mɔtaʀ, -aʀd] NM/F biker; (*policier*) motorcycle cop

mot-dièse [modjɛz] NM (*Inform: Twitter*) hashtag

motel [mɔtɛl] NM motel

★**moteur, -trice** [mɔtœʀ, -tʀis] ADJ (*Anat, Physiol*) motor; (*Tech*) driving; (*Auto*): **à 4 roues motrices** 4-wheel drive ▶ NM engine, motor; (*fig*) mover, mainspring; **à ~** power-driven, motor *cpd*; **~ (à)**

deux temps two-stroke engine; **~ à explosion** internal combustion engine; **~ à réaction** jet engine; **~ de recherche** search engine; **~ thermique** combustion engine

motif [mɔtif] NM (*cause*) motive; (*décoratif*) design, pattern, motif; (*d'un tableau*) subject, motif; (*Mus*) figure, motif; **sans ~** *adj* groundless ■ **motifs** NMPL (*Jur*) grounds *pl*

motion [mosjɔ̃] NF motion; **~ de censure** motion of censure, vote of no confidence

motivant, e [mɔtivɑ̃, -ɑ̃t] ADJ (*salaire*) attractive; (*travail*) rewarding

motivation [mɔtivasjɔ̃] NF motivation

motivé, e [mɔtive] ADJ (*acte*) justified; (*personne*) motivated

motiver [mɔtive] /1/ VT (*justifier*) to justify, account for; (*Admin, Jur, Psych*) to motivate

★**moto** [moto] NF (*motor*)bike; **~ verte** *ou* **de trial** trail (BRIT) *ou* dirt (US) bike

moto-cross [mɔtɔkʀɔs] NM motocross

motoculteur [mɔtɔkyltœʀ] NM (motorized) cultivator

motocyclette [mɔtɔsiklɛt] NF motorbike, motorcycle

motocyclisme [mɔtɔsiklism] NM motorcycle racing

motocycliste [mɔtɔsiklist] NMF motorcyclist

motoneige [mɔtɔnɛʒ] NF snow bike

motorisé, e [mɔtɔʀize] ADJ (*troupe*) motorized; (*personne*) having one's own transport

motrice [mɔtʀis] ADJ F *voir* **moteur**

motricité [mɔtʀisite] NF motivity

motte [mɔt] NF: **~ de terre** lump of earth, clod (of earth); **~ de gazon** turf, sod; **~ de beurre** lump of butter

motus [mɔtys] EXCL: **~ (et bouche cousue)!** mum's the word!

mou, mol, molle [mu, mɔl] ADJ soft; (*péj: visage, traits*) flabby; (: *geste*) limp; (: *personne*) weak; (: *résistance, protestations*) feeble; **avoir les jambes molles** to be weak at the knees ▶ NM (*homme mou*) wimp; (*abats*) lights *pl*, lungs *pl*; (*de la corde*): **avoir du ~** to be slack; **donner du ~ à qch** to slacken sth, loosen sth

moucharabieh [muʃaʀabje] NM wooden lattice, moucharaby

mouchard, e [muʃaʀ, -aʀd] NM/F (*péj: Scol*) sneak; (: *Police*) stool pigeon, grass (BRIT) ▶ NM (*appareil*) control device; (: *de camion*) tachograph

moucharder [muʃaʀde] VI (*fam*) to inform, grass (*fam*), squeal (*fam*)

★**mouche** [muʃ] NF fly; (*Escrime*) button; (*de taffetas*) patch; **prendre la ~** to go into a huff; **faire ~** to score a bull's-eye

moucher [muʃe] /1/ VT (*enfant*) to blow the nose of; (*chandelle*) to snuff (out) ■ **se moucher** VPR to blow one's nose

moucheron [muʃʀɔ̃] NM midge

moucheté, e [muʃ(ə)te] ADJ (*cheval*) dappled; (*laine*) flecked; (*Escrime*) buttoned

★**mouchoir** [muʃwaʀ] NM handkerchief, hanky; **~ en papier** tissue, paper hanky

moudre [mudʀ] /47/ VT to grind

m

moue [mu] NF pout; **faire la ~** to pout; (*fig*) to pull a face

mouette [mwɛt] NF (sea)gull

moufette, mouffette [mufɛt] NF skunk

moufle [mufl] NF (*gant*) mitt(en); (*Tech*) pulley block

mouflet [muflɛ] NM (*fam*) kid (*fam*)

mouflon [mufl5] NM mouf(f)lon

moufter [mufte] VI (*fam*): **ne pas ~** to keep one's mouth shut; **il n'a pas moufté quand le principal est venu lui parler en personne** he kept his mouth shut when the headmaster came to speak to him in person; **sans ~** (*accepter, obéir*) without batting an eyelid

mouillage [mujaʒ] NM (*Navig: lieu*) anchorage, moorings pl

mouillé, e [muje] ADJ wet

mouiller [muje] /1/ VT (*humecter*) to wet, moisten; (*tremper*): **~ qn/qch** to make sb/sth wet; (*Culin: ragoût*) to add stock *ou* wine to; (*couper, diluer*) to water down; (*mine etc*) to lay; **~ l'ancre** to drop *ou* cast anchor ▶ VI (*Navig*) to lie *ou* be at anchor ■ **se mouiller** VPR to get wet; (*fam: prendre des risques*) to commit o.s; to get (o.s.) involved

mouillette [mujɛt] NF (bread) finger

mouillure [mujyʀ] NF wet *no pl*; (*tache*) wet patch

mouise [mwiz] NF (*fam*): **être dans la ~** to be up the creek (*fam*); (*financièrement*) to be stony broke (*fam*); **c'est la ~** it's a bugger (*fam*)

moulage [mulaʒ] NM moulding (BRIT), molding (US); casting; (*objet*) cast

moulais *etc* [mule] VB *voir* **moudre**

moulant, e [mulɑ̃, -ɑ̃t] ADJ figure-hugging

★**moule** [mul] VB *voir* **moudre** ▶ NF (*mollusque*) mussel ▶ NM (*creux, Culin*) mould (BRIT), mold (US); (*modèle plein*) cast; **~ à gâteau** cake tin (BRIT) *ou* pan (US); **~ à gaufre** waffle iron; **~ à tarte** pie *ou* flan dish

moulent [mul] VB *voir* **moudre**; **mouler**

mouler [mule] /1/ VT (*brique*) to mould (BRIT), mold (US); (*statue*) to cast; (*visage, bas-relief*) to make a cast of; (*lettre*) to shape with care; (*vêtement*) to hug, fit closely round; **~ qch sur** (*fig*) to model sth on

moulin [mulɛ̃] NM mill; (*fam*) engine; **~ à café** coffee mill; **~ à eau** watermill; **~ à légumes** (vegetable) shredder; **~ à paroles** (*fig*) chatterbox; **~ à poivre** pepper mill; **~ à prières** prayer wheel; **~ à vent** windmill

mouliner [muline] /1/ VT to shred

moulinet [mulinɛ] NM (*de treuil*) winch; (*de canne à pêche*) reel; (*mouvement*): **faire des moulinets avec qch** to whirl sth around

moulinette® [mulinɛt] NF (vegetable) shredder

moulons *etc* [mul5] VB *voir* **moudre**

moulu, e [muly] PP *de* **moudre** ▶ ADJ (*café*) ground

moulure [mulyʀ] NF (*ornement*) moulding (BRIT), molding (US)

moumoute [mumut] NF (*fam: perruque*) wig

mourant, e [muʀɑ̃, -ɑ̃t] VB *voir* **mourir** ▶ ADJ dying ▶ NM/F dying man/woman

★**mourir** [muʀiʀ] /1/ VI to die; (*civilisation*) to die out; **~ assassiné** to be murdered; **~ de froid/faim/**

vieillesse to die of exposure/hunger/old age; **~ de faim/d'ennui** (*fig*) to be starving/be bored to death; **~ d'envie de faire** to be dying to do; **s'ennuyer à ~** to be bored to death

mouroir [muʀwaʀ] NM (*péj*) place where people are left to die

mouron [muʀ5] NM: **se faire du ~** (*fam*) to worry, fret

mousquetaire [muskətɛʀ] NM musketeer

mousqueton [muskət5] NM (*fusil*) carbine; (*anneau*) snap-link, karabiner

moussant, e [musɑ̃, -ɑ̃t] ADJ foaming; **bain ~** foam *ou* bubble bath, bath foam

mousse [mus] NF (*Bot*) moss; (*de savon*) lather; (*écume: sur eau, bière*) froth, foam; (: *shampooing*) lather; (*de champagne*) bubbles pl; (*Culin*) mousse; (*en caoutchouc etc*) foam; **bain (de) ~** bubble bath; **bas ~** stretch stockings; **balle ~** foam ball; **~ carbonique** (fire-fighting) foam; **~ de nylon** nylon foam; (*tissu*) stretch nylon; **~ à raser** shaving foam ▶ NM (*Navig*) ship's boy

mousseline [muslin] NF (*Textiles*) muslin; chiffon; **pommes ~** (*Culin*) creamed potatoes

mousser [muse] /1/ VI (*bière, détergent*) to foam; (*savon*) to lather

mousseron [musʀ5] NM St. George's Mushroom

mousseux, -euse [musø, -øz] ADJ (*chocolat*) frothy; (*eau*) foamy, frothy; (*vin*) sparkling ▶ NM: **(vin) ~** sparkling wine

mousson [mus5] NM monsoon

moussu, e [musy] ADJ mossy

★**moustache** [mustaʃ] NF moustache ■ **moustaches** NFPL (*d'animal*) whiskers pl

moustachu, e [mustaʃy] ADJ with a moustache

moustiquaire [mustikɛʀ] NF (*rideau*) mosquito net; (*chassis*) mosquito screen

★**moustique** [mustik] NM mosquito; **~ tigre** tiger mosquito

moût [mu] NM (*de vin*) must; (*de bière*) wort

★**moutarde** [mutaʀd] NF mustard ▶ ADJ INV mustard(-coloured)

moutardier [mutaʀdje] NM mustard jar

★**mouton** [mut5] NM (*Zool, péj*) sheep inv; (*peau*) sheepskin; (*Culin*) mutton

mouture [mutyʀ] NF grinding; (*péj*) rehash

mouvance [muvɑ̃s] NF movements pl

mouvant, e [muvɑ̃, -ɑ̃t] ADJ unsettled; changing; shifting

★**mouvement** [muvmɑ̃] NM (*gén, aussi: mécanisme*) movement; (*ligne courbe*) contours pl; (*fig: tumulte, agitation*) activity, bustle; (: *impulsion*) impulse; reaction; (*geste*) gesture; (*Mus: rythme*) tempo; **en ~** in motion; on the move; **mettre qch en ~** to set sth in motion, set sth going; **~ d'humeur** fit *ou* burst of temper; **~ d'opinion** trend of (public) opinion; **le ~ perpétuel** perpetual motion

mouvementé, e [muvmɑ̃te] ADJ (*vie, poursuite*) eventful; (*réunion*) turbulent

mouvoir [muvwaʀ] /27/ VT (*levier, membre*) to move; (*machine*) to drive ■ **se mouvoir** VPR to move

★**moyen, ne** [mwajɛ̃, -ɛn] ADJ average; (*tailles, prix*) medium; (*de grandeur moyenne*) medium-sized; **très ~** (*résultats*) pretty poor; **M~ Âge** Middle Ages;

moyenne entreprise (*Comm*) medium-sized firm ▸ NM (*façon*) means *sg*, way; **au ~ de** by means of; **y a-t-il ~ de …?** is it possible to …?; **can one …?; par quel ~?** how?, which way?, by which means?; **par tous les moyens** by every possible means, every possible way; **~ de locomotion/d'expression** means of transport/expression; **~ de transport** means of transport ▸ NF average; (*Statistique*) mean; (*Scol: à l'examen*) pass mark; (*Auto*) average speed; **en moyenne** on (an) average; **faire la moyenne** to work out the average; **moyenne d'âge** average age; **faire la moyenne** to work out the average; **au-dessus de la moyenne** (*résultats*) above-average; **être au-dessus de la moyenne** to be above average ▪ **moyens** NMPL (*capacités*) means; **je n'en ai pas les moyens** I can't afford it; **avec les moyens du bord** (*fig*) with what's available *ou* what comes to hand; **employer les grands moyens** to resort to drastic measures; **par ses propres moyens** all by oneself

moyenâgeux, -euse [mwajɛnaʒø, -øz] ADJ medieval

moyen-courrier [mwajɛ̃kurje] NM (*Aviat*) medium-haul aircraft

moyennant [mwajɛnɑ̃] PRÉP (*somme*) for; (*service, conditions*) in return for; (*travail, effort*) with

moyennement [mwajɛnmɑ̃] ADV fairly, moderately; **il a ~ réussi** he did fairly *ou* moderately well

Moyen-Orient [mwajɛnɔrjɑ̃] NM: **le ~** the Middle East

moyeu, x [mwajø] NM hub

mozambicain, e [mɔzɑ̃bikɛ̃, -ɛn] ADJ Mozambican

Mozambique [mɔzɑ̃bik] NM: **le ~** Mozambique

MRAP SIGLE M (= *Mouvement contre le racisme et pour l'amitié entre les peuples*) anti-racism organization

ms ABR (= *manuscrit*) MS., ms

MSF SIGLE MPL (= *Médecins sans frontières*) medical aid charity

MST SIGLE F (= *maladie sexuellement transmissible*) STD (= *sexually transmitted disease*)

mû, mue [my] PP *de* **mouvoir**

mucosité [mykozite] NF mucus *no pl*

mucoviscidose [mykovisidoz] NF cystic fibrosis

mucus [mykys] NM mucus *no pl*

mue [my] PP *de* **mouvoir** ▸ NF moulting (BRIT), molting (US); sloughing; breaking of the voice

muer [mɥe] /**1**/ VI (*oiseau, mammifère*) to moult (BRIT), molt (US); (*serpent*) to slough (its skin); (*jeune garçon*): **il mue** his voice is breaking ▪ **se muer** VPR: **se ~ en** to transform into

muet, te [mɥɛ, -ɛt] ADJ with a speech impairment; (*fig*): **~ d'admiration** *etc* speechless with admiration *etc*; (*joie, douleur, Ciné*) silent; (*Ling: lettre*) silent, mute; (*carte*) blank ▸ NM: **le ~** (*Ciné*) the silent cinema *ou* (*esp US*) movies

mufle [myfl] NM muzzle; (*goujat*) boor ▸ ADJ boorish

muflerie [myfləri] NF boorishness

mugir [myʒir] /**2**/ VI (*bœuf*) to bellow; (*vache*) to low, moo; (*fig*) to howl

mugissement [myʒismɑ̃] NM (*voir mugir*) bellowing; lowing, mooing; howling

muguet [mygɛ] NM (*Bot*) lily of the valley; (*Méd*) thrush

mulâtre, -tresse [mylɑtr, -trɛs] NM/F mulatto (!)

mule [myl] NF (*Zool*) (she-)mule

mules [myl] NFPL (*pantoufles*) mules

mulet [mylɛ] NM (*Zool*) (he-)mule; (*poisson*) mullet

muletier, -ière [myl(ə)tje, -jɛr] ADJ: **sentier** *ou* **chemin ~** mule track

mulot [mylo] NM fieldmouse

multicarte [myltikart] ADJ: **VRP ~** rep acting for several firms

multicolore [myltikɔlɔr] ADJ multicoloured (BRIT), multicolored (US)

multicoque [myltikɔk] NM multihull

multiculturel, le [myltikyltyrɛl] ADJ multicultural

multidisciplinaire [myltidisiplinɛr] ADJ multidisciplinary

multiforme [myltifɔrm] ADJ many-sided

multilatéral, e, -aux [myltilateral, -o] ADJ multilateral

multimédia [myltimedja] ADJ (*produits, encyclopédie*) multimedia ▸ NM: **le ~** multimedia

multimilliardaire [myltimiljardɛr], **multimillionnaire** [myltimiljɔnɛr] ADJ, NMF multimillionaire

multinational, e, -aux [myltinasjɔnal, -o] ADJ, NF multinational

multiple [myltipl] ADJ multiple, numerous; (*varié*) many, manifold ▸ NM (*Math*) multiple

multiplex [myltiplɛks] NM (*Radio*) live link-up

multiplicateur [myltiplikatœr] NM multiplier

multiplication [myltiplikasjɔ̃] NF multiplication

multiplicité [myltiplisite] NF multiplicity

multiplier [myltiplije] /**7**/ VT to multiply ▪ **se multiplier** VPR to multiply; (*fig: personne*) to be everywhere at once

multiprogrammation [myltiprɔgramasjɔ̃] NF (*Inform*) multiprogramming

multipropriété [myltiprɔprijete] NF timesharing *no pl*

multirécidiviste [myltiresidivist] ADJ: **délinquant ~** persistent offender ▸ NM/F persistent offender

multirisque [myltirisk] ADJ: **assurance ~** multiple-risk insurance

multisalles [myltisal] ADJ INV: **(cinéma) ~** multiplex (cinema)

multitâche [myltitaʃ] ADJ (*aussi Inform*) multitasking; **être ~** to multitask

multitraitement [myltitrɛtmɑ̃] NM (*Inform*) multiprocessing

multitude [myltityd] NF multitude; mass; **une ~ de** a vast number of, a multitude of

Munich [mynik] N Munich

munichois, e [mynikwa, -waz] ADJ *ou* from Munich

municipal, e, -aux [mynisipal, -o] ADJ (*élections, stade*) municipal; (*conseil*) town cpd; **piscine/bibliothèque municipale** public swimming pool/library

m

municipalité [mynisipalite] NF (*corps municipal*) town council, corporation; (*commune*) town, municipality

munificence [mynifisɑ̃s] NF munificence

munir [myniʀ] /2/ VT: ~ **qn/qch de** to equip sb/sth with ■ **se munir** VPR: **se ~ de** to provide o.s. with

munitions [mynisjɔ̃] NFPL ammunition *sg*

muqueuse [mykøz] NF mucous membrane

★**mur** [myʀ] NM wall; (*fig*) stone *ou* brick wall; **faire le ~** (*interne, soldat*) to jump the wall; ~ **(payant)** (*Inform*) paywall; ~ **du son** sound barrier

★**mûr, e** [myʀ] ADJ ripe; (*personne*) mature ▶ NF (*de la ronce*) blackberry; (*du mûrier*) mulberry

muraille [myʀɑj] NF (high) wall

mural, e, -aux [myʀal, -o] ADJ wall *cpd* ▶ NM (*Art*) mural

mûre [myʀ] NF blackberry

mûrement [myʀmɑ̃] ADV: **ayant ~ réfléchi** having given the matter much thought

murène [myʀɛn] NF moray (eel)

murer [myʀe] /1/ VT (*enclos*) to wall (in); (*porte, issue*) to wall up; (*personne*) to wall up *ou* in ■ **se murer** VPR: **se ~ dans le silence** to retreat into silence

muret [myʀɛ] NM low wall

mûrier [myʀje] NM mulberry tree; (*ronce*) blackberry bush

mûrir [myʀiʀ] /2/ VI (*fruit, blé*) to ripen; (*abcès, furoncle*) to come to a head; (*fig: idée, personne*) to mature; (*projet*) to develop ▶ VT (*fruit, blé*) to ripen; (*personne*) to (make) mature; (*pensée, projet*) to nurture

murmure [myʀmyʀ] NM murmur ■ **murmures** NMPL (*plaintes*) murmurings, mutterings

murmurer [myʀmyʀe] /1/ VI to murmur; (*se plaindre*) to mutter, grumble

mus *etc* [my] VB *voir* **mouvoir**

musaraigne [myzaʀɛɲ] NF shrew

musarder [myzaʀde] /1/ VI to idle (about); (*en marchant*) to dawdle (along)

musc [mysk] NM musk

muscade [myskad] NF (*aussi:* **noix (de) muscade**) nutmeg

muscat [myska] NM (*raisin*) muscat grape; (*vin*) muscatel (wine)

muscle [myskl] NM muscle

musclé, e [myskle] ADJ (*personne, corps*) muscular; (*fig: politique, régime etc*) strong-arm *cpd*

muscler [myskle] /1/ VT to develop the muscles of

musculaire [myskyleʀ] ADJ muscular

musculation [myskylasjɔ̃] NF: **exercices de ~** muscle-developing exercises

musculature [myskylatyʀ] NF muscle structure, muscles *pl*, musculature

muse [myz] NF muse

museau, x [myzo] NM muzzle; (*Culin*) brawn

musée [myze] NM museum; (*de peinture*) art gallery

museler [myz(ə)le] /4/ VT to muzzle

muselière [myzəljɛʀ] NF muzzle

musette [myzɛt] NF (*sac*) lunch bag ▶ ADJ INV (*orchestre etc*) accordion *cpd*

muséum [myzeɔm] NM museum

musical, e, -aux [myzikal, -o] ADJ musical

musicalement [myzikalmɑ̃] ADV musically

musicalité [myzikalite] NF (*de mot, vers*) musicality

music-hall [myzikol] NM (*salle*) variety theatre; (*genre*) variety

★**musicien, ne** [myzisjɛ̃, -ɛn] ADJ musical ▶ NM/F musician

musicologie [myzikɔlɔʒi] NF musicology

★**musique** [myzik] NF music; (*fanfare*) band; **faire de la ~** to make music; (*jouer d'un instrument*) to play an instrument; ~ **de chambre** chamber music; ~ **de fond** background music

musqué, e [myske] ADJ musky

must [mœst] NM must

★**musulman, e** [myzylmɑ̃, -an] ADJ, NM/F Moslem, Muslim

mutant, e [mytɑ̃, -ɑ̃t] NM/F mutant

mutation [mytasjɔ̃] NF (*Admin*) transfer; (*Bio*) mutation

muter [myte] /1/ VT (*Admin*) to transfer, move

mutilation [mytilasjɔ̃] NF mutilation

mutilé, e [mytile] NM/F person with a disability (*through loss of limbs*); ~ **de guerre** disabled ex-serviceman; **grand ~** person with a severe disability

mutiler [mytile] /1/ VT to mutilate, maim; (*fig*) to mutilate, deface

mutin, e [mytɛ̃, -in] ADJ (*enfant, air, ton*) mischievous, impish ▶ NM/F (*Mil, Navig*) mutineer

mutiner [mytine] /1/: **se mutiner** VPR to mutiny

mutinerie [mytinʀi] NF mutiny

mutisme [mytism] NM silence

mutualiste [mytɥalist] ADJ: **société ~** mutual benefit society, ≈ Friendly Society

mutualité [mytɥalite] NF (*assurance*) mutual (benefit) insurance scheme

mutuel, le [mytɥɛl] ADJ mutual ▶ NF mutual benefit society

Additional insurance covers most health care costs that are not covered by basic national health insurance. It is based on the principle of solidarity. The **mutuelles**, which individuals can choose freely, are becoming proportionally more important as the amounts reimbursed by national health insurance decline.

---

mutuellement [mytɥɛlmɑ̃] ADV each other, one another

Myanmar [mjanmaʀ] NM Myanmar

mycose [mikoz] NF mycosis, fungal infection

mygale [migal] NF tarantula

myocarde [mjɔkaʀd] NM *voir* **infarctus**

myopathe [mjɔpat] ADJ (*atteint de myopathie*) suffering from myopathy; (*atteint de myopathie primitive progressive*) suffering from muscular dystrophy ▶ NMF person suffering from muscular dystrophy

myopathie [mjɔpati] NF myopathy; (*aussi:* **myopathie primitive progressive**) muscular dystrophy

myope [mjɔp] ADJ short-sighted

myopie [mjɔpi] NF short-sightedness, myopia

myosotis [mjɔzɔtis] NM forget-me-not

myriade [miRjad] NF myriad

myrtille [miRtij] NF blueberry, bilberry (BRIT)

mystère [mistɛR] NM mystery

mystérieusement [misteRjøzmɑ̃] ADV mysteriously

mystérieux, -euse [misteRjø, -øz] ADJ mysterious

mysticisme [mistisism] NM mysticism

mystificateur, -trice [mistifikatœR, -tRis] NM/F hoaxer, practical joker

mystification [mistifikasjɔ̃] NF (tromperie, mensonge) hoax; (mythe) mystification

mystifier [mistifje] /7/ VT to fool, take in; (tromper) to mystify

mystique [mistik] ADJ mystic, mystical ▶ NMF mystic

mythe [mit] NM myth

mythifier [mitifje] /7/ VT to turn into a myth, mythologize

mythique [mitik] ADJ mythical

mythologie [mitɔlɔʒi] NF mythology

mythologique [mitɔlɔʒik] ADJ mythological

mythomane [mitɔman] ADJ, NMF mythomaniac

mythomanie [mitɔmani] NF mythomania

mytiliculture [mitilikyltyR] NF mussel farming

m

Nn

N, n [ɛn] NM INV N, n ▶ ABR (= *nord*) N; **N comme Nicolas** N for Nelly (BRIT) *ou* Nan (US)

n' [n] ADV *voir* **ne**

n° ABR (*numéro*) no

nabot [nabo] NM (*péj*) dwarf (!)

nacelle [nasɛl] NF (*de ballon*) basket

nacre [nakʀ] NF mother-of-pearl

nacré, e [nakʀe] ADJ pearly

nage [naʒ] NF swimming; (*manière*) style of swimming, stroke; **traverser/s'éloigner à la ~** to swim across/away; **en ~** bathed in sweat; **~ indienne** sidestroke; **~ libre** freestyle; **~ papillon** butterfly

nageoire [naʒwaʀ] NF fin

★**nager** [naʒe] /3/ VI to swim; (*fig: ne rien comprendre*) to be all at sea; **~ dans** to be swimming in; (*vêtements*) to be lost in; **~ dans le bonheur** to be overjoyed

nageur, -euse [naʒœʀ, -øz] NM/F swimmer

naguère [nagɛʀ] ADV (*il y a peu de temps*) not long ago; (*autrefois*) formerly

naïade [najad] NF naiad

naïf, -ïve [naif, naiv] ADJ naïve

nain, e [nɛ̃, nɛn] ADJ, NM/F (*péj*) person of small stature

Nairobi [naiʀɔbi] N Nairobi

nais [nɛ], **naissais** *etc* [nɛsɛ] VB *voir* **naître**

★**naissance** [nɛsɑ̃s] NF birth; **donner ~ à** to give birth to; (*fig*) to give rise to; **prendre ~** to originate; **aveugle de ~** born blind; **Français de ~** French by birth; **à la ~ des cheveux** at the roots of the hair; **lieu de ~** place of birth

naissant, e [nɛsɑ̃, -ɑ̃t] VB *voir* **naître** ▶ ADJ budding, incipient; (*jour*) dawning

naît [nɛ] VB *voir* **naître**

naître [nɛtʀ] /59/ VI to be born; (*conflit, complications*): **~ de** to arise from, be born out of; **~ à** (*amour, poésie*) to awaken to; **je suis né en 1960** I was born in 1960; **il naît plus de filles que de garçons** there are more girls born than boys; **faire ~** (*fig*) to give rise to, arouse

naïvement [naivmɑ̃] ADV naïvely

naïveté [naivte] NF naivety

Namibie [namibi] NF: **la ~** Namibia

nana [nana] NF (*fam: fille*) bird (BRIT), chick

nancéien, ne [nɑ̃sejɛ̃, -jɛn] ADJ from Nancy

nanisme [nanism] NM dwarfism

nanoparticule [nanopaʀtikyl] NF nanoparticle

nanosciences [nanosjɑ̃s] NFPL nanosciences

nanotechnologies [nanotɛknɔlɔʒi] NFPL nano-technologies

nantais, e [nɑ̃tɛ, -ɛz] ADJ of *ou* from Nantes

nantir [nɑ̃tiʀ] /2/ VT: **~ qn de** to provide sb with; **les nantis** (*péj*) the well-to-do

napalm [napalm] NM napalm

naphtaline [naftalin] NF: **boules de ~** mothballs

Naples [napl] N Naples

napolitain, e [napɔlitɛ̃, -ɛn] ADJ Neapolitan; **tranche napolitaine** Neapolitan ice cream

nappage [napaʒ] NM (*couche*) coating

nappe [nap] NF tablecloth; (*fig*) sheet; (*de pétrole, gaz*) layer; **~ de mazout** oil slick; **~ (phréatique)** water table

napper [nape] /1/ VT: **~ qch de** to coat sth with

napperon [napʀɔ̃] NM table-mat; **~ individuel** place mat

naquit [naki] VB *voir* **naître**

narcisse [naʀsis] NM narcissus

narcissique [naʀsisik] ADJ narcissistic

narcissisme [naʀsisism] NM narcissism

narcodollars [naʀkodɔlaʀ] NMPL drug money *no pl*

narcolepsie [naʀkɔlɛpsi] NF narcolepsy

narcotique [naʀkɔtik] ADJ, NM narcotic

narcotrafic [naʀkotʀafik] NM narco-trafficking

narcotrafiquant [naʀkotʀafikɑ̃] NM narco-trafficker

narguer [naʀge] /1/ VT to taunt

narine [naʀin] NF nostril

narquois, e [naʀkwa, -waz] ADJ derisive, mocking

narrateur, -trice [naʀatœʀ, -tʀis] NM/F narrator

narratif, -ive [naʀatif, -iv] ADJ narrative

narration [naʀasjɔ̃] NF narration, narrative; (*Scol*) essay

narrer [naʀe] /1/ VT to tell the story of, recount

narval [naʀval] NM narwhal

NASA [naza] SIGLE F (= *National Aeronautics and Space Administration*) NASA

nasal, e, -aux [nazal, -o] ADJ nasal

nase, naze [naz] ADJ (*fam*) knackered (*fam*)

naseau, x [nazo] NM nostril

nasillard, e [nazijaʀ, -aʀd] ADJ nasal

nasiller [nazije] /1/ VI to speak with a (nasal) twang

nasse [nas] NF fish-trap

natal, e [natal] ADJ native

nataliste [natalist] ADJ supporting a rising birth rate

natalité [natalite] NF birth rate

★**natation** [natasjɔ̃] NF swimming; **faire de la ~** to go swimming (*regularly*)

natif, -ive [natif, -iv] ADJ native ▸ NM/F: **~ numérique** digital native

nation [nasjɔ̃] NF nation; **les Nations unies (NU)** the United Nations (UN)

★**national, e, -aux** [nasjɔnal, -o] ADJ national; **obsèques nationales** state funeral ▸ NF: **(route) nationale** ≈ A road (BRIT), ≈ state highway (US)

nationalisation [nasjɔnalizasjɔ̃] NF nationalization

nationaliser [nasjɔnalize] /1/ VT to nationalize

nationalisme [nasjɔnalism] NM nationalism

nationaliste [nasjɔnalist] ADJ, NMF nationalist

nationalité [nasjɔnalite] NF nationality; **de ~ française** of French nationality

nativité [nativite] NF (*tableau, sculpture*) nativity scene

natte [nat] NF (*tapis*) mat; (*cheveux*) plait

natter [nate] /1/ VT (*cheveux*) to plait

naturalisation [natyralizasjɔ̃] NF naturalization

naturaliser [natyralize] /1/ VT to naturalize; (*empailler*) to stuff

naturalisme [natyralism] NM naturalism

naturaliste [natyralist] NMF naturalist; (*empailleur*) taxidermist

★**nature** [natyr] NF nature; **payer en ~** to pay in kind; **peint d'après ~** painted from life; **être de ~ à faire qch** (*propre à*) to be the sort of thing (*ou* person) to do sth; **~ morte** still-life ▸ ADJ (*Culin*) plain, without seasoning or sweetening; (*café, thé: sans lait*) black; (: *sans sucre*) without sugar; (*yaourt*) natural

★**naturel, le** [natyrɛl] ADJ natural ▸ NM naturalness; (*caractère*) disposition, nature; (*autochtone*) native; **au ~** (*Culin*) in water; in its own juices

naturellement [natyrɛlmɑ̃] ADV naturally; (*bien sûr*) of course

naturisme [natyrism] NM naturism

naturiste [natyrist] NMF naturist

naufrage [nofraʒ] NM (ship)wreck; (*fig*) wreck; **faire ~** to be shipwrecked

naufragé, e [nofraʒe] NM/F shipwreck victim, castaway

nauséabond, e [nozeabɔ̃, -ɔ̃d] ADJ foul, nauseous

nausée [noze] NF nausea; **avoir la ~** to feel sick; **avoir des nausées** to have waves of nausea, feel nauseous *ou* sick

nauséeux, -euse [noseø, øz] ADJ nauseous; **état ~** nausea

★**nautique** [notik] ADJ nautical, water *cpd*; **sports nautiques** water sports

nautisme [notism] NM water sports *pl*

naval, e [naval] ADJ naval; (*industrie*) shipbuilding

navarin [navarɛ̃] NM navarin, mutton stew

navarrais, e [navarɛ, -ɛz] ADJ Navarrese

navet [navɛ] NM turnip; (*péj: film*) third-rate film

navette [navɛt] NF shuttle; (*en car etc*) shuttle (service); **faire la ~ (entre)** to go to and fro (between), shuttle (between); **~ spatiale** space shuttle

navigabilité [navigabilite] NF (*d'un navire*) seaworthiness; (*d'un avion*) airworthiness

navigable [navigabl] ADJ navigable

navigant, e [navigɑ̃, -ɑ̃t] ADJ (*Aviat: personnel*) flying ▸ NM/F: **les navigants** the flying staff *ou* personnel

navigateur [navigatœr] NM (*Navig*) seafarer, sailor; (*Aviat*) navigator; (*Inform*) browser

navigation [navigasjɔ̃] NF navigation, sailing; (*Comm*) shipping; **compagnie de ~** shipping company; **~ spatiale** space navigation

naviguer [navige] /1/ VI to navigate, sail; **~ sur Internet** to browse the internet

navire [navir] NM ship; **~ de guerre** warship; **~ marchand** merchantman

navire-citerne [navirsitɛrn] (*pl* **navires-citernes**) NM tanker

navire-hôpital [navirɔpital] (*pl* **navires-hôpitaux** [-o]) NM hospital ship

navrant, e [navrɑ̃, -ɑ̃t] ADJ (*affligeant*) upsetting; (*consternant*) annoying

navré, e [navre] ADJ (*désolé: personne*) sorry; **l'air ~** (*annoncer, regarder*) unhappily; **je suis ~ de faire** I'm so sorry for doing; **je suis ~ que** (+ *subjonctif*) I'm so sorry that; **il était ~ de ce qu'il voyait** he was saddened by what he saw

navrer [navre] /1/ VT to upset, distress

nazaréen, ne [nazareɛ̃, -ɛn] ADJ Nazarene

Nazareth [nazarɛt] N Nazareth

nazi, e [nazi] ADJ Nazi ▸ NM/F Nazi

nazisme [nazism] NM Nazism

NB ABR (= *nota bene*) NB

nbr. ABR = **nombreux**

nbses ABR = **nombreuses**

ND SIGLE F = **Notre Dame**

NDA SIGLE F = **note de l'auteur**

NDE SIGLE F = **note de l'éditeur**

NDLR SIGLE F = **note de la rédaction**

NDT SIGLE F = **note du traducteur**

★**ne, n'** [nə, n] ADV *voir* **pas¹**; **plus²**; **jamais** *etc*; (*sans valeur négative: non traduit*): **c'est plus loin que je ne le croyais** it's further than I thought

★**né, e** [ne] PP *de* **naître** ▸ ADJ: **un comédien né** a born comedian; **né en 1960** born in 1960; **née Scott** née Scott; **né de ... et de ...** son/daughter of ... and of ...; **né d'une mère française** having a French mother; **né pour commander** born to lead

néanmoins [neɑ̃mwɛ̃] ADV nevertheless, yet

néant [neɑ̃] NM nothingness; **réduire à ~** to bring to nought; (*espoir*) to dash

nébuleux, -euse [nebylø, -øz] ADJ (*ciel*) cloudy; (*fig*) nebulous ▸ NF (*Astronomie*) nebula; (*fig*) complex web

nébuliser [nebylize] /1/ VT (*liquide*) to spray

nébulosité [nebylozite] NF cloud cover; **~ variable** cloudy in places

nécessaire [nesesɛr] ADJ necessary ▸ NM necessary; (*sac*) kit; **faire le ~** to do the necessary; **n'emporter que le strict ~** to take only what is strictly necessary; **~ de couture** sewing kit; **~ de toilette** toilet bag; **~ de voyage** overnight bag

nécessairement [nesesɛrmɑ̃] ADV necessarily

n

297

nécessité [nesesite] NF necessity; **se trouver dans la ~ de faire qch** to find it necessary to do sth; **par ~** out of necessity

nécessiter [nesesite] /1/ VT to require

nécessiteux, -euse [nesesitø, -øz] ADJ needy

nec plus ultra [nekplysyltra] NM: **le ~ de** the last word in

nécrologie [nekrɔlɔʒi] NF obituary

nécrologique [nekrɔlɔʒik] ADJ: **article ~** obituary; **rubrique ~** obituary column

nécromancie [nekrɔmɑ̃si] NF necromancy

nécromancien, ne [nekrɔmɑ̃sjɛ̃, -jɛn] NM/F necromancer

nécropole [nekrɔpɔl] NF necropolis

nécrose [nekroz] NF necrosis

nécrosé, e [nekroze] ADJ necrosed

nectar [nɛktar] NM nectar

nectarine [nɛktarin] NF nectarine

néerlandais, e [neɛrlɑ̃dɛ, -ɛz] ADJ Dutch, of the Netherlands ▶ NM (Ling) Dutch ▶ NM/F: **Néerlandais, e** Dutchman/-woman; **les N~** the Dutch

nef [nɛf] NF (d'église) nave

néfaste [nefast] ADJ (nuisible) harmful; (funeste) ill-fated

négatif, -ive [negatif, -iv] ADJ negative ▶ NM (Photo) negative

négation [negasjɔ̃] NF denial; (Ling) negation

négationnisme [negasjɔnism] NM negationism

négationniste [negasjɔnist] ADJ (auteur, ouvrage) negationist ▶ NMF negationist

négativement [negativmɑ̃] ADV: **répondre ~** to give a negative response

négligé, e [negliʒe] ADJ (en désordre) slovenly ▶ NM (tenue) negligee

négligeable [negliʒabl] ADJ insignificant, negligible

négligemment [negliʒamɑ̃] ADV carelessly

négligence [negliʒɑ̃s] NF carelessness no pl; (faute) careless omission

négligent, e [negliʒɑ̃, -ɑ̃t] ADJ careless; (Jur etc) negligent

négliger [negliʒe] /3/ VT (épouse, jardin) to neglect; (tenue) to be careless about; (avis, précautions) to disregard, overlook; **~ de faire** to fail to do, not bother to do ■ **se négliger** VPR to neglect o.s.

négoce [negɔs] NM trade

négociable [negɔsjabl] ADJ negotiable

négociant, e [negɔsjɑ̃, -jɑ̃t] NM/F merchant

négociateur [negɔsjatœr] NM negotiator

négociation [negɔsjasjɔ̃] NF negotiation; **négociations collectives** collective bargaining sg

négocier [negɔsje] /7/ VI, VT to negotiate

nègre [nɛgr] NM (péj) Negro (!); (péj: écrivain) ghost writer ▶ ADJ (péj) Negro (!)

négresse [negrɛs] NF (péj) Negress (!)

négrier [negrije] NM (fig) slave driver

négroïde [negrɔid] ADJ negroid

★**neige** [nɛʒ] NF snow; **battre les œufs en ~** (Culin) to whip ou beat the egg whites until stiff; **~ carbonique** dry ice; **~ fondue** (par terre) slush; (qui tombe) sleet; **~ poudreuse** powdery snow

★**neiger** [neʒe] /3/ VI to snow

neigeux, -euse [nɛʒø, -øz] ADJ snowy, snow-covered

nématode [nematɔd] NM nematode

nénuphar [nenyfar] NM water-lily

néo-calédonien, ne [neɔkaledɔnjɛ̃, -ɛn] ADJ New Caledonian ▶ NM/F: **Néo-calédonien, ne** New Caledonian

néocapitalisme [neokapitalism] NM neocapitalism

néoclassique [neoklasik] ADJ neoclassical, neoclassical

néocolonialisme [neokɔlɔnjalism] NM neocolonialism

néocolonialiste [neokɔlɔnjalist] ADJ neocolonial

néolithique [neɔlitik] ADJ, NM Neolithic

néologisme [neɔlɔʒism] NM neologism

néon [neɔ̃] NM neon

néonatal, e, néo-natal, e [neonatal] ADJ neonatal, neo-natal

néonazi, e [neonazi] ADJ, NM/F neo-Nazi

néophyte [neofit] NMF novice

néo-zélandais, e [neozelɑ̃dɛ, -ɛz] ADJ New Zealand cpd ▶ NM/F: **Néo-zélandais, e** New Zealander

Népal [nepal] NM: **le ~** Nepal

népalais, e [nepalɛ, -ɛz] ADJ Nepalese, Nepali ▶ NM (Ling) Nepalese, Nepali ▶ NM/F: **Népalais, e** Nepalese, Nepali

néphrétique [nefretik] ADJ (Méd: colique) nephritic

néphrite [nefrit] NF (Méd) nephritis

népotisme [nepɔtism] NM nepotism

nerf [nɛr] NM nerve; (fig) spirit; (: forces) stamina ■ **nerfs** NMPL nerves; **être** ou **vivre sur les nerfs** to live on one's nerves; **être à bout de nerfs** to be at the end of one's tether; **passer ses nerfs sur qn** to take it out on sb

nerveusement [nɛrvøzmɑ̃] ADV nervously

★**nerveux, -euse** [nɛrvø, -øz] ADJ nervous; (cheval) highly-strung; (irritable) touchy, nervy; (voiture) nippy, responsive; (tendineux) sinewy

nervosité [nɛrvozite] NF nervousness; (émotivité) excitability, tenseness

nervure [nɛrvyr] NF (de feuille) vein; (Archit, Tech) rib

n'est-ce pas [nɛspɑ] ADV isn't it?, won't you? etc (selon le verbe qui précède); **c'est bon, ~ ?** it's good, isn't it?; **il a peur, ~ ?** he's afraid, isn't he?; **~ que c'est bon?** don't you think it's good?; **lui, ~, il peut se le permettre** he, of course, can afford to do that, can't he?

Net [nɛt] NM (Internet): **le ~** the Net

net, nette [nɛt] ADJ (sans équivoque, distinct) clear; (photo) sharp; (évident) definite; (amélioration, différence) marked, distinct; (propre) neat, clean; (Comm: prix, salaire, poids) net; **faire place nette** to make a clean sweep; **~ d'impôt** after tax ▶ ADV (refuser) flatly; **s'arrêter ~** to stop dead; **la lame a cassé ~** the blade snapped clean through ▶ NM: **mettre au ~** to copy out

netiquette [netiket] NF netiquette

nettement [nɛtmɑ̃] ADV (distinctement) clearly; (évidemment) definitely; (incontestablement) decidedly; (*avec comparatif, superlatif*): **~ mieux** definitely *ou* clearly better

netteté [nɛtte] NF clearness

nettoie *etc* [netwa] VB *voir* **nettoyer**

nettoiement [netwamɑ̃] NM (*Admin*) cleaning; **service du ~** refuse collection

nettoierai *etc* [netwaʀe] VB *voir* **nettoyer**

nettoyage [netwajaʒ] NM cleaning; **~ à sec** dry cleaning

nettoyant [netwajɑ̃] NM (*produit*) cleaning agent

★**nettoyer** [netwaje] /8/ VT to clean; (*fig*) to clean out

★**neuf¹** [nœf] NUM nine

neuf², **neuve** [nœf, nœv] ADJ new ▶ NM: **repeindre à ~** to redecorate; **remettre à ~** to do up (as good as new), refurbish; **n'acheter que du ~** to buy everything new; **quoi de ~?** what's new?

neurasthénie [nøʀasteni] NF neurasthenia

neurasthénique [nøʀastenik] ADJ neurasthenic

neurobiologie [nøʀobjɔlɔʒi] NF neurobiology

neurochirurgie [nøʀoʃiʀyʀʒi] NF neurosurgery

neurochirurgien [nøʀoʃiʀyʀʒjɛ̃] NM neurosurgeon

neuroleptique [nøʀɔlɛptik] ADJ neuroleptic

neurologie [nøʀɔlɔʒi] NF neurology

neurologique [nøʀɔlɔʒik] ADJ neurological

neurologue [nøʀɔlɔg] NMF neurologist

neurone [nøʀɔn] NM neuron(e)

neuropsychiatre [nøʀopsikjatʀ] NMF neuropsychiatrist

neuropsychiatrie [nøʀopsikjatʀi] NF neuropsychiatry

neurosciences [nøʀosjɑ̃s] NFPL neuroscience *sg*

neutralisation [nøtʀalizasjɔ̃] NF neutralization

neutraliser [nøtʀalize] /1/ VT to neutralize

neutralisme [nøtʀalism] NM neutralism

neutraliste [nøtʀalist] ADJ neutralist

neutralité [nøtʀalite] NF neutrality

neutre [nøtʀ] ADJ neutral; **~ en carbone** carbon neutral ▶ NM (*Ling*) neuter

neutrino [nøtʀino] NM neutrino

neutron [nøtʀɔ̃] NM neutron

neuve [nœv] ADJ F *voir* **neuf²**

neuvième [nœvjɛm] NUM ninth

névé [neve] NM névé

★**neveu, x** [n(ə)vø] NM nephew

névralgie [nevʀalʒi] NF neuralgia

névralgique [nevʀalʒik] ADJ (*fig: sensible*) sensitive; **centre ~** nerve centre

névrite [nevʀit] NF neuritis

névrose [nevʀoz] NF neurosis

névrosé, e [nevʀoze] ADJ, NM/F neurotic

névrotique [nevʀɔtik] ADJ neurotic

New York [njujɔʀk] N New York

new-yorkais, e [njujɔʀkɛ, -ɛz] ADJ of *ou* from New York, New York *cpd* ▶ NM/F: **New-Yorkais, e** New Yorker

★**nez** [ne] NM nose; **rire au ~ de qn** to laugh in sb's face; **avoir du ~** to have flair; **avoir le ~ fin** to have foresight; **~ à ~ avec** face to face with; **à vue de ~** roughly

NF SIGLE MPL = **nouveaux francs** ▶ SIGLE F (*Industrie*: = *norme française*) industrial standard

★**ni** [ni] CONJ: **ni ... ni** neither ... nor; **je n'aime ni les lentilles ni les épinards** I like neither lentils nor spinach; **il n'a dit ni oui ni non** he didn't say either yes or no; **elles ne sont venues ni l'une ni l'autre** neither of them came; **il n'a rien vu ni entendu** he didn't see or hear anything

Niagara [njagaʀa] NM: **les chutes du ~** the Niagara Falls

niais, e [njɛ, njɛz] ADJ silly, thick

niaiserie [njɛzʀi] NF gullibility; (*action, propos, futilité*) silliness

Nicaragua [nikaʀagwa] NM: **le ~** Nicaragua

nicaraguayen, ne [nikaʀagwajɛ̃, -ɛn] ADJ Nicaraguan ▶ NM/F: **Nicaraguayen, ne** Nicaraguan

Nice [nis] N Nice

niche [niʃ] NF (*du chien*) kennel; (*de mur*) recess, niche; (*farce*) trick

nichée [niʃe] NF brood, nest

nicher [niʃe] /1/ VI to nest ▪ **se nicher** VPR: **se ~ dans** (*personne: se blottir*) to snuggle into; (*: se cacher*) to hide in; (*objet*) to lodge itself in

nichon [niʃɔ̃] NM (*fam*) boob, tit

nickel [nikɛl] NM nickel

niçois, e [niswa, -waz] ADJ of *ou* from Nice; (*Culin*) Nicoise

nicotine [nikɔtin] NF nicotine

nid [ni] NM nest; (*fig: repaire etc*) den, lair; **~ d'abeilles** (*Couture, Textiles*) honeycomb stitch; **~ de poule** pothole

nièce [njɛs] NF niece

nième [ɛnjɛm] ADJ: **la ~ fois** the nth *ou* umpteenth time

nier [nje] /7/ VT to deny

nigaud, e [nigo, -od] NM/F booby, fool

Niger [niʒɛʀ] NM: **le ~** Niger; (*fleuve*) the Niger

Nigéria [niʒeʀja] NM Nigeria

nigérian, e [niʒeʀjɑ̃, -an] ADJ Nigerian ▶ NM/F: **Nigérian, e** Nigerian

nigérien, ne [niʒeʀjɛ̃, -ɛn] ADJ of *ou* from Niger

night-club [najtklœb] NM nightclub

nihilisme [niilism] NM nihilism

nihiliste [niilist] ADJ nihilist, nihilistic

Nil [nil] NM: **le ~** the Nile

★**n'importe** [nɛ̃pɔʀt] ADV: **n'importe!** no matter!; **n'importe qui/quoi/où** anybody/anything/anywhere; **n'importe quoi!** (*fam: désapprobation*) what rubbish!; **n'importe quand** any time; **n'importe quel/quelle** any; **n'importe lequel/laquelle** any (one); **n'importe comment** (*sans soin*) carelessly; **n'importe comment, il part ce soir** he's leaving tonight in any case

nippes [nip] NFPL (*fam*) togs

nippon, e *ou* **ne** [nipɔ̃, -ɔn] ADJ Japanese

nique [nik] NF: **faire la ~ à** to thumb one's nose at (*fig*)

niquer [nike] VT (!: *arnaquer*) to shaft (!), screw (!); (: *baiser*) to screw (!), shag (BRIT!)

nitouche [nituʃ] NF (*péj*): **c'est une sainte ~** she looks as if butter wouldn't melt in her mouth

nitrate [nitʀat] NM nitrate

nitrique [nitʀik] ADJ: **acide ~** nitric acid

nitroglycérine [nitroɡliseʁin] NF nitroglycerin(e)

★**niveau, X** [nivo] NM level; (des élèves, études) standard; **au ~ de** at the level of; (personne) on a level with; **de ~ (avec)** level (with); **le ~ de la mer** sea level; **~ (à bulle)** spirit level; **~ (d'eau)** water level; **~ de vie** standard of living

niveler [niv(ə)le] /4/ VT to level

niveleuse [niv(ə)løz] NF (Tech) grader

nivellement [nivɛlmɑ̃] NM levelling

nivernais, e [nivɛʁnɛ, -ɛz] ADJ of ou from Nevers (and region) ▶ NM/F: **Nivernais, e** inhabitant ou native of Nevers (and region)

NL SIGLE F = **nouvelle lune**

nobiliaire [nɔbiljɛʁ] ADJ F voir **particule**

noble [nɔbl] ADJ noble; (de qualité: métal etc) precious ▶ NMF noble(man/-woman)

noblement [nɔbləmɑ̃] ADV (agir) nobly

noblesse [nɔblɛs] NF (classe sociale) nobility; (d'une action etc) nobleness

noce [nɔs] NF wedding; (gens) wedding party (ou guests pl); **il l'a épousée en secondes noces** she was his second wife; **faire la ~** (fam) to go on a binge; **noces d'or/d'argent/de diamant** golden/silver/diamond wedding

noceur [nɔsœʁ] NM (fam): **c'est un sacré ~** he's a real party animal

nocif, -ive [nɔsif, -iv] ADJ harmful, noxious

nocivité [nɔsivite] NF (de substance) toxicity; (fig) harmfulness

noctambule [nɔktɑ̃byl] NMF night-bird

nocturne [nɔktyʁn] ADJ nocturnal ▶ NF (Sport) floodlit fixture; (d'un magasin) late opening

nodule [nɔdyl] NM (Méd) nodule

Noël [nɔɛl] NM Christmas; **la (fête de) ~** Christmas time

nœud [nø] NM (de corde, du bois, Navig) knot; (ruban) bow; (fig: liens) bond, tie; (: d'une question) crux; (: Théât etc): **le ~ de l'action** the web of events; **~ coulant** noose; **~ gordien** Gordian knot; **~ papillon** bow tie

noie etc [nwa] VB voir **noyer**

★**noir, e** [nwaʁ] ADJ black; (obscur, sombre) dark ▶ NM/F: **un N~/une Noire** a black man/woman ▶ NM: **dans le ~** in the dark; **il fait ~** it is dark; **au ~** adv (acheter, vendre) on the black market; **travail au ~** undeclared work, illegal work; **travailler au ~** to work in the black economy ▶ NF (Mus) crotchet (BRIT), quarter note (US)

noirâtre [nwaʁɑtʁ] ADJ (teinte) blackish

noirceur [nwaʁsœʁ] NF blackness; darkness

noircir [nwaʁsiʁ] /2/ VT, VI to blacken

noise [nwaz] NF: **chercher ~ à** to try and pick a quarrel with

noisetier [nwaz(ə)tje] NM hazel (tree)

noisette [nwazɛt] NF hazelnut; (morceau: de beurre etc) small knob ▶ ADJ INV (yeux) hazel

★**noix** [nwa] NF walnut; (fam) twit; (Culin): **une ~ de beurre** a knob of butter; **à la ~** (fam) worthless; **~ de cajou** cashew nut; **~ de coco** coconut; **~ (de) muscade** nutmeg; **~ de veau** (Culin) round fillet of veal

★**nom** [nɔ̃] NM name; (Ling) noun; **connaître qn de ~**

to know sb by name; **au ~ de** in the name of; **~ d'une pipe** ou **d'un chien!** (fam) for goodness' sake!; **~ de Dieu!** (!) bloody hell! (BRIT); **~ commun/propre** common/proper noun; **~ composé** (Ling) compound noun; **~ déposé** trade name; **~ d'emprunt** assumed name; **~ de famille** surname; **~ de fichier** file name; **~ de jeune fille** maiden name; **~ d'utilisateur** username

nomade [nɔmad] ADJ nomadic ▶ NMF nomad

nomadisme [nɔmadism] NM (mode de vie) nomadism; (mode de travail) mobile working

★**nombre** [nɔ̃bʁ] NM number; **venir en ~** to come in large numbers; **ils sont au ~ de trois** there are three of them; **au ~ de mes amis** among my friends; **sans ~** countless; **(bon) ~ de** (beaucoup, plusieurs) a (large) number of; **depuis ~ d'années** for many years; **~ premier/entier** prime/whole number

★**nombreux, -euse** [nɔ̃bʁø, -øz] ADJ many, numerous; (avec nom sg: foule etc) large; **peu ~** few; small; **de ~ cas** many cases

nombril [nɔ̃bʁi(l)] NM navel

nombrilisme [nɔ̃bʁilism] NM navel-gazing, self-absorption

nombriliste [nɔ̃bʁilist] ADJ self-absorbed

nomenclature [nɔmɑ̃klatyʁ] NF wordlist; list of items

nominal, e, -aux [nɔminal, -o] ADJ nominal; (appel, liste) of names

nominatif, -ive [nɔminatif, -iv] NM (Ling) nominative ▶ ADJ: **liste nominative** list of names; **carte nominative** calling card; **titre ~** registered name

nomination [nɔminasjɔ̃] NF nomination

nommément [nɔmemɑ̃] ADV (désigner) by name

nommer [nɔme] /1/ VT (baptiser) to name, give a name to; (qualifier) to call; (mentionner) to name, give the name of; (élire) to appoint, nominate ■ **se nommer** VPR: **il se nomme Pascal** his name's Pascal, he's called Pascal

nomophobe [nɔmɔfɔb] ADJ nomophobic ▶ NMF nomophobe

★**non** [nɔ̃] ADV (réponse) no; (suivi d'un adjectif, adverbe) not; **Paul est venu, ~?** Paul came, didn't he?; **répondre** ou **dire que ~** to say no; **~ pas que** not that; **~ plus: moi ~ plus** neither do I, I don't either; **je préférerais que ~** I would prefer not; **il se trouve que ~** perhaps not; **je pense que ~** I don't think so; **~ mais!** well really!; **~ mais des fois!** you must be joking!; **~ alcoolisé** non-alcoholic; **~ loin/seulement** not far/only

nonagénaire [nɔnaʒenɛʁ] NMF nonagenarian

non-agression [nɔnaɡʁesjɔ̃] NF: **pacte de ~** non-aggression pact

non alcoolisé, e [nɔnalkɔlize] ADJ non-alcoholic

nonante [nɔnɑ̃t] NUM (BELGIQUE, SUISSE) ninety

non-assistance [nɔnasistɑ̃s] NF (Jur): **~ à personne en danger** failure to render assistance to a person in danger

nonce [nɔ̃s] NM (Rel) nuncio

nonchalamment [nɔ̃ʃalamɑ̃] ADV nonchalantly

nonchalance [nɔ̃ʃalɑ̃s] NF nonchalance, casualness

nonchalant, e [nɔ̃ʃalɑ̃, -ɑ̃t] ADJ nonchalant, casual

non-conformisme [nɔ̃kɔ̃fɔʀmism] NM nonconformism

non-conformiste [nɔ̃kɔ̃fɔʀmist] ADJ, NMF nonconformist

non-conformité [nɔ̃kɔ̃fɔʀmite] NF nonconformity

non-croyant, e [nɔ̃kʀwajɑ̃, -ɑ̃t] NM/F (Rel) non-believer

non-engagé, e [nɔ̃ɑ̃gaʒe] ADJ non-aligned

★**non-fumeur, -euse** [nɔ̃fymœʀ, -øz] NM/F non-smoker

non-ingérence [nɔ̃ɛ̃ʒeʀɑ̃s] NF non-interference

non-initié, e [nɔ̃ninisje] NM/F lay person; **les non-initiés** the uninitiated

non-inscrit, e [nɔ̃ɛ̃skri, -it] NM/F (Pol: député) independent

non-intervention [nɔ̃ɛ̃tɛʀvɑ̃sjɔ̃] NF non-intervention

non-lieu [nɔ̃ljø] NM: **il y a eu ~** the case was dismissed

nonne [nɔn] NF nun

nonobstant [nɔnɔpstɑ̃] PRÉP notwithstanding

non-paiement [nɔ̃pɛmɑ̃] NM non-payment

non-prolifération [nɔ̃pʀɔliferasjɔ̃] NF non-proliferation

non-résident [nɔ̃residɑ̃] NM (Écon) non-resident

non-retour [nɔ̃ʀətuʀ] NM: **point de ~** point of no return

non-sens [nɔ̃sɑ̃s] NM absurdity

non-spécialiste [nɔ̃spesjalist] NMF non-specialist

non-stop [nɔnstɔp] ADJ INV nonstop

non-syndiqué, e [nɔ̃sɛ̃dike] NM/F non-union member

non-violence [nɔ̃vjɔlɑ̃s] NF nonviolence

non-violent, e [nɔ̃vjɔlɑ̃, -ɑ̃t] ADJ non-violent

non-voyant, e [nɔ̃vwajɔ̃, ɑ̃t] NM/F blind person

★**nord** [nɔʀ] NM North; **au ~** (situation) in the north; (direction) to the north; **au ~ de** north of, to the north of; **perdre le ~** to lose one's way (fig) ▶ ADJ INV northern; north

nord-africain, e [nɔʀafʀikɛ̃, -ɛn] ADJ North African ▶ NM/F: **Nord-Africain, e** North African

nord-américain, e [nɔʀameʀikɛ̃, -ɛn] ADJ North American ▶ NM/F: **Nord-Américain, e** North American

nord-coréen, ne [nɔʀkɔʀeɛ̃, -ɛn] ADJ North Korean ▶ NM/F: **Nord-Coréen, ne** North Korean

nord-est [nɔʀɛst] NM North-East

nordique [nɔʀdik] ADJ (pays) Nordic; (langues) Scandinavian, Nordic ▶ NMF: **Nordique** Scandinavian

nord-ouest [nɔʀwɛst] NM North-West

nord-vietnamien, ne [nɔʀvjɛtnamjɛ̃, -ɛn] ADJ North Vietnamese ▶ NM/F: **Nord-Vietnamien, ne** North Vietnamese

noria [nɔʀja] NF (machine) noria

★**normal, e, -aux** [nɔʀmal, -o] ADJ normal; **c'est tout à fait ~** it's perfectly natural; **vous trouvez ça - ?** does it seem right to you? ▶ NF: **la normale** the norm, the average

★**normalement** [nɔʀmalmɑ̃] ADV (en général) normally; (comme prévu): **-, il le fera demain** he

should be doing it tomorrow, he's supposed to do it tomorrow

normalien, ne [nɔʀmaljɛ̃, -ɛn] NM/F student of École normale supérieure

normalisation [nɔʀmalizasjɔ̃] NF standardization; normalization

normaliser [nɔʀmalize] /1/ VT (Comm, Tech) to standardize; (Pol) to normalize

normalité [nɔʀmalite] NF normality

normand, e [nɔʀmɑ̃, -ɑ̃d] ADJ (de Normandie) Norman ▶ NM/F: **Normand, e** (de Normandie) Norman

★**Normandie** [nɔʀmɑ̃di] NF: **la ~** Normandy

norme [nɔʀm] NF norm; (Tech) standard

Norvège [nɔʀvɛʒ] NF: **la ~** Norway

norvégien, ne [nɔʀveʒjɛ̃, -ɛn] ADJ Norwegian ▶ NM (Ling) Norwegian ▶ NM/F: **Norvégien, ne** Norwegian

★**nos** [no] ADJ POSS voir **notre**

nosocomial, e, -aux [nozɔkɔmjal, -o] ADJ (infection) nosocomial

nostalgie [nɔstalʒi] NF nostalgia

nostalgique [nɔstalʒik] ADJ nostalgic

notable [nɔtabl] ADJ notable, noteworthy; (marqué) noticeable, marked ▶ NM prominent citizen

notablement [nɔtabləmɑ̃] ADV notably; (sensiblement) noticeably

notaire [nɔtɛʀ] NM notary; solicitor

notamment [nɔtamɑ̃] ADV in particular, among others

notariat [nɔtaʀja] NM profession of notary (ou solicitor)

notarié, e [nɔtaʀje] ADJ: **acte ~** deed drawn up by a notary (ou solicitor)

notation [nɔtasjɔ̃] NF notation

★**note** [nɔt] NF (écrite, Mus) note; (Scol) mark (BRIT), grade; (facture) bill; **prendre des notes** to take notes; **prendre ~ de** to note; (par écrit) to note, write down; **dans la ~** exactly right; **forcer la ~** to exaggerate; **une ~ de tristesse/de gaieté** a sad/happy note; **~ de service** memorandum

noté, e [nɔte] ADJ: **être bien/mal ~** (employé etc) to have a good/bad record

noter [nɔte] /1/ VT (écrire) to write down, note; (remarquer) to note, notice; (Scol, Admin: donner une appréciation: devoir) to mark, give a grade to; **notez bien que ...** (please) note that ...

notice [nɔtis] NF summary, short article; (brochure): **~ explicative** explanatory leaflet, instruction booklet

notification [nɔtifikasjɔ̃] NF notification

notifier [nɔtifje] /7/ VT: **~ qch à qn** to notify sb of sth, notify sth to sb

notion [nɔsjɔ̃] NF notion, idea ■ **notions** NFPL (rudiments) rudiments

notoire [nɔtwaʀ] ADJ widely known; (en mal) notorious; **le fait est ~** the fact is common knowledge

notoirement [nɔtwaʀmɑ̃] ADV (insuffisant) notoriously

notoriété [nɔtɔʀjete] NF: **c'est de ~ publique** it's common knowledge

★**notre** [nɔtʀ] (pl **nos** [no]) ADJ POSS our

301

nôtre [notʀ] PRON: **le/la ~** ours; **les nôtres** ours; (*alliés etc*) our own people; **soyez des nôtres** join us ▸ ADJ ours

nouba [nuba] NF (*fam*): **faire la ~** to live it up

noué, e [nwe] ADJ: **avoir la gorge nouée** to have a lump in one's throat; **avoir l'estomac ~** to have a knot in one's stomach

nouer [nwe] /**1**/ VT to tie, knot; (*fig: alliance etc*) to strike up; **~ la conversation** to start a conversation ■ **se nouer** VPR: **c'est là où l'intrigue se noue** it's at that point that the strands of the plot come together; **ma gorge se noua** a lump came to my throat

noueux, -euse [nwø, -øz] ADJ gnarled

nougat [nuga] NM nougat

nougatine [nugatin] NF kind of nougat

nouille [nuj] NF (*fam*) noodle (BRIT), fathead ■ **nouilles** NFPL (*pâtes*) noodles; pasta *sg*

nounou [nunu] NF nanny

nounours [nunurs] NM teddy (bear)

nourri, e [nuʀi] ADJ (*feu etc*) sustained

nourrice [nuʀis] NF ≈ child-minder; (*autrefois*) wet-nurse

nourricier, -ère [nuʀisje, -jɛʀ] ADJ sustaining

nourrir [nuʀiʀ] /**2**/ VT to feed; (*fig: espoir*) to harbour, nurse; **logé nourri** with board and lodging; **~ au sein** to breast-feed ■ **se nourrir** VPR: **se ~ de légumes** to live on vegetables

nourrissant, e [nuʀisɑ̃, -ɑ̃t] ADJ nourishing, nutritious

nourrisson [nuʀisɔ̃] NM (unweaned) infant

★**nourriture** [nuʀityʀ] NF food

★**nous** [nu] PRON (*sujet*) we; (*objet*) us

nous-mêmes [numɛm] PRON ourselves

★**nouveau, nouvel, -elle, x** [nuvo, -ɛl] ADJ new; (*original*) novel; **de ~, à ~** again; **Nouvel An** New Year; **~ venu, nouvelle venue** newcomer; **nouveaux mariés** newly-weds; **nouvelle vague** new wave ▸ NM/F new pupil (*ou* employee) ▸ NM: **il y a du ~** there's something new ▸ NF (*piece of*) news *sg*; (*Littérature*) short story ■ **nouvelles** NFPL (*Presse, TV*) news; **je suis sans nouvelles de lui** I haven't heard from him

---

News s'emploie avec un verbe au singulier, même lorsqu'il traduit un pluriel français.
Les nouvelles sont préoccupantes. **The news *is* worrying.**
Pour traduire *une nouvelle*, il faut dire soit **a piece of news**, soit **(some) news**.
J'ai une nouvelle à vous annoncer. **I have some news for you.**
une nouvelle étonnante **a surprising piece of news**

---

nouveau-né, e [nuvone] NM/F newborn (baby)

nouveauté [nuvote] NF novelty; (*chose nouvelle*) innovation, something new; (*Comm*) new film (*ou* book *ou* creation *etc*)

nouvel, -elle [nuvɛl] ADJ, NF voir **nouveau**

Nouvelle-Angleterre [nuvɛlɑ̃glətɛʀ] NF: **la ~** New England

Nouvelle-Calédonie [nuvɛlkaledɔni] NF: **la ~** New Caledonia

Nouvelle-Écosse [nuvɛlekɔs] NF: **la ~** Nova Scotia

Nouvelle-Galles du Sud [nuvɛlgaldysyd] NF: **la ~** New South Wales

Nouvelle-Guinée [nuvɛlgine] NF: **la ~** New Guinea

nouvellement [nuvɛlmɑ̃] ADV (*arrivé*) recently, newly

Nouvelle-Orléans [nuvɛlɔʀleɑ̃] NF: **la ~** New Orleans

Nouvelles-Hébrides [nuvɛlzebʀid] NFPL: **les ~** the New Hebrides

Nouvelle-Zélande [nuvɛlzelɑ̃d] NF: **la ~** New Zealand

nouvelliste [nuvelist] NMF editor *ou* writer of short stories

novateur, -trice [nɔvatœʀ, -tʀis] ADJ innovative ▸ NM/F innovator

★**novembre** [nɔvɑ̃bʀ] NM November; *see note; voir aussi* **juillet**

Le 11 novembre is a public holiday in France and commemorates those who died for France in all wars.

---

novice [nɔvis] ADJ inexperienced ▸ NMF novice

noviciat [nɔvisja] NM (*Rel*) noviciate

noyade [nwajad] NF drowning *no pl*

noyau, x [nwajo] NM (*de fruit*) stone; (*Bio, Physique*) nucleus; (*Élec, Géo, fig: centre*) core; (*fig: d'artistes etc*) group; (: *de résistants etc*) cell

noyautage [nwajota3] NM (*Pol*) infiltration

noyauter [nwajote] /**1**/ VT to infiltrate

noyé, e [nwaje] NM/F drowning (*ou* drowned) man/woman ▸ ADJ (*fig: dépassé*) out of one's depth

★**noyer** [nwaje] /**8**/ NM walnut (tree); (*bois*) walnut ▸ VT to drown; (*fig*) to flood; to submerge; (*Auto: moteur*) to flood; **~ son chagrin** to drown one's sorrows; **~ le poisson** to duck the issue ■ **se noyer** VPR to be drowned, drown; (*suicide*) to drown o.s.

NSP SIGLE M (*Rel*) = **Notre Saint Père**; (*dans les sondages:* = *ne sais pas*) don't know

NT SIGLE M (= *Nouveau Testament*) NT

NTIC FPL (= *nouvelles technologies de l'information et de la communication*) NICT (= *new information and communication technologies*)

nu, e [ny] ADJ naked; (*membres*) naked, bare; (*chambre, fil, plaine*) bare; **tout nu** stark naked; **se mettre nu** to strip; **mettre à nu** to bare ▸ NM (*Art*) nude; **le nu intégral** total nudity

★**nuage** [nɥaʒ] NM (*aussi Inform*) cloud; **être dans les nuages** (*distrait*) to have one's head in the clouds; **informatique en ~** cloud computing; **~ de lait** drop of milk

★**nuageux, -euse** [nɥaʒø, -øz] ADJ cloudy

nuance [nɥɑ̃s] NF (*de couleur, sens*) shade; **il y a une ~ (entre)** there's a slight difference (between); **une ~ de tristesse** a tinge of sadness

nuancé, e [nɥɑ̃se] ADJ (*opinion*) finely-shaded, subtly differing; **être ~ dans ses opinions** to have finely-shaded opinions

nuancer [nɥɑ̃se] /**3**/ VT (*pensée, opinion*) to qualify

nuancier [nɥɑ̃sje] NM colour chart (BRIT), color chart (US)

nubile [nybil] ADJ nubile

nucléaire [nyklɛɛʀ] ADJ nuclear ▶ NM: **le ~** nuclear power

nudisme [nydism] NM nudism

nudiste [nydist] ADJ, NMF nudist

nudité [nydite] NF nudity, nakedness; bareness

nuée [nɥe] NF: **une ~ de** a cloud *ou* host *ou* swarm of

nues [ny] NFPL: **tomber des ~** to be taken aback; **porter qn aux ~** to praise sb to the skies

nui [nɥi] PP *de* nuire

nuire [nɥiʀ] /38/ VI to be harmful; **~ à** to harm, do damage to

nuisance [nɥizɑ̃s] NF nuisance ■ **nuisances** NFPL pollution *sg*

nuisette [nɥizɛt] NF very short nightie

nuisible [nɥizibl] ADJ harmful; **(animal) ~** pest

nuisis *etc* [nɥizi] VB *voir* nuire

★**nuit** [nɥi] NF night; **payer sa ~** to pay for one's overnight accommodation; **il fait ~** it's dark; **cette ~** (*hier*) last night; (*aujourd'hui*) tonight; **de ~** (*vol, service*) night *cpd*; **~ blanche** sleepless night; **~ de noces** wedding night; **~ de Noël** Christmas Eve

nuitamment [nɥitamɑ̃] ADV by night

nuitée [nɥite] NF overnight stay

★**nul, nulle** [nyl] ADJ (*aucun*) no; (*minime*) nil, nonexistent; (*non valable*) null; (*péj*) useless, hopeless; **résultat ~**, **match ~** draw; **nulle part** *adv* nowhere ▶ PRON none, no one

nullement [nylmɑ̃] ADV by no means

nullité [nylite] NF nullity; (*péj*) hopelessness; (*: personne*) hopeless individual, nonentity

numéraire [nymeʀɛʀ] NM cash; metal currency

numéral, e, -aux [nymeʀal, -o] ADJ numeral

numérateur [nymeʀatœʀ] NM numerator

numération [nymeʀasjɔ̃] NF: **~ décimale/binaire** decimal/binary notation; **~ globulaire** blood count

numérique [nymeʀik] ADJ numerical; (*Inform*, TV: *affichage, son, télévision*) digital

numériquement [nymeʀikmɑ̃] ADV numerically; (*Inform*) digitally

numérisation [nymeʀizasjɔ̃] NF (*Inform*) digitization

numériser [nymeʀize] /1/ VT (*Inform*) to digitize

numéro [nymeʀo] NM number; (*spectacle*) act, turn; (*Presse*) issue, number; **faire** *ou* **composer un ~** to dial a number; **~ d'identification personnel** personal identification number (PIN); **~ d'immatriculation** *ou* **minéralogique** *ou* **de police** registration (BRIT) *ou* license (US) number; **~ de téléphone** (tele)phone number; **~ vert** ≈ Freefone® number (BRIT), ≈ toll-free number (US)

numérologie [nymeʀɔlɔʒi] NF numerology

numérotage [nymeʀɔtaʒ] NM numbering

numérotation [nymeʀɔtasjɔ̃] NF numeration

numéroter [nymeʀɔte] /1/ VT to number

numerus clausus [nymeʀysklozys] NM INV restriction *ou* limitation of numbers

numismate [nymismat] NMF numismatist, coin collector

numismatique [nymismatik] NF numismatics *sg*

nunuche [nynyʃ] (*fam*) ADJ silly ▶ NF ninny (*fam*)

nu-pieds [nypje] NM sandal ▶ ADJ INV barefoot

nuptial, e, -aux [nypsjal, -o] ADJ nuptial; wedding *cpd*

nuptialité [nypsjalite] NF: **taux de ~** marriage rate

nuque [nyk] NF nape of the neck

nu-tête [nytɛt] ADJ INV bareheaded

nutriment [nytʀimɑ̃] NM nutriment

nutritif, -ive [nytʀitif, -iv] ADJ (*besoins, valeur*) nutritional; (*aliment*) nutritious, nourishing

nutrition [nytʀisjɔ̃] NF nutrition

nutritionnel, le [nytʀisjɔnɛl] ADJ nutritional

nutritionniste [nytʀisjɔnist] NMF nutritionist

nylon® [nilɔ̃] NM nylon

nymphe [nɛ̃f] NF (*Mythologie*) nymph

nymphéa [nɛ̃fea] NM Nymphaea

nymphette [nɛ̃fɛt] NF nymphet

nymphomane [nɛ̃fɔman] ADJ, NF nymphomaniac

nymphomanie [nɛ̃fɔmani] NF nymphomania

n

Oo

O, o [o] NM INV O, o ▶ ABR (= *ouest*) W; **O comme Oscar** O for Oliver (BRIT) *ou* Oboe (US)

oasis [ɔazis] NM OU F oasis

obédience [ɔbedjɑ̃s] NF allegiance

obéir [ɔbeiʀ] /2/ VI to obey; **~ à** to obey; (*moteur, véhicule*) to respond to

obéissance [ɔbeisɑ̃s] NF obedience

obéissant, e [ɔbeisɑ̃, -ɑ̃t] ADJ obedient

obélisque [ɔbelisk] NM obelisk

obèse [ɔbɛz] ADJ obese

obésité [ɔbezite] NF obesity

objecter [ɔbʒɛkte] /1/ VT (*prétexter*) to plead, put forward as an excuse; **~ qch à** (*argument*) to put forward sth against; **~ (à qn) que** to object (to sb) that

objecteur [ɔbʒɛktœʀ] NM: **~ de conscience** conscientious objector

objectif, ive [ɔbʒɛktif, -iv] ADJ objective ▶ NM (*Optique, Photo*) lens *sg*; (*Mil, fig*) objective; **~ grand angulaire/à focale variable** wide-angle/zoom lens

objection [ɔbʒɛksjɔ̃] NF objection; **~ de conscience** conscientious objection

objectivement [ɔbʒɛktivmɑ̃] ADV objectively

objectivité [ɔbʒɛktivite] NF objectivity

★**objet** [ɔbʒɛ] NM (*chose*) object; (*d'une discussion, recherche*) subject; **être** *ou* **faire l'~ de** (*discussion*) to be the subject of; (*soins*) to be given *ou* shown; **sans ~** *adj* purposeless; (*sans fondement*) groundless; **~ d'art** objet d'art; **objets personnels** personal items; **objets de toilette** toiletries; **objets trouvés** lost property *sg* (BRIT), lost-and-found *sg* (US); **objets de valeur** valuables

obligataire [ɔbligatɛʀ] ADJ bond *cpd* ▶ NMF bondholder, debenture holder

obligation [ɔbligasjɔ̃] NF obligation; (*gén pl: devoir*) duty; (*Comm*) bond, debenture; **sans ~ d'achat** with no obligation (to buy); **être dans l'~ de faire** to be obliged to do; **avoir l'~ de faire** to be under an obligation to do; **obligations familiales** family obligations *ou* responsibilities; **obligations militaires** military obligations *ou* duties

★**obligatoire** [ɔbligatwaʀ] ADJ compulsory, obligatory

obligatoirement [ɔbligatwaʀmɑ̃] ADV compulsorily; (*fatalement*) necessarily; (*fam: sans aucun doute*) inevitably

obligé, e [ɔbliʒe] ADJ (*redevable*): **être très ~ à qn** to be most obliged to sb; (*contraint*): **je suis (bien) ~ (de le faire)** I have to (do it); (*nécessaire: conséquence*) necessary; **c'est ~ !** it's inevitable!

obligeamment [ɔbliʒamɑ̃] ADV obligingly

obligeance [ɔbliʒɑ̃s] NF: **avoir l'~ de** to be kind *ou* good enough to

obligeant, e [ɔbliʒɑ̃, -ɑ̃t] ADJ obliging; kind

★**obliger** [ɔbliʒe] /3/ VT (*contraindre*): **~ qn à faire** to force *ou* oblige sb to do; (*Jur: engager*) to bind; (*rendre service à*) to oblige; **je suis bien obligé (de le faire)** I have to (do it)

oblique [ɔblik] ADJ oblique; **regard ~** sidelong glance; **en ~** *adv* diagonally

obliquer [ɔblike] /1/ VI: **~ vers** to turn off towards

oblitération [ɔbliteʀasjɔ̃] NF cancelling *no pl*, cancellation; obstruction

oblitérer [ɔbliteʀe] /6/ VT (*timbre-poste*) to cancel; (*Méd: canal, vaisseau*) to obstruct

oblong, oblongue [ɔblɔ̃, ɔblɔ̃g] ADJ oblong

obnubiler [ɔbnybile] /1/ VT to obsess

obole [ɔbɔl] NF offering

obscène [ɔpsɛn] ADJ obscene

obscénité [ɔpsenite] NF obscenity

obscur, e [ɔpskyʀ] ADJ (*sombre*) dark; (*fig: raisons*) obscure; (: *sentiment, malaise*) vague; (: *personne, vie*) humble, lowly

obscurantisme [ɔpskyʀɑ̃tism] NM obscurantism

obscurcir [ɔpskyʀsiʀ] /2/ VT to darken; (*fig*) to obscure ◼ **s'obscurcir** VPR to grow dark

obscurément [ɔpskyʀemɑ̃] ADV (*sentir*) vaguely

obscurité [ɔpskyʀite] NF darkness; **dans l'~** in the dark, in darkness; (*anonymat, médiocrité*) in obscurity

obsédant, e [ɔpsedɑ̃, -ɑ̃t] ADJ obsessive

obsédé, e [ɔpsede] NM/F fanatic; **~ sexuel** sex maniac

obséder [ɔpsede] /6/ VT to obsess, haunt

obsèques [ɔpsɛk] NFPL funeral *sg*

obséquieux, -euse [ɔpsekjø, -øz] ADJ obsequious

observable [ɔpsɛʀvabl] ADJ (*phénomènes, critères*) observable

observance [ɔpsɛʀvɑ̃s] NF observance

observateur, -trice [ɔpsɛʀvatœʀ, -tʀis] ADJ observant, perceptive ▶ NM/F observer

observation [ɔpsɛʀvasjɔ̃] NF observation; (*d'un*

règlement etc) observance; (commentaire) observation, remark; (reproche) reproof; **en ~** (Méd) under observation

observatoire [ɔpsɛrvatwar] NM observatory; (lieu élevé) observation post, vantage point

observer [ɔpsɛrve] /1/ VT (regarder) to observe, watch; (examiner) to examine; (scientifiquement, aussi: règlement, jeûne etc) to observe; (surveiller) to watch; (remarquer) to observe, notice; **faire ~ qch à qn** (dire) to point out sth to sb ■ **s'observer** VPR (se surveiller) to keep a check on o.s.

obsession [ɔpsesjɔ̃] NF obsession; **avoir l'~ de** to have an obsession with

obsessionnel, le [ɔpsesjɔnɛl] ADJ obsessive

obsidienne [ɔpsidjɛn] NF (roche) obsidian

obsolescent, e [ɔpsɔlesɑ̃, -ɑ̃t] ADJ obsolescent

obsolète [ɔpsɔlɛt] ADJ obsolete

obstacle [ɔpstakl] NM obstacle; (Équitation) jump, hurdle; **faire ~ à** (lumière) to block out; (projet) to hinder, put obstacles in the path of; **obstacles antichars** tank defences

obstétricien, ne [ɔpstetrisjɛ̃, -ɛn] NM/F obstetrician

obstétrique [ɔpstetrik] NF obstetrics sg

obstination [ɔpstinasjɔ̃] NF obstinacy

obstiné, e [ɔpstine] ADJ obstinate

obstinément [ɔpstinemɑ̃] ADV obstinately

obstiner [ɔpstine] /1/: **s'obstiner** VPR to insist, dig one's heels in; **s'~ à faire** to persist (obstinately) in doing; **s'~ sur qch** to keep working at sth, labour away at sth

obstruction [ɔpstryksjɔ̃] NF obstruction, blockage; (Sport) obstruction; **faire de l'~** (fig) to be obstructive

obstruer [ɔpstrye] /1/ VT to block, obstruct ■ **s'obstruer** VPR to become blocked

obtempérer [ɔptɑ̃pere] /6/ VI to obey; **~ à** to obey, comply with

obtenir [ɔptənir] /22/ VT to obtain, get; (total) to arrive at, reach; (résultat) to achieve, obtain; **~ de pouvoir faire** to obtain permission to do; **~ qch à qn** to obtain sth for sb; **~ de qn qu'il fasse** to get sb to agree to do(ing)

obtention [ɔptɑ̃sjɔ̃] NF obtaining

obtenu, e [ɔpt(ə)ny] PP de **obtenir**

obtiendrai [ɔptjɛ̃dre], **obtiens** [ɔptjɛ̃], **obtint** etc [ɔptɛ̃] VB voir **obtenir**

obturateur [ɔptyratœr] NM (Photo) shutter; **~ à rideau** focal plane shutter

obturation [ɔptyrasjɔ̃] NF closing (up); **~ (dentaire)** filling; **vitesse d'~** (Photo) shutter speed

obturer [ɔptyre] /1/ VT to close (up); (dent) to fill

obtus, e [ɔpty, -yz] ADJ obtuse

obus [ɔby] NM shell; **~ explosif** high-explosive shell; **~ incendiaire** incendiary device, fire bomb

obvier [ɔbvje] /7/: **~ à** vt to obviate

OC SIGLE FPL (= ondes courtes) SW

occase [ɔkaz] NF (fam: occasion) bargain

★**occasion** [ɔkazjɔ̃] NF (aubaine, possibilité) opportunity; (circonstance) occasion; (Comm: article non neuf) secondhand buy; (: acquisition avantageuse) bargain; **à plusieurs occasions** on several occasions; **à la première ~** at the first ou earliest opportunity; **avoir l'~ de faire** to have the opportunity to do; **être l'~ de** to occasion, give rise to; **à l'~** adv sometimes, on occasions; (un jour) some time; **à l'~ de** on the occasion of; **d'~** adj, adv secondhand

occasionnel, le [ɔkazjɔnɛl] ADJ (fortuit) chance cpd; (non régulier) occasional; (: travail) casual

occasionnellement [ɔkazjɔnɛlmɑ̃] ADV occasionally, from time to time

occasionner [ɔkazjɔne] /1/ VT to cause, bring about; **~ qch à qn** to cause sb sth

occident [ɔksidɑ̃] NM: **l'O~** the West

occidental, e, -aux [ɔksidɑ̃tal, -o] ADJ western; (Pol) Western ▶ NM/F Westerner

occidentaliser [ɔksidɑ̃talize] /1/ VT (coutumes, mœurs) to westernize

occiput [ɔksipyt] NM back of the head, occiput

occire [ɔksir] VT to slay

occitan, e [ɔksitɑ̃, -an] ADJ of the langue d'oc, of Provençal French

occlusion [ɔklyzjɔ̃] NF: **~ intestinale** obstruction of the bowel

occulte [ɔkylt] ADJ occult, supernatural

occulter [ɔkylte] /1/ VT (fig) to overshadow

occultisme [ɔkyltism] NM occultism

occupant, e [ɔkypɑ̃, -ɑ̃t] ADJ occupying ▶ NM/F (d'un appartement) occupier, occupant; (d'un véhicule) occupant ▶ NM (Mil) occupying forces pl; (Pol: d'usine etc) occupier

occupation [ɔkypasjɔ̃] NF occupation; **l'O~** the Occupation (of France)

occupationnel, le [ɔkypasjɔnɛl] ADJ: **thérapie occupationnelle** occupational therapy

occupé, e [ɔkype] ADJ (Mil, Pol) occupied; (personne: affairé, pris) busy; (esprit: absorbé) occupied; (place, sièges) taken; (toilettes) engaged; **la ligne est occupée** the line's engaged (BRIT) ou busy (US)

occuper [ɔkype] /1/ VT to occupy; (poste, fonction) to hold; (main-d'œuvre) to employ; **ça occupe trop de place** it takes up too much room ■ **s'occuper** VPR: **s'~ (à qch)** to occupy o.s. ou keep o.s. busy (with sth); **s'~ de** (être responsable de) to be in charge of; (se charger de: affaire) to take charge of, deal with; (: clients etc) to attend to; (s'intéresser à, pratique: politique etc) to be involved in

occurrence [ɔkyrɑ̃s] NF: **en l'~** in this case

OCDE SIGLE F (= Organisation de coopération et de développement économique) OECD

océan [ɔseɑ̃] NM ocean; **l'~ Indien** the Indian Ocean

Océanie [ɔseani] NF: **l'~** Oceania, South Sea Islands

océanique [ɔseanik] ADJ oceanic

océanographe [ɔseanɔgraf] NMF oceanographer

océanographie [ɔseanɔgrafi] NF oceanography

océanologie [ɔseanɔlɔʒi] NF oceanology

ocelot [ɔs(ə)lo] NM (Zool) ocelot; (fourrure) ocelot fur

ocre [ɔkr] ADJ INV ochre

octane [ɔktan] NM octane

octante [ɔktɑ̃t] NUM (BELGIQUE, SUISSE) eighty

octave [ɔktav] NF octave

o

octet [ɔktɛ] NM byte

★**octobre** [ɔktɔbʀ] NM October; *voir aussi* **juillet**

octogénaire [ɔktɔʒenɛʀ] ADJ, NMF octogenarian

octogonal, e, -aux [ɔktɔgɔnal, -o] ADJ octagonal

octogone [ɔktɔgɔn] NM octagon

octroi [ɔktʀwa] NM granting

octroyer [ɔktʀwaje] /8/ VT: **~ qch à qn** to grant sth to sb, grant sb sth

oculaire [ɔkylɛʀ] ADJ ocular, eye *cpd* ▶ NM (*de microscope*) eyepiece

oculiste [ɔkylist] NMF eye specialist, oculist

ode [ɔd] NF ode

★**odeur** [ɔdœʀ] NF smell

odieusement [ɔdjøzmɑ̃] ADV odiously

odieux, -euse [ɔdjø, -øz] ADJ odious, hateful

odontologie [ɔdɔ̃tɔlɔʒi] NF odontology

odorant, e [ɔdɔʀɑ̃, -ɑ̃t] ADJ sweet-smelling, fragrant

odorat [ɔdɔʀa] NM (sense of) smell; **avoir l'~ fin** to have a keen sense of smell

odoriférant, e [ɔdɔʀifeʀɑ̃, -ɑ̃t] ADJ sweet-smelling, fragrant

odyssée [ɔdise] NF odyssey

OEA SIGLE F (= *Organisation des États américains*) OAS

œcuménique [ekymenik] ADJ ecumenical

œdème [edɛm] NM oedema (BRIT), edema (US)

œil [œj] (*pl* **yeux** [jø]) NM eye; **avoir un ~ poché** *ou* **au beurre noir** to have a black eye; **à l'~** (*fam*) for free; **à l'~ nu** with the naked eye; **tenir qn à l'~** to keep an eye *ou* a watch on sb; **avoir l'~ à** to keep an eye on; **faire de l'~ à qn** to make eyes at sb; **voir qch d'un bon/mauvais ~** to view sth in a favourable/an unfavourable light; **à l'~ vif** with a lively expression; **à mes/ses yeux** in my/his eyes; **de ses propres yeux** with his own eyes; **fermer les yeux (sur)** (*fig*) to turn a blind eye (to); **les yeux fermés** (*aussi fig*) with one's eyes shut; **ouvrir l'~** (*fig*) to keep one's eyes open *ou* an eye out; **fermer l'~** to get a moment's sleep; **~ pour ~, dent pour dent** an eye for an eye, a tooth for a tooth; **pour les beaux yeux de qn** (*fig*) for love of sb; **~ de verre** glass eye

œil-de-bœuf [œjdəbœf] (*pl* **œils-de-bœuf**) NM bull's-eye (window)

œillade [œjad] NF: **lancer une ~ à qn** to wink at sb, give sb a wink; **faire des œillades à** to make eyes at

œillères [œjɛʀ] NFPL blinkers (BRIT), blinders (US); **avoir des ~** (*fig*) to be blinkered, wear blinders

œillet [œjɛ] NM (*Bot*) carnation; (*trou*) eyelet

œnologue [enɔlɔg] NMF wine expert

œsophage [ezɔfaʒ] NM oesophagus (BRIT), esophagus (US)

œstrogène [ɛstʀɔʒɛn] ADJ oestrogen (BRIT), estrogen (US)

œuf [œf] NM egg; **étouffer dans l'~** to nip in the bud; **~ à la coque/dur/mollet** boiled/hard-boiled/soft-boiled egg; **~ au plat/poché** fried/poached egg; **œufs brouillés** scrambled eggs; **~ de Pâques** Easter egg; **à repriser** darning egg

œuvre [œvʀ] NF (*tâche*) task, undertaking; (*ouvrage achevé, livre, tableau etc*) work; (*ensemble de la production artistique*) works *pl*; (*organisation charitable*) charity; **être/se mettre à l'~** to be at/get (down) to work; **mettre en ~** (*moyens*) to make use of; (*plan, loi, projet etc*) to implement; **~ d'art** work of art ▶ NM (*d'un artiste*) works *pl*; (*Constr*): **le gros ~** the shell ■ **œuvres** NFPL (*actes*) deeds, works; **bonnes œuvres** good works *ou* deeds; **œuvres de bienfaisance** charitable works

OFCE SIGLE M (= *Observatoire français des conjonctures économiques*) economic research institute

offensant, e [ɔfɑ̃sɑ̃, -ɑ̃t] ADJ offensive, insulting

offense [ɔfɑ̃s] NF (*affront*) insult; (*Rel: péché*) transgression, trespass

offenser [ɔfɑ̃se] /1/ VT to offend, hurt; (*principes, Dieu*) to offend against ■ **s'offenser de** VPR to take offence (BRIT) *ou* offense (US) at

offensif, -ive [ɔfɑ̃sif, -iv] ADJ (*armes, guerre*) offensive ▶ NF offensive; (*fig: du froid, de l'hiver*) onslaught; **passer à l'offensive** to go into the attack *ou* offensive

offert, e [ɔfɛʀ, -ɛʀt] PP *de* **offrir**

offertoire [ɔfɛʀtwaʀ] NM offertory

office [ɔfis] NM (*charge*) office; (*agence*) bureau, agency; (*Rel*) service; **faire ~ de** to act as; to do duty as; **d'~** *adv* automatically; **bons offices** (*Pol*) good offices; **~ du tourisme** tourist office ▶ NM OU F (*pièce*) pantry

officialiser [ɔfisjalize] /1/ VT to make official

officiel, le [ɔfisjɛl] ADJ, NM/F official

officiellement [ɔfisjɛlmɑ̃] ADV officially

officier [ɔfisje] /7/ NM; **~ de l'état-civil** registrar; **~ ministériel** member of the legal profession; **~ de police** ≈ police officer ▶ VI (*Rel*) to officiate

officieusement [ɔfisjøzmɑ̃] ADV unofficially

officieux, -euse [ɔfisjø, -øz] ADJ unofficial

> **officieux** does not mean *officious*.

officinal, e, -aux [ɔfisinal, -o] ADJ: **plantes officinales** medicinal plants

officine [ɔfisin] NF (*de pharmacie*) dispensary; (*Admin: pharmacie*) pharmacy; (*gén péj: bureau*) agency, office

offrais *etc* [ɔfʀɛ] VB *voir* **offrir**

offrande [ɔfʀɑ̃d] NF offering

offrant [ɔfʀɑ̃] NM: **au plus ~** to the highest bidder

offre [ɔfʀ] VB *voir* **offrir** ▶ NF offer; (*aux enchères*) bid; (*Admin: soumission*) tender; (*Écon*): **l'~ et la demande** supply and demand; **~ d'emploi** job advertised; **«offres d'emploi»** "situations vacant"; **~ publique d'achat** takeover bid; **offres de service** offer of service

★**offrir** [ɔfʀiʀ] /18/ VT: **~ qch à qn** to offer sth to sb, offer sb sth; (*faire cadeau*) to give sth to sb, give sb sth; **~ (à qn) de faire qch** to offer to do sth (for sb); **~ à boire à qn** (*chez soi*) to offer sb a drink; **je vous offre un verre** I'll buy you a drink ■ **s'offrir** VPR (*se présenter: occasion, paysage*) to present itself; (*se payer: vacances, voiture*) to treat o.s. to; **s'~ à faire qch** to offer *ou* volunteer to do sth; **s'~ comme guide/en otage** to offer one's services as (a) guide/offer o.s. as (a) hostage; **s'~ aux regards** (*personne*) to expose o.s. to the public gaze

offset [ɔfsɛt] NM offset (printing)

offusquer [ɔfyske] /**1**/ VT to offend ▪ **s'offusquer de** VPR to take offence (BRIT) ou offense (US) at, be offended by

ogive [ɔʒiv] NF (Archit) diagonal rib; (d'obus, de missile) nose cone; **voûte en ~** rib vault; **arc en ~** lancet arch; **~ nucléaire** nuclear warhead

OGM SIGLE M (= organisme génétiquement modifié) GMO (= genetically modified organism); **culture ~** GM crop

ogre [ɔgʀ] NM ogre

oh [o] EXCL oh!; **oh là là !** oh (dear)!; **pousser des oh ! et des ah !** to gasp with admiration

oie [wa] NF (Zool) goose; **~ blanche** (fig) young innocent

★**oignon** [ɔɲɔ̃] NM (Culin) onion; (de tulipe etc: bulbe) bulb; (Méd) bunion; **ce ne sont pas tes oignons** (fam) that's none of your business

oindre [wɛ̃dʀ] /**49**/ VT to anoint

★**oiseau, x** [wazo] NM bird; **~ de proie** bird of prey

oiseau-mouche [wazomuʃ] (pl **oiseaux-mouches**) NM hummingbird

oiseleur [waz(ə)lœʀ] NM bird-catcher

oiselier, -ière [wazəlje, -jɛʀ] NM/F bird-seller

oisellerie [wazɛlʀi] NF bird shop

oiseux, -euse [wazø, -øz] ADJ pointless, idle; (sans valeur, importance) trivial

oisif, -ive [wazif, -iv] ADJ idle ▶ NM/F (péj) man/lady of leisure

oisillon [wazijɔ̃] NM little ou baby bird

oisiveté [wazivte] NF idleness

OIT SIGLE F (= Organisation internationale du travail) ILO

OK [oke] EXCL OK!, all right!

OL SIGLE FPL (= ondes longues) LW

oléagineux, -euse [ɔleaʒinø, -øz] ADJ oleaginous, oil-producing

oléiculture [ɔleikyltyʀ] NF olive growing

oléoduc [ɔleɔdyk] NM (oil) pipeline

olfactif, -ive [ɔlfaktif, -iv] ADJ olfactory

olibrius [ɔlibʀijys] NM oddball

oligarchie [ɔligaʀʃi] NF oligarchy

oligo-élément [ɔligɔelemɑ̃] NM trace element

oligopole [ɔligɔpɔl] NM oligopoly

olivâtre [ɔlivɑtʀ] ADJ olive-greenish; (teint) sallow

olive [ɔliv] NF (Bot) olive ▶ ADJ INV olive-green

oliveraie [ɔlivʀɛ] NF olive grove

olivette [ɔlivɛt] NF (tomate allongée) plum tomato

olivier [ɔlivje] NM olive (tree); (bois) olive (wood)

olographe [ɔlɔgʀaf] ADJ: **testament ~** will written, dated and signed by the testator

OLP SIGLE F (= Organisation de libération de la Palestine) PLO

olympiade [ɔlɛ̃pjad] NF (période) Olympiad; **les olympiades** (jeux) the Olympiad sg

olympien, ne [ɔlɛ̃pjɛ̃, -ɛn] ADJ Olympian, of Olympian aloofness

olympique [ɔlɛ̃pik] ADJ Olympic

OM SIGLE FPL (= ondes moyennes) MW

Oman [ɔman] N Oman; **le sultanat d'~** the Sultanate of Oman

ombilical, e, -aux [ɔ̃bilikal, -o] ADJ umbilical

ombrage [ɔ̃bʀaʒ] NM (ombre) (leafy) shade; (fig): **prendre ~ de** to take umbrage at; **faire** ou **porter ~ à qn** to offend sb

ombragé, e [ɔ̃bʀaʒe] ADJ shaded, shady

ombrageux, -euse [ɔ̃bʀaʒø, -øz] ADJ (cheval) skittish, nervous; (personne) touchy, easily offended

★**ombre** [ɔ̃bʀ] NF (espace non ensoleillé) shade; (ombre portée, tache) shadow; **à l'~** in the shade; (fam: en prison) behind bars; **à l'~ de** in the shade of; (tout près de, fig) in the shadow of; **tu me fais de l'~** you're in my light; **ça nous donne de l'~** it gives us (some) shade; **il n'y a pas l'~ d'un doute** there's not the shadow of a doubt; **dans l'~** in the shade; (fig) in the dark; **vivre dans l'~** (fig) to live in obscurity; **laisser dans l'~** (fig) to leave in the dark; **~ à paupières** eye shadow; **~ portée** shadow; **ombres chinoises** (spectacle) shadow show sg

ombrelle [ɔ̃bʀɛl] NF parasol, sunshade

ombrer [ɔ̃bʀe] /**1**/ VT to shade

OMC SIGLE F (= organisation mondiale du commerce) WTO

★**omelette** [ɔmlɛt] NF omelette; **~ baveuse** runny omelette; **~ au fromage/au jambon** cheese/ham omelette; **~ aux herbes** omelette with herbs; **~ norvégienne** baked Alaska

omerta [ɔmɛʀta] NF code of silence; **briser l'~** to break the code of silence

omettre [ɔmɛtʀ] /**56**/ VT to omit, leave out; **~ de faire** to fail ou omit to do

omis, e [ɔmi, -iz] PP de **omettre**

omission [ɔmisjɔ̃] NF omission

omnibus [ɔmnibys] NM slow ou stopping train

omnipotent, e [ɔmnipɔtɑ̃, -ɑ̃t] ADJ omnipotent

omnipraticien, ne [ɔmnipʀatisjɛ̃, -ɛn] NM/F (Méd) general practitioner

omniprésent, e [ɔmnipʀezɑ̃, -ɑ̃t] ADJ omnipresent

omniscient, e [ɔmnisjɑ̃, -ɑ̃t] ADJ omniscient

omnisports [ɔmnispɔʀ] ADJ INV (club) general sports cpd; (salle) multi-purpose cpd; (terrain) all-purpose cpd

omnium [ɔmnjɔm] NM (Comm) corporation; (Cyclisme) omnium; (Courses) open handicap

omnivore [ɔmnivɔʀ] ADJ omnivorous

omoplate [ɔmɔplat] NF shoulder blade

OMS SIGLE F (= Organisation mondiale de la santé) WHO

---

on [ɔ̃]

PRON **1** (indéterminé) you, one; **on peut le faire ainsi** you ou one can do it like this, it can be done like this; **on dit que ...** they say that ..., it is said that ...

2 (quelqu'un): **on les a attaqués** they were attacked; **on vous demande au téléphone** there's a phone call for you, you're wanted on the phone; **on frappe à la porte** someone's knocking at the door

3 (*nous*) we; **on va y aller demain** we're going tomorrow
4 (*les gens*) they; **autrefois, on croyait ...** they used to believe ...
5: **on ne peut plus** *adv*: **on ne peut plus stupide** as stupid as can be

onagre [ɔnagʀ] NF (*plante*) evening primrose

once [ɔ̃s] NF: **une ~ de** an ounce of

★**oncle** [ɔ̃kl] NM uncle

oncologue [ɔ̃kɔlɔg] NMF (*médecin*) oncologist

onction [ɔ̃ksjɔ̃] NF *voir* **extrême-onction**

onctueux, -euse [ɔ̃ktɥø, -øz] ADJ creamy, smooth; (*fig*) smooth, unctuous

onde [ɔ̃d] NF (*Physique*) wave; **sur l'~** on the waters; **sur les ondes** on the radio; **mettre en ondes** to produce for the radio; **~ de choc** shock wave; **ondes courtes (OC)** short wave *sg*; **petites ondes (PO)** medium wave *sg*; **ondes moyennes (OM)** medium wave *sg*; **grandes ondes (GO), ondes longues (OL)** long wave *sg*; **ondes sonores** sound waves

ondée [ɔ̃de] NF shower

on-dit [ɔ̃di] NM INV rumour

ondoyer [ɔ̃dwaje] **/8/** VI to ripple, wave ▶ VT (*Rel*) to baptize (*in an emergency*)

ondulant, e [ɔ̃dylɑ̃, -ɑ̃t] ADJ (*démarche*) swaying; (*ligne*) undulating

ondulation [ɔ̃dylasjɔ̃] NF undulation; wave

ondulatoire [ɔ̃dylatwaʀ] ADJ (*Science*) wave *cpd*; **la mécanique ~** wave mechanics

ondulé, e [ɔ̃dyle] ADJ undulating; wavy

onduler [ɔ̃dyle] **/1/** VI to undulate; (*cheveux*) to wave

onéreux, -euse [ɔneʀø, -øz] ADJ costly; **à titre ~** in return for payment

ONF SIGLE M (= *Office national des forêts*) ≈ Forestry Commission (BRIT), ≈ National Forest Service (US)

ONG SIGLE F (= *organisation non gouvernementale*) NGO

★**ongle** [ɔ̃gl] NM (*Anat*) nail; **manger** *ou* **ronger ses ongles** to bite one's nails; **se faire les ongles** to do one's nails

onglet [ɔ̃glɛ] NM (*rainure*) (thumbnail) groove; (*bande de papier*) tab; (*Internet*) tab; **navigation par onglets** tab browsing

onguent [ɔ̃gɑ̃] NM ointment

onirique [ɔniʀik] ADJ dreamlike, dream *cpd*

onirisme [ɔniʀism] NM dreams *pl*

onomatopée [ɔnɔmatɔpe] NF onomatopoeia

ont [ɔ̃] VB *voir* **avoir**

ontarien, ne [ɔ̃taʀjɛ̃, -ɛn] ADJ Ontarian

ONU [ɔny] SIGLE F (= *Organisation des Nations unies*) UN(O)

ONUAA SIGLE F (= *Organisation des Nations unies pour l'alimentation et l'agriculture*) FAO (= *Food and Agriculture Organization*)

onusien, ne [ɔnyzjɛ̃, -ɛn] ADJ of the UN(O), of the United Nations (Organization)

onyx [ɔniks] NM onyx

★**onze** [ɔ̃z] NUM eleven

onzième [ɔ̃zjɛm] NUM eleventh

op [ɔp] NF (*opération*): **salle d'op** (operating) theatre

OPA SIGLE F = **offre publique d'achat**

opacité [ɔpasite] NF opaqueness

opale [ɔpal] NF opal

opalescent, e [ɔpalesɑ̃, -ɑ̃t] ADJ opalescent

opalin, e [ɔpalɛ̃, -in] ADJ, NF opaline

opaque [ɔpak] ADJ (*vitre, verre*) opaque; (*brouillard, nuit*) impenetrable

OPE SIGLE F (= *offre publique d'échange*) take-over bid where bidder offers shares in his company in exchange for shares in target company

OPEP [ɔpɛp] SIGLE F (= *Organisation des pays exportateurs de pétrole*) OPEC

opéra [ɔpeʀa] NM opera; (*édifice*) opera house

opérable [ɔpeʀabl] ADJ operable

opéra-comique [ɔpeʀakɔmik] (*pl* **opéras-comiques**) NM light opera, opéra comique

opérant, e [ɔpeʀɑ̃, -ɑ̃t] ADJ (*mesure*) effective

opérateur, -trice [ɔpeʀatœʀ, -tʀis] NM/F operator; **~ (de prise de vues)** cameraman

opération [ɔpeʀasjɔ̃] NF operation; (*Comm*) dealing; **salle/table d'~** operating theatre/table; **~ de sauvetage** rescue operation; **~ à cœur ouvert** open-heart surgery *no pl*

opérationnel, le [ɔpeʀasjɔnɛl] ADJ operational

opératoire [ɔpeʀatwaʀ] ADJ (*manœuvre, méthode*) operating; (*choc etc*) post-operative

opéré, e [ɔpeʀe] NM/F post-operative patient

opérer [ɔpeʀe] **/6/** VT (*Méd*) to operate on; (*faire, exécuter*) to carry out, make; **se faire ~** to have an operation; **se faire ~ des amygdales/du cœur** to have one's tonsils out/have a heart operation ▶ VI (*remède: faire effet*) to act, work; (*procéder*) to proceed; (*Méd*) to operate ■ **s'opérer** VPR (*avoir lieu*) to occur, take place

opérette [ɔpeʀɛt] NF operetta, light opera

ophtalmique [ɔftalmik] ADJ ophthalmic

ophtalmo [ɔftalmo] NMF (*fam: ophtalmologue*) ophthalmologist

ophtalmologie [ɔftalmɔlɔʒi] NF ophthalmology

ophtalmologue [ɔftalmɔlɔg] NMF ophthalmologist

opiacé, e [ɔpjase] ADJ opiate

opiner [ɔpine] **/1/** VI: **~ de la tête** to nod assent ▶ VT: **~ à** to consent to

opiniâtre [ɔpinjɑtʀ] ADJ stubborn

opiniâtreté [ɔpinjɑtʀəte] NF stubbornness

★**opinion** [ɔpinjɔ̃] NF opinion; **l'~ (publique)** public opinion; **avoir bonne/mauvaise ~ de** to have a high/low opinion of

opiomane [ɔpjɔman] NMF opium addict

opium [ɔpjɔm] NM opium

OPJ SIGLE M (= *officier de police judiciaire*) ≈ DC (= *Detective Constable*)

opportun, e [ɔpɔʀtœ̃, -yn] ADJ timely, opportune; **en temps ~** at the appropriate time

opportunément [ɔpɔʀtynemɑ̃] ADV opportunely

opportunisme [ɔpɔʀtynism] NM opportunism

opportuniste [ɔpɔʀtynist] ADJ, NMF opportunist

opportunité [ɔpɔʀtynite] NF timeliness, opportuneness

opposant, e [ɔpozɑ̃, -ɑ̃t] ADJ opposing ▶ NM/F opponent

opposé, e [ɔpoze] ADJ (direction, rive) opposite; (faction) opposing; (couleurs) contrasting; (opinions, intérêts) conflicting; (contre): ~ **à** opposed to, against; **être ~ à** to be opposed to ▶ NM: **l'~** the other ou opposite side (ou direction); (contraire) the opposite; **à l'~** (fig) on the other hand; **à l'~ de** on the other ou opposite side from; (fig) contrary to, unlike

opposer [ɔpoze] /1/ VT (meubles, objets) to place opposite each other; (personnes, armées, équipes) to oppose; (couleurs, termes, tons) to contrast; (comparer: livres, avantages) to contrast; ~ **qch à** (comme obstacle, défense) to set sth against; (comme objection) to put sth forward against; (en contraste) to set sth opposite; to match sth with ■ **s'opposer** VPR (équipes) to confront each other; (opinions) to conflict; (couleurs, styles) to contrast; **s'~ à** (interdire, empêcher) to oppose; (tenir tête à) to rebel against; **sa religion s'y oppose** it's against his religion; **s'~ à ce que qn fasse** to be opposed to sb's doing

opposition [ɔpozisjɔ̃] NF opposition; **par ~** in contrast; **par ~ à** as opposed to, in contrast with; **entrer en ~ avec** to come into conflict with; **être en ~ avec** (idées, conduite) to be at variance with; **faire ~ à un chèque** to stop a cheque

oppressant, e [ɔpʀesɑ̃, -ɑ̃t] ADJ oppressive

oppresser [ɔpʀese] /1/ VT to oppress; **se sentir oppressé** to feel breathless

oppresseur [ɔpʀesœʀ] NM oppressor

oppressif, -ive [ɔpʀesif, -iv] ADJ oppressive

oppression [ɔpʀesjɔ̃] NF oppression; (malaise) feeling of suffocation

opprimer [ɔpʀime] /1/ VT (asservir: peuple, faibles) to oppress; (étouffer: liberté, opinion) to suppress, stifle; (suj: chaleur etc) to suffocate, oppress

opprobre [ɔpʀɔbʀ] NM disgrace

opter [ɔpte] /1/ VI: ~ **pour** to opt for; ~ **entre** to choose between

★**opticien, ne** [ɔptisjɛ̃, -ɛn] NM/F optician

optimal, e, -aux [ɔptimal, -o] ADJ optimal

optimisation [ɔptimizasjɔ̃] NF optimization

optimiser [ɔptimize] /1/ VT to optimize

optimisme [ɔptimism] NM optimism

★**optimiste** [ɔptimist] ADJ optimistic ▶ NMF optimist

optimum [ɔptimɔm] ADJ, NM optimum

★**option** [ɔpsjɔ̃] NF option; (Auto: supplément) optional extra; **matière à ~** (Scol) optional subject (BRIT), elective (US); **prendre une ~ sur** to take (out) an option on; ~ **par défaut** (Inform) default (option)

optionnel, le [ɔpsjɔnɛl] ADJ optional

optique [ɔptik] ADJ (nerf) optic; (verres) optical ▶ NF (Photo: lentilles etc) optics pl; (science, industrie) optics sg; (fig: manière de voir) perspective

opulence [ɔpylɑ̃s] NF wealth, opulence

opulent, e [ɔpylɑ̃, -ɑ̃t] ADJ wealthy, opulent; (formes, poitrine) ample, generous

opuscule [ɔpyskyl] NM booklet

OPV SIGLE F (= offre publique de vente) public offer of sale

★**or** [ɔʀ] NM gold; **d'or** (fig) golden; **en or** gold cpd; (occasion) golden; **un mari/enfant en or** a treasure; **une affaire en or** (achat) a real bargain; (commerce) a gold mine; **plaqué or** gold-plated; **or noir** black gold ▶ CONJ now, but; **il croyait gagner or il a perdu** he was sure he would win and yet he lost

oracle [ɔʀakl] NM oracle

★**orage** [ɔʀaʒ] NM (thunder)storm

★**orageux, -euse** [ɔʀaʒø, -øz] ADJ stormy

oraison [ɔʀezɔ̃] NF orison, prayer; ~ **funèbre** funeral oration

★**oral, e, -aux** [ɔʀal, -o] ADJ (déposition, promesse) oral, verbal; (Méd): **par voie orale** by mouth, orally ▶ NM (Scol) oral

oralement [ɔʀalmɑ̃] ADV orally

oralité [ɔʀalite] NF the spoken word, orality

★**orange** [ɔʀɑ̃ʒ] ADJ INV, NF orange; ~ **sanguine** blood orange; ~ **pressée** freshly-squeezed orange juice

orangé, e [ɔʀɑ̃ʒe] ADJ orangey, orange-coloured

orangeade [ɔʀɑ̃ʒad] NF orangeade

oranger [ɔʀɑ̃ʒe] NM orange tree

orangeraie [ɔʀɑ̃ʒʀɛ] NF orange grove

orangerie [ɔʀɑ̃ʒʀi] NF orangery

orang-outan, orang-outang [ɔʀɑ̃utɑ̃] (pl **orangs-outans** ou **orangs-outangs**) NM orangutan

orateur [ɔʀatœʀ] NM speaker; orator

oratoire [ɔʀatwaʀ] NM (lieu, chapelle) oratory; (au bord du chemin) wayside shrine ▶ ADJ oratorical

oratorio [ɔʀatɔʀjo] NM oratorio

orbital, e, -aux [ɔʀbital, -o] ADJ orbital; **station orbitale** space station

orbite [ɔʀbit] NF (Anat) (eye-)socket; (Astronomie) orbit; **mettre sur ~** to put into orbit; (fig) to launch; **dans l'~ de** (fig) within the sphere of influence of

orbiter [ɔʀbite] VI (Astronomie): ~ **autour de** to orbit

Orcades [ɔʀkad] NFPL: **les ~** the Orkneys, the Orkney Islands

orchestral, e, -aux [ɔʀkɛstʀal, -o] ADJ orchestral

orchestrateur, -trice [ɔʀkɛstʀatœʀ, -tʀis] NM/F orchestrator

orchestration [ɔʀkɛstʀasjɔ̃] NF orchestration

★**orchestre** [ɔʀkɛstʀ] NM orchestra; (de jazz, danse) band; (places) stalls pl (BRIT), orchestra (US)

orchestrer [ɔʀkɛstʀe] /1/ VT (Mus) to orchestrate; (fig) to mount, stage-manage

orchidée [ɔʀkide] NF orchid

★**ordinaire** [ɔʀdinɛʀ] ADJ ordinary; (coutumier: maladresse etc) usual; (de tous les jours) everyday; (modèle, qualité) standard; (péj: commun) common ▶ NM ordinary; (menus) everyday fare; **d'~** usually, normally; **à l'~** usually, ordinarily; **comme à l'~** as usual ▶ NF (essence) ≈ two-star (petrol) (BRIT), ≈ regular (gas) (US)

ordinairement [ɔʀdinɛʀmɑ̃] ADV ordinarily, usually

ordinal, e, -aux [ɔʀdinal, -o] ADJ ordinal

★**ordinateur** [ɔʀdinatœʀ] NM computer; **mettre sur ~** to computerize, put on computer; **~ de bureau** desktop computer; **~ individuel** ou **personnel** personal computer; **~ portable** laptop (computer)

ordination [ɔʀdinasjɔ̃] NF ordination

★**ordonnance** [ɔʀdɔnɑ̃s] NF (Méd) prescription; (groupement, disposition) layout; (Jur) order; (Mil) orderly, batman (BRIT); **d'~** (Mil) regulation cpd; **officier d'~** aide-de-camp

ordonnancement [ɔʀdɔnɑ̃smɑ̃] NM (agencement) arrangement, layout; (Tech: de production, tâches) scheduling; (Inform: de paquets) sequencing

ordonnateur, -trice [ɔʀdɔnatœʀ, -tʀis] NM/F (d'une cérémonie, fête) organizer; **~ des pompes funèbres** funeral director

ordonné, e [ɔʀdɔne] ADJ tidy, orderly; (Math) ordered ▸ NF (Math) Y-axis, ordinate

ordonner [ɔʀdɔne] /1/ VT (agencer) to organize, arrange; (meubles, appartement) to lay out, arrange; (donner un ordre): **~ à qn de faire** to order sb to do; (Math) to (arrange in) order; (Rel) to ordain; (Méd) to prescribe; (Jur) to order ▪ **s'ordonner** VPR (faits) to organize themselves

★**ordre** [ɔʀdʀ] NM (gén) order; (propreté et soin) orderliness, tidiness; (association professionnelle, honorifique) association; (Comm): **à l'~ de** payable to; (nature): **d'~ pratique** of a practical nature; **avoir de l'~** to be tidy ou orderly; **mettre en ~** to tidy (up), put in order; **mettre bon ~ à** to put to rights, sort out; **procéder par ~** to take things one at a time; **par ~ alphabétique/d'importance** in alphabetical order/in order of importance; **rappeler qn à l'~** to call sb to order; **jusqu'à nouvel ~** until further notice; **dans le même ~ d'idées** in this connection; **par ~ d'entrée en scène** in order of appearance; **un ~ de grandeur** some idea of the size (ou amount); **de premier ~** first-rate; **~ de grève** strike call; **~ du jour** (d'une réunion) agenda; (Mil) order of the day; **à l'~ du jour** on the agenda; (fig) topical; (Mil: citer) in dispatches; **~ de mission** (Mil) orders pl; **~ public** law and order; **~ de route** marching orders pl ▪ **ordres** NMPL (Rel) holy orders; **être aux ordres de qn/sous les ordres de qn** to be at sb's disposal/under sb's command

ordure [ɔʀdyʀ] NF filth no pl; (propos, écrit) obscenity, (piece of) filth ▪ **ordures** NFPL (balayures, déchets) rubbish sg, refuse sg; **ordures ménagères** household refuse

ordurier, -ière [ɔʀdyʀje, -jɛʀ] ADJ lewd, filthy

★**oreille** [ɔʀɛj] NF (Anat) ear; (Tech: d'un écrou) wing; **avoir de l'~** to have a good ear (for music); **avoir l'~ fine** to have good ou sharp ears; **l'~ basse** crestfallen, dejected; **se faire tirer l'~** to take a lot of persuading; **dire qch à l'~ de qn** to have a word in sb's ear (about sth)

★**oreiller** [ɔʀeje] NM pillow

oreillette [ɔʀɛjɛt] NF (Anat) auricle

oreillons [ɔʀɛjɔ̃] NMPL mumps sg

ores [ɔʀ]: **d'~ et déjà** adv already

orfèvre [ɔʀfɛvʀ] NM goldsmith; silversmith

orfèvrerie [ɔʀfɛvʀəʀi] NF (art, métier) goldsmith's (ou silversmith's) trade; (ouvrage) (silver ou gold) plate

orfraie [ɔʀfʀɛ] NM white-tailed eagle; **pousser**

des cris d'~ to yell at the top of one's voice

organe [ɔʀgan] NM organ; (véhicule, instrument) instrument; (voix) voice; (porte-parole) representative, mouthpiece; **organes de commande** (Tech) controls; **organes de transmission** (Tech) transmission system sg

organigramme [ɔʀganigʀam] NM (hiérarchique, structure) organization chart; (des opérations) flow chart

organique [ɔʀganik] ADJ organic

organisateur, -trice [ɔʀganizatœʀ, -tʀis] NM/F organizer

organisation [ɔʀganizasjɔ̃] NF organization; **O~ des Nations unies (ONU)** United Nations (Organization) (UN(O)); **O~ mondiale de la santé (OMS)** World Health Organization (WHO); **O~ du traité de l'Atlantique Nord (OTAN)** North Atlantic Treaty Organization (NATO)

organisationnel, le [ɔʀganizasjɔnɛl] ADJ organizational

★**organiser** [ɔʀganize] /1/ VT to organize; (mettre sur pied: service etc) to set up ▪ **s'organiser** VPR to get organized

organisme [ɔʀganism] NM (Bio) organism; (corps humain) body; (Admin, Pol etc) body, organism

organiste [ɔʀganist] NMF organist

orgasme [ɔʀgasm] NM orgasm, climax

orge [ɔʀʒ] NF barley

orgeat [ɔʀʒa] NM: **sirop d'~** barley water

orgelet [ɔʀʒəlɛ] NM sty(e)

orgie [ɔʀʒi] NF orgy

orgue [ɔʀg] NM organ; **~ de Barbarie** barrel ou street organ ▪ **orgues** NFPL organ sg

orgueil [ɔʀgœj] NM pride

orgueilleux, -euse [ɔʀgœjø, -øz] ADJ proud

Orient [ɔʀjɑ̃] NM: **l'~** the East, the Orient

orientable [ɔʀjɑ̃tabl] ADJ (phare, lampe etc) adjustable

oriental, e, -aux [ɔʀjɑ̃tal, -o] ADJ (langue, produit) oriental, eastern; (frontière) eastern ▸ NM/F: **Oriental, e** Oriental

orientation [ɔʀjɑ̃tasjɔ̃] NF positioning; adjustment; (de recherches) orientation; direction; (d'une maison etc) aspect; (d'un journal) leanings pl; **avoir le sens de l'~** to have a (good) sense of direction; **course d'~** orienteering exercise; **~ professionnelle** careers advice ou guidance; (service) careers advisory service

orienté, e [ɔʀjɑ̃te] ADJ (fig: article, journal) slanted; **bien/mal ~** (appartement) well/badly positioned; **~ au sud** facing south, with a southern aspect

orienter [ɔʀjɑ̃te] /1/ VT (situer) to position; (placer, disposer: pièce mobile) to adjust, position; (tourner: antenne) to direct, turn; (voyageur, touriste, recherches) to direct; (fig: élève) to orientate ▪ **s'orienter** VPR (se repérer) to find one's bearings; **s'~ vers** (fig) to turn towards

orienteur, -euse [ɔʀjɑ̃tœʀ, -øz] NM/F (Scol) careers adviser

orifice [ɔʀifis] NM opening, orifice

oriflamme [ɔʀiflam] NF banner, standard

origan [ɔʀigɑ̃] NM oregano

originaire [ɔʀiʒinɛʀ] ADJ original; **être ~ de** (pays, *lieu*) to be a native of; (*provenir de*) to originate from; to be native to

★**original, e, -aux** [ɔʀiʒinal, -o] ADJ original; (*bizarre*) eccentric ▶ NM/F (*fam: excentrique*) eccentric; (: *fantaisiste*) joker ▶ NM (*document etc, Art*) original; (*dactylographie*) top copy

originalité [ɔʀiʒinalite] NF (*d'un nouveau modèle*) originality *no pl*; (*excentricité, bizarrerie*) eccentricity

origine [ɔʀiʒin] NF origin; (*d'un message, appel téléphonique*) source; (*d'une révolution, réussite*) root; **d'~** (*pays*) of origin; (*pneus etc*) original; (*bureau postal*) dispatching; **d'~ française** of French origin; **dès l'~** at *ou* from the outset; **à l'~** originally; **avoir son ~ dans** to have its origins in, originate in ■ **origines** NFPL (*d'une personne*) origins

originel, le [ɔʀiʒinɛl] ADJ original

originellement [ɔʀiʒinɛlmɑ̃] ADV (*à l'origine*) originally; (*dès l'origine*) from the beginning

oripeaux [ɔʀipo] NMPL rags

ORL SIGLE F (= *oto-rhino-laryngologie*) ENT; **être en ~** (*malade*) to be in the ENT hospital *ou* department ▶ SIGLE MF (= *oto-rhino-laryngologiste*) ENT specialist

orme [ɔʀm] NM elm

orné, e [ɔʀne] ADJ ornate; **~ de** adorned *ou* decorated with

ornement [ɔʀnəmɑ̃] NM ornament; (*fig*) embellishment, adornment; **ornements sacerdotaux** vestments

ornemental, e, -aux [ɔʀnəmɑ̃tal, -o] ADJ ornamental

ornementer [ɔʀnəmɑ̃te] /1/ VT to ornament

orner [ɔʀne] /1/ VT to decorate, adorn; **~ qch de** to decorate sth with

ornière [ɔʀnjɛʀ] NF rut; (*fig*): **sortir de l'~** (*routine*) to get out of the rut; (*impasse*) to get out of a spot

ornithologie [ɔʀnitɔlɔʒi] NF ornithology

ornithologue [ɔʀnitɔlɔg] NMF ornithologist; **~ amateur** birdwatcher

orphelin, e [ɔʀfəlɛ̃, -in] ADJ orphan(ed); **~ de père/mère** fatherless/motherless ▶ NM/F orphan

orphelinat [ɔʀfəlina] NM orphanage

ORSEC [ɔʀsɛk] SIGLE F = **Organisation de la réponse de sécurité civile**; **le plan ~** *disaster contingency plan*

ORSECRAD [ɔʀsɛkʀad] SIGLE M = **ORSEC en cas d'accident nucléaire**

orteil [ɔʀtɛj] NM toe; **gros ~** big toe

orthodontiste [ɔʀtɔdɔ̃tist] NMF orthodontist

orthodoxe [ɔʀtɔdɔks] ADJ orthodox

orthodoxie [ɔʀtɔdɔksi] NF orthodoxy

orthogénie [ɔʀtɔʒeni] NF family planning

orthographe [ɔʀtɔgʀaf] NF spelling

orthographier [ɔʀtɔgʀafje] /7/ VT to spell; **mal orthographié** misspelt

orthopédie [ɔʀtɔpedi] NF orthopaedics *sg* (BRIT), orthopedics *sg* (US)

orthopédique [ɔʀtɔpedik] ADJ orthopaedic (BRIT), orthopedic (US)

orthopédiste [ɔʀtɔpedist] NMF orthopaedic (BRIT) *ou* orthopedic (US) specialist

orthophonie [ɔʀtɔfɔni] NF (*Méd*) speech therapy; (*Ling*) correct pronunciation

orthophoniste [ɔʀtɔfɔnist] NMF speech therapist

ortie [ɔʀti] NF (stinging) nettle; **~ blanche** white dead-nettle

★**os** [ɔs] NM bone; **sans os** (*Boucherie*) off the bone, boned; **os à moelle** marrowbone

oscillation [ɔsilasjɔ̃] NF oscillation ■ **oscillations** NFPL (*fig*) fluctuations

osciller [ɔsile] /1/ VI (*pendule*) to swing; (*au vent etc*) to rock; (*Tech*) to oscillate; (*fig*): **~ entre** to waver *ou* fluctuate between

osé, e [oze] ADJ daring, bold

oseille [ozɛj] NF sorrel

★**oser** [oze] /1/ VI, VT to dare; **~ faire** to dare (to) do

osier [ozje] NM (*Bot*) willow; **d'~, en ~** wicker(work) *cpd*

Oslo [ɔslo] N Oslo

osmose [ɔsmoz] NF osmosis

ossature [ɔsatyʀ] NF (*Anat: squelette*) frame, skeletal structure; (: *du visage*) bone structure; (*fig*) framework

osselet [ɔslɛ] NM (*Anat*) ossicle; **jouer aux osselets** to play jacks

ossements [ɔsmɑ̃] NMPL bones

osseux, -euse [ɔsø, -øz] ADJ bony; (*tissu, maladie, greffe*) bone *cpd*

ossifier [ɔsifje] /7/: **s'ossifier** VPR to ossify

ossuaire [ɔsɥɛʀ] NM ossuary

Ostende [ɔstɑ̃d] N Ostend

ostensible [ɔstɑ̃sibl] ADJ conspicuous

ostensiblement [ɔstɑ̃sibləmɑ̃] ADV conspicuously

ostensoir [ɔstɑ̃swaʀ] NM monstrance

ostentation [ɔstɑ̃tasjɔ̃] NF ostentation; **faire ~ de** to parade, make a display of

ostentatoire [ɔstɑ̃tatwaʀ] ADJ ostentatious

ostraciser [ɔstʀasize] VT to ostracize

ostracisme [ɔstʀasism] NM ostracism; **frapper d'~** to ostracize

ostréicole [ɔstʀeikɔl] ADJ oyster *cpd*

ostréiculteur, -trice [ɔstʀeikyltœʀ, -tʀis] NM/F oyster farmer, oyster grower

ostréiculture [ɔstʀeikyltyʀ] NF oyster-farming

otage [ɔtaʒ] NM hostage; **prendre qn en ~** to take sb hostage

OTAN [ɔtɑ̃] SIGLE F (= *Organisation du traité de l'Atlantique Nord*) NATO

otarie [ɔtaʀi] NF sea-lion

ôter [ote] /1/ VT to remove; (*soustraire*) to take away; **~ qch à qn** to take sth (away) from sb; **~ qch de** to remove sth from; **six ôté de dix égale quatre** six from ten equals *ou* is four

otite [ɔtit] NF ear infection

oto-rhino [ɔtoʀino], **oto-rhino-laryngologiste** [ɔtoʀinolaʀɛ̃gɔlɔʒist] NMF ear, nose and throat specialist

ottomane [ɔtɔman] NF ottoman

o

★**ou** [u] CONJ or; **ou ... ou** either ... or; **ou bien** or (else)

---

où [u]

PRON RELATIF **1** (*position, situation*) where, that (*souvent omis*); **la chambre où il était** the room (that) he was in, the room where he was; **la ville où je l'ai rencontré** the town where I met him; **la pièce d'où il est sorti** the room he came out of; **le village d'où je viens** the village I come from; **les villes par où il est passé** the towns he went through
2 (*temps, état*) that (*souvent omis*); **le jour où il est parti** the day (that) he left; **au prix où c'est** at the price it is
▶ ADV **1** (*interrogation*) where; **où est-il/va-t-il?** where is he/is he going?; **par où?** which way?; **d'où vient que ...?** how come ...?
2 (*position*) where; **je sais où il est** I know where he is; **où que l'on aille** wherever you go

---

ouah ['wa] EXCL woof!; (*fam: admiratif*) wow!

ouais [wɛ] EXCL yeah

ouate [wat] NF cotton wool (BRIT), cotton (US); (*bourre*) padding, wadding; **~ (hydrophile)** cotton wool (BRIT), (absorbent) cotton (US)

ouaté, e [wate] ADJ cotton-wool; (*doublé*) padded; (*fig: atmosphère*) cocoon-like; (: *pas, bruit*) muffled

oubli [ubli] NM (*acte*): **l'~ de** forgetting; (*trou de mémoire*) lapse of memory; (*étourderie*) forgetfulness *no pl*; (*négligence*) omission, oversight; (*absence de souvenirs*) oblivion; **~ de soi** self-effacement, self-negation; **tomber dans l'~** to sink into oblivion; **le droit à l'~** (*Internet, Méd*) the right to be forgotten

★**oublier** [ublije] /**7**/ VT (*gén*) to forget; (*ne pas voir: erreurs etc*) to miss; (*ne pas mettre: virgule, nom*) to leave out, forget; (*laisser quelque part: chapeau etc*) to leave behind; **~ l'heure** to forget (about) the time ■ **s'oublier** VPR to forget o.s.; (*enfant, animal*) to have an accident (*euphemism*)

oubliettes [ublijɛt] NFPL dungeon *sg*; (**jeter**) **aux ~** (*fig*) (to put) completely out of mind

oublieux, -euse [ublijø, -øz] ADJ forgetful

oued [wed] NM wadi

★**ouest** [wɛst] NM west; **à l'~** in the west; (*direction*) (to the) west, westwards; **à l'~ de** (to the) west of; **vent d'~** westerly wind ▶ ADJ INV west; (*région*) western

ouest-allemand, e [wɛstalmã, -ãd] ADJ West German

ouf [uf] EXCL phew!

Ouganda [ugãda] NM: **l'~** Uganda

ougandais, e [ugãdɛ, -ɛz] ADJ Ugandan

★**oui** [wi] yes; **répondre (par) ~** to answer yes; **mais ~, bien sûr** yes, of course; **je pense que ~** I think so; **pour un ~ ou pour un non** for no apparent reason

ouï-dire [widir]: **par ~** *adv* by hearsay

ouïe [wi] NF hearing ■ **ouïes** NFPL (*de poisson*) gills; (*de violon*) sound-hole *sg*

ouïr [wir] /**10**/ VT to hear; **avoir ouï dire que** to have heard it said that

ouistiti [wistiti] NM marmoset

oukase [ukaz] NM (Hist) ukase; (*fig: décision arbitraire*) edict

ouragan [uragã] NM hurricane; (*fig*) storm

Oural [ural] NM: **l'~** (*fleuve*) the Ural; (*aussi:* **les monts Oural**) the Urals, the Ural Mountains

ourdir [urdir] /**2**/ VT (*complot*) to hatch

ourdou, e [urdu] ADJ Urdu ▶ NM (Ling) Urdu

ourlé, e [urle] ADJ hemmed; (*fig*) rimmed

ourler [urle] /**1**/ VT to hem

ourlet [urlɛ] NM hem; (*de l'oreille*) rim; **faire un ~ à** to hem

★**ours** [urs] NM bear; **~ brun/blanc** brown/polar bear; **~ marin** fur seal; **~ mal léché** uncouth fellow; **~ (en peluche)** teddy (bear)

ourse [urs] NF (Zool) she-bear; **la Grande/Petite O~** the Great/Little Bear, Ursa Major/Minor

oursin [ursɛ̃] NM sea urchin

ourson [ursɔ̃] NM (bear-)cub

ouste [ust] EXCL hop it!

★**outil** [uti] NM tool

outillage [utijaʒ] NM set of tools; (*d'atelier*) equipment *no pl*

outiller [utije] /**1**/ VT (*ouvrier, usine*) to equip

outrage [utraʒ] NM insult; **faire subir les derniers outrages à** (*femme*) to ravish; **~ aux bonnes mœurs** (Jur) outrage to public decency; **~ à magistrat** (Jur) contempt of court; **~ à la pudeur** (Jur) indecent behaviour *no pl*

outragé, e [utraʒe] ADJ offended; outraged

outrageant, e [utraʒã, -ãt] ADJ offensive

outrager [utraʒe] /**3**/ VT to offend gravely; (*fig: contrevenir à*) to outrage, insult

outrageusement [utraʒøzmã] ADV outrageously

outrance [utrãs] NF excessiveness *no pl*, excess; **à ~** *adv* excessively, to excess

outrancier, -ière [utrãsje, -jɛr] ADJ extreme

outre [utr] NF goatskin, water skin ▶ PRÉP besides; **en ~** besides, moreover; **~ que** apart from the fact that; **~ mesure** to excess; (*manger, boire*) immoderately ▶ ADV: **passer ~** to carry on regardless; **passer ~ à** to disregard, take no notice of

outré, e [utre] ADJ (*flatterie, éloge*) excessive, exaggerated; (*indigné, scandalisé*) outraged

outre-Atlantique [utratlãtik] ADV across the Atlantic

outrecuidance [utrəkɥidãs] NF presumptuousness *no pl*

outre-Manche [utrəmãʃ] ADV across the Channel

outremer [utrəmɛr] ADJ INV ultramarine

outre-mer [utrəmɛr] ADV overseas; **d'~** overseas

outrepasser [utrəpase] /**1**/ VT to go beyond, exceed

outrer [utre] /**1**/ VT (*pensée, attitude*) to exaggerate; (*indigner: personne*) to outrage

outre-Rhin [utrərɛ̃] ADV across the Rhine, in Germany

outsider [awtsajdœr] NM outsider

★**ouvert, e** [uvɛr, -ɛrt] PP *de* **ouvrir** ▶ ADJ open; (*robinet, gaz etc*) on; **à bras ouverts** with open arms

ouvertement [uvɛrtəmã] ADV openly

ouverture [uvɛʀtyʀ] NF opening; (*Mus*) overture; (*Pol*): **l'~** the widening of the political spectrum; (*Photo*): **~ (du diaphragme)** aperture; **~ d'esprit** open-mindedness; **heures d'~** (*Comm*) opening hours; **jours d'~** (*Comm*) days of opening ■ **ouvertures** NFPL (*propositions*) overtures

ouvrable [uvʀabl] ADJ: **jour ~** working day, weekday; **heures ouvrables** business hours

ouvrage [uvʀaʒ] NM (*tâche, de tricot etc, Mil*) work *no pl*; (*objet: Couture, Art*) (piece of) work; (*texte, livre*) work; **panier** *ou* **corbeille à ~** work basket; **~ d'art** (*Génie Civil*) bridge or tunnel *etc*

ouvragé, e [uvʀaʒe] ADJ finely embroidered (*ou* worked *ou* carved)

ouvrant, e [uvʀɑ̃, -ɑ̃t] VB *voir* **ouvrir** ▶ ADJ: **toit ~** sunroof

ouvré, e [uvʀe] ADJ finely-worked; **jour ~** working day

ouvre-boîte(s) [uvʀəbwat] NM INV tin (BRIT) *ou* can opener

ouvre-bouteille(s) [uvʀəbutɛj] NM INV bottle-opener

ouvreuse [uvʀøz] NF usherette

★**ouvrier, -ière** [uvʀije, -jɛʀ] NM/F worker; **~ agricole** farmworker; **~ qualifié** skilled worker; **~ spécialisé** semiskilled worker; **~ d'usine** factory worker ▶ NF (*Zool*) worker (bee) ▶ ADJ workingclass; (*problèmes, conflit*) industrial; (*mouvement*) labour *cpd* (BRIT), labor *cpd* (US); (*revendications*) workers'; **classe ouvrière** working class

★**ouvrir** [uvʀiʀ] /**18**/ VT (*gén*) to open; (*brèche, passage*) to open up; (*commencer l'exploitation de, créer*) to open (up); (*eau, électricité, chauffage, robinet*) to turn on; (*Méd: abcès*) to open up, cut open; **~ l'appétit à qn** to whet sb's appetite; **~ des horizons** to open up new horizons; **~ l'esprit** to broaden one's horizons; **~ une session** (*Inform*) to log in ▶ VI to open; to open up; (*Cartes*): **~ à trèfle** to open in clubs; **~ sur** to open onto ■ **s'ouvrir** VPR to open; **s'~** (*art etc*) to open one's mind to; **s'~ à qn (de qch)** to open one's heart to sb (about sth); **s'~ les veines** to slash *ou* cut one's wrists

ouvroir [uvʀwaʀ] NM workroom, sewing room

ovaire [ɔvɛʀ] NM ovary

ovale [ɔval] ADJ oval

ovation [ɔvasjɔ̃] NF ovation

ovationner [ɔvasjɔne] /**1**/ VT: **~ qn** to give sb an ovation

ovin, e [ɔvɛ̃, -in] ADJ ovine

OVNI [ɔvni] SIGLE M (= *objet volant non identifié*) UFO

ovoïde [ɔvɔid] ADJ egg-shaped

ovulation [ɔvylasjɔ̃] NF (*Physiol*) ovulation

ovule [ɔvyl] NM (*Physiol*) ovum; (*Méd*) pessary

oxfordien, ne [ɔksfɔʀdjɛ̃, -ɛn] ADJ Oxonian ▶ NM/F: **Oxfordien, ne** Oxonian

oxydable [ɔksidabl] ADJ liable to rust

oxyde [ɔksid] NM oxide; **~ de carbone** carbon monoxide

oxyder [ɔkside] /**1**/: **s'oxyder** VPR to become oxidized

oxygène [ɔksiʒɛn] NM oxygen

oxygéné, e [ɔksiʒene] ADJ: **eau oxygénée** hydrogen peroxide; **cheveux oxygénés** bleached hair

ozone [ozon] NM ozone; **trou dans la couche d'~** hole in the ozone layer

O

313

Pp

P, p [pe] NM INV P, p ► ABR (= *Père*) Fr; (= *page*) p; **P comme Pierre** P for Peter

PA SIGLE FPL = **les petites annonces**

PAC SIGLE F (= *Politique agricole commune*) CAP

PACA [paka] SIGLE F (*région*: = *Provence-Alpes-Côte d'Azur*) administrative region in south-east France; **en ~** in Provence-Alpes-Côte d'Azur

pacage [pakaʒ] NM grazing, pasture

pacemaker [pɛsmɛkœʀ] NM pacemaker

pachyderme [paʃidɛʀm] NM pachyderm; elephant

pacificateur, -trice [pasifikatœʀ, -tʀis] ADJ pacificatory

pacification [pasifikasjɔ̃] NF pacification

pacifier [pasifje] /7/ VT to pacify

pacifique [pasifik] ADJ (*personne*) peaceable; (*intentions, coexistence*) peaceful ► NM: **le P~, l'océan P~** the Pacific (Ocean)

pacifiquement [pasifikmɑ̃] ADV peaceably; peacefully

pacifisme [pasifism] NM pacifism

pacifiste [pasifist] NMF pacifist

pack [pak] NM pack

pacotille [pakɔtij] NF (*péj*) cheap junk *pl*; **de ~** cheap

Pacs [paks] SIGLE M (= *pacte civil de solidarité*) ≈ civil partnership

> The *Pacte civil de solidarité*, or **Pacs**, is a contract entered into by two single people of 18 or over, allowing them to formally and legally register their relationship and enter into a civil partnership. The parties can be a man and a woman or two people of the same sex. The contract carries with it the mutual obligation to take care of each other and provide each other with financial support. Although it carries rights similar to those of married couples, it is less advantageous in certain areas, for instance as far as inheritance is concerned.

pacsé, e [pakse] ADJ: **être ~** ≈ to have registered a civil partnership ► NM/F *person who has registered a civil partnership*

pacser [pakse] /1/: **se pacser** VPR ≈ to form a civil partnership

pacte [pakt] NM pact, treaty

pactiser [paktize] /1/ VI: **~ avec** to come to terms with

pactole [paktɔl] NM gold mine (*fig*)

paddock [padɔk] NM paddock

Padoue [padu] N Padua

PAF SIGLE F (= *Police de l'air et des frontières*) police authority responsible for civil aviation, border control etc ► SIGLE M (= *paysage audiovisuel français*) French broadcasting

pagaie [pagɛ] NF paddle

pagaille [pagaj] NF (*fam*) mess, shambles *sg*; **il y en a en ~** there are loads *ou* heaps of them

paganisme [paganism] NM paganism

pagayer [pageje] /8/ VI to paddle

★**page** [paʒ] NF page; (*passage: d'un roman*) passage; **mettre en pages** to make up (into pages); **mise en ~** layout; **à la ~** (*fig*) up-to-date; **~ d'accueil** (*Inform*) home page; **~ blanche** blank page; **~ de garde** endpaper; **~ Web** web page ► NM page (boy)

page-écran [paʒekʀɑ̃] (*pl* **pages-écrans**) NF (*Inform*) screen page

pagination [paʒinasjɔ̃] NF pagination

paginer [paʒine] /1/ VT to paginate

pagne [paɲ] NM loincloth

pagode [pagɔd] NF pagoda

paie [pɛ] NF = **paye**

paiement [pɛmɑ̃] NM = **payement**

païen, ne [pajɛ̃, -ɛn] ADJ, NM/F pagan, heathen

paillard, e [pajaʀ, -aʀd] ADJ bawdy

paillasse [pajas] NF (*matelas*) straw mattress; (*d'un évier*) draining board

paillasson [pajasɔ̃] NM doormat

paille [paj] NF straw; (*défaut*) flaw; **être sur la ~** to be ruined; **~ de fer** steel wool

paillé, e [paje] ADJ with a straw seat

pailleté, e [paj(ə)te] ADJ sequined

paillette [pajet] NF speck, flake ■ **paillettes** NFPL (*décoratives*) sequins, spangles; **lessive en paillettes** soapflakes *pl*

★**pain** [pɛ̃] NM (*substance*) bread; (*unité*) loaf (of bread); (*morceau*): **~ de cire** etc bar of wax etc; (*Culin*): **~ de poisson/légumes** fish/vegetable loaf; **petit ~** (bread) roll; **~ bis/complet** brown/wholemeal (BRIT) *ou* wholewheat (US) bread; **~ de campagne** farmhouse bread; **~ d'épice** ≈ gingerbread; **~ grillé** toast; **~ de mie** sandwich loaf; **~ perdu** French toast; **~ de seigle** rye bread; **~ de sucre** sugar loaf; **~ au chocolat** pain au chocolat; **~ aux raisins** currant pastry

pair, e [pɛR] ADJ (*nombre*) even ▶ NM peer; **aller de ~ (avec)** to go hand in hand *ou* together (with); **au ~** (*Finance*) at par; **valeur au ~** par value; **jeune fille au ~** au pair

★**paire** [pɛR] NF pair; **une ~ de lunettes/tenailles** a pair of glasses/pincers; **les deux font la ~** they are two of a kind

pais [pɛ] VB *voir* **paître**

paisible [pezibl] ADJ peaceful, quiet

paisiblement [peziblǝmɑ̃] ADV peacefully, quietly

paître [pɛtR] /57/ VI to graze

★**paix** [pɛ] NF peace; (*fig*) peacefulness, peace; **faire la ~ avec** to make peace with; **avoir la ~** to have peace (and quiet); **fiche-lui la ~ !** (*fam*) leave him alone!

Pakistan [pakistɑ̃] NM: **le ~** Pakistan

pakistanais, e [pakistanɛ, -ɛz] ADJ Pakistani

PAL SIGLE M (= *Phase Alternation Line*) PAL

palabrer [palabRe] /1/ VI to argue endlessly

palabres [palabR] NFPL endless arguments

palace [palas] NM luxury hotel

★**palais** [palɛ] NM palace; (*Anat*) palate; **le P~ Bourbon** *the seat of the French National Assembly*; **le P~ de l'Élysée** the Élysée Palace; **~ des expositions** exhibition centre (BRIT) *ou* center (US); **le P~ de Justice** the Law Courts *pl*

palan [palɑ̃] NM hoist

pale [pal] NF (*d'hélice, de rame*) blade; (*de roue*) paddle

★**pâle** [pɑl] ADJ pale; (*fig*): **une ~ imitation** a pale imitation; **bleu ~** pale blue; **~ de colère** white *ou* pale with anger

palefrenier [palfRǝnje] NM groom (*for horses*)

paléontologie [paleɔ̃tɔlɔʒi] NF paleontology

paléontologiste [paleɔ̃tɔlɔʒist], **paléontologue** [paleɔ̃tɔlɔg] NMF paleontologist

Palerme [palɛRm] N Palermo

Palestine [palɛstin] NF: **la ~** Palestine

palestinien, ne [palɛstinjɛ̃, -ɛn] ADJ Palestinian ▶ NM/F: **Palestinien, ne** Palestinian

palet [palɛ] NM disc; (*Hockey*) puck

paletot [palto] NM (*short*) coat

palette [palɛt] NF (*de peintre*) palette; (*de produits*) range

palétuvier [paletyvje] NM mangrove

pâleur [pɑlœR] NF paleness

palier [palje] NM (*d'escalier*) landing; (*fig*) level, plateau; (: *phase stable*) levelling (BRIT) *ou* leveling (US) off, new level; (*Tech*) bearing; **nos voisins de ~** our neighbo(u)rs across the landing (BRIT) *ou* the hall (US); **en ~** *adv* level; **par paliers** in stages

palière [paljɛR] ADJ F landing *cpd*

pâlir [pɑliR] /2/ VI to turn *ou* go pale; (*couleur*) to fade; **faire ~ qn** (*de jalousie*) to make sb green (with envy)

palissade [palisad] NF fence

palissandre [palisɑ̃dR] NM rosewood

palliatif [paljatif] NM palliative; (*expédient*) stopgap measure

pallier [palje] /7/ VT: **~ (à)** to offset, make up for

palmarès [palmaRɛs] NM record (of achievements); (*Scol*) prize list; (*Sport*) list of winners

palme [palm] NF (*Bot*) palm leaf; (*symbole*) palm; (*de plongeur*) flipper; **palmes (académiques)** *decoration for services to education*

palmé, e [palme] ADJ (*pattes*) webbed

palmeraie [palmǝRɛ] NF palm grove

palmier [palmje] NM palm tree; (*gâteau*) *heart-shaped biscuit made of flaky pastry*

palmipède [palmipɛd] NM palmiped, webfooted bird

palois, e [palwa, -waz] ADJ of *ou* from Pau ▶ NM/F: **Palois, e** inhabitant *ou* native of Pau

palombe [palɔ̃b] NF woodpigeon, ringdove

pâlot, te [pɑlo, -ɔt] ADJ pale, peaky

palourde [paluRd] NF clam

palpable [palpabl] ADJ tangible, palpable

palper [palpe] /1/ VT to feel, finger

palpitant, e [palpitɑ̃, -ɑ̃t] ADJ thrilling, gripping

palpitation [palpitasjɔ̃] NF palpitation

palpiter [palpite] /1/ VI (*cœur, pouls*) to beat; (: *plus fort*) to pound, throb; (*narines, chair*) to quiver

paludisme [palydism] NM malaria

palustre [palystR] ADJ (*coquillage etc*) marsh *cpd*; (*fièvre*) malarial

pâmer [pɑme] /1/: **se pâmer** VPR to swoon; (*fig*): **se ~ devant** to go into raptures over

pâmoison [pɑmwazɔ̃] NF: **tomber en ~** to swoon

pampa [pɑ̃pa] NF pampas *pl*

pamphlet [pɑ̃flɛ] NM lampoon, satirical tract

pamphlétaire [pɑ̃fletɛR] NMF lampoonist

★**pamplemousse** [pɑ̃plǝmus] NM grapefruit

pan [pɑ̃] NM section, piece; (*côté: d'un prisme, d'une tour*) side, face; **~ de chemise** shirt tail; **~ de mur** section of wall ▶ EXCL bang!

panacée [panase] NF panacea

panachage [panaʃaʒ] NM blend, mix; (*Pol*) *voting for candidates from different parties instead of for the set list of one party*

panache [panaʃ] NM plume; (*fig*) spirit, panache

panaché, e [panaʃe] ADJ: **œillet ~** variegated carnation; **glace panachée** mixed ice cream; **salade panachée** mixed salad ▶ NM (*bière*) shandy

panais [panɛ] NM parsnip

Panama [panama] NM: **le ~** Panama

panaméen, ne [panameɛ̃, -ɛn] ADJ Panamanian ▶ NM/F: **Panaméen, ne** Panamanian

panaris [panaRi] NM whitlow

pancarte [pɑ̃kaRt] NF sign, notice; (*dans un défilé*) placard

pancréas [pɑ̃kReas] NM pancreas

panda [pɑ̃da] NM panda

pandémie [pɑ̃demi] NF pandemic

pané, e [pane] ADJ fried in breadcrumbs

panégyrique [paneʒiRik] NM: **faire le ~ de qn** to extol sb's merits *ou* virtues

★**panier** [panje] NM basket; (*à diapositives*) magazine; **mettre au ~** to chuck away; **~ de crabes**: **c'est un ~ de crabes** (*fig*) they're constantly at one another's throats; **~ percé** (*fig*) spendthrift; **~ à provisions** shopping basket; **~ à salade** (*Culin*) salad shaker; (*Police*) paddy wagon, police van

315

panier-repas [panjeʀ(ə)pɑ] (*pl* **paniers-repas**) NM packed lunch

panification [panifikasjɔ̃] NF bread-making

panique [panik] ADJ panicky ▸ NF panic

paniquer [panike] /1/ VI to panic

★**panne** [pan] NF (*d'un mécanisme, moteur*) breakdown; **être/tomber en ~** to have broken down/break down; **être en ~ d'essence** *ou* **en ~ sèche** to have run out of petrol (BRIT) *ou* gas (US); **mettre en ~** (*Navig*) to bring to; **~ d'électricité** *ou* **de courant** power *ou* electrical failure

★**panneau, x** [pano] NM (*écriteau*) sign, notice; (*de boiserie, de tapisserie etc*) panel; **tomber dans le ~** (*fig*) to walk into the trap; **~ d'affichage** notice (BRIT) *ou* bulletin (US) board; **~ électoral** board for election poster; **~ indicateur** signpost; **~ publicitaire** hoarding (BRIT), billboard (US); **~ de signalisation** roadsign; **~ solaire** solar panel

panonceau, x [panɔ̃so] NM (*de magasin etc*) sign; (*de médecin etc*) plaque

panoplie [panɔpli] NF (*jouet*) outfit; (*d'armes*) display; (*fig*) array

panorama [panɔrama] NM (*vue*) all-round view, panorama; (*peinture*) panorama; (*fig: étude complète*) complete overview

panoramique [panɔramik] ADJ panoramic; (*carrosserie*) with panoramic windows ▸ NM (*Ciné, TV*) panoramic shot

panse [pɑ̃s] NF paunch

★**pansement** [pɑ̃smɑ̃] NM dressing, bandage; **~ adhésif** sticking plaster (BRIT), bandaid® (US)

panser [pɑ̃se] /1/ VT (*plaie*) to dress, bandage; (*bras*) to put a dressing on, bandage; (*cheval*) to groom

pantacourt [pɑ̃takur] NM cropped trousers *pl* (BRIT) *ou* pants *pl* (US)

★**pantalon** [pɑ̃talɔ̃] NM trousers *pl* (BRIT), pants *pl* (US), pair of trousers *ou* pants; **~ de ski** ski pants *pl*

pantalonnade [pɑ̃talɔnad] NF slapstick (comedy)

pantelant, e [pɑ̃t(ə)lɑ̃, -ɑ̃t] ADJ gasping for breath, panting

panthère [pɑ̃tɛr] NF panther

pantin [pɑ̃tɛ̃] NM (*jouet*) jumping jack; (*péj: personne*) puppet

pantois, e [pɑ̃twa, -waz] ADJ M: **rester ~** to be flabbergasted

pantomime [pɑ̃tɔmim] NF mime; (*pièce*) mime show; (*péj*) fuss, carry-on

pantouflard, e [pɑ̃tuflar, -ard] ADJ (*péj*) stay-at-home

★**pantoufle** [pɑ̃tufl] NF slipper

panure [panyr] NF breadcrumbs *pl*

PAO SIGLE F (= *publication assistée par ordinateur*) DTP

paon [pɑ̃] NM peacock

★**papa** [papa] NM dad(dy)

papauté [papote] NF papacy

papaye [papaj] NF papaya, pawpaw

pape [pap] NM pope

paperasse [papras] NF (*péj*) bumf *no pl*; papers *pl*; forms *pl*

paperasserie [paprasri] NF (*péj*) red tape *no pl*; paperwork *no pl*

★**papeterie** [papɛtri] NF (*fabrication du papier*) papermaking (industry); (*usine*) paper mill; (*magasin*) stationer's (shop) (BRIT), stationery store (US); (*articles*) stationery

papetier, -ière [pap(ə)tje, -jɛr] NM/F papermaker; stationer

papetier-libraire [pap(ə)tjɛlibrɛr] (*pl* **papetiers-libraires**) NM bookseller and stationer

papi [papi] NM (*fam*) granddad

★**papier** [papje] NM paper; (*feuille*) sheet *ou* piece of paper; (*article*) article; (*écrit officiel*) document; **sur le ~** (*théoriquement*) on paper; **noircir du ~** to write page after page; **~ couché/glacé** art/glazed paper; **~ (d')aluminium** aluminium (BRIT) *ou* aluminum (US) foil, tinfoil; **~ d'Arménie** incense paper; **~ bible** India *ou* bible paper; **~ de brouillon** rough *ou* scrap paper; **~ bulle** manil(l)a paper; **~ buvard** blotting paper; **~ calque** tracing paper; **~ carbone** carbon paper; **~ collant** Sellotape® (BRIT), Scotch tape® (US), sticky tape; **~ en continu** continuous stationery; **~ à dessin** drawing paper; **~ d'emballage** wrapping paper; **~ gommé** gummed paper; **~ hygiénique** *ou* **(de) toilette** toilet paper; **~ journal** newsprint; (*pour emballer*) newspaper; **~ à lettres** writing paper, notepaper; **~ mâché** papier-mâché; **~ machine** typing paper; **~ peint** wallpaper; **~ pelure** India paper; **~ à pliage accordéon** fanfold paper; **~ de soie** tissue paper; **~ thermique** thermal paper; **~ de tournesol** litmus paper; **~ de verre** sandpaper ■ **papiers** NMPL (*aussi*: **papiers d'identité**) (identity) papers

papier-filtre [papjefiltr] (*pl* **papiers-filtres**) NM filter paper

papier-monnaie [papjemɔnɛ] (*pl* **papiers-monnaies**) NM paper money

papille [papij] NF: **papilles gustatives** taste buds

papillon [papijɔ̃] NM butterfly; (*fam: contravention*) (parking) ticket; (*Tech: écrou*) wing *ou* butterfly nut; **~ de nuit** moth

papillonner [papijɔne] /1/ VI to flit from one thing (*ou* person) to another

papillote [papijɔt] NF (*pour cheveux*) curlpaper; (*de gigot*) (paper) frill; **en ~** cooked in tinfoil *ou* baking parchment

papilloter [papijɔte] /1/ VI (*yeux*) to blink; (*paupières*) to flutter; (*lumière*) to flicker

papotage [papɔtaʒ] NM chitchat

papoter [papɔte] /1/ VI to chatter

papou, e [papu] ADJ Papuan

Papouasie-Nouvelle-Guinée [papwazinuvɛlgine] NF: **la ~** Papua-New-Guinea

paprika [paprika] NM paprika

papyrus [papirys] NM papyrus

pâque [pɑk] NF: **la ~** Passover; *voir aussi* **Pâques**

paquebot [pak(ə)bo] NM liner

pâquerette [pakrɛt] NF daisy

Pâques [pɑk] NFPL Easter; **faire ses ~** to do one's Easter duties; **l'île de ~** Easter Island

In France, Easter eggs (**œufs de Pâques**) are said to be brought by the Easter bells, or *cloches de Pâques*, which fly from Rome and drop the eggs in people's gardens.

★paquet [pakɛ] NM packet; (*colis*) parcel; (*ballot*) bundle; (*dans négociations*) package (deal); (*fig: tas*): **~ de pile** ou heap of; **mettre le ~** (*fam*) to give one's all; **~ de mer** big wave; **~ fiscal** fiscal package, tax package ▪ **paquets** NMPL (*bagages*) bags

paquetage [pak(ə)taʒ] NM (*Mil*) kit, pack

paquet-cadeau [pakɛkado] (*pl* **paquets-cadeaux**) NM gift-wrapped parcel; **je vous fais un ~?** shall I (gift-)wrap it for you?

★par [paʀ] PRÉP by; **finir** *etc* **~** to end *etc* with; **~ amour** out of love; **passer ~ Lyon/la côte** to go via ou through Lyons/along by the coast; **~ la fenêtre** (*jeter, regarder*) out of the window; **trois ~ jour/personne** three a ou per day/head; **deux ~ deux** two at a time; (*marcher etc*) in twos; **~ où?** which way?; **~ ici** this way; (*dans le coin*) round here; **par-ci, par-là** here and there; **~ temps de pluie** in wet weather

para [paʀa] NM (*parachutiste*) para

parabole [paʀabɔl] NF (*Rel*) parable; (*Géom*) parabola

parabolique [paʀabɔlik] ADJ parabolic; **antenne ~** satellite dish

parachever [paʀaʃ(ə)ve] /5/ VT to perfect

parachutage [paʀaʃytaʒ] NM (*de soldats, vivres*) parachuting-in; **nous sommes contre le ~ d'un candidat parisien dans notre circonscription** (*Pol, fig*) we are against a Parisian candidate being landed on us

parachute [paʀaʃyt] NM parachute

parachuter [paʀaʃyte] /1/ VT (*soldat etc*) to parachute; (*fig*) to pitchfork; **il a été parachuté à la tête de l'entreprise** he was brought in from outside as head of the company

parachutisme [paʀaʃytism] NM parachuting

parachutiste [paʀaʃytist] NMF parachutist; (*Mil*) paratrooper

parade [paʀad] NF (*spectacle, défilé*) parade; (*Escrime, Boxe*) parry; (*ostentation*): **faire ~ de** to display, show off; (*défense, riposte*): **trouver la ~ à une attaque** to find the answer to an attack; **de ~** *adj* ceremonial

parader [paʀade] /1/ VI to swagger (around), show off

paradis [paʀadi] NM heaven, paradise; **P~ terrestre** (*Rel*) Garden of Eden; (*fig*) heaven on earth

paradisiaque [paʀadizjak] ADJ heavenly, divine

paradoxal, e, -aux [paʀadɔksal, -o] ADJ paradoxical

paradoxalement [paʀadɔksalmɑ̃] ADV paradoxically

paradoxe [paʀadɔks] NM paradox

parafe [paʀaf] NM = **paraphe**

parafer [paʀafe] VT = **parapher**

paraffine [paʀafin] NF paraffin; paraffin wax

paraffiné, e [paʀafine] ADJ: **papier ~** wax(ed) paper

parafoudre [paʀafudʀ] NM (*Élec*) lightning conductor

parages [paʀaʒ] NMPL (*Navig*) waters; **dans les ~ (de)** in the area ou vicinity (of)

paragraphe [paʀagʀaf] NM paragraph

Paraguay [paʀagwɛ] NM: **le ~** Paraguay

paraguayen, ne [paʀagwajɛ̃, -ɛn] ADJ Paraguayan ▶ NM/F: **Paraguayen, ne** Paraguayan

paraître [paʀɛtʀ] /57/ VB COPULE to seem, look, appear; **il ne paraît pas son âge** he doesn't look his age ▶ VI to appear; (*être visible*) to show; (*Presse, Édition*) to be published, come out, appear; (*briller*) to show off; **laisser ~ qch** to let sth show; **~ en justice** to appear before the court(s); **~ en scène/en public/à l'écran** to appear on stage/in public/on the screen ▶ VB IMPERS: **il paraît que** it seems ou appears that; **il me paraît que** it seems to me that; **il paraît absurde de** it seems absurd to

parallèle [paʀalɛl] ADJ parallel; (*police, marché*) unofficial; (*société, énergie*) alternative ▶ NM (*comparaison*): **faire un ~ entre** to draw a parallel between; (*Géo*) parallel; **mettre en ~** (*choses opposées*) to compare; (*choses semblables*) to parallel ▶ NF parallel (line); **en ~** in parallel

parallèlement [paʀalɛlmɑ̃] ADV in parallel; (*fig: en même temps*) at the same time

parallélépipède [paʀalelepiped] NM parallelepiped

parallélisme [paʀalelism] NM parallelism; (*Auto*) wheel alignment

parallélogramme [paʀalelɔgʀam] NM parallelogram

paralympique [paʀalɛ̃pik] ADJ Paralympic; **Jeux paralympiques** Paralympics, Paralympic Games

paralyser [paʀalize] /1/ VT to paralyze

paralysie [paʀalizi] NF paralysis

paralytique [paʀalitik] ADJ, NMF paralytic

paramédical, e, -aux [paʀamedikal, -o] ADJ paramedical; **personnel ~** paramedics *pl*, paramedical workers *pl*

paramétrage [paʀametʀaʒ] NM (*de logiciel, installation*) configuration

paramètre [paʀametʀ] NM parameter

paramétrer [paʀametʀe] VT (*logiciel, installation*) to configure

paramilitaire [paʀamilitɛʀ] ADJ paramilitary

paranoïa [paʀanɔja] NF paranoia

paranoïaque [paʀanɔjak] NMF paranoiac

paranormal, e, -aux [paʀanɔʀmal, -o] ADJ paranormal

parapet [paʀapɛ] NM parapet

parapharmacie [paʀafaʀmasi] NF (*industrie, produits*) over-the-counter drugs and personal hygiene products; (*boutique*) chemist's (BRIT), drugstore (US); **disponible en ~** available in chemists, sold in chemists

paraphe [paʀaf] NM (*trait*) flourish; (*signature*) initials *pl*; signature

parapher [paʀafe] /1/ VT to initial; to sign

paraphrase [paʀafʀɑz] NF paraphrase

paraphraser [paʀafʀɑze] /1/ VT to paraphrase

paraplégie [paʀapleʒi] NF paraplegia

paraplégique [paʀapleʒik] ADJ, NMF paraplegic

★parapluie [paʀaplɥi] NM umbrella; **~ atomique** ou **nucléaire** nuclear umbrella; **~ pliant** telescopic umbrella

P

parapsychique [paʀapsiʃik] ADJ parapsychological

parapsychologie [paʀapsikɔlɔʒi] NF parapsychology

parapublic, -ique [paʀapyblik] ADJ partly state-controlled

parascolaire [paʀaskɔlɛʀ] ADJ extracurricular

parasitaire [paʀazitɛʀ] ADJ parasitic(al)

parasite [paʀazit] NM parasite ▸ ADJ (Bot, Bio) parasitic(al) ∎ **parasites** NMPL (Tél) interference sg

parasitisme [paʀazitism] NM parasitism

★**parasol** [paʀasɔl] NM parasol, sunshade

paratonnerre [paʀatɔnɛʀ] NM lightning conductor

paravent [paʀavɑ̃] NM folding screen; (fig) screen

★**parc** [paʀk] NM (public) park, gardens pl; (de château etc) grounds pl; (pour le bétail) pen, enclosure; (d'enfant) playpen; (Mil: entrepôt) depot; (ensemble d'unités) stock; (de voitures etc) fleet; ~ **d'attractions** amusement park; ~ **automobile** (d'un pays) number of cars on the roads; ~ **éolien** wind farm; ~ **à huîtres** oyster bed; ~ **national** national park; ~ **naturel** nature reserve; ~ **de stationnement** car park; ~ **à thème** theme park; ~ **zoologique** zoological gardens pl

parcelle [paʀsɛl] NF fragment, scrap; (de terrain) plot, parcel

parcelliser [paʀselize] /1/ VT to divide ou split up

★**parce que** [paʀs(ə)kə] CONJ because

parchemin [paʀʃəmɛ̃] NM parchment

parcheminé, e [paʀʃəmine] ADJ wrinkled; (papier) with a parchment finish

parcimonie [paʀsimɔni] NF parsimony, parsimoniousness

parcimonieux, -euse [paʀsimɔnjø, -øz] ADJ parsimonious, miserly

parc(o)mètre [paʀk(ɔ)mɛtʀ] NM parking meter

parcotrain [paʀkɔtʀɛ̃] NM station car park (BRIT) ou parking lot (US), park-and-ride car park (BRIT)

parcourir [paʀkuʀiʀ] /11/ VT (trajet, distance) to cover; (article, livre) to skim ou glance through; (lieu) to go all over, travel up and down; (suj: frisson, vibration) to run through; ~ **des yeux** to run one's eye over

parcours [paʀkuʀ] VB voir **parcourir** ▸ NM (trajet) journey; (itinéraire) route; (Sport: terrain) course; (: tour) round; run; lap; ~ **du combattant** assault course

parcouru, e [paʀkuʀy] PP de **parcourir**

par-delà [paʀdəla] PRÉP beyond

par-dessous [paʀd(ə)su] PRÉP, ADV under(neath)

pardessus [paʀdəsy] NM overcoat

par-dessus [paʀd(ə)sy] PRÉP over (the top of); ~ **le marché** what's more, into the bargain; ~ **tout** above all; **en avoir ~ la tête** to have had enough ▸ ADV over (the top)

par-devant [paʀd(ə)vɑ̃] PRÉP in the presence of, before; ~ **notaire** in the presence of a notary ▸ ADV (boutonner) at the front; (passer) round the front; (entrer) the front way

★**pardon** [paʀdɔ̃] NM forgiveness no pl; **demander ~ à qn (de)** to apologize to sb (for); **je vous demande ~** I'm sorry; (pour interpeller) excuse me;

(demander de répéter) (I beg your) pardon? (BRIT), pardon me? (US) ▸ EXCL (excuses) (I'm) sorry; (pour interpeller etc) excuse me

pardonnable [paʀdɔnabl] ADJ forgivable, excusable

pardonner [paʀdɔne] /1/ VT to forgive; ~ **qch à qn** to forgive sb for sth; **qui ne pardonne pas** (maladie, erreur) fatal

paré, e [paʀe] ADJ ready, prepared

pare-balles [paʀbal] ADJ INV bulletproof

pare-boue [paʀbu] NM INV mudflap

★**pare-brise** [paʀbʀiz] NM INV windscreen (BRIT), windshield (US)

pare-chocs [paʀʃɔk] NM INV bumper (BRIT), fender (US)

pare-étincelles [paʀetɛ̃sɛl] NM INV fireguard

pare-feu [paʀfø] NM INV (de foyer) fireguard; (Inform) firewall ▸ ADJ INV: **portes ~** fire (resistant) doors

★**pareil, le** [paʀɛj] ADJ (identique) the same, alike; (similaire) similar; (tel): **un courage/livre ~** such courage/a book, courage/a book like this; **de pareils livres** such books; **j'en veux un ~** I'd like one just like it; **rien de ~** no (ou any) such thing, nothing (ou anything) like it; ~ **à** the same as; similar to; **en ~ cas** in such a case ▸ ADV: **habillés** ~ dressed the same (way), dressed alike; **faire ~** to do the same (thing) ▸ NMF: **ne pas avoir son (sa) ~(le)** to be second to none; **sans ~** unparalleled, unequalled; **ses pareils** one's fellow men; one's peers ▸ NM: **c'est du ~ au même** it comes to the same thing, it's six (of one) and half-a-dozen (of the other) ▸ NF: **rendre la pareille à qn** to pay sb back in his ou her own coin

pareillement [paʀɛjmɑ̃] ADV the same, alike; in such a way; (également) likewise

parement [paʀmɑ̃] NM (Constr, revers d'un col, d'une manche) facing; (Rel): ~ **d'autel** antependium

parent, e [paʀɑ̃, -ɑ̃t] NM/F: **un/une ~(e)** a relative ou relation; ~ **unique** single ou lone parent ▸ ADJ: **être ~ de** to be related to ∎ **parents** NMPL (père et mère) parents; (famille, proches) relatives, relations; **parents par alliance** relatives ou relations by marriage; **parents en ligne directe** blood relatives ou relations

parental, e, -aux [paʀɑ̃tal, -o] ADJ parental

parentalité [paʀɑ̃talite] NF parenthood

parenté [paʀɑ̃te] NF (lien) relationship; (personnes) relatives pl, relations pl

parenthèse [paʀɑ̃tɛz] NF (ponctuation) bracket, parenthesis; (Math) bracket; (digression) parenthesis, digression; **ouvrir/fermer la ~** to open/close brackets; **entre parenthèses** in brackets; (fig) incidentally

parer [paʀe] /1/ VT to adorn; (Culin) to dress, trim; (éviter) to ward off; ~ **à** (danger) to ward off; (inconvénient) to deal with; ~ **à toute éventualité** to be ready for every eventuality; ~ **au plus pressé** to attend to what's most urgent ∎ **se parer** VPR: **se ~ de** (fig: qualité, titre) to assume

pare-soleil [paʀsɔlɛj] NM INV sun visor

paresse [paʀɛs] NF laziness

paresser [paʀese] /1/ VI to laze around

paresseusement [paʀɛsøzmɑ̃] ADV lazily; sluggishly

★**paresseux, -euse** [paʀɛsø, -øz] ADJ lazy; (fig) slow, sluggish ▸ NM (Zool) sloth

parfaire [paʀfɛʀ] /60/ VT to perfect, complete

★**parfait, e** [paʀfɛ, -ɛt] PP de **parfaire** ▸ ADJ perfect ▸ NM (Ling) perfect (tense); (Culin) parfait ▸ EXCL perfect

parfaitement [paʀfɛtmɑ̃] ADV perfectly ▸ EXCL absolutely

★**parfois** [paʀfwa] ADV sometimes

★**parfum** [paʀfœ̃] NM (produit) perfume, scent; (odeur: de fleur) scent, fragrance; (: de tabac, vin) aroma; (goût: de glace, milk-shake) flavour (BRIT), flavor (US)

parfumé, e [paʀfyme] ADJ (fleur, fruit) fragrant; (papier à lettres etc) scented; (femme) wearing perfume ou scent, perfumed; (aromatisé): **~ au café** coffee-flavoured (BRIT) ou -flavored (US)

parfumer [paʀfyme] /1/ VT (odeur, bouquet) to perfume; (mouchoir) to put scent ou perfume on; (crème, gâteau) to flavour (BRIT), flavor (US) ■ **se parfumer** VPR to put on (some) perfume ou scent; (d'habitude) to use perfume ou scent

★**parfumerie** [paʀfymʀi] NF (commerce) perfumery; (produits) perfumes; (boutique) perfume shop (BRIT) ou store (US)

pari [paʀi] NM bet, wager; (Sport) bet; **~ mutuel urbain (PMU)** system of betting on horses

paria [paʀja] NM pariah, outcast

parier [paʀje] /7/ VT to bet; **j'aurais parié que si/non** I'd have said he (ou you etc) would/wouldn't

parieur [paʀjœʀ] NM (turfiste etc) punter

★**Paris** [paʀi] N Paris

★**parisien, ne** [paʀizjɛ̃, -ɛn] ADJ Parisian; (Géo, Admin) Paris cpd ▸ NM/F: **Parisien, ne** Parisian

paritaire [paʀitɛʀ] ADJ: **commission ~** joint commission

parité [paʀite] NF parity; **~ de change** (Écon) exchange parity; **~ hommes-femmes** (Pol) balanced representation of men and women

parjure [paʀʒyʀ] NM (faux serment) false oath, perjury; (violation de serment) breach of oath, perjury ▸ NMF perjurer

parjurer [paʀʒyʀe] /1/: **se parjurer** VPR to perjure o.s.

parka [paʀka] NF parka

★**parking** [paʀkiŋ] NM (lieu) car park (BRIT), parking lot (US); **parking-relais** park and ride

parlant, e [paʀlɑ̃, -ɑ̃t] ADJ (fig) graphic, vivid; (comparaison, preuve) eloquent; (Ciné) talking ▸ ADV: **généralement ~** generally speaking

parlé, e [paʀle] ADJ: **langue parlée** spoken language

parlement [paʀləmɑ̃] NM parliament; **le P~ européen** the European Parliament

parlementaire [paʀləmɑ̃tɛʀ] ADJ parliamentary ▸ NMF (député) ≈ Member of Parliament (BRIT) ou Congress (US); parliamentarian; (négociateur) negotiator, mediator

parlementarisme [paʀləmɑ̃taʀism] NM parliamentary government

parlementer [paʀləmɑ̃te] /1/ VI (ennemis) to negotiate, parley; (s'entretenir, discuter) to argue at length, have lengthy talks

★**parler** [paʀle] /1/ VI to speak, talk; (avouer) to talk; **~ pour qn** (intercéder) to speak for sb; **~ en l'air** to say the first thing that comes into one's head; **~ en français** to speak in French; **~ en dormant/ du nez** to talk in one's sleep/through one's nose; **tu parles!** you must be joking!; (bien sûr) you bet! ▸ VT: **~ affaires** to talk business; **~ (le) français** to speak French; **~ (à qn) de** to talk ou speak (to sb) about; **n'en parlons plus!** let's forget it!; **sans ~ de** not to mention, to say nothing of ■ **se parler** VPR to talk, to talk to each other; **on vient de se ~ au téléphone** we were just talking on the phone ▸ NM speech; dialect

> Quand on emploie **talk**, on met l'accent sur le fait qu'il y a une conversation entre deux ou plusieurs personnes, tandis que **speak** décrit plus spécifiquement le fait d'émettre des sons. Il est donc logique de dire **to speak French/English**. **Speak** étant d'un registre légèrement plus soutenu que **talk**, il s'emploie plus volontiers pour faire une demande polie.
> *Pourrais-je parler à monsieur Sylvester ?* **May I speak to Mr Sylvester?**

parleur [paʀlœʀ] NM: **beau ~** fine talker

parloir [paʀlwaʀ] NM (d'une prison, d'un hôpital) visiting room; (Rel) parlour (BRIT), parlor (US)

parlote [paʀlɔt] NF chitchat

Parme [paʀm] N Parma

parme [paʀm(ə)] ADJ violet (blue)

parmesan [paʀməzɑ̃] NM Parmesan (cheese)

★**parmi** [paʀmi] PRÉP among(st)

parodie [paʀɔdi] NF parody

parodier [paʀɔdje] /7/ VT (œuvre, auteur) to parody

paroi [paʀwa] NF wall; (cloison) partition; **~ rocheuse** rock face

paroisse [paʀwas] NF parish

paroissial, e, -aux [paʀwasjal, -o] ADJ parish cpd

paroissien, ne [paʀwasjɛ̃, -ɛn] NM/F parishioner ▸ NM prayer book

parole [paʀɔl] NF (mot, promesse) word; (faculté): **la ~** speech; **la bonne ~** (Rel) the word of God; **tenir ~** to keep one's word; **avoir la ~** to have the floor; **n'avoir qu'une ~** to be true to one's word; **donner la ~ à qn** to hand over to sb; **prendre la ~** to speak; **demander la ~** to ask for permission to speak; **perdre la ~** to lose the power of speech; (fig) to lose one's tongue; **je le crois sur ~** I'll take his word for it, I'll take him at his word; **temps de ~** (TV, Radio etc) discussion time; **ma ~!** my word!, good heavens!; **~ d'honneur** word of honour (BRIT) ou honor (US) ■ **paroles** NFPL (Mus) words, lyrics

parolier, -ière [paʀɔlje, -jɛʀ] NM/F lyricist; (Opéra) librettist

paroxysme [paʀɔksism] NM height, paroxysm

parpaing [paʀpɛ̃] NM breeze block (BRIT), cinder block (US)

parquer [paʀke] /1/ VT (voiture, matériel) to park; (bestiaux) to pen (in ou up); (prisonniers) to pack in

P

parquet [paʀkɛ] NM (parquet) floor; (Jur: bureau) public prosecutor's office; **le ~ (général)** (magistrats) ≈ the Bench

parqueter [paʀkəte] /4/ VT to lay a parquet floor in

parrain [paʀɛ̃] NM godfather; (d'un navire) namer; (d'un nouvel adhérent) sponsor, proposer

parrainage [paʀɛnaʒ] NM sponsorship

parrainer [paʀene] /1/ VT (nouvel adhérent) to sponsor, propose; (entreprise) to promote, sponsor

parricide [paʀisid] NMF parricide

pars [paʀ] VB voir **partir**

parsemer [paʀsəme] /5/ VT (feuilles, papiers) to be scattered over; **~ qch de** to scatter sth with

parsi, e [paʀsi] ADJ Parsee

★**part** [paʀ] VB voir **partir** ▶ NF (qui revient à qn) share; (fraction, partie) part; (de gâteau, fromage) portion; (Finance) (non-voting) share; **prendre ~ à** (débat etc) to take part in; (soucis, douleur de qn) to share in; **faire ~ de qch à qn** to announce sth to sb, inform sb of sth; **pour ma ~** as for me, as far as I'm concerned; **à ~ entière** adj full; **de la ~ de** (au nom de) on behalf of; (donné par) from; **c'est de la ~ de qui ?** (au téléphone) who's calling ou speaking (please)?; **de toute(s) ~(s)** from all sides ou quarters; **de ~ et d'autre** on both sides, on either side; **de ~ en ~** right through; **d'une ~ ... d'autre ~** on the one hand ... on the other hand; **d'autre ~** (de plus) moreover; **nulle/autre/quelque ~** nowhere/elsewhere/somewhere; **à ~** adv separately; (de côté) aside; prép apart from, except for; adj exceptional, special; **prendre qch en bonne/mauvaise ~** to take sth well/badly; **faire la ~ des choses** to make allowances; **faire la ~ du feu** (fig) to cut one's losses; **faire la ~ (trop) belle à qn** to give sb more than his (ou her) share

part. ABR = **particulier**

partage [paʀtaʒ] NM sharing (out) no pl, share-out; dividing up; (Pol: de suffrages) share; **recevoir qch en ~** to receive sth as one's share ou lot; **sans ~** undivided; **~ de fichiers** (Inform) file sharing

partagé, e [paʀtaʒe] ADJ (opinions etc) divided; (amour) shared; **être ~ entre** to be shared between; **être ~ sur** to be divided about

★**partager** [paʀtaʒe] /3/ VT to share; (distribuer, répartir) to share (out); (morceler, diviser) to divide (up) ■ **se partager** VPR (héritage etc) to share between themselves (ou ourselves etc)

partance [paʀtɑ̃s]: **en ~** adv outbound, due to leave; **en ~ pour** (bound) for

partant, e [paʀtɑ̃, -ɑ̃t] VB voir **partir** ▶ ADJ: **être ~ pour qch** (d'accord pour) to be quite ready for sth ▶ NM (Sport) starter; (Hippisme) runner

★**partenaire** [paʀtənɛʀ] NMF partner; **partenaires sociaux** management and workforce

parterre [paʀtɛʀ] NM (de fleurs) (flower) bed, border; (Théât) stalls pl

parti [paʀti] NM (Pol) party; (décision) course of action; (personne à marier) match; **tirer ~ de** to take advantage of, turn to good account; **prendre le ~ de faire** to make up one's mind to do, resolve to do; **prendre le ~ de qn** to stand up for sb, side with sb; **prendre ~ (pour/contre)** to take sides ou

a stand (for/against); **prendre son ~ de** to come to terms with; **~ pris** bias

partial, e, -aux [paʀsjal, -o] ADJ biased, partial

partialement [paʀsjalmɑ̃] ADV in a biased way

partialité [paʀsjalite] NF bias, partiality

participant, e [paʀtisipɑ̃, -ɑ̃t] NM/F participant; (à un concours) entrant; (d'une société) member

participation [paʀtisipasjɔ̃] NF participation; (financière) contribution; sharing; (Comm) interest; **la ~ aux bénéfices** profit-sharing; **la ~ ouvrière** worker participation; « **avec la ~ de ...** » "featuring ..."

participe [paʀtisip] NM participle; **~ passé/présent** past/present participle

★**participer** [paʀtisipe] /1/: **~ à** vt (course, réunion) to take part in; (profits etc) to share in; (frais etc) to contribute to; (entreprise: financièrement) to cooperate in; (chagrin, succès de qn) to share (in); **~ de** vt to partake of

particulariser [paʀtikylaʀize] /1/: **se particulariser** VPR to mark o.s. out

particularisme [paʀtikylaʀism] NM sense of identity

particularité [paʀtikylaʀite] NF particularity; (distinctive) characteristic, feature

particule [paʀtikyl] NF particle; **~ (nobiliaire)** nobiliary particle; **particules fines** fine particulate matter

★**particulier, -ière** [paʀtikylje, -jɛʀ] ADJ (personnel, privé) private; (étrange) peculiar, odd; (spécial) special, particular; (caractéristique) characteristic, distinctive; (spécifique) particular; **~ à** peculiar to; **en ~** adv (surtout) in particular, particularly; (à part) separately; (en privé) in private ▶ NM (individu: Admin) private individual; « **~ vend ...** » (Comm) "for sale privately ...", "for sale by owner ..." (US)

particulièrement [paʀtikyljɛʀmɑ̃] ADV particularly

★**partie** [paʀti] NF (gén) part; (profession, spécialité) field, subject; (Jur etc: protagonistes) party; (de cartes, tennis etc) game; (fig: lutte, combat) struggle, fight; **une ~ de campagne/de pêche** an outing in the country/a fishing party ou trip; **en ~** adv partly, in part; **faire ~ de** to belong to; (chose) to be part of; **prendre qn à ~** to take sb to task; (malmener) to set on sb; **en grande ~** largely, in the main; **ce n'est que ~ remise** it will be for another time ou the next time; **avoir ~ liée avec qn** to be in league with sb; **~ civile** (Jur) party claiming damages in a criminal case

partiel, le [paʀsjɛl] ADJ partial ▶ NM (Scol) class exam

partiellement [paʀsjɛlmɑ̃] ADV partially, partly

★**partir** [paʀtiʀ] /16/ VI (gén) to go; (quitter) to go, leave; (s'éloigner) to go ou drive etc away ou off; (moteur) to start; (pétard) to go off; (bouchon) to come out; (bouton) to come off; (tache) to go, come out; **~ de** (lieu: quitter) to leave; (: commencer à) to start from; (date) to run ou start from; **~ pour/à** (lieu, pays etc) to leave for/go off to; **à ~ de** from

partisan, e [paʀtizɑ̃, -an] NM/F partisan; (d'un parti, régime etc) supporter ▶ ADJ (lutte, querelle) partisan, one-sided; **être ~ de qch/faire** to be in favour (BRIT) ou favor (US) of sth/doing

partitif, -ive [paʀtitif, -iv] ADJ: **article ~** partitive article

partition [paʀtisjɔ̃] NF (Mus) score

★**partout** [paʀtu] ADV everywhere; **~ où il allait** everywhere ou wherever he went; **trente ~** (Tennis) thirty all

paru [paʀy] PP de **paraître**

parure [paʀyʀ] NF (bijoux etc) finery no pl; jewellery no pl (BRIT), jewelry no pl (US); (assortiment) set

parus etc [paʀy] VB voir **paraître**

parution [paʀysjɔ̃] NF publication, appearance

parvenir [paʀvəniʀ] /22/: **~ à** vt (atteindre) to reach; (obtenir, arriver à) to attain; (réussir) **~ à faire** to manage to do, succeed in doing; **faire ~ qch à qn** to have sth sent to sb

parvenu, e [paʀvəny] PP de **parvenir** ▸ NM/F (péj) parvenu, upstart

parviendrai [paʀvjɛ̃dʀe], **parviens** etc [paʀvjɛ̃] VB voir **parvenir**

parvis [paʀvi] NM square (in front of a church)

---

pas¹ [pa]

ADV **1** (en corrélation avec ne, non etc) not; **il ne pleure pas** (habituellement) he does not ou doesn't cry; (maintenant) he's not ou isn't crying; **je ne mange pas de viande** I don't ou do not eat meat; **il n'a pas pleuré/ne pleurera pas** he did not ou didn't/will not ou won't cry; **ils n'ont pas de voiture/d'enfants** they haven't got a car/any children, they have no car/children; **il m'a dit de ne pas le faire** he told me not to do it; **non pas que ...** not that ...

2 (employé sans ne etc): **pas moi** not me, not I, I don't (ou can't etc); **elle travaille, (mais) lui pas** ou **pas lui** she works but he doesn't ou does not; **une pomme pas mûre** an apple which isn't ripe; **pas plus tard qu'hier** only yesterday; **pas du tout** not at all; **pas de sucre, merci** no sugar, thanks; **ceci est à vous ou pas?** is this yours or not?, is this yours or isn't it?

3: **pas mal** (joli: personne, maison) not bad; **pas mal fait** not badly done ou made; **comment ça va? — pas mal** how are things? — not bad; **pas mal de** quite a lot of

pas² [pa] NM (démarche) tread; (enjambée, Danse, fig: étape) step; (bruit) (foot)step; (trace) footprint; (allure, mesure) pace; (d'un cheval) walk; (Tech: de vis, d'écrou) thread; **~ à ~** step by step; **au ~** at a walking pace; **de ce ~** (à l'instant même) straightaway, at once; **marcher à grands ~** to stride along; **mettre qn au ~** to bring sb to heel; **au ~ de gymnastique/de course** at a jog trot/at a run; **à ~ de loup** stealthily; **faire les cent ~** to pace up and down; **faire le premier ~** to make the first move; **retourner** ou **revenir sur ses ~** to retrace one's steps; **se tirer d'un mauvais ~** to get o.s. out of a tight spot; **sur le ~ de la porte** on the doorstep; **le ~ de Calais** (détroit) the Straits pl of Dover; **~ de porte** (fig) key money

pascal, e, -aux [paskal, -o] ADJ Easter cpd

passable [pasabl] ADJ passable, tolerable

passablement [pasabləmã] ADV (pas trop mal) reasonably well; (beaucoup) quite a lot

passade [pasad] NF passing fancy, whim

★**passage** [pasaʒ] NM (fait de passer) voir **passer**; (lieu, prix de la traversée, extrait de livre etc) passage; (chemin) way; (itinéraire): **sur le ~ du cortège** along the route of the procession; **« laissez/n'obstruez pas le ~ »** "keep clear/do not obstruct"; **au ~** (en passant) as I (ou he etc) went by; **de ~** (touristes) passing through; (amants etc) casual; **~ clouté** pedestrian crossing; **« ~ interdit »** "no entry"; **~ à niveau** level (crossing); **«~ protégé»** right of way over secondary road(s) on your right; **~ souterrain** subway (BRIT), underpass; **~ à tabac** beating-up; **~ à vide** (fig) bad patch

★**passager, -ère** [pasaʒe, -ɛʀ] ADJ passing; (hôte) short-stay cpd ▸ NM/F passenger; **~ clandestin** stowaway

passagèrement [pasaʒɛʀmã] ADV temporarily, for a short time

★**passant, e** [pasã, -ãt] ADJ (rue, endroit) busy ▸ NM/F passer-by ▸ NM (pour ceinture etc) loop

passation [pasasjɔ̃] NF (Jur: d'un acte) signing; **~ des pouvoirs** transfer ou handover of power

passe [pas] NF (Sport, magnétique) pass; (Navig) channel; **être en ~ de faire** to be on the way to doing; **être dans une mauvaise ~** (fig) to be going through a bad patch; **être dans une bonne ~** (fig) to be in a healthy situation; **~ d'armes** (fig) heated exchange ▸ NM (passe-partout) master ou skeleton key

★**passé, e** [pase] ADJ (événement, temps) past; (dernier: semaine etc) last; (couleur, tapisserie) faded; **il est midi ~** it's gone (BRIT) ou past twelve; **~ de mode** out of fashion ▸ NM past; (Ling) past (tense); **~ composé** perfect (tense); **~ simple** past historic ▸ PRÉP after

passe-droit [pasdʀwa] NM special privilege

passéiste [paseist] ADJ backward-looking

passementerie [pasmãtʀi] NF trimmings pl

passe-montagne [pasmɔ̃taɲ] NM balaclava

passe-partout [paspaʀtu] NM INV master ou skeleton key ▸ ADJ INV all-purpose

passe-passe [paspas] NM: **tour de ~** trick, sleight of hand no pl

passe-plat [paspla] NM serving hatch

★**passeport** [paspɔʀ] NM passport

★**passer** [pase] /1/ VI (se rendre, aller) to go; (voiture, piétons: défiler) to pass (by), go by; (faire une halte rapide: facteur, laitier etc) to come, call; (: pour rendre visite) to call ou drop in; (courant, air, lumière, franchir un obstacle etc) to get through; (accusé, projet de loi): **~ devant** to come before; (film, émission) to be on; (temps, jours) to pass, go by; (liquide, café) to go through; (être digéré, avalé) to go down; (couleur, papier) to fade; (mode) to die out; (douleur) to pass, go away; (Cartes) to pass; (Scol): **~ dans la classe supérieure** to go up (to the next class); (devenir): **~ président** to be appointed ou become president; **en passant** in passing; **remarquer qch en passant** to notice sth in passing; **~ par** to go through; **passez devant/par ici** go in front/this way; **~ sur** (faute, détail inutile) to pass over; **~ dans les mœurs/l'usage** to become the custom/normal usage; **~ avant qch/qn** (fig) to come before sth/sb; **laisser ~** (air, lumière, personne) to let through; (occasion) to let slip, miss; (erreur) to overlook; **faire ~ à qn le goût de qch** to take the taste out of his (ou her) taste for sth; **~ à la radio/fouille** to be X-rayed/searched; **~ à la** radio/télévision to be on the radio/on television; **~ à table** to sit down to eat; **~ au salon** to go through to ou into the sitting room; **~ à l'opposition** to go over to the opposition; **~ aux aveux** to confess, make a confession; **~ à l'action** to go into action; **~ pour riche** to be taken for a rich man; **il passait pour avoir** he was said to have; **faire ~ qn/qch pour** to make sb/sth out to be; **passe encore de le penser, mais de le dire !** it's one thing to think it, but to say it!; **passons !** let's say no more (about it); **et j'en passe !** and that's not all!; **~ en seconde, ~ la seconde** (Auto) to change into second ▶ VT (frontière, rivière etc) to cross; (douane) to go through; (examen) to sit, take; (visite médicale etc) to have; (journée, temps) to spend; (donner): **~ qch à qn** (sel etc) to pass sth to sb; (prêter) to lend sb sth; (lettre, message) to pass sth on to sb; (tolérer) to let sb get away with sth; (transmettre) to pass sth on to sb; (enfiler: vêtement) to slip on; (faire entrer, mettre): **(faire) ~ qch dans/par** to get sth into/through; (café) to pour the water on; (thé, soupe) to strain; (film, pièce) to show, put on; (disque) to play, put on; (commande) to place; (marché, accord) to agree on; **~ un coup de fil à qn** (fam) to give sb a ring; **faire ~** (message) to get sth across; **~ son tour** to miss one's turn; **~ qch en fraude** to smuggle sth in (ou out); **~ la main par la portière** to stick one's hand out of the door; **~ le balai/l'aspirateur** to sweep up/hoover; **~ commande/la parole à qn** to hand over to sb; **je vous passe M. Dupont** I'm putting you through to Mr Dupont; (je lui passe l'appareil) here is Mr Dupont, I'll hand you over to Mr Dupont; **~ prendre** to (come and) collect; **se passer** VPR (avoir lieu: scène, action) to take place; (se dérouler: entretien etc) to go; (arriver): **que s'est-il passé ?** what happened?; (s'écouler: semaine etc) to pass, go by; **se ~ de** to go ou do without; **se ~ les mains sous l'eau/de l'eau sur le visage** to put one's hands under the tap/ run water over one's face

passereau, x [pasʁo] NM sparrow

passerelle [pasʁɛl] NF footbridge; (de navire, avion) gangway; (Navig): **~ (de commandement)** bridge

★**passe-temps** [pastɑ̃] NM INV pastime

passette [pasɛt] NF (tea-)strainer

passeur, -euse [pasœʁ, -øz] NM/F smuggler

passible [pasibl] ADJ: **~ de** liable to

passif, -ive [pasif, -iv] ADJ passive ▶ NM (Ling) passive; (Comm) liabilities pl

★**passion** [pasjɔ̃] NF passion; **avoir la ~ de** to have a passion for; **fruit de la ~** passion fruit

★**passionnant, e** [pasjɔnɑ̃, -ɑ̃t] ADJ fascinating

passionné, e [pasjɔne] ADJ (personne, tempérament) passionate; (description, récit) impassioned; **être ~ de** ou **pour qch** to have a passion for sth ▶ NM/F: **c'est un ~ d'échecs** he's a chess fanatic

passionnel, le [pasjɔnɛl] ADJ of passion

passionnément [pasjɔnemɑ̃] ADV passionately

passionner [pasjɔne] /1/ VT (personne) to fascinate, grip; (débat, discussion) to inflame ▪ **se passionner** VPR: **se ~ pour** to take an avid interest in; to have a passion for

passivement [pasivmɑ̃] ADV passively

passivité [pasivite] NF passivity, passiveness

passoire [paswaʁ] NF sieve; (à légumes) colander; (à thé) strainer

---

pastel [pastɛl] NM, ADJ INV (Art) pastel

pastèque [pastɛk] NF watermelon

pasteur [pastœʁ] NM (protestant) minister, pastor

pasteurisation [pastœʁizasjɔ̃] NF pasteurization

pasteurisé, e [pastœʁize] ADJ pasteurized

pasteuriser [pastœʁize] /1/ VT to pasteurize

pastiche [pastiʃ] NM pastiche

★**pastille** [pastij] NF (à sucer) lozenge, pastille; (de papier etc) (small) disc (BRIT) ou disk (US); **pastilles pour la toux** cough drops ou lozenges

pastis [pastis] NM anise-flavoured alcoholic drink

pastoral, e, -aux [pastɔʁal, -o] ADJ pastoral

patagon, ne [patagɔ̃, -on] ADJ Patagonian

Patagonie [patagɔni] NF: **la ~** Patagonia

patate [patat] NF (fam) spud (fam); **~ douce** sweet potato

pataud, e [pato, -od] ADJ lumbering

patauger [patoʒe] /3/ VI (pour s'amuser) to splash about; (avec effort) to wade about; (fig) to flounder; **~ dans** (en marchant) to wade through

patch [patʃ] NM nicotine patch

patchouli [patʃuli] NM patchouli

patchwork [patʃwœʁk] NM patchwork

pâte [pɑt] NF (à tarte) pastry; (à pain) dough; (à frire) batter; (substance molle) paste; cream; **fromage à ~ dure/molle** hard/soft cheese; **~ d'amandes** almond paste, marzipan; **~ brisée** shortcrust (BRIT) ou pie crust (US) pastry; **~ à choux/feuilletée** choux/puff ou flaky (BRIT) pastry; **~ de fruits** crystallized fruit no pl; **~ à modeler** modelling (BRIT) ou modeling (US) clay, Plasticine® (BRIT); **~ à papier** paper pulp ▪ **pâtes** NFPL (macaronis etc) pasta sg

pâté [pate] NM (charcuterie, terrine) pâté; (tache) ink blot; (de sable) sandpie; **~ (en croûte)** ≈ meat pie; **~ de foie** liver pâté; **~ de maisons** block (of houses)

pâtée [pate] NF mash, feed

patelin [patlɛ̃] NM little place

patente [patɑ̃t] NF (Comm) trading licence (BRIT) ou license (US)

patenté, e [patɑ̃te] ADJ (Comm) licensed; (fig: attitré) registered, (officially) recognized

patère [patɛʁ] NF (coat-)peg

paternalisme [patɛʁnalism] NM paternalism

paternaliste [patɛʁnalist] ADJ paternalistic

paternel, le [patɛʁnɛl] ADJ (amour, soins) fatherly; (ligne, autorité) paternal

paternité [patɛʁnite] NF paternity, fatherhood

pâteux, -euse [patø, -øz] ADJ thick; pasty; **avoir la bouche** ou **langue pâteuse** to have a furred (BRIT) ou coated tongue

pathétique [patetik] ADJ pathetic, moving

pathologie [patɔlɔʒi] NF pathology

pathologique [patɔlɔʒik] ADJ pathological

patibulaire [patibylɛʁ] ADJ sinister

patiemment [pasjamɑ̃] ADV patiently

patience [pasjɑ̃s] NF patience; **être à bout de ~** to have run out of patience; **perdre/prendre ~** to lose (one's)/have patience

★**patient, e** [pasjɑ̃, -ɑ̃t] ADJ, NM/F patient

patienter [pasjɑ̃te] /1/ vi to wait

★**patin** [patɛ̃] NM skate; (*sport*) skating; (*de traîneau, luge*) runner; (*pièce de tissu*) cloth pad (*used as slippers to protect polished floor*); ~ **(de frein)** brake block; **patins (à glace)** (ice) skates; **patins à roulettes** roller skates

★**patinage** [patinaʒ] NM skating; ~ **artistique/de vitesse** figure/speed skating

patine [patin] NF sheen

★**patiner** [patine] /1/ vi to skate; (*embrayage*) to slip; (*roue, voiture*) to spin ■ **se patiner** VPR (*meuble, cuir*) to acquire a sheen, become polished

patineur, -euse [patinœʀ, -øz] NM/F skater

★**patinoire** [patinwaʀ] NF skating rink, (ice) rink

patio [patjo] NM patio

pâtir [pɑtiʀ] /2/: ~ **de** vt to suffer because of

pâtisserie [pɑtisʀi] NF (*boutique*) cake shop, pâtisserie; (*à la maison*) pastry- *ou* cake-making, baking ■ **pâtisseries** NFPL (*gâteaux*) pastries, cakes

pâtissier, -ière [pɑtisje, -jɛʀ] NM/F pastry chef; confectioner

patois [patwa] NM dialect, patois

patraque [patʀak] ADJ (*fam*) peaky, off-colour (BRIT), off-color (US)

patriarche [patʀijaʀʃ] NM patriarch

patrie [patʀi] NF homeland

patrimoine [patʀimwan] NM inheritance, patrimony; (*culture*) heritage; ~ **génétique** *ou* **héréditaire** genetic inheritance

patriote [patʀijɔt] ADJ patriotic ▸ NMF patriot

patriotique [patʀijɔtik] ADJ patriotic

patriotisme [patʀijɔtism] NM patriotism

★**patron, ne** [patʀɔ̃, -ɔn] NM/F (*chef*) boss, manager (manageress); (*propriétaire*) owner, proprietor (proprietress); (*employeur*) employer; (*Méd*) = senior consultant; (*Rel*) patron saint; ~ **de thèse** supervisor (of postgraduate thesis) ▸ NM (*Couture*) pattern

> The French word **patron** is not usually translated by the English word *patron*.

patronage [patʀɔnaʒ] NM patronage; (*organisation, club*) (parish) youth club; (parish) children's club

patronal, e, -aux [patʀɔnal, -o] ADJ (*syndicat, intérêts*) employers'

patronat [patʀɔna] NM employers pl

patronner [patʀɔne] /1/ vt to sponsor, support

patronyme [patʀɔnim] NM name

patronymique [patʀɔnimik] ADJ: **nom ~** patronymic (name)

patrouille [patʀuj] NF patrol

patrouiller [patʀuje] /1/ vi to patrol, be on patrol

patrouilleur [patʀujœʀ] NM (*Aviat*) scout (plane); (*Navig*) patrol boat

★**patte** [pat] NF (*jambe*) leg; (*pied: de chien, chat*) paw; (: *d'oiseau*) foot; (*languette*) strap; (: *de poche*) flap; (*favoris*) sideburn; **pattes (de lapin)** (short) sideburns; **à pattes d'éléphant** *adj* (*pantalon*) flared; **pattes de mouche** (*fig*) spidery scrawl *sg*; **pattes d'oie** (*fig*) crow's feet

pattemouille [patmuj] NF damp cloth (*for ironing*)

pâturage [pɑtyʀaʒ] NM pasture

pâture [pɑtyʀ] NF food

paume [pom] NF palm

paumé, e [pome] NM/F (*fam*) drop-out (*fam*)

paumer [pome] /1/ vt (*fam*) to lose

paupérisation [popeʀizasjɔ̃] NF pauperization

paupérisme [popeʀism] NM pauperism

paupière [popjɛʀ] NF eyelid

paupiette [popjɛt] NF: **paupiettes de veau** veal olives

★**pause** [poz] NF (*arrêt*) break; (*en parlant, Mus*) pause; ~ **de midi** lunch break

pause-café [pozkafe] (*pl* **pauses-café**) NF coffee break

pause-repas [pozʀ(ə)pa] (*pl* **pauses-repas**) NF lunch break

★**pauvre** [povʀ] ADJ poor; ~ **en calcium** low in calcium ▸ NMF poor man/woman; **les pauvres** the poor

pauvrement [povʀəmɑ̃] ADV poorly

pauvreté [povʀəte] NF (*état*) poverty; ~ **énergétique** fuel poverty

pavage [pavaʒ] NM paving; cobbles *pl*

pavaner [pavane] /1/: **se pavaner** VPR to strut about

pavé, e [pave] ADJ (*cour*) paved; (*rue*) cobbled ▸ NM (*bloc*) paving stone, cobblestone; (*pavage*) paving; (*bifteck*) slab of steak; (*fam: livre*) hefty tome; **être sur le ~** (*sans domicile*) to be on the streets; (*sans emploi*) to be out of a job; ~ **numérique** (*Inform*) keypad

pavillon [pavijɔ̃] NM (*de banlieue*) small (detached) house; (*kiosque*) lodge; pavilion; (*d'hôpital*) ward; (*Mus: de cor etc*) bell; (*Anat: de l'oreille*) pavilion, pinna; (*Navig*) flag; ~ **de complaisance** flag of convenience

pavoiser [pavwaze] /1/ vt to deck with flags ▸ vi to put out flags; (*fig*) to rejoice, exult

pavot [pavo] NM poppy

payable [pejabl] ADJ payable

payant, e [pejɑ̃, -ɑ̃t] ADJ (*spectateurs etc*) paying; (*billet*) that you pay for, to be paid for; (*fig: entreprise*) profitable; (*effort*) which pays off; **c'est ~** you have to pay, there is a charge

paye [pɛj] NF pay, wages *pl*

payement [pɛjmɑ̃] NM payment

★**payer** [peje] /8/ vt (*créancier, employé, loyer*) to pay; (*achat, réparations, fig: faute*) to pay for; **être bien/mal payé** to be well/badly paid; **il me l'a fait ~ 10 euros** he charged me 10 euros for it; ~ **qn de** (*ses efforts, peines*) to reward sb for; ~ **qch à qn** to buy sth for sb, buy sb sth; **ils nous ont payé le voyage** they paid for our trip; ~ **cher qch** to pay dear(ly) for sth ▸ vi to pay; (*métier*) to be well-paid, pay; (*effort, tactique etc*) to pay off; ~ **de sa personne** to give of oneself; ~ **d'audace** to act with great daring; **cela ne paie pas de mine** it doesn't look much ■ **se payer** VPR: **se ~ qch** to buy o.s. sth; **se ~ de mots** to shoot one's mouth off; **se ~ la tête de qn** to take the mickey out of sb (BRIT), make a fool of sb; (*duper*) to take sb for a ride

payeur, -euse [pejœʀ, -øz] ADJ (*organisme, bureau*) payments *cpd* ▸ NM/F payer

★**pays** [pei] NM (*territoire, habitants*) country, land; (*région*) region; (*village*) village; **du ~** adj local; **le ~ de Galles** Wales

★**paysage** [peizaʒ] NM landscape

paysager, -ère [peizaʒe, -ɛʀ] ADJ (*jardin, parc*) landscaped

paysagiste [peizaʒist] NMF (*de jardin*) landscape gardener; (*Art*) landscapist, landscape painter

paysan, ne [peizã, -an] NM/F countryman/-woman; farmer; (*péj*) peasant ▶ ADJ (*rural*) country cpd; (*agricole*) farming, farmers'

paysannat [peizana] NM peasantry

★**Pays-Bas** [peiba] NMPL: **les ~** the Netherlands

★**PC** SIGLE M (*Pol*) = **parti communiste**; (*Inform*: = *personal computer*) PC; (*Constr*) = **permis de construire**; (*Mil*) = **poste de commandement**; (= *prêt conventionné*) type of loan for house purchase

pcc ABR (= *pour copie conforme*) cc

Pce ABR = **prince**

Pcesse ABR = **princesse**

PDA SIGLE M (= *personal digital assistant*) PDA

p de p ABR = **pas de porte**

PDG SIGLE M = **président directeur général**

p.-ê. ABR = **peut-être**

PEA SIGLE M (= *plan d'épargne en actions*) building society savings plan

péage [peaʒ] NM toll; (*endroit*) tollgate; **pont à ~** toll bridge

★**peau, x** [po] NF skin; (*cuir*): **gants de ~** leather gloves; **être bien/mal dans sa ~** to be at ease/ill-at-ease; **se mettre dans la ~ de qn** to put o.s. in sb's place ou shoes; **faire ~ neuve** (*se renouveler*) to change one's image; **~ de chamois** (*chiffon*) chamois leather, shammy; **~ d'orange** orange peel

peaufiner [pofine] /1/ VT to polish (up)

peccadille [pekadij] NF trifle, peccadillo

péché [peʃe] NM sin; **~ mignon** weakness

pêche [pɛʃ] NF (*sport, activité*) fishing; (*poissons pêchés*) catch; (*fruit*) peach; **~ à la ~** to go fishing; **avoir la ~** (*fam*) to be on (top) form; **~ à la ligne** (*en rivière*) angling; **~ sous-marine** deep-sea fishing

pêche-abricot [pɛʃabriko] (*pl* **pêches-abricots**) NF yellow peach

pécher [peʃe] /6/ VI (*Rel*) to sin; (*fig: personne*) to err; (: *chose*) to be flawed; **~ contre la bienséance** to break the rules of good behaviour

pêcher [peʃe] /1/ VI to go fishing; (*en rivière*) to go angling; **~ au chalut** to trawl ▶ VT (*attraper*) to catch, land; (*chercher*) to fish for ▶ NM peach tree

pêcheur, -eresse [peʃœr, peʃrɛs] NM/F sinner

pêcheur [peʃœr] NM fisherman; (*à la ligne*) angler; **~ de perles** pearl diver

pectine [pɛktin] NF pectin

pectoral, e, -aux [pɛktɔral, -o] ADJ (*Anat*) pectoral; (*sirop*) throat cpd, cough cpd ▶ NMPL pectoral muscles

pécule [pekyl] NM savings pl, nest egg; (*d'un détenu*) earnings pl (*paid on release*)

pécuniaire [pekynjɛr] ADJ financial

pédagogie [pedagɔʒi] NF educational methods pl, pedagogy

pédagogique [pedagɔʒik] ADJ educational; **formation ~** teacher training

pédagogue [pedagɔg] NMF teacher, education(al)ist

pédale [pedal] NF pedal; **mettre la ~ douce** to soft-pedal

pédaler [pedale] /1/ VI to pedal

pédalier [pedalje] NM pedal and gear mechanism

pédalo [pedalo] NM pedalo, pedal-boat

pédant, e [pedã, -ãt] ADJ pedantic ▶ NM/F pedant

pédantisme [pedãtism] NM pedantry

pédéraste [pederast] NM homosexual, pederast

pédérastie [pederasti] NF homosexuality, pederasty

pédestre [pedɛstr] ADJ: **tourisme ~** hiking; **randonnée ~** (*activité*) rambling; (*excursion*) ramble; **sentier ~** pedestrian footpath

pédiatre [pedjatr] NMF paediatrician (BRIT), pediatrician ou pediatrist (US), child specialist

pédiatrie [pedjatri] NF paediatrics sg (BRIT), pediatrics sg (US)

pédicure [pedikyr] NMF chiropodist, podiatrist

pedigree [pedigre] NM pedigree

peeling [piliŋ] NM peel (*skin treatment*)

PEEP SIGLE F = **Fédération des parents d'élèves de l'enseignement public**

pègre [pɛgr] NF underworld

peignais *etc* [pɛɲe] VB *voir* **peindre**; **peigner**

★**peigne** [pɛɲ] VB *voir* **peindre**; **peigner** ▶ NM comb

peigné, e [pɛɲe] ADJ: **laine peignée** wool worsted; combed wool

peignée [pɛɲe] NF (*fam*) beating (*fam*); **flanquer une ~ à qn** to give sb a beating

peigner [pɛɲe] /1/ VT to comb (the hair of) ■ **se peigner** VPR to comb one's hair

peignez *etc* [pɛɲe] VB *voir* **peindre**; **peigner**

peignoir [pɛɲwar] NM dressing gown; **~ de bain** bathrobe; **~ de plage** beach robe

peignons [pɛɲɔ̃] VB *voir* **peindre**; **peigner**

peinard, e [penar, -ard] ADJ (*emploi*) cushy (BRIT), easy; (*personne*): **on est ~ ici** we're left in peace here

★**peindre** [pɛdr] /52/ VT to paint; (*fig*) to portray, depict

★**peine** [pɛn] NF (*affliction*) sorrow, sadness no pl; (*mal, effort*) trouble no pl, effort; (*difficulté*) difficulty; (*punition, châtiment*) punishment; (*Jur*) sentence; **faire de la ~ à qn** to distress ou upset sb; **prendre la ~ de faire** to go to the trouble of doing; **se donner de la ~** to make an effort; **ce n'est pas la ~ de faire** there's no point in doing, it's not worth doing; **ce n'est pas la ~ que vous fassiez** there's no point (in) you doing; **avoir de la ~ à faire** to have difficulty doing; **donnez-vous** ou **veuillez vous donner la ~ d'entrer** please do come in; **c'est ~ perdue** it's a waste of time (and effort); **à ~** adv scarcely, hardly, barely; **à ~ ... que** hardly ... than, no sooner ... than; **c'est à ~ si ...** it's (ou it was) a job to ...; **sous ~:** **sous ~ d'être puni** for fear of being punished; **défense d'afficher sous ~ d'amende** billposters

will be fined; **~ capitale** capital punishment;
~ de mort death sentence *ou* penalty

Hardly et **scarcely** s'emploient devant le verbe
principal et après un auxiliaire ou un modal.
Scarcely est moins courant que **hardly**.
Il pouvait à peine parler après l'accident. **He could
hardly speak after the accident.**
Devant un chiffre, on utilise le plus souvent
barely.
Le garçon avait à peine 10 ans. **The boy was barely
10 years old.**

---

peiner [pene] /1/ VI to work hard; to struggle;
(moteur, voiture) to labour (BRIT), labor (US) ▶ VT to
grieve, sadden

peint, e [pɛ̃, pɛ̃t] PP *de* **peindre**

★**peintre** [pɛ̃tʀ] NM painter; **~ en bâtiment** house
painter, painter and decorator; **~ d'enseignes**
signwriter

★**peinture** [pɛ̃tyʀ] NF painting; *(couche de couleur,
couleur)* paint; *(surfaces peintes: aussi:* **peintures**)
paintwork; **je ne peux pas le voir en ~** I can't
stand the sight of him; **~ mate/brillante** matt/
gloss paint; **« ~ fraîche »** "wet paint"

peinturluré, e [pɛ̃tyʀlyʀe] ADJ *(visage)* garishly
made-up

péjoratif, -ive [peʒɔʀatif, -iv] ADJ pejorative,
derogatory

Pékin [pekɛ̃] N Beijing

pékinois, e [pekinwa, -waz] ADJ Pekin(g)ese ▶ NM
(chien) peke, pekin(g)ese; *(Ling)* Mandarin,
Pekin(g)ese ▶ NM/F: **Pékinois, e** Pekin(g)ese

PEL SIGLE M *(= plan d'épargne logement) savings scheme
providing lower-interest mortgages*

pelade [pəlad] NF alopecia

pelage [pəlaʒ] NM coat, fur

pelé, e [pəle] ADJ *(chien)* hairless; *(vêtement)* threadbare; *(terrain)* bare

pêle-mêle [pɛlmɛl] ADV higgledy-piggledy

peler [pəle] /5/ VT, VI to peel

pèlerin [pɛlʀɛ̃] NM pilgrim

pèlerinage [pɛlʀinaʒ] NM *(voyage)* pilgrimage;
(lieu) place of pilgrimage, shrine

pèlerine [pɛlʀin] NF cape

pélican [pelikɑ̃] NM pelican

pelisse [pəlis] NF fur-lined cloak

pelle [pɛl] NF shovel; *(d'enfant, de terrassier)* spade; **~
à gâteau** cake slice; **~ mécanique** mechanical
digger

pelletée [pɛlte] NF shovelful; spadeful

pelleter [pɛlte] /4/ VT to shovel (up)

pelleteuse [pɛltøz] NF mechanical digger, excavator

pelletier [pɛltje] NM furrier

pellicule [pelikyl] NF film ■ **pellicules** NFPL *(dans
les cheveux)* dandruff *sg*

Péloponnèse [pelɔpɔnɛz] NM: **le ~** the Pelopon-
nese

pelote [p(ə)lɔt] NF *(de fil, laine)* ball; *(d'épingles)* pin
cushion; **~ basque** pelota

peloter [p(ə)lɔte] /1/ VT *(fam)* to feel (up) ■ **se peloter** VPR to pet

peloton [p(ə)lɔtɔ̃] NM *(groupe: de personnes)* group;
(: de pompiers, gendarmes) squad; *(: Sport)* pack; *(de
laine)* ball; **~ d'exécution** firing squad

pelotonner [p(ə)lɔtɔne] /1/: **se pelotonner** VPR to
curl (o.s.) up

★**pelouse** [p(ə)luz] NF lawn; *(Hippisme) spectating
area inside racetrack*

peluche [p(ə)lyʃ] NF *(bit of)* fluff; **animal en ~**
soft toy, fluffy animal; **chien/lapin en ~** fluffy
dog/rabbit

pelucher [p(ə)lyʃe] /1/ VI to become fluffy, fluff
up

pelucheux, -euse [p(ə)lyʃø, -øz] ADJ fluffy

pelure [p(ə)lyʀ] NF peeling, peel *no pl*; **~ d'oignon**
onion skin

pénal, e, -aux [penal, -o] ADJ penal

pénalisation [penalizasjɔ̃] NF *(Sport)* sanction,
penalty

pénaliser [penalize] /1/ VT to penalize

pénaliste [penalist] NMF criminal lawyer

pénalité [penalite] NF penalty

penalty, -ies [penalti, -z] NM *(Sport)* penalty
(kick)

pénard, e [penaʀ, -aʀd] ADJ = **peinard**

pénates [penat] NMPL: **regagner ses ~** to return
to the bosom of one's family

penaud, e [pəno, -od] ADJ sheepish, contrite

penchant [pɑ̃ʃɑ̃] NM: **un ~ à faire/à qch** a tendency to do/to sth; **un ~ pour qch** a liking *ou* fondness for sth

penché, e [pɑ̃ʃe] ADJ slanting

★**pencher** [pɑ̃ʃe] /1/ VI to tilt, lean over; **~ pour** to be
inclined to favour (BRIT) *ou* favor (US) ▶ VT to tilt
■ **se pencher** VPR to lean over; *(se baisser)* to bend
down; **se ~ sur** to bend over; *(fig: problème)* to look
into; **se ~ au dehors** to lean out

pendable [pɑ̃dabl] ADJ: **tour ~** rotten trick; **c'est
un cas ~ !** he (*ou* she) deserves to be shot!

pendaison [pɑ̃dɛzɔ̃] NF hanging

★**pendant, e** [pɑ̃dɑ̃, -ɑ̃t] ADJ hanging (out); *(Admin,
Jur)* pending ▶ NM counterpart; matching piece;
faire ~ à to match; to be the counterpart of; **pen-
dants d'oreilles** drop *ou* pendant earrings ▶ PRÉP
(au cours de) during; *(indiquant la durée)* for; **~ que**
while

pendeloque [pɑ̃d(ə)lɔk] NF pendant

pendentif [pɑ̃dɑ̃tif] NM pendant

penderie [pɑ̃dʀi] NF wardrobe; *(placard)* walk-in
cupboard

pendiller [pɑ̃dije] /1/ VI to flap (about)

pendre [pɑ̃dʀ] /41/ VT, VI to hang; **~ à** to hang
(down) from; **~ qch à** *(mur)* to hang sth (up) on;
(plafond) to hang sth (up) from ■ **se pendre** VPR:
se ~ (à) *(se suicider)* to hang o.s. (on); **se ~ à** *(se suspendre)* to hang from

---

Le prétérit et le participe passé de **hang** *est*
hung, *sauf quand on parle d'un meurtre ou d'un
suicide ; dans ce cas, le prétérit et le participe
passé est* **hanged**.
Ses longs cheveux pendaient dans son dos. **His long
hair hung down his back.**
Elle s'est pendue. **She hanged herself.**

---

pendu, e [pãdy] PP *de* **pendre** ▶ NM/F hanged man (*ou* woman)

pendulaire [pãdylɛʀ] ADJ pendular, of a pendulum

★**pendule** [pãdyl] NF clock ▶ NM pendulum

pendulette [pãdylɛt] NF small clock

pêne [pɛn] NM bolt

pénétrant, e [penetʀã, -ãt] ADJ (*air, froid*) biting; (*pluie*) that soaks right through you; (*fig: odeur*) noticeable; (*œil, regard*) piercing; (*clairvoyant, perspicace*) perceptive ▶ NF (*route*) expressway

pénétration [penetʀasjɔ̃] NF (*fig: d'idées etc*) penetration; (*perspicacité*) perception

pénétré, e [penetʀe] ADJ (*air, ton*) earnest; **être ~ de soi-même/son importance** to be full of oneself/one's own importance

pénétrer [penetʀe] **/6/** VI to come *ou* get in; **~ dans** to enter; (*suj: froid, projectile*) to penetrate (*: air, eau*) to come into, get into ▶ VT to penetrate; (*mystère, secret*) to fathom, penetrate ■ **se pénétrer** VPR: **se ~ de qch** to get sth firmly set in one's mind

pénible [penibl] ADJ (*astreignant*) hard; (*affligeant*) painful; (*personne, caractère*) tiresome; **il m'est ~ de ...** I'm sorry to ...

péniblement [peniblǝmã] ADV with difficulty

péniche [peniʃ] NF barge; **~ de débarquement** landing craft *inv*

pénicilline [penisilin] NF penicillin

péninsulaire [penɛ̃sylɛʀ] ADJ peninsular

péninsule [penɛ̃syl] NF peninsula

pénis [penis] NM penis

pénitence [penitãs] NF (*repentir*) penitence; (*peine*) penance; (*punition, châtiment*) punishment; **mettre un enfant en ~** to make a child stand in the corner; **faire ~** to do a penance

pénitencier [penitãsje] NM prison, penitentiary (*US*)

pénitent, e [penitã, -ãt] ADJ penitent

pénitentiaire [penitãsjɛʀ] ADJ prison *cpd*, penitentiary (*US*)

pénombre [penɔ̃bʀ] NF (*faible clarté*) half-light; (*obscurité*) darkness

pensable [pãsabl] ADJ: **ce n'est pas ~** it's unthinkable

pensant, e [pãsã, -ãt] ADJ: **bien ~** right-thinking

pense-bête [pãsbɛt] NM aide-mémoire, mnemonic device

pensée [pãse] NF thought; (*démarche, doctrine*) thinking *no pl*; (*Bot*) pansy; **se représenter qch par la ~** to conjure up a mental picture of sth; **en ~** in one's mind

★**penser** [pãse] **/1/** VI to think; **~ à** (*prévoir*) to think of; (*songer à: ami, vacances*) to think of *ou* about; **~ à faire qch** to think of doing sth; **faire ~ à** to remind one of; **n'y pensons plus** let's forget it; **vous n'y pensez pas!** don't let it bother you!; **sans ~ à mal** without meaning any harm ▶ VT to think; (*concevoir: problème, machine*) to think out; **~ faire qch** to be thinking of doing sth, intend to do sth; **je le pense aussi** I think so too; **je pense que oui/non** I think so/don't think so

penseur [pãsœʀ] NM thinker; **libre ~** free-thinker

pensif, -ive [pãsif, -iv] ADJ pensive, thoughtful

pension [pãsjɔ̃] NF (*allocation*) pension; (*prix du logement*) board and lodging, bed and board; (*maison particulière*) boarding house; (*hôtel*) guest-house, hotel; (*école*) boarding school; **prendre ~ chez** to take board and lodging at; **prendre qn en ~** to take sb (in) as a lodger; **mettre en ~** to send to boarding school; **~ alimentaire** (*d'étudiant*) living allowance; (*de divorcée*) maintenance allowance; alimony; **~ complète** full board; **~ de famille** boarding house, guesthouse; **~ de guerre/d'invalidité** war/disability pension

pensionnaire [pãsjɔnɛʀ] NMF (*Scol*) boarder; guest

> **pensionnaire** does not mean *pensioner*.

pensionnat [pãsjɔna] NM boarding school

pensionné, e [pãsjɔne] NM/F pensioner

pensivement [pãsivmã] ADV pensively, thoughtfully

pensum [pɛ̃sɔm] NM (*Scol*) punishment exercise; (*fig*) chore

pentagone [pɛ̃tagɔn] NM pentagon; **le P~** the Pentagon

pentathlon [pɛ̃tatlɔ̃] NM pentathlon

★**pente** [pãt] NF slope; **en ~** *adj* sloping

Pentecôte [pãtkot] NF: **la ~** Whitsun (*BRIT*), Pentecost; (*dimanche*) Whitsunday (*BRIT*); **lundi de ~** Whit Monday (*BRIT*)

pénurie [penyʀi] NF shortage; **~ de main-d'œuvre** undermanning

PEP [pɛp] SIGLE M (= *plan d'épargne populaire*) individual savings plan

pépé [pepe] NM (*fam*) grandad

pépée [pepe] NF (*fam: femme*) bird (*BRIT fam*), chick (*US fam*)

pépère [pepɛʀ] (*fam*) ADJ cushy (*fam*); quiet ▶ NM grandad

pépier [pepje] **/7/** VI to chirp, tweet

pépin [pepɛ̃] NM (*Bot: graine*) pip; (*fam: ennui*) snag, hitch; (*: parapluie*) brolly (*BRIT*), umbrella

pépinière [pepinjɛʀ] NF nursery; (*fig*) nest, breeding-ground

pépiniériste [pepinjeʀist] NM nurseryman

pépite [pepit] NF nugget

péplum [peplɔm] NM (*film*) epic (*set in Roman times*); (*Hist*) peplum

PEPS ABR (= *premier entré premier sorti*) first in first out

péquenaud, e [pɛkno, od] NM/F yokel (*BRIT*), hick (*US*)

PER [pɛʀ] SIGLE M (= *plan d'épargne retraite*) type of personal pension plan

perçant, e [pɛʀsã, -ãt] ADJ (*vue, regard, yeux*) sharp, keen; (*cri, voix*) piercing, shrill

percée [pɛʀse] NF (*trouée*) opening; (*Mil, Comm: fig*) breakthrough; (*Sport*) break

perce-neige [pɛʀsǝnɛʒ] NM OU F INV snowdrop

perce-oreille [pɛʀsɔʀɛj] NM earwig

percepteur, -trice [pɛʀsɛptœʀ, -tʀis] NM/F tax collector

perceptible [pɛʀsɛptibl] ADJ (*son, différence*) perceptible; (*impôt*) payable, collectable

perception [pɛʀsɛpsjɔ̃] NF perception; (*d'impôts etc*) collection; (*bureau*) tax (collector's) office

percer [pɛʀse] /**3**/ vt to pierce; (*ouverture etc*) to make; (*mystère, énigme*) to penetrate; ~ **une dent** to cut a tooth ▸ vi to come through; (*réussir*) to break through

perceuse [pɛʀsøz] NF drill; ~ **à percussion** hammer drill

percevable [pɛʀsəvabl] ADJ collectable, payable

percevoir [pɛʀsəvwaʀ] /**28**/ vt (*distinguer*) to perceive, detect; (*taxe, impôt*) to collect; (*revenu, indemnité*) to receive

perche [pɛʀʃ] NF (*bâton*) pole; (*Zool*) perch; ~ **à selfie** selfie stick; ~ **à son** (sound) boom

percher [pɛʀʃe] /**1**/ vt to perch; ~ **qch sur** to perch sth on ▪ **se percher** VPR (*oiseau*) to perch

perchiste [pɛʀʃist] NMF (*Sport*) pole vaulter; (*TV etc*) boom operator

perchoir [pɛʀʃwaʀ] NM perch; (*fig*) presidency of the French National Assembly

perclus, e [pɛʀkly, -yz] ADJ: ~ **de** (*rhumatismes*) crippled with

perçois *etc* [pɛʀswa] VB *voir* **percevoir**

percolateur [pɛʀkɔlatœʀ] NM percolator

perçu, e [pɛʀsy] PP *de* **percevoir**

percussion [pɛʀkysjɔ̃] NF percussion

percussionniste [pɛʀkysjɔnist] NMF percussionist

percutant, e [pɛʀkytɑ̃, -ɑ̃t] ADJ (*article etc*) resounding, forceful

percuter [pɛʀkyte] /**1**/ vt to strike; (*véhicule*) to crash into ▸ vi: ~ **contre** to crash into

percuteur [pɛʀkytœʀ] NM firing pin, hammer

perdant, e [pɛʀdɑ̃, -ɑ̃t] NM/F loser ▸ ADJ losing

perdition [pɛʀdisjɔ̃] NF (*morale*) ruin; **en** ~ (*Navig*) in distress; **lieu de** ~ den of vice

★**perdre** [pɛʀdʀ] /**41**/ vt to lose; (*gaspiller: temps, argent*) to waste; (: *occasion*) to waste, miss; (*personne*) to ruin; **il ne perd rien pour attendre** he's got it coming to him ▸ vi to lose; (*sur une vente etc*) to lose out; (*récipient*) to leak ▪ **se perdre** VPR (*s'égarer*) to get lost, lose one's way; (*fig: se gâter*) to go to waste; (*disparaître*) to disappear, vanish; **je me suis perdu** (*et je le suis encore*) I'm lost; (*et je ne le suis plus*) I got lost

perdreau, x [pɛʀdʀo] NM (young) partridge

perdrix [pɛʀdʀi] NF partridge

perdu, e [pɛʀdy] PP *de* **perdre** ▸ ADJ (*enfant, cause, objet*) lost; (*isolé*) out-of-the-way; (*Comm: emballage*) non-returnable; (*récolte etc*) ruined; (*malade*): **il est** ~ there's no hope left for him; **à vos moments perdus** in your spare time

père [pɛʀ] NM father; **de** ~ **en fils** from father to son; ~ **de famille** father; family man; **mon** ~ (*Rel*) Father; **le** ~ **Noël** Father Christmas ▪ **pères** NMPL (*ancêtres*) forefathers

pérégrinations [peʀegʀinasjɔ̃] NFPL travels

péremption [peʀɑ̃psjɔ̃] NF: **date de** ~ expiry date

péremptoire [peʀɑ̃ptwaʀ] ADJ peremptory

pérenne [peʀɛn] ADJ (*agriculture, emplois*) sustainable

pérenniser [peʀenize] vt (*emplois, ressources*) to ensure the continued existence of

pérennité [peʀenite] NF durability, lasting quality

péréquation [peʀekwasjɔ̃] NF (*des salaires*) realignment; (*des prix, impôts*) equalization

perfectible [pɛʀfɛktibl] ADJ perfectible

perfection [pɛʀfɛksjɔ̃] NF perfection; **à la** ~ *adv* to perfection

perfectionné, e [pɛʀfɛksjɔne] ADJ sophisticated

perfectionnement [pɛʀfɛksjɔnmɑ̃] NM improvement

perfectionner [pɛʀfɛksjɔne] /**1**/ vt to improve, perfect ▪ **se perfectionner** VPR (*dans un sport, une matière*) to improve; **se** ~ **en anglais** to improve one's English

perfectionniste [pɛʀfɛksjɔnist] NMF perfectionist

perfide [pɛʀfid] ADJ perfidious, treacherous

perfidie [pɛʀfidi] NF treachery

perforant, e [pɛʀfɔʀɑ̃, -ɑ̃t] ADJ (*balle*) armour-piercing (BRIT), armor-piercing (US)

perforateur, -trice [pɛʀfɔʀatœʀ, -tʀis] NM/F punch-card operator ▸ NM (*perceuse*) borer; drill ▸ NF (*perceuse*) borer; drill; (*pour cartes*) card-punch; (*de bureau*) punch

perforation [pɛʀfɔʀasjɔ̃] NF perforation; punching; (*trou*) hole

perforatrice [pɛʀfɔʀatʀis] NF *voir* **perforateur**

perforé, e [pɛʀfɔʀe] ADJ: **bande** ~ punched tape; **carte** ~ punch card

perforer [pɛʀfɔʀe] /**1**/ vt to perforate, punch a hole (*ou* holes) in; (*ticket, bande, carte*) to punch

perforeuse [pɛʀfɔʀøz] NF (*machine*) (card) punch; (*personne*) card punch operator

performance [pɛʀfɔʀmɑ̃s] NF performance

performant, e [pɛʀfɔʀmɑ̃, -ɑ̃t] ADJ (*Écon: produit, entreprise*) high-return *cpd*; (*Tech*): **très** ~ (*appareil, machine*) high-performance *cpd*

perfusion [pɛʀfyzjɔ̃] NF perfusion; **faire une** ~ **à qn** to put sb on a drip

péricliter [peʀiklite] /**1**/ vi to go downhill

péridurale [peʀidyʀal] NF epidural

périgourdin, e [peʀiguʀdɛ̃, -in] ADJ of *ou* from the Périgord

péril [peʀil] NM peril; **au** ~ **de sa vie** at the risk of his (*ou* her) life; **à ses risques et périls** at his (*ou* her) own risk

périlleux, -euse [peʀijø, -øz] ADJ perilous

périmé, e [peʀime] ADJ (out)dated; (*Admin*) out-of-date, expired

périmètre [peʀimɛtʀ] NM perimeter

périnatal, e [peʀinatal] ADJ perinatal

période [peʀjɔd] NF period

périodique [peʀjɔdik] ADJ (*phases*) periodic; (*publication*) periodical; (*Math: fraction*) recurring; **garniture** *ou* **serviette** ~ sanitary towel (BRIT) *ou* napkin (US) ▸ NM periodical

périodiquement [peʀjɔdikmɑ̃] ADV periodically

péripéties [peʀipesi] NFPL events, episodes

périphérie [peʀifeʀi] NF periphery; (*d'une ville*) outskirts *pl*

périphérique [peʀifeʀik] ADJ (*quartiers*) outlying; (*Anat, Tech*) peripheral; (*station de radio*) operating from a neighbouring country ▸ NM (*Inform*) peripheral; (*Auto*): (**boulevard**) ~ ring road (BRIT), beltway (US)

périphrase [peʀifʀɑz] NF circumlocution

périple [peʀipl] NM journey

périr [peʀiʀ] /**2**/ VI to die, perish

périscolaire [peʀiskɔlɛʀ] ADJ extracurricular

périscope [peʀiskɔp] NM periscope

périssable [peʀisabl] ADJ perishable

péristyle [peʀistil] NM peristyle

péritonite [peʀitɔnit] NF peritonitis

perle [pɛʀl] NF pearl; (*de plastique, métal, sueur*) bead; (*personne, chose*) gem, treasure; (*erreur*) gem, howler

perlé, e [pɛʀle] ADJ (*rire*) rippling, tinkling; (*travail*) exquisite; (*orge*) pearl *cpd*; **grève perlée** go-slow, selective strike (action)

perler [pɛʀle] /**1**/ VI to form in droplets

perlier, -ière [pɛʀlje, -jɛʀ] ADJ pearl *cpd*

permanence [pɛʀmanɑ̃s] NF permanence; (*local*) (duty) office, strike headquarters; (*service des urgences*) emergency service; (*Scol*) study room; **assurer une ~** (*service public, bureaux*) to operate *ou* maintain a basic service; **être de ~** to be on call *ou* duty; **en ~** *adv* (*toujours*) permanently; (*continûment*) continuously

permanent, e [pɛʀmanɑ̃, -ɑ̃t] ADJ permanent; (*spectacle*) continuous; (*armée, comité*) standing ▶ NF perm ▶ NM/F (*d'un syndicat, parti*) paid official

perméable [pɛʀmeabl] ADJ (*terrain*) permeable; **~ à** (*fig*) receptive *ou* open to

★**permettre** [pɛʀmɛtʀ] /**56**/ VT to allow, permit; **~ à qn de faire/qch** to allow sb to do/sth; **permettez ! excuse me!** ■ **se permettre** VPR: **se ~ de faire qch** to take the liberty of doing sth

★**permis, e** [pɛʀmi, -iz] PP *de* **permettre** ▶ NM permit, licence (BRIT), license (US); **~ de chasse** hunting permit; **~ (de conduire)** (driving) licence (BRIT), (driver's) license (US); **~ de construire** planning permission (BRIT), building permit (US); **~ d'inhumer** burial certificate; **~ poids lourds** ≈ HGV (driving) licence (BRIT), ≈ class E (driver's) license (US); **~ de séjour** residence permit; **~ de travail** work permit

permissif, -ive [pɛʀmisif, -iv] ADJ permissive

★**permission** [pɛʀmisjɔ̃] NF permission; (*Mil*) leave; (: *papier*) pass; **en ~** on leave; **avoir la ~ de faire** to have permission to do, be allowed to do

permissionnaire [pɛʀmisjɔnɛʀ] NM soldier on leave

permutable [pɛʀmytabl] ADJ which can be changed *ou* switched around

permuter [pɛʀmyte] /**1**/ VT to change *ou* switch around ▶ VI to change, swap

pernicieux, -euse [pɛʀnisjø, -øz] ADJ pernicious

péroné [peʀɔne] NM fibula

pérorer [peʀɔʀe] /**1**/ VI to hold forth

Pérou [peʀu] NM: **le ~** Peru

perpendiculaire [pɛʀpɑ̃dikylɛʀ] ADJ, NF perpendicular

perpendiculairement [pɛʀpɑ̃dikylɛʀmɑ̃] ADV perpendicularly

perpète [pɛʀpɛt] NF: **à ~** (*fam: loin*) miles away (: *longtemps*) forever

perpétrer [pɛʀpetʀe] /**6**/ VT to perpetrate

perpétuel, le [pɛʀpetɥɛl] ADJ perpetual, constant; (*Admin etc*) permanent; for life

perpétuellement [pɛʀpetɥɛlmɑ̃] ADV perpetually, constantly

perpétuer [pɛʀpetɥe] /**1**/ VT to perpetuate ■ **se perpétuer** VPR (*usage, injustice*) to be perpetuated; (*espèces*) to survive

perpétuité [pɛʀpetɥite] NF: **à ~** for life; **être condamné à ~** to be sentenced to life imprisonment, receive a life sentence

perplexe [pɛʀplɛks] ADJ perplexed, puzzled

perplexité [pɛʀplɛksite] NF perplexity

perquisition [pɛʀkizisjɔ̃] NF (police) search

perquisitionner [pɛʀkizisjɔne] /**1**/ VI to carry out a search

perron [peʀɔ̃] NM steps *pl* (*in front of mansion etc*)

★**perroquet** [peʀɔkɛ] NM parrot

★**perruche** [peʀyʃ] NF budgerigar (BRIT), budgie (BRIT), parakeet (US)

perruque [peʀyk] NF wig

persan, e [pɛʀsɑ̃, -an] ADJ Persian ▶ NM (*Ling*) Persian

perse [pɛʀs] ADJ Persian ▶ NM (*Ling*) Persian ▶ NMF: **Perse** Persian ▶ NF: **la P~** Persia

persécuter [pɛʀsekyte] /**1**/ VT to persecute

persécution [pɛʀsekysjɔ̃] NF persecution

persévérance [pɛʀseveʀɑ̃s] NF perseverance

persévérant, e [pɛʀseveʀɑ̃, -ɑ̃t] ADJ persevering

persévérer [pɛʀseveʀe] /**6**/ VI to persevere; **~ à croire que** to continue to believe that

persiennes [pɛʀsjɛn] NFPL (slatted) shutters

persiflage [pɛʀsiflaʒ] NM mockery *no pl*

persifleur, -euse [pɛʀsiflœʀ, -øz] ADJ mocking

persil [pɛʀsi] NM parsley

persillé, e [pɛʀsije] ADJ (sprinkled) with parsley; (*fromage*) veined; (*viande*) marbled, with fat running through

Persique [pɛʀsik] ADJ: **le golfe ~** the (Persian) Gulf

persistance [pɛʀsistɑ̃s] NF persistence

persistant, e [pɛʀsistɑ̃, -ɑ̃t] ADJ persistent; (*feuilles*) evergreen; **à feuillage ~** evergreen

persister [pɛʀsiste] /**1**/ VI to persist; **~ à faire qch** to persist in doing sth

★**personnage** [pɛʀsɔnaʒ] NM (*notable*) personality; figure; (*individu*) character, individual; (*Théât: de roman, film*) character; (*Peinture*) figure

personnaliser [pɛʀsɔnalize] /**1**/ VT to personalize; (*appartement*) to give a personal touch to; (*véhicule, téléphone*) to customize

personnalité [pɛʀsɔnalite] NF personality; (*personnage*) prominent figure

★**personne** [pɛʀsɔn] NF person; **10 euros par ~** 10 euros per person *ou* a head; **en ~** personally, in person; **~ âgée** elderly person; **~ à charge** (*Jur*) dependent; **~ morale** *ou* **civile** (*Jur*) legal entity ▶ PRON nobody, no one; (*avec négation en anglais*) anybody, anyone; **il n'y a ~** there's nobody in *ou* there, there isn't anybody in *ou* there ■ **personnes** NFPL people *pl*

★**personnel, le** [pɛʀsɔnɛl] ADJ personal; (*égoïste: personne*) selfish, self-centred; (*idée, opinion*): **j'ai des idées personnelles à ce sujet** I have my own ideas about that ▶ NM personnel, staff; **service du ~** personnel department

personnellement [pɛʀsɔnɛlmɑ̃] ADV personally

personnification [pɛʀsɔnifikasjɔ̃] NF personification

personnifier [pɛʀsɔnifje] /**7**/ VT to personify; to typify; **c'est l'honnêteté personnifiée** he (ou she etc) is honesty personified

perspective [pɛʀspɛktiv] NF (Art) perspective; (vue, coup d'œil) view; (point de vue) viewpoint, angle; (chose escomptée, envisagée) prospect; **en ~** in prospect

perspicace [pɛʀspikas] ADJ clear-sighted, gifted with (ou showing) insight

perspicacité [pɛʀspikasite] NF insight, perspicacity

persuader [pɛʀsɥade] /**1**/ VT: **~ qn (de/de faire)** to persuade sb (of/to do); **j'en suis persuadé** I'm quite sure ou convinced (of it)

persuasif, -ive [pɛʀsɥazif, -iv] ADJ persuasive

persuasion [pɛʀsɥazjɔ̃] NF persuasion

★**perte** [pɛʀt] NF loss; (de temps) waste; (fig: morale) ruin; **à ~** (Comm) at a loss; **à ~ de vue** as far as the eye can (ou could) see; (fig) interminably; **en pure ~** for absolutely nothing; **courir à sa ~** to be on the road to ruin; **être en ~ de vitesse** (fig) to be losing momentum; **avec ~ et fracas** forcibly; **~ de chaleur** heat loss; **~ sèche** dead loss ■ **pertes** NFPL losses; **pertes blanches** (vaginal) discharge sg

pertinemment [pɛʀtinamɑ̃] ADV to the point; (savoir) perfectly well, full well

pertinence [pɛʀtinɑ̃s] NF pertinence, relevance; discernment

pertinent, e [pɛʀtinɑ̃, -ɑ̃t] ADJ (remarque) apt, pertinent, relevant; (analyse) discerning, judicious

perturbateur, -trice [pɛʀtyʀbatœʀ, -tʀis] ADJ disruptive

perturbation [pɛʀtyʀbasjɔ̃] NF (dans un service public) disruption; (agitation, trouble) perturbation; **~ (atmosphérique)** atmospheric disturbance

perturber [pɛʀtyʀbe] /**1**/ VT to disrupt; (Psych) to perturb, disturb

péruvien, ne [peʀyvjɛ̃, -ɛn] ADJ Peruvian ▶ NM/F: **Péruvien, ne** Peruvian

pervenche [pɛʀvɑ̃ʃ] NF periwinkle; (fam) traffic warden (BRIT), meter maid (US)

pervers, e [pɛʀvɛʀ, -ɛʀs] ADJ perverted, depraved; (malfaisant) perverse

perversion [pɛʀvɛʀsjɔ̃] NF perversion

perversité [pɛʀvɛʀsite] NF depravity; perversity

perverti, e [pɛʀvɛʀti] NM/F pervert

pervertir [pɛʀvɛʀtiʀ] /**2**/ VT to pervert

pesage [pəzaʒ] NM weighing; (Hippisme: action) weigh-in; (: salle) weighing room; (: enceinte) enclosure

pesamment [pəzamɑ̃] ADV heavily

pesant, e [pəzɑ̃, -ɑ̃t] ADJ heavy; (fig: présence) burdensome ▶ NM: **valoir son ~ de** to be worth one's weight in

pesanteur [pəzɑ̃tœʀ] NF gravity

pèse-bébé [pɛzbebe] NM (baby) scales pl

pesée [pəze] NF weighing; (Boxe) weigh-in; (pression) pressure

pèse-lettre [pɛzlɛtʀ] NM letter scales pl

pèse-personne [pɛzpɛʀsɔn] NM (bathroom) scales pl

★**peser** [pəze] /**5**/ VT to weigh; (considérer, comparer) to weigh up ▶ VI to be heavy; (fig: avoir de l'importance) to carry weight; **~ sur** (levier, bouton) to press, push; (fig: accabler) to lie heavy on (: influencer) to influence; **~ à qn** to weigh heavy on sb

pessaire [pesɛʀ] NM pessary

pessimisme [pesimism] NM pessimism

★**pessimiste** [pesimist] ADJ pessimistic ▶ NMF pessimist

peste [pɛst] NF plague; (fig) pest, nuisance

pester [pɛste] /**1**/ VI: **~ contre** to curse

pesticide [pɛstisid] NM pesticide

pestiféré, e [pɛstifere] NM/F plague victim

pestilentiel, le [pɛstilɑ̃sjɛl] ADJ foul

pet [pɛ] NM (!) fart (!)

pétale [petal] NM petal

pétanque [petɑ̃k] NF type of bowls

pétaradant, e [petaʀadɑ̃, -ɑ̃t] ADJ spluttering

pétarade [petaʀad] NF backfiring no pl

pétarader [petaʀade] /**1**/ VI to backfire

pétard [petaʀ] NM (feu d'artifice) banger (BRIT), firecracker; (de cotillon) cracker; (Rail) detonator

pétasse [petas] NF (!: femme) slut (!)

pétaudière [petodjɛʀ] NF bedlam; **être une ~** to be bedlam

pet-de-nonne [pɛd(ə)nɔn] (pl **pets-de-nonne**) NM ≈ choux bun

pété, e [pete] ADJ (fam: cassé: objet) bust (fam), knackered (BRIT fam); (: ivre): **être ~** to be out of it (fam), be pissed (BRIT fam)

péter [pete] /**6**/ VI (fam: casser, sauter) to burst; to bust; (!) to fart (!); **~ une durite ou un fusible ou un plomb** (s'emporter) to blow a gasket (fam) ■ **se péter** VPR (fam: bras, jambe) to do in (fam); **se ~ la gueule** (tomber) to take a header (fam)

pète-sec [pɛtsɛk] ADJ INV (fam) abrupt, sharp(-tongued)

pétillant, e [petijɑ̃, -ɑ̃t] ADJ (eau) sparkling

pétiller [petije] /**1**/ VI (flamme, bois) to crackle; (mousse, champagne) to bubble; (pierre, métal) to glisten; (yeux) to sparkle; (fig): **~ d'esprit** to sparkle with wit

★**petit, e** [p(ə)ti, -it] ADJ (gén) small; (avec nuance affective) little; (main, objet, colline, en âge: enfant) small, little; (mince, fin: personne, taille, pluie) slight; (voyage) short, little; (bruit etc) faint, slight; (mesquin) mean; (peu important) minor; **en ~** in miniature; **~ à ~** bit by bit, gradually; **~(e) ami(e)** boyfriend/girlfriend; **les petites annonces** the small ads; **~ déjeuner** breakfast; **~ doigt** little finger; **le ~ écran** the small screen; **~ four** petit four; **~ pain** (bread) roll; **petite monnaie** small change; **petite vérole** smallpox; **petits pois** petit pois pl, garden peas; **petites gens** people of modest means ▶ NM/F (petit enfant) little one, child; **mon ~** son; little one; **ma petite** dear; little one; **pauvre ~(e)** poor little thing ■ **petits** NMPL (d'un animal) young pl; **faire des petits** to have kittens (ou puppies etc); **la classe des petits** the infant class; **pour petits et grands** for children and adults; **les tout-petits** toddlers

petit-beurre [pətibœʀ] (pl **petits-beurre**) NM sweet butter biscuit (BRIT) ou cookie (US)

petit-bourgeois, petite-bourgeoise [pətiburʒwa, pətitburʒwaz] (pl **petit(e)s-bourgeois(es)**) ADJ (péj) petit-bourgeois, middle-class

★**petite-fille** [pətitfij] (pl **petites-filles**) NF granddaughter

petitement [pətitmɑ̃] ADV poorly; meanly; **être logé ~** to be in cramped accommodation

petitesse [p(ə)titɛs] NF smallness; (d'un salaire, de revenus) modestness; (mesquinerie) meanness

★**petit-fils** [pətifis] (pl **petits-fils**) NM grandson

pétition [petisjɔ̃] NF petition; **faire signer une ~** to get up a petition

pétitionnaire [petisjɔnɛʀ] NMF petitioner

pétitionner [petisjɔne] /**1**/ VI to petition

petit-lait [pətilɛ] (pl **petits-laits**) NM whey no pl

petit-nègre [pətinɛgʀ] NM (péj) pidgin French

★**petits-enfants** [pətizɑ̃fɑ̃] NMPL grandchildren

petit-suisse [pətisɥis] (pl **petits-suisses**) NM small individual pot of cream cheese

pétoche [petɔʃ] NF (fam): **avoir la ~** to be scared out of one's wits

pétoire [petwaʀ] NF (fam: tromblon) old gun

peton [pətɔ̃] NM (fam: pied) foot

pétoncle [petɔ̃kl] NM scallop

pétri, e [petri] ADJ: **~ d'orgueil** filled with pride

pétrifier [petrifje] /**7**/ VT to petrify; (fig) to paralyze, transfix

pétrin [petrɛ̃] NM kneading-trough; (fig): **dans le ~ in a jam** ou fix

pétrir [petriʀ] /**2**/ VT to knead

pétrissage [petrisaʒ] NM kneading

pétrochimie [petrɔʃimi] NF petrochemistry

pétrochimique [petrɔʃimik] ADJ petrochemical

pétrodollar [petrɔdɔlaʀ] NM petrodollar

pétrole [petrɔl] NM oil; (aussi: **pétrole lampant**: pour lampe, réchaud etc) paraffin (BRIT), kerosene (US)

pétrolette [petrɔlɛt] NF (fam: cyclomoteur) moped

pétrolier, -ière [petrɔlje, -jɛʀ] ADJ oil cpd; (pays) oil-producing ▶ NM (navire) oil tanker; (financier) oilman; (technicien) petroleum engineer

pétrolifère [petrɔlifɛʀ] ADJ oil(-bearing)

pétulant, e [petylɑ̃, -ɑ̃t] ADJ exuberant

pétunia [petynja] NM petunia

---

peu [pø]

ADV **1** (modifiant verbe: adjectif: adverbe): **il boit peu** he doesn't drink (very) much; **il est peu bavard** he's not very talkative; **peu avant/après** shortly before/afterwards; **pour peu qu'il fasse** if he should do, if by any chance he does

2 (modifiant nom): **peu de: peu de gens/d'arbres** few ou not (very) many people/trees; **il a peu d'espoir** he hasn't (got) much hope, he has little hope; **pour peu de temps** for (only) a short while; **à peu de frais** for very little cost; **c'est peu de chose** it's nothing

3: **peu à peu** little by little; **à peu près** just about, more or less; **à peu près 10 kg/10 euros** approximately 10 kg/10 euros

▶ NM **1**: **le peu de gens qui** the few people who; **le peu de sable qui** what little sand, the little sand which

2: **un peu** a little; **un petit peu** a little bit; **un peu d'espoir** a little hope; **elle est un peu bavarde** she's rather talkative; **un peu plus de** slightly more than; **un peu moins de** slightly less than; (avec pluriel) slightly fewer than; **pour un peu il ..., un peu plus et il ...** he very nearly ou all but ...; **essayez un peu!** have a go!, just try it!

▶ PRON: **peu le savent** few know (it); **avant** ou **sous peu** shortly, before long; **depuis peu** for a short ou little while; (au passé) a short ou little while ago; **de peu** (only) just; **il est de peu mon cadet** he's just a little ou bit younger than me

---

Bien que **little** (+ nom singulier) et **few** (+ nom pluriel) soient possibles, l'anglais utilise plus volontiers une construction négative pour traduire peu de: **not much/not many** (mot à mot pas beaucoup de).

J'ai peu de travail en ce moment. **I don't have much work at the moment.**

Peu de gens sont au courant. **Not many people know about it.**

Avec un adjectif ou un verbe, la construction négative est également l'option la plus courante.

C'est une expression peu courante. **It isn't a very common expression.**

Elle a peu changé. **She hasn't changed much.**

---

peuplade [pœplad] NF (horde, tribu) tribe, people

peuple [pœpl] NM people; (masse): **un ~ de vacanciers** a crowd of holiday-makers; **il y a du ~** (fam) there are a lot of people

peuplé, e [pœple] ADJ: **très/peu ~** densely/sparsely populated

peuplement [pœpləmɑ̃] NM (de pays, territoire) population, populating; **colonie de ~** settlement

peupler [pœple] /**1**/ VT (pays, région) to populate; (étang) to stock; (hommes, poissons) to inhabit; (fig: imagination, rêves) to fill ■ **se peupler** VPR (ville, région) to become populated; (fig: s'animer) to fill (up), be filled

peuplier [pøplije] NM poplar (tree)

★**peur** [pœʀ] NF fear; **avoir ~ (de/de faire/que)** to be frightened ou afraid (of/of doing/that); **prendre ~** to take fright; **faire ~ à** to frighten; **de ~ de/que** for fear of/that; **j'ai ~ qu'il ne soit trop tard** I'm afraid it might be too late; **j'ai ~ qu'il (ne) vienne (pas)** I'm afraid he may (not) come

peureux, -euse [pœʀø, -øz] ADJ fearful, timorous

peut [pø] VB voir **pouvoir**

peut-être [pøtɛtʀ] ADV perhaps, maybe; **~ que** perhaps, maybe; **~ bien qu'il fera/est** he may well do/be

peuvent [pœv], **peux** etc [pø] VB voir **pouvoir**

p. ex. ABR (= par exemple) e.g.

pèze [pɛz] NM (fam: argent) dosh (BRIT fam), dough (fam)

phacochère [fakɔʃɛʀ] NM warthog

phagocyter [fagɔsite] VT (*Bio*) to ingest by phagocytosis; (*fig: concurrent, entreprise*) to swallow up

phalange [falɑ̃ʒ] NF (*Anat*) phalanx; (*Mil: fig*) phalanx

phallique [falik] ADJ phallic

phallocrate [falɔkʀat] NM male chauvinist

phallocratie [falɔkʀasi] NF male chauvinism

phallus [falys] NM phallus

pharaon [faʀaɔ̃] NM Pharaoh

pharaonique [faʀaɔnik] ADJ (*Hist*) Pharaonic; (*fig: gigantesque*) colossal; **un projet ~** a colossal project

★**phare** [faʀ] NM (*en mer*) lighthouse; (*d'aéroport*) beacon; (*de véhicule*) headlight, headlamp (BRIT); **se mettre en phares, mettre ses phares** to put on one's headlights; **phares de recul** reversing (BRIT) *ou* back-up (US) lights ▶ ADJ: **produit ~** leading product

pharmaceutique [faʀmasøtik] ADJ pharmaceutic(al)

★**pharmacie** [faʀmasi] NF (*science*) pharmacology; (*magasin*) chemist's (BRIT), pharmacy; (*officine*) dispensary; (*produits*) pharmaceuticals *pl*; (*armoire*) medicine chest *ou* cupboard, first-aid cupboard

★**pharmacien, ne** [faʀmasjɛ̃, -ɛn] NM/F pharmacist, chemist (BRIT)

pharmacodépendance [faʀmakodepɑ̃dɑ̃s] NF prescription drug addiction

pharmacologie [faʀmakɔlɔʒi] NF pharmacology

pharmacopée [faʀmakɔpe] NF pharmacopoeia

pharyngite [faʀɛ̃ʒit] NF pharyngitis *no pl*

pharynx [faʀɛ̃ks] NM pharynx

phase [faz] NF phase

phénoménal, e, -aux [fenɔmenal, -o] ADJ phenomenal

phénomène [fenɔmɛn] NM phenomenon; (*monstre*) freak

phénoménologie [fenɔmenɔlɔʒi] NF phenomenology

phéromone [feʀɔmɔn] NF pheromone

philanthrope [filɑ̃tʀɔp] NMF philanthropist

philanthropie [filɑ̃tʀɔpi] NF philanthropy

philanthropique [filɑ̃tʀɔpik] ADJ philanthropic

philatélie [filateli] NF philately, stamp collecting

philatélique [filatelik] ADJ philatelic

philatéliste [filatelist] NMF philatelist, stamp collector

philharmonique [filaʀmɔnik] ADJ philharmonic

philippin, e [filipɛ̃, -in] ADJ Filipino

Philippines [filipin] NFPL: **les ~** the Philippines

philistin [filistɛ̃] NM philistine

philo [filo] NF (*fam:* = *philosophie*) philosophy

philologie [filɔlɔʒi] NF philology

philosophal, e [filɔzɔfal] ADJ: **la pierre philosophale** the philosopher's stone

philosophe [filɔzɔf] NMF philosopher ▶ ADJ philosophical

philosopher [filɔzɔfe] /1/ VI to philosophize

philosophie [filɔzɔfi] NF philosophy

philosophique [filɔzɔfik] ADJ philosophical

philosophiquement [filɔzɔfikmɑ̃] ADV philosophically

philtre [filtʀ] NM philtre, love potion

phlébite [flebit] NF phlebitis

phlébologue [flebɔlɔg] NMF vein specialist

phobie [fɔbi] NF phobia

phocéen, ne [fɔseɛ̃, -ɛn] ADJ (*marseillais*) Marseille *cpd*; **la cité phocéenne** Marseille

phonétique [fɔnetik] ADJ phonetic ▶ NF phonetics *sg*

phonétiquement [fɔnetikmɑ̃] ADV phonetically

phonique [fɔnik] ADJ (*isolation, protection*) sound *cpd*

phonographe [fɔnɔgʀaf] NM (wind-up) gramophone

phoque [fɔk] NM seal; (*fourrure*) sealskin

phosphate [fɔsfat] NM phosphate

phosphaté, e [fɔsfate] ADJ phosphate-enriched

phosphore [fɔsfɔʀ] NM phosphorus

phosphoré, e [fɔsfɔʀe] ADJ phosphorous

phosphorescent, e [fɔsfɔʀesɑ̃, -ɑ̃t] ADJ luminous

phosphorique [fɔsfɔʀik] ADJ: **acide ~** phosphoric acid

★**photo** [fɔto] NF (*photographie*) photo; **en ~** on a photo; **prendre en ~** to take a photo of; **aimer la/faire de la ~** to like photography/taking photos; **~ en couleurs** colour photo; **~ d'identité** passport photo ▶ ADJ: **appareil/pellicule ~** camera/film

photo... [fɔto] PRÉFIXE photo...

photocomposition [fɔtokɔ̃pozisjɔ̃] NF photocomposition, phototypesetting

★**photocopie** [fɔtɔkɔpi] NF (*procédé*) photocopying; (*document*) photocopy

photocopier [fɔtɔkɔpje] /7/ VT to photocopy

photocopieur [fɔtɔkɔpjœʀ] NM, **photocopieuse** [fɔtɔkɔpjøz] NF (photo)copier

photo-électrique [fɔtoelɛktʀik] ADJ photoelectric

photo-finish [fɔtofiniʃ] (*pl* **photos-finish**) NF (*photo*) photo finish picture; **il y a eu ~ pour la troisième place** there was a photo finish for third place

photogénique [fɔtɔʒenik] ADJ photogenic

★**photographe** [fɔtɔgʀaf] NMF photographer

★**photographie** [fɔtɔgʀafi] NF (*procédé, technique*) photography; (*cliché*) photograph; **faire de la ~** to do photography as a hobby; (*comme métier*) to be a photographer

photographier [fɔtɔgʀafje] /7/ VT to photograph, take a photograph *ou* photographs of

photographique [fɔtɔgʀafik] ADJ photographic

photogravure [fɔtɔgʀavyʀ] NF photoengraving

photomaton® [fɔtɔmatɔ̃] NM photo-booth, photomat

photomontage [fɔtɔmɔ̃taʒ] NM photomontage

photon [fɔtɔ̃] NM photon

photophone [fɔtɔfɔn] NM camera phone

photophore [fɔtɔfɔʀ] NM (*pour bougie*) glass tealight holder

photoreportage [fɔtɔʀəpɔʀtaʒ] NM (*journalisme*) photojournalism; (*reportage*) photo report

photoreporter [fɔtɔʀəpɔʀtɛʀ] NMF photojournalist

photo-robot [fɔtɔʀɔbo] (*pl* **photos-robots**) NF Identikit® (picture)

photosensible [fɔtɔsɑ̃sibl] ADJ photosensitive

photostat [fɔtɔsta] NM photostat

photosynthèse [fɔtosɛ̃tɛz] NF photosynthesis

photothérapie [fɔtoteʀapi] NF phototherapy

photovoltaïque [fɔtovɔltaik] ADJ (*cellule*) photovoltaic

★**phrase** [fʀɑz] NF (Ling) sentence; (*propos, Mus*) phrase ■ **phrases** NFPL (*péj*) flowery language *sg*

phrasé [fʀɑze] NM phrasing

phraséologie [fʀɑzeɔlɔʒi] NF phraseology; (*rhétorique*) flowery language

phraseur, -euse [fʀɑzœʀ, -øz] NM/F: **c'est un ~** he uses such flowery language

phréatique [fʀeatik] ADJ *voir* **nappe**

phrygien, ne [fʀiʒjɛ̃, -ɛn] ADJ: **bonnet ~** Phrygian cap

phtisie [ftizi] NF consumption

phylloxéra [filɔkseʀa] NM phylloxera

physicien, ne [fizisjɛ̃, -ɛn] NM/F physicist

physiologie [fizjɔlɔʒi] NF physiology

physiologique [fizjɔlɔʒik] ADJ physiological

physiologiquement [fizjɔlɔʒikmɑ̃] ADV physiologically

physiologiste [fizjɔlɔʒist] NMF physiologist

physionomie [fizjɔnɔmi] NF face; (*d'un paysage etc*) physiognomy

physionomiste [fizjɔnɔmist] NMF (*de boîte de nuit*) bouncer ▶ ADJ: **être ~** to have a good memory for faces

physiothérapeute [fizjoteʀapøt] NMF physiotherapist (Brit), physical therapist (US)

physiothérapie [fizjoteʀapi] NF natural medicine, alternative medicine

★**physique** [fizik] ADJ physical ▶ NM physique; **au ~** physically ▶ NF physics *sg*

physiquement [fizikmɑ̃] ADV physically

phytoplancton [fitoplɑ̃ktɔ̃] NM phytoplankton

phytothérapie [fitoteʀapi] NF herbal medicine

piaffer [pjafe] /1/ VI to stamp

piaillement [pjajmɑ̃] NM squawking *no pl*

piailler [pjaje] /1/ VI to squawk

pianiste [pjanist] NMF pianist

★**piano** [pjano] NM piano; **à queue** grand piano

pianoter [pjanɔte] /1/ VI to tinkle away (at the piano); (*tapoter*): **~ sur** to drum one's fingers on

piaule [pjol] NF (*fam*) pad

piauler [pjole] /1/ VI (*enfant*) to whimper; (*oiseau*) to cheep

PIB SIGLE M (= *produit intérieur brut*) GDP

pic [pik] NM (*instrument*) pick(axe); (*montagne*) peak; (*Zool*) woodpecker; **à ~** adv vertically; (*fig: tomber, arriver*) just at the right time; **couler à ~** (*bateau*) to go straight down; **~ à glace** ice pick

picard, e [pikaʀ, -aʀd] ADJ of *ou* from Picardy

Picardie [pikaʀdi] NF: **la ~** Picardy

picaresque [pikaʀɛsk] ADJ picaresque

piccolo [pikɔlo] NM piccolo

pichenette [piʃnɛt] NF flick

pichet [piʃɛ] NM jug

pickpocket [pikpɔkɛt] NM pickpocket

pick-up [pikœp] NM record player

picoler [pikɔle] /1/ (*fam*) VI to drink, booze (*fam*); **~ dur, ~ sec** to knock it back (*fam*); **on a un peu picolé hier soir** we were knocking it back a bit last night ▶ VT to drink, knock back (*fam*)

picorer [pikɔʀe] /1/ VT to peck

picot [piko] NM sprocket; **entraînement par roue à picots** sprocket feed

picotement [pikɔtmɑ̃] NM smarting *no pl*, prickling *no pl*

picoter [pikɔte] /1/ VT (*oiseau*) to peck ▶ VI (*irriter*) to smart, prickle

pictogramme [piktɔgʀam] NM pictogram

pictural, e, -aux [piktyʀal, -o] ADJ pictorial

pie [pi] NF magpie; (*fig*) chatterbox ▶ ADJ INV: **cheval ~** piebald; **vache ~** black and white cow

pièce [pjɛs] NF (*d'un logement*) room; (*Théât*) play; (*de mécanisme, machine*) part; (*de monnaie*) coin; (*Couture*) patch; (*document*) document; (*de drap, fragment, d'une collection*) piece; (*de bétail*) head; **mettre en pièces** to smash to pieces; **deux euros ~** two euros each; **vendre à la ~** to sell separately *ou* individually; **travailler/payer à la ~** to do piecework/pay piece rate; **c'est inventé de toutes pièces** it's a complete fabrication; **un maillot une ~** a one-piece swimsuit; **un deux-pièces cuisine** a two-room(ed) flat (Brit) *ou* apartment (US) with kitchen; **tout d'une ~** (*personne: franc*) blunt; (*: sans souplesse*) inflexible; **à conviction** exhibit; **~ d'eau** ornamental lake *ou* pond; **~ d'identité**: **avez-vous une ~ d'identité?** have you got any (means of) identification?; **~ jointe** (Inform) attachment; **~ montée** tiered cake; **~ de rechange** spare (part); **~ de résistance** pièce de résistance; (*plat*) main dish; **pièces détachées** spares, (spare) parts; **en pièces détachées** (*à monter*) in kit form; **pièces justificatives** supporting documents

piécette [pjesɛt] NF small coin

★**pied** [pje] NM foot; (*de verre*) stem; (*de table*) leg; (*de lampe*) base; (*plante*) plant; **pieds nus** barefoot; **à ~** on foot; **à ~ sec** without getting one's feet wet; **à ~ d'œuvre** ready to start (work); **au ~ de la lettre** literally; **au ~ levé** at a moment's notice; **de ~ en cap** from head to foot; **en ~** (*portrait*) full-length; **avoir ~** to be able to touch the bottom, not to be out of one's depth; **avoir le ~ marin** to be a good sailor; **perdre ~** to lose one's footing; (*fig*) to get out of one's depth; **sur ~** (Agr) on the stalk, uncut; (*debout, rétabli*) up and about; **mettre sur ~** (*entreprise*) to set up; **mettre à ~** to suspend; to lay off; **mettre qn au ~ du mur** to get sb with his (*ou* her) back to the wall; **sur le ~ de guerre** ready for action; **sur un ~ d'égalité** on an equal footing; **sur ~ d'intervention** on stand-by; **faire du ~ à qn** (*prévenir*) to give sb a (warning) kick; (*galamment*) to play footsie with sb; **mettre les pieds quelque part** to set foot somewhere; **faire des pieds et des mains** (*fig*) to move heaven and earth, pull out all the stops; **c'est le ~!** (*fam*) it's brilliant!; **mettre les pieds dans le plat** (*fam*) to put one's foot in it; **il se débrouille comme un ~** (*fam*) he's completely useless; **se lever du bon ~/du ~ gauche** to get out of bed on the right/wrong side; **~ de lit** footboard; **faire un ~ de nez à** to thumb one's nose at; **~ de vigne** vine

pied-à-terre [pjetatɛʀ] NM INV pied-à-terre

pied-bot [pjebo] (*pl* **pieds-bots**) NM person with a club foot

pied-de-biche [pjedbiʃ] (*pl* **pieds-de-biche**) NM claw; (*Couture*) presser foot

pied-de-poule [pjedpul] ADJ INV hound's-tooth

piédestal, -aux [pjedɛstal, -o] NM pedestal

pied-noir [pjenwaʀ] (*pl* **pieds-noirs**) NMF Algerian-born French national

piège [pjɛʒ] NM trap; **prendre au ~** to trap

piéger [pjeʒe] /3, 6/ VT (*animal, fig*) to trap; (*avec une bombe*) to booby-trap; **lettre/voiture piégée** letter-/car-bomb

piercing [pjɛʀsiŋ] NM piercing

pierraille [pjɛʀaj] NF loose stones *pl*

★**pierre** [pjɛʀ] NF stone; **première ~** (*d'un édifice*) foundation stone; **mur de pierres sèches** drystone wall; **faire d'une ~ deux coups** to kill two birds with one stone; **~ à briquet** flint; **~ fine** semiprecious stone; **~ ponce** pumice stone; **~ de taille** freestone *no pl*; **~ tombale** tombstone, gravestone; **~ de touche** touchstone

pierreries [pjɛʀʀi] NFPL gems, precious stones

pierreux, -euse [pjɛʀø, -øz] ADJ stony

piété [pjete] NF piety

piétinement [pjetinmɑ̃] NM stamping *no pl*

piétiner [pjetine] /1/ VI (*trépigner*) to stamp (one's foot); (*marquer le pas*) to stand about; (*fig*) to be at a standstill ▸ VT to trample on

piéton, ne [pjetɔ̃, -ɔn] NM/F pedestrian ▸ ADJ pedestrian *cpd*

piétonnier, -ière [pjetɔnje, -jɛʀ] ADJ pedestrian *cpd*

piètre [pjɛtʀ] ADJ poor, mediocre

pieu, x [pjø] NM (*piquet*) post; (*pointu*) stake; (*fam: lit*) bed

pieusement [pjøzmɑ̃] ADV piously

pieuvre [pjœvʀ] NF octopus

pieux, -euse [pjø, -øz] ADJ pious

pif [pif] NM (*fam*) conk (BRIT), beak; **au ~** *voir* **pifomètre**

piffer [pife] /1/ VT (*fam*): **je ne peux pas le ~** I can't stand him

pifomètre [pifɔmɛtʀ] NM (*fam*): **choisir** *etc* **au ~** to follow one's nose when choosing *etc*

pige [piʒ] NF piecework rate

pigeon [piʒɔ̃] NM pigeon; **~ voyageur** homing pigeon

pigeonnant, e [piʒɔnɑ̃, -ɑ̃t] ADJ full, well-developed

pigeonneau, x [piʒɔno] NM young pigeon

pigeonner [piʒɔne] VT (*fam: duper*): **~ qn** to take sb for a ride (*fam*); **se faire ~** to be taken for a ride (*fam*)

pigeonnier [piʒɔnje] NM pigeon loft, dovecot(e)

piger [piʒe] /3/ (*fam*) VI to get it ▸ VT to get, understand

pigiste [piʒist] NMF (*typographe*) typesetter on piecework; (*journaliste*) freelance journalist (*paid by the line*)

pigment [pigmɑ̃] NM pigment

pigmentation [pigmɑ̃tasjɔ̃] NF pigmentation

pignon [piɲɔ̃] NM (*de mur*) gable; (*d'engrenage*) cog(wheel), gearwheel; (*graine*) pine kernel; **avoir ~ sur rue** (*fig*) to have a prosperous business

★**pile** [pil] NF (*tas, pilier*) pile; (*Élec*) battery ▸ ADJ: **le côté ~** tails; **jouer à ~ ou face** to toss for it; **~ ou face?** heads or tails? ▸ ADV (*net, brusquement*) dead; (*à temps, à point nommé*) just at the right time; **à deux heures ~** at two on the dot

piler [pile] /1/ VT to crush, pound

pileux, -euse [pilø, -øz] ADJ: **système ~** (body) hair

pilier [pilje] NM (*colonne, support*) pillar; (*personne*) mainstay; (*Rugby*) prop (forward)

pillage [pijaʒ] NM pillaging, plundering, looting

pillard, e [pijaʀ, -aʀd] NM/F looter, plunderer

piller [pije] /1/ VT to pillage, plunder, loot

pilleur, -euse [pijœʀ, -øz] NM/F looter

pilon [pilɔ̃] NM (*instrument*) pestle; (*de volaille*) drumstick; **mettre un livre au ~** to pulp a book

pilonnage [pilɔnaʒ] NM (*bombardement*) bombardment; (*de livre*) pulping; **~ médiatique** (*fig*) media hype

pilonner [pilɔne] /1/ VT to pound

pilori [pilɔʀi] NM: **mettre** *ou* **clouer au ~** to pillory

pilotage [pilɔtaʒ] NM piloting; flying; **~ automatique** automatic piloting; **~ sans visibilité** blind flying

★**pilote** [pilɔt] NMF pilot; (*de char, voiture*) driver; **~ de chasse/d'essai/de ligne** fighter/test/airline pilot; **~ de course** racing driver ▸ ADJ pilot *cpd*; **usine/ferme ~** experimental factory/farm

piloter [pilɔte] /1/ VT (*navire*) to pilot; (*avion*) to fly; (*automobile*) to drive; (*fig*): **~ qn** to guide sb round

pilotis [pilɔti] NM pile; stilt

★**pilule** [pilyl] NF pill; **prendre la ~** to be on the pill; **~ du lendemain** morning-after pill

pimbêche [pɛ̃bɛʃ] NF (*péj*) stuck-up girl

piment [pimɑ̃] NM (*Bot*) pepper, capsicum; (*fig*) spice, piquancy; **~ rouge** (*Culin*) chilli

pimenté, e [pimɑ̃te] ADJ (*plat*) hot, spicy

pimenter [pimɑ̃te] /1/ VT (*plat*) to add spice to, to spice up; (*fig*) to add *ou* give spice to

pimpant, e [pɛ̃pɑ̃, -ɑ̃t] ADJ spruce

pin [pɛ̃] NM pine (tree); (*bois*) pine(wood)

pinacle [pinakl] NM: **porter qn au ~** (*fig*) to praise sb to the skies

pinailler [pinaje] VI (*fam*) to quibble; **~ sur qch** to quibble over *ou* about sth

pinailleur, euse [pinajœʀ, -øz] (*fam*) ADJ nit-picking ▸ NM/F nit-picker

pinard [pinaʀ] NM (*fam*) (cheap) wine, plonk (BRIT)

pince [pɛ̃s] NF (*outil*) pliers *pl*; (*de homard, crabe*) pincer, claw; (*Couture: pli*) dart; **~ à sucre/glace** sugar/ice tongs *pl*; **~ à épiler** tweezers *pl*; **~ à linge**

clothes peg (BRIT) *ou* pin (US); **~ universelle** (universal) pliers *pl*; **pinces de cycliste** bicycle clips

pincé, e [pɛ̃se] ADJ (*air*) stiff; (*mince: bouche*) pinched ▶ NF (*de sel, épice*) pinch; (*fig: de malice*) touch

pinceau, x [pɛ̃so] NM (paint)brush

pincement [pɛ̃smɑ̃] NM: **~ au cœur** twinge of regret

pince-monseigneur (*pl* **pinces-monseigneur**) [pɛ̃smɔ̃seɲœʀ] NF crowbar

pince-nez [pɛ̃sne] NM INV pince-nez

pincer [pɛ̃se] /**3**/ VT (*Mus: cordes*) to pluck; (*Couture*) to dart, put darts in; (*fam*) to nab ■ **se pincer** VPR: **se ~ le doigt** to squeeze *ou* nip one's finger; **se ~ le nez** to hold one's nose

pince-sans-rire [pɛ̃sɑ̃ʀiʀ] ADJ INV deadpan

pincettes [pɛ̃sɛt] NFPL tweezers; (*pour le feu*) (fire) tongs

pinçon [pɛ̃sɔ̃] NM pinch mark

pinède [pined] NF pinewood, pine forest

pingouin [pɛ̃gwɛ̃] NM penguin

★**ping-pong** [piɳpɔ̃g] NM table tennis

pingre [pɛ̃gʀ] ADJ stingy

pingrerie [pɛ̃gʀəʀi] NF stinginess

pinson [pɛ̃sɔ̃] NM chaffinch

pintade [pɛ̃tad] NF guinea-fowl

pinte [pɛ̃t] NF pint

pin up [pinœp] NF INV pin-up (girl)

pioche [pjɔʃ] NF pickaxe

piocher [pjɔʃe] /**1**/ VT to dig up (with a pickaxe); (*fam*) to swot (BRIT) *ou* grind (US) at; **~ dans** to dig into

piolet [pjɔlɛ] NM ice axe

pion, ne [pjɔ̃, pjɔn] NM/F (*Scol*) student paid to supervise schoolchildren ▶ NM (*Échecs*) pawn; (*Dames*) piece, draught (BRIT), checker (US)

pioncer [pjɔ̃se] VI (*fam: dormir*) to sleep, to kip (BRIT *fam*)

pionnier [pjɔnje] NM pioneer

pipe [pip] NF pipe; **fumer la** *ou* **une ~** to smoke a pipe; **~ de bruyère** briar pipe

pipeau, x [pipo] NM (reed-)pipe

pipe-line [piplin] NM pipeline

piper [pipe] /**1**/ VT (*dé*) to load; (*carte*) to mark; **sans ~ mot** (*fam*) without a squeak; **les dés sont pipés** (*fig*) the dice are loaded

pipette [pipɛt] NF pipette

pipi [pipi] NM (*fam*): **faire ~** to have a wee

pipole [pipɔl] NMF (*presse, événement*) celebrity ▶ ADJ *ou* ADJ INV: **la presse ~** the celebrity press; **les magazines pipoles** *ou* **~** celebrity magazines

★**piquant, e** [pikɑ̃, -ɑ̃t] ADJ (*barbe, rosier etc*) prickly; (*saveur, sauce*) hot, pungent; (*fig: détail*) tillating; (: *mordant, caustique*) biting ▶ NM (*épine*) thorn, prickle; (*de hérisson*) quill, spine; (*fig*) spiciness, spice

pique [pik] NF (*arme*) pike; **envoyer** *ou* **lancer des piques à qn** (*fig*) to make cutting remarks to sb ▶ NM (*Cartes: couleur*) spades *pl*; (: *carte*) spade

piqué, e [pike] ADJ (*Couture*) (machine-)stitched; quilted; (*livre, glace*) mildewed; (*vin*) sour; (*Mus:*

note) staccato; (*fam: personne*) nuts ▶ NM (*Aviat*) dive; (*Textiles*) piqué

pique-assiette [pikasjɛt] NMF (*péj*) scrounger, sponger

pique-fleurs [pikflœʀ] NM INV flower holder

★**pique-nique** [piknik] NM picnic

pique-niquer [piknike] /**1**/ VI to (have a) picnic

pique-niqueur, -euse [piknikœʀ, -øz] NM/F picnicker

★**piquer** [pike] /**1**/ VT (*percer*) to prick; (*Méd*) to give an injection to; (: *animal blessé etc*) to put to sleep; (*insecte, fumée, ortie*) to sting; (*moustique*) to bite; (*poivre*) to burn; (*froid*) to bite; (*Couture*) to machine (stitch); (*intérêt etc*) to arouse; (*fam: prendre*) to pick up; (: *voler*) to pinch; (: *arrêter*) to nab; (*planter*): **~ qch dans** to stick sth into; (*fixer*): **~ qch à** *ou* **sur** to pin sth onto; **~ une tête** (*plonger*) to dive headfirst; **~ un galop/un cent mètres** to break into a gallop/put on a sprint; **~ une crise** to throw a fit; **~ au vif** (*fig*) to sting ▶ VI (*oiseau, avion*) to go into a dive; (*saveur*) to be pungent; to be sour; **~ sur** to swoop down on; to head straight for; **~ du nez** (*avion*) to go into a nose-dive ■ **se piquer** VPR (*avec une aiguille*) to prick o.s.; (*se faire une piqûre*) to inject o.s.; (*se vexer*) to get annoyed; **se ~ de faire** to pride o.s. on doing

piquet [pikɛ] NM (*pieu*) post, stake; (*de tente*) peg; **mettre un élève au ~** to make a pupil stand in the corner; **~ de grève** (strike) picket; **~ d'incendie** fire-fighting squad

piqueté, e [pikte] ADJ: **~ de** dotted with

piquette [pikɛt] NF (*fam*) cheap wine, plonk (BRIT)

piqûre [pikyʀ] NF (*d'épingle*) prick; (*d'ortie*) sting; (*de moustique*) bite; (*Méd*) injection, shot (US); (*Couture*) (straight) stitch; straight stitching; (*de ver*) hole; (*tache*) (spot of) mildew; **faire une ~ à qn** to give sb an injection

piranha [piʀana] NM piranha

piratage [piʀataʒ] NM (*Inform*) piracy

pirate [piʀat] ADJ pirate *cpd* ▶ NM pirate; (*fig: escroc*) crook, shark; (*Inform*) hacker; **~ de l'air** hijacker

pirater [piʀate] /**1**/ (*Inform*) VI to hack ▶ VT to hack into

piraterie [piʀatʀi] NF (act of) piracy; **~ aérienne** hijacking

★**pire** [piʀ] ADJ (*comparatif*) worse; (*superlatif*): **le (la) ~ ...** the worst ... ▶ NM: **le ~ (de)** the worst (of); **au ~** at (the very) worst

Pirée [piʀe] N Piraeus

pirogue [piʀɔg] NF dugout (canoe)

pirouette [piʀwɛt] NF pirouette; (*fig: volte-face*) about-turn

pis [pi] NM (*de vache*) udder; (*pire*): **le ~** the worst ▶ ADJ INV, ADV worse; **qui ~ est** what is worse; **au ~ aller** if the worst comes to the worst, at worst; **de mal en ~** from bad to worse

pis-aller [pizale] NM INV stopgap

pisciculture [pisikyltyʀ] NF fish farming

★**piscine** [pisin] NF (swimming) pool; **~ couverte** indoor (swimming) pool

Pise [piz] N Pisa

pissaladière [pisaladjɛʀ] NF *onion, anchovy and olive pizza*

pisse [pis] NF (!) piss (*fam*)

pissenlit [pisɑ̃li] NM dandelion

pisser [pise] /1/ VI (!) to piss (fam)

pissotière [pisɔtjɛʀ] NF (fam) public urinal

pistache [pistaʃ] NF pistachio (nut)

pistard [pistaʀ] NM (Cyclisme) track cyclist

★**piste** [pist] NF (d'un animal, sentier) track, trail; (indice) lead; (de stade, de magnétophone) track; (de cirque) ring; (de danse) floor; (de patinage) rink; (de ski) run; (Aviat) runway; ~ **cavalière** bridle path; ~ **cyclable** cycle track, bikeway (US); ~ **sonore** sound track

pister [piste] /1/ VT to track, trail

pisteur [pistœʀ] NM (Ski) member of the ski patrol

pistil [pistil] NM pistil

pistolet [pistɔlɛ] NM (arme) pistol, gun; (à peinture) spray gun; ~ **à bouchon/air comprimé** popgun/airgun; ~ **à eau** water pistol

pistolet-mitrailleur (pl **pistolets-mitrailleurs**) [pistɔlɛmitʀajœʀ] NM submachine gun

piston [pistɔ̃] NM (Tech) piston; (Mus) valve; (fam: appui) string-pulling; **avoir du** ~ (fam) to have friends in the right places

pistonner [pistɔne] /1/ VT (fam: candidat) to pull strings for

pistou [pistu] NM pesto

pitance [pitɑ̃s] NF (péj) (means of) sustenance

piteusement [pitøzmɑ̃] ADV (échouer) miserably

piteux, -euse [pitø, -øz] ADJ pitiful, sorry (avant le nom); **en** ~ **état** in a sorry state

pitié [pitje] NF pity; **sans** ~ adj pitiless, merciless; **faire** ~ to inspire pity; **il me fait** ~ I pity him, I feel sorry for him; **avoir** ~ **de** (compassion) to pity, feel sorry for; (merci) to have pity ou mercy on; **par** ~ **!** for pity's sake!

piton [pitɔ̃] NM (clou) peg, bolt; ~ **rocheux** rocky outcrop

pitoyable [pitwajabl] ADJ pitiful

pitre [pitʀ] NM clown

pitrerie [pitʀəʀi] NF tomfoolery no pl

★**pittoresque** [pitɔʀɛsk] ADJ picturesque; (expression, détail) colourful (BRIT), colorful (US)

pivert [pivɛʀ] NM green woodpecker

pivoine [pivwan] NF peony

pivot [pivo] NM pivot; (d'une dent) post

pivoter [pivɔte] /1/ VI (fauteuil) to swivel; (porte) to revolve; ~ **sur ses talons** to swing round

pixel [piksɛl] NM pixel

pixélisation [pikselizasjɔ̃], **pixellisation** [pikselizasjɔ̃] NF (Inform) pixelation

pixéliser [pikselize], **pixelliser** [pikselize] VT, VI (Inform) to pixelate

★**pizza** [pidza] NF pizza

PJ SIGLE F (= police judiciaire) ≈ CID (BRIT), ≈ FBI (US) ▶ SIGLE FPL (= pièces jointes) encl

PL SIGLE M (Auto) = **poids lourd**

Pl. ABR = **place**

placage [plakaʒ] NM (bois) veneer

★**placard** [plakaʀ] NM (armoire) cupboard; (affiche) poster, notice; (Typo) galley; ~ **publicitaire** display advertisement

placarder [plakaʀde] /1/ VT (affiche) to put up; (mur) to stick posters on

★**place** [plas] NF (emplacement, situation, classement) place; (de ville, village) square; (espace libre) room, space; (de parking) space; (siège: de train, cinéma, voiture) seat; (prix: au cinéma etc) price; (: dans un bus, taxi) fare; (emploi) job; ~ **financière/boursière** money/stock market; **en** ~ (mettre) in its place; **de** ~ **en** ~, **par places** here and there, in places; **sur** ~ on the spot; **faire** ~ **à** to give way to; **faire de la** ~ **à** to make room for; **ça prend de la** ~ it takes up a lot of room ou space; **prendre** ~ to take one's place; **remettre qn à sa** ~ to put sb in his (ou her) place; **ne pas rester** ou **tenir en** ~ to be always on the go; **à la** ~ **de** in place of, instead of; **à votre** ~ ... if I were you ...; **se mettre à la** ~ **de qn** to put o.s. in sb's place ou in sb's shoes; **une quatre places** (Auto) a four-seater; **il y a 20 places assises/debout** there are 20 seats/there is standing room for 20; ~ **forte** fortified town; ~ **d'honneur** place (ou seat) of honour (BRIT) ou honor (US)

placé, e [plase] ADJ (Hippisme) placed; **haut** ~ (fig) high-ranking; **être bien/mal** ~ to be well/badly placed; (spectateur) to have a good/bad seat; **être bien/mal** ~ **pour faire** to be in/not to be in a position to do; **il est bien** ~ **pour le savoir** he is in a position to know

placebo [plasebo] NM placebo

placement [plasmɑ̃] NM placing; (Finance) investment; **agence** ou **bureau de** ~ employment agency

placenta [plasɛ̃ta] NM placenta

placer [plase] /3/ VT to place, put; (convive, spectateur) to seat; (capital, argent) to place, invest; (dans la conversation) to put ou get in; ~ **qn chez** to get sb a job at (ou with); **se** ~ **au premier rang** to go and stand (ou sit) in the first row

placide [plasid] ADJ placid

placidité [plasidite] NF placidity

placier, -ière [plasje, -jɛʀ] NM/F commercial rep(resentative), salesman/woman

Placoplâtre® [plakoplatʀ] NM plasterboard

★**plafond** [plafɔ̃] NM ceiling

plafonnement [plafɔnmɑ̃] NM (limite imposée): **un** ~ **des aides** an upper limit on aid; **instaurer un** ~ **de** to set a ceiling on

plafonner [plafɔne] /1/ VT (pièce) to put a ceiling (up) in ▶ VI to reach one's (ou a) ceiling

plafonnier [plafɔnje] NM ceiling light; (Auto) interior light

★**plage** [plaʒ] NF beach; (station) (seaside) resort; (fig) band, bracket; (de disque) track; ~ **arrière** (Auto) parcel ou back shelf

plagiaire [plaʒjɛʀ] NMF plagiarist

plagiat [plaʒja] NM plagiarism

plagier [plaʒje] /7/ VT to plagiarize

plagiste [plaʒist] NMF beach attendant

plaid [plɛd] NM (tartan) car rug, lap robe (US)

plaidant, e [plɛdɑ̃, -ɑ̃t] ADJ (Jur) litigant

plaider [plede] /1/ VI (avocat) to plead; (plaignant) to go to court, litigate; ~ **pour** (fig) to speak for ▶ VT (Jur) to plead

plaider-coupable, plaider coupable [pledekupabl] NM (Jur) guilty plea

plaideur, -euse [plɛdœʀ, -øz] NM/F (Jur) litigant

P

335

plaidoirie [plɛdwaʀi] NF (Jur) speech for the defence (BRIT) ou defense (US)

plaidoyer [plɛdwaje] NM (Jur) speech for the defence (BRIT) ou defense (US); (fig) plea

plaie [plɛ] NF wound

plaignant, e [plɛɲɑ̃, -ɑ̃t] VB voir **plaindre** ▶ NM/F plaintiff

★**plaindre** [plɛ̃dʀ] /52/ VT to pity, feel sorry for ▪ se **plaindre** VPR (gémir) to moan; (protester, rouspéter): **se ~ (à qn) (de)** to complain (to sb) (about); **se ~ de** (souffrir) to complain of

plaine [plɛn] NF plain

plain-pied [plɛ̃pje] ADV: **de ~** at street-level; (fig) straight; **de ~ (avec)** on the same level (as)

plaint, e [plɛ̃, -ɛ̃t] PP de **plaindre** ▶ NF (gémissement) moan, groan; (doléance) complaint; **porter plainte** to lodge a complaint

plaintif, -ive [plɛ̃tif, -iv] ADJ plaintive

★**plaire** [plɛʀ] /54/ VI to be a success, be successful; to please; **cela me plaît** I like it; **ça plaît beaucoup aux jeunes** it's very popular with young people; **essayer de ~ à qn** (en étant serviable etc) to try and please sb; **elle plaît aux hommes** she's a success with men, men like her ▶ VB IMPERS: **ce qu'il vous plaira** what(ever) you like ou wish; **s'il vous plaît, s'il te plaît** please ▪ **se plaire** VPR: **se ~ quelque part** to like being somewhere, like it somewhere; **se ~ à faire** to take pleasure in doing

plaisamment [plɛzamɑ̃] ADV pleasantly

plaisance [plɛzɑ̃s] NF (aussi: **navigation de plaisance**) (pleasure) sailing, yachting

plaisancier [plɛzɑ̃sje] NM amateur sailor, yachting enthusiast

plaisant, e [plɛzɑ̃, -ɑ̃t] ADJ pleasant; (histoire, anecdote) amusing

plaisanter [plɛzɑ̃te] /1/ VI to joke; **pour ~** for a joke; **on ne plaisante pas avec cela** that's no joking matter; **tu plaisantes!** you're joking ou kidding! ▶ VT (personne) to tease, make fun of

★**plaisanterie** [plɛzɑ̃tʀi] NF joke; joking no pl

plaisantin [plɛzɑ̃tɛ̃] NM joker; (fumiste) fly-by-night

plaise etc [plɛz] VB voir **plaire**

★**plaisir** [pleziʀ] NM pleasure; **faire ~ à qn** (délibérément) to be nice to sb, please sb; **ça me fait ~** (cadeau, nouvelle etc) I'm delighted ou very pleased with this; **j'espère que ça te fera ~** I hope you'll like it; **prendre ~ à/à faire** to take pleasure in/in doing; **j'ai le ~ de ...** it is with great pleasure that I ...; **M. et Mme X ont le ~ de vous faire part de ...** M. and Mme X are pleased to announce ...; **se faire un ~ de faire qch** to be (only too) pleased to do sth; **faites-moi le ~ de ...** would you mind ..., would you be kind enough to ...; **à ~** freely; for the sake of it; **au ~ (de vous revoir)** (I hope to) see you again; **pour le** ou **pour son** ou **par ~** for pleasure

plaît [plɛ] VB voir **plaire**

★**plan, e** [plɑ̃, -an] ADJ flat ▶ NM plan; (Géom) plane; (fig) level, plane; (Ciné) shot; **au premier/second ~** in the foreground/middle distance; **mettre qch au premier ~** (fig) to consider sth to be of primary importance; **sur le ~ sexuel** sexually, as far as sex is concerned; **laisser/rester en ~** to abandon/be abandoned; **~ d'action** plan of action; **~ direc-**

teur (Écon) master plan; **~ d'eau** lake; pond; **~ de travail** worktop, work surface; **~ de vol** (Aviat) flight plan

★**planche** [plɑ̃ʃ] NF (pièce de bois) plank, (wooden) board; (illustration) plate; (de salades, radis, poireaux) bed; (d'un plongeoir) (diving) board; **les planches** (Théât) the boards; **en planches** adj wooden; **faire la ~** (dans l'eau) to float on one's back; **avoir du pain sur la ~** to have one's work cut out; **~ à découper** chopping board; **~ à dessin** drawing board; **~ à pain** breadboard; **~ à repasser** ironing board; **~ (à roulettes)** (planche) skateboard; (sport) skateboarding; **~ de salut** (fig) lifeline; **~ à voile** (planche) windsurfer, sailboard; (sport) windsurfing

plancher [plɑ̃ʃe] NM floor; (planches) floorboards pl; (fig) minimum level ▶ VI to work hard

planchiste [plɑ̃ʃist] NMF windsurfer

plancton [plɑ̃ktɔ̃] NM plankton

planer [plane] /1/ VI (oiseau, avion) to glide; (fumée, vapeur) to float, hover; (drogué) to be (on a) high; (fam: rêveur) to have one's head in the clouds; **~ sur** (danger) to hang over; to hover above

planétaire [planetɛʀ] ADJ planetary

planétarium [planetaʀjɔm] NM planetarium

planète [planɛt] NF planet

planeur [planœʀ] NM glider

planification [planifikasjɔ̃] NF (economic) planning

planifier [planifje] /7/ VT to plan

planisphère [planisfɛʀ] NM planisphere

planning [planiŋ] NM programme (BRIT), program (US), schedule; **~ familial** family planning

planque [plɑ̃k] NF (fam: combine, filon) cushy (BRIT) ou easy number; (: cachette) hideout

planquer [plɑ̃ke] /1/ (fam) VT to hide (away), stash away ▪ **se planquer** VPR to hide

plant [plɑ̃] NM seedling, young plant

plantage [plɑ̃taʒ] NM (d'ordinateur) crash

plantaire [plɑ̃tɛʀ] ADJ voir **voûte**

★**plante** [plɑ̃t] NF plant; **~ d'appartement** house ou pot plant; **~ du pied** sole (of the foot); **~ verte** house plant

planter [plɑ̃te] /1/ VT (plante) to plant; (enfoncer) to hammer ou drive in; (tente) to put up, pitch; (drapeau, échelle, décors) to put up; (fam: mettre) to dump; (: abandonner): **~ là** to ditch; **~ qch dans** to hammer ou drive sth into; to stick sth into ▪ **se planter** VPR (fam: se tromper) to get it wrong; **se ~ dans** to sink into; to get stuck in; **se ~ devant** to plant o.s. in front of

planteur [plɑ̃tœʀ] NM planter

plantigrade [plɑ̃tigʀad] NM, ADJ plantigrade

planton [plɑ̃tɔ̃] NM orderly

plantureux, -euse [plɑ̃tyʀø, -øz] ADJ (repas) copious, lavish; (femme) buxom

plaquage [plakaʒ] NM (Rugby) tackle

plaque [plak] NF plate; (de verre) sheet; (de verglas, d'eczéma) patch; (dentaire) plaque; (avec inscription) plaque; **~ (minéralogique** ou **de police** ou **d'immatriculation)** number (BRIT) ou license (US) plate; **~ de beurre** slab of butter; **~ chauffante** hotplate; **~ de chocolat** bar of chocolate; **~ de cuisson** hob; **~ d'identité** identity disc; **~ tournante** (fig) centre (BRIT), center (US)

plaqué, e [plake] ADJ: **~ or/argent** gold-/silver-plated; **~ acajou** with a mahogany veneer ▶ NM: **~ or/argent** gold/silver plate

plaquer [plake] /1/ VT (bijou) to plate; (bois) to veneer; (aplatir): **~ qch sur/contre** to make sth stick ou cling to; (Rugby) to bring down; (fam: laisser tomber) to drop, ditch; **~ qn contre** to pin sb to ■ **se plaquer** VPR: **se ~ contre** to flatten o.s. against

plaquette [plakɛt] NF tablet; (de chocolat) bar; (de beurre) slab, packet; (livre) small volume; (Méd: de pilules, gélules) pack, packet; **~ de frein** (Auto) brake pad

plasma [plasma] NM plasma

plastic [plastik] NM plastic explosive

plasticien, ne [plastisjɛ̃, -jɛn] NM/F (artiste) visual artist ▶ ADJ: **artiste ~** visual artist

plastifié, e [plastifje] ADJ plastic-coated

plastifier [plastifje] /7/ VT (document, photo) to laminate

plastiquage [plastikaʒ] NM bombing, bomb attack

★**plastique** [plastik] ADJ plastic ▶ NM plastic ▶ NF plastic arts pl; (d'une statue) modelling

plastiquer [plastike] /1/ VT to blow up

plastiqueur [plastikœr] NM terrorist (planting a plastic bomb)

plastron [plastrɔ̃] NM shirt front

plastronner [plastrɔne] /1/ VI to swagger

plasturgie [plastyrʒi] NF plastics manufacturing

★**plat, e** [pla, -at] ADJ flat; (fade: vin) flat-tasting, insipid; (personne, livre) dull; (style) flat, dull; **à ~ ventre** adv face down; (tomber) flat on one's face; **à ~ adj** (pneu, batterie) flat; (fam: fatigué) dead beat, tired out ▶ NM (récipient, Culin) dish; (d'un repas) course; **le premier ~** the first course; (partie plate): **le ~ de la main** the flat of the hand; (: d'une route) flat (part); **~ cuisiné** ready meal; **~ du jour** dish of the day; **~ principal** ou **de résistance** main course; **plats préparés** convenience food(s)

platane [platan] NM plane tree

★**plateau, x** [plato] NM (support) tray; (d'une table) top; (d'une balance) pan; (Géo) plateau; (de tourne-disques) turntable; (Ciné) set; (TV): **nous avons deux journalistes sur le ~ ce soir** we have two journalists with us tonight; **~ à fromages** cheeseboard

plateau-repas (pl **plateaux-repas**) [platoRəpa] NM tray meal, TV dinner

plate-bande (pl **plates-bandes**) [platbɑ̃d] NF flower bed

platée [plate] NF dish(ful)

plate-forme (pl **plates-formes**) [platfɔrm] NF platform; **~ de forage/pétrolière** drilling/oil rig

platine [platin] NM platinum ▶ NF (d'un tourne-disque) turntable; **~ disque/cassette** record/cassette deck; **~ laser** ou **compact-disc** compact disc (player)

platitude [platityd] NF platitude

platonique [platɔnik] ADJ platonic

plâtras [platra] NM rubble no pl

plâtre [platr] NM (matériau) plaster; (statue) plaster statue; (Méd) (plaster) cast; **avoir un bras dans le ~** to have an arm in plaster ■ **plâtres** NMPL plasterwork sg

plâtrer [platre] /1/ VT to plaster; (Méd) to set ou put in a (plaster) cast

plâtrier [platrije] NM plasterer

plausibilité [plozibilite] NF plausibility

plausible [plozibl] ADJ plausible

play-back [plɛbak] NM miming

play-boy [plɛbɔj] NM playboy

plébiscite [plebisit] NM plebiscite

plébisciter [plebisite] /1/ VT (approuver) to give overwhelming support to; (élire) to elect by an overwhelming majority

plectre [plɛktr] NM plectrum

pléiade [plejad] NF (groupe) host; **toute une ~ de** a whole host of

★**plein, e** [plɛ̃, plɛn] ADJ full; (porte, roue) solid; (chienne, jument) big (with young); **~ de** full of; **avoir les mains pleines** to have one's hands full; **à pleines mains** (ramasser) in handfuls; (empoigner) firmly; **à ~ régime** at maximum revs; (fig) at full speed; **à ~ temps** full-time; **en ~ air** in the open air; **jeux en ~ air** outdoor games; **en pleine mer** on the open sea; **en ~ soleil** in direct sunlight; **en pleine nuit/rue** in the middle of the night/street; **en ~ milieu** right in the middle; **en ~ jour** in broad daylight ▶ NM: **faire le ~ (d'essence)** to fill up (with petrol (BRIT) ou gas (US)); **faire le ~ de voix** to get the maximum number of votes possible; **les pleins** the downstrokes (in handwriting) ▶ PRÉP: **avoir de l'argent ~ les poches** to have loads of money; **en ~ sur** right on; **en avoir ~ le dos** (fam) to have had it up to here

pleinement [plɛnmɑ̃] ADV fully; to the full

plein-emploi [plɛnɑ̃plwa] NM full employment

plénière [plenjɛr] ADJ F: **assemblée ~** plenary assembly

plénipotentiaire [plenipɔtɑ̃sjɛr] NM plenipotentiary

plénitude [plenityd] NF fullness

pléthore [pletɔr] NF: **~ de** overabundance ou plethora of

pléthorique [pletɔrik] ADJ (classes) overcrowded; (documentation) excessive

★**pleurer** [plœre] /1/ VI to cry; (yeux) to water; **~ sur** to lament (over), bemoan; **~ de rire** to cry with laughter ▶ VT to mourn (for)

pleurésie [plœrezi] NF pleurisy

pleureuse [plœrøz] NF professional mourner

pleurnichard, e [plœrniʃar, -ard] ADJ (personne, ton) whining

pleurnicher [plœrniʃe] /1/ VI to snivel, whine

pleurote [plœrɔt] NM (Bot) oyster mushroom

pleurs [plœr] NMPL: **en ~** in tears

pleut [plø] VB voir **pleuvoir**

pleutre [pløtr] ADJ cowardly

pleuvait etc [pløvɛ] VB voir **pleuvoir**

pleuviner [pløvine] /1/ VB IMPERS to drizzle

★pleuvoir [pløvwaʀ] /**23**/ VB IMPERS to rain; **il pleut** it's raining; **il pleut des cordes** ou **à verse** ou **à torrents** it's pouring (down), it's raining cats and dogs ▶ VI (fig: coups) to rain down; (critiques, invitations) to shower down

pleuvra etc [pløvʀa] VB voir **pleuvoir**

plexiglas® [pleksiglɑs] NM Perspex® (BRIT), Plexiglas® (US)

pli [pli] NM fold; (de jupe) pleat; (de pantalon) crease; (aussi: **faux pli**) crease; (enveloppe) envelope; (lettre) letter; (Cartes) trick; **prendre le ~ de faire** to get into the habit of doing; **ça ne fait pas un ~ !** don't you worry!; **~ d'aisance** inverted pleat

pliable [plijabl] ADJ pliable, flexible

pliage [plijaʒ] NM folding; (Art) origami

pliant, e [plijɑ̃, -ɑ̃t] ADJ folding ▶ NM folding stool, campstool

★plier [plije] /**7**/ VT to fold; (pour ranger) to fold up; (table pliante) to fold down; (genou, bras) to bend ▶ VI to bend; (fig) to yield; **~ bagages** (fig) to pack up (and go) ■ **se plier** VPR: **se ~ à** to submit to

plinthe [plɛ̃t] NF skirting board

plissé, e [plise] ADJ (jupe, robe) pleated; (peau) wrinkled; (Géo) folded ▶ NM (Couture) pleats pl

plissement [plismɑ̃] NM (Géo) fold

plisser [plise] /**1**/ VT (chiffonner: papier, étoffe) to crease; (rider: yeux) to screw up; (: front) to furrow, wrinkle; (: bouche) to pucker; (jupe) to put pleats in ■ **se plisser** VPR (vêtement, étoffe) to crease

pliure [plijyʀ] NF (du bras, genou) bend; (d'un ourlet) fold

plomb [plɔ̃] NM (métal) lead; (d'une cartouche) (lead) shot; (Pêche) sinker; (sceau) (lead) seal; (Élec) fuse; **de ~** (soleil) blazing; **sans ~** (essence) unleaded; **sommeil de ~** heavy ou very deep sleep; **mettre à ~** to plumb

plombage [plɔ̃baʒ] NM (de dent) filling

plombémie [plɔ̃bemi] NF blood lead

plomber [plɔ̃be] /**1**/ VT (dent) to fill (BRIT), stop (US); (fam: compromettre: finances, comptes, relations) to compromise; (canne, ligne) to weight (with lead); (colis, wagon) to put a lead seal on; (Tech: mur) to plumb; (Inform) to protect; **~ l'ambiance** to spoil the atmosphere

plomberie [plɔ̃bʀi] NF plumbing

★plombier [plɔ̃bje] NM plumber

plonge [plɔ̃ʒ] NF: **faire la ~** to be a washer-up (BRIT) ou dishwasher (person)

plongeant, e [plɔ̃ʒɑ̃, -ɑ̃t] ADJ (vue) from above; (tir, décolleté) plunging

plongée [plɔ̃ʒe] NF (Sport) diving no pl; (: sans scaphandre) skin diving; (de sous-marin) submersion, dive; **en ~** (sous-marin) submerged; (prise de vue) high angle; **~ sous-marine** diving

plongeoir [plɔ̃ʒwaʀ] NM diving board

plongeon [plɔ̃ʒɔ̃] NM dive

★plonger [plɔ̃ʒe] /**3**/ VI to dive; **~ dans un sommeil profond** to sink straight into a deep sleep ▶ VT: **~ qch dans** to plunge sth into; **~ qn dans l'embarras** to throw sb into a state of confusion ■ **se plonger** VPR: **se ~ dans** (études, lecture) to bury ou immerse o.s. in; **se ~ dans un livre** to get absorbed in a book

plongeur, -euse [plɔ̃ʒœʀ, -øz] NM/F diver; (de café) washer-up (BRIT), dishwasher (person)

plot [plo] NM (Élec) contact

plouc [pluk] NMF (fam, péj) yokel

ploutocratie [plutɔkʀasi] NF plutocracy

ploutocratique [plutɔkʀatik] ADJ plutocratic

ployer [plwaje] /**8**/ VT to bend ▶ VI to bend; (plancher) to sag

plu [ply] PP de **plaire**; **pleuvoir**

★pluie [plɥi] NF rain; (averse, ondée): **une ~ brève** a shower; (fig): **~ de** shower of; **une ~ fine** fine rain; **retomber en ~** to shower down; **sous la ~** in the rain

plumage [plymaʒ] NM plumage no pl, feathers pl

★plume [plym] NF feather; (pour écrire) (pen) nib; (fig) pen; **dessin à la ~** a pen and ink drawing

plumeau, x [plymo] NM feather duster

plumer [plyme] /**1**/ VT to pluck

plumet [plymɛ] NM plume

plumier [plymje] NM pencil box

★plupart [plypaʀ]: **la ~** pron the majority, most (of them); **la ~ des** most, the majority of; **la ~ du temps/d'entre nous** most of the time/of us; **pour la ~** adv for the most part, mostly

pluralisme [plyʀalism] NM pluralism

pluraliste [plyʀalist] ADJ pluralist

pluralité [plyʀalite] NF plurality

pluriannuel, le [plyʀianɥɛl] ADJ long-term

pluridisciplinaire [plyʀidisiplinɛʀ] ADJ multidisciplinary

pluriel [plyʀjɛl] NM plural; **au ~** in the plural

pluriethnique [plyʀiɛtnik] ADJ multi-ethnic

★plus¹ [ply] VB voir **plaire**

---

plus² [ply]

ADV **1** (forme négative): **ne ... plus** no more, no longer; **je n'ai plus d'argent** I've got no more money ou no money left; **il ne travaille plus** he's no longer working, he doesn't work any more

2 [ply, (+voyelle) plyz] (comparatif) more, ...+er; (superlatif): **le plus** the most, the ...+est; **plus grand/intelligent (que)** bigger/more intelligent (than); **le plus grand/intelligent** the biggest/most intelligent; **tout au plus** at the very most

3 (davantage) [plys, (+voyelle) plyz] more; **il travaille plus (que)** he works more (than); **plus il travaille, plus il est heureux** the more he works, the happier he is; **plus de pain** more bread; **plus de 10 personnes/trois heures/quatre kilos** more than ou over 10 people/three hours/four kilos; **trois heures de plus que** three hours more than; **plus de minuit** after ou past midnight; **de plus** what's more, moreover; **il a trois ans de plus que moi** he's three years older than me; **trois kilos en plus** three kilos more; **en plus de** in addition to; **de plus en plus** more and more; **en plus de cela ...** what is more ...; **plus ou moins** more or less; **ni plus ni moins** no more, no less; **sans plus** (but) no more than that, (but) that's all; **qui plus est** what is more

▶ PRÉP [plys]: **quatre plus deux** four plus two

★plusieurs [plyzjœʀ] ADJ, PRON several; **ils sont ~** there are several of them

plus-que-parfait [plyskəpaʀfɛ] NM pluperfect, past perfect

plus-value [plyvaly] NF (*d'un bien*) appreciation; (*bénéfice*) capital gain; (*budgétaire*) surplus

plut [ply] VB *voir* **plaire; pleuvoir**

plutonium [plytɔnjɔm] NM plutonium

plutôt [plyto] ADV rather; **je ferais ~ ceci** I'd rather *ou* sooner do this; **fais ~ comme ça** try this way instead; **~ que (de) faire** rather than *ou* instead of doing

pluvial, e, -aux [plyvjal, -o] ADJ (*eaux*) rain *cpd*

pluvieux, -euse [plyvjø, -øz] ADJ rainy, wet

pluviométrie [plyvjɔmetʀi] NF recorded rainfall

pluviosité [plyvjɔzite] NF rainfall

PM SIGLE F = **Police militaire**

p.m. ABR (= *pour mémoire*) for the record

PMA [peema] SIGLE NMPL (= *pays les moins avancés*) LDCs (= *least developed countries*) ▶ SIGLE F = **procréation médicalement assistée**

PME SIGLE FPL (= *petites et moyennes entreprises*) small businesses

PMI SIGLE FPL = **petites et moyennes industries** ▶ SIGLE F = **protection maternelle et infantile**

PMU SIGLE M (= *pari mutuel urbain*) betting agency

The **PMU** (*pari mutuel urbain*) is a government-regulated network of betting counters run from bars displaying the *PMU* sign or online. Punters buy fixed-price tickets predicting winners or finishing positions in horse races. The traditional bet is the *tiercé*, a triple bet, although other multiple bets (*quarté* and so on) are becoming increasingly popular.

PNB SIGLE M (= *produit national brut*) GNP

★pneu [pnø] NM (*de roue*) tyre (BRIT), tire (US); (*message*) letter sent by pneumatic tube

pneumatique [pnømatik] ADJ pneumatic; (*gonflable*) inflatable ▶ NM tyre (BRIT), tire (US)

pneumonie [pnømɔni] NF pneumonia

pneumopathie [pnømopati] NF acute respiratory disease

PO SIGLE FPL (= *petites ondes*) MW

po [po] ABR *voir* **science**

Pô [po] NM: **le Pô** the Po

p.o. ABR (= *par ordre*) p.p. (*on letters etc*)

★poche [pɔʃ] NF pocket; (*déformation*): **faire une/des ~(s)** to bag; (*sous les yeux*) bag, pouch; (*Zool*) pouch; **de ~** pocket *cpd*; **en être de sa ~** to be out of pocket; **c'est dans la ~** it's in the bag; **argent de ~** pocket money ▶ NM (*livre de poche*) (pocket-size) paperback

poché, e [pɔʃe] ADJ: **œuf ~** poached egg; **œil ~** black eye

pocher [pɔʃe] /**1**/ VT (*Culin*) to poach; (*Art*) to sketch ▶ VI (*vêtement*) to bag

poche-revolver [pɔʃʀəvɔlvɛʀ] (*pl* **poches-revolver**) NF hip pocket

pochette [pɔʃɛt] NF (*de timbres*) wallet, envelope; (*d'aiguilles etc*) case; (*sac: de femme*) clutch bag, purse; (: *d'homme*) bag; (*sur veston*) breast pocket; (*mouchoir*) breast pocket handkerchief; **~ d'allu-mettes** book of matches; **~ de disque** record sleeve; **~ surprise** lucky bag

pochoir [pɔʃwaʀ] NM (*Art: cache*) stencil; (: *tampon*) transfer

podcast [pɔdkast] NM (*Inform*) podcast

podcaster [pɔdkaste] /**1**/ VI (*Inform*) to podcast

podium [pɔdjɔm] NM podium

podologue [pɔdɔlɔg] NMF podiatrist

poêle [pwal] NM stove ▶ NF: **~ (à frire)** frying pan

poêlée [pwale] NF: **une ~ de** a frying pan full of

poêler [pwale] VT to fry

poêlon [pwalɔ̃] NM casserole

poème [pɔɛm] NM poem

poésie [pɔezi] NF (*poème*) poem; (*art*): **la ~** poetry

poète [pɔɛt] NM poet; (*fig*) dreamer ▶ ADJ poetic

poétesse [pɔetɛs] NF poetess

poétique [pɔetik] ADJ poetic

pognon [pɔɲɔ̃] NM (*fam: argent*) dough

★poids [pwa] NM weight; (*Sport*) shot; **vendre au ~** to sell by weight; **de ~** adj (*argument etc*) weighty; **perdre/prendre du ~** to lose/put on weight; **faire le ~** (*fig*) to measure up; **~ plume/mouche/coq/moyen** (*Boxe*) feather/fly/bantam/middleweight; **~ et haltères** weight lifting *sg*; **~ lourd** (*Boxe*) heavyweight; (*camion: aussi*: **PL**) (big) lorry (BRIT), truck (US); (*Admin*) large goods vehicle (BRIT), truck (US); **~ mort** dead weight; **~ utile** net weight

poignant, e [pwaɲɑ̃, -ɑ̃t] ADJ poignant, harrowing

poignard [pwaɲaʀ] NM dagger

poignarder [pwaɲaʀde] /**1**/ VT to stab, knife

poigne [pwaɲ] NF grip; (*fig*) firm-handedness; **à ~** firm-handed; **avoir de la ~** (*fig*) to rule with a firm hand

poignée [pwaɲe] NF (*de sel etc, fig*) handful; (*de couvercle, porte*) handle; **~ de main** handshake

★poignet [pwaɲɛ] NM (*Anat*) wrist; (*de chemise*) cuff

poil [pwal] NM (*Anat*) hair; (*de pinceau, brosse*) bristle; (*de tapis, tissu*) strand; (*pelage*) coat; (*ensemble des poils*): **avoir du ~ sur la poitrine** to have hair(s) on one's chest, have a hairy chest; **à ~** adj (*fam*) starkers; **au ~** adj (*fam*) hunky-dory; **de tout ~** of all kinds; **être de bon/mauvais ~** (*fam*) to be in a good/bad mood; **~ à gratter** itching powder

poilant, e [pwalɑ̃, -ɑ̃t] ADJ (*fam*) uproarious

poilu, e [pwaly] ADJ hairy

poinçon [pwɛ̃sɔ̃] NM awl; bodkin; (*marque*) hallmark

poinçonner [pwɛ̃sɔne] /**1**/ VT (*marchandise*) to stamp; (*bijou etc*) to hallmark; (*billet, ticket*) to punch, clip

poinçonneuse [pwɛ̃sɔnøz] NF (*outil*) punch

poindre [pwɛ̃dʀ] /**49**/ VI (*fleur*) to come up; (*aube*) to break; (*jour*) to dawn

★poing [pwɛ̃] NM fist; **coup de ~** punch; **dormir à poings fermés** to sleep soundly

★point [pwɛ̃] VB *voir* **poindre** ▶ NM (*marque, signe*) dot; (*de ponctuation*) full stop, period (US); (*moment, de score etc, fig: question*) point; (*endroit*) spot; (*Couture, Tricot*) stitch; **faire le ~** (*Navig*) to take a bearing; (*fig*) to take stock (of the situation); **faire le ~ sur** to review; **en tout ~** in every respect; **sur le ~ de**

faire (just) about to do; **au ~ que, à tel ~ que** so much so that; **mettre au ~** (*mécanisme, procédé*) to develop; (*appareil photo*) to focus; (*affaire*) to settle; **à ~** (*Culin: viande*) medium; **à ~ (nommé)** just at the right time; **~ de croix/tige/chaînette** (*Couture*) cross/stem/chain stitch; **~ mousse/jersey** (*Tricot*) garter/stocking stitch; **~ de départ/d'arrivée/d'arrêt** departure/arrival/stopping point; **~ chaud** (*Mil, Pol*) hot spot; **~ de chute** landing place; (*fig*) stopping-off point; **~ (de côté)** stitch (*pain*); **~ culminant** summit; (*fig*) height, climax; **~ d'eau** spring, water point; **~ d'exclamation** exclamation mark; **~ faible** weak spot; **~ final** full stop, period (*US*); **~ d'interrogation** question mark; **~ mort** (*Finance*) break-even point; **au ~ mort** (*Auto*) in neutral; (*affaire, entreprise*) at a standstill; **~ noir** (*sur le visage*) blackhead; (*Auto*) accident black spot; **~ de non-retour** point of no return; **~ de repère** landmark; (*dans le temps*) point of reference; **~ de vente** retail outlet; **~ de vue** viewpoint; (*fig: opinion*) point of view; **du ~ de vue de** from the point of view of; **points cardinaux** points of the compass, cardinal points; **points de suspension** suspension points ▶ ADV **= pas¹; ne ... ~** not (at all)

pointage [pwɛtaʒ] NM ticking off; checking in

pointe [pwɛt] NF point; (*de la côte*) headland; (*allusion*) dig; sally; (*clou*) tack ■ **pointes** NFPL (*Danse*) points, points shoes; **une ~ d'ail/d'accent** a touch *ou* hint of garlic/of an accent; **être à la ~ de** (*fig*) to be in the forefront of; **faire** *ou* **pousser une ~ jusqu'à ...** to press on as far as ...; **sur la ~ des pieds** on tiptoe; **en ~** *adv* (*tailler*) into a point; *adj* pointed, tapered; **de ~** *adj* (*technique, technologie etc*) leading, cutting-edge (*: vitesse*) maximum, top; **heures/jours de ~** peak hours/days; **faire du 180 en ~** (*Auto*) to have a top *ou* maximum speed of 180; **faire des pointes** (*Danse*) to dance on points; **~ d'asperge** asparagus tip; **~ de courant** surge (of current); **~ de vitesse** burst of speed

pointer [pwɛte] /1/ VT (*cocher*) to tick off (*BRIT*), to check off (*US*); (*diriger: canon, longue-vue, doigt*): **~ vers qch, ~ sur qch** to point at sth; (*Mus: note*) to dot; **~ les oreilles** (*chien*) to prick up its ears ▶ VI (*employé*) to clock in *ou* on; (*pousses*) to come through; (*jour*) to break ■ **se pointer** VPR (*fam: arriver, apparaître*) to turn up

pointeur, -euse [pwɛtœʀ, -øz] NM/F time-keeper ▶ NF timeclock ▶ NM (*Inform*) cursor

pointillé [pwɛtije] NM (*trait*) dotted line; (*Art*) stippling *no pl*

pointilleux, -euse [pwɛtijø, -øz] ADJ particular, pernickety

pointu, e [pwɛty] ADJ pointed; (*clou*) sharp; (*voix*) shrill; (*analyse*) precise

★**pointure** [pwɛtyʀ] NF size

point-virgule (*pl* **points-virgules**) [pwɛviʀgyl] NM semi-colon

★**poire** [pwaʀ] NF pear; (*fam, péj*) mug; **~ électrique** (*pear-shaped*) switch; **~ à injections** syringe

★**poireau, x** [pwaʀo] NM leek

poireauter [pwaʀote] /1/ VI (*fam*) to hang about (waiting)

poirier [pwaʀje] NM pear tree; (*Sport*): **faire le ~** to do a headstand

★**pois** [pwa] NM (*Bot*) pea; (*sur une étoffe*) dot, spot; **à ~** (*cravate etc*) spotted, polka-dot *cpd*; **~ chiche** chickpea; **~ de senteur** sweet pea; **~ cassés** split peas

poison [pwazɔ̃] NM poison

poisse [pwas] NF rotten luck

poisser [pwase] /1/ VT to make sticky

poisseux, -euse [pwasø, -øz] ADJ sticky

★**poisson** [pwasɔ̃] NM fish *gén inv*; **les Poissons** (*Astrologie: signe*) Pisces, the Fish; **être des Poissons** to be Pisces; **pêcher** *ou* **prendre du ~** *ou* **des poissons** to fish; **~ d'avril** April fool; (*blague*) April Fools' Day trick; **~ rouge** goldfish

The traditional April Fools' Day prank in France involves attaching a cut-out paper fish, known as a **poisson d'avril**, to the back of one's victim without being caught. In modern-day France people often play practical jokes on each other and say *'Poisson d'avril!'* to the victim when the joke is revealed. Hoax news stories are often reported on TV and in the press, and companies may advertise fake products as part of the joke.

poisson-chat (*pl* **poissons-chats**) [pwasɔ̃ʃa] NM catfish

★**poissonnerie** [pwasɔnʀi] NF fishmonger's (*BRIT*), fish store (*US*)

poissonneux, -euse [pwasɔnø, -øz] ADJ abounding in fish

poissonnier, -ière [pwasɔnje, -jɛʀ] NM/F fishmonger (*BRIT*), fish merchant (*US*) ▶ NF (*ustensile*) fish kettle

poisson-scie (*pl* **poissons-scies**) [pwasɔsi] NM sawfish

poitevin, e [pwat(ə)vɛ̃, -in] ADJ (*région*) of *ou* from Poitou; (*ville*) of *ou* from Poitiers

poitrail [pwatʀaj] NM (*d'un cheval etc*) breast

★**poitrine** [pwatʀin] NF (*Anat*) chest; (*seins*) bust, bosom; (*Culin*) breast; **~ de bœuf** brisket

★**poivre** [pwavʀ] NM pepper; **~ en grains/moulu** whole/ground pepper; **~ de cayenne** cayenne (pepper); **~ et sel** *adj* (*cheveux*) pepper-and-salt

poivré, e [pwavʀe] ADJ peppery

poivrer [pwavʀe] /1/ VT to pepper

poivrier [pwavʀije] NM (*Bot*) pepper plant

poivrière [pwavʀijɛʀ] NF pepperpot, pepper shaker (*US*)

★**poivron** [pwavʀɔ̃] NM pepper, capsicum; **~ vert/rouge** green/red pepper

poivrot, e [pwavʀo, -ɔt] NM/F (*fam: ivrogne*) wino (*fam*)

poix [pwa] NF pitch (*tar*)

poker [pɔkɛʀ] NM: **le ~** poker; **partie de ~** (*fig*) gamble; **~ d'as** four aces

polaire [pɔlɛʀ] ADJ polar

polar [pɔlaʀ] NM (*fam*) detective novel

polarisation [pɔlaʀizasjɔ̃] NF polarization; (*fig*) focusing

polariser [pɔlaʀize] /1/ VT to polarize; (*fig: attirer*) to attract; (*: réunir, concentrer*) to focus; **être polarisé sur** (*personne*) to be completely bound up with *ou* absorbed by

pôle [pol] NM (*Géo, Élec*) pole; **le ~ Nord/Sud** the North/South Pole; **~ d'attraction** (*fig*) centre of attraction; **P~ Emploi** employment office

polémique [polemik] ADJ controversial, polemic(al) ▸ NF controversy

polémiquer [polemike] /1/ VI to be involved in controversy

polémiste [polemist] NMF polemist, polemicist

★**poli, e** [poli] ADJ polite; (*lisse*) smooth; polished

★**police** [polis] NF police; (*discipline*) : **assurer la ~ de** ou **dans** to keep order in; **peine de simple ~** *sentence given by a magistrate's or police court*; **~ (d'assurance)** (insurance) policy; **~ (de caractères)** (*Typo, Inform*) font, typeface; **~ judiciaire (PJ)** ≈ Criminal Investigation Department (CID) (BRIT), ≈ Federal Bureau of Investigation (FBI) (US); **~ des mœurs** ≈ vice squad; **~ secours** ≈ emergency services *pl* (BRIT), ≈ paramedics *pl* (US)

> En anglais britannique, le mot **police** peut fonctionner comme un singulier ou un pluriel selon que l'accent est mis sur le corps en général ou sur ses membres. Le verbe qui suit peut donc être au singulier ou au pluriel.
> *La police est chargée de faire régner l'ordre.* **The police is responsible for maintaining law and order.**
> *La police a arrêté vingt manifestants.* **The police *have* arrested twenty demonstrators.**

policé, e [polise] ADJ civilized

polichinelle [poliʃinɛl] NM Punch; (*péj*) buffoon; **secret de ~** open secret

★**policier, -ière** [polisje, -jɛʀ] ADJ police *cpd* ▸ NM policeman; (*aussi:* **roman policier**) detective novel

policlinique [poliklinik] NF ≈ outpatients *sg* (clinic)

poliment [polimɑ̃] ADV politely

polio [poljo] NF (*aussi:* **poliomyélite**) polio ▸ NMF (*aussi:* **poliomyélitique**) polio patient ou case

poliomyélite [poljomjelit] NF poliomyelitis

poliomyélitique [poljomjelitik] NMF polio patient ou case

polir [poliʀ] /2/ VT to polish

polisson, ne [polisɔ̃, -ɔn] ADJ naughty

politesse [polites] NF politeness; **rendre la ~ à qn** to return sb's favour (BRIT) ou favor (US) ■ **politesses** NFPL (exchange of) courtesies

politicard [politikaʀ] NM (*péj*) politico, political schemer

politicien, ne [politisjɛ̃, -ɛn] ADJ political ▸ NM/F (*péj*) politician

★**politique** [politik] ADJ political ▸ NF (*science, activité*) politics *sg*; (*principes, tactique*) policy, policies *pl*; **~ étrangère/intérieure** foreign/domestic policy ▸ NM (*politicien*) politician

politique-fiction [politikfiksjɔ̃] (*pl* **politiques-fictions**) NF political fiction

politiquement [politikmɑ̃] ADV politically; **~ correct** politically correct

politisation [politizasjɔ̃] NF politicization

politiser [politize] /1/ VT to politicize ■ **se politiser** VPR (*débat*) to become politicized

politologue [politɔlɔg] NMF political commentator

pollen [polɛn] NM pollen

polluant, e [polɥɑ̃, -ɑ̃t] ADJ polluting; **non ~** non-polluting ▸ NM polluting agent, pollutant

★**polluer** [polɥe] /1/ VT to pollute

pollueur, -euse [polɥœʀ, -øz] NM/F polluter

★**pollution** [polysjɔ̃] NF pollution

polo [polo] NM (*sport*) polo; (*tricot*) polo shirt

★**Pologne** [polɔɲ] NF: **la ~** Poland

★**polonais, e** [polɔnɛ, -ɛz] ADJ Polish ▸ NM (*Ling*) Polish ▸ NM/F: **Polonais, e** Pole

poltron, ne [poltrɔ̃, -ɔn] ADJ cowardly

poly... [poli] PRÉFIXE poly...

polyamide [poliamid] NF polyamide

polychrome [polikʀom] ADJ polychrome, polychromatic

polyclinique [poliklinik] NF (private) clinic (*treating different illnesses*)

polycopie [polikɔpi] NF (*procédé*) duplicating; (*reproduction*) duplicated copy

polycopié, e [polikɔpje] ADJ duplicated ▸ NM handout, duplicated notes *pl*

polycopier [polikɔpje] /7/ VT to duplicate

polyculture [polikyltyʀ] NF mixed farming

polyester [poliɛstɛʀ] NM polyester

polyéthylène [polietilɛn] NM polyethylene

polygame [poligam] ADJ polygamous

polygamie [poligami] NF polygamy

polyglotte [poliglɔt] ADJ polyglot

polygone [poligɔn] NM polygon

polymère [polimɛʀ] NM polymer

polymorphe [polimɔʀf] ADJ polymorphous

Polynésie [polinezi] NF: **la ~** Polynesia; **la ~ française** French Polynesia

polynésien, ne [polinezjɛ̃, -ɛn] ADJ Polynesian

polynôme [polinom] NM polynomial

polype [polip] NM polyp

polyphonie [polifɔni] NF (*Mus: technique*) polyphony; (: *chant*) polyphony

polyphonique [polifɔnik] ADJ (*Mus*) polyphonic

polysémie [polisemi] NF polysemy

polysémique [polisemik] ADJ polysemous

polystyrène [polistiʀɛn] NM polystyrene

polytechnicien, ne [politɛknisjɛ̃, -ɛn] NM/F *student or former student of the École polytechnique*

Polytechnique [politɛknik] NF: (**École**) **~** *prestigious military academy producing high-ranking officers and engineers*

polyuréthane [poliyʀetan] NM polyurethane

polyvalent, e [polivalɑ̃, -ɑ̃t] ADJ (*vaccin*) polyvalent; (*personne*) versatile; (*rôle*) varied; (*salle*) multipurpose ▸ NM ≈ tax inspector

pomélo [pomelo] NM pomelo, grapefruit

pommade [pomad] NF ointment, cream

★**pomme** [pom] NF (*Bot*) apple; (*boule décorative*) knob; (*pomme de terre*): **steak pommes (frites)** steak and chips (BRIT) ou (French) fries (US); **tomber dans les pommes** (*fam*) to pass out; **~ d'Adam** Adam's apple; **pommes allumettes** French fries (*thin-cut*); **~ d'arrosoir** (sprinkler) rose; **~ de pin** pine ou fir cone; **~ de terre** potato; **pommes vapeur** boiled potatoes

pommé, e [pɔme] ADJ (*chou etc*) firm

pommeau, x [pɔmo] NM (*boule*) knob; (*de selle*) pommel

pommelé, e [pɔm(ə)le] ADJ: **gris ~** dapple grey

pommette [pɔmɛt] NF cheekbone

pommier [pɔmje] NM apple tree

pompe [pɔ̃p] NF pump; (*faste*) pomp (and ceremony); **~ à eau/essence** water/petrol pump; **~ à huile** oil pump; **~ à incendie** fire engine (*apparatus*); **pompes funèbres** undertaker's *sg*, funeral parlour *sg* (BRIT), mortician's *sg* (US)

Pompéi [pɔ̃pei] N Pompeii

pompéien, ne [pɔ̃pejɛ̃, -ɛn] ADJ Pompeiian

pomper [pɔ̃pe] /1/ VT to pump; (*évacuer*) to pump out; (*aspirer*) to pump up; (*absorber*) to soak up ▶ VI to pump

pompeusement [pɔ̃pøzmɑ̃] ADV pompously

pompeux, -euse [pɔ̃pø, -øz] ADJ pompous

★**pompier** [pɔ̃pje] NM fireman ▶ ADJ M (*style*) pretentious, pompous

pompiste [pɔ̃pist] NMF petrol (BRIT) *ou* gas (US) pump attendant

pompon [pɔ̃pɔ̃] NM pompom, bobble

pomponner [pɔ̃pɔne] /1/ VT to titivate (BRIT), dress up

ponçage [pɔ̃saʒ] NM sanding

ponce [pɔ̃s] NF: **pierre ~** pumice stone

poncer [pɔ̃se] /3/ VT to sand (down)

ponceuse [pɔ̃søz] NF sander

poncif [pɔ̃sif] NM cliché

ponction [pɔ̃ksjɔ̃] NF (*d'argent etc*) withdrawal; **~ lombaire** lumbar puncture

ponctionner [pɔ̃ksjɔne] VT (*fonds, ressources*) to draw off; (*personne, organisme*) to tax

ponctualité [pɔ̃ktɥalite] NF punctuality

ponctuation [pɔ̃ktɥasjɔ̃] NF punctuation

ponctuel, le [pɔ̃ktɥɛl] ADJ (*à l'heure, Tech*) punctual; (*fig: opération etc*) one-off, single; (*scrupuleux*) punctilious, meticulous

ponctuellement [pɔ̃ktɥɛlmɑ̃] ADV punctually; punctiliously, meticulously

ponctuer [pɔ̃ktɥe] /1/ VT to punctuate; (*Mus*) to phrase

pondéré, e [pɔ̃dere] ADJ level-headed, composed

pondérer [pɔ̃dere] /6/ VT to balance

pondeuse [pɔ̃døz] NF layer, laying hen

pondre [pɔ̃dʀ] /41/ VT to lay; (*fig*) to produce ▶ VI to lay

poney [pɔnɛ] NM pony

pongiste [pɔ̃ʒist] NMF table tennis player

★**pont** [pɔ̃] NM bridge; (*Auto*): **~ arrière/avant** rear/front axle; (*Navig*) deck; **faire le ~** to take an extra day off; **faire un ~ d'or à qn** to offer sb a fortune to take a job; **~ aérien** airlift; **~ basculant** bascule bridge; **~ d'envol** flight deck; **~ élévateur** hydraulic ramp; **~ de graissage** ramp (*in garage*); **~ à péage** tollbridge; **~ roulant** travelling crane; **~ suspendu** suspension bridge; **~ tournant** swing bridge; **Ponts et Chaussées** highways department

The expression **faire le pont** refers to the practice of taking a Monday or Friday off to make a long weekend if a public holiday falls on a Tuesday or Thursday. This is very common at the time of the Ascension Day holiday, which always falls on a Thursday.

pontage [pɔ̃taʒ] NM: **~ coronarien** coronary bypass

ponte [pɔ̃t] NF laying; (*œufs pondus*) clutch ▶ NM (*fam*) big shot

pontife [pɔ̃tif] NM pontiff

pontifiant, e [pɔ̃tifjɑ̃, -jɑ̃t] ADJ (*personne, propos*) pontificating

pontificat [pɔ̃tifika] NM (*papauté*) pontificate; (*durée*) pontificate

pontifier [pɔ̃tifje] /7/ VI to pontificate

pont-levis (*pl* **ponts-levis**) [pɔ̃lvi] NM drawbridge

ponton [pɔ̃tɔ̃] NM pontoon (*on water*)

pop [pɔp] ADJ INV pop ▶ NF: **la ~** pop (music)

pop-corn [pɔpkɔʀn] NM popcorn

popeline [pɔplin] NF poplin

populace [pɔpylas] NF (*péj*) rabble

★**populaire** [pɔpylɛʀ] ADJ popular; (*manifestation*) mass *cpd*, of the people; (*milieux, clientèle*) working-class; (*Ling: mot etc*) used by the lower classes (of society)

populariser [pɔpylarize] /1/ VT to popularize

popularité [pɔpylarite] NF popularity

population [pɔpylasjɔ̃] NF population; **~ active/agricole** working/farming population

populeux, -euse [pɔpylø, -øz] ADJ densely populated

populisme [pɔpylism] NM populism

populiste [pɔpylist] ADJ populist

★**porc** [pɔʀ] NM (*Zool*) pig; (*Culin*) pork; (*peau*) pigskin

porcelaine [pɔʀsəlɛn] NF (*substance*) porcelain, china; (*objet*) piece of china(ware)

porcelet [pɔʀsəlɛ] NM piglet

porc-épic (*pl* **porcs-épics**) [pɔʀkepik] NM porcupine

porche [pɔʀʃ] NM porch

porcher, -ère [pɔʀʃe, -ɛʀ] NM/F pig-keeper

porcherie [pɔʀʃəʀi] NF pigsty

porcin, e [pɔʀsɛ̃, -in] ADJ (*race*) porcine; (*élevage*) pig *cpd*; (*fig*) piglike

pore [pɔʀ] NM pore

poreux, -euse [pɔʀø, -øz] ADJ porous

porno [pɔʀno] ADJ porno ▶ NM porn

pornographie [pɔʀnɔgʀafi] NF pornography

pornographique [pɔʀnɔgʀafik] ADJ pornographic

porosité [pɔʀozite] NF (*de matériau, roche*) porosity

★**port** [pɔʀ] NM (*Navig*) harbour (BRIT), harbor (US), port; (*ville, Inform*) port; (*de l'uniforme etc*) wearing; (*pour lettre*) postage; (*pour colis, aussi: posture*) carriage; **~ de commerce/de pêche** commercial/fishing port; **arriver à bon ~** to arrive safe and sound; **~ d'arme** (*Jur*) carrying of a firearm; **~ d'attache** (*Navig*) port of registry; (*fig*) home base; **~ d'escale** port of call; **~ franc** free port; **~ payé** postage paid

★**portable** [pɔʀtabl] ADJ (*vêtement*) wearable; (*portatif*) portable; (*téléphone*) mobile (BRIT), cell (US) ▶NM (*Inform*) laptop (computer); (*téléphone*) mobile (phone) (BRIT), cell (phone) (US)

portail [pɔʀtaj] NM gate; (*de cathédrale*) portal

portant, e [pɔʀtɑ̃, -ɑ̃t] ADJ (*murs*) structural, supporting; (*roues*) running; **bien/mal ~** in good/poor health

portatif, -ive [pɔʀtatif, -iv] ADJ portable

★**porte** [pɔʀt] NF door; (*de ville, forteresse, Ski*) gate; **mettre à la ~** to throw out; **prendre la ~** to leave, go away; **à ma/sa ~** (*tout près*) on my/his (ou her) doorstep; **~ (d'embarquement)** (*Aviat*) (departure) gate; **~ d'entrée** front door; **~ à ~** nm door-to-door selling; **~ de secours** emergency exit; **~ de service** service entrance

porté, e [pɔʀte] ADJ: **être ~ à faire qch** to be apt ou inclined to do sth; **être ~ sur qch** to be partial to sth

porte-à-faux [pɔʀtafo] NM: **en ~** cantilevered; (*fig*) in an awkward position

porte-aiguilles [pɔʀteguij] NM INV needle case

porte-avions [pɔʀtavjɔ̃] NM INV aircraft carrier

porte-bagages [pɔʀt(ə)bagaʒ] NM INV luggage rack (ou basket etc)

porte-bébé [pɔʀt(ə)bebe] NM baby sling ou carrier

porte-bonheur [pɔʀt(ə)bɔnœʀ] NM INV lucky charm

porte-bouteilles [pɔʀt(ə)butɛj] NM INV bottle carrier; (*à casiers*) wine rack

porte-cartes [pɔʀt(ə)kaʀt] NM INV (*de cartes d'identité*) card holder; (*de cartes géographiques*) map wallet

porte-cigarettes [pɔʀt(ə)sigaʀɛt] NM INV cigarette case

porte-clefs [pɔʀt(ə)kle] NM INV key ring

porte-conteneurs [pɔʀt(ə)kɔ̃t(ə)nœʀ] NM INV container ship

porte-couteau, x [pɔʀt(ə)kuto] NM knife rest

porte-crayon [pɔʀt(ə)kʀɛjɔ̃] NM pencil holder

porte-documents [pɔʀt(ə)dɔkymɑ̃] NM INV attaché ou document case

porte-drapeau, x [pɔʀt(ə)dʀapo] NM standard bearer

portée [pɔʀte] NF (*d'une arme*) range; (*fig: importance*) impact, import; (: *capacités*) scope, capability; (*de chatte etc*) litter; (*Mus*) stave, staff; **à/hors de ~ (de)** within/out of reach (of); **à ~ de (la) main** within (arm's) reach; **à ~ de voix** within earshot; **à la ~ de qn** (*fig*) at sb's level, within sb's capabilities; **à la ~ de toutes les bourses** to suit every pocket, within everyone's means

portefaix [pɔʀtəfɛ] NM INV porter

porte-fenêtre (*pl* **portes-fenêtres**) [pɔʀt(ə)fənɛtʀ] NF French window

★**portefeuille** [pɔʀtəfœj] NM wallet; (*Pol, Bourse*) portfolio; **faire un lit en ~** to make an apple-pie bed

porte-jarretelles [pɔʀt(ə)ʒaʀtɛl] NM INV suspender belt (BRIT), garter belt (US)

porte-jupe [pɔʀtəʒyp] NM skirt hanger

portemanteau, x [pɔʀt(ə)mɑ̃to] NM coat rack; (*cintre*) coat hanger

porte-mine [pɔʀtəmin] NM propelling (BRIT) ou mechanical (US) pencil

★**porte-monnaie** [pɔʀt(ə)mɔnɛ] NM INV purse (BRIT), coin purse (US)

porte-parapluies [pɔʀt(ə)paʀaplɥi] NM umbrella stand

porte-parole [pɔʀt(ə)paʀɔl] NM INV spokesperson

porte-plume [pɔʀtaplym] NM INV penholder

★**porter** [pɔʀte] /1/ VT (*charge ou sac etc, aussi: fœtus*) to carry; (*sur soi: vêtement, barbe, bague*) to wear; (*fig: responsabilité etc*) to bear, carry; (*inscription, marque, titre, patronyme, arbre, fruits, fleurs*) to bear; (*coup*) to deal; (*attention*) to turn; (*jugement*) to pass; (*apporter*): **~ qch quelque part/à qn** to take sth somewhere/to sb; (*inscrire*): **~ qch sur** to put sth down on; to enter sth in; **elle portait le nom de Rosalie** she was called Rosalie; **~ qn au pouvoir** to bring sb to power; **~ bonheur à qn** to bring sb luck; **~ qn à croire** to lead sb to believe; **~ son âge** to look one's age; **~ un toast** to drink a toast; **~ de l'argent au crédit d'un compte** to credit an account with some money; **se faire ~ malade** to report sick; **~ la main à son chapeau** to raise one's hand to one's hat; **~ son effort sur** to direct one's efforts towards; **~ un fait à la connaissance de qn** to bring a fact to sb's attention ou notice ▶VI (*voix, regard, canon*) to carry; (*coup, argument*) to hit home; **~ sur** (*peser*) to rest on; (*accent*) to fall on; (*conférence etc*) to concern; (*heurter*) to strike ■ **se porter** VPR (*se sentir*): **se ~ bien/mal** to be well/unwell; (*aller*): **se ~ vers** to go towards; **se ~ partie civile** to associate in a court action with the public prosecutor; **se ~ garant de qch** to guarantee sth, vouch for sth; **se ~ candidat à la députation** ≈ to stand for Parliament (BRIT), ≈ run for Congress (US)

porte-savon [pɔʀt(ə)savɔ̃] NM soap dish

porte-serviettes [pɔʀt(ə)sɛʀvjɛt] NM INV towel rail

portes-ouvertes [pɔʀtuvɛʀt] ADJ INV: **journée ~** open day

porteur, -euse [pɔʀtœʀ, -øz] ADJ (*Comm*) strong, promising; (*nouvelle, chèque etc*): **être ~ de** to be the bearer of ▶NM/F (*de messages*) bearer ▶NM (*de bagages*) porter; (*Comm: de chèque*) bearer; (: *d'actions*) holder; **(avion) gros ~** wide-bodied aircraft, jumbo (jet)

porte-voix [pɔʀtəvwa] NM INV megaphone, loudhailer (BRIT)

portier [pɔʀtje] NM doorman, commissionnaire (BRIT)

portière [pɔʀtjɛʀ] NF door

portillon [pɔʀtijɔ̃] NM gate

portion [pɔʀsjɔ̃] NF (*part*) portion, share; (*partie*) portion, section

portique [pɔʀtik] NM (*Sport*) crossbar; (*Archit*) portico; (*Rail*) gantry

porto [pɔʀto] NM port (wine)

portoricain, e [pɔʀtɔʀikɛ̃, -ɛn] ADJ Puerto Rican

Porto Rico [pɔʀtɔʀiko] NF Puerto Rico

portrait [pɔʀtʀɛ] NM portrait; (*photographie*) photograph; **elle est le ~ de sa mère** (*fig*) she's the image of her mother

portraitiste [pɔʀtʀetist] NMF portrait painter

P

portrait-robot [pɔʀtʀɛʀɔbo] (*pl* **portraits-robots**) NM Identikit® *ou* Photo-fit® (BRIT) picture

portuaire [pɔʀtɥɛʀ] ADJ port *cpd*, harbour *cpd* (BRIT), harbor *cpd* (US)

★**portugais, e** [pɔʀtyge, -ez] ADJ Portuguese ▶ NM (*Ling*) Portuguese ▶ NM/F: **Portugais, e** Portuguese

★**Portugal** [pɔʀtygal] NM: **le ~** Portugal

POS SIGLE M (= *plan d'occupation des sols*) zoning ordinances *ou* regulations

pose [poz] NF (*de moquette, carrelage*) laying; (*de rideaux, papier peint*) hanging; (*attitude, d'un modèle*) pose; (*Photo*) exposure

posé, e [poze] ADJ calm, unruffled

posément [pozemã] ADV calmly

posemètre [pozmɛtʀ] NM exposure meter

★**poser** [poze] /1/ VT (*place*) to put down, put; (*moquette, carrelage*) to lay; (*rideaux, papier peint*) to hang; (*Math: chiffre*) to put (down); (*question*) to ask; (*principe, conditions*) to lay *ou* set down; (*problème*) to formulate; (*difficulté*) to pose; (*personne: mettre en valeur*) to give standing to; **~ qch (sur)** to put sth down (on); **~ qch sur qch/quelque part** to put sth on sth/somewhere; **~ son** *ou* **un regard sur qn/qch** to turn one's gaze on sb/sth; **~ sa candidature à un poste** to apply for a post; (*Pol*) to put o.s. up (BRIT) *ou* run (US) for election ▶ VI (*modèle*) to pose; to sit ■ **se poser** VPR (*oiseau, avion*) to land; (*question*) to arise; **se ~ en** to pass o.s. off as, pose as

poseur, -euse [pozœʀ, -øz] NM/F (*péj*) show-off, poseur; **~ de parquets/carrelages** floor/tile layer

★**positif, -ive** [pozitif, -iv] ADJ positive

position [pozisjɔ̃] NF position; **prendre ~** (*fig*) to take a stand

positionnement [pozisjɔnmã] NM (*disposition, localisation aussi Comm*) positioning; **un ~ habile sur le marché** clever positioning in the market; **le ~ d'un produit** the positioning of a product

positionner [pozisjɔne] /1/ VT to position; (*compte en banque*) to calculate the balance of ■ **se positionner** VPR (*se placer*) to position o.s.; (*troupes*) to take up one's position; (*prendre parti*) to take one's stand; (*Comm: entreprise, produit*) to position itself

positivement [pozitivmã] ADV positively

positiver [pozitive] VI to think positively

posologie [pozɔlɔʒi] NF directions *pl* for use, dosage

possédant, e [pɔsedã, -ãt] ADJ (*classe*) wealthy ▶ NM/F: **les possédants** the haves, the wealthy

possédé, e [pɔsede] NM/F person possessed

posséder [pɔsede] /6/ VT to own, possess; (*qualité, talent*) to have, possess; (*bien connaître: métier, langue*) to have mastered, have a thorough knowledge of; (*sexuellement, aussi: suj, colère*) to possess; (*fam: duper*) to take in

possesseur [pɔsesœʀ] NM owner

possessif, -ive [pɔsesif, -iv] ADJ, NM (*Ling*) possessive

possession [pɔsesjɔ̃] NF ownership *no pl*; possession; **être en ~ de qch** to be in possession of sth; **prendre ~ de qch** to take possession of sth

possessivité [pɔsesivite] NF possessiveness

possibilité [pɔsibilite] NF possibility; **avoir la ~ de faire** to be in a position to do; to have the opportunity to do ■ **possibilités** NFPL (*moyens*) means; (*potentiel*) potential *sg*

★**possible** [pɔsibl] ADJ possible; (*projet, entreprise*) feasible; **(ce n'est) pas ~!** impossible!; **le plus/moins de livres ~** as many/few books as possible; **le plus vite ~** as quickly as possible; **dès que ~** as soon as possible ▶ NM: **faire son ~** to do all one can, do one's utmost; **gentil** *etc* **au ~** as nice *etc* as it is possible to be

post [pɔst] NM (*Inform*) post

postal, e, -aux [pɔstal, -o] ADJ postal, post office *cpd*; **sac ~** mailbag, postbag (BRIT)

postdater [pɔstdate] /1/ VT to postdate

postdoctoral, e, -aux [pɔstdɔktɔral, -o] ADJ post-doctoral

postdoctorant, e [pɔstdɔktɔrã, -ãt] NM/F post-doctoral student

★**poste¹** [pɔst] NF (*service*) post, postal service; (*administration, bureau*) post office; **mettre à la ~** to mail, to post (BRIT); **~ restante** poste restante (BRIT), general delivery (US) ■ **postes** NFPL post office *sg*; **agent** *ou* **employé des postes** post office worker

poste² [pɔst] NM (*fonction, Mil*) post; (*Tél*) extension; (*de radio etc*) set; (*de budget*) item; **~ de commandement** (*Mil etc*) headquarters; **~ de contrôle** checkpoint; **~ de douane** customs post; **~ émetteur** transmitting set; **~ d'essence** filling station; **~ d'incendie** fire point; **~ de péage** tollgate; **~ de pilotage** cockpit, flight deck; **~ (de police)** police station; **~ de radio/de télévision** radio/television set; **~ de secours** first-aid post; **~ de travail** work station

★**poster** /1/ VT [pɔste] (*Inform*) to post ▶ NM [pɔstɛʀ] poster ■ **se poster** VPR to position o.s.

postérieur, e [pɔsterjœʀ] ADJ (*date*) later; (*partie*) back ▶ NM (*fam*) behind

postérieurement [pɔsterjœʀmã] ADV later, subsequently; **~ à** after

posteriori [pɔsterjɔri]: **a ~** *adv* with hindsight, a posteriori

postérité [pɔsterite] NF posterity

postface [pɔstfas] NF appendix

posthume [pɔstym] ADJ posthumous

postiche [pɔstiʃ] ADJ false ▶ NM hairpiece

postier, -ière [pɔstje, -jɛʀ] NM/F post office worker

postillon [pɔstijɔ̃] NM: **envoyer des postillons** to ■ splutter

postillonner [pɔstijɔne] /1/ VI to splutter

postmoderne [pɔstmɔdɛʀn] ADJ post-modern

postmodernisme [pɔstmɔdɛʀnism] NM post-modernism

postnatal, e, post-natal, e [pɔstnatal] ADJ postnatal

postopératoire [pɔstɔperatwaʀ] ADJ post-operative

postproduction [pɔstprɔdyksjɔ̃] NF post-production

postscolaire [pɔstskɔlɛʀ] ADJ further, continuing

post-scriptum [pɔstskʀiptɔm] NM INV postscript

postsynchronisation [pɔstsēkrɔnizasjɔ̃] NF dubbing

postsynchroniser [pɔstsēkrɔnize] /1/ VT to dub

postulant, e [pɔstylɑ̃, -ɑ̃t] NM/F (candidat) applicant; (Rel) postulant

postulat [pɔstyla] NM postulate

postuler [pɔstyle] /1/ VT (emploi) to apply for, put in for ▸ VI: **~ à** ou **pour un emploi** to apply for a job

posture [pɔstyr] NF posture, position; (fig) position

★**pot** [po] NM (en verre) jar; (en terre) pot; (en plastique, carton) carton; (en métal) tin; (fam: chance) luck; **avoir du ~** (fam) to be lucky; **boire** ou **prendre un ~** (fam) to have a drink; **petit ~ (pour bébé)** (jar of) baby food; **découvrir le ~ aux roses** to find out what's been going on; **~ catalytique** catalytic converter; **~ (de chambre)** (chamber)pot; **~ d'échappement** exhaust pipe (BRIT), tail pipe (US); **~ de fleurs** plant pot, flowerpot; (plante) pot plant; **~ à tabac** tobacco jar

★**potable** [pɔtabl] ADJ (fig: boisson) drinkable; (: travail, devoir) decent; **eau (non) ~** (not) drinking water

potache [pɔtaʃ] NM schoolboy

★**potage** [pɔtaʒ] NM soup

potager, -ère [pɔtaʒe, -ɛr] ADJ (plante) edible, vegetable cpd; **(jardin) ~** kitchen ou vegetable garden

potasse [pɔtas] NF potassium hydroxide; (engrais) potash

potasser [pɔtase] /1/ VT (fam) to swot up (BRIT), cram

potassium [pɔtasjɔm] NM potassium

pot-au-feu [pɔtofø] NM INV (beef) stew; (viande) stewing beef ▸ ADJ (fam: personne) stay-at-home

pot-de-vin [podvē] (pl **pots-de-vin**) NM bribe

pote [pɔt] NM (fam) mate (BRIT), pal

poteau, x [pɔto] NM post; **~ de départ/d'arrivée** starting/finishing post; **~ (d'exécution)** execution post, stake; **~ indicateur** signpost; **~ télégraphique** telegraph pole; **poteaux (de but)** goal-posts

potée [pɔte] NF hotpot (of pork and cabbage)

potelé, e [pɔt(ə)le] ADJ plump, chubby

potence [pɔtɑ̃s] NF gallows sg; **en ~** T-shaped

potentat [pɔtɑ̃ta] NM potentate; (fig: péj) despot

potentiel, le [pɔtɑ̃sjɛl] ADJ, NM potential

potentiellement [pɔtɑ̃sjɛlmɑ̃] ADV potentially

potentiomètre [pɔtɑ̃sjɔmɛtr] NM potentiometer

poterie [pɔtri] NF (fabrication) pottery; (objet) piece of pottery

potiche [pɔtiʃ] NF large vase

potier, -ière [pɔtje, -jɛr] NM/F potter

potins [pɔtē] NMPL gossip sg

potion [posjɔ̃] NF potion

potiron [pɔtirɔ̃] NM pumpkin

pot-pourri [popuri] (pl **pots-pourris**) NM (Mus) medley

pou, x [pu] NM louse

pouah [pwa] EXCL ugh!, yuk!

★**poubelle** [pubɛl] NF (dust)bin (BRIT), garbage can (US)

pouce [pus] NM thumb; **se tourner** ou **se rouler les pouces** (fig) to twiddle one's thumbs; **manger sur le ~** to eat on the run, snatch something to eat

★**poudre** [pudr] NF powder; (fard) (face) powder; (explosif) gunpowder; **en ~: café en ~** instant coffee; **savon en ~** soap powder; **lait en ~** dried ou powdered milk; **à canon** gunpowder; **à éternuer** sneezing powder; **à récurer** scouring powder; **~ de riz** face powder

poudrer [pudre] /1/ VT to powder

poudreux, -euse [pudrø, -øz] ADJ dusty; (neige) powdery, powder cpd

poudrier [pudrije] NM (powder) compact

poudrière [pudrijɛr] NF powder magazine; (fig) powder keg

pouf [puf] NM pouffe

pouffer [pufe] /1/ VI: **~ (de rire)** to burst out laughing

pouffiasse [pufjas] NF (fam) fat cow; (prostituée) tart

pouilleux, -euse [pujø, -øz] ADJ flea-ridden; (fig) seedy

poujadisme [puʒadism] NM (Hist) Poujadism (conservative reactionary movement founded to protect the business interests of small traders in 1950s France); (péj) reactionary petit-bourgeois attitudes

poujadiste [puʒadist] NMF, ADJ (Hist) Poujadist; (péj) petit-bourgeois reactionary

poulailler [pulaje] NM henhouse; (Théât): **le ~** the gods sg

poulain [pulē] NM foal; (fig) protégé

poularde [pulard] NF fatted chicken

★**poule** [pul] NF (Zool) hen; (Culin) (boiling) fowl; (Sport) (round-robin) tournament; (Rugby) group; (fam) bird (BRIT), chick, broad (US); (fam: prostituée) tart; **~ d'eau** moorhen; **~ mouillée** coward; **~ pondeuse** laying hen, layer; **~ au riz** boiled chicken and rice

★**poulet** [pulε] NM chicken; (fam) cop

poulette [pulεt] NF (jeune poule) pullet

pouliche [puliʃ] NF filly

poulie [puli] NF pulley

poulpe [pulp] NM octopus

pouls [pu] NM pulse; **prendre le ~ de qn** to take sb's pulse

★**poumon** [pumɔ̃] NM lung; **~ d'acier** ou **artificiel** iron ou artificial lung

poupe [pup] NF stern; **en ~** astern

poupée [pupe] NF doll; **jouer à la ~** to play with one's doll (ou dolls); **de ~** (très petit): **jardin de ~** doll's garden, pocket-handkerchief-sized garden

poupin, e [pupē, -in] ADJ chubby

poupon [pupɔ̃] NM babe-in-arms

pouponner [pupɔne] /1/ VI to fuss (around)

pouponnière [pupɔnjɛr] NF crèche, day nursery

★**pour** [pur] PRÉP for; **~ faire** (so as) to do, in order to do; **~ avoir fait** for having done; **~ que** so that, in order that; **fermé ~ (cause de) travaux** closed for refurbishment ou alterations; **c'est ~ ça que ...** that's why ...; **~ quoi faire?** what for?; **~ moi** (à mon avis, pour ma part) for my part, personally; **~ riche qu'il soit** rich though he may be; **~ 20 euros**

p

345

d'essence 20 euros' worth of petrol (Brit) ou gas (US); **~ cent** per cent; **~ ce qui est de** as for; **y être ~ quelque chose** to have something to do with it ▶ NM: **le ~ et le contre** the pros and cons

★**pourboire** [puʀbwaʀ] NM tip

pourcentage [puʀsɑ̃taʒ] NM percentage; **travailler au ~** to work on commission

pourchasser [puʀʃase] /1/ VT to pursue

pourfendeur [puʀfɑ̃dœʀ] NM sworn opponent

pourfendre [puʀfɑ̃dʀ] /41/ VT to assail

pourlécher [puʀleʃe] /6/: **se pourlécher** VPR to lick one's lips

pourparlers [puʀpaʀle] NMPL talks, negotiations; **être en ~ avec** to be having talks with

pourpre [puʀpʀ] ADJ crimson

★**pourquoi** [puʀkwa] ADV, CONJ why ▶ NM INV: **le ~ (de)** the why and wherefore (of)

pourrai etc [puʀe] VB voir **pouvoir**

pourri, e [puʀi] ADJ rotten; (roche, pierre) crumbling; (temps, climat) filthy, foul ▶ NM: **sentir le ~** to smell rotten

pourriel [puʀjɛl] NM (Inform) spam

pourrir [puʀiʀ] /2/ VI to rot; (fruit) to go rotten ou bad; (fig: situation) to deteriorate ▶ VT to rot; (fig: corrompre: personne) to corrupt; (: gâter: enfant) to spoil thoroughly

pourrissement [puʀismɑ̃] NM deterioration

pourriture [puʀityʀ] NF rot

pourrons etc [puʀɔ̃] VB voir **pouvoir**

poursuis etc [puʀsɥi] VB voir **poursuivre**

poursuite [puʀsɥit] NF pursuit, chase; (course) **~** track race; (fig) chase ■ **poursuites** NFPL (Jur) legal proceedings

poursuivant, e [puʀsɥivɑ̃, -ɑ̃t] VB voir **poursuivre** ▶ NM/F pursuer; (Jur) plaintiff

poursuivre [puʀsɥivʀ] /40/ VT to pursue, chase (after); (relancer) to hound, harry; (obséder) to haunt; (Jur) to bring proceedings against, prosecute; (: au civil) to sue; (but) to strive towards; (voyage, études) to carry on with, continue ▶ VI to carry on, go on ■ **se poursuivre** VPR to go on, continue

★**pourtant** [puʀtɑ̃] ADV yet; **mais ~** but nevertheless, but even so; **c'est ~ facile** (and) yet it's easy

pourtour [puʀtuʀ] NM perimeter

pourvoi [puʀvwa] NM appeal

pourvoir [puʀvwaʀ] /25/ VT (emploi) to fill; **~ qch/ qn de** to equip sth/sb with ▶ VI: **~ à** to provide for ■ **se pourvoir** VPR (Jur): **se ~ en cassation** to take one's case to the Court of Appeal

pourvoyeur, -euse [puʀvwajœʀ, -øz] NM/F supplier

pourvu, e [puʀvy] PP de **pourvoir** ▶ ADJ: **~ de** equipped with ▶ CONJ: **~ que** (si) provided that, so long as; (espérons que) let's hope (that)

pousse [pus] NF growth; (bourgeon) shoot

poussé, e [puse] ADJ sophisticated, advanced; (moteur) souped-up

pousse-café [puskafe] NM (after-dinner) liqueur

poussée [puse] NF thrust; (coup) push; (Méd: d'acné) eruption; (fig: prix) upsurge

pousse-pousse [puspus] NM INV rickshaw

★**pousser** [puse] /1/ VT to push; (moteur, voiture) to drive hard; (émettre: cri etc) to give; (stimuler: élève) to urge on; to drive hard; (poursuivre: études, discussion) to carry on; **~ qn à faire qch** (inciter) to urge ou press sb to do sth; (acculer) to drive sb to do sth; **~ le dévouement** etc **jusqu'à ...** to take devotion etc as far as ... ▶ VI to push; (croître) to grow; (aller): **~ plus loin** to push on a bit further; **faire ~** (plante) to grow ■ **se pousser** VPR to move over

poussette [pusɛt] NF (voiture d'enfant) pushchair (Brit), stroller (US)

poussette-canne [pusɛtkan] (pl **poussettes-cannes**) NF baby buggy (Brit), (folding) stroller (US)

poussier [pusje] NM coal dust

poussière [pusjɛʀ] NF dust; (grain) speck of dust; **et des poussières** (fig) and a bit; **~ de charbon** coal dust

poussiéreux, -euse [pusjeʀø, -øz] ADJ dusty

poussif, -ive [pusif, -iv] ADJ wheezy, wheezing

poussin [pusɛ̃] NM chick

poussoir [puswaʀ] NM button

poutre [putʀ] NF beam; (en fer, ciment armé) girder; **poutres apparentes** exposed beams

poutrelle [putʀɛl] NF (petite poutre) small beam; (barre d'acier) girder

---

pouvoir [puvwaʀ]

/33/ NM power; (dirigeants): **le pouvoir** those in power; **les pouvoirs publics** the authorities; **avoir pouvoir de faire** (autorisation) to have (the) authority to do; (droit) to have the right to do; **pouvoir absolu** absolute power; **pouvoir absorbant** absorbency; **pouvoir d'achat** purchasing power; **pouvoir calorifique** calorific value

▶ VB AUX **1** (être en état de) can, be able to; **je ne peux pas le réparer** I can't ou I am not able to repair it; **déçu de ne pas pouvoir le faire** disappointed not to be able to do it

2 (avoir la permission de) can, may, be allowed to; **vous pouvez aller au cinéma** you can ou may go to the cinema (Brit) ou movies (US)

3 (probabilité, hypothèse) may, might, could; **il a pu avoir un accident** he may ou might ou could have had an accident; **il aurait pu le dire!** he might ou could have said (so)!

4 (expressions): **tu ne peux pas savoir!** you have no idea!; **tu peux le dire!** you can say that again!

▶ VB IMPERS may, might, could; **il peut arriver que** it may ou might ou could happen that; **il pourrait pleuvoir** it might rain

▶ VT **1** can, be able to; **j'ai fait tout ce que j'ai pu** I did all I could; **je n'en peux plus** (épuisé) I'm exhausted; (à bout) I can't take any more

2 (vb +adj ou adv comparatif): **je me porte on ne peut mieux** I'm absolutely fine, I couldn't be better; **elle est on ne peut plus gentille** she couldn't be nicer, she's as nice as can be

■ **se pouvoir** VPR: **il se peut que** it may ou might be that; **cela se pourrait** that's quite possible

---

PP SIGLE F (= préventive de la pellagre: vitamine) niacin ▶ ABR (= pages) pp

p.p.c.m. SIGLE M (*Math*: = *plus petit commun multiple*) LCM (= *lowest common multiple*)

PQ SIGLE F (CANADA: = *province de Québec*) PQ

PR SIGLE F = **poste restante**

Pr ABR = **professeur**

pr ABR = **pour**

pragmatique [pʀagmatik] ADJ pragmatic

pragmatisme [pʀagmatism] NM pragmatism

Prague [pʀag] N Prague

prairie [pʀeʀi] NF meadow

praline [pʀalin] NF (*bonbon*) sugared almond; (*au chocolat*) praline

praliné, e [pʀaline] ADJ (*amande*) sugared; (*chocolat, glace*) praline *cpd*

praticable [pʀatikabl] ADJ (*route etc*) passable, practicable; (*projet*) practicable

praticien, ne [pʀatisjɛ̃, -ɛn] NM/F practitioner

pratiquant, e [pʀatikɑ̃, -ɑ̃t] ADJ practising (BRIT), practicing (US) ▶ NM/F (*regular*) churchgoer

★**pratique** [pʀatik] NF practice; **dans la ~** in (actual) practice; **mettre en ~** to put into practice ▶ ADJ practical; (*commode: horaire etc*) convenient; (: *outil*) handy, useful

pratiquement [pʀatikmɑ̃] ADV (*dans la pratique*) in practice; (*pour ainsi dire*) practically, virtually

pratiquer [pʀatike] /1/ VT to practise (BRIT), practice (US); (*l'équitation, la pêche*) to go in for; (*le golf, le football*) to play; (*appliquer: méthode, théorie*) to apply; (*intervention, opération*) to carry out; (*ouverture, abri*) to make ▶ VI (*Rel*) to be a churchgoer

pré [pʀe] NM meadow

préado [pʀeado] NMF (*fam*) pre-teen

préadolescent, e [pʀeadɔlesɑ̃, -ɑ̃t] NM/F pre-teenager, pre-teen ▶ ADJ pre-teenage, pre-teen

préalable [pʀealabl] ADJ preliminary; **condition ~ (de)** precondition (for), prerequisite (for); **sans avis ~** without prior ou previous notice; **au ~** first, beforehand

préalablement [pʀealabləmɑ̃] ADV first, beforehand

Préalpes [pʀealp] NFPL: **les ~** the Pre-Alps

préalpin, e [pʀealpɛ̃, -in] ADJ of the Pre-Alps

préambule [pʀeɑ̃byl] NM preamble; (*fig*) prelude; **sans ~** straight away

préau, x [pʀeo] NM (*d'une cour d'école*) covered playground; (*d'un monastère, d'une prison*) inner courtyard

préavis [pʀeavi] NM notice; **~ de congé** notice; **communication avec ~** (*Tél*) personal ou person-to-person call

prébende [pʀebɑ̃d] NF (*péj*) remuneration

précaire [pʀekɛʀ] ADJ (*situation*) precarious; (*Écon: emplois*) lacking security

précarisation [pʀekaʀizasjɔ̃] NF (*d'emploi*) casualization; **dans ce secteur la ~ tend à devenir la règle** in this industry casual labour is becoming the norm

précarisé, e [pʀekaʀize] ADJ lacking job security

précarité [pʀekaʀite] NF (*de situation*) precariousness; (*Pol, Écon*): **la ~ (de l'emploi)** job insecurity, lack of job security

précaution [pʀekosjɔ̃] NF precaution; **avec ~** cautiously; **le principe de ~** the precautionary principle; **prendre des** ou **ses précautions** to take precautions; **par ~** as a precaution; **pour plus de ~** to be on the safe side; **précautions oratoires** carefully phrased remarks

précautionneusement [pʀekosjɔnøzmɑ̃] ADV (*prudemment*) cautiously; (*soigneusement*) carefully

précautionneux, -euse [pʀekosjɔnø, -øz] ADJ (*prudent*) cautious; (*soigneux*) careful

précédemment [pʀesedamɑ̃] ADV before, previously

précédent, e [pʀesedɑ̃, -ɑ̃t] ADJ previous; **le jour ~** the day before, the previous day ▶ NM precedent; **sans ~** unprecedented

précéder [pʀesede] /6/ VT to precede; (*marcher ou rouler devant*) to be in front of; (*arriver avant*) to get ahead of

précepte [pʀesɛpt] NM precept

précepteur, -trice [pʀesɛptœʀ, -tʀis] NM/F (*private*) tutor

préchauffage [pʀeʃofaʒ] NM (*de four*) preheating; (*de moteur*) warming up

préchauffer [pʀeʃofe] /1/ VT (*four*) to preheat; (*moteur*) to warm up

prêcher [pʀeʃe] /1/ VT, VI to preach

prêcheur, -euse [pʀɛʃœʀ, -øz] ADJ moralizing ▶ NM/F (*Rel*) preacher; (*fig*) moralizer

précieusement [pʀesjøzmɑ̃] ADV (*avec soin*) carefully; (*conserver*) preciously

précieux, -euse [pʀesjø, -øz] ADJ precious; (*collaborateur, conseils*) invaluable; (*style, écrivain*) précieux, precious

préciosité [pʀesjozite] NF preciosity, preciousness

précipice [pʀesipis] NM drop, chasm; (*fig*) abyss; **au bord du ~** at the edge of the precipice

précipitamment [pʀesipitamɑ̃] ADV hurriedly, hastily

précipitation [pʀesipitasjɔ̃] NF (*hâte*) haste ▪ **précipitations (atmosphériques)** NFPL precipitation *sg*

précipité, e [pʀesipite] ADJ (*respiration*) fast; (*pas*) hurried; (*départ*) hasty

précipiter [pʀesipite] /1/ VT (*hâter: marche*) to quicken; (: *départ*) to hasten; **~ qn/qch du haut de** (*faire tomber*) to throw ou hurl sb/sth off ou from ▪ **se précipiter** VPR (*événements*) to move faster; (*respiration*) to speed up; **se ~ sur/vers** to rush at/towards; **se ~ au-devant de qn** to throw o.s. before sb

précis, e [pʀesi, -iz] ADJ precise; (*tir, mesures*) accurate, precise; **à 4 heures précises** at 4 o'clock sharp ▶ NM handbook

précisément [pʀesizemɑ̃] ADV precisely; **ma vie n'est pas ~ distrayante** my life is not exactly entertaining

préciser [pʀesize] /1/ VT (*expliquer*) to be more specific about, clarify; (*spécifier*) to state, specify ▪ **se préciser** VPR to become clear(er)

précision [pʀesizjɔ̃] NF precision; accuracy; (*détail*) point ou detail (*made clear or to be clarified*)

précoce [pʀekɔs] ADJ early; (*enfant*) precocious; (*calvitie*) premature

précocité [pʀekɔsite] NF earliness; precociousness

préconçu, e [pʀekɔ̃sy] ADJ preconceived

préconiser [pʀekɔnize] /1/ VT to advocate

précontraint, e [pʀekɔ̃tʀɛ̃, -ɛ̃t] ADJ: **béton ~** prestressed concrete

précuit, e [pʀekɥi, -it] ADJ precooked

précurseur [pʀekyʀsœʀ] ADJ M precursory ▶ NM forerunner, precursor

prédateur [pʀedatœʀ] NM predator

prédation [pʀedasjɔ̃] NF (Bio) predation

prédécesseur [pʀedesesœʀ] NM predecessor

prédécoupé, e [pʀedekupe] ADJ pre-cut

prédestiné, e [pʀedɛstine] ADJ predestined; **être ~ à** to be predestined to; **au nom ~** aptly named

prédestiner [pʀedɛstine] /1/ VT: **~ qn à qch/à faire** to predestine sb for sth/to do

prédicateur [pʀedikatœʀ] NM preacher

prédiction [pʀediksjɔ̃] NF prediction

prédilection [pʀedilɛksjɔ̃] NF: **avoir une ~ pour** to be partial to; **de ~** favourite (BRIT), favorite (US)

prédire [pʀediʀ] /37/ VT to predict

prédisposer [pʀedispoze] /1/ VT: **~ qn à qch/à faire** to predispose sb to sth/to do

prédisposition [pʀedispozisjɔ̃] NF predisposition

prédit, e [pʀedi, -it] PP de **prédire**

prédominance [pʀedɔminɑ̃s] NF predominance

prédominant, e [pʀedɔminɑ̃, -ɑ̃t] ADJ predominant; prevailing

prédominer [pʀedɔmine] /1/ VI to predominate; (avis) to prevail

pré-électoral, e, -aux [pʀeelɛktɔʀal, -o] ADJ pre-election cpd

pré-emballé, e [pʀeɑ̃bale] ADJ pre-packed

prééminent, e [pʀeeminɑ̃, -ɑ̃t] ADJ pre-eminent

préempter [pʀeɑ̃pte] VT (Jur: fig) to pre-empt

préemption [pʀeɑ̃psjɔ̃] NF: **droit de ~** (Jur) pre-emptive right

pré-encollé, e [pʀeɑ̃kɔle] ADJ pre-pasted

préétabli, e [pʀeetabli] ADJ pre-established

préexistant, e [pʀeɛgzistɑ̃, -ɑ̃t] ADJ pre-existing

préfabriqué, e [pʀefabʀike] ADJ prefabricated; (péj: sourire) artificial ▶ NM prefabricated material

préface [pʀefas] NF preface

préfacer [pʀefase] /3/ VT to write a preface for

préfectoral, e, -aux [pʀefɛktɔʀal, -o] ADJ prefectorial

préfecture [pʀefɛktyʀ] NF prefecture; **~ de police** police headquarters

---

The **préfecture** is the administrative headquarters of the *département*. The *préfet*, a senior civil servant appointed by the government, is responsible for putting government policy into practice and for maintaining law and order and public safety. France's regions, each comprising a number of *départements*, also have a *préfet de région*.

---

préférable [pʀefeʀabl] ADJ preferable

préféré, e [pʀefeʀe] ADJ, NM/F favourite (BRIT), favorite (US)

préférence [pʀefeʀɑ̃s] NF preference; **de ~** preferably; **de ou par ~ à** in preference to, rather than; **donner la ~ à qn** to give preference to sb; **par ordre de ~** in order of preference; **obtenir la ~ sur** to have preference over

préférentiel, le [pʀefeʀɑ̃sjɛl] ADJ preferential

préférer [pʀefeʀe] /6/ VT: **~ qn/qch (à)** to prefer sb/sth (to), like sb/sth better (than); **~ faire** to prefer to do; **je préférerais du thé** I would rather have tea, I'd prefer tea

préfet [pʀefɛ] NM prefect; **~ de police** ≈ Chief Constable (BRIT), ≈ Police Commissioner (US)

préfigurer [pʀefigyʀe] /1/ VT to prefigure

préfixe [pʀefiks] NM prefix

préhension [pʀeɑ̃sjɔ̃] NF prehension

préhistoire [pʀeistwaʀ] NF prehistory

préhistorique [pʀeistɔʀik] ADJ prehistoric

préinscription [pʀeɛ̃skʀipsjɔ̃] NF (Admin) pre-registration

préinstallé, e [pʀeɛ̃stale] ADJ (logiciel, appli) preinstalled

préjudice [pʀeʒydis] NM (matériel) loss; (moral) harm no pl; **porter ~ à** to harm, be detrimental to; **au ~ de** at the expense of

préjudiciable [pʀeʒydisjabl] ADJ: **~ à** prejudicial ou harmful to

préjugé [pʀeʒyʒe] NM prejudice; **avoir un ~ contre** to be prejudiced against; **bénéficier d'un ~ favorable** to be viewed favourably

préjuger [pʀeʒyʒe] /3/: **~ de** vt to prejudge

prélasser [pʀelɑse] /1/: **se prélasser** VPR to lounge

prélat [pʀela] NM prelate

prélavage [pʀelavaʒ] NM pre-wash

prélèvement [pʀelɛvmɑ̃] NM (montant) deduction; withdrawal; **faire un ~ de sang** to take a blood sample; **les paiements par ~** payment by direct debit

prélever [pʀel(ə)ve] /5/ VT (échantillon) to take; **~ (sur)** (argent) to deduct (from) (: sur son compte) to withdraw (from)

préliminaire [pʀeliminɛʀ] ADJ preliminary ■ **préliminaires** NMPL preliminaries; (négociations) preliminary talks

prélude [pʀelyd] NM prelude; (avant le concert) warm-up

préluder [pʀelyde]: **~ à qch** vt to be the prelude to sth

prématuré, e [pʀematyʀe] ADJ premature; (retraite) early ▶ NM premature baby

prématurément [pʀematyʀemɑ̃] ADV prematurely

prématurité [pʀematyʀite] NF premature birth

préméditation [pʀemeditasjɔ̃] NF: **avec ~** adj premeditated; adv with intent

préméditer [pʀemedite] /1/ VT to premeditate, plan

prémices [pʀemis] NFPL beginnings

★**premier, -ière** [pʀəmje, -jɛʀ] ADJ first; (rang) front; (branche, marche, grade) bottom; (fig: fondamental) basic; prime; (en importance) first, foremost; **au ~ abord** at first sight; **au ou du ~ coup** at the first attempt ou go; **de ~ ordre** first-class, first-rate; **de première qualité, de ~ choix** best *ou* top quality; **de première importance** of the highest importance; **de première nécessité** absolutely essential; **le ~ venu** the first person to come along; **enfant du ~ lit** child of a first marriage; **en ~ lieu** in the first place; **le ~ âge** (*d'un enfant*) the first three months (of life); **P~ ministre** Prime Minister ▶ NM (*premier étage*) first (BRIT); *ou* second (US) floor; **jeune ~** leading man; **le ~ de l'an** New Year's Day ▶ NF (*Auto*) first (gear); (*Rail, Aviat etc*) first class; (*Scol*) year 12 (BRIT), eleventh grade (US); (*Théât*) first night; (*Ciné*) première; (*exploit*) first

premièrement [prəmjɛrmɑ̃] ADV firstly

première-née [prəmjɛrne] (*pl* **premières-nées**) NF first-born

premier-né [prəmjene] (*pl* **premiers-nés**) NM first-born

prémisse [premis] NF premise

prémolaire [premɔlɛr] NF premolar

prémonition [premɔnisjɔ̃] NF premonition

prémonitoire [premɔnitwar] ADJ premonitory

prémunir [premynir] /2/: **se prémunir** VPR: **se ~ contre** to protect o.s. from, guard against

prenant, e [prənɑ̃, -ɑ̃t] VB *voir* **prendre** ▶ ADJ absorbing, engrossing

prénatal, e [prenatal] ADJ (*Méd*) antenatal; (*allocation*) maternity *cpd*

★**prendre** [prɑ̃dr] /58/ VT to take; (*repas*) to have; (*aller chercher*) to get, fetch; (*se procurer*) to get; (*réserver: place*) to book; (*acquérir: du poids, de la valeur*) to put on, gain; (*malfaiteur, poisson*) to catch; (*passager*) to pick up; (*personnel, aussi: couleur, goût*) to take on, (*locataire*) to take in; (*traiter: enfant, problème*) to handle; (*voix, ton*) to put on; (*prélever: pourcentage, argent*) to take off; (*ôter*): **~ qch à** to take sth from; **~ froid** to catch cold; **~ son origine** *ou* **sa source** (*mot*) to originate; (*rivière*) to begin; **~ qn pour** to take sb for; **~ qn en sympathie/horreur** to get to like/loathe sb; **à tout ~** all things considered ▶ VI (*liquide, ciment*) to set; (*greffe, vaccin*) to take; (*mensonge*) to be successful; (*feu: foyer*) to go; (: *incendie*) to start; (*allumette*) to light; (*se diriger*): **~ à gauche** to turn (to the) left; **~ sur soi de faire qch** to take it upon o.s. to do sth ■ **se prendre** VPR: **se ~ pour** to think one is; **s'en ~ à** (*agresser*) to set about; (*passer sa colère sur*) to take it out on; (*critiquer*) to attack; (*remettre en question*) to challenge; **s'y ~** (*procéder*) to set about it; **s'y ~ à l'avance** to see to it in advance; **s'y ~ à deux fois** to try twice, make two attempts; **se ~ d'amitié/d'affection pour** to befriend/become fond of; **se ~ les doigts dans** to get one's fingers caught in

preneur, -euse [prənœr, -øz] NM/F: **être ~** to be willing to buy; **trouver ~** to find a buyer

preniez [prənje] VB *voir* **prendre**

prenne *etc* [prɛn] VB *voir* **prendre**

prénom [prenɔ̃] NM first name

prénommer [prenɔme] /1/: **se prénommer** VPR: **elle se prénomme Claude** her (first) name is Claude

prénuptial, e, -aux [prenypsjal, -o] ADJ premarital

préoccupant, e [preɔkypɑ̃, -ɑ̃t] ADJ worrying

préoccupation [preɔkypasjɔ̃] NF (*souci*) concern; (*idée fixe*) preoccupation

préoccupé, e [preɔkype] ADJ concerned; preoccupied

préoccuper [preɔkype] /1/ VT (*tourmenter, tracasser*) to concern; (*absorber, obséder*) to preoccupy ■ **se préoccuper** VPR: **se ~ de qch** to be concerned about sth; to show concern about sth

préparateur, -trice [preparatœr, -tris] NM/F assistant

préparatifs [preparatif] NMPL preparations

préparation [preparasjɔ̃] NF preparation; (*Scol*) piece of homework

préparatoire [preparatwar] ADJ preparatory

préparer [prepare] /1/ VT to prepare; (*café, repas*) to make; (*examen*) to prepare for; (*voyage, entreprise*) to plan; **~ qch à qn** (*surprise etc*) to have sth in store for sb; **~ qn à qch** (*nouvelle etc*) to prepare sb for sth ■ **se préparer** VPR (*orage, tragédie*) to brew, be in the air; **se ~ (à qch/à faire)** to prepare (o.s.) *ou* get ready (for sth/to do)

prépayé, e [prepeje] ADJ prepaid; **carte téléphonique prépayée** prepaid phonecard

prépondérance [prepɔ̃derɑ̃s] NF: **~ (sur)** predominance (over)

prépondérant, e [prepɔ̃derɑ̃, -ɑ̃t] ADJ major, dominating; **voix prépondérante** casting vote

préposé, e [prepoze] ADJ: **~ à** in charge of ▶ NM/F (*gén: employé*) employee; (*Admin: facteur*) postman/woman (BRIT), mailman/woman (US); (*de la douane etc*) official; (*de vestiaire*) attendant

préposer [prepoze] /1/ VT: **~ qn à qch** to appoint sb to sth

préposition [prepozisjɔ̃] NF preposition

préquel NM, **préquelle** NF [prekɛl] prequel

prérentrée [prerɑ̃tre] NF *in-service training period before start of school term*

préretraite [prer(ə)trɛt] NF early retirement

prérogative [prerɔgativ] NF prerogative

près [prɛ] ADV near, close; **~ de** *prép* near (to), close to; (*environ*) nearly, almost; **~ d'ici** near here; **de ~** closely; **à cinq kg ~** to within about five kg; **à cela ~ que** apart from the fact that; **je ne suis pas ~ de lui pardonner** I'm nowhere near ready to forgive him; **on n'est pas à un jour ~** one day (either way) won't make any difference, we're not going to quibble over the odd day; **il n'est pas à 10 minutes ~** he can spare 10 minutes

présage [preza3] NM omen

présager [preza3e] /3/ VT (*prévoir*) to foresee; (*annoncer*) to portend

pré-salé (*pl* **prés-salés**) [presale] NM (*Culin*) salt-marsh lamb

presbyte [presbit] ADJ long-sighted (BRIT), far-sighted (US)

presbytère [presbiter] NM presbytery

presbytérien, ne [presbiterjɛ̃, -ɛn] ADJ, NM/F Presbyterian

presbytie [presbisi] NF long-sightedness (BRIT), far-sightedness (US)

prescience [presjɑ̃s] NF prescience, foresight

préscolaire [preskɔlɛr] ADJ preschool *cpd*

349

prescripteur, -trice [pʀɛskʀiptœʀ, -tʀis] ADJ (*Méd*): **médecin ~** prescribing doctor; (*rôle, pouvoir*) controlling ▸ NM/F (*Méd*) prescribing doctor

prescription [pʀɛskʀipsjɔ̃] NF (*instruction*) order, instruction; (*Méd, Jur*) prescription

prescrire [pʀɛskʀiʀ] /39/ VT to prescribe ■ **se prescrire** VPR (*Jur*) to lapse

prescrit, e [pʀɛskʀi, -it] PP de **prescrire** ▸ ADJ (*date etc*) stipulated

préséance [pʀeseɑ̃s] NF precedence *no pl*

présélection [pʀeselɛksjɔ̃] NF (*de candidats*) shortlisting; **effectuer une ~** to draw up a shortlist

présélectionner [pʀeselɛksjɔne] /1/ VT to preselect; (*dispositif*) to preset; (*candidats*) to make an initial selection from among, short-list

présence [pʀezɑ̃s] NF presence; (*au bureau etc*) attendance; **en ~** face to face; **en ~ de** in (the) presence of; (*fig*) in the face of; **faire acte de ~** to put in a token appearance; **~ d'esprit** presence of mind

présent, e [pʀezɑ̃, -ɑ̃t] ADJ present; **la présente lettre/loi** this letter/law ▸ NM present; **à ~** now, at present; **dès à ~** here and now; **jusqu'à ~** up till now, until now; **à ~ que** now that ▸ NM/F: **les présents** (*personnes*) those present ▸ NF (*Comm: lettre*): **la présente** this letter

présentable [pʀezɑ̃tabl] ADJ presentable

présentateur, -trice [pʀezɑ̃tatœʀ, -tʀis] NM/F presenter

présentation [pʀezɑ̃tasjɔ̃] NF presentation; (*de nouveau venu*) introduction; (*allure*) appearance; **faire les présentations** to do the introductions

présenter [pʀezɑ̃te] /1/ VT to present; (*invité, candidat*) to introduce; (*félicitations, condoléances*) to offer; (*montrer: billet, pièce d'identité*) to show, produce; (*faire inscrire: candidat*) to put forward; (*soumettre*) to submit; **~ qn à** to introduce sb to; **je vous présente Nadine** this is Nadine ▸ VI: **~ mal/bien** to have an unattractive/a pleasing appearance ■ **se présenter** VPR (*sur convocation*) to report, come; (*se faire connaître*) to come forward; (*à une élection*) to stand; (*occasion*) to arise; **se ~ à un examen** to sit an exam; **se ~ bien/mal** (*situation*) to look good/not too good

présentoir [pʀezɑ̃twaʀ] NM (*étagère*) display shelf; (*vitrine*) showcase; (*étal*) display stand

préservatif [pʀezɛʀvatif] NM condom, sheath

préservation [pʀezɛʀvasjɔ̃] NF protection, preservation

préserver [pʀezɛʀve] /1/ VT: **~ de** (*protéger*) to protect from; (*sauver*) to save from

présidence [pʀezidɑ̃s] NF presidency; chairmanship

président [pʀezidɑ̃] NM (*Pol*) president; (*d'une assemblée, Comm*) chairman; **~ directeur général** chairman and managing director (BRIT), chief executive officer (US); **~ du jury** (*Jur*) foreman of the jury; (*d'examen*) chief examiner

The **président de la République** is the French head of state, elected for a five-year term by direct universal suffrage. He appoints the Prime Minister and, on the latter's recommendation, the members of the French government. He presides over the *Conseil des ministres*, enacts laws and is the commander-in-chief of the French armed forces. He has the power to dissolve the *Assemblée nationale* and, in an emergency, can exercise special powers.

présidente [pʀezidɑ̃t] NF president; (*femme du président*) president's wife; (*d'une réunion*) chairwoman

présidentiable [pʀezidɑ̃sjabl] NMF potential president ▸ ADJ: **être ~** to be a possible *ou* potential president

présidentiel, le [pʀezidɑ̃sjɛl] ADJ presidential ■ **présidentielles** NFPL presidential election(s)

présider [pʀezide] /1/ VT to preside over; (*dîner*) to be the guest of honour (BRIT) *ou* honor (US) at; **~ à** VT to direct; to govern

présomption [pʀezɔ̃psjɔ̃] NF presumption

présomptueux, -euse [pʀezɔ̃ptɥø, -øz] ADJ presumptuous

★**presque** [pʀɛsk] ADV almost, nearly; **~ rien** hardly anything; **~ pas** hardly (at all); **~ pas de** hardly any; **personne, ou ~** next to nobody, hardly anyone; **la ~ totalité (de)** almost *ou* nearly all

> *Presque* peut se traduire par **almost** ou **nearly** dans les phrases affirmatives, mais pour traduire une phrase française négative il est plus courant d'utiliser **hardly**. **Hardly** n'est jamais suivi d'un autre mot négatif.
> *Tu n'as presque rien mangé!* **You hardly ate anything!**
> *Il ne se trompe presque jamais.* **He hardly ever makes a mistake**.

presqu'île [pʀɛskil] NF peninsula

pressage [pʀesaʒ] NM (*de disque, raisin, olives*) pressing

pressant, e [pʀesɑ̃, -ɑ̃t] ADJ urgent; (*personne*) insistent; **se faire ~** to become insistent

presse [pʀɛs] NF press; (*affluence*): **heures de ~** busy times; **sous ~** gone to press; **mettre sous ~** to send to press; **avoir une bonne/mauvaise ~** to have a good/bad press; **~ féminine** women's magazines *pl*; **~ d'information** quality newspapers *pl*

★**pressé, e** [pʀese] ADJ in a hurry; (*air*) hurried; (*besogne*) urgent; **être ~ de faire qch** to be in a hurry to do sth; **orange pressée** freshly squeezed orange juice ▸ NM: **aller au plus ~** to see to first things first

presse-agrumes [pʀɛsagʀym] NM INV juicer

presse-citron [pʀɛssitʀɔ̃] NM INV lemon squeezer

presse-fruits [pʀɛsfʀɥi] NM INV lemon squeezer

pressentiment [pʀesɑ̃timɑ̃] NM foreboding, premonition

pressentir [pʀesɑ̃tiʀ] /16/ VT to sense; (*prendre contact avec*) to approach

presse-papiers [pʀɛspapje] NM INV paperweight

presse-purée [pʀɛspyʀe] NM INV potato masher

presser [pʀese] /1/ VT (*fruit, éponge*) to squeeze; (*interrupteur, bouton*) to press, push; (*allure, affaire*) to speed up; (*débiteur etc*) to press; (*inciter*): **~ qn de faire** to urge *ou* press sb to do; **~ le pas** to quicken one's step; **~ qn entre ses bras** to squeeze sb tight ▸ VI to be urgent; **rien ne presse** there's no hurry;

le temps presse there's not much time ■ **se presser** VPR *(se hâter)* to hurry (up); *(se grouper)* to crowd; **se ~ contre qn** to squeeze up against sb

pressing [prɛsiŋ] NM *(repassage)* steam-pressing; *(magasin)* dry-cleaner's

pression [prɛsjɔ̃] NF pressure; *(bouton)* press stud (BRIT), snap fastener (US); *(fam: bière)* draught beer; **faire ~ sur** to put pressure on; **sous ~** pressurized, under pressure; *(fig)* keyed up; **~ artérielle** blood pressure

pressoir [prɛswar] NM *(wine ou oil etc)* press

pressurer [prɛsyre] /1/ VT *(fig)* to squeeze

pressurisation [prɛsyrizasjɔ̃] NF pressurization

pressurisé, e [prɛsyrize] ADJ pressurized

prestance [prɛstɑ̃s] NF presence, imposing bearing

prestataire [prɛstatɛr] NMF person receiving benefits; *(Comm):* **~ de services** provider of services

prestation [prɛstasjɔ̃] NF *(allocation)* benefit; *(d'une assurance)* cover *no pl*; *(d'une entreprise)* service provided; *(d'un joueur, artiste)* performance; **~ de serment** taking the oath; **~ de service** provision of a service; **prestations familiales** ≈ child benefit

preste [prɛst] ADJ nimble

prestement [prɛstəmɑ̃] ADV nimbly

prestidigitateur, -trice [prɛstidiʒitatœr, -tris] NM/F conjurer

prestidigitation [prɛstidiʒitasjɔ̃] NF conjuring

prestige [prɛstiʒ] NM prestige

prestigieux, -euse [prɛstiʒjø, -øz] ADJ prestigious

présumer [prezyme] /1/ VT: **~ que** to presume *ou* assume that; **~ de** to overrate; **~ qn coupable** to presume sb guilty

présupposé [presypoze] NM presupposition

présupposer [presypoze] /1/ VT to presuppose

présupposition [presypozisjɔ̃] NF presupposition

présure [prezyr] NF rennet

prêt, e [prɛ, prɛt] ADJ ready; **~ à faire** ready to do; **~ à tout** ready for anything ▶ NM lending *no pl*; *(somme prêtée)* loan; **~ sur gages** pawnbroking *no pl*

prêt-à-porter [prɛtaporte] *(pl* **prêts-à-porter)** NM ready-to-wear *ou* off-the-peg (BRIT) clothes *pl*

prétendant [pretɑ̃dɑ̃] NM pretender; *(d'une femme)* suitor

prétendre [pretɑ̃dr] /41/ VT *(affirmer):* **~ que** to claim that; **~ faire qch** *(avoir l'intention de)* to mean *ou* intend to do sth; **~ à** *(droit, titre)* to lay claim to

prétendu, e [pretɑ̃dy] ADJ *(supposé)* so-called

prétendument [pretɑ̃dymɑ̃] ADV allegedly

prête-nom [prɛtnɔ̃] NM *(péj)* figurehead; *(Comm etc)* dummy

prétentieux, -euse [pretɑ̃sjø, -øz] ADJ pretentious

prétention [pretɑ̃sjɔ̃] NF pretentiousness; *(exigence, ambition)* claim; **sans ~** unpretentious

prêter [prete] /1/ VT: **~ qch à qn** *(livres, argent)* to lend sth to sb; *(caractère, propos)* to attribute sth to sb; **~ à** *(commentaires etc)* to be open to, give rise to;

~ assistance à to give help to; **~ attention** to pay attention; **~ serment** to take the oath; **~ l'oreille** to listen ■ **se prêter** VPR *(tissu, cuir)* to give; **se ~ à** to lend o.s. to; *(manigances etc)* to go along with

prêteur, -euse [prɛtœr, -øz] NM/F moneylender; **~ sur gages** pawnbroker

prétexte [pretɛkst] NM pretext, excuse; **sous aucun ~** on no account; **sous (le) ~ que/de** on the pretext that/of

prétexter [pretɛkste] /1/ VT to give as a pretext *ou* an excuse

prétoire [pretwar] NM court

prêtre [prɛtr] NM priest

prêtre-ouvrier [prɛtruvrije] *(pl* **prêtres-ouvriers)** NM worker-priest

prêtrise [prɛtriz] NF priesthood

preuve [prœv] NF proof; *(indice)* proof, evidence *no pl*; **jusqu'à ~ du contraire** until proved otherwise; **faire ~ de** to show; **faire ses preuves** to prove o.s.; **~ matérielle** material evidence

prévaloir [prevalwar] /29/ VI to prevail ■ **se prévaloir** VPR: **se ~ de** VT to take advantage of; *(tirer vanité de)* to pride o.s. on

prévarication [prevarikasjɔ̃] NF maladministration

prévaut *etc* [prevo] VB *voir* **prévaloir**

prévenance [prev(ə)nɑ̃s] NF thoughtfulness *sg* ■ **prévenances** NFPL consideration *sg*

prévenant, e [prev(ə)nɑ̃, -ɑ̃t] ADJ thoughtful, kind

prévenir [prev(ə)nir] /22/ VT *(éviter: catastrophe etc)* to avoid, prevent; *(anticiper: désirs, besoins)* to anticipate; **~ qn (de)** *(avertir)* to warn sb (about); *(informer)* to tell *ou* inform sb (about); **~ qn contre** *(influencer)* to prejudice sb against

préventif, -ive [prevɑ̃tif, -iv] ADJ preventive

prévention [prevɑ̃sjɔ̃] NF prevention; *(préjugé)* prejudice; *(Jur)* custody, detention; **~ routière** road safety

préventivement [prevɑ̃tivmɑ̃] ADV preventively

prévenu, e [prev(ə)ny] NM/F *(Jur)* defendant, accused

prévisible [previzibl] ADJ foreseeable

prévision [previzjɔ̃] NF: **prévisions** predictions; forecast *sg*; **prévisions météorologiques** *ou* **du temps** weather forecast *sg*; **en ~ de** in anticipation of

prévisionnel, le [previzjɔnɛl] ADJ concerned with future requirements

prévit *etc* [previ] VB *voir* **prévoir**

prévoir [prevwar] /24/ VT *(deviner)* to foresee; *(s'attendre à)* to expect, reckon on; *(prévenir)* to anticipate; *(organiser: voyage)* to plan; *(préparer, réserver)* to allow

prévoyance [prevwajɑ̃s] NF foresight; **société/ caisse de ~** provident society/contingency fund

prévoyant, e [prevwajɑ̃, -ɑ̃t] VB *voir* **prévoir** ▶ ADJ gifted with *(ou* showing) foresight, far-sighted

prévu, e [prevy] PP *de* **prévoir** ▶ ADJ: **comme ~** as planned; **~ pour quatre personnes** designed for four people; **~ pour 10 h** scheduled for 10 o'clock

PRG SIGLE M (= *Parti Radical de Gauche*) political party

prier [pʀije] /7/ vɪ to pray ▸ vᴛ (*Dieu*) to pray to; (*implorer*) to beg; (*demander*): **~ qn de faire** to ask sb to do; **~ qn à dîner** to invite sb to dinner; **se faire ~** to need coaxing *ou* persuading; **je vous en prie** (*allez-y*) please do; (*de rien*) don't mention it; **je vous prie de faire** please (would you) do

prière [pʀijɛʀ] ɴꜰ prayer; (*demande instante*) plea, entreaty; **« ~ de faire … »** "please do …"

★**primaire** [pʀimɛʀ] ᴀᴅᴊ primary; (*péj: personne*) simple-minded; (: *idées*) simplistic ▸ ɴᴍ (*Scol*) primary education

primauté [pʀimote] ɴꜰ (*fig*) primacy

prime [pʀim] ɴꜰ (*bonification*) bonus; (*subside*) allowance; (*Comm: cadeau*) free gift; (*Assurances, Bourse*) premium; **~ de risque** danger money *no pl*; **~ de transport** travel allowance ▸ ᴀᴅᴊ: **de ~ abord** at first glance

primer [pʀime] /1/ vᴛ (*l'emporter sur*) to prevail over; (*récompenser*) to award a prize to ▸ vɪ to dominate, prevail

primesautier, -ière [pʀimsotje, -jɛʀ] ᴀᴅᴊ impulsive

primeur [pʀimœʀ] ɴꜰ: **avoir la ~ de** to be the first to hear (*ou see etc*) ■ **primeurs** ɴꜰᴘʟ (*fruits, légumes*) early fruits and vegetables; **marchand de primeurs** greengrocer (*Bʀɪᴛ*), produce dealer (*US*)

primevère [pʀimvɛʀ] ɴꜰ primrose

primipare [pʀimipaʀ] ɴꜰ primipara

primitif, -ive [pʀimitif, -iv] ᴀᴅᴊ primitive; (*originel*) original ▸ ɴᴍ/ꜰ primitive

primo [pʀimo] ᴀᴅᴠ first (of all), firstly

primordial, e, -aux [pʀimɔʀdjal, -o] ᴀᴅᴊ essential, primordial

prince [pʀɛ̃s] ɴᴍ prince; **~ charmant** Prince Charming; **~ de Galles** *n inv* (*tissu*) Prince of Wales check; **~ héritier** crown prince

princesse [pʀɛ̃sɛs] ɴꜰ princess

princier, -ière [pʀɛ̃sje, -jɛʀ] ᴀᴅᴊ princely

★**principal, e, -aux** [pʀɛ̃sipal, -o] ᴀᴅᴊ principal, main; (**proposition) principale** (*Ling*) main clause ▸ ɴᴍ/ꜰ (*Scol*) head (teacher) (*Bʀɪᴛ*), principal (*US*) ▸ ɴᴍ (*essentiel*) main thing

principalement [pʀɛ̃sipalmɑ̃] ᴀᴅᴠ principally, mainly

principauté [pʀɛ̃sipote] ɴꜰ principality

principe [pʀɛ̃sip] ɴᴍ principle; **partir du ~ que** to work on the principle *ou* assumption that; **pour le ~** on principle, for the sake of it; **de ~** *adj* (*hostilité*) automatic; (*accord*) in principle; **par ~** on principle; **en ~** (*habituellement*) as a rule; (*théoriquement*) in principle

printanier, -ière [pʀɛ̃tanje, -jɛʀ] ᴀᴅᴊ spring, spring-like

★**printemps** [pʀɛ̃tɑ̃] ɴᴍ spring; **au ~** in spring

priori [pʀijɔʀi]: **a ~** *adv* at first glance, initially; a priori

prioritaire [pʀijɔʀitɛʀ] ᴀᴅᴊ having priority; (*Auto*) having right of way; (*Inform*) foreground

prioritairement [pʀijɔʀitɛʀmɑ̃] ᴀᴅᴠ (*en priorité*) as a priority

priorité [pʀijɔʀite] ɴꜰ priority; (*Auto*): **avoir la ~ (sur)** to have right of way (over); **~ à droite** right of way to vehicles coming from the right; **en ~** as a (matter of) priority

pris, e [pʀi, pʀiz] ᴘᴘ *de* **prendre** ▸ ᴀᴅᴊ (*place*) taken; (*billets*) sold; (*journée, mains*) full; (*personne*) busy; (*crème, ciment*) set; **avoir le nez/la gorge ~(e)** to have a stuffy nose/a bad throat; **être ~ de peur/ de fatigue/de panique** to be stricken with fear/ overcome with fatigue/panic-stricken

★**prise** [pʀiz] ɴꜰ (*d'une ville*) capture; (*Pêche, Chasse*) catch; (*de judo ou catch, point d'appui ou pour empoigner*) hold; (*Élec: fiche*) plug; (: *femelle*) socket; (: *au mur*) point; **en ~** (*Auto*) in gear; **être aux prises avec** to be grappling with; to be battling with; **lâcher ~** to let go; **donner ~ à** (*fig*) to give rise to; **avoir ~ sur qn** to have a hold over sb; **~ en charge** (*taxe*) pickup charge; (*par la sécurité sociale*) undertaking to reimburse costs; **~ de contact** initial meeting, first contact; **~ de courant** power point; **~ d'eau** water (supply) point; tap; **~ multiple** adaptor; **~ d'otages** hostage-taking; **~ à partie** (*Jur*) action against a judge; **~ péritel** SCART socket; **~ de sang** blood test; **~ de son** sound recording; **~ de tabac** pinch of snuff; **~ de terre** earth; **~ de vue** (*photo*) shot; **~ de vue(s)** (*action*) filming, shooting

prisé, e [pʀize] ᴀᴅᴊ: **très ~** greatly prized

priser [pʀize] /1/ vᴛ (*tabac, héroïne*) to take; (*estimer*) to prize, value ▸ vɪ to take snuff

prisme [pʀism] ɴᴍ prism

★**prison** [pʀizɔ̃] ɴꜰ prison; **aller/être en ~** to go to/ be in prison *ou* jail; **faire de la ~** to serve time; **être condamné à cinq ans de ~** to be sentenced to five years' imprisonment *ou* five years in prison

> Quand les mots **prison** et **jail** désignent l'institution en général, il ne sont jamais précédés de l'article défini. Ce n'est pas le cas quand ils désignent plus précisément le bâtiment.
> *La vie après la prison n'est pas facile.* **Life after prison isn't easy.**
> *Il travaille à la prison.* **He works at the prison.**

★**prisonnier, -ière** [pʀizɔnje, -jɛʀ] ɴᴍ/ꜰ prisoner ▸ ᴀᴅᴊ captive; **faire qn ~** to take sb prisoner

prit [pʀi] ᴠʙ *voir* **prendre**

privatif, -ive [pʀivatif, -iv] ᴀᴅᴊ (*jardin etc*) private; (*peine*) which deprives one of one's liberties

privations [pʀivasjɔ̃] ɴꜰᴘʟ privations, hardships

privatisation [pʀivatizasjɔ̃] ɴꜰ privatization

privatiser [pʀivatize] /1/ vᴛ to privatize

privautés [pʀivote] ɴꜰᴘʟ liberties

privé, e [pʀive] ᴀᴅᴊ private; (*dépourvu*): **~ de** without, lacking; (*en punition*): **tu es ~ de télé !** no TV for you! ▸ ɴᴍ (*Comm*) private sector; **en ~**, **dans le ~** in private

priver [pʀive] /1/ vᴛ: **~ qn de** to deprive sb of; **se ~ de** to go *ou* do without; **ne pas se ~ de faire** not to refrain from doing

privilège [pʀivilɛʒ] ɴᴍ privilege

privilégié, e [pʀivileʒje] ᴀᴅᴊ privileged

privilégier [pʀivileʒje] /7/ vᴛ to favour (*Bʀɪᴛ*), favor (*US*)

★**prix** [pʀi] ɴᴍ (*valeur*) price; (*récompense, Scol*) prize; **mettre à ~** to set a reserve (*Bʀɪᴛ*) *ou* an upset (*US*) price on; **au ~ fort** at a very high price; **acheter qch à ~ d'or** to pay a (small) fortune for sth; **hors de ~** exorbitantly priced; **à aucun ~** not at any price; **à tout ~** at all costs; **grand ~** (*Sport*) Grand

Prix; **~ d'achat/de vente/de revient** purchasing/selling/cost price; **~ conseillé** manufacturer's recommended price (MRP)

pro [pʀo] NM (= *professionnel*) pro

proactif, -ive [pʀoaktif, -iv] ADJ proactive

probabilité [pʀobabilite] NF probability; **selon toute ~** in all probability

probable [pʀobabl] ADJ likely, probable

★**probablement** [pʀobabləmɑ̃] ADV probably

probant, e [pʀobɑ̃, -ɑ̃t] ADJ convincing

probatoire [pʀobatwaʀ] ADJ (*examen, test*) preliminary; (*stage*) probationary, trial *cpd*

probité [pʀobite] NF integrity, probity

problématique [pʀoblematik] ADJ problematic(al) ▶ NF problematics *sg*; (*problème*) problem

problème [pʀoblɛm] NM problem

procédé [pʀosede] NM (*méthode*) process; (*comportement*) behaviour *no pl* (BRIT), behavior *no pl* (US)

procéder [pʀosede] /**6**/ VI to proceed; (*moralement*) to behave; **~ à** VT to carry out

procédure [pʀosedyʀ] NF (*Admin, Jur*) procedure

procédurier, -ière [pʀosedyʀje, -jɛʀ] ADJ (*domaine, cadre*) procedural; (*personne*) litigious; **avoir l'esprit ~** to be of a litigious temperament ▶ NM/F (*spécialiste*) procedural expert; (*péj*) litigious person

procès [pʀosɛ] NM (*Jur*) trial; (: *poursuites*) proceedings *pl*; **être en ~ avec** to be involved in a lawsuit with; **faire le ~ de qn/qch** (*fig*) to put sb/sth on trial; **sans autre forme de ~** without further ado

processeur [pʀosesœʀ] NM processor

procession [pʀosesjɔ̃] NF procession

processus [pʀosesys] NM process

procès-verbal, -aux [pʀosɛvɛʀbal, -o] NM (*constat*) statement; (*de réunion*) minutes *pl*; (*aussi*: **PV**): **avoir un ~** to get a parking ticket, to be booked

★**prochain, e** [pʀoʃɛ̃, -ɛn] ADJ next; (*proche: départ, arrivée*) impending; near; **la prochaine fois/ semaine prochaine** next time/week; **à la prochaine!** (*fam*), **à la prochaine fois!** see you!, see you next time!; **un ~ jour** (some day) soon ▶ NM fellow man

prochainement [pʀoʃɛnmɑ̃] ADV soon, shortly

proche [pʀoʃ] ADJ nearby, near; (*dans le temps*) imminent; close at hand; (*parent, ami*) close; **être ~ (de)** to be near, be close (to); **de ~ en ~** gradually ■ **proches** NMPL (*parents*) close relatives, next of kin; (*amis*): **l'un de ses proches** one of those close to him (*ou* her)

Proche-Orient [pʀoʃoʀjɑ̃] NM: **le ~** the Near East

proclamation [pʀoklamasjɔ̃] NF proclamation

proclamer [pʀoklame] /**1**/ VT to proclaim; (*résultat d'un examen*) to announce

procréation [pʀokʀeasjɔ̃] NF procreation; **~ médicalement assistée, assistance médicale à la ~** assisted reproduction

procréer [pʀokʀee] /**1**/ VT to procreate

procuration [pʀokyʀasjɔ̃] NF proxy; power of attorney; **voter par ~** to vote by proxy

procurer [pʀokyʀe] /**1**/ VT (*fournir*): **~ qch à qn** (*obtenir*) to get *ou* obtain sth for sb; (*plaisir etc*) to bring *ou* give sb sth ■ **se procurer** VPR to get

procureur [pʀokyʀœʀ] NM public prosecutor; **~ général** public prosecutor (*in appeal court*)

prodigalité [pʀodigalite] NF (*générosité*) generosity; (*extravagance*) extravagance, wastefulness

prodige [pʀodiʒ] NM (*miracle, merveille*) marvel, wonder; (*personne*) prodigy

prodigieusement [pʀodiʒjøzmɑ̃] ADV prodigiously, phenomenally

prodigieux, -euse [pʀodiʒjø, -øz] ADJ prodigious; phenomenal

prodigue [pʀodig] ADJ (*généreux*) generous; (*dépensier*) extravagant, wasteful; **fils ~** prodigal son

prodiguer [pʀodige] /**1**/ VT (*argent, biens*) to be lavish with; (*soins, attentions*): **~ qch à qn** to lavish sth on sb

producteur, -trice [pʀodyktœʀ, -tʀis] ADJ: **~ de blé** (*pays, région*) wheat-producing; **société productrice** (*Ciné*) film *ou* movie company ▶ NM/F producer

productif, -ive [pʀodyktif, -iv] ADJ productive

production [pʀodyksjɔ̃] NF (*gén*) production; (*rendement*) output; (*produits*) products *pl*, goods *pl*; (*œuvres*): **la ~ dramatique du XVIIe siècle** the plays of the 17th century

productiviste [pʀodyktivist] ADJ productivist

productivité [pʀodyktivite] NF productivity

★**produire** [pʀodɥiʀ] /**38**/ VT, VI to produce ■ **se produire** VPR (*acteur*) to perform, appear; (*événement*) to happen, occur

★**produit, e** [pʀodɥi, -it] PP *de* **produire** ▶ NM (*gén*) product; **~ chimique** chemical; **~ d'entretien** cleaning product; **~ national brut (PNB)** gross national product (GNP); **~ net** net profit; **~ (pour la) vaisselle** washing-up (BRIT) *ou* dish-washing (US) liquid; **~ des ventes** income from sales; **produits agricoles** farm produce *sg*; **produits alimentaires** foodstuffs; **produits de beauté** beauty products, cosmetics

proéminent, e [pʀoeminɑ̃, -ɑ̃t] ADJ prominent

★**prof** [pʀof] NMF (*fam*: = *professeur*) teacher; professor; lecturer

prof. [pʀof] ABR = **professeur**; **professionnel**

profanation [pʀofanasjɔ̃] NF (*de cimetière*) desecration

profane [pʀofan] ADJ (*Rel*) secular; (*ignorant, non initié*) uninitiated ▶ NMF layman

profaner [pʀofane] /**1**/ VT to desecrate; (*fig: sentiment*) to defile; (: *talent*) to debase

proférer [pʀofeʀe] /**6**/ VT to utter

professer [pʀofese] /**1**/ VT to profess

★**professeur, e** [pʀofesœʀ] NM/F teacher; (*titulaire d'une chaire*) professor; **~ (de faculté)** (university) lecturer

★**profession** [pʀofesjɔ̃] NF (*libérale*) profession; (*gén*) occupation; **faire ~ de** (*opinion, religion*) to profess; **de ~** by profession; **« sans ~ »** "unemployed"; (*femme mariée*) "housewife"

professionnaliser [pʀofesjonalize] VT to professionalize ■ **se professionnaliser** VPR to become professionalized

professionnalisme [pʀofesjonalism] NM professionalism

★**professionnel, le** [pʀofesjonɛl] ADJ professional ▶ NM/F professional; (*ouvrier qualifié*) skilled worker

professoral, e, -aux [pʀofesoʀal, -o] ADJ professorial; **le corps ~** the teaching profession

professorat [pʀɔfɛsɔʀa] NM: **le ~** the teaching profession

profil [pʀɔfil] NM profile; (*d'une voiture*) line, contour; **de ~** in profile

profilé, e [pʀɔfile] ADJ shaped; (*aile etc*) streamlined

profiler [pʀɔfile] /**1**/ VT to streamline ■ **se profiler** VPR (*arbre, tour*) to stand out, be silhouetted

profit [pʀɔfi] NM (*avantage*) benefit, advantage; (*Comm, Finance*) profit; **au ~ de** in aid of; **tirer** *ou* **retirer ~ de** to profit from; **mettre à ~** to take advantage of; to turn to good account; **profits et pertes** (*Comm*) profit and loss(es)

profitabilité [pʀɔfitabilite] NF profitability

profitable [pʀɔfitabl] ADJ (*utile*) beneficial; (*lucratif*) profitable

profiter [pʀɔfite] /**1**/ VI: **~ de** (*situation, occasion*) to take advantage of; (*vacances, jeunesse etc*) to make the most of; **~ de ce que ...** to take advantage of the fact that ...; **~ à** to be of benefit to, benefit; to be profitable to

profiteur, -euse [pʀɔfitœʀ, -øz] NM/F (*péj*) profiteer

★**profond, e** [pʀɔfɔ̃, -ɔ̃d] ADJ deep; (*méditation, mépris*) profound; **peu ~** (*eau, vallée, puits*) shallow; (*coupure*) superficial; **au plus ~ de** in the depths of, at the (very) bottom of; **la France profonde** the heartlands of France

profondément [pʀɔfɔ̃demã] ADV deeply; profoundly; **il dort ~** he is sound asleep

★**profondeur** [pʀɔfɔ̃dœʀ] NF depth; **l'eau a quelle ~ ?** how deep is the water?

profusément [pʀɔfyzemã] ADV profusely

profusion [pʀɔfyzjɔ̃] NF profusion; **à ~** in plenty

progéniture [pʀɔʒenityʀ] NF offspring *inv*

progiciel [pʀɔʒisjɛl] NM (*Inform*) (software) package; **~ d'application** applications package, applications software *no pl*

progouvernemental, e, -aux [pʀɔguvɛʀnəmãtal, -o] ADJ pro-government *cpd*

programmable [pʀɔgʀamabl] ADJ programmable

programmateur, -trice [pʀɔgʀamatœʀ, -tʀis] NM/F (*Ciné, TV*) programme (BRIT) *ou* program (US) planner ▸ NM (*de machine à laver etc*) timer

programmation [pʀɔgʀamasjɔ̃] NF programming

★**programme** [pʀɔgʀam] NM programme (BRIT), program (US); (*TV, Radio*) program(me)s *pl*; (*Scol*) syllabus, curriculum; (*Inform*) program; **au ~ de ce soir** (*TV*) among tonight's program(me)s

programmé, e [pʀɔgʀame] ADJ: **enseignement ~** programmed learning

programmer [pʀɔgʀame] /**1**/ VT (*TV, Radio*) to put on, show; (*organiser, prévoir: émission*) to schedule; (*Inform*) to program

★**programmeur, -euse** [pʀɔgʀamœʀ, -øz] NM/F (computer) programmer

progrès [pʀɔgʀɛ] NM progress *no pl*; **faire des/être en ~** to make/be making progress

progresser [pʀɔgʀese] /**1**/ VI to progress; (*troupes etc*) to make headway *ou* progress

progressif, -ive [pʀɔgʀesif, -iv] ADJ progressive

progression [pʀɔgʀesjɔ̃] NF progression; (*d'une troupe etc*) advance, progress

progressiste [pʀɔgʀesist] ADJ progressive

progressivement [pʀɔgʀesivmã] ADV progressively

prohiber [pʀɔibe] /**1**/ VT to prohibit, ban

prohibitif, -ive [pʀɔibitif, -iv] ADJ prohibitive

prohibition [pʀɔibisjɔ̃] NF ban, prohibition; (*Hist*) Prohibition

proie [pʀwa] NF prey *no pl*; **être la ~ de** to fall prey to; **être en ~ à** (*doutes, sentiment*) to be prey to; (*douleur, mal*) to be suffering

★**projecteur** [pʀɔʒɛktœʀ] NM projector; (*de théâtre, cirque*) spotlight

projectile [pʀɔʒɛktil] NM missile; (*d'arme*) projectile, bullet (*ou* shell *etc*)

projection [pʀɔʒɛksjɔ̃] NF projection; (*séance*) showing; **conférence avec projections** lecture with slides (*ou* a film)

projectionniste [pʀɔʒɛksjɔnist] NMF (*Ciné*) projectionist

★**projet** [pʀɔʒɛ] NM plan; (*ébauche*) draft; **faire des projets** to make plans; **~ de loi** bill

projeter [pʀɔʒ(ə)te] /**4**/ VT (*envisager*) to plan; (*film, photos*) to project; (*passer*) to show; (*ombre, lueur*) to throw, cast, project; (*jeter*) to throw up (*ou* off *ou* out); **~ de faire qch** to plan to do sth

prolétaire [pʀɔletɛʀ] ADJ, NMF proletarian

prolétariat [pʀɔletaʀja] NM proletariat

prolétarien, ne [pʀɔletaʀjɛ̃, -ɛn] ADJ proletarian

prolifération [pʀɔliferasjɔ̃] NF proliferation

proliférer [pʀɔlifeʀe] /**6**/ VI to proliferate

prolifique [pʀɔlifik] ADJ prolific

prolixe [pʀɔliks] ADJ verbose

prolo [pʀɔlo] NMF (*fam*: = prolétaire) prole (*péj*)

prologue [pʀɔlɔg] NM prologue

prolongateur [pʀɔlɔ̃gatœʀ] NM (*Élec*) extension cable

prolongation [pʀɔlɔ̃gasjɔ̃] NF prolongation; extension ■ **prolongations** NFPL (*Football*) extra time *sg*

prolongement [pʀɔlɔ̃ʒmã] NM extension; **dans le ~ de** running on from ■ **prolongements** NMPL (*fig*) repercussions, effects

prolonger [pʀɔlɔ̃ʒe] /**3**/ VT (*débat, séjour*) to prolong; (*délai, billet, rue*) to extend; (*chose*) to be a continuation *ou* an extension of ■ **se prolonger** VPR to go on

★**promenade** [pʀɔm(ə)nad] NF walk (*ou* drive *ou* ride); **faire une ~** to go for a walk; **une ~ (à pied)/ en voiture/à vélo** a walk/drive/(bicycle) ride

★**promener** [pʀɔm(ə)ne] /**5**/ VT (*personne, chien*) to take out for a walk; (*fig*) to carry around; to trail round; (*doigts, regard*): **~ qch sur** to run sth over ■ **se promener** VPR (*à pied*) to go for (*ou* be out for) a walk; (*en voiture*) to go for (*ou* be out for) a drive; (*fig*): **se ~ sur** to wander over

promeneur, -euse [pʀɔm(ə)nœʀ, -øz] NM/F walker, stroller

promenoir [pʀɔm(ə)nwaʀ] NM gallery, (covered) walkway

promesse [pʀɔmɛs] NF promise; **~ d'achat** commitment to buy

prometteur, -euse [pʀɔmɛtœʀ, -øz] ADJ promising

★**promettre** [pʀɔmɛtʀ] /56/ VT to promise; **~ à qn de faire** to promise sb that one will do ▶ VI (*récolte, arbre*) to look promising; (*enfant, musicien*) to be promising ■ **se promettre** VPR: **se ~ de faire** to resolve *ou* mean to do

promeus *etc* [pʀɔmø] VB *voir* **promouvoir**

promis, e [pʀɔmi, -iz] PP *de* **promettre** ▶ ADJ: **être ~ à qch** (*destiné*) to be destined for sth

promiscuité [pʀɔmiskɥite] NF crowding; lack of privacy

promit [pʀɔmi] VB *voir* **promettre**

promo [pʀɔmo] NF (*fam: Scol: promotion*) year (BRIT), class; **~ 95** the class of 95

promontoire [pʀɔmɔ̃twaʀ] NM headland

promoteur, -trice [pʀɔmɔtœʀ, -tʀis] NM/F (*instigateur*) instigator, promoter; **~ (immobilier)** property developer (BRIT), real estate promoter (US)

promotion [pʀɔmosjɔ̃] NF (*avancement*) promotion; (*Scol*) year (BRIT), class; **en ~** (*Comm*) on promotion, on (special) offer

promotionnel, le [pʀɔmɔsjɔnɛl] ADJ (*article*) on promotion, on (special) offer; (*vente*) promotional

promouvoir [pʀɔmuvwaʀ] /27/ VT to promote

prompt, e [pʀɔ̃, pʀɔ̃t] ADJ swift, rapid; (*intervention, changement*) sudden; **~ à faire qch** quick to do sth

promptement [pʀɔ̃ptəmɑ̃] ADV swiftly

prompteur® [pʀɔ̃ptœʀ] NM Autocue® (BRIT), Teleprompter® (US)

promptitude [pʀɔ̃(p)tityd] NF swiftness, rapidity

promu, e [pʀɔmy] PP *de* **promouvoir**

promulgation [pʀɔmylgasjɔ̃] NF (*de loi*) promulgation

promulguer [pʀɔmylge] /1/ VT to promulgate

prôner [pʀone] /1/ VT (*louer*) to laud, extol; (*préconiser*) to advocate, commend

pronom [pʀɔnɔ̃] NM pronoun

pronominal, e, -aux [pʀɔnɔminal, -o] ADJ pronominal; (*verbe*) reflexive, pronominal

prononçable [pʀɔnɔ̃sabl] ADJ pronounceable; **difficilement ~** hard to pronounce

prononcé, e [pʀɔnɔ̃se] ADJ pronounced, marked

★**prononcer** [pʀɔnɔ̃se] /3/ VT (*son, mot, jugement*) to pronounce; (*dire*) to utter; (*discours*) to deliver ▶ VI (*Jur*) to deliver *ou* give a verdict; **~ bien/mal** to have good/poor pronunciation ■ **se prononcer** VPR (*mot*) to be pronounced; **se ~ (sur)** (*se décider*) to reach a decision (on *ou* about), give a verdict (on); **se ~ contre** to come down against; **ça se prononce comment ?** how do you pronounce this?

prononciation [pʀɔnɔ̃sjasjɔ̃] NF pronunciation

pronostic [pʀɔnɔstik] NM (*Méd*) prognosis; (*fig: aussi:* **pronostics**) forecast

pronostiquer [pʀɔnɔstike] /1/ VT (*Méd*) to prognosticate; (*annoncer, prévoir*) to forecast, foretell

pronostiqueur, -euse [pʀɔnɔstikœʀ, -øz] NM/F forecaster

propagande [pʀɔpagɑ̃d] NF propaganda; **faire de la ~ pour qch** to plug *ou* push sth

propagandiste [pʀɔpagɑ̃dist] NMF propagandist

propagation [pʀɔpagasjɔ̃] NF propagation

propager [pʀɔpaʒe] /3/ VT to spread ■ **se propager** VPR to spread; (*Physique*) to be propagated

propane [pʀɔpan] NM propane

propension [pʀɔpɑ̃sjɔ̃] NF: **~ à qch** propensity for sth; **~ à faire qch** propensity to do sth

prophète, prophétesse [pʀɔfɛt, pʀɔfetɛs] NM/F prophet(ess)

prophétie [pʀɔfesi] NF prophecy

prophétique [pʀɔfetik] ADJ prophetic

prophétiser [pʀɔfetize] /1/ VT to prophesy

prophylactique [pʀɔfilaktik] ADJ prophylactic

prophylaxie [pʀɔfilaksi] NF prophylaxis

propice [pʀɔpis] ADJ favourable (BRIT), favorable (US)

proportion [pʀɔpɔʀsjɔ̃] NF proportion; **il n'y a aucune ~ entre le prix demandé et le prix réel** the asking price bears no relation to the real price; **à ~ de** proportionally to, in proportion to; **en ~ (de)** in proportion (to); **hors de ~** out of proportion; **toute(s) ~(s) gardée(s)** making due allowance(s)

proportionnalité [pʀɔpɔʀsjɔnalite] NF proportionality; (*de système électoral*) proportional representation

proportionné, e [pʀɔpɔʀsjɔne] ADJ: **bien ~** well-proportioned; **~ à** proportionate to

proportionnel, le [pʀɔpɔʀsjɔnɛl] ADJ proportional; **~ à** proportional to ▶ NF proportional representation

proportionnellement [pʀɔpɔʀsjɔnɛlmɑ̃] ADV proportionally, proportionately

proportionner [pʀɔpɔʀsjɔne] /1/ VT: **~ qch à** to proportion *ou* adjust sth to

propos [pʀɔpo] NM (*paroles*) talk *no pl*, remark; (*intention, but*) intention, aim; (*sujet*): **à quel ~ ?** what about?; **à ~ de** about, regarding; **à tout ~** for no reason at all; **à ce ~** on that subject, in this connection; **à ~** *adv* by the way; (*opportunément*) (just) at the right moment; **hors de ~, mal à ~** *adv* at the wrong moment

★**proposer** [pʀɔpoze] /1/ VT (*loi, motion*) to propose; (*candidat*) to nominate, put forward; **~ qch (à qn)/de faire** (*suggérer*) to suggest sth (to sb)/doing, propose sth (to sb)/to do; (*offrir*) to offer (sb) sth/to do ■ **se proposer** VPR: **se ~ (pour faire)** to offer one's services (to do); **se ~ de faire** to intend *ou* propose to do

★**proposition** [pʀɔpozisjɔ̃] NF suggestion; proposal; offer; (*Ling*) clause; **sur la ~ de** at the suggestion of; **~ de loi** private bill

★**propre** [pʀɔpʀ] ADJ clean; (*net*) neat, tidy; (*qui ne salit pas: chien, chat*) house-trained; (: *enfant*) toilet-trained; (*fig: honnête*) honest; (*possessif*) own; (*sens*) literal; (*particulier*): **~ à** peculiar to, characteristic of; (*approprié*): **~ à** suitable *ou* appropriate for; (*de nature à*): **~ à faire** likely to do, that will do ▶ NM: **recopier au ~** to make a fair copy of; (*particularité*): **le ~ de** the peculiarity of, the distinctive feature of; **au ~** (*Ling*) literally; **appartenir à qn en ~** to belong to sb (exclusively); **~ à rien** *nmf* (*péj*) good-for-nothing

proprement [pʀɔpʀəmɑ̃] ADV (avec propreté) cleanly; neatly, tidily; **à ~ parler** strictly speaking; **le village ~ dit** the actual village, the village itself

propret, te [pʀɔpʀɛ, -ɛt] ADJ neat and tidy, spick-and-span

propreté [pʀɔpʀəte] NF cleanliness, cleanness; neatness, tidiness

propriétaire [pʀɔpʀijetɛʀ] NMF owner; (d'hôtel etc) proprietor(-tress), owner; (pour le locataire) landlord(-lady); **~ (immobilier)** house-owner; householder; **~ récoltant** grower; **~ (terrien)** landowner

propriété [pʀɔpʀijete] NF (droit) ownership; (objet, immeuble etc) property gén no pl; (villa) residence, property; (terres) property gén no pl, land gén no pl; (qualité, Chimie, Math) property; (correction) appropriateness, suitability; **~ artistique et littéraire** artistic and literary copyright; **~ industrielle** patent rights pl

proprio [pʀɔpʀijo] NMF (fam: propriétaire) landlord(-lady)

propulser [pʀɔpylse] /1/ VT (missile) to propel; (projeter) to hurl, fling

propulseur [pʀɔpylsœʀ] ADJ M propulsive ▶ NM propulsion unit; **~ d'appoint** booster; **~ à hélice** propeller; **~ à réaction** jet engine

propulsion [pʀɔpylsjɔ̃] NF propulsion

prorata [pʀɔʀata] NM INV: **au ~ de** in proportion to, on the basis of

prorogation [pʀɔʀɔgasjɔ̃] NF deferment; extension; adjournment

proroger [pʀɔʀɔʒe] /3/ VT to put back, defer; (prolonger) to extend; (assemblée) to adjourn, prorogue

prosaïque [pʀɔzaik] ADJ mundane, prosaic

prosaïquement [pʀɔzaikmɑ̃] ADV prosaically; **plus ~** more prosaically

proscription [pʀɔskʀipsjɔ̃] NF banishment; (interdiction) banning; prohibition

proscrire [pʀɔskʀiʀ] /39/ VT (bannir) to banish; (interdire) to ban, prohibit

prose [pʀoz] NF prose (style)

prosélyte [pʀɔzelit] NMF proselyte, convert

prospecter [pʀɔspɛkte] /1/ VT to prospect; (Comm) to canvass

prospecteur, -trice [pʀɔspɛktœʀ, -tʀis] NM/F (d'or) prospector; (Comm) canvasser

prospecteur-placier [pʀɔspɛktœʀplasje] (pl **prospecteurs-placiers**) NM placement officer

prospectif, -ive [pʀɔspɛktif, -iv] ADJ prospective

prospection [pʀɔspɛksjɔ̃] NF (pétrolière, minière) prospecting; (de marchés) exploration

prospectus [pʀɔspɛktys] NM (feuille) leaflet; (dépliant) brochure, leaflet

prospère [pʀɔspɛʀ] ADJ prosperous; (santé, entreprise) thriving, flourishing

prospérer [pʀɔspeʀe] /6/ VI to thrive

prospérité [pʀɔspeʀite] NF prosperity

prostate [pʀɔstat] NF prostate (gland)

prosterner [pʀɔstɛʀne] /1/: **se prosterner** VPR to bow low, prostrate o.s.

prostitué, e [pʀɔstitɥe] NM male prostitute ▶ NF prostitute

prostituer [pʀɔstitɥe]: **se prostituer** VPR to work as a prostitute

prostitution [pʀɔstitysjɔ̃] NF prostitution

prostré, e [pʀɔstʀe] ADJ prostrate

protagoniste [pʀɔtagɔnist] NMF protagonist

protecteur, -trice [pʀɔtɛktœʀ, -tʀis] ADJ protective; (air, ton: péj) patronizing ▶ NM/F (défenseur) protector; (des arts) patron

protection [pʀɔtɛksjɔ̃] NF protection; (d'un personnage influent: aide) patronage; **écran de ~** protective screen; **~ civile** state-financed civilian rescue service; **~ maternelle et infantile** social service concerned with child welfare

protectionnisme [pʀɔtɛksjɔnism] NM protectionism

protectionniste [pʀɔtɛksjɔnist] ADJ protectionist

protectorat [pʀɔtɛktɔʀa] NM protectorate; **sous ~ français** under French protectorate

protégé, e [pʀɔteʒe] NM/F protégé(e)

protège-cahier [pʀɔtɛʒkaje] NM exercise book cover

protéger [pʀɔteʒe] /6, 3/ VT to protect; (aider, patronner: personne, arts) to be a patron of; (: carrière) to further ■ **se protéger** VPR: **se ~ (de/contre)** to protect o.s. (from)

protège-slip [pʀɔtɛʒslip] NM panty liner

protéine [pʀɔtein] NF protein

protestant, e [pʀɔtɛstɑ̃, -ɑ̃t] ADJ, NM/F Protestant

protestantisme [pʀɔtɛstɑ̃tism] NM Protestantism

protestataire [pʀɔtɛstatɛʀ] NMF protestor

protestation [pʀɔtɛstasjɔ̃] NF (plainte) protest; (déclaration) protestation, profession

protester [pʀɔtɛste] /1/ VI: **~ (contre)** to protest (against ou about); **~ de** (son innocence, sa loyauté) to protest

prothèse [pʀɔtɛz] NF artificial limb, prosthesis; **~ dentaire** (appareil) denture; (science) dental engineering

protocolaire [pʀɔtɔkɔlɛʀ] ADJ formal; (questions, règles) of protocol

protocole [pʀɔtɔkɔl] NM protocol; (fig) etiquette; **~ d'accord** draft treaty; **~ opératoire** (Méd) operating procedure

proton [pʀɔtɔ̃] NM proton

prototype [pʀɔtɔtip] NM prototype

protubérance [pʀɔtybeʀɑ̃s] NF bulge, protuberance

protubérant, e [pʀɔtybeʀɑ̃, -ɑ̃t] ADJ protruding, bulging, protuberant

proue [pʀu] NF bow(s pl), prow

prouesse [pʀuɛs] NF feat

prouvé [pʀuve] ADJ: **scientifiquement ~** scientifically proven; **c'est ~** it's a proven fact

prouver [pʀuve] /1/ VT to prove

provenance [pʀɔv(ə)nɑ̃s] NF origin; (de mot, coutume) source; **avion en ~ de** plane (arriving) from

provençal, e, -aux [pʀɔvɑ̃sal, -o] ADJ Provençal ▶ NM (Ling) Provençal

Provence [pʀɔvɑ̃s] NF: **la ~** Provence

provenir [pʀɔv(ə)niʀ] /**22**/: **~ de** vt to come from; (*résulter de*) to be due to, be the result of

proverbe [pʀɔvɛʀb] NM proverb

proverbial, e, -aux [pʀɔvɛʀbjal, -o] ADJ proverbial

providence [pʀɔvidɑ̃s] NF: **la ~** providence

providentiel, le [pʀɔvidɑ̃sjɛl] ADJ providential

province [pʀɔvɛ̃s] NF province

provincial, e, -aux [pʀɔvɛ̃sjal, -o] ADJ, NM/F provincial

★**proviseur** [pʀɔvizœʀ] NM ≈ head (teacher) (BRIT), ≈ principal (US)

★**provision** [pʀɔvizjɔ̃] NF (*réserve*) stock, supply; (*avance*: *à un avocat*) retainer, retaining fee; (*Comm*) funds pl (in account); reserve; **faire ~ de** to stock up with ■ **provisions** NFPL (*vivres*) provisions, food no pl; **placard** ou **armoire à provisions** food cupboard

provisionnel, le [pʀɔvizjɔnɛl] ADJ *voir* tiers

★**provisoire** [pʀɔvizwaʀ] ADJ temporary; (*Jur*) provisional; **mise en liberté ~** release on bail

provisoirement [pʀɔvizwaʀmɑ̃] ADV temporarily, for the time being

provocant, e [pʀɔvɔkɑ̃, -ɑ̃t] ADJ provocative

provocateur, -trice [pʀɔvɔkatœʀ, -tʀis] ADJ provocative ▶ NM (*meneur*) agitator

provocation [pʀɔvɔkasjɔ̃] NF provocation

provoquer [pʀɔvɔke] /**1**/ VT (*défier*) to provoke; (*causer*) to cause, bring about; (: *curiosité*) to arouse, give rise to; (: *aveux*) to prompt, elicit; (*inciter*): **~ qn à** to incite sb to

prox. ABR = **proximité**

proxénète [pʀɔksenɛt] NMF procurer

proxénétisme [pʀɔksenetism] NM procuring

proximité [pʀɔksimite] NF nearness, closeness, proximity; (*dans le temps*) imminence, closeness; **à ~** near ou close by; **à ~ de** near (to), close to

prude [pʀyd] ADJ prudish

prudemment [pʀydamɑ̃] ADV carefully; cautiously; prudently; wisely, sensibly

prudence [pʀydɑ̃s] NF carefulness; caution; prudence; **avec ~** carefully; cautiously; wisely; **par (mesure de) ~** as a precaution

prudent, e [pʀydɑ̃, -ɑ̃t] ADJ (*pas téméraire*) careful, cautious, prudent; (: *en général*) safety-conscious; (*sage, conseillé*) wise, sensible; (*réservé*) cautious; **c'est plus ~** it's wiser; **ce n'est pas ~** it's risky; it's not sensible; **soyez ~** take care, be careful

★**prune** [pʀyn] NF plum

pruneau, x [pʀyno] NM prune

prunelle [pʀynɛl] NF pupil; (*œil*) eye; (*Bot*) sloe; (*eau-de-vie*) sloe gin

prunier [pʀynje] NM plum tree

prurit [pʀyʀit] NM (*Méd*) pruritus

Prusse [pʀys] NF: **la ~** Prussia

PS SIGLE M = **parti socialiste**; (= *post-scriptum*) PS

psalmodier [psalmɔdje] /**7**/ VT to chant; (*fig*) to drone out

psaume [psom] NM psalm

pseudonyme [psødɔnim] NM (*gén*) false name; (*d'écrivain*) pseudonym, pen name; (*de comédien*) stage name

PSIG SIGLE M (= *Peloton de surveillance et d'intervention de gendarmerie*) type of police commando squad

psoriasis [psɔʀjazis] NM psoriasis

psy [psi] NMF (*fam*: = *psychiatre, psychologue*) shrink

psychanalyse [psikanaliz] NF psychoanalysis

psychanalyser [psikanalize] /**1**/ VT to psychoanalyze; **se faire ~** to undergo (psycho)analysis

psychanalyste [psikanalist] NMF psychoanalyst

psychanalytique [psikanalitik] ADJ psychoanalytical

psyché [psiʃe] NF psyche

psychédélique [psikedelik] ADJ psychedelic

psychiatre [psikjatʀ] NMF psychiatrist

psychiatrie [psikjatʀi] NF psychiatry

psychiatrique [psikjatʀik] ADJ psychiatric; (*hôpital*) mental, psychiatric

psychique [psiʃik] ADJ psychological

psychisme [psiʃism] NM psyche

psychologie [psikɔlɔʒi] NF psychology

psychologique [psikɔlɔʒik] ADJ psychological

psychologiquement [psikɔlɔʒikmɑ̃] ADV psychologically

psychologue [psikɔlɔg] NMF psychologist; **être ~** (*fig*) to be a good psychologist

psychomoteur, -trice [psikɔmɔtœʀ, -tʀis] ADJ psychomotor

psychopathe [psikɔpat] NMF psychopath

psychopédagogie [psikɔpedagɔʒi] NF educational psychology

psychose [psikoz] NF (*Méd*) psychosis; (*obsession, idée fixe*) obsessive fear

psychosomatique [psikɔsɔmatik] ADJ psychosomatic

psychothérapie [psikɔteʀapi] NF psychotherapy

psychotique [psikɔtik] ADJ psychotic

Pte ABR = **porte**

pte ABR = **pointe**) pt

PTMA SIGLE M (= *poids total maximum autorisé*) maximum loaded weight

PTT SIGLE FPL (= *Postes, Télégraphes et Téléphone*) formerly the French post office and telecommunications service

pu [py] PP *de* **pouvoir**

puant, e [pɥɑ̃, pɥɑ̃t] ADJ (*nauséabond*) stinking, foul; (*odieux, prétentieux*) pompous

puanteur [pɥɑ̃tœʀ] NF stink, stench

pub [pyb] NF (*fam*) (= *publicité*): **la ~** advertising; **une ~** an ad

pubalgie [pybalʒi] NF groin strain

pubère [pybɛʀ] ADJ pubescent

puberté [pybɛʀte] NF puberty

pubis [pybis] NM (*bas-ventre*) pubes pl; (*os*) pubis

publiable [pyblijabl] ADJ publishable

★**public, -ique** [pyblik] ADJ public; (*école, instruction*) state cpd; (*scrutin*) open ▶ NM public; (*assistance*) audience; **en ~** in public; **le grand ~** the general public

publication [pyblikasjɔ̃] NF publication

publiciste [pyblisist] NMF advertising executive

publicitaire [pyblisitɛʀ] ADJ advertising cpd; (film, voiture) publicity cpd; (vente) promotional; **rédacteur ~** copywriter ▶ NMF advertising executive

publicité [pyblisite] NF (méthode, profession) advertising; (annonce) advertisement; (révélations) publicity

publier [pyblije] /7/ VT to publish; (nouvelle) to publicize, make public

publipostage [pyblipostaʒ] NM mailshot, (mass) mailing

publique [pyblik] ADJ F voir **public**

publiquement [pyblikmã] ADV publicly

puce [pys] NF flea; (Inform) chip; **carte à ~** smart card; **(marché aux) puces** flea market sg; **mettre la ~ à l'oreille de qn** to give sb something to think about

puceau, x [pyso] ADJ M (fam): **être ~** to be a virgin

pucelle [pysɛl] ADJ F (fam): **être ~** to be a virgin

puceron [pys(ə)ʀɔ̃] NM aphid

pudding [pudiŋ] NM (à base de pain rassis) bread pudding; (plum-pudding) Christmas pudding, plum pudding

pudeur [pydœʀ] NF modesty

pudibond, e [pydibɔ̃, -ɔ̃d] ADJ prudish

pudique [pydik] ADJ (chaste) modest; (discret) discreet

pudiquement [pydikmã] ADV modestly

puer [pɥe] /1/ (péj) VI to stink ▶ VT to stink of, reek of

puériculteur, -trice [pɥeʀikyltœʀ, -tʀis] NM/F (aussi: **infirmier puériculteur, infirmière puéricultrice**) nursery nurse

puériculture [pɥeʀikyltyʀ] NF infant care

puéril, e [pɥeʀil] ADJ childish

puérilement [pɥeʀilmã] ADV childishly

puérilité [pɥeʀilite] NF childishness; (acte, idée) childish thing

pugilat [pyʒila] NM (fist) fight

pugnace [pygnas] ADJ pugnacious

pugnacité [pygnasite] NF pugnacity

★**puis** [pɥi] VB voir **pouvoir** ▶ ADV (ensuite) then; (dans une énumération) next; (en outre): **et ~** and (then); **et ~ (après ou quoi)?** so (what)?

puisard [pɥizaʀ] NM (égout) cesspool

puiser [pɥize] /1/ VT: **~ (dans)** to draw (from); **~ dans qch** to dip into sth

★**puisque** [pɥisk] CONJ since; (valeur intensive): **~ je te le dis!** I'm telling you!

puissamment [pɥisamã] ADV powerfully

★**puissance** [pɥisãs] NF power; **en ~** adj potential; **deux (à la) ~ cinq** two to the power (of) five

puissant, e [pɥisã, -ãt] ADJ powerful

puisse etc [pɥis] VB voir **pouvoir**

puits [pɥi] NM well; **~ artésien** artesian well; **~ de mine** mine shaft; **~ de science** fount of knowledge

★**pull(-over)** [pyl(ɔvœʀ)] NM sweater, jumper (BRIT)

pulluler [pylyle] /1/ VI to swarm; (fig: erreurs) to abound, proliferate

pulmonaire [pylmɔnɛʀ] ADJ lung cpd; (artère) pulmonary

pulpe [pylp] NF pulp

pulpeux, -euse [pylpø, -øz] ADJ (bouche) fleshy; (femme) curvaceous

pulsation [pylsasjɔ̃] NF (Méd) beat

pulsé [pylse] ADJ M: **chauffage à air ~** warm air heating

pulser [pylse] VT (air) to pump (out) ▶ VI: **ça pulse** (fam: musique, spectacle) it has a real vibe (fam)

pulsion [pylsjɔ̃] NF (Psych) drive, urge

pulvérisateur [pylveʀizatœʀ] NM spray

pulvérisation [pylveʀizasjɔ̃] NF spraying

pulvériser [pylveʀize] /1/ VT (solide) to pulverize; (liquide) to spray; (fig: anéantir: adversaire) to pulverize; (: record) to smash, shatter; (: argument) to demolish

puma [pyma] NM puma, cougar

punaise [pynɛz] NF (Zool) bug; (clou) drawing pin (BRIT), thumb tack (US)

punaiser [pyneze] VT (affiche) to pin up, tack up (US)

punch [pɔ̃ʃ] NM (boisson) punch; (Boxe) [pœnʃ] punching ability; (fig) punch

punching-ball [pœnʃiŋbol] NM punchball

★**punir** [pyniʀ] /2/ VT to punish; **~ qn de qch** to punish sb for sth

punitif, -ive [pynitif, -iv] ADJ punitive

punition [pynisjɔ̃] NF punishment

punk [pœ̃k] ADJ INV, NMF, NM punk

pupille [pypij] NF (Anat) pupil ▶ NMF (enfant) ward; **~ de l'État** child in care; **~ de la Nation** war orphan

pupitre [pypitʀ] NM (Scol) desk; (Rel) lectern; (de chef d'orchestre) rostrum; **~ de commande** control panel

pur, e [pyʀ] ADJ pure; (vin) undiluted; (whisky) neat; (intentions) honourable (BRIT), honorable (US); **en pure perte** fruitlessly, to no avail; **c'est de la folie pure** it's sheer madness ▶ NM (personne) hardliner

purée [pyʀe] NF: **~ (de pommes de terre)** ≈ mashed potatoes pl; **~ de marrons** chestnut purée; **~ de pois** (fig) peasoup(er)

purement [pyʀmã] ADV purely

pureté [pyʀte] NF purity

purgatif [pyʀgatif] NM purgative, purge

purgatoire [pyʀgatwaʀ] NM purgatory

purge [pyʀʒ] NF (Pol) purge; (Méd) purging no pl; purge

purger [pyʀʒe] /3/ VT (radiateur) to flush (out), drain; (circuit hydraulique) to bleed; (Méd, Pol) to purge; (Jur: peine) to serve

purification [pyʀifikasjɔ̃] NF (de l'eau) purification; **~ ethnique** ethnic cleansing

purifier [pyʀifje] /7/ VT to purify; (Tech: métal) to refine

purin [pyʀɛ̃] NM liquid manure

puriste [pyʀist] NMF purist

puritain, e [pyʀitɛ̃, -ɛn] ADJ, NM/F Puritan

puritanisme [pyʀitanism] NM Puritanism

pur-sang [pyʀsã] NM INV thoroughbred, purebred

purulent, e [pyʀylã, -ãt] ADJ purulent

pus [py] VB *voir* **pouvoir** ▶ NM pus

pusillanime [pyzilanim] ADJ fainthearted

pustule [pystyl] NF pustule

putain [pytɛ̃] NF (!) whore (!); **ce/cette ~ de ...** this bloody (BRIT) *ou* goddamn (US)... (!)

pute [pyt] NF (!) whore

putois [pytwa] NM polecat; **crier comme un ~** to yell one's head off

putréfaction [pytrefaksjɔ̃] NF putrefaction

putréfier [pytrefje] /7/ VT to putrefy, rot ▪ **se putréfier** VPR to putrefy, rot

putride [pytrid] ADJ putrid

putsch [putʃ] NM (*Pol*) putsch

puzzle [pœzl] NM jigsaw (puzzle)

PV SIGLE M = **procès-verbal**

PVC SIGLE F (= *polychlorure de vinyle*) PVC

Px ABR = **prix**

pygmée [pigme] NM pygmy

★**pyjama** [piʒama] NM pyjamas *pl* (BRIT), pajamas *pl* (US)

pylône [pilon] NM pylon

pyramide [piramid] NF pyramid

pyrénéen, ne [pireneɛ̃, -ɛn] ADJ Pyrenean

Pyrénées [pirene] NFPL: **les ~** the Pyrenees

pyrex® [pirɛks] NM Pyrex®

pyrogravure [pirɔgravyr] NF poker-work

pyromane [pirɔman] NMF arsonist

pyrotechnique [pirɔteknik] ADJ (*effets*) pyrotechnic; **spectacle ~** firework display

python [pitɔ̃] NM python

p

Qq

Q, q [ky] NM INV Q, q ▸ ABR (= *quintal*) q; **Q comme Quintal** Q for Queen

Qatar [katar] NM: **le ~** Qatar

QCM SIGLE M (= *questionnaire à choix multiples*) multiple-choice test

QG SIGLE M (= *quartier général*) HQ

QHS SIGLE M (= *quartier de haute sécurité*) high-security wing *ou* prison

QI SIGLE M (= *quotient intellectuel*) IQ

QPPV SIGLE M = **quartier prioritaire de la politique de la ville**

qqch. ABR (= *quelque chose*) sth

qqe ABR = **quelque**

qqes ABR = **quelques**

qqn ABR (= *quelqu'un*) sb, s.o.

quad [kwad] NM quad bike

quadra [k(w)adra] NMF (*fam*: = *quadragénaire*) person in his (*ou* her) forties; **les quadras** forty somethings (*fam*)

quadragénaire [kadraʒenɛr] NMF (*de quarante ans*) forty-year-old; (*de quarante à cinquante ans*) man/woman in his/her forties

quadrangulaire [kwadrãgylɛr] ADJ quadrangular

quadrature [kwadratyr] NF: **c'est la ~ du cercle** it's like trying to square the circle

quadrichromie [kwadrikrɔmi] NF four-colour (BRIT) *ou* -color (US) printing

quadrilatère [k(w)adrilatɛr] NM (*Géom, Mil*) quadrilateral; (*terrain*) four-sided area

quadrillage [kadrijaʒ] NM (*lignes etc*) square pattern, criss-cross pattern

quadrillé, e [kadrije] ADJ (*papier*) squared

quadriller [kadrije] /1/ VT (*papier*) to mark out in squares; (*Police: ville, région etc*) to keep under tight control, be positioned throughout

quadrimoteur [k(w)adrimɔtœr] NM four-engined plane

quadripartite [kwadripartit] ADJ (*entre pays*) four-power; (*entre partis*) four-party

quadriphonie [kadrifɔni] NF quadraphony

quadriréacteur [k(w)adrireaktœr] NM four-engined jet

quadrupède [k(w)adrypɛd] NM quadruped

quadruple [k(w)adrypl] NM: **le ~ de** four times as much as

quadrupler [k(w)adryple] /1/ VT, VI to quadruple, increase fourfold

quadruplés, -ées [k(w)adryple] NM/FPL quadruplets, quads

★**quai** [ke] NM (*de port*) quay; (*de gare*) platform; (*de cours d'eau, canal*) embankment; **être à ~** (*navire*) to be alongside; (*train*) to be in the station; **le Q~ d'Orsay** offices of the French Ministry for Foreign Affairs; **le Q~ des Orfèvres** central police headquarters

qualifiable [kalifjabl] ADJ: **ce n'est pas ~** it defies description

qualificatif, -ive [kalifikatif, -iv] ADJ (*Ling*) qualifying ▸ NM (*terme*) term; (*Ling*) qualifier

qualification [kalifikasjõ] NF qualification

qualifié, e [kalifje] ADJ qualified; (*main-d'œuvre*) skilled; **être ~ pour** to be qualified for

qualifier [kalifje] /7/ VT to qualify; (*appeler*): **~ qch/qn de** to describe sth/sb as ▪ **se qualifier** VPR (*Sport*) to qualify

qualitatif, -ive [kalitatif, -iv] ADJ qualitative

qualité [kalite] NF quality; (*titre, fonction*) position; **en ~ de** in one's capacity as; **ès qualités** in an official capacity; **avoir ~ pour** to have authority to; **de ~** *adj* quality *cpd*; **rapport qualité-prix** value (for money)

★**quand** [kã] CONJ, ADV when; **~ je serai riche** when I'm rich; **~ même** (*cependant, pourtant*) nevertheless; (*tout de même*) all the same; **~ même, il exagère !** really, he overdoes it!; **~ bien même** even though

quant [kã] **~ à** *prép* (*pour ce qui est de*) as for, as to; (*au sujet de*) regarding

quant-à-soi [kãtaswa] NM: **rester sur son ~** to remain aloof

quantième [kãtjɛm] NM date, day (of the month)

quantifiable [kãtifjabl] ADJ quantifiable

quantifier [kãtifje] /7/ VT to quantify

quantique [k(w)ãtik] ADJ (*mécanique, physique*) quantum

quantitatif, -ive [kãtitatif, -iv] ADJ quantitative

quantitativement [kãtitativmã] ADV quantitatively

quantité [kãtite] NF quantity, amount; (*Science*) quantity; **une** *ou* **des ~(s) de** (*grand nombre*) a great deal of; a lot of; **en grande ~** in large quantities; **en quantités industrielles** in vast amounts; **du travail en ~** a great deal of work; **~ de** many

quarantaine [karãtɛn] NF (*isolement*) quarantine; **une ~ (de)** forty or so, about forty; **avoir la ~** (*âge*) to be around forty; **mettre en ~** to put into quarantine; (*fig*) to send to Coventry (Brit), ostracize

★**quarante** [kaʀɑ̃t] NUM forty

quarantième [kaʀɑ̃tjɛm] NUM fortieth

quark [kwaʀk] NM quark

★**quart** [kaʀ] NM (*fraction*) quarter; (*surveillance*) watch; (*partie*): **un ~ de poulet/fromage** a chicken quarter/a quarter of a cheese; **un ~ de beurre** a quarter kilo of butter; ≈ a half pound of butter; **un ~ de vin** a quarter litre of wine; **une livre un ~** *ou* **et ~** one and a quarter pounds; **le ~ de** a quarter of; **~ d'heure** quarter of an hour; **deux heures et** *ou* **un ~** (a) quarter past two, (a) quarter after two (US); **il est le ~** it's (a) quarter past *ou* after (US); **une heure moins le ~** (a) quarter to one, (a) quarter of one (US); **il est moins le ~** it's (a) quarter to; **être de/prendre le ~** to keep/take the watch; **~ de tour** quarter turn; **au ~ de tour** (*fig*) straight off; **quarts de finale** (*Sport*) quarter finals

quarté [kaʀte] NM (*Courses*) system of forecast betting giving first four horses

quarteron [kaʀtəʀɔ̃] NM (*péj*) small bunch, handful

quartette [kwaʀtɛt] NM quartet(te)

★**quartier** [kaʀtje] NM (*de ville*) district, area; (*de bœuf, de la lune*) quarter; (*de fruit, fromage*) piece; **cinéma/salle de ~** local cinema/hall; **avoir ~ libre** to be free; (*Mil*) to have leave from barracks; **ne pas faire de ~** to spare no one, give no quarter; **~ commerçant/résidentiel** shopping/residential area; **~ général (QG)** headquarters (HQ) ◾ **quartiers** NMPL (*Mil*) quarters

quartier-maître [kaʀtjemɛtʀ] (*pl* **quartiers-maîtres**) NM ≈ leading seaman

quartz [kwaʀts] NM quartz

quasi [kazi] ADV almost, nearly ▸ PRÉFIXE: **quasi-certitude** near certainty

quasiment [kazimɑ̃] ADV almost, (very) nearly; **~ jamais** hardly ever

quaternaire [kwatɛʀnɛʀ] ADJ (*Géo*) Quaternary

★**quatorze** [katɔʀz] NUM fourteen

quatorzième [katɔʀzjɛm] NUM fourteenth

quatrain [katʀɛ̃] NM quatrain

★**quatre** [katʀ] NUM four; **à ~ pattes** on all fours; **tiré à ~ épingles** dressed up to the nines; **faire les ~ cent coups** to be a bit wild; **se mettre en ~ pour qn** to go out of one's way for sb; **~ à ~** (*monter, descendre*) four at a time; **à ~ mains** (*jouer*) four-handed

quatre-vingt-dix [katʀəvɛ̃dis] NUM ninety

★**quatre-vingts** [katʀəvɛ̃] NUM eighty

quatre-vingt-un NUM eighty-one

quatrième [katʀijɛm] NUM fourth ▸ NF (*Scol*) year 9 (Brit), eighth grade (US)

quatrièmement [katʀijɛmmɑ̃] ADV fourthly

quatuor [kwatɥɔʀ] NM quartet(te)

---

que [kə]

CONJ **1** (*introduisant complétive*) that; **il sait que tu es là** he knows (that) you're here; **je veux que tu acceptes** I want you to accept; **il a dit que oui** he said he would (*ou* it was *etc*)

2 (*reprise d'autres conjonctions*): **quand il rentrera et qu'il aura mangé** when he gets back and

(when) he has eaten; **si vous y allez ou que vous …** if you go there or if you …

3 (*en tête de phrase: hypothèse, souhait etc*): **qu'il le veuille ou non** whether he likes it or not; **qu'il fasse ce qu'il voudra !** let him do as he pleases!

4 (*but*): **tenez-le qu'il ne tombe pas** hold it so (that) it doesn't fall

5 (*après comparatif*) than; as; *voir aussi* **plus²**; **aussi**; **autant** *etc*

6 (*seulement*): **ne … que** only; **il ne boit que de l'eau** he only drinks water

7 (*temps*): **elle venait à peine de sortir qu'il se mit à pleuvoir** she had just gone out when it started to rain, no sooner had she gone out than it started to rain; **il y a quatre ans qu'il est parti** it is four years since he left, he left four years ago

▸ ADV (*exclamation*): **qu'il** *ou* **qu'est-ce qu'il est bête/court vite !** he's so silly!/he runs so fast!; **que de livres !** what a lot of books!

▸ PRON **1** (*relatif: personne*) whom; (: *chose*) that, which; **l'homme que je vois** the man (whom) I see; **le livre que tu vois** the book (that *ou* which) you see; **un jour que j'étais …** a day when I was …

2 (*interrogatif*) what; **que fais-tu ?**, **qu'est-ce que tu fais ?** what are you doing?; **qu'est-ce que c'est ?** what is it?, what's that?; **que faire ?** what can one do?; **que préfères-tu, celui-ci ou celui-là ?** which (one) do you prefer, this one or that one?

Québec [kebɛk] N (*ville*) Quebec ▸ NM: **le ~** Quebec (Province)

québécisme [kebesism] NM *word used in Quebec*

québécois, e [kebekwa, -waz] ADJ Quebec *cpd* ▸ NM (*Ling*) Quebec French ▸ NM/F: **Québécois, e** Quebecois, Quebec(k)er

---

quel, quelle [kɛl]

ADJ **1** (*interrogatif: personne*) who; (: *chose*) what; which; **quel est cet homme ?** who is this man?; **quel est ce livre ?** what is this book?; **quel livre/homme ?** what book/man?; (*parmi un certain choix*) which book/man?; **quels acteurs préférez-vous ?** which actors do you prefer?; **dans quels pays êtes-vous allé ?** which *ou* what countries did you go to?

2 (*exclamatif*): **quelle surprise/coïncidence !** what a surprise/coincidence!

3: **quel que soit le coupable** whoever is guilty; **quel que soit votre avis** whatever your opinion (may be)

---

quelconque [kɛlkɔ̃k] ADJ (*médiocre: repas*) indifferent, poor; (*sans attrait*) ordinary, plain; (*indéfini*): **un ami/prétexte ~** some friend/pretext or other; **un livre ~ suffira** any book will do; **pour une raison ~** for some reason (or other)

---

quelque [kɛlk]

ADJ **1** (*au singulier*) some; (*au pluriel*) a few, some; (*tournure interrogative*) any; **quelque espoir** some hope; **il a quelques amis** he has a few *ou* some friends; **a-t-il quelques amis ?** does he have any friends?; **les quelques livres qui** the few books which; **20 kg et quelque(s)** a bit over 20 kg;

il habite à quelque distance d'ici he lives some distance *ou* way (away) from here **2**: **quelque ... que** whatever, whichever; **quelque livre qu'il choisisse** whatever (*ou* whichever) book he chooses; **par quelque temps qu'il fasse** whatever the weather **3**: **quelque chose** something; (*tournure interrogative*) anything; **quelque chose d'autre** something else; anything else; **y être pour quelque chose** to have something to do with it; **faire quelque chose à qn** to have an effect on sb, do something to sb; **quelque part** somewhere; anywhere; **en quelque sorte** as it were ▶ ADV **1** (*environ*): **quelque 100 mètres** some 100 metres **2**: **quelque peu** rather, somewhat

★**quelquefois** [kɛlkəfwa] ADV sometimes

★**quelques-uns, -unes** [kɛlkəzœ̃, -yn] PRON some, a few; **~ des lecteurs** some of the readers

★**quelqu'un** [kɛlkœ̃] PRON someone, somebody; (*+ tournure interrogative ou négative*) anyone, anybody; **quelqu'un d'autre** someone *ou* somebody else; anybody else

Someone/somebody et anybody/anybody sont suivis d'un verbe au singulier, mais le possessif qui s'y rapporte doit être au pluriel. *Quelqu'un a écrit son nom sur le mur.* **Somebody has written their name on the wall**. *Est-ce que quelqu'un a apporté sa carte de crédit ?* **Has anyone brought their credit card?**

quémander [kemãde] /1/ VT to beg for

qu'en-dira-t-on [kɑ̃diratɔ̃] NM INV: **le qu'en-dira-t-on** gossip, what people say

quenelle [kənɛl] NF quenelle

quenotte [kənɔt] NF (*fam*) toothy-peg (*fam*)

quenouille [kənuj] NF distaff

querelle [kərɛl] NF quarrel; **chercher ~ à qn** to pick a quarrel with sb

quereller [kərele] /1/: **se quereller** VPR to quarrel

querelleur, -euse [kərɛlœr, -øz] ADJ quarrelsome

quérir [kerir] VT (*liter*) to seek; **aller ~** to go in quest of

qu'est-ce que [kɛskə] *voir* **que**

qu'est-ce qui [kɛski] *voir* **qui**

★**question** [kɛstjɔ̃] NF (*gén*) question; (*fig*) matter; issue; **il a été ~ de** we (*ou* they) spoke about; **il est ~ de les emprisonner** there's talk of them being jailed; **c'est une ~ de temps** it's a matter *ou* question of time; **de quoi est-il ~ ?** what is it about?; **il n'en est pas ~** there's no question of it; **en ~** in question; **hors de ~** out of the question; **je ne me suis jamais posé la ~** I've never thought about it; **(re)mettre en ~** (*autorité, science*) to question; **poser la ~ de confiance** (*Pol*) to ask for a vote of confidence; **~ piège** (*d'apparence facile*) trick question; (*pour nuire*) loaded question; **~ subsidiaire** tiebreaker

questionnaire [kɛstjɔnɛr] NM questionnaire

questionnement [kɛstjɔnmã] NM (*réflexion*) questioning

questionner [kɛstjɔne] /1/ VT to question

quête [kɛt] NF (*collecte*) collection; (*recherche*) quest, search; **faire la ~** (*à l'église*) to take the collection;

(*artiste*) to pass the hat round; **se mettre en ~ de qch** to go in search of sth

quêter [kete] /1/ VI (*à l'église*) to take the collection; (*dans la rue*) to collect money (for charity) ▶ VT to seek

quetsche [kwɛtʃ] NF damson

★**queue** [kø] NF tail; (*fig: du classement*) bottom; (: *de poêle*) handle; (: *de fruit, feuille*) stalk; (: *de train, colonne, file*) rear; (*file: de personnes*) queue (BRIT), line (US); **en ~ (de train)** at the rear (of the train); **faire la ~** to queue (up) (BRIT), line up (US); **se mettre à la ~** to join the queue *ou* line; **histoire sans ~ ni tête** cock and bull story; **à la ~ leu leu** in single file; (*fig*) one after the other; **~ de cheval** ponytail; **~ de poisson: faire une ~ de poisson à qn** (*Auto*) to cut in front of sb; **finir en ~ de poisson** (*film*) to come to an abrupt end

queue-de-pie [kødpi] (*pl* **queues-de-pie**) NF (*habit*) tails *pl*, tail coat

queux [kø] ADJ M *voir* **maître**

---

qui [ki]

PRON **1** (*interrogatif: personne*) who; (: *avec préposition*) whom; (: *chose, animal*) which, that; (: *interrogatif indirect: sujet*): **je me demande qui est là** I wonder who is there; (: *objet*): **elle ne sait à qui se plaindre** she doesn't know who to *ou* to whom to complain; (: *chose*): **qu'est-ce qui est sur la table?** what is on the table?; **qui est-ce qui ?** who?; **qui est-ce que ?** who?; **à qui est ce sac ?** whose bag is this?; **à qui parlais-tu ?** who were you talking to?, to whom were you talking?; **chez qui allez-vous ?** whose house are you going to?

2 (*relatif: personne*) who; (*+prép*) whom; **l'ami de qui je vous ai parlé** the friend I told you about; **la dame chez qui je suis allé** the lady whose house I went to

3 (*sans antécédent*): **amenez qui vous voulez** bring who you like; **qui que ce soit** whoever it may be

quiche [kiʃ] NF quiche; **~ lorraine** quiche Lorraine

quiconque [kikɔ̃k] PRON (*celui qui*) whoever, anyone who; (*n'importe qui, personne*) anyone, anybody

quidam [k(ɥ)idam] NM (*humoristique*) fellow

quiétude [kjetyd] NF (*d'un lieu*) quiet, tranquillity; (*d'une personne*) peace (of mind), serenity; **en toute ~** in complete peace; (*mentale*) with complete peace of mind

quignon [kiɲɔ̃] NM: **~ de pain** (*croûton*) crust of bread; (*morceau*) hunk of bread

quille [kij] NF bowling, skittle (BRIT); (*Navig: d'un bateau*) keel; **(jeu de) quilles** skittles *sg* (BRIT), bowling (US)

quincaillerie [kɛ̃kajri] NF (*ustensiles, métier*) hardware, ironmongery (BRIT); (*magasin*) hardware shop *ou* store (US), ironmonger's (BRIT)

quincaillier, -ière [kɛ̃kaje, -jɛr] NM/F hardware dealer, ironmonger (BRIT)

quinconce [kɛ̃kɔ̃s] NM: **en ~** in staggered rows

quinine [kinin] NF quinine

quinqua [kɛ̃ka] NMF (*fam: = quinquagénaire*) person in his (*ou* her) fifties; **les quinquas** fifty somethings (*fam*)

quinquagénaire [kɛ̃kaʒenɛʀ] NMF (*de cinquante ans*) fifty-year old; (*de cinquante à soixante ans*) man/woman in his/her fifties

quinquennal, e, -aux [kɛ̃kenal, -o] ADJ five-year, quinquennial

quinquennat [kɛ̃kena] NM *five year term of office (of French President)*

quinquina [kɛ̃kina] NM cinchona

quintal, -aux [kɛ̃tal, -o] NM quintal (*100 kg*)

quinte [kɛ̃t] NF: **~ (de toux)** coughing fit

quinté [kɛ̃te] NM (*Courses*) system of forecast betting giving first five horses

quintessence [kɛ̃tesɑ̃s] NF quintessence, very essence

quintette [kɛ̃tɛt] NM quintet(te)

quintuple [kɛ̃typl] NM: **le ~ de** five times as much as

quintupler [kɛ̃typle] /1/ VT, VI to increase fivefold

quintuplés, -ées [kɛ̃typle] NM/FPL quintuplets, quins

quinzaine [kɛ̃zɛn] NF: **une ~ (de)** about fifteen, fifteen or so; **une ~ (de jours)** (*deux semaines*) a fortnight (BRIT), two weeks; **~ publicitaire** *ou* **commerciale** (two-week) sale

★**quinze** [kɛ̃z] NUM fifteen; **demain en ~** a fortnight (BRIT) *ou* two weeks tomorrow; **dans ~ jours** in a fortnight('s time) (BRIT), in two weeks(' time)

quinzième [kɛ̃zjɛm] NUM fifteenth

quiproquo [kipʀɔko] NM (*méprise sur une personne*) mistake; (*malentendu sur un sujet*) misunderstanding; (*Théât*) (case of) mistaken identity

Quito [kito] N Quito

quittance [kitɑ̃s] NF (*reçu*) receipt; (*facture*) bill

quitte [kit] ADJ: **être ~ envers qn** to be no longer in sb's debt; (*fig*) to be quits with sb; **être ~ de** (*obligation*) to be clear of; **en être ~ à bon compte** to have got off lightly; **~ à faire** even if it means doing; **~ ou double** (*jeu*) double or quits; (*fig*) **c'est du ~ ou double** it's a big risk

★**quitter** [kite] /1/ VT to leave; (*espoir, illusion*) to give up; (*vêtement*) to take off; **ne pas ~ qn d'une semelle** to stick to sb like glue ▶ VI: **ne quittez pas** (*au téléphone*) hold the line ■ **se quitter** VPR (*couples, interlocuteurs*) to part

quitus [kitys] NM final discharge; **donner ~ à** to discharge

qui-vive [kiviv] NM INV: **être sur le ~** to be on the alert

---

quoi [kwa]

PRON INTERROG **1** what; **quoi de neuf ?** what's new?; **quoi ?** (*qu'est-ce que tu dis ?*) what?

2 (*avec prép*): **à quoi tu penses ?** what are you thinking about?; **de quoi parlez-vous ?** what are you talking about?; **à quoi bon ?** what's the use?

▶ PRON RELATIF: **as-tu de quoi écrire ?** do you have anything to write with?; **il n'a pas de quoi se l'acheter** he can't afford it, he hasn't got the money to buy it; **il y a de quoi être fier** that's something to be proud of; **il n'y a pas de quoi** (please) don't mention it; **il n'y a pas de quoi rire** there's nothing to laugh about

▶ PRON (*locutions*): **quoi qu'il arrive** whatever happens; **quoi qu'il en soit** be that as it may; **quoi que ce soit** anything at all; **en quoi puis-je vous aider ?** how can I help you?; **et puis quoi encore !** what(ever) next!; **quoi faire ?** what's to be done?; **sans quoi** (*ou sinon*) otherwise

▶ EXCL what!

---

quoique [kwak] CONJ (al)though

quolibet [kɔlibɛ] NM gibe, jeer

quorum [kɔʀɔm] NM quorum

quota [kwɔta] NM quota

quote-part [kɔtpaʀ] (*pl* quotes-parts) NF share

★**quotidien, ne** [kɔtidjɛ̃, -ɛn] ADJ (*journalier*) daily; (*banal*) ordinary, everyday ▶ NM (*journal*) daily (paper); (*vie quotidienne*) daily life, day-to-day existence; **les grands quotidiens** the big (national) dailies

quotidiennement [kɔtidjɛnmɑ̃] ADV daily, every day

quotient [kɔsjɑ̃] NM (*Math*) quotient; **~ intellectuel (QI)** intelligence quotient (IQ)

quotité [kɔtite] NF (*Finance*) quota

q

Rr

R, r [εR] NM INV R, r ▸ ABR = **route**; **rue**; **R comme Raoul** R for Robert (BRIT) ou Roger (US)

rab [Rab] NM (*fam: nourriture*) extra, more; **est-ce qu'il y a du ~ ?** are there any seconds?

rabâcher [Rabaʃe] /1/ vi to harp on ▸ vt to keep on repeating

rabais [Rabɛ] NM reduction, discount; **au ~** at a reduction ou discount

rabaisser [Rabese] /1/ vt (*rabattre: prix*) to reduce; (*dénigrer*) to belittle

rabane [Raban] NF raffia (matting)

Rabat [Raba(t)] N Rabat

rabat [Raba] vB *voir* **rabattre** ▸ NM flap

rabat-joie [Rabaʒwa] NMF INV killjoy (BRIT), spoilsport

rabattable [Rabatabl] ADJ (*banquette, siège*) folding

rabatteur, -euse [Rabatœr, -øz] NM/F (*de gibier*) beater; (*péj*) tout

rabattre [RabatR] /41/ vt (*couvercle, siège*) to pull down; (*fam*) to turn down; (*couture*) to stitch down; (*gibier*) to drive; (*somme d'un prix*) to deduct, take off; (*orgueil, prétentions*) to humble; (*Tricot*) to decrease; (*déduire*) to reduce ■ **se rabattre** VPR (*bords, couvercle*) to fall shut; (*véhicule, coureur*) to cut in; **se ~ sur** (*accepter*) to fall back on

rabattu, e [Rabaty] PP *de* **rabattre** ▸ ADJ turned down

rabbin [Rabɛ̃] NM rabbi

rabiot [Rabjo] NM = **rab**

rabique [Rabik] ADJ rabies cpd

râble [Rɑbl] NM back; (*Culin*) saddle

râblé, e [Rɑble] ADJ broad-backed, stocky

rabot [Rabo] NM plane

raboter [Rabɔte] /1/ vt to plane (down)

raboteux, -euse [Rabɔtø, -øz] ADJ uneven, rough

rabougri, e [Rabugri] ADJ stunted

rabrouer [Rabrue] /1/ vt to snub, rebuff

★**racaille** [Rakaj] NF (*péj*) rabble, riffraff

raccommodage [Rakɔmɔdaʒ] NM mending *no pl*, repairing *no pl*; darning *no pl*

raccommoder [Rakɔmɔde] /1/ vt to mend, repair; (*chaussette etc*) to darn; (*fam: réconcilier: amis, ménage*) to bring together again ■ **se raccommoder** VPR: **se ~ (avec)** (*fam*) to patch it up (with)

raccompagner [Rakɔ̃paɲe] /1/ vt to take ou see back

raccord [RakɔR] NM link; **~ de maçonnerie** pointing *no pl*; **~ de peinture** join; (*retouche*) touch-up

raccordement [Rakɔrdəmɑ̃] NM joining up; connection

raccorder [Rakɔrde] /1/ vt to join (up), link up; (*pont etc*) to connect, link; **~ au réseau du téléphone** to connect to the telephone service ■ **se raccorder à** VPR to join up with; (*fig: se rattacher à*) to tie in with

raccourci [Rakursi] NM short cut; **en ~** in brief

raccourcir [RakursiR] /2/ vt to shorten ▸ vi (*vêtement*) to shrink; (*jours*) to grow shorter, draw in

raccourcissement [Rakursismɑ̃] NM (*de durée, longueur*) shortening

raccroc [RakRo]: **par ~** *adv* by chance

★**raccrocher** [RakRoʃe] /1/ vt (*tableau, vêtement*) to hang back up; (*récepteur*) to put down; (*fig: affaire*) to save ▸ vi (*Tél*) to hang up, ring off; **ne raccrochez pas** (*Tél*) hold on, don't hang up ■ **se raccrocher à** VPR to cling to, hang on to

race [Ras] NF race; (*d'animaux, fig: espèce*) breed; (*ascendance, origine*) stock, race; **de ~** *adj* purebred, pedigree

racé, e [Rase] ADJ thoroughbred

rachat [Raʃa] NM buying; (*du même objet*) buying back; redemption; atonement

racheter [Raʃ(ə)te] /5/ vt (*article perdu*) to buy another; (*davantage*) to buy more; (*après avoir vendu*) to buy back; (*d'occasion*) to buy; (*Comm: part, firme*) to buy up; (*pension, rente*) to redeem; (*Rel: pécheur*) to redeem; (*péché*) to atone for, expiate; (*mauvaise conduite, oubli, défaut*) to make up for; **~ du lait/ trois œufs** to buy more milk/another three eggs ou three more eggs ■ **se racheter** VPR (*Rel*) to redeem o.s.; (*gén*) to make amends, make up for it

rachidien, ne [Raʃidjɛ̃, -jen] ADJ (*bulbe, canal*) spinal

rachitique [Raʃitik] ADJ suffering from rickets; (*fig*) scraggy, scrawny

rachitisme [Raʃitism] NM rickets *sg*

racial, e, -aux [Rasjal, -o] ADJ racial

racine [Rasin] NF root; (*fig: attache*) roots *pl*; **~ carrée/cubique** square/cube root; **prendre ~** (*fig*) to take root; to put down roots

★**racisme** [Rasism] NM racism

raciste [Rasist] ADJ, NMF racist

racket [Rakɛt] NM racketeering *no pl*

racketter [Rakete] vt to extort money from

racketteur, -euse [Rakɛtœr, -øz] NM/F racketeer

raclée [ʀɑkle] NF (fam) hiding, thrashing

raclement [ʀɑkləmɑ̃] NM (bruit) scraping (noise)

racler [ʀɑkle] /1/ VT (os, plat) to scrape; (tache, boue) to scrape off; (fig: instrument) to scrape on; (chose: frotter contre) to scrape (against); **se ~ la gorge** to clear one's throat

raclette [ʀɑklɛt] NF (Culin) raclette (Swiss cheese dish)

racloir [ʀɑklwaʀ] NM (outil) scraper

racolage [ʀakɔlaʒ] NM soliciting; touting

racoler [ʀakɔle] /1/ VT (attirer: prostituée) to solicit; (: parti, marchand) to tout for; (attraper) to pick up

racoleur, -euse [ʀakɔlœʀ, -øz] ADJ (péj) lurid ▸ NM (péj: de clients) tout ▸ NF streetwalker

racontars [ʀakɔ̃taʀ] NMPL stories, gossip sg

★**raconter** [ʀakɔ̃te] /1/ VT: **~ (à qn)** (décrire) to relate (to sb), tell (sb) about; (dire) to tell (sb); **~ une histoire** to tell a story

racorni, e [ʀakɔʀni] ADJ hard(ened)

racornir [ʀakɔʀniʀ] /2/ VT to harden

radar [ʀadaʀ] NM radar; **système ~** radar system; **écran ~** radar screen; **~ (automatique)** (Auto) speed camera

rade [ʀad] NF (natural) harbour; **en ~ de Toulon** in Toulon harbour; **rester en ~** (fig) to be left stranded

radeau, x [ʀado] NM raft; **~ de sauvetage** life raft

radial, e, -aux [ʀadjal, -o] ADJ radial

radiant, e [ʀadjɑ̃, -ɑ̃t] ADJ radiant

★**radiateur** [ʀadjatœʀ] NM radiator, heater; (Auto) radiator; **~ électrique/à gaz** electric/gas heater ou fire

radiation [ʀadjasjɔ̃] NF (d'un nom etc) striking off no pl; (Physique) radiation

radical, e, -aux [ʀadikal, -o] ADJ radical ▸ NM (Ling) stem; (Math) root sign; (Pol) radical

radicalement [ʀadikalmɑ̃] ADV radically, completely

radicalisation [ʀadikalizasjɔ̃] NF (durcissement) radicalization

radicaliser [ʀadikalize] /1/ VT (durcir: opinions etc) to harden ▪ **se radicaliser** VPR (mouvement etc) to become more radical

radicalisme [ʀadikalism] NM (Pol) radicalism

radier [ʀadje] /7/ VT to strike off

radiesthésie [ʀadjɛstezi] NF divination (by radiation)

radiesthésiste [ʀadjɛstezist] NMF diviner

radieux, -euse [ʀadjø, -øz] ADJ (visage, personne) radiant; (journée, soleil) brilliant, glorious

radin, e [ʀadɛ̃, -in] ADJ (fam) stingy (fam)

radinerie [ʀadinʀi] NF stinginess (fam)

★**radio** [ʀadjo] NF radio; (Méd) X-ray; **à la ~** on the radio; **avoir la ~** to have a radio; **passer à la ~** to be on the radio; **se faire faire une ~/une ~ des poumons** to have an X-ray/a chest X-ray ▸ NM (personne) radio operator

radio... [ʀadjo] PRÉFIXE radio...

radioactif, -ive [ʀadjoaktif, -iv] ADJ radioactive

radioactivité [ʀadjoaktivite] NF radioactivity

radioamateur [ʀadjoamatœʀ] NM (radio) ham

radiobalise [ʀadjobaliz] NF radio beacon

radiocassette [ʀadjokasɛt] NF cassette radio

radiodiffuser [ʀadjodifyze] /1/ VT to broadcast

radiodiffusion [ʀadjodifyzjɔ̃] NF (radio) broadcasting

radioélectrique [ʀadjoelɛktʀik] ADJ radio cpd

radiographie [ʀadjogʀafi] NF radiography; (photo) X-ray photograph, radiograph

radiographier [ʀadjogʀafje] /7/ VT to X-ray; **se faire ~** to have an X-ray

radioguidage [ʀadjogidaʒ] NM (Navig, Aviat) radio control; (Auto) (broadcast of) traffic information

radioguider [ʀadjogide] /1/ VT (Navig, Aviat) to guide by radio, control by radio

radiologie [ʀadjolɔʒi] NF radiology **radiologique** [ʀadjolɔʒik] ADJ radiological

radiologue [ʀadjolɔg] NMF radiologist

radiophare [ʀadjofaʀ] NM radio beacon

radiophonique [ʀadjofɔnik] ADJ radio cpd; **programme/émission/jeu ~** radio programme/broadcast/game

radioreportage [ʀadjoʀ(ə)pɔʀtaʒ] NM radio report

radio-réveil [ʀadjoʀevɛj] (pl **radios-réveils**) NM radio alarm (clock)

radioscopie [ʀadjoskɔpi] NF radioscopy

radio-taxi [ʀadjotaksi] NM radio taxi

radiotéléphone [ʀadjotelefɔn] NM radio telephone

radiotélescope [ʀadjotelɛskɔp] NM radio telescope

radiotélévisé, e [ʀadjotelevize] ADJ broadcast on radio and television

radiothérapie [ʀadjoteʀapi] NF radiotherapy

radis [ʀadi] NM radish; **~ noir** black radish

radium [ʀadjɔm] NM radium

radius [ʀadjys] NM (Anat) radius

radoter [ʀadɔte] /1/ VI to ramble on

radoub [ʀadu] NM: **bassin** ou **cale de ~** dry dock

radouber [ʀadube] /1/ VT to repair, refit

radoucir [ʀadusiʀ] /2/: **se radoucir** VPR (se réchauffer) to become milder; (se calmer) to calm down; to soften

radoucissement [ʀadusismɑ̃] NM milder period, better weather

rafale [ʀafal] NF (vent) gust (of wind); (de balles, d'applaudissements) burst; **~ de mitrailleuse** burst of machine-gun fire

raffermir [ʀafɛʀmiʀ] /2/ VT (tissus, muscle) to firm up; (fig) to strengthen ▪ **se raffermir** VPR (tissus, muscle) to firm up; (fig) to strengthen

raffermissement [ʀafɛʀmismɑ̃] NM (fig) strengthening

raffinage [ʀafinaʒ] NM refining

raffiné, e [ʀafine] ADJ refined

raffinement [ʀafinmɑ̃] NM refinement

raffiner [ʀafine] /1/ VT to refine

raffinerie [ʀafinʀi] NF refinery

raffoler [ʀafɔle] /1/: **~ de** vt to be very keen on

raffut [ʀafy] NM (fam) row, racket

rafiot [ʀafjo] NM tub

r

365

rafistolage [Rafistɔlaʒ] NM (fam) patching up, makeshift repair

rafistoler [Rafistɔle] /1/ VT (fam) to patch up

rafle [Rɑfl] NF (de police) roundup, raid

rafler [Rɑfle] /1/ VT (fam) to swipe, nick

rafraîchir [RafReʃiR] /2/ VT (atmosphère, température) to cool (down); (boisson) to chill; (air, eau) to freshen up; (fig: rénover) to brighten up; **~ la mémoire à qn** to refresh sb's memory ▸ VI: **mettre du vin/une boisson à ~** to chill wine/a drink ■ **se rafraîchir** VPR to grow cooler; (personne: en se lavant) to freshen up; (en buvant etc) to refresh o.s.

rafraîchissant, e [RafReʃisɑ̃, -ɑ̃t] ADJ refreshing

rafraîchissement [RafReʃismɑ̃] NM cooling; (boisson) cool drink ■ **rafraîchissements** NMPL (boissons, fruits etc) refreshments

ragaillardir [Ragajardir] /2/ VT (fam) to perk ou buck up

rage [Raʒ] NF (Méd): **la ~** rabies; (fureur) rage, fury; **faire ~** to rage; **~ de dents** (raging) toothache

rageant, e [Raʒɑ̃, -ɑ̃t] ADJ infuriating

rager [Raʒe] /3/ VI to fume (with rage); **faire ~ qn** to enrage sb, make sb furious

rageur, -euse [Raʒœr, -øz] ADJ raging, fuming; ill-tempered

rageusement [Raʒøzmɑ̃] ADV furiously

raglan [Raglɑ̃] ADJ INV raglan

ragot [Rago] NM (fam) malicious gossip no pl

ragoût [Ragu] NM (plat) stew

ragoûtant, e [Ragutɑ̃, -ɑ̃t] ADJ: **peu ~** unpalatable

rai [Rɛ] NM: **un ~ de soleil/lumière** a shaft of sunlight/light

raï [Raj] NM Raï music

raid [Rɛd] NM (Mil) raid; (attaque aérienne) air raid; (Sport) long-distance trek

★**raide** [Rɛd] ADJ (tendu) taut, tight; (escarpé) steep; (droit: cheveux) straight; (ankylosé, dur, guindé) stiff; (fam: cher) steep, stiff; (: sans argent) flat broke ▸ ADV (en pente) steeply; **~ mort** stone dead

raideur [Rɛdœr] NF steepness; (rigidité) stiffness; **avec ~** (répondre) stiffly, abruptly

raidillon [Redijɔ̃] NM steep path

raidir [Redir] /2/ VT (muscles) to stiffen; (câble) to pull taut, tighten ■ **se raidir** VPR to stiffen; to become taut; (personne: se crisper) to tense up; (: se préparer moralement) to brace o.s.; (fig: devenir intransigeant) to harden

raidissement [Redismɑ̃] NM stiffening; tightening; hardening

raie [Rɛ] NF (Zool) skate, ray; (rayure) stripe; (des cheveux) parting

raifort [Refɔr] NM horseradish

rail [Rɑj] NM (barre d'acier) rail; (chemins de fer) railways pl (BRIT), railroads pl (US); **les rails** (la voie ferrée) the rails, the track sg; **par ~** by rail; **~ conducteur** live ou conductor rail

railler [Raje] /1/ VT to scoff at, jeer at

raillerie [Rajri] NF mockery

railleur, -euse [Rajœr, -øz] ADJ mocking

rail-route [Rajrut] (pl **rails-routes**) NM road-rail

rainurage [Renyraʒ] NM (Auto) uneven road surface

rainure [Renyr] NF groove; slot

rais [Rɛ] NM INV = **rai**

★**raisin** [Rezɛ̃] NM (aussi: **raisins**) grapes pl; (variété): **~ blanc/noir** white (ou green)/black grape; **~ muscat** muscat grape; **raisins secs** raisins

★**raison** [Rezɔ̃] NF reason; **avoir ~** to be right; **donner ~ à qn** (personne) to agree with sb; (fait) to prove sb right; **avoir ~ de qn/qch** to get the better of sb/sth; **se faire une ~** to learn to live with it; **perdre la ~** to become insane; (fig) to take leave of one's senses; **recouvrer la ~** to come to one's senses; **ramener qn à la ~** to make sb see sense; **demander ~ à qn de** (affront etc) to demand satisfaction from sb for; **entendre ~** to listen to reason, see reason; **plus que de ~** too much, more than is reasonable; **~ de plus** all the more reason; **à plus forte ~** all the more so; **sans ~** for no reason; **en ~ de** (à cause de) because of; (à proportion de) in proportion to; **à ~ de** at the rate of; **~ d'État** reason of state; **~ d'être** raison d'être; **~ sociale** corporate name

raisonnable [Rezɔnabl] ADJ reasonable, sensible

raisonnablement [Rezɔnabləmɑ̃] ADV reasonably

raisonné, e [Rezɔne] ADJ reasoned

raisonnement [Rezɔnmɑ̃] NM reasoning; arguing; argument

raisonner [Rezɔne] /1/ VI (penser) to reason; (argumenter, discuter) to argue ▸ VT (personne) to reason with; (attitude: justifier) to reason out ■ **se raisonner** VPR to reason with oneself

raisonneur, -euse [Rezɔnœr, -øz] ADJ (péj) quibbling

rajeunir [Raʒœnir] /2/ VT (cure) to rejuvenate; (fig: rafraîchir) to brighten up; (: moderniser) to give a new look to; (: en recrutant) to inject new blood into; **~ qn** (coiffure, robe) to make sb look younger ▸ VI (personne) to feel (ou look) younger; (entreprise, quartier) to be modernized

rajeunissement [Raʒœnismɑ̃] NM (de population, effectifs): **des mesures gouvernementales en faveur du ~ des effectifs** government measures to bring down the average age of the workforce; (personne, aspect) rejuvenation; **méthodes de ~ de la peau** ways of rejuvenating one's skin

rajout [Raʒu] NM addition

rajouter [Raʒute] /1/ VT (commentaire) to add; **~ du sel/un œuf** to add some more salt/another egg; **~ que** to add that; **en ~** to lay it on thick

rajustement [Raʒystəmɑ̃] NM adjustment

rajuster [Raʒyste] /1/ VT (vêtement) to straighten, tidy; (salaires) to adjust; (machine) to readjust ■ **se rajuster** VPR to tidy ou straighten o.s. up

râle [Rɑl] NM groan; **~ d'agonie** death rattle

ralenti [Ralɑ̃ti] NM: **au ~** (Ciné) in slow motion; (fig) at a slower pace; **tourner au ~** (Auto) to tick over, idle

★**ralentir** [Ralɑ̃tir] /2/ VT, VI to slow down ■ **se ralentir** VPR to slow down

ralentissement [Ralɑ̃tismɑ̃] NM slowing down

ralentisseur [Ralɑ̃tisœr] NM speed bump

râler [Rɑle] /1/ VI to groan; (fam) to grouse, moan (and groan)

râleur, -euse [ʀɑlœʀ, -øz] *(fam)* NM/F moaner
▶ ADJ: **être ~** to be a moaner

ralliement [ʀalimɑ̃] NM *(rassemblement)* rallying; *(adhésion: à une cause, une opinion)* winning over; **point/signe de ~** rallying point/sign

rallier [ʀalje] **/7/** VT *(rassembler)* to rally; *(rejoindre)* to rejoin; *(gagner à sa cause)* to win over ■ **se rallier à** VPR *(avis)* to come over ou round to

rallonge [ʀalɔ̃ʒ] NF *(de table)* (extra) leaf; *(Élec)* extension (cable ou flex); *(fig: de crédit)* extension; *(argent)* extra *no pl*

rallongement [ʀalɔ̃ʒmɑ̃] NM *(de durée, piste)* extension

rallonger [ʀalɔ̃ʒe] **/3/** VT to lengthen

rallumer [ʀalyme] **/1/** VT to light up again, relight; *(fig)* to revive ■ **se rallumer** VPR *(lumière)* to come on again

rallye [ʀali] NM rally; *(Pol)* march

ramadan [ʀamadɑ̃] NM Ramadan; **faire le ~** to observe Ramadan

ramages [ʀamaʒ] NMPL *(dessin)* leaf pattern *sg*; *(chants)* songs

ramassage [ʀamasaʒ] NM: **~ scolaire** school bus service

ramassé, e [ʀamase] ADJ *(trapu)* squat, stocky; *(concis: expression etc)* compact

ramasse-miettes [ʀamasmjɛt] NM INV table-tidy

ramasse-monnaie [ʀamasmɔnɛ] NM INV change-tray

★**ramasser** [ʀamase] **/1/** VT *(objet tombé ou par terre)* to pick up; *(recueillir: copies, ordures)* to collect; *(récolter)* to gather; *(: pommes de terre)* to lift ■ **se ramasser** VPR *(sur soi-même)* to huddle up; to crouch

ramasseur, -euse [ʀamasœʀ, -øz] NM/F: **~ de balles** ball boy *(ou girl)*

ramassis [ʀamasi] NM *(péj: de voyous)* bunch; *(: de choses)* jumble

rambarde [ʀɑ̃baʀd] NF guardrail

rame [ʀam] NF *(aviron)* oar; *(de métro)* train; *(de papier)* ream; **~ de haricots** bean support; **faire force de rames** to row hard

rameau, X [ʀamo] NM (small) branch; *(fig)* branch; **les Rameaux** *(Rel)* Palm Sunday *sg*

ramener [ʀam(ə)ne] **/5/** VT to bring back; *(reconduire)* to take back; **~ qch sur** *(rabattre: couverture, visière)* to pull sth back over; **~ qch à** *(réduire à, Math)* to reduce sth to; **~ qn à la vie/raison** to bring sb back to life/bring sb to his *(ou her)* senses ■ **se ramener** VPR *(fam)* to roll ou turn up; **se ~ à** *(se réduire à)* to come ou boil down to

ramequin [ʀamkɛ̃] NM ramekin

★**ramer** [ʀame] **/1/** VI to row

rameur, -euse [ʀamœʀ, -øz] NM/F rower

rameuter [ʀamøte] **/1/** VT to gather together

ramier [ʀamje] NM: **(pigeon) ~** woodpigeon

ramification [ʀamifikasjɔ̃] NF ramification

ramifié, e [ʀamifje] ADJ *(organisation, réseau)*: **un réseau d'agences fortement ~** a network of agencies with many branches; *(tige)* branched; **un arbre très ~** a tree with many branches

ramifier [ʀamifje] **/7/**: **se ramifier** VPR: **se ~ (en)** *(tige, secte, réseau)* to branch out (into); *(veines, nerfs)* to ramify

ramolli, e [ʀamɔli] ADJ soft

ramollir [ʀamɔliʀ] **/2/** VT to soften ■ **se ramollir** VPR *(os, tissus)* to get ou go soft; *(beurre, asphalte)* to soften

ramollissement [ʀamɔlismɑ̃] NM *(d'os, beurre, asphalte)* softening; *(fig: de croissance)* slowdown

ramonage [ʀamɔnaʒ] NM (chimney-)sweeping

ramoner [ʀamɔne] **/1/** VT *(cheminée)* to sweep; *(pipe)* to clean

ramoneur [ʀamɔnœʀ] NM (chimney) sweep

rampe [ʀɑ̃p] NF *(d'escalier)* banister(s *pl*); *(dans un garage, d'un terrain)* ramp; *(lampes: lumineuse, de balisage)* floodlights *pl*; **la ~** *(Théât)* the footlights *pl*; **passer la ~** *(toucher le public)* to get across to the audience; **~ de lancement** launching pad

ramper [ʀɑ̃pe] **/1/** VI *(reptile, animal)* to crawl; *(plante)* to creep

rancard [ʀɑ̃kaʀ] NM *(fam: rendez-vous)* date; *(: renseignement)* tip

rancarder [ʀɑ̃kaʀde] *(fam)* VT to give information to ■ **se rancarder** VPR to find out (about)

rancart [ʀɑ̃kaʀ] NM: **mettre au ~** *(article, projet)* to scrap; *(personne)* to put on the scrapheap

rance [ʀɑ̃s] ADJ rancid

rancir [ʀɑ̃siʀ] **/2/** VI to go off, go rancid

rancœur [ʀɑ̃kœʀ] NF rancour *(Brit)*, rancor *(US)*, resentment

rançon [ʀɑ̃sɔ̃] NF ransom; **la ~ du succès** *etc (fig)* the price of success *etc*

rançonner [ʀɑ̃sɔne] **/1/** VT to hold to ransom

rancune [ʀɑ̃kyn] NF grudge, rancour *(Brit)*, rancor *(US)*; **garder ~ à qn (de qch)** to bear sb a grudge (for sth); **sans ~!** no hard feelings!

rancunier, -ière [ʀɑ̃kynje, -jɛʀ] ADJ vindictive, spiteful

randonnée [ʀɑ̃dɔne] NF ride; *(à pied)* walk, ramble; *(en montagne)* hike; **la ~** *(activité)* hiking, walking; **une ~ à cheval** a horse ride

randonneur, -euse [ʀɑ̃dɔnœʀ, -øz] NM/F hiker

rang [ʀɑ̃] NM *(rangée)* row; *(de perles)* row, string, rope; *(grade, condition sociale, classement)* rank; **se mettre en rangs/sur un ~** to get into ou form rows/a line; **sur trois rangs** (lined up) three deep; **se mettre en rangs par quatre** to form fours ou rows of four; **au premier ~** in the first row; *(fig)* ranking first; **rentrer dans le ~** to get into line; **au ~ de** *(au nombre de)* among (the ranks of); **avoir ~ de** to hold the rank of ■ **rangs** NMPL *(Mil)* ranks; **se mettre sur les rangs** *(fig)* to get into the running

rangé, e [ʀɑ̃ʒe] ADJ *(vie)* well-ordered; *(personne)* orderly, steady ▶ NF row

rangement [ʀɑ̃ʒmɑ̃] NM tidying-up, putting-away; **faire des rangements** to tidy up

★**ranger** [ʀɑ̃ʒe] **/3/** VT *(classer, grouper)* to order, arrange; *(mettre à sa place)* to put away; *(voiture dans la rue)* to park; *(mettre de l'ordre dans)* to tidy up; *(arranger, disposer: en cercle etc)* to arrange; **~ qn/qch parmi** *(fig: classer)* to rank sb/sth among ■ **se ranger** VPR *(se placer, se disposer: autour d'une table etc)* to take one's place, sit round; *(véhicule, conducteur)* s'écarter) to pull over ou in; *(: s'arrêter)* to pull in; *(piéton)* to step aside; *(s'assagir)* to settle down; **se ~ à** *(avis)* to come round to, fall in with

ranimer [ʀanime] /1/ VT (*personne évanouie*) to bring round; (*revigorer: forces, courage*) to restore; (*réconforter: troupes etc*) to kindle new life in; (*douleur, souvenir*) to revive; (*feu*) to rekindle

rap [ʀap] NM rap (music)

rapace [ʀapas] NM bird of prey; ~ **diurne/nocturne** diurnal/nocturnal bird of prey ▸ ADJ (*péj*) rapacious, grasping

rapacité [ʀapasite] NF rapacity, greed

rapatrié, e [ʀapatʀije] NM/F repatriate (*esp French North African settler*)

rapatriement [ʀapatʀimɑ̃] NM repatriation

rapatrier [ʀapatʀije] /7/ VT to repatriate; (*capitaux*) to bring (back) into the country

râpe [ʀɑp] NF (*Culin*) grater; (*à bois*) rasp

râpé, e [ʀɑpe] ADJ (*tissu*) threadbare; (*Culin*) grated

râper [ʀɑpe] /1/ VT (*Culin*) to grate; (*gratter, râcler*) to rasp

rapetasser [ʀap(ə)tase] /1/ VT (*fam*) to patch up

rapetisser [ʀap(ə)tise] /1/ VT: ~ **qch** to shorten sth; to make sth look smaller ▸ VI to shrink

râpeux, -euse [ʀɑpø, -øz] ADJ rough

raphia [ʀafja] NM raffia

★**rapide** [ʀapid] ADJ fast; (*prompt: intelligence, coup d'œil, mouvement*) quick ▸ NM express (train); (*de cours d'eau*) rapid

★**rapidement** [ʀapidmɑ̃] ADV fast; quickly

rapidité [ʀapidite] NF speed; quickness

rapiécer [ʀapjese] /3, 6/ VT to patch

rapine [ʀapin] NF (*vol*) stealing, theft; (: *en temps de guerre*) plundering; **vivre de ~** (*vagabond, délinquant*) to steal for a living; (*bande armée*) to live by plundering

rappel [ʀapel] NM (*d'un ambassadeur, Mil*) recall; (*Théât*) curtain call; (*Méd: vaccination*) booster; (*Admin: de salaire*) back pay *no pl*; (*d'une aventure, d'un nom*) reminder; (*de limitation de vitesse: sur écriteau*) speed limit sign (*reminder*); (*Tech*) return; (*Navig*) sitting out; (*Alpinisme: aussi:* **rappel de corde**) abseiling *no pl*, roping down *no pl*; abseil; ~ **à l'ordre** call to order

★**rappeler** [ʀap(ə)le] /4/ VT (*pour faire revenir, retéléphoner*) to call back; (*ambassadeur, Mil*) to recall; (*acteur*) to call back (onto the stage); (*faire se souvenir*): ~ **qch à qn** to remind sb of sth; ~ **qn à la vie** to bring sb back to life; **ça rappelle la Provence** it's reminiscent of Provence, it reminds you of Provence ∎ **se rappeler** VPR (*se souvenir de*) to remember, recall; **se ~ que...** to remember that...

rappelle *etc* [ʀapel] VB *voir* **rappeler**

rappeur, -euse [ʀapœʀ, -øz] NM/F rapper

rappliquer [ʀaplike] /1/ VI (*fam*) to turn up

rapport [ʀapɔʀ] NM (*compte rendu*) report; (*profit*) yield, return; revenue; (*lien, analogie*) relationship; (*corrélation*) connection; (*proportion: Math, Tech*) ratio; **avoir ~ à** to have something to do with, concern; **être en ~ avec** (*corrélation*) to be related to; **être/se mettre en ~ avec qn** to be/get in touch with sb; **par ~ à** (*comparé à*) in relation to; (*à propos de*) with regard to; **sous le ~ de** from the point of view of; ~ **qualité-prix** value (for money) ∎ **rapports** NMPL (*entre personnes, pays*) relations; **sous tous (les) rapports** in all respects; **rapports (sexuels)** (sexual) intercourse *sg*

rapporté, e [ʀapɔʀte] ADJ: **pièce rapportée** (*Couture*) patch

rapporter [ʀapɔʀte] /1/ VT (*rendre, ramener*) to bring back; (*apporter davantage*) to bring more; (*Couture*) to sew on; (*investissement*) to yield; (: *activité*) to bring in; (*relater*) to report; (*Jur: annuler*) to revoke; ~ **qch à** (*fig: rattacher*) to relate sth to ▸ VI (*investissement*) to give a good return *ou* yield; (*activité*) to be very profitable; (*péj: moucharder*) to tell ∎ **se rapporter à** VPR (*correspondre à*) to relate to; **s'en ~ à** to rely on

rapporteur, -euse [ʀapɔʀtœʀ, -øz] NM/F (*de procès, commission*) reporter; (*péj*) telltale ▸ NM (*Géom*) protractor

rapproché, e [ʀapʀɔʃe] ADJ (*proche*) near, close at hand; **rapprochés** (*l'un de l'autre*) at close intervals

rapprochement [ʀapʀɔʃmɑ̃] NM (*réconciliation: de nations, familles*) reconciliation; (*analogie, rapport*) parallel

rapprocher [ʀapʀɔʃe] /1/ VT (*deux objets*) to bring closer together; (*réunir: ennemis, partis etc*) to bring together; (*comparer*) to establish a parallel between; (*chaise d'une table*): ~ **qch (de)** to bring sth closer (to) ∎ **se rapprocher** VPR to draw closer *ou* nearer; (*fig: familles, pays*) to come together; to come closer together; **se ~ de** to come closer to; (*présenter une analogie avec*) to be close to

rapt [ʀapt] NM abduction

raquette [ʀaket] NF (*de tennis*) racket; (*de ping-pong*) bat; (*à neige*) snowshoe

★**rare** [ʀɑʀ] ADJ rare; (*main-d'œuvre, denrées*) scarce; (*cheveux, herbe*) sparse; **il est ~ que** it's rare that, it's unusual that; **se faire ~** to become scarce; (*fig: personne*) to make oneself scarce

raréfaction [ʀaʀefaksjɔ̃] NF scarcity; (*de l'air*) rarefaction

raréfier [ʀaʀefje] /7/: **se raréfier** VPR to grow scarce; (*air*) to rarefy

★**rarement** [ʀaʀmɑ̃] ADV rarely, seldom

rareté [ʀaʀte] NF rarity; scarcity

rarissime [ʀaʀisim] ADJ extremely rare

RAS ABR = **rien à signaler**

ras, e [ʀɑ, ʀɑz] ADJ (*tête, cheveux*) close-cropped; (*poil, herbe*) short; (*mesure, cuillère*) level; **faire table rase** to make a clean sweep; **en rase campagne** in open country; **à ~ bords** to the brim; **au ~ de** level with; **~ du cou** *adj* (*pull, robe*) crew-neck ▸ ADV (*couper*) short; **en avoir ~ le bol** (*fam*) to be fed up

rasade [ʀazad] NF glassful

rasant, e [ʀazɑ̃, -ɑ̃t] ADJ (*Mil: balle, tir*) grazing; (*fam*) boring

rascasse [ʀaskas] NF (*Zool*) scorpion fish

rasé, e [ʀaze] ADJ: ~ **de frais** freshly shaven; ~ **de près** close-shaven

rase-mottes [ʀazmɔt] NM INV: **faire du ~** to hedgehop; **vol en ~** hedgehopping

★**raser** [ʀaze] /1/ VT (*barbe, cheveux*) to shave off; (*menton, personne*) to shave; (*fam: ennuyer*) to bore; (*démolir*) to raze (to the ground); (*frôler*) to graze, skim ∎ **se raser** VPR to shave; (*fam*) to be bored (to tears)

★**rasoir** [ʀazwaʀ] NM razor; ~ **électrique** electric shaver *ou* razor; ~ **mécanique** *ou* **de sûreté** safety razor

rassasié, e [ʀasazje] ADJ (*repu: personne*) full, satisfied; (*fig: curiosité, désir*) satisfied; **être ~** to be full, have eaten one's fill ▶ PP de **rassasier**

rassasier [ʀasazje] /**7**/ VT to satisfy ■ **se rassasier** VPR to eat one's fill; **se ~ de qch** to eat one's fill of sth

rassemblement [ʀasɑ̃bləmɑ̃] NM (*groupe*) gathering; (*Pol*) union; association; (*Mil*): **le ~** parade

rassembler [ʀasɑ̃ble] /**1**/ VT (*réunir*) to assemble, gather; (*regrouper, amasser: documents, notes*) to gather together, collect; **~ ses idées/ses esprits/son courage** to collect one's thoughts/gather one's wits/screw up one's courage ■ **se rassembler** VPR to gather

rasseoir [ʀaswaʀ] /**26**/: **se rasseoir** VPR to sit back down, to sit down again

rasséréné, e [ʀaseʀene] ADJ (*personne*) calm, calmer

rasséréner [ʀaseʀene] VT (*personne*) to calm down ■ **se rasséréner** VPR to calm down

rassir [ʀasiʀ] /**2**/ VI to go stale

rassis, e [ʀasi, -iz] ADJ (*pain*) stale

rassurant, e [ʀasyʀɑ̃, -ɑ̃t] ADJ (*nouvelles etc*) reassuring

rassuré, e [ʀasyʀe] ADJ: **ne pas être très ~** to be rather ill at ease

rassurer [ʀasyʀe] /**1**/ VT to reassure ■ **se rassurer** VPR to be reassured; **rassure-toi** don't worry

rat [ʀa] NM rat; **~ d'hôtel** hotel thief; **~ musqué** muskrat

ratage [ʀataʒ] NM failure

ratatiné, e [ʀatatine] ADJ (*pomme*) shrivelled (up); (*personne*) wrinkled

ratatiner [ʀatatine] /**1**/ VT to shrivel; (*peau*) to wrinkle ■ **se ratatiner** VPR to shrivel; to become wrinkled

ratatouille [ʀatatuj] NF (*Culin*) ratatouille

rate [ʀat] NF female rat; (*Anat*) spleen

raté, e [ʀate] ADJ (*tentative*) unsuccessful, failed ▶ NM/F (*fam: personne*) failure ▶ NM misfiring *no pl*

râteau, x [ʀɑto] NM rake

râtelier [ʀɑtəlje] NM rack; (*fam*) false teeth *pl*

★**rater** [ʀate] /**1**/ VI (*ne pas partir: coup de feu*) to fail to go off; (*affaire, projet etc*) to go wrong, fail ▶ VT (*cible, train, occasion*) to miss; (*démonstration, plat*) to spoil; (*examen*) to fail; **~ son coup** to fail, not to bring it off

raticide [ʀatisid] NM rat poison

ratification [ʀatifikasjɔ̃] NF ratification

ratifier [ʀatifje] /**7**/ VT to ratify

ratio [ʀasjo] NM ratio

ration [ʀasjɔ̃] NF ration; (*fig*) share; **~ alimentaire** food intake

rationalisation [ʀasjɔnalizasjɔ̃] NF rationalization

rationaliser [ʀasjɔnalize] /**1**/ VT to rationalize

rationalité [ʀasjɔnalite] NF rationality

rationnel, le [ʀasjɔnɛl] ADJ rational

rationnellement [ʀasjɔnɛlmɑ̃] ADV rationally

rationnement [ʀasjɔnmɑ̃] NM rationing; **ticket de ~** ration coupon

rationner [ʀasjɔne] /**1**/ VT to ration; (*personne*) to put on rations ■ **se rationner** VPR to ration o.s.

ratisser [ʀatise] /**1**/ VT (*allée*) to rake; (*feuilles*) to rake up; (*armée, police*) to comb; **~ large** to cast one's net wide

raton [ʀatɔ̃] NM: **~ laveur** raccoon

RATP SIGLE F (= *Régie autonome des transports parisiens*) Paris transport authority

rattachement [ʀataʃmɑ̃] NM (*de territoire*) incorporation; (*Admin: d'employé, personnel*) attachment

rattacher [ʀataʃe] /**1**/ VT (*animal, cheveux*) to tie up again; **~ qch à** to join sth to, unite sth with; **~ qn à** to tie sb to ■ **se rattacher: se ~ à** (*avoir un lien avec*) to be linked *ou* connected with

rattrapage [ʀatʀapaʒ] NM (*Scol*) remedial classes *pl*; (*Écon*) catching up

rattraper [ʀatʀape] /**1**/ VT (*fugitif*) to recapture; (*retenir, empêcher de tomber*) to catch (hold of); (*atteindre, rejoindre*) to catch up with; (*réparer: erreur*) to make up for; **~ son retard/le temps perdu** to make up (for) lost time ■ **se rattraper** VPR (*regagner: du temps*) to make up for lost time; (: *de l'argent etc*) to make good one's losses; (*réparer une gaffe etc*) to make up for it; **se ~ (à)** (*se raccrocher*) to stop o.s. falling (by catching hold of)

rature [ʀatyʀ] NF deletion, erasure

raturer [ʀatyʀe] /**1**/ VT to cross out, delete, erase

rauque [ʀok] ADJ raucous; (*voix*) hoarse

ravagé, e [ʀavaʒe] ADJ (*visage*) harrowed

ravager [ʀavaʒe] /**3**/ VT to devastate, ravage

ravages [ʀavaʒ] NMPL ravages; **faire des ~** to wreak havoc; (*fig: séducteur*) to break hearts

ravageur, euse [ʀavaʒœʀ, -øz] ADJ (*destructeur*) destructive; (*fig: humour*) scathing; (: *sourire*) devastating

ravalement [ʀavalmɑ̃] NM restoration

ravaler [ʀavale] /**1**/ VT (*mur, façade*) to restore; (*déprécier*) to lower; (*avaler de nouveau*) to swallow again; **~ sa colère/son dégoût** to stifle one's anger/swallow one's distaste

ravaudage [ʀavodaʒ] NM (*de chaussettes*) mending

ravauder [ʀavode] /**1**/ VT to repair, mend

rave [ʀav] NF (*Bot*) root vegetable

raveur, -euse [ʀɛvœʀ, -øz] NM/F raver

ravi, e [ʀavi] ADJ delighted; **être ~ de/que** to be delighted with/that

ravier [ʀavje] NM hors d'œuvre dish

ravigote [ʀavigɔt] ADJ: **sauce ~** oil and vinegar dressing with shallots

ravigoter [ʀavigɔte] /**1**/ VT (*fam*) to buck up

ravin [ʀavɛ̃] NM gully, ravine

ravine [ʀavin] NF gully

raviner [ʀavine] /**1**/ VT to furrow, gully

raviolis [ʀavjɔli] NMPL ravioli *sg*

ravir [ʀaviʀ] /**2**/ VT (*enchanter*) to delight; (*enlever*): **~ qch à qn** to rob sb of sth; **à ~** *adv* delightfully, beautifully; **être beau à ~** to be ravishingly beautiful

raviser [ʀavize] /**1**/: **se raviser** VPR to change one's mind

ravissant, e [ʀavisɑ̃, -ɑ̃t] ADJ delightful

ravissement [ʀavismɑ̃] NM (*enchantement, délice*) rapture

r

369

ravisseur, -euse [ʀavisœʀ, -øz] NM/F abductor, kidnapper

ravitaillement [ʀavitɑjmɑ̃] NM resupplying; refuelling; (*provisions*) supplies *pl*; **aller au ~** to go for fresh supplies; **~ en vol** (*Aviat*) in-flight refuelling

ravitailler [ʀavitaje] /1/ VT (*en vivres, munitions*) to provide with fresh supplies; (*véhicule*) to refuel ■ **se ravitailler** VPR to get fresh supplies

raviver [ʀavive] /1/ VT (*feu*) to rekindle, revive; (*douleur*) to revive; (*couleurs*) to brighten up

ravoir [ʀavwaʀ] /34/ VT to get back

rayé, e [ʀeje] ADJ (*à rayures*) striped; (*éraflé*) scratched

rayer [ʀeje] /8/ VT (*érafler*) to scratch; (*barrer*) to cross *ou* score out; (*d'une liste: radier*) to cross *ou* strike off

★**rayon** [ʀɛjɔ̃] NM (*de soleil etc*) ray; (*Géom*) radius; (*de roue*) spoke; (*étagère*) shelf; (*de grand magasin*) department; (*fig: domaine*) responsibility, concern; (*de ruche*) (honey)comb; **dans un ~ de** within a radius of; **~ d'action** range; **~ de braquage** (*Auto*) turning circle; **~ laser** laser beam; **~ de soleil** sunbeam, ray of sunlight *ou* sunshine ■ **rayons** NMPL (*radiothérapie*) radiation; **rayons X** X-rays

rayonnage [ʀɛjɔnaʒ] NM set of shelves

rayonnant, e [ʀɛjɔnɑ̃, -ɑ̃t] ADJ radiant

rayonne [ʀɛjɔn] NF rayon

rayonnement [ʀɛjɔnmɑ̃] NM radiation; (*fig: éclat*) radiance; (*influence: d'une culture*) influence

rayonner [ʀɛjɔne] /1/ VI (*chaleur, énergie*) to radiate; (*fig: émotion*) to shine forth; (*: visage, personne*) to be radiant; (*avenues, axes*) to radiate; (*touriste*) to go touring (*from one base*)

rayure [ʀejyʀ] NF (*motif*) stripe; (*éraflure*) scratch; (*rainure, d'un fusil*) groove; **à rayures** striped

raz-de-marée [ʀɑdmaʀe] NM INV tidal wave

razzia [ʀazja] NF raid, foray

RBE SIGLE M (= *revenu brut d'exploitation*) gross profit (*of a farm*)

R-D SIGLE F (= *Recherche-Développement*) R & D

RDA SIGLE F (*Hist*: = *République démocratique allemande*) GDR

RDB SIGLE M (= *revenu disponible brut*) total disposable income

rdc ABR = **rez-de-chaussée**

ré [ʀe] NM (*Mus*) D; (*en chantant la gamme*) re

réabonnement [ʀeabɔnmɑ̃] NM renewal of subscription

réabonner [ʀeabɔne] /1/ VT: **~ qn (à)** to renew sb's subscription (to) ■ **se réabonner** VPR: **se ~ (à)** to renew one's subscription (to)

réac [ʀeak] ADJ, NMF (*fam*: = *réactionnaire*) reactionary

réacteur [ʀeaktœʀ] NM jet engine; **~ nucléaire** nuclear reactor

réactif [ʀeaktif] NM reagent

réaction [ʀeaksjɔ̃] NF reaction; **par ~** jet-propelled; **avion/moteur à ~** jet (plane)/jet engine; **~ en chaîne** chain reaction

réactionnaire [ʀeaksjɔnɛʀ] ADJ, NMF reactionary

réactiver [ʀeaktive] VT (*relancer: marché, controverse*) to revive; (*: projet*) to restart; (*machine, compte*) to reactivate

réactivité [ʀeaktivite] NF (*Physique, Chimie: de métaux*) reactivity; (*capacité à réagir*) responsiveness

réactualiser [ʀeaktɥalize] /1/ VT to update, bring up to date

réadaptation [ʀeadaptasjɔ̃] NF readjustment; (*Méd*) rehabilitation

réadapter [ʀeadapte] /1/ VT to readjust; (*Méd*) to rehabilitate ■ **se réadapter (à)** VPR to readjust (to)

réaffirmation [ʀeafiʀmasjɔ̃] NF reaffirmation

réaffirmer [ʀeafiʀme] /1/ VT to reaffirm, reassert

réagir [ʀeaʒiʀ] /2/ VI to react

réajuster [ʀeaʒyste] /1/ VT = **rajuster**

réalisable [ʀealizabl] ADJ (*projet, plan*) feasible; (*Comm: valeur*) realizable

réalisateur, -trice [ʀealizatœʀ, -tʀis] NM/F (*TV, Ciné*) director

réalisation [ʀealizasjɔ̃] NF carrying out; realization; fulfilment; achievement; (*TV, Ciné*) production; (*œuvre*) production, work; (*création*) creation; **en cours de ~** under way

réaliser [ʀealize] /1/ VT (*projet, opération*) to carry out, realize; (*rêve, souhait*) to realize, fulfil; (*exploit*) to achieve; (*achat, vente*) to make; (*TV, Ciné*) to produce; (*se rendre compte de, Comm: bien, capital*) to realize ■ **se réaliser** VPR to be realized

réalisme [ʀealism] NM realism

réaliste [ʀealist] ADJ realistic; (*peintre, roman*) realist ▶ NMF realist

réalité [ʀealite] NF reality; **en ~** in (actual) fact; **dans la ~** in reality; **~ augmentée** augmented reality; **~ virtuelle** virtual reality

réaménager [ʀeamenaʒe] VT (*lieu*) to refurbish; (*horaires, calendrier*) to reorganize; (*règlement, texte*) to rework

réanimation [ʀeanimasjɔ̃] NF (*Méd*) resuscitation; **service de ~** intensive care unit

réanimer [ʀeanime] /1/ VT (*Méd*) to resuscitate

réapparaître [ʀeapaʀɛtʀ] /57/ VI to reappear

réapparition [ʀeapaʀisjɔ̃] NF reappearance

réappropriation [ʀeapʀɔpʀijasjɔ̃] NF (*objet*) recovery, reappropriation; (*fig: de patrimoine*) taking back; (*: de mémoire*) recovery

réapprovisionner [ʀeapʀɔvizjɔne] /1/ VT (*magasin*) to restock ■ **se réapprovisionner** VPR: **se ~ (en)** to restock (with)

réarmement [ʀeaʀməmɑ̃] NM rearmament

réarmer [ʀeaʀme] /1/ VT (*arme*) to reload ▶ VI (*état*) to rearm

réassortiment [ʀeasɔʀtimɑ̃] NM (*Comm*) restocking

réassortir [ʀeasɔʀtiʀ] /2/ VT to match up; (*Comm*) to restock

réassurance [ʀeasyʀɑ̃s] NF reinsurance

réassurer [ʀeasyʀe] /1/ VT to reinsure

réassureur [ʀeasyʀœʀ] NM reinsurer

rebaptiser [ʀ(ə)batize] /1/ VT (*rue*) to rename

rébarbatif, -ive [ʀebaʀbatif, -iv] ADJ forbidding; (*style*) off-putting (BRIT), daunting

rebattre [R(ə)batR] /41/ VT: ~ **les oreilles à qn de qch** to keep harping on to sb about sth

rebattu, e [R(ə)baty] PP de **rebattre** ▶ ADJ hackneyed

rebelle [Rəbɛl] NMF rebel ▶ ADJ (*troupes*) rebel; (*enfant*) rebellious; (*mèche etc*) unruly; ~ **à qch** unamenable to sth; ~ **à faire** unwilling to do

rebeller [R(ə)bele] /1/: **se rebeller** VPR to rebel

rébellion [Rebeljɔ̃] NF rebellion; (*rebelles*) rebel forces pl

rebiffer [R(ə)bife] /1/: **se rebiffer** VPR to fight back

reboisement [R(ə)bwazmɑ̃] NM reafforestation

reboiser [R(ə)bwaze] /1/ VT to replant with trees, reafforest

rebond [R(ə)bɔ̃] NM (*voir rebondir*) bounce; rebound

rebondi, e [R(ə)bɔ̃di] ADJ (*ventre*) rounded; (*joues*) chubby, well-rounded

rebondir [R(ə)bɔ̃diR] /2/ VI (*ballon: au sol*) to bounce; (: *contre un mur*) to rebound; (*fig: procès, action, conversation*) to get moving again, be suddenly revived

rebondissement [Rəbɔ̃dis(ə)mɑ̃] NM new development

rebonjour [Rəbɔ̃ʒuR] EXCL hello again

rebord [R(ə)bɔR] NM edge; **le ~ de la fenêtre** the windowsill

reboucher [R(ə)buʃe] /1/ VT (*flacon*) to put the stopper ou top back on, recork; (*trou*) to stop up

rebours [R(ə)buR] : **à ~** adv the wrong way

rebouteux, -euse [Rəbutø, -øz] NM/F (*péj*) bonesetter

reboutonner [R(ə)butɔne] /1/ VT (*vêtement*) to button up (again)

rebrousse-poil [RəbRuspwal] : **à ~** adv the wrong way

rebrousser [R(ə)bRuse] /1/ VT (*cheveux, poils*) to brush back, brush up; ~ **chemin** to turn back

rebuffade [R(ə)byfad] NF rebuff

rébus [Rebys] NM INV (*jeu d'esprit*) rebus; (*fig*) puzzle

rebut [Rəby] NM: **mettre au ~** to scrap, discard

rebutant, e [R(ə)bytɑ̃, -ɑ̃t] ADJ (*travail, démarche*) off-putting, disagreeable

rebuter [R(ə)byte] /1/ VT to put off

recadrage [R(ə)kadraʒ] NM (*de programme, objectifs*) refocusing; (*Photo, Ciné*) cropping

récalcitrant, e [Rekalsitrɑ̃, -ɑ̃t] ADJ refractory, recalcitrant

recaler [R(ə)kale] /1/ VT (*Scol*) to fail

récapitulatif, -ive [Rekapitylatif, -iv] ADJ (*liste, tableau*) summary cpd, that sums up

récapituler [Rekapityle] /1/ VT to recapitulate; (*résumer*) to sum up

recel [Rəsɛl] NM receiving (stolen goods)

receler [R(ə)səle] /5/ VT (*produit d'un vol*) to receive; (*malfaiteur*) to harbour; (*fig*) to conceal

receleur, -euse [R(ə)sələʀ, -øz] NM/F receiver

récemment [Resamɑ̃] ADV recently

recensement [R(ə)sɑ̃smɑ̃] NM census; inventory

recenser [R(ə)sɑ̃se] /1/ VT (*population*) to take a census of; (*inventorier*) to make an inventory of; (*dénombrer*) to list

récent, e [Resɑ̃, -ɑ̃t] ADJ recent

recentrer [R(ə)sɑ̃tre] VT (*Pol*) to move towards the centre (BRIT) ou center (US)

récépissé [Resepise] NM receipt

réceptacle [Reseptakl] NM (*où les choses aboutissent*) recipient; (*où les choses sont stockées*) repository; (*Bot*) receptacle

récepteur, -trice [ResɛptœR, -tRis] ADJ receiving ▶ NM receiver; ~ **(de radio)** radio set ou receiver

réceptif, -ive [Resɛptif, -iv] ADJ: ~ **(à)** receptive (to)

réception [Resɛpsjɔ̃] NF receiving no pl; (*d'une marchandise, commande*) receipt; (*accueil*) reception, welcome; (*bureau*) reception (desk); (*réunion mondaine*) reception, party; (*pièces*) reception rooms pl; (*Sport: après un saut*) landing; (*du ballon*) catching no pl; **jour/heures de ~** day/hours for receiving visitors (*ou* students *etc*)

réceptionnaire [ResɛpsjɔnɛR] NMF receiving clerk

réceptionner [Resɛpsjɔne] /1/ VT (*Comm*) to take delivery of; (*Sport: ballon*) to catch (and control)

réceptionniste [Resɛpsjɔnist] NMF receptionist

réceptivité [Reseptivite] NF (*à une influence*) receptiveness; (*à une maladie*) susceptibility

récessif, -ive [Resesif, -iv] ADJ (*Bio*) recessive

récession [Resesjɔ̃] NF recession

★**recette** [R(ə)sɛt] NF (*Culin*) recipe; (*fig*) formula, recipe; (*Comm*) takings pl; (*Admin: bureau*) tax ou revenue office; **faire ~** (*spectacle, exposition*) to be a winner ■ **recettes** NFPL (*Comm: rentrées*) receipts

recevabilité [R(ə)səvabilite] NF (*Admin: de dossier, plainte*) admissibility

recevable [R(ə)səvabl] ADJ (*Admin: dossier, plainte*) admissible; (*argument*) acceptable

receveur, -euse [R(ə)səvœR, -øz] NM/F (*des contributions*) tax collector; (*des postes*) postmaster/mistress; (*d'autobus*) conductor/conductress; (*Méd: de sang, organe*) recipient

★**recevoir** [R(ə)səvwaR] /28/ VT to receive; (*lettre, prime*) to receive, get; (*client, patient, représentant*) to see; (*jour, soleil, pièce*) to get; (*Scol: candidat*) to pass; ~ **qn à dîner** to invite sb to dinner ▶ VI to receive visitors; to give parties; to see patients *etc*; **il reçoit de 8 à 10** he's at home from 8 to 10, he will see visitors from 8 to 10; (*docteur, dentiste etc*) he sees patients from 8 to 10 ■ **se recevoir** VPR (*athlète*) to land

rechange [R(ə)ʃɑ̃ʒ] : **de ~** adj (*pièces, roue*) spare; (*fig: solution*) alternative; **des vêtements de ~** a change of clothes

rechaper [R(ə)ʃape] /1/ VT to remould (BRIT), remold (US), retread

réchapper [Reʃape] /1/: ~ **de** ou **à** vt (*accident, maladie*) to come through; **va-t-il en ~ ?** is he going to get over it?, is he going to come through (it)?

recharge [R(ə)ʃaRʒ] NF refill

rechargeable [R(ə)ʃaRʒabl] ADJ (*briquet, stylo*) refillable; (*batterie*) rechargeable

recharger [R(ə)ʃaRʒe] /3/ VT (*camion, fusil, appareil photo*) to reload; (*briquet, stylo*) to refill; (*batterie*) to recharge

réchaud [Reʃo] NM (*portable*) stove, plate-warmer

réchauffé [Reʃofe] NM (*nourriture*) reheated food; (*fig*) stale news (*ou* joke *etc*)

réchauffement [ʁeʃofmɑ̃] NM warming (up); **le ~ de la planète** global warming

réchauffer [ʁeʃofe] /1/ VT (plat) to reheat; (mains, personne) to warm ■ **se réchauffer** VPR (température) to get warmer; (personne) to warm o.s. (up); **se ~ les doigts** to warm (up) one's fingers

rêche [ʁɛʃ] ADJ rough

★**recherche** [ʁ(ə)ʃɛʁʃ] NF (action): **la ~ de** the search for; (raffinement) affectedness, studied elegance; (scientifique etc): **la ~** research; **être/se mettre à la ~ de** to be/go in search of ■ **recherches** NFPL (de la police) investigations; (scientifiques) research sg

recherché, e [ʁ(ə)ʃɛʁʃe] ADJ (rare, demandé) much sought-after; (entouré: acteur, femme) in demand; (raffiné) studied, affected; (tenue) elegant

rechercher [ʁ(ə)ʃɛʁʃe] /1/ VT (objet égaré, personne) to look for, search for; (témoins, coupable, main-d'œuvre) to look for; (causes d'un phénomène, nouveau procédé) to try to find; (bonheur etc, l'amitié de qn) to seek; **« ~ et remplacer »** (Inform) "find and replace"

rechigner [ʁ(ə)ʃiɲe] /1/ VI: **~ (à)** to balk (at)

rechute [ʁ(ə)ʃyt] NF (Méd) relapse; (dans le péché, le vice) lapse; **faire une ~** to have a relapse

rechuter [ʁ(ə)ʃyte] /1/ VI (Méd) to relapse

récidive [residiv] NF (Jur) second (ou subsequent) offence; (fig) repetition; (Méd) recurrence

récidiver [residive] /1/ VI to commit a second (ou subsequent) offence; (fig) to do it again

récidiviste [residivist] NMF second (ou habitual) offender, recidivist

récif [resif] NM reef

récipiendaire [resipjɑ̃dɛʁ] NM (d'un diplôme) recipient; (d'une société) newly elected member

récipient [resipjɑ̃] NM container

réciprocité [resipʁɔsite] NF reciprocity

réciproque [resipʁɔk] ADJ reciprocal ▶ NF: **la ~** (l'inverse) the converse

réciproquement [resipʁɔkmɑ̃] ADV reciprocally; **et ~** and vice versa

récit [resi] NM (action de narrer) telling; (conte, histoire) story

récital [resital] NM recital

récitant, e [resitɑ̃, -ɑ̃t] NM/F narrator

récitation [resitasjɔ̃] NF recitation

réciter [resite] /1/ VT to recite

réclamation [ʁeklamasjɔ̃] NF complaint ■ **réclamations** NFPL (bureau) complaints department sg

réclame [ʁeklam] NF: **la ~** advertising; **une ~** an ad(vertisement), an advert (BRIT); **faire de la ~ (pour qch/qn)** to advertise (sth/sb); **article en ~** special offer

réclamer [ʁeklame] /1/ VT (aide, nourriture etc) to ask for; (revendiquer: dû, part, indemnité) to claim, demand; (nécessiter) to demand, require ▶ VI to complain ■ **se réclamer de** VPR to identify with

reclassement [ʁ(ə)klasmɑ̃] NM reclassifying; regrading; rehabilitation

reclasser [ʁ(ə)klase] /1/ VT (fiches, dossiers) to reclassify; (fig: fonctionnaire etc) to regrade; (: ouvrier licencié) to place, rehabilitate

reclus, e [ʁəkly, -yz] NM/F recluse

réclusion [ʁeklyzjɔ̃] NF imprisonment; **~ à perpétuité** life imprisonment

recoiffer [ʁ(ə)kwafe] /1/ VT: **~ un enfant** to do a child's hair again ■ **se recoiffer** VPR to do one's hair again

recoin [ʁəkwɛ̃] NM nook, corner; (fig) hidden recess

reçois etc [ʁəswa] VB voir **recevoir**

reçoive etc [ʁəswav] VB voir **recevoir**

recoller [ʁ(ə)kɔle] /1/ VT (enveloppe) to stick back down

récoltant, e [ʁekɔltɑ̃, -ɑ̃t] NM/F grower, farmer ▶ ADJ voir **propriétaire**

récolte [ʁekɔlt] NF harvesting, gathering; (produits) harvest, crop; (fig) crop, collection; (: d'observations) findings

récolter [ʁekɔlte] /1/ VT to harvest, gather (in); (fig) to get

recommandable [ʁ(ə)kɔmɑ̃dabl] ADJ commendable; **peu ~** not very commendable

recommandation [ʁ(ə)kɔmɑ̃dasjɔ̃] NF recommendation

recommandé [ʁ(ə)kɔmɑ̃de] NM (méthode etc) recommended; **en ~** (Postes) by registered mail

recommander [ʁ(ə)kɔmɑ̃de] /1/ VT to recommend; (qualités etc) to commend; (Postes) to register; **~ qch à qn** to recommend sth to sb; **~ à qn de faire** to recommend sb to do; **~ qn auprès de qn** ou **à qn** to recommend sb to sb; **il est recommandé de faire …** it is recommended that one does …; **se ~ à qn** to commend o.s. to sb; **se ~ de qn** to give sb's name as a reference

recommencer [ʁ(ə)kɔmɑ̃se] /3/ VT (reprendre: lutte, séance) to resume, start again; (refaire: travail, explications) to start afresh, start (over) again; (récidiver: erreur) to make again ▶ VI to start again; (récidiver) to do it again; **~ à faire** to start doing again; **ne recommence pas !** don't do that again!

récompense [ʁekɔ̃pɑ̃s] NF reward; (prix) award; **recevoir qch en ~** to get sth as a reward, be rewarded with sth

récompenser [ʁekɔ̃pɑ̃se] /1/ VT: **~ qn (de** ou **pour)** to reward sb (for)

réconciliation [ʁekɔ̃siljasjɔ̃] NF reconciliation

réconcilier [ʁekɔ̃silje] /7/ VT to reconcile; **~ qn avec qn** to reconcile sb with sb; **~ qn avec qch** to reconcile sb to sth ■ **se réconcilier (avec)** VPR to be reconciled (with)

reconductible [ʁ(ə)kɔ̃dyktibl] ADJ (Jur: contrat, bail) renewable

reconduction [ʁ(ə)kɔ̃dyksjɔ̃] NF renewal; (Pol: d'une politique) continuation

reconduire [ʁ(ə)kɔ̃dɥiʁ] /38/ VT (raccompagner) to take ou see back; (: à la porte) to show out; (: à son domicile) to see home, take home; (Jur, Pol: renouveler) to renew

réconfort [ʁekɔ̃fɔʁ] NM comfort

réconfortant, e [ʁekɔ̃fɔʁtɑ̃, -ɑ̃t] ADJ (idée, paroles) comforting; (boisson) fortifying

réconforter [ʁekɔ̃fɔʁte] /1/ VT (consoler) to comfort; (revigorer) to fortify

reconnais etc [ʁ(ə)kɔne] VB voir **reconnaître**

reconnaissable [ʁ(ə)kɔnɛsabl] ADJ recognizable

reconnaissais [ʁ(ə)kɔnɛse] VB voir **reconnaître**

reconnaissance [ʁ(ə)kɔnɛsɑ̃s] NF (action de reconnaître) recognition; acknowledgement; (gratitude)

gratitude, gratefulness; (Mil) reconnaissance, recce; **en ~** (Mil) on reconnaissance; **~ de dette** acknowledgement of a debt, IOU

★**reconnaissant, e** [ʀ(ə)kɔnɛsɑ̃, -ɑ̃t] vb voir **reconnaître** ▶ADJ grateful; **je vous serais ~ de bien vouloir** I should be most grateful if you would (kindly)

reconnaître [ʀ(ə)kɔnɛtʀ] **/57/** vt to recognize; (Mil: lieu) to reconnoitre; (Jur: enfant, dette, droit) to acknowledge; **~ que** to admit ou acknowledge that; **~ qn/qch à** (l'identifier grâce à) to recognize sb/ sth by; **je lui reconnais certaines qualités** I recognize certain qualities in him; **se ~ quelque part** (s'y retrouver) to find one's way around (a place)

reconnu, e [ʀ(ə)kɔny] PP de **reconnaître** ▶ADJ (indiscuté, connu) recognized

reconquérir [ʀ(ə)kɔ̃keʀiʀ] **/21/** vt to reconquer, recapture; (sa dignité etc) to recover

reconquête [ʀ(ə)kɔ̃kɛt] NF recapture; recovery

reconsidérer [ʀ(ə)kɔ̃sidere] **/6/** vt to reconsider

reconstituant, e [ʀ(ə)kɔ̃stitɥɑ̃, -ɑ̃t] ADJ (régime) strength-building ▶NM tonic, pick-me-up

reconstituer [ʀ(ə)kɔ̃stitɥe] **/1/** vt (monument ancien) to recreate, build a replica of; (fresque, vase brisé) to piece together, reconstitute; (événement, accident) to reconstruct; (fortune, patrimoine) to rebuild; (Bio: tissus etc) to regenerate

reconstitution [ʀ(ə)kɔ̃stitysjɔ̃] NF (d'un accident etc) reconstruction

reconstruction [ʀ(ə)kɔ̃stʀyksjɔ̃] NF rebuilding, reconstruction

reconstruire [ʀ(ə)kɔ̃stʀɥiʀ] **/38/** vt to rebuild, reconstruct

recontacter [ʀ(ə)kɔ̃takte] vt to contact again, get back in touch with

reconversion [ʀ(ə)kɔ̃vɛʀsjɔ̃] NF (du personnel) redeployment **reconvertir** [ʀ(ə)kɔ̃vɛʀtiʀ] **/2/** vt (usine) to reconvert; (personnel, troupes etc) to redeploy; **se ~ dans** (un métier, une branche) to move into, be redeployed into

recopier [ʀ(ə)kɔpje] **/7/** vt (transcrire) to copy out again, write out again; (mettre au propre: devoir) to make a clean ou fair copy of

record [ʀ(ə)kɔʀ] NM, ADJ record; **~ du monde** world record

recoucher [ʀ(ə)kuʃe] **/1/** vt (enfant) to put back to bed

recoudre [ʀ(ə)kudʀ] **/48/** vt (bouton) to sew back on; (plaie, incision) to sew (back) up, stitch up

recoupement [ʀ(ə)kupmɑ̃] NM: **faire un ~** ou **des recoupements** to cross-check; **par ~** by cross-checking

recouper [ʀ(ə)kupe] **/1/** vt (tranche) to cut again; (vêtement) to recut ▶vi (Cartes) to cut again ■ **se recouper** vpr (témoignages) to tie ou match up

recourais etc [ʀəkuʀɛ] vb voir **recourir**

recourbé, e [ʀ(ə)kuʀbe] ADJ curved; hooked; bent

recourber [ʀ(ə)kuʀbe] **/1/** vt (branche, tige de métal) to bend ■ **se recourber** vpr to curve (up), bend (up)

recourir [ʀ(ə)kuʀiʀ] **/11/** vt: **~ à** (ami, agence) to turn ou appeal to; (force, ruse, emprunt) to resort to, have recourse to ▶vi (courir de nouveau) to run again; (refaire une course) to race again

recours [ʀ(ə)kuʀ] vb voir **recourir** ▶NM (Jur) appeal; **avoir ~ à** = recourir à; **en dernier ~** as a last resort; **sans ~** final; with no way out; **~ en grâce** plea for clemency (ou pardon)

recouru, e [ʀəkuʀy] PP de **recourir**

recousu, e [ʀəkuzy] PP de **recoudre**

recouvert, e [ʀəkuvɛʀ, -ɛʀt] PP de **recouvrir**

recouvrable [ʀ(ə)kuvʀabl] ADJ (somme) recoverable

recouvrais etc [ʀəkuvʀɛ] vb voir **recouvrer; recouvrir**

recouvrement [ʀ(ə)kuvʀəmɑ̃] NM recovery

recouvrer [ʀ(ə)kuvʀe] **/1/** vt (vue, santé etc) to recover, regain; (impôts) to collect; (créance) to recover

recouvrir [ʀ(ə)kuvʀiʀ] **/18/** vt (couvrir à nouveau) to re-cover; (couvrir entièrement aussi fig) to cover; (cacher, masquer) to conceal, hide ■ **se recouvrir** vpr (se superposer) to overlap

recracher [ʀ(ə)kʀaʃe] **/1/** vt to spit out

récréatif, -ive [ʀekʀeatif, -iv] ADJ of entertainment; recreational

récréation [ʀekʀeasjɔ̃] NF recreation, entertainment; (Scol) break

recréditer [ʀ(ə)kʀedite] vt (compte, carte) to recredit

recréer [ʀ(ə)kʀee] **/1/** vt to recreate

récrier [ʀekʀije] **/7/**: **se récrier** vpr to exclaim

récriminations [ʀekʀiminasjɔ̃] NFPL remonstrations, complaints

récriminer [ʀekʀimine] **/1/** vi: **~ contre qn/qch** to remonstrate against sb/sth

recroquevillé, e [ʀ(ə)kʀɔk(ə)vije] ADJ (personne) curled up; (feuilles) shrivelled up, curled up

recroqueviller [ʀ(ə)kʀɔk(ə)vije] **/1/**: **se recroqueviller** vpr (feuilles) to shrivel ou curl up; (personne) to huddle up

recru, e [ʀəkʀy] ADJ: **~ de fatigue** exhausted ▶NF recruit

recrudescence [ʀ(ə)kʀydesɑ̃s] NF fresh outbreak

recrue [ʀəkʀy] NF recruit; **une nouvelle ~** a new recruit

recrutement [ʀ(ə)kʀytmɑ̃] NM recruiting, recruitment

recruter [ʀ(ə)kʀyte] **/1/** vt to recruit

recruteur, -euse [ʀ(ə)kʀytœʀ, -øz] NM/F recruiter

rectal, e, -aux [ʀɛktal, -o] ADJ: **par voie rectale** rectally

rectangle [ʀɛktɑ̃gl] NM rectangle

rectangulaire [ʀɛktɑ̃gylɛʀ] ADJ rectangular

recteur [ʀɛktœʀ] NM ≈ (regional) director of education (Brit), ≈ state superintendent of education (US)

rectificatif, -ive [ʀɛktifikatif, -iv] ADJ corrected ▶NM correction

rectification [ʀɛktifikasjɔ̃] NF correction

rectifier [ʀɛktifje] **/7/** vt (tracé, virage) to straighten; (calcul, adresse) to correct; (erreur, faute) to rectify, put right

rectiligne [ʀɛktiliɲ] ADJ straight; (Géom) rectilinear

r

rectitude [ʀɛktityd] NF rectitude, uprightness

recto [ʀɛkto] NM front (of a sheet of paper); **~ verso** on both sides (of the page)

rectorat [ʀɛktɔʀa] NM (fonction) position of recteur; (bureau) recteur's office; voir aussi **recteur**

rectum [ʀɛktɔm] NM rectum

reçu, e [ʀ(ə)sy] PP de **recevoir** ▶ ADJ (candidat) successful; (admis, consacré) accepted; **être ~** (à un examen) to pass; **être bien/mal ~** to be well/badly received ▶ NM (Comm) receipt

recueil [ʀəkœj] NM collection

recueillement [ʀ(ə)kœjmɑ̃] NM meditation, contemplation

recueilli, e [ʀ(ə)kœji] ADJ contemplative

recueillir [ʀ(ə)kœjiʀ] /12/ VT to collect; (voix, suffrages) to win; (accueillir: réfugiés, chat) to take in ■ **se recueillir** VPR to gather one's thoughts; to meditate

recuire [ʀ(ə)kɥiʀ] /38/ VI: **faire ~** to recook

recul [ʀ(ə)kyl] NM retreat; recession; (déclin) decline; (éloignement) distance; (d'arme à feu) recoil, kick; **avoir un mouvement de ~** to recoil, step back; **prendre du ~** to stand back; **être en ~** to be on the decline; **avec le ~** with the passing of time, in retrospect

reculade [ʀ(ə)kylad] NF (péj) climb-down

reculé, e [ʀ(ə)kyle] ADJ remote

★**reculer** [ʀ(ə)kyle] /1/ VI to move back, back away; (Auto) to reverse, back (up); (fig: civilisation, épidémie) to be on the decline; (: se dérober) to shrink back; **~ devant** (danger, difficulté) to shrink from; **~ pour mieux sauter** (fig) to take a step back to see the bigger picture ▶ VT to move back; (véhicule) to reverse, back (up); (fig: possibilités, limites) to extend; (: date, décision) to postpone

reculons [ʀ(ə)kylɔ̃]: **à ~** adv backwards

récupérable [ʀekypeʀabl] ADJ (créance) recoverable; (heures) which can be made up; (ferraille) salvageable

récupérateur, -trice [ʀekypeʀatœʀ, -tʀis] NM/F (de métaux) scrap merchant ▶ ADJ (Football): **milieu ~** central midfielder

récupération [ʀekypeʀasjɔ̃] NF (de métaux etc) salvage, reprocessing; (Pol) hijacking (of policies)

récupérer [ʀekypeʀe] /6/ VT (rentrer en possession de) to recover, get back; (: forces) to recover; (déchets etc) to salvage (for reprocessing); (remplacer: journée, heures de travail) to make up; (délinquant etc) to rehabilitate; (Pol) to hijack (policies) ▶ VI to recover

récurer [ʀekyʀe] /1/ VT to scour; **poudre à ~** scouring powder

récurrence [ʀekyʀɑ̃s] NF recurrence

récurrent, e [ʀekyʀɑ̃, -ɑ̃t] ADJ (problème) recurrent

reçus etc [ʀəsy] VB voir **recevoir**

récusable [ʀekyzabl] ADJ (témoin) challengeable; (témoignage) impugnable

récusation [ʀekyzasjɔ̃] NF (Jur: d'idée, principe) challenge

récuser [ʀekyze] /1/ VT to challenge ■ **se récuser** VPR to decline to give an opinion

reçut [ʀ(ə)sy] VB voir **recevoir**

recyclable [ʀ(ə)siklabl] ADJ recyclable

recyclage [ʀ(ə)siklaʒ] NM reorientation; retrain-

ing; recycling; **cours de ~** retraining course

★**recycler** [ʀ(ə)sikle] /1/ VT (Scol) to reorientate; (employés) to retrain; (matériau) to recycle ■ **se recycler** VPR to retrain; to go on a retraining course

rédacteur, -trice [ʀedaktœʀ, -tʀis] NM/F (journaliste) writer; subeditor; (d'ouvrage de référence) editor, compiler; **~ en chef** chief editor; **~ publicitaire** copywriter

rédaction [ʀedaksjɔ̃] NF writing; (rédacteurs) editorial staff; (bureau) editorial office(s); (Scol: devoir) essay, composition

rédactionnel, le [ʀedaksjɔnɛl] ADJ (Presse: équipe, ligne) editorial; (capacités) writing; **d'excellentes capacités rédactionnelles** excellent writing skills

reddition [ʀedisjɔ̃] NF surrender

redécoller [ʀ(ə)dekɔle] VI (avion, ventes) to take off again

redécouvrir [ʀ(ə)dekuvʀiʀ] VT to rediscover

redéfinir [ʀ(ə)definiʀ] /2/ VT to redefine

redéfinition [ʀ(ə)definisjɔ̃] NF redefinition

redemander [ʀədmɑ̃de] /1/ VT (renseignement) to ask again for; (objet prêté): **~ qch** to ask for sth back; **~ de** (nourriture) to ask for more (ou another)

redémarrage [ʀ(ə)demaʀaʒ] NM (de machine: aussi: Inform) restarting; (fig): **un ~ de qch** (industrie, activité) an upturn in sth

redémarrer [ʀ(ə)demaʀe] /1/ VI (véhicule) to start again, get going again; (ordinateur) to restart; (fig: industrie) to get going again

rédemption [ʀedɑ̃psjɔ̃] NF redemption

redéploiement [ʀ(ə)deplwamɑ̃] NM redeployment

redescendre [ʀ(ə)desɑ̃dʀ] /41/ VI (à nouveau) to go back down; (après la montée) to go down (again) ▶ VT (pente etc) to go down

redevable [ʀ(ə)dəvabl] ADJ: **être ~ de qch à qn** (somme) to owe sb sth; (fig) to be indebted to sb for sth

redevance [ʀ(ə)dəvɑ̃s] NF (Tél) rental charge; (TV) licence (BRIT) ou license (US) fee

redevenir [ʀ(ə)dəv(ə)niʀ] /22/ VI to become again

rédhibitoire [ʀedibitwaʀ] ADJ: **vice ~** (Jur) latent defect in merchandise that renders the sales contract void; (fig: défaut) crippling

rediffuser [ʀ(ə)difyze] /1/ VT (Radio, TV) to repeat, broadcast again

rediffusion [ʀ(ə)difyzjɔ̃] NF repeat (programme)

rédiger [ʀediʒe] /3/ VT to write; (contrat) to draw up

redire [ʀ(ə)diʀ] /37/ VT to repeat; **trouver à ~ à** to find fault with

redistribuer [ʀ(ə)distʀibɥe] /1/ VT (cartes etc) to deal again; (richesses, revenus) to redistribute; (tâches) to reallocate

redistribution [ʀ(ə)distʀibysjɔ̃] NF (de richesses, revenus) redistribution; (de tâches) reallocation; **~ des cartes** new deal; (fig) new situation; (politique) new order

redite [ʀ(ə)dit] NF (needless) repetition

redondance [ʀ(ə)dɔ̃dɑ̃s] NF redundancy

redondant, e [ʀədɔ̃dɑ̃, ɑ̃t] ADJ redundant

redonner [ʀ(ə)dɔne] /**1**/ VT (*restituer*) to give back, return; (*du courage, des forces*) to restore

redorer [ʀ(ə)dɔʀe] VT to regild; **~ son blason** (*fig*) to restore one's image

redoublant, e [ʀ(ə)dublɑ̃, -ɑ̃t] NM/F (*Scol*) student repeating a year

redoublé, e [ʀαduble] ADJ: **à coups redoublés** even harder, twice as hard

redoublement [ʀ(ə)dublǝmɑ̃] NM (*Scol*) repeating a year; (*intensification*): **~ d'effort/d'attention** increased effort/attention; (*Ling*: *de lettre*) doubling

★**redoubler** [ʀ(ə)duble] /**1**/ VI (*tempête, violence*) to intensify, get even stronger ou fiercer *etc*; (*Scol*) to repeat a year; **le vent redouble de violence** the wind is blowing twice as hard; **~ de patience/prudence** to be doubly patient/careful ▶ VT (*Scol*: *classe*) to repeat; (*Ling*: *lettre*) to double

redoutable [ʀ(ə)dutabl] ADJ formidable, fearsome

redouter [ʀ(ə)dute] /**1**/ VT to fear; (*appréhender*) to dread; **~ de faire** to dread doing

redoux [ʀαdu] NM milder spell

redressement [ʀ(ə)dʀɛsmɑ̃] NM (*économique*) recovery; (*de l'économie etc*) putting right; **maison de ~** reformatory; **~ fiscal** repayment of back taxes

redresser [ʀ(ə)dʀese] /**1**/ VT (*arbre, mât*) to set upright, right; (*pièce tordue*) to straighten out; (*Aviat, Auto*) to straighten up; (*situation, économie*) to put right; **~ (les roues)** (*Auto*) to straighten up ■ **se redresser** VPR (*objet penché*) to right itself; to straighten up; (*personne*) to sit (*ou stand*) up; to sit (*ou stand*) up straight; (*fig: pays, situation*) to recover

redresseur [ʀ(ə)dʀesœʀ] NM: **~ de torts** righter of wrongs

réducteur, -trice [ʀedyktœʀ, -tʀis] ADJ simplistic

réduction [ʀedyksjɔ̃] NF reduction; **en ~** *adv* in miniature, scaled-down

réduire [ʀedɥiʀ] /**38**/ VT (*gén, Culin, Math*) to reduce; (*prix, dépenses*) to cut, reduce; (*carte*) to scale down, reduce; (*Méd: fracture*) to set; **~ qn/qch à** to reduce sb/sth to ■ **se réduire** VPR: **se ~ à** (*revenir à*) to boil down to; **se ~ en** (*se transformer en*) to be reduced to; **en être réduit à** to be reduced to

réduit, e [ʀedɥi, -it] PP *de* **réduire** ▶ ADJ (*prix, tarif, échelle*) reduced; (*mécanisme*) scaled-down; (*vitesse*) reduced ▶ NM tiny room; recess

redynamiser [ʀ(ə)dinamize] VT to make more dynamic

rééchelonnement [ʀeeʃ(ə)lɔnmɑ̃] NM (*de dette*) rescheduling

rééchelonner [ʀeeʃ(ə)lɔne] VT (*dette*) to reschedule

rééditer [ʀeedite] /**1**/ VT to republish; (*fig: exploit*) to repeat

réédition [ʀeedisjɔ̃] NF new edition

rééducation [ʀeedykasjɔ̃] NF (*d'un membre*) re-education; (*de délinquants, d'un blessé*) rehabilitation; **~ de la parole** speech therapy; **centre de ~** physiotherapy centre (*BRIT*) ou physical therapy center (*US*)

rééduquer [ʀeedyke] /**1**/ VT to re-educate; to rehabilitate

réel, le [ʀeel] ADJ real ▶ NM: **le ~** reality

réélection [ʀeelɛksjɔ̃] NF re-election

rééligible [ʀeeliʒibl] ADJ re-eligible

réélire [ʀeeliʀ] /**43**/ VT to re-elect

réellement [ʀeelmɑ̃] ADV really

réembaucher [ʀeɑ̃boʃe] /**1**/ VT to take on again

réemploi [ʀeɑ̃plwa] NM = **remploi**

réemployer [ʀeɑ̃plwaje] /**8**/ VT (*méthode, produit*) to re-use; (*argent*) to reinvest; (*personnel, employé*) to re-employ

rééquilibrer [ʀeekilibʀe] /**1**/ VT (*budget*) to balance (again)

réescompte [ʀeeskɔ̃t] NM rediscount

réessayer [ʀeeseje] /**8**/ VT to try on again

réévaluation [ʀeevalɥasjɔ̃] NF revaluation

réévaluer [ʀeevalɥe] /**1**/ VT to revalue

réexamen [ʀeegzamɛ̃] NM (*de dossier*) re-examination; (*de demande*) reconsideration

réexaminer [ʀeegzamine] /**1**/ VT (*dossier*) to re-examine; (*demande*) to reconsider

réexpédier [ʀeekspedje] /**7**/ VT (*à l'envoyeur*) to return, send back; (*au destinataire*) to send on, forward

réexporter [ʀeekspɔʀte] /**1**/ VT to re-export

réf. ABR = **référence(s)**; **V/~** Your ref

refaire [ʀ(ə)fɛʀ] /**60**/ VT (*faire de nouveau, recommencer*) to do again; (*sport*) to take up again; (*réparer, restaurer*) to do up ■ **se refaire** (*en argent*) to make up one's losses; **se ~ une santé** to recuperate; **se ~ qch** (*se réhabituer à*) to get used to sth again

refasse *etc* [ʀəfas] VB *voir* **refaire**

réfection [ʀefɛksjɔ̃] NF repair; **en ~** under repair

réfectoire [ʀefɛktwaʀ] NM refectory

referai *etc* [ʀ(ə)fʀe] VB *voir* **refaire**

référé [ʀefeʀe] NM (*Jur*) emergency interim proceedings ou ruling

référence [ʀefeʀɑ̃s] NF reference; **faire ~ à** to refer to; **ouvrage de ~** reference work; **ce n'est pas une ~** (*fig*) that's no recommendation ■ **références** NFPL (*recommandations*) reference *sg*

référencement [ʀefeʀɑ̃smɑ̃] NM (*Internet: de site Web*) referencing

référencer [ʀefeʀɑ̃se] VT (*Internet: site Web, produit*) to reference

référendum [ʀefeʀɑ̃dɔm] NM referendum

référer [ʀefeʀe] /**6**/: **~ à** VT to refer to, relate to; **en ~ à qn** to refer the matter to sb ■ **se référer** VPR: **se ~ à** to refer to

refermer [ʀ(ə)fɛʀme] /**1**/ VT to close again, shut again ■ **se refermer** VPR (*porte*) to close ou shut (again)

refiler [ʀ(ə)file] /**1**/ VT (*fam*): **~ qch à qn** to palm (*BRIT*) ou fob sth off on sb; to pass sth on to sb

refit *etc* [ʀəfi] VB *voir* **refaire**

réfléchi, e [ʀefleʃi] ADJ (*caractère*) thoughtful; (*action*) well-thought-out; (*Ling*) reflexive; **c'est tout ~** my mind's made up

réfléchir [ʀefleʃiʀ] /**2**/ VT to reflect ▶ VI to think; **~ à** ou **sur** to think about

r

375

réflecteur [ʀeflɛktœʀ] NM (*Auto*) reflector

reflet [ʀ(ə)flɛ] NM reflection; (*sur l'eau etc*) sheen *no pl*, glint ■ **reflets** NMPL gleam *sg*

refléter [ʀ(ə)flete] /6/ VT to reflect ■ **se refléter** VPR to be reflected

refleurir [ʀ(ə)flœʀiʀ] VI (*plante*) to flower again; (*fig*) to flourish again

réflex [ʀeflɛks] ADJ INV (*Photo*) reflex

réflexe [ʀeflɛks] ADJ, NM reflex; **~ conditionné** conditioned reflex

réflexion [ʀeflɛksjɔ̃] NF (*de la lumière etc, pensée*) reflection; (*fait de penser*) thought; (*remarque*) remark; **sans ~** without thinking; **~ faite, à la ~, après ~** on reflection; **délai de ~** cooling-off period; **groupe de ~** think tank ■ **réflexions** NFPL (*méditations*) thought *sg*, reflection *sg*

réflexologie [ʀeflɛksɔlɔʒi] NF reflexology

refluer [ʀ(ə)flye] /1/ VI to flow back; (*foule*) to surge back

reflux [ʀəfly] NM (*de la mer*) ebb; (*fig*) backward surge

refondation [ʀ(ə)fɔ̃dasjɔ̃] NF (*de parti, institution*) reorganization

refondre [ʀ(ə)fɔ̃dʀ] /41/ VT (*texte*) to revise; (*système*) to overhaul

refont [ʀ(ə)fɔ̃] VB *voir* **refaire**

refonte [ʀ(ə)fɔ̃t] NF (*de texte*) reworking

reformater [ʀ(ə)fɔʀmate] /1/ VT to reformat

réformateur, -trice [ʀefɔʀmatœʀ, -tʀis] NM/F reformer ▶ ADJ (*mesures*) reforming

Réformation [ʀefɔʀmasjɔ̃] NF: **la ~** the Reformation

réforme [ʀefɔʀm] NF reform; (*Mil*) declaration of unfitness for service; discharge (*on health grounds*); (*Rel*): **la R~** the Reformation

réformé, e [ʀefɔʀme] ADJ, NM/F (*Rel*) Protestant

reformer [ʀ(ə)fɔʀme] /1/ VT to reform; **~ les rangs** (*Mil*) to fall in again ■ **se reformer** VPR to reform

réformer [ʀefɔʀme] /1/ VT to reform; (*Mil: recrue*) to declare unfit for service; (: *soldat*) to discharge, invalid out; (*matériel*) to scrap

réformisme [ʀefɔʀmism] NM reformism, policy of reform

réformiste [ʀefɔʀmist] ADJ, NMF (*Pol*) reformist

reformuler [ʀ(ə)fɔʀmyle] VT (*question*) to reword, rephrase; (*redéfinir*) to reformulate

refoulé, e [ʀ(ə)fule] ADJ (*Psych*) repressed

refoulement [ʀ(ə)fulmɑ̃] NM (*d'une armée*) driving back; (*Psych*) repression

refouler [ʀ(ə)fule] /1/ VT (*envahisseurs*) to drive back, repulse; (*liquide, larmes*) to force back; (*fig*) to suppress; (*Psych: désir, colère*) to repress

réfractaire [ʀefʀaktɛʀ] ADJ (*minerai*) refractory; (*brique*) fire *cpd*; (*maladie*) which is resistant to treatment; (*prêtre*) nonjuring; **soldat ~** draft evader; **être ~ à** to resist

réfracter [ʀefʀakte] /1/ VT to refract

réfraction [ʀefʀaksjɔ̃] NF refraction

refrain [ʀ(ə)fʀɛ̃] NM (*Mus*) refrain, chorus; (*air, fig*) tune

refréner, réfréner [ʀəfʀene, ʀefʀene] /6/ VT to curb, check

réfrigérant, e [ʀefʀiʒeʀɑ̃, -ɑ̃t] ADJ refrigerant, cooling

réfrigérateur [ʀefʀiʒeʀatœʀ] NM refrigerator; **réfrigérateur-congélateur** fridge-freezer (BRIT), refrigerator and freezer (US)

réfrigération [ʀefʀiʒeʀasjɔ̃] NF refrigeration

réfrigéré, e [ʀefʀiʒeʀe] ADJ (*camion, wagon*) refrigerated

réfrigérer [ʀefʀiʒeʀe] /6/ VT to refrigerate; (*fam: glacer aussi fig*) to cool

refroidir [ʀ(ə)fʀwadiʀ] /2/ VT to cool; (*fig*) to have a cooling effect on; (: *personne*) to put off ▶ VI to cool (down) ■ **se refroidir** VPR (*prendre froid*) to catch a chill; (*temps*) to get cooler ou colder; (*fig: ardeur*) to cool (off)

refroidissement [ʀ(ə)fʀwadismɑ̃] NM cooling; (*grippe etc*) chill

refuge [ʀ(ə)fyʒ] NM refuge; (*pour piétons*) (traffic) island; **demander ~ à qn** to ask sb for refuge

réfugié, e [ʀefyʒje] ADJ, NM/F refugee

réfugier [ʀefyʒje] /7/: **se réfugier** VPR to take refuge

refus [ʀ(ə)fy] NM refusal; **ce n'est pas de ~** I won't say no, it's very welcome

★**refuser** [ʀ(ə)fyze] /1/ VT to refuse; (*Scol: candidat*) to fail; **~ qch à qn/de faire** to refuse sb sth/to do; **~ du monde** to have to turn people away ▶ VI to refuse ■ **se refuser** VPR: **se ~ à qch** ou **à faire qch** to refuse to do sth; **il ne se refuse rien** he doesn't stint himself; **se ~ à qn** to refuse sb

réfutable [ʀefytabl] ADJ refutable

réfuter [ʀefyte] /1/ VT to refute

regagner [ʀ(ə)ɡaɲe] /1/ VT (*argent, faveur*) to win back; (*lieu*) to get back to; **~ le temps perdu** to make up for lost time; **~ du terrain** to regain ground

regain [ʀəɡɛ̃] NM (*herbe*) second crop of hay; (*renouveau*): **~ de qch** renewed sth

régal [ʀeɡal] NM treat; **un ~ pour les yeux** a pleasure ou delight to look at

régalade [ʀeɡalad] ADV: **à la ~** from the bottle (*held away from the lips*)

régaler [ʀeɡale] /1/ VT: **~ qn** to treat sb to a delicious meal; **~ qn de** to treat sb to ■ **se régaler** VPR to have a delicious meal; (*fig*) to enjoy o.s.

régalien, ne [ʀeɡaljɛ̃, -jɛn] ADJ sovereign

regard [ʀ(ə)ɡaʀ] NM (*coup d'œil*) look, glance; (*expression*) look (in one's eye); **parcourir/menacer du ~** to cast an eye over/look threateningly at; **au ~ de** (*loi, morale*) from the point of view of; **en ~** (*vis à vis*) opposite; **en ~ de** in comparison with

regardant, e [ʀ(ə)ɡaʀdɑ̃, -ɑ̃t] ADJ: **très/peu ~ (sur)** quite fussy/very free (about); (*économe*) very tight-fisted/quite generous (with)

★**regarder** [ʀ(ə)ɡaʀde] /1/ VT (*examiner, observer, lire*) to look at; (*film, télévision, match*) to watch; (*envisager: situation, avenir*) to view; (*être orienté vers*): **~ (vers)** to face; (*concerner*) to concern; **~ (qch) dans le dictionnaire** to look (sth up) in the dictionary; **cela me regarde** it concerns me, it's my business ▶ VI to look; **~ par la fenêtre** to look out of the window; **~ à** (*dépense, qualité*) to be fussy with ou over; **dépenser sans ~** to spend freely; **ne pas ~ à la dépense** to spare no expense ■ **se regarder**

VPR: **se ~ dans les yeux** to look into each other's eyes; **se ~ en chiens de faïence** to glare at each other

régate NF, **régates** NFPL [Regat] regatta

régénérateur, -trice [Reʒeneratœr, -tris] ADJ regenerative

régénérer [Reʒenere] /6/ VT to regenerate; (*fig*) to revive ■ **se régénérer** VPR (*cellules*) to regenerate

régent [Reʒɑ̃] NM regent

régenter [Reʒɑ̃te] /1/ VT to rule over; to dictate to

régie [Reʒi] NF (*Comm, Industrie*) state-owned company; (*Théât, Ciné*) production; (*Radio, TV*) control room; **la ~ de l'État** state control

regimber [R(ə)ʒɛ̃be] /1/ VI to balk, jib

régime [Reʒim] NM (*Pol*) régime; (*Admin: carcéral, fiscal etc*) system; (*Méd*) diet; (*Tech*) (engine) speed; (*fig*) rate, pace; (*de bananes, dattes*) bunch; **se mettre au/suivre un ~** to go on/be on a diet; **~ sans sel** salt-free diet; **à bas/haut ~** (*Auto*) at low/high revs; **à plein ~** flat out, at full speed; **~ matrimonial** marriage settlement

régiment [Reʒimɑ̃] NM (*Mil: unité*) regiment; (*fig: fam*): **un ~ de** an army of; **un copain de ~** a pal from military service *ou* (one's) army days

région [Reʒjɔ̃] NF region; **la ~ parisienne** the Paris area

régional, e, -aux [Reʒjɔnal, -o] ADJ regional

régionalisation [Reʒjɔnalizasjɔ̃] NF regionalisation

régionalisme [Reʒjɔnalism] NM regionalism

régir [Reʒir] /2/ VT to govern

régisseur [Reʒisœr] NM (*d'un domaine*) steward; (*Ciné, TV*) assistant director; (*Théât*) stage manager

registre [Rəʒistr] NM (*livre*) register; logbook; ledger; (*Mus, Ling*) register; (*d'orgue*) stop; **~ de comptabilité** ledger; **~ de l'état civil** register of births, marriages and deaths

réglable [Reglabl] ADJ (*siège, flamme etc*) adjustable; (*achat*) payable

réglage [Reglaʒ] NM (*d'un mécanisme, d'une machine*) adjustment; (*d'un moteur*) tuning

règle [Regl] NF (*instrument*) ruler; (*loi, prescription*) rule; **avoir pour ~ de** to make it a rule that *ou* to; **en ~** (*papiers d'identité*) in order; **être/se mettre en ~** to be/put o.s. straight with the authorities; **en ~ générale** as a (general) rule; **être la ~** to be the rule; **être de ~** to be usual; **~ à calcul** slide rule; **~ de trois** (*Math*) rule of three ■ **règles** NFPL (*Physiol*) period *sg*

réglé, e [Regle] ADJ well-ordered; stable, steady; (*papier*) ruled; (*arrangé*) settled

règlement [Rɛgləmɑ̃] NM settling; (*paiement*) settlement; (*arrêté*) regulation; (*règles, statuts*) regulations *pl*, rules *pl*; **~ à la commande** cash with order; **~ de compte(s)** settling of scores; **~ en espèces/par chèque** payment in cash/by cheque; **~ intérieur** (*Scol*) school rules *pl*; (*Admin*) by-laws *pl*; **~ judiciaire** compulsory liquidation

réglementaire [Rɛgləmɑ̃tɛr] ADJ conforming to the regulations; (*tenue, uniforme*) regulation *cpd*

réglementation [Rɛgləmɑ̃tasjɔ̃] NF regulation, control; (*règlements*) regulations *pl*

réglementer [Rɛgləmɑ̃te] /1/ VT to regulate, control

régler [Regle] /6/ VT (*mécanisme, machine*) to regulate, adjust; (*moteur*) to tune; (*thermostat*) to set, adjust; (*emploi du temps*) to organize, plan; (*question, conflit, facture, dette*) to settle; (*fournisseur*) to settle up with, pay; (*papier*) to rule; **~ qch sur** to model sth on; **~ son compte à qn** to sort sb out, settle sb; **~ un compte** to settle a score ■ **se régler** VPR (*mécanisme, thermostat*) to be set; **ça se règle comment ?** how do you set it?

réglisse [Reglis] NM OU F liquorice; **bâton de ~** liquorice stick

règne [Rɛɲ] NM (*d'un roi etc, fig*) reign; (*Bio*): **le ~ végétal/animal** the vegetable/animal kingdom

régner [Reɲe] /6/ VI (*roi*) to rule, reign; (*fig*) to reign

regonfler [R(ə)gɔ̃fle] /1/ VT (*ballon, pneu*) to reinflate, blow up again

regorger [R(ə)gɔrʒe] /3/ VI to overflow; **~ de** to overflow with, be bursting with

régresser [Regrese] /1/ VI (*phénomène*) to decline; (*enfant, malade*) to regress

régressif, -ive [Regresif, -iv] ADJ regressive

régression [Regresjɔ̃] NF decline; regression; **être en ~** to be on the decline

regret [R(ə)grɛ] NM regret; **à ~** with regret; **avec ~** regretfully; **sans ~** with no regrets; **être au ~ de devoir/ne pas pouvoir faire** to regret to have to/that one is unable to do; **j'ai le ~ de vous informer que ...** I regret to inform you that ...

regrettable [R(ə)grɛtabl] ADJ regrettable

★**regretter** [R(ə)grɛte] /1/ VT to regret; (*personne*) to miss; **~ d'avoir fait** to regret doing; **~ que** to regret that, be sorry that; **non, je regrette** no, I'm sorry

regroupement [R(ə)grupmɑ̃] NM grouping together; (*groupe*) group

regrouper [R(ə)grupe] /1/ VT (*grouper*) to group together; (*contenir*) to include, comprise ■ **se regrouper** VPR to gather (together)

régularisation [Regylarizasjɔ̃] NF (*de papiers, passeport*) putting in order; (*de sa situation: par le mariage*) regularization; (*d'un mécanisme*) regulation

régulariser [Regylarize] /1/ VT (*fonctionnement, trafic*) to regulate; (*passeport, papiers*) to put in order; (*sa situation*) to straighten out, regularize

régularité [Regylarite] NF regularity

régulateur, -trice [Regylatœr, -tris] ADJ regulating ▸ NM (*Tech*): **~ de vitesse/de température** speed/temperature regulator

régulation [Regylasjɔ̃] NF (*du trafic*) regulation; **~ des naissances** birth control

réguler [Regyle] VT (*marché, température*) to regulate

régulier, -ière [Regylje, -jɛr] ADJ (*gén*) regular; (*vitesse, qualité*) steady; (*répartition, pression*) even; (*Transports: ligne, service*) scheduled, regular; (*légal, réglementaire*) lawful, in order; (*fam: correct*) straight, on the level

régulièrement [Regyljɛrmɑ̃] ADV regularly; steadily; evenly; normally

régurgiter [Regyrʒite] /1/ VT to regurgitate

réhabiliter [Reabilite] /1/ VT to rehabilitate; (*fig*) to restore to favour (BRIT) *ou* favor (US)

r

réhabituer [ʀeabitɥe] /1/ VT: **se ~ à qch/à faire qch** to get used to sth again/to doing sth again

rehausser [ʀəose] /1/ VT (*relever*) to heighten, raise; (*fig: souligner*) to set off, enhance

réhydrater [ʀeidʀate] VT to rehydrate

réimporter [ʀeɛ̃pɔʀte] /1/ VT to reimport

réimposer [ʀeɛ̃poze] /1/ VT (*Finance*) to reimpose; to tax again

réimpression [ʀeɛ̃pʀesjɔ̃] NF reprinting; (*ouvrage*) reprint

réimprimer [ʀeɛ̃pʀime] /1/ VT to reprint

Reims [ʀɛ̃s] N Rheims

rein [ʀɛ̃] NM kidney; **~ artificiel** kidney machine ■ **reins** NMPL (*dos*) lower back *sg*; **avoir mal aux reins** to have backache

réincarnation [ʀeɛ̃kaʀnasjɔ̃] NF reincarnation

réincarner [ʀeɛ̃kaʀne] /1/: **se réincarner** VPR to be reincarnated

★**reine** [ʀɛn] NF queen

reine-claude [ʀɛnklod] (*pl* **reines-claudes**) NF greengage

reinette [ʀɛnɛt] NF rennet, pippin

réinitialisation [ʀeinisjalizasjɔ̃] NF (*Inform*) reset

réinitialiser [ʀeinisjalize] VT (*Inform*) to reset

réinjecter [ʀeɛ̃ʒɛkte] VT (*ressources, argent aussi Méd*) to reinject

réinscriptible [ʀeɛ̃skʀiptibl] ADJ (*CD, DVD*) rewritable

réinscription [ʀeɛ̃skʀipsjɔ̃] NF re-enrolment

réinscrire [ʀeɛ̃skʀiʀ] VT: **~ qn** (*à l'école, à l'université*) to re-enrol sb; (*sur une liste, un registre*) to put sb's name down again ■ **se réinscrire** VPR (*à l'école, à l'université*) to re-enrol; (*sur une liste*) to put one's name down again

réinsérer [ʀeɛ̃seʀe] /6/ VT (*délinquant, handicapé etc*) to rehabilitate

réinsertion [ʀeɛ̃sɛʀsjɔ̃] NF (*de délinquant, handicapé*) rehabilitation

réinstallation [ʀeɛ̃stalasjɔ̃] NF (*de personne, famille*) relocation, resettlement; (*de locaux*) refitting; (*Inform*) reinstallation

réinstaller [ʀeɛ̃stale] VT (*locaux*) to refit; (*personne, famille*) to relocate, resettle; (*direction*) to reinstate; (*Inform*) to reinstall ■ **se réinstaller** VPR (*personne, famille*) to move back; (*firme*) to relocate; (*doute, inquiétude*) to settle in again

réintégration [ʀeɛ̃tegʀasjɔ̃] NF (*de salarié, fonctionnaire*) reinstatement

réintégrer [ʀeɛ̃tegʀe] /6/ VT (*lieu*) to return to; (*salarié, fonctionnaire*) to reinstate

réintroduction [ʀeɛ̃tʀɔdyksjɔ̃] NF (*d'espèce, de pratique*) reintroduction

réintroduire [ʀeɛ̃tʀɔdɥiʀ] VT (*espèce, pratique*) to reintroduce

réinventer [ʀeɛ̃vɑ̃te] VT to reinvent

réitérer [ʀeiteʀe] /6/ VT to repeat, reiterate

rejaillir [ʀ(ə)ʒajiʀ] /2/ VI to splash up; to fall upon; **~ sur** to splash up onto; (*fig: scandale*) to rebound on; (: *gloire*) to be reflected on

rejet [ʀɔʒɛ] NM (*action, aussi Méd*) rejection; (*Poésie*) enjambement, rejet; (*Bot*) shoot

rejeter [ʀəʒ(ə)te] /4/ VT (*relancer*) to throw back; (*vomir*) to bring ou throw up; (*écarter*) to reject; (*déverser*) to throw out, discharge; (*reporter*): **~ un mot à la fin d'une phrase** to transpose a word to the end of a sentence; **~ la tête/les épaules en arrière** to throw one's head/pull one's shoulders back; **~ la responsabilité de qch sur qn** to lay the responsibility for sth at sb's door ■ **se rejeter** VPR: **se ~ en arrière** to jump back

rejeton [ʀəʒ(ə)tɔ̃] NM offspring

rejette *etc* [ʀ(ə)ʒɛt] VB *voir* **rejeter**

rejoignais *etc* [ʀ(ə)ʒwaɲɛ] VB *voir* **rejoindre**

rejoindre [ʀ(ə)ʒwɛ̃dʀ] /49/ VT (*famille, régiment*) to rejoin, return to; (*lieu*) to get (back) to; (*route etc*) to meet, join; (*rattraper*) to catch up (with); **je te rejoins au café** I'll see ou meet you at the café ■ **se rejoindre** VPR to meet

réjoui, e [ʀeʒwi] ADJ joyous

réjouir [ʀeʒwiʀ] /2/ VT to delight ■ **se réjouir** VPR to be delighted; **se ~ de qch/de faire** to be delighted about sth/to do; **se ~ que** to be delighted that

réjouissances [ʀeʒwisɑ̃s] NFPL (*joie*) rejoicing *sg*; (*fête*) festivities, merry-making *sg*

réjouissant, e [ʀeʒwisɑ̃, -ɑ̃t] ADJ heartening, delightful

relâche [ʀəlɑʃ]: **faire ~** VI (*navire*) to put into port; (*Théât, Ciné*) to be closed; **c'est le jour de ~** (*Théât, Ciné*) it's closed today; **sans ~** *adv* without respite ou a break

relâché, e [ʀ(ə)lɑʃe] ADJ loose, lax

relâchement [ʀ(ə)lɑʃmɑ̃] NM (*d'un prisonnier*) release; (*de la discipline, musculaire*) relaxation

relâcher [ʀ(ə)lɑʃe] /1/ VT (*ressort, prisonnier*) to release; (*étreinte, cordes*) to loosen; (*discipline*) to relax ► VI (*Navig*) to put into port ■ **se relâcher** VPR to loosen; (*discipline*) to become slack ou lax; (*élève etc*) to slacken off

relais [ʀ(ə)lɛ] NM (*Sport*): **(course de) ~** relay (race); (*Radio, TV*) relay; (*intermédiaire*) go-between; **équipe de ~** shift team; (*Sport*) relay team; **prendre le ~ (de)** to take over (from); **~ de poste** post house, coaching inn; **~ routier** ≈ transport café (*BRIT*), ≈ truck stop (*US*)

relance [ʀəlɑ̃s] NF boosting, revival; (*Écon*) reflation

relancer [ʀ(ə)lɑ̃se] /3/ VT (*balle*) to throw back (again); (*moteur*) to restart; (*fig*) to boost, revive; (*personne*): **~ qn** to pester sb; to get on to sb again

relater [ʀ(ə)late] /1/ VT to relate, recount

relatif, -ive [ʀ(ə)latif, -iv] ADJ relative

relation [ʀ(ə)lasjɔ̃] NF (*récit*) account, report; (*rapport*) relation(ship); (*connaissance*) acquaintance; **être/entrer en ~(s) avec** to be in contact ou be dealing/get in contact with; **mettre qn en ~(s) avec** to put sb in touch with ■ **relations** NFPL (*rapports*) relations; relationship; (*connaissances*) connections; **relations internationales** international relations; **relations publiques** public relations; **relations (sexuelles)** sexual relations, (sexual) intercourse *sg*

relationnel, le [ʀ(ə)lasjɔnɛl] ADJ (*problèmes*) interpersonal

relativement [ʀ(ə)lativmɑ̃] ADV relatively; **~ à** in relation to

relativiser [ʀəlativize] /**1**/ ᴠᴛ to see in relation to; to put into context

relativité [ʀ(ə)lativite] ɴꜰ relativity

relax [ʀəlaks] ᴀᴅᴊ ɪɴᴠ, **relaxe** [ʀəlaks] ᴀᴅᴊ relaxed, informal, casual; easy-going; **(fauteuil-)relax** *nm* reclining chair

relaxant, e [ʀ(ə)laksã, -ãt] ᴀᴅᴊ *(cure, médicament)* relaxant; *(ambiance)* relaxing

relaxation [ʀ(ə)laksasjɔ̃] ɴꜰ relaxation

relaxer [ʀəlakse] /**1**/ ᴠᴛ to relax; *(Jur)* to discharge ▪ **se relaxer** ᴠᴘʀ to relax

relayer [ʀ(ə)leje] /**8**/ ᴠᴛ *(collaborateur, coureur etc)* to relieve, take over from; *(Radio, TV)* to relay ▪ **se relayer** ᴠᴘʀ *(dans une activité)* to take it in turns

relecture [ʀ(ə)lɛktyʀ] ɴꜰ rereading

relégation [ʀ(ə)legasjɔ̃] ɴꜰ *(Sport)* relegation

reléguer [ʀ(ə)lege] /**6**/ ᴠᴛ to relegate; **~ au second plan** to push into the background

relent [ʀəlã] ɴᴍ, **relents** ɴᴍᴘʟ stench *sg*

relevé, e [ʀəl(ə)ve] ᴀᴅᴊ *(bord de chapeau)* turned-up; *(manches)* rolled-up; *(fig: style)* elevated; *(: sauce)* highly-seasoned ▸ ɴᴍ *(lecture)* reading; *(de cotes)* plotting; *(liste)* statement; list; *(facture)* account; **~ bancaire** *ou* **de compte** bank statement; **~ d'identité bancaire** bank account details

relève [ʀəlɛv] ɴꜰ *(personne)* relief; *(équipe)* relief team *(ou* troops *pl)*; **prendre la ~** to take over

relèvement [ʀ(ə)lɛvmã] ɴᴍ *(d'un taux, niveau)* raising

relever [ʀəl(ə)ve] /**5**/ ᴠᴛ *(statue, meuble)* to stand up again; *(personne tombée)* to help up; *(vitre, plafond, niveau de vie)* to raise; *(pays, économie, entreprise)* to put back on its feet; *(col)* to turn up; *(style, conversation)* to elevate; *(plat, sauce)* to season; *(sentinelle, équipe)* to relieve; *(souligner: fautes, points)* to pick out; *(constater: traces etc)* to find, pick up; *(répliquer à: remarque)* to react to, reply to; *(: défi)* to accept, take up; *(noter: adresse etc)* to take down, note; *(: plan)* to sketch; *(: cotes etc)* to plot; *(compteur)* to read; *(ramasser: cahiers, copies)* to collect, take in; **~ qn de** *(vœux)* to release sb from; *(fonctions)* to relieve sb of; **~ la tête** to look up; to hold up one's head ▸ ᴠɪ: **~ de** *vt (maladie)* to be recovering from; *(être du ressort de)* to be a matter for; *(Admin: dépendre de)* to come under; *(fig)* to pertain to ▪ **se relever** ᴠᴘʀ *(se remettre debout)* to get up; *(fig)*: **se ~ (de)** to recover (from)

relief [ʀəljɛf] ɴᴍ relief; *(de pneu)* tread pattern; **en ~** in relief; *(photographie)* three-dimensional; **mettre en ~** *(fig)* to bring out, highlight ▪ **reliefs** ɴᴍᴘʟ *(restes)* remains

relier [ʀəlje] /**7**/ ᴠᴛ to link up; *(livre)* to bind; **~ qch à** to link sth to; **livre relié cuir** leather-bound book

relieur, -euse [ʀəljœʀ, -øz] ɴᴍ/ꜰ (book)binder

religieusement [ʀ(ə)liʒjøzmã] ᴀᴅᴠ religiously; *(enterré, mariés)* in church; **vivre ~** to lead a religious life

★**religieux, -euse** [ʀ(ə)liʒjø, -øz] ᴀᴅᴊ religious ▸ ɴᴍ monk ▸ ɴꜰ nun; *(gâteau)* cream puff

★**religion** [ʀ(ə)liʒjɔ̃] ɴꜰ religion; *(piété, dévotion)* faith; **entrer en ~** to take one's vows

reliquaire [ʀəlikɛʀ] ɴᴍ reliquary

reliquat [ʀəlika] ɴᴍ *(d'une somme)* balance; *(Jur: de succession)* residue

relique [ʀəlik] ɴꜰ relic

relire [ʀ(ə)liʀ] /**43**/ ᴠᴛ *(à nouveau)* to reread, read again; *(vérifier)* to read over ▪ **se relire** ᴠᴘʀ to read through what one has written

reliure [ʀəljyʀ] ɴꜰ binding; *(art, métier)*: **la ~** bookbinding

reloger [ʀ(ə)lɔʒe] /**3**/ ᴠᴛ *(locataires, sinistrés)* to rehouse

relooker [ʀəluke] /**1**/ ᴠᴛ: **~ qn** to give sb a makeover

relooking [ʀ(ə)lukiŋ] ɴᴍ *(fam: de personne, entreprise)* makeover; *(: de produit)* repackaging

relu, e [ʀəly] ᴘᴘ *de* **relire**

reluire [ʀ(ə)lɥiʀ] /**38**/ ᴠɪ to gleam

reluisant, e [ʀ(ə)lɥizã, -ãt] ᴠʙ *voir* **reluire** ▸ ᴀᴅᴊ gleaming; **peu ~** *(fig)* unattractive; unsavoury (Bʀɪᴛ), unsavory (US)

reluquer [ʀ(ə)lyke] /**1**/ ᴠᴛ *(fam)* to eye (up), ogle

remâcher [ʀ(ə)maʃe] /**1**/ ᴠᴛ to chew *ou* ruminate over

remailler [ʀ(ə)maje] /**1**/ ᴠᴛ *(tricot)* to darn; *(filet)* to mend

remake [ʀimɛk] ɴᴍ *(Ciné)* remake

remaniement [ʀ(ə)manimã] ɴᴍ: **~ ministériel** Cabinet reshuffle

remanier [ʀ(ə)manje] /**7**/ ᴠᴛ to reshape, recast; *(Pol)* to reshuffle

remariage [ʀ(ə)maʀjaʒ] ɴᴍ second marriage

remarier [ʀ(ə)maʀje] /**7**/: **se remarier** ᴠᴘʀ to remarry, get married again

remarquable [ʀ(ə)maʀkabl] ᴀᴅᴊ remarkable

remarquablement [ʀ(ə)maʀkabləmã] ᴀᴅᴠ remarkably

remarque [ʀ(ə)maʀk] ɴꜰ remark; *(écrite)* note

★**remarquer** [ʀ(ə)maʀke] /**1**/ ᴠᴛ *(voir)* to notice; *(dire)*: **~ que** to remark that; **se faire ~** to draw attention to o.s.; **faire ~ (à qn) que** to point out (to sb) that; **faire ~ qch (à qn)** to point sth out (to sb); **remarquez, ...** mind you, ... ▪ **se remarquer** ᴠᴘʀ to be noticeable

remastériser [ʀ(ə)masterize] ᴠᴛ *(album, film)* to remaster

remballer [ʀãbale] /**1**/ ᴠᴛ to wrap up (again); *(dans un carton)* to pack up (again)

rembarrer [ʀãbaʀe] /**1**/ ᴠᴛ: **~ qn** *(repousser)* to rebuff sb; *(remettre à sa place)* to put sb in his *(ou* her) place

remblai [ʀãblɛ] ɴᴍ embankment

remblayer [ʀãbleje] /**8**/ ᴠᴛ to bank up; *(fossé)* to fill in

rembobiner [ʀãbɔbine] /**1**/ ᴠᴛ to rewind

rembourrage [ʀãbuʀaʒ] ɴᴍ stuffing; padding

rembourré, e [ʀãbuʀe] ᴀᴅᴊ padded

rembourrer [ʀãbuʀe] /**1**/ ᴠᴛ to stuff; *(dossier, vêtement, souliers)* to pad

remboursable [ʀãbuʀsabl] ᴀᴅᴊ repayable

remboursement [ʀãbuʀsəmã] ɴᴍ *(de dette, d'emprunt)* repayment; *(de frais)* refund; **envoi contre ~** cash on delivery

★**rembourser** [ʀãbuʀse] /**1**/ ᴠᴛ to pay back, repay; *(frais, billet etc)* to refund; **se faire ~** to get a refund

rembrunir [ʀãbʀyniʀ] /**2**/: **se rembrunir** ᴠᴘʀ to grow sombre (Bʀɪᴛ) *ou* somber (US)

r

remède [ʀ(ə)mɛd] NM (*médicament*) medicine; (*traitement, fig*) remedy, cure; **trouver un ~ à** (*Méd, fig*) to find a cure for

remédier [ʀ(ə)medje] /7/: **~ à** VT to remedy

remembrement [ʀ(ə)mãbʀəmã] NM (*Agr*) regrouping of lands

remémorer [ʀ(ə)memɔʀe] /1/: **se remémorer** VPR to recall, recollect

remerciements [ʀ(ə)mɛʀsimã] NMPL thanks; **(avec) tous mes ~** (with) grateful *ou* many thanks

★**remercier** [ʀ(ə)mɛʀsje] /7/ VT to thank; (*congédier*) to dismiss; **~ qn de/d'avoir fait** to thank sb for/ for having done; **non, je vous remercie** no thank you

remettre [ʀ(ə)mɛtʀ] /56/ VT (*vêtement*): **~ qch** to put sth back on, put sth on again; (*replacer*): **~ qch quelque part** to put sth back somewhere; (*ajouter*): **~ du sel/un sucre** to add more salt/ another lump of sugar; (*ajourner*): **~ qch (à)** to postpone sth *ou* put sth off (until); **~ qn** (*rétablir: personne*) to set sb back on his (*ou* her) feet; **~ qch à qn** (*rendre, restituer*) to give sth back to sb, return sth to sb; (*confier: paquet, argent*) to hand sth over to sb, deliver sth to sb; (*donner: lettre, clé etc*) to hand over sth to sb; (: *prix, décoration*) to present sb with sth; **~ une pendule à l'heure** to put a clock right; **~ un moteur/une machine en marche** to get an engine/a machine going again; **~ en état/en ordre** to repair/sort out; **~ en cause/question** to challenge, to call into question; **~ sa démission** to hand in one's notice; **~ qch à neuf** to make sth as good as new; **~ qn à sa place** (*fig*) to put sb in his (*ou* her) place ◼ **se remettre** VPR to get better, recover; **se ~ de** to recover from, get over; **s'en ~ à** to leave it (up) to; **se ~ à faire/qch** to start doing/ sth again

réminiscence [ʀeminisãs] NF reminiscence

remis, e [ʀəmi, -iz] PP *de* **remettre**

remise [ʀ(ə)miz] NF (*de lettre*) delivery; (*de décoration*) presentation; (*rabais*) discount; (*local*) shed; **~ à neuf** restoration; **~ de fonds** remittance; **une ~ de 10%** a 10% discount; **~ en cause** calling into question, challenging; **~ en jeu** (*Football*) throw-in; **~ en marche** starting up again; **~ en ordre** sorting out; **~ en question** calling into question, challenging

remiser [ʀ(ə)mize] /1/ VT to put away

rémission [ʀemisjɔ̃] NF (*Méd*) remission; **sans ~** *adj* irremediable *adv* unremittingly

remobiliser [ʀ(ə)mɔbilize] VT (*électorat, communauté*) to rally; **~ les troupes** (*fig*) to rally the troops

remodeler [ʀ(ə)mɔd(ə)le] /5/ VT to remodel; (*fig: restructurer*) to restructure

rémois, e [ʀemwa, -waz] ADJ of *ou* from Reims ▶ NM/F: **Rémois, e** inhabitant *ou* native of Reims

remontant [ʀ(ə)mɔ̃tã] NM tonic, pick-me-up

remontée [ʀ(ə)mɔ̃te] NF rising; ascent; **remontées mécaniques** (*Ski*) ski lifts, ski tows

remonte-pente [ʀ(ə)mɔ̃tpãt] NM ski lift, ski tow

remonter [ʀ(ə)mɔ̃te] /1/ VI (*à nouveau*) to go back up; (*à cheval*) to remount; (*après une descente*) to go up (again); (*prix, température*) to go up again; (*en voiture*) to get back in; (*jupe*) to ride up; **~ à** (*dater de*)

to date *ou* go back to; **~ en voiture** to get back into the car ▶ VT (*pente*) to go up; (*fleuve*) to sail (*ou* swim *etc*) up; (*manches, pantalon*) to roll up; (*fam*) to turn up; (*niveau, limite*) to raise; (*fig: personne*) to buck up; (*moteur, meuble*) to put back together, reassemble; (*garde-robe etc*) to renew, replenish; (*montre, mécanisme*) to wind up; **~ le moral à qn** to cheer sb up, to raise sb's spirits

remontoir [ʀ(ə)mɔ̃twaʀ] NM winding mechanism, winder

remontrance [ʀ(ə)mɔ̃tʀãs] NF reproof, reprimand

remontrer [ʀ(ə)mɔ̃tʀe] /1/ VT (*montrer de nouveau*): **~ qch (à qn)** to show sth again (to sb); (*fig*) **en ~ à** to prove one's superiority over

remords [ʀ(ə)mɔʀ] NM remorse *no pl*; **avoir des ~** to feel remorse, be conscience-stricken

remorque [ʀ(ə)mɔʀk] NF trailer; **prendre/être en ~** to tow/be on tow; **être à la ~** (*fig*) to tag along (behind)

remorquer [ʀ(ə)mɔʀke] /1/ VT to tow

remorqueur [ʀ(ə)mɔʀkœʀ] NM tug(boat)

rémoulade [ʀemulad] NF dressing with mustard and herbs

rémouleur [ʀemulœʀ] NM (knife- *ou* scissor-) grinder

remous [ʀəmu] NM (*d'un navire*) (back)wash *no pl*; (*de rivière*) swirl, eddy *pl*; (*fig*) stir *sg*

rempailler [ʀãpaje] /1/ VT to reseat (*with straw*)

rempart [ʀãpaʀ] NM rampart; **faire à qn un ~ de son corps** to shield sb with one's (own) body

remparts [ʀãpaʀ] NMPL walls, ramparts

rempiler [ʀãpile] /1/ VT (*dossiers, livres etc*) to pile up again ▶ VI (*Mil: fam*) to join up again

remplaçant, e [ʀãplasã, -ãt] NM/F replacement, substitute, stand-in; (*Théât*) understudy; (*Scol*) supply (BRIT) *ou* substitute (US) teacher

remplacement [ʀãplasmã] NM replacement; (*job*) replacement work *no pl*; (*suppléance: Scol*) supply (BRIT) *ou* substitute (US) teaching; **assurer le ~ de qn** (*remplaçant*) to stand in *ou* substitute for sb; **faire des remplacements** (*professeur*) to do supply (BRIT) *ou* substitute (US) teaching; (*médecin*) to do locum work; (*secrétaire*) to temp

★**remplacer** [ʀãplase] /3/ VT to replace; (*prendre temporairement la place de*) to stand in for; (*tenir lieu de*) to take the place of, act as a substitute for; **~ qch/qn par** to replace sth/sb with

rempli, e [ʀãpli] ADJ (*emploi du temps*) full, busy; **~ de** full of, filled with

★**remplir** [ʀãpliʀ] /2/ VT to fill (up); (*questionnaire*) to fill in (BRIT) *ou* out (US); (*obligations, fonction, condition*) to fulfil; **~ qch de** to fill sth with ◼ **se remplir** VPR to fill up

remplissage [ʀãplisaʒ] NM (*fig: péj*) padding

remploi [ʀãplwa] NM re-use

rempocher [ʀãpɔʃe] /1/ VT to put back into one's pocket

remporter [ʀãpɔʀte] /1/ VT (*marchandise*) to take away; (*fig*) to win, achieve

rempoter [ʀãpɔte] /1/ VT to repot

remuant, e [ʀəmɥã, -ãt] ADJ restless

remue-ménage [ʀ(ə)mymenaʒ] NM INV commotion

remuer [ʀəmɥe] /**1**/ ᵥᴛ to move; (café, sauce) to stir ▶ ᵥɪ to move; (fig: opposants) to show signs of unrest ■ **se remuer** ᵥᴘʀ to move; (se démener) to stir o.s.; (fam: s'activer) to get a move on

rémunérateur, -trice [ʀemyneʀatœʀ, -tʀis] ᴀᴅᴊ remunerative, lucrative

rémunération [ʀemyneʀasjɔ̃] ɴꜰ remuneration

rémunérer [ʀemyneʀe] /**6**/ ᵥᴛ to remunerate, pay

renâcler [ʀ(ə)nɑkle] /**1**/ ᵥɪ to snort; (fig) to grumble, balk

renaissance [ʀ(ə)nɛsɑ̃s] ɴꜰ rebirth, revival; **la R~** the Renaissance

renaître [ʀ(ə)nɛtʀ] /**59**/ ᵥɪ to be revived; **~ à la vie** to take on a new lease of life; **~ à l'espoir** to find fresh hope

rénal, e, -aux [ʀenal, -o] ᴀᴅᴊ renal, kidney cpd

★**renard** [ʀ(ə)naʀ] ɴᴍ fox

renardeau, x [ʀ(ə)naʀdo] ɴᴍ fox cub

rencard [ʀɑ̃kaʀ] ɴᴍ = **rancard**

rencart [ʀɑ̃kaʀ] ɴᴍ = **rancart**

renchérir [ʀɑ̃ʃeʀiʀ] /**2**/ ᵥɪ to become more expensive; (fig): **~ (sur)** (en paroles) to add something (to)

renchérissement [ʀɑ̃ʃeʀismɑ̃] ɴᴍ increase (in the cost ou price of)

rencontre [ʀɑ̃kɔ̃tʀ] ɴꜰ (de cours d'eau) confluence; (de véhicules) collision; (entrevue, congrès, match etc) meeting; (imprévue) encounter; **faire la ~ de qn** to meet sb; **aller à la ~ de qn** to go and meet sb; **amours de ~** casual love affairs

★**rencontrer** [ʀɑ̃kɔ̃tʀe] /**1**/ ᵥᴛ to meet; (mot, expression) to come across; (difficultés) to meet with ■ **se rencontrer** ᵥᴘʀ to meet; (véhicules) to collide

rendement [ʀɑ̃dmɑ̃] ɴᴍ (d'un travailleur, d'une machine) output; (d'une culture, d'un champ) yield; (d'un investissement) return; **à plein ~** at full capacity

★**rendez-vous** [ʀɑ̃devu] ɴᴍ (rencontre) appointment; (: d'amoureux) date; (lieu) meeting place; **donner ~ à qn** to arrange to meet sb; **recevoir sur ~** to have an appointment system; **fixer un ~ à qn** to give sb an appointment; **avoir/prendre ~ (avec)** to have/make an appointment (with); **prendre ~ chez le médecin** to make an appointment with the doctor; **~ spatial** ou **orbital** docking (in space)

rendormir [ʀɑ̃dɔʀmiʀ] /**16**/: **se rendormir** ᵥᴘʀ to go back to sleep

★**rendre** [ʀɑ̃dʀ] /**41**/ ᵥᴛ (livre, argent etc) to give back, return; (otages, visite, politesse, invitation, Jur: verdict) to return; (honneurs) to pay; (sang, aliments) to bring up; (sons, instrument) to produce, make; (exprimer, traduire) to render; (jugement) to pronounce, render; (faire devenir): **~ qn célèbre/qch possible** to make sb famous/sth possible; **~ la vue/la santé à qn** to restore sb's sight/health; **~ la liberté à qn** to set sb free; **~ la monnaie** to give change ■ **se rendre** ᵥᴘʀ (capituler) to surrender, give o.s. up; (aller): **se ~ quelque part** to go somewhere; **se ~ à** (arguments etc) to bow to; (ordres) to comply with; **se ~ compte de qch** to realize sth; **se ~ insupportable/malade** to become unbearable/make o.s. ill

rendu, e [ʀɑ̃dy] ᴘᴘ de **rendre** ▶ ᴀᴅᴊ (fatigué) exhausted

renégat, e [ʀənega, -at] ɴᴍ/ꜰ renegade

renégocier [ʀənegɔsje] /**7**/ ᵥᴛ to renegotiate

rênes [ʀɛn] ɴꜰᴘʟ reins

renfermé, e [ʀɑ̃fɛʀme] ᴀᴅᴊ (fig) withdrawn ▶ ɴᴍ: **sentir le ~** to smell stuffy

renfermer [ʀɑ̃fɛʀme] /**1**/ ᵥᴛ to contain ■ **se renfermer (sur soi-même)** ᵥᴘʀ to withdraw into o.s.

renfiler [ʀɑ̃file] /**1**/ ᵥᴛ (collier) to rethread; (pull) to slip on

renflé, e [ʀɑ̃fle] ᴀᴅᴊ bulging, bulbous

renflement [ʀɑ̃fləmɑ̃] ɴᴍ bulge

renflouement [ʀɑ̃flumɑ̃] ɴᴍ (d'épave) raising, refloating; (fig: de commerce, affaire) bailing out

renflouer [ʀɑ̃flue] /**1**/ ᵥᴛ (épave) to raise, refloat; (fig: commerce, affaire) to bail out; **~ les caisses** to refill the coffers

renfoncement [ʀɑ̃fɔ̃smɑ̃] ɴᴍ recess

renforcer [ʀɑ̃fɔʀse] /**3**/ ᵥᴛ to reinforce; **~ qn dans ses opinions** to confirm sb's opinion

renfort [ʀɑ̃fɔʀ] ɴᴍ: **renforts** nmpl reinforcements; **en ~** as a back-up; **à grand ~ de** with a great deal of

renfrogné, e [ʀɑ̃fʀɔɲe] ᴀᴅᴊ sullen, scowling

renfrogner [ʀɑ̃fʀɔɲe] /**1**/: **se renfrogner** ᵥᴘʀ to scowl

rengager [ʀɑ̃gaʒe] /**3**/ ᵥᴛ (personnel) to take on again ■ **se rengager** ᵥᴘʀ (Mil) to re-enlist

rengaine [ʀɑ̃gɛn] ɴꜰ (péj) old tune

rengainer [ʀɑ̃gene] /**1**/ ᵥᴛ (revolver) to put back in its holster; (épée) to sheathe; (fam: compliment, discours) to save, withhold

rengorger [ʀɑ̃gɔʀʒe] /**3**/: **se rengorger** ᵥᴘʀ (fig) to puff o.s. up

renier [ʀənje] /**7**/ ᵥᴛ (parents) to disown, repudiate; (engagements) to go back on; (foi) to renounce

renifler [ʀ(ə)nifle] /**1**/ ᵥɪ to sniff ▶ ᵥᴛ (odeur, tabac) to sniff

rennais, e [ʀɛnɛ, -ɛz] ᴀᴅᴊ of ou from Rennes ▶ ɴᴍ/ꜰ: **Rennais, e** inhabitant ou native of Rennes

renne [ʀɛn] ɴᴍ reindeer inv

renom [ʀənɔ̃] ɴᴍ reputation; (célébrité) renown; **vin de grand ~** celebrated ou highly renowned wine

renommé, e [ʀ(ə)nɔme] ᴀᴅᴊ celebrated, renowned ▶ ɴꜰ fame

renoncement [ʀ(ə)nɔ̃smɑ̃] ɴᴍ abnegation, renunciation

★**renoncer** [ʀ(ə)nɔ̃se] /**3**/: **~ à** ᵥᴛ to give up; **~ à faire** to give up the idea of doing; **j'y renonce !** I give up!

renouer [ʀənwe] /**1**/ ᵥᴛ (cravate etc) to retie; (fig: conversation, liaison) to renew, resume; **~ avec** (tradition) to revive; (habitude) to take up again; **~ avec qn** to take up with sb again

renouveau, x [ʀ(ə)nuvo] ɴᴍ revival; **~ de succès** renewed success

★**renouvelable** [ʀ(ə)nuv(ə)labl] ᴀᴅᴊ (contrat, bail, énergie) renewable; (expérience) which can be repeated

renouveler [ʀ(ə)nuv(ə)le] /**4**/ ᵥᴛ (contrat, bail) to renew; (exploit, méfait) to repeat ■ **se renouveler**

r

VPR (*incident*) to recur, happen again, be repeated; (*cellules etc*) to be renewed *ou* replaced; (*artiste, écrivain*) to try something new

renouvellement [R(ə)nuvɛlmɑ̃] NM renewal; recurrence

rénovation [Renɔvasjɔ̃] NF renovation; restoration; reform(ing); redevelopment

rénover [Renɔve] /**1**/ VT (*immeuble*) to renovate, do up; (*meuble*) to restore; (*enseignement*) to reform; (*quartier*) to redevelop

★**renseignement** [Rɑ̃sɛɲmɑ̃] NM information *no pl*, piece of information; (*Mil*) intelligence *no pl*; **prendre des renseignements sur** to make inquiries about, ask for information about; **(guichet des) renseignements** information desk; **(service des) renseignements** (*Tél*) directory inquiries (BRIT), information (US); **service de renseignements** (*Mil*) intelligence service; **les renseignements généraux** = the secret police

★**renseigner** [Rɑ̃sɛɲe] /**1**/ VT: **~ qn (sur)** to give information to sb (about) ■ **se renseigner** VPR to ask for information, make inquiries

rentabiliser [Rɑ̃tabilize] /**1**/ VT (*capitaux, production*) to make profitable

rentabilité [Rɑ̃tabilite] NF profitability; cost-effectiveness; (*d'un investissement*) return; **seuil de ~** break-even point

rentable [Rɑ̃tabl] ADJ profitable; cost-effective

rente [Rɑ̃t] NF income; (*pension*) pension; (*titre*) government stock *ou* bond; **~ viagère** life annuity

rentier, -ière [Rɑ̃tje, -jɛR] NM/F person of private *ou* independent means

rentrée [Rɑ̃tRe] NF: **~ (d'argent)** cash *no pl* coming in; **la ~ (des classes** *ou* **scolaire)** the start of the new school year; **la ~ (parlementaire)** the reopening *ou* reassembly of parliament

La rentrée in September each year has wider connotations than just the start of the new school year. It is also the time when political and social life picks up again after the long summer break, and so is an important point in the French calendar. The *rentrée littéraire* marks the start of the new publishing season, with books by leading writers usually published in September and October.

★**rentrer** [Rɑ̃tRe] /**1**/ VI (*entrer de nouveau*) to go (*ou* come) back in; (*entrer*) to go (*ou* come) in; (*revenir chez soi*) to go (*ou* come) (back) home; (*air, clou: pénétrer*) to go in; (*revenu, argent*) to come in; **~ dans** to go (*ou* come) back into; to go (*ou* come) into; (*famille, patrie*) to go back *ou* return to; (*heurter*) to crash into; (*appartenir à*) to be included in (: *catégorie etc*) to fall into; **~ dans l'ordre** to get back to normal; **~ dans ses frais** to recover one's expenses *ou* initial outlay ▶ VT (*foins*) to bring in; (*véhicule*) to put away; (*chemise dans pantalon etc*) to tuck in; (*griffes*) to draw in; (*train d'atterrissage*) to raise; (*fig: larmes, colère etc*) to hold back; **~ le ventre** to pull in one's stomach

renverrai *etc* [Rɑ̃veRe] VB *voir* **renvoyer**

renversant, e [Rɑ̃vɛRsɑ̃, -ɑ̃t] ADJ amazing, astounding

renverse [Rɑ̃vɛRs]: **à la ~** *adv* backwards

renversé, e [Rɑ̃vɛRse] ADJ (*écriture*) backhand; (*image*) reversed; (*stupéfait*) staggered

renversement [Rɑ̃vɛRsəmɑ̃] NM (*d'un régime, des traditions*) overthrow; **~ de la situation** reversal of the situation

★**renverser** [Rɑ̃vɛRse] /**1**/ VT (*faire tomber: chaise, verre*) to knock over, overturn; (: *piéton*) to knock down; (: *liquide, contenu*) to spill, upset; (*retourner: verre, image*) to turn upside down, invert; (: *ordre des mots etc*) to reverse; (*fig: gouvernement etc*) to overthrow; (*stupéfier*) to bowl over, stagger; **~ la tête/le corps (en arrière)** to tip one's head back/throw oneself back; **~ la vapeur** (*fig*) to change course ■ **se renverser** VPR (*verre, vase*) to fall over; to overturn; (*contenu*) to spill; **se ~ (en arrière)** to lean back

renvoi [Rɑ̃vwa] NM (*d'employé*) dismissal; return; reflection; postponement; (*d'élève*) expulsion; (*référence*) cross-reference; (*éructation*) belch

★**renvoyer** [Rɑ̃vwaje] /**8**/ VT to send back; (*employé*) to dismiss; (*Tennis*) to return; (*élève: définitivement*) to expel; (*lumière*) to reflect; (*son*) to echo; (*ajourner*): **~ qch (à)** to postpone sth (until); **~ qch à qn** (*rendre*) to return sth to sb; **~ qn à** (*fig*) to refer sb to

réorganisation [ReɔRganizasjɔ̃] NF reorganization

réorganiser [ReɔRganize] /**1**/ VT to reorganize

réorienter [ReɔRjɑ̃te] /**1**/ VT to reorient(ate), redirect

réouverture [ReuvɛRtyR] NF reopening

repaire [R(ə)pɛR] NM den

repaître [RəpɛtR] /**57**/ VT to feast; to feed ■ **se repaître** VPR: **se ~ de** (*animal*) to feed on; (*fig*) to wallow *ou* revel in

répandre [RepɑdR] /**41**/ VT (*renverser*) to spill; (*étaler, diffuser*) to spread; (*lumière*) to shed; (*chaleur, odeur*) to give off ■ **se répandre** VPR to spill; to spread; **se ~ en** (*injures etc*) to pour out

répandu, e [Repɑdy] PP *de* **répandre** ▶ ADJ (*opinion, usage*) widespread

réparable [RepaRabl] ADJ (*montre etc*) repairable; (*perte etc*) which can be made up for

reparaître [R(ə)paRɛtR] /**57**/ VI to reappear

réparateur, -trice [RepaRatœR, -tRis] NM/F repairer

réparation [RepaRasjɔ̃] NF repairing *no pl*, repair; **en ~** (*machine etc*) under repair; **demander à qn ~ de** (*offense etc*) to ask sb to make amends for

réparer [RepaRe] /**1**/ VT to repair; (*fig: offense*) to make up for, atone for; (: *oubli, erreur*) to put right

reparler [R(ə)paRle] /**1**/ VI: **~ de qn/qch** to talk about sb/sth again; **~ à qn** to speak to sb again

repars *etc* [Rəpar] VB *voir* **repartir**

répartie, repartie [Reparti] NF retort; **avoir de la ~** to be quick at repartee, to be always ready with a reply

repartir [RəpaRtiR] /**16**/ VI to set off again; (*voyageur*) to leave again; (*fig*) to get going again, pick up again; **~ à zéro** to start from scratch

répartir [RepaRtiR] /**2**/ VT (*pour attribuer*) to share out; (*pour disperser, disposer*) to divide up; (*poids, chaleur*) to distribute; **~ sur** (*étaler: dans le temps*) to spread over; (*classer, diviser*): **~ en** to divide into, split up into ■ **se répartir** VPR (*travail, rôles*) to share out between themselves

répartiteur, -trice [ʀepaʀtitœʀ, -tʀis] NM
(Auto: d'ABS) distributor; (Méd) distributor; (Tél)
main distribution frame ▸ NM/F (distributeur) distributor

répartition [ʀepaʀtisjɔ̃] NF sharing out; dividing
up; (des richesses etc) distribution

reparution [ʀ(ə)paʀysjɔ̃] NF (de livre) republica-
tion

★**repas** [ʀ(ə)pɑ] NM meal; **à l'heure des ~** at meal-
times

repassable [ʀ(ə)pasabl] ADJ (vêtement) ironable;
non ~ non-ironable

repassage [ʀ(ə)pasaʒ] NM ironing

★**repasser** [ʀ(ə)pase] /1/ VI to come (ou go) back ▸ VT
(vêtement, tissu) to iron; (examen) to retake, resit;
(film) to show again; (lame) to sharpen; (leçon, rôle:
revoir) to go over (again); (plat, pain): **~ qch à qn** to
pass sth back to sb

repasseuse [ʀ(ə)pasøz] NF (machine) ironing
machine

repayer [ʀ(ə)peje] /8/ VT to pay again

repêchage [ʀ(ə)pɛʃaʒ] NM (Scol): **question de ~**
question to give candidates a second chance

repêcher [ʀ(ə)peʃe] /1/ VT (noyé) to recover the
body of, fish out; (fam: candidat) to pass (by inflating
marks); to give a second chance to

repeindre [ʀ(ə)pɛ̃dʀ] /52/ VT to repaint

repenser [ʀ(ə)pɑ̃se] VT (question, organisation) to
rethink; (événement) to take a fresh look at ▸ VI: **~ à
qch** (se remémorer) to think about sth again

repentance [ʀ(ə)pɑ̃tɑ̃s] NF repentance; **faire
acte de ~** to show repentance

repentant, e [ʀ(ə)pɑ̃tɑ̃, -ɑ̃t] ADJ, NM/F repentant

repenti, e [ʀ(ə)pɑ̃ti] ADJ repentant ▸ NM/F (ancien
mafieux) pentito, former mafioso turned police witness

repentir [ʀ(ə)pɑ̃tiʀ] /16/ NM repentance ■ **se
repentir** VPR to repent; **se ~ d'avoir fait qch**
(regretter) to regret having done sth

repérable [ʀ(ə)peʀabl] ADJ noticeable; **être ~ à
qch** to be easy to spot because of sth

repérage [ʀ(ə)peʀaʒ] NM (d'objectif, lieux) reconnaissance

répercussions [ʀepɛʀkysjɔ̃] NFPL repercussions

répercuter [ʀepɛʀkyte] /1/ VT (réfléchir, renvoyer:
son, voix) to reflect; (faire transmettre: consignes,
charges etc) to pass on ■ **se répercuter** VPR (bruit)
to reverberate; **se ~ sur** (fig) to have repercussions on

repère [ʀ(ə)pɛʀ] NM mark; (monument etc) landmark; **(point de) ~** point of reference

repérer [ʀ(ə)peʀe] /6/ VT (erreur, connaissance) to
spot; (abri, ennemi) to locate; **se faire ~** to be spotted ■ **se repérer** VPR to get one's bearings

répertoire [ʀepɛʀtwaʀ] NM (liste) (alphabetical)
list; (carnet) index notebook; (Inform) directory; (de
carnet) thumb index; (indicateur) directory, index;
(d'un théâtre, artiste) repertoire

répertorier [ʀepɛʀtɔʀje] /7/ VT to itemize, list

répéter [ʀepete] /6/ VT to repeat; (préparer: leçon) to
learn, go over; (Théât) to rehearse ■ **se répéter**
VPR (redire) to repeat o.s.; (se reproduire) to be
repeated, recur

répéteur [ʀepetœʀ] NM (Tél) repeater

répétitif, -ive [ʀepetitif, -iv] ADJ repetitive

répétition [ʀepetisjɔ̃] NF repetition; (Théât)
rehearsal; **armes à ~** repeater weapons; **~ générale** final dress rehearsal ■ **répétitions** NFPL
(leçons) private coaching sg

répétitivité [ʀepetitivite] NF repetitiveness

repeuplement [ʀ(ə)pœpləmɑ̃] NM (de village,
région) repopulation; (de forêt) replanting; (de
rivière) restocking

repeupler [ʀ(ə)pœple] /1/ VT to repopulate; (forêt)
to replant; (rivière) to restock

repiquage [ʀ(ə)pikaʒ] NM pricking out, planting
out; re-recording

repiquer [ʀ(ə)pike] /1/ VT (plants) to prick out,
plant out; (enregistrement) to re-record

répit [ʀepi] NM respite; **sans ~** without letting up

replacer [ʀ(ə)plase] /3/ VT to replace, put back

replanter [ʀ(ə)plɑ̃te] /1/ VT to replant

replat [ʀəpla] NM ledge

replâtrer [ʀ(ə)plɑtʀe] /1/ VT (mur) to replaster

replet, -ète [ʀəplɛ, -ɛt] ADJ chubby, fat

repli [ʀəpli] NM (d'une étoffe) fold; (Mil, fig) withdrawal

replier [ʀ(ə)plije] /7/ VT (rabattre) to fold down ou
over ■ **se replier** VPR (armée) to withdraw, fall
back; **se ~ sur soi-même** to withdraw into oneself

réplique [ʀeplik] NF (repartie, fig) reply; (objection)
retort; (Théât) line; (copie) replica; **donner la ~ à** to
play opposite; **sans ~** adj no-nonsense; irrefutable

répliquer [ʀeplike] /1/ VI to reply; (avec impertinence) to answer back; (riposter) to retaliate

replonger [ʀ(ə)plɔ̃ʒe] /3/ VT: **~ qch dans** to plunge
sth back into ■ **se replonger** VPR: **se ~ dans** (journal etc) to immerse o.s. in again

répondant, e [ʀepɔ̃dɑ̃, -ɑ̃t] NM/F (garant) guarantor, surety

répondeur [ʀepɔ̃dœʀ] NM: **~ (automatique)** (Tél)
answering machine

répondre [ʀepɔ̃dʀ] /41/ VI to answer, reply; (freins,
mécanisme) to respond; **~ à** vt to reply to, answer;
(invitation, convocation) to reply to; (affection, salut)
to return; (provocation, mécanisme etc) to respond to;
(correspondre à: besoin) to answer; (: conditions) to
meet; (: description) to match; **~ à qn** (avec impertinence) to answer sb back; **~ que** to answer ou reply
that; **~ de** to answer for

réponse [ʀepɔ̃s] NF answer, reply; **avec ~ payée**
(Postes) reply-paid, post-paid (US); **avoir ~ à tout**
to have an answer for everything; **en ~ à** in reply
to; **carte-/bulletin-réponse** reply card/slip

report [ʀapɔʀ] NM postponement; transfer;
~ d'incorporation (Mil) deferment

reportage [ʀ(ə)pɔʀtaʒ] NM (bref) report; (écrit: documentaire) story; article; (en direct) commentary;
(genre, activité): **le ~** reporting

reporter[1] [ʀ(ə)pɔʀtɛʀ] NMF reporter

reporter[2] [ʀ(ə)pɔʀte] VT (total): **~ qch sur** to carry
sth forward ou over to; (ajourner): **~ qch (à)** to postpone sth (until); (transférer): **~ qch sur** to transfer
sth to ■ **se reporter** VPR: **se ~ à** (époque) to think
back to; (document) to refer to

repos [ʀ(ə)po] NM rest; (fig) peace (and quiet);
(mental) peace of mind; (Mil): **~!** (stand) at ease!;

r

en ~ at rest; **au ~** at rest; (soldat) at ease; **de tout ~** safe; **ce n'est pas de tout ~!** it's no picnic!

reposant, e [ʀ(ə)pozɑ̃, -ɑ̃t] ADJ restful; (sommeil) refreshing

repose [ʀ(ə)poz] NF refitting

reposé, e [ʀ(ə)poze] ADJ fresh, rested; **à tête reposée** with a clear head

repose-pied [ʀəpozpje] NM footrest

★**reposer** [ʀ(ə)poze] /1/ VT (verre, livre) to put down; (rideaux, carreaux) to put back; (délasser) to rest; (problème) to reformulate ▶ VI (liquide, pâte) to settle, rest; **laisser ~** (pâte) to leave to stand; **ici repose ...** (personne) here lies ...; **~ sur** to be built on; (fig) to rest on ■ **se reposer** VPR to rest; **se ~ sur qn** to rely on sb

repositionnement [ʀ(ə)pozisjɔnmɑ̃] NM (stratégique, commercial) repositioning

repositionner [ʀ(ə)pozisjɔne]: **se repositionner** VPR (firme) to reposition itself

repoussant, e [ʀ(ə)pusɑ̃, -ɑ̃t] ADJ repulsive

repoussé, e [ʀ(ə)puse] ADJ (cuir) embossed (by hand)

repousser [ʀ(ə)puse] /1/ VI to grow again ▶ VT to repel, repulse; (offre) to turn down, reject; (tiroir, personne) to push back; (différer) to put back

répréhensible [ʀepʀeɑ̃sibl] ADJ reprehensible

★**reprendre** [ʀ(ə)pʀɑ̃dʀ] /58/ VT (prisonnier, ville) to recapture; (objet prêté, donné) to take back; (Comm: article usagé) to take back; to take in part exchange; (: firme, entreprise) to take over; (emprunter: argument, idée) to take up, use; (refaire: article etc) to go over again; (jupe etc) to alter; (émission, pièce) to put on again; (réprimander) to tell off; (corriger) to correct; (travail, promenade) to resume; (chercher): **je viendrai te ~ à 4 h** I'll come and fetch you ou I'll come back for you at 4; (se resservir de): **~ du pain/un œuf** to take (ou eat) more bread/another egg; **~ des forces** to recover one's strength; **~ courage** to take new heart; **~ ses habitudes/sa liberté** to get back into one's old habits/regain one's freedom; **~ la route** to resume one's journey, set off again; **~ connaissance** to come to, regain consciousness; **~ haleine** ou **son souffle** to get one's breath back; **~ la parole** to speak again ▶ VI (classes, pluie) to start (up) again; (activités, travaux, combats) to resume, start (up) again; (affaires, industrie) to pick up; (dire): **reprit-il** he went on ■ **se reprendre** VPR (se ressaisir) to recover, pull o.s. together; **s'y ~** to make another attempt

repreneur [ʀ(ə)pʀənœʀ] NM company fixer ou doctor

reprenne etc [ʀ(ə)pʀɛn] VB voir **reprendre**

représailles [ʀ(ə)pʀezaj] NFPL reprisals, retaliation sg

représentant, e [ʀ(ə)pʀezɑ̃tɑ̃, -ɑ̃t] NM/F representative

représentatif, -ive [ʀ(ə)pʀezɑ̃tatif, -iv] ADJ representative

représentation [ʀ(ə)pʀezɑ̃tasjɔ̃] NF representation; (symbole, image) representation; (spectacle) performance; **la ~** (Comm) commercial travelling; sales representation; **frais de ~** (d'un diplomate) entertainment allowance

représenter [ʀ(ə)pʀezɑ̃te] /1/ VT to represent; (donner: pièce, opéra) to perform ■ **se représenter**

VPR (se figurer) to imagine; to visualize; **se ~ à** (Pol) to stand (BRIT) ou run (US) for; (Scol) to resit

répressif, -ive [ʀepʀesif, -iv] ADJ repressive

répression [ʀepʀesjɔ̃] NF suppression; repression; (Pol): **la ~** repression; **mesures de ~** repressive measures

réprimande [ʀepʀimɑ̃d] NF reprimand, rebuke

réprimander [ʀepʀimɑ̃de] /1/ VT to reprimand, rebuke

réprimer [ʀepʀime] /1/ VT (émotions) to suppress; (peuple etc) to repress

repris, e [ʀ(ə)pʀi, -iz] PP de **reprendre** ▶ NM: **~ de justice** ex-prisoner, ex-convict

reprise [ʀ(ə)pʀiz] NF (recommencement) resumption; (économique) recovery; (TV) repeat; (Ciné) rerun; (Boxe etc) round; (Auto) acceleration no pl; (Comm) trade-in, part exchange; (de location) sum asked for any extras or improvements made to the property; (raccommodage) darn, mend; **la ~ des hostilités** the resumption of hostilities; **à plusieurs reprises** on several occasions, several times

repriser [ʀ(ə)pʀize] /1/ VT (chaussette, lainage) to darn; (tissu) to mend; **aiguille/coton à ~** darning needle/thread

réprobateur, -trice [ʀepʀɔbatœʀ, -tʀis] ADJ reproving

réprobation [ʀepʀɔbasjɔ̃] NF reprobation

reproche [ʀ(ə)pʀɔʃ] NM (remontrance) reproach; **ton/air de ~** reproachful tone/look; **faire des reproches à qn** to reproach sb; **faire ~ à qn de qch** to reproach sb for sth; **sans ~(s)** beyond ou above reproach

reprocher [ʀ(ə)pʀɔʃe] /1/ VT: **~ qch à qn** to reproach ou blame sb for sth; **~ qch à** (machine, théorie) to have sth against; **se ~ qch/d'avoir fait qch** to blame o.s. for sth/for doing sth

reproducteur, -trice [ʀ(ə)pʀɔdyktœʀ, -tʀis] ADJ reproductive

reproductif, -ive [ʀ(ə)pʀɔdyktif, -iv] ADJ reproductive

reproduction [ʀ(ə)pʀɔdyksjɔ̃] NF reproduction; **~ interdite** all rights (of reproduction) reserved

reproduire [ʀ(ə)pʀɔdɥiʀ] /38/ VT to reproduce ■ **se reproduire** VPR (Bio) to reproduce; (recommencer) to recur, re-occur

reprographie [ʀ(ə)pʀɔgʀafi] NF (photo)copying

réprouvé, e [ʀepʀuve] NM/F reprobate

réprouver [ʀepʀuve] /1/ VT to reprove

reptation [ʀɛptasjɔ̃] NF crawling

reptile [ʀɛptil] NM reptile

repu, e [ʀəpy] PP de **repaître** ▶ ADJ satisfied, sated

républicain, e [ʀepyblikɛ̃, -ɛn] ADJ, NM/F republican

république [ʀepyblik] NF republic; **R~ arabe du Yémen** Yemen Arab Republic; **R~ Centrafricaine** Central African Republic; **R~ de Corée** South Korea; **R~ dominicaine** Dominican Republic; **R~ d'Irlande** Irish Republic, Eire; **R~ populaire de Chine** People's Republic of China; **R~ populaire démocratique de Corée** Democratic People's Republic of Korea; **R~ populaire du Yémen** People's Democratic Republic of Yemen

répudiation [ʀepydjasjɔ̃] NF (de femme) repudiation; (de doctrine) renunciation

répudier [ʀepydje] **/7/** VT *(femme)* to repudiate; *(doctrine)* to renounce

répugnance [ʀepyɲɑ̃s] NF repugnance, loathing; **avoir** ou **éprouver de la ~ pour** *(médicament, comportement, travail etc)* to have an aversion to; **avoir** ou **éprouver de la ~ à faire qch** to be loath ou reluctant to do sth

répugnant, e [ʀepyɲɑ̃, -ɑ̃t] ADJ repulsive, loathsome

répugner [ʀepyɲe] **/1/**: **~ à** VT: **~ à qn** to repel ou disgust sb; **~ à faire** to be loath ou reluctant to do

répulsion [ʀepylsjɔ̃] NF repulsion

réputation [ʀepytasjɔ̃] NF reputation; **avoir la ~ d'être ...** to have a reputation for being ...; **connaître qn/qch de ~** to know sb/sth by reputation; **de ~ mondiale** world-renowned

réputé, e [ʀepyte] ADJ renowned; **être ~ pour** to have a reputation for, be renowned for

requérir [ʀəkeʀiʀ] **/21/** VT *(nécessiter)* to require, call for; *(au nom de la loi)* to call upon; *(Jur: peine)* to call for, demand

requête [ʀəkɛt] NF request, petition; *(Jur)* petition

requiem [ʀekɥijɛm] NM requiem

requiers *etc* [ʀəkjɛʀ] VB *voir* **requérir**

requin [ʀəkɛ̃] NM shark

requinquer [ʀ(ə)kɛ̃ke] **/1/** VT to perk up, pep up

requis, e [ʀəki, -iz] PP *de* **requérir** ▸ ADJ required

réquisition [ʀekizisjɔ̃] NF requisition

réquisitionner [ʀekizisjɔne] **/1/** VT to requisition

réquisitoire [ʀekizitwaʀ] NM *(Jur)* closing speech for the prosecution; **~ contre** *(fig)* indictment of

RER SIGLE M (= *Réseau express régional*) Greater Paris high-speed train service

rescapé, e [ʀɛskape] NM/F survivor

rescousse [ʀɛskus] NF: **aller à la ~ de qn** to go to sb's aid ou rescue; **appeler qn à la ~** to call on sb for help

réseau, x [ʀezo] NM network; **~ social** social network

réseautage [ʀezotaʒ] NM social networking

réséda [ʀezeda] NM *(Bot)* reseda, mignonette

réservation [ʀezɛʀvasjɔ̃] NF reservation; booking

réserve [ʀezɛʀv] NF *(retenue)* reserve; *(entrepôt)* storeroom; *(restriction, aussi: d'Indiens)* reservation; *(de pêche, chasse)* preserve; *(restrictions)*: **faire des réserves** to have reservations; **officier de ~** reserve officer; **sous toutes réserves** with all reserve; *(dire)* with reservations; **sous ~ de** subject to; **sans ~** *adv* unreservedly; **en ~** in reserve; **de ~** *(provisions etc)* in reserve

réservé, e [ʀezɛʀve] ADJ *(discret)* reserved; *(chasse, pêche)* private; **~ à** ou **pour** reserved for

réserver [ʀezɛʀve] **/1/** VT *(gén)* to reserve; *(chambre, billet etc)* to book, reserve; *(mettre de côté, garder)*: **~ qch pour** ou **à** to keep ou save sth for; **~ qch à qn** to reserve ou book sth for sb; *(fig: destiner)* to have sth in store for sb; **se ~ le droit de faire** to reserve the right to do

réserviste [ʀezɛʀvist] NMF reservist

réservoir [ʀezɛʀvwaʀ] NM tank

résidence [ʀezidɑ̃s] NF residence; **~ principale/secondaire** main/second home; **~ universitaire** hall of residence (BRIT), dormitory (US); **(en) ~ surveillée** (under) house arrest

résident, e [ʀezidɑ̃, -ɑ̃t] NM/F *(ressortissant)* foreign resident; *(d'un immeuble)* resident ▸ ADJ *(Inform)* resident

résidentiel, le [ʀezidɑ̃sjɛl] ADJ residential

résider [ʀezide] **/1/** VI: **~ à** ou **dans** ou **en** to reside in; **~ dans** *(fig)* to lie in

résidu [ʀezidy] NM residue *no pl*

résiduel, le [ʀeziduɛl] ADJ residual

résignation [ʀeziɲasjɔ̃] NF resignation

résigné, e [ʀeziɲe] ADJ resigned

résigner [ʀeziɲe] **/1/** VT to relinquish, resign ■ **se résigner** VPR: **se ~ (à qch/à faire)** to resign o.s. (to sth/doing)

résiliable [ʀeziljabl] ADJ which can be terminated

résiliation [ʀeziljasjɔ̃] NF *(de contrat, abonnement)* termination

résilier [ʀezilje] **/7/** VT to terminate

résille [ʀezij] NF (hair)net

résine [ʀezin] NF resin

résiné, e [ʀezine] ADJ: **vin ~** retsina

résineux, -euse [ʀezinø, -øz] ADJ resinous ▸ NM coniferous tree

résistance [ʀezistɑ̃s] NF resistance; *(de réchaud, bouilloire: fil)* element

résistant, e [ʀezistɑ̃, -ɑ̃t] ADJ *(personne)* robust, tough; *(matériau)* strong, hard-wearing ▸ NM/F *(patriote)* Resistance worker ou fighter

résister [ʀeziste] **/1/** VI to resist; **~ à** VT *(assaut, tentation)* to resist; *(effort, souffrance)* to withstand; *(matériau, plante)* to withstand, stand up to; *(personne: désobéir à)* to stand up to, oppose

résolu, e [ʀezɔly] PP *de* **résoudre** ▸ ADJ *(ferme)* resolute; **être ~ à qch/faire** to be set upon sth/doing

résolument [ʀezɔlymɑ̃] ADV resolutely, steadfastly; **~ contre qch** firmly against sth

résolution [ʀezɔlysjɔ̃] NF solving; *(fermeté, décision, Inform)* resolution; *(d'un problème)* solution; **prendre la ~ de** to make a resolution to

résolvais *etc* [ʀezɔlvɛ] VB *voir* **résoudre**

résonance [ʀezɔnɑ̃s] NF resonance

résonner [ʀezɔne] **/1/** VI *(cloche, pas)* to reverberate, resound; *(salle)* to be resonant; **~ de** to resound with

résorber [ʀezɔʀbe] **/1/** VT *(chômage, déficit)* to reduce ■ **se résorber** VPR *(Méd)* to be resorbed; *(fig: chômage, déficit)* to be brought down

résorption [ʀezɔʀpsjɔ̃] NF *(de chômage, déficit)* reduction

résoudre [ʀezudʀ] **/51/** VT to solve; **~ qn à faire qch** to get sb to make up his (ou her) mind to do sth; **~ de faire** to resolve to do; **se ~ à faire** to bring o.s. to do

respect [ʀɛspɛ] NM respect; **tenir en ~** to keep at bay; **présenter ses respects à qn** to pay one's respects to sb

respectabilité [ʀɛspɛktabilite] NF respectability

respectable [ʀɛspɛktabl] ADJ respectable

r

★**respecter** [ʀɛspɛkte] /**1**/ vт to respect; **faire ~** to enforce ◾ **se respecter** vPR to respect o.s.; **le lexicographe qui se respecte** (*fig*) any self-respecting lexicographer

respectif, -ive [ʀɛspɛktif, -iv] ADJ respective

respectivement [ʀɛspɛktivmã] ADV respectively

respectueusement [ʀɛspɛktɥøzmã] ADV respectfully

respectueux, -euse [ʀɛspɛktɥø, -øz] ADJ respectful; **~ de** respectful of

respirable [ʀɛspiʀabl] ADJ: **peu ~** unbreathable

respiration [ʀɛspiʀasjõ] NF breathing *no pl*; **faire une ~ complète** to breathe in and out; **retenir sa ~** to hold one's breath; **~ artificielle** artificial respiration

respiratoire [ʀɛspiʀatwaʀ] ADJ respiratory

★**respirer** [ʀɛspiʀe] /**1**/ vI to breathe; (*fig: se reposer*) to get one's breath, have a break; (: *être soulagé*) to breathe again ▸ vт to breathe (in), inhale; (*manifester: santé, calme etc*) to exude

resplendir [ʀɛsplãdiʀ] /**2**/ vI to shine; (*fig*): **~ (de)** to be radiant (with)

resplendissant, e [ʀɛsplãdisã, -ãt] ADJ radiant

responsabiliser [ʀɛspõsabilize] vт to give a sense of responsibility to

responsabilité [ʀɛspõsabilite] NF responsibility; (*légale*) liability; **refuser la ~ de** to deny responsibility (*ou* liability) for; **prendre ses responsabilités** to assume responsibility for one's actions; **~ civile** civil liability; **~ pénale/morale/collective** criminal/moral/collective responsibility

★**responsable** [ʀɛspõsabl] ADJ responsible; **~ de** responsible for; (*légalement: de dégâts etc*) liable for; (*chargé de*) in charge of, responsible for ▸ NMF (*personne coupable*) person responsible; (*du ravitaillement etc*) person in charge; (*de parti, syndicat*) official

resquiller [ʀɛskije] /**1**/ vI (*au cinéma, au stade*) to get in on the sly; (*dans le train*) to fiddle a free ride

resquilleur, -euse [ʀɛskijœʀ, -øz] NM/F (*qui n'est pas invité*) gatecrasher; (*qui ne paie pas*) fare dodger

ressac [ʀəsak] NM backwash

ressaisir [ʀ(ə)seziʀ] /**2**/: **se ressaisir** vPR to regain one's self-control; (*équipe sportive*) to rally

ressasser [ʀ(ə)sase] /**1**/ vт (*remâcher*) to keep turning over; (*redire*) to keep trotting out

ressemblance [ʀ(ə)sãblãs] NF (*visuelle*) resemblance, similarity, likeness; (: *Art*) likeness; (*analogie, trait commun*) similarity

ressemblant, e [ʀ(ə)sãblã, -ãt] ADJ (*portrait*) lifelike, true to life

★**ressembler** [ʀ(ə)sãble] /**1**/: **~ à** vт to be like, resemble; (*visuellement*) to look like ◾ **se ressembler** vPR to be (*ou* look) alike

ressemeler [ʀ(ə)sam(ə)le] /**4**/ vт to (re)sole

ressens *etc* [ʀ(ə)sã] vв *voir* **ressentir**

ressentiment [ʀ(ə)sãtimã] NM resentment

ressentir [ʀ(ə)sãtiʀ] /**16**/ vт to feel; **se ~ de** to feel (*ou* show) the effects of

resserre [ʀəsɛʀ] NF shed

resserrement [ʀ(ə)sɛʀmã] NM narrowing; strengthening; (*goulet*) narrow part

resserrer [ʀ(ə)seʀe] /**1**/ vт (*pores*) to close; (*nœud, boulon*) to tighten (up); (*fig: liens*) to strengthen ◾ **se resserrer** vPR (*route, vallée*) to narrow; (*liens*) to strengthen; **se ~ (autour de)** to draw closer (around), close in (on)

ressers *etc* [ʀ(ə)sɛʀ] vв *voir* **resservir**

resservir [ʀ(ə)sɛʀviʀ] /**14**/ vI to do *ou* serve again ▸ vт: **~ qch (à qn)** to serve sth up again (to sb); **~ de qch (à qn)** to serve (sb) a second helping of sth; **~ qn (d'un plat)** to give sb a second helping (of a dish) ◾ **se resservir** vPR: **se ~ de** (*plat*) to take a second helping of; (*outil etc*) to use again

ressort [ʀəsɔʀ] vв *voir* **ressortir** ▸ NM (*pièce*) spring; (*force morale*) spirit; **en dernier ~** as a last resort; **être du ~ de** to fall within the competence of

ressortir [ʀəsɔʀtiʀ] /**16**/ vI to go (*ou* come) out (again); (*contraster*) to stand out; **~ de** (*résulter de*): **il ressort de ceci que** it emerges from this that; **~ à** (*Jur*) to come under the jurisdiction of; (*Admin*) to be the concern of; **faire ~** (*fig: souligner*) to bring out

ressortissant, e [ʀ(ə)sɔʀtisã, -ãt] NM/F national

ressouder [ʀ(ə)sude] /**1**/ vт to solder together again

ressource [ʀ(ə)suʀs] NF: **avoir la ~ de** to have the possibility of; **leur seule ~ était de** the only course open to them was to ◾ **ressources** NFPL resources; (*fig*) possibilities; **ressources d'énergie** energy resources

ressourcer [ʀ(ə)suʀse]: **se ressourcer** vPR (*se régénérer*) to recharge one's batteries

ressurgir [ʀ(ə)syʀʒiʀ] vI = **resurgir**

ressusciter [ʀesysite] /**1**/ vт to resuscitate, restore to life; (*fig*) to revive, bring back ▸ vI to rise (from the dead); (*fig: pays*) to come back to life

restant, e [ʀɛstã, -ãt] ADJ remaining ▸ NM: **le ~ (de)** the remainder (of); **un ~ de** (*de trop*) some leftover; (*fig*) a remnant *ou* last trace of

restau [ʀɛsto] NM (*fam*) restaurant

★**restaurant** [ʀɛstoʀã] NM restaurant; **manger au ~** to eat out; **~ d'entreprise** staff canteen *ou* cafeteria (*US*); **~ universitaire** university refectory *ou* cafeteria (*US*)

restaurateur, -trice [ʀɛstoʀatœʀ, -tʀis] NM/F restaurant owner, restaurateur; (*de tableaux*) restorer

restauration [ʀɛstoʀasjõ] NF restoration; (*hôtellerie*) catering; **~ rapide** fast food

restaurer [ʀɛstoʀe] /**1**/ vт to restore ◾ **se restaurer** vPR to have something to eat

restoroute [ʀɛstoʀut] NM = **restoroute**

★**reste** [ʀɛst] NM (*Math*) remainder; (*restant*): **le ~ (de)** the rest (of); (*de trop*): **un ~ (de)** some leftover; (*vestige*): **un ~ de** a remnant *ou* last trace of; **avoir du temps de ~** to have time to spare; **ne voulant pas être en ~** not wishing to be outdone; **partir sans attendre** *ou* **demander son ~** (*fig*) to leave without waiting to hear more; **du ~**, **au ~** adv besides, moreover; **pour le ~**, **quant au ~** adv as for the rest ◾ **restes** NMPL leftovers; (*d'une cité etc, dépouille mortelle*) remains

★**rester** [ʀɛste] /**1**/ vI (*dans un lieu, un état, une position*) to stay, remain; (*subsister*) to remain, be left; (*durer*)

to last, live on; **en ~ à** (*stade, menaces*) to go no further than, only go as far as; **restons-en là** let's leave it at that; **~ sur une impression** to retain an impression; **il a failli y ~** he nearly met his end ▶ VB IMPERS: **il reste du pain/deux œufs** there's some bread/there are two eggs left (over); **il reste du temps/10 minutes** there's some time/there are 10 minutes left; **il me reste assez de temps** I have enough time left; **il ne me reste plus qu'à ...** I've just got to ...; **voilà tout ce qui (me) reste** that's all I've got left; **ce qui reste à faire** what remains to be done; **ce qui me reste à faire** what remains for me to do; **(il) reste à savoir/établir si ...** it remains to be seen/established if *ou* whether ...; **il n'en reste pas moins que ...** the fact remains that ..., it's nevertheless a fact that ...

rester does not mean *to rest*.

restituer [Rɛstitɥe] /1/ VT (*objet, somme*): **~ qch (à qn)** to return *ou* restore sth (to sb); (*énergie*) to release; (*son*) to reproduce

restitution [Rɛstitysjɔ̃] NF restoration

resto [Rɛsto] NM (*fam*) restaurant

restoroute [Rɛstɔʀut] NM motorway (BRIT) *ou* highway (US) restaurant

restreindre [Rɛstʀɛ̃dʀ] /52/ VT to restrict, limit ■ **se restreindre** VPR (*dans ses dépenses etc*) to cut down; (*champ de recherches*) to narrow

restreint, e [Rɛstʀɛ̃, -ɛ̃t] PP *de* **restreindre** ▶ ADJ restricted, limited

restrictif, -ive [Rɛstʀiktif, -iv] ADJ restrictive, limiting

restriction [Rɛstʀiksjɔ̃] NF restriction; (*condition*) qualification; **sans ~** *adv* unreservedly ■ **restrictions** NFPL (*rationnement*) restrictions; (*mentales*) reservations

restructuration [Rəstʀyktyʀasjɔ̃] NF restructuring

restructurer [Rəstʀyktyʀe] /1/ VT to restructure

résultante [Rezyltɑ̃t] NF (*conséquence*) result, consequence

résultat [Rezylta] NM result; (*conséquence*) outcome *no pl*, result; (*d'élection etc*) results *pl* ■ **résultats** NMPL (*d'une enquête*) findings; **résultats sportifs** sports results

résulter [Rezylte] /1/: **~ de** *vt* to result from, be the result of; **il résulte de ceci que ...** the result of this is that ...

résumé [Rezyme] NM summary, résumé; **faire le ~ de** to summarize; **en ~** *adv* in brief; (*pour conclure*) to sum up

résumer [Rezyme] /1/ VT (*texte*) to summarize; (*récapituler*) to sum up; (*fig*) to epitomize, typify ■ **se résumer** VPR (*personne*) to sum up (one's ideas); **se ~ à** to come down to

résurgence [Rezyʀʒɑ̃s] NF resurgence

resurgir [R(ə)syʀʒiʀ] /2/ VI to reappear, re-emerge

résurrection [RezyʀɛksjG̃] NF resurrection; (*fig*) revival

rétablir [RetabliʀR] /2/ VT to restore, re-establish; (*personne: traitement*): **~ qn** to restore sb to health, help sb recover; (*Admin*): **~ qn dans son emploi/ ses droits** to reinstate sb in his (*ou* her) post/ restore sb's rights ■ **se rétablir** VPR (*guérir*) to

recover; (*silence, calme*) to return, be restored; (*Gym etc*): **se ~ (sur)** to pull o.s. up (onto)

rétablissement [Retablismɑ̃] NM restoring; (*guérison*) recovery; (*Gym*) pull-up

rétamer [Retame] /1/ VT to re-coat ■ **se rétamer** VPR (*fam: tomber*) to take a tumble (*fam*), come a cropper (BRIT *fam*)

rétameur [Retamœʀ] NM tinker

retaper [R(ə)tape] /1/ VT (*maison, voiture etc*) to do up; (*fam: revigorer*) to buck up; (*redactylographier*) to retype

★**retard** [R(ə)taʀ] NM (*d'une personne attendue*) lateness *no pl*; (*sur l'horaire, un programme, une échéance*) delay; (*fig*! : *scolaire, mental etc*) learning difficulty; **être en ~** (*pays*) to be backward; (*dans paiement, travail*) to be behind; **en ~ (de deux heures)** (two hours) late; **désolé d'être en ~** sorry I'm late; **avoir un ~ de deux km** (*Sport*) to be two km behind; **rattraper son ~** to catch up; **avoir du ~** to be late; (*sur un programme*) to be behind (schedule); **prendre du ~** (*train, avion*) to be delayed; (*montre*) to lose (time); **sans ~** *adv* without delay; **~ à l'allumage** (*Auto*) retarded spark; **~ scolaire** learning difficulty

retardataire [R(ə)taʀdatɛʀ] ADJ late; (*idées*) backward (*péj*) ▶ NMF latecomer; child with a learning difficulty

retardé, e [R(ə)taʀde] ADJ backward

retardement [R(ə)taʀdəmɑ̃]: **à ~** *adj* delayed action *cpd*; **bombe à ~** time bomb

retarder [R(ə)taʀde] /1/ VT to delay; (*horloge*) to put back; (*sur un horaire*): **~ qn (d'une heure)** to delay sb (an hour); (*sur un programme*): **~ qn (de trois mois)** to set sb back *ou* delay sb (three months); (*départ, date*): **~ qch (de deux jours)** to put sth back (two days), delay sth (for *ou* by two days) ▶ VI (*montre*) to be slow; (: *habituellement*) to lose (time); **je retarde (d'une heure)** I'm (an hour) slow

retendre [R(ə)tɑ̃dʀ] /41/ VT (*câble etc*) to stretch again; (*Mus: cordes*) to retighten

retenir [Rət(ə)niʀ] /22/ VT (*garder, retarder*) to keep, detain; (*maintenir: objet qui glisse, fig: colère, larmes, rire*) to hold back; (: *objet suspendu*) to hold; (: *chaleur, odeur*) to retain; (*se rappeler*) to retain; (*réserver*) to reserve; (*accepter*) to accept; (*fig: empêcher d'agir*): **~ qn (de faire)** to hold sb back (from doing); (*prélever*): **~ qch (sur)** to deduct sth (from) ■ **se retenir** VPR (*euphémisme*) to hold on; (*se raccrocher*): **se ~ à** to hold onto; (*se contenir*): **se ~ de faire** to restrain o.s. from doing

rétention [Retɑ̃sjɔ̃] NF: **~ d'urine** urine retention

retentir [R(ə)tɑ̃tiʀ] /2/ VI to ring out; (*salle*): **~ de** to ring *ou* resound with; **~ sur** *vt* (*fig*) to have an effect upon

retentissant, e [R(ə)tɑ̃tisɑ̃, -ɑ̃t] ADJ resounding; (*fig*) impact-making

retentissement [R(ə)tɑ̃tismɑ̃] NM (*retombées*) repercussions *pl*; effect, impact

retenu, e [Rət(ə)ny] PP *de* **retenir** ▶ ADJ (*place*) reserved; (*personne: empêché*) held up; (*propos: contenu, discret*) restrained ▶ NF (*prélèvement*) deduction; (*Math*) number to carry over; (*Scol*) detention; (*modération*) (self-)restraint; (*réserve*) reserve, reticence; (*Auto*) tailback

r

387

réticence [Retisɑ̃s] NF reticence *no pl*, reluctance *no pl*; **sans ~** without hesitation

réticent, e [Retisɑ̃, -ɑ̃t] ADJ reticent, reluctant

retiendrai [Rətjɛ̃dRe], **retiens** *etc* [Rətjɛ̃] VB *voir* **retenir**

rétif, -ive [Retif, -iv] ADJ restive

rétine [Retin] NF retina

retint *etc* [Rətɛ̃] VB *voir* **retenir**

retiré, e [R(ə)tiRe] ADJ (*solitaire*) secluded; (*éloigné*) remote

★**retirer** [R(ə)tiRe] /1/ VT (*argent, plainte*) to withdraw; (*vêtement*) to take off, remove; (*reprendre: billets*) to collect, pick up; (*enlever*): **~ qch à qn** to take sth from sb; (*extraire*): **~ qn/qch de** to take sb away from/sth out of, remove sb/sth from; **~ des avantages de** to derive advantages from ■ **se retirer** VPR (*partir, reculer*) to withdraw; (*prendre sa retraite*) to retire; **se ~ de** to withdraw from; to retire from

retombées [Rətɔ̃be] NFPL (*radioactives*) fallout *sg*; (*fig*) fallout; spin-offs

retomber [R(ə)tɔ̃be] /1/ VI (*à nouveau*) to fall again; (*atterrir: après un saut etc*) to land; (*tomber, redescendre*) to fall back; (*pendre*) to fall, hang (down); (*rechuter*): **~ malade** to fall ill again; (*échoir*): **~ sur qn** to fall on sb

retoquer [R(ə)tɔke] /1/ VT to reject; **se faire ~** (*à un examen*) to fail; (*à un poste*) to be turned down

retordre [R(ə)tɔRdR] /41/ VT: **donner du fil à ~ à qn** to make life difficult for sb

rétorquer [Retɔrke] /1/ VT: **~ (à qn) que** to retort (to sb) that

retors, e [Rətɔr, -ɔrs] ADJ wily

rétorsion [Retɔrsjɔ̃] NF: **mesures de ~** reprisals

retouche [R(ə)tuʃ] NF touching up *no pl*; (*sur vêtement*) alteration; **faire une ~** *ou* **des retouches à** to touch up

retoucher [R(ə)tuʃe] /1/ VT (*photographie, tableau*) to touch up; (*texte, vêtement*) to alter

★**retour** [R(ə)tuR] NM return; **au ~** (*en arrivant*) when we (*ou* they *etc*) get (*ou* got) back; (*en route*) on the way back; **pendant le ~** on the way *ou* journey back; **à mon/ton ~** on my/your return; **au ~ de** on the return of; **être de ~ (de)** to be back (from); **de ~ à .../chez moi** back at .../back home; **quand serons-nous de ~?** when do we get back?; **en ~** *adv* in return; **par ~ du courrier** by return of post; **par un juste ~ des choses** by a favourable twist of fate; **match ~** return match; **~ en arrière** (*Ciné*) flashback; (*mesure*) backward step; **~ de bâton** kickback; **~ de chariot** carriage return; **~ à l'envoyeur** (*Postes*) return to sender; **~ de flamme** backfire; **~ (automatique) à la ligne** (*Inform*) wordwrap; **~ de manivelle** (*fig*) backfire; **~ offensif** renewed attack; **~ aux sources** (*fig*) return to basics

retournement [R(ə)tuRnəmɑ̃] NM (*d'une personne: revirement*) turning (round); **~ de la situation** reversal of the situation

★**retourner** [R(ə)tuRne] /1/ VT (*dans l'autre sens: matelas, crêpe*) to turn (over); (: *caisse*) to turn upside down; (: *sac, vêtement*) to turn inside out; (*fig: argument*) to turn back; (*en remuant: terre, sol, foin*) to turn over; (*émouvoir: personne*) to shake; (*renvoyer, restituer*): **~ qch à qn** to return sth to sb; **~ sa veste** (*fig*) to change sides ▶ VI (*aller, revenir*): **~ quelque part/à** to go back *ou* return somewhere/to; **~ à** (*état, activité*) to return to, go back to; **savoir de quoi il retourne** to know what it is all about; **~ en arrière** *ou* **sur ses pas** to turn back, retrace one's steps; **~ aux sources** to go back to basics ■ **se retourner** VPR to turn over; (*tourner la tête*) to turn round; **s'en ~** to go back; **se ~ contre** (*fig*) to turn against

retracer [R(ə)tRase] /3/ VT to relate, recount

rétractable [Retraktabl] ADJ (*poignée, toit*) retractable

rétracter [Retrakte] /1/ VT to retract ■ **se rétracter** VPR to retract

retraduire [R(ə)tRadɥiR] /38/ VT to translate again; (*dans la langue de départ*) to translate back

retrait [R(ə)tRɛ] NM (*d'argent*) withdrawal; collection; (*rétrécissement*) shrinkage; **en ~** *adj* set back; **écrire en ~** to indent; **~ du permis (de conduire)** disqualification from driving (BRIT), revocation of driver's license (US)

★**retraite** [R(ə)tRɛt] NF (*d'une armée, Rel, refuge*) retreat; (*d'un employé*) retirement; (*revenu*) (retirement) pension; **être/mettre à la ~** to be retired/pension off *ou* retire; **prendre sa ~** to retire; **~ anticipée** early retirement; **~ aux flambeaux** torchlight tattoo

retraité, e [R(ə)tRete] ADJ retired ▶ NM/F (old age) pensioner

retraitement [R(ə)tRɛtmɑ̃] NM reprocessing

retraiter [R(ə)tRete] /1/ VT to reprocess

retranchement [R(ə)tRɑ̃ʃmɑ̃] NM entrenchment; **pousser qn dans ses derniers retranchements** to drive sb into a corner

retrancher [R(ə)tRɑ̃ʃe] /1/ VT (*passage, détails*) to take out, remove; (*couper*) to cut off; **~ qch de** (*nombre, somme*) to take *ou* deduct sth from; **se ~ derrière/dans** to entrench o.s. behind/in; (*fig*) to take refuge behind/in

retranscription [R(ə)tRɑ̃skRipsjɔ̃] NF (*d'entretien, débat*) retranscription

retranscrire [R(ə)tRɑ̃skRiR] /39/ VT to retranscribe

retransmettre [R(ə)tRɑ̃smɛtR] /56/ VT (*Radio*) to broadcast, relay; (*TV*) to show

retransmission [R(ə)tRɑ̃smisjɔ̃] NF broadcast; showing

retravailler [R(ə)tRavaje] /1/ VI to start work again ▶ VT to work on again

retraverser [R(ə)tRavɛRse] /1/ VT (*dans l'autre sens*) to cross back over

rétréci, e [Retresi] ADJ (*idées, esprit*) narrow

rétrécir [RetResiR] /2/ VT (*vêtement*) to take in ▶ VI to shrink ■ **se rétrécir** VPR (*route, vallée*) to narrow

rétrécissement [Retresismɑ̃] NM narrowing

retremper [R(ə)tRɑ̃pe] /1/: **se retremper** VPR: **se ~ dans** (*fig*) to reimmerse o.s. in

rétribuer [Retribɥe] /1/ VT (*travail*) to pay for; (*personne*) to pay

rétribution [Retribysjɔ̃] NF payment

rétro [RetRo] ADJ old-style; **la mode ~** vintage *ou* retro fashion ▶ NM (*rétroviseur*) (rear-view) mirror

rétroactif, -ive [RetRoaktif, -iv] ADJ retroactive

rétroactivement [RetRoaktivmɑ̃] ADV retroactively

rétroactivité [ʀetʀoaktivite] NF retroactivity

rétrocéder [ʀetʀɔsede] /6/ VT to retrocede

rétrocession [ʀetʀɔsesjɔ̃] NF retrocession

rétroéclairage [ʀetʀoeklɛʀaʒ] NM (*Tech*) back-lighting

rétroéclairé, e [ʀetʀoeklɛʀe] ADJ (*Tech*) back-lit

rétrofusée [ʀetʀɔfyze] NF retrorocket

rétrogradation [ʀetʀɔgʀadasjɔ̃] NF (*aussi Sport*) demotion

rétrograde [ʀetʀɔgʀad] ADJ reactionary, backward-looking

rétrograder [ʀetʀɔgʀade] /1/ VI (*Auto*) to change down; (*au classement*): **à la cinquième place** to slip back to fifth place

rétroprojecteur [ʀetʀopʀɔʒɛktœʀ] NM overhead projector

rétrospectif, -ive [ʀetʀɔspɛktif, -iv] ADJ retrospective ▶ NF (*Art*) retrospective; (*Ciné*) season, retrospective

rétrospectivement [ʀetʀɔspɛktivmɑ̃] ADV in retrospect

retroussé, e [ʀ(ə)tʀuse] ADJ: **nez** turned-up nose

retrousser [ʀ(ə)tʀuse] /1/ VT to roll up; (*fig: nez*) to wrinkle; (: *lèvres*) to curl **se retrousser** VPR: **se les manches** (*fig*) to roll up one's sleeves

retrouvailles [ʀ(ə)tʀuvaj] NFPL reunion *sg*

★**retrouver** [ʀ(ə)tʀuve] /1/ VT (*fugitif, objet perdu*) to find; (*occasion*) to find again; (*calme, santé*) to regain; (*reconnaître: expression, style*) to recognize; (*revoir*) to see again; (*rejoindre*) to meet (again), join **se retrouver** VPR: **se** to meet; (*s'orienter*) to find one's way; **se quelque part** to find o.s. somewhere; to end up somewhere; **se seul/sans argent** to find o.s. alone/with no money; **se dans** (*calculs, dossiers, désordre*) to make sense of; **s'y** (*y voir clair*) to make sense of it; (*rentrer dans ses frais*) to break even

rétroviral, e, -aux [ʀetʀoviʀal, -o] ADJ retroviral

rétrovirus [ʀetʀoviʀys] NM retrovirus

rétroviseur [ʀetʀovizœʀ] NM (rear-view) mirror

retweet [ʀətwit] NM (*Inform: Twitter*) retweet

retweeter [ʀətwite] /1/ VT (*Inform: Twitter*) to retweet

réunifier [ʀeynifje] /7/ VT to reunify

Réunion [ʀeynjɔ̃] NF: **la , l'île de la** Réunion

réunion [ʀeynjɔ̃] NF bringing together; joining; (*séance*) meeting

réunionite, réunionnite [ʀeynjɔnit] NF mania for meetings, meetingitis (*fam*)

réunionnais, e [ʀeynjɔnɛ, -ɛz] ADJ of *ou* from Réunion

réunir [ʀeyniʀ] /2/ VT (*convoquer*) to call together; (*rassembler*) to gather together; (*inviter: amis, famille*) to have round, have in; (*cumuler: qualités etc*) to combine; (*rapprocher: ennemis*) to bring together (again), reunite; (*rattacher: parties*) to join (together) **se réunir** VPR (*se rencontrer*) to meet; (*s'allier*) to unite

réussi, e [ʀeysi] ADJ successful

réussir [ʀeysiʀ] /2/ VI to succeed, be successful; (*à un examen*) to pass; (*plante, culture*) to thrive, do

well; **à faire** to succeed in doing; **à qn** to go right for sb; (*être bénéfique à*) to agree with sb; **le travail/le mariage lui réussit** work/married life agrees with him ▶ VT to make a success of; to bring off

réussite [ʀeysit] NF success; (*Cartes*) patience

réutilisable [ʀeytilizabl] ADJ reusable

réutilisation [ʀeytilizasjɔ̃] NF reuse

réutiliser [ʀeytilize] /1/ VT to re-use

revaloir [ʀ(ə)valwaʀ] /29/ VT: **je vous revaudrai cela** I'll repay you some day; (*en mal*) I'll pay you back for this

revalorisation [ʀ(ə)valɔʀizasjɔ̃] NF revaluation; raising

revaloriser [ʀ(ə)valɔʀize] /1/ VT (*monnaie*) to revalue; (*salaires, pensions*) to raise the level of; (*institution, tradition*) to reassert the value of

revanchard, e [ʀ(ə)vɑ̃ʃaʀ, -aʀd] ADJ vengeful

revanche [ʀ(ə)vɑ̃ʃ] NF revenge; (*sport*) revenge match; **prendre sa (sur)** to take one's revenge (on); **en (par contre)** on the other hand; (*en compensation*) in return

rêvasser [ʀɛvase] /1/ VI to daydream

rêve [ʀɛv] NM dream; (*activité psychique*): **le** dreaming; **de** dream *cpd*; **faire un** to have a dream; **éveillé** daydreaming *no pl*, daydream

rêvé, e [ʀeve] ADJ (*endroit, mari etc*) ideal

revêche [ʀəvɛʃ] ADJ surly, sour-tempered

réveil [ʀevɛj] NM (*d'un dormeur*) waking *no pl*; (*fig*) awakening; (*pendule*) alarm (clock); **au** when I (*ou tu etc*) wake (*ou* woke) up, on waking (up); **sonner le** (*Mil*) to sound the reveille

réveille-matin [ʀevɛjmatɛ̃] NM INV alarm clock

réveiller [ʀeveje] /1/ VT (*personne*) to wake up; (*fig*) to awaken, revive **se réveiller** VPR to wake up; (*fig*) to be revived, reawaken

réveillon [ʀevɛjɔ̃] NM Christmas Eve; (*de la Saint-Sylvestre*) New Year's Eve; Christmas Eve (*ou* New Year's Eve) party *ou* dinner

réveillonner [ʀevɛjɔne] /1/ VI to celebrate Christmas Eve (*ou* New Year's Eve)

révélateur, -trice [ʀevelatœʀ, -tʀis] ADJ: **(de qch)** revealing (sth) ▶ NM (*Photo*) developer

révélation [ʀevelasjɔ̃] NF revelation

révéler [ʀevele] /6/ VT (*gén*) to reveal; (*divulguer*) to disclose, reveal; (*dénoter*) to reveal, show; (*faire connaître au public*): **qn/qch** to make sb/sth widely known, bring sb/sth to the public's notice **se révéler** VPR to be revealed, reveal itself; **se facile/faux** to prove (to be) easy/false; **se cruel/un allié sûr** to show o.s. to be cruel/a trustworthy ally

revenant, e [ʀ(ə)vənɑ̃, -ɑ̃t] NM/F ghost

revendeur, -euse [ʀ(ə)vɑ̃dœʀ, -øz] NM/F (*détaillant*) retailer; (*d'occasions*) secondhand dealer; (*de drogue*) (drug-)dealer

revendicatif, -ive [ʀ(ə)vɑ̃dikatif, -iv] ADJ (*mouvement*) protest *cpd*

revendication [ʀ(ə)vɑ̃dikasjɔ̃] NF claim, demand; **journée de** day of action (in support of one's claims)

revendiquer [ʀ(ə)vɑ̃dike] /1/ VT to claim, demand; (*responsabilité*) to claim ▶ VI to agitate in favour of one's claims

r

revendre [ʀ(ə)vɑ̃dʀ] /**41**/ VT (d'occasion) to resell; (détailler) to sell; (vendre davantage de): **~ du sucre/ un foulard/deux bagues** to sell more sugar/ another scarf/another two rings; **à ~** adv (en abondance) to spare

★**revenir** [ʀəv(ə)niʀ] /**22**/ VI to come back; **faire ~** (Culin) to brown; **~ cher/à 100 euros (à qn)** to cost (sb) a lot/100 euros; **~ à** (reprendre: études, projet) to return to, go back to; (équivaloir à) to amount to; **~ à qn** (rumeur, nouvelle) to get back to sb, reach sb's ears; (part, honneur) to go to sb, be sb's; (souvenir, nom) to come back to sb; **~ de** (fig: maladie, étonnement) to recover from; **~ sur** (question, sujet) to go back over; (engagement) to go back on; **~ à la charge** to return to the attack; **~ à soi** to come round; **je n'en reviens pas** I can't get over it; **~ sur ses pas** to retrace one's steps; **cela revient à dire que/au même** it amounts to saying that/to the same thing; **~ de loin** (fig) to have been at death's door

revente [ʀ(ə)vɑ̃t] NF resale

revenu, e [ʀəv(ə)ny] PP de **revenir** ▶ NM income; (de l'État) revenue; (d'un capital) yield; **~ national brut** gross national income ■ **revenus** NMPL income sg

rêver [ʀeve] /**1**/ VI, VT to dream; (rêvasser) to (day)dream; **~ de** (voir en rêve) to dream of ou about; **~ de qch/de faire** to dream of sth/of doing; **~ à** to dream of

réverbération [ʀevɛʀbeʀasjɔ̃] NF reflection

réverbère [ʀevɛʀbɛʀ] NM street lamp ou light

réverbérer [ʀevɛʀbeʀe] /**6**/ VT to reflect

reverdir [ʀ(ə)vɛʀdiʀ] /**2**/ VI (arbre etc) to turn green again

révérence [ʀeveʀɑ̃s] NF (vénération) reverence; (salut: d'homme) bow; (: de femme) curtsey

révérencieux, -euse [ʀeveʀɑ̃sjø, -øz] ADJ reverent

révérend, e [ʀeveʀɑ̃, -ɑ̃d] ADJ: **le ~ père Pascal** the Reverend Father Pascal

révérer [ʀeveʀe] /**6**/ VT to revere

rêverie [ʀɛvʀi] NF daydreaming no pl, daydream

reverrai etc [ʀəvɛʀe] VB voir **revoir**

revers [ʀ(ə)vɛʀ] NM (de feuille, main) back; (d'étoffe) wrong side; (de pièce, médaille) back, reverse; (Tennis, Ping-Pong) backhand; (de veston) lapel; (de pantalon) turn-up (BRIT), cuff (US); (fig: échec) set-back; **~ de fortune** reverse of fortune; **d'un ~ de main** with the back of one's hand; **le ~ de la médaille** (fig) the other side of the coin; **prendre à ~** (Mil) to take from the rear

reverser [ʀ(ə)vɛʀse] /**1**/ VT (reporter: somme etc): **~ sur** to put back into; (liquide) **~ (dans)** to pour some more (into)

réversibilité [ʀevɛʀsibilite] NF reversibility

réversible [ʀevɛʀsibl] ADJ reversible

revêtement [ʀ(ə)vɛtmɑ̃] NM (de paroi) facing; (des sols) flooring; (de chaussée) surface; (de tuyau etc: enduit) coating

revêtir [ʀ(ə)vɛtiʀ] /**20**/ VT (habit) to don, put on; (prendre: importance, apparence) to take on; **~ qn de** to dress sb in; (fig) to endow ou invest sb with; **~ qch de** to cover sth with; (fig) to cloak sth in; **~ d'un visa** to append a visa to

rêveur, -euse [ʀɛvœʀ, -øz] ADJ dreamy ▶ NM/F dreamer

rêveusement [ʀɛvøzmɑ̃] ADV dreamily

reviendrai etc [ʀəvjɛ̃dʀe] VB voir **revenir**

revienne etc [ʀəvjɛn] VB voir **revenir**

revient [ʀəvjɛ̃] VB voir **revenir** ▶ NM: **prix de ~** cost price

revigorant, e [ʀ(ə)vigɔʀɑ̃, -ɑ̃t] ADJ (climat, bain) invigorating; (intellectuellement) refreshing

revigorer [ʀ(ə)vigɔʀe] /**1**/ VT (air frais) to invigorate, refresh; (repas, boisson) to revive, buck up

revint etc [ʀəvɛ̃] VB voir **revenir**

revirement [ʀ(ə)viʀmɑ̃] NM change of mind; (d'une situation) reversal

revis etc [ʀəvi] VB voir **revoir**

révisable [ʀevizabl] ADJ (procès, taux etc) reviewable, subject to review

réviser [ʀevize] /**1**/ VT (texte, Scol: matière) to revise; (comptes) to audit; (machine, installation, moteur) to overhaul, service; (Jur: procès) to review

révision [ʀevizjɔ̃] NF revision; auditing no pl; (de voiture) overhaul, servicing no pl; review; **conseil de ~** (Mil) recruiting board; **faire ses révisions** (Scol) to do one's revision (BRIT), revise (BRIT), review (US); **la ~ des 10 000 km** (Auto) the 10,000 km service

révisionnisme [ʀevizjɔnism] NM revisionism

révisionniste [ʀevizjɔnist] ADJ, NMF revisionist

revisiter [ʀ(ə)vizite] VT (œuvre, auteur) to revisit

revisser [ʀ(ə)vise] /**1**/ VT to screw back again

revit [ʀəvi] VB voir **revoir**

revitalisant, e [ʀ(ə)vitalizɑ̃, -ɑ̃t] ADJ (effet, crème) revitalizing ▶ NM (cosmétique) revitalizer

revitalisation [ʀ(ə)vitalizasjɔ̃] NF revitalization

revitaliser [ʀ(ə)vitalize] /**1**/ VT to revitalize

revivifier [ʀ(ə)vivifje] /**7**/ VT to revitalize

revivre [ʀ(ə)vivʀ] /**46**/ VI (reprendre des forces) to come alive again; (traditions) to be revived; **faire ~** (mode, institution, usage) to bring back to life ▶ VT (épreuve, moment) to relive

révocable [ʀevɔkabl] ADJ (délégué) dismissible; (contrat) revocable

révocation [ʀevɔkasjɔ̃] NF dismissal; revocation

★**revoir** [ʀ(ə)vwaʀ] /**30**/ VT to see again; (réviser) to revise (BRIT), review (US) ▶ NM: **au ~** goodbye; **dire au ~ à qn** to say goodbye to sb ■ **se revoir** VPR (amis) to meet (again), see each other again

révoltant, e [ʀevɔltɑ̃, -ɑ̃t] ADJ revolting, appalling

révolte [ʀevɔlt] NF rebellion, revolt

révolter [ʀevɔlte] /**1**/ VT to revolt, outrage ■ **se révolter** VPR: **se ~ (contre)** to rebel (against); **se ~ (à)** to be outraged (by)

révolu, e [ʀevɔly] ADJ past; (Admin): **âgé de 18 ans révolus** over 18 years of age; **après trois ans révolus** when three full years have passed

révolution [ʀevɔlysjɔ̃] NF revolution; **être en ~** (pays etc) to be in revolt; **la ~ industrielle** the industrial revolution

révolutionnaire [ʀevɔlysjɔnɛʀ] ADJ, NMF revolutionary

révolutionner [ʀevɔlysjɔne] /**1**/ VT to revolutionize; (fig) to stir up

revolver [ʀevɔlvɛʀ] NM gun; (à barillet) revolver

révoquer [ʀevɔke] /**1**/ VT (fonctionnaire) to dismiss, remove from office; (arrêt, contrat) to revoke

revoyais etc [ʀəvwajɛ] VB voir **revoir**

revu, e [ʀəvy] PP de **revoir ▶** NF (périodique) magazine; (inventaire) review; (Mil: défilé) review, march
past; (inspection) inspection, review; (de music-hall)
variety show; (pièce satirique) revue; **passer en
revue** (troupes) to review, inspect; (fig: mentalement) to review, to go through; (Sport: défense) to
get past, beat; **revue de presse** press review

révulsé, e [ʀevylse] ADJ (yeux) rolled upwards;
(visage) contorted

Reykjavik [ʀekjavik] N Reykjavik

rez-de-chaussée [ʀed(ə)ʃose] NM INV ground
floor (BRIT), first floor (US)

rez-de-jardin [ʀed(ə)ʒaʀdɛ̃] NM INV garden level

RF SIGLE F = **République française**

RFA SIGLE F (= République fédérale d'Allemagne) FRG

RFO SIGLE F (= Radio-Télévision Française d'Outre-mer)
French overseas broadcasting service

rhabiller [ʀabije] /1/: **se rhabiller** VPR to get
dressed again, put one's clothes on again

rhapsodie [ʀapsɔdi] NF rhapsody

rhéostat [ʀeɔsta] NM rheostat

rhésus [ʀezys] ADJ INV, NM rhesus; **~ positif/néga-
tif** rhesus positive/negative

rhétorique [ʀetɔʀik] NF rhetoric ▶ ADJ rhetorical

★**Rhin** [ʀɛ̃] NM: **le ~** the Rhine

rhinite [ʀinit] NF rhinitis

rhinocéros [ʀinɔseʀɔs] NM rhinoceros

rhinopharyngite [ʀinɔfaʀɛ̃ʒit] NF throat infection

rhodanien, ne [ʀɔdanjɛ̃, -ɛn] ADJ Rhône cpd, of ou
from the Rhône

Rhodes [ʀɔd] N: (**l'île de) ~** Rhodes

Rhodésie [ʀɔdezi] NF (Hist): **la ~** Rhodesia

rhodésien, ne [ʀɔdezjɛ̃, -ɛn] ADJ (Hist) Rhodesian

rhododendron [ʀɔdɔdɛ̃dʀɔ̃] NM rhododendron

Rhône [ʀon] NM: **le ~** the Rhone

rhubarbe [ʀybaʀb] NF rhubarb

rhum [ʀɔm] NM rum

rhumatisant, e [ʀymatizɑ̃, -ɑ̃t] ADJ, NM/F rheumatic

rhumatismal, e, -aux [ʀymatismal, -o] ADJ
rheumatic

rhumatisme [ʀymatism] NM rheumatism no pl

rhumatologie [ʀymatɔlɔʒi] NF rheumatology

rhumatologue [ʀymatɔlɔg] NMF rheumatologist

★**rhume** [ʀym] NM cold; **~ de cerveau** head cold;
le ~ des foins hay fever

rhumerie [ʀɔmʀi] NF (distillerie) rum distillery

RI SIGLE M (Mil) = **régiment d'infanterie**

ri [ʀi] PP de **rire**

riant, e [ʀjɑ̃, -ɑ̃t] VB voir **rire** ▶ ADJ smiling, cheerful; (campagne, paysage) pleasant

RIB SIGLE M = **relevé d'identité bancaire**

ribambelle [ʀibɑ̃bɛl] NF: **une ~ de** a herd ou
swarm of

ricain, e [ʀikɛ̃, -ɛn] ADJ (fam) Yank, Yankee

ricanement [ʀikanmɑ̃] NM snigger; giggle

ricaner [ʀikane] /1/ VI (avec méchanceté) to snigger;
(bêtement, avec gêne) to giggle

★**riche** [ʀiʃ] ADJ (gén) rich; (personne, pays) rich,
wealthy; **~ en** rich in; **~ de** full of; rich in

richement [ʀiʃmɑ̃] ADV richly

richesse [ʀiʃɛs] NF wealth; (fig: de sol, musée etc)
richness; **~ en vitamines** high vitamin content
■ **richesses** NFPL (ressources, argent) wealth sg; (fig:
trésors) treasures

richissime [ʀiʃisim] ADJ extremely rich ou
wealthy

ricin [ʀisɛ̃] NM: **huile de ~** castor oil

ricocher [ʀikɔʃe] /1/ VI: **~ (sur)** to rebound (off);
(sur l'eau) to bounce (on ou off); **faire ~** (galet) to
skim

ricochet [ʀikɔʃɛ] NM rebound; bounce; **faire ~** to
rebound, bounce; (fig) to rebound; **faire des rico-
chets** to skip stones; **par ~** adv on the rebound;
(fig) as an indirect result

rictus [ʀiktys] NM grin, (snarling) grimace

ride [ʀid] NF wrinkle; (fig) ripple

ridé, e [ʀide] ADJ wrinkled

★**rideau, x** [ʀido] NM curtain; **tirer/ouvrir les
rideaux** to draw/open the curtains; **~ de fer** (lit)
metal shutter; **le ~ de fer** (Pol) the Iron Curtain

ridelle [ʀidɛl] NF slatted side (of truck)

rider [ʀide] /1/ VT to wrinkle; (fig) to ripple, ruffle
the surface of ■ **se rider** VPR to become wrinkled

★**ridicule** [ʀidikyl] ADJ ridiculous ▶ NM ridiculous-
ness no pl; (travers: gén pl) absurdities pl; **le ~** ridicule; **tourner en ~** to ridicule

ridiculement [ʀidikylmɑ̃] ADV ridiculously

ridiculiser [ʀidikylize] /1/ VT to ridicule ■ **se ridiculiser** VPR to make a fool of o.s.

ridule [ʀidyl] NF (euph: ride) little wrinkle

rie etc [ʀi] VB voir **rire**

---

rien [ʀjɛ̃]

PRON **1: (ne) … rien** nothing; (tournure négative)
anything; **qu'est-ce que vous avez? — rien**
what have you got? — nothing; **il n'a rien dit/
fait** he said/did nothing, he hasn't said/done
anything; **n'avoir peur de rien** to be afraid ou
frightened of nothing, not to be afraid ou
frightened of anything; **il n'a rien** (n'est pas
blessé) he's all right; **ça ne fait rien** it doesn't
matter; **il n'y est pour rien** he's got nothing to
do with it

2 (quelque chose): **a-t-il jamais rien fait pour
nous?** has he ever done anything for us?

3: **rien de**: **rien d'intéressant** nothing interesting; **rien d'autre** nothing else; **rien du tout**
nothing at all; **il n'a rien d'un champion** he's
no champion, there's nothing of the champion about him

4: **rien que** just, only; nothing but; **rien que
pour lui faire plaisir** only ou just to please him;
rien que la vérité nothing but the truth; **rien
que cela** that alone

▶ EXCL: **de rien!** not at all!, don't mention it!;
il n'en est rien! nothing of the sort!; **rien à
faire!** it's no good!, it's no use!

▶ NM: **un petit rien** (cadeau) a little something;
des riens trivia pl; **un rien de** a hint of; **en un
rien de temps** in no time at all; **avoir peur d'un
rien** to be frightened of the slightest thing

r

rieur, -euse [ʀjœʀ, -øz] ADJ cheerful

rigide [ʀiʒid] ADJ stiff; (fig) rigid; (moralement) strict

rigidifier [ʀiʒidifje] VT (matériau, pièce) to stiffen; (péj: système, organisation) to make more rigid; (rendre plus strict: règlement) to make more strict ■ **se rigidifier** VPR (matériau) to stiffen

rigidité [ʀiʒidite] NF stiffness; **la ~ cadavérique** rigor mortis

rigolade [ʀigɔlad] NF: **la ~** fun; (fig): **c'est de la ~** it's a big farce; (c'est facile) it's a cinch

rigolard, e [ʀigɔlaʀ, -aʀd] ADJ (personne) fun-loving; (air, ton) jokey

rigole [ʀigɔl] NF (conduit) channel; (filet d'eau) rivulet

rigoler [ʀigɔle] /1/ VI (rire) to laugh; (s'amuser) to have (some) fun; (plaisanter) to be joking ou kidding

★**rigolo, rigolote** [ʀigɔlo, -ɔt] ADJ (fam) funny ▶ NM/F comic; (péj) fraud, phoney

rigorisme [ʀigɔʀism] NM (moral) rigorism

rigoriste [ʀigɔʀist] ADJ rigorist

rigoureusement [ʀiguʀøzmɑ̃] ADV rigorously; **~ vrai/interdit** strictly true/forbidden

rigoureux, -euse [ʀiguʀø, -øz] ADJ (morale) rigorous, strict; (personne) stern, strict; (climat, châtiment) rigorous, harsh, severe; (interdiction, neutralité) strict; (preuves, analyse, méthode) rigorous

rigueur [ʀigœʀ] NF rigour (BRIT), rigor (US); strictness; harshness; **« tenue de soirée de ~ »** "evening dress (to be worn)"; **être de ~** to be the usual thing, be the rule; **à la ~** at a pinch; possibly; **tenir ~ à qn de qch** to hold sth against sb

riions etc [ʀijɔ̃] VB voir **rire**

rillettes [ʀijɛt] NFPL ≈ potted meat sg (made from pork or goose)

rime [ʀim] NF rhyme; **n'avoir ni ~ ni raison** to have neither rhyme nor reason

rimer [ʀime] /1/ VI: **~ (avec)** to rhyme (with); **ne ~ à rien** not to make sense

Rimmel® [ʀimɛl] NM mascara

rinçage [ʀɛ̃saʒ] NM rinsing (out); (opération) rinse

rince-doigts [ʀɛ̃sdwa] NM INV finger-bowl

rincer [ʀɛ̃se] /3/ VT to rinse; (récipient) to rinse out; **se ~ la bouche** to rinse one's mouth out

ring [ʀiŋ] NM (boxing) ring; **monter sur le ~** (aussi fig) to enter the ring; (faire carrière de boxeur) to take up boxing

ringard, e [ʀɛ̃gaʀ, -aʀd] ADJ (fam, péj) square (fam)

ringardisation [ʀɛ̃gaʀdizasjɔ̃] NF (fam, péj): **être en voie de ~** (personne) to become square (fam); (chose) to become passé

ringardise [ʀɛ̃gaʀdiz] NF (fam, péj: de personne) squareness (fam)

Rio de Janeiro [ʀiodʒanɛʀo] N Rio de Janeiro

rions [ʀiɔ̃] VB voir **rire**

ripaille [ʀipaj] NF: **faire ~** to feast

riper [ʀipe] /1/ VI to slip, slide

ripoliné, e [ʀipɔline] ADJ enamel-painted

ripoliner [ʀipɔline] VT (peindre) to paint; (remettre à neuf) to give a face-lift to

riposte [ʀipɔst] NF retort, riposte; (fig) counter-attack, reprisal

riposter [ʀipɔste] /1/ VI to retaliate; **~ à** to counter; to reply to ▶ VT: **~ que** to retort that

ripper [ʀipe] /1/ VT (Inform) to rip

★**rire** [ʀiʀ] /36/ VI to laugh; (se divertir) to have fun; (plaisanter) to joke; **~ de** to laugh at; **tu veux ~ !** you must be joking!; **~ aux éclats/aux larmes** to roar with laughter/laugh until one cries; **~ jaune** to force oneself to laugh; **~ sous cape** to laugh up one's sleeve; **~ au nez de qn** to laugh in sb's face; **pour ~** (pas sérieusement) for a joke ou a laugh ▶ NM laugh; **le ~** laughter ■ **se rire de** VPR to make light of

ris [ʀi] VB voir **rire** ▶ NM: **~ de veau** (calf) sweetbread

risée [ʀize] NF: **être la ~ de** to be the laughing stock of

risette [ʀizɛt] NF: **faire ~ (à)** to give a nice little smile (to)

risible [ʀizibl] ADJ laughable, ridiculous

★**risque** [ʀisk] NM risk; **le ~** danger; **l'attrait du ~** the lure of danger; **prendre des risques** to take risks; **à ses risques et périls** at his (ou her) own risk; **au ~ de** at the risk of; **~ d'incendie** fire risk; **~ calculé** calculated risk

risqué, e [ʀiske] ADJ risky; (plaisanterie) risqué, daring

★**risquer** [ʀiske] /1/ VT to risk; (allusion, question) to venture, hazard; **tu risques qu'on te renvoie** you risk being dismissed; **ça ne risque rien** it's quite safe; **il risque de se tuer** he could get ou risks getting himself killed; **il a risqué de se tuer** he almost got himself killed; **ce qui risque de se produire** what might ou could well happen; **il ne risque pas de recommencer** there's no chance of him doing that again; **~ le tout pour le tout** to risk the lot ■ **se risquer** VPR: **se ~ dans** (s'aventurer) to venture into; **se ~ à faire** (tenter) to dare to do

risque-tout [ʀiskətu] NMF INV daredevil

rissoler [ʀisɔle] /1/ VI, VT: **(faire) ~** to brown

ristourne [ʀistuʀn] NF rebate; discount

rit etc [ʀi] VB voir **rire**

rite [ʀit] NM rite; (fig) ritual

ritournelle [ʀituʀnɛl] NF (fig) tune; **c'est toujours la même ~** (fam) it's always the same old story

rituel, le [ʀitɥɛl] ADJ, NM ritual

rituellement [ʀitɥɛlmɑ̃] ADV religiously

riv. ABR (= rivière) R

rivage [ʀivaʒ] NM shore

rival, e, -aux [ʀival, -o] ADJ, NM/F rival; **sans ~** adj unrivalled

rivaliser [ʀivalize] /1/ VI: **~ avec** to rival, vie with; (être comparable) to hold its own against, compare with; **~ avec qn de** (élégance etc) to vie with ou rival sb in

rivalité [ʀivalite] NF rivalry

rive [ʀiv] NF shore; (de fleuve) bank

river [ʀive] /1/ VT (clou, pointe) to clinch; (plaques) to rivet together; **être rivé sur/à** to be riveted on/to

riverain, e [ʀiv(ə)ʀɛ̃, -ɛn] ADJ riverside cpd; lakeside cpd; roadside cpd ▶ NM/F riverside (ou lakeside) resident; (d'une route) local ou roadside resident

rivet [Rivɛ] NM rivet

riveter [Riv(ə)te] /4/ VT to rivet (together)

Riviera [Rivjɛra] NF: **la ~ (italienne)** the Italian Riviera

rivière [RivjɛR] NF river; **~ de diamants** diamond rivière

rixe [Riks] NF brawl, scuffle

Riyad [Rijad] N Riyadh

★**riz** [Ri] NM rice; **~ au lait** ≈ rice pudding

rizicole [Rizikɔl] ADJ (région) rice-growing; (production) rice cpd

riziculture [RizikyltyR] NF rice growing

rizière [RizjɛR] NF paddy field

RMC SIGLE F = **Radio Monte Carlo**

RN SIGLE F = **route nationale**

★**robe** [Rɔb] NF dress; (de juge, d'ecclésiastique) robe; (de professeur) gown; (pelage) coat; **~ de soirée/de mariée** evening/wedding dress; **~ de baptême** christening robe; **~ de chambre** dressing gown; **~ de grossesse** maternity dress

★**robinet** [Rɔbinɛ] NM tap (BRIT), faucet (US); **~ du gaz** gas tap; **~ mélangeur** mixer tap

robinetterie [Rɔbinɛtri] NF taps pl, plumbing

roboratif, -ive [Rɔbɔratif, -iv] ADJ bracing, invigorating

robot [Rɔbo] NM robot; **~ de cuisine** food processor

robotique [Rɔbɔtik] NF robotics sg

robotiser [Rɔbɔtize] /1/ VT (personne, travailleur) to turn into a robot; (monde, vie) to automate

robuste [Rɔbyst] ADJ robust, sturdy

robustesse [Rɔbystɛs] NF robustness, sturdiness

roc [Rɔk] NM rock

rocade [Rɔkad] NF (Auto) bypass

rocaille [Rɔkaj] NF (pierres) loose stones pl; (terrain) rocky ou stony ground; (jardin) rockery, rock garden ▶ ADJ (style) rocaille

rocailleux, -euse [Rɔkajø, -øz] ADJ rocky, stony; (voix) harsh

rocambolesque [Rɔkɑ̃bɔlɛsk] ADJ fantastic, incredible

roche [Rɔʃ] NF rock

★**rocher** [Rɔʃe] NM rock; (Anat) petrosal bone

rochet [Rɔʃɛ] NM: **roue à ~** ratchet wheel

rocheux, -euse [Rɔʃø, -øz] ADJ rocky; **les (montagnes) Rocheuses** the Rockies, the Rocky Mountains

★**rock** [Rɔk], **rock and roll** [RɔkɛnRɔl] NM (musique) rock(-'n'-roll); (danse) rock

rocker [Rɔkœr] NM (chanteur) rock musician; (adepte) rock fan

rocking-chair [Rɔkiŋ(t)ʃɛr] NM rocking chair

rococo [Rɔkɔko] NM INV rococo ▶ ADJ INV rococo

rodage [Rɔdaʒ] NM (Auto) running in (BRIT), breaking in (US); **en ~** running ou breaking in

rodé, e [Rɔde] ADJ (Auto) run in (BRIT), broken in (US); (personne): **être ~ à qch** to have got the hang of sth

rodéo [Rɔdeo] NM rodeo

roder [Rɔde] /1/ VT (moteur, voiture) to run in (BRIT), break in (US); **~ un spectacle** to iron out the initial problems of a show

rôder [Rode] /1/ VI to roam ou wander about; (de façon suspecte) to lurk (about ou around)

rôdeur, -euse [Rodœr, -øz] NM/F prowler

rodomontades [Rɔdɔmɔ̃tad] NFPL bragging sg; sabre rattling sg

rogatoire [Rɔgatwar] ADJ: **commission ~** letters rogatory

rogne [Rɔɲ] NF: **être en ~** to be mad ou in a temper; **se mettre en ~** to get mad ou in a temper

rogner [Rɔɲe] /1/ VT to trim; (fig) to whittle down; **~ sur** (fig) to cut down ou back on

rognons [Rɔɲɔ̃] NMPL kidneys

rognures [Rɔɲyr] NFPL trimmings

rogue [Rɔg] ADJ arrogant

★**roi** [Rwa] NM king; **les Rois mages** the Three Wise Men, the Magi; **le jour** ou **la fête des Rois, les Rois** Twelfth Night

> The **fête des Rois** is celebrated on Twelfth Night (6 January), the date on which many Christians commemorate Jesus being visited by the Three Wise Men. People eat galette des Rois, a cake in which a porcelain charm (la fève) is hidden. Whoever finds the charm is king or queen for the day and gets to wear the golden paper crown that French bakeries usually provide with each cake.

roitelet [Rwat(ə)lɛ] NM wren; (péj) kinglet

rôle [Rol] NM role; (contribution) part

rollers [Rɔlœr] NMPL Rollerblades®

rollmops [Rɔlmɔps] NM rollmop

ROM [Rɔm] SIGLE F (= mémoire morte) ROM (= read-only memory)

rom [Rɔm] ADJ (populations) Romany ▶ NM/F: **Rom** Romany

romain, e [Rɔmɛ̃, -ɛn] ADJ Roman ▶ NM/F: **Romain, e** Roman ▶ NF (laitue) cos (lettuce)

★**roman, e** [Rɔmɑ̃, -an] ADJ (Archit) Romanesque; (Ling) Romance cpd, Romanic ▶ NM novel; **~ d'amour** love story; **~ d'espionnage** spy novel; **~ noir** thriller; **~ policier** detective novel

romance [Rɔmɑ̃s] NF ballad

romancer [Rɔmɑ̃se] /3/ VT to romanticize

romanche [Rɔmɑ̃ʃ] ADJ, NM Romansh

romancier, -ière [Rɔmɑ̃sje, -jɛr] NM/F novelist

romand, e [Rɔmɑ̃, -ɑ̃d] ADJ of ou from French-speaking Switzerland ▶ NM/F: **Romand, e** French-speaking Swiss

romanesque [Rɔmanɛsk] ADJ (fantastique) fantastic; (amours, aventures) storybook cpd; (sentimental: personne) romantic; (Littérature) novelistic

roman-feuilleton [Rɔmɑ̃fœjtɔ̃] (pl **romans-feuilletons**) NM serialized novel

roman-fleuve [Rɔmɑ̃flœv] (pl **romans-fleuves**) NM saga, roman-fleuve

romanichel, le [Rɔmaniʃɛl] NM/F gipsy (péj)

roman-photo [Rɔmɑ̃foto] (pl **romans-photos**) NM (romantic) picture story

★**romantique** [Rɔmɑ̃tik] ADJ romantic

romantisme [Rɔmɑ̃tism] NM romanticism

romarin [Rɔmarɛ̃] NM rosemary

rombière [Rɔ̃bjɛr] NF (péj) old bag

Rome [Rɔm] N Rome

rompre [ʀɔ̃pʀ] **/41/** vt to break; (*entretien, fiançailles*) to break off; **à tout ~** *adv* wildly; **applaudir à tout ~** to bring the house down, applaud wildly; **rompez (les rangs) !** (*Mil*) dismiss!, fall out! ▶ vi (*fiancés*) to break it off; **~ avec** to break with ■ **se rompre** vpr to break; (*Méd*) to burst, rupture; **se ~ les os** *ou* **le cou** to break one's neck

rompu, e [ʀɔ̃py] pp *de* **rompre** ▶ adj (*fourbu*) exhausted, worn out; **~ à** with wide experience of; inured to

romsteck [ʀɔ̃mstɛk] NM rump steak *no pl*

ronce [ʀɔ̃s] NF (*Bot*) bramble branch; (*Menuiserie*): **~ de noyer** burr walnut ■ **ronces** NFPL brambles, thorns

ronchon [ʀɔ̃ʃɔ̃] ADJ INV (*fam*) grumpy

ronchonner [ʀɔ̃ʃɔne] **/1/** vi (*fam*) to grouse, grouch

★**rond, e** [ʀɔ̃, ʀɔ̃d] ADJ round; (*joues, mollets*) well-rounded; (*fam: ivre*) tight; (*sincère, décidé*): **être ~ en affaires** to be on the level in business, do an honest deal; **pour faire un compte ~** to make (it) a round figure, to round (it) off; **avoir le dos ~** to be round-shouldered ▶ NM (*cercle*) ring; (*fam: sou*): **je n'ai plus un ~** I haven't a penny left; **en ~** (*s'asseoir, danser*) in a ring; **faire des ronds de jambe** to bow and scrape; **~ de serviette** napkin ring ▶ NF (*gén: de surveillance*) rounds pl, patrol; (*danse*) round (dance); (*Mus*) semibreve (*Brit*), whole note (*US*); **à la ronde** (*alentour*): **à 10 km à la ronde** for 10 km round; **passer qch à la ronde** to pass sth (a)round ▶ ADV: **tourner ~** (*moteur*) to run smoothly; **ça ne tourne pas ~** (*fig*) there's something not quite right about it

rond-de-cuir [ʀɔ̃dkɥiʀ] (*pl* **ronds-de-cuir**) NM (*péj*) penpusher

rondelet, te [ʀɔ̃dlɛ, -ɛt] ADJ plump; (*fig: somme*) tidy; (: *bourse*) well-lined, fat

rondelle [ʀɔ̃dɛl] NF (*Tech*) washer; (*tranche*) slice, round

rondement [ʀɔ̃dmɑ̃] ADV (*avec décision*) briskly; (*loyalement*) frankly

rondeur [ʀɔ̃dœʀ] NF (*d'un bras, des formes*) plumpness; (*bonhomie*) friendly straightforwardness ■ **rondeurs** NFPL (*d'une femme*) curves

rondin [ʀɔ̃dɛ̃] NM log

rondouillard, e [ʀɔ̃dujar, ard] ADJ (*fam*) tubby

★**rond-point** [ʀɔ̃pwɛ̃] (*pl* **ronds-points**) NM roundabout (*Brit*), traffic circle (*US*)

ronéotyper [ʀɔneɔtipe] vt to roneo

ronflant, e [ʀɔ̃flɑ̃, -ɑ̃t] ADJ (*péj*) high-flown, grand

ronflement [ʀɔ̃fləmɑ̃] NM snore, snoring *no pl*

ronfler [ʀɔ̃fle] **/1/** vi to snore; (*moteur, poêle*) to hum; (: *plus fort*) to roar

ronger [ʀɔ̃ʒe] **/3/** vt to gnaw (at); (*vers, rouille*) to eat into; **~ son frein** to champ (at) the bit ■ **se ronger** vpr: **se ~ de souci, se ~ les sangs** to worry o.s. sick, fret; **se ~ les ongles** to bite one's nails

rongeur, -euse [ʀɔ̃ʒœʀ, -øz] NM/F rodent

ronronnement [ʀɔ̃ʀɔnmɑ̃] NM purring; (*bruit*) purr

ronronner [ʀɔ̃ʀɔne] **/1/** vi to purr

roque [ʀɔk] NM (*Échecs*) castling

roquefort [ʀɔkfɔʀ] NM Roquefort

roquer [ʀɔke] **/1/** vi (*Échecs*) to castle

roquet [ʀɔkɛ] NM yappy little lap-dog

roquette [ʀɔkɛt] NF (*Mil*) rocket; (*salade*) rocket (*Brit*), arugula (*US*); **~ antichar** antitank rocket

rosace [ʀozas] NF (*vitrail*) rose window, rosace; (*motif: de plafond etc*) rose

rosaire [ʀozɛʀ] NM rosary

rosbif [ʀɔsbif] NM: **du ~** roasting beef; (*cuit*) roast beef; **un ~** a joint of (roasting) beef

★**rose** [ʀoz] NF rose; (*vitrail*) rose window; **~ des vents** compass card ▶ ADJ pink; **~ bonbon** *adj inv* candy pink

rosé, e [ʀoze] ADJ pinkish; **(vin) ~** rosé (wine)

roseau, x [ʀozo] NM reed

rosée [ʀoze] ADJ F *voir* **rosé** ▶ NF dew; **goutte de ~** dewdrop

roseraie [ʀozʀɛ] NF rose garden; (*plantation*) rose nursery

rosette [ʀozɛt] NF rosette (*gen of the Légion d'honneur*)

rosier [ʀozje] NM rosebush, rose tree

rosir [ʀoziʀ] **/2/** vi to go pink

rosse [ʀɔs] NF (*péj: cheval*) nag ▶ ADJ nasty, vicious

rosser [ʀɔse] **/1/** vt (*fam*) to thrash

rossignol [ʀɔsiɲɔl] NM (*Zool*) nightingale; (*crochet*) picklock

rot [ʀo] NM (*fam*) burp, belch

rotatif, -ive [ʀɔtatif, -iv] ADJ rotary ▶ NF rotary press

rotation [ʀɔtasjɔ̃] NF rotation; (*fig*) swap-around, (*renouvellement*) turnover; **par ~** on a rota (*Brit*) *ou* rotation (*US*) basis; **~ des cultures** crop rotation; **~ des stocks** stock (*Brit*) *ou* inventory (*US*) rotation

rotatoire [ʀɔtatwaʀ] ADJ: **mouvement ~** rotary movement

roter [ʀɔte] **/1/** vi (*fam*) to burp, belch

rôti [ʀoti] NM: **du ~** roasting meat; (*cuit*) roast meat; **un ~ de bœuf/porc** a joint of beef/pork

rotin [ʀɔtɛ̃] NM rattan (cane); **fauteuil en ~** cane (arm)chair

rôtir [ʀotiʀ] **/2/** vt (*aussi:* **faire rôtir**) to roast ▶ vi to roast ■ **se rôtir** vpr: **se ~ au soleil** to bask in the sun

rôtisserie [ʀotisʀi] NF (*restaurant*) steakhouse; (*comptoir*) roast meat counter; (*magasin, traiteur*) roast meat shop (*Brit*) *ou* store (*US*)

rôtissoire [ʀotiswaʀ] NF (roasting) spit

rotonde [ʀɔtɔ̃d] NF (*Archit*) rotunda; (*Rail*) engine shed

rotondité [ʀɔtɔ̃dite] NF roundness

rotor [ʀɔtɔʀ] NM rotor

Rotterdam [ʀɔtɛʀdam] N Rotterdam

rotule [ʀɔtyl] NF kneecap, patella

roturier, -ière [ʀɔtyʀje, -jɛʀ] NM/F commoner

rouage [ʀwaʒ] NM cog(wheel), gearwheel; (*de montre*) part; (*fig*) cog ■ **rouages** NMPL (*fig*) internal structure *sg*; **les rouages de l'État** the wheels of State

Rouanda [ʀwɑ̃da] NM: **le ~** Rwanda

roubaisien, ne [ʀubezjɛ̃, -ɛn] ADJ of *ou* from Roubaix

roublard, e [ʀublaʀ, -aʀd] ADJ (*péj*) crafty, wily

roublardise [Rublaʀdiz] NF (*péj*) craftiness

rouble [Rubl] NM rouble

roucoulement [Rukulmã] NM (*de pigeons, fig*) coo, cooing

roucouler [Rukule] /1/ VI to coo; (*fig: péj*) to warble; (: *amoureux*) to bill and coo

★**roue** [Ru] NF wheel; **faire la ~** (*paon*) to spread *ou* fan its tail; (*Gym*) to do a cartwheel; **descendre en ~ libre** to freewheel *ou* coast down; **pousser à la ~** to put one's shoulder to the wheel; **grande ~** (*à la foire*) big wheel; **~ à aubes** paddle wheel; **~ dentée** cogwheel; **~ de secours** spare wheel

roué, e [Rwe] ADJ wily

rouelle [Rwɛl] NF (*viande*) round steak (*cut across the leg*)

rouennais, e [Rwanɛ, -ɛz] ADJ *ou* from Rouen

rouer [Rwe] /1/ VT: **~ qn de coups** to give sb a thrashing

rouet [Rwɛ] NM spinning wheel

★**rouge** [Ruʒ] ADJ red; **sur la liste ~** (*Tél*) ex-directory (BRIT), unlisted (US); **~ de honte/colère** red with shame/anger ▶ NM red; (*fard*) rouge; **(vin) ~** red wine; **passer au ~** (*signal*) to go red; (*automobiliste*) to go through a red light; **porter au ~** (*métal*) to bring to red heat; **~ à joue** blusher; **~ (à lèvres)** lipstick ▶ ADV: **se fâcher tout/voir ~** to blow one's top/see red ▶ NMF red

rougeâtre [Ruʒɑtʀ] ADJ reddish

rougeaud, e [Ruʒo, -od] ADJ (*teint*) red; (*personne*) red-faced

rouge-gorge [Ruʒgɔʀʒ] (*pl* **rouges-gorges**) NM robin (redbreast)

rougeoiement [Ruʒwamã] NM reddish glow

rougeole [Ruʒɔl] NF measles *sg*

rougeoyant, e [Ruʒwajã, -ãt] ADJ (*ciel, braises*) glowing; (*aube, reflets*) glowing red

rougeoyer [Ruʒwaje] /8/ VI to glow red

rouget [Ruʒɛ] NM mullet

rougeur [Ruʒœʀ] NF redness; (*du visage*) red face ▪ **rougeurs** NFPL (*Méd*) red blotches

rougir [Ruʒiʀ] /2/ VI to turn red; (*de honte, timidité*) to blush, flush; (*de plaisir, colère*) to flush; (*fraise, tomate*) to go *ou* turn red; (*ciel*) to redden

rouille [Ruj] ADJ INV rust-coloured, rusty ▶ NF rust; (*Culin*) spicy Provençal sauce served with fish dishes

rouillé, e [Ruje] ADJ rusty

rouiller [Ruje] /1/ VT to rust, go rusty ▪ **se rouiller** VPR to rust; (*fig: mentalement*) to become rusty; (: *physiquement*) to grow stiff

roulade [Rulad] NF (*Gym*) roll; (*Culin*) rolled meat *no pl*; (*Mus*) roulade, run

roulage [Rulaʒ] NM (*transport*) haulage

roulant, e [Rulã, -ãt] ADJ (*meuble*) on wheels; (*surface, trottoir, tapis*) moving; **matériel ~** (*Rail*) rolling stock; **escalier ~** escalator; **personnel ~** (*Rail*) train crews *pl*

roulé, e [Rule] ADJ: **bien roulée** (*fam: femme*) shapely, curvy

rouleau, x [Rulo] NM (*de papier, tissu, pièces de monnaie, Sport*) roll; (*de machine à écrire*) roller, platen; (*à mise en plis, à peinture, vague*) roller; **être au bout du ~** (*fig*) to be at the end of the line; **~ compresseur** steamroller; **~ à pâtisserie** rolling pin; **~ de pellicule** roll of film

roulé-boulé [Rulebule] (*pl* **roulés-boulés**) N (*Sport*) roll

roulement [Rulmã] NM (*bruit*) rumbling *no pl*, rumble; (*rotation*) rotation; turnover; (*de capitaux*) circulation; **par ~** on a rota (BRIT) *ou* rotation (US) basis; **~ (à billes)** ball bearings *pl*; **~ de tambour** drum roll; **~ d'yeux** roll(ing) of the eyes

★**rouler** [Rule] /1/ VT to roll; (*papier, tapis*) to roll up; (*Culin: pâte*) to roll out; (*fam: duper*) to do, con; **~ sa bosse** (*fam*) to get around; **~ qn dans la farine** (*fam*) to con sb; **~ les épaules/hanches** to sway one's shoulders/wiggle one's hips; **~ les « r »** to roll one's r's ▶ VI (*bille, boule*) to roll; (*voiture, train*) to go, run; (*automobiliste*) to drive; (*cycliste*) to ride; (*bateau*) to roll; (*tonnerre*) to rumble, roll; (*dégringoler*): **~ en bas de** to roll down; **~ sur** (*conversation*) to turn on; **~ sur l'or** to be rolling in money, be rolling in it ▪ **se rouler** VPR: **se ~ dans** (*boue*) to roll in; (*couverture*) to roll o.s. (up) in

roulette [Rulɛt] NF (*de table, fauteuil*) castor; (*de dentiste*) drill; (*de pâtissier*) pastry wheel; (*jeu*): **la ~** roulette; **à roulettes** on castors; **la ~ russe** Russian roulette; **ça a marché comme sur des roulettes** (*fam*) it went off very smoothly

roulis [Ruli] NM roll(ing)

roulotte [Rulɔt] NF caravan

roumain, e [Rumɛ̃, -ɛn] ADJ Romanian ▶ NM (*Ling*) Romanian ▶ NM/F: **Roumain, e** Romanian

Roumanie [Rumani] NF: **la ~** Romania

round [Raund] NM (*de combat, négociations*) round

roupiller [Rupije] /1/ VI (*fam*) to sleep

rouquin, e [Rukɛ̃, -in] NM/F (*péj*) redhead

rouspéter [Ruspete] /6/ VI (*fam*) to moan, grouse

rousse [Rus] ADJ F *voir* **roux**

roussette [Rusɛt] NF (*poisson*) spotted dogfish; (*chauve-souris*) flying fox; (*grenouille*) common frog

rousseur [Rusœʀ] NF: **tache de ~** freckle

roussi [Rusi] NM: **ça sent le ~** there's a smell of burning; (*fig*) I can smell trouble

roussir [Rusiʀ] /2/ VT to scorch ▶ VI (*feuilles*) to go *ou* turn brown; **faire ~** (*Culin*) to brown

routage [Rutaʒ] NM (collective) mailing

routard, e [Rutaʀ, -aʀd] NM/F traveller

★**route** [Rut] NF road; (*fig: chemin*) way; (*itinéraire, parcours*) route; (*fig: voie*) road, path; **par (la) ~** by road; **il y a trois heures de ~** it's a three-hour ride *ou* journey; **en ~** ADV on the way; **en ~ !** let's go!; **en cours de ~** en route; **mettre en ~** to start up; **se mettre en ~** to set off; **faire ~ vers** to head towards; **faire fausse ~** (*fig*) to be on the wrong track; **~ nationale** ≈ A-road (BRIT), ≈ state highway (US)

routeur [Rutœʀ] NM (*Inform*) router

★**routier, -ière** [Rutje, -jɛʀ] ADJ road *cpd*; **carte routière** road map ▶ NM (*camionneur*) (long-distance) lorry (BRIT) *ou* truck (US) driver; (*restaurant*) ≈ transport café (BRIT), ≈ truck stop (US); (*scout*) ≈ rover; (*cycliste*) road racer; **vieux ~** old stager ▶ NF (*voiture*) touring car

routine [Rutin] NF routine; **visite/contrôle de ~** routine visit/check

routinier, -ière [Rutinje, -jɛʀ] ADJ (*péj: travail*) humdrum, routine; (: *personne*) addicted to routine; **c'est un ~** he's a creature of habit

rouvert, e [RuvɛR, -ɛRt] PP *de* **rouvrir**

rouvrir [ʀuvʀiʀ] /**18**/ vt, vi to reopen, open again ■ **se rouvrir** vpr (*blessure*) to open up again

★**roux, rousse** [ʀu, ʀus] adj red; (*personne*) red-haired ▶ nm/f redhead ▶ nm (*Culin*) roux

royal, e, -aux [ʀwajal, -o] adj royal; (*fig*) fit for a king, princely; blissful; thorough

royalement [ʀwajalmɑ̃] adv royally

royaliste [ʀwajalist] adj, nmf royalist

royaume [ʀwajom] nm kingdom; (*fig*) realm; **le ~ des cieux** the kingdom of heaven

Royaume-Uni [ʀwajomyni] nm: **le ~** the United Kingdom

royauté [ʀwajote] nf (*dignité*) kingship; (*régime*) monarchy

RP sigle f = **la région parisienne** ▶ sigle fpl (= *relations publiques*) PR

RSA sigle m (= *revenu de solidarité active*) ≈ income support (*Brit*), ≈ welfare (*US*)

RSVP abr (= *répondez s'il vous plaît*) R.S.V.P.

RTB sigle f = **Radio-Télévision belge**

Rte abr = **route**

RTL sigle f = **Radio-Télévision Luxembourg**

RTT sigle f = **réduction du temps de travail**

> The **RTT** (*Réduction du temps de travail*) is a system designed to ensure that French employees do not work more than 35 hours a week. If companies cannot simply reduce their staff's number of hours from the 39 hours that used to be the norm, they can, under this system, either grant days in lieu (*jours de RTT*) or pay the extra hours as overtime.

RU [ʀy] sigle m = **restaurant universitaire**

ruade [ʀɥad] nf kick

Ruanda [ʀwɑ̃da] nm: **le ~** Rwanda

ruban [ʀybɑ̃] nm (*gén*) ribbon; (*pour ourlet, couture*) binding; (*de téléscripteur etc*) tape; (*d'acier*) strip; **~ adhésif** adhesive tape; **~ carbone** carbon ribbon

rubéole [ʀybeɔl] nf German measles *sg*, rubella

rubicond, e [ʀybikɔ̃, -ɔ̃d] adj rubicund, ruddy

rubis [ʀybi] nm ruby; (*Horlogerie*) jewel; **payer ~ sur l'ongle** to pay cash on the nail

rubrique [ʀybʀik] nf (*titre, catégorie*) heading, rubric; (*Presse: article*) column

ruche [ʀyʃ] nf hive

rucher [ʀyʃe] nm apiary

rude [ʀyd] adj (*barbe, toile*) rough; (*métier, tâche*) hard, tough; (*climat*) severe, harsh; (*bourru*) harsh, rough; (*fruste: manières*) rugged, tough; (*fam: fameux*) jolly good; **être mis à ~ épreuve** to be put through the mill

rudement [ʀydmɑ̃] adv (*tomber, frapper*) hard; (*traiter, reprocher*) harshly; (*fam: très*) terribly; (: *beaucoup*) terribly hard

rudesse [ʀydɛs] nf roughness; toughness; severity; harshness

rudimentaire [ʀydimɑ̃tɛʀ] adj rudimentary, basic

rudiments [ʀydimɑ̃] nmpl rudiments; basic knowledge *sg*; basic principles; **avoir des ~ d'anglais** to have a smattering of English

rudoyer [ʀydwaje] /**8**/ vt to treat harshly

★**rue** [ʀy] nf street; **être/jeter qn à la ~** to be on the streets/throw sb out onto the street

ruée [ʀɥe] nf rush; **la ~ vers l'or** the gold rush

ruelle [ʀɥɛl] nf alley(way)

ruer [ʀɥe] /**1**/ vi (*cheval*) to kick out; **~ dans les brancards** to become rebellious ■ **se ruer** vpr: **se ~ sur** to pounce on; **se ~ vers/dans/hors de** to rush *ou* dash towards/into/out of

★**rugby** [ʀygbi] nm rugby (football); **~ à treize/quinze** rugby league/union

rugbyman [ʀygbiman] nm rugby player

rugbywoman [ʀygbiwuman] nf rugby player

rugir [ʀyʒiʀ] /**2**/ vi to roar

rugissement [ʀyʒismɑ̃] nm roar, roaring *no pl*

rugosité [ʀygozite] nf roughness; (*aspérité*) rough patch

rugueux, -euse [ʀygø, -øz] adj rough

ruine [ʀɥin] nf ruin; **tomber en ~** to fall into ruin(s) ■ **ruines** nfpl ruins

ruiner [ʀɥine] /**1**/ vt to ruin

ruineux, -euse [ʀɥinø, -øz] adj ruinously expensive; extravagant

ruisseau, x [ʀɥiso] nm stream, brook; (*caniveau*) gutter; **ruisseaux de larmes/sang** (*fig*) floods of tears/streams of blood

ruisselant, e [ʀɥis(ə)lɑ̃, -ɑ̃t] adj streaming

ruisseler [ʀɥis(ə)le] /**4**/ vi to stream; **~ (d'eau)** to be streaming (with water); **~ de lumière** to stream with light

ruissellement [ʀɥisɛlmɑ̃] nm streaming; **~ de lumière** stream of light

rumeur [ʀymœʀ] nf (*bruit confus*) rumbling; hubbub *no pl*; (*protestation*) murmur(ing); (*nouvelle*) rumour (*Brit*), rumor (*US*)

ruminant [ʀyminɑ̃] nm (*Zool*) ruminant

ruminer [ʀymine] /**1**/ vt (*herbe*) to ruminate; (*fig*) to ruminate on *ou* over, chew over ▶ vi (*vache*) to chew the cud, ruminate

rumsteck [ʀɔmstɛk] nm = **romsteck**

rupestre [ʀypɛstʀ] adj (*plante*) rock *cpd*; (*art*) wall *cpd*

rupin, e [ʀypɛ̃, -in] (*fam, péj*) adj (*personne*) filthy rich (*fam*); (*quartier, appartement*) posh (*Brit fam*), swanky (*fam*) ▶ nm/f (*personne*) rich person; **les rupins** the rich folk

rupture [ʀyptyʀ] nf (*de câble, digue*) breaking; (*de tendon*) rupture, tearing; (*de négociations etc*) breakdown; (*de contrat*) breach; (*dans continuité*) break; (*séparation, désunion*) break-up, split; **en ~ de ban** at odds with authority; **en ~ de stock** (*Comm*) out of stock

rural, e, -aux [ʀyʀal, -o] adj rural, country *cpd* ▶ nmpl: **les ruraux** country people

ruralité [ʀyʀalite] nf rurality

ruse [ʀyz] nf: **la ~** cunning, craftiness; (*pour tromper*) trickery; **une ~** a trick, a ruse; **par ~** by trickery

rusé, e [ʀyze] adj cunning, crafty

ruser [ʀyze] vi to use cunning; **~ avec** (*personne, loi, autorité*) to get round

rush [ʀœʃ] nm (*précipitation, ruée*) rush; (*Sport*) final burst ■ **rushes** nmpl (*Ciné*) rushes

★**russe** [ʀys] ADJ Russian ▶ NM (*Ling*) Russian ▶ NMF:
Russe Russian

★**Russie** [ʀysi] NF: **la ~** Russia; **la ~ blanche** White
Russia; **la ~ soviétique** Soviet Russia

rustine [ʀystin] NF repair patch (*for bicycle inner tube*)

rustique [ʀystik] ADJ rustic; (*plante*) hardy

rustre [ʀystʀ] NM boor

rut [ʀyt] NM: **être en ~** (*animal domestique*) to be in *ou* on heat; (*animal sauvage*) to be rutting

rutabaga [ʀytabaga] NM swede

rutilant, e [ʀytilɑ̃, -ɑ̃t] ADJ gleaming

RV SIGLE M = **rendez-vous**

Rwanda [ʀwɑ̃da] NM: **le ~** Rwanda

rwandais, e [ʀwɑ̃dɛ, -ɛz] ADJ Rwandan ▶ NM/F:
Rwandais, e Rwandan

rythme [ʀitm] NM rhythm; (*vitesse*) rate; (: *de la vie*) pace, tempo; **au ~ de 10 par jour** at the rate of 10 a day

rythmé, e [ʀitme] ADJ rhythmic(al)

rythmer [ʀitme] /1/ VT to give rhythm to

rythmique [ʀitmik] ADJ rhythmic(al) ▶ NF rhythmics *sg*

r

Ss

S, s [ɛs] NM INV S, s ▸ ABR (= *sud*) S; (= *seconde*) sec; (= *siècle*) c., century; **S comme Suzanne** S for Sugar

S/ ABR = **sur¹**

★**s'** [s] PRON *voir* **se**

SA SIGLE F = **société anonyme**; (= *Son Altesse*) HH

★**sa** [sa] ADJ POSS *voir* **son¹**

sabbatique [sabatik] ADJ: **année ~** sabbatical year

★**sable** [sabl] NM sand; **sables mouvants** quicksand(s)

sablé [sable] ADJ (*allée*) sandy; **pâte sablée** (*Culin*) shortbread dough ▸ NM shortbread biscuit

sabler [sable] /1/ VT to sand; (*contre le verglas*) to grit; **~ le champagne** to drink champagne

sableux, -euse [sablø, -øz] ADJ sandy

sablier [sablije] NM hourglass; (*de cuisine*) egg timer

sablière [sablijɛʀ] NF sand quarry

sablonneux, -euse [sablɔnø, -øz] ADJ sandy

saborder [sabɔʀde] /1/ VT (*navire*) to scuttle; (*fig*) to wind up, shut down

sabot [sabo] NM clog; (*de cheval, bœuf*) hoof; **~ (de Denver)** (wheel) clamp (BRIT), Denver boot (US); **~ de frein** brake shoe

sabotage [sabɔtaʒ] NM sabotage

saboter [sabɔte] /1/ VT (*travail, morceau de musique*) to botch, make a mess of; (*machine, installation, négociation etc*) to sabotage

saboteur, -euse [sabɔtœʀ, -øz] NM/F saboteur

sabre [sabʀ] NM sabre; **le ~** (*fig*) the sword, the army

sabrer [sabʀe] /1/ VT to cut down

★**sac** [sak] NM bag; (*à charbon etc*) sack; (*pillage*) sack(ing); **mettre à ~** to sack; **~ à provisions/de voyage** shopping/overnight *ou* travel bag; **~ de couchage** sleeping bag; **à dos** backpack, rucksack; **~ à main** handbag; **~ de plage** beach bag

saccade [sakad] NF jerk; **par saccades** jerkily; haltingly

saccadé, e [sakade] ADJ jerky; (*respiration*) spasmodic

saccage [sakaʒ] NM havoc

saccager [sakaʒe] /3/ VT (*piller*) to sack, lay waste; (*dévaster*) to create havoc in, wreck

saccharine [sakaʀin] NF saccharin(e)

saccharose [sakaʀoz] NM sucrose

SACEM [sasɛm] SIGLE F (= *Société des auteurs, compositeurs et éditeurs de musique*) body responsible for collecting and distributing royalties

sacerdoce [sasɛʀdɔs] NM priesthood; (*fig*) calling, vocation

sacerdotal, e, -aux [sasɛʀdɔtal, -o] ADJ priestly, sacerdotal

sachant *etc* [saʃɑ̃] VB *voir* **savoir**

sache *etc* [saʃ] VB *voir* **savoir**

sachet [saʃɛ] NM (small) bag; (*de lavande, poudre, shampooing*) sachet; **thé en sachets** tea bags; **~ de thé** tea bag; **du potage en ~** packet soup

sacoche [sakɔʃ] NF (*gén*) bag; (*de bicyclette*) saddlebag; (*du facteur*) (post)bag; (*d'outils*) toolbag

sacquer [sake] /1/ VT (*fam: employé*) to sack; (: *élève: mal noter*) to give low marks (BRIT) *ou* grades (US)

sacraliser [sakʀalize] /1/ VT to make sacred

sacre [sakʀ] NM coronation; consecration

sacré, e [sakʀe] ADJ sacred; (*fam: satané*) blasted; (: *fameux*): **un ~ ...** a heck of a ...; (*Anat*) sacral

sacrement [sakʀəmɑ̃] NM sacrament; **les derniers sacrements** the last rites

sacrer [sakʀe] /1/ VT (*roi*) to crown; (*évêque*) to consecrate ▸ VI to curse, swear

sacrifice [sakʀifis] NM sacrifice; **faire le ~ de** to sacrifice

sacrificiel, le [sakʀifisjɛl] ADJ sacrificial

sacrifier [sakʀifje] /7/ VT to sacrifice; **~ à** to conform to; **articles sacrifiés** (*Comm*) items sold at rock-bottom *ou* give-away prices ■ **se sacrifier** VPR to sacrifice o.s.

sacrilège [sakʀilɛʒ] NM sacrilege ▸ ADJ sacrilegious

sacristain [sakʀistɛ̃] NM sexton; sacristan

sacristie [sakʀisti] NF sacristy; (*culte protestant*) vestry

sacro-saint, e [sakʀosɛ̃, -ɛ̃t] ADJ sacrosanct

sadique [sadik] ADJ sadistic ▸ NMF sadist

sadisme [sadism] NM sadism

sadomasochisme [sadɔmazɔʃism] NM sadomasochism

sadomasochiste [sadɔmazɔʃist] NMF sadomasochist

safari [safaʀi] NM safari; **faire un ~** to go on safari

safari-photo [safaʀifɔto] (*pl* **safaris-photos**) NM photographic safari

SAFER [safɛʀ] SIGLE F (= *Société d'aménagement foncier et d'établissement rural*) organization with the right to buy land in order to retain it for agricultural use

safran [safʀɑ̃] NM saffron

saga [saga] NF saga

sagace [sagas] ADJ sagacious, shrewd

sagacité [sagasite] NF sagacity, shrewdness

sagaie [sagɛ] NF assegai

★**sage** [saʒ] ADJ wise; (enfant) good ▶ NM wise man; sage

sage-femme [saʒfam] (pl **sages-femmes**) NF midwife

sagement [saʒmɑ̃] ADV (raisonnablement) wisely, sensibly; (tranquillement) quietly

sagesse [saʒɛs] NF wisdom

Sagittaire [saʒitɛʀ] NM: **le ~** Sagittarius, the Archer; **être du ~** to be Sagittarius

Sahara [saaʀa] NM: **le ~** the Sahara (Desert); **le ~ occidental** (pays) Western Sahara

saharien, ne [saaʀjɛ̃, -ɛn] ADJ Saharan ▶ NF safari jacket

Sahel [saɛl] NM: **le ~** the Sahel

sahélien, ne [saeljɛ̃, -ɛn] ADJ Sahelian

★**saignant, e** [sɛɲɑ̃, -ɑ̃t] ADJ (viande) rare; (blessure, plaie) bleeding

saignée [seɲe] NF (Méd) bleeding no pl, bloodletting no pl; (fig: Mil) heavy losses pl; (: prélèvement) savage cut; **la ~ du bras** the bend of the arm

saignement [sɛɲmɑ̃] NM bleeding; **~ de nez** nosebleed

★**saigner** [seɲe] /1/ VI to bleed; **~ du nez** to have a nosebleed ▶ VT to bleed; (animal) to bleed to death; **~ qn à blanc** (fig) to bleed sb white

Saigon [sajgɔ̃] N Saigon

saillant, e [sajɑ̃, -ɑ̃t] ADJ (pommettes, menton) prominent; (corniche etc) projecting; (fig) salient, outstanding

saillie [saji] NF (sur un mur etc) projection; (trait d'esprit) witticism; (accouplement) covering, serving; **faire ~** to project, stick out; **en ~, formant ~** projecting, overhanging

saillir [sajiʀ] /13/ VI to project, stick out; (veine, muscle) to bulge ▶ VT (Agr) to cover, serve

★**sain, e** [sɛ̃, sɛn] ADJ healthy; (dents, constitution) healthy, sound; (lectures) wholesome; **~ et sauf** safe and sound, unharmed; **~ d'esprit** sound in mind, sane

saindoux [sɛ̃du] NM lard

sainement [sɛnmɑ̃] ADV (vivre) healthily; (raisonner) soundly

saint, e [sɛ̃, sɛ̃t] ADJ holy; (fig) saintly; **la Sainte Vierge** the Blessed Virgin ▶ NM/F saint

saint-bernard [sɛ̃bɛʀnaʀ] NM (chien) St Bernard

Sainte-Hélène [sɛ̃telɛn] NF St Helena

Sainte-Lucie [sɛ̃tlysi] NF Saint Lucia

Saint-Esprit [sɛ̃tɛspʀi] NM: **le ~** the Holy Spirit ou Ghost

sainteté [sɛ̃te] NF holiness; saintliness

Saint-Laurent [sɛ̃lɔʀɑ̃] NM: **le ~** the St Lawrence

Saint-Marin [sɛ̃maʀɛ̃] NM: **le ~** San Marino

Saint-Père [sɛ̃pɛʀ] (pl **Saints-Pères**) NM: **le ~** the Holy Father, the Pontiff

Saint-Pierre [sɛ̃pjɛʀ] NM Saint Peter; (église) Saint Peter's

Saint-Pierre-et-Miquelon [sɛ̃pjɛʀemiklɔ̃] N Saint Pierre and Miquelon

Saint-Siège [sɛ̃sjɛʒ] NM: **le ~** the Holy See

Saint-Sylvestre [sɛ̃silvɛstʀ] NF: **la ~** New Year's Eve

Saint-Thomas [sɛ̃tɔma] NF Saint Thomas

Saint-Vincent et les Grenadines [sɛ̃vɛ̃sɑ̃elegʀənadin] NM St Vincent and the Grenadines

sais etc [sɛ] VB voir **savoir**

saisie [sezi] NF seizure; **à la ~** (texte) being keyed; **~ (de données)** (data) capture

saisine [sezin] NF (Jur) submission of a case to the court

saisir [seziʀ] /2/ VT to take hold of, grab; (fig: occasion) to seize; (comprendre) to grasp; (entendre) to get, catch; (émotions) to take hold of, come over; (Inform) to capture, key; (Culin) to fry quickly; (Jur: biens, publication) to seize; (: juridiction): **~ un tribunal d'une affaire** to submit ou refer a case to a court; **être saisi** (frappé de) to be overcome ■ **se saisir** VPR: **se ~ de** to seize

saisissant, e [sezisɑ̃, -ɑ̃t] ADJ startling, striking; (froid) biting

saisissement [sezismɑ̃] NM: **muet/figé de ~** speechless/frozen with emotion

★**saison** [sɛzɔ̃] NF season; **la belle/mauvaise ~** the summer/winter months; **être de ~** to be in season; **en/hors ~** in/out of season; **haute/basse/morte ~** high/low/slack season; **la ~ des pluies/des amours** the rainy/mating season

saisonnier, -ière [sɛzɔnje, -jɛʀ] ADJ seasonal ▶ NM (travailleur) seasonal worker; (vacancier) seasonal holidaymaker (BRIT) ou vacationer (US)

sait [sɛ] VB voir **savoir**

salace [salas] ADJ salacious

★**salade** [salad] NF (Bot) lettuce etc (generic term); (Culin) (green) salad; (fam: confusion) tangle, muddle; **haricots en ~** bean salad; **~ composée** mixed salad; **~ de concombres** cucumber salad; **~ de fruits** fruit salad; **~ niçoise** salade niçoise; **~ russe** Russian salad; **~ de tomates** tomato salad; **~ verte** green salad ■ **salades** NFPL (fam): **raconter des salades** to tell tales (fam)

saladier [saladje] NM (salad) bowl

★**salaire** [salɛʀ] NM (annuel, mensuel) salary; (hebdomadaire, journalier) pay, wages pl; (fig) reward; **~ de base** basic salary (ou wage); **~ de misère** starvation wage; **~ minimum interprofessionnel de croissance** index-linked guaranteed minimum wage

salaison [salɛzɔ̃] NF salting ■ **salaisons** NFPL salt meat sg

salamandre [salamɑ̃dʀ] NF salamander

salami [salami] NM salami

salant [salɑ̃] ADJ M: **marais ~** salt pan

salarial, e, -aux [salaʀjal, -o] ADJ salary cpd, wage(s) cpd

salariat [salaʀja] NM salaried staff

salarié, e [salaʀje] ADJ salaried; wage-earning ▶ NM/F salaried employee; wage-earner

salaud [salo] NM (!) sod (!), bastard (!)

★**sale** [sal] ADJ dirty, filthy

S

★**salé, e** [sale] ADJ (*liquide, saveur, mer, goût*) salty; (*Culin: amandes, beurre etc*) salted; (: *gâteaux*) savoury; (*fig: grivois*) spicy, juicy; (: *note, facture*) steep, stiff ▶ NM (*porc salé*) salt pork; **petit ~** = boiling bacon

salement [salmã] ADV (*manger etc*) dirtily, messily

saler [sale] /1/ VT to salt

saleté [salte] NF (*état*) dirtiness; (*crasse*) dirt, filth; (*tache etc*) dirt *no pl*, piece of dirt, dirty mark; (*fig: tour*) filthy trick; (: *chose sans valeur*) rubbish *no pl*; (: *obscénité*) filth *no pl*; (: *microbe etc*) bug; **vivre dans la ~** to live in squalor

salière [saljɛʀ] NF saltcellar

saligaud [saligo] NM (!) bastard (!), sod (!)

salin, e [salɛ̃, -in] ADJ saline ▶ NF saltworks *sg*

salinité [salinite] NF salinity, salt-content

★**salir** [saliʀ] /2/ VT to (make) dirty; (*fig*) to soil the reputation of ▪ **se salir** VPR to get dirty

salissant, e [salisã, -ãt] ADJ (*tissu*) which shows the dirt; (*métier*) dirty, messy

salissure [salisyʀ] NF dirt *no pl*; (*tache*) dirty mark

salive [saliv] NF saliva

saliver [salive] /1/ VI to salivate

★**salle** [sal] NF room; (*d'hôpital*) ward; (*de restaurant*) dining room; (*d'un cinéma*) auditorium; (: *public*) audience; **faire ~ comble** to have a full house; **~ d'armes** (*pour l'escrime*) arms room; **~ d'attente** waiting room; **~ de bain(s)** bathroom; **~ de bal** ballroom; **~ de cinéma** auditorium; cinema (BRIT), movie theater (US); **~ de classe** classroom; **~ commune** (*d'hôpital*) ward; **~ de concert** concert hall; **~ de consultation** consulting room (BRIT), office (US); **~ de danse** dance hall; **~ de douches** shower-room; **~ d'eau** shower-room; **~ d'embarquement** (*à l'aéroport*) departure lounge; **~ d'exposition** showroom; **~ de jeux** games room; (*pour enfants*) playroom; **~ des machines** engine room; **~ à manger** dining room; (*mobilier*) dining room suite; **~ obscure** cinema (BRIT), movie theater (US); **~ d'opération** (*d'hôpital*) operating theatre (BRIT), operating room (US); **~ des professeurs** staffroom; **~ de projection** projection room; **~ de séjour** living room; **~ de spectacle** auditorium; **~ des ventes** saleroom

salmonellose [salmɔnɛloz] NF (*Méd*) salmonella poisoning

Salomon [salɔmɔ̃]: **les îles ~** the Solomon Islands

★**salon** [salɔ̃] NM lounge, sitting room; (*mobilier*) lounge suite; (*exposition*) exhibition, show; (*mondain, littéraire*) salon; **~ de coiffure** hairdressing salon; **~ de discussion** (*Inform*) chatroom; **~ de thé** tearoom

salopard [salɔpaʀ] NM (!) bastard (!)

salope [salɔp] NF (!) bitch (!)

saloper [salɔpe] /1/ VT (!) to muck up, mess up

saloperie [salɔpʀi] NF (!) filth *no pl*; (: *action*) dirty trick; (: *chose sans valeur*) piece of junk

salopette [salɔpɛt] NF dungarees *pl*; (*d'ouvrier*) overall(s)

salpêtre [salpɛtʀ] NM saltpetre

salsifis [salsifi] NM salsify, oyster plant

saltimbanque [saltɛ̃bãk] NMF (travelling) acrobat

salubre [salybʀ] ADJ healthy, salubrious

salubrité [salybʀite] NF healthiness, salubrity; **~ publique** public health

saluer [salɥe] /1/ VT (*pour dire bonjour, fig*) to greet; (*pour dire au revoir*) to take one's leave; (*Mil*) to salute

★**salut** [saly] NM (*sauvegarde*) safety; (*Rel*) salvation; (*geste*) wave; (*parole*) greeting; (*Mil*) salute ▶ EXCL (*fam: pour dire bonjour*) hi (there); (: *pour dire au revoir*) see you!, bye!

salutaire [salytɛʀ] ADJ (*remède*) beneficial; (*conseils*) salutary

salutations [salytasjɔ̃] NFPL greetings; **recevez mes ~ distinguées** *ou* **respectueuses** yours faithfully

salutiste [salytist] NMF Salvationist

Salvador [salvadɔʀ] NM: **le ~** El Salvador

salve [salv] NF salvo; volley of shots; **~ d'applaudissements** burst of applause

Samarie [samaʀi] NF: **la ~** Samaria

samaritain [samaʀitɛ̃] NM: **le bon S~** the Good Samaritan

★**samedi** [samdi] NM Saturday; *voir aussi* **lundi**

Samoa [samɔa] NFPL: **les (îles) ~** Samoa, the Samoan Islands

★**SAMU** [samy] SIGLE M (= *service d'assistance médicale d'urgence*) = ambulance (service) (BRIT), = paramedics (US)

sanatorium [sanatɔʀjɔm] NM sanatorium

sanctifier [sãktifje] /7/ VT to sanctify

sanction [sãksjɔ̃] NF sanction; (*fig*) penalty; **prendre des sanctions contre** to impose sanctions on

sanctionner [sãksjɔne] /1/ VT (*loi, usage*) to sanction; (*punir*) to punish

sanctuaire [sãktɥɛʀ] NM sanctuary

★**sandale** [sãdal] NF sandal; **sandales à lanières** strappy sandals

sandalette [sãdalɛt] NF sandal

sandow® [sãdo] NM luggage elastic

★**sandwich** [sãdwitʃ] NM sandwich; **pris en ~** sandwiched

sandwicherie [sãdwitʃʀi] NF sandwich bar

★**sang** [sã] NM blood; **en ~** covered in blood; **jusqu'au ~** (*mordre, pincer*) till the blood comes; **se faire du mauvais ~** to fret, get in a state

sang-froid [sãfʀwa] NM calm, sangfroid; **garder/perdre/reprendre son ~** to keep/lose/regain one's cool; **de ~** in cold blood

sanglant, e [sãglã, -ãt] ADJ bloody, covered in blood; (*combat*) bloody; (*fig: reproche, affront*) cruel

sangle [sãgl] NF strap ▪ **sangles** NFPL (*pour lit etc*) webbing *sg*

sangler [sãgle] /1/ VT to strap up; (*animal*) to girth

sanglier [sãglije] NM (wild) boar

sanglot [sãglo] NM sob

sangloter [sãglɔte] /1/ VI to sob

sangsue [sãsy] NF leech

sanguin, e [sãgɛ̃, -in] ADJ blood *cpd*; (*fig*) fiery ▶ NF blood orange; (*Art*) red pencil drawing

sanguinaire [sãginɛʀ] ADJ (*animal, personne*) bloodthirsty; (*lutte*) bloody

sanguinolent, e [sɑ̃ginɔlɑ̃, -ɑ̃t] ADJ streaked with blood

Sanisette® [sanizɛt] NF coin-operated public lavatory

sanitaire [sanitɛʀ] ADJ health cpd; **installation/ appareil ~** bathroom plumbing/appliance ■ **sanitaires** NMPL (salle de bain et w.-c.) bathroom sg

★**sans** [sɑ̃] PRÉP without; **~ qu'il s'en aperçoive** without him ou his noticing; **~ scrupules** unscrupulous; **~ manches** sleeveless; **un pull ~ manches** a sleeveless sweater ou jumper (BRIT); **~ faute** without fail; **~ arrêt** without a break; **~ ça** (fam) otherwise

sans-abri [sɑ̃zabʀi] NMF INV homeless person; **les ~** the homeless

sans-emploi [sɑ̃zɑ̃plwa] NMF INV unemployed person; **les ~** the unemployed

sans-façon [sɑ̃fasɔ̃] ADJ INV flippant; free and easy

sans-gêne [sɑ̃ʒɛn] ADJ INV inconsiderate ▶ NM INV (attitude) lack of consideration

sans-logis [sɑ̃lɔʒi] NMPL homeless

sans-papiers [sɑ̃papje] NMF undocumented migrant

sans-souci [sɑ̃susi] ADJ INV carefree

sans-travail [sɑ̃tʀavaj] NMPL unemployed, jobless

santal [sɑ̃tal] NM sandal(wood)

santé [sɑ̃te] NF health; **avoir une ~ de fer** to be bursting with health; **être en bonne ~** to be in good health, be healthy; **boire à la ~ de qn** to drink (to) sb's health; **« à la ~ de »** "here's to"; **à ta** ou **votre ~!** cheers!; **service de ~** (dans un port etc) quarantine service; **la ~ publique** public health

Santiago [sɑ̃tjago], **Santiago du Chili** [sɑ̃tjagodyʃili] N Santiago (de Chile)

santon [sɑ̃tɔ̃] NM ornamental figure at a Christmas crib

saoudien, ne [saudjɛ̃, -ɛn] ADJ Saudi (Arabian) ▶ NM/F: **Saoudien, ne** Saudi (Arabian)

saoul, e [su, sul] ADJ = **soûl**

sape [sap] NF: **travail de ~** (Mil) sap; (fig) insidious undermining process ou work ■ **sapes** NFPL (fam) gear sg, togs

saper [sape] /1/ VT to undermine, sap ■ **se saper** VPR (fam) to dress

sapeur [sapœʀ] NM sapper

★**sapeur-pompier** [sapœʀpɔ̃pje] (pl **sapeurs-pompiers**) NM fire fighter

saphir [safiʀ] NM sapphire; (d'électrophone) needle, sapphire

sapin [sapɛ̃] NM fir (tree); (bois) fir; **~ de Noël** Christmas tree

sapinière [sapinjɛʀ] NF fir plantation ou forest

saquer [sake] VT (fam: renvoyer) to sack (BRIT), to can (US); (: supporter): **je ne peux pas le ~** I can't stand him

SAR SIGLE F (= Son Altesse Royale) HRH

sarabande [saʀabɑ̃d] NF saraband; (fig) hullabaloo; whirl

sarbacane [saʀbakan] NF blowpipe, blowgun; (jouet) peashooter

sarcasme [saʀkasm] NM sarcasm no pl; (propos) piece of sarcasm

sarcastique [saʀkastik] ADJ sarcastic

sarcastiquement [saʀkastikmɑ̃] ADV sarcastically

sarclage [saʀklaʒ] NM weeding

sarcler [saʀkle] /1/ VT to weed

sarcloir [saʀklwaʀ] NM (weeding) hoe, spud

sarcophage [saʀkɔfaʒ] NM sarcophagus

Sardaigne [saʀdɛɲ] NF: **la ~** Sardinia

sarde [saʀd] ADJ Sardinian

★**sardine** [saʀdin] NF sardine; **sardines à l'huile** sardines in oil

sardinerie [saʀdinʀi] NF sardine cannery

sardinier, -ière [saʀdinje, -jɛʀ] ADJ (pêche, industrie) sardine cpd ▶ NM (bateau) sardine boat

sardonique [saʀdɔnik] ADJ sardonic

sari [saʀi] NM sari

SARL [saʀl] SIGLE F (= société à responsabilité limitée) ≈ plc (BRIT), ≈ Inc. (US)

sarment [saʀmɑ̃] NM: **~ (de vigne)** vine shoot

sarrasin [saʀazɛ̃] NM buckwheat

sarrau [saʀo] NM smock

Sarre [saʀ] NF: **la ~** the Saar

sarriette [saʀjɛt] NF savory

sarrois, e [saʀwa, -waz] ADJ Saar cpd ▶ NM/F: **Sarrois, e** inhabitant ou native of the Saar

sas [sas] NM (de sous-marin, d'engin spatial) airlock; (d'écluse) lock

satané, e [satane] ADJ (fam) blasted

satanique [satanik] ADJ satanic, fiendish

sataniste [satanist] ADJ, NMF Satanist

satelliser [satelize] /1/ VT (fusée) to put into orbit; (fig: pays) to make into a satellite

★**satellite** [satelit] NM satellite; **pays ~** satellite country

satellite-espion [satelitɛspjɔ̃] (pl **satellites-espions**) NM spy satellite

satellite-observatoire [satelitɔpsɛʀvatwaʀ] (pl **satellites-observatoires**) NM observation satellite

satellite-relais [satelitʀəlɛ] (pl **satellites-relais**) NM (TV) relay satellite

satiété [sasjete]: **à ~** adv to one's heart's content; (répéter) ad nauseam

satin [satɛ̃] NM satin

satiné, e [satine] ADJ satiny; (peau) satin-smooth

satinette [satinɛt] NF satinet, sateen

satire [satiʀ] NF satire; **faire la ~** to satirize

satirique [satiʀik] ADJ satirical

satiriser [satiʀize] /1/ VT to satirize

satiriste [satiʀist] NMF satirist

satisfaction [satisfaksjɔ̃] NF satisfaction; **à ma grande ~** to my great satisfaction; **obtenir ~** to obtain ou get satisfaction; **donner ~ (à)** to give satisfaction (to)

satisfaire [satisfɛʀ] /60/ VT to satisfy; **~ à** (engagement) to fulfil; (revendications, conditions) to meet, satisfy ■ **se satisfaire de** VPR to be satisfied ou content with

S

satisfaisant, e [satisfəzɑ̃, -ɑ̃t] VB *voir* **satisfaire**
▶ ADJ (*acceptable*) satisfactory; (*qui fait plaisir*) satisfying

satisfait, e [satisfɛ, -ɛt] PP *de* **satisfaire** ▶ ADJ satisfied; **~ de** happy *ou* satisfied with

satisfasse [satisfas], **satisferai** *etc* [satisfʁe] VB *voir* **satisfaire**

saturation [satyʁasjɔ̃] NF saturation; **arriver à ~** to reach saturation point

saturer [satyʁe] /1/ VT to saturate; **~ qn/qch de** to saturate sb/sth with

saturnisme [satyʁnism] NM (*Méd*) lead poisoning

satyre [satiʁ] NM satyr; (*péj*) lecher

★**sauce** [sos] NF sauce; (*avec un rôti*) gravy; **en ~** in a sauce; **~ blanche** white sauce; **~ chasseur** sauce chasseur; **~ tomate** tomato sauce

saucer [sose] /3/ VT (*assiette*) to soak up the sauce from

saucière [sosjɛʁ] NF sauce boat; gravy boat

★**saucisse** [sosis] NF sausage

★**saucisson** [sosisɔ̃] NM (slicing) sausage; **~ à l'ail** garlic sausage

saucissonner [sosisɔne] /1/ VT to cut up, slice ▶ VI to picnic

★**sauf¹** [sof] PRÉP except; **~ si** (*à moins que*) unless; **~ avis contraire** unless you hear to the contrary; **~ empêchement** barring (any) problems; **~ erreur** if I'm not mistaken; **~ imprévu** unless anything unforeseen arises, barring accidents

sauf², sauve [sof, sov] ADJ unharmed, unhurt; (*fig: honneur*) intact, saved; **laisser la vie sauve à qn** to spare sb's life

sauf-conduit [sofkɔ̃dɥi] NM safe-conduct

sauge [soʒ] NF sage

saugrenu, e [sogʁəny] ADJ preposterous, ludicrous

saule [sol] NM willow (tree); **~ pleureur** weeping willow

saumâtre [somɑtʁ] ADJ briny; (*désagréable: plaisanterie*) unsavoury (BRIT), unsavory (US)

★**saumon** [somɔ̃] NM salmon *inv*; **~ fumé** (*Culin*) smoked salmon ▶ ADJ INV salmon (pink)

saumoné, e [somɔne] ADJ: **truite saumonée** salmon trout

saumure [somyʁ] NF brine

sauna [sona] NM sauna

saupoudrer [sopudʁe] /1/ VT: **~ qch de** to sprinkle sth with

saupoudreuse [sopudʁøz] NF dredger

saur [sɔʁ] ADJ M: **hareng ~** smoked *ou* red herring, kipper

saurai *etc* [sɔʁe] VB *voir* **savoir**

saut [so] NM jump; (*discipline sportive*) jumping; **faire un ~** to (make a) jump *ou* leap; **faire un ~ chez qn** to pop over to sb's (place); **au ~ du lit** on getting out of bed; **~ en hauteur/longueur** high/long jump; **~ à la corde** skipping; **~ de page/ligne** (*Inform*) page/line break; **~ en parachute** parachuting *no pl*; **~ à la perche** pole vaulting; **~ à l'élastique** bungee jumping; **~ périlleux** somersault

saute [sot] NF: **~ de vent/température** sudden change of wind direction/in the temperature;

avoir des **sautes d'humeur** to have sudden changes of mood

sauté, e [sote] ADJ (*Culin*) sauté ▶ NM: **~ de veau** sauté of veal

saute-mouton [sotmutɔ̃] NM: **jouer à ~** to play leapfrog

★**sauter** [sote] /1/ VI to jump, leap; (*exploser*) to blow up, explode; (: *fusibles*) to blow; (*se rompre*) to snap, burst; (*se détacher*) to pop out (*ou* off); **faire ~** to blow up; to burst open; (*Culin*) to sauté; **~ à pieds joints/à cloche-pied** to make a standing jump/ to hop; **~ en parachute** to make a parachute jump; **~ à la corde** to skip; **~ de joie** to jump for joy; **~ de colère** to be hopping with rage *ou* hopping mad; **~ au cou de qn** to fly into sb's arms; **~ sur une occasion** to jump at an opportunity; **~ aux yeux** to be quite obvious; **~ au plafond** (*fig*) to hit the roof ▶ VT to jump (over), leap (over); (*fig: omettre*) to skip, miss (out)

sauterelle [sotʁɛl] NF grasshopper

sauterie [sotʁi] NF party, hop

sauternes [sotɛʁn] NM Sauternes

sauteur, -euse [sotœʁ, -øz] NM/F (*athlète*) jumper; **~ à la perche** pole vaulter; **~ à skis** ski jumper ▶ NF (*poêle*) shallow pan

sautillement [sotijmɑ̃] NM hopping; skipping

sautiller [sotije] /1/ VI (*oiseau*) to hop; (*enfant*) to skip

sautoir [sotwaʁ] NM chain; (*Sport: emplacement*) jumping pit; **~ (de perles)** string of pearls

★**sauvage** [sovaʒ] ADJ (*gén*) wild; (*peuplade*) savage; (*farouche*) unsociable; (*barbare*) wild, savage; (*non officiel*) unauthorized, unofficial; **faire du camping ~** to camp in the wild ▶ NM/F savage; (*timide*) unsociable type, recluse

sauvagement [sovaʒmɑ̃] ADV savagely

sauvageon, ne [sovaʒɔ̃, -ɔn] NM/F little savage

sauvagerie [sovaʒʁi] NF wildness, savagery; unsociability

sauve [sov] ADJ F *voir* **sauf²**

sauvegarde [sovgaʁd] NF safeguard; **sous la ~ de** under the protection of; **fichier de ~** (*Inform*) backup file

★**sauvegarder** [sovgaʁde] /1/ VT to safeguard; (*Inform: enregistrer*) to save; (: *copier*) to back up

sauve-qui-peut [sovkipø] NM INV stampede, mad rush ▶ EXCL run for your life!

★**sauver** [sove] /1/ VT to save; (*porter secours à*) to rescue; (*récupérer*) to salvage, rescue; **~ qn de** to save sb from; **~ la vie à qn** to save sb's life; **~ les apparences** to keep up appearances ■ **se sauver** VPR (*s'enfuir*) to run away; (*fam: partir*) to be off

sauvetage [sov(ə)taʒ] NM rescue; (*de banque, d'entreprise*) bailout; **~ en montagne** mountain rescue; **ceinture de ~** lifebelt (BRIT), life preserver (US); **brassière** *ou* **gilet de ~** life jacket (BRIT), life vest (US)

sauveteur [sov(ə)tœʁ] NM rescuer

sauvette [sovɛt]: **à la ~** *adv* (*vendre*) without authorization; (*se marier etc*) hastily, hurriedly; **vente à la ~** (unauthorized) street trading, (street) peddling

sauveur [sovœʁ] NM saviour (BRIT), savior (US)

SAV SIGLE M = **service après-vente**

savais etc [save] VB voir **savoir**

savamment [savamɑ̃] ADV (avec érudition) learnedly; (habilement) skilfully, cleverly

savane [savan] NF savannah

savant, e [savɑ̃, -ɑ̃t] ADJ scholarly, learned; **animal ~** performing animal ▸ NM/F scientist

savate [savat] NF worn-out shoe; (Sport) French boxing

saveur [savœʀ] NF flavour (BRIT), flavor (US); (fig) savour (BRIT), savor (US)

Savoie [savwa] NF: **la ~** Savoy

★**savoir** [savwaʀ] /32/ VT to know; (être capable de): **il sait nager** he knows how to swim, he can swim; **il est petit : tu ne peux pas ~!** you won't believe how small he is!; **vous n'êtes pas sans ~ que** you are not ou will not be unaware of the fact that; **je crois ~ que ...** I believe that ..., I think I know that ...; **je n'en sais rien** I (really) don't know; **à ~ (que)** that is, namely; **faire ~ qch à qn** to let sb know sth, inform sb about sth; **pas que je sache** not as far as I know; **sans le ~** adv unknowingly, unwittingly; **en ~ long** to know a lot ▸ NM knowledge ▪ **se savoir** VPR (être connu) to be known; **se ~ malade/incurable** to know that one is ill/incurably ill

savoir-faire [savwaʀfɛʀ] NM INV know-how

> The French word **savoir-faire** is not translated by savoir-faire as used in English.

savoir-vivre [savwaʀvivʀ] NM INV: **le ~** savoir-faire, good manners pl

★**savon** [savɔ̃] NM (produit) soap; (morceau) bar ou tablet of soap; **passer un ~ à qn** (fam) to give sb a good dressing-down

savonner [savɔne] /1/ VT to soap

savonnerie [savɔnʀi] NF soap factory

savonnette [savɔnɛt] NF bar of soap

savonneux, -euse [savɔnø, -øz] ADJ soapy

savons [savɔ̃] VB voir **savoir**

savourer [savuʀe] /1/ VT to savour (BRIT), savor (US)

★**savoureux, -euse** [savuʀø, -øz] ADJ tasty; (fig: anecdote) spicy, juicy

savoyard, e [savwajaʀ, -aʀd] ADJ Savoyard

Saxe [saks] NF: **la ~** Saxony

saxo [saksɔ] NM (fam) sax

saxophone [saksɔfɔn] NM saxophone

saxophoniste [saksɔfɔnist] NMF saxophonist, sax(ophone) player

saynète [sɛnɛt] NF playlet

SBB SIGLE F (= Schweizerische Bundesbahn) Swiss federal railways

sbire [sbiʀ] NM (péj) henchman

sc. ABR = **scène**

s/c ABR = sous couvert de) ≈ c/o

scabreux, -euse [skabʀø, -øz] ADJ risky; (indécent) improper, shocking

scalp [skalp] NM (trophée) scalp

scalpel [skalpɛl] NM scalpel

scalper [skalpe] /1/ VT to scalp

scampi [skɑ̃pi] NMPL scampi

scandale [skɑ̃dal] NM scandal; **faire un ~** (scène) to make a scene; (Jur) to create a disturbance; **faire ~** to scandalize people; **au grand ~ de ...** to the great indignation of ...

scandaleusement [skɑ̃daløzmɑ̃] ADV scandalously, outrageously

scandaleux, -euse [skɑ̃dalø, -øz] ADJ scandalous, outrageous

scandaliser [skɑ̃dalize] /1/ VT to scandalize ▪ **se scandaliser** VPR: **se ~ (de)** to be scandalized (by)

scander [skɑ̃de] /1/ VT (vers) to scan; (mots, syllabes) to stress separately; (slogans) to chant

scandinave [skɑ̃dinav] ADJ Scandinavian ▸ NMF: **Scandinave** Scandinavian

Scandinavie [skɑ̃dinavi] NF: **la ~** Scandinavia

scanner [skanɛʀ] NM (Méd) scanner

scanographie [skanɔgʀafi] NF (Méd) scanning; (image) scan

scansion [skɑ̃sjɔ̃] NF scansion

scaphandre [skafɑ̃dʀ] NM (de plongeur) diving suit; (de cosmonaute) spacesuit; **~ autonome** aqualung

scaphandrier [skafɑ̃dʀije] NM diver

scarabée [skaʀabe] NM beetle

scarification [skaʀifikasjɔ̃] NF scarification

scarlatine [skaʀlatin] NF scarlet fever

scarole [skaʀɔl] NF endive

scatologique [skatɔlɔʒik] ADJ scatological, lavatorial

sceau, x [so] NM seal; (fig) stamp, mark; **sous le ~ du secret** under the seal of secrecy

scélérat, e [seleʀa, -at] NM/F villain, blackguard ▸ ADJ villainous, blackguardly

sceller [sele] /1/ VT to seal

scellés [sele] NMPL seals

scénario [senaʀjo] NM (Ciné) screenplay, script; (: idée, plan) scenario; (fig) pattern; scenario

scénariste [senaʀist] NMF scriptwriter

scène [sɛn] NF (gén) scene; (estrade, fig: théâtre) stage; **entrer en ~** to come on stage; **mettre en ~** (Théât) to stage; (Ciné) to direct; (fig) to present, introduce; **sur le devant de la ~** (en pleine actualité) in the forefront; **porter à la ~** to adapt for the stage; **faire une ~ (à qn)** to make a scene (with sb); **~ de ménage** domestic squabble ou quarrel

scénique [senik] ADJ (effets) theatrical; (art) scenic

scénographie [senɔgʀafi] NF (Théât) stage design

scepticisme [sɛptisism] NM scepticism

sceptique [sɛptik] ADJ sceptical ▸ NMF sceptic

sceptre [sɛptʀ] NM sceptre

schéma [ʃema] NM (diagramme) diagram, sketch; (fig) outline

schématique [ʃematik] ADJ diagrammatic(al), schematic; (fig) oversimplified

schématiquement [ʃematikmɑ̃] ADV schematically, diagrammatically

schématisation [ʃematizasjɔ̃] NF schematization; oversimplification

schématiser [ʃematize] /1/ VT to schematize; to (over)simplify

schismatique [ʃismatik] ADJ schismatic

schisme [ʃism] NM schism; rift, split

schiste [ʃist] NM schist

S

schizophrène [skizɔfʀɛn] NMF schizophrenic

schizophrénie [skizɔfʀeni] NF schizophrenia

sciatique [sjatik] ADJ: **nerf ~** sciatic nerve ▶ NF sciatica

scie [si] NF saw; (*fam: rengaine*) classic song; (: *personne*) bore; **~ à bois** wood saw; **~ circulaire** circular saw; **~ à découper** fretsaw; **~ à métaux** hacksaw; **~ sauteuse** jigsaw

sciemment [sjamɑ̃] ADV knowingly, wittingly

★**science** [sjɑ̃s] NF science; (*savoir*) knowledge; (*savoir-faire*) art, skill; **sciences économiques** economics; **sciences humaines/sociales** social sciences; **sciences naturelles** (*Scol*) natural science *sg*, biology *sg*; **sciences po** political science *ou* studies *pl*

★**science-fiction** [sjɑ̃sfiksjɔ̃] (*pl* **sciences-fictions**) NF science fiction

★**scientifique** [sjɑ̃tifik] ADJ scientific ▶ NMF (*savant*) scientist; (*étudiant*) science student

scientifiquement [sjɑ̃tifikmɑ̃] ADV scientifically

Scientologie® [sjɑ̃tɔlɔʒi] NF (*secte*) Scientology®

scientologue [sjɑ̃tɔlɔg] NMF (*adepte de la Scientologie*) Scientologist

scier [sje] /**7**/ VT to saw; (*retrancher*) to saw off

scierie [siʀi] NF sawmill

scieur [sjœʀ] NM: **~ de long** pit sawyer

Scilly [sili]: **les îles ~** the Scilly Isles, the Scillies, the Isles of Scilly

scinder [sɛ̃de] /**1**/ VT to split (up) ■ **se scinder** VPR to split (up)

scintillant, e [sɛ̃tijɑ̃, -ɑ̃t] ADJ sparkling

scintillement [sɛ̃tijmɑ̃] NM sparkling *no pl*

scintiller [sɛ̃tije] /**1**/ VI to sparkle; (*étoile*) to twinkle

scission [sisjɔ̃] NF split

sciure [sjyʀ] NF: **~ (de bois)** sawdust

sclérose [skleʀoz] NF sclerosis; (*fig*) ossification; **~ en plaques (SEP)** multiple sclerosis (MS)

sclérosé, e [skleʀoze] ADJ sclerosed, sclerotic; ossified

scléroser [skleʀoze] /**1**/: **se scléroser** VPR to become sclerosed; (*fig*) to become ossified

★**scolaire** [skɔlɛʀ] ADJ school *cpd*; (*péj*) scholastic; **l'année ~** the school year; (*à l'université*) the academic year; **en âge ~** of school age

scolarisation [skɔlaʀizasjɔ̃] NF (*d'un enfant*) schooling; **la ~ d'une région** the provision of schooling in a region; **le taux de ~** the proportion of children in full-time education

scolariser [skɔlaʀize] /**1**/ VT to provide with schooling

scolarité [skɔlaʀite] NF schooling; **frais de ~** school fees (BRIT), tuition (US)

scolastique [skɔlastik] ADJ (*péj*) scholastic

scoliose [skɔljoz] NF curvature of the spine, scoliosis

scolopendre [skɔlɔpɑ̃dʀ] NF (*Zool*) centipede; (*Bot*) hart's-tongue

scoop [skup] NM (*Presse*) scoop, exclusive

scooter [skutœʀ] NM (motor) scooter

scorbut [skɔʀbyt] NM scurvy

score [skɔʀ] NM score; (*électoral etc*) result

scories [skɔʀi] NFPL scoria *pl*

scorpion [skɔʀpjɔ̃] NM (*signe*): **le S~** Scorpio, the Scorpion; **être du S~** to be Scorpio

scotch [skɔtʃ] NM (*whisky*) scotch, whisky; **Scotch**® (*adhésif*) Sellotape® (BRIT), Scotch tape® (US)

scotché, e [skɔtʃe] ADJ (*fam*): **il reste des heures ~ devant la télévision** he spends hours glued to the television; **je suis resté ~** (*stupéfait*) I was flabbergasted

scotcher [skɔtʃe] /**1**/ VT to sellotape® (BRIT), scotch-tape® (US); (*fam: stupéfier*) to blow away

scoubidou [skubidu] NM *a plait woven from multicoloured plastic threads*

scoumoune [skumun] NF (*fam*) tough luck; **avoir la ~** to be jinxed

scout, e [skut] ADJ, NM scout

scoutisme [skutism] NM (*boy*) scout movement; (*activités*) scouting

scribe [skʀib] NM scribe; (*péj*) penpusher

scribouillard [skʀibujaʀ] NM penpusher

script [skʀipt] NM (*écriture*) printing; (*Ciné*) (shooting) script

scripte [skʀipt] NF continuity girl

script-girl [skʀiptgœʀl] NF continuity girl

scriptural, e, -aux [skʀiptyʀal, -o] ADJ: **monnaie scripturale** bank money

scrotum [skʀɔtɔm] NM scrotum

scrupule [skʀypyl] NM scruple; **être sans scrupules** to be unscrupulous; **se faire un ~ de qch** to have scruples *ou* qualms about doing sth

scrupuleusement [skʀypyløzmɑ̃] ADV scrupulously

scrupuleux, -euse [skʀypylø, -øz] ADJ scrupulous

scrutateur, -trice [skʀytatœʀ, -tʀis] ADJ searching ▶ NM/F scrutineer

scruter [skʀyte] /**1**/ VT to scrutinize, search; (*l'obscurité*) to peer into; (*motifs, comportement*) to examine, scrutinize

scrutin [skʀytɛ̃] NM (*vote*) ballot; (*ensemble des opérations*) poll; **~ proportionnel/majoritaire** election on a proportional/majority basis; **~ à deux tours** poll with two ballots *ou* rounds; **~ de liste** list system

sculpter [skylte] /**1**/ VT to sculpt; (*érosion*) to carve

★**sculpteur** [skyltœʀ] NM sculptor

sculptural, e, -aux [skyltyʀal, -o] ADJ sculptural; (*fig*) statuesque

★**sculpture** [skyltyʀ] NF sculpture; **~ sur bois** wood carving

sdb. ABR = **salle de bain**

★**SDF** SIGLE M (= *sans domicile fixe*) homeless person; **les ~** the homeless

SE SIGLE F (= *Son Excellence*) HE

---

se, s' [sə, s]

PRON **1** (*emploi réfléchi*) oneself; (: *masc*) himself; (: *fém*) herself; (: *sujet non humain*) itself; (: *pl*) themselves; **se voir comme l'on est** to see o.s. as one is; **se savonner** to soap o.s.

2 (*réciproque*) one another, each other; **ils s'aiment** they love one another *ou* each other

3 (*passif*): **cela se répare facilement** it is easily repaired
4 (*possessif*): **se casser la jambe/se laver les mains** to break one's leg/wash one's hands

séance [seɑ̃s] NF (*d'assemblée, récréative*) meeting, session; (*de tribunal*) sitting, session; (*musicale, Ciné, Théât*) performance; **ouvrir/lever la ~** to open/close the meeting; **~ tenante** forthwith

séant, e [seɑ̃, -ɑ̃t] ADJ seemly, fitting ▶ NM posterior

★**seau, x** [so] NM bucket, pail; **~ à glace** ice bucket

sébum [sebɔm] NM sebum

★**sec, sèche** [sɛk, sɛʃ] ADJ dry; (*raisins, figues*) dried; (*insensible: cœur, personne*) hard, cold; (*maigre, décharné*) spare, lean; (*réponse, ton*) sharp, curt; (*démarrage*) sharp, sudden; **à pied ~** without getting one's feet wet ▶ NM: **tenir au ~** to keep in a dry place; **à ~** *adj* (*puits*) dried up; (*à court d'argent*) broke ▶ ADV hard; (*démarrer*) sharply; **boire ~** to be a heavy drinker; **je le bois ~** I drink it straight *ou* neat

SECAM [sekam] SIGLE M (= *procédé séquentiel à mémoire*) SECAM

sécante [sekɑ̃t] NF secant

sécateur [sekatœʀ] NM secateurs *pl* (BRIT), shears *pl*, pair of secateurs *ou* shears

sécession [sesesjɔ̃] NF: **faire ~** to secede; **la guerre de S~** the American Civil War

séchage [seʃaʒ] NM drying; (*de bois*) seasoning

sèche [sɛʃ] ADJ F *voir* **sec** ▶ NF (*fam*) cigarette, fag (BRIT)

sèche-cheveux [sɛʃʃəvø] NM INV hair dryer

sèche-linge [sɛʃlɛ̃ʒ] NM INV tumble dryer

sèche-mains [sɛʃmɛ̃] NM INV hand drier

sèchement [sɛʃmɑ̃] ADV (*frapper etc*) sharply; (*répliquer etc*) drily, sharply

sécher [seʃe] /6/ VT to dry; (*dessécher: peau, blé*) to dry (out); (: *étang*) to dry up; (*bois*) to season; (*fam: classe, cours*) to skip, miss ▶ VI to dry; to dry out; to dry up; (*fam: candidat*) to be stumped ■ **se sécher** VPR (*après le bain*) to dry o.s.

sécheresse [sɛʃʀɛs] NF dryness; (*absence de pluie*) drought

séchoir [seʃwaʀ] NM drier

★**second, e** [s(ə)gɔ̃, -ɔ̃d] ADJ second; **en ~** in second place; **doué de seconde vue** having (the gift of) second sight; **trouver son ~ souffle** (*Sport, fig*) to get one's second wind; **être dans un état ~** to be in a daze (*ou* trance); **de seconde main** second-hand ▶ NM (*assistant*) second in command; (*étage*) second floor (BRIT), third floor (US); (*Navig*) first mate ▶ NF (*unité de temps*) second; (*Scol*) ≈ year 11 (BRIT), ≈ tenth grade (US); (*Rail*) second class; **voyager en seconde** to travel second-class

★**secondaire** [s(ə)gɔ̃dɛʀ] ADJ secondary

seconder [s(ə)gɔ̃de] /1/ VT to assist; (*favoriser*) to back

★**secouer** [s(ə)kwe] /1/ VT to shake; (*passagers*) to rock; (*traumatiser*) to shake (up); **~ la tête** to shake one's head; **~ la poussière d'un tapis** to shake the dust off a carpet ■ **se secouer** VPR (*chien*) to shake itself; (*fam: se démener*) to give o.s. a shake

secourable [s(ə)kuʀabl] ADJ helpful

secourir [s(ə)kuʀiʀ] /11/ VT (*aller sauver*) to (go and) rescue; (*prodiguer des soins à*) to help, assist; (*venir en aide à*) to assist, aid

secourisme [s(ə)kuʀism] NM (*premiers soins*) first aid; (*sauvetage*) life saving

secouriste [s(ə)kuʀist] NMF first-aid worker

secourons *etc* [səkuʀɔ̃] VB *voir* **secourir**

★**secours** [s(ə)kuʀ] VB *voir* **secourir** ▶ NM help, aid, assistance; **cela lui a été d'un grand ~** this was a great help to him; **au ~!** help!; **appeler au ~** to shout ou call for help; **appeler qn à son ~** to call sb to one's assistance; **porter ~ à qn** to give sb assistance, help sb ▶ NMPL aid *sg*; **les premiers ~** first aid *sg*; **le ~ en montagne** mountain rescue; *see note*

Emergency phone numbers can be dialled free from public phones. For the police (*la police*) dial 17; for medical services (*le SAMU*) dial 15; for the fire brigade (*les pompiers*), dial 18.

secouru, e [səkuʀy] PP *de* **secourir**

secousse [s(ə)kus] NF jolt, bump; (*électrique*) shock; (*fig: psychologique*) jolt, shock; **~ sismique** *ou* **tellurique** earth tremor

★**secret, -ète** [səkʀɛ, -ɛt] ADJ secret; (*fig: renfermé*) reticent, reserved ▶ NM secret; (*discrétion absolue*): **le ~** secrecy; **en ~** in secret, secretly; **au ~** in solitary confinement; **~ de fabrication** trade secret; **~ professionnel** professional secrecy

secrétaire [s(ə)kʀetɛʀ] NMF secretary; **~ d'ambassade** embassy secretary; **~ de direction** private *ou* personal secretary; **~ d'État** ≈ junior minister; **~ général(e)** Secretary-General; (*Comm*) company secretary; **~ de mairie** town clerk; **~ médical(e)** medical secretary; **~ de rédaction** sub-editor ▶ NM (*meuble*) writing desk, secretaire

secrétariat [s(ə)kʀetaʀja] NM (*profession*) secretarial work; (*bureau: d'entreprise, d'école*) (secretary's) office; (: *d'organisation internationale*) secretariat; (*Pol etc: fonction*) secretaryship, office of Secretary

secrètement [səkʀɛtmɑ̃] ADV secretly

sécréter [sekʀete] /6/ VT to secrete

sécrétion [sekʀesjɔ̃] NF secretion

sectaire [sɛktɛʀ] ADJ sectarian, bigoted

sectarisme [sɛktaʀism] NM sectarianism

secte [sɛkt] NF sect

secteur [sɛktœʀ] NM sector; (*Admin*) district; (*Élec*): **branché sur le ~** plugged into the mains (supply); **fonctionne sur pile et ~** battery or mains operated; **le ~ privé/public** (*Écon*) the private/public sector; **le ~ primaire/tertiaire** the primary/tertiary sector

section [sɛksjɔ̃] NF section; (*de parcours d'autobus*) fare stage; (*Mil: unité*) platoon; **~ rythmique** rhythm section

sectionner [sɛksjɔne] /1/ VT to sever ■ **se sectionner** VPR to be severed

sectionneur [sɛksjɔnœʀ] NM (*Élec*) isolation switch

sectoriel, le [sɛktɔʀjɛl] ADJ sector-based

sectorisation [sɛktɔʀizasjɔ̃] NF division into sectors

sectoriser [sɛktɔʀize] /1/ VT to divide into sectors

S

sécu [seky] NF (fam: = sécurité sociale) ≈ benefits (BRIT), ≈ Welfare (US)

séculaire [sekylɛʀ] ADJ secular; (très vieux) age-old

séculariser [sekylaʀize] /1/ VT to secularize

séculier, -ière [sekylje, -jɛʀ] ADJ secular

sécurisant, e [sekyʀizɑ̃, -ɑ̃t] ADJ secure, giving a sense of security

sécuriser [sekyʀize] /1/ VT to give a sense of security to

sécurité [sekyʀite] NF (absence de troubles) security; (absence de danger) safety; **impression de ~** sense of security; **la ~ internationale** international security; **système de ~** security (ou safety) system; **être en ~** to be safe; **la ~ de l'emploi** job security; **la ~ routière** road safety; **la ~ sociale** ≈ Social Security (BRIT), ≈ Welfare (US)

sédatif, -ive [sedatif, -iv] ADJ, NM sedative

sédentaire [sedɑ̃tɛʀ] ADJ sedentary

sédentarisation [sedɑ̃taʀizasjɔ̃] NF settlement

sédentariser [sedɑ̃taʀize] VT (Bédouins) to settle (forcibly) ■ **se sédentariser** VPR to settle

sédiment [sedimɑ̃] NM sediment ■ **sédiments** NMPL (alluvions) sediment sg

sédimentaire [sedimɑ̃tɛʀ] ADJ sedimentary

sédimentation [sedimɑ̃tasjɔ̃] NF sedimentation

séditieux, -euse [sedisjø, -øz] ADJ insurgent; seditious

sédition [sedisjɔ̃] NF insurrection; sedition

séducteur, -trice [sedyktœʀ, -tʀis] ADJ seductive ▶ NM/F seducer (seductress)

séduction [sedyksjɔ̃] NF seduction; (charme, attrait) appeal, charm

séduire [sedɥiʀ] /38/ VT to charm; (femme: abuser de) to seduce; (chose) to appeal to

séduisant, e [sedɥizɑ̃, -ɑ̃t] VB voir **séduire** ▶ ADJ (femme) seductive; (homme, offre) very attractive

séduit, e [sedɥi, -it] PP de **séduire**

séfarade, sépharade [sefaʀad] ADJ Sephardic ▶ NMF Sephardi, Sephardic Jew

segment [sɛgmɑ̃] NM segment; (Auto): **~ (de piston)** piston ring; (Auto) brake shoe

segmenter [sɛgmɑ̃te] /1/ VT to segment ■ **se segmenter** VPR to segment

ségrégation [segʀegasjɔ̃] NF segregation

ségrégationnisme [segʀegasjɔnism] NM segregationism

ségrégationniste [segʀegasjɔnist] ADJ segregationist

seiche [sɛʃ] NF cuttlefish

séide [seid] NM (péj) henchman

seigle [sɛgl] NM rye

seigneur [sɛɲœʀ] NM lord; **le S~** the Lord

seigneurial, e, -aux [sɛɲœʀjal, -o] ADJ lordly, stately

sein [sɛ̃] NM breast; (entrailles) womb; **au ~ de** prép (équipe, institution) within; (flots, bonheur) in the midst of; **donner le ~ à** (bébé) to feed (at the breast); to breast-feed; **nourrir au ~** to breast-feed

Seine [sɛn] NF: **la ~** the Seine

séisme [seism] NM earthquake

séismique etc [seismik] ADJ voir **sismique** etc

★**seize** [sɛz] NUM sixteen

seizième [sɛzjɛm] NUM sixteenth

séjour [seʒuʀ] NM stay; (pièce) living room

séjourner [seʒuʀne] /1/ VI to stay

★**sel** [sɛl] NM salt; (fig) wit; (: piquant) spice; **~ de cuisine/de table** cooking/table salt; **~ gemme** rock salt; **sels de bain** bath salts

sélect, e [selɛkt] ADJ select

sélectif, -ive [selɛktif, -iv] ADJ selective

sélection [selɛksjɔ̃] NF selection; **faire/opérer une ~ parmi** to make a selection from among; **épreuve de ~** (Sport) trial (for selection); **~ naturelle** natural selection; **~ professionnelle** professional recruitment

sélectionné, e [selɛksjɔne] ADJ (joueur) selected; (produit) specially selected

sélectionner [selɛksjɔne] /1/ VT to select

sélectionneur, -euse [selɛksjɔnœʀ, -øz] NM/F selector

sélectivement [selɛktivmɑ̃] ADV selectively

sélectivité [selɛktivite] NF selectivity

★**self** [sɛlf] NM (fam) self-service

selfie [sɛlfi] NM selfie

self-service [sɛlfsɛʀvis] ADJ self-service ▶ NM self-service (restaurant); (magasin) self-service shop (BRIT) ou store (US)

selle [sɛl] NF saddle; **aller à la ~** (Méd) to have a bowel movement; **se mettre en ~** to mount, get into the saddle ■ **selles** NFPL (Méd) stools

seller [sele] /1/ VT to saddle

sellette [sɛlɛt] NF: **être sur la ~** to be in the hot seat

sellier [selje] NM saddler

★**selon** [s(ə)lɔ̃] PRÉP according to; (en se conformant à) in accordance with; **~ moi** as I see it; **~ que** according to, depending on whether

SEm SIGLE F (= Son Éminence) HE

semailles [s(ə)maj] NFPL sowing sg

★**semaine** [s(ə)mɛn] NF week; (salaire) week's wages ou pay, weekly wages ou pay; **en ~** during the week, on weekdays; **à la petite ~** from day to day; **la ~ sainte** Holy Week

semainier [s(ə)menje] NM (bracelet) bracelet made up of seven bands; (calendrier) desk diary; (meuble) chest of (seven) drawers

sémantique [semɑ̃tik] ADJ semantic ▶ NF semantics sg

sémaphore [semafɔʀ] NM (Rail) semaphore signal

semblable [sɑ̃blabl] ADJ similar; (de ce genre): **de semblables mésaventures** such mishaps; **~ à** similar to, like ▶ NM fellow creature ou man

semblant [sɑ̃blɑ̃] NM: **un ~ de vérité** a semblance of truth; **faire ~ (de faire)** to pretend (to do)

★**sembler** [sɑ̃ble] /1/ VB COPULE to seem; **~ être** to seem to be ▶ VB IMPERS: **il semble (bien) que/inutile de** it (really) seems ou appears that/useless to; **il me semble (bien) que** it (really) seems to me that, I (really) think that; **il me semble le connaître** I think ou I've a feeling I know him; **comme bon lui semble** as he (ou she) sees fit; **me semble-t-il, à ce qu'il me semble** it seems to me, to my mind

semelle [s(ə)mɛl] NF sole; (*intérieure*) insole, inner sole; **battre la ~** to stamp one's feet (to keep them warm); (*fig*) to hang around (waiting); **semelles compensées** platform soles

semence [s(ə)mãs] NF (*graine*) seed; (*clou*) tack

semer [s(ə)me] /5/ VT to sow; (*fig: éparpiller*) to scatter; (: *confusion*) to spread; (*fam: poursuivants*) to lose, shake off; **~ la discorde parmi** to sow discord among; **semé de** (*difficultés*) riddled with

semestre [s(ə)mɛstʀ] NM half-year; (*Scol*) semester

semestriel, le [s(ə)mɛstʀijɛl] ADJ half-yearly; semestral

semeur, -euse [s(ə)mœʀ, -øz] NM/F sower

semi-automatique [səmiɔtɔmatik] ADJ semiautomatic

semiconducteur [səmikɔ̃dyktœʀ] NM semiconductor

semi-conserve [səmikɔ̃sɛʀv(ə)] NF semi-perishable foodstuff

semi-fini [səmifini] ADJ M (*produit*) semi-finished

semi-liberté [səmilibɛʀte] NF (*Jur*) partial release from prison (*in order to follow a profession or undergo medical treatment*)

sémillant, e [semijɑ̃, -ɑ̃t] ADJ vivacious; dashing

séminaire [seminɛʀ] NM seminar; (*Rel*) seminary; **~ en ligne** webinar

séminariste [seminaʀist] NM seminarist

sémiologie [semjɔlɔʒi] NF semiology

semi-public, -ique [səmipyblik] ADJ (*Jur*) semipublic

semi-remorque [səmiʀəmɔʀk] NF trailer ▶ NM articulated lorry (BRIT), semi(trailer) (US)

semis [s(ə)mi] NM (*terrain*) seedbed, seed plot; (*plante*) seedling

sémite [semit] ADJ Semitic

sémitique [semitik] ADJ Semitic

semoir [səmwaʀ] NM seed-bag; seeder

semonce [səmɔ̃s] NF: **un coup de ~** a shot across the bows

semoule [s(ə)mul] NF semolina; **~ de riz** ground rice

sempiternel, le [sɛ̃pitɛʀnɛl] ADJ eternal, never-ending

sénat [sena] NM senate

The **Sénat** is the upper house of the French parliament and is housed in the *Palais du Luxembourg* in Paris. Every three years one half of its members, called *sénateurs*, are elected for a six-year term by an electoral college consisting of the *députés* and other elected representatives. The *Sénat* has a wide range of powers but can be overridden by the lower house, the *Assemblée nationale*, in the event of dispute.

sénateur, -trice [senatœʀ, -tʀis] NM/F senator

sénatorial, e, -aux [senatɔʀjal, -o] ADJ senatorial, Senate *cpd*

Sénégal [senegal] NM: **le ~** Senegal

sénégalais, e [senegalɛ, -ɛz] ADJ Senegalese

sénevé [sɛnve] NM (*Bot*) mustard; (*graine*) mustard seed

sénile [senil] ADJ senile

sénilité [senilite] NF senility

senior [senjɔʀ] NMF (*Sport*) senior

★**sens** [sɑ̃s] VB *voir* **sentir** ▶ NM (*Physiol: instinct*) sense; (*signification*) meaning, sense; (*direction*) direction, way ▶ NMPL (*sensualité*) senses; **reprendre ses ~** to regain consciousness; **avoir le ~ des affaires/de la mesure** to have business sense/a sense of moderation; **ça n'a pas de ~** that doesn't make (any) sense; **en dépit du bon ~** contrary to all good sense; **tomber sous le ~** to stand to reason, be perfectly obvious; **en un ~, dans un ~** in a sense; **en ce ~ que** in the sense that; **à mon ~** to my mind; **dans le ~ des aiguilles d'une montre** clockwise; **dans le ~ contraire des aiguilles d'une montre** anticlockwise; **dans le ~ de la longueur/largeur** lengthways/widthways; **dans le mauvais ~** (*aller*) the wrong way; in the wrong direction; **bon ~** good sense; **~ commun** common sense; **~ dessus dessous** upside down; **~ interdit, ~ unique** one-way street

sensass [sɑ̃sas] ADJ INV (*fam*) fantastic

sensation [sɑ̃sasjɔ̃] NF sensation; **faire ~** to cause a sensation, create a stir; **à ~** (*péj*) sensational

sensationnalisme [sɑ̃sasjɔnalism] NM sensationalism

sensationnel, le [sɑ̃sasjɔnɛl] ADJ sensational, fantastic

sensé, e [sɑ̃se] ADJ sensible

sensibilisation [sɑ̃sibilizasjɔ̃] NF consciousness-raising; **une campagne de ~ de l'opinion** a campaign to raise public awareness

sensibiliser [sɑ̃sibilize] /1/ VT to make aware of; **être sensibilisé(e) à** to have been made aware of; **~ qn (à)** to make sb sensitive (to); to make sb aware (of)

sensibilité [sɑ̃sibilite] NF sensitivity; (*affectivité, émotivité*) sensitivity, sensibility

★**sensible** [sɑ̃sibl] ADJ sensitive; (*aux sens*) perceptible; (*appréciable: différence, progrès*) appreciable, noticeable; (*quartier*) problem *cpd*; **~ à** sensitive to

sensiblement [sɑ̃sibləmɑ̃] ADV (*notablement*) appreciably, noticeably; (*à peu près*): **ils ont ~ le même poids** they weigh approximately the same

sensiblerie [sɑ̃sibləʀi] NF sentimentality; squeamishness

sensitif, -ive [sɑ̃sitif, -iv] ADJ (*nerf*) sensory; (*personne*) oversensitive

sensoriel, le [sɑ̃sɔʀjɛl] ADJ sensory, sensorial

sensualité [sɑ̃sɥalite] NF sensuality, sensuousness

sensuel, le [sɑ̃sɥɛl] ADJ (*personne*) sensual; (*musique*) sensuous

sent [sɑ̃] VB *voir* **sentir**

sente [sɑ̃t] NF path

sentence [sɑ̃tɑ̃s] NF (*Jur: jugement*) sentence; (*adage*) maxim

sentencieusement [sɑ̃tɑ̃sjøzmɑ̃] ADV sententiously

sentencieux, -euse [sɑ̃tɑ̃sjø, -øz] ADJ sententious

senteur [sɑ̃tœʀ] NF scent, perfume

senti, e [sɑ̃ti] ADJ: **bien ~** (*mots etc*) well-chosen

★**sentier** [sɑ̃tje] NM path

★**sentiment** [sɑ̃timɑ̃] NM feeling; (*conscience, impression*): **avoir le ~ de/que** to be aware of/have the feeling that; **recevez mes sentiments respectueux** (*personne nommée*) yours sincerely; (*personne non nommée*) yours faithfully; **faire du ~** (*péj*) to be sentimental; **si vous me prenez par les sentiments** if you appeal to my feelings

sentimental, e, -aux [sɑ̃timɑ̃tal, -o] ADJ sentimental; (*vie, aventure*) love *cpd*

sentimentalisme [sɑ̃timɑ̃talism] NM sentimentalism

sentimentalité [sɑ̃timɑ̃talite] NF sentimentality

sentinelle [sɑ̃tinɛl] NF sentry; **en ~** standing guard; (*soldat: en faction*) on sentry duty

★**sentir** [sɑ̃tiʀ] /**16**/ VT (*par l'odorat*) to smell; (*par le goût*) to taste; (*au toucher, fig*) to feel; (*répandre une odeur de*) to smell of; (: *ressemblance*) to smell like; (*avoir la saveur de*) to taste of; to taste like; (*fig: dénoter, annoncer*) to be indicative of; to smack of; to foreshadow; **il ne peut pas le ~** (*fam*) he can't stand him ▶ VI to smell; **~ mauvais** to smell bad ■ **se sentir** VPR: **se ~ bien** to feel good; **se ~ mal** (*être indisposé*) to feel unwell ou ill; **je ne me sens pas bien** I don't feel well; **se ~ le courage/la force de faire** to feel brave/strong enough to do; **ne plus se ~ de joie** to be beside o.s. with joy

seoir [swaʀ] /**26**/: **~ à** vt to become, befit; **comme il (leur) sied** as it is fitting (to them)

Séoul [seul] N Seoul

SEP SIGLE F (= *sclérose en plaques*) MS

séparation [separasjɔ̃] NF separation; (*cloison*) division, partition; **~ de biens** division of property (*in marriage settlement*); **~ de corps** legal separation

séparatisme [separatism] NM separatism

séparatiste [separatist] ADJ, NMF (*Pol*) separatist

séparé, e [separe] ADJ (*appartements, pouvoirs*) separate; (*époux*) separated; **~ de** separate from; separated from

séparément [separemɑ̃] ADV separately

séparer [separe] /**1**/ VT (*gén*) to separate; (*désunir: divergences etc*) to divide; to drive apart; (: *différences, obstacles*) to stand between; (*détacher*): **~ qch de** to pull sth (off) from; (*dissocier*) to distinguish between; (*diviser*): to divide sth (up) with; **~ une pièce en deux** to divide a room into two ■ **se séparer** VPR (*époux*) to separate, part; (*prendre congé: amis etc*) to part, leave each other; (: *adversaires*) to separate; (*se diviser: route, tige etc*) to divide; (*se détacher*): **se ~ (de)** to split off (from); to come off; **se ~ de** (*époux*) to separate ou part from; (*employé, objet personnel*) to part with

sépharade [sefaʀad] ADJ, NMF *voir* **séfarade**

sépia [sepja] NF sepia

★**sept** [sɛt] NUM seven

septante [sɛptɑ̃t] NUM (BELGIQUE, SUISSE) seventy

★**septembre** [sɛptɑ̃bʀ] NM September; *voir aussi* **juillet**

septennal, e, -aux [sɛptenal, -o] ADJ seven-year; (*festival*) seven-year, septennial

septennat [sɛptena] NM seven-year term (of office)

septentrional, e, -aux [sɛptɑ̃tʀijɔnal, -o] ADJ northern

septicémie [sɛptisemi] NF blood poisoning, septicaemia

septième [sɛtjɛm] NUM seventh; **être au ~ ciel** to be on cloud nine

septique [sɛptik] ADJ: **fosse ~** septic tank; **choc ~** septic shock

septuagénaire [sɛptɥaʒenɛʀ] ADJ, NMF septuagenarian

sépulcral, e, -aux [sepylkʀal, -o] ADJ (*voix*) sepulchral

sépulcre [sepylkʀ] NM sepulchre

sépulture [sepyltyʀ] NF burial; (*tombeau*) burial place, grave

séquelles [sekɛl] NFPL after-effects; (*fig*) aftermath *sg*; consequences

séquençage [sekɑ̃saʒ] NM (*de génome*) sequencing

séquence [sekɑ̃s] NF sequence

séquencer [sekɑ̃se] VT (*génome, production*) to sequence

séquentiel, le [sekɑ̃sjɛl] ADJ sequential

séquestration [sekɛstʀasjɔ̃] NF illegal confinement; impounding

séquestre [sekɛstʀ] NM impoundment; **mettre sous ~** to impound

séquestrer [sekɛstʀe] /**1**/ VT (*personne*) to confine illegally; (*biens*) to impound

séquoia [sekɔja] NM sequoia

serai *etc* [səʀe] VB *voir* **être**

sérail [seʀaj] NM seraglio; harem; **rentrer au ~** to return to the fold

serbe [sɛʀb] ADJ Serbian ▶ NM (*Ling*) Serbian ▶ NMF: **Serbe** Serb

Serbie [sɛʀbi] NF: **la ~** Serbia

serbo-croate [sɛʀbɔkʀɔat] ADJ Serbo-Croat, Serbo-Croatian ▶ NM (*Ling*) Serbo-Croat

serein, e [səʀɛ̃, -ɛn] ADJ serene; (*jugement*) dispassionate

sereinement [səʀɛnmɑ̃] ADV serenely

sérénade [seʀenad] NF serenade; (*fam*) hullabaloo

sérénité [seʀenite] NF serenity

serez [səʀe] VB *voir* **être**

serf, serve [sɛʀ, sɛʀv] NM/F serf

serfouette [sɛʀfwɛt] NF weeding hoe

serge [sɛʀʒ] NF serge

sergent [sɛʀʒɑ̃] NM sergeant

sergent-chef [sɛʀʒɑ̃ʃɛf] (*pl* **sergents-chefs**) NM staff sergeant

sergent-major [sɛʀʒɑ̃maʒɔʀ] (*pl* **sergents-majors**) NM = quartermaster sergeant

sériciculture [seʀisikyltyʀ] NF silkworm breeding, sericulture

série [seʀi] NF (*de questions, d'accidents, TV*) series *inv*; (*de clés, casseroles, outils*) set; (*catégorie: Sport*) rank; class; **en ~** in quick succession; (*Comm*) mass *cpd*; **de ~** adj (*voiture*) standard; **hors ~** (*Comm*) custombuilt; (*fig*) outstanding; **imprimante ~** (*Inform*) serial printer; **soldes de fin de séries** end of line special offers; **~ noire** nm (crime) thriller; nf (*suite de malheurs*) run of bad luck

sérier [seʀje] /**7**/ VT to classify, sort out

sérieusement [seʀjøzmɑ̃] ADV seriously; reliably; responsibly; **il parle ~** he's serious, he means it; **~ ?** seriously?

sérieux, -euse [seʀjø, -øz] ADJ serious; (*élève, employé*) reliable, responsible; (*client, maison*) reliable, dependable; (*offre, proposition*) genuine, serious; (*grave, sévère*) serious, solemn; (*maladie, situation*) serious, grave; (*important*) considerable; **ce n'est pas ~** (*raisonnable*) that's not on ▸ ADV (*fam*): **il s'est marié — sérieux ?** he got married — seriously? ▸ NM seriousness; (*d'une entreprise etc*) reliability; **garder son ~** to keep a straight face; **manquer de ~** not to be very responsible (*ou* reliable); **prendre qch/qn au ~** to take sth/sb seriously

sérigraphie [seʀigʀafi] NF silk screen printing

serin [s(ə)ʀɛ̃] NM canary

seriner [s(ə)ʀine] /**1**/ VT: **~ qch à qn** to drum sth into sb

seringue [s(ə)ʀɛ̃g] NF syringe

serions *etc* [səʀjɔ̃] VB *voir* **être**

serment [seʀmɑ̃] NM (*juré*) oath; (*promesse*) pledge, vow; **prêter ~** to take the (*ou* an) oath; **faire le ~ de** to take a vow to, swear to; **sous ~** on *ou* under oath

sermon [seʀmɔ̃] NM sermon; (*péj*) sermon, lecture

sermonner [seʀmɔne] /**1**/ VT to lecture

sérologie [seʀɔlɔʒi] NF serology

séronégatif, -ive [seʀonegatif, -iv] ADJ HIV negative

séropositif, -ive [seʀopozitif, -iv] ADJ HIV positive

séropositivité [seʀopozitivite] NF HIV positivity, seropositivity

sérotonine [seʀɔtɔnin] NF serotonin

serpe [seʀp] NF billhook

★**serpent** [seʀpɑ̃] NM snake; **~ à sonnettes** rattlesnake; **~ monétaire (européen)** (European) monetary snake

serpenter [seʀpɑ̃te] /**1**/ VI to wind

serpentin [seʀpɑ̃tɛ̃] NM (*tube*) coil; (*ruban*) streamer

serpillière [seʀpijɛʀ] NF floorcloth

serpolet [seʀpɔlɛ] NM wild thyme

serrage [seʀaʒ] NM tightening; **collier de ~** clamp

serre [seʀ] NF (*Agr*) greenhouse; **~ chaude** hothouse; **~ froide** unheated greenhouse ■ **serres** NFPL (*griffes*) claws, talons

serré, e [seʀe] ADJ (*tissu*) closely woven; (*réseau*) dense; (*écriture*) close; (*habits*) tight; (*fig: lutte, match*) tight, close-fought; (*passagers etc*) (tightly) packed; (*café*) strong; **avoir la gorge serrée** to have a lump in one's throat; **avoir le cœur ~** to have a heavy heart ▸ ADV: **jouer ~** to play it close, play a close game; **écrire ~** to have cramped handwriting

serre-livres [seʀlivʀ] NM INV book ends *pl*

serrement [seʀmɑ̃] NM: **~ de main** handshake; **~ de cœur** pang of anguish

★**serrer** [seʀe] /**1**/ VT (*tenir*) to grip *ou* hold tight; (*comprimer, coincer*) to squeeze; (*poings, mâchoires*) to clench; (*vêtement*) to be too tight for; to fit tightly; (*rapprocher*) to close up, move closer together; (*ceinture, nœud, frein, vis*) to tighten; **~ la main à qn** to shake sb's hand; **~ qn dans ses bras** to hug sb,

clasp sb in one's arms; **~ la gorge à qn** (*chagrin*) to bring a lump to sb's throat; **~ les dents** to clench *ou* grit one's teeth; **~ qn de près** to follow close behind sb; **~ le trottoir** to hug the kerb; **~ sa droite** to keep well to the right; **~ la vis à qn** to crack down harder on sb; **~ les rangs** to close ranks ▸ VI: **~ à droite** to keep to the right; to move into the right-hand lane ■ **se serrer** VPR (*se rapprocher*) to squeeze up; **se ~ contre qn** to huddle up to sb; **se ~ les coudes** to stick together, back one another up; **se ~ la ceinture** to tighten one's belt

serre-tête [seʀtɛt] NM (*bandeau*) headband; (*bonnet*) skullcap

★**serrure** [seʀyʀ] NF lock

serrurerie [seʀyʀʀi] NF (*métier*) locksmith's trade; (*ferronnerie*) ironwork; **~ d'art** ornamental ironwork

serrurier [seʀyʀje] NM locksmith

sers, sert [seʀ] VB *voir* **servir**

sertir [seʀtiʀ] /**2**/ VT (*pierre*) to set; (*pièces métalliques*) to crimp

sérum [seʀɔm] NM serum; **~ antivenimeux** snakebite serum; **~ sanguin** (blood) serum

servage [seʀvaʒ] NM serfdom

servant [seʀvɑ̃] NM server

servante [seʀvɑ̃t] NF (maid)servant

serve [seʀv] NF *voir* **serf** ▸ VB *voir* **servir**

★**serveur, -euse** [seʀvœʀ, -øz] NM/F waiter (waitress) ▸ NM (*Inform*) server ▸ ADJ: **centre ~** (*Inform*) service centre

servi, e [seʀvi] ADJ: **être bien ~** to get a large helping (*ou* helpings); **vous êtes ~?** are you being served?

serviable [seʀvjabl] ADJ obliging, willing to help

★**service** [seʀvis] NM (*gén*) service; (*série de repas*): **premier ~** first sitting; (*pourboire*) service (charge); (*assortiment de vaisselle*) set, service; (*linge de table*) set; (*bureau: de la vente etc*) department, section; (*travail*): **pendant le ~** on duty; **faire le ~** to serve; **être en ~ chez qn** (*domestique*) to be in sb's service; **être au ~ de** (*patron, patrie*) to be in the service of; **être au ~ de qn** (*collaborateur, voiture*) to be at sb's service; **porte de ~** tradesman's entrance; **rendre ~ à qn** to help sb; (*objet: s'avérer utile*) to come in useful *ou* handy for sb; **il aime rendre ~** he likes to help; **rendre un ~ à qn** to do sb a favour; **heures de ~** hours of duty; **être de ~** to be on duty; **reprendre du ~** to get back into action; **avoir 25 ans de ~** to have completed 25 years' service; **être/mettre en ~** to be in/put into service *ou* operation; **~ compris/non compris** service included/not included, inclusive/exclusive of service; **hors ~** not in use; out of order; **~ à thé/café** tea/coffee set *ou* service; **~ après-vente** after-sales service; **en ~ commandé** on an official assignment; **~ funèbre** funeral service; **~ militaire** military service; **~ d'ordre** police (*ou* stewards) in charge of maintaining order ■ **services** NMPL (*travail, Écon*) services; **services publics** public services, (public) utilities; **services secrets** secret service *sg*; **services sociaux** social services

★**serviette** [seʀvjɛt] NF (*de table*) (table) napkin, serviette; (*de toilette*) towel; (*porte-documents*) briefcase; **~ éponge** terry towel; **~ hygiénique** sanitary towel (BRIT) *ou* napkin (US)

servile [sɛʀvil] ADJ servile

servilement [sɛʀvilmɑ̃] ADV slavishly

★**servir** [sɛʀviʀ] /**14**/ VT (gén) to serve; (dîneur: au restaurant) to wait on; (client: au magasin) to serve, attend to; (fig: aider) ~ **qn** to aid sb; to serve sb's interests; to stand sb in good stead; (Comm: rente) to pay; (s'approvisionner) **vous êtes servi?** are you being served?; **sers-toi!** help yourself!; ~ **qch à qn** to serve sb with sth, help sb to sth; **qu'est-ce que je vous sers?** what can I get you?; ~ **à qn** (diplôme, livre) to be of use to sb; ~ **à qch/à faire** (outil etc) to be used for sth/for doing; **ça peut** ~ **it** may come in handy; **à quoi cela sert-il (de faire)?** what's the use (of doing)?; **ça ne sert à rien** it's no use; ~ **(à qn) de ...** to serve as ... (for sb); ~ **à dîner (à qn)** to serve dinner (to sb); **ça m'a servi pour faire** it was useful to me when I did; I used it to do ▸ VI (Tennis) to serve; (Cartes) to deal; (être militaire) to serve ■ **se servir** VPR (prendre d'un plat) to help o.s.; **se** ~ **chez** to shop at; **se** ~ **de** (plat) to help o.s. to; (voiture, outil, relations) to use

serviteur [sɛʀvitœʀ] NM servant

servitude [sɛʀvityd] NF servitude; (fig) constraint; (Jur) easement

servofrein [sɛʀvɔfʀɛ̃] NM servo(-assisted) brake

servomécanisme [sɛʀvɔmekanism] NM servo system

★**ses** [se] ADJ POSS voir **son¹**

sésame [sezam] NM (Bot) sesame; (graine) sesame seed

session [sesjɔ̃] NF session

set [sɛt] NM set; (napperon) placemat; ~ **de table** set of placemats

seuil [sœj] NM doorstep; (fig) threshold; **sur le** ~ **de la maison** in the doorway of his (ou her etc) house, on his (ou her etc) doorstep; **au** ~ **de** (fig) on the threshold ou brink ou edge of; ~ **de rentabilité** (Comm) breakeven point

★**seul, e** [sœl] ADJ (sans compagnie) alone; (avec nuance affective: isolé) lonely; (unique): **un** ~ **livre** only one book, a single book; **le** ~ **livre** the only book; **d'un** ~ **coup** (soudainement) all at once; (à la fois) in one go; (vivre) alone, on one's own; **faire qch (tout)** ~ to do sth (all) on one's own ou (all) by oneself; ~ **ce livre, ce livre** ~ this book alone, only this book; **à lui (tout)** ~ single-handed, on his own; **se sentir** ~ to feel lonely; **parler tout** ~ to talk to oneself ▸ NM/F: **il en reste un(e)** ~**(e)** there's only one left; **pas un(e)** ~**(e)** not a single; ~ **à** ~ in private

★**seulement** [sœlmɑ̃] ADV only; ~ **cinq, cinq** ~ only five; ~ **eux** only them, them alone; ~ **hier/à 10h** only yesterday/at 10 o'clock; **il consent,** ~ **il demande des garanties** he agrees, only he wants guarantees; **non** ~ **... mais aussi** ou **encore** not only ... but also

sève [sɛv] NF sap

sévère [sevɛʀ] ADJ severe

sévèrement [sevɛʀmɑ̃] ADV severely

sévérité [severite] NF severity

sévices [sevis] NMPL (physical) cruelty sg, ill treatment sg

Séville [sevil] N Seville

sévir [seviʀ] /**2**/ VI (punir) to use harsh measures, crack down; (fléau) to rage, be rampant; ~ **contre** (abus) to deal ruthlessly with, crack down on

sevrage [səvʀaʒ] NM weaning; deprivation; (d'un toxicomane) withdrawal

sevrer [səvʀe] /**5**/ VT to wean; (fig): ~ **qn de** to deprive sb of

sexagénaire [sɛgzaʒenɛʀ] ADJ, NMF sexagenarian

SExc SIGLE F (= Son Excellence) HE

★**sexe** [sɛks] NM sex; (organe mâle) member

sexisme [sɛksism] NM sexism

sexiste [sɛksist] ADJ, NM sexist

sexologie [sɛksɔlɔʒi] NF sexology

sexologue [sɛksɔlɔg] NMF sexologist, sex specialist

sextant [sɛkstɑ̃] NM sextant

sexto [sɛksto] NM sext; **envoyer un** ~ **à qn** to sext sb

sexualité [sɛksɥalite] NF sexuality

sexué, e [sɛksɥe] ADJ sexual

sexuel, le [sɛksɥɛl] ADJ sexual; **acte** ~ sex act

sexuellement [sɛksɥɛlmɑ̃] ADV sexually

sexy [sɛksi] ADJ sexy ▸ ADV: **s'habiller** ~ to dress sexily

seyait [sejɛ] VB voir **seoir**

seyant, e [sejɑ̃, -ɑ̃t] VB voir **seoir** ▸ ADJ becoming

Seychelles [seʃɛl] NFPL: **les** ~ the Seychelles

SG SIGLE MF = **secrétaire général(e)**

SGEN SIGLE M (= Syndicat général de l'éducation nationale) teachers' trade union

shaker [ʃekœʀ] NM (cocktail) shaker

shampoing [ʃɑ̃pwɛ̃] NM = **shampooing**

shampooiner [ʃɑ̃pwine] /**1**/ VT to shampoo

shampooineur, -euse [ʃɑ̃pwinœʀ, -øz] NM/F (personne) junior (who does the shampooing)

★**shampo(o)ing** [ʃɑ̃pwɛ̃] NM shampoo; **se faire un** ~ to shampoo one's hair; ~ **colorant** (colour) rinse; ~ **traitant** medicated shampoo

shampouiner [ʃɑ̃pwine] NM = **shampooiner**

shampouineur, -euse [ʃɑ̃pwinœʀ, -øz] NM/F = **shampooineur**

Shetland [ʃɛtlɑ̃d] N: **les îles** ~ the Shetland Islands, Shetland

shetland [ʃɛtlɑ̃d] NM (laine) Shetland wool; (aussi: **pull shetland**) Shetland sweater ou jumper (BRIT); (poney) Shetland pony

shiite [ʃiit] ADJ, NMF Shiite; voir **chiite**

shit [ʃit] NM (fam) hash (fam)

shoot [ʃut] NM (Football) shot

shooter [ʃute] /**1**/ VI (Football) to shoot ■ **se shooter** VPR (drogué) to mainline

shopping [ʃɔpiŋ] NM: **faire du** ~ to go shopping

short [ʃɔʀt] NM (pair of) shorts pl

SI SIGLE M = **syndicat d'initiative**

---

si [si]

ADV **1** (oui) yes; « **Paul n'est pas venu** » — « **si!** » "Paul hasn't come" — "Yes he has!"; **je vous assure que si** I assure you he did/she is etc
2 (tellement) so; **si gentil/rapidement** so kind/fast; **(tant et) si bien que** so much so that; **si rapide qu'il soit** however fast he may be
▸ CONJ **1** if; **si tu veux** if you want; **je me demande si** I wonder if ou whether; **si j'étais toi** if I were you; **si seulement** if only; **si ce n'est que** apart from; **une des plus belles, si ce n'est la plus belle** one of the most beautiful, if not THE most

beautiful; **s'il est aimable, eux par contre ...**
while ou whereas he's nice, they (on the other
hand) ...
▶ NM (*Mus*) B; (: *en chantant la gamme*) ti

siamois, e [sjamwa, -waz] ADJ Siamese; **frères/
sœurs ~(es)** Siamese twins

Sibérie [sibeʀi] NF: **la ~** Siberia

sibérien, ne [sibeʀjɛ̃, -ɛn] ADJ Siberian ▶ NM/F:
Sibérien, ne Siberian

sibyllin, e [sibilɛ̃, -in] ADJ sibylline

SICAV [sikav] SIGLE F (= *société d'investissement à capital variable*) open-ended investment trust or a share in
such a trust

Sicile [sisil] NF: **la ~** Sicily

sicilien, ne [sisiljɛ̃, -ɛn] ADJ Sicilian

★**sida** [sida] NM (= *syndrome immuno-déficitaire acquis*)
AIDS *sg*

sidéral, e, -aux [sideʀal, -o] ADJ sideral

sidérant, e [sideʀɑ̃, -ɑ̃t] ADJ staggering

sidéré, e [sideʀe] ADJ staggered

sidérurgie [sideʀyʀʒi] NF steel industry

sidérurgique [sideʀyʀʒik] ADJ steel *cpd*

sidérurgiste [sideʀyʀʒist] NMF steel worker

siècle [sjɛkl] NM century; (*époque*): **le ~ des
lumières/de l'atome** the age of enlightenment/
atomic age; (*Rel*): **le ~** the world

sied [sje] VB *voir* **seoir**

siège [sjɛʒ] NM seat; (*d'entreprise*) head office; (*d'organisation*) headquarters *pl*; (*Mil*) siege; **lever le ~**
to raise the siege; **mettre le ~ devant** to besiege;
présentation par le ~ (*Méd*) breech presentation;
~ avant/arrière (*Auto*) front/back seat; **~ baquet**
bucket seat; **~ social** registered office

siéger [sjeʒe] /**3, 6**/ VI (*assemblée, tribunal*) to sit;
(*résider, se trouver*) to lie, be located

sien, ne [sjɛ̃, sjɛn] PRON: **le (la) ~(ne), les ~(ne)s**
(*d'un homme*) his; (*d'une femme*) hers; (*d'une chose*)
its; **y mettre du ~** to pull one's weight; **faire des
siennes** (*fam*) to be up to one's (usual) tricks; **les
siens** (*sa famille*) one's family

siérait *etc* [sjeʀɛ] VB *voir* **seoir**

Sierra Leone [sjeʀaleɔn] NF: **la ~** Sierra Leone

sieste [sjɛst] NF (afternoon) snooze ou nap, siesta;
faire la ~ to have a snooze ou nap

sieur [sjœʀ] NM: **le ~ Thomas** Mr Thomas; (*en plaisantant*) Master Thomas

sifflant, e [siflɑ̃, -ɑ̃t] ADJ (*bruit*) whistling; (*toux*)
wheezing; (**consonne**) **sifflante** (*Ling*) sibilant

sifflement [sifləmɑ̃] NM whistle, whistling *no pl*;
wheezing *no pl*; hissing *no pl*

★**siffler** [sifle] /**1**/ VI (*gén*) to whistle; (*avec un sifflet*)
to blow (on) one's whistle; (*en respirant*) to
wheeze; (*serpent, vapeur*) to hiss ▶ VT (*chanson*) to
whistle; (*chien etc*) to whistle for; (*fille*) to whistle
at; (*pièce, orateur*) to hiss, boo; (*faute*) to blow one's
whistle at; (*fin du match, départ*) to blow one's
whistle for; (*fam: verre, bouteille*) to guzzle, knock
back (BRIT)

sifflet [siflɛ] NM whistle; **coup de ~** whistle ▪ **sif-
flets** NMPL (*de mécontentement*) whistles, boos

siffloter [siflɔte] /**1**/ VI, VT to whistle

sigle [sigl] NM acronym, (set of) initials *pl*

signal, -aux [siɲal, -o] NM (*signe convenu, appareil*)
signal; (*indice, écriteau*) sign; **donner le ~ de** to give
the signal for; **~ d'alarme** alarm signal; **~ d'alerte/
de détresse** warning/distress signal; **~ horaire**
time signal; **~ optique/sonore** warning light/
sound; visual/acoustic signal; **signaux (lumineux)** (*Auto*) traffic signals; **signaux routiers**
road signs; (*lumineux*) traffic lights

signalement [siɲalmɑ̃] NM description, particulars *pl*

signaler [siɲale] /**1**/ VT to indicate; to announce;
(*vol, perte*) to report; (*personne: faire un signe*) to
signal; (*être l'indice de*) to indicate; **~ qch à qn
que** to point out sth to sb/to sb that; **~ qn à la
police** to bring sb to the notice of the police; **se ~
par** to distinguish o.s. by; **se ~ à l'attention de qn**
to attract sb's attention

signalétique [siɲaletik] ADJ: **fiche ~** identification sheet

signalisation [siɲalizasjɔ̃] NF signalling, signposting; signals *pl*; roadsigns *pl*; **panneau de ~**
roadsign

signaliser [siɲalize] /**1**/ VT to put up roadsigns on;
to put signals on

signataire [siɲatɛʀ] NMF signatory

★**signature** [siɲatyʀ] NF signature; (*action*) signing

★**signe** [siɲ] NM sign; (*Typo*) mark; **ne pas donner ~
de vie** to give no sign of life; **c'est bon ~** it's a
good sign; **c'est ~ que** it's a sign that; **faire un ~
de la main/tête** to give a sign with one's hand/
shake one's head; **faire ~ à qn** (*fig: contacter*) to get
in touch with sb; **faire ~ à qn d'entrer** to motion
(to) sb to come in; **en ~ de** as a sign ou mark of; **le
~ de la croix** the sign of the Cross; **~ de ponctuation** punctuation mark; **~ du zodiaque** sign of
the zodiac; **signes particuliers** distinguishing
marks

★**signer** [siɲe] /**1**/ VT to sign ▪ **se signer** VPR to cross
o.s.

signet [siɲɛ] NM bookmark

significatif, -ive [siɲifikatif, -iv] ADJ significant

signification [siɲifikasjɔ̃] NF meaning

signifier [siɲifje] /**7**/ VT (*vouloir dire*) to mean, signify; (*faire connaître*): **~ qch (à qn)** to make sth
known (to sb); (*Jur*): **~ qch à qn** to serve notice of
sth on sb

silence [silɑ̃s] NM silence; (*Mus*) rest; **garder le ~
(sur qch)** to keep silent (about sth), say nothing
(about sth); **passer sous ~** to pass over (in silence);
réduire au ~ to silence

silencieusement [silɑ̃sjøzmɑ̃] ADV silently

silencieux, -euse [silɑ̃sjø, -øz] ADJ quiet, silent
▶ NM silencer (BRIT), muffler (US)

silex [silɛks] NM flint

silhouette [silwɛt] NF outline, silhouette; (*lignes,
contour*) outline; (*figure*) figure

silice [silis] NF silica

siliceux, -euse [silisø, -øz] ADJ (*terrain*) chalky

silicium [silisjɔm] NM silicon; **plaquette de ~** silicon chip

silicone [silikon] NF silicone

silicose [silikoz] NF silicosis, dust disease

sillage [sijaʒ] NM wake; (*fig*) trail; **dans le ~ de** (*fig*)
in the wake of

S

sillon [sijɔ̃] NM (d'un champ) furrow; (de disque) groove

sillonner [sijɔne] /1/ VT (creuser) to furrow; (traverser) to criss-cross, cross

silo [silo] NM silo

silure [silyʀ] NM catfish

simagrées [simagʀe] NFPL fuss sg; airs and graces

simiesque [simjɛsk] ADJ monkey-like, simian

similaire [similɛʀ] ADJ similar

similarité [similaʀite] NF similarity

simili [simili] NM imitation; (Typo) half-tone ▶ NF half-tone engraving

simili... [simili] PRÉFIXE imitation cpd, artificial

similicuir [similikɥiʀ] NM imitation leather

similigravure [similigʀavyʀ] NF half-tone engraving

similitude [similityd] NF similarity

★**simple** [sɛ̃pl] ADJ (gén) simple; (non multiple) single; **~ soldat** private; **un ~ particulier** an ordinary citizen; **une ~ formalité** a mere formality; **dans le plus ~ appareil** in one's birthday suit ▶ NM: **cela varie du ~ au double** it can double, it can double the price etc; **~ messieurs/dames** nm (Tennis) men's/ladies' singles sg ▶ NMF: **~ d'esprit** simpleton ▪ **simples** NMPL (Méd) medicinal plants

simplement [sɛ̃pləmɑ̃] ADV simply

simplet, te [sɛ̃plɛ, -ɛt] ADJ (personne) simple-minded

simplicité [sɛ̃plisite] NF simplicity; **en toute ~** quite simply

simplification [sɛ̃plifikasjɔ̃] NF simplification

simplifier [sɛ̃plifje] /7/ VT to simplify

simpliste [sɛ̃plist] ADJ simplistic

simulacre [simylakʀ] NM enactment; (péj): **un ~ de** a pretence of, a sham

simulateur, -trice [simylatœʀ, -tʀis] NM/F shammer, pretender; (qui se prétend malade) malingerer ▶ NM: **~ de vol** flight simulator

simulation [simylasjɔ̃] NF shamming, simulation; malingering

simuler [simyle] /1/ VT to sham, simulate

simultané, e [simyltane] ADJ simultaneous

simultanéité [simyltaneite] NF simultaneity

simultanément [simyltanemɑ̃] ADV simultaneously

Sinaï [sinai] NM: **le ~** Sinai

sinapisme [sinapism] NM (Méd) mustard poultice

sincère [sɛ̃sɛʀ] ADJ sincere; genuine; heartfelt; **mes sincères condoléances** my deepest sympathy

sincèrement [sɛ̃sɛʀmɑ̃] ADV sincerely; genuinely

sincérité [sɛ̃seʀite] NF sincerity; **en toute ~** in all sincerity

sinécure [sinekyʀ] NF sinecure

sine die [sinedje] ADV sine die, indefinitely

sine qua non [sinekwanɔn] ADJ: **condition ~** indispensable condition

Singapour [sɛ̃gapuʀ] NM: **le ~** Singapore

★**singe** [sɛ̃ʒ] NM monkey; (de grande taille) ape

singer [sɛ̃ʒe] /3/ VT to ape, mimic

singeries [sɛ̃ʒʀi] NFPL antics; (simagrées) airs and graces

singulariser [sɛ̃gylaʀize] /1/ VT to mark out ▪ **se singulariser** VPR to call attention to o.s.

singularité [sɛ̃gylaʀite] NF peculiarity

singulier, -ière [sɛ̃gylje, -jɛʀ] ADJ remarkable, singular; (Ling) singular ▶ NM singular

singulièrement [sɛ̃gyljɛʀmɑ̃] ADV singularly, remarkably

sinistre [sinistʀ] ADJ sinister; (intensif): **un ~ imbécile** an absolute idiot ▶ NM (incendie) blaze; (catastrophe) disaster; (Assurances) damage (giving rise to a claim)

sinistré, e [sinistʀe] ADJ disaster-stricken ▶ NM/F disaster victim

sinistrose [sinistʀoz] NF pessimism

sino... [sino] PRÉFIXE: **sino-indien** Sino-Indian, Chinese-Indian

sinon [sinɔ̃] CONJ (autrement, sans quoi) otherwise, or else; (sauf) except, other than; (si ce n'est) if not

sinueux, -euse [sinɥø, -øz] ADJ winding; (fig) tortuous

sinuosité [sinɥozite] NF (de route) twists and turns pl ▪ **sinuosités** NFPL (de route, cours d'eau) winding sg, curves; **les sinuosités de son raisonnement** (fig) his (ou her) tortuous train of thought

sinus [sinys] NM (Anat) sinus; (Géom) sine

sinusite [sinyzit] NF sinusitis, sinus infection

sinusoïdal, e, -aux [sinyzɔidal, -o] ADJ sinusoidal

sinusoïde [sinyzɔid] NF sinusoid

sionisme [sjɔnism] NM Zionism

sioniste [sjɔnist] ADJ, NMF Zionist

siphon [sifɔ̃] NM (tube, d'eau gazeuse) siphon; (d'évier etc) U-bend

siphonnage [sifɔnaʒ] NM (de bac) draining; (d'eau, essence aussi fig: de fonds, ressources) siphoning off

siphonner [sifɔne] /1/ VT (bac) to drain; (eau, essence: aussi fig: fonds, ressources) to siphon off; **~ un réservoir d'essence** to siphon off the petrol (BRIT) ou gas (US) from a tank

sire [siʀ] NM (titre): **S~** Sire; **un triste ~** an unsavoury individual

sirène [siʀɛn] NF siren; **~ d'alarme** fire alarm; (pendant la guerre) air-raid siren

★**sirop** [siʀo] NM (à diluer: de fruit etc) syrup, cordial (BRIT); (boisson) fruit drink; (pharmaceutique) syrup, mixture; **~ de menthe** mint syrup ou cordial; **~ contre la toux** cough syrup ou mixture

siroter [siʀɔte] /1/ VT to sip

sirupeux, -euse [siʀypø, -øz] ADJ syrupy

sis, e [si, siz] ADJ: **~ rue de la Paix** located in the rue de la Paix

sisal [sizal] NM (Bot) sisal

sismique [sismik] ADJ seismic

sismographe [sismɔgʀaf] NM seismograph

sismologie [sismɔlɔʒi] NF seismology

sitar [sitaʀ] NM sitar

site [sit] NM (paysage, environnement) setting; (d'une ville etc: emplacement) site; **~ (pittoresque)** beauty spot; **sites touristiques** tourist attractions; **sites naturels/historiques** natural/historic sites; **~ web** (Inform) website

sitôt [sito] ADV: **~ parti** as soon as he (ou she etc) had left; **~ après** straight after; **pas de ~** not for a long time; **~ (après) que** as soon as

★**situation** [sitɥasjɔ̃] NF (gén) situation; (d'un édifice, d'une ville) situation, position; (emplacement) location; **être en ~ de faire qch** to be in a position to do sth; **~ de famille** marital status

situé, e [sitɥe] ADJ: **bien ~** well situated, in a good location; **~ à/près de** situated at/near

situer [sitɥe] /1/ VT to site, situate; (en pensée) to set, place ■ **se situer** VPR: **se ~ à/près de** to be situated at/near

SIVOM [sivɔm] SIGLE M (= Syndicat intercommunal à vocation multiple) association of "communes"

★**six** [sis] NUM six

sixième [sizjɛm] NUM sixth ▶ NF (Scol: classe) year 7 (BRIT), sixth grade (US); **en ~** in year 7 (BRIT), in sixth grade (US)

skaï® [skaj] NM ≈ Leatherette®

skate [sket], **skate-board** [sketbɔʀd] NM (sport) skateboarding; (planche) skateboard

skateur, -euse [sketœʀ, øz] NM/F, **skater** [sketœʀ] NMF skateboarder

sketch [skɛtʃ] NM (variety) sketch

★**ski** [ski] NM (objet) ski; (sport) skiing; **faire du ~** to ski; **~ alpin** Alpine skiing; **~ court** short ski; **~ évolutif** short ski method; **~ de fond** cross-country skiing; **~ nautique** water-skiing; **~ de piste** downhill skiing; **~ de randonnée** cross-country skiing

skiable [skjabl] ADJ (neige, pente) skiable; voir aussi **domaine**

ski-bob [skibɔb] NM skibob

★**skier** [skje] /7/ VI to ski

skieur, -euse [skjœʀ, -øz] NM/F skier

skif, skiff [skif] NM skiff

slalom [slalɔm] NM slalom; **faire du ~ entre** to slalom between

slalomer [slalɔme] /1/ VI (entre des obstacles) to weave in and out; (Ski) to slalom

slalomeur, -euse [slalɔmœʀ, -øz] NM/F (Ski) slalom skier

slam [slam] NM slam poetry

slave [slav] ADJ Slav(onic), Slavic ▶ NM (Ling) Slavonic ▶ NMF: **Slave** Slav

★**slip** [slip] NM (sous-vêtement) underpants pl, pants pl (BRIT), briefs pl; (de bain: d'homme) trunks pl; (: du bikini) (bikini) briefs pl

slogan [slɔgɑ̃] NM slogan

slovaque [slɔvak] ADJ Slovak ▶ NM (Ling) Slovak ▶ NMF: **Slovaque** Slovak

Slovaquie [slɔvaki] NF: **la ~** Slovakia

slovène [slɔvɛn] ADJ Slovene ▶ NM (Ling) Slovene ▶ NMF: **Slovène** Slovene

Slovénie [slɔveni] NF: **la ~** Slovenia

slow [slo] NM (danse) slow number

SM SIGLE F (= Sa Majesté) HM

smartphone [smaʀtfɔn] NM (Inform) smartphone

smash [smaʃ] NM (Tennis, Volley-ball) smash

smasher [smaʃe] /1/ VI to smash the ball ▶ VT (balle) to smash

SMIC [smik] SIGLE M = **salaire minimum interprofessionnel de croissance**

In France, the **SMIC** (salaire minimum interprofessionnel de croissance) is the minimum hourly rate which workers over the age of 18 must legally be paid. It is index-linked and is raised on 1 January of every year as well as whenever the cost-of-living index goes above 2%.

smicard, e [smikaʀ, -aʀd] NM/F minimum wage earner

smocks [smɔk] NMPL (Couture) smocking no pl

smoking [smɔkiŋ] NM dinner ou evening suit

SMS SIGLE M (service: = short message service) SMS; (: message) text (message)

SMUR [smyʀ] SIGLE M (= service médical d'urgence et de réanimation) specialist mobile emergency unit

snack [snak] NM snack bar

SNC ABR = **service non compris**

SNCB SIGLE F (= Société nationale des chemins de fer belges) Belgian railways

★**SNCF** SIGLE F (= Société nationale des chemins de fer français) French railways

SNES [snɛs] SIGLE M (= Syndicat national de l'enseignement secondaire) secondary teachers' union

SNE-sup [ɛsɛnəsyp] SIGLE M (= Syndicat national de l'enseignement supérieur) university teachers' union

SNJ SIGLE M (= Syndicat national des journalistes) journalists' union

snob [snɔb] ADJ snobbish ▶ NMF snob

snober [snɔbe] /1/ VT: **~ qn** to give sb the cold shoulder, treat sb with disdain

snobinard, e [snɔbinaʀ, -aʀd] NM/F snooty ou stuck-up person

snobisme [snɔbism] NM snobbery, snobbishness

snowboard [snobɔʀd] NM (sport) snowboarding; (planche) snowboard

snowboarder [snobɔʀdœʀ] NMF = **snowboardeur**

snowboardeur, -euse [snobɔʀdœʀ, -øz] NM/F, **snowboarder** [snobɔʀdœʀ] NMF snowboarder

SNSM SIGLE F (= Société nationale de sauvetage en mer) national sea-rescue association

s.o. ABR (= sans objet) no longer applicable

sobre [sɔbʀ] ADJ (personne) temperate, abstemious; (élégance, style) restrained, sober; **~ de** (gestes, compliments) sparing of

sobrement [sɔbʀəmɑ̃] ADV in moderation, abstemiously; soberly

sobriété [sɔbʀijete] NF temperance, abstemiousness; sobriety

sobriquet [sɔbʀikɛ] NM nickname

soc [sɔk] NM ploughshare

sociabilité [sɔsjabilite] NF sociability

sociable [sɔsjabl] ADJ sociable

★**social, e, -aux** [sɔsjal, -o] ADJ social

socialement [sɔsjalmɑ̃] ADV socially

socialisant, e [sɔsjalizɑ̃, -ɑ̃t] ADJ with socialist tendencies

socialisation [sɔsjalizasjɔ̃] NF socialisation

socialiser [sɔsjalize] /1/ VT to socialize

S

socialisme [sɔsjalism] NM socialism

socialiste [sɔsjalist] ADJ, NMF socialist

sociétaire [sɔsjetɛʀ] NMF member

société [sɔsjete] NF society; (d'abeilles, de fourmis) colony; (sportive) club; (Comm) company; **la bonne ~** polite society; **se plaire dans la ~ de** to enjoy the society of; **l'archipel de la S~** the Society Islands; **la ~ d'abondance/de consommation** the affluent/consumer society; **~ par actions** joint stock company; **~ anonyme** ≈ limited company (BRIT), ≈ incorporated company (US); **~ d'investissement à capital variable** ≈ investment trust (BRIT), ≈ mutual fund (US); **~ à responsabilité limitée** type of limited liability company (with non-negotiable shares); **~ savante** learned society; **~ de services** service company

socioculturel, le [sɔsjokyltyʀɛl] ADJ sociocultural

socio-économique [sɔsjoekɔnɔmik] ADJ socio-economic

socio-éducatif, -ive [sɔsjoedykatif, -iv] ADJ socio-educational

sociolinguistique [sɔsjolɛ̃ɡɥistik] ADJ sociolinguistic

sociologie [sɔsjɔlɔʒi] NF sociology

sociologique [sɔsjɔlɔʒik] ADJ sociological

sociologue [sɔsjɔlɔɡ] NMF sociologist

socio-professionnel, le [sɔsjopʀɔfesjɔnɛl] ADJ socioprofessional

socle [sɔkl] NM (de colonne, statue) plinth, pedestal; (de lampe) base

socquette [sɔkɛt] NF ankle sock

socratique [sɔkʀatik] ADJ (tradition) Socratic

soda [sɔda] NM (boisson) fizzy drink, soda (US)

sodium [sɔdjɔm] NM sodium

sodomie [sɔdɔmi] NF sodomy; buggery

sodomiser [sɔdɔmize] /1/ VT to sodomize; to bugger

sœur [sœʀ] NF sister; (religieuse) nun, sister; **~ Élisabeth** (Rel) Sister Elizabeth; **~ de lait** foster sister

sofa [sɔfa] NM sofa

Sofia [sɔfja] N Sofia

SOFRES [sɔfʀɛs] SIGLE F (= Société française d'enquête par sondage) company which conducts opinion polls

soi [swa] PRON oneself; **en ~** (intrinsèquement) in itself; **cela va de ~ that** ou it goes without saying, it stands to reason

soi-disant [swadizã] ADJ INV so-called ▶ ADV supposedly

★**soie** [swa] NF silk; (de porc, sanglier: poil) bristle

soient [swa] VB voir être

soierie [swaʀi] NF (industrie) silk trade; (tissu) silk

★**soif** [swaf] NF thirst; (fig): **~ de** thirst ou craving for; **avoir ~** to be thirsty; **donner ~ à qn** to make sb thirsty

soignant, e [swaɲã, -ãt] ADJ: **le personnel ~** the nursing staff; voir aussi **aide-soignant**

soigné, e [swaɲe] ADJ (tenue) well-groomed, neat; (travail) careful, meticulous; (fam) whopping; stiff

★**soigner** [swaɲe] /1/ VT (malade, maladie: docteur) to treat; (: infirmière, mère) to nurse, look after; (blessé) to tend; (travail, détails) to take care over; (jardin, chevelure, invités) to look after ■ **se soigner** VPR: **soigne-toi bien !** take good care of yourself!

soigneur [swaɲœʀ] NM (Cyclisme, Football) trainer; (Boxe) second

soigneusement [swaɲøzmã] ADV carefully

soigneux, -euse [swaɲø, -øz] ADJ (propre) tidy, neat; (méticuleux) painstaking, careful; **~ de** careful with

soi-même [swamɛm] PRON oneself

★**soin** [swɛ̃] NM (application) care; (propreté, ordre) tidiness, neatness; (responsabilité): **le ~ de qch** the care of sth; **avoir** ou **prendre ~ de** to take care of, look after; **avoir** ou **prendre ~ de faire** to take care to do; **faire qch avec (grand) ~** to do sth (very) carefully; **sans ~** adj careless; untidy ■ **soins** NMPL (à un malade, blessé) treatment sg, medical attention sg; (attentions, prévenance) care and attention sg; (hygiène) care sg; **soins de la chevelure/de beauté** hair/skin care; **soins du corps/ménage** body care/housekeeping, running a home; **les premiers soins** first aid sg; **aux bons soins de** c/o, care of; **être aux petits soins pour qn** to wait on sb hand and foot, see to sb's every need; **confier qn aux soins de qn** to hand sb over to sb's care

★**soir** [swaʀ] NM, ADV evening; **le ~** in the evening(s); **ce ~** this evening, tonight; **à ce ~ !** see you this evening (ou tonight)!; **la veille au ~** the previous evening; **sept/dix heures du ~** seven in the evening/ten at night; **le repas/journal du ~** the evening meal/newspaper; **dimanche ~** Sunday evening; **hier ~** yesterday evening; **demain ~** tomorrow evening, tomorrow night

soirée [swaʀe] NF evening; (réception) party; **donner en ~** (film, pièce) to give an evening performance of

soit [swa] VB voir être ▶ CONJ (à savoir) namely, to wit; (ou): **~ ... ~** either ... or; **~ que ... ~ que** ou **ou que** whether ... or whether ▶ ADV so be it, very well; **~ un triangle ABC** let ABC be a triangle

soixantaine [swasãtɛn] NF: **une ~ (de)** sixty or so, about sixty; **avoir la ~** (âge) to be around sixty

★**soixante** [swasãt] NUM sixty

soixante-dix [swasãtdis] NUM seventy

soixante-dixième [swasãtdizjɛm] NUM seventieth

soixante-huitard, e [swazãtɥitaʀ, -aʀd] ADJ relating to the demonstrations of May 1968 ▶ NM/F participant in the demonstrations of May 1968

soixantième [swasãtjɛm] NUM sixtieth

soja [sɔʒa] NM soya; (graines) soya beans pl; **germes de ~** beansprouts

★**sol** [sɔl] NM ground; (de logement) floor; (revêtement) flooring no pl; (territoire, Agr, Géo) soil; (Mus) G; (: en chantant la gamme) so(h)

solaire [sɔlɛʀ] ADJ (énergie etc) solar; (crème etc) sun cpd

solarium [sɔlaʀjɔm] NM solarium

★**soldat** [sɔlda] NM soldier; **S~ inconnu** Unknown Warrior ou Soldier; **~ de plomb** tin ou toy soldier

soldatesque [sɔldatɛsk] NF rabble of soldiers

★**solde** [sɔld] NF (Mil) pay; **à la ~ de qn** (péj) in sb's pay ▶ NM (Comm) balance; **~ créditeur/débiteur** credit/debit balance; **~ à payer** balance outstanding; **en** ~ at sale price ■ **soldes** NMPL (*Comm*) sales; (*articles*) sale goods

solder [sɔlde] /**1**/ VT (*compte*) to settle; (*marchandise*) to sell at sale price, sell off; **se ~ par** (*fig*) to end in; **article soldé (à) 10 euros** item reduced to 10 euros

soldeur, -euse [sɔldœʀ, -øz] NM/F (*Comm*) discounter

sole [sɔl] NF sole *inv* (*fish*)

★**soleil** [sɔlɛj] NM sun; (*lumière*) sun(light); (*temps ensoleillé*) sun(shine); (*feu d'artifice*) Catherine wheel; (*d'acrobate*) grand circle; (*Bot*) sunflower; **il y a** *ou* **il fait du** ~ it's sunny; **au** ~ in the sun; **en plein** ~ in full sun; **le** ~ **levant/couchant** the rising/setting sun; **le** ~ **de minuit** the midnight sun

solennel, le [sɔlanɛl] ADJ solemn; ceremonial

solennellement [sɔlanɛlmɑ̃] ADV solemnly

solennité [sɔlanite] NF (*d'une fête*) solemnity ■ **solennités** NFPL (*formalités*) formalities

solénoïde [sɔlenɔid] NM (*Élec*) solenoid

solfège [sɔlfɛʒ] NM music theory; (*exercices*) sight reading, sight singing

solfier [sɔlfje] /**7**/ VT: ~ **un morceau** to sing a piece using the sol-fa

soli [sɔli] NMPL *de* **solo**

solidaire [sɔlidɛʀ] ADJ: **être solidaires** (*personnes*) to show solidarity, stand *ou* stick together; (*pièces mécaniques*) interdependent; (*Jur: engagement*) binding on all parties; (: *débiteurs*) jointly liable; **être** ~ **de** (*collègues*) to stand by; (*mécanisme*) to be bound up with, be dependent on

solidairement [sɔlidɛʀmɑ̃] ADV jointly

solidariser [sɔlidaʀize] /**1**/: **se solidariser avec** VPR to show solidarity with

solidarité [sɔlidaʀite] NF (*entre personnes*) solidarity; (*de mécanisme, phénomènes*) interdependence; **par ~ (avec)** (*cesser le travail etc*) in sympathy (with)

solide [sɔlid] ADJ solid; (*mur, maison, meuble*) solid, sturdy; (*connaissances, argument*) sound; (*personne*) robust, sturdy; (*estomac*) strong; **avoir les reins solides** (*fig*) to be in a good financial position; to have sound financial backing ▶ NM solid

solidement [sɔlidmɑ̃] ADV solidly; (*fermement*) firmly

solidification [sɔlidifikasjɔ̃] NF solidification

solidifier [sɔlidifje] /**7**/ VT to solidify ■ **se solidifier** VPR to solidify

solidité [sɔlidite] NF solidity; sturdiness

soliloque [sɔlilɔk] NM soliloquy

soliste [sɔlist] NMF soloist

solitaire [sɔlitɛʀ] ADJ (*sans compagnie*) solitary, lonely; (*isolé*) solitary, isolated, lone; (*lieu*) lonely ▶ NMF (*ermite*) recluse; (*fig: ours*) loner ▶ NM (*diamant, jeu*) solitaire

solitude [sɔlityd] NF loneliness; (*paix*) solitude

solive [sɔliv] NF joist

sollicitations [sɔlisitasjɔ̃] NFPL (*requêtes*) entreaties, appeals; (*attractions*) enticements; (*Tech*) stress *sg*

solliciter [sɔlisite] /**1**/ VT (*personne*) to appeal to; (*emploi, faveur*) to seek; (*moteur*) to prompt; (*occupations, attractions etc*): ~ **qn** to appeal to sb's curiosity *etc*; to entice sb; to make demands on sb's time; ~ **qn de faire** to appeal to sb *ou* request sb to do

sollicitude [sɔlisityd] NF concern

solo [sɔlo] (*pl* **soli** [sɔli]) NM (*Mus*) solo

sol-sol [sɔlsɔl] ADJ INV surface-to-surface

solstice [sɔlstis] NM solstice; ~ **d'hiver/d'été** winter/summer solstice

solubilisé, e [sɔlybilize] ADJ soluble

solubilité [sɔlybilite] NF solubility

soluble [sɔlybl] ADJ (*sucre, cachet*) soluble; (*problème etc*) soluble, solvable

soluté [sɔlyte] NM solution

solution [sɔlysjɔ̃] NF solution; ~ **de continuité** gap, break; ~ **de facilité** easy way out

solutionner [sɔlysjɔne] /**1**/ VT to solve, find a solution for

solvabilité [sɔlvabilite] NF solvency

solvable [sɔlvabl] ADJ solvent

solvant [sɔlvɑ̃] NM solvent

Somalie [sɔmali] NF: **la** ~ Somalia

somalien, ne [sɔmaljɛ̃, -ɛn] ADJ Somalian

somatique [sɔmatik] ADJ somatic

sombre [sɔ̃bʀ] ADJ dark; (*fig*) sombre, gloomy; (*sinistre*) awful, dreadful

sombrer [sɔ̃bʀe] /**1**/ VI (*bateau*) to sink, go down; ~ **corps et biens** to go down with all hands; ~ **dans** (*misère, désespoir*) to sink into

sommaire [sɔmɛʀ] ADJ (*simple*) basic; (*expéditif*) summary; **exécution** ~ summary execution ▶ NM summary; **faire le** ~ **de** to make a summary of, summarize

sommairement [sɔmɛʀmɑ̃] ADV basically; summarily

sommation [sɔmasjɔ̃] NF (*Jur*) summons *sg*; (*avant de faire feu*) warning

somme [sɔm] NF (*Math*) sum; (*fig*) amount; (*argent*) sum, amount; **faire la** ~ **de** to add up; **en** ~, ~ **toute** *adv* all in all ▶ NM: **faire un** ~ to have a (short) nap

★**sommeil** [sɔmɛj] NM sleep; **avoir** ~ to be sleepy; **avoir le** ~ **léger** to be a light sleeper; **en** ~ (*fig*) dormant

sommeiller [sɔmeje] /**1**/ VI to doze; (*fig*) to lie dormant

sommelier [sɔməlje] NM wine waiter

sommer [sɔme] /**1**/ VT: ~ **qn de faire** to command *ou* order sb to do; (*Jur*) to summon sb to do

sommes [sɔm] VB *voir* **être**; *voir aussi* **somme**

★**sommet** [sɔmɛ] NM top; (*d'une montagne*) summit, top; (*fig: de la perfection, gloire*) height; (*Géom: d'angle*) vertex; (*conférence*) summit (conference); **atteindre des sommets** (*élégance*) to reach new heights; (*bêtise, égoïsme*) to reach new depths

sommier [sɔmje] NM bed base, bedspring (*US*); (*Admin: registre*) register; ~ **à ressorts** (interior sprung) divan base (*BRIT*), box spring (*US*); ~ **à lattes** slatted bed base *ou* bedspring (*US*)

sommité [sɔmite] NF prominent person, leading light

somnambule [sɔmnɑ̃byl] NMF sleepwalker

somnambulisme [sɔmnɑ̃bylism] NM sleepwalking

somnifère [sɔmnifɛʀ] NM sleeping drug; (*comprimé*) sleeping pill *ou* tablet

somnolence [sɔmnɔlɑ̃s] NF drowsiness

S

somnolent, e [sɔmnɔlã, -ãt] ADJ sleepy, drowsy

somnoler [sɔmnɔle] /1/ VI to doze

somptuaire [sɔ̃ptɥɛʀ] ADJ: **lois somptuaires** sumptuary laws; **dépenses somptuaires** extravagant expenditure *sg*

somptueusement [sɔ̃ptɥøzmã] ADV sumptuously

somptueux, -euse [sɔ̃ptɥø, -øz] ADJ sumptuous; *(cadeau)* lavish

somptuosité [sɔ̃ptɥozite] NF sumptuousness; *(d'un cadeau)* lavishness

★**son¹, sa** [sɔ̃, sa] *(pl* **ses** [se]*)* ADJ POSS *(antécédent humain: masculin)* his; *(: féminin)* her; *(: valeur indéfinie)* one's, his (her); *(: non humain)* its; *voir* **il**

son² [sɔ̃] NM *(son)* sound; *(de blé etc)* bran; **~ et lumière** *adj inv* son et lumière

sonar [sɔnaʀ] NM *(Navig)* sonar

sonate [sɔnat] NF sonata

★**sondage** [sɔ̃daʒ] NM *(de terrain)* boring, drilling; *(de mer, atmosphère)* sounding; probe; *(enquête)* survey, sounding out of opinion; **~ (d'opinion)** (opinion) poll

sonde [sɔ̃d] NF *(Navig)* lead *ou* sounding line; *(Météorologie)* sonde; *(Méd)* probe; catheter; *(: d'alimentation)* feeding tube; *(Tech)* borer, driller; *(: de forage, sondage)* drill; *(pour fouiller etc)* probe; **~ à avalanche** pole *(for probing snow and locating victims)*; **~ spatiale** probe

sonder [sɔ̃de] /1/ VT *(Navig)* to sound; *(atmosphère, plaie, bagages etc)* to probe; *(Tech)* to bore, drill; *(fig: personne)* to sound out; *(: opinion)* to probe; **le terrain** *(fig)* to see how the land lies

songe [sɔ̃ʒ] NM dream

songer [sɔ̃ʒe] /3/ VI to dream; **~ à** *(rêver à)* to think over, muse over; *(penser à)* to think of; *(envisager)* to contemplate, think of, consider; **~ que** to consider that; to think that

songerie [sɔ̃ʒʀi] NF reverie

songeur, -euse [sɔ̃ʒœʀ, -øz] ADJ pensive; **ça me laisse ~** that makes me wonder

sonnailles [sɔnaj] NFPL jingle of bells

sonnant, e [sɔnã, -ãt] ADJ: **en espèces sonnantes et trébuchantes** in coin of the realm; **à huit heures sonnantes** on the stroke of eight

sonné, e [sɔne] ADJ *(fam)* cracked; *(passé)*: **il est midi ~** it's gone twelve; **il a quarante ans bien sonnés** he's well into his forties

★**sonner** [sɔne] /1/ VI *(retentir)* to ring; *(donner une impression)* to sound; **~ bien/mal/creux** to sound good/bad/hollow; **~ faux** *(instrument)* to sound out of tune; *(rire)* to ring false; **minuit vient de ~** midnight has just struck; **~ chez qn** to ring sb's doorbell, ring at sb's door ▶ VT *(cloche)* to ring; *(glas, tocsin)* to sound; *(portier, infirmière)* to ring for; *(messe)* to ring the bell for; *(fam: choc, coup)* to knock out; **~ du clairon** to sound the bugle; **~ les heures** to strike the hours

sonnerie [sɔnʀi] NF *(son)* ringing; *(sonnette)* bell; *(mécanisme d'horloge)* striking mechanism; *(de portable)* ringtone; **~ d'alarme** alarm bell; **~ de clairon** bugle call

sonnet [sɔnɛ] NM sonnet

sonnette [sɔnɛt] NF bell; **~ d'alarme** alarm bell; **~ de nuit** night-bell

sono [sɔno] NF *(= sonorisation)* PA (system); *(d'une discothèque)* sound system

sonore [sɔnɔʀ] ADJ *(voix)* sonorous, ringing; *(salle, métal)* resonant; *(ondes, film, signal)* sound *cpd*; *(Ling)* voiced; **effets sonores** sound effects

sonorisation [sɔnɔʀizasjɔ̃] NF *(équipement: de salle de conférences)* public address system, PA system; *(: de discothèque)* sound system

sonoriser [sɔnɔʀize] /1/ VT *(film, spectacle)* to add the sound track to; *(salle)* to fit with a public address system

sonorité [sɔnɔʀite] NF *(de piano, violon)* tone; *(de voix, mot)* sonority; *(d'une salle)* resonance, acoustics *pl*

sonothèque [sɔnɔtɛk] NF sound library

sont [sɔ̃] VB *voir* **être**

sophisme [sɔfism] NM sophism

sophiste [sɔfist] NMF sophist

sophistication [sɔfistikasjɔ̃] NF sophistication

sophistiqué, e [sɔfistike] ADJ sophisticated

sophrologie [sɔfʀɔlɔʒi] NF sophrology

soporifique [sɔpɔʀifik] ADJ soporific

soprano [sɔpʀano] NMF soprano

sorbet [sɔʀbɛ] NM water ice, sorbet

sorbetière [sɔʀbətjɛʀ] NF ice-cream maker

sorbier [sɔʀbje] NM service tree

sorcellerie [sɔʀsɛlʀi] NF witchcraft *no pl*, sorcery *no pl*

sorcier, -ière [sɔʀsje, -jɛʀ] NM/F wizard, sorcerer *(witch ou sorceress)* ▶ ADJ: **ce n'est pas ~** *(fam)* it's not rocket science

sordide [sɔʀdid] ADJ *(lieu)* squalid; *(action)* sordid

sorgho [sɔʀgo] NM sorghum

Sorlingues [sɔʀlɛ̃g] NFPL: **les (îles) ~** the Scilly Isles, the Isles of Scilly, the Scillies

sornettes [sɔʀnɛt] NFPL twaddle *sg*

sort [sɔʀ] VB *voir* **sortir** ▶ NM *(fortune, destinée)* fate; *(condition, situation)* lot; *(magique)*: **jeter un ~** to cast a spell; **un coup du ~** a blow dealt by fate; **le ~ en est jeté** the die is cast; **tirer au ~** to draw lots; **tirer qch au ~** to draw lots for sth

sortable [sɔʀtabl] ADJ: **il n'est pas ~** you can't take him anywhere

sortant, e [sɔʀtã, -ãt] VB *voir* **sortir** ▶ ADJ *(numéro)* which comes up *(in a draw etc)*; *(député, président)* outgoing

★**sorte** [sɔʀt] VB *voir* **sortir** ▶ NF sort, kind; **une ~ de** a sort of; **de la ~** *adv* in that way; **en quelque ~** in a way; **de ~ à** so as to, in order to; **de (telle) ~ que**, **en ~ que** *(de manière que)* so that; *(si bien que)* so much so that; **faire en ~ que** to see to it that

★**sortie** [sɔʀti] NF *(issue)* way out, exit; *(Mil)* sortie; *(fig: verbale)* outburst; *(: parole incongrue)* odd remark; *(d'un gaz, de l'eau)* outlet; *(promenade)* outing; *(le soir: au restaurant etc)* night out; *(de produits)* export; *(de capitaux)* outflow; *(Inform)* output; *(d'imprimante)* printout; *(Comm: d'un disque)* release; *(: d'un livre)* publication; *(: d'un modèle)* launch; **à sa ~** as he *(ou* she) went out *ou* left; **à la ~ de ce nouveau modèle** when this new model comes *(ou* came) out, when they bring *(ou* brought) out this new model; **à la ~ de l'école/l'usine** *(moment)* after school/work; when school/the factory comes out; (*lieu*) at the school/factory gates; **~ de bain** (*vêtement*) bathrobe; **« ~ de camions »** "vehicle exit"; **~ papier** hard copy; **~ de secours** emergency exit ■ **sorties** NFPL (*Comm: somme*) items of expenditure; outgoings

sortilège [sɔʀtilɛʒ] NM (magic) spell

★**sortir** [sɔʀtiʀ] /**16**/ VI (*gén*) to come out; (*partir, se promener, aller au spectacle etc*) to go out; (*bourgeon, plante, numéro gagnant*) to come up; **~ avec qn** to be going out with sb; **~ de** (*gén*) to go out of; to go (*ou* come) out of, leave; (*rainure etc*) to come out of; (*maladie*) to get over; (*époque*) to get through; (*cadre, compétence*) to be outside; (*provenir de: famille etc*) to come from; **~ de table** to leave the table; **~ du système** (*Inform*) to log out; **~ de ses gonds** (*fig*) to fly off the handle ▸ VT (*gén*) to take out; (*produit, ouvrage, modèle*) to bring out; (*fam: dire: boniments, incongruités*) to come out with; (*Inform*) to output; (: *sur papier*) to print out; (*fam: expulser*) to throw out; **~ qch de** to take sth out of; **~ qn d'embarras** to get sb out of trouble ▸ NM: **au ~ de l'hiver/l'enfance** as winter/childhood nears its end ■ **se sortir de** VPR (*affaire, situation*) to get out of; **s'en ~** (*malade*) to pull through; (*d'une difficulté etc*) to come through all right; to get through, be able to manage

SOS SIGLE M mayday, SOS

sosie [sɔzi] NM double

sot, sotte [so, sɔt] ADJ silly, foolish ▸ NM/F fool

sottement [sɔtmɑ̃] ADV foolishly

sottise [sɔtiz] NF silliness *no pl*, foolishness *no pl*; (*propos, acte*) silly *ou* foolish thing (to do *ou* say)

sou [su] NM: **près de ses sous** tight-fisted; **sans le ~** penniless; **~ à ~** penny by penny; **pas un ~ de bon sens** not a scrap *ou* an ounce of good sense; **de quatre sous** worthless

souahéli [swaeli] NM (*Ling*) Swahili

soubassement [subɑsmɑ̃] NM base

soubresaut [subʀəso] NM (*de peur etc*) start; (*cahot: d'un véhicule*) jolt

soubrette [subʀɛt] NF soubrette, maidservant

souche [suʃ] NF (*d'arbre*) stump; (*de carnet*) counterfoil (BRIT), stub; **dormir comme une ~** to sleep like a log; **de vieille ~** of old stock

★**souci** [susi] NM (*inquiétude*) worry; (*préoccupation*) concern; (*Bot*) marigold; **se faire du ~** to worry; **avoir (le) ~ de** to have concern for; **par ~ de** for the sake of, out of concern for

soucier [susje] /**7**/: **se soucier de** VPR to care about

soucieux, -euse [susjø, -øz] ADJ concerned, worried; **~ de** concerned about; **peu ~ de/que** caring little about/whether

soucoupe [sukup] NF saucer; **~ volante** flying saucer

★**soudain, e** [sudɛ̃, -ɛn] ADJ (*douleur, mort*) sudden ▸ ADV suddenly, all of a sudden

soudainement [sudɛnmɑ̃] ADV suddenly

soudaineté [sudɛnte] NF suddenness

Soudan [sudɑ̃] NM: **le ~** Sudan; **le ~ du Sud** South Sudan

soudanais, e [sudanɛ, -ɛz] ADJ Sudanese

soude [sud] NF soda

soudé, e [sude] ADJ (*fig: pétales, organes*) joined (together)

souder [sude] /**1**/ VT (*avec fil à souder*) to solder; (*par soudure autogène*) to weld; (*fig*) to bind *ou* knit together; to fuse (together) ■ **se souder** VPR (*os*) to knit (together)

soudeur, -euse [sudœʀ, -øz] NM/F (*ouvrier*) welder

soudoyer [sudwaje] /**8**/ VT (*péj*) to bribe, buy over

soudure [sudyʀ] NF soldering; welding; (*joint*) soldered joint; weld; **faire la ~** (*Comm*) to fill a gap; (*fig: assurer une transition*) to bridge the gap

souffert, e [sufɛʀ, -ɛʀt] PP *de* **souffrir**

soufflage [suflaʒ] NM (*du verre*) glass-blowing

souffle [sufl] NM (*en expirant*) breath; (*en soufflant*) puff, blow; (*respiration*) breathing; (*d'explosion, de ventilateur*) blast; (*du vent*) blowing; (*fig*) inspiration; **retenir son ~** to hold one's breath; **avoir du/manquer de ~** to have a lot of puff/be short of breath; **être à bout de ~** to be out of breath; **avoir le ~ court** to be short-winded; **un ~ d'air** *ou* **de vent** a breath of air, a puff of wind; **~ au cœur** (*Méd*) heart murmur

soufflé, e [sufle] ADJ (*Culin*) soufflé; (*fam: ahuri, stupéfié*) staggered ▸ NM (*Culin*) soufflé

★**souffler** [sufle] /**1**/ VI (*gén*) to blow; (*haleter*) to puff (and blow); **laisser ~ qn** (*fig*) to give sb a breather ▸ VT (*feu, bougie*) to blow out; (*chasser: poussière etc*) to blow away; (*Tech: verre*) to blow; (*explosion*) to destroy (with its blast); (*dire*): **~ qch à qn** to whisper sth to sb; (*fam: voler*): **~ qch à qn** to pinch sth from sb; **~ son rôle à qn** to prompt sb; **ne pas ~ mot** not to breathe a word

soufflerie [sufləʀi] NF (*Tech, Science*) wind tunnel; (*d'orgue*) bellows *pl*; **essai en ~** wind tunnel tests

soufflet [suflɛ] NM (*pour attiser*) bellows *pl*; (*entre wagons*) vestibule; (*Couture*) gusset; (*gifle: liter*) slap (in the face)

souffleur, -euse [suflœʀ, -øz] NM/F (*Théât*) prompter; (*Tech*) glass-blower

souffrance [sufʀɑ̃s] NF suffering; **en ~** (*marchandise*) awaiting delivery; (*affaire*) pending

souffrant, e [sufʀɑ̃, -ɑ̃t] ADJ unwell

souffre-douleur [sufʀədulœʀ] NM INV whipping boy (BRIT), butt, underdog

souffreteux, -euse [sufʀətø, -øz] ADJ sickly

souffrir [sufʀiʀ] /**18**/ VI to suffer; (*éprouver des douleurs*) to be in pain; **~ de** (*maladie, froid*) to suffer from; **~ des dents** to have trouble with one's teeth; **faire ~ qn** (*personne*) to make sb suffer (: *dents, blessure etc*) to hurt sb ▸ VT to suffer, endure; (*supporter*) to bear, stand; (*admettre: exception etc*) to allow *ou* admit of; **ne pas pouvoir ~ qch/que ...** not to be able to endure *ou* bear sth/that ...; **ne ~ aucune exception** to suffer no exception; **elle ne peut pas le ~** she can't stand *ou* bear him

soufisme [sufism] NM Sufism

soufre [sufʀ] NM sulphur (BRIT), sulfur (US)

soufrer [sufʀe] /**1**/ VT (*vignes*) to treat with sulphur (BRIT) *ou* sulfur (US)

souhait [swɛ] NM wish; **tous nos souhaits de** good wishes *ou* our best wishes for; **tous nos souhaits pour la nouvelle année** (our) best wishes for the New Year; **riche** *etc* **à ~** as rich *etc* as one could wish; **à vos souhaits !** bless you!

souhaitable [swɛtabl] ADJ desirable

souhaiter [swete] /1/ VT to wish for; **~ le bonjour à qn** to bid sb good day; **~ la bonne année à qn** to wish sb a happy New Year; **~ que** to hope that; **il est à ~ que** it is to be hoped that

souiller [suje] /1/ VT to dirty, soil; (fig) to sully, tarnish

souillure [sujyʀ] NF stain

soûl, e [su, sul] ADJ drunk; **~ de musique/plaisirs** (fig) drunk with music/pleasure ▶ NM: **tout son ~** to one's heart's content

soulagement [sulaʒmã] NM relief

soulager [sulaʒe] /3/ VT to relieve; **~ qn de** to relieve sb of

soûler [sule] /1/ VT: **~ qn** to get sb drunk; (boisson) to make sb drunk; (fig) to make sb's head spin ou reel ▪ **se soûler** VPR to get drunk; **se ~ de** (fig) to intoxicate o.s. with

soûlerie [sulʀi] NF (péj) drunken binge

soulèvement [sulɛvmã] NM uprising; (Géo) upthrust

★**soulever** [sul(ə)ve] /5/ VT to lift; (vagues, poussière) to send up; (peuple) to stir up (to revolt); (enthousiasme) to arouse; (question, débat, protestations, difficultés) to raise; **cela me soulève le cœur** it makes me feel sick ▪ **se soulever** VPR (peuple) to rise up; (personne couchée) to lift o.s. up; (couvercle etc) to lift

soulier [sulje] NM shoe; **souliers bas** low-heeled shoes; **souliers plats/à talons** flat/heeled shoes

★**souligner** [suliɲe] /1/ VT to underline; (fig) to emphasize, stress

soumettre [sumɛtʀ] /56/ VT (pays) to subject, subjugate; (rebelles) to put down, subdue; **~ qn/qch à** to subject sb/sth to; **~ qch à qn** (projet etc) to submit sth to sb; **se ~ (à)** (se rendre, obéir) to submit (to); **se ~ à** (formalités etc) to submit to; (régime etc) to submit o.s. to

soumis, e [sumi, -iz] PP de **soumettre** ▶ ADJ submissive; **revenus ~ à l'impôt** taxable income

soumission [sumisjɔ̃] NF (voir se soumettre) submission; (docilité) submissiveness; (Comm) tender

soumissionner [sumisjɔne] /1/ VT (Comm: travaux) to bid for, tender for

soupape [supap] NF valve; **~ de sûreté** safety valve

soupçon [supsɔ̃] NM suspicion; (petite quantité): **un ~ de** a hint ou touch of; **avoir ~ de** to suspect; **au dessus de tout ~** above (all) suspicion

soupçonner [supsɔne] /1/ VT to suspect; **~ qn de qch/d'être** to suspect sb of sth/of being

soupçonneux, -euse [supsɔnø, -øz] ADJ suspicious

★**soupe** [sup] NF soup; **~ au lait** adj inv quick-tempered; **~ à l'oignon/de poisson** onion/fish soup; **~ populaire** soup kitchen

soupente [supãt] NF (mansarde) attic; (placard) cupboard (BRIT) ou closet (US) under the stairs

souper [supe] /1/ VI to have supper; **avoir soupé de** (fam) to be sick and tired of ▶ NM supper

soupeser [supəze] /5/ VT to weigh in one's hand(s), feel the weight of; (fig) to weigh up

soupière [supjɛʀ] NF (soup) tureen

soupir [supiʀ] NM sigh; (Mus) crotchet rest (BRIT), quarter note rest (US); **rendre le dernier ~** to breathe one's last; **pousser un ~ de soulagement** to heave a sigh of relief

soupirail, -aux [supiʀaj, -o] NM (small) basement window

soupirant [supiʀã] NM (péj) suitor, wooer

soupirer [supiʀe] /1/ VI to sigh; **~ après qch** to yearn for sth

souple [supl] ADJ supple; (fam) soft; (fig: règlement, caractère) flexible; (: démarche, taille) lithe, supple

souplesse [suplɛs] NF suppleness; (de caractère) flexibility

souquer [suke] VI to pull hard at the oars

sourate [suʀat] NF (de Coran) sura

source [suʀs] NF (point d'eau) spring; (d'un cours d'eau, fig) source; **prendre sa ~ à/dans** (cours d'eau) to have its source at/in; **tenir qch de bonne ~/de ~ sûre** to have sth on good authority/from a reliable source; **~ thermale/d'eau minérale** hot ou thermal/mineral spring

sourcier, -ière [suʀsje, -jɛʀ] NM/F water diviner

sourcil [suʀsij] NM (eye)brow

sourcilière [suʀsiljɛʀ] ADJ F voir **arcade**

sourciller [suʀsije] /1/ VI: **sans ~** without turning a hair ou batting an eyelid

sourcilleux, -euse [suʀsijø, -øz] ADJ (hautain, sévère) haughty, supercilious; (pointilleux) finicky, pernickety

★**sourd, e** [suʀ, suʀd] ADJ deaf; (bruit, voix) muffled; (couleur) muted; (douleur) dull; (lutte) silent, hidden; (Ling) voiceless; **être ~ à** to be deaf to; **faire la sourde oreille** to turn a deaf ear ▶ NM/F deaf person

sourdement [suʀdəmã] ADV (avec un bruit sourd) dully; (secrètement) silently

sourdine [suʀdin] NF (Mus) mute; **en ~** adv softly, quietly; **mettre une ~ à** (fig) to tone down

sourd-muet, sourde-muette [suʀmyɛ, suʀdmyɛt] ADJ with a speech and hearing impairment

sourdre [suʀdʀ] VI (eau) to spring up; (fig) to rise

souriant, e [suʀjã, -ãt] VB voir **sourire** ▶ ADJ cheerful

souricière [suʀisjɛʀ] NF mousetrap; (fig) trap

sourie etc [suʀi] VB voir **sourire**

★**sourire** [suʀiʀ] /36/ NM smile; **faire un ~ à qn** to give sb a smile; **garder le ~** to keep smiling ▶ VI to smile; **~ à qn** to smile at sb; (fig: plaire à) to appeal to sb (: chance) to smile on sb

★**souris** [suʀi] NF (aussi Inform) mouse

sournois, e [suʀnwa, -waz] ADJ deceitful, underhand

sournoisement [suʀnwazmã] ADV deceitfully

sournoiserie [suʀnwazʀi] NF deceitfulness, underhandedness

★**sous** [su] PRÉP (gén) under; **~ la pluie/le soleil** in the rain/sunshine; **~ mes yeux** before my eyes; **~ terre** adj, adv underground; **~ l'influence/l'action de** under the influence of/by the action of; **~ antibiotiques/perfusion** on antibiotics/a drip (BRIT) ou an IV (US); **~ cet angle/ce rapport** from this angle/in this respect; **~ vide** adj, adv vacuum-packed; **~ peu** adv shortly, before long

★**sous...** [su, (+vowel) suz] PRÉFIXE sub-; under...

sous-alimentation [suzalimãtasjɔ̃] NF undernourishment

sous-alimenté, e [suzalimɑ̃te] ADJ undernourished

sous-bois [subwa] NM INV undergrowth

sous-catégorie [sukategɔʀi] NF subcategory

sous-chef [suʃɛf] NM deputy chief, second in command; **~ de bureau** deputy head clerk

sous-comité [sukɔmite] NM subcommittee

sous-commission [sukɔmisjɔ̃] NF subcommittee

sous-continent [sukɔ̃tinɑ̃] NM subcontinent

sous-couche [sukuʃ] NF (*de peinture*) undercoat

souscripteur, -trice [suskʀiptœʀ, -tʀis] NM/F subscriber

souscription [suskʀipsjɔ̃] NF subscription; **offert en ~** available on subscription

souscrire [suskʀiʀ] /**39**/: **~ à** vt to subscribe to

sous-cutané, e [sukytane] ADJ subcutaneous

sous-développé, e [sudevlɔpe] ADJ underdeveloped

sous-développement [sudevlɔpmɑ̃] NM underdevelopment

sous-directeur, -trice [sudiʀɛktœʀ, -tʀis] NM/F assistant manager

sous-effectif [suzefɛktif] NM understaffing; **être en ~** to be understaffed

sous-emploi [suzɑ̃plwa] NM underemployment

sous-employé, e [suzɑ̃plwaje] ADJ underemployed

sous-ensemble [suzɑ̃sɑ̃bl] NM subset

sous-entendre [suzɑ̃tɑ̃dʀ] /**41**/ VT to imply, infer

sous-entendu, e [suzɑ̃tɑ̃dy] ADJ implied; (*Ling*) understood ▸ NM innuendo, insinuation

sous-équipé, e [suzekipe] ADJ under-equipped; **~ en infrastructures industrielles** (*Écon: pays, région*) with an insufficient industrial infrastructure

sous-estimer [suzɛstime] /**1**/ VT to underestimate

sous-exploiter [suzɛksplwate] /**1**/ VT to underexploit

sous-exposer [suzɛkspoze] /**1**/ VT to underexpose

sous-fifre [sufifʀ] NM (*péj*) underling

sous-gonflage [sugɔ̃flaʒ] NM (*de pneu*) under-inflation

sous-groupe [sugʀup] NM subgroup

sous-homme [suzɔm] NM sub-human

sous-investissement [suzɛ̃vɛstismɑ̃] NM underinvestment

sous-jacent, e [suʒasɑ̃, -ɑ̃t] ADJ underlying

sous-lieutenant [suljøtnɑ̃] NM sub-lieutenant

sous-locataire [sulɔkatɛʀ] NMF subtenant

sous-location [sulɔkasjɔ̃] NF subletting

sous-louer [sulwe] /**1**/ VT to sublet

sous-main [sumɛ̃] NM desk blotter; **en ~** adv secretly

sous-marin, e [sumaʀɛ̃, -in] ADJ (*flore, volcan*) submarine; (*navigation, pêche, explosif*) underwater ▸ NM submarine

sous-médicalisé, e [sumedikalize] ADJ lacking adequate medical care

sous-nappe [sunap] NF undercloth

sous-officier [suzɔfisje] NM ≈ non-commissioned officer (NCO)

sous-ordre [suzɔʀdʀ] NM subordinate; **créancier en ~** creditor's creditor

sous-payé, e [supeje] ADJ underpaid

sous-préfecture [supʀefɛktyʀ] NF sub-prefecture

sous-préfet [supʀefɛ] NM sub-prefect

sous-production [supʀɔdyksjɔ̃] NF underproduction

sous-produit [supʀɔdɥi] NM by-product; (*fig: péj*) pale imitation

sous-programme [supʀɔgʀam] NM (*Inform*) sub-routine

sous-pull [supul] NM thin polo-neck sweater *ou* jumper

sous-secrétaire [susəkʀetɛʀ] NM: **~ d'État** Under-Secretary of State

soussigné, e [susiɲe] ADJ: **je ~** I the undersigned

★**sous-sol** [susɔl] NM basement; (*Géo*) subsoil

sous-tasse [sutas] NF saucer

sous-tendre [sutɑ̃dʀ] /**41**/ VT to underlie

★**sous-titre** [sutitʀ] NM subtitle

★**sous-titré, e** [sutitʀe] ADJ with subtitles

soustraction [sustʀaksjɔ̃] NF subtraction

soustraire [sustʀɛʀ] /**50**/ VT to subtract, take away; (*dérober*): **~ qch à qn** to remove sth from sb; **~ qn à** (*danger*) to shield sb from; **se ~ à** (*autorité, obligation, devoir*) to elude, escape from

sous-traitance [sutʀɛtɑ̃s] NF subcontracting

sous-traitant [sutʀɛtɑ̃] NM subcontractor

sous-traiter [sutʀete] /**1**/ VT, VI to subcontract

soustrayais etc [sustʀeje] VB voir **soustraire**

sous-verre [suvɛʀ] NM INV glass mount

sous-vêtement [suvɛtmɑ̃] NM undergarment, item of underwear ▪ **sous-vêtements** NMPL underwear sg

soutane [sutan] NF cassock, soutane

soute [sut] NF hold; **~ à bagages** baggage hold

soutenable [sut(ə)nabl] ADJ (*opinion*) tenable, defensible

soutenance [sut(ə)nɑ̃s] NF: **~ de thèse** ≈ viva (voce) (*Brit*), defense (*US*)

soutènement [sutɛnmɑ̃] NM: **mur de ~** retaining wall

souteneur [sut(ə)nœʀ] NM procurer

soutenir [sut(ə)niʀ] /**22**/ VT to support; (*assaut, choc, regard*) to stand up to, withstand; (*intérêt, effort*) to keep up; (*assurer*): **~ que** to maintain that; **~ la comparaison avec** to bear *ou* stand comparison with; **~ le regard de qn** to be able to look sb in the face ▪ **se soutenir** VPR (*dans l'eau etc*) to hold o.s. up; (*être soutenable: point de vue*) to be tenable; (*s'aider mutuellement*) to stand by each other

soutenu, e [sut(ə)ny] PP de **soutenir** ▸ ADJ (*efforts*) sustained, unflagging; (*style*) elevated; (*couleur*) strong

★**souterrain, e** [sutɛʀɛ̃, -ɛn] ADJ underground; (*fig*) subterranean ▸ NM underground passage

soutien [sutjɛ̃] NM support; **apporter son ~ à** to lend one's support to; **~ de famille** breadwinner

soutiendrai etc [sutjɛ̃dʀe] VB voir **soutenir**

★**soutien-gorge** [sutjɛ̃gɔʀʒ] (*pl* **soutiens-gorge**) NM bra; (*de maillot de bain*) top

soutiens [sutjɛ̃], **soutint** etc [sutɛ̃] VB voir **soutenir**

419

soutif [sutif] NM (*fam: soutien-gorge*) bra

soutirer [sutiʀe] /1/ VT: ~ **qch à qn** to squeeze *ou* get sth out of sb

souvenance [suv(ə)nɑ̃s] NF: **avoir ~ de** to recollect

★**souvenir** [suv(ə)niʀ] /22/ NM (*réminiscence*) memory; (*cadeau*) souvenir, keepsake; (*de voyage*) souvenir; **garder le ~ de** to retain the memory of; **en ~ de** in memory *ou* remembrance of; **avec mes affectueux/meilleurs souvenirs, ...** with love from, .../regards, ... ■ **se souvenir** VPR: **se ~ de** to remember; **se ~ que** to remember that

★**souvent** [suvɑ̃] ADV often; **peu ~** seldom, infrequently; **le plus ~** more often than not, most often

souvenu, e [suvəny] PP = **se souvenir**

souverain, e [suv(ə)ʀɛ̃, -ɛn] ADJ sovereign; (*fig: mépris*) supreme ▶ NM/F sovereign, monarch

souverainement [suv(ə)ʀɛnmɑ̃] ADV (*sans appel*) with sovereign power; (*extrêmement*) supremely, intensely

souveraineté [suv(ə)ʀɛnte] NF sovereignty

souverainiste [suv(ə)ʀenist] NMF (*Pol*) partisan of sovereignty; (*au Québec*) partisan of Quebec sovereignty

souviendrai [suvjɛ̃dʀe], **souviens** [suvjɛ̃], **souvint** *etc* [suvɛ̃] VB *voir* **souvenir**

soviétique [sɔvjetik] (*Hist*) ADJ Soviet ▶ NMF: **Soviétique** Soviet citizen

soviétologue [sɔvjetɔlɔg] NMF Kremlinologist

soyeux, -euse [swajø, -øz] ADJ silky

soyez *etc* [swaje] VB *voir* **être**

soyons *etc* [swajɔ̃] VB *voir* **être**

SPA SIGLE F (= *Société protectrice des animaux*) ≈ RSPCA (BRIT), ≈ SPCA (US)

★**spacieux, -euse** [spasjø, -øz] ADJ spacious; roomy

spaciosité [spasjozite] NF spaciousness

★**spaghettis** [spageti] NMPL spaghetti *sg*

spammer [spame] VT, VI (*Inform*) to spam

sparadrap [spaʀadʀa] NM adhesive *ou* sticking (BRIT) plaster, bandaid® (US)

Sparte [spaʀt] NF Sparta

spartiate [spaʀsjat] ADJ Spartan ■ **spartiates** NFPL (*sandales*) gladiator sandals

spasme [spazm] NM spasm

spasmodique [spazmɔdik] ADJ spasmodic

spasmophilie [spasmɔfili] NF spasmophilia

spatial, e, -aux [spasjal, -o] ADJ (*Aviat*) space *cpd*; (*Psych*) spatial

spationaute [spasjonot] NMF astronaut

spatule [spatyl] NF (*ustensile*) slice; spatula; (*bout*) tip

speaker, ine [spikœʀ, -kʀin] NM/F announcer

spécial, e, -aux [spesjal, -o] ADJ special; (*bizarre*) peculiar

spécialement [spesjalmɑ̃] ADV especially, particularly; (*tout exprès*) specially; **pas ~** not particularly

spécialisation [spesjalizasjɔ̃] NF specialization

spécialisé, e [spesjalize] ADJ specialized; **ordinateur ~** dedicated computer

spécialiser [spesjalize] /1/: **se spécialiser** VPR to specialize

spécialiste [spesjalist] NMF specialist

spécialité [spesjalite] NF speciality; (*Scol*) special field; **~ pharmaceutique** patent medicine

spécieux, -euse [spesjø, -øz] ADJ specious

spécification [spesifikasjɔ̃] NF specification

spécificité [spesifisite] NF specificity

spécifier [spesifje] /7/ VT to specify, state

spécifique [spesifik] ADJ specific

spécifiquement [spesifikmɑ̃] ADV (*typiquement*) typically; (*tout exprès*) specifically

spécimen [spesimɛn] NM specimen; (*revue etc*) specimen *ou* sample copy

★**spectacle** [spɛktakl] NM (*tableau, scène*) sight; (*représentation*) show; (*industrie*) show business, entertainment; **se donner en ~** (*péj*) to make a spectacle *ou* an exhibition of o.s.; **pièce/revue à grand ~** spectacular (play/revue); **au ~ de ...** at the sight of ...

spectaculaire [spɛktakylɛʀ] ADJ spectacular

spectateur, -trice [spɛktatœʀ, -tʀis] NM/F (*Ciné etc*) member of the audience; (*Sport*) spectator; (*d'un événement*) onlooker, witness

spectre [spɛktʀ] NM (*fantôme, fig*) spectre; (*Physique*) spectrum; **~ solaire** solar spectrum

spéculateur, -trice [spekylatœʀ, -tʀis] NM/F speculator

spéculatif, -ive [spekylatif, -iv] ADJ speculative

spéculation [spekylasjɔ̃] NF speculation

spéculer [spekyle] /1/ VI to speculate; **~ sur** (*Comm*) to speculate in; (*réfléchir*) to speculate on; (*tabler sur*) to bank *ou* rely on

speedé, e [spide] ADJ (*fam: personne: agité*) hyper (*fam*); (: *rapide, accéléré*) speeded up

spéléologie [speleɔlɔʒi] NF (*étude*) speleology; (*activité*) potholing

spéléologue [speleɔlɔg] NMF speleologist; potholer

spermatozoïde [spɛʀmatozɔid] NM sperm, spermatozoon

sperme [spɛʀm] NM semen, sperm

spermicide [spɛʀmisid] ADJ, NM spermicide

sphère [sfɛʀ] NF sphere

sphérique [sferik] ADJ spherical

sphincter [sfɛ̃ktɛʀ] NM sphincter

sphinx [sfɛ̃ks] NM INV sphinx; (*Zool*) hawkmoth

spiral, -aux [spiʀal, -o] NM hairspring

spirale [spiʀal] NF spiral; **en ~** in a spiral

spire [spiʀ] NF (*d'une spirale*) turn; (*d'une coquille*) whorl

spiritisme [spiʀitism] NM spiritualism, spiritism

spiritualité [spiʀitɥalite] NF spirituality

spirituel, le [spiʀitɥɛl] ADJ spiritual; (*fin, piquant*) witty; **musique spirituelle** sacred music; **concert ~** concert of sacred music

spirituellement [spiʀitɥɛlmɑ̃] ADV spiritually; wittily

spiritueux [spiʀitɥø] NM spirit

splendeur [splɑ̃dœʀ] NF splendour (BRIT), splendor (US)

★**splendide** [splɑ̃did] ADJ splendid, magnificent

spoliation [spɔljasjɔ̃] NF (*de bien, droit*) despoliation

spolier [spɔlje] /7/ VT: **~ qn (de)** to despoil sb (of)

spongieux, -euse [spɔ̃ʒjø, -øz] ADJ spongy

sponsor [spɔ̃sɔʀ] NM sponsor

sponsoriser [spɔ̃sɔʀize] /1/ VT to sponsor

spontané, e [spɔ̃tane] ADJ spontaneous

spontanéité [spɔ̃taneite] NF spontaneity

spontanément [spɔ̃tanemɑ̃] ADV spontaneously

sporadique [spɔʀadik] ADJ sporadic

sporadiquement [spɔʀadikmɑ̃] ADV sporadically

★**sport** [spɔʀ] NM sport; **faire du ~** to do sport; **~ individuel/d'équipe** individual/team sport; **~ de combat** combat sport; **sports d'hiver** winter sports ▶ ADJ INV (*vêtement*) casual; (*fair-play*) sporting

★**sportif, -ive** [spɔʀtif, -iv] ADJ (*journal, association, épreuve*) sports cpd; (*allure, démarche*) athletic; (*attitude, esprit*) sporting; **les résultats sportifs** the sports results

sportivement [spɔʀtivmɑ̃] ADV sportingly

sportivité [spɔʀtivite] NF sportsmanship

spot [spɔt] NM (*lampe*) spot(light); (*annonce*): **~ (publicitaire)** commercial (break)

spray [spʀɛ] NM spray, aerosol

sprint [spʀint] NM sprint; **piquer un ~** to put on a (final) spurt

sprinter [spʀintœʀ] NMF sprinter ▶ /1/ VI [spʀinte] to sprint

sprinteur, -euse [spʀintœʀ, øz] NM/F sprinter

squale [skwal] NM (*type of*) shark

square [skwaʀ] NM public garden(s)

squash [skwaʃ] NM squash

squat [skwat] NM (*lieu*) squat

squatter [skwatœʀ] NMF squatter ▶ /1/VT [skwate] to squat

squatteur, -euse [skwatœʀ, øz] NM/F squatter

squelette [skəlɛt] NM skeleton

squelettique [skəletik] ADJ scrawny; (*fig*) skimpy

SRAS [sʀas] SIGLE M (= *syndrome respiratoire aigu sévère*) SARS

Sri Lanka [sʀilɑ̃ka] NM: **le ~** Sri Lanka

sri-lankais, e, sri lankais, e [sʀilɑ̃kɛ, -ɛz] ADJ Sri-Lankan ▶ NM/F: **Sri-Lankais, e** Sri Lankan

SS SIGLE F = **la sécurité sociale**; (= *Sa Sainteté*) HH

SS ABR = **sous**

SSR SIGLE F (= *Société suisse romande*) the Swiss French-language broadcasting company

St, Ste ABR (= *Saint(e)*) St

stabilisateur, -trice [stabilizatœʀ, -tʀis] ADJ stabilizing ▶ NM stabilizer; (*d'un véhicule*) anti-roll device; (*d'un avion*) tailplane

stabiliser [stabilize] /1/ VT to stabilize; (*terrain*) to consolidate

stabilité [stabilite] NF stability

stable [stabl] ADJ stable, steady

★**stade** [stad] NM (*Sport*) stadium; (*phase, niveau*) stage

stadier [stadje] NM steward (*working in a stadium*), stage

★**stage** [staʒ] NM training period; (*cours*) training course; (*d'avocat stagiaire*) articles pl; **~ en entreprise** internship, work experience placement (BRIT); **~ de formation (professionnelle)** vocational (training) course; **~ de perfectionnement** advanced training course

★**stagiaire** [staʒjɛʀ] NMF, ADJ trainee, intern

stagnant, e [stagnɑ̃, -ɑ̃t] ADJ stagnant

stagnation [stagnasjɔ̃] NF stagnation

stagner [stagne] /1/ VI to stagnate

stalactite [stalaktit] NF stalactite

stalagmite [stalagmit] NF stalagmite

stalle [stal] NF stall, box

stambouliote [stɑ̃buljɔt] ADJ from Istanbul ▶ NMF: **Stambouliote** person from Istanbul

stand [stɑ̃d] NM (*d'exposition*) stand; (*de foire*) stall; **~ de tir** (*à la foire, Sport*) shooting range; **~ de ravitaillement** pit

standard [stɑ̃daʀ] ADJ INV standard ▶ NM (*type, norme*) standard; (*téléphonique*) switchboard

standardisation [stɑ̃daʀdizasjɔ̃] NF standardization

standardiser [stɑ̃daʀdize] /1/ VT to standardize

standardiste [stɑ̃daʀdist] NMF switchboard operator

standing [stɑ̃diŋ] NM standing; **de grand ~** luxury; **immeuble de grand ~** block of luxury flats (BRIT), condo(minium) (US)

star [staʀ] NF star

starlette [staʀlɛt] NF starlet

starter [staʀtɛʀ] NM (*Auto*) choke; (*Sport: personne*) starter; **mettre le ~** to pull out the choke

start-up [staʀtəp] NF (*Comm*) start-up

★**station** [stasjɔ̃] NF station; (*de bus*) stop; (*de villégiature*) resort; (*posture*): **la ~ debout** standing, an upright posture; **~ balnéaire** seaside resort; **~ de graissage** lubrication bay; **~ de lavage** carwash; **~ de ski** ski resort; **~ de sports d'hiver** winter sports resort; **~ de taxis** taxi rank (BRIT) *ou* stand (US); **~ thermale** thermal spa; **~ de travail** workstation

stationnaire [stasjɔnɛʀ] ADJ stationary

stationnement [stasjɔnmɑ̃] NM parking; **zone de ~ interdit** no parking area; **~ alterné** parking on alternate sides

★**stationner** [stasjɔne] /1/ VI to park

★**station-service** [stasjɔ̃sɛʀvis] (*pl* **stations-service**) NF service station

statique [statik] ADJ static

statisticien, ne [statistisjɛ̃, -ɛn] NM/F statistician

statistique [statistik] NF (*science*) statistics sg; (*rapport, étude*) statistic ▶ ADJ statistical ■ **statistiques** NFPL (*données*) statistics pl

statistiquement [statistikmɑ̃] ADV statistically

statuaire [statɥɛʀ] NF, ADJ statuary

statue [staty] NF statue

statuer [statɥe] /1/ VI: **~ sur** to rule on, give a ruling on

statuette [statɥɛt] NF statuette

statu quo [statykwo] NM status quo

stature [statyʀ] NF stature; **de haute ~** of great stature

statut [staty] NM status ■ **statuts** NMPL (*Jur, Admin*) statutes

statutaire [statɥtɛʀ] ADJ statutory

statutairement [statɥtɛʀmɑ̃] ADV statutorily

S

Sté ABR (= *société*) SOC

★**steak** [stɛk] NM steak; **~ haché** hamburger

stèle [stɛl] NF stela, stele

stellaire [stelɛʀ] ADJ stellar

stencil [stɛnsil] NM stencil

sténo [stenɔ] NMF (*aussi:* **sténographe**) shorthand typist (*BRIT*), stenographer (*US*) ▶ NF (*aussi:* **sténographie**) shorthand; **prendre en ~** to take down in shorthand

sténodactylo [stenɔdaktilo] NMF shorthand typist (*BRIT*), stenographer (*US*)

sténodactylographie [stenɔdaktilɔgrafi] NF shorthand typing (*BRIT*), stenography (*US*)

sténographe [stenɔgraf] NMF shorthand typist (*BRIT*), stenographer (*US*)

sténographie [stenɔgrafi] NF shorthand

sténographier [stenɔgrafje] /**7**/ VT to take down in shorthand

sténographique [stenɔgrafik] ADJ shorthand *cpd*

stentor [stɑ̃tɔʀ] NM: **voix de ~** stentorian voice

step® [stɛp] NM step aerobics® *sg*, step Reebok®

stéphanois, e [stefanwa, -waz] ADJ of *ou* from Saint-Étienne

steppe [stɛp] NF steppe

stère [stɛʀ] NM stere

stéréo NF (*aussi:* **stéréophonie**) stereo; **émission en ~** stereo broadcast ▶ ADJ (*aussi:* **stéréophonique**) stereo

stéréophonie [stereɔfɔni] NF stereo(phony)

stéréophonique [stereɔfɔnik] ADJ stereo(phonic)

stéréoscope [stereɔskɔp] NM stereoscope

stéréoscopique [stereɔskɔpik] ADJ stereoscopic

stéréotype [stereɔtip] NM stereotype

stéréotypé, e [stereɔtipe] ADJ stereotyped

stérile [steril] ADJ sterile; (*terre*) barren; (*fig*) fruitless, futile

stérilement [sterilmɑ̃] ADV fruitlessly

stérilet [sterilɛ] NM coil, loop

stérilisateur [sterilizatœʀ] NM sterilizer

stérilisation [sterilizasjɔ̃] NF sterilization

stériliser [sterilize] /**1**/ VT to sterilize

stérilité [sterilite] NF sterility

sterne [stɛʀn] NF (*oiseau*) tern

sternum [stɛʀnɔm] NM breastbone, sternum

stéroïde [steʀɔid] NM steroid

stéthoscope [stetɔskɔp] NM stethoscope

steward [stiwaʀt] NM air steward

stick [stik] NM stick

stigmates [stigmat] NMPL scars, marks; (*Rel*) stigmata *pl*

stigmatisation [stigmatizasjɔ̃] NM/F stigmatization

stigmatiser [stigmatize] /**1**/ VT to denounce, stigmatize

stimulant, e [stimylɑ̃, -ɑ̃t] ADJ stimulating ▶ NM (*Méd*) stimulant; (*fig*) stimulus, incentive

stimulateur [stimylatœʀ] NM: **~ cardiaque** pacemaker

stimulation [stimylasjɔ̃] NF stimulation

stimuler [stimyle] /**1**/ VT to stimulate

stimulus [stimylys] NM (*pl* **stimuli** [stimyli]) stimulus

stipulation [stipylasjɔ̃] NF stipulation

stipuler [stipyle] /**1**/ VT to stipulate, specify

stock [stɔk] NM stock; **en ~** in stock

stockage [stɔkaʒ] NM stocking; storage

stocker [stɔke] /**1**/ VT to stock; (*déchets*) to store

Stockholm [stɔkɔlm] N Stockholm

stockiste [stɔkist] NM stockist

stoïcien, ne [stɔisjɛ̃, -jɛn] NM/F, ADJ Stoic

stoïcisme [stɔisism] NM stoicism

stoïque [stɔik] ADJ stoic, stoical

stoïquement [stɔikmɑ̃] ADV stoically

stomacal, e, -aux [stɔmakal, -o] ADJ gastric, stomach *cpd*

stomatologie [stɔmatɔlɔʒi] NF stomatology

stomatologue [stɔmatɔlɔg] NMF stomatologist

stop [stɔp] NM (*Auto: écriteau*) stop sign; (*: signal*) brake-light; (*dans un télégramme*) stop; **faire du ~** (*fam*) to hitch(hike) ▶ EXCL stop!

stoppage [stɔpaʒ] NM invisible mending

stopper [stɔpe] /**1**/ VT to stop, halt; (*Couture*) to mend ▶ VI to stop, halt

store [stɔʀ] NM blind; (*de magasin*) shade, awning

strabisme [strabism] NM squint(ing)

strangulation [strɑ̃gylasjɔ̃] NF strangulation

strapontin [strapɔ̃tɛ̃] NM jump *ou* foldaway seat

Strasbourg [strazbur] N Strasbourg

strasbourgeois, e [strazburʒwa, -waz] ADJ of *ou* from Strasbourg ▶ NM/F: **Strasbourgeois, e** person from Strasbourg

strass [stras] NM paste, strass

stratagème [strataʒɛm] NM stratagem

strate [strat] NF (*Géo*) stratum, layer

stratège [strateʒ] NM strategist

stratégie [strateʒi] NF strategy

stratégique [strateʒik] ADJ strategic

stratégiquement [strateʒikmɑ̃] ADV strategically

stratification [stratifikasjɔ̃] NF (*Géol, Statistique*) stratification

stratifié, e [stratifje] ADJ (*Géo*) stratified; (*Tech*) laminated

stratosphère [stratɔsfɛʀ] NF stratosphere

streptocoque [strɛptɔkɔk] NM streptococcus

stress [stres] NM INV stress

stressant, e [stresɑ̃, -ɑ̃t] ADJ stressful

stressé, e [strese] ADJ (*personne*) stressed

stresser [strese] /**1**/ VT to stress (out)

stretching [stretʃiŋ] NM (*Sport*) stretching

strict, e [strikt] ADJ strict; (*tenue, décor*) severe, plain; **son droit le plus ~** his most basic right; **dans la plus stricte intimité** strictly in private; **le ~ nécessaire/minimum** the bare essentials/minimum

strictement [striktəmɑ̃] ADV strictly; plainly

strident, e [stridɑ̃, -ɑ̃t] ADJ shrill, strident

stridulations [stridylasjɔ̃] NFPL stridulations, chirrings

strie [stri] NF streak; (*Anat, Géo*) stria

strier [stʀije] /**7**/ vt to streak; to striate

string [stʀiŋ] NM thong, G-string

strip-tease [stʀiptiz] NM striptease

strip-teaseuse [stʀiptizøz] NF stripper, strip-tease artist

striures [stʀijyʀ] NFPL streaking *sg*

strophe [stʀɔf] NF verse, stanza

structure [stʀyktyʀ] NF structure; **structures d'accueil/touristiques** reception/tourist facilities

structurel, le [stʀyktyʀɛl] ADJ (*réforme, problème*) structural

structurer [stʀyktyʀe] /**1**/ vt to structure

strychnine [stʀiknin] NF strychnine

stuc [styk] NM stucco

studette [stydɛt] NF small studio flat (BRIT), small studio apartment (BRIT)

studieusement [stydjøzmã] ADV studiously

studieux, -euse [stydjø, -øz] ADJ (*élève*) studious; (*vacances*) study *cpd*

★**studio** [stydjo] NM (*logement*) studio flat (BRIT) *ou* apartment (US); (*d'artiste, TV etc*) studio

stupéfaction [stypefaksjɔ̃] NF stupefaction, astonishment

stupéfait, e [stypefɛ, -ɛt] ADJ astonished

stupéfiant, e [stypefjã, -ãt] ADJ (*étonnant*) astonishing ▸ NM (*Méd*) drug, narcotic

stupéfier [stypefje] /**7**/ vt to stupefy; (*étonner*) astonish

stupeur [stypœʀ] NF (*inertie, insensibilité*) stupor; (*étonnement*) astonishment

★**stupide** [stypid] ADJ stupid; (*hébété*) stunned

stupidement [stypidmã] ADV stupidly

stupidité [stypidite] NF stupidity *no pl*; (*parole, acte*) stupid thing (to say *ou* do)

stups [styp] NMPL drugs, narcotics; **brigade des ~** drug squad (BRIT), narcotics unit (US)

★**style** [stil] NM style; **meuble/robe de ~** piece of period furniture/period dress; **~ de vie** lifestyle

stylé, e [stile] ADJ well-trained

stylet [stile] NM (*poignard*) stiletto; (*Chirurgie*) stylet

stylisé, e [stilize] ADJ stylized

stylisme [stilism] NM (*Mode*) fashion design; (*Industrie*) design

styliste [stilist] NMF stylist; designer

stylistique [stilistik] NF stylistics *sg* ▸ ADJ stylistic

★**stylo** [stilo] NM: **~ (à encre)** (fountain) pen; **~ (à) bille** ballpoint pen

stylo-feutre [stilɔføtʀ] (*pl* **stylos-feutres**) NM felt-tip pen

su, e [sy] PP *de* **savoir** ▸ NM: **au su de** with the knowledge of

suaire [sɥɛʀ] NM shroud

suant, e [sɥã, -ãt] ADJ sweaty

suave [sɥav] ADJ (*odeur*) sweet; (*voix*) suave, smooth; (*coloris*) soft, mellow

subalterne [sybaltɛʀn] ADJ (*employé, officier*) junior; (*rôle*) subordinate, subsidiary ▸ NMF subordinate, inferior

subaquatique [sybakwatik] ADJ subaquatic

subconscient [sybkɔ̃sjã] NM subconscious

subculture [sybkyltyʀ] ADJ subculture

subdiviser [sybdivize] /**1**/ vt to subdivide

subdivision [sybdivizjɔ̃] NF subdivision

subir [sybiʀ] /**2**/ vt (*affront, dégâts, mauvais traitements*) to suffer; (*influence, charme*) to be under, be subjected to; (*traitement, opération, châtiment*) to undergo; (*personne*) to suffer, be subjected to

subit, e [sybi, -it] ADJ sudden

subitement [sybitmã] ADV suddenly, all of a sudden

subjectif, -ive [sybʒɛktif, -iv] ADJ subjective

subjectivement [sybʒɛktivmã] ADV subjectively

subjectivité [sybʒɛktivite] NF subjectivity

subjonctif [sybʒɔ̃ktif] NM subjunctive

subjuguer [sybʒyge] /**1**/ vt to subjugate

sublime [syblim] ADJ sublime

sublimer [syblime] /**1**/ vt to sublimate

subliminal, e, -aux [sybliminal, -o] ADJ (*message*) subliminal

submergé, e [sybmɛʀʒe] ADJ submerged; **~ de** (*fig*) snowed under with; overwhelmed with

submerger [sybmɛʀʒe] /**3**/ vt to submerge; (*foule*) to engulf; (*fig*) to overwhelm

submersible [sybmɛʀsibl] NM submarine

subodorer [sybodɔʀe] /**1**/ vt to detect, sense

subordination [sybɔʀdinasjɔ̃] NF subordination

subordonné, e [sybɔʀdɔne] ADJ, NM/F subordinate; **~ à** (*personne*) subordinate to; (*résultats etc*) subject to, depending on

subordonner [sybɔʀdɔne] /**1**/ vt: **~ qn/qch à** to subordinate sb/sth to

subornation [sybɔʀnasjɔ̃] NF bribing

suborner [sybɔʀne] /**1**/ vt to bribe

subrepticement [sybʀɛptismã] ADV surreptitiously

subroger [sybʀɔʒe] /**3**/ vt (*Jur*) to subrogate

subside [sypsid] NM grant

subsidiaire [sypsidjɛʀ] ADJ subsidiary; **question ~** deciding question

subsistance [sybzistãs] NF subsistence; **pourvoir à la ~ de qn** to keep sb, provide for sb's subsistence *ou* keep

subsister [sybziste] /**1**/ vi (*rester*) to remain, subsist; (*vivre*) to live; (*survivre*) to live on

subsonique [sybsonik] ADJ subsonic

substance [sypstãs] NF substance; **en ~** in substance

substantiel, le [sypstãsjɛl] ADJ substantial

substantif [sypstãtif] NM noun, substantive

substantiver [sypstãtive] /**1**/ vt to nominalize

substituer [sypstitɥe] /**1**/ vt: **~ qn/qch à** to substitute sb/sth for; **se ~ à qn** (*représenter*) to substitute for sb; (*évincer*) to substitute o.s. for sb

substitut [sypstity] NM (*Jur*) deputy public prosecutor; (*succédané*) substitute

substitution [sypstitysjɔ̃] NF substitution

substrat [sypstʀatɔm] NM (*Géol*) substratum; (*Chimie*) substrate

subterfuge [sybtɛʀfyʒ] NM subterfuge

subtil, e [syptil] ADJ subtle

S

423

subtilement [syptilmɑ̃] ADV subtly

subtiliser [syptilize] /1/ VT: **~ qch (à qn)** to spirit sth away (from sb)

subtilité [syptilite] NF subtlety

subtropical, e, -aux [sybtʀɔpikal, -o] ADJ subtropical

suburbain, e [sybyʀbɛ̃, -ɛn] ADJ suburban

subvenir [sybvəniʀ] /22/: **~ à** vt to meet

subvention [sybvɑ̃sjɔ̃] NF subsidy, grant

subventionner [sybvɑ̃sjɔne] /1/ VT to subsidize

subversif, -ive [sybvɛʀsif, -iv] ADJ subversive

subversion [sybvɛʀsjɔ̃] NF subversion

suc [syk] NM (Bot) sap; (de viande, fruit) juice; **sucs gastriques** gastric juices

succédané [syksedane] NM substitute

succéder [syksede] /6/: **~ à** vt (directeur, roi etc) to succeed; (venir après: dans une série) to follow, succeed ■ **se succéder** VPR (accidents, années) to follow one another

succès [syksɛ] NM success; **avec ~** successfully; **sans ~** unsuccessfully; **avoir du ~** to be a success, be successful; **à ~** successful; **livre à ~** bestseller; **~ de librairie** bestseller

successeur [syksesœʀ] NM successor

successif, -ive [syksesif, -iv] ADJ successive

succession [syksesjɔ̃] NF (série, Pol) succession; (Jur: patrimoine) estate, inheritance; **prendre la ~ de** (directeur) to succeed, take over from; (entreprise) to take over

successivement [syksesivmɑ̃] ADV successively

succinct, e [syksɛ̃, -ɛ̃t] ADJ succinct

succinctement [syksɛ̃tmɑ̃] ADV succinctly

succion [syksjɔ̃] NF: **bruit de ~** sucking noise

succomber [sykɔ̃be] /1/ VI to die, succumb; (fig): **~ à** to succumb to, give way to

succulent, e [sykylɑ̃, -ɑ̃t] ADJ delicious

succursale [sykyʀsal] NF branch; **magasin à succursales multiples** chain ou multiple store

sucer [syse] /3/ VT to suck

sucette [sysɛt] NF (bonbon) lollipop; (de bébé) dummy (BRIT), comforter, pacifier (US)

suçoter [sysɔte] /1/ VT to suck

★**sucre** [sykʀ] NM (substance) sugar; (morceau) lump of sugar, sugar lump ou cube; **~ de canne/betterave** cane/beet sugar; **~ en morceaux/cristallisé/en poudre** lump ou cube/granulated/caster sugar (BRIT), superfine sugar (US); **~ glace** icing sugar (BRIT), confectioner's sugar (US); **~ d'orge** barley sugar

★**sucré, e** [sykʀe] ADJ (produit alimentaire) sweetened; (au goût) sweet; (péj) sugary, honeyed

sucrer [sykʀe] /1/ VT (thé, café) to sweeten, put sugar in ■ **se sucrer** VPR (fam) to line one's pocket(s)

sucrerie [sykʀəʀi] NF (usine) sugar refinery ■ **sucreries** NFPL (bonbons) sweets (BRIT), candy (US), sweet things

sucrette [sykʀɛt] NF sweetener

sucrier, -ière [sykʀije, -jɛʀ] ADJ (industrie) sugar cpd; (région) sugar-producing ▶ NM (fabricant) sugar producer; (récipient) sugar bowl ou basin

★**sud** [syd] NM: **le ~** the south; **au ~** (situation) in the south; (direction) to the south; **au ~ de** (to the) south of ▶ ADJ INV south; (côte) south, southern

sud-africain, e [sydafʀikɛ̃, -ɛn] ADJ South African ▶ NM/F: **Sud-Africain, e** South African

sud-américain, e [sydameʀikɛ̃, -ɛn] ADJ South American ▶ NM/F: **Sud-Américain, e** South American

sudation [sydasjɔ̃] NF sweating, sudation

sud-coréen, ne [sydkɔʀeɛ̃, -ɛn] ADJ South Korean ▶ NM/F: **Sud-Coréen, ne** South Korean

sud-est [sydɛst] NM, ADJ INV south-east

sud-ouest [sydwɛst] NM, ADJ INV south-west

sud-vietnamien, ne [sydvjɛtnamjɛ̃, -ɛn] ADJ South Vietnamese ▶ NM/F: **Sud-Vietnamien, ne** South Vietnamese

Suède [sɥɛd] NF: **la ~** Sweden

suédois, e [sɥedwa, -waz] ADJ Swedish ▶ NM (Ling) Swedish ▶ NM/F: **Suédois, e** Swede

suer [sɥe] /1/ VI to sweat; (suinter) to ooze; **~ à grosses gouttes** to sweat profusely ▶ VT (fig) to exude

sueur [sɥœʀ] NF sweat; **en ~** sweating, in a sweat; **avoir des sueurs froides** to be in a cold sweat

★**suffire** [syfiʀ] /37/ VI (être assez): **~ (à qn/pour qch/pour faire)** to be enough ou sufficient (for sb/for sth/to do); **cela lui suffit** he's (ou she's) content with this, this is enough for him (ou her); **cela suffit pour les irriter/qu'ils se fâchent** it's enough to annoy them/for them to get angry; **ça suffit !** that's enough!, that'll do! ■ **se suffire** VPR to be self-sufficient ▶ VB IMPERS: **il suffit d'une négligence/qu'on oublie pour que ...** it only takes one act of carelessness/one only needs to forget for ...

★**suffisamment** [syfizamɑ̃] ADV sufficiently, enough; **~ de** sufficient, enough

suffisance [syfizɑ̃s] NF (vanité) self-importance, bumptiousness; (quantité): **en ~** in plenty

suffisant, e [syfizɑ̃, -ɑ̃t] ADJ (temps, ressources) sufficient; (résultats) satisfactory; (vaniteux) self-important, bumptious

suffisons etc [syfizɔ̃] VB voir **suffire**

suffixe [syfiks] NM suffix

suffocant, e [syfɔkɑ̃, -ɑ̃t] ADJ (étouffant) suffocating; (stupéfiant) staggering

suffocation [syfɔkasjɔ̃] NF suffocation

suffoquer [syfɔke] /1/ VT to choke, suffocate; (stupéfier) to stagger, astound ▶ VI to choke, suffocate; **~ de colère/d'indignation** to choke with anger/indignation

suffrage [syfʀaʒ] NM (Pol: voix) vote; (du public etc) approval no pl; **~ universel/direct/indirect** universal/direct/indirect suffrage; **suffrages exprimés** valid votes

suggérer [syɡʒeʀe] /6/ VT to suggest; **~ que/de faire** to suggest that/doing

suggestif, -ive [syɡʒɛstif, -iv] ADJ suggestive

suggestion [syɡʒɛstjɔ̃] NF suggestion

suggestivité [syɡʒɛstivite] NF suggestiveness, suggestive nature

suicidaire [sɥisidɛʀ] ADJ suicidal

suicide [sɥisid] NM suicide ▶ ADJ: **opération ~** suicide mission

suicidé, e [sɥiside] NM/F suicide

suicider [sɥiside] /1/: **se suicider** VPR to commit suicide

suie [sɥi] NF soot

suif [sɥif] NM tallow

suintement [sɥɛ̃tmã] NM (de plaie) oozing; (d'eau) seepage

suinter [sɥɛ̃te] /1/ VI (plaie) to ooze

suis [sɥi] VB voir **être**; **suivre**

★**suisse** [sɥis] ADJ Swiss; ~ **romand** Swiss French ▶ NM (bedeau) ≈ verger ▶ NMF: **Suisse** Swiss inv ▶ NF: **la S~** Switzerland; **la S~ romande/allemande** French-speaking/German-speaking Switzerland

suisse-allemand, e [sɥisalmã, -ãd] ADJ, NM/F Swiss German

Suissesse [sɥisɛs] NF Swiss (woman ou girl)

suit [sɥi] VB voir **suivre**

suite [sɥit] NF (continuation: d'énumération etc) rest, remainder; (: de feuilleton) continuation; (: second film etc sur le même thème) sequel; (série) series, succession; (Math) series sg; (conséquence) result; (ordre, liaison logique) coherence; (appartement, Mus) suite; (escorte) retinue, suite; **une ~ de** (de maisons, succès) a series ou succession of; **prendre la ~ de** (directeur etc) to succeed, take over from; **donner ~ à** (requête, projet) to follow up; **faire ~ à** to follow; **~ à votre lettre du** further to your letter of the; **sans ~** adj incoherent, disjointed; adv incoherently, disjointedly; **de ~** adv (d'affilée) in succession; (immédiatement) at once; **par la ~** afterwards, subsequently; **à la ~** adv one after the other; **à la ~ de** (derrière) behind; (en conséquence de) following; **par ~ de** owing to, as a result of; **avoir de la ~ dans les idées** to show great singleness of purpose; **attendre la ~ des événements** to (wait and) see what happens ■ **suites** NFPL (d'une maladie etc) effects

★**suivant, e** [sɥivã, -ãt] VB voir **suivre** ▶ ADJ next, following; (ci-après): **l'exercice ~** the following exercise ▶ PRÉP (selon) according to; **~ que** according to whether ▶ NM: **au ~!** next!

suive etc [sɥiv] VB voir **suivre**

suiveur, -euse [sɥivœr] NM/F (aussi réseaux sociaux) follower; (Cyclisme) (official) follower; (péj) (camp) follower

suivi, e [sɥivi] PP de **suivre** ▶ ADJ (régulier) regular; (Comm: article) in general production; (effort, qualité) consistent; (cohérent) coherent; **très/peu ~** (cours) well-/poorly-attended; (mode) widely/not widely adopted; (feuilleton etc) widely/not widely followed ▶ NM follow-up

suivisme [sɥivism] NM tendency to follow the herd

suiviste [sɥivist] ADJ that follows the herd ▶ NMF person who follows the herd

★**suivre** [sɥivr] /40/ VT (gén) to follow; (Scol: cours) to attend; (: leçon) to follow, attend to; (: programme) to keep up with; (Comm: article) to continue to stock ▶ VI to follow; (élève: écouter) to attend, pay attention; (: assimiler le programme) to keep up, follow ■ **se suivre** VPR (accidents, personnes, voitures etc) to follow one after the other; (raisonnement) to be coherent; **~ des yeux** to follow with one's eyes; **faire ~** (lettre) to forward; **~ son cours** (enquête etc) to run ou take its course; **« à ~ »** "to be continued"

★**sujet, te** [syʒɛ, -ɛt] ADJ: **être ~ à** (accidents) to be prone to; (vertige etc) to be liable ou subject to; **~ à caution** questionable ▶ NM/F (d'un souverain) subject ▶ NM subject; **un ~ de dispute/discorde/mécontentement** a cause for argument/dissension/dissatisfaction; **c'est à quel ~?** what is it about?; **avoir ~ de se plaindre** to have cause for complaint; **au ~ de** prép about; **~ de conversation** topic ou subject of conversation; **~ d'examen** (Scol) examination question; examination paper; **~ d'expérience** (Bio etc) experimental subject

sujétion [syʒesjɔ̃] NF subjection; (fig) constraint

sulfater [sylfate] /1/ VT to spray with copper sulphate

sulfureux, -euse [sylfyrø, -øz] ADJ sulphurous (BRIT), sulfurous (US)

sulfurique [sylfyrik] ADJ: **acide ~** sulphuric (BRIT) ou sulfuric (US) acid

sulfurisé, e [sylfyrize] ADJ: **papier ~** greaseproof (BRIT) ou wax (US) paper

sultan [syltã] NM sultan

sultanat [syltana] NM sultanate

Sumatra [symatra] NF Sumatra

summum [sɔmɔm] NM: **le ~ de** the height of

sunnite [synit] ADJ Sunni ▶ NMF Sunnite

★**super** [sypɛr] ADJ INV great, fantastic ▶ NM (= supercarburant) ≈ 4-star (BRIT), ≈ premium (US)

superbe [sypɛrb] ADJ magnificent, superb ▶ NF arrogance

superbement [sypɛrbəmã] ADV superbly

supercarburant [sypɛrkarbyrã] NM ≈ 4-star petrol (BRIT), ≈ premium gas (US)

supercherie [sypɛrʃəri] NF trick, trickery no pl; (fraude) fraud

supérette [sypɛrɛt] NF minimarket

superfétatoire [sypɛrfetatwar] ADJ superfluous

superficialité [sypɛrfisjalite] NF superficiality

superficie [sypɛrfisi] NF (surface) area; (fig) surface

superficiel, le [sypɛrfisjɛl] ADJ superficial

superficiellement [sypɛrfisjɛlmã] ADV superficially

superflu, e [sypɛrfly] ADJ superfluous ▶ NM: **le ~** the superfluous

superforme [sypɛrfɔrm] NF (fam) top form, excellent shape

super-grand [sypɛrgrã] NM superpower

super-huit [sypɛrɥit] ADJ INV: **camera/film ~** super-eight camera/film

supérieur, e [syperjœr] ADJ (lèvre, étages, classes) upper; **~ (à)** (plus élevé: température, niveau) higher (than); (meilleur: qualité, produit) superior (to); (excellent, hautain) superior; **Mère supérieure** Mother Superior; **à l'étage ~** on the next floor up; **~ en nombre** superior in number ▶ NM/F superior

supérieurement [syperjœrmã] ADV exceptionally well; (avec adjectif) exceptionally

supériorité [syperjɔrite] NF superiority

superlatif [sypɛrlatif] NM superlative

supermarché [sypɛrmarʃe] NM supermarket

supernova [sypɛrnɔva] NF supernova

superposable [sypɛrpozabl] ADJ (figures) that may be superimposed; (lits) stackable

S

superposer [sypɛʀpoze] /1/ VT to superpose; (meubles, caisses) to stack; (faire chevaucher) to superimpose; **lits superposés** bunk beds ■ **se superposer** VPR (images, souvenirs) to be superimposed

superposition [sypɛʀpozisjɔ̃] NF superposition; superimposition

superpréfet [sypɛʀpʀefɛ] NM prefect in charge of a region

superproduction [sypɛʀpʀɔdyksjɔ̃] NF (film) spectacular

superpuissance [sypɛʀpɥisɑ̃s] NF superpower

supersonique [sypɛʀsɔnik] ADJ supersonic

superstitieux, -euse [sypɛʀstisjø, -øz] ADJ superstitious

superstition [sypɛʀstisjɔ̃] NF superstition

superstructure [sypɛʀstʀyktyʀ] NF superstructure

supertanker [sypɛʀtɑ̃kœʀ] NM supertanker

superviser [sypɛʀvize] /1/ VT to supervise

supervision [sypɛʀvizjɔ̃] NF supervision

suppl. ABR = **supplément**

supplanter [syplɑ̃te] /1/ VT to supplant

suppléance [sypleɑ̃s] NF (poste) supply post (BRIT), substitute teacher's post (US)

suppléant, e [sypleɑ̃, -ɑ̃t] ADJ (juge, fonctionnaire) deputy cpd; (professeur) supply cpd (BRIT), substitute cpd (US); **médecin ~** locum ▶ NM/F deputy; (professeur) supply (BRIT) ou substitute (US) teacher

suppléer [syplee] /1/ VT (ajouter: mot manquant etc) to supply, provide; (compenser: lacune) to fill in; (: défaut) to make up for; (remplacer: professeur) to stand in for; (: juge) to deputize for; **~ à** VT to make up for; to substitute for

supplément [syplemɑ̃] NM supplement; **un ~ de travail** extra ou additional work; **un ~ de pain** etc an extra portion of bread etc; **un ~ de 10 euros** a supplement of 10 euros, an extra ou additional 10 euros; **ceci est en ~** (au menu etc) this is extra, there is an extra charge for this; **le vin est en ~** wine is extra; **payer un ~** to pay an additional charge; **~ d'information** additional information

supplémentaire [syplemɑ̃tɛʀ] ADJ additional, further; (train, bus) relief cpd, extra

supplémentation [syplemɑ̃tasjɔ̃] NF: **la ~ nutritionnelle** food supplements

supplétif, -ive [sypletif, -iv] ADJ (Mil) auxiliary

suppliant, e [syplijɑ̃, -ɑ̃t] ADJ imploring

supplication [syplikasjɔ̃] NF (Rel) supplication ■ **supplications** NFPL (adjurations) pleas, entreaties

supplice [syplis] NM (peine corporelle) torture no pl; form of torture; (douleur physique, morale) torture, agony; **être au ~** to be in agony

supplicier [syplisje] VT to torture

supplier [syplije] /7/ VT to implore, beseech

supplique [syplik] NF petition

support [sypɔʀ] NM support; (pour livre, outils) stand; **~ audiovisuel** audio-visual aid; **~ publicitaire** advertising medium

supportable [sypɔʀtabl] ADJ (douleur, température) bearable; (procédé, conduite) tolerable

★**supporter¹** [sypɔʀtœʀ] NMF, **supporteur, -trice** [sypɔʀtœʀ, tʀis] NM/F (Sport, Pol) supporter, fan

supporter² [sypɔʀte] VT (poids, poussée, Sport: concurrent, équipe) to support; (conséquences, épreuve) to bear, endure; (défauts, personne) to tolerate, put up with; (chose, chaleur etc) to withstand; (personne, chaleur, vin) to take

supposé, e [sypoze] ADJ (nombre) estimated; (auteur) supposed

supposément [sypozemɑ̃] ADV supposedly

★**supposer** [sypoze] /1/ VT to suppose; (impliquer) to presuppose; **en supposant** ou **à ~ que** supposing (that)

supposition [sypozisjɔ̃] NF supposition

suppositoire [sypozitwaʀ] NM suppository

suppôt [sypo] NM (péj) henchman

suppression [sypʀesjɔ̃] NF removal; deletion; cancellation; suppression

supprimer [sypʀime] /1/ VT (cloison, cause, anxiété) to remove; (clause, mot) to delete; (congés, service d'autobus etc) to cancel; (publication, article) to suppress; (emplois, privilèges, témoin gênant) to do away with; **~ qch à qn** to deprive sb of sth

suppurer [sypyʀe] /1/ VI to suppurate

supputations [sypytasjɔ̃] NFPL calculations, reckonings

supputer [sypyte] /1/ VT to calculate, reckon

supraconducteur, -trice [sypʀakɔ̃dyktœʀ, -tʀis] ADJ (matériau) superconductive ▶ NM superconductor

supranational, e, -aux [sypʀanasjɔnal, -o] ADJ supranational

suprématie [sypʀemasi] NF supremacy

suprême [sypʀɛm] ADJ supreme

suprêmement [sypʀɛmmɑ̃] ADV supremely

---

sur¹ [syʀ]

PRÉP **1** (position) on; (: par-dessus) over; (: au-dessus) above; **pose-le sur la table** put it on the table; **je n'ai pas d'argent sur moi** I haven't any money on me

2 (direction) towards; **en allant sur Paris** going towards Paris; **sur votre droite** on ou to your right

3 (à propos de) on, about; **un livre/une conférence sur Balzac** a book/lecture on ou about Balzac

4 (proportion, mesures) out of; by; **un sur 10** one in 10; (Scol) one out of 10; **sur 20, deux sont venus** out of 20, two came; **4 m sur 2** 4 m by 2; **avoir accident sur accident** to have one accident after another

5 (cause) **sur sa recommandation** on ou at his recommendation; **sur son invitation** at his invitation

6: sur ce adv whereupon; **sur ce, il faut que je vous quitte** and now I must leave you

---

sur², e [syʀ] ADJ sour

★**sûr, e** [syʀ] ADJ sure, certain; (digne de confiance) reliable; (sans danger) safe; **peu ~** unreliable; **~ de qch** sure ou certain of sth; **être ~ de qn** to be sure of sb; **~ et certain** absolutely certain; **~ de soi** self-assured, self-confident; **le plus ~ est de** the safest thing is to

surabondance [syʀabɔ̃dɑ̃s] NF overabundance

surabondant, e [syʀabɔ̃dɑ̃, -ɑ̃t] ADJ overabundant

surabonder [syʀabɔ̃de] /**1**/ VI to be overabundant; **~ de** to abound with, have an overabundance of

suractivité [syʀaktivite] NF hyperactivity

suraigu, ë [syʀegy] ADJ very shrill

surajouter [syʀaʒute] /**1**/ VT: **~ qch à** to add sth to

suralimentation [syʀalimɑ̃tasjɔ̃] NF overfeeding; (Tech: d'un moteur) supercharging

suralimenté, e [syʀalimɑ̃te] ADJ (personne) overfed; (moteur) supercharged

suranné, e [syʀane] ADJ outdated, outmoded

surarmement [syʀaʀməmɑ̃] NM (excess) stockpiling of arms ou weapons

surbaissé, e [syʀbese] ADJ lowered, low

surbooké, e [syʀbuke] ADJ (fam: personne): **être ~** to have too many demands on one's time; (vol) overbooked

surcapacité [syʀkapasite] NF overcapacity

surcharge [syʀʃaʀʒ] NF (de passagers, marchandises) excess load; (de détails, d'ornements) overabundance, excess; (correction) alteration; (Postes) surcharge; **prendre des passagers en ~** to take on excess ou extra passengers; **~ de bagages** excess luggage; **~ de travail** extra work

surchargé, e [syʀʃaʀʒe] ADJ (décoration, style) overelaborate, overfussy; (voiture, emploi du temps) overloaded

surcharger [syʀʃaʀʒe] /**3**/ VT to overload; (timbre-poste) to surcharge; (décoration) to overdo

surchauffe [syʀʃof] NF overheating; **en ~** (moteur, économie) overheating

surchauffé, e [syʀʃofe] ADJ (salle) overheated; (fig: imagination) overactive; (: ambiance) frenetic; (: économie) overheated

surchauffer [syʀʃofe] VI, VT to overheat

surchoix [syʀʃwa] ADJ INV top-quality

surclasser [syʀklase] /**1**/ VT to outclass

surconsommation [syʀkɔ̃sɔmasjɔ̃] NF (Écon) overconsumption

surcoté, e [syʀkɔte] ADJ overpriced

surcouper [syʀkupe] /**1**/ VT to overtrump

surcoût [syʀku] NM additional cost

surcroît [syʀkʀwa] NM: **~ de qch** additional sth; **par ou de ~** moreover; **en ~** in addition

surdimensionné, e [syʀdimɑ̃sjɔne] ADJ outsize; **un ego ~** an outsize ego

surdi-mutité, surdimutité [syʀdimytite] NF hearing and speech impairment

surdité [syʀdite] NF deafness; **atteint de ~ totale** profoundly deaf

surdose [syʀdoz] NF (lit, fig) overdose

surdoué, e [syʀdwe] ADJ gifted

sureau, x [syʀo] NM elder (tree)

sureffectif [syʀefɛktif] NM overmanning

surélever [syʀel(ə)ve] /**5**/ VT to raise, heighten

sûrement [syʀmɑ̃] ADV reliably; (sans risques) safely, securely; (certainement) certainly; **~ pas** certainly not

suremploi [syʀɑ̃plwa] NM (Écon) overemployment

surenchère [syʀɑ̃ʃɛʀ] NF (aux enchères) higher bid; (sur prix fixe) overbid; (fig) overstatement; outbidding tactics pl; **~ de violence** build-up of violence; **~ électorale** political (ou electoral) one-upmanship

surenchérir [syʀɑ̃ʃeʀiʀ] /**2**/ VI to bid higher; to raise one's bid; (fig) to try and outbid each other

surendetté, e [syʀɑ̃dete] ADJ (personne, entreprise, pays) over-indebted, overindebted

surendettement [syʀɑ̃dɛtmɑ̃] NM over-indebtedness, overindebtedness

surent [syʀ] VB voir **savoir**

surentraîné, e [syʀɑ̃tʀene] ADJ overtrained

suréquipé, e [syʀekipe] ADJ overequipped

surestimer [syʀɛstime] /**1**/ VT (tableau) to overvalue; (possibilité, personne) to overestimate

sûreté [syʀte] NF (voir sûr: exactitude: de renseignements etc) reliability; (sécurité) safety; (d'un geste) steadiness; (Jur) guaranty, surety; **mettre en ~** to put in a safe place; **pour plus de ~** as an extra precaution; **to be on the safe side; la ~ de l'État** State security; **la S~ (nationale)** division of the Ministère de l'Intérieur heading all police forces except the gendarmerie and the Paris préfecture de police

surévaluation [syʀevalɥasjɔ̃] NF (de monnaie) overvaluation; (de recettes, marché) overvaluing

surévaluer [syʀevalɥe] VT (importance, capacité) to overestimate; (monnaie, recettes, marché) to overvalue

surexcité, e [syʀɛksite] ADJ overexcited

surexciter [syʀɛksite] /**1**/ VT (personne) to overexcite

surexploitation [syʀɛksplwatasjɔ̃] NF (de ressources) over-exploitation; (d'idée, thème) overuse, excessive use; (de main d'œuvre) exploitation

surexploiter [syʀɛksplwate] /**1**/ VT to over-exploit

surexposer [syʀɛkspoze] /**1**/ VT to overexpose

surf [sœʀf] NM surfing; **faire du ~** to go surfing

surface [syʀfas] NF surface; (superficie) surface area; **une grande ~** a supermarket; **faire ~** to surface; **en ~** adv near the surface; (fig) superficially; **la pièce fait 100 m² de ~** the room has a surface area of 100m²; **~ de réparation** (Sport) penalty area; **~ porteuse ou de sustentation** (Aviat) aerofoil

surfacturation [syʀfaktyʀasjɔ̃] NF overbilling

surfait, e [syʀfɛ, -ɛt] ADJ overrated

★**surfer** [sœʀfe] /**1**/ VI to surf; **~ sur Internet** to surf ou browse the internet

surfeur, -euse [sœʀfœʀ, -øz] NM/F surfer

surfiler [syʀfile] /**1**/ VT (Couture) to oversew

surfin, e [syʀfɛ̃, -in] ADJ superfine

surgélateur [syʀʒelatœʀ] NM deep freeze

surgélation [syʀʒelasjɔ̃] NF deep-freezing

surgelé, e [syʀʒale] ADJ (deep-)frozen ▶ NM: **les surgelés** (deep-)frozen food

surgeler [syʀʒale] /**5**/ VT to (deep-)freeze

surgir [syʀʒiʀ] /**2**/ VI (personne, véhicule) to appear suddenly; (jaillir) to shoot up; (montagne etc) to rise up, loom up; (fig: problème, conflit) to arise

surhomme [syʀɔm] NM superman

surhumain, e [syʀymɛ̃, -ɛn] ADJ superhuman

surimposer [syʀɛ̃poze] /**1**/ VT to overtax

surimpression [syʀɛ̃pʀesjɔ̃] NF (Photo) double exposure; **en ~** superimposed

surimprimer [syʀɛ̃pʀime] /1/ vт to overstrike, overprint

Surinam [syʀinam] NM: **le ~** Surinam

surinfection [syʀɛ̃fɛksjɔ̃] NF (*Méd*) secondary infection

surjet [syʀʒɛ] NM (*Couture*) overcast seam

surjouer [syʀʒwe] vт (*rôle, émotion*) to overact ▸ vı to overact

sur-le-champ [syʀləʃɑ̃] ADV immediately

surlendemain [syʀlɑ̃d(ə)mɛ̃] NM: **le ~ (soir)** two days later (in the evening); **le ~ de** two days after

surligner [syʀliɲe] vт to highlight

surligneur [syʀliɲœʀ] NM (*feutre*) highlighter (pen)

surmenage [syʀmənaʒ] NM overwork; **le ~ intellectuel** mental fatigue

surmené, e [syʀməne] ADJ overworked

surmener [syʀməne] /5/ vт to overwork ■ **se surmener** vPR to overwork

surmonter [syʀmɔ̃te] /1/ vт (*coupole etc*) to surmount, top; (*vaincre*) to overcome, surmount; (*être au-dessus de*) to top

surmortalité [syʀmɔʀtalite] NF excess death rate

surmultiplié, e [syʀmyltiplije] ADJ, NF: **(vitesse) surmultipliée** overdrive

surnager [syʀnaʒe] /3/ vı to float

surnaturel, le [syʀnatyʀɛl] ADJ, NM supernatural

surnom [syʀnɔ̃] NM nickname

surnombre [syʀnɔ̃bʀ] NM: **être en ~** to be too many (*ou* one too many)

surnommer [syʀnɔme] /1/ vт to nickname

surnuméraire [syʀnymeʀɛʀ] NMF supernumerary

suroît [syʀwa] NM sou'wester

surpasser [syʀpɑse] /1/ vт to surpass ■ **se surpasser** vPR to surpass o.s., excel o.s.

surpayer [syʀpeje] /8/ vт (*personne*) to overpay; (*article etc*) to pay too much for

surpeuplé, e [syʀpœple] ADJ overpopulated

surpeuplement [syʀpœpləmɑ̃] NM overpopulation

surpiquer [syʀpike] /1/ vт (*Couture*) to overstitch

surpiqûre [syʀpikyʀ] NF (*Couture*) overstitching

surplace [syʀplas] NM: **faire du ~** to mark time

surplis [syʀpli] NM surplice

surplomb [syʀplɔ̃] NM overhang; **en ~** overhanging

surplomber [syʀplɔ̃be] /1/ vı to be overhanging ▸ vт to overhang; (*dominer*) to tower above

surplus [syʀply] NM (*Comm*) surplus; (*reste*): **~ de bois** wood left over; **au ~** moreover; **~ américains** American army surplus *sg*

surpoids [syʀpwa] NM excess weight; **être en ~** to be overweight

surpopulation [syʀpɔpylasjɔ̃] NF overpopulation

surprenant, e [syʀpʀənɑ̃, -ɑ̃t] vB *voir* **surprendre** ▸ ADJ amazing

surprendre [syʀpʀɑ̃dʀ] /58/ vт (*étonner, prendre à l'improviste*) to amaze, surprise; (*secret*) to discover; (*tomber sur: intrus etc*) to catch; (*fig*) to detect; to chance *ou* happen upon; (*clin d'œil*) to intercept; (*conversation*) to overhear; (*orage, nuit etc*) to catch out, take by surprise; **~ la vigilance/bonne foi de qn** to catch sb out/betray sb's good faith; **se ~ à faire** to catch *ou* find o.s. doing

surprime [syʀpʀim] NF additional premium

★**surpris, e** [syʀpʀi, -iz] PP *de* **surprendre** ▸ ADJ: **~ (de/que)** amazed *ou* surprised (at/that)

★**surprise** [syʀpʀiz] NF surprise; **faire une ~ à qn** to give sb a surprise; **voyage sans surprises** uneventful journey; **par ~** by surprise

surprise-partie [syʀpʀizpaʀti] (*pl* **surprises-parties**) NF party

surprit [syʀpʀi] vB *voir* **surprendre**

surproduction [syʀpʀɔdyksjɔ̃] NF overproduction

surpuissant, e [syʀpɥisɑ̃, -ɑ̃t] ADJ ultra-powerful

surréaliste [syʀʀealist] ADJ, NMF surrealist

surrégime [syʀʀeʒim] NM (*moteur*) over-revving; **tourner en ~** to over-rev; (*fig*) to go into overdrive

surréservation [syʀʀezɛʀvasjɔ̃] NF overbooking

sursaut [syʀso] NM start, jump; **~ de** (*énergie, indignation*) sudden fit *ou* burst of; **en ~** *adv* with a start

sursauter [syʀsote] /1/ vı to (give a) start, jump

surseoir [syʀswaʀ] /26/: **~ à** vt to defer; (*Jur*) to stay

sursis [syʀsi] NM (*Jur: gén*) suspended sentence; (: *à l'exécution capitale aussi fig*) reprieve; (*Mil*): **~ (d'appel ou d'incorporation)** deferment; **condamné à cinq mois (de prison) avec ~** given a five-month suspended (prison) sentence

sursitaire [syʀsitɛʀ] NM (*Mil*) deferred conscript

sursois [syʀswa], **sursoyais** *etc* [syʀswaje] vB *voir* **surseoir**

surtaxe [syʀtaks] NF surcharge

surtaxé, e [syʀtakse] ADJ (*Tél: appel, numéro*) premium-rate

surtaxer [syʀtakse] vт to put a surcharge on

surtension [syʀtɑ̃sjɔ̃] NF (*Élec*) overvoltage

★**surtout** [syʀtu] ADV (*avant tout, d'abord*) above all; (*spécialement, particulièrement*) especially; **il aime le sport, ~ le rugby** he likes sport, especially rugby; **cet été, il a ~ fait de la pêche** this summer he went fishing more than anything (else); **~ pas d'histoires!** no fuss now!; **~, ne dites rien!** whatever you do, don't say anything!; **~ pas!** certainly *ou* definitely not!; **~ que …** especially as …

survécu, e [syʀveky] PP *de* **survivre**

surveillance [syʀvejɑ̃s] NF watch; (*Police, Mil*) surveillance; **sous ~ médicale** under medical supervision; **la ~ du territoire** internal security; *voir aussi* DGSI

★**surveillant, e** [syʀvejɑ̃, -ɑ̃t] NM/F (*de prison*) warder; (*Scol*) monitor; (*de travaux*) supervisor, overseer

★**surveiller** [syʀveje] /1/ vт (*enfant, élèves, bagages*) to watch, keep an eye on; (*malade*) to watch over; (*prisonnier, suspect*) to keep (a) watch on; (*territoire, bâtiment*) to (keep) watch over; (*travaux, cuisson*) to supervise; (*Scol: examen*) to invigilate; **~ son langage/sa ligne** to watch one's language/figure ■ **se surveiller** vPR to keep a check *ou* watch on o.s.

survenir [syʀvəniʀ] /22/ vı (*incident, retards*) to occur, arise; (*événement*) to take place; (*personne*) to appear, arrive

survenu, e [syʀv(ə)ny] PP *de* **survenir**

survêt [syʀvɛt], **survêtement** [syʀvɛtmɑ̃] NM tracksuit (BRIT), sweat suit (US)

survie [syʀvi] NF survival; (Rel) afterlife; **équipement de ~** survival equipment; **une ~ de quelques mois** a few more months of life

surviens [syʀvjɛ̃], **survint** *etc* [syʀvɛ̃] VB *voir* **survenir**

survit *etc* [syʀvi] VB *voir* **survivre**

survitaminé, e [syʀvitamine] ADJ (fam) supercharged

survitrage [syʀvitʀaʒ] NM double-glazing

survivance [syʀvivɑ̃s] NF relic

survivant, e [syʀvivɑ̃, -ɑ̃t] VB *voir* **survivre** ▶ NM/F survivor

survivre [syʀvivʀ] /46/ VI to survive; **~ à** VT (accident etc) to survive; (personne) to outlive; **la victime a peu de chance de ~** the victim has little hope of survival

survol [syʀvɔl] NM flying over

survoler [syʀvɔle] /1/ VT to fly over; (fig: livre) to skim through; (: question, problèmes) to skim over

survolté, e [syʀvɔlte] ADJ (Élec) stepped up, boosted; (fig) worked up

sus [sy(s)]: **en ~ de** prép in addition to, over and above; **en ~** adv in addition; **~ à** excl: **~ au tyran!** at the tyrant!; *voir* **savoir**

susceptibilité [sysɛptibilite] NF sensitivity *no pl*

susceptible [sysɛptibl] ADJ touchy, sensitive; **~ de faire** (capacité) able to do; (probabilité) liable to do; **~ d'amélioration** *ou* **d'être amélioré** that can be improved, open to improvement

susciter [sysite] /1/ VT (admiration) to arouse; (obstacles, ennuis): **~ (à qn)** to create (for sb)

susdit, e [sysdi, -dit] ADJ foresaid

susmentionné, e [sysmɑ̃sjɔne] ADJ abovementioned

susnommé, e [sysnɔme] ADJ above-named

suspect, e [syspɛ(kt), -ɛkt] ADJ suspicious; (témoignage, opinions, vin etc) suspect; **peu ~ de** unlikely to be suspected of ▶ NM/F suspect

suspecter [syspɛkte] /1/ VT to suspect; (honnêteté de qn) to question, have one's suspicions about; **~ qn d'être/d'avoir fait qch** to suspect sb of being/having done sth

suspendre [syspɑ̃dʀ] /41/ VT (interrompre, démettre) to suspend; (remettre) to defer; (accrocher: vêtement): **~ qch (à)** to hang sth up (on); (fixer: lustre etc): **~ qch à** to hang sth from ■ **se suspendre** VPR: **se ~ à** to hang from

suspendu, e [syspɑ̃dy] PP *de* **suspendre** ▶ ADJ (accroché): **~ à** hanging on (ou from); (perché): **~ audessus de** suspended over; **bien/mal ~** (Auto) with good/poor suspension; **être ~ aux lèvres de qn** to hang upon sb's every word

suspens [syspɑ̃]: **en ~** adv (affaire) in abeyance; **tenir en ~** to keep in suspense

suspense [syspɑ̃s] NM suspense

suspension [syspɑ̃sjɔ̃] NF suspension; deferment; (Auto) suspension; (lustre) pendant light fitting; **en ~** in suspension, suspended; **~ d'audience** adjournment

suspicieux, -euse [syspisjø, -øz] ADJ suspicious

suspicion [syspisjɔ̃] NF suspicion

sustentation [systɑ̃tasjɔ̃] NF (Aviat) lift; **base** *ou* **polygone de ~** support polygon

sustenter [systɑ̃te] /1/: **se sustenter** VPR to take sustenance

susurrer [sysyʀe] /1/ VT to whisper

sut [sy] VB *voir* **savoir**

suture [sytyʀ] NF: **point de ~** stitch

suturer [sytyʀe] /1/ VT to stitch up, suture

suzeraineté [syz(ə)ʀɛnte] NF suzerainty

svelte [svɛlt] ADJ slender, svelte

SVP ABR (= s'il vous plaît) please

SVT SIGLE NF (Scol: = Sciences de la vie et de la Terre) natural sciences

swahili [swaili] NM (Ling) Swahili

Swaziland [swazilɑ̃d] NM: **le ~** Swaziland

★**sweat** [swit] NM (fam) sweatshirt

sweat-shirt [switʃœʀt] (pl **sweat-shirts**) NM sweatshirt

syllabe [silab] NF syllable

sylphide [silfid] NF (fig): **sa taille de ~** her sylph-like figure

sylvestre [silvɛstʀ] ADJ: **pin ~** Scots pine, Scotch fir

sylvicole [silvikɔl] ADJ forestry *cpd*

sylviculteur [silvikyltœʀ] NM forester

sylviculture [silvikyltyʀ] NF forestry, sylviculture

symbiose [sɛ̃bjoz] NF symbiosis; **en ~ avec qch** in symbiosis with sth

symbole [sɛ̃bɔl] NM symbol

symbolique [sɛ̃bɔlik] ADJ symbolic; (geste, offrande) token *cpd*; (salaire, dommages-intérêts) nominal

symboliquement [sɛ̃bɔlikmɑ̃] ADV symbolically

symboliser [sɛ̃bɔlize] /1/ VT to symbolize

symétrie [simetʀi] NF symmetry

symétrique [simetʀik] ADJ symmetrical

symétriquement [simetʀikmɑ̃] ADV symmetrically

★**sympa** [sɛ̃pa] ADJ INV (fam) = **sympathique** nice; friendly; good; **sois ~, prête-le moi** be a pal and lend it to me

sympathie [sɛ̃pati] NF (inclination) liking; (affinité) fellow feeling; (condoléances) sympathy; **accueillir avec ~** (projet) to receive favourably; **avoir de la ~ pour qn** to like sb, have a liking for sb; **témoignages de ~** expressions of sympathy; **croyez à toute ma ~** you have my deepest sympathy

★**sympathique** [sɛ̃patik] ADJ (personne, figure) nice, friendly, likeable; (geste) friendly; (livre) good; (déjeuner) nice; (réunion, endroit) pleasant, nice

sympathique does not mean *sympathetic*.

sympathisant, e [sɛ̃patizɑ̃, -ɑ̃t] NM/F sympathizer

sympathiser [sɛ̃patize] /1/ VI (voisins etc: s'entendre) to get on (BRIT) ou along (US) (well); (: se fréquenter) to socialize, see each other; **~ avec** to get on ou along (well) with, to see, socialize with

symphonie [sɛ̃fɔni] NF symphony

symphonique [sɛ̃fɔnik] ADJ (orchestre, concert) symphony *cpd*; (musique) symphonic

symposium [sɛ̃pozjɔm] NM symposium

symptomatique [sɛ̃ptɔmatik] ADJ symptomatic

symptôme [sɛ̃ptom] NM symptom

synagogue [sinagɔg] NF synagogue

synchrone [sɛ̃krɔn] ADJ synchronous

synchronique [sɛ̃krɔnik] ADJ: **tableau ~** synchronic table of events

synchronisation [sɛ̃krɔnizasjɔ̃] NF synchronization; (Auto): **~ des vitesses** synchromesh

synchronisé, e [sɛ̃krɔnize] ADJ synchronized

synchroniser [sɛ̃krɔnize] /1/ VT to synchronize

syncope [sɛ̃kɔp] NF (Méd) blackout; (Mus) syncopation; **tomber en ~** to faint, pass out

syncopé, e [sɛ̃kɔpe] ADJ syncopated

syndic [sɛ̃dik] NM managing agent

syndical, e, -aux [sɛ̃dikal, -o] ADJ (trade-)union cpd; **centrale syndicale** group of affiliated trade unions

syndicalisme [sɛ̃dikalism] NM (mouvement) trade unionism; (activités) union(ist) activities pl

syndicaliste [sɛ̃dikalist] NMF trade unionist

syndicat [sɛ̃dika] NM (d'ouvriers, employés) (trade(s)) union; (autre association d'intérêts) union, association; **~ d'initiative** tourist office ou bureau; **~ patronal** employers' syndicate, federation of employers; **~ de propriétaires** association of property owners

syndiqué, e [sɛ̃dike] ADJ belonging to a (trade) union; **non ~** non-union

syndiquer [sɛ̃dike] /1/: **se syndiquer** VPR to form a trade union; (adhérer) to join a trade union

syndrome [sɛ̃drom] NM syndrome; **~ prémenstruel** premenstrual syndrome (PMS)

synergie [sinɛrʒi] NF synergy

synode [sinɔd] NM synod

synonyme [sinɔnim] ADJ synonymous; **~ de** synonymous with ▶ NM synonym

synopsis [sinɔpsis] NMF synopsis

synoptique [sinɔptik] ADJ: **tableau ~** synoptic table

synovie [sinɔvi] NF synovia; **épanchement de ~** water on the knee

syntaxe [sɛ̃taks] NF syntax

synthèse [sɛ̃tɛz] NF synthesis; **faire la ~ de** to synthesize

synthétique [sɛ̃tetik] ADJ synthetic

synthétiser [sɛ̃tetize] /1/ VT to synthesize

synthétiseur [sɛ̃tetizœr] NM (Mus) synthesizer

syphilis [sifilis] NF syphilis

Syrie [siri] NF: **la ~** Syria

syrien, ne [siʁjɛ̃, -ɛn] ADJ Syrian ▶ NM/F: **Syrien, ne** Syrian

systématique [sistematik] ADJ systematic

systématiquement [sistematikmɑ̃] ADV systematically

systématisation [sistematizasjɔ̃] NF systematization

systématiser [sistematize] /1/ VT to systematize

système [sistɛm] NM system; **le ~ D** resourcefulness; **~ décimal** decimal system; **~ expert** expert system; **~ d'exploitation** (Inform) operating system; **~ immunitaire** immune system; **~ métrique** metric system; **~ solaire** solar system

systémique [sistemik] ADJ systemic

Tt

T, t [te] NM INV T, t; **T comme Thérèse** T for Tommy
► ABR (= *tonne*) t

★**t'** [t] PRON *voir* **te**

★**ta** [ta] ADJ POSS *voir* **ton¹**

★**tabac** [taba] NM tobacco; (*aussi:* **débit** *ou* **bureau de tabac**) tobacconist's (shop); **passer qn à ~** (*fam*) to beat sb up; **faire un ~** (*fam*) to be a big hit; **~ blond/brun** light/dark tobacco; **~ gris** shag; **~ à priser** snuff ► ADJ INV: **(couleur) ~** buff, tobacco *cpd*

tabagie [tabaʒi] NF smoke den

tabagique [tabaʒik] ADJ (*dépendance*) nicotine, tobacco *cpd*; (*consommation*) tobacco *cpd*

tabagisme [tabaʒism] NM nicotine addiction; **~ passif** passive smoking

tabassage [tabasaʒ] NM (*fam*) beating up

tabasser [tabase] /1/ VT (*fam*) to beat up

tabatière [tabatjɛʀ] NF snuffbox

tabernacle [tabɛʀnakl] NM tabernacle

★**table** [tabl] NF table; **avoir une bonne ~** to keep a good table; **à ~!** dinner *etc* is ready!; **se mettre à ~** to sit down to eat; (*fig: fam*) to come clean; **mettre** *ou* **dresser/desservir la ~** to lay *ou* set/clear the table; **faire ~ rase de** to make a clean sweep of; **~ à repasser** ironing board; **~ basse** coffee table; **~ de cuisson** (*à l'électricité*) hob, hotplate; (*au gaz*) hob, gas ring; **~ d'écoute** wire-tapping set; **~ d'harmonie** sounding board; **~ d'hôte** set menu; **~ de lecture** turntable; **~ des matières** (table of) contents *pl*; **~ de multiplication** multiplication table; **~ des négociations** negotiating table; **~ de nuit** *ou* **chevet** bedside table; **~ d'orientation** viewpoint indicator; **~ ronde** (*débat*) round table; **~ roulante** (tea) trolley (BRIT), tea wagon (US); **~ de toilette** washstand; **~ traçante** (*Inform*) plotter

★**tableau, x** [tablo] NM (*Art*) painting; (*reproduction, fig*) picture; (*panneau*) board; (*schéma*) table, chart; **~ blanc** whiteboard; **~ blanc interactif** interactive whiteboard; **~ d'affichage** notice board; **~ de bord** dashboard; (*Aviat*) instrument panel; **~ de chasse** tally; **~ de contrôle** console, control panel; **~ de maître** masterpiece; **~ noir** blackboard

tablée [table] NF (*personnes*) table

tabler [table] /1/ VI: **~ sur** to count *ou* bank on

tablette [tablɛt] NF (*planche*) shelf; (*Inform*) tablet; **~ de chocolat** bar of chocolate

tableur [tablœʀ] NM (*Inform*) spreadsheet

tablier [tablije] NM apron; (*de pont*) roadway; (*de cheminée*) (flue-)shutter

tabou, e [tabu] ADJ, NM taboo

taboulé [tabule] NM tabbouleh

tabouret [tabuʀɛ] NM stool

tabulateur [tabylatœʀ] NM (*Tech*) tabulator

tac [tak] NM: **du ~ au ~** tit for tat

★**tache** [taʃ] NF (*saleté*) stain, mark; (*Art, de couleur, lumière*) spot; splash, patch; **faire ~ d'huile** to spread, gain ground; **~ de rousseur** *ou* **de son** freckle; **~ de vin** (*sur la peau*) strawberry mark

★**tâche** [taʃ] NF task; **travailler à la ~** to do piece-work

tacher [taʃe] /1/ VT to stain, mark; (*fig*) to sully, stain ■ **se tacher** VPR (*fruits*) to become marked

tâcher [taʃe] /1/ VI: **~ de faire** to try to do, endeavour (BRIT) *ou* endeavor (US) to do

tâcheron [taʃ(ə)ʀɔ̃] NM (*fig*) drudge

tacheté, e [taʃte] ADJ: **~ de** speckled *ou* spotted with

tachisme [taʃism] NM (*Peinture*) tachisme

tachycardie [takikaʀdi] NF tachycardia

tachygraphe [takigʀaf] NM tachograph

tachymètre [takimɛtʀ] NM tachometer

tacite [tasit] ADJ tacit

tacitement [tasitmɑ̃] ADV tacitly

taciturne [tasityʀn] ADJ taciturn

tacle [takl] NM (*Football*) tackle; **~ par derrière** tackle from behind

tacler [takle] VT (*Football*) to tackle

tacot [tako] NM (*péj: voiture*) banger (BRIT), clunker (US)

tact [takt] NM tact; **avoir du ~** to be tactful, have tact

tacticien, ne [taktisjɛ̃, -ɛn] NM/F tactician

tactile [taktil] ADJ tactile; **affichage ~** touch-sensitive display; *voir aussi* **écran**

tactique [taktik] ADJ tactical ► NF (*technique*) tactics *sg*; (*plan*) tactic

Tadjikistan [tadʒikistɑ̃] NM Tajikistan

taffetas [tafta] NM taffeta

Tage [taʒ] NM: **le ~** the (river) Tagus

taguer [tage] VT to graffiti, put graffiti on

tagueur, -euse [tagœʀ, -øz] NM/F graffiti artist, graffitist

Tahiti [taiti] NF Tahiti

tahitien, ne [taisjɛ̃, -ɛn] ADJ Tahitian

taie [tɛ] NF: **~ (d'oreiller)** pillowslip, pillowcase

taïga [tajga] NF taiga

t

taillader [tɑjade] /**1**/ VT to gash

★**taille** [tɑj] NF cutting; (*d'arbre*) pruning; (*milieu du corps*) waist; (*hauteur*) height; (*grandeur*) size; **de ~ à faire** capable of doing; **de ~** *adj* sizeable; **quelle ~ faites- vous?** what size are you?

taillé, e [tɑje] ADJ (*moustache, ongles, arbre*) trimmed; **~ pour** (*fait pour, apte à*) cut out for; tailor-made for; **~ en pointe** sharpened to a point

★**taille-crayon(s)** [tɑjkʀɛjɔ̃] NM INV pencil sharpener

tailler [tɑje] /**1**/ VT (*pierre, diamant*) to cut; (*arbre, plante*) to prune; (*vêtement*) to cut out; (*crayon*) to sharpen ▶ VI: **~ dans** (*chair, bois*) to cut into; **~ grand/petit** to be on the large/small side ■ **se tailler** VPR (*ongles, barbe*) to trim, cut; (*fig: réputation*) to gain, win; (*fam: s'enfuir*) to beat it

tailleur, -euse [tɑjœʀ, -øz] NM/F: **~ de diamants** diamond-cutter ▶ NM (*couturier*) tailor; (*vêtement*) suit, costume; **en ~** (*assis*) cross-legged

tailleur-pantalon [tɑjœʀpɑ̃talɔ̃] (*pl* **tailleurs-pantalons**) NM trouser suit (BRIT), pantsuit (US)

taillis [tɑji] NM copse

tain [tɛ̃] NM silvering; **glace sans ~** two-way mirror

★**taire** [tɛʀ] /**54**/ VT to keep to o.s., conceal ▶ VI: **faire ~ qn** to make sb be quiet; (*fig*) to silence sb ■ **se taire** VPR (*s'arrêter de parler*) to fall silent, stop talking; (*ne pas parler*) to be silent ou quiet; (*s'abstenir de s'exprimer*) to keep quiet; (*bruit, voix*) to disappear; **tais-toi!**, **taisez-vous!** be quiet!

taiseux, -euse [tɛzø, øz] ADJ (*fam*) silent, uncommunicative ▶ NM/F reserved ou quiet person

Taiwan [tajwan] NF Taiwan

tajine [taʒin] NM tagine, tajine

talc [talk] NM talc, talcum powder

talé, e [tale] ADJ (*fruit*) bruised

talent [talɑ̃] NM talent; **avoir du ~** to be talented, have talent

talentueux, -euse [talɑ̃tɥø, -øz] ADJ talented

talion [taljɔ̃] NM: **la loi du ~** an eye for an eye

talisman [talismɑ̃] NM talisman

talkie-walkie [tɔkiwɔki] (*pl* **talkies-walkies**) NM walkie-talkie

taloche [talɔʃ] NF (*fam: claque*) slap; (*Tech*) plaster float

★**talon** [talɔ̃] NM heel; (*de chèque, billet*) stub, counterfoil (BRIT); **talons plats/aiguilles** flat/stiletto heels; **être sur les talons de qn** to be on sb's heels; **tourner les talons** to turn on one's heel; **montrer les talons** (*fig*) to show a clean pair of heels

talonnade [talɔnad] NF (*Football*) back heel

talonner [talɔne] /**1**/ VT to follow hard behind; (*fig*) to hound; (*Rugby*) to heel

talonnette [talɔnɛt] NF (*de chaussure*) heelpiece; (*de pantalon*) stirrup

talonneur [talɔnœʀ] NM (*Rugby*) hooker

talquer [talke] /**1**/ VT to put talc(um powder) on

talus [taly] NM embankment; **~ de remblai/ déblai** embankment/excavation slope

tamarin [tamaʀɛ̃] NM (*Bot*) tamarind

tambour [tɑ̃buʀ] NM (*Mus, Tech*) drum; (*musicien*) drummer; (*porte*) revolving door(s *pl*); **sans ~ ni trompette** unobtrusively

tambourin [tɑ̃buʀɛ̃] NM tambourine

tambouriner [tɑ̃buʀine] /**1**/ VI: **~ contre** to drum against ou on

tambour-major [tɑ̃buʀmaʒɔʀ] (*pl* **tambours-majors**) NM drum major

tamis [tami] NM sieve

★**Tamise** [tamiz] NF: **la ~** the Thames

tamisé, e [tamize] ADJ (*fig*) subdued, soft

tamiser [tamize] /**1**/ VT to sieve, sift

tampon [tɑ̃pɔ̃] NM (*de coton, d'ouate*) pad; (*aussi:* **tampon hygiénique** ou **périodique**) tampon; (*amortisseur, Inform: aussi:* **mémoire tampon**) buffer; (*bouchon*) plug, stopper; (*cachet, timbre*) stamp; (*Chimie*) buffer; **~ buvard** blotter; **~ encreur** inking pad; **~ (à récurer)** scouring pad

tamponné, e [tɑ̃pɔne] ADJ: **solution tamponnée** buffer solution

tamponner [tɑ̃pɔne] /**1**/ VT (*timbres*) to stamp; (*heurter*) to crash ou ram into; (*essuyer*) to mop up ■ **se tamponner** VPR (*voitures*) to crash (into each other)

tamponneuse [tɑ̃pɔnøz] ADJ F: **autos tamponneuses** dodgems, bumper cars

tam-tam [tamtam] NM tomtom

tancer [tɑ̃se] /**3**/ VT to scold

tanche [tɑ̃ʃ] NF tench

tandem [tɑ̃dɛm] NM tandem; (*fig*) duo, pair

tandis [tɑ̃di]: **~ que** *conj* while

tangage [tɑ̃gaʒ] NM pitching (and tossing)

tangent, e [tɑ̃ʒɑ̃, -ɑ̃t] ADJ (*Math*): **~ à** tangential (to); (*de justesse: fam*) close ▶ NF (*Math*) tangent

Tanger [tɑ̃ʒe] N Tangier

tango [tɑ̃go] NM (*Mus*) tango ▶ ADJ INV (*couleur*) dark orange

tanguer [tɑ̃ge] /**1**/ VI to pitch (and toss)

tanière [tanjɛʀ] NF lair, den

tanin [tanɛ̃] NM tannin

tank [tɑ̃k] NM tank

tanker [tɑ̃kɛʀ] NM tanker

tankini [tɑ̃kini] NM tankini

tanné, e [tane] ADJ weather-beaten

tanner [tane] /**1**/ VT to tan

tannerie [tanʀi] NF tannery

tanneur [tanœʀ] NM tanner

tant [tɑ̃] ADV so much; **~ de** (*sable, eau*) so much; (*gens, livres*) so many; **~ que** *conj* as long as; **~ que** (*comparatif*) as much as; **~ mieux** that's great; (*avec une certaine réserve*) so much the better; **~ mieux pour lui** good for him; **~ pis** too bad; (*conciliant*) never mind; **un ~ soit peu** (*un peu*) a little bit; (*même un peu*) (even) remotely; **~ bien que mal** as well as can be expected; **~ s'en faut** far from it, not by a long way

★**tante** [tɑ̃t] NF aunt

tantinet [tɑ̃tinɛ]: **un ~** *adv* a tiny bit

tantôt [tɑ̃to] ADV (*parfois*): **tantôt ... tantôt** now ... now; (*cet après-midi*) this afternoon

Tanzanie [tɑ̃zani] NF: **la ~** Tanzania

tanzanien, ne [tɑ̃zanjɛ̃, -ɛn] ADJ Tanzanian

TAO SIGLE F (= *traduction assistée par ordinateur*) MAT (= *machine-aided translation*)

taon [tɑ̃] NM horsefly, gadfly

tapage [tapaʒ] NM uproar, din; (fig) fuss, row; **~ nocturne** (Jur) disturbance of the peace (at night)

tapageur, -euse [tapaʒœʀ, -øz] ADJ (bruyant: enfants etc) noisy; (voyant: toilette) loud, flashy; (publicité) obtrusive

tape [tap] NF slap

tape-à-l'œil [tapalœj] ADJ INV flashy, showy

tapenade [tap(ə)nad] NF (Culin) tapenade

★**taper** [tape] /1/ VT (personne) to clout; (porte) to bang, slam; (enfant) to slap; (dactylographier) to type (out); (Inform) to key(board); (fam: emprunter): **~ qn de 10 euros** to touch sb for 10 euros, cadge 10 euros off sb ▶ VI (soleil) to beat down; **~ sur qn** to thump sb; (fig) to run sb down; **~ sur qch** (clou etc) to hit sth; (table etc) to bang on sth; **~ à** (porte etc) to knock on; **~ dans** (se servir) to dig into; **~ des mains/pieds** to clap one's hands/stamp one's feet; **~ (à la machine)** to type ■ **se taper** VPR (fam: travail) to get landed with; (: boire, manger) to down

tapette [tapɛt] NF: **~ à souris** mousetrap; (pour insectes) fly swatter; (fam: homosexuel) fairy (fam), poofter (fam); (petite tape) little tap

tapi, e [tapi] ADJ: **~ dans/derrière** (blotti) crouching ou cowering in/behind; (caché) hidden away in/behind

tapinois [tapinwa]: **en ~** adv stealthily

tapioca [tapjɔka] NM tapioca

tapir [tapiʀ] /2/: **se tapir** VPR to hide away

★**tapis** [tapi] NM carpet; (petit) rug; (de table) cloth; **mettre sur le ~** (fig) to bring up for discussion; **aller au ~** (Boxe) to go down; **envoyer au ~** (Boxe) to floor; **~ roulant** conveyor belt; (pour piétons) moving walkway; (pour bagages) carousel; **~ de sol** (de tente) groundsheet; **~ de souris** (Inform) mouse mat

tapis-brosse [tapibʀɔs] NM doormat

tapisser [tapise] /1/ VT (avec du papier peint) to paper; (recouvrir): **~ qch (de)** to cover sth (with)

tapisserie [tapisʀi] NF (tenture, broderie) tapestry; (: travail) tapestry-making; (: ouvrage) tapestry work; (papier peint) wallpaper; (fig): **faire ~** to sit out, be a wallflower

tapissier, -ière [tapisje, -jɛʀ] NM/F: **tapissier-décorateur** interior decorator

tapoter [tapote] /1/ VT (joue, main) to pat; (objet) to tap

taquet [takɛ] NM (cale) wedge; (cheville) peg

taquin, e [takɛ̃, -in] ADJ teasing

taquiner [takine] /1/ VT to tease

taquinerie [takinʀi] NF teasing no pl

tarabiscoté, e [taʀabiskɔte] ADJ over-ornate, fussy

tarabuster [taʀabyste] /1/ VT to bother, worry

tarama [taʀama] NM (Culin) taramasalata

tarauder [taʀode] /1/ VT (Tech) to tap; to thread; (fig) to pierce

★**tard** [taʀ] ADV late; **plus ~** later (on); **au plus ~** at the latest; **il est trop ~** it's too late ▶ NM: **sur le ~** (à une heure avancée) late in the day; (vers la fin de la vie) late in life

tarder [taʀde] /1/ VI (chose) to be a long time coming; (personne): **~ à faire** to delay doing; **il me tarde d'être** I am longing to be; **sans (plus) ~** without (further) delay

tardif, -ive [taʀdif, -iv] ADJ (heure, repas, fruit) late; (talent, goût) late in developing

tardivement [taʀdivmɑ̃] ADV late

tare [taʀ] NF (Comm) tare; (fig) defect; blemish

taré, e [taʀe] NM/F cretin

targette [taʀʒɛt] NF (verrou) bolt

targuer [taʀge] /1/: **se targuer de** VPR to boast about

★**tarif** [taʀif] NM: **~ des consommations** price list; **tarifs postaux/douaniers** postal/customs rates; **~ des taxis** taxi fares; **~ plein/réduit** (train) full/reduced fare; (téléphone) peak/off-peak rate; **voyager à plein ~/à ~ réduit** to travel at full/reduced fare

tarifaire [taʀifɛʀ] ADJ (voir tarif) relating to price lists etc

tarifé, e [taʀife] ADJ: **~ 10 euros** priced at 10 euros

tarifer [taʀife] /1/ VT to fix the price ou rate for

tarification [taʀifikasjɔ̃] NF fixing of a price scale

tarir [taʀiʀ] /2/ VI to dry up, run dry ▶ VT to dry up ■ **se tarir** VPR (source) to dry up, run dry; (ressources) to dry up

tarmac [taʀmak] NM tarmac

tarot [taʀo] NM tarot card; (jeu) (set of) tarot cards; **jouer au ~** to play tarot

tartan [taʀtɑ̃] NM tartan; **en ~** tartan cpd

tartare [taʀtaʀ] ADJ (Culin) tartar(e)

★**tarte** [taʀt] NF tart; **~ aux pommes/à la crème** apple/custard tart; **~ Tatin ≈** apple upside-down tart

tartelette [taʀtəlɛt] NF tartlet

★**tartine** [taʀtin] NF slice of bread (and butter (ou jam)); **~ de miel** slice of bread and honey; **~ beurrée** slice of bread and butter

tartiner [taʀtine] /1/ VT to spread; **fromage à ~** cheese spread

tartre [taʀtʀ] NM (des dents) tartar; (de chaudière) fur, scale

★**tas** [tɑ] NM heap, pile; **un ~ de** (fig) heaps of, lots of; **en ~** in a heap ou pile; **dans le ~** (fig) in the crowd; among them; **formé sur le ~** trained on the job

Tasmanie [tasmani] NF: **la ~** Tasmania

tasmanien, ne [tasmanjɛ̃, -ɛn] ADJ Tasmanian

★**tasse** [tɑs] NF cup; **boire la ~** (en se baignant) to swallow a mouthful; **~ à café/thé** coffee/teacup

tassé, e [tɑse] ADJ: **bien ~** (café etc) strong

tasseau, x [tɑso] NM length of wood

tassement [tɑsmɑ̃] NM (de vertèbres) compression; (Écon, Pol: ralentissement) fall-off, slowdown; (Bourse) dullness

tasser [tɑse] /1/ VT (terre, neige) to pack down; (entasser): **~ qch dans** to cram sth into ■ **se tasser** VPR (terrain) to settle; (s'affaisser) to settle; (personne: avec l'âge) to shrink; (fig) to sort itself out, settle down

tata [tata] NF aunt

tâter [tɑte] /1/ VT to feel; (fig) to try out; **~ de** (prison etc) to have a taste of; **~ le terrain** (fig) to test the ground ■ **se tâter** VPR (hésiter) to be in two minds

tatillon, ne [tatijɔ̃, -ɔn] ADJ pernickety

tâtonnement [tɑtɔnmɑ̃] NM: **par tâtonnements** (fig) by trial and error

433

tâtonner [tɑtɔne] /1/ vi to grope one's way along; (fig) to grope around (in the dark)

tâtons [tɑtɔ̃]: **à ~** adv: **chercher/avancer à ~** to grope around for/grope one's way forward

tatouage [tatwaʒ] NM tattooing; (dessin) tattoo

tatouer [tatwe] /1/ VT to tattoo

taudis [todi] NM hovel, slum

taulard, e [tolaʀ, -aʀd] NM/F (fam) ex con (fam), jailbird (fam)

taule [tol] NF (fam) nick (BRIT), jail

taupe [top] NF mole; (peau) moleskin

taupinière [topinjɛʀ] NF molehill

taureau, x [tɔʀo] NM bull; (signe): **le T~** Taurus, the Bull; **être du T~** to be Taurus

taurillon [tɔʀijɔ̃] NM bull-calf

tauromachie [tɔʀɔmaʃi] NF bullfighting

tautologie [totɔlɔʒi] NF tautology

tautologique [totɔlɔʒik] ADJ tautological

taux [to] NM rate; (d'alcool) level; **~ d'escompte** discount rate; **~ d'intérêt** interest rate; **~ de mortalité** mortality rate

tavelé, e [tav(ə)le] ADJ marked

taverne [tavɛʀn] NF inn, tavern

taxable [taksabl] ADJ taxable

taxation [taksasjɔ̃] NF taxation; (Tél) charges pl

taxe [taks] NF tax; (douanière) duty; **toutes taxes comprises** inclusive of tax; **la boutique hors taxes** the duty-free shop; **~ de base** (Tél) unit charge; **~ de séjour** tourist tax; **~ à** ou **sur la valeur ajoutée** value added tax

taxer [takse] /1/ VT (personne) to tax; (produit) to put a tax on, tax; **~ qn de qch** (qualifier) to call sb sth; (accuser) to accuse sb of sth, tax sb with sth

★**taxi** [taksi] NM taxi; (chauffeur: fam) taxi driver

taxidermie [taksidɛʀmi] NF taxidermy

taxidermiste [taksidɛʀmist] NMF taxidermist

taximètre [taksimɛtʀ] NM (taxi)meter

taxiphone [taksifɔn] NM pay phone

TB ABR = **très bien; très bon**

tbe ABR (= très bon état) VGC, vgc

Tchad [tʃad] NM: **le ~** Chad

tchadien, ne [tʃadjɛ̃, -ɛn] ADJ Chad(ian), of ou from Chad

tchao [tʃao] EXCL (fam) bye(-bye)!

tchécoslovaque [tʃekɔslɔvak] (Hist) ADJ Czechoslovak(ian) ▶NMF: **Tchécoslovaque** Czechoslovak(ian)

Tchécoslovaquie [tʃekɔslɔvaki] NF (Hist): **la ~** Czechoslovakia

tchèque [tʃɛk] ADJ Czech; **la République ~** the Czech Republic ▶NM (Ling) Czech ▶NMF: **Tchèque** Czech

Tchéquie [tʃeki] NF Czechia

tchétchène [tʃetʃɛn] ADJ Chechen ▶NM (langue) Chechen ▶NMF: **Tchétchène** Chechen

Tchétchénie [tʃetʃeni] NF: **la ~** Chechnya

TCS SIGLE M (= Touring Club de Suisse) ≈ AA ou RAC (BRIT), ≈ AAA (US)

TD SIGLE MPL = **travaux dirigés**

★**te, t'** [tə, t] PRON you; (réfléchi) yourself

té [te] NM T-square

★**technicien, ne** [tɛknisjɛ̃, -ɛn] NM/F technician

technicisation [tɛknisizasjɔ̃] NF increasing technicality

technicité [tɛknisite] NF technical nature

technico-commercial, e, -aux [tɛknikokɔmɛʀsjal, -o] ADJ: **agent ~** sales technician

★**technique** [tɛknik] ADJ technical ▶ NF technique

techniquement [tɛknikmɑ̃] ADV technically

techno [tɛkno] NF (fam: Mus): **la (musique) ~** techno (music); = **technologie**

technocrate [tɛknɔkʀat] NMF technocrat

technocratie [tɛknɔkʀasi] NF technocracy

technocratique [tɛknɔkʀatik] ADJ technocratic

★**technologie** [tɛknɔlɔʒi] NF technology

technologique [tɛknɔlɔʒik] ADJ technological

technologue [tɛknɔlɔg] NMF technologist

teck [tɛk] NM teak

teckel [tekɛl] NM dachshund

tectonique [tɛktɔnik] NF (Géol) tectonics sg ▶ ADJ tectonic

tee [ti] NM tee

tee-shirt [tiʃœʀt] NM T-shirt, tee-shirt

Téhéran [teeʀɑ̃] N Teheran

teigne [tɛɲ] VB voir **teindre** ▶ NF (Zool) moth; (Méd) ringworm

teigneux, -euse [tɛɲø, -øz] ADJ (péj) nasty, scabby

teindre [tɛ̃dʀ] /52/ VT to dye ■ **se teindre** VPR: **se ~ (les cheveux)** to dye one's hair

teint, e [tɛ̃, tɛ̃t] PP de **teindre** ▶ ADJ dyed ▶ NM (du visage: permanent) complexion, colouring (BRIT), coloring (US); (: momentané) colour (BRIT), color (US); **bon ~** adj inv (couleur) fast; (tissu) colourfast; (fig: personne) staunch; **grand ~** adj inv colourfast ▶ NF (nuance) shade; (couleur) colour (BRIT), color (US); **une très jolie teinte** a very pretty colour; **une teinte dans les bleus** a bluey shade; (fig): **une teinte de** a hint of

teinté, e [tɛ̃te] ADJ (verres) tinted; (bois) stained; **~ acajou** mahogany-stained; **~ de** (fig) tinged with

teinter [tɛ̃te] /1/ VT (verre) to tint; (bois) to stain; **~ qch de** (fig) to tinge sth with

teinture [tɛ̃tyʀ] NF dyeing; (substance) dye; (Méd): **~ d'iode** tincture of iodine

teinturerie [tɛ̃tyʀʀi] NF dry cleaner's

teinturier, -ière [tɛ̃tyʀje, -jɛʀ] NM/F dry cleaner

tel, telle [tɛl] ADJ (pareil) such; (comme): **~ un/ des ...** like a/like ...; (indéfini) such-and-such a, a given; (intensif): **un ~/de tels ...** such (a)/such ...; **venez ~ jour** come on such-and-such a day; **rien de ~** nothing like it, no such thing; **~ que** conj like, such as; **~ quel** as it is ou stands (ou was etc)

tél. ABR = **téléphone**

Tel Aviv [tɛlaviv] N Tel Aviv

télé [tele] NF (fam: télévision) TV, telly (BRIT); **à la ~** on TV ou telly

téléachat [teleaʃa] NM teleshopping

télébenne [telebɛn] NMF telecabine, gondola

télécabine [telekabin] NMF (benne) cable car

télécarte [telekaʀt] NF phonecard

téléchargeable [teleʃaʀʒabl] ADJ downloadable

téléchargement [teleʃaʀʒɛmã] NM (*action*) downloading; (*fichier*) download

télécharger [teleʃaʀʒe] /3/ VT (*Inform: recevoir*) to download; (: *transmettre*) to upload

télécom [telekɔm] ABR (= *télécommunication*) ≈ telecom

télécommande [telekɔmãd] NF remote control

télécommander [telekɔmãde] /1/ VT to operate by remote control, radio-control

télécommunications [telekɔmynikasjɔ̃] NFPL telecommunications

téléconférence [telekɔ̃feʀãs] NF teleconference

télécopie [telekɔpi] NF fax, telefax

télécopieur [telekɔpjœʀ] NM fax (machine)

télédéclaration [teledeklaʀasjɔ̃] NF online tax filing

télédétection [teledetɛksjɔ̃] NF remote sensing

télédiffuser [teledifyze] /1/ VT to broadcast (on television)

télédiffusion [teledifyzjɔ̃] NF television broadcasting

télédistribution [teledistʀibysjɔ̃] NF cable TV

téléenseignement [teleãsɛɲmã] NM distance teaching (*ou* learning)

téléférique [telefeʀik] NM = **téléphérique**

téléfilm [telefilm] NM film made for TV, TV film

télégénique [teleʒenik] ADJ telegenic

télégramme [telegʀam] NM telegram

télégraphe [telegʀaf] NM telegraph

télégraphie [telegʀafi] NF telegraphy

télégraphier [telegʀafje] /7/ VT to telegraph, cable

télégraphique [telegʀafik] ADJ telegraph *cpd*, telegraphic; (*fig*) telegraphic

télégraphiste [telegʀafist] NMF telegraphist

téléguider [telegide] /1/ VT to operate by remote control, radio-control

téléinformatique [teleɛ̃fɔʀmatik] NF remote access computing

téléjournal, -aux [teleʒuʀnal, -o] NM television news magazine programme

télémarketing [telemaʀketiŋ] NM telemarketing

télématique [telematik] NF telematics *sg* ▸ ADJ telematic

téléobjectif [teleɔbʒɛktif] NM telephoto lens *sg*

téléopérateur, -trice [teleɔpeʀatœʀ, -tʀis] NM/F call-centre operator

télépaiement [telepɛmã] NM online payment

télépathie [telepati] NF telepathy

télépéage [telepeaʒ] NM electronic toll system

téléphérique [telefeʀik] NM cable-car

téléphone [telefɔn] NM telephone; **avoir le ~** to be on the (tele)phone; **au ~** on the phone; **~ arabe** bush telegraph; **~ à carte** cardphone; **~ avec appareil photo** camera phone; **~ fixe** landline; **~ mobile** *ou* **portable** mobile (phone) (BRIT), cell (phone) (US); **~ rouge** hotline; **~ sans fil** cordless (tele)phone

téléphoner [telefɔne] /1/ VI to telephone; to make a phone call ▸ VT to telephone; **~ à** to phone, ring up, call up

téléphonie [telefɔni] NF telephony; **~ fixe** landline telephone services

téléphonique [telefɔnik] ADJ (tele)phone *cpd*, phone *cpd*; **cabine ~** call box (BRIT), (tele)phone box (BRIT) *ou* booth; **conversation/appel ~** (tele)phone conversation/call

téléphoniste [telefɔnist] NMF telephonist, telephone operator; (*d'entreprise*) switchboard operator

téléport [telepɔʀ] NM teleport

téléprompteur [telepʀɔ̃ptœʀ] NM Autocue®, teleprompter

téléprospection [telepʀɔspɛksjɔ̃] NF telesales

téléréalité [teleʀealite] NF reality TV

télescopage [telɛskɔpaʒ] NM crash

télescope [telɛskɔp] NM telescope

télescoper [telɛskɔpe] /1/ VT to smash up ▪ **se télescoper** VPR (*véhicules*) to concertina, crash into each other

télescopique [telɛskɔpik] ADJ telescopic

téléscripteur [teleskʀiptœʀ] NM teleprinter

télésiège [telesjɛʒ] NM chairlift

téléski [teleski] NM ski-tow; **~ à archets** T-bar tow; **~ à perche** button lift

téléspectateur, -trice [telespɛktatœʀ, -tʀis] NM/F (television) viewer

télésurveillance [telesyʀvɛjãs] NF TV surveillance

télétexte® [teletɛkst] NM Teletext®

téléthon [teletɔ̃] NM telethon

télétraitement [teletʀɛtmã] NM remote processing

télétransmission [teletʀãsmisjɔ̃] NF remote transmission

télétravail NM teleworking, telecommuting

télétravailleur, -euse [teletʀavajœʀ, -øz] NM/F teleworker, telecommuter

télétype [teletip] NM teleprinter

télévente [televãt] NF telesales

télévisé [televize] ADJ (*droits, journal*) television *cpd*, TV *cpd*; (*débat*) televised

téléviser [televize] /1/ VT to televise

téléviseur [televizœʀ] NM television set

télévision [televizjɔ̃] NF television; **(poste de) ~** television (set); **avoir la ~** to have a television; **à la ~** on television; **~ numérique** digital TV; **~ par câble/satellite** cable/satellite television

télévisuel, le [televizɥɛl] ADJ (*droits, publicité*) television *cpd*, TV *cpd*

télex [telɛks] NM telex

télexer [telɛkse] /1/ VT to telex

télexiste [telɛksist] NMF telex operator

telle [tɛl] ADJ F *voir* **tel**

★**tellement** [telmã] ADV (*tant*) so much; (*si*) so; **~ plus grand (que)** so much bigger (than); **~ de** (*sable, eau*) so much; (*gens, livres*) so many; **il s'est endormi ~ il était fatigué** he was so tired (that) he fell asleep; **pas ~** not really; **pas ~ fort/lentement** not (all) that strong/slowly; **il ne mange pas ~** he doesn't eat (all that) much

tellurique [telyʀik] ADJ: **secousse ~** earth tremor; **planète ~** telluric planet

téloche [telɔʃ] NF (*fam*) TV, telly (BRIT *fam*)

téméraire – tenir

téméraire [temeʀɛʀ] ADJ reckless, rash

témérité [temerite] NF recklessness, rashness

témoignage [temwaɲaʒ] NM (Jur: *déclaration*) testimony *no pl*, evidence *no pl*; (*: faits*) evidence *no pl*; (*gén: rapport, récit*) account; (*fig: d'affection etc*) token, mark; (*geste*) expression

témoigner [temwaɲe] /1/ VT (*manifester: intérêt, gratitude*) to show; **~ que** to testify that; (*fig: démontrer*) to reveal that, testify the fact that; **~ de** (*confirmer*) to bear witness to, testify to ▸ VI (*Jur*) to testify, give evidence

témoin [temwɛ̃] NM witness; (*fig*) testimony; (*Sport*) baton; (*Constr*) telltale; **~ le fait que ...** (as) witness the fact that ...; **être ~ de** (*voir*) to witness; **prendre à ~** to call to witness; **~ à charge** witness for the prosecution; **~ de connexion** (*Internet*) cookie; **T~ de Jehovah** Jehovah's Witness; **~ de moralité** character reference; **~ oculaire** eyewitness ▸ ADJ control *cpd*, test *cpd*; **appartement-témoin** show flat (BRIT), model apartment (US)

tempe [tɑ̃p] NF (*Anat*) temple

tempérament [tɑ̃peʀamɑ̃] NM temperament, disposition; (*santé*) constitution; **à ~** (*vente*) on deferred (payment) terms; (*achat*) by instalments, hire purchase *cpd*; **avoir du ~** to be hot-blooded

tempérance [tɑ̃peʀɑ̃s] NF temperance; **société de ~** temperance society

tempérant, e [tɑ̃peʀɑ̃, -ɑ̃t] ADJ temperate

température [tɑ̃peʀatyʀ] NF temperature; **prendre la ~ de** to take the temperature of; (*fig*) to gauge the feeling of; **avoir** *ou* **faire de la ~** to be running *ou* have a temperature

tempéré, e [tɑ̃peʀe] ADJ temperate

tempérer [tɑ̃peʀe] /6/ VT to temper

tempête [tɑ̃pɛt] NF storm; **~ de sable/neige** sand/snowstorm; **vent de ~** gale

tempêter [tɑ̃pete] /1/ VI to rant and rave

temple [tɑ̃pl] NM temple; (*protestant*) church

tempo [tɛmpo] NM tempo

temporaire [tɑ̃pɔʀɛʀ] ADJ temporary

temporairement [tɑ̃pɔʀɛʀmɑ̃] ADV temporarily

temporel, le [tɑ̃pɔʀɛl] ADJ temporal

temporisateur, -trice [tɑ̃pɔʀizatœʀ, -tʀis] ADJ temporizing, delaying

temporisation [tɑ̃pɔʀizasjɔ̃] NF temporizing, playing for time

temporiser [tɑ̃pɔʀize] /1/ VI to temporize, play for time

★**temps** [tɑ̃] NM (*atmosphérique*) weather; (*durée*) time; (*époque*) time, times *pl*; (*Ling*) tense; (*Mus*) beat; (*Tech*) stroke; **un ~ de chien** (*fam*) rotten weather; **quel ~ fait-il?** what's the weather like?; **il fait beau/mauvais ~** the weather is fine/bad; **avoir le ~/tout le ~/juste le ~** to have time/plenty of time/just enough time; **les ~ changent/sont durs** times are changing/hard; **avoir fait son ~** (*fig*) to have had its (*ou* his *etc*) day; **en ~ de paix/guerre** in peacetime/wartime; **en ~ utile** *ou* **voulu** in due time *ou* course; **ces derniers ~** lately; **dans quelque ~** in a (little) while; **de ~ en ~, de ~ à autre** from time to time, now and again; **en même ~** at the same time; **à ~** (*partir, arriver*) in

time; **à ~ complet, à plein ~** *adv, adj* full-time; **à ~ partiel, à mi-temps** *adv, adj* part-time; **dans le ~** at one time; **de tout ~** always; **du ~ que** at the time when, in the days when; **dans le** *ou* **du** *ou* **au ~ où** at the time when; **pendant ce ~** in the meantime; **~ d'accès** (*Inform*) access time; **~ d'arrêt** pause, halt; **~ libre** free *ou* spare time; **~ mort** (*Sport*) stoppage (time); (*Comm*) slack period; **~ partagé** (*Inform*) time-sharing; **~ réel** (*Inform*) real time

tenable [t(ə)nabl] ADJ bearable

tenace [tənas] ADJ tenacious, persistent

ténacité [tenasite] NF tenacity, persistence

tenailler [tənaje] /1/ VT (*fig*) to torment, torture

tenailles [tənaj] NFPL pincers

tenais *etc* [t(ə)nɛ] VB *voir* **tenir**

tenancier, -ière [tənɑ̃sje, -jɛʀ] NM/F (*d'hôtel, de bistro*) manager (manageress)

tenant, e [tənɑ̃, -ɑ̃t] ADJ F *voir* **séance** ▸ NM/F (*Sport*): **~ du titre** title-holder ▸ NM: **d'un seul ~** in one piece; **les tenants et les aboutissants** (*fig*) the ins and outs

tendance [tɑ̃dɑ̃s] NF (*opinions*) leanings *pl*, sympathies *pl*; (*inclination*) tendency; (*évolution*) trend; **~ à la hausse/baisse** upward/downward trend; **avoir ~ à** to have a tendency to, tend to ▸ ADJ INV (*fam*) trendy

tendanciel, le [tɑ̃dɑ̃sjɛl] ADJ (*baisse, évolution*) underlying

tendancieux, -euse [tɑ̃dɑ̃sjø, -øz] ADJ tendentious

tendeur [tɑ̃dœʀ] NM (*de vélo*) chain-adjuster; (*de câble*) wire-strainer; (*de tente*) runner; (*attache*) elastic strap

tendinite [tɑ̃dinit] NF tendinitis, tendonitis

tendon [tɑ̃dɔ̃] NM tendon, sinew; **~ d'Achille** Achilles' tendon

tendre [tɑ̃dʀ] /41/ ADJ (*viande, légumes*) tender; (*bois, roche, couleur*) soft; (*affectueux*) tender, loving ▸ VT (*élastique, peau*) to stretch, draw tight; (*corde*) to tighten; (*muscle*) to tense; (*donner*): **~ qch à qn** to hold sth out to sb; (*offrir*) to offer sth sth; (*fig: piège*) to set, lay; **~ l'oreille** to prick up one's ears; **la main/le bras** to hold out one's hand/stretch out one's arm; **~ la perche à qn** (*fig*) to throw sb a line; **~ à qch/à faire** to tend towards sth/to do ▪ **se tendre** VPR (*corde*) to tighten; (*relations*) to become strained

tendrement [tɑ̃dʀəmɑ̃] ADV tenderly, lovingly

tendresse [tɑ̃dʀɛs] NF tenderness ▪ **tendresses** NFPL (*caresses etc*) tenderness *no pl*, caresses

tendu, e [tɑ̃dy] PP *de* **tendre** ▸ ADJ (*corde*) tight; (*muscles*) tensed; (*relations*) strained; **~ de soie** hung with silk, with silk hangings

ténèbres [tenɛbʀ] NFPL darkness *sg*

ténébreux, -euse [tenebʀø, -øz] ADJ obscure, mysterious; (*personne*) saturnine

Ténérife [teneʀif] NF Tenerife

teneur [tənœʀ] NF content, substance; (*d'une lettre*) terms *pl*, content; **~ en cuivre** copper content

ténia [tenja] NM tapeworm

★**tenir** [t(ə)niʀ] /22/ VT to hold; (*magasin, hôtel*) to run; (*promesse*) to keep; **~ à** VT (*personne, objet*) to be attached to, care about (*ou* for); (*réputation*) to care about; (*avoir pour cause*) to be due to, stem from; **~ à faire** to want to do, be keen to do; **~ à ce que qn fasse qch** to be anxious that sb should do sth; **~ de** to partake of; (*ressembler à*) to take after; **ça ne tient qu'à lui** it is entirely up to him; **~ qn pour** to take sb for; **~ qch de qn** (*histoire*) to have heard *ou* learnt sth from sb; (*qualité, défaut*) to have inherited *ou* got sth from sb; **~ compte de qch** to take sth into account; **~ les comptes** to keep the books; **~ un rôle** to play a part; **~ de la place** to take up space *ou* room; **~ l'alcool** to be able to hold a drink; **~ le coup** to hold out; **un manteau qui tient chaud** a warm coat; **~ prêt** to have ready; **~ sa langue** (*fig*) to hold one's tongue; **~ au chaud/à l'abri** to keep hot/under shelter *ou* cover; **tiens** (*ou* **tenez**), **voilà le stylo** there's the pen!; **tiens, voilà Alain!** look, here's Alain!; **tiens ?** (*surprise*) really? ▶ vi to hold; (*neige, gel*) to last; (*survivre*) to survive; **~ dans** to fit into; **~ bon** to stand *ou* hold fast; **~ trois jours/deux mois** (*résister*) to hold out *ou* last three days/two months ■ **se tenir** VPR (*avoir lieu*) to be held, take place; (*être: personne*) to stand; **se ~ droit** to stand up (*ou* sit up) straight; **bien se ~** to behave well; **se ~ à qch** to hold on to sth; **s'en ~ à qch** to confine o.s. to sth; to stick to sth; **tiens-toi bien!** (*pour informer*) brace yourself!, take a deep breath!

★**tennis** [tenis] NM tennis; (*aussi:* **court de tennis**) tennis court; **~ de table** table tennis ▶ NMPL OU FPL (*aussi:* **chaussures de tennis**) tennis *ou* gym shoes

tennisman [tenisman] NM tennis player

ténor [tenɔʀ] NM tenor

tension [tɑ̃sjɔ̃] NF tension; (*fig: des relations, de la situation*) tension; (: *concentration, effort*) strain; (*Méd*) blood pressure; **faire** *ou* **avoir de la ~** to have high blood pressure; **~ nerveuse/raciale** nervous/racial tension

tentaculaire [tɑ̃takylɛʀ] ADJ (*fig*) sprawling

tentacule [tɑ̃takyl] NM tentacle

tentant, e [tɑ̃tɑ̃, -ɑ̃t] ADJ tempting

tentateur, -trice [tɑ̃tatœʀ, -tʀis] ADJ tempting ▶ NM (*Rel*) tempter

tentation [tɑ̃tasjɔ̃] NF temptation

tentative [tɑ̃tativ] NF attempt, bid; **~ d'évasion** escape bid; **~ de suicide** suicide attempt

★**tente** [tɑ̃t] NF tent; **~ à oxygène** oxygen tent

tenter [tɑ̃te] /1/ VT (*éprouver, attirer*) to tempt; (*essayer*): **~ qch/de faire** to attempt *ou* try sth/to do; **être tenté de** to be tempted to; **~ sa chance** to try one's luck

tenture [tɑ̃tyʀ] NF hanging

tenu, e [t(ə)ny] PP *de* **tenir** ▶ ADJ: **bien ~** (*maison, comptes*) well-kept; **être ~ de faire** to be under an obligation to do ▶ NF (*action de tenir: de commerce*) running; (: *de registre, comptes*) keeping; (: *de réunion*) holding; (*vêtements*) outfit; **elle portait une tenue très élégante** she was very elegantly dressed, she was wearing a very elegant outfit; (*allure vestimentaire*) dress *no pl*, appearance; **sa tenue laissait à désirer** his appearance left a lot to be desired; **une tenue correcte est exigée** appropriate clothing must be worn; (*comportement*) manners *pl*, behaviour (BRIT), behavior (US); (*d'une maison*) upkeep; **être en tenue** to be dressed (up); **se mettre en tenue** to dress (up); **en grande tenue** in full dress; **en petite tenue**

scantily dressed *ou* clad; **avoir de la tenue** to have good manners; (*journal*) to have a high standard; **tenue de combat** combat gear *ou* dress; **tenue de pompier** fireman's uniform; **tenue de route** (*Auto*) road-holding; **tenue de soirée** evening dress; **tenue de sport/voyage** sports/travelling clothes *pl ou* gear *no pl*

ténu, e [teny] ADJ (*indice, nuance*) tenuous, subtle; (*fil, objet*) fine; (*voix*) thin

TER SIGLE M (= *Train Express Régional*) local train

ter [tɛʀ] ADV: **16** ~ 16b *ou* B

térébenthine [teʀebɑ̃tin] NF: **(essence de) ~** (oil of) turpentine

tergal® [tɛʀgal] NM Terylene®

tergiversations [tɛʀʒivɛʀsasjɔ̃] NFPL shilly-shallying *no pl*

tergiverser [tɛʀʒivɛʀse] /1/ VI to shilly-shally

terme [tɛʀm] NM term; (*fin*) end; **être en bons/mauvais termes avec qn** to be on good/bad terms with sb; **vente/achat à ~** (*Comm*) forward sale/purchase; **au ~ de** at the end of; **en d'autres termes** in other words; **moyen ~** (*solution intermédiaire*) middle course; **à court/long ~** adj short-/long-term *ou* -range; adv in the short/long term; **à ~** (*Méd*) adj full-term; adv sooner or later, eventually; (*Méd*) at term; **avant ~** (*Méd*) adj premature; adv prematurely; **mettre un ~ à** to put an end *ou* a stop to; **toucher à son ~** to be nearing its end

terminaison [tɛʀminɛzɔ̃] NF (*Ling*) ending

terminal, e, -aux [tɛʀminal, -o] ADJ (*partie, phase*) final; (*Méd*) terminal ▶ NM terminal ▶ NF (*Scol*) ≈ year 13 (BRIT), ≈ twelfth grade (US)

★**terminer** [tɛʀmine] /1/ VT to end; (*travail, repas*) to finish ■ **se terminer** VPR to end; **se ~ par** to end with

terminologie [tɛʀminɔlɔʒi] NF terminology

terminologique [tɛʀminɔlɔʒik] ADJ terminological

terminologue [tɛʀminɔlɔg] NMF terminologist

terminus [tɛʀminys] NM terminus; **~!** all change!

termite [tɛʀmit] NM termite, white ant

termitière [tɛʀmitjɛʀ] NF ant-hill

ternaire [tɛʀnɛʀ] ADJ compound

terne [tɛʀn] ADJ dull

ternir [tɛʀniʀ] /2/ VT to dull; (*fig*) to sully, tarnish ■ **se ternir** VPR to become dull

★**terrain** [teʀɛ̃] NM (*sol, fig*) ground; (*Comm: étendue de terre*) land *no pl*; (: *parcelle*) plot (of land); (: *à bâtir*) site; **sur le ~** (*fig*) on the field; **~ de football/rugby** football/rugby pitch (BRIT) *ou* field (US); **~ d'atterrissage** landing strip; **~ d'aviation** airfield; **~ de camping** campsite; **un ~ d'entente** an area of agreement; **~ de golf** golf course; **~ de jeu** (*pour les petits*) playground; (*Sport*) games field; **~ de sport** sports ground; **~ vague** waste ground *no pl*

terrarium [teʀaʀjɔm] NM terrarium

★**terrasse** [teʀas] NF terrace; (*de café*) pavement area, terrasse; **à la ~** (*café*) outside

terrassement [teʀasmɑ̃] NM earth-moving, earthworks *pl*; embankment

terrasser [teʀase] /1/ VT (*adversaire*) to floor, bring down; (*maladie etc*) to lay low

terrassier [teʀasje] NM navvy, roadworker

★**terre** [tɛʀ] NF (*gén, aussi Élec*) earth; (*Astronomie*): **la T~** the Earth; (*substance*) soil, earth; (*opposé à mer*) land *no pl*; (*contrée*) land; **travail de la ~** work on the land; **en ~** (*pipe, poterie*) clay *cpd*; **mettre en ~** (*plante etc*) to plant; (*personne: enterrer*) to bury; **à ou par ~** (*mettre, être, s'asseoir*) on the ground (*ou* floor); (*jeter, tomber*) to the ground, down; **~ à ~** *adj inv* down-to-earth, matter-of-fact; **la T~ Adélie** Adélie Coast *ou* Land; **~ de bruyère** (heath-)peat; **~ cuite** earthenware; terracotta; **la ~ ferme** dry land, terra firma; **la T~ de Feu** Tierra del Fuego; **~ glaise** clay; **la T~ promise** the Promised Land; **la T~ Sainte** the Holy Land ▪ **terres** NFPL (*terrains*) lands, land *sg*

terreau [teʀo] NM compost

terre-neuve [tɛʀnœv] NM INV (*chien*) Newfoundland dog ▶NF: **Terre-Neuve** Newfoundland

terre-neuvien, ne [tɛʀnœvjɛ̃, -jɛn] ADJ from Newfoundland ▶NM/F: **Terre-Neuvien, ne** Newfoundlander

terre-plein [tɛʀplɛ̃] NM platform; (*sur chaussée*) central reservation

terrer [teʀe] /1/: **se terrer** VPR to hide away; to go to ground

terrestre [teʀɛstʀ] ADJ (*surface*) earth's, of the earth; (*Bot, Zool, Mil*) land *cpd*; (*Rel*) earthly, worldly

terreur [teʀœʀ] NF terror *no pl*, fear

terreux, -euse [teʀø, -øz] ADJ muddy; (*goût*) earthy

★**terrible** [teʀibl] ADJ terrible, dreadful; (*fam: fantastique*) terrific; **pas ~** nothing special

terriblement [teʀibləmɑ̃] ADV (*très*) terribly, awfully

terrien, ne [teʀjɛ̃, -ɛn] ADJ: **propriétaire ~** landowner ▶NM/F countryman/woman, man/ woman of the soil; (*non martien etc*) earthling; (*non marin*) landsman

terrier [teʀje] NM burrow, hole; (*chien*) terrier

terrifiant, e [teʀifjɑ̃, -ɑ̃t] ADJ (*effrayant*) terrifying; (*extraordinaire*) terrible, awful

terrifier [teʀifje] /7/ VT to terrify

terril [teʀil] NM slag heap

terrine [teʀin] NF (*récipient*) terrine; (*Culin*) pâté

territoire [teʀitwaʀ] NM territory; **T~ des Afars et des Issas** French Territory of Afars and Issas

territorial, e, -aux [teʀitɔʀjal, -o] ADJ territorial; **eaux territoriales** territorial waters; **armée territoriale** regional defence force, ≈ Territorial Army (BRIT); **collectivités territoriales** local and regional authorities

terroir [teʀwaʀ] NM (*Agr*) soil; (*région*) region; **accent du ~** country *ou* rural accent

terroriser [teʀɔʀize] /1/ VT to terrorize

terrorisme [teʀɔʀism] NM terrorism

terroriste [teʀɔʀist] NMF terrorist

tertiaire [tɛʀsjɛʀ] ADJ tertiary ▶ NM (*Écon*) tertiary sector, service industries *pl*

tertiarisation [tɛʀsjaʀizasjɔ̃] NF expansion *ou* development of the service sector

tertiariser [tɛʀsjaʀize]: **se tertiariser** VPR to have expand the service industries

tertio [tɛʀsjo] ADV thirdly

tertre [tɛʀtʀ] NM hillock, mound

★**tes** [te] ADJ POSS *voir* **ton¹**

tessiture [tesityʀ] NF (*Mus*) range

tesson [tesɔ̃] NM: **~ de bouteille** piece of broken bottle

test [tɛst] NM test; **~ de grossesse** pregnancy test

testament [tɛstamɑ̃] NM (*Jur*) will; (*fig*) legacy; (*Rel*): **T~** Testament; **faire son ~** to make one's will

testamentaire [tɛstamɑ̃tɛʀ] ADJ of a will

tester [tɛste] /1/ VT to test

testeur [tɛstœʀ] NM (*personne*) tester; (*instrument*) tester

testicule [tɛstikyl] NM testicle

testostérone [tɛstɔsteʀɔn] NF testosterone

tétanie [tetani] NF tetany

tétaniser [tetanize] VT to tetanize ▪ **se tétaniser** VPR to become tetanized

tétanos [tetanos] NM tetanus

têtard [tɛtaʀ] NM tadpole

tête [tɛt] NF head; (*cheveux*) hair *no pl*; (*visage*) face; (*longueur*): **gagner d'une (courte) ~** to win by a (short) head; (*Football*) header; **de ~** *adj* (*wagon etc*) front *cpd*; (*concurrent*) leading; *adv* (*calculer*) in one's head, mentally; **par ~** (*par personne*) per head; **se mettre en ~ que** to get it into one's head that; **se mettre en ~ de faire** to take it into one's head to do; **prendre la ~ de qch** to take the lead in sth; **perdre la ~** (*fig: s'affoler*) to lose one's head; (: *devenir fou*) to go off one's head; **ça ne va pas, la ~?** (*fam*) are you crazy?; **tenir ~ à qn** to stand up to *ou* defy sb; **la ~ en bas** with one's head down; **la ~ la première** (*tomber*) head-first; **la ~ basse** hanging one's head; **avoir la ~ dure** (*fig*) to be thickheaded; **faire une ~** (*Football*) to head the ball; **faire la ~** (*fig*) to sulk; **en ~** (*Sport*) in the lead; at the front *ou* head; **à la ~ de** at the head of; **à ~ reposée** in a more leisurely moment; **n'en faire qu'à sa ~** to do as one pleases; **en avoir pardessus la ~** to be fed up; **en ~ à ~** in private, alone together; **de la ~ aux pieds** from head to toe; **~ d'affiche** (*Théât etc*) top of the bill; **~ de bétail** head *inv* of cattle; **~ brûlée** desperado; **~ chercheuse** homing device; **~ d'enregistrement** recording head; **~ d'impression** printhead; **~ de lecture** (playback) head; **~ de ligne** (*Transports*) start of the line; **~ de liste** (*Pol*) chief candidate; **~ de mort** skull and crossbones; **~ de pont** (*Mil*) bridge- *ou* beachhead; **~ de série** (*Tennis*) seeded player, seed; **~ de Turc** (*fig*) whipping boy (BRIT), butt; **~ de veau** (*Culin*) calf's head

tête-à-queue [tɛtakø] NM INV: **faire un ~** to spin round

tête-à-tête [tɛtatɛt] NM INV tête-à-tête; (*service*) breakfast set for two; **en ~** in private, alone together

tête-bêche [tɛtbɛʃ] ADV head to tail

tétée [tete] NF (*action*) sucking; (*repas*) feed

téter [tete] /6/ VT: **~ (sa mère)** to suck at one's mother's breast, feed

tétine [tetin] NF teat; (*sucette*) dummy (BRIT), pacifier (US)

téton [tetɔ̃] NM breast

tétralogie [tetralɔʒi] NF tetralogy

têtu, e [tety] ADJ stubborn, pigheaded

★**texte** [tɛkst] NM text; (*morceau choisi*) passage; (*Scol: d'un devoir*) subject, topic; **apprendre son ~** (*Théât*) to learn one's lines; **un ~ de loi** the wording of a law

texter [tɛkste] /1/ VI, VT to text

textile [tɛkstil] ADJ textile *cpd* ▸ NM textile; (*industrie*) textile industry

Texto® [tɛksto] NM text (message)

texto [tɛksto] ADV (*fam*) word for word

textoter [tɛkstɔte] /1/ VI, VT to text

textuel, le [tɛkstɥɛl] ADJ literal, word for word

textuellement [tɛkstɥɛlmɑ̃] ADV literally

texture [tɛkstyʀ] NF texture; (*fig: d'un texte, livre*) feel

texturé [tɛkstyʀe] ADJ (*matériau, vin*) textured

TF1 SIGLE F (= *Télévision française 1*) TV channel

TG SIGLE F = **trésorerie générale**

TGI SIGLE M = **tribunal de grande instance**

★**TGV** SIGLE M = **train à grande vitesse**

thaï, e [taj] ADJ Thai ▸ NM (*Ling*) Thai

thaïlandais, e [tajlɑ̃dɛ, -ɛz] ADJ Thai ▸ NM/F: **Thaïlandais, e** Thai

Thaïlande [tajlɑ̃d] NF: **la ~** Thailand

thalasso [talaso] NF (*fam*) = **thalassothérapie**

thalassothérapie [talasɔteʀapi] NF thalassotherapy

thé [te] NM tea; (*réunion*) tea party; **prendre le ~** to have tea; **~ au lait/citron** tea with milk/lemon; **faire le ~** to make the tea

théâtral, e, -aux [teɑtʀal, -o] ADJ theatrical

théâtre [teɑtʀ] NM theatre; (*techniques, genre*) drama, theatre; (*activité*) stage, theatre; (*œuvres*) plays *pl*, dramatic works *pl*; (*péj*) histrionics *pl*, playacting; (*fig: lieu*): **le ~ de** the scene of; **faire du ~** (*en professionnel*) to be on the stage; (*en amateur*) to act; **~ filmé** filmed stage productions *pl*

thébain, e [tebɛ̃, -ɛn] ADJ Theban

Thèbes [tɛb] N Thebes

théière [tejɛʀ] NF teapot

théine [tein] NF theine

théisme [teism] NM theism

thématique [tematik] ADJ thematic

thème [tɛm] NM theme; (*Scol: traduction*) prose (composition); **~ astral** birth chart

théocratie [teɔkʀasi] NF theocracy

théologie [teɔlɔʒi] NF theology

théologien, ne [teɔlɔʒjɛ̃, -ɛn] NM theologian

théologique [teɔlɔʒik] ADJ theological

théorème [teɔʀɛm] NM theorem

théoricien, ne [teɔʀisjɛ̃, -ɛn] NM/F theoretician, theorist

théorie [teɔʀi] NF theory; **en ~** in theory

théorique [teɔʀik] ADJ theoretical

théoriquement [teɔʀikmɑ̃] ADV theoretically

théorisation [teɔʀizasjɔ̃] NF theorization

théoriser [teɔʀize] /1/ VI to theorize

thérapeutique [teʀapøtik] ADJ therapeutic ▸ NF (*Méd: branche*) therapeutics *sg*; (*: traitement*) therapy

thérapie [teʀapi] NF therapy; **~ de groupe** group therapy

thermal, e, -aux [tɛʀmal, -o] ADJ thermal; **station thermale** spa; **cure thermale** water cure

thermes [tɛʀm] NMPL thermal baths; (*romains*) thermae *pl*

thermique [tɛʀmik] ADJ (*énergie*) thermic; (*unité*) thermal

thermodynamique [tɛʀmɔdinamik] NF thermodynamics *sg*

thermoélectrique [tɛʀmoelɛktʀik] ADJ thermoelectric

thermomètre [tɛʀmɔmɛtʀ] NM thermometer

thermonucléaire [tɛʀmɔnykleɛʀ] ADJ thermonuclear

thermorégulateur, -trice [tɛʀmɔʀegylatœʀ, -tʀis] ADJ thermotaxic

thermos® [tɛʀmos] NM OU F: **(bouteille) ~** vacuum *ou* Thermos® flask (*BRIT*) *ou* bottle (*US*)

thermostat [tɛʀmɔsta] NM thermostat

thermostatique [tɛʀmɔstatik] ADJ thermostatic

thésard, e [tezaʀ, -aʀd] NM/F person preparing a thesis

thésauriser [tezɔʀize] /1/ VI to hoard money

thèse [tɛz] NF thesis

Thessalie [tesali] NF: **la ~** Thessaly

thibaude [tibod] NF carpet underlay

★**thon** [tɔ̃] NM tuna (fish)

thonier [tɔnje] NM tuna boat

thoracique [tɔʀasik] ADJ thoracic

thorax [tɔʀaks] NM thorax

thriller [sʀilœʀ] NM thriller

thrombose [tʀɔ̃boz] NF thrombosis

thune [tyn] NF (*fam*) money, dough (*fam*)

thym [tɛ̃] NM thyme

thyroïde [tiʀɔid] NF thyroid (gland)

thyroïdien, -ienne [tiʀɔidjɛ̃, -jɛn] ADJ thyroid *cpd*

TI SIGLE M = **tribunal d'instance**

tiare [tjaʀ] NF tiara

Tibet [tibɛ] NM: **le ~** Tibet

tibétain, e [tibetɛ̃, -ɛn] ADJ Tibetan

tibia [tibja] NM shin; (*os*) shinbone, tibia

Tibre [tibʀ] NM: **le ~** the Tiber

TIC SIGLE FPL (= *technologies de l'information et de la communication*) ICT *sg*

tic [tik] NM tic, (nervous) twitch; (*de langage etc*) mannerism

★**ticket** [tikɛ] NM ticket; **~ de caisse** till receipt; **~ modérateur** patient's contribution towards medical costs; **~ de quai** platform ticket; **~ repas** luncheon voucher

tic-tac [tiktak] NM INV tick-tock

tictaquer [tiktake] /1/ VI to tick (away)

tiède [tjɛd] ADJ (*bière etc*) lukewarm; (*thé, café etc*) tepid; (*bain, accueil, sentiment*) lukewarm; (*vent, air*) mild, warm ▸ ADV: **boire ~** to drink things lukewarm

tièdement [tjɛdmɑ̃] ADV coolly, half-heartedly

tiédeur [tjedœʀ] NF lukewarmness; (*du vent, de l'air*) mildness

tiédir [tjediʀ] /2/ VI (*se réchauffer*) to grow warmer; (*refroidir*) to cool

t

tien, tienne [tjɛ̃, tjɛn] PRON: **le (la) ~(ne)** yours; **les ~(ne)s** yours; **à la tienne!** cheers!

tiendrai etc [tjɛ̃dʀe] VB voir **tenir**

tienne [tjɛn] VB voir **tenir** ▶ PRON voir **tien**

tiens [tjɛ̃] VB, EXCL voir **tenir**

tierce [tjɛʀs] ADJ F, NF voir **tiers**

tiercé [tjɛʀse] NM system of forecast betting giving first three horses

★**tiers, tierce** [tjɛʀ, tjɛʀs] ADJ third; **une tierce personne** a third party; **le ~ monde** the third world ▶ NM (Jur) third party; (fraction) third; **~ payant** direct payment by insurers of medical expenses; **~ provisionnel** interim payment of tax; **assurance au ~** third-party insurance ▶ NF (Mus) third; (Cartes) tierce

tifs [tif] NMPL (fam) hair

TIG SIGLE M = **travail d'intérêt général**

tige [tiʒ] NF stem; (baguette) rod

tignasse [tiɲas] NF (péj) shock ou mop of hair

Tigre [tigʀ] NM: **le ~** the Tigris

★**tigre** [tigʀ] NM tiger

tigré, e [tigʀe] ADJ (rayé) striped; (tacheté) spotted; (chat) tabby

tigresse [tigʀɛs] NF tigress

tilde [tild(e)] NM tilde

tilleul [tijœl] NM lime (tree), linden (tree); (boisson) lime(-blossom) tea

tilt [tilt] NM: **faire ~** (fig: inspirer) to ring a bell

timbale [tɛ̃bal] NF (metal) tumbler ■ **timbales** NFPL (Mus) timpani, kettledrums

timbrage [tɛ̃bʀaʒ] NM: **dispensé de ~** post(age) paid

★**timbre** [tɛ̃bʀ] NM (tampon) stamp; (aussi: **timbre-poste**) (postage) stamp; (cachet de la poste) postmark; (sonnette) bell; (Mus: de voix, instrument) timbre, tone; **~ anti-tabac** nicotine patch; **~ dateur** date stamp

timbré, e [tɛ̃bʀe] ADJ (enveloppe) stamped; (voix) resonant; (fam: fou) cracked, nuts

timbrer [tɛ̃bʀe] /1/ VT to stamp

★**timide** [timid] ADJ (emprunté) shy, timid; (timoré) timid, timorous

timidement [timidmɑ̃] ADV shyly; timidly

timidité [timidite] NF shyness; timidity

timing [tajmiŋ] NM timing

timonerie [timɔnʀi] NF wheelhouse

timonier [timɔnje] NM helmsman

timoré, e [timɔʀe] ADJ timorous

Timor oriental [ˈtimɔʀˈɔʀjɑ̃tal] NF East Timor

tint etc [tɛ̃] VB voir **tenir**

tintamarre [tɛ̃tamaʀ] NM din, uproar

tintement [tɛ̃tmɑ̃] NM ringing, chiming; **tintements d'oreilles** ringing in the ears

tinter [tɛ̃te] /1/ VI to ring, chime; (argent, clés) to jingle

TIP SIGLE M (= titre interbancaire de paiement) ≈ payment slip

tipi [tipi] NM teepee, tipi

Tipp-Ex® [tipɛks] NM Tipp-Ex®

tique [tik] NF tick (insect)

tiquer [tike] /1/ VI (personne) to make a face

TIR SIGLE MPL (= Transports internationaux routiers) TIR

tir [tiʀ] NM (sport) shooting; (fait ou manière de tirer) firing no pl; (Football) shot; (rafale) fire; (stand) shooting gallery; **~ d'obus/de mitraillette** shell/machine gun fire; **~ à l'arc** archery; **~ de barrage** barrage fire; **~ au fusil** (rifle) shooting; **~ au pigeon** (d'argile) clay pigeon shooting

tirade [tiʀad] NF tirade

tirage [tiʀaʒ] NM (action) printing; (Photo) print; (Inform) printout; (de journal) circulation; (de livre) (print-)run; edition; (de cheminée) draught (BRIT), draft (US); (de loterie) draw; (fig: désaccord) friction; **~ au sort** drawing lots

tiraillement [tiʀɑjmɑ̃] NM (douleur) sharp pain; (fig: doutes) agony no pl of indecision; (conflits) friction no pl

tirailler [tiʀɑje] /1/ VT to pull at, tug at; (fig) to gnaw at ▶ VI to fire at random

tirailleur [tiʀɑjœʀ] NM skirmisher

tirant [tiʀɑ̃] NM: **~ d'eau** draught (BRIT), draft (US)

tire [tiʀ] NF: **vol à la ~** pickpocketing

tiré, e [tiʀe] ADJ (visage, traits) drawn; **~ par les cheveux** far-fetched ▶ NM (Comm) drawee; **~ à part** off-print

tire-au-flanc [tiʀoflɑ̃] NM INV (péj) skiver

★**tire-bouchon** [tiʀbuʃɔ̃] NM corkscrew

tire-bouchonner [tiʀbuʃɔne] /1/ VT to twirl

tire-d'aile [tiʀdɛl]: **à tire-d'aile** adv swiftly

tire-fesses [tiʀfɛs] NM INV ski-tow

tire-lait [tiʀlɛ] NM INV breast-pump

tire-larigot [tiʀlaʀigo]: **à ~** adv as much as one likes, to one's heart's content

tirelire [tiʀliʀ] NF moneybox

★**tirer** [tiʀe] /1/ VT (gén) to pull; (tracer: ligne, trait) to draw, trace; (fermer: volet, porte, trappe) to pull to, close; (: rideau) to draw; (choisir: carte, conclusion: Comm: chèque) to draw; (en faisant feu: balle, coup) to fire; (: animal) to shoot; (journal, livre, photo) to print; (Football: corner etc) to take; **~ qch de** to get sth out of; (extraire) to extract sth from; **~ son nom de** to take ou get its name from; **~ la langue** to stick out one's tongue; **~ qn de** (embarras etc) to help ou get sb out of; **~ qch au clair** to clear sth up; **~ parti de** to take advantage of; **~ profit de** to profit from; **~ les cartes** to read ou tell the cards ▶ VI (faire feu) to fire; (faire du tir, Football) to shoot; (cheminée) to draw; **~ sur** (corde, poignée) to pull on ou at; (faire feu sur) to shoot ou fire at; (pipe) to draw on; (fig: avoisiner) to verge ou border on; **~ six mètres** (Navig) to draw six metres of water; **~ à l'arc/la carabine** to shoot with a bow and arrow/with a rifle; **~ en longueur** to drag on; **~ à sa fin** to be drawing to an end; **~ au sort** to draw lots ■ **se tirer** VPR (fam) to push off; **s'en ~** (éviter le pire) to get off; (survivre) to pull through; (se débrouiller) to manage

tiret [tiʀɛ] NM dash; (en fin de ligne) hyphen

tireur [tiʀœʀ] NM gunman; (Comm) drawer; **bon ~** good shot; **~ d'élite** marksman; **~ de cartes** fortune-teller

★**tiroir** [tiʀwaʀ] NM drawer

tiroir-caisse [tiʀwaʀkɛs] (pl **tiroirs-caisses**) NM till

tisane [tizan] NF herb tea

tison [tizɔ̃] NM brand

tisonner [tizɔne] /**1**/ vт to poke

tisonnier [tizɔnje] ɴм poker

tissage [tisaʒ] ɴм weaving *no pl*

tisser [tise] /**1**/ vт to weave

tisserand, e [tisʀɑ̃, -ɑ̃d] ɴм/ꜰ weaver

★**tissu¹** [tisy] ɴм fabric, material, cloth *no pl*; (*fig*) fabric; (*Anat, Bio*) tissue; ~ **de mensonges** web of lies

tissu², e [tisy] ADJ (*liter*): ~ **de** woven through with

tissu-éponge [tisyepɔ̃ʒ] (*pl* **tissus-éponges**) ɴм (terry) towelling *no pl*

titan [titɑ̃] ɴм (*géant*) titan; **travail de** ~ Herculean task

titane [titan] ɴм titanium

titanesque [titanɛsk] ADJ titanic

titiller [titile] /**1**/ vт to titillate

titrage [titʀaʒ] ɴм (*d'un film*) titling; (*d'un alcool*) determination of alcohol content

titraille [titʀaj] ɴꜰ (*Typo*) headlines

★**titre** [titʀ] ɴм (*gén*) title; (*de journal*) headline; (*diplôme*) qualification; (*Comm*) security; (*Chimie*) titre; **en** ~ (*champion, responsable*) official, recognized; **à juste** ~ with just cause, rightly; **à quel** ~ ? on what grounds?; **à aucun** ~ on no account; **au même** ~ (**que**) in the same way (as); **au** ~ **de la coopération** *etc* in the name of cooperation *etc*; **à** ~ **d'exemple** as an *ou* by way of an example; **à** ~ **exceptionnel** exceptionally; **à** ~ **d'information** for (your) information; **à** ~ **gracieux** free of charge; **à** ~ **d'essai** on a trial basis; **à** ~ **privé** in a private capacity; ~ **courant** running head; ~ **de propriété** title deed; ~ **de transport** ticket

titré, e [titʀe] ADJ (*livre, film*) entitled; (*personne*) titled

titrer [titʀe] /**1**/ vт (*Chimie*) to titrate; to assay; (*Presse*) to run as a headline; (*vin*): ~ **10°** to be 10° proof

titubant, e [titybɑ̃, -ɑ̃t] ADJ staggering, reeling

tituber [titybe] /**1**/ vi to stagger *ou* reel (along)

titulaire [titylɛʀ] ADJ (*Admin*) appointed, with tenure ▶ ɴмꜰ (*Admin*) incumbent; (*de permis*) holder; **être** ~ **de** (*diplôme, permis*) to hold

titularisation [titylaʀizasjɔ̃] ɴꜰ granting of tenure

titulariser [titylaʀize] /**1**/ vт to give tenure to

TMS [teemɛs] SIGLE MPL (= *troubles musculosquelettiques*) MSDs (= *musculoskeletal disorders*)

TNP SIGLE M = **Théâtre national populaire**

TNT SIGLE M (= *Trinitrotoluène*) TNT ▶ SIGLE F (= *Télévision numérique terrestre*) digital television

toast [tost] ɴм slice *ou* piece of toast; (*de bienvenue*) (welcoming) toast; **porter un** ~ **à qn** to propose *ou* drink a toast to sb

toboggan [tɔbɔgɑ̃] ɴм toboggan; (*jeu*) slide; (*Auto*) flyover (BʀɪT), overpass (US); ~ **de secours** (*Aviat*) escape chute

TOC [tɔk] SIGLE M (= *trouble obsessionnel compulsif*) OCD (= *obsessive compulsive disorder*)

toc [tɔk] ɴм: **en** ~ imitation *cpd* ▶ EXCL: **toc, toc** knock knock

tocsin [tɔksɛ̃] ɴм alarm (bell)

toge [tɔʒ] ɴꜰ toga; (*de juge*) gown

Togo [tɔgo] ɴм: **le** ~ Togo

togolais, e [tɔgɔlɛ, -ɛz] ADJ Togolese

tohu-bohu [tɔybɔy] ɴм (*désordre*) confusion; (*tumulte*) commotion

★**toi** [twa] PRON you; ~, **tu l'as fait ?** did YOU do it?

toile [twal] ɴꜰ (*matériau*) cloth *no pl*; (*bâche*) piece of canvas; (*tableau*) canvas; **grosse** ~ canvas; **de** *ou* **en** ~ (*pantalon*) cotton; (*sac*) canvas; **tisser sa** ~ (*araignée*) to spin its web; ~ **d'araignée** spider's web; (*au plafond etc: à enlever*) cobweb; **la T~** (*Internet*) the Web; ~ **cirée** oilcloth; ~ **émeri** emery cloth; ~ **de fond** (*fig*) backdrop; ~ **de jute** hessian; ~ **de lin** linen; ~ **de tente** canvas

toilettage [twalɛtaʒ] ɴм grooming *no pl*; (*d'un texte*) tidying up

toilette [twalɛt] ɴꜰ wash; (*s'habiller et se préparer*) getting ready, washing and dressing; (*habits*) outfit; dress *no pl*; **faire sa** ~ to have a wash, get washed; **faire la** ~ **de** (*animal*) to groom; (*voiture etc*) to clean, wash; (*texte*) to tidy up; **articles de** ~ toiletries; ~ **intime** personal hygiene ■ **toilettes** ɴꜰPL toilet *sg*; **les toilettes des dames/messieurs** the ladies'/gents' (toilets) (BʀɪT), the ladies'/men's (rest)room (US)

toiletter [twalete] vт (*animal*) to groom; (*texte, loi*) to tidy up

toi-même [twamɛm] PRON yourself

toise [twaz] ɴꜰ: **passer à la** ~ to have one's height measured

toiser [twaze] /**1**/ vт to eye up and down

toison [twazɔ̃] ɴꜰ (*de mouton*) fleece; (*cheveux*) mane

★**toit** [twa] ɴм roof; ~ **ouvrant** sun roof

toiture [twatyʀ] ɴꜰ roof

Tokyo [tɔkjo] ɴ Tokyo

tôle [tol] ɴꜰ sheet metal *no pl*; (*plaque*) steel (*ou* iron) sheet; ~ **d'acier** sheet steel *no pl*; ~ **ondulée** corrugated iron ■ **tôles** ɴꜰPL (*carrosserie*) bodywork *sg* (BʀɪT), body *sg*; panels

Tolède [tɔlɛd] ɴ Toledo

tolérable [tɔleʀabl] ADJ tolerable, bearable

tolérance [tɔleʀɑ̃s] ɴꜰ tolerance; (*hors taxe*) allowance

tolérant, e [tɔleʀɑ̃, -ɑ̃t] ADJ tolerant

tolérer [tɔleʀe] /**6**/ vт to tolerate; (*Admin: hors taxe etc*) to allow

tôlerie [tolʀi] ɴꜰ sheet metal manufacture; (*atelier*) sheet metal workshop; (*ensemble des tôles*) panels *pl*

tollé [tɔle] ɴм: **un** ~ (**de protestations**) a general outcry

TOM [tɔm] SIGLE ɴм(PL) = **territoire(s) d'outre-mer**

★**tomate** [tɔmat] ɴꜰ tomato; **tomates farcies** stuffed tomatoes

tombal, e [tɔ̃bal] ADJ: **pierre tombale** tombstone, gravestone

tombant, e [tɔ̃bɑ̃, -ɑ̃t] ADJ (*fig*) drooping, sloping

tombe [tɔ̃b] ɴꜰ (*sépulture*) grave; (*avec monument*) tomb

tombeau, x [tɔ̃bo] ɴм tomb; **à** ~ **ouvert** at breakneck speed

tombée [tɔ̃be] ɴꜰ: **à la** ~ **du jour** *ou* **de la nuit** at the close of day, at nightfall

★**tomber** [tɔ̃be] /**1**/ vi to fall; (fièvre, vent) to drop; **laisser ~** (objet) to drop; (personne) to let down; (activité) to give up; **laisse ~ !** forget it!; **faire ~** to knock over; **~ sur** (rencontrer) to come across; (attaquer) to set about; **~ de fatigue/sommeil** to drop from exhaustion/be falling asleep on one's feet; **~ à l'eau** (fig: projet etc) to fall through; **~ en panne** to break down; **~ juste** (opération, calcul) to come out right; **~ en ruine** to fall into ruins; **ça tombe bien/mal** (fig) that's come at the right/wrong time; **il est bien/mal tombé** (fig) he's been lucky/unlucky ▸ VT: **~ la veste** to slip off one's jacket

tombereau, x [tɔ̃bʀo] NM tipcart

tombeur [tɔ̃bœʀ] NM (péj) Casanova

tombola [tɔ̃bɔla] NF raffle

Tombouctou [tɔ̃buktu] N Timbuktu

tome [tɔm] NM volume

tomette, tommette [tɔmɛt] NF hexagonal terracotta floor tile

tomographie [tɔmɔgʀafi] NF tomography

★**ton¹, ta** [tɔ̃, ta] (pl **tes** [te]) ADJ POSS your

ton² [tɔ̃] NM (gén) tone; (Mus) key; (couleur) shade, tone; (de la voix: hauteur) pitch; **donner le ~** to set the tone; **élever** ou **hausser le ~** to raise one's voice; **de bon ~** in good taste; **si vous le prenez sur ce ~** if you're going to take it like that; **~ sur ~** in matching shades

tonal, e [tɔnal] ADJ tonal

tonalité [tɔnalite] NF (au téléphone) dialling tone; (Mus) tonality; (: ton) key; (fig) tone

tondeuse [tɔ̃døz] NF (à gazon) (lawn)mower; (du coiffeur) clippers pl; (pour la tonte) shears pl

tondre [tɔ̃dʀ] /**41**/ VT (pelouse, herbe) to mow; (haie) to cut, clip; (mouton, toison) to shear; (cheveux) to crop

tondu, e [tɔ̃dy] PP de **tondre** ▸ ADJ (cheveux) cropped; (mouton, crâne) shorn

Tonga [tɔ̃ga] NM: **les îles ~** Tonga

tongs [tɔ̃g] NFPL flip-flops (BRIT), thongs (US)

tonicité [tɔnisite] NF (Méd: des tissus) tone; (fig: de l'air, la mer) bracing effect

tonifiant, e [tɔnifjɑ̃, -ɑ̃t] ADJ invigorating, revivifying

tonifier [tɔnifje] /**7**/ VT (air, eau) to invigorate; (peau, organisme) to tone up

tonique [tɔnik] ADJ fortifying; (personne) dynamic ▸ NMF tonic

tonitruant, e [tɔnitʀyɑ̃, -ɑ̃t] ADJ: **voix tonitruante** thundering voice

Tonkin [tɔ̃kɛ̃] NM: **le ~** Tonkin, Tongking

tonkinois, e [tɔ̃kinwa, -waz] ADJ Tonkinese

tonnage [tɔnaʒ] NM tonnage

tonnant, e [tɔnɑ̃, -ɑ̃t] ADJ thunderous

tonne [tɔn] NF metric ton, tonne

tonneau, x [tɔno] NM (à vin, cidre) barrel; (Navig) ton; **faire des tonneaux** (voiture, avion) to roll over

tonnelet [tɔnlɛ] NM keg

tonnelier [tɔnəlje] NM cooper

tonnelle [tɔnɛl] NF bower, arbour (BRIT), arbor (US)

tonnellerie [tɔnɛlʀi] NF (secteur, activité) cooperage, barrel-making; (entreprise) cooper, barrel-maker

tonner [tɔne] /**1**/ vi to thunder; (parler avec véhémence): **~ contre qn/qch** to inveigh against sb/sth; **il tonne** it is thundering, there's some thunder

★**tonnerre** [tɔnɛʀ] NM thunder; **coup de ~** (fig) thunderbolt, bolt from the blue; **un ~ d'applaudissements** thunderous applause; **du ~** adj (fam) terrific

tonsure [tɔ̃syʀ] NF bald patch; (de moine) tonsure

tonte [tɔ̃t] NF shearing

tonton [tɔ̃tɔ̃] NM uncle

tonus [tɔnys] NM energy; (des muscles) tone; (d'une personne) dynamism

top [tɔp] NM: **au troisième ~** at the third stroke ▸ ADJ INV: **~ secret** top secret ▸ EXCL go!

topaze [tɔpaz] NF topaz

toper [tɔpe] /**1**/ vi: **tope/topez là !** it's a deal!, you're on!

topinambour [tɔpinɑ̃buʀ] NM Jerusalem artichoke

topo [tɔpo] NM (discours, exposé) talk; (fam) spiel

topographie [tɔpɔgʀafi] NF topography

topographique [tɔpɔgʀafik] ADJ topographical

topologie [tɔpɔlɔʒi] NF topology

toponyme [tɔpɔnim] NM place name, toponym

toponymie [tɔpɔnimi] NF study of place names, toponymy

toquade [tɔkad] NF fad, craze

toque [tɔk] NF (de fourrure) fur hat; **~ de jockey/juge** jockey's/judge's cap; **~ de cuisinier** chef's hat

toqué, e [tɔke] ADJ (fam) touched, cracked

torche [tɔʀʃ] NF torch; **se mettre en ~** (parachute) to candle

torcher [tɔʀʃe] /**1**/ VT (fam) to wipe ■ **se torcher** VPR: **se ~ le cul** (!) to wipe one's arse (BRIT !), to wipe one's ass (US !)

torchère [tɔʀʃɛʀ] NF flare

torchis [tɔʀʃi] NM cob (building material)

torchon [tɔʀʃɔ̃] NM cloth, duster; (à vaisselle) tea towel ou cloth

tordre [tɔʀdʀ] /**41**/ VT (chiffon) to wring; (barre, fig: visage) to twist ■ **se tordre** VPR (barre) to bend; (roue) to twist, buckle; (ver, serpent) to writhe; **se ~ le poignet/la cheville** to twist one's wrist/ankle; **se ~ de douleur/rire** to writhe in pain/be doubled up with laughter

tordu, e [tɔʀdy] PP de **tordre** ▸ ADJ (fig) warped, twisted; (fig) crazy

torero [tɔʀeʀo] NM bullfighter

tornade [tɔʀnad] NF tornado

toron [tɔʀɔ̃] NM strand (of rope)

Toronto [tɔʀɔ̃to] N Toronto

torontois, e [tɔʀɔ̃twa, -waz] ADJ Torontonian ▸ NM/F: **Torontois, e** Torontonian

torpeur [tɔʀpœʀ] NF torpor, drowsiness

torpillage [tɔʀpijaʒ] NM (de bateau, projet) torpedoing

torpille [tɔʀpij] NF torpedo

torpiller [tɔʀpije] /**1**/ VT to torpedo

torpilleur [tɔʀpijœʀ] NM torpedo boat

torréfacteur [tɔʀefaktœʀ] NM (entreprise) coffee merchant

torréfaction [tɔʀefaksjɔ̃] NF roasting

torréfier [tɔʀefje] /7/ VT to roast

torrent [tɔʀɑ̃] NM torrent, mountain stream; *(fig)*: **un ~ de** a torrent *ou* flood of; **il pleut à torrents** the rain is lashing down

torrentiel, le [tɔʀɑ̃sjɛl] ADJ torrential

torride [tɔʀid] ADJ torrid

tors, e [tɔʀ, tɔʀs(ə)] ADJ twisted

torsade [tɔʀsad] NF twist; *(Archit)* cable moulding (BRIT) *ou* molding (US); **un pull à torsades** a cable sweater

torsadé [tɔʀsade] ADJ twisted

torsader [tɔʀsade] /1/ VT to twist

torse [tɔʀs] NM chest; *(Anat, Sculpture)* torso; *(poitrine)* chest; **~ nu** stripped to the waist

torsion [tɔʀsjɔ̃] NF *(action)* twisting; *(Tech, Physique)* torsion

★**tort** [tɔʀ] NM *(défaut)* fault; *(préjudice)* wrong *no pl*; **avoir ~** to be wrong; **être dans son ~** to be in the wrong; **donner ~ à qn** to lay the blame on sb; *(fig)* to prove sb wrong; **causer du ~ à** to harm; to be harmful *ou* detrimental to; **en ~** in the wrong, at fault; **à ~** wrongly; **à ~ ou à raison** rightly or wrongly; **à ~ et à travers** wildly ■ **torts** NMPL *(Jur)* fault *sg*

torte [tɔʀt] ADJ F *voir* **tors**

torticolis [tɔʀtikɔli] NM stiff neck

tortiller [tɔʀtije] /1/ VT *(corde, mouchoir)* to twist; *(doigts)* to twiddle; *(moustache)* to twirl ■ **se tortiller** VPR to wriggle, squirm; *(en dansant)* to wiggle

tortionnaire [tɔʀsjɔnɛʀ] NM torturer

★**tortue** [tɔʀty] NF tortoise; *(fig)* slowcoach (BRIT), slowpoke (US); *(d'eau douce)* terrapin; *(d'eau de mer)* turtle

tortueux, -euse [tɔʀtɥø, -øz] ADJ *(rue)* twisting; *(fig)* tortuous

torture [tɔʀtyʀ] NF torture

torturer [tɔʀtyʀe] /1/ VT to torture; *(fig)* to torment

torve [tɔʀv] ADJ: **regard ~** menacing *ou* grim look

toscan, e [tɔskɑ̃, -an] ADJ Tuscan

Toscane [tɔskan] NF: **la ~** Tuscany

tôt [to] ADV early; **~ ou tard** sooner or later; **si ~** so early; *(déjà)* so soon; **au plus ~** at the earliest, as soon as possible; **plus ~** earlier; **il eut ~ fait de faire …** he soon did …

total, e, -aux [tɔtal, -o] ADJ, NM total; **au ~** in total *ou* all; *(fig)* all in all, on the whole; **faire le ~** to work out the total

totalement [tɔtalmɑ̃] ADV totally, completely

totalisateur [tɔtalizatœʀ] NM adding machine

totaliser [tɔtalize] /1/ VT to total (up)

totalitaire [tɔtalitɛʀ] ADJ totalitarian

totalitarisme [tɔtalitaʀism] NM totalitarianism

totalité [tɔtalite] NF: **la ~ de**: **la ~ des élèves** all (of) the pupils; **la ~ de la population/classe** the whole population/class; **en ~** entirely

totem [tɔtɛm] NM totem

touareg [twaʀɛg] ADJ Tuareg, Touareg ▶ NM *(Ling)* Tuareg, Touareg ▶ NMF, NMF INV: **T~** Tuareg, Touareg

toubib [tubib] NM *(fam)* doctor

toucan [tukɑ̃] NM toucan

touchant, e [tuʃɑ̃, -ɑ̃t] ADJ touching

touche [tuʃ] NF *(de piano, de machine à écrire)* key; *(de violon)* fingerboard; *(de télécommande etc)* key, button; *(de téléphone)* button; *(Peinture etc)* stroke, touch; *(fig: de couleur, nostalgie)* touch, hint; *(Rugby)* line-out; *(Football: aussi:* **remise en touche***)* throw-in; *(aussi:* **ligne de touche***)* touch-line; *(Escrime)* hit; **en ~** in *(ou* into*)* touch; **avoir une drôle de ~** to look a sight; **~ de commande/de fonction/de retour** *(Inform)* control/function/ return key; **~ dièse** *(de téléphone, clavier)* hash key; **~ à effleurement** *ou* **sensitive** touch-sensitive control *ou* key

touche-à-tout [tuʃatu] NM INV *(péj: gén: enfant)* meddler; *(fig: inventeur etc)* dabbler

★**toucher** [tuʃe] /1/ NM touch; **au ~** to the touch; by the feel ▶ VT to touch; *(palper)* to feel; *(atteindre: d'un coup de feu etc)* to hit; *(affecter)* to touch, affect; *(concerner)* to concern, affect; *(contacter)* to reach, contact; *(recevoir: récompense)* to receive, get; *(: salaire)* to draw, get; *(: chèque)* to cash; *(aborder: problème, sujet)* to touch on; **~ à** to touch; *(modifier)* to touch, tamper *ou* meddle with; *(traiter de, concerner)* to have to do with, concern; **je vais lui en ~ un mot** I'll have a word with him about it; **~ au but** *(fig)* to near one's goal; **~ à sa fin** to be drawing to a close ■ **se toucher** VPR *(être en contact)* to touch

touffe [tuf] NF tuft

touffu, e [tufy] ADJ thick, dense; *(fig)* complex, involved

★**toujours** [tuʒuʀ] ADV always; *(encore)* still; *(constamment)* forever; **depuis ~** always; **essaie ~** (you can) try anyway; **pour ~** forever; **~ est-il que** the fact remains that; **~ plus** more and more

toulonnais, e [tulɔnɛ, -ɛz] ADJ *of ou* from Toulon

toulousain, e [tuluzɛ̃, -ɛn] ADJ *of ou* from Toulouse

toundra [tundʀa] NF tundra

toupet [tupɛ] NM quiff (BRIT), tuft; *(fam)* nerve, cheek (BRIT)

toupie [tupi] NF *(spinning)* top

★**tour** [tuʀ] NF tower; *(immeuble)* high-rise block (BRIT) *ou* building (US), tower block (BRIT); *(Échecs)* castle, rook; **~ de contrôle** control tower; **la ~ Eiffel** the Eiffel Tower ▶ NM *(excursion: à pied)* stroll, walk; *(: en voiture etc)* run, ride; *(Sport: aussi:* **tour de piste***)* lap; *(d'être servi ou de jouer etc, tournure, de vis ou clef)* turn; *(de roue etc)* revolution; *(Pol: aussi:* **tour de scrutin***)* ballot; *(ruse, de prestidigitation, de cartes)* trick; *(de potier)* wheel; *(à bois, métaux)* lathe; *(circonférence)*: **de 3 m de ~** 3 m round, with a circumference *ou* girth of 3 m; **faire le ~ de** to go (a)round; *(à pied)* to walk (a)round; *(fig)* to review; **faire le ~ de l'Europe** to tour Europe; **faire un ~** to go for a walk; *(en voiture etc)* to go for a ride; **faire 2 tours** to go (a)round twice; *(hélice etc)* to turn *ou* revolve twice; **fermer à double ~** vi to double-lock the door; **c'est au ~ de Renée** it's Renée's turn; **à ~ de rôle**, **~ à ~** in turn; **à ~ de bras** with all one's strength; *(fig)* non-stop, relentlessly; **~ de taille/ tête** waist/head measurement; **~ de chant** song recital; **le T~ de France** the Tour de France; **~ de force** tour de force; **~ de garde** spell of duty; **un 33 tours** an LP; **un 45 tours** a single; **~ d'horizon** *(fig)* general survey; **~ de lit** valance; **~ de main** dexterity, knack; **en un ~ de main** (as) quick as a flash; **~ de passe-passe** trick, sleight of hand; **~ de reins** sprained back

The **Tour de France** is an annual road race for professional cyclists. It takes about three weeks to complete and is divided into daily stages, or *étapes*, that vary in length from around 55km to more than 200km and which are over terrain of varying levels of difficulty. The leading cyclist wears a yellow jersey, the *maillot jaune*. The route varies; it is not usually confined to France but always ends in Paris. In addition, there are a number of time trials.

tourangeau, -elle, x [tuʀɑ̃ʒo, -ɛl] ADJ *(de la région)* of *ou* from Touraine; *(de la ville)* of *ou* from Tours

tourbe [tuʀb] NF peat

tourbeux, -euse [tuʀbø, -øz] ADJ peaty

tourbière [tuʀbjɛʀ] NF peat-bog

tourbillon [tuʀbijɔ̃] NM whirlwind; *(d'eau)* whirlpool; *(fig)* whirl, swirl

tourbillonner [tuʀbijɔne] /1/ VI to whirl, swirl; *(objet, personne)* to whirl *ou* twirl round

tourelle [tuʀɛl] NF turret

★**tourisme** [tuʀism] NM tourism; **agence de ~** tourist agency; **avion/voiture de ~** private plane/car; **faire du ~** to go touring; *(en ville)* to go sightseeing

tourista [tuʀista] NF *(fam)* = **turista**

★**touriste** [tuʀist] NMF tourist

★**touristique** [tuʀistik] ADJ tourist *cpd*; *(région)* touristic *(péj)*, with tourist appeal

tourment [tuʀmɑ̃] NM torment

tourmente [tuʀmɑ̃t] NF storm

tourmenté, e [tuʀmɑ̃te] ADJ tormented, tortured; *(mer, période)* turbulent

tourmenter [tuʀmɑ̃te] /1/ VT to torment ▪ **se tourmenter** VPR to fret, worry o.s.

tournage [tuʀnaʒ] NM *(d'un film)* shooting

tournant, e [tuʀnɑ̃, -ɑ̃t] ADJ *(feu, scène)* revolving; *(chemin)* winding; *(escalier)* spiral *cpd*; *(mouvement)* circling ▸ NM *(de route)* bend (BRIT), curve (US); *(fig)* turning point; *voir* **plaque**; **grève**

tourné, e [tuʀne] ADJ *(lait, vin)* sour, off; *(Menuiserie: bois)* turned; **bien ~** *(compliment)* well-phrased; *(femme)* shapely; **mal ~** *(lettre)* badly expressed; **avoir l'esprit mal ~** to have a dirty mind

tournebroche [tuʀnəbʀɔʃ] NM roasting spit

tourne-disque [tuʀnədisk] NM record player

tournedos [tuʀnədo] NM tournedos

tournée [tuʀne] NF *(du facteur etc)* round; *(d'artiste, politicien)* tour; *(au café)* round (of drinks); **faire la ~ de** to go (a)round

tournemain [tuʀnəmɛ̃]: **en un ~** *adv* in a flash

★**tourner** [tuʀne] /1/ VT to turn; *(sauce, mélange)* to stir; *(contourner)* to get (a)round; *(Ciné: faire les prises de vues)* to shoot; *(: produire)* to make; **~ le dos à** *(aussi fig: mouvement)* to turn one's back on; *(: position)* to have one's back to; **~ la tête** to look away; **~ la tête à qn** *(fig)* to go to sb's head; **~ la page** *(fig)* to turn the page ▸ VI to turn; *(moteur)* to run; *(compteur)* to tick away; *(lait etc)* to turn (sour); *(fig: chance, vie)* to turn out; **bien ~** to turn out well;

mal ~ to go wrong; **~ autour de** to go (a)round; *(planète)* to revolve (a)round; *(péj)* to hang (a) round; **~ autour du pot** *(fig)* to go (a)round in circles; **~ à/en** to turn into; **~ à la pluie/au rouge** to turn rainy/red; **~ en ridicule** to ridicule; **~ court** to come to a sudden end; **~ de l'œil** to pass out ▪ **se tourner** VPR to turn (a)round; **se ~ vers** to turn to; to turn towards; **se ~ les pouces** to twiddle one's thumbs

tournesol [tuʀnəsɔl] NM sunflower

tourneur [tuʀnœʀ] NM turner; lathe-operator

tournevis [tuʀnəvis] NM screwdriver

tourniquer [tuʀnike] /1/ VI to go (a)round in circles

tourniquet [tuʀnikɛ] NM *(pour arroser)* sprinkler; *(portillon)* turnstile; *(présentoir)* revolving stand, spinner; *(Chirurgie)* tourniquet

tournis [tuʀni] NM: **avoir/donner le ~** to feel/make dizzy

tournoi [tuʀnwa] NM tournament

tournoyer [tuʀnwaje] /8/ VI *(oiseau)* to wheel (a)round; *(fumée)* to swirl (a)round

tournure [tuʀnyʀ] NF *(Ling: syntaxe)* turn of phrase; form; *(d'une phrase)* phrasing; **la ~ de qch** *(évolution)* the way sth is developing; *(aspect)* the look of sth; **la ~ des événements** the turn of events; **prendre ~** to take shape; **~ d'esprit** turn *ou* cast of mind

tour-opérateur [tuʀɔpeʀatœʀ] NM tour operator

tourte [tuʀt] NF pie

tourteau, x [tuʀto] NM *(Agr)* oilcake, cattle-cake; *(Zool)* edible crab

tourtereau, x [tuʀtəʀo] NM baby turtledove; **des tourtereaux** *(fig: un couple d'amoureux)* lovebirds

tourterelle [tuʀtəʀɛl] NF turtledove

tourtière [tuʀtjɛʀ] NF pie dish *ou* plate

tous [tu, tus] ADJ, PRON *voir* **tout**

★**Toussaint** [tusɛ̃] NF: **la ~** All Saints' Day

La Toussaint, or All Saints' Day, which falls on 1 November, is a public holiday in France. People traditionally visit the graves of friends and relatives to lay chrysanthemums on them.

★**tousser** [tuse] /1/ VI to cough

toussotement [tusɔtmɑ̃] NM slight cough

toussoter [tusɔte] /1/ VI to have a slight cough; *(pour avertir)* to give a slight cough

---

tout, e [tu, tut]

(mpl **tous** [tus], *fpl* **toutes** [tut]*)* ADJ **1** *(avec article singulier)* all; **tout le lait** all the milk; **toute la nuit** all night, the whole night; **tout le livre** the whole book; **tout un pain** a whole loaf; **tout le temps** all the time, the whole time; **c'est tout le contraire** it's quite the opposite; **c'est toute une affaire** *ou* **histoire** it's quite a business, it's a whole rigmarole

2 *(avec article pluriel)* every all; **tous les livres** all the books; **toutes les nuits** every night; **toutes les fois** every time; **toutes les trois/deux semaines** every third/other *ou* second week, every three/two weeks; **tous les deux** both *ou*

each of us (*ou* them *ou* you); **toutes les trois** all three of us (*ou* them *ou* you)

3 (*sans article*): **à tout âge** at any age; **pour toute nourriture, il avait …** his only food was …; **de tous côtés, de toutes parts** from everywhere, from every side

▶ PRON everything, all; **il a tout fait** he's done everything; **je les vois tous** I can see them all *ou* all of them; **nous y sommes tous allés** all of us went, we all went; **c'est tout** that's all; **en tout** in all; **en tout et pour tout** all in all; **tout ce qu'il sait** all he knows; **c'était tout ce qu'il y a de chic** it was the last word *ou* the ultimate in chic

▶ NM whole; **le tout** all of it (*ou* them); **le tout est de …** the main thing is to …; **pas du tout** not at all; **elle a tout d'une mère/d'une intrigante** she's a real *ou* true mother/schemer; **du tout au tout** utterly

▶ ADV **1** (*très, complètement*) very; **tout près** *ou* **à côté** very near; **le tout premier** the very first; **tout seul** all alone; **il était tout rouge** he was really *ou* all red; **parler tout bas** to speak very quietly; **le livre tout entier** the whole book; **tout en haut** right at the top; **tout droit** straight ahead

2: **tout en** while; **tout en travaillant** while working, as he *etc* works

3: **tout d'abord** first of all; **tout à coup** suddenly; **tout à fait** absolutely; **tout à fait !** exactly!; **tout à l'heure** a short while ago; (*futur*) in a short while, shortly; **à tout à l'heure !** see you later!; **il répondit tout court que non** he just answered no (and that was all); **tout de même** all the same; **tout le monde** everybody, everyone; **tout ou rien** all or nothing; **tout simplement** quite simply; **tout de suite** immediately, straight away

---

Everyone et everybody sont suivis d'un verbe au singulier, mais le possessif qui s'y rapporte doit être au pluriel.
Est-ce que tout le monde a fini ses devoirs ? Has **everybody finished** *their* **homework?**

---

tout-à-l'égout [tutalegu] NM INV mains drainage

toutefois [tutfwa] ADV however

toutes [tut] ADJ, PRON *voir* **tout**

toutou [tutu] NM (*fam*) doggie

tout-petit [tup(ə)ti] NM toddler

tout-puissant, toute-puissante [tupɥisã, tutpɥisãt] ADJ all-powerful, omnipotent

tout-terrain [tuterɛ̃] ADJ INV: **vélo ~** mountain bike; **véhicule ~** four-wheel drive

tout-venant [tuv(ə)nã] NM: **le ~** everyday stuff

toux [tu] NF cough

toxémie [tɔksemi] NF toxaemia (BRIT), toxemia (US)

toxicité [tɔksisite] NF toxicity

toxico [tɔksiko] NMF (*fam*: *toxicomane*) junkie (*fam*), addict

toxicologie [tɔksikɔlɔʒi] NF toxicology

toxicologique [tɔksikɔlɔʒik] ADJ (*analyse, résultat*) toxicology cpd, toxicological; (*laboratoire*) toxicology cpd

★**toxicomane** [tɔksikɔman] NMF drug addict

toxicomanie [tɔksikɔmani] NF drug addiction

toxine [tɔksin] NF toxin

toxique [tɔksik] ADJ toxic, poisonous

toxoplasmose [tɔksoplasmoz] NF toxoplasmosis

TP SIGLE MPL = **travaux pratiques; travaux publics**
▶ SIGLE M = **trésor (public)**

TPG SIGLE M = **Trésorier-payeur général**

tps ABR = **temps**

trac [trak] NM (*aux examens*) nerves *pl*; (*Théât*) stage fright; **avoir le ~** (*aux examens*) to get an attack of nerves; (*Théât*) to have stage fright; **tout à ~** all of a sudden

traçabilité [trasabilite] NF traceability

traçable [trasabl] ADJ traceable

traçant, e [trasɑ̃, -ɑ̃t] ADJ: **table traçante** (*Inform*) (graph) plotter

tracas [traka] NM bother *no pl*, worry *no pl*

tracasser [trakase] /1/ VT to worry, bother; (*harceler*) to harass ■ **se tracasser** VPR to worry (o.s.), fret

tracasserie [trakasri] NF annoyance *no pl*; harassment *no pl*

tracassier, -ière [trakasje, -jɛr] ADJ irksome

trace [tras] NF (*empreintes*) tracks *pl*; (*marques*: *fig*) mark; (*restes, vestige*) trace; (*indice*) sign; (*aussi*: **suivre à la trace**) to track; **traces de pas** footprints

tracé [trase] NM (*contour*) line; (*plan*) layout

tracer [trase] /3/ VT to draw; (*mot*) to trace; (*piste*) to open up; (*fig*: *chemin*) to show

traceur [trasœr] NM (*Inform*) plotter

trachée [traʃe], **trachée-artère** [traʃeartɛr] NF windpipe, trachea

trachéite [trakeit] NF tracheitis

trachéotomie [trakeɔtɔmi] NF tracheotomy

tract [trakt] NM tract, pamphlet; (*publicitaire*) handout

tractations [traktasjɔ̃] NFPL dealings, bargaining *sg*

tracter [trakte] /1/ VT to tow

tracteur [traktœr] NM tractor

traction [traksjɔ̃] NF traction; (*Gym*) pull-up; **~ avant/arrière** front-wheel/rear-wheel drive; **~ électrique** electric(al) traction *ou* haulage

tractopelle [traktɔpɛl] NM digger

trad. ABR (= *traduit*) translated; (= *traduction*) translation; (= *traducteur*) translator

trader [trɛdœr] NM, **tradeur, -euse** [trɛdœr, -øz] NM/F (*entreprise*) broker; (*personne*) trader

tradition [tradisjɔ̃] NF tradition

traditionalisme [tradisjɔnalism] NM traditionalism

traditionaliste [tradisjɔnalist] ADJ, NMF traditionalist

traditionnel, le [tradisjɔnɛl] ADJ traditional

traditionnellement [tradisjɔnɛlmã] ADV traditionally

★**traducteur, -trice** [tradyktœr, -tris] NM/F translator

traduction [tradyksjɔ̃] NF translation

★**traduire** [tʀadɥiʀ] /38/ VT to translate; (*exprimer*) to convey, render; **se ~ par** to find expression in; **~ en français** to translate into French; **~ en justice** to bring before the courts

traduis *etc* [tʀadɥi] VB *voir* **traduire**

traduisible [tʀadɥizibl] ADJ translatable

traduit, e [tʀadɥi, -it] PP *de* **traduire**

trafic [tʀafik] NM traffic; **~ d'armes** arms dealing; **~ de drogue** drug peddling

trafiquant, e [tʀafikã, -ãt] NM/F trafficker; (*d'armes*) dealer

trafiquer [tʀafike] /1/ VT (*péj: vin*) to doctor; (: *moteur, document*) to tamper with ▶ VI to traffic, be engaged in trafficking

tragédie [tʀaʒedi] NF tragedy

tragédien, ne [tʀaʒedjɛ̃, -ɛn] NM/F tragedian/ tragedienne

tragi-comique [tʀaʒikɔmik] ADJ tragi-comic

tragique [tʀaʒik] ADJ tragic ▶ NM: **prendre qch au ~** to make a tragedy out of sth

tragiquement [tʀaʒikmã] ADV tragically

trahir [tʀaiʀ] /2/ VT to betray; (*fig*) to give away, reveal ■ **se trahir** VPR to betray o.s., give o.s. away

trahison [tʀaizɔ̃] NF betrayal; (*Jur*) treason

traie *etc* [tʀɛ] VB *voir* **traire**

★**train** [tʀɛ̃] NM (*Rail*) train; (*allure*) pace; (*fig: ensemble*) set; **être en ~ de faire qch** to be doing sth; **mettre qch en ~** to get sth under way; **mettre qn en ~** to put sb in good spirits; **se mettre en ~** (*commencer*) to get started; (*faire de la gymnastique*) to warm up; **se sentir en ~** to feel in good form; **aller bon ~** to make good progress; **~ avant/arrière** front-wheel/rear-wheel axle unit; **~ à grande vitesse** high-speed train; **~ d'atterrissage** undercarriage; **~ autos-couchettes** car-sleeper train; **~ électrique** (*jouet*) (electric) train set; **~ de pneus** set of tyres ou tires; **~ de vie** style of living

traînailler [tʀenaje] /1/ VI = **traînasser**

traînant, e [tʀenã, -ãt] ADJ (*voix, ton*) drawling

traînard, e [tʀenaʀ, -aʀd] NM/F (*péj*) slowcoach (BRIT), slowpoke (US)

traînasser [tʀenase] /1/ VI to dawdle

traîne [tʀɛn] NF (*de robe*) train; **être à la ~** to be in tow; (*en arrière*) to lag behind; (*en désordre*) to be lying around

traîneau, x [tʀeno] NM sleigh, sledge

traînée [tʀene] NF streak, trail; (*péj*) slut (!)

traîner [tʀene] /1/ VT (*remorque*) to pull; (*enfant, chien*) to drag ou trail along; (*maladie*): **il traîne un rhume depuis l'hiver** he has a cold which has been dragging on since winter; **~ qn au cinéma** to drag sb to the cinema; **~ les pieds** to drag one's feet ▶ VI (*robe, manteau*) to trail; (*être en désordre*) to lie around; (*marcher lentement*) to dawdle (along); (*vagabonder*) to hang about; (*agir lentement*) to idle about; (*durer*) to drag on; **~ par terre** to trail on the ground; **~ en longueur** to drag out ■ **se traîner** VPR (*ramper*) to crawl along; **se ~ par terre** to crawl (on the ground); (*marcher avec difficulté*) to drag o.s. along; (*durer*) to drag on

training [tʀeniŋ] NM (*pull*) tracksuit top; (*chaussure*) trainer (BRIT), sneaker (US)

train-train [tʀɛ̃tʀɛ̃] NM humdrum routine

traire [tʀɛʀ] /50/ VT to milk

trait, e [tʀɛ, -ɛt] PP *de* **traire** ▶ NM (*ligne*) line; (*de dessin*) stroke; (*caractéristique*) feature, trait; (*flèche: vieilli*) dart, arrow; shaft; **d'un ~** (*boire*) in one gulp; **de ~** *adj* (*animal*) draught (BRIT), draft (US); **avoir ~ à** to concern; **~ pour ~** line for line; **~ de caractère** characteristic, trait; **~ d'esprit** flash of wit; **~ de génie** brainwave; **~ d'union** hyphen; (*fig*) link ■ **traits** NMPL (*du visage*) features

traitable [tʀɛtabl] ADJ (*personne*) accommodating; (*sujet*) manageable

traitant, e [tʀɛtã, -ãt] ADJ: **votre médecin ~** your usual ou family doctor; **shampo(o)ing ~** medicated shampoo; **crème traitante** conditioning cream, conditioner

traite [tʀɛt] NF (*Comm*) draft; (*Agr*) milking; (*trajet*) stretch; **d'une (seule) ~** without stopping (once); **la ~ des noirs** the slave trade; **la ~ des blanches** the white slave trade

traité [tʀete] NM treaty

traitement [tʀɛtmã] NM treatment; processing; (*salaire*) salary; **suivre un ~** to undergo treatment; **mauvais ~** ill-treatment; **~ de données** ou **de l'information** (*Inform*) data processing; **~ hormono-supplétif** hormone replacement therapy; **~ par lots** (*Inform*) batch processing; **~ de texte** (*Inform*) word processing; (*logiciel*) word processing package

traiter [tʀete] /1/ VT (*gén*) to treat; (*Tech: matériaux*) to process, treat; (*Inform*) to process; (*affaire*) to deal with, handle; (*qualifier*): **~ qn d'idiot** to call sb a fool; **bien/mal ~** to treat well/ill-treat ▶ VI to deal; **~ de** to deal with

traiteur [tʀɛtœʀ] NM caterer

traître, -esse [tʀɛtʀ, -tʀɛs] ADJ (*dangereux*) treacherous ▶ NM/F traitor (traitress); **prendre qn en ~** to make an insidious attack on sb

traîtrise [tʀetʀiz] NF treachery

trajectoire [tʀaʒɛktwaʀ] NF trajectory, path

★**trajet** [tʀaʒɛ] NM (*parcours, voyage*) journey; (*itinéraire*) route; (*fig*) path, course; (*distance à parcourir*) distance; **il y a une heure de ~** the journey takes one hour

tralala [tʀalala] NM (*péj*) fuss

tram [tʀam] NM tram (BRIT), streetcar (US)

trame [tʀam] NF (*de tissu*) weft; (*fig*) framework; texture; (*Typo*) screen

tramer [tʀame] /1/ VT to plot, hatch

traminot [tʀamino] NM tramway worker

tramontane [tʀamɔ̃tan] NF tramontane (*cold, dry south-southwesterly wind*)

trampoline [tʀãpolin], **trampolino** [tʀãpolino] NM trampoline; (*Sport*) trampolining

tramway [tʀamwɛ] NM tram(way); (*voiture*) tram(car) (BRIT), streetcar (US)

tranchant, e [tʀãʃã, -ãt] ADJ sharp; (*fig: personne*) peremptory; (: *couleurs*) striking ▶ NM (*d'un couteau*) cutting edge; (*de la main*) edge; **à double ~** (*argument, procédé*) double-edged

★**tranche** [tʀãʃ] NF (*morceau*) slice; (*arête*) edge; (*partie*) section; (*série*) block; (*d'impôts, revenus etc*) bracket; (*loterie*) issue; **~ d'âge/de salaires** age/ wage bracket; **~ (de silicium)** wafer

tranché, e [tʀãʃe] ADJ (*couleurs*) distinct, sharply contrasted; (*opinions*) clear-cut, definite ▶ NF trench

trancher [tʀɑ̃ʃe] /1/ vt to cut, sever; (fig: résoudre) to settle ▶ vi to be decisive; (entre deux choses) to settle the argument; ~ **avec** qch to contrast sharply with

tranchet [tʀɑ̃ʃɛ] NM knife

tranchoir [tʀɑ̃ʃwaʀ] NM chopper

★**tranquille** [tʀɑ̃kil] ADJ calm, quiet; (enfant, élève) quiet; (rassuré) easy in one's mind, with one's mind at rest; **se tenir** ~ (enfant) to be quiet; **avoir la conscience** ~ to have an easy conscience; **laisse-moi/laisse-ça** ~ leave me/it alone

tranquillement [tʀɑ̃kilmɑ̃] ADV calmly

tranquillisant, e [tʀɑ̃kiliza, -ɑ̃t] ADJ (nouvelle) reassuring ▶ NM tranquillizer

tranquilliser [tʀɑ̃kilize] /1/ vt to reassure ■ **se tranquilliser** VPR to calm (o.s.) down

tranquillité [tʀɑ̃kilite] NF quietness, peace (and quiet); **en toute** ~ with complete peace of mind; ~ **d'esprit** peace of mind

transaction [tʀɑ̃zaksjɔ̃] NF (Comm) transaction, deal

transactionnel, le [tʀɑ̃zaksjɔnɛl] ADJ (Jur: indemnité) compromise cpd; (Inform, Psych) transactional

transafricain, e [tʀɑ̃safʀikɛ̃, -ɛn] ADJ transafrican

transalpin, e [tʀɑ̃zalpɛ̃, -in] ADJ transalpine

transaméricain, e [tʀɑ̃zamerikɛ̃, -ɛn] ADJ transamerican

transat [tʀɑ̃zat] NM deckchair ▶ NF = **course transatlantique**

transatlantique [tʀɑ̃zatlɑ̃tik] ADJ transatlantic ▶ NM transatlantic liner

transbahuter [tʀɑ̃sbayte] vt (fam) to cart (fam)

transborder [tʀɑ̃sbɔʀde] /1/ vt to tran(s)ship

transbordeur [tʀɑ̃sbɔʀdœʀ] NM (aussi: **navire transbordeur**) ferry

transcendant, e [tʀɑ̃sɑ̃dɑ̃, -ɑ̃t] ADJ (Philosophie, Math) transcendental; (supérieur) transcendent

transcodeur [tʀɑ̃skɔdœʀ] NM compiler

transcontinental, e, -aux [tʀɑ̃skɔ̃tinɑ̃tal, -o] ADJ transcontinental

transcription [tʀɑ̃skʀipsjɔ̃] NF transcription

transcrire [tʀɑ̃skʀiʀ] /39/ vt to transcribe

transe [tʀɑ̃s] NF: **entrer en** ~ to go into a trance ■ **transes** NFPL agony sg

transept [tʀɑ̃sɛpt] NM (Archit) transept

transférable [tʀɑ̃sfeʀabl] ADJ transferable

transfèrement [tʀɑ̃sfɛʀmɑ̃] NM transfer

transférer [tʀɑ̃sfeʀe] /6/ vt to transfer

transfert [tʀɑ̃sfɛʀ] NM transfer

transfiguration [tʀɑ̃sfigyʀasjɔ̃] NF transformation, transfiguration

transfigurer [tʀɑ̃sfigyʀe] /1/ vt to transform

transfo [tʀɑ̃sfo] NM (= transformateur) transformer

transformable [tʀɑ̃sfɔʀmabl] ADJ convertible

transformateur [tʀɑ̃sfɔʀmatœʀ] NM transformer

transformation [tʀɑ̃sfɔʀmasjɔ̃] NF change, alteration; (radicale) transformation; (Rugby) conversion; **industries de** ~ processing industries ■ **transformations** NFPL (travaux) alterations

transformer [tʀɑ̃sfɔʀme] /1/ vt to change; (radicalement) to transform, alter ("alter" implique un changement moins radical); (vêtement) alter; (matière première, appartement, Rugby) to convert; ~ **en** to transform into; to turn into; to convert into ■ **se transformer** VPR to be transformed; to alter

---

The French word **transformer** is very often not translated by *to transform*.

---

transfrontalier, -ière [tʀɑ̃sfʀɔ̃talje, -jɛʀ] ADJ cross-border

transfuge [tʀɑ̃sfyʒ] NM renegade

transfuser [tʀɑ̃sfyze] /1/ vt to transfuse

transfusion [tʀɑ̃sfyzjɔ̃] NF: ~ **sanguine** blood transfusion

transgénérationnel, le [tʀɑ̃sʒeneʀasjɔnɛl] ADJ transgenerational

transgénique [tʀɑ̃sʒenik] ADJ transgenic

transgresser [tʀɑ̃sgʀese] /1/ vt to contravene, disobey

transgression [tʀɑ̃sgʀesjɔ̃] NF (de loi) breaking, contravention; (de tabou) breaking

transhumance [tʀɑ̃zymɑ̃s] NF transhumance, seasonal move to new pastures

transhumanisme [tʀɑ̃symanism] NM transhumanism

transi, e [tʀɑ̃zi] ADJ numb (with cold), chilled to the bone

transiger [tʀɑ̃ziʒe] /3/ vi to compromise, come to an agreement; ~ **sur** ou **avec** qch to compromise on sth

transistor [tʀɑ̃zistɔʀ] NM transistor

transistorisé, e [tʀɑ̃zistɔʀize] ADJ transistorized

transit [tʀɑ̃zit] NM transit; **de** ~ transit cpd; **en** ~ in transit

transitaire [tʀɑ̃ziteʀ] NMF forwarding agent

transiter [tʀɑ̃zite] /1/ vi to pass in transit

transitif, -ive [tʀɑ̃zitif, -iv] ADJ transitive

transition [tʀɑ̃zisjɔ̃] NF transition; **de** ~ transitional

transitoire [tʀɑ̃zitwaʀ] ADJ (mesure, gouvernement) transitional, provisional; (fugitif) transient

translucide [tʀɑ̃slysid] ADJ translucent

transmet etc [tʀɑ̃smɛ] VB voir **transmettre**

transmettais etc [tʀɑ̃smɛtɛ] VB voir **transmettre**

transmetteur [tʀɑ̃smɛtœʀ] NM transmitter

transmettre [tʀɑ̃smɛtʀ] /56/ vt (passer): ~ **qch à qn** to pass sth on to sb; (Tech, Tél, Méd) to transmit; (TV, Radio: retransmettre) to broadcast

transmis, e [tʀɑ̃smi, -iz] PP de **transmettre**

transmissible [tʀɑ̃smisibl] ADJ transmissible

transmission [tʀɑ̃smisjɔ̃] NF transmission, passing on; (Auto) transmission; ~ **de données** (Inform) data transmission; ~ **de pensée** thought transmission ■ **transmissions** NFPL (Mil) ≈ signals corps sg

transnational, e, -aux [tʀɑ̃snasjɔnal, -o] ADJ transnational

transocéanien, ne [tʀɑ̃zɔseanjɛ̃, -ɛn], **transocéanique** [tʀɑ̃zɔseanik] ADJ transoceanic

transparaître [tʀɑ̃spaʀɛtʀ] /57/ vi to show (through)

transparence [tʀɑ̃spaʀɑ̃s] NF transparency; **par** ~ (regarder) against the light; (voir) showing through

transparent, e [tʀɑ̃spaʀɑ̃, -ɑ̃t] ADJ transparent

transpercer [tʀɑ̃spɛʀse] /3/ VT (froid, pluie) to go through, pierce; (balle) to go through

transpiration [tʀɑ̃spiʀasjɔ̃] NF perspiration

transpirer [tʀɑ̃spiʀe] /1/ VI to perspire; (information, nouvelle) to come to light

transplant [tʀɑ̃splɑ̃] NM transplant

transplantation [tʀɑ̃splɑ̃tasjɔ̃] NF transplant

transplanter [tʀɑ̃splɑ̃te] /1/ VT (Méd, Bot) to transplant; (personne) to uproot, move

transport [tʀɑ̃spɔʀ] NM transport; (émotions): ~ **de colère** fit of rage; ~ **de joie** transport of delight; ~ **de voyageurs/marchandises** passenger/goods transportation; **transports en commun** public transport sg; **transports routiers** haulage (BRIT), trucking (US)

transportable [tʀɑ̃spɔʀtabl] ADJ (marchandises) transportable; (malade) fit (enough) to be moved

transporter [tʀɑ̃spɔʀte] /1/ VT to carry, move; (Comm) to transport, convey; (fig): ~ **qn (de joie)** to send sb into raptures; **se ~ quelque part** (fig) to let one's imagination carry one away (somewhere)

transporteur [tʀɑ̃spɔʀtœʀ] NM haulage contractor (BRIT), trucker (US)

transposer [tʀɑ̃spoze] /1/ VT to transpose

transposition [tʀɑ̃spozisjɔ̃] NF transposition

transrhénan, e [tʀɑ̃sʀenɑ̃, -an] ADJ transrhenane

transsaharien, ne [tʀɑ̃ssaaʀjɛ̃, -ɛn] ADJ trans-Saharan

transsexuel, le [tʀɑ̃ssɛksɥɛl] ADJ, NM/F transsexual

transsibérien, ne [tʀɑ̃ssibeʀjɛ̃, -ɛn] ADJ trans-Siberian

transvaser [tʀɑ̃svaze] /1/ VT to decant

transversal, e, -aux [tʀɑ̃svɛʀsal, -o] ADJ transverse, cross(-); (route etc) cross-country; (mur, chemin, rue) running at right angles; (Auto): **axe ~** main cross-country road (BRIT) ou highway (US); **coupe transversale** cross section

transversalement [tʀɑ̃svɛʀsalmɑ̃] ADV crosswise

trapèze [tʀapɛz] NM (Géom) trapezium; (au cirque) trapeze

trapéziste [tʀapezist] NMF trapeze artist

trapézoïdal, e [tʀapezɔidal] ADJ trapezoid

trappe [tʀap] NF (de cave, grenier) trap door; (piège) trap

trappeur [tʀapœʀ] NM trapper, fur trader

trapu, e [tʀapy] ADJ squat, stocky

traquenard [tʀaknaʀ] NM trap

traquer [tʀake] /1/ VT to track down; (harceler) to hound

traumatisant, e [tʀomatizɑ̃, -ɑ̃t] ADJ traumatic

traumatiser [tʀomatize] /1/ VT to traumatize

traumatisme [tʀomatism] NM traumatism

traumatologie [tʀomatɔlɔʒi] NF branch of medicine concerned with accidents

★**travail, -aux** [tʀavaj, -o] NM (gén) work; (tâche, métier) work no pl, job; (Écon, Méd) labour (BRIT), labor (US); (Inform) job; **être/entrer en ~** (Méd) to be in/go into labour; **être sans ~** (employé) to be out of work, be unemployed; ~ **d'intérêt général** ≈ community service; ~ **au noir** moonlighting; ~ **posté** shiftwork ∎ **travaux** NMPL (de réparation, agricoles etc) work sg; (sur route) roadworks (BRIT); (de construction) building (work) sg; **travaux des champs** farm work sg; **travaux dirigés** (Scol) supervised practical work sg; **travaux forcés** hard labour sg; **travaux manuels** (Scol) handicrafts; **travaux ménagers** housework sg; **travaux pratiques** (gén) practical work pl; (en laboratoire) lab work pl (BRIT), lab (US); **travaux publics** ≈ public works sg

travaillé, e [tʀavaje] ADJ (style) polished

★**travailler** [tʀavaje] /1/ VI to work; (bois) to warp ▶ VT (bois, métal) to work; (pâte) to knead; (objet d'art, discipline, fig: influencer) to work on; **cela le travaille** it is on his mind; ~ **la terre** to work the land; ~ **son piano** to do one's piano practice; ~ **à** to work on; (fig: contribuer à) to work towards; ~ **à faire** to endeavour (BRIT) ou endeavor (US) to do

★**travailleur, -euse** [tʀavajœʀ, -øz] ADJ hard-working ▶ NM/F worker; ~ **de force** labourer (BRIT), laborer (US); ~ **intellectuel** non-manual worker; ~ **social** social worker; **travailleuse familiale** home help

travailliste [tʀavajist] ADJ ≈ Labour cpd ▶ NMF member of the Labour party

travaux [tʀavo] NMPL voir **travail**

travée [tʀave] NF row; (Archit) bay; span

traveller's [tʀavlœʀs], **traveller's chèque** [tʀavlœʀsʃɛk] NM traveller's cheque

travelling [tʀavliŋ] NM (chariot) dolly; (technique) tracking; ~ **optique** zoom shots pl

travelo [tʀavlo] NM (fam) (drag) queen

travers [tʀavɛʀ] NM fault, failing; **à ~** adv through; **au ~ (de)** through; **en ~ (de)** across; **de ~** adj (nez, bouche) crooked; (chapeau) askew; **regarder de ~** (fig) to look askance at; **comprendre de ~** to misunderstand

traverse [tʀavɛʀs] NF (de voie ferrée) sleeper; **chemin de ~** shortcut

traversée [tʀavɛʀse] NF crossing

★**traverser** [tʀavɛʀse] /1/ VT (gén) to cross; (ville, tunnel: aussi: percer, fig) to go through; (ligne, trait) to run across

traversin [tʀavɛʀsɛ̃] NM bolster

travesti [tʀavɛsti] NM (comme mode de vie) transvestite; (artiste de cabaret) female impersonator, drag artist; (costume) fancy dress

travestir [tʀavɛstiʀ] /2/ VT (vérité) to misrepresent ∎ **se travestir** VPR (se costumer) to dress up; (artiste) to put on drag; (Psych) to dress as a woman

trayais etc [tʀɛje] VB voir **traire**

trayeuse [tʀɛjøz] NF milking machine

trébucher [tʀebyʃe] /1/ VI: ~ **(sur)** to stumble (over), trip (over)

trèfle [tʀɛfl] NM (Bot) clover; (Cartes: couleur) clubs pl; (: carte) club; ~ **à quatre feuilles** four-leaf clover

treillage [tʀɛjaʒ] NM lattice work

treille [tʀɛj] NF (tonnelle) vine arbour (BRIT) ou arbor (US); (vigne) climbing vine

treillis [tʀɛji] NM (métallique) wire-mesh; (toile) canvas; (Mil: tenue) combat uniform; (: pantalon) combat trousers pl

★**treize** [tʀɛz] NUM thirteen

treizième [tʀɛzjɛm] NUM thirteenth; *see note*

The **treizième mois** is an end-of-year bonus roughly corresponding to one month's salary. For many employees it is a standard part of their salary package.

tréma [tʀema] NM diaeresis

tremblant, e [tʀɑ̃blɑ̃, -ɑ̃t] ADJ trembling, shaking

tremble [tʀɑ̃bl] NM (*Bot*) aspen

tremblé, e [tʀɑ̃ble] ADJ shaky

tremblement [tʀɑ̃bləmɑ̃] NM trembling *no pl*, shaking *no pl*, shivering *no pl*; **~ de terre** earthquake

★**trembler** [tʀɑ̃ble] /**1**/ VI to tremble, shake; **~ de** (*froid, fièvre*) to shiver *ou* tremble with; (*peur*) to shake *ou* tremble with; **~ pour qn** to fear for sb

tremblotant, e [tʀɑ̃blɔtɑ̃, -ɑ̃t] ADJ trembling

trembloter [tʀɑ̃blɔte] /**1**/ VI to tremble *ou* shake slightly

trémolo [tʀemɔlo] NM (*d'un instrument*) tremolo; (*de la voix*) quaver

trémousser [tʀemuse] /**1**/: **se trémousser** VPR to jig about, wriggle about

trempe [tʀɑ̃p] NF (*fig*): **de cette/sa ~** of this/his calibre (BRIT) *ou* caliber (US)

trempé, e [tʀɑ̃pe] ADJ soaking (wet), drenched; (*Tech*): **acier ~** tempered steel

★**tremper** [tʀɑ̃pe] /**1**/ VT to soak, drench; (*aussi:* **faire tremper, mettre à tremper**) to soak; **se faire ~** to get soaked *ou* drenched ▶ VI to soak; (*fig*): **~ dans** to be involved in *ou* have a hand in ■ **se tremper** VPR to have a quick dip

trempette [tʀɑ̃pɛt] NF: **faire ~** to go paddling

tremplin [tʀɑ̃plɛ̃] NM springboard; (*Ski*) ski jump

trentaine [tʀɑ̃tɛn] NF (*âge*): **avoir la ~** to be around thirty; **une ~ (de)** thirty or so, about thirty

★**trente** [tʀɑ̃t] NUM thirty; **voir trente-six chandelles** (*fig*) to see stars; **être/se mettre sur son ~ et un** to be wearing/put on one's Sunday best; **trente-trois tours** *nm* long-playing record, LP

trentième [tʀɑ̃tjɛm] NUM thirtieth

trépanation [tʀepanasjɔ̃] NF trepan

trépaner [tʀepane] /**1**/ VT to trepan, trephine

trépasser [tʀepase] /**1**/ VI to pass away

trépidant, e [tʀepidɑ̃, -ɑ̃t] ADJ (*fig: rythme*) pulsating; (*: vie*) hectic

trépidation [tʀepidasjɔ̃] NF (*d'une machine, d'un moteur*) vibration; (*fig: de la vie*) whirl

trépider [tʀepide] /**1**/ VI to vibrate

trépied [tʀepje] NM (*d'appareil*) tripod; (*meuble*) trivet

trépignement [tʀepiɲmɑ̃] NM stamping (of feet)

trépigner [tʀepiɲe] /**1**/ VI to stamp (one's feet)

très [tʀɛ] ADV very; **~ beau/bien** very beautiful/well; **~ critiqué** much criticized; **~ industrialisé** highly industrialized; **j'ai ~ faim** I'm very hungry

trésor [tʀezɔʀ] NM treasure; (*Admin*) finances *pl*; (*d'une organisation*) funds *pl*; **~ (public)** public revenue; (*service*) public revenue office

trésorerie [tʀezɔʀʀi] NF (*fonds*) funds *pl*; (*gestion*) accounts *pl*; (*bureaux*) accounts department;

(*poste*) treasurership; **difficultés de ~** cash problems, shortage of cash *ou* funds; **~ générale** local government finance office

trésorier, -ière [tʀezɔʀje, -jɛʀ] NM/F treasurer

Trésorier-payeur [tʀezɔʀjepejœʀ] (*pl* **Trésoriers-payeurs**) NM: **~ général** paymaster

tressaillement [tʀesajmɑ̃] NM shiver, shudder; quiver

tressaillir [tʀesajiʀ] /**13**/ VI (*de peur etc*) to shiver, shudder; (*de joie*) to quiver

tressauter [tʀesote] /**1**/ VI to start, jump

tresse [tʀɛs] NF (*de cheveux*) braid, plait; (*cordon, galon*) braid

tresser [tʀese] /**1**/ VT (*cheveux*) to braid, plait; (*fil, jonc*) to plait; (*corbeille*) to weave; (*corde*) to twist

tréteau, x [tʀeto] NM trestle; **les tréteaux** (*fig: Théât*) the boards

treuil [tʀœj] NM winch

trêve [tʀɛv] NF (*Mil, Pol*) truce; (*fig*) respite; **sans ~** unremittingly; **~ de ...** enough of this ...; **les États de la T~** the Trucial States

tri [tʀi] NM (*voir trier*) sorting (out) *no pl*; selection; screening; (*Inform*) sort; (*Postes: action*) sorting; **faire le ~ (de)** to sort out; **le (bureau de) ~** (*Postes*) the sorting office

triade [tʀijad] NF (*groupe, gang*) triad

triage [tʀijaʒ] NM (*Rail*) shunting; (*gare*) marshalling yard

trial [tʀijal] NM (*Sport*) scrambling

triangle [tʀijɑ̃gl] NM triangle; **~ isocèle/équilatéral** isosceles/equilateral triangle; **~ rectangle** right-angled triangle

triangulaire [tʀijɑ̃gylɛʀ] ADJ triangular

triathlon [tʀi(j)atlɔ̃] NM triathlon

tribal, e, -aux [tʀibal, -o] ADJ tribal

tribord [tʀibɔʀ] NM: **à ~** to starboard, on the starboard side

tribu [tʀiby] NF tribe

tribulations [tʀibylasjɔ̃] NFPL tribulations, trials

tribunal, -aux [tʀibynal, -o] NM (*Jur*) court; (*Mil*) tribunal; **~ de police/pour enfants** police/juvenile court; **~ d'instance** ≈ magistrates' court (BRIT), ≈ district court (US); **~ de grande instance** ≈ High Court (BRIT), ≈ Supreme Court (US)

tribune [tʀibyn] NF (*estrade*) platform, rostrum; (*débat*) forum; (*d'église, de tribunal*) gallery; (*de stade*) stand; **~ libre** (*Presse*) opinion column

tribut [tʀiby] NM tribute

tributaire [tʀibytɛʀ] ADJ: **être ~ de** to be dependent on; (*Géo*) to be a tributary of

tricentenaire [tʀisɑ̃t(ə)nɛʀ] NM tercentenary, tricentennial

triche [tʀiʃ] NF (*fam*): **la ~** cheating

★**tricher** [tʀiʃe] /**1**/ VI to cheat

tricherie [tʀiʃʀi] NF cheating *no pl*

tricheur, -euse [tʀiʃœʀ, -øz] NM/F cheat

trichromie [tʀikʀɔmi] NF three-colour (BRIT) *ou* -color (US) printing

tricolore [tʀikɔlɔʀ] ADJ three-coloured (BRIT), three-colored (US); (*français: drapeau*) red, white and blue; (*: équipe etc*) French

tricot [tʀiko] NM (*technique, ouvrage*) knitting *no pl*; (*tissu*) knitted fabric; (*vêtement*) jersey, sweater; **~ de corps**, **~ de peau** vest (BRIT), undershirt (US)

tricoté, e [tʀikɔte] ADJ knitted

tricoter [tʀikɔte] /1/ VT to knit; **machine/aiguille à ~** knitting machine/needle (BRIT) *ou* pin (US)

trictrac [tʀiktʀak] NM backgammon

tricycle [tʀisikl] NM tricycle

tridimensionnel, le [tʀidimãsjɔnɛl] ADJ three-dimensional

triennal, e, -aux [tʀiɛnal, -o] ADJ (*prix, foire, élection*) three-yearly; (*charge, mandat, plan*) three-year

trier [tʀije] /7/ VT (*classer*) to sort (out); (*choisir*) to select; (*visiteurs*) to screen; (*Postes, Inform, fruits*) to sort

trieur, -euse [tʀijœʀ, -øz] NM/F sorter

triglycéride [tʀigliseʀid] NM triglyceride; **taux de triglycérides** triglyceride levels

trigonométrie [tʀigɔnɔmetʀi] NF trigonometry

trigonométrique [tʀigɔnɔmetʀik] ADJ trigonometric

trilingue [tʀilɛ̃g] ADJ trilingual

trilogie [tʀilɔʒi] NF trilogy

trimaran [tʀimaʀã] NM trimaran

trimbaler [tʀɛ̃bale] /1/ VT to cart around, trail along

trimer [tʀime] /1/ VI to slave away

★**trimestre** [tʀimɛstʀ] NM (*Scol*) term; (*Comm*) quarter

trimestriel, le [tʀimɛstʀijɛl] ADJ quarterly; (*Scol*) end-of-term

trimoteur [tʀimɔtœʀ] NM three-engined aircraft

tringle [tʀɛ̃gl] NF rod

Trinité [tʀinite] NF Trinity

Trinité et Tobago [tʀiniteetɔbago] NF Trinidad and Tobago

trinquer [tʀɛ̃ke] /1/ VI to clink glasses; (*fam*) to cop it; **~ à qch/la santé de qn** to drink to sth/sb

trio [tʀijo] NM trio

triolet [tʀijɔlɛ] NM (*Mus*) triplet

triolisme [tʀi(j)ɔlism] NM troilism, threesomes *pl*

triomphal, e, -aux [tʀijɔ̃fal, -o] ADJ triumphant, triumphal

triomphalement [tʀijɔ̃falmã] ADV triumphantly

triomphalisme [tʀijɔ̃falism] NM triumphalism

triomphaliste [tʀijɔ̃falist] ADJ triumphalist

triomphant, e [tʀijɔ̃fã, -ãt] ADJ triumphant

triomphateur, -trice [tʀijɔ̃fatœʀ, -tʀis] NM/F (*triumphant*) victor

triomphe [tʀijɔ̃f] NM triumph; **être reçu/porté en ~** to be given a triumphant welcome/be carried shoulder-high in triumph

triompher [tʀijɔ̃fe] /1/ VI to triumph, win; **~ de** to triumph over, overcome

tripartite [tʀipaʀtit], **triparti, e** [tʀipaʀti] ADJ (*accord, assemblée*) tripartite, three-party

triperie [tʀipʀi] NF tripe shop

tripes [tʀip] NFPL (*Culin*) tripe *sg*; (*fam*) guts

triphasé, e [tʀifaze] ADJ three-phase

triplace [tʀiplas] ADJ three-seater *cpd*

triple [tʀipl] ADJ (*à trois éléments*) triple; (*trois fois plus grand*) treble; **en ~ exemplaire** in triplicate; **~ saut** (*Sport*) triple jump ▶ NM: **le ~ (de)** (*comparaison*) three times as much (as)

triplé [tʀiple] NM hat-trick (BRIT), triple success

triplement [tʀipləmã] ADV (*à un degré triple*) three times over; (*de trois façons*) in three ways; (*pour trois raisons*) on three counts ▶ NM trebling, threefold increase

tripler [tʀiple] /1/ VI, VT to triple, treble, increase threefold

triplés, -ées [tʀiple] NM/FPL triplets

triplex [tʀiplɛks] NM (*appartement*) three-floor apartment; (*verre*) Triplex® (BRIT), safety glass

tripode [tʀipɔd] ADJ with three legs ▶ NM (*Tech*) tripod; (*fig*) triumvirate

Tripoli [tʀipɔli] N Tripoli

triporteur [tʀipɔʀtœʀ] NM delivery tricycle

tripot [tʀipo] NM (*péj*) dive

tripotage [tʀipɔtaʒ] NM (*fam, péj*) jiggery-pokery

tripotée [tʀipɔte] NF (*fam: grand nombre*) hordes *pl*

tripoter [tʀipɔte] /1/ VT (*fam: manipuler*) to fiddle with, finger; (: *personne*) to feel up (*fam*), grope (*fam*)

tripous, tripoux [tʀipu] NMPL braised sheep's tripe with herbs and vegetable flavourings

triptyque [tʀiptik] NM triptych

trique [tʀik] NF cudgel

trisannuel, le [tʀizanɥɛl] ADJ triennial

trisomie [tʀizɔmi] NF Down's syndrome

trisomique [tʀizɔmik] ADJ with Down's Syndrome; **être ~** to have Down's Syndrome ▶ NMF person with Down's syndrome

★**triste** [tʀist] ADJ sad; (*couleur, temps, journée*) dreary; (*péj*): **~ personnage/affaire** sorry individual/affair; **c'est pas ~ !** (*fam*) it's something else!

tristement [tʀistəmã] ADV sadly

tristesse [tʀistɛs] NF sadness

trithérapie [tʀiteʀapi] NF triple therapy, triple combination therapy

triton [tʀitɔ̃] NM triton

triturateur [tʀityʀatœʀ] NM (*machine*) grinder, grinding machine

triturer [tʀityʀe] /1/ VT (*pâte*) to knead; (*objets*) to manipulate

triumvirat [tʀijɔmviʀa] NM triumvirate

trivial, e, -aux [tʀivjal, -o] ADJ coarse, crude; (*commun*) mundane

trivialité [tʀivjalite] NF coarseness, crudeness; mundaneness

troc [tʀɔk] NM (*Écon*) barter; (*transaction*) exchange, swap

troène [tʀɔɛn] NM privet

troglodyte [tʀɔglɔdit] NMF cave dweller, troglodyte

trognon [tʀɔɲɔ̃] NM (*de fruit*) core; (*de légume*) stalk

★**trois** [tʀwa] NUM three

trois-huit [tʀwaɥit] NMPL: **faire les ~** to work eight-hour shifts (round the clock)

troisième [tʀwazjɛm] NUM third; **le ~ âge** (*période de vie*) one's retirement years; (*personnes âgées*) senior citizens *pl* ▶ NF (*Scol*) year 10 (BRIT), ninth grade (US)

troisièmement [tRwazjɛmmã] ADV thirdly

trois quarts [tRwakaR] NMPL: **les ~ de** three-quarters of

trois-quarts [tRwakaR] NMPL (*Rugby: joueur*) three-quarter; (*aussi:* **manteau trois quarts**) three-quarter-length coat

troll [tRɔl] NM, **trolleur, -euse** [tRɔlœR, -øz] NM/F (*Inform*) troll

troller [tRɔle] VI (*Internet*) to troll

trolleybus [tRɔlɛbys] NM trolley bus

trombe [tRɔ̃b] NF waterspout; **des trombes d'eau** a downpour; **en ~** (*arriver, passer*) like a whirlwind

trombine [tRɔ̃bin] NF (*fam: tête*) face, mug (*fam*)

trombinoscope [tRɔ̃binɔskɔp] NM (*fam*) group photo

trombone [tRɔ̃bɔn] NM (*Mus*) trombone; (*de bureau*) paper clip; **~ à coulisse** slide trombone

tromboniste [tRɔ̃bɔnist] NMF trombonist

trompe [tRɔ̃p] NF (*d'éléphant*) trunk; (*Mus*) trumpet, horn; **~ d'Eustache** Eustachian tube; **trompes utérines** Fallopian tubes

trompe-l'œil [tRɔ̃plœj] NM: **en trompe-l'œil** in trompe-l'œil style

★**tromper** [tRɔ̃pe] /1/ VT to deceive; (*fig: espoir, attente*) to disappoint; (*vigilance, poursuivants*) to elude ▪ **se tromper** VPR to make a mistake, be mistaken; **se ~ de voiture/jour** to take the wrong car/get the day wrong; **se ~ de 3 cm/20 euros** to be out by 3 cm/20 euros

tromperie [tRɔ̃pRi] NF deception, trickery *no pl*

★**trompette** [tRɔ̃pɛt] NF trumpet; **en ~** (*nez*) turned-up

trompettiste [tRɔ̃petist] NMF trumpet player

trompeur, -euse [tRɔ̃pœR, -øz] ADJ deceptive, misleading

tronc [tRɔ̃] NM (*Bot, Anat*) trunk; (*d'église*) collection box; **~ d'arbre** tree trunk; **~ commun** (*Scol*) common-core syllabus; **~ de cône** truncated cone

tronche [tRɔ̃ʃ] NF (*fam*) mug, face

tronçon [tRɔ̃sɔ̃] NM section

tronçonner [tRɔ̃sɔne] /1/ VT (*arbre*) to saw up; (*pierre*) to cut up

tronçonneuse [tRɔ̃sɔnøz] NF chainsaw

trône [tRon] NM throne; **monter sur le ~** to ascend the throne

trôner [tRone] /1/ VI (*fig*) to have (*ou* take) pride of place (*BRIT*), have the place of honour (*BRIT*) *ou* honor (*US*)

tronqué, e [tRɔ̃ke] ADJ (*Science: forme, séquence*) truncated; (*citation*) shortened

tronquer [tRɔ̃ke] /1/ VT to truncate; (*fig*) to curtail

★**trop** [tRo] ADV too; (*avec verbe*) too much; (*aussi:* **trop nombreux**) too many; (*aussi:* **trop souvent**) too often; **~ peu (nombreux)** too few; **~ longtemps** (for) too long; **~ de** (*nombre*) too many; (*quantité*) too much; **de ~, en ~: des livres en ~** a few books too many, a few extra books; **du lait en ~** too much milk; **trois livres/cinq euros de ~** three books too many/five euros too much; **ça coûte ~ cher** it's too expensive

trophée [tRofe] NM trophy

tropical, e, -aux [tRɔpikal, -o] ADJ tropical

tropique [tRɔpik] NM tropic; **~ du Cancer/Capricorne** Tropic of Cancer/Capricorn ▪ **tropiques** NMPL tropics

trop-plein [tRoplɛ̃] NM (*tuyau*) overflow *ou* outlet (pipe); (*liquide*) overflow

troquer [tRɔke] /1/ VT: **~ qch contre** to barter *ou* trade sth for; (*fig*) to swap sth for

troquet [tRɔkɛ] NM (*fam*) bar

trot [tRo] NM trot; **aller au ~** to trot along; **partir au ~** to set off at a trot

trotskiste, trotskyste [tRɔtskist] ADJ, NMF Trotskyite, Trotskyist

trotter [tRɔte] /1/ VI to trot; (*fig*) to scamper along (*ou* about)

trotteuse [tRɔtøz] NF (*de montre*) second hand

trottiner [tRɔtine] /1/ VI (*fig*) to scamper along (*ou* about)

trottinette [tRɔtinɛt] NF (child's) scooter

★**trottoir** [tRɔtwaR] NM pavement (*BRIT*), sidewalk (*US*); **faire le ~** (*péj*) to walk the streets; **~ roulant** moving walkway, travelator

★**trou** [tRu] NM hole; (*fig*) gap; (*Comm*) deficit; **~ d'aération** (air) vent; **~ d'air** air pocket; **~ de mémoire** blank, lapse of memory; **~ noir** black hole; **~ de la serrure** keyhole

troubadour [tRubaduR] NM (*Hist*) troubadour; (*fig: bohème*) bohemian

troublant, e [tRublã, -ãt] ADJ disturbing

trouble [tRubl] ADJ (*liquide*) cloudy; (*image, photo*) blurred; (*mémoire*) indistinct, hazy; (*affaire*) shady, murky ▸ ADV indistinctly; **voir ~** to have blurred vision ▸ NM (*désarroi*) distress, agitation; (*émoi sensuel*) turmoil, agitation; (*embarras*) confusion; (*zizanie*) unrest, discord ▪ **troubles** NMPL (*Pol*) disturbances, troubles, unrest *sg*; (*Méd*) trouble *sg*, disorders; **troubles de la personnalité** personality problems; **troubles de la vision** eye trouble

trouble-fête [tRublfɛt] NMF INV spoilsport

troubler [tRuble] /1/ VT (*embarrasser*) to confuse, disconcert; (*émouvoir*) to agitate; to disturb; to perturb; (*perturber: ordre etc*) to disrupt, disturb; (*: liquide*) to make cloudy; (*intriguer*) to bother; **~ l'ordre public** to cause a breach of the peace ▪ **se troubler** VPR (*personne*) to become flustered *ou* confused

troué, e [tRue] ADJ with a hole (*ou* holes) in it ▸ NF (*dans une masse*) gap; (*Mil*) breach

trouer [tRue] /1/ VT to make a hole (*ou* holes) in; (*fig*) to pierce

troufion [tRufjɔ̃] NM (*fam*) soldier, squaddie (*BRIT*), GI (*US*)

trouillard, e [tRujaR, -aRd] (*fam*) NM/F coward, chicken (*fam*) ▸ ADJ cowardly, chicken (*fam*)

trouille [tRuj] NF (*fam*): **avoir la ~** to be scared stiff, be scared out of one's wits

trouillomètre [tRujɔmɛtR] NM (*fam*): **avoir le ~ à zéro** to be scared stiff

troupe [tRup] NF (*Mil*) troop; (*groupe*) troop, group; **la ~** (*Mil: l'armée*) the army; (*: les simples soldats*) the troops *pl*; **~ (de théâtre)** (theatrical) company; **troupes de choc** shock troops

troupeau, x [tRupo] NM (*de moutons*) flock; (*de vaches*) herd

★**trousse** [tʀus] NF case, kit; (d'écolier) pencil case; (de docteur) instrument case; **aux trousses de** (fig) on the heels ou tail of; **~ à outils** toolkit; **~ de toilette** toilet bag

trousseau, x [tʀuso] NM (de mariée) trousseau; **~ de clefs** bunch of keys

trouvaille [tʀuvaj] NF find; (fig: idée, expression etc) brainwave

trouvé, e [tʀuve] ADJ: **tout ~** ready-made

★**trouver** [tʀuve] /1/ VT to find; (rendre visite): **aller/venir ~ qn** to go/come and see sb ■ **se trouver** VPR (être) to be; (être soudain) to find o.s.; **je trouve que** I find ou think that; **~ à boire/critiquer** to find something to drink/criticize; **~ asile/refuge** to find refuge/shelter; **se ~ être/avoir** to happen to be/have; **il se trouve que** it happens that, it turns out that; **se ~ bien** to feel well; **se ~ mal** to pass out

truand [tʀyɑ̃] NM villain, crook

truander [tʀyɑ̃de] /1/ (fam) VI to cheat, do ▶ VT: **se faire ~** to be swindled

trublion [tʀyblijɔ̃] NM troublemaker

★**truc** [tʀyk] NM (astuce) way, device; (de cinéma, prestidigitateur) trick effect; (chose) thing; (machin) thingumajig, whatsit (BRIT); **avoir le ~** to have the knack; **c'est pas son** (ou **mon** etc) **~** (fam) it's not really his (ou my etc) thing

trucage [tʀykaʒ] NM = **truquage**

truchement [tʀyʃmɑ̃] NM: **par le ~ de qn** through (the intervention of) sb

trucider [tʀyside] /1/ VT (fam) to do in, bump off

truculence [tʀykylɑ̃s] NF colourfulness (BRIT), colorfulness (US)

truculent, e [tʀykylɑ̃, -ɑ̃t] ADJ colourful (BRIT), colorful (US)

truelle [tʀyɛl] NF trowel

truffe [tʀyf] NF truffle; (nez) nose

truffé, e [tʀyfe] ADJ (Culin) garnished with truffles; voir aussi **truffer**

truffer [tʀyfe] /1/ VT (Culin) to garnish with truffles; **truffé de** (citations) peppered with; (fautes) riddled with; (pièges) bristling with

truie [tʀɥi] NF sow

truisme [tʀyism] NM truism

★**truite** [tʀɥit] NF trout inv

truquage [tʀykaʒ] NM fixing; (Ciné) special effects pl

truquer [tʀyke] /1/ VT (élections, serrure, dés) to fix; (Ciné) to use special effects in

trust [tʀœst] NM (Comm) trust

truster [tʀœste] /1/ VT (Comm) to monopolize

ts ABR = **tous**

tsar [dzaʀ] NM tsar

tsé-tsé [tsetse] (pl **tsétsés** ou **~**) NF: **mouche ~** tsetse fly

★**t-shirt** [tiʃœʀt] (pl **t-shirts**) NM T-shirt

tsigane [tsigan] ADJ, NM,F = **tzigane**

TSVP ABR (= tournez s'il vous plaît) PTO

TT, TTA SIGLE M (= transit temporaire (autorisé)) vehicle registration for cars etc bought in France for export tax-free by non-residents

tt ABR = **tout**

TTC ABR (= toutes taxes comprises) inclusive of tax

ttes ABR = **toutes**

TU SIGLE M = **temps universel**

★**tu**[1] [ty] PRON you ▶ NM: **employer le tu** to use the "tu" form

tu[2]**, e** [ty] PP de **taire**

tuant, e [tɥɑ̃, -ɑ̃t] ADJ (épuisant) killing; (énervant) infuriating

tuba [tyba] NM (Mus) tuba; (Sport) snorkel

tubage [tybaʒ] NM (Méd) intubation

tube [tyb] NM tube; (de canalisation, métallique etc) pipe; (chanson, disque) hit song ou record; **~ digestif** alimentary canal, digestive tract; **~ à essai** test tube

tuberculeux, -euse [tybɛʀkylø, -øz] ADJ tubercular ▶ NM/F tuberculosis ou TB patient

tuberculose [tybɛʀkyloz] NF tuberculosis, TB

tubulaire [tybylɛʀ] ADJ tubular

tubulure [tybylyʀ] NF pipe; piping no pl; (Auto): **~ d'échappement/d'admission** exhaust/inlet manifold

tué, e [tɥe] NM/F: **cinq tués** five killed ou dead

tue-mouche [tymuʃ] ADJ: **papier ~(s)** flypaper

★**tuer** [tɥe] /1/ VT to kill ■ **se tuer** VPR (se suicider) to kill o.s.; (dans un accident) to be killed; **se ~ au travail** (fig) to work o.s. to death

tuerie [tyʀi] NF slaughter no pl, massacre; (fam: délice): **c'est une ~**! it's a killer!

tue-tête [tytɛt]: **à ~** adv at the top of one's voice

tueur [tɥœʀ] NM killer; **~ à gages** hired killer

tuile [tɥil] NF tile; (fam) spot of bad luck, blow

tulipe [tylip] NF tulip

tulle [tyl] NM tulle

tuméfié, e [tymefje] ADJ puffy, swollen

tumeur [tymœʀ] NF growth, tumour (BRIT), tumor (US)

tumulte [tymylt] NM commotion, hubbub

tumultueux, -euse [tymyltɥø, -øz] ADJ stormy, turbulent

tumulus [tymylys] NM burial mound, tumulus

tuner [tynɛʀ] NM tuner

tungstène [tœ̃kstɛn] NM tungsten

tunique [tynik] NF tunic; (de femme) smock, tunic

Tunis [tynis] N Tunis

★**Tunisie** [tynizi] NF: **la ~** Tunisia

★**tunisien, ne** [tynizjɛ̃, -ɛn] ADJ Tunisian ▶ NM/F: **Tunisien, ne** Tunisian

tunisois, e [tynizwa, -waz] ADJ of ou from Tunis

★**tunnel** [tynɛl] NM tunnel; **le ~ sous la Manche** the Channel Tunnel

turban [tyʀbɑ̃] NM turban

turbin [tyʀbɛ̃] NM (fam) work no pl

turbine [tyʀbin] NF turbine

turbo [tyʀbo] NM turbo; **un moteur ~** a turbo (-charged) engine

turbomoteur [tyʀbɔmɔtœʀ] NM turbo(-boosted) engine

turbopropulseur [tyʀbɔpʀɔpylsœʀ] NM turboprop

turboréacteur [tyʀbɔʀeaktœʀ] NM turbojet

turbot [tyʀbo] NM turbot

turbotrain [tyʀbɔtʀɛ̃] NM turbotrain

turbulences [tyʀbylɑ̃s] NFPL (Aviat) turbulence sg

turbulent, e [tyʀbylɑ̃, -ɑ̃t] ADJ boisterous, unruly

turc, turque [tyʀk] ADJ Turkish; (w.-c.) seatless ▶ NM (Ling) Turkish ▶ NM/F: **Turc, Turque** Turk/ Turkish woman ▶ NF: **à la turque** adv (assis) cross-legged; adj (toilettes, w.-c.) seatless

turf [tyʀf] NM racing

turfiste [tyʀfist] NMF racegoer

turista [tuʀista] NF (fam) Montezuma's revenge, Delhi belly

Turks et Caïques [tyʀkekaik], **Turks et Caicos** [tyʀkekaikɔs] NFPL Turks and Caicos Islands

turpitude [tyʀpityd] NF base act, baseness no pl

turque [tyʀk] ADJ F, NF voir **turc**

Turquie [tyʀki] NF: **la ~** Turkey

turquoise [tyʀkwaz] NF, ADJ INV turquoise

tus etc [ty] VB voir **taire**

tut etc [ty] VB voir **taire**

tutélaire [tytelɛʀ] ADJ (puissance) protecting

tutelle [tytɛl] NF (Jur) guardianship; (Pol) trusteeship; **sous la ~ de** (fig) under the supervision of

tuteur, -trice [tytœʀ, -tʀis] NM/F (Jur) guardian; (de plante) stake, support

tuto [tyto] NM (fam: = tutoriel) tutorial

tutoiement [tytwamɑ̃] NM use of familiar "tu" form

tutoriel [tytɔʀjɛl] NM tutorial

★**tutoyer** [tytwaje] /8/ VT: **~ qn** to address sb as "tu"

tutti quanti [tutikwɑti] NMPL: **et ~** and all the rest (of them)

tutu [tyty] NM (Danse) tutu

tuyau, x [tɥijo] NM pipe; (flexible) tube; (fam: conseil) tip; (: mise au courant) gen no pl; **~ d'arrosage** hosepipe; **~ d'échappement** exhaust pipe; **~ d'incendie** fire hose

tuyauté, e [tɥijote] ADJ fluted

tuyauter [tɥijɔte] VT (fam) to give a tip to

tuyauterie [tɥijotʀi] NF piping no pl

tuyère [tɥijɛʀ] NF nozzle

TV [teve] NF TV, telly (BRIT)

★**TVA** SIGLE F (= taxe à ou sur la valeur ajoutée) VAT

TVHD SIGLE F (= télévision haute définition) HDTV

tweed [twid] NM tweed

tweet [twit] NM (Inform: Twitter) tweet

tweeter [twite] /1/ VI (Inform: Twitter) to tweet

tweetos [twitos] NMF INV = **twittos**

tweetosphère [twitosfɛʀ] NF = **twittosphère**

twittos [twitos] NMF INV Twitterer

twittosphère [twitosfɛʀ] NF Twittersphere

tympan [tɛ̃pɑ̃] NM (Anat) eardrum

type [tip] NM type; (personne, chose, représentant) classic example, epitome; (fam) chap, guy; **avoir le ~ nordique** to be Nordic-looking ▶ ADJ typical, standard

typé, e [tipe] ADJ ethnic (euphémisme)

typhoïde [tifɔid] NF typhoid (fever)

typhon [tifɔ̃] NM typhoon

typhus [tifys] NM typhus (fever)

typique [tipik] ADJ typical

typiquement [tipikmɑ̃] ADV typically

typographe [tipɔgʀaf] NMF typographer

typographie [tipɔgʀafi] NF typography; (procédé) letterpress (printing)

typographique [tipɔgʀafik] ADJ typographical; letterpress cpd

typologie [tipɔlɔʒi] NF typology

tyran [tiʀɑ̃] NM tyrant

tyrannie [tiʀani] NF tyranny

tyrannique [tiʀanik] ADJ tyrannical

tyranniser [tiʀanize] /1/ VT to tyrannize

Tyrol [tiʀɔl] NM: **le ~** the Tyrol

tyrolien, ne [tiʀɔljɛ̃, -ɛn] ADJ Tyrolean ▶ NF (câble) zip line

tzar [dzaʀ] NM = **tsar**

tzigane [dzigan] ADJ gipsy (péj), tzigane ▶ NMF (Hungarian) gipsy, Tzigane

t

Uu

U, u [y] NM INV U, u; **U comme Ursule** U for Uncle
ubériser [ybeʀize] /1/ VT to uberize
ubiquité [ybikɥite] NF: **avoir le don d'~** ʊɔ be everywhere at once, be ubiquitous
ubuesque [ybyɛsk] ADJ (*situation, projet, idée*) ludicrous; (*personne*) Ubuesque
uchronie [ykʀɔni] NF uchronia
UDI SIGLE M (= *Union des Démocrates et Indépendants*) political party
UE SIGLE F (= *Union européenne*) EU
UEFA [yefa] SIGLE F (= *Union of European Football Associations*) UEFA
UEM SIGLE F (= *Union économique et monétaire*) EMU
UER SIGLE F (= *unité d'enseignement et de recherche*) old title of UFR; (= *Union européenne de radio-télévision*) EBU
UFC SIGLE F (= *Union fédérale des consommateurs*) national consumer group
UFR SIGLE F (= *unité de formation et de recherche*) ≈ university department
UHF SIGLE F (= *ultra-haute fréquence*) UHF
UHT ABR (= *ultra-haute température*) UHT
UIT SIGLE F (= *Union internationale des télécommunications*) ITU (= *International Telecommunications Union*)
Ukraine [ykʀɛn] NF: **l'~** the Ukraine
ukrainien, ne [ykʀɛnjɛ̃, -ɛn] ADJ Ukrainian ▶ NM (*Ling*) Ukrainian ▶ NM/F: **Ukrainien, ne** Ukrainian
ukulélé [jukulele] NM ukelele
ulcère [ylsɛʀ] NM ulcer; **~ à l'estomac** stomach ulcer
ulcéré, e [ylseʀe] ADJ (*excédé*) sickened
ulcérer [ylseʀe] /6/ VT (*Méd*) to ulcerate; (*fig*) to sicken, appal
ulcéreux, -euse [ylseʀø, -øz] ADJ (*plaie, lésion*) ulcerous; (*membre*) ulcerated
uléma [ylema] NM (*Rel*) ulema
ULM SIGLE M (= *ultra léger motorisé*) microlight
ulna [ylna] NM (*Anat*) ulna
ultérieur, e [ylteʀjœʀ] ADJ later, subsequent; **remis à une date ultérieure** postponed to a later date
ultérieurement [ylteʀjœʀmã] ADV later, subsequently
ultimatum [yltimatɔm] NM ultimatum
ultime [yltim] ADJ final
ultra [yltʀa] PRÉFIXE ultra ▶ NMF ultra

ultramoderne [yltʀamɔdɛʀn] ADJ ultra-modern
ultra-rapide [yltʀaʀapid] ADJ ultra-fast
ultra-sensible [yltʀasɑ̃sibl] ADJ (*Photo*) high-speed
ultrason, ultra-son [yltʀasɔ̃] NM ultrasound *no pl* ▪ **ultra(-)sons** NMPL ultrasonics
ultraviolet, ultra-violet, te [yltʀavjɔlɛ, -ɛt] ADJ ultraviolet ▶ NM: **les ultra(-)violets** ultraviolet rays
ululer [ylyle] /1/ VI = hululer
UME SIGLE F (= *Union monétaire européenne*) EMU

---

un, une [œ̃, yn]

ART INDÉF a; (*devant voyelle*) an; **un garçon/vieillard** a boy/an old man; **une fille** a girl
▶ PRON one; **l'un des meilleurs** one of the best; **l'un ..., l'autre** (the) one ..., the other; **les uns ..., les autres** some ..., others; **l'un et l'autre** both (of them); **l'un ou l'autre** either (of them); **l'un l'autre, les uns les autres** each other, one another; **pas un seul** not a single one; **un par un** one by one
▶ NUM one; **une pomme seulement** one apple only, just one apple
▶ NF: **la une** (*Presse*) the front page

---

unanime [ynanim] ADJ unanimous; **ils sont unanimes (à penser que)** they are unanimous (in thinking that)
unanimement [ynanimmã] ADV (*par tous*) unanimously; (*d'un commun accord*) with one accord
unanimité [ynanimite] NF unanimity; **à l'~** unanimously; **faire l'~** to be approved unanimously
underground [œndœʀgʀawnd] ADJ, NM underground
UNEDIC [ynedik] SIGLE F = **Union Nationale pour l'Emploi dans l'Industrie et le Commerce**
UNEF [ynɛf] SIGLE F = **Union nationale des étudiants de France**
UNESCO [ynɛsko] SIGLE F (= *United Nations Educational, Scientific and Cultural Organization*) UNESCO
Unetelle [yntɛl] NF *voir* Untel
UNI SIGLE F = **Union nationale inter-universitaire**
uni, e [yni] ADJ (*ton, tissu*) plain; (*surface*) smooth, even; (*famille*) close(-knit); (*pays*) united
UNICEF [ynisɛf] SIGLE MF (= *United Nations International Children's Emergency Fund*) UNICEF
unicellulaire [yniselylɛʀ] ADJ (*Bio: organisme, algue*) unicellular

unidirectionnel, le [ynidiʀɛksjɔnɛl] ADJ unidirectional, one-way

unième [ynjɛm] NUM: **vingt/trente et ~** twenty-/thirty-first; **cent ~** (one) hundred and first

unificateur, -trice [ynifikatœʀ, -tʀis] ADJ unifying

unification [ynifikasjɔ̃] NF uniting; unification; standardization

unifier [ynifje] /7/ VT to unite, unify; (*systèmes*) to standardize, unify ■**s'unifier** VPR to become united

★**uniforme** [ynifɔʀm] ADJ (*mouvement*) regular, uniform; (*surface, ton*) even; (*objets, maisons*) uniform; (*fig: vie, conduite*) unchanging ▸ NM uniform; **être sous l'~** (*Mil*) to be serving

uniformément [ynifɔʀmemɑ̃] ADV uniformly

uniformisation [ynifɔʀmizasjɔ̃] NF standardization

uniformiser [ynifɔʀmize] /1/ VT to make uniform; (*systèmes*) to standardize

uniformité [ynifɔʀmite] NF regularity; uniformity; evenness

unijambiste [yniʒɑ̃bist] NMF one-legged man/woman

unilatéral, e, -aux [ynilateʀal, -o] ADJ unilateral; **stationnement ~** parking on one side only

unilatéralement [ynilateʀalmɑ̃] ADV unilaterally

uninominal, e, -aux [yninɔminal, -o] ADJ uncontested

union [ynjɔ̃] NF union; **~ conjugale** union of marriage; **~ de consommateurs** consumers' association; **~ libre** free love; **vivre en ~ libre** (*en concubinage*) to cohabit; **l'U~ européenne** the European Union; **l'U~ des Républiques socialistes soviétiques (URSS)** the Union of Soviet Socialist Republics (USSR); **l'U~ soviétique** the Soviet Union

unique [ynik] ADJ (*seul*) only; (*exceptionnel*) unique; **un prix/système ~** a single price/system; **ménage à salaire ~** one-salary family; **route à voie ~** single-lane road; **fils/fille ~** only son/daughter, only child; **sens ~** one-way street; **~ en France** the only one of its kind in France

uniquement [ynikmɑ̃] ADV only, solely; (*juste*) only, merely

unir [yniʀ] /2/ VT (*nations*) to unite; (*éléments, couleurs*) to combine; (*en mariage*) to unite, join together; **~ qch à** to unite sth with; to combine sth with ■**s'unir** VPR to unite; (*en mariage*) to be joined together; **s'~ à** *ou* **avec** to unite with

unisexe [yniseks] ADJ unisex

unisson [ynisɔ̃]: **à l'~** *adv* in unison

unitaire [ynitɛʀ] ADJ unitary; (*Pol*) unitarian; **prix ~** unit price

unité [ynite] NF (*harmonie, cohésion*) unity; (*Comm, Mil, de mesure, Math*) unit; **~ centrale de traitement** central processing unit; **~ de valeur** (*university*) course, credit

univers [ynivɛʀ] NM universe

universalisation [ynivɛʀsalizasjɔ̃] NF universalization

universaliser [ynivɛʀsalize] /1/ VT to universalize

universaliste [ynivɛʀsalist] ADJ (*Philosophie*) universalist

universalité [ynivɛʀsalite] NF universality

universel, le [ynivɛʀsɛl] ADJ universal; (*esprit*) all-embracing

universellement [ynivɛʀsɛlmɑ̃] ADV universally

universitaire [ynivɛʀsitɛʀ] ADJ university *cpd*; (*diplôme, études*) academic, university *cpd* ▸ NMF academic

université [ynivɛʀsite] NF university

univoque [ynivɔk] ADJ unambiguous; (*Math*) one-to-one

UNR SIGLE F (= *Union pour la nouvelle république*) *former political party*

UNSS SIGLE F = **Union nationale de sport scolaire**

Untel, Unetelle [œ̃tɛl, yntɛl] NM/F: **Monsieur ~** Mr so-and-so

uppercut [ypɛʀkyt] NM (*Boxe*) uppercut; (*fig*) blow

uranium [yʀanjɔm] NM uranium

urbain, e [yʀbɛ̃, -ɛn] ADJ urban, city *cpd*, town *cpd*; (*poli*) urbane

urbanisation [yʀbanizasjɔ̃] NF urbanization

urbaniser [yʀbanize] /1/ VT to urbanize

urbanisme [yʀbanism] NM town planning

urbaniste [yʀbanist] NMF town planner

urbanité [yʀbanite] NF urbanity

urée [yʀe] NF urea

urémie [yʀemi] NF uraemia (*Brit*), uremia (*US*)

★**urgence** [yʀʒɑ̃s] NF urgency; (*Méd etc*) emergency; **d'~** *adj* emergency *cpd*; *adv* as a matter of urgency; **en cas d'~** in case of emergency; **service des urgences** emergency service

★**urgent, e** [yʀʒɑ̃, -ɑ̃t] ADJ urgent

urgentiste [yʀʒɑ̃tist] NMF A&E doctor (*Brit*), emergency physician (*US*)

urinaire [yʀinɛʀ] ADJ urinary

urinal, -aux [yʀinal, -o] NM (bed) urinal

urine [yʀin] NF urine

uriner [yʀine] /1/ VI to urinate

urinoir [yʀinwaʀ] NM (public) urinal

URL SIGLE F (*Inform*: = *Uniform Resource Locator*) URL; **adresse ~** URL

urne [yʀn] NF (*électorale*) ballot box; (*vase*) urn; **aller aux urnes** (*voter*) to go to the polls

urologie [yʀɔlɔʒi] NF urology

URSS [yʀs] SIGLE F (*Hist*: = *Union des Républiques Socialistes Soviétiques*) USSR

URSSAF [yʀsaf] SIGLE F (= *Union pour le recouvrement de la sécurité sociale et des allocations familiales*) *administrative body responsible for social security funds and payments*

urticaire [yʀtikɛʀ] NF nettle rash, urticaria

Uruguay [yʀygwɛ] NM: **l'~** Uruguay

uruguayen, ne [yʀygwajɛ̃, -ɛn] ADJ Uruguayan ▸ NM/F: **Uruguayen, ne** Uruguayan

us [ys] NMPL: **us et coutumes** (habits and) customs

USA SIGLE MPL (= *United States of America*) USA

usage [yzaʒ] NM (*emploi, utilisation*) use; (*coutume*) custom; (*éducation*) (good) manners *pl*, (good) breeding; (*Ling*): **l'~** usage; **faire ~ de** (*pouvoir, droit*) to exercise; **avoir l'~ de** to have the use of; **à l'~** *adv* with use; **à l'~ de** (*pour*) for (use of); **en ~** in use; **hors d'~** out of service; **à ~ interne** (*Méd*) to be

u

455

taken (internally); **à ~ externe** (*Méd*) for external use only

usagé, e [yzaʒe] ADJ (*usé*) worn; (*d'occasion*) used

usager, -ère [yzaʒe, -ɛʀ] NM/F user

usant, e [yzɑ̃, -ɑ̃t] ADJ (*fatigant*) wearing

USB SIGLE M (*Inform*: = *Universal Serial Bus*) USB; **clé ~** USB stick; **port ~** USB port

usé, e [yze] ADJ worn (down *ou* out *ou* away); ruined; (*banal: argument etc*) hackneyed

user [yze] /1/ VT (*outil*) to wear down; (*vêtement*) to wear out; (*matière*) to wear away; (*consommer: charbon etc*) to use; (*fig: santé*) to ruin; (: *personne*) to wear out; **~ de** (*moyen, procédé*) to use, employ; (*droit*) to exercise ▪ **s'user** VPR to wear; (*tissu, vêtement*) to wear out; (*fig*) to decline; **s'~ à la tâche** to wear o.s. out with work

usinage [yzinaʒ] NM (*de pièce, bois, métal*) machining; (*fabrication*) manufacture

★**usine** [yzin] NF factory; **~ atomique** nuclear power plant; **~ à gaz** gasworks *sg*; **~ marémotrice** tidal power station

usiner [yzine] /1/ VT (*Tech*) to machine; (*fabriquer*) to manufacture

usité, e [yzite] ADJ in common use, common; **peu ~** rarely used

ustensile [ystɑ̃sil] NM implement; **~ de cuisine** kitchen utensil

usuel, le [yzɥɛl] ADJ everyday, common

usufruit [yzyfrɥi] NM usufruct

usufruitier, -ière [yzyfrɥitje, -jɛʀ] NM/F, ADJ usufructuary

usuraire [yzyʀɛʀ] ADJ usurious

usure [yzyʀ] NF wear; worn state; (*de l'usurier*) usury; **avoir qn à l'~** to wear sb down; **~ normale** fair wear and tear

usurier, -ière [yzyʀje, -jɛʀ] NM/F usurer

usurpateur, -trice [yzyʀpatœʀ, -tʀis] NM/F usurper

usurpation [yzyʀpasjɔ̃] NF usurpation

usurper [yzyʀpe] /1/ VT to usurp

ut [yt] NM (*Mus*) C

UTA SIGLE F = **Union des transporteurs aériens**

utérin, e [yteʀɛ̃, -in] ADJ uterine

utérus [yteʀys] NM uterus, womb

★**utile** [ytil] ADJ useful; **~ à qn/qch** of use to sb/sth

utilement [ytilmɑ̃] ADV usefully

utilisable [ytilizabl] ADJ usable

utilisateur, -trice [ytilizatœʀ, -tʀis] NM/F user

utilisation [ytilizasjɔ̃] NF use

★**utiliser** [ytilize] /1/ VT to use

utilitaire [ytilitɛʀ] ADJ utilitarian; (*objets*) practical ▶ NM (*Inform*) utility

utilité [ytilite] NF usefulness *no pl*; use; **jouer les utilités** (*Théât*) to play bit parts; **reconnu d'~ publique** state-approved; **c'est d'une grande ~** it's extremely useful; **il n'y a aucune ~ à ...** there's no use in ...; **de peu d'~** of little use *ou* help

utopie [ytɔpi] NF (*idée, conception*) utopian idea *ou* view; (*société etc idéale*) utopia

utopique [ytɔpik] ADJ utopian

utopiste [ytɔpist] NMF utopian

UV SIGLE F (*Scol*) = **unité de valeur** ▶ SIGLE MPL (= *ultra-violets*) UV

uvule [yvyl] NF uvula

Vv

V, v [ve] NM INV V, v; **V comme Victor** V for Victor; **en V** V-shaped; **encolure en V** V-neck; **décolleté en V** V(-)neckline ▶ ABR (= *voir, verset*) v; *nm* (= *vers*) l.; *prép* (= *vers*) toward(s)

V° ABR = **verso**

va [va] VB *voir* **aller**

vacance [vakɑ̃s] NF (*Admin*) vacancy ◼ **vacances** NFPL holiday(s) (BRIT), vacation *sg* (US); **les grandes vacances** the summer holidays *ou* vacation; **prendre des/ses vacances** to take a holiday *ou* vacation/one's holiday *ou* vacation; **aller en vacances** to go on holiday *ou* vacation

vacancier, -ière [vakɑ̃sje, -jɛʀ] NM/F holiday-maker (BRIT), vacationer (US)

vacant, e [vakɑ̃, -ɑ̃t] ADJ vacant

vacarme [vakaʀm] NM row, din

vacataire [vakatɛʀ] NMF temporary (employee); (*enseignement*) supply (BRIT) *ou* substitute (US) teacher; (*Université*) part-time temporary lecturer

vaccin [vaksɛ̃] NM vaccine; (*opération*) vaccination

vaccination [vaksinasjɔ̃] NF vaccination

vacciner [vaksine] /1/ VT to vaccinate; (*fig*) to make immune; **être vacciné** (*fig*) to be immune

★**vache** [vaʃ] NF (*Zool*) cow; (*cuir*) cowhide; **~ à eau** (canvas) water bag; **(manger de la) ~ enragée** (to go through) hard times; **~ à lait** (*péj*) mug, sucker; **~ laitière** dairy cow; **période de vaches maigres** lean times *pl*, lean period ▶ ADJ (*fam*) rotten, mean

vachement [vaʃmɑ̃] ADV (*fam*) damned, really

vacher, -ère [vaʃe, -ɛʀ] NM/F cowherd

vacherie [vaʃʀi] NF (*fam*) meanness *no pl*; (: *action*) dirty trick; (: *propos*) nasty remark

vacherin [vaʃʀɛ̃] NM (*fromage*) vacherin cheese; (*gâteau*): **~ glacé** vacherin (*type of cream gâteau*)

vachette [vaʃɛt] NF calfskin

vacillant, e [vasijɑ̃, -ɑ̃t] ADJ (*jambes*) wobbly; (*lumière*) flickering; (*pouvoir*) faltering; (*santé*) failing

vacillement [vasijmɑ̃] NM (*de pouvoir*) faltering; (*de lumière, flamme*) flickering

vaciller [vasije] /1/ VI (*personne, jambes*) to sway, wobble; (*bougie, lumière*) to flicker; (*fig: pouvoir*) falter; (: *santé*) to fail; **~ dans ses réponses** to falter in one's replies; **~ dans ses résolutions** to waver in one's resolutions

vacuité [vakɥite] NF emptiness, vacuity

vade-mecum [vademekɔm] NM INV pocketbook

vadrouille [vadʀuj] NF: **être/partir en ~** to be on/go for a wander

vadrouiller [vadʀuje] /1/ VI to wander around *ou* about

VAE SIGLE F (= *Validation des acquis de l'expérience*) accreditation for work experience, that can count towards a qualification ▶ SIGLE M (= *vélo (à assistance) électrique*) e-bike

va-et-vient [vaevjɛ̃] NM INV (*de pièce mobile*) to and fro (*ou* up and down) movement; (*de personnes, véhicules*) comings and goings *pl*, to-ings and fro-ings *pl*; (*Élec*) two-way switch

vagabond, e [vagabɔ̃, -ɔ̃d] ADJ wandering; (*imagination*) roaming, roving ▶ NM (*rôdeur*) tramp, vagrant; (*voyageur*) wanderer

vagabondage [vagabɔ̃daʒ] NM roaming, wandering; (*Jur*) vagrancy

vagabonder [vagabɔ̃de] /1/ VI to roam, wander

vagin [vaʒɛ̃] NM vagina

vaginal, e, -aux [vaʒinal, -o] ADJ vaginal

vagissement [vaʒismɑ̃] NM cry (*of newborn baby*)

★**vague** [vag] NF wave; **~ d'assaut** (*Mil*) wave of assault; **~ de chaleur** heatwave; **~ de fond** ground swell; **~ de froid** cold spell ▶ ADJ vague; (*regard*) faraway; (*manteau, robe*) loose(-fitting); (*quelconque*): **un ~ bureau/cousin** some office/cousin or other ▶ NM: **être dans le ~** to be rather in the dark; **rester dans le ~** to keep things rather vague; **regarder dans le ~** to gaze into space; **~ à l'âme** vague melancholy

vaguelette [vaglɛt] NF ripple

vaguement [vagmɑ̃] ADV vaguely

vahiné [vaine] NF Tahitian woman, wahine

vaillamment [vajamɑ̃] ADV bravely, gallantly

vaillance [vajɑ̃s] NF courage, bravery

vaillant, e [vajɑ̃, -ɑ̃t] ADJ (*courageux*) brave, gallant; (*robuste*) vigorous, hale and hearty; **n'avoir plus un sou ~** to be penniless

vaille [vaj] VB *voir* **valoir**

vain, e [vɛ̃, vɛn] ADJ vain; **en ~** *adv* in vain

vaincre [vɛ̃kʀ] /42/ VT to defeat; (*fig*) to conquer, overcome

vaincu, e [vɛ̃ky] PP *de* **vaincre** ▶ NM/F defeated party

vainement [vɛnmɑ̃] ADV vainly

vainquais *etc* [vɛ̃kɛ] VB *voir* **vaincre**

vainqueur [vɛ̃kœʀ] NM victor; (*Sport*) winner ▶ ADJ M victorious

vais [vɛ] VB *voir* **aller**

v

vaisseau, x [vɛso] NM (Anat) vessel; (Navig) ship, vessel; **~ spatial** spaceship

vaisselier [vɛsəlje] NM dresser

★**vaisselle** [vɛsɛl] NF (service) crockery; (plats etc à laver) (dirty) dishes pl; **faire la ~** to do the washing-up (BRIT) ou the dishes

val [val] (pl **vaux** ou **vals**) NM valley

valable [valabl] ADJ valid; (acceptable) decent, worthwhile

valablement [valabləmɑ̃] ADV legitimately; (de façon satisfaisante) satisfactorily

Valence [valɑ̃s] N (en Espagne) Valencia; (en France) Valence

valent etc [val] VB voir **valoir**

valériane [valerjan] NF (Bot) valerian

valet [valɛ] NM valet; (péj) lackey; (Cartes) jack, knave (BRIT); **~ de chambre** manservant, valet; **~ de ferme** farmhand; **~ de pied** footman

★**valeur** [valœR] NF (gén) value; (mérite) worth, merit; (Comm: titre) security; **mettre en ~** (bien) to exploit; (terrain, région) to develop; (fig) to highlight; to show off to advantage; **avoir de la ~** to be valuable; **prendre de la ~** to go up ou gain in value; **sans ~** worthless; **~ absolue** absolute value; **~ d'échange** exchange value; **~ nominale** face value ▪ **valeurs** NFPL (morales) values; **valeurs mobilières** transferable securities

valeureux, -euse [valœRø, -øz] ADJ valorous

validation [validasjɔ̃] NF validation

valide [valid] ADJ (en bonne santé) fit, well; (indemne) able-bodied, fit; (valable) valid

valider [valide] /1/ VT to validate

validité [validite] NF validity

valions etc [valjɔ̃] VB voir **valoir**

★**valise** [valiz] NF (suit)case; **faire sa ~** to pack one's (suit)case; **la ~ (diplomatique)** the diplomatic bag

vallée [vale] NF valley

vallon [valɔ̃] NM small valley

vallonné, e [valɔne] ADJ undulating

vallonnement [valɔnmɑ̃] NM undulation

★**valoir** [valwaR] /29/ VI (être valable) to hold, apply; **faire ~** (droits, prérogatives) to assert; (domaine, capitaux) to exploit; **faire ~ que** to point out that; **se faire ~** to make the most of o.s.; **à ~ on account; à ~ sur** to be deducted from; **vaille que vaille** somehow or other; **cela ne me dit rien qui vaille** I don't like the look of it at all ▸ VT (prix, valeur, effort) to be worth; (causer): **~ qch à qn** to earn sb sth; **~ la peine** to be worth the trouble, be worth it; **ce climat ne me vaut rien** this climate doesn't suit me; **ça ne vaut rien** it's worthless; **que vaut ce candidat?** how good is this applicant? ▸ VB IMPERS: **il vaut mieux se taire** it's better to say nothing; **il vaut mieux que je fasse comme ceci** it's better if I do like this ▪ **se valoir** VPR to be of equal merit; (péj) to be two of a kind

valorisable [valɔRizabl] ADJ (Écologie: déchet) reusable; (Écon: produit, ressource) that can be made use of; (Finance) that can be put to work

valorisant, e [valɔRizɑ̃, -ɑ̃t] ADJ (image, rôle) positive; (travail, emploi) worthwhile

valorisation [valɔRizasjɔ̃] NF (economic) development; increased standing; (Écologie): **la ~ des déchets** waste repurposing

valoriser [valɔRize] /1/ VT (Écon) to develop (the economy of); (produit) to increase the value of; (Psych) to increase the standing of; (fig) to highlight, bring out

valse [vals] NF waltz; **c'est la ~ des étiquettes** the prices don't stay the same from one moment to the next

valser [valse] /1/ VI to waltz; **aller ~** (fig) to go flying

valu, e [valy] PP de **valoir**

valve [valv] NF valve

vamp [vɑ̃p] NF vamp

vampire [vɑ̃piR] NM vampire

vampiriser [vɑ̃piRize] VT to suck the blood out of (fig)

vampirisme [vɑ̃piRism] NM vampirism

van [vɑ̃] NM horse box (BRIT) ou trailer (US)

vandale [vɑ̃dal] NMF vandal

vandaliser [vɑ̃dalize] VT to vandalize

★**vandalisme** [vɑ̃dalism] NM vandalism

★**vanille** [vanij] NF vanilla; **glace à la ~** vanilla ice cream

vanillé, e [vanije] ADJ vanilla cpd

vanité [vanite] NF vanity

vaniteux, -euse [vanitø, -øz] ADJ vain, conceited

vanity-case [vanitikez] NM vanity case

vanne [van] NF gate; (fam: remarque) dig, (nasty) crack; **lancer une ~ à qn** to have a go at sb (BRIT), knock sb

vanné [vane] ADJ (fam: fatigué) worn out, knackered (BRIT fam)

vanneau, x [vano] NM lapwing

vanner [vane] /1/ VT to winnow

vannerie [vanRi] NF basketwork

vantail, -aux [vɑ̃taj, -o] NM door, leaf

vantard, e [vɑ̃taR, -aRd] ADJ boastful

vantardise [vɑ̃taRdiz] NF boastfulness no pl; boast

vanter [vɑ̃te] /1/ VT to speak highly of, praise ▪ **se vanter** VPR to boast, brag; **se ~ de** to pride o.s. on; (péj) to boast of

Vanuatu [vanwatu] NM: **le ~** Vanuatu

va-nu-pieds [vanypje] NMF INV tramp, beggar

vapeur [vapœR] NF steam; (émanation) vapour (BRIT), vapor (US), fumes pl; (brouillard, buée) haze; **à ~** steam-powered, steam cpd; **à toute ~** full steam ahead; (fig) at full tilt; **renverser la ~** to reverse engines; (fig) to backtrack, backpedal; **cuit à la ~** steamed ▪ **vapeurs** NFPL (bouffées) vapours, vapors

vapocuiseur [vapɔkyizœR] NM pressure cooker

vaporeux, -euse [vapɔRø, -øz] ADJ (flou) hazy, misty; (léger) filmy, gossamer cpd

vaporisateur [vapɔRizatœR] NM spray

vaporisation [vapɔRizasjɔ̃] NF (de parfum, liquide) spray; (Chimie) vaporization

vaporiser [vapɔRize] /1/ VT (Chimie) to vaporize; (parfum etc) to spray

vapoter [vapɔte] /1/ VI to smoke an e-cigarette

vaquer [vake] /1/ VI (Admin) to be on vacation; **~ à ses occupations** to attend to one's affairs, go about one's business

varappe [vaʀap] NF rock climbing

varappeur, -euse [vaʀapœʀ, -øz] NM/F (rock) climber

varech [vaʀɛk] NM wrack, varec

vareuse [vaʀøz] NF (blouson) pea jacket; (d'uniforme) tunic

variabilité [vaʀjabilite] NF variability

variable [vaʀjabl] ADJ variable; (temps, humeur) changeable; (Tech: à plusieurs positions etc) adaptable; (Ling) inflectional; (divers: résultats) varied, various ▶ NF (Inform, Math) variable

variante [vaʀjɑ̃t] NF variant

variation [vaʀjasjɔ̃] NF variation; changing no pl, change; (Mus) variation

varice [vaʀis] NF varicose vein

varicelle [vaʀisɛl] NF chickenpox

varié, e [vaʀje] ADJ varied; (divers) various; **hors-d'œuvre variés** selection of hors d'œuvres

varier [vaʀje] /**7**/ VI to vary; (temps, humeur) to change ▶ VT to vary

variété [vaʀjete] NF variety; **spectacle de variétés** variety show

variole [vaʀjɔl] NF smallpox

variqueux, -euse [vaʀikø, -øz] ADJ varicose

Varsovie [vaʀsɔvi] N Warsaw

vas [va] VB voir **aller**; **vas-y !** go on!

vasculaire [vaskylɛʀ] ADJ vascular

★**vase** [vaz] NM vase; **en ~ clos** in isolation; **~ de nuit** chamberpot; **vases communicants** communicating vessels ▶ NF silt, mud

vasectomie [vazɛktɔmi] NF vasectomy

vaseline [vaz(ə)lin] NF Vaseline®

vaseux, -euse [vazø, -øz] ADJ silty, muddy; (fig: confus) woolly, hazy; (: fatigué) peaky; (: étourdi) woozy

vasistas [vazistas] NM fanlight

vasodilatateur, -trice [vazodilatatœʀ, -tʀis] NM, ADJ vasodilator

vasque [vask] NF (bassin) basin; (coupe) bowl

vassal, e, -aux [vasal, -o] NM/F vassal

vassaliser [vasalize] VT (soumettre) to subjugate

vaste [vast] ADJ vast, immense

Vatican [vatikɑ̃] NM: **le ~** the Vatican

vaticiner [vatisine] /**1**/ VI (péj) to make pompous predictions

va-tout [vatu] NM: **jouer son ~** to stake one's all

vaudeville [vod(ə)vil] NM vaudeville, light comedy

vaudrai etc [vodʀe] VB voir **valoir**

vau-l'eau [volo]: **à vau-l'eau** adv with the current; **s'en aller à vau-l'eau** (fig: projets) to be adrift

vaurien, ne [voʀjɛ̃, -ɛn] NM/F good-for-nothing, guttersnipe

vaut [vo] VB voir **valoir**

vautour [votuʀ] NM vulture

vautrer [votʀe] /**1**/: **se vautrer** VPR: **se ~ dans** to wallow in; **se ~ sur** to sprawl on

vaux [vo] PL de **val** ▶ VB voir **valoir**

va-vite [vavit]: **à la ~** adv in a rush

vd ABR = **vend**

VDQS SIGLE M (= vin délimité de qualité supérieure) label guaranteeing quality of wine

vds ABR = **vends**

★**veau, x** [vo] NM (Zool) calf; (Culin) veal; (peau) calfskin; **tuer le ~ gras** to kill the fatted calf

vecteur [vɛktœʀ] NM vector; (Mil, Bio) carrier

vécu, e [veky] PP de **vivre** ▶ ADJ real(-life)

vedettariat [vədɛtaʀja] NM stardom; (attitude) acting like a star

★**vedette** [vədɛt] NF (artiste etc) star; (canot) patrol boat; (police) launch; **avoir la ~** to top the bill, get star billing; **mettre qn en ~** (Ciné etc) to give sb the starring role; (fig) to push sb into the limelight; **voler la ~ à qn** to steal the show from sb

végane [vegan] ADJ, NMF vegan

végétal, e, -aux [veʒetal, -o] ADJ vegetable ▶ NM vegetable, plant

végétalien, ne [veʒetaljɛ̃, -ɛn] ADJ, NM/F vegan

végétalisé, e [veʒetalize] ADJ: **toit/mur ~** green roof/wall, planted roof/wall

végétalisme [veʒetalism] NM veganism

végétarien, ne [veʒetaʀjɛ̃, -ɛn] ADJ, NM/F vegetarian

végétarisme [veʒetaʀism] NM vegetarianism

végétatif, -ive [veʒetatif, -iv] ADJ: **une vie végétative** a vegetable existence

végétation [veʒetasjɔ̃] NF vegetation ▪ **végétations** NFPL (Méd) adenoids

végéter [veʒete] /**6**/ VI (fig) to vegetate

véhémence [veemɑ̃s] NF vehemence

véhément, e [veemɑ̃, -ɑ̃t] ADJ vehement

véhicule [veikyl] NM vehicle; **~ utilitaire** commercial vehicle

véhiculer [veikyle] /**1**/ VT (personnes, marchandises) to transport, convey; (fig: idées, substances) to convey, serve as a vehicle for

★**veille** [vɛj] NF (garde) watch; (Psych) wakefulness; (jour): **la ~** the day before, the previous day; **la ~ au soir** the previous evening; **la ~ de** the day before; **la ~ de Noël** Christmas Eve; **la ~ du jour de l'An** New Year's Eve; **à la ~ de** on the eve of; **l'état de ~** the waking state

veillée [veje] NF (soirée) evening; (réunion) evening gathering; **~ d'armes** night before combat; (fig) vigil; **~ (funèbre)** wake; **~ (mortuaire)** watch

veiller [veje] /**1**/ VI (rester debout) to stay ou sit up; (ne pas dormir) to be awake; (être de garde) to be on watch; (être vigilant) to be watchful; **~ sur** to keep a watch ou an eye on ▶ VT (malade, mort) to watch over, sit up with; **~ à** to attend to, see to; **~ à ce que** to make sure that, see to it that

veilleur [vejœʀ] NM: **~ de nuit** night watchman

veilleuse [vejøz] NF (lampe) night light; (Auto) sidelight; (flamme) pilot light; **en ~** adj (lampe) dimmed; (fig: affaire) shelved, set aside

veinard, e [venaʀ, -aʀd] NM/F (fam) lucky devil

★**veine** [vɛn] NF (Anat, du bois etc) vein; (filon) vein, seam; (inspiration) inspiration; **avoir de la ~** (fam: chance) to be lucky

veiné, e [vene] ADJ veined; (bois) grained

veineux, -euse [venø, -øz] ADJ venous

Velcro® [vɛlkʀo] NM Velcro®

vêler [vele] /**1**/ VI to calve

vélin [velɛ̃] NM: **(papier) ~** vellum (paper)

V

459

véliplanchiste [veliplɑ̃ʃist] NMF windsurfer

velléitaire [veleitɛʀ] ADJ irresolute, indecisive

velléités [veleite] NFPL vague impulses

vélo [velo] NM bike, cycle; **faire du ~** to go cycling

véloce [velɔs] ADJ swift

vélocité [velɔsite] NF (Mus) nimbleness, swiftness; (vitesse) velocity

vélodrome [velɔdʀɔm] NM velodrome

vélomoteur [velɔmɔtœʀ] NM moped

véloski [veloski] NM skibob

velours [v(ə)luʀ] NM velvet; **~ côtelé** corduroy

velouté, e [vəlute] ADJ (au toucher) velvety; (à la vue) soft, mellow; (au goût) smooth, mellow ▶ NM: **~ d'asperges/de tomates** cream of asparagus/tomato soup

velouteux, -euse [vəlutø, -øz] ADJ velvety

velu, e [vəly] ADJ hairy

venais etc [vənɛ] VB voir **venir**

venaison [vənɛzɔ̃] NF venison

vénal, e, -aux [venal, -o] ADJ venal

vénalité [venalite] NF venality

venant [v(ə)nɑ̃]: **à tout ~** adv to all and sundry

vendable [vɑ̃dabl] ADJ saleable, marketable

vendange [vɑ̃dɑ̃ʒ] NF (opération, période: aussi: **vendanges**) grape harvest; (raisins) grape crop, grapes pl

vendanger [vɑ̃dɑ̃ʒe] /3/ VI to harvest the grapes

vendangeur, -euse [vɑ̃dɑ̃ʒœʀ, -øz] NM/F grape-picker

vendéen, ne [vɑ̃deɛ̃, -ɛn] ADJ of ou from the Vendée

vendetta [vɑ̃deta] NF vendetta

★**vendeur, -euse** [vɑ̃dœʀ, -øz] NM/F (de magasin) shop ou sales assistant (BRIT), sales clerk (US); (Comm) salesman/woman; **~ de journaux** newspaper seller ▶ NM (Jur) vendor, seller

★**vendre** [vɑ̃dʀ] /41/ VT to sell; **~ qch à qn** to sell sb sth; **cela se vend à la douzaine** these are sold by the dozen; **« à ~ »** "for sale"

★**vendredi** [vɑ̃dʀədi] NM Friday; **V~ saint** Good Friday; voir aussi **lundi**

vendu, e [vɑ̃dy] PP de **vendre** ▶ ADJ (péj) corrupt

venelle [vənɛl] NF alley

vénéneux, -euse [venenø, -øz] ADJ poisonous

vénérable [veneʀabl] ADJ venerable

vénération [veneʀasjɔ̃] NF veneration

vénérer [veneʀe] /6/ VT to venerate

vénerie [vɛnʀi] NF hunting

vénérien, ne [veneʀjɛ̃, -ɛn] ADJ venereal

Venezuela [venezɥela] NM: **le ~** Venezuela

vénézuélien, ne [venezɥeljɛ̃, -ɛn] ADJ Venezuelan ▶ NM/F: **Vénézuélien, ne** Venezuelan

vengeance [vɑ̃ʒɑ̃s] NF vengeance no pl, revenge no pl; (acte) act of vengeance ou revenge

venger [vɑ̃ʒe] /3/ VT to avenge ■ **se venger** VPR to avenge o.s.; (par rancune) to take revenge; **se ~ de qch** to avenge o.s. for sth; to take one's revenge for sth; **se ~ de qn** to take revenge on sb; **se ~ sur** to wreak vengeance upon; to take revenge on; to take it out on

vengeur, -eresse [ʒ(ə)ʀɛs, -ʒʀɛs] ADJ vengeful ▶ NM/F avenger

véniel, le [venjɛl] ADJ venial

venimeux, -euse [vənimø, -øz] ADJ poisonous, venomous; (fig: haineux) venomous, vicious

venin [vənɛ̃] NM venom, poison; (fig) venom

★**venir** [v(ə)niʀ] /22/ VI to come; **~ de** to come from; **~ de faire: je viens d'y aller/de le voir** I've just been there/seen him; **s'il vient à pleuvoir** if it should rain, if it happens to rain; **j'en viens à croire que** I am coming to believe that; **où veux-tu en ~?** what are you getting at?; **il en est venu à mendier** he has been reduced to begging; **en ~ aux mains** to come to blows; **les années/générations à ~** the years/generations to come; **il me vient une idée** an idea has just occurred to me; **il me vient des soupçons** I'm beginning to be suspicious; **je te vois ~** I know what you're after; **faire ~** (docteur, plombier) to call (out); **d'où vient que ...?** how is it that ...?; **~ au monde** to come into the world

Venise [vəniz] N Venice

vénitien, ne [venisjɛ̃, -ɛn] ADJ Venetian

★**vent** [vɑ̃] NM wind; **il y a du ~** it's windy; **c'est du ~** it's all hot air; **au ~** to windward; **sous le ~** to leeward; **avoir le ~ debout/arrière** to head into the wind/have the wind astern; **dans le ~** (fam) trendy; **prendre le ~** (fig) to see which way the wind blows; **avoir ~ de** to get wind of; **contre vents et marées** come hell or high water

vente [vɑ̃t] NF sale; **la ~** (activité) selling; (secteur) sales pl; **mettre en ~** to put on sale; (objets personnels) to put up for sale; **~ aux enchères** auction sale; **~ de charité** jumble (BRIT) ou rummage (US) sale; **~ par correspondance (VPC)** mail-order selling

venté, e [vɑ̃te] ADJ windswept, windy

venter [vɑ̃te] /1/ VB IMPERS: **il vente** the wind is blowing

venteux, -euse [vɑ̃tø, -øz] ADJ windswept, windy

ventilateur [vɑ̃tilatœʀ] NM fan

ventilation [vɑ̃tilasjɔ̃] NF ventilation

ventiler [vɑ̃tile] /1/ VT to ventilate; (total, statistiques) to break down

ventouse [vɑ̃tuz] NF (ampoule) cupping glass; (de caoutchouc) suction pad; (Zool) sucker

★**ventre** [vɑ̃tʀ] NM (Anat) stomach; (fig) belly; **prendre du ~** to be getting a paunch; **avoir mal au ~** to have (a) stomach ache

ventricule [vɑ̃tʀikyl] NM ventricle

ventriloque [vɑ̃tʀilɔk] NMF ventriloquist

ventripotent, e [vɑ̃tʀipɔtɑ̃, -ɑ̃t] ADJ potbellied

ventru, e [vɑ̃tʀy] ADJ potbellied

venu, e [v(ə)ny] PP de **venir** ▶ ADJ: **être mal ~ à** ou **de faire** to have no grounds for doing, be in no position to do; **mal ~** ill-timed, unwelcome; **bien ~** timely, welcome ▶ NF coming

vêpres [vɛpʀ] NFPL vespers

ver [vɛʀ] NM worm; (des fruits etc) maggot; (du bois) woodworm no pl; **~ blanc** white grub; **~ luisant** glow-worm; **~ à soie** silkworm; **~ solitaire** tapeworm; **~ de terre** earthworm

véracité [veʀasite] NF veracity

véranda [veʀɑ̃da] NF veranda(h)

verbal, e, -aux [vɛʀbal, -o] ADJ verbal

verbalement [vɛʀbalmɑ̃] ADV verbally

verbalisation [vɛʀbalizasjɔ̃] NF (*par la police*) booking, reporting (of minor offences); (*Psych*) verbalization; **la ~ des contrevenants** the booking of offenders

verbaliser [vɛʀbalize] /**1**/ VI (*Police*) to book *ou* report an offender; (*Psych*) to verbalize

verbe [vɛʀb] NM (*Ling*) verb; (*voix*): **avoir le ~ sonore** to have a sonorous tone (of voice); **la magie du ~** the magic of language *ou* the word; **le V~** (*Rel*) the Word

verbeux, -euse [vɛʀbø, -øz] ADJ verbose, wordy

verbiage [vɛʀbjaʒ] NM verbiage

verbosité [vɛʀbozite] NF verbosity

verdâtre [vɛʀdɑtʀ] ADJ greenish

verdeur [vɛʀdœʀ] NF (*vigueur*) vigour (*BRIT*), vigor (*US*), vitality; (*crudité*) forthrightness; (*défaut de maturité*) tartness, sharpness

verdict [vɛʀdik(t)] NM verdict

verdir [vɛʀdiʀ] /**2**/ VI, VT to turn green

verdoyant, e [vɛʀdwajɑ̃, -ɑ̃t] ADJ green, verdant

verdure [vɛʀdyʀ] NF (*arbres, feuillages*) greenery; (*légumes verts*) green vegetables *pl*, greens *pl*

véreux, -euse [veʀø, -øz] ADJ worm-eaten; (*malhonnête*) shady, corrupt

verge [vɛʀʒ] NF (*Anat*) penis; (*baguette*) stick, cane

verger [vɛʀʒe] NM orchard

vergetures [vɛʀʒətyʀ] NFPL stretch marks

verglacé, e [vɛʀglase] ADJ icy, iced-over

verglas [vɛʀglɑ] NM (black) ice

vergogne [vɛʀgɔɲ]: **sans ~** *adv* shamelessly

véridique [veʀidik] ADJ truthful

vérifiable [veʀifjabl] ADJ (*faits, chiffres*) verifiable

vérificateur, -trice [veʀifikatœʀ, -tʀis] NM/F controller, checker; **~ des comptes** (*Finance*) auditor ▶ NF (*machine*) verifier

vérification [veʀifikasjɔ̃] NF checking *no pl*, check; **~ d'identité** identity check

vérifier [veʀifje] /**7**/ VT to check; (*corroborer*) to confirm, bear out ▪ **se vérifier** VPR to be confirmed *ou* verified

vérin [veʀɛ̃] NM jack

véritable [veʀitabl] ADJ real; (*ami, amour*) true; **un ~ désastre** an absolute disaster

véritablement [veʀitabləmɑ̃] ADV (*effectivement*) really; (*absolument*) absolutely

vérité [veʀite] NF truth; (*d'un portrait*) lifelikeness; (*sincérité*) truthfulness, sincerity; **en ~, à la ~** to tell the truth

verjus [vɛʀʒy] NM (*Culin*) verjuice (*juice of unripe grapes*)

verlan [vɛʀlɑ̃] NM (back) slang

> **Verlan** is a form of slang first popularized in the 1950s. It consists of inverting a word's syllables, the term *verlan* itself coming from *l'envers* (*à l'envers* = back to front). Typical examples are *féca* (*café*), *ripou* (*pourri*), *meuf* (*femme*), and *beur* (*Arabe*). Verlan has enjoyed new mainstream popularity since the 1990s as it is frequently used in French rap and hip-hop, with many musicians coming from the Paris *banlieues* where *verlan* is commonly used.

vermeil, le [vɛʀmɛj] ADJ bright red, ruby red ▶ NM (*substance*) vermeil

vermicelles [vɛʀmisɛl] NMPL vermicelli *sg*

vermifuge [vɛʀmifyʒ] NM: **poudre ~** worm powder

vermillon [vɛʀmijɔ̃] ADJ INV vermilion, scarlet

vermine [vɛʀmin] NF vermin *pl*

vermoulu, e [vɛʀmuly] ADJ worm-eaten, with woodworm

vermout, vermouth [vɛʀmut] NM vermouth

vernaculaire [vɛʀnakylɛʀ] ADJ (*tradition, savoir, texte*) popular; (*Bio*) vernacular, common; **langue ~** vernacular

verni [vɛʀni] ADJ varnished; glazed; (*fam*) lucky; **cuir ~** patent leather; **souliers vernis** patent (leather) shoes

vernir [vɛʀniʀ] /**2**/ VT (*bois, tableau, ongles*) to varnish; (*poterie*) to glaze

vernis [vɛʀni] NM (*enduit*) varnish; glaze; (*fig*) veneer; **~ à ongles** nail varnish (*BRIT*) *ou* polish

vernissage [vɛʀnisaʒ] NM varnishing; glazing; (*d'une exposition*) preview

vernisser [vɛʀnise] /**1**/ VT to glaze

vérole [veʀɔl] NF (*variole*) smallpox; (*fam: syphilis*) pox

Vérone [veʀɔn] N Verona

verrai *etc* [veʀe] VB *voir* **voir**

★**verre** [vɛʀ] NM glass; (*de lunettes*) lens *sg*; **boire** *ou* **prendre un ~** to have a drink; **~ à vin/à liqueur** wine/liqueur glass; **~ à dents** tooth mug; **~ dépoli** frosted glass; **~ de lampe** lamp glass *ou* chimney; **~ de montre** watch glass; **~ à pied** stemmed glass ▪ **verres** NMPL (*lunettes*) glasses; **verres de contact** contact lenses; **verres fumés** tinted lenses

verrerie [vɛʀʀi] NF (*fabrique*) glassworks *sg*; (*activité*) glass-making, glass-working; (*objets*) glassware

verrier [vɛʀje] NM glass-blower

verrière [vɛʀjɛʀ] NF (*grand vitrage*) window; (*toit vitré*) glass roof

verrons *etc* [vɛʀɔ̃] VB *voir* **voir**

verroterie [vɛʀɔtʀi] NF glass beads *pl*, glass jewellery (*BRIT*) *ou* jewelry (*US*)

verrou [vɛʀu] NM (*targette*) bolt; (*fig*) constriction; **mettre le ~** to bolt the door; **mettre qn sous les verrous** to put sb behind bars

verrouillage [vɛʀujaʒ] NM (*dispositif*) locking mechanism; **~ central** *ou* **centralisé** (*Auto*) central locking

verrouiller [vɛʀuje] /**1**/ VT to bolt; to lock; (*Mil: brèche*) to close

verrue [vɛʀy] NF wart; (*plantaire*) verruca; (*fig*) eyesore

★**vers** [vɛʀ] NM line ▶ NMPL (*poésie*) verse *sg* ▶ PRÉP (*en direction de*) toward(s); (*près de*) about, around

versant [vɛʀsɑ̃] NM slopes *pl*, side

versatile [vɛʀsatil] ADJ fickle, changeable

versatilité [vɛʀsatilite] NF (*inconstance*) fickleness

verse [vɛʀs]: **à ~** *adv*: **il pleut à ~** it's pouring (with rain)

versé, e [vɛʀse] ADJ: **être ~ dans** (*science*) to be (well-)versed in

Verseau [vɛʀso] NM: **le ~** Aquarius, the water-carrier; **être du ~** to be Aquarius

V

versement [vɛʀsəmɑ̃] NM payment; (*sur un compte*) deposit, remittance; **en trois versements** in three instalments

★**verser** [vɛʀse] /1/ VT (*liquide, grains*) to pour; (*larmes, sang*) to shed; (*argent*) to pay; (*soldat: affecter*): ~ **qn dans** to assign sb to; ~ **sur un compte** to pay into an account ▶ VI (*véhicule*) to overturn; (*fig*): ~ **dans** to lapse into

verset [vɛʀse] NM verse; versicle

verseur [vɛʀsœʀ] ADJ M *voir* **bec**; **bouchon**

versification [vɛʀsifikasjɔ̃] NF versification

versifier [vɛʀsifje] /7/ VT to put into verse ▶ VI to versify, write verse

version [vɛʀsjɔ̃] NF version; (*Scol*) translation (*into the mother tongue*); **film en ~ originale** film in the original language

verso [vɛʀso] NM back; **voir au ~** see over(leaf)

★**vert, e** [vɛʀ, vɛʀt] ADJ green; (*écologique: croissance, économie*) green; (*vin*) young; (*vigoureux*) sprightly; (*cru*) forthright; ~ **bouteille** *adj inv* bottle-green; ~ **d'eau** *adj inv* sea-green; ~ **pomme** *adj inv* apple-green ▶ NM green; **les Verts** (*Pol*) the Greens ▶ NFPL: **en dire des vertes et des pas mûres** to say some pretty spicy things; **il en a vu des vertes et des pas mûres** he's seen a thing or two

vert-de-gris [vɛʀdəgʀi] NM verdigris ▶ ADJ INV grey(ish)-green

vertébral, e, -aux [vɛʀtebʀal, -o] ADJ back *cpd*; *voir* **colonne**

vertèbre [vɛʀtɛbʀ] NF vertebra

vertébré, e [vɛʀtebʀe] ADJ, NM vertebrate

vertement [vɛʀtəmɑ̃] ADV (*réprimander*) sharply

vertical, e, -aux [vɛʀtikal, -o] ADJ vertical

verticale [vɛʀtikal] NF vertical; **à la ~** *adv* vertically

verticalement [vɛʀtikalmɑ̃] ADV vertically

verticalité [vɛʀtikalite] NF verticalness, verticality

vertige [vɛʀtiʒ] NM (*peur du vide*) vertigo; (*étourdissement*) dizzy spell; (*fig*) fever; **ça me donne le ~** it makes me dizzy; (*fig*) it makes my head spin

vertigineux, -euse [vɛʀtiʒinø, -øz] ADJ (*hausse, vitesse*) breathtaking; (*altitude, gorge*) breathtakingly high (*ou* deep)

vertu [vɛʀty] NF virtue; **une ~** a saint, a paragon of virtue; **avoir la ~ de faire** to have the virtue of doing; **en ~ de** *prép* in accordance with

vertueusement [vɛʀtɥøzmɑ̃] ADV virtuously

vertueux, -euse [vɛʀtɥø, -øz] ADJ virtuous

verve [vɛʀv] NF witty eloquence; **être en ~** to be in brilliant form

verveine [vɛʀvɛn] NF (*Bot*) verbena, vervain; (*infusion*) verbena tea

vésicule [vezikyl] NF vesicle; ~ **biliaire** gall-bladder

vespasienne [vɛspazjɛn] NF urinal

vespéral, e, -aux [vɛspeʀal, -o] ADJ vespertine, evening *cpd*

vessie [vesi] NF bladder

★**veste** [vɛst] NF jacket; ~ **droite/croisée** single-/double-breasted jacket; **retourner sa ~** (*fig*) to change sides

★**vestiaire** [vɛstjɛʀ] NM (*au théâtre etc*) cloakroom; (*de stade etc*) changing-room (BRIT), locker-room (US); (*métallique*) **(armoire)** ~ locker

★**vestibule** [vɛstibyl] NM hall

vestige [vɛstiʒ] NM (*objet*) relic; (*fragment*) trace; (*fig*) remnant, vestige ■ **vestiges** NMPL (*d'une ville*) remains; (*d'une civilisation, du passé*) remnants, relics

vestimentaire [vɛstimɑ̃tɛʀ] ADJ (*dépenses*) clothing; (*élégance*) sartorial

veston [vɛstɔ̃] NM jacket

Vésuve [vezyv] NM: **le ~** Vesuvius

vêtais *etc* [vɛtɛ] VB *voir* **vêtir**

vêtement [vɛtmɑ̃] NM garment, item of clothing; (*Comm*): **le ~** the clothing industry ■ **vêtements** NMPL clothes; **vêtements de sport** sportswear *sg*, sports clothes

vétéran [veteʀɑ̃] NM veteran

vétérinaire [veteʀinɛʀ] ADJ veterinary ▶ NMF vet, veterinary surgeon (BRIT), veterinarian (US)

vétille [vetij] NF trifle, triviality

vétilleux, -euse [vetijø, -øz] ADJ punctilious

vêtir [vetiʀ] /20/ VT to clothe, dress ■ **se vêtir** VPR to dress (o.s.)

vêtit *etc* [veti] VB *voir* **vêtir**

vétiver [vetiveʀ] NM (*Bot*) vetiver

veto [veto] NM veto; **droit de ~** right of veto; **mettre** *ou* **opposer un ~ à** to veto

vêtu, e [vety] PP *de* **vêtir** ▶ ADJ: ~ **de** dressed in, wearing; **chaudement ~** warmly dressed

vétuste [vetyst] ADJ ancient, timeworn

vétusté [vetyste] NF age, dilapidation

★**veuf, veuve** [vœf, vœv] ADJ widowed ▶ NM widower ▶ NF widow

veuille [vœj], **veuillez** *etc* [vœje] VB *voir* **vouloir**

veule [vøl] ADJ spineless

veulent *etc* [vœl] VB *voir* **vouloir**

veulerie [vølʀi] NF spinelessness

veut [vø] VB *voir* **vouloir**

veuvage [vœvaʒ] NM widowhood

★**veuve** [vœv] ADJ F, NF *voir* **veuf**

veux [vø] VB *voir* **vouloir**

vexant, e [vɛksɑ̃, -ɑ̃t] ADJ (*contrariant*) annoying; (*blessant*) upsetting

vexation [vɛksasjɔ̃] NF humiliation

vexatoire [vɛksatwaʀ] ADJ: **mesures vexatoires** harassment *sg*

vexé [vɛkse] ADJ (*offensé*) offended, hurt; (*contrarié*) annoyed

vexer [vɛkse] /1/ VT to hurt, upset ■ **se vexer** VPR to be offended, get upset

VF SIGLE F (*Ciné*) = **version française**

VHF SIGLE F (= *Very High Frequency*) VHF

via [vja] PRÉP via

viabiliser [vjabilize] /1/ VT to provide with services (*water etc*)

viabilité [vjabilite] NF viability; (*d'un chemin*) practicability

viable [vjabl] ADJ viable; (*économie, industrie etc*) sustainable

viaduc [vjadyk] NM viaduct

viager, -ère [vjaʒe, -ɛʀ] ADJ: **rente viagère** life annuity ▶ NM: **mettre en ~** to sell in return for a life annuity

★**viande** [vjɑ̃d] NF meat; **je ne mange pas de ~** I don't eat meat

viatique [vjatik] NM (*Rel*) viaticum; (*fig*) provisions *pl ou* money for the journey

vibrant, e [vibʀɑ̃, -ɑ̃t] ADJ vibrating; (*voix*) vibrant; (*émouvant*) emotive

vibraphone [vibʀafɔn] NM vibraphone, vibes *pl*

vibraphoniste [vibʀafɔnist] NMF vibraphone player

vibration [vibʀasjɔ̃] NF vibration

vibratoire [vibʀatwaʀ] ADJ vibratory

vibrer [vibʀe] /1/ VI to vibrate; (*son, voix*) to be vibrant; (*fig*) to be stirred; **faire ~** to (cause to) vibrate; to stir, thrill

vibreur [vibʀœʀ] NM (*de téléphone portable*) vibrate facility ▶ ADJ: **mettre son téléphone en mode ~** to put one's phone on vibrate

vibromasseur [vibʀɔmasœʀ] NM vibrator

vicaire [vikɛʀ] NM curate

vice [vis] NM vice; (*défaut*) fault; **~ caché** (*Comm*) latent *ou* inherent defect; **~ de forme** legal flaw *ou* irregularity

vice... [vis] PRÉFIXE vice-

vice-consul [viskɔ̃syl] NM vice-consul

vice-présidence [vispʀezidɑ̃s] NF (*d'un pays*) vice-presidency; (*d'une société*) vice-presidency, vice-chairmanship (BRIT)

vice-président, e [vispʀezidɑ̃, -ɑ̃t] NM/F vice-president; vice-chairman

vice-roi [visʀwa] NM viceroy

vice-versa [visevɛʀsa] ADV vice versa

vichy [viʃi] NM (*toile*) gingham; (*eau*) Vichy water; **carottes V~** boiled carrots

vichyssois, e [viʃiswa, -waz] ADJ of *ou* from Vichy, Vichy *cpd* ▶ NF (*Culin: soupe*) vichyssoise, *cream of leek and potato soup* ▶ NM/F: **Vichyssois, e** native *ou* inhabitant of Vichy

vicié, e [visje] ADJ (*air*) polluted, tainted; (*Jur*) invalidated

vicier [visje] /7/ VT (*Jur*) to invalidate

vicieux, -euse [visjø, -øz] ADJ (*pervers*) dirty (-minded); (*méchant*) nasty; (*fautif*) incorrect, wrong ▶ NM/F lecher

vicinal, e, -aux [visinal, -o] ADJ: **chemin ~** byroad, byway

vicissitudes [visisityd] NFPL (trials and) tribulations

vicomte [vikɔ̃t] NM viscount

vicomtesse [vikɔ̃tɛs] NF viscountess

★**victime** [viktim] NF victim; (*d'accident*) casualty; **être (la) ~ de** to be the victim of; **être ~ d'une attaque/d'un accident** to suffer a stroke/be involved in an accident

victimisation [viktimizasjɔ̃] NF victimization

victimiser [viktimize] VT to victimize

victoire [viktwaʀ] NF victory

victorieusement [viktɔʀjøzmɑ̃] ADV triumphantly, victoriously

victorieux, -euse [viktɔʀjø, -øz] ADJ victorious; (*sourire, attitude*) triumphant

victuailles [viktɥaj] NFPL provisions

vidange [vidɑ̃ʒ] NF (*d'un fossé, réservoir*) emptying; (*Auto*) oil change; (*de lavabo: bonde*) waste outlet; **faire la ~** (*Auto*) to change the oil, do an oil change; **tuyau de ~** drainage pipe ■ **vidanges** NFPL (*matières*) sewage *sg*

vidanger [vidɑ̃ʒe] /3/ VT to empty; **faire ~ la voiture** to have the oil changed in one's car

★**vide** [vid] ADJ empty; **~ de** empty of; (*de sens etc*) devoid of ▶ NM (*Physique*) vacuum; (*espace*) (empty) space, gap; (*sous soi*) drop; (*futilité, néant*) void; **sous ~** in a vacuum; **emballé sous ~** vacuum-packed; **regarder dans le ~** to stare into space; **avoir peur du ~** to be afraid of heights; **parler dans le ~** to waste one's breath; **faire le ~** (*dans son esprit*) to empty one's mind; **faire le ~ autour de qn** to isolate sb; **à ~** (*sans occupants*) empty; (*sans charge*) unladen; (*Tech*) without gripping *ou* being in gear

vidé, e [vide] ADJ (*épuisé*) done in, all in

vidéaste [videast] NMF video maker

vidéo [video] NF, ADJ INV video; **cassette ~** video cassette; **~ inverse** reverse video

vidéocassette [videokasɛt] NF video cassette

vidéoclip [videoklip] NM music video

vidéoclub [videoklœb] NM video club

vidéoconférence [videokɔ̃feʀɑ̃s] NF video conference

vidéodisque [videodisk] NM videodisc

vidéoprojecteur [videopʀɔʒɛktœʀ] NM video projector

vidéoprotection [videopʀɔtɛksjɔ̃] NF video surveillance

vide-ordures [vidɔʀdyʀ] NM INV (rubbish) chute

vidéosurveillance [videosyʀvɛjɑ̃s] NF video surveillance

vidéotex® [videotɛks] NM teletext

vidéothèque [videotɛk] NF video library

vide-poches [vidpɔʃ] NM tidy; (*Auto*) glove compartment

vide-pomme [vidpɔm] NM apple-corer

★**vider** [vide] /1/ VT to empty; (*Culin: volaille, poisson*) to gut, clean out; (*régler: querelle*) to settle; (*fatiguer*) to wear out; (*fam: expulser*) to throw out, chuck out; **~ les lieux** to quit *ou* vacate the premises ■ **se vider** VPR to empty

videur [vidœʀ] NM (*de boîte de nuit*) bouncer

★**vie** [vi] NF life; **être en ~** to be alive; **sans ~** lifeless; **à ~** for life; **membre à ~** life member; **dans la ~ courante** in everyday life; **avoir la ~ dure** to have nine lives; to die hard; **mener la ~ dure à qn** to make life a misery for sb; **que faites-vous dans la ~?** what do you do?

vieil [vjɛj] ADJ M *voir* **vieux**

vieillard [vjɛjaʀ] NM old man; **les vieillards** old people, the elderly

★**vieille** [vjɛj] ADJ F, NF *voir* **vieux**

vieilleries [vjɛjʀi] NFPL old things *ou* stuff *sg*

vieillesse [vjɛjɛs] NF old age; (*vieillards*): **la ~** old people, elderly people

vieilli, e [vjeji] ADJ (*marqué par l'âge*) aged; (*suranné*) dated

vieillir [vjejiʀ] /2/ VI (*prendre de l'âge*) to grow old; (*population, vin*) to age; (*doctrine, auteur*) to become dated; **il a beaucoup vieilli** he has aged a lot ▸ VT to age ◼ **se vieillir** VPR to make o.s. look older

vieillissement [vjɛjismɑ̃] NM growing old; ageing

vieillot, te [vjɛjo, -ɔt] ADJ antiquated, quaint

vielle [vjɛl] NF hurdy-gurdy

viendrai etc [vjɛ̃dʀe] VB voir **venir**

Vienne [vjɛn] N (en Autriche) Vienna

vienne [vjɛn], **viens** etc [vjɛ̃] VB voir **venir**

viennois, e [vjɛnwa, -waz] ADJ Viennese ▸ NM/F: **Viennois, e** Viennese

viennoiseries [vjɛnwazʀi] NFPL pastries

viens [vjɛ̃] VB voir **venir**

vierge [vjɛʀʒ] ADJ virgin; (film) blank; (page) clean, blank; (jeune fille): **être ~** to be a virgin; **~ de** (sans) free from, unsullied by ▸ NF virgin; (signe): **la V~** Virgo, the Virgin; **être de la V~** to be Virgo

Viêtnam, Vietnam [vjɛtnam] NM: **le ~** Vietnam

vietnamien, ne [vjɛtnamjɛ̃, -ɛn] ADJ Vietnamese ▸ NM (Ling) Vietnamese ▸ NM/F: **Vietnamien, ne** Vietnamese

★**vieux, vieil, vieille** [vjø, vjɛj] ADJ old; **vieille fille** spinster (péj); **~ garçon** bachelor; **~ jeu** adj inv old-fashioned; **vieil or** adj inv old gold; **~ rose** adj inv old rose; **se faire ~** to be old, be getting on ▸ NM/F old man/woman; **un petit ~** a little old man; **mon ~/ ma vieille** (fam) old man/girl; **pauvre ~** poor old soul ▸ NMPL: **les ~** (péj) old people; (fam: parents) the old folk ou ones ▸ NM: **prendre un coup de ~** to age overnight; **un ~ de la vieille** one of the old brigade

★**vif, vive** [vif, viv] ADJ (animé) lively; (alerte) sharp, quick; (brusque) sharp, brusque; (aigu) sharp; (lumière, couleur) brilliant; (air) crisp; (vent, émotion) keen; (froid) bitter; (fort: regret, déception) great, deep; (vivant): **brûlé ~** burnt alive; **eau vive** running water; **de vive voix** personally; **avoir l'esprit ~** to be quick-witted; **piquer qn au ~** to cut sb to the quick; **tailler dans le ~** to cut into the living flesh; **à ~** (plaie) open; **avoir les nerfs à ~** to be on edge; **sur le ~** (Art) from life; **entrer dans le ~ du sujet** to get to the very heart of the matter

vif-argent [vifaʀʒɑ̃] NM INV quicksilver

vigie [viʒi] NF (matelot) look-out; (poste) look-out post, crow's nest

vigilance [viʒilɑ̃s] NF vigilance

vigilant, e [viʒilɑ̃, -ɑ̃t] ADJ vigilant

vigile [viʒil] NM (veilleur de nuit) (night) watchman; (police privée) vigilante

vigne [viɲ] NF (plante) vine; (plantation) vineyard; **~ vierge** Virginia creeper

vigneron [viɲ(ə)ʀɔ̃] NM wine grower

vignette [viɲɛt] NF (motif) vignette; (de marque) manufacturer's label ou seal; (petite illustration) (small) illustration; (pour voiture) ≈ (road) tax disc (BRIT), ≈ license plate sticker (US); (sur médicament) price label (on medicines for reimbursement by Social Security)

vignoble [viɲɔbl] NM (plantation) vineyard; (vignes d'une région) vineyards pl

vigoureusement [viguʀøzmɑ̃] ADV vigorously

vigoureux, -euse [viguʀø, -øz] ADJ vigorous, robust

vigueur [vigœʀ] NF vigour (BRIT), vigor (US); **être/ entrer en ~** to be in/come into force; **en ~** current

VIH SIGLE M (= virus de l'immunodéficience humaine) HIV

vil, e [vil] ADJ vile, base; **à ~ prix** at a very low price

vilain, e [vilɛ̃, -ɛn] ADJ (laid) ugly; (affaire, blessure) nasty; (pas sage: enfant) naughty; **~ mot** bad word ▸ NM (paysan) villein, villain; **ça va tourner au ~** things are going to turn nasty

vilainement [vilɛnmɑ̃] ADV badly

vilebrequin [vilbʀəkɛ̃] NM (outil) (bit-)brace; (Auto) crankshaft

vilenie [vil(ə)ni] NF vileness no pl, baseness no pl

vilipender [vilipɑ̃de] /1/ VT to revile, vilify

villa [vila] NF (detached) house; **~ en multipro- priété** time-share villa

★**village** [vilaʒ] NM village; **~ de toile** tent village; **~ de vacances** holiday village

villageois, e [vilaʒwa, -waz] ADJ village cpd ▸ NM/F villager

★**ville** [vil] NF town; (importante) city; (administration): **la ~** ≈ the (town) council; **aller en ~** to go to town; **habiter en ~** to live in town; **~ jumelée** twin town; **~ d'eaux** spa; **~ nouvelle** new town

ville-champignon [vilʃɑ̃piɲɔ̃] (pl **villes- champignons**) NF boom town

ville-dortoir [vildɔʀtwaʀ] (pl **villes-dortoirs**) NF dormitory town

villégiature [vileʒjatyʀ] NF (séjour) holiday; (lieu) (holiday) resort

★**vin** [vɛ̃] NM wine; **avoir le ~ gai/triste** to get happy/ miserable after a few drinks; **~ blanc/rosé/ rouge** white/rosé/red wine; **~ d'honneur** reception (with wine and snacks); **~ de messe** altar wine; **~ ordinaire** ou **de table** table wine; **~ de pays** local wine; voir aussi **AOC; VDQS**

★**vinaigre** [vinɛgʀ] NM vinegar; **tourner au ~** (fig) to turn sour; **~ de vin/d'alcool** wine/spirit vinegar

vinaigrette [vinɛgʀɛt] NF vinaigrette, French dressing

vinaigrier [vinɛgʀije] NM (fabricant) vinegar-maker; (flacon) vinegar cruet ou bottle

vinasse [vinas] NF (péj) cheap wine, plonk (BRIT)

vindicatif, -ive [vɛ̃dikatif, -iv] ADJ vindictive

vindicte [vɛ̃dikt] NF: **désigner qn à la ~ publique** to expose sb to public condemnation

vineux, -euse [vino, -øz] ADJ win(e)y

★**vingt** [vɛ̃, vɛ̃t] (2nd pron used when followed by a vowel) NUM twenty; **vingt-quatre heures sur vingt- quatre** twenty-four hours a day, round the clock

★**vingtaine** [vɛ̃tɛn] NF: **une ~ (de)** around twenty, twenty or so

vingtième [vɛ̃tjɛm] NUM twentieth

vinicole [vinikɔl] ADJ (production) wine cpd; (région) wine-growing

vinification [vinifikasjɔ̃] NF wine-making, wine production; (des sucres) vinification

vinifier [vinifje] VT (raisin, cépage) to vinify

vins etc [vɛ̃] VB voir **venir**

vinyle [vinil] NM vinyl

viol [vjɔl] NM (d'une femme) rape; (d'un lieu sacré) violation

violacé, e [vjɔlase] ADJ purplish, mauvish

violation [vjɔlasjɔ̃] NF desecration; violation; (d'un droit) breach

violemment [vjɔlamɑ̃] ADV violently

violence [vjɔlɑ̃s] NF violence; **faire ~ à qn** to do violence to sb; **se faire ~** to force o.s.; **~ conjugale** domestic violence, intimate partner violence (US) ◼ **violences** NFPL acts of violence

violent, e [vjɔlɑ̃, -ɑ̃t] ADJ violent; (remède) drastic; (besoin, désir) intense, urgent

violenter [vjɔlɑ̃te] VT to assault (sexually)

violer [vjɔle] /1/ VT (femme) to rape; (sépulture) to desecrate, violate; (loi, traité) to violate

★**violet, te** [vjɔlɛ, -ɛt] ADJ, NM purple, mauve ▶ NF (fleur) violet

violeur [vjɔlœʀ] NM rapist

violine [vjɔlin] NF deep purple

★**violon** [vjɔlɔ̃] NM violin; (dans la musique folklorique etc) fiddle; (fam: prison) slammer, nick (BRIT); **premier ~** first violin; **~ d'Ingres** (artistic) hobby

violoncelle [vjɔlɔ̃sɛl] NM cello

violoncelliste [vjɔlɔ̃selist] NMF cellist

violoniste [vjɔlɔnist] NMF violinist, violin-player; (folklorique etc) fiddler

VIP SIGLE M (= Very Important Person) VIP

vipère [vipɛʀ] NF viper, adder

★**virage** [viʀaʒ] NM (d'un véhicule) turn; (d'une route, piste) bend; (Chimie) change in colour (BRIT) ou color (US); (de cuti-réaction) positive reaction; (Photo) toning; (fig: Pol) about-turn; **prendre un ~** to go into a bend, take a bend; **~ sans visibilité** blind bend

viral, e, -aux [viʀal, -o] ADJ (aussi Inform) viral

virée [viʀe] NF (courte) run; (: à pied) walk; (longue) hike, trip, walking tour

virelangue [viʀlɑ̃g] NM tongue twister

virement [viʀmɑ̃] NM (Comm) transfer; **~ bancaire** bank (credit) transfer; **~ postal** Post office credit transfer

virent [viʀ] VB voir **voir**

virer [viʀe] /1/ VT (Comm) to transfer; (Photo) to tone; (fam: renvoyer) to sack, boot out ▶ VI to turn; (Chimie) to change colour (BRIT) ou color (US); (cuti-réaction) to come up positive; (Photo) to tone; **~ au bleu** to turn blue; **~ de bord** to tack; (fig) to change tack; **~ sur l'aile** to bank

virevolte [viʀvɔlt] NF twirl; (d'avis, d'opinion) about-turn

virevolter [viʀvɔlte] /1/ VI to twirl around

virginal, e, -aux [viʀʒinal, -o] ADJ virginal

virginité [viʀʒinite] NF virginity; (fig) purity

virgule [viʀgyl] NF comma; (Math) point; **quatre ~ deux** four point two; **~ flottante** floating decimal

viril, e [viʀil] ADJ (propre à l'homme) masculine; (énergique, courageux) manly, virile

viriliser [viʀilize] /1/ VT to make (more) manly ou masculine

virilité [viʀilite] NF (attributs masculins) masculinity; (fermeté, courage) manliness; (sexuelle) virility

virologie [viʀɔlɔʒi] NF virology

virtualité [viʀtɥalite] NF virtuality; potentiality

virtuel, le [viʀtɥɛl] ADJ potential; (théorique) virtual

virtuellement [viʀtɥɛlmɑ̃] ADV potentially; (presque) virtually

virtuose [viʀtɥoz] NMF (Mus) virtuoso; (gén) master

virtuosité [viʀtɥozite] NF virtuosity; masterliness, masterful skills pl

virulence [viʀylɑ̃s] NF virulence

virulent, e [viʀylɑ̃, -ɑ̃t] ADJ virulent

virus [viʀys] NM virus

vis VB [vi] voir **voir**; **vivre** ▶ NF [vis] screw; **~ à tête plate/ronde** flat-headed/round-headed screw; **~ platinées** (Auto) (contact) points; **~ sans fin** worm, endless screw

visa [viza] NM (sceau) stamp; (validation de passeport) visa; **~ de censure** (censor's) certificate

★**visage** [vizaʒ] NM face; **à ~ découvert** (franchement) openly

visagiste [vizaʒist] NMF beautician

vis-à-vis [vizavi] ADV face to face; **~ de** prép opposite; (fig) towards, vis-à-vis ▶ NM person opposite; house etc opposite; **en ~** facing ou opposite each other; **sans ~** (immeuble) with an open outlook

viscéral, e, -aux [viseral, -o] ADJ (fig) deep-seated, deep-rooted

viscéralement [viseralmɑ̃] ADV (attaché) deeply; (opposé) virulently

viscères [visɛʀ] NMPL intestines, entrails

viscose [viskoz] NF viscose

viscosité [viskozite] NF viscosity

visée [vize] NF (avec une arme) aiming; (Arpentage) sighting ◼ **visées** NFPL (intentions) designs; **avoir des visées sur qn/qch** to have designs on sb/sth

viser [vize] /1/ VI to aim ▶ VT to aim at; (concerner) to be aimed ou directed at; (apposer un visa sur) to stamp, visa; **~ à qch/faire** to aim at sth/at doing ou to do

viseur [vizœʀ] NM (d'arme) sights pl; (Photo) viewfinder

visibilité [vizibilite] NF visibility; **sans ~** (pilotage, virage) blind cpd

visible [vizibl] ADJ visible; (disponible): **est-il ~ ?** can he see me?, will he see visitors?

visiblement [vizibləmɑ̃] ADV visibly, obviously

visière [vizjɛʀ] NF (de casquette) peak; (qui s'attache) eyeshade

visioconférence [vizjokɔ̃feʀɑ̃s] NF video conference

vision [vizjɔ̃] NF vision; (sens) (eye)sight, vision; (fait de voir): **la ~ de** the sight of; **première ~** (Ciné) first showing

visionnage [vizjɔnaʒ] NM viewing

visionnaire [vizjɔnɛʀ] ADJ, NMF visionary

visionner [vizjɔne] /1/ VT to view

visionneuse [vizjɔnøz] NF viewer

visiophone [vizjɔfɔn] NM videophone

★**visite** [vizit] NF visit; (visiteur) visitor; (touristique: d'un musée ou ville) tour; (Comm: de représentant) call; (expertise, d'inspection) inspection; (médicale, à domicile) visit, call; **~ médicale** medical examination (Mil: d'entrée) medicals pl; (: quotidienne) sick parade; **~ accompagnée** ou **guidée** guided tour; **faire une ~ à qn** to call on sb, pay sb a visit; **rendre ~ à qn** to visit sb, pay sb a visit; **être en ~ (chez qn)** to be visiting (sb); **avoir de la ~** to have visitors;

V

heures de ~ (*hôpital, prison*) visiting hours; **le droit de ~** (*Jur: aux enfants*) right of access, access; **~ de douane** customs inspection *ou* examination

★**visiter** [vizite] /**1**/ VT to visit; (*musée, ville*) to visit, go round

visiteur, -euse [vizitœʀ, -øz] NM/F visitor; **~ des douanes** customs inspector; **~ médical** medical rep(resentative); **~ de prison** prison visitor

vison [vizɔ̃] NM mink

visqueux, -euse [viskø, -øz] ADJ viscous; (*péj*) gooey; (: *manières*) slimy

vissage [visaʒ] NM screwing

visser [vise] /**1**/ VT: **~ qch** (*fixer, serrer*) to screw sth on

visu [vizy]: **de ~** adv with one's own eyes

visualisation [vizɥalizasjɔ̃] NF (*Inform*) display; **écran de ~** visual display unit (VDU)

visualiser [vizɥalize] /**1**/ VT to visualize; (*Inform*) to display, bring up on screen

visuel, le [vizɥɛl] ADJ visual

visuellement [vizɥɛlmɑ̃] ADV visually

vit [vi] VB *voir* vivre; voir

vital, e, -aux [vital, -o] ADJ vital

vitalité [vitalite] NF vitality

★**vitamine** [vitamin] NF vitamin

vitaminé, e [vitamine] ADJ with (added) vitamins

vitaminique [vitaminik] ADJ vitamin *cpd*

★**vite** [vit] ADV (*rapidement*) quickly, fast; (*sans délai*) quickly; soon; **~!** quick!; **faire ~** (*agir rapidement*) to act fast; (*se dépêcher*) to be quick; **ce sera ~ fini** this will soon be finished; **viens ~** come quick(ly)

★**vitesse** [vites] NF speed; (*Auto: dispositif*) gear; **faire de la ~** to drive fast *ou* at speed; **prendre qn de ~** to outstrip sb, get ahead of sb; **prendre de la ~** to pick up *ou* gather speed; **à toute ~** at full *ou* top speed; **en perte de ~** (*avion*) losing lift; (*fig*) losing momentum; **changer de ~** (*Auto*) to change gear; **~ acquise** momentum; **~ de croisière** cruising speed; **~ de pointe** top speed; **~ du son** speed of sound; **en ~** quickly; *see note*

The **limitation de vitesse**, or speed limit, in France is 50 km/h in built-up areas, 90 km/h on main roads (80 km/h when it is raining), 110 km/h on 4-lane roads with central reservations (100 km/h when it is raining), and 130 km/h on motorways (110 km/h when it is raining).

viticole [vitikɔl] ADJ (*industrie*) wine *cpd*; (*région*) wine-growing

viticulteur [vitikyltœʀ] NM wine grower

viticulture [vitikyltyʀ] NF wine growing

vitrage [vitʀaʒ] NM (*cloison*) glass partition; (*toit*) glass roof; (*rideau*) net curtain; **double ~** double glazing

vitrail, -aux [vitʀaj, -o] NM stained-glass window

vitre [vitʀ] NF (window) pane; (*de portière, voiture*) window

vitré, e [vitʀe] ADJ glass *cpd*

vitrer [vitʀe] /**1**/ VT to glaze

vitreux, -euse [vitʀø, -øz] ADJ vitreous; (*terne*) glassy

vitrier [vitʀije] NM glazier

vitrification [vitʀifikasjɔ̃] NF (*de parquet*) varnishing; (*de sable*) vitrification

vitrifier [vitʀifje] /**7**/ VT to vitrify; (*parquet*) to glaze

★**vitrine** [vitʀin] NF (*devanture*) (shop) window; (*étalage*) display; (*petite armoire*) display cabinet; **en ~** in the window, on display; **~ publicitaire** display case, showcase

vitriol [vitʀijɔl] NM vitriol; **au ~** (*fig*) vitriolic

vitupérations [vitypeʀasjɔ̃] NFPL invective *sg*

vitupérer [vitypeʀe] /**6**/ VI to rant and rave; **~ contre** to rail against

vivable [vivabl] ADJ (*maison*) fit to live in; (*personne*): **il n'est pas ~** he's impossible to live with

vivace ADJ [vivas] (*arbre, plante*) hardy; (*fig*) enduring ▶ ADV [vivatʃe] (*Mus*) vivace

vivacité [vivasite] NF (*voir vif*) liveliness, vivacity; sharpness; brilliance

vivant, e [vivɑ̃, -ɑ̃t] VB *voir* vivre ▶ ADJ (*qui vit*) living, alive; (*animé*) lively; (*preuve, exemple*) living; (*langue*) modern ▶ NM: **du ~ de qn** in sb's lifetime; **les vivants et les morts** the living and the dead

vivarium [vivaʀjɔm] NM vivarium

vivats [viva] NMPL cheers

vive [viv] ADJ F *voir* vif ▶ VB *voir* vivre ▶ EXCL: **~ le roi!** long live the king!; **~ les vacances!** hurrah for the holidays!

vivement [vivmɑ̃] ADV vivaciously; sharply ▶ EXCL: **~ les vacances!** I can't wait for the holidays!, roll on the holidays!

viveur [vivœʀ] NM (*péj*) high liver, pleasure-seeker

vivier [vivje] NM (*au restaurant etc*) fish tank; (*étang*) fishpond

vivifiant, e [vivifjɑ̃, -ɑ̃t] ADJ invigorating

vivifier [vivifje] /**7**/ VT to invigorate; (*fig: souvenirs, sentiments*) to liven up, enliven

vivions [vivjɔ̃] VB *voir* vivre

vivipare [vivipaʀ] ADJ viviparous

vivisection [viviseksjɔ̃] NF vivisection

vivoter [vivɔte] /**1**/ VI (*personne*) to scrape a living, get by; (*fig: affaire etc*) to struggle along

★**vivre** [vivʀ] /**46**/ VI to live; **il vit encore** he is still alive; **se laisser ~** to take life as it comes; **ne plus ~** (*être anxieux*) to live on one's nerves; **il a vécu** (*eu une vie aventureuse*) he has seen life; **ce régime a vécu** this regime has had its day; **être facile à ~** to be easy to get on with; **faire ~ qn** (*pourvoir à sa subsistance*) to provide (a living) for sb; **~ mal** (*chichement*) to have a meagre existence; **~ de** (*salaire etc*) to live on ▶ VT to live ∎ **vivres** NMPL provisions, food supplies

vivrier, -ière [vivʀije, -jɛʀ] ADJ food-producing *cpd*

vlan [vlɑ̃] EXCL wham!, bang!

VO SIGLE F (*Ciné*) = **version originale**; **voir un film en VO** to see a film in its original language

vocable [vɔkabl] NM term

★**vocabulaire** [vɔkabylɛʀ] NM vocabulary

vocal, e, -aux [vɔkal, -o] ADJ vocal

vocalique [vɔkalik] ADJ vocalic, vowel *cpd*

vocalise [vɔkaliz] NF singing exercise

vocaliser [vɔkalize] /1/ vi (Ling) to vocalize; (Mus) to do one's singing exercises

vocaliste [vɔkalist] NMF vocalist

vocation [vɔkasjɔ̃] NF vocation, calling; **avoir la ~** to have a vocation

vociférations [vɔsiferasjɔ̃] NFPL cries of rage, screams

vociférer [vɔsifere] /6/ vi, vt to scream

vodka [vɔdka] NF vodka

vœu, x [vø] NM wish; (à Dieu) vow; **faire ~ de** to take a vow of; **avec tous nos vœux** with every good wish ou our best wishes; **meilleurs vœux** best wishes; (sur une carte de nouvel an) "Season's Greetings"; **vœux de bonheur** best wishes for your future happiness; **vœux de bonne année** best wishes for the New Year

vogue [vɔg] NF fashion, vogue; **en ~** in fashion, in vogue

voguer [vɔge] /1/ vi to sail

voici [vwasi] PRÉP (pour introduire, désigner) here is (+ sg); here are (+ pl); **et ~ que ...** and now it (ou he etc) ...; **il est parti ~ trois ans** he left three years ago; **~ une semaine que je l'ai vue** it's a week since I've seen her; **me ~** here I am; **«~!»** (en offrant etc) "here ou there you are!"; voir aussi **voilà**

★**voie** [vwa] vb voir voir ▶ NF way; (Rail) track, line; (Auto) lane; **par ~ buccale** ou **orale** orally; **par ~ rectale** rectally; **suivre la ~ hiérarchique** to go through official channels; **ouvrir/montrer la ~** to open up/show the way; **être en bonne ~** to be shaping up ou going well; **mettre qn sur la ~** to put sb on the right track; **être en ~ d'achèvement/de rénovation** to be nearing completion/ in the process of renovation; **à ~ étroite** narrow-gauge; **à ~ unique** single-track; **route à deux/trois voies** two-/three-lane road; **par la ~ aérienne/ maritime** by air/sea; **~ d'eau** (Navig) leak; **~ express** expressway; **~ de fait** (Jur) assault (and battery); **~ ferrée** track; railway line (BRIT), railroad (US); **par ~ ferrée** by rail, by railroad; **~ de garage** (Rail) siding; **la ~ lactée** the Milky Way; **~ navigable** waterway; **~ prioritaire** (Auto) road with right of way; **~ privée** private road; **la ~ publique** the public highway

voilà [vwala] PRÉP (en désignant) there is (+ sg); there are (+ pl); **les ~** ou **voici** here ou there they are; **en ~ ou voici un** here's one, there's one; **voici mon frère et ~ ma sœur** this is my brother and that's my sister; **~ ou voici deux ans** two years ago; **~ ou voici deux ans que** it's two years since; **et ~!** there we are!; **~ tout** that's all; **«~!»** (en offrant etc) "there ou here you are!"; **tiens! ~ Paul** look! there's Paul

voilage [vwalaʒ] NM (rideau) net curtain; (tissu) net

★**voile** [vwal] NM veil; (tissu léger) net; **prendre le ~** to take the veil; **~ du palais** soft palate, velum; **~ au poumon** shadow on the lung ▶ NF sail; (sport) sailing; **mettre à la ~** to set sail

voiler [vwale] /1/ vt to veil; (Photo) to fog; (fausser: roue) to buckle; (: bois) to warp ■ **se voiler** VPR (lune, regard) to mist over; (ciel) to grow hazy; (voix) to become husky; (roue, disque) to buckle; (planche) to warp; **se ~ la face** to hide one's face

voilette [vwalɛt] NF (hat) veil

voilier [vwalje] NM sailing ship; (de plaisance) sailing boat

voilure [vwalyʀ] NF (de voilier) sails pl; (d'avion) aerofoils pl (BRIT), airfoils pl (US); (de parachute) canopy

★**voir** [vwaʀ] /30/ vt to see; **~ à faire qch** to see to it that sth is done; **~ venir** (fig) to wait and see; **faire ~ qch à qn** to show sb sth; **en faire ~ à qn** (fig) to give sb a hard time; **ne pas pouvoir ~ qn** (fig) not to be able to stand sb; **regardez ~** just look; **montrez ~** show (me); **dites ~** tell me; **voyons!** let's see now; (indignation etc) come (along) now!; **c'est à ~!** we'll see!; **c'est ce qu'on va ~!** we'll see about that!; **avoir quelque chose à ~ avec** to have something to do with; **ça n'a rien à ~ avec lui** that has nothing to do with him ▶ vi to see; **~ loin** (fig) to be far-sighted ■ **se voir** VPR: **cela se voit** (c'est visible) that's obvious, it shows; (cela arrive) it happens; **se ~ critiquer/transformer** to be criticized/transformed

voire [vwaʀ] ADV indeed; nay; or even

voirie [vwaʀi] NF highway maintenance; (administration) highways department; (enlèvement des ordures) refuse (BRIT) ou garbage (US) collection

vois [vwa] vb voir voir

★**voisin, e** [vwazɛ̃, -in] ADJ (proche) neighbouring (BRIT), neighboring (US); (contigu) next; (ressemblant) connected ▶ NM/F neighbour (BRIT), neighbor (US); (de table, de dortoir etc) person next to me (ou him etc); **~ de palier** neighbo(u)r across the landing (BRIT) ou hall (US)

voisinage [vwazinaʒ] NM (proximité) proximity; (environs) vicinity; (quartier, voisins) neighbourhood (BRIT), neighborhood (US); **relations de bon ~** neighbo(u)rly terms

voisiner [vwazine] /1/ vi: **~ avec** to be side by side with

voit [vwa] vb voir voir

★**voiture** [vwatyʀ] NF car; (wagon) coach, carriage; **en ~!** all aboard!; **~ à bras** handcart; **~ d'enfant** pram (BRIT), baby carriage (US); **~ d'infirme** invalid carriage; **~ de course** racing car; **~ de sport** sports car

voiture-lit [vwatyʀli] (pl **voitures-lits**) NF sleeper

voiture-restaurant [vwatyʀʀɛstɔʀɑ̃] (pl **voitures-restaurants**) NF dining car

★**voix** [vwa] NF voice; (Pol) vote; **la ~ de la conscience/ raison** the voice of conscience/reason; **à haute ~** aloud; **à ~ basse** in a low voice; **faire la grosse ~** to speak gruffly; **avoir de la ~** to have a good voice; **rester sans ~** to be speechless; **~ de basse/ténor** etc bass/tenor etc voice; **à deux/quatre ~** (Mus) in two/four parts; **avoir ~ au chapitre** to have a say in the matter; **mettre aux ~** to put to the vote; **~ off** voice-over

★**vol** [vɔl] NM (mode de locomotion) flying; (trajet, voyage, groupe d'oiseaux) flight; (mode d'appropriation) theft, stealing; (larcin) theft; **à ~ d'oiseau** as the crow flies; **au ~: attraper qch au ~** to catch sth as it flies past; **saisir une remarque au ~** to pick up a passing remark; **prendre son ~** to take flight; **de haut ~** (fig) of the highest order; **en ~** in flight; **~ avec effraction** breaking and entering no pl, break-in; **~ à l'étalage** shoplifting no pl; **~ libre** hang-gliding; **~ à main armée** armed robbery; **~ de nuit** night flight; **~ régulier** scheduled flight; **~ plané** (Aviat) glide, gliding no pl; **~ à la tire** pick-pocketing no pl; **~ à voile** gliding

vol. ABR (= *volume*) vol

volage [vɔlaʒ] ADJ fickle

volaille [vɔlɑj] NF (*oiseaux*) poultry *pl*; (*viande*) poultry *no pl*; (*oiseau*) fowl

volailler [vɔlɑje] NM poulterer

volant, e [vɔlɑ̃, -ɑ̃t] ADJ flying; *voir* **feuille** *etc*; **le personnel ~** (*Aviat*) the flight staff ▸ NM (*d'automobile*) (steering) wheel; (*de commande*) wheel; (*objet lancé*) shuttlecock; (*jeu*) battledore and shuttlecock; (*bande de tissu*) flounce; (*feuillet détachable*) tear-off portion; **~ de sécurité** (*fig*) reserve, margin, safeguard

volatil, e [vɔlatil] ADJ volatile

volatile [vɔlatil] NM (*volaille*) bird; (*tout oiseau*) winged creature

volatiliser [vɔlatilize] /1/: **se volatiliser** VPR (*Chimie*) to volatilize; (*fig*) to vanish into thin air

volatilité [vɔlatilite] NF (*Physique, Écon*) volatility

vol-au-vent [vɔlovɑ̃] NM INV vol-au-vent

volcan [vɔlkɑ̃] NM volcano; (*fig: personne*) hothead

volcanique [vɔlkanik] ADJ volcanic; (*fig: tempérament*) volatile

volcanologie [vɔlkanɔlɔʒi] NF vulcanology

volcanologue [vɔlkanɔlɔg] NMF vulcanologist

volée [vɔle] NF (*groupe d'oiseaux*) flight, flock; (*Tennis*) volley; **~ de coups/de flèches** volley of blows/arrows; **à la ~: rattraper à la ~** to catch in midair; **lancer à la ~** to fling about; **semer à la ~** to (sow) broadcast; **à toute ~** (*sonner les cloches*) vigorously; (*lancer un projectile*) with full force; **de haute ~** (*fig*) of the highest order

★**voler** [vɔle] /1/ VI (*avion, oiseau, fig*) to fly; (*voleur*) to steal; **~ en éclats** to smash to smithereens; **~ de ses propres ailes** (*fig*) to stand on one's own two feet; **~ au vent** to fly in the wind ▸ VT (*objet*) to steal; (*personne*) to rob; **~ qch à qn** to steal sth from sb; **on m'a volé mon portefeuille** my wallet (BRIT) *ou* billfold (US) has been stolen; **il ne l'a pas volé!** he asked for it!

★**volet** [vɔlɛ] NM (*de fenêtre*) shutter; (*Aviat*) flap; (*de feuillet, document*) section; (*fig: d'un plan*) facet; **trié sur le ~** hand-picked

voleter [vɔl(ə)te] /4/ VI to flutter (about)

★**voleur, -euse** [vɔlœR, -øz] NM/F thief; **« au ~ ! »** "stop thief!" ▸ ADJ thieving

volière [vɔljɛR] NF aviary

★**volley** [vɔlɛ], **volley-ball** [vɔlɛbol] NM volleyball

volleyer [vɔleje] VT (*Tennis: balle*) to volley

volleyeur, -euse [vɔlɛjœR, -øz] NM/F volleyball player

volontaire [vɔlɔ̃tɛR] ADJ (*acte, activité*) voluntary; (*délibéré*) deliberate; (*caractère, personne: décidé*) self-willed ▸ NMF volunteer

volontairement [vɔlɔ̃tɛRmɑ̃] ADV voluntarily; deliberately

volontariat [vɔlɔ̃taRja] NM voluntary service

volontarisme [vɔlɔ̃taRism] NM voluntarism

volontariste [vɔlɔ̃taRist] ADJ, NMF voluntarist

volonté [vɔlɔ̃te] NF (*faculté de vouloir*) will; (*énergie, fermeté*) will(power); (*souhait, désir*) wish; **se servir/boire à ~** to take/drink as much as one likes; **bonne ~** goodwill, willingness; **mauvaise ~** lack of goodwill, unwillingness

volontiers [vɔlɔ̃tje] ADV (*de bonne grâce*) willingly; (*avec plaisir*) willingly, gladly; (*habituellement, souvent*) readily, willingly; **« voulez-vous dîner chez nous ? » — « ~ ! »** "would you like to eat with us?" —"I'd love to *ou* with pleasure!"

volt [vɔlt] NM volt

voltage [vɔltaʒ] NM voltage

volte-face [vɔltəfas] NF INV about-turn; (*fig*) about-turn, U-turn; **faire ~** to do an about-turn; to do a U-turn

voltige [vɔltiʒ] NF (*Équitation*) trick riding; (*au cirque*) acrobatics *sg*; (*Aviat*) (aerial) acrobatics *sg*; **numéro de haute ~** acrobatic act

voltiger [vɔltiʒe] /3/ VI to flutter (about)

voltigeur [vɔltiʒœR] NM (*au cirque*) acrobat; (*Mil*) light infantryman

voltmètre [vɔltmɛtR] NM voltmeter

volubile [vɔlybil] ADJ voluble

volubilis [vɔlybilis] NM convolvulus

volubilité [vɔlybilite] NF volubility

volume [vɔlym] NM volume; (*Géom: solide*) solid

volumétrique [vɔlymetRik] ADJ volumetric

volumineux, -euse [vɔlyminø, -øz] ADJ voluminous, bulky

volumique [vɔlymik] ADJ (*Physique*): **masse ~** density

volupté [vɔlypte] NF sensual delight *ou* pleasure

voluptueusement [vɔlyptɥøzmɑ̃] ADV voluptuously

voluptueux, -euse [vɔlyptɥø, -øz] ADJ voluptuous

volute [vɔlyt] NF (*Archit*) volute; **~ de fumée** curl of smoke

vomi [vɔmi] NM vomit

★**vomir** [vɔmiR] /2/ VI to vomit, be sick ▸ VT to vomit, bring up; (*fig*) to belch out, spew out; (*exécrer*) to loathe, abhor

vomissements [vɔmismɑ̃] NMPL (*action*) vomiting *no pl*; **des ~** vomit *sg*

vomissure [vɔmisyR] NF vomit *no pl*

vomitif [vɔmitif] NM emetic

vont [vɔ̃] VB *voir* **aller**

vorace [vɔRas] ADJ voracious

voracement [vɔRasmɑ̃] ADV voraciously

voracité [vɔRasite] NF voracity

★**vos** [vo] ADJ POSS *voir* **votre**

Vosges [voʒ] NFPL: **les ~** the Vosges

vosgien, ne [voʒjɛ̃, -ɛn] ADJ *ou* from the Vosges ▸ NM/F inhabitant *ou* native of the Vosges

VOST SIGLE F (*Ciné: = version originale sous-titrée*) subtitled version

votant, e [vɔtɑ̃, -ɑ̃t] NM/F voter

vote [vɔt] NM vote; **~ par correspondance/procuration** postal/proxy vote; **~ à main levée** vote by show of hands; **~ secret, ~ à bulletins secrets** secret ballot

voter [vɔte] /1/ VI to vote ▸ VT (*loi, décision*) to vote for

votif, -ive [vɔtif, -iv] ADJ votive

★**votre** [vɔtR] (*pl* **vos** [vo]) ADJ POSS your

vôtre [votʀ] PRON: **le ~, la ~, les vôtres** yours; **les vôtres** (fig) your family ou folks; **à la ~** (toast) your (good) health!

voudrai etc [vudʀe] VB voir **vouloir**

voué, e [vwe] ADJ: **à** doomed to, destined for

vouer [vwe] /1/ VT: **~ qch à** (Dieu/un saint) to dedicate sth to; **~ sa vie/son temps à** (étude, cause etc) to devote one's life/time to; **~ une haine/amitié éternelle à qn** to vow undying hatred/friendship to sb

---

vouloir [vulwaʀ]

/31/ VT **1** (exiger, désirer) to want; **vouloir faire/que qn fasse** to want to do/sb to do; **voulez-vous du thé ?** would you like ou do you want some tea?; **vouloir qch à qn** to wish sth for sb; **que me veut-il ?** what does he want with me?; **que veux-tu que je te dise ?** what do you want me to say?; **sans le vouloir** (involontairement) without meaning to, unintentionally; **je voudrais ceci/faire** I would ou I'd like this/to do; **le hasard a voulu que ...** as fate would have it, ...; **la tradition veut que ...** tradition demands that ...
2 (consentir): **je veux bien** (bonne volonté) I'll be happy to; (concession) fair enough, that's fine; **oui, si on veut** (en quelque sorte) yes, if you like; **comme tu veux** as you wish; (en quelque sorte) if you like; **veuillez attendre** please wait; **veuillez agréer ...** (formule épistolaire) yours faithfully **3**: **en vouloir** (être ambitieux) to be out to win; **en vouloir à qn** to bear sb a grudge; **je lui en veux d'avoir fait ça** I resent his having done that; **s'en vouloir (de)** to be annoyed with o.s. (for); **il en veut à mon argent** he's after my money **4**: **vouloir de** to want; **l'entreprise ne veut plus de lui** the firm doesn't want him any more; **elle ne veut pas de son aide** she doesn't want his help **5**: **vouloir dire** to mean

▶ NM: **le bon vouloir de qn** sb's goodwill; sb's pleasure

■ **se vouloir** VPR **1** (avec attribut): **il se veut dynamique** he likes to think he's dynamic; **... qui se veut moderne ...** which purports to be modern **2**: **s'en vouloir** to be cross with o.s.; **s'en vouloir de qch** to be cross with o.s. for sth; **il s'en veut d'avoir laissé passer cette occasion** he's cross with himself for letting this opportunity slip by

---

voulu, e [vuly] PP de **vouloir** ▶ ADJ (requis) required, requisite; (délibéré) deliberate, intentional

voulus etc [vuly] VB voir **vouloir**

★**vous** [vu] PRON you; (objet indirect) (to) you; (réfléchi: sg) yourself; (: pl) yourselves; (réciproque) each other; **vous-même** yourself; **vous-mêmes** yourselves ▶ NM: **employer le ~** (vouvoyer) to use the "vous" form

voûte [vut] NF vault; **la ~ céleste** the vault of heaven; **~ du palais** (Anat) roof of the mouth; **~ plantaire** arch (of the foot)

voûté, e [vute] ADJ vaulted, arched; (dos, personne) bent, stooped

voûter [vute] /1/ VT (Archit) to arch, vault ■ **se voûter** VPR (dos, personne) to become stooped

vouvoiement [vuvwamɑ̃] NM use of the formal "vous" form

vouvoyer [vuvwaje] /8/ VT: **~ qn** to address sb as "vous"

★**voyage** [vwajaʒ] NM journey, trip; (fait de voyager): **le ~, les voyages** travel(ling); **partir/être en ~** to go off/be away on a journey ou trip; **faire un ~** to go on ou make a trip ou journey; **faire bon ~** to have a good journey; **les gens du ~** travelling people; **~ d'agrément/d'affaires** pleasure/business trip; **~ de noces** honeymoon; **~ organisé** package tour

> Ne confondez pas **journey**, **trip** et **travel**.
> **Journey** désigne le déplacement lui-même, qui est souvent long : un voyage de plus de 3 000 kilomètres **a journey of over 2,000 miles**
> **Trip**, lui comprend le déplacement, le séjour (généralement court) et le retour au point de départ. Il s'emploie plus couramment en anglais américain qu'en anglais britannique : un voyage d'affaires à Milan **a business trip to Milan**
> **Travel** est réservé aux voyages en général. Il n'est jamais précédé d'un article.
> Les voyages forment la jeunesse. **Travel broadens the mind.**

★**voyager** [vwajaʒe] /3/ VI to travel

★**voyageur, -euse** [vwajaʒœʀ, -øz] NM/F traveller; (passager) passenger ▶ ADJ (tempérament) nomadic, wayfaring; **~ (de commerce)** commercial traveller

voyagiste [vwajaʒist] NM tour operator

voyais etc [vwaje] VB voir **voir**

voyance [vwajɑ̃s] NF clairvoyance

voyant, e [vwajɑ̃, -ɑ̃t] ADJ (couleur) loud, gaudy ▶ NM/F (personne qui voit) sighted person ▶ NM (signal) (warning) light ▶ NF clairvoyant

voyelle [vwajɛl] NF vowel

voyeur, -euse [vwajœʀ, -øz] NM/F voyeur; peeping Tom

voyeurisme [vwajœʀism] NM voyeurism

voyeuriste [vwajœʀist] ADJ (fig) voyeuristic

voyons etc [vwajɔ̃] VB voir **voir**

★**voyou** [vwaju] NM lout, hoodlum; (enfant) guttersnipe

voyoucratie [vwajukʀasi] NF yob rule

VPC SIGLE F (= vente par correspondance) mail-order selling

vrac [vʀak]: **en ~** adv loose; (Comm) in bulk

★**vrai, e** [vʀe] ADJ (véridique: récit, faits) true; (non factice, authentique) real; **à ~ dire** to tell the truth; **il est ~ que** it is true that ▶ NM: **le ~** the truth; **être dans le ~** to be right

★**vraiment** [vʀemɑ̃] ADV really

vraisemblable [vʀesɑ̃blabl] ADJ (plausible) likely; (excuse) plausible; (probable) likely, probable

vraisemblablement [vʀesɑ̃blabləmɑ̃] ADV in all likelihood, very likely

vraisemblance [vʀesɑ̃blɑ̃s] NF likelihood, plausibility; (romanesque) verisimilitude; **selon toute ~** in all likelihood

vraquier [vʀakje] NM freighter

vrille [vʀij] NF (de plante) tendril; (outil) gimlet; (spirale) spiral; (Aviat) spin

V

vriller [vʀije] /1/ vt to bore into, pierce

vrombir [vʀɔ̃biʀ] /2/ vi to hum

vrombissant, e [vʀɔ̃bisɑ̃, -ɑ̃t] adj humming

vrombissement [vʀɔ̃bismɑ̃] nm hum(ming)

VRP sigle m (= *voyageur, représentant, placier*) (sales) rep (*fam*)

★**VTT** sigle m (= *vélo tout-terrain*) mountain bike

vu¹ [vy] prép (*en raison de*) in view of; **vu que** in view of the fact that

vu², e [vy] pp de **voir** ▶ adj: **bien/mal vu** (*personne*) well/poorly thought of; (*conduite*) good/bad form; **ni vu ni connu** what the eye doesn't see …, no one will be any the wiser; **c'est tout vu** it's a foregone conclusion ▶ nm: **au vu et au su de tous** openly and publicly

★**vue** [vy] nf (*sens, faculté*) (eye)sight; (*panorama, image, photo*) view; (*spectacle*) sight; **la ~ de** (*spectacle*) the sight of; **perdre la ~** to lose one's (eye)sight; **perdre de ~** to lose sight of; **à la ~ de tous** in full view of everybody; **hors de ~** out of sight; **à première ~** at first sight; **connaître de ~** to know by sight; **à ~** (*Comm*) at sight; **tirer à ~** to shoot on sight; **à ~ d'œil** adv visibly; (*à première vue*) at a quick glance; **avoir ~ sur** to have a view of; **en ~** (*visible*) in sight; (*Comm: célèbre*) in the public eye; **avoir qch en ~** (*intentions*) to have one's sights on sth; **en ~ de faire** with the intention of doing, with a view to doing; **~ d'ensemble** overall view;

~ de l'esprit theoretical view ■ **vues** nfpl (*idées*) views; (*dessein*) designs

vulcanisation [vylkanizasjɔ̃] nf vulcanization

vulcaniser [vylkanize] /1/ vt to vulcanize

vulcanologie [vylkanɔlɔʒi] nf = **volcanologie**

vulcanologue [vylkanɔlɔg] nmf = **volcanologue**

vulgaire [vylgɛʀ] adj (*grossier*) vulgar, coarse; (*trivial*) commonplace, mundane; (*péj: quelconque*): **de vulgaires touristes/chaises de cuisine** ordinary tourists/kitchen chairs; (*Bot, Zool: non latin*) common

vulgairement [vylgɛʀmɑ̃] adv vulgarly, coarsely; (*communément*) commonly

vulgarisation [vylgaʀizasjɔ̃] nf: **ouvrage de ~** popular work

vulgariser [vylgaʀize] /1/ vt to popularize

vulgarité [vylgaʀite] nf vulgarity, coarseness

vulgate [vylgat] nf (*Rel*): **la V~** the Vulgate; (*fig*) orthodoxy

vulnérabilité [vylneʀabilite] nf vulnerability

vulnérable [vylneʀabl] adj vulnerable

vulve [vylv] nf vulva

vumètre [vymɛtʀ] nm recording level gauge

Vve abr = **veuve**

VVF sigle m (= *village vacances famille*) state-subsidized holiday village

VX abr = **vieux**

Ww

W, w [dubləve] NM INV W, w ▸ ABR (= *watt*) W; **W comme William** W for William

★**wagon** [vagɔ̃] NM (*de voyageurs*) carriage; (*de marchandises*) truck, wagon

wagon-citerne [vagɔ̃sitɛʀn] (*pl* **wagons-citernes**) NM tanker

wagon-lit [vagɔ̃li] (*pl* **wagons-lits**) NM sleeper, sleeping car

wagonnet [vagɔnɛ] NM small truck

wagon-poste [vagɔ̃pɔst] (*pl* **wagons-postes**) NM mail van

wagon-restaurant [vagɔ̃ʀɛstɔʀɑ̃] (*pl* **wagons-restaurants**) NM restaurant *ou* dining car

Walkman® [wɔkman] NM Walkman®, personal stereo

Wallis et Futuna [walisefytyna] N: **les îles ~** the Wallis and Futuna Islands

wallon, ne [walɔ̃, -ɔn] ADJ Walloon ▸ NM (*Ling*) Walloon ▸ NM/F: **Wallon, ne** Walloon

Wallonie [walɔni] NF: **la ~** French-speaking (part of) Belgium

water-polo [watɛʀpɔlo] NM water polo

waters [watɛʀ] NMPL toilet *sg*, loo *sg* (BRIT)

watt [wat] NM watt

WC [vese] NMPL toilet *sg*, lavatory *sg*

Web [wɛb] NM INV: **le ~** the (World Wide) Web

webcam [wɛbkam] NF webcam

webdesign [wɛbdizajn] NM web design

webdesigner [wɛbdizajnœʀ] NMF web designer

webmaster [wɛbmastœʀ], **webmestre** [wɛbmɛstʀ] NMF webmaster

webzine [wɛbzin] NM webzine

★**week-end** [wikɛnd] NM weekend

★**western** [wɛstɛʀn] NM western

Westphalie [vɛsfali] NF: **la ~** Westphalia

whisky [wiski] (*pl* **whiskies**) NM whisky

white-spirit [wajtspiʀit] NM white spirit

widget [widʒɛt] NM (*Inform*) widget

wifi, Wi-Fi [wifi] NM INV (= *wireless fidelity*) wifi, Wi-Fi

wishbone [wiʃbon] NM (*d'une planche à voile*) wishbone

wok [wɔk] NM wok

WWW SIGLE M (= *World Wide Web*) WWW

w

X, x [iks] NM INV X, x; **plainte contre X** (*Jur*) action against person or persons unknown; **X comme Xavier** X for Xmas ▶ SIGLE M: **l'X** the *École polytechnique* (*prestigious engineering college in France*)

xénogreffe [gzenogʀɛf] NF heterograft, xenograft

xénophobe [gzenɔfɔb] ADJ xenophobic ▶ NMF xenophobe

xénophobie [gzenɔfɔbi] NF xenophobia

xérès [gzeʀɛs] NM sherry

xylographie [gzilɔgʀafi] NF xylography; (*image*) xylograph

xylophone [gzilɔfɔn] NM xylophone

Yy

★**Y, y** [igʀɛk] NM INV Y, y; **Y comme Yvonne** Y for Yellow (BRIT) ou Yoke (US)

★**y** [i] ADV (à cet endroit) there; (dessus) on it (ou them); (dedans) in it (ou them) ▶ PRON (about ou on ou of) it (vérifier la syntaxe du verbe employé); **j'y pense** I'm thinking about it; **ça y est!** that's it!; voir aussi **aller; avoir**

yacht [jɔt] NM yacht

yack ['jak] NM yak

★**yaourt** [jauʀt] NM yogurt; **~ nature/aux fruits** plain/fruit yogurt

yaourtière [jauʀtjɛʀ] NF yoghurt-maker

Yémen [jemɛn] NM: **le ~** Yemen

yéménite [jemenit] ADJ Yemeni

★**yeux** [jø] NMPL de **œil**

★**yoga** [jɔga] NM yoga

yoghourt [jɔgurt] NM = **yaourt**

yogi ['jɔgi] NM yogi

yole [jɔl] NF skiff

yorkshire ['jɔʀkʃœʀ] NM (Zool) Yorkshire terrier

yougoslave [jugɔslav] (Hist) ADJ Yugoslav(ian) ▶ NMF: **Yougoslave** Yugoslav(ian)

Yougoslavie [jugɔslavi] NF: **la ~** Yugoslavia; **l'ex-Yougoslavie** the former Yugoslavia

yourte ['juʀt] NF yurt

youtubeur, -euse [jutybœʀ, -øz] NM/F YouTuber

youyou [juju] NM dinghy

yo-yo [jojo] NM INV yo-yo

yucca [juka] NM yucca (tree ou plant)

yuppie ['jupi] NMF yuppie

Zz

Z, z [zɛd] NM INV Z, z; **Z comme Zoé** Z for Zebra

ZAC [zak] SIGLE F (= *zone d'aménagement concerté*) urban development zone

ZAD [zad] SIGLE F (= *zone d'aménagement différé*) future development zone; (= *zone à défendre*) site *occupied by activists trying to stop future development from taking place*

zadiste [zadist] NMF *protester who occupies a ZAD (zone à défendre)*

Zaïre [zaiʀ] NM: **le ~** (*Hist*) Zaïre

zaïrois, e [zaiʀwa, -waz] (*Hist*) ADJ Zairian ▶ NM/F: **Zaïrois, e** Zairian

Zambèze [zɑ̃bɛz] NM: **le ~** the Zambezi

Zambie [zɑ̃bi] NF: **la ~** Zambia

zambien, ne [zɑ̃bjɛ̃, -ɛn] ADJ Zambian ▶ NM/F: **Zambien, ne** Zambian

zapette, zappette [zapɛt] NF zapper (*fam*), remote control

zapper [zape] /1/ VI to zap

zapping [zapiŋ] NM: **faire du ~** to flick through the channels

zèbre [zɛbʀ(ə)] NM (*Zool*) zebra

zébré, e [zebre] ADJ striped, streaked

zébrure [zebʀyʀ] NF stripe, streak

zélateur, -trice [zelatœʀ, -tʀis] NM/F partisan, zealot

zèle [zɛl] NM zeal, diligence, assiduousness; **faire du ~** (*péj*) to be over-zealous

zélé, e [zele] ADJ zealous

zen [zɛn] NM (*Rel*) Zen ▶ ADJ (*Rel*) Zen; (*calme: personne*) who has a Zen-like calm

zénith [zenit] NM zenith

ZEP [zɛp] SIGLE F (= *zone d'éducation prioritaire*) *area targeted for special help in education*

zéro [zero] NM zero, nought (*Brit*); **au-dessous de ~** below zero (Centigrade), below freezing; **partir de ~** to start from scratch; **réduire à ~** to reduce to nothing; **trois (buts) à ~** three (goals) to) nil

> En anglais britannique parlé, **nought** est plus courant que **zero** : *zéro virgule cinq* **nought point five**.
> Dans les numéros de téléphone, *zéro* se dit soit **zero**, soit **o** [əu].

zeste [zɛst] NM peel, zest; **un ~ de citron** a piece of lemon peel

zézaiement [zezɛmɑ̃] NM lisp

zézayer [zezeje] /8/ VI to have a lisp

ZI SIGLE F = **zone industrielle**

zibeline [ziblin] NF sable

ZIF [zif] SIGLE F (= *zone d'intervention foncière*) intervention zone

zigouiller [ziguje] /1/ VT (*fam*) to do in

zigzag [zigzag] NM zigzag

zigzaguer [zigzage] /1/ VI to zigzag (along)

Zimbabwe [zimbabwe] NM: **le ~** Zimbabwe

zimbabwéen, ne [zimbabweɛ̃, -ɛn] ADJ Zimbabwean

zinc [zɛ̃g] NM (*Chimie*) zinc; (*comptoir*) bar, counter

zinguer [zɛ̃ge] /1/ VT to cover with zinc

zingueur [zɛ̃gœʀ] NM zinc worker

zip [zip] NM (*de vêtement*) zip (*Brit*), zipper (*US*) ▶ ADJ (*Inform*): **fichier ~** zip file

zippé, e [zipe] ADJ (*vêtement*) zip-up; (*Inform: fichier*) zipped

zipper [zipe] /1/ VT (*Inform*) to zip

zircon [ziʀkɔ̃] NM zircon

zizanie [zizani] NF: **semer la ~** to stir up ill-feeling

zizi [zizi] NM (*fam*) willy (*Brit*), peter (*US*)

zodiacal, e, -aux [zɔdjakal, -o] ADJ (*signe*) of the zodiac

zodiaque [zɔdjak] NM zodiac

zona [zona] NM shingles *sg*

zonage [zonaʒ] NM (*Admin*) zoning

zonard, e [zonaʀ, -aʀd] NM/F (*fam*) (young) hooligan *ou* thug

zone [zon] NF zone, area; **la ~** (*quartiers pauvres*) the slums; **de seconde ~** (*fig*) second-rate; **~ d'action** (*Mil*) sphere of activity; **~ blanche** (*Tél*) dead zone; **~ bleue** ≈ restricted parking area; **~ d'extension** *ou* **d'urbanisation** urban development area; **~ franche** free zone; **~ industrielle** industrial estate; **~ piétonne** pedestrian precinct; **~ résidentielle** residential area; **~ tampon** buffer zone

zoner [zone] /1/ VI (*fam*) to hang around

★**zoo** [zoo] NM zoo

zoologie [zɔɔlɔʒi] NF zoology

zoologique [zɔɔlɔʒik] ADJ zoological

zoologiste [zɔɔlɔʒist] NMF zoologist

zoom [zum] NM (*Photo*) zoom (lens)

zoomer [zume] VI: **~ sur qch** to zoom in on sth

zozoter [zɔzɔte] vi to lisp
ZUP [zyp] SIGLE F (= *zone à urbaniser en priorité*) = **ZAC**

Zurich [zyʀik] N Zürich
★**zut** [zyt] EXCL dash (it)! (*BRIT*), nuts! (*US*)

Aa

★ **A, a¹** [eɪ] N (*letter*) A, a *m*; (*Scol: mark*) A; (*Mus*): **A** la *m*;
A for Andrew, A for Able (US) A comme Anatole;
A shares *npl* (BRIT *Stock Exchange*) actions *fpl* prio-
ritaires

---

a² [eɪ, ə]

(*before vowel and silent h* **an**) INDEF ART **1** un(e); **a
book** un livre; **an apple** une pomme; **she's a
doctor** elle est médecin
2 (*instead of the number "one"*) un(e); **a year ago** il y
a un an; **a hundred/thousand** *etc* **pounds** cent/
mille *etc* livres
3 (*in expressing ratios, prices etc*): **three a day/week**
trois par jour/semaine; **10 km an hour** 10 km à
l'heure; **£5 a person** 5 livres par personne; **30p
a kilo** 30p le kilo

---

a. ABBR = **acre**

A2 N (BRIT *Scol*) deuxième partie de l'examen équivalent
au baccalauréat

AA N ABBR (BRIT: = *Automobile Association*) ≈ ACF *m*;
(US: = *Associate in/of Arts*) diplôme universitaire;
(= *Alcoholics Anonymous*) AA; (= *anti-aircraft*) AA

AAA N ABBR (= *American Automobile Association*) ≈ ACF
m; (BRIT) = **Amateur Athletics Association**

A & E N ABBR (BRIT: = *Accident and Emergency (Department)*) service *m* des urgences, urgences *fpl*

A & R N ABBR (*Mus*) = **artists and repertoire**; **~ man**
découvreur *m* de talent

AASCU N ABBR (US) = **American Association of
State Colleges and Universities**

AAUP N ABBR (= *American Association of University Pro-
fessors*) syndicat universitaire

AB ABBR (BRIT) = **able-bodied seaman**; (CANADA)
= **Alberta**

aback [əˈbæk] ADV: **to be taken ~** être déconte-
nancé(e)

abacus [ˈæbəkəs] (*pl* **abaci** [-saɪ]) N boulier *m*

abalone [æbəˈləʊnɪ] N (*shellfish*) ormeau *m*

★ **abandon** [əˈbændən] VT abandonner; **to ~ ship**
évacuer le navire ▸ N abandon *m*

abandoned [əˈbændənd] ADJ (*child, house etc*)
abandonné(e); (*unrestrained*) sans retenue

abase [əˈbeɪs] VT: **to ~ o.s. (so far as to do)**
s'abaisser (à faire)

abashed [əˈbæʃt] ADJ confus(e), embarrassé(e)

abate [əˈbeɪt] VI s'apaiser, se calmer

abatement [əˈbeɪtmənt] N: **noise ~** lutte *f* contre
le bruit

abattoir [ˈæbətwɑːʳ] N (BRIT) abattoir *m*

abbey [ˈæbɪ] N abbaye *f*

abbot [ˈæbət] N père supérieur

abbreviate [əˈbriːvɪeɪt] VT abréger

abbreviation [əbriːvɪˈeɪʃən] N abréviation *f*

ABC N ABBR (= *American Broadcasting Company*) chaîne
de télévision

abdicate [ˈæbdɪkeɪt] VT, VI abdiquer

abdication [æbdɪˈkeɪʃən] N abdication *f*

abdomen [ˈæbdəmən] N abdomen *m*

abdominal [æbˈdɔmɪnl] ADJ abdominal(e)

abduct [æbˈdʌkt] VT enlever

abduction [æbˈdʌkʃən] N enlèvement *m*

abductor [æbˈdʌktəʳ] N ravisseur(-euse); **child ~**
kidnappeur *m* (d'enfants)

Aberdonian [æbəˈdəʊnɪən] ADJ d'Aberdeen ▸ N
habitant(e) d'Aberdeen, natif(-ive) d'Aberdeen

aberration [æbəˈreɪʃən] N anomalie *f*; **in a
moment of mental ~** dans un moment d'égarement

abet [əˈbɛt] VT *see* **aid**

abeyance [əˈbeɪəns] N: **in ~** (*law*) en désuétude;
(*matter*) en suspens

abhor [əbˈhɔːʳ] VT abhorrer, exécrer

abhorrent [əbˈhɔrənt] ADJ odieux(-euse), exécrable

abide [əˈbaɪd] VT souffrir, supporter; **I can't ~ it/
him** je ne le supporte pas
▸ **abide by** VT FUS observer, respecter

abiding [əˈbaɪdɪŋ] ADJ (*memory etc*) durable

★ **ability** [əˈbɪlɪtɪ] N compétence *f*; capacité *f*; (*skill*)
talent *m*; **to the best of my ~** de mon mieux

abject [ˈæbdʒɛkt] ADJ (*poverty*) sordide; (*coward*)
méprisable; **an ~ apology** les excuses les plus
plates

ablaze [əˈbleɪz] ADJ en feu, en flammes; **~ with
light** resplendissant de lumière

★ **able** [ˈeɪbl] ADJ compétent(e); **to be ~ to do sth**
pouvoir faire qch, être capable de faire qch

able-bodied [ˈeɪblˈbɔdɪd] ADJ robuste; **~ seaman**
(BRIT) matelot breveté

ably [ˈeɪblɪ] ADV avec compétence *or* talent, habilement

ABM N ABBR = **anti-ballistic missile**

abnormal [æbˈnɔːməl] ADJ anormal(e)

abnormality [æbnɔːˈmælɪtɪ] N (*condition*) caractère anormal; (*instance*) anomalie *f*

aboard [ə'bɔːd] ADV à bord ▶ PREP à bord de; (train) dans

abode [ə'bəud] N (old) demeure f; (Law): **of no fixed ~** sans domicile fixe

abolish [ə'bɒlɪʃ] VT abolir

abolition [æbə'lɪʃən] N abolition f

abominable [ə'bɒmɪnəbl] ADJ abominable

Aboriginal [æbə'rɪdʒɪnəl] (in Australia) N aborigène mf (d'Australie) ▶ ADJ (art, people) aborigène

aboriginal [æbə'rɪdʒɪnəl] ADJ (native, indigenous) autochtone

Aborigine [æbə'rɪdʒɪnɪ] N (in Australia) aborigène mf (d'Australie)

aborigine [æbə'rɪdʒɪnɪ] N aborigène mf

abort [ə'bɔːt] VT (Med) faire avorter; (Comput, fig) abandonner

abortion [ə'bɔːʃən] N avortement m; **to have an ~** se faire avorter

abortionist [ə'bɔːʃənɪst] N avorteur(-euse)

abortive [ə'bɔːtɪv] ADJ manqué(e)

abound [ə'baund] VI abonder; **to ~ in** abonder en, regorger de

---

about [ə'baut]

ADV **1** (approximately) environ, à peu près; **about a hundred/thousand** etc environ cent/mille etc, une centaine (de)/un millier (de) etc; **it takes about 10 hours** ça prend environ or à peu près 10 heures; **at about 2 o'clock** vers 2 heures; **I've just about finished** j'ai presque fini
2 (referring to place) çà et là, de-ci de-là; **to run about** courir çà et là; **to walk about** se promener, aller et venir; **is Paul about?** (BRIT) est-ce que Paul est là?; **it's about here** c'est par ici, c'est dans les parages; **they left all their things lying about** ils ont laissé traîner toutes leurs affaires
3: **to be about to do sth** être sur le point de faire qch; **I'm not about to do all that for nothing** (inf) je ne vais quand même pas faire tout ça pour rien
4 (opposite): **it's the other way about** (BRIT) c'est l'inverse
▶ PREP **1** (relating to) au sujet de, à propos de; **a book about London** un livre sur Londres; **what is it about?** de quoi s'agit-il?; **we talked about it** nous en avons parlé; **do something about it!** faites quelque chose!; **what** or **how about doing this?** et si nous faisions ceci?
2 (referring to place) dans; **to walk about the town** se promener dans la ville

---

about-turn [əbaut'təːn], **about-face** [əbaut'feɪs] N (U-turn) volte-face f; (Mil) demi-tour m; **to do an ~** (U-turn) faire volte-face; (Mil) faire un demi-tour

★**above** [ə'bʌv] ADV au-dessus; **mentioned ~** mentionné ci-dessus ▶ PREP au-dessus de; (more than) plus de; **costing ~ £10** coûtant plus de 10 livres; **~ all** par-dessus tout, surtout

aboveboard [əbʌv'bɔːd] ADJ franc (franche), loyal(e); honnête

abrasion [ə'breɪʒən] N frottement m; (on skin) écorchure f

abrasive [ə'breɪzɪv] ADJ abrasif(-ive); (fig) caustique, agressif(-ive)

abreast [ə'brest] ADV de front; **to keep ~ of** se tenir au courant de

abridge [ə'brɪdʒ] VT abréger

★**abroad** [ə'brɔːd] ADV à l'étranger; **there is a rumour ~ that ...** (fig) le bruit court que ...

abrupt [ə'brʌpt] ADJ (steep, blunt) abrupt(e); (sudden, gruff) brusque

abruptly [ə'brʌptlɪ] ADV (speak, end) brusquement

abs [æbz] NPL (inf: abdominal muscles) abdos mpl

abscess ['æbsɛs] N abcès m

abscond [əb'skɒnd] VI disparaître, s'enfuir

abseil ['æbseɪl] (BRIT) VI descendre en rappel; **to ~ down a cliff** descendre en rappel une falaise

★**absence** ['æbsəns] N absence f; **in the ~ of** (person) en l'absence de; (thing) faute de

★**absent** ['æbsənt] ADJ absent(e); **~ without leave (AWOL)** (Mil) en absence irrégulière

absentee [æbsən'tiː] N absent(e)

absenteeism [æbsən'tiːɪzəm] N absentéisme m

absent-minded [æbsənt'maɪndɪd] ADJ distrait(e)

absent-mindedness [æbsənt'maɪndɪdnɪs] N distraction f

absolute ['æbsəluːt] ADJ absolu(e)

★**absolutely** [æbsə'luːtlɪ] ADV absolument

absolve [əb'zɒlv] VT: **to ~ sb (from)** (sin etc) absoudre qn (de); **to ~ sb from** (oath) délier qn de

absorb [əb'zɔːb] VT absorber; **to be absorbed in a book** être plongé(e) dans un livre

absorbent [əb'zɔːbənt] ADJ absorbant(e)

absorbent cotton N (US) coton m hydrophile

absorbing [əb'zɔːbɪŋ] ADJ absorbant(e); (book, film etc) captivant(e)

absorption [əb'sɔːpʃən] N absorption f

abstain [əb'steɪn] VI: **to ~ (from)** s'abstenir (de)

abstemious [əb'stiːmɪəs] ADJ sobre, frugal(e)

abstention [əb'stenʃən] N abstention f

abstinence ['æbstɪnəns] N abstinence f

abstract ADJ ['æbstrækt] abstrait(e) ▶ N (summary) résumé m ▶ VT [æb'strækt] extraire

abstruse [æb'struːs] ADJ abstrus(e)

absurd [əb'səːd] ADJ absurde

absurdity [əb'səːdɪtɪ] N absurdité f

ABTA ['æbtə] N ABBR = **Association of British Travel Agents**

Abu Dhabi ['æbuː'dɑːbɪ] N Ab(o)u Dhabi m

abundance [ə'bʌndəns] N abondance f

abundant [ə'bʌndənt] ADJ abondant(e)

★**abuse** N [ə'bjuːs] (insults) insultes fpl, injures fpl; (ill-treatment) mauvais traitements mpl; (of power etc) abus m; **to be open to ~** se prêter à des abus ▶ VT [ə'bjuːz] (insult) insulter; (ill-treat) malmener; (power etc) abuser de

abuser [ə'bjuːzəʳ] N (of victim, child) auteur m de sévices, auteur m de maltraitances; (of drugs) toxicomane mf; (of alcohol) ivrogne mf

abusive [ə'bjuːsɪv] ADJ grossier(-ière), injurieux(-euse)

abysmal [ə'bɪzməl] ADJ exécrable; (ignorance etc) sans bornes

abyss [ə'bɪs] N abîme *m*, gouffre *m*

AC N ABBR (*US*) = **athletic club**

a/c ABBR (*Banking etc*) = **account; account current**

acacia [ə'keɪʃə] N (*also:* **acacia tree**) acacia *m*

★**academic** [ækə'dɛmɪk] ADJ universitaire; (*person: scholarly*) intellectuel(le); (*pej: issue*) oiseux(-euse), purement théorique; **~ freedom** liberté *f* académique ▸ N universitaire *mf*

academic year N (*University*) année *f* universitaire; (*Scol*) année scolaire

academy [ə'kædəmɪ] N (*learned body*) académie *f*; (*school*) collège *m*; **military/naval ~** école militaire/navale; **~ of music** conservatoire *m*

ACAS ['eɪkæs] N ABBR (*BRIT*: = *Advisory, Conciliation and Arbitration Service*) organisme de conciliation et d'arbitrage des conflits du travail

accede [æk'siːd] VI: **to ~ to** (*request, throne*) accéder à

accelerate [æk'sɛləreɪt] VT, VI accélérer

acceleration [æksɛlə'reɪʃən] N accélération *f*

accelerator [æk'sɛləreɪtə^r] N (*BRIT*) accélérateur *m*

★**accent** ['æksɛnt] N accent *m*

accentuate [æk'sɛntjueɪt] VT (*syllable*) accentuer; (*need, difference etc*) souligner

★**accept** [ək'sɛpt] VT accepter

★**acceptable** [ək'sɛptəbl] ADJ acceptable

acceptance [ək'sɛptəns] N acceptation *f*; **to meet with general ~** être favorablement accueilli par tous

★**access** ['æksɛs] N accès *m*; **to have ~ to** (*information, library etc*) avoir accès à, pouvoir utiliser or consulter; (*person*) avoir accès auprès de; **the burglars gained ~ through a window** les cambrio-leurs sont entrés par une fenêtre ▸ VT (*Comput*) accéder à

accessibility [əksɛsə'bɪlɪtɪ] N accessibilité *f*

accessible [æk'sɛsəbl] ADJ accessible

accession [æk'sɛʃən] N accession *f*; (*of king*) avènement *m*; (*to library*) acquisition *f*

accessorize [æk'sɛsəraɪz] VT (*clothes, furniture*) accessoiriser

accessory [æk'sɛsərɪ] N accessoire *m*; **toilet accessories** (*BRIT*) articles *mpl* de toilette; **~ to** (*Law*) accessoire à

access road N voie *f* d'accès; (*to motorway*) bretelle *f* de raccordement

access time N (*Comput*) temps *m* d'accès

★**accident** ['æksɪdənt] N accident *m*; (*chance*) hasard *m*; **to meet with** ■ **have an ~** avoir un accident; **I've had an ~** j'ai eu un accident; **accidents at work** accidents du travail; **by ~** (*by chance*) par hasard; (*not deliberately*) accidentellement

accidental [æksɪ'dɛntl] ADJ accidentel(le)

accidentally [æksɪ'dɛntəlɪ] ADV accidentellement

Accident and Emergency Department N (*BRIT*) service *m* des urgences

accident insurance N assurance *f* accident

accident-prone ['æksɪdəntprəun] ADJ sujet(te) aux accidents

acclaim [ə'kleɪm] VT acclamer ▸ N acclamations *fpl*

acclamation [æklə'meɪʃən] N (*approval*) acclamation *f*; (*applause*) ovation *f*

acclimatize [ə'klaɪmətaɪz], (*US*) **acclimate** [ə'klaɪmət] VT: **to become acclimatized** s'acclimater

accolade ['ækəleɪd] N accolade *f*; (*fig*) marque *f* d'honneur

accommodate [ə'kɔmədeɪt] VT loger, recevoir; (*oblige, help*) obliger; (*car etc*) contenir; (*adapt*): **to ~ one's plans to** adapter ses projets à

accommodating [ə'kɔmədeɪtɪŋ] ADJ obligeant(e), arrangeant(e)

★**accommodation** N, (*US*) **accommodations** NPL [əkɔmə'deɪʃən(z)] logement *m*; **he's found ~** il a trouvé à se loger; **"~ to let"** (*BRIT*) « appartement or studio *etc* à louer »; **they have ~ for 500** ils peuvent recevoir 500 personnes, il y a de la place pour 500 personnes; **the hall has seating ~ for 600** (*BRIT*) la salle contient 600 places assises

accompaniment [ə'kʌmpənɪmənt] N accompagnement *m*

accompanist [ə'kʌmpənɪst] N accompagnateur(-trice)

accompany [ə'kʌmpənɪ] VT accompagner

accomplice [ə'kʌmplɪs] N complice *mf*

accomplish [ə'kʌmplɪʃ] VT accomplir

accomplished [ə'kʌmplɪʃt] ADJ accompli(e)

accomplishment [ə'kʌmplɪʃmənt] N (*skill: gen pl*) talent *m*; (*completion*) accomplissement *m*; (*achievement*) réussite *f*

accord [ə'kɔːd] N accord *m*; **of his own ~** de son plein gré; **with one ~** d'un commun accord ▸ VT accorder

accordance [ə'kɔːdəns] N: **in ~ with** conformément à

according [ə'kɔːdɪŋ]: **~ to** prep selon; **~ to plan** comme prévu

accordingly [ə'kɔːdɪŋlɪ] ADV (*appropriately*) en conséquence; (*as a result*) par conséquent

accordion [ə'kɔːdɪən] N accordéon *m*

accost [ə'kɔst] VT accoster, aborder

★**account** [ə'kaunt] N (*Comm*) compte *m*; (*report*) compte rendu, récit *m*; **"~ payee only"** (*BRIT*) « chèque non endossable »; **to keep an ~ of** noter; **to bring sb to ~ for sth/for having done sth** amener qn à rendre compte de qch/d'avoir fait qch; **by all accounts** au dire de tous; **of little ~** de peu d'importance; **of no ~** sans importance; **on ~** en acompte; **to buy sth on ~** acheter qch à crédit; **on no ~** en aucun cas; **on ~ of** à cause de; **to take into ~, take ~ of** tenir compte de ■ **accounts** NPL (*Comm: records*) comptabilité *f*, comptes
▸ **account for** VT FUS (*explain*) expliquer, rendre compte de; (*represent*) représenter; **all the children were accounted for** aucun enfant ne manquait; **four people are still not accounted for** on n'a toujours pas retrouvé quatre personnes

accountability [əkauntə'bɪlɪtɪ] N responsabilité *f*; (*financial, political*) transparence *f*

accountable [ə'kauntəbl] ADJ: **~ (for/to)** responsable (de/devant)

accountancy [ə'kauntənsɪ] N comptabilité *f*

accountant [ə'kauntənt] N comptable *mf*

accounting [ə'kauntɪŋ] N comptabilité *f*

accounting period N exercice financier, période f comptable

account number N numéro m de compte

account payable N compte m fournisseurs

account receivable N compte m clients

accreditation [əkredɪ'teɪʃən] N (of qualification, institution) habilitation f; (of diplomat, journalist, representative) accréditation f

accredited [ə'kredɪtɪd] ADJ (person) accrédité(e)

accretion [ə'kri:ʃən] N accroissement m

accrual [ə'kru:əl] N accumulation f

accrue [ə'kru:] VI s'accroître; (mount up) s'accumuler; **to ~ to** s'ajouter à; **accrued interest** intérêt couru

accumulate [ə'kju:mjuleɪt] VT accumuler, amasser ▶ VI s'accumuler, s'amasser

accumulation [əkju:mju'leɪʃən] N accumulation f

accuracy ['ækjurəsɪ] N exactitude f, précision f

★**accurate** ['ækjurɪt] ADJ exact(e), précis(e); (device) précis

accurately ['ækjurɪtlɪ] ADV avec précision

accusation [ækju'zeɪʃən] N accusation f

accusative [ə'kju:zətɪv] N (Ling) accusatif m

accusatory [ə'kju:zətərɪ, ækju'zeɪtərɪ] ADJ accusateur(-trice)

★**accuse** [ə'kju:z] VT: **to ~ sb (of sth)** accuser qn (de qch)

accused [ə'kju:zd] N (Law) accusé(e)

accuser [ə'kju:zə'] N accusateur(-trice)

accusing [ə'kju:zɪŋ] ADJ accusateur(-trice)

accusingly [ə'kju:zɪŋlɪ] ADV (say, ask) d'un ton accusateur; (look, point) d'un air accusateur

accustom [ə'kʌstəm] VT accoutumer, habituer; **to ~ o.s. to sth** s'habituer à qch

accustomed [ə'kʌstəmd] ADJ (usual) habituel(le); **~ to** habitué(e) or accoutumé(e) à

AC/DC ABBR = **alternating current/direct current**

ACE [eɪs] N ABBR = **American Council on Education**

ace [eɪs] N as m; **within an ~ of** (Brit) à deux doigts or un cheveu de

acerbic [ə'sə:bɪk] ADJ (also fig) acerbe

acetate ['æsɪteɪt] N acétate m

★**ache** [eɪk] N mal m, douleur f; **I've got stomach ~** or (US) **a stomach ~** j'ai mal à l'estomac ▶ VI (be sore) faire mal, être douloureux(-euse); (yearn): **to ~ to do sth** mourir d'envie de faire qch; **my head aches** j'ai mal à la tête; **I'm aching all over** j'ai mal partout

★**achieve** [ə'tʃi:v] VT (aim) atteindre; (victory, success) remporter, obtenir; (task) accomplir

★**achievement** [ə'tʃi:vmənt] N exploit m, réussite f; (of aims) réalisation f

achiever [ə'tʃi:və'] N: **to be a high ~** être très doué(e); **a way to keep low achievers from dropping out** un moyen de maintenir les moins doués dans le système

Achilles heel [ə'kɪli:z-] N talon m d'Achille

★**acid** ['æsɪd] N, ADJ acide m

acidic [ə'sɪdɪk] ADJ acide

acidity [ə'sɪdɪtɪ] N acidité f

acid rain N pluies fpl acides

acid test N (fig) épreuve décisive

acknowledge [ək'nɔlɪdʒ] VT (also: **acknowledge receipt of**) accuser réception de; (fact) reconnaître

acknowledgement [ək'nɔlɪdʒmənt] N (of letter) accusé m de réception ■ **acknowledgements** NPL (in book) remerciements mpl

ACLU N ABBR (= American Civil Liberties Union) ligue des droits de l'homme

acme ['ækmɪ] N point culminant

acne ['æknɪ] N acné m

acorn ['eɪkɔ:n] N gland m

acoustic [ə'ku:stɪk] ADJ acoustique

acoustics [ə'ku:stɪks] N, NPL acoustique f

acquaint [ə'kweɪnt] VT: **to ~ sb with sth** mettre qn au courant de qch; **to be acquainted with** (person) connaître; (fact) savoir

acquaintance [ə'kweɪntəns] N connaissance f; **to make sb's ~** faire la connaissance de qn

acquiesce [ækwɪ'es] VI (agree): **to ~ (in)** acquiescer (à)

acquiescent [ækwɪ'esənt] ADJ consentant(e)

acquire [ə'kwaɪə'] VT acquérir

acquired [ə'kwaɪəd] ADJ acquis(e); **an ~ taste** un goût acquis

acquisition [ækwɪ'zɪʃən] N acquisition f

acquisitive [ə'kwɪzɪtɪv] ADJ qui a l'instinct de possession or le goût de la propriété

acquit [ə'kwɪt] VT acquitter; **to ~ o.s. well** s'en tirer très honorablement

acquittal [ə'kwɪtl] N acquittement m

acre ['eɪkə'] N acre f (= 4 047 m²)

acreage ['eɪkərɪdʒ] N superficie f

acrid ['ækrɪd] ADJ (smell) âcre; (fig) mordant(e)

acrimonious [ækrɪ'məunɪəs] ADJ acrimonieux(-euse), aigre

acrimoniously [ækrɪ'məunɪəslɪ] ADV (end, break up) avec acrimonie

acrimony ['ækrɪmənɪ] N acrimonie f

acrobat ['ækrəbæt] N acrobate mf

acrobatic [ækrə'bætɪk] ADJ acrobatique

acrobatics [ækrə'bætɪks] N, NPL acrobatie f

acronym ['ækrənɪm] N acronyme m

Acropolis [ə'krɔpəlɪs] N: **the ~** l'Acropole f

acrosport ['ækrəspɔ:t] N acrosport m

★**across** [ə'krɔs] PREP (on the other side) de l'autre côté de; (crosswise) en travers de; **to walk ~ the road** traverser la route; **to take sb ~ the road** faire traverser la route à qn; **the bridge ~ Lake Washington** le pont qui traverse le Lac Washington ▶ ADV de l'autre côté; en travers; **to run/swim ~** traverser en courant/à la nage; **to walk ~ to the window** aller à la fenêtre; **the lake is 12 km ~** le lac fait 12 km de large; **~ from** en face de; **to get sth ~ (to sb)** faire comprendre qch (à qn)

acrylic [ə'krɪlɪk] N, ADJ acrylique m

ACT N ABBR (= American College Test) examen de fin d'études secondaires

★**act** [ækt] N acte m, action f; (Theat: part of play) acte; (: of performer) numéro m; (Law) loi f; **to catch sb in the ~** prendre qn sur le fait or en flagrant délit;

it's only an ~ c'est du cinéma; ~ **of God** (*Law*) catastrophe naturelle ▶ vɪ agir; (*Theat*) jouer; (*pretend*) jouer la comédie; **to ~ as** servir de; **it acts as a deterrent** cela a un effet dissuasif; **acting in my capacity as chairman, I ...** en ma qualité de président, je ... ▶ vᴛ (*role*) jouer, tenir; **to ~ Hamlet** (*Bʀɪᴛ*) tenir *or* jouer le rôle d'Hamlet; **to ~ the fool** (*Bʀɪᴛ*) faire l'idiot

▶ **act on** vᴛ ꜰᴜs: **to ~ on sth** agir sur la base de qch

▶ **act out** vᴛ (*event*) raconter en mimant; (*fantasies*) réaliser

▶ **act up** vɪ (*inf: person*) se conduire mal; (*: knee, back, injury*) jouer des tours; (*: machine*) être capricieux(-euse)

acting ['æktɪŋ] ᴀᴅᴊ suppléant(e), par intérim; **he is the ~ manager** il remplace (provisoirement) le directeur ▶ ɴ (*of actor*) jeu *m*; (*activity*): **to do some ~** faire du théâtre (*or* du cinéma)

★**action** ['ækʃən] ɴ action *f*; (*Mil*) combat(s) *m(pl)*; (*Law*) procès *m*, action en justice; **to bring an ~ against sb** (*Law*) poursuivre qn en justice, intenter un procès contre qn; **killed in ~** (*Mil*) tué au champ d'honneur; **out of ~** hors de combat; (*machine etc*) hors d'usage; **to take ~** agir, prendre des mesures; **to put a plan into ~** mettre un projet à exécution ▶ vᴛ (*Comm*) mettre en œuvre

action plan ɴ (*also*: **plan of action**) plan *m* d'action

action replay ɴ (*Bʀɪᴛ TV*) ralenti *m*

activate ['æktɪveɪt] vᴛ (*mechanism*) actionner, faire fonctionner; (*Chem, Physics*) activer

activation [æktɪ'veɪʃən] ɴ (*of mechanism, also Chem*) activation *f*

★**active** ['æktɪv] ᴀᴅᴊ actif(-ive); (*volcano*) en activité; **to play an ~ part in** jouer un rôle actif dans

active duty ɴ (*US Mil*) campagne *f*

actively ['æktɪvlɪ] ᴀᴅᴠ activement; (*discourage*) vivement

active partner ɴ (*Comm*) associé(e)

active service ɴ (*Bʀɪᴛ Mil*) campagne *f*

activism ['æktɪvɪzəm] ɴ activisme *m*; **political ~** activisme politique; **environmental ~** militantisme *m* écologique

activist ['æktɪvɪst] ɴ activiste *mf*

★**activity** [æk'tɪvɪtɪ] ɴ activité *f*

activity holiday ɴ vacances actives

★**actor** ['æktər] ɴ acteur *m*

★**actress** ['æktrɪs] ɴ actrice *f*

★**actual** ['æktjuəl] ᴀᴅᴊ réel(le), véritable; (*emphatic use*) lui-même (elle-même)

---

actual ne veut pas dire *actuel*.

---

actuality [æktju'ælɪtɪ] ɴ (*reality*) réalité *f*; (*formal: fact*) fait *m*; (*: condition*) situation *f* réelle; **in ~** en réalité

★**actually** ['æktjuəlɪ] ᴀᴅᴠ réellement, véritablement; (*in fact*) en fait

---

actually ne veut pas dire *actuellement*.

---

actuarial [æktju'ɛərɪəl] ᴀᴅᴊ actuariel(le)

actuary ['æktjuərɪ] ɴ actuaire *m*

actuate ['æktjueɪt] vᴛ déclencher, actionner

acuity [ə'kju:ɪtɪ] ɴ acuité *f*

acumen ['ækjumən] ɴ perspicacité *f*; **business ~** sens *m* des affaires

acupressure ['ækjuprɛʃər] ɴ acupressing *m*

acupuncture ['ækjupʌŋktʃər] ɴ acuponcture *f*

acute [ə'kju:t] ᴀᴅᴊ (*severe: crisis, shortage*) grave; (*: embarrassment*) profond(e); (*illness, accent*) aigu(ë); (*mind, observer*) subtil(e)

acutely [ə'kju:tlɪ] ᴀᴅᴠ (*keenly: aware*) profondément; (*: feel*) vivement; (*intensely: embarrassing*) extrêmement

AD ᴀᴅᴠ ᴀʙʙʀ (= *Anno Domini*) ap. J.-C. ▶ ɴ ᴀʙʙʀ (*US Mil*) = **active duty**

★**ad** [æd] ɴ ᴀʙʙʀ = **advertisement**

adage ['ædɪdʒ] ɴ adage *m*; **the old ~ that ...** le vieil adage selon lequel ...

adamant ['ædəmənt] ᴀᴅᴊ inflexible

Adam's apple ['ædəmz-] ɴ pomme *f* d'Adam

adapt [ə'dæpt] vᴛ adapter ▶ vɪ: **to ~ (to)** s'adapter (à)

adaptability [ədæptə'bɪlɪtɪ] ɴ faculté *f* d'adaptation

adaptable [ə'dæptəbl] ᴀᴅᴊ (*device*) adaptable; (*person*) qui s'adapte facilement

adaptation [ædæp'teɪʃən] ɴ adaptation *f*

adapter, adaptor [ə'dæptər] ɴ (*Elec*) adaptateur *m*; (*for several plugs*) prise *f* multiple

adaptive [ə'dæptɪv] ᴀᴅᴊ (*adaptable*) qui a une grande capacité d'adaptation

ADC ɴ ᴀʙʙʀ (*Mil*) = **aide-de-camp**; (*US*: = *Aid to Dependent Children*) aide pour enfants assistés

ADD ɴ ᴀʙʙʀ (= *attention deficit disorder*) TDA *m*

★**add** [æd] vᴛ ajouter; (*figures: also:* **add up**) additionner ▶ vɪ: **to ~ to** (*increase*) ajouter à, accroître; **it doesn't ~ up** (*fig*) cela ne rime à rien

▶ **add on** vᴛ ajouter

▶ **add up to** vᴛ ꜰᴜs (*Math*) s'élever à; (*fig: mean*) signifier; **it doesn't ~ up to much** ça n'est pas grand-chose

added ['ædɪd] ᴀᴅᴊ (*extra: advantage, benefit*) supplémentaire; (*sugar, vitamins*) ajouté(e)

adder ['ædər] ɴ vipère *f*

addict ['ædɪkt] ɴ toxicomane *mf*; (*fig*) fanatique *mf*; **heroin ~** héroïnomane *mf*; **drug ~** drogué(e)

addicted [ə'dɪktɪd] ᴀᴅᴊ: **to be ~ to** (*drink, drugs*) être adonné(e) à; (*fig: football etc*) être un(e) fanatique de

addiction [ə'dɪkʃən] ɴ (*Med*) dépendance *f*

addictive [ə'dɪktɪv] ᴀᴅᴊ qui crée une dépendance

adding machine ['ædɪŋ-] ɴ machine *f* à calculer

Addis Ababa ['ædɪs'æbəbə] ɴ Addis Abeba, Addis Ababa

★**addition** [ə'dɪʃən] ɴ (*adding up*) addition *f*; (*thing added*) ajout *m*; **in ~** de plus, de surcroît; **in ~ to** en plus de

additional [ə'dɪʃənl] ᴀᴅᴊ supplémentaire

additionally [ə'dɪʃənəlɪ] ᴀᴅᴠ (*moreover, to a greater extent*) de plus, en outre

additive ['ædɪtɪv] ɴ additif *m*

★**address** [ə'drɛs] ɴ adresse *f*; (*talk*) discours *m*, allocution *f*; **my ~ is ...** mon adresse, c'est ...; **form of ~** titre *m*; **what form of ~ do you use for ...?** comment s'adresse-t-on à ...?; **absolute/relative ~** (*Comput*) adresse absolue/relative ▶ vᴛ adresser; (*speak to*) s'adresser à; **to ~ (o.s. to) sth** (*problem, issue*) aborder qch

address book N carnet *m* d'adresses

addressee [ædrɛ'siː] N destinataire *mf*

Aden ['eɪdən] N: **Gulf of ~** Golfe *m* d'Aden

adenoids ['ædɪnɔɪdz] NPL végétations *fpl*

adept [ə'dɛpt] ADJ: **~ at** expert(e) à *or* en

adequate ['ædɪkwɪt] ADJ (*enough*) suffisant(e); (*satisfactory*) satisfaisant(e); **to feel ~ to the task** se sentir à la hauteur de la tâche

adequately ['ædɪkwɪtlɪ] ADV de façon adéquate

ADHD N ABBR (= *attention deficit hyperactivity disorder*) TDAH *m*

adhere [əd'hɪə'] VI: **to ~ to** adhérer à; (*fig: rule, decision*) se tenir à

adherence [əd'hɪərəns] N (*to rule, agreement, belief*) adhésion *f*; **~ to sth** adhésion à qch

adhesion [əd'hiːʒən] N adhésion *f*

adhesive [əd'hiːzɪv] ADJ adhésif(-ive) ▶ N adhésif *m*

adhesive tape N (BRIT) ruban *m* adhésif; (*US Med*) sparadrap *m*

ad hoc [æd'hɔk] ADJ (*decision*) de circonstance; (*committee*) ad hoc

ad infinitum ['ædɪnfɪ'naɪtəm] ADV à l'infini

adjacent [ə'dʒeɪsənt] ADJ adjacent(e), contigu(ë); **~ to** adjacent à

★**adjective** ['ædʒɛktɪv] N adjectif *m*

adjoin [ə'dʒɔɪn] VT jouxter

adjoining [ə'dʒɔɪnɪŋ] ADJ voisin(e), adjacent(e), attenant(e) ▶ PREP voisin de, adjacent à

adjourn [ə'dʒəːn] VT ajourner; **to ~ a meeting till the following week** reporter une réunion à la semaine suivante ▶ VI suspendre la séance; lever la séance; clore la session; (*go*) se retirer; **they adjourned to the pub** (BRIT *inf*) ils ont filé au pub

adjournment [ə'dʒəːnmənt] N (*period*) ajournement *m*

Adjt ABBR (*Mil*: = *adjutant*) Adj

adjudicate [ə'dʒuːdɪkeɪt] VT (*contest*) juger; (*claim*) statuer (sur) ▶ VI se prononcer

adjudication [ədʒuːdɪ'keɪʃən] N (*Law*) jugement *m*

adjudicator [ə'dʒuːdɪkeɪtə'] N juge *mf*

adjust [ə'dʒʌst] VT (*machine*) ajuster, régler; (*prices, wages*) rajuster ▶ VI: **to ~ (to)** s'adapter (à)

adjustable [ə'dʒʌstəbl] ADJ réglable

adjuster [ə'dʒʌstə'] N *see* **loss**

adjustment [ə'dʒʌstmənt] N (*of machine*) ajustage *m*, réglage *m*; (*of prices, wages*) rajustement *m*; (*of person*) adaptation *f*

adjutant ['ædʒətənt] N adjudant *m*

ad-lib [æd'lɪb] VT, VI improviser ▶ N improvisation *f* ▶ ADV: **ad lib** à volonté, à discrétion

adman ['ædmæn] N (*irreg*) (*inf*) publicitaire *m*

admin ['ædmɪn] N ABBR (*inf*) = **administration**

administer [əd'mɪnɪstə'] VT administrer; (*justice*) rendre

★**administration** [ədmɪnɪs'treɪʃən] N (*management*) administration *f*; (*government*) gouvernement *m*

administrative [əd'mɪnɪstrətɪv] ADJ administratif(-ive)

administrator [əd'mɪnɪstreɪtə'] N administrateur(-trice)

admirable ['ædmərəbl] ADJ admirable

admirably ['ædmɪrəblɪ] ADV admirablement

admiral ['ædmərəl] N amiral *m*

Admiralty ['ædmərəltɪ] N (BRIT: *also*: **Admiralty Board**) ministère *m* de la Marine

admiration [ædmə'reɪʃən] N admiration *f*

★**admire** [əd'maɪə'] VT admirer

admirer [əd'maɪərə'] N (*fan*) admirateur(-trice)

admiring [əd'maɪərɪŋ] ADJ admiratif(-ive)

admiringly [əd'maɪərɪŋlɪ] ADV (*say, look*) avec admiration

admissible [əd'mɪsəbl] ADJ acceptable, admissible; (*evidence*) recevable

admission [əd'mɪʃən] N admission *f*; (*to exhibition, night club etc*) entrée *f*; (*confession*) aveu *m*; "**~ free**", "**free ~**" « entrée libre »; **by his own ~** de son propre aveu

admission charge N droits *mpl* d'admission

★**admit** [əd'mɪt] VT laisser entrer; admettre; (*agree*) reconnaître, admettre; (*crime*) reconnaître avoir commis; "**children not admitted**" « entrée interdite aux enfants »; **this ticket admits two** ce billet est valable pour deux personnes; **I must ~ that …** je dois admettre *or* reconnaître que …
  ▶ **admit of** VT FUS admettre, permettre
  ▶ **admit to** VT FUS reconnaître, avouer

admittance [əd'mɪtəns] N admission *f*, (droit *m* d')entrée *f*; "**no ~**" « défense d'entrer »

admittedly [əd'mɪtɪdlɪ] ADV il faut en convenir

admonish [əd'mɔnɪʃ] VT donner un avertissement à; réprimander

admonishment [əd'mɔnɪʃmənt] N réprimande *f*

ad nauseam [æd'nɔːzɪæm] ADV à satiété

ado [ə'duː] N: **without (any) more ~** sans plus de cérémonies

adolescence [ædəu'lɛsns] N adolescence *f*

adolescent [ædəu'lɛsnt] ADJ, N adolescent(e)

★**adopt** [ə'dɔpt] VT adopter

★**adopted** [ə'dɔptɪd] ADJ adoptif(-ive), adopté(e)

adoption [ə'dɔpʃən] N adoption *f*

adoptive [ə'dɔptɪv] ADJ (*child, parents, family*) adoptif(-ive); (*country, home*) d'adoption, adoptif(-ive)

adorable [ə'dɔːrəbl] ADJ adorable

adoration [ædɔː'reɪʃən] N adoration *f*

adore [ə'dɔː'] VT adorer

adoring [ə'dɔːrɪŋ] ADJ: **his ~ wife** sa femme qui est en adoration devant lui

adoringly [ə'dɔːrɪŋlɪ] ADV avec adoration

adorn [ə'dɔːn] VT orner

adornment [ə'dɔːnmənt] N ornement *m*

ADP N ABBR = **automatic data processing**

adrenalin, adrenaline [ə'drɛnəlɪn] N adrénaline *f*; **to get the ~ going** faire monter le taux d'adrénaline

Adriatic [eɪdrɪ'ætɪk] N: **the ~ (Sea)** la mer Adriatique, l'Adriatique *f*

adrift [ə'drɪft] ADV à la dérive; **to come ~** (*boat*) aller à la dérive; (*wire, rope, fastening etc*) se défaire

adroit [ə'drɔɪt] ADJ adroit(e), habile

ADSL N ABBR (= *asymmetric digital subscriber line*) ADSL *m*

ADT ABBR (*US*: = *Atlantic Daylight Time*) *heure d'été de New York*

adulation ['ædjuleɪʃən] N adulation *f*

★**adult** ['ædʌlt] N adulte *mf* ▶ ADJ (*grown-up*) adulte; (*for adults*) pour adultes

adult education N éducation *f* des adultes

adulterate [ə'dʌltəreɪt] VT frelater, falsifier

adulterer [ə'dʌltərər] N homme *m* adultère

adulteress [ə'dʌltərɪs] N femme *f* adultère

adulterous [ə'dʌltərəs] ADJ adultère

adultery [ə'dʌltərɪ] N adultère *m*

adulthood ['ædʌlthud] N âge *m* adulte

★**advance** [əd'vɑːns] N avance *f*; **in ~** (*prepare, notify, decide*) à l'avance; (*pay*) d'avance; **do I need to book in ~?** est-ce qu'il faut réserver à l'avance ?; **to make advances to sb** (*gen*) faire des propositions à qn; (*amorously*) faire des avances à qn ▶ VT avancer ▶ VI s'avancer ▶ CPD: **~ booking** location *f*; **~ notice**, **~ warning** préavis *m*; (*verbal*) avertissement *m*

★**advanced** [əd'vɑːnst] ADJ avancé(e); (*Scol: studies*) supérieur(e); **~ in years** d'un âge avancé

advancement [əd'vɑːnsmənt] N avancement *m*

★**advantage** [əd'vɑːntɪdʒ] N (*also Tennis*) avantage *m*; **to take ~ of** (*person*) exploiter; (*opportunity*) profiter de; **it's to our ~** c'est notre intérêt; **it's to our ~ to ...** nous avons intérêt à ...

advantaged [əd'vɑːntɪdʒd] ADJ avantagé(e)

advantageous [ædvən'teɪdʒəs] ADJ avantageux(-euse)

advent ['ædvɛnt] N avènement *m*, venue *f*; **A~** (*Rel*) Avent *m*

Advent calendar N calendrier *m* de l'Avent

★**adventure** [əd'vɛntʃər] N aventure *f*

adventure playground N aire *f* de jeux

adventurer [əd'vɛntʃərər] N aventurier(-ière)

adventuresome [əd'vɛntʃəsəm] (*US*) ADJ aventureux(-euse)

adventurous [əd'vɛntʃərəs] ADJ aventureux(-euse)

adverb ['ædvə:b] N adverbe *m*

adversarial [ædvə'sɛərɪəl] ADJ antagonique

adversary ['ædvəsərɪ] N adversaire *m(f)*

adverse ['ædvə:s] ADJ adverse; (*effect*) négatif(-ive); (*weather, publicity*) mauvais(e); (*wind*) contraire; **~ to** hostile à; **in ~ circumstances** dans l'adversité

adversely ['ædvə:slɪ] ADV: **to affect sth ~** avoir un effet négatif sur qch

adversity [əd'və:sɪtɪ] N adversité *f*

advert ['ædvə:t] N (*BRIT*) = **advertisement**

★**advertise** ['ædvətaɪz] VI faire de la publicité *or* de la réclame; (*in classified ads etc*) mettre une annonce; **to ~ for** (*staff*) recruter par (voie d') annonce ▶ VT faire de la publicité *or* de la réclame pour; (*in classified ads etc*) mettre une annonce pour vendre

advertisement [əd'və:tɪsmənt] N publicité *f*, réclame *f*; (*in classified ads etc*) annonce *f*

advertiser ['ædvətaɪzər] N annonceur *m*

advertising ['ædvətaɪzɪŋ] N publicité *f*

advertising agency N agence *f* de publicité

advertising campaign N campagne *f* de publicité

★**advice** [əd'vaɪs] N conseils *mpl*; (*notification*) avis *m*; **a piece of ~** un conseil; **to ask (sb) for ~** demander conseil (à qn); **to take legal ~** consulter un avocat

advice note N (*BRIT*) avis *m* d'expédition

advisable [əd'vaɪzəbl] ADJ recommandable, indiqué(e)

★**advise** [əd'vaɪz] VT conseiller; **to ~ sb of sth** aviser *or* informer qn de qch; **to ~ sb against sth/doing sth** déconseiller qch/conseiller de ne pas faire qch; **you would be well/ill advised to go** vous feriez mieux d'y aller/de ne pas y aller, vous auriez intérêt à y aller/à ne pas y aller

advisedly [əd'vaɪzɪdlɪ] ADV (*deliberately*) délibérément

adviser, advisor [əd'vaɪzər] N conseiller(-ère)

advisory [əd'vaɪzərɪ] ADJ consultatif(-ive); **in an ~ capacity** à titre consultatif

advocacy ['ædvəkəsɪ] N plaidoyer *m*; **sb's ~ of sth** le plaidoyer de qn en faveur de qch

advocate N ['ædvəkɪt] (*lawyer*) avocat(e) (plaidant(e)); (*upholder*) défenseur *m*, avocat(e); **to be an ~ of** être partisan(e) de ▶ VT ['ædvəkeɪt] recommander, prôner

advt. ABBR = **advertisement**

AEA N ABBR (*BRIT*: = *Atomic Energy Authority*) ≈ AEN *f* (= *Agence pour l'énergie nucléaire*)

AEC N ABBR (*US*: = *Atomic Energy Commission*) CEA *m* (= *Commissariat à l'énergie atomique*)

Aegean [i:'dʒi:ən] N, ADJ: **the ~ (Sea)** la mer Égée, l'Égée *f*

aegis ['i:dʒɪs] N: **under the ~ of** sous l'égide de

aeon ['i:ən] N éternité *f*

aerial ['ɛərɪəl] N antenne *f* ▶ ADJ aérien(ne)

aerobatics [ɛərəu'bætɪks] NPL acrobaties aériennes

aerobic [ɛə'rəubɪk] ADJ aérobie

★**aerobics** [ɛə'rəubɪks] N aérobic *m*

aerodrome ['ɛərədrəum] N (*BRIT*) aérodrome *m*

aerodynamic [ɛərəudaɪ'næmɪk] ADJ aérodynamique

aerodynamics [ɛərəudaɪ'næmɪks] N aérodynamique *f*

aeronautical [ɛərə'nɔ:tɪkl] ADJ (*engineer, research*) aéronautique; **~ engineering** aéronautique *f*

aeronautics [ɛərə'nɔ:tɪks] N aéronautique *f*

★**aeroplane** ['ɛərəpleɪn] N (*BRIT*) avion *m*

aerosol ['ɛərəsɔl] N aérosol *m*

aerospace industry ['ɛərəuspeɪs-] N (*industrie*) aérospatiale *f*

aesthete ['i:sθi:t] N esthète *mf*

aesthetic [ɪs'θɛtɪk] ADJ esthétique

aesthetics [ɪs'θɛtɪks] N esthétique *f*

afar [ə'fɑ:r] ADV: **from ~** de loin

AFB N ABBR (*US*) = **Air Force Base**

AFDC N ABBR (*US*: = *Aid to Families with Dependent Children*) *aide pour enfants assistés*

affable [ˈæfəbl] ADJ affable

★**affair** [əˈfɛəʳ] N affaire f; (also: **love affair**) liaison f; aventure f ■ **affairs** NPL (business) affaires

★**affect** [əˈfɛkt] VT affecter; (subj: disease) atteindre

affectation [æfɛkˈteɪʃən] N affectation f

affected [əˈfɛktɪd] ADJ affecté(e)

affecting [əˈfɛktɪŋ] ADJ (story, music) touchant(e), émouvant(e)

affection [əˈfɛkʃən] N affection f

affectionate [əˈfɛkʃənɪt] ADJ affectueux(-euse)

affectionately [əˈfɛkʃənɪtlɪ] ADV affectueusement

affidavit [æfɪˈdeɪvɪt] N (Law) déclaration écrite sous serment

affiliated [əˈfɪlɪeɪtɪd] ADJ affilié(e); **~ company** filiale f

affiliation [əfɪlɪˈeɪʃən] N affiliation f; **~ with sth**, **~ to sth** affiliation à qch; **political affiliations** attaches fpl politiques

affinity [əˈfɪnɪtɪ] N affinité f

affirm [əˈfəːm] VT affirmer

affirmation [æfəˈmeɪʃən] N affirmation f, assertion f

affirmative [əˈfəːmətɪv] ADJ affirmatif(-ive) ▶ N: **in the ~** dans or par l'affirmative

affix [əˈfɪks] VT apposer, ajouter

afflict [əˈflɪkt] VT affliger

affliction [əˈflɪkʃən] N affliction f

affluence [ˈæfluəns] N aisance f, opulence f

affluent [ˈæfluənt] ADJ opulent(e); (person, family, surroundings) aisé(e), riche; **the ~ society** la société d'abondance

★**afford** [əˈfɔːd] VT (goods etc) avoir les moyens d'acheter or d'entretenir; (behaviour) se permettre; (provide) fournir, procurer; **can we ~ a car?** avons-nous de quoi acheter or les moyens d'acheter une voiture ?; **I can't ~ the time** je n'ai vraiment pas le temps

affordability [əfɔːdəˈbɪlɪtɪ] N accessibilité m des prix

affordable [əˈfɔːdəbl] ADJ abordable

affray [əˈfreɪ] N (BRIT Law) échauffourée f, rixe f

affront [əˈfrʌnt] N affront m

affronted [əˈfrʌntɪd] ADJ insulté(e)

Afghan [ˈæfgæn] ADJ afghan(e) ▶ N Afghan(e)

Afghanistan [æfˈgænɪstæn] N Afghanistan m

aficionado [əfɪʃəˈnɑːdəʊ] N passionné(e); **an ~ of sth** un(e) passionné(e) de qch

afield [əˈfiːld] ADV: **far ~** loin

aflame [əˈfleɪm] ADJ (grass, forest) en flammes; (with colour) flamboyant(e); (with emotion: heart) embrasé(e); (: face) en feu

AFL-CIO N ABBR (= American Federation of Labor and Congress of Industrial Organizations) confédération syndicale

afloat [əˈfləʊt] ADJ à flot ▶ ADV: **to stay ~** surnager; **to keep/get a business ~** maintenir à flot/lancer une affaire

afoot [əˈfʊt] ADV: **there is something ~** il se prépare quelque chose

aforementioned [əˈfɔːmɛnʃənd], **aforesaid** [əˈfɔːsɛd] ADJ susdit(e), susmentionné(e)

★**afraid** [əˈfreɪd] ADJ effrayé(e); **to be ~ of** or **to** avoir peur de; **I am ~ that** je crains que + sub; **I'm ~ so/not** oui/non, malheureusement

afresh [əˈfrɛʃ] ADV de nouveau

★**Africa** [ˈæfrɪkə] N Afrique f

African [ˈæfrɪkən] ADJ africain(e) ▶ N Africain(e)

African-American [ˈæfrɪkənəˈmɛrɪkən] ADJ afro-américain(e) ▶ N Afro-Américain(e)

Afrikaans [æfrɪˈkɑːns] N afrikaans m

Afrikaner [æfrɪˈkɑːnəʳ] N Afrikaner mf

Afro [ˈæfrəʊ] ADJ (hair, wig) afro ▶ N (hairstyle) coiffure f afro

Afro-American [ˈæfrəʊəˈmɛrɪkən] ADJ afro-américain(e)

AFT N ABBR (= American Federation of Teachers) syndicat enseignant

aft [ɑːft] ADV à l'arrière, vers l'arrière

★**after** [ˈɑːftəʳ] PREP, ADV après; **~ dinner** après (le) dîner; **the day ~ tomorrow** après-demain; **it's quarter ~ two** (US) il est deux heures et quart; **to name sb ~ sb** donner à qn le nom de qn; **to ask ~ sb** demander des nouvelles de qn; **what/who are you ~?** que/qui cherchez-vous ?; **the police are ~ him** la police est à ses trousses; **~ you!** après vous !; **~ all** après tout ▶ CONJ après que, après avoir or être + pp; **~ having done/~ he left** après avoir fait/ après son départ

> Reword phrases such as *after finishing* or *after I'd finished* as *after having finished* before translating them into French: *after finishing* **après avoir fini**.

afterbirth [ˈɑːftəbəːθ] N placenta m

aftercare [ˈɑːftəkɛəʳ] N (BRIT Med) post-cure f

after-effects [ˈɑːftərɪfɛkts] NPL (of disaster, radiation, drink etc) répercussions fpl; (of illness) séquelles fpl, suites fpl

afterlife [ˈɑːftəlaɪf] N vie f après la mort

aftermarket [ˈɑːftəmɑːkɪt] N (for cars) marché m des accessoires; (Stock Exchange) marché secondaire

aftermath [ˈɑːftəmɑːθ] N conséquences fpl; **in the ~ of** dans les mois or années etc qui suivirent, au lendemain de

★**afternoon** [ɑːftəˈnuːn] N après-midi mf; **good ~!** bonjour !; (goodbye) au revoir !

> L'**afternoon tea** est une sorte de goûter assez consistant dont l'apparition date du XIXe siècle, parmi les Anglaises de la haute société qui se réunissaient chez l'une ou l'autre pour prendre le thé. L'*afternoon tea* est toujours répandu, même si de nos jours on se retrouve plutôt entre amies dans un hôtel ou un café, le plus souvent pour une occasion particulière. Au menu de l'*afternoon tea* classique : petits sandwiches au pain de mie, *scones* avec crème et confiture, assortiment de pâtisseries, thé ou café.

afterparty [ˈɑːftəpɑːtɪ] N after m

afters [ˈɑːftəz] N (BRIT inf: dessert) dessert m

after-sales service [ɑːftəˈseɪlz-] N service m après-vente, SAV m

after-shave ['ɑːfəʃeɪv], **after-shave lotion** N lotion f après-rasage

aftershock ['ɑːftəʃɔk] N réplique f (sismique)

aftersun (cream/lotion) ['ɑːftəsʌn-] N après-soleil m inv

aftertaste ['ɑːftəteɪst] N arrière-goût m

afterthought ['ɑːftəθɔːt] N: **I had an ~** il m'est venu une idée après coup

★**afterwards** ['ɑːftəwədz], (US) **afterward** ['ɑːftəwəd] ADV après

afterword ['ɑːftəwəːd] N postface f

★**again** [ə'gɛn] ADV de nouveau, encore (une fois); **to do sth ~** refaire qch; **not ... ~** ne ... plus; **~ and ~** à plusieurs reprises; **he's opened it ~** il l'a rouvert, il l'a de nouveau or l'a encore ouvert; **now and ~** de temps à autre

★**against** [ə'gɛnst] PREP contre; (compared to) par rapport à; **~ a blue background** sur un fond bleu; **(as) ~** (BRIT) contre

agape [ə'geɪp] ADJ: **with her mouth ~** bouche bée

★**age** [eɪdʒ] N âge m; **what ~ is he?** quel âge a-t-il ?; **he is 20 years of ~** il a 20 ans; **under ~** mineur(e); **to come of ~** atteindre sa majorité; **it's been ages since I saw you** ça fait une éternité que je ne t'ai pas vu ▶ VT, VI vieillir

★**aged** ADJ [eɪdʒd] âgé(e); **~ 10** âgé de 10 ans ▶ NPL ['eɪdʒɪd]: **the ~** les personnes âgées

age group N tranche f d'âge; **the 40 to 50 ~** la tranche d'âge des 40 à 50 ans

ageing ['eɪdʒɪŋ] ADJ vieillissant(e)

ageism ['eɪdʒɪzəm] N âgisme m

ageless ['eɪdʒlɪs] ADJ sans âge

age limit N limite f d'âge

agency ['eɪdʒənsɪ] N agence f; **through** or **by the ~ of** par l'entremise or l'action de

★**agenda** [ə'dʒɛndə] N ordre m du jour; **on the ~** à l'ordre du jour

agenda ne veut pas dire agenda.

★**agent** ['eɪdʒənt] N agent m; (firm) concessionnaire m

agglomeration [əglɔmə'reɪʃən] N agglomérat m

aggravate ['æɡrəveɪt] VT (situation) aggraver; (annoy) exaspérer, agacer

aggravating ['æɡrəveɪtɪŋ] ADJ (annoying) exaspérant(e)

aggravation [æɡrə'veɪʃən] N agacements mpl

aggregate ['æɡrɪɡɪt] N ensemble m, total m; **on ~** (Sport) au total des points

aggregator ['æɡrɪɡeɪtə'] N agrégateur m

aggression [ə'ɡrɛʃən] N agression f

★**aggressive** [ə'ɡrɛsɪv] ADJ agressif(-ive)

aggressiveness [ə'ɡrɛsɪvnɪs] N agressivité f

aggressor [ə'ɡrɛsə'] N agresseur m

aggrieved [ə'ɡriːvd] ADJ chagriné(e), affligé(e)

aggro ['æɡrəu] N (BRIT inf: physical) grabuge m; (: hassle) embêtements mpl

aghast [ə'ɡɑːst] ADJ consterné(e), atterré(e)

agile ['ædʒaɪl] ADJ agile

agility [ə'dʒɪlɪtɪ] N agilité f, souplesse f

agitate ['ædʒɪteɪt] VT (person) perturber ▶ VI faire de l'agitation (politique); **to ~ for** faire campagne pour

agitated ['ædʒɪteɪtɪd] ADJ perturbé(e)

agitation [ædʒɪ'teɪʃən] N (distress) agitation f; (political) campagne f; **in a state of ~** dans tous ses états

agitator ['ædʒɪteɪtə'] N agitateur(-trice) (politique)

AGM N ABBR (= annual general meeting) AG f

agnostic [æɡ'nɔstɪk] ADJ, N agnostique mf

agnosticism [æɡ'nɔstɪsɪzm] N agnosticisme m

★**ago** [ə'ɡəu] ADV: **two days ~** il y a deux jours; **not long ~** il n'y a pas longtemps; **as long ~ as 1960** déjà en 1960; **how long ~?** il y a combien de temps (de cela) ?

agog [ə'ɡɔɡ] ADJ: **(all) ~** en émoi

agonize ['æɡənaɪz] VI: **he agonized over the problem** ce problème lui a causé bien du tourment

agonizing ['æɡənaɪzɪŋ] ADJ angoissant(e); (cry) déchirant(e)

agony ['æɡənɪ] N (pain) douleur f atroce; (distress) angoisse f; **to be in ~** souffrir le martyre

agony aunt N (BRIT inf) journaliste qui tient la rubrique du courrier du cœur

agony column N courrier m du cœur

agoraphobia [æɡərə'fəubɪə] N agoraphobie f

agoraphobic [æɡərə'fəubɪk] ADJ, N agoraphobe mf

agrarian [ə'ɡrɛərɪən] ADJ agraire

★**agree** [ə'ɡriː] VT (price) convenir de; **to ~ that** (admit) convenir or reconnaître que; **it was agreed that ...** il a été convenu que ...; **to ~ to do** accepter de or consentir à faire ▶ VI: **to ~ with** (person) être d'accord avec; (statements etc) concorder avec; (Ling) s'accorder avec; **to ~ to sth** consentir à qch; **they ~ on this** ils sont d'accord sur ce point; **they agreed on going/a price** ils se mirent d'accord pour y aller/sur un prix; **garlic doesn't ~ with me** je ne supporte pas l'ail

agreeable [ə'ɡriːəbl] ADJ (pleasant) agréable; (willing) consentant(e), d'accord; **are you ~ to this?** est-ce que vous êtes d'accord ?

agreeably [ə'ɡriːəblɪ] ADV agréablement; **to be ~ surprised** être agréablement surpris(e)

agreed [ə'ɡriːd] ADJ (time, place) convenu(e); **to be ~** être d'accord

★**agreement** [ə'ɡriːmənt] N accord m; **in ~** d'accord; **by mutual ~** d'un commun accord

agribusiness ['æɡrɪbɪznɪs] N agro-industrie f, agribusiness m

agricultural [æɡrɪ'kʌltʃərəl] ADJ agricole

★**agriculture** ['æɡrɪkʌltʃə'] N agriculture f

agritourism [æɡrɪ'tuərɪzm] N tourisme m vert, agritourisme m

agroforestry [æɡrəu'fɔrɪstrɪ] N agroforesterie f

agrofuel ['æɡrəufjuəl] N agrocarburant m

agronomist [ə'ɡrɔnəmɪst] N agronome mf

aground [ə'ɡraund] ADV: **to run ~** s'échouer

★**ahead** [ə'hɛd] ADV en avant; devant; **go right** or **straight ~** (direction) allez tout droit; **go ~!** (permission) allez-y !; **~ of** devant; (fig: schedule etc) en avance sur; **~ of time** en avance; **they were (right) ~ of us** ils nous précédaient (de peu), ils étaient (juste) devant nous

ahoy [ə'hɔɪ] EXCL ohé !; **ship ~!** ohé du navire !

AI N ABBR = **Amnesty International**; (*Comput*) = **artificial intelligence**

AID N ABBR (= *artificial insemination by donor*) IAD *f*; (US: = *Agency for International Development*) agence pour le développement international

★**aid** [eɪd] N aide *f*; (*device*) appareil *m*; **with the ~ of** avec l'aide de; **in ~ of** en faveur de ▸ VT aider; **to ~ and abet** (*Law*) se faire le complice de

aide [eɪd] N (*person*) assistant(e)

aide-de-camp [eɪddə'kɔm] N aide *m* de camp

aide-memoire [eɪdmɛm'wɑːʳ] N aide-mémoire *m inv*

★**AIDS** [eɪdz] N ABBR (= *acquired immune (or immuno-) deficiency syndrome*) SIDA *m*

AIH N ABBR (= *artificial insemination by husband*) IAC *f*

ailing ['eɪlɪŋ] ADJ (*person*) souffreteux(euse); (*economy*) malade

ailment ['eɪlmənt] N affection *f*

★**aim** [eɪm] N (*objective*) but *m*; (*skill*): **his ~ is bad** il vise mal ▸ VI (*also*: **to take aim**) viser; **to ~ at** viser; (*fig*) viser (à); avoir pour but *or* ambition; **to ~ to do** avoir l'intention de faire ▸ VT: **to ~ sth (at)** (*gun, camera*) braquer *or* pointer qch (sur); (*missile*) lancer qch (à *or* contre *or* en direction de); (*remark, blow*) destiner *or* adresser qch (à)

aimless ['eɪmlɪs] ADJ sans but

aimlessly ['eɪmlɪslɪ] ADV sans but

ain't [eɪnt] (*inf*) = **am not; aren't; isn't**

★**air** [ɛəʳ] N air *m*; **to throw sth into the ~** (*ball etc*) jeter qch en l'air; **by ~** par avion; **to be on the ~** (*Radio, TV: programme*) être diffusé(e); (: *station*) émettre ▸ VT aérer; (*idea, grievance, views*) mettre sur le tapis; (*knowledge*) faire étalage de ▸ CPD (*currents, attack etc*) aérien(ne)

airbag ['ɛəbæg] N airbag *m*

air base N base aérienne

airbed ['ɛəbed] N (BRIT) matelas *m* pneumatique

airborne ['ɛəbɔːn] ADJ (*plane*) en vol; (*troops*) aéroporté(e); (*particles*) dans l'air; **as soon as the plane was ~** dès que l'avion eut décollé

airbrush ['ɛəbrʌʃ] VT (*photograph, picture*) retoucher à l'aérographe
▸ **airbrush out** VT (*from picture*) effacer à l'aérographe; (*fig*) balayer

air cargo N fret aérien

★**air-conditioned** ['ɛəkən'dɪʃənd] ADJ climatisé(e), à air conditionné

air conditioning [-kən'dɪʃnɪŋ] N climatisation *f*

air-cooled ['ɛəkuːld] ADJ à refroidissement à air

aircraft ['ɛəkrɑːft] N INV avion *m*

aircraft carrier N porte-avions *m inv*

aircrew ['ɛəkruː] N équipage *m* (*d'un avion*)

air cushion N coussin *m* d'air

airdrome ['ɛədrəum] N (US) aérodrome *m*

air-drop ['ɛədrɔp] N (*of supplies*) parachutage *m* ▸ VT (*food, supplies*) parachuter; **the US air-dropped supplies into Bosnia** les États-Unis ont parachuté des vivres en Bosnie

airfare ['ɛəfɛəʳ] N prix *m* du billet d'avion

airfield ['ɛəfiːld] N terrain *m* d'aviation

air force N armée *f* de l'air

air freight N fret aérien

air freshener [-'frɛʃnəʳ] N désodorisant *m*

airgun ['ɛəgʌn] N fusil *m* à air comprimé

air hostess N (BRIT) hôtesse *f* de l'air

airily ['ɛərɪlɪ] ADV d'un air dégagé

airing ['ɛərɪŋ] N: **to give an ~ to** aérer; (*fig: ideas, views etc*) mettre sur le tapis

airing cupboard N (BRIT) placard qui contient la chaudière et dans lequel on met le linge à sécher

airless ['ɛəlɪs] ADJ (*room*) sans air; (*day, afternoon*) étouffant(e)

air letter N (BRIT) aérogramme *m*

airlift ['ɛəlɪft] N pont aérien
▸ **airlift in** VT (*food, supplies*) acheminer par pont aérien
▸ **airlift out** VT (*person, refugees*) évacuer par pont aérien

★**airline** ['ɛəlaɪn] N ligne aérienne, compagnie aérienne

airliner ['ɛəlaɪnəʳ] N avion *m* de ligne

airlock ['ɛəlɔk] N sas *m*

★**airmail** ['ɛəmeɪl] N: **by ~** par avion

airman ['ɛəmən] N (*irreg*) aviateur *m*

air mattress N matelas *m* pneumatique

air mile N air mile *m*

airplane ['ɛəpleɪn] N (US) avion *m*

airplay ['ɛəpleɪ] N temps *m* de diffusion à la radio; **our first single got a lot of ~** notre premier single est beaucoup passé à la radio

air pocket N trou *m* d'air

★**airport** ['ɛəpɔːt] N aéroport *m*

air raid N attaque aérienne

air rifle N carabine *f* à air comprimé

airship ['ɛəʃɪp] N dirigeable *m*

air show ['ɛəʃəu] N (*display*) meeting *m* aérien; (*trade exhibition*) salon *m* de l'aéronautique

airsick ['ɛəsɪk] ADJ: **to be ~** avoir le mal de l'air

airspace ['ɛəspeɪs] N espace *m* aérien

airspeed ['ɛəspiːd] N vitesse relative

air strike N attaque *f* aérienne

airstrip ['ɛəstrɪp] N terrain *m* d'atterrissage

air terminal N aérogare *f*

airtight ['ɛətaɪt] ADJ hermétique

air time N (*Radio, TV*) temps *m* d'antenne

air-traffic control ['ɛətræfɪk-] N contrôle *m* de la navigation aérienne

air-traffic controller N aiguilleur *m* du ciel

airwaves ['ɛəweɪvz] NPL ondes *fpl*; **on the ~** sur les ondes

airway ['ɛəweɪ] N (*Aviat*) voie aérienne ■ **airways** NPL (*Anat*) voies aériennes

airworthy ['ɛəwəːðɪ] ADJ en état de navigation

airy ['ɛərɪ] ADJ bien aéré(e); (*manners*) dégagé(e)

aisle [aɪl] N (*of church: central*) allée *f* centrale; (: *side*) nef *f* latérale, bas-côté *m*; (*in theatre, supermarket*) allée; (*on plane*) couloir *m*

aisle seat N place *f* côté couloir

ajar [ə'dʒɑːʳ] ADJ entrouvert(e)

AK ABBR (US) = **Alaska**

aka ABBR (= *also known as*) alias

akimbo [ə'kɪmbəʊ] ADJ: **with arms ~** les poings sur les hanches, les mains sur les hanches

akin [ə'kɪn] ADJ: **~ to** semblable à, du même ordre que

AL ABBR (*US*) = **Alabama**

ALA N ABBR = **American Library Association**

Ala. ABBR (*US*) = **Alabama**

alabaster ['æləbɑːstəʳ] N albâtre *m* ▸ CPD (*figure, vase*) en albâtre; (*skin, neck*) d'albâtre

à la carte [ælæ'kɑːt] ADV à la carte

alacrity [ə'lækrɪtɪ] N: **with ~** avec empressement, promptement

★**alarm** [ə'lɑːm] N alarme *f* ▸ VT alarmer

alarm call N coup *m* de fil pour réveiller; **could I have an ~ at 7 am, please?** pouvez-vous me réveiller à 7 heures, s'il vous plaît?

alarm clock N réveille-matin *m inv*, réveil *m*

alarmed [ə'lɑːmd] ADJ (*frightened*) alarmé(e); (*protected by an alarm*) protégé(e) par un système d'alarme; **to become ~** prendre peur

alarming [ə'lɑːmɪŋ] ADJ alarmant(e)

alarmingly [ə'lɑːmɪŋlɪ] ADV d'une manière alarmante; **~ close** dangereusement proche; **~ quickly** à une vitesse inquiétante

alarmist [ə'lɑːmɪst] N alarmiste *mf*

alas [ə'læs] EXCL hélas

Alas. ABBR (*US*) = **Alaska**

Alaska [ə'læskə] N Alaska *m*

Albania [æl'beɪnɪə] N Albanie *f*

Albanian [æl'beɪnɪən] ADJ albanais(e) ▸ N Albanais(e); (*Ling*) albanais *m*

albatross ['ælbətrɔs] N albatros *m*

albeit [ɔːl'biːɪt] CONJ bien que + *sub*, encore que + *sub*

albino [æl'biːnəʊ] ADJ, N albinos *mf*

★**album** ['ælbəm] N album *m*

albumen ['ælbjumɪn] N albumine *f*; (*of egg*) albumen *m*

alchemist ['ælkəmɪst] N alchimiste *mf*

alchemy ['ælkɪmɪ] N alchimie *f*

★**alcohol** ['ælkəhɔl] N alcool *m*

alcohol-free ['ælkəhɔlfriː] ADJ sans alcool

alcoholic [ælkə'hɔlɪk] ADJ, N alcoolique *mf*

alcoholism ['ælkəhɔlɪzəm] N alcoolisme *m*

alcopop ['ælkəpɔp] N alcopop *m*

alcove ['ælkəʊv] N alcôve *f*

Ald. ABBR = **alderman**

alder ['ɔːldəʳ] N aulne *m*

alderman ['ɔːldəmən] N (*irreg*) conseiller municipal (*en Angleterre*)

ale [eɪl] N bière *f*

alert [ə'lɜːt] ADJ alerte, vif (vive); (*watchful*) vigilant(e) ▸ N alerte *f*; **on the ~** sur le qui-vive; (*Mil*) en état d'alerte ▸ VT alerter; **to ~ sb (to sth)** attirer l'attention de qn (sur qch); **to ~ sb to the dangers of sth** avertir qn des dangers de qch

alertness [ə'lɜːtnɪs] N vivacité *f*

Aleutian Islands [ə'luːʃən-] NPL îles Aléoutiennes

A level N ABBR (*BRIT*: = *Advanced level*) ≈ baccalauréat *m*; *voir article*

Les **A levels** (*Advanced levels*) sont les épreuves de fin d'études secondaires en Angleterre, au pays de Galles et en Irlande du Nord. La préparation se fait en deux ans, la première année étant elle-même sanctionnée par une série d'examens, les AS (*Advanced Subsidiary exams*). Les A levels sont beaucoup plus spécialisés que le baccalauréat puisqu'ils ne comportent qu'entre trois et cinq matières. Les notes obtenues déterminent si le candidat pourra entreprendre des études supérieures et, si c'est le cas, s'il sera accepté par l'université de son choix.

Alexandria [ælɪg'zɑːndrɪə] N Alexandrie

alfalfa [æl'fælfə] N luzerne *f*

alfresco [æl'freskəʊ] ADJ, ADV en plein air

algae ['ældʒiː] N algues *fpl*

algebra ['ældʒɪbrə] N algèbre *m*

Algeria [æl'dʒɪərɪə] N Algérie *f*

Algerian [æl'dʒɪərɪən] ADJ algérien(ne) ▸ N Algérien(ne)

Algiers [æl'dʒɪəz] N Alger

algorithm ['ælgərɪðəm] N algorithme *m*

alias ['eɪlɪəs] ADV alias ▸ N faux nom, nom d'emprunt

alibi ['ælɪbaɪ] N alibi *m*

alien ['eɪlɪən] N (*from abroad*) étranger(-ère); (*from outer space*) extraterrestre *mf* ▸ ADJ: **~ (to)** étranger(-ère) (à)

alienate ['eɪlɪəneɪt] VT aliéner; (*subj: person*) s'aliéner

alienated ['eɪlɪəneɪtɪd] ADJ aliéné(e); **to feel ~ (from sb/sth)** se sentir étranger(-ère) (à qn/qch)

alienation [eɪlɪə'neɪʃən] N aliénation *f*

alight [ə'laɪt] ADJ, ADV en feu ▸ VI mettre pied à terre; (*passenger*) descendre; (*bird*) se poser

align [ə'laɪn] VT aligner

alignment [ə'laɪnmənt] N alignement *m*; **it's out of ~ (with)** ce n'est pas aligné (avec)

alike [ə'laɪk] ADJ semblable, pareil(le); **to look ~** se ressembler ▸ ADV de même

alimony ['ælɪmənɪ] N (*payment*) pension *f* alimentaire

★**alive** [ə'laɪv] ADJ vivant(e); (*active*) plein(e) de vie; **~ with** grouillant(e) de; **~ to** sensible à

alkali ['ælkəlaɪ] N alcali *m*

alkaline ['ælkəlaɪn] ADJ alcalin(e)

all [ɔːl]

ADJ (*singular*) tout(e); (*plural*) tous (toutes); **all day** toute la journée; **all night** toute la nuit; **all men** tous les hommes; **all five** tous les cinq; **all the food** toute la nourriture; **all the books** tous les livres; **all the time** tout le temps; **all his life** toute sa vie

▸ PRON **1** tout; **I ate it all, I ate all of it** j'ai tout mangé; **all of us went** nous y sommes tous allés; **all of the boys went** tous les garçons y sont allés; **is that all?** c'est tout?; (*in shop*) ce sera tout?

2 (*in phrases*): **above all** surtout, par-dessus tout; **after all** après tout; **at all**: **not at all** (*in answer to question*) pas du tout; (*in answer to thanks*) je vous en prie !; **I'm not at all tired** je ne suis pas du tout fatigué(e); **anything at all will do** n'importe quoi fera l'affaire; **all in all** tout bien considéré, en fin de compte
▶ ADV: **all alone** tout(e) seul(e); **it's not as hard as all that** ce n'est pas si difficile que ça; **all the more/the better** d'autant plus/mieux; **all but** presque, pratiquement; **to be all in** (*BRIT inf*) être complètement à plat; **the score is 2 all** le score est de 2 partout

Allah ['ælə] N Allah *m*

all-around [ɔːlə'raʊnd] ADJ (*US*) = **all-round**

allay [ə'leɪ] VT (*fears*) apaiser, calmer

all clear N (*also fig*) fin *f* d'alerte

allegation [ælɪ'ɡeɪʃən] N allégation *f*

allege [ə'lɛdʒ] VT alléguer, prétendre; **he is alleged to have said** il aurait dit

alleged [ə'lɛdʒd] ADJ prétendu(e)

allegedly [ə'lɛdʒɪdlɪ] ADV à ce que l'on prétend, paraît-il

allegiance [ə'liːdʒəns] N fidélité *f*, obéissance *f*

allegorical [ælɪ'ɡɒrɪkl] ADJ allégorique

allegory ['ælɪɡərɪ] N allégorie *f*

alleluia [ælɪ'luːjə] EXCL = **hallelujah**

all-embracing ['ɔːlɪm'breɪsɪŋ] ADJ universel(le)

allergen ['ælədʒɛn] N allergène *m*

★**allergic** [ə'lɜːdʒɪk] ADJ: **~ to** allergique à; **I'm ~ to penicillin** je suis allergique à la pénicilline

allergy ['ælədʒɪ] N allergie *f*

alleviate [ə'liːvɪeɪt] VT (*suffering*) soulager, adoucir; (*symptoms*) atténuer; (*poverty*) réduire

alleviation [əliːvɪ'eɪʃən] N (*of pain, suffering*) soulagement *m*; (*of symptoms*) atténuation *f*; (*of poverty*) réduction *f*

alley ['ælɪ] N ruelle *f*; (*in garden*) allée *f*

alleyway ['ælɪweɪ] N ruelle *f*

alliance [ə'laɪəns] N alliance *f*

allied ['ælaɪd] ADJ allié(e)

alligator ['ælɪɡeɪtə'] N alligator *m*

all-important ['ɔːlɪm'pɔːtənt] ADJ capital(e), crucial(e)

all-in ['ɔːlɪn] ADJ, ADV (*BRIT: charge*) tout compris

all-in wrestling N (*BRIT*) catch *m*

alliteration [əlɪtə'reɪʃən] N allitération *f*

all-night ['ɔːl'naɪt] ADJ ouvert(e) *or* qui dure toute la nuit

allocate ['æləkeɪt] VT (*share out*) répartir, distribuer; **to ~ sth to** (*duties*) assigner *or* attribuer qch à; (*sum, time*) allouer qch à; **to ~ sth for** affecter qch à

allocation [ælə'keɪʃən] N répartition *f*; attribution *f*; allocation *f*; affectation *f*; (*money*) crédit(s) *m*(*pl*), somme(s) allouée(s)

allot [ə'lɒt] VT (*share out*) répartir, distribuer; **to ~ sth to** (*time*) allouer qch à; (*duties*) assigner qch à; **in the allotted time** dans le temps imparti

allotment [ə'lɒtmənt] N (*share*) part *f*; (*garden*) lopin *m* de terre (*loué à la municipalité*)

all-out ['ɔːlaut] ADJ (*effort etc*) total(e)

★**allow** [ə'lau] VT (*practice, behaviour*) permettre, autoriser; (*sum to spend etc*) accorder, allouer; (*sum, time estimated*) compter, prévoir; (*claim, goal*) admettre; (*concede*): **to ~ that** convenir que; **to ~ sb to do** permettre à qn de faire, autoriser qn à faire; **he is allowed to ...** on lui permet de ...; **smoking is not allowed** il est interdit de fumer; **we must ~ three days for the journey** il faut compter trois jours pour le voyage
▶ **allow for** VT FUS tenir compte de

allowable [ə'lauəbl] ADJ (*permissible*) admissible; (*non-taxed: costs, expenses*) déductible

allowance [ə'lauəns] N (*money received*) allocation *f*; (: *from parent etc*) subside *m*; (: *for expenses*) indemnité *f*; (*US: pocket money*) argent *m* de poche; (*Tax*) somme *f* déductible du revenu imposable, abattement *m*; **to make allowances for** (*person*) essayer de comprendre; (*thing*) tenir compte de

alloy ['ælɔɪ] N alliage *m*

★**all right** ADV (*feel, work*) bien; (*as answer*) d'accord

all-round ['ɔːl'raund] ADJ compétent(e) dans tous les domaines; (*athlete etc*) complet(-ète)

all-rounder [ɔːl'raundə'] N (*BRIT*): **to be a good ~** être doué(e) en tout

allspice ['ɔːlspaɪs] N poivre *m* de la Jamaïque

all-time ['ɔːl'taɪm] ADJ (*record*) sans précédent, absolu(e)

allude [ə'luːd] VI: **to ~ to** faire allusion à

allure [ə'luə'] N (*attraction: of place, event*) attrait *m*; (: *of person*) charme *m*; **sexual ~** pouvoir *m* de séduction

alluring [ə'luərɪŋ] ADJ séduisant(e), alléchant(e)

allusion [ə'luːʒən] N allusion *f*

alluvial [ə'luːvɪəl] ADJ (*soil, plain*) alluvial(e); (*deposits*) alluvionnaire

alluvium [ə'luːvɪəm] N alluvions *fpl*

ally N ['ælaɪ] allié *m* ▶ VT [ə'laɪ]: **to ~ o.s. with** s'allier avec

alma mater ['ælmə'mɑːtə'] N (*formal: school, university*) alma mater *f inv*; (*US: official song*) hymne *m*

almanac, almanack ['ɔːlmənæk] N almanach *m*

almighty [ɔːl'maɪtɪ] ADJ tout(e)-puissant(e); (*tremendous*) énorme

almond ['ɑːmənd] N amande *f*

★**almost** ['ɔːlməust] ADV presque; **he ~ fell** il a failli tomber

alms [ɑːmz] N aumône(s) *f*(*pl*)

aloft [ə'lɒft] ADV en haut, en l'air; (*Naut*) dans la mâture

★**alone** [ə'ləun] ADJ, ADV seul(e); **to leave sb ~** laisser qn tranquille; **to leave sth ~** ne pas toucher à qch; **let ~ ...** sans parler de ...; encore moins ...

★**along** [ə'lɒŋ] PREP le long de ▶ ADV: **is he coming ~ with us?** vient-il avec nous ?; **he was hopping/limping ~** il venait *or* avançait en sautillant/boitant; **~ with** avec, en plus de; (*person*) en compagnie de; **all ~** (*all the time*) depuis le début

alongside [ələŋ'saɪd] PREP (*along*) le long de; (*beside*) à côté de ▶ ADV bord à bord; côte à côte;

we brought our boat ~ (of a pier, shore etc) nous avons accosté

aloof [ə'lu:f] ADJ distant(e) ▶ ADV à distance, à l'écart; **to stand ~** se tenir à l'écart or à distance

aloofness [ə'lu:fnɪs] N réserve (hautaine), attitude distante

★**aloud** [ə'laud] ADV à haute voix

★**alphabet** ['ælfəbɛt] N alphabet m

alphabetical [ælfə'bɛtɪkl] ADJ alphabétique; **in ~ order** par ordre alphabétique

alphabetically [ælfə'bɛtɪklɪ] ADV par ordre alphabétique

alphanumeric [ælfənju:'mɛrɪk] ADJ alphanumérique

alpine ['ælpaɪn] ADJ alpin(e), alpestre; **~ hut** cabane f or refuge m de montagne; **~ pasture** pâturage m (de montagne); **~ skiing** ski alpin

★**Alps** [ælps] NPL: **the ~** les Alpes fpl

★**already** [ɔ:l'rɛdɪ] ADV déjà

alright ['ɔ:l'raɪt] ADV = **all right**

Alsace [æl'sæs] N Alsace f

Alsatian [æl'seɪʃən] ADJ alsacien(ne), d'Alsace ▶ N Alsacien(ne); (BRIT: dog) berger allemand

★**also** ['ɔ:lsəu] ADV aussi

Alta. ABBR (CANADA) = **Alberta**

altar ['ɔltə'] N autel m

alter ['ɔltə'] VT, VI changer

alteration [ɔltə'reɪʃən] N changement m, modification f; **timetable subject to ~** horaires sujets à modifications **alterations** NPL (Sewing) retouches fpl; (Archit) modifications fpl

altercation [ɔltə'keɪʃən] N altercation f

alternate ADJ [ɔl'tə:nɪt] alterné(e), alternant(e), alternatif(-ive); (US) = **alternative**; **on ~ days** un jour sur deux, tous les deux jours ▶ VI ['ɔltə:neɪt] alterner; **to ~ with** alterner avec

alternately [ɔl'tə:nɪtlɪ] ADV alternativement, en alternant

alternating ['ɔltə:neɪtɪŋ] ADJ (current) alternatif(-ive)

★**alternative** [ɔl'tə:nətɪv] ADJ (solution, plan) autre, de remplacement; (energy) doux (douce); (lifestyle) parallèle ▶ N (choice) alternative f; (other possibility) autre possibilité f

alternatively [ɔl'tə:nətɪvlɪ] ADV: **~ one could ...** une autre or l'autre solution serait de ...

alternative medicine N médecines fpl parallèles or douces

alternator ['ɔltə:neɪtə'] N (Aut) alternateur m

★**although** [ɔ:l'ðəu] CONJ bien que + sub

altitude ['æltɪtju:d] N altitude f

alto ['æltəu] N (female) contralto m; (male) haute-contre f

altogether [ɔ:ltə'gɛðə'] ADV entièrement, tout à fait; (on the whole) tout compte fait; (in all) en tout; **how much is that ~?** ça fait combien en tout?

altruism ['æltruɪzəm] N altruisme m

altruistic [æltru'ɪstɪk] ADJ altruiste

aluminium [ælju'mɪnɪəm], (US) **aluminum** [ə'lu:mɪnəm] N aluminium m

alumna [ə'lʌmnə] (pl **alumnae** [-ni:]) N (US Scol) ancienne élève; (University) ancienne étudiante

alumnus [ə'lʌmnəs] (pl **alumni** [-naɪ]) N (US Scol) ancien élève; (University) ancien étudiant

★**always** ['ɔ:lweɪz] ADV toujours

Alzheimer's ['æltshaɪməz], **Alzheimer's disease** N maladie f d'Alzheimer

AM ABBR = **amplitude modulation** ▶ N ABBR (= Assembly Member) député m au Parlement gallois

am [æm] VB see **be**

a.m. ADV ABBR (= ante meridiem) du matin

AMA N ABBR = **American Medical Association**

amalgam [ə'mælgəm] N amalgame m

amalgamate [ə'mælgəmeɪt] VT, VI fusionner

amalgamation [əmælgə'meɪʃən] N fusion f; (Comm) fusionnement m

amass [ə'mæs] VT amasser

amateur ['æmətə'] N amateur(-trice) ▶ ADJ (Sport) amateur inv; **~ dramatics** le théâtre amateur

amateurish ['æmətərɪʃ] ADJ (pej) d'amateur, un peu amateur

amaze [ə'meɪz] VT stupéfier

amazed [ə'meɪzd] ADJ stupéfait(e); **to be ~ (at)** être stupéfait(e) (de)

amazement [ə'meɪzmənt] N surprise f, étonnement m

★**amazing** [ə'meɪzɪŋ] ADJ étonnant(e), incroyable; (bargain, offer) exceptionnel(le)

amazingly [ə'meɪzɪŋlɪ] ADV incroyablement

Amazon ['æməzən] N (Geo, Mythology) Amazone f ▶ CPD amazonien(ne), de l'Amazone; **the ~ basin** le bassin de l'Amazone; **the ~ jungle** la forêt amazonienne

Amazonian [æmə'zəunɪən] ADJ amazonien(ne)

ambassador [æm'bæsədə'] N ambassadeur m

amber ['æmbə'] N ambre m; **at ~** (BRIT Aut) à l'orange

ambidextrous [æmbɪ'dɛkstrəs] ADJ ambidextre

ambience ['æmbɪəns] N ambiance f

ambient ['æmbɪənt] ADJ ambiant(e)

ambiguity [æmbɪ'gjuɪt] N ambiguïté f

ambiguous [æm'bɪgjuəs] ADJ ambigu(ë)

ambit ['æmbɪt] N (formal) étendue f; **to be** or **fall within the ~ of sth** relever de qch; **to be** or **fall outside the ~ of sth** ne pas être du ressort de qch

★**ambition** [æm'bɪʃən] N ambition f

ambitious [æm'bɪʃəs] ADJ ambitieux(-euse)

ambivalence [æm'bɪvələns] N ambivalence f

ambivalent [æm'bɪvələnt] ADJ (attitude) ambivalent(e)

amble ['æmbl] VI (also: **to amble along**) aller d'un pas tranquille

★**ambulance** ['æmbjuləns] N ambulance f; **call an ~!** appelez une ambulance!

ambush ['æmbuʃ] N embuscade f ▶ VT tendre une embuscade à

ameba [ə'mi:bə] N (US) = **amoeba**

ameliorate [ə'mi:lɪəreɪt] VT améliorer

amen ['ɑ:'mɛn] EXCL amen

amenable [ə'mi:nəbl] ADJ: **~ to** (advice etc) disposé(e) à écouter or suivre; **~ to the law** responsable devant la loi

amend [əˈmɛnd] VT (law) amender; (text) corriger; (habits) réformer ▶ VI s'amender, se corriger; **to make amends** réparer ses torts, faire amende honorable

amendment [əˈmɛndmənt] N (to law) amendement m; (to text) correction f

amenities [əˈmiːnɪtɪz] NPL aménagements mpl, équipements mpl

amenity [əˈmiːnɪtɪ] N charme m, agrément m

★**America** [əˈmɛrɪkə] N Amérique f

American [əˈmɛrɪkən] ADJ américain(e) ▶ N Américain(e)

American football N (BRIT) football m américain

Americanize [əˈmɛrɪkənaɪz] VT américaniser

amethyst [ˈæmɪθɪst] N améthyste f

Amex [ˈæmɛks] N ABBR = **American Stock Exchange**

amiable [ˈeɪmɪəbl] ADJ aimable, affable

amicable [ˈæmɪkəbl] ADJ amical(e); (Law) à l'amiable

amicably [ˈæmɪkəblɪ] ADV amicalement

amid [əˈmɪd], **amidst** [əˈmɪdst] PREP parmi, au milieu de

amiss [əˈmɪs] ADJ, ADV: **there's something ~** il y a quelque chose qui ne va pas or qui cloche; **to take sth ~** prendre qch mal or de travers

ammo [ˈæməʊ] N ABBR (inf) = **ammunition**

ammonia [əˈməʊnɪə] N (gas) ammoniac m; (liquid) ammoniaque f

ammunition [æmjuˈnɪʃən] N munitions fpl; (fig) arguments mpl

ammunition dump N dépôt m de munitions

amnesia [æmˈniːzɪə] N amnésie f

amnesty [ˈæmnɪstɪ] N amnistie f; **to grant an ~ to** accorder une amnistie à

Amnesty International N Amnesty International

amoeba, (US) **ameba** [əˈmiːbə] N amibe f

amok [əˈmɔk] ADV: **to run ~** être pris(e) d'un accès de folie furieuse

★**among** [əˈmʌŋ], **amongst** [əˈmʌŋst] PREP parmi, entre

amoral [æˈmɔrəl] ADJ amoral(e)

amorous [ˈæmərəs] ADJ amoureux(-euse)

amorphous [əˈmɔːfəs] ADJ amorphe

amortization [əmɔːtaɪˈzeɪʃən] N (Comm) amortissement m

★**amount** [əˈmaʊnt] N (sum of money) somme f; (total) montant m; (quantity) quantité f; nombre m; **the total ~** (of money) le montant total ▶ VI: **to ~ to** (total) s'élever à; (be same as) équivaloir à, revenir à; **this amounts to a refusal** cela équivaut à un refus

amp [æmp], **ampère** [ˈæmpɛəʳ] N ampère m; **a 13 ~ plug** une fiche de 13 A

ampersand [ˈæmpəsænd] N signe &, « et » commercial

amphetamine [æmˈfɛtəmiːn] N amphétamine f

amphibian [æmˈfɪbɪən] N batracien m

amphibious [æmˈfɪbɪəs] ADJ amphibie

amphitheatre, (US) **amphitheater** [ˈæmfɪθɪətəʳ] N amphithéâtre m

ample [ˈæmpl] ADJ ample, spacieux(-euse); (enough): **this is ~** c'est largement suffisant; **to have ~ time/room** avoir bien assez de temps/place, avoir largement le temps/la place

amplifier [ˈæmplɪfaɪəʳ] N amplificateur m

amplify [ˈæmplɪfaɪ] VT amplifier

amply [ˈæmplɪ] ADV amplement, largement

ampoule, (US) **ampule** [ˈæmpuːl] N (Med) ampoule f

amputate [ˈæmpjuteɪt] VT amputer

amputation [æmpjuˈteɪʃən] N amputation f

amputee [æmpjuˈtiː] N amputé(e)

Amsterdam [ˈæmstədæm] N Amsterdam

amt ABBR = **amount**

Amtrak [ˈæmtræk] (US) N société mixte de transports ferroviaires interurbains pour voyageurs

amuck [əˈmʌk] ADV = **amok**

amulet [ˈæmjulət] N amulette f

amuse [əˈmjuːz] VT amuser; **to ~ o.s. with sth/by doing sth** se divertir avec qch/à faire qch; **to be amused at** être amusé par; **he was not amused** il n'a pas apprécié

amusement [əˈmjuːzmənt] N amusement m; (pastime) distraction f

amusement arcade N salle f de jeu

amusement park N parc m d'attractions

amusing [əˈmjuːzɪŋ] ADJ amusant(e), divertissant(e)

an [æn, ən, n] INDEF ART see **a**

ANA N ABBR = **American Newspaper Association**; **American Nurses Association**

anachronism [əˈnækrənɪzəm] N anachronisme m

anachronistic [ənækrəˈnɪstɪk] ADJ anachronique

anaemia, (US) **anemia** [əˈniːmɪə] N anémie f

anaemic, (US) **anemic** [əˈniːmɪk] ADJ anémique

anaerobic [ænɛəˈrəʊbɪk] ADJ (animal, process) anaérobie; (exercise) d'anaérobie

anaesthetic, (US) **anesthetic** [ænɪsˈθɛtɪk] ADJ, N anesthésique m; **under the ~** sous anesthésie; **local/general ~** anesthésie locale/générale

anaesthetist, (US) **anesthetist** [æˈniːsθɪtɪst] N anesthésiste mf

anaesthetize, (US) **anesthetize** [əˈniːsθətaɪz] VT anesthésier

anagram [ˈænəgræm] N anagramme m

anal [ˈeɪnl] ADJ anal(e)

analgesic [ænælˈdʒiːzɪk] ADJ, N analgésique m

analog, analogue [ˈænəlɒg] ADJ (watch, computer) analogique

analogous [əˈnæləgəs] ADJ: **~ (to or with)** analogue (à)

analogy [əˈnælədʒɪ] N analogie f; **to draw an ~ between** établir une analogie entre

analyse, (US) **analyze** [ˈænəlaɪz] VT analyser

analysis [əˈnæləsɪs] (pl **analyses** [-siːz]) N analyse f; **in the last ~** en dernière analyse

analyst [ˈænəlɪst] N (political analyst etc) analyste mf; (US) psychanalyste mf

analytic [ænəˈlɪtɪk], **analytical** [ænəˈlɪtɪkl] ADJ analytique

analyze ['ænəlaɪz] VT (US) = **analyse**

anarchic [æ'nɑːkɪk] ADJ anarchique

anarchist ['ænəkɪst] ADJ, N anarchiste mf

anarchy ['ænəkɪ] N anarchie f

anathema [ə'næθɪmə] N: **it is ~ to him** il a cela en abomination

anatomical [ænə'tɔmɪkl] ADJ anatomique

anatomy [ə'nætəmɪ] N anatomie f

ANC N ABBR (= African National Congress) ANC m

ancestor ['ænsɪstə^r] N ancêtre m, aïeul m

ancestral [æn'sɛstrəl] ADJ ancestral(e)

ancestry ['ænsɪstrɪ] N ancêtres mpl; ascendance f

anchor ['æŋkə^r] N ancre f; **to weigh ~** lever l'ancre ▶ VI (also: **to drop anchor**) jeter l'ancre, mouiller ▶ VT mettre à l'ancre; (fig): **to ~ sth to** fixer qch à

anchorage ['æŋkərɪdʒ] N mouillage m, ancrage m

anchor man, anchor woman N (irreg) (TV, Radio) présentateur(-trice)

anchovy ['æntʃəvɪ] N anchois m

ancient ['eɪnʃənt] ADJ ancien(ne), antique; (person) d'un âge vénérable; (car) antédiluvien(ne); **~ monument** monument m historique

ancillary [æn'sɪlərɪ] ADJ auxiliaire

★**and** [ænd] CONJ et; **~ so on** et ainsi de suite; **try ~ come** tâchez de venir; **come ~ sit here** venez vous asseoir ici; **he talked ~ talked** il a parlé pendant des heures; **better ~ better** de mieux en mieux; **more ~ more** de plus en plus

Andes ['ændiːz] NPL: **the ~** les Andes fpl

Andorra [æn'dɔːrə] N (principauté f d')Andorre f

androgynous [æn'drɔdʒɪnəs] ADJ androgyne

android ['ændrɔɪd] N androïde m

anecdotal [ænɪk'dəutl] ADJ (account) anecdotique; **~ evidence** témoignages mpl

anecdote ['ænɪkdəut] N anecdote f

anemia [ə'niːmɪə] N (US) = **anaemia** etc

anemic [ə'niːmɪk] ADJ (US) = **anaemic**

anemone [ə'nɛmənɪ] N (Bot) anémone f; **sea ~** anémone de mer

anesthesiologist [ænɪsθiːzɪ'ɔlədʒɪst] N (US) anesthésiste mf

anesthetic [ænɪs'θɛtɪk] N, ADJ (US) = **anaesthetic**

anesthetist [æ'niːsθɪtɪst] N = **anaesthetist**

anesthetize [ə'niːsθətaɪz] VT (US) = **anaesthetize**

anew [ə'njuː] ADV à nouveau

★**angel** ['eɪndʒəl] N ange m

angel dust N poussière f d'ange

angelic [æn'dʒɛlɪk] ADJ angélique

★**anger** ['æŋgə^r] N colère f ▶ VT mettre en colère, irriter

angina [æn'dʒaɪnə] N angine f de poitrine

★**angle** ['æŋgl] N angle m; **from their ~** de leur point de vue ▶ VI: **to ~ for** (trout) pêcher; (compliments) chercher

angler ['æŋglə^r] N pêcheur(-euse) à la ligne

Anglican ['æŋglɪkən] ADJ, N anglican(e)

anglicize ['æŋglɪsaɪz] VT angliciser

angling ['æŋglɪŋ] N pêche f à la ligne

Anglo- ['æŋgləu] PREFIX anglo(-)

Anglo-French ['æŋgləu'frɛntʃ] ADJ anglo-français(e)

Anglo-Saxon ['æŋgləu'sæksən] ADJ, N anglo-saxon(ne)

Angola [æŋ'gəulə] N Angola m

Angolan [æŋ'gəulən] ADJ angolais(e) ▶ N Angolais(e)

angrily ['æŋgrɪlɪ] ADV avec colère

★**angry** ['æŋgrɪ] ADJ en colère, furieux(-euse); (wound) enflammé(e); **to be ~ with sb/at sth** être furieux contre qn/de qch; **to get ~** se fâcher, se mettre en colère; **to make sb ~** mettre qn en colère

angst [æŋst] N angoisse f

anguish ['æŋgwɪʃ] N angoisse f

anguished ['æŋgwɪʃt] ADJ (mentally) angoissé(e); (physically) plein(e) de souffrance

angular ['æŋgjulə] ADJ anguleux(-euse)

★**animal** ['ænɪməl] N animal m ▶ ADJ animal(e)

animal rights NPL droits mpl de l'animal

animate VT ['ænɪmeɪt] animer ▶ ADJ ['ænɪmɪt] animé(e), vivant(e)

animated ['ænɪmeɪtɪd] ADJ animé(e)

animation [ænɪ'meɪʃən] N (of person) entrain m; (of street, Cine) animation f

animator ['ænɪmeɪtə^r] N (for films, cartoons) animateur(-trice)

animosity [ænɪ'mɔsɪtɪ] N animosité f

aniseed ['ænɪsiːd] N anis m

Ankara ['æŋkərə] N Ankara

ankle ['æŋkl] N cheville f

ankle socks NPL socquettes fpl

annals ['ænəlz] NPL annales fpl; **in the ~ of sth** dans les annales de qch

annex N ['ænɛks] (BRIT: also: **annexe**) annexe f ▶ VT [ə'nɛks] annexer

annexation [ænɛks'eɪʃən] N annexion f

annihilate [ə'naɪəleɪt] VT annihiler, anéantir

annihilation [ənaɪə'leɪʃən] N anéantissement m

★**anniversary** [ænɪ'vəːsərɪ] N anniversaire m

anniversary dinner N dîner commémoratif or anniversaire

annotate ['ænəteɪt] VT annoter

annotation [ænə'teɪʃən] N annotation f

★**announce** [ə'nauns] VT annoncer; (birth, death) faire part de; **he announced that he wasn't going** il a déclaré qu'il n'irait pas

announcement [ə'naunsmənt] N annonce f; (for births etc: in newspaper) avis m de faire-part; (: letter, card) faire-part m; **I'd like to make an ~** j'ai une communication à faire

announcer [ə'naunsə^r] N (Radio, TV: between programmes) speaker(ine); (: in a programme) présentateur(-trice)

annoy [ə'nɔɪ] VT agacer, ennuyer, contrarier; **to be annoyed (at sth/with sb)** être en colère or irrité (contre qch/qn); **don't get annoyed!** ne vous fâchez pas !

annoyance [ə'nɔɪəns] N mécontentement m, contrariété f

★**annoying** [ə'nɔɪɪŋ] ADJ agaçant(e), contrariant(e)

491

★**annual** ['ænjuəl] ADJ annuel(le) ▶ N (Bot) plante annuelle; (book) album m

annual general meeting N (BRIT) assemblée générale annuelle

annually ['ænjuəlɪ] ADV annuellement

annual report N rapport annuel

annuity [ə'njuːɪtɪ] N rente f; **life ~** rente viagère

annul [ə'nʌl] VT annuler; (law) abroger

annulment [ə'nʌlmənt] N annulation f; abrogation f

annum ['ænəm] N see **per**

Annunciation [ənʌnsɪ'eɪʃən] N Annonciation f

anode ['ænəud] N anode f

anodyne ['ænədaɪn] ADJ anodin(e)

anoint [ə'nɔɪnt] VT oindre

anomalous [ə'nɔmələs] ADJ anormal(e)

anomaly [ə'nɔməlɪ] N anomalie f

anon [ə'nɔn] ADV (literary) sous peu

anon. [ə'nɔn] ABBR = **anonymous**

anonymity [ænə'nɪmɪtɪ] N anonymat m

anonymous [ə'nɔnɪməs] ADJ anonyme; **to remain ~** garder l'anonymat

anonymously [ə'nɔnɪməslɪ] ADV anonymement

anorak ['ænəræk] N anorak m

anorexia [ænə'rɛksɪə] N (also: **anorexia nervosa**) anorexie f

anorexic [ænə'rɛksɪk] ADJ, N anorexique mf

★**another** [ə'nʌðə'] ADJ: **~ book** (one more) un autre livre, encore un livre, un livre de plus; (a different one) un autre livre; **~ drink?** encore un verre ?; **in ~ five years** dans cinq ans ▶ PRON un(e) autre, encore un(e), un(e) de plus; see also **one**

ANSI ['ænsɪ] N ABBR (= American National Standards Institution) ANSI m (= Institut américain de normalisation)

★**answer** ['ɑːnsə'] N réponse f; (to problem) solution f; **in ~ to your letter** suite à or en réponse à votre lettre ▶ VI répondre ▶ VT (reply to) répondre à; (problem) résoudre; (prayer) exaucer; **to ~ the phone** répondre (au téléphone); **to ~ the bell** or **the door** aller or venir ouvrir (la porte)
▶ **answer back** VI répondre, répliquer
▶ **answer for** VT FUS répondre de, se porter garant de; (crime, one's actions) répondre de
▶ **answer to** VT FUS (description) répondre or correspondre à

answerable ['ɑːnsərəbl] ADJ: **~ (to sb/for sth)** responsable (devant qn/de qch); **I am ~ to no-one** je n'ai de comptes à rendre à personne

answering machine ['ɑːnsərɪŋ-] N répondeur m

answerphone ['ɑːnsəfəun] N (esp BRIT) répondeur m (téléphonique)

ant [ænt] N fourmi f

ANTA N ABBR = **American National Theater and Academy**

antacid [ænt'æsɪd] N alcalin m ▶ CPD (tablet, medication) antiacide

antagonism [æn'tægənɪzəm] N antagonisme m

antagonist [æn'tægənɪst] N antagoniste mf, adversaire mf

antagonistic [æntægə'nɪstɪk] ADJ (attitude, feelings) hostile

antagonize [æn'tægənaɪz] VT éveiller l'hostilité de, contrarier

Antarctic [ænt'ɑːktɪk] ADJ antarctique, austral(e) ▶ N: **the ~** l'Antarctique m

Antarctica [ænt'ɑːktɪkə] N Antarctique m, Terres Australes

Antarctic Circle N cercle m Antarctique

Antarctic Ocean N océan m Antarctique or Austral

ante ['æntɪ] N: **to up the ~** faire monter les enjeux

ante... ['æntɪ] PREFIX anté..., anti..., pré...

anteater ['æntiːtə'] N fourmilier m, tamanoir m

antecedent [æntɪ'siːdənt] N antécédent m

antechamber ['æntɪtʃeɪmbə'] N antichambre f

antelope ['æntɪləup] N antilope f

antenatal [æntɪ'neɪtl] ADJ prénatal(e)

antenatal clinic N service m de consultation prénatale

antenna [æn'tɛnə] (pl **antennae** [-niː]) N antenne f

anteroom ['æntɪruːm] N antichambre f

anthem ['ænθəm] N motet m; **national ~** hymne national

ant-hill ['ænthɪl] N fourmilière f

anthology [æn'θɔlədʒɪ] N anthologie f

anthrax ['ænθræks] N anthrax m

anthropologist [ænθrə'pɔlədʒɪst] N anthropologue mf

anthropology [ænθrə'pɔlədʒɪ] N anthropologie f

anthropomorphic [ænθrəpə'mɔːfɪk] ADJ anthropomorphique

anthropomorphism [ænθrəpə'mɔːfɪzəm] N anthropomorphisme m

anti ['æntɪ] PREFIX anti-

anti-aircraft [æntɪ'ɛəkrɑːft] ADJ antiaérien(ne)

anti-aircraft defence N défense f contre avions, DCA f

anti-allergenic [æntɪælə'dʒɛnɪk] ADJ antiallergène

antiballistic [æntɪbə'lɪstɪk] ADJ antibalistique

antibiotic [æntɪbaɪ'ɔtɪk] ADJ, N antibiotique m

antibody ['æntɪbɔdɪ] N anticorps m

anticipate [æn'tɪsɪpeɪt] VT s'attendre à, prévoir; (wishes, request) aller au devant de, devancer; **this is worse than I anticipated** c'est pire que je ne pensais; **as anticipated** comme prévu

anticipation [æntɪsɪ'peɪʃən] N attente f; **thanking you in ~** en vous remerciant d'avance, avec mes remerciements anticipés

anticlimax [æntɪ'klaɪmæks] N déception f

anticlockwise [æntɪ'klɔkwaɪz] (BRIT) ADV dans le sens inverse des aiguilles d'une montre

antics ['æntɪks] NPL singeries fpl

anticyclone [æntɪ'saɪkləun] N anticyclone m

antidepressant [æntɪdɪ'prɛsnt] N antidépresseur m

antidote ['æntɪdəut] N antidote m, contrepoison m

antifreeze ['æntɪfriːz] N antigel m

antigen ['æntɪdʒən] N antigène m

anti-globalization [æntɪgləʊbəlaɪ'zeɪʃən] N antimondialisation f

Antigua and Barbuda [æn'tiːgə ænd bɑː'buːdə] N Antigua-et-Barbuda f

anti-hero ['æntɪhɪərəʊ] N antihéros m

antihistamine [æntɪ'hɪstəmɪn] N antihistaminique m

Antilles [æn'tɪliːz] NPL: **the ~** les Antilles fpl

antimatter ['æntɪmætəʳ] N antimatière f

antioxidant [æntɪ'ɒksɪdənt] N antioxydant(e)

antipathy [æn'tɪpəθɪ] N antipathie f

antiperspirant [æntɪ'pəːspɪrənt] N déodorant m

Antipodean [æntɪpə'diːən] ADJ australien(ne) et néo-zélandais(e), d'Australie et de Nouvelle-Zélande

Antipodes [æn'tɪpədiːz] NPL: **the ~** l'Australie f et la Nouvelle-Zélande

antiquarian [æntɪ'kwɛərɪən] ADJ: **~ bookshop** librairie f d'ouvrages anciens ▶ N expert m en objets or livres anciens; amateur m d'antiquités

antiquated ['æntɪkweɪtɪd] ADJ vieilli(e), suranné(e), vieillot(te)

★**antique** [æn'tiːk] N (ornament) objet m d'art ancien; (furniture) meuble ancien ▶ ADJ ancien(ne); (pre-mediaeval) antique

antique dealer N antiquaire mf

antique shop N magasin m d'antiquités

antiquity [æn'tɪkwɪtɪ] N antiquité f

anti-retroviral [æntɪretrəʊ'vaɪərəl] (Med) N antirétroviral m ▶ ADJ antirétroviral(e)

anti-Semitic [æntɪsɪ'mɪtɪk] ADJ antisémite

anti-Semitism [æntɪ'semɪtɪzəm] N antisémitisme m

antiseptic [æntɪ'septɪk] ADJ, N antiseptique m

antisocial [æntɪ'səʊʃəl] ADJ (unfriendly) peu liant(e), insociable; (against society) antisocial(e)

antitank [æntɪ'tæŋk] ADJ antichar

antithesis [æn'tɪθɪsɪs] (pl **antitheses** [-siːz]) N antithèse f

antitrust [æntɪ'trʌst] ADJ: **~ legislation** loi f antitrust

antiviral [æntɪ'vaɪərəl] ADJ (Med) antiviral

antivirus [æntɪ'vaɪərəs] ADJ (Comput) antivirus inv; **~ software** (logiciel m) antivirus m inv

anti-war [æntɪ'wɔːʳ] ADJ antiguerre

antlers ['æntləz] NPL bois mpl, ramure f

antonym ['æntənɪm] N antonyme m

Antwerp ['æntwəːp] N Anvers

anus ['eɪnəs] N anus m

anvil ['ænvɪl] N enclume f

anxiety [æŋ'zaɪətɪ] N anxiété f; (keenness): **~ to do** grand désir or impatience f de faire

anxious ['æŋkʃəs] ADJ (très) inquiet(-ète); (always worried) anxieux(-euse); (worrying) angoissant(e); **~ to do/that** (keen) qui tient beaucoup à faire/à ce que + sub; impatient(e) de faire/que + sub; **I'm very ~ about you** je me fais beaucoup de souci pour toi

anxiously ['æŋkʃəslɪ] ADV anxieusement

---

any ['enɪ]

ADJ **1** (in questions etc: singular) du, de l', de la; (: plural) des; **do you have any butter/children/ink?** avez-vous du beurre/des enfants/de l'encre?

2 (with negative) de, d'; **I don't have any money/books** je n'ai pas d'argent/de livres; **without any difficulty** sans aucune difficulté

3 (no matter which) n'importe quel(le); (each and every) tout(e), chaque; **choose any book you like** vous pouvez choisir n'importe quel livre; **any teacher you ask will tell you** n'importe quel professeur vous le dira

4 (in phrases): **in any case** de toute façon; **any day now** d'un jour à l'autre; **at any moment** à tout moment, d'un instant à l'autre; **at any rate** en tout cas; **any time** n'importe quand; **he might come (at) any time** il pourrait venir n'importe quand; **come (at) any time** venez quand vous voulez

▶ PRON **1** (in questions etc) en; **have you got any?** est-ce que vous en avez?; **can any of you sing?** est-ce que parmi vous il y en a qui savent chanter?

2 (with negative) en; **I don't have any (of them)** je n'en ai pas, je n'en ai aucun

3 (no matter which one(s)) n'importe lequel (or laquelle); (anybody) n'importe qui; **take any of those books (you like)** vous pouvez prendre n'importe lequel de ces livres

▶ ADV **1** (in questions etc): **do you want any more soup/sandwiches?** voulez-vous encore de la soupe/des sandwichs?; **are you feeling any better?** est-ce que vous vous sentez mieux?

2 (with negative): **I can't hear him any more** je ne l'entends plus; **don't wait any longer** n'attendez pas plus longtemps

---

★**anybody** ['enɪbɒdɪ] PRON n'importe qui; (in interrogative sentences) quelqu'un; (in negative sentences): **I don't see ~** je ne vois personne; **if ~ should phone ...** si quelqu'un téléphone ...

anyhow ['enɪhaʊ] ADV quoi qu'il en soit; (haphazardly) n'importe comment; **do it ~ you like** faites-le comme vous voulez; **she leaves things just ~** elle laisse tout traîner; **I shall go ~** j'irai de toute façon

anymore [enɪ'mɔːʳ] ADV ne ... plus

★**anyone** ['enɪwʌn] PRON = anybody

anyplace ['enɪpleɪs] ADV (US) = anywhere

★**anything** ['enɪθɪŋ] PRON (no matter what) n'importe quoi; (in questions) quelque chose; (with negative) ne ... rien; **I don't want ~** je ne veux rien; **can you see ~?** tu vois quelque chose?; **if ~ happens to me ...** s'il m'arrive quoi que ce soit ...; **you can say ~ you like** vous pouvez dire ce que vous voulez; **~ will do** n'importe quoi fera l'affaire; **he'll eat ~** il mange de tout; **~ else?** (in shop) avec ceci?; **it can cost ~ between £15 and £20** (BRIT) ça peut coûter dans les 15 à 20 livres

anytime ['enɪtaɪm] ADV (at any moment) d'un moment à l'autre; (whenever) n'importe quand

★**anyway** ['enɪweɪ] ADV de toute façon; **I couldn't come even if I wanted to** de toute façon, je ne pourrais pas venir même si je le voulais; **I shall go ~** j'irai quand même; **why are you phoning, ~?** au fait, pourquoi tu me téléphones?

★**anywhere** [ˈɛnɪwɛəʳ] ADV n'importe où; (in interrogative sentences) quelque part; (in negative sentences): **I can't see him ~** je ne le vois nulle part; **can you see him ~?** tu le vois quelque part ?; **put the books down ~** pose les livres n'importe où; **~ in the world** (no matter where) n'importe où dans le monde

Anzac [ˈænzæk] N ABBR (= Australia-New Zealand Army Corps) soldat du corps ANZAC

Anzac Day N voir article

> **Anzac Day** est le 25 avril, jour férié en Australie et en Nouvelle-Zélande commémorant le débarquement des soldats du corps ANZAC (Australia and New Zealand Army Corps) à Gallipoli en 1915, pendant la Première Guerre mondiale. Ce fut la plus célèbre des campagnes du corps ANZAC.

aorta [eɪˈɔːtə] N aorte f

★**apart** [əˈpɑːt] ADV (to one side) à part; de côté; à l'écart; (separately) séparément; **to take/pull ~** démonter; **10 miles/a long way ~** à 10 miles/très éloignés l'un de l'autre; **they are living ~** ils sont séparés; **~ from** prep à part, excepté

apartheid [əˈpɑːteɪt] N apartheid m

★**apartment** [əˈpɑːtmənt] N (US) appartement m, logement m; (room) chambre f

apartment block, (US) **apartment building** N immeuble m, maison f divisée en appartements

apathetic [æpəˈθɛtɪk] ADJ apathique, indifférent(e)

apathy [ˈæpəθɪ] N apathie f, indifférence f

APB N ABBR (US: = all points bulletin) expression de la police signifiant « découvrir et appréhender le suspect »

ape [eɪp] N (grand) singe ▸ VT singer

Apennines [ˈæpənaɪnz] NPL: **the ~** les Apennins mpl

aperitif [əˈpɛrɪtif] N apéritif m

aperture [ˈæpətjuəʳ] N orifice m, ouverture f; (Phot) ouverture (du diaphragme)

apex [ˈeɪpɛks] N sommet m

aphid [ˈeɪfɪd] N puceron m

aphorism [ˈæfərɪzəm] N aphorisme m

aphrodisiac [æfrəʊˈdɪzɪæk] ADJ, N aphrodisiaque m

API N ABBR = **American Press Institute**

apiece [əˈpiːs] ADV (for each person) chacun(e), par tête; (for each item) chacun(e), la pièce

aplenty [əˈplɛntɪ] ADV en abondance

aplomb [əˈplɔm] N sang-froid m, assurance f

apocalypse [əˈpɔkəlɪps] N apocalypse f

apocalyptic [əpɔkəˈlɪptɪk] ADJ apocalyptique

apocryphal [əˈpɔkrɪfl] ADJ apocryphe

apolitical [eɪpəˈlɪtɪkl] ADJ apolitique

apologetic [əpɔləˈdʒɛtɪk] ADJ (tone, letter) d'excuse; **to be very ~ about** s'excuser vivement de

apologetically [əpɔləˈdʒɛtɪklɪ] ADV (say) en s'excusant

apologist [əˈpɔlədʒɪst] N apologiste mf; **an ~ for sb** un apologiste de qn

★**apologize** [əˈpɔlədʒaɪz] VI: **to ~ (for sth to sb)** s'excuser (de qch auprès de qn), présenter des excuses (à qn pour qch)

apology [əˈpɔlədʒɪ] N excuses fpl; **to send one's apologies** envoyer une lettre or un mot d'excuse, s'excuser (de ne pas pouvoir venir); **please accept my apologies** vous voudriez bien m'excuser

> **apology** ne veut pas dire apologie.

apoplectic [æpəˈplɛktɪk] ADJ (Med) apoplectique; (inf): **~ with rage** fou (folle) de rage

apoplexy [ˈæpəplɛksɪ] N apoplexie f

apostle [əˈpɔsl] N apôtre m

★**apostrophe** [əˈpɔstrəfɪ] N apostrophe f

apotheosis [əpɔθɪˈəʊsɪs] (formal) N (epitome) quintessence f; (high point) apothéose f; **the ~ of sth** l'exemple même de qch

app [æp] N ABBR (inf: Comput: = application) appli f

appal, (US) **appall** [əˈpɔːl] VT consterner, atterrer; horrifier

Appalachian Mountains [æpəˈleɪʃən-] NPL: **the ~ les** (monts mpl) Appalaches mpl

appalling [əˈpɔːlɪŋ] ADJ épouvantable; (stupidity) consternant(e); **she's an ~ cook** c'est une très mauvaise cuisinière

apparatus [æpəˈreɪtəs] N appareil m, dispositif m; (in gymnasium) agrès mpl

apparel [əˈpærl] N habillement m, confection f

apparent [əˈpærənt] ADJ apparent(e); **it is ~ that** il est évident que

★**apparently** [əˈpærəntlɪ] ADV apparemment

apparition [æpəˈrɪʃən] N apparition f

appeal [əˈpiːl] VI (Law) faire or interjeter appel; **to ~ for** demander (instamment); implorer; **to ~ to** (beg) faire appel à; (be attractive) plaire à; **to ~ to sb for mercy** implorer la pitié de qn, prier or adjurer qn d'avoir pitié; **it doesn't ~ to me** cela ne m'attire pas ▸ N (Law) appel m; (request) appel; prière f; (charm) attrait m, charme m; **right of ~** droit m de recours

appealing [əˈpiːlɪŋ] ADJ (attractive) attrayant(e); (touching) attendrissant(e)

★**appear** [əˈpɪəʳ] VI apparaître, se montrer; (Law) comparaître; (publication) paraître, sortir, être publié(e); (seem) paraître, sembler; **it would ~ that** il semble que; **to ~ in Hamlet** jouer dans Hamlet; **to ~ on TV** passer à la télé

★**appearance** [əˈpɪərəns] N apparition f; parution f; (look, aspect) apparence f, aspect m; **to put in** or **make an ~** faire acte de présence; **by order of ~** (Theat) par ordre d'entrée en scène; **to keep up appearances** sauver les apparences; **to all appearances** selon toute apparence

appease [əˈpiːz] VT apaiser, calmer

appeasement [əˈpiːzmənt] N (Pol) apaisement m

appellant [əˈpɛlənt] N appelant(e)

append [əˈpɛnd] VT (Comput) ajouter (à la fin d'un fichier)

appendage [əˈpɛndɪdʒ] N appendice m

appendices [əˈpɛndɪsiːz] NPL of **appendix**

appendicitis [əpɛndɪˈsaɪtɪs] N appendicite f

appendix [əˈpɛndɪks] (pl **appendices** [-siːz]) N appendice m; **to have one's ~ out** se faire opérer de l'appendicite

appetite ['æpɪtaɪt] N appétit m; **that walk has given me an ~** cette promenade m'a ouvert l'appétit

appetizer ['æpɪtaɪzə'] N (food) amuse-gueule m; (drink) apéritif m

appetizing ['æpɪtaɪzɪŋ] ADJ appétissant(e)

applaud [ə'plɔːd] VT, VI applaudir

applause [ə'plɔːz] N applaudissements mpl

★**apple** ['æpl] N pomme f; (also: **apple tree**) pommier m; **it's the ~ of my eye** j'y tiens comme à la prunelle de mes yeux

applecart ['æplkɑːt] N: **to upset the ~** tout chambouler

apple pie N tarte f aux pommes

applet ['æplɪt] N (Comput) appliquette f, microprogramme m

apple turnover N chausson m aux pommes

appliance [ə'plaɪəns] N appareil m; **electrical appliances** l'électroménager m

applicable [ə'plɪkəbl] ADJ applicable; **the law is ~ from January** la loi entre en vigueur au mois de janvier; **to be ~ to** (relevant) valoir pour

applicant ['æplɪkənt] N: **~ (for)** (Admin: for benefit etc) demandeur(-euse) (de); (: for post) candidat(e) (à)

★**application** [æplɪ'keɪʃən] N application f; (for a job, a grant etc) demande f; candidature f; (Comput) application, (logiciel m) applicatif m; **on ~** sur demande

application form N formulaire m de demande

application program N (Comput) (logiciel m) applicatif m

applications package N (Comput) progiciel m d'application

applicator ['æplɪkeɪtə'] N applicateur m

applied [ə'plaɪd] ADJ appliqué(e); **~ arts** arts décoratifs

appliqued, appliquéd [ə'pliːkeɪd] ADJ (design, cushion) en appliqué

★**apply** [ə'plaɪ] VT: **to ~ (to)** (paint, ointment) appliquer (sur); (rule, theory, technique) appliquer (à); **to ~ the brakes** actionner les freins, freiner; **to ~ o.s. to** s'appliquer à ▶ VI: **to ~ to** (ask) s'adresser à; (be suitable for, relevant to) s'appliquer à, être valable pour; **to ~ (for)** (permit, grant) faire une demande (en vue d'obtenir); (job) poser sa candidature (pour), faire une demande d'emploi (concernant)

appoint [ə'pɔɪnt] VT (to post) nommer, engager; (date, place) fixer, désigner

appointed [ə'pɔɪntɪd] ADJ: **at the ~ time or hour** à l'heure convenue

appointee [əpɔɪn'tiː] N personne nommée; candidat retenu

★**appointment** [ə'pɔɪntmənt] N (to post) nomination f; (job) poste m; (arrangement to meet) rendez-vous m; **to have an ~** avoir un rendez-vous; **to make an ~ (with)** prendre rendez-vous (avec); **I'd like to make an ~** je voudrais prendre rendez-vous; **"appointments (vacant)"** (Press) « offres d'emploi »; **by ~** sur rendez-vous

apportion [ə'pɔːʃən] VT (share out) répartir, distribuer; **to ~ sth to sb** attribuer or assigner or allouer qch à qn

apposite ['æpəzɪt] ADJ (formal) pertinent(e)

appraisal [ə'preɪzl] N évaluation f

appraise [ə'preɪz] VT (value) estimer; (situation etc) évaluer

appreciable [ə'priːʃəbl] ADJ appréciable

appreciably [ə'priːʃəblɪ] ADV sensiblement, de façon appréciable

★**appreciate** [ə'priːʃɪeɪt] VT (like) apprécier, faire cas de; (be grateful for) être reconnaissant(e) de; (assess) évaluer; (be aware of) comprendre, se rendre compte de; **I ~ your help** je vous remercie pour votre aide ▶ VI (Finance) prendre de la valeur

appreciation [əpriːʃɪ'eɪʃən] N appréciation f, (gratitude) reconnaissance f; (Finance) hausse f, valorisation f

appreciative [ə'priːʃɪətɪv] ADJ (person) sensible; (comment) élogieux(-euse)

apprehend [æprɪ'hɛnd] VT appréhender, arrêter; (understand) comprendre

apprehension [æprɪ'hɛnʃən] N appréhension f, inquiétude f

apprehensive [æprɪ'hɛnsɪv] ADJ inquiet(-ète), appréhensif(-ive)

apprentice [ə'prɛntɪs] N apprenti m ▶ VT: **to be apprenticed to** être en apprentissage chez

apprenticeship [ə'prɛntɪsʃɪp] N apprentissage m; **to serve one's ~** faire son apprentissage

apprise [ə'praɪz] VT (formal) informer; **to ~ sb of sth** informer qn de qch

appro. ['æprəʊ] ABBR (BRIT Comm: inf) = approval

★**approach** [ə'prəʊtʃ] VI approcher ▶ VT (come near) approcher de; (ask, apply to) s'adresser à; (subject, passer-by) aborder; **to ~ sb about sth** aller or venir voir qn pour qch ▶ N approche f; accès m, abord m; démarche f (auprès de qn); (intellectual) démarche f

approachable [ə'prəʊtʃəbl] ADJ accessible

approach road N voie f d'accès

approbation [æprə'beɪʃən] N approbation f

★**appropriate** ADJ [ə'prəʊprɪɪt] (tool etc) qui convient, approprié(e); (moment, remark) opportun(e); **~ for or to** approprié à; **it would not be ~ for me to comment** il ne me serait pas approprié de commenter ▶ VT [ə'prəʊprɪeɪt] (take) s'approprier; (allot): **to ~ sth for** affecter qch à

appropriately [ə'prəʊprɪtlɪ] ADV pertinemment, avec à-propos

appropriation [əprəʊprɪ'eɪʃən] N dotation f, affectation f

approval [ə'pruːvəl] N approbation f; **to meet with sb's ~** (proposal etc) recueillir l'assentiment de qn; **on ~** (Comm) à l'examen

★**approve** [ə'pruːv] VT approuver
▶ **approve of** VT FUS (thing) approuver; (person): **they don't ~ of her** ils n'ont pas bonne opinion d'elle

approved school [ə'pruːvd-] N (BRIT) centre m d'éducation surveillée

approvingly [ə'pruːvɪŋlɪ] ADV d'un air approbateur

approx. ABBR (= approximately) env

approximate ADJ [ə'prɒksɪmɪt] approximatif(-ive) ▶ VT [ə'prɒksɪmeɪt] se rapprocher de; être proche de

approximately [əˈprɒksɪmɪtlɪ] ADV approximativement

approximation [əprɒksɪˈmeɪʃən] N approximation f

APR N ABBR (= *Annual Percentage Rate*) taux (d'intérêt) annuel

Apr. ABBR = **April**

apres-ski, après-ski [æpreɪˈskiː] N après-ski m

apricot [ˈeɪprɪkɒt] N abricot m

★**April** [ˈeɪprəl] N avril m; **~ fool!** poisson d'avril !; *see also* **July**

April Fools' Day N le premier avril

> **April Fools' Day**, le 1er avril, est l'occasion de faire des farces de toutes sortes. Les victimes de ces farces sont les *April fools*. Traditionnellement, on n'est censé faire des farces que jusqu'à midi.

apron [ˈeɪprən] N tablier m; (*Aviat*) aire f de stationnement

apropos [æprəˈpəʊ] PREP (*also*: **apropos of**) à propos de ▸ ADJ (*appropriate*) approprié(e)

apse [æps] N (*Archit*) abside f

apt [æpt] ADJ (*suitable*) approprié(e); **~ (at)** (*able*) doué(e) (pour); apte (à); **~ to do** (*likely*) susceptible de faire; ayant tendance à faire

apt. ABBR (= *apartment*) appt

aptitude [ˈæptɪtjuːd] N aptitude f

aptitude test N test m d'aptitude

aptly [ˈæptlɪ] ADV (*fort*) à propos

aqualung [ˈækwəlʌŋ] N scaphandre m autonome

aquamarine [ækwəməˈriːn] N (*stone*) aiguemarine f; (*colour*) bleu-vert m inv ▸ ADJ (*in colour*) bleu-vert inv

aquarium [əˈkwɛərɪəm] N aquarium m

Aquarius [əˈkwɛərɪəs] N le Verseau; **to be ~** être du Verseau

aquatic [əˈkwætɪk] ADJ aquatique; (*sport*) nautique

aqueduct [ˈækwɪdʌkt] N aqueduc m

aqueous [ˈeɪkwɪəs] ADJ (*solution, cream*) aqueux(-euse)

aquifer [ˈækwɪfəʳ] N aquifère m

aquiline [ˈækwɪlaɪn] ADJ (*nose, profile*) aquilin(e)

AR ABBR (*US*) = **Arkansas**

ARA N ABBR (*BRIT*) = **Associate of the Royal Academy**

Arab [ˈærəb] N Arabe mf ▸ ADJ arabe

Arabia [əˈreɪbɪə] N Arabie f

Arabian [əˈreɪbɪən] ADJ arabe

Arabian Desert N désert m d'Arabie

Arabian Sea N mer f d'Arabie

Arabic [ˈærəbɪk] ADJ, N arabe m

Arabic numerals NPL chiffres mpl arabes

arable [ˈærəbl] ADJ arable

ARAM N ABBR (*BRIT*) = **Associate of the Royal Academy of Music**

arbiter [ˈɑːbɪtəʳ] N arbitre m

arbitrage [ˈɑːbɪtrɑːʒ] N (*Finance*) arbitrage m

arbitrary [ˈɑːbɪtrərɪ] ADJ arbitraire

arbitrate [ˈɑːbɪtreɪt] VI arbitrer; trancher

arbitration [ɑːbɪˈtreɪʃən] N arbitrage m; **the dispute went to ~** le litige a été soumis à arbitrage

arbitrator [ˈɑːbɪtreɪtəʳ] N arbitre m, médiateur(-trice)

arboretum [ɑːbəˈriːtəm] N arboretum m

arbour [ˈɑːbəʳ] N tonnelle f

ARC N ABBR = **American Red Cross**

arc [ɑːk] N arc m

arcade [ɑːˈkeɪd] N arcade f; (*passage with shops*) passage m, galerie f; (*with games*) salle f de jeu

arcane [ɑːˈkeɪn] ADJ (*formal: world*) obscur(e); (: *knowledge*) ésotérique

arch [ɑːtʃ] N arche f; (*of foot*) cambrure f, voûte f plantaire; **pointed ~** ogive f ▸ VT arquer, cambrer ▸ ADJ malicieux(-euse) ▸ PREFIX: **~(-)** achevé(e); par excellence

archaeological, (*US*) **archeological** [ɑːkɪəˈlɒdʒɪkl] ADJ archéologique

archaeologist, (*US*) **archeologist** [ɑːkɪˈɒlədʒɪst] N archéologue mf

archaeology, (*US*) **archeology** [ɑːkɪˈɒlədʒɪ] N archéologie f

archaic [ɑːˈkeɪɪk] ADJ archaïque

archangel [ˈɑːkeɪndʒəl] N archange m

archbishop [ɑːtʃˈbɪʃəp] N archevêque m

archdeacon [ɑːtʃˈdiːkən] N archidiacre m

archdiocese [ɑːtʃˈdaɪəsɪs] N archidiocèse m

archenemy [ɑːtʃˈɛnɪmɪ] N ennemi m de toujours or par excellence

archeology *etc* [ɑːkɪˈɒlədʒɪ] N (*US*) = **archaeology**

archer [ˈɑːtʃəʳ] N archer m

archery [ˈɑːtʃərɪ] N tir m à l'arc

archetypal [ˈɑːkɪtaɪpəl] ADJ archétype

archetype [ˈɑːkɪtaɪp] N prototype m, archétype m

archipelago [ɑːkɪˈpɛlɪgəʊ] N archipel m

architect [ˈɑːkɪtɛkt] N architecte m

architectural [ɑːkɪˈtɛktʃərəl] ADJ architectural(e)

architecturally [ɑːkɪˈtɛktʃərəlɪ] ADV du point de vue de l'architecture

architecture [ˈɑːkɪtɛktʃəʳ] N architecture f

archive [ˈɑːkaɪv] N (*often pl*) archives fpl

archive file N (*Comput*) fichier m d'archives

archives [ˈɑːkaɪvz] NPL archives fpl

archivist [ˈɑːkɪvɪst] N archiviste mf

archway [ˈɑːtʃweɪ] N voûte f, porche voûté or cintré

ARCM N ABBR (*BRIT*) = **Associate of the Royal College of Music**

Arctic [ˈɑːktɪk] ADJ arctique ▸ N: **the ~** l'Arctique m

Arctic Circle N cercle m Arctique

Arctic Ocean N océan m Arctique

ardent [ˈɑːdənt] ADJ fervent(e)

ardour, (*US*) **ardor** [ˈɑːdəʳ] N ardeur f

arduous [ˈɑːdjuəs] ADJ ardu(e)

are [ɑːʳ] VB *see* **be**

★**area** [ˈɛərɪə] N (*Geom*) superficie f; (*zone*) région f; (: *smaller*) secteur m; (*in room*) coin m; (*knowledge, research*) domaine m; **the London ~** la région londonienne

area code (*US*) N (*Tel*) indicatif *m* de zone

arena [əˈriːnə] N arène *f*

aren't [ɑːnt] = **are not**

Argentina [ɑːdʒənˈtiːnə] N Argentine *f*

Argentinian [ɑːdʒənˈtɪnɪən] ADJ argentin(e) ▶ N Argentin(e)

argon [ˈɑːgɔn] N argon *m*

arguable [ˈɑːgjuəbl] ADJ discutable, contestable; **it is ~ whether** on peut se demander si

arguably [ˈɑːgjuəblɪ] ADV: **it is ~ ...** on peut soutenir que c'est ...

★**argue** [ˈɑːgjuː] VI (*quarrel*) se disputer; (*reason*) argumenter; **to ~ about sth (with sb)** se disputer (avec qn) au sujet de qch; **to ~ that** objecter *or* alléguer que, donner comme argument que ▶ VT (*debate: case, matter*) débattre

★**argument** [ˈɑːgjumənt] N (*quarrel*) dispute *f*, discussion *f*; (*reasons*) argument *m*; (*debate*) discussion, controverse *f*; **~ for/against** argument pour/contre

argumentative [ɑːgjuˈmɛntətɪv] ADJ ergoteur(-euse), raisonneur(-euse)

aria [ˈɑːrɪə] N aria *f*

ARIBA [əˈriːbə] N ABBR (*BRIT*) = **Associate of the Royal Institute of British Architects**

arid [ˈærɪd] ADJ aride

aridity [əˈrɪdɪtɪ] N aridité *f*

Aries [ˈɛərɪz] N le Bélier; **to be ~** être du Bélier

arise [əˈraɪz] (*pt* **arose** [əˈrəuz], *pp* **arisen** [əˈrɪzn]) VI survenir, se présenter; **to ~ from** résulter de; **should the need ~** en cas de besoin

aristocracy [ærɪsˈtɔkrəsɪ] N aristocratie *f*

aristocrat [ˈærɪstəkræt] N aristocrate *mf*

aristocratic [ærɪstəˈkrætɪk] ADJ aristocratique

arithmetic [əˈrɪθmətɪk] N arithmétique *f*

arithmetical [ærɪθˈmɛtɪkl] ADJ arithmétique

ark [ɑːk] N: **Noah's A~** l'Arche *f* de Noé

★**arm** [ɑːm] N bras *m*; **~ in ~** bras dessus bras dessous ▶ VT armer ■ **arms** NPL (*weapons, Heraldry*) armes *fpl*

Armageddon [ɑːməˈgɛdən] N Armaggedon *m*

armaments [ˈɑːməmənts] NPL (*weapons*) armement *m*

armband [ˈɑːmbænd] N brassard *m*

armchair [ˈɑːmtʃɛəʳ] N fauteuil *m*

armed [ɑːmd] ADJ armé(e)

armed forces NPL: **the ~** les forces armées

armed robbery N vol *m* à main armée

Armenia [ɑːˈmiːnɪə] N Arménie *f*

Armenian [ɑːˈmiːnɪən] ADJ arménien(ne) ▶ N Arménien(ne); (*Ling*) arménien *m*

armful [ˈɑːmful] N brassée *f*

armistice [ˈɑːmɪstɪs] N armistice *m*

armour, (*US*) **armor** [ˈɑːməʳ] N armure *f*; (*also:* **armour-plating**) blindage *m*; (*Mil: tanks*) blindés *mpl*

armoured car, (*US*) **armored car** [ˈɑːməd-] N véhicule blindé

armoury, (*US*) **armory** [ˈɑːmərɪ] N arsenal *m*

armpit [ˈɑːmpɪt] N aisselle *f*

armrest [ˈɑːmrɛst] N accoudoir *m*

arms control N contrôle *m* des armements

arms race N course *f* aux armements

★**army** [ˈɑːmɪ] N armée *f*

A road N (*BRIT*) ≈ route nationale

aroma [əˈrəumə] N arôme *m*

aromatherapist [ərəuməˈθɛrəpɪst] N aromathérapeute *mf*

aromatherapy [ərəuməˈθɛrəpɪ] N aromathérapie *f*

aromatic [ærəˈmætɪk] ADJ aromatique

arose [əˈrəuz] PT *of* **arise**

★**around** [əˈraund] ADV (*tout*) autour; (*nearby*) dans les parages; **is he ~?** est-il dans les parages *or* là ? ▶ PREP autour de; (*near*) près de; (*fig: about*) environ; (: *date, time*) vers

arousal [əˈrauzəl] N (*sexual*) excitation sexuelle, éveil *m*

arouse [əˈrauz] VT (*sleeper*) éveiller; (*curiosity, passions*) éveiller, susciter; (*anger*) exciter

aroused [əˈrauzd] ADJ (*sexually*) excité(e)

arraign [əˈreɪn] VT (*Law*) traduire en justice; **to be arraigned on charges of sth** être inculpé(e) de qch

★**arrange** [əˈreɪndʒ] VT arranger; (*programme*) arrêter, convenir de; **to ~ to do sth** prévoir de faire qch; **it was arranged that ...** il a été convenu que ..., il a été décidé que ... ▶ VI: **we have arranged for a car to pick you up** nous avons prévu qu'une voiture vienne vous prendre

arrangement [əˈreɪndʒmənt] N arrangement *m*; **to come to an ~ (with sb)** se mettre d'accord (avec qn); **home deliveries by ~** livraison à domicile sur demande ■ **arrangements** NPL (*plans etc*) arrangements *mpl*, dispositions *fpl*; **I'll make arrangements for you to be met** je vous enverrai chercher

arrant [ˈærənt] ADJ: **he's talking ~ nonsense** il raconte vraiment n'importe quoi

array [əˈreɪ] N (*of objects*) déploiement *m*, étalage *m*; (*Math, Comput*) tableau *m*

arrayed [əˈreɪd] ADJ (*arranged: objects*) disposé(e); (*Mil*): **to be ~ against sb** être déployé(e) contre qn; (*literary: dressed*): **~ in sth** paré(e) de qch

arrears [əˈrɪəz] NPL arriéré *m*; **to be in ~ with one's rent** devoir un arriéré de loyer, être en retard pour le paiement de son loyer

★**arrest** [əˈrɛst] VT arrêter; (*sb's attention*) retenir, attirer ▶ N arrestation *f*; **under ~** en état d'arrestation

arresting [əˈrɛstɪŋ] ADJ (*fig: beauty*) saisissant(e); (: *charm, candour*) désarmant(e)

arrival [əˈraɪvl] N arrivée *f*; (*Comm*) arrivage *m*; (*person*) arrivant(e); **new ~** nouveau venu/nouvelle venue; (*baby*) nouveau-né(e)

★**arrive** [əˈraɪv] VI arriver

▶ **arrive at** VT FUS (*decision, solution*) parvenir à

arrogance [ˈærəgəns] N arrogance *f*

arrogant [ˈærəgənt] ADJ arrogant(e)

arrogantly [ˈærəgəntlɪ] ADV (*claim*) avec arrogance

arrow [ˈærəu] N flèche *f*

arrowhead ['ærəuhɛd] N pointe f de flèche

arse [ɑ:s] N (BRIT inf!) cul m (!)

arsehole ['ɑ:shəul] N (BRIT inf!) connard m (!)

arsenal ['ɑ:sɪnl] N arsenal m

arsenic ['ɑ:snɪk] N arsenic m

arson ['ɑ:sn] N incendie criminel

arsonist ['ɑ:sənɪst] N incendiaire mf

★**art** [ɑ:t] N art m; (craft) métier m; **work of ~** œuvre f d'art ■ **Arts** NPL (Scol) les lettres fpl

art college N école f des beaux-arts

Art Deco [ɑ:t'dɛkəu] N art m déco

artefact ['ɑ:tɪfækt] N objet fabriqué

arterial [ɑ:'tɪərɪəl] ADJ (Anat) artériel(le); (road etc) à grande circulation

arteriosclerosis [ɑ:tɪərɪəusklɛ'rəusɪs] N artériosclérose f

artery ['ɑ:tərɪ] N artère f

artful ['ɑ:tful] ADJ rusé(e)

art gallery N musée m d'art; (saleroom) galerie f de peinture

art-house ['ɑ:thaus] ADJ (film, classic) d'art et d'essai

arthritic [ɑ:'θrɪtɪk] ADJ arthritique

arthritis [ɑ:'θraɪtɪs] N arthrite f

artichoke ['ɑ:tɪtʃəuk] N artichaut m; **Jerusalem ~** topinambour m

★**article** ['ɑ:tɪkl] N article m; **articles of clothing** vêtements mpl ■ **articles** NPL (training) ≈ stage m

articled ['ɑ:tɪkld] ADJ (clerk) stagiaire; **to be ~ to sb** être stagiaire chez qn

articles of association NPL (Comm) statuts mpl d'une société

articulacy [ɑ:'tɪkjuləsɪ] N (of person) éloquence f; (of speech) articulation f

articulate ADJ [ɑ:'tɪkjulɪt] (person) qui s'exprime clairement et aisément; (speech) bien articulé(e), prononcé(e) clairement ▶ VI [ɑ:'tɪkjuleɪt] articuler, parler distinctement ▶ VT articuler

articulated lorry [ɑ:'tɪkjuleɪtɪd-] N (BRIT) (camion m) semi-remorque m

artifact ['ɑ:tɪfækt] N (US) objet fabriqué

artifice ['ɑ:tɪfɪs] N ruse f

artificial [ɑ:tɪ'fɪʃəl] ADJ artificiel(le)

artificial insemination [-ɪnsɛmɪ'neɪʃən] N insémination artificielle

artificial intelligence N intelligence artificielle

artificial respiration N respiration artificielle

artillery [ɑ:'tɪlərɪ] N artillerie f

artisan ['ɑ:tɪzæn] N artisan(e)

★**artist** ['ɑ:tɪst] N artiste mf

artiste [ɑ:'ti:st] (esp BRIT) N artiste mf; **a cabaret ~** un artiste de cabaret

artistic [ɑ:'tɪstɪk] ADJ artistique

artistry ['ɑ:tɪstrɪ] N art m, talent m

artless ['ɑ:tlɪs] ADJ naïf (naïve), simple, ingénu(e)

Art Nouveau [ɑ:tnu:'vəu] N art m inv nouveau ▶ CPD (work, building) art nouveau inv

arts [ɑ:ts] NPL (Scol) lettres fpl

art school N ≈ école f des beaux-arts

artsy ['ɑ:tsɪ] ADJ (inf: person) qui se donne le genre artiste; (: film, photograph) de style artiste prétentieux

artwork ['ɑ:twə:k] N maquette f (prête pour la photogravure)

ARV N ABBR (= American Revised Version) traduction américaine de la Bible

AS N ABBR (US Scol: = Associate in or of Science) diplôme universitaire ▶ ABBR (US) = **American Samoa**

---

as [æz]

CONJ **1** (time: moment) comme, alors que; (: duration) tandis que; **he came in as I was leaving** il est arrivé comme je partais; **as the years went by** à mesure que les années passaient; **as from tomorrow** à partir de demain

2 (because) comme, puisque; **he left early as he had to be home by 10** comme il or puisqu'il devait être de retour avant 10h, il est parti de bonne heure

3 (referring to manner, way) comme; **do as you wish** faites comme vous voudrez; **as she said** comme elle disait

▶ ADV **1** (in comparisons): **as big as** aussi grand que; **twice as big as** deux fois plus grand que; **big as it is** si grand que ce soit; **much as I like them, I …** je les aime bien, mais je …; **as much** or **many as** autant que; **as much money/many books as** autant d'argent/de livres que; **as soon as** dès que

2 (concerning): **as for** or **to that** quant à cela, pour ce qui est de cela

3: **as if** or **though** comme si; **he looked as if he was ill** il avait l'air d'être malade; see also **long**; **such**; **well**

▶ PREP (in the capacity of) en tant que, en qualité de; **he works as a driver** il travaille comme chauffeur; **as chairman of the company, he …** en tant que président de la société, il …; **dressed up as a cowboy** déguisé en cow-boy; **he gave me it as a present** il me l'a offert, il m'en a fait cadeau

---

ASA N ABBR (= American Standards Association) association de normalisation

a.s.a.p. ABBR = **as soon as possible**

asbestos [æz'bestəs] N asbeste m, amiante m

ASBO ['æzbəu] N ABBR (BRIT: = Antisocial Behaviour Order) décision de justice visant à empêcher une personne reconnue coupable d'incivilités de récidiver en restreignant sa liberté de mouvement ou d'action

ascend [ə'sɛnd] VT gravir

ascendancy [ə'sɛndənsɪ] N ascendant m

ascendant [ə'sɛndənt] N: **to be in the ~** monter

ascending [ə'sɛndɪŋ] ADJ (spiral, scale) croissant(e); **in ~ order** par ordre croissant

ascension [ə'sɛnʃən] N: **the A~** (Rel) l'Ascension f

Ascension Island N île f de l'Ascension

ascent [ə'sɛnt] N (climb) ascension f

ascertain [æsə'teɪn] VT s'assurer de, vérifier; établir

ascetic [ə'sɛtɪk] ADJ ascétique

asceticism [ə'sɛtɪsɪzəm] N ascétisme m

ASCII ['æski:] N ABBR (= American Standard Code for Information Interchange) ASCII

ascribe [ə'skraɪb] VT: **to ~ sth to** attribuer qch à; (blame) imputer qch à

ASE N ABBR = **American Stock Exchange**

asexual [eɪ'sɛkʃʊəl] ADJ (*reproduction*) asexuel(le), asexué(e); (*relationship*) platonique; (*creature, plant*) asexué(e)

ASH [æʃ] N ABBR (BRIT: = *Action on Smoking and Health*) *ligue anti-tabac*

ash [æʃ] N (*dust*) cendre *f*; (*also*: **ash tree**) frêne *m*

ashamed [ə'ʃeɪmd] ADJ honteux(-euse), confus(e); **to be ~ of** avoir honte de; **to be ~ (of o.s.) for having done** avoir honte d'avoir fait

ash blond, ash blonde ADJ blond(e) cendré(e)

ashen ['æʃən] ADJ (*pale*) cendreux(-euse), blême

ashore [ə'ʃɔːʳ] ADV à terre; **to go ~** aller à terre, débarquer

ashtray ['æʃtreɪ] N cendrier *m*

Ash Wednesday N mercredi *m* des Cendres

★**Asia** ['eɪʃə] N Asie *f*

Asia Minor N Asie Mineure

Asian ['eɪʃən] N (*from Asia*) Asiatique *mf*; (BRIT: *from Indian subcontinent*) Indo-Pakistanais(e) ▸ ADJ asiatique; indo-pakistanais(e)

Asiatic [eɪsɪ'ætɪk] ADJ asiatique

aside [ə'saɪd] ADV de côté; à l'écart; **~ from** prep à part, excepté ▸ N aparté *m*

★**ask** [ɑːsk] VT demander; (*invite*) inviter; **to ~ sb sth/ to do sth** demander à qn qch/de faire qch; **to ~ sb the time** demander l'heure à qn; **to ~ sb about sth** questionner qn au sujet de qch; se renseigner auprès de qn au sujet de qch; **to ~ (sb) a question** poser une question (à qn); **to ~ sb out to dinner** inviter qn au restaurant ▸ VI demander; **to ~ about the price** s'informer du prix, se renseigner au sujet du prix
  ▸ **ask after** VT FUS demander des nouvelles de
  ▸ **ask for** VT FUS demander; **it's just asking for trouble** *or* **for it** ce serait chercher des ennuis

askance [ə'skɑːns] ADV: **to look ~ at sb** regarder qn de travers *or* d'un œil désapprobateur

askew [ə'skjuː] ADV de travers, de guingois

asking price ['ɑːskɪŋ-] N prix demandé

★**asleep** [ə'sliːp] ADJ endormi(e); **to be ~** dormir, être endormi; **to fall ~** s'endormir

ASLEF ['æzlɛf] N ABBR (BRIT: = *Associated Society of Locomotive Engineers and Firemen*) *syndicat de cheminots*

AS level N ABBR (= *Advanced Subsidiary level*) *première partie de l'examen équivalent au baccalauréat*

asp [æsp] N aspic *m*

asparagus [əs'pærəgəs] N asperges *fpl*

asparagus tips NPL pointes *fpl* d'asperges

ASPCA N ABBR (= *American Society for the Prevention of Cruelty to Animals*) ≈ SPA *f*

★**aspect** ['æspɛkt] N aspect *m*; (*direction in which a building etc faces*) orientation *f*, exposition *f*

aspen ['æspən] N (*tree*) tremble *m*

aspersions [əs'pəːʃənz] NPL: **to cast ~ on** dénigrer

asphalt ['æsfælt] N asphalte *m*

asphyxia [æs'fɪksɪə] N asphyxie *f*

asphyxiate [æs'fɪksɪeɪt] VT asphyxier

asphyxiation [æsfɪksɪ'eɪʃən] N asphyxie *f*

aspiration [æspə'reɪʃən] N aspiration *f* ▸ NPL (*hopes, ambition*) aspirations *fpl*

aspire [əs'paɪəʳ] VI: **to ~ to** aspirer à

aspirin ['æsprɪn] N aspirine *f*

aspiring [əs'paɪərɪŋ] ADJ (*artist, writer*) en herbe; (*manager*) potentiel(le)

ass [æs] N âne *m*; (*inf*) imbécile *mf*; (*US inf!*) cul *m* (!)

assail [ə'seɪl] VT assaillir

assailant [ə'seɪlənt] N agresseur *m*; assaillant *m*

assassin [ə'sæsɪn] N assassin *m*

assassinate [ə'sæsɪneɪt] VT assassiner

assassination [əsæsɪ'neɪʃən] N assassinat *m*

assault [ə'sɔːlt] N (*Mil*) assaut *m*; (*gen: attack*) agression *f*; (*Law*): **~ (and battery)** voies *fpl* de fait, coups *mpl* et blessures *fpl* ▸ VT attaquer; (*sexually*) violenter

assemble [ə'sɛmbl] VT assembler ▸ VI s'assembler, se rassembler

assembly [ə'sɛmblɪ] N (*meeting*) rassemblement *m*; (*parliament*) assemblée *f*; (*construction*) assemblage *m*

assembly language N (*Comput*) langage *m* d'assemblage

assembly line N chaîne *f* de montage

assemblyman [ə'sɛmblɪmən] N (*irreg*) membre *m* d'une assemblée législative

assemblywoman [ə'sɛmblɪwumən] N (*irreg*) membre *m* d'une assemblée législative

assent [ə'sɛnt] N assentiment *m*, consentement *m* ▸ VI: **to ~ (to sth)** donner son assentiment (à qch), consentir (à qch)

assert [ə'səːt] VT affirmer, déclarer; établir; (*authority*) faire valoir; (*innocence*) protester de; **to ~ o.s.** s'imposer

assertion [ə'səːʃən] N assertion *f*, affirmation *f*

assertive [ə'səːtɪv] ADJ assuré(e); péremptoire

assertiveness [ə'səːtɪvnɪs] N assurance *f* ▸ CPD (*class, training*) d'affirmation de la personnalité

assess [ə'sɛs] VT évaluer, estimer; (*tax, damages*) établir *or* fixer le montant de; (*property etc: for tax*) calculer la valeur imposable de; (*person*) juger la valeur de

assessment [ə'sɛsmənt] N évaluation *f*, estimation *f*; (*of tax*) fixation *f*; (*of property*) calcul *m* de la valeur imposable; (*judgment*): **~ (of)** jugement *m* *or* opinion *f* (sur)

assessor [ə'sɛsəʳ] N expert *m* (*en matière d'impôt et d'assurance*)

asset ['æsɛt] N avantage *m*, atout *m*; (*person*) atout **assets** NPL (*Comm*) capital *m*; avoir(s) *m(pl)*; actif *m*

asset-stripping ['æsɛtstrɪpɪŋ] N (*Comm*) récupération *f* (et démantèlement *m*) d'une entreprise en difficulté

asshole ['æʃhəul] N (*US!*) con(ne) (!), connard(e) (!)

assiduous [ə'sɪdjuəs] ADJ assidu(e)

assign [ə'saɪn] VT (*date*) fixer, arrêter; **to ~ sth to** (*task*) assigner qch à; (*resources*) affecter qch à; (*cause, meaning*) attribuer qch à

assignation [æsɪg'neɪʃən] N (*formal, hum*) rendez-vous *m*

assignment [ə'saɪnmənt] N (*task*) mission *f*; (*homework*) devoir *m*

assimilate [əˈsɪmɪleɪt] VT assimiler

assimilation [əsɪmɪˈleɪʃən] N assimilation f

assist [əˈsɪst] VT aider, assister; (injured person etc) secourir

assistance [əˈsɪstəns] N aide f, assistance f; secours mpl

★**assistant** [əˈsɪstənt] N assistant(e), adjoint(e); (BRIT: also: **shop assistant**) vendeur(-euse)

assistant manager N sous-directeur m

assizes [əˈsaɪzɪz] NPL assises fpl

associate ADJ, N [əˈsəuʃɪɪt] associé(e); ~ **director** directeur adjoint ▶ VT [əˈsəuʃɪeɪt] associer; **associated company** société affiliée ▶ VI [əˈsəuʃɪeɪt]: **to ~ with sb** fréquenter qn

association [əsəuʃɪˈeɪʃən] N association f; **in ~ with** en collaboration avec

association football N (BRIT) football m

assorted [əˈsɔːtɪd] ADJ assorti(e); **in ~ sizes** en plusieurs tailles

assortment [əˈsɔːtmənt] N assortiment m; (of people) mélange m

Asst. ABBR = **assistant**

assuage [əˈsweɪdʒ] VT (grief, pain) soulager; (thirst, appetite) assouvir

assume [əˈsjuːm] VT supposer; (responsibilities etc) assumer; (attitude, name) prendre, adopter

assumed name [əˈsjuːmd-] N nom m d'emprunt

assumption [əˈsʌmpʃən] N supposition f, hypothèse f; (of power) assomption f, prise f; **on the ~ that** dans l'hypothèse où; (on condition that) à condition que

assurance [əˈʃuərəns] N assurance f; **I can give you no assurances** je ne peux rien vous garantir

assure [əˈʃuə^r] VT assurer

assured [əˈʃuəd] ADJ assuré(e)

assuredly [əˈʃuərɪdlɪ] ADV assurément

AST ABBR (US: = Atlantic Standard Time) heure d'hiver de New York

asterisk [ˈæstərɪsk] N astérisque m

astern [əˈstəːn] ADV à l'arrière

asteroid [ˈæstərɔɪd] N astéroïde m

★**asthma** [ˈæsmə] N asthme m

asthmatic [æsˈmætɪk] ADJ, N asthmatique mf

astigmatism [əˈstɪgmətɪzəm] N astigmatisme m

astir [əˈstəː^r] ADV en émoi

astonish [əˈstɔnɪʃ] VT étonner, stupéfier

astonished [əˈstɔnɪʃt] ADJ étonné(e); **to be ~ at** être étonné(e) de

astonishing [əˈstɔnɪʃɪŋ] ADJ étonnant(e), stupéfiant(e); **I find it ~ that ...** je trouve incroyable que ... + sub

astonishingly [əˈstɔnɪʃɪŋlɪ] ADV incroyablement

astonishment [əˈstɔnɪʃmənt] N (grand) étonnement, stupéfaction f

astound [əˈstaund] VT stupéfier, sidérer

astounded [əˈstaundɪd] ADJ abasourdi(e), stupéfait(e); **to be ~ at sth** être abasourdi(e) par qch, être stupéfait(e) par qch

astounding [əˈstaundɪŋ] ADJ stupéfiant(e), étonnant(e)

astray [əˈstreɪ] ADV: **to go ~** s'égarer; (fig) quitter le droit chemin; **to lead ~** (morally) détourner du droit chemin; **to go ~ in one's calculations** faire fausse route dans ses calculs

astride [əˈstraɪd] ADV à cheval ▶ PREP à cheval sur

astringent [əˈstrɪndʒənt] ADJ astringent(e) ▶ N astringent m

astrologer [əˈstrɔlədʒə^r] N astrologue mf

astrological [æstrəˈlɔdʒɪkl] ADJ astrologique

astrology [əˈstrɔlədʒɪ] N astrologie f

astronaut [ˈæstrənɔːt] N astronaute mf

astronomer [əˈstrɔnəmə^r] N astronome mf

astronomical [æstrəˈnɔmɪkl] ADJ astronomique

astronomy [əˈstrɔnəmɪ] N astronomie f

astroparticle [ˈæstrəupɑːtɪkl] N astroparticule f

astrophysicist [æstrəuˈfɪzɪsɪst] N astrophysicien(-ienne)

astrophysics [æstrəuˈfɪzɪks] N astrophysique f

astute [əsˈtjuːt] ADJ astucieux(-euse), malin(-igne)

asunder [əˈsʌndə^r] ADV: **to tear ~** déchirer

ASV N ABBR (= American Standard Version) traduction de la Bible

asylum [əˈsaɪləm] N asile m; **to seek political ~** demander l'asile politique

asylum seeker [-siːkə^r] N demandeur(-euse) d'asile

asymmetric [eɪsɪˈmɛtrɪk], **asymmetrical** [eɪsɪˈmɛtrɪkl] ADJ asymétrique

asymmetry [eɪˈsɪmətrɪ] N asymétrie f

---

at [æt]

PREP **1** (referring to position, direction) à; **at the top** au sommet; **at home/school** à la maison or chez soi/à l'école; **at the baker's** à la boulangerie, chez le boulanger; **to look at sth** regarder qch

2 (referring to time): **at 4 o'clock** à 4 heures; **at Christmas** à Noël; **at night** la nuit; **at times** par moments, parfois

3 (referring to rates, speed etc) à; **at £1 a kilo** le kilo; **two at a time** deux à la fois; **at 50 km/h** à 50 km/h; **at full speed** à toute vitesse

4 (referring to manner): **at a stroke** d'un seul coup; **at peace** en paix

5 (referring to activity): **to be at work** (in the office etc) être au travail; (working) travailler; **to play at cowboys** jouer aux cow-boys; **to be good at sth** être bon en qch

6 (referring to cause): **shocked/surprised/ annoyed at sth** choqué par/étonné de/agacé par qch; **I went at his suggestion** j'y suis allé sur son conseil

▶ N (@ symbol) arobase f

---

atavistic [ætəˈvɪstɪk] ADJ (formal) atavique

ate [eɪt] PT of **eat**

atheism [ˈeɪθɪɪzəm] N athéisme m

atheist [ˈeɪθɪɪst] N athée mf

Athenian [əˈθiːnɪən] ADJ athénien(ne) ▶ N Athénien(ne)

Athens [ˈæθɪnz] N Athènes

★**athlete** [ˈæθliːt] N athlète mf

athletic [æθˈlɛtɪk] ADJ athlétique

athletics [æθ'letɪks] N athlétisme m

atishoo [ə'tɪʃuː] EXCL atchoum !

★**Atlantic** [ət'læntɪk] ADJ atlantique ▶N: **the ~ (Ocean)** l'(océan m) Atlantique m

★**atlas** ['ætləs] N atlas m

Atlas Mountains NPL: **the ~** les monts mpl de l'Atlas, l'Atlas m

ATM N ABBR (= Automated Telling Machine) guichet m automatique

atmosphere ['ætməsfɪə'] N (air) atmosphère f; (fig: of place etc) atmosphère, ambiance f

atmospheric [ætməs'ferɪk] ADJ atmosphérique

atmospherics [ætməs'ferɪks] N (Radio) parasites mpl

atoll ['ætɔl] N atoll m

atom ['ætəm] N atome m

atom bomb, atomic bomb N bombe f atomique

atomic [ə'tɔmɪk] ADJ atomique

atomizer ['ætəmaɪzə'] N atomiseur m

atonal [eɪ'təunl] ADJ atonal(e)

atone [ə'təun] VI: **to ~ for** expier, racheter

atonement [ə'təunmənt] N expiation f

atop [ə'tɔp] PREP (literary) au sommet de, sur

ATP N ABBR (= Association of Tennis Professionals) ATP f (= Association des joueurs de tennis professionnels)

atrium ['eɪtrɪəm] N atrium m

atrocious [ə'trəuʃəs] ADJ (very bad) atroce, exécrable

atrocity [ə'trɔsɪtɪ] N atrocité f

atrophy ['ætrəfɪ] N atrophie f ▶VT atrophier ▶VI s'atrophier

★**attach** [ə'tætʃ] VT (gen) attacher; (document, letter) joindre; (employee, troops) affecter; **to be attached to sb/sth** (to like) être attaché à qn/qch; **to ~ a file to an email** joindre un fichier à un e-mail; **the attached letter** la lettre ci-jointe

attaché [ə'tæʃeɪ] N attaché m

attaché case [ə'tæʃeɪ-] N mallette f, attaché-case m

attachment [ə'tætʃmənt] N (tool) accessoire m; (Comput) fichier m joint; (love): **~ (to)** affection f (pour), attachement m (à)

★**attack** [ə'tæk] VT attaquer; (task etc) s'attaquer à ▶N attaque f; **heart ~** crise f cardiaque

attacker [ə'tækə'] N attaquant m; agresseur m

attain [ə'teɪn] VT (also: **to attain to**) parvenir à, atteindre; (knowledge) acquérir

attainable [ə'teɪnəbl] (goal) accessible

attainment [ə'teɪnmənt] N (achievement: of aim) réalisation f, obtention f; (skill) connaissance f; (of school pupil) résultat m

★**attempt** [ə'tempt] N tentative f; **to make an ~ on sb's life** attenter à la vie de qn; **he made no ~ to help** il n'a rien fait pour m'aider or l'aider etc ▶VT essayer, tenter

attempted [ə'temptɪd] ADJ: **~ murder/suicide/theft** tentative f de meurtre/suicide/vol

★**attend** [ə'tend] VT (course) suivre; (meeting, talk) assister à; (school, church) aller à, fréquenter; (patient) soigner, s'occuper de

▶**attend on, attend upon** VT FUS (person) servir, être au service de

▶**attend to** VT FUS (needs, affairs etc) s'occuper de; (customer) s'occuper de, servir

attendance [ə'tendəns] N (being present) présence f; (people present) assistance f

attendant [ə'tendənt] N employé(e); gardien(ne) ▶ADJ concomitant(e), qui accompagne or s'ensuit

attendee [ətɛn'diː] (esp US) N participant(e)

★**attention** [ə'tenʃən] N attention f; (Mil): **at ~** au garde-à-vous; **for the ~ of** (Admin) à l'attention de; **it has come to my ~ that ...** je constate que ... ▶EXCL (Mil) garde-à-vous ! ■**attentions** NPL attentions fpl, prévenances fpl

attentive [ə'tentɪv] ADJ attentif(-ive); (kind) prévenant(e)

attentively [ə'tentɪvlɪ] ADV attentivement, avec attention

attenuate [ə'tenjueɪt] VT atténuer ▶VI s'atténuer

attest [ə'test] VI: **to ~ to** témoigner de, attester de

attic ['ætɪk] N grenier m, combles mpl

attire [ə'taɪə'] N habit m, atours mpl

attired [ə'taɪəd] ADJ (formal) vêtu(e) (formal); **~ in** vêtu(e) de

attitude ['ætɪtjuːd] N (behaviour) attitude f, manière f; (posture) pose f, attitude; (view): **~ (to)** attitude (envers)

attorney [ə'təːnɪ] N (US: lawyer) avocat m; (having proxy) mandataire m; **power of ~** procuration f

Attorney General N (BRIT) ≈ procureur général; (US) ≈ garde m des Sceaux, ministre m de la Justice

attract [ə'trækt] VT attirer

attracted [ə'træktɪd] ADJ: **to be ~ to sb/sth** être attiré(e) par qn/qch

attraction [ə'trækʃən] N (gen pl: pleasant things) attraction f, attrait m; (Physics) attraction; (fig: towards sb, sth) attirance f

★**attractive** [ə'træktɪv] ADJ séduisant(e), attrayant(e)

attractiveness [ə'træktɪvnɪs] N (of place, region) charme m; (of person) beauté f, charme m; (of scheme, price) attrait m

attribute N ['ætrɪbjuːt] attribut m ▶VT [ə'trɪbjuːt]: **to ~ sth to** attribuer qch à

attribution [ætrɪ'bjuːʃən] N attribution f

attrition [ə'trɪʃən] N: **war of ~** guerre f d'usure

attuned [ə'tjuːnd] ADJ: **~ to** (feeling, needs) à l'écoute de; (sound) accoutumé(e) à

Atty. Gen. ABBR = **Attorney General**

ATV N ABBR (= all terrain vehicle) véhicule m tout-terrain

atypical [eɪ'tɪpɪkl] ADJ atypique

aubergine ['əubəʒiːn] N aubergine f

auburn ['ɔːbən] ADJ auburn inv, châtain roux inv

auction ['ɔːkʃən] N (also: **sale by auction**) vente f aux enchères ▶VT (also: **to sell by auction**) vendre aux enchères; (also: **to put up for auction**) mettre aux enchères

auctioneer [ɔːkʃə'nɪə'] N commissaire-priseur m

auction room N salle f des ventes

audacious [ɔːˈdeɪʃəs] ADJ impudent(e); audacieux(-euse), intrépide

audacity [ɔːˈdæsɪtɪ] N impudence f; audace f

audible [ˈɔːdɪbl] ADJ audible

★**audience** [ˈɔːdɪəns] N (people) assistance f, public m; (on radio) auditeurs mpl; (at theatre) spectateurs mpl; (interview) audience f

audio [ˈɔːdɪəu] ADJ (equipment) audio inv

audiotape [ˈɔːdɪəuteɪp] N (magnetic tape) bande f audio inv; (US: cassette) cassette f ▶ VT (US) enregistrer sur cassette

audiovisual [ɔːdɪəuˈvɪzjuəl] ADJ audio-visuel(le); **~ aids** supports or moyens audiovisuels

audit [ˈɔːdɪt] N vérification f des comptes, apurement m ▶ VT vérifier, apurer

audition [ɔːˈdɪʃən] N audition f ▶ VI auditionner

auditor [ˈɔːdɪtəʳ] N vérificateur(-trice) des comptes

auditorium [ɔːdɪˈtɔːrɪəm] N auditorium m, salle f de concert or de spectacle

auditory [ˈɔːdɪtrɪ] ADJ auditif(-ive)

Aug. ABBR = **August**

augment [ɔːgˈmɛnt] VT, VI augmenter

augur [ˈɔːgəʳ] VT (be a sign of) présager, annoncer ▶ VI: **it augurs well** c'est bon signe or de bon augure, cela s'annonce bien

★**August** [ˈɔːgəst] N août m; see also **July**

august [ɔːˈgʌst] ADJ majestueux(-euse), imposant(e)

aunt [ɑːnt] N tante f

auntie, aunty [ˈɑːntɪ] N DIMINUTIVE of **aunt**

★**au pair** [ˈəuˈpɛəʳ] N (also: **au pair girl**) jeune fille f au pair

aura [ˈɔːrə] N atmosphère f; (of person) aura f

aural [ˈɔːrəl] ADJ (at school: comprehension, test) oral(e)

auspices [ˈɔːspɪsɪz] NPL: **under the ~ of** sous les auspices de

auspicious [ɔːsˈpɪʃəs] ADJ de bon augure, propice

Aussie [ˈɒzɪ] ADJ, N (inf) Aussie mf

austere [ɒsˈtɪəʳ] ADJ austère

austerity [ɒsˈtɛrɪtɪ] N austérité f

Australasia [ɒstrəˈleɪzɪə] N Australasie f

★**Australia** [ɒsˈtreɪlɪə] N Australie f

Australian [ɒsˈtreɪlɪən] ADJ australien(ne) ▶ N Australien(ne)

★**Austria** [ˈɒstrɪə] N Autriche f

Austrian [ˈɒstrɪən] ADJ autrichien(ne) ▶ N Autrichien(ne)

auteur [ɔːˈtəːʳ] N (film director) grand(e) réalisateur(-trice)

authentic [ɔːˈθɛntɪk] ADJ authentique

authenticate [ɔːˈθɛntɪkeɪt] VT établir l'authenticité de

authentication [ɔːθɛntɪˈkeɪʃən] N authentification f

authenticity [ɔːθɛnˈtɪsɪtɪ] N authenticité f

★**author** [ˈɔːθəʳ] N auteur(e)

authorial [ɔːˈθɔːrɪəl] ADJ (voice, intention) de l'auteur

authoritarian [ɔːθɒrɪˈtɛərɪən] ADJ autoritaire

authoritarianism [ɔːθɒrɪˈtɛərɪənɪzəm] N autoritarisme m

authoritative [ɔːˈθɒrɪtətɪv] ADJ (account) digne de foi; (study, treatise) qui fait autorité; (manner) autoritaire

authority [ɔːˈθɒrɪtɪ] N autorité f; (permission) autorisation (formelle); **the authorities** les autorités fpl, l'administration f; **to have ~ to do sth** être habilité à faire qch

authorization [ɔːθəraɪˈzeɪʃən] N autorisation f **authorize** [ˈɔːθəraɪz] VT autoriser

authorized capital [ˈɔːθəraɪzd-] N (Comm) capital social

authorship [ˈɔːθəʃɪp] N paternité f (littéraire etc)

autism [ˈɔːtɪzəm] N autisme m

autistic [ɔːˈtɪstɪk] ADJ autiste, autistique

auto [ˈɔːtəu] N (US) auto f, voiture f

autobiographical [ˈɔːtəbaɪəˈɡræfɪkl] ADJ autobiographique

autobiography [ɔːtəbaɪˈɒɡrəfɪ] N autobiographie f

autocracy [ɔːˈtɒkrəsɪ] N autocratie f

autocrat [ˈɔːtəkræt] N autocrate mf

autocratic [ɔːtəˈkrætɪk] ADJ autocratique

Autocue® [ˈɔːtəukjuː] (BRIT) N prompteur m

autograph [ˈɔːtəɡrɑːf] N autographe m ▶ VT signer, dédicacer

autoimmune [ɔːtəuɪˈmjuːn] ADJ auto-immune

automaker [ˈɔːtəumeɪkəʳ] N (US) constructeur m automobile

automat [ˈɔːtəmæt] N (vending machine) distributeur m (automatique); (US: place) cafétéria f avec distributeurs automatiques

automate [ˈɔːtəmeɪt] VT automatiser

automated [ˈɔːtəmeɪtɪd] ADJ automatisé(e)

★**automatic** [ɔːtəˈmætɪk] ADJ automatique ▶ N (gun) automatique m; (washing machine) lave-linge m automatique; (car) voiture f à transmission automatique

automatically [ɔːtəˈmætɪklɪ] ADV automatiquement

automatic data processing N traitement m automatique des données

automation [ɔːtəˈmeɪʃən] N automatisation f

automaton [ɔːˈtɒmətən] (pl **automata** [-tə]) N automate m

automobile [ˈɔːtəməbiːl] N (US) automobile f

automotive [ɔːtəˈməutɪv] ADJ (industry, parts) automobile

autonomous [ɔːˈtɒnəməs] ADJ autonome

autonomy [ɔːˈtɒnəmɪ] N autonomie f

autopilot [ˈɔːtəupaɪlət] N pilote m automatique; **to be on ~** (plane) être sur pilote automatique; (fig) marcher au radar

autopsy [ˈɔːtɒpsɪ] N autopsie f

★**autumn** [ˈɔːtəm] N automne m

autumnal [ɔːˈtʌmnəl] ADJ (colour) automnal(e); (weather) d'automne

auxiliary [ɔːgˈzɪlɪərɪ] ADJ, N auxiliaire mf

AV N ABBR (= Authorized Version) traduction anglaise de la Bible ▶ ABBR = **audiovisual**

Av. ABBR (= avenue) Av

avail [əˈveɪl] vt: **to ~ o.s. of** user de; profiter de ▶ N: **to no ~** sans résultat, en vain, en pure perte

availability [əveɪləˈbɪlɪtɪ] N disponibilité f

★**available** [əˈveɪləbl] ADJ disponible; **every ~ means** tous les moyens possibles or à sa (or notre etc) disposition; **is the manager ~?** est-ce que le directeur peut (me) recevoir?; (on phone) pourrais-je parler au directeur?; **to make sth ~ to sb** mettre qch à la disposition de qn

avalanche [ˈævəlɑːnʃ] N avalanche f

avant-garde [ˈævɒ̃ˈɡɑːd] ADJ d'avant-garde

avarice [ˈævərɪs] N avarice f

avaricious [ævəˈrɪʃəs] ADJ âpre au gain

avatar [ˈævətɑːʳ] N (Comput) avatar m

avdp. ABBR = **avoirdupois**

Ave. ABBR (= avenue) Av

avenge [əˈvɛndʒ] vt venger

avenger [əˈvɛndʒəʳ] N vengeur(-eresse)

avenue [ˈævənjuː] N avenue f; (fig) moyen m

aver [əˈvɜːʳ] vt (formal) affirmer

★**average** [ˈævərɪdʒ] N moyenne f; **on ~** en moyenne; **above/below (the) ~** au-dessus/en-dessous de la moyenne ▶ ADJ moyen(ne) ▶ vt (a certain figure) atteindre or faire etc en moyenne ▶ **average out** vi: **to ~ out at** représenter en moyenne, donner une moyenne de

averse [əˈvɜːs] ADJ: **to be ~ to sth/doing** éprouver une forte répugnance envers qch/à faire; **I wouldn't be ~ to a drink** un petit verre ne serait pas de refus, je ne dirais pas non à un petit verre

aversion [əˈvɜːʃən] N aversion f, répugnance f

avert [əˈvɜːt] vt (danger) prévenir, écarter; (one's eyes) détourner

aviary [ˈeɪvɪərɪ] N volière f

aviation [eɪvɪˈeɪʃən] N aviation f

aviator [ˈeɪvɪeɪtəʳ] N aviateur(-trice)

avid [ˈævɪd] ADJ avide

avidly [ˈævɪdlɪ] ADV avidement, avec avidité

avionics [eɪvɪˈɒnɪks] N avionique f

avocado [ævəˈkɑːdəʊ] N (BRIT: also: **avocado pear**) avocat m

★**avoid** [əˈvɔɪd] vt éviter

avoidable [əˈvɔɪdəbl] ADJ évitable

avoidance [əˈvɔɪdəns] N le fait d'éviter

avowed [əˈvaʊd] ADJ déclaré(e)

AVP N ABBR (US) = **assistant vice-president**

AWACS [ˈeɪwæks] N ABBR (= airborne warning and control system) AWACS (système aéroporté d'alerte et de contrôle)

await [əˈweɪt] vt attendre; **awaiting attention/delivery** (Comm) en souffrance; **long awaited** tant attendu(e)

awake [əˈweɪk] (pt **awoke** [əˈwəʊk], pp **awoken** [əˈwəʊkən]) ADJ éveillé(e); (fig) en éveil; **to be ~** être réveillé(e); **he was still ~** il ne dormait pas encore; **~ to** conscient de ▶ vt éveiller ▶ vi s'éveiller

awaken [əˈweɪkən] (literary) vi: **to ~ to sth** (become aware of) prendre conscience de qch; (wake up) s'éveiller ▶ vt (wake up: person) réveiller; (interest) éveiller

awakening [əˈweɪknɪŋ] N réveil m

award [əˈwɔːd] N (for bravery) récompense f; (prize) prix m; (Law: damages) dommages-intérêts mpl ▶ vt (prize) décerner; (Law: damages) accorder

award ceremony N cérémonie f de remise des prix

aware [əˈwɛəʳ] ADJ: **~ of** (conscious) conscient(e) de; (informed) au courant de; **to become ~ of/that** prendre conscience de/que; se rendre compte de/que; **politically/socially ~** sensibilisé(e) aux or ayant pris conscience des problèmes politiques/sociaux; **I am fully ~ that** je me rends parfaitement compte que

awareness [əˈwɛənɪs] N conscience f, connaissance f; **to develop people's ~ (of)** sensibiliser le public (à)

awash [əˈwɒʃ] ADJ recouvert(e) (d'eau); **~ with** inondé(e) de

★**away** [əˈweɪ] ADV (au) loin; (movement): **she went ~** elle est partie; **far ~** (au) loin; **two kilometres ~** à (une distance de) deux kilomètres, à deux kilomètres de distance; **two hours ~ by car** à deux heures de voiture or de route; **the holiday was two weeks ~** il restait deux semaines jusqu'aux vacances; **~ from** loin de; **to take sth ~ from sth** (subtract) ôter qch de qch; **to take sth ~ from sb** prendre qch à qn; **to work/pedal ~** travailler/pédaler à cœur joie; **to fade ~** (colour) s'estomper; (sound) s'affaiblir ▶ ADJ (not in, not here) absent(e); **he's ~ for a week** il est parti (pour) une semaine; **he's ~ in Milan** il est (parti) à Milan

away game, away match N (Sport) match m à l'extérieur

awe [ɔː] N respect mêlé de crainte, effroi mêlé d'admiration

awe-inspiring [ˈɔːɪnspaɪərɪŋ], **awesome** [ˈɔːsəm] ADJ impressionnant(e)

awesome [ˈɔːsəm] (US) ADJ (inf: excellent) génial(e)

awestruck [ˈɔːstrʌk] ADJ frappé(e) d'effroi

★**awful** [ˈɔːfəl] ADJ affreux(-euse); **an ~ lot of** énormément de

awfully [ˈɔːfəlɪ] ADV (very) terriblement, vraiment

awhile [əˈwaɪl] ADV un moment, quelque temps

awkward [ˈɔːkwəd] ADJ (clumsy) gauche, maladroit(e); (inconvenient) peu pratique; (embarrassing) gênant; **I can't talk just now, it's a bit ~** je ne peux pas parler tout de suite, c'est un peu difficile

awkwardness [ˈɔːkwədnɪs] N (embarrassment) gêne f

awl [ɔːl] N alêne f

awning [ˈɔːnɪŋ] N (of tent) auvent m; (of shop) store m; (of hotel etc) marquise f (de toile)

awoke [əˈwəʊk] PT of **awake**

awoken [əˈwəʊkən] PP of **awake**

AWOL [ˈeɪwɒl] ABBR (Mil) = **absent without leave**

awry [əˈraɪ] ADV, ADJ de travers; **to go ~** mal tourner

axe, (US) **ax** [æks] N hache f; **to have an ~ to grind** (fig) prêcher pour son saint ▶ vt (employee) renvoyer; (project etc) abandonner; (jobs) supprimer

axes [ˈæksiːz] NPL of **axis**

axiom [ˈæksɪəm] N axiome m

axiomatic [æksɪəuˈmætɪk] ADJ axiomatique

axis [ˈæksɪs] (pl **axes** [-siːz]) N axe m

axle [ˈæksl] N (*also*: **axle-tree**) essieu *m*
ay, aye [aɪ] EXCL (*yes*) oui ▸ N: **the ay(e)s** les oui
ayatollah [aɪəˈtɒlə] N ayatollah *m*
AYH N ABBR = **American Youth Hostels**
AZ ABBR (*US*) = **Arizona**
azalea [əˈzeɪlɪə] N azalée *f*
Azerbaijan [æzəbaɪˈdʒɑːn] N Azerbaïdjan *m*

Azerbaijani [æzəbaɪˈdʒɑːnɪ], **Azeri** [əˈzɛərɪ] ADJ azerbaïdjanais(e) ▸ N Azerbaïdjanais(e)
Azores [əˈzɔːz] NPL: **the ~** les Açores *fpl*
AZT N ABBR (= *azidothymidine*) AZT *f*
Aztec [ˈæztɛk] ADJ aztèque ▸ N Aztèque *mf*
azure [ˈeɪʒəʳ] ADJ azuré(e)

B, b [bi:] N (letter) B, b m; (Scol: mark) B; (Mus): **B** si m; **B for Benjamin**, (US) **B for Baker** B comme Berthe; **B road** n (BRIT Aut) route départementale

b. ABBR = **born**

B2B ['bi:tə'bi:] ADJ ABBR, N ABBR (= business to business) b2b m

B2C ['bi:tə'si:] ADJ ABBR, N ABBR (= business to consumer) b2c m

B4 [bi:'fɔ:ʳ] ABBR (in text message, e-mail: = before) avant

BA ABBR = **British Academy**; (Scol) = **Bachelor of Arts**

babble ['bæbl] VI babiller ▶ N babillage m

babe [beɪb] N (esp US inf: term of address) ma poule; (woman) canon m (inf), super nana f (inf); (old: baby) bébé m

baboon [bə'bu:n] N babouin m

★**baby** ['beɪbɪ] N bébé m

baby boomer ['beɪbibu:məʳ] N enfant mf du baby-boom

baby carriage N (US) voiture f d'enfant

baby food N aliments mpl pour bébé(s)

baby grand N (also: **baby grand piano**) (piano m) demi-queue m

babyish ['beɪbɪʃ] ADJ enfantin(e), de bébé

baby-minder ['beɪbɪmaɪndəʳ] N (BRIT) gardienne f (d'enfants)

baby-sit ['beɪbɪsɪt] VI garder les enfants

baby-sitter ['beɪbɪsɪtəʳ] N baby-sitter mf

baby talk N langage m bébé

baby wipe N lingette f (pour bébé)

baccalaureate [bækə'lɔ:rɪət] N baccalauréat m; **international ~** baccalauréat international

bachelor ['bætʃələʳ] N célibataire m; **B~ of Arts/ Science (BA/BSc)** ≈ licencié(e) ès or en lettres/ sciences; **B~ of Arts/Science degree (BA/BSc)** n ≈ licence f ès or en lettres/sciences

> Un **Bachelor's degree** est un diplôme accordé au terme de trois ou quatre années d'études universitaires. Les Bachelor's degrees les plus courants sont le BA (Bachelor of Arts), le BSc (Bachelor of Science) ou BS aux États-Unis, le BEd (Bachelor of Education) et le LLB (Bachelor of Laws).

bachelor party N (US) enterrement m de vie de garçon

bacillus [bə'sɪləs] N bacille m

★**back** [bæk] N (of person, horse) dos m; (of hand) dos, revers m; (of house, car, train) arrière m; (of chair) dossier m; (of page) verso m; (Football) arrière m; **can the people at the ~ hear me properly?** est-ce que les gens du fond m'entendent?; **to have one's ~ to the wall** (fig) être au pied du mur; **to break the ~ of a job** (BRIT) faire le gros d'un travail; **~ to front** à l'envers ▶ VT (financially) soutenir (financièrement); (candidate: also: **back up**) soutenir, appuyer; (horse: at races) parier or miser sur; (car) (faire) reculer ▶ VI reculer; (car etc) faire marche arrière ▶ ADJ (in compounds) de derrière, à l'arrière; **~ seat/wheel** (Aut) siège m/ roue f arrière inv; **~ payments/rent** arriéré m de paiements/loyer; **~ garden/room** jardin/ pièce sur l'arrière; **to take a ~ seat** (fig) se contenter d'un second rôle, être relégué(e) au second plan ▶ ADV (not forward) en arrière; (returned): **he's ~** il est rentré, il est de retour; **when will you be ~?** quand seras-tu de retour?; **he ran ~** il est revenu en courant; **throw the ball ~** renvoie la balle; **can I have it ~?** puis-je le ravoir?, peux-tu me le rendre?; **he called ~** (again) il a rappelé

▶ **back down** VI rabattre de ses prétentions

▶ **back on to** VT FUS: **the house backs on to the golf course** la maison donne derrière sur le terrain de golf

▶ **back out** VI (of promise) se dédire

▶ **back up** VT (person) soutenir; (Comput) faire une copie de sauvegarde de

backache ['bækeɪk] N mal m au dos

backbencher [bæk'bentʃəʳ] N (BRIT) membre du parlement sans portefeuille

back benches NPL (BRIT) voir article

> Le terme **back benches** désigne les bancs les plus éloignés de l'allée centrale de la Chambre des communes. Les députés qui occupent ces bancs sont les backbenchers et n'ont pas de portefeuille ministériel.

backbiting ['bækbaɪtɪŋ] N médisance(s) f(pl)

backbone ['bækbəun] N colonne vertébrale, épine dorsale; **he's the ~ of the organization** c'est sur lui que repose l'organisation

back-breaking ['bækbreɪkɪŋ] ADJ (work, labour) éreintant(e)

back burner [bæk'bə:nəʳ] N: **on the ~** en veilleuse

backchat ['bæktʃæt] N (BRIT inf) impertinences fpl

backcloth ['bækklɔθ] N (BRIT) toile f de fond

backcomb ['bækkəum] VT (BRIT) crêper

back country (US) N: **the ~** la campagne f profonde

backdate [bæk'deɪt] VT (letter) antidater; **backdated pay rise** augmentation f avec effet rétroactif

back door N porte f de derrière

backdrop ['bækdrɔp] N = **backcloth**

backer ['bækər] N partisan m; (Comm) commanditaire m

backfire [bæk'faɪər] VI (Aut) pétarader; (plans) mal tourner

backgammon ['bækgæmən] N trictrac m

★**background** ['bækgraund] N arrière-plan m; (of events) situation f, conjoncture f; (basic knowledge) éléments mpl de base; (experience) formation f; **family ~** milieu familial ▶ CPD (noise, music) de fond; **~ reading** lecture(s) générale(s) (sur un sujet)

backhand ['bækhænd] N (Tennis: also: **backhand stroke**) revers m

backhanded ['bæk'hændɪd] ADJ (fig) déloyal(e); équivoque

backhander ['bæk'hændər] N (BRIT: bribe) pot-de-vin m

backing ['bækɪŋ] N (fig) soutien m, appui m; (Comm) soutien (financier); (Mus) accompagnement m

backlash ['bæklæʃ] N contre-coup m, répercussion f

backless ['bæklɪs] ADJ (dress, top) dos nu inv

backlog ['bæklɔg] N: **~ of work** travail m en retard

back number N (of magazine etc) vieux numéro

backpack ['bækpæk] N sac m à dos

backpacker ['bækpækər] N randonneur(-euse)

back pain N mal m de dos

back pay N rappel m de salaire

backpedal ['bækpɛdl] VI (fig) faire marche arrière

backrest ['bækrɛst] N dossier m

backroom ['bækrum] N (place: lit) pièce f du fond; (: fig) coulisses fpl ▶ CPD (pej: deal, negotiations) dans les coulisses; **~ team** équipe qui travaille dans les coulisses

backseat driver ['bæksi:t-] N passager qui donne des conseils au conducteur

backside ['bæksaɪd] N (inf) derrière m, postérieur m

back-slapping ['bækslæpɪŋ] N (cordiality) cordialité f; (congratulating) félicitations fpl

backslash ['bækslæʃ] N barre oblique inversée

backslide ['bækslaɪd] VI retomber dans l'erreur

backspace ['bækspeɪs] VI (in typing) appuyer sur la touche retour

backstage [bæk'steɪdʒ] ADV dans les coulisses

back-street ['bækstri:t] ADJ (abortion) clandestin(e); **~ abortionist** avorteur(-euse) (clandestin)

backstroke ['bækstrəuk] N dos crawlé

backtrack ['bæktræk] VI (fig) = **backpedal**

backup ['bækʌp] ADJ (train, plane) supplémentaire, de réserve; (Comput) de sauvegarde ▶ N (support) appui m, soutien m; (Comput: also: **backup file**) sauvegarde f

★**backward** ['bækwəd] ADJ (movement) en arrière; (measure) rétrograde; (person, country) arriéré(e), attardé(e); (shy) hésitant(e); **~ and forward movement** mouvement de va-et-vient

backward-looking ['bækwədlukɪŋ] ADJ rétrograde

★**backwards** ['bækwədz] ADV (move, go) en arrière; (read a list) à l'envers, à rebours; (fall) à la renverse; (walk) à reculons; (in time) en arrière, vers le passé; **to know sth ~** or (US) **~ and forwards** (inf) connaître qch sur le bout des doigts

backwash ['bækwɔʃ] N (repercussions) contrecoup m; **in the ~ of sth** à la suite de qch

backwater ['bækwɔ:tər] N (fig) coin reculé; bled perdu

backwoods ['bækwudz] NPL coin m reculé; **the ~ of** le fin fond de ▶ CPD (town, area) reculé(e)

backyard [bæk'jɑ:d] N arrière-cour f

★**bacon** ['beɪkən] N bacon m, lard m

bacteria [bæk'tɪərɪə] NPL bactéries fpl

bacterial [bæk'tɪərɪəl] ADJ bactérien(ne)

bacteriology [bæktɪərɪ'ɔlədʒɪ] N bactériologie f

bacterium [bæk'tɪərɪəm] N of **bacteria**

★**bad** [bæd] ADJ mauvais(e); (child) vilain(e); (mistake, accident) grave; (meat, food) gâté(e), avarié(e); **his ~ leg** sa jambe malade; **to go ~** (meat, food) se gâter; (milk) tourner; **to have a ~ time of it** traverser une mauvaise passe; **I feel ~ about it** (guilty) j'ai un peu mauvaise conscience; **~ debt** créance douteuse; **in ~ faith** de mauvaise foi

bad cheque, (US) **bad check** N chèque m en bois

baddie, baddy ['bædɪ] N (inf: Cine etc) méchant m

bade [bæd] PT of **bid**

badge [bædʒ] N insigne m; (of police officer) plaque f; (stick-on, sew-on) badge m

badger ['bædʒər] N blaireau m ▶ VT harceler

badinage ['bædɪnɑːʒ] N (literary) badinage m

★**badly** ['bædlɪ] ADV (work, dress etc) mal; **to reflect ~ on sb** donner une mauvaise image de qn; **~ wounded** grièvement blessé; **he needs it ~** il en a un absolument besoin; **things are going ~** les choses vont mal; **~ off** adj, adv dans la gêne

bad-mannered ['bæd'mænəd] ADJ mal élevé(e)

badminton ['bædmɪntən] N badminton m

bad-mouth ['bæd'mauθ] VT (inf) débiner

bad-tempered ['bæd'tɛmpəd] ADJ (by nature) ayant mauvais caractère; (on one occasion) de mauvaise humeur

baffle ['bæfl] VT (puzzle) laisser perplexe

baffled ['bæfld] ADJ perplexe; **to be ~ by sth** être dérouté(e) par qch

baffling ['bæflɪŋ] ADJ déroutant(e), déconcertant(e)

★**bag** [bæg] N sac m; (of hunter) gibecière f, chasse f; **bags of** (inf: lots of) des tas de; **to pack one's bags** faire ses valises or bagages; **bags under the eyes** poches fpl sous les yeux ▶ VT (inf: take) empocher; s'approprier; (Tech) mettre en sacs

bagful ['bægful] N plein sac

baggage ['bægɪdʒ] N bagages mpl

baggage allowance N franchise f de bagages

baggage reclaim N (at airport) livraison f des bagages

b

baggy ['bægɪ] ADJ avachi(e), qui fait des poches

Baghdad [bæg'dæd] N Bagdad

bag lady N (inf) clocharde f

bagpipes ['bægpaɪps] NPL cornemuse f

bag-snatcher ['bægsnætʃəʳ] N (BRIT) voleur(-euse) à l'arraché

bag-snatching ['bægsnætʃɪŋ] N (BRIT) vol m à l'arraché

baguette [bæ'gɛt] N baguette f

Bahamas [bə'hɑːməz] NPL: **the ~** les Bahamas fpl

Bahrain [bɑː'reɪn] N Bahreïn m

bail [beɪl] N caution f; **to be released on ~** être libéré(e) sous caution ▸ VT (prisoner: also: **grant bail to**) mettre en liberté sous caution; (boat: also: **bail out**) écoper; see **bale**
▸ **bail out** VT (prisoner) payer la caution de

bailiff ['beɪlɪf] N huissier m

bailout ['beɪlaʊt] N sauvetage m (de banque, d'entreprise)

bait [beɪt] N appât m ▸ VT appâter; (fig: tease) tourmenter

★**bake** [beɪk] VT (faire) cuire au four ▸ VI (bread etc) cuire (au four); (make cakes etc) faire de la pâtisserie

baked beans [beɪkt-] NPL haricots blancs à la sauce tomate

baked potato N pomme f de terre en robe des champs

★**baker** ['beɪkəʳ] N boulanger(-ère)

bakery ['beɪkərɪ] N boulangerie f; boulangerie industrielle

baking ['beɪkɪŋ] N (process) cuisson f

baking powder N levure f (chimique)

baking tin N (for cake) moule m à gâteaux; (for meat) plat m pour le four

baking tray N plaque f à gâteaux

balaclava [bælə'klɑːvə] N (also: **balaclava helmet**) passe-montagne m

★**balance** ['bæləns] N équilibre m; (Comm: sum) solde m; (remainder) reste m; (scales) balance f; **~ of trade/payments** balance commerciale/des comptes or paiements; **~ carried forward** solde m à reporter; **~ brought forward** solde reporté ▸ VT mettre or faire tenir en équilibre; (pros and cons) peser; (budget) équilibrer; (account) balancer; (compensate) compenser, contrebalancer; **to ~ the books** arrêter les comptes, dresser le bilan

balanced ['bælənst] ADJ (personality, diet) équilibré(e); (report) objectif(-ive)

balance sheet N bilan m

★**balcony** ['bælkənɪ] N balcon m; **do you have a room with a ~?** avez-vous une chambre avec balcon?

bald [bɔːld] ADJ chauve; (tyre) lisse

balding ['bɔːldɪŋ] ADJ aux cheveux clairsemés

baldness ['bɔːldnɪs] N calvitie f

bale [beɪl] N balle f, ballot m
▸ **bale out** VI (of a plane) sauter en parachute ▸ VT (Naut: water, boat) écoper

Balearic Islands [bælɪ'ærɪk-] NPL: **the ~** les (îles fpl) Baléares fpl

baleful ['beɪlful] ADJ funeste, maléfique

balk [bɔːk] VI: **to ~ (at)** (person) regimber (contre); (horse) se dérober (devant)

Balkan ['bɔːlkən] ADJ balkanique ▸ N: **the Balkans** les Balkans mpl

★**ball** [bɔːl] N boule f; (football) ballon m; (for tennis, golf) balle f; (dance) bal m; **to play ~** jouer au ballon (or à la balle); (fig) coopérer; **to be on the ~** (fig: competent) être à la hauteur; (: alert) être éveillé(e), être vif (vive); **to start the ~ rolling** (fig) commencer; **the ~ is in their court** (fig) la balle est dans leur camp

ballad ['bæləd] N ballade f

ballast ['bæləst] N lest m

ball bearings N roulement m à billes

ball cock N robinet m à flotteur

ballerina [bælə'riːnə] N ballerine f

ballet ['bæleɪ] N ballet m; (art) danse f (classique)

ballet dancer N danseur(-euse) de ballet

ballet shoe N chausson m de danse

ball game N (tennis, baseball) jeu m de balle; (football, basketball) jeu m de ballon; (US: baseball match) match m de base-ball; (fig: situation) course f; **a (whole) different ~** une (tout) autre histoire

ballgown ['bɔːlgaun] N robe f de bal

ballistic [bə'lɪstɪk] ADJ balistique

ballistics [bə'lɪstɪks] N balistique f

★**balloon** [bə'luːn] N ballon m; (in comic strip) bulle f ▸ VI gonfler

balloonist [bə'luːnɪst] N aéronaute mf

ballot ['bælət] N scrutin m

ballot box N urne f (électorale)

ballot paper N bulletin m de vote

ballot rigging ['bælətrɪgɪŋ] N fraude f électorale

ballpark ['bɔːlpɑːk] N (US) stade m de base-ball

ballpark figure N (inf) chiffre approximatif

ballplayer ['bɔːlpleɪəʳ] (US) N joueur(-euse) de base-ball

ballpoint ['bɔːlpɔɪnt], **ballpoint pen** N stylo m à bille

ballroom ['bɔːlrum] N salle f de bal

balls [bɔːlz] NPL (inf!) couilles fpl (!)

ballsy ['bɔːlzɪ] ADJ (inf: person, behaviour) gonflé(e)

ballyhoo ['bælɪhuː] N bruit m

balm [bɑːm] N baume m

balmy ['bɑːmɪ] ADJ (breeze, air) doux (douce); (BRIT inf) = **barmy**

baloney [bə'launɪ] N (inf: esp US) balivernes fpl

BALPA ['bælpə] N ABBR (= British Airline Pilots' Association) syndicat des pilotes de ligne

balsa ['bɔːlsə], **balsa wood** N balsa m

balsam ['bɔːlsəm] N baume m

balsamic [bɔːl'sæmɪk] N (also: **balsamic vinegar**) vinaigre m balsamique

Baltic [bɔːltɪk] ADJ, N: **the ~ (Sea)** la (mer) Baltique

balustrade [bæləs'treɪd] N balustrade f

bamboo [bæm'buː] N bambou m

bamboozle [bæm'buːzl] VT (inf) embobiner

★**ban** [bæn] N interdiction f ▸ VT interdire; **he was banned from driving** (BRIT) on lui a retiré le permis (de conduire)

banal [bə'nɑːl] ADJ banal(e)

banality [bə'nælɪtɪ] N banalité f

★**banana** [bə'nɑːnə] N banane f

★**band** [bænd] N bande f; (at a dance) orchestre m; (Mil) musique f, fanfare f
▸ **band together** VI se liguer

bandage ['bændɪdʒ] N bandage m, pansement m
▸ VT (wound, leg) mettre un pansement or un bandage sur; (person) mettre un pansement or un bandage à

Band-Aid® ['bændeɪd] N (US) pansement adhésif

bandanna, bandana [bæn'dænə] N bandana m

B & B N ABBR = **bed and breakfast**

bandit ['bændɪt] N bandit m

band leader ['bændliːdə'] N chef m d'orchestre

bandstand ['bændstænd] N kiosque m (à musique)

bandwagon ['bændwægən] N: **to jump on the ~** (fig) monter dans or prendre le train en marche

bandwidth ['bændwɪdθ] N largeur f de bande

bandy ['bændɪ] VT (jokes, insults) échanger
▸ **bandy about** VT employer à tout bout de champ or à tort et à travers

bandy-legged ['bændɪ'lɛgɪd] ADJ aux jambes arquées

bane [beɪn] N: **it** (or **he** etc) **is the ~ of my life** c'est (or il est etc) le drame de ma vie

bang [bæŋ] N détonation f; (of door) claquement m; (blow) coup (violent) ▸ VT frapper (violemment); (door) claquer ▸ VI détoner; claquer; **to ~ at the door** cogner à la porte; **to ~ into sth** se cogner contre qch ▸ ADV: **to be ~ on time** (BRIT inf) être à l'heure pile
▸ **bang on about** VT FUS (BRIT inf) radoter sur
▸ **bang up** VT (BRIT inf: in prison) coffrer (inf); **to be banged up in a cell** être coincé(e) (inf) dans une cellule

banger ['bæŋə'] N (BRIT inf: car: also: **old banger**) (vieux) tacot m; (inf: sausage) saucisse f; (firework) pétard m

Bangkok [bæŋ'kɔk] N Bangkok

Bangladesh [bæŋglə'dɛʃ] N Bangladesh m

Bangladeshi [bæŋglə'dɛʃɪ] ADJ du Bangladesh
▸ N habitant(e) du Bangladesh

bangle ['bæŋgl] N bracelet m

bang-on ['bæŋ'ɔn] ADJ (BRIT inf) au poil (inf); **to be ~ with sth** être au poil (inf) avec qch

bangs [bæŋz] NPL (US: fringe) frange f

banish ['bænɪʃ] VT bannir

banishment ['bænɪʃmənt] N bannissement m

banister ['bænɪstə'] N, **banisters** ['bænɪstəz] NPL rampe f (d'escalier)

banjo ['bændʒəu] N (pl **banjoes** or **banjos**) banjo m

★**bank** [bæŋk] N banque f; (of river, lake) bord m, rive f; (of earth) talus m, remblai m ▸ VI (Aviat) virer sur l'aile; (Comm): **they ~ with Pitt's** leur banque or banquier est Pitt's
▸ **bank on** VT FUS miser or tabler sur

bank account N compte m en banque

bank balance N solde m bancaire

bank card (BRIT) N carte f d'identité bancaire

bank charges NPL (BRIT) frais mpl de banque

bank draft N traite f bancaire

★**banker** ['bæŋkə'] N banquier(-ère); **~'s card** (BRIT) carte f d'identité bancaire; **~'s order** (BRIT) ordre m de virement

bank giro N paiement m par virement

bank holiday N (BRIT) jour férié (où les banques sont fermées)

Le terme **bank holiday** s'applique au Royaume-Uni aux jours fériés pendant lesquels les banques (et généralement les petits commerces) sont fermées. Les principaux bank holidays à part Noël et Pâques se situent au mois de mai et fin août, et, contrairement aux pays de tradition catholique, ne coïncident pas avec des fêtes religieuses.

banking ['bæŋkɪŋ] N opérations fpl bancaires; profession f de banquier

banking hours NPL heures fpl d'ouverture des banques

bank loan N prêt m bancaire

bank manager N directeur m d'agence (bancaire)

banknote ['bæŋknəut] N billet m de banque

bank rate N taux m de l'escompte

bankroll ['bæŋkrəul] VT financer

bankrupt ['bæŋkrʌpt] N failli(e) ▸ ADJ en faillite; **to go ~** faire faillite

bankruptcy ['bæŋkrʌptsɪ] N faillite f

bank statement N relevé m de compte

banner ['bænə'] N bannière f

bannister ['bænɪstə'] N, **bannisters** ['bænɪstəz] NPL = **banister**

banns [bænz] NPL bans mpl (de mariage)

banquet ['bæŋkwɪt] N banquet m, festin m

bantam-weight ['bæntəmweɪt] N poids m coq inv

banter ['bæntə'] N badinage m

baobab ['beɪəubæb] N baobab m

bap [bæp] N (BRIT: roll) petit pain m

baptism ['bæptɪzəm] N baptême m

baptismal [bæp'tɪzməl] ADJ de baptême

Baptist ['bæptɪst] N baptiste mf

baptize [bæp'taɪz] VT baptiser

★**bar** [bɑː'] N (pub) bar m; (counter) comptoir m, bar; (rod: of metal etc) barre f; (: of window etc) barreau m; (of chocolate) tablette f, plaque f; (fig: obstacle) obstacle m; (prohibition) mesure f d'exclusion; (Mus) mesure f; **~ of soap** savonnette f; **behind bars** (prisoner) derrière les barreaux; **the B~** (Law) le barreau ▸ VT (road) barrer; (window) munir de barreaux; (person) exclure; (activity) interdire
▸ PREP: **~ none** sans exception

Barbados [bɑː'beɪdɔs] N Barbade f

barbarian [bɑː'bɛərɪən] ADJ, N barbare mf

barbaric [bɑː'bærɪk] ADJ barbare

barbarism ['bɑːbərɪzəm] N barbarie f

barbarity [bɑː'bærɪtɪ] N barbarie f

barbarous ['bɑːbərəs] ADJ barbare, cruel(le)

★**barbecue** ['bɑːbɪkjuː] N barbecue m

barbed ['bɑːbd] ADJ (comment, criticism) acéré(e)

barbed wire N fil m de fer barbelé

barber ['bɑːbə'] N coiffeur m (pour hommes)

barber's (shop) ['bɑːbəz-], (US) **barber shop** N salon m de coiffure (pour hommes); **to go to the barber's** aller chez le coiffeur

barbie ['bɑːbɪ] N (BRIT, AUSTRALIA inf: barbecue) barbecue m

barbiturate [bɑːˈbɪtjurɪt] N barbiturique m

Barcelona [bɑːsəˈləunə] N Barcelone

bar chart N diagramme m en bâtons

bar code N code m à barres, code-barre m

bard [bɑːd] N (literary) poète m

★**bare** [bɛə'] ADJ nu(e); **the ~ essentials** le strict nécessaire ▶ VT mettre à nu, dénuder; (teeth) montrer

bareback ['bɛəbæk] ADV à cru, sans selle

barefaced ['bɛəfeɪst] ADJ impudent(e), effronté(e)

barefoot ['bɛəfut] ADJ, ADV nu-pieds, (les) pieds nus

bareheaded [bɛəˈhɛdɪd] ADJ, ADV nu-tête, (la) tête nue

barely ['bɛəlɪ] ADV à peine

Barents Sea ['bærənts-] N: **the ~** la mer de Barents

★**bargain** ['bɑːgɪn] N (transaction) marché m; (good buy) affaire f, occasion f; **into the ~** par-dessus le marché ▶ VI (haggle) marchander; (negotiate) négocier, traiter
▶ **bargain for** VT FUS: **he got more than he bargained for!** il en a eu pour son argent !
▶ **bargain on** VT FUS (expect) s'attendre à; **to ~ on sth happening** s'attendre à ce que qch arrive

bargain-basement CPD (prices, rates) de bazar

bargain hunter N personne f à l'affût des bonnes occasions

bargaining ['bɑːgənɪŋ] N marchandage m; négociations fpl

bargaining position N: **to be in a weak/strong ~** être en mauvaise/bonne position pour négocier

barge [bɑːdʒ] N péniche f
▶ **barge in** VI (walk in) faire irruption; (interrupt talk) intervenir mal à propos
▶ **barge into** VT FUS rentrer dans
▶ **barge past** VT FUS bousculer en passant ▶ VI foncer

baritone ['bærɪtəun] N baryton m

barium meal ['bɛərɪəm-] N (bouillie f de) sulfate m de baryum

bark [bɑːk] N (of tree) écorce f; (of dog) aboiement m ▶ VI aboyer

barking mad, barking ['bɑːkɪŋ] ADJ (BRIT inf) complètement cinglé(e) (inf)

barley ['bɑːlɪ] N orge f

barley sugar N sucre m d'orge

barmaid ['bɑːmeɪd] N serveuse f (de bar), barmaid f

barman ['bɑːmən] N (irreg) serveur m (de bar), barman m

bar meal N repas m de bistrot; **to go for a ~** aller manger au bistrot

barmy ['bɑːmɪ] ADJ (BRIT inf) timbré(e), cinglé(e)

barn [bɑːn] N grange f

barnacle ['bɑːnəkl] N anatife m, bernache f

barn owl N chouette-effraie f, chat-huant m

barnyard ['bɑːnjɑːd] N basse-cour f ▶ CPD (animal) de basse-cour

barometer [bəˈrɔmɪtə'] N baromètre m

baron ['bærən] N baron m; **the press/oil barons** les magnats mpl or barons mpl de la presse/du pétrole

baroness ['bærənɪs] N baronne f

baronet ['bærənət] (BRIT) N baronnet m

baronial [bəˈrəunɪəl] ADJ seigneurial(e)

baroque [bəˈrɔk] ADJ baroque ▶ N: **the ~** le baroque

barrack ['bærək] VT (BRIT) chahuter

barracking ['bærəkɪŋ] N (BRIT): **to give sb a ~** chahuter qn

barracks ['bærəks] NPL caserne f

barrage ['bærɑːʒ] N (Mil) tir m de barrage; (dam) barrage m; (of criticism) feu m

barrel ['bærəl] N tonneau m; (of gun) canon m

barrel organ N orgue m de Barbarie

barren ['bærən] ADJ stérile; (hills) aride

barrette [bəˈrɛt] (US) N barrette f

barricade [bærɪˈkeɪd] N barricade f ▶ VT barricader

barrier ['bærɪə'] N barrière f; (BRIT: also: **crash barrier**) rail m de sécurité

barrier cream N (BRIT) crème protectrice

barring ['bɑːrɪŋ] PREP sauf

barrister ['bærɪstə'] N (BRIT) avocat (plaidant)

> En Angleterre, un **barrister**, que l'on appelle également *barrister-at-law*, est un avocat qui représente ses clients devant la cour et plaide pour eux. Pour devenir *barrister*, l'inscription auprès de l'une des quatre *Inns of Court* londoniennes est obligatoire. Ces associations professionnelles remplissent une fonction de conseil et de soutien financier auprès de leurs membres.

barrow ['bærəu] N (cart) charrette f à bras

barstool ['bɑːstuːl] N tabouret m de bar

Bart. ABBR (BRIT) = **baronet**

bartender ['bɑːtɛndə'] N (US) serveur m (de bar), barman m

barter ['bɑːtə'] N échange m, troc m ▶ VT: **to ~ sth for** échanger qch contre

base [beɪs] N base f ▶ VT (troops): **to be based at** être basé(e) à; (opinion, belief): **to ~ sth on** baser or fonder qch sur; **I'm based in London** je suis basé(e) à Londres; **coffee-based** à base de café; **a Paris-based firm** une maison opérant de Paris or dont le siège est à Paris ▶ ADJ vil(e), bas(se)

★**baseball** ['beɪsbɔːl] N base-ball m

baseball cap N casquette f de base-ball

baseboard ['beɪsbɔːd] N (US) plinthe f

base camp N camp m de base

Basel [bɑːl] N = **Basle**

baseless ['beɪslɪs] ADJ (accusation, rumour) sans fondement

baseline ['beɪslaɪn] N (Tennis) ligne f de fond

★**basement** ['beɪsmənt] N sous-sol m

base rate N taux m de base

bases ['beɪsɪz] NPL of **base**

bash [bæʃ] VT (inf) frapper, cogner; **bashed in** adj enfoncé(e), défoncé(e) ▶ N: **I'll have a ~ (at it)** (BRIT inf) je vais essayer un coup
▶ **bash up** VT (inf: car) bousiller; (: BRIT: person) tabasser

bashful ['bæʃful] ADJ timide; modeste

bashing ['bæʃɪŋ] N (inf) raclée f

BASIC ['beɪsɪk] N (Comput) BASIC m

basic ['beɪsɪk] ADJ (precautions, rules) élémentaire; (principles, research) fondamental(e); (vocabulary, salary) de base; (minimal) réduit(e) au minimum, rudimentaire

★**basically** ['beɪsɪklɪ] ADV (in fact) en fait; (essentially) fondamentalement

basic rate N (of tax) première tranche d'imposition

basics ['beɪsɪks] NPL: **the ~** l'essentiel m

basil ['bæzl] N basilic m

basilica [bə'zɪlɪkə] N basilique f

basin ['beɪsn] N (vessel, also Geo) cuvette f, bassin m; (BRIT: for food) bol m; (: bigger) saladier m; (also: **washbasin**) lavabo m

basis ['beɪsɪs] (pl **bases** [-siːz]) N base f; **on a part-time/trial ~** à temps partiel/à l'essai; **on the ~ of what you've said** d'après or compte tenu de ce que vous dites

bask [bɑːsk] VI: **to ~ in the sun** se chauffer au soleil

★**basket** ['bɑːskɪt] N corbeille f; (with handle) panier m

★**basketball** ['bɑːskɪtbɔːl] N basket-ball m

basketball player N basketteur(-euse)

Basle [bɑːl] N Bâle

basmati rice [bəz'mætɪ-] N riz m basmati

Basque [bæsk] ADJ basque; **the ~ Country** le Pays basque ▶ N Basque mf

bass [beɪs] N (Mus) basse f

bass clef N clé f de fa

bass drum N grosse caisse f

bassoon [bə'suːn] N basson m

bastard ['bɑːstəd] N enfant naturel(le), bâtard(e); (!) salaud m (!)

bastardized ['bɑːstədaɪzd] ADJ bâtard(e)

baste [beɪst] VT (Culin) arroser; (Sewing) bâtir, faufiler

bastion ['bæstɪən] N bastion m; **a ~ of sth** un bastion de qch

★**bat** [bæt] N (animal) chauve-souris f; (for baseball etc) batte f; (BRIT: for table tennis) raquette f; **off one's own ~** de sa propre initiative ▶ VT: **he didn't ~ an eyelid** il n'a pas sourcillé or bronché

batch [bætʃ] N (of bread) fournée f; (of papers) liasse f; (of applicants, letters) paquet m; (of work) monceau m; (of goods) lot m

bated ['beɪtɪd] ADJ: **with ~ breath** en retenant son souffle

★**bath** [bɑːθ] (pl **baths** [bɑːðz]) N bain m; (bathtub) baignoire f; **to have a ~** prendre un bain; see also **baths** ▶ VT baigner, donner un bain à

bathe [beɪð] VI se baigner ▶ VT baigner; (wound etc) laver

bather ['beɪðə'] N baigneur(-euse)

bathing ['beɪðɪŋ] N baignade f

bathing cap N bonnet m de bain

bathing costume, (US) **bathing suit** N maillot m (de bain)

bathmat ['bɑːθmæt] N tapis m de bain

bathrobe ['bɑːθrəub] N peignoir m de bain

★**bathroom** ['bɑːθrum] N salle f de bains

baths [bɑːðz] NPL (BRIT: also: **swimming baths**) piscine f

bath towel N serviette f de bain

bathtub ['bɑːθtʌb] N baignoire f

bath water N eau f du bain

batik [bə'tiːk] N batik m ▶ CPD (scarf, skirt) en batik

batman ['bætmən] N (irreg) (BRIT Mil) ordonnance f

baton ['bætən] N bâton m; (Mus) baguette f; (club) matraque f

batsman ['bætsmən] N (irreg) batteur m

battalion [bə'tælɪən] N bataillon m

batten ['bætn] N (Carpentry) latte f; (Naut: on sail) latte de voile
▶ **batten down** VT (Naut): **to ~ down the hatches** fermer les écoutilles

batter ['bætə'] VT battre ▶ N pâte f à frire

battered ['bætəd] ADJ (hat, pan) cabossé(e); (wife, child) battu(e); **a refuge for ~ wives** un centre d'accueil pour femmes battues

battering ['bætərɪŋ] N (violence) violences fpl physiques; **to take a ~** souffrir

battering ram ['bætərɪŋ-] N bélier m (fig)

battery ['bætrɪ] N (for torch, radio) pile f; (Aut, Mil) batterie f

battery charger N chargeur m

battery farming N élevage m en batterie

battery-operated ['bætərɪ'ɔpəreɪtɪd], **battery-powered** ['bætərɪ'pauəd] ADJ à piles, à pile

★**battle** ['bætl] N bataille f, combat m; **that's half the ~** (fig) c'est déjà bien; **it's a** or **we're fighting a losing ~** (fig) c'est perdu d'avance, c'est peine perdue ▶ VI se battre, lutter

battle dress N tenue f de campagne or d'assaut

battlefield ['bætlfiːld] N champ m de bataille

battleground ['bætlgraund] N champ m de bataille

battlements ['bætlmənts] NPL remparts mpl

battleship ['bætlʃɪp] N cuirassé m

batty ['bætɪ] ADJ (inf: person) toqué(e); (: idea, behaviour) loufoque

bauble ['bɔːbl] N babiole f

baulk [bɔːlk] VI = **balk**

bauxite ['bɔːksaɪt] N bauxite f

Bavaria [bə'veərɪə] N Bavière f

Bavarian [bə'veərɪən] ADJ bavarois(e) ▶ N Bavarois(e)

bawdy ['bɔːdɪ] ADJ paillard(e)

bawl [bɔːl] VI hurler, brailler

bay [beɪ] N (of sea) baie f; (BRIT: for parking) place f de stationnement; (: for loading) aire f de chargement; (*horse*) bai(e); **B~ of Biscay** golfe *m* de Gascogne; **to hold sb at ~** tenir qn à distance *or* en échec

bay leaf N laurier *m*

bayonet ['beɪənɪt] N baïonnette *f*

bay tree N laurier *m*

bay window N baie vitrée

bazaar [bə'zɑːr] N (*shop, market*) bazar *m*; (*sale*) vente *f* de charité

bazooka [bə'zuːkə] N bazooka *m*

BB N ABBR (BRIT.: = *Boys' Brigade*) mouvement de garçons

BBB N ABBR (US: = *Better Business Bureau*) organisme de défense du consommateur

BBC N ABBR (= *British Broadcasting Corporation*) office de la radiodiffusion et télévision britannique

La **BBC** est un organisme centralisé dont les membres, nommés par l'État, gèrent les chaînes de télévision publiques (*BBC*1, qui présente des émissions d'intérêt général, et *BBC*2 plutôt orientée vers les émissions plus culturelles, ainsi que les chaînes numériques et en ligne) et les stations de radio publiques. Bien que sa programmation ne soit pas contrôlée par l'État, la *BBC* est responsable devant le parlement quant au contenu des émissions qu'elle diffuse. Par ailleurs, la *BBC* offre un service mondial de diffusion d'émissions, en anglais et dans 28 autres langues, appelé *BBC World Service*. La *BBC* ne diffuse pas de publicité car elle est financée par la redevance télé et par l'exportation d'émissions.

BBQ N ABBR (= *barbecue*) barbecue *m*

BC ADV ABBR (= *before Christ*) av. J.-C. ▶ ABBR (CANADA) = **British Columbia**

BCE ADV ABBR (*Before Common Era*) AEC

BCG N ABBR (= *Bacillus Calmette-Guérin*) BCG *m*

BD N ABBR (= *Bachelor of Divinity*) diplôme universitaire

B/D ABBR = **bank draft**

BDS N ABBR (= *Bachelor of Dental Surgery*) diplôme universitaire

---

be [biː]

(*pt* **was** [wɔz], **were** [wəːr], *pp* **been** [biːn]) AUX VB **1** (*with present participle: forming continuous tenses*): **what are you doing?** que faites-vous ?; **they're coming tomorrow** ils viennent demain; **I've been waiting for you for 2 hours** je t'attends depuis 2 heures

2 (*with pp: forming passives*) être; **to be killed** être tué(e); **the box had been opened** la boîte avait été ouverte; **he was nowhere to be seen** on ne le voyait nulle part

3 (*in tag questions*): **it was fun, wasn't it?** c'était drôle, n'est-ce pas ?; **he's good-looking, isn't he?** il est beau, n'est-ce pas ?; **she's back, is she?** elle est rentrée, n'est-ce pas or alors ?

4 (+*to* +*infinitive*): **the house is to be sold** (*necessity*) la maison doit être vendue; (*future*) la maison va être vendue; **he's not to open it** il ne doit pas l'ouvrir; **am I to understand that ...?** dois-je comprendre que ... ?; **he was to have come yesterday** il devait venir hier

5 (*possibility: supposition*): **if I were you, I ...** à votre place, je ..., si j'étais vous, je ...

▶ VB + COMPLEMENT **1** (*gen*) être; **I'm English** je suis anglais(e); **I'm tired** je suis fatigué(e); **I'm hot/cold** j'ai chaud/froid; **he's a doctor** il est médecin; **be careful/good/quiet!** faites attention/soyez sages/taisez-vous !; **2 and 2 are 4** 2 et 2 font 4

2 (*of health*) aller; **how are you?** comment allez-vous ?; **I'm better now** je vais mieux maintenant; **he's fine now** il va bien maintenant; **he's very ill** il est très malade

3 (*of age*) avoir; **how old are you?** quel âge avez-vous ?; **I'm sixteen (years old)** j'ai seize ans

4 (*cost*) coûter; **how much was the meal?** combien a coûté le repas ?; **that'll be £5, please** ça fera 5 livres, s'il vous plaît; **this shirt is £17** cette chemise coûte 17 livres

▶ VI **1** (*exist, occur etc*) être, exister; **the prettiest girl that ever was** la fille la plus jolie qui ait jamais existé; **is there a God?** y a-t-il un dieu ?; **be that as it may** quoi qu'il en soit; **so be it** soit

2 (*referring to place*) se trouver; **I won't be here tomorrow** je ne serai pas là demain; **Edinburgh is in Scotland** Édimbourg est or se trouve en Écosse

3 (*referring to movement*) aller; **where have you been?** où êtes-vous allé(s) ?

▶ IMPERS VB **1** (*referring to time*) être; **it's 5 o'clock** il est 5 heures; **it's the 28th of April** c'est le 28 avril

2 (*referring to distance*): **it's 10 km to the village** le village est à 10 km

3 (*referring to the weather*) faire; **it's too hot/cold** il fait trop chaud/froid; **it's windy today** il y a du vent aujourd'hui

4 (*emphatic*): **it's me/the postman** c'est moi/le facteur; **it was Maria who paid the bill** c'est Maria qui a payé la note

B/E ABBR = **bill of exchange**

★**beach** [biːtʃ] N plage *f* ▶ VT échouer

beachcomber ['biːtʃkəʊmər] N ramasseur(-euse) d'épaves; (*fig*) bon(ne) à rien

beachfront ['biːtʃfrʌnt] CPD (*café, hotel*) en front de mer

beachwear ['biːtʃwɛər] N tenues *fpl* de plage

beacon ['biːkən] N (*lighthouse*) fanal *m*; (*marker*) balise *f*; (*also*: **radio beacon**) radiophare *m*

bead [biːd] N perle *f*; (*of dew, sweat*) goutte *f* ■ **beads** NPL (*necklace*) collier *m*

beaded ['biːdɪd] ADJ (*dress, cushion*) orné(e) de perles; **his forehead was ~ with sweat** la sueur perlait sur son front

beady ['biːdɪ] ADJ: **~ eyes** yeux *mpl* de fouine

beagle ['biːgl] N beagle *m*

beak [biːk] N bec *m*

beaker ['biːkər] N gobelet *m*

beam [biːm] N (*Archit*) poutre *f*; (*of light*) rayon *m*; (*Radio*) faisceau *m* radio; **to drive on full** or **main** or (*US*) **high ~** rouler en pleins phares ▶ VI rayonner

beaming ['biːmɪŋ] ADJ (*sun, smile*) radieux(-euse)

bean [biːn] N haricot *m*; (*of coffee*) grain *m*

beanbag ['biːnbæg] N fauteuil *m* poire

bean counter N (*pej*) comptable *mf*

beanpole ['biːnpəʊl] N (*inf*) perche *f*

beansprouts ['biːnsprauts] NPL pousses *fpl* or germes *mpl* de soja

★**bear** [bɛəʳ] (pt **bore** [bɔːʳ], pp **borne** [bɔːn]) N ours m; (Stock Exchange) baissier m ▶ VT porter; (endure) supporter; (traces, signs) porter; (Comm: interest) rapporter; **to ~ the responsibility of** assumer la responsabilité de; **to ~ comparison with** soutenir la comparaison avec; **I can't ~ him** je ne peux pas le supporter or souffrir ▶ VI: **to ~ right/left** obliquer à droite/gauche, se diriger vers la droite/gauche; **to bring pressure to ~ on sb** faire pression sur qn
  ▶ **bear down** VI (rush towards): **to ~ down on sb/sth** se ruer sur qn/qch
  ▶ **bear out** VT (theory, suspicion) confirmer
  ▶ **bear up** VI supporter, tenir le coup; **he bore up well** il a tenu le coup
  ▶ **bear with** VT FUS (sb's moods, temper) supporter; **~ with me a minute** un moment, s'il vous plaît
bearable [ˈbɛərəbl] ADJ supportable
beard [bɪəd] N barbe f
bearded [ˈbɪədɪd] ADJ barbu(e)
bearer [ˈbɛərəʳ] N porteur m; (of passport etc) titulaire mf
bearing [ˈbɛərɪŋ] N maintien m, allure f; (connection) rapport m; **to take a ~** faire le point; **to find one's bearings** s'orienter ■ **(ball) bearings** NPL (Tech) roulement m (à billes)
bearskin [ˈbɛəskɪn] N (hat) bonnet m à poil; (skin) peau f d'ours
beast [biːst] N bête f; (inf: person) brute f
beastly [ˈbiːstlɪ] ADJ infect(e)

★**beat** [biːt] (pt **~**, pp **beaten** [ˈbiːtn]) N battement m; (Mus) temps m, mesure f; (of police officer) ronde f ▶ VT, VI battre; **to ~ it** (inf) ficher le camp; **that beats everything!** c'est le comble !; **to ~ about the bush** tourner autour du pot
  ▶ **beat down** VT (door) enfoncer; (price) faire baisser; (seller) faire descendre ▶ VI (rain) tambouriner; (sun) taper
  ▶ **beat off** VT repousser
  ▶ **beat up** VT (eggs) battre; (inf: person) tabasser
beaten [ˈbiːtən] PP **beat** ▶ ADJ (trampled) battu(e); **off the ~ track** hors des chemins or sentiers battus
beater [ˈbiːtəʳ] N (for eggs, cream) fouet m, batteur m
beatific [biːəˈtɪfɪk] ADJ (literary: smile) béat(e)
beatification [biːætɪfɪˈkeɪʃən] N béatification f
beating [ˈbiːtɪŋ] N raclée f
beat-up [ˈbiːtˈʌp] ADJ (inf) déglingué(e)
beautician [bjuːˈtɪʃən] N esthéticien(ne)
★**beautiful** [ˈbjuːtɪful] ADJ beau (belle)
beautifully [ˈbjuːtɪflɪ] ADV admirablement
beautify [ˈbjuːtɪfaɪ] VT embellir
★**beauty** [ˈbjuːtɪ] N beauté f; **the ~ of it is that …** le plus beau, c'est que …
beauty contest N concours m de beauté
beauty parlour, (US) **beauty parlor** N institut m de beauté
beauty queen N reine f de beauté
beauty salon N institut m de beauté
beauty sleep N: **I need my ~** j'ai besoin de faire un gros dodo
beauty spot N (on skin) grain m de beauté; (BRIT Tourism) site naturel (d'une grande beauté)

beaver [ˈbiːvəʳ] N castor m
  ▶ **beaver away** VI travailler d'arrache-pied
becalmed [bɪˈkɑːmd] ADJ immobilisé(e) par le calme plat
became [bɪˈkeɪm] PT of **become**
★**because** [bɪˈkɔz] CONJ parce que; **~ of** prep à cause de
beck [bɛk] N: **to be at sb's ~ and call** être à l'entière disposition de qn
beckon [ˈbɛkən] VT (also: **beckon to**) faire signe (de venir) à
★**become** [bɪˈkʌm] VI (irreg: like **come**) devenir; **to ~ fat/thin** grossir/maigrir; **to ~ angry** se mettre en colère; **it became known that** on apprit que; **what has ~ of him?** qu'est-il devenu ?
becoming [bɪˈkʌmɪŋ] ADJ (behaviour) convenable, bienséant(e); (clothes) seyant(e)
BECTU [ˈbɛktu] N ABBR (BRIT) = **Broadcasting, Entertainment, Cinematographic and Theatre Union**
BEd N ABBR (= Bachelor of Education) diplôme d'aptitude à l'enseignement
★**bed** [bɛd] N lit m; (of flowers) parterre m; (of coal, clay) couche f; (of sea, lake) fond m; **to go to ~** aller se coucher
  ▶ **bed down** VI se coucher
bed and breakfast N (terms) chambre et petit déjeuner; (place) ≈ chambre f d'hôte

Un **bed and breakfast** est une petite pension dans une maison particulière ou une ferme, où l'on peut louer une chambre avec petit déjeuner pour un prix souvent inférieur à celui d'un hôtel. Ces établissements sont communément appelés B&B et sont signalés par une pancarte dans le jardin ou au-dessus de la porte.

bedbug [ˈbɛdbʌg] N punaise f
bedclothes [ˈbɛdkləuðz] NPL couvertures fpl et draps mpl
bedcover [ˈbɛdkʌvəʳ] N couvre-lit m, dessus-de-lit m
bedding [ˈbɛdɪŋ] N literie f
bedevil [bɪˈdɛvl] VT (harass) harceler; **to be bedevilled by** être victime de
bedfellow [ˈbɛdfɛləu] N: **they are strange bedfellows** (fig) ça fait un drôle de mélange
bedlam [ˈbɛdləm] N chahut m, cirque m
bed linen N draps mpl de lit (et taies fpl d'oreillers), literie f
Bedouin [ˈbɛduɪn] N Bédouin(e) ▶ ADJ bédouin(e)
bedpan [ˈbɛdpæn] N bassin m (hygiénique)
bedpost [ˈbɛdpəust] N colonne f de lit
bedraggled [bɪˈdrægld] ADJ dépenaillé(e), les vêtements en désordre
bedridden [ˈbɛdrɪdn] ADJ cloué(e) au lit
bedrock [ˈbɛdrɔk] N (fig) principes essentiels or de base, essentiel m; (Geo) roche f en place, socle m
bedroll [ˈbɛdrəul] N couchage m
★**bedroom** [ˈbɛdrum] N chambre f (à coucher)
bed settee N canapé-lit m
bedside [ˈbɛdsaɪd] N: **at sb's ~** au chevet de qn ▶ CPD (book, lamp) de chevet

bedside lamp N lampe f de chevet

bedside table N table f de chevet

bedsit ['bɛdsɪt], **bedsitter** ['bɛdsɪtə'] N (BRIT) chambre meublée, studio m

bedsore ['bɛdsɔː'] N escarre f

bedspread ['bɛdsprɛd] N couvre-lit m, dessus-de-lit m

bedstead ['bɛdstɛd] N châlit m

★**bedtime** ['bɛdtaɪm] N: **it's ~** c'est l'heure de se coucher

bedwetting ['bɛdwɛtɪŋ] N incontinence f nocturne

bee [biː] N abeille f; **to have a ~ in one's bonnet (about sth)** être obnubilé(e) (par qch)

Beeb [biːb] N (BRIT inf): **the ~** la BBC

beech [biːtʃ] N hêtre m

★**beef** [biːf] N bœuf m; **roast ~** rosbif m
▶ **beef up** VT (inf: support) renforcer; (: essay) étoffer

★**beefburger** ['biːfbə:gə'] N hamburger m

beefcake ['biːfkeɪk] N (inf) armoire f à glace (inf), malabar m (inf)

Beefeater ['biːfiːtə'] N hallebardier m (de la tour de Londres)

beefsteak ['biːfsteɪk] N bifteck m, steak m

beefy ['biːfɪ] ADJ (person) costaud(e)

beehive ['biːhaɪv] N ruche f

beekeeper ['biːkiːpə'] N apiculteur(-trice)

bee-keeping ['biːkiːpɪŋ] N apiculture f

beeline ['biːlaɪn] N: **to make a ~ for** se diriger tout droit vers

been [biːn] PP of **be**

beep [biːp] N bip m

beeper ['biːpə'] N (pager) bip m

★**beer** [bɪə'] N bière f

beer belly N (inf) bedaine f (de buveur de bière)

beer can N canette f de bière

beer garden N (BRIT) jardin m d'un pub (où l'on peut emmener ses consommations)

beermat ['bɪəmæt] N dessous m de verre

beeswax ['biːzwæks] N cire f d'abeille

beet [biːt] N (vegetable) betterave f; (US: also: **red beet**) betterave (potagère)

beetle ['biːtl] N scarabée m, coléoptère m

beetroot ['biːtruːt] N (BRIT) betterave f

befall [bɪ'fɔːl] VI, VT (irreg: like **fall**) advenir (à)

befit [bɪ'fɪt] VT seoir à

★**before** [bɪ'fɔː'] PREP (of time) avant; (of space) devant
▶ CONJ avant que + sub; avant de; **~ she goes** avant qu'elle (ne) parte; **~ going** avant de partir ▶ ADV avant; **the week ~** la semaine précédente or d'avant; **I've seen it ~** je l'ai déjà vu; **I've never seen it ~** c'est la première fois que je le vois

beforehand [bɪ'fɔːhænd] ADV au préalable, à l'avance

befriend [bɪ'frɛnd] VT venir en aide à; traiter en ami

befuddled [bɪ'fʌdld] ADJ: **to be ~** avoir les idées brouillées

beg [bɛg] VI mendier ▶ VT mendier; (favour) quémander, solliciter; (forgiveness, mercy etc)

demander; (entreat) supplier; **to ~ sb to do sth** supplier qn de faire qch; **I ~ your pardon** (apologizing) excusez-moi; (not hearing) pardon ?; **that begs the question of …** cela soulève la question de …, cela suppose réglée la question de …; see also **pardon**

began [bɪ'gæn] PT of **begin**

beget [bɪ'gɛt] (pt **begot** [bɪ'gɔt], pp **begotten** [bɪ'gɔtn]) VT engendrer

beggar ['bɛgə'] N (also: **beggarman, beggarwoman**) mendiant(e)

★**begin** [bɪ'gɪn] (pt **began** [bɪ'gæn], pp **begun** [bɪ'gʌn]) VT, VI commencer; **to ~ doing** or **to do sth** commencer à faire qch; **beginning (from) Monday** à partir de lundi; **I can't ~ to thank you** je ne saurais vous remercier; **to ~ with** d'abord, pour commencer

beginner [bɪ'gɪnə'] N débutant(e)

★**beginning** [bɪ'gɪnɪŋ] N commencement m, début m; **right from the ~** dès le début

begonia [bɪ'gəunɪə] N bégonia m

begot [bɪ'gɔt] PT of **beget**

begotten [bɪ'gɔtn] PP of **beget**

begrudge [bɪ'grʌdʒ] VT: **to ~ sb sth** envier qch à qn; donner qch à contrecœur or à regret à qn

beguile [bɪ'gaɪl] VT (enchant) enjôler

beguiling [bɪ'gaɪlɪŋ] ADJ (charming) séduisant(e), enchanteur(-eresse)

begun [bɪ'gʌn] PP of **begin**

★**behalf** [bɪ'hɑːf] N: **on ~ of**, (US) **in ~ of** (representing) de la part de; au nom de; (for benefit of) pour le compte de; **on my/his ~** de ma/sa part

★**behave** [bɪ'heɪv] VI se conduire, se comporter; (well: also: **behave o.s.**) se conduire bien or comme il faut

behaviour, (US) **behavior** [bɪ'heɪvjə'] N comportement m, conduite f

behavioural, (US) **behavioral** [bɪ'heɪvjərəl] ADJ de comportement, comportemental(e)

behead [bɪ'hɛd] VT décapiter

beheld [bɪ'hɛld] PT, PP of **behold**

behest [bɪ'hɛst] N: **at sb's ~**, **at the ~ of sb** sur l'ordre de qn

★**behind** [bɪ'haɪnd] PREP derrière; (time) en retard sur; (supporting): **to be ~ sb** soutenir qn; **~ the scenes** dans les coulisses ▶ ADV derrière; en retard; **to leave sth ~** (forget) oublier de prendre qch; **to be ~ with sth** être en retard dans qch ▶ N derrière m

behold [bɪ'həuld] VT (irreg: like **hold**) apercevoir, voir

beholden [bɪ'həuldən] ADJ: **~ to** redevable à

behove [bɪ'həuv], (US) **behoove** [bɪ'huːv] VT incomber; **it behoves us to …** il nous incombe de …

beige [beɪʒ] ADJ beige

Beijing ['beɪ'dʒɪŋ] N Pékin m

being ['biːɪŋ] N être m; **to come into ~** prendre naissance

Beirut [beɪ'ruːt] N Beyrouth

bejewelled, (US) **bejeweled** [bɪ'dʒuːəld] ADJ (woman) paré(e) de bijoux; (crown, tiara) incrusté(e) de joyaux

Belarus [belə'rus] N Biélorussie f, Bélarus m

Belarussian [belə'rʌʃən] ADJ biélorusse ▶ N Biélorusse mf; (Ling) biélorusse m

belated [bɪ'leɪtɪd] ADJ tardif(-ive)

belatedly [bɪ'leɪtɪdlɪ] ADV tardivement, avec retard

belch [beltʃ] VI avoir un renvoi, roter ▶ VT (smoke etc: also: **belch out**) vomir, cracher

beleaguered [bɪ'li:gɪd] ADJ (city) assiégé(e); (army) cerné(e); (fig) sollicité(e) de toutes parts

Belfast ['bɛlfɑ:st] N Belfast

belfry ['bɛlfrɪ] N beffroi m

★**Belgian** ['bɛldʒən] ADJ belge, de Belgique ▶ N Belge mf

★**Belgium** ['bɛldʒəm] N Belgique f

Belgrade [bɛl'greɪd] N Belgrade

belie [bɪ'laɪ] VT démentir; (give false impression of) occulter

belief [bɪ'li:f] N (opinion) conviction f; (trust, faith) foi f; (acceptance as true) croyance f; **it's beyond ~** c'est incroyable; **in the ~ that** dans l'idée que

believable [bɪ'li:vəbl] ADJ croyable

★**believe** [bɪ'li:v] VT, VI croire, estimer; **to ~ in** (God) croire en; (ghosts, method) croire à; **I don't ~ in corporal punishment** je ne suis pas partisan des châtiments corporels; **he is believed to be abroad** il serait à l'étranger

believer [bɪ'li:və°] N (in idea, activity) partisan(e); **~ in** partisan(e) de; (Rel) croyant(e)

belittle [bɪ'lɪtl] VT déprécier, rabaisser

Belize [bɛ'li:z] N Bélize m

★**bell** [bɛl] N cloche f; (small) clochette f, grelot m; (on door) sonnette f; (electric) sonnerie f; **that rings a ~** (fig) cela me rappelle qch

bell-bottoms ['bɛlbɔtəmz] NPL pantalon m à pattes d'éléphant

bellboy ['bɛlbɔɪ], (US) **bellhop** ['bɛlhɔp] N groom m, chasseur m

bellicose ['bɛlɪkəus] ADJ (literary) belliqueux(-euse)

belligerence [bɪ'lɪdʒərəns] N belligérance f

belligerent [bɪ'lɪdʒərənt] ADJ (person) agressif(-ive); (nation) belligérant(e)

bellow ['bɛləu] VI (bull) meugler; (person) brailler ▶ VT (orders) hurler

bellows ['bɛləuz] NPL soufflet m

bell pepper N (esp US) poivron m

bell push N (BRIT) bouton m de sonnette

belly ['bɛlɪ] N ventre m

bellyache ['bɛlɪeɪk] (inf) N colique f ▶ VI ronchonner

belly button N (inf) nombril m

bellyful ['bɛlɪful] N (inf): **I've had a ~** j'en ai ras le bol

★**belong** [bɪ'lɔŋ] VI: **to ~ to** appartenir à; (club etc) faire partie de; **this book belongs here** ce livre va ici, la place de ce livre est ici

belonging [bɪ'lɔŋɪŋ] N: **sense of ~** sentiment m d'appartenance

belongings [bɪ'lɔŋɪŋz] NPL affaires fpl, possessions fpl; **personal ~** effets personnels

Belorussia [bɛlə'rʌʃə] N Biélorussie f

Belorussian [bɛlə'rʌʃən] ADJ, N = **Belarussian**

beloved [bɪ'lʌvɪd] ADJ (bien-)aimé(e), chéri(e) ▶ N bien-aimé(e)

★**below** [bɪ'ləu] PREP sous, au-dessous de; **temperatures ~ normal** températures inférieures à la normale ▶ ADV en dessous; en contre-bas; **see ~** voir plus bas or plus loin or ci-dessous

belt [bɛlt] N ceinture f; (Tech) courroie f; **industrial ~** zone industrielle ▶ VT (thrash) donner une raclée à ▶ VI (BRIT inf) filer (à toutes jambes)
  ▶ **belt out** VT (song) chanter à tue-tête or à pleins poumons
  ▶ **belt up** VI (BRIT inf) la boucler

beltway ['bɛltweɪ] N (US Aut) route f de ceinture; (: motorway) périphérique m

bemoan [bɪ'məun] VT se lamenter sur

bemused [bɪ'mju:zd] ADJ perplexe, médusé(e)

bemusement [bɪ'mju:zmənt] N perplexité f

bench [bentʃ] N banc m; (in workshop) établi m; **the B~** (Law: judges) la magistrature, la Cour

benchmark ['bentʃmɑ:k] N référence f ▶ VT évaluer (par comparaison); **to ~ sth against sth** comparer qch à qch

bend [bend] (pt, pp **bent** [bent]) VT courber; (leg, arm) plier ▶ VI se courber ▶ N (in road) virage m, tournant m; (in pipe, river) coude m
  ▶ **bend down** VI se baisser
  ▶ **bend over** VI se pencher

bends [bendz] NPL (Med) maladie f des caissons

bendy ['bendɪ] ADJ (toy, wire) flexible; (river) sinueux(-euse)

★**beneath** [bɪ'ni:θ] PREP sous, au-dessous de; (unworthy of) indigne de ▶ ADV dessous, au-dessous, en bas

benefactor ['bɛnɪfæktə°] N bienfaiteur m

benefactress ['bɛnɪfæktrɪs] N bienfaitrice f

beneficial [bɛnɪ'fɪʃəl] ADJ: **~ (to)** salutaire (pour), bénéfique (à)

beneficiary [bɛnɪ'fɪʃərɪ] N (Law) bénéficiaire mf

★**benefit** ['bɛnɪfɪt] N avantage m, profit m; (allowance of money) allocation f ▶ VT faire du bien à, profiter à ▶ VI: **he'll ~ from it** cela lui fera du bien, il y gagnera or s'en trouvera bien

benefit performance N représentation f or gala m de bienfaisance

Benelux ['bɛnɪlʌks] N Bénélux m

benevolence [bɪ'nɛvələns] N bienveillance f

benevolent [bɪ'nɛvələnt] ADJ bienveillant(e)

BEng N ABBR (= Bachelor of Engineering) diplôme universitaire

Bengali [bɛn'gɔ:lɪ] ADJ bengali f inv ▶ N (person) Bengali mf; (language) bengali m

benighted [bɪ'naɪtɪd] ADJ (literary: ignorant) ignorant(e); (: unfortunate) maudit(e)

benign [bɪ'naɪn] ADJ (person, smile) bienveillant(e), affable; (Med) bénin(-igne)

Benin [bɛ'ni:n] N Bénin m

bent [bent] PT, PP of **bend** ▶ N inclination f, penchant m ▶ ADJ (wire, pipe) coudé(e); (inf: dishonest) véreux(-euse); **to be ~ on** être résolu(e) à

benzene ['bɛnzi:n] N benzène m

bequeath [bɪ'kwi:ð] VT léguer

bequest [bɪ'kwɛst] N legs m

berate [bɪˈreɪt] VT réprimander; **to ~ sb for sth** réprimander qn pour qch

bereaved [bɪˈriːvd] N: **the ~** la famille du disparu ▸ ADJ endeuillé(e)

bereavement [bɪˈriːvmənt] N deuil *m*

bereft [bɪˈrɛft] ADJ (*lonely*) perdu(e); **to be ~ of sth** être dépourvu(e) de qch

beret [ˈbɛreɪ] N béret *m*

Bering Sea [ˈbeɪrɪŋ-] N: **the ~** la mer de Béring

berk [bəːk] N (*BRIT pej*) andouille *f*

Berlin [bəːˈlɪn] N Berlin; **East/West ~** Berlin Est/Ouest

berm [bəːm] N (*US Aut*) accotement *m*

Bermuda [bəːˈmjuːdə] N Bermudes *fpl*

Bermuda shorts NPL bermuda *m*

Bern [bəːn] N Berne

berry [ˈbɛrɪ] N baie *f*

berserk [bəˈsəːk] ADJ: **to go ~** être pris(e) d'une rage incontrôlable; se déchaîner

berth [bəːθ] N (*bed*) couchette *f*; (*for ship*) poste *m* d'amarrage, mouillage *m*; **to give sb a wide ~** (*fig*) éviter qn ▸ VI (*in harbour*) venir à quai; (*at anchor*) mouiller

beseech [bɪˈsiːtʃ] (*pt, pp* **besought** [-ˈsɔːt]) VT implorer, supplier

beseeching [bɪˈsiːtʃɪŋ] ADJ (*expression, tone*) suppliant(e)

beset [bɪˈsɛt] (*pt, pp* **~**) VT assaillir ▸ ADJ: **~ with** semé(e) de

besetting [bɪˈsɛtɪŋ] ADJ: **his ~ sin** son vice, son gros défaut

★**beside** [bɪˈsaɪd] PREP à côté de; (*compared with*) par rapport à; **that's ~ the point** ça n'a rien à voir; **to be ~ o.s. (with anger)** être hors de soi

besides [bɪˈsaɪdz] ADV en outre, de plus ▸ PREP en plus de; (*except*) excepté

besiege [bɪˈsiːdʒ] VT (*town*) assiéger; (*fig*) assaillir

besmirch [bɪˈsməːtʃ] VT (*reputation*) ternir, entacher; **to ~ sb** diffamer qn

besotted [bɪˈsɔtɪd] ADJ (*BRIT*): **~ with** entiché(e) de

besought [bɪˈsɔːt] PT, PP *of* **beseech**

bespectacled [bɪˈspɛktɪkld] ADJ à lunettes

bespoke [bɪˈspəuk] ADJ (*BRIT: garment*) fait(e) sur mesure; **~ tailor** tailleur *m* à façon

★**best** [bɛst] ADJ meilleur(e); **the ~ thing to do is ...** le mieux, c'est de ...; **the ~ part of** (*quantity*) le plus clair de, la plus grande partie de ▸ ADV le mieux ▸ N: **at ~** au mieux; **to do one's ~** faire de son mieux; **to make the ~ of sth** s'accommoder de qch (du mieux que l'on peut); **to the ~ of my knowledge** pour autant que je sache; **to the ~ of my ability** du mieux que je pourrai; **he's not exactly patient at the ~ of times** il n'est jamais spécialement patient

best-before date [bɛstbɪˈfɔː-] N date *f* de limite d'utilisation *or* de consommation

best man N (*irreg*) garçon *m* d'honneur

bestow [bɪˈstəu] VT accorder; (*title*) conférer

bestseller [ˈbɛstˈsɛləʳ] N best-seller *m*, succès *m* de librairie

bet [bɛt] (*pt, pp* **~** *or* **betted** [ˈbɛtɪd]) VT, VI parier; **to ~ sb sth** parier qch à qn ▸ N pari *m*; **it's a safe ~** (*fig*) il y a de fortes chances

beta [ˈbiːtə] ADJ, N bêta *adj*, *m inv*

Bethlehem [ˈbɛθlɪhɛm] N Bethléem

betide [bɪˈtaɪd] VT: **woe ~** malheur à

betray [bɪˈtreɪ] VT trahir

betrayal [bɪˈtreɪəl] N trahison *f*

betrothed [bɪˈtrəuðd] ADJ, N (*old*) fiancé(e)

★**better** [ˈbɛtəʳ] ADJ meilleur(e); **that's ~!** c'est mieux !; **to get ~** (*Med*) aller mieux; (*improve*) s'améliorer ▸ ADV mieux; **I had ~ go** il faut que je m'en aille; **you had ~ do it** vous feriez mieux de le faire; **he thought ~ of it** il s'est ravisé; **~ off** *adj* plus à l'aise financièrement; (*fig*) **you'd be ~ off this way** vous vous en trouveriez mieux ainsi, ce serait mieux *or* plus pratique ainsi ▸ VT améliorer ▸ N: **to get the ~ of** triompher de, l'emporter sur; **a change for the ~** une amélioration

betterment [ˈbɛtəmənt] N amélioration *f*

betting [ˈbɛtɪŋ] N paris *mpl*

betting shop N (*BRIT*) bureau *m* de paris

★**between** [bɪˈtwiːn] PREP entre; **the road ~ here and London** la route d'ici à Londres; **we only had 5 ~ us** nous n'en avions que 5 en tout ▸ ADV au milieu, dans l'intervalle

bevel [ˈbɛvəl] N (*also:* **bevel edge**) biseau *m*

beverage [ˈbɛvərɪdʒ] N boisson *f* (*gén sans alcool*)

bevy [ˈbɛvɪ] N: **a ~ of** un essaim *or* une volée de

bewail [bɪˈweɪl] VT se lamenter sur

beware [bɪˈwɛəʳ] VT, VI: **to ~ (of)** prendre garde (à); **"~ of the dog"** « (attention) chien méchant »

bewildered [bɪˈwɪldəd] ADJ dérouté(e), ahuri(e)

bewildering [bɪˈwɪldrɪŋ] ADJ déroutant(e), ahurissant(e)

bewitch [bɪˈwɪtʃ] VT ensorceler; **to be bewitched by sth/sb** être captivé(e) par qch/qn

bewitching [bɪˈwɪtʃɪŋ] ADJ enchanteur(-eresse)

★**beyond** [bɪˈjɔnd] PREP (*in space, time*) au-delà de; (*exceeding*) au-dessus de; **~ doubt** hors de doute; **~ repair** irréparable ▸ ADV au-delà

b/f ABBR = **brought forward**

BFPO N ABBR (= *British Forces Post Office*) *service postal de l'armée*

bhaji [ˈbɑːdʒi] N bhaji *m* (*beignet indien aux légumes*)

bhp N ABBR (*Aut*: = *brake horsepower*) puissance *f* aux freins

Bhutan [buːˈtɑːn] N Bhoutan *m*

bi... [baɪ] PREFIX bi...

biannual [baɪˈænjuəl] ADJ semestriel(le)

bias [ˈbaɪəs] N (*prejudice*) préjugé *m*, parti pris *m*; (*preference*) prévention *f*

biased, biassed [ˈbaɪəst] ADJ partial(e), montrant un parti pris; **to be bias(s)ed against** avoir un préjugé contre

biathlon [baɪˈæθlən] N biathlon *m*

bib [bɪb] N bavoir *m*, bavette *f*

★**Bible** [ˈbaɪbl] N Bible *f*

Bible Belt N (*in the US*): **the ~** la ceinture de la Bible (*région du Sud profond où le protestantisme évangélique est prédominant*)

biblical [ˈbɪblɪkl] ADJ biblique

bibliography [bɪblɪ'ɔgrəfɪ] N bibliographie f

bicarbonate of soda [baɪ'kɑ:bənɪt-] N bicarbonate m de soude

bicentenary [baɪsɛn'ti:nərɪ], **bicentennial** [baɪsɛn'tɛnɪəl] N bicentenaire m

biceps ['baɪsɛps] N biceps m

bicker ['bɪkə'] VI se chamailler

bickering ['bɪkərɪŋ] N (political) querelles fpl; (of neighbours, family) chamailleries fpl

★**bicycle** ['baɪsɪkl] N bicyclette f

bicycle path, bicycle track N piste f cyclable

bicycle pump N pompe f à vélo

bid [bɪd] N offre f; (at auction) enchère f; (attempt) tentative f ▶ VI (pt, pp ~) faire une enchère or offre ▶ VT (pt **bade** [bæd], pp **bidden** ['bɪdn]) faire une enchère or offre de; **to ~ sb good day** souhaiter le bonjour à qn

bidden ['bɪdn] PP of **bid**

bidder ['bɪdə'] N: **the highest ~** le plus offrant

bidding ['bɪdɪŋ] N enchères fpl

bide [baɪd] VT: **to ~ one's time** attendre son heure

bidet ['bi:deɪ] N bidet m

bidirectional ['baɪdɪ'rɛkʃənl] ADJ bidirectionnel(le)

biennial [baɪ'ɛnɪəl] ADJ biennal(e), bisannuel(le) ▶ N biennale f; (plant) plante bisannuelle

bier [bɪə'] N bière f (cercueil)

bifocals [baɪ'fəuklz] NPL lunettes fpl à double foyer

★**big** [bɪg] ADJ (in height: person, building, tree) grand(e); (in bulk, amount: person, parcel, book) gros(se); **to do things in a ~ way** faire les choses en grand

bigamist ['bɪgəmɪst] N bigame mf

bigamy ['bɪgəmɪ] N bigamie f

Big Apple N voir article

> Si l'on sait que **The Big Apple** désigne la ville de New York (apple est en réalité un terme d'argot signifiant grande ville), on connaît moins les surnoms donnés aux autres grandes villes américaines. Chicago est surnommée Windy City, peut-être à cause des rafales soufflant du lac Michigan, La Nouvelle-Orléans doit son sobriquet de Big Easy à son style de vie décontracté, et l'industrie automobile a donné à Detroit son surnom de Motown.

big bang theory N théorie f du big bang

big dipper [-'dɪpə'] N montagnes fpl russes

big end N (Aut) tête f de bielle

biggish ['bɪgɪʃ] ADJ (see big) assez grand(e), assez gros(se)

bigheaded ['bɪg'hɛdɪd] ADJ prétentieux(-euse)

big-hearted ['bɪg'hɑ:tɪd] ADJ au grand cœur

bigot ['bɪgət] N fanatique mf, sectaire mf

bigoted ['bɪgətɪd] ADJ fanatique, sectaire

bigotry ['bɪgətrɪ] N fanatisme m, sectarisme m

big picture N: **the ~** la situation dans son ensemble

big time, big-time (inf) ADJ (football, investment) de première catégorie f ▶ N: **to hit the ~** percer ▶ ADV (US) de manière très spectaculaire

big toe N gros orteil

big top N grand chapiteau

big wheel N (at fair) grande roue

bigwig ['bɪgwɪg] N (inf) grosse légume, huile f

★**bike** [baɪk] N (bicycle) vélo m; (motorbike) moto f, bécane f

bike lane N piste f cyclable

biker ['baɪkə'] N (motorcyclist) motard(e); (US: cyclist) cycliste mf

bikini [bɪ'ki:nɪ] N bikini m

bilateral [baɪ'lætərl] ADJ bilatéral(e)

bilberry ['bɪlbərɪ] N myrtille f

bile [baɪl] N bile f

bilingual [baɪ'lɪŋgwəl] ADJ bilingue

bilious ['bɪlɪəs] ADJ bilieux(-euse); (fig) maussade, irritable

★**bill** [bɪl] N note f, facture f; (in restaurant) addition f, note f; (Pol) projet m de loi; (US: banknote) billet m (de banque); (notice) affiche f; (of bird) bec m; (Theat): **on the ~** à l'affiche; **may I have the ~ please?** (est-ce que je peux avoir) l'addition, s'il vous plaît ?; **put it on my ~** mettez-le sur mon compte; **"post no bills"** « défense d'afficher »; **to fit** or **fill the ~** (fig) faire l'affaire; **~ of exchange** lettre f de change; **~ of lading** connaissement m; **~ of sale** contrat m de vente ▶ VT (item) facturer; (customer) remettre la facture à

billboard ['bɪlbɔ:d] N (US) panneau m d'affichage

billet ['bɪlɪt] N cantonnement m (chez l'habitant) ▶ VT (troops) cantonner

billfold ['bɪlfəuld] N (US) portefeuille m

billiards ['bɪljədz] N billard m

billing ['bɪlɪŋ] N (of performer) affiche f

★**billion** ['bɪljən] N (BRIT) billion m (million de millions); (US) milliard m

billionaire [bɪljə'nɛə'] N milliardaire mf

billow ['bɪləu] N nuage m ▶ VI (smoke) s'élever en nuage; (sail) se gonfler

billy goat ['bɪlɪgəut] N bouc m

bimbo ['bɪmbəu] N (pej) bimbo f, ravissante idiote f

bimonthly [baɪ'mʌnθlɪ] (BRIT) ADJ bimestriel(le)

bin [bɪn] N boîte f; (BRIT: also: **dustbin, litter bin**) poubelle f; (for coal) coffre m

binary ['baɪnərɪ] ADJ binaire

bind [baɪnd] (pt, pp **bound** [baund]) VT attacher; (book) relier; (oblige) obliger, contraindre ▶ N (inf: nuisance) scie f
▶ **bind over** VT (Law) mettre en liberté conditionnelle
▶ **bind up** VT (wound) panser; **to be bound up in** (work, research etc) être complètement absorbé par, être accroché par; **to be bound up with** (person) être accroché à

binder ['baɪndə'] N (file) classeur m

binding ['baɪndɪŋ] N (of book) reliure f ▶ ADJ (contract) qui constitue une obligation

bindweed ['baɪndwi:d] N liseron m

binge [bɪndʒ] N (inf): **to go on a ~** faire la bringue

binge-watch ['bɪndʒwɔtʃ] VT regarder non stop

bingo ['bɪŋgəu] N sorte de jeu de loto pratiqué dans des établissements publics

bin liner N sac m poubelle

binoculars [bɪ'nɔkjuləz] NPL jumelles fpl

biochemical [baɪəu'kɛmɪkl] ADJ biochimique

biochemist [baɪəʊ'kɛmɪst] N biochimiste mf
biochemistry [baɪə'kɛmɪstrɪ] N biochimie f
biodegradable ['baɪəʊdɪ'greɪdəbl] ADJ biodégradable
biodiesel ['baɪəʊdiːzl] N biogazole m, biodiesel m
biodiversity ['baɪəʊdaɪ'vəːsɪtɪ] N biodiversité f
bioengineering [baɪəʊendʒɪ'nɪərɪŋ] N (genetic engineering) génie m génétique; (Med) bio-ingénierie f
biofuel ['baɪəʊfjuəl] N biocarburant m
biographer [baɪ'ɔgrəfə'] N biographe mf
biographic [baɪə'græfɪk], **biographical** [baɪə'græfɪkl] ADJ biographique
biography [baɪ'ɔgrəfɪ] N biographie f
bioinformatics [baɪəʊɪnfə'mætɪks] N bioinformatique f
biological [baɪə'lɔdʒɪkl] ADJ biologique
biological clock N horloge f physiologique
biologist [baɪ'ɔlədʒɪst] N biologiste mf
★**biology** [baɪ'ɔlədʒɪ] N biologie f
biomedical [baɪəʊ'mɛdɪkl] ADJ biomédical(e)
biometric [baɪə'mɛtrɪk] ADJ biométrique
bionic [baɪ'ɔnɪk] ADJ bionique
biophysics ['baɪəʊ'fɪzɪks] N biophysique f
biopic ['baɪəʊpɪk] N film m biographique
biopsy ['baɪɔpsɪ] N biopsie f
biosecurity ['baɪəʊsɪ'kjuərɪtɪ] N biosécurité f
biosphere ['baɪəsfɪə'] N biosphère f
biotech ['baɪəʊtɛk] N biotechnologie f ▸ CPD (industry, shares) biotechnologique; (company) de biotechnologie
biotechnology ['baɪəʊtɛk'nɔlədʒɪ] N biotechnologie f
bioterrorism [baɪəʊ'tɛrərɪzəm] N bioterrorisme m
bioterrorist [baɪəʊ'tɛrərɪst] N bioterroriste mf ▸ CPD (attack) bioterroriste
bipartisan [baɪpɑːtɪ'zæn] ADJ biparti(e), bipartite
biped ['baɪpɛd] N bipède m
bipolar [baɪ'pəʊlə'] ADJ bipolaire
birch [bəːtʃ] N bouleau m
★**bird** [bəːd] N oiseau m; (BRIT pej: girl) nana f
birdcage ['bəːdkeɪdʒ] N cage f à oiseaux
birder ['bəːdə'] N passionné(e) m/f d'oiseaux, ornithologue mf amateur(-trice)
bird flu N grippe f aviaire
birdie ['bəːdɪ] (Golf) N birdie m; **to get a ~** faire un birdie ▸ VT: **to ~ a hole** faire un birdie
bird of prey N oiseau m de proie
bird's-eye view ['bəːdzaɪ-] N vue f à vol d'oiseau; (fig) vue d'ensemble or générale
birdsong ['bəːdsɔŋ] N chant m des oiseaux
bird watcher [-wɔtʃə'] N ornithologue mf amateur(-trice)
birdwatching ['bəːdwɔtʃɪŋ] N ornithologie f (d'amateur)
Biro® ['baɪərəʊ] N stylo m à bille
★**birth** [bəːθ] N naissance f; **to give ~ to** donner naissance à, mettre au monde; (animal) mettre bas

birth certificate N acte m de naissance
birth control N (policy) limitation f des naissances; (methods) méthode(s) contraceptive(s)
birthdate ['bəːθdeɪt] N date f de naissance
★**birthday** ['bəːθdeɪ] N anniversaire m ▸ CPD (cake, card etc) d'anniversaire
birthmark ['bəːθmɑːk] N envie f, tache f de vin
birthplace ['bəːθpleɪs] N lieu m de naissance
birth rate N (taux m de) natalité f
birthright ['bəːθraɪt] N droit m de naissance
Biscay ['bɪskeɪ] N: **the Bay of ~** le golfe de Gascogne
★**biscuit** ['bɪskɪt] N (BRIT) biscuit m; (US) petit pain au lait
bisect [baɪ'sɛkt] VT couper or diviser en deux
bisexual [baɪ'sɛksjuəl] ADJ, N bisexuel(le)
bishop ['bɪʃəp] N évêque m; (Chess) fou m
bison ['baɪsən] N pl inv (esp BRIT) bison m
bistro ['biːstrəʊ] N petit restaurant m, bistrot m
★**bit** [bɪt] PT of **bite** ▸ N morceau m; (Comput) bit m, élément m binaire; (of tool) mèche f; (of horse) mors m; **a ~ of** un peu de; **a ~ mad/dangerous** un peu fou/risqué; **~ by ~** petit à petit; **to come to bits** (break) tomber en morceaux, se déglinguer; **bring all your bits and pieces** apporte toutes tes affaires; **to do one's ~** y mettre du sien
bitch [bɪtʃ] N (dog) chienne f; (!) salope f (!), garce f
bitchy ['bɪtʃɪ] ADJ (inf) vache
bitcoin ['bɪtkɔɪn] N (Comput) bitcoin m
★**bite** [baɪt] (pt **bit** [bɪt], pp **bitten** ['bɪtn]) VT, VI mordre; (insect) piquer; **to ~ one's nails** se ronger les ongles ▸ N morsure f; (insect bite) piqûre f; (mouthful) bouchée f; **let's have a ~ (to eat)** mangeons un morceau
biting ['baɪtɪŋ] ADJ mordant(e)
bit-map ['bɪtmæp] N (Comput) mode point m; (also: **bit-map image**) image f en mode point
bit part N (Theat) petit rôle
bitten ['bɪtn] PP of **bite**
★**bitter** ['bɪtə'] ADJ amer(-ère); (criticism) cinglant(e); (icy: weather, wind) glacial(e); **to the ~ end** jusqu'au bout ▸ N (BRIT: beer) bière f (à forte teneur en houblon)
bitterly ['bɪtəlɪ] ADV (complain, weep) amèrement; (oppose, criticise) durement, âprement; (jealous, disappointed) horriblement; **it's ~ cold** il fait un froid de loup
bitterness ['bɪtənɪs] N amertume f; goût amer
bittersweet ['bɪtəswiːt] ADJ aigre-doux (douce)
bitty ['bɪtɪ] ADJ (BRIT inf) décousu(e)
bitumen ['bɪtjumɪn] N bitume m
bivouac ['bɪvuæk] N bivouac m
bizarre [bɪ'zɑː'] ADJ bizarre
BL N ABBR (= Bachelor of Law(s), Bachelor of Letters) diplôme universitaire; (US: = Bachelor of Literature) diplôme universitaire
bl ABBR = **bill of lading**
blab [blæb] VI jaser, trop parler ▸ VT (also: **blab out**) laisser échapper, aller raconter
★**black** [blæk] ADJ noir(e); **to give sb a ~ eye** pocher l'œil à qn, faire un œil au beurre noir à qn; **~ and blue** (bruised) couvert(e) de bleus ▸ N (colour) noir m;

b

517

to be in the ~ (*in credit*) avoir un compte créditeur; **there it is in ~ and white** (*fig*) c'est écrit noir sur blanc ▶ VT (*shoes*) cirer; (*BRIT Industry*) boycotter
▶ **black out** VI (*faint*) s'évanouir

black belt N (*Judo etc*) ceinture noire; **he's a ~** il est ceinture noire

blackberry ['blækbəri] N mûre f

blackbird ['blækbə:d] N merle m

blackboard ['blækbɔ:d] N tableau noir

black box N (*Aviat*) boîte noire

black coffee N café noir

Black Country N (*BRIT*): **the ~** le Pays Noir (*dans les Midlands*)

blackcurrant ['blæk'kʌrənt] N cassis m

black economy N (*BRIT*) travail m au noir

blacken ['blækn] VT noircir

Black Forest N: **the ~** la Forêt Noire

blackhead ['blækhɛd] N point noir

black hole N (*Astronomy*) trou noir

black humour, (*US*) **black humor** N humour m noir

black ice N verglas m

blackjack ['blækdʒæk] N (*Cards*) vingt-et-un m; (*US: truncheon*) matraque f

blackleg ['blæklɛg] N (*BRIT*) briseur(-euse) de grève, jaune mf

blacklist ['blæklɪst] N liste noire ▶ VT mettre sur la liste noire

blackmail ['blækmeɪl] N chantage m ▶ VT faire chanter, soumettre au chantage

blackmailer ['blækmeɪlə'] N maître chanteur m

black market N marché noir

blackout ['blækaut] N panne f d'électricité; (*in wartime*) black-out m; (*TV*) interruption f d'émission; (*fainting*) syncope f

black pepper N poivre noir

black pudding N boudin (noir)

Black Sea N: **the ~** la mer Noire

black sheep N brebis galeuse

blacksmith ['blæksmɪθ] N forgeron m

black spot N (*Aut*) point noir

black-tie ADJ (*dinner, function*) en tenue de soirée, habillé(e)

bladder ['blædə'] N vessie f

blade [bleɪd] N lame f; (*of oar*) plat m; (*of propeller*) pale f; **a ~ of grass** un brin d'herbe

blag [blæg] VT (*BRIT inf*) obtenir à l'esbroufe

blame [bleɪm] N faute f, blâme m ▶ VT: **to ~ sb/sth for sth** attribuer à qn/qch la responsabilité de qch; reprocher qch à qn/qch; **who's to ~?** qui est le fautif or coupable or responsable ?; **I'm not to ~** ce n'est pas ma faute

blameless ['bleɪmlɪs] ADJ irréprochable

blanch [blɑ:ntʃ] VI (*person, face*) blêmir ▶ VT (*Culin*) blanchir

bland [blænd] ADJ affable; (*taste, food*) doux (douce), fade

blank [blæŋk] ADJ blanc (blanche); (*look*) sans expression, dénué(e) d'expression ▶ N espace m vide, blanc m; (*cartridge*) cartouche f à blanc;

his mind was a ~ il avait la tête vide; **we drew a ~** (*fig*) nous n'avons abouti à rien

blank cheque, (*US*) **blank check** N chèque m en blanc; **to give sb a ~ to do ...** (*fig*) donner carte blanche à qn pour faire ...

★**blanket** ['blæŋkɪt] N couverture f; (*of snow, cloud*) couche f ▶ ADJ (*statement, agreement*) global(e), de portée générale; **to give ~ cover** (*insurance policy*) couvrir tous les risques

blare [blɛə'] VI (*brass band, horns, radio*) beugler

blarney ['blɑ:nɪ] N boniment m

blasé ['blɑ:zeɪ] ADJ blasé(e)

blasphemous ['blæsfɪməs] ADJ (*words*) blasphématoire; (*person*) blasphémateur(-trice)

blasphemy ['blæsfɪmɪ] N blasphème m

blast [blɑ:st] N explosion f; (*shock wave*) souffle m; (*of air, steam*) bouffée f; **(at) full ~** (*play music etc*) à plein volume ▶ VT faire sauter or exploser ▶ EXCL (*BRIT inf*) zut !
▶ **blast off** VI (*Space*) décoller

blasted ['blɑ:stɪd] ADJ (*inf: damned*) fichu(e)

blast-off ['blɑ:stɔf] N (*Space*) lancement m

blatant ['bleɪtənt] ADJ flagrant(e), criant(e)

blatantly ['bleɪtəntlɪ] ADV ouvertement; **it's ~ obvious** c'est l'évidence même

blaze [bleɪz] N (*fire*) incendie m; (*flames: of fire, sun etc*) embrasement m; (*: in hearth*) flamme f, flambée f; (*fig*) flamboiement m; **in a ~ of publicity** à grand renfort de publicité ▶ VI (*fire*) flamber; (*fig*) flamboyer, resplendir ▶ VT: **to ~ a trail** (*fig*) montrer la voie

blazer ['bleɪzə'] N blazer m

bleach [bli:tʃ] N (*also*: **household bleach**) eau f de Javel ▶ VT (*linen*) blanchir

bleached [bli:tʃt] ADJ (*hair*) oxygéné(e), décoloré(e)

bleachers ['bli:tʃəz] NPL (*US Sport*) gradins mpl (*en plein soleil*)

bleak [bli:k] ADJ morne, désolé(e); (*weather*) triste, maussade; (*smile*) lugubre; (*prospect, future*) morose

bleary-eyed ['blɪərɪ'aɪd] ADJ aux yeux pleins de sommeil

bleat [bli:t] N bêlement m ▶ VI bêler

bled [blɛd] PT, PP of **bleed**

bleed [bli:d] (*pt, pp* **bled** [blɛd]) VT saigner; (*brakes, radiator*) purger ▶ VI saigner; **my nose is bleeding** je saigne du nez

bleep [bli:p] N (*Radio, TV*) top m; (*of pocket device*) bip m ▶ VI émettre des signaux ▶ VT (*doctor etc*) appeler (*au moyen d'un bip*)

bleeper ['bli:pə'] N (*of doctor etc*) bip m

blemish ['blɛmɪʃ] N défaut m; (*on reputation*) tache f

blend [blɛnd] N mélange m ▶ VT mélanger ▶ VI (*colours etc: also*: **blend in**) se mélanger, se fondre, s'allier

blender ['blɛndə'] N (*Culin*) mixeur m

bless [blɛs] (*pt, pp* **blessed** or **blest** [blɛst]) VT bénir; **to be blessed with** avoir le bonheur de jouir de or d'avoir; **~ you!** (*after sneeze*) à tes souhaits !

blessed ['blɛsɪd] ADJ (*Rel: holy*) béni(e); (*: happy*) bienheureux(-euse); **it rains every ~ day** il ne se passe pas de jour sans qu'il ne pleuve

blessing ['blɛsɪŋ] N bénédiction f; (godsend) bienfait m; **to count one's blessings** s'estimer heureux; **it was a ~ in disguise** c'est un bien pour un mal

blew [blu:] PT of **blow**

blight [blaɪt] N (of plants) rouille f ▶ VT (hopes etc) anéantir, briser

blimey ['blaɪmɪ] EXCL (BRIT inf) mince alors !

★**blind** [blaɪnd] ADJ aveugle; **to turn a ~ eye (on or to)** fermer les yeux (sur) ▶ N (for window) store m ▶ VT aveugler; **~ people** les aveugles mpl

blind alley N impasse f

blind corner N (BRIT) virage m sans visibilité

blind date N rendez-vous galant (avec un(e) inconnu(e))

blinders ['blaɪndəz] (US) NPL œillères fpl

blindfold ['blaɪndfəʊld] N bandeau m ▶ ADJ, ADV les yeux bandés ▶ VT bander les yeux à

blinding ['blaɪndɪŋ] ADJ (light, flash) aveuglant(e); (pain) fulgurant(e)

blindly ['blaɪndlɪ] ADV aveuglément

blindness ['blaɪndnɪs] N cécité f; (fig) aveuglement m

blind spot N (Aut etc) angle m aveugle; (fig) angle mort

bling ['blɪŋ], **bling bling** N (inf: also: **bling-bling jewellery**) quincaillerie f (inf)

blink [blɪŋk] VI cligner des yeux; (light) clignoter ▶ N: **the TV's on the ~** (inf) la télé ne va pas tarder à nous lâcher

blinkered ['blɪŋkəd] ADJ (BRIT: person) qui a l'esprit borné; (: approach) borné(e); (: view) étroit(e)

blinkers ['blɪŋkəz] NPL œillères fpl

blinking ['blɪŋkɪŋ] ADJ (BRIT inf): **this ~ ...** ce fichu or sacré ...

blip [blɪp] N (on radar etc) spot m; (on graph) petite aberration; (fig) petite anomalie (passagère)

bliss [blɪs] N félicité f, bonheur m sans mélange

blissful ['blɪsful] ADJ (event, day) merveilleux(-euse); (smile) de bonheur; **a ~ sigh** un soupir d'aise; **in ~ ignorance** dans une ignorance béate

blissfully ['blɪsfulɪ] ADV (smile) béatement; (happy) merveilleusement

blister ['blɪstə'] N (on skin) ampoule f, cloque f; (on paintwork) boursouflure f ▶ VI (paint) se boursoufler, se cloquer

blistering ['blɪstərɪŋ] ADJ (hot: heat, day) torride; (: sun) brûlant(e); (angry: attack) cinglant(e); (fast: pace) foudroyant(e)

BLit, BLitt N ABBR (= Bachelor of Literature) diplôme universitaire

blithely ['blaɪðlɪ] ADV (unconcernedly) tranquillement; (joyfully) gaiement

blithering ['blɪðərɪŋ] ADJ (inf): **this ~ idiot** cet espèce d'idiot

blitz [blɪts] N bombardement (aérien); **to have a ~ on sth** (fig) s'attaquer à qch

blizzard ['blɪzəd] N blizzard m, tempête f de neige

BLM N ABBR (US: = Bureau of Land Management) ≈ les domaines

bloated ['bləʊtɪd] ADJ (face) bouffi(e); (stomach, person) gonflé(e)

blob [blɔb] N (drop) goutte f; (stain, spot) tache f

bloc [blɔk] N (Pol) bloc m

★**block** [blɔk] N bloc m; (in pipes) obstruction f; (toy) cube m; (of buildings) pâté m (de maisons); **~ of flats** (BRIT) immeuble (locatif); **3 blocks from here** à trois rues d'ici; **mental ~** blocage m; **~ and tackle** (Tech) palan m ▶ VT bloquer; (fig) faire obstacle à; (Comput) grouper; **the sink is blocked** l'évier est bouché
▶ **block off** VT boucher, condamner
▶ **block out** VT (memories) refouler
▶ **block up** VT boucher

blockade [blɔ'keɪd] N blocus m ▶ VT faire le blocus de

blockage ['blɔkɪdʒ] N obstruction f

block booking N réservation f en bloc

blockbuster ['blɔkbʌstə'] N (film, book) grand succès

block capitals NPL majuscules fpl d'imprimerie

blockhead ['blɔkhɛd] N imbécile mf

block letters NPL majuscules fpl

block release N (BRIT) congé m de formation

block vote N (BRIT) vote m de délégation

blog [blɔg] N blog m, blogue m ▶ VI bloguer

blogger ['blɔgə'] N blogueur(-euse)

blogging ['blɔgɪŋ] N blogging m

blogosphere ['blɔgəsfɪə'] N blogosphère f

blogpost ['blɔgpəʊst] N post m de blog

bloke [bləʊk] N (BRIT inf) type m

blond, blonde [blɔnd] ADJ, N blond(e)

★**blood** [blʌd] N sang m

blood bank N banque f du sang

blood count N numération f globulaire

bloodcurdling ['blʌdkə:dlɪŋ] ADJ à vous glacer le sang

blood donor N donneur(-euse) de sang

blood group N groupe sanguin

bloodhound ['blʌdhaund] N limier m

bloodless ['blʌdlɪs] ADJ (victory) sans effusion de sang; (pale) anémié(e)

bloodletting ['blʌdlɛtɪŋ] N (Med) saignée f; (fig) effusion f de sang, représailles fpl

bloodline ['blʌdlaɪn] N lignée f

blood poisoning N empoisonnement m du sang

blood pressure N tension (artérielle); **to have high/low~** faire de l'hypertension/l'hypotension

blood relation, blood relative N parent(e) (par le sang)

bloodshed ['blʌdʃɛd] N effusion f de sang, carnage m

bloodshot ['blʌdʃɔt] ADJ: **~ eyes** yeux injectés de sang

blood sports NPL sports mpl sanguinaires

bloodstain ['blʌdsteɪn] N tache f de sang

bloodstained ['blʌdsteɪnd] ADJ taché(e) de sang

bloodstream ['blʌdstri:m] N sang m, système sanguin

blood test N analyse f de sang

bloodthirsty ['blʌdθə:stɪ] ADJ sanguinaire

blood transfusion N transfusion f de sang

blood type N groupe sanguin

b

blood vessel N vaisseau sanguin

bloody ['blʌdɪ] ADJ sanglant(e); (BRIT inf!): **this ~ ...** ce foutu ..., ce putain de ... (!) ▶ ADV: **~ strong/ good** (BRIT inf!) vachement or sacrément fort/ bon

bloody-minded ['blʌdɪ'maɪndɪd] ADJ (BRIT inf) contrariant(e), obstiné(e)

bloom [blu:m] N fleur f; (fig) épanouissement m ▶ VI être en fleur; (fig) s'épanouir; être florissant(e)

blooming ['blu:mɪŋ] ADJ (inf): **this ~ ...** ce fichu or sacré ...

blooper ['blu:pəʳ] N (inf: esp US) gaffe f

blossom ['blɔsəm] N fleur(s) f(pl) ▶ VI être en fleurs; (fig) s'épanouir; **to ~ into** (fig) devenir

blot [blɔt] N tache f; **to be a ~ on the landscape** gâcher le paysage ▶ VT tacher; (ink) sécher; **to ~ one's copy book** (fig) faire un impair
▶ **blot out** VT (memories) effacer; (view) cacher, masquer; (nation, city) annihiler

blotch [blɔtʃ] N tache f

blotchy ['blɔtʃɪ] ADJ (complexion) couvert(e) de marbrures

blotting paper ['blɔtɪŋ-] N buvard m

blotto ['blɔtəu] ADJ (inf) bourré(e)

★**blouse** [blauz] N (feminine garment) chemisier m, corsage m

★**blow** [bləu] (pt **blew** [blu:], pp **blown** [bləun]) N coup m; **to come to blows** en venir aux coups ▶ VI souffler ▶ VT (glass) souffler; (instrument) jouer de; (fuse) faire sauter; **to ~ one's nose** se moucher; **to ~ a whistle** siffler
▶ **blow away** VI s'envoler ▶ VT chasser, faire s'envoler
▶ **blow down** VT faire tomber, renverser
▶ **blow off** VI s'envoler ▶ VT (hat) emporter; (ship): **to ~ off course** faire dévier
▶ **blow out** VI (fire, flame) s'éteindre; (tyre) éclater; (fuse) sauter
▶ **blow over** VI s'apaiser
▶ **blow up** VI exploser, sauter ▶ VT faire sauter; (tyre) gonfler; (Phot) agrandir

blow-dry ['bləudraɪ] N (hairstyle) brushing m ▶ VT faire un brushing à

blowlamp ['bləulæmp] N (BRIT) chalumeau m

blown [bləun] PP of **blow**

blowout ['bləuaut] N (of tyre) éclatement m; (BRIT inf: big meal) gueuleton m

blowtorch ['bləutɔ:tʃ] N chalumeau m

blowzy ['blauzɪ] ADJ (BRIT) peu soigné(e)

BLS N ABBR (US) = **Bureau of Labor Statistics**

blubber ['blʌbəʳ] N blanc m de baleine ▶ VI (pej) pleurer comme un veau

bludgeon ['blʌdʒən] N gourdin m, trique f

★**blue** [blu:] ADJ bleu(e); (depressed) triste; **~ film/joke** film m/histoire f pornographique; **(only) once in a ~ moon** tous les trente-six du mois; **out of the ~** (fig) à l'improviste, sans qu'on s'y attende

blue baby N enfant bleu(e)

bluebell ['blu:bɛl] N jacinthe f des bois

blueberry ['blu:bərɪ] N myrtille f, airelle f

bluebottle ['blu:bɔtl] N mouche f à viande

blue cheese N (fromage) bleu m

blue-chip ['blu:tʃɪp] ADJ: **~ investment** investissement m de premier ordre

blue-collar worker ['blu:kɔləʳ-] N ouvrier(-ère) col bleu

blue jeans NPL blue-jeans mpl

blueprint ['blu:prɪnt] N bleu m; (fig) projet m, plan directeur

blues [blu:z] NPL: **the ~** (Mus) le blues; **to have the ~** (inf: feeling) avoir le cafard

bluff [blʌf] VI bluffer ▶ N bluff m; (cliff) promontoire m, falaise f; **to call sb's ~** mettre qn au défi d'exécuter ses menaces ▶ ADJ (person) bourru(e), brusque

blunder ['blʌndəʳ] N gaffe f, bévue f ▶ VI faire une gaffe or une bévue; **to ~ into sb/sth** buter contre qn/qch

blunt [blʌnt] ADJ (knife) émoussé(e), peu tranchant(e); (pencil) mal taillé(e); (person) brusque, ne mâchant pas ses mots; **~ instrument** (Law) instrument contondant ▶ VT émousser

bluntly ['blʌntlɪ] ADV carrément, sans prendre de gants

bluntness ['blʌntnɪs] N (of person) brusquerie f, franchise brutale

blur [bləːʳ] N (shape): **to become a ~** devenir flou ▶ VT brouiller, rendre flou(e)

blurb [bləːb] N (for book) texte m de présentation; (pej) baratin m

blurred [bləːd] ADJ flou(e)

blurt [bləːt]: **to ~ out** VT (reveal) lâcher; (say) balbutier, dire d'une voix entrecoupée

blush [blʌʃ] VI rougir ▶ N rougeur f

blusher ['blʌʃəʳ] N rouge m à joues

bluster ['blʌstəʳ] N paroles fpl en l'air; (boasting) fanfaronnades fpl; (threats) menaces fpl en l'air ▶ VI parler en l'air; fanfaronner

blustering ['blʌstərɪŋ] ADJ fanfaron(ne)

blustery ['blʌstərɪ] ADJ (weather) à bourrasques

Blvd ABBR (= boulevard) Bd

BM N ABBR = **British Museum**; (Scol: = Bachelor of Medicine) diplôme universitaire

BMA N ABBR = **British Medical Association**

BMI N ABBR (= body mass index) IMC m

BMJ N ABBR = **British Medical Journal**

BMus N ABBR (= Bachelor of Music) diplôme universitaire

BMX N ABBR (= bicycle motocross) BMX m

bn ABBR = **billion**

BO N ABBR (inf: = body odour) odeurs corporelles; (US) = **box office**

boar [bɔːʳ] N sanglier m

★**board** [bɔːd] N (wooden) planche f; (on wall) panneau m; (for chess etc) plateau m; (cardboard) carton m; (committee) conseil m, comité m; (in firm) conseil d'administration; (Naut, Aviat): **on ~** à bord; **full ~** (BRIT) pension complète; **half ~** (BRIT) demi-pension f; **with ~ and lodging** logé nourri; **~ and lodging** n chambre f avec pension; **above ~** (fig) régulier(-ère); **across the ~** (fig: adv) systématiquement (: adj) de portée générale; **to go by the ~** (hopes, principles) être abandonné(e); (be unimportant) compter pour rien, n'avoir aucune importance ▶ VT (ship) monter à bord de; (train) monter dans

▶ **board up** VT (*door*) condamner (*au moyen de planches, de tôle*)

boarder ['bɔːdəʳ] N pensionnaire *mf*; (*Scol*) interne *mf*, pensionnaire

board game N jeu *m* de société

boarding card ['bɔːdɪŋ-] N (*Aviat, Naut*) carte *f* d'embarquement

boarding house ['bɔːdɪŋ-] N pension *f*

boarding party ['bɔːdɪŋ-] N section *f* d'abordage

boarding pass ['bɔːdɪŋ-] N (*BRIT*) = **boarding card**

boarding school ['bɔːdɪŋ-] N internat *m*, pensionnat *m*

board meeting N réunion *f* du conseil d'administration

board room N salle *f* du conseil d'administration

boardwalk ['bɔːdwɔːk] N (*US*) cheminement *m* en planches

boast [bəust] VI: **to ~ (about** *or* **of)** se vanter (de) ▶ VT s'enorgueillir de ▶ N vantardise *f*; sujet *m* d'orgueil *or* de fierté

boastful ['bəustful] ADJ vantard(e)

boastfulness ['bəustfulnɪs] N vantardise *f*

★ **boat** [bəut] N bateau *m*; (*small*) canot *m*; barque *f*; **to go by ~** aller en bateau; **to be in the same ~** (*fig*) être logé à la même enseigne

boater ['bəutəʳ] N (*hat*) canotier *m*

boathouse ['bəuthaus] N hangar *m* à bateau

boating ['bəutɪŋ] N canotage *m*

boat people NPL boat people *mpl*

boatswain ['bəusn] N maître *m* d'équipage

boatyard ['bəutjɑːd] N chantier *m* naval

bob [bɔb] VI (*boat, cork on water: also:* **bob up and down**) danser, se balancer ▶ N (*BRIT inf*) = **shilling**
▶ **bob up** VI surgir *or* apparaître brusquement

bobbed [bɔbd] ADJ (*hair*) coupé(e) au carré

bobbin ['bɔbɪn] N bobine *f*; (*of sewing machine*) navette *f*

bobble ['bɔbl] N (*BRIT: of hat*) pompon *m*; (*for hair*) élastique *m* à cheveux

bobby ['bɔbɪ] N (*BRIT inf*) ≈ agent *m* (de police)

bobby pin ['bɔbɪ-] N (*US*) pince *f* à cheveux

bobsled ['bɔbslɛd] N (*esp US: sledge*) bob *m*; (*: sport*) bobsleigh *m*

bobsleigh ['bɔbsleɪ] N bob *m*

bode [bəud] VI: **to ~ well/ill (for)** être de bon/mauvais augure (pour)

bodice ['bɔdɪs] N corsage *m*

bodily ['bɔdɪlɪ] ADJ corporel(le); (*pain, comfort*) physique; (*needs*) matériel(le) ▶ ADV (*carry, lift*) dans ses bras

★ **body** ['bɔdɪ] N corps *m*; (*of car*) carrosserie *f*; (*of plane*) fuselage *m*; (*fig: society*) organe *m*, organisme *m*; (*: quantity*) ensemble *m*, masse *f*; (*of wine*) corps *m*; (*also:* **body stocking**) body *m*, justaucorps *m*; **ruling ~** organe directeur; **in a ~** en masse, ensemble; (*speak*) comme un seul et même homme

body blow N (*fig*) coup dur, choc *m*

bodybuilder ['bɔdɪbɪldəʳ] N culturiste *mf*

body-building ['bɔdɪbɪldɪŋ] N body-building *m*, culturisme *m*

bodyguard ['bɔdɪgɑːd] N garde *mf* du corps

body language N langage *m* du corps

body odour, (*US*) **body odor** N odeur *f* corporelle

body repairs NPL travaux *mpl* de carrosserie

body search N fouille *f* (corporelle); **to carry out a ~ on sb** fouiller qn; **to submit to** *or* **undergo a ~** se faire fouiller

bodywork ['bɔdɪwəːk] N carrosserie *f*

boffin ['bɔfɪn] N (*BRIT*) savant *m*

bog [bɔg] N tourbière *f* ▶ VT: **to get bogged down (in)** (*fig*) s'enliser (dans)

boggle ['bɔgl] VI: **the mind boggles** c'est incroyable, on en reste sidéré

boggy ['bɔgɪ] ADJ marécageux(-euse)

bogie ['bəugɪ] N bogie *m*

Bogotá [bəugə'tɑː] N Bogotá

bogus ['bəugəs] ADJ bidon *inv*; fantôme

Bohemia [bəu'hiːmɪə] N Bohême *f*

Bohemian [bəu'hiːmɪən] ADJ bohémien(ne) ▶ N Bohémien(ne); (*gipsy: also:* **bohemian**) bohémien(ne)

★ **boil** [bɔɪl] VT (faire) bouillir ▶ VI bouillir ▶ N (*Med*) furoncle *m*; **to come to the** *or* (*US*) **a ~** bouillir; **to bring to the** *or* (*US*) **a ~** porter à ébullition
▶ **boil down** VI (*fig*): **to ~ down to** se réduire *or* ramener à
▶ **boil over** VI déborder

boiled egg N œuf *m* à la coque

boiler ['bɔɪləʳ] N chaudière *f*

boiler suit N (*BRIT*) bleu *m* de travail, combinaison *f*

boiling ['bɔɪlɪŋ] ADJ: **I'm ~ (hot)** (*inf*) je crève de chaud

boiling point N point *m* d'ébullition

boil-in-the-bag [bɔɪlɪnðə'bæg] ADJ (*rice etc*) en sachet cuisson

boisterous ['bɔɪstərəs] ADJ bruyant(e), tapageur(-euse)

bold [bəuld] ADJ (*fearless: person*) hardi(e), intrépide; (*move, reform*) audacieux(-euse); (*pej: impudent*) effronté(e); (*striking: colour*) vif (vive); (*: pattern*) voyant(e)

boldly ['bəuldlɪ] ADV (*fearlessly*) audacieusement, hardiment; (*look, announce, say*) avec assurance; (*patterned, coloured*) de façon voyante, de manière voyante

boldness ['bəuldnɪs] N hardiesse *f*, audace *f*; aplomb *m*, effronterie *f*

bold type N (*Typ*) caractères *mpl* gras

Bolivia [bə'lɪvɪə] N Bolivie *f*

Bolivian [bə'lɪvɪən] ADJ bolivien(ne) ▶ N Bolivien(ne)

bollard ['bɔləd] N (*Naut*) bitte *f* d'amarrage; (*BRIT Aut*) borne lumineuse *or* de signalisation

bollocks ['bɔləks] (*BRIT inf!*) EXCL quelles conneries *fpl*! ▶ NPL couilles *fpl* (!)

Bollywood ['bɔlɪwud] N Bollywood *m*

bolshy ['bɔlʃɪ] ADJ (*inf*) râleur(-euse); **to be in a ~ mood** être peu coopératif(-ive)

bolster ['bəulstəʳ] N traversin *m*
▶ **bolster up** VT soutenir

bolt [bəʊlt] N verrou m; (with nut) boulon m; **a ~ from the blue** (fig) un coup de tonnerre dans un ciel bleu ▸ ADV: **~ upright** droit(e) comme un piquet ▸ VT (door) verrouiller; (food) engloutir ▸ VI se sauver, filer (comme une flèche); (horse) s'emballer

★**bomb** [bɒm] N bombe f ▸ VT bombarder

bombard [bɒmˈbɑːd] VT bombarder

bombardment [bɒmˈbɑːdmənt] N bombardement m

bombastic [bɒmˈbæstɪk] ADJ grandiloquent(e), pompeux(-euse)

bomb disposal N: **~ unit** section f de déminage; **~ expert** artificier m

bomber [ˈbɒmə[r]] N caporal m d'artillerie; (Aviat) bombardier m; (terrorist) poseur m de bombes

bombing [ˈbɒmɪŋ] N bombardement m

bomb scare N alerte f à la bombe

bombshell [ˈbɒmʃɛl] N obus m; (fig) bombe f

bomb site N zone f de bombardement

bona fide [ˈbəʊnəˈfaɪdɪ] ADJ de bonne foi; (offer) sérieux(-euse)

bonanza [bəˈnænzə] N filon m

bond [bɒnd] N lien m; (binding promise) engagement m, obligation f; (Finance) obligation; **in ~** (of goods) en entrepôt ▪ **bonds** NPL (chains) chaînes fpl

bondage [ˈbɒndɪdʒ] N esclavage m

bonded warehouse [ˈbɒndɪd-] N entrepôt m sous douanes

bonding [ˈbɒndɪŋ] N (formation f de) liens mpl affectifs

★**bone** [bəʊn] N os m; (of fish) arête f ▸ VT désosser; ôter les arêtes de

bone china N porcelaine f tendre

bone-dry [ˈbəʊnˈdraɪ] ADJ absolument sec (sèche)

bone idle ADJ fainéant(e)

bone marrow N moelle osseuse

boner [ˈbəʊnə[r]] N (US) gaffe f, bourde f

bonfire [ˈbɒnfaɪə[r]] N feu m (de joie); (for rubbish) feu

bonk [bɒŋk] (inf) VT s'envoyer (!), sauter (!) ▸ VI s'envoyer en l'air (!)

bonkers [ˈbɒŋkəz] ADJ (BRIT inf) cinglé(e), dingue

Bonn [bɒn] N Bonn

bonnet [ˈbɒnɪt] N bonnet m; (BRIT: of car) capot m

bonny [ˈbɒnɪ] ADJ (SCOTTISH) joli(e)

bonsai [ˈbɒnsaɪ] ADJ (tree) bonsaï ▸ N (tree) bonsaï m; (art) l'art m du bonsaï

bonus [ˈbəʊnəs] N (money) prime f; (advantage) avantage m

bony [ˈbəʊnɪ] ADJ (arm, face, Med: tissue) osseux(-euse); (thin: person) squelettique; (meat) plein(e) d'os; (fish) plein d'arêtes

boo [buː] EXCL hou !, peuh ! ▸ VT huer ▸ N huée f

boob [buːb] N (inf: breast) nichon m; (: BRIT: mistake) gaffe f

booby prize [ˈbuːbɪ-] N timbale f (ironic)

booby trap [ˈbuːbɪ-] N guet-apens m

booby-trapped [ˈbuːbɪtræpt] ADJ piégé(e)

booing [ˈbuːɪŋ] N huées fpl

★**book** [bʊk] N livre m; (of stamps, tickets etc) carnet m; **by the ~** à la lettre, selon les règles; **to throw the**

~ at sb passer un savon à qn ▸ VT (ticket) prendre; (seat, room) réserver; (football player) prendre le nom de, donner un carton à; (driver) dresser un procès-verbal à; **I booked a table in the name of ...** j'ai réservé une table au nom de ... ▪ **books** NPL (Comm) comptes mpl, comptabilité f; **to keep the books** tenir la comptabilité
▸ **book in** VI (BRIT: at hotel) prendre sa chambre
▸ **book up** VT réserver; **all seats are booked up** tout est pris, c'est complet; **the hotel is booked up** l'hôtel est complet

bookable [ˈbʊkəbl] ADJ: **seats are ~** on peut réserver ses places

bookcase [ˈbʊkkeɪs] N bibliothèque f (meuble)

book ends NPL serre-livres m inv

bookie [ˈbʊkɪ] N (inf) book m, bookmaker m

booking [ˈbʊkɪŋ] N (BRIT) réservation f; **I confirmed my ~ by fax/email** j'ai confirmé ma réservation par fax/e-mail

booking office N (BRIT) bureau m de location

bookish [ˈbʊkɪʃ] ADJ (studious) studieux(-euse); (book-loving) qui aime lire

book-keeping [ˈbʊkˈkiːpɪŋ] N comptabilité f

booklet [ˈbʊklɪt] N brochure f

bookmaker [ˈbʊkmeɪkə[r]] N bookmaker m

bookmark [ˈbʊkmɑːk] N (for book) marque-page m; (Comput) signet m

bookseller [ˈbʊksɛlə[r]] N libraire mf

bookshelf [ˈbʊkʃɛlf] N (single) étagère f (à livres); (bookcase) bibliothèque f; **bookshelves** rayons mpl (de bibliothèque)

★**bookshop** [ˈbʊkʃɒp], **bookstore** [ˈbʊkstɔː[r]] N librairie f

bookstall [ˈbʊkstɔːl] N kiosque m à journaux

book store N = **bookshop**

book token N bon-cadeau m (pour un livre)

book value N valeur f comptable

bookworm [ˈbʊkwɜːm] N dévoreur(-euse) de livres

boom [buːm] N (noise) grondement m; (in prices, population) forte augmentation; (busy period) boom m, vague f de prospérité ▸ VI gronder; prospérer
▸ **boom out** VI résonner ▸ VT hurler

boomerang [ˈbuːməræŋ] N boomerang m

boom town N ville f en plein essor

boon [buːn] N bénédiction f, grand avantage

boorish [ˈbʊərɪʃ] ADJ grossier(-ère), rustre

boost [buːst] N stimulant m, remontant m; **to give a ~ to sb's spirits** or **to sb** remonter le moral à qn ▸ VT stimuler

booster [ˈbuːstə[r]] N (TV) amplificateur m (de signal); (Elec) survolteur m; (Med: vaccine) rappel m; (also: **booster rocket**) booster m

booster seat N (Aut: for children) siège m rehausseur

★**boot** [buːt] N botte f; (for hiking) chaussure f (de marche); (ankle boot) bottine f; (BRIT: of car) coffre m; **to give sb the ~** (inf) flanquer qn dehors, virer qn; **to ~** (in addition) par-dessus le marché, en plus
▸ **boot up** VT FUS faire démarrer, mettre en route
▸ VI (computer) démarrer

booth [buːð] N (at fair) baraque (foraine); (of telephone etc) cabine f; (also: **voting booth**) isoloir m

bootlace ['buːtleɪs] N lacet m (de chaussure)

bootleg ['buːtlɛg] ADJ de contrebande; **~ record** enregistrement m pirate

bootlegger ['buːtlɛgə'] N pirate m (qui se livre à l'enregistrement et à la vente de contenue audiovisuel)

booty ['buːtɪ] N butin m

booze [buːz] (inf) N boissons fpl alcooliques, alcool m ▶ VI boire, picoler

boozer ['buːzə'] N (inf: person): **he's a ~** il picole pas mal; (: BRIT: pub): pub m

borax ['bɔːræks] N borax m

★**border** ['bɔːdə'] N bordure f; bord m; (of a country) frontière f; **the Borders** la région frontière entre l'Écosse et l'Angleterre
  ▶ **border on** VT FUS être voisin(e) de, toucher à

borderline ['bɔːdəlaɪn] N (fig) ligne f de démarcation ▶ ADJ: **~ case** cas m limite

bore [bɔː'] PT of **bear** ▶ VT (person) ennuyer, raser; (hole) percer; (well, tunnel) creuser ▶ N (person) raseur(-euse); (boring thing) barbe f; (of gun) calibre m

★**bored** ['bɔːd] ADJ: **to be ~** s'ennuyer; **he's ~ to tears** or **to death** or **stiff** il s'ennuie à mourir

boredom ['bɔːdəm] N ennui m

borehole ['bɔːhəul] N trou m de sonde

★**boring** ['bɔːrɪŋ] ADJ ennuyeux(-euse)

★**born** [bɔːn] ADJ: **to be ~** naître; **I was ~ in 1960** je suis né en 1960; **~ blind** aveugle de naissance; **a ~ comedian** un comédien-né

born-again [bɔːnə'gɛn] ADJ: **~ Christian** ≈ évangéliste mf

borne [bɔːn] PP of **bear**

Borneo ['bɔːnɪəu] N Bornéo f

borough ['bʌrə] N municipalité f

★**borrow** ['bɔrəu] VT: **to ~ sth (from sb)** emprunter qch (à qn); **may I ~ your car?** est-ce que je peux vous emprunter votre voiture ?

borrower ['bɔrəuə'] N emprunteur(-euse)

borrowing ['bɔrəuɪŋ] N emprunt(s) mpl

borstal ['bɔːstl] N (BRIT) ≈ maison f de correction

Bosnia ['bɔznɪə] N Bosnie f

Bosnia and Herzegovina ['bɔznɪə ənd hɛrtsə-'gəuviːnə] N Bosnie-Herzégovine f

Bosnian ['bɔznɪən] ADJ bosniaque, bosnien(ne) ▶ N Bosniaque mf, Bosnien(ne)

bosom ['buzəm] N poitrine f; (fig) sein m

bosom friend N ami(e) intime

★**boss** [bɔs] N patron(ne) ▶ VT (also: **boss about, boss around**) mener à la baguette

bossy ['bɔsɪ] ADJ autoritaire

bosun ['bəusn] N maître m d'équipage

bot ['bɔt] N (Comput) bot m

botanical [bə'tænɪkl] ADJ botanique

botanist ['bɔtənɪst] N botaniste mf

botany ['bɔtənɪ] N botanique f

botch [bɔtʃ] VT (also: **botch up**) saboter, bâcler

★**both** [bəuθ] ADJ les deux, l'un(e) et l'autre ▶ PRON: **~ (of them)** les deux, tous (toutes) (les) deux, l'un(e) et l'autre; **~ of us went, we ~ went** nous y sommes allés tous les deux ▶ ADV: **~ A and B** A et B; **they sell ~ the fabric and the finished curtains** ils vendent (et) le tissu et les rideaux

(finis), ils vendent à la fois le tissu et les rideaux (finis)

★**bother** ['bɔðə'] VT (worry) tracasser; (needle, bait) importuner, ennuyer; (disturb) déranger; **to ~ doing** prendre la peine de faire; **I'm sorry to ~ you** excusez-moi de vous déranger ▶ VI (also: **bother o.s.**) se tracasser, se faire du souci; **please don't ~** ne vous dérangez pas; **don't ~** ce n'est pas la peine ▶ N (trouble) ennuis mpl; **it is a ~ to have to do** c'est vraiment ennuyeux d'avoir à faire; **it's no ~** aucun problème ▶ EXCL zut !

bothered ['bɔðəd] ADJ inquiet(-ète); **I'm not ~** ça m'est égal

bothersome ['bɔðəsəm] ADJ (old) ennuyeux(-euse)

Botox® ['bəutɔks] N Botox m; **~ injections** injections fpl de Botox

Botswana [bɔt'swɑːnə] N Botswana m

★**bottle** ['bɔtl] N bouteille f; (baby's) biberon m; (of perfume, medicine) flacon m; **~ of wine/milk** bouteille de vin/lait; **wine/milk ~** bouteille à vin/lait ▶ VT mettre en bouteille(s)
  ▶ **bottle up** VT refouler, contenir

bottle bank N conteneur m (de bouteilles)

bottleneck ['bɔtlnɛk] N (in traffic) bouchon m; (in production) goulet m d'étranglement

bottle-opener ['bɔtləupnə'] N ouvre-bouteille m

★**bottom** ['bɔtəm] N (of container, sea etc) fond m; (buttocks) derrière m; (of page, list) bas m; (of chair) siège m; (of mountain, tree, hill) pied m; **to get to the ~ of sth** (fig) découvrir le fin fond de qch ▶ ADJ (shelf, step) du bas
  ▶ **bottom out** VI (recession, price) atteindre son point le plus bas

bottomless ['bɔtəmlɪs] ADJ sans fond, insondable

bottom line N: **the ~ is that …** l'essentiel, c'est que …

botulism ['bɔtjulɪzəm] N botulisme m

bougainvillea, bougainvillaea [buːgən'vɪlɪə] N bougainvillée f, bougainvillier m

bough [bau] N branche f, rameau m

bought [bɔːt] PT, PP of **buy**

boulder ['bəuldə'] N gros rocher (gén lisse, arrondi)

boulevard ['buːləvɑː'd] N boulevard m

bounce [bauns] VI (ball) rebondir; (cheque) être refusé (étant sans provision); (also: **to bounce forward/out**) bondir, s'élancer ▶ VT faire rebondir ▶ N (rebound) rebond m; **he's got plenty of ~** (fig) il est plein d'entrain or d'allant
  ▶ **bounce back** VI (team, competitor) faire un retour en force

bouncer ['baunsə'] N (inf: at dance, club) videur m

bouncing ['baunsɪŋ] ADJ (baby) plein(e) de santé

bouncy ['baunsɪ] ADJ (lively: person) dynamique; (ball, toy) élastique

bound [baund] PT, PP of **bind** ▶ N (gen pl) limite f; (leap) bond m; **out of bounds** dont l'accès est interdit ▶ VI (leap) bondir ▶ VT (limit) borner ▶ ADJ: **to be ~ to do sth** (obliged) être obligé(e) or avoir obligation de faire qch; **he's ~ to fail** (likely) il est sûr d'échouer, son échec est inévitable or assuré; **~ by** (law, regulation) engagé(e) par; **~ for** à destination de

523

boundary ['baʊndrɪ] N frontière f

boundless ['baʊndlɪs] ADJ illimité(e), sans bornes

bountiful ['baʊntɪful] ADJ (person) généreux(-euse); (God) bienfaiteur(-trice); (supply) ample

bounty ['baʊntɪ] N (generosity) générosité f

bouquet ['baʊkeɪ] N bouquet m

bourbon ['bʊəbən] N (US: also: **bourbon whiskey**) bourbon m

bourgeois ['bʊəʒwɑː] ADJ, N bourgeois(e)

bourgeoisie ['bʊəʒwɑːziː] N bourgeoisie f

bout [baʊt] N période f; (of malaria etc) accès m, crise f, attaque f; (Boxing etc) combat m, match m

boutique [buːˈtiːk] N boutique f

bovine ['bəʊvaɪn] ADJ bovin(e)

bow¹ [bəʊ] N nœud m; (weapon) arc m; (Mus) archet m

bow² [baʊ] N (with body) révérence f, inclination f (du buste or corps); (Naut: also: **bows**) proue f ▶ vɪ faire une révérence, s'incliner; (yield): **to ~ to** or **before** s'incliner devant, se soumettre à; **to ~ to the inevitable** accepter l'inévitable or l'inéluctable
  ▶ **bow out** vɪ tirer sa révérence; **to ~ out of sth** se retirer de qch

bowels [baʊəlz] NPL intestins mpl; (fig) entrailles fpl

bower ['baʊə^r] N (literary: in garden) tonnelle f

★**bowl** [bəʊl] N (for eating) bol m; (for washing) cuvette f; (ball) boule f; (of pipe) fourneau m ▶ vɪ (Cricket) lancer (la balle)
  ▶ **bowl out** vᴛ (Cricket) éliminer par lancer direct
  ▶ **bowl over** vᴛ ꜰᴜs (fig) renverser

bow-legged ['bəʊ'lɛgɪd] ADJ aux jambes arquées

bowler ['bəʊlə^r] N joueur m de boules; (Cricket) lanceur m (de la balle); (BRIT: also: **bowler hat**) (chapeau m) melon m

bowlful ['bəʊlful] N bol m

bowling ['bəʊlɪŋ] N (game) jeu m de boules, jeu de quilles

bowling alley N bowling m

bowling green N terrain m de boules (gazonné et carré)

bowls [bəʊlz] N (jeu m de) boules fpl

bow tie [bəʊ-] N nœud m papillon

★**box** [bɔks] N boîte f; (also: **cardboard box**) carton m; (crate) caisse f; (Theat) loge f ▶ vᴛ mettre en boîte; (Sport) boxer avec ▶ vɪ boxer, faire de la boxe
  ▶ **box in** vᴛ ꜰᴜs coincer

boxer ['bɔksə^r] N (person) boxeur(-euse); (dog) boxer m

boxer shorts NPL caleçon m

boxing ['bɔksɪŋ] N (sport) boxe f

Boxing Day N (BRIT) le lendemain de Noël

> **Boxing Day** est le lendemain de Noël, férié en Grande-Bretagne. Ce nom vient d'une coutume du XIXe siècle qui consistait à donner des cadeaux de Noël (dans des boîtes) à ses employés, son personnel de maison etc le 26 décembre.

boxing gloves NPL gants mpl de boxe

boxing ring N ring m

box number N (for advertisements) numéro m d'annonce

box office N bureau m de location

box room N débarras m; chambrette f

box set N (TV) coffret m

★**boy** [bɔɪ] N garçon m

boy band N boys band m

boycott ['bɔɪkɔt] N boycottage m ▶ vᴛ boycotter

★**boyfriend** ['bɔɪfrɛnd] N (petit) ami

boyhood ['bɔɪhʊd] N enfance f

boyish ['bɔɪɪʃ] ADJ d'enfant, de garçon; **to look ~** (man: appear youthful) faire jeune

bozo ['bəʊzəʊ] N (inf) andouille f (inf)

bp ABBR = **bishop**

bps N ABBR (= bits per second) bits mpl par seconde

BR ABBR = **British Rail**

Br. ABBR (Rel) = **brother**

bra [brɑː] N soutien-gorge m

brace [breɪs] N (support) attache f, agrafe f; (BRIT also: **braces**: on teeth) appareil m (dentaire); (tool) vilebrequin m; (Typ: also: **brace bracket**) accolade f ▶ vᴛ (support) consolider, soutenir; **to ~ o.s.** (fig) se préparer mentalement ■ **braces** NPL (BRIT: for trousers) bretelles fpl

bracelet ['breɪslɪt] N bracelet m

bracing ['breɪsɪŋ] ADJ tonifiant(e), tonique

bracken ['brækən] N fougère f

bracket ['brækɪt] N (Tech) tasseau m, support m; (group) classe f, tranche f; (also: **brace bracket**) accolade f; (also: **round bracket**) parenthèse f; (also: **square bracket**) crochet m; **income ~** tranche f des revenus; **in brackets** entre parenthèses or crochets ▶ vᴛ mettre entre parenthèses; (fig: also: **bracket together**) regrouper

brackish ['brækɪʃ] ADJ (water) saumâtre

brag [bræg] vɪ se vanter

braid [breɪd] N (trimming) galon m; (of hair) tresse f, natte f ▶ vᴛ (hair) tresser

Braille [breɪl] N braille m

★**brain** [breɪn] N cerveau m ■ **brains** NPL (intellect, food) cervelle f; **he's got brains** il est intelligent

brainchild ['breɪntʃaɪld] N trouvaille (personnelle), invention f

braindead ['breɪndɛd] ADJ (Med) dans un coma dépassé; (inf) demeuré(e)

brain haemorrhage, (US) **brain hemorrhage** N hémorragie f cérébrale

brainless ['breɪnlɪs] ADJ sans cervelle, stupide

brainpower ['breɪnpaʊə^r] N intelligence f

brainstorm ['breɪnstɔːm] N (fig) moment m d'égarement; (US: brainwave) idée f de génie

brainstorming ['breɪnstɔːmɪŋ] N brainstorming m, remue-méninges m

brainwash ['breɪnwɔʃ] vᴛ faire subir un lavage de cerveau à

brainwave ['breɪnweɪv] N idée f de génie

brainy ['breɪnɪ] ADJ intelligent(e), doué(e)

braise [breɪz] vᴛ braiser

brake [breɪk] N frein m ▶ vᴛ, vɪ freiner

brake light N feu m de stop

brake pedal N pédale f de frein

bramble ['bræmbl] N ronces fpl; (fruit) mûre f

bran [bræn] N son m

★**branch** [brɑːntʃ] N branche f; (Comm) succursale f; (: of bank) agence f; (of association) section locale ▶ VI bifurquer
▶ **branch off** VI (road) bifurquer
▶ **branch out** VI diversifier ses activités; **to ~ out into** étendre ses activités à

branch line N (Rail) bifurcation f, embranchement m

branch manager N directeur(-trice) de succursale (or d'agence)

brand [brænd] N marque (commerciale) ▶ VT (cattle) marquer (au fer rouge); (fig: pej): **to ~ sb a communist** etc traiter or qualifier qn de communiste etc

branded ['brændɪd] ADJ (BRIT: product) de marque

branding ['brændɪŋ] N branding m, marquage m

brandish ['brændɪʃ] VT brandir

brand name N nom m de marque

brand-new ['brænd'njuː] ADJ tout(e) neuf (neuve), flambant neuf (neuve)

brandy ['brændɪ] N cognac m, fine f

brash [bræʃ] ADJ effronté(e)

Brasilia [brə'zɪlɪə] N Brasilia

brass [brɑːs] N cuivre m (jaune), laiton m; **the ~** (Mus) les cuivres

brass band N fanfare f

brassiere ['bræsɪə'] N soutien-gorge m

brass tacks NPL: **to get down to ~** en venir au fait

brat [bræt] N (pej) mioche mf, môme mf

bravado [brə'vɑːdəu] N bravade f

★**brave** [breɪv] ADJ courageux(-euse), brave ▶ N guerrier indien ▶ VT braver, affronter

bravery ['breɪvərɪ] N bravoure f, courage m

bravo [brɑː'vəu] EXCL (old) bravo

brawl [brɔːl] N rixe f, bagarre f ▶ VI se bagarrer

brawn [brɔːn] N muscle m; (meat) fromage m de tête

brawny ['brɔːnɪ] ADJ musclé(e), costaud(e)

bray [breɪ] N braiement m ▶ VI braire

brazen ['breɪzn] ADJ impudent(e), effronté(e) ▶ VT: **to ~ it out** payer d'effronterie, crâner

brazenly ['breɪzənlɪ] ADV impudemment, effrontément

brazier ['breɪzɪə'] N brasero m

Brazil [brə'zɪl] N Brésil m

Brazilian [brə'zɪljən] ADJ brésilien(ne) ▶ N Brésilien(ne)

Brazil nut N noix f du Brésil

breach [briːtʃ] VT ouvrir une brèche dans ▶ N (gap) brèche f; (estrangement) brouille f; (breaking): **~ of contract** rupture f de contrat; **~ of the peace** attentat m à l'ordre public; **~ of trust** abus m de confiance

★**bread** [bred] N pain m; (inf: money) fric m; **~ and butter** n tartines (beurrées); (fig) subsistance f; **to earn one's daily ~** gagner son pain; **to know which side one's ~ is buttered (on)** savoir où est son avantage or intérêt

breadbin ['bredbɪn] N (BRIT) boîte f or huche f à pain

breadboard ['bredbɔːd] N planche f à pain; (Comput) montage expérimental

breadbox ['bredbɒks] N (US) boîte f or huche f à pain

breadcrumbs ['bredkrʌmz] NPL miettes fpl de pain; (Culin) chapelure f, panure f

breaded ['bredɪd] ADJ pané(e)

breadfruit ['bredfruːt] N fruit m de l'arbre à pain

breadline ['bredlaɪn] N: **to be on the ~** être sans le sou or dans l'indigence

breadth [bretθ] N largeur f

breadwinner ['bredwɪnə'] N soutien m de famille

★**break** [breɪk] (pt **broke** [brəuk], pp **broken** ['brəukən]) VT casser, briser; (promise) rompre; (law) violer; **to ~ one's leg** etc se casser la jambe etc; **to ~ a record** battre un record; **to ~ the news to sb** annoncer la nouvelle à qn ▶ VI se casser, se briser; (weather) tourner; (storm) éclater; (day) se lever; **to ~ with sb** rompre avec qn; **to ~ even** rentrer dans ses frais; **to ~ free** or **loose** se dégager, s'échapper ▶ N (gap) brèche f; (fracture) cassure f; (rest) interruption f, arrêt m; (: short) pause f; (: at school) récréation f; (chance) chance f, occasion f favorable; **to take a ~** (few minutes) faire une pause, s'arrêter cinq minutes; (holiday) prendre un peu de repos; **without a ~** sans interruption, sans arrêt
▶ **break away** VI (from other people) se détacher; **to ~ away from sth** (idea, tradition) rompre avec qch
▶ **break down** VT (door etc) enfoncer; (resistance) venir à bout de; (figures, data) décomposer, analyser ▶ VI s'effondrer; (Med) faire une dépression (nerveuse); (Aut) tomber en panne; **my car has broken down** ma voiture est en panne
▶ **break in** VT (horse etc) dresser ▶ VI (burglar) entrer par effraction; (interrupt) interrompre
▶ **break into** VT FUS (house) s'introduire or pénétrer par effraction dans
▶ **break off** VI (speaker) s'interrompre; (branch) se rompre ▶ VT (talks, engagement) rompre
▶ **break open** VT (door etc) forcer, fracturer
▶ **break out** VI éclater, se déclarer; (prisoner) s'évader; **to ~ out in spots** se couvrir de boutons
▶ **break through** VI: **the sun broke through** le soleil a fait son apparition ▶ VT FUS (defences, barrier) franchir; (crowd) se frayer un passage à travers
▶ **break up** VI (partnership) cesser, prendre fin; (marriage) se briser; (crowd, meeting) se séparer; (ship) se disloquer; (Scol: pupils) être en vacances; (line) couper; **the line's** or **you're breaking up** ça coupe ▶ VT fracasser, casser; (fight etc) interrompre, faire cesser; (marriage) désunir

breakable ['breɪkəbl] ADJ cassable, fragile ▶ N: **breakables** objets mpl fragiles

breakage ['breɪkɪdʒ] N casse f; **to pay for breakages** payer la casse

breakaway ['breɪkəweɪ] ADJ (group etc) dissident(e)

breakdown ['breɪkdaun] N (Aut) panne f; (in communications, marriage) rupture f; (Med: also: **nervous breakdown**) dépression (nerveuse); (of figures) ventilation f, répartition f

breakdown service N (BRIT) service m de dépannage

breakdown van, (US) **breakdown truck** N dépanneuse f

breaker ['breɪkə'] N brisant m

breakeven ['breɪk'iːvn] CPD: **~ chart** graphique m de rentabilité; **~ point** seuil m de rentabilité

★**breakfast** ['brɛkfəst] N petit déjeuner m; **what time is ~?** le petit déjeuner est à quelle heure ?

breakfast cereal N céréales fpl

break-in ['breɪkɪn] N cambriolage m

breaking and entering ['breɪkɪŋən'ɛntərɪŋ] N (Law) effraction f

breaking point ['breɪkɪŋ-] N limites fpl

breakneck ['breɪknɛk] ADJ: **at ~ speed** (develop, happen) à la vitesse grand V; **to drive at ~ speed** rouler à tombeau ouvert

breakout ['breɪkaut] N évasion f

breakthrough ['breɪkθruː] N percée f

break-up ['breɪkʌp] N (of partnership, marriage) rupture f

break-up value N (Comm) valeur f de liquidation

breakwater ['breɪkwɔːtə'] N brise-lames m inv, digue f

breast [brɛst] N (of woman) sein m; (chest) poitrine f; (of chicken, turkey) blanc m

breastbone ['brɛstbəun] N sternum m

breast-feed ['brɛstfiːd] VT, VI (irreg: like **feed**) allaiter

breast milk N lait m maternel

breast pocket N poche f (de) poitrine

breast-stroke ['brɛststrəuk] N brasse f

★**breath** [brɛθ] N haleine f, souffle m; **to go out for a ~ of air** sortir prendre l'air; **to take a deep ~** respirer à fond; **out of ~** à bout de souffle, essoufflé(e)

breathable ['briːðəbl] ADJ (fabric) aéré(e)

breathalyse ['brɛəlaɪz] VT faire subir un alcootest à

Breathalyser® ['brɛθəlaɪzə'] (BRIT) N alcootest m

★**breathe** [briːð] VT, VI respirer; **I won't ~ a word about it** je n'en soufflerai pas mot, je n'en dirai rien à personne

▶ **breathe in** VI inspirer ▶ VT aspirer

▶ **breathe out** VT, VI expirer

breather ['briːðə'] N moment m de repos or de répit

breathing ['briːðɪŋ] N respiration f

breathing space N (fig) (moment m de) répit m

breathless ['brɛθlɪs] ADJ essoufflé(e), haletant(e), oppressé(e); **~ with excitement** le souffle coupé par l'émotion

breathtaking ['brɛθteɪkɪŋ] ADJ stupéfiant(e), à vous couper le souffle

breath test N alcootest m

bred [brɛd] PT, PP of **breed**

-bred [brɛd] SUFFIX: **well/ill-bred** bien/mal élevé(e)

breeches ['brɪtʃɪz, 'brɪːtʃɪz] NPL (old) culotte f

breed [briːd] (pt, pp **bred** [brɛd]) VT élever, faire l'élevage de; (fig: hate, suspicion) engendrer ▶ VI se reproduire ▶ N race f, variété f

breeder ['briːdə'] N (person) éleveur m; (Physics: also: **breeder reactor**) (réacteur m) surrégénérateur m

breeding ['briːdɪŋ] N reproduction f; élevage m; (upbringing) éducation f

breeze [briːz] N brise f

▶ **breeze in** VI entrer d'un air dégagé

breeze-block ['briːzblɔk] N (BRIT) parpaing m

breezy ['briːzɪ] ADJ (day, weather) venteux(-euse); (manner) désinvolte; (person) jovial(e)

brethren ['brɛðrɪn] NPL (old) frères mpl

Breton ['brɛtən] ADJ breton(ne) ▶ N Breton(ne); (Ling) breton m

brevity ['brɛvɪtɪ] N brièveté f

brew [bruː] VT (tea) faire infuser; (beer) brasser; (plot) tramer, préparer ▶ VI (tea) infuser; (beer) fermenter; (fig) se préparer, couver

brewer ['bruːə'] N brasseur m

brewery ['bruːərɪ] N brasserie f (fabrique)

brewing ['bruːɪŋ] N brassage m

Brexit ['brɛksɪt] N Brexit m, le retrait du Royaume-Uni de l'Union européenne; **hard/soft ~** Brexit dur/mou

briar ['braɪə'] N (thorny bush) ronces fpl; (wild rose) églantine f

bribe [braɪb] N pot-de-vin m ▶ VT acheter; soudoyer; **to ~ sb to do sth** soudoyer qn pour qu'il fasse qch

bribery ['braɪbərɪ] N corruption f

bric-a-brac ['brɪkəbræk] N bric-à-brac m

brick [brɪk] N brique f

brickbat ['brɪkbæt] N violente critique f

bricklayer ['brɪkleɪə'] N maçon m

brickwork ['brɪkwəːk] N briquetage m, maçonnerie f

brickworks ['brɪkwəːks] N briqueterie f

bridal ['braɪdl] ADJ nuptial(e); **~ party** noce f

bride [braɪd] N mariée f, épouse f

bridegroom ['braɪdgruːm] N marié m, époux m

bridesmaid ['braɪdzmeɪd] N demoiselle f d'honneur

★**bridge** [brɪdʒ] N pont m; (Naut) passerelle f (de commandement); (of nose) arête f; (Cards, Dentistry) bridge m ▶ VT (river) construire un pont sur; (gap) combler

bridging loan ['brɪdʒɪŋ-] N (BRIT) prêt m relais

bridle ['braɪdl] N bride f ▶ VT refréner, mettre la bride à; (horse) brider

bridle path N piste or allée cavalière

brief [briːf] ADJ bref (brève) ▶ N (Law) dossier m, cause f; (gen) tâche f; **in ~ ...** (en) bref ... ▶ VT mettre au courant; (Mil) donner des instructions à ▶ **briefs** NPL slip m

briefcase ['briːfkeɪs] N serviette f; porte-documents m inv

briefing ['briːfɪŋ] N instructions fpl; (Press) briefing m

briefly ['briːflɪ] ADV brièvement; (visit) en coup de vent; **to glimpse ~** entrevoir

briefness ['briːfnɪs] N brièveté f

Brig. ABBR = **brigadier**

brigade [brɪ'geɪd] N (Mil) brigade f

brigadier [brɪgə'dɪə'] N brigadier général

★**bright** [braɪt] ADJ brillant(e); (room, weather) clair(e); (person: clever) intelligent(e), doué(e); (: cheerful) gai(e); (idea) génial(e); (colour) vif (vive); **to look on the ~ side** regarder le bon côté des choses

brighten ['braɪtn], **brighten up** VT (*room*) éclaircir; égayer ▶ VI s'éclaircir; (*person*) retrouver un peu de sa gaieté

brightly ['braɪtlɪ] ADV brillamment

brill [brɪl] ADJ (*BRIT inf*) super *inv*

brilliance ['brɪljəns] N éclat *m*; (*fig: of person*) brio *m*

★**brilliant** ['brɪljənt] ADJ brillant(e); (*light, sunshine*) éclatant(e); (*inf: great*) super

brim [brɪm] N bord *m*

brimful ['brɪm'ful] ADJ plein(e) à ras bord; (*fig*) débordant(e)

brine [braɪn] N eau salée; (*Culin*) saumure *f*

★**bring** [brɪŋ] (*pt, pp* **brought** [brɔːt]) VT (*thing*) apporter; (*person*) amener; **to ~ sth to an end** mettre fin à qch; **I can't ~ myself to fire him** je ne peux me résoudre à le mettre à la porte
  ▶ **bring about** VT provoquer, entraîner
  ▶ **bring along** VT (*thing*) apporter; (*person*) amener
  ▶ **bring back** VT rapporter; (*person*) ramener
  ▶ **bring down** VT (*lower*) abaisser; (*shoot down*) abattre; (*government*) faire s'effondrer
  ▶ **bring forward** VT avancer; (*Book-keeping*) reporter
  ▶ **bring in** VT (*person*) faire entrer; (*object*) rentrer; (*Pol: legislation*) introduire; (*Law: verdict*) rendre; (*produce: income*) rapporter
  ▶ **bring off** VT (*task, plan*) réussir, mener à bien; (*deal*) mener à bien
  ▶ **bring on** VT (*illness, attack*) provoquer; (*player, substitute*) amener
  ▶ **bring out** VT sortir; (*meaning*) faire ressortir, mettre en relief; (*new product, book*) sortir
  ▶ **bring round**, **bring to** VT (*unconscious person*) ranimer
  ▶ **bring up** VT élever; (*carry up*) monter; (*question*) soulever; (*food: vomit*) vomir, rendre

brink [brɪŋk] N bord *m*; **on the ~ of doing** sur le point de faire, à deux doigts de faire; **she was on the ~ of tears** elle était au bord des larmes

brinkmanship ['brɪŋkmənʃɪp] N politique *f* de la corde raide

brisk [brɪsk] ADJ vif (vive); (*abrupt*) brusque; (*trade etc*) actif(-ive); **to go for a ~ walk** se promener d'un bon pas; **business is ~** les affaires marchent (bien)

bristle ['brɪsl] N poil *m* ▶ VI se hérisser; **bristling with** hérissé(e) de

bristly ['brɪslɪ] ADJ (*beard, hair*) hérissé(e); **your chin's all ~** ton menton gratte

Brit [brɪt] N ABBR (*inf: = British person*) Britannique *mf*

★**Britain** ['brɪtən] N (*also:* **Great Britain**) la Grande-Bretagne; **in ~** en Grande-Bretagne

★**British** ['brɪtɪʃ] ADJ britannique ▶ NPL: **the ~** les Britanniques *mpl*

British Isles NPL: **the ~** les îles *fpl* Britanniques

British Rail N compagnie ferroviaire britannique, ≈ SNCF *f*

British Summer Time N heure *f* d'été britannique

Briton ['brɪtən] N Britannique *mf*

★**Brittany** ['brɪtənɪ] N Bretagne *f*

brittle ['brɪtl] ADJ cassant(e), fragile

Bro. ABBR (*Rel*) = **brother**

broach [brəutʃ] VT (*subject*) aborder

broad [brɔːd] ADJ large; (*distinction*) général(e); (*accent*) prononcé(e); **~ hint** allusion transparente; **in ~ daylight** en plein jour; **the ~ outlines** les grandes lignes ▶ N (*US pej*) nana *f*

B road N (*BRIT*) ≈ route départementale

broadband ['brɔːdbænd] N (internet *m* à) haut débit *m*

broad bean N fève *f*

broadcast ['brɔːdkɑːst] (*pt, pp* ~) N émission *f* ▶ VT (*Radio*) radiodiffuser; (*TV*) téléviser ▶ VI émettre

broadcaster ['brɔːdkɑːstər] N personnalité *f* de la radio *or* de la télévision

broadcasting ['brɔːdkɑːstɪŋ] N radiodiffusion *f*; télévision *f*

broadcasting station N station *f* de radio (*or* de télévision)

broaden ['brɔːdn] VT élargir; **to ~ one's mind** élargir ses horizons ▶ VI s'élargir

broadly ['brɔːdlɪ] ADV en gros, généralement

broad-minded ['brɔːd'maɪndɪd] ADJ large d'esprit

broadsheet ['brɔːdʃiːt] N (*BRIT*) journal *m* grand format

broadside ['brɔːdsaɪd] N (*attack*) attaque *f* violente *or* virulente; **~ on** *adv* par le travers

brocade [brə'keɪd] N brocart *m*

★**broccoli** ['brɔkəlɪ] N brocoli *m*

brochure ['brəuʃjuər] N prospectus *m*, dépliant *m*

brogue [brəug] N (*accent*) accent régional; (*shoe*) (*sorte de*) chaussure basse de cuir épais

broil [brɔɪl] VT (*US*) rôtir

broiler ['brɔɪlər] N (*US: fowl*) poulet *m* (à rôtir); (*: grill*) gril *m*

broke [brəuk] PT *of* **break** ▶ ADJ (*inf*) fauché(e); **to go ~** (*business*) faire faillite

broken ['brəukn] PP *of* **break** ▶ ADJ (*stick, leg etc*) cassé(e); (*machine: also:* **broken down**) fichu(e); (*promise, vow*) rompu(e); **a ~ marriage** un couple dissocié; **a ~ home** un foyer désuni; **in ~ French/English** dans un français/anglais approximatif *or* hésitant

broken-down ['brəukn'daun] ADJ (*car*) en panne; (*machine*) fichu(e); (*house*) en ruines

broken-hearted ['brəukn'hɑːtɪd] ADJ (ayant) le cœur brisé

broker ['brəukər] N courtier *m*

brokerage ['brəukrɪdʒ] N courtage *m*

brolly ['brɔlɪ] N (*BRIT inf*) pépin *m*, parapluie *m*

bromance ['brəumæns] N (*inf*) amitié forte entre deux hommes hétérosexuels

bronchitis [brɔŋ'kaɪtɪs] N bronchite *f*

bronze [brɔnz] N bronze *m*

bronzed ['brɔnzd] ADJ bronzé(e), hâlé(e)

brooch ['brəutʃ] N broche *f*

brood [bruːd] N couvée *f* ▶ VI (*hen, storm*) couver; (*person*) méditer (sombrement), ruminer

broody ['bruːdɪ] ADJ (*fig*) taciturne, mélancolique

brook [bruk] N ruisseau *m*

broom [brum] N balai *m*; (*Bot*) genêt *m*

broomstick ['brumstɪk] N manche *m* à balai

Bros. ABBR (*Comm*: = *brothers*) Frères

broth [brɔθ] N bouillon *m* de viande et de légumes

brothel [ˈbrɔθl] N maison close, bordel *m*

★**brother** [ˈbrʌðəʳ] N frère *m*

brotherhood [ˈbrʌðəhud] N fraternité *f*

brother-in-law [ˈbrʌðərɪnˈlɔ:ʳ] N beau-frère *m*

brotherly [ˈbrʌðəlɪ] ADJ fraternel(le)

brought [brɔ:t] PT, PP *of* **bring**

brouhaha [ˈbru:hɑ:hɑ:] N brouhaha *m*

brow [brau] N front *m*; (*rare: eyebrow*) sourcil *m*; (*of hill*) sommet *m*

browbeat [ˈbraubi:t] VT (*irreg: like* **beat**) intimider, brusquer

★**brown** [braun] ADJ brun(e), marron *inv*; (*hair*) châtain *inv*; (*tanned*) bronzé(e); (*rice, bread, flour*) complet(-ète); **to go ~** (*person*) bronzer; (*leaves*) jaunir ▶ N (*colour*) brun *m*, marron *m* ▶ VT brunir; (*Culin*) faire dorer, faire roussir

brown bread N pain *m* bis

Brownie [ˈbraunɪ] N jeannette *f* éclaireuse (cadette)

brown paper N papier *m* d'emballage, papier kraft

brown rice N riz *m* complet

brown sugar N cassonade *f*

browse [brauz] VI (*in shop*) regarder (*sans acheter*); (*among books*) bouquiner, feuilleter les livres; (*animal*) paître; **to ~ through a book** feuilleter un livre

browser [ˈbrauzəʳ] N (*Comput*) navigateur *m*

bruise [bru:z] N bleu *m*, ecchymose *f*, contusion *f* ▶ VT contusionner, meurtrir; **to ~ one's arm** se faire un bleu au bras ▶ VI (*fruit*) se taler, se meurtrir

bruised [bru:zd] ADJ contusionné(e)

bruiser [ˈbru:zəʳ] N (*inf*) cogneur(-euse)

bruising [ˈbru:zɪŋ] ADJ (*experience*) douloureux(-euse); (*campaign, encounter*) éprouvant(e) ▶ N bleus *mpl*, contusions *fpl*

Brum [brʌm] N ABBR, **Brummagem** [ˈbrʌmədʒəm] N (*inf*) Birmingham

Brummie [ˈbrʌmɪ] N (*inf*) habitant(e) de Birmingham; natif(-ive) de Birmingham

brunch [brʌntʃ] N brunch *m*

Brunei [bruːˈnaɪ, ˈbruːnaɪ] N Brunei *m*

brunette [bruːˈnet] N (*femme*) brune

brunt [brʌnt] N: **the ~ of** (*attack, criticism etc*) le plus gros de

★**brush** [brʌʃ] N brosse *f*; (*for painting*) pinceau *m*; (*for shaving*) blaireau *m*; (*quarrel*) accrochage *m*, prise *f* de bec; **to have a ~ with sb** s'accrocher avec qn; **to have a ~ with the police** avoir maille à partir avec la police ▶ VT brosser; (*also*: **brush past**, **brush against**) effleurer, frôler
▶ **brush aside** VT écarter, balayer
▶ **brush off** VT (*remove: thing*) enlever; (*person*) envoyer balader
▶ **brush up** VT (*knowledge*) rafraîchir, réviser

brushed [brʌʃt] ADJ (*Tech: steel, chrome etc*) brossé(e); (: *nylon, denim etc*) gratté(e)

brush-off [ˈbrʌʃɔf] N (*inf*): **to give sb the ~** envoyer qn promener

brushwood [ˈbrʌʃwud] N broussailles *fpl*, taillis *m*

brusque [bruːsk] ADJ (*person, manner*) brusque, cassant(e); (*tone*) sec (sèche), cassant(e)

★**Brussels** [ˈbrʌslz] N Bruxelles

Brussels sprout N chou *m* de Bruxelles

brutal [ˈbruːtl] ADJ brutal(e)

brutality [bruːˈtælɪtɪ] N brutalité *f*

brutalize [ˈbruːtəlaɪz] VT (*harden*) rendre brutal(e); (*ill-treat*) brutaliser

brute [bruːt] N brute *f* ▶ ADJ: **by ~ force** par la force

brutish [ˈbruːtɪʃ] ADJ grossier(-ère), brutal(e)

BS N ABBR (*US*: = *Bachelor of Science*) diplôme universitaire

bs ABBR = **bill of sale**

BSA N ABBR = **Boy Scouts of America**

BSc N ABBR (*University*) = **Bachelor of Science**

BSE N ABBR (= *bovine spongiform encephalopathy*) ESB *f*, BSE *f*

BSI N ABBR (= *British Standards Institution*) association de normalisation

BST ABBR (= *British Summer Time*) heure *f* d'été

btu N ABBR (= *British thermal unit*) btu (= 1,054, 2 *joules*)

btw, BTW ABBR (= *by the way*) au fait, à propos

bubble [ˈbʌbl] N bulle *f* ▶ VI bouillonner, faire des bulles; (*sparkle, fig*) pétiller

bubble bath N bain moussant

bubble gum N chewing-gum *m*

bubble jet printer [ˈbʌbldʒet-] N imprimante *f* à bulle d'encre

bubbly [ˈbʌblɪ] ADJ (*drink*) pétillant(e); (*person*) plein(e) de vitalité ▶ N (*inf*) champ *m*

Bucharest [buːkəˈrest] N Bucarest

buck [bʌk] N mâle *m* (*d'un lapin, lièvre, daim etc*); (*US inf*) dollar *m*; **to pass the ~ (to sb)** se décharger de la responsabilité (sur qn) ▶ VI ruer, lancer une ruade
▶ **buck up** VI (*cheer up*) reprendre du poil de la bête, se remonter ▶ VT: **to ~ one's ideas up** se reprendre

bucket [ˈbʌkɪt] N seau *m* ▶ VI (*Brit inf*): **the rain is bucketing (down)** il pleut à verse

bucketful [ˈbʌkɪtful] N plein seau *m*

bucket list N liste *f* de choses à faire avant de mourir

Buckingham Palace [ˈbʌkɪŋəm-] N le palais de Buckingham

> **Buckingham Palace** est la résidence officielle londonienne du souverain britannique depuis 1762. Construit en 1703, il fut à l'origine le palais du duc de Buckingham. Il a été partiellement reconstruit au début du XXe siècle.

buckle [ˈbʌkl] N boucle *f* ▶ VT (*belt etc*) boucler, attacher ▶ VI (*warp*) tordre, gauchir; (: *wheel*) se voiler
▶ **buckle down** VI s'y mettre

buckskin [ˈbʌkskɪn] N peau *f* de daim

buckwheat [ˈbʌkwiːt] N (*grain*) sarrasin *m*; (*flour*) farine *f* de blé noir

bucolic [bjuːˈkɔlɪk] ADJ (*setting, scene*) pastoral; (*poetry, poet*) bucolique

bud [bʌd] N bourgeon m; (of flower) bouton m ▶ vi bourgeonner; (flower) éclore

Buddha ['budə] N Bouddha m

Buddhism ['budɪzəm] N bouddhisme m

Buddhist ['budɪst] ADJ, N bouddhiste mf

budding ['bʌdɪŋ] ADJ (flower) en bouton; (poet etc) en herbe; (passion etc) naissant(e)

buddy ['bʌdɪ] N (US) copain m

budge [bʌdʒ] VT faire bouger ▶ vi bouger

budgerigar ['bʌdʒərɪgɑːʳ] N perruche f

★**budget** ['bʌdʒɪt] N budget m; **I'm on a tight ~** je dois faire attention à mon budget ▶ vi: **to ~ for sth** inscrire qch au budget

budget airline N compagnie f aérienne low cost

budgetary ['bʌdʒɪtrɪ] ADJ budgétaire

budgeting ['bʌdʒɪtɪŋ] N prévisions fpl budgétaires

budgie ['bʌdʒɪ] N = **budgerigar**

Buenos Aires ['bweɪnɔs'aɪrɪz] N Buenos Aires

buff [bʌf] ADJ (couleur f) chamois m ▶ N (inf: enthusiast) mordu(e)

buffalo ['bʌfələu] (pl ~ or **buffaloes**) N (BRIT) buffle m; (US) bison m

buffer ['bʌfəʳ] N tampon m; (Comput) mémoire f tampon ▶ vt, vi (Comput) mettre en mémoire tampon

buffering ['bʌfərɪŋ] N (Comput) mise f en mémoire tampon

buffer state N état m tampon

buffer zone N zone f tampon

buffet N ['bufeɪ] (food: BRIT: bar) buffet m ▶ vt ['bʌfɪt] (wind, storm) secouer; (government, economy) secouer, ébranler

buffet car N (BRIT Rail) voiture-bar f

buffeting ['bʌfɪtɪŋ] N (of wind, seas) assaut m; (attack) rebuffade f; **to take a ~** essuyer une rebuffade

buffet lunch N lunch m

buffoon [bə'fuːn] N bouffon m, pitre m

bug [bʌg] N (bedbug etc) punaise f; (esp US: any insect) insecte m, bestiole f; (fig: germ) virus m, microbe m; (spy device) dispositif m d'écoute (électronique), micro clandestin; (Comput: of program) erreur f; (: of equipment) défaut m; **I've got the travel ~** (fig) j'ai le virus du voyage ▶ vt (room) poser des micros dans; (inf: annoy) embêter

bugbear ['bʌgbɛəʳ] N cauchemar m, bête noire

bugger ['bʌgəʳ] (inf!) N salaud m (!), connard m (!) ▶ vi: **~ off!** tire-toi ! (!) ▶ EXCL: **~!** (also: **bugger it!**) merde ! (!)

buggered ['bʌgəd] ADJ (BRIT inf!: broken) foutu(e); **I'll be ~ if ...** je préfère plutôt crever

bugging ['bʌgɪŋ] N (surveillance) utilisation f d'appareils d'écoute ▶ CPD (device, equipment) d'écoute (clandestine)

buggy ['bʌgɪ] N poussette f

bugle ['bjuːgl] N clairon m

bugler ['bjuːgləʳ] N (joueur m de) clairon m

★**build** [bɪld] (pt, pp **built** [bɪlt]) N (of person) carrure f, charpente f ▶ vt construire, bâtir
 ▶ **build on** vt FUS (fig) tirer parti de, partir de

▶ **build up** vt accumuler, amasser; (business) développer; (reputation) bâtir

builder ['bɪldəʳ] N entrepreneur m

★**building** ['bɪldɪŋ] N (trade) construction f; (structure) bâtiment m, construction f; (: residential, offices) immeuble m

building contractor N entrepreneur m (en bâtiment)

building industry N (industrie f du) bâtiment m

building site N chantier m (de construction)

building society N (BRIT) société f de crédit immobilier

> Une **building society** est une mutuelle dont les épargnants et les emprunteurs sont les propriétaires. Ces mutuelles offrent principalement deux services : des comptes épargne et des prêts, notamment immobiliers. Les building societies ont eu jusqu'en 1985 le quasi-monopole des comptes épargne et des prêts immobiliers, mais les banques ont maintenant une part importante de ce marché.

building trade N = **building industry**

build-up ['bɪldʌp] N (of gas etc) accumulation f; (publicity): **to give sb/sth a good ~** faire de la pub pour qn/qch

built [bɪlt] PT, PP of **build**

built-in ['bɪlt'ɪn] ADJ (cupboard) encastré(e); (device) incorporé(e); intégré(e)

built-up ['bɪltʌp] ADJ: **~ area** agglomération (urbaine); zone urbanisée

bulb [bʌlb] N (Bot) bulbe m, oignon m; (Elec) ampoule f

bulbous ['bʌlbəs] ADJ bulbeux(-euse)

Bulgaria [bʌl'gɛərɪə] N Bulgarie f

Bulgarian [bʌl'gɛərɪən] ADJ bulgare ▶ N Bulgare mf; (Ling) bulgare m

bulge [bʌldʒ] N renflement m, gonflement m; (in birth rate, sales) brusque augmentation f ▶ vi faire saillie; présenter un renflement; (pocket, file): **to be bulging with** être plein(e) à craquer de

bulimia [bə'lɪmɪə] N boulimie f

bulimic [bjuː'lɪmɪk] ADJ, N boulimique mf

bulk [bʌlk] N masse f, volume m; **in ~** (Comm) en gros, en vrac; **the ~ of** la plus grande or grosse partie de
 ▶ **bulk up** vt épaissir ▶ vi prendre de l'épaisseur

bulk buying [-'baɪɪŋ] N achat m en gros

bulk carrier N cargo m

bulkhead ['bʌlkhɛd] N cloison f (étanche)

bulky ['bʌlkɪ] ADJ volumineux(-euse), encombrant(e)

bull [bul] N taureau m; (male elephant, whale) mâle m; (Stock Exchange) haussier m; (Rel) bulle f

bulldog ['buldɔg] N bouledogue m

bulldoze ['buldəuz] vt passer or raser au bulldozer; **I was bulldozed into doing it** (fig: inf) on m'a forcé la main

bulldozer ['buldəuzəʳ] N bulldozer m

bullet ['bulɪt] N balle f (de fusil etc)

bulletin ['bulɪtɪn] N bulletin m, communiqué m; (also: **news bulletin**) (bulletin d')informations fpl

bulletin board N (*Comput*) messagerie f (électronique)

bulletproof [ˈbʊlɪtpruːf] ADJ à l'épreuve des balles; **~ vest** gilet m pare-balles

bullfight [ˈbʊlfaɪt] N corrida f, course f de taureaux

bullfighter [ˈbʊlfaɪtəʳ] N torero m

bullfighting [ˈbʊlfaɪtɪŋ] N tauromachie f

bullfinch [ˈbʊlfɪntʃ] N bouvreuil m

bullion [ˈbʊljən] N or m or argent m en lingots

bullish [ˈbʊlɪʃ] ADJ (*on stock market: mood*) haussier(-ière); (*optimistic*): **to be ~ about sth** être optimiste au sujet de qch

bullock [ˈbʊlək] N bœuf m

bullring [ˈbʊlrɪŋ] N arène f

bull's-eye [ˈbʊlzaɪ] N centre m (*de la cible*)

bullshit [ˈbʊlʃɪt] (*inf!*) N connerie(s) f(pl) (!) ▸ VT raconter des conneries à (!) ▸ VI déconner (!)

bully [ˈbʊlɪ] N brute f, tyran m ▸ VT tyranniser, rudoyer; (*frighten*) intimider

bullying [ˈbʊlɪɪŋ] N brimades fpl

bulwark [ˈbʊlwək] N rempart m

bum [bʌm] N (*inf: Brit: backside*) derrière m; (*esp US: tramp*) vagabond(e), traîne-savates mf; (: *idler*) glandeur m
▸ **bum around** VI (*inf*) vagabonder

bumblebee [ˈbʌmblbiː] N bourdon m

bumbling [ˈbʌmblɪŋ] ADJ empoté(e)

bumf [bʌmf] N (*inf: forms etc*) paperasses fpl

bummer [ˈbʌməʳ] N (*inf*): **what a ~!** quelle poisse !; **a ~ of a day** une journée pourrie

bump [bʌmp] N (*blow*) coup m, choc m; (*jolt*) cahot m; (*on road etc, on head*) bosse f ▸ VT heurter, cogner; (*car*) emboutir
▸ **bump along** VI avancer en cahotant
▸ **bump into** VT FUS rentrer dans, tamponner; (*inf: meet*) tomber sur
▸ **bump up** VT (*inf: amount, price*) faire grimper

bumper [ˈbʌmpəʳ] N pare-chocs m inv ▸ ADJ: **~ crop/harvest** récolte/moisson exceptionnelle

bumper cars NPL (*US*) autos tamponneuses

bumph [bʌmf] N = **bumf**

bumptious [ˈbʌmpʃəs] ADJ suffisant(e), prétentieux(-euse)

bumpy [ˈbʌmpɪ] ADJ (*road*) cahoteux(-euse); **it was a ~ flight/ride** on a été secoués dans l'avion/la voiture

bun [bʌn] N (*cake*) petit gâteau; (*bread*) petit pain au lait; (*of hair*) chignon m

★**bunch** [bʌntʃ] N (*of flowers*) bouquet m; (*of keys*) trousseau m; (*of bananas*) régime m; (*of people*) groupe m; **~ of grapes** grappe f de raisin ■ **bunches** NPL (*in hair*) couettes fpl

bundle [ˈbʌndl] N paquet m ▸ VT (*also*: **bundle up**) faire un paquet de; (*put*): **to ~ sth/sb into** fourrer or enfourner qch/qn dans
▸ **bundle off** VT (*person*) faire sortir (en toute hâte); expédier
▸ **bundle out** VT éjecter, sortir (sans ménagements)

bun fight N (*Brit inf*) réception f; (*tea party*) thé m

bung [bʌŋ] N bonde f, bouchon m ▸ VT (*Brit: throw: also*: **bung into**) flanquer; (*also*: **bung up**: *pipe, hole*)

boucher; **my nose is bunged up** (*inf*) j'ai le nez bouché

bungalow [ˈbʌŋgələʊ] N bungalow m

bungee jumping [ˈbʌndʒiːˈdʒʌmpɪŋ] N saut m à l'élastique

bungle [ˈbʌŋgl] VT bâcler, gâcher

bungling [ˈbʌŋglɪŋ] ADJ maladroit(e)

bunion [ˈbʌnjən] N oignon m (*au pied*)

bunk [bʌŋk] N couchette f; (*Brit inf*): **to do a ~** mettre les bouts or les voiles
▸ **bunk off** VI (*Brit inf: Scol*) sécher (les cours); **I'll ~ off at 3 o'clock this afternoon** je vais mettre les bouts or les voiles à 3 heures cet après-midi

bunk beds NPL lits superposés

bunker [ˈbʌŋkəʳ] N (*coal store*) soute f à charbon; (*Mil, Golf*) bunker m

bunkum [ˈbʌŋkəm] N (*inf*) foutaises fpl (*inf*), foutaise f (*inf*)

bunny [ˈbʌnɪ] N (*also*: **bunny rabbit**) lapin m

bunny girl N (*Brit*) hôtesse de cabaret

bunny hill N (*US Ski*) piste f pour débutants

bunting [ˈbʌntɪŋ] N pavoisement m, drapeaux mpl

buoy [bɔɪ] N bouée f
▸ **buoy up** VT faire flotter; (*fig*) soutenir, épauler

buoyancy [ˈbɔɪənsɪ] N (*of ship*) flottabilité f

buoyant [ˈbɔɪənt] ADJ (*ship*) flottable; (*carefree*) gai(e), plein(e) d'entrain; (*Comm: market, economy*) actif(-ive); (: *prices, currency*) soutenu(e)

burble [ˈbəːbl] VI (*water, river*) murmurer; (*person*) marmonner; **to ~ on about sth** radoter sur (le thème de) qch ▸ VT (*say*) marmonner

burden [ˈbəːdn] N fardeau m, charge f; **to be a ~ to sb** être un fardeau pour qn ▸ VT charger; (*oppress*) accabler, surcharger

burdened [ˈbəːdənd] ADJ: **~ with** (*loaded with*) chargé(e) de qch; (*debt, guilt*) accablé(e) de

burdensome [ˈbəːdənsəm] ADJ lourd(e)

bureau [ˈbjʊərəʊ] (*pl* **bureaux** [-z]) N (*Brit: writing desk*) bureau m, secrétaire m; (*US: chest of drawers*) commode f; (*office*) bureau, office m

bureaucracy [bjʊəˈrɔkrəsɪ] N bureaucratie f

bureaucrat [ˈbjʊərəkræt] N bureaucrate mf, rond-de-cuir m

bureaucratic [bjʊərəˈkrætɪk] ADJ bureaucratique

bureau de change [-dəˈʃɒnʒ] (*pl* **bureaux de change**) N bureau m de change

bureaux [ˈbjʊərəʊz] NPL of **bureau**

burgeon [ˈbəːdʒən] VI (*fig*) être en expansion rapide

★**burger** [ˈbəːgəʳ] N hamburger m

burglar [ˈbəːgləʳ] N cambrioleur(-euse)

burglar alarm N sonnerie f d'alarme

burglarize [ˈbəːgləraɪz] VT (*US*) cambrioler

burglary [ˈbəːglərɪ] N cambriolage m

burgle [ˈbəːgl] VT cambrioler

Burgundy [ˈbəːgəndɪ] N Bourgogne f

burgundy [ˈbəːgəndɪ] ADJ (*wine-coloured*) bordeaux inv ▸ N (*colour*) bordeaux m; (*wine*) bourgogne m

burial [ˈbɛrɪəl] N enterrement m

burial ground N cimetière m

burkha [ˈbəːkə] N = **burqa**

Burkina Faso [bəːˈkiːnəˈfæsəu] N Burkina Faso m

burlesque [bəːˈlɛsk] N parodie f

burly [ˈbəːlɪ] ADJ de forte carrure, costaud(e)

Burma [ˈbəːmə] N Birmanie f; see also **Myanmar**

Burmese [bəːˈmiːz] ADJ birman(e), de Birmanie
▶ N (pl inv) Birman(e); (Ling) birman m

★**burn** [bəːn] (pt, pp **burned** [bəːnd] or **burnt** [bəːnt])
VT, VI brûler; **the cigarette burnt a hole in her dress** la cigarette a fait un trou dans sa robe; **I've burnt myself!** je me suis brûlé(e) ! ▶ N brûlure f
▶ **burn down** VT incendier, détruire par le feu
▶ **burn out** VT (writer etc): **to ~ o.s. out** s'user (à force de travailler)
▶ **burn up** VI (satellite) se désintégrer ▶ VT (calories) brûler

burner [ˈbəːnəʳ] N brûleur m

burning [ˈbəːnɪŋ] ADJ (building, forest) en flammes; (issue, question) brûlant(e); (ambition) dévorant(e)

burnish [ˈbəːnɪʃ] VT polir

burnished [ˈbəːnɪʃt] ADJ (literary) aux reflets dorés

burnout [ˈbəːnaut] N (inf) épuisement f

Burns' Night [bəːnz-] N fête écossaise à la mémoire du poète Robert Burns

Burns' Night est une fête qui a lieu, le 25 janvier, à la mémoire du poète écossais Robert Burns (1759–1796). A cette occasion, les Écossais du monde entier organisent un souper, en général arrosé de whisky. Le plat principal est toujours le _haggis_, servi avec de la purée de pommes de terre et de la purée de rutabagas. On apporte le _haggis_ à table au son des cornemuses et le repas est ponctué de chansons et de poèmes de Burns interprétés par les convives.

burnt [bəːnt] PT, PP of **burn**

burnt sugar N (BRIT) caramel m

burp [bəːp] (inf) ▶ N rot m ▶ VI roter

burqa [ˈbəːkə] N burqa f, burka f

burrow [ˈbʌrəu] N terrier m ▶ VT creuser ▶ VI (rabbit) creuser un terrier; (rummage) fouiller

bursar [ˈbəːsəʳ] N économe mf; (BRIT: student) boursier(-ère)

bursary [ˈbəːsərɪ] N (BRIT) bourse f (d'études)

burst [bəːst] (pt, pp ~) VT faire éclater; **to ~ its banks** (river) sortir de son lit; **the river has ~ its banks** le cours d'eau est sorti de son lit ▶ VI éclater; (tyre) crever; **to ~ into flames** s'enflammer soudainement; **to ~ out laughing** éclater de rire; **to ~ into tears** fondre en larmes; **to ~ open** s'ouvrir violemment or soudainement; **to be bursting with** (container) être plein(e) (à craquer) de, regorger de; (fig) être débordant(e) de ▶ N explosion f; (also: **burst pipe**) fuite f (due à une rupture); **a ~ of enthusiasm/energy** un accès d'enthousiasme/d'énergie; **~ of laughter** éclat m de rire; **a ~ of applause** une salve d'applaudissements; **a ~ of gunfire** une rafale de tir; **a ~ of speed** une pointe de vitesse ▶ ADJ: **~ blood vessel** rupture f de vaisseau sanguin
▶ **burst into** VT FUS (room etc) faire irruption dans
▶ **burst out of** VT FUS sortir précipitamment de

Burundi [bəˈrundɪ] N Burundi m

★**bury** [ˈbɛrɪ] VT enterrer; **to ~ one's face in one's hands** se couvrir le visage de ses mains; **to ~ one's head in the sand** (fig) pratiquer la politique de l'autruche; **to ~ the hatchet** (fig) enterrer la hache de guerre

★**bus** [bʌs] (pl **buses** [ˈbʌsɪz]) N (auto) bus m

busboy [ˈbʌsbɔɪ] N (US) aide-serveur m

bus conductor N receveur(-euse) de bus

bush [buʃ] N buisson m; (scrub land) brousse f; **to beat about the ~** tourner autour du pot

bushed [buʃt] ADJ (inf) crevé(e), claqué(e)

bushel [ˈbuʃl] N boisseau m

bushfire [ˈbuʃfaɪəʳ] N feu m de brousse

bushy [ˈbuʃɪ] ADJ broussailleux(-euse), touffu(e)

busily [ˈbɪzɪlɪ] ADV: **to be ~ doing sth** s'affairer à faire qch

★**business** [ˈbɪznɪs] N (matter, firm) affaire f; (trading) affaires fpl; (job, duty) travail m; **to be away on ~** être en déplacement d'affaires; **I'm here on ~** je suis là pour affaires; **he's in the insurance ~** il est dans les assurances; **to do ~ with sb** traiter avec qn; **it's none of my ~** cela ne me regarde pas, ce ne sont pas mes affaires; **he means ~** il ne plaisante pas, il est sérieux

business address N adresse professionnelle or au bureau

business card N carte f de visite (professionnelle)

business class N (on plane) classe f affaires

businesslike [ˈbɪznɪslaɪk] ADJ sérieux(-euse), efficace

★**businessman** [ˈbɪznɪsmən] N (irreg) homme m d'affaires

business trip N voyage m d'affaires

★**businesswoman** [ˈbɪznɪswumən] N (irreg) femme f d'affaires

busk [ˈbʌsk] VI (BRIT: play) jouer dans la rue; (: sing) chanter dans la rue

busker [ˈbʌskəʳ] N (BRIT) artiste ambulant(e)

bus lane N (BRIT) voie réservée aux autobus

bus pass N carte f de bus

bus shelter N abribus m

bus station N gare routière

bus stop N arrêt m d'autobus

bust [bʌst] N buste m; (measurement) tour m de poitrine ▶ ADJ (inf: broken) fichu(e), fini(e); **to go ~** (inf) faire faillite ▶ VT (inf: Police: arrest) pincer

bustier [ˈbʌstɪəʳ] N bustier m

bustle [ˈbʌsl] N remue-ménage m, affairement m ▶ VI s'affairer, se démener

bustling [ˈbʌslɪŋ] ADJ (person) affairé(e); (town) très animé(e)

bust-up [ˈbʌstʌp] N (BRIT inf) engueulade f

busty [ˈbʌstɪ] ADJ (inf) à la poitrine plantureuse

★**busy** [ˈbɪzɪ] ADJ occupé(e); (shop, street) très fréquenté(e); (US: telephone, line) occupé; **he's a ~ man** (normally) c'est un homme très pris; (temporarily) il est très pris ▶ VT: **to ~ o.s.** s'occuper

busybody [ˈbɪzɪbɔdɪ] N mouche f du coche, âme f charitable

busy signal N (US) tonalité f occupé inv

but [bʌt]

CONJ mais; **I'd love to come, but I'm busy** j'aimerais venir mais je suis occupé; **he's not English but French** il n'est pas anglais mais français; **but that's far too expensive!** mais c'est bien trop cher !

▶ PREP (apart from, except) sauf, excepté; **nothing but** rien d'autre que; **we've had nothing but trouble** nous n'avons eu que des ennuis; **no-one but him can do it** lui seul peut le faire; **who but a lunatic would do such a thing?** qui sinon un fou ferait une chose pareille ?; **but for you/your help** sans toi/ton aide; **anything but that** tout sauf or excepté ça, tout mais pas ça; **the last but one** (BRIT) l'avant-dernier(-ère)

▶ ADV (just, only) ne ... que; **she's but a child** elle n'est qu'une enfant; **had I but known** si seulement j'avais su; **I can but try** je peux toujours essayer; **all but finished** pratiquement terminé; **anything but finished** tout sauf fini, très loin d'être fini

butane ['bjuːteɪn] N (also: **butane gas**) butane m

butch [butʃ] ADJ (inf: woman: pej) costaude, masculine; (: man) costaud, viril

★**butcher** ['butʃəʳ] N boucher m ▶ VT massacrer; (cattle etc for meat) tuer

★**butcher's** ['butʃəz], **butcher's shop** N boucherie f

butler ['bʌtləʳ] N maître m d'hôtel

butt [bʌt] N (cask) gros tonneau; (thick end) (gros) bout; (of gun) crosse f; (of cigarette) mégot m; (BRIT fig: target) cible f ▶ VT donner un coup de tête à ▶ **butt in** VI (interrupt) interrompre

★**butter** ['bʌtəʳ] N beurre m ▶ VT beurrer

buttercup ['bʌtəkʌp] N bouton m d'or

butter dish N beurrier m

butterfingers ['bʌtəfɪŋgəz] N (inf) maladroit(e)

butterfly ['bʌtəflaɪ] N papillon m; (Swimming: also: **butterfly stroke**) brasse f papillon

buttermilk ['bʌtəmɪlk] N babeurre m

butterscotch ['bʌtəskɔtʃ] N caramel m dur (au beurre) ▶ CPD (sauce) au caramel

buttocks ['bʌtəks] NPL fesses fpl

★**button** ['bʌtn] N bouton m; (US: badge) pin m ▶ VT (also: **button up**) boutonner ▶ VI se boutonner

buttonhole ['bʌtnhəul] N boutonnière f ▶ VT accrocher, arrêter, retenir

buttress ['bʌtrɪs] N contrefort m

buxom ['bʌksəm] ADJ aux formes avantageuses or épanouies, bien galbé(e)

★**buy** [baɪ] (pt, pp bought [bɔːt]) VT acheter; (Comm: company) (r)acheter; **where can I ~ some postcards?** où est-ce que je peux acheter des cartes postales ?; **to ~ sb sth/sth from sb** acheter qch à qn; **to ~ sb a drink** offrir un verre or à boire à qn; **can I ~ you a drink?** je vous offre un verre ? ▶ N achat m; **that was a good/bad ~** c'était un bon/mauvais achat

▶ **buy back** VT racheter

▶ **buy in** VT (BRIT: goods) acheter, faire venir

▶ **buy into** VT FUS (BRIT Comm) acheter des actions de

▶ **buy off** VT (inf: bribe) acheter

▶ **buy out** VT (partner) désintéresser; (business) racheter

▶ **buy up** VT acheter en bloc, rafler

buyer ['baɪəʳ] N acheteur(-euse); **~'s market** marché m favorable aux acheteurs

buy-out ['baɪaut] N (Comm) rachat m (d'entreprise)

buzz [bʌz] N bourdonnement m; (inf: phone call): **to give sb a ~** passer un coup de fil à qn ▶ VI bourdonner; **my head is buzzing** j'ai la tête qui bourdonne ▶ VT (call on intercom) appeler; (with buzzer) sonner; (Aviat: plane, building) raser

▶ **buzz off** VI (inf) s'en aller, ficher le camp

buzzard ['bʌzəd] N buse f

buzzer ['bʌzəʳ] N timbre m électrique

buzz word N (inf) mot m à la mode or dans le vent

by [baɪ]

PREP **1** (referring to cause, agent) par, de; **killed by lightning** tué par la foudre; **surrounded by a fence** entouré d'une barrière; **a painting by Picasso** un tableau de Picasso

2 (referring to method: manner: means): **by bus/car** en autobus/voiture; **by train** par le or en train; **to pay by cheque** payer par chèque; **by moonlight/candlelight** à la lueur de la lune/d'une bougie; **by saving hard, he ...** à force d'économiser, il ...

3 (via, through) par; **we came by Dover** nous sommes venus par Douvres

4 (close to, past) à côté de; **the house by the school** la maison à côté de l'école; **a holiday by the sea** des vacances au bord de la mer; **she sat by his bed** elle était assise à son chevet; **she went by me** elle est passée à côté de moi; **I go by the post office every day** je passe devant la poste tous les jours

5 (with time: not later than) avant; (: during): **by daylight** à la lumière du jour; **by night** la nuit, de nuit; **by 4 o'clock** avant 4 heures; **by this time tomorrow** d'ici demain à la même heure; **by the time I got here it was too late** lorsque je suis arrivé il était déjà trop tard

6 (amount) à; **by the kilo/metre** au kilo/au mètre; **paid by the hour** payé à l'heure; **to increase** etc **by the hour** augmenter etc d'heure en heure

7 (Math: measure): **to divide/multiply by 3** diviser/multiplier par 3; **a room 3 metres by 4** une pièce de 3 mètres sur 4; **it's broader by a metre** c'est plus large d'un mètre; **the bullet missed him by inches** la balle est passée à quelques centimètres de lui; **one by one** une à un; **little by little** petit à petit, peu à peu

8 (according to) d'après, selon; **it's 3 o'clock by my watch** il est 3 heures à ma montre; **it's all right by me** je n'ai rien contre

9: **(all) by oneself** etc tout(e) seul(e)

▶ ADV **1** see go; pass etc

2: **by and by** un peu plus tard, bientôt; **by and large** dans l'ensemble

★**bye** [baɪ], **bye-bye** ['baɪ'baɪ] EXCL au revoir !, salut !

bye-law ['baɪlɔː] N = **by-law**

by-election ['baɪɪlekʃən] N (BRIT) élection (législative) partielle

Byelorussia [bjɛləuˈrʌʃə] N Biélorussie f

Byelorussian [bjɛləuˈrʌʃən] ADJ, N = **Belorussian**

bygone [ˈbaɪɡɔn] ADJ passé(e) ▶ N: **let bygones be bygones** passons l'éponge, oublions le passé

by-law [ˈbaɪlɔː] N arrêté municipal

bypass [ˈbaɪpɑːs] N rocade f; (Med) pontage m ▶ VT éviter

by-product [ˈbaɪprɔdʌkt] N sous-produit m, dérivé m; (fig) conséquence f secondaire, retombée f

byre [ˈbaɪəʳ] N (BRIT) étable f (à vaches)

bystander [ˈbaɪstændəʳ] N spectateur(-trice), badaud(e)

byte [baɪt] N (Comput) octet m

byway [ˈbaɪweɪ] N chemin détourné

byword [ˈbaɪwəːd] N: **to be a ~ for** être synonyme de (fig)

by-your-leave [ˈbaɪjɔːˈliːv] N: **without so much as a ~** sans même demander la permission

b

Cc

C¹, c [si:] N (letter) C, c m; (Scol: mark) C; (Mus): **C** do m; **C for Charlie** C comme Célestin

C² ABBR (= Celsius, centigrade) C

C ABBR (= century) s.; (US etc) = **cent**; (= circa) v.

CA N ABBR = **Central America**; (BRIT) = **chartered accountant** ▸ ABBR (US) = **California**

ca. ABBR (= circa) v

c/a ABBR = **credit account**; **current account**

CAA N ABBR (BRIT) = **Civil Aviation Authority**; (US: = Civil Aeronautics Authority) direction de l'aviation civile

CAB N ABBR (BRIT) = **Citizens' Advice Bureau**

cab [kæb] N taxi m; (of train, truck) cabine f; (horse-drawn) fiacre m

cabaret ['kæbəreɪ] N attractions fpl; (show) spectacle m de cabaret

★**cabbage** ['kæbɪdʒ] N chou m

cabbie, cabby ['kæbɪ] N (inf) taxi m, chauffeur m de taxi

cab driver N chauffeur m de taxi

cabin ['kæbɪn] N (house) cabane f, hutte f; (on ship) cabine f; (on plane) compartiment m

cabin crew N (Aviat) équipage m

cabin cruiser N yacht m (à moteur)

cabinet ['kæbɪnɪt] N (Pol) cabinet m; (furniture) petit meuble à tiroirs et rayons; (also: **display cabinet**) vitrine f, petite armoire vitrée

cabinet-maker ['kæbɪnɪt'meɪkəʳ] N ébéniste mf

cabinet minister N ministre mf (membre du cabinet)

★**cable** ['keɪbl] N câble m ▸ VT câbler, télégraphier

cable car N téléphérique m

cablegram ['keɪblgræm] N câblogramme m

cable railway N (BRIT) funiculaire m

cable television N télévision f par câble

cache [kæʃ] N cachette f; **a ~ of food** etc un dépôt secret de provisions etc, une cachette contenant des provisions etc

cachet ['kæʃeɪ] N (of position, place) prestige m; (of thing) cachet m

cackle ['kækl] VI caqueter

cacophony [kə'kɔfənɪ] N cacophonie f

cactus ['kæktəs] (pl **cacti** [-taɪ]) N cactus m

CAD N ABBR (= computer-aided design) CAO f

cad [kæd] N (old) mufle m, goujat m

cadaver [kə'dævəʳ] N cadavre m

caddie ['kædɪ] N caddie m

cadet [kə'dɛt] N (Mil) élève mf officier; **police ~** élève agent de police

cadge [kædʒ] VT (inf) se faire donner; **to ~ a meal (off sb)** se faire inviter à manger (par qn)

cadmium ['kædmɪəm] N cadmium m

cadre ['kædrɪ] N cadre m

Caesarean, (US) **Cesarean** [si:'zɛərɪən] ADJ: **~ (section)** césarienne f

Caesar salad [si:zə-] N salade f césar

CAF ABBR (BRIT: = cost and freight) C et F

café ['kæfeɪ] N ≈ café(-restaurant) m (sans alcool)

cafeteria [kæfɪ'tɪərɪə] N cafétéria f

caffeine ['kæfi:n] N caféine f

cage [keɪdʒ] N cage f ▸ VT mettre en cage

caged [keɪdʒd] ADJ en cage

cagey ['keɪdʒɪ] ADJ (inf) réticent(e), méfiant(e)

cagoule [kə'gu:l] N K-way® m

cahoots [kə'hu:ts] N (inf): **to be in ~ (with)** être de mèche (avec)

CAI N ABBR (= computer-aided instruction) EAO m

cairn [kɛən] N cairn m

Cairo ['kaɪərəu] N Le Caire

cajole [kə'dʒəul] VT couvrir de flatteries or de gentillesses

Cajun ['keɪdʒən] ADJ cajun inv ▸ N (person) Cajun mf; (language) cajun m

★**cake** [keɪk] N gâteau m; **~ of soap** savonnette f; **it's a piece of ~** (inf) c'est un jeu d'enfant; **he wants to have his ~ and eat it (too)** (fig) il veut avoir le beurre et l'argent du beurre ?

caked [keɪkt] ADJ: **~ with** raidi(e) par, couvert(e) d'une croûte de

cake shop N pâtisserie f

cakewalk ['keɪkwɔ:k] N (dance) cake-walk; (fig) promenade f de santé

calamitous [kə'læmɪtəs] ADJ catastrophique, désastreux(-euse)

calamity [kə'læmɪtɪ] N calamité f, désastre m

calcium ['kælsɪəm] N calcium m

calculate ['kælkjuleɪt] VT calculer; (estimate: chances, effect) évaluer
▸ **calculate on** VT FUS: **to ~ on sth/on doing sth** compter sur qch/faire qch

calculated ['kælkjuleɪtɪd] ADJ (insult, action) délibéré(e); **a ~ risk** un risque pris en toute connaissance de cause

calculating ['kælkjuleɪtɪŋ] ADJ calculateur(-trice)

calculation [kælkjuˈleɪʃən] N calcul m

★**calculator** [ˈkælkjuleɪtəʳ] N machine f à calculer, calculatrice f

calculus [ˈkælkjuləs] N analyse f (mathématique), calcul infinitésimal; **integral/differential ~** calcul intégral/différentiel

calendar [ˈkæləndəʳ] N calendrier m

calendar year N année civile

★**calf** [kɑːf] (pl **calves** [kɑːvz]) N (of cow) veau m; (of other animals) petit m; (also: **calfskin**) veau m, vachette f; (Anat) mollet m

calfskin [ˈkɑːfskɪn] N (cuir m de) veau m, (cuir de) vachette f ► CPD en veau

caliber [ˈkælɪbəʳ] N (US) = **calibre**

calibrate [ˈkælɪbreɪt] VT (gun etc) calibrer; (scale of measuring instrument) étalonner

calibre, (US) **caliber** [ˈkælɪbəʳ] N calibre m

calico [ˈkælɪkəu] N (BRIT) calicot m; (US) indienne f

California [kælɪˈfɔːnɪə] N Californie f

calipers [ˈkælɪpəz] NPL (US) = **callipers**

calisthenics [kælɪsˈθɛnɪks] NPL = **callisthenics**

★**call** [kɔːl] VT (gen, also Tel) appeler; (announce: flight) annoncer; (: meeting) convoquer; (: strike) lancer; **to be called** s'appeler; **she's called Suzanne** elle s'appelle Suzanne ► VI appeler; (visit: also: **call in**, **call round**) passer; **who is calling?** (Tel) qui est à l'appareil ?; **London calling** (Radio) ici Londres ► N (shout) appel m, cri m; (summons: for flight etc, fig: lure) appel; (visit) visite f; (also: **telephone call**) coup m de téléphone; communication f; **please give me a ~ at 7** appelez-moi à 7 heures; **to make a ~** téléphoner, passer un coup de fil; **can I make a ~ from here?** est-ce que je peux téléphoner d'ici ?; **to pay a ~ on sb** rendre visite à qn, passer voir qn; **to be on ~** être de permanence; **there's not much ~ for these items** ces articles ne sont pas très demandés
  ► **call at** VT FUS (ship) faire escale à; (train) s'arrêter à
  ► **call back** VI (return) repasser; (Tel) rappeler; **can you call back later?** pouvez-vous rappeler plus tard ? ► VT (Tel) rappeler
  ► **call for** VT FUS (demand) demander; (fetch) passer prendre
  ► **call in** VT (doctor, expert, police) appeler, faire venir
  ► **call off** VT annuler; **the strike was called off** l'ordre de grève a été levé
  ► **call on** VT FUS (visit) rendre visite à, passer voir; (request): **to ~ on sb to do** inviter qn à faire
  ► **call out** VI pousser un cri or des cris ► VT (doctor, police, troops) appeler
  ► **call up** VT (Mil) appeler, mobiliser; (Tel) appeler

callback [ˈkɔːlbæk] N (interview) deuxième entrevue f; (audition) deuxième audition f

call box N (BRIT) cabine f téléphonique

call centre, (US) **call center** N centre m d'appels

caller [ˈkɔːləʳ] N (Tel) personne f qui appelle; (visitor) visiteur m; **hold the line, ~!** (Tel) ne quittez pas, Monsieur (or Madame) !

call girl N call-girl f

calligraphy [kəˈlɪgrəfɪ] N calligraphie f

call-in [ˈkɔːlɪn] N (US Radio, TV) programme m à ligne ouverte

calling [ˈkɔːlɪŋ] N vocation f; (trade, occupation) état m

calling card N (US) carte f de visite

callipers, (US) **calipers** [ˈkælɪpəz] NPL (Math) compas m; (Med) étrier m

callisthenics, calisthenics [kælɪsˈθɛnɪks] NPL gymnastique suédoise, gymnastique f rythmique

callous [ˈkæləs] ADJ dur(e), insensible

calloused, callused [ˈkæləst] ADJ calleux(-euse)

callousness [ˈkæləsnɪs] N dureté f, manque m de cœur, insensibilité f

call-out charge, call-out fee [ˈkɔːlaut-] N frais mpl de déplacement

callow [ˈkæləu] ADJ sans expérience (de la vie)

★**calm** [kɑːm] ADJ calme ► N calme m ► VT calmer, apaiser
  ► **calm down** VI se calmer, s'apaiser ► VT calmer, apaiser

calmly [ˈkɑːmlɪ] ADV calmement, avec calme

calmness [ˈkɑːmnɪs] N calme m

Calor gas® [ˈkælə-] N (BRIT) butane m, butagaz® m

calorie [ˈkælərɪ] N calorie f; **low ~ product** produit m pauvre en calories

calve [kɑːv] VI vêler, mettre bas

calves [kɑːvz] NPL of **calf**

CAM N ABBR (= computer-aided manufacturing) FAO f

camber [ˈkæmbəʳ] N (of road) bombement m

Cambodia [kæmˈbəudɪə] N Cambodge m

Cambodian [kæmˈbəudɪən] ADJ cambodgien(ne) ► N Cambodgien(ne)

camcorder [ˈkæmkɔːdəʳ] N caméscope m

came [keɪm] PT of **come**

camel [ˈkæməl] N chameau m

camellia [kəˈmiːlɪə] N camélia m

cameo [ˈkæmɪəu] N camée m

★**camera** [ˈkæmərə] N appareil photo m; (Cine, TV) caméra f; **digital ~** appareil numérique; **in ~** à huis clos, en privé

cameraman [ˈkæmərəmæn] N (irreg) caméraman m

camera phone N téléphone m avec appareil photo

Cameroon, Cameroun [kæməˈruːn] N Cameroun m

camisole [ˈkæmɪsəul] N caraco m

camomile [ˈkæməmaɪl] N camomille f

camouflage [ˈkæməflɑːʒ] N camouflage m ► VT camoufler

★**camp** [kæmp] N camp m ► VI camper ► ADJ (man) efféminé(e)

★**campaign** [kæmˈpeɪn] N (Mil, Pol) campagne f ► VI (also fig) faire campagne; **to ~ for/against** militer pour/contre

campaigner [kæmˈpeɪnəʳ] N: **~ for** partisan(e) de; **~ against** opposant(e) à

camp bed N (BRIT) lit m de camp

camper [ˈkæmpəʳ] N campeur(-euse); (vehicle) camping-car m

★**camping** [ˈkæmpɪŋ] N camping m; **to go ~** faire du camping

camping gas® N butane m

★**campsite** [ˈkæmpsaɪt] N (terrain m de) camping m

campus [ˈkæmpəs] N campus m

camshaft ['kæmʃɑːft] N arbre *m* à came

★**can¹** [kæn] N (*of milk, oil, water*) bidon *m*; (*tin*) boîte *f* (de conserve) ▶ VT (*food*) mettre en conserve; (*US inf: woman*) mettre à la porte; **a ~ of beer** une canette de bière; **he had to carry the ~** (*BRIT inf*) on lui a fait porter le chapeau

---

can² [kæn]

(*negative* **cannot** ['kænɔt], **can't** [kɑːnt], *conditional, pt* **could** [kud]) AUX VB **1** (*be able to*) pouvoir; **you can do it if you try** vous pouvez le faire si vous essayez; **I can't hear you** je ne t'entends pas

2 (*know how to*) savoir; **I can swim/play tennis/drive** je sais nager/jouer au tennis/conduire; **can you speak French?** parlez-vous français ?

3 (*may*) pouvoir; **can I use your phone?** puis-je me servir de votre téléphone ?

4 (*expressing disbelief, puzzlement etc*): **it can't be true!** ce n'est pas possible !; **what CAN he want?** qu'est-ce qu'il peut bien vouloir ?

5 (*expressing possibility, suggestion etc*): **he could be in the library** il est peut-être dans la bibliothèque; **she could have been delayed** il se peut qu'elle ait été retardée; **they could have forgotten** ils ont pu oublier

---

can is not translated with French verbs such as **voir, entendre, comprendre** and **se souvenir de**.
I can see her! **Je la vois !**
I can't understand him. **Je ne le comprends pas.**

★**Canada** ['kænədə] N Canada *m*

★**Canadian** [kə'neɪdɪən] ADJ canadien(ne) ▶ N Canadien(ne)

canal [kə'næl] N canal *m*

canary [kə'nɛərɪ] N canari *m*, serin *m*

Canary Islands, Canaries [kə'nɛərɪz] NPL: **the ~** les (îles *fpl*) Canaries *fpl*

Canberra ['kænbərə] N Canberra

★**cancel** ['kænsəl] VT annuler; (*train*) supprimer; (*party, appointment*) décommander; (*cross out*) barrer, rayer; (*stamp*) oblitérer; (*cheque*) faire opposition à; **I would like to ~ my booking** je voudrais annuler ma réservation

▶ **cancel out** VT annuler; **they ~ each other out** ils s'annulent

cancellation [kænsə'leɪʃən] N annulation *f*; suppression *f*; oblitération *f*; (*booking*) réservation annulée, client *etc* qui s'est décommandé; (*person*) client *etc* qui s'est décommandé

★**Cancer** ['kænsər] N (*Astrology*) le Cancer; **to be ~** être du Cancer

cancer ['kænsər] N cancer *m*

cancerous ['kænsrəs] ADJ cancéreux(-euse)

cancer patient N cancéreux(-euse)

cancer research N recherche *f* contre le cancer

C & F ABBR (*BRIT: = cost and freight*) C et F

candid ['kændɪd] ADJ (très) franc (franche), sincère

candidacy ['kændɪdəsɪ] N candidature *f*

★**candidate** ['kændɪdeɪt] N candidat(e)

candidature ['kændɪdətʃər] N (*BRIT*) = **candidacy**

candied ['kændɪd] ADJ confit(e); **~ apple** (*US*) pomme caramélisée

candle ['kændl] N bougie *f*; (*of tallow*) chandelle *f*; (*in church*) cierge *m*

candlelight ['kændllaɪt] N: **by ~** à la lumière d'une bougie; (*dinner*) aux chandelles

candlelit ['kændllɪt] ADJ (*room, table*) éclairé(e) à la bougie (*or* aux chandelles)

candlestick ['kændlstɪk] N (*also*: **candle holder**) bougeoir *m*; (: *bigger, ornate*) chandelier *m*

candour, (*US*) **candor** ['kændər] N (grande) franchise *or* sincérité

C & W N ABBR = **country and western**

candy ['kændɪ] N sucre candi; (*US*) bonbon *m*

candy bar (*US*) N barre *f* chocolatée

candyfloss ['kændɪflɔs] N (*BRIT*) barbe *f* à papa

candy store N (*US*) confiserie *f*

cane [keɪn] N canne *f*; (*for baskets, chairs etc*) rotin *m* ▶ VT (*BRIT Scol*) administrer des coups de bâton à

canine ['kænaɪn] ADJ canin(e)

canister ['kænɪstər] N boîte *f* (*gén en métal*); (*of gas*) bombe *f*

cannabis ['kænəbɪs] N (*drug*) cannabis *m*; (*cannabis plant*) chanvre indien

canned ['kænd] ADJ (*food*) en boîte, en conserve; (*inf: music*) enregistré(e); (*BRIT inf: drunk*) bourré(e); (*US inf: worker*) mis(e) à la porte

cannibal ['kænɪbəl] N cannibale *mf*, anthropophage *mf*

cannibalism ['kænɪbəlɪzəm] N cannibalisme *m*, anthropophagie *f*

cannon ['kænən] (*pl* **~** *or* **cannons**) N (*gun*) canon *m*

cannonball ['kænənbɔːl] N boulet *m* de canon

cannon fodder N chair *f* à canon

cannot ['kænɔt] = **can not**

canny ['kænɪ] ADJ madré(e), finaud(e)

canoe [kə'nuː] N pirogue *f*; (*Sport*) canoë *m*

canoeing [kə'nuːɪŋ] N canoë *m*

canoeist [kə'nuːɪst] N canoéiste *mf*

canon ['kænən] N (*clergyman*) chanoine *m*; (*standard*) canon *m*

canonize ['kænənaɪz] VT canoniser

can-opener [-'əupnər] N ouvre-boîte *m*

canopy ['kænəpɪ] N baldaquin *m*; dais *m*

cant [kænt] N jargon *m* ▶ VT, VI pencher

can't [kɑːnt] = **can not**

cantankerous [kæn'tæŋkərəs] ADJ querelleur(-euse), acariâtre

canteen [kæn'tiːn] N (*eating place*) cantine *f*; (*BRIT: of cutlery*) ménagère *f*

canter ['kæntər] N petit galop ▶ VI aller au petit galop

cantilever ['kæntɪliːvər] N porte-à-faux *m inv*

Cantonese [kæntə'niːz] ADJ cantonais(e) ▶ N (*person*) Cantonais(e); (*language*) cantonais *m*

canvas ['kænvəs] N (*gen*) toile *f*; **under ~** (*camping*) sous la tente; (*Naut*) toutes voiles dehors

canvass ['kænvəs] VI (*Pol*): **to ~ for** faire campagne pour ▶ VT (*Pol: district*) faire la tournée électorale dans; (: *person*) solliciter le suffrage de; (*Comm: district*) prospecter; (: *citizens, opinions*) sonder

canvasser [ˈkænvəsəʳ] N (Pol) agent électoral; (Comm) démarcheur m

canvassing [ˈkænvəsɪŋ] N (Pol) prospection électorale, démarchage électoral; (Comm) démarchage, prospection

canyon [ˈkænjən] N cañon m, gorge (profonde)

CAP N ABBR (= Common Agricultural Policy) PAC f

★**cap** [kæp] N casquette f; (for swimming) bonnet m de bain; (of pen) capuchon m; (of bottle) capsule f; (BRIT: contraceptive: also: **Dutch cap**) diaphragme m; (Football) sélection f pour l'équipe nationale ▶ VT capsuler; (outdo) surpasser; (put limit on) plafonner; **capped with** coiffé(e) de; **and to ~ it all, he ...** (BRIT) pour couronner le tout, il ...

capability [keɪpəˈbɪlɪtɪ] N aptitude f, capacité f

★**capable** [ˈkeɪpəbl] ADJ capable; **~ of** (interpretation etc) susceptible de

capably [ˈkeɪpəblɪ] ADV avec compétence

capacious [kəˈpeɪʃəs] ADJ vaste

capacity [kəˈpæsɪtɪ] N (of container) capacité f, contenance f; (ability) aptitude f; **filled to ~** plein(e); **in his ~ as** en sa qualité de; **in an advisory ~** à titre consultatif; **to work at full ~** travailler à plein rendement

cape [keɪp] N (garment) cape f; (Geo) cap m

Cape of Good Hope N cap m de Bonne Espérance

caper [ˈkeɪpəʳ] N (Culin: gen pl) câpre f; (prank) farce f

Cape Town N Le Cap

Cape Verde [keɪpˈvɜːd] N Cap-Vert m

capita [ˈkæpɪtə] N see **per capita**

★**capital** [ˈkæpɪtl] N (also: **capital city**) capitale f; (money) capital m; (also: **capital letter**) majuscule f

capital account N balance f des capitaux; (of country) compte capital

capital allowance N provision f pour amortissement

capital assets NPL immobilisations fpl

capital expenditure N dépenses fpl d'équipement

capital gains tax N impôt m sur les plus-values

capital goods N biens mpl d'équipement

capital-intensive [ˈkæpɪtlɪnˈtensɪv] ADJ à forte proportion de capitaux

capitalism [ˈkæpɪtəlɪzəm] N capitalisme m

capitalist [ˈkæpɪtəlɪst] ADJ, N capitaliste mf

capitalize [ˈkæpɪtəlaɪz] VT (provide with capital) financer
▶ **capitalize on** VT FUS (fig) profiter de

capital punishment N peine capitale

capital transfer tax N (BRIT) impôt m sur le transfert de propriété

Capitol [ˈkæpɪtl] N: **the ~** le Capitole

> Le **Capitol** est le siège du *Congress*, à Washington D.C. Il est situé sur *Capitol Hill*, dont le nom désigne par métonymie le *Congress* lui-même.

capitulate [kəˈpɪtjuleɪt] VI capituler

capitulation [kəpɪtjuˈleɪʃən] N capitulation f

cappuccino [kæpəˈtʃiːnəu] N cappuccino m

capricious [kəˈprɪʃəs] ADJ capricieux(-euse), fantasque

Capricorn [ˈkæprɪkɔːn] N (Astrology) le Capricorne; **to be ~** être du Capricorne

caps [kæps] ABBR = **capital letters**

capsize [kæpˈsaɪz] VT faire chavirer ▶ VI chavirer

capstan [ˈkæpstən] N cabestan m

capsule [ˈkæpsjuːl] N capsule f

Capt. ABBR (= captain) Cne

★**captain** [ˈkæptɪn] N capitaine m ▶ VT commander, être le capitaine de

★**caption** [ˈkæpʃən] N légende f

captivate [ˈkæptɪveɪt] VT captiver, fasciner

captive [ˈkæptɪv] ADJ, N captif(-ive)

captivity [kæpˈtɪvɪtɪ] N captivité f

captor [ˈkæptəʳ] N (unlawful) ravisseur m; (lawful): **his captors** les gens (or ceux etc) qui l'ont arrêté

capture [ˈkæptʃəʳ] VT (prisoner, animal) capturer; (town) prendre; (attention) capter; (Comput) saisir ▶ N capture f; (of data) saisie f de données

★**car** [kɑːʳ] N voiture f, auto f; (US Rail) wagon m, voiture; **by ~** en voiture

carafe [kəˈræf] N carafe f

carafe wine N (in restaurant) ≈ vin ouvert

caramel [ˈkærəməl] N caramel m

carat [ˈkærət] N carat m; **18 ~ gold** or m à 18 carats

★**caravan** [ˈkærəvæn] N caravane f

caravan site N (BRIT) camping m pour caravanes

caraway [ˈkærəweɪ] N: **~ seed** graine f de carvi, carvi m

carb [kɑːb] N (inf: carbohydrate) glucide m; **a low-carb diet** un régime pauvre en glucides

carbohydrate [kɑːbəuˈhaɪdreɪt] N (Chem) glucide m, hydrate m de carbone ■ **carbohydrates** NPL (food) farineux mpl, féculents mpl

carbolic acid [kɑːˈbɔlɪk-] N phénol m

car bomb N voiture piégée

carbon [ˈkɑːbən] N carbone m

carbonated [ˈkɑːbəneɪtɪd] ADJ (drink) gazeux(-euse)

carbon copy N carbone m

carbon credit N crédit m carbone

carbon dioxide [-daɪˈɔksaɪd] N gaz m carbonique, dioxyde m de carbone

carbon footprint N empreinte f carbone

carbon monoxide [-mɔˈnɔksaɪd] N oxyde m de carbone

carbon-neutral [kɑːbnˈnjuːtrəl] ADJ neutre en carbone

carbon offset N compensation f carbone; **~ credit** crédit m de compensation carbone

carbon paper N papier m carbone

carbon ribbon N ruban m carbone

car boot sale N (BRIT) vide-grenier m

carburettor, (US) **carburetor** [kɑːbjuˈretəʳ] N carburateur m

carcass [ˈkɑːkəs] N carcasse f

carcinogen [kɑːˈsɪnədʒən] N substance f cancérigène

carcinogenic [kɑːsɪnəˈdʒenɪk] ADJ cancérigène

★**card** [kɑːd] N carte f; (material) carton m; (membership card) carte d'adhérent; **to play cards** jouer aux cartes

cardamom ['kɑːdəməm] N cardamome f

★cardboard ['kɑːdbɔːd] N carton m

cardboard box N (boîte f en) carton m

cardboard city N endroit de la ville où dorment les SDF dans des boîtes en carton

card-carrying member ['kɑːdkærɪŋ-] N membre encarté

card game N jeu m de cartes

cardiac ['kɑːdɪæk] ADJ cardiaque

cardigan ['kɑːdɪgən] N cardigan m

cardinal ['kɑːdml] ADJ cardinal(e); (importance) capital(e) ▶ N cardinal m

card index N fichier m (alphabétique)

cardiologist [kɑːdɪˈɔlədʒɪst] N cardiologue mf

cardiology [kɑːdɪˈɔlədʒɪ] N cardiologie f

cardphone ['kɑːdfəun] N téléphone m à carte (magnétique)

cardsharp ['kɑːdʃɑːp] N tricheur(-euse) professionnel(le)

card vote N (BRIT) vote m de délégués

CARE [kɛəʳ] N ABBR (= Cooperative for American Relief Everywhere) association charitable

★care [kɛəʳ] N soin m, attention f; (worry) souci m; in sb's ~ à la garde de qn, confié à qn; ~ of (on letter) chez; "with ~" « fragile »; to take ~ (to do) faire attention (à faire); to take ~ of s'occuper de; the child has been taken into ~ l'enfant a été placé en institution ▶ VI: to ~ about (feel interest for) se soucier de, s'intéresser à; (person: love) être attaché(e) à; would you ~ to/for …? voulez-vous …?; I wouldn't ~ to do it je n'aimerais pas le faire; I don't ~ ça m'est bien égal, peu m'importe; I couldn't ~ less cela m'est complètement égal, je m'en fiche complètement
▶ care for VT FUS s'occuper de; (like) aimer

careen [kəˈriːn] VI (ship) donner de la bande ▶ VT caréner, mettre en carène

★career [kəˈrɪəʳ] N carrière f ▶ VI (also: career along) aller à toute allure

career girl N jeune fille f or femme f ambitieuse

careers officer N conseiller(-ère) d'orientation (professionnelle)

career woman N (irreg) femme f ambitieuse

carefree ['kɛəfriː] ADJ sans souci, insouciant(e)

★careful ['kɛəful] ADJ soigneux(-euse); (cautious) prudent(e); (be) ~! (fais) attention !; to be ~ with one's money regarder à la dépense

carefully ['kɛəfəlɪ] ADV avec soin, soigneusement; prudemment

caregiver ['kɛəgɪvəʳ] N (US: professional) travailleur social; (unpaid) personne qui s'occupe d'un proche qui est malade

careless ['kɛəlɪs] ADJ négligent(e); (heedless) insouciant(e)

carelessly ['kɛəlɪslɪ] ADV négligemment; avec insouciance

carelessness ['kɛəlɪsnɪs] N manque m de soin, négligence f; insouciance f

carer ['kɛərəʳ] N (professional) travailleur social; (unpaid) personne qui s'occupe d'un proche qui est malade

caress [kəˈres] N caresse f ▶ VT caresser

★caretaker ['kɛəteɪkəʳ] N gardien(ne), concierge mf

caretaker government N (BRIT) gouvernement m intérimaire

car-ferry ['kɑːferɪ] N (on sea) ferry(-boat) m; (on river) bac m

cargo ['kɑːgəu] (pl cargoes) N cargaison f, chargement m

cargo boat N cargo m

cargo plane N avion-cargo m

car hire N (BRIT) location f de voitures

Caribbean [kærɪˈbiːən] N (islands) les Antilles fpl, les Caraïbes fpl; (sea) la mer des Antilles or des Caraïbes ▶ ADJ antillais(e), des Caraïbes; the ~ Sea la mer des Antilles or des Caraïbes

caricature ['kærɪkətjuəʳ] N caricature f

caring ['kɛərɪŋ] ADJ (person) bienveillant(e); (society, organization) humanitaire

car maker N constructeur m automobile

carnage ['kɑːnɪdʒ] N carnage m

carnal ['kɑːnl] ADJ charnel(le)

carnation [kɑːˈneɪʃən] N œillet m

carnival ['kɑːnɪvl] N (public celebration) carnaval m; (US: funfair) fête foraine

carnivore ['kɑːnɪvɔːʳ] N (animal) carnivore m; (person) carnivore mf

carnivorous [kɑːˈnɪvərəs] ADJ carnivore, carnassier(-ière)

carol ['kærəl] N: (Christmas) ~ chant m de Noël

carouse [kəˈrauz] VI faire la bringue

carousel [kærəˈsɛl] N (for luggage) carrousel m; (US) manège m

carp [kɑːp] N (fish) carpe f
▶ carp at VT FUS critiquer

★car park (BRIT) N parking m, parc m de stationnement

carpenter ['kɑːpɪntəʳ] N charpentier m; (joiner) menuisier m

carpentry ['kɑːpɪntrɪ] N charpenterie f, métier m de charpentier; (woodwork: at school etc) menuiserie f

★carpet ['kɑːpɪt] N tapis m; fitted ~ (BRIT) moquette f ▶ VT recouvrir (d'un tapis)

carpet bombing N bombardement intensif

carpet slippers NPL pantoufles fpl

carpet sweeper N balai m mécanique

car phone N téléphone m de voiture

car pool N (arrangement) covoiturage m; (stock of cars) parc m de voitures de fonction ▶ VI (esp US, AUSTRALIA) pratiquer le covoiturage

carport ['kɑːpɔːt] N auvent m pour voitures

car rental N (US) location f de voitures

carriage ['kærɪdʒ] N (BRIT Rail) wagon m; (horse-drawn) voiture f; (of goods) transport m; (: cost) port m; (of typewriter) chariot m; (bearing) maintien m, port m; ~ forward port dû; ~ free franco de port; ~ paid (en) port payé

carriage return N retour m à la ligne

carriageway ['kærɪdʒweɪ] N (BRIT: part of road) chaussée f

carrier ['kærɪəʳ] N transporteur m, camionneur m; (company) entreprise f de transport; (Med) porteur(-euse); (Naut) porte-avions m inv

carrier bag N (BRIT) sac m en papier or en plastique

carrier pigeon N pigeon voyageur

carrion ['kærɪən] N charogne f

★**carrot** ['kærət] N carotte f

★**carry** ['kærɪ] VT (subj: person) porter; (: vehicle) transporter; (a motion, bill) voter, adopter; (Math: figure) retenir; (Comm: interest) rapporter; (involve: responsibilities etc) comporter, impliquer; (Med: disease) être porteur de; **to get carried away** (fig) s'emballer, s'enthousiasmer; **this loan carries 10% interest** ce prêt est à 10% (d'intérêt) ▶ VI (sound) porter
▶ **carry forward** VT (gen, Book-keeping) reporter
▶ **carry on** VI (continue) continuer; (inf: make a fuss) faire des histoires; **to ~ on with sth/doing** continuer qch/à faire ▶ VT (conduct: business) diriger; (: conversation) entretenir; (continue: business, conversation) continuer
▶ **carry out** VT (orders) exécuter; (investigation) effectuer; (idea, threat) mettre à exécution

carrycot ['kærɪkɔt] N (BRIT) porte-bébé m

carry-on ['kærɪ'ɔn] N (inf: fuss) histoires fpl; (: annoying behaviour) cirque m, cinéma m

cart [kɑːt] N charrette f ▶ VT (inf) transporter

carte blanche ['kɑːt'blɑ̃ʃ] N: **to give sb ~** donner carte blanche à qn

cartel [kɑː'tɛl] N (Comm) cartel m

cartilage ['kɑːtɪlɪdʒ] N cartilage m

cartographer [kɑː'tɔɡrəfər] N cartographe mf

cartography [kɑː'tɔɡrəfɪ] N cartographie f

carton ['kɑːtən] N (box) carton m; (of yogurt) pot m (en carton); (of cigarettes) cartouche f

★**cartoon** [kɑː'tuːn] N (Press) dessin m (humoristique); (satirical) caricature f; (comic strip) bande dessinée; (Cine) dessin animé

cartoonist [kɑː'tuːnɪst] N dessinateur(-trice) humoristique; caricaturiste mf; auteur de bandes dessinées; auteur m de dessins animés

cartridge ['kɑːtrɪdʒ] N (for gun, pen) cartouche f; (for camera) chargeur m; (music tape) cassette f; (of record player) cellule f

cartwheel ['kɑːtwiːl] N roue f; **to turn a ~** faire la roue

carve [kɑːv] VT (meat: also: **carve up**) découper; (wood, stone) tailler, sculpter

carving ['kɑːvɪŋ] N (in wood etc) sculpture f

carving knife N couteau m à découper

car wash N station f de lavage (de voitures)

Casablanca [kæsə'blæŋkə] N Casablanca f

cascade [kæs'keɪd] N cascade f ▶ VI tomber en cascade

★**case** [keɪs] N cas m; (Law) affaire f, procès m; (box) caisse f, boîte f; (for glasses) étui m; (BRIT: also: **suitcase**) valise f; (Typ): **lower/upper ~** minuscule f/ majuscule f; **to have a good ~** avoir de bons arguments; **there's a strong ~ for reform** il y aurait lieu d'engager une réforme; **in ~ of** en cas de; **in ~ he** au cas où il; **just in ~** à tout hasard; **in any ~** en tout cas, de toute façon

case history N (Med) dossier médical, antécédents médicaux

caseload ['keɪsləud] N (of doctor, social worker) nombre m de dossiers

case study N étude f de cas

caseworker ['keɪswəːkər] N assistant(e) social(e)

★**cash** [kæʃ] N argent m; (Comm) (argent) liquide m, numéraire m; liquidités fpl; (in payment) argent comptant, espèces fpl; **to pay (in) ~** payer (en argent) comptant or en espèces; **~ with order/on delivery** (Comm) payable or paiement à la commande/livraison; **to be short of ~** être à court d'argent; **I haven't got any ~** je n'ai pas de liquide ▶ VT encaisser
▶ **cash in** VT (insurance policy etc) toucher
▶ **cash in on** VT FUS profiter de

cash account N compte m caisse

cash and carry N libre-service m de gros, cash and carry m inv

cashback ['kæʃbæk] N (discount) remise f; (at supermarket etc) retrait m à la caisse

cashbook ['kæʃbuk] N livre m de caisse

cash box N caisse f

cash card N carte f de retrait

cash desk N (BRIT) caisse f

cash discount N escompte m de caisse (pour paiement au comptant), remise f au comptant

cash dispenser N distributeur m automatique de billets

cashew [kæ'ʃuː] N (also: **cashew nut**) noix f de cajou

cash flow N cash-flow m, marge brute d'autofinancement

cashier [kæ'ʃɪər] N caissier(-ère) ▶ VT (Mil) destituer, casser

cashless ['kæʃlɪs] ADJ sans cash

cashmere ['kæʃmɪər] N cachemire m

cash payment N paiement comptant, versement m en espèces

cash point N distributeur m automatique de billets

cash price N prix comptant

cash register N caisse enregistreuse

cash sale N vente f au comptant

casing ['keɪsɪŋ] N revêtement (protecteur), enveloppe (protectrice)

casino [kə'siːnəu] N casino m

cask [kɑːsk] N tonneau m

casket ['kɑːskɪt] N coffret m; (US: coffin) cercueil m

Caspian Sea ['kæspɪən-] N: **the ~** la mer Caspienne

cassava [kə'sɑːvə] N manioc m

casserole ['kæsərəul] N (pot) cocotte f; (food) ragoût m (en cocotte)

cassette [kæ'sɛt] N cassette f

cassette deck N platine f cassette

cassette player N lecteur m de cassettes

cassette recorder N magnétophone m à cassettes

cassock ['kæsək] N soutane f

cast [kɑːst] (vb: pt, pp **~**) VT (throw) jeter; (shadow: lit) projeter; (: fig) jeter; (glance) jeter; (shed) perdre; se dépouiller de; (metal) couler, fondre; **to ~ sb as Hamlet** attribuer à qn le rôle d'Hamlet; **to ~ one's vote** voter, exprimer son suffrage; **to ~ doubt on** jeter un doute sur ▶ N (Theat) distribution f; (mould) moule m; (also: **plaster cast**) plâtre m

539

▶ **cast aside** vt (*reject*) rejeter
▶ **cast off** vi (*Naut*) larguer les amarres; (*Knitting*) arrêter les mailles ▶ vt (*Knitting*) arrêter
▶ **cast on** (*Knitting*) vt monter ▶ vi monter les mailles

castanets [kæstə'nɛts] NPL castagnettes *fpl*

castaway ['kɑːstəweɪ] N naufragé(e)

caste [kɑːst] N caste *f*, classe sociale

caster sugar ['kɑːstə-] N (*BRIT*) sucre *m* semoule

castigate ['kæstɪgeɪt] vt (*formal*) fustiger

casting ['kɑːstɪŋ] N (*of actor*) casting *m*

casting vote N (*BRIT*) voix prépondérante (*pour départager*)

cast iron N fonte *f*

cast-iron ['kɑːstaɪən] ADJ (*lit*) de or en fonte; (*fig: will*) de fer; (: *alibi*) en béton

★**castle** ['kɑːsl] N château *m*; (*fortress*) château-fort *m*; (*Chess*) tour *f*

cast-offs ['kɑːstɔfs] NPL vêtements *mpl* dont on ne veut plus

castor ['kɑːstə-] N (*wheel*) roulette *f*

castor oil N huile *f* de ricin

castrate [kæs'treɪt] vt châtrer

casual ['kæʒjul] ADJ (*by chance*) de hasard, fait(e) au hasard, fortuit(e); (*irregular: work etc*) temporaire; (*unconcerned*) désinvolte; **~ wear** vêtements *mpl* sport *inv*

casual labour N main-d'œuvre *f* temporaire

casually ['kæʒjulɪ] ADV avec désinvolture, négligemment; (*by chance*) fortuitement

★**casualty** ['kæʒjultɪ] N accidenté(e), blessé(e); (*dead*) victime *f*, mort(e); (*BRIT Med: department*) urgences *fpl*; **heavy casualties** lourdes pertes

casualty ward N (*BRIT*) service *m* des urgences

★**cat** [kæt] N chat *m*

cataclysmic [kætə'klɪzmɪk] ADJ cataclysmique

catacombs ['kætəkuːmz] NPL catacombes *fpl*

Catalan ['kætələn] ADJ catalan(e) ▶ N Catalan(e)

catalogue, (*US*) **catalog** ['kætəlɔg] N catalogue *m* ▶ vt cataloguer

catalyst ['kætəlɪst] N catalyseur *m*

catalytic converter [kætə'lɪtɪkkən'vɜːtə-] N pot *m* catalytique

catamaran [kætəmə'ræn] N catamaran *m*

catapult ['kætəpʌlt] N lance-pierres *m inv*, fronde *f*; (*Hist*) catapulte *f*

cataract ['kætərækt] N (*also Med*) cataracte *f*

catarrh [kə'tɑː-] N rhume *m* chronique, catarrhe *f*

catastrophe [kə'tæstrəfɪ] N catastrophe *f*

catastrophic [kætə'strɔfɪk] ADJ catastrophique

catcall ['kætkɔːl] N (*at meeting etc*) sifflet *m*

★**catch** [kætʃ] (*pt*, *pp* **caught** [kɔːt]) vt (*ball, train, thief, cold*) attraper; (*person: by surprise*) prendre, surprendre; (*understand*) saisir; (*get entangled*) accrocher; **to ~ sb's attention** *or* **eye** attirer l'attention de qn; **to ~ fire** prendre feu; **to ~ sight of** apercevoir ▶ vi (*fire*) prendre; (*get entangled*) s'accrocher ▶ N (*fish etc*) prise *f*; (*thief etc*) capture *f*; (*hidden problem*) attrape *f*; (*Tech*) loquet *m*; cliquet *m*; **to play ~** jouer à chat; (*with ball*) jouer à attraper le ballon ▶ **catch on** vi (*become popular*) prendre; (*understand*): **to ~ on (to sth)** saisir (qch)

▶ **catch out** vt (*BRIT fig: with trick question*) prendre en défaut
▶ **catch up** vi (*with work*) se rattraper, combler son retard ▶ vt (*also: catch up with*) rattraper
▶ **catch up on** vt (*news*) se remettre au courant de; (*sleep*) rattraper son retard de

catch-22 ['kætʃtwɛntɪ'tuː] N: **it's a ~ situation** c'est (une situation) sans issue

catching ['kætʃɪŋ] ADJ (*Med*) contagieux(-euse)

catchment area ['kætʃmənt-] N (*BRIT Scol*) aire *f* de recrutement; (*Geo*) bassin *m* hydrographique

catch phrase N slogan *m*, expression toute faite

catchy ['kætʃɪ] ADJ (*tune*) facile à retenir

catechism ['kætɪkɪzəm] N catéchisme *m*

categoric [kætɪ'gɔrɪk], **categorical** [kætɪ'gɔrɪkl] ADJ catégorique

categorically [kætɪ'gɔrɪklɪ] ADV catégoriquement

categorize ['kætɪgəraɪz] vt classer par catégories

category ['kætɪgərɪ] N catégorie *f*

cater ['keɪtə-] vi: **to ~ for** (*BRIT: needs*) satisfaire, pourvoir à; (: *readers, consumers*) s'adresser à, pourvoir aux besoins de; (: *Comm: parties etc*) préparer des repas pour

caterer ['keɪtərə-] N traiteur *m*; fournisseur *m*

catering ['keɪtərɪŋ] N restauration *f*; approvisionnement *m*, ravitaillement *m*

caterpillar ['kætəpɪlə-] N chenille *f* ▶ CPD (*vehicle*) à chenille; **~ track** N chenille *f*

catfight ['kætfaɪt] N (*between women*) crêpage *m* de chignon

cat flap N chatière *f*

cathartic [kə'θɑːtɪk] ADJ cathartique

cathedral [kə'θiːdrəl] N cathédrale *f*

Catherine wheel ['kæθrɪn-] N soleil *m*

catheter ['kæθɪtə-] N cathéter *m*

cathode ['kæθəud] N cathode *f*

cathode ray tube N tube *m* cathodique

Catholic ['kæθəlɪk] (*Rel*) ADJ, N catholique *mf*

catholic ['kæθəlɪk] ADJ (*wide-ranging*) éclectique; universel(le); libéral(e)

Catholicism [kə'θɔlɪsɪzəm] N (*Rel*) catholicisme *m*

catnap ['kætnæp] N (*inf*) (petit) somme

catsup ['kætsəp] N (*US*) ketchup *m*

cattery ['kætərɪ] N (*BRIT*) pension *f* pour chats

cattle ['kætl] NPL bétail *m*, bestiaux *mpl*

catty ['kætɪ] ADJ méchant(e)

catwalk ['kætwɔːk] N passerelle *f*; (*for models*) podium *m* (*de défilé de mode*)

Caucasian [kɔː'keɪzɪən] ADJ, N caucasien(ne)

Caucasus ['kɔːkəsəs] N Caucase *m*

caucus ['kɔːkəs] N (*US Pol*) comité électoral (*pour désigner des candidats*); (*BRIT Pol: group*) comité local (*d'un parti politique*)

caught [kɔːt] PT, PP of **catch**

cauldron ['kɔːldrən] N chaudron *m*

★**cauliflower** ['kɔlɪflauə-] N chou-fleur *m*

causal ['kɔːzəl] ADJ causal(e)

★**cause** [kɔːz] N cause *f*; **there is no ~ for concern** il n'y a pas lieu de s'inquiéter ▶ vt causer; **to ~ sth to be done** faire faire qch; **to ~ sb to do sth** faire faire qch à qn

causeway ['kɔːzweɪ] N chaussée (surélevée)

caustic ['kɔːstɪk] ADJ caustique

caution ['kɔːʃən] N prudence f; (warning) avertissement m ▸ VT avertir, donner un avertissement à

cautious ['kɔːʃəs] ADJ prudent(e)

cautiously ['kɔːʃəslɪ] ADV prudemment, avec prudence

cautiousness ['kɔːʃəsnɪs] N prudence f

cavalcade [kævəl'keɪd] N cortège m

cavalier [kævə'lɪər] ADJ cavalier(-ère), désinvolte ▸ N (knight) cavalier m

cavalry ['kævəlrɪ] N cavalerie f

★**cave** [keɪv] N caverne f, grotte f ▸ VI: **to go caving** faire de la spéléo(logie)
▸ **cave in** VI (roof etc) s'effondrer

> Le mot anglais **cave** ne veut pas dire cave.

caveat ['kævɪæt] N mise f en garde

caveman ['keɪvmæn] N (irreg) homme m des cavernes

cavern ['kævən] N caverne f

cavernous ['kævənəs] ADJ immense

caviar, caviare ['kævɪɑːr] N caviar m

cavity ['kævɪtɪ] N cavité f; (Med) carie f

cavity wall insulation N isolation f des murs creux

cavort [kə'vɔːt] VI cabrioler, faire des cabrioles

cayenne [keɪ'ɛn] N (also: **cayenne pepper**) poivre m de cayenne

CBC N ABBR (= Canadian Broadcasting Corporation) organisme de radiodiffusion

CBE N ABBR (= Companion of (the Order of) the British Empire) titre honorifique

CBI N ABBR (= Confederation of British Industry) = MEDEF m (= Mouvement des entreprises de France)

CC ABBR (BRIT) = **county council**

cc ABBR (= cubic centimetre) cm³; (on letter etc: = carbon copy) cc

CCA N ABBR (US: = Circuit Court of Appeals) cour f d'appel itinérante

CCTV N ABBR = **closed-circuit television**

CCTV camera N caméra f de vidéosurveillance

CCU N ABBR (US: = coronary care unit) unité f de soins cardiologiques

★**CD** N ABBR (= compact disc) CD m; (Mil: BRIT) = **Civil Defence (Corps)**; (: US) = **Civil Defense** ▸ ABBR (BRIT: = Corps Diplomatique) CD

CD burner N graveur m de CD

CDC N ABBR (US) = **center for disease control**

★**CD player** N platine f laser

Cdr. ABBR (= commander) Cdt

★**CD-ROM** [siːdiːˈrɔm] N ABBR (= compact disc read-only memory) CD-ROM m inv

CDT ABBR (US: = Central Daylight Time) heure d'été du centre

CDW N ABBR = **collision damage waiver**

CD writer N graveur m de CD

CE ABBR = **Common Era**

cease [siːs] VT, VI cesser

★**ceasefire** ['siːsfaɪər] N cessez-le-feu m

ceaseless ['siːslɪs] ADJ incessant(e), continuel(le)

ceaselessly ['siːslɪslɪ] ADV (work, campaign) sans cesse; (complain) continuellement **CED** N ABBR (US) = **Committee for Economic Development**

cedar ['siːdər] N cèdre m

cede [siːd] VT céder

cedilla [sɪ'dɪlə] N cédille f

CEEB N ABBR (US: = College Entrance Examination Board) commission d'admission dans l'enseignement supérieur

ceilidh ['keɪlɪ] N bal m folklorique écossais or irlandais

★**ceiling** ['siːlɪŋ] N (also fig) plafond m

celeb [sɪ'lɛb] N (inf: celebrity) célébrité f

★**celebrate** ['sɛlɪbreɪt] VT, VI célébrer

celebrated ['sɛlɪbreɪtɪd] ADJ célèbre

celebration [sɛlɪ'breɪʃən] N célébration f

celebratory ['sɛləbreɪtərɪ] ADJ (meal) de fête; **let's have a ~ drink!** prenons un verre pour fêter ça !

celebrity [sɪ'lɛbrɪtɪ] N célébrité f

celeriac [sə'lɛrɪæk] N céleri(-rave) m

celery ['sɛlərɪ] N céleri m (en branches)

celestial [sɪ'lɛstɪəl] ADJ céleste

celiac ['siːlɪæk] ADJ (US) = **coeliac**

celibacy ['sɛlɪbəsɪ] N célibat m

celibate ['sɛlɪbət] ADJ (life, priest) célibataire; (lay person) chaste

★**cell** [sɛl] N (gen) cellule f; (Elec) élément m (de pile)

★**cellar** ['sɛlər] N cave f

cellist ['tʃɛlɪst] N violoncelliste mf

cellmate ['sɛlmeɪt] N compagnon (compagne) de cellule

cello ['tʃɛləʊ] N violoncelle m

Cellophane® ['sɛləfeɪn] N cellophane® f

cellphone ['sɛlfəʊn] N (téléphone m) portable m, mobile m

cell tower N (US Tel) antenne-relais f

cellular ['sɛljʊlər] ADJ cellulaire

cellular phone (esp US) N (téléphone m) portable m, mobile m

cellulite ['sɛljʊlaɪt] N cellulite f

cellulose ['sɛljʊləʊs] N cellulose f

Celsius ['sɛlsɪəs] ADJ Celsius inv

Celt [kɛlt, sɛlt] N Celte mf

Celtic ['kɛltɪk, 'sɛltɪk] ADJ celte, celtique ▸ N (Ling) celtique m

cement [sə'mɛnt] N ciment m ▸ VT cimenter

cement mixer N bétonnière f

cemetery ['sɛmɪtrɪ] N cimetière m

cenotaph ['sɛnətɑːf] N cénotaphe m

censor ['sɛnsər] N censeur m ▸ VT censurer

censorious [sɛn'sɔːrɪəs] ADJ (formal) sévère

censorship ['sɛnsəʃɪp] N censure f

censure ['sɛnʃər] VT blâmer, critiquer

census ['sɛnsəs] N recensement m

★**cent** [sɛnt] N (unit of dollar, euro) cent m (= un centième du dollar, de l'euro); see also **per cent**

centenarian [sɛntɪ'nɛərɪən] N centenaire mf

centenary [sɛn'tiːnərɪ], (US) **centennial** [sɛn'tɛnɪəl] N centenaire m

center etc ['sɛntə] N, VT (US) = **centre** etc

★**centigrade** ['sɛntɪgreɪd] ADJ centigrade

centilitre, (US) centiliter ['sɛntɪliːtəʳ] N centilitre m

centimetre, (US) centimeter ['sɛntɪmiːtəʳ] N centimètre m

centipede ['sɛntɪpiːd] N mille-pattes m inv

★central ['sɛntrəl] ADJ central(e)

Central African Republic N République Centrafricaine

Central America N Amérique centrale

★central heating N chauffage central

centralize ['sɛntrəlaɪz] VT centraliser

centrally ['sɛntrəlɪ] ADV (placed) au centre; (located) dans le centre

central processing unit N (Comput) unité centrale (de traitement)

central reservation N (BRIT Aut) terre-plein central

★centre, (US) center ['sɛntəʳ] N centre m ▶ VT centrer; (Phot) cadrer; (concentrate): to ~ (on) centrer (sur)

centrefold, (US) centerfold ['sɛntəfəuld] N (Press) pages centrales détachables (avec photo de pin up)

centre-forward ['sɛntəfɔːwəd] N (Sport) avant-centre m

centre-half ['sɛntəhɑːf] N (Sport) demi-centre m

centrepiece, (US) centerpiece ['sɛntəpiːs] N milieu m de table; (fig) pièce maîtresse

centre spread N (BRIT) publicité f en double page

centre-stage [sɛntəsteɪdʒ] N: to take ~ occuper le centre de la scène

centrifugal [sɛnˈtrɪfjugl] ADJ centrifuge

centrifuge ['sɛntrɪfjuːʒ] N centrifugeuse f

centrist ['sɛntrɪst] ADJ, N centriste mf

★century ['sɛntjurɪ] N siècle m; in the twentieth ~ au vingtième siècle

CEO N ABBR = chief executive officer

ceramic [sɪˈræmɪk] ADJ céramique

ceramics [sɪˈræmɪks] N céramique f

★cereal ['siːrɪəl] N céréale f

cerebral ['sɛrɪbrəl] ADJ cérébral(e)

ceremonial [sɛrɪˈməunɪəl] N cérémonial m; (rite) rituel m

★ceremony ['sɛrɪmənɪ] N cérémonie f; to stand on ~ faire des façons

cerise [səˈriːz, səˈriːs] ADJ (couleur) cerise inv ▶ N rouge m cerise

cert [səːt] N (BRIT inf): it's a dead ~ ça ne fait pas un pli

★certain ['səːtən] ADJ certain(e); to make ~ of s'assurer de; for ~ certainement, sûrement

★certainly ['səːtənlɪ] ADV certainement

certainty ['səːtəntɪ] N certitude f

★certificate [səˈtɪfɪkɪt] N certificat m

certified letter ['səːtɪfaɪd-] N (US) lettre recommandée

certified public accountant ['səːtɪfaɪd-] N (US) expert-comptable m

certify ['səːtɪfaɪ] VT certifier; (award diploma to) conférer un diplôme etc à; (declare insane) déclarer malade mental(e) ▶ VI: to ~ to attester

cervical ['səːvɪkl] ADJ: ~ cancer cancer m du col de l'utérus; ~ smear frottis vaginal

cervix ['səːvɪks] N col m de l'utérus

Cesarean [siːˈzɛərɪən] ADJ, N (US) = Caesarean

cessation [səˈseɪʃən] N cessation f, arrêt m

cesspit ['sɛspɪt] N fosse f d'aisance

CET ABBR (= Central European Time) heure d'Europe centrale

Ceylon [sɪˈlɔn] N Ceylan m

cf. ABBR (= compare) cf.

c/f ABBR (Comm) = carried forward

CFC N ABBR (= chlorofluorocarbon) CFC m

CG N ABBR (US) = coastguard

cg ABBR (= centigram) cg

CGI N ABBR (= computer-generated imagery) images fpl de synthèse

CH N ABBR (BRIT: = Companion of Honour) titre honorifique

ch ABBR (BRIT: = central heating) cc

ch. ABBR (= chapter) chap

Chad [tʃæd] N Tchad m

chafe [tʃeɪf] VT irriter, frotter contre ▶ VI (fig): to ~ against se rebiffer contre, regimber contre

chaffinch ['tʃæfɪntʃ] N pinson m

chagrin ['ʃægrɪn] N contrariété f, déception f

★chain [tʃeɪn] N (gen) chaîne f ▶ VT (also: chain up) enchaîner, attacher (avec une chaîne)

chain reaction N réaction f en chaîne

chain-smoke ['tʃeɪnsməuk] VI fumer cigarette sur cigarette

chain store N magasin m à succursales multiples

★chair [tʃɛəʳ] N chaise f; (armchair) fauteuil m; (of university) chaire f; (of meeting) présidence f; the ~ (US: electric chair) la chaise électrique ▶ VT (meeting) présider

chairlift ['tʃɛəlɪft] N télésiège m

★chairman ['tʃɛəmən] N (irreg) président m

chairmanship ['tʃɛəmənʃɪp] N présidence f

chairperson ['tʃɛəpəːsn] N président(e)

chairwoman ['tʃɛəwumən] N (irreg) présidente f

chalet ['ʃæleɪ] N chalet m

chalice ['tʃælɪs] N calice m

chalk [tʃɔːk] N craie f
▶ chalk up VT écrire à la craie; (fig: success etc) remporter

★challenge ['tʃælɪndʒ] N défi m ▶ VT défier; (statement, right) mettre en question, contester; to ~ sb to a fight/game inviter qn à se battre/à jouer (sous forme d'un défi); to ~ sb to do mettre qn au défi de faire

challenger ['tʃælɪndʒəʳ] N (Sport) challenger m

challenging ['tʃælɪndʒɪŋ] ADJ (task, career) qui représente un défi or une gageure; (tone, look) de défi, provocateur(-trice)

chamber ['tʃeɪmbəʳ] N chambre f; (BRIT Law: gen pl) cabinet m; ~ of commerce chambre de commerce

chambermaid ['tʃeɪmbəmeɪd] N femme f de chambre

chamber music N musique f de chambre

chamberpot ['tʃeɪmbəpɔt] N pot m de chambre

chameleon [kəˈmiːlɪən] N caméléon m

chamois [ˈʃæmwɑː] N chamois m

chamois leather [ˈʃæmɪ-] N peau f de chamois

champ [tʃæmp] N (inf: champion) champion(ne)

champagne [ʃæmˈpeɪn] N champagne m

champers [ˈʃæmpəz] N (inf) champ m

★**champion** [ˈtʃæmpɪən] N (also of cause) champion(ne) ▶ VT défendre

★**championship** [ˈtʃæmpɪənʃɪp] N championnat m

★**chance** [tʃɑːns] N (luck) hasard m; (opportunity) occasion f, possibilité f; (hope, likelihood) chance f; (risk) risque m; **there is little ~ of his coming** il est peu probable or il y a peu de chances qu'il vienne; **to take a ~** prendre un risque; **it's the ~ of a lifetime** c'est une occasion unique; **by ~** par hasard ▶ VT (risk) risquer; (happen): **to ~ to do** faire par hasard; **to ~ doing** se risquer à faire qch; **to ~ it** risquer le coup, essayer ▶ ADJ fortuit(e), de hasard

▶ **chance on, chance upon** VT FUS (person) tomber sur, rencontrer par hasard; (thing) trouver par hasard

chancel [ˈtʃɑːnsəl] N chœur m

chancellor [ˈtʃɑːnsələ] N chancelier m

Chancellor of the Exchequer [-ɪksˈtʃɛkə] (BRIT) N chancelier m de l'Échiquier

chandelier [ʃændəˈlɪə] N lustre m

★**change** [tʃeɪndʒ] VT (alter, replace: Comm: money) changer; (switch, substitute: hands, trains, clothes, one's name etc) changer de; (transform): **to ~ sb into** changer or transformer qn en; **where can I ~ some money?** où est-ce que je peux changer de l'argent?; **to ~ gear** (Aut) changer de vitesse; **to ~ one's mind** changer d'avis ▶ VI (gen) changer; (change clothes) se changer; (be transformed): **to ~ into** se changer or transformer en; **she changed into an old skirt** elle (s'est changée et) a enfilé une vieille jupe ▶ N changement m; (money) monnaie f; **a ~ of clothes** des vêtements de rechange; **for a ~** pour changer; **small ~** petite monnaie; **to give sb ~ for** or **of £10** faire à qn la monnaie de 10 livres; **do you have ~ for £10?** vous avez la monnaie de 10 livres?; **keep the ~!** gardez la monnaie!

▶ **change over** VI (swap) échanger; (change: drivers etc) changer; (change sides: players etc) changer de côté; **to ~ over from sth to sth** passer de qch à qch

> Use **changement** to refer to a change in something: *a change of plan* **un changement de programme**. The French word **change** is a financial term meaning *exchange*.

changeable [ˈtʃeɪndʒəbl] ADJ (weather) variable; (person) d'humeur changeante

change machine N distributeur m de monnaie

changeover [ˈtʃeɪndʒəʊvə] N (to new system) changement m, passage m

changing [ˈtʃeɪndʒɪŋ] ADJ changeant(e)

changing room N (BRIT: in shop) salon m d'essayage; (: Sport) vestiaire m

★**channel** [ˈtʃænl] N (TV) chaîne f; (waveband, groove, fig: medium) canal m; (of river, sea) chenal m; **through the usual channels** en suivant la filière habituelle; **green/red ~** (Customs) couloir m or sortie f «rien à déclarer»/»marchandises à déclarer»; **the (English) C~** la Manche ▶ VT canaliser; (fig: interest, energies): **to ~ into** diriger vers

channel-hopping [ˈtʃænlˈhɔpɪŋ] N (TV) zapping m

Channel Islands NPL: **the ~** les îles fpl Anglo-Normandes

channel-surf [ˈtʃænlsɜːf] VI (esp US) zapper

Channel Tunnel N: **the ~** le tunnel sous la Manche

chant [tʃɑːnt] N chant m; mélopée f; (Rel) psalmodie f ▶ VT chanter, scander; psalmodier

Chanukah [ˈhɑːnəkə] N = **Hanukkah**

★**chaos** [ˈkeɪɔs] N chaos m

chaos theory N théorie f du chaos

chaotic [keɪˈɔtɪk] ADJ chaotique

chap [tʃæp] N (BRIT inf: man) type m; (term of address): **old ~** mon vieux ▶ VT (skin) gercer, crevasser

chapel [ˈtʃæpl] N chapelle f

chaperone, chaperon [ˈʃæpərəun] N chaperon m ▶ VT chaperonner

chaplain [ˈtʃæplɪn] N aumônier m

chapped [tʃæpt] ADJ (skin, lips) gercé(e)

★**chapter** [ˈtʃæptə] N chapitre m

char [tʃɑː] VT (burn) carboniser ▶ VI (BRIT: cleaner) faire des ménages ▶ N (BRIT) = **charlady**

★**character** [ˈkærɪktə] N caractère m; (in novel, film) personnage m; (eccentric person) numéro m, phénomène m; **a person of good ~** une personne bien

character code N (Comput) code m de caractère

characteristic [ˈkærɪktəˈrɪstɪk] ADJ, N caractéristique (f)

characterize [ˈkærɪktəraɪz] VT caractériser; **to ~ (as)** définir (comme)

charade [ʃəˈrɑːd] N charade f

charcoal [ˈtʃɑːkəul] N charbon m de bois; (Art) charbon

★**charge** [tʃɑːdʒ] N (accusation) accusation f; (Law) inculpation f; (cost) prix (demandé); (of gun, battery, Mil: attack) charge f; **is there a ~?** doit-on payer?; **there's no ~** c'est gratuit, on ne fait pas payer; **extra ~** supplément m; **to be in ~ of** être responsable de, s'occuper de; **to take ~ of** se charger de; **to have ~ of** avoir la charge de qn ▶ VT (gun, battery, Mil: enemy) charger; (customer, sum) faire payer; (Law): **to ~ sb (with)** inculper qn (de); **how much do you ~ for this repair?** combien demandez-vous pour cette réparation?; **they charged us £10 for the meal** ils nous ont fait payer le repas 10 livres, ils nous ont compté 10 livres pour le repas; **to ~ an expense (up) to sb** mettre une dépense sur le compte de qn; **~ it to my account** facturez-le sur mon compte ▶ VI (gen with: up, along etc) foncer; **to ~ in/out** entrer/sortir en trombe; **to ~ down/up** dévaler/grimper à toute allure ▪ **charges** NPL (costs) frais mpl; **to reverse the charges** (BRIT Tel) téléphoner en PCV; **bank/labour charges** frais de banque/main-d'œuvre

▶ **charge up** VT (battery) charger, recharger

charge account N compte m client

charge card N carte f de client (émise par un grand magasin)

chargehand [ˈtʃɑːdʒhænd] N (BRIT) chef m

C

d'équipe

charger ['tʃɑːdʒəʳ] N (*also*: **battery charger**) chargeur *m*; (*old*: *warhorse*) cheval *m* de bataille

char-grilled [tʃɑːˈɡrɪld] ADJ (BRIT) grillé(e) au feu de bois

chariot ['tʃærɪət] N char *m*

charisma [kəˈrɪzmə] N charisme *m*

charismatic [kærɪzˈmætɪk] ADJ charismatique

charitable ['tʃærɪtəbl] ADJ charitable

★**charity** ['tʃærɪtɪ] N charité *f*; (*organization*) institution *f* charitable *or* de bienfaisance, œuvre *f* (de charité)

charity shop N (BRIT) boutique vendant des articles d'occasion au profit d'une organisation caritative

charlady ['tʃɑːleɪdɪ] N (BRIT) femme *f* de ménage

charlatan ['ʃɑːlətən] N charlatan *m*

charm [tʃɑːm] N charme *m*; (*on bracelet*) breloque *f* ▶ VT charmer, enchanter

charm bracelet N bracelet *m* à breloques

charming ['tʃɑːmɪŋ] ADJ charmant(e)

★**chart** [tʃɑːt] N tableau *m*, diagramme *m*; graphique *m*; (*map*) carte marine; (*weather chart*) carte *f* du temps ▶ VT dresser *or* établir la carte de; (*sales, progress*) établir la courbe de ■ **charts** NPL (*Mus*) hit-parade *m*; **to be in the charts** (*record, pop group*) figurer au hit-parade

charter ['tʃɑːtəʳ] VT (*plane*) affréter ▶ N (*document*) charte *f*; **on ~** (*plane*) affrété(e)

chartered accountant ['tʃɑːtəd-] N (BRIT) expert-comptable (experte-comptable)

charter flight N charter *m*

charwoman ['tʃɑːwumən] N (*irreg*) = **charlady**

★**chase** [tʃeɪs] VT poursuivre, pourchasser; (*also*: **chase away**) chasser ▶ N poursuite *f*, chasse *f*
▶ **chase down** VT (US) = **chase up**
▶ **chase up** VT (BRIT: *person*) relancer; (: *information*) rechercher

chasm ['kæzəm] N gouffre *m*, abîme *m*

chassis ['ʃæsɪ] N châssis *m*

chaste ['tʃeɪst] ADJ (*old*: *person, kiss*) chaste

chastened ['tʃeɪsnd] ADJ assagi(e), rappelé(e) à la raison

chastening ['tʃeɪsnɪŋ] ADJ qui fait réfléchir

chastise [tʃæsˈtaɪz] VT punir, châtier; corriger

chastity ['tʃæstɪtɪ] N chasteté *f*

★**chat** [tʃæt] VI (*also*: **have a chat**) bavarder, causer; (: *on Internet*) chatter ▶ N conversation *f*; (*on Internet*) chat *m*
▶ **chat up** VT (BRIT *inf*) baratiner

chatline ['tʃætlaɪn] N numéro téléphonique qui permet de bavarder avec plusieurs personnes en même temps

chat room N (*Internet*) salon *m* de discussion

chat show N (BRIT) talk-show *m*

chattel ['tʃætl] N *see* **good**

chatter ['tʃætəʳ] VI (*person*) bavarder, papoter; **my teeth are chattering** je claque des dents ▶ N bavardage *m*, papotage *m*

chatterbox ['tʃætəbɔks] N moulin *m* à paroles, babillard(e)

chattering classes ['tʃætərɪŋ-] NPL: **the ~** (*pej*) les intellos *mpl*

chatty ['tʃætɪ] ADJ (*style*) familier(-ière); (*person*) enclin(e) à bavarder *or* au papotage

chauffeur ['ʃəufəʳ] N chauffeur *m* (de maître)

chauvinism ['ʃəuvɪnɪzəm] N (*also*: **male chauvinism**) phallocratie *f*, machisme *m*; (*nationalism*) chauvinisme *m*

chauvinist ['ʃəuvɪnɪst] N (*also*: **male chauvinist**) phallocrate *m*, macho *m*; (*nationalist*) chauvin(e)

chauvinistic [ʃəuvɪˈnɪstɪk] ADJ (*sexist*) machiste; (*nationalistic*) chauvin(e)

chav [tʃæv] N (*pej*) ≈ caillera *m* (!)

ChE ABBR = **chemical engineer**

★**cheap** [tʃiːp] ADJ bon marché *inv*, pas cher (chère); (*reduced*: *ticket*) à prix réduit; (: *fare*) réduit(e); (*joke*) facile, d'un goût douteux; (*poor quality*) à bon marché, de qualité médiocre; **can you recommend a ~ hotel/restaurant, please?** pourriez-vous m'indiquer un hôtel/restaurant bon marché ?; **cheaper** *adj* moins cher (chère) ▶ ADV à bon marché, pour pas cher

cheap day return N (BRIT) billet *m* d'aller et retour réduit (*valable pour la journée*)

cheapen ['tʃiːpn] VT rabaisser, déprécier

cheaply ['tʃiːplɪ] ADV à bon marché, à bon compte

cheapskate ['tʃiːpskeɪt] ADJ, N (*inf*) radin(e)

cheat [tʃiːt] VI tricher; (*in exam*) copier ▶ VT tromper, duper; (*rob*): **to ~ sb out of sth** escroquer qch à qn ▶ N tricheur(-euse); escroc *m*; (*trick*) duperie *f*, tromperie *f*
▶ **cheat on** VT FUS tromper

cheating ['tʃiːtɪŋ] N tricherie *f*

cheat sheet N (US: *in exam*) antisèche *f*

Chechen ['tʃetʃen] ADJ tchétchène ▶ N (*person*) Tchétchène *mf*; (*language*) tchétchène *m*

Chechnya [tʃɪtʃˈnjɑː] N Tchétchénie *f*

★**check** [tʃek] VT vérifier; (*passport, ticket*) contrôler; (*halt*) enrayer; (*restrain*) maîtriser ▶ VI (*official etc*) se renseigner; **to ~ with sb** demander à qn ▶ N vérification *f*; contrôle *m*; (*curb*) frein *m*; (BRIT: *bill*) addition *f*; (US) = **cheque**; (*pattern*: *gen pl*) carreaux *mpl*; **to keep a ~ on sb/sth** surveiller qn/qch ▶ ADJ (*also*: **checked**: *pattern, cloth*) à carreaux
▶ **check in** VI (*in hotel*) remplir sa fiche (d'hôtel); (*at airport*) se présenter à l'enregistrement ▶ VT (*luggage*) (faire) enregistrer
▶ **check off** VT (*tick off*) cocher
▶ **check out** VI (*in hotel*) régler sa note ▶ VT (*luggage*) retirer; (*investigate*: *story*) vérifier; (: *person*) prendre des renseignements sur
▶ **check up** VI: **to ~ up (on sth)** vérifier (qch); **to ~ up on sb** se renseigner sur le compte de qn

checkbook ['tʃekbuk] N (US) = **chequebook**

checked ['tʃekt] ADJ (*pattern, cloth*) à carreaux

checkered ['tʃekəd] ADJ (US) = **chequered**

checkers ['tʃekəz] N (US) jeu *m* de dames

check guarantee card N (US) carte *f* d'identité bancaire

check-in ['tʃekɪn] N (*at airport*: *also*: **check-in desk**) enregistrement *m*

checking account ['tʃekɪŋ-] N (US) compte courant

checklist ['tʃeklɪst] N liste *f* de contrôle

checkmate ['tʃekmeɪt] N échec et mat *m*

checkout ['tʃekaut] N (*in supermarket*) caisse *f*

checkpoint ['tʃɛkpɔɪnt] N contrôle m

checkroom ['tʃɛkruːm] (US) N consigne f

checkup ['tʃɛkʌp] N (Med) examen médical, check-up m

cheddar ['tʃɛdəʳ] N (also: **cheddar cheese**) cheddar m

cheek [tʃiːk] N joue f; (impudence) toupet m, culot m; **what a ~!** quel toupet!

cheekbone ['tʃiːkbəʊn] N pommette f

★**cheeky** ['tʃiːkɪ] ADJ effronté(e), culotté(e)

cheep [tʃiːp] N (of bird) piaulement m ▶ VI piauler

★**cheer** [tʃɪəʳ] VT acclamer, applaudir; (gladden) réjouir, réconforter ▶ VI applaudir ▶ N (gen pl) acclamations fpl, applaudissements mpl; bravos mpl, hourras mpl; **cheers!** à la vôtre!
 ▶ **cheer on** VT encourager (par des cris etc)
 ▶ **cheer up** VI se dérider, reprendre courage ▶ VT remonter le moral à or de, dérider, égayer

★**cheerful** ['tʃɪəful] ADJ gai(e), joyeux(-euse)

cheerfully ['tʃɪəfulɪ] ADV (say, greet) gaiement; (blithely: ignore, admit) allégrement; (without hesitation) sans la moindre hésitation

cheerfulness ['tʃɪəfulnɪs] N gaieté f, bonne humeur

cheerio [tʃɪərɪ'əʊ] EXCL (BRIT) salut!, au revoir!

cheerleader ['tʃɪəliːdəʳ] N membre d'un groupe de majorettes qui chantent et dansent pour soutenir leur équipe pendant les matchs de football américain

cheerless ['tʃɪəlɪs] ADJ sombre, triste

cheery ['tʃɪərɪ] ADJ (wave, smile) gai(e); (person) joyeux(-euse)

★**cheese** [tʃiːz] N fromage m

cheeseboard ['tʃiːzbɔːd] N plateau m à fromages; (with cheese on it) plateau m de fromages

cheeseburger ['tʃiːzbɜːgəʳ] N cheeseburger m

cheesecake ['tʃiːzkeɪk] N cheesecake m

cheesy ['tʃiːzɪ] ADJ (biscuit, sauce) au fromage; (inf: tasteless) ringard(e)

cheetah ['tʃiːtə] N guépard m

★**chef** [ʃɛf] N chef (cuisinier)

★**chemical** ['kɛmɪkl] ADJ chimique ▶ N produit m chimique

★**chemist** ['kɛmɪst] N (BRIT: pharmacist) pharmacien(ne); (scientist) chimiste mf

★**chemistry** ['kɛmɪstrɪ] N chimie f

chemist's ['kɛmɪsts], **chemist's shop** N (BRIT) pharmacie f

chemo ['kiːməʊ] N (chemotherapy) chimio f

chemotherapy [kiːməʊ'θerəpɪ] N chimiothérapie f

cheque, (US) **check** [tʃɛk] N chèque m; **to pay by ~** payer par chèque

chequebook, (US) **checkbook** ['tʃɛkbuk] N chéquier m, carnet m de chèques

cheque card N (BRIT) carte f (d'identité) bancaire

chequered, (US) **checkered** ['tʃɛkəd] ADJ (fig) varié(e)

cherish ['tʃɛrɪʃ] VT (person, memory) chérir; (hope) caresser; (right, value) entretenir

cherished ['tʃɛrɪʃt] ADJ (dream, belief, memory) cher (chère); (possession) précieux(-euse)

cheroot [ʃə'ruːt] N cigare m de Manille

★**cherry** ['tʃɛrɪ] N cerise f; (also: **cherry tree**) cerisier m

cherub ['tʃɛrəb] N chérubin m

chess [tʃɛs] N échecs mpl

chessboard ['tʃɛsbɔːd] N échiquier m

chessman ['tʃɛsmən] N (irreg) pièce f (de jeu d'échecs)

chessplayer ['tʃɛspleɪəʳ] N joueur(-euse) d'échecs

★**chest** [tʃɛst] N poitrine f; (box) coffre m, caisse f; **to get sth off one's ~** (inf) vider son sac

chest measurement N tour m de poitrine

chestnut ['tʃɛsnʌt] N châtaigne f; (also: **chestnut tree**) châtaignier m; (colour) châtain m ▶ ADJ (hair) châtain inv; (horse) alezan

chest of drawers N commode f

chesty ['tʃɛstɪ] ADJ (cough) de poitrine

chevron ['ʃɛvrən] N (on sign) flèche f; (stripe: of officer) chevron m

chew [tʃuː] VT mâcher

chewing gum ['tʃuːɪŋ-] N chewing-gum m

chewy ['tʃuːɪ] ADJ (meat, bread) difficile à mâcher

chic [ʃiːk] ADJ chic inv, élégant(e)

chicanery [ʃɪ'keɪnərɪ] N (formal: political, financial) chicane f

chick [tʃɪk] N poussin m; (inf) fille f

★**chicken** ['tʃɪkɪn] N poulet m; (inf: coward) poule mouillée
 ▶ **chicken out** VI (inf) se dégonfler

chicken feed N (fig) broutilles fpl, bagatelle f

chickenpox ['tʃɪkɪnpɔks] N varicelle f

chickpea ['tʃɪkpiː] N pois m chiche

chicory ['tʃɪkərɪ] N chicorée f; (salad) endive f

chide [tʃaɪd] VT réprimander, gronder

★**chief** [tʃiːf] N chef m; **C~ of Staff** (Mil) chef d'État-major ▶ ADJ principal(e)

chief constable N (BRIT) ≈ préfet m de police

chief executive, (US) **chief executive officer** N directeur(-trice) général(e)

chiefly ['tʃiːflɪ] ADV principalement, surtout

chiffon ['ʃɪfɔn] N mousseline f de soie

chihuahua [tʃɪ'wɑːwə] N chihuahua m

chilblain ['tʃɪlbleɪn] N engelure f

★**child** [tʃaɪld] (pl **children** ['tʃɪldrən]) N enfant mf

child abuse N maltraitance f d'enfants; (sexual) abus mpl sexuels sur des enfants

childbearing ['tʃaɪldbɛərɪŋ] ADJ: **of ~ age** en âge d'avoir des enfants

child benefit N (BRIT) ≈ allocations familiales

childbirth ['tʃaɪldbɜːθ] N accouchement m

childcare ['tʃaɪldkɛəʳ] N garde f des enfants (pour les parents qui travaillent)

childhood ['tʃaɪldhud] N enfance f

childish ['tʃaɪldɪʃ] ADJ puéril(e), enfantin(e)

childishly ['tʃaɪldɪʃlɪ] ADV (pej: behave) d'une manière puérile; (excited, pleased) comme un enfant

child labour, (US) **child labor** N (practice) travail m des enfants; (workers) main-d'œuvre enfantine

childless ['tʃaɪldlɪs] ADJ sans enfants

childlike ['tʃaɪldlaɪk] ADJ innocent(e), pur(e)

child minder N (BRIT) garde f d'enfants

C

child prodigy N enfant mf prodige

★**children** [ˈtʃɪldrən] NPL of **child**

children's home [ˈtʃɪldrənz-] N ≈ foyer m d'accueil (pour enfants)

Chile [ˈtʃɪlɪ] N Chili m

Chilean [ˈtʃɪlɪən] ADJ chilien(ne) ▶ N Chilien(ne)

chili, chilli [ˈtʃɪlɪ] N piment m (rouge)

chill [tʃɪl] N (of water) froid m; (of air) fraîcheur f; (Med) refroidissement m, coup m de froid ▶ ADJ froid(e), glacial(e) ▶ VT (person) faire frissonner; refroidir; (Culin) mettre au frais, rafraîchir; **"serve chilled"** « à servir frais »
▶ **chill out** VI (inf: esp US) se relaxer

chilling [ˈtʃɪlɪŋ] ADJ (wind) frais (fraîche), froid(e); (look, smile) glacé(e); (thought) qui donne le frisson

chillingly [ˈtʃɪlɪŋlɪ] ADV (similiar, familiar) qui fait froid dans le dos

chilly [ˈtʃɪlɪ] ADJ froid(e), glacé(e); (sensitive to cold) frileux(-euse); **to feel ~** avoir froid

chime [tʃaɪm] N carillon m ▶ VI carillonner, sonner

chimera [kaɪˈmɪərə] N chimère f

chimney [ˈtʃɪmnɪ] N cheminée f

chimney sweep N ramoneur m

chimp [tʃɪmp] N (inf: chimpanzee) chimpanzé m

chimpanzee [tʃɪmpænˈziː] N chimpanzé m

chin [tʃɪn] N menton m

★**China** [ˈtʃaɪnə] N Chine f

china [ˈtʃaɪnə] N (material) porcelaine f; (crockery) (vaiselle f en) porcelaine

Chinese [tʃaɪˈniːz] ADJ chinois(e) ▶ N (pl inv) Chinois(e); (Ling) chinois m

chink [tʃɪŋk] N (opening) fente f, fissure f; (noise) tintement m

chintz [tʃɪnts] N chintz m; **~ curtains** rideaux mpl de chintz

chinwag [ˈtʃɪnwæg] N (Brit inf): **to have a ~** tailler une bavette

★**chip** [tʃɪp] N (gen pl: Culin: Brit) frite f; (: US: also: **potato chip**) chip f; (of wood) copeau m; (of glass, stone) éclat m; (also: **microchip**) puce f; (in gambling) fiche f; **when the chips are down** (fig) au moment critique ▶ VT (cup, plate) ébrécher
▶ **chip in** VI (inf) mettre son grain de sel

chip and PIN N carte f à puce; **~ machine** machine f à carte (à puce)

chipboard [ˈtʃɪpbɔːd] N aggloméré m, panneau m de particules

chipmunk [ˈtʃɪpmʌŋk] N suisse m (animal)

chippings [ˈtʃɪpɪŋz] NPL: **loose ~** gravillons mpl

chippy, chippie [ˈtʃɪpɪ] N (Brit inf) friterie f

chip shop N (Brit) friterie f

Un **chip shop**, que l'on appelle également un fish-and-chip shop, est un magasin où l'on vend des plats à emporter. Les chip shops sont d'ailleurs à l'origine des takeaways. On y achète en particulier du poisson frit et des frites, mais on y trouve également des plats traditionnels britanniques (steak pies, saucisses, etc). Tous les plats étaient à l'origine emballés dans du papier journal. Dans certains de ces magasins, on peut s'asseoir pour consommer sur place.

---

chiropodist [kɪˈrɔpədɪst] N (Brit) pédicure mf

chiropractor [ˈkaɪərəpræktər] N chiropracteur(-trice)

chirp [tʃəːp] N pépiement m, gazouillis m; (of crickets) stridulation f ▶ VI pépier, gazouiller; chanter, striduler

chirpy [ˈtʃəːpɪ] ADJ (inf) plein(e) d'entrain, tout guilleret(te)

chisel [ˈtʃɪzl] N ciseau m

chit [tʃɪt] N mot m, note f

chitchat [ˈtʃɪttʃæt] N bavardage m, papotage m

chivalrous [ˈʃɪvələrəs] ADJ chevaleresque

chivalry [ˈʃɪvəlrɪ] N chevalerie f; esprit m chevaleresque

chives [tʃaɪvz] NPL ciboulette f, civette f

chloride [ˈklɔːraɪd] N chlorure m

chlorinate [ˈklɔrɪneɪt] VT chlorer

chlorine [ˈklɔːriːn] N chlore m

chloroform [ˈklɔrəfɔːm] N chloroforme m

chlorophyll [ˈklɔrəfɪl] N chlorophylle f

choc-ice [ˈtʃɔkaɪs] N (Brit) esquimau® m

chock [tʃɔk] N cale f

chock-a-block [ˈtʃɔkəˈblɔk], **chock-full** [tʃɔkˈful] ADJ plein(e) à craquer

★**chocolate** [ˈtʃɔklɪt] N chocolat m

★**choice** [tʃɔɪs] N choix m; **by** or **from ~** par choix; **a wide ~** un grand choix ▶ ADJ de choix

choir [ˈkwaɪər] N chœur m, chorale f

choirboy [ˈkwaɪəbɔɪ] N jeune choriste m, petit chanteur

choke [tʃəuk] VI étouffer ▶ VT étrangler; étouffer; (block) boucher, obstruer ▶ N (Aut) starter m

cholera [ˈkɔlərə] N choléra m

cholesterol [kəˈlɛstərɔl] N cholestérol m

chook [tʃuk] N (Australia, New Zealand inf) poule f

★**choose** [tʃuːz] (pt **chose** [tʃəuz], pp **chosen** [ˈtʃəuzn]) VT choisir; **to ~ to do** décider de faire, juger bon de faire ▶ VI: **to ~ between** choisir entre; **to ~ from** choisir parmi

choosy [ˈtʃuːzɪ] ADJ: **(to be) ~** (faire le) difficile

chop [tʃɔp] VT (wood) couper (à la hache); (Culin: also: **chop up**) couper (fin), émincer, hacher (en morceaux) ▶ N coup m (de hache, du tranchant de la main); (Culin) côtelette f; **to get the ~** (Brit inf: project) tomber à l'eau; (: person: be sacked) se faire renvoyer
▶ **chop down** VT (tree) abattre
▶ **chop off** VT trancher

chopper [ˈtʃɔpə] N (helicopter) hélicoptère m, hélico m

choppy [ˈtʃɔpɪ] ADJ (sea) un peu agité(e)

chops [tʃɔps] NPL (jaws) mâchoires fpl; babines fpl

chopsticks [ˈtʃɔpstɪks] NPL baguettes fpl

choral [ˈkɔːrəl] ADJ choral(e), chanté(e) en chœur

chord [kɔːd] N (Mus) accord m

chore [tʃɔːʳ] N travail m de routine; **household chores** taches fpl ménagères

choreograph [ˈkɔrɪəgrɑːf] VT, VI chorégraphier

choreographer [kɔrɪˈɔgrəfəʳ] N chorégraphe mf

choreography [kɔrɪˈɔgrəfɪ] N chorégraphie f

chorister [ˈkɔrɪstəʳ] N choriste mf

chortle ['tʃɔ:tl] VI glousser

chorus ['kɔ:rəs] N chœur m; (repeated part of song, also fig) refrain m

chose [tʃəuz] PT of **choose**

chosen ['tʃəuzn] PP of **choose**

chow [tʃau] N (dog) chow-chow m

chowder ['tʃaudəʳ] N soupe f de poisson

Christ [kraɪst] N Christ m

christen ['krɪsn] VT baptiser

christening ['krɪsnɪŋ] N baptême m

Christian ['krɪstɪən] ADJ, N chrétien(ne)

Christianity [krɪstɪ'ænɪtɪ] N christianisme m

Christian name N prénom m

★**Christmas** ['krɪsməs] N Noël mf; **happy** or **merry ~!** joyeux Noël!

Christmas card N carte f de Noël

Christmas carol N chant m de Noël

Christmas Day N le jour de Noël

Christmas Eve N la veille de Noël; la nuit de Noël

Christmas Island N île f Christmas

Christmas pudding N Christmas pudding m

Christmas tree N arbre m de Noël

chrome [krəum] N chrome m

chromium ['krəumɪəm] N chrome m; (also: **chromium plating**) chromage m

chromosome ['krəuməsəum] N chromosome m

chronic ['krɒnɪk] ADJ chronique; (fig: liar, smoker) invétéré(e)

chronicle ['krɒnɪkl] N chronique f

chronological [krɒnə'lɒdʒɪkl] ADJ chronologique

chronologically [krɒnə'lɒdʒɪklɪ] ADV chronologiquement, par ordre chronologique

chronology [krə'nɒlədʒɪ] N chronologie f

chronometer [krə'nɒmɪtəʳ] N chronomètre m

chrysanthemum [krɪ'sænθəməm] N chrysanthème m

chubby ['tʃʌbɪ] ADJ potelé(e), rondelet(te)

chuck [tʃʌk] VT (inf) lancer, jeter; (job) lâcher; (person) plaquer
▶ **chuck out** VT (inf: person) flanquer dehors or à la porte; (: rubbish etc) jeter

chuckle ['tʃʌkl] VI glousser

chuffed [tʃʌft] ADJ (BRIT inf): **to be ~ about sth** être content(e) de qch

chug [tʃʌg] VI faire teuf-teuf; souffler

chugger ['tʃʌgəʳ] N (inf) personne travaillant pour une association caritative, qui aborde les gens dans la rue pour leur demander de faire un don régulier

chum [tʃʌm] N (inf) copain (copine)

chump ['tʃʌmp] N (inf) imbécile mf, crétin(e)

chunk [tʃʌŋk] N gros morceau; (of bread) quignon m

chunky ['tʃʌŋkɪ] ADJ (furniture etc) massif(-ive); (person) trapu(e); (knitwear) en grosse laine

Chunnel ['tʃʌnəl] N = **Channel Tunnel**

★**church** [tʃəːtʃ] N église f; **the C~ of England** l'Église anglicane

churchgoer ['tʃəːtʃɡəuəʳ] N pratiquant(e)

churchyard ['tʃəːtʃjɑːd] N cimetière m

churlish ['tʃəːlɪʃ] ADJ grossier(-ère); hargneux(-euse)

churn [tʃəːn] N (for butter) baratte f; (also: **milk churn**) (grand) bidon à lait
▶ **churn out** VT débiter

chute [ʃuːt] N goulotte f; (also: **rubbish chute**) vide-ordures m inv; (BRIT: children's slide) toboggan m

chutney ['tʃʌtnɪ] N chutney m

CIA N ABBR (= Central Intelligence Agency) CIA f

CID N ABBR (= Criminal Investigation Department) ≈ P.J. f

cider ['saɪdəʳ] N cidre m

CIF ABBR (= cost, insurance and freight) CAF

cigar [sɪ'ɡɑːʳ] N cigare m

★**cigarette** [sɪɡə'ret] N cigarette f

cigarette case N étui m à cigarettes

cigarette end N mégot m

cigarette holder N fume-cigarettes m inv

cigarette lighter N briquet m

C-in-C ABBR = **commander-in-chief**

cinch [sɪntʃ] N (inf): **it's a ~** c'est du gâteau, c'est l'enfance de l'art

Cinderella [sɪndə'relə] N Cendrillon

cine-camera ['sɪnɪ'kæmərə] N (BRIT) caméra f

cine-film ['sɪnɪfɪlm] N (BRIT) film m

★**cinema** ['sɪnəmə] N cinéma m

cinematic [sɪnə'mætɪk] ADJ cinématographique

cine-projector ['sɪnɪprə'dʒektəʳ] N (BRIT) projecteur m de cinéma

cinnamon ['sɪnəmən] N cannelle f

cipher ['saɪfəʳ] N code secret; (fig: faceless employee etc) numéro m; **in ~** codé(e)

circa ['səːkə] PREP circa, environ

★**circle** ['səːkl] N cercle m; (in cinema) balcon m ▶ VI faire or décrire des cercles ▶ VT (surround) entourer, encercler; (move round) faire le tour de, tourner autour de

circuit ['səːkɪt] N circuit m; (lap) tour m

circuit board N plaquette f

circuitous [səː'kjuɪtəs] ADJ indirect(e), qui fait un détour

circular ['səːkjuləʳ] ADJ circulaire ▶ N circulaire f; (as advertisement) prospectus m

circulate ['səːkjuleɪt] VI circuler ▶ VT faire circuler

circulation [səːkju'leɪʃən] N circulation f; (of newspaper) tirage m

circulatory [səːkju'leɪtərɪ] ADJ circulatoire

circumcise ['səːkəmsaɪz] VT (male) circoncire; (female) exciser

circumcision [səːkəm'sɪʒən] N (of male) circoncision f; (of female) excision f

circumference [sə'kʌmfərəns] N circonférence f

circumflex ['səːkəmfleks] N (also: **circumflex accent**) accent m circonflexe

circumnavigate [səːkəm'nævɪɡeɪt] VT (island) contourner; **to ~ the world** faire le tour du monde en bateau

circumscribe ['səːkəmskraɪb] VT circonscrire

circumspect ['səːkəmspekt] ADJ circonspect(e)

circumstances ['səːkəmstənsɪz] NPL circonstances fpl; (financial condition) moyens mpl, situation financière; **in** or **under the ~** dans ces conditions; **under no ~** en aucun cas, sous aucun prétexte

circumstantial [sə:kəm'stænʃl] ADJ (report, statement) circonstancié(e); **~ evidence** preuve indirecte

circumvent [sə:kəm'vɛnt] VT (rule etc) tourner

circus ['sə:kəs] N cirque m; (also: **Circus**: in place names) place f

cirrhosis [sɪ'rəʊsɪs] N (also: **cirrhosis of the liver**) cirrhose f (du foie)

CIS N ABBR (= Commonwealth of Independent States) CEI f

cissy ['sɪsɪ] N = **sissy**

cistern ['sɪstən] N réservoir m (d'eau); (in toilet) réservoir de la chasse d'eau

citadel ['sɪtədəl, 'sɪtədɛl] N citadelle f

citation [saɪ'teɪʃən] N citation f; (US) P.-V. m

cite [saɪt] VT citer

★**citizen** ['sɪtɪzn] N (Pol) citoyen(ne); (resident): **the citizens of this town** les habitants de cette ville

Citizens' Advice Bureau ['sɪtɪznz-] N (BRIT) ≈ Centre communal d'action sociale

citizenship ['sɪtɪznʃɪp] N citoyenneté f; (BRIT Scol) ≈ éducation f civique

citric ['sɪtrɪk] ADJ: **~ acid** acide m citrique

citrus fruits ['sɪtrəs-] NPL agrumes mpl

★**city** ['sɪtɪ] N (grande) ville f; **the C~** la Cité de Londres (centre des affaires)

city centre N centre-ville m

City Hall N (US) ≈ hôtel m de ville

city technology college N (BRIT) établissement m d'enseignement technologique (situé dans un quartier défavorisé)

civic ['sɪvɪk] ADJ civique; (authorities) municipal(e)

civic centre N (BRIT) centre administratif (municipal)

civil ['sɪvɪl] ADJ civil(e); (polite) poli(e), civil(e)

civil engineer N ingénieur civil

civil engineering N génie civil, travaux publics

civilian [sɪ'vɪlɪən] ADJ, N civil(e)

civility [sɪ'vɪlɪtɪ] N courtoisie f

civilization [sɪvɪlaɪ'zeɪʃən] N civilisation f

civilized ['sɪvɪlaɪzd] ADJ civilisé(e); (fig) où règnent les bonnes manières, empreint(e) d'une courtoisie de bon ton

civil law N code civil; (study) droit civil

civil liberties NPL libertés fpl civiques

civil partnership N ≈ PACS m

civil rights NPL droits mpl civiques

civil servant N fonctionnaire mf

Civil Service N fonction publique, administration f

civil war N guerre civile

civvies ['sɪvɪz] NPL (inf): **in ~** en civil

CJD N ABBR (= Creutzfeldt-Jakob disease) MCJ f

cl ABBR (= centilitre) cl

clad [klæd] ADJ: **~ in** habillé(e) de, vêtu(e) de

cladding ['klædɪŋ] N (of building) revêtement m

★**claim** [kleɪm] VT (rights etc) revendiquer; (compensation) réclamer; (assert) déclarer, prétendre ▶ VI (for insurance) faire une déclaration de sinistre ▶ N revendication f; prétention f; (right) droit m; (for expenses) note f de frais; **(insurance) ~** demande f d'indemnisation, déclaration f de sinistre; **to put in a ~ for** (pay rise etc) demander

claimant ['kleɪmənt] N (Admin, Law) requérant(e)

claim form N (gen) formulaire m de demande

clairvoyant [klɛə'vɔɪənt] N voyant(e), extralucide mf

clam [klæm] N palourde f
▶ **clam up** VI (inf) la boucler

clamber ['klæmbər] VI grimper, se hisser

clammy ['klæmɪ] ADJ humide et froid(e) (au toucher), moite

clamour, (US) **clamor** ['klæmər] N (noise) clameurs fpl; (protest) protestations bruyantes ▶ VI: **to ~ for sth** réclamer qch à grands cris

clamp [klæmp] N crampon m; (on workbench) valet m; (on car) sabot m de Denver ▶ VT attacher; (car) mettre un sabot à
▶ **clamp down on** VT FUS sévir contre, prendre des mesures draconiennes à l'égard de

clampdown ['klæmpdaʊn] N: **there has been a ~ on ...** des mesures énergiques ont été prises contre ...

clan [klæn] N clan m

clandestine [klæn'dɛstɪn] ADJ clandestin(e)

clang [klæŋ] N bruit m or fracas m métallique ▶ VI émettre un bruit or fracas métallique

clanger ['klæŋər] N (BRIT inf): **to drop a ~** faire une boulette

clank [klæŋk] VI cliqueter ▶ N cliquetis m

clansman ['klænzmən] N (irreg) membre m d'un clan (écossais)

clap [klæp] VI applaudir ▶ VT: **to ~ one's hands** battre des mains ▶ N claquement m; tape f; **a ~ of thunder** un coup de tonnerre

clapboard ['klæpbɔ:d] N (wooden) planche f à clin ▶ CPD (building, wall) à clins

clapping ['klæpɪŋ] N applaudissements mpl

claptrap ['klæptræp] N (inf) baratin m

claret ['klærət] N (vin m de) bordeaux m (rouge)

clarification [klærɪfɪ'keɪʃən] N (fig) clarification f, éclaircissement m

clarify ['klærɪfaɪ] VT clarifier

clarinet [klærɪ'nɛt] N clarinette f

clarity ['klærɪtɪ] N clarté f

clash [klæʃ] N (sound) choc m, fracas m; (with police) affrontement m; (fig) conflit m ▶ VI se heurter; être or entrer en conflit; (inf) clasher; (colours) jurer; (dates, events) tomber en même temps

clasp [klɑ:sp] N (of necklace, bag) fermoir m ▶ VT serrer, étreindre

★**class** [klɑ:s] N (gen) classe f; (group, category) catégorie f ▶ VT classer, classifier

class-conscious ['klɑ:s'kɔnʃəs] ADJ conscient(e) de son appartenance sociale

class consciousness N conscience f de classe

classic ['klæsɪk] ADJ classique ▶ N (author, work) classique m; (race etc) classique f

classical ['klæsɪkl] ADJ classique

classics ['klæsɪks] NPL (Scol) lettres fpl classiques

classification [klæsɪfɪ'keɪʃən] N classification f

classified ['klæsɪfaɪd] ADJ (information) secret(-ète); **~ ads** petites annonces

classify ['klæsɪfaɪ] VT classifier, classer

classless society ['klɑ:slɪs-] N société f sans classes

classmate ['klɑːsmeɪt] N camarade *mf* de classe

classroom ['klɑːsrum] N (salle *f* de) classe *f*

classroom assistant N assistant(e) d'éducation

classy ['klɑːsɪ] ADJ (*inf*) classe (*inf*)

clatter ['klætə'] N cliquetis *m* ▸ VI cliqueter

clause [klɔːz] N clause *f*; (*Ling*) proposition *f*

claustrophobia [klɔːstrə'fəubɪə] N claustrophobie *f*

claustrophobic [klɔːstrə'fəubɪk] ADJ (*person*) claustrophobe; (*place*) où l'on se sent claustrophobe

claw [klɔː] N griffe *f*; (*of bird of prey*) serre *f*; (*of lobster*) pince *f* ▸ VT griffer; déchirer
  ▸ **claw back** VT récupérer

clay [kleɪ] N argile *f*

★**clean** [kliːn] ADJ propre; (*clear, smooth*) net(te); (*record, reputation*) sans tache; (*joke, story*) correct(e); **~ driving licence** or (*US*) **record** permis où n'est portée aucune indication de contravention ▸ VT nettoyer; **to ~ one's teeth** se laver les dents ▸ ADV: **he ~ forgot** il a complètement oublié; **to come ~** (*inf: admit guilt*) se mettre à table
  ▸ **clean off** VT enlever
  ▸ **clean out** VT nettoyer (à fond)
  ▸ **clean up** VT nettoyer; (*fig*) remettre de l'ordre dans ▸ VI (*fig: make profit*): **to ~ up on** faire son beurre avec

clean-cut ['kliːn'kʌt] ADJ (*man*) soigné; (*situation etc*) bien délimité(e), net(te), clair(e)

cleaner ['kliːnə'] N (*person*) nettoyeur(-euse), femme *f* de ménage; (*also:* **dry cleaner**) teinturier(-ière); (*product*) détachant *m*

cleaner's ['kliːnə'z] N (*also:* **dry cleaner's**) teinturier *m*

cleaning ['kliːnɪŋ] N nettoyage *m*

cleaning lady N femme *f* de ménage

cleanliness ['klɛnlɪnɪs] N propreté *f*

cleanly ['kliːnlɪ] ADV proprement; nettement

cleanse [klɛnz] VT nettoyer; purifier

cleanser ['klɛnzə'] N détergent *m*; (*for face*) démaquillant *m*

clean-shaven ['kliːn'ʃeɪvn] ADJ rasé(e) de près

cleansing department ['klɛnzɪŋ-] N (*BRIT*) service *m* de voirie

clean sweep N: **to make a ~** (*Sport*) rafler tous les prix

clean technology N technologie *f* propre

clean-up ['kliːnʌp] N nettoyage *m*

★**clear** [klɪə'] ADJ clair(e); (*glass, plastic*) transparent(e); (*road, way*) libre, dégagé(e); (*profit, majority*) net(te); (*conscience*) tranquille; (*sky*) frais (fraîche); (*sky*) dégagé(e); **to make o.s. ~** se faire bien comprendre; **to make it ~ to sb that ...** bien faire comprendre à qn que ...; **I have a ~ day tomorrow** (*BRIT*) je n'ai rien de prévu demain ▸ VT (*road*) dégager, déblayer; (*table*) débarrasser; (*room etc: of people*) faire évacuer; (*woodland*) défricher; (*cheque*) compenser; (*Comm: goods*) liquider; (*Law: suspect*) innocenter; (*obstacle*) franchir or sauter sans heurter; **to ~ the table** débarrasser la table, desservir; **to ~ one's throat** s'éclaircir la gorge; **to ~ a profit** faire un bénéfice net ▸ VI (*weather*) s'éclaircir; (*fog*) se dissiper ▸ ADV:

~ of à distance de, à l'écart de; **to keep ~ of sb/sth** éviter qn/qch ▸ N: **to be in the ~** (*out of debt*) être dégagé(e) de toute dette; (*out of suspicion*) être lavé(e) de tout soupçon; (*out of danger*) être hors de danger
  ▸ **clear away** VT (*things, clothes etc*) enlever, retirer; **to ~ away the dishes** débarrasser la table
  ▸ **clear off** VI (*inf: leave*) dégager
  ▸ **clear up** VI s'éclaircir, se dissiper ▸ VT ranger, mettre en ordre; (*mystery*) éclaircir, résoudre

clearance ['klɪərəns] N (*removal*) déblayage *m*; (*free space*) dégagement *m*; (*permission*) autorisation *f*

clearance sale N (*Comm*) liquidation *f*

clear-cut ['klɪə'kʌt] ADJ précis(e), nettement défini(e)

clearing ['klɪərɪŋ] N (*in forest*) clairière *f*; (*BRIT Banking*) compensation *f*, clearing *m*

clearing bank N (*BRIT*) banque *f* qui appartient à une chambre de compensation

clearly ['klɪəlɪ] ADV clairement; (*obviously*) de toute évidence

clearway ['klɪəweɪ] N (*BRIT*) route *f* à stationnement interdit

cleavage ['kliːvɪdʒ] N (*of dress*) décolleté *m*

cleaver ['kliːvə'] N fendoir *m*, couperet *m*

clef [klɛf] N (*Mus*) clé *f*

cleft [klɛft] N (*in rock*) crevasse *f*, fissure *f*

clemency ['klɛmənsɪ] N clémence *f*

clement ['klɛmənt] ADJ (*weather*) clément(e)

clementine ['klɛməntaɪn] N clémentine *f*

clench [klɛntʃ] VT serrer

clergy ['klɜːdʒɪ] N clergé *m*

clergyman ['klɜːdʒɪmən] N (*irreg*) ecclésiastique *m*

cleric ['klɛrɪk] N ecclésiastique *m*

clerical ['klɛrɪkl] ADJ de bureau, d'employé de bureau; (*Rel*) clérical(e), du clergé

clerk [klɑːk, (*US*) klɜːrk] N (*BRIT*) employé(e) de bureau; (*US: salesman/woman*) vendeur(-euse); **C~ of Court** (*Law*) greffier(-ière) (du tribunal)

★**clever** ['klɛvə'] ADJ (*intelligent*) intelligent(e); (*skilful*) habile, adroit(e); (*device, arrangement*) ingénieux(-euse), astucieux(-euse)

cleverly ['klɛvəlɪ] ADV (*skilfully*) habilement; (*craftily*) astucieusement

clew [kluː] N (*US*) = **clue**

cliché ['kliːʃeɪ] N cliché *m*

click [klɪk] N (*Comput*) clic *m* ▸ VI faire un bruit sec or un déclic; (*Comput*) cliquer; **to ~ on an icon** cliquer sur une icône ▸ VT: **to ~ one's tongue** faire claquer sa langue; **to ~ one's heels** claquer des talons

clickable ['klɪkəbl] ADJ (*Comput*) cliquable

★**client** ['klaɪənt] N client(e)

clientele [kliːɔːn'tɛl] N clientèle *f*

cliff [klɪf] N falaise *f*

cliffhanger ['klɪfhæŋə'] N (*TV, fig*) histoire pleine de suspense

clifftop ['klɪftɔp] N sommet *m* d'une falaise

climactic [klaɪ'mæktɪk] ADJ à son point culminant, culminant(e)

★**climate** ['klaɪmɪt] N climat *m*

climate change N changement *m* climatique

climatic [klaɪˈmætɪk] ADJ climatique

climatologist [klaɪmɔˈtɔlədʒɪst] N climatologue mf

climax [ˈklaɪmæks] N apogée m, point culminant; (sexual) orgasme m

★**climb** [klaɪm] VI grimper, monter; (plane) prendre de l'altitude; **to ~ over a wall** passer par-dessus un mur ▶ VT (stairs) monter; (mountain) escalader; (tree) grimper à ▶ N montée f, escalade f
▶ **climb down** VI (re)descendre; (BRIT fig) rabattre de ses prétentions

climb-down [ˈklaɪmdaun] N (BRIT) reculade f

climber [ˈklaɪmə'] N (also: **rock climber**) grimpeur(-euse), varappeur(-euse); (plant) plante grimpante

climbing [ˈklaɪmɪŋ] N (also: **rock climbing**) escalade f, varappe f

clinch [klɪntʃ] VT (deal) conclure, sceller

clincher [ˈklɪntʃə'] N: **that was the ~** c'est ce qui a fait pencher la balance

cling [klɪŋ] (pt, pp **clung** [klʌŋ]) VI: **to ~ (to)** se cramponner (à), s'accrocher (à); (clothes) coller (à)

clingfilm® [ˈklɪŋfɪlm] N film m alimentaire

clingy [ˈklɪŋɪ] ADJ (child) dépendant(e); (adult) collant(e); (clothes) moulant(e)

clinic [ˈklɪnɪk] N clinique f; centre médical; (session: Med) consultation(s) f(pl), séance(s) f(pl); (: Sport) séance(s) de perfectionnement

clinical [ˈklɪnɪkl] ADJ clinique; (fig) froid(e)

clinician [klɪˈnɪʃən] N clinicien(ne)

clink [klɪŋk] VI tinter, cliqueter

clip [klɪp] N (for hair) barrette f; (also: **paper clip**) trombone m; (BRIT: also: **bulldog clip**) pince f de bureau; (holding hose etc) collier m or bague f (métallique) de serrage; (TV, Cine) clip m ▶ VT (papers: also: **clip together**) attacher; (hair, nails) couper; (hedge) tailler

clipboard [ˈklɪpbɔːd] N (board) écritoire m à pince; (Comput) bloc-notes m

clippers [ˈklɪpəz] NPL tondeuse f; (also: **nail clippers**) coupe-ongles m inv

clipping [ˈklɪpɪŋ] N (from newspaper) coupure f de journal

clique [kliːk] N clique f, coterie f

cloak [kləuk] N grande cape ▶ VT (fig) masquer, cacher

cloakroom [ˈkləukrum] N (for coats etc) vestiaire m; (BRIT: W.C.) toilettes fpl

clobber [ˈklɔbə'] (inf) N (BRIT) barda m (inf) ▶ VT (hit) frapper; (affect): **to be clobbered by sth** être mis(e) à mal par qch

★**clock** [klɔk] N (large) horloge f; (small) pendule f; **round the ~** (work etc) vingt-quatre heures sur vingt-quatre; **to sleep round the ~** or **the ~ round** faire le tour du cadran; **30,000 on the ~** (BRIT Aut) 30 000 milles au compteur; **to work against the ~** faire la course contre la montre
▶ **clock in, clock on** (BRIT) VI (with card) pointer (en arrivant); (start work) commencer à travailler
▶ **clock off, clock out** (BRIT) VI (with card) pointer (en partant); (leave work) quitter le travail
▶ **clock up** VT (miles, hours etc) faire

clock tower N clocher m

clockwise [ˈklɔkwaɪz] ADV dans le sens des aiguilles d'une montre

clockwork [ˈklɔkwəːk] N rouages mpl, mécanisme m; (of clock) mouvement m (d'horlogerie) ▶ ADJ (toy, train) mécanique

clog [klɔg] N sabot m ▶ VT boucher, encrasser ▶ VI (also: **clog up**) se boucher, s'encrasser

cloister [ˈklɔɪstə'] N cloître m

clone [kləun] N clone m ▶ VT cloner

★**close¹** [kləus] ADJ (writing, texture) serré(e); (contact, link, watch) étroit(e); (examination) attentif(-ive), minutieux(-euse); (contest) très serré(e); (weather) lourd(e), étouffant(e); (room) mal aéré(e); (near): **~ (to)** près (de), proche (de); **how ~ is Edinburgh to Glasgow?** combien de kilomètres y a-t-il entre Édimbourg et Glasgow?; **a ~ friend** un ami intime; **to have a ~ shave** (fig) l'échapper belle; **at ~ quarters** tout près, à côté ▶ ADV près, à proximité; **~ to** prep près de; **~ by, ~ at hand** adj, adv tout(e) près

close² [kləuz] VT fermer; (bargain, deal) conclure ▶ VI (shop etc) fermer; (lid, door etc) se fermer; (end) se terminer, se conclure; **what time do you ~?** à quelle heure fermez-vous? ▶ N (end) conclusion f; **to bring sth to a ~** mettre fin à qch
▶ **close down** VT, VI fermer (définitivement)
▶ **close in** VI (hunters) approcher; (night, fog) tomber; **to ~ in on sb** cerner qn
▶ **close off** VT (area) boucler

★**closed** [kləuzd] ADJ (shop etc) fermé(e); (road) fermé à la circulation

closed-circuit [ˈkləuzdˈsəːkɪt] ADJ: **~ television** (système m de) vidéosurveillance f

closed shop N organisation f qui n'admet que des travailleurs syndiqués

close-knit [ˈkləusˈnɪt] ADJ (family, community) très uni(e)

closely [ˈkləuslɪ] ADV (examine, watch) de près; **we are ~ related** nous sommes proches parents; **a ~ guarded secret** un secret bien gardé

close season [kləuz-] N (BRIT: Hunting) fermeture f de la chasse/pêche; (: Football) trêve f

closet [ˈklɔzɪt] N (cupboard) placard m, réduit m

close-up [ˈkləusʌp] N gros plan

closing [ˈkləuzɪŋ] ADJ (stages, remarks) final(e); **~ price** (Stock Exchange) cours m de clôture

closing time N heure f de fermeture

closure [ˈkləuʒə'] N fermeture f

clot [klɔt] N (of blood, milk) caillot m; (inf: person) ballot m ▶ VI (blood) former des caillots; (: external bleeding) se coaguler

cloth [klɔθ] N (material) tissu m, étoffe f; (BRIT: also: **tea cloth**) torchon m; lavette f; (also: **tablecloth**) nappe f

clothe [kləuð] VT habiller, vêtir

clothed [kləuðd] ADJ habillé(e); **~ in sth** (dressed) vêtu(e) de qch

★**clothes** [kləuðz] NPL vêtements mpl, habits mpl; **to put one's ~ on** s'habiller; **to take one's ~ off** enlever ses vêtements

clothes brush N brosse f à habits

clothes line N corde f (à linge)

clothes peg, (US) **clothes pin** N pince f à linge

clothing [ˈkləuðɪŋ] N = **clothes**

clotted cream [ˈklɔtɪd-] N (BRIT) crème caillée

★**cloud** [klaud] N (*also Comput*) nuage *m*; **every ~ has a silver lining** (*proverb*) à quelque chose malheur est bon (*proverbe*) ▶ VT (*liquid*) troubler; **to ~ the issue** brouiller les cartes
▶ **cloud over** VI se couvrir; (*fig*) s'assombrir

cloudburst ['klaudbə:st] N violente averse

cloud computing N (*Comput*) cloud computing *m*, informatique *f* en nuage

cloud-cuckoo-land ['klaud'kuku:'lænd] N (*BRIT*) monde *m* imaginaire

cloudless ['klaudlıs] ADJ sans nuages

cloudy ['klaudı] ADJ nuageux(-euse), couvert(e); (*liquid*) trouble

clout [klaut] N (*blow*) taloche *f*; (*fig*) pouvoir *m* ▶ VT flanquer une taloche à

clove [kləuv] N clou *m* de girofle; **a ~ of garlic** une gousse d'ail

clover ['kləuvə'] N trèfle *m*

cloverleaf ['kləuvəli:f] N feuille *f* de trèfle; (*Aut*) croisement *m* en trèfle

clown [klaun] N clown *m* ▶ VI (*also*: **clown about**, **clown around**) faire le clown

cloying ['klɔıɪŋ] ADJ (*taste, smell*) écœurant(e)

★**club** [klʌb] N (*society*) club *m*; (*weapon*) massue *f*, matraque *f*; (*also*: **golf club**) club ▶ VT matraquer ▶ VI: **to ~ together** s'associer ■ **clubs** NPL (*Cards*) trèfle *m*

clubbing ['klʌbıŋ] N sorties *fpl* en boîte (*inf*); **to go ~** sortir en boîte

club car N (*US Rail*) wagon-restaurant *m*

club class N (*Aviat*) classe *f* club

clubhouse ['klʌbhaus] N pavillon *m*

club soda N (*US*) eau *f* de seltz

cluck [klʌk] VI glousser

clue [klu:] N indice *m*; (*in crosswords*) définition *f*; **I haven't a ~** je n'en ai pas la moindre idée

clued up, (*US*) **clued in** [klu:d-] ADJ (*inf*) (vachement) calé(e)

clueless ['klu:lıs] ADJ (*inf*): **to be ~ about sth** ne rien connaître à qch; **I'm ~ about computers** je ne connais rien aux ordinateurs

clump [klʌmp] N: **~ of trees** bouquet *m* d'arbres

clumsy ['klʌmzı] ADJ (*person*) gauche, maladroit(e); (*object*) malcommode, peu maniable

clung [klʌŋ] PT, PP *of* **cling**

cluster ['klʌstə'] N (*petit*) groupe *m*; (*of flowers*) grappe *f* ▶ VI se rassembler

clutch [klʌtʃ] N (*Aut*) embrayage *m*; (*grasp*): **clutches** étreinte *f*, prise *f* ▶ VT (*grasp*) agripper; (*hold tightly*) serrer fort; (*hold on to*) se cramponner à

clutter ['klʌtə'] VT (*also*: **clutter up**) encombrer ▶ N désordre *m*, fouillis *m*

cm ABBR (= *centimetre*) cm

CNAA N ABBR (*BRIT*: = *Council for National Academic Awards*) *organisme non universitaire délivrant des diplômes*

CND N ABBR = **Campaign for Nuclear Disarmament**

CO N ABBR (= *commanding officer*) Cdt; (*BRIT*) = **Commonwealth Office** ▶ ABBR (*US*) = **Colorado**

Co. ABBR = **company, county**

c/o ABBR (= *care of*) c/o, aux bons soins de

★**coach** [kəutʃ] N (*bus*) autocar *m*; (*horse-drawn*) diligence *f*; (*of train*) voiture *f*, wagon *m*; (*Sport: trainer*) entraîneur(-euse); (*school: tutor*) répétiteur(-trice) ▶ VT (*Sport*) entraîner; (*student*) donner des leçons particulières à

coachload ['kəutʃləud] N (*BRIT*: *party*) bus *m*; **coachloads of** (*hordes of*) des hordes *fpl* de

coach station N (*BRIT*) gare routière

coach trip N excursion *f* en car

coagulate [kəu'ægjuleıt] VT coaguler ▶ VI se coaguler

★**coal** [kəul] N charbon *m*

coal face N front *m* de taille

coalfield ['kəulfi:ld] N bassin houiller

coalition [kəuə'lıʃən] N coalition *f*

coalman ['kəulmən] N (*irreg*) charbonnier *m*, marchand *m* de charbon

coal mine N mine *f* de charbon

coarse [kɔ:s] ADJ grossier(-ère), rude; (*vulgar*) vulgaire

★**coast** [kəust] N côte *f* ▶ VI (*car, cycle*) descendre en roue libre

coastal ['kəustl] ADJ côtier(-ère)

coaster ['kəustə'] N (*Naut*) caboteur *m*; (*for glass*) dessous *m* de verre

coastguard ['kəustgɑ:d] N garde-côte *m*

coastline ['kəustlaın] N côte *f*, littoral *m*

★**coat** [kəut] N (*garment*) manteau *m*; (*of animal*) pelage *m*, poil *m*; (*of paint*) couche *f*; **~ of arms** *n* blason *m*, armoiries *fpl* ▶ VT (*with dirt, plastic*) couvrir; (*with varnish, sealant*) enduire; (*with metal*) revêtir

coated ['kəutıd] ADJ recouvert(e); **to be ~ with sth** être recouvert(e) de qch

coat hanger N cintre *m*

coating ['kəutıŋ] N couche *f*, enduit *m*

co-author ['kəu'ɔ:θə'] N co-auteur *m*

coax [kəuks] VT persuader par des cajoleries

cob [kɔb] N *see* **corn**

cobbled ['kɔbld] ADJ pavé(e)

cobbler ['kɔblə'] N cordonnier *m*

cobbles, cobblestones ['kɔblz, 'kɔblstəunz] NPL pavés (ronds)

cobble together VT bricoler

COBOL ['kəubɔl] N COBOL *m*

cobra ['kəubrə] N cobra *m*

cobweb ['kɔbwɛb] N toile *f* d'araignée

cocaine [kə'keın] N cocaïne *f*

cock [kɔk] N (*rooster*) coq *m*; (*male bird*) mâle *m* ▶ VT (*gun*) armer; **to ~ one's ears** (*fig*) dresser l'oreille

cock-a-hoop [kɔkə'hu:p] ADJ jubilant(e)

cockatoo [kɔkə'tu:] N cacatoès *m*

cockerel ['kɔkərl] N jeune coq *m*

cock-eyed ['kɔkaıd] ADJ (*fig*) de travers; qui louche; qui ne tient pas debout (*fig*)

cockle ['kɔkl] N coque *f*

cockney ['kɔknı] N cockney *mf* (*habitant des quartiers populaires de l'East End de Londres*), ≈ faubourien(ne)

cockpit ['kɔkpıt] N (*in aircraft*) poste *m* de pilotage, cockpit *m*

cockroach ['kɔkrəutʃ] N cafard m, cancrelat m

cocktail ['kɔkteɪl] N cocktail m; **prawn ~**, (US) **shrimp ~** cocktail de crevettes

cocktail cabinet N (meuble-)bar m

cocktail party N cocktail m

cocktail shaker [-'ʃeɪkə'] N shaker m

cocky ['kɔkɪ] ADJ trop sûr(e) de soi

cocoa ['kəukəu] N cacao m

coconut ['kəukənʌt] N noix f de coco

cocoon [kə'ku:n] N cocon m

COD ABBR = **cash on delivery**; (US) = **collect on delivery**

cod [kɔd] N morue fraîche, cabillaud m

★**code** [kəud] N code m; (Tel: area code) indicatif m; **~ of behaviour** règles fpl de conduite; **~ of practice** règlements mpl et usages mpl ▸ VT, VI (Comput) coder

coded ['kəudɪd] ADJ (lit: information, signal) codé(e); (fig: language) voilé(e)

codeine ['kəudi:n] N codéine f

coder ['kəudə'] N (computer programmer) codeur(-euse)

code word N mot m de passe

codger ['kɔdʒə'] N: **an old ~** (BRIT pej) un drôle de vieux bonhomme

codicil ['kɔdɪsɪl] N codicille m

codify ['kəudɪfaɪ] VT codifier

cod-liver oil ['kɔdlɪvər-] N huile f de foie de morue

co-driver ['kəu'draɪvə'] N (in race) copilote mf; (of lorry) deuxième chauffeur m

co-ed ['kəu'ed] ADJ ABBR = **coeducational** ▸ N ABBR (US: female student) étudiante d'une université mixte; (BRIT: school) école f mixte

coeducational ['kəuɛdju'keɪʃənl] ADJ mixte

coeliac, (US) **celiac** ['si:lɪæk] ADJ cœliaque

coerce [kəu'ə:s] VT contraindre

coercion [kəu'ə:ʃən] N contrainte f

coercive [kəu'ə:sɪv] ADJ coercitif(-ive)

coexist [kəuɪg'zɪst] VI coexister

coexistence ['kəuɪg'zɪstəns] N coexistence f

C of C N ABBR = **chamber of commerce**

C of E N ABBR = **Church of England**

★**coffee** ['kɔfɪ] N café m; **white ~**, (US) **~ with cream** (café-)crème m

coffee bar N (BRIT) café m

coffee bean N grain m de café

coffee break N pause-café f

coffee cake N (US) ≈ petit pain aux raisins

coffee cup N tasse f à café

coffee maker N cafetière f

coffeepot ['kɔfɪpɔt] N cafetière f

coffee shop N café m

coffee table N (petite) table basse

coffin ['kɔfɪn] N cercueil m

C of I N ABBR = **Church of Ireland**

C of S N ABBR = **Church of Scotland**

cog [kɔg] N (wheel) roue dentée; (tooth) dent f (d'engrenage)

cogent ['kəudʒənt] ADJ puissant(e), convaincant(e)

cognac ['kɔnjæk] N cognac m

cognitive ['kɔgnɪtɪv] ADJ cognitif(-ive)

cognizance ['kɔgnɪzəns] N (formal) connaissance f; **to take ~ of sth** prendre connaissance de qch

cognizant ['kɔgnɪzənt] ADJ (formal) conscient(e)

cogwheel ['kɔgwi:l] N roue dentée

cohabit [kəu'hæbɪt] VI (formal): **to ~ (with sb)** cohabiter (avec qn)

cohabitation [kəuhæbɪ'teɪʃən] N concubinage m, vie f maritale

coherence [kəu'hɪərəns] N cohérence f

coherent [kəu'hɪərənt] ADJ cohérent(e)

cohesion [kəu'hi:ʒən] N cohésion f

cohesive [kəu'hi:sɪv] ADJ (fig) cohésif(-ive)

cohort ['kəuhɔ:t] N (group) groupe m; (supporter) acolyte m

COI N ABBR (BRIT: = Central Office of Information) service d'information gouvernemental

coil [kɔɪl] N rouleau m, bobine f; (one loop) anneau m, spire f; (of smoke) volute f; (contraceptive) stérilet m ▸ VT enrouler

coin [kɔɪn] N pièce f (de monnaie) ▸ VT (word) inventer

coinage ['kɔɪnɪdʒ] N monnaie f, système m monétaire

coinbox ['kɔɪnbɔks] N (BRIT) cabine f téléphonique

coincide [kəun'saɪd] VI coïncider

coincidence [kəu'ɪnsɪdəns] N coïncidence f

coincidental [kəuɪnsɪ'dɛntəl] ADJ (resemblance, event) fortuit(e); **it is ~ that ...** c'est une coïncidence si or que...

coincidentally [kəuɪnsɪ'dɛntəlɪ] ADV par coïncidence

coin-operated ['kɔɪn'ɔpəreɪtɪd] ADJ (machine, launderette) automatique

coir ['kɔɪə'] N coco m

★**Coke®** [kəuk] N coca m

coke [kəuk] N (coal) coke m

Col. ABBR (= colonel) Col; (US) = **Colorado**

COLA N ABBR (US: = cost-of-living adjustment) réajustement (des salaires, indemnités etc) en fonction du coût de la vie

colander ['kɔləndə'] N passoire f (à légumes)

★**cold** [kəuld] ADJ froid(e); **it's ~** il fait froid; **to be ~** (person) avoir froid; **in ~ blood** de sang-froid; **to have ~ feet** avoir froid aux pieds; (fig) avoir la frousse or la trouille; **to give sb the ~ shoulder** battre froid à qn ▸ N froid m; (Med) rhume m; **to catch a ~, to catch ~** s'enrhumer, attraper un rhume

cold-blooded ['kəuld'blʌdɪd] ADJ (Zool) à sang froid

cold call N appel m de démarchage ▸ VT démarcher par téléphone

cold cream N crème f de soins

coldly ['kəuldlɪ] ADV froidement

coldness ['kəuldnɪs] N froideur f

cold sore N bouton m de fièvre

cold sweat N: **to be in a ~ (about sth)** avoir des sueurs froides (au sujet de qch)

cold turkey N (inf) manque m; **to go ~** être en manque

Cold War N: **the ~** la guerre froide

coleslaw ['kəulslɔ:] N sorte de salade de chou cru

colic ['kɒlɪk] N colique(s) f(pl)

colicky ['kɒlɪkɪ] ADJ qui souffre de coliques

collaborate [kə'læbəreɪt] VI collaborer

collaboration [kəlæbə'reɪʃən] N collaboration f

collaborative [kə'læbərətɪv] ADJ (project) en collaboration

collaborator [kə'læbəreɪtə'] N collaborateur(-trice)

collage [kɒ'lɑ:ʒ] N (Art) collage m

collagen ['kɒlədʒən] N collagène m

★collapse [kə'læps] VI s'effondrer, s'écrouler; (Med) avoir un malaise ▶ N effondrement m, écroulement m; (of government) chute f

collapsible [kə'læpsəbl] ADJ pliant(e), télescopique

collar ['kɒlə'] N (of coat, shirt) col m; (for dog) collier m; (Tech) collier, bague f ▶ VT (inf: person) pincer

collarbone ['kɒləbəun] N clavicule f

collate [kɒ'leɪt] VT collationner

collateral [kə'lætərl] N nantissement m

collation [kə'leɪʃən] N collation f

★colleague ['kɒli:g] N collègue mf

★collect [kə'lɛkt] VT rassembler; (pick up) ramasser; (as a hobby) collectionner; (Brit: call for) (passer) prendre; (mail) faire la levée de, ramasser; (money owed) encaisser; (donations, subscriptions) recueillir; **to ~ one's thoughts** réfléchir, réunir ses idées ▶ VI (people) se rassembler; (dust, dirt) s'amasser; **~ on delivery (COD)** (US Comm) payable or paiement à la livraison ▶ ADV: **to call ~** (US Tel) téléphoner en PCV

collected [kə'lɛktɪd] ADJ: **~ works** œuvres complètes

★collection [kə'lɛkʃən] N collection f; (of mail) levée f; (for money) collecte f, quête f

collective [kə'lɛktɪv] ADJ collectif(-ive) ▶ N collectif m

collective bargaining N convention collective

collector [kə'lɛktə'] N collectionneur(-euse); (of taxes) percepteur(-trice); (of rent, cash) encaisseur(-euse); **~'s item** or **piece** pièce f de collection

★college ['kɒlɪdʒ] N collège m; (of technology, agriculture etc) institut m; **to go to ~** faire des études supérieures; **~ of education** ≈ école normale

collide [kə'laɪd] VI: **to ~ (with)** entrer en collision (avec)

collie ['kɒlɪ] N (dog) colley m

colliery ['kɒlɪərɪ] N (Brit) mine f de charbon, houillère f

collision [kə'lɪʒən] N collision f, heurt m; **to be on a ~ course** aller droit à la collision; (fig) aller vers l'affrontement

collision damage waiver N (Insurance) rachat m de franchise

colloquial [kə'ləukwɪəl] ADJ familier(-ère)

collude [kə'lu:d] VI (pej) s'associer; **to ~ to do sth** s'associer pour faire qch; **to ~ in sth** être de mèche dans qch

collusion [kə'lu:ʒən] N collusion f; **in ~ with** en complicité avec

cologne [kə'ləun] N (also: **eau de Cologne**) eau f de cologne

Colombia [kə'lɒmbɪə] N Colombie f

Colombian [kə'lɒmbɪən] ADJ colombien(ne) ▶ N Colombien(ne)

colon ['kəulən] N (sign) deux-points m; (Med) côlon m

colonel ['kə:nl] N colonel m

colonial [kə'ləunɪəl] ADJ colonial(e)

colonialism [kə'ləunɪəlɪzəm] N colonialisme m

colonize ['kɒlənaɪz] VT coloniser

colonnade [kɒlə'neɪd] N colonnade f

colony ['kɒlənɪ] N colonie f

color etc ['kʌlə'] N (US) = **colour** etc

Colorado beetle [kɒlə'rɑ:dəu-] N doryphore m

colossal [kə'lɒsl] ADJ colossal(e)

colostomy [kə'lɒstəmɪ] N colostomie f

colour, (US) **color** ['kʌlə'] N couleur f; **I'd like a different ~** je le voudrais dans un autre coloris ▶ VT colorer; (dye) teindre; (paint) peindre; (with crayons) colorier; (news) fausser, exagérer ▶ VI (blush) rougir ▶ CPD (film, photograph, television) en couleur
■ **colours** NPL (of party, club) couleurs fpl
▶ **colour in** VT colorier

colour bar, (US) N discrimination raciale (dans un établissement etc)

colour-blind, (US) **color-blind** ['kʌləblaɪnd] ADJ daltonien(ne)

coloured, (US) **colored** ['kʌləd] ADJ (glass, water) coloré(e); (!: person, race) de couleur; **brightly ~** aux couleurs vives

colour film, (US) **color film** N (for camera) pellicule f (en) couleur

colourful, (US) **colorful** ['kʌləful] ADJ coloré(e), vif (vive); (personality) pittoresque, haut(e) en couleurs

colourfully, (US) **colorfully** ['kʌləfulɪ] ADV (dressed, painted) en couleurs vives; (described) de façon pittoresque

colouring, (US) **coloring** ['kʌlərɪŋ] N colorant m; (complexion) teint m

colouring book, (US) **coloring book** N album m à colorier

colour scheme, (US) **color scheme** N combinaison f de(s) couleur(s)

colour supplement N (Brit Press) supplément m magazine

colour television, (US) **color television** N télévision f (en) couleur

colt [kəult] N poulain m

column ['kɒləm] N colonne f; (fashion column, sports column etc) rubrique f; **the editorial ~** l'éditorial m

columnist ['kɒləmnɪst] N rédacteur(-trice) d'une rubrique

coma ['kəumə] N coma m

comatose ['kəumətəus, 'kəumətəuz] ADJ (in a coma) comateux(-euse); (inf: asleep) comateux

★comb [kəum] N peigne m ▶ VT (hair) peigner; (area) ratisser, passer au peigne fin

combat ['kɒmbæt] N combat m ▶ VT combattre, lutter contre

combat fatigues NPL treillis m

combative ['kɒmbətɪv] ADJ combatif(-ive)

★combination [kɒmbɪ'neɪʃən] N (gen) combinaison f

combination lock N serrure f à combinaison

★combine VT [kəm'baɪn] combiner; **to ~ sth with sth** (one quality with another) joindre or allier qch à qch; **a combined effort** un effort conjugué

▶ VI s'associer; (*Chem*) se combiner ▶ N ['kɔmbaɪn] association *f*; (*Econ*) trust *m*; (*also:* **combine harvester**) moissonneuse-batteuse(-lieuse) *f*
combine harvester N moissonneuse-batteuse(-lieuse) *f*
combo ['kɔmbəu] N (*Jazz etc*) groupe *m* de musiciens
combustible [kəm'bʌstɪbl] ADJ combustible
combustion [kəm'bʌstʃən] N combustion *f*

---

come [kʌm]

(*pt* came [keɪm], *pp* come [kʌm]) VI **1** (*movement towards*) venir; **to come running** arriver en courant; **he's come here to work** il est venu ici pour travailler; **come with me** suivez-moi; **to come into sight** *or* **view** apparaître
2 (*arrive*) arriver; **to come home** rentrer (chez soi *or* à la maison); **we've just come from Paris** nous arrivons de Paris; **coming!** j'arrive !
3 (*reach*): **to come to** (*decision etc*) parvenir à, arriver à; **the bill came to £40** la note s'est élevée à 40 livres; **if it comes to it** s'il le faut, dans le pire des cas
4 (*occur*): **an idea came to me** il m'est venu une idée; **what might come of it** ce qui pourrait en résulter, ce qui pourrait advenir *or* se produire
5 (*be, become*): **to come loose/undone** se défaire/desserrer; **I've come to like him** j'ai fini par bien l'aimer
6 (*inf: sexually*) jouir
▶ **come about** VI se produire, arriver
▶ **come across** VT FUS rencontrer par hasard, tomber sur ▶ VI: **to come across well/badly** faire une bonne/mauvaise impression
▶ **come along** VI (BRIT: *pupil, work*) faire des progrès, avancer; **come along!** viens !; allons !, allez !
▶ **come apart** VI s'en aller en morceaux; se détacher
▶ **come away** VI partir, s'en aller; (*become detached*) se détacher
▶ **come back** VI revenir; (*reply*): **can I come back to you on that one?** est-ce qu'on peut revenir là-dessus plus tard ?
▶ **come by** VT FUS (*acquire*) obtenir, se procurer
▶ **come down** VI descendre; (*prices*) baisser; (*buildings*) s'écrouler; (*: be demolished*) être démoli(e)
▶ **come forward** VI s'avancer; (*make o.s. known*) se présenter, s'annoncer
▶ **come from** VT FUS (*source*) venir de; (*place*) venir de, être originaire de
▶ **come in** VI entrer; (*train*) arriver; (*fashion*) entrer en vogue; (*on deal etc*) participer
▶ **come in for** VT FUS (*criticism etc*) être l'objet de
▶ **come into** VT FUS (*money*) hériter de
▶ **come off** VI (*button*) se détacher; (*attempt*) réussir
▶ **come on** VI (*lights, electricity*) s'allumer; (*central heating*) se mettre en marche; (*pupil, work, project*) faire des progrès, avancer; **come on!** viens !; allons !, allez !
▶ **come out** VI sortir; (*sun*) se montrer; (*book*) paraître; (*stain*) s'enlever; (*strike*) cesser le travail, se mettre en grève
▶ **come over** VT FUS: **I don't know what's come over him!** je ne sais pas ce qui lui a pris !
▶ **come round** VI (*after faint, operation*) revenir à soi, reprendre connaissance

▶ **come through** VI (*survive*) s'en sortir; (*telephone call*): **the call came through** l'appel est bien parvenu
▶ **come to** VI revenir à soi ▶ VT (*add up to: amount*): **how much does it come to?** ça fait combien ?
▶ **come under** VT FUS (*heading*) se trouver sous; (*influence*) subir
▶ **come up** VI monter; (*sun*) se lever; (*problem*) se poser; (*event*) survenir; (*in conversation*) être soulevé
▶ **come up against** VT FUS (*resistance, difficulties*) rencontrer
▶ **come upon** VT FUS tomber sur
▶ **come up to** VT FUS arriver à; **the film didn't come up to our expectations** le film nous a déçus
▶ **come up with** VT FUS (*money*) fournir; **he came up with an idea** il a eu une idée, il a proposé quelque chose

---

comeback ['kʌmbæk] N (*Theat*) rentrée *f*; (*reaction*) réaction *f*; (*response*) réponse *f*
Comecon ['kɔmɪkɔn] N ABBR (= *Council for Mutual Economic Aid*) COMECON *m*
comedian [kə'miːdɪən] N (*comic*) comique *m*; (*Theat*) comédien(ne)
comedic [kə'miːdɪk] ADJ (*formal*) comique
comedienne [kəmiːdɪ'ɛn] N comique *f*
comedown ['kʌmdaun] N déchéance *f*
★**comedy** ['kɔmɪdɪ] N comédie *f*; (*humour*) comique *m*
comet ['kɔmɪt] N comète *f*
comeuppance [kʌm'ʌpəns] N: **to get one's ~** recevoir ce qu'on mérite
comfort ['kʌmfət] N confort *m*, bien-être *m*; (*solace*) consolation *f*, réconfort *m* ▶ VT consoler, réconforter
★**comfortable** ['kʌmfətəbl] ADJ confortable; (*person*) à l'aise; (*financially*) aisé(e); (*patient*) dont l'état est stationnaire; **I don't feel very ~ about it** cela m'inquiète un peu
comfortably ['kʌmfətəblɪ] ADV (*sit*) confortablement; (*live*) à l'aise
comforter ['kʌmfətə'] N (*US*) édredon *m*
comforting ['kʌmfətɪŋ] ADJ (*thought, words*) réconfortant(e)
comforts ['kʌmfəts] NPL aises *fpl*
comfort station N (*US*) toilettes *fpl*
comfy ['kʌmfɪ] ADJ (*inf: clothes, chair*) confortable; **to be ~** (*person*) être à l'aise
comic ['kɔmɪk] ADJ (*also:* **comical**) comique ▶ N (*person*) comique *m*; (BRIT: *magazine: for children*) magazine *m* de bandes dessinées *or* de BD; (*: for adults*) illustré *m*
comical ['kɔmɪkl] ADJ amusant(e)
comic book N (US: *for children*) magazine *m* de bandes dessinées *or* de BD; (*: for adults*) illustré *m*
comic strip N bande dessinée
coming ['kʌmɪŋ] N arrivée *f* ▶ ADJ (*next*) prochain(e); (*future*) à venir; **in the ~ weeks** dans les prochaines semaines
Comintern ['kɔmɪntəːn] N Comintern *m*
comma ['kɔmə] N virgule *f*
★**command** [kə'mɑːnd] N ordre *m*, commandement *m*; (*Mil: authority*) commandement; (*mastery*)

maîtrise f; (*Comput*) commande f; **to have/take ~ of** avoir/prendre le commandement de; **to have at one's ~** (*money, resources etc*) disposer de ▶ VT (*troops*) commander; (*be able to get*) (pouvoir) disposer de, avoir à sa disposition; (*deserve*) avoir droit à; **to ~ sb to do** donner l'ordre *or* commander à qn de faire

command economy N économie planifiée

commandeer [kɔmənˈdɪəʳ] VT réquisitionner (par la force)

commander [kəˈmɑːndəʳ] N chef m; (*Mil*) commandant m

commander-in-chief [kəˈmɑːndərɪnˈtʃiːf] N (*Mil*) commandant m en chef

commanding [kəˈmɑːndɪŋ] ADJ (*appearance*) imposant(e); (*voice, tone*) autoritaire; (*lead, position*) dominant(e)

commanding officer N commandant m

commandment [kəˈmɑːndmənt] N (*Rel*) commandement m

command module N (*Space*) module m de commande

commando [kəˈmɑːndəu] N commando m; membre m d'un commando

commemorate [kəˈmeməreɪt] VT commémorer

commemoration [kəmeməˈreɪʃən] N commémoration f

commemorative [kəˈmemərətɪv] ADJ commémoratif(-ive)

commence [kəˈmens] VT, VI commencer

commencement [kəˈmensmənt] N (*start*) commencement m; (*US: graduation*) remise f des diplômes

commend [kəˈmend] VT louer; (*recommend*) recommander

commendable [kəˈmendəbl] ADJ louable

commendation [kɔmenˈdeɪʃən] N éloge m; recommandation f

commensurate [kəˈmenʃərɪt] ADJ: **~ with/to** en rapport avec/selon

★**comment** [ˈkɔment] N commentaire m; **"no ~"** « je n'ai rien à déclarer » ▶ VI faire des remarques *or* commentaires; **to ~ on** faire des remarques sur ▶ VT: **to ~ that** faire remarquer que

commentary [ˈkɔməntəri] N commentaire m; (*Sport*) reportage m (en direct)

commentate [ˈkɔmənteɪt] VI faire le commentaire; **to ~ on sth** (*match, one-off event*) faire le commentaire de qch; (*series of events*) couvrir qch, faire un reportage sur qch

commentator [ˈkɔmənteɪtəʳ] N commentateur(-trice); (*Sport*) reporter m

commerce [ˈkɔməːs] N commerce m

★**commercial** [kəˈməːʃəl] ADJ commercial(e) ▶ N (*Radio, TV*) annonce f publicitaire, spot m (publicitaire)

commercial bank N banque f d'affaires

commercial break N (*Radio, TV*) spot m (publicitaire)

commercial college N école f de commerce

commercialism [kəˈməːʃəlɪzəm] N mercantilisme m

commercialization [kəˈməːʃəlaɪzeɪʃən] N commercialisation f

commercialize [kəˈməːʃəlaɪz] VT commercialiser

commercially [kəˈməːʃəlɪ] ADV (*viable*) commercialement; (*available*) dans le commerce; (*produce*) à échelle commerciale

commercial television N chaînes fpl privées (financées par la publicité)

commercial traveller N voyageur(-euse) de commerce

commercial vehicle N véhicule m utilitaire

commiserate [kəˈmɪzəreɪt] VI: **to ~ with sb** témoigner de la sympathie pour qn

★**commission** [kəˈmɪʃən] N (*committee, fee*) commission f; (*order for work of art etc*) commande f; **out of ~** (*Naut*) hors de service; (*machine*) hors service; **I get 10% ~** je reçois une commission de 10%; **~ of inquiry** (*BRIT*) commission d'enquête ▶ VT (*Mil*) nommer (à un commandement); (*work of art*) commander, charger un artiste de l'exécution de

commissionaire [kəmɪʃəˈnɛəʳ] N (*BRIT: at shop, cinema etc*) portier m (en uniforme)

commissioner [kəˈmɪʃənəʳ] N membre m d'une commission; (*Police*) préfet m (de police)

★**commit** [kəˈmɪt] VT (*act*) commettre; (*resources*) consacrer; (*to sb's care*) confier (à); **to ~ o.s. (to do)** s'engager (à faire); **to ~ suicide** se suicider; **to ~ to writing** coucher par écrit; **to ~ sb for trial** traduire qn en justice

commitment [kəˈmɪtmənt] N engagement m; (*obligation*) responsabilité(s) fpl

committed [kəˈmɪtɪd] ADJ (*writer, politician etc*) engagé(e)

★**committee** [kəˈmɪtɪ] N comité m; commission f; **to be on a ~** siéger dans un comité *or* une commission)

committee meeting N réunion f de comité *or* commission

commodity [kəˈmɔdɪtɪ] N produit m, marchandise f, article m; (*food*) denrée f

commodity exchange N bourse f de marchandises

★**common** [ˈkɔmən] ADJ (*gen*) commun(e); (*usual*) courant(e); **in ~ use** d'un usage courant; **it's ~ knowledge that** il est bien connu *or* notoire que; **to the ~ good** pour le bien de tous, dans l'intérêt général ▶ N terrain communal; **in ~** en commun

common cold N: **the ~** le rhume

common denominator N dénominateur commun

commoner [ˈkɔmənəʳ] N roturier(-ière)

common ground N (*fig*) terrain m d'entente

common land N terrain communal

common law N droit coutumier

common-law [ˈkɔmənlɔː] ADJ: **~ wife** épouse f de facto

commonly [ˈkɔmənlɪ] ADV communément, généralement; couramment

Common Market N Marché commun

commonplace [ˈkɔmənpleɪs] ADJ banal(e), ordinaire

common room N salle commune; (*Scol*) salle f des professeurs

Commons ['kɔmənz] NPL (*Brit Pol*): **the (House of)** ~ la chambre des Communes

common sense N bon sens

Commonwealth ['kɔmənwɛlθ] N: **the** ~ le Commonwealth

Le **Commonwealth** regroupe 52 États indépendants et plusieurs territoires qui reconnaissent tous le souverain britannique comme dirigeant de cette association. Il fut formé en 1949 dans un souci de cohésion après le démantèlement de l'Empire britannique. Depuis 1930, les Jeux du Commonwealth ont lieu tous les quatre ans dans l'un des pays de l'organisation.

commotion [kə'məuʃən] N désordre *m*, tumulte *m*

communal ['kɔmju:nl] ADJ (*life*) communautaire; (*for common use*) commun(e)

commune N ['kɔmju:n] (*group*) communauté *f* ▶ VI [kə'mju:n]: **to ~ with** converser intimement avec; (*nature*) communier avec

communicable [kə'mju:nɪkəbl] ADJ (*disease*) transmissible

★**communicate** [kə'mju:nɪkeɪt] VT communiquer, transmettre ▶ VI: **to ~ (with)** communiquer (avec)

★**communication** [kəmju:nɪ'keɪʃən] N communication *f*

communication cord N (*Brit*) sonnette *f* d'alarme

communications network N réseau *m* de communications

communications satellite N satellite *m* de télécommunications

communicative [kə'mju:nɪkətɪv] ADJ communicatif(-ive)

communicator [kə'mju:nɪkeɪtə'] N communicateur(-trice)

communion [kə'mju:nɪən] N (*also*: **Holy Communion**) communion *f*

communism ['kɔmjunɪzəm] N communisme *m*

★**communist** ['kɔmjunɪst] ADJ, N communiste *mf*

★**community** [kə'mju:nɪtɪ] N communauté *f*

community centre, (US) **community center** N foyer socio-éducatif, centre *m* de loisirs

community chest N (US) fonds commun

community health centre, (US) **community health center** N centre médico-social

community service N ≈ travail *m* d'intérêt général, TIG *m*

community spirit N solidarité *f*

commutation ticket [kɔmju'teɪʃən-] N (US) carte *f* d'abonnement

commute [kə'mju:t] VI faire le trajet journalier (*de son domicile à un lieu de travail assez éloigné*) ▶ VT (*Law*) commuer; (*Math*: *terms etc*) opérer la commutation de

commuter [kə'mju:tə'] N banlieusard(e) (*qui fait un trajet journalier pour se rendre à son travail*)

Comoros ['kɔmərəuz, kə'mɔ:rəuz] NPL Comores *fpl*

compact ADJ [kəm'pækt] compact(e) ▶ N ['kɔmpækt] contrat *m*, entente *f*; (*also*: **powder compact**) poudrier *m*

compact disc N disque compact

compact disc player N lecteur *m* de disques compacts

companion [kəm'pænjən] N compagnon (compagne)

companionship [kəm'pænjənʃɪp] N camaraderie *f*

companionway [kəm'pænjənweɪ] N (*Naut*) escalier *m* des cabines

★**company** ['kʌmpənɪ] N (*also* Comm, Mil, Theat) compagnie *f*; **he's good** ~ il est d'une compagnie agréable; **we have** ~ nous avons de la visite; **to keep sb** ~ tenir compagnie à qn; **to part** ~ **with** se séparer de; **Smith and C**~ Smith et Compagnie

company car N voiture *f* de fonction

company director N administrateur(-trice)

company secretary N (*Brit Comm*) secrétaire général (*d'une société*)

comparable ['kɔmpərəbl] ADJ comparable

comparative [kəm'pærətɪv] ADJ (*study*) comparatif(-ive); (*relative*) relatif(-ive)

comparatively [kəm'pærətɪvlɪ] ADV (*relatively*) relativement

★**compare** [kəm'pɛə'] VT: **to ~ sth/sb with** *or* **to** comparer qch/qn avec *or* à; **compared with** *or* **to** par rapport à ▶ VI: **to ~ (with)** se comparer (à); être comparable (à); **how do the prices ~?** comment sont les prix ?, est-ce que les prix sont comparables ?

★**comparison** [kəm'pærɪsn] N comparaison *f*; **in ~ (with)** en comparaison (de)

compartment [kəm'pɑ:tmənt] N (*also Rail*) compartiment *m*; **a non-smoking** ~ un compartiment non-fumeurs

compass ['kʌmpəs] N boussole *f*; **within the** ~ **of** dans les limites de ■ **compasses** NPL (*Math*) compas *m*

compassion [kəm'pæʃən] N compassion *f*, humanité *f*

compassionate [kəm'pæʃənɪt] ADJ accessible à la compassion, au cœur charitable et bienveillant; **on ~ grounds** pour raisons personnelles *or* de famille

compassionate leave N congé exceptionnel (*pour raisons de famille*)

compassionately [kəm'pæʃənətlɪ] ADV avec compassion

compatibility [kəmpætɪ'bɪlɪtɪ] N compatibilité *f*

compatible [kəm'pætɪbl] ADJ compatible

compatriot [kəm'pætrɪət] N compatriote *mf*

compel [kəm'pɛl] VT contraindre, obliger

compelling [kəm'pɛlɪŋ] ADJ (*fig*: *argument*) irrésistible

compendium [kəm'pɛndɪəm] N (*summary*) abrégé *m*

compensate ['kɔmpənseɪt] VT indemniser, dédommager ▶ VI: **to ~ for** compenser

compensation [kɔmpən'seɪʃən] N compensation *f*; (*money*) dédommagement *m*, indemnité *f*

compensatory [kɔmpən'seɪtərɪ] ADJ (*damages*, *payments*) compensateur(-trice); (*measures*, *programme*) compensatoire

compere ['kɔmpɛə'] N présentateur(-trice), animateur(-trice)

★**compete** [kəm'piːt] vi (take part) concourir; (vie):
to ~ (with) rivaliser (avec), faire concurrence (à)

competence ['kɔmpɪtəns] n compétence f

competency ['kɔmpɪtənsɪ] n compétence f

competent ['kɔmpɪtənt] adj compétent(e), capable

competing [kəm'piːtɪŋ] adj (ideas, theories) opposé(e); (companies) concurrent(e)

★**competition** [kɔmpɪ'tɪʃən] n (contest) compétition f, concours m; (Econ) concurrence f; **in ~ with** en concurrence avec

★**competitive** [kəm'petɪtɪv] adj (price, product) concurrentiel(le), compétitif(-ive); (sports, tennis) de compétition; **to be ~** (person) avoir l'esprit de compétition

competitive examination n concours m

competitiveness [kəm'petɪtɪvnɪs] n (ambition) esprit m de compétition; (of price, product) compétitivité f

★**competitor** [kəm'petɪtəʳ] n concurrent(e)

compile [kəm'paɪl] vt compiler

complacency [kəm'pleɪsnsɪ] n contentement m de soi, autosatisfaction f

complacent [kəm'pleɪsnt] adj (trop) content(e) de soi

★**complain** [kəm'pleɪn] vi: **to ~ (about)** se plaindre (de); (in shop etc) réclamer (au sujet de)
▶ **complain of** vt fus (Med) se plaindre de

complainant [kəm'pleɪnənt] n (Law) plaignant(e)

★**complaint** [kəm'pleɪnt] n plainte f; (in shop etc) réclamation f; (Med) affection f

complement n ['kɔmplɪmənt] n complément m; (esp of ship's crew etc) effectif complet ▶ vt (enhance) compléter

complementary [kɔmplɪ'mentərɪ] adj complémentaire

★**complete** [kəm'pliːt] adj complet(-ète); (finished) achevé(e) ▶ vt achever, parachever; (set, group) compléter; (a form) remplir

★**completely** [kəm'pliːtlɪ] adv complètement

completion [kəm'pliːʃən] n achèvement m; (of contract) exécution f; **to be nearing ~** être presque terminé

complex ['kɔmpleks] adj complexe ▶ n (Psych, buildings etc) complexe m

complexion [kəm'plekʃən] n (of face) teint m; (of event etc) aspect m, caractère m

complexity [kəm'pleksɪtɪ] n complexité f

compliance [kəm'plaɪəns] n (submission) docilité f; (agreement): **~ with** le fait de se conformer à; **in ~ with** en conformité avec, conformément à

compliant [kəm'plaɪənt] adj docile, très accommodant(e)

complicate ['kɔmplɪkeɪt] vt compliquer

★**complicated** ['kɔmplɪkeɪtɪd] adj compliqué(e)

complication [kɔmplɪ'keɪʃən] n complication f

complicit [kəm'plɪsɪt] adj complice; **to be ~ in sth** être complice de qch

complicity [kəm'plɪsɪtɪ] n complicité f

compliment n ['kɔmplɪmənt] compliment m; **to pay sb a ~** faire or adresser un compliment à qn
▶ vt ['kɔmplɪment] complimenter; **to ~ sb (on**

sth/on doing sth) féliciter qn (pour qch/de faire qch) ▪ **compliments** npl compliments mpl, hommages mpl; vœux mpl

complimentary [kɔmplɪ'mentərɪ] adj flatteur(-euse); (free) à titre gracieux

complimentary ticket n billet m de faveur

compliments slip n fiche f de transmission

comply [kəm'plaɪ] vi: **to ~ with** se soumettre à, se conformer à

component [kəm'pəunənt] adj composant(e), constituant(e) ▶ n composant m, élément m

compose [kəm'pəuz] vt composer; (form): **to be composed of** se composer de; **to ~ o.s.** se calmer, se maîtriser; **to ~ one's features** prendre une contenance

composed [kəm'pəuzd] adj calme, posé(e)

composer [kəm'pəuzəʳ] n (Mus) compositeur(-trice)

composite ['kɔmpəzɪt] adj composite; (Bot, Math) composé(e)

composition [kɔmpə'zɪʃən] n composition f

compost ['kɔmpɔst] n compost m

composure [kəm'pəuʒəʳ] n calme m, maîtrise f de soi

compound n ['kɔmpaund] (Chem, Ling) composé m; (enclosure) enclos m, enceinte f ▶ adj ['kɔmpaund] composé(e); (fracture) compliqué(e) ▶ vt [kəm'paund] (fig: problem etc) aggraver

compound fracture n fracture compliquée

compound interest n intérêt composé

comprehend [kɔmprɪ'hend] vt comprendre

comprehensible [kɔmprɪ'hensɪbl] adj compréhensible

comprehension [kɔmprɪ'henʃən] n compréhension f

comprehensive [kɔmprɪ'hensɪv] adj (très) complet(-ète); **~ policy** (Insurance) assurance f tous risques

---

Be careful not to translate comprehensive by the
French word compréhensif.

---

comprehensive [kɔmprɪ'hensɪv], **comprehensive school** n (Brit) école secondaire non sélective

comprehensively [kɔmprɪ'hensɪvlɪ] adv (reject, destroy, rebuild) complètement; (beat, defeat) à plate couture

compress vt [kəm'pres] comprimer; (text, information) condenser ▶ n ['kɔmpres] (Med) compresse f

compression [kəm'preʃən] n compression f

compressor [kəm'presəʳ] n compresseur m

comprise [kəm'praɪz] vt comprendre; (constitute) constituer, représenter

★**compromise** ['kɔmprəmaɪz] n compromis m
▶ vt compromettre ▶ vi transiger, accepter un compromis ▶ cpd (decision, solution) de compromis

compromising ['kɔmprəmaɪzɪŋ] adj compromettant(e)

compulsion [kəm'pʌlʃən] n contrainte f, force f; **under ~** sous la contrainte

compulsive [kəmˈpʌlsɪv] ADJ (Psych) compulsif(-ive); (book, film etc) captivant(e); **he's a ~ smoker** c'est un fumeur invétéré

compulsory [kəmˈpʌlsərɪ] ADJ obligatoire

compulsory purchase N expropriation f

compunction [kəmˈpʌŋkʃən] N scrupule m; **to have no ~ about doing sth** n'avoir aucun scrupule à faire qch

computation [kɔmpjuˈteɪʃən] N calcul m

computational [kɔmpjuˈteɪʃənəl] ADJ (methods) informatique

compute [kəmˈpjuːt] VT calculer

★**computer** [kəmˈpjuːtəʳ] N ordinateur m; (mechanical) calculatrice f

★**computer game** N jeu m vidéo

computer-generated [kəmˈpjuːtəˈdʒɛnəreɪtɪd] ADJ de synthèse

computerize [kəmˈpjuːtəraɪz] VT (data) traiter par ordinateur; (system, office) informatiser

computer language N langage m machine or informatique

computer literate ADJ initié(e) à l'informatique

computer peripheral N périphérique m

computer program N programme m informatique

computer programmer N programmeur(-euse)

computer programming N programmation f

computer science N informatique f

computer scientist N informaticien(ne)

computer studies NPL informatique f

computing [kəmˈpjuːtɪŋ] N informatique f

comrade [ˈkɔmrɪd] N camarade mf

comradeship [ˈkɔmrɪdʃɪp] N camaraderie f **Comsat** [ˈkɔmsæt] N ABBR = **communications satellite**

con [kɔn] VT duper; (cheat) escroquer; **to ~ sb into doing sth** tromper qn pour lui faire faire qch ▸ N escroquerie f

concave [ˈkɔnˈkeɪv] ADJ concave

conceal [kənˈsiːl] VT cacher, dissimuler

concealment [kənˈsiːlmənt] N (of person, stolen goods) recel m; (of information, documents) dissimulation f

concede [kənˈsiːd] VT concéder ▸ VI céder

conceit [kənˈsiːt] N vanité f, suffisance f, prétention f

conceited [kənˈsiːtɪd] ADJ vaniteux(-euse), suffisant(e)

conceivable [kənˈsiːvəbl] ADJ concevable, imaginable; **it is ~ that** il est concevable que

conceivably [kənˈsiːvəblɪ] ADV: **he may ~ be right** il n'est pas impossible qu'il ait raison

conceive [kənˈsiːv] VT, VI concevoir; **to ~ of sth/of doing sth** imaginer qch/de faire qch

★**concentrate** [ˈkɔnsəntreɪt] VI se concentrer ▸ VT concentrer

concentration [kɔnsənˈtreɪʃən] N concentration f

concentration camp N camp m de concentration

concentric [kɔnˈsɛntrɪk] ADJ concentrique

concept [ˈkɔnsɛpt] N concept m

conception [kənˈsɛpʃən] N conception f; (idea) idée f

conceptual [kənˈsɛptjuəl] ADJ conceptuel(le)

conceptualize [kənˈsɛptʃuəlaɪz] VT concevoir, conceptualiser

concern [kənˈsəːn] N affaire f; (Comm) entreprise f, firme f; (anxiety) inquiétude f, souci m ▸ VT (worry) inquiéter; (involve) concerner; (relate to) se rapporter à; **to be concerned (about)** s'inquiéter (de), être inquiet(-ète) (au sujet de); **"to whom it may ~"** « à qui de droit »; **as far as I am concerned** en ce qui me concerne; **to be concerned with** (person: involved with) s'occuper de; **the department concerned** (under discussion) le service en question; (involved) le service concerné

concerning [kənˈsəːnɪŋ] PREP en ce qui concerne, à propos de

★**concert** [ˈkɔnsət] N concert m; **in ~** à l'unisson, en chœur; ensemble

concerted [kənˈsəːtɪd] ADJ concerté(e)

concertgoer [ˈkɔnsətgəuəʳ] N (regular) amateur(-trice) de concerts

concert hall N salle f de concert

concertina [kɔnsəˈtiːnə] N concertina m ▸ VI se télescoper, se caramboler

concerto [kənˈtʃəːtəu] N concerto m

concession [kənˈsɛʃən] N (compromise) concession f; (reduced price) réduction f; **tax ~** dégrèvement fiscal; **"concessions"** tarif réduit

concessionaire [kənsɛʃəˈnɛəʳ] N concessionnaire mf

concessionary [kənˈsɛʃənrɪ] ADJ (ticket, fare) à tarif réduit

conciliate [kənˈsɪlɪeɪt] VT apaiser ▸ VI concilier

conciliation [kənsɪlɪˈeɪʃən] N conciliation f, apaisement m

conciliator [kənˈsɪlɪeɪtəʳ] N conciliateur(-trice)

conciliatory [kənˈsɪlɪətrɪ] ADJ conciliateur(-trice); conciliant(e)

concise [kənˈsaɪs] ADJ concis(e)

conclave [ˈkɔnkleɪv] N assemblée secrète; (Rel) conclave m

conclude [kənˈkluːd] VT conclure ▸ VI (speaker) conclure; (events): **to ~ (with)** se terminer (par)

concluding [kənˈkluːdɪŋ] ADJ (remarks etc) final(e)

conclusion [kənˈkluːʒən] N conclusion f; **to come to the ~ that** (en) conclure que

conclusive [kənˈkluːsɪv] ADJ concluant(e), définitif(-ive)

conclusively [kənˈkluːsɪvlɪ] ADV de façon concluante; **to prove sth ~** prouver qch de façon probante

concoct [kənˈkɔkt] VT confectionner, composer

concoction [kənˈkɔkʃən] N (food, drink) mélange m

concord [ˈkɔnkɔːd] N (harmony) harmonie f; (treaty) accord m

concourse [ˈkɔnkɔːs] N (hall) hall m, salle f des pas perdus; (crowd) affluence f; multitude f

concrete [ˈkɔnkriːt] N béton m ▸ ADJ concret(-ète); (Constr) en béton

concretely [ˈkɔnkriːtlɪ] ADV concrètement

concrete mixer N bétonnière f

concur [kən'kɜː^r] vi être d'accord

concurrently [kən'kʌrntlɪ] ADV simultanément

concussed [kən'kʌst] ADJ (Med) commotionné(e)

concussion [kən'kʌʃən] N (Med) commotion (cérébrale)

condemn [kən'dɛm] vt condamner

condemnation [kɔndɛm'neɪʃən] N condamnation f

condensation [kɔndɛn'seɪʃən] N condensation f

condense [kən'dɛns] vi se condenser ▸vt condenser

condensed milk [kən'dɛnst-] N lait concentré (sucré)

condescend [kɔndɪ'sɛnd] vi condescendre, s'abaisser; **to ~ to do sth** daigner faire qch

condescending [kɔndɪ'sɛndɪŋ] ADJ condescendant(e)

condiment ['kɔndɪmənt] N condiment m

★**condition** [kən'dɪʃən] N condition f; (disease) maladie f; **in good/poor ~** en bon/mauvais état; **a heart ~** une maladie cardiaque; **weather conditions** conditions fpl météorologiques; **on ~ that** à condition que + sub, à condition de ▸vt déterminer, conditionner

conditional [kən'dɪʃənl] ADJ conditionnel(le); **to be ~ upon** dépendre de

conditioner [kən'dɪʃənə^r] N (for hair) baume démêlant; (for fabrics) assouplissant m

conditioning [kən'dɪʃənɪŋ] N (of person) conditionnement m; (of hair) traitement m

condo ['kɔndəu] N (US inf) = **condominium**

condolences [kən'dəulənsɪz] NPL condoléances fpl

condom ['kɔndəm] N préservatif m

condominium [kɔndə'mɪnɪəm] N (US: building) immeuble m (en copropriété); (: rooms) appartement m (dans un immeuble en copropriété)

condone [kən'dəun] vt fermer les yeux sur, approuver (tacitement)

conducive [kən'djuːsɪv] ADJ **~ to** favorable à, qui contribue à

conduct N ['kɔndʌkt] conduite f ▸vt [kən'dʌkt] conduire; (manage) mener, diriger; (Mus) diriger; **to ~ o.s.** se conduire, se comporter

conductivity [kɔndʌk'tɪvɪtɪ] N (Elec) conductivité f

conductor [kən'dʌktə^r] N (of orchestra) chef m d'orchestre; (on bus) receveur m; (US: on train) chef de train; (Elec) conducteur m

conductress [kən'dʌktrɪs] N (on bus) receveuse f

conduit ['kɔndɪt] N conduit m, tuyau m; tube m

cone [kəun] N cône m; (for ice-cream) cornet m; (Bot) pomme f de pin, cône

confectioner [kən'fɛkʃənə^r] N (of cakes) pâtissier(-ière); (of sweets) confiseur(-euse); **~'s (shop)** confiserie-pâtisserie f

confectionery [kən'fɛkʃənrɪ] N (sweets) confiserie f; (cakes) pâtisserie f

confederate [kən'fɛdrɪt] ADJ confédéré(e) ▸N (pej) acolyte m; (US Hist) confédéré(e)

confederation [kənfɛdə'reɪʃən] N confédération f

confer [kən'fɜː^r] vt: **to ~ sth on** conférer qch à ▸vi conférer, s'entretenir; **to ~ (with sb about sth)** s'entretenir (de qch avec qn)

conference ['kɔnfərns] N conférence f; **to be in ~** être en réunion or en conférence

conference room N salle f de conférence

confess [kən'fɛs] vt confesser, avouer ▸vi (admit sth) avouer; (Rel) se confesser

confession [kən'fɛʃən] N confession f

confessional [kən'fɛʃənl] N confessional m

confessor [kən'fɛsə^r] N confesseur m

confetti [kən'fɛtɪ] N confettis mpl

confidant [kɔnfɪ'dænt] N confident m

confidante [kɔnfɪ'dænt] N confidente f

confide [kən'faɪd] vi: **to ~ in** s'ouvrir à, se confier à

★**confidence** ['kɔnfɪdns] N confiance f; (also: **self-confidence**) assurance f, confiance en soi; (secret) confidence f; **to have (every) ~ that** être certain que; **motion of no ~** motion f de censure; **in ~** (speak, write) en confidence, confidentiellement; **to tell sb sth in strict ~** dire qch à qn en toute confidence

confidence trick N escroquerie f

confident ['kɔnfɪdənt] ADJ (self-assured) sûr(e) de soi; (sure) sûr(e)

confidential [kɔnfɪ'dɛnʃəl] ADJ confidentiel(le)

confidentiality ['kɔnfɪdɛnʃɪ'ælɪtɪ] N confidentialité f

confidentially [kɔnfɪ'dɛnʃəlɪ] ADV (secretly) confidentiellement; (quietly: say, speak) sur un ton confidentiel

configuration [kənfɪgju'reɪʃən] N (also Comput) configuration f

configure [kən'fɪgə^r] vt (Comput) configurer

confine [kən'faɪn] vt limiter, borner; (shut up) confiner, enfermer; **to ~ o.s. to doing sth/to sth** se contenter de faire qch/se limiter à qch

confined [kən'faɪnd] ADJ (space) restreint(e), réduit(e)

confinement [kən'faɪnmənt] N emprisonnement m, détention f; (Mil) consigne f (au quartier); (Med) accouchement m

confines ['kɔnfaɪnz] NPL confins mpl, bornes fpl

★**confirm** [kən'fɜːm] vt (report, Rel) confirmer; (appointment) ratifier

confirmation [kɔnfə'meɪʃən] N confirmation f; ratification f

confirmed [kən'fɜːmd] ADJ invétéré(e), incorrigible

confiscate ['kɔnfɪskeɪt] vt confisquer

confiscation [kɔnfɪs'keɪʃən] N confiscation f

conflagration [kɔnflə'greɪʃən] N incendie m; (fig) conflagration f

conflict N ['kɔnflɪkt] conflit m, lutte f ▸vi [kən'flɪkt] être or entrer en conflit; (opinions) s'opposer, se heurter

conflicting [kən'flɪktɪŋ] ADJ contradictoire

confluence ['kɔnfluəns] N confluence f

conform [kən'fɔːm] vi: **to ~ (to)** se conformer (à)

conformist [kən'fɔːmɪst] N (gen, Rel) conformiste mf

conformity [kən'fɔːmɪtɪ] N conformisme m; **in ~ with** conformément à

confound [kən'faund] vt confondre; (amaze) rendre perplexe

confounded [kən'faundɪd] ADJ maudit(e), sacré(e)

confront [kən'frʌnt] VT (*two people*) confronter; (*enemy, danger*) affronter, faire face à; (*problem*) faire face à

confrontation [kɔnfrən'teɪʃən] N confrontation *f*

confrontational [kɔnfrən'teɪʃənl] ADJ conflictuel(le)

confuse [kən'fjuːz] VT (*person*) troubler; (*situation*) embrouiller; (*one thing with another*) confondre

confused [kən'fjuːzd] ADJ (*person*) dérouté(e), désorienté(e); (*situation*) embrouillé(e)

confusing [kən'fjuːzɪŋ] ADJ peu clair(e), déroutant(e)

confusion [kən'fjuːʒən] N confusion *f*

congeal [kən'dʒiːl] VI (*oil*) se figer; (*blood*) se coaguler

congenial [kən'dʒiːnɪəl] ADJ sympathique, agréable

congenital [kən'dʒɛnɪtl] ADJ congénital(e)

conger eel ['kɔŋgər-] N congre *m*, anguille *f* de roche

congested [kən'dʒɛstɪd] ADJ (*Med*) congestionné(e); (*fig*) surpeuplé(e); congestionné; bloqué(e); (*telephone lines*) encombré(e)

congestion [kən'dʒɛstʃən] N (*Med*) congestion *f*; (*fig: traffic*) encombrement *m*

conglomerate [kən'glɔmərɪt] N (*Comm*) conglomérat *m*

conglomeration [kənglɔmə'reɪʃən] N groupement *m*; agglomération *f*

Congo ['kɔŋgəu] N (*state*) (république *f* du) Congo

congratulate [kən'grætjuleɪt] VT: **to ~ sb (on)** féliciter qn (de)

★**congratulations** [kəngrætju'leɪʃənz] NPL: **~ (on)** félicitations *fpl* (pour) ▶ EXCL: **~!** (toutes mes) félicitations !

congratulatory [kəngrætʃu'leɪtərɪ] ADJ (*message, letter*) de félicitations

congregate ['kɔŋgrɪgeɪt] VI se rassembler, se réunir

congregation [kɔŋgrɪ'geɪʃən] N assemblée *f* (des fidèles)

congress ['kɔŋgrɛs] N congrès *m*; (*Pol*): **C~** Congrès *m*

> Le **Congress** est le parlement des États-Unis. Il comprend la *House of Representatives* et le *Senate*. Représentants et sénateurs sont élus au suffrage universel direct. Le Congrès se réunit au *Capitol*, à Washington D.C.

congressional [kən'grɛʃənl] ADJ (*Pol: policy, action, leader*) du Congrès

congressman ['kɔŋgrɛsmən] N (*irreg*) (*Pol*) membre *m* du Congrès

congresswoman ['kɔŋgrɛswumən] N (*irreg*) (*Pol*) membre *m* du Congrès

conical ['kɔnɪkl] ADJ (*de forme*) conique

conifer ['kɔnɪfər] N conifère *m*

coniferous [kə'nɪfərəs] ADJ (*forest*) de conifères

conjecture [kən'dʒɛktʃər] N conjecture *f* ▶ VT, VI conjecturer

conjugal ['kɔndʒugl] ADJ conjugal(e)

conjugate ['kɔndʒugeɪt] VT conjuguer

conjugation [kɔndʒə'geɪʃən] N conjugaison *f*

conjunction [kən'dʒʌŋkʃən] N conjonction *f*; **in ~ with** (conjointement) avec

conjunctivitis [kəndʒʌŋktɪ'vaɪtɪs] N conjonctivite *f*

conjure VT ['kʌndʒər] (*by magic*) faire apparaître (par la prestidigitation); [kən'dʒuər] conjurer, supplier ▶ VI ['kʌndʒər] faire des tours de passe-passe

▶ **conjure up** VT (*ghost, spirit*) faire apparaître; (*memories*) évoquer

conjurer ['kʌndʒərər] N prestidigitateur(-trice), illusionniste *mf*

conjuring trick ['kʌndʒərɪŋ-] N tour *m* de prestidigitation

conker ['kɔŋkər] N (*BRIT*) marron *m* (d'Inde)

conk out [kɔŋk-] VI (*inf*) tomber *or* rester en panne

conman ['kɔnmæn] N (*irreg*) escroc *m*

connect [kə'nɛkt] VT joindre, relier; (*Elec*) connecter; (*Tel: caller*) mettre en connexion; (*: subscriber*) brancher; (*fig*) établir un rapport entre, faire un rapprochement entre; **I am trying to ~ you** (*Tel*) j'essaie d'obtenir votre communication ▶ VI (*train*): **to ~ with** assurer la correspondance avec

connected [kə'nɛktɪd] ADJ (*electrical devices*) relié(e); (*associated: people, events*) associé(e); (*causally linked*) lié(e); **to be ~ with sth** (*person*) être associé(e) à qch; (*problem, condition*) être lié(e) à qch

connecting flight N (*vol m* de) correspondance *f*

★**connection** [kə'nɛkʃən] N relation *f*, lien *m*; (*Elec*) connexion *f*; (*Tel*) communication *f*; (*train etc*) correspondance *f*; **in ~ with** à propos de; **what is the ~ between them?** quel est le lien entre eux ?; **business connections** relations d'affaires; **to miss/make one's ~** (*train etc*) rater/avoir sa correspondance

connection charge, connection fee N frais *mpl* de raccordement

connectivity [kɔnɛk'tɪvətɪ] N (*Comput*) connectivité *f*

connexion [kə'nɛkʃən] N (*BRIT*) = **connection**

conning tower ['kɔnɪŋ-] N kiosque *m* (*de sous-marin*)

connivance [kə'naɪvəns] N connivence *f*; **with the ~ of sb** avec l'accord tacite de qn, avec la connivence de qn

connive [kə'naɪv] VI: **to ~ with sb to do sth** être de connivence avec qn pour faire qch; **to ~ at** se faire le complice de

conniving [kə'naɪvɪŋ] ADJ intrigant(e)

connoisseur [kɔnɪ'səːr] N connaisseur(-euse)

connotation [kɔnə'teɪʃən] N connotation *f*, implication *f*

connubial [kə'njuːbɪəl] ADJ conjugal(e)

conquer ['kɔŋkər] VT conquérir; (*feelings*) vaincre, surmonter

conqueror ['kɔŋkərər] N conquérant(e), vainqueur *m*

conquest ['kɔŋkwɛst] N conquête *f*

cons [kɔnz] NPL *see* **convenience**; **pro**

conscience ['kɔnʃəns] N conscience *f*; **in all ~** en conscience

conscientious [kɔnʃɪ'ɛnʃəs] ADJ consciencieux(-euse); (*scruple, objection*) de conscience

conscientiously [kɒnʃɪ'ɛnʃəslɪ] ADV consciencieusement

conscientious objector N objecteur *m* de conscience

★**conscious** ['kɒnʃəs] ADJ conscient(e); (*deliberate: insult, error*) délibéré(e); **to become ~ of sth/that** prendre conscience de qch/que

consciousness ['kɒnʃəsnɪs] N conscience *f*; (*Med*) connaissance *f*; **to lose/regain ~** perdre/reprendre connaissance

conscript ['kɒnskrɪpt] N conscrit *m*

conscription [kən'skrɪpʃən] N conscription *f*

consecrate ['kɒnsɪkreɪt] VT consacrer

consecutive [kən'sɛkjʊtɪv] ADJ consécutif(-ive); **on three ~ occasions** trois fois de suite

consecutively [kən'sɛkjʊtɪvlɪ] ADV consécutivement

consensual [kən'sɛnsjuəl] ADJ (*approach, decision*) consensuel(le); (*sex*) consenti(e)

consensus [kən'sɛnsəs] N consensus *m*; **the ~ (of opinion)** le consensus (d'opinion)

consent [kən'sɛnt] N consentement *m*; **age of ~** âge nubile (légal); **by common ~** d'un commun accord ▸ VI: **to ~ (to)** consentir (à)

consenting adults [kən'sɛntɪŋ-] NPL personnes consentantes

★**consequence** ['kɒnsɪkwəns] N suites *fpl*, conséquence *f*; (*significance*) importance *f*; **in ~** en conséquence, par conséquent

consequent ['kɒnsɪkwənt] ADJ résultant(e)

consequently ['kɒnsɪkwəntlɪ] ADV par conséquent, donc

conservation [kɒnsə'veɪʃən] N préservation *f*, protection *f*; (*also:* **nature conservation**) défense *f* de l'environnement; **energy ~** économies *fpl* d'énergie

conservationist [kɒnsə'veɪʃnɪst] N protecteur(-trice) de la nature

Conservative [kən'sə:vətɪv] ADJ, N (*BRIT Pol*) conservateur(-trice); **the ~ Party** le parti conservateur

★**conservative** [kən'sə:vətɪv] ADJ conservateur(-trice); (*cautious*) prudent(e)

conservatory [kən'sə:vətrɪ] N (*room*) jardin *m* d'hiver; (*Mus*) conservatoire *m*

conserve [kən'sə:v] VT conserver, préserver; (*supplies, energy*) économiser ▸ N confiture *f*, conserve *f* (de fruits)

★**consider** [kən'sɪdə'] VT (*study*) considérer, réfléchir à; (*take into account*) penser à, prendre en considération; (*regard, judge*) considérer, estimer; **to ~ doing sth** envisager de faire qch; **~ yourself lucky** estimez-vous heureux; **all things considered** (toute) réflexion faite

considerable [kən'sɪdərəbl] ADJ considérable

considerably [kən'sɪdərəblɪ] ADV nettement

considerate [kən'sɪdərɪt] ADJ prévenant(e), plein(e) d'égards

consideration [kənsɪdə'reɪʃən] N considération *f*; (*reward*) rétribution *f*, rémunération *f*; **out of ~ for** par égard pour; **under ~** à l'étude; **my first ~ is my family** ma famille passe avant tout le reste

considered [kən'sɪdəd] ADJ: **it is my ~ opinion that …** après avoir mûrement réfléchi, je pense que …

considering [kən'sɪdərɪŋ] PREP: **~ (that)** étant donné (que)

consign [kən'saɪn] VT expédier, livrer

consignee [kɒnsaɪ'ni:] N destinataire *mf*

consignment [kən'saɪnmənt] N arrivage *m*, envoi *m*

consignment note N (*Comm*) bordereau *m* d'expédition

consignor [kən'saɪnə'] N expéditeur(-trice)

consist [kən'sɪst] VI: **to ~ of** consister en, se composer de

consistency [kən'sɪstənsɪ] N (*thickness*) consistance *f*; (*fig*) cohérence *f*

consistent [kən'sɪstənt] ADJ logique, cohérent(e); **~ with** compatible avec, en accord avec

consistently [kən'sɪstəntlɪ] ADV (*always*) toujours

consolation [kɒnsə'leɪʃən] N consolation *f*

console¹ [kən'səul] VT consoler

console² ['kɒnsəul] N console *f*

consolidate [kən'sɒlɪdeɪt] VT consolider

consolidation [kənsɒlɪ'deɪʃən] N (*of power, position*) consolidation *f*; (*amalgamation: of groups, firms*) fusion *f*

consols ['kɒnsɒlz] NPL (*BRIT Stock Exchange*) rente *f* d'État

consommé [kən'sɒmeɪ] N consommé *m*

consonant ['kɒnsənənt] N consonne *f*

consort N ['kɒnsɔ:t] époux (épouse); **prince ~** prince *m* consort ▸ VI [kən'sɔ:t] (*often pej*): **to ~ with sb** frayer avec qn

consortium [kən'sɔ:tɪəm] N consortium *m*, comptoir *m*

conspicuous [kən'spɪkjuəs] ADJ voyant(e), qui attire l'attention; **to make o.s. ~** se faire remarquer

conspiracy [kən'spɪrəsɪ] N conspiration *f*, complot *m*

conspirator [kən'spɪrətə'] N conspirateur(-trice)

conspiratorial [kən'spɪrə'tɔ:rɪəl] ADJ (*behaviour*) de conspirateur; (*glance*) conspirateur(-trice)

conspire [kən'spaɪə'] VI conspirer, comploter

constable ['kʌnstəbl] N (*BRIT*) ≈ agent *m* de police, gendarme *m*; **chief ~** ≈ préfet *m* de police

constabulary [kən'stæbjulərɪ] N ≈ police *f*, gendarmerie *f*

★**constant** ['kɒnstənt] ADJ constant(e); incessant(e)

constantly ['kɒnstəntlɪ] ADV constamment, sans cesse

constellation [kɒnstə'leɪʃən] N constellation *f*

consternation [kɒnstə'neɪʃən] N consternation *f*

constipated ['kɒnstɪpeɪtɪd] ADJ constipé(e)

constipation [kɒnstɪ'peɪʃən] N constipation *f*

constituency [kən'stɪtjuənsɪ] N (*Pol: area*) circonscription électorale; (*: electors*) électorat *m*

constituency party N section locale (d'un parti)

constituent [kən'stɪtjuənt] N électeur(-trice); (*part*) élément constitutif, composant *m*

constitute ['kɒnstɪtju:t] VT constituer

constitution [kɔnstɪ'tju:ʃən] N constitution f

constitutional [kɔnstɪ'tju:ʃənl] ADJ constitutionnel(le)

constitutional monarchy N monarchie constitutionnelle

constrain [kən'streɪn] VT contraindre, forcer

constrained [kən'streɪnd] ADJ contraint(e), gêné(e)

constraint [kən'streɪnt] N contrainte f; (embarrassment) gêne f

constrict [kən'strɪkt] VT rétrécir, resserrer; gêner, limiter

construct [kən'strʌkt] VT construire

construction [kən'strʌkʃən] N construction f; (fig: interpretation) interprétation f; **under ~** (building etc) en construction

construction industry N (industrie f du) bâtiment

constructive [kən'strʌktɪv] ADJ constructif(-ive)

construe [kən'stru:] VT analyser, expliquer

consul ['kɔnsl] N consul m

consular ['kɔnsjulə'] ADJ consulaire

consulate ['kɔnsjulɪt] N consulat m

★**consult** [kən'sʌlt] VT consulter; **to ~ sb (about sth)** consulter qn (à propos de qch)

consultancy [kən'sʌltənsɪ] N service m de conseils

consultancy fee N honoraires mpl d'expert

consultant [kən'sʌltənt] N (Med) médecin consultant; (other specialist) consultant m, (expert-)conseil m; **legal/management ~** conseiller m juridique/en gestion ▶ CPD: **~ engineer** n ingénieur-conseil mf; **~ paediatrician** n pédiatre mf

consultation [kɔnsəl'teɪʃən] N consultation f; **in ~ with** en consultation avec

consultative [kən'sʌltətɪv] ADJ consultatif(-ive)

consulting room [kən'sʌltɪŋ-] N (BRIT) cabinet m de consultation

consume [kən'sju:m] VT consommer; (subj: flames, hatred, desire) consumer; **to be consumed with hatred** être dévoré par la haine; **to be consumed with desire** brûler de désir

★**consumer** [kən'sju:mə'] N consommateur(-trice); (of electricity, gas etc) usager m

consumer credit N crédit m aux consommateurs

consumer durables NPL biens mpl de consommation durables

consumer goods NPL biens mpl de consommation

consumerism [kən'sju:mərɪzəm] N (consumer protection) défense f du consommateur; (Econ) consumérisme m

consumerist [kən'sju:mərɪst] ADJ (pej: society) consumériste

consumer society N société f de consommation

consumer watchdog N organisme m pour la défense des consommateurs

consummate ['kɔnsəmeɪt] VT consommer

consummation [kɔnsə'meɪʃən] N consommation f

consumption [kən'sʌmpʃən] N consommation f; **not fit for human ~** non comestible

cont. ABBR (= continued) suite

★**contact** ['kɔntækt] N contact m; (person) connaissance f, relation f; **to be in ~ with sb/sth** être en contact avec qn/qch; **business contacts** relations fpl d'affaires, contacts mpl ▶ CPD: **~ number** numéro m de téléphone ▶ VT se mettre en contact or en rapport avec

contact lenses NPL verres mpl de contact

contactless ['kɔntæktlɪs] ADJ sans contact

contagion [kən'teɪdʒən] N contagion f

contagious [kən'teɪdʒəs] ADJ contagieux(-euse)

★**contain** [kən'teɪn] VT contenir; **to ~ o.s.** se contenir, se maîtriser

container [kən'teɪnə'] N récipient m; (for shipping etc) conteneur m

containerize [kən'teɪnəraɪz] VT conteneuriser

container ship N porte-conteneurs m inv

containment [kən'teɪnmənt] N (policy) endiguement m; (of fire, disease) maîtrise f

contaminate [kən'tæmɪneɪt] VT contaminer

contamination [kəntæmɪ'neɪʃən] N contamination f

contemplate ['kɔntəmpleɪt] VT contempler; (consider) envisager

contemplation [kɔntəm'pleɪʃən] N contemplation f

contemporaneous [kəntempə'reɪnɪəs] ADJ contemporain(e)

contemporary [kən'tempərərɪ] ADJ contemporain(e); (design, wallpaper) moderne ▶ N contemporain(e)

contempt [kən'tempt] N mépris m, dédain m; **~ of court** (Law) outrage m à l'autorité de la justice

contemptible [kən'temptəbl] ADJ méprisable, vil(e)

contemptuous [kən'temptjuəs] ADJ dédaigneux(-euse), méprisant(e)

contemptuously [kən'temptjuəslɪ] ADV (say) avec mépris

contend [kən'tend] VT: **to ~ that** soutenir or prétendre que ▶ VI: **to ~ with** (compete) rivaliser avec; (struggle) lutter avec; **to have to ~ with** (be faced with) avoir affaire à, être aux prises avec

contender [kən'tendə'] N prétendant(e); candidat(e)

content ADJ [kən'tent] content(e), satisfait(e); **to be ~ with** se contenter de ▶ VT [kən'tent] contenter, satisfaire; **to ~ o.s. with sth/with doing sth** se contenter de qch/de faire qch ▶ N ['kɔntent] (also Comput) contenu m; (of fat, moisture) teneur f ▪ **contents** NPL (of container etc) contenu m; **(table of) contents** table f des matières

contented [kən'tentɪd] ADJ content(e), satisfait(e)

contentedly [kən'tentɪdlɪ] ADV avec un sentiment de (profonde) satisfaction

contention [kən'tenʃən] N dispute f, contestation f; (argument) assertion f, affirmation f; **bone of ~** sujet m de discorde

contentious [kən'tenʃəs] ADJ querelleur(-euse); litigieux(-euse)

contentment [kən'tɛntmənt] N contentement m, satisfaction f

★**contest** N ['kɔntɛst] combat m, lutte f; (*competition*) concours m ▶ VT [kən'tɛst] contester, discuter; (*compete for*) disputer; (*Law*) attaquer

contestant [kən'tɛstənt] N concurrent(e); (*in fight*) adversaire mf

★**context** ['kɔntɛkst] N contexte m; **in/out of ~** dans le/hors contexte

contiguous [kən'tɪgjuəs] ADJ (*formal*) contigu(ë); **to be ~ with sth** être contigu(ë) à qch, être attenant(e) à qch

★**continent** ['kɔntɪnənt] N continent m; **the C~** (*BRIT*) l'Europe continentale; **on the C~** en Europe (continentale)

continental [kɔntɪ'nɛntl] ADJ continental(e) ▶ N (*BRIT*) Européen(ne) (continental(e))

continental breakfast N petit déjeuner m continental

continental quilt N (*BRIT*) couette f

contingency [kən'tɪndʒənsɪ] N éventualité f, événement imprévu

contingency plan N plan m d'urgence

contingent [kən'tɪndʒənt] ADJ contingent(e); **to be ~ upon** dépendre de ▶ N contingent m

continual [kən'tɪnjuəl] ADJ continuel(le)

continually [kən'tɪnjuəlɪ] ADV continuellement, sans cesse

continuance [kən'tɪnjuəns] N (*of situation*) continuation f; (*of species*) continuité f

continuation [kəntɪnju'eɪʃən] N continuation f; (*after interruption*) reprise f; (*of story*) suite f

★**continue** [kən'tɪnju:] VI continuer ▶ VT continuer; (*start again*) reprendre; **to be continued** (*story*) à suivre; **continued on page 10** suite page 10

continuing education [kən'tɪnjuɪŋ-] N formation permanente or continue

continuity [kɔntɪ'nju:ɪtɪ] N continuité f; (*TV*) enchaînement m; (*Cine*) script m

continuity girl N (*Cine*) script-girl f

continuous [kən'tɪnjuəs] ADJ continu(e), permanent(e); (*Ling*) progressif(-ive); **~ performance** (*Cine*) séance permanente; **~ stationery** (*Comput*) papier m en continu

continuous assessment N (*BRIT*) contrôle continu

continuously [kən'tɪnjuəslɪ] ADV (*repeatedly*) continuellement; (*uninterruptedly*) sans interruption

contort [kən'tɔ:t] VT tordre, crisper

contortion [kən'tɔ:ʃən] N crispation f, torsion f; (*of acrobat*) contorsion f

contortionist [kən'tɔ:ʃənɪst] N contorsionniste mf

contour ['kɔntuə'] N contour m, profil m; (*also:* **contour line**) courbe f de niveau

contraband ['kɔntrəbænd] N contrebande f ▶ ADJ de contrebande

contraception [kɔntrə'sɛpʃən] N contraception f

contraceptive [kɔntrə'sɛptɪv] ADJ contraceptif(-ive), anticonceptionnel(le) ▶ N contraceptif m

★**contract** N ['kɔntrækt] contrat m; **~ of employment/service** contrat de travail/de service ▶ CPD (*price, date*) contractuel(le); (*work*) à forfait

▶ VI [kən'trækt] (*become smaller*) se contracter, se resserrer; **to ~ to do sth** (*Comm*) s'engager (par contrat) à faire qch ▶ VT contracter

▶ **contract in** VI s'engager (par contrat); (*BRIT Admin*) s'affilier au régime de retraite complémentaire

▶ **contract out** VI se dégager; (*BRIT Admin*) opter pour la non-affiliation au régime de retraite complémentaire

contraction [kən'trækʃən] N contraction f; (*Ling*) forme contractée

contractor [kən'træktə'] N entrepreneur(-euse)

contractual [kən'træktʃuəl] ADJ contractuel(le)

contractually [kən'træktʃuəlɪ] ADV contractuellement

contradict [kɔntrə'dɪkt] VT contredire; (*be contrary to*) démentir, être en contradiction avec

contradiction [kɔntrə'dɪkʃən] N contradiction f; **to be in ~ with** contredire, être en contradiction avec

contradictory [kɔntrə'dɪktərɪ] ADJ contradictoire

contraflow ['kɔntrəfləu] N (*Aut*) **~ lane** voie f à contresens; **there's a ~ system in operation on ...** une voie a été mise en sens inverse sur ...

contraindication ['kɔntraɪndɪ'keɪʃən] N (*Med*) contre-indication f

contralto [kən'træltəu] N contralto m

contraption [kən'træpʃən] N (*pej*) machin m, truc m

contrary[1] ['kɔntrərɪ] ADJ contraire, opposé(e) ▶ N contraire m; **on the ~** au contraire; **unless you hear to the ~** sauf avis contraire ▶ ADV: **~ to what we thought** contrairement à ce que nous pensions

contrary[2] [kən'trɛərɪ] ADJ (*perverse*) contrariant(e), entêté(e)

★**contrast** N ['kɔntrɑ:st] contraste m; **in ~ to** or **with** contrairement à, par opposition à ▶ VT [kən'trɑ:st] mettre en contraste, contraster

contrasting [kən'trɑ:stɪŋ] ADJ opposé(e), contrasté(e)

contravene [kɔntrə'vi:n] VT enfreindre, violer, contrevenir à

contravention [kɔntrə'vɛnʃən] N: **~ (of)** infraction f (à)

★**contribute** [kən'trɪbju:t] VI contribuer; **to ~ to** (*gen*) contribuer à; (*newspaper*) collaborer à; (*discussion*) prendre part à ▶ VT: **to ~ £10/an article to** donner 10 livres/un article à

★**contribution** [kɔntrɪ'bju:ʃən] N contribution f; (*BRIT: for social security*) cotisation f; (*to publication*) article m

contributor [kən'trɪbjutə'] N (*to newspaper*) collaborateur(-trice); (*of money, goods*) donateur(-trice)

contributory [kən'trɪbjutərɪ] ADJ (*cause*) annexe; **it was a ~ factor in ...** ce facteur a contribué à ...

contributory pension scheme N (*BRIT*) régime m de retraite salariale

contrite ['kɔntraɪt] ADJ contrit(e)

contrition [kən'trɪʃən] N remords m

contrivance [kən'traɪvəns] N (*scheme*) machination f, combinaison f; (*device*) appareil m, dispositif m

contrive [kən'traɪv] VT combiner, inventer ▶ VI: **to ~ to do** s'arranger pour faire, trouver le moyen de faire

contrived [kən'traɪvd] ADJ (pej: not spontaneous) forcé(e); (: unconvincing: plot) tiré(e) par les cheveux

★**control** [kən'trəʊl] VT (process, machinery) commander; (temper) maîtriser; (disease) enrayer; (check) contrôler; **to ~ o.s.** se contrôler ▶ N maîtrise f; (power) autorité f; **to take ~ of** se rendre maître de; (Comm) acquérir une participation majoritaire dans; **to be in ~ of** être maître de, maîtriser; (in charge of) être responsable de; **everything is under ~** j'ai (or il a etc) la situation en main; **the car went out of ~** j'ai (or il a etc) perdu le contrôle de la voiture; **beyond our ~** indépendant(e) de notre volonté ■ **controls** NPL (of machine etc) commandes fpl; (on radio) boutons mpl de réglage

control key N (Comput) touche f contrôle

controlled drug, controlled substance N substance f inscrite au tableau

controller [kən'trəʊlər] N contrôleur(-euse)

controlling interest [kən'trəʊlɪŋ-] N (Comm) participation f majoritaire

control panel N (on aircraft, ship, TV etc) tableau m de commandes

control point N (poste m de) contrôle m

control room N (Naut, Mil) salle f des commandes; (Radio, TV) régie f

control tower N (Aviat) tour f de contrôle

control unit N (Comput) unité f de contrôle

★**controversial** [kɒntrə'vəːʃl] ADJ discutable, controversé(e)

controversy ['kɒntrəvəːsɪ] N controverse f, polémique f

conundrum [kə'nʌndrəm] N énigme f

conurbation [kɒnə'beɪʃən] N conurbation f

convalesce [kɒnvə'lɛs] VI relever de maladie, se remettre (d'une maladie)

convalescence [kɒnvə'lɛsns] N convalescence f

convalescent [kɒnvə'lɛsnt] ADJ, N convalescent(e)

convector [kən'vɛktər] N radiateur m à convection, appareil m de chauffage par convection

convene [kən'viːn] VT convoquer, assembler ▶ VI se réunir, s'assembler

convener, convenor [kən'viːnər] N responsable mf des convocations

convenience [kən'viːnɪəns] N commodité f; **at your ~** quand or comme cela vous convient; **at your earliest ~** (Comm) dans les meilleurs délais, le plus tôt possible; **all modern conveniences, all mod cons** (BRIT) avec tout le confort moderne, tout confort

convenience foods NPL plats cuisinés

convenient [kən'viːnɪənt] ADJ commode; **if it is ~ to you** si cela vous convient, si cela ne vous dérange pas

conveniently [kən'viːnɪəntlɪ] ADV (happen) à pic; (situated) commodément

convent ['kɒnvənt] N couvent m

convention [kən'vɛnʃən] N convention f; (custom) usage m

conventional [kən'vɛnʃənl] ADJ conventionnel(le)

conventionally [kən'vɛnʃənlɪ] ADV (dress, produce) de manière conventionnelle; (beautiful, handsome) classiquement

convent school N couvent m

converge [kən'vəːdʒ] VI converger

convergence [kən'vəːdʒəns] N convergence f

conversant [kən'vəːsnt] ADJ: **to be ~ with** s'y connaître en; être au courant de

★**conversation** [kɒnvə'seɪʃən] N conversation f

conversational [kɒnvə'seɪʃənl] ADJ de la conversation; (Comput) conversationnel(le)

conversationalist [kɒnvə'seɪʃnəlɪst] N brillant(e) causeur(-euse)

converse N ['kɒnvəːs] contraire m, inverse m ▶ VI [kən'vəːs]: **to ~ (with sb about sth)** s'entretenir (avec qn de qch)

conversely [kɒn'vəːslɪ] ADV inversement, réciproquement

conversion [kən'vəːʃən] N conversion f; (BRIT: of house) transformation f, aménagement m; (Rugby) transformation f

conversion table N table f de conversion

convert VT [kən'vəːt] (Rel, Comm) convertir; (alter) transformer; (house) aménager; (Rugby) transformer ▶ N ['kɒnvəːt] converti(e)

converter [kən'vəːtər] N convertisseur m

convertible [kən'vəːtəbl] ADJ convertible ▶ N (voiture f) décapotable f

convex ['kɒn'vɛks] ADJ convexe

convey [kən'veɪ] VT transporter; (thanks) transmettre; (idea) communiquer

conveyance [kən'veɪəns] N (of goods) transport m de marchandises; (vehicle) moyen m de transport

conveyancing [kən'veɪənsɪŋ] N (Law) rédaction f des actes de cession de propriété

conveyor belt [kən'veɪər-] N convoyeur m tapis roulant

convict VT [kən'vɪkt] déclarer (or reconnaître) coupable ▶ N ['kɒnvɪkt] forçat m, convict m

conviction [kən'vɪkʃən] N (Law) condamnation f; (belief) conviction f

★**convince** [kən'vɪns] VT convaincre, persuader; **to ~ sb (of sth/that)** persuader qn (de qch/que)

convinced [kən'vɪnst] ADJ: **~ of/that** convaincu(e) de/que

convincing [kən'vɪnsɪŋ] ADJ persuasif(-ive), convaincant(e)

convincingly [kən'vɪnsɪŋlɪ] ADV de façon convaincante

convivial [kən'vɪvɪəl] ADJ joyeux(-euse), plein(e) d'entrain

convoluted ['kɒnvəluːtɪd] ADJ (shape) tarabiscoté(e); (argument) compliqué(e)

convoy ['kɒnvɔɪ] N convoi m

convulse [kən'vʌls] VT ébranler; **to be convulsed with laughter** se tordre de rire

convulsion [kən'vʌlʃən] N convulsion f

COO N ABBR (= chief operating officer) président(e)

coo [kuː] VI roucouler

★**cook** [kuk] VT (faire) cuire ▶ VI cuire; (person) faire la cuisine ▶ N cuisinier(-ière)
  ▶ **cook up** VT (inf: excuse, story) inventer

cookbook ['kukbuk] N livre m de cuisine

★**cooker** ['kukə^r] N cuisinière f

cookery ['kukərı] N cuisine f

cookery book N (Brit) = **cookbook**

cookie ['kukı] N (US) biscuit m, petit gâteau sec; (Comput) cookie m, témoin m de connexion

cooking ['kukıŋ] N cuisine f ▸ CPD (apples, chocolate) à cuire; (utensils, salt) de cuisine

cookout ['kukaut] N (US) barbecue m

cookware ['kukwɛə^r] N batterie f de cuisine

★**cool** [ku:l] ADJ frais (fraîche); (not afraid) calme; (unfriendly) froid(e); (impertinent) effronté(e); (inf: trendy) cool inv (inf); (: great) super inv (inf); **it's ~** (weather) il fait frais; **to keep sth ~** or **in a ~ place** garder or conserver qch au frais ▸ VT, VI rafraîchir, refroidir
   ▸ **cool down** VI refroidir; (fig: person, situation) se calmer
   ▸ **cool off** VI (become calmer) se calmer; (lose enthusiasm) perdre son enthousiasme

coolant ['ku:lənt] N liquide m de refroidissement

cool box, (US) **cooler** ['ku:lə^r] N boîte f isotherme

cooling ['ku:lıŋ] ADJ (breeze) rafraîchissant(e)

cooling tower N refroidisseur m

coolly ['ku:lı] ADV (calmly) calmement; (audaciously) sans se gêner; (unenthusiastically) froidement

coolness ['ku:lnıs] N fraîcheur f; sang-froid m, calme m; froideur f

coop [ku:p] N poulailler m
   ▸ **coop up** VT (fig) cloîtrer, enfermer

co-op ['kəuɔp] N ABBR (= cooperative (society)) coop f

cooperate [kəu'ɔpəreıt] VI coopérer, collaborer

cooperation [kəuɔpə'reıʃən] N coopération f, collaboration f

cooperative [kəu'ɔpərətıv] ADJ coopératif(-ive)
   ▸ N coopérative f

coopt [kəu'ɔpt] VT: **to ~ sb onto a committee** coopter qn pour faire partie d'un comité

coordinate VT [kəu'ɔ:dıneıt] coordonner ▸ N [kəu'ɔdınət] (Math) coordonnée f ■ **coordinates** NPL (clothes) ensemble m, coordonnés mpl

coordination [kəuɔ:dı'neıʃən] N coordination f

coordinator [kəu'ɔ:dıneıtə^r] N coordinateur(-trice)

coot [ku:t] N foulque f

co-ownership ['kəu'əunəʃıp] N copropriété f

cop [kɔp] N (inf) flic m

coparent [kəu'pɛərənt] N coparent m ▸ VT élever en coparentalité

coparenting [kəu'pɛərəntıŋ] N coparentalité f

cope [kəup] VI s'en sortir, tenir le coup; **to ~ with** (problem) faire face à; (take care of) s'occuper de

Copenhagen ['kəupn'heıgən] N Copenhague

copier ['kɔpıə^r] N (also: **photocopier**) copieur m

co-pilot ['kəu'paılət] N copilote mf

copious ['kəupıəs] ADJ copieux(-euse), abondant(e)

copper ['kɔpə^r] N cuivre m; (Brit inf: police officer) flic m ■ **coppers** NPL (Brit) petite monnaie

coppice ['kɔpıs], **copse** [kɔps] N taillis m

copulate ['kɔpjuleıt] VI copuler

★**copy** ['kɔpı] N copie f; (book etc) exemplaire m; (material: for printing) copie f; **rough ~** (gen) premier jet; (Scol) brouillon m; **fair ~** version définitive; propre m; **to make good ~** (Press) faire un bon sujet d'article ▸ VT copier; (imitate) imiter
   ▸ **copy out** VT copier

copycat ['kɔpıkæt] N (pej) copieur(-euse)

copyright ['kɔpıraıt] N droit m d'auteur, copyright m; **~ reserved** tous droits (de reproduction) réservés

copy typist N dactylo mf

copywriter ['kɔpıraıtə^r] N rédacteur(-trice) publicitaire

coracle ['kɔrəkl] N coracle m

coral ['kɔrəl] N corail m

coral reef N récif m de corail

Coral Sea N: **the ~** la mer de Corail

cord [kɔːd] N corde f; (fabric) velours côtelé; (Elec) cordon m (d'alimentation), fil m (électrique) ■ **cords** NPL (trousers) pantalon m de velours côtelé

cordial ['kɔːdıəl] ADJ cordial(e), chaleureux(-euse)
   ▸ N sirop m; cordial m

cordially ['kɔːdıəlı] ADV chaleureusement

cordless ['kɔːdlıs] ADJ sans fil

cordon ['kɔːdn] N cordon m
   ▸ **cordon off** VT (area) interdire l'accès à; (crowd) tenir à l'écart

corduroy ['kɔːdərɔı] N velours côtelé

CORE [kɔː^r] N ABBR (US) = **Congress of Racial Equality**

core [kɔː^r] N (of fruit) trognon m, cœur m; (Tech: also of earth) noyau m; (: of nuclear reactor) cœur m; (fig: of problem etc) cœur; **rotten to the ~** complètement pourri ▸ VT enlever le trognon or le cœur de

Corfu [kɔː'fuː] N Corfou

coriander [kɔrı'ændə^r] N coriandre f

cork [kɔːk] N (material) liège m; (of bottle) bouchon m

corkage ['kɔːkıdʒ] N droit payé par le client qui apporte sa propre bouteille de vin

corked [kɔːkt], (US) **corky** ['kɔːkı] ADJ (wine) qui sent le bouchon

corkscrew ['kɔːkskruː] N tire-bouchon m

cormorant ['kɔːmərnt] N cormoran m

corn [kɔːn] N (Brit: wheat) blé m; (US: maize) maïs m; (on foot) cor m; **~ on the cob** (Culin) épi m de maïs au naturel

cornea ['kɔːnıə] N cornée f

corned beef ['kɔːnd-] N corned-beef m

★**corner** ['kɔːnə^r] N coin m; (in road) tournant m, virage m; (Football: also: **corner kick**) corner m; **to cut corners** (fig) prendre des raccourcis ▸ VT (trap: prey) acculer; (fig) coincer; (Comm: market) accaparer ▸ VI prendre un virage

corner flag N (Football) piquet m de coin

corner kick N (Football) corner m

corner shop (Brit) N magasin m du coin

cornerstone ['kɔːnəstəun] N pierre f angulaire

cornet ['kɔːnıt] N (Mus) cornet m à pistons; (Brit: of ice-cream) cornet (de glace)

cornfield ['kɔːnfiːld] N (Brit: field of wheat) champ m de blé; (US: field of maize) champ m de maïs

cornflakes ['kɔːnfleıks] NPL cornflakes mpl

cornflour [ˈkɔːnflauəʳ] N (*Brit*) farine *f* de maïs, maïzena® *f*

cornflower [ˈkɔːnflauəʳ] N bleuet *m*, barbeau *m*

cornice [ˈkɔːnɪs] N corniche *f*

Cornish [ˈkɔːnɪʃ] ADJ de Cornouailles, cornouaillais(e)

corn oil N huile *f* de maïs

cornstarch [ˈkɔːnstɑːtʃ] N (*US*) farine *f* de maïs, maïzena® *f*

cornucopia [kɔːnjuˈkəupɪə] N corne *f* d'abondance

Cornwall [ˈkɔːnwəl] N Cornouailles *f*

corny [ˈkɔːnɪ] ADJ (*inf*) rebattu(e), galvaudé(e)

corollary [kəˈrɔlərɪ] N corollaire *m*

coronary [ˈkɔrənərɪ] N: **~ (thrombosis)** infarctus *m* (du myocarde), thrombose *f* coronaire

coronation [kɔrəˈneɪʃən] N couronnement *m*

coroner [ˈkɔrənəʳ] N coroner *m*, *officier de police judiciaire chargé de déterminer les causes d'un décès*

coronet [ˈkɔrənɪt] N couronne *f*

Corp. ABBR = **corporation**

corporal [ˈkɔːpərl] N caporal *m*, brigadier *m* ▶ ADJ: **~ punishment** châtiment corporel

corporate [ˈkɔːpərɪt] ADJ (*action, ownership*) en commun; (*Comm*) de la société

corporate hospitality N *arrangement selon lequel une société offre des places de théâtre, concert etc à ses clients*

corporate identity, corporate image N (*of organization*) image *f* de la société

corporation [kɔːpəˈreɪʃən] N (*of town*) municipalité *f*, conseil municipal; (*Comm*) société *f*

corporation tax N ≈ impôt *m* sur les bénéfices

corps [kɔːʳ] (*pl* ~ [kɔːz]) N corps *m*; **the diplomatic ~** le corps diplomatique; **the press ~** la presse

corpse [kɔːps] N cadavre *m*

corpulent [ˈkɔːpjulənt] ADJ (*literary*) corpulent(e)

corpuscle [ˈkɔːpʌsl] N corpuscule *m*

corral [kəˈrɑːl] N corral *m*

★**correct** [kəˈrɛkt] ADJ (*accurate*) correct(e), exact(e); (*proper*) correct, convenable; **you are ~** vous avez raison ▶ VT corriger

correction [kəˈrɛkʃən] N correction *f*

correctional [kəˈrɛkʃənəl] ADJ (*esp US*) correctionnel(le)

correctly [kəˈrɛktlɪ] ADV (*right*) correctement; **quite ~, she ...** à fort juste titre, elle ...

correlate [ˈkɔrɪleɪt] VT mettre en corrélation ▶ VI: **to ~ with** correspondre à

correlation [kɔrɪˈleɪʃən] N corrélation *f*

correspond [kɔrɪsˈpɔnd] VI correspondre; **to ~ to sth** (*be equivalent to*) correspondre à qch

correspondence [kɔrɪsˈpɔndəns] N correspondance *f*

correspondence course N cours *m* par correspondance

correspondent [kɔrɪsˈpɔndənt] N correspondant(e)

corresponding [kɔrɪsˈpɔndɪŋ] ADJ correspondant(e)

correspondingly [kɔrɪsˈpɔndɪŋlɪ] ADV (*proportionately*) proportionnellement

corridor [ˈkɔrɪdɔːʳ] N couloir *m*, corridor *m*

corroborate [kəˈrɔbəreit] VT corroborer, confirmer

corroboration [kərɔbəˈreɪʃən] N confirmation *f*

corrode [kəˈrəud] VT corroder, ronger ▶ VI se corroder

corrosion [kəˈrəuʒən] N corrosion *f*

corrosive [kəˈrəuzɪv] ADJ corrosif(-ive)

corrugated [ˈkɔrəgeitɪd] ADJ plissé(e); ondulé(e)

corrugated iron N tôle ondulée

corrupt [kəˈrʌpt] ADJ corrompu(e); (*Comput*) altéré(e); **~ practices** (*dishonesty, bribery*) malversation *f* ▶ VT corrompre; (*Comput*) altérer

corruption [kəˈrʌpʃən] N corruption *f*; (*Comput*) altération *f* (de données)

corset [ˈkɔːsɪt] N corset *m*

Corsica [ˈkɔːsɪkə] N Corse *f*

Corsican [ˈkɔːsɪkən] ADJ corse ▶ N Corse *mf*

cortège [kɔːˈteɪʒ] N cortège *m* (*gén funèbre*)

cortex [ˈkɔːtɛks] (*pl* **cortices** [ˈkɔːtɪsiːz]) N (*of brain*) cortex *m*

cortisone [ˈkɔːtɪzəun] N cortisone *f*

coruscating [ˈkɔrəskeitɪŋ] ADJ scintillant(e)

cosh [kɔʃ] N (*Brit*) matraque *f*

cosignatory [ˈkəuˈsɪgnətərɪ] N cosignataire *mf*

cosiness [ˈkəuzɪnɪs] N atmosphère douillette, confort *m*

cos lettuce [ˈkɔs-] N (*Brit*) (laitue *f*) romaine *f*

cosmetic [kɔzˈmɛtɪk] N produit *m* de beauté, cosmétique *m* ▶ ADJ (*preparation*) cosmétique; (*fig: reforms*) symbolique, superficiel(le)

cosmetic surgery N chirurgie *f* esthétique

cosmic [ˈkɔzmɪk] ADJ cosmique

cosmonaut [ˈkɔzmənɔːt] N cosmonaute *mf*

cosmopolitan [kɔzməˈpɔlɪtn] ADJ cosmopolite

cosmos [ˈkɔzmɔs] N cosmos *m*

cosset [ˈkɔsɪt] VT choyer, dorloter

★**cost** [kɔst] N coût *m*; **at all costs** coûte que coûte, à tout prix ▶ VT (*pt, pp* ~: *money*) coûter; (*pt, pp* **costed**: *estimate cost of*) établir *or* calculer le prix de revient de; **how much does it ~?** combien ça coûte ?; **it costs £5/too much** cela coûte 5 livres/ trop cher; **what will it ~ to have it repaired?** combien cela coûtera de le faire réparer ?; **to ~ sb time/effort** demander du temps/un effort à qn; **it ~ him his life/job** ça lui a coûté la vie/ son emploi ▪ **costs** NPL (*Comm*) frais *mpl*; (*Law*) dépens *mpl*

cost accountant N analyste *mf* de coûts

co-star [ˈkəustɑːʳ] N partenaire *mf*

Costa Rica [ˈkɔstəˈriːkə] N Costa Rica *m*

cost centre N centre *m* de coût

cost control N contrôle *m* des coûts

cost-effective [ˈkɔstɪˈfɛktɪv] ADJ rentable

cost-effectiveness [ˈkɔstɪˈfɛktɪvnɪs] N rentabilité *f*

costing [ˈkɔstɪŋ] N calcul *m* du prix de revient

costly [ˈkɔstlɪ] ADJ coûteux(-euse)

cost of living [ˈkɔstəvˈlɪvɪŋ] N coût *m* de la vie ▶ CPD: **~ allowance** indemnité *f* de vie chère; **~ index** indice *m* du coût de la vie

cost price N (*Brit*) prix coûtant *or* de revient

costume [ˈkɔstjuːm] N costume m; (lady's suit) tailleur m; (BRIT: also: **swimming costume**) maillot m (de bain)

costume jewellery N (BRIT) bijoux mpl de fantaisie

cosy, (US) **cozy** [ˈkəʊzɪ] ADJ (room, bed) douillet(te); (scarf, gloves) bien chaud(e); (atmosphere) chaleureux(-euse); **to be ~** (person) être bien (au chaud)

cot [kɔt] N (BRIT: child's) lit m d'enfant, petit lit; (US: campbed) lit de camp

cot death N mort subite du nourrisson

Cotswolds [ˈkɔtswəʊldz] NPL: **the ~** région de collines du Gloucestershire

★**cottage** [ˈkɔtɪdʒ] N petite maison (à la campagne), cottage m

cottage cheese N fromage blanc (maigre)

cottage industry N industrie familiale or artisanale

cottage pie N ≈ hachis m Parmentier

★**cotton** [ˈkɔtn] N coton m; (thread) fil m (de coton)
▶ CPD (dress, sheet) de coton; **a ~ shirt** une chemise de coton
  ▶ **cotton on** VI (inf): **to ~ on (to sth)** piger (qch)

cotton bud N (BRIT) coton-tige® m

cotton candy N (US) barbe f à papa

cotton wool N (BRIT) ouate f, coton m hydrophile

couch [kautʃ] N canapé m; divan m; (doctor's) table f d'examen; (psychiatrist's) divan ▶ VT formuler, exprimer

couchette [kuːˈʃet] N couchette f

couch potato N (inf) mollasson(ne) (qui passe son temps devant la télé)

couchsurfing [ˈkautʃsəːfɪŋ] N couchsurfing m, hébergement temporaire gratuit chez un particulier

★**cough** [kɔf] VI tousser ▶ N toux f; **I've got a ~** j'ai la toux, je tousse
  ▶ **cough up** (inf) VT FUS (money) raquer (inf); cracher (inf) ▶ VI (pay money) raquer (inf)

cough drop N pastille f pour or contre la toux

cough mixture N sirop m pour la toux

cough sweet N pastille f pour or contre la toux

cough syrup N sirop m pour la toux

★**could** [kud] PT of **can²**

couldn't = **could not**

★**council** [ˈkaunsl] N conseil m; **city** or **town ~** conseil municipal; **C~ of Europe** Conseil de l'Europe

council estate N (BRIT) (quartier m or zone f de) logements loués à/par la municipalité

council house N (BRIT) maison f (à loyer modéré) louée par la municipalité

councillor, (US) **councilor** [ˈkaunslə^r] N conseiller(-ère)

council tax N (BRIT) impôts locaux

counsel [ˈkaunsl] N conseil m; (lawyer) avocat(e); **~ for the defence/the prosecution** (avocat de la) défense/avocat du ministère public ▶ VT: **to ~ (sb to do sth)** conseiller (à qn de faire qch)

counselling, (US) **counseling** [ˈkaunslɪŋ] N (Psych) aide psychosociale

counsellor, (US) **counselor** [ˈkaunslə^r] N conseiller(-ère); (US Law) avocat m

★**count** [kaunt] VT compter; **not counting the children** sans compter les enfants; **10 counting him** 10 avec lui, 10 en le comptant; **to ~ the cost of** établir le coût de; **~ yourself lucky** estimez-vous heureux ▶ VI compter; **to ~ (up) to 10** compter jusqu'à 10; **it counts for very little** cela n'a pas beaucoup d'importance ▶ N compte m; (nobleman) comte m; **to keep ~ of sth** tenir le compte de qch
  ▶ **count in** VT (inf): **to ~ sb in (on sth)** inclure qn (dans qch)
  ▶ **count on** VT FUS compter sur; **to ~ on doing sth** compter faire qch
  ▶ **count up** VT compter, additionner

countdown [ˈkauntdaun] N compte m à rebours

countenance [ˈkauntɪnəns] N expression f ▶ VT approuver

★**counter** [ˈkauntə^r] N comptoir m; (in post office, bank) guichet m; (in game) jeton m; **to buy under the ~** (fig) acheter sous le manteau or en sous-main ▶ VT aller à l'encontre de, opposer; (blow) parer; **to ~ sth with sth/by doing sth** contrer or riposter à qch par qch/en faisant qch ▶ ADV: **~ to** à l'encontre de; contrairement à

counteract [ˈkauntərˈækt] VT neutraliser, contrebalancer

counterattack [ˈkauntərəˈtæk] N contre-attaque f ▶ VI contre-attaquer

counterbalance [ˈkauntəˈbæləns] VT contrebalancer, faire contrepoids à

counterbid [ˈkauntəbɪd] N surenchère f, suroffre f ▶ VT surenchérir de, faire une suroffre de

counterclockwise [ˈkauntəˈklɔkwaɪz] ADV (US) en sens inverse des aiguilles d'une montre

counter-espionage [ˈkauntərˈespɪɑnɑːʒ] N contre-espionnage m

counterfeit [ˈkauntəfɪt] N faux m, contrefaçon f ▶ VT contrefaire ▶ ADJ faux (fausse)

counterfoil [ˈkauntəfɔɪl] N talon m, souche f

counterintelligence [ˈkauntərɪnˈtelɪdʒəns] N contre-espionnage m

countermand [ˈkauntəmɑːnd] VT annuler

countermeasure [ˈkauntəmeʒə^r] N contre-mesure f

counteroffensive [ˈkauntərəˈfensɪv] N contre-offensive f

counterpane [ˈkauntəpeɪn] N dessus-de-lit m

counterpart [ˈkauntəpɑːt] N (of document etc) double m; (of person) homologue mf

counterproductive [ˈkauntəprəˈdʌktɪv] ADJ contre-productif(-ive)

counterproposal [ˈkauntəprəˈpəuzl] N contre-proposition f

counter-revolutionary [ˈkauntərevəˈluːʃənrɪ] ADJ, N contre-révolutionnaire mf

countersign [ˈkauntəsam] VT contresigner

countersink [ˈkauntəsɪŋk] VT (hole) fraiser

countertenor [ˈkauntətenə^r] N haute-contre m

counterterrorism [kauntəˈterərɪzəm] N contre-terrorisme m

countertop [ˈkauntətɔp] N (US: worktop) plan m de travail

counterweight [ˈkauntəweɪt] N contrepoids m ▶ VT contrebalancer

countess ['kauntıs] N comtesse f

countless ['kauntlıs] ADJ innombrable

countrified ['kʌntrıfaıd] ADJ rustique, à l'air campagnard

★**country** ['kʌntrı] N pays m; (native land) patrie f; (as opposed to town) campagne f; (region) région f, pays; **in the ~** à la campagne; **mountainous ~** pays de montagne, région montagneuse

country and western, country and western music N musique f country

country dancing N (BRIT) danse f folklorique

country house N manoir m, (petit) château

countryman ['kʌntrımən] N (irreg) (compatriot) compatriote m; (country dweller) habitant m de la campagne, campagnard m

★**countryside** ['kʌntrısaıd] N campagne f

countrywide ['kʌntrı'waıd] ADJ s'étendant à l'ensemble du pays; (problem) à l'échelle nationale ▶ ADV à travers or dans tout le pays

countrywoman ['kʌntrıwumən] N (irreg) (compatriot) compatriote f; (country dweller) habitante f de la campagne, campagnarde f

★**county** ['kauntı] N comté m

county council N (BRIT) ≈ conseil régional

county town N (BRIT) chef-lieu m

coup [ku:] (pl **coups** [ku:z]) N (achievement) beau coup; (also: **coup d'état**) coup d'État

coupé [ku:'peı] N (Aut) coupé m

★**couple** ['kʌpl] N couple m; **a ~ of** (two) deux; (a few) deux ou trois ▶ VT (carriages) atteler; (Tech) coupler; (ideas, names) associer

couplet ['kʌplıt] N distique m

coupling ['kʌplıŋ] N (Rail) attelage m

coupon ['ku:pɔn] N (voucher) bon m de réduction; (detachable form) coupon m détachable, coupon-réponse m; (Finance) coupon

★**courage** ['kʌrıdʒ] N courage m

courageous [kə'reıdʒəs] ADJ courageux(-euse)

courgette [kuə'ʒɛt] N (BRIT) courgette f

courier ['kurıə'] N messager m, courrier m; (for tourists) accompagnateur(-trice)

★**course** [kɔ:s] N cours m; (of ship) route f; (for golf) terrain m; (part of meal) plat m; **first ~** entrée f; **of ~** adv bien sûr; **(no,) of ~ not!** bien sûr que non !, évidemment que non !; **in the ~ of** au cours de; **in the ~ of the next few days** au cours des prochains jours; **in due ~** en temps utile or voulu; **~ (of action)** parti m, ligne f de conduite; **the best ~ would be to ...** le mieux serait de ...; **we have no other ~ but to ...** nous n'avons pas d'autre solution que de ...; **~ of lectures** série f de conférences; **~ of treatment** (Med) traitement m

coursework ['kɔ:swə:k] N (students' work) devoirs mpl; (continuous assessment) contrôle m continu

★**court** [kɔ:t] N cour f; (Law) cour, tribunal m; (Tennis) court m; **out of ~** (Law: settle) à l'amiable; **to take ~ to ~** actionner or poursuivre en justice; **~ of appeal** cour d'appel ▶ VT (woman) courtiser, faire la cour à; (fig: favour, popularity) rechercher; (: death, disaster) courir après, flirter avec

courteous [kə'tıəs] ADJ courtois(e), poli(e)

courtesan [kɔ:tı'zæn] N courtisane f

courtesy ['kə:təsı] N courtoisie f, politesse f; **(by) ~ of** avec l'aimable autorisation de

courtesy bus, courtesy coach N navette gratuite

courtesy light N (Aut) plafonnier m

courthouse ['kɔ:thaus] N (US) palais m de justice

courtier ['kɔ:tıə'] N courtisan m, dame f de cour

court martial (pl **courts martial**) N cour martiale, conseil m de guerre

courtroom ['kɔ:trum] N salle f de tribunal

court shoe N escarpin m

courtyard ['kɔ:tjɑ:d] N cour f

★**cousin** ['kʌzn] N cousin(e); **first ~** cousin(e) germain(e)

couturier [ku'tjuərıeı] N grand couturier m

cove [kəuv] N petite baie, anse f

covenant ['kʌvənənt] N contrat m, engagement m ▶ VT: **to ~ £200 per year to a charity** s'engager à verser 200 livres par an à une œuvre de bienfaisance

Coventry ['kɔvəntrı] N: **to send sb to ~** (BRIT fig) mettre qn en quarantaine

★**cover** ['kʌvə'] VT couvrir; (Press: report on) faire un reportage sur; (feelings, mistake) cacher; (include) englober; (discuss) traiter; **£10 will ~ everything** 10 livres suffiront (pour tout payer) ▶ N (of book, Comm) couverture f; (of pan) couvercle m; (over furniture) housse f; (shelter) abri m; **to take ~** se mettre à l'abri; **under ~** à l'abri; **under ~ of darkness** à la faveur de la nuit; **under separate ~** (Comm) sous pli séparé ▪ **covers** NPL (on bed) couvertures ▶ **cover up** VT (truth, facts) occulter; (person, object): **to ~ up (with)** couvrir (de) ▶ VI: **to ~ up for sb** (fig) couvrir qn

coverage ['kʌvərıdʒ] N (in media) reportage m; (Insurance) couverture f

cover charge N couvert m (supplément à payer)

covered ['kʌvəd] ADJ couvert(e); **to be ~ in or with sth** être couvert(e) de qch

covering ['kʌvərıŋ] N couverture f, enveloppe f

covering letter, (US) **cover letter** N lettre explicative

cover note N (Insurance) police f provisoire

cover price N prix m de l'exemplaire

covert ['kʌvət] ADJ (threat) voilé(e), caché(e); (attack) indirect(e); (glance) furtif(-ive)

covertly ['kʌvətlı] ADV (work, operate) secrètement; (watch) à la dérobée; **to film sb ~** filmer qn à son insu

cover-up ['kʌvərʌp] N tentative f pour étouffer une affaire

covet ['kʌvıt] VT convoiter

★**cow** [kau] N vache f ▶ CPD femelle ▶ VT effrayer, intimider

coward ['kauəd] N lâche mf

cowardice ['kauədıs] N lâcheté f

cowardly ['kauədlı] ADJ lâche

cowboy ['kaubɔı] N cow-boy m

cower ['kauə'] VI se recroqueviller; trembler

cowhide ['kauhaıd] N cuir m de vache ▶ CPD (boots, bag, chair) en cuir de vache

cowl [kaul] N (hood) capuchon m

cowpat ['kaupæt] N bouse f de vache

cowshed ['kauʃed] N étable f

cowslip ['kauslɪp] N (Bot) (fleur f de) coucou m

cox [kɔks] N (of rowing boat) barreur(-euse)

coxswain ['kɔksən] N (of lifeboat) timonier m

coy [kɔɪ] ADJ (shy) faussement effarouché(e) or timide; (coquettish: smile) séducteur(-trice); (evasive) évasif(-ive)

coyly ['kɔɪlɪ] ADV (coquettishly) avec coquetterie; (euphemistically) euphémiquement; (evasively) évasivement

coyote [kɔɪ'əutɪ] N coyote m

cozy ['kəuzɪ] ADJ (US) = **cosy**

CP N ABBR (= Communist Party) PC m

cp. ABBR (= compare) cf.

CPA N ABBR (US) = **certified public accountant**

CPI N ABBR (= Consumer Price Index) IPC m

Cpl. ABBR (= corporal) C/C

CP/M N ABBR (= Central Program for Microprocessors) CP/M m

CPR N ABBR (= cardiopulmonary resuscitation) RCP f

c.p.s. ABBR (= characters per second) caractères/seconde

CPSA N ABBR (BRIT: = Civil and Public Services Association) syndicat de la fonction publique

CPU N ABBR = **central processing unit**

cr. ABBR = **credit; creditor**

crab [kræb] N crabe m

crab apple N pomme f sauvage

★**crack** [kræk] N (split) fente f, fissure f; (in cup, bone) fêlure f; (in wall) lézarde f; (noise) craquement m, coup (sec); (joke) plaisanterie f; (inf: attempt): **to have a ~ (at sth)** essayer (qch); (also: **crack cocaine**) crack m; (IRISH inf: craic) ambiance f ▶ VT fendre, fissurer; fêler; lézarder; (whip) faire claquer; (nut) casser; (problem) résoudre, trouver la clef de; (code) déchiffrer; **to ~ jokes** (inf) raconter des blagues ▶ VI: **to get cracking** (inf) s'y mettre, se magner (inf) ▶ CPD (athlete) de première classe, d'élite
  ▶ **crack down on** VT FUS (crime) sévir contre, réprimer; (spending) mettre un frein à
  ▶ **crack up** VI être au bout du rouleau, flancher

crack cocaine N crack m

crackdown ['krækdaun] N: **~ (on)** (on crime) répression f (de); (on spending) restrictions fpl (de)

cracked [krækt] ADJ (cup, bone) fêlé(e); (broken) cassé(e); (wall) lézardé(e); (surface) craquelé(e); (inf) toqué(e), timbré(e)

cracker ['krækər] N (also: **Christmas cracker**) pétard m; (biscuit) biscuit (salé), craquelin m; **a ~ of a ...** (BRIT inf) un(e) ... formidable; **he's crackers** (BRIT inf) il est cinglé

crackle ['krækl] VI crépiter, grésiller

crackling ['kræklɪŋ] N crépitement m, grésillement m; (on radio, telephone) grésillement m, friture f; (of pork) couenne f

crackpot ['krækpɔt] N (inf) tordu(e)

cradle ['kreɪdl] N berceau m ▶ VT (child) bercer; (object) tenir dans ses bras

craft [krɑːft] N métier (artisanal); (cunning) ruse f, astuce f; (boat: pl inv) embarcation f, barque f; (plane: pl inv) appareil m

craftsman ['krɑːftsmən] N (irreg) artisan m

craftsmanship ['krɑːftsmənʃɪp] N métier m, habileté f

craftswoman ['krɑːftswumən] N (irreg) artisane f

crafty ['krɑːftɪ] ADJ rusé(e), malin(-igne), astucieux(-euse)

crag [kræg] N rocher escarpé

craggy ['krægɪ] ADJ (cliff) escarpé(e); (face) anguleux(-euse)

craic [kræk] N (IRISH inf) ambiance f

cram [kræm] VT: **to ~ sth with** (fill) bourrer qch de; **to ~ sth into** (put) fourrer qch dans ▶ VI (for exams) bachoter

crammed [kræmd] ADJ: **to be ~ with sth** être bourré(e) de qch; **to be ~ into sth** être entassé(e) dans qch

cramming ['kræmɪŋ] N (for exams) bachotage m

cramp [kræmp] N crampe f; **I've got ~ in my leg** j'ai une crampe à la jambe ▶ VT gêner, entraver

cramped [kræmpt] ADJ à l'étroit, très serré(e)

crampon ['kræmpən] N crampon m

cranberry ['krænbərɪ] N canneberge f

crane [kreɪn] N grue f ▶ VI, VT: **to ~ forward, to ~ one's neck** allonger le cou

cranefly ['kreɪnflaɪ] N tipule f

cranium ['kreɪnɪəm] (pl **crania** ['kreɪnɪə]) N boîte crânienne

crank [kræŋk] N manivelle f; (person) excentrique mf

crankshaft ['kræŋkʃɑːft] N vilebrequin m

cranky ['kræŋkɪ] ADJ excentrique, loufoque; (bad-tempered) grincheux(-euse), revêche

cranny ['krænɪ] N see **nook**

crap [kræp] N (inf!: nonsense) conneries fpl (!); (: excrement) merde f (!); **the party was ~** la fête était merdique (!); **to have a ~** chier (!)

crappy ['kræpɪ] ADJ (inf!) merdique (!)

★**crash** [kræʃ] N (noise) fracas m; (of car, plane) collision f; (of business) faillite f; (Stock Exchange) krach m ▶ VT (plane) écraser; **he crashed the car into a wall** il s'est écrasé contre un mur avec sa voiture ▶ VI (plane) s'écraser; (two cars) se percuter, s'emboutir; (business) s'effondrer; **to ~ into** se jeter or se fracasser contre

crash barrier N (BRIT Aut) rail m de sécurité

crash course N cours intensif

crash helmet N casque (protecteur)

crash landing N atterrissage forcé or en catastrophe

crass [kræs] ADJ grossier(-ière), crasse

crate [kreɪt] N cageot m; (for bottles) caisse f

crater ['kreɪtər] N cratère m

cravat [krə'væt] N foulard (noué autour du cou)

crave [kreɪv] VT, VI: **to ~ (for)** avoir un besoin physiologique de, avoir une envie irrésistible de

craving ['kreɪvɪŋ] N: **~ (for)** (for food, cigarettes etc) envie f irrésistible de

crawl [krɔːl] VI ramper; (vehicle) avancer au pas; **to ~ on one's hands and knees** aller à quatre pattes; **to ~ to sb** (inf) faire de la lèche à qn (inf) ▶ N (Swimming) crawl m

crawler lane [ˈkrɔːləˌ] N (BRIT Aut) file f or voie f pour véhicules lents

crawling [ˈkrɔːlɪŋ] ADJ: **to be ~ with** (pej) grouiller de

crayfish [ˈkreɪfɪʃ] N (pl inv: freshwater) écrevisse f; (: saltwater) langoustine f

crayon [ˈkreɪən] N crayon m (de couleur)

craze [kreɪz] N engouement m

crazed [kreɪzd] ADJ (look, person) affolé(e); (pottery, glaze) craquelé(e)

craziness [ˈkreɪzɪnɪs] N folie f

★**crazy** [ˈkreɪzɪ] ADJ fou (folle); **to go ~** devenir fou; **to be ~ about sb/sth** (inf) être fou de qn/qch

crazy paving N (BRIT) dallage irrégulier (en pierres plates)

CRB N ABBR (BRIT) = **Criminal Records Bureau**

creak [kriːk] VI (hinge) grincer; (floor, shoes) craquer

creaky [ˈkriːkɪ] ADJ (door) grinçant(e); (floorboard) qui craque; (old-fashioned) vieillot(te)

★**cream** [kriːm] N crème f; **whipped ~** crème fouettée ▶ ADJ (colour) crème inv
▶ **cream off** VT (fig) prélever

cream cake N (petit) gâteau à la crème

cream cheese N fromage m à la crème, fromage blanc

creamery [ˈkriːmərɪ] N (shop) crémerie f; (factory) laiterie f

creamy [ˈkriːmɪ] ADJ crémeux(-euse)

crease [kriːs] N pli m ▶ VT froisser, chiffonner ▶ VI se froisser, se chiffonner

crease-resistant [ˈkriːsrɪzɪstənt] ADJ infroissable

★**create** [kriːˈeɪt] VT créer; (impression, fuss) faire

creation [kriːˈeɪʃən] N création f

creationism [kriːˈeɪʃənɪzəm] N créationnisme m

★**creative** [kriːˈeɪtɪv] ADJ créatif(-ive)

creatively [kriːˈeɪtɪvlɪ] ADV de façon créative

creativity [kriːeɪˈtɪvɪtɪ] N créativité f

creator [kriːˈeɪtəʳ] N créateur(-trice)

creature [ˈkriːtʃəʳ] N créature f

creature comforts NPL petit confort

crèche [krɛʃ] N garderie f, crèche f

credence [ˈkriːdns] N croyance f, foi f

credentials [krɪˈdɛnʃlz] NPL (references) références fpl; (identity papers) pièce f d'identité; (letters of reference) pièces justificatives

credibility [krɛdɪˈbɪlɪtɪ] N crédibilité f

credible [ˈkrɛdɪbl] ADJ digne de foi, crédible

★**credit** [ˈkrɛdɪt] N crédit m; (recognition) honneur m; (Scol) unité f de valeur; **to be in ~** (person, bank account) être créditeur(-trice); **on ~** à crédit; **to one's ~** à son honneur; à son actif; **to take the ~ for** s'attribuer le mérite de; **it does him ~** cela lui fait honneur ▶ VT (Comm) créditer; (believe: also: **give credit to**) ajouter foi à, croire; **to ~ sb with** (fig) prêter or attribuer à qn; **to ~ £5 to sb** créditer (le compte de) qn de 5 livres ■ **credits** NPL (Cine) générique m

creditable [ˈkrɛdɪtəbl] ADJ honorable, estimable

credit account N compte m client

credit agency N (BRIT) agence f de renseignements commerciaux

credit balance N solde créditeur

credit bureau N (US) agence f de renseignements commerciaux

credit card N carte f de crédit; **do you take ~s?** acceptez-vous les cartes de crédit ?

credit control N suivi m des factures

credit crunch N crise f du crédit

credit facilities NPL facilités fpl de paiement

credit limit N limite f de crédit

credit note N (BRIT) avoir m

creditor [ˈkrɛdɪtəʳ] N créancier(-ière)

credit rating N indice m de solvabilité

credit transfer N virement m

creditworthiness [ˈkrɛdɪtwəːðɪnɪs] N solvabilité f

creditworthy [ˈkrɛdɪtwəːðɪ] ADJ solvable

credulity [krɪˈdjuːlɪtɪ] N crédulité f

credulous [ˈkrɛdʒuləs] ADJ crédule

creed [kriːd] N croyance f; credo m, principes mpl

creek [kriːk] N (inlet) crique f, anse f; (US: stream) ruisseau m, petit cours d'eau

creel [kriːl] N panier m de pêche; (also: **lobster creel**) panier à homards

creep [kriːp] N (pt, pp **crept** [krɛpt]) VI ramper; (silently) se faufiler, se glisser; (plant) grimper; **to ~ up on sb** s'approcher furtivement de qn ▶ N (pej: flatterer) lèche-botte m; **he's a ~** (pej) c'est un type puant; **it gives me the creeps** (inf) cela me fait froid dans le dos

creeper [ˈkriːpəʳ] N plante grimpante

creepers [ˈkriːpəz] NPL (US: for baby) barboteuse f

creepy [ˈkriːpɪ] ADJ (frightening) qui fait frissonner, qui donne la chair de poule

creepy-crawly [ˈkriːpɪˈkrɔːlɪ] N (inf) bestiole f

cremate [krɪˈmeɪt] VT incinérer

cremation [krɪˈmeɪʃən] N incinération f

crematorium [krɛməˈtɔːrɪəm] (pl **crematoria** [-ˈtɔːrɪə]) N four m crématoire

creosote [ˈkrɪəsəut] N créosote f

crepe [kreɪp] N crêpe m

crepe bandage N (BRIT) bande f Velpeau®

crepe paper N papier m crépon

crept [krɛpt] PT, PP of **creep**

crescendo [krɪˈʃɛndəu] N crescendo m

crescent [ˈkrɛsnt] N croissant m; (street) rue f (en arc de cercle)

cress [krɛs] N cresson m

crest [krɛst] N crête f; (of helmet) cimier m; (of coat of arms) timbre m

crestfallen [ˈkrɛstfɔːlən] ADJ déconfit(e), découragé(e)

Crete [kriːt] N Crète f

crevasse [krɪˈvæs] N crevasse f

crevice [ˈkrɛvɪs] N fissure f, lézarde f, fente f

crew [kruː] N équipage m; (Cine) équipe f (de tournage); (gang) équipe f

crew-cut [ˈkruːkʌt] N: **to have a ~** avoir les cheveux en brosse

crewman [ˈkruːmən] N (irreg) membre m de l'équipage

crew-neck [ˈkruːnɛk] N col ras

crib [krɪb] N lit m d'enfant; (for baby) berceau m ▶ VT (inf) copier

cribbage ['krɪbɪdʒ] N sorte de jeu de cartes

crib sheet N (BRIT: in exam) antisèche f

crick [krɪk] N crampe f; **~ in the neck** torticolis m

★**cricket** ['krɪkɪt] N (insect) grillon m, cri-cri m inv; (game) cricket m

cricketer ['krɪkɪtər] N joueur m de cricket

★**crime** [kraɪm] N crime m; **minor ~** délit mineur, infraction mineure

crime wave N poussée f de la criminalité

crime writer N auteur mf de romans policiers

★**criminal** ['krɪmɪnl] ADJ, N criminel(le)

criminality [krɪmɪ'nælɪtɪ] N criminalité f

criminalize ['krɪmɪnəlaɪz] VT criminaliser

criminally ['krɪmɪnəlɪ] ADV (responsible, liable) pénalement; (fig: expensive, underpaid) scandaleusement; **~ irresponsible** d'une irresponsabilité criminelle

criminology [krɪmɪ'nɔlədʒɪ] N criminologie f

crimp [krɪmp] VT friser, frisotter

crimson ['krɪmzn] ADJ cramoisi(e)

cringe [krɪndʒ] VI avoir un mouvement de recul; (fig) s'humilier, ramper

crinkle ['krɪŋkl] VT froisser, chiffonner

cripple ['krɪpl] N (!) boiteux(-euse), infirme mf ▶ VT (person) estropier, paralyser; (ship, plane) immobiliser; (production, exports) paralyser; **crippled with rheumatism** perclus(e) de rhumatismes

crippling ['krɪplɪŋ] ADJ (disease) handicapant(e); (taxation, debts) écrasant(e)

★**crisis** ['kraɪsɪs] (pl **crises** [-siːz]) N crise f

crisp [krɪsp] ADJ croquant(e); (weather) vif (vive); (manner etc) brusque

★**crisps** [krɪsps] NPL (BRIT) (pommes fpl) chips fpl

crispy ['krɪspɪ] ADJ croustillant(e)

crisscross ['krɪskrɔs] ADJ entrecroisé(e), en croisillons; **~ pattern** croisillons mpl ▶ VT sillonner

criterion [kraɪ'tɪərɪən] (pl **criteria** [-'tɪərɪə]) N critère m

★**critic** ['krɪtɪk] N critique mf

critical ['krɪtɪkl] ADJ critique; **to be ~ of sb/sth** critiquer qn/qch

critically ['krɪtɪklɪ] ADV (examine) d'un œil critique; (speak) sévèrement; **~ ill** gravement malade

★**criticism** ['krɪtɪsɪzəm] N critique f

★**criticize** ['krɪtɪsaɪz] VT critiquer

critique [krɪ'tiːk] N critique f

croak [krəuk] VI (frog) coasser; (raven) croasser

Croat ['krəuæt] ADJ, N = **Croatian**

Croatia [krəu'eɪʃə] N Croatie f

Croatian [krəu'eɪʃən] ADJ croate ▶ N Croate mf; (Ling) croate m

crochet ['krəuʃeɪ] N travail m au crochet

crock [krɔk] N cruche f; (inf: also: **old crock**) épave f

crockery ['krɔkərɪ] N vaisselle f

crocodile ['krɔkədaɪl] N crocodile m

crocus ['krəukəs] N crocus m

croft [krɔft] N (BRIT) petite ferme

crofter ['krɔftər] N (BRIT) fermier m

croissant ['krwasɔŋ] N croissant m

crone [krəun] N vieille bique, (vieille) sorcière

crony ['krəunɪ] N copain (copine)

cronyism ['krəuniːzəm] N copinage m; **political ~** copinage politique

crook [kruk] N (inf) escroc m; (of shepherd) houlette f

crooked ['krukɪd] ADJ courbé(e), tordu(e); (action) malhonnête

★**crop** [krɔp] N (produce) culture f; (amount produced) récolte f; (riding crop) cravache f; (of bird) jabot m ▶ VT (hair) tondre; (animals, grass) brouter
  ▶ **crop up** VI surgir, se présenter, survenir

cropped [krɔpt] ADJ (hair) coupé(e) court; (top) petit(e); (trousers) court(e)

cropper ['krɔpər] N: **to come a ~** (inf) faire la culbute, s'étaler

crop spraying [-'spreɪɪŋ] N pulvérisation f des cultures

croquet ['krəukeɪ] N croquet m

★**cross** [krɔs] N croix f; (Biol) croisement m ▶ VT (street etc) traverser; (arms, legs, Biol) croiser; (cheque) barrer; (thwart: person, plan) contrarier; **to ~ o.s.** se signer, faire le signe de (la) croix; **we have a crossed line** (BRIT: on telephone) il y a des interférences; **they've got their lines crossed** (fig) il y a un malentendu entre eux ▶ VI: **the boat crosses from ... to ...** le bateau fait la traversée de ... à ... ▶ ADJ en colère, fâché(e); **to be/get ~ with sb (about sth)** être en colère/(se) fâcher contre qn (à propos de qch)
  ▶ **cross off, cross out** VT barrer, rayer
  ▶ **cross over** VI traverser

crossbar ['krɔsbɑːr] N barre transversale

crossbow ['krɔsbəu] N arbalète f

crossbreed ['krɔsbriːd] N hybride m

cross-Channel ferry ['krɔs'tʃænl-] N ferry m qui fait la traversée de la Manche

cross-check ['krɔstʃɛk] N recoupement m ▶ VI vérifier par recoupement

cross-country ['krɔs'kʌntrɪ], **cross-country race** N cross(-country) m

cross-dressing [krɔs'drɛsɪŋ] N travestisme m

cross-examination ['krɔsɪgzæmɪ'neɪʃən] N (Law) examen m contradictoire (d'un témoin)

cross-examine ['krɔsɪg'zæmɪn] VT (Law) faire subir un examen contradictoire à

cross-eyed ['krɔsaɪd] ADJ qui louche

crossfire ['krɔsfaɪər] N feux croisés

★**crossing** ['krɔsɪŋ] N croisement m, carrefour m; (sea passage) traversée f; (also: **pedestrian crossing**) passage clouté; **how long does the ~ take?** combien de temps dure la traversée ?

crossing guard N (US) contractuel qui fait traverser la rue aux enfants

crossing point N poste frontalier

crossover ['krɔsəuvər] N hybride m

cross-purposes ['krɔs'pəːpəsɪz] NPL: **to be at ~ with sb** comprendre qn de travers; **we're (talking) at ~** on ne parle pas de la même chose

cross-question ['krɔs'kwɛstʃən] VT faire subir un interrogatoire à

cross-reference ['krɔs'refrəns] N renvoi m, référence f

★**crossroads** ['krɔsrəudz] N carrefour m

cross section N (Biol) coupe transversale; (in population) échantillon m

cross-stitch ['krɔsstɪtʃ] N point m de croix

crosswalk ['krɔswɔːk] N (US) passage clouté

crosswind ['krɔswɪnd] N vent m de travers

crosswise ['krɔswaɪz] ADV en travers

crossword ['krɔswəːd] N mots mpl croisés

crotch [krɔtʃ] N (of garment) entrejambe m; (Anat) entrecuisse m

crotchet ['krɔtʃɪt] N (Mus) noire f

crotchety ['krɔtʃɪtɪ] ADJ (person) grognon(ne), grincheux(-euse)

crouch [krautʃ] VI s'accroupir; (hide) se tapir; (before springing) se ramasser

croup [kruːp] N (Med) croup m

crouton ['kruːtɔn] N croûton m

crow [krəu] N (bird) corneille f; (of cock) chant m du coq, cocorico m ▶ VI (cock) chanter; (fig) pavoiser, chanter victoire

crowbar ['krəubɑːʳ] N levier m

★**crowd** [kraud] N foule f; **crowds of people** une foule de gens ▶ VT (streets) se presser dans; (pavements) se presser sur ▶ VI affluer, s'attrouper, s'entasser
　　▶ **crowd into** VT FUS (room, building, bus) s'entasser dans; (square) s'attrouper sur

crowded ['kraudɪd] ADJ bondé(e), plein(e); **~ with** plein de

crowdfunding ['kraudfʌndɪŋ] N crowdfunding m, financement m participatif

crowd scene N (Cine, Theat) scène f de foule

crowdsource ['kraudsɔːs] VT crowdsourcer

crowdsourcing ['kraudsɔːsɪŋ] N crowdsourcing m, externalisation ouverte

★**crown** [kraun] N couronne f; (of head) sommet m de la tête, calotte crânienne; (of hat) fond m; (of hill) sommet m ▶ VT (also tooth) couronner

crown court N (BRIT) ≈ Cour f d'assises

En Angleterre et au pays de Galles, une **crown court** est une cour de justice où sont jugées, en présence d'un jury, les affaires très graves comme le meurtre, l'homicide, le viol et le vol. Tous les crimes et tous les délits, quel que soit leur degré de gravité, doivent d'abord passer devant une *magistrates' court*. Il existe environ 90 *crown courts*.

crowning ['kraunɪŋ] ADJ (achievement, glory) suprême

crown jewels NPL joyaux mpl de la Couronne

crown prince N prince héritier

crow's-feet ['krəuzfiːt] NPL pattes fpl d'oie (fig)

crow's-nest ['krəuznest] N (on sailing-ship) nid m de pie

crucial ['kruːʃl] ADJ crucial(e), décisif(-ive); **~ to** essentiel(le) à

crucifix ['kruːsɪfɪks] N crucifix m

crucifixion [kruːsɪ'fɪkʃən] N crucifiement m, crucifixion f

crucify ['kruːsɪfaɪ] VT crucifier, mettre en croix; (fig) crucifier

crude [kruːd] ADJ (materials) brut(e); non raffiné(e); (basic) rudimentaire, sommaire; (vulgar) cru(e), grossier(-ière) ▶ N (also: **crude oil**) (pétrole) brut m

cruel ['kruəl] ADJ cruel(le)

cruelly ['kruːəlɪ] ADV cruellement

cruelty ['kruəltɪ] N cruauté f

cruet ['kruːɪt] N (BRIT: for salt and pepper) service m à condiments; (US: for oil and vinegar) huilier m; vinaigrier m

cruise [kruːz] N croisière f ▶ VI (ship) croiser; (car) rouler; (aircraft) voler; (taxi) être en maraude

cruise missile N missile m de croisière

cruiser ['kruːzəʳ] N croiseur m

cruising speed ['kruːzɪŋ-] N vitesse f de croisière

crumb [krʌm] N miette f

crumble ['krʌmbl] VT émietter ▶ VI s'émietter; (plaster etc) s'effriter; (land, earth) s'ébouler; (building) s'écrouler, crouler; (fig) s'effondrer

crumbly ['krʌmblɪ] ADJ friable

crummy ['krʌmɪ] ADJ (inf) minable; (: unwell) mal fichu(e), patraque

crumpet ['krʌmpɪt] N petite crêpe (épaisse)

crumple ['krʌmpl] VT froisser, friper

crunch [krʌntʃ] VT croquer; (underfoot) faire craquer, écraser; faire crisser ▶ N (fig) instant m or moment m critique, moment de vérité

crunchy ['krʌntʃɪ] ADJ croquant(e), croustillant(e)

crusade [kruː'seɪd] N croisade f ▶ VI (fig): **to ~ for/ against** partir en croisade pour/contre

crusader [kruː'seɪdəʳ] N croisé m; **~ (for)** (fig) champion m (de)

crush [krʌʃ] N (crowd) foule f, cohue f; (love): **to have a ~ on sb** avoir le béguin pour qn; (drink): **lemon ~** citron pressé ▶ VT écraser; (crumple) froisser; (grind, break up: garlic, ice) piler; (: grapes) presser; (hopes) anéantir

crush barrier N (BRIT) barrière f de sécurité

crushing ['krʌʃɪŋ] ADJ écrasant(e)

crust [krʌst] N croûte f

crustacean [krʌs'teɪʃən] N crustacé m

crusty ['krʌstɪ] ADJ (bread) croustillant(e); (inf: person) revêche, bourru(e); (: remark) irrité(e)

crutch [krʌtʃ] N béquille f; (Tech) support m; (of garment) entrejambe m; (Anat) entrecuisse m

crux [krʌks] N point crucial

★**cry** [kraɪ] VI pleurer; (shout: also: **cry out**) crier; **why are you crying?** pourquoi pleures-tu ?; **to ~ for help** appeler à l'aide ▶ N cri m; **she had a good ~** elle a pleuré un bon coup; **it's a far ~ from ...** (fig) on est loin de ...
　　▶ **cry off** VI se dédire; se décommander
　　▶ **cry out** VI (call out, shout) pousser un cri ▶ VT crier

crybaby ['kraɪbeɪbɪ] N (inf) pleurnichard(e) (inf)

crying ['kraɪɪŋ] ADJ (fig) criant(e), flagrant(e)

cryogenics [kraɪəu'dʒenɪks] N cryogénie f

crypt [krɪpt] N crypte f

cryptic ['krɪptɪk] ADJ énigmatique

crystal ['krɪstl] N cristal m

crystal-clear ['krɪstl'klɪəʳ] ADJ clair(e) comme de l'eau de roche

crystallize ['krɪstəlaɪz] VT cristalliser; **crystallized fruits** (BRIT) fruits confits ▶ VI (se) cristalliser

CSA N ABBR = **Confederate States of America**; (BRIT: = Child Support Agency) organisme pour la protection des enfants de parents séparés, qui contrôle le versement des pensions alimentaires.

CSC N ABBR (= Civil Service Commission) commission de recrutement des fonctionnaires

CS gas N (BRIT) gaz m C.S.

CST ABBR (US: = Central Standard Time) fuseau horaire

CT ABBR (US) = **Connecticut**

ct ABBR = **carat**

CTC N ABBR (BRIT) = **city technology college**

CT scanner N ABBR (Med: = computerized tomography scanner) scanner m, tomodensitomètre m

cu. ABBR = **cubic**

cub [kʌb] N petit m (d'un animal); (also: **cub scout**) louveteau m

Cuba ['kju:bə] N Cuba m

Cuban ['kju:bən] ADJ cubain(e) ▶ N Cubain(e)

cubbyhole ['kʌbɪhəul] N cagibi m

cube [kju:b] N cube m ▶ VT (Math) élever au cube

cube root N racine f cubique

cubic ['kju:bɪk] ADJ cubique; **~ metre** etc mètre m etc cube; **~ capacity** (Aut) cylindrée f

cubicle ['kju:bɪkl] N (in hospital) box m; (at pool) cabine f

cuckoo ['kuku] N coucou m

cuckoo clock N (pendule f à) coucou m

★**cucumber** ['kju:kʌmbəʳ] N concombre m

cud [kʌd] N: **to chew the ~** ruminer

cuddle ['kʌdl] VT câliner, caresser ▶ VI se blottir l'un contre l'autre ▶ N câlin; **to give sb a ~** faire un câlin à qn
▶ **cuddle up** VI: **to ~ up with** or **to sb** se blottir contre qn

cuddly ['kʌdlɪ] ADJ câlin(e)

cudgel ['kʌdʒl] N gourdin m ▶ VT: **to ~ one's brains** se creuser la tête

cue [kju:] N queue f de billard; (Theat etc) signal m

cuff [kʌf] N (BRIT: of shirt, coat etc) poignet m, manchette f; (US: on trousers) revers m; (blow) gifle f; **off the ~** adv à l'improviste ▶ VT gifler

cufflinks ['kʌflɪŋks] N boutons m de manchette

cu. ft. ABBR = **cubic feet**

cu. in. ABBR = **cubic inches**

cuisine [kwɪ'zi:n] N cuisine f, art m culinaire

cul-de-sac ['kʌldəsæk] N cul-de-sac m, impasse f

culinary ['kʌlɪnərɪ] ADJ culinaire

cull [kʌl] VT sélectionner; (kill selectively) pratiquer l'abattage sélectif de ▶ N (of animals) abattage sélectif

culminate ['kʌlmɪneɪt] VI: **to ~ in** finir or se terminer par; (lead to) mener à

culmination [kʌlmɪ'neɪʃən] N point culminant

culottes [kju:'lɔts] NPL jupe-culotte f

culpability [kʌlpə'bɪlɪtɪ] N culpabilité f

culpable ['kʌlpəbl] ADJ coupable

culprit ['kʌlprɪt] N coupable mf

cult [kʌlt] N culte m

cult figure N idole f

cultivate ['kʌltɪveɪt] VT (also fig) cultiver

cultivation [kʌltɪ'veɪʃən] N culture f

cultural ['kʌltʃərəl] ADJ culturel(le)

★**culture** ['kʌltʃəʳ] N (also fig) culture f

cultured ['kʌltʃəd] ADJ cultivé(e) (fig)

culvert ['kʌlvət] N caniveau m

cumbersome ['kʌmbəsəm] ADJ encombrant(e), embarrassant(e)

cumin ['kʌmɪn] N (spice) cumin m

cumulative ['kju:mjulətɪv] ADJ cumulatif(-ive)

cunning ['kʌnɪŋ] N ruse f, astuce f ▶ ADJ rusé(e), malin(-igne); (clever: device, idea) astucieux(-euse)

cunt [kʌnt] N (inf!) chatte f (!); (insult) salaud m (!), salope f (!)

★**cup** [kʌp] N tasse f; (prize, event) coupe f; (of bra) bonnet m; **a ~ of tea** une tasse de thé

★**cupboard** ['kʌbəd] N placard m

cupcake ['kʌpkeɪk] N petit gâteau m

cup final N (BRIT Football) finale f de la coupe

cupful ['kʌpful] N tasse f

Cupid ['kju:pɪd] N Cupidon m; (figurine) amour m

cupidity [kju:'pɪdɪtɪ] N cupidité f

cupola ['kju:pələ] N coupole f

cuppa ['kʌpə] N (BRIT inf) tasse f de thé

cup tie ['kʌptaɪ] N (BRIT Football) match m de coupe

curable ['kjuərəbl] ADJ guérissable, curable

curate ['kjuərɪt] N vicaire m

curator [kjuə'reɪtəʳ] N conservateur(-trice) (d'un musée etc)

curb [kə:b] VT refréner, mettre un frein à; (expenditure) limiter, juguler ▶ N (fig) frein m; (US) bord m du trottoir

curd cheese N = fromage blanc

curdle ['kə:dl] VI (se) cailler

curds [kə:dz] NPL lait caillé

cure [kjuəʳ] VT guérir; (Culin: salt) saler; (: smoke) fumer; (: dry) sécher; **to be cured of sth** être guéri de qch ▶ N remède m

cure-all ['kjuərɔ:l] N (also fig) panacée f

curfew ['kə:fju:] N couvre-feu m

curio ['kjuərɪəu] N bibelot m, curiosité f

curiosity [kjuərɪ'ɔsɪtɪ] N curiosité f

★**curious** ['kjuərɪəs] ADJ curieux(-euse); **I'm ~ about him** il m'intrigue

curiously ['kjuərɪəslɪ] ADV curieusement; (inquisitively) avec curiosité; **~ enough, ...** bizarrement, ...

curl [kə:l] N boucle f (de cheveux); (of smoke etc) volute f ▶ VT, VI boucler; (tightly) friser
▶ **curl up** VI s'enrouler; (person) se pelotonner

curler ['kə:ləʳ] N bigoudi m, rouleau m; (Sport) joueur(-euse) de curling

curlew ['kə:lu:] N courlis m

curling ['kə:lɪŋ] N (sport) curling m

curling tongs, (US) **curling irons** NPL fer m à friser

curly ['kə:lɪ] ADJ bouclé(e); (tightly curled) frisé(e)

573

currant ['kʌrnt] N raisin m de Corinthe, raisin sec; (fruit) groseille f

★**currency** ['kʌrnsɪ] N monnaie f; **foreign ~** devises étrangères, monnaie étrangère; **to gain ~** (fig) s'accréditer

current ['kʌrnt] N courant m; **direct/alternating ~** (Elec) courant continu/alternatif ▸ ADJ (common) courant(e); (tendency, price, event) actuel(le); **the ~ issue of a magazine** le dernier numéro d'un magazine; **in ~ use** d'usage courant

current account N (BRIT) compte courant

current affairs NPL (questions fpl d')actualité f

current assets NPL (Comm) actif m disponible

current liabilities NPL (Comm) passif m exigible

currently ['kʌrntlɪ] ADV actuellement

curriculum [kə'rɪkjuləm] (pl **curriculums** or **curricula** [-lə]) N programme m d'études

curriculum vitae [-'viːtaɪ] N curriculum vitae (CV) m

curry ['kʌrɪ] N curry m; **chicken ~** curry de poulet, poulet m au curry ▸ VT: **to ~ favour with** chercher à gagner la faveur or à s'attirer les bonnes grâces de

curry powder N poudre f de curry

curse [kəːs] VI jurer, blasphémer ▸ VT maudire ▸ N (spell) malédiction f; (problem, scourge) fléau m; (swearword) juron m

cursor ['kəːsər] N (Comput) curseur m

cursory ['kəːsərɪ] ADJ superficiel(le), hâtif(-ive)

curt [kəːt] ADJ brusque, sec (sèche)

curtail [kəː'teɪl] VT (visit etc) écourter; (expenses etc) réduire

★**curtain** ['kəːtn] N rideau m; **to draw the curtains** (together) fermer or tirer les rideaux; (apart) ouvrir les rideaux

curtain call N (Theat) rappel m

curtsey, curtsy ['kəːtsɪ] N révérence f ▸ VI faire une révérence

curvaceous [kəː'veɪʃəs] ADJ plantureux(-euse)

curvature ['kəːvətʃər] N courbure f

curve [kəːv] N courbe f; (in the road) tournant m, virage m ▸ VT courber ▸ VI se courber; (road) faire une courbe

curved [kəːvd] ADJ courbe

cushion ['kuʃən] N coussin m ▸ VT (seat) rembourrer; (fall, shock) amortir

cushy ['kuʃɪ] ADJ (inf): **a ~ job** un boulot de tout repos; **to have a ~ time** se la couler douce

cusp [kʌsp] N: **to be on the ~ of sth** être à l'orée de qch

custard ['kʌstəd] N (for pouring) crème anglaise

custard powder N (BRIT) ≈ crème anglaise instantanée

custodial sentence [kʌs'təudɪəl-] N peine f de prison

custodian [kʌs'təudɪən] N gardien(ne); (of collection etc) conservateur(-trice)

custody ['kʌstədɪ] N (of child) garde f; (for offenders) détention préventive; **to take sb into ~** placer qn en détention préventive; **in the ~ of** sous la garde de

custom ['kʌstəm] N coutume f, usage m; (Law) droit coutumier, coutume; (Comm) clientèle f

customary ['kʌstəmərɪ] ADJ habituel(le); **it is ~ to do it** l'usage veut qu'on le fasse

custom-built ['kʌstəm'bɪlt] ADJ see **custom-made**

★**customer** ['kʌstəmər] N client(e); **he's an awkward ~** (inf) ce n'est pas quelqu'un de facile

customer profile N profil m du client

customize ['kʌstəmaɪz] VT personnaliser; customiser

customized ['kʌstəmaɪzd] ADJ personnalisé(e); (car etc) construit(e) sur commande

custom-made ['kʌstəm'meɪd] ADJ (clothes) fait(e) sur mesure; (other goods: also: **custom-built**) hors série, fait(e) sur commande

customs ['kʌstəmz] NPL douane f; **to go through (the) ~** passer la douane

Customs and Excise N (BRIT) administration f des douanes

customs officer N douanier(-ière)

★**cut** [kʌt] (pt, pp **~**) VT couper; (meat) découper; (shape, make) tailler; couper; creuser; graver; (reduce) réduire; (inf: lecture, appointment) manquer; **to ~ teeth** (baby) faire ses dents; **to ~ a tooth** percer une dent; **to ~ one's finger** se couper le doigt; **to get one's hair ~** se faire couper les cheveux; **I've ~ myself** je me suis coupé; **to ~ sth short** couper court à qch; **to ~ sb dead** ignorer (complètement) qn ▸ VI (intersect) se couper ▸ N (gen) coupure f; (of clothes) coupe f; (of jewel) taille f; (in salary etc) réduction f; (of meat) morceau m
  ▸ **cut back** VT (plants) tailler; (production, expenditure) réduire
  ▸ **cut down** VT (tree) abattre; (reduce) réduire; **to ~ sb down to size** (fig) remettre qn à sa place
  ▸ **cut down on** VT FUS réduire
  ▸ **cut in** VI (interrupt: conversation): **to ~ in (on)** couper la parole (à); (Aut) faire une queue de poisson
  ▸ **cut off** VT couper; (fig) isoler; **we've been ~ off** (Tel) nous avons été coupés
  ▸ **cut out** VT (picture etc) découper; (remove) supprimer
  ▸ **cut up** VT découper

cut-and-dried ['kʌtən'draɪd] ADJ (also: **cut-and-dry**) tout(e) fait(e), tout(e) décidé(e)

cutaway ['kʌtəweɪ] ADJ, N: **~ (drawing)** écorché m

cutback ['kʌtbæk] N réduction f

cute [kjuːt] ADJ mignon(ne), adorable; (clever) rusé(e), astucieux(-euse)

cut glass N cristal taillé

cuticle ['kjuːtɪkl] N (on nail) cuticule f; **~ remover** repousse-peaux m inv

cutlery ['kʌtlərɪ] N couverts mpl; (trade) coutellerie f

cutlet ['kʌtlɪt] N côtelette f

cutoff ['kʌtɔf] N (also: **cutoff point**) seuil-limite m

cutoff switch N interrupteur m

cutout ['kʌtaut] N coupe-circuit m inv; (paper figure) découpage m

cut-price ['kʌt'praɪs], (US) **cut-rate** ['kʌt'reɪt] ADJ au rabais, à prix réduit

cut-throat ['kʌtθrəut] N assassin m ▸ ADJ: **~ competition** concurrence f sauvage

cutting ['kʌtɪŋ] ADJ tranchant(e), coupant(e); (fig) cinglant(e) ▸ N (BRIT: from newspaper) coupure f (de journal); (from plant) bouture f; (Rail) tranchée f; (Cine) montage m

cutting edge N (of knife) tranchant m; **on** or **at the ~ of** à la pointe de

cutting-edge [kʌtɪŋ'ɛdʒ] ADJ (technology, research) de pointe

cuttlefish ['kʌtlfɪʃ] N seiche f

cut-up ['kʌtʌp] ADJ affecté(e), démoralisé(e)

★**CV** N ABBR = **curriculum vitae**

cwo ABBR (Comm) = **cash with order**

cwt ABBR = **hundredweight**

cyanide ['saɪənaɪd] N cyanure m

cyberattack ['saɪbərətæk] N cyber-attaque f

cyberbully ['saɪbəbulɪ] N cyberharceleur(-euse)

cyberbullying ['saɪbəbulɪŋ] N cyberharcèlement m

cybercafé ['saɪbəkæfeɪ] N cybercafé m

cybercrime ['saɪbəkraɪm] N cybercriminalité f

cybernetics [saɪbə'nɛtɪks] N cybernétique f

cybersecurity [saɪbəsɪ'kjʊrɪtɪ] N cyber-sécurité f

cyberspace ['saɪbəspeɪs] N cyberespace m

cybersquatting ['saɪbəskwɔtɪŋ] N cybersquatting m

cyberterrorism [saɪbə'tɛrərɪzəm] N cyberterrorisme m

cyborg ['saɪbɔːg] N cyborg m

cyclamen ['sɪkləmən] N cyclamen m

★**cycle** ['saɪkl] N cycle m; (bicycle) bicyclette f, vélo m ▶ VI faire de la bicyclette

cycle hire N location f de vélos

cycle lane, cycle path N piste f cyclable

cycle race N course f cycliste

cycle rack N râtelier m à bicyclette

cyclical ['sɪklɪkl, 'saɪklɪkl] ADJ cyclique

cycling ['saɪklɪŋ] N cyclisme m; **to go on a ~ holiday** (BRIT) faire du cyclotourisme

cyclist ['saɪklɪst] N cycliste mf

cyclone ['saɪkləun] N cyclone m

cygnet ['sɪgnɪt] N jeune cygne m

cylinder ['sɪlɪndəʳ] N cylindre m

cylinder capacity N cylindrée f

cylinder head N culasse f

cymbals ['sɪmblz] NPL cymbales fpl

cynic ['sɪnɪk] N cynique mf

cynical ['sɪnɪkl] ADJ cynique

cynicism ['sɪnɪsɪzəm] N cynisme m

CYO N ABBR (US: = Catholic Youth Organization) ≈ JC f

cypress ['saɪprɪs] N cyprès m

Cypriot ['sɪprɪət] ADJ cypriote, chypriote ▶ N Cypriote mf, Chypriote mf

Cyprus ['saɪprəs] N Chypre f

cyst [sɪst] N kyste m

cystitis [sɪs'taɪtɪs] N cystite f

CZ N ABBR (US: = Central Zone) zone du canal de Panama

czar [zɑːʳ] N tsar m

Czech [tʃɛk] ADJ tchèque ▶ N Tchèque mf; (Ling) tchèque m

Czechia ['tʃɛkɪə] N (Czech Republic) Tchéquie f

Czechoslovak [tʃɛkə'sləuvæk] ADJ, N (Hist) = **Czechoslovakian**

Czechoslovakia [tʃɛkəslə'vækɪə] N (Hist) Tchécoslovaquie f

Czechoslovakian [tʃɛkəslə'vækɪən] (Hist) ADJ tchécoslovaque ▶ N Tchécoslovaque mf

Czech Republic N: **the ~** la République tchèque

Dd

D¹, d¹ [di:] N (*letter*) D, d *m*; (*Mus*): **D** ré *m*; **D for David**, (*US*) **D for Dog** D comme Désirée

D² ABBR (*US Pol*) = **democrat; democratic**

d² ABBR (*Brit old*) = **penny**

d. ABBR = **died**

DA N ABBR (*US*) = **district attorney**

DAB N ABBR (= *digital audio broadcasting*) DAB *m*

dab [dæb] VT (*eyes, wound*) tamponner; (*paint, cream*) appliquer (par petites touches *or* rapidement) ▶ N: **a ~ of paint** un petit coup de peinture

dabble ['dæbl] VI: **to ~ in** faire *or* se mêler *or* s'occuper un peu de

Dacca ['dækə] N Dacca

dachshund ['dækshund] N teckel *m*

★**dad, daddy** [dæd, 'dædɪ] N papa *m*

daddy-long-legs [dædɪ'lɔŋlegz] N tipule *f*; faucheux *m*

daffodil ['dæfədɪl] N jonquille *f*

daft [dɑ:ft] ADJ (*inf*) idiot(e), stupide; **to be ~ about** être toqué(e) *or* mordu(e) de

dagger ['dægə*ʳ*] N poignard *m*; **to be at daggers drawn with sb** être à couteaux tirés avec qn; **to look daggers at sb** foudroyer qn du regard

dahlia ['deɪljə] N dahlia *m*

★**daily** ['deɪlɪ] ADJ quotidien(ne), journalier(-ière) ▶ N quotidien *m*; (*Brit: servant*) femme *f* de ménage (à la journée) ▶ ADV tous les jours; **twice ~** deux fois par jour

dainty ['deɪntɪ] ADJ délicat(e), mignon(ne)

dairy ['dεərɪ] N (*shop*) crémerie *f*, laiterie *f*; (*on farm*) laiterie *f* ▶ ADJ laitier(-ière)

dairy cow N vache laitière

dairy farm N exploitation *f* pratiquant l'élevage laitier

dairy produce N produits laitiers

dairy products NPL produits laitiers

dais ['deɪɪs] N estrade *f*

daisy ['deɪzɪ] N pâquerette *f*

Dakar ['dækə] N Dakar

dale [deɪl] N vallon *m*

dalliance ['dælɪəns] N (*with person*) badinage amoureux; (*with idea, thing*) flirt *m*

dally ['dælɪ] VI musarder, flâner

dalmatian [dæl'meɪʃən] N (*dog*) dalmatien(ne)

dam [dæm] N (*wall*) barrage *m*; (*water*) réservoir *m*, lac *m* de retenue ▶ VT endiguer

★**damage** ['dæmɪdʒ] N dégâts *mpl*, dommages *mpl*; (*fig*) tort *m*; **~ to property** dégâts matériels ▶ VT endommager, abîmer; (*fig*) faire du tort à ■ **damages** NPL (*Law*) dommages-intérêts *mpl*; **to pay £5000 in damages** payer 5000 livres de dommages-intérêts

damage limitation N: **an exercise in ~** une opération visant à limiter les dégâts

damaging ['dæmɪdʒɪŋ] ADJ: **~ (to)** préjudiciable (à), nuisible (à)

Damascus [də'mɑ:skəs] N Damas

dame [deɪm] N (*title*) titre porté par une femme décorée de l'ordre de l'Empire britannique ou d'un ordre de chevalerie, *titre porté par la femme ou la veuve d'un chevalier ou baronnet*; (*US inf*) nana *f*; (*Theat*) vieille dame (*rôle comique joué par un homme*)

damn [dæm] VT condamner; (*curse*) maudire ▶ N (*inf*): **I don't give a ~** je m'en fous ▶ ADJ (*inf*: *also*: **damned**): **this ~ ...** ce sacré *or* foutu ... ▶ EXCL: **~!** (*also*: **damn it!**) zut !

damnable ['dæmnəbl] ADJ (*inf*: *behaviour*) odieux(-euse), détestable; (*: weather*) épouvantable, abominable

damnation [dæm'neɪʃən] N (*Rel*) damnation *f* ▶ EXCL (*inf*) malédiction !, merde !

damning ['dæmɪŋ] ADJ (*evidence*) accablant(e)

damp [dæmp] ADJ humide ▶ N humidité *f* ▶ VT (*also*: **dampen**: *cloth, rag*) humecter; (*: enthusiasm etc*) refroidir

dampcourse ['dæmpkɔ:s] N couche isolante (contre l'humidité)

dampener ['dæmpnə*ʳ*] N: **to put a ~ on sth** gâcher qch

damper ['dæmpə*ʳ*] N (*Mus*) étouffoir *m*; (*of fire*) registre *m*; **to put a ~ on sth** (*fig*) gâcher qch

dampness ['dæmpnɪs] N humidité *f*

damson ['dæmzən] N prune *f* de Damas

★**dance** [dɑ:ns] N danse *f*; (*ball*) bal *m* ▶ VI danser; **to ~ about** sautiller, gambader

dance floor N piste *f* de danse

dance hall N salle *f* de bal, dancing *m*

dancer ['dɑ:nsə*ʳ*] N danseur(-euse)

dancing ['dɑ:nsɪŋ] N danse *f*

D and C N ABBR (*Med*: = *dilation and curettage*) curetage *m*

dandelion ['dændɪlaɪən] N pissenlit *m*

dandruff ['dændrəf] N pellicules *fpl*

D & T N ABBR (*Brit Scol*) = **design and technology**

dandy ['dændɪ] N dandy *m*, élégant *m* ▶ ADJ (*US inf*) fantastique, super

Dane [deɪn] N Danois(e)

★**danger** [ˈdeɪndʒəʳ] N danger m; ~! (on sign) danger !; **there is a ~ of fire** il y a (un) risque d'incendie; **in ~** en danger; **he was in ~ of falling** il risquait de tomber; **out of ~** hors de danger

danger list N (Med): **on the ~** dans un état critique

danger money N (BRIT) prime f de risque

★**dangerous** [ˈdeɪndʒrəs] ADJ dangereux(-euse)

dangerously [ˈdeɪndʒrəslɪ] ADV dangereusement; **~ ill** très gravement malade, en danger de mort

danger zone N zone dangereuse

dangle [ˈdæŋgl] VT balancer; (fig) faire miroiter ▶ VI pendre, se balancer

★**Danish** [ˈdeɪnɪʃ] ADJ danois(e) ▶ N (Ling) danois m

Danish pastry N feuilleté m (recouvert d'un glaçage et fourré aux fruits etc)

dank [dæŋk] ADJ froid(e) et humide

Danube [ˈdænjuːb] N: **the ~** le Danube

dapper [ˈdæpəʳ] ADJ pimpant(e)

dappled [ˈdæpld] ADJ (horse) pommelé(e); **to be ~ with sunlight** être tacheté(e) de lumière

Dardanelles [dɑːdəˈnɛlz] NPL Dardanelles fpl

dare [dɛəʳ] VT: **to ~ sb to do** défier qn or mettre qn au défi de faire ▶ AUX VB: **to ~ (to) do sth** oser faire qch; **I daren't tell him** (BRIT) je n'ose pas le lui dire; **I ~ say he'll turn up** il est probable qu'il viendra

daredevil [ˈdɛədɛvl] N casse-cou m inv

Dar-es-Salaam [dɑːrɛssəˈlɑːm] N Dar-es-Salaam, Dar-es-Salam

daring [ˈdɛərɪŋ] ADJ hardi(e), audacieux(-euse) ▶ N audace f, hardiesse f

★**dark** [dɑːk] ADJ (night, room) obscur(e), sombre; (colour, complexion) foncé(e); (fig) sombre; **it is/is getting ~** il fait nuit/commence à faire nuit ▶ N: **in the ~** dans le noir; **to be in the ~ about** (fig) ignorer tout de; **after ~** après la tombée de la nuit

darken [ˈdɑːkn] VT obscurcir, assombrir ▶ VI s'obscurcir, s'assombrir

darkened [ˈdɑːknd] ADJ (house, room) plongé(e) dans l'obscurité

dark glasses NPL lunettes noires

dark horse N (fig): **he's a ~** on ne sait pas grand-chose de lui

darkly [ˈdɑːklɪ] ADV (gloomily) mélancoliquement; (in a sinister way) lugubrement

darkness [ˈdɑːknɪs] N obscurité f

darkroom [ˈdɑːkrum] N chambre noire

darling [ˈdɑːlɪŋ] ADJ, N chéri(e)

darn [dɑːn] VT repriser

dart [dɑːt] N fléchette f; (in sewing) pince f ▶ VI: **to ~ towards** (also: **make a dart towards**) se précipiter or s'élancer vers; **to ~ away/along** partir/passer comme une flèche

dartboard [ˈdɑːtbɔːd] N cible f (de jeu de fléchettes)

darts [dɑːts] N jeu m de fléchettes

dash [dæʃ] N (sign) tiret m; (small quantity) goutte f, larme f; **a ~ of soda** un peu d'eau gazeuse ▶ VT (throw) jeter or lancer violemment; (hopes) anéantir ▶ VI: **to ~ towards** (also: **make a dash towards**) se précipiter or se ruer vers

▶ **dash away** VI partir à toute allure

▶ **dash off** VI = **dash away**

dashboard [ˈdæʃbɔːd] N (Aut) tableau m de bord

dashing [ˈdæʃɪŋ] ADJ fringant(e)

dastardly [ˈdæstədlɪ] ADJ lâche

DAT N ABBR (= digital audio tape) cassette f audio digitale

★**data** [ˈdeɪtə] NPL données fpl

database [ˈdeɪtəbeɪs] N base f de données

data capture N saisie f de données

data processing N traitement m des données

data transmission N transmission f de données

★**date** [deɪt] N date f; (with sb) rendez-vous m; (fruit) datte f; **what's the ~ today?** quelle date sommes-nous aujourd'hui ?; **~ of birth** date de naissance; **closing ~** date de clôture; **to ~** adv à ce jour; **out of ~** périmé(e); **up to ~** à la page, mis(e) à jour, moderne; **to bring up to ~** (correspondence, information) mettre à jour; (method) moderniser; (person) mettre au courant ▶ VT dater; (person) sortir avec; **letter dated 5th July** or (US) **July 5th** lettre (datée) du 5 juillet

▶ **date back to** VT FUS dater de

▶ **date from** VT FUS dater de

dated [ˈdeɪtɪd] ADJ démodé(e)

dateline [ˈdeɪtlaɪn] N ligne f de changement de date

date rape N viol m (à l'issue d'un rendez-vous galant)

date stamp N timbre-dateur m

dating [ˈdeɪtɪŋ] ADJ (service) de rencontres

daub [dɔːb] VT barbouiller

★**daughter** [ˈdɔːtəʳ] N fille f

daughter-in-law [ˈdɔːtərɪnlɔː] N belle-fille f, bru f

daunt [dɔːnt] VT intimider, décourager

daunting [ˈdɔːntɪŋ] ADJ décourageant(e), intimidant(e)

dauntless [ˈdɔːntlɪs] ADJ intrépide

dawdle [ˈdɔːdl] VI traîner, lambiner; **to ~ over one's work** traînasser or lambiner sur son travail

dawn [dɔːn] N aube f, aurore f; **at ~** à l'aube; **from ~ to dusk** du matin au soir ▶ VI (day) se lever, poindre; (fig) naître, se faire jour; **it dawned on him that ...** il lui vint à l'esprit que ...

dawn chorus N (BRIT) chant m des oiseaux à l'aube

★**day** [deɪ] N jour m; (as duration) journée f; (period of time, age) époque f, temps m; **the ~ before** la veille, le jour précédent; **the ~ after, the following ~** le lendemain, le jour suivant; **the ~ before yesterday** avant-hier; **the ~ after tomorrow** après-demain; **(on) the ~ that ...** le jour où ...; **~ by ~** jour après jour; **by ~** de jour; **paid by the ~** payé(e) à la journée; **these days, in the present ~** de nos jours, à l'heure actuelle

---

Use **jour** to mean the whole 24-hour period: *We stayed there for three days.* **Nous y sommes restés trois jours**. The word **journée** refers to the time while you are awake: *I spent all day at home.* **J'ai passé toute la journée chez moi**.

daybook ['deɪbuk] N (BRIT) main courante, brouillard m, journal m

day boy N (Scol) externe m

daybreak ['deɪbreɪk] N point m du jour

day-care centre ['deɪkɛə-] N (for elderly etc) centre m d'accueil de jour; (for children) garderie f

daydream ['deɪdri:m] N rêverie f ▶ vi rêver (tout éveillé)

day girl N (Scol) externe f

daylight ['deɪlaɪt] N (lumière f du) jour m

daylight robbery N: **it's ~** (fig: inf) c'est du vol caractérisé or manifeste

daylight saving time N (US) heure f d'été

day release N: **to be on ~** avoir une journée de congé pour formation professionnelle

day return N (BRIT) billet m d'aller-retour (valable pour la journée)

day shift N équipe f de jour

daytime ['deɪtaɪm] N jour m, journée f

day-to-day ['deɪtə'deɪ] ADJ (routine, expenses) journalier(-ière); **on a ~ basis** au jour le jour

day trip N excursion f (d'une journée)

day tripper N excursionniste mf

daze [deɪz] VT (drug) hébéter; (blow) étourdir ▶ N: **in a ~** hébété(e), étourdi(e)

dazed [deɪzd] ADJ abruti(e)

dazzle ['dæzl] VT éblouir, aveugler

dazzling ['dæzlɪŋ] ADJ (light) aveuglant(e), éblouissant(e); (fig) éblouissant(e)

DC ABBR (Elec) = **direct current**; (US) = **District of Columbia**

DD N ABBR (= Doctor of Divinity) titre universitaire

dd. ABBR (Comm) = **delivered**

D/D ABBR = **direct debit**

D-day ['di:deɪ] N le jour J

DDS N ABBR (US: = Doctor of Dental Science) titre universitaire; (BRIT: = Doctor of Dental Surgery) titre universitaire

DDT N ABBR (= dichlorodiphenyl trichloroethane) DDT m

DE ABBR (US) = **Delaware**

DEA N ABBR (US: = Drug Enforcement Administration) ≈ brigade f des stupéfiants

deacon ['di:kən] N diacre m

★**dead** [dɛd] ADJ mort(e); (numb) engourdi(e), insensible; (battery) à plat; **he was shot ~** il a été tué d'un coup de revolver; **the line is ~** (Tel) la ligne est coupée ▶ ADV (completely) absolument, complètement; (exactly) juste; **~ on time** à l'heure pile; **~ tired** éreinté(e), complètement fourbu(e); **to stop ~** s'arrêter pile or net ■ **the dead** NPL les morts

deadbeat ['dɛdbi:t] N (esp US inf) bon(ne) à rien

dead beat ADJ (inf) claqué(e), crevé(e)

deaden ['dɛdn] VT (blow, sound) amortir; (make numb) endormir, rendre insensible

dead end N impasse f

dead-end ['dɛdɛnd] ADJ: **a ~ job** un emploi or poste sans avenir

dead heat N (Sport): **to finish in a ~** terminer ex aequo

dead-letter office [dɛd'lɛtər-] N ≈ centre m de recherche du courrier

★**deadline** ['dɛdlaɪn] N date f or heure f limite; **to work to a ~** avoir des délais stricts à respecter

deadlock ['dɛdlɔk] N impasse f

deadlocked ['dɛdlɔkt] ADJ: **to be ~** (negotiations) être au point mort; (people) être dans l'impasse

dead loss N (inf): **to be a ~** (person) n'être bon(ne) à rien; (thing) ne rien valoir

deadly ['dɛdlɪ] ADJ mortel(le); (weapon) meurtrier(-ière); **~ dull** ennuyeux(-euse) à mourir, mortellement ennuyeux

deadpan ['dɛdpæn] ADJ impassible; (humour) pince-sans-rire m

Dead Sea N: **the ~** la mer Morte

★**deaf** [dɛf] ADJ sourd(e); **to turn a ~ ear to sth** faire la sourde oreille à qch

deaf-aid ['dɛfeɪd] N (BRIT) appareil auditif

deaf-and-dumb ['dɛfən'dʌm] (!) ADJ sourd(e)-muet(te); **~ alphabet** alphabet m des sourds-muets

deafen ['dɛfn] VT rendre sourd(e); (fig) assourdir

deafening ['dɛfnɪŋ] ADJ assourdissant(e)

deaf-mute ['dɛfmju:t] N (!) sourd(e)-muet(te)

deafness ['dɛfnɪs] N surdité f

★**deal** [di:l] (pt, pp **dealt** [dɛlt]) N affaire f, marché m; **to strike a ~ with sb** faire or conclure un marché avec qn; **it's a ~!** (inf) marché conclu !, tope là !, topez là !; **he got a bad ~ from them** ils ont mal agi envers lui; **he got a fair ~ from them** ils ont agi loyalement envers lui; **a good ~** (a lot) beaucoup; **a good ~ of, a great ~ of** beaucoup de, énormément de ▶ VT (blow) porter; (cards) distribuer ▶ vi (deal cards) donner; **it's your turn to ~** c'est à toi de donner
▶ **deal in** VT FUS (Comm) faire le commerce de, être dans le commerce de
▶ **deal out** VT (cards) distribuer; (punishment) donner
▶ **deal with** VT FUS (Comm) traiter avec; (handle) s'occuper or se charger de; (be about: book etc) traiter de

dealbreaker ['di:lbreɪkər] N: **it was a ~** cela a fait capoter l'affaire

dealer ['di:lər] N (Comm) marchand m; (Cards) donneur m

dealership ['di:ləʃɪp] N concession f

dealings ['di:lɪŋz] NPL (in goods, shares) opérations fpl, transactions fpl; (relations) relations fpl, rapports mpl

dealt [dɛlt] PT, PP of **deal**

dean [di:n] N (Rel, BRIT Scol) doyen m; (US Scol) conseiller principal (conseillère principale) d'éducation

★**dear** [dɪər] ADJ cher (chère); (expensive) cher, coûteux(-euse); **D~ Sir/Madam** (in letter) Monsieur/Madame; **D~ Mr/Mrs X** Cher Monsieur/Chère Madame X ▶ N: **my ~** mon cher (ma chère) ▶ EXCL: **~ me!** mon Dieu !

dearest ['dɪərɪst] N chéri(e) ▶ ADJ: **D~ Paul/Maria** Mon cher Paul/Ma chère Maria; **my ~ hope** mon plus grand espoir; **my ~ wish** mon vœu le plus cher

dearly ['dɪəlɪ] ADV (love) tendrement; (pay) cher

dearth [də:θ] N disette f, pénurie f

★**death** [dɛθ] N mort f; (Admin) décès m

deathbed ['dɛθbɛd] N lit m de mort
death certificate N acte m de décès
death knell N mort f; **to sound the ~ of sth** sonner le glas pour qch
deathly ['dɛθlɪ] ADJ de mort ▶ ADV comme la mort
death penalty N peine f de mort
death rate N taux m de mortalité
death row [-'rəu] N (US) quartier m des condamnés à mort; **to be on ~** être condamné à la peine de mort
death sentence N condamnation f à mort
death squad N escadron m de la mort
death throes NPL agonie f; **a society in its ~** une société agonisante
death toll N nombre m de morts
death trap N endroit or véhicule etc dangereux
deb [dɛb] N ABBR (inf) = **debutante**
debacle [deɪ'bɑːkl] N (BRIT: fiasco) fiasco m; (military) débâcle f
debar [dɪ'bɑːʳ] VT: **to ~ sb from a club** etc exclure qn d'un club etc; **to ~ sb from doing** interdire à qn de faire
debase [dɪ'beɪs] VT (currency) déprécier, dévaloriser; (person) abaisser, avilir
debatable [dɪ'beɪtəbl] ADJ discutable, contestable; **it is ~ whether** ... il est douteux que ...
debate [dɪ'beɪt] N discussion f, débat m ▶ VT discuter, débattre ▶ VI (consider): **to ~ whether** se demander si
debauched [dɪ'bɔːtʃt] ADJ (old: society) de débauchés, dépravé(e); **a ~ lifestyle** une vie de débauché(e)
debauchery [dɪ'bɔːtʃərɪ] N débauche f
debenture [dɪ'bɛntʃəʳ] N (Comm) obligation f
debilitate [dɪ'bɪlɪteɪt] VT débiliter
debilitating [dɪ'bɪlɪteɪtɪŋ] ADJ débilitant(e)
debit ['dɛbɪt] N débit m ▶ VT: **to ~ a sum to sb** or **to sb's account** porter une somme au débit de qn, débiter qn d'une somme
debit balance N solde débiteur
debit card N carte f de paiement
debit note N note f de débit
debrief [diː'briːf] VT demander un compte rendu de fin de mission à
debriefing [diː'briːfɪŋ] N compte rendu m
debris ['dɛbriː] N débris mpl, décombres mpl
debt [dɛt] N dette f; **to be in ~** avoir des dettes, être endetté(e); **bad ~** créance f irrécouvrable
debt collector N agent m de recouvrements
debtor ['dɛtəʳ] N débiteur(-trice)
debug [diː'bʌg] VT (Comput) déboguer
debunk [diː'bʌŋk] VT (inf: theory, claim) montrer le ridicule de
debut ['deɪbjuː] N début(s) m(pl)
debutante ['dɛbjutænt] N débutante f
Dec. ABBR (= December) déc
★**decade** ['dɛkeɪd] N décennie f, décade f
decadence ['dɛkədəns] N décadence f
decadent ['dɛkədənt] ADJ décadent(e)
decaf ['diːkæf] N (inf) déca m

decaffeinated [dɪ'kæfɪneɪtɪd] ADJ décaféiné(e)
decamp [dɪ'kæmp] VI (inf) décamper, filer
decant [dɪ'kænt] VT (wine) décanter
decanter [dɪ'kæntəʳ] N carafe f
decapitate [dɪ'kæpɪteɪt] VT décapiter
decarbonize [diː'kɑːbənaɪz] VT (Aut) décalaminer
decathlon [dɪ'kæθlən] N décathlon m
decay [dɪ'keɪ] N (of food, wood etc) décomposition f, pourriture f; (of building) délabrement m; (fig) déclin m; (also: **tooth decay**) carie f (dentaire) ▶ VI (rot) se décomposer, pourrir; (teeth) se carier; (fig: city, district, building) se délabrer; (: civilization) décliner; (: system) tomber en ruine
decease [dɪ'siːs] N décès m
deceased [dɪ'siːst] N: **the ~** le (la) défunt(e)
deceit [dɪ'siːt] N tromperie f, supercherie f
deceitful [dɪ'siːtful] ADJ trompeur(-euse)
deceive [dɪ'siːv] VT tromper; **to ~ o.s.** s'abuser

to deceive ne veut pas dire _décevoir_.

decelerate [diː'sɛləreɪt] VT, VI ralentir
★**December** [dɪ'sɛmbəʳ] N décembre m; see also **July**
decency ['diːsənsɪ] N décence f
decent ['diːsənt] ADJ (proper) décent(e), convenable; **they were very ~ about it** ils se sont montrés très chics
decently ['diːsəntlɪ] ADV (respectably) décemment, convenablement; (kindly) décemment
decentralization [diːsɛntrəlaɪ'zeɪʃən] N décentralisation f
decentralize [diː'sɛntrəlaɪz] VT décentraliser
deception [dɪ'sɛpʃən] N tromperie f

deception ne veut pas dire _déception_.

deceptive [dɪ'sɛptɪv] ADJ trompeur(-euse)
decibel ['dɛsɪbɛl] N décibel m
★**decide** [dɪ'saɪd] VT (subj: person) décider; (question, argument) trancher, régler; **to ~ to do/that** décider de faire/que ▶ VI se décider, décider; **to ~ on** décider, se décider pour; **to ~ on doing** décider de faire; **to ~ against doing** décider de ne pas faire
decided [dɪ'saɪdɪd] ADJ (resolute) résolu(e), décidé(e); (clear, definite) net(te), marqué(e)
decidedly [dɪ'saɪdɪdlɪ] ADV résolument; incontestablement, nettement
deciding [dɪ'saɪdɪŋ] ADJ décisif(-ive)
deciduous [dɪ'sɪdjuəs] ADJ à feuilles caduques
decimal ['dɛsɪməl] ADJ décimal(e); **to three ~ places** (jusqu')à la troisième décimale ▶ N décimale f
decimalize ['dɛsɪməlaɪz] VT (BRIT) décimaliser
decimal point N ≈ virgule f
decimate ['dɛsɪmeɪt] VT décimer
decimation [dɛsɪ'meɪʃən] N (reduction) décimation f; (destruction) destruction f
decipher [dɪ'saɪfəʳ] VT déchiffrer
★**decision** [dɪ'sɪʒən] N décision f; **to make a ~** prendre une décision
decisive [dɪ'saɪsɪv] ADJ décisif(-ive); (influence) décisif, déterminant(e); (manner, person) décidé(e), catégorique; (reply) ferme, catégorique

decisiveness [dɪ'saɪsɪvnɪs] N (of person) esprit m de décision

★**deck** [dɛk] N (Naut) pont m; (of cards) jeu m; (record deck) platine f; (of bus): **top ~** impériale f; **to go up on ~** monter sur le pont; **below ~** dans l'entrepont

deckchair ['dɛktʃɛəʳ] N chaise longue

deck hand N matelot m

declaration [dɛklə'reɪʃən] N déclaration f

declare [dɪ'klɛəʳ] VT déclarer

declassify [di:'klæsɪfaɪ] VT rendre accessible au public or à tous

decline [dɪ'klaɪn] N (decay) déclin m; (lessening) baisse f; **~ in living standards** baisse du niveau de vie ▸ VT refuser, décliner; **to ~ to do sth** refuser (poliment) de faire qch ▸ VI décliner; (business) baisser

declutch ['di:'klʌtʃ] VI (BRIT) débrayer

declutter [di:'klʌtər] VT désencombrer

decode [di:'kəʊd] VT décoder

decoder [di:'kəʊdəʳ] N (Comput, TV) décodeur m

decommission [di:kə'mɪʃən] VT mettre hors service

decompose [di:kəm'pəʊz] VI se décomposer

decomposition [di:kɒmpə'zɪʃən] N décomposition f

decompression [di:kəm'prɛʃən] N décompression f

decompression chamber N caisson m de décompression

decongestant [di:kən'dʒɛstənt] N décongestif m

deconstruct [di:kən'strʌkt] VT déconstruire

decontaminate [di:kən'tæmɪneɪt] VT décontaminer

decontrol [di:kən'trəʊl] VT (prices etc) libérer

décor ['deɪkɔ:ʳ] N décor m

★**decorate** ['dɛkəreɪt] VT (adorn, give a medal to) décorer; (paint and paper) peindre et tapisser

decorating ['dɛkəreɪtɪŋ] N (painting and papering) peinture f et tapisserie f

decoration [dɛkə'reɪʃən] N (medal etc, adornment) décoration f

decorative ['dɛkərətɪv] ADJ décoratif(-ive)

decorator ['dɛkəreɪtəʳ] N peintre m en bâtiment

decorum [dɪ'kɔ:rəm] N décorum m, bienséance f

decoy ['di:kɔɪ] N piège m; **they used him as a ~ for the enemy** ils se sont servis de lui pour attirer l'ennemi

decrease N ['di:kri:s] diminution f; **to be on the ~** diminuer, être en diminution ▸ VT, VI [di:'kri:s] diminuer

decreasing [di:'kri:sɪŋ] ADJ en voie de diminution

decree [dɪ'kri:] N (Pol, Rel) décret m; (Law) arrêt m, jugement m; **~ absolute** jugement définitif (de divorce); **~ nisi** jugement provisoire de divorce ▸ VT: **to ~ (that)** décréter (que), ordonner (que)

decrepit [dɪ'krɛpɪt] ADJ (person) décrépit(e); (building) délabré(e)

decriminalization [di:krɪmɪnəlaɪˈzeɪʃən] N dépénalisation f

decriminalize [di:'krɪmɪnəlaɪz] VT dépénaliser

decry [dɪ'kraɪ] VT condamner ouvertement, déplorer; (disparage) dénigrer, décrier

decrypt [di:'krɪpt] VT (Comput, Tel) décrypter

dedicate ['dɛdɪkeɪt] VT consacrer; (book etc) dédier

dedicated ['dɛdɪkeɪtɪd] ADJ (person) dévoué(e); (Comput) spécialisé(e), dédié(e); **~ word processor** station f de traitement de texte

dedication [dɛdɪ'keɪʃən] N (devotion) dévouement m; (in book) dédicace f

deduce [dɪ'dju:s] VT déduire, conclure

deduct [dɪ'dʌkt] VT: **to ~ sth (from)** déduire qch (de), retrancher qch (de); (from wage etc) prélever qch (sur), retenir qch (sur)

deduction [dɪ'dʌkʃən] N (deducting, deducing) déduction f; (from wage etc) prélèvement m, retenue f

deductive [dɪ'dʌktɪv] ADJ déductif(-ive)

deed [di:d] N action f, acte m; (Law) acte notarié, contrat m; **~ of covenant** (acte m de) donation f

deem [di:m] VT (formal) juger, estimer; **to ~ it wise to do** juger bon de faire

★**deep** [di:p] ADJ (water, sigh, sorrow, thoughts) profond(e); (voice) grave; **how ~ is the water?** l'eau a quelle profondeur ?; **he took a ~ breath** il inspira profondément, il prit son souffle ▸ ADV: **~ in snow** recouvert(e) d'une épaisse couche de neige; **spectators stood 20 ~** il y avait 20 rangs de spectateurs; **knee-deep in water** dans l'eau jusqu'aux genoux; **4 metres ~** de 4 mètres de profondeur

deepen ['di:pn] VT (hole) approfondir ▸ VI s'approfondir; (darkness) s'épaissir

deepfreeze ['di:p'fri:z] N congélateur m ▸ VT surgeler

deep-fry ['di:p'fraɪ] VT faire frire (dans une friteuse)

deeply ['di:plɪ] ADV profondément; (dig) en profondeur; (regret, interested) vivement

deep-rooted ['di:p'ru:tɪd] ADJ (prejudice) profondément enraciné(e); (affection) profond(e); (habit) invétéré(e)

deep-sea ['di:p'si:] ADJ: **~ diver** plongeur sous-marin; **~ diving** plongée sous-marine; **~ fishing** pêche hauturière

deep-seated ['di:p'si:tɪd] ADJ (belief) profondément enraciné(e)

deep-set ['di:p'sɛt] ADJ (eyes) enfoncé(e)

deep vein thrombosis N thrombose f veineuse profonde

deer [dɪəʳ] N pl inv: **the ~** les cervidés mpl; **(red) ~** cerf m; **(fallow) ~** daim m; **(roe) ~** chevreuil m

deerskin ['dɪəskɪn] N peau f de daim

deerstalker ['dɪəstɔ:kəʳ] N (person) chasseur m de cerf; (hat) casquette f à la Sherlock Holmes

deface [dɪ'feɪs] VT dégrader; barbouiller; rendre illisible

de facto [deɪ'fæktəʊ] ADJ de fait ▸ ADV de facto

defamation [dɛfə'meɪʃən] N diffamation f

defamatory [dɪ'fæmətrɪ] ADJ diffamatoire, diffamant(e)

default [dɪ'fɔ:lt] N (Law) faire défaut; (gen) manquer à ses engagements; **to ~ on a debt** ne pas s'acquitter d'une dette ▸ N (Comput: also: **default**

value) valeur f par défaut; **by ~** (Law) par défaut, par contumace; (Sport) par forfait

defaulter [dɪˈfɔːltəʳ] N (on debt) débiteur défaillant

default option N (Comput) option f par défaut

★**defeat** [dɪˈfiːt] N défaite f ▶ VT (team, opponents) battre; (fig: plans, efforts) faire échouer

defeatism [dɪˈfiːtɪzəm] N défaitisme m

defeatist [dɪˈfiːtɪst] ADJ, N défaitiste mf

defecate [ˈdɛfəkeɪt] VI déféquer

defect N [ˈdiːfɛkt] défaut m; **physical ~** malformation f, vice m de conformation; **mental ~** anomalie or déficience mentale ▶ VI [dɪˈfɛkt]: **to ~ to the enemy/the West** passer à l'ennemi/l'Ouest

defection [dɪˈfɛkʃən] N défection f

defective [dɪˈfɛktɪv] ADJ défectueux(-euse)

defector [dɪˈfɛktəʳ] N transfuge mf

★**defence**, (US) **defense** [dɪˈfɛns] N défense f; **in ~ of** pour défendre; **witness for the ~** témoin m à décharge; **the Ministry of D~**, (US) **the Department of Defense** le ministère de la Défense nationale

defenceless, (US) **defenseless** [dɪˈfɛnslɪs] ADJ sans défense

★**defend** [dɪˈfɛnd] VT défendre; (decision, action, opinion) justifier, défendre

defendant [dɪˈfɛndənt] N défendeur(-eresse); (in criminal case) accusé(e), prévenu(e)

defender [dɪˈfɛndəʳ] N défenseur m

defending champion [dɪˈfɛndɪŋ-] N (Sport) champion(ne) en titre

defending counsel [dɪˈfɛndɪŋ-] N (Law) avocat m de la défense

defense [ˈdiːfɛns] N (US) = **defence**

defensible [dɪˈfɛnsɪbl] ADJ défendable; **morally ~** moralement défendable

defensive [dɪˈfɛnsɪv] ADJ défensif(-ive) ▶ N défensive f; **on the ~** sur la défensive

defensively [dɪˈfɛnsɪvlɪ] ADV (play) défensivement; (say) sur la défensive

defer [dɪˈfɜːʳ] VT (postpone) différer, ajourner ▶ VI (submit): **to ~ to sb/sth** déférer à qn/qch, s'en remettre à qn/qch

deference [ˈdɛfərəns] N déférence f, égards mpl; **out of** or **in ~ to** par déférence or égards pour

deferential [dɛfəˈrɛnʃl] ADJ déférent(e)

defiance [dɪˈfaɪəns] N défi m; **in ~ of** au mépris de

defiant [dɪˈfaɪənt] ADJ provocant(e), de défi; (person) rebelle, intraitable

defiantly [dɪˈfaɪəntlɪ] ADV d'un air (or d'un ton) de défi

defibrillator [diːˈfɪbrɪleɪtəʳ] N défibrillateur m

deficiency [dɪˈfɪʃənsɪ] N (lack) insuffisance f; (: Med) carence f; (flaw) faiblesse f; (Comm) déficit m, découvert m

deficiency disease N maladie f de carence

deficient [dɪˈfɪʃənt] ADJ (inadequate) insuffisant(e); (defective) défectueux(-euse); **to be ~ in** manquer de

deficit [ˈdɛfɪsɪt] N déficit m

defile [dɪˈfaɪl] VT souiller ▶ VI défiler

define [dɪˈfaɪn] VT définir

definite [ˈdɛfɪnɪt] ADJ (fixed) défini(e), (bien) déterminé(e); (clear, obvious) net(te), manifeste; (Ling) défini(e); (certain) sûr(e); **he was ~ about it** il a été catégorique; il était sûr de son fait

★**definitely** [ˈdɛfɪnɪtlɪ] ADV sans aucun doute

definition [dɛfɪˈnɪʃən] N définition f; (clearness) netteté f

definitive [dɪˈfɪnɪtɪv] ADJ définitif(-ive)

definitively [dɪˈfɪnɪtɪvlɪ] ADV de façon absolue

deflate [dɪˈfleɪt] VT dégonfler; (pompous person) rabattre le caquet à; (Econ) provoquer la déflation de; (: prices) faire tomber or baisser

deflated [dɪˈfleɪtɪd] ADJ (person) découragé(e)

deflation [dɪˈfleɪʃən] N (Econ) déflation f

deflationary [dɪˈfleɪʃənrɪ] ADJ (Econ) déflationniste

deflect [dɪˈflɛkt] VT détourner, faire dévier

defog [diːˈfɔg] VT (US Aut) désembuer

defogger [diːˈfɔgəʳ] N (US Aut) dispositif m anti-buée inv

deforest [diːˈfɔrɪst] VT déforester

deforestation [diːfɔrɪˈsteɪʃən] N déforestation f

deform [dɪˈfɔːm] VT déformer

deformed [dɪˈfɔːmd] ADJ difforme

deformity [dɪˈfɔːmɪtɪ] N difformité f

DEFRA [ˈdɛfrə] N ABBR (Brit: = Department for Environment, Food and Rural Affairs) ≈ ministère m de l'agriculture

defraud [dɪˈfrɔːd] VT frauder; **to ~ sb of sth** soutirer qch malhonnêtement à qn; escroquer qch à qn; frustrer qn de qch

defray [dɪˈfreɪ] VT: **to ~ sb's expenses** défrayer qn (de ses frais), rembourser or payer à qn ses frais

defriend [diːˈfrɛnd] VT (Internet) supprimer de sa liste d'amis

defrost [diːˈfrɔst] VT (fridge) dégivrer; (frozen food) décongeler

deft [dɛft] ADJ adroit(e), preste

deftly [ˈdɛftlɪ] ADV adroitement

defunct [dɪˈfʌŋkt] ADJ défunt(e)

defuse [diːˈfjuːz] VT désamorcer

defy [dɪˈfaɪ] VT défier; (efforts etc) résister à; **it defies description** cela défie toute description

degenerate VI [dɪˈdʒɛnəreɪt] dégénérer ▶ ADJ [dɪˈdʒɛnərɪt] dégénéré(e)

degenerative [dɪˈdʒɛnərətɪv] ADJ dégénératif(-ive)

degradation [dɛgrəˈdeɪʃən] N dégradation f

degrade [dɪˈgreɪd] VT dégrader

degrading [dɪˈgreɪdɪŋ] ADJ dégradant(e)

★**degree** [dɪˈgriː] N degré m; (Scol) diplôme m (universitaire); **10 degrees below (zero)** 10 degrés au-dessous de zéro; **a (first) ~ in maths** (Brit) une licence en maths; **a considerable ~ of risk** un facteur or élément considérable de risque; **by degrees** (gradually) par degrés; **to some ~, to a certain ~** jusqu'à un certain point, dans une certaine mesure

dehumanize [diːˈhjuːmənaɪz] VT déshumaniser

dehumanizing [diːˈhjuːmənaɪzɪŋ] ADJ déshumanisant(e)

dehumidifier [di:hju'mɪdɪfaɪəʳ] N déshumidificateur m

dehydrated [di:haɪ'dreɪtɪd] ADJ déshydraté(e); (milk, eggs) en poudre

dehydration [di:haɪ'dreɪʃən] N déshydratation f

de-ice ['di:'aɪs] VT (windscreen) dégivrer

de-icer ['di:'aɪsəʳ] N dégivreur m

deign [deɪn] VI: **to ~ to do** daigner faire

deity ['di:ɪtɪ] N divinité f; dieu m, déesse f

déjà vu [deɪʒɑ:'vu:] N: **I had a sense of ~** j'ai eu une impression de déjà-vu

dejected [dɪ'dʒɛktɪd] ADJ abattu(e), déprimé(e)

dejection [dɪ'dʒɛkʃən] N abattement m, découragement m

de jure [deɪ'dʒuəreɪ] ADJ, ADV (Law) de jure

Del. ABBR (US) = Delaware

del. ABBR = delete

★**delay** [dɪ'leɪ] VT (journey, operation) retarder, différer; (traveller, train) retarder; (payment) différer; **to be delayed** être en retard ▶ VI s'attarder ▶ N délai m, retard m; **without ~** sans délai, sans tarder

delayed-action [dɪ'leɪd'ækʃən] ADJ à retardement

delectable [dɪ'lɛktəbl] ADJ délicieux(-euse)

delegate N ['dɛlɪgɪt] délégué(e) ▶ VT ['dɛlɪgeɪt] déléguer; **to ~ sth to sb/sb to do sth** déléguer qch à qn/qn pour faire qch

delegation [dɛlɪ'geɪʃən] N délégation f

delete [dɪ'li:t] VT (word) rayer, supprimer; (Comput: file) effacer; (: message) supprimer

deletion [dɪ'li:ʃən] N (in written text) rature f; (in electronic text) suppression f

Delhi ['dɛlɪ] N Delhi

deli ['dɛlɪ] N épicerie fine

deliberate ADJ [dɪ'lɪbərɪt] (intentional) délibéré(e); (slow) mesuré(e) ▶ VI [dɪ'lɪbəreɪt] délibérer, réfléchir

deliberately [dɪ'lɪbərɪtlɪ] ADV (on purpose) exprès, délibérément

deliberation [dɪlɪbə'reɪʃən] N délibération f, réflexion f; (gen pl: discussion) délibérations, débats mpl

deliberative [dɪ'lɪbərətɪv] ADJ délibérant(e)

delicacy ['dɛlɪkəsɪ] N délicatesse f; (choice food) mets fin or délicat, friandise f

delicate ['dɛlɪkɪt] ADJ délicat(e)

delicately ['dɛlɪkɪtlɪ] ADV délicatement; (act, express) avec délicatesse, avec tact

delicatessen [dɛlɪkə'tɛsn] N épicerie fine

delicious [dɪ'lɪʃəs] ADJ délicieux(-euse), exquis(e)

deliciously [dɪ'lɪʃəslɪ] ADV délicieusement

delight [dɪ'laɪt] N (grande) joie, grand plaisir; **she's a ~ to work with** c'est un plaisir de travailler avec elle; **a ~ to the eyes** un régal or plaisir pour les yeux; **to take ~ in** prendre grand plaisir à; **to be the ~ of** faire les délices or la joie de ▶ VT enchanter

★**delighted** [dɪ'laɪtɪd] ADJ: **~ (at or with sth)** ravi(e) (de qch); **to be ~ to do sth/that** être enchanté(e) or ravi(e) de faire qch/que; **I'd be ~** j'en serais enchanté or ravi

delightful [dɪ'laɪtful] ADJ (person) charmant(e), adorable; (place, meal, evening) merveilleux(-euse)

delightfully [dɪ'laɪtfulɪ] ADV délicieusement

delimit [di:'lɪmɪt] VT délimiter

delineate [dɪ'lɪnɪeɪt] VT tracer, esquisser; (fig) dépeindre, décrire

delinquency [dɪ'lɪŋkwənsɪ] N délinquance f

delinquent [dɪ'lɪŋkwənt] ADJ, N délinquant(e)

delirious [dɪ'lɪrɪəs] ADJ (Med: fig) délirant(e); **to be ~** délirer

deliriously [dɪ'lɪrɪəslɪ] ADV: **~ happy** fou (folle) de joie

delirium [dɪ'lɪrɪəm] N délire m

★**deliver** [dɪ'lɪvəʳ] VT (mail) distribuer; (goods) livrer; (message) remettre; (speech) prononcer; (warning, ultimatum) lancer; (free) délivrer; (Med: baby) mettre au monde; (: woman) accoucher; **to ~ the goods** (fig) tenir ses promesses

deliverables [dɪ'lɪvərəblz] NPL livrables mpl

deliverance [dɪ'lɪvrəns] N délivrance f, libération f

delivery [dɪ'lɪvərɪ] N (of mail) distribution f; (of goods) livraison f; (of speaker) élocution f; (Med) accouchement m; **to take ~ of** prendre livraison de

delivery note N bon m de livraison

delivery van, (US) **delivery truck** N fourgonnette f or camionnette f de livraison

delta ['dɛltə] N delta m

delude [dɪ'lu:d] VT tromper, leurrer; **to ~ o.s.** se leurrer, se faire des illusions

deluge ['dɛlju:dʒ] N déluge m ▶ VT (fig): **to ~ (with)** inonder (de)

delusion [dɪ'lu:ʒən] N illusion f; **to have delusions of grandeur** être un peu mégalomane

de luxe [də'lʌks] ADJ de luxe

delve [dɛlv] VI: **to ~ into** fouiller dans

Dem. ABBR (US Pol) = democrat; democratic

demagogue ['dɛməgɔg] N démagogue mf

★**demand** [dɪ'mɑ:nd] VT réclamer, exiger; (need) exiger, requérir; **to ~ sth (from or of sb)** exiger qch (de qn), réclamer qch (à qn) ▶ N exigence f; (claim) revendication f; (Econ) demande f; **in ~** demandé(e), recherché(e); **on ~** sur demande; (TV) à la carte

to demand ne veut pas dire demander.

demanding [dɪ'mɑ:ndɪŋ] ADJ (person) exigeant(e); (work) astreignant(e)

demarcation [di:mɑ:'keɪʃən] N démarcation f

demarcation dispute N (Industry) conflit m d'attributions

demean [dɪ'mi:n] VT: **to ~ o.s.** s'abaisser

demeaning [dɪ'mi:nɪŋ] ADJ dégradant(e)

demeanour, (US) **demeanor** [dɪ'mi:nəʳ] N comportement m; maintien m

demented [dɪ'mɛntɪd] ADJ dément(e), fou (folle)

dementia [dɪ'mɛnʃə] N démence f

demerger [di:'mə:dʒəʳ] N (BRIT) scission f

demilitarized zone [di:'mɪlɪtəraɪzd-] N zone démilitarisée

demise [dɪ'maɪz] N décès m

demist [di:'mɪst] VT (BRIT Aut) désembuer

demister [di:'mɪstə^r] N (*Brit Aut*) dispositif *m* anti-buée *inv*

demo ['dɛməʊ] N ABBR (*inf*) = **demonstration**; (*protest*) manif *f*; (*Comput*) démonstration *f*

demobilize [di:'məʊbɪlaɪz] VT démobiliser

★**democracy** [dɪ'mɔkrəsɪ] N démocratie *f*

democrat ['dɛməkræt] N démocrate *mf*

★**democratic** [dɛmə'krætɪk] ADJ démocratique; **the D- Party** (*US*) le parti démocrate

democratically [dɛmə'krætɪkəlɪ] ADV démocratiquement

democratization [dɪ'mɔkrətaɪzeɪʃən] N démocratisation *f*

democratize [dɪ'mɔkrətaɪz] VT démocratiser

demographic [dɛmə'græfɪk] ADJ démographique ▶ N (*group*) tranche *f* de population ▪ **demographics** NPL données *fpl* démographiques

demography [dɪ'mɔgrəfɪ] N démographie *f*

demolish [dɪ'mɔlɪʃ] VT démolir

demolition [dɛmə'lɪʃən] N démolition *f*

demon ['di:mən] N démon *m* ▶ CPD: **a - squash player** un crack en squash; **a - driver** un fou du volant

demonic [dɪ'mɔnɪk] ADJ (*forces, grin*) démoniaque; (*energy, drive, ability*) redoutable

demonize ['di:mənaɪz] VT diaboliser

demonstrably ['dɛmənstrəblɪ, dɪ'mɔnstrəblɪ] ADV (*true, false*) manifestement

★**demonstrate** ['dɛmənstreɪt] VT démontrer, prouver; (*show*) faire une démonstration de ▶ VI: **to - (for/against)** manifester (en faveur de/contre)

★**demonstration** [dɛmən'streɪʃən] N démonstration *f*; (*Pol etc*) manifestation *f*; **to hold a -** (*Pol etc*) organiser une manifestation, manifester

demonstrative [dɪ'mɔnstrətɪv] ADJ démonstratif(-ive)

demonstrator ['dɛmənstreɪtə^r] N (*Pol etc*) manifestant(e); (*Comm: salesperson*) vendeur(-euse); (*: car, computer etc*) modèle *m* de démonstration

demoralize [dɪ'mɔrəlaɪz] VT démoraliser

demote [dɪ'məʊt] VT rétrograder

demotion [dɪ'məʊʃən] N rétrogradation *f*

demur [dɪ'mə:^r] VI: **to - (at sth)** hésiter (devant qch); (*object*) élever des objections (contre qch) ▶ N: **without -** sans hésiter; sans faire de difficultés

demure [dɪ'mjʊə^r] ADJ sage, réservé(e), d'une modestie affectée

demurrage [dɪ'mʌrɪdʒ] N droits *mpl* de magasinage, surestarie *f*

demutualize [di:'mju:tʃuəlaɪz] VI (*Brit*) se démutualiser

demystify [di:'mɪstɪfaɪ] VT démystifier

den [dɛn] N (*of lion*) tanière *f*; (*room*) repaire *m*

denationalization [di:næʃnəlaɪ'zeɪʃən] N dénationalisation *f*

denationalize [di:'næʃnəlaɪz] VT dénationaliser

denial [dɪ'naɪəl] N (*of accusation*) démenti *m*; (*of rights, guilt, truth*) dénégation *f*

denier ['dɛnɪə^r] N denier *m*; **15 - stockings** bas de 15 deniers

denigrate ['dɛnɪgreɪt] VT dénigrer

denim ['dɛnɪm] N jean *m* ▪ **denims** NPL (blue-) jeans *mpl*

denim jacket N veste *f* en jean

denizen ['dɛnɪzn] N (*inhabitant*) habitant(e); (*foreigner*) étranger(-ère)

★**Denmark** ['dɛnmɑ:k] N Danemark *m*

denomination [dɪnɔmɪ'neɪʃən] N (*money*) valeur *f*; (*Rel*) confession *f*; culte *m*

denominator [dɪ'nɔmɪneɪtə^r] N dénominateur *m*

denote [dɪ'nəʊt] VT dénoter

denouement, dénouement [deɪ'nu:mɔn] N dénouement *m*

denounce [dɪ'naʊns] VT dénoncer

dense [dɛns] ADJ dense; (*inf: stupid*) obtus(e), dur(e) *or* lent(e) à la comprenette

densely ['dɛnslɪ] ADV: **- wooded** couvert(e) d'épaisses forêts; **- populated** à forte densité (de population), très peuplé(e)

density ['dɛnsɪtɪ] N densité *f*

dent [dɛnt] N bosse *f*; **to make a - in sth** (*car*) faire une bosse dans qch; **to make a - in one's savings** entamer ses économies ▶ VT (*make a dent in*) cabosser

dental ['dɛntl] ADJ dentaire

dental floss [-flɔs] N fil *m* dentaire

dental surgeon N (chirurgien(ne)-)dentiste

dental surgery N cabinet *m* de dentiste

dented ['dɛntɪd] ADJ cabossé(e)

★**dentist** ['dɛntɪst] N dentiste *mf*; **-'s surgery** (*Brit*) cabinet *m* de dentiste

dentistry ['dɛntɪstrɪ] N art *m* dentaire

dentures ['dɛntʃəz] NPL dentier *msg*

denunciation [dɪnʌnsɪ'eɪʃən] N dénonciation *f*

deny [dɪ'naɪ] VT nier; (*refuse*) refuser; (*disown*) renier; **he denies having said it** il nie l'avoir dit

deodorant [di:'əʊdərənt] N désodorisant *m*, déodorant *m*

dep. ABBR = **departs**; **departure**

depart [dɪ'pɑ:t] VI partir; **to - from** (*leave*) quitter, partir de; (*fig: differ from*) s'écarter de

departed [dɪ'pɑ:tɪd] ADJ (*dead*) défunt(e); **the (dear) -** le défunt/la défunte/les défunts

★**department** [dɪ'pɑ:tmənt] N (*Comm*) rayon *m*; (*Scol*) section *f*; (*Pol*) ministère *m*, département *m*; **that's not my -** (*fig*) ce n'est pas mon domaine *or* ma compétence, ce n'est pas mon rayon; **D- of State** (*US*) Département d'État

departmental [di:pɑ:t'mɛntl] ADJ d'une *or* de la section; d'un *or* du ministère, d'un *or* du département; **- manager** chef *m* de service; (*in shop*) chef de rayon

department store N grand magasin

★**departure** [dɪ'pɑ:tʃə^r] N départ *m*; (*fig*): **- from** écart *m* par rapport à; **a new -** une nouvelle voie

departure lounge N salle *f* de départ

★**depend** [dɪ'pɛnd] VI: **to - (up)on** dépendre de; (*rely on*) compter sur; (*financially*) dépendre (financièrement) de, être à la charge de; **it depends** cela dépend; **depending on the result ...** selon le résultat ...

dependable [dɪ'pɛndəbl] ADJ sûr(e), digne de confiance

d

dependant [dɪˈpɛndənt] N personne f à charge

dependence [dɪˈpɛndəns] N dépendance f

dependency [dɪˈpɛndənsɪ] N (country) colonie f; (on person, thing) dépendance f; **drug ~** dépendance à la drogue f

dependent [dɪˈpɛndənt] ADJ: **to be ~ (on)** dépendre (de) ▶ N = **dependant**

depict [dɪˈpɪkt] VT (in picture) représenter; (in words) (dé)peindre, décrire

depiction [dɪˈpɪkʃən] N (in picture) représentation f; (in words) description f

depilatory [dɪˈpɪlətrɪ] N (also: **depilatory cream**) dépilatoire m, crème f à épiler

deplete [dɪˈpliːt] VT réduire

depleted [dɪˈpliːtɪd] ADJ (considérablement) réduit(e) or diminué(e)

depletion [dɪˈpliːʃən] N diminution f; **ozone ~** diminution de la couche d'ozone

deplorable [dɪˈplɔːrəbl] ADJ déplorable, lamentable

deplore [dɪˈplɔːʳ] VT déplorer

deploy [dɪˈplɔɪ] VT déployer

deployment [dɪˈplɔɪmənt] N déploiement m

depopulate [diːˈpɔpjuleɪt] VT dépeupler

depopulation [ˈdiːpɔpjuˈleɪʃən] N dépopulation f, dépeuplement m

deport [dɪˈpɔːt] VT déporter, expulser

deportation [diːpɔːˈteɪʃən] N déportation f, expulsion f

deportation order N arrêté m d'expulsion

deportee [diːpɔːˈtiː] N déporté(e)

deportment [dɪˈpɔːtmənt] N maintien m, tenue f

depose [dɪˈpəuz] VT déposer

★**deposit** [dɪˈpɔzɪt] N (Chem, Comm, Geo) dépôt m; (of ore, oil) gisement m; (part payment) arrhes fpl, acompte m; (on bottle etc) consigne f; (for hired goods etc) cautionnement m, garantie f; **to put down a ~ of £50** verser 50 livres d'arrhes or d'acompte; laisser 50 livres en garantie ▶ VT déposer; (valuables) mettre or laisser en dépôt

deposit account N compte m sur livret

depositor [dɪˈpɔzɪtəʳ] N déposant(e)

depository [dɪˈpɔzɪtərɪ] N (person) dépositaire mf; (place) dépôt m

depot [ˈdɛpəu] N dépôt m; (US Rail) gare f

depraved [dɪˈpreɪvd] ADJ dépravé(e), perverti(e)

depravity [dɪˈprævɪtɪ] N dépravation f

deprecate [ˈdɛprɪkeɪt] VT désapprouver

deprecating [ˈdɛprɪkeɪtɪŋ] ADJ (disapproving) désapprobateur(-trice); (apologetic): **a ~ smile** un sourire d'excuse

depreciate [dɪˈpriːʃɪeɪt] VT déprécier ▶ VI se déprécier, se dévaloriser

depreciation [dɪpriːʃɪˈeɪʃən] N dépréciation f

depress [dɪˈprɛs] VT déprimer; (press down) appuyer sur, abaisser; (wages etc) faire baisser

depressant [dɪˈprɛsnt] N (Med) dépresseur m

depressed [dɪˈprɛst] ADJ déprimé(e), abattu(e); (area) en déclin, touché(e) par le sous-emploi; (Comm: market, trade) maussade; **to get ~** se démoraliser, se laisser abattre

depressing [dɪˈprɛsɪŋ] ADJ déprimant(e)

depression [dɪˈprɛʃən] N (Econ) dépression f

depressive [dɪˈprɛsɪv] ADJ, N (Med) dépressif(-ive)

deprivation [dɛprɪˈveɪʃən] N privation f; (loss) perte f

deprive [dɪˈpraɪv] VT: **to ~ sb of** priver qn de

deprived [dɪˈpraɪvd] ADJ déshérité(e)

dept. ABBR (= department) dép, dépt

★**depth** [dɛpθ] N profondeur f; **in the depths of** au fond de; au cœur de; au plus profond de; **to be in the depths of despair** être au plus profond du désespoir; **at a ~ of 3 metres** à 3 mètres de profondeur; **to be out of one's ~** (BRIT: swimmer) ne plus avoir pied; (fig) être dépassé(e), nager; **to study sth in ~** étudier qch en profondeur

depth charge N grenade sous-marine

deputation [dɛpjuˈteɪʃən] N députation f, délégation f

deputize [ˈdɛpjutaɪz] VI: **to ~ for** assurer l'intérim de

deputy [ˈdɛpjutɪ] N (replacement) suppléant(e), intérimaire mf; (second in command) adjoint(e); (Pol) député m; (US: also: **deputy sheriff**) shérif adjoint ▶ ADJ: **~ chairman** vice-président m; **~ head** (Scol) directeur(-trice) adjoint(e), sous-directeur(-trice); **~ leader** (BRIT Pol) vice-président(e), secrétaire adjoint(e)

derail [dɪˈreɪl] VT faire dérailler; **to be derailed** dérailler

derailment [dɪˈreɪlmənt] N déraillement m

deranged [dɪˈreɪndʒd] ADJ: **to be (mentally) ~** avoir le cerveau dérangé

derby [ˈdəːrbɪ] N (US) (chapeau m) melon m

deregulate [dɪˈrɛgjuleɪt] VT libérer, dérégler, déréguler

deregulation [dɪrɛgjuˈleɪʃən] N libération f, déréglement m

derelict [ˈdɛrɪlɪkt] ADJ abandonné(e), à l'abandon

deride [dɪˈraɪd] VT railler

derision [dɪˈrɪʒən] N dérision f

derisive [dɪˈraɪsɪv] ADJ moqueur(-euse), railleur(-euse)

derisory [dɪˈraɪsərɪ] ADJ (sum) dérisoire; (smile, person) moqueur(-euse), railleur(-euse)

derivation [dɛrɪˈveɪʃən] N dérivation f

derivative [dɪˈrɪvətɪv] N dérivé m ▶ ADJ dérivé(e)

derive [dɪˈraɪv] VT: **to ~ sth from** tirer qch de; trouver qch dans ▶ VI: **to ~ from** provenir de, dériver de

dermatitis [dəːməˈtaɪtɪs] N dermatite f

dermatologist [dəːməˈtɔlədʒɪst] N dermatologue mf

dermatology [dəːməˈtɔlədʒɪ] N dermatologie f

derogatory [dɪˈrɔgətərɪ] ADJ désobligeant(e), péjoratif(-ive)

derrick [ˈdɛrɪk] N mât m de charge, derrick m

derv [dəːv] N (BRIT) gas-oil m, diesel m

DES N ABBR (BRIT) = Department of Education and Science) ministère de l'éducation nationale et des sciences

desalination [diːsælɪˈneɪʃən] N dessalement m, dessalage m

descend [dɪˈsɛnd] VT, VI descendre; **to ~ from** descendre de, être issu(e) de; **to ~ to** s'abaisser à;

in descending order of importance par ordre d'importance décroissante
▸ **descend (up)on** VT FUS (enemy, angry person) tomber or sauter sur; (misfortune) s'abattre sur; (gloom, silence) envahir; **visitors descended (up)on us** des gens sont arrivés chez nous à l'improviste

descendant [dɪˈsɛndənt] N descendant(e)

descended [dɪˈsɛndɪd] ADJ: **to be ~ from sb** descendre de qn

descending [dɪˈsɛndɪŋ] ADJ: **in ~ order** par ordre décroissant

descent [dɪˈsɛnt] N descente f; (origin) origine f

★**describe** [dɪsˈkraɪb] VT décrire

★**description** [dɪsˈkrɪpʃən] N description f; (sort) sorte f, espèce f; **of every ~** de toutes sortes

descriptive [dɪsˈkrɪptɪv] ADJ descriptif(-ive)

desecrate [ˈdɛsɪkreɪt] VT profaner

desecration [dɛsɪˈkreɪʃən] N profanation f

desegregation [diːsɛɡrɪˈɡeɪʃən] N déségrégation f

★**desert** N [ˈdɛzət] désert m ▸ VT [dɪˈzəːt] déserter, abandonner ▸ VI (Mil) déserter

deserted [dɪˈzəːtɪd] ADJ désert(e)

deserter [dɪˈzəːtə']̓ N déserteur m

desertification [dɪzəːtɪfɪˈkeɪʃən] N désertification f

desertion [dɪˈzəːʃən] N désertion f

desert island N île déserte

deserts [dɪˈzəːts] NPL: **to get one's just ~** n'avoir que ce qu'on mérite

★**deserve** [dɪˈzəːv] VT mériter

deservedly [dɪˈzəːvɪdlɪ] ADV à juste titre, à bon droit

deserving [dɪˈzəːvɪŋ] ADJ (person) méritant(e); (action, cause) méritoire

desiccated [ˈdɛsɪkeɪtɪd] ADJ séché(e)

★**design** [dɪˈzaɪn] N (sketch) plan m, dessin m; (layout, shape) conception f, ligne f; (pattern) dessin, motif(s) m(pl); (of dress, car) modèle m; (art) design m, stylisme m; (intention) dessein m; **to have designs on** avoir des visées sur; **industrial ~** esthétique industrielle ▸ VT dessiner; (plan) concevoir; **well-designed** adj bien conçu(e)

design and technology N (BRIT Scol) technologie f

designate VT [ˈdɛzɪɡneɪt] désigner ▸ ADJ [ˈdɛzɪɡnɪt] désigné(e)

designation [dɛzɪɡˈneɪʃən] N désignation f

★**designer** [dɪˈzaɪnə'] N (Archit, Art) dessinateur(-trice); (Industry) concepteur(-trice), designer mf; (Fashion) styliste mf

desirability [dɪzaɪərəˈbɪlɪtɪ] N avantage m; attrait m

desirable [dɪˈzaɪərəbl] ADJ (property, location, purchase) attrayant(e); **it is ~ that** il est souhaitable que

desire [dɪˈzaɪə'] N désir m ▸ VT désirer, vouloir; **to ~ to do sth/that** désirer faire qch/que

desirous [dɪˈzaɪərəs] ADJ: **~ of** désireux(-euse) de

desist [dɪˈzɪst, dɪˈsɪst] VI cesser; **to ~ from sth** cesser qch; **to ~ from doing sth** cesser de faire qch

★**desk** [dɛsk] N (in office) bureau m; (for pupil) pupitre m; (BRIT: in shop, restaurant) caisse f; (in hotel, at airport) réception f

desktop [ˈdɛsktɔp] N bureau m ▸ ADJ de bureau; **~ computer** ordinateur m de bureau

desktop publishing N publication assistée par ordinateur, PAO f

desolate [ˈdɛsəlɪt] ADJ désolé(e)

desolation [dɛsəˈleɪʃən] N désolation f

despair [dɪsˈpɛə'] N désespoir m; **to be in ~** être au désespoir ▸ VI: **to ~ of** désespérer de

despatch [dɪsˈpætʃ] N, VT = **dispatch**

★**desperate** [ˈdɛspərɪt] ADJ désespéré(e); (fugitive) prêt(e) à tout; (measures) désespéré, extrême; **to be ~ for sth/to do sth** avoir désespérément besoin de qch/de faire qch; **we are getting ~** nous commençons à désespérer

desperately [ˈdɛspərɪtlɪ] ADV désespérément; (very) terriblement, extrêmement; **~ ill** très gravement malade

desperation [dɛspəˈreɪʃən] N désespoir m; **in (sheer) ~** en désespoir de cause

despicable [dɪsˈpɪkəbl] ADJ méprisable

despise [dɪsˈpaɪz] VT mépriser, dédaigner

★**despite** [dɪsˈpaɪt] PREP malgré, en dépit de

despondent [dɪsˈpɔndənt] ADJ découragé(e), abattu(e)

despot [ˈdɛspɔt] N despote mf

despotic [dɛˈspɔtɪk] ADJ despotique

dessert [dɪˈzəːt] N dessert m

dessertspoon [dɪˈzəːtspuːn] N cuiller f à dessert

destabilize [diːˈsteɪbɪlaɪz] VT déstabiliser

destination [dɛstɪˈneɪʃən] N destination f

destine [ˈdɛstɪn] VT destiner

destined [ˈdɛstɪnd] ADJ: **to be ~ to do sth** être destiné(e) à faire qch; **~ for London** à destination de Londres

destiny [ˈdɛstɪnɪ] N destinée f, destin m

destitute [ˈdɛstɪtjuːt] ADJ misérable, dans la misère; **to be left ~** être plongé(e) dans la misère; **the ~** les indigents

destitution [dɛstɪˈtjuːʃən] N dénuement m, indigence f

de-stress [diːˈstrɛs] VI, VT déstresser (inf)

★**destroy** [dɪsˈtrɔɪ] VT détruire; (injured horse) abattre; (dog) faire piquer

destroyer [dɪsˈtrɔɪə'] N (Naut) contre-torpilleur m

destruction [dɪsˈtrʌkʃən] N destruction f

destructive [dɪsˈtrʌktɪv] ADJ destructeur(-trice)

desultory [ˈdɛsəltərɪ] ADJ (reading, conversation) décousu(e); (contact) irrégulier(-ière)

detach [dɪˈtætʃ] VT détacher

detachable [dɪˈtætʃəbl] ADJ amovible, détachable

detached [dɪˈtætʃt] ADJ (attitude) détaché(e)

detached house N pavillon m maison(nette) (individuelle)

detachment [dɪˈtætʃmənt] N (Mil) détachement m; (fig) détachement, indifférence f

★**detail** [ˈdiːteɪl] N détail m; (Mil) détachement m; **in ~** en détail; **to go into ~(s)** entrer dans les détails ▸ VT raconter en détail, énumérer; (Mil): **to ~ sb (for)** affecter qn (à), détacher qn (pour)

detailed [ˈdiːteɪld] ADJ détaillé(e)

detain [dɪˈteɪn] VT retenir; (in captivity) détenir; (in hospital) hospitaliser

detainee [diːteɪˈniː] N détenu(e)

detect [dɪˈtɛkt] VT déceler, percevoir; (Med, Police) dépister; (Mil, Radar, Tech) détecter

detection [dɪˈtɛkʃən] N découverte f; (Med, Police) dépistage m; (Mil, Radar, Tech) détection f; **to escape ~** échapper aux recherches, éviter d'être découvert(e); (mistake) passer inaperçu(e); **crime ~** le dépistage des criminels

★**detective** [dɪˈtɛktɪv] N agent m de la sûreté, policier m; **private ~** détective privé

detective story N roman policier

detector [dɪˈtɛktəʳ] N détecteur m

détente [deɪˈtɑːnt] N détente f

★**detention** [dɪˈtɛnʃən] N détention f; (Scol) retenue f, consigne f

deter [dɪˈtəːʳ] VT dissuader

detergent [dɪˈtəːdʒənt] N détersif m, détergent m

deteriorate [dɪˈtɪərɪəreɪt] VI se détériorer, se dégrader

deterioration [dɪtɪərɪəˈreɪʃən] N détérioration f

determinant [dɪˈtəːmɪnənt] N déterminant m

determination [dɪtəːmɪˈneɪʃən] N détermination f

determine [dɪˈtəːmɪn] VT déterminer; **to ~ to do** résoudre de faire, se déterminer à faire

determined [dɪˈtəːmɪnd] ADJ (person) déterminé(e), décidé(e); (quantity) déterminé, établi(e); (effort) très gros(se); **~ to do** bien décidé à faire

determinism [dɪˈtəːmɪnɪzəm] N déterminisme m

deterrence [dɪˈtɛrəns] N dissuasion f

deterrent [dɪˈtɛrənt] N effet m de dissuasion; force f de dissuasion; **to act as a ~** avoir un effet dissuasif

detest [dɪˈtɛst] VT détester, avoir horreur de

detestable [dɪˈtɛstəbl] ADJ détestable, odieux(-euse)

detonate [ˈdɛtəneɪt] VI exploser ▶ VT faire exploser or détoner

detonator [ˈdɛtəneɪtəʳ] N détonateur m

detour [ˈdiːtuəʳ] N détour m; (US Aut: diversion) déviation f

detox [ˈdiːtɔks] VI se détoxifier ▶ VT (body) détoxifier ▶ N détox f

detoxification [diːtɔksɪfɪˈkeɪʃən] N détox f

detoxify [diːˈtɔksɪfaɪ] VI se détoxifier ▶ VT (body) détoxifier

detract [dɪˈtrækt] VT: **to ~ from** (quality, pleasure) diminuer; (reputation) porter atteinte à

detractor [dɪˈtræktəʳ] N détracteur(-trice)

detriment [ˈdɛtrɪmənt] N: **to the ~ of** au détriment de, au préjudice de; **without ~ to** sans porter atteinte or préjudice à, sans conséquences fâcheuses pour

detrimental [dɛtrɪˈmɛntl] ADJ: **~ to** préjudiciable or nuisible à

deuce [djuːs] N (Tennis) égalité f

devaluation [diːvæljuˈeɪʃən] N dévaluation f

devalue [diːˈvæljuː] VT dévaluer

devastate [ˈdɛvəsteɪt] VT dévaster; **he was devastated by the news** cette nouvelle lui a porté un coup terrible

devastating [ˈdɛvəsteɪtɪŋ] ADJ dévastateur(-trice); (news) accablant(e)

devastation [dɛvəsˈteɪʃən] N dévastation f

★**develop** [dɪˈvɛləp] VT (gen) développer; (disease) commencer à souffrir de; (habit) contracter; (resources) mettre en valeur, exploiter; (land) aménager; **can you ~ this film?** pouvez-vous développer cette pellicule ?; **to ~ a taste for sth** prendre goût à qch ▶ VI se développer; (situation, disease: evolve) évoluer; (facts, symptoms: appear) se manifester, se produire; **to ~ into** devenir

developer [dɪˈvɛləpəʳ] N (Phot) révélateur m; (of land) promoteur m; (also: **property developer**) promoteur immobilier

developing [dɪˈvɛləpɪŋ] ADJ (world) en voie de développement

developing country N pays m en voie de développement

development [dɪˈvɛləpmənt] N développement m; (of land) exploitation f; (new fact, event) rebondissement m, fait(s) nouveau(x)

development area N zone f à urbaniser

deviate [ˈdiːvɪeɪt] VI: **to ~ (from)** dévier (de)

deviation [diːvɪˈeɪʃən] N déviation f

device [dɪˈvaɪs] N (scheme) moyen m, expédient m; (apparatus) appareil m, dispositif m; **explosive ~** engin explosif; **improvised explosive ~** engin explosif improvisé

devil [ˈdɛvl] N diable m; démon m

devilish [ˈdɛvlɪʃ] ADJ diabolique

devil-may-care [ˈdɛvlmeɪˈkɛəʳ] ADJ je-m'en-foutiste

devil's advocate N: **to play ~** se faire l'avocat du diable

devious [ˈdiːvɪəs] ADJ (means) détourné(e); (person) sournois(e), dissimulé(e)

devise [dɪˈvaɪz] VT imaginer, concevoir

devoid [dɪˈvɔɪd] ADJ: **~ of** dépourvu(e) de, dénué(e) de

devolution [diːvəˈluːʃən] N (Pol) décentralisation f

devolve [dɪˈvɔlv] VI: **to ~ (up)on** retomber sur

devote [dɪˈvəut] VT: **to ~ sth to** consacrer qch à

devoted [dɪˈvəutɪd] ADJ dévoué(e); **to be ~ to** être dévoué(e) or très attaché(e) à; (book etc) être consacré(e) à

devotee [dɛvəuˈtiː] N (Rel) adepte mf; (Mus, Sport) fervent(e)

devotion [dɪˈvəuʃən] N dévouement m, attachement m; (Rel) dévotion f, piété f

devour [dɪˈvauəʳ] VT dévorer

devout [dɪˈvaut] ADJ pieux(-euse), dévot(e)

dew [djuː] N rosée f

dexterity [dɛksˈtɛrɪtɪ] N dextérité f, adresse f

DfE N ABBR (BRIT: = Department for Education) Ministère de l'éducation

dg ABBR (= decigram) dg

diabetes [daɪəˈbiːtiːz] N diabète m

diabetic [daɪəˈbɛtɪk] N diabétique mf ▶ ADJ (person) diabétique; (chocolate, jam) pour diabétiques

diabolical [daɪə'bɒlɪkl] ADJ diabolique; (inf: dreadful) infernal(e), atroce

diagnose [daɪəg'nəuz] VT diagnostiquer

diagnosis [daɪəg'nəusɪs] (pl **diagnoses** [-si:z]) N diagnostic m

diagnostic [daɪəg'nɒstɪk] ADJ diagnostique

diagonal [daɪ'ægənl] ADJ diagonal(e) ▶ N diagonale f

diagram ['daɪəgræm] N diagramme m, schéma m

dial ['daɪəl] N cadran m ▶ VT (number) faire, composer; **to ~ a wrong number** faire un faux numéro; **can I ~ London direct?** puis-je or est-ce que je peux avoir Londres par l'automatique ?

dial. ABBR = **dialect**

dialect ['daɪəlɛkt] N dialecte m

dialling code ['daɪəlɪŋ-], (US) **dial code** N indicatif m (téléphonique); **what's the ~ for Paris?** quel est l'indicatif de Paris ?

dialling tone ['daɪəlɪŋ-], (US) **dial tone** N tonalité f

dialogue, (US) **dialog** ['daɪəlɒg] N dialogue m

dialogue box, dialog box N (Comput) boîte f de dialogue

dialysis [daɪ'ælɪsɪs] N dialyse f

diameter [daɪ'æmɪtə^r] N diamètre m

diametrically [daɪə'mɛtrɪklɪ] ADV: **~ opposed (to)** diamétralement opposé(e) (à)

diamond ['daɪəmənd] N diamant m; (shape) losange m ▪ **diamonds** NPL (Cards) carreau m

diamond ring N bague f de diamant(s)

diaper ['daɪəpə^r] N (US) couche f

diaphanous [daɪ'æfənəs] ADJ diaphane

diaphragm ['daɪəfræm] N diaphragme m

diarrhoea, (US) **diarrhea** [daɪə'ri:ə] N diarrhée f

★**diary** ['daɪərɪ] N (daily account) journal m; (book) agenda m; **to keep a ~** tenir un journal

diaspora [daɪ'æspərə] N diaspora f; **the Irish ~** la diaspora irlandaise

diatribe ['daɪətraɪb] N diatribe f

dice [daɪs] N (pl inv) dé m ▶ VT (Culin) couper en dés or en cubes

dicey ['daɪsɪ] ADJ (inf): **it's a bit ~** c'est un peu risqué

dichotomy [daɪ'kɔtəmɪ] N dichotomie f

dickhead ['dɪkhɛd] N (Brit !) tête f de nœud (!)

Dictaphone® ['dɪktəfəun] N Dictaphone® m

dictate VT [dɪk'teɪt] dicter ▶ VI: **to ~ to** (person) imposer sa volonté à, régenter; **I won't be dictated to** je n'ai d'ordres à recevoir de personne ▶ N ['dɪkteɪt] injonction f

dictation [dɪk'teɪʃən] N dictée f; **at ~ speed** à une vitesse de dictée

dictator [dɪk'teɪtə^r] N dictateur m

dictatorial [dɪktə'tɔ:rɪəl] ADJ dictatorial(e)

dictatorship [dɪk'teɪtəʃɪp] N dictature f

diction ['dɪkʃən] N diction f, élocution f

★**dictionary** ['dɪkʃənrɪ] N dictionnaire m

did [dɪd] PT of **do**

didactic [daɪ'dæktɪk] ADJ didactique

diddle ['dɪdl] VT (esp Brit inf: con) rouler ▶ VI (US inf): **to ~ with sth** (fiddle) tripatouiller qch; **to ~ around** (waste time) traînasser

didn't ['dɪdnt] = **did not**

★**die** [daɪ] N (pl **dice**) dé m; (pl **dies**) coin m; matrice f; étampe f ▶ VI mourir; **to ~ of** or **from** mourir de; **to be dying** être mourant(e); **to be dying for sth** avoir une envie folle de qch; **to be dying to do sth** mourir d'envie de faire qch

▶ **die away** VI s'éteindre

▶ **die down** VI se calmer, s'apaiser

▶ **die out** VI disparaître, s'éteindre

diehard ['daɪhɑ:d] N réactionnaire mf, jusqu'au-boutiste mf

diesel ['di:zl] N (vehicle) diesel m; (also: **diesel oil**) carburant m diesel, gas-oil m

diesel engine N moteur m diesel

diesel fuel, diesel oil N carburant m diesel

★**diet** ['daɪət] N alimentation f; (restricted food) régime m; **to live on a ~ of** se nourrir de ▶ VI (also: **be on a diet**) suivre un régime

dietary ['daɪətrɪ] ADJ (habits, advice) diététique; (fat, fibre) alimentaire

dietician [daɪə'tɪʃən] N diététicien(ne)

differ ['dɪfə^r] VI: **to ~ from sth** (be different) être différent(e) de qch, différer de qch; **to ~ from sb over sth** ne pas être d'accord avec qn au sujet de qch

★**difference** ['dɪfrəns] N différence f; (quarrel) différend m, désaccord m; **it makes no ~ to me** cela m'est égal, cela m'est indifférent; **to settle one's differences** résoudre la situation

★**different** ['dɪfrənt] ADJ différent(e)

differential [dɪfə'rɛnʃəl] N (Aut, wages) différentiel m

differentiate [dɪfə'rɛnʃɪeɪt] VT différencier ▶ VI se différencier; **to ~ between** faire une différence entre

differentiation [dɪfərɛnʃɪ'eɪʃən] N différenciation f

differently ['dɪfrəntlɪ] ADV différemment

★**difficult** ['dɪfɪkəlt] ADJ difficile; **~ to understand** difficile à comprendre

★**difficulty** ['dɪfɪkəltɪ] N difficulté f; **to have difficulties with** avoir des ennuis or problèmes avec; **to be in ~** avoir des difficultés, avoir des problèmes

diffidence ['dɪfɪdəns] N manque m de confiance en soi, manque d'assurance

diffident ['dɪfɪdənt] ADJ qui manque de confiance or d'assurance, peu sûr(e) de soi

diffuse ADJ [dɪ'fju:s] diffus(e) ▶ VT [dɪ'fju:z] diffuser, répandre

diffusion [dɪ'fju:ʒən] N diffusion f

★**dig** [dɪg] (pt, pp **dug** [dʌg]) VT (hole) creuser; (garden) bêcher; **to ~ one's nails into** enfoncer ses ongles dans ▶ VI: **to ~ into** (snow, soil) creuser; **to ~ into one's pockets for sth** fouiller dans ses poches pour chercher or prendre qch ▶ N (prod) coup m de coude; (fig: remark) coup de griffe or de patte; (Archaeology) fouille f

▶ **dig in** VI (Mil) se retrancher; (fig) tenir bon, se braquer; (inf: eat) attaquer (un repas or un plat etc) ▶ VT (compost) bien mélanger à la bêche; (knife, claw) enfoncer; **to ~ in one's heels** (fig) se braquer, se buter

▶ **dig out** VT (survivors, car from snow) sortir or dégager (à coups de pelles or pioches)

▶ **dig up** VT déterrer

digest VT [daɪˈdʒɛst] digérer ▸ N [ˈdaɪdʒɛst] sommaire *m*, résumé *m*

digestible [dɪˈdʒɛstəbl] ADJ digestible

digestion [dɪˈdʒɛstʃən] N digestion *f*

digestive [dɪˈdʒɛstɪv] ADJ digestif(-ive)

digger [ˈdɪgəʳ] N (*machine*) excavateur *m*, excavatrice *f*

digit [ˈdɪdʒɪt] N (*number*) chiffre *m* (*de o à 9*); (*finger*) doigt *m*

digital [ˈdɪdʒɪtl] ADJ (*system, recording, radio*) numérique; (*watch*) à affichage numérique

digital camera N appareil *m* photo numérique

digital compact cassette N cassette *f* numérique

digitally [ˈdɪdʒɪtəlɪ] ADV numériquement

digital TV N télévision *f* numérique

digitize [ˈdɪdʒɪtaɪz] VT numériser

dignified [ˈdɪgnɪfaɪd] ADJ digne

dignitary [ˈdɪgnɪtərɪ] N dignitaire *m*

dignity [ˈdɪgnɪtɪ] N dignité *f*

digress [daɪˈgrɛs] VI: **to ~ from** s'écarter de, s'éloigner de

digression [daɪˈgrɛʃən] N digression *f*

digs [dɪgz] NPL (*BRIT inf*) piaule *f*, chambre meublée

diktat [ˈdɪktæt] N diktat *m*

dilapidated [dɪˈlæpɪdeɪtɪd] ADJ délabré(e)

dilate [daɪˈleɪt] VT dilater ▸ VI se dilater

dilatory [ˈdɪlətərɪ] ADJ dilatoire

dilemma [daɪˈlɛmə] N dilemme *m*; **to be in a ~** être pris dans un dilemme

diligence [ˈdɪlɪdʒəns] N assiduité *f*, application *f*; **with ~** avec assiduité

diligent [ˈdɪlɪdʒənt] ADJ (*worker, student*) appliqué(e), assidu(e); (*work*) assidu(e)

dill [dɪl] N aneth *m*

dilly-dally [ˈdɪlɪˈdælɪ] VI hésiter, tergiverser; traînasser, lambiner

dilute [daɪˈluːt] VT diluer ▸ ADJ dilué(e)

dilution [daɪˈluːʃən] N (*of solution, substance*) dilution *f*; (*of quality, value*) affaiblissement *m*

dim [dɪm] ADJ (*light, eyesight*) faible; (*memory, outline*) vague, indécis(e); (*room*) sombre; (*inf: stupid*) borné(e), obtus(e); **to take a ~ view of sth** voir qch d'un mauvais œil ▸ VT (*light*) réduire, baisser; (*US Aut*) mettre en code, baisser

dime [daɪm] N (*US*) pièce *f* de 10 cents

dimension [daɪˈmɛnʃən] N dimension *f*

-dimensional [dɪˈmɛnʃənl] ADJ SUFFIX: **two-dimensional** à deux dimensions

diminish [dɪˈmɪnɪʃ] VT, VI diminuer

diminished [dɪˈmɪnɪʃt] ADJ: **~ responsibility** (*Law*) responsabilité atténuée

diminutive [dɪˈmɪnjutɪv] ADJ minuscule, tout(e) petit(e) ▸ N (*Ling*) diminutif *m*

dimly [ˈdɪmlɪ] ADV faiblement; vaguement

dimmer [ˈdɪməʳ] N (*also:* **dimmer switch**) variateur *m* ■ **dimmers** NPL (*US Aut:* dipped headlights) phares *mpl* code *inv*, codes *mpl*; (*parking lights*) feux *mpl* de position

dimple [ˈdɪmpl] N fossette *f*

dim-witted [ˈdɪmˈwɪtɪd] ADJ (*inf*) stupide, borné(e)

din [dɪn] N vacarme *m* ▸ VT: **to ~ sth into sb** (*inf*) enfoncer qch dans la tête *or* la caboche de qn

dine [daɪn] VI dîner
▸ **dine out** VI (*at restaurant*) aller au restaurant

diner [ˈdaɪnəʳ] N (*person*) dîneur(-euse); (*Rail*) = **dining car**; (*US: eating place*) petit restaurant

dinghy [ˈdɪŋgɪ] N youyou *m*; (*inflatable*) canot *m* pneumatique; (*also:* **sailing dinghy**) voilier *m*, dériveur *m*

dingo [ˈdɪŋgəu] N dingo *m*

dingy [ˈdɪndʒɪ] ADJ miteux(-euse), minable

dining car [ˈdaɪnɪŋ-] N (*BRIT*) voiture-restaurant *f*, wagon-restaurant *m*

dining room [ˈdaɪnɪŋ-] N salle *f* à manger

dining table [daɪnɪŋ-] N table *f* de (la) salle à manger

dinkum [ˈdɪŋkʌm] ADJ (*AUSTRALIA, NEW ZEALAND inf*) vrai(e); **fair ~** vrai(e)

★**dinner** [ˈdɪnəʳ] N (*evening meal*) dîner *m*; (*lunch*) déjeuner *m*; (*public*) banquet *m*; **~'s ready!** à table !

dinner jacket N smoking *m*

dinner party N dîner *m*

dinner time N (*evening*) heure *f* du dîner; (*midday*) heure du déjeuner

dinosaur [ˈdaɪnəsɔːʳ] N dinosaure *m*

dint [dɪnt] N: **by ~ of (doing) sth** à force de (faire) qch

diocese [ˈdaɪəsɪs] N diocèse *m*

dioxide [daɪˈɔksaɪd] N dioxyde *m*

dip [dɪp] N (*slope*) déclivité *f*; (*in sea*) baignade *f*, bain *m*; (*Culin*) ≈ sauce *f* ▸ VT tremper, plonger; (*BRIT Aut: lights*) mettre en code, baisser ▸ VI plonger
▸ **dip into** VT FUS (*book*) parcourir; (*savings*) puiser dans

Dip. ABBR (*BRIT*) = **diploma**

diphtheria [dɪfˈθɪərɪə] N diphtérie *f*

diphthong [ˈdɪfθɔŋ] N diphtongue *f*

diploma [dɪˈpləumə] N diplôme *m*

diplomacy [dɪˈpləuməsɪ] N diplomatie *f*

diplomat [ˈdɪpləmæt] N diplomate *mf*

diplomatic [dɪpləˈmætɪk] ADJ diplomatique; **to break off ~ relations (with)** rompre les relations diplomatiques (avec)

diplomatic corps N corps *m* diplomatique

diplomatic immunity N immunité *f* diplomatique

dipstick [ˈdɪpstɪk] N (*BRIT Aut*) jauge *f* de niveau d'huile

dipswitch [ˈdɪpswɪtʃ] N (*BRIT Aut*) commutateur *m* de code

dire [daɪəʳ] ADJ (*poverty*) extrême; (*awful*) affreux(-euse)

★**direct** [daɪˈrɛkt] ADJ direct(e); (*manner, person*) direct, franc (franche) ▸ VT (*tell way*) diriger, orienter; (*letter, remark*) adresser; (*Cine, TV*) réaliser; (*Theat*) mettre en scène; (*order*): **to ~ sb to do sth** ordonner à qn de faire qch; **can you ~ me to ...?** pouvez-vous m'indiquer le chemin de ...? ▸ ADV directement

direct cost N (*Comm*) coût *m* variable

direct current N (*Elec*) courant continu

direct debit N (*BRIT Banking*) prélèvement *m* automatique

direct dialling N (*Tel*) automatique *m*

direct hit N (*Mil*) coup *m* au but, touché *m*

★**direction** [dɪˈrɛkʃən] N direction *f*; (*Theat*) mise *f* en scène; (*Cine, TV*) réalisation *f*; **sense of ~** sens *m* de l'orientation; **in the ~ of** dans la direction de, vers ▪ **directions** NPL (*to a place*) indications *fpl*; **directions for use** mode *m* d'emploi; **to ask for directions** demander sa route *or* son chemin

directive [dɪˈrɛktɪv] N directive *f*; **a government ~** une directive du gouvernement

direct labour N main-d'œuvre directe; employés municipaux

directly [dɪˈrɛktlɪ] ADV (*in straight line*) directement, tout droit; (*at once*) tout de suite, immédiatement

direct mail N vente *f* par publicité directe

direct mailshot N (*BRIT*) publicité postale

directness [dɪˈrɛktnɪs] N (*of person, speech*) franchise *f*

★**director** [dɪˈrɛktəʳ] N directeur *m*; (*board member*) administrateur *m*; (*Theat*) metteur *m* en scène; (*Cine, TV*) réalisateur(-trice); **D~ of Public Prosecutions** (*BRIT*) ≈ procureur général

directorship [dɪˈrɛktəʃɪp] N poste *m* de directeur, fonction *f* de directeur

directory [dɪˈrɛktərɪ] N annuaire *m*; (*also*: **street directory**) indicateur *m* de rues; (*also*: **trade directory**) annuaire du commerce; (*Comput*) répertoire *m*

directory enquiries, (*US*) **directory assistance** N (*Tel*: *service*) renseignements *mpl*

dirt [dəːt] N saleté *f*; (*mud*) boue *f*; **to treat sb like ~** traiter qn comme un chien

dirt-cheap [ˈdəːtˈtʃiːp] ADJ (ne) coûtant presque rien

dirt road N chemin non macadamisé *or* non revêtu

★**dirty** [ˈdəːtɪ] ADJ sale; (*joke*) cochon(ne); **~ story** histoire cochonne; **~ trick** coup tordu ▪ VT salir

disability [dɪsəˈbɪlɪtɪ] N invalidité *f*, infirmité *f*

disability allowance N allocation *f* d'invalidité *or* d'infirmité

disable [dɪsˈeɪbl] VT (*illness, accident*) rendre *or* laisser infirme; (*tank, gun*) mettre hors d'action

disabled [dɪsˈeɪbld] ADJ handicapé(e); (*maimed*) mutilé(e); (*through illness, old age*) impotent(e)

disabling [dɪˈseɪblɪŋ] ADJ handicapant(e)

disabuse [dɪsəˈbjuːz] VT détromper; **to ~ sb of sth** détromper qn de qch

disadvantage [dɪsədˈvɑːntɪdʒ] N désavantage *m*, inconvénient *m*

disadvantaged [dɪsədˈvɑːntɪdʒd] ADJ (*person*) désavantagé(e)

disadvantageous [dɪsædvɑːnˈteɪdʒəs] ADJ désavantageux(-euse)

disaffected [dɪsəˈfɛktɪd] ADJ: **~ (to or towards)** mécontent(e) (de)

disaffection [dɪsəˈfɛkʃən] N désaffection *f*, mécontentement *m*

disagree [dɪsəˈɡriː] VI (*differ*) ne pas concorder; (*be against, think otherwise*): **to ~ (with)** ne pas être

d'accord (avec); **garlic disagrees with me** l'ail ne me convient pas, je ne supporte pas l'ail

disagreeable [dɪsəˈɡriːəbl] ADJ désagréable

disagreement [dɪsəˈɡriːmənt] N désaccord *m*, différend *m*

disallow [dɪsəˈlau] VT rejeter, désavouer; (*BRIT Football*: *goal*) refuser

★**disappear** [dɪsəˈpɪəʳ] VI disparaître

disappearance [dɪsəˈpɪərəns] N disparition *f*

disappoint [dɪsəˈpɔɪnt] VT décevoir

★**disappointed** [dɪsəˈpɔɪntɪd] ADJ déçu(e)

disappointing [dɪsəˈpɔɪntɪŋ] ADJ décevant(e)

disappointingly [dɪsəˈpɔɪntɪŋlɪ] ADV: **~ slow** d'une lenteur décevante; **~, ...** à ma (*or* notre *etc*) grande déception, ..., à la grande déception de tous, ...

disappointment [dɪsəˈpɔɪntmənt] N déception *f*

disapproval [dɪsəˈpruːvəl] N désapprobation *f*

disapprove [dɪsəˈpruːv] VI: **to ~ of** désapprouver

disapproving [dɪsəˈpruːvɪŋ] ADJ désapprobateur(-trice), de désapprobation

disarm [dɪsˈɑːm] VT désarmer

disarmament [dɪsˈɑːməmənt] N désarmement *m*

disarming [dɪsˈɑːmɪŋ] ADJ (*smile*) désarmant(e)

disarray [dɪsəˈreɪ] N désordre *m*, confusion *f*; **in ~** (*troops*) en déroute; (*thoughts*) embrouillé(e); (*clothes*) en désordre; **to throw into ~** semer la confusion *or* le désordre dans (*or* parmi)

disassemble [dɪsəˈsɛmbl] VT (*formal*: *machine, weapon*) démonter

disassociate [dɪsəˈsəuʃɪeɪt] VT dissocier; **to ~ o.s. from sth/sb** se dissocier de qch/qn

★**disaster** [dɪˈzɑːstəʳ] N catastrophe *f*, désastre *m*

disastrous [dɪˈzɑːstrəs] ADJ désastreux(-euse)

disastrously [dɪˈzɑːstrəslɪ] ADV (*high, low, late*) terriblement; **to go ~ wrong** tourner au désastre

disband [dɪsˈbænd] VT démobiliser; disperser ▶ VI se séparer; se disperser

disbelief [dɪsbəˈliːf] N incrédulité *f*; **in ~** avec incrédulité

disbelieve [dɪsbəˈliːv] VT (*person*) ne pas croire; (*story*) mettre en doute; **I don't ~ you** je veux bien vous croire

disbursement [dɪsˈbəːsmənt] N (*formal*: *act*) déboursement *m*; (: *sum paid*) débours *m*

disc [dɪsk] N disque *m*; (*Comput*) = **disk**

discard [dɪsˈkɑːd] VT (*old things*) se débarrasser de, mettre au rencart *or* au rebut; (*fig*) écarter, renoncer à

disc brake N frein *m* à disque

discern [dɪˈsəːn] VT discerner, distinguer

discernible [dɪˈsəːnəbl] ADJ discernable, perceptible; (*object*) visible

discerning [dɪˈsəːnɪŋ] ADJ judicieux(-euse), perspicace

discharge VT [dɪsˈtʃɑːdʒ] (*duties*) s'acquitter de; (*settle*: *debt*) s'acquitter de, régler; (*waste etc*) déverser; décharger; (*Elec, Med*) émettre; (*patient*) renvoyer (chez lui); (*employee, soldier*) congédier, licencier; (*defendant*) relaxer, élargir; **to ~ one's gun** faire feu; **discharged bankrupt** failli(e), réhabilité(e) ▶ N [ˈdɪstʃɑːdʒ] (*Elec, Med*) émission *f*;

(*also:* **vaginal discharge**) pertes blanches; (*dismissal*) renvoi *m*, licenciement *m*, élargissement *m*

disciple [dɪ'saɪpl] N disciple *mf*

disciplinarian [dɪsɪplɪ'nɛərɪən] N: **to be a ~** être strict(e) en matière de discipline

disciplinary ['dɪsɪplɪnərɪ] ADJ disciplinaire; **to take ~ action against sb** prendre des mesures disciplinaires à l'encontre de qn

★**discipline** ['dɪsɪplɪn] N discipline *f* ▶ VT discipliner; (*punish*) punir; **to ~ o.s. to do sth** s'imposer *or* s'astreindre à une discipline pour faire qch

disc jockey N disque-jockey *m* (DJ)

disclaim [dɪs'kleɪm] VT désavouer, dénier

disclaimer [dɪs'kleɪmə^r] N démenti *m*, dénégation *f*; **to issue a ~** publier un démenti

disclose [dɪs'kləʊz] VT révéler, divulguer

disclosure [dɪs'kləʊʒə^r] N révélation *f*, divulgation *f*

disco ['dɪskəʊ] N ABBR discothèque *f*

discolour, (*US*) **discolor** [dɪs'kʌlə^r] VT décolorer; (*sth white*) jaunir ▶ VI se décolorer; jaunir

discolouration, (*US*) **discoloration** [dɪskʌlə-'reɪʃən] N décoloration *f*; jaunissement *m*

discoloured, (*US*) **discolored** [dɪs'kʌləd] ADJ décoloré(e), jauni(e)

discomfiture [dɪs'kʌmfɪtʃə^r] N embarras *m*

discomfort [dɪs'kʌmfət] N malaise *m*, gêne *f*; (*lack of comfort*) manque *m* de confort

disconcert [dɪskən'sə:t] VT déconcerter, décontenancer

disconcerting [dɪskən'sə:tɪŋ] ADJ déconcertant(e)

disconnect [dɪskə'nɛkt] VT détacher; (*Elec, Radio*) débrancher; (*gas, water*) couper

disconnected [dɪskə'nɛktɪd] ADJ (*speech, thoughts*) décousu(e), peu cohérent(e)

disconnection [dɪskə'nɛkʃən] N (*of water, electricity, telephone*) coupure *f*; (*between people, organizations*) séparation *f*

disconsolate [dɪs'kɔnsəlɪt] ADJ inconsolable

discontent [dɪskən'tɛnt] N mécontentement *m*

discontented [dɪskən'tɛntɪd] ADJ mécontent(e)

discontinue [dɪskən'tɪnjuː] VT cesser, interrompre; **"discontinued"** (*Comm*) « fin de série »

discord ['dɪskɔːd] N discorde *f*, dissension *f*; (*Mus*) dissonance *f*

discordant [dɪs'kɔːdənt] ADJ discordant(e), dissonant(e)

★**discount** N ['dɪskaʊnt] remise *f*, rabais *m*; **to give sb a ~ on sth** faire une remise *or* un rabais à qn sur qch; **~ for cash** escompte *f* au comptant; **at a ~** avec une remise *or* réduction, au rabais ▶ VT [dɪs'kaʊnt] (*report etc*) ne pas tenir compte de

discount house N (*Finance*) banque *f* d'escompte; (*Comm: also:* **discount store**) magasin *m* de discount

discount rate N taux *m* de remise

discourage [dɪs'kʌrɪdʒ] VT (*dishearten*) décourager; (*dissuade, deter*) dissuader, décourager

discouraged [dɪs'kʌrɪdʒd] ADJ découragé(e); **don't be ~** ne te décourage pas

discouragement [dɪs'kʌrɪdʒmənt] N (*depression*) découragement *m*; **to act as a ~ to sb** dissuader qn

discouraging [dɪs'kʌrɪdʒɪŋ] ADJ décourageant(e)

discourse N ['dɪskɔːs] (*communication*) conversation *m*; (*speech*) discours *m*; (*written piece*) dissertation *f* ▶ VI [dɪs'kɔːs] (*formal*) discourir; **to ~ on sth** discourir sur qch

discourteous [dɪs'kəːtɪəs] ADJ incivil(e), discourtois(e)

★**discover** [dɪs'kʌvə^r] VT découvrir

discovery [dɪs'kʌvərɪ] N découverte *f*

discredit [dɪs'krɛdɪt] VT (*idea*) mettre en doute; (*person*) discréditer ▶ N discrédit *m*

discreet [dɪ'skriːt] ADJ discret(-ète)

discreetly [dɪ'skriːtlɪ] ADV discrètement

discrepancy [dɪ'skrɛpənsɪ] N divergence *f*, contradiction *f*

discrete [dɪs'kriːt] ADJ distinct(e), séparé(e)

discretion [dɪ'skrɛʃən] N discrétion *f*; **at the ~ of** à la discrétion de; **use your own ~** à vous de juger

discretionary [dɪ'skrɛʃənrɪ] ADJ (*powers*) discrétionnaire

discriminate [dɪ'skrɪmɪneɪt] VI: **to ~ between** établir une distinction entre, faire la différence entre; **to ~ against** pratiquer une discrimination contre

discriminating [dɪ'skrɪmɪneɪtɪŋ] ADJ qui a du discernement

discrimination [dɪskrɪmɪ'neɪʃən] N discrimination *f*; (*judgment*) discernement *m*; **racial/sexual ~** discrimination raciale/sexuelle

discriminatory [dɪ'skrɪmɪnətərɪ] ADJ discriminatoire

discus ['dɪskəs] N disque *m*

★**discuss** [dɪ'skʌs] VT discuter de; (*debate*) discuter

★**discussion** [dɪ'skʌʃən] N discussion *f*; **under ~** en discussion

disdain [dɪs'deɪn] N dédain *m*

disdainful [dɪs'deɪnful] ADJ dédaigneux(-euse); **to be ~ of sb/sth** dédaigner qn/qch

disease [dɪ'ziːz] N maladie *f*

diseased [dɪ'ziːzd] ADJ malade

disembark [dɪsɪm'baːk] VT, VI débarquer

disembarkation [dɪsɛmbaː'keɪʃən] N débarquement *m*

disembodied [dɪsɪm'bɔdɪd] ADJ désincarné(e)

disembowel [dɪsɪm'bauəl] VT éviscérer, étriper

disempower [dɪsɪm'pauə^r] VT (*person, group*) priver de son autonomie

disenchanted [dɪsɪn'tʃɑːntɪd] ADJ: **~** désenchanté(e), désabusé(e); **to be ~ with sb/sth** être déçu(e) par qn/qch

disenchantment [dɪsɪn'tʃɑːntmənt] N désillusion *f*; **there's growing ~ with the government** de plus en plus de gens sont déçus par le gouvernement

disenfranchise [dɪsɪn'fræntʃaɪz] VT priver du droit de vote; (*Comm*) retirer la franchise à

disengage [dɪsɪn'geɪdʒ] VT dégager; (*Tech*) déclencher; **to ~ the clutch** (*Aut*) débrayer

disentangle [dɪsɪn'tæŋgl] VT démêler

disfavour, (US) **disfavor** [dɪs'feɪvəʳ] N défaveur f; disgrâce f

disfigure [dɪs'fɪgəʳ] VT défigurer

disgorge [dɪs'gɔːdʒ] VT déverser

disgrace [dɪs'greɪs] N honte f; (disfavour) disgrâce f ▶ VT déshonorer, couvrir de honte

disgraced [dɪs'greɪst] ADJ disgracié(e)

disgraceful [dɪs'greɪsful] ADJ scandaleux(-euse), honteux(-euse)

disgruntled [dɪs'grʌntld] ADJ mécontent(e)

disguise [dɪs'gaɪz] N déguisement m; **in ~** déguisé(e) ▶ VT déguiser; (voice) déguiser, contrefaire; (feelings etc) masquer, dissimuler; **to ~ o.s. as** se déguiser en; **there's no disguising the fact that …** on ne peut pas se dissimuler que …

disguised [dɪs'gaɪzd] ADJ (in disguise) déguisé(e); (veiled: criticism, anger) dissimulé(e); **to be ~ as sb/sth** être déguisé(e) en qn/qch

disgust [dɪs'gʌst] N dégoût m, aversion f ▶ VT dégoûter, écœurer

disgusted [dɪs'gʌstɪd] ADJ dégoûté(e), écœuré(e)

disgusting [dɪs'gʌstɪŋ] ADJ dégoûtant(e), révoltant(e)

★**dish** [dɪʃ] N plat m; **to do** or **wash the dishes** faire la vaisselle
▶ **dish out** VT distribuer
▶ **dish up** VT servir; (facts, statistics) sortir, débiter

dishcloth ['dɪʃklɔθ] N (for drying) torchon m; (for washing) lavette f

dishearten [dɪs'hɑːtn] VT décourager

disheartening [dɪs'hɑːtnɪŋ] ADJ décourageant(e)

dishevelled, (US) **disheveled** [dɪ'ʃɛvəld] ADJ ébouriffé(e), décoiffé(e), débraillé(e)

dishonest [dɪs'ɔnɪst] ADJ malhonnête

dishonesty [dɪs'ɔnɪstɪ] N malhonnêteté f

dishonour, (US) **dishonor** [dɪs'ɔnəʳ] N déshonneur m

dishonourable, (US) **dishonorable** [dɪs'ɔnərəbl] ADJ déshonorant(e)

dish soap N (US) produit m pour la vaisselle

dishtowel ['dɪʃtauəl] N (US) torchon m (à vaisselle)

dishwasher ['dɪʃwɔʃəʳ] N lave-vaisselle m; (person) plongeur(-euse)

dishwater ['dɪʃwɔːtəʳ] N eau f de vaisselle; **as dull as ~** ennuyeux(-euse) comme la pluie

dishy ['dɪʃɪ] ADJ (BRIT old) séduisant(e), sexy inv

disillusion [dɪsɪ'luːʒən] VT désabuser, désenchanter ▶ N désenchantement m

disillusioned [dɪsɪ'luːʒənd] ADJ désabusé(e), désenchanté(e); **to become ~ (with sth/sb)** perdre ses illusions (sur qch/qn)

disillusionment [dɪsɪ'luːʒənmənt] N désillusion f; **~ with sth/sb** désillusion envers qch/qn

disincentive [dɪsɪn'sɛntɪv] N: **it's a ~** c'est démotivant; **to be a ~ to sb** démotiver qn

disinclined [dɪsɪn'klaɪnd] ADJ: **to be ~ to do sth** être peu disposé(e) or peu enclin(e) à faire qch

disinfect [dɪsɪn'fɛkt] VT désinfecter

disinfectant [dɪsɪn'fɛktənt] N désinfectant m

disinflation [dɪsɪn'fleɪʃən] N désinflation f

disinformation [dɪsɪnfə'meɪʃən] N désinformation f

disingenuous [dɪsɪn'dʒɛnjuəs] ADJ peu sincère; **it is ~ to do …** ce n'est pas sincère de faire …

disingenuously [dɪsɪn'dʒɛnjuəslɪ] ADV de manière peu sincère

disinherit [dɪsɪn'hɛrɪt] VT déshériter

disintegrate [dɪs'ɪntɪgreɪt] VI se désintégrer

disintegration [dɪsɪntɪ'greɪʃən] N (of object) désintégration f; (of substance, relationship, nation) désagrégation f

disinterested [dɪs'ɪntrəstɪd] ADJ désintéressé(e)

disjointed [dɪs'dʒɔɪntɪd] ADJ décousu(e), incohérent(e)

disk [dɪsk] N (Comput) disquette f; **single-/double-sided ~** disquette une face/double face

disk drive N lecteur m de disquette

diskette [dɪs'kɛt] N (Comput) disquette f

disk operating system N système m d'exploitation à disques

dislike [dɪs'laɪk] N aversion f, antipathie f; **to take a ~ to sb/sth** prendre qn/qch en grippe ▶ VT ne pas aimer; **I ~ the idea** l'idée me déplaît

dislocate ['dɪsləkeɪt] VT (shoulder, ankle) disloquer, déboîter; (service) désorganiser; (system, process) bouleverser; **he has dislocated his shoulder** il s'est disloqué l'épaule

dislocation [dɪslə'keɪʃən] N (of shoulder, ankle) dislocation f, déboîtement m; (of system, process, service) bouleversement m

dislodge [dɪs'lɔdʒ] VT déplacer, faire bouger; (enemy) déloger

disloyal [dɪs'lɔɪəl] ADJ déloyal(e)

dismal ['dɪzml] ADJ (gloomy) lugubre, maussade; (very bad) lamentable

dismally ['dɪzməlɪ] ADV (fail, perform) lamentablement

dismantle [dɪs'mæntl] VT démonter; (fort, warship) démanteler

dismast [dɪs'mɑːst] VT démâter

dismay [dɪs'meɪ] N consternation f; **much to my ~** à ma grande consternation, à ma grande inquiétude ▶ VT consterner

dismiss [dɪs'mɪs] VT congédier, renvoyer; (idea) écarter; (Law) rejeter ▶ VI (Mil) rompre les rangs

dismissal [dɪs'mɪsl] N renvoi m

dismissive [dɪs'mɪsɪv] ADJ dédaigneux(-euse); **to be ~ of sth** faire peu de cas de qch

dismount [dɪs'maunt] VI mettre pied à terre

disobedience [dɪsə'biːdɪəns] N désobéissance f

disobedient [dɪsə'biːdɪənt] ADJ désobéissant(e), indiscipliné(e)

disobey [dɪsə'beɪ] VT désobéir à; (rule) transgresser, enfreindre

disorder [dɪs'ɔːdəʳ] N (Med) troubles mpl; (mess) désordre m; (rioting) désordres mpl; **a kidney ~** une maladie des reins; **in ~** en désordre; **civil ~** désordre m public

disordered [dɪs'ɔːdəd] ADJ (messy) en désordre; (mind, behaviour) dérangé(e), déséquilibré(e)

disorderly [dɪs'ɔːdəlɪ] ADJ (room) en désordre; (behaviour, retreat, crowd) désordonné(e)

disorderly conduct N (Law) conduite f contraire aux bonnes mœurs

disorganized [dɪsˈɔːɡənaɪzd] ADJ désorganisé(e)

disorientated [dɪsˈɔːrɪenteɪtɪd] ADJ désorienté(e)

disown [dɪsˈəʊn] VT renier

disparaging [dɪsˈpærɪdʒɪŋ] ADJ désobligeant(e); **to be ~ about sb/sth** faire des remarques désobligeantes sur qn/qch

disparate [ˈdɪspərɪt] ADJ disparate

disparity [dɪsˈpærɪtɪ] N disparité f

dispassionate [dɪsˈpæʃənət] ADJ calme, froid(e), impartial(e), objectif(-ive)

dispatch [dɪsˈpætʃ] VT expédier, envoyer; (deal with: business) régler, en finir avec ▶ N envoi m, expédition f; (Mil, Press) dépêche f

dispatch department N service m des expéditions

dispatch rider N (Mil) estafette f

dispel [dɪsˈpɛl] VT dissiper, chasser

dispensary [dɪsˈpɛnsərɪ] N pharmacie f; (in chemist's) officine f

dispense [dɪsˈpɛns] VT distribuer, administrer; (medicine) préparer (et vendre); **to ~ sb from** dispenser qn de
   ▶ **dispense with** VT FUS se passer de; (make unnecessary) rendre superflu(e)

dispenser [dɪsˈpɛnsəʳ] N (device) distributeur m

dispensing chemist [dɪsˈpɛnsɪŋ-] N (BRIT) pharmacie f

dispersal [dɪsˈpəːsl] N dispersion f; (Admin) déconcentration f

disperse [dɪsˈpəːs] VT disperser; (knowledge) disséminer ▶ VI se disperser

dispirited [dɪsˈpɪrɪtɪd] ADJ découragé(e), déprimé(e)

dispiriting [dɪˈspɪrɪtɪŋ] ADJ décourageant(e)

displace [dɪsˈpleɪs] VT déplacer

displaced person [dɪsˈpleɪst-] N (Pol) personne déplacée

displacement [dɪsˈpleɪsmənt] N déplacement m

display [dɪsˈpleɪ] N (of goods) étalage m; affichage m; (Comput: information) visualisation f; (: device) visuel m; (of feeling) manifestation f; (pej) ostentation f; (show, spectacle) spectacle m; (military display) parade f militaire; **on ~** (exhibits) exposé(e), exhibé(e); (goods) à l'étalage ▶ VT montrer; (goods) mettre à l'étalage, exposer; (results, departure times) afficher; (pej) faire étalage de

display advertising N publicité rédactionnelle

displease [dɪsˈpliːz] VT mécontenter, contrarier; **displeased with** mécontent(e) de

displeasure [dɪsˈplɛʒəʳ] N mécontentement m

disposable [dɪsˈpəʊzəbl] ADJ (pack etc) jetable; (income) disponible; **~ nappy** (BRIT) couche f à jeter, couche-culotte f

disposal [dɪsˈpəʊzl] N (of rubbish) évacuation f, destruction f; (of property etc: by selling) vente f; (: by giving away) cession f; (availability, arrangement) disposition f; **at one's ~** à sa disposition; **to put sth at sb's ~** mettre qch à la disposition de qn

dispose [dɪsˈpəʊz] VT disposer ▶ VI: **~ of** (time, money) disposer de; (unwanted goods) se débarrasser de, se défaire de; (Comm: stock) écouler, vendre; (problem) expédier

disposed [dɪsˈpəʊzd] ADJ: **~ to do** disposé(e) à faire

disposition [dɪspəˈzɪʃən] N disposition f; (temperament) naturel m

dispossess [dɪspəˈzɛs] VT: **to ~ sb (of)** déposséder qn (de)

disproportion [dɪsprəˈpɔːʃən] N disproportion f

disproportionate [dɪsprəˈpɔːʃənət] ADJ disproportionné(e)

disproportionately [dɪsprəˈpɔːʃənətlɪ] ADV: **~ high** disproportionné(e)

disprove [dɪsˈpruːv] VT réfuter

dispute [dɪsˈpjuːt] N discussion f; (also: **industrial dispute**) conflit m; **to be in** or **under ~** (matter) être en discussion; (territory) être contesté(e) ▶ VT (question) contester; (matter) discuter; (victory) disputer

disputed [dɪˈspjuːtɪd] ADJ (territory, region, border) contesté(e)

disqualification [dɪskwɒlɪfɪˈkeɪʃən] N disqualification f; **~ (from driving)** (BRIT) retrait m du permis (de conduire)

disqualify [dɪsˈkwɒlɪfaɪ] VT (Sport) disqualifier; **to ~ sb for sth/from doing** (status, situation) rendre qn inapte à qch/à faire; (authority) signifier à qn l'interdiction de qch/de faire; **to ~ sb (from driving)** (BRIT) retirer à qn son permis (de conduire)

disquiet [dɪsˈkwaɪət] N inquiétude f, trouble m

disquieting [dɪsˈkwaɪətɪŋ] ADJ inquiétant(e), alarmant(e)

disregard [dɪsrɪˈɡɑːd] VT ne pas tenir compte de ▶ N: **~ (for)** (feelings) indifférence f (pour), insensibilité f (à); (danger, money) mépris m (pour)

disrepair [dɪsrɪˈpɛəʳ] N mauvais état; **to fall into ~** (building) tomber en ruine; (street) se dégrader

disreputable [dɪsˈrɛpjutəbl] ADJ (person) de mauvaise réputation, peu recommandable; (behaviour) déshonorant(e); (area) mal famé(e), louche

disrepute [dɪsrɪˈpjuːt] N déshonneur m, discrédit m; **to bring into ~** faire tomber dans le discrédit

disrespect [dɪsrɪˈspɛkt] N manque m de respect; **~ for sb/sth** manque de respect envers qn/qch

disrespectful [dɪsrɪˈspɛktful] ADJ irrespectueux(-euse); **to be ~ to sb** (person) manquer de respect à qn

disrupt [dɪsˈrʌpt] VT (plans, meeting, lesson) perturber, déranger

disruption [dɪsˈrʌpʃən] N perturbation f, dérangement m

disruptive [dɪsˈrʌptɪv] ADJ perturbateur(-trice)

diss [dɪs] VT (inf) débiner (inf)

dissatisfaction [dɪssætɪsˈfækʃən] N mécontentement m, insatisfaction f

dissatisfied [dɪsˈsætɪsfaɪd] ADJ: **~ (with)** insatisfait(e) (de)

dissect [daɪˈsɛkt] VT (body, issue, theory) disséquer; (account, book, report) éplucher

dissection [daɪˈsɛkʃən] N (of body, issue, theory) dissection f; (of account, book, report) épluchage m

disseminate [dɪˈsɛmɪneɪt] VT (information, facts) disséminer, propager; (knowledge) diffuser

dissemination [dɪsɛmɪˈneɪʃən] N (of information, facts, ideas) dissémination f, propagation f; (of knowledge) diffusion f

dissent [dɪˈsɛnt] N dissentiment m, différence f d'opinion

dissenter [dɪ'sɛntə^r] N (Rel, Pol etc) dissident(e)

dissenting [dɪ'sɛntɪŋ] ADJ contestataire

dissertation [dɪsə'teɪʃən] N (Scol) mémoire m

disservice [dɪs'sə:vɪs] N: **to do sb a ~** rendre un mauvais service à qn; desservir qn

dissident ['dɪsɪdnt] ADJ, N dissident(e)

dissimilar [dɪ'sɪmɪlə^r] ADJ: **~ (to)** dissemblable (à), différent(e) (de)

dissipate ['dɪsɪpeɪt] VT dissiper; (energy, efforts) disperser

dissipated ['dɪsɪpeɪtɪd] ADJ dissolu(e), débauché(e)

dissociate [dɪ'səʊʃɪeɪt] VT dissocier; **to ~ o.s. from sb/sth** se dissocier de qn/qch

dissolute ['dɪsəlu:t] ADJ débauché(e), dissolu(e)

dissolution [dɪsə'lu:ʃən] N dissolution f

dissolve [dɪ'zɔlv] VT dissoudre ▶ VI se dissoudre, fondre; (fig) disparaître; **to ~ in(to) tears** fondre en larmes

dissuade [dɪ'sweɪd] VT: **to ~ sb (from)** dissuader qn (de)

★**distance** ['dɪstns] N distance f; **what's the ~ to London?** à quelle distance se trouve Londres ?; **it's within walking ~** on peut y aller à pied; **in the ~** au loin

distant ['dɪstnt] ADJ lointain(e), éloigné(e); (manner) distant(e), froid(e)

distaste [dɪs'teɪst] N dégoût m

distasteful [dɪs'teɪstful] ADJ déplaisant(e), désagréable

Dist. Atty. ABBR (US) = **district attorney**

distemper [dɪs'tɛmpə^r] N (paint) détrempe f, badigeon m; (of dogs) maladie f de Carré

distended [dɪs'tɛndɪd] ADJ (stomach) dilaté(e)

distil, (US) **distill** [dɪs'tɪl] VT (whisky, water) distiller; (thoughts, ideas) condenser

distillation [dɪstɪ'leɪʃən] N (of whisky, water) distillation f; (of thoughts, ideas) condensé m

distillery [dɪs'tɪlərɪ] N distillerie f

distinct [dɪs'tɪŋkt] ADJ distinct(e); (clear) marqué(e); **as ~ from** par opposition à, en contraste avec

distinction [dɪs'tɪŋkʃən] N distinction f; (in exam) mention f très bien; **to draw a ~ between** faire une distinction entre; **a writer of ~** un écrivain réputé

distinctive [dɪs'tɪŋktɪv] ADJ (style, feature, character) distinctif(-ive); (taste, smell) caractéristique

distinctively [dɪ'stɪŋktɪvlɪ] ADV (typically: American, British) typiquement; (decorated) de façon particulière

distinctly [dɪs'tɪŋktlɪ] ADV distinctement; (specify) expressément

distinguish [dɪs'tɪŋgwɪʃ] VT distinguer; **to ~ o.s.** se distinguer ▶ VI: **to ~ between** (concepts) distinguer entre, faire une distinction entre

distinguishable [dɪ'stɪŋgwɪʃəbl] ADJ (recognizable) reconnaissable; (discernible: sound) perceptible; (: shape) visible; **to be ~ by sth** être reconnaissable par qch, se distinguer par qch

distinguished [dɪs'tɪŋgwɪʃt] ADJ (eminent, refined) distingué(e); (career) remarquable, brillant(e)

distinguishing [dɪs'tɪŋgwɪʃɪŋ] ADJ (feature) distinctif(-ive), caractéristique

distort [dɪs'tɔ:t] VT déformer

distorted [dɪ'stɔ:tɪd] ADJ (picture, image, sound) déformé(e); (view, idea) faussé(e)

distortion [dɪs'tɔ:ʃən] N déformation f

distract [dɪs'trækt] VT distraire, déranger

distracted [dɪs'træktɪd] ADJ (not concentrating) distrait(e); (worried) affolé(e)

distractedly [dɪ'stræktɪdlɪ] ADV distraitement

distraction [dɪs'trækʃən] N distraction f, dérangement m; **to drive sb to ~** rendre qn fou (folle)

distraught [dɪs'trɔ:t] ADJ éperdu(e)

distress [dɪs'trɛs] N détresse f; (pain) douleur f; **in ~** (ship) en perdition; (plane) en détresse ▶ VT bouleverser

distressed [dɪ'strɛst] ADJ (upset) bouleversé(e); (poor) dans le besoin; (artificially aged: denim) vieilli(e); **to be ~ about sth** être bouleversé(e) par qch; **~ area** (BRIT) zone sinistrée

distressing [dɪs'trɛsɪŋ] ADJ douloureux(-euse), pénible, affligeant(e)

distress signal N signal m de détresse

distribute [dɪs'trɪbju:t] VT distribuer

distribution [dɪstrɪ'bju:ʃən] N distribution f

distribution cost N coût m de distribution

distributor [dɪs'trɪbjutə^r] N (gen: Tech) distributeur m; (Comm) concessionnaire mf

★**district** ['dɪstrɪkt] N (of country) région f; (of town) quartier m; (Admin) district m

district attorney N (US) ≈ procureur mf de la République

district council N (BRIT) ≈ conseil municipal

district nurse N (BRIT) infirmière visiteuse

distrust [dɪs'trʌst] N méfiance f, doute m ▶ VT se méfier de

distrustful [dɪs'trʌstful] ADJ méfiant(e)

disturb [dɪs'tə:b] VT troubler; (inconvenience) déranger; **sorry to ~ you** excusez-moi de vous déranger

disturbance [dɪs'tə:bəns] N dérangement m; (political etc) troubles mpl; (by drunks etc) tapage m; **to cause a ~** troubler l'ordre public; **~ of the peace** (Law) tapage injurieux or nocturne

disturbed [dɪs'tə:bd] ADJ (worried, upset) agité(e), troublé(e); **to be emotionally ~** avoir des problèmes affectifs

disturbing [dɪs'tə:bɪŋ] ADJ troublant(e), inquiétant(e)

disunited [dɪsju'naɪtɪd] ADJ désuni(e)

disunity [dɪs'ju:nɪtɪ] N désunion f

disuse [dɪs'ju:s] N: **to fall into ~** tomber en désuétude

disused [dɪs'ju:zd] ADJ désaffecté(e)

ditch [dɪtʃ] N fossé m; (for irrigation) rigole f ▶ VT (inf) abandonner; (person) plaquer

dither ['dɪðə^r] VI hésiter

ditto ['dɪtəu] ADV idem

ditty ['dɪtɪ] N chansonnette f

diuretic [daɪjuə'rɛtɪk] ADJ, N diurétique m

diva ['di:və] N diva f

divan [dɪ'væn] N divan m

divan bed N divan-lit m

dive [daɪv] N plongeon m; (of submarine) plongée f; (Aviat) piqué m; (pej: café, bar etc) bouge m ▸ VI plonger; **to ~ into** (bag etc) plonger la main dans; (place) se précipiter dans

diver ['daɪvəʳ] N plongeur(-euse)

diverge [daɪ'vɜːdʒ] VI diverger

divergence [daɪ'vɜːdʒəns] N divergence f; **a ~ of opinion** une divergence d'opinions

divergent [daɪ'vɜːdʒənt] ADJ divergent(e)

diverse [daɪ'vɜːs] ADJ divers(e)

diversification [daɪvɜːsɪfɪ'keɪʃən] N diversification f

diversify [daɪ'vɜːsɪfaɪ] VT diversifier

diversion [daɪ'vɜːʃən] N (BRIT Aut) déviation f; (distraction, Mil) diversion f

diversionary [daɪ'vɜːʃənrɪ] ADJ (activity, attack) de diversion; **~ tactic** manœuvre f de diversion

diversity [daɪ'vɜːsɪtɪ] N diversité f, variété f

divert [daɪ'vɜːt] VT (BRIT: traffic) dévier; (plane) dérouter; (train, river) détourner; (amuse) divertir

divest [daɪ'vest] VT: **to ~ sb of** dépouiller qn de

★**divide** [dɪ'vaɪd] VT (quantity, number) diviser; (separate) séparer; **40 divided by 5** 40 divisé par 5; **to ~ people into groups** diviser or repartir des personnes en groupes; **to ~ sth between** or **among** partager or répartir entre ▸ VI se diviser
  ▸ **divide out** VT: **to ~ out (between** or **among)** distribuer or répartir (entre)
  ▸ **divide up** VT (group, country) diviser; (share: money, possessions) partager; **to ~ sth up into** diviser qch en

divided [dɪ'vaɪdɪd] ADJ (fig: country, couple) désuni(e); (opinions) partagé(e)

divided highway N (US) route f à quatre voies

divided skirt N jupe-culotte f

dividend ['dɪvɪdend] N dividende m

dividend cover N rapport m dividendes-résultat

dividers [dɪ'vaɪdəz] NPL compas m à pointes sèches; (between pages) feuillets mpl intercalaires

divine [dɪ'vaɪn] ADJ divin(e) ▸ VT (future) prédire; (truth) deviner, entrevoir; (water, metal) détecter la présence de (par l'intermédiaire de la radiesthésie)

diving ['daɪvɪŋ] N plongée (sous-marine)

diving board N plongeoir m

diving suit N scaphandre m

divinity [dɪ'vɪnɪtɪ] N divinité f; (as study) théologie f

division [dɪ'vɪʒən] N division f; (BRIT Football) division; (separation) séparation f; (Comm) service m; (BRIT Pol) vote m; (also: **division of labour**) division du travail

divisive [dɪ'vaɪsɪv] ADJ qui entraîne la division, clivant(e)

divorce [dɪ'vɔːs] N divorce m ▸ VT divorcer d'avec

★**divorced** [dɪ'vɔːst] ADJ divorcé(e)

divorcee [dɪvɔː'siː] N divorcé(e)

divot ['dɪvət] N (Golf) motte f de gazon

divulge [daɪ'vʌldʒ] VT divulguer, révéler

Diwali [dɪ'wɑːlɪ], **Divali** [dɪ'vɑːlɪ] N Dipavali m

★**DIY** ADJ, N ABBR (BRIT) = **do-it-yourself**

dizziness ['dɪzɪnɪs] N vertige m, étourdissement m

dizzy ['dɪzɪ] ADJ (height) vertigineux(-euse); **to make sb ~** donner le vertige à qn; **I feel ~** la tête me tourne, j'ai la tête qui tourne

dizzying ['dɪzɪŋ] ADJ (height, speed) vertigineux(-euse)

DJ N ABBR = **disc jockey**

d.j. N ABBR = **dinner jacket**

Djakarta [dʒə'kɑːtə] N Djakarta

DJIA N ABBR (US Stock Exchange) = **Dow-Jones Industrial Average**

Djibouti [dʒɪ'buːtɪ] N Djibouti

dl ABBR (= decilitre) dl

DLit, DLitt N ABBR (= Doctor of Literature, Doctor of Letters) titre universitaire

DMus N ABBR (= Doctor of Music) titre universitaire

DMZ N ABBR = **demilitarized zone**

DNA N ABBR (= deoxyribonucleic acid) ADN m

DNA fingerprinting [-'fɪŋɡəprɪntɪŋ] N technique f des empreintes génétiques

---

do [duː]

(pt **did** [dɪd], pp **done** [dʌn]) N (inf: party etc) soirée f, fête f; (: formal gathering) réception f

▸ AUX VB **1** (in negative constructions) non traduit; **I don't understand** je ne comprends pas

2 (to form questions) non traduit; **didn't you know?** vous ne le saviez pas ?; **what do you think?** qu'en pensez-vous ?; **why didn't you come?** pourquoi n'êtes-vous pas venu ?

3 (for emphasis: in polite expressions): **people do make mistakes sometimes** on peut toujours se tromper; **she does seem rather late** je trouve qu'elle est bien en retard; **do sit down/ help yourself** asseyez-vous/servez-vous je vous en prie; **do take care!** faites bien attention à vous !; **I DO wish I could go** j'aimerais tant y aller; **but I DO like it!** mais si, je l'aime !

4 (used to avoid repeating vb): **she swims better than I do** elle nage mieux que moi; **do you agree? — yes, I do/no I don't** vous êtes d'accord ? — oui/non; **she lives in Glasgow — so do I** elle habite Glasgow — moi aussi; **he didn't like it and neither did we** il n'a pas aimé ça, et nous non plus; **who broke it? — I did** qui l'a cassé ? — c'est moi; **he asked me to help him and I did** il m'a demandé de l'aider, et c'est ce que j'ai fait

5 (in question tags): **you like him, don't you?** vous l'aimez bien, n'est-ce pas ?; **he laughed, didn't he?** il a ri, n'est-ce pas ?; **I don't know him, do I?** je ne crois pas le connaître

▸ VT **1** (gen: carry out, perform etc) faire; (: visit: city, museum) faire, visiter; **what are you doing tonight?** qu'est-ce que vous faites ce soir ?; **what do you do?** (job) que faites-vous dans la vie ?; **what did he do with the cat?** qu'a-t-il fait du chat ?; **what can I do for you?** que puis-je faire pour vous ?; **to do the cooking/washing-up** faire la cuisine/la vaisselle; **to do one's teeth/hair/nails** se brosser les dents/se coiffer/ se faire les ongles

2 (Aut etc: distance) faire; (: speed) faire du; **we've done 200 km already** nous avons déjà fait 200 km; **the car was doing 100** la voiture faisait du 100 (à l'heure); **he can do 100 in that car** il peut faire du 100 (à l'heure) dans cette voiture-là

▸ VI **1** (act, behave) faire; **do as I do** faites comme moi

2 (get on, fare) marcher; **the firm is doing well**

l'entreprise marche bien; **he's doing well/ badly at school** ça marche bien/mal pour lui à l'école; **how do you do?** comment allez-vous ?; (on being introduced) enchanté(e) !
3 (suit) aller; **will it do?** est-ce que ça ira ?
4 (be sufficient) suffire, aller; **will £10 do?** est-ce que 10 livres suffiront ?; **that'll do** ça suffit, ça ira; **that'll do!** (in annoyance) ça va or suffit comme ça !; **to make do (with)** se contenter (de)
▸ **do away with** VT FUS abolir; (inf: kill) supprimer
▸ **do for** VT FUS (BRIT inf: clean for) faire le ménage chez
▸ **do up** VT (laces, dress) attacher; (buttons) boutonner; (zip) fermer; (renovate: room) refaire; (: house) remettre à neuf; **to do o.s. up** se faire beau (belle)
▸ **do with** VT FUS (need): **I could do with a drink/ some help** quelque chose à boire/un peu d'aide ne serait pas de refus; **it could do with a wash** ça ne lui ferait pas de mal d'être lavé; (be connected with): **that has nothing to do with you** cela ne vous concerne pas; **I won't have anything to do with it** je ne veux pas m'en mêler; **what has that got to do with it?** quel est le rapport ?, qu'est-ce que cela vient faire là-dedans ?
▸ **do without** VI s'en passer; **if you're late for tea then you'll do without** si vous êtes en retard pour le dîner il faudra vous en passer
▸ VT FUS se passer de; **I can do without a car** je peux me passer de voiture

do. ABBR (= ditto) d
DOA ABBR (= dead on arrival) décédé(e) à l'admission
doable ['du:əbl] ADJ faisable
d.o.b. ABBR = **date of birth**
doc [dɔk] N (inf) toubib m
docile ['dəusaɪl] ADJ docile
dock [dɔk] N dock m; (wharf) quai m; (Law) banc m des accusés ▸ VI se mettre à quai; (Space) s'arrimer ▸ VT: **they docked a third of his wages** ils lui ont retenu or décompté un tiers de son salaire
  ■ **docks** NPL (Naut) docks
dock dues NPL droits mpl de bassin
docker ['dɔkəʳ] N docker m
docket ['dɔkɪt] N bordereau m; (on parcel etc) étiquette f or fiche f (décrivant le contenu d'un paquet etc)
dockside ['dɔksaɪd] N docks mpl
dockyard ['dɔkjɑːd] N chantier m de construction navale
★**doctor** ['dɔktəʳ] N médecin m, docteur m; (PhD etc) docteur; **call a ~!** appelez un docteur or un médecin !; **~'s office** (US) cabinet m de consultation ▸ VT (cat) couper; (interfere with: food) altérer; (: drink) frelater; (: text, document) arranger
doctoral ['dɔktərəl] ADJ (thesis, research) doctoral(e); (student, degree) de doctorat
doctorate ['dɔktərɪt] N doctorat m

Le **doctorate** est le diplôme universitaire le plus prestigieux. Décerné après soutenance d'une thèse devant un jury, il est l'aboutissement de trois années de recherche au minimum. Le doctorate le plus répandu est le PhD (Doctor of Philosophy), pour les lettres, les sciences et l'ingénierie, bien qu'il existe également d'autres doctorats spécialisés (en musique, en droit, etc) ; voir Bachelor's degree, Master's degree

Doctor of Philosophy N (degree) doctorat m; (person) titulaire mf d'un doctorat
doctrine ['dɔktrɪn] N (belief) doctrine f; (US: government policy) politique f; **the ~ that ...** la doctrine selon laquelle ...
docudrama ['dɔkjudrɑːmə] N docudrame m
document N ['dɔkjumənt] document m ▸ VT ['dɔkjumɛnt] documenter
documentary [dɔkju'mɛntərɪ] ADJ, N documentaire m
documentation [dɔkjumən'teɪʃən] N documentation f
docusoap ['dɔkjusəup] N feuilleton-documentaire m
DOD N ABBR (US) = **Department of Defense**
doddering ['dɔdərɪŋ] ADJ (senile) gâteux(-euse)
doddery ['dɔdərɪ] ADJ branlant(e)
doddle ['dɔdl] N: **it's a ~** (inf) c'est simple comme bonjour, c'est du gâteau
Dodecanese [dəudekə'niːz] N, **Dodecanese Islands** NPL Dodécanèse m
dodge [dɔdʒ] N truc m; combine f ▸ VT esquiver, éviter ▸ VI faire un saut de côté; (Sport) faire une esquive; **to ~ out of the way** s'esquiver; **to ~ through the traffic** se faufiler or faire de savantes manœuvres entre les voitures
Dodgems® ['dɔdʒəmz] NPL (BRIT) autos tamponneuses
dodgy ['dɔdʒɪ] ADJ (BRIT inf: uncertain) douteux(-euse); (: shady) louche
DOE N ABBR (BRIT) = **Department of the Environment**; (US) = **Department of Energy**
doe [dəu] N (deer) biche f; (rabbit) lapine f
does [dʌz] VB see **do**
★**doesn't** ['dʌznt] = **does not**
★**dog** [dɔg] N chien(ne); **to go to the dogs** (nation etc) aller à vau-l'eau ▸ VT (follow closely) suivre de près, ne pas lâcher d'une semelle; (fig: memory etc) poursuivre, harceler
dog biscuits NPL biscuits mpl pour chien
dog collar N collier m de chien; (fig) faux-col m d'ecclésiastique
dog-eared ['dɔgɪəd] ADJ corné(e)
dogfight ['dɔgfaɪt] N (between competitors) bagarre f; (between planes) combat m tournoyant
dog food N nourriture f pour les chiens or le chien
dogged ['dɔgɪd] ADJ obstiné(e), opiniâtre
doggy ['dɔgɪ] N (inf) toutou m
doggy bag N petit sac pour emporter les restes
doghouse ['dɔghaus] N (US) niche f, chenil m; **to be in the ~** (inf) ne pas être en odeur de sainteté
dogma ['dɔgmə] N dogme m
dogmatic [dɔg'mætɪk] ADJ dogmatique
do-gooder ['du:gudəʳ] N (pej) faiseur(-euse) de bonnes œuvres
dogsbody ['dɔgzbɔdɪ] N (BRIT) bonne f à tout faire, tâcheron m
doily ['dɔɪlɪ] N dessus m d'assiette
doing ['duɪŋ] N: **this is your ~** c'est votre travail, c'est vous qui avez fait ça
doings ['duɪŋz] NPL activités fpl
do-it-yourself ['duːɪtjɔː'sɛlf] N bricolage m

doldrums ['dɔldrəmz] NPL: **to be in the ~** avoir le cafard; être dans le marasme

dole [dəul] N (*BRIT: payment*) allocation f de chômage; **on the ~** au chômage
▸ **dole out** VT donner au compte-goutte

doleful ['dəulful] ADJ triste, lugubre

doll [dɔl] N poupée f
▸ **doll up** VT: **to ~ o.s. up** se faire beau (belle)

★**dollar** ['dɔlə'] N dollar m

dollop ['dɔləp] N (*of butter, cheese*) bon morceau; (*of cream*) bonne cuillerée

dolly ['dɔlɪ] N poupée f

dolphin ['dɔlfɪn] N dauphin m

domain [də'meɪn] N (*also fig*) domaine m

dome [dəum] N dôme m

★**domestic** [də'mestɪk] ADJ (*duty, happiness*) familial(e); (*policy, affairs, flight*) intérieur(e); (*news*) national(e); (*animal*) domestique

domesticated [də'mestɪkeɪtɪd] ADJ domestiqué(e); (*pej*) d'intérieur; **he's very ~** il participe volontiers aux tâches ménagères; question ménage, il est très organisé

domesticity [dəumes'tɪsɪtɪ] N vie f de famille

domestic servant N domestique mf

domicile ['dɔmɪsaɪl] N domicile m

dominance ['dɔmɪnəns] N domination f; **~ over sb** domination sur qn

dominant ['dɔmɪnənt] ADJ dominant(e)

dominate ['dɔmɪneɪt] VT dominer

domination [dɔmɪ'neɪʃən] N domination f

domineering [dɔmɪ'nɪərɪŋ] ADJ dominateur(-trice), autoritaire

Dominica [dɔmɪ'niːkə, də'mɪnɪkə] N Dominique f

Dominican Republic [də'mɪnɪkən-] N République dominicaine

dominion [də'mɪnɪən] N domination f; territoire m; dominion m

domino ['dɔmɪnəu] (*pl dominoes*) N domino m

dominoes ['dɔmɪnəuz] N (*game*) dominos mpl

don [dɔn] N (*BRIT*) professeur m d'université ▸ VT revêtir

donate [də'neɪt] VT faire don de, donner

donation [də'neɪʃən] N donation f, don m

★**done** [dʌn] PP *of* **do**

dongle ['dɔŋgl] N (*Comput*) dongle m

donkey ['dɔŋkɪ] N âne m

donkey-work ['dɔŋkɪwəːk] N (*BRIT inf*) le gros du travail, le plus dur (du travail)

donor ['dəunə'] N (*of blood etc*) donneur(-euse); (*to charity*) donateur(-trice)

donor card N carte f de don d'organes

★**don't** [dəunt] = **do not**

donut ['dəunʌt] N (*US*) = **doughnut**

doodle ['duːdl] N griffonnage m, gribouillage m ▸ VI griffonner, gribouiller

doom [duːm] N (*fate*) destin m; (*ruin*) ruine f ▸ VT: **to be doomed to failure** être voué(e) à l'échec

doomsday ['duːmzdeɪ] N le Jugement dernier

★**door** [dɔː'] N porte f; (*Rail, car*) portière f; **to go from ~ to ~** aller de porte en porte

doorbell ['dɔːbɛl] N sonnette f

door handle N poignée f de porte; (*of car*) poignée de portière

doorknob ['dɔːnɔb] N poignée f or bouton m de porte

doorman ['dɔːmən] N (*irreg*) (*in hotel*) portier m; (*in block of flats*) concierge m

doormat ['dɔːmæt] N paillasson m

doorpost ['dɔːpəust] N montant m de porte

doorstep ['dɔːstɛp] N pas m de (la) porte, seuil m

door-to-door ['dɔːtə'dɔː'] ADJ: **~ selling** vente f à domicile

doorway ['dɔːweɪ] N (embrasure f de) porte f

dope [dəup] N (*inf: drug*) drogue f; (: *person*) andouille f; (: *information*) tuyaux mpl, rancards mpl ▸ VT (*horse etc*) doper

dopey ['dəupɪ] ADJ (*inf*) à moitié endormi(e)

doping ['dəupɪŋ] (*Sport*) N dopage m ▸ CPD (*offence, allegation, test*) de dopage

dormant ['dɔːmənt] ADJ assoupi(e), en veilleuse; (*rule, law*) inappliqué(e)

dormer ['dɔːmə'] N (*also:* **dormer window**) lucarne f

dormice ['dɔːmaɪs] NPL *of* **dormouse**

dormitory ['dɔːmɪtrɪ] N (*BRIT*) dortoir m; (*US: hall of residence*) résidence f universitaire

dormouse ['dɔːmaus] (*pl dormice* [-maɪs]) N loir m

DOS [dɔs] N ABBR (= *disk operating system*) DOS m

dosage ['dəusɪdʒ] N dose f; dosage m; (*on label*) posologie f

dose [dəus] N dose f; (*BRIT: bout*) attaque f; **a ~ of flu** une belle *or* bonne grippe ▸ VT: **to ~ o.s.** se bourrer de médicaments

dosh [dɔʃ] N (*inf*) fric m

dosser ['dɔsə'] N (*BRIT pej*) clochard(e)

doss house ['dɔs-] N (*BRIT*) asile m de nuit

dossier ['dɔsɪeɪ] N dossier m

DOT N ABBR (*US*) = **Department of Transportation**

dot [dɔt] N point m; (*on material*) pois m; **on the ~** à l'heure tapante ▸ VT: **dotted with** parsemé(e) de

dotcom N point com m, pointcom m

dot command N (*Comput*) commande précédée d'un point

dote [dəut]: **to ~ on** VT *fus* être fou (folle) de

dot-matrix printer [dɔt'meɪtrɪks-] N imprimante matricielle

dotted line ['dɔtɪd-] N ligne pointillée; (*Aut*) ligne discontinue; **to sign on the ~** signer à l'endroit indiqué *or* sur la ligne pointillée; (*fig*) donner son consentement

dotty ['dɔtɪ] ADJ (*inf*) loufoque, farfelu(e)

★**double** ['dʌbl] ADJ double; **~ five two six (5526)** (*BRIT Tel*) cinquante-cinq – vingt-six; **it's spelt with a ~ "l"** ça s'écrit avec deux « l » ▸ ADV (*fold*) en deux; (*twice*): **to cost ~ (sth)** coûter le double (de qch) *or* deux fois plus (que qch) ▸ N double m; (*Cine*) doublure f; **on the ~, at the ~** au pas de course ▸ VT doubler; (*fold*) plier en deux ▸ VI doubler; (*have two uses*): **to ~ as** servir aussi de
▸ **double back** VI (*person*) revenir sur ses pas
▸ **double up** VI (*bend over*) se courber, se plier; (*share room*) partager la chambre

double bass N contrebasse f

double bed N grand lit

double-breasted [ˈdʌblˈbrɛstɪd] ADJ croisé(e)

double-check [ˈdʌblˈtʃɛk] VT, VI revérifier

double-click [ˈdʌblˈklɪk] VI (*Comput*) double-cliquer

double-clutch [ˈdʌblˈklʌtʃ] VI (*US*) faire un double débrayage

double cream N (*BRIT*) crème fraîche épaisse

double-cross [ˈdʌblˈkrɔs] VT doubler, trahir

double-decker [ˈdʌblˈdɛkəʳ] N autobus *m* à impériale

double declutch VI (*BRIT*) faire un double débrayage

double exposure N (*Phot*) surimpression *f*

double glazing N (*BRIT*) double vitrage *m*

double-page [ˈdʌblpeɪdʒ] ADJ: **~ spread** publicité *f* en double page

double parking N stationnement *m* en double file

double room N chambre *f* pour deux

doubles [ˈdʌblz] N (*Tennis*) double *m*

double whammy [-ˈwæmɪ] N (*inf*) double contretemps *m*

double yellow lines NPL (*BRIT Aut*) double bande *jaune marquant l'interdiction de stationner*

doubly [ˈdʌblɪ] ADV doublement, deux fois plus

★**doubt** [daut] N doute *m*; **no ~** sans doute; **without (a) ~** sans aucun doute; **beyond ~** *adv* indubitablement; *adj* indubitable ▸ VT douter de; **I ~ it very much** j'en doute fort; **to ~ that** douter que + *sub*

doubtful [ˈdautful] ADJ douteux(-euse); (*person*) incertain(e); **to be ~ about sth** avoir des doutes sur qch, ne pas être convaincu de qch; **I'm a bit ~** je n'en suis pas certain *or* sûr

doubtless [ˈdautlɪs] ADV sans doute, sûrement

dough [dəu] N pâte *f*; (*inf: money*) fric *m*, pognon *m*

doughnut, (*US*) **donut** [ˈdəunʌt] N beignet *m*

dour [duəʳ] ADJ austère

douse [dauz] VT (*with water*) tremper, inonder; (*flames*) éteindre

dove [dʌv] N colombe *f*

dovecote, dovecot [ˈdʌvkɔt] N pigeonnier *m*

Dover [ˈdəuvəʳ] N Douvres

dovetail [ˈdʌvteɪl] N: **~ joint** assemblage *m* à queue d'aronde ▸ VI (*fig*) concorder

dowager [ˈdauədʒəʳ] N douairière *f*

dowdy [ˈdaudɪ] ADJ démodé(e), mal fagoté(e)

Dow-Jones average [ˈdauˈdʒəunz-] N (*US*) indice *m* Dow-Jones

★**down** [daun] N (*fluff*) duvet *m*; (*hill*) colline (dénudée) ▸ ADV en bas, vers le bas; (*on the ground*) par terre; **to fall ~** tomber; **she's going ~ to Bristol** elle descend à Bristol; **to write sth ~** écrire qch; **~ there** là-bas (en bas), là au fond; **~ here** ici en bas; **the price of meat is ~** le prix de la viande a baissé; **I've got it ~ in my diary** c'est inscrit dans mon agenda; **to pay £2 ~** verser 2 livres d'arrhes *or* en acompte; **England is two goals ~** l'Angleterre a deux buts de retard; **~ with X!** à bas X! ▸ PREP en bas de; (*along*) le long de; **to walk ~ a hill** descendre une colline; **to run ~ the street**

descendre la rue en courant ▸ VT (*enemy*) abattre; (*inf: drink*) siffler; **to ~ tools** (*BRIT*) cesser le travail

down-and-out [ˈdaunəndaut] N (*tramp*) clochard(e)

down-at-heel [ˈdaunətˈhiːl] ADJ (*fig*) miteux(-euse)

downbeat [ˈdaunbiːt] N (*Mus*) temps frappé ▸ ADJ sombre, négatif(-ive)

downcast [ˈdaunkɑːst] ADJ démoralisé(e)

downer [ˈdaunəʳ] N (*inf: drug*) tranquillisant *m*; **to be on a ~** (*depressed*) flipper

downfall [ˈdaunfɔːl] N chute *f*; ruine *f*

downgrade [ˈdaungreɪd] VT déclasser

downhearted [ˈdaunˈhɑːtɪd] ADJ découragé(e)

downhill [ˈdaunˈhɪl] ADV (*face, look*) en aval, vers l'aval; (*roll, go*) vers le bas, en bas; **to go ~** descendre; (*business*) péricliter, aller à vau-l'eau ▸ N (*Ski: also:* **downhill race**) descente *f*

Downing Street [ˈdaunɪŋ-] N (*BRIT*): **10 ~** *résidence du Premier ministre*

> **Downing Street** est une rue de Westminster (à Londres) où se trouvent la résidence officielle du Premier ministre (au numéro 10) et celle du ministre des Finances (au numéro 11). L'expression *Downing Street* est souvent utilisée pour désigner le gouvernement britannique.

★**download** [ˈdaunləud] (*Comput*) N téléchargement *m* ▸ VT télécharger

downloadable [daunˈləudəbl] ADJ (*Comput*) téléchargeable

down-market [ˈdaunˈmɑːkɪt] ADJ (*product*) bas de gamme *inv*

down payment N acompte *m*

downplay [ˈdaunpleɪ] VT (*US*) minimiser (l'importance de)

downpour [ˈdaunpɔːʳ] N pluie torrentielle, déluge *m*

downright [ˈdaunraɪt] ADJ (*lie etc*) effronté(e); (*refusal*) catégorique

Downs [daunz] NPL (*BRIT*): **the ~** *collines crayeuses du sud-est de l'Angleterre*

downscale [ˈdaunskeɪl] VT (*production*) réduire; (*plans*) revoir à la baisse ▸ VI (*company, sector*) réduire son activité

downside [ˈdaunsaɪd] N inconvénient *m*; **the ~ of sth** l'inconvénient de qch

downsize [ˈdaunsaɪz] VT (*company, industry*) dégraisser

downsizing [ˈdaunsaɪzɪŋ] N (*of company, industry*) dégraissage *m*

Down's syndrome [daunz-] N mongolisme *m*, trisomie *f*; **a ~ baby** un bébé mongolien *or* trisomique

★**downstairs** [ˈdaunˈstɛəz] ADV (*on or to ground floor*) au rez-de-chaussée; (*on or to floor below*) à l'étage inférieur; **to come ~, to go ~** descendre (l'escalier)

downstream [ˈdaunˈstriːm] ADV en aval

downtime [ˈdauntaɪm] N (*of machine etc*) temps mort; (*of person*) temps d'arrêt

down-to-earth [ˈdauntuˈəːθ] ADJ terre à terre *inv*

downtown ['daun'taun] ADV en ville ▶ ADJ (US): ~ **Chicago** le centre commerçant de Chicago

downtrodden ['dauntrɔdn] ADJ opprimé(e)

downturn ['dauntəːn] N (slump) récession f

down under ADV en Australie or Nouvelle-Zélande

downward ['daunwəd] ADJ, ADV vers le bas; **a ~ trend** une tendance à la baisse, une diminution progressive

downwards ['daunwədz] ADV vers le bas

dowry ['dauri] N dot f

doyen ['dɔiən] N doyen m

doyenne [dɔi'ɛn] N doyenne f

doz. ABBR = **dozen**

doze [dəuz] VI sommeiller
  ▶ **doze off** VI s'assoupir

★**dozen** ['dʌzn] N douzaine f; **a ~ books** une douzaine de livres; **8op a ~** 8op la douzaine; **dozens of** des centaines de

DPh, DPhil N ABBR (= Doctor of Philosophy) titre universitaire

DPP N ABBR (BRIT) = **Director of Public Prosecutions**

DPT N ABBR (Med: = diphtheria, pertussis, tetanus) DCT m

DPW N ABBR (US) = **Department of Public Works**

dr ABBR (Comm) = **debtor**

Dr. ABBR (= doctor) Dr; (in street names) = **drive**

drab [dræb] ADJ terne, morne

draconian [drə'kəuniən] ADJ draconien(ne)

★**draft** [drɑːft] N (of letter, school work) brouillon m; (of literary work) ébauche f; (of contract, document) version f préliminaire; (Comm) traite f; (US Mil) contingent m; (: call-up) conscription f ▶ VT faire le brouillon de; (document, report) rédiger une version préliminaire de; (Mil: send) détacher; see also **draught**
  ▶ **draft in** VT (worker, player) affecter

draftsman etc ['drɑːftsmən] (US) N (irreg) = **draughtsman** etc

drafty etc ['drɑːftɪ] (US) N = **draughty** etc

drag [dræg] VT traîner; (river) draguer; **to ~ and drop** (Comput) glisser-déposer ▶ VI traîner ▶ N (Aviat, Naut) résistance f; (inf) casse-pieds mf; (: women's clothing): **in ~** (en) travesti
  ▶ **drag away** VT: **to ~ away (from)** arracher or emmener de force (de)
  ▶ **drag on** VI s'éterniser
  ▶ **drag out** VT (process) faire traîner; **to ~ sth out of sb** soutirer qch à qn

dragnet ['drægnɛt] N drège f; (fig) piège m, filets mpl

dragon ['drægn] N dragon m

dragonfly ['drægnflaɪ] N libellule f

dragoon [drə'guːn] N (cavalryman) dragon m ▶ VT: **to ~ sb into doing sth** (BRIT) forcer qn à faire qch

★**drain** [dreɪn] N égout m; (on resources) saignée f ▶ VT (land, marshes, vegetables) drainer, assécher; (vegetables) égoutter; (reservoir etc) vider; **to feel drained** (of energy, emotion) être épuisé(e) ▶ VI (water) s'écouler

drainage ['dreɪnɪdʒ] N (system) système m d'égouts; (act) drainage m

draining ['dreɪnɪŋ] ADJ épuisant(e); **emotionally ~** épuisant(e) moralement

draining board ['dreɪnɪŋ-], (US) **drainboard** ['dreɪnbɔːd] N égouttoir m

drainpipe ['dreɪnpaɪp] N tuyau m d'écoulement

drake [dreɪk] N canard m (mâle)

dram [dræm] N petit verre

★**drama** ['drɑːmə] N (art) théâtre m, art m dramatique; (play) pièce f; (event) drame m

★**dramatic** [drə'mætɪk] ADJ (Theat) dramatique; (impressive) spectaculaire

dramatically [drə'mætɪklɪ] ADV de façon spectaculaire

dramatist ['dræmətɪst] N auteur m dramatique

dramatization [dræmətaɪ'zeɪʃən] N (of book, story) adaptation f pour la scène/télévision/radio

dramatize ['dræmətaɪz] VT (events etc) dramatiser; (adapt) adapter pour la télévision (or pour l'écran)

drank [dræŋk] PT of **drink**

drape [dreɪp] VT draper ■ **drapes** NPL (US) rideaux mpl

draper ['dreɪpəʳ] N (BRIT) marchand(e) de nouveautés

drastic ['dræstɪk] ADJ (measures) d'urgence, énergique; (change) radical(e)

drastically ['dræstɪklɪ] ADV radicalement

draught, (US) **draft** [drɑːft] N courant m d'air; (of chimney) tirage m; (Naut) tirant m d'eau; **on ~** (beer) à la pression

draught beer N bière f (à la) pression

draughtboard ['drɑːftbɔːd] N (BRIT) damier m

draughts [drɑːfts] N (BRIT: game) (jeu m de) dames fpl

draughtsman, (US) **draftsman** ['drɑːftsmən] N (irreg) dessinateur(-trice) (industriel(le))

draughtsmanship, (US) **draftsmanship** ['drɑːftsmənʃɪp] N (technique) dessin industriel; (art) graphisme m

★**draughty**, (US) **drafty** ['drɑːftɪ] ADJ plein(e) de courants d'air

★**draw** [drɔː] (pt drew [druː], pp drawn [drɔːn]) VT tirer; (picture) dessiner; (attract) attirer; (line, circle) tracer; (money) retirer; (wages) toucher; (comparison, distinction): **to ~ (between)** faire (entre) ▶ VI (Sport) faire match nul; (move, come): **to ~ to a close** toucher à or tirer à sa fin; **to ~ near** s'approcher; approcher ▶ N match nul; (lottery) loterie f; (picking of ticket) tirage m au sort
  ▶ **draw back** VI (move back): **to ~ back (from)** reculer (de)
  ▶ **draw in** VI (BRIT: car) s'arrêter le long du trottoir; (train) entrer en gare or dans la station
  ▶ **draw on** VT (resources) faire appel à; (imagination, person) avoir recours à, faire appel à
  ▶ **draw out** VI (lengthen) s'allonger ▶ VT (money) retirer
  ▶ **draw up** VI (stop) s'arrêter ▶ VT (document) établir, dresser; (plan) formuler, dessiner; (chair) approcher

drawback ['drɔːbæk] N inconvénient m, désavantage m

drawbridge ['drɔːbrɪdʒ] N pont-levis m

drawee [drɔː'iː] N tiré m

drawer N [drɔːʳ] tiroir m; (of cheque) ['drɔːəʳ] tireur m

★**drawing** ['drɔːɪŋ] N dessin m

drawing board N planche f à dessin

drawing pin N (BRIT) punaise f

drawing room N salon m

drawl [drɔːl] N accent traînant

drawn [drɔ:n] PP *of* **draw** ▶ ADJ (*haggard*) tiré(e), crispé(e)

drawstring ['drɔ:strɪŋ] N cordon *m*

DRC N ABBR (= *Democratic Republic of the Congo*) RDC *f*

dread [drɛd] N épouvante *f*, effroi *m* ▶ VT redouter, appréhender

dreadful ['drɛdful] ADJ épouvantable, affreux(-euse)

dreadfully ['drɛdfulɪ] ADV (*very badly: behave, treat*) très mal; (*very: ill, worried*) affreusement; (*very much: miss*) terriblement

dreadlocks ['drɛdlɔks] NPL dreadlocks *fpl*

★**dream** [dri:m] (*pt, pp* **dreamed** [dri:md] *or* **dreamt** [drɛmt]) N rêve *m*; **to have a ~ about sb/sth** rêver à qn/qch; **sweet dreams!** faites de beaux rêves !
▶ VT, VI rêver
▶ **dream up** VT inventer

dreamer ['dri:mə'] N rêveur(-euse)

dreamt [drɛmt] PT, PP *of* **dream**

dreamy ['dri:mɪ] ADJ (*absent-minded*) rêveur(-euse)

dreary ['drɪərɪ] ADJ triste; monotone

dredge [drɛdʒ] VT draguer
▶ **dredge up** VT draguer; (*fig: unpleasant facts*) (faire) ressortir

dredger ['drɛdʒə'] N (*ship*) dragueur *m*; (*machine*) drague *f*; (BRIT: *also*: **sugar dredger**) saupoudreuse *f*

dregs [drɛgz] NPL lie *f*

drench [drɛntʃ] VT tremper; **drenched to the skin** trempé(e) jusqu'aux os

★**dress** [drɛs] N robe *f*; (*clothing*) habillement *m*, tenue *f* ▶ VT habiller; (*wound*) panser; (*food*) préparer; **to ~ o.s.**, **to get dressed** s'habiller; **to ~ a shop window** faire l'étalage *or* la vitrine ▶ VI: **she dresses very well** elle s'habille très bien
▶ **dress up** VI s'habiller; (*in fancy dress*) se déguiser

dressage ['drɛsɑ:ʒ] N dressage *m*

dress circle N (BRIT) premier balcon

dress designer N modéliste *mf*, dessinateur(-trice) de mode

dresser ['drɛsə'] N (*Theat*) habilleur(-euse); (*also*: **window dresser**) étalagiste *mf*; (*furniture*) vaisselier *m*; (: US) coiffeuse *f*, commode *f*

dressing ['drɛsɪŋ] N (*Med*) pansement *m*; (*Culin*) sauce *f*, assaisonnement *m*

dressing gown N (BRIT) robe *f* de chambre

dressing room N (*Theat*) loge *f*; (*Sport*) vestiaire *m*

dressing table N coiffeuse *f*

dressmaker ['drɛsmeɪkə'] N couturière *f*

dressmaking ['drɛsmeɪkɪŋ] N couture *f*; travaux *mpl* de couture

dress rehearsal N (répétition *f*) générale *f*

dress shirt N chemise *f* à plastron

dressy ['drɛsɪ] ADJ (*inf: clothes*) (qui fait) habillé(e)

drew [dru:] PT *of* **draw**

dribble ['drɪbl] VI tomber goutte à goutte; (*baby*) baver ▶ VT (*ball*) dribbler

dried [draɪd] ADJ (*fruit, beans*) sec (sèche); (*eggs, milk*) en poudre

drier ['draɪə'] N = **dryer**

drift [drɪft] N (*of current etc*) force *f*; direction *f*; (*of sand etc*) amoncellement *m*; (*of snow*) rafale *f*; coulée *f*; (*on ground*) congère *f*; (*general meaning*) sens général; **I get** *or* **catch your ~** je vois en gros ce que vous voulez dire ▶ VI (*boat*) aller à la dérive, dériver; (*sand, snow*) s'amonceler, s'entasser; **to let things ~** laisser les choses aller à la dérive; **to ~ apart** (*friends, lovers*) s'éloigner l'un de l'autre

drifter ['drɪftə'] N personne *f* sans but dans la vie

driftwood ['drɪftwud] N bois flotté

drill [drɪl] N perceuse *f*; (*bit*) foret *m*; (*of dentist*) roulette *f*, fraise *f*; (*Mil*) exercice *m* ▶ VT percer; (*troops*) entraîner; (*pupils: in grammar*) faire faire des exercices à ▶ VI (*for oil*) faire un *or* des forage(s)

drilling ['drɪlɪŋ] N (*for oil*) forage *m*

drilling rig N (*on land*) tour *f* (de forage), derrick *m*; (*at sea*) plate-forme *f* de forage

drily ['draɪlɪ] ADV = **dryly**

★**drink** [drɪŋk] (*pt* **drank** [dræŋk], *pp* **drunk** [drʌŋk]) N boisson *f*; (*alcoholic*) verre *m*; **to have a ~** boire quelque chose; boire un verre; **a ~ of water** un verre d'eau; **would you like a ~?** tu veux boire quelque chose ?; **we had drinks before lunch** on a pris l'apéritif ▶ VT, VI boire
▶ **drink in** VT (*fresh air*) inspirer profondément; (*story*) avaler, ne pas perdre une miette de; (*sight*) se remplir la vue de
▶ **drink to** VT FUS (*success, sb's memory*) boire à
▶ **drink up** VI finir *or* vider son verre ▶ VT finir

drinkable ['drɪŋkəbl] ADJ (*not dangerous*) potable; (*palatable*) buvable

drink-driving ['drɪŋk'draɪvɪŋ] N conduite *f* en état d'ivresse

drinker ['drɪŋkə'] N buveur(-euse)

drinking ['drɪŋkɪŋ] N (*drunkenness*) boisson *f*, alcoolisme *m*

drinking fountain N (*in park etc*) fontaine publique; (*in building*) jet *m* d'eau potable

drinking water N eau *f* potable

drink problem N: **to have a ~** trop boire

drip [drɪp] N (*drop*) goutte *f*; (*sound: of water etc*) bruit *m* de l'eau qui tombe goutte à goutte; (*Med: device*) goutte-à-goutte *m inv*; (: *liquid*) perfusion *f*; (*inf: person*) lavette *f*, nouille *f* ▶ VI tomber goutte à goutte; (*tap*) goutter; (*washing*) s'égoutter; (*wall*) suinter

drip-dry ['drɪp'draɪ] ADJ (*shirt*) sans repassage

drip-feed ['drɪpfi:d] VT alimenter au goutte-à-goutte *or* par perfusion

dripping ['drɪpɪŋ] N graisse *f* de rôti ▶ ADJ: **~ wet** trempé(e)

★**drive** [draɪv] (*pt* **drove** [drəuv], *pp* **driven** ['drɪvn]) N promenade *f* *or* trajet *m* en voiture; (*also*: **driveway**) allée *f*; (*energy*) dynamisme *m*, énergie *f*; (*Psych*) besoin *m*, pulsion *f*; (*push*) effort (concerté), campagne *f*; (*Sport*) drive *m*; (*Tech*) entraînement *m*; traction *f*; transmission *f*; (*Comput: also:* **disk drive**) lecteur *m* de disques; **to go for a ~** aller faire une promenade en voiture; **it's 3 hours' ~ from London** Londres est à 3 heures de route; **left-/right-hand ~** (*Aut*) conduite *f* à gauche/droite; **front-/rear-wheel ~** (*Aut*) traction *f* avant/arrière ▶ VT conduire; (*nail*) enfoncer; (*push*) chasser, pousser; (*Tech: motor*) actionner; entraîner; **to ~ sb to (do) sth** pousser *or* conduire qn à (faire) qch; **to ~ sb mad** rendre qn fou (folle) ▶ VI (*be at the wheel*) conduire; (*travel by car*) aller en voiture

▶ **drive at** VT FUS (fig: intend, mean) vouloir dire, en venir à

▶ **drive away** VT (customers, friends) faire fuir

▶ **drive on** VI poursuivre sa route, continuer; (after stopping) reprendre sa route, repartir ▶ VT (incite, encourage) inciter

▶ **drive out** VT (force out) chasser

drive-by ['draɪvbaɪ] N (also: **drive-by shooting**) tentative d'assassinat par coups de feu tirés d'une voiture

drive-in ['draɪvɪn] ADJ, N (esp US) drive-in m

drive-in window N (US) guichet-auto m

drivel ['drɪvl] N (inf) idioties fpl, imbécillités fpl

driven ['drɪvn] PP of **drive**

★**driver** ['draɪvə^r] N conducteur(-trice); (of taxi, bus) chauffeur m

driver's license N (US) permis m de conduire

driveway ['draɪvweɪ] N allée f

driving ['draɪvɪŋ] ADJ: ~ **rain** pluie battante ▶ N conduite f

driving force N locomotive f, élément m dynamique

driving instructor N moniteur(-trice) d'autoécole

driving lesson N leçon f de conduite

driving licence N (BRIT) permis m de conduire

driving school N auto-école f

driving test N examen m du permis de conduire

drizzle ['drɪzl] N bruine f, crachin m ▶ VI bruiner

drizzly ['drɪzlɪ] ADJ (weather, day) de crachin

droll [drəʊl] ADJ drôle

dromedary ['drɒmədərɪ] N dromadaire m

drone [drəʊn] VI (bee) bourdonner; (engine etc) ronronner; (also: **drone on**) parler d'une voix monocorde ▶ N bourdonnement m; ronronnement m; (male bee) faux-bourdon m

drool [druːl] VI baver; **to ~ over sb/sth** (fig) baver d'admiration or être en extase devant qn/qch

droop [druːp] VI (flower) commencer à se faner; (shoulders, head) tomber

★**drop** [drɒp] N (of liquid) goutte f; (fall) baisse f; (: in salary) réduction f; (also: **parachute drop**) saut m; (of cliff) dénivellation f; à-pic m; **a ~ of 10%** une baisse (or réduction) de 10% ▶ VT laisser tomber; (voice, eyes, price) baisser; (passenger) déposer; **to ~ anchor** jeter l'ancre; **to ~ sb a line** mettre un mot à qn ▶ VI (wind, temperature, price, voice) tomber; (numbers, attendance) diminuer ■ **drops** NPL (Med) gouttes fpl; **cough drops** pastilles fpl pour la toux

▶ **drop by** VI (call in) passer

▶ **drop in** VI (inf: visit): **to ~ in (on)** faire un saut (chez), passer (chez)

▶ **drop off** VI (sleep) s'assoupir ▶ VT (passenger) déposer; **to ~ sb off** déposer qn

▶ **drop out** VI (withdraw) se retirer; (student etc) abandonner, décrocher

drop-down menu ['drɒpdaʊn-] N menu m déroulant

droplet ['drɒplɪt] N gouttelette f

dropout ['drɒpaʊt] N (from society) marginal(e); (from university) (étudiant(e)) décrocheur(-euse)

dropper ['drɒpə^r] N (Med etc) compte-gouttes m inv

droppings ['drɒpɪŋz] NPL crottes fpl

dross [drɒs] N déchets mpl; rebut m

drought [draʊt] N sécheresse f

drove [drəʊv] PT of **drive** ▶ N: **droves of people** une foule de gens

drown [draʊn] VT noyer; (also: **drown out**: sound) couvrir, étouffer ▶ VI se noyer

drowse [draʊz] VI somnoler

drowsiness ['draʊzɪnɪs] N somnolence f

drowsy ['draʊzɪ] ADJ somnolent(e)

drudge [drʌdʒ] N bête f de somme (fig)

drudgery ['drʌdʒərɪ] N corvée f

★**drug** [drʌg] N médicament m; (narcotic) drogue f; **to be on drugs** se droguer; **he's on drugs** il se drogue; (Med) il est sous médication ▶ VT droguer

drug addict N toxicomane mf

drug dealer N revendeur(-euse) de drogue

drug-driving ['drʌg'draɪvɪŋ] N conduite f sous l'emprise de stupéfiants

druggist ['drʌgɪst] N (US) pharmacien(ne)-droguiste

drug peddler N revendeur(-euse) de drogue

drugs test, drug test N contrôle m antidopage

drugstore ['drʌgstɔː^r] N (US) pharmacie-droguerie f, drugstore m

Druid ['druːɪd] N druide mf

★**drum** [drʌm] N tambour m; (for oil, petrol) bidon m ▶ VT: **to ~ one's fingers on the table** pianoter or tambouriner sur la table ■ **drums** NPL (Mus) batterie f

▶ **drum up** VT (enthusiasm, support) susciter, rallier

drummer ['drʌmə^r] N (joueur m de) tambour m; (in rock band, in jazz band) batteur m

drum roll N roulement m de tambour

drumstick ['drʌmstɪk] N (Mus) baguette f de tambour; (of chicken) pilon m

drunk [drʌŋk] PP of **drink** ▶ ADJ ivre, soûl(e); **to get ~** s'enivrer, se soûler ▶ N (also: **drunkard**) ivrogne mf

drunkard ['drʌŋkəd] N ivrogne mf

drunken ['drʌŋkən] ADJ ivre, soûl(e); (rage, stupor) ivrogne, d'ivrogne; **~ driving** conduite f en état d'ivresse

drunkenness ['drʌŋkənnɪs] N ivresse f; ivrognerie f

★**dry** [draɪ] ADJ sec (sèche); (day) sans pluie; (humour) pince-sans-rire; (uninteresting) aride, rébarbatif(-ive); **on ~ land** sur la terre ferme ▶ VT sécher; (clothes) faire sécher; **to ~ one's hands/hair/eyes** se sécher les mains/les cheveux/les yeux ▶ VI sécher

▶ **dry off** VI, VT sécher

▶ **dry up** VI (river, supplies) se tarir; (speaker) sécher, rester sec

dry-clean ['draɪ'kliːn] VT nettoyer à sec

dry-cleaner ['draɪ'kliːnə^r] N teinturier m

dry-cleaner's ['draɪ'kliːnəz] N teinturerie f

dry-cleaning ['draɪ'kliːnɪŋ] N (process) nettoyage m à sec

dry dock N (Naut) cale sèche, bassin m de radoub

dryer ['draɪə^r] N (tumble-dryer) sèche-linge m inv; (for hair) sèche-cheveux m inv

dry goods NPL (Comm) textiles mpl, mercerie f

dry goods store N (US) magasin m de nouveautés

dry ice N neige f carbonique

dryly ['draɪlɪ] ADV sèchement, d'un ton sec

dryness ['draɪnɪs] N sécheresse f

dry rot N pourriture sèche (du bois)

dry run N (fig) essai m

dry ski slope N piste (de ski) artificielle

DSc N ABBR (= Doctor of Science) titre universitaire

DST ABBR (US: = Daylight Saving Time) heure d'été

DT N ABBR (Comput) = **data transmission**

DTP N ABBR (= desktop publishing) PAO f

DT's [diː'tiːz] N ABBR (inf: = delirium tremens) delirium tremens m

dual ['djuəl] ADJ double

dual carriageway N (BRIT) quatre voie f, voie express

dual-control ['djuəlkən'trəul] ADJ à doubles commandes

dual nationality N double nationalité f

dual-purpose ['djuəl'pəːpəs] ADJ à double emploi

dubbed [dʌbd] ADJ (Cine) doublé(e); (nicknamed) surnommé(e)

dubious ['djuːbɪəs] ADJ hésitant(e), incertain(e); (reputation, company) douteux(-euse); **I'm very ~ about it** j'ai des doutes sur la question, je n'en suis pas sûr du tout

Dublin ['dʌblɪn] N Dublin

Dubliner ['dʌblɪnəʳ] N habitant(e) de Dublin, originaire mf de Dublin

duchess ['dʌtʃɪs] N duchesse f

duchy ['dʌtʃɪ] N duché m

★**duck** [dʌk] N canard m ▸ VI se baisser vivement, baisser subitement la tête ▸ VT plonger dans l'eau

duckling ['dʌklɪŋ] N caneton m

duct [dʌkt] N conduite f, canalisation f; (Anat) conduit m

dud [dʌd] N (shell) obus non éclaté; (object, tool): **it's a ~** c'est de la camelote, ça ne marche pas ▸ ADJ (BRIT: cheque) sans provision; (: note, coin) faux (fausse)

dude [duːd] N (US inf) mec m (inf)

★**due** [djuː] ADJ (money, payment) dû (~); (expected) attendu(e); (fitting) qui convient; **~ to** (because of) en raison de; (caused by) dû à; **in ~ course** en temps utile or voulu; (in the end) finalement; **the rent is ~ on the 30th** il faut payer le loyer le 30; **the train is ~ at 8 a.m.** le train est attendu à 8 h; **she is ~ back tomorrow** elle doit rentrer demain; **he is ~ £10** on lui doit 10 livres; **I am ~ 6 days' leave** j'ai droit à 6 jours de congé ▸ N dû m; **to give sb his** or **her ~** être juste envers qn ▸ ADV: **~ north** droit vers le nord ■ **dues** NPL (for club, union) cotisation f; (in harbour) droits mpl (de port)

due date N date f d'échéance

duel ['djuəl] N duel m

duet [djuː'ɛt] N duo m

duff [dʌf] ADJ (BRIT inf) nullard(e), nul(le)

duffel bag, duffle bag ['dʌfl-] N sac marin

duffel coat, duffle coat ['dʌfl-] N duffel-coat m

duffer ['dʌfəʳ] N (inf) nullard(e)

dug [dʌg] PT, PP of **dig**

dugout ['dʌgaut] N (Sport) banc m de touche

DUI N ABBR (US: = driving under (the) influence (of alcohol)) CEI (= conduite en état d'ivresse)

duke [djuːk] N duc m

dukedom ['djuːkdəm] N (title) titre m de duc; (land) duché m

dull [dʌl] ADJ (boring) ennuyeux(-euse); (slow) borné(e); (not bright) morne, terne; (sound, pain) sourd(e); (weather, day) gris(e), maussade; (blade) émoussé(e) ▸ VT (pain, grief) atténuer; (mind, senses) engourdir

duly ['djuːlɪ] ADV (on time) en temps voulu; (as expected) comme il se doit

dumb [dʌm] ADJ (inf: stupid) bête; **to be struck ~** (fig) rester abasourdi(e), être sidéré(e) ▸ **dumb down** VT niveler par le bas

dumbbell ['dʌmbɛl] N (Sport) haltère m

dumbfounded [dʌm'faundɪd] ADJ sidéré(e)

dumbstruck ['dʌmstrʌk] ADJ sans voix; **to be ~** rester sans voix

dummy ['dʌmɪ] N (tailor's model) mannequin m; (mock-up) factice m, maquette f; (Sport) feinte f; (BRIT: for baby) tétine f ▸ ADJ faux (fausse), factice

dummy run N essai m

★**dump** [dʌmp] N tas m d'ordures; (also: **rubbish dump**) décharge (publique); (Mil) dépôt m; (Comput) listage m (de la mémoire); (inf: place) trou m; **to be (down) in the dumps** (inf) avoir le cafard, broyer du noir ▸ VT (put down) déposer; déverser; (get rid of) se débarrasser de; (Comput) lister; (Comm: goods) vendre à perte (sur le marché extérieur)

dumping ['dʌmpɪŋ] N (Econ) dumping m; (of rubbish): **"no ~"** « décharge interdite »

dumpling ['dʌmplɪŋ] N boulette f (de pâte)

Dumpster® ['dʌmpstəʳ] N (US) benne f (à ordures)

dumpy ['dʌmpɪ] ADJ courtaud(e), boulot(te)

dunce [dʌns] N âne m, cancre m

dune [djuːn] N dune f

dung [dʌŋ] N fumier m

dungarees [dʌŋgə'riːz] NPL bleu(s) m(pl); (for child, woman) salopette f

dungeon ['dʌndʒən] N cachot m

dunk [dʌŋk] VT tremper

Dunkirk [dʌn'kəːk] N Dunkerque

duo ['djuːəu] N (gen, Mus) duo m

duodenal [djuːəu'diːnl] ADJ duodénal(e); **~ ulcer** ulcère m du duodénum

dupe [djuːp] N dupe f ▸ VT duper, tromper

duplex ['djuːplɛks] N (US: also: **duplex apartment**) duplex m

duplicate N ['djuːplɪkət] double m, copie exacte; (copy of letter etc) duplicata m; **in ~** en deux exemplaires, en double ▸ ADJ (copy) en double; **~ key** double m de la (or d'une) clé ▸ VT ['djuːplɪkeɪt] faire un double de; (on machine) polycopier

duplicating machine ['djuːplɪkeɪtɪŋ-], **duplicator** ['djuːplɪkeɪtəʳ] N duplicateur m

duplication [djuːplɪ'keɪʃən] N (of effort) répétition f

duplicity [djuː'plɪsɪtɪ] N duplicité f, fausseté f

durability [djuərə'bɪlɪtɪ] N solidité f; durabilité f

durable ['djuərəbl] ADJ durable; (clothes, metal) résistant(e), solide

duration [djuə'reɪʃən] N durée f

duress [djuə'rɛs] N: **under ~** sous la contrainte

Durex® ['djuərɛks] N (BRIT) préservatif (masculin)

★**during** ['djuərɪŋ] PREP pendant, au cours de

dusk [dʌsk] N crépuscule *m*

dusky ['dʌskɪ] ADJ sombre

★**dust** [dʌst] N poussière *f* ▶ VT (*furniture*) essuyer, épousseter; (*cake etc*): **to ~ with** saupoudrer de ▶ **dust off** VT (*also fig*) dépoussiérer

★**dustbin** ['dʌstbɪn] N (BRIT) poubelle *f*

duster ['dʌstər] N chiffon *m*

dusting ['dʌstɪŋ] N: **to do the ~** faire les poussières; **I hate ~!** je déteste faire les poussières !

dust jacket N jacquette *f*

dustman ['dʌstmən] N (*irreg*) (BRIT) boueux *m*, éboueur *m*

dustpan ['dʌstpæn] N pelle *f* à poussière

dusty ['dʌstɪ] ADJ poussiéreux(-euse)

★**Dutch** [dʌtʃ] ADJ hollandais(e), néerlandais(e) ▶ N (*Ling*) hollandais *m*, néerlandais *m* ▶ ADV: **to go ~** *or* **dutch** (*inf*) partager les frais ■ **the Dutch** NPL les Hollandais, les Néerlandais

Dutch auction N enchères *fpl* à la baisse

Dutchman ['dʌtʃmən] N (*irreg*) Hollandais *m*

Dutchwoman ['dʌtʃwumən] N (*irreg*) Hollandaise *f*

dutiable ['dju:tɪəbl] ADJ taxable, soumis(e) à des droits de douane

dutiful ['dju:tɪful] ADJ (*child*) respectueux(-euse); (*husband, wife*) plein(e) d'égards, prévenant(e); (*employee*) consciencieux(-euse)

★**duty** ['dju:tɪ] N devoir *m*; (*tax*) droit *m*, taxe *f*; **to make it one's ~ to do sth** se faire un devoir de faire qch; **to pay ~ on sth** payer un droit *or* une taxe sur qch; **on ~** de service; (*at night etc*) de garde; **off ~** libre, pas de service *or* de garde ■ **duties** NPL fonctions *fpl*

duty-free ['dju:tɪ'fri:] ADJ exempté(e) de douane, hors-taxe; **~ shop** boutique *f* hors-taxe

duty officer N (*Mil etc*) officier *m* de permanence

★**duvet** ['du:veɪ] N (BRIT) couette *f*

DV ABBR (= *Deo volente*) si Dieu le veut

★**DVD** N ABBR (= *digital versatile or video disc*) DVD *m*

DVD burner N graveur *m* de DVD

★**DVD player** N lecteur *m* de DVD

DVD writer N graveur *m* de DVD

DVLA N ABBR (BRIT: = *Driver and Vehicle Licensing Agency*) service qui délivre les cartes grises et les permis de conduire

DVM N ABBR (US: = *Doctor of Veterinary Medicine*) titre universitaire

DVT N ABBR = **deep vein thrombosis**

dwarf [dwɔ:f] (*pl* **dwarves** [dwɔ:vz]) N (!) nain(e) ▶ VT écraser

dwell [dwɛl] (*pt, pp* **dwelt** [dwɛlt]) VI demeurer ▶ **dwell on** VT FUS s'étendre sur

dweller ['dwɛlər] N habitant(e)

dwelling ['dwɛlɪŋ] N habitation *f*, demeure *f*

dwelt [dwɛlt] PT, PP *of* **dwell**

dwindle ['dwɪndl] VI diminuer, décroître

dwindling ['dwɪndlɪŋ] ADJ décroissant(e), en diminution

DWP N ABBR (BRIT) = **Department of Work and Pensions**

dye [daɪ] N teinture *f*; **hair ~** teinture pour les cheveux ▶ VT teindre

dyestuffs ['daɪstʌfs] NPL colorants *mpl*

dying ['daɪɪŋ] ADJ mourant(e), agonisant(e)

dyke [daɪk] N (*embankment*) digue *f*

dynamic [daɪ'næmɪk] ADJ dynamique

dynamics [daɪ'næmɪks] N, NPL dynamique *f*

dynamism ['daɪnəmɪzəm] N dynamisme *m*

dynamite ['daɪnəmaɪt] N dynamite *f* ▶ VT dynamiter, faire sauter à la dynamite

dynamo ['daɪnəməu] N dynamo *f*

dynastic [dɪ'næstɪk] ADJ dynastique

dynasty ['dɪnəstɪ] N dynastie *f*

dysentery ['dɪsntrɪ] N dysenterie *f*

dysfunctional [dɪs'fʌŋkʃənl] ADJ dysfonctionnel(le)

dyslexia [dɪs'lɛksɪə] N dyslexie *f*

dyslexic [dɪs'lɛksɪk] ADJ dyslexique

dyspepsia [dɪs'pɛpsɪə] N dyspepsie *f*

dyspraxia [dɪs'præksɪə] N dyspraxie *f*

dystrophy ['dɪstrəfɪ] N dystrophie *f*; **muscular ~** dystrophie musculaire

Ee

E, e [iː] N (letter) E, e m; (Mus): **E** mi m; **E for Edward**, (US) **E for Easy** E comme Eugène ▶ ABBR (= east) E ▶ N ABBR (Drugs): **ecstasy**

ea. ABBR = **each**

E.A. N ABBR (US: = educational age) niveau scolaire

★**each** [iːtʃ] ADJ chaque; **~ day** chaque jour, tous les jours; **~ one** chacun(e); **~ other** l'un l'autre; **they hate ~ other** ils se détestent (mutuellement); **you are jealous of ~ other** vous êtes jaloux l'un de l'autre ▶ PRON chacun(e); **they have 2 books ~** ils ont 2 livres chacun; **they cost £5 ~** ils coûtent 5 livres (la) pièce; **~ of us** chacun(e) de nous

eager ['iːɡəʳ] ADJ (person, buyer) empressé(e); (lover) ardent(e), passionné(e); (keen: pupil, worker) enthousiaste; **to be ~ to do sth** (impatient) brûler de faire qch; (keen) désirer vivement faire qch; **to be ~ for** (event) désirer vivement; (vengeance, affection, information) être avide de

eagerly ['iːɡəlɪ] ADV (ask) avec impatience; **~ awaited** tant attendu(e)

eagle ['iːɡl] N aigle m

E & OE ABBR = **errors and omissions excepted**

★**ear** [ɪəʳ] N oreille f; (of corn) épi m; **up to one's ears in debt** endetté(e) jusqu'au cou

earache ['ɪəreɪk] N mal m aux oreilles

eardrum ['ɪədrʌm] N tympan m

earful ['ɪəful] N (inf): **to give sb an ~** passer un savon à qn

earl [əːl] N comte m

★**earlier** ['əːlɪəʳ] ADJ (date etc) plus rapproché(e); (edition etc) plus ancien(ne), antérieur(e) ▶ ADV plus tôt

★**early** ['əːlɪ] ADV tôt, de bonne heure; (ahead of time) en avance; (near the beginning) au début; **~ in the morning** tôt le matin; **~ in the spring/19th century** au début or commencement du printemps/19ème siècle ▶ ADJ précoce, qui se manifeste (or se fait) tôt or de bonne heure; (Christians, settlers) premier(-ière); (reply) rapide; (death) prématuré(e); (work) de jeunesse; **you're ~!** tu es en avance !; **to have an ~ night/start** se coucher/partir tôt or de bonne heure; **take the ~ train** prenez le premier train; **in the ~ spring/19th century** au début or commencement du printemps/19ème siècle; **she's in her ~ forties** elle a un peu plus de quarante ans or de la quarantaine; **at your earliest convenience** (Comm) dans les meilleurs délais

early retirement N retraite anticipée

early warning system N système m de première alerte

earmark ['ɪəmɑːk] VT: **to ~ sth for** réserver or destiner qch à

★**earn** [əːn] VT gagner; (Comm: yield) rapporter; **to ~ one's living** gagner sa vie; **this earned him much praise, he earned much praise for this** ceci lui a valu de nombreux éloges; **he's earned his rest/reward** il mérite or a bien mérité or a bien gagné son repos/sa récompense

earned income [əːnd-] N revenu m du travail

earner ['əːnəʳ] N (person): **a high ~** un(e) salarié(e) aux revenus élevés; (product) source f de revenus; **to be a nice little ~** (BRIT inf) bien rapporter

earnest ['əːnɪst] ADJ sérieux(-euse) ▶ N (also: **earnest money**) acompte m, arrhes fpl; **in ~** adv sérieusement, pour de bon

earnestly ['əːnɪstlɪ] ADV (seriously: say) avec le plus grand sérieux; (sincerely: hope, wish) sincèrement

★**earnings** ['əːnɪŋz] NPL salaire m; gains mpl; (of company etc) profits mpl, bénéfices mpl

ear, nose and throat specialist N oto-rhino-laryngologiste mf

earphones ['ɪəfəunz] NPL écouteurs mpl

earplugs ['ɪəplʌgz] NPL boules fpl Quiès®; (to keep out water) protège-tympans mpl

earring ['ɪərɪŋ] N boucle f d'oreille

earshot ['ɪəʃɔt] N: **out of/within ~** hors de portée/à portée de voix

★**earth** [əːθ] N (gen, also BRIT Elec) terre f; (of fox etc) terrier m ▶ VT (BRIT Elec) relier à la terre

earthenware ['əːθnwɛəʳ] N poterie f; faïence f ▶ ADJ de or en faïence

earthly ['əːθlɪ] ADJ terrestre; (also: **earthly paradise**) paradis m terrestre; **there is no ~ reason to think that …** il n'y a absolument aucune raison or pas la moindre raison de penser que …

earthquake ['əːθkweɪk] N tremblement m de terre, séisme m

earth-shattering ['əːθʃætərɪŋ] ADJ stupéfiant(e)

earth tremor N secousse f sismique

earthworks ['əːθwəːks] NPL travaux mpl de terrassement

earthy ['əːθɪ] ADJ (fig) terre à terre inv, truculent(e)

earwax ['ɪəwæks] N cérumen m

earwig ['ɪəwɪg] N perce-oreille m

ease [iːz] N facilité f, aisance f; (comfort) bien-être m; **with ~** sans difficulté, aisément; **life of ~** vie oisive; **at ~** à l'aise; (*Mil*) au repos ▸ VT (*soothe: mind*) tranquilliser; (*reduce: pain, problem*) atténuer; (*: tension*) réduire; (*loosen*) relâcher, détendre; (*help pass*): **to ~ sth in/out** faire pénétrer/sortir qch délicatement or avec douceur, faciliter la pénétration/la sortie de qch ▸ VI (*situation*) se détendre

▸ **ease off, ease up** VI diminuer; (*slow down*) ralentir; (*relax*) se détendre

easel ['i:zl] N chevalet m

★**easily** ['i:zɪlɪ] ADV facilement; (*by far*) de loin

easiness ['i:sɪnɪs] N facilité f; (*of manner*) aisance f; nonchalance f

★**east** [i:st] N est m; **the E~** l'Orient m; (*Pol*) les pays mpl de l'Est ▸ ADJ (*wind*) d'est; (*side*) est inv ▸ ADV à l'est, vers l'est

eastbound ['i:stbaund] ADJ en direction de l'est; (*carriageway*) est inv

Easter ['i:stəʳ] N Pâques fpl ▸ ADJ (*holidays*) de Pâques, pascal(e)

Easter egg N œuf m de Pâques

Easter Island N île f de Pâques

easterly ['i:stəlɪ] ADJ d'est

Easter Monday N le lundi de Pâques

★**eastern** ['i:stən] ADJ de l'est, oriental(e); **E~ Europe** l'Europe de l'Est; **the E~ bloc** (*Pol*) les pays mpl de l'est

Easter Sunday N le dimanche de Pâques

East Germany N (*formerly*) Allemagne f de l'Est

East Timor ['i:st'i:mɔ:] N Timor m oriental

eastward ['i:stwəd], **eastwards** ['i:stwədz] ADV vers l'est, à l'est

★**easy** ['i:zɪ] ADJ facile; (*manner*) aisé(e); **to have an ~ life** avoir la vie facile; **payment on ~ terms** (*Comm*) facilités fpl de paiement; **I'm ~** (*inf*) ça m'est égal ▸ ADV: **to take it** or **things ~** ne pas se fatiguer; (*not worry*) ne pas (trop) s'en faire; **that's easier said than done** c'est plus facile à dire qu'à faire, c'est vite dit

easy chair N fauteuil m

easy-going ['i:zɪ'gəuɪŋ] ADJ accommodant(e), facile à vivre

easy touch N (*inf*): **he's an ~** c'est une bonne poire

★**eat** [i:t] (*pt* **ate** [eɪt], *pp* **eaten** ['i:tn]) VT, VI manger; **can we have something to ~?** est-ce qu'on peut manger quelque chose?

▸ **eat away** VT (*sea*) saper, éroder; (*acid*) ronger, corroder

▸ **eat away at, eat into** VT FUS ronger, attaquer

▸ **eat out** VI manger au restaurant

▸ **eat up** VT (*food*) finir (de manger); **it eats up electricity** ça bouffe du courant, ça consomme beaucoup d'électricité

eatable ['i:təbl] ADJ mangeable; (*safe to eat*) comestible

eaten ['i:tn] PP of **eat**

eau de Cologne ['əudəkə'ləun] N eau f de Cologne

eaves [i:vz] NPL avant-toit m

eavesdrop ['i:vzdrɔp] VI: **to ~ (on)** écouter de façon indiscrète

ebb [ɛb] N reflux m; **the ~ and flow** le flux et le reflux; **to be at a low ~** (*fig*) être bien bas(se), ne

pas aller bien fort ▸ VI refluer; (*fig: also:* **ebb away**) décliner

ebb tide N marée descendante, reflux m

e-bike ['i:baɪk] N VAE m

ebony ['ɛbənɪ] N ébène f

e-book ['i:buk] N livre m électronique

ebullient [ɪ'bʌlɪənt] ADJ exubérant(e)

e-business ['i:bɪznɪs] N (*company*) entreprise f électronique; (*commerce*) commerce m électronique

e-card ['i:kɑ:d] N carte f virtuelle

ECB N ABBR (= *European Central Bank*) BCE f (= *Banque centrale européenne*)

eccentric [ɪk'sɛntrɪk] ADJ, N excentrique mf

ecclesiastic [ɪkli:zɪ'æstɪk], **ecclesiastical** [ɪkli:zɪ'æstɪkl] ADJ ecclésiastique

ECG N ABBR = **electrocardiogram**

echelon ['ɛʃəlɔn] N échelon m; **the upper echelons of** les plus hauts échelons de

★**echo** ['ɛkəu] (*pl* **echoes**) N écho m ▸ VT répéter; faire chorus avec ▸ VI résonner; faire écho

e-cigarette ['i:sɪgə'rɛt] N cigarette f électronique

éclair ['eɪkleəʳ] N éclair m (*Culin*)

eclectic [ɪ'klɛktɪk] ADJ (*collection*) hétéroclite; (*tastes*) éclectique

eclipse [ɪ'klɪps] N éclipse f ▸ VT éclipser

eco- ['i:kəu] PREFIX éco-

eco-friendly [i:kəu'frɛndlɪ] ADJ non nuisible à l'environnement

ecological [i:kə'lɔdʒɪkəl] ADJ écologique

ecologist [ɪ'kɔlədʒɪst] N écologiste mf

ecology [ɪ'kɔlədʒɪ] N écologie f

e-commerce ['i:kɔmə:s] N commerce m électronique

★**economic** [i:kə'nɔmɪk] ADJ économique; (*profitable*) rentable

economical [i:kə'nɔmɪkl] ADJ économique; (*person*) économe

economically [i:kə'nɔmɪklɪ] ADV économiquement

★**economics** [i:kə'nɔmɪks] N (*Scol*) économie f politique ▸ NPL (*of project etc*) côté m or aspect m économique

economist [ɪ'kɔnəmɪst] N économiste mf

economize [ɪ'kɔnəmaɪz] VI économiser, faire des économies

★**economy** [ɪ'kɔnəmɪ] N économie f; **economies of scale** économies d'échelle

economy class N (*Aviat*) classe f touriste

economy class syndrome N syndrome m de la classe économique

economy size N taille f économique

ecosystem ['i:kəusɪstəm] N écosystème m

eco-tourism [i:kəu'tuərɪzəm] N écotourisme m

ecstasy ['ɛkstəsɪ] N extase f; (*Drugs*) ecstasy m; **to go into ecstasies over** s'extasier sur

ecstatic [ɛks'tætɪk] ADJ extatique, en extase

ECT N ABBR = **electroconvulsive therapy**

Ecuador ['ɛkwədɔ:ʳ] N Équateur m

ecumenical [i:kju'mɛnɪkl] ADJ œcuménique

eczema ['ɛksɪmə] N eczéma m

eddy ['ɛdɪ] N tourbillon m

★**edge** [ɛdʒ] N bord m; (of knife etc) tranchant m, fil m; **on ~** (fig) crispé(e), tendu(e); **to have the ~ on** (fig) l'emporter (de justesse) sur, être légèrement meilleur que ▶ VT border ▶ VI: **to ~ forward** avancer petit à petit; **to ~ away from** s'éloigner furtivement de

edged [ɛdʒd] ADJ: **~ with** bordé(e) de

edgeways ['ɛdʒweɪz] ADV latéralement; **he couldn't get a word in ~** il ne pouvait pas placer un mot

edging ['ɛdʒɪŋ] N bordure f

edgy ['ɛdʒɪ] ADJ crispé(e), tendu(e)

edible ['ɛdɪbl] ADJ comestible; (meal) mangeable

edict ['i:dɪkt] N décret m

edifice ['ɛdɪfɪs] N édifice m

edifying ['ɛdɪfaɪɪŋ] ADJ édifiant(e)

Edinburgh ['ɛdɪnbərə] N Édimbourg

Le Festival d'Édimbourg (**Edinburgh Festival**), qui se tient chaque année durant trois semaines au mois d'août, est l'un des grands festivals culturels européens. Il est réputé pour son programme officiel, mais aussi pour son festival off (the Fringe) qui propose des spectacles de théâtre, de musique, de comédie et de danse aussi bien traditionnels que résolument d'avant-garde. Pendant la durée du Festival se tient par ailleurs, sur l'esplanade du château, un grand spectacle de musique militaire, le Military Tattoo.

edit ['ɛdɪt] VT (report, essay) préparer; (sb else's text, computer file) éditer; (editor, magazine, newspaper) être le rédacteur or la rédactrice en chef de; (film) monter
▶ **edit out** VT couper

editable ['ɛdɪtəbl] ADJ (text) éditable, modifiable

editing ['ɛdɪtɪŋ] N (of own article, manuscript) préparation f; (of sb else's text) édition f; (of film, programme) montage m ▶ CPD (Comput: package, software, tools) d'édition

edition [ɪ'dɪʃən] N édition f

★**editor** ['ɛdɪtə'] N (of newspaper) rédacteur(-trice), rédacteur(-trice) en chef; (of sb's work) éditeur(-trice); (also: **film editor**) monteur(-euse); **political/foreign ~** rédacteur politique/au service étranger

editorial [ɛdɪ'tɔːrɪəl] ADJ de la rédaction, éditorial(e); **the ~ staff** la rédaction ▶ N éditorial m

EDP N ABBR = **electronic data processing**

EDT ABBR (US: = Eastern Daylight Time) heure d'été de New York

educate ['ɛdjukeɪt] VT (teach) instruire; (bring up) éduquer; **educated at …** qui a fait ses études à …

educated ['ɛdjukeɪtɪd] ADJ (person) cultivé(e)

educated guess N supposition éclairée

★**education** [ɛdju'keɪʃən] N éducation f; (studies) études fpl; (teaching) enseignement m, instruction f; (at university: subject etc) pédagogie f; **primary** or (US) **elementary/secondary ~** instruction f primaire/secondaire

★**educational** [ɛdju'keɪʃənl] ADJ (toy, system) éducatif(-ive); (theory, method) pédagogique; (institution) d'enseignement; (attainments, background) scolaire; (useful) instructif(-ive); **~ technology** technologie f de l'enseignement

educationally [ɛdju'keɪʃnəlɪ] ADV (subnormal, disadvantaged) sur le plan éducatif; (sound, valuable) du point de vue pédagogique

edutainment [ɛdju'teɪnmənt] N jeux mpl éducatifs

Edwardian [ɛd'wɔːdɪən] ADJ de l'époque du roi Édouard VII, des années 1900

EEG N ABBR = **electroencephalogram**

eel [i:l] N anguille f

EENT N ABBR (US Med) = **eye, ear, nose and throat**

EEOC N ABBR (US) = **Equal Employment Opportunity Commission**

eerie ['ɪərɪ] ADJ inquiétant(e), spectral(e), surnaturel(le)

EET ABBR (= Eastern European Time) HEO (= heure d'Europe orientale)

★**effect** [ɪ'fɛkt] N effet m; **to have an ~ on sb/sth** avoir or produire un effet sur qn/qch; **to take ~** (Law) entrer en vigueur, prendre effet; (drug) agir, faire son effet; **to put into ~** (plan) mettre en application or à exécution; **in ~** en fait; **his letter is to the ~ that …** sa lettre nous apprend que …
▶ VT effectuer ■ **effects** NPL (Theat) effets mpl; (property) effets, affaires fpl

★**effective** [ɪ'fɛktɪv] ADJ efficace; (striking: display, outfit) frappant(e), qui produit or fait de l'effet; (actual) véritable; **to become ~** (Law) entrer en vigueur, prendre effet; **~ date** date f d'effet or d'entrée en vigueur

effectively [ɪ'fɛktɪvlɪ] ADV efficacement; (strikingly) d'une manière frappante, avec beaucoup d'effet; (in reality) effectivement, en fait

effectiveness [ɪ'fɛktɪvnɪs] N efficacité f

effeminate [ɪ'fɛmɪnɪt] ADJ efféminé(e)

effervescent [ɛfə'vɛsnt] ADJ effervescent(e)

efficacious [ɛfɪ'keɪʃəs] ADJ efficace

efficacy ['ɛfɪkəsɪ] N efficacité f

efficiency [ɪ'fɪʃənsɪ] N efficacité f; (of machine, car) rendement m

efficiency apartment N (US) studio m avec coin cuisine

★**efficient** [ɪ'fɪʃənt] ADJ efficace; (machine, car) d'un bon rendement

efficiently [ɪ'fɪʃəntlɪ] ADV efficacement

effigy ['ɛfɪdʒɪ] N effigie f

effluent ['ɛfluənt] N effluent m

★**effort** ['ɛfət] N effort m; **to make an ~ to do sth** faire or fournir un effort pour faire qch

effortless ['ɛfətlɪs] ADJ sans effort, aisé(e); (achievement) facile

effrontery [ɪ'frʌntərɪ] N effronterie f

effusive [ɪ'fjuːsɪv] ADJ (person) expansif(-ive); (welcome) chaleureux(-euse)

EFL N ABBR (Scol) = **English as a Foreign Language**

EFTA ['ɛftə] N ABBR (= European Free Trade Association) AELE f (= Association européenne de libre-échange)

e.g. ADV ABBR (= exempli gratia) par exemple, p. ex.

egalitarian [ɪgælɪ'tɛərɪən] ADJ égalitaire

★egg [ɛg] N œuf m; **hard-boiled/soft-boiled ~** œuf dur/à la coque
  ▶ **egg on** VT pousser

eggcup ['ɛgkʌp] N coquetier m

egghead ['ɛghɛd] N (inf) intello mf(inf)

eggnog ['ɛgnɔg] N lait m de poule

egg plant ['ɛgplɑ:nt] N (US) aubergine f

eggshell ['ɛgʃɛl] N coquille f d'œuf ▶ ADJ (colour) blanc cassé inv

egg-timer ['ɛgtaɪmə'] N sablier m

egg white N blanc m d'œuf

egg yolk N jaune m d'œuf

ego ['iːgəu] N (self-esteem) amour-propre m; (Psych) moi m

egocentric [iːgəu'sɛntrɪk, ɛgəu'sɛntrɪk] ADJ égocentrique

egoism ['ɛgəuɪzəm] N égoïsme m

egoist ['ɛgəuɪst] N égoïste mf

egoistic [iːgəu'ɪstɪk, ɛgəu'ɪstɪk] ADJ égoïste

egotism ['ɛgəutɪzəm] N égotisme m

egotist ['ɛgəutɪst] N égocentrique mf

egotistic [iːgə'tɪstɪk, ɛgə'tɪstɪk], **egotistical** [iːgə'tɪstɪkl, ɛgə'tɪstɪkl] ADJ égotiste

ego trip N: **to be on an ~** être en plein délire d'autosatisfaction

Egypt ['iːdʒɪpt] N Égypte f

Egyptian [ɪ'dʒɪpʃən] ADJ égyptien(ne) ▶ N Égyptien(ne)

EHIC N ABBR (= European Health Insurance Card) CEAM f

Eid ['iːd] N (also: **Eid-al-Fitr, Eid-ul-Fitr**) Aïd m

eiderdown ['aɪdədaun] N édredon m

Eiffel Tower ['aɪfəl-] N tour f Eiffel

★eight [eɪt] NUM huit

★eighteen [eɪ'tiːn] NUM dix-huit

★eighteenth [eɪ'tiːnθ] NUM dix-huitième

★eighth [eɪtθ] NUM huitième

eightieth ['eɪtɪθ] NUM quatre-vingtième

★eighty ['eɪtɪ] NUM quatre-vingt(s)

★Eire ['ɛərə] N République f d'Irlande

EIS N ABBR (= Educational Institute of Scotland) syndicat enseignant

eisteddfod [aɪ'stɛdvəd] N au Pays de Galles, fête lors de laquelle on dispute des concours de musique et de poésie en gallois

★either ['aɪðə'] ADJ l'un ou l'autre; (both, each) chaque; **on ~ side** de chaque côté ▶ PRON: **~ (of them)** l'un ou l'autre; **I don't like ~** je n'aime ni l'un ni l'autre; **which bike do you want? — ~ will do** quel vélo voulez-vous ? — n'importe lequel ▶ ADV non plus; **no, I don't ~** moi non plus ▶ CONJ: **~ good or bad** ou bon ou mauvais, soit bon soit mauvais; **answer with ~ yes or no** répondez par oui ou par non; **I haven't seen ~ one or the other** je n'ai vu ni l'un ni l'autre

ejaculate [ɪ'dʒækjuleɪt] VI (Physiol) éjaculer ▶ VT (literary: exclaim) s'exclamer, s'écrier

ejaculation [ɪdʒækju'leɪʃən] N (Physiol) éjaculation f

eject [ɪ'dʒɛkt] VT (tenant etc) expulser; (object) éjecter ▶ VI (pilot) s'éjecter

ejector seat [ɪ'dʒɛktə-] N siège m éjectable

eke [iːk]: **to ~ out** VT faire durer; augmenter

EKG N ABBR (US) = **electrocardiogram**

el [ɛl] N ABBR (US inf) = **elevated railroad**

elaborate ADJ [ɪ'læbərɪt] (system, procedure) compliqué(e); (dinner, scheme) élaboré(e); (costume, jewellery) recherché(e) ▶ VT [ɪ'læbəreɪt] élaborer ▶ VI entrer dans les détails

elaborately [ɪ'læbərɪtlɪ] ADV (in detail: planned) avec minutie; (richly: decorated, costumed) avec recherche

élan, elan [eɪ'lɑːn] N (literary): **to do sth with ~** faire qch avec entrain

elapse [ɪ'læps] VI s'écouler, passer

elastic [ɪ'læstɪk] ADJ, N élastique m

elasticated [ɪ'læstɪkeɪtɪd] ADJ (BRIT) à élastique

elastic band N (BRIT) élastique m

elasticity [ɪlæs'tɪsɪtɪ] N élasticité f

elated [ɪ'leɪtɪd] ADJ transporté(e) de joie

elation [ɪ'leɪʃən] N (grande) joie, allégresse f

elbow ['ɛlbəu] N coude m ▶ VT: **to ~ one's way through the crowd** se frayer un passage à travers la foule (en jouant des coudes)

elbow grease N: **to use a bit of ~** mettre de l'huile de coude

★elder ['ɛldə'] ADJ aîné(e) ▶ N (tree) sureau m; **one's elders** ses aînés

elderberry ['ɛldəbɛrɪ] N (berry) baie f de sureau; (tree) sureau m

★elderly ['ɛldəlɪ] ADJ âgé(e); **~ people** les personnes âgées

elder statesman N (irreg) vétéran m de la politique

★eldest ['ɛldɪst] ADJ, N: **the ~ (child)** l'aîné(e) (des enfants)

elect [ɪ'lɛkt] VT élire; (choose): **to ~ to do** choisir de faire ▶ ADJ: **the president ~** le président désigné

★election [ɪ'lɛkʃən] N élection f; **to hold an ~** procéder à une élection

election campaign N campagne électorale

electioneering [ɪlɛkʃə'nɪərɪŋ] N propagande électorale, manœuvres électorales

elective [ɪ'lɛktɪv] ADJ électif(-ive) ▶ N (US) cours m facultatif

elector [ɪ'lɛktə'] N électeur(-trice)

electoral [ɪ'lɛktərəl] ADJ électoral(e)

electoral college N collège électoral

electoral roll N (BRIT) liste électorale

electorate [ɪ'lɛktərɪt] N électorat m

★electric [ɪ'lɛktrɪk] ADJ électrique

electrical [ɪ'lɛktrɪkl] ADJ électrique

electrical engineer N ingénieur électricien

electrical failure N panne f d'électricité or de courant

electric blanket N couverture chauffante

electric blue ADJ, N bleu électrique m inv

electric chair N chaise f électrique

electric cooker N cuisinière f électrique

electric current N courant m électrique

electric fire N (BRIT) radiateur m électrique

electrician [ɪlɛk'trɪʃən] N électricien *m*

★**electricity** [ɪlɛk'trɪsɪtɪ] N électricité *f*; **to switch on/off the ~** rétablir/couper le courant

electricity board N (*BRIT*) ≈ agence régionale de l'E.D.F.

electric light N lumière *f* électrique

electrics [ɪ'lɛktrɪks] NPL (*BRIT*) installation *f* électrique

electric shock N choc *m* or décharge *f* électrique

electrify [ɪ'lɛktrɪfaɪ] VT (*Rail*) électrifier; (*audience*) électriser

electro... [ɪ'lɛktrəʊ] PREFIX électro...

electrocardiogram [ɪlɛktrəʊ'kɑːdɪəgræm] N électrocardiogramme *m*

electro-convulsive therapy [ɪlɛktrəʊkən-'vʌlsɪv-] N électrochocs *mpl*

electrocute [ɪ'lɛktrəkjuːt] VT électrocuter

electrode [ɪ'lɛktrəʊd] N électrode *f*

electroencephalogram [ɪlɛktrəʊen'sɛfələgræm] N électroencéphalogramme *m*

electrolysis [ɪlɛk'trɒlɪsɪs] N électrolyse *f*

electromagnetic [ɪ'lɛktrəmæg'nɛtɪk] ADJ électromagnétique

electron [ɪ'lɛktrɒn] N électron *m*

★**electronic** [ɪlɛk'trɒnɪk] ADJ électronique

electronically [ɪlɛk'trɒnɪklɪ] ADV électroniquement

electronic data processing N traitement *m* électronique des données

electronic mail N courrier *m* électronique

electronics [ɪlɛk'trɒnɪks] N électronique *f*

electron microscope N microscope *m* électronique

electroplated [ɪ'lɛktrə'pleɪtɪd] ADJ plaqué(e) or doré(e) or argenté(e) par galvanoplastie

electrotherapy [ɪlɛktrə'θɛrəpɪ] N électrothérapie *f*

elegance ['ɛlɪgəns] N élégance *f*

★**elegant** ['ɛlɪgənt] ADJ élégant(e)

elegantly ['ɛlɪgəntlɪ] ADV (*dressed, furnished*) avec élégance; (*designed, shaped*) élégamment; **~ simple** d'une élégante simplicité

elegy ['ɛlɪdʒɪ] N élégie *f*

element ['ɛlɪmənt] N (*gen*) élément *m*; (*of heater, kettle etc*) résistance *f*

elementary [ɛlɪ'mɛntərɪ] ADJ élémentaire; (*school, education*) primaire

elementary school N (*US*) école *f* primaire

Aux États-Unis et au Canada, une **elementary school** (également appelée *grade school* ou *grammar school* aux États-Unis) est une école publique où les enfants passent les six à huit premières années de leur scolarité.

★**elephant** ['ɛlɪfənt] N éléphant *m*

elevate ['ɛlɪveɪt] VT élever **elevated railroad** ['ɛlɪveɪtɪd-] N (*US*) métro *m* aérien

elevation [ɛlɪ'veɪʃən] N élévation *f*; (*height*) altitude *f*

elevator ['ɛlɪveɪtə'] N (*in warehouse etc*) élévateur *m*, monte-charge *m inv*; (*US: lift*) ascenseur *m*

★**eleven** [ɪ'lɛvn] NUM onze

elevenses [ɪ'lɛvnzɪz] NPL (*BRIT*) ≈ pause-café *f*

★**eleventh** [ɪ'lɛvnθ] NUM onzième; **at the ~ hour** (*fig*) à la dernière minute

elf [ɛlf] (*pl* **elves** [ɛlvz]) N lutin *m*

elfin ['ɛlfɪn] ADJ (*face*) délicat(e)

elicit [ɪ'lɪsɪt] VT: **to ~ (from)** obtenir (de); tirer (de)

eligibility [ɛlɪdʒɪ'bɪlɪtɪ] N: **~ (for sth)** (*membership, job*) admissibilité *f* (à qch); (*benefits*) droit *m* (à qch); **~ to do sth** droit de faire qch

eligible ['ɛlɪdʒəbl] ADJ (*for compensation, benefits*) éligible; (*for membership*) admissible; **an ~ young man** un beau parti; **to be ~ for sth** remplir les conditions requises pour qch; **~ for a pension** ayant droit à la retraite

eliminate [ɪ'lɪmɪneɪt] VT éliminer

elimination [ɪlɪmɪ'neɪʃən] N élimination *f*; **by process of ~** par élimination

elite, élite [ɪ'liːt] ADJ (*group, athlete*) d'élite; (*institution*) prestigieux(-euse) ▶ N: **the ~** l'élite *f*

elitist [ɛ'liːtɪst] ADJ (*pej*) élitiste

elixir [ɪ'lɪksə'] N (*literary*) élixir *m*

Elizabethan [ɪlɪzə'biːθən] ADJ élisabéthain(e)

ellipse [ɪ'lɪps] N ellipse *f*

elliptical [ɪ'lɪptɪkl] ADJ elliptique

elm [ɛlm] N orme *m*

elocution [ɛlə'kjuːʃən] N élocution *f*

elongated ['iːlɒŋgeɪtɪd] ADJ étiré(e), allongé(e)

elope [ɪ'ləʊp] VI (*lovers*) s'enfuir (ensemble)

elopement [ɪ'ləʊpmənt] N fugue amoureuse

eloquence ['ɛləkwəns] N éloquence *f*

eloquent ['ɛləkwənt] ADJ éloquent(e)

eloquently ['ɛləkwəntlɪ] ADV (*speak, write*) avec éloquence

El Salvador [ɛl 'sælvədɔː] N Salvador *m*

★**else** [ɛls] ADV d'autre; **something ~** quelque chose d'autre, autre chose; **somewhere ~** ailleurs, autre part; **everywhere ~** partout ailleurs; **everyone ~** tous les autres; **nothing ~** rien d'autre; **is there anything ~ I can do?** est-ce que je peux faire quelque chose d'autre?; **where ~?** à quel autre endroit?; **little ~** pas grand-chose d'autre

elsewhere [ɛls'wɛə'] ADV ailleurs, autre part

ELT N ABBR (*Scol*) = **English Language Teaching**

elucidate [ɪ'luːsɪdeɪt] VT élucider

elude [ɪ'luːd] VT échapper à; (*question*) éluder

elusive [ɪ'luːsɪv] ADJ insaisissable; (*answer*) évasif(-ive)

elves [ɛlvz] NPL *of* **elf**

emaciated [ɪ'meɪsɪeɪtɪd] ADJ émacié(e), décharné(e)

★**email** ['iːmeɪl] N ABBR (= *electronic mail*) (e-)mail *m*, courriel *m* ▶ VT: **to ~ sb** envoyer un (e-)mail *or* un courriel à qn

email account N compte *m* (e-)mail

email address N adresse *f* (e-)mail *or* électronique

emanate ['ɛməneɪt] VI: **to ~ from** émaner de

emancipate [ɪ'mænsɪpeɪt] VT émanciper

emancipation [ɪmænsɪˈpeɪʃən] N émancipation f
emasculate [ɪˈmæskjuleɪt] VT émasculer
embalm [ɪmˈbɑːm] VT embaumer
embankment [ɪmˈbæŋkmənt] N (of road, railway) remblai m, talus m; (of river) berge f, quai m; (dyke) digue f
embargo [ɪmˈbɑːgəu] (pl **embargoes**) N (Comm, Naut) embargo m; (prohibition) interdiction f; **to put an ~ on sth** mettre l'embargo sur qch ▶ VT frapper d'embargo, mettre l'embargo sur
embark [ɪmˈbɑːk] VI embarquer; **to ~ on** (ship) (s') embarquer à bord de or sur; (journey etc) commencer, entreprendre; (fig) se lancer or s'embarquer dans ▶ VT embarquer
embarkation [ɛmbɑːˈkeɪʃən] N embarquement m
embarkation card N carte f d'embarquement
embarrass [ɪmˈbærəs] VT embarrasser, gêner
★**embarrassed** [ɪmˈbærəst] ADJ gêné(e); **to be ~** être gêné(e)
embarrassing [ɪmˈbærəsɪŋ] ADJ gênant(e), embarrassant(e)
embarrassment [ɪmˈbærəsmənt] N embarras m, gêne f; (embarrassing thing, person) source f d'embarras
★**embassy** [ˈɛmbəsɪ] N ambassade f; **the French E~** l'ambassade de France
embed [ɪmˈbɛd] VT (object) enfoncer; (values, attitudes) ancrer; **to ~ itself in sth** (object) s'enfoncer dans qch; (bullet) se loger dans qch
embedded [ɪmˈbɛdɪd] ADJ (object) enfoncé(e); **to be ~ in sth** (thorn) être enfoncé(e) dans qch; (bullet) être logé(e) dans qch; (value, attitude) être ancré(e) dans qch
embellish [ɪmˈbɛlɪʃ] VT embellir; enjoliver
embers [ˈɛmbəz] NPL braise f
embezzle [ɪmˈbɛzl] VT détourner
embezzlement [ɪmˈbɛzlmənt] N détournement m (de fonds)
embezzler [ɪmˈbɛzləʳ] N escroc m
embitter [ɪmˈbɪtəʳ] VT aigrir; envenimer
emblazoned [ɪmˈbleɪzənd] ADJ: **to be ~ with sth** être armorié(e) de qch; **to be ~ on sth** être inscrit(e) sur qch
emblem [ˈɛmbləm] N emblème m
emblematic [ɛmbləˈmætɪk] ADJ emblématique
embodiment [ɪmˈbɔdɪmənt] N personnification f, incarnation f
embody [ɪmˈbɔdɪ] VT (features) réunir, comprendre; (ideas) formuler, exprimer
embolden [ɪmˈbəuldn] VT enhardir
embolism [ˈɛmbəlɪzəm] N embolie f
embossed [ɪmˈbɔst] ADJ repoussé(e), gaufré(e); **~ with** où figure(nt) en relief
embrace [ɪmˈbreɪs] VT embrasser, étreindre; (include) embrasser, couvrir, comprendre ▶ VI s'embrasser, s'étreindre ▶ N étreinte f
embroider [ɪmˈbrɔɪdəʳ] VT broder; (fig: story) enjoliver
embroidery [ɪmˈbrɔɪdərɪ] N broderie f
embroil [ɪmˈbrɔɪl] VT: **to become embroiled (in**

sth) se retrouver mêlé(e) (à qch), se laisser entraîner (dans qch)
embryo [ˈɛmbrɪəu] N (also fig) embryon m
embryonic [ɛmbrɪˈɔnɪk] ADJ (idea, organization) à l'état embryonnaire, embryonnaire; (Biol) embryonnaire
emcee [ɛmˈsiː] N maître m de cérémonie
emend [ɪˈmɛnd] VT (text) corriger
emerald [ˈɛmərəld] N émeraude f
emerge [ɪˈmɜːdʒ] VI apparaître; (from room, car) surgir; (from sleep, imprisonment) sortir; **it emerges that** (BRIT) il ressort que
emergence [ɪˈmɜːdʒəns] N apparition f; (of nation) naissance f
★**emergency** [ɪˈmɜːdʒənsɪ] N (crisis) cas m d'urgence; (Med) urgence f; **in an ~** en cas d'urgence; **state of ~** état m d'urgence
emergency brake (US) N frein m à main
emergency exit N sortie f de secours
emergency landing N atterrissage forcé
emergency lane N (US Aut) accotement stabilisé
emergency road service N (US) service m de dépannage
emergency room N (US Med) urgences fpl
emergency services NPL: **the ~** (fire, police, ambulance) les services mpl d'urgence
emergency stop N (BRIT Aut) arrêt m d'urgence
emergent [ɪˈmɜːdʒənt] ADJ: **~ nation** pays m en voie de développement
emeritus [ɪˈmɛrɪtəs] ADJ émérite
emery board [ˈɛmərɪ-] N lime f à ongles (en carton émerisé)
emery paper [ˈɛmərɪ-] N papier m (d')émeri
emetic [ɪˈmɛtɪk] N vomitif m, émétique m
emigrant [ˈɛmɪgrənt] N émigrant(e)
emigrate [ˈɛmɪgreɪt] VI émigrer
emigration [ɛmɪˈgreɪʃən] N émigration f
émigré [ˈɛmɪgreɪ] N émigré(e)
eminence [ˈɛmɪnəns] N éminence f
eminent [ˈɛmɪnənt] ADJ éminent(e)
eminently [ˈɛmɪnəntlɪ] ADV éminemment, admirablement
emir [ɛˈmɪəʳ] N émir m
emissary [ˈɛmɪsərɪ] N émissaire m
emissions [ɪˈmɪʃənz] NPL émissions fpl
emit [ɪˈmɪt] VT émettre
emoji [ɪˈməudʒɪ] N émoji m
emolument [ɪˈmɔljumənt] N (often pl: formal) émoluments mpl; (fee) honoraires mpl; (salary) traitement m
emoticon [ɪˈməutɪkɔn] N (Comput) émoticone m
emotion [ɪˈməuʃən] N sentiment m; (as opposed to reason) émotion f, sentiments
★**emotional** [ɪˈməuʃənl] ADJ (person) émotif(-ive), très sensible; (needs) affectif(-ive); (scene) émouvant(e); (tone, speech) qui fait appel aux sentiments
emotionally [ɪˈməuʃnəlɪ] ADV (behave) émotivement; (be involved) affectivement; (speak) avec émotion; **~ disturbed** qui souffre de troubles de l'affectivité
emotive [ɪˈməutɪv] ADJ émotif(-ive); **~ power**

capacité f d'émouvoir or de toucher

empathize ['ɛmpəθaɪz] vɪ se montrer compréhensif(-ive); **to ~ with sb** comprendre ce que ressent qn

empathy ['ɛmpəθɪ] ɴ communion f d'idées or de sentiments, empathie f; **to feel ~ with sb** se mettre à la place de qn

emperor ['ɛmpərəʳ] ɴ empereur m

emphasis ['ɛmfəsɪs] (pl **emphases** [-siːz]) ɴ accent m; **to lay** or **place ~ on sth** (fig) mettre l'accent sur, insister sur; **the ~ is on reading** la lecture tient une place primordiale, on accorde une importance particulière à la lecture

★**emphasize** ['ɛmfəsaɪz] vᴛ (syllable, word, point) appuyer or insister sur; (feature) souligner, accentuer

emphatic [ɛm'fætɪk] ᴀᴅᴊ (strong) énergique, vigoureux(-euse); (unambiguous, clear) catégorique

emphatically [ɛm'fætɪklɪ] ᴀᴅᴠ avec vigueur or énergie; catégoriquement

emphysema [ɛmfɪ'siːmə] ɴ emphysème m

empire ['ɛmpaɪəʳ] ɴ empire m

empirical [ɛm'pɪrɪkl] ᴀᴅᴊ empirique

empirically [ɪm'pɪrɪklɪ] ᴀᴅᴠ de manière empirique, empiriquement; **~ based** fondé(e) sur l'expérience

★**employ** [ɪm'plɔɪ] vᴛ employer; **he's employed in a bank** il est employé de banque, il travaille dans une banque

★**employee** [ɪmplɔɪ'iː] ɴ employé(e)

★**employer** [ɪm'plɔɪəʳ] ɴ employeur(-euse)

★**employment** [ɪm'plɔɪmənt] ɴ emploi m; **to find ~** trouver un emploi or du travail; **without ~** au chômage, sans emploi; **place of ~** lieu m de travail

employment agency ɴ agence f or bureau m de placement

employment exchange ɴ (ʙʀɪᴛ) agence f pour l'emploi

emporium [ɛm'pɔːrɪəm] (pl **emporia** [ɛm'pɔːrɪə]) ɴ grand magasin m; **food ~** grand magasin d'alimentation

empower [ɪm'pauəʳ] vᴛ (strengthen: person, group) responsabiliser; **to ~ sb to do** autoriser or habiliter qn à faire

empowerment [ɪm'pauəmənt] ɴ responsabilisation f

empress ['ɛmprɪs] ɴ impératrice f

emptiness ['ɛmptɪnɪs] ɴ vide m; (of area) aspect m désertique

★**empty** ['ɛmptɪ] ᴀᴅᴊ vide; (street, area) désert(e); (threat, promise) en l'air, vain(e); **on an ~ stomach** à jeun ▶ ɴ (bottle) bouteille f vide ▶ vᴛ vider ▶ vɪ se vider; (liquid) s'écouler; **to ~ into** (river) se jeter dans, se déverser dans

empty-handed [ɛmptɪ'hændɪd] ᴀᴅᴊ les mains vides

empty-headed [ɛmptɪ'hɛdɪd] ᴀᴅᴊ écervelé(e), qui n'a rien dans la tête

EMT ɴ ᴀʙʙʀ = **emergency medical technician**

EMU ɴ ᴀʙʙʀ (= European Monetary Union) UME f

emu ['iːmjuː] (pl **~** or **emus**) ɴ émeu m

emulate ['ɛmjuleɪt] vᴛ rivaliser avec, imiter

emulsion [ɪ'mʌlʃən] ɴ émulsion f; (also: **emulsion paint**) peinture mate

enable [ɪ'neɪbl] vᴛ **to ~ sb to do** permettre à qn de faire, donner à qn la possibilité de faire

enact [ɪ'nækt] vᴛ (Law) promulguer; (play, scene) jouer, représenter

enactment [ɪn'æktmənt] ɴ (Law) promulgation f; (of play, story) représentation f

enamel [ɪ'næml] ɴ émail m; (also: **enamel paint**) (peinture f) laque f

enamelled, (US) **enameled** [ɪ'næməld] ᴀᴅᴊ (steel, gold) émaillé(e); (bath, bowl) en émail

enamoured, (US) **enamored** [ɪ'næməd] ᴀᴅᴊ **~ of** amoureux(-euse) de; (idea) enchanté(e) par

enc. ᴀʙʙʀ (on letters etc: = enclosed, enclosure) PJ, ci-joint

encampment [ɪn'kæmpmənt] ɴ campement m

encapsulate [ɪn'kæpsjuleɪt] vᴛ (mood, spirit) incarner; (views, ideas) résumer

encased [ɪn'keɪst] ᴀᴅᴊ **~ in** enfermé(e) dans, recouvert(e) de

enchant [ɪn'tʃɑːnt] vᴛ enchanter

enchanting [ɪn'tʃɑːntɪŋ] ᴀᴅᴊ ravissant(e), enchanteur(-eresse)

encircle [ɪn'sɜːkl] vᴛ entourer, encercler

encl. ᴀʙʙʀ (on letters etc: = enclosed) ci-joint(e); (= enclosure) PJ f

enclave ['ɛŋkleɪv] ɴ enclave f

enclose [ɪn'kləuz] vᴛ (land) clôturer; (space, object) entourer; (letter etc) joindre (à); **please find enclosed** veuillez trouver ci-joint

enclosure [ɪn'kləuʒəʳ] ɴ enceinte f; (in letter etc) annexe f

encode [ɪn'kəud] vᴛ coder

encoder [ɪn'kəudəʳ] ɴ (Comput) encodeur m

encompass [ɪn'kʌmpəs] vᴛ encercler, entourer; (include) contenir, inclure

encore [ɔŋ'kɔːʳ] ᴇxᴄʟ, ɴ bis m

encounter [ɪn'kauntəʳ] ɴ rencontre f ▶ vᴛ rencontrer

★**encourage** [ɪn'kʌrɪdʒ] vᴛ encourager; (industry, growth) favoriser; **to ~ sb to do sth** encourager qn à faire qch

encouragement [ɪn'kʌrɪdʒmənt] ɴ encouragement m

encouraging [ɪn'kʌrɪdʒɪŋ] ᴀᴅᴊ encourageant(e)

encroach [ɪn'krəutʃ] vɪ **to ~ (up)on** empiéter sur

encroachment [ɪn'krəutʃmənt] ɴ empiètement m

encrusted [ɪn'krʌstɪd] ᴀᴅᴊ **~ (with)** incrusté(e) (de)

encrypt [ɪn'krɪpt] vᴛ crypter

encryption [ɪn'krɪpʃən] ɴ cryptage m ▶ ᴄᴘᴅ (technology, code) de cryptage

encumbered [ɪn'kʌmbəd] ᴀᴅᴊ encombré(e); **to be ~ with** (luggage) être encombré(e) de; (debts) être criblé(e) de; (rules, regulations) être surchargé(e) de

encyclopaedia, encyclopedia [ɛnsaɪkləu'piːdɪə] ɴ encyclopédie f

encyclopaedic, encyclopedic [ɪnsaɪklə'piːdɪk] ᴀᴅᴊ encyclopédique

★**end** [ɛnd] ɴ fin f; (of table, street, rope etc) bout m, extrémité f; (of pointed object) pointe f; (of town) bout; (Sport) côté m; **from - to -** d'un bout à l'autre; **to come to an -** prendre fin; **to be at an -** être fini(e), être terminé(e); **in the -** finalement; **on -** (object) debout, dressé(e); **to stand on -** (hair) se dresser sur la tête; **for 5 hours on -** durant 5 heures d'affilée or de suite; **for hours on -** pendant des heures (et des heures); **at the - of the day** (BRIT fig) en fin de compte; **to this -, with this - in view** à cette fin, dans ce but ▶ VT terminer; (also: **to bring to an end, to put an end to**) mettre fin à ▶ VI se terminer, finir

▶ **end up** VI: **to - up in** (condition) finir or se terminer par; (place) finir or aboutir à

endanger [ɪn'deɪndʒəʳ] VT mettre en danger; **an endangered species** une espèce en voie de disparition

endear [ɪn'dɪəʳ] VT: **to - o.s. to sb** se faire aimer de qn

endearing [ɪn'dɪərɪŋ] ADJ attachant(e)

endearment [ɪn'dɪəmənt] N: **to whisper endearments** murmurer des mots or choses tendres; **term of -** terme m d'affection

endeavour, (US) **endeavor** [ɪn'dɛvəʳ] N effort m; (attempt) tentative f ▶ VT: **to - to do** tenter or s'efforcer de faire

endemic [ɛn'dɛmɪk] ADJ endémique

endgame ['ɛndgeɪm] N (Chess, fig) fin f de partie

ending ['ɛndɪŋ] N dénouement m, conclusion f; (Ling) terminaison f

endive ['ɛndaɪv] N (curly) chicorée f; (smooth, flat) endive f

endless ['ɛndlɪs] ADJ (interminable: journey, war) sans fin, interminable; (unlimited: patience, resources) inépuisable, sans limites; (: possibilities) illimité(e)

endlessly ['ɛndlɪslɪ] ADV (talk, repeat) continuellement; (infinitely): **to be - patient** être d'une patience infinie; **it's - fascinating** cela ne cesse pas de me fasciner

endorse [ɪn'dɔːs] VT (cheque) endosser; (approve) appuyer, approuver, sanctionner

endorsee [ɪndɔː'siː] N bénéficiaire mf, endossataire mf

endorsement [ɪn'dɔːsmənt] N (approval) appui m, aval m; (signature) endossement m; (BRIT: on driving licence) contravention f (portée au permis de conduire)

endorser [ɪn'dɔːsəʳ] N avaliste m, endosseur m

endow [ɪn'dau] VT (provide with money) faire une donation à, doter; (equip): **to - with** gratifier de, doter de

endowment [ɪn'daumənt] N dotation f

endowment mortgage N hypothèque liée à une assurance-vie

endowment policy N assurance f à capital différé

end product N (Industry) produit fini; (fig) résultat m, aboutissement m

end result N résultat final

endurable [ɪn'djuərəbl] ADJ supportable

endurance [ɪn'djuərəns] N endurance f

endurance test N test m d'endurance

endure [ɪn'djuəʳ] VT (bear) supporter, endurer ▶ VI (last) durer

enduring [ɪn'djuərɪŋ] ADJ (appeal, influence) constant(e); (legacy, love) durable; (image, memory) tenace

end user N (Comput) utilisateur final

enema ['ɛnɪmə] N (Med) lavement m

★**enemy** ['ɛnəmɪ] ADJ, N ennemi(e); **to make an - of sb** se faire un(e) ennemi(e) de qn, se mettre qn à dos

energetic [ɛnə'dʒɛtɪk] ADJ énergique; (activity) très actif(-ive), qui fait se dépenser (physiquement)

energize ['ɛnədʒaɪz] VT stimuler, motiver; **to be energized** être plein(e) d'énergie

energizing ['ɛnədʒaɪzɪŋ] ADJ stimulant(e)

★**energy** ['ɛnədʒɪ] N énergie f; **Department of E- ministère** m de l'Énergie

energy crisis N crise f de l'énergie

energy drink N boisson f énergisante

energy-efficient ['ɛnədʒɪ'fɪʃənt] ADJ économe en énergie

energy-saving ['ɛnədʒɪseɪvɪŋ] ADJ (policy) d'économie d'énergie; (device) qui permet de réaliser des économies d'énergie

enervating ['ɛnəveɪtɪŋ] ADJ débilitant(e), affaiblissant(e)

enforce [ɪn'fɔːs] VT (law) appliquer, faire respecter

enforced [ɪn'fɔːst] ADJ forcé(e)

enforcement [ɪn'fɔːsmənt] N (of law, rule) application f

enfranchise [ɪn'fræntʃaɪz] VT accorder le droit de vote à; (set free) affranchir

engage [ɪn'geɪdʒ] VT engager; (Mil) engager le combat avec; (lawyer) prendre; **to - sb in conversation** engager la conversation avec qn ▶ VI (Tech) s'enclencher, s'engrener; **to - in** se lancer dans

★**engaged** [ɪn'geɪdʒd] ADJ (BRIT: busy, in use) occupé(e); (betrothed) fiancé(e); **to get -** se fiancer; **the line's -** la ligne est occupée; **he is - in research/a survey** il fait de la recherche/une enquête

engaged tone N (BRIT Tel) tonalité f occupé inv

engagement [ɪn'geɪdʒmənt] N (undertaking) obligation f, engagement m; (appointment) rendez-vous m inv; (to marry) fiançailles fpl; (Mil) combat m; **I have a previous -** j'ai déjà un rendez-vous, je suis déjà pris(e)

engagement ring N bague f de fiançailles

engaging [ɪn'geɪdʒɪŋ] ADJ engageant(e), attirant(e)

engender [ɪn'dʒɛndəʳ] VT produire, causer

engine ['ɛndʒɪn] N (Aut) moteur m; (Rail) locomotive f **engine driver** N (BRIT: of train) mécanicien m

★**engineer** [ɛndʒɪ'nɪəʳ] N ingénieur m; (BRIT: repairer) dépanneur m; (Navy, US Rail) mécanicien m; **civil/ mechanical -** ingénieur des Travaux Publics or des Ponts et Chaussées/mécanicien

★**engineering** [ɛndʒɪ'nɪərɪŋ] N engineering m, ingénierie f; (of bridges, ships) génie m; (of machine) mécanique f ▶ CPD: **- works** or **factory** atelier m de construction mécanique

engine failure N panne f

engine trouble N ennuis mpl mécaniques

★**England** ['ɪŋglənd] N Angleterre f

★**English** ['ɪŋglɪʃ] ADJ anglais(e) ▶ N (*Ling*) anglais *m*; **an ~ speaker** un anglophone ▶ NPL: **the ~** les Anglais *mpl*

English Channel N: **the ~** la Manche

★**Englishman** ['ɪŋglɪʃmən] N (*irreg*) Anglais *m*

English-speaking ['ɪŋglɪʃspi:kɪŋ] ADJ qui parle anglais; anglophone

★**Englishwoman** ['ɪŋglɪʃwumən] N (*irreg*) Anglaise *f*

engrave [ɪn'greɪv] VT graver

engraving [ɪn'greɪvɪŋ] N gravure *f*

engrossed [ɪn'grəʊst] ADJ: **~ in** absorbé(e) par, plongé(e) dans

engulf [ɪn'gʌlf] VT engloutir

enhance [ɪn'hɑːns] VT rehausser, mettre en valeur; (*position*) améliorer; (*reputation*) accroître

enhancement [ɪn'hɑːnsmənt] N (*of quality, appearance, condition*) amélioration *f*; (*to pension, salary*) majoration *f*; **image ~** retouche *f* d'images; **breast ~** augmentation *f* mammaire

enigma [ɪ'nɪgmə] N énigme *f*

enigmatic [ɛnɪg'mætɪk] ADJ énigmatique

★**enjoy** [ɪn'dʒɔɪ] VT aimer, prendre plaisir à; (*have benefit of: health, fortune*) jouir de; (*: success*) connaître; **to ~ o.s.** s'amuser

enjoyable [ɪn'dʒɔɪəbl] ADJ agréable

enjoyment [ɪn'dʒɔɪmənt] N plaisir *m*

enlarge [ɪn'lɑːdʒ] VT accroître; (*Phot*) agrandir ▶ VI: **to ~ on** (*subject*) s'étendre sur

enlarged [ɪn'lɑːdʒd] ADJ (*edition*) augmenté(e); (*Med: organ, gland*) anormalement gros(se), hypertrophié(e)

enlargement [ɪn'lɑːdʒmənt] N (*Phot*) agrandissement *m*

enlighten [ɪn'laɪtn] VT éclairer

enlightened [ɪn'laɪtnd] ADJ éclairé(e)

enlightening [ɪn'laɪtnɪŋ] ADJ instructif(-ive), révélateur(-trice)

enlightenment [ɪn'laɪtnmənt] N édification *f*; éclaircissements *mpl*; (*Hist*): **the E~** ≈ le Siècle des lumières

enlist [ɪn'lɪst] VT recruter; (*support*) s'assurer; **enlisted man** (*US Mil*) simple soldat *m* ▶ VI s'engager

enliven [ɪn'laɪvn] VT animer, égayer

en masse [ɔn'mæs] ADV en masse

enmity ['ɛnmɪtɪ] N inimitié *f*

ennoble [ɪ'nəʊbl] VT (*with title*) anoblir

enormity [ɪ'nɔːmɪtɪ] N énormité *f*

★**enormous** [ɪ'nɔːməs] ADJ énorme

enormously [ɪ'nɔːməslɪ] ADV (*increase*) dans des proportions énormes; (*rich*) extrêmement

★**enough** [ɪ'nʌf] ADJ: **~ time/books** assez *or* suffisamment de temps/livres ▶ ADV: **big ~** assez *or* suffisamment grand; **he has not worked ~** il n'a pas assez *or* suffisamment travaillé, il n'a pas travaillé assez *or* suffisamment; **it's hot ~ (as it is)!** il fait assez chaud comme ça !; **he was kind ~ to lend me the money** il a eu la gentillesse de me prêter l'argent; **... which, funnily** *or* **oddly** *or* **strangely ~ ...** qui, chose curieuse, ... ▶ PRON: **have you got ~?** (en) avez-vous assez ?; **~ to eat** assez à manger; **will five be ~?** est-ce que cinq suffiront ?, est-ce qu'il y en aura assez avec cinq ?; **(that's) ~!** ça suffit !, assez !; **that's ~, thanks** cela suffit *or* c'est assez, merci; **I've had ~!** je n'en peux plus !; **I've had ~ of him** j'en ai assez de lui

enquire [ɪn'kwaɪə'] VT, VI = **inquire**

enquiry [ɪn'kwaɪərɪ] N = **inquiry**

enrage [ɪn'reɪdʒ] VT mettre en fureur *or* en rage, rendre furieux(-euse)

enraged [ɪn'reɪdʒd] ADJ furieux(-euse); **to be ~ at sb/by sth** être furieux(-euse) contre qn/à cause de qch

enrich [ɪn'rɪtʃ] VT enrichir

enrichment [ɪn'rɪtʃmənt] N enrichissement *m*

enrol, (*US*) **enroll** [ɪn'rəʊl] VT inscrire ▶ VI s'inscrire

enrolment, (*US*) **enrollment** [ɪn'rəʊlmənt] N inscription *f*

en route [ɔn'ruːt] ADV en route, en chemin; **~ for** *or* **to** en route vers, à destination de

ensconced [ɪn'skɔnst] ADJ: **~ in** bien calé(e) dans

enshrine [ɪn'ʃraɪn] VT (*fig*) préserver

ensign N (*Naut*) ['ɛnsən] enseigne *f*, pavillon *m*; (*Mil*) ['ɛnsaɪn] porte-étendard *m*

enslave [ɪn'sleɪv] VT asservir

ensue [ɪn'sjuː] VI s'ensuivre, résulter

en suite ['ɔnswiːt] ADJ: **with ~ bathroom** avec salle de bains en attenante

ensure [ɪn'ʃuə'] VT assurer, garantir; **to ~ that** s'assurer que

ENT N ABBR (= *Ear, Nose and Throat*) ORL *f*

entail [ɪn'teɪl] VT entraîner, nécessiter

entangle [ɪn'tæŋgl] VT emmêler, embrouiller; **to become entangled in sth** (*fig*) se laisser entraîner *or* empêtrer dans qch

★**enter** ['ɛntə'] VT (*room*) entrer dans, pénétrer dans; (*club, army*) entrer à; (*profession*) embrasser; (*competition*) s'inscrire à *or* pour; (*sb for a competition*) (faire) inscrire; (*write down*) inscrire, noter; (*Comput*) entrer, introduire ▶ VI entrer
▶ **enter for** VT FUS s'inscrire à, se présenter pour *or* à
▶ **enter into** VT FUS (*explanation*) se lancer dans; (*negotiations*) entamer; (*debate*) prendre part à; (*agreement*) conclure
▶ **enter on** VT FUS commencer
▶ **enter up** VT inscrire
▶ **enter upon** VT FUS = **enter on**

enteritis [ɛntə'raɪtɪs] N entérite *f*

enterprise ['ɛntəpraɪz] N (*company, undertaking*) entreprise *f*; (*initiative*) (esprit *m* d')initiative *f*; **free ~** libre entreprise; **private ~** entreprise privée

enterprising ['ɛntəpraɪzɪŋ] ADJ entreprenant(e), dynamique; (*scheme*) audacieux(-euse)

★**entertain** [ɛntə'teɪn] VT amuser, distraire; (*invite*) recevoir (à dîner); (*idea, plan*) envisager

entertainer [ɛntə'teɪnə'] N artiste *mf* de variétés

entertaining [ɛntə'teɪnɪŋ] ADJ amusant(e), distrayant(e) ▶ N: **to do a lot of ~** beaucoup recevoir

entertainment [ɛntə'teɪnmənt] N (*amusement*) distraction *f*, divertissement *m*, amusement *m*; (*show*) spectacle *m*

entertainment allowance N frais *mpl* de

représentation

enthralled [ɪnˈθrɔːld] ADJ captivé(e)

enthralling [ɪnˈθrɔːlɪŋ] ADJ captivant(e), enchanteur(-eresse)

enthuse [ɪnˈθuːz] VI: **to ~ about** or **over** parler avec enthousiasme de

★**enthusiasm** [ɪnˈθuːzɪæzəm] N enthousiasme m

enthusiast [ɪnˈθuːzɪæst] N enthousiaste mf; **a jazz** etc **~** un fervent or passionné du jazz etc

enthusiastic [ɪnθuːzɪˈæstɪk] ADJ enthousiaste; **to be ~ about** être enthousiasmé(e) par

enthusiastically [ɪnθjuːzeˈæstɪklɪ] ADV avec enthousiasme

entice [ɪnˈtaɪs] VT attirer, séduire

enticing [ɪnˈtaɪsɪŋ] ADJ (person, offer) séduisant(e); (food) alléchant(e)

entire [ɪnˈtaɪəʳ] ADJ (tout) entier(-ère)

entirely [ɪnˈtaɪəlɪ] ADV entièrement, complètement

entirety [ɪnˈtaɪərətɪ] N: **in its ~** dans sa totalité

entitle [ɪnˈtaɪtl] VT (allow): **to ~ sb to do** donner (le) droit à qn de faire; **to ~ sb to sth** donner droit à qch à qn

entitled [ɪnˈtaɪtld] ADJ (book) intitulé(e); **to be ~ to do** avoir le droit de faire

entitlement [ɪnˈtaɪtlmənt] N droit m; **~ to** (benefit, leave) droit à

entity [ˈɛntɪtɪ] N entité f

entourage [ˈɔntuɾɑːʒ] N entourage m

entrails [ˈɛntreɪlz] NPL entrailles fpl

★**entrance** N [ˈɛntrəns] entrée f; **where's the ~?** où est l'entrée?; **to gain ~ to** (university etc) être admis à ▸ VT [ɛnˈtrɑːns] enchanter, ravir

entrance examination N examen m d'entrée or d'admission

entrance fee N (to museum etc) prix m d'entrée; (to join club etc) droit m d'inscription

entrance ramp N (US Aut) bretelle f d'accès

entrancing [ɪnˈtrɑːnsɪŋ] ADJ enchanteur(-eresse), ravissant(e)

entrant [ˈɛntrənt] N (in race etc) participant(e), concurrent(e); (BRIT: in exam) candidat(e)

entreat [ɛnˈtriːt] VT supplier

entreaty [ɛnˈtriːtɪ] N supplication f, prière f

entrée [ˈɔntreɪ] N (Culin) entrée f

entrenched [ɪnˈtrɛntʃt] ADJ retranché(e)

entrepreneur [ɔntrəprəˈnəːʳ] N entrepreneur m

entrepreneurial [ɔntrəprəˈnəːrɪəl] ADJ animé(e) d'un esprit d'entreprise

entrepreneurship [ɔntrəprəˈnəːʃɪp] N esprit m d'entreprise

entrust [ɪnˈtrʌst] VT: **to ~ sth to** confier qch à

★**entry** [ˈɛntrɪ] N entrée f; (in register, diary) inscription f; (in ledger) écriture f; **"no ~"** « défense d'entrer », « entrée interdite »; (Aut) « sens interdit »; **single/double ~ book-keeping** comptabilité f en partie simple/double

entry form N feuille f d'inscription

entry phone N (BRIT) interphone m (à l'entrée d'un immeuble)

entwine [ɪnˈtwaɪn] VT entrelacer

E-number [ˈiːnʌmbəʳ] N additif m (alimentaire)

enumerate [ɪˈnjuːməreɪt] VT énumérer

enunciate [ɪˈnʌnsɪeɪt] VT énoncer; prononcer

envelop [ɪnˈvɛləp] VT envelopper

envelope [ˈɛnvələup] N enveloppe f

enviable [ˈɛnvɪəbl] ADJ enviable

envious [ˈɛnvɪəs] ADJ envieux(-euse)

★**environment** [ɪnˈvaɪənmənt] N (social, moral) milieu m; (natural world): **the ~** l'environnement m; **Department of the E~** (BRIT) ministère de l'Équipement et de l'Aménagement du territoire

★**environmental** [ɪnvaɪənˈmɛntl] ADJ (of surroundings) du milieu; (issue, disaster) écologique; **~ studies** (in school etc) écologie f

environmentalist [ɪnvaɪənˈmɛntəlɪst] N écologiste mf

environmentally [ɪnvaɪənˈmɛntəlɪ] ADV: **~ sound/ friendly** qui ne nuit pas à l'environnement

Environmental Protection Agency N (US) ≈ ministère m de l'Environnement

envisage [ɪnˈvɪzɪdʒ] VT (imagine) envisager; (foresee) prévoir

envision [ɪnˈvɪʒən] VT envisager, concevoir

envoy [ˈɛnvɔɪ] N envoyé(e); (diplomat) ministre m plénipotentiaire

envy [ˈɛnvɪ] N envie f ▸ VT envier; **to ~ sb sth** envier qch à qn

enzyme [ˈɛnzaɪm] N enzyme m

EPA N ABBR (US) = **Environmental Protection Agency**

ephemeral [ɪˈfɛmərəl] ADJ éphémère

epic [ˈɛpɪk] N épopée f ▸ ADJ épique

epicentre, (US) **epicenter** [ˈɛpɪsɛntəʳ] N épicentre m

epidemic [ɛpɪˈdɛmɪk] N épidémie f

epidural [ɛpɪˈdjuərəl] N péridurale f

epilepsy [ˈɛpɪlɛpsɪ] N épilepsie f

epileptic [ɛpɪˈlɛptɪk] ADJ, N épileptique mf

epileptic fit N crise f d'épilepsie

epilogue [ˈɛpɪlɔg] N épilogue m

Epiphany [ɪˈpɪfənɪ] N Épiphanie f

episcopal [ɪˈpɪskəpl] ADJ épiscopal(e)

episode [ˈɛpɪsəud] N épisode m

episodic [ɛpɪˈsɔdɪk] ADJ épisodique

epistle [ɪˈpɪsl] N épître f

epitaph [ˈɛpɪtɑːf] N épitaphe f

epithet [ˈɛpɪθɛt] N épithète f

epitome [ɪˈpɪtəmɪ] N (fig) quintessence f, type m

epitomize [ɪˈpɪtəmaɪz] VT (fig) illustrer, incarner

epoch [ˈiːpɔk] N époque f, ère f

epoch-making [ˈiːpɔkmeɪkɪŋ] ADJ qui fait époque

eponymous [ɪˈpɔnɪməs] ADJ de ce or du même nom, éponyme

★**equal** [ˈiːkwl] ADJ égal(e); **~ to** (task) à la hauteur de; **~ to doing** de taille à or capable de faire ▸ N égal(e) ▸ VT égaler

Equal and Human Rights Commission, (US) **Equal Employment Opportunity Commission** N commission pour la non discrimination dans l'emploi

equality [iːˈkwɔlɪtɪ] N égalité f

equalize [ˈiːkwəlaɪz] VT, VI (Sport) égaliser

equalizer [ˈiːkwəlaɪzəʳ] N (Sport) but égalisateur

equally [ˈiːkwəlɪ] ADV également; (share) en parts égales; (treat) de la même façon; (pay) autant; (just as) tout aussi; **they are ~ clever** ils sont tout aussi intelligents

equal sign, equals sign N signe m d'égalité

equanimity [ɛkwəˈnɪmɪtɪ] N égalité f d'humeur

equate [ɪˈkweɪt] VT: **to ~ sth with** comparer qch à; assimiler qch à; **to ~ sth to** mettre qch en équation avec; égaler qch à
▶ **equate to** VT FUS (equal) être égal à; (mean) signifier

equation [ɪˈkweɪʃən] N (Math) équation f

equator [ɪˈkweɪtəʳ] N équateur m

Equatorial Guinea [ɛkwəˈtɔːrɪəl-] N Guinée équatoriale

equestrian [ɪˈkwɛstrɪən] ADJ équestre ▶ N écuyer(-ère), cavalier(-ère)

equilibrium [iːkwɪˈlɪbrɪəm] N équilibre m

equine [ˈɛkwaɪn] ADJ équin(e)

equinox [ˈiːkwɪnɔks] N équinoxe m

equip [ɪˈkwɪp] VT équiper; **to ~ sb/sth with** équiper ou munir qn/qch de; **he is well equipped for the job** il a les compétences or les qualités requises pour ce travail

★**equipment** [ɪˈkwɪpmənt] N équipement m; (electrical etc) appareillage m, installation f

equitable [ˈɛkwɪtəbl] ADJ équitable

equities [ˈɛkwɪtɪz] NPL (BRIT Comm) actions cotées en Bourse

equity [ˈɛkwɪtɪ] N équité f

equity capital N capitaux mpl propres

★**equivalent** [ɪˈkwɪvələnt] ADJ équivalent(e); **to be ~ to** équivaloir à, être équivalent(e) à ▶ N équivalent m

equivocal [ɪˈkwɪvəkl] ADJ équivoque; (open to suspicion) douteux(-euse)

equivocate [ɪˈkwɪvəkeɪt] VI user de faux-fuyants; éviter de répondre

equivocation [ɪkwɪvəˈkeɪʃən] N équivoque f

ER ABBR (BRIT: = Elizabeth Regina) la reine Élisabeth; (US Med: = emergency room) urgences fpl

ERA N ABBR (US Pol: = Equal Rights Amendment) amendement sur l'égalité des droits des femmes

era [ˈɪərə] N ère f, époque f

eradicate [ɪˈrædɪkeɪt] VT éliminer

eradication [ɪrædɪˈkeɪʃən] N éradication f

erase [ɪˈreɪz] VT effacer

eraser [ɪˈreɪzəʳ] N gomme f

e-reader, eReader [ˈiːriːdəʳ] N liseuse f

erect [ɪˈrɛkt] ADJ droit(e) ▶ VT construire; (monument) ériger, élever; (tent etc) dresser

erection [ɪˈrɛkʃən] N (Physiol) érection f; (of building) construction f; (of machinery etc) installation f

ergonomics [əːɡəˈnɔmɪks] N ergonomie f

ERISA N ABBR (US: = Employee Retirement Income Security Act) loi sur les pensions de retraite

Eritrea [ɛrɪˈtreɪə] N Érythrée f

ERM N ABBR (= Exchange Rate Mechanism) mécanisme m des taux de change

ermine [ˈəːmɪn] N hermine f

ERNIE [ˈəːnɪ] N ABBR (BRIT: = Electronic Random Number Indicator Equipment) ordinateur servant au tirage des bons à lots gagnants

erode [ɪˈrəud] VT éroder; (metal) ronger

erogenous zone [ɪˈrɔdʒənəs-] N zone f érogène

erosion [ɪˈrəuʒən] N érosion f

erotic [ɪˈrɔtɪk] ADJ érotique

erotica [ɪˈrɔtɪkə] NPL art m érotique

eroticism [ɪˈrɔtɪsɪzəm] N érotisme m

err [əːʳ] VI se tromper; (Rel) pécher

errand [ˈɛrənd] N course f, commission f; **to run errands** faire des courses; **~ of mercy** mission f de charité, acte m charitable

errand boy N garçon m de courses

errant [ˈɛrənt] ADJ (unfaithful: husband) infidèle; (son, child) délinquant(e)

erratic [ɪˈrætɪk] ADJ irrégulier(-ière), inconstant(e)

erroneous [ɪˈrəunɪəs] ADJ erroné(e)

erroneously [ɪˈrəunɪəslɪ] ADV erronément

★**error** [ˈɛrəʳ] N erreur f; **typing/spelling ~** faute f de frappe/d'orthographe; **in ~** par erreur, par méprise; **errors and omissions excepted** sauf erreur ou omission

error message N (Comput) message m d'erreur

erstwhile [ˈəːstwaɪl] ADJ précédent(e), d'autrefois

erudite [ˈɛrjudaɪt] ADJ savant(e)

erupt [ɪˈrʌpt] VI entrer en éruption; (fig) éclater, exploser

eruption [ɪˈrʌpʃən] N éruption f; (of anger, violence) explosion f

ESA N ABBR (= European Space Agency) ASE f (= Agence spatiale européenne)

escalate [ˈɛskəleɪt] VI s'intensifier; (costs) monter en flèche

escalation [ɛskəˈleɪʃən] N escalade f

escalation clause N clause f d'indexation

escalator [ˈɛskəleɪtəʳ] N escalier roulant

escapade [ɛskəˈpeɪd] N fredaine f; équipée f

★**escape** [ɪˈskeɪp] N évasion f, fuite f; (of gas etc) fuite; (Tech) échappement m ▶ VI s'échapper, fuir; (from jail) s'évader; (fig) s'en tirer, en réchapper; (leak) fuir, s'échapper; **to ~ from** (person) échapper à; (place) s'échapper de; (fig) fuir; **to ~ to** (another place) fuir à, s'enfuir à; **to ~ to safety** se réfugier dans or gagner un endroit sûr ▶ VT échapper à; **to ~ notice** passer inaperçu(e); **his name escapes me** son nom m'échappe

escape artist N virtuose mf de l'évasion

escape clause N clause f dérogatoire

escapee [ɪskeɪˈpiː] N évadé(e)

escape key N (Comput) touche f d'échappement

escape route N (from fire) issue f de secours; (of prisoners etc) voie empruntée pour s'échapper

escapism [ɪˈskeɪpɪzəm] N évasion f (fig)

escapist [ɪˈskeɪpɪst] ADJ (literature) d'évasion ▶ N personne f qui se réfugie hors de la réalité

escapologist [ɛskəˈpɔlədʒɪst] N (BRIT) = **escape artist**

escarpment [ɪsˈkɑːpmənt] N escarpement m

eschew [ɪsˈtʃuː] VT éviter

escort VT [ɪˈskɔːt] escorter ▸ N [ˈeskɔːt] (Mil) escorte f; (to dance etc): her ~ son compagnon or cavalier; his ~ sa compagne

escort agency N bureau m d'hôtesses

Eskimo [ˈeskɪməʊ] (often !) ADJ esquimau(de), eskimo ▸ N Esquimau(de); (Ling) esquimau m

ESL N ABBR (Scol) = English as a Second Language

esophagus [iːˈsɒfəɡəs] N (US) = oesophagus

esoteric [ɛsəˈtɛrɪk] ADJ ésotérique

ESP N ABBR = extrasensory perception; (Scol) = English for Special Purposes

esp. ABBR = especially

★**especially** [ɪˈspeʃəlɪ] ADV (particularly) particulièrement; (above all) surtout

espionage [ˈɛspɪənɑːʒ] N espionnage m

esplanade [ɛspləˈneɪd] N esplanade f

espouse [ɪˈspaʊz] VT épouser, embrasser

espresso [ɛˈspresəʊ] N expresso m

Esquire [ɪˈskwaɪəʳ] N (BRIT: abbr Esq.): J. Brown, ~ Monsieur J. Brown

essay [ˈeseɪ] N (Scol) dissertation f; (Literature) essai m; (attempt) tentative f

essence [ˈɛsns] N essence f; (Culin) extrait m; in ~ en substance; speed is of the ~ l'essentiel, c'est la rapidité

★**essential** [ɪˈsenʃl] ADJ essentiel(le); (basic) fondamental(e); it is ~ that il est essentiel or primordial que ■ **essentials** NPL éléments essentiels

essentially [ɪˈsenʃəlɪ] ADV essentiellement

EST ABBR (US: = Eastern Standard Time) heure d'hiver de New York

est. ABBR = established; estimate(d)

establish [ɪˈstæblɪʃ] VT établir; (business) fonder, créer; (one's power etc) asseoir, affermir

established [ɪˈstæblɪʃt] ADJ bien établi(e)

establishment [ɪˈstæblɪʃmənt] N établissement m; (founding) création f; (institution) établissement; the E~ les pouvoirs établis; l'ordre établi

estate [ɪˈsteɪt] N (land) domaine m, propriété f; (Law) biens mpl, succession f; (BRIT: also: **housing estate**) lotissement m

estate agency N (BRIT) agence immobilière

estate agent N (BRIT) agent immobilier

estate car N (BRIT) break m

esteem [ɪˈstiːm] N estime f; to hold sb in high ~ tenir qn en haute estime ▸ VT estimer; apprécier

esthetic [ɪsˈθɛtɪk] ADJ (US) = aesthetic

★**estimate** N [ˈestɪmət] estimation f; (Comm) devis m; to give sb an ~ of faire or donner un devis à qn pour; at a rough ~ approximativement ▸ VT [ˈestɪmeɪt] estimer ▸ VI (BRIT Comm): **to ~ for** estimer, faire une estimation de; (bid for) faire un devis pour

estimated [ˈestɪmeɪtɪd] ADJ (quantity, value) estimé(e); there are an ~ 90,000 gangsters in the country on estime à 90,000 le nombre de malfaiteurs dans le pays

estimation [estɪˈmeɪʃən] N opinion f; estime f; in my ~ à mon avis, selon moi

Estonia [ɛˈstəʊnɪə] N Estonie f

Estonian [ɛˈstəʊnɪən] ADJ estonien(ne) ▸ N Estonien(ne); (Ling) estonien m

estranged [ɪsˈtreɪndʒd] ADJ (couple) séparé(e); (husband, wife) dont on s'est séparé(e)

estrangement [ɪsˈtreɪndʒmənt] N (from wife, family) séparation f

estrogen [ˈiːstrəudʒən] N (US) = oestrogen

estuary [ˈestjʊərɪ] N estuaire m

ET N ABBR (BRIT: = Employment Training) formation professionnelle pour les demandeurs d'emploi ▸ ABBR (US: = Eastern Time) heure de New York

ETA N ABBR (= estimated time of arrival) HPA f (= heure probable d'arrivée)

e-tailer [ˈiːteɪləʳ] N détaillant(e) électronique

et al. ABBR (= et alii) et coll

★**etc** ABBR (= et cetera) etc

etch [ɛtʃ] VT graver à l'eau forte

etching [ˈetʃɪŋ] N eau-forte f

ETD N ABBR (= estimated time of departure) HPD f (= heure probable de départ)

eternal [ɪˈtəːnl] ADJ éternel(le)

eternity [ɪˈtəːnɪtɪ] N éternité f

ethanol [ˈeθənɒl] N alcool m éthylique

ether [ˈiːθəʳ] N éther m

ethereal [ɪˈθɪərɪəl] ADJ éthéré(e)

Ethernet® [ˈiːθənet] N Ethernet® m

ethical [ˈeθɪkl] ADJ (moral: aspect, consideration) moral(e); (morally acceptable) éthique; ~ investment placements mpl éthiques

ethically [ˈeθɪklɪ] ADV (dubious, satisfactory) d'un point de vue éthique; (behave, invest) conformément à l'éthique

ethics [ˈeθɪks] N éthique f ▸ NPL moralité f

Ethiopia [iːθɪˈəʊpɪə] N Éthiopie f

Ethiopian [iːθɪˈəʊpɪən] ADJ éthiopien(ne) ▸ N Éthiopien(ne)

★**ethnic** [ˈeθnɪk] ADJ ethnique; (clothes, food) folklorique, exotique, propre aux minorités ethniques non-occidentales

ethnic cleansing [-ˈklenzɪŋ] N purification f ethnique

ethnicity [eθˈnɪsɪtɪ] N ethnicité f

ethnic minority N minorité f ethnique

ethnology [eθˈnɒlədʒɪ] N ethnologie f

ethos [ˈiːθɒs] N (système m de) valeurs fpl

e-ticket [ˈiːtɪkɪt] N billet m électronique

etiquette [ˈetɪket] N convenances fpl, étiquette f

ETV N ABBR (US: = Educational Television) télévision scolaire

etymology [etɪˈmɒlədʒɪ] N étymologie f

EU N ABBR (= European Union) UE f

eucalyptus [juːkəˈlɪptəs] N eucalyptus m

eugenics [juːˈdʒenɪks] N eugénisme m

eulogy [ˈjuːlədʒɪ] N éloge m

euphemism [ˈjuːfəmɪzəm] N euphémisme m

euphemistic [juːfəˈmɪstɪk] ADJ euphémique

euphoria [juːˈfɔːrɪə] N euphorie f

euphoric [juːˈfɔrɪk] ADJ euphorique

Eurasia [juəˈreɪʃə] N Eurasie f

Eurasian [juəˈreɪʃən] ADJ eurasien(ne); (continent) eurasiatique ▸ N Eurasien(ne)

Euratom [juəˈrætəm] N ABBR (= European Atomic Energy Community) EURATOM f

eureka [juˈriːkə] EXCL eurêka

★**euro** [ˈjuərəu] N (*currency*) euro *m*

Euro- [ˈjuərəu] PREFIX euro-

Eurocrat [ˈjuərəukræt] N eurocrate *mf*

Euroland [ˈjuərəulænd] N Euroland *m*

★**Europe** [ˈjuərəp] N Europe *f*

★**European** [juərəˈpiːən] ADJ européen(ne) ▶ N Européen(ne)

European Community N Communauté européenne

European Court of Justice N Cour *f* de Justice de la CEE

European Union N Union européenne

Euro-sceptic [ˈjuərəuskɛptɪk] N eurosceptique *mf*

Eurostar® [ˈjuərəustɑːʳ] N Eurostar® *m*

eurozone [ˈjuərəuzəun] N zone *f* euro

euthanasia [juːθəˈneɪzɪə] N euthanasie *f*

euthanize [ˈjuːθənaɪz] VT euthanasier

evacuate [ɪˈvækjueɪt] VT évacuer

evacuation [ɪvækjuˈeɪʃən] N évacuation *f*

evacuee [ɪvækjuˈiː] N évacué(e)

evade [ɪˈveɪd] VT échapper à; (*question etc*) éluder; (*duties*) se dérober à

evaluate [ɪˈvæljueɪt] VT évaluer

evaluation [ɪvæljuˈeɪʃən] N évaluation *f*

evangelical [iːvænˈdʒɛlɪkl] ADJ (*Christian, group*) évangélique; (*zeal, fervour*) fanatique

evangelist [ɪˈvændʒəlɪst] N évangéliste *m*

evangelize [ɪˈvændʒəlaɪz] VT évangéliser, prêcher l'Évangile à

evaporate [ɪˈvæpəreɪt] VI s'évaporer; (*fig: hopes, fear*) s'envoler; (: *anger*) se dissiper ▶ VT faire évaporer

evaporated milk [ɪˈvæpəreɪtɪd-] N lait condensé (non sucré)

evaporation [ɪvæpəˈreɪʃən] N évaporation *f*

evasion [ɪˈveɪʒən] N dérobade *f*; (*excuse*) fauxfuyant *m*

evasive [ɪˈveɪsɪv] ADJ évasif(-ive)

eve [iːv] N: **on the ~ of** à la veille de

★**even** [ˈiːvn] ADJ (*level, smooth*) régulier(-ière); (*equal*) égal(e); (*number*) pair(e); **to break ~** s'y retrouver, équilibrer ses comptes; **to get ~ with sb** prendre sa revanche sur qn ▶ ADV même; **~ if** même si + *indic*; **~ though** quand (bien) même + *cond*, alors même que + *cond*; **~ more** encore plus; **~ faster** encore plus vite; **~ so** quand même; **not ~** pas même; **~ he was there** même lui était là; **~ on Sundays** même le dimanche
▶ **even out** VI s'égaliser

even-handed [iːvnˈhændɪd] ADJ équitable

★**evening** [ˈiːvnɪŋ] N soir *m*; (*as duration, event*) soirée *f*; **in the ~** le soir; **this ~** ce soir; **tomorrow/yesterday ~** demain/hier soir

evening class N cours *m* du soir

evening dress N (*man's*) tenue *f* de soirée, smoking *m*; (*woman's*) robe *f* de soirée

evenly [ˈiːvnlɪ] ADV uniformément, également; (*space*) régulièrement

evensong [ˈiːvnsɔŋ] N office *m* du soir

★**event** [ɪˈvɛnt] N événement *m*; (*Sport*) épreuve *f*; **in the course of events** par la suite; **in the ~ of** en cas de; **in the ~** en réalité, en fait; **at all events**, (BRIT) **in any ~** en tout cas, de toute manière

eventful [ɪˈvɛntful] ADJ mouvementé(e)

eventing [ɪˈvɛntɪŋ] N (*Horse-Riding*) concours complet (*équitation*)

eventual [ɪˈvɛntʃuəl] ADJ final(e)

eventuality [ɪvɛntʃuˈælɪtɪ] N possibilité *f*, éventualité *f*

★**eventually** [ɪˈvɛntʃuəlɪ] ADV finalement

★**ever** [ˈɛvəʳ] ADV jamais; (*at all times*) toujours; **why ~ not?** mais enfin, pourquoi pas ?; **the best ~** le meilleur qu'on ait jamais vu; **have you ~ seen it?** l'as-tu déjà vu ?, as-tu eu l'occasion or t'est-il arrivé de le voir ?; **did you ~ meet him?** est-ce qu'il vous est arrivé de le rencontrer ?; **have you ~ been there?** y êtes-vous déjà allé ?; **for ~** pour toujours; **hardly ~** ne ... presque jamais; **~ since** (*as adv*) depuis; (*as conj*) depuis que; **~ so pretty** si joli; **thank you ~ so much** merci mille fois

Everest [ˈɛvərɪst] N (*also:* **Mount Everest**) le mont Everest, l'Everest *m*

evergreen [ˈɛvəgriːn] N arbre *m* à feuilles persistantes

everlasting [ɛvəˈlɑːstɪŋ] ADJ éternel(le)

---

every [ˈɛvrɪ]

ADJ 1 (*each*) chaque; **every one of them** tous (sans exception); **every shop in town was closed** tous les magasins en ville étaient fermés

2 (*all possible*) tous (toutes) les; **I gave you every assistance** j'ai fait tout mon possible pour vous aider; **I have every confidence in him** j'ai entièrement *or* pleinement confiance en lui; **we wish you every success** nous vous souhaitons beaucoup de succès

3 (*showing recurrence*) tous les; **every day** tous les jours, chaque jour; **every other car** une voiture sur deux; **every other/third day** tous les deux/trois jours; **every now and then** de temps en temps

---

★**everybody** PRON = **everyone**

everyday [ˈɛvrɪdeɪ] ADJ (*expression*) courant(e), d'usage courant; (*use*) courant; (*clothes, life*) de tous les jours; (*occurrence, problem*) quotidien(ne)

★**everyone** [ˈɛvrɪwʌn] PRON tout le monde, tous *pl*; **~ knows about it** tout le monde le sait; **~ else** tous les autres

★**everything** [ˈɛvrɪθɪŋ] PRON tout; **~ is ready** tout est prêt; **he did ~ possible** il a fait tout son possible

★**everywhere** [ˈɛvrɪwɛəʳ] ADV partout; **~ you go you meet ...** où qu'on aille on rencontre ...

evict [ɪˈvɪkt] VT expulser

eviction [ɪˈvɪkʃən] N expulsion *f*

eviction notice N préavis *m* d'expulsion

evidence [ˈɛvɪdns] N (*proof*) preuve(s) *f(pl)*; (*of witness*) témoignage *m*; (*sign*): **to show ~ of** donner des signes de; **to give ~** témoigner, déposer; **in ~** (*obvious*) en évidence; en vue

evidence se traduit rarement par *évidence*.

evident [ˈɛvɪdnt] ADJ évident(e)

evidently [ˈɛvɪdntlɪ] ADV de toute évidence; (*apparently*) apparemment

evil ['iːvl] ADJ mauvais(e) ▸ N mal m

evince [ɪ'vɪns] VT manifester

evocation [iːvə'keɪʃən] N évocation f

evocative [ɪ'vɒkətɪv] ADJ évocateur(-trice)

evoke [ɪ'vəuk] VT évoquer; (admiration) susciter

evolution [iːvə'luːʃən] N évolution f

evolutionary [iːvə'luːʃənrɪ] ADJ (process) d'évolution; (theory) de l'évolution; **~ change** évolution f

evolve [ɪ'vɒlv] VT élaborer ▸ VI évoluer, se transformer

ewe [juː] N brebis f

ex [ɛks] N (inf): **my ex** mon ex

ex- [ɛks] PREFIX (former: husband, president etc) ex-; (out of): **the price ex-works** le prix départ usine

exacerbate [ɪg'zæsəbeɪt] VT (pain) exacerber, accentuer; (fig) aggraver

★**exact** [ɪg'zækt] ADJ exact(e) ▸ VT: **to ~ sth (from)** (signature, confession) extorquer qch (à); (apology) exiger qch (de)

exacting [ɪg'zæktɪŋ] ADJ exigeant(e); (work) fatigant(e)

exactitude [ɪg'zæktɪtjuːd] N exactitude f, précision f

★**exactly** [ɪg'zæktlɪ] ADV exactement; **~!** parfaitement !, précisément !

exaggerate [ɪg'zædʒəreɪt] VT, VI exagérer

exaggeration [ɪgzædʒə'reɪʃən] N exagération f

exalted [ɪg'zɔːltɪd] ADJ (rank) élevé(e); (person) haut placé(e); (elated) exalté(e)

★**exam** [ɪg'zæm] N ABBR (Scol) = **examination**

examination [ɪgzæmɪ'neɪʃən] N (Scol, Med) examen m; **to take** or **sit an ~** (BRIT) passer un examen; **the matter is under ~** la question est à l'examen

examine [ɪg'zæmɪn] VT (gen) examiner; (Scol, Law: person) interroger; (inspect: machine, premises) inspecter; (: passport) contrôler; (: luggage) fouiller

examiner [ɪg'zæmɪnəʳ] N examinateur(-trice)

★**example** [ɪg'zɑːmpl] N exemple m; **for ~** par exemple; **to set a good/bad ~** donner le bon/mauvais exemple

exasperate [ɪg'zɑːspəreɪt] VT exaspérer, agacer

exasperated [ɪg'zɑːspəreɪtɪd] ADJ exaspéré(e)

exasperating [ɪg'zɑːspəreɪtɪŋ] ADJ exaspérant(e)

exasperation [ɪgzɑːspə'reɪʃən] N exaspération f, irritation f

excavate ['ɛkskəveɪt] VT (site) fouiller, excaver; (object) mettre au jour

excavation [ɛkskə'veɪʃən] N excavation f

excavator ['ɛkskəveɪtəʳ] N excavateur m, excavatrice f

exceed [ɪk'siːd] VT dépasser; (one's powers) outrepasser

exceedingly [ɪk'siːdɪŋlɪ] ADV extrêmement

excel [ɪk'sɛl] VI exceller ▸ VT surpasser; **to ~ o.s.** se surpasser

excellence ['ɛksələns] N excellence f

Excellency ['ɛksələnsɪ] N: **His ~** son Excellence f

★**excellent** ['ɛksələnt] ADJ excellent(e)

★**except** [ɪk'sɛpt] PREP (also: **except for, excepting**) sauf, excepté, à l'exception de; **~ if/when** sauf si/

quand; **~ that** excepté que, si ce n'est que ▸ VT excepter

exception [ɪk'sɛpʃən] N exception f; **to take ~ to** s'offusquer de; **with the ~ of** à l'exception de

exceptional [ɪk'sɛpʃənl] ADJ exceptionnel(le)

exceptionally [ɪk'sɛpʃənəlɪ] ADV exceptionnellement

excerpt ['ɛksəːpt] N extrait m

excess [ɪk'sɛs] N excès m; **in ~ of** plus de

excess baggage N excédent m de bagages

excess fare N supplément m

excessive [ɪk'sɛsɪv] ADJ excessif(-ive)

excessively [ɪk'sɛsɪvlɪ] ADV (long, large) excessivement; (drink) avec excès

excess supply N suroffre f, offre f excédentaire

★**exchange** [ɪks'tʃeɪndʒ] N échange m; (also: **telephone exchange**) central m; **in ~ for** en échange de; **foreign ~** (Comm) change m ▸ VT: **to ~ (for)** échanger (contre); **could I ~ this, please?** est-ce que je peux échanger ceci, s'il vous plaît ?

exchange control N contrôle m des changes

exchange market N marché m des changes

★**exchange rate** N taux m de change

Exchequer [ɪks'tʃɛkəʳ] N (BRIT): **the ~** l'Échiquier m, ≈ le ministère m des Finances

excisable [ɪk'saɪzəbl] ADJ taxable

excise N ['ɛksaɪz] taxe f ▸ VT [ɛk'saɪz] exciser

excise duties NPL impôts indirects

excitable [ɪk'saɪtəbl] ADJ excitable, nerveux(-euse)

excite [ɪk'saɪt] VT exciter

★**excited** [ɪk'saɪtɪd] ADJ (tout (toute)) excité(e); **to get ~** s'exciter

excitement [ɪk'saɪtmənt] N excitation f

★**exciting** [ɪk'saɪtɪŋ] ADJ passionnant(e)

excl. ABBR = **excluding; exclusive (of)**

exclaim [ɪk'skleɪm] VI s'exclamer

exclamation [ɛksklə'meɪʃən] N exclamation f

exclamation mark, (US) **exclamation point** N point m d'exclamation

exclude [ɪk'skluːd] VT exclure

excluding [ɪk'skluːdɪŋ] PREP: **~ VAT** la TVA non comprise

exclusion [ɪk'skluːʒən] N exclusion f; **to the ~ of** à l'exclusion de

exclusion clause N clause f d'exclusion

exclusion zone N zone interdite

exclusive [ɪk'skluːsɪv] ADJ exclusif(-ive); (club, district) sélect(e); (item of news) en exclusivité; **~ rights** (Comm) exclusivité f ▸ ADV (Comm) exclusivement, non inclus; **~ of VAT** TVA non comprise; **~ of postage** (les) frais de poste non compris; **from 1st to 15th March ~** du 1er au 15 mars exclusivement or exclu

exclusively [ɪk'skluːsɪvlɪ] ADV exclusivement

excommunicate [ɛkskə'mjuːnɪkeɪt] VT excommunier

excrement ['ɛkskrəmənt] N excrément m

excruciating [ɪk'skruːʃɪeɪtɪŋ] ADJ (pain) atroce, déchirant(e); (embarrassing) pénible

excursion [ɪk'skəːʃən] N excursion f

excursion ticket N billet m tarif excursion

excusable [ɪkˈskjuːzəbl] ADJ excusable

★**excuse** N [ɪkˈskjuːs] excuse f; **to make excuses for sb** trouver des excuses à qn ▸ VT [ɪkˈskjuːz] (forgive) excuser; (justify) excuser, justifier; **to ~ sb from** (activity) dispenser qn de; **~ me!** excusez-moi!, pardon!; **now if you will ~ me, ...** maintenant, si vous (le) permettez ...; **to ~ o.s. for sth/for doing sth** s'excuser de/d'avoir fait qch

ex-directory [ˈɛksdɪˈrɛktərɪ] ADJ (BRIT) sur la liste rouge

executable [ˈɛksɪkjuːtəbl] ADJ (Comput) exécutable

execute [ˈɛksɪkjuːt] VT exécuter

execution [ɛksɪˈkjuːʃən] N exécution f

executioner [ɛksɪˈkjuːʃənəʳ] N bourreau m

executive [ɪgˈzɛkjutɪv] N (person) cadre m; (managing group) bureau m; (Pol) exécutif m ▸ ADJ exécutif(-ive); (position, job) de cadre; (secretary) de direction; (offices) de la direction; (car, plane) de fonction

executive director N administrateur(-trice)

executor [ɪgˈzɛkjutəʳ] N exécuteur(-trice) testamentaire

exemplary [ɪgˈzɛmplərɪ] ADJ exemplaire

exemplify [ɪgˈzɛmplɪfaɪ] VT illustrer

exempt [ɪgˈzɛmpt] ADJ: **~ from** exempté(e) or dispensé(e) de ▸ VT: **to ~ sb from** exempter or dispenser qn de

exemption [ɪgˈzɛmpʃən] N exemption f, dispense f

★**exercise** [ˈɛksəsaɪz] N exercice m ▸ VT exercer; (patience etc) faire preuve de; (dog) promener ▸ VI (also: **to take exercise**) prendre de l'exercice

exercise bike N vélo m d'appartement

exercise book N cahier m

exert [ɪgˈzəːt] VT exercer, employer; (strength, force) employer; **to ~ o.s.** se dépenser

exertion [ɪgˈzəːʃən] N effort m

exfoliate [ɛksˈfəulɪeɪt] VT exfolier

ex gratia [ɛksˈɡreɪʃə] ADJ: **~ payment** gratification f

exhale [ɛksˈheɪl] VT (breathe out) expirer; exhaler ▸ VI expirer

exhaust [ɪgˈzɔːst] N (also: **exhaust fumes**) gaz mpl d'échappement; (also: **exhaust pipe**) tuyau m d'échappement ▸ VT épuiser; **to ~ o.s.** s'épuiser

★**exhausted** [ɪgˈzɔːstɪd] ADJ épuisé(e)

exhausting [ɪgˈzɔːstɪŋ] ADJ épuisant(e)

exhaustion [ɪgˈzɔːstʃən] N épuisement m; **nervous ~** fatigue nerveuse

exhaustive [ɪgˈzɔːstɪv] ADJ très complet(-ète)

exhibit [ɪgˈzɪbɪt] N (Art) objet exposé, pièce exposée; (Law) pièce à conviction ▸ VT (Art) exposer; (courage, skill) faire preuve de

★**exhibition** [ɛksɪˈbɪʃən] N exposition f; **~ of temper** manifestation f de colère

exhibitionist [ɛksɪˈbɪʃənɪst] N exhibitionniste mf

exhibitor [ɪgˈzɪbɪtəʳ] N exposant(e)

exhilarated [ɪgˈzɪləreɪtɪd] ADJ euphorique

exhilarating [ɪgˈzɪləreɪtɪŋ] ADJ grisant(e), stimulant(e)

exhilaration [ɪgzɪləˈreɪʃən] N euphorie f, ivresse f

exhort [ɪgˈzɔːt] VT exhorter

exhumation [ɛksjuːˈmeɪʃən] N exhumation f

exhume [ɛksˈhjuːm] VT exhumer

ex-husband [ɛksˈhʌzbənd] N ex-mari m

exile [ˈɛksaɪl] N exil m; (person) exilé(e); **in ~** en exil ▸ VT exiler

exist [ɪgˈzɪst] VI exister

existence [ɪgˈzɪstəns] N existence f; **to be in ~** exister

existentialism [ɛgzɪsˈtɛnʃəlɪzəm] N existentialisme m

existing [ɪgˈzɪstɪŋ] ADJ (laws) existant(e); (system, regime) actuel(le)

★**exit** [ˈɛksɪt] N sortie f; **where's the ~?** où est la sortie? ▸ VI (Comput, Theat) sortir

exit poll N sondage m (fait à la sortie de l'isoloir)

exit ramp N (US Aut) bretelle f d'accès

exit visa N visa m de sortie

exodus [ˈɛksədəs] N exode m

ex officio [ˈɛksəˈfɪʃɪəu] ADJ, ADV d'office, de droit

exonerate [ɪgˈzɔnəreɪt] VT: **to ~ from** disculper de

exorbitant [ɪgˈzɔːbɪtnt] ADJ (price) exorbitant(e), excessif(-ive); (demands) exorbitant(e), démesuré(e)

exorcize [ˈɛksɔːsaɪz] VT exorciser

exotic [ɪgˈzɔtɪk] ADJ exotique

expand [ɪkˈspænd] VT (area) agrandir; (quantity) accroître; (influence etc) étendre ▸ VI (population, production) s'accroître; (trade, etc) se développer, s'accroître; (gas, metal) se dilater, dilater; **to ~ on** (notes, story etc) développer

expanse [ɪkˈspæns] N étendue f

expansion [ɪkˈspænʃən] N (territorial, economic) expansion f; (of trade, influence etc) développement m; (of production) accroissement m; (of population) croissance f; (of gas, metal) expansion, dilatation f

expansionism [ɪkˈspænʃənɪzəm] N expansionnisme m

expansionist [ɪkˈspænʃənɪst] ADJ expansionniste

expansive [ɪkˈspænsɪv] ADJ (area) étendu(e); (person, also Econ) expansif(-ive); **to be in ~ mood** être d'humeur joviale

expat [ɛksˈpæt] N (BRIT inf) expatrié(e)

expatriate N [ɛksˈpætrɪət] expatrié(e) ▸ VT [ɛksˈpætrɪeɪt] expatrier, exiler

★**expect** [ɪkˈspɛkt] VT (anticipate) s'attendre à, s'attendre à ce que + sub; (count on) compter sur, escompter; (hope for) espérer; (require) demander, exiger; (suppose) supposer; (await: also baby) attendre; **to ~ sb to do** (anticipate) s'attendre à ce que qn fasse; (demand) attendre de qn qu'il fasse; **to ~ to do sth** penser or compter faire qch, s'attendre à faire qch; **as expected** comme prévu ▸ VI: **to be expecting** (pregnant woman) être enceinte; **I ~ so** je crois que oui, je crois bien

expectancy [ɪkˈspɛktənsɪ] N attente f; **life ~** espérance f de vie

expectant [ɪkˈspɛktənt] ADJ qui attend (quelque chose); **~ mother** future maman

expectantly [ɪkˈspɛktntlɪ] ADV (look, listen) avec l'air d'attendre quelque chose

expectation [ɛkspɛkˈteɪʃən] N (hope) attente f, espérance(s) f(pl); (belief) attente; **in ~ of** dans l'attente de, en prévision de; **against** or **contrary**

to all ~(s) contre toute attente, contrairement à ce qu'on attendait; **to come** or **live up to sb's expectations** répondre à l'attente or aux espérances de qn

expedience [ɛkˈspiːdɪəns], **expediency** [ɛkˈspiːdɪənsɪ] N opportunité f; convenance f (du moment); **for the sake of ~** parce que c'est (or c'était) plus simple or plus commode

expedient [ɪkˈspiːdɪənt] ADJ indiqué(e), opportun(e), commode ▶ N expédient m

expedite [ˈɛkspɪdaɪt] VT hâter; expédier

expedition [ɛkspəˈdɪʃən] N expédition f

expeditionary force [ɛkspəˈdɪʃənrɪ-] N corps m expéditionnaire

expeditious [ɛkspəˈdɪʃəs] ADJ expéditif(-ive), prompt(e)

expel [ɪkˈspɛl] VT chasser, expulser; (Scol) renvoyer, exclure

expend [ɪkˈspɛnd] VT consacrer; (use up) dépenser

expendable [ɪkˈspɛndəbl] ADJ remplaçable

expenditure [ɪkˈspɛndɪtʃəʳ] N (act of spending) dépense f; (money spent) dépenses

expense [ɪkˈspɛns] N (high cost) coût m; (spending) dépense f, frais mpl; **to go to the ~ of** faire la dépense de; **at great/little ~** à grands/peu de frais; **at the ~ of** aux frais de; (fig) aux dépens de ∎ **expenses** NPL frais mpl; dépenses

expense account N (note f de) frais mpl

★**expensive** [ɪkˈspɛnsɪv] ADJ cher (chère), coûteux(-euse); **to be ~** coûter cher; **it's too ~** ça coûte trop cher; **~ tastes** goûts mpl de luxe

★**experience** [ɪkˈspɪərɪəns] N expérience f; **to know by ~** savoir par expérience ▶ VT connaître; (feeling) éprouver

experienced [ɪkˈspɪərɪənst] ADJ expérimenté(e)

experiment [ɪkˈspɛrɪmənt] N expérience f; **to perform** or **carry out an ~** faire une expérience; **as an ~** à titre d'expérience ▶ VI faire une expérience; **to ~ with** expérimenter

experimental [ɪkspɛrɪˈmɛntl] ADJ expérimental(e)

experimentation [ɪkspɛrɪmɛnˈteɪʃən] N expérimentation f

★**expert** [ˈɛkspəːt] ADJ expert(e); **to be ~ in** or **at doing sth** être spécialiste de qch; **~ witness** (Law) expert m ▶ N expert m; **an ~ on sth** un spécialiste de qch

expertise [ɛkspəːˈtiːz] N (grande) compétence

expertly [ˈɛkspəːtlɪ] ADV habilement

expire [ɪkˈspaɪəʳ] VI expirer

expiry [ɪkˈspaɪərɪ] N expiration f

expiry date N date f d'expiration; (on label) à utiliser avant …

★**explain** [ɪkˈspleɪn] VT expliquer
▶ **explain away** VT justifier, excuser

explanation [ɛkspləˈneɪʃən] N explication f; **to find an ~ for sth** trouver une explication à qch

explanatory [ɪkˈsplænətrɪ] ADJ explicatif(-ive)

expletive [ɪkˈspliːtɪv] N juron m

explicit [ɪkˈsplɪsɪt] ADJ explicite; (definite) formel(le)

★**explode** [ɪkˈspləud] VI exploser ▶ VT faire exploser; (fig: theory) démolir; **to ~ a myth** détruire un mythe

exploit N [ˈɛksplɔɪt] exploit m ▶ VT [ɪkˈsplɔɪt] exploiter

exploitation [ɛksplɔɪˈteɪʃən] N exploitation f

exploitative [ɪkˈsplɔɪtətɪv] ADJ (pej: relationship, behaviour) fondé(e) sur l'exploitation d'autrui

exploration [ɛkspləˈreɪʃən] N exploration f

exploratory [ɪkˈsplɔrətrɪ] ADJ (fig: talks) préliminaire; **~ operation** (Med) intervention f (à visée) exploratrice

explore [ɪkˈsplɔːʳ] VT explorer; (possibilities) étudier, examiner

explorer [ɪkˈsplɔːrəʳ] N explorateur(-trice)

★**explosion** [ɪkˈspləuʒən] N explosion f

explosive [ɪkˈspləusɪv] ADJ explosif(-ive) ▶ N explosif m

exponent [ɪkˈspəunənt] N (of school of thought etc) interprète m, représentant m; (Math) exposant m

exponential [ɛkspəˈnɛnʃəl] ADJ exponentiel(le)

exponentially [ɛkspəˈnɛnʃəlɪ] ADV de manière exponentielle

export VT [ɪkˈspɔːt] exporter ▶ N [ˈɛkspɔːt] exportation f ▶ CPD [ˈɛkspɔːt] d'exportation

exportation [ɛkspɔːˈteɪʃən] N exportation f

exporter [ɛkˈspɔːtəʳ] N exportateur m

export licence N licence f d'exportation

expose [ɪkˈspəuz] VT exposer; (unmask) démasquer, dévoiler; **to ~ o.s.** (Law) commettre un outrage à la pudeur

exposed [ɪkˈspəuzd] ADJ (land, house) exposé(e); (Elec: wire) à nu; (pipe, beam) apparent(e)

exposition [ɛkspəˈzɪʃən] N exposition f

exposure [ɪkˈspəuʒəʳ] N exposition f; (publicity) couverture f; (Phot: speed) (temps m de) pose f; (: shot) pose; **suffering from ~** (Med) souffrant des effets du froid et de l'épuisement; **to die of ~** (Med) mourir de froid

exposure meter N posemètre m

expound [ɪkˈspaund] VT exposer, expliquer

★**express** [ɪkˈsprɛs] ADJ (definite) formel(le), exprès(-esse); (BRIT: letter etc) exprès inv ▶ N (train) rapide m ▶ ADV (send) exprès ▶ VT exprimer; **to ~ o.s.** s'exprimer

★**expression** [ɪkˈsprɛʃən] N expression f

expressionism [ɪkˈsprɛʃənɪzəm] N expressionnisme m

expressive [ɪkˈsprɛsɪv] ADJ expressif(-ive)

expressly [ɪkˈsprɛslɪ] ADV expressément, formellement

expressway [ɪkˈsprɛsweɪ] N (US) voie f express (à plusieurs files)

expropriate [ɪksˈprəuprɪeɪt] VT exproprier

expulsion [ɪkˈspʌlʃən] N expulsion f; renvoi m

exquisite [ɛkˈskwɪzɪt] ADJ exquis(e)

ex-serviceman [ˈɛksˈsəːvɪsmən] N (irreg) ancien combattant

ext. ABBR (Tel) = **extension**

extemporize [ɪkˈstɛmpəraɪz] VI improviser

extend [ɪkˈstɛnd] VT (visit, street) prolonger; (deadline) reporter, remettre; (building) agrandir; (offer) présenter, offrir; (Comm: credit) accorder; (hand, arm) tendre ▶ VI (land) s'étendre

extension [ɪkˈstɛnʃən] N (of visit, street) prolongation f; (of building) agrandissement m; (building) annexe f; (to wire, table) rallonge f; (telephone: in offices) poste m; (: in private house) téléphone m supplémentaire; **~ 3718** (Tel) poste 3718

extension cable, extension lead N (Elec) rallonge f

extensive [ɪkˈstɛnsɪv] ADJ étendu(e), vaste; (damage, alterations) considérable; (inquiries) approfondi(e); (use) largement répandu(e)

extensively [ɪkˈstɛnsɪvlɪ] ADV (altered, damaged etc) considérablement; **he's travelled ~** il a beaucoup voyagé

★**extent** [ɪkˈstɛnt] N étendue f; (degree: of damage, loss) importance f; **to some ~** dans une certaine mesure; **to a certain ~** dans une certaine mesure, jusqu'à un certain point; **to a large ~** en grande partie; **to the ~ of ...** au point de ...; **to what ~?** dans quelle mesure ?, jusqu'à quel point ?; **to such an ~ that ...** à tel point que ...

extenuating [ɪkˈstɛnjueɪtɪŋ] ADJ: **~ circumstances** circonstances atténuantes

exterior [ɛkˈstɪərɪəʳ] ADJ extérieur(e) ▶ N extérieur m

exterminate [ɪkˈstəːmɪneɪt] VT exterminer

extermination [ɪkstəːmɪˈneɪʃən] N extermination f

external [ɛkˈstəːnl] ADJ externe; **for ~ use only** (Med) à usage externe ▶ N: **the externals** les apparences fpl

externally [ɛkˈstəːnəlɪ] ADV extérieurement

extinct [ɪkˈstɪŋkt] ADJ (volcano) éteint(e); (species) disparu(e)

extinction [ɪkˈstɪŋkʃən] N extinction f

extinguish [ɪkˈstɪŋgwɪʃ] VT éteindre

extinguisher [ɪkˈstɪŋgwɪʃəʳ] N extincteur m

extol, (US) **extoll** [ɪkˈstəul] VT (merits) chanter, prôner; (person) chanter les louanges de

extort [ɪkˈstɔːt] VT: **to ~ sth (from)** extorquer qch (à)

extortion [ɪkˈstɔːʃən] N extorsion f

extortionate [ɪkˈstɔːʃnɪt] ADJ exorbitant(e)

extortionist [ɪkˈstɔːʃnɪst] N extorqueur(-euse)

★**extra** [ˈɛkstrə] ADJ supplémentaire, de plus; **breakfast is ~** il y a un supplément pour le petit déjeuner ▶ ADV (in addition) en plus; **wine will cost ~** le vin sera en supplément; **~ large sizes** très grandes tailles ▶ N supplément m; (perk) à-coté m; (Cine, Theat) figurant(e)

extra... [ˈɛkstrə] PREFIX extra...

extract VT [ɪkˈstrækt] extraire; (tooth) arracher; (money, promise) soutirer ▶ N [ˈɛkstrækt] extrait m

extraction [ɪkˈstrækʃən] N extraction f

extractor fan [ɪkˈstræktə-] N exhausteur m, ventilateur m extracteur

extracurricular [ɛkstrəkəˈrɪkjuləʳ] ADJ (Scol) parascolaire

extradite [ˈɛkstrədaɪt] VT extrader

extradition [ɛkstrəˈdɪʃən] N extradition f

extramarital [ɛkstrəˈmærɪtl] ADJ extraconjugal(e)

extramural [ɛkstrəˈmjuərəl] ADJ hors-faculté inv

extraneous [ɛkˈstreɪnɪəs] ADJ: **~ to** étranger(-ère) à

extraordinarily [ɪkˈstrɔːdənrɪlɪ] ADV (exceptionally) extraordinairement

★**extraordinary** [ɪkˈstrɔːdnrɪ] ADJ extraordinaire; **the ~ thing is that ...** le plus étrange or étonnant c'est que ...

extraordinary general meeting N assemblée f générale extraordinaire

extrapolate [ɪkˈstræpəleɪt] VT, VI extrapoler; **to ~ from sth** extrapoler à partir de qch

extrapolation [ɪkstræpəˈleɪʃən] N extrapolation f

extrasensory perception [ˈɛkstrəsɛnsərɪ-] N perception f extrasensorielle

extraterrestrial [ɛkstrətɪˈrɛstrɪəl] ADJ extraterrestre

extra time N (Football) prolongations fpl

extravagance [ɪkˈstrævəgəns] N (excessive spending) prodigalités fpl; (thing bought) folie f, dépense excessive

extravagant [ɪkˈstrævəgənt] ADJ extravagant(e); (in spending: person) prodigue, dépensier(-ière); (: tastes) dispendieux(-euse)

extravaganza [ɪkstrævəˈgænzə] N spectacle m somptueux

★**extreme** [ɪkˈstriːm] ADJ, N extrême m; **the ~ left/right** (Pol) l'extrême gauche f/droite f; **extremes of temperature** différences fpl extrêmes de température

★**extremely** [ɪkˈstriːmlɪ] ADV extrêmement

extremism [ɪkˈstriːmɪzəm] N extrémisme m

extremist [ɪkˈstriːmɪst] ADJ, N extrémiste mf

extremity [ɪkˈstrɛmɪtɪ] N extrémité f

extricate [ˈɛkstrɪkeɪt] VT: **to ~ sth (from)** dégager qch (de)

extrovert [ˈɛkstrəvəːt] N extraverti(e)

exuberance [ɪɡˈzjuːbərəns] N exubérance f

exuberant [ɪɡˈzjuːbərənt] ADJ exubérant(e)

exude [ɪɡˈzjuːd] VT exsuder; (fig) respirer; **the charm etc he exudes** le charme etc qui émane de lui

exult [ɪɡˈzʌlt] VI exulter, jubiler

exultant [ɪɡˈzʌltənt] ADJ (shout, expression) de triomphe; **to be ~** jubiler, triompher

exultation [ɛɡzʌlˈteɪʃən] N exultation f, jubilation f

ex-wife [ɛksˈwaɪf] N ex-femme f

★**eye** [aɪ] N œil m; (of needle) trou m, chas m; **as far as the ~ can see** à perte de vue; **to keep an ~ on** surveiller; **to have an ~ for sth** avoir l'œil pour qch; **in the public ~** en vue; **with an ~ to doing sth** (BRIT) en vue de faire qch; **there's more to this than meets the ~** ce n'est pas aussi simple que cela paraît ▶ VT examiner

eyeball [ˈaɪbɔːl] N globe m oculaire

eyebath [ˈaɪbɑːθ] N (BRIT) œillère f (pour bains d'œil)

eyebrow [ˈaɪbrau] N sourcil m

eyebrow pencil N crayon m à sourcils

eye-catching [ˈaɪkætʃɪŋ] ADJ voyant(e), accrocheur(-euse)

eye cup N (US) = **eyebath**

eye drops NPL gouttes fpl pour les yeux

eyeful [ˈaɪful] N: **to get an ~ (of sth)** se rincer l'œil (en voyant qch)

eyeglass [ˈaɪglɑːs] N monocle m

eyelash [ˈaɪlæʃ] N cil m

eyelet [ˈaɪlɪt] N œillet m

eye-level [ˈaɪlɛvl] ADJ en hauteur

eyelid [ˈaɪlɪd] N paupière f

eyeliner [ˈaɪlaɪnəʳ] N eye-liner m

eye-opener [ˈaɪəʊpnəʳ] N révélation f

eye shadow N ombre f à paupières

eyesight [ˈaɪsaɪt] N vue f

eyesore [ˈaɪsɔːʳ] N horreur f, chose f qui dépare or enlaidit

eyestrain [ˈaɪstreɪn] N: **to get ~** se fatiguer la vue or les yeux

eyewash [ˈaɪwɒʃ] N bain m d'œil; (fig) frime f

eye witness N témoin m oculaire

eyrie [ˈɪərɪ] N aire f

F¹, f [ɛf] N (*letter*) F, f m; (*Mus*): **F** fa m; **F for Frederick**, (*US*) **F for Fox** F comme François

F² ABBR (= *Fahrenheit*) F

FA N ABBR (BRIT: = *Football Association*) fédération de football

FAA N ABBR (*US*) = **Federal Aviation Administration**

fable ['feɪbl] N fable f

fabric ['fæbrɪk] N tissu m ▶ CPD: **~ ribbon** (*for typewriter*) ruban m (en) tissu

> fabric ne veut pas dire *fabrique*.

fabricate ['fæbrɪkeɪt] VT fabriquer, inventer

fabrication [fæbrɪ'keɪʃən] N fabrication f, invention f

fabulous ['fæbjʊləs] ADJ (*inf: wonderful: food, prize*) formidable, sensationnel(le); (: *figure*) sensationnel(le); (*wealth*) fabuleux(-euse)

fabulously ['fæbjʊləslɪ] ADV (*rich, wealthy*) fabuleusement; (*successful, beautiful*) incroyablement

façade [fə'sɑːd] N façade f

★**face** [feɪs] N visage m, figure f; (*expression*) air m; grimace f; (*of clock*) cadran m; (*of cliff*) paroi f; (*of mountain*) face f; (*of building*) façade f; (*side, surface*) face; **~ down** (*person*) à plat ventre; (*card*) face en dessous; **to lose/save ~** perdre/sauver la face; **to pull a ~** faire une grimace; **in the ~ of** (*difficulties etc*) face à, devant; **on the ~ of it** à première vue; **~ to ~** face à face ▶ VT faire face à; (*facts etc*) accepter
> ▶ **face up to** VT FUS faire face à, affronter

Facebook® ['feɪsbʊk] N Facebook® m ▶ VT: **to facebook sb** envoyer un message sur Facebook à qn

face cloth N (BRIT) gant m de toilette

face cream N crème f pour le visage

faceless ['feɪslɪs] ADJ anonyme

face lift N lifting m; (*of façade etc*) ravalement m, retapage m

face pack N (BRIT) masque m (de beauté)

face powder N poudre f (pour le visage)

face-saving ['feɪseɪvɪŋ] ADJ qui sauve la face

facet ['fæsɪt] N facette f

facetious [fə'siːʃəs] ADJ facétieux(-euse)

face-to-face ['feɪstə'feɪs] ADV face à face

face value N (*of coin*) valeur nominale; **to take sth at ~** (*fig*) prendre qch pour argent comptant

facia ['feɪʃə] N = **fascia**

facial ['feɪʃl] ADJ facial(e) ▶ N soin complet du visage

facile ['fæsaɪl] ADJ facile

facilitate [fə'sɪlɪteɪt] VT faciliter

facilitator [fə'sɪlɪteɪtə'] N (*in negotiations*) facilitateur(-trice); (*educational*) animateur(-trice)

facilities [fə'sɪlɪtɪz] NPL installations fpl, équipement m; **credit ~** facilités fpl de paiement

facility [fə'sɪlɪtɪ] N facilité f

facing ['feɪsɪŋ] PREP face à, en face de ▶ N (*of wall etc*) revêtement m; (*Sewing*) revers m

facsimile [fæk'sɪmɪlɪ] N (*exact replica*) facsimilé m; (*also:* **facsimile machine**) télécopieur m; (*transmitted document*) télécopie f

★**fact** [fækt] N fait m; **in ~** en fait; **to know for a ~ that ...** savoir pertinemment que ...

fact-finding ['fæktfaɪndɪŋ] ADJ: **a ~ tour** *or* **mission** une mission d'enquête

faction ['fækʃən] N faction f

factional ['fækʃənl] ADJ de factions

factor ['fæktə'] N facteur m; (*of sun cream*) indice m (de protection); (*Comm*) factor m, société f d'affacturage; (: *agent*) dépositaire mf; **safety ~** facteur de sécurité; **I'd like a ~ 15 suntan lotion** je voudrais une crème solaire d'indice 15 ▶ VI faire du factoring
> ▶ **factor in** VT prendre en compte; **to ~ sth in to** prendre qch en compte dans

★**factory** ['fæktərɪ] N usine f, fabrique f

factory farming N (BRIT) élevage industriel

factory floor N: **the ~** (*workers*) les ouvriers mpl; (*workshop*) l'usine f; **on the ~** dans les ateliers

factory ship N navire-usine m

factual ['fæktjʊəl] ADJ basé(e) sur les faits

faculty ['fækəltɪ] N faculté f; (*US: teaching staff*) corps enseignant

fad [fæd] N (*personal*) manie f; (*craze*) engouement m

fade [feɪd] VI (*fabric, wallpaper*) se décolorer, passer; (*colour*) passer, pâlir; (*light, sound*) s'affaiblir, disparaître; (*flower*) se faner
> ▶ **fade away** VI (*sound*) s'affaiblir
> ▶ **fade in** VT (*picture*) ouvrir en fondu; (*sound*) monter progressivement
> ▶ **fade out** VT (*picture*) fermer en fondu; (*sound*) baisser progressivement

faded ['feɪdɪd] ADJ (*blue, green*) passé(e); (*fabric, object*) décoloré(e); (*jeans*) délavé(e); (*photograph*) jauni(e)

faeces, (*US*) **feces** ['fiːsiːz] NPL fèces fpl

fag [fæg] N (BRIT inf: *cigarette*) clope f; (: *chore*): **what a ~!** quelle corvée !; (*US !: gay*) pédé m

fag end N (BRIT inf) mégot m

fagged out [fægd-] ADJ (BRIT inf) crevé(e)

Fahrenheit ['fɑːrənhaɪt] N Fahrenheit m inv

★**fail** [feɪl] VT (exam) échouer à; (candidate) recaler; (subj: courage, memory) faire défaut à; **to ~ to do sth** (neglect) négliger de or ne pas faire qch; (be unable) ne pas arriver or parvenir à faire qch ▶ VI échouer; (supplies) manquer; (eyesight, health, light: also: **be failing**) baisser, s'affaiblir; (brakes) lâcher ▶ N: **without ~** à coup sûr; sans faute

failed [feɪld] ADJ (attempt, marriage) raté(e)

failing ['feɪlɪŋ] N défaut m ▶ PREP faute de; **~ that** à défaut, sinon

failsafe ['feɪlseɪf] ADJ (device etc) à sûreté intégrée

★**failure** ['feɪljər] N échec m; (person) raté(e); (mechanical etc) défaillance f; **his ~ to turn up** le fait de n'être pas venu or qu'il ne soit pas venu

faint [feɪnt] ADJ faible; (recollection) vague; (mark) à peine visible; (smell, breeze, trace) léger(-ère); **to feel ~** défaillir ▶ N évanouissement m ▶ VI s'évanouir

faintest ['feɪntɪst] ADJ: **I haven't the ~ idea** je n'en ai pas la moindre idée

faint-hearted [feɪnt'hɑːtɪd] ADJ pusillanime

faintly ['feɪntlɪ] ADV faiblement; (vaguely) vaguement

faintness ['feɪntnɪs] N faiblesse f

★**fair** [fɛər] ADJ équitable, juste; (reasonable) correct(e), honnête; (hair) blond(e); (skin, complexion) pâle, blanc (blanche); (weather) beau (belle); (good enough) assez bon(ne); (sizeable) considérable; **it's not ~!** ce n'est pas juste!; **a ~ amount of** une quantité considérable de ▶ ADV: **to play ~** jouer franc jeu ▶ N foire f; (BRIT: funfair) fête (foraine); (also: **trade fair**) foire(-exposition) commerciale

fair copy N copie f au propre, corrigé m

fair game N: **to be ~ (for)** être une cible légitime (pour)

fairground ['fɛəgraund] N champ m de foire

fair-haired [fɛə'hɛəd] ADJ (person) aux cheveux clairs, blond(e)

★**fairly** ['fɛəlɪ] ADV (justly) équitablement; (quite) assez; **I'm ~ sure** j'en suis quasiment or presque sûr

fairness ['fɛənɪs] N (of trial etc) justice f, équité f; (of person) sens m de la justice; **in all ~** en toute justice

fair play N fair play m

fair trade N commerce m équitable

fairway ['fɛəweɪ] N (Golf) fairway m

fairy ['fɛərɪ] N fée f

fairy godmother N bonne fée

fairy lights NPL (BRIT) guirlande f électrique

fairy tale N conte m de fées

★**faith** [feɪθ] N foi f; (trust) confiance f; (sect) culte m, religion f; **to have ~ in sb/sth** avoir confiance en qn/qch

faithful ['feɪθful] ADJ fidèle

faithfully ['feɪθfəlɪ] ADV fidèlement; **yours ~** (BRIT: in letters) veuillez agréer l'expression de mes salutations les plus distinguées

faith healer N guérisseur(-euse)

fake [feɪk] N (painting etc) faux m; (photo) trucage m; (person) imposteur m; **his illness is a ~** sa maladie est une comédie or de la simulation ▶ ADJ faux (fausse) ▶ VT (emotions) simuler; (painting) faire un faux de; (photo) truquer; (story) fabriquer

fake news N fake news f inv, information truquée diffusée par les médias traditionnels ou les réseaux sociaux

falcon ['fɔːlkən] N faucon m

Falkland Islands ['fɔːlklənd-] NPL: **the ~** les Malouines fpl, les îles fpl Falkland

★**fall** [fɔːl] (pt **fell** [fɛl], pp **fallen** ['fɔːlən]) N chute f; (decrease) baisse f; (US: autumn) automne m; **a ~ of snow** (BRIT) une chute de neige ▶ VI tomber; (price, temperature, dollar) baisser; **to ~ flat** (on one's face) tomber de tout son long, s'étaler; (joke) tomber à plat; (plan) échouer; **to ~ short of** (sb's expectations) ne pas répondre à ■ **falls** NPL (waterfall) chute f d'eau, cascade f

▶ **fall apart** VI (object) tomber en morceaux; (inf: emotionally) craquer

▶ **fall back** VI reculer, se retirer

▶ **fall back on** VT FUS se rabattre sur; **to have something to ~ back on** (money etc) avoir quelque chose en réserve; (job etc) avoir une solution de rechange

▶ **fall behind** VI prendre du retard

▶ **fall down** VI (person) tomber; (building) s'effondrer, s'écrouler

▶ **fall for** VT FUS (trick) se laisser prendre à; (person) tomber amoureux(-euse) de

▶ **fall in** VI s'effondrer; (Mil) se mettre en rangs

▶ **fall in with** VT FUS (sb's plans etc) accepter

▶ **fall off** VI tomber; (diminish) baisser, diminuer

▶ **fall out** VI (friends etc) se brouiller; (hair, teeth) tomber

▶ **fall over** VI tomber (par terre)

▶ **fall through** VI (plan, project) tomber à l'eau

fallacious [fə'leɪʃəs] ADJ (formal) fallacieux(-euse)

fallacy ['fæləsɪ] N erreur f, illusion f

fallback ['fɔːlbæk] ADJ: **~ position** position f de repli

fallen ['fɔːlən] PP of **fall**

fallible ['fæləbl] ADJ faillible

fallopian tube [fə'ləupɪən-] N (Anat) trompe f de Fallope

fallout ['fɔːlaut] N retombées (radioactives)

fallout shelter N abri m anti-atomique

fallow ['fæləu] ADJ en jachère; en friche

★**false** [fɔːls] ADJ faux (fausse); **under ~ pretences** sous un faux prétexte

false alarm N fausse alerte

falsehood ['fɔːlshud] N mensonge m

falsely ['fɔːlslɪ] ADV (accuse) à tort

false teeth NPL (BRIT) fausses dents, dentier m

falsify ['fɔːlsɪfaɪ] VT falsifier; (accounts) maquiller

falter ['fɔːltər] VI (when speaking) hésiter; (when walking) chanceler, vaciller

faltering ['fɔːltərɪŋ] ADJ (voice, speech, steps) hésitant(e); (economy, process) chancelant(e)

fame [feɪm] N renommée f, renom m

famed [feɪmd] ADJ célèbre; **to be ~ for sth** être célèbre pour qch

familial [fə'mɪlɪəl] ADJ familial(e)

★**familiar** [fə'mɪlɪər] ADJ familier(-ière); **to be ~ with sth** connaître qch; **to make o.s. ~ with sth** se familiariser avec qch; **to be on ~ terms with sb** bien connaître qn

familiarity [fəmɪlɪˈærɪtɪ] N familiarité f

familiarize [fəˈmɪlɪəraɪz] VT familiariser; **to ~ o.s. with** se familiariser avec

★**family** [ˈfæmɪlɪ] N famille f

family allowance N (BRIT) allocations familiales

family business N entreprise familiale

family credit N (BRIT) complément familial

family doctor N médecin m de famille

family life N vie f de famille

family man N (irreg) père m de famille

family planning N planning familial

family planning clinic N centre m de planning familial

family tree N arbre m généalogique

famine [ˈfæmɪn] N famine f

famished [ˈfæmɪʃt] ADJ affamé(e); **I'm ~!** (inf) je meurs de faim !

★**famous** [ˈfeɪməs] ADJ célèbre

famously [ˈfeɪməslɪ] ADV (get on) fameusement, à merveille

★**fan** [fæn] N (folding) éventail m; (Elec) ventilateur m; (person) fan m, admirateur(-trice); (Sport) supporter mf ▶ VT éventer; (fire, quarrel) attiser
▶ **fan out** VI se déployer (en éventail)

fanatic [fəˈnætɪk] N fanatique mf

fanatical [fəˈnætɪkl] ADJ fanatique

fanaticism [fəˈnætɪsɪzəm] N fanatisme m; **religious ~** le fanatisme religieux

fan belt N courroie f de ventilateur

fancied [ˈfænsɪd] ADJ imaginaire

fanciful [ˈfænsɪful] ADJ fantaisiste

fan club N fan-club m

fancy [ˈfænsɪ] N (whim) fantaisie f, envie f; (imagination) imagination f; **to take a ~ to** se prendre d'affection pour; s'enticher de; **it took** or **caught my ~** ça m'a plu; **when the ~ takes him** quand ça lui prend ▶ ADJ (luxury) de luxe; (elaborate: jewellery, packaging) fantaisie inv; (showy) tape-à-l'œil inv; (pretentious: words) recherché(e) ▶ VT (feel like, want) avoir envie de; (imagine) imaginer; **to ~ that ...** se figurer or s'imaginer que ...; **he fancies her** elle lui plaît

fancy dress N déguisement m, travesti m

fancy-dress ball [ˈfænsɪdres-] N bal masqué or costumé

fancy goods NPL articles mpl (de) fantaisie

fanfare [ˈfænfɛəʳ] N fanfare f (musique)

fanfold paper [ˈfænfəuld-] N papier m à pliage accordéon

fang [fæŋ] N croc m; (of snake) crochet m **fan heater** N (BRIT) radiateur soufflant

fanlight [ˈfænlaɪt] N imposte f

fanny [ˈfænɪ] N (BRIT inf!) chatte f (!); (US inf) cul m (!)

fantasize [ˈfæntəsaɪz] VI fantasmer

★**fantastic** [fænˈtæstɪk] ADJ fantastique

fantasy [ˈfæntəsɪ] N imagination f, fantaisie f; (unreality) fantasme m

fanzine [ˈfænziːn] N fanzine m

FAO N ABBR (= Food and Agriculture Organization) FAO f

FAQ N ABBR (= frequently asked question) FAQ f inv, faq f inv ▶ ABBR (= free alongside quay) FLQ

★**far** [fɑːʳ] ADJ (distant) lointain(e), éloigné(e); **the ~ side/end** l'autre côté/bout; **the ~ left/right** (Pol) l'extrême gauche f/droite f ▶ ADV loin; **is it ~ to London?** est-ce qu'on est loin de Londres ?; **it's not ~ (from here)** ce n'est pas loin (d'ici); **~ away, ~ off** au loin, dans le lointain; **~ better** beaucoup mieux; **~ from** loin de; **by ~** de loin, de beaucoup; **as ~ back as the 13th century** dès le 13e siècle; **go as ~ as the bridge** allez jusqu'au pont; **as ~ as I know** pour autant que je sache; **how ~ is it to ...?** combien y a-t-il jusqu'à ...?; **as ~ as possible** dans la mesure du possible; **how ~ have you got with your work?** où en êtes-vous dans votre travail ?

faraway [ˈfɑːrəweɪ] ADJ lointain(e); (look) absent(e)

farce [fɑːs] N farce f

farcical [ˈfɑːsɪkl] ADJ grotesque

★**fare** [fɛəʳ] N (on trains, buses) prix m du billet; (in taxi) prix de la course; (passenger in taxi) client m; (food) table f, chère f; **half ~** demi-tarif; **full ~** plein tarif ▶ VI se débrouiller

Far East N: **the ~** l'Extrême-Orient m

farewell [fɛəˈwel] EXCL, N adieu m ▶ CPD (party etc) d'adieux

far-fetched [fɑːˈfetʃt] ADJ exagéré(e), poussé(e)

★**farm** [fɑːm] N ferme f ▶ VT cultiver
▶ **farm out** VT (work etc) distribuer

★**farmer** [ˈfɑːməʳ] N fermier(-ière), cultivateur (-trice)

farmers' market N marché m fermier

farmhand [ˈfɑːmhænd] N ouvrier(-ière) agricole

farmhouse [ˈfɑːmhaus] N (maison f de) ferme f

farming [ˈfɑːmɪŋ] N agriculture f; (of animals) élevage m; **intensive ~** culture intensive; **sheep ~** élevage du mouton

farm labourer N = **farmhand**

farmland [ˈfɑːmlænd] N terres cultivées or arables

farm produce N produits mpl agricoles

farm worker N = **farmhand**

farmyard [ˈfɑːmjɑːd] N cour f de ferme

Faroe Islands [ˈfɛərəu-], **Faroes** [ˈfɛərəuz] NPL: **the ~** les îles fpl Féroé or Faeroe

far-reaching [fɑːˈriːtʃɪŋ] ADJ d'une grande portée

farrier [ˈfærɪəʳ] N maréchal-ferrant m

far-sighted [fɑːˈsaɪtɪd] ADJ presbyte; (fig) prévoyant(e), qui voit loin

fart [fɑːt] (inf!) N pet m ▶ VI péter

farther [ˈfɑːðəʳ] ADV plus loin ▶ ADJ plus éloigné(e), plus lointain(e)

farthest [ˈfɑːðɪst] SUPERLATIVE of **far**

FAS ABBR (BRIT: = free alongside ship) FLB

fascia [ˈfeɪʃə] N (Aut) (garniture f du) tableau m de bord

fascinate [ˈfæsɪneɪt] VT fasciner, captiver

fascinated [ˈfæsɪneɪtɪd] ADJ fasciné(e)

fascinating [ˈfæsɪneɪtɪŋ] ADJ fascinant(e)

fascination [fæsɪˈneɪʃən] N fascination f

fascism [ˈfæʃɪzəm] N fascisme m

fascist [ˈfæʃɪst] ADJ, N fasciste mf

★**fashion** [ˈfæʃən] N mode f; (manner) façon f, manière f; **in ~** à la mode; **out of ~** démodé(e);

in the Greek ~ à la grecque; **after a ~** *(finish, manage etc)* tant bien que mal ▶ VT façonner

fashionable ['fæʃnəbl] ADJ à la mode

fashion designer N (grand(e)) couturier(-ière)

fashionista [fæʃə'nɪstɑ] N fashionista *mf*

fashion show N défilé *m* de mannequins *or* de mode

★**fast** [fɑːst] ADJ rapide; *(clock)*: **to be ~** avancer; *(dye, colour)* grand *or* bon teint *inv*; **my watch is 5 minutes ~** ma montre avance de 5 minutes; **to make a boat ~** (BRIT) amarrer un bateau ▶ ADV vite, rapidement; *(stuck, held)* solidement; **~ asleep** profondément endormi; **as ~ as I can** aussi vite que je peux ▶ N jeûne *m* ▶ VI jeûner

fasten ['fɑːsn] VT attacher, fixer; *(coat)* attacher, fermer ▶ VI se fermer, s'attacher
▶ **fasten on, fasten upon** VT FUS *(idea)* se cramponner à

fastener ['fɑːsnəʳ], **fastening** ['fɑːsnɪŋ] N fermeture *f*, attache *f*; (BRIT: *zip fastener*) fermeture éclair® *inv or* à glissière

fast food N fast food *m*, restauration *f* rapide

fastidious [fæs'tɪdɪəs] ADJ exigeant(e), difficile

fast lane N (*Aut: in Britain*) voie *f* de droite

fast-track ['fɑːsttræk] VT *(student, employee)* faire suivre un programme accéléré à; *(bring forward: event)* avancer ▶ CPD *(promotion, scheme)* accéléré(e)

★**fat** [fæt] ADJ gros(se) ▶ N graisse *f*; *(on meat)* gras *m*; *(for cooking)* matière grasse; **to live off the ~ of the land** vivre grassement

fatal ['feɪtl] ADJ *(mistake)* fatal(e); *(injury)* mortel(le)

fatalism ['feɪtəlɪzəm] N fatalisme *m*

fatalistic [feɪtə'lɪstɪk] ADJ fataliste; **to be ~ about sth** être fataliste quant à qch

fatality [fə'tælɪtɪ] N *(road death etc)* victime *f*, décès *m*

fatally ['feɪtəlɪ] ADV fatalement; *(injured)* mortellement

fate [feɪt] N destin *m*; *(of person)* sort *m*; **to meet one's ~** trouver la mort

fated ['feɪtɪd] ADJ *(person)* condamné(e); *(project)* voué(e) à l'échec

fateful ['feɪtful] ADJ fatidique

fat-free ['fæt'friː] ADJ sans matières grasses

★**father** ['fɑːðəʳ] N père *m*

Father Christmas N le Père Noël

fatherhood ['fɑːðəhud] N paternité *f*

father-in-law ['fɑːðərɪnlɔː] N beau-père *m*

fatherland ['fɑːðəlænd] N (mère *f*) patrie *f*

fatherly ['fɑːðəlɪ] ADJ paternel(le)

fathom ['fæðəm] N brasse *f* (= *1828 mm*) ▶ VT *(mystery)* sonder, pénétrer

fatigue [fə'tiːg] N fatigue *f*; (Mil) corvée *f*; **metal ~** fatigue du métal

fatness ['fætnɪs] N corpulence *f*, grosseur *f*

fatten ['fætn] VT, VI engraisser

fattening ['fætnɪŋ] ADJ *(food)* qui fait grossir; **chocolate is ~** le chocolat fait grossir

fatty ['fætɪ] ADJ *(food)* gras(se) ▶ N *(pej)* gros (grosse)

fatuous ['fætjuəs] ADJ stupide

fatwa, fatwah ['fætwɑː] N fatwa *f*

faucet ['fɔːsɪt] N (US) robinet *m*

★**fault** [fɔːlt] N faute *f*; *(defect)* défaut *m*; (Geo) faille *f*; **it's my ~** c'est de ma faute; **to find ~ with** trouver à redire *or* à critiquer à; **at ~** fautif(-ive), coupable; **to a ~** à l'excès ▶ VT trouver des défauts à, prendre en défaut

faultless ['fɔːltlɪs] ADJ impeccable; irréprochable

faulty ['fɔːltɪ] ADJ défectueux(-euse)

fauna ['fɔːnə] N faune *f*

faux pas ['fəu'pɑː] N impair *m*, bévue *f*, gaffe *f*

favour, (US) **favor** ['feɪvəʳ] N faveur *f*; *(help)* service *m*; **to do sb a ~** rendre un service à qn; **in ~ of** en faveur de; **to be in ~ of sth/of doing sth** être partisan de qch/de faire qch; **to find ~ with sb** trouver grâce aux yeux de qn ▶ VT *(proposition)* être en faveur de; *(pupil etc)* favoriser; *(team, horse)* donner gagnant

favourable, (US) **favorable** ['feɪvrəbl] ADJ favorable; *(price)* avantageux(-euse)

favourably, (US) **favorably** ['feɪvrəblɪ] ADV favorablement

favourite, (US) **favorite** ['feɪvrɪt] ADJ, N favori(te)

favouritism, (US) **favoritism** ['feɪvrɪtɪzəm] N favoritisme *m*

fawn [fɔːn] N *(deer)* faon *m* ▶ ADJ *(also: **fawn-coloured**)* fauve ▶ VI: **to ~ (up)on** flatter servilement

fax [fæks] N *(document)* télécopie *f*; *(machine)* télécopieur *m* ▶ VT envoyer par télécopie

FBI N ABBR (US: = *Federal Bureau of Investigation*) FBI *m*

FCC N ABBR (US) = **Federal Communications Commission**

FCO N ABBR (BRIT: = *Foreign and Commonwealth Office*) ministère des Affaires étrangères et du Commonwealth

FD N ABBR (US) = **fire department**

FDA N ABBR (US) = *Food and Drug Administration*) office de contrôle des produits pharmaceutiques et alimentaires

FE N ABBR = **further education**

★**fear** [fɪəʳ] N crainte *f*, peur *f*; **~ of heights** vertige *m*; **for ~ of** de peur que + *sub or* de + *infinitive* ▶ VT craindre; **to ~ that** craindre que ▶ VI: **to ~ for** craindre pour

fearful ['fɪəful] ADJ craintif(-ive); *(sight, noise)* affreux(-euse), épouvantable; **to be ~ of** avoir peur de, craindre

fearfully ['fɪəfəlɪ] ADV *(timidly)* craintivement; *(old: very)* affreusement

fearless ['fɪəlɪs] ADJ intrépide, sans peur

fearsome ['fɪəsəm] ADJ *(opponent)* redoutable; *(sight)* épouvantable

feasibility [fiːzə'bɪlɪtɪ] N *(of plan)* possibilité *f* de réalisation, faisabilité *f*

feasibility study N étude *f* de faisabilité

feasible ['fiːzəbl] ADJ faisable, réalisable

feast [fiːst] N festin *m*, banquet *m*; (Rel: *also: **feast day**)* fête *f* ▶ VI festoyer; **to ~ on** se régaler de

feat [fiːt] N exploit *m*, prouesse *f*

feather ['feðəʳ] N plume *f* ▶ VT: **to ~ one's nest** *(fig)* faire sa pelote ▶ CPD *(bed etc)* de plumes

feather-weight ['feðəweɪt] N poids *m* plume *inv*

★**feature** ['fiːtʃəʳ] N caractéristique *f*; *(article)* chronique *f*, rubrique *f*; **a (special) ~ on sth/sb** un reportage sur qch/qn ▸ VT (*film*) avoir pour vedette(s) ▸ VI figurer (en bonne place); **it featured prominently in ...** cela a figuré en bonne place sur or dans ... **features** NPL (*of face*) traits *mpl*

feature film N long métrage

featureless ['fi:tʃəlıs] ADJ anonyme, sans traits distinctifs

Feb. ABBR (= *February*) fév

★**February** ['februərı] N février m; *see also* **July**

feces ['fi:si:z] NPL (*US*) = **faeces**

feckless ['fɛklıs] ADJ inepte

Fed ABBR (*US*) = **federal; federation**

fed [fɛd] PT, PP *of* **feed**

Fed. [fɛd] N ABBR (*US inf*) = **Federal Reserve Board**

federal ['fɛdərəl] ADJ fédéral(e)

federalism ['fɛdərəlızəm] N fédéralisme m

federalist ['fɛdərəlıst] ADJ, N fédéraliste mf

Federal Reserve Board N (*US*) organe de contrôle de la banque centrale américaine

Federal Trade Commission N (*US*) organisme de protection contre les pratiques commerciales abusives

federation [fɛdə'reıʃən] N fédération f

fed up ADJ: **to be ~ (with)** en avoir marre or plein le dos (de)

fee [fi:] N rémunération f; (*of doctor, lawyer*) honoraires *mpl*; (*of school, college etc*) frais *mpl* de scolarité; (*for examination*) droits *mpl*; **entrance/membership ~** droit d'entrée/d'inscription; **for a small ~** pour une somme modique

feeble ['fi:bl] ADJ faible; (*attempt, excuse*) pauvre; (*joke*) piteux(-euse)

feeble-minded ['fi:bl'maındıd] ADJ faible d'esprit

★**feed** [fi:d] (*pt, pp* **fed** [fɛd]) N (*of baby*) tétée f; (*of animal*) nourriture f, pâture f; (*on printer*) mécanisme m d'alimentation ▸ VT (*person*) nourrir; (*BRIT: baby: breastfeed*) allaiter; (*: with bottle*) donner le biberon à; (*horse etc*) donner à manger à; (*machine*) alimenter; (*data etc*) **to ~ sth into** enregistrer qch dans
▸ **feed back** VT (*results*) donner en retour
▸ **feed on** VT FUS se nourrir de
▸ **feed through** VI (*be felt*) se faire ressentir; **to ~ through to sb/sth** (*impact on*) se répercuter sur qn/qch

feedback ['fi:dbæk] N (*Elec*) effet m Larsen; (*from person*) réactions *fpl*

feeder ['fi:dər] N (*bib*) bavette f

feeding bottle ['fi:dıŋ-] N (*BRIT*) biberon m

★**feel** [fi:l] (*pt, pp* **felt** [fɛlt]) N (*sensation*) sensation f; (*impression*) impression f; **to get the ~ of sth** (*fig*) s'habituer à qch ▸ VT (*touch*) toucher; (*explore*) tâter, palper; (*cold, pain*) sentir; (*grief, anger*) ressentir, éprouver; (*think, believe*): **to ~ (that)** trouver que; **I ~ that you ought to do it** il me semble que vous devriez le faire ▸ VI: **to ~ hungry/cold** avoir faim/froid; **to ~ lonely/better** se sentir seul/mieux; **I don't ~ well** je ne me sens pas bien; **to ~ sorry for** avoir pitié de; **it feels soft** c'est doux au toucher; **it feels colder here** je trouve qu'il fait plus froid ici; **it feels like velvet** on dirait du velours, ça ressemble au velours; **to ~ like** (*want*) avoir envie de; **to ~ about** or **around** fouiller, tâtonner

▸ **feel for** VT FUS (*feel sorry for*) plaindre; (*grope for*) chercher à tâtons

feeler ['fi:lər] N (*of insect*) antenne f; (*fig*): **to put out a ~** or **feelers** tâter le terrain

feel-good ['fi:lgud] ADJ (*film*) qui réchauffe le cœur

★**feeling** ['fi:lıŋ] N (*physical*) sensation f; (*emotion, impression*) sentiment m; **to hurt sb's feelings** froisser qn; **feelings ran high about it** cela a déchaîné les passions; **what are your feelings about the matter?** quel est votre sentiment sur cette question ?; **my ~ is that ...** j'estime que ...; **I have a ~ that ...** j'ai l'impression que ...

fee-paying school ['fi:peıŋ-] N établissement (d'enseignement) privé

feet [fi:t] NPL *of* **foot**

feign [feın] VT feindre, simuler

feisty ['faıstı] ADJ fougueux(-euse)

felicitous [fı'lısıtəs] ADJ heureux(-euse)

fell [fɛl] PT *of* **fall** ▸ VT (*tree*) abattre ▸ N (*BRIT: mountain*) montagne f; (*: moorland*): **the fells** la lande ▸ ADJ: **with one ~ blow** d'un seul coup

fellow ['fɛləu] N type m; (*comrade*) compagnon m; (*of learned society*) membre m; (*of university*) universitaire mf (*membre du conseil*) ▸ CPD: **their ~ prisoners/students** leurs camarades prisonniers/étudiants; **his ~ workers** ses collègues *mpl* (de travail)

fellow citizen N concitoyen(ne)

fellow countryman N (*irreg*) compatriote m

fellow feeling N sympathie f

fellow men NPL semblables *mpl*

fellowship ['fɛləuʃıp] N (*society*) association f; (*comradeship*) amitié f, camaraderie f; (*Scol*) sorte de bourse universitaire

fellow traveller N compagnon (compagne) de route; (*Pol*) communisant(e)

fell-walking ['fɛlwɔ:kıŋ] N (*BRIT*) randonnée f en montagne

felon ['fɛlən] N (*Law*) criminel(le)

felony ['fɛlənı] N crime m, forfait m

felt [fɛlt] PT, PP *of* **feel** ▸ N feutre m

felt-tip [fɛlt'tıp] N (*also*: **felt-tip pen**) stylo-feutre m

★**female** ['fi:meıl] N (*Zool*) femelle f; (*pej: woman*) bonne femme f ▸ ADJ (*Biol, Elec*) femelle; (*sex, character*) féminin(e); (*vote etc*) des femmes; (*child etc*) du sexe féminin; **male and ~ students** étudiants et étudiantes

female impersonator N (*Theat*) travesti m

feminine ['fɛmının] ADJ féminin(e) ▸ N féminin m

femininity [fɛmı'nınıtı] N féminité f

feminism ['fɛmınızəm] N féminisme m

feminist ['fɛmınıst] N féministe mf

fen [fɛn] N (*BRIT*): **the Fens** les plaines *fpl* du Norfolk (*anciennement marécageuses*)

★**fence** [fɛns] N barrière f; (*Sport*) obstacle m; (*inf: person*) receleur(-euse); **to sit on the ~** (*fig*) ne pas se mouiller ▸ VT (*also*: **fence in**) clôturer ▸ VI faire de l'escrime

fencing ['fɛnsıŋ] N (*sport*) escrime m

fend [fɛnd] VI: **to ~ for o.s.** se débrouiller (tout seul)
▸ **fend off** VT (*attack etc*) parer; (*questions*) éluder

625

fender ['fɛndə'] N garde-feu m inv; (on boat) défense f; (US: of car) aile f

feng shui [fʌŋ'ʃweɪ] N feng shui m inv

fennel ['fɛnl] N fenouil m

feral ['fɛrəl] ADJ sauvage

ferment vɪ [fə'mɛnt] fermenter ▶ N ['fəːmɛnt] (fig) agitation f, effervescence f

fermentation [fəːmɛn'teɪʃən] N fermentation f

fern [fəːn] N fougère f

ferocious [fə'rəʊʃəs] ADJ féroce

ferociously [fə'rəʊʃəslɪ] ADV violemment

ferocity [fə'rɔsɪtɪ] N férocité f

ferret ['fɛrɪt] N furet m
  ▶ **ferret about, ferret around** vɪ fureter
  ▶ **ferret out** vT dénicher

Ferris wheel ['fɛrɪs-] N (US) grande roue f

ferry ['fɛrɪ] N (small) bac m; (large: also: **ferryboat**) ferry(-boat m) m ▶ vT transporter; **to ~ sth/sb across** or **over** faire traverser qch/qn

ferryman ['fɛrɪmən] N (irreg) passeur m

fertile ['fəːtaɪl] ADJ fertile; (Biol) fécond(e); **~ period** période f de fécondité

fertility [fə'tɪlɪtɪ] N fertilité f; fécondité f

fertility drug N médicament m contre la stérilité

fertilize ['fəːtɪlaɪz] vT fertiliser; (Biol) féconder

fertilizer ['fəːtɪlaɪzə'] N engrais m

fervent ['fəːvənt] ADJ fervent(e), ardent(e)

fervently ['fəːvəntlɪ] ADV ardemment

fervour, (US) **fervor** ['fəːvə'] N ferveur f

fester ['fɛstə'] vɪ suppurer

★**festival** ['fɛstɪvəl] N (Rel) fête f; (Art, Mus) festival m

festive ['fɛstɪv] ADJ de fête; **the ~ season** (BRIT: Christmas) la période des fêtes

festivities [fɛs'tɪvɪtɪz] NPL réjouissances fpl

festoon [fɛs'tuːn] vT: **to ~ with** orner de

fetal ['fiːtəl] ADJ (US) = **foetal**

fetch [fɛtʃ] vT aller chercher; (BRIT: sell for) rapporter; **how much did it ~?** ça a atteint quel prix ?
  ▶ **fetch up** vɪ (BRIT) se retrouver

fetching ['fɛtʃɪŋ] ADJ charmant(e)

fête [feɪt] N fête f, kermesse f

fetid ['fɛtɪd] ADJ fétide

fetish ['fɛtɪʃ] N fétiche m

fetter ['fɛtə'] vT entraver

fetters ['fɛtəz] NPL chaînes fpl

fettle ['fɛtl] N (BRIT): **in fine ~** en bonne forme

fetus ['fiːtəs] N (US) = **foetus**

feud [fjuːd] N querelle f, dispute f; **a family ~** une querelle de famille ▶ vɪ se quereller, se disputer

feudal ['fjuːdl] ADJ féodal(e)

feudalism ['fjuːdəlɪzəm] N féodalité f

fever ['fiːvə'] N fièvre f; **he has a ~** il a de la fièvre

fevered ['fiːvəd] ADJ (activity, anticipation) fébrile; (excitement) frénétique; (brow) brûlant(e) de fièvre

feverish ['fiːvərɪʃ] ADJ (Med) fiévreux(-euse), fébrile; (frantic: activity) fébrile; (: excitement) frénétique

★**few** [fjuː] ADJ (not many) peu de; **a ~** (+ noun) quelques; **quite a ~ ...** (+ noun) un certain nombre de ..., pas mal de ...; **in the next ~ days** dans les jours qui viennent; **in the past ~ days** ces derniers jours;

every ~ days/months tous les deux ou trois jours/mois; **a ~ more ...** encore quelques ..., quelques ... de plus ▶ PRON peu; **a ~ quelques-uns(-unes)**; **~ succeed** il y en a peu qui réussissent, (bien) peu réussissent; **they were ~** ils étaient peu (nombreux), il y en avait peu; **I know a ~** j'en connais quelques-uns; **a ~ of the teachers** quelques-uns des professeurs; **a ~ of us** quelques-uns d'entre nous

fewer ['fjuːə'] ADJ moins de; **there are ~ buses on Sundays** il y a moins de bus le dimanche; **they are ~ now** il y en a moins maintenant, ils sont moins (nombreux) maintenant ▶ PRON moins; **no ~ than** pas moins de

fewest ['fjuːɪst] ADJ le moins nombreux

FFA N ABBR = **Future Farmers of America**

FH ABBR (BRIT) = **fire hydrant**

FHA N ABBR (US: = Federal Housing Administration) office fédéral du logement

fiancé [fɪ'ɔŋseɪ] N fiancé m

fiancée [fɪ'ɔŋseɪ] N fiancée f

fiasco [fɪ'æskəʊ] N fiasco m

fib [fɪb] N bobard m

fibre, (US) **fiber** ['faɪbə'] N fibre f

fibreboard, (US) **fiberboard** ['faɪbəbɔːd] N panneau m de fibres

fibreglass, (US) **Fiberglass**® ['faɪbəglɑːs] N fibre f de verre

fibre optic, (US) **fiber optic** CPD (cable) en fibre f optique

fibrositis [faɪbrə'saɪtɪs] N aponévrosite f

FICA N ABBR (US) = **Federal Insurance Contributions Act**

fickle ['fɪkl] ADJ inconstant(e), volage, capricieux(-euse)

fiction ['fɪkʃən] N romans mpl, littérature f romanesque; (invention) fiction f

fictional ['fɪkʃənl] ADJ fictif(-ive)

fictionalize ['fɪkʃnəlaɪz] vT romancer

fictitious [fɪk'tɪʃəs] ADJ fictif(-ive), imaginaire

fiddle ['fɪdl] N (Mus) violon m; (cheating) combine f; escroquerie f; **tax ~** fraude fiscale, combine pour échapper au fisc; **to work a ~** traficoter ▶ vT (BRIT: accounts) falsifier, maquiller
  ▶ **fiddle with** vT FUS tripoter

fiddler ['fɪdlə'] N violoniste mf

fiddly ['fɪdlɪ] ADJ (task) minutieux(-euse)

fidelity [fɪ'dɛlɪtɪ] N fidélité f

fidget ['fɪdʒɪt] vɪ se trémousser, remuer

fidgety ['fɪdʒɪtɪ] ADJ agité(e), qui a la bougeotte

fiduciary [fɪ'djuːʃɪərɪ] N agent m fiduciaire

★**field** [fiːld] N champ m; (fig) domaine m, champ; (Sport: ground) terrain m; (Comput) champ, zone f; **to lead the ~** (Sport, Comm) dominer; **the children had a ~ day** (fig) c'était un grand jour pour les enfants

fielder ['fiːldə'] N joueur(-euse) de champ

field glasses NPL jumelles fpl

field hospital N antenne chirurgicale

field marshal N maréchal m

fieldwork ['fiːldwəːk] N travaux mpl pratiques (or recherches fpl) sur le terrain

fiend [fiːnd] N démon *m*

fiendish ['fiːndɪʃ] ADJ diabolique; (*problem, task*) infernal(e)

fiendishly ['fiːndɪʃli] ADV (*clever*) extrêmement; (*difficult, complicated*) abominablement

★**fierce** [fɪəs] ADJ (*look, animal*) féroce, sauvage; (*wind, attack, person*) (très) violent(e); (*fighting, enemy*) acharné(e)

fiercely ['fɪəsli] ADV (*say*) d'un ton féroce; (*fight, compete*) avec acharnement; (*loyal, proud*) profondément; (*ambitious*) redoutablement

fiery ['faɪərɪ] ADJ ardent(e), brûlant(e), fougueux(-euse)

FIFA ['fiːfə] N ABBR (= *Fédération Internationale de Football Association*) FIFA *f*

★**fifteen** [fɪf'tiːn] NUM quinze

★**fifteenth** [fɪf'tiːnθ] NUM quinzième

★**fifth** [fɪfθ] NUM cinquième ▶ N (*Aut: also:* **fifth gear**) cinquième *f*

fiftieth ['fɪftɪɪθ] NUM cinquantième

★**fifty** ['fɪftɪ] NUM cinquante

fifty-fifty ['fɪftɪ'fɪftɪ] ADV moitié-moitié; **to share ~ with sb** partager moitié-moitié avec qn ▶ ADJ: **to have a ~ chance (of success)** avoir une chance sur deux (de réussir)

fig [fɪg] N figue *f*

★**fight** [faɪt] (*pt, pp* **fought** [fɔːt]) N (*between persons*) bagarre *f*; (*argument*) dispute *f*; (*Mil*) combat *m*; (*against cancer etc*) lutte *f* ▶ VT se battre contre; (*cancer, alcoholism, emotion*) combattre, lutter contre; (*election*) se présenter à; (*Law: case*) défendre ▶ VI se battre; (*argue*) se disputer; (*fig*): **to ~ (for/against)** lutter (pour/contre)
▶ **fight back** VI rendre les coups; (*after illness*) reprendre le dessus ▶ VT (*tears*) réprimer
▶ **fight off** VT repousser; (*disease, sleep, urge*) lutter contre

fighter ['faɪtə'] N lutteur *m*; (*fig: plane*) chasseur *m*

fighter pilot N pilote *m* de chasse

fighting ['faɪtɪŋ] N combats *mpl*; (*brawls*) bagarres *fpl*

figment ['fɪgmənt] N: **a ~ of the imagination** une invention

figurative ['fɪgjʊrətɪv] ADJ figuré(e)

figuratively ['fɪgjʊrətɪvlɪ] ADV au sens figuré

★**figure** ['fɪgə'] N (*Drawing, Geom*) figure *f*; (*number*) chiffre *m*; (*body, outline*) silhouette *f*; (*person's shape*) ligne *f*, formes *fpl*; (*person*) personnage *m*; **public ~** personnalité *f*; **~ of speech** figure *f* de rhétorique ▶ VT (*US: think*) supposer ▶ VI (*appear*) figurer; (*US: make sense*) s'expliquer
▶ **figure on** VT FUS (*US*): **to ~ on doing** compter faire
▶ **figure out** VT (*understand*) arriver à comprendre; (*plan*) calculer

figurehead ['fɪgəhɛd] N (*Naut*) figure *f* de proue; (*pej*) prête-nom *m*

figure skating N figures imposées (*en patinage*), patinage *m* artistique

Fiji ['fiːdʒiː] N, **Fiji Islands** NPL (îles *fpl*) Fi(d)ji *fpl*

filament ['fɪləmənt] N filament *m*

filch [fɪltʃ] VT (*inf: steal*) voler, chiper

★**file** [faɪl] N (*tool*) lime *f*; (*dossier*) dossier *m*; (*folder*) dossier, chemise *f*; (*: binder*) classeur *m*; (*Comput*) fichier *m*; (*row*) file *f* ▶ VT (*nails, wood*) limer; (*papers*) classer; (*Law: claim*) faire enregistrer; déposer; **to ~ a suit against sb** (*Law*) intenter un procès à qn ▶ VI: **to ~ in/out** entrer/sortir l'un derrière l'autre; **to ~ past** défiler devant

file name N (*Comput*) nom *m* de fichier

file sharing [-ʃɛərɪŋ] N (*Comput*) partage *m* de fichiers

filibuster ['fɪlɪbʌstə'] (*esp US Pol*) N (*also:* **filibusterer**) obstructionniste *mf* ▶ VI faire de l'obstructionnisme

filing ['faɪlɪŋ] N (travaux *mpl* de) classement *m* ■ **filings** NPL limaille *f*

filing cabinet N classeur *m* (*meuble*)

filing clerk N documentaliste *mf*

Filipino [fɪlɪ'piːnəʊ] ADJ philippin(e) ▶ N (*person*) Philippin(e); (*Ling*) tagalog *m*

★**fill** [fɪl] VT remplir; (*vacancy*) pourvoir à; **to ~ with** remplir de ▶ N: **to eat one's ~** manger à sa faim
▶ **fill in** VT (*hole*) boucher; (*form*) remplir; (*details, report*) compléter
▶ **fill out** VT (*form, receipt*) remplir
▶ **fill up** VT remplir; **~ it up, please** (*Aut*) le plein, s'il vous plaît ▶ VI (*Aut*) faire le plein

filled [fɪld] ADJ: **~ with** (*full of*) rempli(e) de

fillet ['fɪlɪt] N filet *m* ▶ VT préparer en filets

fillet steak N filet *m* de bœuf, tournedos *m*

filling ['fɪlɪŋ] N (*Culin*) garniture *f*, farce *f*; (*for tooth*) plombage *m*

filling station N station-service *f*, station *f* d'essence

fillip ['fɪlɪp] N coup *m* de fouet (*fig*)

filly ['fɪlɪ] N pouliche *f*

★**film** [fɪlm] N film *m*; (*Phot*) pellicule *f*, film; (*of powder, liquid*) couche *f*, pellicule; **I'd like a 36-exposure ~** je voudrais une pellicule de 36 poses ▶ VT (*scene*) filmer ▶ VI tourner

filming ['fɪlmɪŋ] N tournage *m*

film-maker ['fɪlmmeɪkə'] N (*esp BRIT*) cinéaste *mf*

film star N vedette *f* de cinéma

filmstrip ['fɪlmstrɪp] N (film *m* pour) projection *f* fixe

film studio N studio *m* (de cinéma)

Filofax® ['faɪləʊfæks] N Filofax® *m*

filter ['fɪltə'] N filtre *m* ▶ VT filtrer
▶ **filter through** VI filtrer; **to ~ through to sb** filtrer jusqu'à qn

filter coffee N café *m* filtre

filter lane N (*BRIT Aut: at traffic lights*) voie *f* de dégagement; (*: on motorway*) voie *f* de sortie

filter tip N bout *m* filtre

filth [fɪlθ] N saleté *f*

filthy ['fɪlθɪ] ADJ sale, dégoûtant(e); (*language*) ordurier(-ière), grossier(-ière)

fin [fɪn] N (*of fish*) nageoire *f*; (*of shark*) aileron *m*; (*of diver*) palme *f*

★**final** ['faɪnl] ADJ final(e), dernier(-ière); (*decision, answer*) définitif(-ive); **~ demand** (*on invoice etc*) dernier rappel ▶ N (*BRIT Sport*) finale *f* ■ **finals** NPL (*US*) (*Scol*) examens *mpl* de dernière année; (*Sport*) finale *f*

finale [fɪ'nɑːlɪ] N finale *m*

finalist ['faɪnəlɪst] N (*Sport*) finaliste *mf*

finalize [ˈfaɪnəlaɪz] vt mettre au point

★**finally** [ˈfaɪnəlɪ] adv (eventually) enfin, finalement; (lastly) en dernier lieu; (irrevocably) définitivement

finance [faɪˈnæns] n finance f ▶ vt financer ■ **finances** npl finances fpl

financial [faɪˈnænʃəl] adj financier(-ière); ~ **statement** bilan m, exercice financier

financially [faɪˈnænʃəlɪ] adv financièrement

financial year n année f budgétaire

financier [faɪˈnænsɪəʳ] n financier m

★**find** [faɪnd] (pt, pp **found** [faʊnd]) vt trouver; (lost object) retrouver; (Law) **to ~ sb guilty** (Law) déclarer qn coupable; **to ~ (some) difficulty in doing sth** avoir du mal à faire qch ▶ n trouvaille f, découverte f
▶ **find out** vt se renseigner sur; (truth, secret) découvrir; (person) démasquer ▶ vi: **to ~ out about** (make enquiries) se renseigner sur; (by chance) apprendre

findings [ˈfaɪndɪŋz] npl (Law) conclusions fpl, verdict m; (of report) constatations fpl

★**fine** [faɪn] adj (weather) beau (belle); (excellent) excellent(e); (thin, subtle, not coarse) fin(e); (acceptable) bien inv; **he's ~** il va bien; **the weather is ~** il fait beau ▶ adv (well) très bien; (small) fin, finement; **you're doing ~** c'est bien, vous vous débrouillez bien; **to cut it ~** calculer un peu juste ▶ n (Law) amende f; contravention f ▶ vt (Law) condamner à une amende; donner une contravention à

fine arts npl beaux-arts mpl

finely [ˈfaɪnlɪ] adv (slice, grate) finement; (well: observed, drawn) bien

fine print n: **the ~** ce qui est imprimé en tout petit

finery [ˈfaɪnərɪ] n parure f

finesse [fɪˈnɛs] n finesse f, élégance f

fine-tooth comb [ˈfaɪntuːθ-] n: **to go through sth with a ~** (fig) passer qch au peigne fin or au crible

★**finger** [ˈfɪŋɡəʳ] n doigt m; **index ~** index m ▶ vt palper, toucher

fingernail [ˈfɪŋɡəneɪl] n ongle m (de la main)

fingerprint [ˈfɪŋɡəprɪnt] n empreinte digitale ▶ vt (person) prendre les empreintes digitales de

fingerstall [ˈfɪŋɡəstɔːl] n doigtier m

fingertip [ˈfɪŋɡətɪp] n bout m du doigt; (fig): **to have sth at one's fingertips** avoir qch à sa disposition; (knowledge) savoir qch sur le bout du doigt

finicky [ˈfɪnɪkɪ] adj tatillon(ne), méticuleux(-euse), minutieux(-euse)

★**finish** [ˈfɪnɪʃ] n fin f; (Sport) arrivée f; (polish etc) finition f ▶ vt finir, terminer; **to ~ doing sth** finir de faire qch ▶ vi finir, se terminer; (session) s'achever; **to ~ third** arriver or terminer troisième; **when does the show ~?** quand est-ce que le spectacle se termine ?
▶ **finish off** vt finir, terminer; (kill) achever
▶ **finish up** vi, vt finir
▶ **finish with** vt fus (girlfriend, boyfriend) quitter

finishing line [ˈfɪnɪʃɪŋ-] n ligne f d'arrivée

finishing school [ˈfɪnɪʃɪŋ-] n institution privée (pour jeunes filles)

finite [ˈfaɪnaɪt] adj fini(e); (verb) conjugué(e)

★**Finland** [ˈfɪnlənd] n Finlande f

Finn [fɪn] n Finnois(e), Finlandais(e)

★**Finnish** [ˈfɪnɪʃ] adj finnois(e), finlandais(e) ▶ n (Ling) finnois m

fiord [fjɔːd] n fjord m

fir [fəːʳ] n sapin m

★**fire** [ˈfaɪəʳ] n feu m; (accidental) incendie m; (heater) radiateur m; ~! au feu !; **on ~** en feu; **to set ~ to sth, set sth on ~** mettre le feu à qch; **insured against ~** assuré contre l'incendie ▶ vt (discharge): **to ~ a gun** tirer un coup de feu; (fig: interest) enflammer, animer; (inf: dismiss) mettre à la porte, renvoyer ▶ vi (shoot) tirer, faire feu ▶ cpd: ~ **hazard**, ~ **risk**: **that's a ~ risk** or **hazard** cela présente un risque d'incendie

fire alarm n avertisseur m d'incendie

firearm [ˈfaɪərɑːm] n arme f à feu

fireball [ˈfaɪəbɔːl] n boule f de feu

fire brigade n pompiers mpl, régiment m de sapeurs-pompiers

fire chief n (US) = **fire master**

fire department n (US) = **fire brigade**

fire door n porte f coupe-feu

fire engine n (Brit) pompe f à incendie

fire escape n escalier m de secours

fire exit n issue f or sortie f de secours

fire extinguisher n extincteur m

firefighter [ˈfaɪəfaɪtəʳ] n pompier m

firefighting [ˈfaɪəfaɪtɪŋ] n (lit) lutte f contre les incendies; (fig) gestion f de crise

fireguard [ˈfaɪəɡɑːd] n (Brit) garde-feu m inv

fire insurance n assurance f incendie

fire master n (Brit) capitaine m des pompiers

fireplace [ˈfaɪəpleɪs] n cheminée f

firepower [ˈfaɪəpauəʳ] n puissance f de feu

fireproof [ˈfaɪəpruːf] adj ignifuge

fire regulations npl consignes fpl en cas d'incendie

fire screen n (decorative) écran m de cheminée; (for protection) garde-feu m inv

fireside [ˈfaɪəsaɪd] n foyer m, coin m du feu

fire station n caserne f de pompiers

fire truck n (US) = **fire engine**

firewall [ˈfaɪəwɔːl] n (Internet) pare-feu m

firewood [ˈfaɪəwud] n bois m de chauffage

fireworks [ˈfaɪəwəːks] npl (display) feu(x) m(pl) d'artifice

firing [ˈfaɪərɪŋ] n (Mil) feu m, tir m

firing line n ligne f de tir; **to be in the ~** (lit) être dans la ligne de tir; (fig) être sous le feu des attaques

firing squad n peloton m d'exécution

★**firm** [fəːm] adj ferme; **it is my ~ belief that ...** je crois fermement que ... ▶ n compagnie f, firme f

firmly [ˈfəːmlɪ] adv fermement

firmness [ˈfəːmnɪs] n fermeté f

★**first** [fəːst] adj premier(-ière); **in the ~ instance** en premier lieu; **I'll do it ~ thing tomorrow** je le ferai tout de suite demain matin ▶ adv (before other people) le premier, la première; (before other *things*) en premier, d'abord; (*when listing reasons etc*) en premier lieu, premièrement; (*in the beginning*) au début; **~ of all** tout d'abord, pour commencer ▶ N (*person: in race*) premier(-ière); (*Brit Scol*) mention *f* très bien; (*Aut: also:* **first gear**) première *f*; **the ~ of January** le premier janvier; **at ~** au commencement, au début

first aid N premiers secours *or* soins

first-aid kit [fəːstˈeɪd-] N trousse *f* à pharmacie

first-class [fəːstˈklɑːs] ADJ (*ticket etc*) de première classe; (*excellent*) excellent(e), exceptionnel(le); (*post*) en tarif prioritaire

first-class mail N courrier *m* rapide

first-hand [fəːstˈhænd] ADJ de première main

first lady N (*US*) femme *f* du président

firstly [ˈfəːstlɪ] ADV premièrement, en premier lieu

first minister N (*in Scotland*) chef *du parlement écossais*

first name N prénom *m*

first night N (*Theat*) première *f*

first-rate [fəːstˈreɪt] ADJ excellent(e)

first-time buyer [ˈfəːstaɪm-] N *personne achetant une maison ou un appartement pour la première fois*

fir tree N sapin *m*

fiscal [ˈfɪskl] ADJ fiscal(e)

fiscal year N exercice financier

★**fish** [fɪʃ] N (*pl inv*) poisson *m*; poissons *mpl*; **~ and chips** poisson frit et frites ▶ VT, VI pêcher; **to ~ a river** pêcher dans une rivière
▶ **fish out** VT (*inf: take out*) sortir; **to ~ sth out of sth** sortir qch de qch

fisherman [ˈfɪʃəmən] N (*irreg*) pêcheur *m*

> The word for *fisherman* has a circumflex accent: *he's a fisherman* **il est pêcheur**. The word **pêcheur** means *sinner*.

fishery [ˈfɪʃərɪ] N pêcherie *f*

fish factory N (*Brit*) conserverie *f* de poissons

fish farm N établissement *m* piscicole

fish fingers NPL (*Brit*) bâtonnets *mpl* de poisson (congelés)

fish hook N hameçon *m*

★**fishing** [ˈfɪʃɪŋ] N pêche *f*; **to go ~** aller à la pêche

fishing boat N barque *f* de pêche

fishing industry N industrie *f* de la pêche

fishing line N ligne *f* (de pêche)

fishing rod N canne *f* à pêche

fishing tackle N attirail *m* de pêche

fish market N marché *m* au poisson

fishmonger [ˈfɪʃmʌŋgə**ʳ**] N (*Brit*) marchand *m* de poisson

fishmonger's [ˈfɪʃmʌŋgəz], **fishmonger's shop** N (*Brit*) poissonnerie *f*

fishnet stockings [ˈfɪʃnɛt-] NPL bas *mpl* résille

fish slice N (*Brit*) pelle *f* à poisson

fish sticks NPL (*US*) = **fish fingers**

fishy [ˈfɪʃɪ] ADJ (*inf*) suspect(e), louche

fission [ˈfɪʃən] N fission *f*; **atomic** *or* **nuclear ~** fission nucléaire

fissure [ˈfɪʃəʳ] N fissure *f*

fist [fɪst] N poing *m*

fistfight [ˈfɪstfaɪt] N pugilat *m*, bagarre *f* (à coups de poing)

★**fit** [fɪt] ADJ (*Med, Sport*) en (bonne) forme; (*proper*) convenable; approprié(e); **~ to** (*ready to*) en état de; **~ for** (*worthy*) digne de; (*capable*) apte à; **to keep ~** se maintenir en forme ▶ VT (*subj: clothes*) aller à; (*adjust*) ajuster; (*put in, attach*) installer, poser; adapter; (*equip*) équiper, garnir, munir; (*suit*) convenir à ▶ VI (*clothes*) aller; (*parts*) s'adapter; (*in space, gap*) entrer, s'adapter ▶ N (*Med*) accès *m*, crise *f*; (*of anger*) accès; (*of hysterics, jealousy*) crise; **this dress is a tight/good ~** cette robe est un peu juste/(me) va très bien; **a ~ of coughing** une quinte de toux; **to have a ~** (*Med*) faire *or* avoir une crise; (*inf*) piquer une crise; **by fits and starts** par à-coups
▶ **fit in** VI (*add up*) cadrer; (*integrate*) s'intégrer; (*to new situation*) s'adapter
▶ **fit into** VT FUS (*group, team*) s'intégrer à; (*space, container*) tenir dans; (*slot*) entrer
▶ **fit out** VT (*Brit: also:* **fit up**) équiper

fitful [ˈfɪtful] ADJ intermittent(e)

fitment [ˈfɪtmənt] N meuble encastré, élément *m*

fitness [ˈfɪtnɪs] N (*Med*) forme *f* physique; (*of remark*) à-propos *m*, justesse *f*

fitness instructor N professeur *mf* de fitness

fitted [ˈfɪtɪd] ADJ (*jacket, shirt*) ajusté(e)

fitted carpet N moquette *f*

fitted kitchen N (*Brit*) cuisine équipée

fitted sheet N drap-housse *m*

fitter [ˈfɪtəʳ] N monteur *m*; (*Dress*) essayeur(-euse)

fitting [ˈfɪtɪŋ] ADJ approprié(e) ▶ N (*of dress*) essayage *m*; (*of piece of equipment*) pose *f*, installation *f*

fitting room N (*in shop*) cabine *f* d'essayage

fittings [ˈfɪtɪŋz] NPL installations *fpl*

★**five** [faɪv] NUM cinq

five-day week [ˈfaɪvdeɪ-] N semaine *f* de cinq jours

fiver [ˈfaɪvəʳ] N (*inf: US*) billet de cinq dollars; (: *Brit*) billet *m* de cinq livres

★**fix** [fɪks] VT (*date, amount etc*) fixer; (*sort out*) arranger; (*mend*) réparer; (*make ready: meal, drink*) préparer; (*inf: game etc*) truquer ▶ N: **to be in a ~** être dans le pétrin
▶ **fix up** VT (*meeting*) arranger; **to ~ sb up with sth** faire avoir qch à qn

fixation [fɪkˈseɪʃən] N (*Psych*) fixation *f*; (*fig*) obsession *f*

★**fixed** [fɪkst] ADJ (*prices etc*) fixe; **there's a ~ charge** il y a un prix forfaitaire; **how are you ~ for money?** (*inf*) question fric, ça va ?

fixed assets NPL immobilisations *fpl*

fixture [ˈfɪkstʃəʳ] N installation *f* (fixe); (*Sport*) rencontre *f* (au programme)

fizz [fɪz] VI pétiller

fizzle [ˈfɪzl] VI pétiller
▶ **fizzle out** VI rater

fizzy [ˈfɪzɪ] ADJ pétillant(e), gazeux(-euse)

fjord [fjɔːd] N = **fiord**

FL, Fla. ABBR (*US*) = **Florida**

flabbergasted [ˈflæbəgɑːstɪd] ADJ sidéré(e), ahuri(e)

flabby [ˈflæbɪ] ADJ mou (molle)

f

629

★**flag** [flæg] N drapeau m; (also: **flagstone**) dalle f; **~ of convenience** pavillon m de complaisance ▶ VI faiblir; fléchir
▶ **flag down** VT héler, faire signe (de s'arrêter) à
▶ **flag up** VT signaler

flagging ['flægɪŋ] ADJ (strength) déclinant(e); (enthusiasm) émoussé(e); (spirits) défaillant(e); (conversation) languissant(e); **he soon revived their ~ spirits** il a rapidement remonté leur moral défaillant

flagon ['flægən] N bonbonne f

flagpole ['flægpəʊl] N mât m

flagrant ['fleɪɡrənt] ADJ flagrant(e)

flagship ['flægʃɪp] N vaisseau m amiral; (fig) produit m vedette

flag stop N (US: for bus) arrêt facultatif

flair [flɛəʳ] N flair m

flak [flæk] N (Mil) tir antiaérien; (inf: criticism) critiques fpl

flake [fleɪk] N (of rust, paint) écaille f; (of snow, soap powder) flocon m ▶ VI (also: **flake off**) s'écailler

flaky ['fleɪkɪ] ADJ (paintwork) écaillé(e); (skin) desquamé(e); (pastry) feuilleté(e)

flamboyant [flæm'bɔɪənt] ADJ flamboyant(e), éclatant(e); (person) haut(e) en couleur

flame [fleɪm] N flamme f

flamingo [flə'mɪŋɡəʊ] N flamant m (rose)

flammable ['flæməbl] ADJ inflammable

flan [flæn] N (BRIT) tarte f

Flanders ['flɑːndəz] N Flandre(s) f(pl)

flange [flændʒ] N boudin m, collerette f

flank [flæŋk] N flanc m ▶ VT flanquer

flannel ['flænl] N (BRIT: also: **face flannel**) gant m de toilette; (fabric) flanelle f; (BRIT inf) baratin m ■ **flannels** NPL pantalon m de flanelle

flap [flæp] N (of pocket, envelope) rabat m ▶ VT (wings) battre (de) ▶ VI (sail, flag) claquer; (inf: also: **be in a flap**) paniquer

flapjack ['flæpdʒæk] N (US: pancake) ≈ crêpe f; (BRIT: biscuit) galette f

flare [flɛəʳ] N (signal) signal lumineux; (Mil) fusée éclairante; (in skirt etc) évasement m ■ **flares** NPL (trousers) pantalon m à pattes d'éléphant
▶ **flare up** VI s'embraser; (fig: person) se mettre en colère, s'emporter; (: revolt) éclater

flared [flɛəd] ADJ (trousers) à jambes évasées; (skirt) évasé(e)

★**flash** [flæʃ] N éclair m; (also: **news flash**) flash m (d'information); (Phot) flash; un éclair; **in a ~** en un clin d'œil ▶ VT (switch on) allumer (brièvement); (direct): **to ~ sth at** braquer qch sur; (flaunt) étaler, exhiber; (send: message) câbler; (smile) lancer; **to ~ one's headlights** faire un appel de phares ▶ VI briller; jeter des éclairs; (light on ambulance etc) clignoter; **he flashed by or past** il passa (devant nous) comme un éclair

flashback ['flæʃbæk] N flashback m, retour m en arrière

flashbulb ['flæʃbʌlb] N ampoule f de flash

flash card N (Scol) carte f (support visuel)

flashcube ['flæʃkjuːb] N cube-flash m

flash drive N (Comput) clé f USB

flasher ['flæʃəʳ] N (Aut) clignotant m

flashlight ['flæʃlaɪt] N lampe f de poche

flashpoint ['flæʃpɔɪnt] N point m d'ignition; (fig): **to be at ~** être sur le point d'exploser

flashy ['flæʃɪ] ADJ (pej) tape-à-l'œil inv, tapageur(-euse)

flask [flɑːsk] N flacon m, bouteille f; (Chem) ballon m; (also: **vacuum flask**) bouteille f thermos®

★**flat** [flæt] ADJ plat(e); (tyre) dégonflé(e), à plat; (beer) éventé(e); (battery) à plat; (denial) catégorique; (Mus) bémol inv; (: voice) faux (fausse); **~ rate of pay** (Comm) salaire m fixe ▶ N (BRIT: apartment) appartement m; (Aut) crevaison f, pneu crevé; (Mus) bémol m ▶ ADV: **~ out** (work) sans relâche; (race) à fond

flat-footed [flæt'fʊtɪd] ADJ: **to be ~** avoir les pieds plats

flatly ['flætlɪ] ADV catégoriquement

flatmate ['flætmeɪt] N (BRIT): **he's my ~** il partage l'appartement avec moi

flatness ['flætnɪs] N (of land) absence f de relief, aspect plat

flat pack N (BRIT) meuble m en kit

flat-screen ['flætskriːn] ADJ à écran plat ▶ N écran plat

flatten ['flætn] VT (also: **flatten out**) aplatir; (crop) coucher; (house, city) raser

flatter ['flætəʳ] VT flatter

flatterer ['flætərəʳ] N flatteur m

flattering ['flætərɪŋ] ADJ flatteur(-euse); (clothes etc) seyant(e)

flattery ['flætərɪ] N flatterie f

flatulence ['flætjʊləns] N flatulence f

flaunt [flɔːnt] VT faire étalage de

flavour, (US) **flavor** ['fleɪvəʳ] N goût m, saveur f; (of ice cream etc) parfum m; **what flavours do you have?** quels parfums avez-vous ?; **to give or add ~ to** donner du goût à, relever ▶ VT parfumer, aromatiser; **vanilla-flavoured** à l'arôme de vanille, vanillé(e)

flavouring, (US) **flavoring** ['fleɪvərɪŋ] N arôme m (synthétique)

flavoursome, (US) **flavorsome** ['fleɪvəsəm] ADJ goûteux(-euse)

flaw [flɔː] N défaut m

flawed [flɔːd] ADJ défectueux(-euse); **to be seriously ~** comporter de sérieux défauts; **to be fundamentally ~** être foncièrement défectueux(-euse)

flawless ['flɔːlɪs] ADJ sans défaut

flawlessly ['flɔːlɪslɪ] ADV parfaitement

flax [flæks] N lin m

flaxen ['flæksən] ADJ blond(e)

flea [fliː] N puce f

flea market N marché m aux puces

fleck [flɛk] N (of dust) particule f; (of mud, paint, colour) tacheture f, moucheture f ▶ VT tacher, éclabousser; **brown flecked with white** brun moucheté de blanc

fled [flɛd] PT, PP of **flee**

fledgeling, fledgling ['flɛdʒlɪŋ] N oisillon m

flee [fliː] (pt, pp **fled** [flɛd]) VT fuir, s'enfuir de ▶ VI fuir, s'enfuir

fleece [fliːs] N (of sheep) toison f; (top) (laine f) polaire f ▶ VT (inf) voler, filouter

fleecy ['fli:sɪ] ADJ *(blanket)* moelleux(-euse); *(cloud)* floconneux(-euse)

fleet [fli:t] N flotte *f*; *(of lorries, cars etc)* parc *m*; convoi *m*

fleeting ['fli:tɪŋ] ADJ fugace, fugitif(-ive); *(visit)* très bref (brève)

Fleet Street N *terme désignant la presse nationale britannique et ses journalistes*

Flemish ['flemɪʃ] ADJ flamand(e) ▶ N *(Ling)* flamand *m*; **the ~** npl les Flamands

flesh [fleʃ] N chair *f*
▶ **flesh out** VT *(story, plan)* développer

flesh wound [-wu:nd] N blessure superficielle

fleshy ['fleʃɪ] ADJ *(person)* grassouillet(te); *(part of body)* rebondi(e); *(plant, fruit)* charnu(e)

flew [flu:] PT of **fly**

flex [fleks] N fil *m* or câble *m* électrique (souple) ▶ VT *(knee)* fléchir; *(muscles)* bander

flexibility [fleksə'bɪlɪtɪ] N flexibilité *f*

★**flexible** ['fleksəbl] ADJ flexible; *(person, schedule)* souple

flexitarian [fleksɪ'tɛərɪən] ADJ, N flexitarien(ne)

flexitime ['fleksɪtaɪm], *(US)* **flextime** ['flekstaɪm] N horaire *m* variable *or* à la carte

flick [flɪk] N petit coup; *(with finger)* chiquenaude *f* ▶ VT donner un petit coup à; *(switch)* appuyer sur
▶ **flick through** VT FUS feuilleter

flicker ['flɪkər] VI *(light, flame)* vaciller ▶ N vacillement *m*; **a ~ of light** une brève lueur

flick knife N *(BRIT)* couteau *m* à cran d'arrêt

flicks [flɪks] NPL *(inf)* ciné *m*

flier N = **flyer**

flies [flaɪz] NPL of **fly**

★**flight** [flaɪt] N vol *m*; *(escape)* fuite *f*; *(also:* **flight of steps)** escalier *m*; **to take ~** prendre la fuite; **to put to ~** mettre en fuite

flight attendant N steward *m*, hôtesse *f* de l'air

flight crew N équipage *m*

flight deck N *(Aviat)* poste *m* de pilotage; *(Naut)* pont *m* d'envol

flight path N trajectoire *f* (de vol)

flight recorder N enregistreur *m* de vol

flimsy ['flɪmzɪ] ADJ *(thin)* peu solide; *(clothes)* trop léger(-ère); *(excuse)* pauvre, mince

flinch [flɪntʃ] VI tressaillir; **to ~ from** se dérober à, reculer devant

fling [flɪŋ] *(pt, pp* flung [flʌŋ]*)* VT jeter, lancer ▶ N *(love affair)* brève liaison, passade *f*

flint [flɪnt] N silex *m*; *(in lighter)* pierre *f* (à briquet)

flip [flɪp] N chiquenaude *f* ▶ VT *(throw)* donner une chiquenaude à; *(switch)* appuyer sur; *(US: pancake)* faire sauter; **to ~ sth over** retourner qch ▶ VI: **to ~ for sth** *(US)* jouer qch à pile ou face
▶ **flip through** VT FUS feuilleter

flip chart N tableau *m* de conférence

flip-flops ['flɪpflɒps] NPL *(esp BRIT)* tongs *fpl*

flippant ['flɪpənt] ADJ désinvolte, irrévérencieux(-euse)

flipper ['flɪpər] N *(of animal)* nageoire *f*; *(for swimmer)* palme *f*

flip side N *(of record)* deuxième face *f*

flirt [flə:t] VI flirter ▶ N flirteur(-euse)

flirtation [flə:'teɪʃən] N flirt *m*

flirtatious [flə:'teɪʃəs] ADJ dragueur(-euse)

flit [flɪt] VI voleter

★**float** [fləut] N flotteur *m*; *(in procession)* char *m*; *(sum of money)* réserve *f* ▶ VI flotter; *(bather)* flotter, faire la planche ▶ VT faire flotter; *(loan, business, idea)* lancer

floating ['fləutɪŋ] ADJ flottant(e); **~ vote** voix flottante; **~ voter** électeur indécis

flock [flɒk] N *(of sheep)* troupeau *m*; *(of birds)* vol *m*; *(of people)* foule *f*

floe [fləu] N *(also:* **ice floe)** iceberg *m*

flog [flɒg] VT fouetter

★**flood** [flʌd] N inondation *f*; *(of letters, refugees etc)* flot *m*; **in ~** en crue ▶ VT inonder; *(Aut: carburettor)* noyer; **to ~ the market** *(Comm)* inonder le marché ▶ VI *(place)* être inondé; *(people)*: **to ~ into** envahir
▶ **flood in** VI affluer

floodgates ['flʌdgeɪts] NPL: **to open the ~ to sth** être la porte ouverte à qch

flooding ['flʌdɪŋ] N inondation *f*

floodlight ['flʌdlaɪt] N projecteur *m* ▶ VT *(irreg: like* **light)** éclairer aux projecteurs, illuminer

floodlit ['flʌdlɪt] PT, PP of **floodlight** ▶ ADJ illuminé(e)

flood tide N marée montante

floodwater ['flʌdwɔ:tər] N eau *f* de la crue

★**floor** [flɔ:ʳ] N sol *m*; *(storey)* étage *m*; *(of sea, valley)* fond *m*; *(fig: at meeting)*: **the ~** l'assemblée *f*, les membres mpl de l'assemblée; **on the ~** par terre; **ground ~**, *(US)* **first ~** rez-de-chaussée *m*; **first ~**, *(US)* **second ~** premier étage; **top ~** dernier étage; **what ~ is it on?** c'est à quel étage ?; **to have the ~** *(speaker)* avoir la parole ▶ VT *(knock down)* terrasser; *(baffle)* désorienter

floorboard ['flɔ:bɔ:d] N planche *f* *(du plancher)*

flooring ['flɔ:rɪŋ] N sol *m*; *(wooden)* plancher *m*; *(material to make floor)* matériau(x) *m(pl)* pour planchers; *(covering)* revêtement *m* de sol

floor lamp N *(US)* lampadaire *m*

floor show N spectacle *m* de variétés

floorwalker ['flɔ:wɔ:kər] N *(esp US)* surveillant *m* (de grand magasin)

flop [flɒp] N fiasco *m* ▶ VI *(fail)* faire fiasco; *(fall)* s'affaler, s'effondrer

floppy ['flɒpɪ] ADJ lâche, flottant(e); **~ hat** chapeau *m* à bords flottants ▶ N *(Comput: also:* **floppy disk)** disquette *f*

floppy disk N disquette *f*, disque *m* souple

flora ['flɔ:rə] N flore *f*

floral ['flɔ:rəl] ADJ floral(e); *(dress)* à fleurs

Florence ['flɒrəns] N Florence

florid ['flɒrɪd] ADJ *(complexion)* fleuri(e); *(style)* plein(e) de fioritures

florist ['flɒrɪst] N fleuriste *mf*

florist's ['flɒrɪsts], **florist's shop** N magasin *m* or boutique *f* de fleuriste

flotation [fləu'teɪʃən] N *(of shares)* émission *f*; *(of company)* lancement *m* (en Bourse)

flotilla [flə'tɪlə] N flottille *f*

flounce [flauns] N volant *m*
▶ **flounce out** VI sortir dans un mouvement d'humeur

flounder ['flaʊndə'] N (Zool) flet m ▸ VI patauger

flour ['flaʊə'] N farine f

flourish ['flʌrɪʃ] VI prospérer ▸ VT brandir ▸ N (gesture) moulinet m; (decoration) fioriture f; (of trumpets) fanfare f

flourishing ['flʌrɪʃɪŋ] ADJ prospère, florissant(e)

flout [flaʊt] VT se moquer de, faire fi de

★**flow** [fləʊ] N (of water, traffic etc) écoulement m; (tide, influx) flux m; (of orders, letters etc) flot m; (of blood, Elec) circulation f; (of river) courant m ▸ VI couler; (traffic) s'écouler; (robes, hair) flotter

flow chart, flow diagram N organigramme m

★**flower** ['flaʊə'] N fleur f; **in ~** en fleur ▸ VI fleurir

flower bed N plate-bande f

flowerpot ['flaʊəpɒt] N pot m (à fleurs)

flowery ['flaʊərɪ] ADJ fleuri(e)

flown [fləʊn] PP of **fly**

fl. oz. ABBR = **fluid ounce**

flu [fluː] N grippe f

fluctuate ['flʌktjʊeɪt] VI varier, fluctuer

fluctuation [flʌktjʊ'eɪʃən] N fluctuation f, variation f

flue [fluː] N conduit m

fluency ['fluːənsɪ] N facilité f, aisance f

fluent ['fluːənt] ADJ (speech, style) coulant(e), aisé(e); **he's a ~ speaker/reader** il s'exprime/lit avec aisance or facilité; **he speaks ~ French, he's ~ in French** il parle couramment français

fluently ['fluːəntlɪ] ADV couramment; avec aisance or facilité

fluff [flʌf] N duvet m; (on jacket, carpet) peluche f

fluffy ['flʌfɪ] ADJ duveteux(-euse); (jacket, carpet) pelucheux(-euse); (toy) en peluche

fluid ['fluːɪd] N fluide m; (in diet) liquide m ▸ ADJ fluide

fluid ounce N (Brit) = 0.028 l ; 0.05 pints

fluke [fluːk] N (inf) coup m de veine

flummox ['flʌməks] VT dérouter, déconcerter

flung [flʌŋ] PT, PP of **fling**

flunky ['flʌŋkɪ] N larbin m

fluorescent [flʊə'resnt] ADJ fluorescent(e)

fluoridation [flʊərɪ'deɪʃən] N fluoration f

fluoride ['flʊəraɪd] N fluor m

fluorine ['flʊəriːn] N fluor m

flurry ['flʌrɪ] N (of snow) rafale f, bourrasque f; **a ~ of activity** un affairement soudain; **a ~ of excitement** une excitation soudaine

flush [flʌʃ] N (on face) rougeur f; (fig: of youth etc) éclat m; (of blood) afflux m; **hot flushes** (Med) bouffées fpl de chaleur ▸ VT nettoyer à grande eau; (also: **flush out**) débusquer; **to ~ the toilet** tirer la chasse (d'eau) ▸ VI rougir ▸ ADJ (inf) en fonds; (level): **~ with** au ras de, de niveau avec

flushed [flʌʃt] ADJ (tout(e)) rouge

fluster ['flʌstə'] N agitation f, trouble m

flustered ['flʌstəd] ADJ énervé(e)

flute [fluːt] N flûte f

flutter ['flʌtə'] N (of panic, excitement) agitation f; (of wings) battement m ▸ VI (bird) battre des ailes, voleter; (person) aller et venir dans une grande agitation

flux [flʌks] N: **in a state of ~** fluctuant sans cesse

★**fly** [flaɪ] (pt **flew** [fluː], pp **flown** [fləʊn]) N (insect) mouche f; (on trousers: also: **flies**) braguette f ▸ VT (plane) piloter; (passengers, cargo) transporter (par avion); (distance) parcourir ▸ VI voler; (passengers) aller en avion; (escape) s'enfuir, fuir; (flag) se déployer; **to ~ open** s'ouvrir brusquement; **to ~ off the handle** s'énerver, s'emporter
▸ **fly away, fly off** VI s'envoler
▸ **fly in** VI (plane) atterrir; **he flew in yesterday** il est arrivé hier (par avion)
▸ **fly into** VT FUS: **to ~ into a rage** se mettre en rage
▸ **fly out** VI partir (par avion)

fly-drive N formule f avion plus voiture

flyer ['flaɪə'] N (pilot) aviateur(-trice); (passenger) passager(-ère) (d'un avion); (handbill) prospectus m

fly-fishing ['flaɪfɪʃɪŋ] N pêche f à la mouche

flying ['flaɪɪŋ] N (activity) aviation f; (action) vol m; **he doesn't like ~** il n'aime pas voyager en avion ▸ ADJ: **~ visit** visite f éclair inv; **with ~ colours** haut la main

flying buttress N arc-boutant m

flying picket N piquet m de grève volant

flying saucer N soucoupe volante

flying squad N (Police) brigade volante

flying start N: **to get off to a ~** faire un excellent départ

flyleaf ['flaɪliːf] N page f de garde

flyover ['flaɪəʊvə'] N (Brit: overpass) pont routier

flypast ['flaɪpɑːst] N défilé aérien

flysheet ['flaɪʃiːt] N (for tent) double toit m

flyweight ['flaɪweɪt] N (Sport) poids m mouche

flywheel ['flaɪwiːl] N volant m (de commande)

FM ABBR (Brit Mil) = **field marshal**; (Radio: = frequency modulation) FM

FMB N ABBR (US) = **Federal Maritime Board**

FMCS N ABBR (US: = Federal Mediation and Conciliation Services) organisme de conciliation en cas de conflits du travail

FO N ABBR (Brit) = **Foreign Office**

foal [fəʊl] N poulain m

foam [fəʊm] N écume f; (on beer) mousse f; (also: **foam rubber**) caoutchouc m mousse; (also: **plastic foam**) mousse cellulaire or de plastique ▸ VI (liquid) écumer; (soapy water) mousser

foam rubber N caoutchouc m mousse

FOB ABBR (= free on board) fob

fob [fɒb] N (also: **watch fob**) chaîne f, ruban m ▸ VT: **to ~ sb off with sth** refiler qch à qn

focal ['fəʊkl] ADJ (also fig) focal(e)

focal point N foyer m; (fig) centre m de l'attention, point focal

★**focus** ['fəʊkəs] N foyer m; (of interest) centre m; **out of/in ~** (picture) flou(e)/net(te); (camera) pas au point/au point ▸ VT (field glasses etc) mettre au point; (light rays) faire converger ▸ VI: **to ~ (on)** (with camera) régler la mise au point (sur); (with eyes) fixer son regard (sur); (fig: concentrate) se concentrer (sur)

fodder ['fɒdə'] N fourrage m

FOE N ABBR (= Friends of the Earth) AT mpl (= Amis de la Terre); (US: = Fraternal Order of Eagles) organisation charitable

foe [fəu] N ennemi *m*

foetal, (*US*) **fetal** [ˈfiːtəl] ADJ fœtal(e)

foetus, (*US*) **fetus** [ˈfiːtəs] N fœtus *m*

★**fog** [fɔg] N brouillard *m*

fogbound [ˈfɔgbaund] ADJ bloqué(e) par le brouillard

★**foggy** [ˈfɔgɪ] ADJ: **it's ~** il y a du brouillard

fog lamp, (*US*) **fog light** N (*Aut*) phare *m* anti-brouillard

foible [ˈfɔɪbl] N faiblesse *f*

foil [fɔɪl] VT déjouer, contrecarrer ▶ N feuille *f* de métal; (*kitchen foil*) papier *m* d'alu(minium); (*Fencing*) fleuret *m*; **to act as a ~ to** (*fig*) servir de repoussoir à

foist [fɔɪst] VT: **to ~ sth on sb** imposer qch à qn

★**fold** [fəuld] N (*bend, crease*) pli *m*; (*Agr*) parc *m* à moutons; (*fig*) bercail *m* ▶ VT plier; **to ~ one's arms** croiser les bras
▶ **fold up** VI (*map etc*) se plier, se replier; (*business*) fermer boutique ▶ VT (*map etc*) plier, replier

folder [ˈfəuldər] N (*for papers*) chemise *f*; (*binder*) classeur *m*; (*brochure*) dépliant *m*; (*Comput*) dossier *m*

folding [ˈfəuldɪŋ] ADJ (*chair, bed*) pliant(e)

foliage [ˈfəulɪdʒ] N feuillage *m*

folk [fəuk] NPL gens *mpl* ▶ CPD folklorique ■ **folks** NPL (*inf: parents*) famille *f*, parents *mpl*

folklore [ˈfəuklɔːr] N folklore *m*

folk music N musique *f* folklorique; (*contemporary*) musique folk, folk *m*

folk song [ˈfəuksɔŋ] N chanson *f* folklorique; (*contemporary*) chanson folk *inv*

folksy [ˈfəuksɪ] ADJ rustique

★**follow** [ˈfɔləu] VT suivre; (*on Twitter*) s'abonner aux tweets de; **to ~ sb's advice** suivre les conseils de qn; **I don't quite ~ you** je ne vous suis plus; **to ~ suit** (*fig*) faire de même ▶ VI suivre; (*result*) s'ensuivre; **to ~ in sb's footsteps** emboîter le pas à qn; (*fig*) suivre les traces de qn; **it follows that ...** il s'ensuit que ...
▶ **follow out** VT (*idea, plan*) poursuivre, mener à terme
▶ **follow through** VT = **follow out**
▶ **follow up** VT (*victory*) tirer parti de; (*letter, offer*) donner suite à; (*case*) suivre

follower [ˈfɔləuər] N disciple *mf*, partisan(e)

★**following** [ˈfɔləuɪŋ] ADJ suivant(e) ▶ N partisans *mpl*, disciples *mpl*

follow-up [ˈfɔləuʌp] N suite *f*; (*on file, case*) suivi *m*

folly [ˈfɔlɪ] N inconscience *f*; sottise *f*; (*building*) folie *f*

foment [fəˈmɛnt] VT fomenter

fond [fɔnd] ADJ (*memory, look*) tendre, affectueux(-euse); (*hopes, dreams*) un peu fou (folle); **to be ~ of** aimer beaucoup

fondle [ˈfɔndl] VT caresser

fondly [ˈfɔndlɪ] ADV (*lovingly*) tendrement; (*naïvely*) naïvement

fondness [ˈfɔndnɪs] N (*for things*) attachement *m*; (*for people*) sentiments affectueux; **a special ~ for** une prédilection pour

font [fɔnt] N (*Rel*) fonts baptismaux; (*Typ*) police *f* de caractères

★**food** [fuːd] N nourriture *f*

food chain N chaîne *f* alimentaire

foodie [ˈfuːdɪ] N (*inf*) gourmet *m*

food mixer N mixeur *m*

food poisoning N intoxication *f* alimentaire

food processor N robot *m* de cuisine

food stamp N (*US*) bon *m* de nourriture (*pour indigents*)

foodstuffs [ˈfuːdstʌfs] NPL denrées *fpl* alimentaires

★**fool** [fuːl] N idiot(e); (*Hist: of king*) bouffon *m*, fou *m*; (*Culin*) mousse *f* de fruits; **to make a ~ of sb** (*ridicule*) ridiculiser qn; (*trick*) avoir or duper qn; **to make a ~ of o.s.** se couvrir de ridicule ▶ VT berner, duper; **you can't ~ me** vous (ne) me la ferez pas, on (ne) me la fait pas ▶ VI (*also:* **fool around**) faire l'idiot or l'imbécile
▶ **fool about**, **fool around** VI (*pej: waste time*) traînailler, glandouiller; (: *behave foolishly*) faire l'idiot or l'imbécile

foolhardy [ˈfuːlhɑːdɪ] ADJ téméraire, imprudent(e)

foolish [ˈfuːlɪʃ] ADJ idiot(e), stupide; (*rash*) imprudent(e)

foolishly [ˈfuːlɪʃlɪ] ADV stupidement

foolishness [ˈfuːlɪʃnɪs] N idiotie *f*, stupidité *f*

foolproof [ˈfuːlpruːf] ADJ (*plan etc*) infaillible

foolscap [ˈfuːlskæp] N ≈ papier *m* ministre

★**foot** [fut] (*pl* **feet** [fiːt]) N pied *m*; (*of animal*) patte *f*; (*measure*) pied (= 30.48 *cm* ; 12 *inches*); **on ~** à pied; **to find one's feet** (*fig*) s'acclimater; **to put one's ~ down** (*Aut*) appuyer sur le champignon; (*say no*) s'imposer ▶ VT (*bill*) casquer, payer

footage [ˈfutɪdʒ] N (*Cine: length*) ≈ métrage *m*; (: *material*) séquences *fpl*

foot-and-mouth [futənd'mauθ], **foot-and-mouth disease** N fièvre aphteuse

★**football** [ˈfutbɔːl] N (*ball*) ballon *m* (de football); (*sport*: Brit) football *m*; (: *US*) football américain

★**footballer** [ˈfutbɔːlər] N (*Brit*) = **football player**

football ground N terrain *m* de football

football match N (*Brit*) match *m* de foot(ball)

football player N footballeur(-euse), joueur(-euse) de football; (*US*) joueur(-euse) de football américain

football pools NPL (*US*) ≈ loto *m* sportif, ≈ pronostics *mpl* (sur les matchs de football)

footbrake [ˈfutbreɪk] N frein *m* à pédale

footbridge [ˈfutbrɪdʒ] N passerelle *f*

footfall [ˈfutfɔːl] N (*footstep*) (bruit *m* de) pas *m*; (*Comm*) fréquentation *f*

foothills [ˈfuthɪlz] NPL contreforts *mpl*

foothold [ˈfuthəuld] N prise *f* (de pied)

footie, footy [ˈfutɪ] N (Brit *inf*) foot *m* (*inf*) ▶ CPD (*season, fan*) de foot (*inf*)

footing [ˈfutɪŋ] N (*fig*) position *f*; **to lose one's ~** perdre pied; **on an equal ~** sur pied d'égalité

footlights [ˈfutlaɪts] NPL rampe *f*

footloose [ˈfutluːs] ADJ libre; **to be ~ and fancy-free** être libre comme l'air

footman [ˈfutmən] N (*irreg*) laquais *m*

footnote [ˈfutnəut] N note *f* (en bas de page)

footpath [ˈfutpɑːθ] N sentier *m*; (*in street*) trottoir *m*

footprint [ˈfutprɪnt] N trace f (de pied)

footrest [ˈfutrest] N marchepied m

footsie [ˈfutsɪ] N (inf): **to play ~ with sb** faire du pied à qn

footsore [ˈfutsɔːr] ADJ: **to be ~** avoir mal aux pieds

footstep [ˈfutstep] N pas m

footstool [ˈfutstuːl] N repose-pied m

footwear [ˈfutwɛər] N chaussures fpl

footwork [ˈfutwɜːk] N (of boxer, footballer) jeu m de jambes; (fig) manœuvre f

footy [ˈfutɪ] N (BRIT inf) = **footie**

FOR ABBR (= free on rail) franco wagon

---

for [fɔːr]

PREP **1** (indicating destination, intention, purpose) pour; **the train for London** le train pour (or à destination de) Londres; **he left for Rome** il est parti pour Rome; **he went for the paper** il est allé chercher le journal; **is this for me?** c'est pour moi ?; **it's time for lunch** c'est l'heure du déjeuner; **what's it for?** ça sert à quoi ?; **what for?** (why?) pourquoi ?; (to what end?) pour quoi faire ?, à quoi bon ?; **for sale** à vendre; **to pray for peace** prier pour la paix

2 (on behalf of, representing) pour; **the MP for Hove** le député de Hove; **to work for sb/sth** travailler pour qn/qch; **I'll ask him for you** je vais lui demander pour toi; **G for George** G comme Georges

3 (because of) pour; **for this reason** pour cette raison; **for fear of being criticized** de peur d'être critiqué

4 (with regard to) pour; **it's cold for July** il fait froid pour juillet; **a gift for languages** un don pour les langues

5 (in exchange for): **I sold it for £5** je l'ai vendu 5 livres; **to pay 50 pence for a ticket** payer un billet 50 pence

6 (in favour of) pour; **are you for or against us?** êtes-vous pour ou contre nous ?; **I'm all for it** je suis tout à fait pour; **vote for X** votez pour X

7 (referring to distance) pendant, sur; **there are roadworks for 5 km** il y a des travaux sur or pendant 5 km; **we walked for miles** nous avons marché pendant des kilomètres

8 (referring to time) pendant; depuis; pour; **he was away for 2 years** il a été absent pendant 2 ans; **she will be away for a month** elle sera absente (pendant) un mois; **it hasn't rained for 3 weeks** ça fait 3 semaines qu'il ne pleut pas, il ne pleut pas depuis 3 semaines; **I have known her for years** je la connais depuis des années; **can you do it for tomorrow?** est-ce que tu peux le faire pour demain ?

9 (with infinitive clauses): **it is not for me to decide** ce n'est pas à moi de décider; **it would be best for you to leave** le mieux serait que vous partiez; **there is still time for you to do it** vous avez encore le temps de le faire; **for this to be possible ...** pour que cela soit possible ...

10 (in spite of): **for all that** malgré cela, néanmoins; **for all his work/efforts** malgré tout son travail/tous ses efforts; **for all his complaints, he's very fond of her** il a beau se plaindre, il l'aime beaucoup

▶ CONJ (since, as: formal) car

When talking about how long something has been happening use **depuis** and the present tense.

I've been learning French for two years. **J'apprends le français depuis deux ans.**

If the action has finished, use **pendant** and the past tense.

I learned French for two years. **J'ai appris le français pendant deux ans.**

---

forage [ˈfɔrɪdʒ] N fourrage m ▶ VI fourrager, fouiller

forage cap N calot m

foray [ˈfɔreɪ] N incursion f

forbad, forbade [fəˈbæd] PT of **forbid**

forbearing [fɔːˈbɛərɪŋ] ADJ patient(e), tolérant(e)

forbid [fəˈbɪd] (pt **forbad** [-ˈbæd] or **forbade** [-ˈbæd], pp **forbidden** [-ˈbɪdn]) VT défendre, interdire; **to ~ sb to do** défendre or interdire à qn de faire

forbidden [fəˈbɪdn] ADJ défendu(e)

forbidding [fəˈbɪdɪŋ] ADJ d'aspect or d'allure sévère or sombre

★**force** [fɔːs] N force f; **in ~** (rule, law, prices) en vigueur; (in large numbers) en force; **to come into ~** entrer en vigueur; **a ~ 5 wind** un vent de force 5; **the sales** — (Comm) la force de vente; **to join forces** unir ses forces ▶ VT forcer; (push) pousser (de force); **to ~ o.s. to do** se forcer à faire; **to ~ sb to do sth** forcer qn à faire ■ **Forces** NPL: **the Forces** (BRIT Mil) les forces armées

▶ **force back** VT (crowd, enemy) repousser; (tears) refouler

▶ **force down** VT (food) se forcer à manger

forced [fɔːst] ADJ forcé(e)

force-feed [ˈfɔːsˈfiːd] VT nourrir de force

forceful [ˈfɔːsful] ADJ énergique

forcemeat [ˈfɔːsmiːt] N (BRIT Culin) farce f

forceps [ˈfɔːseps] NPL forceps m

forcibly [ˈfɔːsəblɪ] ADV par la force, de force; (vigorously) énergiquement

ford [fɔːd] N gué m ▶ VT passer à gué

fore [fɔːr] N: **to the ~** en évidence; **to come to the ~** se faire remarquer

forearm [ˈfɔːrɑːm] N avant-bras m inv

forebear [ˈfɔːbɛər] N ancêtre m

foreboding [fɔːˈbəudɪŋ] N pressentiment m (néfaste)

★**forecast** [ˈfɔːkɑːst] N prévision f; (also: **weather forecast**) prévisions fpl météorologiques, météo f ▶ VT (irreg: like **cast**) prévoir

forecaster [ˈfɔːkɑːstər] N (also: **weather forecaster**) météorologiste mf; (economic) prévisionniste mf

foreclose [fɔːˈkləuz] VT (Law: also: **foreclose on**) saisir

foreclosure [fɔːˈkləuʒər] N saisie f du bien hypothéqué

forecourt [ˈfɔːkɔːt] N (of garage) devant m

foredeck [ˈfɔːdek] N pont m avant

forefathers [ˈfɔːfɑːðəz] NPL ancêtres mpl

forefinger [ˈfɔːfɪŋgər] N index m

forefront [ˈfɔːfrʌnt] N: **in the ~ of** au premier rang or plan de

forego [fɔː'gəu] vt (*irreg: like* **go**) renoncer à

foregoing ['fɔː'gəuɪŋ] ADJ susmentionné(e) ▶ N: **the ~** ce qui précède

foregone ['fɔːgɔn] ADJ: **it's a ~ conclusion** c'est à prévoir, c'est couru d'avance

foreground ['fɔːgraund] N premier plan ▶ CPD (*Comput*) prioritaire

forehand ['fɔːhænd] N (*Tennis*) coup droit

forehead ['fɔrɪd] N front *m*

★**foreign** ['fɔrɪn] ADJ étranger(-ère); (*trade*) extérieur(e); (*travel*) à l'étranger

foreign body N corps étranger

foreign currency N devises étrangères

★**foreigner** ['fɔrɪnə'] N étranger(-ère)

foreign exchange N (*system*) change *m*; (*money*) devises *fpl*

foreign exchange market N marché *m* des devises

foreign exchange rate N cours *m* des devises

foreign investment N investissement *m* à l'étranger

Foreign Office N (*Brit*) ministère *m* des Affaires étrangères

Foreign Secretary N (*Brit*) ministre *m* des Affaires étrangères

foreknowledge [fɔː'nɔlɪdʒ] N: **to have ~ of sth** savoir qch à l'avance

foreleg ['fɔːlɛg] N patte *f* de devant, jambe antérieure

foreman ['fɔːmən] N (*irreg*) (*in construction*) contremaître *m*; (*Law: of jury*) président *m* (du jury)

foremost ['fɔːməust] ADJ le (la) plus en vue, premier(-ière) ▶ ADV: **first and ~** avant tout, tout d'abord

forename ['fɔːneɪm] N prénom *m*

forensic [fə'rɛnsɪk] ADJ: **~ medicine** médecine légale; **~ expert** expert *m* de la police, expert légiste

foreplay ['fɔːpleɪ] N stimulation *f* érotique, prélude *m*

forerunner ['fɔːrʌnə'] N précurseur *m*

foresee [fɔː'siː] vt (*irreg: like* **see**) prévoir

foreseeable [fɔː'siːəbl] ADJ prévisible

foreseen [fɔː'siːn] PP of **foresee**

foreshadow [fɔː'ʃædəu] vt présager, annoncer, laisser prévoir

foreshore ['fɔːʃɔː'] N laisse *f* de mer

foreshorten [fɔː'ʃɔːtn] vt (*figure, scene*) réduire, faire en raccourci

foresight ['fɔːsaɪt] N prévoyance *f*

foreskin ['fɔːskɪn] N (*Anat*) prépuce *m*

★**forest** ['fɔrɪst] N forêt *f*

forestall [fɔː'stɔːl] vt devancer

forested ['fɔrɪstɪd] ADJ boisé(e); **thickly ~** très boisé

forestry ['fɔrɪstrɪ] N sylviculture *f*

foretaste ['fɔːteɪst] N avant-goût *m*

foretell [fɔː'tɛl] vt (*irreg: like* **tell**) prédire

forethought ['fɔːθɔːt] N prévoyance *f*

foretold [fɔː'təuld] PT, PP of **foretell**

forever [fə'rɛvə'] ADV pour toujours; (*fig: endlessly*) continuellement

forewarn [fɔː'wɔːn] vt avertir

forewent [fɔː'wɛnt] PT of **forego**

foreword ['fɔːwəːd] N avant-propos *m inv*

forfeit ['fɔːfɪt] N prix *m*, rançon *f* ▶ vt perdre; (*one's life, health*) payer de

forgave [fə'geɪv] PT of **forgive**

forge [fɔːdʒ] N forge *f* ▶ vt (*signature*) contrefaire; (*wrought iron*) forger; **to ~ documents/a will** fabriquer de faux papiers/un faux testament; **to ~ money** (*Brit*) fabriquer de la fausse monnaie ▶ **forge ahead** vi pousser de l'avant, prendre de l'avance

forged [fɔːdʒd] ADJ faux (fausse)

forger ['fɔːdʒə'] N faussaire *m*

forgery ['fɔːdʒərɪ] N faux *m*, contrefaçon *f*

★**forget** [fə'gɛt] (*pt* **forgot** [-'gɔt], *pp* **forgotten** [-'gɔtn]) vt, vi oublier; **to ~ to do sth** oublier de faire qch; **to ~ about sth** (*accidentally*) oublier qch; (*on purpose*) ne plus penser à qch; **I've forgotten my key/passport** j'ai oublié ma clé/mon passeport

forgetful [fə'gɛtful] ADJ distrait(e), étourdi(e); **~ of** oublieux(-euse) de

forgetfulness [fə'gɛtfulnɪs] N tendance *f* aux oublis; (*oblivion*) oubli *m*

forget-me-not [fə'gɛtmɪnɔt] N myosotis *m*

forgettable [fə'gɛtəbl] ADJ (*film, year*) peu mémorable; (*person, face*) ordinaire

forgivable [fə'gɪvəbl] ADJ pardonnable

★**forgive** [fə'gɪv] vt (*irreg: like* **give**) pardonner; **to ~ sb for sth/for doing sth** pardonner qch à qn/à qn de faire qch

forgiveness [fə'gɪvnɪs] N pardon *m*

forgiving [fə'gɪvɪŋ] ADJ indulgent(e)

forgo [fɔː'gəu] (*pt* **forwent** [-'wɛnt], *pp* **forgone** [-'gɔn]) vt = **forego**

forgot [fə'gɔt] PT of **forget**

forgotten [fə'gɔtn] PP of **forget**

fork [fɔːk] N (*for eating*) fourchette *f*; (*for gardening*) fourche *f*; (*of roads*) bifurcation *f*; (*of railways*) embranchement *m* ▶ vi (*road*) bifurquer ▶ **fork out** (*inf*) vt (*pay*) allonger, se fendre de ▶ vi casquer

forked [fɔːkt] ADJ (*lightning*) en zigzags, ramifié(e)

fork-lift truck ['fɔːklɪft-] N chariot élévateur

forlorn [fə'lɔːn] ADJ (*person*) délaissé(e); (*deserted*) abandonné(e); (*hope, attempt*) désespéré(e)

★**form** [fɔːm] N forme *f*; (*Scol*) classe *f*; (*questionnaire*) formulaire *m*; **in the ~ of** sous forme de; **to be on good ~** (*Sport, fig*) être en forme; **on top ~** en pleine forme ▶ vt former; (*habit*) contracter; **to ~ part of sth** faire partie de qch

★**formal** ['fɔːməl] ADJ (*offer, receipt*) en bonne et due forme; (*person*) cérémonieux(-euse), à cheval sur les convenances; (*occasion, dinner*) officiel(le); (*garden*) à la française; (*Art, Philosophy*) formel(le); (*clothes*) de soirée

formaldehyde [fɔː'mældɪhaɪd] N formaldéhyde *m*

formality [fɔː'mælɪtɪ] N formalité *f*, cérémonie(s) *f(pl)*

formalize ['fɔːməlaɪz] vt officialiser

formally ['fɔːməlɪ] ADV officiellement; formellement; cérémonieusement

format ['fɔːmæt] N format m ▸ VT (Comput) formater

formation [fɔːˈmeɪʃən] N formation f

formative ['fɔːmətɪv] ADJ: ~ **years** années fpl d'apprentissage (fig) or de formation (d'un enfant, d'un adolescent)

formatting ['fɔːmætɪŋ] N (Comput) formatage m

★**former** ['fɔːmər] ADJ ancien(ne); (before n) précédent(e); **the ~ ... the latter** le premier ... le second, celui-là ... celui-ci; **the ~ president** l'ex-président; **the ~ Yugoslavia/Soviet Union** l'ex Yougoslavie/Union Soviétique

formerly ['fɔːməlɪ] ADV autrefois

form feed N (on printer) alimentation f en feuilles

Formica® [fɔːˈmaɪkə] N formica® m

formidable ['fɔːmɪdəbl] ADJ redoutable

formula ['fɔːmjulə] N formule f; **F~ One** (Aut) Formule un

formulaic [fɔːmjuˈleɪk] ADJ convenu(e)

formulate ['fɔːmjuleɪt] VT formuler

fornicate ['fɔːnɪkeɪt] VI forniquer

forsake [fəˈseɪk] (pt **forsook** [-ˈsuk], pp **forsaken** [-ˈseɪkən]) VT abandonner

fort [fɔːt] N fort m; **to hold the ~** (fig) assurer la permanence

forte ['fɔːtɪ] N (point) fort m

★**forth** [fɔːθ] ADV en avant; **to go back and ~** aller et venir; **and so ~** et ainsi de suite

forthcoming [fɔːθˈkʌmɪŋ] ADJ qui va paraître or avoir lieu prochainement; (character) ouvert(e), communicatif(-ive); (available) disponible

forthright ['fɔːθraɪt] ADJ franc (franche), direct(e)

forthwith [fɔːθˈwɪθ] ADV sur le champ

fortieth ['fɔːtɪɪθ] NUM quarantième

fortification [fɔːtɪfɪˈkeɪʃən] N fortification f

fortified wine ['fɔːtɪfaɪd-] N vin liquoreux or de liqueur

fortify ['fɔːtɪfaɪ] VT (city) fortifier; (person) remonter

fortitude ['fɔːtɪtjuːd] N courage m, force f d'âme

fortnight ['fɔːtnaɪt] N (BRIT) quinzaine f, quinze jours mpl; **it's a ~ since ...** il y a quinze jours que ...

fortnightly ['fɔːtnaɪtlɪ] ADJ bimensuel(le) ▸ ADV tous les quinze jours

FORTRAN ['fɔːtræn] N FORTRAN m

fortress ['fɔːtrɪs] N forteresse f

fortuitous [fɔːˈtjuːɪtəs] ADJ fortuit(e)

fortunate ['fɔːtʃənɪt] ADJ heureux(-euse); (person) chanceux(-euse); **to be ~** avoir de la chance; **it is ~ that** c'est une chance que, il est heureux que

fortunately ['fɔːtʃənɪtlɪ] ADV heureusement, par bonheur

★**fortune** ['fɔːtʃən] N chance f; (wealth) fortune f; **to make a ~** faire fortune

fortune-teller ['fɔːtʃəntɛlər] N diseuse f de bonne aventure

★**forty** ['fɔːtɪ] NUM quarante

forum ['fɔːrəm] N forum m, tribune f

★**forward** ['fɔːwəd] ADJ (movement, position) en avant, vers l'avant; (not shy) effronté(e); (in time) en avance; (Comm: delivery, sales, exchange) à terme; **~ planning** planification f à long terme ▸ ADV (also: **forwards**) en avant; **to look ~ to sth** atten-

dre qch avec impatience; **to move ~** avancer ▸ N (Sport) avant m ▸ VT (letter) faire suivre; (parcel, goods) expédier; (fig) promouvoir, favoriser; **"please ~"** « prière de faire suivre »

forwarding address ['fɔːwədɪŋ-] N adresse f de réexpédition

forward slash N barre f oblique

forwent [fɔːˈwɛnt] PT of **forgo**

fossick ['fɒsɪk] VI (AUSTRALIA, NEW ZEALAND inf) chercher; **to ~ around for** fouiner (inf) pour trouver

fossil ['fɒsl] ADJ, N fossile m; **~ fuel** combustible m fossile

fossilized ['fɒsəlaɪzd] ADJ (bones) fossilisé(e)

foster ['fɒstər] VT (encourage) encourager, favoriser; (child) élever (sans adopter)

foster brother N frère m de lait

foster child N (irreg) enfant élevé dans une famille d'accueil

foster mother N mère adoptive; mère nourricière

foster parent N parent qui élève un enfant sans l'adopter

foster sister N sœur f de lait

fought [fɔːt] PT, PP of **fight**

foul [faul] ADJ (weather, smell, food) infect(e); (language) ordurier(-ière); (deed) infâme; **he's got a ~ temper** il a un caractère de chien ▸ N (Football) faute f ▸ VT (dirty) salir, encrasser; (football player) commettre une faute sur; (entangle: anchor, propeller) emmêler

foul play N (Sport) jeu déloyal; (Law) acte criminel; **~ is not suspected** la mort (or l'incendie etc) n'a pas de causes suspectes, on écarte l'hypothèse d'un meurtre (or d'un acte criminel)

found [faund] PT, PP of **find** ▸ VT (establish) fonder

foundation [faunˈdeɪʃən] N (act) fondation f; (base) fondement m; (also: **foundation cream**) fond m de teint ■ **foundations** NPL (of building) fondations; **to lay the foundations** (fig) poser les fondements

foundation stone N première pierre

founder ['faundər] N fondateur m ▸ VI couler, sombrer

founding ['faundɪŋ] ADJ: ~ **fathers** (esp US) pères mpl fondateurs; **~ member** membre m fondateur

foundry ['faundrɪ] N fonderie f

fount [faunt] N source f; (Typ) fonte f

★**fountain** ['fauntɪn] N fontaine f

fountain pen N stylo m (à encre)

★**four** [fɔːr] NUM quatre; **on all fours** à quatre pattes

four-by-four [fɔːbaɪˈfɔːr] N (Aut) 4x4 m

four-letter word ['fɔːlɛtə-] N obscénité f, gros mot

four-poster ['fɔːˈpəustər] N (also: **four-poster bed**) lit m à baldaquin

foursome ['fɔːsəm] N partie f à quatre; sortie f à quatre

★**fourteen** [fɔːˈtiːn] NUM quatorze

★**fourteenth** [fɔːˈtiːnθ] NUM quatorzième

★**fourth** [fɔːθ] NUM quatrième ▸ N (Aut: also: **fourth gear**) quatrième f

four-wheel drive ['fɔ:wi:l-] N (Aut: car) voiture f à quatre roues motrices; **with ~** à quatre roues motrices

fowl [faul] N volaille f

★**fox** [fɔks] N renard m ▶ VT mystifier

fox fur N renard m

foxglove ['fɔksglʌv] N (Bot) digitale f

fox-hunting ['fɔkshʌntɪŋ] N chasse f au renard

foyer ['fɔɪeɪ] N (in hotel) vestibule m; (Theat) foyer m

FP N ABBR (BRIT) = **former pupil**; (US) = **fireplug**

FPA N ABBR (BRIT) = **Family Planning Association**

Fr. ABBR (Rel: = father) P; (= friar) F

fr. ABBR (= franc) F

fracas ['fræka:] N bagarre f

fracking ['frækɪŋ] N fracturation f hydraulique

fractal ['fræktəl] N fractale f

fraction ['frækʃən] N fraction f

fractional ['frækʃənəl] ADJ infime

fractionally ['frækʃnəlɪ] ADV: **~ smaller etc** un poil plus petit etc

fractious ['frækʃəs] ADJ grincheux(-euse)

fracture ['fræktʃəʳ] N fracture f ▶ VT fracturer

fragile ['frædʒaɪl] ADJ fragile

fragility [frə'dʒɪlɪtɪ] N fragilité f

fragment ['frægmənt] N fragment m

fragmentary ['frægməntərɪ] ADJ fragmentaire

fragmented [fræg'mɛntɪd] ADJ (divided) divisé(e)

fragrance ['freɪgrəns] N parfum m

fragrant ['freɪgrənt] ADJ parfumé(e), odorant(e)

frail [freɪl] ADJ fragile, délicat(e); (person) frêle

frailty ['freɪltɪ] N (weakness) faiblesse f; (poor health) fragilité f

★**frame** [freɪm] N (of building) charpente f; (of human, animal) charpente, ossature f; (of picture) cadre m; (of door, window) encadrement m, chambranle m; (of spectacles: also: **frames**) monture f; **~ of mind** disposition f d'esprit ▶ VT (picture) encadrer; (theory, plan) construire, élaborer; **to ~ sb** (inf) monter un coup contre qn

framework ['freɪmwə:k] N structure f

★**France** [fra:ns] N la France; **in ~** en France

franchise ['fræntʃaɪz] N (Pol) droit m de vote; (Comm) franchise f

franchisee [fræntʃaɪ'zi:] N franchisé m

franchiser ['fræntʃaɪzəʳ] N franchiseur m

Francophone ['fræŋkəufəun] N francophone mf

frank [fræŋk] ADJ franc (franche) ▶ VT (letter) affranchir

Frankfurt ['fræŋkfə:t] N Francfort

franking machine ['fræŋkɪŋ-] N machine f à affranchir

frankly ['fræŋklɪ] ADV franchement

frankness ['fræŋknɪs] N franchise f

frantic ['fræntɪk] ADJ (hectic) frénétique; (need, desire) effréné(e); (distraught) hors de soi

frantically ['fræntɪklɪ] ADV frénétiquement

fraternal [frə'tə:nl] ADJ fraternel(le)

fraternity [frə'tə:nɪtɪ] N (club) communauté f, confrérie f; (spirit) fraternité f

fraternize ['frætənaɪz] VI fraterniser

fraud [frɔ:d] N supercherie f, fraude f, tromperie f; (person) imposteur m

fraud squad N service m de la répression des fraudes

fraudster ['frɔ:dstəʳ] N (esp BRIT) fraudeur(-euse)

fraudulent ['frɔ:djulənt] ADJ frauduleux(-euse)

fraudulently ['frɔ:djuləntlɪ] ADV frauduleusement

fraught [frɔ:t] ADJ (tense: person) très tendu(e); (: situation) pénible; **~ with** (difficulties etc) chargé(e) de, plein(e) de

fray [freɪ] N bagarre f; (Mil) combat m ▶ VT effilocher ▶ VI s'effilocher; **tempers were frayed** les gens commençaient à s'énerver; **her nerves were frayed** elle était à bout de nerfs

FRB N ABBR (US) = **Federal Reserve Board**

FRCM N ABBR (BRIT) = **Fellow of the Royal College of Music**

FRCO N ABBR (BRIT) = **Fellow of the Royal College of Organists**

FRCP N ABBR (BRIT) = **Fellow of the Royal College of Physicians**

FRCS N ABBR (BRIT) = **Fellow of the Royal College of Surgeons**

freak [fri:k] N (eccentric person) phénomène m; (unusual event) hasard m extraordinaire; (pej: fanatic): **health food ~** fana mf or obsédé(e) de l'alimentation saine ▶ ADJ (storm) exceptionnel(le); (accident) bizarre

  ▶ **freak out** VI (inf: drop out) se marginaliser; (: on drugs) se défoncer

freakish ['fri:kɪʃ] ADJ insolite, anormal(e)

freckle ['frɛkl] N tache f de rousseur

freckled ['frɛkld] ADJ plein(e) de taches de rousseur

★**free** [fri:] ADJ libre; (gratis) gratuit(e); (liberal) généreux(-euse), large; **is this seat ~?** la place est libre ?; **to give sb a ~ hand** donner carte blanche à qn; **~ and easy** sans façon, décontracté(e); **admission ~** entrée libre ▶ VT (prisoner etc) libérer; (jammed object or person) dégager ▶ ADV: **~ (of charge)** gratuitement

  ▶ **free up** VT dégager

freebie ['fri:bɪ] N (inf): **it's a ~** c'est gratuit

★**freedom** ['fri:dəm] N liberté f

freedom fighter N combattant m de la liberté

free enterprise N libre entreprise f

Freefone® ['fri:fəun] N numéro vert

free-for-all ['fri:fərɔ:l] N mêlée générale

free gift N prime f

freehold ['fri:həuld] N propriété foncière libre

free kick N (Sport) coup franc

freelance ['fri:la:ns] ADJ (journalist etc) indépendant(e), free-lance inv; (work) en free-lance ▶ ADV en free-lance

freelancer ['fri:la:nsəʳ] N travailleur(-euse) indépendant(e), free-lance mf

freeloader ['fri:ləudəʳ] N (pej) parasite m

freely ['fri:lɪ] ADV librement; (liberally) libéralement

free-market economy [fri:'ma:kɪt-] N économie f de marché

freemason ['fri:meɪsn] N franc-maçon m

f

freemasonry ['friːmeɪsnrɪ] N franc-maçonnerie f

Freepost® ['friːpəust] N (BRIT) port payé

free-range [friː'reɪndʒ] ADJ (egg) de ferme; (chicken) fermier

free sample N échantillon gratuit

free speech N liberté f d'expression

freestyle ['friːstaɪl] ADJ (swimming, wrestling) libre; ~ **skiing** ski acrobatique; ~ **event** (in swimming) épreuve libre; (in skiing) épreuve f acrobatique

free trade N libre-échange m

Freeview® ['friːvjuː] N (BRIT) télévision f numérique terrestre, ≈ TNT f

freeware ['friːwɛəʳ] N (Comput) freeware m, graticiel m

freeway ['friːweɪ] N (US) autoroute f

freewheel [friː'wiːl] VI descendre en roue libre

freewheeling [friː'wiːlɪŋ] ADJ indépendant(e), libre

free will N libre arbitre m; **of one's own** ~ de son plein gré

★**freeze** [friːz] (pt **froze** [frəuz], pp **frozen** ['frəuzn]) VI geler ▶ VT geler; (food) congeler; (prices, salaries) bloquer, geler ▶ N gel m; (of prices, salaries) blocage m
▶ **freeze over** VI (river) geler; (windscreen) se couvrir de givre or de glace
▶ **freeze up** VI geler

freeze-dried ['friːzdraɪd] ADJ lyophilisé(e)

★**freezer** ['friːzəʳ] N congélateur m

★**freezing** ['friːzɪŋ] ADJ: ~ **(cold)** (room etc) glacial(e); (person, hands) gelé(e), glacé(e); **it's** ~ il fait un froid glacial ▶ N: **3 degrees below** ~ 3 degrés au-dessous de zéro

freezing point N point m de congélation

freight [freɪt] N (goods) fret m, cargaison f; (money charged) fret, prix m du transport; ~ **forward** port dû; ~ **inward** port payé par le destinataire

freighter ['freɪtəʳ] N (Naut) cargo m

freight forwarder [-'fɔːwədəʳ] N transitaire m

freight train N (US) train m de marchandises

★**French** [frɛntʃ] ADJ français(e) ▶ N (Ling) français m; **what's the** ~ **for ...?** comment dit-on ... en français ?; **the** ~ npl les Français

French bean N (BRIT) haricot vert

French bread N pain m français

French Canadian ADJ canadien(ne) français(e) ▶ N Canadien(ne) français(e)

French dressing N (Culin) vinaigrette f

French fried potatoes, (US) **French fries** NPL (pommes de terre fpl) frites fpl

French Guiana [-gaɪ'ænə] N Guyane française

French horn N (Mus) cor m (d'harmonie)

French kiss N baiser profond

French loaf N ≈ pain m, ≈ parisien m

★**Frenchman** ['frɛntʃmən] N (irreg) Français m

French Riviera N: **the** ~ la Côte d'Azur

French stick N ≈ baguette f

French window N porte-fenêtre f

★**Frenchwoman** ['frɛntʃwumən] N (irreg) Française f

frenetic [frə'nɛtɪk] ADJ frénétique

frenzied ['frɛnzɪd] ADJ (activity) frénétique; (attack) déchaîné(e)

frenzy ['frɛnzɪ] N frénésie f

frequency ['friːkwənsɪ] N fréquence f

frequency modulation N modulation f de fréquence

★**frequent** ADJ ['friːkwənt] fréquent(e) ▶ VT [frɪ'kwɛnt] fréquenter

frequently ['friːkwəntlɪ] ADV fréquemment

fresco ['frɛskəu] N fresque f

★**fresh** [frɛʃ] ADJ frais (fraîche); (new) nouveau (nouvelle); (cheeky) familier(-ière), culotté(e); **to make a** ~ **start** prendre un nouveau départ

freshen ['frɛʃən] VI (wind, air) fraîchir
▶ **freshen up** VI faire un brin de toilette

freshener ['frɛʃnəʳ] N: **air** ~ désodorisant m; **skin** ~ astringent m

fresher ['frɛʃəʳ] N (BRIT University: inf) bizuth m, étudiant(e) de première année

freshly ['frɛʃlɪ] ADV nouvellement, récemment

freshman ['frɛʃmən] N (irreg) (US) = **fresher**

freshness ['frɛʃnɪs] N fraîcheur f

freshwater ['frɛʃwɔːtəʳ] ADJ (fish) d'eau douce

fret [frɛt] VI s'agiter, se tracasser

fretful ['frɛtful] ADJ (child) grincheux(-euse)

Freudian ['frɔɪdɪən] ADJ freudien(ne); ~ **slip** lapsus m

FRG N ABBR (= Federal Republic of Germany) RFA f

Fri. ABBR (= Friday) ve.

friar ['fraɪəʳ] N moine m, frère m

friction ['frɪkʃən] N friction f, frottement m

friction feed N (on printer) entraînement m par friction

★**Friday** ['fraɪdɪ] N vendredi m; see also **Tuesday**

★**fridge** [frɪdʒ] N (BRIT) frigo m, frigidaire® m

fridge-freezer ['frɪdʒ'friːzəʳ] N réfrigérateur-congélateur m

fried [fraɪd] PT, PP of **fry** ▶ ADJ frit(e); ~ **egg** œuf m sur le plat

★**friend** [frɛnd] N ami(e); **to make friends with** se lier (d'amitié) avec ▶ VT (Internet) ajouter comme ami(e)

friendliness ['frɛndlɪnɪs] N attitude amicale

★**friendly** ['frɛndlɪ] ADJ amical(e); (kind) sympathique, gentil(le); (place) accueillant(e); (Pol: country) ami(e); **to be** ~ **with** être ami(e) avec; **to be** ~ **to** être bien disposé(e) à l'égard de ▶ N (also: **friendly match**) match amical

friendly fire N: **they were killed by** ~ ils sont morts sous les tirs de leur propre camp

friendly society N société f mutualiste

★**friendship** ['frɛndʃɪp] N amitié f

fries [fraɪz] NPL (esp US) = **chips**

frieze [friːz] N frise f, bordure f

frigate ['frɪgɪt] N (Naut: modern) frégate f

fright [fraɪt] N peur f, effroi m; **to give sb a** ~ faire peur à qn; **to take** ~ prendre peur, s'effrayer; **she looks a** ~ elle a l'air d'un épouvantail

frighten ['fraɪtn] VT effrayer, faire peur à
▶ **frighten away, frighten off** VT (birds, children etc) faire fuir, effaroucher

★**frightened** ['fraɪtnd] ADJ: **to be** ~ **(of)** avoir peur (de)

frightening ['fraɪtnɪŋ] ADJ effrayant(e)

frightful ['fraɪtful] ADJ affreux(-euse)

frightfully ['fraɪtfəlɪ] ADV affreusement

frigid ['frɪdʒɪd] ADJ frigide

frigidity [frɪ'dʒɪdɪtɪ] N frigidité f

frill [frɪl] N (of dress) volant m; (of shirt) jabot m; **without frills** (fig) sans manières

frilly ['frɪlɪ] ADJ à fanfreluches

fringe [frɪndʒ] N (BRIT: of hair) frange f; (edge: of forest etc) bordure f; (fig): **on the ~** en marge

fringe benefits NPL avantages sociaux or en nature

fringe theatre N théâtre m d'avant-garde

Frisbee® ['frɪzbɪ] N Frisbee® m

frisk [frɪsk] VT fouiller

frisky ['frɪskɪ] ADJ vif (vive), sémillant(e)

frisson ['friːsɔ̃ː] N (literary) frisson m

fritter ['frɪtə'] N beignet m
  ▶ **fritter away** VT gaspiller

frivolity [frɪ'vɔlɪtɪ] N frivolité f

frivolous ['frɪvələs] ADJ frivole

frizzy ['frɪzɪ] ADJ crépu(e)

fro [frəu] ADV see **to**

frock [frɔk] N robe f

★**frog** [frɔg] N grenouille f; **to have a ~ in one's throat** avoir un chat dans la gorge

frogman ['frɔgmən] N (irreg) homme-grenouille m

frogmarch ['frɔgmaːtʃ] VT (BRIT): **to ~ sb in/out** faire entrer/sortir qn de force

frolic ['frɔlɪk] N ébats mpl ▶ VI folâtrer, batifoler

---

from [frɔm]

PREP **1** (indicating starting place, origin etc) de; **where do you come from?, where are you from?** d'où venez-vous ?; **where has he come from?** d'où arrive-t-il ?; **from London to Paris** de Londres à Paris; **to escape from sb/sth** échapper à qn/qch; **a letter/telephone call from my sister** une lettre/un appel de ma sœur; **to drink from the bottle** boire à (même) la bouteille; **tell him from me that ...** dites-lui de ma part que ...

2 (indicating time) (à partir) de; **from one o'clock to or until or till two** d'une heure à deux heures; **from January (on)** à partir de janvier

3 (indicating distance) de; **the hotel is one kilometre from the beach** l'hôtel est à un kilomètre de la plage

4 (indicating price, number etc) de; **prices range from £10 to £50** les prix varient entre 10 livres et 50 livres; **the interest rate was increased from 9% to 10%** le taux d'intérêt est passé de 9% à 10%

5 (indicating difference) de; **he can't tell red from green** il ne peut pas distinguer le rouge du vert; **to be different from sb/sth** être différent de qn/qch

6 (because of, on the basis of): **from what he says** d'après ce qu'il dit; **weak from hunger** affaibli par la faim

---

frond [frɔnd] N fronde f

★**front** [frʌnt] N (of house, dress) devant m; (of coach, train) avant m; (of book) couverture f; (promenade: also: **sea front**) bord m de mer; (Mil, Pol, Meteorology) front m; (fig: appearances) contenance f, façade f; **in ~ (of)** devant ▶ ADJ de devant; (page, row) premier(-ière); (seat, wheel) avant inv ▶ VI: **to ~ onto sth** donner sur qch

frontage ['frʌntɪdʒ] N façade f; (of shop) devanture f

frontal ['frʌntl] ADJ frontal(e)

front bench N (BRIT Pol) voir article

Le **front bench** est, dans l'enceinte de la Chambre des communes, le banc réservé au gouvernement, à la droite du Speaker, ou au cabinet fantôme, à sa gauche. Les front benches du gouvernement et de l'opposition se font face. Par extension, l'expression front bench désigne les dirigeants des groupes parlementaires de la majorité et de l'opposition, qui sont appelés frontbenchers par opposition aux autres députés, les backbenchers.

frontbencher [frʌnt'bentʃə'] N (BRIT: government minister) ministre m; (: shadow minister) membre m du cabinet fantôme

front desk N (US: in hotel, at doctor's) réception f

front door N porte f d'entrée; (of car) portière f avant

frontier [frʌn'tɪə'] N frontière f

frontispiece ['frʌntɪspiːs] N frontispice m

front page N première page

front room N (BRIT) pièce f de devant, salon m

front runner N (fig) favori(te)

front-wheel drive ['frʌntwiːl-] N traction f avant

★**frost** [frɔst] N gel m, gelée f; (also: **hoarfrost**) givre m

frostbite ['frɔstbaɪt] N gelures fpl

frostbitten ['frɔstbɪtən] ADJ gelé(e)

frosted ['frɔstɪd] ADJ (glass) dépoli(e); (esp US: cake) glacé(e)

frosting ['frɔstɪŋ] N (esp US: on cake) glaçage m

★**frosty** ['frɔstɪ] ADJ (window) couvert(e) de givre; (weather, welcome) glacial(e)

froth [frɔθ] N mousse f; écume f

frothy ['frɔθɪ] ADJ mousseux(-euse)

frown [fraun] N froncement m de sourcils ▶ VI froncer les sourcils
  ▶ **frown on** VT (fig) désapprouver

froze [frəuz] PT of **freeze**

★**frozen** ['frəuzn] PP of **freeze** ▶ ADJ (food) congelé(e); (person: also assets) gelé(e)

FRS N ABBR (BRIT: = Fellow of the Royal Society) membre de l'Académie des sciences; (US: = Federal Reserve System) banque centrale américaine

fructose ['frʌktəuz] N fructose m

frugal ['fruːgl] ADJ frugal(e)

★**fruit** [fruːt] N (pl inv) fruit m

fruiterer ['fruːtərə'] N fruitier m, marchand(e) de fruits; **~'s (shop)** fruiterie f

fruit fly N mouche f du vinaigre, drosophile f

fruitful ['fruːtful] ADJ fructueux(-euse); (plant, soil) fécond(e)

fruition [fruː'ɪʃən] N: **to come to ~** se réaliser

fruit juice N jus m de fruit

fruitless ['fru:tlɪs] ADJ (fig) vain(e), infructueux(-euse)

fruit machine N (BRIT) machine f à sous

fruit salad N salade f de fruits

frump [frʌmp] N mocheté f

frustrate [frʌs'treɪt] VT frustrer; (plot, plans) faire échouer

frustrated [frʌs'treɪtɪd] ADJ frustré(e)

frustrating [frʌs'treɪtɪŋ] ADJ (job) frustrant(e); (day) démoralisant(e)

frustration [frʌs'treɪʃən] N frustration f

★**fry** [fraɪ] (pt, pp **fried** [-d]) VT (faire) frire ▶ N: **small ~** le menu fretin

frying pan ['fraɪɪŋ-] N poêle f (à frire)

FT N ABBR (BRIT: = Financial Times) journal financier

ft. ABBR = **foot; feet**

FTC N ABBR (US) = **Federal Trade Commission**

FTSE 100 (Share) Index ['futsɪ-] N ABBR (= Financial Times Stock Exchange 100 (Share) Index) indice m Footsie des cent grandes valeurs

fuchsia ['fju:ʃə] N fuchsia m

fuck [fʌk] VT, VI (inf!) baiser (!); **~ off!** fous le camp! (!) ▶ **fuck up** VT (inf!) foutre la merde dans (inf)

fucking ['fʌkɪŋ] (inf!) ADJ putain de (inf) ▶ ADV (stupid, expensive) carrément (inf)

fuddled ['fʌdld] ADJ (muddled) embrouillé(e), confus(e)

fuddy-duddy ['fʌdɪdʌdɪ] ADJ (pej) vieux jeu inv, ringard(e)

fudge [fʌdʒ] N (Culin) sorte de confiserie à base de sucre, de beurre et de lait ▶ VT (issue, problem) esquiver

★**fuel** ['fjuəl] N (for heating) combustible m; (for engine) carburant m

fuel oil N mazout m

fuel poverty N pauvreté f énergétique

fuel pump N (Aut) pompe f d'alimentation

fuel tank N cuve f à mazout, citerne f; (in vehicle) réservoir m de or à carburant

fug [fʌg] N (BRIT) puanteur f, odeur f de renfermé

fugitive ['fju:dʒɪtɪv] N fugitif(-ive)

fulfil, (US) **fulfill** [ful'fɪl] VT (function, condition) remplir; (order) exécuter; (wish, desire) satisfaire, réaliser

fulfilled [ful'fɪld] ADJ (person) comblé(e), épanoui(e)

fulfilling [ful'fɪlɪŋ] ADJ profondément satisfaisant(e)

fulfilment, (US) **fulfillment** [ful'fɪlmənt] N (of wishes) réalisation f

★**full** [ful] ADJ plein(e); (details, hotel, bus) complet(-ète); (price) fort(e), normal(e); (busy: day) chargé(e); (skirt) ample, large; **~ (up)** (hotel etc) complet(-ète); **I'm ~ (up)** j'ai bien mangé; **~ employment/fare** plein emploi/tarif; **a ~ two hours** deux bonnes heures; **at ~ speed** à toute vitesse ▶ ADV: **to know ~ well that** savoir fort bien que ▶ N: **in ~** (reproduce, quote, pay) intégralement; (write name etc) en toutes lettres

fullback ['fulbæk] N (Rugby, Football) arrière m

full-blooded [ful'blʌdɪd] ADJ (vigorous) vigoureux(-euse)

full board N (esp BRIT) pension complète

full-cream ['ful'kri:m] ADJ: **~ milk** (BRIT) lait entier

full-grown ['ful'grəun] ADJ arrivé(e) à maturité, adulte

full-length ['ful'lɛŋθ] ADJ (portrait) en pied; (coat) long(ue); **~ film** long métrage

full moon N pleine lune

fullness ['fulnɪs] N (of garment) ampleur f; (after eating) rassasiement m; **in the ~ of time** avec le temps

full-scale ['fulskeɪl] ADJ (model) grandeur nature inv; (search, retreat) complet(-ète), total(e)

full-sized ['ful'saɪzd] ADJ (portrait etc) grandeur nature inv

full stop N point m

full-time ['ful'taɪm] ADJ, ADV (work) à plein temps ▶ N (Sport) fin f du match

fully ['fulɪ] ADV entièrement, complètement; (at least): **~ as big** au moins aussi grand

fully-fledged ['fulɪ'flɛdʒd] ADJ (teacher, barrister) diplômé(e); (citizen, member) à part entière

fulsome ['fulsəm] ADJ (pej: praise) excessif(-ive); (: manner) exagéré(e)

fumble ['fʌmbl] VI fouiller, tâtonner ▶ VT (ball) mal réceptionner, cafouiller ▶ **fumble for** VT fouiller pour trouver ▶ **fumble with** VT FUS tripoter

fume [fju:m] VI (rage) rager

fumes [fju:mz] NPL vapeurs fpl, émanations fpl, gaz mpl

fumigate ['fju:mɪgeɪt] VT désinfecter (par fumigation)

★**fun** [fʌn] N amusement m, divertissement m; **to have ~** s'amuser; **for ~** pour rire; **it's not much ~** ce n'est pas très drôle or amusant; **to make ~ of** se moquer de

function ['fʌŋkʃən] N fonction f; (reception, dinner) cérémonie f, soirée officielle ▶ VI fonctionner; **to ~ as** faire office de

functional ['fʌŋkʃənl] ADJ fonctionnel(le)

functionality [fʌŋkʃə'nælɪtɪ] N fonctionnalité f

function key N (Comput) touche f de fonction

fund [fʌnd] N caisse f, fonds m; (source, store) source f, mine f ■ **funds** NPL (money) fonds mpl

fundamental [fʌndə'mɛntl] ADJ fondamental(e) ■ **fundamentals** NPL principes mpl de base

fundamentalism [fʌndə'mɛntəlɪzəm] N intégrisme m

fundamentalist [fʌndə'mɛntəlɪst] N intégriste mf

fundamentally [fʌndə'mɛntəlɪ] ADV fondamentalement

funding ['fʌndɪŋ] N financement m

fund-raising ['fʌndreɪzɪŋ] N collecte f de fonds

funeral ['fju:nərəl] N enterrement m; (more formal occasion) obsèques fpl

funeral director N entrepreneur m des pompes funèbres

funeral parlour N (BRIT) dépôt m mortuaire

funeral service N service m funèbre

funereal [fju:'nɪərɪəl] ADJ lugubre, funèbre

funfair ['fʌnfɛəʳ] N (BRIT) fête (foraine)

fungal ['fʌŋgəl] ADJ fongique

fungus ['fʌŋgəs] (pl **fungi** [-gaɪ]) N champignon m; (mould) moisissure f

funicular [fjuː'nɪkjʊləʳ] N (also: **funicular railway**) funiculaire m

funky ['fʌŋkɪ] ADJ (music) funky inv; (inf: excellent) super inv

funnel ['fʌnl] N entonnoir m; (of ship) cheminée f

funnily ['fʌnɪlɪ] ADV drôlement; (strangely) curieusement

★**funny** ['fʌnɪ] ADJ amusant(e), drôle; (strange) curieux(-euse), bizarre

funny bone N endroit sensible du coude

fun run N course f de fond (pour amateurs)

fur [fəːʳ] N fourrure f; (BRIT: in kettle etc) (dépôt m de) tartre m

fur coat N manteau m de fourrure

furious ['fjʊərɪəs] ADJ furieux(-euse); (effort) acharné(e); **to be ~ with sb** être dans une fureur noire contre qn

furiously ['fjʊərɪəslɪ] ADV furieusement; avec acharnement

furl [fəːl] VT rouler; (Naut) ferler

furlong ['fəːlɔŋ] N = 201.17 m (terme d'hippisme)

furlough ['fəːləʊ] N permission f, congé m

furnace ['fəːnɪs] N fourneau m

furnish ['fəːnɪʃ] VT meubler; (supply) fournir; **furnished flat** or (US) **apartment** meublé m

furnishings ['fəːnɪʃɪŋz] NPL mobilier m, articles mpl d'ameublement

★**furniture** ['fəːnɪtʃəʳ] N meubles mpl, mobilier m; **piece of ~** meuble

furniture polish N encaustique f

furore [fjʊə'rɔːrɪ] N (protests) protestations fpl

furrier ['fʌrɪəʳ] N fourreur m

furrow ['fʌrəʊ] N sillon m

furry ['fəːrɪ] ADJ (animal) à fourrure; (toy) en peluche

★**further** ['fəːðəʳ] ADJ supplémentaire, autre; nouveau (nouvelle); **how much ~ is it?** quelle distance or combien reste-t-il à parcourir ?; **until ~ notice** jusqu'à nouvel ordre or avis ▶ ADV plus loin; (more) davantage; (moreover) de plus; **~ to your letter of …** (Comm) suite à votre lettre du … ▶ VT faire avancer or progresser, promouvoir

further education N enseignement m postscolaire (recyclage, formation professionnelle)

furthermore [fəːðə'mɔːʳ] ADV de plus, en outre

furthermost ['fəːðəməʊst] ADJ le (la) plus éloigné(e)

furthest ['fəːðɪst] SUPERLATIVE of **far**

furtive ['fəːtɪv] ADJ furtif(-ive)

fury ['fjʊərɪ] N fureur f

fuse, (US) **fuze** [fjuːz] N fusible m; (for bomb etc) amorce f, détonateur m; **a ~ has blown** un fusible a sauté ▶ VT, VI (metal) fondre; (fig) fusionner; (BRIT Elec) **to ~ the lights** faire sauter les fusibles or les plombs

fuse box N boîte f à fusibles

fuselage ['fjuːzəlɑːʒ] N fuselage m

fuse wire N fusible m

fusillade [fjuːzɪ'leɪd] N fusillade f; (fig) feu roulant

fusion ['fjuːʒən] N fusion f

fuss [fʌs] N (anxiety, excitement) chichis mpl, façons fpl; (commotion) tapage m; (complaining, trouble) histoire(s) f(pl); **to make a ~** faire des façons (or des histoires); **to make a ~ of sb** dorloter qn ▶ VI faire des histoires ▶ VT (person) embêter
▶ **fuss over** VT FUS (person) dorloter

fusspot ['fʌspɔt] N (inf): **don't be such a ~!** ne fais pas tant d'histoires !

fussy ['fʌsɪ] ADJ (person) tatillon(ne), difficile, chichiteux(-euse); (dress, style) tarabiscoté(e); **I'm not ~** (inf) ça m'est égal

fusty ['fʌstɪ] ADJ (old-fashioned) vieillot(te); (smell) de renfermé or moisi

futile ['fjuːtaɪl] ADJ futile

futility [fjuː'tɪlɪtɪ] N futilité f

futon ['fuːtɒn] N futon m

★**future** ['fjuːtʃəʳ] ADJ futur(e) ▶ N avenir m; (Ling) futur m; **in (the) ~** à l'avenir; **in the near/immediate ~** dans un avenir proche/immédiat ■ **futures** NPL (Comm) opérations fpl à terme

futuristic [fjuːtʃə'rɪstɪk] ADJ futuriste

fuze [fjuːz] N, VT, VI (US) = **fuse**

fuzz [fʌz] N (on body, face) duvet m ▶ NPL: **the ~** (inf) les flics (inf)

fuzzy ['fʌzɪ] ADJ (Phot) flou(e); (hair) crépu(e)

fwd. ABBR = **forward**

FY ABBR = **fiscal year**

FYI ABBR = **for your information**

Gg

G¹, g [dʒiː] N (*letter*) G, g *m*; (*Mus*): **G** sol *m*; **G for George** G comme Gaston

G² N ABBR (*BRIT Scol*: = *good*) b (= *bien*); (*US Cine*: = *general (audience)*) ≈ tous publics

g. ABBR (= *gram*) g; (= *gravity*) g

G8 N ABBR (*Pol*: = *Group of Eight*) G8 *m*

G20 N ABBR (*Pol*: = *Group of Twenty*) G20 *m*

GA ABBR (*US*) = **Georgia**

gab [gæb] N (*inf*): **to have the gift of the ~** avoir la langue bien pendue

gabble ['gæbl] VI bredouiller, jacasser

gaberdine [gæbə'diːn] N gabardine *f*

gable ['geɪbl] N pignon *m*

Gabon [gə'bɔn] N Gabon *m*

gad about [gæd-] VI (*inf*) se balader

gadget ['gædʒɪt] N gadget *m*

Gaelic ['geɪlɪk] ADJ, N (*Ling*) gaélique *m*

gaffe [gæf] N gaffe *f*

gaffer ['gæfə] N (*BRIT: foreman*) contremaître *m*; (: *inf: boss*) patron *m*

gag [gæg] N (*on mouth*) bâillon *m*; (*joke*) gag *m* ▶ VT (*prisoner etc*) bâillonner ▶ VI (*choke*) étouffer

gaga ['gɑːgɑː] ADJ: **to go ~** devenir gaga or gâteux(-euse)

gaggle ['gægl] N troupeau *m*

gaiety ['geɪɪtɪ] N gaieté *f*

gaily ['geɪlɪ] ADV gaiement

gain [geɪn] N (*improvement*) gain *m*; (*profit*) gain, profit *m* ▶ VT gagner; **to ~ 3lbs (in weight)** prendre 3 livres; **to ~ ground** gagner du terrain ▶ VI (*watch*) avancer; **to ~ from/by** gagner de/à; **to ~ on sb** (*catch up*) rattraper qn

gainful ['geɪnful] ADJ profitable, lucratif(-ive)

gainfully ['geɪnfəlɪ] ADV: **to be ~ employed** avoir un emploi rémunéré

gainsay [geɪn'seɪ] VT (*irreg: like* **say**) contredire; nier

gait [geɪt] N démarche *f*

gal. ABBR = **gallon**

gala ['gɑːlə] N gala *m*; **swimming ~** grand concours de natation

galactic [gə'læktɪk] ADJ galactique

Galápagos [gə'læpəgəs] NPL: **the ~ (Islands)** les (îles *fpl*) Galapagos *fpl*

galaxy ['gæləksɪ] N galaxie *f*

gale [geɪl] N coup *m* de vent; **~ force 10** vent *m* de force 10

gall [gɔːl] N (*Anat*) bile *f*; (*fig*) effronterie *f* ▶ VT ulcérer, irriter

gall. ABBR = **gallon**

gallant ['gælənt] ADJ vaillant(e), brave; (*towards ladies*) empressé(e), galant(e)

gallantly ['gæləntlɪ] ADV (*bravely*) courageusement; (*valiantly*) vaillamment; (*chivalrously*) galamment

gallantry ['gæləntrɪ] N bravoure *f*, vaillance *f*; empressement *m*, galanterie *f*

gall bladder N vésicule *f* biliaire

galleon ['gælɪən] N galion *m*

gallery ['gælərɪ] N galerie *f*; (*also:* **art gallery**) musée *m*; (: *private*) galerie; (*for spectators*) tribune *f*; (: *in theatre*) dernier balcon

galley ['gælɪ] N (*ship's kitchen*) cambuse *f*; (*ship*) galère *f*; (*also:* **galley proof**) placard *m*, galée *f*

Gallic ['gælɪk] ADJ (*of Gaul*) gaulois(e); (*French*) français(e)

galling ['gɔːlɪŋ] ADJ irritant(e)

gallon ['gæln] N gallon *m* (*Brit* = 4.543 l; *US* = 3.785 l)

gallop ['gæləp] N galop *m* ▶ VI galoper; **galloping inflation** inflation galopante

gallows ['gæləuz] N potence *f*

gallstone ['gɔːlstəun] N calcul *m* (biliaire)

Gallup Poll ['gæləp-] N sondage *m* Gallup

galore [gə'lɔː] ADV en abondance, à gogo

galvanize ['gælvənaɪz] VT galvaniser; (*fig*): **to ~ sb into action** galvaniser qn

Gambia ['gæmbɪə] N Gambie *f*

gambit ['gæmbɪt] N (*fig*): **(opening) ~** manœuvre *f* stratégique

gamble ['gæmbl] N pari *m*, risque calculé ▶ VT, VI jouer; **to ~ on the Stock Exchange** jouer en *or* à la Bourse; **to ~ on** (*fig*) miser sur
▶ **gamble away** VT perdre au jeu

gambler ['gæmblə] N joueur *m*

gambling ['gæmblɪŋ] N jeu *m*

gambol ['gæmbl] VI gambader

★**game** [geɪm] N jeu *m*; (*event*) match *m*; (*of tennis, chess, cards*) partie *f*; (*Hunting*) gibier *m*; **a ~ of football/tennis** une partie de football/tennis; **big ~** gros gibier ▶ ADJ brave; (*willing*): **to be ~ (for)** être prêt(e) (à *or* pour) ■ **games** NPL (*Scol*) sport *m*; (*sport event*) jeux

game bird N gibier *m* à plume

gamekeeper ['geɪmkiːpə] N garde-chasse *m*

gamely ['geɪmlɪ] ADV vaillamment

gamer ['geɪməʳ] N joueur(-euse) de jeux vidéos

game reserve N réserve animalière

games console N console f de jeux vidéo

game show N jeu télévisé

gamesmanship ['geɪmzmənʃɪp] N roublardise f

gaming ['geɪmɪŋ] N jeu m, jeux mpl d'argent; (video games) jeux mpl vidéos

gammon ['gæmən] N (bacon) quartier m de lard fumé; (ham) jambon fumé or salé

gamut ['gæmət] N gamme f

G&T N ABBR gin m inv tonic m

★**gang** [gæŋ] N bande f, groupe m; (of workmen) équipe f
  ▶ **gang up** VI: **to ~ up on sb** se liguer contre qn

Ganges ['gændʒiːz] N: **the ~** le Gange

gangland ['gæŋlænd] ADJ: **~ killer** tueur professionnel du milieu; **~ boss** chef m de gang

gangling ['gæŋglɪŋ], **gangly** ['gæŋgli] ADJ dégingandé(e)

gangplank ['gæŋplæŋk] N passerelle f

gangrene ['gæŋgriːn] N gangrène f

gangster ['gæŋstəʳ] N gangster m, bandit m

gangway ['gæŋweɪ] N passerelle f; (BRIT: of bus) couloir central

gantry ['gæntrɪ] N portique m; (for rocket) tour f de lancement

GAO N ABBR (US: = General Accounting Office) ≈ Cour f des comptes

gaol [dʒeɪl] N, VT (BRIT) = **jail**

gap [gæp] N trou m; (in time) intervalle m; (fig) lacune f; vide m; (difference): **~ (between)** écart m (entre)

gape [geɪp] VI (person) être or rester bouche bée; (hole, shirt) être ouvert(e)

gaping ['geɪpɪŋ] ADJ (hole) béant(e)

gap year N année que certains étudiants prennent pour voyager ou pour travailler avant d'entrer à l'université

garage ['gæraːʒ] N garage m

garage sale N vide-grenier m

garb [gaːb] N tenue f, costume m

garbage ['gaːbɪdʒ] N (US: rubbish) ordures fpl, détritus mpl; (inf: nonsense) âneries fpl

garbage can N (US) poubelle f, boîte f à ordures

garbage collector N (US) éboueur m

garbage disposal, garbage disposal unit N broyeur m d'ordures

garbage truck N (US) camion m (de ramassage des ordures), benne f à ordures

garbled ['gaːbld] ADJ déformé(e), faussé(e)

★**garden** ['gaːdn] N jardin m ▶ VI jardiner
  ■ **gardens** NPL (public) jardin public; (private) parc m

garden centre (BRIT) N pépinière f, jardinerie f

garden city N (BRIT) cité-jardin f

gardener ['gaːdnəʳ] N jardinier m

gardening ['gaːdnɪŋ] N jardinage m

gargantuan [gaːˈgæntjuən] ADJ gargantuesque

gargle ['gaːgl] VI se gargariser ▶ N gargarisme m

gargoyle ['gaːgɔɪl] N gargouille f

garish ['gɛərɪʃ] ADJ criard(e), voyant(e)

garland ['gaːlənd] N guirlande f; couronne f

garlic ['gaːlɪk] N ail m

garment ['gaːmənt] N vêtement m

garner ['gaːnəʳ] VT engranger, amasser

garnish ['gaːnɪʃ] (Culin) VT garnir ▶ N décoration f

garret ['gærɪt] N mansarde f

garrison ['gærɪsn] N garnison f ▶ VT mettre en garnison, stationner

garrulous ['gærjuləs] ADJ volubile, loquace

garter ['gaːtəʳ] N jarretière f; (US: suspender) jarretelle f

garter belt N (US) porte-jarretelles m inv

★**gas** [gæs] N gaz m; (US: gasoline) essence f; **I can smell ~** ça sent le gaz; **to be given ~** (as anaesthetic) se faire endormir ▶ VT asphyxier; (Mil) gazer

Gascony ['gæskənɪ] N Gascogne f

gas cooker N (BRIT) cuisinière f à gaz

gas cylinder N bouteille f de gaz

gaseous ['gæsɪəs] ADJ gazeux(-euse)

gas fire N (BRIT) radiateur m à gaz

gas-fired ['gæsfaɪəd] ADJ au gaz

gash [gæʃ] N entaille f; (on face) balafre f ▶ VT taillader; balafrer

gasket ['gæskɪt] N (Aut) joint m de culasse

gas mask N masque m à gaz

gas meter N compteur m à gaz

gasoline ['gæsəliːn] N (US) essence f

gasp [gaːsp] N halètement m; (of shock etc): **she gave a small ~ of pain** la douleur lui coupa le souffle ▶ VI haleter; (fig) avoir le souffle coupé
  ▶ **gasp out** VT (say) dire dans un souffle or d'une voix entrecoupée

gas pedal N (US) accélérateur m

gas ring N brûleur m

gas station N (US) station-service f

gas stove N réchaud m à gaz; (cooker) cuisinière f à gaz

gassy ['gæsɪ] ADJ gazeux(-euse)

gas tank N (US Aut) réservoir m d'essence

gas tap N bouton m (de cuisinière à gaz); (on pipe) robinet m à gaz

gastric ['gæstrɪk] ADJ gastrique

gastric band N (Med) anneau m gastrique

gastric ulcer N ulcère m de l'estomac

gastroenteritis ['gæstrəuɛntə'raɪtɪs] N gastro-entérite f

gastrointestinal [gæstrəuɪn'tɛstɪnəl] ADJ gastro-intestinal(e)

gastronomic [gæstrə'nɔmɪk] ADJ gastronomique

gastronomy [gæs'trɔnəmɪ] N gastronomie f

gasworks ['gæswəːks] N, NPL usine f à gaz

★**gate** [geɪt] N (of garden) portail m; (of field, at level crossing) barrière f; (of building, town, at airport) porte f; (of lock) vanne f

gateau ['gætəu] (pl **gateaux** [-z]) N gros gâteau à la crème

gatecrash ['geɪtkræʃ] VT s'introduire sans invitation dans

gatecrasher ['geɪtkræʃəʳ] N intrus(e)

gated community ['geɪtɪd-] N quartier enclos dont l'entrée est gardée; ≈ quartier m sécurisé

gatehouse ['geɪthaus] N loge f

gatekeeper ['geɪtkiːpəʳ] N gardien(-ienne)

gateway ['geɪtweɪ] N porte f

gather ['gæðəʳ] vt (flowers, fruit) cueillir; (pick up) ramasser; (assemble: objects) rassembler; (: people) réunir; (: information) recueillir; (understand) comprendre; (Sewing) froncer; **to ~ (from/that)** conclure or déduire (de/que); **to ~ speed** prendre de la vitesse ▶ vi (assemble) se rassembler; (dust) s'amasser; (clouds) s'amonceler; **as far as I can ~** d'après ce que je comprends

gathering ['gæðərɪŋ] N rassemblement m

gauche [gəʊʃ] ADJ gauche, maladroit(e)

gaudy ['gɔːdɪ] ADJ voyant(e)

gauge [geɪdʒ] N (standard measure) calibre m; (Rail) écartement m; (instrument) jauge f; **petrol ~**, (US) **gas ~** jauge d'essence ▶ vt jauger; (fig: sb's capabilities, character) juger de; **to ~ the right moment** calculer le moment propice

Gaul [gɔːl] N (country) Gaule f; (person) Gaulois(e)

gaunt [gɔːnt] ADJ décharné(e); (grim, desolate) désolé(e)

gauntlet ['gɔːntlɪt] N (fig): **to throw down the ~** jeter le gant; **to run the ~ through an angry crowd** se frayer un passage à travers une foule hostile or entre deux haies de manifestants etc hostiles

gauze [gɔːz] N gaze f

gave [geɪv] PT of **give**

gavel ['gævəl] N marteau m (de commissaire-priseur, de magistrat, etc)

gawk [gɔːk] vi (inf) rester bouche bée; **to ~ at sb/sth** regarder qn/qch bouche bée

gawky ['gɔːkɪ] ADJ dégingandé(e), godiche

gawp [gɔːp] vi: **to ~ at** regarder bouche bée

gay [geɪ] ADJ homosexuel(le); (old: cheerful) gai(e), réjoui(e); (colour) gai, vif (vive); **~ marriage** mariage homosexuel

gaze [geɪz] N regard m fixe ▶ vi: **to ~ at** fixer du regard

gazebo [gə'ziːbəu] N belvédère m

gazelle [gə'zɛl] N gazelle f

gazette [gə'zɛt] N (newspaper) gazette f; (official publication) journal officiel

gazetteer [gæzə'tɪəʳ] N dictionnaire m géographique

gazump [gə'zʌmp] vi (Brit) revenir sur une promesse de vente pour accepter un prix plus élevé

GB ABBR = **Great Britain**

GBH N ABBR (Brit Law: inf) = **grievous bodily harm**

GC N ABBR (Brit: = George Cross) distinction honorifique

GCE N ABBR (Brit) = **General Certificate of Education**

GCHQ N ABBR (Brit: = Government Communications Headquarters) centre d'interception des télécommunications étrangères

★**GCSE** N ABBR (Brit: = General Certificate of Secondary Education) examen passé vers l'âge de 16 ans sanctionnant les connaissances de l'élève; **she's got eight GCSEs** elle a réussi dans huit matières aux épreuves du GCSE

Les GCSE (General Certificate of Secondary Education) sont des épreuves passées dans plusieurs matières par les jeunes Anglais, Gallois et Irlandais du Nord vers l'âge de 16 ans. La réussite à ces épreuves est une condition à remplir pour ceux qui souhaitent continuer leurs études et passer les A levels dans les matières en question (voir A level). Les résultats obtenus aux GCSE sont également importants pour ceux qui terminent leur scolarité à ce stade et souhaitent trouver un emploi. Le nombre de matières est généralement compris entre 8 et 11, certaines, comme l'anglais, les maths et les sciences, étant obligatoires pour tous les étudiants.

Gdns. ABBR = **gardens**

GDP N ABBR = **gross domestic product**

GDR N ABBR (old: = German Democratic Republic) RDA f

gear [gɪəʳ] N matériel m, équipement m; (Tech) engrenage m; (Aut) vitesse f; **top** or (US) **high/low ~** quatrième (or cinquième)/première vitesse; **in ~** en prise; **out of ~** au point mort ▶ vt (fig: adapt) adapter; **our service is geared to meet the needs of people with disabilities** notre service répond de façon spécifique aux besoins des handicapés
  ▶ **gear up** vi: **to ~ up (to do)** se préparer (à faire)
  ▶ **gear up for** vt se préparer pour

gear box N boîte f de vitesse

gear lever N levier m de vitesse

gear shift N (US) = **gear lever**

gear stick (Brit) N = **gear lever**

GED N ABBR (US Scol) = **general educational development**

gee [dʒiː] EXCL (US inf) ça alors

geek [giːk] N (inf: nerd) allumé(e) (inf); (: also: **computer geek**) crack m (inf) en informatique

geese [giːs] NPL of **goose**

geezer ['giːzəʳ] N (Brit inf) mec m

Geiger counter ['gaɪgə-] N compteur m Geiger

gel [dʒɛl] N gelée f; (Chem) colloïde m

gelatin, gelatine ['dʒɛlətiːn] N gélatine f

gelding ['gɛldɪŋ] N hongre m

gelignite ['dʒɛlɪgnaɪt] N plastic m

gem [dʒɛm] N pierre précieuse

Gemini ['dʒɛmɪnaɪ] N les Gémeaux mpl; **to be ~** être des Gémeaux

gemstone ['dʒɛmstəun] N pierre f précieuse

gen [dʒɛn] N (Brit inf): **to give sb the ~ on sth** mettre qn au courant de qch

Gen. ABBR (Mil: = General) Gal

gen. ABBR (= general, generally) gén

gender ['dʒɛndəʳ] N genre m; (person's sex) sexe m

gender-fluid [dʒɛndə'fluːɪd] ADJ (person) dont l'identité de genre est fluide

gene [dʒiːn] N (Biol) gène m

genealogy [dʒiːnɪ'ælədʒɪ] N généalogie f

★**general** ['dʒɛnərl] N général m; **in ~** en général ▶ ADJ général(e); **the ~ public** le grand public; **~ audit** (Comm) vérification annuelle

general anaesthetic, (US) **general anesthetic** N anesthésie générale

general delivery N poste restante

general election N élection(s) législative(s)

generalization ['dʒɛnrəlaɪ'zeɪʃən] N généralisation f

generalize ['dʒɛnrəlaɪz] VI généraliser

general knowledge N connaissances générales

★**generally** ['dʒɛnrəlɪ] ADV généralement

general manager N directeur général

general practitioner N généraliste mf

general store N épicerie f

general strike N grève générale

generate ['dʒɛnəreɪt] VT engendrer; (electricity) produire

★**generation** [dʒɛnə'reɪʃən] N génération f; (of electricity etc) production f

generator ['dʒɛnəreɪtə'] N générateur m

generic [dʒɪ'nɛrɪk] ADJ générique

generosity [dʒɛnə'rɔsɪtɪ] N générosité f

★**generous** ['dʒɛnərəs] ADJ généreux(-euse); (copious) copieux(-euse)

generously ['dʒɛnərəslɪ] ADV généreusement; (plentifully) abondamment

genesis ['dʒɛnɪsɪs] N genèse f

genetic [dʒɪ'nɛtɪk] ADJ génétique; **~ engineering** ingénierie m génétique; **~ fingerprinting** système m d'empreinte génétique

genetically modified ADJ (food etc) génétiquement modifié(e)

geneticist [dʒɪ'nɛtɪsɪst] N généticien(-ienne)

genetics [dʒɪ'nɛtɪks] N génétique f

Geneva [dʒɪ'niːvə] N Genève; **Lake ~** le lac Léman

genial ['dʒiːnɪəl] ADJ cordial(e), chaleureux(-euse); (climate) clément(e)

genie ['dʒiːnɪ] N génie m, djinn m

genitals ['dʒɛnɪtlz] NPL organes génitaux

genitive ['dʒɛnɪtɪv] N génitif m

genius ['dʒiːnɪəs] N génie m

Genoa ['dʒɛnəuə] N Gênes

genocidal [dʒɛnə'saɪdl] ADJ génocide

genocide ['dʒɛnəusaɪd] N génocide m

genome ['dʒiːnəum] N génome m

genre ['ʒɔnrə] N genre m

gent [dʒɛnt] N ABBR (BRIT inf) = **gentleman**

genteel [dʒɛn'tiːl] ADJ de bon ton, distingué(e)

Gentile ['dʒɛntaɪl] N gentil(e)

★**gentle** ['dʒɛntl] ADJ doux (douce); (breeze, touch) léger(-ère)

★**gentleman** ['dʒɛntlmən] N (irreg) monsieur m; (well-bred man) gentleman m; **~'s agreement** gentleman's agreement m

gentlemanly ['dʒɛntlmənlɪ] ADJ bien élevé(e)

gentleness ['dʒɛntlnɪs] N douceur f

gently ['dʒɛntlɪ] ADV doucement

gentry ['dʒɛntrɪ] N petite noblesse

gents [dʒɛnts] N W.-C. mpl (pour hommes)

★**genuine** ['dʒɛnjuɪn] ADJ véritable, authentique; (person, emotion) sincère

genuinely ['dʒɛnjuɪnlɪ] ADV sincèrement, vraiment

genus ['dʒiːnəs] N (pl **genera** ['dʒɛnərə]) N genre m

geographer [dʒɪ'ɔgrəfə'] N géographe mf

geographic [dʒɪə'græfɪk], **geographical** [dʒɪə'græfɪkl] ADJ géographique

geographically [dʒɪə'græfɪklɪ] ADV géographiquement

geography [dʒɪ'ɔgrəfɪ] N géographie f

geolocate [dʒiː'ələu'keɪt] VT géolocaliser

geolocation [dʒiː'ələu'keɪʃən] N géolocalisation f

geological [dʒɪə'lɔdʒɪkl] ADJ géologique

geologist [dʒɪ'ɔlədʒɪst] N géologue mf

geology [dʒɪ'ɔlədʒɪ] N géologie f

geometric [dʒɪə'mɛtrɪk], **geometrical** [dʒɪə'mɛtrɪkl] ADJ géométrique

geometry [dʒɪ'ɔmətrɪ] N géométrie f

geophysicist [dʒiː'əu'fɪzɪsɪst] N géophysicien(-ienne)

geopolitical [dʒiː'əupə'lɪtɪkl] ADJ géopolitique

Geordie ['dʒɔːdɪ] N (inf) habitant(e) de Tyneside; originaire mf de Tyneside

Georgia ['dʒɔːdʒə] N Géorgie f

Georgian ['dʒɔːdʒən] ADJ (Geo) géorgien(ne) ▶ N Géorgien(ne); (Ling) géorgien m

geranium [dʒɪ'reɪnɪəm] N géranium m

gerbil ['dʒɜːbɪl] N gerbille f

geriatric [dʒɛrɪ'ætrɪk] ADJ gériatrique ▶ N patient(e) gériatrique

germ [dʒɜːm] N (Med) microbe m; (Biol, fig) germe m

★**German** ['dʒɜːmən] ADJ allemand(e) ▶ N Allemand(e); (Ling) allemand m

germane [dʒɜː'meɪn] ADJ (formal): **~ (to)** se rapportant (à)

German measles N rubéole f

★**Germany** ['dʒɜːmənɪ] N Allemagne f

germinate ['dʒɜːmɪneɪt] VI germer ▶ VT faire germer

germination [dʒɜː'mɪ'neɪʃən] N germination f

germ warfare N guerre f bactériologique

gerrymandering ['dʒɛrɪmændərɪŋ] N tripotage m du découpage électoral

gestation [dʒɛs'teɪʃən] N gestation f

gesticulate [dʒɛs'tɪkjuleɪt] VI gesticuler

gesture ['dʒɛstjə'] N geste m; **as a ~ of friendship** en témoignage d'amitié

---

get [gɛt]

(pt, pp **got** [gɔt], US pp **gotten** ['gɔtn]) VI 1 (become, be) devenir; **to get old/tired** devenir vieux/fatigué, vieillir/se fatiguer; **to get drunk** s'enivrer; **to get ready/washed/shaved etc** se préparer/laver/raser etc; **to get killed** se faire tuer; **to get dirty** se salir; **to get married** se marier; **when do I get paid?** quand est-ce que je serai payé ?; **it's getting late** il se fait tard

2 (go): **to get to/from** aller à/de; **to get home** rentrer chez soi; **how did you get here?** comment es-tu arrivé ici ?; **he got across the bridge/under the fence** il a traversé le pont/est passé au-dessous de la barrière

3 (begin) commencer or se mettre à; **to get to know sb** apprendre à connaître qn; **I'm getting to like him** je commence à l'apprécier; **let's get going** or **started** allons-y

4 (modal aux vb): **you've got to do it** il faut que

vous le fassiez; **I've got to tell the police** je dois le dire à la police

▶ VT **1: to get sth done** (*do*) faire qch; (*have done*) faire qch; **to get sth/sb ready** préparer qch/qn; **to get one's hair cut** se faire couper les cheveux; **to get the car going** or **to go** (faire) démarrer la voiture; **to get sb to do sth** faire faire qch à qn; **to get sb drunk** enivrer qn

2 (*obtain: money, permission, results*) obtenir, avoir; (*buy*) acheter; (*find: job, flat*) trouver; (*fetch: person, doctor, object*) aller chercher; **to get sth for sb** procurer qch à qn; **get me Mr Jones, please** (*on phone*) passez-moi Mr Jones, s'il vous plaît; **can I get you a drink?** est-ce que je peux vous servir à boire ?

3 (*receive: present, letter*) recevoir, avoir; (*acquire: reputation*) avoir; (: *prize*) obtenir; **what did you get for your birthday?** qu'est-ce que tu as eu pour ton anniversaire ?; **how much did you get for the painting?** combien avez-vous vendu le tableau ?

4 (*catch*) prendre, saisir, attraper; (*hit: target etc*) atteindre; **to get sb by the arm/throat** prendre or saisir or attraper qn par le bras/à la gorge; **get him!** arrête-le ! ; **the bullet got him in the leg** il a pris la balle dans la jambe; **he really gets me!** il me porte sur les nerfs !

5 (*take, move*): **to get sth to sb** faire parvenir qch à qn; **do you think we'll get it through the door?** on arrivera à le faire passer par la porte ?; **I'll get you there somehow** je me débrouillerai pour t'y emmener

6 (*catch, take: plane, bus etc*) prendre; **where do I get the train for Birmingham?** où prend-on le train pour Birmingham ?

7 (*understand*) comprendre, saisir; (*hear*) entendre; **I've got it!** j'ai compris !; **I don't get your meaning** je ne vois or comprends pas ce que vous voulez dire; **I didn't get your name** je n'ai pas entendu votre nom

8 (*have, possess*): **to have got** avoir; **how many have you got?** vous en avez combien ?

9 (*illness*) avoir; **I've got a cold** j'ai le rhume; **she got pneumonia and died** elle a fait une pneumonie et en est morte

▶ **get about** VI se déplacer; (*news*) se répandre

▶ **get across** VT: **to get across (to)** (*message, meaning*) faire passer (à) ▶ VI: **to get across (to)** (*speaker*) se faire comprendre (par)

▶ **get ahead** VI (*succeed*) réussir

▶ **get along** VI (*agree*) s'entendre; (*depart*) s'en aller; (*manage*) = **get by**

▶ **get around** VI (*news*) circuler; (*person*) se déplacer; **to get around to sth** avoir le temps de faire qch ▶ VT (*problem, rule*) contourner

▶ **get at** VT FUS (*attack*) s'en prendre à; (*reach*) attraper, atteindre; **what are you getting at?** à quoi voulez-vous en venir ?

▶ **get away** VI partir, s'en aller; (*escape*) s'échapper

▶ **get away with** VT FUS (*punishment*) en être quitte pour; (*crime etc*) se faire pardonner

▶ **get back** VI (*return*) rentrer; **to get back to** (*start again*) retourner or revenir à ▶ VT récupérer, recouvrer; (*contact again*) recontacter; **when do we get back?** quand serons-nous de retour ?

▶ **get back at** VT FUS (*inf*): **to get back at sb** rendre la monnaie de sa pièce à qn

▶ **get by** VI (*pass*) passer; (*manage*) se débrouiller; **I can get by in Dutch** je me débrouille en hollandais

▶ **get down** VI, VT FUS descendre ▶ VT descendre; (*depress*) déprimer

▶ **get down to** VT FUS (*work*) se mettre à (faire); **to get down to business** passer aux choses sérieuses

▶ **get in** VI entrer; (*arrive home*) rentrer; (*train*) arriver ▶ VT (*bring in: harvest*) rentrer; (: *coal*) faire rentrer; (: *supplies*) faire des provisions de

▶ **get into** VT FUS entrer dans; (*car, train etc*) monter dans; (*clothes*) mettre, enfiler, endosser; **to get into bed/a rage** se mettre au lit/en colère

▶ **get off** VI (*from train etc*) descendre; (*depart: person, car*) s'en aller; (*escape*) s'en tirer ▶ VT (*remove: clothes, stain*) enlever; (*send off*) expédier; (*have as leave: day, time*): **we got 2 days off** nous avons eu 2 jours de congé ▶ VT FUS (*train, bus*) descendre de; **where do I get off?** où est-ce que je dois descendre ?; **to get off to a good start** (*fig*) prendre un bon départ

▶ **get on** VI (*at exam etc*) se débrouiller; (*agree*): **to get on (with)** s'entendre (avec); **how are you getting on?** comment ça va ? ▶ VT FUS monter dans; (*horse*) monter sur

▶ **get on to** VT FUS (BRIT: *deal with: problem*) s'occuper de; (: *contact: person*) contacter

▶ **get out** VI sortir; (*of vehicle*) descendre; (*news etc*) s'ébruiter ▶ VT sortir

▶ **get out of** VT FUS sortir de; (*duty etc*) échapper à, se soustraire à

▶ **get over** VT FUS (*illness*) se remettre de ▶ VT (*communicate: idea etc*) communiquer; (*finish*): **let's get it over (with)** finissons-en

▶ **get round** VI: **to get round to doing sth** se mettre (finalement) à faire qch ▶ VT FUS contourner; (*fig: person*) entortiller

▶ **get through** VI (*Tel*) avoir la communication; **to get through to sb** atteindre qn ▶ VT FUS (*finish: work, book*) finir, terminer

▶ **get together** VI se réunir ▶ VT rassembler

▶ **get up** VI (*rise*) se lever ▶ VT FUS monter

▶ **get up to** VT FUS (*reach*) arriver à; (*prank etc*) faire

getaway [ˈɡɛtəweɪ] N fuite *f*

getaway car N voiture prévue pour prendre la fuite

get-together [ˈɡɛttəɡɛðəʳ] N petite réunion, petite fête

get-up [ˈɡɛtʌp] N (*inf: outfit*) accoutrement *m*

get-well card [ɡɛtˈwɛl-] N carte *f* de vœux de bon rétablissement

geyser [ˈɡiːzəʳ] N chauffe-eau *m inv*; (*Geo*) geyser *m*

Ghana [ˈɡɑːnə] N Ghana *m*

Ghanaian [ɡɑːˈneɪən] ADJ ghanéen(ne) ▶ N Ghanéen(ne)

ghastly [ˈɡɑːstlɪ] ADJ atroce, horrible; (*pale*) livide, blême

ghee [ɡiː] N beurre *m* clarifié

gherkin [ˈɡəːkɪn] N cornichon *m*

ghetto [ˈɡɛtəu] N ghetto *m*

ghetto blaster [-blɑːstəʳ] N (*inf*) gros radiocassette

ghost [ɡəust] N fantôme *m*, revenant *m* ▶ VT (*sb else's book*) écrire

ghostly [ˈɡəustlɪ] ADJ fantomatique

ghostwriter [ˈɡəustraɪtəʳ] N nègre *m* (*fig: pej*)

ghoul [ɡuːl] N (*ghost*) vampire *m*

ghoulish ['gu:lɪʃ] ADJ (*tastes etc*) morbide

GHQ N ABBR (*Mil*: = *general headquarters*) GQG *m*

GHz ABBR = **gigahertz**

GI N ABBR (*US inf*: = *government issue*) soldat de l'armée américaine, GI *m*

★**giant** ['dʒaɪənt] N géant(e) ▶ ADJ géant(e), énorme; **~ (size) packet** paquet géant

giant killer N (*Sport*) équipe inconnue qui remporte un match contre une équipe renommée

gibber ['dʒɪbəʳ] VI émettre des sons inintelligibles

gibberish ['dʒɪbərɪʃ] N charabia *m*

gibbon ['gɪbən] N gibbon *m*

gibe [dʒaɪb] N sarcasme *m* ▶ VI: **to ~ at** railler

giblets ['dʒɪblɪts] NPL abats *mpl*

Gibraltar [dʒɪ'brɔːltəʳ] N Gibraltar *m*

giddiness ['gɪdɪnɪs] N vertige *m*

giddy ['gɪdɪ] ADJ (*dizzy*): **to be** (*or* **feel**) **~** avoir le vertige; (*height*) vertigineux(-euse); (*thoughtless*) sot(te), étourdi(e)

★**gift** [gɪft] N cadeau *m*, présent *m*; (*donation, talent*) don *m*; (*Comm: also*: **free gift**) cadeau(-réclame) *m*; **to have a ~ for sth** avoir des dons pour *or* le don de qch

gifted ['gɪftɪd] ADJ doué(e)

gift shop, (*US*) **gift store** N boutique *f* de cadeaux

gift token, gift voucher N chèque-cadeau *m*

gig [gɪg] N (*inf: concert*) concert *m*

gigabyte ['gɪgəbaɪt] N gigaoctet *m*

gigantic [dʒaɪ'gæntɪk] ADJ gigantesque

gig economy N (*inf*) économie *f* reposant sur le travail indépendant

giggle ['gɪgl] VI glousser, ricaner sottement ▶ N petit rire *m* bête

giggly ['gɪglɪ] ADJ: **~ teenage girls** des adolescentes qui gloussent sans arrêt

GIGO ['gaɪgəu] ABBR (*Comput: inf*: = *garbage in, garbage out*) qualité d'entrée = qualité de sortie

gild [gɪld] VT dorer

gill [dʒɪl] N (*measure*) = 0.25 *pints* (Brit = 0.148 l; US = 0.118 l)

gills [gɪlz] NPL (*of fish*) ouïes *fpl*, branchies *fpl*

gilt [gɪlt] N dorure *f* ▶ ADJ doré(e)

gilt-edged ['gɪltɛdʒd] ADJ (*stocks, securities*) de premier ordre

gimlet ['gɪmlɪt] N vrille *f*

gimmick ['gɪmɪk] N truc *m*; **sales ~** astuce *f* pour faire vendre

gimmicky ['gɪmɪkɪ] ADJ (*inf*) fantaisiste

gin [dʒɪn] N gin *m*

ginger ['dʒɪndʒəʳ] N gingembre *m*
▶ **ginger up** VT secouer; animer

ginger ale, ginger beer N boisson gazeuse au gingembre

gingerbread ['dʒɪndʒəbred] N pain *m* d'épices

ginger group N (*BRIT*) groupe *m* de pression

ginger-haired ['dʒɪndʒə'heəd] ADJ roux (rousse)

gingerly ['dʒɪndʒəlɪ] ADV avec précaution

gingham ['gɪŋəm] N vichy *m*

ginseng ['dʒɪnsɛŋ] N ginseng *m*

gipsy ['dʒɪpsɪ] N = **gypsy**

★**giraffe** [dʒɪ'rɑːf] N girafe *f*

girder ['gəːdəʳ] N poutrelle *f*

girdle ['gəːdl] N (*corset*) gaine *f* ▶ VT ceindre

★**girl** [gəːl] N fille *f*, fillette *f*; (*young unmarried woman*) jeune fille; (*daughter*) fille; **an English ~** une jeune Anglaise; **a little English ~** une petite Anglaise

girl band N girls band *m*

★**girlfriend** ['gəːlfrɛnd] N (*female friend*) amie *f*; (*romantic partner*) petite amie

Girl Guide N (*BRIT*) éclaireuse *f*; (*Roman Catholic*) guide *f*

girlish ['gəːlɪʃ] ADJ de jeune fille

Girl Scout N (*US*) = **Girl Guide**

Giro ['dʒaɪrəu] N: **the National ~** (*BRIT*) ≈ les comptes chèques postaux

giro ['dʒaɪrəu] N (*bank giro*) virement *m* bancaire; (*post office giro*) mandat *m*

girth [gəːθ] N circonférence *f*; (*of horse*) sangle *f*

gist [dʒɪst] N essentiel *m*

★**give** [gɪv] (*pt* **gave** [geɪv], *pp* **given** ['gɪvn]) N (*of fabric*) élasticité *f* ▶ VT donner; **to ~ sb sth, ~ sth to sb** donner qch à qn; (*gift*) offrir qch à qn; (*message*) transmettre qch à qn; **to ~ sb a call/kiss** appeler/embrasser qn; **to ~ a cry/sigh** pousser un cri/un soupir; **how much did you ~ for it?** combien (l') avez-vous payé ?; **12 o'clock, ~ or take a few minutes** midi, à quelques minutes près; **to ~ way** céder; (*BRIT Aut*) donner la priorité ▶ VI (*break*) céder; (*stretch: fabric*) se prêter
▶ **give away** VT donner; (*give free*) faire cadeau de; (*betray*) trahir, donner; (*disclose*) révéler; (*bride*) conduire à l'autel
▶ **give back** VT rendre
▶ **give in** VI céder ▶ VT donner
▶ **give off** VT dégager
▶ **give out** VT (*food etc*) distribuer; (*news*) annoncer ▶ VI (*be exhausted: supplies*) s'épuiser; (*fail*) lâcher
▶ **give up** VI renoncer ▶ VT renoncer à; **to ~ up smoking** arrêter de fumer; **to ~ o.s. up** se rendre

give-and-take ['gɪvənd'teɪk] N concessions mutuelles

giveaway ['gɪvəweɪ] N (*inf*): **her expression was a ~** son expression la trahissait; **the exam was a ~!** cet examen, c'était du gâteau ! ▶ CPD: **~ prices** prix sacrifiés

given ['gɪvn] PP *of* **give** ▶ ADJ (*fixed: time, amount*) donné(e), déterminé(e) ▶ CONJ: **~ the circumstances …** étant donné les circonstances …, vu les circonstances …; **~ that …** étant donné que …

giver ['gɪvəʳ] N (*of aid*) donateur(-trice)

gizmo ['gɪzməu] N (*inf*) truc *m*

glacial ['gleɪsɪəl] ADJ (*Geo*) glaciaire; (*wind, weather*) glacial(e)

glacier ['glæsɪəʳ] N glacier *m*

★**glad** [glæd] ADJ content(e); **to be ~ about sth/that** être heureux(-euse) *or* bien content de qch/que; **I was ~ of his help** j'étais bien content de (pouvoir compter sur) son aide *or* qu'il m'aide

gladden ['glædn] VT réjouir

glade [gleɪd] N clairière *f*

gladioli [glædɪ'əulaɪ] NPL glaïeuls *mpl*

gladly ['glædlɪ] ADV volontiers

glamorous ['glæmərəs] ADJ (*person*) séduisant(e); (*job*) prestigieux(-euse)

g

glamour, (US) **glamor** ['glæmə'] N éclat m, prestige m

glance [glɑːns] N coup m d'œil ▶ VI: **to ~ at** jeter un coup d'œil à
▶ **glance off** VT FUS (bullet) ricocher sur

glancing ['glɑːnsɪŋ] ADJ (blow) oblique

gland [glænd] N glande f

glandular ['glændjulə'] ADJ: **~ fever** (BRIT) mononucléose infectieuse

glare [glɛə'] N (of anger) regard furieux; (of light) lumière éblouissante; (of publicity) feux mpl ▶ VI briller d'un éclat aveuglant; **to ~ at** lancer un regard or des regards furieux à

glaring ['glɛərɪŋ] ADJ (mistake) criant(e), qui saute aux yeux

glasnost ['glæznɒst] N glasnost f

★**glass** [glɑːs] N verre m; (also: **looking glass**) miroir m ▪ **glasses** NPL (spectacles) lunettes fpl

glass-blowing ['glɑːsbləuɪŋ] N soufflage m (du verre)

glass ceiling N (fig) plafond dans l'échelle hiérarchique au-dessus duquel les femmes ou les membres d'une minorité ethnique ne semblent pouvoir s'élever

glass fibre N fibre f de verre

glasshouse ['glɑːshaus] N serre f

glassware ['glɑːswɛə'] N verrerie f

glassy ['glɑːsɪ] ADJ (eyes) vitreux(-euse)

Glaswegian [glæs'wiːdʒən] ADJ de Glasgow ▶ N habitant(e) de Glasgow, natif(-ive) de Glasgow

glaucoma [glɔː'kəumə] N glaucome m

glaze [gleɪz] VT (door) vitrer; (pottery) vernir; (Culin) glacer ▶ N vernis m; (Culin) glaçage m

glazed [gleɪzd] ADJ (eye) vitreux(-euse); (pottery) verni(e); (tiles) vitrifié(e)

glazier ['gleɪzɪə'] N vitrier m

gleam [gliːm] N lueur f; **a ~ of hope** une lueur d'espoir ▶ VI luire, briller

gleaming ['gliːmɪŋ] ADJ luisant(e)

glean [gliːn] VT (information) recueillir

glee [gliː] N joie f

gleeful ['gliːful] ADJ joyeux(-euse)

glen [glɛn] N vallée f

glib [glɪb] ADJ qui a du bagou; facile

glide [glaɪd] VI glisser; (Aviat, bird) planer ▶ N glissement m; vol plané

glider ['glaɪdə'] N (Aviat) planeur m

gliding ['glaɪdɪŋ] N (Aviat) vol m à voile

glimmer ['glɪmə'] VI luire ▶ N lueur f

glimpse [glɪmps] N vision passagère, aperçu m; **to catch a ~ of** entrevoir ▶ VT entrevoir, apercevoir

glint [glɪnt] N éclair m ▶ VI étinceler

glisten ['glɪsn] VI briller, luire

glitch [glɪtʃ] N (inf) pépin m; **a technical ~** un pépin technique

glitter ['glɪtə'] VI (metal, light) scintiller, briller; (eyes) briller ▶ N scintillement m; (on decorations, cards) paillettes fpl

glittering ['glɪtərɪŋ] ADJ (sparkling) étincelant(e); (eyes, career) brillant(e); (occasion) somptueux(-euse)

glitz [glɪts] N (inf) faste m

glitzy ['glɪtsɪ] ADJ (inf) fastueux(-euse)

gloat [gləut] VI: **to ~ (over)** jubiler (à propos de)

★**global** ['gləubl] ADJ (world-wide) mondial(e); (overall) global(e)

globalization [gləublaɪ'zeɪʃən] N mondialisation f

globally ['gləubəlɪ] ADV mondialement

global warming [-'wɔːmɪŋ] N réchauffement m de la planète

globe [gləub] N globe m

globe-trotter ['gləubtrɒtə'] N globe-trotter m

globule ['glɒbjuːl] N (Anat) globule m; (of water etc) gouttelette f

gloom [gluːm] N obscurité f; (sadness) tristesse f, mélancolie f

gloomily ['gluːmɪlɪ] ADV (say, speak) d'un air sombre

gloomy ['gluːmɪ] ADJ (person) morose, sombre; (place, outlook) sombre; **to feel ~** se sentir morose

glorification [glɔːrɪfɪ'keɪʃən] N glorification f

glorified ['glɔːrɪfaɪd] ADJ: **I'm just a ~ secretary** je ne suis guère mieux qu'une simple secrétaire

glorify ['glɔːrɪfaɪ] VT glorifier

glorious ['glɔːrɪəs] ADJ glorieux(-euse); (beautiful) splendide

glory ['glɔːrɪ] N gloire f; splendeur f ▶ VI: **to ~ in** se glorifier de

glory hole N (inf) capharnaüm m

gloss [glɒs] N (shine) brillant m, vernis m; (also: **gloss paint**) peinture brillante
▶ **gloss over** VT FUS glisser sur

glossary ['glɒsərɪ] N glossaire m, lexique m

glossy ['glɒsɪ] ADJ brillant(e), luisant(e) ▶ N (also: **glossy magazine**) revue f de luxe

glove [glʌv] N gant m

glove compartment N (Aut) boîte f à gants, vide-poches m inv

gloved [glʌvd] ADJ ganté(e)

glow [gləu] VI rougeoyer; (face) rayonner; (eyes) briller ▶ N rougeoiement m

glower ['glauə'] VI lancer des regards mauvais

glowing ['gləuɪŋ] ADJ (fire) rougeoyant(e); (complexion) éclatant(e); (report, description etc) dithyrambique

glow-worm ['gləuwəːm] N ver luisant

glucose ['gluːkəus] N glucose m

glue [gluː] N colle f ▶ VT coller

glue-sniffing ['gluːsnɪfɪŋ] N inhalation f de colle

glum [glʌm] ADJ sombre, morose

glumly ['glʌmlɪ] ADV (say) d'un air sombre

glut [glʌt] N surabondance f ▶ VT rassasier; (market) encombrer

glute [gluːt] N (inf) fessier m

gluten ['gluːtən] N gluten m

glutinous ['gluːtɪnəs] ADJ visqueux(-euse)

glutton ['glʌtn] N glouton(ne); **a ~ for work** un bourreau de travail

gluttonous ['glʌtənəs] ADJ glouton(ne)

gluttony ['glʌtənɪ] N gloutonnerie f; (sin) gourmandise f

glycerin, glycerine ['glɪsəriːn] N glycérine f

GM ABBR (= *genetically modified*) génétiquement modifié(e)

gm ABBR (= *gram*) g

GMAT ['dʒiːmæt] N ABBR (US: = *Graduate Management Admissions Test*) examen d'admission dans le *2e* cycle de l'enseignement supérieur

GM crop N culture f OGM

GM foods N aliments *mpl* génétiquement modifiés

GMO N ABBR (= *genetically modified organism*) OGM *m*

GMT ABBR (= *Greenwich Mean Time*) GMT

gnarled [nɑːld] ADJ noueux(-euse)

gnash [næʃ] VT: **to ~ one's teeth** grincer des dents

gnat [næt] N moucheron *m*

gnaw [nɔː] VT ronger

gnome [nəum] N gnome *m*, lutin *m*

GNP N ABBR = **gross national product**

★**go** [gəu] VI (*pt* **went** [wɛnt], *pp* **gone** [gɒn]) aller; (*depart*) partir, s'en aller; (*work*) marcher; (*break*) céder; (*time*) passer; (*be sold*): **to go for £10** se vendre 10 livres; (*become*): **to go pale/mouldy** pâlir/moisir; **to go by car/on foot** aller en voiture/à pied; **he's going to do it** il va le faire, il est sur le point de le faire; **to go for a walk** aller se promener; **to go dancing/shopping** aller danser/faire les courses; **to go looking for sb/sth** aller *or* partir à la recherche de qn/qch; **to go to sleep** s'endormir; **to go and see sb, go to see sb** aller voir qn; **how is it going?** comment ça marche ?; **how did it go?** comment est-ce que ça s'est passé ?; **to go round the back/by the shop** passer par derrière/devant le magasin; **my voice has gone** j'ai une extinction de voix; **the cake is all gone** il n'y a plus de gâteau; **I'll take whatever is going** (BRIT) je prendrai ce qu'il y a (*or* ce que vous avez); **... to go** (US: *food*) ... à emporter ▸ N (*pl* **goes**): **to have a go (at)** essayer (de faire); **to be on the go** être en mouvement; **whose go is it?** à qui est-ce de jouer ?

▸ **go about** VI (*also:* **go around**) aller çà et là; (*:rumour*) se répandre ▸ VT FUS: **how do I go about this?** comment dois-je m'y prendre (pour faire ceci) ?; **to go about one's business** s'occuper de ses affaires

▸ **go after** VT FUS (*pursue*) poursuivre, courir après; (*job, record etc*) essayer d'obtenir

▸ **go against** VT FUS (*be unfavourable to*) être défavorable à; (*be contrary to*) être contraire à

▸ **go ahead** VI (*make progress*) avancer; (*take place*) avoir lieu; (*get going*) y aller

▸ **go along** VI aller, avancer; **as you go along (with your work)** au fur et à mesure (de votre travail); **to go along with** (*accompany*) accompagner; (*agree with: idea*) être d'accord sur; (*:person*) suivre ▸ VT FUS (*street*) parcourir

▸ **go away** VI partir, s'en aller

▸ **go back** VI rentrer; revenir; (*go again*) retourner

▸ **go back on** VT FUS (*promise*) revenir sur

▸ **go back to** VT FUS (*task, activity*) reprendre; **to go back to work** reprendre le travail

▸ **go by** VI (*years, time*) passer, s'écouler ▸ VT FUS s'en tenir à; (*believe*) en croire

▸ **go down** VI descendre; (*number, price, amount*) baisser; (*ship*) couler; (*sun*) se coucher; **that should go down well with him** (*fig*) ça devrait lui plaire ▸ VT FUS descendre

▸ **go for** VT FUS (*fetch*) aller chercher; (*like*) aimer; (*attack*) s'en prendre à; attaquer

▸ **go in** VI entrer

▸ **go in for** VT FUS (*competition*) se présenter à; (*like*) aimer

▸ **go into** VT FUS entrer dans; (*investigate*) étudier, examiner; (*embark on*) se lancer dans

▸ **go off** VI partir, s'en aller; (*food*) se gâter; (*milk*) tourner; (*bomb*) sauter; (*alarm clock*) sonner; (*alarm*) se déclencher; (*lights etc*) s'éteindre; (*event*) se dérouler; **the gun went off** le coup est parti; **to go off to sleep** s'endormir; **the party went off well** la fête s'est bien passée *or* était très réussie ▸ VT FUS ne plus aimer, ne plus avoir envie de

▸ **go on** VI continuer; (*happen*) se passer; (*lights*) s'allumer; **to go on doing** continuer à faire; **what's going on here?** qu'est-ce qui se passe ici ? ▸ VT FUS (*be guided by: evidence etc*) se fonder sur

▸ **go on at** VT FUS (*nag*) tomber sur le dos de

▸ **go on with** VT FUS poursuivre, continuer

▸ **go out** VI sortir; (*fire, light*) s'éteindre; (*tide*) descendre; **to go out with sb** sortir avec qn

▸ **go over** VI (*ship*) chavirer ▸ VT FUS (*check*) revoir, vérifier; **to go over sth in one's mind** repasser qch dans son esprit

▸ **go past** VT FUS: **to go past sth** passer devant qch

▸ **go round** VI (*circulate: news, rumour*) circuler; (*revolve*) tourner; (*suffice*) suffire (pour tout le monde); (*visit*): **to go round to sb's** passer chez qn; aller chez qn; (*make a detour*): **to go round (by)** faire un détour (par)

▸ **go through** VT FUS (*town etc*) traverser; (*search through*) fouiller; (*suffer*) subir; (*examine: list, book*) lire *or* regarder en détail, éplucher; (*perform: lesson*) réciter; (*: formalities*) remplir; (*: programme*) exécuter

▸ **go through with** VT FUS (*plan, crime*) aller jusqu'au bout de

▸ **go under** VI (*sink, also fig*) couler; (*: person*) succomber

▸ **go up** VI monter; (*price*) augmenter; (*also:* **go up in flames**) flamber, s'enflammer brusquement ▸ VT FUS monter, gravir

▸ **go with** VT FUS aller avec

▸ **go without** VT FUS se passer de

goad [gəud] VT aiguillonner

go-ahead ['gəuəhed] ADJ dynamique, entreprenant(e) ▸ N feu vert

★**goal** [gəul] N but *m*

goal difference N différence f de buts

goalie ['gəuli] N (*inf*) goal *m*

goalkeeper ['gəulkiːpər] N gardien *m* de but

goalkeeping ['gəulkiːpɪŋ] N jeu *m* du gardien de but

goal kick N coup *m* de pied de renvoi (aux six mètres)

goalless ['gəullɪs] ADJ (*draw*) sans but marqué

goal-post ['gəulpəust] N poteau *m* de but

goat [gəut] N chèvre f

goatee [gəu'tiː] N bouc *m*

gob [gɒb] N (BRIT *inf*) gueule f (*inf*)

gobble ['gɒbl] VT (*also:* **gobble down, gobble up**) engloutir

gobbledygook, gobbledegook ['gɒbldiguːk] N (*inf*) charabia *m*

g

go-between [ˈgəʊbɪtwiːn] N médiateur *m*

Gobi Desert [ˈgəʊbɪ-] N désert *m* de Gobi

goblet [ˈgɒblɪt] N coupe *f*

goblin [ˈgɒblɪn] N lutin *m*

gobsmacked [ˈgɒbsmækt] ADJ (*Brit inf*) estomaqué(e) (*inf*)

go-cart [ˈgəʊkɑːt] N kart *m* ▸ CPD: **~ racing** karting *m*

★**god** [gɒd] N dieu *m*; **God** Dieu

god-awful [gɒdˈɔːfəl] ADJ (*inf*) franchement atroce

godchild [ˈgɒdtʃaɪld] N (*irreg*) filleul(e)

goddamn, goddam [ˈgɒddæm] EXCL (*esp US inf*): **~ (it)!** nom de Dieu ! ▸ ADJ (*also:* **goddamned**) fichu(e) ▸ ADV sacrément

goddaughter [ˈgɒdɔːtəʳ] N filleule *f*

goddess [ˈgɒdɪs] N déesse *f*

godfather [ˈgɒdfɑːðəʳ] N parrain *m*

god-fearing [ˈgɒdfɪərɪŋ] ADJ croyant(e)

god-forsaken [ˈgɒdfəseɪkən] ADJ maudit(e)

godless [ˈgɒdlɪs] ADJ impie

godmother [ˈgɒdmʌðəʳ] N marraine *f*

godparents [ˈgɒdpɛərənts] NPL: **the ~** le parrain et la marraine

godsend [ˈgɒdsɛnd] N aubaine *f*

godson [ˈgɒdsʌn] N filleul *m*

goes [gəʊz] VB *see* **go**

gofer [ˈgəʊfəʳ] N (*inf*) coursier(-ière)

go-getter [ˈgəʊgɛtəʳ] N arriviste *mf*

goggle [ˈgɒgl] VI: **to ~ at** regarder avec des yeux ronds

goggles [ˈgɒglz] NPL (*for skiing etc*) lunettes (protectrices); (*for swimming*) lunettes de piscine

going [ˈgəʊɪŋ] N (*conditions*) état *m* du terrain; **it was slow ~** les progrès étaient lents, ça n'avançait pas vite ▸ ADJ: **the ~ rate** le tarif (en vigueur); **a ~ concern** une affaire prospère

going-over [ˈgəʊɪŋˈəʊvəʳ] N (*inf*) vérification *f*, révision *f*; (*beating*) passage *m* à tabac

goings-on [ˈgəʊɪŋzˈɒn] NPL (*inf*) manigances *fpl*

go-kart [ˈgəʊkɑːt] N = **go-cart**

★**gold** [gəʊld] N or *m* ▸ ADJ en or; (*reserves*) d'or

golden [ˈgəʊldən] ADJ (*made of gold*) en or; (*gold in colour*) doré(e)

golden age N âge *m* d'or

golden handshake N (*Brit*) prime *f* de départ

golden rule N règle *f* d'or

goldfish [ˈgəʊldfɪʃ] N poisson *m* rouge

gold leaf N or *m* en feuille

gold medal N (*Sport*) médaille *f* d'or

goldmine [ˈgəʊldmaɪn] N mine *f* d'or

gold-plated [ˈgəʊldˈpleɪtɪd] ADJ plaqué(e) or *inv*

goldsmith [ˈgəʊldsmɪθ] N orfèvre *m*

gold standard N étalon-or *m*

★**golf** [gɒlf] N golf *m*

golf ball N balle *f* de golf; (*on typewriter*) boule *f*

golf club N club *m* de golf; (*stick*) club *m*, crosse *f* de golf

golf course N terrain *m* de golf

golfer [ˈgɒlfəʳ] N joueur(-euse) de golf

golfing [ˈgɒlfɪŋ] N golf *m*

gondola [ˈgɒndələ] N gondole *f*

gondolier [gɒndəˈlɪəʳ] N gondolier *m*

★**gone** [gɒn] PP *of* **go** ▸ ADJ parti(e)

goner [ˈgɒnəʳ] N (*inf*): **to be a ~** être fichu(e) *or* foutu(e)

gong [gɒŋ] N gong *m*

gonna [ˈgɒnə] = **going to**

gonorrhoea, (US) **gonorrhea** [gɒnəˈrɪə] N blennorragie *f*

goo [guː] N (*inf*) pâte *f* visqueuse

★**good** [gʊd] ADJ bon(ne); (*kind*) gentil(le); (*child*) sage; (*weather*) beau (belle); **~!** bon !, très bien !; **to be ~ at** être bon en; **to be ~ for** être bon pour; **it's ~ for you** c'est bon pour vous; **she is ~ with children/her hands** elle sait bien s'occuper des enfants/sait se servir de ses mains; **to feel ~** se sentir bien; **it's a ~ thing you were there** heureusement que vous étiez là; **it's ~ to see you** ça me fait plaisir de vous voir, je suis content de vous voir; **~ morning/afternoon!** bonjour !; **~ evening!** bonsoir !; **~ night!** bonsoir !; (*on going to bed*) bonne nuit !; **would you be ~ enough to …?** auriez-vous la bonté *or* l'amabilité de … ?; **that's very ~ of you** c'est très gentil de votre part; **to make ~** (*deficit*) combler; (*losses*) compenser; **a ~ deal (of)** beaucoup (de); **a ~ many** beaucoup (de); **~ N** bien *m*; **he's up to no ~** il prépare quelque mauvais coup; **it's no ~ complaining** cela ne sert à rien de se plaindre; **is this any ~?** (*will it do?*) est-ce que ceci fera l'affaire ?, est-ce que cela peut vous rendre service ?; (*what's it like?*) qu'est-ce que ça vaut ?; **for the common ~** dans l'intérêt commun; **for ~** (*for ever*) pour de bon, une fois pour toutes ▪ **goods** NPL marchandise *f*, articles *mpl*; (*Comm etc*) marchandises; **goods and chattels** biens *mpl* et effets *mpl*

goodbye [gʊdˈbaɪ] EXCL au revoir !; **to say ~ to sb** dire au revoir à qn

good faith N bonne foi

good-for-nothing [ˈgʊdfənʌθɪŋ] ADJ bon(ne) *or* propre à rien

Good Friday N Vendredi saint

good-humoured [ˈgʊdˈhjuːməd] ADJ (*person*) jovial(e); (*remark, joke*) sans malice

goodies [ˈgʊdɪz] NPL (*inf*): **a little bag of ~** un sachet de petits cadeaux

good-looking [ˈgʊdˈlʊkɪŋ] ADJ beau (belle), bien *inv*

good-natured [ˈgʊdˈneɪtʃəd] ADJ (*person*) qui a un bon naturel; (*discussion*) enjoué(e)

goodness [ˈgʊdnɪs] N (*of person*) bonté *f*; **for ~ sake!** je vous en prie !; **~ gracious!** mon Dieu !

goods train N (*Brit*) train *m* de marchandises

goodwill [gʊdˈwɪl] N bonne volonté; (*Comm*) réputation *f* (auprès de la clientèle)

goody-goody [ˈgʊdɪgʊdɪ] N (*pej*) petit saint, sainte nitouche

gooey [ˈguːɪ] ADJ (*inf*) gluant(e)

Google® [ˈguːgl] N Google® *m* ▸ VT: **to google** (*word, name*) chercher sur Google

goose [guːs] N (*pl* **geese** [giːs]) N oie *f*

gooseberry [ˈguːzbərɪ] N groseille *f* à maquereau; **to play ~** (*Brit*) tenir la chandelle

goose bumps NPL chair *f* de poule

gooseflesh [ˈguːsfleʃ] N, **goose pimples** NPL chair *f* de poule

goose step N (*Mil*) pas *m* de l'oie

GOP N ABBR (*US Pol: inf: = Grand Old Party*) parti républicain

gopher ['gəufə^r] N = **gofer**

gore [gɔː^r] VT encorner ▶ N sang *m*

gorge [gɔːdʒ] N gorge *f* ▶ VT: **to ~ o.s. (on)** se gorger (de)

gorgeous ['gɔːdʒəs] ADJ splendide, superbe

gorilla [gə'rɪlə] N gorille *m*

gormless ['gɔːmlɪs] ADJ (*BRIT inf*) lourdaud(e)

gorse [gɔːs] N ajoncs *mpl*

gory ['gɔːrɪ] ADJ sanglant(e)

gosh [gɔʃ] EXCL (*inf*) mince alors !

go-slow ['gəu'sləu] N (*BRIT*) grève perlée

gospel ['gɔspl] N évangile *m*

gossamer ['gɔsəmə^r] N (*cobweb*) fils *mpl* de la vierge; (*light fabric*) étoffe très légère

gossip ['gɔsɪp] N (*chat*) bavardages *mpl*; (*malicious*) commérage *m*, cancans *mpl*; (*person*) commère *f*; **a piece of ~** un ragot, un racontar ▶ VI bavarder; cancaner, faire des commérages

gossip column N (*Press*) échos *mpl*

★**got** [gɔt] PT, PP of **get**

Gothic ['gɔθɪk] ADJ gothique

gotta ['gɔtə] = **has got to**; = **have got to**

gotten ['gɔtn] (*US*) PP of **get**

gouge [gaudʒ] VT (*also*: **gouge out**: *hole etc*) évider; (*initials*) tailler; **to ~ sb's eyes out** crever les yeux à qn

gourd [guəd] N calebasse *f*, gourde *f*

gourmet ['guəmeɪ] N gourmet *m*, gastronome *mf*

gout [gaut] N goutte *f*

govern ['gʌvən] VT (*gen, Ling*) gouverner; (*influence*) déterminer

governance ['gʌvənəns] N (*formal: of country*) gouvernement *m*; (: *of company, organization*) gestion *f*

governess ['gʌvənɪs] N gouvernante *f*

governing ['gʌvənɪŋ] ADJ (*Pol*) au pouvoir, au gouvernement; **~ body** conseil *m* d'administration

★**government** ['gʌvnmənt] N gouvernement *m*; (*BRIT: ministers*) ministère *m* ▶ CPD de l'État

governmental [gʌvn'mentl] ADJ gouvernemental(e)

government housing N (*US*) logements sociaux

government stock N titres *mpl* d'État

governor ['gʌvənə^r] N (*of colony, state, bank*) gouverneur *m*; (*of school, hospital etc*) administrateur(-trice); (*BRIT: of prison*) directeur(-trice)

Govt ABBR (= *government*) gvt

gown [gaun] N robe *f*; (*of teacher, BRIT: of judge*) toge *f*

★**GP** N ABBR (*Med*) = **general practitioner**; **who's your GP?** qui est votre médecin traitant ?

GPO N ABBR (*BRIT old*) = **General Post Office**; (*US*) = **Government Printing Office**

GPS N ABBR (= *global positioning system*) GPS *m*

gr. ABBR (*Comm*) = **gross**

★**grab** [græb] VT saisir, empoigner; (*property, power*) se saisir de ▶ VI: **to ~ at** essayer de saisir

grace [greɪs] N grâce *f*; **5 days' ~** un répit de 5 jours; **to say ~** dire le bénédicité; (*after meal*) dire les grâces; **with a good/bad ~** de bonne/mauvaise grâce; **his sense of humour is his saving ~** il se rachète par son sens de l'humour ▶ VT (*honour*) honorer; (*adorn*) orner

graceful ['greɪsful] ADJ (*person, movement*) gracieux(-euse), élégant(e); (*polite*) élégant(e)

gracefully ['greɪsfulɪ] ADV (*move*) gracieusement; (*politely*) élégamment

gracious ['greɪʃəs] ADJ (*kind*) charmant(e), bienveillant(e); (*polite*) courtois(e); (*elegant*) plein(e) d'élégance, d'une grande élégance; (*formal: pardon etc*) miséricordieux(-euse) ▶ EXCL: **(good) ~!** mon Dieu !

graciously ['greɪʃəslɪ] ADV (*politely*) courtoisement

gradation [grə'deɪʃən] N gradation *f*

★**grade** [greɪd] N (*Comm: quality*) qualité *f*; (: *size*) calibre *m*; (: *type*) catégorie *f*; (*in hierarchy*) grade *m*, échelon *m*; (*Scol*) note *f*; (*US: school class*) classe *f*; (: *gradient*) pente *f*; **to make the ~** (*fig*) réussir ▶ VT classer; (*by size*) calibrer; graduer

grade crossing N (*US*) passage *m* à niveau

grade school N (*US*) école *f* primaire

gradient ['greɪdɪənt] N inclinaison *f*, pente *f*; (*Geom*) gradient *m*

gradual ['grædjuəl] ADJ graduel(le), progressif(-ive)

★**gradually** ['grædjuəlɪ] ADV peu à peu, graduellement

★**graduate** N ['grædjuɪt] diplômé(e) d'université; (*US: of high school*) diplômé(e) de fin d'études ▶ VI ['grædjueɪt] obtenir un diplôme d'université (*or* de fin d'études)

graduated pension ['grædjueɪtɪd-] N retraite calculée en fonction des derniers salaires

graduation [grædju'eɪʃən] N cérémonie *f* de remise des diplômes

graffiti [grə'fiːtɪ] NPL graffiti *mpl*; **~ artist** graffeur(-euse)

graft [grɑːft] N (*Agr, Med*) greffe *f*; (*bribery*) corruption *f*; **hard ~** (*BRIT inf*) boulot acharné ▶ VT greffer

Grail [greɪl] N: **the ~** le Graal

grain [greɪn] N (*single piece*) grain *m*; (*no pl: cereals*) céréales *fpl*; (*US: corn*) blé *m*; (*of wood*) fibre *f*; **it goes against the ~** cela va à l'encontre de sa (*or* ma *etc*) nature

grainy ['greɪnɪ] ADJ (*film, photograph*) qui a du grain; (*surface*) granuleux(-euse)

gram [græm] N gramme *m*

grammar ['græmə^r] N grammaire *f*

grammar school N (*BRIT*) école secondaire accessible sur concours d'entrée

grammatical [grə'mætɪkl] ADJ grammatical(e)

gramme [græm] N = **gram**

gramophone ['græməfəun] N (*BRIT*) gramophone *m*

gran [græn] N (*BRIT inf*) mamie *f* (*inf*), mémé *f* (*inf*); **my ~** (*young child speaking*) ma mamie *or* mémé; (*older child or adult speaking*) ma grand-mère

granary ['grænərɪ] N grenier *m*

grand [grænd] ADJ magnifique, splendide; (*terrific*) magnifique, formidable; (*gesture etc*) noble ▶ N (*inf: thousand*) mille livres *fpl* (*or* dollars *mpl*)

grandad ['grændæd] N (inf) = **granddad**

★**grandchild** ['græntʃaɪld] N petit-fils m, petite-fille f ■ **grandchildren** NPL petits-enfants

granddad ['grændæd] N (inf) papy m (inf), papi m (inf), pépé m (inf); **my ~** (young child speaking) mon papy or papi or pépé; (older child or adult speaking) mon grand-père

★**granddaughter** ['grændɔːtəʳ] N petite-fille f

grandeur ['grændjəʳ] N magnificence f, splendeur f; (of position etc) éminence f

★**grandfather** ['grændfɑːðəʳ] N grand-père m

grandiose ['grændɪəus] ADJ grandiose; (pej) pompeux(-euse)

grand jury N (US) jury m d'accusation (formé de 12 à 23 jurés)

grandma ['grænmɑː] N (inf) = **gran**

★**grandmother** ['grænmʌðəʳ] N grand-mère f

grandpa ['grænpɑː] N (inf) = **granddad**

★**grandparents** ['grændpɛərənts] NPL grands-parents mpl

grand piano N piano m à queue

Grand Prix ['grɒŋ'priː] N (Aut) grand prix automobile

grand slam N grand chelem m

★**grandson** ['grænsʌn] N petit-fils m

grandstand ['grændstænd] N (Sport) tribune f

grandstanding ['grændstændɪŋ] N (pej) démagogie f

grand total N total général

granite ['grænɪt] N granit m

granny ['grænɪ] N (inf) = **gran**

grant [grɑːnt] VT accorder; (a request) accéder à; (admit) concéder; **to take sth for granted** considérer qch comme acquis; **to take sb for granted** considérer qn comme faisant partie du décor; **to ~ that** admettre que ▸ N (Scol) bourse f; (Admin) subside m, subvention f

granular ['grænjuləʳ] ADJ granulaire; (detailed) détaillé(e)

granulated ['grænjuleɪtɪd] ADJ: **~ sugar** sucre m en poudre

granule ['grænjuːl] N granule m

★**grape** [greɪp] N raisin m; **a bunch of grapes** une grappe de raisin

grapefruit ['greɪpfruːt] N pamplemousse m

grapevine ['greɪpvaɪn] N vigne f; **I heard it on the ~** (fig) je l'ai appris par le téléphone arabe

graph [grɑːf] N graphique m, courbe f

graphic ['græfɪk] ADJ graphique; (vivid) vivant(e)

graphic designer N graphiste mf

graphic equalizer N égaliseur m graphique

graphics ['græfɪks] N (art) arts mpl graphiques; (process) graphisme m ▸ NPL (drawings) illustrations fpl

graphite ['græfaɪt] N graphite m

graph paper N papier millimétré

grapple ['græpl] VI: **to ~ with** être aux prises avec

grappling iron ['græplɪŋ-] N (Naut) grappin m

grasp [grɑːsp] VT saisir, empoigner; (understand) saisir, comprendre ▸ N (grip) prise f; (fig) compréhension f, connaissance f; **to have sth within**
one's **~** avoir qch à sa portée; **to have a good ~ of sth** (fig) bien comprendre qch
▸ **grasp at** VT FUS (rope etc) essayer de saisir; (fig: opportunity) sauter sur

grasping ['grɑːspɪŋ] ADJ avide

★**grass** [grɑːs] N herbe f; (lawn) gazon m; (BRIT inf: informer) mouchard(e); (: ex-terrorist) balanceur(-euse)

grasshopper ['grɑːshɔpəʳ] N sauterelle f

grassland ['grɑːslænd] N prairie f

grass roots NPL (fig) base f

grass snake N couleuvre f

grassy ['grɑːsɪ] ADJ herbeux(-euse)

grate [greɪt] N grille f de cheminée ▸ VI grincer ▸ VT (Culin) râper

grateful ['greɪtful] ADJ reconnaissant(e)

gratefully ['greɪtfəlɪ] ADV avec reconnaissance

grater ['greɪtəʳ] N râpe f

gratification [grætɪfɪ'keɪʃən] N satisfaction f

gratify ['grætɪfaɪ] VT faire plaisir à; (whim) satisfaire

gratifying ['grætɪfaɪɪŋ] ADJ agréable, satisfaisant(e)

grating ['greɪtɪŋ] N (iron bars) grille f ▸ ADJ (noise) grinçant(e)

gratitude ['grætɪtjuːd] N gratitude f

gratuitous [grə'tjuːɪtəs] ADJ gratuit(e)

gratuity [grə'tjuːɪtɪ] N pourboire m

grave [greɪv] N tombe f ▸ ADJ grave, sérieux(-euse)

gravedigger ['greɪvdɪgəʳ] N fossoyeur m

gravel ['grævl] N gravier m

gravely ['greɪvlɪ] ADV gravement, sérieusement; **~ ill** gravement malade

gravestone ['greɪvstəun] N pierre tombale

graveyard ['greɪvjɑːd] N cimetière m

gravitas ['grævɪtæs] N sérieux m

gravitate ['grævɪteɪt] VI graviter

gravitational [grævɪ'teɪʃənəl] N (Physics: field, force) de gravitation

gravity ['grævɪtɪ] N (Physics) gravité f; pesanteur f; (seriousness) gravité, sérieux m

gravy ['greɪvɪ] N jus m (de viande), sauce f (au jus de viande)

gravy boat N saucière f

gravy train N (inf): **to ride the ~** avoir une bonne planque

gray etc [greɪ] ADJ (US) = **grey** etc

graze [greɪz] VI paître, brouter ▸ VT (touch lightly) frôler, effleurer; (scrape) écorcher ▸ N écorchure f

grazed [greɪzd] ADJ (arm, knee) écorché(e)

grazing ['greɪzɪŋ] N (pasture) pâturage m

grease [griːs] N (fat) graisse f; (lubricant) lubrifiant m ▸ VT graisser; lubrifier; **to ~ the skids** (US fig) huiler les rouages

grease gun N graisseur m

greasepaint ['griːspeɪnt] N produits mpl de maquillage

greaseproof paper ['griːspruːf-] N (BRIT) papier sulfurisé

greasy ['griːsɪ] ADJ gras(se), graisseux(-euse); (hands, clothes) graisseux; (BRIT: road, surface) glissant(e)

★**great** [greɪt] ADJ grand(e); (*heat, pain etc*) très fort(e), intense; (*inf*) formidable; **they're ~ friends** ils sont très amis, ce sont de grands amis; **we had a ~ time** nous nous sommes bien amusés; **it was ~!** c'était fantastique *or* super!; **the ~ thing is that ...** ce qu'il y a de vraiment bien c'est que ...

Great Barrier Reef N: **the ~** la Grande Barrière

★**Great Britain** N Grande-Bretagne *f*

> Bien qu'il soit courant d'utiliser indifféremment **Great Britain** (Grande-Bretagne) et *United Kingdom* (Royaume-Uni), ces deux termes ne recouvrent pas les mêmes réalités. *Great Britain* désigne l'ensemble composé de l'Angleterre, du pays de Galles et de l'Écosse, né en 1707 de l'union de deux royaumes. Le Royaume-Uni, quant à lui, comprend la Grande-Bretagne plus l'Irlande du Nord.

great-grandchild [greɪt'ɡræntʃaɪld] (*pl* **-children** [-tʃɪldrən]) N arrière-petit(e)-enfant

great-grandfather [greɪt'ɡrænfɑːðəʳ] N arrière-grand-père *m*

great-grandmother [greɪt'ɡrænmʌðəʳ] N arrière-grand-mère *f*

Great Lakes NPL: **the ~** les Grands Lacs

greatly ['greɪtlɪ] ADV très, grandement; (*with verbs*) beaucoup

greatness ['greɪtnɪs] N grandeur *f*

Grecian ['griːʃən] ADJ grec (grecque)

★**Greece** [griːs] N Grèce *f*

greed [griːd] N (*also*: **greediness**) avidité *f*; (*for food*) gourmandise *f*

greedily ['griːdɪlɪ] ADV avidement; avec gourmandise

greedy ['griːdɪ] ADJ avide; (*for food*) gourmand(e)

Greek [griːk] ADJ grec (grecque) ▶ N Grec (Grecque); (*Ling*) grec *m*; **ancient/modern ~** grec classique/moderne

★**green** [griːn] ADJ vert(e); (*inexperienced*) (bien) jeune, naïf(-ïve); (*ecological: product etc*) écologique; **to have ~ fingers** *or* (US) **a ~ thumb** (*fig*) avoir le pouce vert; **G~** (*Pol*) écologiste *mf*; **the G~ Party** le parti écologiste ▶ N (*colour*) vert *m*; (*on golf course*) green *m*; (*stretch of grass*) pelouse *f*; (*also*: **village green**) ≈ place *f* du village ■ **greens** NPL (*vegetables*) légumes verts

green belt N (*round town*) ceinture verte

green card N (*Aut*) carte verte; (*US: work permit*) permis *m* de travail

greenery ['griːnərɪ] N verdure *f*

greenfly ['griːnflaɪ] N (BRIT) puceron *m*

greengage ['griːnɡeɪdʒ] N reine-claude *f*

greengrocer ['griːnɡrəʊsəʳ] N (BRIT) marchand *m* de fruits et légumes

★**greengrocer's** ['griːnɡrəʊsəz], **greengrocer's shop** N magasin *m* de fruits et légumes

greenhouse ['griːnhaʊs] N serre *f*

greenhouse effect N: **the ~** l'effet *m* de serre

greenhouse gas N gaz *m* contribuant à l'effet de serre

greenish ['griːnɪʃ] ADJ verdâtre

Greenland ['griːnlənd] N Groenland *m*

Greenlander ['griːnləndəʳ] N Groenlandais(e)

green light N: **to give sb/sth the ~** donner le feu vert à qn/qch

green pepper N poivron (vert)

green pound N (*Econ*) livre verte

green salad N salade verte

green tax N écotaxe *f*

greet [griːt] VT accueillir

greeting ['griːtɪŋ] N salutation *f*; **Christmas/birthday greetings** souhaits *mpl* de Noël/de bon anniversaire

greetings card N carte *f* de vœux

gregarious [ɡrəˈɡɛərɪəs] ADJ grégaire, sociable

Grenada [ɡrɛˈneɪdə] N Grenade *f*

grenade [ɡrəˈneɪd] N (*also*: **hand grenade**) grenade *f*

grew [ɡruː] PT of **grow**

★**grey**, (US) **gray** [ɡreɪ] ADJ gris(e); (*dismal*) sombre; **to go ~** (commencer à) grisonner

grey area, (US) **gray area** N zone *f* floue

grey-haired, (US) **gray-haired** [ɡreɪˈhɛəd] ADJ aux cheveux gris

greyhound ['ɡreɪhaʊnd] N lévrier *m*

greying, (US) **graying** ['ɡreɪɪŋ] ADJ (*hair, person*) grisonnant(e)

grey matter, (US) **gray matter** N (*inf*) matière *f* grise

grey squirrel, (US) **gray squirrel** N écureuil *m* gris, petit-gris *m*

grey vote, (US) **gray vote** N vote *m* des seniors

grid [ɡrɪd] N grille *f*; (*Elec*) réseau *m*; (*US Aut*) intersection *f* (*matérialisée par des marques au sol*); **off-grid** hors-réseau

griddle ['ɡrɪdl] N (*on cooker*) plaque chauffante

gridiron ['ɡrɪdaɪən] N gril *m*

gridlock ['ɡrɪdlɔk] N (*traffic jam*) embouteillage *m*

gridlocked ['ɡrɪdlɔkt] ADJ: **to be ~** (*roads*) être bloqué par un embouteillage; (*talks etc*) être suspendu

grief [ɡriːf] N chagrin *m*, douleur *f*; **to come to ~** (*plan*) échouer; (*person*) avoir un malheur

grievance ['ɡriːvəns] N doléance *f*, grief *m*; (*cause for complaint*) grief

grieve [ɡriːv] VI avoir du chagrin; se désoler; **to ~ for sb** pleurer qn; **to ~ at** se désoler de; pleurer ▶ VT faire de la peine à, affliger

grievous ['ɡriːvəs] ADJ grave, cruel(le); **~ bodily harm** (*Law*) coups *mpl* et blessures *fpl*

grill [ɡrɪl] N (*on cooker*) gril *m*; (*also*: **mixed grill**) grillade(s) *f(pl)*; (*also*: **grillroom**) rôtisserie *f* ▶ VT (*Culin*) griller; (*inf: question*) interroger longuement, cuisiner

grille [ɡrɪl] N grillage *m*; (*Aut*) calandre *f*

grillroom ['ɡrɪlrum] N rôtisserie *f*

grim [ɡrɪm] ADJ sinistre, lugubre; (*serious, stern*) sévère

grimace [ɡrɪˈmeɪs] N grimace *f* ▶ VI grimacer, faire une grimace

grime [ɡraɪm] N crasse *f*

grimly ['ɡrɪmlɪ] ADV (*say*) d'un air sévère

grimy ['ɡraɪmɪ] ADJ crasseux(-euse)

grin [ɡrɪn] N large sourire *m* ▶ VI sourire; **to ~ (at)** faire un grand sourire (à)

g

grind [graɪnd] (*pt, pp* **ground** [graʊnd]) vᴛ écraser; (*coffee, pepper etc*) moudre; (*US: meat*) hacher; (*make sharp*) aiguiser; (*polish: gem, lens*) polir; **to ~ one's teeth** grincer des dents ▶ vɪ (*car gears*) grincer; **to ~ to a halt** (*vehicle*) s'arrêter dans un grincement de freins; (*fig*) s'arrêter, s'immobiliser ▶ N (*work*) corvée f; **the daily ~** (*inf*) le train-train quotidien

grinder [ˈgraɪndəʳ] N (*machine: for coffee*) moulin m (à café); (*: for waste disposal etc*) broyeur m

grinding [ˈgraɪndɪŋ] ADJ (*poverty, difficulty*) écrasant(e); **to come to a ~ halt** s'arrêter net

grindstone [ˈgraɪndstəʊn] N: **to keep one's nose to the ~** travailler sans relâche

grip [grɪp] N (*handclasp*) poigne f; (*control*) prise f; (*handle*) poignée f; (*holdall*) sac m de voyage; **to lose one's ~** lâcher prise; (*fig*) perdre les pédales, être dépassé(e); **to come to grips with** se colleter avec, en venir aux prises avec ▶ vᴛ saisir, empoigner; (*viewer, reader*) captiver; **to ~ the road** (*Aut*) adhérer à la route

gripe [graɪp] N (*Med*) coliques fpl; (*inf: complaint*) ronchonnement m, rouspétance f ▶ vɪ (*inf*) râler

gripping [ˈgrɪpɪŋ] ADJ prenant(e), palpitant(e)

grisly [ˈgrɪzlɪ] ADJ sinistre, macabre

grist [grɪst] N (*fig*): **it's (all) ~ to his mill** ça t'arrange, ça apporte de l'eau à son moulin

gristle [ˈgrɪsl] N cartilage m (*de poulet etc*)

grit [grɪt] N gravillon m; (*courage*) cran m; **to have a piece of ~ in one's eye** avoir une poussière or saleté dans l'œil ▶ vᴛ (*road*) sabler; **to ~ one's teeth** serrer les dents

grits [grɪts] NPL (*US*) gruau m de maïs

gritty [ˈgrɪtɪ] ADJ (*surface*) recouvert(e) de gravier; (*texture*) graveleux(-euse); (*realistic: description*) réaliste

grizzle [ˈgrɪzl] vɪ (*Brit*) pleurnicher

grizzly [ˈgrɪzlɪ] N (*also*: **grizzly bear**) grizzli m, ours gris

groan [grəʊn] N (*of pain*) gémissement m; (*of disapproval, dismay*) grognement m ▶ vɪ gémir; grogner

grocer [ˈgrəʊsəʳ] N épicier m

groceries [ˈgrəʊsərɪz] NPL provisions fpl

grocer's (shop) [ˈgrəʊsəz-], **grocery** [ˈgrəʊsərɪ] N épicerie f

grog [grɒg] N grog m

groggy [ˈgrɒgɪ] ADJ groggy inv

groin [grɔɪn] N aine f

groom [gruːm] N (*for horses*) palefrenier m; (*also*: **bridegroom**) marié m ▶ vᴛ (*horse*) panser; (*fig*): **to ~ sb for** former qn pour

grooming [ˈgruːmɪŋ] N (*personal care*) toilette f; (*between monkeys*) épouillage m; (*on Internet*) utilisation de services de rencontres en ligne par des adultes cherchant à séduire des mineurs

groove [gruːv] N sillon m, rainure f

grope [grəʊp] vɪ tâtonner; **to ~ for** chercher à tâtons

gross [grəʊs] ADJ grossier(-ière); (*Comm*) brut(e) ▶ N pl inv (*twelve dozen*) grosse f ▶ vᴛ (*Comm*): **to ~ £500,000** gagner 500 000 livres avant impôt

gross domestic product N produit brut intérieur

grossly [ˈgrəʊslɪ] ADV (*greatly*) très, grandement

gross national product N produit national brut

grotesque [grəˈtɛsk] ADJ grotesque

grotto [ˈgrɒtəʊ] N grotte f

grotty [ˈgrɒtɪ] ADJ (*Brit inf*) minable

grouch [graʊtʃ] (*inf*) vɪ rouspéter ▶ N (*person*) rouspéteur(-euse)

★**ground** [graʊnd] PT, PP *of* **grind** ▶ N sol m, terre f; (*land*) terrain m, terres fpl; (*Sport*) terrain; (*reason: gen pl*) raison f; (*US: also*: **ground wire**) terre f; **on the ~, to the ~** par terre; **below ~** sous terre; **to gain/lose ~** gagner/perdre du terrain; **common ~** terrain d'entente; **he covered a lot of ~ in his lecture** sa conférence a traité un grand nombre de questions *or* la question en profondeur ▶ vᴛ (*plane*) empêcher de décoller, retenir au sol; (*US Elec*) équiper d'une prise de terre, mettre à la terre ▶ vɪ (*ship*) s'échouer ▶ ADJ (*coffee etc*) moulu(e); (*US: meat*) haché(e) ■ **grounds** NPL (*gardens etc*) parc m, domaine m; (*of coffee*) marc m

groundbreaking [ˈgraʊndbreɪkɪŋ] ADJ révolutionnaire

ground cloth N (*US*) = **groundsheet**

ground control N (*Aviat, Space*) centre m de contrôle (au sol)

ground floor N (*Brit*) rez-de-chaussée m

groundhog [ˈgraʊndhɒg] N marmotte f commune

grounding [ˈgraʊndɪŋ] N (*in education*) connaissances fpl de base

groundless [ˈgraʊndlɪs] ADJ sans fondement

groundnut [ˈgraʊndnʌt] N arachide f

ground rent N (*Brit*) fermage m

ground rules NPL: **the ~** les principes mpl de base

groundsheet [ˈgraʊndʃiːt] N (*Brit*) tapis m de sol

groundsman [ˈgraʊndzmən] (*irreg*), (*US*) **groundskeeper** [ˈgraʊndzkiːpəʳ] N (*Sport*) gardien m de stade

ground staff N équipage m au sol

groundswell [ˈgraʊndswɛl] N lame f or vague f de fond

ground-to-air [ˈgraʊntuˈɛəʳ] ADJ (*Mil*) sol-air inv

ground-to-ground [ˈgraʊntəˈgraʊnd] ADJ (*Mil*) sol-sol inv

groundwater [ˈgraʊndwɔːtəʳ] N nappe f phréatique

groundwork [ˈgraʊndwəːk] N préparation f

★**group** [gruːp] N groupe m ▶ vᴛ (*also*: **group together**) grouper ▶ vɪ (*also*: **group together**) se grouper

group chat N discussion f de groupe

groupie [ˈgruːpɪ] N groupie f

grouping [ˈgruːpɪŋ] N groupement m

group therapy N thérapie f de groupe

grouse [graʊs] N pl inv (*bird*) grouse f (*sorte de coq de bruyère*) ▶ vɪ (*complain*) rouspéter, râler

grove [grəʊv] N bosquet m

grovel [ˈgrɒvl] vɪ (*fig*): **to ~ (before)** ramper (devant)

★**grow** [grəʊ] (*pt* **grew** [gruː], *pp* **grown** [grəʊn]) vɪ (*plant*) pousser, croître; (*person*) grandir; (*increase*) augmenter, se développer; (*become*) devenir; **to ~ rich/weak** s'enrichir/s'affaiblir ▶ vᴛ cultiver, faire pousser; (*hair, beard*) laisser pousser
  ▶ **grow apart** vɪ (*fig*) se détacher (l'un de l'autre)
  ▶ **grow away from** vᴛ FUS (*fig*) s'éloigner de

▶ **grow into** vi (*become*) se transformer en ▶ vt fus (*clothes*) devenir assez grand pour mettre

▶ **grow on** vt fus: **that painting is growing on me** je finirai par aimer ce tableau

▶ **grow out of** vt fus (*clothes*) devenir trop grand pour; (*habit*) perdre (avec le temps); **he'll ~ out of it** ça lui passera

▶ **grow up** vi grandir

grower ['grəuə'] N producteur m; (*Agr*) cultivateur(-trice)

growing ['grəuıŋ] ADJ (*fear, amount*) croissant(e), grandissant(e); **~ pains** (*Med*) fièvre f de croissance; (*fig*) difficultés fpl de croissance

growl [graul] vi grogner

grown [grəun] PP *of* **grow** ▶ ADJ adulte

grown-up [grəun'ʌp] N adulte mf, grande personne

growth [grəuθ] N croissance f, développement m; (*what has grown*) pousse f; poussée f; (*Med*) grosseur f, tumeur f

growth rate N taux m de croissance

GRSM N ABBR (*BRIT*) = **Graduate of the Royal Schools of Music**

grub [grʌb] N larve f; (*inf: food*) bouffe f

grubby ['grʌbı] ADJ crasseux(-euse)

grudge [grʌdʒ] N rancune f; **to bear sb a ~ (for)** garder rancune or en vouloir à qn (de) ▶ vt: **to ~ sb sth** (*in giving*) donner qch à qn à contre-cœur; (*resent*) reprocher qch à qn; **he grudges spending** il rechigne à dépenser

grudging ['grʌdʒıŋ] ADJ (*respect, admiration*) accordé(e) à contre-cœur

grudgingly ['grʌdʒıŋlı] ADV à contre-cœur, de mauvaise grâce

gruelling, (*US*) **grueling** ['gruəlıŋ] ADJ exténuant(e)

gruesome ['gru:səm] ADJ horrible

gruff [grʌf] ADJ bourru(e)

grumble ['grʌmbl] vi rouspéter, ronchonner

grumpy ['grʌmpı] ADJ grincheux(-euse)

grunge [grʌndʒ] N (*Mus: style*) grunge m

grunt [grʌnt] vi grogner ▶ N grognement m

G-string ['dʒi:strıŋ] N (*garment*) cache-sexe m inv

GSUSA N ABBR = **Girl Scouts of the United States of America**

GU ABBR (*US*) = **Guam**

guarantee [gærən'ti:] N garantie f ▶ vt garantir; **he can't ~ (that) he'll come** il n'est pas absolument certain de pouvoir venir

guaranteed [gærən'ti:d] ADJ (*income, success*) garanti(e); **articles of this kind are ~ to cause anxiety** des articles de ce genre vont à coup sûr provoquer des inquiétudes

guarantor [gærən'tɔ:'] N garant(e)

★**guard** [gɑ:d] N garde f, surveillance f; (*squad: Boxing, Fencing*) garde f; (*one man*) garde m; (*BRIT Rail*) chef m de train; (*safety device: on machine*) dispositif m de sûreté; (*also:* **fireguard**) garde-feu m inv; **to be on one's ~** (*fig*) être sur ses gardes ▶ vt garder, surveiller; (*protect*): **to ~ sb/sth (against or from)** protéger qn/qch (contre)

▶ **guard against** vi: **to ~ against doing sth** se garder de faire qch

guard dog N chien m de garde

guarded ['gɑ:dıd] ADJ (*fig*) prudent(e)

guardian ['gɑ:dıən] N gardien(ne); (*of minor*) tuteur(-trice)

guard's van ['gɑ:dz-] N (*BRIT Rail*) fourgon m

Guatemala [gwɑ:tı'mɑ:lə] N Guatémala m

Guernsey ['gə:nzı] N Guernesey mf

guerrilla [gə'rılə] N guérillero m

guerrilla warfare N guérilla f

★**guess** [ges] vi deviner; **to keep sb guessing** laisser qn dans le doute or l'incertitude, tenir qn en haleine ▶ vt deviner; (*estimate*) évaluer; (*US*) croire, penser ▶ N supposition f, hypothèse f; **to take** or **have a ~** essayer de deviner

guesstimate ['gestımıt] N (*inf*) estimation f

guesswork ['geswə:k] N hypothèse f; **I got the answer by ~** j'ai deviné la réponse

★**guest** [gest] N invité(e); (*in hotel*) client(e); **be my ~** (*inf*) faites comme chez vous

guest house N pension f

guest of honour, (*US*) **guest of honor** N invité(e) d'honneur

guest room N chambre f d'amis

guff [gʌf] N (*inf*) bêtises fpl

guffaw [gʌ'fɔ:] N gros rire ▶ vi pouffer de rire

guidance ['gaıdəns] N (*advice*) conseils mpl; **under the ~ of** conseillé(e) or encadré(e) par, sous la conduite de; **vocational ~** orientation professionnelle; **marriage ~** conseils conjugaux

★**guide** [gaıd] N (*person*) guide mf; (*book*) guide m; (*also:* **Girl Guide**) éclaireuse f; (*: Roman Catholic*) guide f; **is there an English-speaking ~?** est-ce que l'un des guides parle anglais ? ▶ vt guider; **to be guided by sb/sth** se laisser guider par qn/qch

guidebook ['gaıdbuk] N guide m; **do you have a ~ in English?** est-ce que vous avez un guide en anglais ?

guided missile ['gaıdıd-] N missile téléguidé

guide dog N chien m d'aveugle

guided tour ['gaıdıd-] N visite guidée; **what time does the ~ start?** la visite guidée commence à quelle heure ?

guidelines ['gaıdlaınz] NPL (*advice*) instructions générales, conseils mpl

guild [gıld] N (*Hist*) corporation f; (*sharing interests*) cercle m, association f

guildhall ['gıldhɔ:l] N (*BRIT*) hôtel m de ville

guile [gaıl] N astuce f

guileless ['gaıllıs] ADJ candide

guillotine ['gıləti:n] N guillotine f; (*for paper*) massicot m

guilt [gılt] N culpabilité f

★**guilty** ['gıltı] ADJ coupable; **to plead ~/not ~** plaider coupable/non coupable; **to feel ~ about doing sth** avoir mauvaise conscience à faire qch

Guinea ['gını] N: **Republic of ~** (République f de) Guinée f

guinea ['gını] N (*BRIT: formerly*) guinée f (= 21 shillings)

Guinea-Bissau ['gınıbı'sau] N Guinée-Bissau f

★**guinea pig** N cobaye m

guise [gaız] N aspect m, apparence f

★**guitar** [gı'tɑ:'] N guitare f

guitarist [gɪ'tɑːrɪst] N guitariste *mf*

gulch [gʌltʃ] N (*US*) ravin *m*

gulf [gʌlf] N golfe *m*; (*abyss*) gouffre *m*; **the (Persian) G~** le golfe Persique

Gulf States NPL: **the ~** (*in Middle East*) les pays *mpl* du Golfe

Gulf Stream N: **the ~** le Gulf Stream

gull [gʌl] N mouette *f*

gullet ['gʌlɪt] N gosier *m*

gullibility [gʌlɪ'bɪlɪtɪ] N crédulité *f*

gullible ['gʌlɪbl] ADJ crédule

gully ['gʌlɪ] N ravin *m*; ravine *f*; couloir *m*

gulp [gʌlp] VI avaler sa salive; (*from emotion*) avoir la gorge serrée, s'étrangler ▸ VT (*also*: **gulp down**) avaler ▸ N (*of drink*) gorgée *f*; **at one ~** d'un seul coup

gum [gʌm] N (*Anat*) gencive *f*; (*glue*) colle *f*; (*sweet*) boule *f* de gomme; (*also*: **chewing-gum**) chewing-gum *m* ▸ VT coller

gumboil ['gʌmbɔɪl] N abcès *m* dentaire

gumboots ['gʌmbuːts] NPL (*BRIT*) bottes *fpl* en caoutchouc

gumption ['gʌmpʃən] N bon sens, jugeote *f*

★**gun** [gʌn] N (*small*) revolver *m*, pistolet *m*; (*rifle*) fusil *m*, carabine *f*; (*cannon*) canon *m*; **to stick to one's guns** (*fig*) ne pas en démordre ▸ VT (*also*: **gun down**) abattre
▸ **gun for** VT FUS: **to be gunning for sb** essayer d'avoir qn

gunboat ['gʌnbəut] N canonnière *f*

gun dog N chien *m* de chasse

gunfight ['gʌnfaɪt] N échange *m* de coups de feu

gunfire ['gʌnfaɪə^r] N fusillade *f*

gung-ho [gʌŋ'həu] ADJ (*inf*) enthousiaste

gunk [gʌŋk] N (*inf*) saleté *f*

gunman ['gʌnmən] N (*irreg*) bandit armé

gunner ['gʌnə^r] N artilleur *m*

gunpoint ['gʌnpɔɪnt] N: **at ~** sous la menace du pistolet (*or* fusil)

gunpowder ['gʌnpaudə^r] N poudre *f* à canon

gunrunner ['gʌnrʌnə^r] N trafiquant *m* d'armes

gunrunning ['gʌnrʌnɪŋ] N trafic *m* d'armes

gunshot ['gʌnʃɔt] N coup *m* de feu; **within ~** à portée de fusil

gunsmith ['gʌnsmɪθ] N armurier *m*

gurgle ['gəːgl] N gargouillis *m* ▸ VI gargouiller

gurney ['gəːnɪ] N (*US*) lit *m* roulant

guru ['guruː] N gourou *m*

gush [gʌʃ] N jaillissement *m*, jet *m* ▸ VI jaillir; (*fig*) se répandre en effusions

gushing ['gʌʃɪŋ] ADJ (*person*) trop exubérant(e) *or* expansif(-ive); (*compliments*) exagéré(e)

gusset ['gʌsɪt] N gousset *m*, soufflet *m*; (*in tights, pants*) entre-jambes *m*

gust [gʌst] N (*of wind*) rafale *f*; (*of smoke*) bouffée *f*

gusto ['gʌstəu] N enthousiasme *m*

gusty ['gʌstɪ] ADJ venteux(-euse); **~ winds** des rafales de vent

gut [gʌt] N intestin *m*, boyau *m*; (*Mus etc*) boyau ▸ VT (*poultry, fish*) vider; (*building*) ne laisser que les murs de ■ **guts** NPL (*inf*: *Anat*) boyaux *mpl*; (: *courage*) cran *m*; **to hate sb's guts** ne pas pouvoir voir qn en peinture *or* sentir qn

gut reaction N réaction instinctive

gutsy ['gʌtsɪ] ADJ (*person*) qui a du cran; (*style*) qui a du punch

gutted ['gʌtɪd] ADJ: **I was ~** (*inf*: *disappointed*) j'étais carrément dégoûté

gutter ['gʌtə^r] N (*of roof*) gouttière *f*; (*in street*) caniveau *m*; (*fig*) ruisseau *m*

gutter press N: **the ~** la presse de bas étage *or* à scandale

guttural ['gʌtərl] ADJ guttural(e)

★**guy** [gaɪ] N (*inf*: *man*) type *m*; (*also*: **guyrope**) corde *f*; (*figure*) effigie *de Guy Fawkes*

Guyana [gaɪ'ænə] N Guyane *f*

Guy Fawkes' Night [gaɪ'fɔːks-] N *voir article*

Guy Fawkes' Night, ou *Bonfire Night*, commémore l'échec du complot (le *Gunpowder Plot*) contre James Ier et son parlement le 5 novembre 1605. L'un des conspirateurs, Guy Fawkes, avait été surpris dans les caves du parlement alors qu'il s'apprêtait à y mettre le feu. Chaque année pour le 5 novembre, beaucoup de Britanniques font un feu de joie et un feu d'artifice dans leur jardin. La plupart des municipalités font de même, mais dans un parc et de façon plus officielle.

guzzle ['gʌzl] VI s'empiffrer ▸ VT avaler gloutonnement

★**gym** [dʒɪm] N (*also*: **gymnasium**) gymnase *m*; (*also*: **gymnastics**) gym *f*

gymkhana [dʒɪm'kɑːnə] N gymkhana *m*

gymnasium [dʒɪm'neɪzɪəm] N gymnase *m*

gymnast ['dʒɪmnæst] N gymnaste *mf*

gymnastics [dʒɪm'næstɪks] N, NPL gymnastique *f*

gym shoes NPL chaussures *fpl* de gym(nastique)

gynaecological, (*US*) **gynecological** [gaɪnɪkə'lɔdʒɪkl] ADJ gynécologique

gynaecologist, (*US*) **gynecologist** [gaɪnɪ'kɔlədʒɪst] N gynécologue *mf*

gynaecology, (*US*) **gynecology** [gaɪnə'kɔlədʒɪ] N gynécologie *f*

gypsy ['dʒɪpsɪ] N gitan(e), bohémien(ne) ▸ CPD: **~ caravan** *n* roulotte *f*

gyrate [dʒaɪ'reɪt] VI tournoyer

Hh

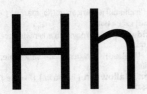

H, h [eɪtʃ] N (letter) H, h m; **H for Harry,** (US) **H for How** H comme Henri

habeas corpus [ˈheɪbɪəsˈkɔːpəs] N (Law) habeas corpus m

haberdashery [hæbəˈdæʃərɪ] N (BRIT) mercerie f

★**habit** [ˈhæbɪt] N habitude f; (costume: Rel) habit m; (: for riding) tenue f d'équitation; **to get out of/into the ~ of doing sth** perdre/prendre l'habitude de faire qch

habitable [ˈhæbɪtəbl] ADJ habitable

habitat [ˈhæbɪtæt] N habitat m

habitation [hæbɪˈteɪʃən] N habitation f

habitual [həˈbɪtjuəl] ADJ habituel(le); (drinker, liar) invétéré(e)

habitually [həˈbɪtjuəlɪ] ADV habituellement, d'habitude

hack [hæk] VT hacher, tailler ▶ N (cut) entaille f; (blow) coup m; (pej: writer) nègre m; (old horse) canasson m
▶**hack into** VT FUS (computer system, network) s'introduire dans

hacker [ˈhækə^r] N (Comput) pirate m (informatique); (: enthusiast) passionné(e) des ordinateurs

hackles [ˈhæklz] NPL: **to make sb's ~ rise** (fig) mettre qn hors de soi

hackney cab [ˈhæknɪ-] N fiacre m

hackneyed [ˈhæknɪd] ADJ usé(e), rebattu(e)

hacksaw [ˈhæksɔː] N scie f à métaux

had [hæd] PT, PP of **have**

haddock [ˈhædək] (pl ~ or **haddocks**) N églefin m; **smoked ~** haddock m

hadn't [ˈhædnt] = **had not**

haematology, (US) **hematology** [ˈhiːməˈtɔlədʒɪ] N hématologie f

haemoglobin, (US) **hemoglobin** [ˈhiːməˈɡləubɪn] N hémoglobine f

haemophilia, (US) **hemophilia** [ˈhiːməˈfɪlɪə] N hémophilie f

haemorrhage, (US) **hemorrhage** [ˈhɛmərɪdʒ] N hémorragie f

haemorrhoids, (US) **hemorrhoids** [ˈhɛmərɔɪdz] NPL hémorroïdes fpl

hag [hæɡ] N (ugly) vieille sorcière; (nasty) chameau m, harpie f; (witch) sorcière

haggard [ˈhæɡəd] ADJ hagard(e), égaré(e)

haggis [ˈhæɡɪs] N plat à base d'abats de mouton, d'avoine et d'épices dont on farcit l'estomac de l'animal et que l'on fait bouillir

haggle [ˈhæɡl] VI marchander; **to ~ over** chicaner sur

haggling [ˈhæɡlɪŋ] N marchandage m

Hague [heɪɡ] N: **The ~** La Haye

hail [heɪl] N grêle f ▶ VT (call) héler; (greet) acclamer ▶ VI grêler; (originate): **he hails from Scotland** il est originaire d'Écosse

hailstone [ˈheɪlstəun] N grêlon m

hailstorm [ˈheɪlstɔːm] N averse f de grêle

★**hair** [hɛə^r] N cheveux mpl; (on body) poils mpl, pilosité f; (of animal) pelage m; (single hair: on head) cheveu m; (: on body, of animal) poil m; **to do one's ~** se coiffer

hairband [ˈhɛəbænd] N (elasticated) bandeau m; (plastic) serre-tête m

hairbrush [ˈhɛəbrʌʃ] N brosse f à cheveux

haircare [ˈhɛəkɛə^r] N soins mpl capillaires ▶ CPD (product) capillaire, pour les cheveux

haircut [ˈhɛəkʌt] N coupe f (de cheveux)

hairdo [ˈhɛəduː] N coiffure f

★**hairdresser** [ˈhɛədrɛsə^r] N coiffeur(-euse)

> Un **coiffeur** is a hairdresser; une **coiffure** is a hairdo.

★**hairdresser's** [ˈhɛədrɛsəz] N salon m de coiffure, coiffeur m

hairdressing [ˈhɛədrɛsɪŋ] N coiffure f

hair dryer N sèche-cheveux m, séchoir m

-haired [hɛəd] SUFFIX: **fair/long-haired** aux cheveux blonds/longs

hair gel N gel m pour cheveux

hairgrip [ˈhɛəɡrɪp] N pince f à cheveux

hairline [ˈhɛəlaɪn] N naissance f des cheveux

hairline fracture N fêlure f

hairnet [ˈhɛənɛt] N résille f

hair oil N huile f capillaire

hairpiece [ˈhɛəpiːs] N postiche m

hairpin [ˈhɛəpɪn] N épingle f à cheveux

hairpin bend, (US) **hairpin curve** N virage m en épingle à cheveux

hair-raising [ˈhɛəreɪzɪŋ] ADJ à (vous) faire dresser les cheveux sur la tête

hair remover N dépilateur m

hair removing cream [-rɪˈmuːvɪŋ-] N crème f dépilatoire

hair spray N laque f (pour les cheveux)

hairstyle [ˈhɛəstaɪl] N coiffure f

h

hairy [ˈhɛərɪ] ADJ poilu(e), chevelu(e); (inf: frightening) effrayant(e)

Haiti [ˈheɪtɪ] N Haïti m

haka [ˈhɑːkə] N (NEW ZEALAND) haka m

hake [heɪk] (pl ~ or **hakes**) N colin m, merlu m

halal [həˈlɑːl] N (also: **halal meat**) viande f halal or hallal ▶ ADJ halal, hallal

halcyon [ˈhælsɪən] ADJ merveilleux(-euse)

hale [heɪl] ADJ: ~ **and hearty** robuste, en pleine santé

★**half** [hɑːf] (pl **halves** [hɑːvz]) N moitié f; (of beer: also: **half pint**) ≈ demi m; (Rail, bus: also: **half fare**) demi-tarif m; (Sport: of match) mi-temps f; (: of ground) moitié (du terrain); **two and a** ~ deux et demi; **a week and a** ~ une semaine et demie; ~ **(of it)** la moitié; ~ **(of)** la moitié de; **to cut sth in** ~ couper qch en deux; **to go halves (with sb)** se mettre de moitié avec qn; ~ **past three** trois heures et demie ▶ ADJ demi(e); ~ **an hour** une demi-heure; ~ **a dozen** une demi-douzaine; ~ **a dozen eggs** une demi-douzaine d'œufs; ~ **a pound** une demi-livre, ≈ 250 g; ~ **the amount of** la moitié de ▶ ADV (à) moitié, à demi; ~ **empty/closed** à moitié vide/fermé(e)

half-back [ˈhɑːfbæk] N (Sport) demi m

half-baked [ˈhɑːfˈbeɪkt] ADJ (inf: idea, scheme) qui ne tient pas debout

half board N (BRIT: in hotel) demi-pension f

half-breed [ˈhɑːfbriːd] N (!) = **half-caste**

half-brother [ˈhɑːfbrʌðəʳ] N demi-frère m

half-caste [ˈhɑːfkɑːst] N (!) métis(se)

half day N demi-journée f

half-dead ADJ à moitié mort(e)

half fare N demi-tarif m

half-hearted [ˈhɑːfˈhɑːtɪd] ADJ tiède, sans enthousiasme

half-hour [hɑːfˈaʊəʳ] N demi-heure f

half-life [ˈhɑːflaɪf] N (Physics) demi-vie f

half-mast [ˈhɑːfˈmɑːst] N: **at** ~ (flag) en berne, à mi-mât

halfpenny [ˈheɪpnɪ] N demi-penny m

half-price [ˈhɑːfˈpraɪs] ADJ à moitié prix ▶ ADV (also: **at half-price**) à moitié prix

half term N (BRIT Scol) vacances fpl (de demi-trimestre)

half-time [hɑːfˈtaɪm] N mi-temps f

halfway [ˈhɑːfˈweɪ] ADV à mi-chemin; **to meet sb** ~ (fig) parvenir à un compromis avec qn; ~ **through sth** au milieu de qch

halfway house N (hostel) centre m de réadaptation (pour anciens prisonniers, malades mentaux etc); (fig): **a** ~ **(between)** une étape intermédiaire (entre)

half-wit [ˈhɑːfwɪt] N (!) idiot(e), imbécile mf

half-yearly [hɑːfˈjɪəlɪ] ADV deux fois par an ▶ ADJ semestriel(le)

halibut [ˈhælɪbət] N (pl inv) flétan m

halitosis [hælɪˈtəʊsɪs] N mauvaise haleine

★**hall** [hɔːl] N salle f; (entrance way: big) hall m; (: small) entrée f; (US: corridor) couloir m; (mansion) château m, manoir m

hallelujah [hælɪˈluːjə] EXCL (also: **alleluia**) alléluia m

hallmark [ˈhɔːlmɑːk] N poinçon m; (fig) marque f

hallo [həˈləʊ] EXCL = **hello**

hall of residence N (BRIT) pavillon m or résidence f universitaire

hallowed [ˈhæləʊd] ADJ (respected) vénérable; (holy) béni(e)

Hallowe'en, Halloween [ˈhæləʊˈiːn] N veille f de la Toussaint

> Fête d'origine païenne, **Hallowe'en** est célébré au Royaume-Uni et aux États-Unis le 31 octobre, veille de la Toussaint. De nombreuses coutumes américaines ont été adoptées par les Britanniques. Ainsi, il est courant de confectionner des lanternes à partir d'une citrouille évidée dans laquelle on a découpé un visage menaçant. Les enfants se déguisent en sorcières, fantômes, etc, et vont de porte en porte quémander des sucreries en menaçant les réfractaires de leur jouer un mauvais tour.

hallucination [həluːsɪˈneɪʃən] N hallucination f

hallucinogenic [həluːsɪnəʊˈdʒɛnɪk] ADJ hallucinogène

hallway [ˈhɔːlweɪ] N (entrance) vestibule m; (corridor) couloir m

halo [ˈheɪləʊ] N (of saint etc) auréole f; (of sun) halo m

halt [hɔːlt] N halte f, arrêt m; **to call a** ~ **to sth** (fig) mettre fin à qch ▶ VT faire arrêter; (progress etc) interrompre ▶ VI faire halte, s'arrêter

halter [ˈhɔːltəʳ] N (for horse) licou m

halterneck [ˈhɔːltənɛk] ADJ (dress) (avec) dos nu inv

halting [ˈhɔːltɪŋ] ADJ hésitant(e)

halve [hɑːv] VT (apple etc) partager or diviser en deux; (reduce by half) réduire de moitié

halves [hɑːvz] NPL of **half**

★**ham** [hæm] N jambon m; (inf: also: **radio ham**) radio-amateur m; (also: **ham actor**) cabotin(e)

Hamburg [ˈhæmbəːg] N Hambourg

★**hamburger** [ˈhæmbəːgəʳ] N hamburger m

ham-fisted [ˈhæmˈfɪstɪd], (US) **ham-handed** [ˈhæmˈhændɪd] ADJ maladroit(e)

hamlet [ˈhæmlɪt] N hameau m

hammer [ˈhæməʳ] N marteau m ▶ VT (nail) enfoncer; (fig) éreinter, démolir; **to** ~ **a point home to sb** faire rentrer qch dans la tête de qn ▶ VI (at door) frapper à coups redoublés
▶ **hammer out** VT (metal) étendre au marteau; (fig: solution) élaborer

hammered [ˈhæməd] ADJ (inf: BRIT: drunk) bourré(e)

hammering [ˈhæmərɪŋ] N (inf: criticism) volée f (inf); (: defeat) raclée f (inf); (knocking) martèlement m

hammock [ˈhæmək] N hamac m

hamper [ˈhæmpəʳ] VT gêner ▶ N panier m (d'osier)

★**hamster** [ˈhæmstəʳ] N hamster m

hamstring [ˈhæmstrɪŋ] N (Anat) tendon m du jarret

★**hand** [hænd] N main f; (of clock) aiguille f; (handwriting) écriture f; (at cards) jeu m; (measurement: of horse) paume f; (worker) ouvrier(-ière); **to give sb a** ~ donner un coup de main à qn; **at** ~ à portée de la main; **in** ~ (situation) en main; (work) en cours; **we have the situation in** ~ nous avons la situation bien en main; **to be on ~** (person) être disponible; (emergency services) se tenir prêt(e) (à intervenir); **to ~** (information etc) sous la main, à portée de la main; **to force sb's ~** forcer la main à qn; **to have a free ~** avoir carte blanche; **to have sth in one's ~** tenir qch à la main; **on the one ~ ..., on the other ~** d'une part ..., d'autre part ▶ vt passer, donner

▶ **hand back** vt : **to ~ sth back (to sb)** (object, property, land) rendre qch (à qn); (power, control) restituer qch (à qn)

▶ **hand down** vt passer; (tradition, heirloom) transmettre; (US: sentence, verdict) prononcer

▶ **hand in** vt remettre

▶ **hand out** vt distribuer

▶ **hand over** vt remettre; (powers etc) transmettre

▶ **hand round** (Brit: information) faire circuler; (: chocolates etc) faire passer

★**handbag** ['hændbæg] N sac m à main

hand baggage N = **hand luggage**

handball ['hændbɔːl] N handball m

handbasin ['hændbeɪsn] N lavabo m

handbook ['hændbuk] N manuel m

handbrake ['hændbreɪk] N frein m à main

h & c ABBR (Brit) = **hot and cold (water)**

hand cream N crème f pour les mains

handcuffs ['hændkʌfs] NPL menottes fpl

handful ['hændful] N poignée f

handgun ['hændgʌn] N arme f de poing

handheld ['hænd'held] ADJ (device) portatif(-ive); (computer) de poche; (camera) de reportage

handicap ['hændɪkæp] N handicap m ▶ vt handicaper

handicraft ['hændɪkrɑːft] N travail m d'artisanat, technique artisanale

handiwork ['hændɪwəːk] N ouvrage m; **this looks like his ~** (pej) ça a tout l'air d'être son œuvre

★**handkerchief** ['hæŋkətʃɪf] N mouchoir m

★**handle** ['hændl] N (of door etc) poignée f; (of cup etc) anse f; (of knife etc) manche m; (of saucepan) queue f; (for winding) manivelle f; **to fly off the ~** s'énerver ▶ vt toucher, manier; (deal with) s'occuper de; (treat: people) prendre ▶ vi: **"~ with care"** « fragile »

handlebar ['hændlbɑːʳ] N, **handlebars** ['hændlbɑːz] NPL guidon m

handler ['hændləʳ] N (of animal) dresseur(-euse); **food ~** personne f qui manipule des aliments

handling ['hændlɪŋ] N (Aut) maniement m; (treatment): **his ~ of the matter** la façon dont il a traité l'affaire

handling charges NPL frais mpl de manutention; (Banking) agios mpl

hand luggage N bagages mpl à main; **one item of ~** un bagage à main

handmade ['hænd'meɪd] ADJ fait(e) à la main

handout ['hændaut] N (money) aide f, don m; (leaflet) prospectus m; (press handout) communiqué m de presse; (at lecture) polycopié m

handover ['hændəuvəʳ] N (of place, country) transfert m; (of company, business) cession f; (of power) passation f

handpick ['hænd'pɪk] vt (staff, successor) trier sur le volet

handpicked ['hænd'pɪkt] ADJ (produce) cueilli(e) à la main; (staff, successor) trié(e) sur le volet

handrail ['hændreɪl] N (on staircase etc) rampe f, main courante

handset ['hændset] N (Tel) combiné m

hands-free [hændz'friː] ADJ mains libres inv ▶ N (also: **hands-free kit**) kit m mains libres inv

handshake ['hændʃeɪk] N poignée f de main; (Comput) établissement m de la liaison

★**handsome** ['hænsəm] ADJ beau (belle); (gift) généreux(-euse); (profit) considérable

> **beau** changes to **bel** before a vowel or a mute 'h': *a handsome man* **un bel homme**.

hands-on [hændz'ɔn] ADJ (training, experience) sur le tas; **she has a very ~ approach** sa politique est de mettre la main à la pâte

handstand ['hændstænd] N: **to do a ~** faire l'arbre droit

hand-to-hand ['hændtə'hænd] ADJ (fighting) corps à corps

hand-to-mouth ['hændtə'mauθ] ADJ (existence) au jour le jour

hand-wash ['hændwɔʃ] vt laver à la main

handwriting ['hændraɪtɪŋ] N écriture f

handwritten ['hændrɪtn] ADJ manuscrit(e), écrit(e) à la main

handy ['hændɪ] ADJ (person) adroit(e); (close at hand) sous la main; (convenient) pratique; **to come in ~** être (or s'avérer) utile

handyman ['hændɪmæn] N (irreg) bricoleur m; (servant) homme m à tout faire

★**hang** [hæŋ] (pt, pp **hung** [hʌŋ]) vt accrocher; (pt, pp **hanged**: criminal) pendre ▶ vi pendre; (hair, drapery) tomber ▶ N: **to get the ~ of (doing) sth** (inf) attraper le coup pour faire qch

▶ **hang about, hang around** vi flâner, traîner

▶ **hang back** vi (hesitate): **to ~ back (from doing)** être réticent(e) (pour faire)

▶ **hang down** vi pendre

▶ **hang on** vi (wait) attendre; **to ~ on to** (keep hold of) ne pas lâcher; (keep) garder ▶ vt FUS (depend on) dépendre de

▶ **hang out** vt (washing) étendre (dehors) ▶ vi pendre; (inf: live) habiter, percher; (: spend time) traîner

▶ **hang round** vi = **hang about**

▶ **hang together** vi (argument etc) se tenir, être cohérent(e)

▶ **hang up** vi (Tel) raccrocher; **to ~ up on sb** (Tel) raccrocher au nez de qn ▶ vt (coat, painting etc) accrocher, suspendre

hangar ['hæŋəʳ] N hangar m

hangdog ['hæŋdɔg] ADJ (look, expression) de chien battu

hanger ['hæŋəʳ] N cintre m, portemanteau m

hanger-on [hæŋər'ɔn] N parasite m

hang-glider ['hæŋglaɪdəʳ] N deltaplane m

hang-gliding ['hæŋglaɪdɪŋ] N vol m libre or sur aile delta

hanging ['hæŋɪŋ] N (execution) pendaison f

hangman ['hæŋmən] N (irreg) bourreau m

hangover ['hæŋəuvəʳ] N (after drinking) gueule f de bois

hang-up ['hæŋʌp] N complexe m

hank [hæŋk] N écheveau m

hanker ['hæŋkə'] VI: **to ~ after** avoir envie de

hankering ['hæŋkərɪŋ] N: **to have a ~ for/to do sth** avoir une grande envie de/de faire qch

hankie, hanky ['hæŋkɪ] N ABBR = **handkerchief**

hanky-panky [hæŋkɪ'pæŋkɪ] N (inf: sexual) galipettes fpl (inf); (: dishonest) entourloupes fpl (inf)

Hanukkah, Hanukah ['hɑːnəkə] N Hanoukka f

haphazard [hæp'hæzəd] ADJ fait(e) au hasard, fait(e) au petit bonheur

hapless ['hæplɪs] ADJ malheureux(-euse)

happen ['hæpən] VI arriver, se passer, se produire; **what's happening?** que se passe-t-il?; **she happened to be free** il s'est trouvé (or se trouvait) qu'elle était libre; **if anything happened to him** s'il lui arrivait quoi que ce soit; **as it happens** justement
  ▶ **happen on, happen upon** VT FUS tomber sur

happening ['hæpnɪŋ] N événement m

happily ['hæpɪlɪ] ADV heureusement; (cheerfully) joyeusement

happiness ['hæpɪnɪs] N bonheur m

★**happy** ['hæpɪ] ADJ heureux(-euse); **~ with** (arrangements etc) satisfait(e) de; **to be ~ to do** faire volontiers; **yes, I'd be ~ to** oui, avec plaisir or (bien) volontiers; **~ birthday!** bon anniversaire !; **~ Christmas/New Year!** joyeux Noël/bonne année !

happy-go-lucky ['hæpɪɡəʊ'lʌkɪ] ADJ insouciant(e)

happy hour N l'heure f de l'apéritif; heure pendant laquelle les consommations sont à prix réduit

harangue [hə'ræŋ] VT haranguer

harass ['hærəs] VT accabler, tourmenter

harassed ['hærəst] ADJ tracassé(e)

harassment ['hærəsmənt] N tracasseries fpl; **sexual ~** harcèlement sexuel

harbinger ['hɑːbɪndʒə'] N (literary) signe m avant-coureur

harbour, (US) **harbor** ['hɑːbə'] N port m ▶VT héberger, abriter; (hopes, suspicions) entretenir; **to ~ a grudge against sb** en vouloir à qn

harbour dues, (US) **harbor dues** NPL droits mpl de port

harbour master, (US) **harbor master** N capitaine m du port

★**hard** [hɑːd] ADJ dur(e); (question, problem) difficile; (facts, evidence) concret(-ète); **~ luck!** pas de veine !; **no ~ feelings!** sans rancune !; **to be ~ of hearing** être dur(e) d'oreille; **to be ~ on sb** être dur(e) avec qn; **I find it ~ to believe that ...** je n'arrive pas à croire que ... ▶ ADV (work) dur; (think, try) sérieusement; **to look ~ at** regarder fixement; (thing) regarder de près; **to drink ~** boire sec; **to be ~ done by** être traité(e) injustement

hard-and-fast ['hɑːdən'fɑːst] ADJ strict(e), absolu(e)

hardback ['hɑːdbæk] N livre relié

hardball ['hɑːdbɔːl] N: **to play ~** (fig) employer les grands moyens

hardboard ['hɑːdbɔːd] N Isorel® m

hard-boiled egg ['hɑːd'bɔɪld-] N œuf dur

hard cash N espèces fpl

hard copy N (Comput) sortie f or copie f papier

hard-core ['hɑːd'kɔː'] ADJ (pornography) (dit(e)) dur(e); (supporters) inconditionnel(le)

hard court N (Tennis) court m en dur

hard disk N (Comput) disque dur

hard drive N (Comput) disque dur

harden ['hɑːdn] VT durcir; (steel) tremper; (fig) endurcir ▶ VI (substance) durcir

hardened ['hɑːdnd] ADJ (criminal) endurci(e); **to be ~ to sth** être endurci(e) à qch, être (devenu(e)) insensible à qch

hardening ['hɑːdənɪŋ] N (of attitude, position) durcissement m

hard-headed ['hɑːd'hedɪd] ADJ réaliste, décidé(e)

hard-hearted ['hɑːd'hɑːtɪd] ADJ dur(e), impitoyable

hard-hitting ['hɑːd'hɪtɪŋ] ADJ (speech, article) sans complaisances

hard labour N travaux forcés

hardline [hɑːd'laɪn] ADJ (communist, republican) pur(e) et dur(e); (policy, stance) jusqu'au-boutiste, intransigeant(e)

hardliner [hɑːd'laɪnə'] N intransigeant(e), dur(e)

hard-luck story [hɑːd'lʌk-] N histoire larmoyante

★**hardly** ['hɑːdlɪ] ADV (scarcely) à peine; (harshly) durement; **it's ~ the case** ce n'est guère le cas; **~ anywhere/ever** presque nulle part/jamais; **I can ~ believe it** j'ai du mal à le croire

hardness ['hɑːdnɪs] N dureté f

hard-nosed ['hɑːd'nəʊzd] ADJ impitoyable, dur(e)

hard-pressed ['hɑːd'prest] ADJ sous pression

hard sell N vente agressive

hardship ['hɑːdʃɪp] N (difficulties) épreuves fpl; (deprivation) privations fpl

hard shoulder N (BRIT Aut) accotement stabilisé

hard-up [hɑːd'ʌp] ADJ (inf) fauché(e)

hardware ['hɑːdwɛə'] N quincaillerie f; (Comput, Mil) matériel m

hardware shop, (US) **hardware store** N quincaillerie f

hard-wearing [hɑːd'wɛərɪŋ] ADJ solide

hard-wired [hɑːd'waɪəd] ADJ (Comput) câblé(e); (into the brain) programmé(e)

hard-won ['hɑːd'wʌn] ADJ (si) durement gagné(e)

hardwood ['hɑːdwʊd] N bois m dur ▶ CPD (floor, flooring) en bois dur; (tree) feuillu(e)

hard-working [hɑːd'wəːkɪŋ] ADJ travailleur(-euse), consciencieux(-euse)

hardy ['hɑːdɪ] ADJ robuste; (plant) résistant(e) au gel

hare [hɛə'] N lièvre m

hare-brained ['hɛəbreɪnd] ADJ farfelu(e), écervelé(e)

harelip ['hɛəlɪp] N (Med) bec-de-lièvre m

harem [hɑː'riːm] N harem m

hark back [hɑːk-] VI: **to ~ to** (en) revenir toujours à

★**harm** [hɑːm] N mal m; (wrong) tort m; **to mean no ~** ne pas avoir de mauvaises intentions; **there's no ~ in trying** on peut toujours essayer; **out of ~'s way** à l'abri du danger, en lieu sûr ▶ VT (person) faire du mal or du tort à; (thing) endommager

harmful ['hɑːmful] ADJ nuisible

harmless ['hɑːmlɪs] ADJ inoffensif(-ive)

harmonic [hɑː'mɔnɪk] ADJ harmonique

harmonica [hɑːˈmɒnɪkə] N harmonica m
harmonics [hɑːˈmɒnɪks] NPL harmoniques mpl or fpl
harmonious [hɑːˈməʊnɪəs] ADJ harmonieux(-euse)
harmonium [hɑːˈməʊnɪəm] N harmonium m
harmonization [hɑːmənaɪˈzeɪʃən] N harmonisation f
harmonize [ˈhɑːmənaɪz] VT harmoniser ▸ VI s'harmoniser
harmony [ˈhɑːmənɪ] N harmonie f
harness [ˈhɑːnɪs] N harnais m ▸ VT (horse) harnacher; (resources) exploiter
harp [hɑːp] N harpe f ▸ VI: **to ~ on about** revenir toujours sur
harpist [ˈhɑːpɪst] N harpiste mf
harpoon [hɑːˈpuːn] N harpon m
harpsichord [ˈhɑːpsɪkɔːd] N clavecin m
harrowing [ˈhærəʊɪŋ] ADJ déchirant(e)
harsh [hɑːʃ] ADJ (hard) dur(e); (severe) sévère; (rough: surface) rugueux(-euse); (unpleasant: sound) discordant(e); (: light) cru(e); (: taste) âpre
harshly [ˈhɑːʃlɪ] ADV durement, sévèrement
harshness [ˈhɑːʃnɪs] N dureté f, sévérité f
harvest [ˈhɑːvɪst] N (of corn) moisson f; (of fruit) récolte f; (of grapes) vendange f ▸ VI, VT moissonner; récolter; vendanger
harvester [ˈhɑːvɪstəʳ] N (machine) moissonneuse f; (also: **combine harvester**) moissonneuse-batteuse(-lieuse) f
has [hæz] VB see **have**
has-been [ˈhæzbiːn] N (inf: person): **he/she's a ~** il/elle a fait son temps or est fini(e)
hash [hæʃ] N (Culin) hachis m; (fig: mess) gâchis m ▸ N ABBR (inf) = **hashish**
hashish [ˈhæʃɪʃ] N haschisch m
hashtag [ˈhæʃtæg] N (on Twitter) mot-dièse m, hashtag m
hasn't [ˈhæznt] = **has not**
hassle [ˈhæsl] N (inf: fuss) histoire(s) f(pl)
haste [heɪst] N hâte f, précipitation f; **in ~** à la hâte, précipitamment
hasten [ˈheɪsn] VT hâter, accélérer ▸ VI se hâter, s'empresser; **I ~ to add that ...** je m'empresse d'ajouter que ...
hastily [ˈheɪstɪlɪ] ADV à la hâte; (leave) précipitamment
hasty [ˈheɪstɪ] ADJ (decision, action) hâtif(-ive); (departure, escape) précipité(e)
★**hat** [hæt] N chapeau m
hatbox [ˈhætbɒks] N carton m à chapeau
hatch [hætʃ] N (Naut: also: **hatchway**) écoutille f; (Brit: also: **service hatch**) passe-plats m inv ▸ VI éclore ▸ VT faire éclore; (fig: scheme) tramer, ourdir
hatchback [ˈhætʃbæk] N (Aut) modèle m avec hayon arrière
hatchet [ˈhætʃɪt] N hachette f
hatchet job N (inf) démolissage m
hatchet man N (irreg) (inf) homme m de main
★**hate** [heɪt] VT haïr, détester; **to ~ to do** or **doing** détester faire; **I ~ to trouble you, but ...** désolé de vous déranger, mais ... ▸ N haine f
hateful [ˈheɪtful] ADJ odieux(-euse), détestable

hater [ˈheɪtəʳ] N: **cop-hater** anti-flic mf; **woman-hater** misogyne mf (haineux(-euse))
hatred [ˈheɪtrɪd] N haine f
hat trick N (Brit Sport, also fig): **to get a ~** réussir trois coups (or gagner trois matchs etc) consécutifs
haughty [ˈhɔːtɪ] ADJ hautain(e), arrogant(e)
haul [hɔːl] VT traîner, tirer; (by lorry) camionner; (Naut) haler ▸ N (of fish) prise f; (of stolen goods etc) butin m
haulage [ˈhɔːlɪdʒ] N transport routier
haulage contractor N (Brit: firm) entreprise f de transport (routier); (: person) transporteur routier
haulier [ˈhɔːlɪəʳ], (US) **hauler** [ˈhɔːləʳ] N transporteur (routier), camionneur m
haunch [hɔːntʃ] N hanche f; **~ of venison** cuissot m de chevreuil
haunt [hɔːnt] VT (subj: ghost, fear) hanter; (: person) fréquenter ▸ N repaire m
haunted [ˈhɔːntɪd] ADJ (castle etc) hanté(e); (look) égaré(e), hagard(e)
haunting [ˈhɔːntɪŋ] ADJ (sight, music) obsédant(e)
Havana [həˈvænə] N La Havane

h

---

have [hæv]

(pt, pp **had** [hæd]) AUX VB **1** (gen) avoir; être; **to have eaten/slept** avoir mangé/dormi; **to have arrived/gone** être arrivé(e)/allé(e); **he has been promoted** il a eu une promotion; **having finished** or **when he had finished, he left** quand il a eu fini, il est parti; **we'd already eaten** nous avions déjà mangé
2 (in tag questions): **you've done it, haven't you?** vous l'avez fait, n'est-ce pas ?
3 (in short answers and questions): **no I haven't!/yes we have!** mais non !/mais si !; **so I have!** ah oui !, oui c'est vrai !; **I've been there before, have you?** j'y suis déjà allé, et vous ?
▸ MODAL AUX VB (be obliged): **to have (got) to do sth** devoir faire qch, être obligé(e) de faire qch; **she has (got) to do it** elle doit le faire, il faut qu'elle le fasse; **you haven't to tell her** vous n'êtes pas obligé de le lui dire; (must not) ne le lui dites surtout pas; **do you have to book?** il faut réserver ?
▸ VT **1** (possess) avoir; **he has (got) blue eyes/dark hair** il a les yeux bleus/les cheveux bruns
2 (referring to meals etc): **to have breakfast** prendre le petit déjeuner; **to have dinner/lunch** dîner/déjeuner; **to have a drink** prendre un verre; **to have a cigarette** fumer une cigarette
3 (receive) avoir, recevoir; (obtain) avoir; **may I have your address?** puis-je avoir votre adresse ?; **you can have it for £5** vous pouvez l'avoir pour 5 livres; **I must have it for tomorrow** il me le faut pour demain; **to have a baby** avoir un bébé
4 (maintain, allow): **I won't have it!** ça ne se passera pas comme ça !; **we can't have that** nous ne tolérerons pas ça
5 (by sb else): **to have sth done** faire faire qch; **to have one's hair cut** se faire couper les cheveux; **to have sb do sth** faire faire qch à qn
6 (experience, suffer): **to have a cold/flu** avoir un rhume/la grippe; **to have an operation** se faire opérer; **she had her bag stolen** elle s'est fait voler son sac

661

7 (+noun): **to have a swim/walk** nager/se promener; **to have a bath/shower** prendre un bain/une douche; **let's have a look** regardons; **to have a meeting** se réunir; **to have a party** organiser une fête; **let me have a try** laissez-moi essayer

8 (inf: dupe) avoir; **he's been had** il s'est fait avoir or rouler

▸ **have on** vт: **to be having sb on** (BRIT inf) faire marcher qn

▸ **have out** vт: **to have it out with sb** (settle a problem etc) s'expliquer (franchement) avec qn

haven ['heɪvn] N port m; (fig) havre m

haven't ['hævnt] = **have not**

haversack ['hævəsæk] N sac m à dos

haves [hævz] NPL (inf): **the ~ and have-nots** les riches et les pauvres

havoc ['hævək] N ravages mpl, dégâts mpl; **to play ~ with** (fig) désorganiser complètement, détraquer

Hawaii [hə'waɪɪ] N (îles fpl) Hawaï m

Hawaiian [hə'waɪən] ADJ hawaïen(ne) ▸ N Hawaïen(ne); (Ling) hawaïen m

hawk [hɔːk] N faucon m ▸ vт (goods for sale) colporter

hawker ['hɔːkəʳ] N colporteur m

hawkish ['hɔːkɪʃ] ADJ belliciste

hawthorn ['hɔːθɔːn] N aubépine f

hay [heɪ] N foin m

hay fever N rhume m des foins

haystack ['heɪstæk] N meule f de foin

haywire ['heɪwaɪəʳ] ADJ (inf): **to go ~** perdre la tête; mal tourner

hazard ['hæzəd] N (risk) danger m, risque m; (chance) hasard m, chance f; **to be a health/fire ~** présenter un risque pour la santé/d'incendie ▸ vт risquer, hasarder; **to ~ a guess** émettre or hasarder une hypothèse

hazardous ['hæzədəs] ADJ hasardeux(-euse), risqué(e)

hazard pay N (US) prime f de risque

hazard warning lights NPL (Aut) feux mpl de détresse

haze [heɪz] N brume f

hazel [heɪzl] N (tree) noisetier m ▸ ADJ (eyes) noisette inv

hazelnut ['heɪzlnʌt] N noisette f

hazy ['heɪzɪ] ADJ brumeux(-euse); (idea) vague; (photograph) flou(e)

H-bomb ['eɪtʃbɔm] N bombe f H

HD ABBR (= high definition) HD (= haute définition)

HDTV N ABBR (= high definition television) TVHD f (= télévision haute-définition)

HE ABBR = **high explosive**; (Rel, Diplomacy) = **His Excellency; Her Excellency**

★**he** [hiː] PRON il; **it is he who …** c'est lui qui …; **here he is** le voici; **he-bear** etc ours etc mâle

★**head** [hɛd] N tête f; (leader) chef m; (of school) directeur(-trice); (of secondary school) proviseur m; **~ first** la tête la première; **~ over heels in love** follement or éperdument amoureux(-euse); **10 euros a or per ~** 10 euros par personne; **to sit at the ~ of the table** présider la tablée; **to have a ~ for business**

avoir des dispositions pour les affaires; **to have no ~ for heights** être sujet(te) au vertige; **to come to a ~** (fig: situation etc) devenir critique ▸ vт (list) être en tête de; (group, company) être à la tête de; **to ~ the ball** faire une tête ■ **heads** NPL (on coin) (le côté) face; **heads or tails** pile ou face

▸ **head back** vı retourner

▸ **head for** vт FUS se diriger vers; (disaster) aller à

▸ **head off** vт (threat, danger) détourner

▸ **head out** vı (person) sortir; **a fishing boat heading out to sea** un bateau de pêcheurs prenant le large

▸ **head up** vт (department, division) diriger; **to ~ up an investigation** mener une enquête

★**headache** ['hɛdeɪk] N mal m de tête; **to have a ~** avoir mal à la tête

headband ['hɛdbænd] N bandeau m

headboard ['hɛdbɔːd] N dosseret m

head-butt ['hɛdbʌt] vт donner un coup de tête à

head cold N rhume m de cerveau

headcount ['hɛdkaunt] N (number present) nombre m de personnes présentes; (number of staff) effectifs mpl; **to do a ~** compter combien il y a de personnes

headdress ['hɛddrɛs] N coiffure f

headed notepaper ['hɛdɪd-] N papier m à lettres à en-tête

header ['hɛdəʳ] N (Football) (coup m de) tête f; (inf: fall) chute f (or plongeon m) la tête la première

head-first ['hɛd'fəːst] ADV (lit) la tête la première

headgear ['hɛdgɪəʳ] N (hat) chapeau m; protective ~ (helmets) casques m

headhunt ['hɛdhʌnt] vт: **she was headhunted** elle a été recrutée par un chasseur de têtes

headhunter ['hɛdhʌntəʳ] N chasseur m de têtes

heading ['hɛdɪŋ] N titre m; (subject title) rubrique f

headlamp ['hɛdlæmp] N (BRIT) = **headlight**

headland ['hɛdlənd] N promontoire m, cap m

headlight ['hɛdlaɪt] N phare m

★**headline** ['hɛdlaɪn] N titre m

headlong ['hɛdlɔŋ] ADV (fall) la tête la première; (rush) tête baissée

headmaster [hɛd'mɑːstəʳ] N directeur m, proviseur m

headmistress [hɛd'mɪstrɪs] N directrice f

head office N siège m, bureau m central

head-on [hɛd'ɔn] ADJ (collision) de plein fouet

headphones ['hɛdfəunz] NPL casque m (à écouteurs)

headquartered [hɛd'kwɔːtəd] ADJ: **to be ~** (business) avoir son siège

★**headquarters** ['hɛdkwɔːtəz] NPL (of business) bureau or siège central; (Mil) quartier général

headrest ['hɛdrɛst] N appui-tête m

headroom ['hɛdrum] N (in car) hauteur f de plafond; (under bridge) hauteur limite; dégagement m

headscarf ['hɛdskɑːf] (pl headscarves [-skɑːvz]) N foulard m

headset ['hɛdsɛt] N = **headphones**

headship ['hɛdʃɪp] N (of school, department) poste m de directeur

head start N (in career, competition): **to have a ~** être avantagé(e) dès le départ; **to give sb a ~** donner à qn une longueur d'avance

headstone ['hɛdstəʊn] N pierre tombale

headstrong ['hɛdstrɒŋ] ADJ têtu(e), entêté(e)

heads-up ['hɛdzʌp] N (inf): **to give sb a ~** donner un tuyau à qn (inf)

headteacher [hɛd'tiːtʃəʳ] N directeur(-trice); (of secondary school) proviseur m

head waiter N maître m d'hôtel

headway ['hɛdweɪ] N: **to make ~** avancer, faire des progrès

headwind ['hɛdwɪnd] N vent m contraire

heady ['hɛdɪ] ADJ capiteux(-euse), enivrant(e)

★**heal** [hiːl] VT, VI guérir

healer ['hiːləʳ] N guérisseur(-euse)

★**health** [hɛlθ] N santé f; **Department of H~** (BRIT, US) ≈ ministère m de la Santé

health care N services médicaux

health centre N (BRIT) centre m de santé

health food N aliment(s) naturel(s)

health food shop N magasin m diététique

healthful ['hɛlθful] ADJ sain(e)

health hazard N risque m pour la santé

Health Service N: **the ~** (BRIT) ≈ la Sécurité Sociale

★**healthy** ['hɛlθɪ] ADJ (person) en bonne santé; (climate, food, attitude etc) sain(e)

heap [hiːp] N tas m, monceau m; **heaps (of)** (inf: lots) des tas (de) ▶ VT (also: **heap up**) entasser, amonceler; **she heaped her plate with cakes** elle a chargé son assiette de gâteaux; **to ~ favours/praise/gifts etc on sb** combler qn de faveurs/d'éloges/de cadeaux etc

heaped ['hiːpt] ADJ: **~ with sth** (surface) recouvert(e) d'une montagne de qch; (dish, bowl) rempli(e) d'une montagne de qch; **add one ~ tablespoon of salt** ajouter une grosse cuillerée à soupe de sel

★**hear** [hɪəʳ] (pt, pp **heard** [həːd]) VT entendre; (news) apprendre; (lecture) assister à, écouter ▶ VI entendre; **to ~ about** entendre parler de; (have news of) avoir des nouvelles de; **did you ~ about the move?** tu es au courant du déménagement ?; **to ~ from sb** recevoir des nouvelles de qn; **I've never heard of that book** je n'ai jamais entendu parler de ce livre
▶ **hear out** VT écouter jusqu'au bout

heard [həːd] PT, PP of **hear**

hearing ['hɪərɪŋ] N (sense) ouïe f; (of witnesses) audition f; (of a case) audience f; (of committee) séance f; **to give sb a ~** (BRIT) écouter ce que qn a à dire

hearing aid N appareil m acoustique

hearing impaired [-ɪm'pɛəd] ADJ malentendant(e) ▶ NPL: **the ~** les malentendants mpl

hearsay ['hɪəseɪ] N on-dit mpl, rumeurs fpl; **by ~** adv par ouï-dire

hearse [həːs] N corbillard m

★**heart** [hɑːt] N cœur m; **at ~** au fond; **by ~** (learn, know) par cœur; **to have a weak ~** avoir le cœur malade, avoir des problèmes de cœur; **to lose/take ~** perdre/prendre courage; **to set one's ~ on sth/on doing sth** vouloir absolument qch/faire qch; **the ~ of the matter** le fond du problème
■ **hearts** NPL (Cards) cœur m

heartache ['hɑːteɪk] N chagrin m, douleur f

heart attack N crise f cardiaque

heartbeat ['hɑːtbiːt] N battement m de cœur

heartbreak ['hɑːtbreɪk] N immense chagrin m

heartbreaking ['hɑːtbreɪkɪŋ] ADJ navrant(e), déchirant(e)

heartbroken ['hɑːtbrəʊkən] ADJ: **to be ~** avoir beaucoup de chagrin

heartburn ['hɑːtbəːn] N brûlures fpl d'estomac

heart disease N maladie f cardiaque

-hearted ['hɑːtɪd] SUFFIX: **kind-hearted** bon(ne), qui a bon cœur

heartening ['hɑːtnɪŋ] ADJ encourageant(e), réconfortant(e)

heart failure N (Med) arrêt m du cœur

heartfelt ['hɑːtfɛlt] ADJ sincère

hearth [hɑːθ] N foyer m, cheminée f

heartily ['hɑːtɪlɪ] ADV chaleureusement; (laugh) de bon cœur; (eat) de bon appétit; **to agree ~** être entièrement d'accord; **to be ~ sick of** (BRIT) en avoir ras le bol de

heartland ['hɑːtlænd] N centre m, cœur m; **France's heartlands** la France profonde

heartless ['hɑːtlɪs] ADJ (person) sans cœur, insensible; (treatment) cruel(le)

heart rate N rythme m cardiaque

heart-rending ['hɑːtrɛndɪŋ] ADJ déchirant(e)

heartstrings ['hɑːtstrɪŋz] NPL: **to tug (at) sb's ~** toucher or faire vibrer les cordes sensibles de qn

heartthrob ['hɑːtθrɒb] N idole f

heart-to-heart ['hɑːttə'hɑːt] ADJ, ADV à cœur ouvert

heart transplant N greffe f du cœur

heartwarming ['hɑːtwɔːmɪŋ] ADJ réconfortant(e)

hearty ['hɑːtɪ] ADJ chaleureux(-euse); (appetite) solide; (dislike) cordial(e); (meal) copieux(-euse)

★**heat** [hiːt] N chaleur f; (fig) ardeur f; feu m; (Sport: also: **qualifying heat**) éliminatoire f ▶ VT chauffer
▶ **heat up** VI (liquid) chauffer; (room) se réchauffer ▶ VT réchauffer

heated ['hiːtɪd] ADJ chauffé(e); (fig) passionné(e), échauffé(e), excité(e)

heater ['hiːtəʳ] N appareil m de chauffage; radiateur m; (in car) chauffage m; (water heater) chauffe-eau m

heath [hiːθ] N (BRIT) lande f

heathen ['hiːðn] ADJ, N païen(ne)

heather ['hɛðəʳ] N bruyère f

heating ['hiːtɪŋ] N chauffage m

heat-resistant ['hiːtrɪzɪstənt] ADJ résistant(e) à la chaleur

heat-seeking ['hiːtsiːkɪŋ] ADJ guidé(e) par infrarouge

heatstroke ['hiːtstrəʊk] N coup m de chaleur

heatwave ['hiːtweɪv] N vague f de chaleur

heave [hiːv] VT soulever (avec effort); **to ~ a sigh** pousser un gros soupir ▶ VI se soulever; (retch) avoir des haut-le-cœur ▶ N (push) poussée f

heaven ['hɛvn] N ciel m, paradis m; (fig) paradis; **~ forbid!** surtout pas !; **thank ~!** Dieu merci !; **for ~'s sake!** (pleading) je vous en prie !; (protesting) mince alors !

heavenly ['hɛvnlɪ] ADJ céleste, divin(e)

heavily ['hɛvɪlɪ] ADV lourdement; (drink, smoke) beaucoup; (sleep, sigh) profondément

h

★**heavy** ['hɛvɪ] ADJ lourd(e); (work, rain, user, eater) gros(se); (drinker, smoker) grand(e); (schedule, week) chargé(e); **it's too ~** c'est trop lourd; **it's ~ going** ça ne va pas tout seul, c'est pénible

heavy cream N (US) crème fraîche épaisse

heavy-duty ['hɛvɪ'djuːtɪ] ADJ à usage intensif

heavy goods vehicle N (BRIT) poids lourd m

heavy-handed ['hɛvɪ'hændɪd] ADJ (fig) maladroit(e), qui manque de tact

heavy metal N (Mus) heavy metal m

heavy-set ['hɛvɪ'sɛt] ADJ (esp US) costaud(e)

heavyweight ['hɛvɪweɪt] N (Sport) poids lourd

Hebrew ['hiːbruː] ADJ hébraïque ▸ N (Ling) hébreu m

Hebrides ['hɛbrɪdiːz] NPL: **the ~** les Hébrides fpl

heck [hɛk] N (inf): **why the ~ ...?** pourquoi diable ... ?; **a ~ of a lot** une sacrée quantité; **he has done a ~ of a lot for us** il a vraiment beaucoup fait pour nous

heckle ['hɛkl] VT, VI chahuter

heckler ['hɛklə'] N interrupteur m; élément perturbateur

heckling ['hɛklɪŋ] N chahut m

hectare ['hɛktɑː'] N (BRIT) hectare m

hectic ['hɛktɪk] ADJ (schedule) très chargé(e); (day) mouvementé(e); (activity) fiévreux(-euse); (lifestyle) trépidant(e)

hectoring ['hɛktərɪŋ] ADJ (tone) autoritaire

he'd [hiːd] = **he would; he had**

hedge [hɛdʒ] N haie f; **as a ~ against inflation** pour se prémunir contre l'inflation ▸ VI se dérober ▸ VT: **to ~ one's bets** (fig) se couvrir
▸ **hedge in** VT entourer d'une haie

hedgehog ['hɛdʒhɔg] N hérisson m

hedgerow ['hɛdʒrəu] N haie(s) f(pl)

hedonism ['hiːdənɪzəm] N hédonisme m

hedonistic [hiːdə'nɪstɪk] ADJ hédoniste

heed [hiːd] VT (also: **take heed of**) tenir compte de, prendre garde à

heedless ['hiːdlɪs] ADJ insouciant(e)

heel [hiːl] N talon m; **to bring to ~** (dog) faire venir à ses pieds; (fig: person) rappeler à l'ordre; **to take to one's heels** (inf) prendre ses jambes à son cou
▸ VT (shoe) retalonner

hefty ['hɛftɪ] ADJ (person) costaud(e); (parcel) lourd(e); (piece, price) gros(se)

hegemony [hɪ'gɛmənɪ] N hégémonie f

heifer ['hɛfə'] N génisse f

★**height** [haɪt] N (of person) taille f, grandeur f; (of object) hauteur f; (of plane, mountain) altitude f; (high ground) hauteur, éminence f; (fig: of glory, fame, power) sommet m; (: of luxury, stupidity) comble m; **at the ~ of summer** au cœur de l'été; **what ~ are you?** combien mesurez-vous ?, quelle est votre taille ?; **of average ~** de taille moyenne; **to be afraid of heights** être sujet(te) au vertige; **it's the ~ of fashion** c'est le dernier cri

heighten ['haɪtn] VT hausser, surélever; (fig) augmenter

heinous ['heɪnəs] ADJ odieux(-euse), atroce

heir [ɛə'] N héritier m

heir apparent N héritier présomptif

heiress ['ɛərɛs] N héritière f

heirloom ['ɛəluːm] N meuble m (or bijou m or tableau m) de famille

heist [haɪst] N (US inf: hold-up) casse m

held [hɛld] PT, PP of **hold**

★**helicopter** ['hɛlɪkɒptə'] N hélicoptère m

helipad ['hɛlɪpæd] N hélistation f

heliport ['hɛlɪpɔːt] N (Aviat) héliport m

helium ['hiːlɪəm] N hélium m

★**hell** [hɛl] N enfer m; **a ~ of a ...** (inf) un(e) sacré(e) ...; **oh ~!** (inf) merde !

he'll [hiːl] = **he will; he shall**

hell-bent [hɛl'bɛnt] ADJ (inf): **to be ~ on doing sth** vouloir à tout prix faire qch

hellish ['hɛlɪʃ] ADJ infernal(e)

★**hello** [hə'ləu] EXCL bonjour !; (to attract attention) hé !; (surprise) tiens !

helm [hɛlm] N (Naut) barre f

helmet ['hɛlmɪt] N casque m

helmsman ['hɛlmzmən] N (irreg) timonier m

★**help** [hɛlp] N aide f; (cleaner etc) femme f de ménage; (assistant etc) employé(e); **with the ~ of** (person) avec l'aide de; (tool etc) à l'aide de; **to be of ~ to sb** être utile à qn ▸ VT, VI aider; **can you ~ me?** pouvez-vous m'aider ?; **can I ~ you?** (in shop) vous désirez ?; **~ yourself** servez-vous; **to ~ sb (to) do sth** aider qn à faire qch; **I can't ~ saying** je ne peux pas m'empêcher de dire; **he can't ~ it** il n'y peut rien ▸ EXCL au secours !
▸ **help out** VI aider ▸ VT: **to ~ sb out** aider qn

help desk N (esp Comput) centre m d'assistance

helper ['hɛlpə'] N aide mf, assistant(e)

helpful ['hɛlpful] ADJ (person) serviable, aimable; (useful) utile

helpfully ['hɛlpfulɪ] ADV aimablement

helping ['hɛlpɪŋ] N portion f

helping hand N coup m de main; **to give sb a ~** prêter main-forte à qn

helpless ['hɛlplɪs] ADJ impuissant(e); (baby) sans défense

helplessly ['hɛlplɪslɪ] ADV (watch) sans pouvoir rien faire

helplessness ['hɛlplɪsnɪs] N impuissance f

helpline ['hɛlplaɪn] N service m d'assistance téléphonique; (free) ≈ numéro vert

Helsinki ['hɛlsɪŋkɪ] N Helsinki

helter-skelter ['hɛltə'skɛltə'] N (BRIT: at amusement park) toboggan m

hem [hɛm] N ourlet m ▸ VT ourler
▸ **hem in** VT cerner; **to feel hemmed in** (fig) avoir l'impression d'étouffer, se sentir oppressé(e) or écrasé(e)

he-man ['hiːmæn] N (irreg) (inf) macho m

hematology ['hiːmə'tɔlədʒɪ] N (US) = **haematology**

hemisphere ['hɛmɪsfɪə'] N hémisphère m

hemlock ['hɛmlɔk] N ciguë f

hemoglobin ['hiːmə'gləubɪn] N (US) = **haemoglobin**

hemophilia ['hiːmə'fɪlɪə] N (US) = **haemophilia**

hemorrhage ['hɛmərɪdʒ] N (US) = **haemorrhage**

hemorrhoids ['hɛmərɔɪdz] NPL (US) = **haemorrhoids**

hemp [hɛmp] N chanvre m

hen [hɛn] N poule f; (female bird) femelle f

hence [hɛns] ADV (therefore) d'où, de là; **2 years ~** d'ici 2 ans

henceforth [hɛns'fɔ:θ] ADV dorénavant

henchman ['hɛntʃmən] N (irreg) (pej) acolyte m, séide m

henna ['hɛnə] N henné m

hen night, hen party N (inf) soirée f entre filles (avant le mariage d'une d'elles)

henpecked ['hɛnpɛkt] ADJ dominé par sa femme

hepatitis [hɛpə'taɪtɪs] N hépatite f

heptathlon [hɛp'tæθlɔn] N heptathlon m

★**her** [hə:ʳ] PRON (direct) la, l' + vowel or h mute; (indirect) lui; (stressed, after prep) elle; **I see ~** je la vois; **give ~ a book** donne-lui un livre; **after ~** après elle ▶ ADJ son (sa), ses pl; see also **me; my**

herald ['hɛrəld] N héraut m ▶ VT annoncer

heraldic [hɛ'rældɪk] ADJ héraldique

heraldry ['hɛrəldrɪ] N héraldique f; (coat of arms) blason m

herb [hə:b] N herbe f ▪ **herbs** NPL fines herbes

herbaceous [hə:'beɪʃəs] ADJ herbacé(e)

herbal ['hə:bl] ADJ à base de plantes

herbalist ['hə:bəlɪst] N herboriste mf

herbal tea N tisane f

herbicide ['hə:bɪsaɪd] N herbicide m

Herculean [hə:kju'li:ən] ADJ (literary) herculéen(ne)

herd [hə:d] N troupeau m; (of wild animals, swine) troupeau, troupe f ▶ VT (drive: animals, people) mener, conduire; (gather) rassembler; **herded together** parqués (comme du bétail)

★**here** [hɪəʳ] ADV ici; (time) alors; **~ is, ~ are** voici; **~'s my sister** voici ma sœur; **~ he/she is** le (la) voici; **~ she comes** la voici qui vient; **come ~!** viens ici !; **~ and there** ici et là ▶ EXCL tiens !, tenez !; (present) présent !

hereabouts ['hɪərə'bauts] ADV par ici, dans les parages

hereafter [hɪər'ɑ:ftəʳ] ADV après, plus tard; ci-après ▶ N: **the ~** l'au-delà m

hereby [hɪə'baɪ] ADV (in letter) par la présente

hereditary [hɪ'rɛdɪtrɪ] ADJ héréditaire

heredity [hɪ'rɛdɪtɪ] N hérédité f

herein [hɪər'ɪn] ADV (in this text) dans le présent texte; **~ lies the problem** de là vient tout le problème

heresy ['hɛrəsɪ] N hérésie f

heretic ['hɛrətɪk] N hérétique mf

heretical [hɪ'rɛtɪkl] ADJ hérétique

herewith [hɪə'wɪð] ADV avec ceci, ci-joint

heritage ['hɛrɪtɪdʒ] N héritage m, patrimoine m; **our national ~** notre patrimoine national

hermetically [hə:'mɛtɪklɪ] ADV hermétique

hermit ['hə:mɪt] N ermite m

hernia ['hə:nɪə] N hernie f

★**hero** ['hɪərəu] (pl heroes) N héros m

heroic [hɪ'rəuɪk] ADJ héroïque

heroin ['hɛrəuɪn] N héroïne f (drogue)

heroin addict N héroïnomane mf

heroine ['hɛrəuɪn] N héroïne f (femme)

heroism ['hɛrəuɪzəm] N héroïsme m

heron ['hɛrən] N héron m

hero worship N culte m (du héros)

herpes ['hə:pi:z] N herpès m

herring ['hɛrɪŋ] N hareng m

★**hers** [hə:z] PRON le (la) sien(ne), les siens (siennes); **a friend of ~** un(e) ami(e) à elle, un(e) de ses ami(e)s; see also **mine¹**

★**herself** [hə:'sɛlf] PRON (reflexive) se; (emphatic) elle-même; (after prep) elle; see also **oneself**

he's [hi:z] = **he is; he has**

hesitant ['hɛzɪtənt] ADJ hésitant(e), indécis(e); **to be ~ about doing sth** hésiter à faire qch

hesitate ['hɛzɪteɪt] VI: **to ~ (about/to do)** hésiter (sur/à faire)

hesitation [hɛzɪ'teɪʃən] N hésitation f; **I have no ~ in saying (that) …** je n'hésiterais pas à dire (que) …

hessian ['hɛsɪən] N (toile f de) jute m

heterogeneous ['hɛtərə'dʒi:nɪəs] ADJ hétérogène

heterosexual ['hɛtərəu'sɛksjuəl] ADJ, N hétérosexuel(le)

het up [hɛt-] ADJ (inf) agité(e), excité(e)

hew [hju:] VT tailler (à la hache)

hex [hɛks] (US) N sort m ▶ VT jeter un sort sur

hexagon ['hɛksəgən] N hexagone m

hexagonal [hɛk'sægənl] ADJ hexagonal(e)

hey [heɪ] EXCL hé !

heyday ['heɪdeɪ] N: **the ~ of** l'âge m d'or de, les beaux jours de

HF N ABBR (= high frequency) HF f

HGV N ABBR = **heavy goods vehicle**

HI ABBR (US) = **Hawaii**

★**hi** [haɪ] EXCL salut !; (to attract attention) hé !

hiatus [haɪ'eɪtəs] N trou m, lacune f; (Ling) hiatus m

hibernate ['haɪbəneɪt] VI hiberner

hibernation [haɪbə'neɪʃən] N hibernation f

hibiscus [hɪ'bɪskəs] N hibiscus m

hiccough, hiccup ['hɪkʌp] VI hoqueter ▶ N hoquet m; **to have (the) hiccoughs** avoir le hoquet

hick [hɪk] N (US pej) plouc m, péquenaud(e)

hid [hɪd] PT of **hide**

hidden ['hɪdn] PP of **hide** ▶ ADJ: **there are no ~ extras** absolument tout est compris dans le prix; **~ agenda** intentions non déclarées

★**hide** [haɪd] (pt **hid** [hɪd], pp **hidden** ['hɪdn]) N (skin) peau f ▶ VT cacher; (feelings, truth) dissimuler; **to ~ sth from sb** cacher qch à qn ▶ VI: **to ~ (from sb)** se cacher (de qn)

hide-and-seek ['haɪdən'si:k] N cache-cache m

hideaway ['haɪdəweɪ] N cachette f

hideous ['hɪdɪəs] ADJ hideux(-euse), atroce

hide-out ['haɪdaut] N cachette f

hiding ['haɪdɪŋ] N (beating) correction f, volée f de coups; **to be in ~** (concealed) se tenir caché(e)

hiding place N cachette f

hierarchy ['haɪərɑ:kɪ] N hiérarchie f

hieroglyphic [haɪərə'glɪfɪk] ADJ hiéroglyphique ▪ **hieroglyphics** NPL hiéroglyphes mpl

hi-fi ['haɪfaɪ] ADJ, N ABBR (= high fidelity) hi-fi f inv

higgledy-piggledy ['hɪgldɪ'pɪgldɪ] ADV pêle-mêle, dans le plus grand désordre

★**high** [haɪ] ADJ haut(e); (speed, respect, number) grand(e); (price) élevé(e); (wind) fort(e), violent(e); (voice) aigu(ë); (inf: person: on drugs) défoncé(e), fait(e); (: on drink) soûl(e), bourré(e); (BRIT Culin: meat, game) faisandé(e); (: spoilt) avarié(e); **20 m** ~ haut(e) de 20 m; **to pay a ~ price for sth** payer cher pour qch ▸ ADV haut, en haut; **~ in the air** haut dans le ciel ▸ N (weather) zone f de haute pression; **exports have reached a new ~** les exportations ont atteint un nouveau record

highball ['haɪbɔ:l] N (US) whisky m à l'eau avec des glaçons

highboy ['haɪbɔɪ] N (US) grande commode

highbrow ['haɪbrau] ADJ, N intellectuel(le)

highchair ['haɪtʃɛəʳ] N (child's) chaise haute

high-class ['haɪ'klɑ:s] ADJ (neighbourhood, hotel) chic inv, de grand standing; (performance etc) de haut niveau

High Court N (Law) cour f suprême

Dans le système juridique d'Angleterre et du pays de Galles, la **High Court** est une cour de droit civil chargée des affaires plus importantes et plus complexes que celles traitées par les county courts. En Écosse en revanche, la High Court (of Justiciary) est la plus haute cour de justice, à laquelle sont soumises les affaires les plus graves comme le meurtre et le viol et où elles sont examinées devant un jury.

higher ['haɪəʳ] ADJ (form of life, study etc) supérieur(e) ▸ ADV plus haut

★**higher education** N études supérieures

highfalutin [haɪfə'lu:tɪn] ADJ (inf) affecté(e)

high finance N la haute finance

high five N high five m; **to give sb a ~** faire or échanger un high five avec qn, taper dans les mains de qn

high-flier, high-flyer [haɪ'flaɪəʳ] N (ambitious) ambitieux(-euse); (gifted) personne particulièrement douée et promise à un avenir brillant

high-flying [haɪ'flaɪɪŋ] ADJ (fig) ambitieux(-euse), de haut niveau

high-handed [haɪ'hændɪd] ADJ très autoritaire; très cavalier(-ière)

high-heeled [haɪ'hi:ld] ADJ à hauts talons

high heels NPL talons hauts, hauts talons

high jump N (Sport) saut m en hauteur

highlands ['haɪləndz] NPL région montagneuse; **the H~** (in Scotland) les Highlands mpl

high-level ['haɪlɛvl] ADJ (talks etc) à un haut niveau; **~ language** (Comput) langage évolué

★**highlight** ['haɪlaɪt] N (fig: of event) point culminant ▸ VT (emphasize) faire ressortir, souligner ▪ **highlights** NPL (in hair) reflets mpl

highlighter ['haɪlaɪtəʳ] N (pen) surligneur (lumineux)

highly ['haɪlɪ] ADV extrêmement, très; (unlikely) fort; (recommended, skilled, qualified) hautement; **~ paid** très bien payé(e); **to speak ~ of** dire beaucoup de bien de

highly strung ADJ nerveux(-euse), toujours tendu(e)

High Mass N grand-messe f

highness ['haɪnɪs] N hauteur f; **His/Her H~** son Altesse f

high-pitched [haɪ'pɪtʃt] ADJ aigu(ë)

high point N: **the ~ (of)** le clou (de), le point culminant (de)

high-powered ['haɪ'pauəd] ADJ (engine) performant(e); (fig: person) dynamique; (: job, businessman) très important(e)

high-pressure ['haɪprɛʃəʳ] ADJ à haute pression

high-profile [haɪ'prəufaɪl] CPD (visible: person, position) très en vue; (influential: role) très influent(e); (talked about: issue) très discuté(e); (of media interest: event) médiatisé(e)

high-rise ['haɪraɪz] N (also: **high-rise block, high-rise building**) tour f (d'habitation)

high school N lycée m; (US) établissement m d'enseignement secondaire

Aux États-Unis, la **high school** se compose de la junior high school, qui correspond au collège, et de la senior high school, qui correspond au lycée. En Grande-Bretagne, les mots high school figurent parfois dans le nom des établissements d'enseignement secondaire; voir elementary school.

high season N (BRIT) haute saison

high spirits NPL pétulance f; **to be in ~** être plein(e) d'entrain

high street N (BRIT) grand-rue f

high-tech ['haɪ'tɛk] ADJ (inf) de pointe

highway ['haɪweɪ] N (BRIT) route f; (US) route nationale; **the information ~** l'autoroute f de l'information

Highway Code N (BRIT) code m de la route

highwayman ['haɪweɪmən] N (irreg) voleur m de grand chemin

hijack ['haɪdʒæk] VT détourner (par la force) ▸ N (also: **hijacking**) détournement m (d'avion)

hijacker ['haɪdʒækəʳ] N auteur m d'un détournement d'avion, pirate m de l'air

hike [haɪk] VI faire des excursions à pied ▸ N excursion f à pied, randonnée f; (inf: in prices etc) augmentation f ▸ VT (inf) augmenter

hiker ['haɪkəʳ] N promeneur(-euse), excursionniste mf

hiking ['haɪkɪŋ] N excursions fpl à pied, randonnée f

hilarious [hɪ'lɛərɪəs] ADJ (behaviour, event) désopilant(e)

hilarity [hɪ'lærɪtɪ] N hilarité f

★**hill** [hɪl] N colline f; (fairly high) montagne f; (on road) côte f

hillbilly ['hɪlbɪlɪ] N (US) montagnard(e) du sud des USA; (pej) péquenaud m

hillock ['hɪlək] N petite colline, butte f

hillside ['hɪlsaɪd] N (flanc m de) coteau m

hill start N (Aut) démarrage m en côte

hilltop ['hɪltɔp] N sommet m de la/d'une colline ▸ CPD (village, building) perché(e) sur une colline

hill walking N randonnée f de basse montagne

hilly ['hɪlɪ] ADJ vallonné(e), montagneux(-euse); (road) à fortes côtes

hilt [hɪlt] N (of sword) garde f; **to the ~** (fig: support) à fond

★**him** [hɪm] PRON (direct) le, l' + vowel or h mute; (stressed, indirect, after prep) lui; **I see ~** je le vois; **give ~ a book** donne-lui un livre; **after ~** après lui; see also **me**

Himalayas [hɪmə'leɪəz] NPL: **the ~** l'Himalaya m

★**himself** [hɪm'sɛlf] PRON (reflexive) se; (emphatic) lui-même; (after prep) lui; see also **oneself**

hind [haɪnd] ADJ de derrière ▸ N biche f

hinder ['hɪndə'] VT gêner; (delay) retarder; (prevent): **to ~ sb from doing** empêcher qn de faire

Hindi ['hɪndi] N hindi m; **to speak ~** parler hindi or l'hindi

hindquarters ['haɪnd'kwɔːtəz] NPL (Zool) arrière-train m

hindrance ['hɪndrəns] N gêne f, obstacle m

hindsight ['haɪndsaɪt] N bon sens après coup; **with (the benefit of) ~** avec du recul, rétrospectivement

Hindu ['hɪndu:] N Hindou(e)

Hinduism ['hɪnduɪzəm] N (Rel) hindouisme m

hinge [hɪndʒ] N charnière f ▸ VI (fig): **to ~ on** dépendre de

★**hint** [hɪnt] N allusion f; (advice) conseil m; (clue) indication f; **to drop a ~** faire une allusion or insinuation; **give me a ~** (clue) mettez-moi sur la voie, donnez-moi une indication ▸ VT: **to ~ that** insinuer que ▸ VI: **to ~ at** faire une allusion à

hinterland ['hɪntəlænd] N arrière-pays m

★**hip** [hɪp] N hanche f; (Bot) fruit m de l'églantier or du rosier

hip flask N flacon m (pour la poche)

hip-hop ['hɪphɔp] N hip hop m

hippie, hippy ['hɪpɪ] N hippie mf

hippo ['hɪpəu] (pl hippos) N hippopotame m

hippopotamus [hɪpə'pɔtəməs] (pl hippopotamuses [hɪpə'pɔtəməsɪs] or hippopotami [hɪpə-'pɔtəmaɪ]) N hippopotame m

hippy ['hɪpɪ] N = **hippie**

hipster ['hɪpstə'] N (inf) hipster mf

★**hire** ['haɪə'] VT (Brit: car, equipment) louer; (worker) embaucher, engager; **I'd like to ~ a car** je voudrais louer une voiture ▸ N location f; **for ~** à louer; (taxi) libre; **on ~** en location
▸ **hire out** VT louer

hire car, hired car ['haɪəd-] N (Brit) voiture f de location

hire purchase N (Brit) achat m (or vente f) à tempérament or crédit; **to buy sth on ~** acheter qch en location-vente

★**his** [hɪz] PRON le (la) sien(ne), les siens (siennes); **this is ~** c'est à lui, c'est le sien; **a friend of ~** un(e) de ses ami(e)s, un(e) ami(e) à lui ▸ ADJ son (sa), ses pl; see also **mine¹**; **my**

> The adjectives **son**, **sa** and **ses** agree with the noun they go with. They do not indicate whether the owner in question is male or female: his father **son père**; his car **sa voiture**; his friends **ses amis**.

Hispanic [hɪs'pænɪk] ADJ (in US) hispano-américain(e) ▸ N Hispano-Américain(e)

hiss [hɪs] VI siffler ▸ N sifflement m

hissy fit [hɪsɪ-] N (inf) crise f; **to throw a ~** piquer une crise

histogram ['hɪstəgræm] N histogramme m

historian [hɪ'stɔːrɪən] N historien(ne)

historic [hɪ'stɔrɪk], **historical** [hɪ'stɔrɪkl] ADJ historique

historically [hɪ'stɔrɪklɪ] ADV historiquement

★**history** ['hɪstərɪ] N histoire f; **medical ~** (of patient) passé médical

histrionics [hɪstrɪ'ɔnɪks] N gestes mpl dramatiques, cinéma m (fig)

★**hit** [hɪt] (pt, pp ~) VT frapper; (knock against) cogner; (reach: target) atteindre, toucher; (collide with: car) entrer en collision avec, heurter; (fig: affect) toucher; (find) tomber sur; **to ~ it off with sb** bien s'entendre avec qn; **to ~ the headlines** être à la une des journaux; **to ~ the road** (inf) se mettre en route ▸ N coup m; (success) coup réussi, succès m; (song) chanson f à succès, tube m; (to website) visite f; (on search engine) résultat m de recherche
▸ **hit back** VI: **to ~ back at sb** prendre sa revanche sur qn
▸ **hit on** VT FUS (answer) trouver (par hasard); (solution) tomber sur (par hasard)
▸ **hit out at** VT FUS envoyer un coup à; (fig) attaquer
▸ **hit upon** VT FUS = **hit on**

hit-and-miss ['hɪtænd'mɪs] ADJ au petit bonheur (la chance)

hit-and-run driver ['hɪtænd'rʌn-] N chauffard m

hitch [hɪtʃ] VT (fasten) accrocher, attacher; (also: **hitch up**) remonter d'une saccade; (: **a lift**) faire du stop ▸ VI faire de l'autostop ▸ N (knot) nœud m; (difficulty) anicroche f, contretemps m; **technical ~** incident m technique
▸ **hitch up** VT (horse, cart) atteler

hitch-hike ['hɪtʃhaɪk] VI faire de l'auto-stop

hitch-hiker ['hɪtʃhaɪkə'] N auto-stoppeur(-euse)

hitch-hiking ['hɪtʃhaɪkɪŋ] N auto-stop m, stop m (inf)

hi-tech ['haɪ'tɛk] ADJ de pointe ▸ N high-tech m

hitherto [hɪðə'tu:] ADV jusqu'ici, jusqu'à présent

hit list N liste noire

hitman ['hɪtmæn] N (irreg) (inf) tueur m à gages

hit-or-miss ['hɪtə'mɪs] ADJ au petit bonheur (la chance); **it's ~ whether …** il est loin d'être certain que … +sub

hit parade N hit parade m

hitter ['hɪtə'] N (in tennis, baseball) frappeur(-euse); **a big** or **heavy ~** (fig) un poids lourd

HIV N ABBR (= human immunodeficiency virus) HIV m, VIH m; **HIV-negative** séronégatif(-ive); **HIV-positive** séropositif(-ive)

hive [haɪv] N ruche f; **the shop was a ~ of activity** (fig) le magasin était une véritable ruche
▸ **hive off** VT (inf) mettre à part, séparer

hl ABBR (= hectolitre) hl

HM ABBR (= His (or) Her Majesty) SM

HMG ABBR (Brit) = Her Majesty's Government; His Majesty's Government

HMI N ABBR (Brit Scol) = His Majesty's Inspector; Her Majesty's Inspector

HMO N ABBR (US: = *health maintenance organization*) organisme médical assurant un forfait entretien de santé

HMS ABBR (BRIT) = **His Majesty's Ship; Her Majesty's Ship**

HMSO N ABBR (BRIT: = *His (or) Her Majesty's Stationery Office*) ≈ Imprimerie nationale

HNC N ABBR (BRIT: = *Higher National Certificate*) ≈ DUT *m*

HND N ABBR (BRIT: = *Higher National Diploma*) ≈ licence *f* de sciences et techniques

hoard [hɔːd] N (*of food*) provisions *fpl*, réserves *fpl*; (*of money*) trésor *m* ▶ VT amasser

hoarding ['hɔːdɪŋ] N (BRIT) panneau *m* d'affichage or publicitaire

hoarfrost ['hɔːfrɒst] N givre *m*

hoarse [hɔːs] ADJ enroué(e)

hoax [həʊks] N canular *m*

hob [hɒb] N plaque chauffante

hobble ['hɒbl] VI boitiller

hobby ['hɒbɪ] N passe-temps favori

hobby-horse ['hɒbɪhɔːs] N cheval *m* à bascule; (*fig*) dada *m*

hobnob ['hɒbnɒb] VI: **to ~ with** frayer avec, fréquenter

hobo ['həʊbəʊ] N (US) vagabond *m*

hock [hɒk] N (BRIT: *wine*) vin *m* du Rhin; (*of animal: Culin*) jarret *m*

hockey ['hɒkɪ] N hockey *m*

hockey stick N crosse *f* de hockey

hocus-pocus ['həʊkəs'pəʊkəs] N (*trickery*) supercherie *f*; (*words: of magician*) formules *fpl* magiques; (: *jargon*) galimatias *m*

hod [hɒd] N oiseau *m*, hotte *f*

hodgepodge ['hɒdʒpɒdʒ] N = **hotchpotch**

hoe [həʊ] N houe *f*, binette *f* ▶ VT (*ground*) biner; (*plants etc*) sarcler

hog [hɒg] N porc (châtré); **to go the whole ~** aller jusqu'au bout ▶ VT (*fig*) accaparer

Hogmanay [hɒgmə'neɪ] N réveillon *m* du jour de l'An, Saint-Sylvestre *f*

La Saint-Sylvestre, ou *New Year's Eve*, se nomme **Hogmanay** en Écosse, où traditionnellement elle faisait l'objet de célébrations plus importantes que Noël. À cette occasion, la famille et les amis se réunissent pour entendre sonner les douze coups de minuit et fêter le *first-footing*, une coutume qui veut qu'on se rende chez ses amis et voisins en apportant quelque chose à boire (du whisky en général) et un morceau de charbon en gage de prospérité pour la nouvelle année.

hogwash ['hɒgwɒʃ] N (*inf*) foutaises *fpl*

hoist [hɔɪst] N palan *m* ▶ VT hisser

hoity-toity [hɔɪtɪ'tɔɪtɪ] ADJ (*inf*) prétentieux(-euse), qui se donne

★**hold** [həʊld] (*pt, pp* **held** [held]) VT tenir; (*contain*) contenir; (*meeting*) tenir; (*keep back*) retenir; (*believe*) maintenir, considérer; (*possess*) avoir; détenir; **~ the line!** (*Tel*) ne quittez pas !; **to ~ one's own** (*fig*) (bien) se défendre; **to ~ office** (*Pol*)

avoir un portefeuille; **he holds the view that ...** il pense or estime que ..., d'après lui ...; **to ~ sb responsible for sth** tenir qn pour responsable de qch ▶ VI (*withstand pressure*) tenir (bon); (*be valid*) valoir; (*on telephone*) attendre; **to ~ firm** or **fast** tenir bon ▶ N prise *f*; (*find*) influence *f*; (*Naut*) cale *f*; **to catch** or **get (a) ~ of** saisir; **to get ~ of** (*find*) trouver; **to get ~ of o.s.** se contrôler

▶ **hold back** VT retenir; (*secret*) cacher; **to ~ sb back from doing sth** empêcher qn de faire qch

▶ **hold down** VT (*person*) maintenir à terre; (*job*) occuper

▶ **hold forth** VI pérorer

▶ **hold off** VT tenir à distance ▶ VI: **if the rain holds off** s'il ne pleut pas, s'il ne se met pas à pleuvoir

▶ **hold on** VI tenir bon; (*wait*) attendre; **~ on!** (*Tel*) ne quittez pas !; **to ~ on to sth** (*grasp*) se cramponner à qch; (*keep*) conserver or garder qch

▶ **hold out** VT offrir ▶ VI (*resist*): **to ~ out (against)** résister (devant), tenir bon (devant)

▶ **hold over** VT (*meeting etc*) ajourner, reporter

▶ **hold up** VT (*raise*) lever; (*support*) soutenir; (*delay*) retarder; (: *traffic*) ralentir; (*rob*) braquer

▶ **hold with** VT FUS apprécier

holdall ['həʊldɔːl] N (BRIT) fourre-tout *m inv*

holder ['həʊldəʳ] N (*container*) support *m*; (*of ticket, record*) détenteur(-trice); (*of office, title, passport etc*) titulaire *mf*

holding ['həʊldɪŋ] N (*share*) intérêts *mpl*; (*farm*) ferme *f*

holding company N holding *m*

hold-up ['həʊldʌp] N (*robbery*) hold-up *m*; (*delay*) retard *m*; (BRIT: *in traffic*) embouteillage *m*

★**hole** [həʊl] N trou *m*; **~ in the heart** (*Med*) communication *f* interventriculaire; **to pick holes (in)** (*fig*) chercher des poux (dans) ▶ VT trouer, faire un trou dans

▶ **hole up** VI se terrer

★**holiday** ['hɒlədɪ] N (BRIT: *vacation*) vacances *fpl*; (*day off*) jour *m* de congé; (*public*) jour férié; **to be on ~** être en vacances; **I'm here on ~** je suis ici en vacances; **tomorrow is a ~** demain c'est fête, on a congé demain

holiday camp N (BRIT: *for children*) colonie *f* de vacances; (: *also:* **holiday centre**) camp *m* de vacances

holiday home N (*rented*) location *f* de vacances; (*owned*) résidence *f* secondaire

holiday job N (BRIT) boulot *m* (*inf*) de vacances

holiday-maker ['hɒlədɪmeɪkəʳ] N (BRIT) vacancier(-ière)

holiday pay N paie *f* des vacances

holiday resort N centre *m* de villégiature or de vacances

holiday season N période *f* des vacances

holiness ['həʊlɪnɪs] N sainteté *f*

holistic [həʊ'lɪstɪk] ADJ holiste, holistique

★**Holland** ['hɒlənd] N Hollande *f*

holler ['hɒləʳ] VI (*inf*) brailler

hollow ['hɒləʊ] ADJ creux(-euse); (*fig*) faux (fausse) ▶ N creux *m*; (*in land*) dépression *f* (de terrain), cuvette *f* ▶ VT: **to ~ out** creuser, évider

holly ['hɒlɪ] N houx *m*

hollyhock ['hɒlɪhɒk] N rose trémière

Hollywood ['hɒlɪwʊd] N Hollywood *m*

holocaust ['hɒləkɔːst] N holocauste *m*

hologram ['hɒləgræm] N hologramme *m*

hols [hɒlz] NPL (*inf*) vacances *fpl*

holster ['həʊlstə^r] N étui *m* de revolver

★**holy** ['həʊlɪ] ADJ saint(e); (*bread, water*) bénit(e); (*ground*) sacré(e)

Holy Communion N la (sainte) communion

Holy Ghost, Holy Spirit N Saint-Esprit *m*

Holy Land N: **the ~** la Terre Sainte

holy orders NPL ordres (majeurs)

homage ['hɒmɪdʒ] N hommage *m*; **to pay ~ to** rendre hommage à

★**home** [həʊm] N foyer *m*, maison *f*; (*country*) pays natal, patrie *f*; (*institution*) maison; **at ~** chez soi, à la maison; **make yourself at ~** faites comme chez vous; **near my ~** près de chez moi ▶ ADJ de famille; (*Econ, Pol*) national(e), intérieur(e); (*Sport: team*) qui reçoit; (: *match, win*) sur leur (*or* notre) terrain ▶ ADV chez soi, à la maison; au pays natal; (*right in: nail etc*) à fond; **to go** (*or* **come**) **~** rentrer (chez soi), rentrer à la maison (*or* au pays); **I'm going ~ on Tuesday** je rentre mardi

▶ **home in on** VT FUS (*missile*) se diriger automatiquement vers *or* sur

home address N domicile permanent

home-brew [həʊm'bruː] N vin *m* (*or* bière *f*) maison

homecoming ['həʊmkʌmɪŋ] N retour *m* (au bercail)

home computer N ordinateur *m* domestique

Home Counties NPL *les comtés autour de Londres*

home economics N économie *f* domestique

home ground N: **to be on ~** être sur son terrain

home-grown ['həʊmgrəʊn] ADJ (*not foreign*) du pays; (*from garden*) du jardin

home help N (*BRIT*) aide-ménagère *f*

homeland ['həʊmlænd] N patrie *f*

★**homeless** ['həʊmlɪs] ADJ sans logis, sans abri; **a ~ person** un sans-abri; **to be made ~** perdre son logement, devenir sans-abri ■ **the homeless** NPL les sans-abri *mpl*

homelessness ['həʊmlɪsnɪs] N problème *m* des sans-abri

home loan N prêt *m* sur hypothèque

homely ['həʊmlɪ] ADJ (*plain*) simple, sans prétention; (*welcoming*) accueillant(e)

home-made [həʊm'meɪd] ADJ fait(e) à la maison

home match N match *m* à domicile

Home Office N (*BRIT*) ministère *m* de l'Intérieur

homeopathy *etc* [həʊmɪ'ɒpəθɪ] N (*US*) = **homeopathy** *etc*

home owner N propriétaire occupant

★**home page** N (*Comput*) page *f* d'accueil

home rule N autonomie *f*

Home Secretary N (*BRIT*) ministre *m* de l'Intérieur

homesick ['həʊmsɪk] ADJ: **to be ~** avoir le mal du pays; (*missing one's family*) s'ennuyer de sa famille

homesickness ['həʊmsɪknɪs] N mal *m* du pays

homestead ['həʊmstɛd] N propriété *f*; (*farm*) ferme *f*

home town N ville natale

home truth N: **to tell sb a few ~s** dire ses quatre vérités à qn

homeward ['həʊmwəd] ADJ (*journey*) du retour
▶ ADV = **homewards**

homewards ['həʊmwədz] ADV vers la maison

★**homework** ['həʊmwəːk] N devoirs *mpl*

homey ['həʊmɪ] ADJ (*esp US: cosy*) simple et accueillant(e)

homicidal [hɒmɪ'saɪdl] ADJ homicide

homicide ['hɒmɪsaɪd] N (*US*) homicide *m*

homily ['hɒmɪlɪ] N homélie *f*

homing ['həʊmɪŋ] ADJ (*device, missile*) à tête chercheuse; **~ pigeon** pigeon voyageur

homoeopath, (*US*) **homeopath** ['həʊmɪəʊpæθ] N homéopathe *mf*

homoeopathic, (*US*) **homeopathic** [həʊmɪəʊ'pæθɪk] ADJ (*medicine*) homéopathique; (*doctor*) homéopathe

homoeopathy, (*US*) **homeopathy** [həʊmɪ'ɒpəθɪ] N homéopathie *f*

homogeneous [hɒməʊ'dʒiːnɪəs] ADJ homogène

homogenize [hə'mɒdʒənaɪz] VT homogénéiser

homophobia [hɒmə'fəʊbɪə] N homophobie *f*

homophobic [hɒmə'fəʊbɪk] ADJ homophobe

homosexual [hɒməʊ'sɛksjuəl] ADJ, N homosexuel(le)

homosexuality [hɒməʊsɛksju'ælɪtɪ] N homosexualité *f*

Hon. ABBR (= *honourable, honorary*) *dans un titre*

Honduras [hɒn'djuərəs] N Honduras *m*

hone [həʊn] N pierre *f* à aiguiser ▶ VT affûter, aiguiser

★**honest** ['ɒnɪst] ADJ honnête; (*sincere*) franc (franche); **to be quite ~ with you …** à dire vrai …

honestly ['ɒnɪstlɪ] ADV honnêtement; franchement

honesty ['ɒnɪstɪ] N honnêteté *f*

honey ['hʌnɪ] N miel *m*; (*inf: darling*) chéri(e)

honeycomb ['hʌnɪkəʊm] N rayon *m* de miel; (*pattern*) nid *m* d'abeilles, motif alvéolé ▶ VT (*fig*): **to ~ with** cribler de

honeymoon ['hʌnɪmuːn] N lune *f* de miel, voyage *m* de noces; **we're on ~** nous sommes en voyage de noces

honeysuckle ['hʌnɪsʌkl] N chèvrefeuille *m*

Hong Kong ['hɔŋ'kɔŋ] N Hong Kong

honk [hɔŋk] N (*Aut*) coup *m* de klaxon ▶ VI klaxonner

Honolulu [hɒnə'luːluː] N Honolulu

honorary ['ɒnərərɪ] ADJ honoraire; (*duty, title*) honorifique; **~ degree** diplôme *m* honoris causa

honour, (*US*) **honor** ['ɒnə^r] VT honorer ▶ N honneur *m*; **in ~ of** en l'honneur de; **to graduate with honours** obtenir sa licence avec mention

honourable, (*US*) **honorable** ['ɒnərəbl] ADJ honorable

honour-bound, (*US*) **honor-bound** ['ɒnə'baʊnd] ADJ: **to be ~ to do** se devoir de faire

honours degree N (*University*) ≈ licence f avec mention

Un **honours degree** est un diplôme universitaire sanctionnant trois années d'études en Angleterre et quatre en Écosse. Les mentions qui l'accompagnent sont, par ordre décroissant : *first class* (très bien/bien), *upper second class* ou 2 :1 (assez bien), *lower second class* ou 2 :2 (passable), et *third class* (diplôme sans mention). Le titulaire d'un *honours degree* est autorisé à mettre un titre à la suite de son nom, par exemple : *Peter Jones BA Hons* ; voir *ordinary degree*.

honours list N (BRIT): **the ~** voir article

L' **honours list** est la liste des citoyens du Royaume-Uni et du Commonwealth auxquels le souverain confère un titre ou une décoration. Cette liste est préparée par le Premier ministre et paraît deux fois par an, au Nouvel An et lors de l'anniversaire officiel du règne du souverain. Des personnes qui se sont distinguées dans le monde des affaires, du sport, des médias et des forces armées, mais également des citoyens "ordinaires" qui se consacrent à des œuvres de charité sont ainsi récompensés.

Hons. ABBR (*Scol*) = **honours degree**

hood [hud] N capuchon m; (*of cooker*) hotte f; (BRIT Aut) capote f; (US Aut) capot m; (*inf*) truand m

hooded ['hudɪd] ADJ (*jacket, coat*) à capuche; (*gunman*) cagoulé(e); (*eyes*) aux paupières tombantes

hoodie ['hudɪ] N (*top*) sweat m à capuche; (*youth*) jeune m à capuche

hoodlum ['hu:dləm] N truand m

hoodwink ['hudwɪŋk] VT tromper

hoof [hu:f] (*pl* hoofs *or* hooves [hu:vz]) N sabot m

★**hook** [huk] N crochet m; (*on dress*) agrafe f; (*for fishing*) hameçon m; **off the ~** (*Tel*) décroché; **~ and eye** agrafe; **by ~ or by crook** de gré ou de force, coûte que coûte ▶ VT accrocher; (*dress*) agrafer; **to be hooked (on)** (*inf*) être accroché(e) (par); (*person*) être dingue (de)
▶ **hook up** VT (*Radio, TV etc*) faire un duplex entre

hooker ['hukər] N (*esp US inf*) pute f (inf)

hooligan ['hu:lɪgən] N hooligan m

hooliganism ['hu:lɪgənɪzəm] N hooliganisme m; **football ~** le hooliganisme dans le football

hoop [hu:p] N cerceau m; (*of barrel*) cercle m

hooray [hə'reɪ, hu'reɪ] EXCL hourra

hoot [hu:t] VI (BRIT Aut) klaxonner; (*siren*) mugir; (*owl*) hululer; **to ~ with laughter** rire aux éclats ▶ VT (*jeer at*) huer ▶ N huée f; coup m de klaxon; mugissement m; hululement m

hooter ['hu:tər] N (BRIT Aut) klaxon m; (*Naut, factory*) sirène f

Hoover® ['hu:vər] (BRIT) N aspirateur m ▶ VT: **to hoover** (*room*) passer l'aspirateur dans; (*carpet*) passer l'aspirateur sur

hooves [hu:vz] NPL *of* hoof

hop [hɔp] VI sauter; (*on one foot*) sauter à cloche-pied; (*bird*) sautiller ▶ N saut m

★**hope** [həup] VT, VI espérer; **I ~ so** je l'espère; **I ~ not** j'espère que non ▶ N espoir m

hopeful ['həupful] ADJ (*person*) plein(e) d'espoir; (*situation*) prometteur(-euse), encourageant(e); **I'm ~ that she'll manage to come** j'ai bon espoir qu'elle pourra venir

hopefully ['həupfulɪ] ADV (*expectantly*) avec espoir, avec optimisme; (*one hopes*) avec un peu de chance; **~, they'll come back** espérons bien qu'ils reviendront

hopeless ['həuplɪs] ADJ désespéré(e), sans espoir; (*useless*) nul(le)

hopelessly ['həuplɪslɪ] ADV (*live etc*) sans espoir; **~ confused** *etc* complètement désorienté *etc*

hops [hɔps] NPL houblon m

horde ['hɔ:d] N horde f

horizon [hə'raɪzn] N horizon m

horizontal [hɔrɪ'zɔntl] ADJ horizontal(e)

hormonal [hɔː'məunl] ADJ hormonal(e)

hormone ['hɔːməun] N hormone f

hormone replacement therapy N hormonothérapie substitutive, traitement hormono-supplétif

horn [hɔ:n] N corne f; (*Mus*) cor m; (*Aut*) klaxon m

horned [hɔ:nd] ADJ (*animal*) à cornes

hornet ['hɔ:nɪt] N frelon m

horny ['hɔ:nɪ] ADJ corné(e); (*hands*) calleux(-euse); (*inf: aroused*) excité(e)

horoscope ['hɔrəskəup] N horoscope m

horrendous [həʹrendəs] ADJ horrible, affreux(-euse)

★**horrible** ['hɔrɪbl] ADJ horrible, affreux(-euse)

horrid ['hɔrɪd] ADJ (*person*) détestable; (*weather, place, smell*) épouvantable

horrific [hə'rɪfɪk] ADJ horrible

horrified ['hɔrɪfaɪd] ADJ horrifié(e); **to be ~ by/at sth** être horrifié(e) par qch

horrify ['hɔrɪfaɪ] VT horrifier

horrifying ['hɔrɪfaɪɪŋ] ADJ horrifiant(e)

★**horror** ['hɔrər] N horreur f

horror film, (*US*) **horror movie** N film m d'épouvante

horror-struck ['hɔrəstrʌk], **horror-stricken** ['hɔrəstrɪkn] ADJ horrifié(e)

hors d'œuvre [ɔː'də:vrə] N hors d'œuvre m

★**horse** [hɔ:s] N cheval m

horseback ['hɔ:sbæk]: **on ~** adj, adv à cheval

horsebox ['hɔ:sbɔks] N van m

horse chestnut N (*nut*) marron m (d'Inde); (*tree*) marronnier m (d'Inde)

horse-drawn ['hɔ:sdrɔ:n] ADJ tiré(e) par des chevaux

horsefly ['hɔ:sflaɪ] N taon m

horseman ['hɔ:smən] N (*irreg*) cavalier m

horsemanship ['hɔ:smənʃɪp] N talents mpl de cavalier

horseplay ['hɔ:spleɪ] N chahut m (*blagues etc*)

horsepower ['hɔ:spauər] N puissance f (en chevaux); (*unit*) cheval-vapeur m (CV)

horse-racing ['hɔ:sreɪsɪŋ] N courses fpl de chevaux

horseradish ['hɔ:srædɪʃ] N raifort m

horse riding N (BRIT) équitation f

horseshoe ['hɔːʃuː] N fer m à cheval

horse show N concours m hippique

horse-trading ['hɔːstreɪdɪŋ] N maquignonnage m

horse trials NPL = **horse show**

horsewhip ['hɔːswɪp] VT cravacher

horsewoman ['hɔːswuman] N (irreg) cavalière f

horsey ['hɔːsɪ] ADJ (inf) féru(e) d'équitation or de cheval; (appearance) chevalin(e)

horticultural [hɔːtɪ'kʌltʃərəl] ADJ horticole

horticulture ['hɔːtɪkʌltʃəʳ] N horticulture f

hose [həuz] N (also: **hosepipe**) tuyau m; (also: **garden hose**) tuyau d'arrosage
▶ **hose down** VT laver au jet

hosepipe ['həuzpaɪp] N tuyau m; (in garden) tuyau d'arrosage; (for fire) tuyau d'incendie

hosiery ['həuzɪərɪ] N (rayon m des) bas mpl

hospice ['hɔspɪs] N hospice m

hospitable ['hɔspɪtəbl] ADJ hospitalier(-ière)

★**hospital** ['hɔspɪtl] N hôpital m; **in ~**, (US) **in the ~** à l'hôpital; **where's the nearest ~?** où est l'hôpital le plus proche ?

hospitality [hɔspɪ'tælɪtɪ] N hospitalité f

hospitalize ['hɔspɪtəlaɪz] VT hospitaliser

host [həust] N hôte m; (in hotel etc) patron m; (TV, Radio) présentateur(-trice), animateur(-trice); (large number): **a ~ of** une foule de; (Rel) hostie f ▶ VT (TV programme) présenter, animer

★**hostage** ['hɔstɪdʒ] N otage m

host country N pays m d'accueil, pays-hôte m

hostel ['hɔstl] N foyer m; (also: **youth hostel**) auberge f de jeunesse

hostelling ['hɔstlɪŋ] N: **to go (youth) ~** faire une virée or randonnée en séjournant dans des auberges de jeunesse

hostess ['həustɪs] N hôtesse f; (BRIT: also: **air hostess**) hôtesse de l'air; (TV, Radio) présentatrice f; (in nightclub) entraîneuse f

hostile ['hɔstaɪl] ADJ hostile

hostile bid N (also: **hostile takeover bid**) OPA f hostile

hostility [hɔ'stɪlɪtɪ] N hostilité f

★**hot** [hɔt] ADJ chaud(e); (as opposed to only warm) très chaud; (spicy) fort(e); (fig: contest) acharné(e); (topic) brûlant(e); (temper) violent(e), passionné(e); **to be ~** (person) avoir chaud; (thing) être (très) chaud; **it's ~** (weather) il fait chaud
▶ **hot up** (BRIT inf) VI (situation) devenir tendu(e); (party) s'animer ▶ VT (pace) accélérer, forcer; (engine) gonfler

hot-air balloon [hɔt'ɛə-] N montgolfière f, ballon m

hotbed ['hɔtbɛd] N (fig) foyer m, pépinière f

hotchpotch ['hɔtʃpɔtʃ] N (BRIT) mélange m hétéroclite

hot dog N hot-dog m

★**hotel** [həu'tɛl] N hôtel m

hotelier [həu'tɛlɪəʳ] N hôtelier(-ière)

hotel industry N industrie hôtelière

hotel room N chambre f d'hôtel

hot flush N (BRIT) bouffée f de chaleur

hotfoot ['hɔtfut] ADV à toute vitesse

hothead ['hɔthɛd] N (fig) tête brûlée

hotheaded [hɔt'hɛdɪd] ADJ impétueux(-euse)

hothouse ['hɔthaus] N serre chaude

hotline ['hɔtlaɪn] N (Pol) téléphone m rouge, ligne directe

hotly ['hɔtlɪ] ADV passionnément, violemment

hotplate ['hɔtpleɪt] N (on cooker) plaque chauffante

hotpot ['hɔtpɔt] N (BRIT Culin) ragoût m

hot potato N (BRIT inf) sujet brûlant; **to drop sb/sth like a ~** laisser tomber qn/qch brusquement

hot seat N (fig) poste chaud

hotspot ['hɔtspɔt] N (Comput: also: **wireless hotspot**) borne f wifi, hotspot m

hot spot N point chaud

hot spring N source thermale

hot-tempered ['hɔt'tɛmpəd] ADJ emporté(e)

hot-water bottle [hɔt'wɔːtə-] N bouillotte f

hot-wire ['hɔtwaɪəʳ] VT (inf: car) démarrer en faisant se toucher les fils de contact

hound [haund] VT poursuivre avec acharnement
▶ N chien courant; **the hounds** la meute

★**hour** ['auəʳ] N heure f; **at 30 miles an ~** ≈ à 50 km à l'heure; **lunch ~** heure du déjeuner; **to pay sb by the ~** payer qn à l'heure

hourglass ['auəglɑːs] N sablier m; **to have an ~ figure** avoir des formes fpl généreuses

hourly ['auəlɪ] ADJ toutes les heures; (rate) horaire; **~ paid** adj payé(e) à l'heure

★**house** [haus] (pl **houses** ['hauzɪz]) N maison f; (Pol) chambre f; (Theat) salle f; auditoire m; **at** (or **to**) **my ~** chez moi; **on the ~** (fig) aux frais de la maison; **the H~ of Commons/des lords** la Chambre des communes/des lords; **the H~ (of Representatives)** (US) la Chambre des représentants ▶ VT [hauz] (person) loger, héberger

Le parlement en Grande-Bretagne est constitué de deux assemblées. La **House of Commons** est présidée par le *Speaker* et composée de plus de 600 députés (les *MPs*) élus au suffrage universel direct. Ceux-ci reçoivent tous un salaire. La Chambre des communes siège environ 175 jours par an. La **House of Lords**, présidée par le *Lord Chancellor*, est composée de lords qui se voient attribuer ce titre à vie par le souverain. Elle peut amender certains projets de loi votés par la *House of Commons*, mais elle n'est pas habilitée à débattre des projets de lois de finances. La *House of Lords* fait également office de juridiction suprême en Angleterre et au pays de Galles.

Aux États-Unis, le parlement, appelé le *Congress*, est constitué du *Senate* et de la **House of Representatives**. Cette dernière comprend 435 membres maximum, le nombre de ces représentants par État étant proportionnel à la densité de population de cet État. Ils sont élus pour deux ans au suffrage universel direct et siègent au *Capitol*, à Washington D.C.

house arrest N assignation f à domicile

houseboat ['hausbəut] N bateau (aménagé en habitation)

housebound ['hausbaund] ADJ confiné(e) chez soi

housebreaking ['hausbreikɪŋ] N cambriolage m (avec effraction)

house-broken ['hausbrəukn] ADJ (US) = **house-trained**

housecoat ['hauskəut] N peignoir m

household ['haushəuld] N (Admin etc) ménage m; (people) famille f, maisonnée f; ~ **name** nom connu de tout le monde

householder ['haushəuldəʳ] N propriétaire mf; (head of house) chef m de famille

househunting ['haushʌntɪŋ] N: **to go ~** se mettre en quête d'une maison (or d'un appartement)

housekeeper ['hauski:pəʳ] N gouvernante f

housekeeping ['hauski:pɪŋ] N (work) ménage m; (also: **housekeeping money**) argent m du ménage; (Comput) gestion f (des disques)

housemate ['hausmeit] N colocataire mf

house-owner ['hausəunəʳ] N propriétaire mf (de maison ou d'appartement)

house-proud ['hauspraud] ADJ qui tient à avoir une maison impeccable

house-to-house ['haustə'haus] ADJ (enquiries etc) chez tous les habitants (du quartier etc)

house-train ['haustrein] VT (pet) apprendre à être propre à

house-trained ['haustreind] ADJ (pet) propre

house-warming ['hauswɔ:mɪŋ] N (also: **house-warming party**) pendaison f de crémaillère

housewife ['hauswaif] N (irreg) ménagère f; femme f au foyer

house wine N cuvée f maison or du patron

housework ['hauswə:k] N (travaux mpl du) ménage m

housing ['hauzɪŋ] N logement m ▶ CPD (problem, shortage) de or du logement

housing association N fondation f charitable fournissant des logements

housing benefit N (BRIT) ≈ allocations fpl logement

housing development, (BRIT) **housing estate** N (blocks of flats) cité f; (houses) lotissement m

hovel ['hɒvl] N taudis m

hover ['hɒvəʳ] VI planer; **to ~ round sb** rôder or tourner autour de qn

hovercraft ['hɒvəkrɑ:ft] N aéroglisseur m, hovercraft m

hoverport ['hɒvəpɔ:t] N hoverport m

★**how** [hau] ADV comment; ~ **are you?** comment allez-vous ?; ~ **do you do?** bonjour; (on being introduced) enchanté(e); ~ **far is it to ...?** combien y a-t-il jusqu'à ... ?; ~ **long have you been here?** depuis combien de temps êtes-vous là ?; ~ **lovely/awful!** que or comme c'est joli/affreux !; ~ **many/much?** combien ?; ~ **much time/many people?** combien de temps/gens ?; ~ **much does it cost?** ça coûte combien ?; ~ **old are you?** quel âge avez-vous ?; ~ **tall is he?** combien mesure-t-il ?; ~ **is school?** ça va à l'école ?; ~ **was the film?** comment était le film ?; ~**'s life?** (inf) comment ça va ?; ~ **about a drink?** si on buvait quelque chose ?; ~ **is it that ...?** comment se fait-il que ... + sub ?

★**however** [hau'evəʳ] CONJ pourtant, cependant ▶ ADV de quelque façon or manière que + sub; (+ adjective) quelque or si ... que + sub; (in questions) comment; ~ **I do it** de quelque manière que je m'y prenne; ~ **cold it is** même s'il fait très froid; ~ **did you do it?** comment y êtes-vous donc arrivé ?

howitzer ['hauitsəʳ] N (Mil) obusier m

howl [haul] N hurlement m ▶ VI hurler; (wind) mugir

howler ['hauləʳ] N gaffe f, bourde f

howling ['haulɪŋ] ADJ: **a ~ wind** or **gale** un vent à décorner les bœufs

HP N ABBR (BRIT) = **hire purchase**

h.p. ABBR (Aut) = **horsepower**

HQ N ABBR (= headquarters) QG m

HR N ABBR (US) = **House of Representatives**

hr ABBR (= hour) h

HRH ABBR (= His (or Her) Royal Highness) SAR

hrs ABBR (= hours) h

HRT N ABBR = **hormone replacement therapy**

HS ABBR (US) = **high school**

HTML N ABBR (= hypertext markup language) HTML m

hub [hʌb] N (of wheel) moyeu m; (fig) centre m, foyer m

hubbub ['hʌbʌb] N brouhaha m

hubby ['hʌbɪ] N (inf) mari m

hubcap [hʌbkæp] N (Aut) enjoliveur m

hubris ['hju:brɪs] N arrogance f

HUD N ABBR (US: = Department of Housing and Urban Development) ministère de l'urbanisme et du logement

huddle ['hʌdl] VI: **to ~ together** se blottir les uns contre les autres

hue [hju:] N teinte f, nuance f; ~ **and cry** n tollé (général), clameur f

huff [hʌf] N: **in a ~** fâché(e); **to take the ~** prendre la mouche

huffy ['hʌfɪ] ADJ (inf) froissé(e)

hug [hʌg] VT serrer dans ses bras; (shore, kerb) serrer ▶ N étreinte f; **to give sb a ~** serrer qn dans ses bras

★**huge** [hju:dʒ] ADJ énorme, immense

hugely ['hju:dʒlɪ] ADV (popular, successful) extrêmement; (enjoy) énormément

hulk [hʌlk] N (ship) vieux rafiot; (car, building) carcasse f; (person) mastodonte m, malabar m

hulking ['hʌlkɪŋ] ADJ balourd(e)

hull [hʌl] N (of ship) coque f; (of nuts) coque f; (of peas) cosse f

hullabaloo ['hʌləbə'lu:] N (inf: noise) tapage m, raffut m

hullo [hə'ləu] EXCL = **hello**

hum [hʌm] VT (tune) fredonner ▶ VI fredonner; (insect) bourdonner; (plane, tool) vrombir ▶ N fredonnement m; bourdonnement m; vrombissement m

★**human** ['hju:mən] ADJ humain(e) ▶ N (also: **human being**) être humain

humane [hju:'mein] ADJ humain(e), humanitaire

humanely [hju:'meinlɪ] ADV (treat) humainement; **to be ~ destroyed** être abattu(e) sans cruauté

humanism ['hju:mənizəm] N humanisme m

humanist ['hjuːmənɪst] N humaniste *mf*
humanitarian [hjuːmænɪ'tɛərɪən] ADJ humanitaire
humanity [hjuː'mænɪtɪ] N humanité *f*
humankind [hjuːmən'kaɪnd] N l'humanité *f*
humanly ['hjuːmənlɪ] ADV humainement
humanoid ['hjuːmənɔɪd] ADJ, N humanoïde *mf*
human rights NPL droits *mpl* de l'homme
humble ['hʌmbl] ADJ humble, modeste ▶ VT humilier
humbled ['hʌmbəld] ADJ empli(e) d'humilité
humbling ['hʌmblɪŋ] ADJ: **to be a ~ experience** être une leçon d'humilité
humbly ['hʌmblɪ] ADV humblement, modestement
humbug ['hʌmbʌg] N fumisterie *f*; (*BRIT: sweet*) bonbon *m* à la menthe
humdrum ['hʌmdrʌm] ADJ monotone, routinier(-ière)
humid ['hjuːmɪd] ADJ humide
humidifier [hjuː'mɪdɪfaɪəʳ] N humidificateur *m*
humidity [hjuː'mɪdɪtɪ] N humidité *f*
humiliate [hjuː'mɪlɪeɪt] VT humilier
humiliating [hjuː'mɪlɪeɪtɪŋ] ADJ humiliant(e)
humiliation [hjuːmɪlɪ'eɪʃən] N humiliation *f*
humility [hjuː'mɪlɪtɪ] N humilité *f*
hummus ['huməs] N houm(m)ous *m*
humorist ['hjuːmərɪst] N humoriste *mf*
humorous ['hjuːmərəs] ADJ humoristique; (*person*) plein(e) d'humour
humour, (*US*) **humor** ['hjuːməʳ] N humour *m*; (*mood*) humeur *f*; **sense of ~** sens *m* de l'humour; **to be in a good/bad ~** être de bonne/mauvaise humeur ▶ VT (*person*) faire plaisir à; se prêter aux caprices de
humourless, (*US*) **humorless** ['huːməlɪs] ADJ dépourvu(e) d'humour
hump [hʌmp] N bosse *f*
humpback ['hʌmpbæk] N bossu(e); (*BRIT: also:* **humpback bridge**) dos-d'âne *m*
humus ['hjuːməs] N humus *m*
hunch [hʌntʃ] N bosse *f*; (*premonition*) intuition *f*; **I have a ~ that** j'ai (comme une vague) idée que
hunchback ['hʌntʃbæk] N bossu(e)
hunched [hʌntʃt] ADJ arrondi(e), voûté(e)
★**hundred** ['hʌndrəd] NUM cent; **about a ~ people** une centaine de personnes; **hundreds of** des centaines de; **I'm a ~ per cent sure** j'en suis absolument certain
hundredth ['hʌndrədθ] NUM centième
hundredweight ['hʌndrɪdweɪt] N (*BRIT*) = 50.8 *kg*; (*US*) = 45.3 *kg*
hung [hʌŋ] PT, PP *of* hang
Hungarian [hʌŋ'gɛərɪən] ADJ hongrois(e) ▶ N Hongrois(e); (*Ling*) hongrois *m*
Hungary ['hʌŋgərɪ] N Hongrie *f*
hunger ['hʌŋgəʳ] N faim *f* ▶ VI: **to ~ for** avoir faim de, désirer ardemment
hunger strike N grève *f* de la faim
hungover [hʌŋ'əuvəʳ] ADJ (*inf*): **to be ~** avoir la gueule de bois

hungrily ['hʌŋgrəlɪ] ADV voracement; (*fig*) avidement
hungry ['hʌŋgrɪ] ADJ affamé(e); **to be ~** avoir faim; **~ for** (*fig*) avide de
hung up ADJ (*inf*) complexé(e), bourré(e) de complexes
hunk [hʌŋk] N gros morceau; (*inf: man*) beau mec
hunker down ['hʌŋkə-] VI (*US: squat*) s'accroupir; (*: lie low*) adopter un profil bas
hunt [hʌnt] VT (*seek*) chercher; (*criminal*) pourchasser; (*Sport*) chasser ▶ VI (*search*): **to ~ for** chercher (partout); (*Sport*) chasser ▶ N (*Sport*) chasse *f* ▶ **hunt down** VT pourchasser
hunter ['hʌntəʳ] N chasseur *m*; (*BRIT: horse*) cheval *m* de chasse
hunting ['hʌntɪŋ] N chasse *f*
hurdle ['həːdl] N (*for fences*) claie *f*; (*Sport*) haie *f*; (*fig*) obstacle *m*
hurdler ['həːdləʳ] N coureur(-euse) de haies
hurl [həːl] VT lancer (avec violence); (*abuse, insults*) lancer
hurling ['həːlɪŋ] N (*Sport*) genre de hockey joué en Irlande
hurly-burly ['həːlɪ'bəːlɪ] N tohu-bohu *m inv*; brouhaha *m*
hurrah, hurray [hu'rɑː, hu'reɪ] EXCL hourra !
hurricane ['hʌrɪkən] N ouragan *m*
hurried ['hʌrɪd] ADJ pressé(e), précipité(e); (*work*) fait(e) à la hâte
hurriedly ['hʌrɪdlɪ] ADV précipitamment, à la hâte
hurry ['hʌrɪ] N hâte *f*, précipitation *f*; **to be in a ~** être pressé(e); **to do sth in a ~** faire qch en vitesse ▶ VI se presser, se dépêcher; **to ~ in/out** entrer/sortir précipitamment; **to ~ home** se dépêcher de rentrer ▶ VT (*person*) faire presser, faire se dépêcher; (*work*) presser
▶ **hurry along** VI marcher d'un pas pressé
▶ **hurry away, hurry off** VI partir précipitamment
▶ **hurry up** VI se dépêcher
★**hurt** [həːt] (*pt, pp ~*) VT (*cause pain to*) faire mal à; (*injure, fig*) blesser; (*damage: business, interests etc*) nuire à; faire du tort à; **I ~ my arm** je me suis fait mal au bras; **to ~ o.s.** se faire mal ▶ VI faire mal; **my arm hurts** j'ai mal au bras; **where does it ~?** où avez-vous mal ?, où est-ce que ça vous fait mal ? ▶ ADJ blessé(e)
hurtful ['həːtful] ADJ (*remark*) blessant(e)
hurtle ['həːtl] VT lancer (de toutes ses forces) ▶ VI: **to ~ past** passer en trombe; **to ~ down** dégringoler
★**husband** ['hʌzbənd] N mari *m*
hush [hʌʃ] N calme *m*, silence *m* ▶ VT faire taire ▶ EXCL **~!** chut !
▶ **hush up** VT (*fact*) étouffer
hushed [hʌʃt] ADJ (*tone, voice*) étouffé(e)
hush-hush [hʌʃ'hʌʃ] ADJ (*inf*) ultra-secret(-ète)
husk [hʌsk] N (*of wheat*) balle *f*; (*of rice, maize*) enveloppe *f*; (*of peas*) cosse *f*
husky ['hʌskɪ] ADJ (*voice*) rauque; (*burly*) costaud(e) ▶ N chien *m* esquimau *or* de traîneau
hustings ['hʌstɪŋz] NPL (*BRIT Pol*) plate-forme électorale
hustle ['hʌsl] VT pousser, bousculer ▶ N bousculade *f*; **~ and bustle** *n* tourbillon *m* (d'activité)

h

hustler [ˈhʌslər] N (inf: sex worker) prostitué(e)

hut [hʌt] N hutte f; (shed) cabane f

hutch [hʌtʃ] N clapier m

hyacinth [ˈhaɪəsɪnθ] N jacinthe f

hybrid [ˈhaɪbrɪd] ADJ, N hybride m

hydrant [ˈhaɪdrənt] N prise f d'eau; (also: **fire hydrant**) bouche f d'incendie

hydraulic [haɪˈdrɔːlɪk] ADJ hydraulique

hydraulics [haɪˈdrɔːlɪks] N hydraulique f

hydrocarbon [haɪdrəuˈkɑːbən] N hydrocarbure m

hydrochloric [ˈhaɪdrəuˈklɔrɪk] ADJ: ~ **acid** acide m chlorhydrique

hydroelectric [ˈhaɪdrəuˈlɛktrɪk] ADJ hydro-électrique

hydrofoil [ˈhaɪdrəfɔɪl] N hydrofoil m

hydrogen [ˈhaɪdrədʒən] N hydrogène m

hydrogen bomb N bombe f à hydrogène

hydrophobia [ˈhaɪdrəˈfəubɪə] N hydrophobie f

hydroplane [ˈhaɪdrəpleɪn] N (seaplane) hydravion m; (jetfoil) hydroglisseur m

hydrotherapy [haɪdrəuˈθɛrəpɪ] N hydrothérapie f

hyena [haɪˈiːnə] N hyène f

hygiene [ˈhaɪdʒiːn] N hygiène f

hygienic [haɪˈdʒiːnɪk] ADJ hygiénique

hygienist [haɪˈdʒiːnɪst] N (also: **dental hygienist**) hygiéniste mf dentaire

hymn [hɪm] N hymne m, cantique m

hype [haɪp] N (inf) matraquage m publicitaire or médiatique

hyperactive [ˈhaɪpərˈæktɪv] ADJ hyperactif(-ive)

hyperactivity [haɪpərækˈtɪvɪtɪ] N hyperactivité f

hyperbole [haɪˈpəːbəlɪ] N hyperbole f

hyperconnected [haɪpəkəˈnɛktɪd] ADJ hyperconnecté(e)

hyperconnectivity [ˈhaɪpəkɔnɛkˈtɪvəti] N hyperconnectivité f

hyperinflation [haɪpərɪnˈfleɪʃən] N hyperinflation f

hyperlink [ˈhaɪpəlɪŋk] N hyperlien m

hypermarket [ˈhaɪpəmɑːkɪt] N (BRIT) hypermarché m

hypertension [ˈhaɪpəˈtɛnʃən] N (Med) hypertension f

hypertext [ˈhaɪpətɛkst] N (Comput) hypertexte m

hyperventilate [haɪpərˈvɛntɪleɪt] VI faire de l'hyperventilation

hyperventilation [haɪpəvɛntɪˈleɪʃən] N hyperventilation f

hyphen [ˈhaɪfn] N trait m d'union

hypnosis [hɪpˈnəusɪs] N hypnose f

hypnotherapist [hɪpnəuˈθɛrəpɪst] N hypnothérapeute mf

hypnotherapy [hɪpnəuˈθɛrəpɪ] N hypnothérapie f

hypnotic [hɪpˈnɔtɪk] ADJ hypnotique

hypnotism [ˈhɪpnətɪzəm] N hypnotisme m

hypnotist [ˈhɪpnətɪst] N hypnotiseur(-euse)

hypnotize [ˈhɪpnətaɪz] VT hypnotiser

hypoallergenic [ˈhaɪpəuæləˈdʒenɪk] ADJ hypoallergénique

hypochondriac [haɪpəˈkɔndrɪæk] N hypocondriaque mf

hypocrisy [hɪˈpɔkrɪsɪ] N hypocrisie f

hypocrite [ˈhɪpəkrɪt] N hypocrite mf

hypocritical [hɪpəˈkrɪtɪkl] ADJ hypocrite

hypodermic [haɪpəˈdəːmɪk] ADJ hypodermique
▶ N (syringe) seringue f hypodermique

hypotenuse [haɪˈpɔtɪnjuːz] N hypoténuse f

hypothermia [haɪpəˈθəːmɪə] N hypothermie f

hypothesis [haɪˈpɔθɪsɪs] (pl **hypotheses** [-siːz]) N hypothèse f

hypothesize [haɪˈpɔθɪsaɪz] VT faire l'hypothèse de; **to ~ that ...** faire l'hypothèse que ...

hypothetical [haɪpəˈθɛtɪkəl] ADJ hypothétique
▶ N hypothèse f

hysterectomy [hɪstəˈrɛktəmɪ] N hystérectomie f

hysteria [hɪˈstɪərɪə] N hystérie f

hysterical [hɪˈstɛrɪkl] ADJ hystérique; (funny) hilarant(e); **to become ~** avoir une crise de nerfs

hysterics [hɪˈstɛrɪks] NPL (violente) crise de nerfs; (laughter) crise de rire; **to be in/have ~** (anger, panic) avoir une crise de nerfs; (laughter) attraper un fou rire

Hz ABBR (= hertz) Hz

I i

I¹, i [aɪ] N (*letter*) I, i *m*; **I for Isaac,** (*US*) **I for Item** I comme Irma

I² [aɪ] PRON je; (*before vowel*) j'; (*stressed*) moi ▶ ABBR (= *island, isle*) I

IA, Ia. ABBR (*US*) = **Iowa**

IAEA N ABBR = **International Atomic Energy Agency**

Iberian [aɪ'bɪərɪən] ADJ ibérique, ibérien(ne)

Iberian Peninsula N: **the ~** la péninsule Ibérique

IBEW N ABBR (*US*: = *International Brotherhood of Electrical Workers*) *syndicat international des électriciens*

i/c ABBR (*BRIT*) = **in charge**

ICBM N ABBR (= *intercontinental ballistic missile*) ICBM *m*, engin *m* balistique à portée intercontinentale

ICC N ABBR (= *International Chamber of Commerce*) CCI *f*

★**ice** [aɪs] N glace *f*; (*on road*) verglas *m*; **to put sth on ~** (*fig*) mettre qch en attente ▶ VT (*cake*) glacer; (*drink*) faire rafraîchir ▶ VI (*also:* **ice over**) geler; (*also:* **ice up**) se givrer

Ice Age N ère *f* glaciaire

ice axe, (*US*) **ice ax** N piolet *m*

iceberg ['aɪsbəːg] N iceberg *m*; **the tip of the ~** (*also fig*) la partie émergée de l'iceberg

icebox ['aɪsbɔks] N (*US*) réfrigérateur *m*; (*BRIT*) compartiment *m* à glace; (*insulated box*) glacière *f*

icebreaker ['aɪsbreɪkə'] N brise-glace *m*

ice bucket N seau *m* à glace

ice-cap ['aɪskæp] N calotte *f* glaciaire

ice-cold [aɪs'kəuld] ADJ glacé(e)

★**ice cream** N glace *f*

ice cube N glaçon *m*

iced [aɪst] ADJ (*drink*) frappé(e); (*coffee, tea, also cake*) glacé(e)

ice hockey N hockey *m* sur glace

Iceland ['aɪslənd] N Islande *f*

Icelander ['aɪsləndə'] N Islandais(e)

Icelandic [aɪs'lændɪk] ADJ islandais(e) ▶ N (*Ling*) islandais *m*

ice lolly N (*BRIT*) esquimau *m*

ice pick N pic *m* à glace

ice rink N patinoire *f*

ice-skate ['aɪsskeɪt] N patin *m* à glace ▶ VI faire du patin à glace

ice skating N patinage *m* (sur glace)

icicle ['aɪsɪkl] N glaçon *m* (*naturel*)

icing ['aɪsɪŋ] N (*Aviat etc*) givrage *m*; (*Culin*) glaçage *m*

icing sugar N (*BRIT*) sucre *m* glace

ICJ N ABBR = **International Court of Justice**

icon ['aɪkɔn] N icône *f*

iconic [aɪ'kɔnɪk] ADJ (*status, figure*) d'icône, emblématique

iconoclastic [aɪkɔnə'klæstɪk] ADJ iconoclaste

iconography [aɪkə'nɔgrəfɪ] N iconographie *f*

ICR N ABBR (*US*) = **Institute for Cancer Research**

ICRC N ABBR (= *International Committee of the Red Cross*) CICR *m*

ICT N ABBR (*BRIT Scol*: = *information and communications technology*) TIC *fpl*

ICU N ABBR = **intensive care unit**

icy ['aɪsɪ] ADJ glacé(e); (*road*) verglacé(e); (*weather, temperature*) glacial(e)

ID ABBR (*US*) = **Idaho**

I'd [aɪd] = **I would; I had**

ID card N carte *f* d'identité

IDD N ABBR (*BRIT Tel*: = *international direct dialling*) *automatique international*

★**idea** [aɪ'dɪə] N idée *f*; **good ~!** bonne idée !; **to have an ~ that ...** avoir idée que ...; **I have no ~** je n'ai pas la moindre idée

★**ideal** [aɪ'dɪəl] N idéal *m* ▶ ADJ idéal(e)

idealist [aɪ'dɪəlɪst] N idéaliste *mf*

idealize [aɪ'dɪəlaɪz] VT idéaliser

ideally [aɪ'dɪəlɪ] ADV (*preferably*) dans l'idéal; (*perfectly*): **he is ~ suited to the job** il est parfait pour ce poste; **~ the book should have ...** l'idéal serait que le livre ait ...

identical [aɪ'dɛntɪkl] ADJ identique

identifiable [aɪdɛntɪ'faɪəbl] ADJ identifiable

identification [aɪdɛntɪfɪ'keɪʃən] N identification *f*; **means of ~** pièce *f* d'identité

★**identify** [aɪ'dɛntɪfaɪ] VT identifier ▶ VI: **to ~ with** s'identifier à

Identikit® [aɪ'dɛntɪkɪt] N: **~ (picture)** portrait-robot *m*

identity [aɪ'dɛntɪtɪ] N identité *f*

identity card N carte *f* d'identité

identity parade N (*BRIT*) parade *f* d'identification

identity theft N usurpation *f* d'identité

ideological [aɪdɪə'lɔdʒɪkl] ADJ idéologique

ideology [aɪdɪ'ɔlədʒɪ] N idéologie *f*

idiocy ['ɪdɪəsɪ] N idiotie f, stupidité f

idiom ['ɪdɪəm] N (language) langue f, idiome m; (phrase) expression f idiomatique; (style) style m

idiomatic [ɪdɪə'mætɪk] ADJ idiomatique

idiosyncrasy [ɪdɪəʊ'sɪŋkrəsɪ] N singularité f

idiosyncratic [ɪdɪəʊsɪŋ'krætɪk] ADJ singulier(-ière); **a highly ~ personality** un personnage des plus singuliers

idiot ['ɪdɪət] N idiot(e), imbécile mf

idiotic [ɪdɪ'ɔtɪk] ADJ idiot(e), bête, stupide

idle ['aɪdl] ADJ (doing nothing) sans occupation, désœuvré(e); (lazy) oisif(-ive), paresseux(-euse); (unemployed) au chômage; (machinery) au repos; (question, pleasures) vain(e), futile; **to lie ~** être arrêté, ne pas fonctionner ▶ VI (engine) tourner au ralenti ▶ **idle away** VT: **to ~ away one's time** passer son temps à ne rien faire

idleness ['aɪdlnɪs] N désœuvrement m; oisiveté f

idler ['aɪdlə^r] N désœuvré(e), oisif(-ive)

idle time N (Comm) temps mort

idol ['aɪdl] N idole f

idolatry [aɪ'dɔlətrɪ] N idolâtrie f

idolize ['aɪdəlaɪz] VT idolâtrer, adorer

idyll, (US) **idyl** ['ɪdəl] N idylle f; **a rural ~** une idylle bucolique

idyllic [ɪ'dɪlɪk] ADJ idyllique

i.e. ABBR (= id est: that is) c. à d., c'est-à-dire

IED [aii'di:] ABBR (= Improvised Explosive Device) EEI m

★**if** [ɪf] CONJ si; **I'd be pleased if you could do it** je serais très heureux si vous pouviez le faire; **if necessary** si nécessaire, le cas échéant; **if so** si c'est le cas; **if not** sinon; **if only I could!** si seulement je pouvais !; **if only he were here** si seulement il était là; **if only to show him my gratitude** ne serait-ce que pour lui témoigner ma gratitude; see also **as**; even ▶ N: **there are a lot of ifs and buts** il y a beaucoup de si mpl et de mais mpl

iffy ['ɪfɪ] ADJ (inf) douteux(-euse)

igloo ['ɪɡlu:] N igloo m

ignite [ɪɡ'naɪt] VT mettre le feu à, enflammer ▶ VI s'enflammer

ignition [ɪɡ'nɪʃən] N (Aut) allumage m; **to switch on/off the ~** mettre/couper le contact

ignition key N (Aut) clé f de contact

ignoble [ɪɡ'nəubl] ADJ ignoble, indigne

ignominious [ɪɡnə'mɪnɪəs] ADJ honteux(-euse), ignominieux(-euse)

ignominy ['ɪɡnəmɪnɪ] N ignominie f

ignoramus [ɪɡnə'reɪməs] N personne f ignare

ignorance ['ɪɡnərəns] N ignorance f; **to keep sb in ~ of sth** tenir qn dans l'ignorance de qch

ignorant ['ɪɡnərənt] ADJ ignorant(e); **to be ~ of** (subject) ne rien connaître en; (events) ne pas être au courant de

★**ignore** [ɪɡ'nɔ:^r] VT ne tenir aucun compte de; (mistake) ne pas relever; (person: pretend to not see) faire semblant de ne pas reconnaître; (: pay no attention to) ignorer

ikon ['aɪkɔn] N = **icon**

IL ABBR (US) = **Illinois**

ILA N ABBR (US: = International Longshoremen's Association) syndicat international des dockers

ilk ['ɪlk] N: **of that ~** (of that type) de cette eau; **and their ~** et consorts

★**ill** [ɪl] ADJ (sick) malade; (bad) mauvais(e); **to be taken ~** tomber malade ▶ N mal m ▶ ADV: **to speak/think ~ of sb** dire/penser du mal de qn

I'll [aɪl] = **I will; I shall**

ill-advised [ɪləd'vaɪzd] ADJ (decision) peu judicieux(-euse); (person) malavisé(e)

ill-at-ease [ɪlət'i:z] ADJ mal à l'aise

ill-considered [ɪlkən'sɪdəd] ADJ (plan) inconsidéré(e), irréfléchi(e)

ill-disposed [ɪldɪs'pəuzd] ADJ: **to be ~ towards sb/ sth** être mal disposé(e) envers qn/qch

ill effects NPL effets mpl adverses

★**illegal** [ɪ'li:ɡl] ADJ illégal(e)

illegally [ɪ'li:ɡəlɪ] ADV illégalement

illegible [ɪ'ledʒɪbl] ADJ illisible

illegitimate [ɪlɪ'dʒɪtɪmət] ADJ illégitime

ill-fated [ɪl'feɪtɪd] ADJ malheureux(-euse); (day) néfaste

ill-favoured, (US) **ill-favored** [ɪl'feɪvəd] ADJ déplaisant(e)

ill feeling N ressentiment m, rancune f

ill-gotten ['ɪlɡɔtn] ADJ (gains etc) mal acquis(e)

ill health N mauvaise santé

illicit [ɪ'lɪsɪt] ADJ illicite

ill-informed [ɪlɪn'fɔ:md] ADJ (judgment) erroné(e); (person) mal renseigné(e)

illiterate [ɪ'lɪtərət] ADJ illettré(e); (letter) plein(e) de fautes

ill-mannered [ɪl'mænəd] ADJ impoli(e), grossier(-ière)

★**illness** ['ɪlnɪs] N maladie f

illogical [ɪ'lɔdʒɪkl] ADJ illogique

ill-suited [ɪl'su:tɪd] ADJ (couple) mal assorti(e); **he is ~ to the job** il n'est pas vraiment fait pour ce travail

ill-timed [ɪl'taɪmd] ADJ inopportun(e)

ill-treat [ɪl'tri:t] VT maltraiter

ill-treatment [ɪl'tri:tmənt] N mauvais traitement

illuminate [ɪ'lu:mɪneɪt] VT (room, street) éclairer; (for special effect) illuminer; **illuminated sign** enseigne lumineuse

illuminating [ɪ'lu:mɪneɪtɪŋ] ADJ éclairant(e)

illumination [ɪlu:mɪ'neɪʃən] N éclairage m; illumination f

illusion [ɪ'lu:ʒən] N illusion f; **to be under the ~ that** avoir l'illusion que

illusive [ɪ'lu:sɪv], **illusory** [ɪ'lu:sərɪ] ADJ illusoire

illustrate ['ɪləstreɪt] VT illustrer

★**illustration** [ɪlə'streɪʃən] N illustration f

illustrator ['ɪləstreɪtə^r] N illustrateur(-trice)

illustrious [ɪ'lʌstrɪəs] ADJ illustre

ill will N malveillance f

ILO N ABBR (= International Labour Organization) OIT f

ILWU N ABBR (US: = International Longshoremen's and Warehousemen's Union) syndicat international des dockers et des magasiniers

IM N ABBR (= instant messaging) messagerie f instantanée ▶ VT envoyer un message instantané à

I'm [aɪm] = **I am**

★**image** ['ɪmɪdʒ] N image f; (*public face*) image de marque

imagery ['ɪmɪdʒərɪ] N images fpl

imaginable [ɪ'mædʒɪnəbl] ADJ imaginable

imaginary [ɪ'mædʒɪnərɪ] ADJ imaginaire

★**imagination** [ɪmædʒɪ'neɪʃən] N imagination f

imaginative [ɪ'mædʒɪnətɪv] ADJ imaginatif(-ive); (*person*) plein(e) d'imagination

★**imagine** [ɪ'mædʒɪn] VT s'imaginer; (*suppose*) imaginer, supposer

imam [ɪ'mɑːm] N imam m

imbalance [ɪm'bæləns] N déséquilibre m

imbecile ['ɪmbəsiːl] N imbécile mf

imbue [ɪm'bjuː] VT: **to ~ sth with** imprégner qch de

IMF N ABBR = **International Monetary Fund**

imitate ['ɪmɪteɪt] VT imiter

imitation [ɪmɪ'teɪʃən] N imitation f

imitator ['ɪmɪteɪtəʳ] N imitateur(-trice)

immaculate [ɪ'mækjulət] ADJ impeccable; (*Rel*) immaculé(e)

immaculately [ɪ'mækjulətlɪ] ADV impeccablement

immaterial [ɪmə'tɪərɪəl] ADJ sans importance, insignifiant(e)

immature [ɪmə'tjuəʳ] ADJ (*fruit*) qui n'est pas mûr(e); (*person*) qui manque de maturité

immaturity [ɪmə'tjuərɪtɪ] N immaturité f

immeasurable [ɪ'mɛʒrəbl] ADJ incommensurable

immediacy [ɪ'miːdɪəsɪ] N (*of events etc*) caractère or rapport immédiat; (*of needs*) urgence f

★**immediate** [ɪ'miːdɪət] ADJ immédiat(e)

★**immediately** [ɪ'miːdɪətlɪ] ADV (*at once*) immédiatement; **~ next to** juste à côté de

immemorial [ɪmɪ'mɔːrɪəl] ADJ (*literary*) immémorial(e); **since time ~** depuis des temps immémoriaux

immense [ɪ'mɛns] ADJ immense, énorme

immensely [ɪ'mɛnslɪ] ADV (*+adj*) extrêmement; (*+vb*) énormément

immensity [ɪ'mɛnsɪtɪ] N immensité f

immerse [ɪ'məːs] VT immerger, plonger; **to ~ sth in** plonger qch dans

immersed [ɪ'məːst] ADJ: **to be ~ in sth** (*in subject, activity*) être plongé(e) dans qch, être absorbé(e) par qch

immersion heater [ɪ'məːʃən-] N (*BRIT*) chauffe-eau m électrique

★**immigrant** ['ɪmɪɡrənt] N immigrant(e); (*already established*) immigré(e)

immigration [ɪmɪ'ɡreɪʃən] N immigration f

immigration authorities NPL service m de l'immigration

immigration laws NPL lois fpl sur l'immigration

imminent ['ɪmɪnənt] ADJ imminent(e)

immobile [ɪ'məubaɪl] ADJ immobile

immobility [ɪməu'bɪlɪtɪ] N immobilité f

immobilize [ɪ'məubɪlaɪz] VT immobiliser

immoderate [ɪ'mɔdərət] ADJ immodéré(e), démesuré(e)

immodest [ɪ'mɔdɪst] ADJ (*indecent*) indécent(e); (*boasting*) pas modeste, présomptueux(-euse)

immoral [ɪ'mɔrl] ADJ immoral(e)

immorality [ɪmɔ'rælɪtɪ] N immoralité f

immortal [ɪ'mɔːtl] ADJ, N immortel(le)

immortality [ɪmɔː'tælɪtɪ] N immortalité f; **to achieve ~** passer à la postérité

immortalize [ɪ'mɔːtlaɪz] VT immortaliser

immovable [ɪ'muːvəbl] ADJ (*object*) fixe; immobilier(-ière); (*person*) inflexible; (*opinion*) immuable

immune [ɪ'mjuːn] ADJ: **~ (to)** immunisé(e) (contre)

immune system N système m immunitaire

immunity [ɪ'mjuːnɪtɪ] N immunité f; **diplomatic ~** immunité diplomatique

immunization [ɪmjunaɪ'zeɪʃən] N immunisation f

immunize ['ɪmjunaɪz] VT immuniser

immutable [ɪ'mjuːtəbl] ADJ immuable

imp [ɪmp] N (*small devil*) lutin m; (*child*) petit diable

impact N ['ɪmpækt] choc m, impact m; (*fig*) impact
▶ **impact on** VT FUS [ɪm'pækt] avoir un réel impact sur

impair [ɪm'pɛəʳ] VT détériorer, diminuer

impaired [ɪm'pɛəd] ADJ (*organ, vision*) abîmé(e), détérioré(e); **his memory/circulation is ~** il a des problèmes de mémoire/circulation; **visually ~** malvoyant(e); **hearing ~** malentendant(e); **mentally/physically ~** intellectuellement/physiquement diminué(e)

impairment [ɪm'pɛəmənt] N handicap m; **a visual ~** un handicap visuel

impale [ɪm'peɪl] VT empaler

impart [ɪm'pɑːt] VT (*make known*) communiquer, transmettre; (*bestow*) confier, donner

impartial [ɪm'pɑːʃl] ADJ impartial(e)

impartiality [ɪmpɑːʃɪ'ælɪtɪ] N impartialité f

impassable [ɪm'pɑːsəbl] ADJ infranchissable; (*road*) impraticable

impasse [æm'pɑːs] N (*fig*) impasse f

impassioned [ɪm'pæʃənd] ADJ passionné(e)

impassive [ɪm'pæsɪv] ADJ impassible

impatience [ɪm'peɪʃəns] N impatience f

impatient [ɪm'peɪʃənt] ADJ impatient(e); **to get** or **grow ~** s'impatienter

impatiently [ɪm'peɪʃəntlɪ] ADV avec impatience

impeach [ɪm'piːtʃ] VT accuser, attaquer; (*public official*) mettre en accusation

impeachment [ɪm'piːtʃmənt] N (*Law*) (mise f en) accusation f

impeccable [ɪm'pɛkəbl] ADJ impeccable, parfait(e)

impeccably [ɪm'pɛkəblɪ] ADV impeccablement

impecunious [ɪmpɪ'kjuːnɪəs] ADJ sans ressources

impede [ɪm'piːd] VT gêner

impediment [ɪm'pɛdɪmənt] N obstacle m; (*also:* **speech impediment**) défaut m d'élocution

impel [ɪm'pɛl] VT (*force*): **to ~ sb (to do sth)** forcer qn (à faire qch)

impending [ɪm'pɛndɪŋ] ADJ imminent(e)

impenetrable [ɪm'pɛnɪtrəbl] ADJ impénétrable

imperative [ɪm'pɛrətɪv] ADJ nécessaire; (need) urgent(e), pressant(e); (tone) impérieux(-euse) ▸ N (Ling) impératif m

imperceptible [ɪmpə'sɛptɪbl] ADJ imperceptible

imperceptibly [ɪmpə'sɛptɪblɪ] ADV imperceptiblement

imperfect [ɪm'pə:fɪkt] ADJ imparfait(e); (goods etc) défectueux(-euse) ▸ N (Ling: also: **imperfect tense**) imparfait m

imperfection [ɪmpə:'fɛkʃən] N imperfection f; défectuosité f

imperial [ɪm'pɪərɪəl] ADJ impérial(e); (BRIT: measure) légal(e)

imperialism [ɪm'pɪərɪəlɪzəm] N impérialisme m

imperil [ɪm'pɛrɪl] VT mettre en péril

imperious [ɪm'pɪərɪəs] ADJ impérieux(-euse)

impersonal [ɪm'pə:sənl] ADJ impersonnel(le)

impersonate [ɪm'pə:səneɪt] VT se faire passer pour; (Theat) imiter

impersonation [ɪmpə:sə'neɪʃən] N (Law) usurpation f d'identité; (Theat) imitation f

impersonator [ɪm'pə:səneɪtər] N imposteur m; (Theat) imitateur(-trice)

impertinence [ɪm'pə:tɪnəns] N impertinence f, insolence f

impertinent [ɪm'pə:tɪnənt] ADJ impertinent(e), insolent(e)

imperturbable [ɪmpə'tə:bəbl] ADJ imperturbable

impervious [ɪm'pə:vɪəs] ADJ imperméable; **~ to** (fig) insensible à; inaccessible à

impetuous [ɪm'pɛtjuəs] ADJ impétueux(-euse), fougueux(-euse)

impetus ['ɪmpətəs] N impulsion f; (of runner) élan m

impinge [ɪm'pɪndʒ]: **to ~ on** vt fus (person) affecter, toucher; (rights) empiéter sur

impish ['ɪmpɪʃ] ADJ espiègle

implacable [ɪm'plækəbl] ADJ implacable

implant [ɪm'plɑ:nt] VT (Med) implanter; (fig: idea, principle) inculquer

implausible [ɪm'plɔ:zɪbl] ADJ peu plausible

implement N ['ɪmplɪmənt] outil m, instrument m; (for cooking) ustensile m ▸ VT ['ɪmplɪment] mettre en œuvre, implémenter

implementation [ɪmplɪmɛn'teɪʃən] N mise f en œuvre, implémentation f

implicate ['ɪmplɪkeɪt] VT impliquer, compromettre

implication [ɪmplɪ'keɪʃən] N implication f; **by ~** indirectement

implicit [ɪm'plɪsɪt] ADJ implicite; (complete) absolu(e), sans réserve

implicitly [ɪm'plɪsɪtlɪ] ADV implicitement; absolument, sans réserve

implode [ɪm'pləud] VI imploser

implore [ɪm'plɔ:r] VT implorer, supplier

imply [ɪm'plaɪ] VT (hint) suggérer, laisser entendre; (mean) indiquer, supposer

impolite [ɪmpə'laɪt] ADJ impoli(e)

imponderable [ɪm'pɒndərəbl] ADJ impondérable

import VT [ɪm'pɔ:t] importer ▸ N ['ɪmpɔ:t] (Comm) importation f; (meaning) portée f, signification f ▸ CPD ['ɪmpɔ:t] (duty, licence etc) d'importation

★**importance** [ɪm'pɔ:tns] N importance f; **to be of great/little ~** avoir beaucoup/peu d'importance

★**important** [ɪm'pɔ:tnt] ADJ important(e); **it is ~ that** il importe que, il est important que; **it's not ~** c'est sans importance, ce n'est pas important

importantly [ɪm'pɔ:tntlɪ] ADV (with an air of importance) d'un air important; (essentially): **but, more ~ ...** mais, (ce qui est) plus important encore ...

importation [ɪmpɔ:'teɪʃən] N importation f

imported [ɪm'pɔ:tɪd] ADJ importé(e), d'importation

importer [ɪm'pɔ:tər] N importateur(-trice)

impose [ɪm'pəuz] VT imposer ▸ VI: **to ~ on sb** abuser de la gentillesse de qn

imposing [ɪm'pəuzɪŋ] ADJ imposant(e), impressionnant(e)

imposition [ɪmpə'zɪʃən] N (of tax etc) imposition f; **to be an ~ on** (person) abuser de la gentillesse or la bonté de

impossibility [ɪmpɔsə'bɪlɪtɪ] N impossibilité f

★**impossible** [ɪm'pɔsɪbl] ADJ impossible; **it is ~ for me to leave** il m'est impossible de partir

impostor [ɪm'pɔstər] N imposteur m

impotence ['ɪmpətns] N impuissance f

impotent ['ɪmpətnt] ADJ impuissant(e)

impound [ɪm'paund] VT confisquer, saisir

impoverished [ɪm'pɒvərɪʃt] ADJ pauvre, appauvri(e)

impracticable [ɪm'præktɪkəbl] ADJ impraticable

impractical [ɪm'præktɪkl] ADJ pas pratique; (person) qui manque d'esprit pratique

imprecise [ɪmprɪ'saɪs] ADJ imprécis(e)

impregnable [ɪm'prɛgnəbl] ADJ (fortress) imprenable; (fig) inattaquable, irréfutable

impregnate ['ɪmprɛgneɪt] VT imprégner; (fertilize) féconder

impresario [ɪmprɪ'sɑ:rɪəu] N impresario m

impress [ɪm'prɛs] VT impressionner, faire impression sur; (mark) imprimer, marquer; **to ~ sth on sb** faire bien comprendre qch à qn

impressed [ɪm'prɛst] ADJ impressionné(e)

impression [ɪm'prɛʃən] N impression f; (of stamp, seal) empreinte f; (imitation) imitation f; **to make a good/bad ~ on sb** faire bonne/mauvaise impression sur qn; **to be under the ~ that** avoir l'impression que

impressionable [ɪm'prɛʃnəbl] ADJ impressionnable, sensible

impressionist [ɪm'prɛʃənɪst] N impressionniste mf

impressionistic [ɪmprɛʃə'nɪstɪk] ADJ impressionniste

impressive [ɪm'prɛsɪv] ADJ impressionnant(e)

imprint ['ɪmprɪnt] N empreinte f; (Publishing) notice f; (: label) nom m (de collection or d'éditeur)

imprinted [ɪm'prɪntɪd] ADJ: **~ on** imprimé(e) sur; (fig) imprimé(e) or gravé(e) dans

imprison [ɪm'prɪzn] VT emprisonner, mettre en prison

imprisonment [ɪm'prɪznmənt] N emprisonnement m; (period): **to sentence sb to 10 years' ~** condamner qn à 10 ans de prison

improbable [ɪmˈprɔbəbl] ADJ improbable; (*excuse*) peu plausible

impromptu [ɪmˈprɔmptjuː] ADJ impromptu(e)
▸ ADV impromptu

improper [ɪmˈprɔpə^r] ADJ (*wrong*) incorrect(e); (*unsuitable*) déplacé(e), de mauvais goût; (*indecent*) indécent(e); (*dishonest*) malhonnête

impropriety [ɪmprəˈpraɪətɪ] N inconvenance f; (*of expression*) impropriété f

★**improve** [ɪmˈpruːv] VT améliorer ▸ VI s'améliorer; (*pupil etc*) faire des progrès
▸ **improve on**, **improve upon** VT FUS (*offer*) enchérir sur

★**improvement** [ɪmˈpruːvmənt] N amélioration f; (*of pupil etc*) progrès m; **to make improvements to** apporter des améliorations à

improvisation [ɪmprəvaɪˈzeɪʃən] N improvisation f

improvise [ˈɪmprəvaɪz] VT, VI improviser

imprudence [ɪmˈpruːdns] N imprudence f

imprudent [ɪmˈpruːdnt] ADJ imprudent(e)

impudent [ˈɪmpjudnt] ADJ impudent(e)

impugn [ɪmˈpjuːn] VT contester, attaquer

impulse [ˈɪmpʌls] N impulsion f; **on ~** impulsivement, sur un coup de tête

impulse buy N achat m d'impulsion

impulsive [ɪmˈpʌlsɪv] ADJ impulsif(-ive)

impunity [ɪmˈpjuːnɪtɪ] N: **with ~** impunément

impure [ɪmˈpjuə^r] ADJ impur(e)

impurity [ɪmˈpjuərɪtɪ] N impureté f

IN ABBR (US) = **Indiana**

---

in [ɪn]

PREP **1** (*indicating place, position*) dans; **in the house/the fridge** dans la maison/le frigo; **in the garden** dans le *or* au jardin; **in town** en ville; **in the country** à la campagne; **in school** à l'école; **in here/there** ici/là

2 (*with place names: of town, region, country*): **in London** à Londres; **in England** en Angleterre; **in Japan** au Japon; **in the United States** aux États-Unis

3 (*indicating time: during*): **in spring** au printemps; **in summer** en été; **in May/2005** en mai/2005; **in the afternoon** (dans) l'après-midi; **at 4 o'clock in the afternoon** à 4 heures de l'après-midi

4 (*indicating time: in the space of*) en; (: *future*) dans; **I did it in 3 hours/days** je l'ai fait en 3 heures/jours; **I'll see you in 2 weeks** *or* **in 2 weeks' time** je te verrai dans 2 semaines; **once in a hundred years** une fois tous les cent ans

5 (*indicating manner etc*) à; **in a loud/soft voice** à voix haute/basse; **in pencil** au crayon; **in writing** par écrit; **in French** en français; **to pay in dollars** payer en dollars; **the boy in the blue shirt** le garçon à *or* avec la chemise bleue

6 (*indicating circumstances*): **in the sun** au soleil; **in the shade** à l'ombre; **in the rain** sous la pluie; **a change in policy** un changement de politique

7 (*indicating mood, state*): **in tears** en larmes; **in anger** sous le coup de la colère; **in despair** au désespoir; **in good condition** en bon état; **to live in luxury** vivre dans le luxe

8 (*with ratios, numbers*): **1 in 10 households,**

---

1 household in 10 1 ménage sur 10; **20 pence in the pound** 20 pence par livre sterling; **they lined up in twos** ils se mirent en rangs (deux) par deux; **in hundreds** par centaines

9 (*referring to people, works*) chez; **the disease is common in children** c'est une maladie courante chez les enfants; **in (the works of) Dickens** chez Dickens, dans (l'œuvre de) Dickens

10 (*indicating profession etc*) dans; **to be in teaching** être dans l'enseignement

11 (*after superlative*) de; **the best pupil in the class** le meilleur élève de la classe

12 (*with present participle*): **in saying this** en disant ceci

▸ ADV: **to be in** (*person: at home, work*) être là; (*train, ship, plane*) être arrivé(e); (*in fashion*) être à la mode; **to ask sb in** inviter qn à entrer; **to run/limp etc in** entrer en courant/boitant *etc*; **their party is in** leur parti est au pouvoir

▸ N: **the ins and outs (of)** (*of proposal, situation etc*) les tenants et aboutissants (de)

---

in. ABBR = **inch; inches**

inability [ɪnəˈbɪlɪtɪ] N incapacité f; **~ to pay** incapacité de payer

inaccessible [ɪnækˈsɛsɪbl] ADJ inaccessible

inaccuracy [ɪnˈækjurəsɪ] N inexactitude f; manque m de précision

inaccurate [ɪnˈækjurət] ADJ inexact(e); (*person*) qui manque de précision

inaction [ɪnˈækʃən] N inaction f, inactivité f

inactivity [ɪnækˈtɪvɪtɪ] N inactivité f

inadequacy [ɪnˈædɪkwəsɪ] N insuffisance f

inadequate [ɪnˈædɪkwət] ADJ (*supply, resources*) insuffisant(e), inadéquat(e); (*person*) qui n'est pas à la hauteur

inadequately [ɪnˈædɪkwətlɪ] ADV (*funded, trained, protected*) insuffisamment

inadmissible [ɪnədˈmɪsəbl] ADJ (*behaviour*) inadmissible; (*Law: evidence*) irrecevable

inadvertent [ɪnədˈvəːtnt] ADJ (*mistake*) commis(e) par inadvertance

inadvertently [ɪnədˈvəːtntlɪ] ADV par mégarde

inadvisable [ɪnədˈvaɪzəbl] ADJ à déconseiller; **it is ~ to** il est déconseillé de

inane [ɪˈneɪn] ADJ inepte, stupide

inanimate [ɪnˈænɪmət] ADJ inanimé(e)

inapplicable [ɪnˈæplɪkəbl] ADJ inapplicable

inappropriate [ɪnəˈprəuprɪət] ADJ inopportun(e), mal à propos; (*word, expression*) impropre

inapt [ɪnˈæpt] ADJ inapte; peu approprié(e)

inaptitude [ɪnˈæptɪtjuːd] N inaptitude f

inarticulate [ɪnɑːˈtɪkjulət] ADJ (*person*) qui s'exprime mal; (*speech*) indistinct(e)

inasmuch [ɪnəzˈmʌtʃ] ADV: **~ as** vu que, en ce sens que

inattention [ɪnəˈtɛnʃən] N manque m d'attention

inattentive [ɪnəˈtɛntɪv] ADJ inattentif(-ive), distrait(e); négligent(e)

inaudible [ɪnˈɔːdɪbl] ADJ inaudible

inaugural [ɪˈnɔːgjurəl] ADJ inaugural(e)

inaugurate [ɪˈnɔːgjureɪt] VT inaugurer; (*president, official*) investir de ses fonctions

inauguration [ɪnɔːgjuˈreɪʃən] N inauguration f; investiture f

inauspicious [ɪnɔːˈspɪʃəs] ADJ peu propice

inauthentic [ɪnɔːˈθentɪk] ADJ (document) non authentique; (person, feeling) artificiel(le)

in-between [ɪnbɪˈtwiːn] ADJ entre les deux

inborn [ɪnˈbɔːn] ADJ (feeling) inné(e); (defect) congénital(e)

inbox [ˈɪnbɒks] N (Comput) boîte f de réception; (US: intray) corbeille f du courrier reçu

inbred [ɪnˈbred] ADJ inné(e), naturel(le); (family) consanguin(e)

inbreeding [ɪnˈbriːdɪŋ] N croisement m d'animaux de même souche; (family) unions consanguines

in-built [ɪnˈbɪlt] ADJ (innate: tendency, feeling) inné(e); (integral: feature, device) intégré(e)

Inc. ABBR = incorporated

Inca [ˈɪŋkə] ADJ (also: **Incan**) inca inv ▸ N Inca mf

incalculable [ɪnˈkælkjuləbl] ADJ incalculable

incandescent [ɪnkænˈdesənt] ADJ (substance, device) incandescent(e); **to be ~ with rage** être vert(e) de rage

incapability [ɪnkeɪpəˈbɪlɪtɪ] N incapacité f

incapable [ɪnˈkeɪpəbl] ADJ: **~ (of)** incapable (de)

incapacitate [ɪnkəˈpæsɪteɪt] VT: **to ~ sb from doing** rendre qn incapable de faire

incapacitated [ɪnkəˈpæsɪteɪtɪd] ADJ (Law) frappé(e) d'incapacité

incapacity [ɪnkəˈpæsɪtɪ] N incapacité f

incarcerate [ɪnˈkɑːsəreɪt] VT incarcérer

incarceration [ɪnkɑːsəˈreɪʃən] N incarcération f

incarnate ADJ [ɪnˈkɑːnɪt] incarné(e) ▸ VT [ˈɪnkɑːneɪt] incarner

incarnation [ɪnkɑːˈneɪʃən] N incarnation f

incendiary [ɪnˈsendɪərɪ] ADJ incendiaire ▸ N (bomb) bombe f incendiaire

incense N [ˈɪnsens] encens m ▸ VT [ɪnˈsens] (anger) mettre en colère

incense burner N encensoir m

incentive [ɪnˈsentɪv] N encouragement m, raison f de se donner de la peine

incentive scheme N système m de primes d'encouragement

inception [ɪnˈsepʃən] N commencement m, début m

incessant [ɪnˈsesnt] ADJ incessant(e)

incessantly [ɪnˈsesntlɪ] ADV sans cesse, constamment

incest [ˈɪnsest] N inceste m

incestuous [ɪnˈsestjuəs] ADJ (lit: relationship) incestueux(-euse); (fig: group, place) fermé(e)

★**inch** [ɪntʃ] N pouce m (= 25 mm; 12 in a foot); **within an ~ of** à deux doigts de; **he wouldn't give an ~** (fig) il n'a pas voulu céder d'un pouce
▸ **inch forward** VI avancer petit à petit

inch tape N (BRIT) centimètre m (de couturière)

incidence [ˈɪnsɪdns] N (of crime, disease) fréquence f

★**incident** [ˈɪnsɪdnt] N incident m; (in book) péripétie f

incidental [ɪnsɪˈdentl] ADJ accessoire; (unplanned) accidentel(le); **~ to** qui accompagne; **~ expenses** faux frais mpl

incidentally [ɪnsɪˈdentəlɪ] ADV (by the way) à propos

incidental music N musique f de fond

incident room N (Police) salle f d'opérations

incinerate [ɪnˈsɪnəreɪt] VT incinérer

incinerator [ɪnˈsɪnəreɪtəʳ] N incinérateur m

incipient [ɪnˈsɪpɪənt] ADJ naissant(e)

incision [ɪnˈsɪʒən] N incision f

incisive [ɪnˈsaɪsɪv] ADJ incisif(-ive), mordant(e)

incisor [ɪnˈsaɪzəʳ] N incisive f

incite [ɪnˈsaɪt] VT inciter, pousser

incitement [ɪnˈsaɪtmənt] N incitation f; **~ to murder** incitation au meurtre

incl. ABBR = including; inclusive (of)

inclement [ɪnˈklemənt] ADJ inclément(e), rigoureux(-euse)

inclination [ɪnklɪˈneɪʃən] N inclination f; (desire) envie f

incline N [ˈɪnklaɪn] pente f, plan incliné ▸ VT [ɪnˈklaɪn] incliner; **to be inclined to do** (want to) être enclin(e) à faire; (have a tendency to do) avoir tendance à faire; **to be well inclined towards sb** être bien disposé(e) à l'égard de qn ▸ VI (surface) s'incliner; **I ~ to the view that …** j'ai tendance à penser que …

★**include** [ɪnˈkluːd] VT inclure, comprendre; **service is/is not included** le service est compris/n'est pas compris

★**including** [ɪnˈkluːdɪŋ] PREP y compris; **~ service** service compris

inclusion [ɪnˈkluːʒən] N inclusion f

inclusive [ɪnˈkluːsɪv] ADJ inclus(e), compris(e); **~ of tax** taxes comprises; **£50 ~ of all surcharges** 50 livres tous frais compris

inclusive terms NPL (BRIT) prix tout compris

incognito [ɪnkɒgˈniːtəʊ] ADV incognito

incoherent [ɪnkəʊˈhɪərənt] ADJ incohérent(e)

income [ˈɪnkʌm] N revenu m; (from property etc) rentes fpl; **gross/net ~** revenu brut/net; **~ and expenditure account** compte m de recettes et de dépenses

income support N (BRIT) ≈ revenu m minimum d'insertion, RMI m

income tax N impôt m sur le revenu

income tax inspector N inspecteur m des contributions directes

income tax return N déclaration f des revenus

incoming [ˈɪnkʌmɪŋ] ADJ (passengers, mail) à l'arrivée; (government, tenant) nouveau (nouvelle); **~ tide** marée montante

incommunicado [ˈɪnkəmjunɪˈkɑːdəʊ] ADJ: **to hold sb ~** tenir qn au secret

incomparable [ɪnˈkɒmpərəbl] ADJ incomparable

incompatible [ɪnkəmˈpætɪbl] ADJ incompatible

incompetence [ɪnˈkɒmpɪtns] N incompétence f, incapacité f

incompetent [ɪnˈkɒmpɪtnt] ADJ incompétent(e), incapable

incomplete [ɪnkəmˈpliːt] ADJ incomplet(-ète)

incomprehensible [ɪnkɒmprɪˈhensɪbl] ADJ incompréhensible

incomprehension [ɪnkɒmprɪˈhenʃən] N incompréhension f

inconceivable [ɪnkən'siːvəbl] ADJ inconcevable

inconclusive [ɪnkən'kluːsɪv] ADJ peu concluant(e); (*argument*) peu convaincant(e)

incongruity [ɪnkɔŋ'gruːɪtɪ] N incongruité *f*

incongruous [ɪn'kɔŋgruəs] ADJ peu approprié(e); (*remark, act*) incongru(e), déplacé(e)

inconsequential [ɪnkɔnsɪ'kwɛnʃl] ADJ sans importance

inconsiderable [ɪnkən'sɪdərəbl] ADJ: **not ~** non négligeable

inconsiderate [ɪnkən'sɪdərət] ADJ (*action*) inconsidéré(e); (*person*) qui manque d'égards

inconsistency [ɪnkən'sɪstənsɪ] N (*of actions etc*) inconséquence *f*; (*of work*) irrégularité *f*; (*of statement etc*) incohérence *f*

inconsistent [ɪnkən'sɪstnt] ADJ qui manque de constance; (*work*) irrégulier(-ière); (*statement*) peu cohérent(e); **~ with** en contradiction avec

inconsolable [ɪnkən'səuləbl] ADJ inconsolable

inconspicuous [ɪnkən'spɪkjuəs] ADJ qui passe inaperçu(e); (*colour, dress*) discret(-ète); **to make o.s. ~** ne pas se faire remarquer

inconstant [ɪn'kɔnstnt] ADJ inconstant(e), variable

incontinence [ɪn'kɔntɪnəns] N incontinence *f*

incontinent [ɪn'kɔntɪnənt] ADJ incontinent(e)

incontrovertible [ɪnkɔntrə'vəːtəbl] ADJ irréfutable

inconvenience [ɪnkən'viːnjəns] N inconvénient *m*; (*trouble*) dérangement *m* ▶ VT déranger; **don't ~ yourself** ne vous dérangez pas

inconvenient [ɪnkən'viːnjənt] ADJ malcommode; (*time, place*) mal choisi(e), qui ne convient pas; (*visitor*) importun(e); **that time is very ~ for me** c'est un moment qui ne me convient pas du tout

incorporate [ɪn'kɔːpəreɪt] VT incorporer; (*contain*) contenir ▶ VI fusionner; (*two firms*) se constituer en société

incorporated [ɪn'kɔːpəreɪtɪd] ADJ: **~ company** (*US*) ≈ société *f* anonyme

incorrect [ɪnkə'rɛkt] ADJ incorrect(e); (*opinion, statement*) inexact(e)

incorrigible [ɪn'kɔrɪdʒɪbl] ADJ incorrigible

incorruptible [ɪnkə'rʌptɪbl] ADJ incorruptible

★**increase** N ['ɪnkriːs] augmentation *f*; **an ~ of 5%** une augmentation de 5%; **to be on the ~** être en augmentation ▶ VI, VT [ɪn'kriːs] augmenter

increasing [ɪn'kriːsɪŋ] ADJ croissant(e)

increasingly [ɪn'kriːsɪŋlɪ] ADV de plus en plus

★**incredible** [ɪn'krɛdɪbl] ADJ incroyable

incredibly [ɪn'krɛdɪblɪ] ADV incroyablement

incredulity [ɪnkrə'djuːlɪtɪ] N incrédulité *f*

incredulous [ɪn'krɛdjuləs] ADJ incrédule

increment ['ɪnkrɪmənt] N augmentation *f*

incremental [ɪnkrɪ'mɛntl] ADJ (*rise, increase*) progressif(-ive); (*cost*) marginal

incriminate [ɪn'krɪmɪneɪt] VT incriminer, compromettre

incriminating [ɪn'krɪmɪneɪtɪŋ] ADJ compromettant(e)

incubate ['ɪnkjubeɪt] VT (*egg*) couver, incuber ▶ VI (*eggs*) couver; (*disease*) couver

incubation [ɪnkju'beɪʃən] N incubation *f*

incubation period N période *f* d'incubation

incubator ['ɪnkjubeɪtəʳ] N incubateur *m*; (*for babies*) couveuse *f*

inculcate ['ɪnkʌlkeɪt] VT: **to ~ sth in sb** inculquer qch à qn

incumbent [ɪn'kʌmbənt] ADJ: **it is ~ on him to ...** il lui appartient de ... ▶ N titulaire *mf*

incur [ɪn'kəːʳ] VT (*expenses*) encourir; (*anger, risk*) s'exposer à; (*debt*) contracter; (*loss*) subir

incurable [ɪn'kjuərəbl] ADJ incurable

incursion [ɪn'kəːʃən] N incursion *f*

indebted [ɪn'dɛtɪd] ADJ: **to be ~ to sb (for)** être redevable à qn (de)

indebtedness [ɪn'dɛtɪdnɪs] N dette *f*

indecency [ɪn'diːsnsɪ] N indécence *f*

indecent [ɪn'diːsnt] ADJ indécent(e), inconvenant(e)

indecent assault N (*BRIT*) attentat *m* à la pudeur

indecent exposure N outrage *m* public à la pudeur

indecipherable [ɪndɪ'saɪfərəbl] ADJ indéchiffrable

indecision [ɪndɪ'sɪʒən] N indécision *f*

indecisive [ɪndɪ'saɪsɪv] ADJ indécis(e); (*discussion*) peu concluant(e)

★**indeed** [ɪn'diːd] ADV (*confirming, agreeing*) en effet, effectivement; (*for emphasis*) vraiment; (*furthermore*) d'ailleurs; **yes ~!** certainement!

indefatigable [ɪndɪ'fætɪgəbl] ADJ infatigable

indefensible [ɪndɪ'fɛnsɪbl] ADJ (*conduct*) indéfendable

indefinable [ɪndɪ'faɪnəbl] ADJ indéfinissable

indefinite [ɪn'dɛfɪnɪt] ADJ indéfini(e); (*answer*) vague; (*period, number*) indéterminé(e)

indefinitely [ɪn'dɛfɪnɪtlɪ] ADV (*wait*) indéfiniment; (*speak*) vaguement, avec imprécision

indelible [ɪn'dɛlɪbl] ADJ indélébile

indelicate [ɪn'dɛlɪkɪt] ADJ (*tactless*) indélicat(e), grossier(-ière); (*not polite*) inconvenant(e), malséant(e)

indemnify [ɪn'dɛmnɪfaɪ] VT indemniser, dédommager

indemnity [ɪn'dɛmnɪtɪ] N (*insurance*) assurance *f*, garantie *f*; (*compensation*) indemnité *f*

indent [ɪn'dɛnt] VT (*text*) commencer en retrait

indentation [ɪndɛn'teɪʃən] N découpure *f*; (*Typ*) alinéa *m*; (*on metal*) bosse *f*

indenture [ɪn'dɛntʃəʳ] N contrat *m* d'emploi-formation

★**independence** [ɪndɪ'pɛndns] N indépendance *f*

Independence Day N (*US*) fête de l'Indépendance américaine

L'**Independence Day** (le 4 juillet) est la fête nationale des États-Unis. Il commémore l'adoption en 1776 de la déclaration d'Indépendance, écrite par Thomas Jefferson et proclamant la séparation des 13 colonies américaines de la Grande-Bretagne.

★**independent** [ɪndɪ'pɛndnt] ADJ indépendant(e); (*radio*) libre; **to become ~** s'affranchir

independently [ɪndɪ'pɛndntlɪ] ADV de façon indépendante; **~ of** indépendamment de

independent school N (*BRIT*) école privée

in-depth ['ındɛpθ] ADJ approfondi(e)

indescribable [ındı'skraıbəbl] ADJ indescriptible

indestructible [ındı'strʌktıbl] ADJ indestructible

indeterminate [ındı'tə:mınıt] ADJ indéterminé(e)

★**index** ['ındɛks] N (pl **indexes** ['ındɛksıs]) (in book) index m; (: in library etc) catalogue m; (pl **indices** ['ındısi:z]) (ratio, sign) indice m

index card N fiche f

index finger N index m

index-linked ['ındɛks'lıŋkt], (US) **indexed** ['ındɛkst] ADJ indexé(e) (sur le coût de la vie etc)

★**India** ['ındıə] N Inde f

Indian ['ındıən] ADJ indien(ne) ▶ N Indien(ne); (**American**) **~** Indien(ne) (d'Amérique)

Indian ink N encre f de Chine

Indian Ocean N: **the ~** l'océan Indien

Indian summer N (fig) été indien, beaux jours en automne

India paper N papier m bible

India rubber N gomme f

★**indicate** ['ındıkeıt] VT indiquer ▶ VI (BRIT Aut): **to ~ left/right** mettre son clignotant à gauche/à droite

indication [ındı'keıʃən] N indication f, signe m

indicative [ın'dıkətıv] ADJ indicatif(-ive); **to be ~ of sth** être symptomatique de qch ▶ N (Ling) indicatif m

indicator ['ındıkeıtə'] N (sign) indicateur m; (Aut) clignotant m

indices ['ındısi:z] NPL of **index**

indict [ın'daıt] VT accuser

indictable [ın'daıtəbl] ADJ (person) passible de poursuites; **~ offence** délit m tombant sous le coup de la loi

indictment [ın'daıtmənt] N accusation f

indifference [ın'dıfrəns] N indifférence f

indifferent [ın'dıfrənt] ADJ indifférent(e); (poor) médiocre, quelconque

indigenous [ın'dıdʒınəs] ADJ indigène

indigestible [ındı'dʒɛstıbl] ADJ indigeste

indigestion [ındı'dʒɛstʃən] N indigestion f, mauvaise digestion

indignant [ın'dıgnənt] ADJ: **~ (at sth/with sb)** indigné(e) (de qch/contre qn)

indignation [ındıg'neıʃən] N indignation f

indignity [ın'dıgnıtı] N indignité f, affront m

indigo ['ındıgəu] ADJ indigo inv ▶ N indigo m

indirect [ındı'rɛkt] ADJ indirect(e)

indirectly [ındı'rɛktlı] ADV indirectement

indiscreet [ındı'skri:t] ADJ indiscret(-ète); (rash) imprudent(e)

indiscretion [ındı'skrɛʃən] N indiscrétion f; (rashness) imprudence f

indiscriminate [ındı'skrımınət] ADJ (person) qui manque de discernement; (admiration) aveugle; (killings) commis(e) au hasard

indispensable [ındı'spɛnsəbl] ADJ indispensable

indisposed [ındı'spəuzd] ADJ (unwell) indisposé(e), souffrant(e)

indisposition [ındıspə'zıʃən] N (illness) indisposition f, malaise m

indisputable [ındı'spju:təbl] ADJ incontestable, indiscutable

indistinct [ındı'stıŋkt] ADJ indistinct(e); (memory, noise) vague

indistinguishable [ındı'stıŋgwıʃəbl] ADJ impossible à distinguer

★**individual** [ındı'vıdjuəl] N individu m ▶ ADJ individuel(le); (characteristic) particulier(-ière), original(e)

individualism [ındı'vıdjuəlızəm] N individualisme m

individualist [ındı'vıdjuəlıst] N individualiste mf

individualistic [ındıvıdjuə'lıstık] ADJ individualiste

individuality [ındıvıdju'ælıtı] N individualité f

individually [ındı'vıdjuəlı] ADV individuellement

indivisible [ındı'vızıbl] ADJ indivisible; (Math) insécable

Indo-China ['ındəu'tʃaınə] N Indochine f

indoctrinate [ın'dɔktrıneıt] VT endoctriner

indoctrination [ındɔktrı'neıʃən] N endoctrinement m

indolent ['ındələnt] ADJ indolent(e), nonchalant(e)

indomitable [ın'dɔmıtəbl] ADJ indomptable

Indonesia [ındə'ni:zıə] N Indonésie f

Indonesian [ındə'ni:zıən] ADJ indonésien(ne) ▶ N Indonésien(ne); (Ling) indonésien m

indoor ['ındɔ:'] ADJ d'intérieur; (plant) d'appartement; (swimming pool) couvert(e); (sport, games) pratiqué(e) en salle

indoors [ın'dɔ:z] ADV à l'intérieur; (at home) à la maison

indubitable [ın'dju:bıtəbl] ADJ indubitable, incontestable

induce [ın'dju:s] VT (persuade) persuader; (bring about) provoquer; (labour) déclencher; **to ~ sb to do sth** inciter or pousser qn à faire qch

inducement [ın'dju:smənt] N incitation f; (incentive) but m; (pej: bribe) pot-de-vin m

induct [ın'dʌkt] VT établir dans ses fonctions; (fig) initier

induction [ın'dʌkʃən] N (Med: of birth) accouchement provoqué

induction course N (BRIT) stage m de mise au courant

indulge [ın'dʌldʒ] VT (whim) céder à, satisfaire; (child) gâter ▶ VI: **to ~ in sth** (luxury) s'offrir qch, se permettre qch; (fantasies etc) se livrer à qch

indulgence [ın'dʌldʒəns] N fantaisie f (que l'on s'offre); (leniency) indulgence f

indulgent [ın'dʌldʒənt] ADJ indulgent(e)

industrial [ın'dʌstrıəl] ADJ industriel(le); (injury) du travail; (dispute) ouvrier(-ière)

industrial action N action revendicative

industrial estate N (BRIT) zone industrielle

industrialist [ın'dʌstrıəlıst] N industriel m

industrialization [ındʌstrıəlaı'zeıʃən] N industrialisation f

industrialize [ın'dʌstrıəlaız] VT industrialiser

industrial park N (US) zone industrielle

industrial relations NPL relations *fpl* dans l'entreprise

industrial tribunal N (BRIT) ≈ conseil *m* de prud'hommes

industrious [ɪn'dʌstrɪəs] ADJ travailleur(-euse)

industry ['ɪndəstrɪ] N industrie *f*; (*diligence*) zèle *m*, application *f*

inebriated [ɪ'ni:brɪeɪtɪd] ADJ ivre

inedible [ɪn'edɪbl] ADJ immangeable; (*plant etc*) non comestible

ineffective [ɪnɪ'fɛktɪv], **ineffectual** [ɪnɪ'fɛktʃuəl] ADJ inefficace; incompétent(e)

inefficiency [ɪnɪ'fɪʃənsɪ] N inefficacité *f*

inefficient [ɪnɪ'fɪʃənt] ADJ inefficace

inelegant [ɪn'elɪgənt] ADJ peu élégant(e), inélégant(e)

ineligible [ɪn'elɪdʒɪbl] ADJ (*candidate*) inéligible; **to be ~ for sth** ne pas avoir droit à qch

inept [ɪ'nept] ADJ inepte

ineptitude [ɪ'neptɪtjuːd] N ineptie *f*

inequality [ɪnɪ'kwɔlɪtɪ] N inégalité *f*

inequitable [ɪn'ekwɪtəbl] ADJ inéquitable, inique

ineradicable [ɪnɪ'rædɪkəbl] ADJ indéracinable, tenace

inert [ɪ'nəːt] ADJ inerte

inertia [ɪ'nəːʃə] N inertie *f*

inertia-reel seat belt [ɪ'nəːʃə'riːl-] N ceinture *f* de sécurité à enrouleur

inescapable [ɪnɪ'skeɪpəbl] ADJ inéluctable, inévitable

inessential [ɪnɪ'senʃl] ADJ superflu(e)

inestimable [ɪn'estɪməbl] ADJ inestimable, incalculable

inevitability [ɪnevɪtə'bɪlɪtɪ] N caractère *m* inévitable

inevitable [ɪn'evɪtəbl] ADJ inévitable

inevitably [ɪn'evɪtəblɪ] ADV inévitablement, fatalement

inexact [ɪnɪg'zækt] ADJ inexact(e)

inexcusable [ɪnɪk'skjuːzəbl] ADJ inexcusable

inexhaustible [ɪnɪg'zɔːstɪbl] ADJ inépuisable

inexorable [ɪn'eksərəbl] ADJ inexorable

inexpensive [ɪnɪk'spensɪv] ADJ bon marché *inv*

inexperience [ɪnɪk'spɪərɪəns] N inexpérience *f*, manque *m* d'expérience

inexperienced [ɪnɪk'spɪərɪənst] ADJ inexpérimenté(e); **to be ~ in sth** manquer d'expérience dans qch

inexplicable [ɪnɪk'splɪkəbl] ADJ inexplicable

inexpressible [ɪnɪk'spresɪbl] ADJ inexprimable; indicible

inextricable [ɪnɪk'strɪkəbl] ADJ inextricable

infallibility [ɪnfælə'bɪlɪtɪ] N infaillibilité *f*

infallible [ɪn'fælɪbl] ADJ infaillible

infamous ['ɪnfəməs] ADJ infâme, abominable

infamy ['ɪnfəmɪ] N infamie *f*

infancy ['ɪnfənsɪ] N petite enfance, bas âge; (*fig*) enfance, débuts *mpl*

infant ['ɪnfənt] N (*baby*) nourrisson *m*; (*young child*) petit(e) enfant

infantile ['ɪnfəntaɪl] ADJ infantile

infant mortality N mortalité *f* infantile

infantry ['ɪnfəntrɪ] N infanterie *f*

infantryman ['ɪnfəntrɪmən] N (*irreg*) fantassin *m*

infant school N (BRIT) classes *fpl* préparatoires (*entre 5 et 7 ans*)

infatuated [ɪn'fætjueɪtɪd] ADJ: **~ with** entiché(e) de; **to become ~ (with sb)** s'enticher (de qn)

infatuation [ɪnfætju'eɪʃən] N toquade *f*; engouement *m*

infect [ɪn'fɛkt] VT (*wound*) infecter; (*person, blood*) contaminer; (*fig, pej*) corrompre; **infected with** (*illness*) atteint(e) de; **to become infected** (*wound*) s'infecter

★**infection** [ɪn'fɛkʃən] N infection *f*; (*contagion*) contagion *f*

infectious [ɪn'fɛkʃəs] ADJ infectieux(-euse); (*also fig*) contagieux(-euse)

infer [ɪn'fəːʳ] VT: **to ~ (from)** conclure (de), déduire (de)

inference ['ɪnfərəns] N conclusion *f*, déduction *f*

inferior [ɪn'fɪərəʳ] ADJ inférieur(e); (*goods*) de qualité inférieure; **to feel ~** avoir un sentiment d'infériorité ▸ N inférieur(e); (*in rank*) subalterne *mf*

inferiority [ɪnfɪərɪ'ɔrɪtɪ] N infériorité *f*

inferiority complex N complexe *m* d'infériorité

infernal [ɪn'fəːnl] ADJ infernal(e)

inferno [ɪn'fəːnəu] N enfer *m*; brasier *m*

infertile [ɪn'fəːtaɪl] ADJ stérile

infertility [ɪnfəː'tɪlɪtɪ] N infertilité *f*, stérilité *f*

infestation [ɪnfe'steɪʃən] N infestation *f*

infested [ɪn'festɪd] ADJ: **~ (with)** infesté(e) (de)

infidelity [ɪnfɪ'delɪtɪ] N infidélité *f*

in-fighting ['ɪnfaɪtɪŋ] N querelles *fpl* internes

infiltrate ['ɪnfɪltreɪt] VT (*troops etc*) faire s'infiltrer; (*enemy line etc*) s'infiltrer dans ▸ VI s'infiltrer

infinite ['ɪnfɪnɪt] ADJ infini(e); (*time, money*) illimité(e)

infinitely ['ɪnfɪnɪtlɪ] ADV infiniment

infinitesimal [ɪnfɪnɪ'tesɪməl] ADJ infinitésimal(e)

infinitive [ɪn'fɪnɪtɪv] N infinitif *m*

infinity [ɪn'fɪnɪtɪ] N infinité *f*; (*also Math*) infini *m*

infirm [ɪn'fəːm] ADJ infirme

infirmary [ɪn'fəːmərɪ] N hôpital *m*; (*in school, factory*) infirmerie *f*

infirmity [ɪn'fəːmɪtɪ] N infirmité *f*

inflamed [ɪn'fleɪmd] ADJ enflammé(e)

inflammable [ɪn'flæməbl] ADJ (BRIT) inflammable

inflammation [ɪnflə'meɪʃən] N inflammation *f*

inflammatory [ɪn'flæmətərɪ] ADJ (*speech*) incendiaire

inflatable [ɪn'fleɪtəbl] ADJ gonflable

inflate [ɪn'fleɪt] VT (*tyre, balloon*) gonfler; (*fig: exaggerate*) grossir, gonfler; (: *increase*) gonfler

inflated [ɪn'fleɪtɪd] ADJ (*style*) enflé(e); (*value*) exagéré(e)

★**inflation** [ɪn'fleɪʃən] N (Econ) inflation *f*

inflationary [ɪn'fleɪʃənərɪ] ADJ inflationniste

inflexible [ɪn'fleksɪbl] ADJ inflexible, rigide

inflict [ɪn'flɪkt] VT: **to ~ on** infliger à

infliction [ɪn'flɪkʃən] N: **without the ~ of pain** sans infliger de douleurs

in-flight ['ɪnflaɪt] ADJ (refuelling) en vol; (service etc) à bord

inflow ['ɪnfləʊ] N afflux m

influence ['ɪnfluəns] N influence f; **under the ~ of** sous l'effet de; **under the ~ of alcohol** en état d'ébriété ▶ VT influencer

influential [ɪnflu'ɛnʃl] ADJ influent(e)

influenza [ɪnflu'ɛnzə] N grippe f

influx ['ɪnflʌks] N afflux m

info ['ɪnfəʊ] N (inf: = information) renseignements mpl

infomercial ['ɪnfəʊməːʃl] (US) N (for product) publi-information f; (Pol) émission où un candidat présente son programme électoral

★**inform** [ɪn'fɔːm] VT: **to ~ sb (of)** informer or avertir qn (de); **to ~ sb about** renseigner qn sur, mettre qn au courant de ▶ VI: **to ~ on sb** dénoncer qn, informer contre qn

informal [ɪn'fɔːml] ADJ (person, manner, party) simple, sans cérémonie; (visit, discussion) dénué(e) de formalités; (announcement, invitation) non officiel(le); (colloquial) familier(-ère); **"dress ~"** « tenue de ville »

informality [ɪnfɔː'mælɪtɪ] N simplicité f, absence f de cérémonie; caractère non officiel

informally [ɪn'fɔːməlɪ] ADV sans cérémonie, en toute simplicité; non officiellement

informant [ɪn'fɔːmənt] N informateur(-trice)

★**information** [ɪnfə'meɪʃən] N information(s) f(pl); renseignements mpl; (knowledge) connaissances fpl; **to get ~ on** se renseigner sur; **a piece of ~** un renseignement; **for your ~** à titre d'information

information bureau N bureau m de renseignements

information desk N accueil m

information office N bureau m de renseignements

information processing N traitement m de l'information

information technology N informatique f

informative [ɪn'fɔːmətɪv] ADJ instructif(-ive)

informed [ɪn'fɔːmd] ADJ (bien) informé(e); **an ~ guess** une hypothèse fondée sur la connaissance des faits

informer [ɪn'fɔːmə^r] N dénonciateur(-trice); (also: **police informer**) indicateur(-trice)

infra dig ['ɪnfrə'dɪg] ADJ ABBR (inf: = infra dignitatem) au-dessous de ma (or sa etc) dignité

infra-red [ɪnfrə'rɛd] ADJ infrarouge

infrastructure ['ɪnfrəstrʌktʃə^r] N infrastructure f

infrequent [ɪn'friːkwənt] ADJ peu fréquent(e), rare

infringe [ɪn'frɪndʒ] VT enfreindre ▶ VI: **to ~ on** empiéter sur

infringement [ɪn'frɪndʒmənt] N: **~ (of)** infraction f (à)

infuriate [ɪn'fjʊərɪeɪt] VT mettre en fureur

infuriating [ɪn'fjʊərɪeɪtɪŋ] ADJ exaspérant(e)

infuse [ɪn'fjuːz] VT: **to ~ sb with sth** (fig) insuffler qch à qn

infusion [ɪn'fjuːʒən] N (tea etc) infusion f

ingenious [ɪn'dʒiːnjəs] ADJ ingénieux(-euse)

ingenuity [ɪndʒɪ'njuːɪtɪ] N ingéniosité f

ingenuous [ɪn'dʒɛnjuəs] ADJ franc (franche), ouvert(e)

ingot ['ɪŋgət] N lingot m

ingrained [ɪn'greɪnd] ADJ enraciné(e)

ingratiate [ɪn'greɪʃɪeɪt] VT: **to ~ o.s. with** s'insinuer dans les bonnes grâces de, se faire bien voir de

ingratiating [ɪn'greɪʃɪeɪtɪŋ] ADJ (smile, speech) insinuant(e); (person) patelin(e)

ingratitude [ɪn'grætɪtjuːd] N ingratitude f

★**ingredient** [ɪn'griːdɪənt] N ingrédient m; (fig) élément m

ingrowing ['ɪngrəʊɪŋ], **ingrown** ['ɪngrəʊn] ADJ: **~ toenail** ongle incarné

inhabit [ɪn'hæbɪt] VT habiter

inhabitable [ɪn'hæbɪtəbl] ADJ habitable

inhabitant [ɪn'hæbɪtnt] N habitant(e)

inhale [ɪn'heɪl] VT inhaler; (perfume) respirer; (smoke) avaler ▶ VI (breathe in) aspirer; (in smoking) avaler la fumée

inhaler [ɪn'heɪlə^r] N inhalateur m

inherent [ɪn'hɪərənt] ADJ: **~ (in or to)** inhérent(e) (à)

inherently [ɪn'hɪərəntlɪ] ADV (easy, difficult) en soi; (lazy) fondamentalement

inherit [ɪn'hɛrɪt] VT hériter (de)

inheritance [ɪn'hɛrɪtəns] N héritage m; (fig): **the situation that was his ~ as president** la situation dont il a hérité en tant que président; **law of ~** droit m de la succession

inhibit [ɪn'hɪbɪt] VT (Psych) inhiber; (growth) freiner; **to ~ sb from doing** empêcher or retenir qn de faire

inhibited [ɪn'hɪbɪtɪd] ADJ (person) inhibé(e)

inhibiting [ɪn'hɪbɪtɪŋ] ADJ gênant(e)

inhibition [ɪnhɪ'bɪʃən] N inhibition f

inhospitable [ɪnhɔs'pɪtəbl] ADJ inhospitalier(-ière)

in-house ['ɪn'haʊs] ADJ (system) interne; (training) effectué(e) sur place or dans le cadre de la compagnie ▶ ADV (train, produce) sur place

inhuman [ɪn'hjuːmən] ADJ inhumain(e)

inhumane [ɪnhjuː'meɪn] ADJ inhumain(e)

inhumanity [ɪnhjuː'mænɪtɪ] N inhumanité f

inimical [ɪ'nɪmɪkl] ADJ: **to be ~ to sth** être antagonique à qch

inimitable [ɪ'nɪmɪtəbl] ADJ inimitable

iniquity [ɪ'nɪkwɪtɪ] N iniquité f

initial [ɪ'nɪʃl] ADJ initial(e) ▶ N initiale f ▶ VT parafer ■ **initials** NPL initiales fpl; (as signature) parafe m

initialize [ɪ'nɪʃəlaɪz] VT (Comput) initialiser

initially [ɪ'nɪʃəlɪ] ADV initialement, au début

initiate [ɪ'nɪʃɪeɪt] VT (start) entreprendre; amorcer; (enterprise) lancer; (person) initier; **to ~ sb into a secret** initier qn à un secret; **to ~ proceedings against sb** (Law) intenter une action à qn, engager des poursuites contre qn

initiation [ɪnɪʃɪ'eɪʃən] N (into secret etc) initiation f

initiative [ɪ'nɪʃətɪv] N initiative f; **to take the ~** prendre l'initiative

inject [ɪn'dʒɛkt] VT (liquid, fig: money) injecter; (person): **to ~ sb with sth** faire une piqûre de qch à qn

injection [ɪnˈdʒɛkʃən] N injection f, piqûre f; **to have an** ~ se faire faire une piqûre

injudicious [ɪndʒuˈdɪʃəs] ADJ peu judicieux(-euse)

injunction [ɪnˈdʒʌŋkʃən] N (*Law*) injonction f, ordre m

injure [ˈɪndʒər] VT blesser; (*wrong*) faire du tort à; (*damage: reputation etc*) compromettre; (: *feelings*) heurter; **to** ~ **o.s.** se blesser

to injure ne veut pas dire *injurier*.

★**injured** [ˈɪndʒəd] ADJ (*person, leg etc*) blessé(e); (*tone, feelings*) offensé(e); ~ **party** (*Law*) partie lésée

injurious [ɪnˈdʒʊərɪəs] ADJ: ~ **(to)** préjudiciable (à)

★**injury** [ˈɪndʒərɪ] N blessure f; (*wrong*) tort m; **to escape without** ~ s'en sortir sain et sauf

injury ne veut pas dire *injure*.

injury time N (*Sport*) arrêts mpl de jeu

injustice [ɪnˈdʒʌstɪs] N injustice f; **you do me an** ~ vous êtes injuste envers moi

ink [ɪŋk] N encre f

ink-jet printer [ˈɪŋkdʒɛt-] N imprimante f à jet d'encre

inkling [ˈɪŋklɪŋ] N soupçon m, vague idée f

inkpad [ˈɪŋkpæd] N tampon m encreur

inky [ˈɪŋkɪ] ADJ taché(e) d'encre

inlaid [ˈɪnleɪd] ADJ incrusté(e); (*table etc*) marqueté(e)

inland ADJ [ˈɪnlənd] intérieur(e); ~ **waterways** canaux mpl et rivières fpl ▶ ADV [ɪnˈlænd] à l'intérieur, dans les terres

Inland Revenue N (*BRIT*) fisc m

in-laws [ˈɪnlɔːz] NPL beaux-parents mpl; belle famille

inlet [ˈɪnlɛt] N (*Geo*) crique f

inlet pipe N (*Tech*) tuyau m d'arrivée

inmate [ˈɪnmeɪt] N (*in prison*) détenu(e); (*in asylum*) interné(e)

inmost [ˈɪnməʊst] ADJ le (la) plus profond(e)

inn [ɪn] N auberge f

innards [ˈɪnədz] NPL (*inf*) entrailles fpl

innate [ɪˈneɪt] ADJ inné(e)

inner [ˈɪnər] ADJ intérieur(e)

inner city N centre m urbain (*souffrant souvent de délabrement, d'embouteillages etc*)

inner-city [ˈɪnəˈsɪtɪ] ADJ (*schools, problems*) de quartiers déshérités

innermost [ˈɪnəməʊst] ADJ le (la) plus profond(e)

inner tube N (*of tyre*) chambre f à air

inning [ˈɪnɪŋ] N (*US Baseball*) tour m de batte ∎ **innings** N (*Cricket*) tour de batte; **he has had a good innings** (*BRIT fig*) il (en) a bien profité

innocence [ˈɪnəsns] N innocence f

★**innocent** [ˈɪnəsnt] ADJ innocent(e)

innocuous [ɪˈnɔkjuəs] ADJ inoffensif(-ive)

innovate [ˈɪnəveɪt] VI innover

innovation [ɪnəʊˈveɪʃən] N innovation f

innovative [ˈɪnəvətɪv] ADJ (*product, idea*) innovant(e); (*person*) novateur(-trice)

innovator [ˈɪnəveɪtər] N novateur(-trice)

innuendo [ɪnjuˈɛndəʊ] (*pl* **innuendoes**) N insinuation f, allusion (malveillante)

innumerable [ɪˈnjuːmrəbl] ADJ innombrable

inoculate [ɪˈnɔkjuleɪt] VT: **to** ~ **sb with sth** inoculer qch à qn; **to** ~ **sb against sth** vacciner qn contre qch

inoculation [ɪnɔkjuˈleɪʃən] N inoculation f

inoffensive [ɪnəˈfɛnsɪv] ADJ inoffensif(-ive)

inoperable [ɪnˈɔprəbl] ADJ inopérable

inopportune [ɪnˈɔpətjuːn] ADJ inopportun(e)

inordinate [ɪnˈɔːdɪnət] ADJ démesuré(e)

inordinately [ɪnˈɔːdɪnətlɪ] ADV démesurément

inorganic [ɪnɔːˈgænɪk] ADJ inorganique

in-patient [ˈɪnpeɪʃənt] N malade hospitalisé(e)

input [ˈɪnput] N (*contribution*) contribution f; (*resources*) ressources fpl; (*Elec*) énergie f, puissance f; (*of machine*) consommation f; (*Comput*) entrée f (de données); (: *data*) données fpl ▶ VT (*Comput*) introduire, entrer

inquest [ˈɪnkwɛst] N enquête (criminelle); (*coroner's*) enquête judiciaire

inquire [ɪnˈkwaɪər] VI demander; **to** ~ **about** s'informer de, se renseigner sur ▶ VT demander; **to** ~ **when/where/whether** demander quand/où/si
▶ **inquire after** VT FUS demander des nouvelles de
▶ **inquire into** VT FUS faire une enquête sur

inquiring [ɪnˈkwaɪərɪŋ] ADJ (*mind*) curieux(-euse), investigateur(-trice)

★**inquiry** [ɪnˈkwaɪərɪ] N demande f de renseignements; (*Law*) enquête f, investigation f; **"inquiries"** « renseignements »; **to hold an** ~ **into sth** enquêter sur qch

inquiry desk N (*BRIT*) guichet m de renseignements

inquiry office N (*BRIT*) bureau m de renseignements

inquisition [ɪnkwɪˈzɪʃən] N enquête f, investigation f; (*Rel*): **the I**~ l'Inquisition f

inquisitive [ɪnˈkwɪzɪtɪv] ADJ curieux(-euse)

inroads [ˈɪnrəʊdz] NPL: **to make** ~ **into** (*savings, supplies*) entamer

insane [ɪnˈseɪn] ADJ fou (folle); (*Med*) aliéné(e)

insanitary [ɪnˈsænɪtərɪ] ADJ insalubre

insanity [ɪnˈsænɪtɪ] N folie f; (*Med*) aliénation (mentale)

insatiable [ɪnˈseɪʃəbl] ADJ insatiable

inscribe [ɪnˈskraɪb] VT inscrire; (*book etc*): **to** ~ **(to sb)** dédicacer (à qn)

inscription [ɪnˈskrɪpʃən] N inscription f; (*in book*) dédicace f

inscrutable [ɪnˈskruːtəbl] ADJ impénétrable

inseam [ˈɪnsiːm] N (*US*): ~ **measurement** hauteur f d'entre-jambe

insect [ˈɪnsɛkt] N insecte m

insect bite N piqûre f d'insecte

insecticide [ɪnˈsɛktɪsaɪd] N insecticide m

insect repellent N crème f anti-insectes

insecure [ɪnsɪˈkjʊər] ADJ (*person*) anxieux(-euse); (*job*) précaire; (*building etc*) peu sûr(e)

insecurity [ɪnsɪˈkjʊərɪtɪ] N insécurité f

insemination [ɪnsɛmɪˈneɪʃən] N insémination f

insensible [ɪnˈsɛnsɪbl] ADJ insensible; (*unconscious*) sans connaissance

insensitive [ɪnˈsɛnsɪtɪv] ADJ insensible

insensitivity [ɪnsɛnsɪˈtɪvɪtɪ] N insensibilité f

inseparable [ɪnˈsɛprəbl] ADJ inséparable

insert VT [ɪnˈsəːt] insérer ▶ N [ˈɪnsəːt] insertion f

insertion [ɪnˈsəːʃən] N insertion f

in-service [ˈɪnˈsəːvɪs] ADJ (training) continu(e); (course) d'initiation; de perfectionnement; de recyclage

inshore ADJ [ˈɪnʃɔːʳ] côtier(-ière) ▶ ADV [ɪnˈʃɔːʳ] près de la côte; vers la côte

★**inside** [ˈɪnˈsaɪd] N intérieur m; (of road: BRIT) côté m gauche (de la route); (: US, Europe etc) côté droit (de la route) ▶ ADJ intérieur(e); ~ **information** renseignements mpl à la source; ~ **story** histoire racontée par un témoin ▶ ADV à l'intérieur, dedans; **to go ~** rentrer ▶ PREP à l'intérieur de; (of time): ~ **10 minutes** en moins de 10 minutes ■ **insides** NPL (inf) intestins mpl

inside forward N (Sport) intérieur m

inside lane N (Aut: in Britain) voie f de gauche; (: in US, Europe) voie f de droite

inside leg measurement N (BRIT) hauteur f d'entre-jambe

inside out ADV à l'envers; (know) à fond; **to turn sth** ~ retourner qch

insider [ɪnˈsaɪdəʳ] N initié(e)

insider dealing, insider trading N (Stock Exchange) délit m d'initiés

insidious [ɪnˈsɪdɪəs] ADJ insidieux(-euse)

insight [ˈɪnsaɪt] N perspicacité f; (glimpse, idea) aperçu m; **to gain an ~ into sth** avoir un aperçu de qch; **to give sb an ~ into sth** donner à qn un aperçu de qch

insightful [ˈɪnsaɪtful] ADJ sagace

insignia [ɪnˈsɪgnɪə] NPL insignes mpl

insignificant [ɪnsɪgˈnɪfɪknt] ADJ insignifiant(e)

insincere [ɪnsɪnˈsɪəʳ] ADJ hypocrite

insincerity [ɪnsɪnˈsɛrɪtɪ] N manque m de sincérité, hypocrisie f

insinuate [ɪnˈsɪnjueɪt] VT insinuer

insinuation [ɪnsɪnjuˈeɪʃən] N insinuation f

insipid [ɪnˈsɪpɪd] ADJ insipide, fade

★**insist** [ɪnˈsɪst] VI insister; **to ~ on doing** insister pour faire; **to ~ on sth** exiger qch; **to ~ that** insister pour que + sub; (claim) maintenir or soutenir que

insistence [ɪnˈsɪstəns] N insistance f

insistent [ɪnˈsɪstənt] ADJ insistant(e), pressant(e); (noise, action) ininterrompu(e)

insistently [ɪnˈsɪstəntlɪ] ADV avec insistance

insofar [ɪnsəʊˈfɑːʳ]: ~ **as** conj dans la mesure où

insole [ˈɪnsəʊl] N semelle intérieure; (fixed part of shoe) première f

insolence [ˈɪnsələns] N insolence f

insolent [ˈɪnsələnt] ADJ insolent(e)

insoluble [ɪnˈsɔljubl] ADJ insoluble

insolvency [ɪnˈsɔlvənsɪ] N insolvabilité f; faillite f

insolvent [ɪnˈsɔlvənt] ADJ insolvable; (bankrupt) en faillite

insomnia [ɪnˈsɔmnɪə] N insomnie f

insomniac [ɪnˈsɔmnɪæk] N insomniaque mf

insouciance [ɪnˈsuːsɪəns] N (formal) insouciance f

inspect [ɪnˈspɛkt] VT inspecter; (BRIT: ticket) contrôler

inspection [ɪnˈspɛkʃən] N inspection f; (BRIT: of tickets) contrôle m

★**inspector** [ɪnˈspɛktəʳ] N inspecteur(-trice); (BRIT: on buses, trains) contrôleur(-euse)

inspiration [ɪnspəˈreɪʃən] N inspiration f

inspirational [ɪnspɪˈreɪʃənl] ADJ (person, leader) charismatique

inspire [ɪnˈspaɪəʳ] VT inspirer

inspired [ɪnˈspaɪəd] ADJ (writer, book etc) inspiré(e); **in an ~ moment** dans un moment d'inspiration

inspiring [ɪnˈspaɪərɪn] ADJ inspirant(e)

inst. ABBR (BRIT Comm) = **instant**

instability [ɪnstəˈbɪlɪtɪ] N instabilité f

install, (US) instal [ɪnˈstɔːl] VT installer

installation [ɪnstəˈleɪʃən] N installation f

installer [ɪnˈstɔːlə] N (Comput) installeur m

installment plan N (US) achat m (or vente f) à tempérament or crédit

instalment, (US) installment [ɪnˈstɔːlmənt] N (payment) acompte m, versement partiel; (of TV serial etc) épisode m; **in instalments** (pay) à tempérament; (receive) en plusieurs fois

★**instance** [ˈɪnstəns] N exemple m; **for ~** par exemple; **in many instances** dans bien des cas; **in that ~** dans ce cas; **in the first ~** tout d'abord, en premier lieu

★**instant** [ˈɪnstənt] N instant m; **the 10th ~** le 10 courant ▶ ADJ immédiat(e), urgent(e); (coffee, food) instantané(e), en poudre

instantaneous [ɪnstənˈteɪnɪəs] ADJ instantané(e)

instantly [ˈɪnstəntlɪ] ADV immédiatement, tout de suite

instant message N message m instantané

instant messaging N messagerie f instantanée

instant replay N (US TV) retour m sur une séquence

★**instead** [ɪnˈstɛd] ADV au lieu de cela; ~ **of** au lieu de; ~ **of sb** à la place de qn

instep [ˈɪnstɛp] N cou-de-pied m; (of shoe) cambrure f

instigate [ˈɪnstɪgeɪt] VT (rebellion, strike, crime) inciter à; (new ideas etc) susciter

instigation [ɪnstɪˈgeɪʃən] N instigation f; **at sb's ~** à l'instigation de qn

instigator [ˈɪnstɪgeɪtəʳ] N instigateur(-trice)

instil [ɪnˈstɪl] VT: **to ~ (into)** inculquer (à); (courage) insuffler (à)

instinct [ˈɪnstɪŋkt] N instinct m

instinctive [ɪnˈstɪŋktɪv] ADJ instinctif(-ive)

instinctively [ɪnˈstɪŋktɪvlɪ] ADV instinctivement

★**institute** [ˈɪnstɪtjuːt] N institut m ▶ VT instituer, établir; (inquiry) ouvrir; (proceedings) entamer

★**institution** [ɪnstɪˈtjuːʃən] N institution f; (school) établissement m (scolaire); (for care) établissement (psychiatrique etc)

institutional [ɪnstɪˈtjuːʃənl] ADJ institutionnel(le); ~ **care** soins fournis par un établissement médico-social

institutionalized [ɪnstɪˈtjuːʃənlaɪzd] ADJ (*racism, corruption*) institutionnalisé(e); **to become ~** (*person*) devenir un(e) perpétuel(le) assisté(e)

instruct [ɪnˈstrʌkt] VT instruire, former; **to ~ sb in sth** enseigner qch à qn; **to ~ sb to do** charger qn *or* ordonner à qn de faire

instruction [ɪnˈstrʌkʃən] N instruction *f* ▪ **instructions** NPL (*orders*) directives *fpl*; **instructions for use** mode *m* d'emploi

instruction book N manuel *m* d'instructions

instructive [ɪnˈstrʌktɪv] ADJ instructif(-ive)

instructor [ɪnˈstrʌktə̞ʳ] N professeur *m*; (*for skiing, driving*) moniteur *m*

★**instrument** [ˈɪnstrumənt] N instrument *m*

instrumental [ɪnstruˈmɛntl] ADJ (*Mus*) instrumental(e); **to be ~ in sth/in doing sth** contribuer à qch/à faire qch

instrumentalist [ɪnstruˈmɛntəlɪst] N instrumentiste *mf*

instrument panel N tableau *m* de bord

insubordinate [ɪnsəˈbɔːdənɪt] ADJ insubordonné(e)

insubordination [ɪnsəbɔːdəˈneɪʃən] N insubordination *f*

insufferable [ɪnˈsʌfrəbl] ADJ insupportable

insufficient [ɪnsəˈfɪʃənt] ADJ insuffisant(e)

insufficiently [ɪnsəˈfɪʃəntlɪ] ADV insuffisamment

insular [ˈɪnsjulə̞ʳ] ADJ insulaire; (*outlook*) étroit(e); (*person*) aux vues étroites

insulate [ˈɪnsjuleɪt] VT isoler; (*against sound*) insonoriser

insulating tape [ˈɪnsjuleɪtɪŋ-] N ruban isolant

insulation [ɪnsjuˈleɪʃən] N isolation *f*; (*against sound*) insonorisation *f*

insulin [ˈɪnsjulɪn] N insuline *f*

insult N [ˈɪnsʌlt] insulte *f*, affront *m* ▶ VT [ɪnˈsʌlt] insulter, faire un affront à

insulting [ɪnˈsʌltɪŋ] ADJ insultant(e), injurieux(-euse)

insuperable [ɪnˈsjuːprəbl] ADJ insurmontable

★**insurance** [ɪnˈʃuərəns] N assurance *f*; **fire/life ~** assurance-incendie/-vie; **to take out ~ (against)** s'assurer (contre)

insurance agent N agent *m* d'assurances

insurance broker N courtier *m* en assurances

insurance company N compagnie *f* or société *f* d'assurances

insurance policy N police *f* d'assurance

insurance premium N prime *f* d'assurance

insure [ɪnˈʃuə̞ʳ] VT assurer; **to ~ (o.s.) against** (*fig*) parer à; **to ~ sb/sb's life** assurer qn/la vie de qn; **to be insured for £5000** être assuré(e) pour 5000 livres

insured [ɪnˈʃuəd] N: **the ~** l'assuré(e)

insurer [ɪnˈʃuərə̞ʳ] N assureur *m*

insurgency [ɪnˈsəːdʒənsɪ] N insurrection *f*

insurgent [ɪnˈsəːdʒənt] ADJ, N insurgé(e)

insurmountable [ɪnsəˈmauntəbl] ADJ insurmontable

insurrection [ɪnsəˈrɛkʃən] N insurrection *f*

intact [ɪnˈtækt] ADJ intact(e)

intake [ˈɪnteɪk] N (*Tech*) admission *f*; (*consumption*) consommation *f*; (BRIT *Scol*): **an ~ of 200 a year** 200 admissions par an

intangible [ɪnˈtændʒɪbl] ADJ intangible; (*assets*) immatériel(le)

integral [ˈɪntɪɡrəl] ADJ (*whole*) intégral(e); (*part*) intégrant(e)

integrate [ˈɪntɪɡreɪt] VT intégrer ▶ VI s'intégrer

integrated circuit [ˈɪntɪɡreɪtɪd-] N (*Comput*) circuit intégré

integration [ɪntɪˈɡreɪʃən] N intégration *f*; **racial ~** intégration raciale

integrity [ɪnˈtɛɡrɪtɪ] N intégrité *f*

intellect [ˈɪntəlɛkt] N intelligence *f*

intellectual [ɪntəˈlɛktjuəl] ADJ, N intellectuel(le)

intellectually [ɪntəˈlɛktjuəlɪ] ADV intellectuellement

intelligence [ɪnˈtɛlɪdʒəns] N intelligence *f*; (*Mil*) informations *fpl*, renseignements *mpl*

intelligence quotient N quotient intellectuel

Intelligence Service N services *mpl* de renseignements

intelligence test N test *m* d'intelligence

★**intelligent** [ɪnˈtɛlɪdʒənt] ADJ intelligent(e)

intelligently [ɪnˈtɛlɪdʒəntlɪ] ADV intelligemment

intelligentsia [ɪntɛlɪˈdʒɛntsɪə] N: **the ~** l'intelligentsia *f*

intelligible [ɪnˈtɛlɪdʒɪbl] ADJ intelligible

intemperate [ɪnˈtɛmpərət] ADJ immodéré(e); (*drinking too much*) adonné(e) à la boisson

★**intend** [ɪnˈtɛnd] VT (*gift etc*): **to ~ sth for** destiner qch à; **to ~ to do** avoir l'intention de faire

intended [ɪnˈtɛndɪd] ADJ (*insult*) intentionnel(le); (*journey*) projeté(e); (*effect*) voulu(e)

★**intense** [ɪnˈtɛns] ADJ intense; (*person*) véhément(e)

intensely [ɪnˈtɛnslɪ] ADV intensément; (*moving*) profondément

intensify [ɪnˈtɛnsɪfaɪ] VT intensifier

intensity [ɪnˈtɛnsɪtɪ] N intensité *f*

intensive [ɪnˈtɛnsɪv] ADJ intensif(-ive)

intensive care N: **to be in ~** être en réanimation

intensive care unit N service *m* de réanimation

intent [ɪnˈtɛnt] N intention *f*; **to all intents and purposes** en fait, pratiquement ▶ ADJ attentif(-ive), absorbé(e); **to be ~ on doing sth** être (bien) décidé à faire qch

intention [ɪnˈtɛnʃən] N intention *f*

intentional [ɪnˈtɛnʃənl] ADJ intentionnel(le), délibéré(e)

intentionally [ɪnˈtɛnʃənlɪ] ADV intentionnellement

intently [ɪnˈtɛntlɪ] ADV attentivement

inter [ɪnˈtəːʳ] VT enterrer

interact [ɪntərˈækt] VI avoir une action réciproque; (*people*) communiquer

interaction [ɪntərˈækʃən] N interaction *f*

interactive [ɪntərˈæktɪv] ADJ (*group*) interactif(-ive); (*Comput*) interactif, conversationnel(le)

interactivity [ɪntərækˈtɪvɪtɪ] N (*Comput*) interactivité *f*

intercede [ɪntəˈsiːd] VI: **to ~ with sb/on behalf of sb** intercéder auprès de qn/en faveur de qn

intercept [ɪntə'sɛpt] VT intercepter; (person) arrêter au passage

interception [ɪntə'sɛpʃən] N interception f

interchange N ['ɪntətʃeɪndʒ] (exchange) échange m; (on motorway) échangeur m ▶ VT [ɪntə'tʃeɪndʒ] échanger; mettre à la place l'un(e) de l'autre

interchangeable [ɪntə'tʃeɪndʒəbl] ADJ interchangeable

intercity [ɪntə'sɪtɪ] ADJ: ~ (train) train m rapide

intercom ['ɪntəkɔm] N interphone m

interconnect [ɪntəkə'nɛkt] VI (rooms) communiquer

intercontinental ['ɪntəkɔntɪ'nɛntl] ADJ intercontinental(e)

intercourse ['ɪntəkɔːs] N rapports mpl; **sexual ~** rapports sexuels

interdependent [ɪntədɪ'pɛndənt] ADJ interdépendant(e)

★**interest** ['ɪntrɪst] N intérêt m; (Comm: stake, share) participation f, intérêts mpl; **compound/simple ~** intérêt composé/simple; **British interests in the Middle East** les intérêts britanniques au Moyen-Orient; **his main ~ is ...** ce qui l'intéresse le plus est ... ▶ VT intéresser

interested ['ɪntrɪstɪd] ADJ intéressé(e); **to be ~ in sth** s'intéresser à qch; **I'm ~ in going** ça m'intéresse d'y aller

interest-free ['ɪntrɪst'friː] ADJ sans intérêt

★**interesting** ['ɪntrɪstɪŋ] ADJ intéressant(e)

interestingly ['ɪntrɪstɪŋlɪ] ADV (it is of interest that) il est intéressant de noter que; (curiously) curieusement; **~ enough, he soon remarried** il est intéressant de noter qu'il s'est remarié peu après

interest rate N taux m d'intérêt

interface ['ɪntəfeɪs] N (Comput) interface f

interfaith [ɪntə'feɪθ] ADJ (relations, dialogue) interreligieux(-euse)

interfere [ɪntə'fɪəʳ] VI: **to ~ in** (quarrel) s'immiscer dans; (other people's business) se mêler de; **to ~ with** (object) tripoter, toucher à; (plans) contrecarrer; (duty) être en conflit avec; **don't ~** mêlez-vous de vos affaires

interference [ɪntə'fɪərəns] N (gen) ingérence f; (Physics) interférence f; (Radio, TV) parasites mpl

interfering [ɪntə'fɪərɪŋ] ADJ importun(e)

interim ['ɪntərɪm] ADJ provisoire; (post) intérimaire ▶ N: **in the ~** dans l'intérim

interior [ɪn'tɪərɪəʳ] N intérieur m ▶ ADJ intérieur(e); (minister, department) de l'intérieur

interior decorator, interior designer N décorateur(-trice) d'intérieur

interior design N architecture f d'intérieur

interjection [ɪntə'dʒɛkʃən] N interjection f

interlock [ɪntə'lɔk] VI s'enclencher ▶ VT enclencher

interloper ['ɪntələupəʳ] N intrus(e)

interlude ['ɪntəluːd] N intervalle m; (Theat) intermède m

intermarry [ɪntə'mærɪ] VI former des alliances entre familles (or tribus); (within same family) former des unions consanguines

intermediary [ɪntə'miːdɪərɪ] N intermédiaire mf

intermediate [ɪntə'miːdɪət] ADJ intermédiaire; (Scol: course, level) moyen(ne)

interment [ɪn'tɜːmənt] N inhumation f, enterrement m

interminable [ɪn'tɜːmɪnəbl] ADJ sans fin, interminable

intermission [ɪntə'mɪʃən] N pause f; (Theat, Cine) entracte m

intermittent [ɪntə'mɪtnt] ADJ intermittent(e)

intermittently [ɪntə'mɪtntlɪ] ADV par intermittence, par intervalles

intern VT [ɪn'tɜːn] interner ▶ N ['ɪntɜːn] (in company) stagiaire mf; (esp US Med) ≈ interne mf

internal [ɪn'tɜːnl] ADJ interne; (dispute, reform etc) intérieur(e); **~ injuries** lésions fpl internes

internalize [ɪn'tɜːnlaɪz] VT (belief, values) intérioriser

internally [ɪn'tɜːnəlɪ] ADV intérieurement; **"not to be taken ~"** « pour usage externe »

Internal Revenue Service N (US) fisc m

★**international** [ɪntə'næʃənl] ADJ international(e) ▶ N (BRIT Sport) international m

International Atomic Energy Agency N Agence Internationale de l'Énergie Atomique

International Court of Justice N Cour internationale de justice

international date line N ligne f de changement de date

internationalist [ɪntə'næʃnəlɪst] ADJ internationaliste

internationally [ɪntə'næʃnəlɪ] ADV dans le monde entier

International Monetary Fund N Fonds monétaire international

international relations NPL relations internationales

internecine [ɪntə'niːsaɪn] ADJ mutuellement destructeur(-trice)

internee [ɪntɜː'niː] N interné(e)

★**internet** [ɪntə'nɛt] N: **the ~** l'Internet m

internet café N cybercafé m

internet connection N connexion f Internet

internet service provider N fournisseur m d'accès à Internet

internet user N internaute mf

internment [ɪn'tɜːnmənt] N internement m

internship [ɪn'tɜːnʃɪp] N (in company) stage m de formation en entreprise; (US Med) ≈ internat m (aux États-Unis, première année de formation clinique avant le passage de l'examen d'État permettant d'exercer)

interpersonal [ɪntəpə:snl] ADJ interpersonnel(le)

interplay ['ɪntəpleɪ] N effet m réciproque, jeu m

Interpol ['ɪntəpɔl] N Interpol m

interpret [ɪn'tɜːprɪt] VT interpréter ▶ VI servir d'interprète

interpretation [ɪntəprɪ'teɪʃən] N interprétation f

interpreter [ɪn'tɜːprɪtəʳ] N interprète mf; **could you act as an ~ for us?** pourriez-vous nous servir d'interprète ?

interpreting [ɪn'tɜːprɪtɪŋ] N (profession) interprétariat m

interpretive [ɪnˈtə:prɪtɪv] ADJ interprétatif(-ive)

interrelated [ɪntərɪˈleɪtɪd] ADJ en corrélation, en rapport étroit

interrogate [ɪnˈterəugeɪt] VT interroger; (*suspect etc*) soumettre à un interrogatoire

interrogation [ɪnterəuˈgeɪʃən] N interrogation f; (*by police*) interrogatoire m

interrogative [ɪntəˈrɔgətɪv] ADJ interrogateur (-trice) ▶ N (*Ling*) interrogatif m

interrogator [ɪnˈterəgeɪtər] N interrogateur(-trice)

interrupt [ɪntəˈrʌpt] VT, VI interrompre

interruption [ɪntəˈrʌpʃən] N interruption f

intersect [ɪntəˈsɛkt] VT couper, croiser; (*Math*) intersecter ▶ VI se croiser, se couper; s'intersecter

intersection [ɪntəˈsɛkʃən] N intersection f; (*of roads*) croisement m

intersperse [ɪntəˈspə:s] VT: **to ~ with** parsemer de

interspersed [ɪntəˈspə:st] ADJ: **~ with** (*in time*) entrecoupé de; (*in space*) alternant avec

interstate [ˈɪntəsteɪt] N (US) autoroute f (qui relie plusieurs États)

intertwine [ɪntəˈtwaɪn] VT entrelacer ▶ VI s'entrelacer

interval [ˈɪntəvl] N intervalle m; (BRIT: *Theat*) entracte m; (: *Sport*) mi-temps f; **bright intervals** (*in weather*) éclaircies fpl; **at intervals** par intervalles

intervene [ɪntəˈvi:n] VI (*time*) s'écouler (entretemps); (*event*) survenir; (*person*) intervenir

intervention [ɪntəˈvɛnʃən] N intervention f

interventionist [ɪntəˈvɛnʃənɪst] ADJ, N interventionniste mf

★**interview** [ˈɪntəvju:] N (*Radio, TV*) interview f; (*for job*) entrevue f ▶ VT interviewer, avoir une entrevue avec

interviewee [ɪntəvjuˈi:] N (*for job*) candidat m (qui passe un entretien); (TV *etc*) invité(e), personne interviewée

interviewer [ˈɪntəvjuər] N (*Radio, TV*) interviewer m

intestate [ɪnˈtɛsteɪt] ADJ intestat f inv

intestinal [ɪnˈtɛstɪnl] ADJ intestinal(e)

intestine [ɪnˈtɛstɪn] N intestin m; **large ~** gros intestin; **small ~** intestin grêle

intimacy [ˈɪntɪməsɪ] N intimité f

intimate ADJ [ˈɪntɪmət] intime; (*friendship*) profond(e); (*knowledge*) approfondi(e) ▶ VT [ˈɪntɪmeɪt] suggérer, laisser entendre; (*announce*) faire savoir

intimately [ˈɪntɪmətlɪ] ADV intimement

intimation [ɪntɪˈmeɪʃən] N annonce f

intimidate [ɪnˈtɪmɪdeɪt] VT intimider

intimidating [ɪnˈtɪmɪdeɪtɪŋ] ADJ intimidant(e)

intimidation [ɪntɪmɪˈdeɪʃən] N intimidation f

★**into** [ˈɪntu] PREP dans; **~ pieces/French** en morceaux/français; **to change pounds ~ dollars** changer des livres en dollars; **3 ~ 9 goes 3** 9 divisé par 3 donne 3; **she's ~ opera** c'est une passionnée d'opéra

intolerable [ɪnˈtɔlərəbl] ADJ intolérable

intolerance [ɪnˈtɔlərns] N intolérance f

intolerant [ɪnˈtɔlərnt] ADJ: **~ (of)** intolérant(e) (de); (*Med*) intolérant (à)

intonation [ɪntəuˈneɪʃən] N intonation f

intoxicate [ɪnˈtɔksɪkeɪt] VT enivrer

intoxicated [ɪnˈtɔksɪkeɪtɪd] ADJ ivre

intoxicating [ɪnˈtɔksɪkeɪtɪŋ] ADJ (*atmosphere, fragrance*) enivrant(e); (*drink*) alcoolisé(e)

intoxication [ɪntɔksɪˈkeɪʃən] N ivresse f

intractable [ɪnˈtræktəbl] ADJ (*child, temper*) indocile, insoumis(e); (*problem*) insoluble; (*illness*) incurable

intranet [ˈɪntrənet] N intranet m

intransigence [ɪnˈtrænsɪdʒəns] N intransigeance f

intransigent [ɪnˈtrænsɪdʒənt] ADJ intransigeant(e)

intransitive [ɪnˈtrænsɪtɪv] ADJ intransitif(-ive)

intra-uterine device [ˈɪntrəˈju:təraɪn-] N dispositif intra-utérin, stérilet m

intravenous [ɪntrəˈvi:nəs] ADJ intraveineux(-euse)

intravenously [ɪntrəˈvi:nəslɪ] ADV par intraveineuse

in-tray [ˈɪntreɪ] N courrier m « arrivée »

intrepid [ɪnˈtrepɪd] ADJ intrépide

intricacy [ˈɪntrɪkəsɪ] N complexité f

intricate [ˈɪntrɪkət] ADJ complexe, compliqué(e)

intrigue [ɪnˈtri:g] N intrigue f ▶ VT intriguer ▶ VI intriguer, comploter

intriguing [ɪnˈtri:gɪŋ] ADJ fascinant(e)

intrinsic [ɪnˈtrɪnsɪk] ADJ intrinsèque

★**introduce** [ɪntrəˈdju:s] VT introduire; (TV *show etc*) présenter; **to ~ sb (to sb)** présenter qn (à qn); **to ~ sb to** (*pastime, technique*) initier qn à; **may I ~ ...?** je vous présente ...

introduction [ɪntrəˈdʌkʃən] N introduction f; (*of person*) présentation f; (*to new experience*) initiation f; **a letter of ~** une lettre de recommandation

introductory [ɪntrəˈdʌktərɪ] ADJ préliminaire, introductif(-ive); **~ remarks** remarques fpl liminaires; **an ~ offer** une offre de lancement

introspection [ɪntrəuˈspɛkʃən] N introspection f

introspective [ɪntrəuˈspɛktɪv] ADJ introspectif(-ive)

introvert [ˈɪntrəuvə:t] ADJ, N introverti(e)

intrude [ɪnˈtru:d] VI (*person*) être importun(e); **to ~ on** or **into** (*conversation etc*) s'immiscer dans; **am I intruding?** est-ce que je vous dérange ?

intruder [ɪnˈtru:dər] N intrus(e)

intrusion [ɪnˈtru:ʒən] N intrusion f

intrusive [ɪnˈtru:sɪv] ADJ importun(e), gênant(e)

intuition [ɪntju:ˈɪʃən] N intuition f

intuitive [ɪnˈtju:ɪtɪv] ADJ intuitif(-ive)

inundate [ˈɪnʌndeɪt] VT: **to ~ with** inonder de

inure [ɪnˈjuər] VT: **to ~ (to)** habituer (à)

invade [ɪnˈveɪd] VT envahir

invader [ɪnˈveɪdər] N envahisseur m

invalid N [ˈɪnvəlɪd] malade mf; (*with disability*) invalide mf ▶ ADJ [ɪnˈvælɪd] (*not valid*) invalide, non valide

invalidate [ɪnˈvælɪdeɪt] VT invalider, annuler

invalid chair [ˈɪnvəlɪd-] N (BRIT) fauteuil m d'infirme

invaluable [ɪnˈvæljuəbl] ADJ inestimable, inappréciable

invariable [ɪnˈvɛərɪəbl] ADJ invariable; (*fig*) immanquable

invariably [ɪnˈvɛərɪəblɪ] ADV invariablement; **she is ~ late** elle est toujours en retard

invasion [ɪnˈveɪʒən] N invasion f

invective [ɪnˈvɛktɪv] N invective f

inveigle [ɪnˈviːgl] VT: **to ~ sb into (doing) sth** amener qn à (faire) qch (par la ruse or la flatterie)

invent [ɪnˈvɛnt] VT inventer

invention [ɪnˈvɛnʃən] N invention f

inventive [ɪnˈvɛntɪv] ADJ inventif(-ive)

inventiveness [ɪnˈvɛntɪvnɪs] N esprit inventif or d'invention

inventor [ɪnˈvɛntər] N inventeur(-trice)

inventory [ˈɪnvəntrɪ] N inventaire m

inventory control N (Comm) contrôle m des stocks

inverse [ɪnˈvəːs] ADJ inverse; **in ~ proportion (to)** inversement proportionnel(le) (à) ▶ N inverse m, contraire m

inversely [ɪnˈvəːslɪ] ADV inversement

invert [ɪnˈvəːt] VT intervertir; (cup, object) retourner

invertebrate [ɪnˈvəːtɪbrət] N invertébré m

inverted commas [ɪnˈvəːtɪd-] NPL (BRIT) guillemets mpl

invest [ɪnˈvɛst] VT investir; (endow): **to ~ sb with sth** conférer qch à qn ▶ VI faire un investissement, investir; **to ~ in** placer de l'argent or investir dans; (fig: acquire) s'offrir, faire l'acquisition de

investigate [ɪnˈvɛstɪgeɪt] VT étudier, examiner; (crime) faire une enquête sur

investigation [ɪnvɛstɪˈgeɪʃən] N examen m; (of crime) enquête f, investigation f

investigative [ɪnˈvɛstɪgeɪtɪv] ADJ: **~ journalism** enquête-reportage f, journalisme m d'enquête

investigator [ɪnˈvɛstɪgeɪtər] N investigateur (-trice); **private ~** détective privé

investiture [ɪnˈvɛstɪtʃər] N investiture f

investment [ɪnˈvɛstmənt] N investissement m, placement m

investment income N revenu m de placement

investment trust N société f d'investissements

investor [ɪnˈvɛstər] N épargnant(e); (shareholder) actionnaire mf

inveterate [ɪnˈvɛtərət] ADJ invétéré(e)

invidious [ɪnˈvɪdɪəs] ADJ injuste; (task) déplaisant(e)

invigilate [ɪnˈvɪdʒɪleɪt] (BRIT) VT surveiller ▶ VI être de surveillance

invigilator [ɪnˈvɪdʒɪleɪtər] N (BRIT) surveillant m (d'examen)

invigorating [ɪnˈvɪgəreɪtɪŋ] ADJ vivifiant(e), stimulant(e)

invincibility [ɪnvɪnsɪˈbɪlɪtɪ] N invincibilité f

invincible [ɪnˈvɪnsɪbl] ADJ invincible

inviolate [ɪnˈvaɪələt] ADJ inviolé(e)

invisible [ɪnˈvɪzɪbl] ADJ invisible

invisible assets NPL (BRIT) actif incorporel

invisible ink N encre f sympathique

invisible mending N stoppage m

★**invitation** [ɪnvɪˈteɪʃən] N invitation f; **by ~ only** sur invitation; **at sb's ~** à la demande de qn

★**invite** [ɪnˈvaɪt] VT inviter; (opinions etc) demander; (trouble) chercher; **to ~ sb (to do)** inviter qn (à faire); **to ~ sb to dinner** inviter qn à dîner
  ▶ **invite out** VT inviter (à sortir)
  ▶ **invite over** VT inviter (chez soi)

invitee [ɪnvaɪˈtiː] N invité(e)

inviting [ɪnˈvaɪtɪŋ] ADJ engageant(e), attrayant(e); (gesture) encourageant(e)

invoice [ˈɪnvɔɪs] N facture f ▶ VT facturer; **to ~ sb for goods** facturer des marchandises à qn

invoke [ɪnˈvəuk] VT invoquer

involuntarily [ˈɪnvɒləntrɪlɪ] ADV involontairement

involuntary [ɪnˈvɒləntrɪ] ADJ involontaire

★**involve** [ɪnˈvɒlv] VT (entail) impliquer; (concern) concerner; (require) nécessiter; **to ~ sb in** (theft etc) impliquer qn dans; (activity, meeting) faire participer qn à

involved [ɪnˈvɒlvd] ADJ (complicated) complexe; **to be ~ in** (take part) participer à; (be engrossed) être plongé(e) dans; **to feel ~** se sentir concerné(e); **to become ~** (in love etc) s'engager

involvement [ɪnˈvɒlvmənt] N (personal role) rôle m; (participation) participation f; (enthusiasm) enthousiasme m; (of resources, funds) mise f en jeu

invulnerable [ɪnˈvʌlnərəbl] ADJ invulnérable

inward [ˈɪnwəd] ADJ (movement) vers l'intérieur; (thought, feeling) profond(e), intime ▶ ADV = **inwards**

inwardly [ˈɪnwədlɪ] ADV (feel, think etc) secrètement, en son for intérieur

inwards [ˈɪnwədz] ADV vers l'intérieur

I/O ABBR (Comput: = input/output) E/S

IOC N ABBR (= International Olympic Committee) CIO m (= Comité international olympique)

iodine [ˈaɪəudiːn] N iode m

IOM ABBR = **Isle of Man**

ion [ˈaɪən] N ion m

Ionian Sea [aɪˈəunɪən-] N: **the ~** la mer Ionienne

ioniser [ˈaɪənaɪzər] N ioniseur m

iota [aɪˈəutə] N (fig) brin m, grain m

IOU N ABBR (= I owe you) reconnaissance f de dette

IOW ABBR (BRIT) = **Isle of Wight**

IPA N ABBR (= International Phonetic Alphabet) API m

iPad® [ˈaɪpæd] N iPad® m

iPhone® [ˈaɪfəun] N iPhone® m

iPlayer® [ˈaɪpleɪər] N service de radiotélévision de rattrapage de la BBC

IPO N ABBR (Stock Exchange: = initial public offering) OPI f (= offre publique initiale)

iPod® [ˈaɪpɒd] N iPod® m

IQ N ABBR (= intelligence quotient) Q.I. m

IRA N ABBR (= Irish Republican Army) IRA f; (US) = **individual retirement account**

Iran [ɪˈrɑːn] N Iran m

Iranian [ɪˈreɪnɪən] ADJ iranien(ne) ▶ N Iranien(ne); (Ling) iranien m

Iraq [ɪˈrɑːk] N Irak m

Iraqi [ɪˈrɑːkɪ] ADJ irakien(ne) ▶ N Irakien(ne)

irascible [ɪˈræsɪbl] ADJ irascible

irate [aɪˈreɪt] ADJ courroucé(e)

ire ['aɪəʳ] N ire f

★**Ireland** ['aɪələnd] N Irlande f; **Republic of ~** République f d'Irlande

iridescent [ɪrɪ'dɛsnt] ADJ (literary) iridescent(e)

iris ['aɪrɪs] (pl **irises** [-ɪz]) N iris m

★**Irish** ['aɪrɪʃ] ADJ irlandais(e) ▶ NPL: **the ~** les Irlandais ▶ N (Ling) irlandais m

★**Irishman** ['aɪrɪʃmən] N (irreg) Irlandais m

Irish Sea N: **the ~** la mer d'Irlande

★**Irishwoman** ['aɪrɪʃwumən] N (irreg) Irlandaise f

irk [ə:k] VT ennuyer

irksome ['ə:ksəm] ADJ ennuyeux(-euse)

IRN N ABBR (= Independent Radio News) agence de presse radiophonique

IRO N ABBR (US) = **International Refugee Organization**

★**iron** ['aɪən] N fer m; (for clothes) fer m à repasser ▶ ADJ de or en fer ▶ VT (clothes) repasser ■ **irons** NPL (chains) fers mpl, chaînes fpl
▶ **iron out** VT (crease) faire disparaître au fer; (fig) aplanir; faire disparaître

Iron Curtain N: **the ~** le rideau de fer

iron foundry N fonderie f de fonte

ironic [aɪ'rɔnɪk], **ironical** [aɪ'rɔnɪkl] ADJ ironique

ironically [aɪ'rɔnɪklɪ] ADV ironiquement

ironing ['aɪənɪŋ] N (activity) repassage m; (clothes: ironed) linge repassé; (: to be ironed) linge à repasser

ironing board N planche f à repasser

ironmonger ['aɪənmʌŋgəʳ] N (BRIT) quincaillier m; **~'s (shop)** quincaillerie f

iron ore N minerai m de fer

ironworks ['aɪənwə:ks] N usine f sidérurgique

irony ['aɪrənɪ] N ironie f

irradiate [ɪ'reɪdɪeɪt] VT irradier

irrational [ɪ'ræʃənl] ADJ irrationnel(le); (person) qui n'est pas rationnel

irreconcilable [ɪrekən'saɪləbl] ADJ irréconciliable; (opinion): **~ with** inconciliable avec

irredeemable [ɪrɪ'di:məbl] ADJ (Comm) non remboursable

irrefutable [ɪrɪ'fju:təbl] ADJ irréfutable

irregular [ɪ'regjuləʳ] ADJ irrégulier(-ière)

irregularity [ɪregju'lærɪtɪ] N irrégularité f

irregularly [ɪ'regjuləlɪ] ADV (occur, eat) sporadiquement; **~ spaced** à intervalles irréguliers; **~ shaped/sized** de forme/taille irrégulière

irrelevance [ɪ'rɛləvəns] N manque m de rapport or d'à-propos

irrelevant [ɪ'rɛləvənt] ADJ sans rapport, hors de propos

irreligious [ɪrɪ'lɪdʒəs] ADJ irréligieux(-euse)

irreparable [ɪ'reprəbl] ADJ irréparable

irreplaceable [ɪrɪ'pleɪsəbl] ADJ irremplaçable

irrepressible [ɪrɪ'presəbl] ADJ irrépressible

irreproachable [ɪrɪ'prəutʃəbl] ADJ irréprochable

irresistible [ɪrɪ'zɪstɪbl] ADJ irrésistible

irresolute [ɪ'rezəlu:t] ADJ irrésolu(e), indécis(e)

irrespective [ɪrɪ'spektɪv]: **~ of** prep sans tenir compte de

irresponsibility [ɪrɪspɔnsɪ'bɪlɪtɪ] N irresponsabilité f

irresponsible [ɪrɪ'spɔnsɪbl] ADJ irresponsable

irresponsibly [ɪrɪ'spɔnsɪblɪ] ADV de manière irresponsable

irretrievable [ɪrɪ'tri:vəbl] ADJ irréparable, irrémédiable; (object) introuvable

irreverent [ɪ'rɛvərnt] ADJ irrévérencieux(-euse)

irreversible [ɪrɪ'və:sɪbl] ADJ irréversible

irrevocable [ɪ'rɛvəkəbl] ADJ irrévocable

irrevocably [ɪ'rɛvəkəblɪ] ADV irrévocablement

irrigate ['ɪrɪgeɪt] VT irriguer

irrigation [ɪrɪ'geɪʃən] N irrigation f

irritable ['ɪrɪtəbl] ADJ irritable

irritant ['ɪrɪtənt] N (substance) irritant m; (annoyance) source f d'irritation

irritate ['ɪrɪteɪt] VT irriter

irritating ['ɪrɪteɪtɪŋ] ADJ irritant(e)

irritation [ɪrɪ'teɪʃən] N irritation f

IRS N ABBR (US) = **Internal Revenue Service**

is [ɪz] VB see **be**

ISA ['aɪsə] N ABBR (BRIT: = Individual Savings Account) plan m d'épargne défiscalisé

ISBN N ABBR (= International Standard Book Number) ISBN m

ISDN N ABBR (= Integrated Services Digital Network) RNIS m

Islam ['ɪzlɑ:m] N Islam m

Islamic [ɪz'lɑ:mɪk] ADJ islamique; **~ fundamentalists** intégristes mpl musulmans

Islamist ['ɪzləmɪst] N islamiste mf

★**island** ['aɪlənd] N île f; (also: **traffic island**) refuge m (pour piétons)

islander ['aɪləndəʳ] N habitant(e) d'une île, insulaire mf

isle [aɪl] N île f

isn't ['ɪznt] = **is not**

isolate ['aɪsəleɪt] VT isoler

isolated ['aɪsəleɪtɪd] ADJ isolé(e)

isolation [aɪsə'leɪʃən] N isolement m

isotope ['aɪsətəup] N isotope m

ISP N ABBR = **Internet Service Provider**

Israel ['ɪzreɪl] N Israël m

Israeli [ɪz'reɪlɪ] ADJ israélien(ne) ▶ N Israélien(ne)

issue ['ɪʃu:] N question f, problème m; (outcome) résultat m, issue f; (of banknotes) émission f; (of newspaper) numéro m; (of book) publication f, parution f; (offspring) descendance f; **at ~** en jeu, en cause; **to avoid the ~** éluder le problème; **to take ~ with sb (over sth)** exprimer son désaccord avec qn (sur qch); **to make an ~ of sth** faire de qch un problème; **to confuse** or **obscure the ~** embrouiller la question ▶ VT (rations, equipment) distribuer; (orders) donner; (statement) publier, faire; (certificate, passport) délivrer; (book) faire paraître; publier; (banknotes, cheques, stamps) émettre, mettre en circulation ▶ VI: **to ~ from** provenir de

Le mot anglais **issue** se traduit rarement par *issue*.

Istanbul [ɪstæn'bu:l] N Istamboul, Istanbul

isthmus ['ɪsməs] N isthme m

★**IT** N ABBR = **information technology**

---

it [ɪt]

PRON **1** (specific: subject) il (elle); (: direct object) le, la, l'; (: indirect object) lui; **it's on the table** c'est or il (or elle) est sur la table; **I can't find it** je n'arrive pas à le trouver; **give it to me** donne-le-moi

2 (after prep): **about/from/of it** en; **I spoke to him about it** je lui en ai parlé; **what did you learn from it?** qu'est-ce que vous en avez retiré ?; **I'm proud of it** j'en suis fier; **I've come from it** j'en viens; **in/to it** y; **put the book in it** mettez-y le livre; **it's on it** c'est dessus; **he agreed to it** il y a consenti; **did you go to it?** (party, concert etc) est-ce que vous y êtes allé(s) ?; **above it, over it** (au-)dessus; **below it, under it** (en-)dessous; **in front of/behind it** devant/derrière

3 (impersonal) il; ce, cela, ça; **it's Friday tomorrow** demain, c'est vendredi or nous sommes vendredi; **it's 6 o'clock** il est 6 heures; **how far is it? — it's 10 miles** c'est loin ? — c'est à 10 miles; **it's 2 hours by train** c'est à 2 heures de train; **who is it? — it's me** qui est-ce ? — c'est moi; **it's raining** il pleut

---

il/elle est is used to translate it is or it's when it refers to a noun.

The bank? It's closed. **La banque ? Elle est fermée.**

c'est is used with pronouns, names, adverbs and conjunctions.

It's him. **C'est lui.**

It's here. **C'est ici.**

It's because… **C'est parce que …**

ITA N ABBR (BRIT: = initial teaching alphabet) alphabet en partie phonétique utilisé pour l'enseignement de la lecture

Italian [ɪˈtæljən] ADJ italien(ne) ▶ N Italien(ne); (Ling) italien m

italic [ɪˈtælɪk] ADJ italique

italics [ɪˈtælɪks] NPL italique m

★**Italy** [ˈɪtəlɪ] N Italie f

itch [ɪtʃ] N démangeaison f ▶ VI (person) éprouver des démangeaisons; (part of body) démanger; **I'm itching to do** l'envie me démange de faire

itchy [ˈɪtʃɪ] ADJ qui démange; **my back is ~** j'ai le dos qui me démange

it'd [ˈɪtd] = **it would**; **it had**

★**item** [ˈaɪtəm] N (gen) article m; (on agenda) question f, point m; (in programme) numéro m; (also: **news item**) nouvelle f; **items of clothing** articles vestimentaires

itemize [ˈaɪtəmaɪz] VT détailler, spécifier

itemized bill [ˈaɪtəmaɪzd-] N facture détaillée

itinerant [ɪˈtɪnərənt] ADJ itinérant(e); (musician) ambulant(e)

itinerary [aɪˈtɪnərərɪ] N itinéraire m

it'll [ˈɪtl] = **it will**; **it shall**

ITN N ABBR (BRIT: = Independent Television News) chaîne de télévision commerciale

★**its** [ɪts] ADJ son (sa), ses pl ▶ PRON le (la) sien(ne), les siens (siennes)

it's [ɪts] = **it is**; **it has**

★**itself** [ɪtˈsɛlf] PRON (reflexive) se; (emphatic) lui-même (elle-même)

ITV N ABBR (BRIT: = Independent Television) chaîne de télévision commerciale

IUD N ABBR = **intra-uterine device**

I've [aɪv] = **I have**

IVF N ABBR (= in vitro fertilization) FIV f (= fécondation in vitro)

ivory [ˈaɪvərɪ] N ivoire m

Ivory Coast N Côte f d'Ivoire

ivory tower N tour f d'ivoire

ivy [ˈaɪvɪ] N lierre m

Ivy League N (US) voir article

L'**Ivy League** regroupe huit universités privées du nord-est des États-Unis, qui comptent parmi les plus anciennes du pays et les plus prestigieuses du monde en raison de l'excellence de leur enseignement. Elles sélectionnent très strictement les candidats à l'entrée et demandent des frais d'inscription très élevés. De nombreuses personnalités du monde politique et culturel américain ont fait leurs études dans les universités de l'Ivy League. Bien que le terme désigne à l'origine une compétition sportive entre les équipes des huit établissements, il a acquis une connotation beaucoup plus large en raison de la rivalité non seulement sportive mais aussi intellectuelle qui les oppose. Il est aujourd'hui synonyme d'excellence et d'élitisme.

J j

J, j [dʒeɪ] N (letter) J, j m; **J for Jack**, (US) **J for Jig** J comme Joseph

JA N ABBR = **judge advocate**

J/A N ABBR = **joint account**

jab [dʒæb] VT: **to ~ sth into** enfoncer or planter qch dans ▶ N coup m; (Med, inf) piqûre f

jabber ['dʒæbəʳ] VT, VI bredouiller, baragouiner

jack [dʒæk] N (Aut) cric m; (Bowls) cochonnet m; (Cards) valet m
▶ **jack in** VT (inf) laisser tomber
▶ **jack up** VT soulever (au cric)

jackal ['dʒækl] N chacal m

jackass ['dʒækæs] N (also fig) âne m

jackdaw ['dʒækdɔː] N choucas m

★**jacket** ['dʒækɪt] N veste f, veston m; (of boiler etc) enveloppe f; (of book) couverture f, jaquette f

jacket potato N pomme f de terre en robe des champs

jack-in-the-box ['dʒækɪnðəbɔks] N diable m à ressort

jackknife ['dʒæknaɪf] N couteau m de poche ▶ VI: **the lorry jackknifed** la remorque (du camion) s'est mise en travers

jack-of-all-trades ['dʒækəv'ɔːltreɪdz] N bricoleur m

jack plug N (BRIT) jack m

jackpot ['dʒækpɔt] N gros lot

Jacuzzi® [dʒə'kuːzɪ] N jacuzzi® m

jade [dʒeɪd] N jade m ▶ CPD (earrings, brooch) de jade

jaded ['dʒeɪdɪd] ADJ éreinté(e), fatigué(e)

JAG N ABBR = **Judge Advocate General**

jagged ['dʒægɪd] ADJ dentelé(e)

jaguar ['dʒægjuəʳ] N jaguar m

★**jail** [dʒeɪl] N prison f ▶ VT emprisonner, mettre en prison

jailbird ['dʒeɪlbəːd] N récidiviste mf

jailbreak ['dʒeɪlbreɪk] N évasion f

jailer ['dʒeɪləʳ] N geôlier(-ière)

jail sentence N peine f de prison

jalopy [dʒə'lɔpɪ] N (inf) vieux clou

jam [dʒæm] N confiture f; (of shoppers etc) cohue f; (also: **traffic jam**) embouteillage m; **to be in a ~** (inf) être dans le pétrin; **to get sb out of a ~** (inf) sortir qn du pétrin ▶ VT (passage etc) encombrer, obstruer; (mechanism, drawer etc) bloquer, coincer; (Radio) brouiller; **to ~ sth into** (stuff) entasser or comprimer qch dans; (thrust) enfoncer qch dans;

the telephone lines are jammed les lignes (téléphoniques) sont encombrées ▶ VI (mechanism, sliding part) se coincer, se bloquer; (gun) s'enrayer

Jamaica [dʒə'meɪkə] N Jamaïque f

Jamaican [dʒə'meɪkən] ADJ jamaïquain(e) ▶ N Jamaïquain(e)

jamb [dʒæm] N jambage m

jam jar N pot m à confiture

jammed [dʒæmd] ADJ (window etc) coincé(e)

jam-packed [dʒæm'pækt] ADJ: **~ (with)** bourré(e) (de)

jam session N jam session f

jangle ['dʒæŋgl] VI cliqueter

janitor ['dʒænɪtəʳ] N (caretaker) concierge m

★**January** ['dʒænjuərɪ] N janvier m; see also **July**

★**Japan** [dʒə'pæn] N Japon m

Japanese [dʒæpə'niːz] ADJ japonais(e) ▶ N (pl inv) Japonais(e); (Ling) japonais m

jar [dʒɑːʳ] N (stone, earthenware) pot m; (glass) bocal m ▶ VI (sound) produire un son grinçant or discordant; (colours etc) détonner, jurer ▶ VT (shake) ébranler, secouer

jargon ['dʒɑːgən] N jargon m

jarring ['dʒɑːrɪŋ] ADJ (sound, colour) discordant(e)

Jas. ABBR = **James**

jasmin, jasmine ['dʒæzmɪn] N jasmin m

jaundice ['dʒɔːndɪs] N jaunisse f

jaundiced ['dʒɔːndɪst] ADJ (fig) envieux(-euse), désapprobateur(-trice)

jaunt [dʒɔːnt] N balade f

jaunty ['dʒɔːntɪ] ADJ enjoué(e), désinvolte

Java ['dʒɑːvə] N Java f

javelin ['dʒævlɪn] N javelot m

jaw [dʒɔː] N mâchoire f

jawbone ['dʒɔːbəun] N maxillaire m

jay [dʒeɪ] N geai m

jaywalker ['dʒeɪwɔːkəʳ] N piéton indiscipliné

★**jazz** [dʒæz] N jazz m
▶ **jazz up** VT animer, égayer

jazz band N orchestre m or groupe m de jazz

jazzy ['dʒæzɪ] ADJ bariolé(e), tapageur(-euse); (beat) de jazz

JCB® N excavatrice f

JCS N ABBR (US) = **Joint Chiefs of Staff**

JD N ABBR (US) titre universitaire; (: = Justice Department) ministère de la Justice

★**jealous** ['dʒɛləs] ADJ jaloux(-ouse)

jealously ['dʒɛləslɪ] ADV jalousement

jealousy ['dʒɛləsɪ] N jalousie f

★**jeans** [dʒiːnz] NPL jean m

Jeep® [dʒiːp] N jeep f

jeer [dʒɪəʳ] VI: **to ~ (at)** huer; se moquer cruellement (de), railler

jeering ['dʒɪərɪŋ] ADJ railleur(-euse), moqueur(-euse) ▶ N huées fpl

jeers [dʒɪəz] NPL huées fpl; sarcasmes mpl

jeggings ['dʒɛgɪŋz] NPL jeggins mpl

Jehovah's Witness [dʒɪ'həuvəz-] N témoin m de Jéhovah

Jell-O® ['dʒɛləu] N (US) gelée f

jelly ['dʒɛlɪ] N (dessert) gelée f; (US: jam) confiture f

jellyfish ['dʒɛlɪfɪʃ] N méduse f

jeopardize ['dʒɛpədaɪz] VT mettre en danger or péril

jeopardy ['dʒɛpədɪ] N: **in ~** en danger or péril

jerk [dʒəːk] N secousse f, saccade f; (of muscle) spasme m; (pej) pauvre type m ▶ VT (shake) donner une secousse à; (pull) tirer brusquement ▶ VI (vehicles) cahoter

jerkin ['dʒəːkɪn] N blouson m

jerky ['dʒəːkɪ] ADJ saccadé(e), cahotant(e)

jerry-built ['dʒɛrɪbɪlt] ADJ de mauvaise qualité

jerry can ['dʒɛrɪ-] N bidon m

★**Jersey** ['dʒəːzɪ] N Jersey f

★**jersey** ['dʒəːzɪ] N tricot m; (fabric) jersey m

Jerusalem [dʒə'ruːsləm] N Jérusalem

jest [dʒɛst] N plaisanterie f; **in ~** en plaisantant

jester ['dʒɛstəʳ] N (Hist) plaisantin m

Jesus ['dʒiːzəs] N Jésus; **~ Christ** Jésus-Christ

jet [dʒɛt] N (of gas, liquid) jet m; (Aut) gicleur m; (Aviat) avion m à réaction; jet m

jet-black ['dʒɛt'blæk] ADJ (d'un noir) de jais

jet engine N moteur m à réaction

jet lag N décalage m horaire

jetsam ['dʒɛtsəm] N objets jetés à la mer (et rejetés sur la côte)

jet-setter ['dʒɛtsɛtəʳ] N membre m du or de la jet set

jet-ski ['dʒɛtskiː] VI faire du jet-ski or scooter des mers

jettison ['dʒɛtɪsn] VT jeter par-dessus bord

jetty ['dʒɛtɪ] N jetée f, digue f

Jew [dʒuː] N Juif m

jewel ['dʒuːəl] N bijou m, joyau m; (in watch) rubis m

jewelled, (US) **jeweled** ['dʒuːəld] ADJ orné(e) de pierreries

jeweller, (US) **jeweler** ['dʒuːələʳ] N bijoutier(-ière), joaillier m

jeweller's, **jeweller's shop** N (BRIT) bijouterie f, joaillerie f

jewellery, (US) **jewelry** ['dʒuːəlrɪ] N bijoux mpl

Jewess ['dʒuːɪs] (pej) N Juive f

Jewish ['dʒuːɪʃ] ADJ juif (juive)

JFK N ABBR (US) = **John Fitzgerald Kennedy International Airport**

jib [dʒɪb] N (Naut) foc m; (of crane) flèche f ▶ VI (horse) regimber; **to ~ at doing sth** rechigner à faire qch

jibe [dʒaɪb] N sarcasme m

jiffy ['dʒɪfɪ] N (inf): **in a ~** en un clin d'œil

jig [dʒɪg] N (dance, tune) gigue m

jiggle ['dʒɪgəl] VT (from side to side) remuer

jigsaw ['dʒɪgsɔː] N (also: **jigsaw puzzle**) puzzle m; (tool) scie sauteuse

jihad [dʒɪ'hæd] N djihad m, jihad m

jihadist [dʒɪ'hædɪst] ADJ, N djihadiste mf

jilbab ['dʒɪlbæb] N jilbab m

jilt [dʒɪlt] VT laisser tomber, plaquer

jingle ['dʒɪŋgl] N (advertising jingle) couplet m publicitaire ▶ VI cliqueter, tinter

jingoism ['dʒɪŋgəuɪzəm] N chauvinisme m

jinx [dʒɪŋks] N (inf) (mauvais) sort

jinxed [dʒɪŋkst] ADJ maudit(e)

jitters ['dʒɪtəz] NPL (inf): **to get the ~** avoir la trouille or la frousse

jittery ['dʒɪtərɪ] ADJ (inf) nerveux(-euse); **to be ~** avoir les nerfs en pelote

jiujitsu [dʒuː'dʒɪtsuː] N jiu-jitsu m

jive [dʒaɪv] VI danser le rock, danser le swing ▶ N rock m, swing m

Jnr ADJ (BRIT: = Junior) jr.

★**job** [dʒɔb] N (chore, task) travail m, tâche f; (employment) emploi m, poste m, place f; **a part-time/full-time ~** un emploi à temps partiel/à plein temps; **he's only doing his ~** il fait son boulot; **it's a good ~ that ...** c'est heureux or c'est une chance que ... + sub; **just the ~!** (c'est) juste or exactement ce qu'il faut !

jobber ['dʒɔbəʳ] N (BRIT Stock Exchange) négociant m en titres

jobbing ['dʒɔbɪŋ] ADJ (BRIT: workman) à la tâche, à la journée

job centre ['dʒɔbsɛntəʳ] N (BRIT) ≈ ANPE f, ≈ Agence nationale pour l'emploi

job creation scheme N plan m pour la création d'emplois

job description N description f du poste

jobless ['dʒɔblɪs] ADJ sans travail, au chômage ▶ NPL: **the ~** les sans-emploi m inv, les chômeurs mpl

job lot N lot m (d'articles divers)

job satisfaction N satisfaction professionnelle

job security N sécurité f de l'emploi

job-share ['dʒɔbʃɛəʳ] (BRIT) N (also: **job share**) partage m de poste ▶ VI partager un poste

job specification N caractéristiques fpl du poste

Jock [dʒɔk] N (pej: Scotsman) Écossais m

jockey ['dʒɔkɪ] N jockey m ▶ VI: **to ~ for position** manœuvrer pour être bien placé

jockey box N (US Aut) boîte f à gants, vide-poches m inv

jockstrap ['dʒɔkstræp] N slip m de sport

jocular ['dʒɔkjuləʳ] ADJ jovial(e), enjoué(e); facétieux(-euse)

jodhpurs ['dʒɔdpəz] NPL jodhpur m, jodhpurs mpl

jog [dʒɔg] VT secouer; **to ~ sb's memory** rafraîchir la mémoire de qn ▶ VI (Sport) faire du jogging; **to ~ along** cahoter; trotter

jogger ['dʒɔgəʳ] N jogger mf

jogging ['dʒɔgɪŋ] N jogging m

john [dʒɔn] N (US inf): **the ~** (toilet) les cabinets mpl

★**join** [dʒɔɪn] VT (*put together*) unir, assembler; (*become member of*) s'inscrire à; (*meet*) rejoindre, retrouver; (*queue*) se joindre à; **will you ~ us for dinner?** vous dînerez bien avec nous ?; **I'll ~ you later** je vous rejoindrai plus tard; **to ~ forces (with)** s'associer (à) ▶ VI (*roads, rivers*) se rejoindre, se rencontrer ▶ N raccord m
▶ **join in** VI se mettre de la partie ▶ VT FUS se mêler à
▶ **join up** VI (*meet*) se rejoindre; (*Mil*) s'engager

joiner ['dʒɔɪnəʳ] N (BRIT) menuisier m

joinery ['dʒɔɪnərɪ] N menuiserie f

★**joint** [dʒɔɪnt] N (Tech) jointure f; joint m; (Anat) articulation f, jointure; (BRIT Culin) rôti m; (inf: place) boîte f; (of cannabis) joint ▶ ADJ commun(e); (committee) mixte, paritaire; (winner) ex aequo; **~ responsibility** coresponsabilité f

joint account N compte joint

jointly ['dʒɔɪntlɪ] ADV ensemble, en commun

joint ownership N copropriété f

joint-stock company ['dʒɔɪntstɔk-] N société f par actions

joint venture N entreprise commune

joist [dʒɔɪst] N solive f

★**joke** [dʒəuk] N plaisanterie f; (also: **practical joke**) farce f; **to play a ~ on** jouer un tour à, faire une farce à ▶ VI plaisanter

joker ['dʒəukəʳ] N plaisantin m, blagueur(-euse); (Cards) joker m

joking ['dʒəukɪŋ] N plaisanterie f

jokingly ['dʒəukɪŋlɪ] ADV pour plaisanter; **half-jokingly** en plaisantant à moitié

jollity ['dʒɔlɪtɪ] N réjouissances fpl, gaieté f

jolly ['dʒɔlɪ] ADJ gai(e), enjoué(e); (enjoyable) amusant(e), plaisant(e) ▶ ADV (BRIT inf) rudement, drôlement; **~ good!** formidable ! ▶ VT (BRIT) **to ~ sb along** amadouer qn, convaincre or entraîner qn à force d'encouragements

jolt [dʒəult] N cahot m, secousse f; (shock) choc m ▶ VT cahoter, secouer

Jordan [dʒɔːdən] N (country) Jordanie f; (river) Jourdain m

Jordanian [dʒɔːˈdeɪnɪən] ADJ jordanien(ne) ▶ N Jordanien(ne)

joss stick ['dʒɔs-] N bâton m d'encens

jostle ['dʒɔsl] VT bousculer, pousser ▶ VI jouer des coudes

jot [dʒɔt] N: **not one ~** pas un brin
▶ **jot down** VT inscrire rapidement, noter

jotter ['dʒɔtəʳ] N (BRIT: exercise book) cahier m (de brouillon); (: pad) bloc-notes m

joule [dʒuːl] N joule m

journal ['dʒəːnl] N journal m

journalese [dʒəːnəˈliːz] N (pej) style m journalistique

journalism ['dʒəːnəlɪzəm] N journalisme m

★**journalist** ['dʒəːnəlɪst] N journaliste mf

journalistic [dʒəːnəˈlɪstɪk] ADJ journalistique

★**journey** ['dʒəːnɪ] N voyage m; (distance covered) trajet m; **the ~ takes two hours** le trajet dure deux heures; **a 5-hour ~** un voyage de 5 heures; **how was your ~?** votre voyage s'est bien passé ? ▶ VI voyager

journey ne veut pas dire *journée*.

jovial ['dʒəuvɪəl] ADJ jovial(e)

jowl [dʒaul] N mâchoire f (inférieure); bajoue f

★**joy** [dʒɔɪ] N joie f

joyful ['dʒɔɪful], **joyous** ['dʒɔɪəs] ADJ joyeux(-euse)

joyride ['dʒɔɪraɪd] VI: **to go joyriding** faire une virée dans une voiture volée

joyrider ['dʒɔɪraɪdəʳ] N voleur(-euse) de voiture (qui fait une virée dans le véhicule volé)

joy stick N (Aviat) manche m à balai; (Comput) manche à balai, manette f (de jeu)

JP N ABBR = **Justice of the Peace**

JPEG ['dʒeɪpeɪg] N JPEG m ▶ CPD: **~ image** image f en format JPEG

Jr ABBR = **junior**

JTPA N ABBR (US: = Job Training Partnership Act) programme gouvernemental de formation

jubilant ['dʒuːbɪlnt] ADJ triomphant(e), réjoui(e)

jubilation [dʒuːbɪˈleɪʃən] N jubilation f

jubilee ['dʒuːbɪliː] N jubilé m; **silver ~** (jubilé du) vingt-cinquième anniversaire

Judaism ['dʒuːdeɪɪzəm] N judaïsme m

★**judge** [dʒʌdʒ] N juge m ▶ VT juger; (estimate: weight, size etc) apprécier; (consider) estimer ▶ VI: **judging** or **to ~ by his expression** d'après son expression; **as far as I can ~** autant que je puisse en juger

judge advocate N (Mil) magistrat m militaire

judgment, judgement ['dʒʌdʒmənt] N jugement m; (punishment) châtiment m; **in my ~** à mon avis; **to pass ~ on** (Law) prononcer un jugement (sur)

judgmental, judgemental [dʒʌdʒˈmentəl] ADJ: **to be ~** être catégorique dans ses jugements; **to be ~ about sb** s'ériger en juge à propos de qn

judicial [dʒuːˈdɪʃl] ADJ judiciaire; (fair) impartial(e)

judiciary [dʒuːˈdɪʃɪərɪ] N (pouvoir m) judiciaire m

judicious [dʒuːˈdɪʃəs] ADJ judicieux(-euse)

judo ['dʒuːdəu] N judo m

jug [dʒʌg] N pot m, cruche f

jugged hare ['dʒʌgd-] N (BRIT) civet m de lièvre

juggernaut ['dʒʌgənɔːt] N (BRIT: huge truck) mastodonte m

juggle ['dʒʌgl] VI jongler

juggler ['dʒʌgləʳ] N jongleur m

Jugoslav ['juːgəuˈslɑːv] ADJ, N = **Yugoslav**

jugular ['dʒʌgjuləʳ] ADJ: **~ (vein)** veine f jugulaire

★**juice** [dʒuːs] N jus m; (inf: petrol): **we've run out of ~** c'est la panne sèche

juicy ['dʒuːsɪ] ADJ juteux(-euse)

jukebox ['dʒuːkbɔks] N juke-box m

Jul. ABBR (= July) juil.

★**July** [dʒuːˈlaɪ] N juillet m; **the first of ~** le premier juillet; **(on) the eleventh of ~** le onze juillet; **in the month of ~** au mois de juillet; **at the beginning/end of ~** au début/à la fin (du mois) de juillet; **at the beginning/end of ~** au début/à la fin juillet; **in the middle of ~** au milieu (du mois) de juillet, à la mi-juillet; **during** the month of ~ pendant le mois de juillet; **in ~ of next year** en juillet de l'année prochaine; **each** or **every ~** tous les ans or chaque année en juillet; **~ was wet this year** il a beaucoup plu cette année en juillet

jumble ['dʒʌmbl] N fouillis m ▶ VT (also: **jumble up, jumble together**) mélanger, brouiller

jumble sale N (BRIT) vente f de charité

jumbo ['dʒʌmbəu] ADJ (also: **jumbo jet**) (avion) gros porteur (à réaction); **~ size** format maxi or extra-grand

★**jump** [dʒʌmp] VI sauter, bondir; (with fear etc) sursauter; (increase) monter en flèche ▶ VT sauter, franchir; **to ~ the queue** (BRIT) passer avant son tour ▶ N saut m, bond m; (with fear etc) sursaut m; (fence) obstacle m
  ▶ **jump about** VI sautiller
  ▶ **jump at** VT FUS (fig) sauter sur; **he jumped at the offer** il s'est empressé d'accepter la proposition
  ▶ **jump down** VI sauter (pour descendre)
  ▶ **jump up** VI se lever (d'un bond)

jumped-up ['dʒʌmptʌp] ADJ (BRIT pej) parvenu(e)

★**jumper** ['dʒʌmpəʳ] N (BRIT: pullover) pull-over m; (US: pinafore dress) robe-chasuble f; (Sport) sauteur(-euse)

jump leads, (US) **jumper cables** NPL câbles mpl de démarrage

jump-start ['dʒʌmpstɑːt] VT (car: push) démarrer en poussant; (: with jump leads) démarrer avec des câbles (de démarrage); (fig: project, situation) faire redémarrer promptement

jumpy ['dʒʌmpɪ] ADJ nerveux(-euse), agité(e)

Jun. ABBR = **June; junior**

junction ['dʒʌŋkʃən] N (BRIT: of roads) carrefour m; (: of rails) embranchement m

juncture ['dʒʌŋktʃəʳ] N: **at this ~** à ce moment-là, sur ces entrefaites

★**June** [dʒuːn] N juin m; see also **July**

jungle ['dʒʌŋgl] N jungle f

junior ['dʒuːnɪəʳ] ADJ, N: **he's ~ to me (by two years), he's my ~ (by two years)** il est mon cadet (de deux ans), il est plus jeune que moi (de deux ans); **he's ~ to me** (seniority) il est en dessous de moi (dans la hiérarchie), j'ai plus d'ancienneté que lui

junior executive N cadre moyen

junior high school N (US) ≈ collège m d'enseignement secondaire; see also **high school**

junior minister N (BRIT) ministre m sous tutelle

junior partner N associé(-adjoint) m

junior school N (BRIT) école f primaire

junior sizes NPL (Comm) tailles fpl fillettes/garçonnets

juniper ['dʒuːnɪpəʳ] N: **~ berry** baie f de genièvre

junk [dʒʌŋk] N (rubbish) camelote f; (cheap goods) bric-à-brac m inv; (ship) jonque f ▶ VT (inf) abandonner, mettre au rancart

junk bond N (Comm) obligation hautement spéculative utilisée dans les OPA agressives

junk dealer N brocanteur(-euse)

junket ['dʒʌŋkɪt] N (Culin) lait caillé; (BRIT inf): **to go on a ~, go junketing** voyager aux frais de la princesse

junk food N snacks vite prêts (sans valeur nutritive)

junkie ['dʒʌŋkɪ] N (inf) junkie m, drogué(e)

junk mail N prospectus mpl; (Comput) messages mpl publicitaires

junk room N (US) débarras m

junk shop N (boutique f de) brocanteur m

Junr ABBR = **junior**

junta ['dʒʌntə] N junte f

Jupiter ['dʒuːpɪtəʳ] N (planet) Jupiter f

jurisdiction [dʒuərɪs'dɪkʃən] N juridiction f; **it falls or comes within/outside our ~** cela est/n'est pas de notre compétence or ressort

jurisprudence [dʒuərɪs'pruːdəns] N jurisprudence f

juror ['dʒuərəʳ] N juré m

★**jury** ['dʒuərɪ] N jury m

jury box N banc m des jurés

juryman ['dʒuərɪmən] N (irreg) = **juror**

★**just** [dʒʌst] ADJ juste ▶ ADV: **he's ~ done it/left** il vient de le faire/partir; **~ as I expected** exactement or précisément comme je m'y attendais; **~ right/two o'clock** exactement or juste ce qu'il faut/deux heures; **we were ~ going** nous partions; **I was ~ about to phone** j'allais téléphoner; **~ as he was leaving** au moment or à l'instant précis où il partait; **~ before/enough/here** juste avant/assez/là; **it's ~ me/a mistake** ce n'est que moi/(rien) qu'une erreur; **~ missed/caught** manqué/attrapé de justesse; **~ listen to this!** écoutez un peu ça !; **~ ask someone the way** vous n'avez qu'à demander votre chemin à quelqu'un; **it's ~ as good** c'est (vraiment) aussi bon; **she's ~ as clever as you** elle est tout aussi intelligente que vous; **it's ~ as well that you ...** heureusement que vous ...; **not ~ now** pas tout de suite; **~ a minute!, ~ one moment!** un instant (s'il vous plaît) !

★**justice** ['dʒʌstɪs] N justice f; (US: judge) juge m de la Cour suprême; **Lord Chief J~** (BRIT) premier président de la cour d'appel; **this photo doesn't do you ~** cette photo ne vous avantage pas

Justice of the Peace N juge m de paix

justifiable [dʒʌstɪ'faɪəbl] ADJ justifiable

justifiably [dʒʌstɪ'faɪəblɪ] ADV légitimement, à juste titre

justification [dʒʌstɪfɪ'keɪʃən] N justification f

★**justify** ['dʒʌstɪfaɪ] VT justifier; **to be justified in doing sth** être en droit de faire qch

justly ['dʒʌstlɪ] ADV avec raison, justement

justness ['dʒʌstnɪs] N justesse f

jut [dʒʌt] VI (also: **jut out**) dépasser, faire saillie

jute [dʒuːt] N jute m

juvenile ['dʒuːvənaɪl] ADJ juvénile; (court, books) pour enfants ▶ N adolescent(e)

juvenile delinquency N délinquance f juvénile

juxtapose ['dʒʌkstəpəuz] VT juxtaposer

juxtaposition ['dʒʌkstəpə'zɪʃən] N juxtaposition f

K k

K, k [keɪ] N (letter) K, k m; **K for King** K comme Kléber ▸ ABBR (= one thousand) K; (BRIT: = Knight) titre honorifique

kaftan ['kæftæn] N cafetan m

Kalahari Desert [kælə'hɑːrɪ-] N désert m de Kalahari

kale [keɪl] N chou frisé

kaleidoscope [kə'laɪdəskəup] N kaléidoscope m

kamikaze [kæmɪ'kɑːzɪ] ADJ kamikaze

Kampala [kæm'pɑːlə] N Kampala

kangaroo [kæŋgə'ruː] N kangourou m

Kans. ABBR (US) = **Kansas**

kaput [kə'put] ADJ (inf) kaput

karaoke [kɑːrə'əukɪ] N karaoké m

karate [kə'rɑːtɪ] N karaté m

karma ['kɑːmə] N karma m

Kashmir [kæʃ'mɪəʳ] N Cachemire m

kayak ['kaɪæk] N kayak m

Kazakhstan [kɑːzɑːk'stæn] N Kazakhstan m

kB ABBR (= kilobyte) Ko m

KC N ABBR (BRIT Law: = King's Counsel) titre donné à certains avocats; see also **QC**

kd ABBR (US: = knocked down) en pièces détachées

kebab [kə'bæb] N kebab m

keel [kiːl] N quille f; **on an even ~** (fig) à flot
▸ **keel over** VI (Naut) chavirer, dessaler; (person) tomber dans les pommes

★**keen** [kiːn] ADJ (eager) plein(e) d'enthousiasme; (interest, desire, competition) vif (vive); (eye, intelligence) pénétrant(e); (edge) effilé(e); **to be ~ to do** or **on doing sth** désirer vivement faire qch, tenir beaucoup à faire qch; **to be ~ on sth/sb** aimer beaucoup qch/qn; **I'm not ~ on going** je ne suis pas chaud pour y aller, je n'ai pas très envie d'y aller

keenly ['kiːnlɪ] ADV (enthusiastically) avec enthousiasme; (feel) vivement, profondément; (look) intensément

keenness ['kiːnnɪs] N (eagerness) enthousiasme m; **~ to do** vif désir de faire

★**keep** [kiːp] (pt, pp kept [kɛpt]) VT (retain, preserve) garder; (hold back) retenir; (shop, accounts, promise, diary) tenir; (support) entretenir, assurer la subsistance de; (a promise) tenir; (chickens, bees, pigs etc) élever; **to ~ sb from doing/sth from happening** empêcher qn de faire or que qn (ne) fasse/que qch (n')arrive; **to ~ sb happy/a place tidy** faire que qn soit content/qu'un endroit reste propre; **to ~ sb waiting** faire attendre qn; **to ~ an appointment** ne pas manquer un rendez-vous; **to ~ a record of sth** prendre note de qch; **to ~ sth to o.s.** garder qch pour soi, tenir qch secret; **to ~ sth from sb** cacher qch à qn; **to ~ time** (clock) être à l'heure, ne pas retarder ▸ VI (food) se conserver; (remain: in a certain state or place) rester; **to ~ doing sth** (continue) continuer à faire qch; (repeatedly) ne pas arrêter de faire qch ▸ N (of castle) donjon m; (food etc): **enough for his ~** assez pour (assurer) sa subsistance; **for keeps** (inf) pour de bon, pour toujours
▸ **keep at** VT FUS: **to ~ at it** persévérer
▸ **keep away** VT: **to ~ sth/sb away from sb** tenir qch/qn éloigné de qn ▸ VI: **to ~ away (from)** ne pas s'approcher (de)
▸ **keep back** VT (crowds, tears, money) retenir; (conceal: information): **to ~ sth back from sb** cacher qch à qn ▸ VI rester en arrière
▸ **keep down** VT (control: prices, spending) empêcher d'augmenter, limiter; (retain: food) garder ▸ VI (person) rester assis(e); rester par terre
▸ **keep in** VT (invalid, child) garder à la maison; (Scol) consigner ▸ VI (inf): **to ~ in with sb** rester en bons termes avec qn
▸ **keep off** VT (dog, person) éloigner; **~ your hands off!** pas touche ! (inf) ▸ VT FUS: **"~ off the grass"** « pelouse interdite » ▸ VI ne pas s'approcher; **if the rain keeps off** s'il ne pleut pas
▸ **keep on** VI continuer; **to ~ on doing** continuer à faire; **don't ~ on about it!** arrête (d'en parler) !
▸ **keep out** VT empêcher d'entrer ▸ VI (stay out) rester en dehors; **"~ out"** « défense d'entrer »
▸ **keep to** VT FUS (plan, speed limit) respecter; (path, road) rester sur
▸ **keep up** VI (fig: in comprehension) suivre; **to ~ up with sb** (in work etc) se maintenir au même niveau que qn; (in race etc) aller aussi vite que qn ▸ VT continuer, maintenir

keeper ['kiːpəʳ] N gardien(ne)

keep-fit [kiːp'fɪt] N gymnastique f (d'entretien)

keeping ['kiːpɪŋ] N (care) garde f; **in ~ with** en harmonie avec

keeps [kiːps] N: **for ~** (inf) pour de bon, pour toujours

keepsake ['kiːpseɪk] N souvenir m

keg [kɛg] N barrique f, tonnelet m

Ken. ABBR (US) = **Kentucky**

kennel ['kɛnl] N niche f ▪ **kennels** NPL (for boarding) chenil m

Kenya ['kɛnjə] N Kenya m

Kenyan ['kɛnjən] ADJ kényan(ne) ▶ N Kényan(ne)

kept [kɛpt] PT, PP of **keep**

kerb [kə:b] N (BRIT) bordure f du trottoir

kerb crawler [-krɔːləʳ] N *personne qui accoste les prostitué(e)s en voiture*

kerbside ['kə:bsaɪd] N (bordure f du) trottoir m

kernel ['kə:nl] N amande f; (fig) noyau m

kerosene ['kɛrəsi:n] N kérosène m

kestrel ['kɛstrəl] N faucon m crécerelle

ketchup ['kɛtʃəp] N ketchup m

kettle ['kɛtl] N bouilloire f

kettling ['kɛtəlɪŋ] N ≈ tactique f de l'encerclement, *tactique policière consistant à encercler des manifestants pour les confiner dans un lieu de façon prolongée*

★**key** [ki:] N (gen, Mus) clé f; (of piano, typewriter) touche f; (on map) légende f; **can I have my ~?** je peux avoir ma clé ? ▶ ADJ (factor, role, area) clé inv; **a ~ issue** un problème fondamental ▶ CPD (vital: position, industry) clé ▶ VT (word) taper
  ▶ **key in** VT (text) rentrer, taper

keyboard ['ki:bɔ:d] N clavier m ▶ VT (text) saisir

keyboarder ['ki:bɔ:dəʳ] N claviste mf

keyed up [ki:d-] ADJ: **to be (all)** ~ être surexcité(e)

keyhole ['ki:həul] N trou m de la serrure

keyhole surgery N *chirurgie très minutieuse où l'incision est minimale*

keynote ['ki:nəut] N (Mus) tonique f; (fig) note dominante

keypad ['ki:pæd] N pavé m numérique; (of smartphone) clavier m

keyring ['ki:rɪŋ] N porte-clés m

keystroke ['ki:strəuk] N frappe f

kg ABBR (= kilogram) K

KGB N ABBR KGB m

khaki ['kɑːkɪ] ADJ, N kaki m

kibbutz [kɪ'buts] N kibboutz m

★**kick** [kɪk] VT donner un coup de pied à; **to ~ the habit** (inf) arrêter ▶ VI (horse) ruer ▶ N coup m de pied; (of rifle) recul m; (inf: thrill): **he does it for kicks** il le fait parce que ça l'excite, il le fait pour le plaisir
  ▶ **kick around** VI (inf) traîner
  ▶ **kick in** VI (start working) se mettre en marche
  ▶ **kick off** VI (Sport) donner le coup d'envoi
  ▶ **kick out** VI (inf) virer (inf); **to ~ sb out of sth** virer qn de qch
  ▶ **kick up** VT: **to ~ up a fuss (about sth)** faire du foin (à propos de qch); **to ~ up a rumpus** faire du scandale

kickback ['kɪkbæk] N (bribe) pot m de vin

kick-off ['kɪkɔf] N (Sport) coup m d'envoi

kick-start ['kɪkstɑːt] N (also: **kick-starter**) lanceur m au pied

★**kid** [kɪd] N (inf: child) gamin(e), gosse mf; (animal, leather) chevreau m ▶ VI (inf) plaisanter, blaguer

kid gloves NPL: **to treat sb with** ~ traiter qn avec ménagement

kidnap ['kɪdnæp] VT enlever, kidnapper

kidnapper ['kɪdnæpəʳ] N ravisseur(-euse)

kidnapping ['kɪdnæpɪŋ] N enlèvement m

kidney ['kɪdnɪ] N (Anat) rein m; (Culin) rognon m

kidney bean N haricot m rouge

kidney machine N (Med) rein artificiel

Kilimanjaro [kɪlɪmən'dʒɑːrəu] N: **Mount ~** Kilimandjaro m

★**kill** [kɪl] VT tuer; (fig) faire échouer; détruire; supprimer; **to ~ time** tuer le temps ▶ N mise f à mort
  ▶ **kill off** VT exterminer; (fig) éliminer

★**killer** ['kɪləʳ] N tueur(-euse); (murderer) meurtrier(-ière)

killer instinct N combativité f; **to have the ~** avoir un tempérament de battant

killing ['kɪlɪŋ] N meurtre m; (of group of people) tuerie f, massacre m; (inf): **to make a ~** se remplir les poches, réussir un beau coup ▶ ADJ (inf) tordant(e)

killjoy ['kɪldʒɔɪ] N rabat-joie m inv

kiln [kɪln] N four m

★**kilo** ['ki:ləu] N kilo m

kilobyte ['ki:ləubaɪt] N (Comput) kilo-octet m

kilogram, kilogramme ['kɪləugræm] N kilogramme m

kilometre, (US) **kilometer** ['kɪləmi:təʳ] N kilomètre m

> When saying how far away something is, the distance is preceded by à.
> *It's ten kilometres from here.* **C'est à dix kilomètres d'ici**.

kilowatt ['kɪləuwɔt] N kilowatt m

kilt [kɪlt] N kilt m

kilter ['kɪltəʳ] N: **out of ~** déréglé(e), détraqué(e)

kimono [kɪ'məunəu] N kimono m

kin [kɪn] N see **next-of-kin**; **kith**

★**kind** [kaɪnd] ADJ gentil(le), aimable; **would you be ~ enough to …?, would you be so ~ as to …?** auriez-vous la gentillesse or l'obligeance de … ?; **it's very ~ of you (to do)** c'est très aimable à vous (de faire) ▶ N sorte f, espèce f; (species) genre m; **to be two of a ~** se ressembler; **in ~** (Comm) en nature; (fig) **to repay sb in ~** rendre la pareille à qn; **~ of** (inf: rather) plutôt; **a ~ of** une sorte de; **what ~ of …?** quelle sorte de … ?

kindergarten ['kɪndəgɑːtn] N jardin m d'enfants

kind-hearted [kaɪnd'hɑːtɪd] ADJ bon(ne)

Kindle® ['kɪndl] N Kindle® m

kindle ['kɪndl] VT allumer, enflammer

kindling ['kɪndlɪŋ] N petit bois

kindly ['kaɪndlɪ] ADJ bienveillant(e), plein(e) de gentillesse ▶ ADV avec bonté; **will you ~ …** auriez-vous la bonté or l'obligeance de …; **he didn't take it ~** il l'a mal pris

kindness ['kaɪndnɪs] N (quality) bonté f, gentillesse f

kindred ['kɪndrɪd] ADJ apparenté(e); **~ spirit** âme f sœur

kinetic [kɪ'nɛtɪk] ADJ cinétique

★**king** [kɪŋ] N roi m

kingdom ['kɪŋdəm] N royaume m

kingfisher ['kɪŋfɪʃəʳ] N martin-pêcheur m

kingpin ['kɪŋpɪn] N (Tech) pivot m; (fig) cheville ouvrière

king-size ['kɪŋsaɪz], **king-sized** ['kɪŋsaɪzd] ADJ (cigarette) (format) extra-long (longue)

king-size bed, king-sized bed N grand lit (de 1,95 m de large)

kink [kɪŋk] N (of rope) entortillement m; (in hair) ondulation f; (inf: fig) aberration f

kinky ['kɪŋkɪ] ADJ (fig) excentrique; (pej) aux goûts spéciaux

kinship ['kɪnʃɪp] N parenté f

kinsman ['kɪnzmən] N (irreg) parent m

kinswoman ['kɪnzwumən] N (irreg) parente f

kiosk ['kiːɔsk] N kiosque m; (BRIT: also: **telephone kiosk**) cabine f (téléphonique); (also: **newspaper kiosk**) kiosque à journaux

kipper ['kɪpəʳ] N hareng fumé et salé

Kirghizia [kəːˈgɪzɪə] N Kirghizistan m

Kiribati [kɪrɪˈbætɪ] N Kiribati fpl

★**kiss** [kɪs] N baiser m ▶ VT embrasser; **to ~ (each other)** s'embrasser; **to ~ sb goodbye** dire au revoir à qn en l'embrassant

kissagram ['kɪsəgræm] N baiser envoyé à l'occasion d'une célébration par l'intermédiaire d'une personne employée à cet effet

kiss of life N (BRIT) bouche à bouche m

kit [kɪt] N équipement m, matériel m; (set of tools etc) trousse f; (for assembly) kit m; **tool ~** nécessaire m à outils
  ▶ **kit out** VT (BRIT) équiper

kitbag ['kɪtbæg] N sac m de voyage or de marin

★**kitchen** ['kɪtʃɪn] N cuisine f

kitchen garden N jardin m potager

kitchen sink N évier m

kitchen unit N (BRIT) élément m de cuisine

kitchenware ['kɪtʃɪnwɛəʳ] N vaisselle f; ustensiles mpl de cuisine

kite [kaɪt] N (toy) cerf-volant m; (Zool) milan m

kith [kɪθ] N: **~ and kin** parents et amis mpl

kitten ['kɪtn] N petit chat, chaton m

kitty ['kɪtɪ] N (money) cagnotte f

kiwi ['kiːwiː] N (also: **kiwi fruit**) kiwi m

KKK N ABBR (US) = **Ku Klux Klan**

Kleenex® ['kliːnɛks] N Kleenex® m

kleptomaniac [klɛptəuˈmeɪnɪæk] N kleptomane mf

km ABBR (= kilometre) km

km/h ABBR (= kilometres per hour) km/h

knack [næk] N: **to have the ~ (of doing)** avoir le coup (pour faire); **there's a ~** il y a un coup à prendre or une combine

knackered ['nækəd] ADJ (inf) crevé(e), nase

knapsack ['næpsæk] N musette f

knave [neɪv] N (Cards) valet m

knead [niːd] VT pétrir

★**knee** [niː] N genou m

kneecap ['niːkæp] N rotule f ▶ VT tirer un coup de feu dans la rotule de

knee-deep ['niːˈdiːp] ADJ: **the water was ~** l'eau arrivait aux genoux

★**kneel** [niːl] (pt, pp **knelt** [nɛlt]) VI (also: **kneel down**) s'agenouiller

kneepad ['niːpæd] N genouillère f

knell [nɛl] N glas m

knelt [nɛlt] PT, PP of **kneel**

knew [njuː] PT of **know**

★**knickers** ['nɪkəz] NPL (BRIT) culotte f (de femme)

knick-knack ['nɪknæk] N colifichet m

★**knife** [naɪf] (pl **knives** [naɪvz]) N couteau m; **~, fork and spoon** couvert m ▶ VT poignarder, frapper d'un coup de couteau

knife-edge ['naɪfɛdʒ] N: **to be on a ~** être sur le fil du rasoir

knifepoint ['naɪfpɔɪnt] N: **at ~** (rape, rob) sous la menace d'un couteau; **to hold sb at ~** tenir qn en respect avec son couteau

knight [naɪt] N chevalier m; (Chess) cavalier m

knighthood ['naɪthud] N chevalerie f; (title): **to get a ~** être fait chevalier

knit [nɪt] VT tricoter; (fig): **to ~ together** unir; **to ~ one's brows** froncer les sourcils ▶ VI tricoter; (broken bones) se ressouder

knitted ['nɪtɪd] ADJ en tricot

knitting ['nɪtɪŋ] N tricot m

knitting machine N machine f à tricoter

knitting needle N aiguille f à tricoter

knitting pattern N modèle m (pour tricot)

knitwear ['nɪtwɛəʳ] N tricots mpl, lainages mpl

knives [naɪvz] NPL of **knife**

knob [nɔb] N bouton m; (BRIT): **a ~ of butter** une noix de beurre

knobbly ['nɔblɪ], (US) **knobby** ['nɔbɪ] ADJ (wood, surface) noueux(-euse); (knees) noueux

★**knock** [nɔk] VT frapper; (bump into) heurter; (force: nail etc): **to ~ a nail into** enfoncer un clou dans; (inf, fig) dénigrer; (make: hole etc): **to ~ a hole in** faire un trou dans, trouer ▶ VI (engine) cogner; (at door etc): **to ~ at/on** frapper à/sur; **he knocked at the door** il frappa à la porte ▶ N coup m
  ▶ **knock down** VT renverser; (price) réduire
  ▶ **knock off** VI (inf: finish) s'arrêter (de travailler) ▶ VT (vase, object) faire tomber; (inf: steal) piquer; (fig: from price etc): **to ~ off £10** faire une remise de 10 livres
  ▶ **knock out** VT assommer; (Boxing) mettre k.-o.; (in competition) éliminer
  ▶ **knock over** VT (object) faire tomber; (pedestrian) renverser

knockdown ['nɔkdaun] ADJ (price) sacrifié(e)

knocker ['nɔkəʳ] N (on door) heurtoir m

knocking ['nɔkɪŋ] N coups mpl

knock-kneed [nɔkˈniːd] ADJ aux genoux cagneux

knockout ['nɔkaut] N (Boxing) knock-out m, K.-O. m; **~ competition** (BRIT) compétition f avec épreuves éliminatoires

knock-up ['nɔkʌp] N (Tennis): **to have a ~** faire des balles

knot [nɔt] N (gen) nœud m; **to tie a ~** faire un nœud ▶ VT nouer

knotty ['nɔtɪ] ADJ (fig) épineux(-euse)

★**know** [nəu] (pt **knew** [njuː], pp **known** [nəun]) VT savoir; (person, place) connaître; **to ~ that** savoir que; **to ~ how to do** savoir faire; **to ~ how to swim** savoir nager; **to get to ~ sth** (fact) apprendre qch; (place) apprendre à connaître qch; **I don't ~ him** je ne le connais pas; **do you ~ where I can …?** savez-vous où je peux … ?; **to ~ right from wrong** savoir distinguer le bon du mauvais ▶ VI savoir; **I don't ~ ~**

k

699

je ne sais pas; **as far as I ~ ...** à ma connaissance ..., autant que je sache ...
▶ **know about** VT FUS (*news, event*) être au courant de; (*subject*) s'y connaître en; **to ~ a lot about sth** bien s'y connaître en qch; **I don't ~ much about computers** je ne m'y connais pas bien en informatique
▶ **know of** VT FUS (*have heard of*) connaître; **no, not that I ~ of** non, pas autant que je sache

know-all ['nəʊ:l] N (*BRIT pej*) je-sais-tout *mf*

know-how ['nəʊhau] N savoir-faire *m*, technique *f*, compétence *f*

knowing ['nəʊɪŋ] ADJ (*look etc*) entendu(e)

knowingly ['nəʊɪŋlɪ] ADV (*on purpose*) sciemment; (*smile, look*) d'un air entendu

know-it-all ['nəʊɪtɔ:l] N (*US*) = **know-all**

★**knowledge** ['nɒlɪdʒ] N connaissance *f*; (*learning*) connaissances, savoir *m*; **to have no ~ of** ignorer; **not to my ~** pas à ma connaissance; **without my ~** à mon insu; **to have a working ~ of French** se débrouiller en français; **it is common ~ that ...** chacun sait que ...; **it has come to my ~ that ...** j'ai appris que ...

knowledgeable ['nɒlɪdʒəbl] ADJ bien informé(e)

known [nəun] PP *of* **know** ▶ ADJ (*thief, facts*) notoire; (*expert*) célèbre

knuckle ['nʌkl] N articulation *f* (des phalanges), jointure *f*
▶ **knuckle down** VI (*inf*) s'y mettre
▶ **knuckle under** VI (*inf*) céder

knuckleduster ['nʌkldʌstə'] N coup-de-poing américain

KO ABBR = **knock out** ▶ N K.-O. *m* ▶ VT mettre K.-O.

koala [kəu'ɑ:lə] N (*also*: **koala bear**) koala *m*

kook [ku:k] N (*US inf*) loufoque *mf*

Koran [kɔ'rɑ:n] N Coran *m*

Korea [kə'rɪə] N Corée *f*; **North/South ~** Corée du Nord/Sud

Korean [kə'rɪən] ADJ coréen(ne) ▶ N Coréen(ne)

kosher ['kəʊʃə'] ADJ kascher *inv*

Kosovar, Kosovan ['kɔsəvɑ:', 'kɔsəvæn] ADJ kosovar(e)

Kosovo ['kɔsɔvəu] N Kosovo *m*

kowtow ['kau'tau] VI: **to ~ to sb** s'aplatir devant qn

Kremlin ['kremlɪn] N: **the ~** le Kremlin

KS ABBR (*US*) = **Kansas**

Kt ABBR (*BRIT*: = *Knight*) titre honorifique

Kuala Lumpur ['kwɑ:lə'lumpuə'] N Kuala Lumpur

kudos ['kju:dɔs] N gloire *f*, lauriers *mpl*

Kurd [kə:d] N Kurde *mf*

Kurdish ['kə:dɪʃ] ADJ kurde ▶ N (*Ling*) kurde *m*

Kuwait [ku'weɪt] N Koweït *m*

Kuwaiti [ku'weɪtɪ] ADJ koweïtien(ne) ▶ N Koweïtien(ne)

kW ABBR (= *kilowatt*) kW

KY, Ky. ABBR (*US*) = **Kentucky**

Kyrgyzstan ['kɪəgɪzstɑ:n] N Kirghizistan *m*

Ll

L¹, l [ɛl] N (letter) L, l m; **L for Lucy**, (US) **L for Love** L comme Louis

L² ABBR (= lake, large) L; (BRIT Aut: = learner) signale un conducteur débutant; (= left) g

l. ABBR (= litre) l

LA N ABBR (US) = **Los Angeles** ▶ ABBR (US) = **Louisiana**

La. ABBR (US) = **Louisiana**

lab [læb] N ABBR (= laboratory) labo m

Lab. ABBR (CANADA) = **Labrador**

★**label** ['leɪbl] N étiquette f; (brand: of record) marque f ▶ VT étiqueter; **to ~ sb a ...** qualifier qn de ...

labor etc ['leɪbər] N (US) = **labour** etc

★**laboratory** [lə'bɔrətəri] N laboratoire m

Labor Day N (US, CANADA) fête f du travail (le premier lundi de septembre)

Aux États-Unis et au Canada, le **Labor Day** est fixé au premier lundi de septembre. Institué par le Congrès en 1894 après avoir été réclamé par les mouvements ouvriers pendant douze ans, il a perdu une grande partie de son caractère politique pour devenir un jour férié assez ordinaire et l'occasion de partir en long week-end avant la rentrée des classes.

laborious [lə'bɔːrɪəs] ADJ laborieux(-euse)

labor union N (US) syndicat m

Labour ['leɪbər] N (BRIT Pol: also: **the Labour Party**) le parti travailliste, les travaillistes mpl

labour, (US) **labor** ['leɪbər] N (work) travail m; (workforce) main-d'œuvre f; (Med) travail, accouchement m; **in ~** (Med) en travail ▶ VI: **to ~ (at)** travailler dur (à), peiner (sur) ▶ VT: **to ~ a point** insister sur un point

labour camp, (US) **labor camp** N camp m de travaux forcés

labour cost, (US) **labor cost** N coût m de la main-d'œuvre; coût de la façon

laboured, (US) **labored** ['leɪbəd] ADJ lourd(e), laborieux(-euse); (breathing) difficile, pénible; (style) lourd, embarrassé(e)

labourer, (US) **laborer** ['leɪbərər] N manœuvre m; **farm ~** ouvrier m agricole

labour force, (US) **labor force** N main-d'œuvre f

labour-intensive, (US) **labor-intensive** [leɪbərɪn'tensɪv] ADJ intensif(-ive) en main-d'œuvre

labour market, (US) **labor market** N marché m du travail

labour pains, (US) **labor pains** NPL douleurs fpl de l'accouchement

labour relations, (US) **labor relations** NPL relations fpl dans l'entreprise

labour-saving, (US) **labor-saving** ['leɪbəseɪvɪŋ] ADJ qui simplifie le travail

labour unrest, (US) **labor unrest** N agitation sociale

labyrinth ['læbɪrɪnθ] N labyrinthe m, dédale m

lace [leɪs] N dentelle f; (of shoe etc) lacet m ▶ VT (shoe: also: **lace up**) lacer; (drink) arroser, corser

lacemaking ['leɪsmeɪkɪŋ] N fabrication f de dentelle

laceration [læsə'reɪʃən] N lacération f

lace-up ['leɪsʌp] ADJ (shoes etc) à lacets

★**lack** [læk] N manque m; **through** or **for ~ of** faute de, par manque de ▶ VT manquer de ▶ VI: **to be lacking** manquer, faire défaut; **to be lacking in** manquer de

lackadaisical [lækə'deɪzɪkl] ADJ nonchalant(e), indolent(e)

lackey ['lækɪ] N (also fig) laquais m

lacklustre ['læklʌstər] ADJ terne

laconic [lə'kɒnɪk] ADJ laconique

lacquer ['lækər] N laque f

lacquered ['lækəd] ADJ laqué(e)

lacrosse [lə'krɒs] N la crosse f, jeu m de la crosse

lacy ['leɪsɪ] ADJ (made of lace) en dentelle; (like lace) comme de la dentelle, qui ressemble à de la dentelle

lad [læd] N garçon m, gars m; (BRIT: in stable etc) lad m

ladder ['lædər] N échelle f; (BRIT: in tights) maille filée f ▶ VT, VI (BRIT: tights) filer

laden ['leɪdn] ADJ: **~ (with)** chargé(e) (de); **fully ~** (truck, ship) en pleine charge

ladle ['leɪdl] N louche f

★**lady** ['leɪdɪ] N dame f; **"ladies and gentlemen ..."** « Mesdames (et) Messieurs ... »; **young ~** jeune fille f; (married) jeune femme f; **L~ Smith** lady Smith; **the ladies' (room)** les toilettes fpl des dames; **a ~ doctor** une doctoresse, une femme médecin

ladybird ['leɪdɪbəːd], (US) **ladybug** ['leɪdɪbʌg] N coccinelle f

lady-in-waiting ['leɪdɪɪn'weɪtɪŋ] N dame f d'honneur

lady-killer ['leɪdɪkɪlər] N don Juan m

ladylike ['leɪdɪlaɪk] ADJ distingué(e)

ladyship ['leɪdɪʃɪp] N: **your L~** Madame la comtesse (or la baronne etc)

lag [læg] N retard m ▸ VI (also: **lag behind**) rester en arrière, traîner; (: fig) rester à la traîne ▸ VT (pipes) calorifuger

lager ['lɑːɡər] N bière blonde

lager lout N (BRIT pej) jeune voyou m (porté sur la boisson)

lagging ['læɡɪŋ] N enveloppe isolante, calorifuge m

lagoon [lə'ɡuːn] N lagune f

Lagos ['leɪɡɔs] N Lagos

laid [leɪd] PT, PP of **lay**

laid back ADJ (inf) relaxe, décontracté(e)

laid up ADJ alité(e)

lain [leɪn] PP of **lie**

lair [lɛər] N tanière f, gîte m

laissez-faire [leseɪ'fɛər] N libéralisme m

laity ['leɪətɪ] N laïques mpl

★**lake** [leɪk] N lac m

Lake District N: **the ~** (BRIT) la région des lacs

lamb [læm] N agneau m

lambast [læm'bæst], (US) **lambaste** [læm'beɪst] VT étriller

lamb chop N côtelette f d'agneau

lambing ['læmɪŋ] N agnelage m

lambskin ['læmskɪn] N (peau f d')agneau m

lambswool ['læmzwul] N laine f d'agneau

lame [leɪm] ADJ (also fig) boiteux(-euse); **~ duck** (fig) canard boiteux

lamely ['leɪmlɪ] ADV (fig) sans conviction

lament [lə'ment] N lamentation f ▸ VT pleurer, se lamenter sur

lamentable ['læməntəbl] ADJ déplorable, lamentable

laminated ['læmɪneɪtɪd] ADJ laminé(e); (windscreen) (en verre) feuilleté

laminator ['læmɪneɪtər] N plastifieuse f

lamp [læmp] N lampe f

lamplight ['læmplaɪt] N: **by ~** à la lumière de la (or d'une) lampe

lampoon [læm'puːn] N pamphlet m

lamppost ['læmppəust] N (BRIT) réverbère m

lampshade ['læmpʃeɪd] N abat-jour m inv

lance [lɑːns] N lance f ▸ VT (Med) inciser

lance corporal N (BRIT) (soldat m de) première classe m

lancet ['lɑːnsɪt] N (Med) bistouri m

Lancs [læŋks] ABBR (BRIT) = **Lancashire**

★**land** [lænd] N (as opposed to sea) terre f (ferme); (country) pays m; (soil) terre; (piece of land) terrain m; (estate) terre(s), domaine(s) m(pl); **to go/travel by ~** se déplacer par voie de terre; **to own ~** être propriétaire foncier ▸ VI (from ship) débarquer; (Aviat) atterrir; (fig: fall) (re-)tomber; **to ~ on one's feet** (also fig) retomber sur ses pieds ▸ VT (passengers, goods) débarquer; (obtain) décrocher; **to ~ sb with sth** (inf) coller qch à qn ▸ **land up** VI atterrir, (finir par) se retrouver

landed gentry ['lændɪd-] N (BRIT) propriétaires terriens or fonciers

landfill site ['lændfɪl-] N centre m d'enfouissement des déchets

landing ['lændɪŋ] N (from ship) débarquement m; (Aviat) atterrissage m; (of staircase) palier m

landing card N carte f de débarquement

landing craft N péniche f de débarquement

landing gear N train m d'atterrissage

landing stage N (BRIT) débarcadère m, embarcadère m

landing strip N piste f d'atterrissage

landlady ['lændleɪdɪ] N propriétaire f, logeuse f; (of pub) patronne f

landline ['lændlaɪn] N ligne f fixe

landlocked ['lændlɔkt] ADJ entouré(e) de terre(s), sans accès à la mer

landlord ['lændlɔːd] N propriétaire m, logeur m; (of pub etc) patron m

landlubber ['lændlʌbər] N terrien(ne)

landmark ['lændmɑːk] N (point m de) repère m; **to be a ~** (fig) faire date or époque

landmine ['lændmaɪn] N mine f terrestre

landowner ['lændəunər] N propriétaire foncier or terrien

★**landscape** ['lænskeɪp] N paysage m

landscape architect, landscape gardener N paysagiste mf

landscaped ['lændskeɪpt] ADJ paysagé(e), paysager inv

landscape painting N (Art) paysage m

landslide ['lændslaɪd] N (Geo) glissement m (de terrain); (fig: Pol) raz-de-marée (électoral)

★**lane** [leɪn] N (in country) chemin m; (in town) ruelle f; (Aut: of road) voie f; (: line of traffic) file f; (in race) couloir m; **shipping ~** route f maritime or de navigation

★**language** ['læŋɡwɪdʒ] N langue f; (way one speaks) langage m; **what languages do you speak?** quelles langues parlez-vous ?; **bad ~** grossièretés fpl, langage grossier

> Use **langue** to refer to a language such as French or English; use **langage** for a way of communicating: everyday language **le langage courant**.

language laboratory N laboratoire m de langues

language school N école f de langue

languid ['læŋɡwɪd] ADJ languissant(e), langoureux(-euse)

languish ['læŋɡwɪʃ] VI languir

lank [læŋk] ADJ (hair) raide et terne

lanky ['læŋkɪ] ADJ grand(e) et maigre, efflanqué(e)

lanolin, lanoline ['lænəlɪn] N lanoline f

lantern ['læntn] N lanterne f

Laos [laus] N Laos m

★**lap** [læp] N (of track) tour m (de piste); (of body): **in** or **on one's ~** sur les genoux ▸ VT (also: **lap up**) laper ▸ VI (waves) clapoter ▸ **lap up** VT (fig) boire comme du petit-lait, se gargariser de; (: lies etc) gober

La Paz [læ'pæz] N La Paz

lap dancing N strip-tease où la danseuse s'asseoit sur les genoux des clients

lapdog ['læpdɔɡ] N chien m d'appartement

lapel [lə'pɛl] N revers m

Lapland ['læplænd] N Laponie f

lapse [læps] N défaillance f; (in behaviour) écart m (de conduite); **~ of time** laps m de temps, intervalle m; **a ~ of memory** un trou de mémoire ▸ vi (Law) cesser d'être en vigueur; (contract) expirer; (pass) être périmé; (subscription) prendre fin; **to ~ into bad habits** prendre de mauvaises habitudes

★**laptop** ['læptɒp], **laptop computer** N (ordinateur m) portable m

larceny ['lɑːsənɪ] N vol m

larch [lɑːtʃ] N mélèze m

lard [lɑːd] N saindoux m

larder ['lɑːdər] N garde-manger m inv

★**large** [lɑːdʒ] ADJ grand(e); (person, animal) gros (grosse); **to make larger** agrandir; **a ~ number of people** beaucoup de gens; **by and ~** en général; **on a ~ scale** sur une grande échelle; **at ~** (free) en liberté; (generally) en général; pour la plupart; see also **by**

Le mot anglais **large** ne veut pas dire large.

★**largely** ['lɑːdʒlɪ] ADV en grande partie; (principally) surtout

large-scale ['lɑːdʒ'skeɪl] ADJ (map, drawing etc) à grande échelle; (fig) important(e)

largesse, (US) **largess** [lɑː'ʒɛs] N largesses fpl

lark [lɑːk] N (bird) alouette f; (joke) blague f, farce f ▸ **lark about** vi faire l'idiot, rigoler

larrikin ['lærɪkɪn] N (AUSTRALIA, NEW ZEALAND inf) fripon m (inf)

larva ['lɑːvə] (pl **larvae** [-iː]) N larve f

laryngitis [lærɪn'dʒaɪtɪs] N laryngite f

larynx ['lærɪŋks] N larynx m

lasagne [lə'zænjə] N lasagne f

lascivious [lə'sɪvɪəs] ADJ lascif(-ive)

laser ['leɪzər] N laser m

laser beam N rayon m laser

laser printer N imprimante f laser

lash [læʃ] N coup m de fouet; (also: **eyelash**) cil m ▸ vt fouetter; (tie) attacher
▸ **lash down** vt attacher, amarrer, arrimer ▸ vi (rain) tomber avec violence
▸ **lash out** vi: **to ~ out (at** or **against sb/sth)** attaquer violemment (qn/qch); **to ~ out (on sth)** (inf: spend) se fendre (de qch)

lashing ['læʃɪŋ] N: **lashings of** (BRIT old: cream etc) des masses de

lass [læs] N (BRIT) (jeune) fille f

lasso [læ'suː] N lasso m ▸ vt prendre au lasso

★**last** [lɑːst] ADJ dernier(-ière); **~ week** la semaine dernière; **~ night** (evening) hier soir; (night) la nuit dernière; **the ~ time** la dernière fois; **the ~ but one** adj l'avant-dernier(-ière) (before noun) ▸ ADV en dernier; (most recently) la dernière fois; (finally) finalement ▸ vi durer; **it lasts (for) 2 hours** ça dure 2 heures ▸ N: **at ~** enfin ▸ PRON: **the ~** (the last one) le dernier (la dernière); (the last ones) les derniers; **the ~ but one** l'avant-dernier(-ière)

last-ditch ['lɑːst'dɪtʃ] ADJ ultime, désespéré(e)

lasting ['lɑːstɪŋ] ADJ durable

lastly ['lɑːstlɪ] ADV en dernier lieu, pour finir

last-minute ['lɑːstmɪnɪt] ADJ de dernière minute

latch [lætʃ] N loquet m
▸ **latch onto** vt FUS (cling to: person, group) s'accrocher à; (: idea) se mettre en tête

latchkey ['lætʃkiː] N clé f (de la porte d'entrée)

★**late** [leɪt] ADJ (not on time) en retard; (far on in day etc) tardif(-ive); (: edition, delivery) dernier(-ière); (recent) récent(e), dernier; (former) ancien(ne); (dead) défunt(e); **to be ~** avoir du retard; **to be 10 minutes ~** avoir 10 minutes de retard; **sorry I'm ~** désolé d'être en retard; **it's too ~** il est trop tard; **in ~ May** vers la fin (du mois) de mai, fin mai; **the ~ Mr X** feu M. X ▸ ADV tard; (behind time, schedule) en retard; **to work ~** travailler tard; **~ in life** sur le tard, à un âge avancé ▸ N: **of ~** (lately) dernièrement

latecomer ['leɪtkʌmər] N retardataire mf

lately ['leɪtlɪ] ADV récemment

lateness ['leɪtnɪs] N (of person) retard m; (of event) heure tardive

latent ['leɪtnt] ADJ latent(e); **~ defect** vice caché

★**later** ['leɪtər] ADJ (date etc) ultérieur(e); (version etc) plus récent(e) ▸ ADV plus tard; **~ on today** plus tard dans la journée

lateral ['lætərl] ADJ latéral(e)

★**latest** ['leɪtɪst] ADJ tout(e) dernier(-ière); **the ~ news** les dernières nouvelles; **at the ~** au plus tard

latex ['leɪtɛks] N latex m

lath [læθ] (pl **laths** [læðz]) N latte f

lathe [leɪð] N tour m

lather ['lɑːðər] N mousse f (de savon) ▸ vt savonner ▸ vi mousser

★**Latin** ['lætɪn] N latin m ▸ ADJ latin(e)

Latin America N Amérique latine

Latin American ADJ latino-américain(e), d'Amérique latine ▸ N Latino-Américain(e)

latitude ['lætɪtjuːd] N (also fig) latitude f

latrine [lə'triːn] N latrines fpl

latte ['lɑːteɪ] N crème m

latter ['lætər] ADJ deuxième, dernier(-ière) ▸ N: **the ~** ce dernier, celui-ci

latterly ['lætəlɪ] ADV dernièrement, récemment

lattice ['lætɪs] N treillis m; treillage m

lattice window N fenêtre treillissée, fenêtre à croisillons

Latvia ['lætvɪə] N Lettonie f

Latvian ['lætvɪən] ADJ letton(ne) ▸ N Letton(ne); (Ling) letton m

laud [lɔːd] vt louer

laudable ['lɔːdəbl] ADJ louable

laudatory ['lɔːdətrɪ] ADJ élogieux(-euse)

★**laugh** [lɑːf] N rire m; **(to do sth) for a ~** (faire qch) pour rire ▸ vi rire
▸ **laugh at** vt FUS se moquer de; (joke) rire de
▸ **laugh off** vt écarter or rejeter par une plaisanterie or par une boutade

laughable ['lɑːfəbl] ADJ risible, ridicule

laughing ['lɑːfɪŋ] ADJ rieur(-euse); **this is no ~ matter** il n'y a pas de quoi rire, ça n'a rien d'amusant

laughing gas N gaz hilarant

laughing stock N: **the ~ of** la risée de

laughter ['lɑ:ftə'] N rire m; (of several people) rires mpl

★**launch** [lɔ:ntʃ] N lancement m; (boat) chaloupe f; (also: **motor launch**) vedette f ▶VT (ship, rocket, plan) lancer
▶ **launch into** VT FUS se lancer dans
▶ **launch out** VI: **to ~ out (into)** se lancer (dans)

launching ['lɔ:ntʃɪŋ] N lancement m

launder ['lɔ:ndə'] VT laver; (fig: money) blanchir

Launderette® [lɔ:n'dret], (US) **Laundromat**® ['lɔ:ndrəmæt] N laverie f (automatique)

laundry ['lɔ:ndrɪ] N (clothes) linge m; (business) blanchisserie f; (room) buanderie f; **to do the ~** faire la lessive

laureate ['lɔ:rɪət] ADJ see **poet laureate**

laurel ['lɔrl] N laurier m; **to rest on one's laurels** se reposer sur ses lauriers

lava ['lɑ:və] N lave f

lavatory ['lævətərɪ] N toilettes fpl

lavatory paper N (BRIT) papier m hygiénique

lavender ['lævəndə'] N lavande f

lavish ['lævɪʃ] ADJ (amount) copieux(-euse); (meal) somptueux(-euse); (hospitality) généreux(-euse); (person: giving freely): **~ with** prodigue de ▶VT: **to ~ sth on sb** prodiguer qch à qn; (money) dépenser qch sans compter pour qn

lavishly ['lævɪʃlɪ] ADV (give, spend) sans compter; (furnished) luxueusement

★**law** [lɔ:] N loi f; (field of study, profession) droit m; **against the ~** contraire à la loi; **to study ~** faire du droit; **to go to ~** (BRIT) avoir recours à la justice; **~ and order** n l'ordre public

law-abiding ['lɔ:əbaɪdɪŋ] ADJ respectueux(-euse) des lois

lawbreaker ['lɔ:breɪkə'] N personne f qui transgresse la loi

law court N tribunal m, cour f de justice

law enforcement CPD (agency, officer) chargé(e) de faire appliquer la loi

lawful ['lɔ:ful] ADJ légal(e), permis(e)

lawfully ['lɔ:fəlɪ] ADV légalement

lawless ['lɔ:lɪs] ADJ (action) illégal(e); (place) sans loi; **~ behaviour** le non-respect des lois

lawlessness ['lɔ:lɪsnɪs] N non-respect m des lois, non-droit m

Law Lord N (BRIT) juge siégant à la Chambre des Lords

lawmaker ['lɔ:meɪkə'] N législateur(-trice)

lawn [lɔ:n] N pelouse f

lawnmower ['lɔ:nməuə'] N tondeuse f à gazon

lawn tennis N tennis m

law school N faculté f de droit

law student N étudiant(e) en droit

lawsuit ['lɔ:su:t] N procès m; **to bring a ~ against** engager des poursuites contre

★**lawyer** ['lɔ:jə'] N (consultant, with company) juriste m; (for sales, wills etc) = notaire m; (partner, in court) = avocat m

lax [læks] ADJ relâché(e)

laxative ['læksətɪv] N laxatif m

laxity ['læksɪtɪ] N relâchement m

★**lay** [leɪ] PT of **lie** ▶ADJ laïque; (not expert) profane ▶VT (pt, pp **laid** [leɪd]) poser, mettre; (eggs) pondre; (trap) tendre; (plans) élaborer; **to ~ the table** mettre la table; **to ~ the facts/one's proposals before sb** présenter les faits/ses propositions à qn; **to get laid** (inf!) baiser (!), se faire baiser (!)
▶ **lay aside, lay by** VT mettre de côté
▶ **lay down** VT poser; (rules etc) établir; **to ~ down the law** (fig) faire la loi
▶ **lay in** VT accumuler, s'approvisionner en
▶ **lay into** VI (inf: attack) tomber sur; (: scold) passer une engueulade à
▶ **lay off** VT (workers) licencier
▶ **lay on** VT (water, gas) mettre, installer; (provide: meal etc) fournir; (paint) étaler
▶ **lay out** VT (design) dessiner, concevoir; (display) disposer; (spend) dépenser
▶ **lay up** VT (store) amasser; (car) remiser; (ship) désarmer; (illness) forcer à s'aliter

layabout ['leɪəbaut] N fainéant(e)

lay-by ['leɪbaɪ] N (BRIT) aire f de stationnement (sur le bas-côté)

lay days NPL (Naut) estarie f

★**layer** ['leɪə'] N couche f ▶ VT disposer en couches

layette [leɪ'ɛt] N layette f

layman ['leɪmən] N (irreg) (Rel) laïque m; (non-expert) profane m

lay-off ['leɪɔf] N licenciement m

layout ['leɪaut] N disposition f, plan m, agencement m; (Press) mise f en page

laze [leɪz] VI paresser

laziness ['leɪzɪnɪs] N paresse f

lazy ['leɪzɪ] ADJ paresseux(-euse)

LB N ABBR (CANADA) = **Labrador**

lb. ABBR (weight) = **pound**

lbw ABBR (Cricket: = leg before wicket) faute dans laquelle le joueur a la jambe devant le guichet

LC N ABBR (US) = **Library of Congress**

lc ABBR (Typ: = lower case) b.d.c.

L/C ABBR = **letter of credit**

LCD N ABBR = **liquid crystal display**

Ld ABBR (BRIT: = lord) titre honorifique

LDS N ABBR (= Licentiate in Dental Surgery) diplôme universitaire; (= Latter-day Saints) Église de Jésus-Christ des Saints du dernier jour

LEA N ABBR (BRIT: = local education authority) services locaux de l'enseignement

★**lead¹** [li:d] (pt, pp **led** [lɛd]) N (front position) tête f; (distance, time ahead) avance f; (clue) piste f; (to battery) raccord m; (Elec) fil m; (for dog) laisse f; (Theat) rôle principal; **to be in the ~** (Sport: in race) mener, être en tête; (: in match) mener (à la marque); **to take the ~** (Sport) passer en tête, prendre la tête; mener; (fig) prendre l'initiative ▶VT (guide) mener, conduire; (induce) amener; (be leader of) être à la tête de; (Sport) être en tête de; (orchestra: BRIT) être le premier violon de; (: US) diriger; **to ~ sb astray** détourner qn du droit chemin; **to ~ sb to believe that ...** amener qn à croire que ...; **to ~ sb to do sth** amener qn à faire qch; **to ~ the way** montrer le chemin ▶VI (Sport) mener, être en tête; **to ~ to** (road, pipe) mener à, conduire à; (result in) conduire à; aboutir à
▶ **lead away** VT emmener
▶ **lead back** VT ramener
▶ **lead off** VI (in game etc) commencer
▶ **lead on** VT (tease) faire marcher; **to ~ sb on to** (induce) amener qn à

▶**lead up to** VT conduire à; (*in conversation*) en venir à

lead² [lɛd] N (*metal*) plomb *m*; (*in pencil*) mine *f*

leaded ['lɛdɪd] ADJ (*windows*) à petits carreaux

leaded petrol N essence *f* au plomb

leaden ['lɛdn] ADJ de or en plomb

★**leader** ['liːdə^r] N (*of team*) chef *m*; (*of party etc*) dirigeant(e), leader *m*; (*Sport: in league*) leader; (: *in race*) coureur *m* de tête; (*in newspaper*) éditorial *m*; **they are leaders in their field** (*fig*) ils sont à la pointe du progrès dans leur domaine; **the L~ of the House** (BRIT) le chef de la majorité ministérielle

leadership ['liːdəʃɪp] N (*position*) direction *f*; **under the ~ of ...** sous la direction de ...; **qualities of ~** qualités *fpl* de chef or de meneur

lead-free ['lɛdfriː] ADJ sans plomb

leading ['liːdɪŋ] ADJ de premier plan; (*main*) principal(e); (*in race*) de tête; **a ~ question** une question tendancieuse; **~ role** rôle prépondérant or de premier plan

leading lady N (*Theat*) vedette (féminine)

leading light N (*person*) sommité *f*, personnalité *f* de premier plan

leading man N (*irreg*) (*Theat*) vedette (masculine)

lead pencil [lɛd-] N crayon noir or à papier

lead poisoning [lɛd-] N saturnisme *m*

lead singer [liːd-] N (*in pop group*) (chanteur *m*) vedette *f*

lead time [liːd-] N (*Comm*) délai *m* de livraison

lead weight [lɛd-] N plomb *m*

★**leaf** [liːf] (*pl* **leaves** [liːvz]) N feuille *f*; (*of table*) rallonge *f*; **to turn over a new ~** changer de conduite or d'existence; **to take a ~ out of sb's book** (*fig*) prendre exemple sur qn
▶**leaf through** VT (*book*) feuilleter

leaflet ['liːflɪt] N prospectus *m*, brochure *f*; (*Pol, Rel*) tract *m*

leafleting ['liːflətɪŋ] N (*for company, for political party*) tractage *m*

leafy ['liːfɪ] ADJ feuillu(e)

★**league** [liːg] N ligue *f*; (*Football*) championnat *m*; (*measure*) lieue *f*; **to be in ~ with** avoir partie liée avec, être de mèche avec

league table N classement *m*

★**leak** [liːk] N (*lit, fig*) fuite *f*; (*in*) infiltration *f* ▶ VI (*pipe, liquid etc*) fuir; (*shoes*) prendre l'eau; (*ship*) faire eau ▶ VT (*liquid*) répandre; (*information*) divulguer
▶**leak out** VI fuir; (*information*) être divulgué(e)

leakage ['liːkɪdʒ] N (*also fig*) fuite *f*

leaky ['liːkɪ] ADJ (*pipe, bucket*) qui fuit, percé(e); (*roof*) qui coule; (*shoe*) qui prend l'eau; (*boat*) qui fait eau

★**lean** [liːn] (*pt, pp* **leaned** [liːnd] *or* **leant** [lɛnt]) ADJ maigre ▶ N (*of meat*) maigre *m* ▶ VT: **to ~ sth on** appuyer qch sur ▶ VI (*slope*) pencher; (*rest*): **to ~ against** s'appuyer contre; être appuyé(e) contre; **to ~ on** s'appuyer sur
▶**lean back** VI se pencher en arrière
▶**lean forward** VI se pencher en avant
▶**lean out** VI: **to ~ out (of)** se pencher au dehors (de)
▶**lean over** VI se pencher

leaning ['liːnɪŋ] ADJ penché(e); **the L~ Tower of Pisa** la tour penchée de Pise ▶ N: **~ (towards)** penchant *m* (pour)

leant [lɛnt] PT, PP *of* **lean**

lean-to ['liːntuː] N appentis *m*

leap [liːp] (*pt, pp* **leaped** [liːpt] *or* **leapt** [lɛpt]) N bond *m*, saut *m* ▶ VI bondir, sauter; **to ~ at an offer** saisir une offre
▶**leap up** VI (*person*) faire un bond; se lever d'un bond

leapfrog ['liːpfrɔg] N jeu *m* de saute-mouton

leapt [lɛpt] PT, PP *of* **leap**

leap year N année *f* bissextile

★**learn** [ləːn] (*pt, pp* **learned** [ləːnd] *or* **learnt** [ləːnt]) VT, VI apprendre; **to ~ (how) to do sth** apprendre à faire qch; **we were sorry to ~ that ...** nous avons appris avec regret que ...; **to ~ about sth** (*Scol*) étudier qch; (*hear, read*) apprendre qch

learned ['ləːnɪd] ADJ érudit(e), savant(e)

learner ['ləːnə^r] N débutant(e); (BRIT: *also*: **learner driver**) (conducteur(-trice)) débutant(e)

learning ['ləːnɪŋ] N savoir *m*

learning difficulties, learning disabilities NPL (*in adults*) difficultés *fpl* d'apprentissage; (*in children*) difficultés *fpl* scolaires

learnt [ləːnt] PP *of* **learn**

lease [liːs] N bail *m*; **on ~** en location ▶ VT louer à bail
▶**lease back** VT vendre en cession-bail

leaseback ['liːsbæk] N cession-bail *f*

leasehold ['liːshəuld] N (*contract*) bail *m* ▶ ADJ loué(e) à bail

leaseholder ['liːshəuldə^r] N preneur *m*

leash [liːʃ] N laisse *f*

★**least** [liːst] ADJ: **the ~** (+ *noun*) le (la) plus petit(e), le (la) moindre; (*smallest amount of*) le moins de; **the ~ money** le moins d'argent ▶ N: **(the) ~** le moins; **at ~** au moins; (*or rather*) du moins; **you could at ~ have written** tu aurais au moins pu écrire; **not in the ~** pas le moins du monde ▶ ADV (+ *verb*) le moins; (+ *adj*): **the ~** le (la) moins; **the ~ expensive** le (la) moins cher (chère); **the ~ possible effort** le moins d'effort possible

★**leather** ['lɛðə^r] N cuir *m* ▶ CPD en or de cuir; **~ goods** maroquinerie *f*

★**leave** [liːv] (*pt, pp* **left** [lɛft]) VT laisser; (*go away from*) quitter; (*forget*) oublier; **to ~ sth to sb** (*money etc*) laisser qch à qn; **to be left** rester; **there's some milk left over** il reste du lait; **to ~ school** quitter l'école, terminer sa scolarité; **~ it to me!** laissez-moi faire!, je m'en occupe! ▶ VI partir, s'en aller; **what time does the train/bus ~?** le train/le bus part à quelle heure? ▶ N (*time off*) congé *m*; (*Mil.: also consent*) permission *f*; **on ~** en permission; **to take one's ~ of** prendre congé de; **~ of absence** *n* congé exceptionnel; (*Mil*) permission spéciale
▶**leave behind** VT (*also fig*) laisser; (*opponent in race*) distancer; (*forget*) laisser, oublier
▶**leave off** VT (*cover, lid, heating*) ne pas (re)mettre; (*light*) ne pas (r)allumer, laisser éteint(e) ▶ VI (BRIT *inf: stop*): **to ~ off (doing sth)** s'arrêter (de faire qch)
▶**leave on** VT (*coat etc*) garder, ne pas enlever; (*lid*) laisser dessus; (*light, fire, cooker*) laisser allumé(e)
▶**leave out** VT oublier, omettre

leaver ['liːvəʳ] N (BRIT: from EU) partisan de la sortie de l'Union européenne

leaves [liːvz] NPL of **leaf**

leavetaking ['liːvteɪkɪŋ] N adieux mpl

Lebanese [lebə'niːz] ADJ libanais(e) ▶ N (pl inv) Libanais(e)

Lebanon ['lebənən] N Liban m

lecherous ['letʃərəs] ADJ lubrique

lectern ['lektəːn] N lutrin m, pupitre m

★**lecture** ['lektʃəʳ] N conférence f; (Scol) cours (magistral); **to give a ~ (on)** faire une conférence (sur), faire un cours (sur) ▶ VI donner des cours; enseigner; **to ~ on** faire un cours (or son cours) sur ▶ VT (scold) sermonner, réprimander

Le mot anglais **lecture** ne veut pas dire lecture.

lecture hall N amphithéâtre m

lecturer ['lektʃərəʳ] N (speaker) conférencier(-ière); (BRIT: at university) professeur m (d'université), prof mf de fac (inf); **assistant ~** (BRIT) ≈ assistant(e); **senior ~** (BRIT) ≈ chargé(e) d'enseignement

lecture theatre N = **lecture hall**

LED N ABBR (= light-emitting diode) LED f, diode électroluminescente

led [led] PT, PP of **lead**[1]

ledge [ledʒ] N (of window, on wall) rebord m; (of mountain) saillie f, corniche f

ledger ['ledʒəʳ] N registre m, grand livre

lee [liː] N côté m sous le vent; **in the ~ of** à l'abri de

leech [liːtʃ] N sangsue f

leek [liːk] N poireau m

leer [lɪəʳ] VI: **to ~ at sb** regarder qn d'un air mauvais or concupiscent, lorgner qn

leeward ['liːwəd] ADJ, ADV sous le vent ▶ N côté m sous le vent; **to ~** sous le vent

leeway ['liːweɪ] N (fig): **to make up ~** rattraper son retard; **to have some ~** avoir une certaine liberté d'action

★**left** [left] PT, PP of **leave** ▶ ADJ (not right) gauche; (remaining): **there are two ~** il en reste deux ▶ ADV à gauche ▶ N gauche f; **on the ~, to the ~** à gauche; **the L~** (Pol) la gauche

left-hand ['lefthænd] ADJ: **the ~ side** la gauche, le côté gauche

left-hand drive N conduite f à gauche; (vehicle) véhicule m avec la conduite à gauche

left-handed [left'hændɪd] ADJ gaucher(-ère); (scissors etc) pour gauchers

leftie ['leftɪ] N (inf) gaucho mf, gauchiste mf

leftist ['leftɪst] ADJ (Pol) gauchiste, de gauche

left-luggage [left'lʌgɪdʒ], **left-luggage office** N (BRIT) consigne f

left-luggage locker N (BRIT) (casier m à) consigne f automatique

left-overs ['leftəuvəz] NPL restes mpl

left wing N (Mil, Sport) aile f gauche; (Pol) gauche f

left-wing ['left'wɪŋ] ADJ (Pol) de gauche

left-winger ['left'wɪŋgəʳ] N (Pol) membre m de la gauche; (Sport) ailier m gauche

lefty ['leftɪ] N (inf) = **leftie**

★**leg** [leg] N jambe f; (of animal) patte f; (of furniture) pied m; (Culin: of chicken) cuisse f; (of journey) étape f; **1st/2nd ~** (Sport) match m aller/retour; (of journey) 1ère/2ème étape; **~ of lamb** (Culin) gigot m d'agneau; **to stretch one's legs** se dégourdir les jambes

legacy ['legəsɪ] N (also fig) héritage m, legs m

★**legal** ['liːgl] ADJ (permitted by law) légal(e); (relating to law) juridique; **to take ~ action** or **proceedings against sb** poursuivre qn en justice

legal adviser N conseiller(-ère) juridique

legal holiday N (US) jour férié

legality [lɪ'gælɪtɪ] N légalité f

legalization [liːgəlaɪ'zeɪʃən] N légalisation f

legalize ['liːgəlaɪz] VT légaliser

legally ['liːgəlɪ] ADV légalement; **~ binding** juridiquement contraignant(e)

legal tender N monnaie légale

legation [lɪ'geɪʃən] N légation f

legend ['ledʒənd] N légende f

legendary ['ledʒəndərɪ] ADJ légendaire

-legged ['legɪd] SUFFIX: **two-legged** à deux pattes (or jambes or pieds)

leggings ['legɪŋz] NPL caleçon m

leggy ['legɪ] ADJ aux longues jambes

legibility [ledʒɪ'bɪlɪtɪ] N lisibilité f

legible ['ledʒəbl] ADJ lisible

legibly ['ledʒəblɪ] ADV lisiblement

legion ['liːdʒən] N légion f

legionnaire [liːdʒə'nɛəʳ] N légionnaire m; **~'s disease** maladie f du légionnaire

legislate ['ledʒɪsleɪt] VI légiférer

legislation [ledʒɪs'leɪʃən] N législation f; **a piece of ~** un texte de loi

legislative ['ledʒɪslətɪv] ADJ législatif(-ive)

legislator ['ledʒɪsleɪtəʳ] N législateur(-trice)

legislature ['ledʒɪslətʃəʳ] N corps législatif

legitimacy [lɪ'dʒɪtɪməsɪ] N légitimité f

legitimate [lɪ'dʒɪtɪmət] ADJ légitime

legitimately [lɪ'dʒɪtɪmətlɪ] ADV légitimement

legitimize [lɪ'dʒɪtɪmaɪz] VT légitimer

legless ['leglɪs] ADJ (BRIT inf) bourré(e)

leg-room ['legruːm] N place f pour les jambes

legume ['legjuːm] N légumineuse f

legwork ['legwəːk] N travail m sur le terrain

leisure ['leʒəʳ] N (free time) temps m libre, loisirs mpl; **at ~** (tout) à loisir; **at your ~** (later) à tête reposée

leisure centre N (BRIT) centre m de loisirs

leisurely ['leʒəlɪ] ADJ tranquille, fait(e) sans se presser

leisure suit N (BRIT) survêtement m (mode)

leisurewear ['leʒəwɛəʳ] N vêtements mpl de loisir(s)

lemon ['lemən] N citron m

lemonade [lemə'neɪd] N (fizzy) limonade f

lemon cheese, lemon curd N crème f de citron

lemon juice N jus m de citron

lemon squeezer [-skwiːzəʳ] N presse-citron m inv

lemon tea N thé m au citron

★**lend** [lɛnd] (*pt, pp* **lent** [lɛnt]) VT: **to ~ sth (to sb)** prêter qch (à qn); **could you ~ me some money?** pourriez-vous me prêter de l'argent?; **to ~ a hand** donner un coup de main

lender ['lɛndə'] N prêteur(-euse)

lending ['lɛndɪŋ] N prêt *m*

lending library N bibliothèque *f* de prêt

★**length** [lɛŋθ] N longueur *f*; (*section: of road, pipe etc*) morceau *m*, bout *m*; **~ of time** durée *f*; **what ~ is it?** quelle longueur fait-il?; **it is 2 metres in ~** cela fait 2 mètres de long; **to fall full ~** tomber de tout son long; **at ~** (*at last*) enfin, à la fin; (*lengthily*) longuement; **to go to any ~(s) to do sth** faire n'importe quoi pour faire qch, ne reculer devant rien pour faire qch

lengthen ['lɛŋθən] VT allonger, prolonger ▶ VI s'allonger

lengthways ['lɛŋθweɪz] ADV dans le sens de la longueur, en long

lengthy ['lɛŋθɪ] ADJ (très) long (longue)

leniency ['liːnɪənsɪ] N indulgence *f*, clémence *f*

lenient ['liːnɪənt] ADJ indulgent(e), clément(e)

leniently ['liːnɪəntlɪ] ADV avec indulgence *or* clémence

★**lens** [lɛnz] N lentille *f*; (*of spectacles*) verre *m*; (*of camera*) objectif *m*

Lent [lɛnt] N carême *m*

lent [lɛnt] PT, PP *of* **lend**

lentil ['lɛntl] N lentille *f*

Leo ['liːəu] N le Lion; **to be ~** être du Lion

leopard ['lɛpəd] N léopard *m*

leotard ['liːətɑːd] N justaucorps *m*

leper ['lɛpə'] N lépreux(-euse)

leper colony N léproserie *f*

leprosy ['lɛprəsɪ] N lèpre *f*

lesbian ['lɛzbɪən] N lesbienne *f* ▶ ADJ lesbien(ne)

lesion ['liːʒən] N (*Med*) lésion *f*

Lesotho [lɪ'suːtuː] N Lesotho *m*

★**less** [lɛs] ADJ moins de ▶ PRON, ADV moins; **~ than that/you** moins que cela/vous; **~ than half** moins de la moitié; **~ than one/a kilo/3 metres** moins de un/d'un kilo/de 3 mètres; **~ than ever** moins que jamais; **~ and ~** de moins en moins; **the ~ he works ...** moins il travaille ... ▶ PREP: **~ tax/10% discount** avant impôt/moins 10% de remise

lessee [lɛ'siː] N locataire *mf* (à bail), preneur(-euse) du bail

lessen ['lɛsn] VI diminuer, s'amoindrir, s'atténuer ▶ VT diminuer, réduire, atténuer

lesser ['lɛsə'] ADJ moindre; **to a ~ extent** *or* **degree** à un degré moindre

★**lesson** ['lɛsn] N leçon *f*; **a maths ~** une leçon *or* un cours de maths; **to give lessons in** donner des cours de; **to teach sb a ~** (*fig*) donner une bonne leçon à qn; **it taught him a ~** (*fig*) cela lui a servi de leçon

lessor ['lɛsɔː', lɛ'sɔː'] N bailleur(-eresse)

lest [lɛst] CONJ de peur de + *infinitive*, de peur que + *sub*

★**let** [lɛt] (*pt, pp ~*) VT laisser; (*BRIT: lease*) louer; **to ~ sb do sth** laisser qn faire qch; **to ~ sb know sth** faire savoir qch à qn, prévenir qn de qch; **he ~ me go** il m'a laissé partir; **~ the water boil and ...** faites

bouillir l'eau et ...; **~'s go** allons-y; **~ him come** qu'il vienne; **"to ~"** (*BRIT*) « à louer »

▶ **let down** VT (*lower*) baisser; (*dress*) rallonger; (*hair*) défaire; (*BRIT: tyre*) dégonfler; (*disappoint*) décevoir

▶ **let go** VI lâcher prise; **to ~ go of sth, to ~ sth go** lâcher qch ▶ VT (*release hold on*) lâcher

▶ **let in** VT laisser entrer; (*visitor etc*) faire entrer; **what have you ~ yourself in for?** à quoi t'es-tu engagé?

▶ **let off** VT (*allow to leave*) laisser partir; (*not punish*) ne pas punir; (*taxi driver, bus driver*) déposer; (*firework etc*) faire partir; (*bomb*) faire exploser; (*smell etc*) dégager; **to ~ off steam** (*fig, inf*) se défouler, décharger sa rate *or* bile

▶ **let on** VI (*inf*): **to ~ on that ....** révéler que ..., dire que ...

▶ **let out** VT laisser sortir; (*dress*) élargir; (*scream*) laisser échapper; (*BRIT: rent out*) louer

▶ **let up** VI diminuer, s'arrêter

let-down ['lɛtdaun] N (*disappointment*) déception *f*

lethal ['liːθl] ADJ mortel(le), fatal(e); (*weapon*) meurtrier(-ère)

lethargic [lɛ'θɑːdʒɪk] ADJ léthargique

lethargy ['lɛθədʒɪ] N léthargie *f*

★**letter** ['lɛtə'] N lettre *f*; **small/capital ~** minuscule *f*/majuscule *f*; **~ of credit** lettre *f* de crédit ■ **letters** NPL (*Literature*) lettres

letter bomb N lettre piégée

letterbox ['lɛtəbɔks] N (*BRIT*) boîte *f* aux *or* à lettres

letterhead ['lɛtəhɛd] N en-tête *m*

lettering ['lɛtərɪŋ] N lettres *fpl*; caractères *mpl*

letter opener N coupe-papier *m*

letterpress ['lɛtəprɛs] N (*method*) typographie *f*

letter quality N qualité *f* « courrier »

letters patent NPL brevet *m* d'invention

lettuce ['lɛtɪs] N laitue *f*, salade *f*

let-up ['lɛtʌp] N répit *m*, détente *f*

leukaemia, (US) **leukemia** [luː'kiːmɪə] N leucémie *f*

★**level** ['lɛvl] N niveau *m*; (*flat place*) terrain plat; (*also*: **spirit level**) niveau à bulle; **on the ~** à l'horizontale; (*fig: honest*) régulier(-ière); **A levels** *npl* (*BRIT*) ≈ baccalauréat *m*; **O levels** *npl* (*BRIT: formerly*) examens passés à l'âge de 16 ans sanctionnant les connaissances de l'élève, ≈ brevet *m* des collèges ▶ ADJ (*flat*) plat(e), plane(e), uni(e); (*horizontal*) horizontal(e); **a ~ spoonful** (*Culin*) une cuillerée rase; **to be ~ with** être au même niveau que ▶ ADV: **to draw ~ with** (*team*) arriver à égalité de points avec, égaliser avec; arriver au même classement que; (*runner, car*) arriver à la hauteur de, rattraper ▶ VT niveler, aplanir; (*gun*) pointer, braquer; (*accusation*): **to ~ (against)** lancer *or* porter (contre) ▶ VI (*inf*): **to ~ with sb** être franc (franche) avec qn

▶ **level off, level out** VI (*prices etc*) se stabiliser ▶ VT (*ground*) aplanir, niveler

level crossing N (*BRIT*) passage *m* à niveau

level-headed [lɛvl'hɛdɪd] ADJ équilibré(e)

levelling, (US) **leveling** ['lɛvlɪŋ] ADJ (*process, effect*) de nivellement

level playing field N: **to compete on a ~** jouer sur un terrain d'égalité

lever ['liːvə'] N levier *m* ▶ VT: **to ~ up/out** soulever/extraire au moyen d'un levier

leverage ['li:vərɪdʒ] N (influence): ~ **(on** or **with)** prise f (sur)

levity ['levɪtɪ] N manque m de sérieux, légèreté f

levy ['levɪ] N taxe f, impôt m ▶ VT (tax) lever; (fine) infliger

lewd [lu:d] ADJ obscène, lubrique

lexicographer [leksɪˈkɔgrəfəʳ] N lexicographe mf

lexicography [leksɪˈkɔgrəfɪ] N lexicographie f

lexicon ['leksɪkən] N lexique m

LGBT N ABBR (= lesbian, gay, bisexual and transgender) LGBT (= lesbiennes, gays, bisexuels et transgenres)

LGV N ABBR (= Large Goods Vehicle) poids lourd

LI ABBR (US) = **Long Island**

liabilities [laɪəˈbɪlətɪz] NPL (Comm) obligations fpl, engagements mpl; (on balance sheet) passif m

liability [laɪəˈbɪlətɪ] N responsabilité f; (handicap) handicap m

liable ['laɪəbl] ADJ (subject): ~ **to** sujet(te) à, passible de; (responsible): ~ **(for)** responsable (de); (likely): ~ **to do** susceptible de faire; **to be ~ to a fine** être passible d'une amende

liaise [li:'eɪz] VI: **to ~ with** assurer la liaison avec

liaison [li:'eɪzɔn] N liaison f

liar ['laɪəʳ] N menteur(-euse)

libel ['laɪbl] N diffamation f; (document) écrit m diffamatoire ▶ VT diffamer

libellous ['laɪbləs] ADJ diffamatoire

★**liberal** ['lɪbərl] ADJ libéral(e); (generous): ~ **with** prodigue de, généreux(-euse) avec ▶ N: **L~** (Pol) libéral(e)

Liberal Democrat N (BRIT) libéral(e)-démocrate

liberalism ['lɪbrəlɪzəm] N libéralisme m

liberality [lɪbəˈrælɪtɪ] N (generosity) générosité f, libéralité f

liberalization [lɪbrəlaɪˈzeɪʃən] N libéralisation f

liberalize ['lɪbrəlaɪz] VT libéraliser

liberally ['lɪbrəlɪ] ADV généreusement

liberal-minded ['lɪbərl'maɪndɪd] ADJ libéral(e), tolérant(e)

liberate ['lɪbəreɪt] VT libérer

liberating ['lɪbəreɪtɪŋ] ADJ libérateur(-trice)

liberation [lɪbəˈreɪʃən] N libération f

liberation theology N théologie f de libération

Liberia [laɪˈbɪərɪə] N Libéria m, Liberia m

Liberian [laɪˈbɪərɪən] ADJ libérien(ne) ▶ N Libérien(ne)

liberty ['lɪbətɪ] N liberté f; **to be at ~** (criminal) être en liberté; **at ~ to do** libre de faire; **to take the ~ of** prendre la liberté de, se permettre de

libido [lɪˈbiːdəu] N libido f

Libra ['liːbrə] N la Balance; **to be ~** être de la Balance

librarian [laɪˈbrɛərɪən] N bibliothécaire mf

★**library** ['laɪbrərɪ] N bibliothèque f

library book N livre m de bibliothèque

libretto [lɪˈbretəu] N livret m

Libya ['lɪbɪə] N Libye f

Libyan ['lɪbɪən] ADJ libyen(ne), de Libye ▶ N Libyen(ne)

lice [laɪs] NPL of **louse**

licence, (US) **license** ['laɪsns] N autorisation f, permis m; (Comm) licence f; (Radio, TV) redevance f; (excessive freedom) licence; **driving ~**, (US) **driver's license** permis m (de conduire); **import ~** licence d'importation; **produced under ~** fabriqué(e) sous licence

licence number N (BRIT Aut) numéro m d'immatriculation

license ['laɪsns] N (US) = **licence** ▶ VT donner une licence à; (car) acheter la vignette de; délivrer la vignette de

licensed ['laɪsnst] ADJ (for alcohol) patenté(e) pour la vente des spiritueux, qui a une patente de débit de boissons; (car) muni(e) de la vignette

licensee [laɪsənˈsiː] N (BRIT: of pub) patron(ne), gérant(e)

license plate N (US Aut) plaque f minéralogique

licensing hours (BRIT) NPL heures fpl d'ouvertures (des pubs)

licentious [laɪˈsenʃəs] ADJ licencieux(-euse)

lichen ['laɪkən] N lichen m

lick [lɪk] VT lécher; (inf: defeat) écraser, flanquer une piquette or raclée à; **to ~ one's lips** (fig) se frotter les mains ▶ N coup m de langue; **a ~ of paint** un petit coup de peinture

licorice ['lɪkərɪʃ] N = **liquorice**

lid [lɪd] N couvercle m; (eyelid) paupière f; **to take the ~ off sth** (fig) exposer or étaler qch au grand jour

lido ['laɪdəu] N piscine f en plein air, complexe m balnéaire

★**lie** [laɪ] N mensonge m; **to tell lies** mentir ▶ VI (pt, pp **lied**) mentir; (pt **lay** [leɪ], pp **lain** [leɪn]) (rest) être étendu(e) or allongé(e) or couché(e); (: in grave) être enterré(e), reposer; (: object: be situated) se trouver, être; **to ~ low** (fig) se cacher, rester caché(e)
   ▶ **lie about, lie around** VI (things) traîner; (BRIT: person) traînasser, flemmarder
   ▶ **lie ahead** VI être à venir
   ▶ **lie back** VI se renverser en arrière
   ▶ **lie down** VI se coucher, s'étendre
   ▶ **lie up** VI (hide) se cacher

Liechtenstein ['lɪktənstaɪn] N Liechtenstein m

lie detector N détecteur m de mensonges

lie-down ['laɪdaun] N (BRIT): **to have a ~** s'allonger, se reposer

lie-in ['laɪɪn] N (BRIT): **to have a ~** faire la grasse matinée

lieu [lu:]: **in ~ of** prep au lieu de, à la place de

Lieut. ABBR (= lieutenant) Lt

lieutenant [lefˈtenənt, (US) luːˈtenənt] N lieutenant m

lieutenant-colonel [lefˈtenəntˈkəːnl, (US) luːtenəntˈkəːnl] N lieutenant-colonel m

★**life** [laɪf] (pl **lives** [laɪvz]) N vie f; **to come to ~** (fig) s'animer; **true to ~** réaliste, fidèle à la réalité; **to paint from ~** peindre d'après nature; **to be sent to prison for ~** être condamné(e) (à la réclusion criminelle) à perpétuité; **country/city ~** la vie à la campagne/à la ville ▶ CPD de vie; de la vie; à vie

life annuity N pension f, rente viagère

life assurance N (BRIT) = **life insurance**

lifebelt ['laɪfbelt] N (BRIT) bouée f de sauvetage

lifeblood ['laɪfblʌd] N (fig) élément m moteur

lifeboat ['laɪfbəut] N canot *m* or chaloupe *f* de sauvetage

lifebuoy ['laɪfbɔɪ] N bouée *f* de sauvetage

life expectancy N espérance *f* de vie

life force N force *f* vitale

lifeguard ['laɪfgɑːd] N surveillant *m* de baignade

life imprisonment N prison *f* à vie; (*Law*) réclusion *f* à perpétuité

life insurance N assurance-vie *f*

life jacket N gilet *m* or ceinture *f* de sauvetage

lifeless ['laɪflɪs] ADJ sans vie, inanimé(e); (*dull*) qui manque de vie or de vigueur

lifelike ['laɪflaɪk] ADJ qui semble vrai(e) or vivant(e), ressemblant(e); (*painting*) réaliste

lifeline ['laɪflaɪn] N corde *f* de sauvetage

lifelong ['laɪflɔŋ] ADJ de toute une vie, de toujours

life preserver [-prɪ'zɜːvə'] N (*US*) gilet *m* or ceinture *f* de sauvetage

lifer ['laɪfə'] N (*inf*) condamné(e) à perpète

life-raft ['laɪfrɑːft] N radeau *m* de sauvetage

life-saver ['laɪfseɪvə'] N surveillant *m* de baignade

life-saving ['laɪfseɪvɪŋ] N sauvetage *m*

life sentence N condamnation *f* à vie or à perpétuité

life-size ['laɪfsaɪz], **life-sized** ['laɪfsaɪzd] ADJ grandeur nature *inv*

life span N (durée *f* de) vie *f*

lifestyle ['laɪfstaɪl] N style *m* de vie

life-support system ['laɪfsəpɔːt-] N (*Med*) respirateur artificiel

lifetime ['laɪftaɪm] N: **in his ~** de son vivant; **the chance of a ~** la chance de ma (*or* sa *etc*) vie, une occasion unique

★**lift** [lɪft] VT soulever, lever; (*end*) supprimer, lever; (*steal*) prendre, voler ▶ VI (*fog*) se lever ▶ N (*BRIT: elevator*) ascenseur *m*; **to give sb a ~** (*BRIT*) emmener *or* prendre qn en voiture; **can you give me a ~ to the station?** pouvez-vous m'emmener à la gare ?
  ▶ **lift off** VI (*rocket, helicopter*) décoller
  ▶ **lift out** VT sortir; (*troops, evacuees etc*) évacuer par avion or hélicoptère
  ▶ **lift up** VT soulever

lift-off ['lɪftɔf] N décollage *m*

ligament ['lɪgəmənt] N ligament *m*

★**light** [laɪt] (*pt, pp* **lighted** ['laɪtɪd] *or* **lit** [lɪt]) N lumière *f*; (*daylight*) lumière, jour *m*; (*lamp*) lampe *f*; (*Aut: rear light*) feu *m*; (: *headlamp*) phare *m*; (*for cigarette etc*) **have you got a ~?** avez-vous du feu ?; **to turn the ~ on/off** allumer/éteindre; **to cast** *or* **shed** *or* **throw ~ on** éclaircir; **to come to ~** être dévoilé(e) or découvert(e); **in the ~ of** à la lumière de; étant donné ▶ VT (*candle, cigarette, fire*) allumer; (*room*) éclairer ▶ ADJ (*room, colour*) clair(e); (*not heavy, also fig*) léger(-ère); (*not strenuous*) peu fatigant(e); **to make ~ of sth** (*fig*) prendre qch à la légère, faire peu de cas de qch ▶ ADV (*travel*) avec peu de bagages ■ **lights** NPL (*traffic lights*) feux *mpl*
  ▶ **light up** VI s'allumer; (*face*) s'éclairer; (*smoke*) allumer une cigarette or une pipe *etc* ▶ VT (*illuminate*) éclairer, illuminer

light bulb N ampoule *f*

lighten ['laɪtn] VI s'éclaircir ▶ VT (*light up*) éclairer; (*make lighter*) éclaircir; (*make less heavy*) alléger

lighter ['laɪtə'] N (*also*: **cigarette lighter**) briquet *m*; (: *in car*) allume-cigare *m inv*; (*boat*) péniche *f*

light-fingered [laɪt'fɪŋɡəd] ADJ chapardeur(-euse)

light-headed [laɪt'hɛdɪd] ADJ étourdi(e), écervelé(e)

light-hearted [laɪt'hɑːtɪd] ADJ gai(e), joyeux(-euse), enjoué(e)

lighthouse ['laɪthaus] N phare *m*

lighting ['laɪtɪŋ] N éclairage *m*; (*in theatre*) éclairages

lighting-up time [laɪtɪŋ'ʌp-] N (*BRIT*) heure officielle de la tombée du jour

lightly ['laɪtlɪ] ADV légèrement; **to get off ~** s'en tirer à bon compte

light meter N (*Phot*) photomètre *m*, cellule *f*

lightness ['laɪtnɪs] N clarté *f*; (*in weight*) légèreté *f*

★**lightning** ['laɪtnɪŋ] N foudre *f*; (*flash*) éclair *m*

lightning conductor, (*US*) **lightning rod** N paratonnerre *m*

lightning strike N (*BRIT*) grève *f* surprise

light pen N crayon *m* optique

lightship ['laɪtʃɪp] N bateau-phare *m*

lightweight ['laɪtweɪt] ADJ (*suit*) léger(-ère) ▶ N (*Boxing*) poids léger

light year N année-lumière *f*

★**like** [laɪk] VT aimer (bien); **I would ~**, **I'd ~** je voudrais, j'aimerais; **would you ~ a coffee?** voulez-vous du café ?; **if you ~** si vous voulez ▶ PREP comme; **to be/look ~ sb/sth** ressembler à qn/qch; **what's he ~?** comment est-il ?; **what's the weather ~?** quel temps fait-il ?; **what does it look ~?** de quoi est-ce que ça a l'air ?; **what does it taste ~?** quel goût est-ce que ça a ?; **that's just ~ him** c'est bien de lui, ça lui ressemble; **something ~ that** quelque chose comme ça; **do it ~ this** fais-le comme ceci; **I feel ~ a drink** je boirais bien quelque chose; **it's nothing ~ ...** ce n'est pas du tout comme ...; **there's nothing ~ ...** il n'y a rien de tel que ... ▶ ADJ semblable, pareil(le) ▶ N: **the ~** un(e) pareil(le) or semblable; le (la) pareil(le); (*pej*) (d')autres du même genre or acabit; **his likes and dislikes** ses goûts *mpl* or préférences *fpl*

> **aimer** can mean *to like* or *to love*. **aimer bien** indicates liking rather than love.
> *I like him but I don't want to go out with him.* **Je l'aime bien mais je ne veux pas sortir avec lui.**

likeable ['laɪkəbl] ADJ sympathique, agréable

likelihood ['laɪklɪhud] N probabilité *f*; **in all ~** selon toute vraisemblance

★**likely** ['laɪklɪ] ADJ (*result, outcome*) probable; (*excuse*) plausible; **he's ~ to leave** il va sûrement partir, il risque fort de partir; **not ~!** (*inf*) pas de danger !

like-minded ['laɪk'maɪndɪd] ADJ de même opinion

liken ['laɪkən] VT: **to ~ sth to** comparer qch à

likeness ['laɪknɪs] N ressemblance *f*

likewise ['laɪkwaɪz] ADV de même, pareillement

liking ['laɪkɪŋ] N (*for person*) affection *f*; (*for thing*) penchant *m*, goût *m*; **to take a ~ to sb** se prendre d'amitié pour qn; **to be to sb's ~** être au goût de qn, plaire à qn

lilac ['laɪlək] N lilas *m* ▶ ADJ lilas *inv*

Lilo® ['laɪləu] N matelas m pneumatique

lilt [lɪlt] N rythme m, cadence f

lilting ['lɪltɪŋ] ADJ aux cadences mélodieuses; chantant(e)

lily ['lɪlɪ] N lis m; **~ of the valley** muguet m

Lima ['liːmə] N Lima

limb [lɪm] N membre m; **to be out on a ~** (fig) être isolé(e)

limber ['lɪmbə^r]: **to ~ up** vi se dégourdir, se mettre en train

limbo ['lɪmbəu] N: **to be in ~** (fig) être tombé(e) dans l'oubli

lime [laɪm] N (tree) tilleul m; (fruit) citron vert, lime f; (Geo) chaux f

lime green N citron m vert ▸ ADJ (also: **lime-green**) couleur citron vert inv

lime juice N jus m de citron vert

limelight ['laɪmlaɪt] N: **in the ~** (fig) en vedette, au premier plan

limerick ['lɪmərɪk] N petit poème humoristique

limestone ['laɪmstəun] N pierre f à chaux; (Geo) calcaire m

★**limit** ['lɪmɪt] N limite f; **weight/speed ~** limite de poids/de vitesse ▸ VT limiter

limitation [lɪmɪ'teɪʃən] N limitation f, restriction f

limited ['lɪmɪtɪd] ADJ limité(e), restreint(e); **~ edition** édition f à tirage limité; **to be ~ to** se limiter à, ne concerner que

limited company, limited liability company N (BRIT) ≈ société f anonyme

limitless ['lɪmɪtlɪs] ADJ illimité(e)

limo ['lɪməu] N (inf) limousine f

limousine ['lɪməziːn] N limousine f

limp [lɪmp] N: **to have a ~** boiter ▸ VI boiter ▸ ADJ mou (molle)

limpet ['lɪmpɪt] N patelle f; **like a ~** (fig) comme une ventouse

limpid ['lɪmpɪd] ADJ limpide

linchpin ['lɪntʃpɪn] N esse f; (fig) pivot m

★**line** [laɪn] N (gen) ligne f; (stroke) trait m; (wrinkle) ride f; (rope) corde f; (wire) fil m; (of poem) vers m; (row, series) rangée f; (of people) file f, queue f; (railway track) voie f; (Comm: series of goods) article(s) m(pl), ligne de produits; (work) métier m; **to stand in ~** (US) faire la queue; **to cut in ~** (US) passer avant son tour; **in his ~ of business** dans sa partie, dans son rayon; **on the right lines** sur la bonne voie; **a new ~ in cosmetics** une nouvelle ligne de produits de beauté; **hold the ~ please** (BRIT Tel) ne quittez pas; **to be in ~ for sth** (fig) être en lice pour qch; **in ~ with** en accord avec, en conformité avec; **in a ~** aligné(e); **to bring sth into ~ with sth** aligner qch sur qch; **to draw the ~ at (doing) sth** (fig) se refuser à (faire) qch; ne pas tolérer or admettre (qu'on fasse) qch; **to take the ~ that ...** être d'avis or de l'opinion que ... ▸ VT (subj: trees, crowd) border; **to ~ (with)** (clothes) doubler (de); (box) garnir or tapisser (de)
▸ **line up** VI s'aligner, se mettre en rang(s); (in queue) faire la queue ▸ VT aligner; (event) prévoir; (find) trouver; **to have sb/sth lined up** avoir qn/qch en vue or de prévu(e)

linear ['lɪnɪə^r] ADJ linéaire

lined [laɪnd] ADJ (paper) réglé(e); (face) marqué(e), ridé(e); (clothes) doublé(e)

lineman ['laɪnmən] N (irreg) (US: Rail) poseur m de rails; (: Tel) ouvrier m de ligne; (: Football) avant m

linen ['lɪnɪn] N linge m (de corps or de maison); (cloth) lin m

line printer N imprimante f (ligne par) ligne

liner ['laɪnə^r] N (ship) paquebot m de ligne; (for bin) sac-poubelle m

linesman ['laɪnzmən] N (irreg) (Tennis) juge m de ligne; (Football) juge de touche

line-up ['laɪnʌp] N (US: queue) file f; (also: **police line-up**) parade f d'identification; (Sport) (composition f de l')équipe f

linger ['lɪŋgə^r] VI s'attarder; traîner; (smell, tradition) persister

lingerie ['lænʒəriː] N lingerie f

lingering ['lɪŋgərɪŋ] ADJ persistant(e); qui subsiste; (death) lent(e)

lingo ['lɪŋgəu] (pl **lingoes**) N (inf) jargon m

linguist ['lɪŋgwɪst] N linguiste mf; **to be a good ~** être doué(e) pour les langues

linguistic [lɪŋ'gwɪstɪk] ADJ linguistique

linguistics [lɪŋ'gwɪstɪks] N linguistique f

lining ['laɪnɪŋ] N doublure f; (Tech) revêtement m; (: of brakes) garniture f

★**link** [lɪŋk] N (connection) lien m, rapport m; (Internet) lien; (of a chain) maillon m; **rail ~** liaison f ferroviaire ▸ VT relier, lier, unir ▪ **links** NPL (Golf) (terrain m de) golf m
▸ **link up** VT relier ▸ VI (people) se rejoindre; (companies etc) s'associer

link-up ['lɪŋkʌp] N lien m, rapport m; (of roads) jonction f, raccordement m; (of spaceships) arrimage m; (Radio, TV) liaison f; (: programme) duplex m

lino ['laɪnəu] N = **linoleum**

linoleum [lɪ'nəuliəm] N linoléum m

linseed oil ['lɪnsiːd-] N huile f de lin

lint [lɪnt] N tissu ouaté (pour pansements)

lintel ['lɪntl] N linteau m

★**lion** ['laɪən] N lion m

lion cub N lionceau m

lioness ['laɪənɪs] N lionne f

★**lip** [lɪp] N lèvre f; (of cup etc) rebord m; (insolence) insolences fpl

liposuction ['lɪpəusʌkʃən] N liposuccion f

lip-read ['lɪpriːd] VI (irreg: like **read**) lire sur les lèvres

lip salve [-sælv] N pommade f pour les lèvres, pommade rosat

lip service N: **to pay ~ to sth** ne reconnaître le mérite de qch que pour la forme or qu'en paroles

lipstick ['lɪpstɪk] N rouge m à lèvres

liquefy ['lɪkwɪfaɪ] VT liquéfier ▸ VI se liquéfier

liqueur [lɪ'kjuə^r] N liqueur f

liquid ['lɪkwɪd] N liquide m ▸ ADJ liquide

liquid assets NPL liquidités fpl, disponibilités fpl

liquidate ['lɪkwɪdeɪt] VT liquider

liquidation [lɪkwɪ'deɪʃən] N liquidation f; **to go into ~** déposer son bilan

liquidator ['lɪkwɪdeɪtə^r] N liquidateur m

liquid crystal display N affichage m à cristaux liquides

liquidity [lɪˈkwɪdɪtɪ] N liquidité f

liquidize [ˈlɪkwɪdaɪz] VT (BRIT Culin) passer au mixer

liquidizer [ˈlɪkwɪdaɪzəʳ] N (BRIT Culin) mixer m

liquor [ˈlɪkəʳ] N spiritueux m, alcool m

liquorice [ˈlɪkərɪʃ] N (BRIT) réglisse m

liquor store N (US) magasin m de vins et spiritueux

Lisbon [ˈlɪzbən] N Lisbonne

lisp [lɪsp] N zézaiement m ▶ VI zézayer

lissom [ˈlɪsəm] ADJ souple, agile

★**list** [lɪst] N liste f; (of ship) inclinaison f; **shopping ~** liste des courses ▶ VT (write down) inscrire; (make list of) faire la liste de; (enumerate) énumérer; (Comput) lister ▶ VI (ship) gîter, donner de la bande

listed building [ˈlɪstɪd-] N (Archit) monument classé

listed company [ˈlɪstɪd-] N société cotée en Bourse

★**listen** [ˈlɪsn] VI écouter; **to ~ to** écouter

listener [ˈlɪsnəʳ] N auditeur(-trice)

listeria [lɪsˈtɪərɪə] N listéria f

listing [ˈlɪstɪŋ] N (Comput) listage m; (: hard copy) liste f, listing m

listless [ˈlɪstlɪs] ADJ indolent(e), apathique

listlessly [ˈlɪstlɪslɪ] ADV avec indolence or apathie

list price N prix m de catalogue

lit [lɪt] PT, PP of **light**

litany [ˈlɪtənɪ] N litanie f

liter [ˈliːtəʳ] N (US) = **litre**

literacy [ˈlɪtərəsɪ] N degré m d'alphabétisation, fait m de savoir lire et écrire; (BRIT Scol) enseignement m de la lecture et de l'écriture; **basic ~ and numeracy** des notions élémentaires de lecture, d'écriture et de calcul

literal [ˈlɪtərl] ADJ littéral(e)

literally [ˈlɪtrəlɪ] ADV littéralement; (really) réellement

literary [ˈlɪtərərɪ] ADJ littéraire

literate [ˈlɪtərət] ADJ qui sait lire et écrire; (educated) instruit(e)

★**literature** [ˈlɪtrɪtʃəʳ] N littérature f; (brochures etc) copie f publicitaire, prospectus mpl

lithe [laɪð] ADJ agile, souple

lithography [lɪˈθɔgrəfɪ] N lithographie f

Lithuania [lɪθjuˈeɪnɪə] N Lituanie f

Lithuanian [lɪθjuˈeɪnɪən] ADJ lituanien(ne) ▶ N Lituanien(ne); (Ling) lituanien m

litigate [ˈlɪtɪgeɪt] VT mettre en litige ▶ VI plaider

litigation [lɪtɪˈgeɪʃən] N litige m; contentieux m

litmus [ˈlɪtməs] N: **~ paper** papier m de tournesol

litre, (US) **liter** [ˈliːtəʳ] N litre m

litter [ˈlɪtəʳ] N (rubbish) détritus mpl; (dirtier) ordures fpl; (young animals) portée f ▶ VT éparpiller; laisser des détritus dans; **littered with** jonché(e) de, couvert(e) de

litter bin N (BRIT) poubelle f

litter lout, (US) **litterbug** [ˈlɪtəbʌg] N personne qui jette des détritus par terre

★**little** [ˈlɪtl] ADJ (small) petit(e); (not much): **~ milk** peu de lait; (some): **a ~** (+ noun) un peu de; **with ~ difficulty** sans trop de difficulté; **a ~ milk** un peu de lait; **a ~ bit** un peu; **for a ~ while** pendant un petit moment ▶ ADV peu; **as ~ as possible** le moins possible; **~ by ~** petit à petit, peu à peu ▶ PRON (not much) peu de choses; (a bit): **a ~** un peu; **to make ~ of** faire peu de cas de; **~ is known about his childhood** on sait peu de choses sur son enfance

little finger N auriculaire m, petit doigt

little-known [ˈlɪtlˈnəun] ADJ peu connu(e)

liturgy [ˈlɪtədʒɪ] N liturgie f

★**live**[1] [laɪv] ADJ (animal) vivant(e), en vie; (wire) sous tension; (broadcast) (transmis(e)) en direct; (issue) d'actualité, brûlant(e); (unexploded) non explosé(e); **~ ammunition** munitions fpl de combat

live[2] [lɪv] VI vivre; (reside) vivre, habiter; **to ~ in London** habiter (à) Londres; **where do you ~?** où habitez-vous?
  ▶ **live down** VT faire oublier (avec le temps)
  ▶ **live in** VI être logé(e) et nourri(e); être interne
  ▶ **live off** VT FUS (land, fish etc) vivre de; (inf: parents etc) vivre aux crochets de
  ▶ **live on** VT FUS (food) vivre de; **to ~ on £50 a week** vivre avec 50 livres par semaine ▶ VI survivre
  ▶ **live out** VI (BRIT: students) être externe ▶ VT: **to ~ out one's days** or **life** passer sa vie
  ▶ **live together** VI vivre ensemble, cohabiter
  ▶ **live up** VT: **to ~ it up** (inf) faire la fête; mener la grande vie
  ▶ **live up to** VT FUS se montrer à la hauteur de

liveblog [ˈlaɪvblɔg] N blog m en direct ▶ VT, VI bloguer en direct

live-in [ˈlɪvɪn] ADJ (nanny) à demeure; **~ partner** concubin(e)

livelihood [ˈlaɪvlɪhud] N moyens mpl d'existence

liveliness [ˈlaɪvlɪnəs] N vivacité f, entrain m

lively [ˈlaɪvlɪ] ADJ vif (vive), plein(e) d'entrain; (place, book) vivant(e)

liven up [ˈlaɪvn-] VT (room etc) égayer; (discussion, evening) animer ▶ VI s'animer

liver [ˈlɪvəʳ] N foie m

liverish [ˈlɪvərɪʃ] ADJ qui a mal au foie; (fig) grincheux(-euse)

Liverpudlian [lɪvəˈpʌdlɪən] ADJ de Liverpool ▶ N habitant(e) de Liverpool; natif(-ive) de Liverpool

livery [ˈlɪvərɪ] N livrée f

lives [laɪvz] NPL of **life**

livestock [ˈlaɪvstɔk] N cheptel m, bétail m

livestream [ˈlaɪvstriːm] N diffusion f en direct sur Internet ▶ VT diffuser en direct sur Internet

live wire [laɪv-] N (lit) fil m sous tension; (inf, fig): **to be a (real) ~** péter le feu

livid [ˈlɪvɪd] ADJ livide, blafard(e); (furious) furieux(-euse), furibond(e)

living [ˈlɪvɪŋ] ADJ vivant(e), en vie; **within ~ memory** de mémoire d'homme ▶ N: **to earn** or **make a ~** gagner sa vie

living conditions NPL conditions fpl de vie

living expenses NPL dépenses courantes

living room N salle f de séjour

living standards NPL niveau m de vie

living wage N salaire m permettant de vivre (décemment)

living will N directives fpl anticipées

lizard ['lɪzəd] N lézard m

llama ['lɑːmə] N lama m

LLB N ABBR (= Bachelor of Laws) titre universitaire

LLD N ABBR (= Doctor of Laws) titre universitaire

LMT ABBR (US: = Local Mean Time) heure locale

★**load** [ləud] N (weight) poids m; (thing carried) chargement m, charge f; (Elec, Tech) charge; **a ~ of, loads of** (fig) un or des tas de, des masses de; **to talk a ~ of rubbish** (inf) dire des bêtises ▶ VT charger; (also: **load up**): **to ~ (with)** (lorry, ship) charger (de); (gun, camera) charger (avec)

loaded ['ləudɪd] ADJ (dice) pipé(e); (question) insidieux(-euse); (inf: rich) bourré(e) de fric; (: drunk) bourré

loading bay ['ləudɪŋ-] N aire f de chargement

loaf [ləuf] (pl **loaves** [ləuvz]) N pain m, miche f ▶ VI (also: **loaf about, loaf around**) fainéanter, traîner

loam [ləum] N terreau m

★**loan** [ləun] N prêt m; **on ~** prêté(e), en prêt; **public ~** emprunt public ▶ VT prêter

loan account N compte m de prêt

loan capital N capital m d'emprunt

loan shark N (pej) usurier m

loath [ləuθ] ADJ: **to be ~ to do** répugner à faire

loathe [ləuð] VT détester, avoir en horreur

loathing ['ləuðɪŋ] N dégoût m, répugnance f

loathsome ['ləuðsəm] ADJ répugnant(e), détestable

loaves [ləuvz] NPL of **loaf**

lob [lɔb] VT (ball) lober

lobby ['lɔbɪ] N hall m, entrée f; (Pol) lobby m, groupe m de pression ▶ VT faire du lobbying auprès de, faire pression sur ▶ VI: **to ~ for sth** faire du lobbying pour qch

lobbying ['lɔbɪɪŋ] N lobbying m

lobbyist ['lɔbɪɪst] N lobbyiste mf, membre mf d'un groupe de pression

lobe [ləub] N lobe m

lobster ['lɔbstər] N homard m

lobster pot N casier m à homards

★**local** ['ləukl] ADJ local(e) ▶ N (BRIT: pub) pub m or café m du coin ■ **the locals** NPL les gens mpl du pays or du coin

local anaesthetic, (US) **local anesthetic** N anesthésie locale

local authority N collectivité locale, municipalité f

local call N (Tel) communication urbaine

local government N administration locale or municipale

locality [ləu'kælɪtɪ] N région f, environs mpl; (position) lieu m

localize ['ləukəlaɪz] VT localiser

locally ['ləukəlɪ] ADV localement; dans les environs or la région

locate [ləu'keɪt] VT (find) trouver, repérer; (situate) situer; **to be located in** être situé à or en

location [ləu'keɪʃən] N emplacement m; **on ~** (Cine) en extérieur

loch [lɔx] N lac m, loch m

★**lock** [lɔk] N (of door, box) serrure f; (of canal) écluse f; (of hair) mèche f, boucle f; **~ stock and barrel** (fig) en bloc; **on full ~** (BRIT Aut) le volant tourné à fond ▶ VT (with key) fermer à clé; (immobilize) bloquer ▶ VI (door etc) fermer à clé; (wheels) se bloquer
  ▶ **lock away** VT (valuables) mettre sous clé; (criminal) mettre sous les verrous, enfermer
  ▶ **lock in** VT enfermer
  ▶ **lock out** VT enfermer dehors; (on purpose) mettre à la porte; (: workers) lock-outer
  ▶ **lock up** VT (person) enfermer; (house) fermer à clé ▶ VI tout fermer (à clé)

lockdown ['lɔkdaun] N: **to be in** or **under ~** (place) faire l'objet de mesures de confinement; **to be on ~** (prisoner) être confiné(e) dans sa or sa cellule

locker ['lɔkər] N casier m; (in station) consigne f automatique

locker-room ['lɔkəruːm] N (US Sport) vestiaire m

locket ['lɔkɪt] N médaillon m

lockjaw ['lɔkdʒɔː] N tétanos m

lockout ['lɔkaut] N (Industry) lock-out m, grève patronale

locksmith ['lɔksmɪθ] N serrurier m

lock-up ['lɔkʌp] N (prison) prison f; (cell) cellule f provisoire; (also: **lock-up garage**) box m

locomotive [ləukə'məutɪv] N locomotive f

locum ['ləukəm] N (Med) suppléant(e) de médecin etc

locust ['ləukəst] N locuste f, sauterelle f

lodge [lɔdʒ] N pavillon m (de gardien); (also: **hunting lodge**) pavillon de chasse; (Freemasonry) loge f ▶ VI (person): **to ~ with** être logé(e) chez, être en pension chez; (bullet) se loger; **to ~ in/between** se loger dans/entre ▶ VT (appeal etc) présenter, déposer; **to ~ a complaint** porter plainte; **to ~ itself in/between** se loger dans/entre

lodger ['lɔdʒər] N locataire mf; (with room and meals) pensionnaire mf

lodging ['lɔdʒɪŋ] N logement m; see also **board**

lodging house N (BRIT) pension f de famille

lodgings ['lɔdʒɪŋz] NPL chambre f, meublé m

loft [lɔft] N grenier m; (apartment) grenier aménagé (en appartement) (gén dans ancien entrepôt ou fabrique)

lofty ['lɔftɪ] ADJ élevé(e); (haughty) hautain(e); (sentiments, aims) noble

★**log** [lɔg] N (of wood) bûche f; (Naut) livre m or journal m de bord; (of car) ≈ carte grise ▶ N ABBR (= logarithm) log m ▶ VT enregistrer
  ▶ **log in, log on** VI (Comput) ouvrir une session, entrer dans le système
  ▶ **log off, log out** VI (Comput) clore une session, sortir du système

logarithm ['lɔgərɪðm] N logarithme m

logbook ['lɔgbuk] N (Naut) livre m or journal m de bord; (Aviat) carnet m de vol; (of lorry driver) carnet de route; (of movement of goods etc) registre m; (of car) ≈ carte grise

log cabin N cabane f en rondins

log fire N feu m de bois

logger ['lɔgər] N bûcheron m

loggerheads ['lɔgəhɛdz] NPL: **at ~ (with)** à couteaux tirés (avec)

logging ['lɔgɪŋ] N exploitation f forestière ▶ CPD (company) d'exploitation f forestière

logic [ˈlɒdʒɪk] N logique f

logical [ˈlɒdʒɪkl] ADJ logique

logically [ˈlɒdʒɪkəlɪ] ADV logiquement

login [ˈlɒgɪn] N (Comput) identifiant m

logistic [lɒˈdʒɪstɪk], **logistical** [lɒˈdʒɪstɪkl] ADJ logistique

logistics [lɒˈdʒɪstɪks] N logistique f

logjam [ˈlɒdʒæm] N: **to break the ~** créer une ouverture dans l'impasse

logo [ˈləʊgəʊ] N logo m

loin [lɔɪn] N (Culin) filet m, longe f ▪ **loins** NPL reins mpl

loin cloth N pagne m

Loire [lwaː] N: **the (River) ~** la Loire

loiter [ˈlɔɪtəʳ] VI s'attarder; **to ~ (about)** traîner, musarder; (pej) rôder

LOL, lol ABBR (inf: = laugh out loud) MDR (= mort(e) de rire)

loll [lɒl] VI (also: **loll about**) se prélasser, fainéanter

lollipop [ˈlɒlɪpɒp] N sucette f

lollipop man/lady (BRIT) N (irreg) contractuel(le) qui fait traverser la rue aux enfants

> Les **lollipop men/ladies** sont employés pour aider les enfants à traverser la rue à proximité des écoles lorsqu'ils entrent en classe et en sortent. On les reconnaît facilement à leur long ciré jaune et à la pancarte ronde avec laquelle ils font signe aux automobilistes de s'arrêter. Ils doivent leur surnom à la forme circulaire de cette pancarte, qui rappelle une sucette.

lollop [ˈlɒləp] VI (BRIT) avancer (or courir) maladroitement

lolly [ˈlɒlɪ] N (inf: ice) esquimau m; (: lollipop) sucette f; (: money) fric m

Lombardy [ˈlɒmbədɪ] N Lombardie f

★**London** [ˈlʌndən] N Londres

★**Londoner** [ˈlʌndənəʳ] N Londonien(ne)

lone [ləʊn] ADJ solitaire

loneliness [ˈləʊnlɪnɪs] N solitude f, isolement m

lonely [ˈləʊnlɪ] ADJ seul(e); (childhood etc) solitaire; (place) solitaire, isolé(e)

lonely hearts ADJ: **~ ad** petite annonce (personnelle); **~ club** club m de rencontres (pour personnes seules)

lone parent N parent m unique

loner [ˈləʊnəʳ] N solitaire mf

lonesome [ˈləʊnsəm] ADJ seul(e), solitaire

★**long** [lɒŋ] ADJ long (longue); **how ~ is this river/course?** quelle est la longueur de ce fleuve/la durée de ce cours ?; **6 metres ~** (long) de 6 mètres; **6 months ~** qui dure 6 mois, de 6 mois; **at ~ last** enfin; **in the ~ run** à la longue; finalement ▶ ADV longtemps; **he had ~ understood that ...** il avait compris depuis longtemps que ...; **all night ~** toute la nuit; **he no longer comes** il ne vient plus; **I can't stand it any longer** je ne peux plus le supporter; **~ before** longtemps avant; **before ~** (+ future) avant peu, dans peu de temps; (+ past) peu de temps après; **~ ago** il y a longtemps; **don't be ~!** fais vite !, dépêche-toi !; **I shan't be ~** je n'en ai pas pour longtemps; **so** or **as ~ as** à condition que + sub ▶ N: **the ~ and the short of it is that ...**

(fig) le fin mot de l'histoire c'est que ... ▶ VI: **to ~ for sth/to do sth** avoir très envie de qch/de faire qch, attendre qch avec impatience/attendre avec impatience de faire qch

long-distance [lɒŋˈdɪstəns] ADJ (race) de fond; (call) interurbain(e)

longer ADV see **long**

longevity [lɒnˈdʒɛvɪtɪ] N (of person) longévité f; (of event, situation) longue durée f

long-haired [ˈlɒŋˈhɛəd] ADJ (person) aux cheveux longs; (animal) aux longs poils

longhand [ˈlɒŋhænd] N écriture normale or courante

long-haul [ˈlɒŋhɔːl] ADJ (flight) long-courrier

longing [ˈlɒŋɪŋ] N désir m, envie f; (nostalgia) nostalgie f ▶ ADJ plein(e) d'envie or de nostalgie

longingly [ˈlɒŋɪŋlɪ] ADV avec désir or nostalgie

longitude [ˈlɒŋgɪtjuːd] N longitude f

long johns NPL caleçons longs

long jump N saut m en longueur

long-life [lɒŋˈlaɪf] ADJ (batteries etc) longue durée inv; (milk) longue conservation

long-lost [ˈlɒŋlɒst] ADJ perdu(e) depuis longtemps

long-playing [ˈlɒŋpleɪɪŋ] ADJ: **~ record (LP)** (disque m) 33 tours m inv

long-range [ˈlɒŋˈreɪndʒ] ADJ à longue portée; (weather forecast) à long terme

longshoreman [ˈlɒŋʃɔːmən] N (irreg) (US) docker m, débardeur m

long-sighted [ˈlɒŋˈsaɪtɪd] ADJ (BRIT) presbyte; (fig) prévoyant(e)

long-standing [ˈlɒŋˈstændɪŋ] ADJ de longue date

long-suffering [lɒŋˈsʌfərɪŋ] ADJ empreint(e) d'une patience résignée; extrêmement patient(e)

long-term [ˈlɒŋtɜːm] ADJ à long terme

longtime [ˈlɒŋtaɪm] ADJ de longue date

long wave N (Radio) grandes ondes, ondes longues

long-winded [lɒŋˈwɪndɪd] ADJ intarissable, interminable

loo [luː] N (BRIT inf) w.-c. mpl, petit coin

loofah [ˈluːfə] N sorte d'éponge végétale

★**look** [lʊk] VI regarder; (seem) sembler, paraître, avoir l'air; (building etc): **to ~ south/on to the sea** donner au sud/sur la mer; **to ~ like** ressembler à; **it looks like him** on dirait que c'est lui; **it looks about 4 metres long** je dirais que ça fait 4 mètres de long; **it looks all right to me** ça me paraît bien; **~ (here)!** (annoyance) écoutez! ▶ N regard m; (appearance) air m, allure f, aspect m; **to have a ~** regarder; **to have a ~ at sth** jeter un coup d'œil à qch; **to have a ~ for sth** chercher qch ▪ **looks** NPL (good looks) physique m, beauté f

▶ **look after** VT FUS s'occuper de, prendre soin de; (luggage etc: watch over) garder, surveiller

▶ **look ahead** VI (lit) regarder devant soi; (fig) penser à l'avenir; **to ~ ahead to sth** envisager qch

▶ **look around** VI regarder autour de soi

▶ **look at** VT FUS regarder; (problem etc) examiner

▶ **look back** VI: **to ~ back at sth/sb** se retourner pour regarder qch/qn; **to ~ back on** (event, period) évoquer, repenser à

▶ **look down on** vt fus (fig) regarder de haut, dédaigner

▶ **look for** vt fus chercher; **we're looking for a hotel/restaurant** nous cherchons un hôtel/restaurant

▶ **look forward to** vt fus attendre avec impatience; **I'm not looking forward to it** cette perspective ne me réjouit guère; **looking forward to hearing from you** (in letter) dans l'attente de vous lire

▶ **look in** vi: **to ~ in on sb** passer voir qn

▶ **look into** vt fus (matter, possibility) examiner, étudier

▶ **look on** vi regarder (en spectateur)

▶ **look out** vi (beware): **to ~ out (for)** prendre garde (à), faire attention (à); **~ out!** attention!

▶ **look out for** vt fus (seek) être à la recherche de; (try to spot) guetter

▶ **look over** vt (essay) jeter un coup d'œil à; (town, building) visiter (rapidement); (person) jeter un coup d'œil à; examiner de la tête aux pieds

▶ **look round** vt fus (house, shop) faire le tour de ▶ vi (turn) regarder derrière soi, se retourner; **to ~ round for sth** chercher qch

▶ **look through** vt (papers, book) examiner; (: briefly) parcourir; (telescope) regarder à travers

▶ **look to** vt fus veiller à; (rely on) compter sur

▶ **look up** vi (situation) s'améliorer ▶ vt (word) chercher; (friend) passer voir

▶ **look up to** vt fus avoir du respect pour

lookalike ['lʊkəlaɪk] N sosie m; **a Marilyn Monroe ~** un sosie de Marilyn Monroe

looking glass ['lʊkɪŋ-] N miroir m

lookout ['lʊkaʊt] N (tower etc) poste m de guet; (person) guetteur m; **to be on the ~ (for)** guetter

look-up table ['lʊkʌp-] N (Comput) table f à consulter

loom [luːm] N métier m à tisser ▶ vi (also: **loom up**) surgir; (: event) paraître imminent(e); (: threaten) menacer

loony ['luːnɪ] ADJ (pej) timbré(e), cinglé(e)

loop [luːp] N boucle f; (contraceptive) stérilet m ▶ vt: **to ~ sth round sth** passer qch autour de qch

loophole ['luːphəʊl] N (fig) porte f de sortie; échappatoire f

★**loose** [luːs] ADJ (knot, screw) desserré(e); (stone) branlant(e); (clothes) vague, ample, lâche; (hair) dénoué(e), épars(e); (not firmly fixed) pas solide; (animal) en liberté, échappé(e); (life) dissolu(e); (morals, discipline) relâché(e); (thinking) peu rigoureux(-euse), vague; (translation) approximatif(-ive); **~ connection** (Elec) mauvais contact; **to be at a ~ end** or (US) **at a ~ ends** (fig) ne pas trop savoir quoi faire; **to tie up ~ ends** (fig) mettre au point or régler les derniers détails ▶ N: **to be on the ~** être en liberté ▶ vt (free: animal) lâcher; (: prisoner) relâcher, libérer; (slacken) détendre, relâcher; desserrer; défaire; donner du mou a; donner du ballant à; (BRIT: arrow) tirer

loose change N petite monnaie

loose chippings [-'tʃɪpɪŋz] NPL (on road) gravillons mpl

loose-fitting ['luːsfɪtɪŋ] ADJ (clothes) ample

loose-leaf ['luːsliːf] ADJ: **~ binder** or **folder** classeur m à feuillets mobiles

loose-limbed [luːs'lɪmd] ADJ agile, souple

loosely ['luːslɪ] ADV sans serrer; (imprecisely) approximativement

loosely-knit ['luːslɪˈnɪt] ADJ élastique

loosen ['luːsn] vt desserrer, relâcher, défaire

▶ **loosen up** vi (before game) s'échauffer; (inf: relax) se détendre, se laisser aller

loot [luːt] N butin m ▶ vt piller

looter ['luːtər] N pillard m, casseur m

looting ['luːtɪŋ] N pillage m

lop [lɒp]: **to ~ off** vt couper, trancher

lop-sided ['lɒp'saɪdɪd] ADJ de travers, asymétrique

loquacious [ləˈkweɪʃəs] ADJ (formal) loquace

lord [lɔːd] N seigneur m; **L~ Smith** lord Smith; **the L~** (Rel) le Seigneur; **my L~** (to noble) Monsieur le comte/le baron; (to judge) Monsieur le juge; (to bishop) Monseigneur; **good L~!** mon Dieu!

lordly ['lɔːdlɪ] ADJ noble, majestueux(-euse); (arrogant) hautain(e)

Lords ['lɔːdz] NPL (BRIT Pol): **the (House of) ~** la Chambre des Lords

lordship ['lɔːdʃɪp] N (BRIT): **your L~** Monsieur le comte (or le baron or le Juge)

lore [lɔːʳ] N tradition(s) f(pl)

lorry ['lɒrɪ] N (BRIT) camion m

lorry driver N (BRIT) camionneur m, routier m

★**lose** [luːz] (pt, pp **lost**) [lɒst]) vt perdre; (opportunity) manquer, perdre; (pursuers) distancer, semer; **I've lost my wallet/passport** j'ai perdu mon portefeuille/passeport; **to ~ time** (clock) retarder; **to ~ no time (in doing sth)** ne pas perdre de temps (à faire qch); see also **lost** ▶ vi perdre; (clock) retarder

▶ **lose out** vi être perdant(e)

loser ['luːzər] N perdant(e); **to be a good/bad ~** être beau/mauvais joueur

★**loss** [lɒs] N perte f; **to cut one's losses** limiter les dégâts; **to make a ~** enregistrer une perte; **to sell sth at a ~** vendre qch à perte; **to be at a ~** être perplexe or embarrassé(e); **to be at a ~ to do** se trouver incapable de faire

loss adjuster N (Insurance) responsable mf de l'évaluation des dommages

loss leader N (Comm) article sacrifié

★**lost** [lɒst] PT, PP of **lose** ▶ ADJ perdu(e); **to get ~** vi (person) se perdre; **my watch has got ~** ma montre est perdue; **I'm ~** je me suis perdu; **~ in thought** perdu dans ses pensées; **~ and found property** (US) objets trouvés; **~ and found** (US) (bureau m des) objets trouvés

lost property N (BRIT) objets trouvés; **~ office** or **department** (bureau m des) objets trouvés

★**lot** [lɒt] N (at auctions, set) lot m; (destiny) sort m, destinée f; **the ~** (everything) le tout; (everyone) tous mpl, toutes fpl; **a ~** beaucoup; **a ~ of** beaucoup de; **lots of** des tas de; **to draw lots (for sth)** tirer (qch) au sort

lotion ['ləʊʃən] N lotion f

lottery ['lɒtərɪ] N loterie f

★**loud** [laʊd] ADJ bruyant(e), sonore; (voice) fort(e); (condemnation etc) vigoureux(-euse); (gaudy) voyant(e), tapageur(-euse) ▶ ADV (speak etc) fort; **out ~** tout haut

loud-hailer [laʊd'heɪlər] N porte-voix m inv

loudly ['laʊdlɪ] ADV fort, bruyamment

loudspeaker [laud'spi:kə^r] N haut-parleur m

lounge [laundʒ] N salon m; (of airport) salle f; (BRIT: also: **lounge bar**) (salle de) café m or bar m ▶ VI (also: **lounge about**, **lounge around**) se prélasser, paresser

lounge bar N (salle f de) bar m

lounge suit N (BRIT) complet m; (: on invitation) « tenue de ville »

louse [laus] (pl **lice** [laɪs]) N pou m
▶ **louse up** [lauz-] VT (inf) gâcher

lousy ['lauzi] ADJ (inf: bad quality) infect(e), moche; **I feel ~** je suis mal fichu(e)

lout [laut] N rustre m, butor m

louvre, (US) **louver** ['lu:və^r] ADJ (door, window) à claire-voie

lovable ['lʌvəbl] ADJ très sympathique; adorable

★**love** [lʌv] N amour m; **to be/fall in ~ with** être/tomber amoureux(-euse) de; **to make ~** faire l'amour; **~ at first sight** le coup de foudre; **to send one's ~ to sb** adresser ses amitiés à qn; **~ from Anne**, **~**, **Anne** affectueusement, Anne; **"15 ~"** (Tennis) « 15 à rien or zéro » ▶ VT aimer; (caringly, kindly) aimer beaucoup; **I ~ you** je t'aime; **I ~ chocolate** j'adore le chocolat; **to ~ to do** aimer beaucoup or adorer faire; **I'd ~ to come** cela me ferait très plaisir (de venir)

love affair N liaison (amoureuse)

love child N (irreg) enfant m f de l'amour

loved ones ['lʌvdwʌnz] NPL proches mpl et amis chers

love-hate relationship [lʌv'heɪt-] N rapport ambigu; **they have a ~** ils s'aiment et se détestent à la fois

love life N vie sentimentale

lovelorn ['lʌvlɔ:n] ADJ qui se languit d'amour

★**lovely** ['lʌvlɪ] ADJ (pretty) ravissant(e); (friend, wife) charmant(e); (holiday, surprise) très agréable, merveilleux(-euse); **we had a ~ time** c'était vraiment très bien, nous avons eu beaucoup de plaisir

lovemaking ['lʌvmeɪkɪŋ] N ébats mpl (amoureux)

lover ['lʌvə^r] N amant m; (person in love) amoureux(-euse); (amateur): **a ~ of** un(e) ami(e) de, un(e) amoureux(-euse) de

lovesick ['lʌvsɪk] ADJ qui se languit d'amour

love song N chanson f d'amour

loving ['lʌvɪŋ] ADJ affectueux(-euse), tendre, aimant(e)

★**low** [ləu] ADJ bas(se); (quality) mauvais(e), inférieur(e); **to feel ~** se sentir déprimé(e); **he's very ~** (ill) il est bien bas or très affaibli; **to be ~ on** (supplies etc) être à court de ▶ ADV bas; **to turn (down) ~** VT baisser ▶ N (Meteorology) dépression f; **to reach a new or an all-time ~** tomber au niveau le plus bas ▶ VI (cow) mugir

low-alcohol [ləu'ælkəhɔl] ADJ à faible teneur en alcool, peu alcoolisé(e)

lowbrow ['ləubrau] ADJ sans prétentions intellectuelles

low-calorie ['ləu'kælərɪ] ADJ hypocalorique

low-carb [ləu'kɑ:b] ADJ (inf) pauvre en glucides

low-cut ['ləukʌt] ADJ (dress) décolleté(e)

low-down ['ləudaun] N (inf): **he gave me the ~ (on it)** il m'a mis au courant ▶ ADJ (mean) méprisable

lower ADJ ['ləuə^r] inférieur(e) ▶ VT ['ləuə^r] baisser; (resistance) diminuer; **to ~ o.s. to** s'abaisser à ▶ VI ['lauə^r] (person, sky, clouds) être menaçant; **to ~ at sb** jeter un regard mauvais or noir à qn

lower sixth (BRIT) N (Scol) première f

low-fat ['ləu'fæt] ADJ maigre

low-key ['ləu'ki:] ADJ modéré(e), discret(-ète)

lowland N, **lowlands** NPL ['ləulənd(z)] plaine(s) f(pl)

low-level ['ləulɛvl] ADJ bas(se); (flying) à basse altitude

low-loader ['ləuləudə^r] N semi-remorque f à plate-forme surbaissée

lowly ['ləulɪ] ADJ humble, modeste

low-lying [ləu'laɪɪŋ] ADJ à faible altitude

low-paid [ləu'peɪd] ADJ mal payé(e), aux salaires bas

low-rise ['ləuraɪz] ADJ bas(se), de faible hauteur

low-tech ['ləutɛk] ADJ sommaire

loyal ['lɔɪəl] ADJ loyal(e), fidèle

loyalist ['lɔɪəlɪst] N loyaliste mf

loyalty ['lɔɪəltɪ] N loyauté f, fidélité f

loyalty card N carte f de fidélité

lozenge ['lɔzɪndʒ] N (Med) pastille f; (Geom) losange m

LP N ABBR = **long-playing record**

LPG N ABBR (= liquid petroleum gas) GPL m

L-plates ['ɛlpleɪts] NPL (BRIT) plaques fpl (obligatoires) d'apprenti conducteur

LPN N ABBR (US: = Licensed Practical Nurse) infirmier(-ière) diplômé(e)

LRAM N ABBR (BRIT) = **Licentiate of the Royal Academy of Music**

LSAT N ABBR (US) = **Law School Admissions Test**

LSD N ABBR (= lysergic acid diethylamide) LSD m; (BRIT: = pounds, shillings and pence) système monétaire en usage en GB jusqu'en 1971

LSE N ABBR = **London School of Economics**

LT ABBR (Elec: = low tension) BT

Lt ABBR (= lieutenant) Lt.

Ltd ABBR (Comm: = limited) ≈ SA

lubricant ['lu:brɪkənt] N lubrifiant m

lubricate ['lu:brɪkeɪt] VT lubrifier, graisser

lucid ['lu:sɪd] ADJ lucide

lucidity [lu:'sɪdɪtɪ] N lucidité f

★**luck** [lʌk] N chance f; **bad ~** malchance f, malheur m; **to be in ~** avoir de la chance; **to be out of ~** ne pas avoir de chance; **good ~!** bonne chance !; **bad or hard or tough ~!** pas de chance !

luckily ['lʌkɪlɪ] ADV heureusement, par bonheur

luckless ['lʌklɪs] ADJ (person) malchanceux(-euse); (trip) marqué(e) par la malchance

★**lucky** ['lʌkɪ] ADJ (person) qui a de la chance; (coincidence) heureux(-euse); (number etc) qui porte bonheur

lucrative ['lu:krətɪv] ADJ lucratif(-ive), rentable, qui rapporte

ludicrous ['lu:dɪkrəs] ADJ ridicule, absurde

ludo ['lu:dəu] N jeu m des petits chevaux

lug [lʌg] VT traîner, tirer

luggage ['lʌgɪdʒ] N bagages mpl; **our ~ hasn't arrived** nos bagages ne sont pas arrivés; **could**

you send someone to collect our ~? pourriez-vous envoyer quelqu'un chercher nos bagages ?

luggage lockers NPL consigne f automatique

luggage rack N (in train) porte-bagages m inv; (: made of string) filet m à bagages; (on car) galerie f

luggage van, (US) **luggage car** N (Rail) fourgon m (à bagages)

lugubrious [lu'gu:brɪəs] ADJ lugubre

lukewarm ['lu:kwɔ:m] ADJ tiède

lull [lʌl] N accalmie f; (in conversation) pause f ▶ VT: **to ~ sb to sleep** bercer qn pour qu'il s'endorme; **to be lulled into a false sense of security** s'endormir dans une fausse sécurité

lullaby ['lʌləbaɪ] N berceuse f

lumbago [lʌm'beɪɡəu] N lumbago m

lumber ['lʌmbəʳ] N (wood) bois m de charpente; (junk) bric-à-brac m inv ▶ VT (BRIT inf): **to ~ sb with sth/sb** coller or refiler qch/qn à qn ▶ VI (also: **lumber about, lumber along**) marcher pesamment

lumberjack ['lʌmbədʒæk] N bûcheron m

lumber room N (BRIT) débarras m

lumber yard N entrepôt m de bois

luminous ['lu:mɪnəs] ADJ lumineux(-euse)

lump [lʌmp] N morceau m; (in sauce) grumeau m; (swelling) grosseur f ▶ VT (also: **lump together**) réunir, mettre en tas

lump sum N somme globale or forfaitaire

lumpy ['lʌmpɪ] ADJ (sauce) qui a des grumeaux; (bed) défoncé(e), peu confortable

lunacy ['lu:nəsɪ] N démence f, folie f

lunar ['lu:nəʳ] ADJ lunaire

lunatic ['lu:nətɪk] N (!) fou (folle), dément(e) ▶ ADJ fou (folle), dément(e)

lunatic asylum N (!) asile m d'aliénés

★**lunch** [lʌntʃ] N déjeuner m; **to invite sb to** or **for ~** inviter qn à déjeuner; **it is his ~ hour** c'est l'heure où il déjeune ▶ VI déjeuner

lunch box N (lit) boîte dans laquelle on transporte son déjeuner; (BRIT inf, fig) engin m (inf)

lunch break, lunch hour N pause f de midi, heure f du déjeuner

luncheon ['lʌntʃən] N déjeuner m

luncheon meat N sorte de saucisson

luncheon voucher N chèque-repas m, ticket-repas m

lunchtime ['lʌntʃtaɪm] N: **it's ~** c'est l'heure du déjeuner

lung [lʌŋ] N poumon m

lung cancer N cancer m du poumon

lunge [lʌndʒ] VI (also: **lunge forward**) faire un mouvement brusque en avant; **to ~ at sb** envoyer or assener un coup à qn

lupin ['lu:pɪn] N lupin m

lurch [lə:tʃ] VI vaciller, tituber ▶ N écart m brusque, embardée f; **to leave sb in the ~** laisser qn se débrouiller or se dépêtrer tout(e) seul(e)

lure [luəʳ] N (attraction) attrait m, charme m; (in hunting) appât m, leurre m ▶ VT attirer or persuader par la ruse

lurid ['luərɪd] ADJ affreux(-euse), atroce

lurk [lə:k] VI se tapir, se cacher

luscious ['lʌʃəs] ADJ succulent(e), appétissant(e)

lush [lʌʃ] ADJ luxuriant(e)

lust [lʌst] N (sexual) désir (sexuel); (Rel) luxure f; (fig): **~ for** soif f de
▶ **lust after** VT FUS convoiter, désirer

luster ['lʌstəʳ] N (US) = **lustre**

lustful ['lʌstful] ADJ lascif(-ive)

lustre, (US) **luster** ['lʌstəʳ] N lustre m, brillant m

lusty ['lʌstɪ] ADJ vigoureux(-euse), robuste

lute [lu:t] N luth m

Luxembourg ['lʌksəmbə:ɡ] N Luxembourg m

luxuriant [lʌɡ'zjuərɪənt] ADJ luxuriant(e)

luxurious [lʌɡ'zjuərɪəs] ADJ luxueux(-euse)

★**luxury** ['lʌkʃərɪ] N luxe m ▶ CPD de luxe

LW ABBR (Radio: = long wave) GO

Lycra® ['laɪkrə] N Lycra® m

lying ['laɪɪŋ] N mensonge(s) m(pl) ▶ ADJ (statement, story) mensonger(-ère), faux (fausse); (person) menteur(-euse)

lynch [lɪntʃ] VT lyncher

lynx [lɪŋks] N lynx m inv

Lyons ['laɪɔn] N Lyon n

lyre ['laɪəʳ] N lyre f

lyric ['lɪrɪk] ADJ lyrique

lyrical ['lɪrɪkl] ADJ lyrique

lyricism ['lɪrɪsɪzəm] N lyrisme m

lyrics ['lɪrɪks] NPL (of song) paroles fpl

Mm

M¹, m [ɛm] N (letter) M, m m; **M for Mary**, (US) **M for Mike** M comme Marcel

M² N ABBR (BRIT) = **motorway**; **the M8** ≈ l'A8 ▶ ABBR (= medium) M

m. ABBR (= metre) m; (= million) M; (= mile) mi

MA N ABBR (Scol) = **Master of Arts** ▶ ABBR (US) = **military academy**; **Massachusetts**

ma [mɑ:] N (inf) maman f

ma'am ['mæm] N (esp US: madam) Madame f

mac [mæk] N (BRIT) imper(méable m) m

macabre [mə'kɑ:brə] ADJ macabre

macaroni [mækə'rəʊnɪ] N macaronis mpl

macaroon [mækə'ru:n] N macaron m

mace [meɪs] N masse f; (spice) macis m

Macedonia [mæsɪ'dəʊnɪə] N Macédoine f

Macedonian [mæsɪ'dəʊnɪən] ADJ macédonien(ne) ▶ N Macédonien(ne); (Ling) macédonien m

machete [mə'ʃɛtɪ] N machette f

Machiavellian [mækɪə'vɛlɪən] ADJ machiavélique

machinations [mækɪ'neɪʃənz] NPL machinations fpl, intrigues fpl

★**machine** [mə'ʃi:n] N machine f ▶ VT (dress etc) coudre à la machine; (Tech) usiner

machine code N (Comput) code m machine

machine gun N mitrailleuse f

machine language N (Comput) langage m machine

machine-readable [mə'ʃi:nri:dəbl] ADJ (Comput) exploitable par une machine

machinery [mə'ʃi:nərɪ] N machinerie f, machines fpl; (fig) mécanisme(s) m(pl)

machine shop N atelier m d'usinage

machine tool N machine-outil f

machine washable ADJ (garment) lavable en machine

machinist [mə'ʃi:nɪst] N machiniste mf

machismo [mæ'kɪzməʊ, mæ'tʃɪzməʊ] N machisme m

macho ['mætʃəʊ] ADJ macho inv

mackerel ['mækrl] N (pl inv) maquereau m

mackintosh ['mækɪntɒʃ] N (BRIT) imperméable m

macro... ['mækrəʊ] PREFIX macro...

macroeconomic [mækrəʊi:kə'nɒmɪk] ADJ macro-économique

macroeconomics [mækrəʊi:kə'nɒmɪks] N macro-économie f

★**mad** [mæd] ADJ fou (folle); (foolish) insensé(e); (angry) furieux(-euse); **to go ~** devenir fou; **to be ~ (keen) about** or **on sth** (inf) être follement passionné de qch, être fou de qch

Madagascar [mædə'gæskəʳ] N Madagascar m

madam ['mædəm] N madame f; **yes ~** oui Madame; **M~ Chairman** Madame la Présidente

madcap ['mædkæp] ADJ (inf) écervelé(e)

mad cow disease N maladie f de la vache folle

madden ['mædn] VT exaspérer

maddening ['mædnɪŋ] ADJ exaspérant(e)

made [meɪd] PT, PP of **make**

Madeira [mə'dɪərə] N (Geo) Madère f; (wine) madère m

made-to-measure ['meɪdtə'mɛʒəʳ] ADJ (BRIT) fait(e) sur mesure

made-up ['meɪdʌp] ADJ (story) inventé(e), fabriqué(e)

madhouse ['mædhaʊs] N (also fig) maison f de fous

madly ['mædlɪ] ADV follement; **~ in love** éperdument amoureux(-euse)

madman ['mædmən] N (irreg) fou m, aliéné m

madness ['mædnɪs] N folie f

Madonna [mə'dɒnə] N (Rel) Madone f

Madrid [mə'drɪd] N Madrid

maelstrom ['meɪlstrəm] N maelström m, tourbillon m

Mafia ['mæfɪə] N maf(f)ia f

mag [mæg] N ABBR (BRIT inf: = magazine) magazine m

★**magazine** [mægə'zi:n] N (Press) magazine m, revue f; (Radio, TV) magazine; (Mil: store) dépôt m, arsenal m; (of firearm) magasin m

magenta [mə'dʒɛntə] ADJ magenta inv ▶ N magenta m

maggot ['mægət] N ver m, asticot m

★**magic** ['mædʒɪk] N magie f ▶ ADJ magique

magical ['mædʒɪkl] ADJ magique; (experience, evening) merveilleux(-euse)

magician [mə'dʒɪʃən] N magicien(ne)

magistrate ['mædʒɪstreɪt] N magistrat m; juge m; **magistrates' court** (BRIT) ≈ tribunal m d'instance

magnanimous [mæg'nænɪməs] ADJ magnanime

magnate ['mægneɪt] N magnat *m*

magnesium [mæg'niːzɪəm] N magnésium *m*

magnet ['mægnɪt] N aimant *m*

magnetic [mæg'netɪk] ADJ magnétique

magnetic disk N (*Comput*) disque *m* magnétique

magnetic tape N bande *f* magnétique

magnetism ['mægnɪtɪzəm] N magnétisme *m*

magnification [mægnɪfɪ'keɪʃən] N grossissement *m*

magnificence [mæg'nɪfɪsns] N magnificence *f*

magnificent [mæg'nɪfɪsnt] ADJ superbe, magnifique; (*splendid: robe, building*) somptueux(-euse), magnifique

magnificently [mæg'nɪfɪsntlɪ] ADV magnifiquement, brillamment

magnify ['mægnɪfaɪ] VT grossir; (*sound*) amplifier

magnifying glass ['mægnɪfaɪɪŋ-] N loupe *f*

magnitude ['mægnɪtjuːd] N ampleur *f*

magnolia [mæg'nəʊlɪə] N magnolia *m*

magpie ['mægpaɪ] N pie *f*

mahogany [mə'hɔgənɪ] N acajou *m* ▸ CPD en (bois d')acajou

maid [meɪd] N bonne *f*; (*in hotel*) femme *f* de chambre; **old ~** (*pej*) vieille fille

maiden [meɪdn] N jeune fille *f* ▸ ADJ (*aunt etc*) non mariée; (*speech, voyage*) inaugural(e)

maiden name N nom *m* de jeune fille

★**mail** [meɪl] N poste *f*; (*letters*) courrier *m*; **by ~** par la poste ▸ VT envoyer (par la poste)

mailbag ['meɪlbæg] N (*sack*) sac postal; (*postman's*) sacoche *f*

mailbox ['meɪlbɔks] N (*US, also Comput*) boîte *f* aux lettres

mailing list ['meɪlɪŋ-] N liste *f* d'adresses

mailman ['meɪlmæn] N (*irreg*) (*US*) facteur *m*

mail-order ['meɪlɔːdəʳ] N vente *f* or achat *m* par correspondance ▸ CPD: **~ firm** or **house** maison *f* de vente par correspondance

mailshot ['meɪlʃɔt] N (*BRIT*) mailing *m*

mail train N train postal

mail truck N (*US Aut*) = **mail van**

mail van N (*BRIT*) (*Aut*) voiture *f* or fourgonnette *f* des postes; (*Rail*) wagon-poste *m*

maim [meɪm] VT mutiler

★**main** [meɪn] ADJ principal(e); **the ~ thing** l'essentiel *m* ▸ N (*pipe*) conduite principale, canalisation *f*; **the mains** (*Elec*) le secteur; **in the ~** dans l'ensemble

main course N (*Culin*) plat *m* principal

mainframe ['meɪnfreɪm] N (*also:* **mainframe computer**) (gros) ordinateur, unité centrale

mainland ['meɪnlənd] N continent *m*

mainline ['meɪnlaɪn] ADJ (*Rail*) de grande ligne ▸ VT (*drugs slang*) se shooter à ▸ VI (*drugs slang*) se shooter

main line N (*Rail*) grande ligne

★**mainly** ['meɪnlɪ] ADV principalement, surtout

main road N grand axe, route nationale

mainstay ['meɪnsteɪ] N (*fig*) pilier *m*

mainstream ['meɪnstriːm] N (*fig*) courant principal

main street N rue *f* principale

★**maintain** [meɪn'teɪn] VT entretenir; (*continue*) maintenir, préserver; (*affirm*) soutenir; **to ~ that ...** soutenir que ...

maintenance ['meɪntənəns] N entretien *m*; (*Law: alimony*) pension *f* alimentaire

maintenance contract N contrat *m* d'entretien

maintenance order N (*Law*) obligation *f* alimentaire

maisonette [meɪzə'nɛt] N (*BRIT*) appartement *m* en duplex

maize [meɪz] N (*BRIT*) maïs *m*

Maj. ABBR (*Mil*) = **major**

majestic [mə'dʒɛstɪk] ADJ majestueux(-euse)

majesty ['mædʒɪstɪ] N majesté *f*; (*title*): **Your M~** Votre Majesté

★**major** ['meɪdʒəʳ] N (*Mil*) commandant *m* ▸ ADJ (*important*) important(e); (*most important*) principal(e); (*Mus*) majeur(e); **a ~ operation** (*Med*) une grosse opération ▸ VI (*US Scol*): **to ~ (in)** se spécialiser (en)

Majorca [mə'jɔːkə] N Majorque *f*

major general N (*Mil*) général *m* de division

★**majority** [mə'dʒɔrɪtɪ] N majorité *f* ▸ CPD (*verdict, holding*) majoritaire

★**make** [meɪk] (*pt, pp* **made** [meɪd]) VT faire; (*manufacture*) faire, fabriquer; (*earn*) gagner; (*decision*) prendre; (*friend*) se faire; (*speech*) faire, prononcer; (*cause to*): **to ~ sb sad** *etc* rendre qn triste *etc*; (*force*): **to ~ sb do sth** obliger qn à faire qch, faire faire qch à qn; (*equal*): **2 and 2 ~ 4** 2 et 2 font 4; **to ~ the bed** faire le lit; **to ~ a fool of sb** (*ridicule*) ridiculiser qn; (*trick*) avoir or duper qn; **to ~ a profit** faire un or des bénéfice(s); **to ~ a loss** essuyer une perte; **to ~ it** (*in time etc*) y arriver; (*succeed*) réussir; **what time do you ~ it?** quelle heure avez-vous ?; **I ~ it £249** d'après mes calculs ça fait 249 livres; **to be made of** être en; **to ~ do with** se contenter de; se débrouiller avec; **to ~ good** VI (*succeed*) faire son chemin, réussir; VT (*deficit*) combler; (*losses*) compenser ▸ N (*manufacture*) fabrication *f*; (*brand*) marque *f*

▸ **make for** VT FUS (*place*) se diriger vers

▸ **make off** VI filer

▸ **make out** VT (*write out: cheque*) faire; (*decipher*) déchiffrer; (*understand*) comprendre; (*see*) distinguer; (*claim, imply*) prétendre, vouloir faire croire; **to ~ out a case for sth** présenter des arguments solides en faveur de qch

▸ **make over** VT (*assign*): **to ~ over (to)** céder (à), transférer (au nom de)

▸ **make up** VT (*invent*) inventer, imaginer; (*constitute*) constituer; (*parcel, bed*) faire; **to be made up of** se composer de ▸ VI se réconcilier; (*with cosmetics*) se maquiller, se farder

▸ **make up for** VT FUS compenser; (*lost time*) rattraper

make-believe ['meɪkbɪliːv] N: **a world of ~** un monde de chimères or d'illusions; **it's just ~** c'est de la fantaisie; c'est une illusion

make-or-break [meɪkɔː'breɪk] ADJ (*issue, game, meeting*) décisif(-ive); **it's ~ time** c'est le moment décisif

makeover ['meɪkəʊvəʳ] N (by beautician) soins mpl de maquillage; (change of image) changement m d'image; **to give sb a ~** relooker qn

★**maker** ['meɪkəʳ] N fabricant m; (of film, programme) réalisateur(-trice)

makeshift ['meɪkʃɪft] ADJ provisoire, improvisé(e)

★**make-up** ['meɪkʌp] N maquillage m

make-up bag N trousse f de maquillage

make-up remover N démaquillant m

making ['meɪkɪŋ] N (fig): **in the ~** en formation or gestation; **to have the makings of** (actor, athlete) avoir l'étoffe de

maladjusted [mælə'dʒʌstɪd] ADJ inadapté(e)

maladministration [mælədmɪnɪ'streɪʃən] N mauvaise gestion f

malaise [mæ'leɪz] N malaise m

malaria [mə'lɛərɪə] N malaria f, paludisme m

Malawi [mə'lɑːwɪ] N Malawi m

Malay [mə'leɪ] ADJ malais(e) ▶ N (person) Malais(e); (language) malais m

Malaya [mə'leɪə] N Malaisie f

Malayan [mə'leɪən] ADJ, N = **Malay**

Malaysia [mə'leɪzɪə] N Malaisie f

Malaysian [mə'leɪzɪən] ADJ malaisien(ne) ▶ N Malaisien(ne)

Maldives ['mɔːldaɪvz] NPL: **the ~** les Maldives fpl

★**male** [meɪl] N (Biol, Elec) mâle m ▶ ADJ (sex, attitude) masculin(e); (animal) mâle; (child etc) du sexe masculin; **~ and female students** étudiants et étudiantes

male chauvinist N phallocrate m

male nurse N infirmier m

malevolence [mə'lɛvələns] N malveillance f

malevolent [mə'lɛvələnt] ADJ malveillant(e)

malfunction [mæl'fʌŋkʃən] N fonctionnement défectueux

Mali ['mɑːlɪ] N Mali m

malice ['mælɪs] N méchanceté f, malveillance f

malicious [mə'lɪʃəs] ADJ méchant(e), malveillant(e); (Law) avec intention criminelle

maliciously [mə'lɪʃəslɪ] ADV avec malveillance

malign [mə'laɪn] VT diffamer, calomnier

malignant [mə'lɪɡnənt] ADJ (Med) malin(-igne)

malinger [mə'lɪŋɡəʳ] VI faire semblant d'être malade

malingerer [mə'lɪŋɡərəʳ] N faux (fausse) malade

mall [mɔːl] N (also: **shopping mall**) centre commercial

mallard ['mælɑːd] N colvert m

malleable ['mælɪəbl] ADJ malléable

mallet ['mælɪt] N maillet m

malnourished [mæl'nʌrɪʃt] ADJ mal nourri(e)

malnutrition [mælnjuː'trɪʃən] N malnutrition f

malpractice [mæl'præktɪs] N faute professionnelle; négligence f

malt [mɔːlt] N malt m ▶ CPD (whisky) pur malt

Malta ['mɔːltə] N Malte f

Maltese [mɔːl'tiːz] ADJ maltais(e) ▶ N (pl inv) Maltais(e); (Ling) maltais m

maltreat [mæl'triːt] VT maltraiter

malware ['mælwɛəʳ] N (Comput) logiciel m malveillant

mammal ['mæml] N mammifère m

mammogram ['mæməɡræm] N mammographie f

mammoth ['mæməθ] N mammouth m ▶ ADJ géant(e), monstre

★**man** [mæn] (pl **men** [mɛn]) N homme m; (Sport) joueur m; (Chess) pièce f; (Draughts) pion m; **an old ~** un vieillard; **~ and wife** mari et femme ▶ VT (Naut: ship) garnir d'hommes; (machine) assurer le fonctionnement de; (Mil: gun) servir; (: post) être de service à

manacles ['mænəklz] NPL menottes fpl

★**manage** ['mænɪdʒ] VI se débrouiller; (succeed) y arriver, réussir ▶ VT (business) gérer; (team, operation) diriger; (control: ship) manier, manœuvrer; (: person) savoir s'y prendre avec; (device, things to do, carry etc) arriver à se débrouiller avec, s'en tirer avec; **to ~ to do** se débrouiller pour faire; (succeed) réussir à faire

manageable ['mænɪdʒəbl] ADJ maniable; (task etc) faisable; (number) raisonnable

★**management** ['mænɪdʒmənt] N (running) administration f, direction f; (people in charge: of business, firm) dirigeants mpl, cadres mpl; (: of hotel, shop, theatre) direction; **"under new ~"** « changement de gérant », « changement de propriétaire »

management accounting N comptabilité f de gestion

management consultant N conseiller(-ère) de direction

★**manager** ['mænɪdʒəʳ] N (of business) directeur m; (of institution etc) administrateur m; (of department, unit) responsable mf, chef m; (of hotel etc) gérant m; (Sport) manager m; (of artist) impresario m; **sales ~** responsable or chef des ventes

★**manageress** [mænɪdʒə'rɛs] N directrice f; (of hotel etc) gérante f

managerial [mænɪ'dʒɪərɪəl] ADJ directorial(e); (skills) de cadre, de gestion; **~ staff** cadres mpl

managing director ['mænɪdʒɪŋ-] N directeur général

Mancunian [mæŋ'kjuːnɪən] ADJ de Manchester ▶ N habitant(e) Manchester; natif(-ive) de Manchester

Mandarin ['mændərɪn] N (language) mandarin m

mandarin ['mændərɪn] N (also: **mandarin orange**) mandarine f; (person) mandarin m

mandate ['mændeɪt] N mandat m

mandatory ['mændətərɪ] ADJ obligatoire; (powers etc) mandataire

mandolin, mandoline ['mændəlɪn] N mandoline f

mane [meɪn] N crinière f

maneuver etc [mə'nuːvəʳ] N (US) = **manoeuvre** etc

manfully ['mænfəlɪ] ADV vaillamment

manganese [mæŋɡə'niːz] N manganèse m

manger ['meɪndʒəʳ] N mangeoire f

mangetout ['mɔnʒ'tuː] N mange-tout m inv

mangle ['mæŋɡl] VT déchiqueter; mutiler ▶ N essoreuse f; calandre f

mango ['mæŋɡəʊ] (pl **mangoes**) N mangue f

m

mangrove ['mæŋgrəuv] N palétuvier m

mangy ['meɪndʒɪ] ADJ galeux(-euse)

manhandle ['mænhændl] VT (*mistreat*) maltraiter, malmener; (*move by hand*) manutentionner

manhole ['mænhəul] N trou m d'homme

manhood ['mænhud] N (*age*) âge m d'homme; (*manliness*) virilité f

man-hour ['mænauəʳ] N heure-homme f, heure f de main-d'œuvre

manhunt ['mænhʌnt] N chasse f à l'homme

mania ['meɪnɪə] N manie f

maniac ['meɪnɪæk] N maniaque mf; (*fig*) fou (folle)

manic ['mænɪk] ADJ maniaque

manic-depressive ['mænɪkdɪ'presɪv] ADJ, N (*Psych*) maniaco-dépressif(-ive)

manicure ['mænɪkjuəʳ] N manucure f ▶ VT (*person*) faire les mains à

manicure set N trousse f à ongles

manifest ['mænɪfest] VT manifester ▶ ADJ manifeste, évident(e) ▶ N (*Aviat, Naut*) manifeste m

manifestation [mænɪfes'teɪʃən] N manifestation f

manifesto [mænɪ'festəu] N (*Pol*) manifeste m

manifold ['mænɪfəuld] ADJ multiple, varié(e) ▶ N (*Aut etc*): **exhaust ~** collecteur m d'échappement

Manila [mə'nɪlə] N Manille, Manila

manila [mə'nɪlə] ADJ: **~ paper** papier m bulle

manipulate [mə'nɪpjuleɪt] VT manipuler; (*system, situation*) exploiter

manipulation [mənɪpju'leɪʃən] N manipulation f

manipulative [mə'nɪpjulətɪv] ADJ manipulateur(-trice)

mankind [mæn'kaɪnd] N humanité f, genre humain

manliness ['mænlɪnɪs] N virilité f

manly ['mænlɪ] ADJ viril(e)

man-made ['mæn'meɪd] ADJ artificiel(le); (*fibre*) synthétique

manna ['mænə] N manne f

manned [mænd] ADJ (*spacecraft, flight*) habité(e)

mannequin ['mænɪkɪn] N mannequin m

★**manner** ['mænəʳ] N manière f, façon f; (*behaviour*) attitude f, comportement m; **all ~ of** toutes sortes de ■ **manners** NPL: (**good**) **manners** (bonnes) manières; **bad manners** mauvaises manières

mannerism ['mænərɪzəm] N particularité f de langage (*or* de comportement), tic m

mannerly ['mænəlɪ] ADJ poli(e), courtois(e)

manoeuvrable, (*US*) **maneuverable** [mə'nu:vrəbl] ADJ facile à manœuvrer

manoeuvre, (*US*) **maneuver** [mə'nu:vəʳ] VT (*move*) manœuvrer; (*manipulate: person*) manipuler; (: *situation*) exploiter; **to ~ sb into doing sth** manipuler qn pour lui faire faire qch ▶ N manœuvre f

manor ['mænəʳ] N (*also:* **manor house**) manoir m

manpower ['mænpauəʳ] N main-d'œuvre f

manservant ['mænsə:vənt] (*pl* **menservants** ['mɛn-]) N domestique m

mansion ['mænʃən] N château m, manoir m

manslaughter ['mænslɔ:təʳ] N homicide m involontaire

mantelpiece ['mæntlpi:s] N cheminée f

mantle ['mæntl] N cape f; (*fig*) manteau m

man-to-man ['mæntə'mæn] ADJ, ADV d'homme à homme

mantra ['mæntrə] N mantra m

manual ['mænjuəl] ADJ manuel(le) ▶ N manuel m

manually ['mænjuəlɪ] ADV manuellement

manual worker N travailleur manuel

★**manufacture** [mænju'fæktʃəʳ] VT fabriquer ▶ N fabrication f

manufactured goods [mænju'fæktʃəd-] NPL produits manufacturés

★**manufacturer** [mænju'fæktʃərəʳ] N fabricant m

manufacturing [mænju'fæktʃərɪŋ] N industrie f ▶ CPD (*sector, output*) industriel(le)

manufacturing industries NPL industries fpl de transformation

manure [mə'njuəʳ] N fumier m; (*artificial*) engrais m

manuscript ['mænjuskrɪpt] N manuscrit m

Manx [mæŋks] ADJ mannois(e), de l'île de Man

★**many** ['menɪ] ADJ beaucoup de, de nombreux(-euses); **how ~ ...?** combien de ... ?; **a great many...** un grand nombre de ...; **too ~ difficulties** trop de difficultés; **twice as ~** deux fois plus de ...; **~ a ...** bien des ..., plus d'un(e) ... ▶ PRON beaucoup, un grand nombre; **how ~?** combien ?; **a great ~** un grand nombre; **twice as ~** deux fois plus

Maori ['mauri] N Maori(e) ▶ ADJ maori(e)

★**map** [mæp] N carte f; (*of town*) plan m; **can you show it to me on the ~?** pouvez-vous me l'indiquer sur la carte ? ▶ VT dresser la carte de ▶ **map out** VT tracer; (*fig: task*) planifier; (: *career, holiday*) organiser, préparer (à l'avance); (: *essay*) faire le plan de

maple ['meɪpl] N érable m

mar [ma:ʳ] VT gâcher, gâter

Mar. ABBR = **March**

marathon ['mærəθən] N marathon m ▶ ADJ: **a ~ session** une séance-marathon

marathon runner N coureur(-euse) de marathon, marathonien(ne)

marauder [mə'rɔ:dəʳ] N maraudeur(-euse)

marble ['ma:bl] N marbre m; (*toy*) bille f ■ **marbles** NPL (*game*) billes

★**March** [ma:tʃ] N mars m; *see also* **July**

★**march** [ma:tʃ] VI marcher au pas; (*demonstrators*) défiler; **to ~ out of/into** etc sortir de/entrer dans etc (*de manière décidée ou impulsive*) ▶ N marche f; (*demonstration*) manifestation f

marcher ['ma:tʃəʳ] N (*demonstrator*) manifestant(e), marcheur(-euse)

marching ['ma:tʃɪŋ] N: **to give sb his ~ orders** (*fig*) renvoyer qn; envoyer promener qn

march-past ['ma:tʃpa:st] N défilé m

mare [meəʳ] N jument f

marg. [ma:dʒ] N ABBR (*inf*) = **margarine**

margarine [ma:dʒə'ri:n] N margarine f

margin ['ma:dʒɪn] N marge f

marginal ['mɑ:dʒɪnl] ADJ marginal(e); **~ seat** (Pol) siège disputé

marginalize ['mɑ:dʒɪnəlaɪz] VT marginaliser

marginally ['mɑ:dʒɪnəlɪ] ADV très légèrement, sensiblement

marigold ['mærɪɡəʊld] N souci m

marijuana [mærɪ'wɑ:nə] N marijuana f

marina [mə'ri:nə] N marina f

marinade N [mærɪ'neɪd] marinade f ▶ VT ['mærɪneɪd] = **marinate**

marinate ['mærɪneɪt] VT (faire) mariner

marine [mə'ri:n] ADJ marin(e) ▶ N fusilier marin; (US) marine m

marine insurance N assurance f maritime

marital ['mærɪtl] ADJ matrimonial(e)

marital status N situation f de famille

maritime ['mærɪtaɪm] ADJ maritime

maritime law N droit m maritime

marjoram ['mɑ:dʒərəm] N marjolaine f

★**mark** [mɑ:k] N marque f; (of skid etc) trace f; (Brit Scol) note f; (Sport) cible f; (currency) mark m; (Brit Tech): **M~ 2/3** 2ème/3ème série f or version f; (oven temperature): **(gas) ~ 4** thermostat m 4; **to be quick off the ~ (in doing)** (fig) ne pas perdre de temps (pour faire); **up to the ~** (in efficiency) à la hauteur; **punctuation marks** signes mpl de ponctuation ▶ VT (Sport: player) marquer; (stain) tacher; (Brit Scol) corriger, noter; **to ~ time** marquer le pas
▶ **mark down** VT (prices, goods) démarquer, réduire le prix de
▶ **mark off** VT (tick off) cocher, pointer
▶ **mark out** VT désigner
▶ **mark up** VT (price) majorer

marked [mɑ:kt] ADJ (obvious) marqué(e), net(te)

markedly ['mɑ:kɪdlɪ] ADV visiblement, manifestement

marker ['mɑ:kəʳ] N (sign) jalon m; (bookmark) signet m

★**market** ['mɑ:kɪt] N marché m; **to be on the ~** être sur le marché; **on the open ~** en vente libre; **to play the ~** jouer à la or spéculer en Bourse ▶ VT (Comm) commercialiser

marketable ['mɑ:kɪtəbl] ADJ commercialisable

market analysis N analyse f de marché

market day N jour m de marché

market demand N besoins mpl du marché

market economy N économie f de marché

market forces NPL tendances fpl du marché

market garden N (Brit) jardin maraîcher

★**marketing** ['mɑ:kɪtɪŋ] N marketing m

marketplace ['mɑ:kɪtpleɪs] N place f du marché; (Comm) marché m

market price N prix marchand

market research N étude f de marché

market value N valeur marchande; valeur du marché

marking ['mɑ:kɪŋ] N (on animal) marque f, tache f; (on road) signalisation f

marksman ['mɑ:ksmən] N (irreg) tireur m d'élite

marksmanship ['mɑ:ksmənʃɪp] N adresse f au tir

mark-up ['mɑ:kʌp] N (Comm: margin) marge f (bénéficiaire); (: increase) majoration f

marmalade ['mɑ:məleɪd] N confiture f d'oranges

maroon [mə'ru:n] VT: **to be marooned** être abandonné(e); (fig) être bloqué(e) ▶ ADJ (colour) bordeaux inv

marquee [mɑ:'ki:] N chapiteau m

marquess, marquis ['mɑ:kwɪs] N marquis m

Marrakech, Marrakesh [mærə'keʃ] N Marrakech

★**marriage** ['mærɪdʒ] N mariage m

marriage bureau N agence matrimoniale

marriage certificate N extrait m d'acte de mariage

marriage guidance, (US) **marriage counseling** N conseils conjugaux

marriage guidance counsellor, (US) **marriage counselor** N conseiller(-ère) conjugal(e)

marriage of convenience N mariage m de convenance

★**married** ['mærɪd] ADJ marié(e); (life, love) conjugal(e)

marrow ['mærəʊ] N (of bone) moelle f; (vegetable) courge f

★**marry** ['mærɪ] VT épouser, se marier avec; (subj: father, priest etc) marier ▶ VI (also: **get married**) se marier

Mars [mɑ:z] N (planet) Mars f

Marseilles [mɑ:'seɪ] N Marseille

marsh [mɑ:ʃ] N marais m, marécage m

marshal ['mɑ:ʃl] N maréchal m; (US: fire, police) = capitaine m; (for demonstration, meeting) membre m du service d'ordre ▶ VT rassembler

marshalling yard ['mɑ:ʃlɪŋ-] N (Rail) gare f de triage

Marshall Islands ['mɑ:ʃəl-] NPL îles fpl Marshall

marshmallow [mɑ:ʃ'mæləʊ] N (Bot) guimauve f; (sweet) (pâte f de) guimauve

marshy ['mɑ:ʃɪ] ADJ marécageux(-euse)

marsupial [mɑ:'su:pɪəl] ADJ marsupial(e) ▶ N marsupial m

martial ['mɑ:ʃl] ADJ martial(e)

martial arts NPL arts martiaux

martial law N loi martiale

Martian ['mɑ:ʃən] N Martien(ne)

martin ['mɑ:tɪn] N (also: **house martin**) martinet m

martyr ['mɑ:təʳ] N martyr(e) ▶ VT martyriser

martyrdom ['mɑ:tədəm] N martyre m

marvel ['mɑ:vl] N merveille f ▶ VI: **to ~ (at)** s'émerveiller (de)

marvellous, (US) **marvelous** ['mɑ:vləs] ADJ merveilleux(-euse)

Marxism ['mɑ:ksɪzəm] N marxisme m

Marxist ['mɑ:ksɪst] ADJ, N marxiste mf

marzipan ['mɑ:zɪpæn] N pâte f d'amandes

mascara [mæs'kɑ:rə] N mascara m

mascot ['mæskət] N mascotte f

masculine ['mæskjulɪn] ADJ masculin(e) ▶ N masculin m

masculinity [mæskju'lɪnɪtɪ] N masculinité f

mash [mæʃ] VT (Culin) faire une purée de

mashed potato N, **mashed potatoes** NPL [mæʃt-] purée f de pommes de terre

★**mask** [mɑːsk] N masque m ▶ VT masquer

masked [mɑːskt] ADJ masqué(e)

masochism [ˈmæsəkɪzəm] N masochisme m

masochist [ˈmæsəkɪst] N masochiste mf

masochistic [mæsəˈkɪstɪk] ADJ masochiste

mason [ˈmeɪsn] N (also: **stonemason**) maçon m; (also: **freemason**) franc-maçon m

masonic [məˈsɒnɪk] ADJ maçonnique

masonry [ˈmeɪsnrɪ] N maçonnerie f

masquerade [mæskəˈreɪd] N bal masqué; (fig) mascarade f ▶ VI: **to ~ as** se faire passer pour

★**mass** [mæs] N multitude f, masse f; (Physics) masse f; (Rel) messe f; **to go to ~** aller à la messe ▶ CPD (communication) de masse; (unemployment) massif(-ive) ▶ VI se masser ■ **masses** NPL: **the masses** les masses; **masses of** (inf) des tas de

massacre [ˈmæsəkəʳ] N massacre m ▶ VT massacrer

massage [ˈmæsɑːʒ] N massage m ▶ VT masser

massage parlour, (US) **massage parlor** N salon m de massage

★**massive** [ˈmæsɪv] ADJ énorme, massif(-ive)

massively [ˈmæsɪvlɪ] ADV (rise, increase) massivement; (popular, important) immensément; **to be ~ successful** remporter un succès immense

mass market N marché m grand public

mass media NPL mass-media mpl

mass meeting N rassemblement m de masse

mass-produce [ˈmæsprəˈdjuːs] VT fabriquer en série

mass production N fabrication f en série

mast [mɑːst] N mât m; (Radio, TV) pylône m

mastectomy [mæsˈtektəmɪ] N mastectomie f

★**master** [ˈmɑːstəʳ] N maître m; (in secondary school) professeur m; (in primary school) instituteur m; (title for boys): **M~ X** Monsieur X; **~ of ceremonies (MC)** n maître des cérémonies; **M~ of Arts/Science (MA/MSc)** n ≈ titulaire mf d'une maîtrise (en lettres/science); **M~ of Arts/Science degree (MA/MSc)** n ≈ maîtrise f; **M~'s degree** n ≈ maîtrise; voir article ▶ VT maîtriser; (learn) apprendre à fond; (understand) posséder parfaitement or à fond

Le **Master's degree** est un diplôme qui suit généralement le Bachelor's degree, bien que certaines universités décernent un Master's au lieu d'un Bachelor's. Il consiste soit à suivre des cours, soit à rédiger un mémoire à partir d'une recherche personnelle, soit encore en un mélange des deux. Les principaux masters sont le MA (Master of Arts) et le MSc (Master of Science), qui comprennent cours et mémoire, et le MLitt (Master of Letters) et le MPhil (Master of Philosophy), qui reposent uniquement sur le mémoire ; voir doctorate.

master disk N (Comput) disque original

masterful [ˈmɑːstəful] ADJ autoritaire, impérieux(-euse)

master key N passe-partout m inv

masterly [ˈmɑːstəlɪ] ADJ magistral(e)

mastermind [ˈmɑːstəmaɪnd] N esprit supérieur ▶ VT diriger, être le cerveau de

masterpiece [ˈmɑːstəpiːs] N chef-d'œuvre m

master plan N stratégie f d'ensemble

master stroke N coup m de maître

mastery [ˈmɑːstərɪ] N maîtrise f; connaissance parfaite

mastiff [ˈmæstɪf] N mastiff m

masturbate [ˈmæstəbeɪt] VI se masturber

masturbation [mæstəˈbeɪʃən] N masturbation f

mat [mæt] N petit tapis; (also: **doormat**) paillasson m; (also: **tablemat**) set m de table ▶ ADJ = **matt**

★**match** [mætʃ] N allumette f; (game) match m, partie f; (fig) égal(e); mariage m; parti m; **to be a good ~** être bien assorti(e) ▶ VT (also: **match up**) assortir; (go well with) aller bien avec, s'assortir à; (equal) égaler, valoir ▶ VI être assorti(e) ▶ **match up** VT assortir

matchbox [ˈmætʃbɒks] N boîte f d'allumettes

matching [ˈmætʃɪŋ] ADJ assorti(e)

matchless [ˈmætʃlɪs] ADJ sans égal

★**mate** [meɪt] N camarade mf de travail; (inf) copain (copine); (animal) partenaire mf, mâle (femelle); (in merchant navy) second m ▶ VI s'accoupler ▶ VT accoupler

★**material** [məˈtɪərɪəl] N (substance) matière f, matériau m; (cloth) tissu m, étoffe f; (information, data) données fpl; **reading ~** de quoi lire, de la lecture ▶ ADJ matériel(le); (relevant: evidence) pertinent(e); (important) essentiel(le) ■ **materials** NPL (equipment) matériaux mpl

materialism [məˈtɪərɪəlɪzəm] N matérialisme m

materialist [məˈtɪərɪəlɪst] ADJ, N matérialiste mf

materialistic [mətɪərɪəˈlɪstɪk] ADJ matérialiste

materialize [məˈtɪərɪəlaɪz] VI se matérialiser, se réaliser

materially [məˈtɪərɪəlɪ] ADV matériellement; essentiellement

maternal [məˈtəːnl] ADJ maternel(le)

maternity [məˈtəːnɪtɪ] N maternité f ▶ CPD de maternité, de grossesse

maternity benefit N prestation f de maternité

maternity dress N robe f de grossesse

maternity hospital N maternité f

maternity leave N congé m de maternité

matey [ˈmeɪtɪ] ADJ (BRIT inf) copain-copain inv

math [mæθ] N (US: = mathematics) maths fpl

mathematical [mæθəˈmætɪkl] ADJ mathématique

mathematician [mæθəməˈtɪʃən] N mathématicien(ne)

mathematics [mæθəˈmætɪks] N mathématiques fpl

maths [mæθs] N ABBR (BRIT: = mathematics) maths fpl

matinée [ˈmætɪneɪ] N matinée f

mating [ˈmeɪtɪŋ] N accouplement m

mating call N appel m du mâle

mating season N saison f des amours

matriarchal [meɪtrɪˈɑːkl] ADJ matriarcal(e)

matrices [ˈmeɪtrɪsiːz] NPL of **matrix**

matriculation [mətrɪkjuˈleɪʃən] N inscription f

matrimonial [mætrɪˈməunɪəl] ADJ matrimonial(e), conjugal(e)

matrimony [ˈmætrɪmənɪ] N mariage m

matrix [ˈmeɪtrɪks] (pl **matrices** [ˈmeɪtrɪsiːz]) N matrice f

matron [ˈmeɪtrən] (in hospital) infirmière-chef f; (in school) infirmière f

matronly [ˈmeɪtrənlɪ] ADJ de matrone; imposant(e)

matt [mæt] ADJ mat(e)

matted [ˈmætɪd] ADJ emmêlé(e)

★**matter** [ˈmætər] N question f; (Physics) matière f, substance f; (content) contenu m, fond m; (Med: pus) pus m; **what's the ~?** qu'est-ce qu'il y a ?, qu'est-ce qui ne va pas ?; **no ~ what** quoi qu'il arrive; **that's another ~** c'est une autre affaire; **as a ~ of course** tout naturellement; **as a ~ of fact** en fait; **it's a ~ of habit** c'est une question d'habitude; **printed ~** imprimés mpl; **reading ~** (BRIT) de quoi lire, de la lecture ▸ VI importer; **it doesn't ~** cela n'a pas d'importance; (I don't mind) cela ne fait rien ■ **matters** NPL (affairs, situation) la situation

matter-of-fact [ˈmætərəvˈfækt] ADJ terre à terre, neutre

matting [ˈmætɪŋ] N natte f

mattress [ˈmætrɪs] N matelas m

mature [məˈtjuər] ADJ mûr(e); (cheese) fait(e); (wine) arrivé(e) à maturité ▸ VI mûrir; (cheese, wine) se faire

mature student N étudiant(e) plus âgé(e) que la moyenne

maturity [məˈtjuərɪtɪ] N maturité f

maudlin [ˈmɔːdlɪn] ADJ larmoyant(e)

maul [mɔːl] VT lacérer

Mauritania [mɔːrɪˈteɪnɪə] N Mauritanie f

Mauritius [məˈrɪʃəs] N l'île f Maurice

mausoleum [mɔːsəˈlɪəm] N mausolée m

mauve [məuv] ADJ mauve

maverick [ˈmævrɪk] N (fig) franc-tireur m, non-conformiste mf

mawkish [ˈmɔːkɪʃ] ADJ (sentimental) mièvre; (insipid) fade

max ABBR = **maximum**

maxim [ˈmæksɪm] N maxime f

maxima [ˈmæksɪmə] NPL of **maximum**

maximize [ˈmæksɪmaɪz] VT (profits etc, chances) maximiser

★**maximum** [ˈmæksɪməm] (pl **maxima** [-mə]) ADJ maximum ▸ N maximum m

★**May** [meɪ] N mai m; see also **July**

★**may** [meɪ] (conditional **might** [maɪt]) VI (indicating possibility): **he ~ come** il se peut qu'il vienne; (be allowed to) **~ I smoke?** puis-je fumer ?; (wishes) **~ God bless you!** (que) Dieu vous bénisse !; **~ I sit here?** vous permettez que je m'assoie ici ?; **he might be there** il pourrait bien y être, il se pourrait qu'il y soit; **you ~ as well go** vous feriez aussi bien d'y aller; **I might as well go** je ferais aussi bien d'y aller, autant y aller; **you might like to try** vous pourriez (peut-être) essayer

★**maybe** [ˈmeɪbiː] ADV peut-être; **~ he'll ...** peut-être qu'il ...; **~ not** peut-être pas

mayday [ˈmeɪdeɪ] N S.O.S. m

May Day N le Premier mai

mayhem [ˈmeɪhɛm] N grabuge m

mayonnaise [meɪəˈneɪz] N mayonnaise f

★**mayor** [mɛər] N maire m

mayoress [ˈmɛərɛs] N (female mayor) maire m; (wife of mayor) épouse f du maire

maypole [ˈmeɪpəul] N mât enrubanné (autour duquel on danse)

maze [meɪz] N labyrinthe m, dédale m

MB ABBR (Comput) = **megabyte**; (CANADA) = **Manitoba**

MBA N ABBR (= Master of Business Administration) titre universitaire

MBBS, MBChB N ABBR (BRIT: = Bachelor of Medicine and Surgery) titre universitaire

MBE N ABBR (BRIT: = Member of the Order of the British Empire) titre honorifique

MBO N ABBR (BRIT) = **management buyout**

MC N ABBR = **master of ceremonies**

MCAT [ˈɛmkæt] N ABBR (US) = **Medical College Admissions Test**

MD N ABBR (= Doctor of Medicine) titre universitaire; (Comm) = **managing director** ▸ ABBR (US) = **Maryland**

MDF N ABBR (= medium-density fibreboard) panneau m MDF, panneau m de fibre de moyenne densité

MDT ABBR (US: = Mountain Daylight Time) heure d'été des Montagnes Rocheuses

ME N ABBR (US: = medical examiner) médecin légiste mf; (Med: = myalgic encephalomyelitis) encéphalomyélite f myalgique ▸ ABBR (US) = **Maine**

★**me** [miː] PRON me, m' + vowel or h mute; (stressed, after prep) moi; **it's me** c'est moi; **he heard me** il m'a entendu; **give me a book** donnez-moi un livre; **it's for me** c'est pour moi

meadow [ˈmɛdəu] N prairie f, pré m

meagre, (US) **meager** [ˈmiːgər] ADJ maigre

★**meal** [miːl] N repas m; (flour) farine f; **to go out for a ~** sortir manger

meals on wheels NPL (BRIT) repas livrés à domicile aux personnes âgées ou handicapées

mealtime [ˈmiːltaɪm] N heure f du repas

mealy-mouthed [ˈmiːlɪmauðd] ADJ mielleux(-euse)

★**mean** [miːn] (pt, pp **meant** [mɛnt]) ADJ (with money) avare, radin(e); (unkind) mesquin(e), méchant(e); (shabby) misérable; (US inf: animal) méchant, vicieux(-euse); (: person) vache; (average) moyen(ne) ▸ VT (signify) signifier, vouloir dire; (refer to) faire allusion à, parler de; (intend): **to ~ to do** avoir l'intention de faire; **to be meant for** être destiné(e) à; **do you ~ it?** vous êtes sérieux ?; **what do you ~?** que voulez-vous dire ? ▸ N moyenne f ■ **means** NPL (way, money) moyens mpl; **by means of** (instrument) au moyen de; **by all means** je vous en prie

meander [mɪˈændər] VI faire des méandres; (fig) flâner

★**meaning** [ˈmiːnɪŋ] N signification f, sens m

meaningful [ˈmiːnɪŋful] ADJ significatif(-ive); (relationship) valable

meaningfully ['miːnɪŋfʊlɪ] ADV (say, add) sur un ton qui en dit long; **to glance ~ at sb** jeter un regard éloquent à qn

meaningless ['miːnɪŋlɪs] ADJ dénué(e) de sens

meanness ['miːnnɪs] N avarice f; mesquinerie f

means test N (Admin) contrôle m des conditions de ressources

meant [mɛnt] PT, PP of **mean**

meantime ['miːntaɪm] ADV (also: **in the mean-time**) pendant ce temps

★**meanwhile** ['miːnwaɪl] ADV = **meantime**

measles ['miːzlz] N rougeole f

measly ['miːzlɪ] ADJ (inf) minable

measurable ['mɛʒərəbl] ADJ mesurable

★**measure** ['mɛʒəʳ] VT, VI mesurer ▶ N mesure f; (ruler) règle (graduée); **a litre ~** un litre; **some ~ of success** un certain succès; **to take measures to do sth** prendre des mesures pour faire qch
▶ **measure up** VI: **to ~ up (to)** être à la hauteur (de)

measured ['mɛʒəd] ADJ mesuré(e)

measurements ['mɛʒəməntz] NPL mesures fpl; **chest/hip ~** tour m de poitrine/hanches; **to take sb's ~** prendre les mesures de qn

★**meat** [miːt] N viande f; **I don't eat ~** je ne mange pas de viande; **cold meats** (BRIT) viandes froides; **crab ~** crabe f

meatball ['miːtbɔːl] N boulette f de viande

meat pie N pâté m en croûte

meaty ['miːtɪ] ADJ (flavour) de viande; (fig: argument, book) étoffé(e), substantiel(le)

Mecca ['mɛkə] N la Mecque; (fig): **a ~ (for)** la Mecque (de)

mechanic [mɪ'kænɪk] N mécanicien m; **can you send a ~?** pouvez-vous nous envoyer un mécanicien ?

mechanical [mɪ'kænɪkl] ADJ mécanique

mechanical engineering N (science) mécanique f; (industry) construction f mécanique

mechanically [mɪ'kænɪklɪ] ADV (react, say) mécaniquement; **~ sound** en bon état mécanique

mechanics [mə'kænɪks] N mécanique f ▶ NPL mécanisme m

mechanism ['mɛkənɪzəm] N mécanisme m

mechanization [mɛkənaɪ'zeɪʃən] N mécanisation f

MEd N ABBR (= Master of Education) titre universitaire

★**medal** ['mɛdl] N médaille f

medallion [mɪ'dælɪən] N médaillon m

medallist, (US) **medalist** ['mɛdlɪst] N (Sport) médaillé(e)

meddle ['mɛdl] VI: **to ~ in** se mêler de, s'occuper de; **to ~ with** toucher à

meddlesome ['mɛdlsəm], **meddling** ['mɛdlɪŋ] ADJ indiscret(-ète), qui se mêle de ce qui ne le (or la) regarde pas; touche-à-tout inv

★**media** ['miːdɪə] NPL media mpl ▶ NPL of **medium**

media circus N (event) battage m médiatique; (group of journalists) cortège m médiatique

mediaeval [mɛdɪ'iːvl] ADJ = **medieval**

median ['miːdɪən] N (US: also: **median strip**) bande médiane

media research N étude f de l'audience

mediate ['miːdɪeɪt] VI servir d'intermédiaire

mediation [miːdɪ'eɪʃən] N médiation f

mediator ['miːdɪeɪtəʳ] N médiateur(-trice)

medic ['mɛdɪk] N (inf: doctor) toubib mf (inf); (: student) carabin m (inf)

Medicaid ['mɛdɪkeɪd] N (US) assistance médicale aux indigents

★**medical** ['mɛdɪkl] ADJ médical(e) ▶ N (also: **medical examination**) visite médicale; (: private) examen médical

medical certificate N certificat médical

medicalize ['mɛdɪkəlaɪz] VT médicaliser

medical student N étudiant(e) en médecine

Medicare ['mɛdɪkɛəʳ] N (US) régime d'assurance maladie

medicated ['mɛdɪkeɪtɪd] ADJ traitant(e), médicamenteux(-euse)

medication [mɛdɪ'keɪʃən] N (drugs etc) médication f

medicinal [mɛ'dɪsɪnl] ADJ médicinal(e)

★**medicine** ['mɛdsɪn] N médecine f; (drug) médicament m

medicine chest N pharmacie f (murale ou portative)

medicine man N (irreg) sorcier m

medieval [mɛdɪ'iːvl] ADJ médiéval(e)

mediocre [miːdɪ'əʊkəʳ] ADJ médiocre

mediocrity [miːdɪ'ɔkrɪtɪ] N médiocrité f

meditate ['mɛdɪteɪt] VI: **to ~ (on)** méditer (sur)

meditation [mɛdɪ'teɪʃən] N méditation f

Mediterranean [mɛdɪtə'reɪnɪən] ADJ méditerranéen(ne); **the ~ (Sea)** la (mer) Méditerranée

★**medium** ['miːdɪəm] ADJ moyen(ne) ▶ N (pl **media** ['miːdɪə]) (means) moyen m; (pl **mediums**: person) médium m; **the happy ~** le juste milieu

medium-dry ['miːdɪəm'draɪ] ADJ demi-sec

medium-sized ['miːdɪəm'saɪzd] ADJ de taille moyenne

medium wave N (Radio) ondes moyennes, petites ondes

medley ['mɛdlɪ] N mélange m

meek [miːk] ADJ doux (douce), humble

★**meet** [miːt] (pt, pp **met** [mɛt]) VT rencontrer; (by arrangement) retrouver, rejoindre; (for the first time) faire la connaissance de; (go and fetch): **I'll ~ you at the station** j'irai te chercher à la gare; (opponent, danger, problem) faire face à; (requirements) satisfaire à, répondre à; (bill, expenses) régler, honorer; **pleased to ~ you!** enchanté !; **nice meeting you** ravi d'avoir fait votre connaissance ▶ VI (friends) se rencontrer; se retrouver; (in session) se réunir; (join: lines, roads) se joindre ▶ N (BRIT Hunting) rendez-vous m de chasse; (US Sport) rencontre f, meeting m
▶ **meet up** VI: **to ~ up with sb** rencontrer qn
▶ **meet with** VT FUS (difficulty) rencontrer; **to ~ with success** être couronné(e) de succès

★**meeting** ['miːtɪŋ] N (of group of people) réunion f; (between individuals) rendez-vous m; (formal) assemblée f; (Sport: rally) rencontre f, meeting m; (interview) entrevue f; **she's at** or **in a ~** (Comm) elle est en réunion; **to call a ~** convoquer une réunion

meeting place N lieu m de (la) réunion; (for appointment) lieu de rendez-vous

mega ['mɛgə] ADV (inf): **he's ~ rich** il est hyper-riche

megabit ['mɛgəbɪt] N (Comput) mégabit m

megabyte ['mɛgəbaɪt] N (Comput) méga-octet m

megalomaniac [mɛgələu'meɪnɪæk] N mégalo-mane mf

megaphone ['mɛgəfəun] N porte-voix m inv

megapixel ['mɛgəpɪksl] N mégapixel m

megastore ['mɛgəstɔ:ʳ] N mégastore m

megaton ['mɛgətʌn] N mégatonne f

megawatt ['mɛgəwɔt] N mégawatt m

meh [mɛ] EXCL bof

melancholy ['mɛlənkəlɪ] N mélancolie f ▶ ADJ mélancolique

melanoma [mɛlə'nəumə] N mélanome m

mellow ['mɛləu] ADJ velouté(e), doux (douce); (colour) riche et profond(e); (fruit) mûr(e) ▶ VI (person) s'adoucir

melodic [mɪ'lɒdɪk] ADJ mélodique

melodious [mɪ'ləudɪəs] ADJ mélodieux(-euse)

melodrama ['mɛləudrɑ:mə] N mélodrame m

melodramatic [mɛlədrə'mætɪk] ADJ mélodrama-tique

melody ['mɛlədɪ] N mélodie f

melon ['mɛlən] N melon m

melt [mɛlt] VI fondre; (become soft) s'amollir; (fig) s'attendrir ▶ VT faire fondre

  ▶ **melt away** VI fondre complètement

  ▶ **melt down** VT fondre

meltdown ['mɛltdaun] N fusion f (du cœur d'un réacteur nucléaire)

melting point ['mɛltɪŋ-] N point m de fusion

melting pot ['mɛltɪŋ-] N (fig) creuset m; **to be in the ~** être encore en discussion

★**member** ['mɛmbəʳ] N membre m; (of club, political party) membre, adhérent(e) ▶ CPD: **~ country/ state** n pays m/état m membre

Member of Parliament N (BRIT) député m

Member of the European Parliament N Eurodéputé m

Member of the House of Representatives N (US) membre m de la Chambre des représent-ants

Member of the Scottish Parliament N (BRIT) député m au Parlement écossais

★**membership** ['mɛmbəʃɪp] N (becoming a member) adhésion f; admission f; (being a member) qualité f de membre, fait m d'être membre; (members) membres mpl, adhérents mpl; (number of members) nombre m des membres or adhérents

membership card N carte f de membre

membrane ['mɛmbreɪn] N membrane f

meme [mi:m] N (Internet) mème m

memento [mə'mɛntəu] N souvenir m

memo ['mɛməu] N note f (de service)

memoir ['mɛmwɑ:ʳ] N mémoire m, étude f
  ■ **memoirs** NPL mémoires

memo pad N bloc-notes m

memorabilia [mɛmrə'bɪlɪə] NPL objets mpl de col-lection; **rock and pop ~** des objets de collection sur le rock et la pop

memorable ['mɛmərəbl] ADJ mémorable

memorandum [mɛmə'rændəm] (pl **memoranda** [-də]) N note f (de service); (Diplomacy) mémoran-dum m

memorial [mɪ'mɔ:rɪəl] N mémorial m ▶ ADJ com-mémoratif(-ive)

Memorial Day N (US) voir article

> **Memorial Day** est un jour férié aux États-Unis, le dernier lundi de mai dans la plupart des États, à la mémoire des soldats américains morts au combat.

memorize ['mɛməraɪz] VT apprendre or retenir par cœur

★**memory** ['mɛmərɪ] N (also Comput) mémoire f; (rec-ollection) souvenir m; **to have a good/bad ~** avoir une bonne/mauvaise mémoire; **loss of ~** perte f de mémoire; **in ~ of** à la mémoire de

memory card N (for digital camera) carte f mé-moire

memory stick N (Comput: flash pen) clé f USB; (: card) carte f mémoire

men [mɛn] NPL of **man**

menace ['mɛnɪs] N menace f; (inf: nuisance) peste f, plaie f; **a public ~** un danger public ▶ VT menacer

menacing ['mɛnɪsɪŋ] ADJ menaçant(e)

menagerie [mɪ'nædʒərɪ] N ménagerie f

mend [mɛnd] VT réparer; (darn) raccommoder, repriser; **to ~ one's ways** s'amender ▶ N reprise f; **on the ~** en voie de guérison

mending ['mɛndɪŋ] N raccommodages mpl

menfolk ['mɛnfəuk] NPL hommes mpl

menial ['mi:nɪəl] ADJ de domestique, inférieur(e); subalterne

meningitis [mɛnɪn'dʒaɪtɪs] N méningite f

menopausal [mɛnə'pɔ:zl] ADJ ménopausé(e)

menopause ['mɛnəpɔ:z] N ménopause f

menservants ['mɛnsə:vənts] NPL of **manservant**

men's room N (US): **the ~** les toilettes fpl pour hommes

menstrual ['mɛnstruəl] ADJ menstruel(le)

menstruate ['mɛnstrueɪt] VI avoir ses règles

menstruation [mɛnstru'eɪʃən] N menstrua-tion f

menswear ['mɛnzwɛəʳ] N vêtements mpl d'hommes

★**mental** ['mɛntl] ADJ mental(e); **~ illness** maladie mentale

mentality [mɛn'tælɪtɪ] N mentalité f

mentally ['mɛntlɪ] ADV: **she is ~ ill** elle souffre d'une maladie mentale

menthol ['mɛnθɒl] N menthol m

★**mention** ['mɛnʃən] N mention f ▶ VT mentionner, faire mention de; **don't ~ it!** je vous en prie, il n'y a pas de quoi!; **I need hardly ~ that ...** est-il besoin de rappeler que ... ?; **not to ~ ..., without mentioning ...** sans parler de ..., sans compter ...

mentor ['mɛntɔ:ʳ] N mentor m ▶ VT servir de mentor à

menu ['mɛnju:] N (set menu, Comput) menu m; (list of dishes) carte f; **could we see the ~?** est-ce qu'on peut voir la carte ?

menu-driven ['mɛnju:drɪvn] ADJ (Comput) piloté(e) par menu

meow [mi'au] VI see **miaow**

MEP N ABBR = **Member of the European Parliament**

mercantile ['mə:kəntaɪl] ADJ marchand(e); (law) commercial(e)

mercenary ['mə:sɪnərɪ] ADJ (person) intéressé(e), mercenaire ▶ N mercenaire m

merchandise ['mə:tʃəndaɪz] N marchandises fpl ▶ VT commercialiser

merchandiser ['mə:tʃəndaɪzər] N marchandiseur m

★**merchant** ['mə:tʃənt] N négociant m, marchand m; **timber/wine ~** négociant en bois/vins, marchand de bois/vins

merchant bank N (BRIT) banque f d'affaires

merchantman ['mə:tʃəntmən] N (irreg) navire marchand

merchant navy, (US) **merchant marine** N marine marchande

merciful ['mə:sɪful] ADJ miséricordieux(-euse), clément(e)

mercifully ['mə:sɪflɪ] ADV avec clémence; (fortunately) par bonheur, Dieu merci

merciless ['mə:sɪlɪs] ADJ impitoyable, sans pitié

mercilessly ['mə:sɪlɪslɪ] ADV impitoyablement

mercurial [mə:'kjuərɪəl] ADJ changeant(e); (lively) vif (vive)

mercury ['mə:kjurɪ] N mercure m

mercy ['mə:sɪ] N pitié f, merci f; (Rel) miséricorde f; **to have ~ on sb** avoir pitié de qn; **at the ~ of** à la merci de

mercy killing N euthanasie f

mere [mɪər] ADJ simple; (chance) pur(e); **a ~ two hours** seulement deux heures

merely ['mɪəlɪ] ADV simplement, purement

merge [mə:dʒ] VT unir; (Comput) fusionner, interclasser ▶ VI (colours, shapes, sounds) se mêler; (roads) se joindre; (Comm) fusionner

merger ['mə:dʒər] N (Comm) fusion f

meridian [mə'rɪdɪən] N méridien m

meringue [mə'ræŋ] N meringue f

merit ['mɛrɪt] N mérite m, valeur f ▶ VT mériter

meritocracy [mɛrɪ'tɔkrəsɪ] N méritocratie f

mermaid ['mə:meɪd] N sirène f

merriment ['mɛrɪmənt] N gaieté f

merry ['mɛrɪ] ADJ gai(e); **M~ Christmas!** joyeux Noël !

merry-go-round ['mɛrɪgəuraund] N manège m

mesh [mɛʃ] N mailles fpl; **wire ~** grillage m (métallique), treillis m (métallique) ▶ VI (gears) s'engrener

mesmerize ['mɛzməraɪz] VT ensorceler, hypnotiser

mesmerizing ['mɛzməraɪzɪŋ] ADJ ensorcelant(e)

★**mess** [mɛs] N désordre m, fouillis m, pagaille f; (muddle: of life) gâchis m; (: of economy) pagaille f;

(dirt) saleté f; (Mil) mess m, cantine f; **to be (in) a ~** être en désordre; **to be/get o.s. in a ~** (fig) être/se mettre dans le pétrin

▶ **mess about, mess around** VI (inf) perdre son temps

▶ **mess about with, mess around with** VT FUS (inf) chambarder, tripoter

▶ **mess up** VT (inf: dirty) salir; (: spoil) gâcher

▶ **mess with** (inf) VT FUS (challenge, confront) se frotter à; (interfere with) toucher à

★**message** ['mɛsɪdʒ] N message m; **can I leave a ~?** est-ce que je peux laisser un message ?; **are there any messages for me?** est-ce que j'ai des messages ?; **to get the ~** (fig, inf) saisir, piger ▶ VT envoyer un message (à); **she messaged me on Facebook** elle m'a envoyé un message sur Facebook

message board N (on Internet) forum m

message switching [-swɪtʃɪŋ] N (Comput) commutation f de messages

messaging ['mɛsɪdʒɪŋ] N messagerie f

messenger ['mɛsɪndʒər] N messager m

Messiah [mɪ'saɪə] N Messie m

Messrs, Messrs. ['mɛsəz] ABBR (on letters: = messieurs) MM

messy ['mɛsɪ] ADJ (dirty) sale; (untidy) en désordre

Met [mɛt] N ABBR (US) = **Metropolitan Opera**

met [mɛt] PT, PP of **meet** ▶ ADJ ABBR (= meteorological) météo inv

metabolic [mɛtə'bɔlɪk] ADJ métabolique

metabolism [mɛ'tæbəlɪzəm] N métabolisme m

★**metal** ['mɛtl] N métal m ▶ CPD en métal ▶ VT empierrer

metallic [mɛ'tælɪk] ADJ métallique

metallurgy [mɛ'tælədʒɪ] N métallurgie f

metalwork ['mɛtlwə:k] N (craft) ferronnerie f

metamorphosis [mɛtə'mɔ:fəsɪs] (pl **metamorphoses** [-si:z]) N métamorphose f

metaphor ['mɛtəfər] N métaphore f

metaphorical [mɛtə'fɔrɪkl] ADJ métaphorique

metaphysical [mɛtə'fɪzɪkl] ADJ métaphysique

metaphysics [mɛtə'fɪzɪks] N métaphysique f

mete [mi:t] **to ~ out** vt fus infliger

meteor ['mi:tɪər] N météore m

meteoric [mi:tɪ'ɔrɪk] ADJ (fig) fulgurant(e)

meteorite ['mi:tɪəraɪt] N météorite mf

meteorological [mi:tɪərə'lɔdʒɪkl] ADJ météorologique

meteorologist [mi:tɪə'rɔlədʒɪst] N météorologue mf

meteorology [mi:tɪə'rɔlədʒɪ] N météorologie f

meter ['mi:tər] N (instrument) compteur m; (also: **parking meter**) parc(o)mètre m; (US: unit) = **metre** ▶ VT (US Post) affranchir à la machine

methane ['mi:θeɪn] N méthane m

★**method** ['mɛθəd] N méthode f; **~ of payment** mode m or modalité f de paiement

methodical [mɪ'θɔdɪkl] ADJ méthodique

Methodist ['mɛθədɪst] ADJ, N méthodiste mf

method of payment N (also: **payment method**) mode m or méthode f de paiement

methodology [mɛθə'dɔlədʒɪ] N méthodologie f

methylated spirit ['mɛθɪleɪtɪd-] N (BRIT) alcool m à brûler

meticulous [mɛ'tɪkjʊləs] ADJ (person) méticuleux(-euse); (care, attention) minutieux(-euse)

meticulously [mə'tɪkjʊləslɪ] ADV (planned, researched) méticuleusement; (detailed) minutieusement

Met Office N (BRIT): **the ~** ≈ la Météorologie nationale

★**metre**, (US) **meter** ['mi:tə'] N mètre m

metric ['mɛtrɪk] ADJ métrique; **to go ~** adopter le système métrique

metrical ['mɛtrɪkl] ADJ métrique

metrication [mɛtrɪ'keɪʃən] N conversion f au système métrique

metric system N système m métrique

metric ton N tonne f

metro ['mɛtrəʊ] N métro m

metronome ['mɛtrənəʊm] N métronome m

metropolis [mɪ'trɔpəlɪs] N métropole f

metropolitan [mɛtrə'pɔlɪtən] ADJ métropolitain(e); **the M~ Police** (BRIT) la police londonienne

mettle ['mɛtl] N courage m

mew [mju:] VI (cat) miauler

mews [mju:z] N (BRIT): **~ cottage** maisonnette aménagée dans une ancienne écurie ou remise

Mexican ['mɛksɪkən] ADJ mexicain(e) ▶ N Mexicain(e)

Mexico ['mɛksɪkəʊ] N Mexique m

Mexico City N Mexico

mezzanine ['mɛtsəni:n] N mezzanine f; (of shops, offices) entresol m

mezzo-soprano [mɛtsəʊsə'prɑːnəʊ] N mezzosoprano f

MFA N ABBR (US: = Master of Fine Arts) titre universitaire

mfr ABBR = **manufacture; manufacturer**

mg ABBR (= milligram) mg

Mgr ABBR (= Monseigneur, Monsignor) Mgr; (= manager) dir

MHR N ABBR (US) = **Member of the House of Representatives**

MHz ABBR (= megahertz) MHz

MI ABBR (US) = **Michigan**

MI5 N ABBR (BRIT: = Military Intelligence 5) ≈ DST f

MI6 N ABBR (BRIT: = Military Intelligence 6) ≈ DGSE f

MIA ABBR (= missing in action) disparu(e) au combat

miaow [mi:'au] VI (also: **meow**) miauler

mice [maɪs] NPL of **mouse**

micro ['maɪkrəʊ] N (also: **microcomputer**) micro(-ordinateur m) m

micro... [maɪkrəʊ] PREFIX micro...

microbe ['maɪkrəʊb] N microbe m

microbiologist [maɪkrəʊbaɪ'ɔlədʒɪst] N microbiologiste mf

microbiology [maɪkrəʊbaɪ'ɔlədʒɪ] N microbiologie f

microblog ['maɪkrəʊblɔg] N microblog m

microbrewery ['maɪkrəʊbruərɪ] N microbrasserie f

microchip ['maɪkrəʊtʃɪp] N (Elec) puce f

microcomputer ['maɪkrəʊkəm'pju:tə'] N micro-ordinateur m

microcosm ['maɪkrəʊkɔzəm] N microcosme m

microeconomics ['maɪkrəui:kə'nɔmɪks] N micro-économie f

microfiche ['maɪkrəufi:ʃ] N microfiche f

microfilm ['maɪkrəufɪlm] N microfilm m ▶ VT microfilmer

microlight ['maɪkrəulaɪt] N ULM m

micrometer [maɪ'krɔmɪtə'] N palmer m, micromètre m

micro-organism [maɪkrəu'ɔːgənɪzəm] N micro-organisme m

microphone ['maɪkrəfəun] N microphone m

microprocessor ['maɪkrəu'prəusɛsə'] N microprocesseur m

microscope ['maɪkrəskəup] N microscope m; **under the ~** au microscope

microscopic [maɪkrə'skɔpɪk] ADJ microscopique

microwave ['maɪkrəuweɪv] N (also: **microwave oven**) (four m à) micro-ondes m ▶ VT cuire au micro-ondes

mid [mɪd] ADJ: **~ May** la mi-mai; **~ afternoon** le milieu de l'après-midi; **in ~ air** en plein ciel; **he's in his ~ thirties** il a dans les trente-cinq ans

midday [mɪd'deɪ] N midi m

★**middle** ['mɪdl] N milieu m; (waist) ceinture f, taille f; **in the ~ of the night** au milieu de la nuit; **I'm in the ~ of reading it** je suis (justement) en train de le lire ▶ ADJ du milieu; (average) moyen(ne)

middle age N tranche d'âge aux limites floues, entre la quarantaine et le début du troisième âge

middle-aged [mɪdl'eɪdʒd] ADJ d'un certain âge, ni vieux ni jeune; (pej: values, outlook) conventionnel(le), rassis(e)

Middle Ages NPL: **the ~** le Moyen Âge

middle class N, **middle classes** NPL: **the ~(es)** ≈ les classes moyennes

middle-class [mɪdl'klɑːs] ADJ bourgeois(e)

Middle East N: **the ~** le Moyen-Orient

Middle Eastern ADJ du Moyen-Orient

middleman ['mɪdlmæn] N (irreg) intermédiaire m

middle management N cadres moyens

middle name N second prénom

middle-of-the-road ['mɪdləvðə'rəud] ADJ (policy) modéré(e), du juste milieu; (music etc) plutôt classique, assez traditionnel(le)

middle school N (US) école pour les enfants de 12 à 14 ans, ≈ collège m; (BRIT) école pour les enfants de 8 à 14 ans

middleweight ['mɪdlweɪt] N (Boxing) poids moyen

middling ['mɪdlɪŋ] ADJ moyen(ne)

midge [mɪdʒ] N moucheron m

midget ['mɪdʒɪt] N (!) nain(e) ▶ ADJ minuscule

midi system ['mɪdɪ-] N chaîne f midi

Midlands ['mɪdləndz] NPL comtés du centre de l'Angleterre

★**midnight** ['mɪdnaɪt] N minuit m; **at ~** à minuit

midpoint ['mɪdpɔɪnt] N (between places, things) point m médian; (middle) milieu m; **the ~ of one's life** la moitié de sa vie

midriff ['mɪdrɪf] N estomac m, taille f

midst [mɪdst] N: **in the ~ of** au milieu de

midsummer [mɪd'sʌmə^r] N milieu m de l'été

Midsummer's Day N Saint-Jean f

midway [mɪd'weɪ] ADJ, ADV: **~** à mi-chemin (entre); **~ through ...** au milieu de ..., en plein(e) ...

midweek [mɪd'wiːk] ADJ du milieu de la semaine ▸ ADV au milieu de la semaine, en pleine semaine

Midwest [mɪd'wɛst] N: **in the ~** dans le Midwest ▸ CPD (town) du Midwest; **the ~ states** les États du Midwest

midwife ['mɪdwaɪf] (pl **midwives** [-vz]) N sage-femme f

midwifery ['mɪdwɪfərɪ] N obstétrique f

midwinter [mɪd'wɪntə^r] N milieu m de l'hiver

miffed [mɪft] ADJ (inf) fâché(e), vexé(e)

★**might** [maɪt] VB see **may** ▸ N puissance f, force f

mighty ['maɪtɪ] ADJ puissant(e) ▸ ADV (inf) rudement

migraine ['miːɡreɪn] N migraine f

migrant ['maɪɡrənt] N (bird, animal) migrateur m; (person) migrant(e); nomade mf ▸ ADJ migrateur(-trice); migrant(e); nomade; (worker) saisonnier(-ière)

migrate [maɪ'ɡreɪt] VI migrer

migration [maɪ'ɡreɪʃən] N migration f

migratory ['maɪɡrətrɪ] ADJ (animal, bird) migrateur(-trice); (pattern, path) migratoire

mike [maɪk] N ABBR (= microphone) micro m

Milan [mɪ'læn] N Milan

★**mild** [maɪld] ADJ doux (douce); (reproach, infection) léger(-ère); (illness) bénin(-igne); (interest) modéré(e); (taste) peu relevé(e) ▸ N bière légère

mildew ['mɪldjuː] N mildiou m

mildly ['maɪldlɪ] ADV doucement; légèrement; **to put it ~** (inf) c'est le moins qu'on puisse dire

mildness ['maɪldnɪs] N douceur f

★**mile** [maɪl] N mil(l)e m (= 1609 m); **to do 30 miles per gallon** ≈ faire 9, 4 litres aux cent

mileage ['maɪlɪdʒ] N distance f en milles, ≈ kilométrage m

mileage allowance N ≈ indemnité f kilométrique

mileometer [maɪ'lɔmɪtə^r] N compteur m kilométrique

milestone ['maɪlstəun] N borne f; (fig) jalon m

milieu ['miːljə:] N milieu m

militancy ['mɪlɪtnsɪ] N militantisme m

militant ['mɪlɪtnt] ADJ, N militant(e)

militarily [mɪlɪ'tɛərɪlɪ] ADV militairement

militarism ['mɪlɪtərɪzəm] N militarisme m

militaristic [mɪlɪtə'rɪstɪk] ADJ militariste

★**military** ['mɪlɪtərɪ] ADJ militaire ▸ N: **the ~** l'armée f, les militaires mpl

military service N service m (militaire or national)

militate ['mɪlɪteɪt] VI: **to ~ against** militer contre

militia [mɪ'lɪʃə] N milice f

★**milk** [mɪlk] N lait m ▸ VT (cow) traire; (fig: person) dépouiller, plumer; (: situation) exploiter à fond

milk chocolate N chocolat m au lait

milk float N (BRIT) voiture f or camionnette f du or de laitier

milking ['mɪlkɪŋ] N traite f

milkman ['mɪlkmən] N (irreg) laitier m

milk shake N milk-shake m

milk tooth N dent f de lait

milk truck N (US) = **milk float**

milky ['mɪlkɪ] ADJ (drink) au lait; (colour) laiteux(-euse)

Milky Way N Voie lactée

mill [mɪl] N moulin m; (factory) usine f, fabrique f; (spinning mill) filature f; (flour mill) minoterie f; (steel mill) aciérie f ▸ VT moudre, broyer ▸ VI (also: **mill about**) grouiller

millennium [mɪ'lɛnɪəm] (pl **millenniums** or **millennia** [-'lɛnɪə]) N millénaire m

millennium bug N bogue m or bug m de l'an 2000

miller ['mɪlə^r] N meunier m

millet ['mɪlɪt] N millet m

milli... ['mɪlɪ] PREFIX milli...

milligram, milligramme ['mɪlɪɡræm] N milligramme m

millilitre, (US) **milliliter** ['mɪlɪliːtə^r] N millilitre m

millimetre, (US) **millimeter** ['mɪlɪmiːtə^r] N millimètre m

milliner ['mɪlɪnə^r] N modiste f

millinery ['mɪlɪnərɪ] N modes fpl

★**million** ['mɪljən] N million m; **a ~ pounds** un million de livres sterling

millionaire [mɪljə'nɛə^r] N millionnaire m

millionth ['mɪljənθ] NUM millionième

millipede ['mɪlɪpiːd] N mille-pattes m inv

millisecond ['mɪlɪsɛkənd] N millième m de seconde

millstone ['mɪlstəun] N meule f

millwheel ['mɪlwiːl] N roue f de moulin

milometer [maɪ'lɔmɪtə^r] N = **mileometer**

mime [maɪm] N mime m ▸ VT, VI mimer

mimic ['mɪmɪk] N imitateur(-trice) ▸ VT, VI imiter, contrefaire

mimicry ['mɪmɪkrɪ] N imitation f; (Zool) mimétisme m

min. ABBR (= minute(s)) mn.; (= minimum) min.

minaret [mɪnə'rɛt] N minaret m

mince [mɪns] VT hacher; **he does not ~ (his) words** il ne mâche pas ses mots ▸ VI (in walking) marcher à petits pas maniérés ▸ N (BRIT Culin) viande hachée, hachis m

mincemeat ['mɪnsmiːt] N hachis de fruits secs utilisés en pâtisserie; (US) viande hachée, hachis m

mince pie N sorte de tarte aux fruits secs

mincer ['mɪnsə^r] N hachoir m

mincing ['mɪnsɪŋ] ADJ affecté(e)

★**mind** [maɪnd] N esprit m; **it is on my ~** cela me préoccupe; **to change one's ~** changer d'avis; **to be in two minds about sth** (BRIT) être indécis(e) or irrésolu(e) en ce qui concerne qch; **to my ~** à mon avis, selon moi; **to be out of one's ~** ne plus avoir toute sa raison; **to keep sth in ~** ne pas oublier qch; **to bear sth in ~** tenir compte de qch; **to have sb/sth in ~** avoir qn/qch en tête; **to have in ~ to do** avoir l'intention de faire; **it went right out of my ~** ça m'est complètement sorti de la tête; **to bring** or **call sth to ~** se rappeler qch; **to make up one's ~** se décider ▸ VT (attend to, look after) s'occuper de; (be careful) faire attention à; (object to): **I don't ~ the noise** je ne crains pas le bruit, le bruit ne me dérange pas; **~ you, ...** remarquez, ...; **"~ the step"** « attention à la marche » ▸ VI: **do you ~ if ...?** est-ce que cela vous gêne si ... ?; **I don't ~** cela ne me dérange pas; (don't care) ça m'est égal; **never ~** peu importe, ça ne fait rien; (don't worry) ne vous en faites pas

mind-boggling ['maɪndbɒɡlɪŋ] ADJ (inf) époustouflant(e), ahurissant(e)

minded ['maɪndɪd] ADJ: **to be ~ to do sth** avoir l'intention de faire qch; **if they were so ~, ...** s'ils le voulaient, ...

-minded ['maɪndɪd] ADJ: **fair-minded** impartial(e); **an industrially-minded nation** une nation orientée vers l'industrie

minder ['maɪndə'] N (child minder) gardienne f; (bodyguard) ange gardien (fig)

mindful ['maɪndful] ADJ: **~ of** attentif(-ive) à, soucieux(-euse) de

mindfulness ['maɪndfulnəs] N pleine conscience f

mindless ['maɪndlɪs] ADJ irréfléchi(e); (violence, crime) insensé(e); (boring: job) idiot(e)

mindset ['maɪndsɛt] N mentalité f

★**mine**[1] [maɪn] PRON le (la) mien(ne), les miens (miennes); **a friend of ~** un de mes amis, un ami à moi; **this book is ~** ce livre est à moi

mine[2] [maɪn] N mine f ▸ VT (coal) extraire; (ship, beach) miner

mine detector N détecteur m de mines

minefield ['maɪnfiːld] N champ m de mines

miner ['maɪnə'] N mineur m

mineral ['mɪnərəl] ADJ minéral(e) ▸ N minéral m ▪ **minerals** NPL (BRIT) (soft drinks) boissons gazeuses (sucrées)

mineralogy [mɪnə'rælədʒɪ] N minéralogie f

mineral water N eau minérale

minesweeper ['maɪnswiːpə'] N dragueur m de mines

mingle ['mɪŋɡl] VT mêler, mélanger ▸ VI: **to ~ with** se mêler à

mingy ['mɪndʒɪ] ADJ (inf) radin(e)

miniature ['mɪnətʃə'] ADJ (en) miniature ▸ N miniature f

minibar ['mɪnɪbɑː'] N minibar m

minibus ['mɪnɪbʌs] N minibus m

minicab ['mɪnɪkæb] N (BRIT) taxi m indépendant

minicomputer ['mɪnɪkəm'pjuːtə'] N miniordinateur m

minim ['mɪnɪm] N (Mus) blanche f

minima ['mɪnɪmə] NPL of **minimum**

minimal ['mɪnɪml] ADJ minimal(e)

minimalism ['mɪnɪməlɪzəm] N minimalisme m

minimalist ['mɪnɪməlɪst] ADJ, N minimaliste mf

minimalistic [mɪnɪməl'ɪstɪk] ADJ minimaliste

minimize ['mɪnɪmaɪz] VT (reduce) réduire au minimum; (play down) minimiser

★**minimum** ['mɪnɪməm] (pl **minima** ['mɪnɪmə]) N minimum m; **to reduce to a ~** réduire au minimum ▸ ADJ minimum

minimum lending rate N (Econ) taux m de crédit minimum

mining ['maɪnɪŋ] N exploitation minière ▸ ADJ minier(-ière); de mineurs

minion ['mɪnjən] N (pej) laquais m; favori(te)

mini-series ['mɪnɪsɪəriːz] N téléfilm m en plusieurs parties

miniskirt ['mɪnɪskəːt] N mini-jupe f

★**minister** ['mɪnɪstə'] N (BRIT Pol) ministre mf; (Rel) pasteur m ▸ VI: **to ~ to sb** donner ses soins à qn; **to ~ to sb's needs** pourvoir aux besoins de qn

ministerial [mɪnɪs'tɪərɪəl] ADJ (BRIT Pol) ministériel(le)

ministry ['mɪnɪstrɪ] N (BRIT Pol) ministère m; (Rel): **to go into the ~** devenir pasteur

mink [mɪŋk] N vison m

mink coat N manteau m de vison

minnow ['mɪnəu] N vairon m

★**minor** ['maɪnə'] ADJ petit(e), de peu d'importance; (Mus, poet, problem) mineur(e) ▸ N (Law) mineur(e)

Minorca [mɪ'nɔːkə] N Minorque f

minority [maɪ'nɔrɪtɪ] N minorité f; **to be in a ~** être en minorité

minster ['mɪnstə'] N église abbatiale

minstrel ['mɪnstrəl] N trouvère m, ménestrel m

mint [mɪnt] N (plant) menthe f; (sweet) bonbon m à la menthe; **the (Royal) M~, the (US) M~** ≈ l'hôtel m de la Monnaie ▸ ADJ: **in ~ condition** à l'état de neuf ▸ VT (coins) battre

mint sauce N sauce f à la menthe

minuet [mɪnju'ɛt] N menuet m

minus ['maɪnəs] N (also: **minus sign**) signe m moins ▸ PREP moins; **12 ~ 6 equals 6** 12 moins 6 égal 6; **~ 24°C** moins 24°C

minuscule ['mɪnəskjuːl] ADJ minuscule

★**minute**[1] ['mɪnɪt] N minute f; (official record) procès-verbal m, compte rendu; **it is 5 minutes past 3** il est 3 heures 5; **wait a ~!** (attendez) un instant !; **at the last ~** à la dernière minute; **up to the ~** (fashion) dernier cri; (news) de dernière minute; (machine, technology) de pointe ▪ **minutes** NPL (of meeting) procès-verbal m, compte rendu

minute[2] [maɪ'njuːt] ADJ minuscule; (detailed) minutieux(-euse); **in ~ detail** par le menu

minute book ['mɪnɪt-] N registre m des procès-verbaux

minute hand ['mɪnɪt-] N aiguille f des minutes

minutely [maɪ'njuːtlɪ] ADV (by a small amount) de peu, de manière infime; (in detail) minutieusement, dans les moindres détails

minutiae [mɪ'njuːʃɪː] NPL menus détails

miracle ['mɪrəkl] N miracle m

miraculous [mɪ'rækjuləs] ADJ miraculeux(-euse)

mirage ['mɪrɑːʒ] N mirage m

mire ['maɪə'] N bourbe f, boue f

★**mirror** ['mɪrə'] N miroir m, glace f; (in car) rétroviseur m ▸ VT refléter

mirror image N image inversée

m

729

mirth [mə:θ] N gaieté f

misadventure [mɪsəd'vɛntʃəʳ] N mésaventure f; **death by ~** (BRIT) décès accidentel

misanthropist [mɪˈzænθrəpɪst] N misanthrope mf

misapply [mɪsəˈplaɪ] VT mal employer

misapprehension ['mɪsæprɪ'hɛnʃən] N malentendu m, méprise f

misappropriate [mɪsəˈprəuprɪeɪt] VT détourner

misappropriation ['mɪsəprəuprɪ'eɪʃən] N escroquerie f, détournement m

misbehave [mɪsbɪˈheɪv] VI mal se conduire

misbehaviour, (US) **misbehavior** [mɪsbɪˈheɪvjəʳ] N mauvaise conduite

misc. ABBR = **miscellaneous**

miscalculate [mɪsˈkælkjuleɪt] VT mal calculer

miscalculation ['mɪskælkjuˈleɪʃən] N erreur f de calcul

miscarriage ['mɪskærɪdʒ] N (Med) fausse couche; **~ of justice** erreur f judiciaire

miscarry [mɪsˈkærɪ] VI (Med) faire une fausse couche; (fail: plans) échouer, mal tourner

miscellaneous [mɪsɪˈleɪnɪəs] ADJ (items, expenses) divers(es); (selection) varié(e)

miscellany [mɪˈsɛlənɪ] N recueil m

mischance [mɪsˈtʃɑːns] N malchance f; **by (some) ~** par malheur

mischief ['mɪstʃɪf] N (naughtiness) sottises fpl; (fun) farce f; (playfulness) espièglerie f; (harm) mal m, dommage m; (maliciousness) méchanceté f

mischievous ['mɪstʃɪvəs] ADJ (playful, naughty) coquin(e), espiègle; (harmful) méchant(e)

miscommunication [mɪskəmju:nɪˈkeɪʃən] N mauvaise communication f

misconception ['mɪskənˈsɛpʃən] N idée fausse

misconduct [mɪsˈkɔndʌkt] N inconduite f; **professional ~** faute professionnelle

misconstrue [mɪskənˈstru:] VT mal interpréter

miscount [mɪsˈkaunt] VT, VI mal compter

misdeed ['mɪsˈdi:d] N méfait m

misdemeanour, (US) **misdemeanor** [mɪsdɪˈmi:nəʳ] N écart m de conduite; infraction f

misdirect [mɪsdɪˈrɛkt] VT (person) mal renseigner; (letter) mal adresser

miser ['maɪzəʳ] N avare mf

miserable ['mɪzərəbl] ADJ (person, expression) malheureux(-euse); (conditions) misérable; (weather) maussade; (offer, donation) minable; (failure) pitoyable; **to feel ~** avoir le cafard

miserably ['mɪzərəblɪ] ADV (smile, answer) tristement; (live, pay) misérablement; (fail) lamentablement

miserly ['maɪzəlɪ] ADJ avare

misery ['mɪzərɪ] N (unhappiness) tristesse f; (pain) souffrances fpl; (wretchedness) misère f

misfire [mɪsˈfaɪəʳ] VI rater; (car engine) avoir des ratés

misfit ['mɪsfɪt] N (person) inadapté(e)

misfortune [mɪsˈfɔːtʃən] N malchance f, malheur m

misgiving [mɪsˈgɪvɪŋ] N (apprehension) craintes fpl; **to have misgivings about sth** avoir des doutes quant à qch

misguided [mɪsˈgaɪdɪd] ADJ malavisé(e)

mishandle [mɪsˈhændl] VT (treat roughly) malmener; (mismanage) mal s'y prendre pour faire or résoudre etc

mishap ['mɪshæp] N mésaventure f

mishear [mɪsˈhɪəʳ] VT, VI (irreg: like **hear**) mal entendre

mishmash ['mɪʃmæʃ] N (inf) fatras m, méli-mélo m

misinform [mɪsɪnˈfɔːm] VT mal renseigner

misinformation [mɪsɪnfəˈmeɪʃən] N informations fpl erronées, information f erronée, fausse information

misinterpret [mɪsɪnˈtə:prɪt] VT mal interpréter

misinterpretation ['mɪsɪntə:prɪ'teɪʃən] N interprétation erronée, contresens m

misjudge [mɪsˈdʒʌdʒ] VT méjuger, se méprendre sur le compte de

mislay [mɪsˈleɪ] VT (irreg: like **lay**) égarer

mislead [mɪsˈli:d] VT (irreg: like **lead**[1]) induire en erreur

misleading [mɪsˈli:dɪŋ] ADJ trompeur(-euse)

misled [mɪsˈlɛd] PT, PP of **mislead**

mismanage [mɪsˈmænɪdʒ] VT mal gérer; mal s'y prendre pour faire or résoudre etc

mismanagement [mɪsˈmænɪdʒmənt] N mauvaise gestion

mismatch ['mɪsmætʃ] N décalage m; **a ~ between requirements and resources** un décalage entre les besoins et les ressources; **a ~ of styles** une discordance des styles

misnomer [mɪsˈnəuməʳ] N terme or qualificatif trompeur or peu approprié

misogynist [mɪˈsɔdʒɪnɪst] N misogyne mf

misogyny [mɪˈsɔdʒɪnɪ] N misogynie f

misplace [mɪsˈpleɪs] VT égarer; **to be misplaced** (trust etc) être mal placé(e)

misprint ['mɪsprɪnt] N faute f d'impression

mispronounce [mɪsprəˈnauns] VT mal prononcer

misquote [mɪsˈkwəut] VT citer erronément or inexactement

misread [mɪsˈri:d] VT (irreg: like **read**) mal lire

misrepresent [mɪsrɛprɪˈzɛnt] VT (person) donner une image inexacte de; (views) déformer

misrepresentation [mɪsrɛprɪzɛnˈteɪʃən] N (of facts, data) déformation f

★**Miss** [mɪs] N Mademoiselle; **Dear ~ Smith** Chère Mademoiselle Smith

★**miss** [mɪs] VT (fail to get, attend, see) manquer, rater; (appointment, class) manquer; (escape, avoid) échapper à, éviter; (notice loss of: money etc) s'apercevoir de l'absence de; (regret the absence of): **I ~ him/it** il/cela me manque; **we missed our train** nous avons raté notre train; **the bus just missed the wall** le bus a évité le mur de justesse; **you're missing the point** vous êtes à côté de la question; **you can't ~ it** vous ne pouvez pas vous tromper ▶ VI manquer ▶ N (shot) coup manqué

▶ **miss out** VT (BRIT) oublier

▶ **miss out on** VT FUS (fun, party) rater, manquer; (chance, bargain) laisser passer

To translate a sentence like *I'm missing my parents* you have to rephrase it as *my parents are missing to me*.
I'm missing my parents. **Mes parents me manquent**.
She's missing her boyfriend. **Son petit ami lui manque**.

missal ['mɪsl] N missel *m*

mis-sell [mɪs'sɛl] VT (*irreg: like* **sell**) vendre de façon abusive

mis-selling [mɪs'sɛlɪŋ] N vente *f* abusive

misshapen [mɪs'ʃeɪpən] ADJ difforme

missile ['mɪsaɪl] N (*Aviat*) missile *m*; (*object thrown*) projectile *m*

missile base N base *f* de missiles

missile launcher [-lɔːntʃəʳ] N lance-missiles *m*

★**missing** ['mɪsɪŋ] ADJ manquant(e); (*after escape, disaster: person*) disparu(e); **to go ~** disparaître; **~ person** personne disparue, disparu(e); **~ in action** (*Mil*) porté(e) disparu(e)

mission ['mɪʃən] N mission *f*; **on a ~ to sb** en mission auprès de qn

missionary ['mɪʃənrɪ] N missionnaire *mf*

mission statement N déclaration *f* d'intention

missive ['mɪsɪv] N missive *f*

misspell ['mɪs'spɛl] VT (*irreg: like* **spell**) mal orthographier

misspent ['mɪs'spɛnt] ADJ: **his ~ youth** sa folle jeunesse

missus ['mɪsɪz] N (*inf: wife*): **my ~, the ~** bobonne *f* (*inf*); (*as address*): **thanks, ~** merci M'dame (*inf*)

mist [mɪst] N brume *f* ▶ VI (*also:* **mist over, mist up**) devenir brumeux(-euse); (: *Brit: windows*) s'embuer

★**mistake** [mɪs'teɪk] N erreur *f*, faute *f*; **by ~** par erreur, par inadvertance; **to make a ~** (*in writing*) faire une faute; (*in calculating etc*) faire une erreur; **there must be some ~** il doit y avoir une erreur, se tromper; **to make a ~ about sb/sth** se tromper sur le compte de qn/sur qch ▶ VT (*irreg: like* **take**) (*meaning*) mal comprendre; (*intentions*) se méprendre sur; **to ~ for** prendre pour

mistaken [mɪs'teɪkən] PP *of* **mistake** ▶ ADJ (*idea etc*) erroné(e); **to be ~** faire erreur, se tromper

mistaken identity N erreur *f* d'identité

mistakenly [mɪs'teɪkənlɪ] ADV par erreur, par mégarde

mister ['mɪstəʳ] N (*inf*) Monsieur *m*; *see* **Mr**

mistletoe ['mɪsltəu] N gui *m*

mistook [mɪs'tuk] PT *of* **mistake**

mistranslation [mɪstræns'leɪʃən] N erreur *f* de traduction, contresens *m*

mistreat [mɪs'triːt] VT maltraiter

mistress ['mɪstrɪs] N maîtresse *f*; (*Brit: in primary school*) institutrice *f*; (: *in secondary school*) professeur *m*

mistrust [mɪs'trʌst] VT se méfier de ▶ N: **~ (of)** méfiance *f* (à l'égard de)

mistrustful [mɪs'trʌstful] ADJ: **~ (of)** méfiant(e) (à l'égard de)

misty ['mɪstɪ] ADJ brumeux(-euse); (*glasses, window*) embué(e)

misty-eyed ['mɪstɪ'aɪd] ADJ les yeux embués de larmes; (*fig*) sentimental(e)

misunderstand [mɪsʌndə'stænd] VT, VI (*irreg: like* **understand**) mal comprendre

misunderstanding ['mɪsʌndə'stændɪŋ] N méprise *f*, malentendu *m*; **there's been a ~** il y a eu un malentendu

misunderstood [mɪsʌndə'stud] PT, PP *of* **misunderstand** ▶ ADJ (*person*) incompris(e)

misuse N [mɪs'juːs] mauvais emploi; (*of power*) abus *m* ▶ VT [mɪs'juːz] mal employer; abuser de

MIT N ABBR (*US*) = **Massachusetts Institute of Technology**

mite [maɪt] N (*small quantity*) grain *m*, miette *f*; (*Brit: small child*) petit(e)

mitigate ['mɪtɪgeɪt] VT atténuer; **mitigating circumstances** circonstances atténuantes

mitigation [mɪtɪ'geɪʃən] N atténuation *f*

mitre, (*US*) **miter** ['maɪtəʳ] N mitre *f*; (*Carpentry*) onglet *m*

mitt [mɪt], **mitten** ['mɪtn] N moufle *f*; (*fingerless*) mitaine *f*

★**mix** [mɪks] VT mélanger; (*sauce, drink etc*) préparer; **to ~ sth with sth** mélanger qch à qch; **to ~ business with pleasure** unir l'utile à l'agréable ▶ VI se mélanger; (*socialize*): **he doesn't ~ well** il est peu sociable ▶ N mélange *m*; **cake ~** préparation *f* pour gâteau

▶ **mix in** VT incorporer, mélanger

▶ **mix up** VT mélanger; (*confuse*) confondre; **to be mixed up in sth** être mêlé(e) à qch *or* impliqué(e) dans qch

★**mixed** [mɪkst] ADJ (*feelings, reactions*) contradictoire; (*school, marriage*) mixte

mixed-ability ['mɪkstə'bɪlɪtɪ] ADJ (*class etc*) sans groupes de niveaux

mixed bag N: **it's a (bit of a) ~** il y a (un peu) de tout

mixed blessing N: **it's a ~** cela a du bon et du mauvais

mixed doubles NPL (*Sport*) double *m* mixte

mixed economy N économie *f* mixte

mixed grill N (*Brit*) assortiment *m* de grillades

mixed marriage N mariage *m* mixte

mixed salad N salade *f* de crudités

mixed-up [mɪkst'ʌp] ADJ (*person*) désorienté(e), embrouillé(e)

mixer ['mɪksəʳ] N (*for food*) batteur *m*, mixeur *m*; (*drink*) boisson gazeuse (*servant à couper un alcool*); (*person*): **he is a good ~** il est très sociable

mixer tap N (robinet *m*) mélangeur *m*

★**mixture** ['mɪkstʃəʳ] N assortiment *m*, mélange *m*; (*Med*) préparation *f*

mix-up ['mɪksʌp] N: **there was a ~** il y a eu confusion

MK ABBR (*Brit Tech*) = **mark**

mk ABBR = **mark**

mkt ABBR = **market**

ml ABBR (= *millilitre(s)*) ml

MLitt ['ɛm'lɪt] N ABBR (= *Master of Literature, Master of Letters*) titre universitaire

MLR N ABBR (*BRIT*) = **minimum lending rate**

mm ABBR (= *millimetre*) mm

MMR N ABBR (= *measles, mumps and rubella*) vaccin *m* ROR (= *rougeole, oreillons, rubéole*)

MN ABBR (*BRIT*) = **Merchant Navy**; (*US*) = **Minnesota**

MO N ABBR (*Med*) = **medical officer**; (*US inf*: = *modus operandi*) méthode *f* ▶ ABBR (*US*) = **Missouri**

m.o. ABBR = **money order**

moan [məun] N gémissement *m* ▶ VI gémir; (*inf*: *complain*): **to ~ (about)** se plaindre (de)

moaner ['məunəʳ] N (*inf*) rouspéteur(-euse), râleur(-euse)

moaning ['məunɪŋ] N gémissements *mpl*

moat [məut] N fossé *m*, douves *fpl*

mob [mɔb] N foule *f*; (*disorderly*) cohue *f*; (*pej*): **the ~** la populace ▶ VT assaillir

mobbing ['mɔbɪŋ] N harcèlement *m* collectif, mobbing *m*

★**mobile** ['məubaɪl] ADJ mobile; **applicants must be ~** (*BRIT*) les candidats devront être prêts à accepter tout déplacement ▶ N (*Art*) mobile *m*; (*BRIT*: *phone*) (téléphone *m*) portable *m*, mobile *m*

mobile home N caravane *f*

★**mobile phone** N (téléphone *m*) portable *m*, mobile *m*

mobile phone mast N (*BRIT Tel*) antenne-relais *f*

mobile shop N (*BRIT*) camion *m* magasin

mobility [məu'bɪlɪtɪ] N mobilité *f*

mobilization [məubɪlaɪ'zeɪʃən] N mobilisation *f*

mobilize ['məubɪlaɪz] VT, VI mobiliser

moccasin ['mɔkəsɪn] N mocassin *m*

mock [mɔk] VT ridiculiser; (*laugh at*) se moquer de ▶ ADJ faux (fausse) ■ **mocks** NPL (*BRIT Scol*) examens blancs

mockery ['mɔkərɪ] N moquerie *f*, raillerie *f*; **to make a ~ of** ridiculiser, tourner en dérision

mocking ['mɔkɪŋ] ADJ moqueur(-euse)

mockingbird ['mɔkɪŋbə:d] N moqueur *m*

mock-up ['mɔkʌp] N maquette *f*

MOD N ABBR (*BRIT*) = **Ministry of Defence**; *see* **defence**

mod [mɔd] ADJ *see* **convenience**

mod cons ['mɔd'kɔnz] NPL ABBR (*BRIT*) = **modern conveniences**; *see* **convenience**

mode [məud] N mode *m*; (*of transport*) moyen *m*

★**model** ['mɔdl] N modèle *m*; (*person: for fashion*) mannequin *m*; (: *for artist*) modèle ▶ VT (*with clay etc*) modeler; **to ~ clothes** présenter des vêtements; **to ~ o.s. on** imiter; **to ~ sb/sth on** modeler qn/qch sur ▶ VI travailler comme mannequin ▶ ADJ (*railway: toy*) modèle réduit *inv*; (*child, factory*) modèle

modelling ['mɔdlɪŋ] N (*profession*) mannequinat *f* ▶ CPD (*contract, career*) de mannequinat

modem ['məudɛm] N modem *m*

★**moderate** ADJ ['mɔdərət] modéré(e); (*amount, change*) peu important(e) ▶ N (*Pol*) modéré(e) ▶ VI ['mɔdəreɪt] se modérer, se calmer ▶ VT ['mɔdəreɪt] modérer

moderately ['mɔdərətlɪ] ADV (*act*) avec modération *or* mesure; (*expensive, difficult*) moyennement;

(*pleased, happy*) raisonnablement, assez; **~ priced** à un prix raisonnable

moderation [mɔdə'reɪʃən] N modération *f*, mesure *f*; **in ~** à dose raisonnable, pris(e) *or* pratiqué(e) modérément

moderator ['mɔdəreɪtəʳ] N (*Rel*): **M~** président *m* (*de l'Assemblée générale de l'Église presbytérienne*); (*Pol*) modérateur *m*

★**modern** ['mɔdən] ADJ moderne

modernity [mɔ'də:nɪtɪ] N modernité *f*

modernization [mɔdənaɪ'zeɪʃən] N modernisation *f*

modernize ['mɔdənaɪz] VT moderniser

modern languages NPL langues vivantes

★**modest** ['mɔdɪst] ADJ modeste

modesty ['mɔdɪstɪ] N modestie *f*

modicum ['mɔdɪkəm] N: **a ~ of** un minimum de

modification [mɔdɪfɪ'keɪʃən] N modification *f*; **to make modifications** faire *or* apporter des modifications

modify ['mɔdɪfaɪ] VT modifier

modish ['məudɪʃ] ADJ à la mode

Mods [mɔdz] N ABBR (*BRIT*: = (*Honour*) *Moderations*) *premier examen universitaire (à Oxford)*

modular ['mɔdjuləʳ] ADJ (*filing, unit*) modulaire

modulate ['mɔdjuleɪt] VT moduler

modulation [mɔdju'leɪʃən] N modulation *f*

module ['mɔdju:l] N module *m*

Mogadishu [mɔgə'dɪʃu:] N Mogadiscio

mogul ['məugl] N (*fig*) nabab *m*; (*Ski*) bosse *f*

MOH N ABBR (*BRIT*) = **Medical Officer of Health**

mohair ['məuhɛəʳ] N mohair *m*

Mohammed [mə'hæmed] N Mahomet *m*

moist [mɔɪst] ADJ humide, moite

moisten ['mɔɪsn] VT humecter, mouiller légèrement

moisture ['mɔɪstʃəʳ] N humidité *f*; (*on glass*) buée *f*

moisturize ['mɔɪstʃəraɪz] VT (*skin*) hydrater

moisturizer ['mɔɪstʃəraɪzəʳ] N crème hydratante

mojo ['məudʒəu] N (*US inf*) mojo *m*, charisme *m*

molar ['məuləʳ] N molaire *f*

molasses [məu'læsɪz] N mélasse *f*

mold *etc* [məuld] N (*US*) = **mould** *etc*

Moldavia [mɔl'deɪvɪə], **Moldova** [mɔl'dəuvə] N Moldavie *f*

Moldavian [mɔl'deɪvɪən], **Moldovan** [mɔl'dəuvən] ADJ moldave

mole [məul] N (*animal, spy*) taupe *f*; (*spot*) grain *m* de beauté

molecular [mə'lɛkjuləʳ] ADJ moléculaire

molecule ['mɔlɪkju:l] N molécule *f*

molehill ['məulhɪl] N taupinière *f*

molest [məu'lɛst] VT (*assault sexually*) attenter à la pudeur de; (*attack*) molester; (*harass*) tracasser

mollusc ['mɔləsk] N mollusque *m*

mollycoddle ['mɔlɪkɔdl] VT chouchouter, couver

Molotov cocktail ['mɔlətɔf-] N cocktail *m* Molotov

molt [məult] VI (*US*) = **moult**

molten ['məultən] ADJ fondu(e); (*rock*) en fusion

mom [mɔm] N (US) = **mum**

★**moment** ['məumənt] N moment m, instant m; (*importance*) importance f; **at the ~** en ce moment; **for the ~** pour l'instant; **in a ~** dans un instant; **"one ~ please"** (Tel) « ne quittez pas »

momentarily ['məuməntrılı] ADV momentanément; (US: *soon*) bientôt

momentary ['məuməntərı] ADJ momentané(e), passager(-ère)

momentous [məu'mɛntəs] ADJ important(e), capital(e)

momentum [məu'mɛntəm] N élan m, vitesse acquise; (*fig*) dynamique f; **to gather ~** prendre de la vitesse; (*fig*) gagner du terrain

mommy ['mɔmı] N (US: *mother*) maman f

Mon. ABBR (= *Monday*) lun.

Monaco ['mɔnəkəu] N Monaco f

monarch ['mɔnək] N monarque m

monarchist ['mɔnəkıst] N monarchiste mf

monarchy ['mɔnəkı] N monarchie f

monastery ['mɔnəstərı] N monastère m

monastic [mə'næstık] ADJ monastique

★**Monday** ['mʌndı] N lundi m; *see also* **Tuesday**

monetarism ['mʌnɪtərɪzəm] N monétarisme m

monetarist ['mʌnɪtərɪst] N monétariste mf

monetary ['mʌnɪtərı] ADJ monétaire

monetization [mʌnɪtaɪ'zeɪʃən] N monétisation f

monetize ['mʌnɪtaɪz] VT monétiser

★**money** ['mʌnı] N argent m; **to make ~** (*person*) gagner de l'argent; (*business*) rapporter; **I've got no ~ left** je n'ai plus d'argent, je n'ai plus un sou

money belt N ceinture-portefeuille f

moneyed ['mʌnıd] ADJ riche

money laundering [-lɔ:ndərıŋ] N blanchiment m d'argent

moneylender ['mʌnılɛndər] N prêteur(-euse)

moneymaker ['mʌnımeıkər] N (BRIT inf: *business*) affaire lucrative

moneymaking ['mʌnımeıkıŋ] ADJ lucratif(-ive), qui rapporte (de l'argent)

money market N marché financier

money order N mandat m

money-spinner ['mʌnıspınər] N (*inf*) mine f d'or (*fig*)

money supply N masse f monétaire

Mongol ['mɔŋgəl] N Mongol(e); (*Ling*) mongol m

Mongolia [mɔŋ'gəulıə] N Mongolie f

Mongolian [mɔŋ'gəulıən] ADJ mongol(e) ▶ N Mongol(e); (*Ling*) mongol m

mongoose ['mɔŋgu:s] N mangouste f

mongrel ['mʌŋgrəl] N (*dog*) bâtard m

monies ['mʌnız] NPL sommes fpl d'argent

★**monitor** ['mɔnıtər] N (TV, Comput) écran m, moniteur m; (BRIT Scol) chef m de classe; (US Scol) surveillant m (d'examen) ▶ VT contrôler; (*foreign station*) être à l'écoute de; (*progress*) suivre de près

monk [mʌŋk] N moine m

★**monkey** ['mʌŋkı] N singe m

monkey nut N (BRIT) cacahuète f

monkey wrench N clé f à molette

mono ['mɔnəu] ADJ mono *inv*

mono... ['mɔnəu] PREFIX mono...

monochrome ['mɔnəkrəum] ADJ monochrome

monocle ['mɔnəkl] N monocle m

monogamous [mə'nɔgəməs] ADJ monogame

monogamy [mə'nɔgəmı] N monogamie f

monogram ['mɔnəgræm] N monogramme m

monolith ['mɔnəlıθ] N monolithe m

monologue ['mɔnəlɔg] N monologue m

monoplane ['mɔnəpleın] N monoplan m

monopolize [mə'nɔpəlaız] VT monopoliser

monopoly [mə'nɔpəlı] N monopole m

monorail ['mɔnəureıl] N monorail m

monosodium glutamate ['mɔnəsəudıəm'glu:təmeıt] N glutamate m de sodium

monosyllabic [mɔnəsı'læbık] ADJ monosyllabique; (*person*) laconique

monosyllable ['mɔnəsıləbl] N monosyllabe m

monotone ['mɔnətəun] N ton m (or voix f) monocorde; **to speak in a ~** parler sur un ton monocorde

monotonous [mə'nɔtənəs] ADJ monotone

monotony [mə'nɔtənı] N monotonie f

monoxide [mɔ'nɔksaıd] N: **carbon ~** oxyde m de carbone

monsoon [mɔn'su:n] N mousson f

monster ['mɔnstər] N monstre m

monstrosity [mɔns'trɔsıtı] N monstruosité f, atrocité f

monstrous ['mɔnstrəs] ADJ (*huge*) gigantesque; (*atrocious*) monstrueux(-euse), atroce

montage [mɔn'tɑ:ʒ] N montage m

Mont Blanc [mɔ̃blɔ̃] N Mont Blanc m

Montenegro [mɔntı'ni:grəu] N Monténégro m

★**month** [mʌnθ] N mois m; **every ~** tous les mois; **300 dollars a ~** 300 dollars par mois

★**monthly** ['mʌnθlı] ADJ mensuel(le) ▶ ADV mensuellement; **twice ~** deux fois par mois ▶ N (*magazine*) mensuel m, publication mensuelle

Montreal [mɔntrı'ɔ:l] N Montréal

monument ['mɔnjumənt] N monument m

monumental [mɔnju'mɛntl] ADJ monumental(e)

monumental mason N marbrier m

moo [mu:] VI meugler, beugler

★**mood** [mu:d] N humeur f, disposition f; **to be in a good/bad ~** être de bonne/mauvaise humeur; **to be in the ~ for** être d'humeur à, avoir envie de

moody ['mu:dı] ADJ (*variable*) d'humeur changeante, lunatique; (*sullen*) morose, maussade

★**moon** [mu:n] N lune f

moonbeam ['mu:nbi:m] N rayon m de lune

moon landing N alunissage m

moonlight ['mu:nlaıt] N clair m de lune ▶ VI travailler au noir

moonlighting ['mu:nlaıtıŋ] N travail m au noir

moonlit ['mu:nlıt] ADJ éclairé(e) par la lune; **a ~ night** une nuit de lune

m

moonshot ['muːnʃɒt] N (*Space*) tir *m* lunaire

moonstruck ['muːnstrʌk] ADJ fou (folle), dérangé(e)

moony ['muːnɪ] ADJ: **to have ~ eyes** avoir l'air dans la lune *or* rêveur

Moor [muə^r] N Maure (Mauresque)

moor [muə^r] N lande *f* ▶ VT (*ship*) amarrer ▶ VI mouiller

moorings ['muərɪŋz] NPL (*chains*) amarres *fpl*; (*place*) mouillage *m*

Moorish ['muərɪʃ] ADJ maure, mauresque

moorland ['muələnd] N lande *f*

moose [muːs] N (*pl inv*) élan *m*

moot [muːt] VT soulever ▶ ADJ: **~ point** point *m* discutable

mop [mɒp] N balai *m* à laver; (*for dishes*) lavette *f* à vaisselle; **~ of hair** tignasse *f* ▶ VT éponger, essuyer
▶ **mop up** VT éponger

mope [məup] VI avoir le cafard, se morfondre
▶ **mope about, mope around** VI broyer du noir, se morfondre

moped ['məupɛd] N cyclomoteur *m*

MOR ADJ ABBR (*Mus*: = *middle-of-the-road*) tous publics

★**moral** ['mɒrl] ADJ moral(e) ▶ N morale *f* ■ **morals** NPL moralité *f*

morale [mɔ'rɑːl] N moral *m*

> In French **la morale** is used for the moral of a story, or to mean *morals*. Use **le moral** for the morale of a person or team.
> *The team's morale is low.*
> **Le moral de l'équipe est bas.**

morality [mə'rælɪtɪ] N moralité *f*

moralize ['mɒrəlaɪz] VI: **to ~ (about)** moraliser (sur)

morally ['mɒrəlɪ] ADV moralement

moral victory N victoire morale

morass [mə'ræs] N marais *m*, marécage *m*

moratorium [mɒrə'tɔːrɪəm] N moratoire *m*

morbid ['mɔːbɪd] ADJ morbide

---

more [mɔː^r]

ADJ **1** (*greater in number etc*) plus (de), davantage (de); **more people/work (than)** plus de gens/de travail (que)
2 (*additional*) encore (de); **do you want (some) more tea?** voulez-vous encore du thé ?; **is there any more wine?** reste-t-il du vin ?; **I have no** *or* **I don't have any more money** je n'ai plus d'argent; **it'll take a few more weeks** ça prendra encore quelques semaines
▶ PRON plus, davantage; **more than 10** plus de 10; **it cost more than we expected** cela a coûté plus que prévu; **I want more** j'en veux plus *or* davantage; **is there any more?** est-ce qu'il en reste ?; **there's no more** il n'y en a plus; **a little more** un peu plus; **many/much more** beaucoup plus, bien davantage
▶ ADV plus; **more dangerous/easily (than)** plus dangereux/facilement (que); **more and more expensive** de plus en plus cher; **more or less**

---

plus ou moins; **more than ever** plus que jamais; **once more** encore une fois, une fois de plus; **and what's more ...** et de plus ..., et qui plus est ...

> When making comparisons, use **plus**.
> *It's more expensive in France.* **En France c'est plus cher.**
> When talking about an additional amount, use **encore**.
> *Would you like some more?* **Vous en voulez encore ?**

moreover [mɔː'rəuvə^r] ADV de plus

morgue [mɔːg] N morgue *f*

MORI ['mɔːrɪ] N ABBR (*BRIT*: = *Market & Opinion Research Institute*) institut de sondage

moribund ['mɒrɪbʌnd] ADJ moribond(e)

★**morning** ['mɔːnɪŋ] N matin *m*; (*as duration*) matinée *f*; **in the ~** le matin; **7 o'clock in the ~** 7 heures du matin; **this ~** ce matin ▶ CPD matinal(e); (*paper*) du matin

morning-after pill ['mɔːnɪŋ'ɑːftə-] N pilule *f* du lendemain

morning sickness N nausées matinales

Moroccan [mə'rɒkən] ADJ marocain(e) ▶ N Marocain(e)

Morocco [mə'rɒkəu] N Maroc *m*

moron ['mɔːrɒn] (!) N idiot(e), minus *mf*

moronic [mə'rɒnɪk] ADJ idiot(e), imbécile

morose [mə'rəus] ADJ morose, maussade

morphine ['mɔːfiːn] N morphine *f*

morris dancing ['mɒrɪs-] N (*BRIT*) danses folkloriques anglaises

Morse [mɔːs] N (*also*: **Morse code**) morse *m*

morsel ['mɔːsl] N bouchée *f*

mortal ['mɔːtl] ADJ, N mortel(le)

mortality [mɔː'tælɪtɪ] N mortalité *f*

mortality rate N (taux *m* de) mortalité *f*

mortar ['mɔːtə^r] N mortier *m*

mortgage ['mɔːgɪdʒ] N hypothèque *f*; (*loan*) prêt *m* (*or* crédit *m*) hypothécaire; **to take out a ~** prendre une hypothèque, faire un emprunt ▶ VT hypothéquer

mortgage company N (*US*) société *f* de crédit immobilier

mortgagee [mɔːgə'dʒiː] N prêteur(-euse) (sur hypothèque)

mortgagor ['mɔːgədʒə^r] N emprunteur(-euse) (sur hypothèque)

mortician [mɔː'tɪʃən] N (*US*) entrepreneur *m* de pompes funèbres

mortified ['mɔːtɪfaɪd] ADJ mort(e) de honte

mortise lock ['mɔːtɪs-] N serrure encastrée

mortuary ['mɔːtjuərɪ] N morgue *f*

mosaic [məu'zeɪɪk] N mosaïque *f*

Moscow ['mɒskəu] N Moscou

Moslem ['mɒzləm] ADJ, N = **Muslim**

mosque [mɒsk] N mosquée *f*

mosquito [mɒs'kiːtəu] (*pl* **mosquitoes**) N moustique *m*

mosquito net N moustiquaire *f*

moss [mɔs] N mousse f

mossy ['mɔsɪ] ADJ moussu(e)

★**most** [məust] ADJ (majority of) la plupart de; (greatest amount of) le plus de; **~ fish** la plupart des poissons ▶ PRON la plupart; **~ of** (with plural) la plupart de; (with singular) la plus grande partie de; **~ of them** la plupart d'entre eux; **~ of the time** la plupart du temps; **at the (very)** au plus; **to make the ~ of** profiter au maximum de ▶ ADV le plus; (very) très, extrêmement; **I saw ~** (more than the others) c'est moi qui en ai vu le plus; **the ~** le plus; **he's the one who talks the ~** c'est lui qui parle le plus; **the ~ beautiful woman in the world** la plus belle femme du monde

> **le/la/les plus** is used with an adjective to make the superlative (the most...). When the French adjective follows the noun the article is repeated: the easiest question **la question la plus facile**.
> When the French adjective goes in front of the noun it is not repeated: the biggest hotels **les plus grands hôtels**.

★**mostly** ['məustlɪ] ADV (chiefly) surtout, principalement; (usually) généralement

MOT N ABBR (BRIT) = Ministry of Transport; **the ~ (test)** visite technique (annuelle) obligatoire des véhicules à moteur

motel [məu'tɛl] N motel m

moth [mɔθ] N papillon m de nuit; (in clothes) mite f

mothball ['mɔθbɔːl] N boule f de naphtaline

moth-eaten ['mɔθiːtn] ADJ mité(e)

★**mother** ['mʌðəʳ] N mère f ▶ VT (pamper, protect) dorloter

mother board N (Comput) carte-mère f

motherhood ['mʌðəhud] N maternité f

mother-in-law ['mʌðərɪnlɔː] N belle-mère f

motherly ['mʌðəlɪ] ADJ maternel(le)

mother-of-pearl ['mʌðərəv'pəːl] N nacre f

Mother's Day N fête f des Mères

mother's help N aide f or auxiliaire f familiale

mother-to-be ['mʌðətə'biː] N future maman

mother tongue N langue maternelle

mothproof ['mɔθpruːf] ADJ traité(e) à l'antimite

motif [məu'tiːf] N motif m

motion ['məuʃən] N mouvement m; (gesture) geste m; (at meeting) motion f; (BRIT: also: **bowel motion**) selles fpl; **to be in ~** (vehicle) être en marche; **to set in ~** mettre en marche; **to go through the motions of doing sth** (fig) faire qch machinalement or sans conviction ▶ VT, VI: **to ~ (to) sb to do** faire signe à qn de faire

motionless ['məuʃənlɪs] ADJ immobile, sans mouvement

motion picture N film m

motivate ['məutɪveɪt] VT motiver

motivated ['məutɪveɪtɪd] ADJ motivé(e)

motivation [məutɪ'veɪʃən] N motivation f

motive ['məutɪv] N motif m, mobile m; **from the best (of) motives** avec les meilleures intentions (du monde) ▶ ADJ moteur(-trice)

motley ['mɔtlɪ] ADJ hétéroclite; bigarré(e), bariolé(e)

★**motor** ['məutəʳ] N moteur m; (BRIT inf: vehicle) auto f ▶ ADJ moteur(-trice)

motorbike ['məutəbaɪk] N moto f

motorboat ['məutəbəut] N bateau m à moteur

motorcade ['məutəkeɪd] N cortège m d'automobiles or de voitures

motorcar ['məutəkɑː] N (BRIT) automobile f

motorcoach ['məutəkəutʃ] N (BRIT) car m

motorcycle ['məutəsaɪkl] N moto f

motorcycle racing N course f de motos

motorcyclist ['məutəsaɪklɪst] N motocycliste mf

motoring ['məutərɪŋ] (BRIT) N tourisme m automobile ▶ ADJ (accident) de voiture, de la route; **~ holiday** vacances fpl en voiture; **~ offence** infraction f au code de la route

motorist ['məutərɪst] N automobiliste mf

motorize ['məutəraɪz] VT motoriser

motor mechanic N mécanicien m garagiste

motor oil N huile f de graissage

motor racing N (BRIT) course f automobile

motor scooter N scooter m

motor trade N secteur m de l'automobile

motor vehicle N véhicule m automobile

motorway ['məutəweɪ] N (BRIT) autoroute f

mottled ['mɔtld] ADJ tacheté(e), marbré(e)

motto ['mɔtəu] (pl **mottoes**) N devise f

mould, (US) **mold** [məuld] N moule m; (mildew) moisissure f ▶ VT mouler, modeler; (fig) façonner

moulder, (US) **molder** ['məuldəʳ] VI (decay) moisir

moulding, (US) **mold** ['məuldɪŋ] N (Archit) moulure f

mouldy, (US) **moldy** ['məuldɪ] ADJ moisi(e); (smell) de moisi

moult, (US) **molt** [məult] VI muer

mound [maund] N monticule m, tertre m

mount [maunt] N (hill) mont m, montagne f; (horse) monture f; (for picture) carton m de montage; (for jewel etc) monture ▶ VT monter; (horse) monter à; (bike) monter sur; (exhibition) organiser, monter; (picture) monter sur carton; (stamp) coller dans un album ▶ VI (inflation, tension) augmenter ▶ **mount up** VI s'élever, monter; (bills, problems, savings) s'accumuler

★**mountain** ['mauntɪn] N montagne f; **to make a ~ out of a molehill** (fig) se faire une montagne d'un rien ▶ CPD de (la) montagne

mountain bike N VTT m, vélo m tout terrain

mountaineer [mauntɪ'nɪəʳ] N alpiniste mf

mountaineering [mauntɪ'nɪərɪŋ] N alpinisme m; **to go ~** faire de l'alpinisme

mountainous ['mauntɪnəs] ADJ montagneux(-euse)

mountain range N chaîne f de montagnes

mountain rescue team N colonne f de secours

mountainside ['mauntɪnsaɪd] N flanc m or versant m de la montagne

mounted ['mauntɪd] ADJ monté(e)

Mount Everest N le mont Everest

mounting ['mauntɪŋ] ADJ (tension, excitement) croissant(e); (ever-increasing): **he ignored his ~ debts**

il ignora les dettes qui s'accumulaient; **in order to cover ~ costs** pour compenser l'augmentation des coûts

mourn [mɔːn] vt pleurer ▶ vi: **to ~ for sb** pleurer qn; **to ~ for sth** se lamenter sur qch

mourner [ˈmɔːnəʳ] N parent(e) or ami(e) du défunt; personne f en deuil or venue rendre hommage au défunt

mournful [ˈmɔːnful] ADJ triste, lugubre

mourning [ˈmɔːnɪŋ] N deuil m; **in ~** en deuil ▶ CPD (dress) de deuil

★**mouse** [maus] (pl **mice** [maɪs]) N (also Comput) souris f

mouse mat N (Comput) tapis m de souris

mousetrap [ˈmaustræp] N souricière f

moussaka [muˈsɑːkə] N moussaka f

mousse [muːs] N mousse f

moustache [məsˈtɑːʃ], (US) **mustache** [ˈmʌstæʃ] N moustache(s) f(pl)

mousy [ˈmausɪ] ADJ (person) effacé(e); (hair) d'un châtain terne

★**mouth** [mauθ] (pl **mouths** [mauðz]) N bouche f; (of dog, cat) gueule f; (of river) embouchure f; (of hole, cave) ouverture f; (of bottle) goulot m; (opening) orifice m

mouthful [ˈmauθful] N bouchée f

mouth organ N harmonica m

mouthpiece [ˈmauθpiːs] N (of musical instrument) bec m, embouchure f; (spokesperson) porte-parole m inv

mouth-to-mouth [ˈmauθtəˈmauθ] ADJ: **~ resuscitation** bouche à bouche m

mouthwash [ˈmauθwɔʃ] N eau f dentifrice

mouth-watering [ˈmauθwɔːtərɪŋ] ADJ qui met l'eau à la bouche

movable [ˈmuːvəbl] ADJ mobile

★**move** [muːv] N (movement) mouvement m; (in game) coup m; (: turn to play) tour m; (change of house) déménagement m; (change of job) changement m d'emploi; **to get a ~ on** se dépêcher, se remuer ▶ vt déplacer, bouger; (emotionally) émouvoir; (Pol: resolution etc) proposer; **can you ~ your car, please?** pouvez-vous déplacer votre voiture, s'il vous plaît ?; **to ~ sb to do sth** pousser or inciter qn à faire qch ▶ vi (gen) bouger, remuer; (traffic) circuler; (also: **move house**) déménager; (in game) jouer; **to ~ towards** se diriger vers
▶ **move about, move around** vi (fidget) remuer; (travel) voyager, se déplacer
▶ **move along** vi se pousser
▶ **move away** vi s'en aller, s'éloigner
▶ **move back** vi revenir, retourner
▶ **move forward** vi avancer ▶ vt avancer; (people) faire avancer
▶ **move in** vi (to a house) emménager; (police, soldiers) intervenir
▶ **move into** vt fus (house) emménager dans
▶ **move off** vi s'éloigner, s'en aller
▶ **move on** vi se remettre en route ▶ vt (onlookers) faire circuler
▶ **move out** vi (of house) déménager
▶ **move over** vi se pousser, se déplacer
▶ **move up** vi avancer; (employee) avoir de l'avancement; (pupil) passer dans la classe supérieure

moveable [muːvəbl] ADJ = **movable**

★**movement** [ˈmuːvmənt] N mouvement m; **~ (of the bowels)** (Med) selles fpl

mover [ˈmuːvəʳ] N auteur m d'une proposition

movie [ˈmuːvɪ] N film m ■ **movies** NPL: **the movies** le cinéma

movie camera N caméra f

moviegoer [ˈmuːvɪgəuəʳ] N (US) cinéphile mf

movie theater (US) N cinéma m

moving [ˈmuːvɪŋ] ADJ en mouvement; (touching) émouvant(e) ▶ N (US) déménagement m

mow [məu] (pt **mowed** [məud], pp **mowed** or **mown** [məun]) vt faucher; (lawn) tondre
▶ **mow down** vt faucher

mower [ˈməuəʳ] N (also: **lawnmower**) tondeuse f à gazon

mown [məun] PP of **mow**

Mozambique [məuzæmˈbiːk] N Mozambique m

★**MP** N ABBR (= Military Police) PM; (BRIT) = **Member of Parliament**; (CANADA) = **Mounted Police**

MP3 N mp3 m

MP3 player N baladeur m numérique, lecteur m mp3

mpg N ABBR (= miles per gallon) (30 mpg = 9,4 l. aux 100 km)

mph ABBR (= miles per hour) (60 mph = 96 km/h)

MPhil [ˈemˈfɪl] N ABBR (US: = Master of Philosophy) titre universitaire

MPS N ABBR (BRIT) = **Member of the Pharmaceutical Society**

★**Mr**, (US) **Mr.** [ˈmɪstəʳ] N: **~ X** Monsieur X, M. X

MRC N ABBR (BRIT: = Medical Research Council) conseil de la recherche médicale

MRCP N ABBR (BRIT) = **Member of the Royal College of Physicians**

MRCS N ABBR (BRIT) = **Member of the Royal College of Surgeons**

MRCVS N ABBR (BRIT) = **Member of the Royal College of Veterinary Surgeons**

★**Mrs**, (US) **Mrs.** [ˈmɪsɪz] N: **~ X** Madame X, Mme X

★**MS** N ABBR (= manuscript) ms; (= multiple sclerosis) SEP f; (US: = Master of Science) titre universitaire ▶ ABBR (US) = **Mississippi**

★**Ms**, (US) **Ms.** [mɪz] N (Miss or Mrs): **Ms X** Madame X, Mme X

Ms est un titre utilisé à la place de Mrs (Mme) ou de Miss (Mlle) pour éviter la distinction traditionnelle entre femmes mariées et femmes non mariées.

MSA N ABBR (US: = Master of Science in Agriculture) titre universitaire

MSc N ABBR = **Master of Science**

MSG N ABBR = **monosodium glutamate**

MSP N ABBR (= Member of the Scottish Parliament) député m au Parlement écossais

MST ABBR (US: = Mountain Standard Time) heure d'hiver des Montagnes Rocheuses

MT N ABBR (= machine translation) TM ▶ ABBR (US) = **Montana**

Mt ABBR (Geo: = mount) Mt

mth ABBR (= *month*) m

MTV N ABBR = **music television**

★**much** [mʌtʃ] ADJ beaucoup de; **~ milk** beaucoup de lait; **we don't have ~ time** nous n'avons pas beaucoup de temps ▶ADV, N, PRON beaucoup; **how ~ is it?** combien est-ce que ça coûte ?; **it's not ~** ce n'est pas beaucoup; **too ~** trop (de); **so ~** tant (de); **I like it very/so ~** j'aime beaucoup/tellement ça; **as ~ as** autant de; **thank you very ~** merci beaucoup; **that's ~ better** c'est beaucoup mieux; **~ to my amazement ...** à mon grand étonnement ...

muck [mʌk] N (*mud*) boue f; (*dirt*) ordures fpl
▶ **muck about** VI (*inf*) faire l'imbécile; (: *waste time*) traînasser; (: *tinker*) bricoler; tripoter
▶ **muck in** VI (BRIT *inf*) donner un coup de main
▶ **muck out** VT (*stable*) nettoyer
▶ **muck up** VT (*inf: ruin*) gâcher, esquinter; (: *dirty*) salir; (: *exam, interview*) se planter à

muckraking [ˈmʌkreɪkɪŋ] N (*fig, inf*) déterrement m d'ordures

mucky [ˈmʌkɪ] ADJ (*dirty*) boueux(-euse), sale

mucus [ˈmjuːkəs] N mucus m

mud [mʌd] N boue f

muddle [ˈmʌdl] N (*mess*) pagaille f, fouillis m; (*mix-up*) confusion f; **to be in a ~** (*person*) ne plus savoir où l'on en est; **to get in a ~** (*while explaining etc*) s'embrouiller ▶VT (*also:* **muddle up**) brouiller, embrouiller
▶ **muddle along** VI aller son chemin tant bien que mal
▶ **muddle through** VI se débrouiller

muddled [ˈmʌdld] ADJ (*person*) perdu(e); (*ideas, approach*) confus(e)

muddle-headed [mʌdlˈhedɪd] ADJ (*person*) à l'esprit embrouillé or confus, dans le brouillard

muddy [ˈmʌdɪ] ADJ boueux(-euse)

mud flats NPL plage f de vase

mudguard [ˈmʌdgɑːd] N garde-boue m inv

mudpack [ˈmʌdpæk] N masque m de beauté

mudslide [ˈmʌdslaɪd] N coulée f de boue

mud-slinging [ˈmʌdslɪŋɪŋ] N médisance f, dénigrement m

muesli [ˈmjuːzlɪ] N muesli m

muezzin [muːˈezɪn] N muezzin m

muff [mʌf] N manchon m ▶VT (*inf: shot, catch etc*) rater, louper; **to ~ it** rater or louper son coup

muffin [ˈmʌfɪn] N (*roll*) petit pain rond et plat; (*cake*) petit gâteau au chocolat ou aux fruits

muffle [ˈmʌfl] VT (*sound*) assourdir, étouffer; (*against cold*) emmitoufler

muffled [ˈmʌfld] ADJ étouffé(e), voilé(e)

muffler [ˈmʌflər] N (*scarf*) cache-nez m inv; (*US Aut*) silencieux m

mufti [ˈmʌftɪ] N: **in ~** en civil

mug [mʌg] N (*cup*) tasse f (sans soucoupe); (: *for beer*) chope f; (*inf: face*) bouille f; (: *fool*) poire f; **it's a ~'s game** (BRIT) c'est bon pour les imbéciles ▶VT (*assault*) agresser
▶ **mug up** VT (BRIT *inf: also:* **mug up on**) bosser, bûcher

mugger [ˈmʌgər] N agresseur m

mugging [ˈmʌgɪŋ] N agression f

muggins [ˈmʌgɪnz] N (*inf*) ma pomme

muggy [ˈmʌgɪ] ADJ lourd(e), moite

mug shot N (*inf: Police*) photo f de criminel; (: *gen: photo*) photo d'identité

mulatto [mjuːˈlætəʊ] (*pl* **mulattoes**) (!) N mulâtre(-tresse)

mulberry [ˈmʌlbrɪ] N (*fruit*) mûre f; (*tree*) mûrier m

mule [mjuːl] N mule f

mull [mʌl]: **to ~ over** VT réfléchir à, ruminer

mullah [ˈmʌlə] N mollah m

mulled [mʌld] ADJ: **~ wine** vin chaud

mullet [ˈmʌlɪt] (*pl* **~**) N (*fish*) mulet m; **red ~** rouget m

multi... [ˈmʌltɪ] PREFIX multi...

multi-access [ˈmʌltɪˈækses] ADJ (*Comput*) à accès multiple

multicoloured, (US) **multicolored** [ˈmʌltɪkʌləd] ADJ multicolore

multicultural [mʌltɪˈkʌltʃərəl] ADJ multiculturel(le)

multiculturalism [mʌltɪˈkʌltʃərəlɪzəm] N multiculturalisme m

multifaceted [mʌltɪˈfæsɪtɪd] ADJ: **he's a ~ performer** c'est un artiste aux multiples talents; **her job is ~** son travail est très varié

multifarious [mʌltɪˈfɛərɪəs] ADJ divers(es), varié(e)

multigrain [ˈmʌltɪgreɪn] ADJ multicéréales

multilateral [mʌltɪˈlætərl] ADJ (*Pol*) multilatéral(e)

multi-level [ˈmʌltɪlevl] ADJ (US) = **multistorey**

multilingual [mʌltɪˈlɪŋgwəl] ADJ (*country*) multilingue, plurilingue; (*person*) polyglotte

multimedia [ˈmʌltɪˈmiːdɪə] ADJ multimédia inv

multimillionaire [mʌltɪmɪljəˈneər] N milliardaire mf

multinational [mʌltɪˈnæʃənl] N multinationale f
▶ADJ multinational(e)

multiple [ˈmʌltɪpl] ADJ multiple ▶N multiple m; (BRIT: *also:* **multiple store**) magasin m à succursales (multiples)

multiple choice (test) N QCM m, questionnaire m à choix multiple

multiple crash N carambolage m

multiple sclerosis [-sklɪˈrəʊsɪs] N sclérose f en plaques

multiplex (cinema) [ˈmʌltɪpleks-] N (cinéma m) multisalles m

multiplication [mʌltɪplɪˈkeɪʃən] N multiplication f

multiplication table N table f de multiplication

multiplicity [mʌltɪˈplɪsɪtɪ] N multiplicité f

multiply [ˈmʌltɪplaɪ] VT multiplier ▶VI se multiplier

multiracial [mʌltɪˈreɪʃl] ADJ multiracial(e)

multistorey [ˈmʌltɪˈstɔːrɪ] ADJ (BRIT: *building*) à étages; (: *car park*) à étages or niveaux multiples

multitask [ˈmʌltɪtɑːsk] VI (*also Comput*) être multitâche

multitasking [ˈmʌltɪtɑːskɪŋ] N (*also Comput*) multitâche m

multitude ['mʌltɪtjuːd] N multitude f

★**mum** [mʌm] N (BRIT) maman f ▶ ADJ: **to keep ~** ne pas souffler mot; **~'s the word!** motus et bouche cousue!

Mumbai [mum'baɪ] N Mumbai

mumble ['mʌmbl] VT, VI marmotter, marmonner

mumbo jumbo ['mʌmbəu-] N (inf) baragouin m, charabia m

mummify ['mʌmɪfaɪ] VT momifier

mummy ['mʌmɪ] N (BRIT: mother) maman f; (embalmed) momie f

mumps [mʌmps] N oreillons mpl

munch [mʌntʃ] VT, VI mâcher

mundane [mʌn'deɪn] ADJ banal(e), terre à terre inv

municipal [mjuː'nɪsɪpl] ADJ municipal(e)

municipality [mjuːnɪsɪ'pælɪtɪ] N municipalité f

munitions [mjuː'nɪʃənz] NPL munitions fpl

mural ['mjuərl] N peinture murale

★**murder** ['məːdəʳ] N meurtre m, assassinat m; **to commit ~** commettre un meurtre ▶ VT assassiner

murderer ['məːdərəʳ] N meurtrier m, assassin m

murderess ['məːdərɪs] N meurtrière f

murderous ['məːdərəs] ADJ meurtrier(-ière)

murk [məːk] N obscurité f

murky ['məːkɪ] ADJ sombre, ténébreux(-euse); (water) trouble

murmur ['məːməʳ] N murmure m; **heart ~** (Med) souffle m au cœur ▶ VT, VI murmurer

MusB, MusBac N ABBR (= Bachelor of Music) titre universitaire

★**muscle** ['mʌsl] N muscle m; (fig) force f ▶ **muscle in** VI s'imposer, s'immiscer

muscular ['mʌskjulaʳ] ADJ musculaire; (person, arm) musclé(e)

muscular dystrophy N dystrophie f musculaire

MusD, MusDoc N ABBR (= Doctor of Music) titre universitaire

muse [mjuːz] VI méditer, songer ▶ N muse f

★**museum** [mjuː'zɪəm] N musée m

mush [mʌʃ] N bouillie f; (pej) sentimentalité f à l'eau de rose

★**mushroom** ['mʌʃrum] N champignon m ▶ VI (fig) pousser comme un (or des) champignon(s)

mushy ['mʌʃɪ] ADJ (vegetables, fruit) en bouillie; (movie etc) à l'eau de rose

★**music** ['mjuːzɪk] N musique f

★**musical** ['mjuːzɪkl] ADJ musical(e); (person) musicien(ne) ▶ N (show) comédie musicale

musical box N = **music box**

musical chairs NPL chaises musicales; (fig): **to play ~** faire des permutations

musical instrument N instrument m de musique

music box N boîte f à musique

music centre N chaîne compacte

music hall N music-hall m

★**musician** [mjuː'zɪʃən] N musicien(ne)

music stand N pupitre m à musique

musk [mʌsk] N musc m

musket ['mʌskɪt] N mousquet m

muskrat ['mʌskræt] N rat musqué

musk rose N (Bot) rose f muscade

Muslim ['mʌzlɪm] ADJ, N musulman(e)

muslin ['mʌzlɪn] N mousseline f

musquash ['mʌskwɔʃ] N loutre f; (fur) rat m d'Amérique, ondatra m

mussel ['mʌsl] N moule f

★**must** [mʌst] AUX VB (obligation): **I ~ do it** je dois le faire, il faut que je le fasse; (probability): **he ~ be there by now** il doit y être maintenant, il y est probablement maintenant; (suggestion, invitation): **you ~ come and see me** il faut que vous veniez me voir; **I ~ have made a mistake** j'ai dû me tromper ▶ N nécessité f, impératif m; **it's a ~** c'est indispensable

mustache ['mʌstæʃ] N (US) = **moustache**

mustard ['mʌstəd] N moutarde f

mustard gas N ypérite f, gaz m moutarde

muster ['mʌstəʳ] VT rassembler; (also: **muster up**: strength, courage) rassembler

mustiness ['mʌstɪnɪs] N odeur f de moisi or de renfermé

mustn't ['mʌsnt] = **must not**

musty ['mʌstɪ] ADJ qui sent le moisi or le renfermé

mutant ['mjuːtənt] ADJ mutant(e) ▶ N mutant m

mutate [mjuː'teɪt] VI subir une mutation

mutation [mjuː'teɪʃən] N mutation f

mute [mjuːt] ADJ muet(te)

muted ['mjuːtɪd] ADJ (noise) sourd(e), assourdi(e); (criticism) voilé(e); (Mus) en sourdine; (: trumpet) bouché(e)

mutilate ['mjuːtɪleɪt] VT mutiler

mutilation [mjuːtɪ'leɪʃən] N mutilation f

mutinous ['mjuːtɪnəs] ADJ (troops) mutiné(e); (attitude) rebelle

mutiny ['mjuːtɪnɪ] N mutinerie f ▶ VI se mutiner

mutter ['mʌtəʳ] VT, VI marmonner, marmotter

mutton ['mʌtn] N mouton m

mutual ['mjuːtʃuəl] ADJ mutuel(le), réciproque; (benefit, interest) commun(e)

mutually ['mjuːtʃuəlɪ] ADV mutuellement, réciproquement

Muzak® ['mjuːzæk] N (often pej) musique f d'ambiance

muzzle ['mʌzl] N museau m; (protective device) muselière f; (of gun) gueule f ▶ VT museler

MVP N ABBR (US Sport) = **most valuable player**

MW ABBR (= medium wave) PO

★**my** [maɪ] ADJ mon (ma), mes pl; **my book/car/gloves** mon livre/ma voiture/mes gants; **I've washed my hair/cut my finger** je me suis lavé les cheveux/coupé le doigt; **is this my pen or yours?** c'est mon stylo ou c'est le vôtre?

Myanmar ['maɪænmɑːʳ] N Myanmar m

myopic [maɪ'ɔpɪk] ADJ myope

myriad ['mɪrɪəd] N myriade f

★**myself** [maɪ'sɛlf] PRON (reflexive) me; (emphatic) moi-même; (after prep) moi; see also **oneself**

mysterious [mɪs'tɪərɪəs] ADJ mystérieux(-euse)

mysteriously [mɪˈstɪəriəslɪ] ADV mystérieusement
★**mystery** [ˈmɪstərɪ] N mystère m
mystery story N roman m à suspense
mystic [ˈmɪstɪk] N mystique mf ▶ ADJ (mysterious) ésotérique
mystical [ˈmɪstɪkl] ADJ mystique
mysticism [ˈmɪstɪsɪzəm] N mysticisme m

mystify [ˈmɪstɪfaɪ] VT (deliberately) mystifier; (puzzle) ébahir
mystique [mɪsˈtiːk] N mystique f
myth [mɪθ] N mythe m
mythical [ˈmɪθɪkl] ADJ mythique
mythological [mɪθəˈlɒdʒɪkl] ADJ mythologique
mythology [mɪˈθɒlədʒɪ] N mythologie f

N n

N¹, n [ɛn] N (letter) N, n m; **N for Nellie,** (US) **N for Nan** N comme Nicolas

N² ABBR (= north) N

'n' [ən] CONJ (inf: and) 'n'; **country 'n' western** country inv; **a country 'n' western song** une chanson country; **a fish 'n' chips restaurant** un fish and chips

NA N ABBR (US: = Narcotics Anonymous) association d'aide aux drogués; (US) = **National Academy**

n/a ABBR (= not applicable) n.a.; (Comm etc) = **no account**

NAACP N ABBR (US) = **National Association for the Advancement of Colored People**

NAAFI ['næfɪ] N ABBR (BRIT: = Navy, Army & Air Force Institute) organisme responsable des magasins et cantines de l'armée

nab [næb] VT (inf) pincer, attraper

NACU N ABBR (US) = **National Association of Colleges and Universities**

nadir ['neɪdɪər] N (Astronomy) nadir m; (fig) fond m, point m extrême

naff [næf] ADJ (BRIT inf) nul(le)

nag [næg] VT (scold) être toujours après, reprendre sans arrêt ▶ N (pej: horse) canasson m; (person): **she's an awful ~** elle est constamment après lui (or eux etc), elle est très casse-pieds

nagging ['nægɪŋ] ADJ (doubt, pain) persistant(e) ▶ N remarques continuelles

nail [neɪl] N (human) ongle m; (metal) clou m; **to pay cash on the ~** (BRIT) payer rubis sur l'ongle ▶ VT clouer; **to ~ sth to sth** clouer qch à qch; **to ~ sb down to a date/price** contraindre qn à accepter or donner une date/un prix

nailbrush ['neɪlbrʌʃ] N brosse f à ongles

nailfile ['neɪlfaɪl] N lime f à ongles

nail polish N vernis m à ongles

nail polish remover N dissolvant m

nail scissors NPL ciseaux mpl à ongles

nail varnish N (BRIT) = **nail polish**

Nairobi [naɪˈrəubɪ] N Nairobi

naïve [naɪˈiːv] ADJ naïf(-ïve)

naïveté [naɪˈiːvteɪ], **naivety** [naɪˈiːvɪtɪ] N naïveté f

naked ['neɪkɪd] ADJ nu(e); **with the ~ eye** à l'œil nu

nakedness ['neɪkɪdnɪs] N nudité f

NAM N ABBR (US) = **National Association of Manufacturers**

★**name** [neɪm] N nom m; (reputation) réputation f; **by ~** par son nom; de nom; **in the ~ of** au nom de; **what's your ~?** comment vous appelez-vous ?, quel est votre nom ?; **my ~ is Peter** je m'appelle Peter; **to take sb's ~ and address** relever l'identité de qn or les nom et adresse de qn; **to make a ~ for o.s.** se faire un nom; **to get (o.s.) a bad ~** se faire une mauvaise réputation; **to call sb names** traiter qn de tous les noms ▶ VT nommer; (identify: accomplice etc) citer; (price, date) fixer, donner

name dropping N mention (pour se faire valoir) du nom de personnalités qu'on connaît (ou prétend connaître)

nameless ['neɪmlɪs] ADJ sans nom; (witness, contributor) anonyme

namely ['neɪmlɪ] ADV à savoir

nameplate ['neɪmpleɪt] N (on door etc) plaque f

namesake ['neɪmseɪk] N homonyme m

Namibia [nɑːˈmɪbɪə] N Namibie f

nan bread [nɑːn-] N nan m

nanny ['nænɪ] N bonne f d'enfants

nanny goat N chèvre f

nanobot ['nænəubɒt] N (Comput) nanorobot m

nanotechnology [nænəutɛkˈnɔlədʒɪ] N nanotechnologie f

nap [næp] N (sleep) (petit) somme ▶ VI: **to be caught napping** être pris(e) à l'improviste or en défaut

napalm ['neɪpɑːm] N napalm m

nape [neɪp] N: **~ of the neck** nuque f

napkin ['næpkɪn] N serviette f (de table)

Naples ['neɪplz] N Naples

Napoleonic [nəpəulɪˈɔnɪk] ADJ napoléonien(ne)

nappy ['næpɪ] N (BRIT) couche f

nappy liner N (BRIT) protège-couche m

nappy rash N: **to have ~** avoir les fesses rouges

narcissistic [nɑːsɪˈsɪstɪk] ADJ narcissique

narcissus [nɑːˈsɪsəs] (pl **narcissi** [-saɪ]) N narcisse m

narcotic [nɑːˈkɔtɪk] N (Med) narcotique m

narcotics [nɑːˈkɔtɪkz] NPL (illegal drugs) stupéfiants mpl

nark [nɑːk] VT (BRIT inf) mettre en rogne

narrate [nəˈreɪt] VT raconter, narrer

narration [nəˈreɪʃən] N narration f

narrative ['nærətɪv] N récit m ▶ ADJ narratif(-ive)

narrator [nəˈreɪtər] N narrateur(-trice)

★narrow ['nærəu] ADJ étroit(e); *(fig)* restreint(e), limité(e); **to have a ~ escape** l'échapper belle ▶ VI *(road)* devenir plus étroit, se rétrécir; *(gap, difference)* se réduire
> **narrow down** VT restreindre

narrow gauge ADJ *(Rail)* à voie étroite

narrowly ['nærəulɪ] ADV: **he ~ missed injury/the tree** il a failli se blesser/rentrer dans l'arbre; **he only ~ missed the target** il a manqué la cible de peu *or* de justesse

narrow-minded [nærəu'maɪndɪd] ADJ à l'esprit étroit, borné(e); *(attitude)* borné(e)

NAS N ABBR *(US)* = **National Academy of Sciences**

NASA ['næsə] N ABBR *(US: = National Aeronautics and Space Administration)* NASA *f*

nasal ['neɪzl] ADJ nasal(e)

Nassau ['næsɔː] N *(in Bahamas)* Nassau

nastily ['nɑːstɪlɪ] ADV *(say, act)* méchamment

nastiness ['nɑːstɪnɪs] N *(of person, remark)* méchanceté *f*

nasturtium [nəs'tɜːʃəm] N capucine *f*

nasty ['nɑːstɪ] ADJ *(person: malicious)* méchant(e); *(: rude)* très désagréable; *(smell)* dégoûtant(e); *(wound, situation)* mauvais(e), vilain(e); *(weather)* affreux(-euse); **to turn ~** *(situation)* mal tourner; *(weather)* se gâter; *(person)* devenir méchant; **it's a ~ business** c'est une sale affaire

NAS/UWT N ABBR *(BRIT: = National Association of Schoolmasters/Union of Women Teachers)* syndicat enseignant

★nation ['neɪʃən] N nation *f*

★national ['næʃənl] ADJ national(e) ▶ N *(abroad)* ressortissant(e); *(when home)* national(e)

national anthem N hymne national

National Curriculum N *(BRIT)* programme scolaire commun à toutes les écoles publiques en Angleterre et au Pays de Galles comprenant dix disciplines

national debt N dette *f* publique

national dress N costume national

National Guard N *(US)* milice *f (de volontaires)*

National Health Service N *(BRIT)* service national de santé, ≈ Sécurité Sociale

Depuis sa création, en 1948, le **National Health Service** (ou, plus couramment, *NHS*) a pour mission de fournir des soins de santé à tous les résidents du Royaume-Uni. Il s'agit du plus grand système de santé public du monde. Financé par les contribuables, il est fondé sur un grand principe : la gratuité des soins de santé pour tous, quels que soient leurs revenus. À quelques exceptions près (notamment les soins dentaires et les médicaments en Angleterre, au pays de Galles et en Irlande du Nord), toutes les prestations, y compris les consultations médicales et les soins hospitaliers, sont gratuites. Chacun des quatre pays du Royaume-Uni possède son propre système, financé et géré de façon indépendante. Souvent en butte aux critiques en raison des temps d'attente pour les opérations chirurgicales et de l'insuffisance des effectifs dans les hôpitaux, le *NHS* fait régulièrement l'objet de réformes visant à améliorer le service fourni.

National Insurance N *(BRIT)* ≈ Sécurité Sociale

Le **National Insurance** est un système de cotisations obligatoires versées par les travailleurs (par prélèvement à la source sur les salaires) et les employeurs du Royaume-Uni afin de contribuer au coût de certaines prestations sociales : retraite, congé maternité, allocations chômage, pension d'invalidité. Introduit en 1911 comme système d'assurance contre la maladie et le chômage, il a été considérablement étendu en 1948.

nationalism ['næʃnəlɪzəm] N nationalisme *m*

nationalist ['næʃnəlɪst] ADJ, N nationaliste *mf*

nationality [næʃə'nælɪtɪ] N nationalité *f*

nationalization [næʃnəlaɪ'zeɪʃən] N nationalisation *f*

nationalize ['næʃnəlaɪz] VT nationaliser

nationally ['næʃnəlɪ] ADV du point de vue national; dans le pays entier

national park N parc national

national press N presse nationale

National Security Council N *(US)* conseil national de sécurité

national service N *(Mil)* service *m* militaire

National Trust N *(BRIT)* ≈ Caisse *f* nationale des monuments historiques et des sites

Le **National Trust** est un organisme indépendant, à but non lucratif, dont la mission est de protéger et de mettre en valeur les monuments et les sites britanniques en raison de leur intérêt historique ou de leur beauté naturelle.

nation state N État-nation *m*

nationwide ['neɪʃənwaɪd] ADJ s'étendant à l'ensemble du pays; *(problem)* à l'échelle du pays entier ▶ ADV à travers *or* dans tout le pays

★native ['neɪtɪv] N habitant(e) du pays, autochtone *mf*; *(!: in colonies)* indigène *mf*; **a ~ of Russia** une personne originaire de Russie ▶ ADJ du pays, indigène; *(country)* natal(e); *(language)* maternel(le); *(ability)* inné(e); **a ~ speaker of French** une personne de langue maternelle française

Native American N Indien(ne) d'Amérique ▶ ADJ amérindien(ne)

native speaker N locuteur natif; *see also* **native**

Nativity [nə'tɪvɪtɪ] N *(Rel)*: **the ~** la Nativité

nativity play N mystère *m or* miracle *m* de la Nativité

NATO ['neɪtəu] N ABBR *(= North Atlantic Treaty Organization)* OTAN *f*

natter ['nætə*r*] VI *(BRIT)* bavarder

★natural ['nætʃrəl] ADJ naturel(le); **to die of ~ causes** mourir d'une mort naturelle

natural childbirth N accouchement *m* sans douleur

natural gas N gaz naturel

natural history N histoire naturelle

naturalism ['nætʃrəlɪzəm] N naturalisme *m*

naturalist ['nætʃrəlɪst] N naturaliste *mf*

naturalization ['nætʃrəlaɪ'zeɪʃən] N naturalisation *f*; acclimatation *f*

naturalize ['nætʃrəlaɪz] VT naturaliser; (plant) acclimater; **to become naturalized** (person) se faire naturaliser

★**naturally** ['nætʃrəlɪ] ADV naturellement

natural resources NPL ressources naturelles

natural selection N sélection naturelle

natural wastage N (Industry) départs naturels et volontaires

★**nature** ['neɪtʃər] N nature f; **by ~** par tempérament, de nature; **documents of a confidential ~** documents à caractère confidentiel

-natured ['neɪtʃəd] SUFFIX: **ill-natured** qui a mauvais caractère

nature reserve N (BRIT) réserve naturelle

nature trail N sentier de découverte de la nature

naturist ['neɪtʃərɪst] N naturiste mf

naught [nɔːt] N = **nought**

naughtiness ['nɔːtɪnɪs] N (of child) désobéissance f; (of story etc) grivoiserie f

naughty ['nɔːtɪ] ADJ (child) vilain(e), pas sage; (story, film) grivois(e)

Nauru [nɑːˈuːruː] N Nauru

nausea ['nɔːsɪə] N nausée f

nauseate ['nɔːsɪeɪt] VT écœurer, donner la nausée à

nauseating ['nɔːsɪeɪtɪŋ] ADJ écœurant(e), dégoûtant(e)

nauseous ['nɔːsɪəs] ADJ nauséabond(e), écœurant(e); (feeling sick): **to be ~** avoir des nausées

nautical ['nɔːtɪkl] ADJ nautique

nautical mile N mille marin (= 1853 m)

naval ['neɪvl] ADJ naval(e)

naval officer N officier m de marine

nave [neɪv] N nef f

navel ['neɪvl] N nombril m

navigable ['nævɪgəbl] ADJ navigable

navigate ['nævɪgeɪt] VT (steer) diriger, piloter ▶ VI naviguer; (Aut) indiquer la route à suivre

navigation [nævɪˈgeɪʃən] N navigation f

navigator ['nævɪgeɪtər] N navigateur m

navvy ['nævɪ] N (BRIT) terrassier m

★**navy** ['neɪvɪ] N marine f; **Department of the N~** (US) ministère m de la Marine

navy-blue ['neɪvɪ'bluː] ADJ bleu marine inv

Nazi ['nɑːtsɪ] ADJ nazi(e) ▶ N Nazi(e)

NB ABBR (= nota bene) NB; (CANADA) = **New Brunswick**

NBA N ABBR (US) = **National Basketball Association; National Boxing Association**

NBC N ABBR (US: = National Broadcasting Company) chaîne de télévision

NBS N ABBR (US: = National Bureau of Standards) office de normalisation

NC ABBR (US) = **North Carolina**

NCC N ABBR (BRIT: = Nature Conservancy Council) organisme de protection de la nature; (US) = **National Council of Churches**

NCO N ABBR = **non-commissioned officer**

ND, N. Dak. ABBR (US) = **North Dakota**

NE ABBR (US) = **Nebraska; New England**

NEA N ABBR (US) = **National Education Association**

neap [niːp] N (also: **neap tide**) mortes-eaux fpl

★**near** [nɪər] ADJ proche; **in the ~ future** dans un proche avenir; **£25,000 or nearest offer** (BRIT) 25 000 livres à débattre ▶ ADV près; **to come ~** s'approcher ▶ PREP (also: **near to**) près de; **~ here/there** près d'ici/non loin de là ▶ VT approcher de

★**nearby** [nɪəˈbaɪ] ADJ proche ▶ ADV tout près, à proximité

Near East N: **the ~** le Proche-Orient

nearer ['nɪərər] ADJ plus proche ▶ ADV plus près

★**nearly** ['nɪəlɪ] ADV presque; **I ~ fell** j'ai failli tomber; **it's not ~ big enough** ce n'est vraiment pas assez grand, c'est loin d'être assez grand

near miss N collision évitée de justesse; (when aiming) coup manqué de peu or de justesse

nearness ['nɪənɪs] N proximité f

nearside ['nɪəsaɪd] (Aut) N (right-hand drive) côté m gauche; (left-hand drive) côté droit ▶ ADJ de gauche; de droite

near-sighted [nɪəˈsaɪtɪd] ADJ myope

★**neat** [niːt] ADJ (person, work) soigné(e); (room etc) bien tenu(e) or rangé(e); (solution, plan) habile; (spirits) pur(e); **I drink it ~** je le bois sec or sans eau

neatly ['niːtlɪ] ADV avec soin or ordre; (skilfully) habilement

neatness ['niːtnɪs] N (tidiness) netteté f; (skilfulness) habileté f

nebulous ['nɛbjuləs] ADJ nébuleux(-euse)

★**necessarily** ['nɛsɪsərɪlɪ] ADV nécessairement; **not ~** pas nécessairement or forcément

★**necessary** ['nɛsɪsrɪ] ADJ nécessaire; **if ~** si besoin est, le cas échéant

necessitate [nɪˈsɛsɪteɪt] VT nécessiter

necessity [nɪˈsɛsɪtɪ] N nécessité f; chose nécessaire or essentielle; **in case of ~** en cas d'urgence

★**neck** [nɛk] N cou m; (of horse, garment) encolure f; (of bottle) goulot m; **~ and ~** à égalité; **to stick one's ~ out** (inf) se mouiller ▶ VI (inf) se peloter

necklace ['nɛklɪs] N collier m

neckline ['nɛklaɪn] N encolure f

necktie ['nɛktaɪ] N (esp US) cravate f

nectar ['nɛktər] N nectar m

nectarine ['nɛktərɪn] N brugnon m, nectarine f

née [neɪ] ADJ: **~ Scott** née Scott

★**need** [niːd] N besoin m; **to be in ~ of** or **have ~ of** avoir besoin de; **£10 will meet my immediate needs** 10 livres suffiront pour mes besoins immédiats; **in case of ~** en cas de besoin, au besoin; **there's no ~ to do ....** il n'y a pas lieu de faire ..., il n'est pas nécessaire de faire ...; **there's no ~ for that** ce n'est pas la peine, cela n'est pas nécessaire ▶ VT avoir besoin de; **to ~ to do** devoir faire; avoir besoin de faire; **you don't ~ to go** vous n'avez pas besoin or vous n'êtes pas obligé de partir; **a signature is needed** il faut une signature

needle ['niːdl] N aiguille f; (on record player) saphir m ▶ VT (inf) asticoter, tourmenter

needlecord ['niːdlkɔːd] N (BRIT) velours m mille-raies

needless ['ni:dlɪs] ADJ inutile; **~ to say, ...** inutile de dire que ...

needlessly ['ni:dlɪslɪ] ADV inutilement

needlework ['ni:dlwə:k] N (activity) travaux mpl d'aiguille; (object) ouvrage m

needn't ['ni:dnt] = **need not**

needy ['ni:dɪ] ADJ nécessiteux(-euse)

negation [nɪ'geɪʃən] N négation f

★**negative** ['negətɪv] N (Phot, Elec) négatif m; (Ling) terme m de négation; **to answer in the ~** répondre par la négative ▸ ADJ négatif(-ive)

negative equity N situation dans laquelle la valeur d'une maison est inférieure à celle du prêt immobilier contracté pour la payer

negatively ['negətɪvlɪ] ADV négativement

negativity [negə'tɪvɪtɪ] N négativité f

neglect [nɪ'glɛkt] VT négliger; (garden) ne pas entretenir; (duty) manquer à; **to ~ to do sth** négliger or omettre de faire qch; **to ~ one's appearance** se négliger ▸ N (of person, duty, garden) le fait de négliger; **(state of) ~** abandon m

neglected [nɪ'glɛktɪd] ADJ négligé(e), à l'abandon

neglectful [nɪ'glɛktful] ADJ (gen) négligent(e); **to be ~ of sb/sth** négliger qn/qch

negligee ['nɛglɪʒeɪ] N déshabillé m

negligence ['nɛglɪdʒəns] N négligence f

negligent ['nɛglɪdʒənt] ADJ négligent(e)

negligently ['nɛglɪdʒəntlɪ] ADV par négligence; (offhandedly) négligemment

negligible ['nɛglɪdʒɪbl] ADJ négligeable

negotiable [nɪ'gəuʃɪəbl] ADJ négociable; **not ~** (cheque) non négociable

★**negotiate** [nɪ'gəuʃɪeɪt] VI négocier; **to ~ with sb for sth** négocier avec qn en vue d'obtenir qch ▸ VT négocier; (Comm) négocier; (obstacle) franchir, négocier; (bend in road) négocier

negotiating table [nɪ'gəuʃɪeɪtɪŋ-] N table f des négociations

negotiation [nɪgəuʃɪ'eɪʃən] N négociation f, pourparlers mpl; **to enter into negotiations with sb** engager des négociations avec qn

negotiator [nɪ'gəuʃɪeɪtə'] N négociateur(-trice)

Negress ['ni:grɪs] N (!) négresse f

Negro ['ni:grəu] (pl **Negroes**) (!) ADJ (gen) noir(e); (music, arts) nègre, noir ▸ N Noir(e)

neigh [neɪ] VI hennir

neighbour, (US) **neighbor** ['neɪbə'] N voisin(e)

neighbourhood, (US) **neighborhood** ['neɪbəhud] N (place) quartier m; (people) voisinage m

neighbourhood watch N (BRIT: also: **neighbourhood watch scheme**) système de surveillance, assuré par les habitants d'un même quartier

neighbouring, (US) **neighboring** ['neɪbərɪŋ] ADJ voisin(e), avoisinant(e)

neighbourly ['neɪbəlɪ] ADJ (US) **neighborly** obligeant(e); (relations) de bon voisinage

★**neither** ['naɪðə'] ADJ, PRON aucun(e) (des deux), ni l'un(e) ni l'autre; **~ of them** ni l'un ni l'autre ▸ CONJ: **~ do I** moi non plus; **I didn't move and ~ did Claude** je n'ai pas bougé, (et) Claude non plus; **~ did I refuse** (et or mais) je n'ai pas non plus refusé ▸ ADV: **~ good nor bad** ni bon ni mauvais

nemesis ['nɛməsɪs] N némésis f

neo... ['ni:əu] PREFIX néo-

neolithic [ni:əu'lɪθɪk] ADJ néolithique

neologism [nɪ'ɔlədʒɪzəm] N néologisme m

neon ['ni:ɔn] N néon m

neonatal [ni:əu'neɪtəl] ADJ néonatal(e)

neon light N lampe f au néon

neon sign N enseigne (lumineuse) au néon

Nepal [nɪ'pɔ:l] N Népal m

★**nephew** ['nɛvju:] N neveu m

nepotism ['nɛpətɪzəm] N népotisme m

nerd [nə:d] N (pej) pauvre mec m, ballot m

★**nerve** [nə:v] N nerf m; (bravery) sang-froid m, courage m; (cheek) aplomb m, toupet m; **to lose one's ~** (self-confidence) perdre son sang-froid ▪ **nerves** NPL (nervousness) nervosité f; **he gets on my nerves** il m'énerve; **to have a fit of nerves** avoir le trac

nerve centre N (Anat) centre nerveux; (fig) centre névralgique

nerve gas N gaz m neuroplégique

nerve-racking ['nə:vrækɪŋ] ADJ angoissant(e)

★**nervous** ['nə:vəs] ADJ nerveux(-euse); (anxious) inquiet(-ète), plein(e) d'appréhension; (timid) intimidé(e)

nervous breakdown N dépression nerveuse

nervously ['nə:vəslɪ] ADV nerveusement

nervousness ['nə:vəsnɪs] N nervosité f; inquiétude f, appréhension f

nervous wreck N (inf): **to be a ~** être une boule de nerfs

nervy ['nə:vɪ] ADJ (inf): **he's very ~** il a les nerfs à fleur de peau or à vif

nest [nɛst] N nid m; **~ of tables** table f gigogne ▸ VI (se) nicher, faire son nid

nest egg N (fig) bas m de laine, magot m

nestle ['nɛsl] VI se blottir

nestling ['nɛstlɪŋ] N oisillon m

★**Net** [nɛt] N (Comput): **the ~** (Internet) le Net

★**net** [nɛt] N filet m; (fabric) tulle f ▸ ADJ net(te) ▸ ADV: **~ of tax** net d'impôt; **he earns £20,000 ~ per year** il gagne 20 000 livres net par an ▸ VT (fish etc) prendre au filet; (money: person) toucher; (: deal, sale) rapporter

netball ['nɛtbɔ:l] N netball m

net curtains NPL voilages mpl

★**Netherlands** ['nɛðələndz] NPL: **the ~** les Pays-Bas mpl

netiquette ['nɛtɪkɛt] N nétiquette f

net profit N bénéfice net

nett [nɛt] ADJ = **net**

netting ['nɛtɪŋ] N (for fence etc) treillis m, grillage m; (fabric) voile m

nettle ['nɛtl] N ortie f

★**network** ['nɛtwə:k] N réseau m ▸ CPD: **there's no ~ coverage here** (Tel) il n'y a pas de réseau ici ▸ VT (Radio, TV) diffuser sur l'ensemble du réseau; (computers) interconnecter ▸ VI créer des réseaux, réseauter

networking ['nɛtwə:kɪŋ] N réseautage m

neuralgia [njuə'rældʒə] N névralgie f

neurological [njuərə'lɔdʒɪkl] ADJ neurologique

743

neurologist [njuə'rɔlədʒɪst] N neurologue *mf*

neurology [njuə'rɔlədʒɪ] N neurologie *f*

neuron ['njuərɔn], **neurone** ['njuərəun] N neurone *m*

neurosis [njuə'rəusɪs] (*pl* **neuroses** [-siːz]) N névrose *f*

neurotic [njuə'rɔtɪk] ADJ, N névrosé(e)

neuter ['njuːtə'] ADJ neutre ▸ N neutre *m* ▸ VT (*cat etc*) châtrer, couper

neutral ['njuːtrəl] ADJ neutre ▸ N (*Aut*) point mort

neutrality [njuː'trælɪtɪ] N neutralité *f*

neutralize ['njuːtrəlaɪz] VT neutraliser

neutron bomb ['njuːtrɔn-] N bombe *f* à neutrons

★**never** ['nɛvə'] ADV (ne ...) jamais; **I ~ went** je ne suis pas allé; **I've ~ been to Spain** je ne suis jamais allé en Espagne; **~ again** plus jamais; **~ in my life** jamais de ma vie; *see also* **mind**

never-ending [nɛvər'ɛndɪŋ] ADJ interminable

nevertheless [nɛvəðə'lɛs] ADV néanmoins, malgré tout

★**new** [njuː] ADJ nouveau (nouvelle); (*brand new*) neuf (neuve); **as good as ~** comme neuf

> **nouveau** changes to **nouvel** before a vowel or a mute 'h': *her new computer* **son nouvel ordinateur**; *a new hotel* **un nouvel hôtel**.

New Age N New Age *m*

newbie ['njuːbɪ] N (*beginner*) newbie *mf*; (*on forum*) nouveau (nouvelle)

newborn ['njuːbɔːn] ADJ nouveau-né(e)

new build N constructions *fpl* nouvelles

newcomer ['njuːkʌmə'] N nouveau venu (nouvelle venue)

new-fangled ['njuːfæŋgld] ADJ (*pej*) ultramoderne (et farfelu(e))

new-found ['njuːfaund] ADJ de fraîche date; (*friend*) nouveau (nouvelle)

Newfoundland ['njuːfənlənd] N Terre-Neuve *f*

New Guinea N Nouvelle-Guinée *f*

newly ['njuːlɪ] ADV nouvellement, récemment

newly-weds ['njuːlɪwɛdz] NPL jeunes mariés *mpl*

new moon N nouvelle lune

newness ['njuːnɪs] N nouveauté *f*; (*of fabric, clothes etc*) état neuf

New Orleans [-'ɔːlənz] N la Nouvelle-Orléans

★**news** [njuːz] N nouvelle(s) *f(pl)*; (*Radio, TV*) informations *fpl*, actualités *fpl*; **a piece of ~** une nouvelle; **good/bad ~** bonne/mauvaise nouvelle; **financial ~** (*Press, Radio, TV*) page financière

news agency N agence *f* de presse

★**newsagent** ['njuːzeɪdʒənt] N (*BRIT*) marchand *m* de journaux

news bulletin N (*Radio, TV*) bulletin *m* d'informations

newscaster ['njuːzkɑːstə'] N (*Radio, TV*) présentateur(-trice)

news flash N flash *m* d'information

newsgroup ['njuːzgruːp] N forum *m* Internet

newsletter ['njuːzlɛtə'] N bulletin *m*

★**newspaper** ['njuːzpeɪpə'] N journal *m*; **daily ~** quotidien *m*; **weekly ~** hebdomadaire *m*

newsprint ['njuːzprɪnt] N papier *m* (de) journal

newsreader ['njuːzriːdə'] N = **newscaster**

newsreel ['njuːzriːl] N actualités (filmées)

newsroom ['njuːzruːm] N (*Press*) salle *f* de rédaction; (*Radio, TV*) studio *m*

news stand N kiosque *m* à journaux

newsworthy ['njuːzwəːðɪ] ADJ: **to be ~** valoir la peine d'être publié

newt [njuːt] N triton *m*

new town N (*BRIT*) ville nouvelle

★**New Year** N Nouvel An; **Happy ~!** Bonne Année !; **to wish sb a happy ~** souhaiter la Bonne Année à qn

New Year's Day N le jour de l'An

New Year's Eve N la Saint-Sylvestre

New Year's resolution N résolution *f* pour la nouvelle année

New York [-'jɔːk] N New York; (*also*: **New York State**) New York *m*

New Zealand [-'ziːlənd] N Nouvelle-Zélande *f* ▸ ADJ néo-zélandais(e)

New Zealander [-'ziːləndə'] N Néo-Zélandais(e)

★**next** [nɛkst] ADJ (*in time*) prochain(e); (*seat, room*) voisin(e), d'à côté; (*meeting, bus stop*) suivant(e); **~ time** la prochaine fois; **the ~ day** le lendemain, le jour suivant *or* d'après; **~ week** la semaine prochaine; **the ~ week** la semaine suivante; **~ year** l'année prochaine; **"turn to the ~ page"** « voir page suivante »; **who's ~?** c'est à qui ? ▸ ADV la fois suivante; la prochaine fois; (*afterwards*) ensuite; **when do we meet ~?** quand nous revoyons-nous ?; **~ to** *prep* à côté de; **~ to nothing** presque rien ▸ PRON: **the week after ~** dans deux semaines; **~ please!** (*at doctor's etc*) au suivant !

next door ADV à côté ▸ ADJ (*neighbour*) d'à côté

next-of-kin ['nɛkstəv'kɪn] N parent *m* le plus proche

NF N ABBR (*BRIT Pol*: = *National Front*) ≈ FN ▸ ABBR (*CANADA*) = **Newfoundland**

NFL N ABBR (*US*) = **National Football League**

NG ABBR (*US*) = **National Guard**

NGO N ABBR (*US*: = *non-governmental organization*) ONG *f*

NH ABBR (*US*) = **New Hampshire**

NHL N ABBR (*US*) = **National Hockey League**

NHS N ABBR (*BRIT*) = **National Health Service**

NI ABBR = **Northern Ireland**; (*BRIT*) = **National Insurance**

Niagara Falls [naɪ'ægərə-] NPL les chutes *fpl* du Niagara

nib [nɪb] N (*of pen*) (bec *m* de) plume *f*

nibble ['nɪbl] VT grignoter

Nicaragua [nɪkə'rægjuə] N Nicaragua *m*

Nicaraguan [nɪkə'rægjuən] ADJ nicaraguayen(ne) ▸ N Nicaraguayen(ne)

★**nice** [naɪs] ADJ (*holiday, trip, taste*) agréable; (*flat, picture*) joli(e); (*person*) gentil(le); (*distinction, point*) subtil(e)

nice-looking ['naɪslukɪŋ] ADJ joli(e)

nicely ['naɪslɪ] ADV agréablement; joliment; gentiment; subtilement; **that will do ~** ce sera parfait

niceties ['naɪsɪtɪz] NPL subtilités *fpl*

niche [niːʃ] N (*Archit*) niche *f*

nick [nɪk] N (*indentation*) encoche *f*; (*wound*) entaille *f*; (BRIT *inf*): **in good ~** en bon état; **in the ~ of time** juste à temps ▶ VT (*cut*): **to ~ o.s.** se couper; (BRIT *inf*: *steal*) faucher, piquer; (: *arrest*) choper, pincer

nickel ['nɪkl] N nickel *m*; (US) pièce *f* de 5 cents

nickname ['nɪkneɪm] N surnom *m* ▶ VT surnommer

Nicosia [nɪkə'siːə] N Nicosie

nicotine ['nɪkətiːn] N nicotine *f*

nicotine patch N timbre *m* anti-tabac, patch *m*

★**niece** [niːs] N nièce *f*

nifty ['nɪftɪ] ADJ (*inf*: *car, jacket*) qui a du chic or de la classe; (: *gadget, tool*) astucieux(-euse)

Niger ['naɪdʒəʳ] N (*country, river*) Niger *m*

Nigeria [naɪ'dʒɪərɪə] N Nigéria *mf*

Nigerian [naɪ'dʒɪərɪən] ADJ nigérien(ne) ▶ N Nigérien(ne)

niggardly ['nɪgədlɪ] ADJ (*person*) parcimonieux(-euse), pingre; (*allowance, amount*) misérable

niggle ['nɪgl] VT tracasser ▶ VI (*find fault*) trouver toujours à redire; (*fuss*) n'être jamais content(e)

niggling ['nɪglɪŋ] ADJ tatillon(ne); (*detail*) insignifiant(e); (*doubt, pain*) persistant(e)

★**night** [naɪt] N nuit *f*; (*evening*) soir *m*; **at ~** la nuit; **by ~** de nuit; **in the ~**, **during the ~** pendant la nuit; **last ~** (*evening*) hier soir; (*night-time*) la nuit dernière; **the ~ before last** avant-hier soir

night-bird ['naɪtbəːd] N oiseau *m* nocturne; (*fig*) couche-tard *m inv*, noctambule *mf*

nightcap ['naɪtkæp] N *boisson prise avant le coucher*

night club N boîte *f* de nuit

nightdress ['naɪtdrɛs] N chemise *f* de nuit

nightfall ['naɪtfɔːl] N tombée *f* de la nuit

nightgown ['naɪtgaun] N (US) chemise *f* de nuit

nightie ['naɪtɪ] N chemise *f* de nuit

nightingale ['naɪtɪŋgeɪl] N rossignol *m*

nightlife ['naɪtlaɪf] N vie *f* nocturne

nightly ['naɪtlɪ] ADJ (*news*) du soir; (*by night*) nocturne ▶ ADV (*every evening*) tous les soirs; (*every night*) toutes les nuits

★**nightmare** ['naɪtmɛəʳ] N cauchemar *m*

night porter N gardien *m* de nuit, concierge *m* de service la nuit

night safe N coffre *m* de nuit

night school N cours *mpl* du soir

nightshade ['naɪtʃeɪd] N: **deadly ~** (*Bot*) belladone *f*

night shift N équipe *f* de nuit

nightspot ['naɪtspɔt] N (*inf*) boîte *f* de nuit

night-time ['naɪttaɪm] N nuit *f*

night watchman N (*irreg*) veilleur *m* de nuit; poste *m* de nuit

nightwear ['naɪtwɛəʳ] N vêtements *mpl* de nuit

nihilism ['naɪɪlɪzəm] N nihilisme *m*

nihilistic [naɪɪ'lɪstɪk] ADJ nihiliste

nil [nɪl] N rien *m*; (BRIT *Sport*) zéro *m*

Nile [naɪl] N: **the ~** le Nil

nimble ['nɪmbl] ADJ agile

nimbyism ['nɪmbɪɪzəm] N syndrome *m* du « pas dans mon jardin », *mobilisation contre des décisions d'aménagement du territoire (par ex. implantation d'une déchetterie, d'une ligne haute tension ou d'un parc éolien).*

★**nine** [naɪn] NUM neuf

★**nineteen** ['naɪn'tiːn] NUM dix-neuf

★**nineteenth** [naɪn'tiːnθ] NUM dix-neuvième

ninetieth ['naɪntɪɪθ] NUM quatre-vingt-dixième

★**ninety** ['naɪntɪ] NUM quatre-vingt-dix

★**ninth** [naɪnθ] NUM neuvième

nip [nɪp] VT pincer ▶ VI (BRIT *inf*): **to ~ out/down/up** sortir/descendre/monter en vitesse; **to ~ into a shop** faire un saut dans un magasin ▶ N pincement *m*; (*drink*) petit verre

nipple ['nɪpl] N (*Anat*) mamelon *m*, bout *m* du sein

nippy ['nɪpɪ] ADJ (BRIT: *person*) alerte, leste; (: *car*) nerveux(-euse)

nit [nɪt] N (*in hair*) lente *f*; (*inf*: *idiot*) imbécile *mf*, crétin(e)

nit-pick ['nɪtpɪk] VI (*inf*) être tatillon(ne)

nitrogen ['naɪtrədʒən] N azote *m*

nitroglycerin, nitroglycerine ['naɪtrəu'glɪsərin] N nitroglycérine *f*

nitty-gritty ['nɪtɪ'grɪtɪ] N (*inf*): **to get down to the ~** en venir au fond du problème

nitwit ['nɪtwɪt] N (*inf*) nigaud(e)

NJ ABBR (US) = **New Jersey**

NLF N ABBR (= *National Liberation Front*) FLN *m*

NLQ ABBR (= *near letter quality*) qualité *f* courrier

NLRB N ABBR (US: = *National Labor Relations Board*) *organisme de protection des travailleurs*

NM, N. Mex. ABBR (US) = **New Mexico**

---

no [nəu]

ADV (*opposite of "yes"*) non; **are you coming? — no (I'm not)** est-ce que vous venez ? — non; **would you like some more? — no thank you** vous en voulez encore ? — non merci

▶ ADJ (*not any*) (ne ...) pas de, (ne ...) aucun(e); **I have no money/books** je n'ai pas d'argent/de livres; **no student would have done it** aucun étudiant ne l'aurait fait; **"no smoking"** « défense de fumer »; **"no dogs"** « les chiens ne sont pas admis »

▶ N (*pl* **noes**) non *m*; **I won't take no for an answer** il n'est pas question de refuser

---

★**no.** ABBR (= *number*) n°

nobble ['nɔbl] VT (BRIT *inf*: *person*: *bribe*) soudoyer, acheter; (: *to speak to*) mettre le grappin sur; (*Racing*: *horse, dog*) droguer (*pour l'empêcher de gagner*)

Nobel prize [nəu'bɛl-] N prix *m* Nobel

nobility [nəu'bɪlɪtɪ] N noblesse *f*

noble ['nəubl] ADJ noble

nobleman ['nəublmən] N (*irreg*) noble *m*

nobly ['nəublɪ] ADV noblement

★**nobody** ['nəubədɪ] PRON (ne ...) personne

no-claims bonus ['nəukleɪmz-] N bonus *m*

nocturnal [nɔk'təːnl] ADJ nocturne

★**nod** [nɔd] VI faire un signe de (la) tête (*affirmatif ou amical*); (*sleep*) somnoler ▶ VT: **to ~ one's head**

n

faire un signe de (la) tête; (in agreement) faire signe que oui; **they nodded their agreement** ils ont acquiescé d'un signe de la tête ▸ N signe m de (la) tête

▸ **nod off** VI s'assoupir

node [nəud] N nœud m; (Anat) nodule m

no-fly zone [nəu'flaɪ-] N zone interdite (aux avions et hélicoptères)

★**noise** [nɔɪz] N bruit m; **I can't sleep for the ~** je n'arrive pas à dormir à cause du bruit

noiseless ['nɔɪzlɪs] ADJ silencieux(-euse)

noisily ['nɔɪzɪlɪ] ADV bruyamment

noisy ['nɔɪzɪ] ADJ bruyant(e)

nomad ['nəumæd] N nomade mf

nomadic [nəu'mædɪk] ADJ nomade

no man's land N no man's land m

nominal ['nɒmɪnl] ADJ (rent, fee) symbolique; (value) nominal(e)

nominate ['nɒmɪneɪt] VT (propose) proposer; (appoint) nommer

nomination [nɒmɪ'neɪʃən] N nomination f

nominee [nɒmɪ'ni:] N candidat agréé; personne nommée

non- [nɒn] PREFIX non-

nonalcoholic [nɒnælkə'hɒlɪk] ADJ non alcoolisé(e)

nonbreakable [nɒn'breɪkəbl] ADJ incassable

nonce word ['nɒns-] N mot créé pour l'occasion

nonchalant ['nɒnʃələnt] ADJ nonchalant(e)

non-commissioned [nɒnkə'mɪʃənd] ADJ: **~ officer** sous-officier m

noncommittal [nɒnkə'mɪtl] ADJ évasif(-ive)

nonconformist [nɒnkən'fɔ:mɪst] N non-conformiste mf ▸ ADJ non-conformiste, dissident(e)

noncooperation ['nɒnkəuɒpə'reɪʃən] N refus m de coopérer, non-coopération f

nondescript ['nɒndɪskrɪpt] ADJ quelconque, indéfinissable

★**none** [nʌn] PRON aucun(e); **~ of you** aucun d'entre vous, personne parmi vous; **I have ~** je n'en ai pas; **I have ~ left** je n'en ai plus; **~ at all** (not one) aucun(e); **how much milk? — ~ at all** combien de lait ? — pas du tout; **he's ~ the worse for it** il ne s'en porte pas plus mal

nonentity [nɒ'nentɪtɪ] N personne insignifiante

nonessential [nɒnɪ'senʃl] ADJ accessoire, super-flu(e) ▸ N: **nonessentials** le superflu

nonetheless ['nʌnðə'les] ADV néanmoins

nonevent [nɒnɪ'vent] N événement manqué

nonexecutive [nɒnɪg'zekjutɪv] ADJ: **~ director** administrateur(-trice), conseiller(-ère) de direction

nonexistent [nɒnɪg'zɪstənt] ADJ inexistant(e)

non-fiction [nɒn'fɪkʃən] N littérature f non romanesque

nonintervention ['nɒnɪntə'venʃən] N non-intervention f

non-nuclear [nɒn'nju:klɪə'] ADJ (weapon) conventionnel(le); (country) non doté(e) de l'arme nucléaire

no-no ['nəunəu] N (inf): **it's a ~** il n'en est pas question

non obst. ABBR (= non obstante: notwithstanding) nonobstant

no-nonsense [nəu'nɒnsəns] ADJ (manner, person) plein(e) de bon sens

nonpayment [nɒn'peɪmənt] N non-paiement m

nonplussed [nɒn'plʌst] ADJ perplexe

non-profit [nɒn'prɒfɪt] ADJ à but non lucratif

non-profit-making [nɒn'prɒfɪtmeɪkɪŋ] ADJ à but non lucratif

non-proliferation [nɒnprəlɪfə'reɪʃən] N non-prolifération f

nonsense ['nɒnsəns] N absurdités fpl, idioties fpl; **~!** ne dites pas d'idioties !; **it is ~ to say that ...** il est absurde de dire que ....

nonsensical [nɒn'sensɪkl] ADJ absurde, qui n'a pas de sens

non-smoker ['nɒn'sməukə'] N non-fumeur m

non-smoking ['nɒn'sməukɪŋ] ADJ non-fumeur

nonstarter [nɒn'stɑ:tə'] N: **it's a ~** c'est voué à l'échec

non-stick ['nɒn'stɪk] ADJ qui n'attache pas

nonstop ['nɒn'stɒp] ADJ direct(e), sans arrêt (or escale) ▸ ADV sans arrêt

nontaxable [nɒn'tæksəbl] ADJ: **~ income** revenu m non imposable

non-U ['nɒn'ju:] ADJ ABBR (BRIT inf: = non-upper class) qui ne se dit (or se fait) pas

non-violent [nɒn'vaɪələnt] ADJ (protest, offender) non violent(e); (crime) commis(e) sans user de violence

nonvolatile [nɒn'vɒlətaɪl] ADJ: **~ memory** (Comput) mémoire rémanente or non volatile

nonvoting [nɒn'vəutɪŋ] ADJ: **~ shares** actions fpl sans droit de vote

non-white ['nɒn'waɪt] ADJ de couleur ▸ N (!) personne f de couleur

noodles ['nu:dlz] NPL nouilles fpl

nook [nuk] N: **nooks and crannies** recoins mpl

noon [nu:n] N midi m

no-one ['nəuwʌn] PRON = **nobody**

noose [nu:s] N nœud coulant; (hangman's) corde f

★**nor** [nɔ:'] CONJ = **neither** ▸ ADV see **neither**

norm [nɔ:m] N norme f

★**normal** ['nɔ:ml] ADJ normal(e) ▸ N: **to return to ~** redevenir normal(e)

normality [nɔ:'mælɪtɪ] N normalité f

★**normally** ['nɔ:məlɪ] ADV normalement

Norman ['nɔ:mən] ADJ, N Normand(e)

Normandy ['nɔ:məndɪ] N Normandie f

Norse [nɔ:s] ADJ (mythology, gods) scandinave ▸ N (language) norrois m

★**north** [nɔ:θ] N nord m ▸ ADJ nord inv; (wind) du nord ▸ ADV au or vers le nord

North Africa N Afrique f du Nord

North African ADJ nord-africain(e), d'Afrique du Nord ▸ N Nord-Africain(e)

North America N Amérique f du Nord

North American N Nord-Américain(e) ▸ ADJ nord-américain(e), d'Amérique du Nord

northbound ['nɔ:θbaund] ADJ (traffic) en direction du nord; (carriageway) nord inv

north-east [nɔ:θ'i:st] N nord-est m

northeastern [nɔ:θ'i:stən] ADJ (du) nord-est inv

northerly ['nɔːðəlɪ] ADJ (*wind, direction*) du nord

★**northern** ['nɔːðən] ADJ du nord, septentrional(e)

northerner ['nɔːðənəʳ] N habitant(e) du nord; **northerners** les gens du nord; **to be a ~** être or venir du nord

★**Northern Ireland** N Irlande *f* du Nord

L'Irlande du Nord (**Northern Ireland**), qui fait partie du Royaume-Uni, se compose de six comtés du nord-est de l'Irlande. Elle est née en 1921 de la division de cette dernière en Irlande du Nord et Irlande du Sud, devenue depuis un État indépendant. La population se composait en majorité d'unionistes, désireux de rester rattachés au Royaume-Uni, avec une importante minorité de républicains, catholiques pour la plupart, partisans d'une Irlande unifiée et indépendante. L'Irlande du Nord a été longtemps marquée par le conflit entre ces deux communautés. De la fin des années 1960 à la fin des années 1990, elle a connu une époque de violence, *The Troubles*, qui a fait des milliers de victimes. L'accord connu sous le nom de *Good Friday Agreement* (accord du Vendredi saint) a marqué une étape importante sur la voie de la paix, même si le sectarisme et la ségrégation religieuse continuent de poser des problèmes.

northernmost ['nɔːðənməʊst] ADJ (*part*) le (la) plus au nord; (*tip*) septentrional(e)

North Korea N Corée *f* du Nord

North Pole N: **the ~** le pôle Nord

North Sea N: **the ~** la mer du Nord

North Sea oil N pétrole *m* de la mer du Nord

northward ['nɔːθwəd], **northwards** ['nɔːθwədz] ADV vers le nord

north-west [nɔːθ'wɛst] N nord-ouest *m*

northwestern ['nɔːθ'wɛstən] ADJ (du) nord-ouest *inv*

★**Norway** ['nɔːweɪ] N Norvège *f*

★**Norwegian** [nɔː'wiːdʒən] ADJ norvégien(ne) ▶ N Norvégien(ne); (*Ling*) norvégien *m*

nos. ABBR (= *numbers*) n^os

★**nose** [nəʊz] N nez *m*; (*of dog, cat*) museau *m*; (*fig*) flair *m*; **to pay through the ~ (for sth)** (*inf*) payer un prix excessif (pour qch) ▶ VI (*also*: **nose one's way**) avancer précautionneusement ▶ **nose about, nose around** VI fouiner or fureter (partout)

nosebleed ['nəʊzbliːd] N saignement *m* de nez

nose-dive ['nəʊzdaɪv] N (descente *f* en) piqué *m*

nose drops NPL gouttes *fpl* pour le nez

nosey ['nəʊzɪ] ADJ (*inf*) curieux(-euse)

nostalgia [nɒs'tældʒɪə] N nostalgie *f*

nostalgic [nɒs'tældʒɪk] ADJ nostalgique

nostril ['nɒstrɪl] N narine *f*; (*of horse*) naseau *m*

nosy ['nəʊzɪ] ADJ (*inf*) = **nosey**

★**not** [nɒt] ADV (ne ...) pas; **he is ~** or **isn't here** il n'est pas ici; **you must ~** or **mustn't do that** tu ne dois pas faire ça; **I hope ~** j'espère que non; **~ at all** pas du tout; (*after thanks*) de rien; **it's too late, isn't it?** c'est trop tard, n'est-ce pas?; **~ yet/now** pas encore/maintenant; *see also* **only**

notable ['nəʊtəbl] ADJ notable

notably ['nəʊtəblɪ] ADV (*particularly*) en particulier; (*markedly*) spécialement

notary ['nəʊtərɪ] N (*also*: **notary public**) notaire *m*

notation [nəʊ'teɪʃən] N notation *f*

notch [nɒtʃ] N encoche *f*
▶ **notch up** VT (*score*) marquer; (*victory*) remporter

★**note** [nəʊt] N note *f*; (*letter*) mot *m*; (*banknote*) billet *m*; **just a quick ~ to let you know ...** juste un mot pour vous dire ...; **to take notes** prendre des notes; **to compare notes** (*fig*) échanger des (or leurs *etc*) impressions; **to take ~ of** prendre note de; **a person of ~** une personne éminente ▶ VT (*also*: **note down**) noter; (*notice*) constater

notebook ['nəʊtbuk] N carnet *m*; (*for shorthand etc*) bloc-notes *m*

note-case ['nəʊtkeɪs] N (BRIT) porte-feuille *m*

noted ['nəʊtɪd] ADJ réputé(e)

notepad ['nəʊtpæd] N bloc-notes *m*

notepaper ['nəʊtpeɪpəʳ] N papier *m* à lettres

noteworthy ['nəʊtwəːðɪ] ADJ remarquable

★**nothing** ['nʌθɪŋ] N rien *m*; **he does ~** il ne fait rien; **~ new** rien de nouveau; **for ~** (*free*) pour rien, gratuitement; (*in vain*) pour rien; **~ at all** rien du tout; **~ much** pas grand-chose

rien can be used by itself.
What's wrong? Nothing. **Qu'est-ce qui ne va pas? Rien.**
If using a verb with **rien**, put **ne** in front of the verb.
He does nothing. **Il ne fait rien.**

★**notice** ['nəʊtɪs] N (*announcement, warning*) avis *m*; (*of leaving*) congé *m*; (BRIT: *review: of play etc*) critique *f*, compte rendu *m*; **without ~** sans préavis; **advance ~** préavis *m*; **to give sb ~ of sth** notifier qn de qch; **at short ~** dans un délai très court; **until further ~** jusqu'à nouvel ordre; **to give ~, hand in one's ~** (*employee*) donner sa démission, démissionner; **to take ~ of** prêter attention à; **to bring sth to sb's ~** porter qch à la connaissance de qn; **it has come to my ~ that ...** on m'a signalé que ...; **to escape** or **avoid ~** (essayer de) passer inaperçu or ne pas se faire remarquer ▶ VT remarquer, s'apercevoir de

noticeable ['nəʊtɪsəbl] ADJ (*difference, improvement*) sensible; (*effect*) visible

noticeably ['nəʊtɪsəblɪ] ADV (*improve, change*) sensiblement; (*visibly*) visiblement

notice board N (BRIT) panneau *m* d'affichage

notification [nəʊtɪfɪ'keɪʃən] N notification *f*

notify ['nəʊtɪfaɪ] VT: **to ~ sth to sb** notifier qch à qn; **to ~ sb of sth** avertir qn de qch

notion ['nəʊʃən] N idée *f*; (*concept*) notion *f*
notions NPL (US: *haberdashery*) mercerie *f*

notoriety [nəʊtə'raɪətɪ] N notoriété *f*

notorious [nəʊ'tɔːrɪəs] ADJ notoire (*souvent en mal*)

notoriously [nəʊ'tɔːrɪəslɪ] ADV notoirement

notwithstanding [nɒtwɪθ'stændɪŋ] ADV néanmoins ▶ PREP en dépit de

nougat ['nuːgɑː] N nougat *m*

nought [nɔːt] N zéro *m*

noun [naʊn] N nom *m*

nourish ['nʌrɪʃ] VT nourrir

nourishing ['nʌrɪʃɪŋ] ADJ nourrissant(e)

nourishment ['nʌrɪʃmənt] N nourriture f

nous [naus] N (BRIT) bon sens m; **to have political/ business ~** être habile en politique/affaires; **to have the ~ to do sth** avoir l'intelligence de faire qch

Nov. ABBR (= November) nov

Nova Scotia ['nəuvə'skəuʃə] N Nouvelle-Écosse f

★**novel** ['nɔvl] N roman m ▸ ADJ nouveau (nouvelle), original(e)

novelist ['nɔvəlɪst] N romancier m

novella [nə'vɛlə] N roman m court

novelty ['nɔvəltɪ] N nouveauté f

★**November** [nəu'vɛmbəʳ] N novembre m; see also **July**

novice ['nɔvɪs] N novice mf

NOW [nau] N ABBR (US) = **National Organization for Women**

★**now** [nau] ADV maintenant; **right ~** tout de suite; **by ~** à l'heure qu'il est; **that's the fashion just ~** c'est la mode en ce moment or maintenant; **I saw her just ~** je viens de la voir, je l'ai vue à l'instant; **I'll read it just ~** je vais le lire à l'instant or dès maintenant; **~ and then, ~ and again** de temps en temps; **from ~ on** dorénavant; **in 3 days from ~** dans or d'ici trois jours; **between ~ and Monday** d'ici (à) lundi; **that's all for ~** c'est tout pour l'instant ▸ CONJ: **~ (that)** maintenant (que)

nowadays ['nauədeɪz] ADV de nos jours

★**nowhere** ['nəuwɛəʳ] ADV (ne ...) nulle part; **~ else** nulle part ailleurs

no-win situation [nəu'wɪn-] N impasse f; **we're in a ~** nous sommes dans l'impasse

noxious ['nɔkʃəs] ADJ toxique

nozzle ['nɔzl] N (of hose) jet m, lance f; (of vacuum cleaner) suceur m

NP N ABBR = **notary public**

nr ABBR (BRIT) = **near**

NS ABBR (CANADA) = **Nova Scotia**

NSC N ABBR (US) = **National Security Council**

NSF N ABBR (US) = **National Science Foundation**

NSPCC N ABBR (BRIT) = **National Society for the Prevention of Cruelty to Children**

NSW ABBR (AUSTRALIA) = **New South Wales**

NT N ABBR (= New Testament) NT m ▸ ABBR (CANADA) = **Northwest Territories**

nth [ɛnθ] ADJ: **for the ~ time** (inf) pour la énième fois

nuance ['nju:ɔ̃:s] N nuance f

nubile ['nju:baɪl] ADJ nubile; (attractive) jeune et désirable

★**nuclear** ['nju:klɪəʳ] ADJ nucléaire

nuclear disarmament N désarmement m nucléaire

nuclear family N famille f nucléaire

nuclear-free zone ['nju:klɪə'fri:-] N zone f où le nucléaire est interdit

nucleus ['nju:klɪəs] (pl nuclei ['nju:klɪaɪ]) N noyau m

nude [nju:d] ADJ nu(e) ▸ N (Art) nu m; **in the ~** (tout(e)) nu(e)

nudge [nʌdʒ] VT donner un (petit) coup de coude à

nudist ['nju:dɪst] N nudiste mf

nudist colony N colonie f de nudistes

nudity ['nju:dɪtɪ] N nudité f

nugget ['nʌgɪt] N pépite f

nuisance ['nju:sns] N: **it's a ~** c'est (très) ennuyeux or gênant; **he's a ~** il est assommant or casse-pieds; **what a ~!** quelle barbe!

NUJ N ABBR (BRIT: = National Union of Journalists) syndicat des journalistes

nuke [nju:k] N (inf) bombe f atomique

null [nʌl] ADJ: **~ and void** nul(le) et non avenu(e)

nullify ['nʌlɪfaɪ] VT invalider

NUM N ABBR (BRIT: = National Union of Mineworkers) syndicat des mineurs

numb [nʌm] ADJ engourdi(e); (with fear) paralysé(e); **~ with cold** engourdi(e) par le froid, transi(e) (de froid); **~ with fear** transi de peur, paralysé(e) par la peur ▸ VT engourdir

★**number** ['nʌmbəʳ] N nombre m; (numeral) chiffre m; (of house, car, telephone, newspaper) numéro m; **a ~ of** un certain nombre de; **they were seven in ~** ils étaient au nombre de sept; **wrong ~** (Tel) mauvais numéro ▸ VT numéroter; (amount to) compter; **to be numbered among** compter parmi; **the staff numbers 20** le nombre d'employés s'élève à or est de 20

numbered account ['nʌmbəd-] N (in bank) compte numéroté

number plate N (BRIT Aut) plaque f minéralogique or d'immatriculation

Number Ten N (BRIT: 10 Downing Street) résidence du Premier ministre

numbness ['nʌmnɪs] N torpeur f; (due to cold) engourdissement m

numbskull ['nʌmskʌl] N (pej) gourde f

numeracy ['nju:mərəsɪ] N notions fpl de calcul; **people who have problems with literacy and ~** les personnes qui ont des difficultés pour lire, écrire et compter

numeral ['nju:mərəl] N chiffre m

numerate ['nju:mərɪt] ADJ (BRIT): **to be ~** savoir compter

numerical [nju:'mɛrɪkl] ADJ numérique

numerous ['nju:mərəs] ADJ nombreux(-euse)

nun [nʌn] N religieuse f, sœur f

nunnery ['nʌnərɪ] N couvent m

nuptial ['nʌpʃəl] ADJ nuptial(e)

★**nurse** [nɜːs] N infirmière f; (also: **nursemaid**) bonne f d'enfants ▸ VT (patient, cold) soigner; (baby: BRIT) bercer (dans ses bras); (: US) allaiter, nourrir; (hope) nourrir

nursery ['nɜːsərɪ] N (room) nursery f; (institution) crèche f, garderie f; (for plants) pépinière f

nursery rhyme N comptine f, chansonnette f pour enfants

nursery school N école maternelle

nursery slope N (BRIT Ski) piste f pour débutants

nursing ['nɜːsɪŋ] N (profession) profession f d'infirmière; (care) soins mpl ▸ ADJ (mother) qui allaite

nursing home N clinique f; (for convalescence) maison f de convalescence or de repos; (for old people) maison de retraite

nurture ['nɜːtʃəʳ] VT élever

NUS N ABBR (BRIT: = National Union of Students) syndicat des étudiants

NUT N ABBR (BRIT: = National Union of Teachers) syndicat enseignant

nut [nʌt] N (of metal) écrou m; (fruit) terme générique désignant les noix, noisettes, etc; (walnut) noix f; (hazelnut) noisette f; (peanut) cacahuète f ▶ ADJ (chocolate etc) aux noisettes; **he's nuts** (inf) il est dingue

nutcase ['nʌtkeɪs] N (inf) dingue mf

nutcrackers ['nʌtkrækəz] NPL casse-noix m inv, casse-noisette(s) m

nutmeg ['nʌtmɛg] N (noix f) muscade f

nutrient ['njuːtrɪənt] ADJ nutritif(-ive) ▶ N substance nutritive

nutrition [njuːˈtrɪʃən] N nutrition f, alimentation f

nutritional [njuːˈtrɪʃənəl] ADJ nutritif(-ive)

nutritionist [njuːˈtrɪʃənɪst] N nutritionniste mf

nutritious [njuːˈtrɪʃəs] ADJ nutritif(-ive), nourrissant(e)

nuts [nʌts] ADJ (inf) dingue

nutshell ['nʌtʃɛl] N coquille f de noix; **in a ~** en un mot

nutter ['nʌtər] N (BRIT inf): **he's a complete ~** il est complètement cinglé

nutty ['nʌtɪ] ADJ (flavour) à la noisette; (inf: person) cinglé(e), dingue

nuzzle ['nʌzl] VI: **to ~ up to** fourrer son nez contre

NV ABBR (US) = **Nevada**

NVQ N ABBR (BRIT) = **National Vocational Qualification**

NWT ABBR (CANADA) = **Northwest Territories**

NY ABBR (US) = **New York**

NYC ABBR (US) = **New York City**

nylon ['naɪlɔn] N nylon m ▶ ADJ de or en nylon ■ **nylons** NPL bas mpl nylon

nymph [nɪmf] N nymphe f

nymphomaniac ['nɪmfəʊ'meɪnɪæk] ADJ, N nymphomane f

NYSE N ABBR (US) = **New York Stock Exchange**

NZ ABBR = **New Zealand**

Oo

O, o [əu] N (*letter*) O, o *m*; (*US Scol*: = *outstanding*) tb (= *très bien*); **O for Oliver**, (*US*) **O for Oboe** O comme Oscar

oaf [əuf] N balourd *m*

oak [əuk] N chêne *m* ▶ CPD de *or* en (bois de) chêne

O&M N ABBR = **organization and method**

OAP N ABBR (*BRIT*) = **old age pensioner**

oar [ɔːʳ] N aviron *m*, rame *f*; **to put** *or* **shove one's ~ in** (*fig, inf*) mettre son grain de sel

oarsman [ˈɔːzmən], **oarswoman** [ˈɔːzwumən] N (*irreg*) rameur(-euse); (*Naut, Sport*) nageur(-euse)

OAS N ABBR (= *Organization of American States*) OEA *f* (= *Organisation des États américains*)

oasis [əuˈeɪsɪs] (*pl* **oases** [əuˈeɪsiːz]) N oasis *f*

oath [əuθ] N serment *m*; (*swear word*) juron *m*; **to take the ~** prêter serment; **on** (*BRIT*) *or* **under ~** sous serment; assermenté(e)

oatmeal [ˈəutmiːl] N flocons *mpl* d'avoine

oats [əuts] N avoine *f*

OAU N ABBR (= *Organization of African Unity*) OUA *f* (= *Organisation de l'unité africaine*)

obdurate [ˈɔbdjurɪt] ADJ obstiné(e), impénitent(e); intraitable

OBE N ABBR (*BRIT*: = *Order of the British Empire*) distinction honorifique

obedience [əˈbiːdɪəns] N obéissance *f*; **in ~ to** conformément à

obedient [əˈbiːdɪənt] ADJ obéissant(e); **to be ~ to sb/sth** obéir à qn/qch

obelisk [ˈɔbɪlɪsk] N obélisque *m*

obese [əuˈbiːs] ADJ obèse

obesity [əuˈbiːsɪtɪ] N obésité *f*

obey [əˈbeɪ] VT obéir à; (*instructions, regulations*) se conformer à ▶ VI obéir

obituary [əˈbɪtjuərɪ] N nécrologie *f*

★**object** N [ˈɔbdʒɪkt] objet *m*; (*purpose*) but *m*, objet; (*Ling*) complément *m* d'objet; **what's the ~ of doing that?** quel est l'intérêt de faire cela ?; **money is no ~** l'argent n'est pas un problème ▶ VI [əbˈdʒɛkt]: **to ~ to** (*attitude*) désapprouver; (*proposal*) protester contre, élever une objection contre; **I ~!** je proteste !; **do you ~ to my smoking?** est-ce que cela vous gêne si je fume ? ▶ VT [əbˈdʒɛkt]: **he objected that ...** il a fait valoir *or* a objecté que ...

objection [əbˈdʒɛkʃən] N objection *f*; (*drawback*) inconvénient *m*; **if you have no ~** si vous n'y voyez pas d'inconvénient; **to make** *or* **raise an ~** élever une objection

objectionable [əbˈdʒɛkʃənəbl] ADJ très désagréable; choquant(e)

★**objective** [əbˈdʒɛktɪv] N objectif *m* ▶ ADJ objectif(-ive)

objectively [əbˈdʒɛktɪvlɪ] ADV objectivement

objectivity [ɔbdʒɪkˈtɪvɪtɪ] N objectivité *f*

object lesson N (*fig*) (bonne) illustration

objector [əbˈdʒɛktəʳ] N opposant(e)

obligation [ɔblɪˈgeɪʃən] N obligation *f*, devoir *m*; (*debt*) dette *f* (de reconnaissance); **"without ~"** « sans engagement »

obligatory [əˈblɪɡətərɪ] ADJ obligatoire

oblige [əˈblaɪdʒ] VT (*force*): **to ~ sb to do** obliger *or* forcer qn à faire; (*do a favour*) rendre service à, obliger; **to be obliged to sb for sth** être obligé(e) à qn de qch; **anything to ~!** (*inf*) (toujours prêt à rendre) service !

obliging [əˈblaɪdʒɪŋ] ADJ obligeant(e), serviable

oblique [əˈbliːk] ADJ oblique; (*allusion*) indirect(e) ▶ N (*BRIT Typ*) barre *f* oblique

obliterate [əˈblɪtəreɪt] VT effacer

oblivion [əˈblɪvɪən] N oubli *m*

oblivious [əˈblɪvɪəs] ADJ: **~ of** oublieux(-euse) de

oblong [ˈɔblɔŋ] ADJ oblong(ue) ▶ N rectangle *m*

obnoxious [əbˈnɔkʃəs] ADJ odieux(-euse); (*smell*) nauséabond(e)

o.b.o. ABBR (*US: in classified ads*: = *or best offer*) ≈ à débattre

oboe [ˈəubəu] N hautbois *m*

oboist [ˈəubəuɪst] N hautboïste *mf*

obscene [əbˈsiːn] ADJ obscène

obscenity [əbˈsɛnɪtɪ] N obscénité *f*

obscure [əbˈskjuəʳ] ADJ obscur(e) ▶ VT obscurcir; (*hide: sun*) cacher

obscurity [əbˈskjuərɪtɪ] N obscurité *f*

obsequious [əbˈsiːkwɪəs] ADJ obséquieux(-euse)

observable [əbˈzəːvəbl] ADJ observable; (*appreciable*) notable

observance [əbˈzəːvns] N observance *f*, observation *f*; **religious observances** observances religieuses

observant [əbˈzəːvnt] ADJ observateur(-trice)

observation [ɔbzəˈveɪʃən] N observation *f*; (*by police etc*) surveillance *f*

observation post N (*Mil*) poste *m* d'observation

observatory [əbˈzəːvətrɪ] N observatoire *m*

observe [əb'zɜː:v] VT observer; (remark) faire observer or remarquer

observer [əb'zɜː:vəʳ] N observateur(-trice)

obsess [əb'sɛs] VT obséder; **to be obsessed by** or **with sb/sth** être obsédé(e) par qn/qch

obsession [əb'sɛʃən] N obsession f

obsessive [əb'sɛsɪv] ADJ obsédant(e)

obsolescence [ɔbsə'lɛsns] N vieillissement m; obsolescence f; **built-in** or **planned ~** (Comm) désuétude calculée

obsolescent [ɔbsə'lɛsnt] ADJ obsolescent(e), en voie d'être périmé(e)

obsolete [ɔbsəli:t] ADJ dépassé(e), périmé(e)

obstacle ['ɔbstəkl] N obstacle m

obstacle race N course f d'obstacles

obstetrician [ɔbstə'trɪʃən] N obstétricien(ne)

obstetrics [ɔb'stɛtrɪks] N obstétrique f

obstinacy ['ɔbstɪnəsɪ] N obstination f

obstinate ['ɔbstɪnɪt] ADJ obstiné(e); (pain, cold) persistant(e)

obstreperous [əb'strɛpərəs] ADJ turbulent(e)

obstruct [əb'strʌkt] VT (block) boucher, obstruer; (halt) arrêter; (hinder) entraver

obstruction [əb'strʌkʃən] N obstruction f; (to plan, progress) obstacle m

obstructive [əb'strʌktɪv] ADJ obstructionniste

obtain [əb'teɪn] VT obtenir ▶ VI avoir cours

obtainable [əb'teɪnəbl] ADJ qu'on peut obtenir

obtrusive [əb'tru:sɪv] ADJ (person) importun(e); (smell) pénétrant(e); (building etc) trop en évidence

obtuse [əb'tju:s] ADJ obtus(e)

obverse ['ɔbvɜ:s] N (of medal, coin) côté m face; (fig) contrepartie f

obviate ['ɔbvɪeɪt] VT parer à, obvier à

★**obvious** ['ɔbvɪəs] ADJ évident(e), manifeste

★**obviously** ['ɔbvɪəslɪ] ADV manifestement; (of course): **~, he ... or he ~ ...** il est bien évident qu'il ...; **~!** bien sûr!; **~ not!** évidemment pas!, bien sûr que non!

OCAS N ABBR (= Organization of Central American States) ODEAC f (= Organisation des États d'Amérique centrale)

★**occasion** [ə'keɪʒən] N occasion f; (event) événement m; **on that ~** à cette occasion; **to rise to the ~** se montrer à la hauteur de la situation ▶ VT occasionner, causer

occasional [ə'keɪʒənl] ADJ pris(e) (or fait(e) etc) de temps en temps; (worker, spending) occasionnel(le)

occasionally [ə'keɪʒənəlɪ] ADV de temps en temps, quelquefois; **very ~** (assez) rarement

occasional table N table décorative

occult [ɔ'kʌlt] ADJ occulte ▶ N: **the ~** le surnaturel

occupancy ['ɔkjupənsɪ] N occupation f

occupant ['ɔkjupənt] N occupant m

occupation [ɔkju'peɪʃən] N occupation f; (job) métier m, profession f; **unfit for ~** (house) impropre à l'habitation

occupational [ɔkju'peɪʃənl] ADJ (accident, disease) du travail; (hazard) du métier

occupational guidance N (BRIT) orientation professionnelle

occupational hazard N risque m du métier

occupational pension N retraite professionnelle

occupational therapy N ergothérapie f

occupier ['ɔkjupaɪəʳ] N occupant(e)

occupy ['ɔkjupaɪ] VT occuper; **to ~ o.s. with** or **by doing** s'occuper à faire; **to be occupied with sth** être occupé avec qch

occur [ə'kɜ:ʳ] VI se produire; (difficulty, opportunity) se présenter; (phenomenon, error) se rencontrer; **to ~ to sb** venir à l'esprit de qn

occurrence [ə'kʌrəns] N (existence) présence f, existence f; (event) cas m, fait m

OCD N ABBR (= obsessive compulsive disorder) TOC m

★**ocean** ['əuʃən] N océan m; **oceans of** (inf) des masses de

ocean bed N fond (sous-)marin

ocean-going ['əuʃəngəuɪŋ] ADJ de haute mer

Oceania [əuʃɪ'eɪnɪə] N Océanie f

ocean liner N paquebot m

oceanographer [əuʃə'nɔgrəfəʳ] N océanographe mf

ochre ['əukəʳ] ADJ ocre

★**o'clock** [ə'klɔk] ADV: **it is 5 o'clock** il est 5 heures

OCR N ABBR = **optical character reader**; **optical character recognition**

Oct. ABBR (= October) oct

octagonal [ɔk'tægənl] ADJ octogonal(e)

octane ['ɔkteɪn] N octane m; **high-octane petrol** or (US) **gas** essence f à indice d'octane élevé

octave ['ɔktɪv] N octave f

★**October** [ɔk'təubəʳ] N octobre m; see also **July**

octogenarian ['ɔktəudʒɪ'nɛərɪən] N octogénaire mf

octopus ['ɔktəpəs] N pieuvre f

★**odd** [ɔd] ADJ (strange) bizarre, curieux(-euse); (number) impair(e); (left over) qui reste, en plus; (not of a set) dépareillé(e); **60-odd** 60 et quelques; **at ~ times** de temps en temps; **the ~ one out** l'exception f

oddball ['ɔdbɔ:l] N (inf) excentrique mf

oddity ['ɔdɪtɪ] N bizarrerie f; (person) excentrique mf

odd-job man [ɔd'dʒɔb-] N (irreg) homme m à tout faire

odd jobs NPL petits travaux divers

oddly ['ɔdlɪ] ADV bizarrement, curieusement

oddments ['ɔdmənts] NPL (BRIT Comm) fins fpl de série

odds [ɔdz] NPL (in betting) cote f; **the ~ are against his coming** il y a peu de chances qu'il vienne; **it makes no ~** cela n'a pas d'importance; **to succeed against all the ~** réussir contre toute attente; **~ and ends** de petites choses; **at ~** en désaccord

odds-on [ɔdz'ɔn] ADJ: **the ~ favourite** le grand favori; **it's ~ that he'll come** il y a toutes les chances or gros à parier qu'il vienne

ode [əud] N ode f

odious ['əudɪəs] ADJ odieux(-euse), détestable

odometer [ɔ'dɔmɪtəʳ] N (US) odomètre m

odour, (US) **odor** ['əʊdə'] N odeur f

odourless, (US) **odorless** ['əʊdəlɪs] ADJ inodore

odyssey ['ɒdɪsɪ] N odyssée f

OECD N ABBR (= Organization for Economic Cooperation and Development) OCDE f (= Organisation de coopération et de développement économique)

oesophagus, (US) **esophagus** [iː'sɒfəgəs] N œsophage m

oestrogen, (US) **estrogen** ['iːstrəʊdʒən] N œstrogène m

---

of [ɒv, əv]

PREP **1** (gen) de; **a friend of ours** un de nos amis; **a boy of 10** un garçon de 10 ans; **that was kind of you** c'était gentil de votre part

2 (expressing quantity, amount, dates etc) de; **a kilo of flour** un kilo de farine; **how much of this do you need?** combien vous en faut-il ?; **there were three of them** (people) ils étaient 3; (objects) il y en avait 3; **three of us went** 3 d'entre nous y sont allés (allées); **the 5th of July** le 5 juillet; **a quarter of 4** (US) 4 heures moins le quart

3 (from, out of) en, de; **a statue of marble** une statue de or en marbre; **made of wood** (fait) en bois

---

Ofcom ['ɒfkɒm] N ABBR (BRIT: = Office of Communications Regulation) organe de régulation de télécommunications

★**off** [ɒf] ADJ, ADV (engine) coupé(e); (light, TV) éteint(e); (tap) fermé(e); (BRIT: food) mauvais(e), avancé(e); (: milk) tourné(e); (absent) absent(e); (cancelled) annulé(e); **the lid was ~** (removed) le couvercle était retiré or n'était pas mis; **to run/drive ~** (away) partir en courant/en voiture; **to be ~** (to leave) partir, s'en aller; **I must be ~** il faut que je file; **to be ~ sick** être absent pour cause de maladie; **a day ~** un jour de congé; **to have an ~ day** n'être pas en forme; **he had his coat ~** il avait enlevé son manteau; **the hook is ~** le crochet s'est détaché; le crochet n'est pas mis; **10% ~** (Comm) 10% de rabais; **it's a long way ~** c'est loin (d'ici); **to be well/badly ~** être bien/mal loti; (financially) être aisé/dans la gêne; **~ and on, on and ~** de temps à autre; **I'm afraid the chicken is ~** (BRIT: not available) je regrette, il n'y a plus de poulet; **that's a bit ~** (fig, inf) c'est un peu fort ▶ PREP de; **5 km ~ (the road)** à 5 km (de la route); **~ the coast** au large de la côte; **a house ~ the main road** une maison à l'écart de la grand-route; **I'm ~ meat** je ne mange plus de viande; je n'aime plus la viande

offal ['ɒfl] N (Culin) abats mpl

offbeat ['ɒfbiːt] ADJ excentrique

off-centre [ɒf'sɛntə'] ADJ décentré(e), excentré(e)

off chance N: **on the ~** à tout hasard

off-colour ['ɒf'kʌlə'] ADJ (BRIT: ill) malade, mal fichu(e); **to feel ~** être mal fichu

off day N (bad day): **to have an ~** avoir un jour sans; (US: holiday) jour m de congé; **he had an ~** il a eu un jour sans, il n'était pas en forme

offence, (US) **offense** [ə'fɛns] N (crime) délit m, infraction f; **to give ~ to** blesser, offenser; **to take ~ at** se vexer de, s'offenser de; **to commit an ~** commettre une infraction

offend [ə'fɛnd] VT (person) offenser, blesser ▶ VI: **to ~ against** (law, rule) contrevenir à, enfreindre

offender [ə'fɛndə'] N délinquant(e); (against regulations) contrevenant(e)

offending [ə'fɛndɪŋ] ADJ incriminé(e)

offense [ə'fɛns] N (US) = **offence**

offensive [ə'fɛnsɪv] ADJ offensant(e), choquant(e); (smell etc) très déplaisant(e); (weapon) offensif(-ive) ▶ N (Mil) offensive f

★**offer** ['ɒfə'] N offre f, proposition f; **to make an ~ for sth** faire une offre pour qch; **"on ~"** (Comm) « en promotion » ▶ VT offrir, proposer; **to ~ sth to sb, ~ sb sth** offrir qch à qn; **to ~ to do sth** proposer de faire qch

offering ['ɒfərɪŋ] N offrande f

offhand [ɒf'hænd] ADJ désinvolte ▶ ADV spontanément; **I can't tell you ~** je ne peux pas vous le dire comme ça

★**office** ['ɒfɪs] N (place) bureau m; (position) charge f, fonction f; **doctor's ~** (US) cabinet (médical); **to take ~** entrer en fonctions; **through his good offices** (fig) grâce à ses bons offices; **O~ of Fair Trading** (BRIT) organisme de protection contre les pratiques commerciales abusives

office automation N bureautique f

office bearer N (of club etc) membre m du bureau

office block, (US) **office building** N immeuble m de bureaux

office boy N garçon m de bureau

office hours NPL heures fpl de bureau; (US Med) heures de consultation

office manager N responsable administratif(-ive)

★**officer** ['ɒfɪsə'] N (Mil etc) officier m; (also: **police officer**) agent m (de police); (of organization) membre m du bureau directeur

office work N travail m de bureau

office worker N employé(e) de bureau

★**official** [ə'fɪʃl] ADJ (authorized) officiel(le) ▶ N officiel m; (civil servant) fonctionnaire mf; (of railways, post office, town hall) employé(e)

officialdom [ə'fɪʃldəm] N bureaucratie f

officially [ə'fɪʃəlɪ] ADV officiellement

official receiver N administrateur m judiciaire, syndic m de faillite

officiate [ə'fɪʃɪeɪt] VI (Rel) officier; **to ~ as Mayor** exercer les fonctions de maire; **to ~ at a marriage** célébrer un mariage

officious [ə'fɪʃəs] ADJ trop empressé(e)

offing ['ɒfɪŋ] N: **in the ~** (fig) en perspective

off-key [ɒf'kiː] ADJ faux (fausse) ▶ ADV faux

off-licence ['ɒflaɪsns] N (BRIT: shop) débit m de vins et de spiritueux

off-limits [ɒf'lɪmɪts] ADJ (esp US) dont l'accès est interdit

off-line [ɒf'laɪn] ADJ (Comput) (en mode) autonome; (: switched off) non connecté(e)

off-load ['ɒfləʊd] VT: **to ~ sth (onto)** (goods) décharger qch (sur); (job) se décharger de qch (sur)

off-peak [ɒf'piːk] ADJ aux heures creuses; (electricity, ticket) au tarif heures creuses

off-putting ['ɔfpʊtɪŋ] ADJ (BRIT: *remark*) rébarbatif(-ive); (*person*) rebutant(e), peu engageant(e)

off-road vehicle ['ɔfrəud-] N véhicule *m* tout-terrain

off-screen [ɔf'skri:n] ADV, ADJ hors écran

off-season [ɔf'si:zn] ADJ, ADV hors-saison *inv*

offset ['ɔfsɛt] VT (*irreg: like* set) (*counteract*) contrebalancer, compenser ▶ N (*also:* offset printing) offset *m*

offshoot ['ɔfʃu:t] N (*fig*) ramification *f*, antenne *f*; (: *of discussion etc*) conséquence *f*

offshore [ɔf'ʃɔ:ʳ] ADJ (*breeze*) de terre; (*island*) proche du littoral; (*fishing*) côtier(-ière); ~ **oilfield** gisement *m* pétrolifère en mer

offside [ɔf'saɪd] N (Aut: *with right-hand drive*) côté droit; (: *with left-hand drive*) côté gauche ▶ ADJ (*Sport*) hors jeu; (Aut: *in Britain*) de droite; (: *in US, Europe*) de gauche

offspring ['ɔfsprɪŋ] N progéniture *f*

offstage [ɔf'steɪdʒ] ADV dans les coulisses

off-the-cuff [ɔfðə'kʌf] ADV au pied levé; de chic

off-the-job ['ɔfðə'dʒɔb] ADJ: ~ **training** formation professionnelle extérieure

off-the-peg ['ɔfðə'pɛg], (US) **off-the-rack** ['ɔfðə'ræk] ADV en prêt-à-porter

off-the-record ['ɔfðə'rɛkɔ:d] ADJ (*remark*) confidentiel(le), sans caractère officiel ▶ ADV officieusement

off-white ['ɔfwaɪt] ADJ blanc cassé *inv*

Ofqual ['ɔfkwɔl] N ABBR (= *Office of Qualifications and Examinations Regulation*) *instance de réglementation des examens et des diplômes en Angleterre et en Irlande du Nord*

★**often** ['ɔfn] ADV souvent; **how ~ do you go?** vous y allez tous les combien?; **every so ~** de temps en temps, de temps à autre; **as ~ as not** la plupart du temps

Ofwat ['ɔfwɔt] N ABBR (BRIT: = *Office of Water Services*) *organisme qui surveille les activités des compagnies des eaux*

ogle ['əugl] VT lorgner

ogre ['əugəʳ] N ogre *m*

OH ABBR (US) = **Ohio**

oh [əu] EXCL ô!, oh!, ah!

OHMS ABBR (BRIT) = **On His/Her Majesty's Service**

★**oil** [ɔɪl] N huile *f*; (*petroleum*) pétrole *m*; (*for central heating*) mazout *m* ▶ VT (*machine*) graisser

oilcan ['ɔɪlkæn] N burette *f* de graissage; (*for storing*) bidon *m* à huile

oil change N vidange *f*

oilfield ['ɔɪlfi:ld] N gisement *m* de pétrole

oil filter N (Aut) filtre *m* à huile

oil-fired ['ɔɪlfaɪəd] ADJ au mazout

oil gauge N jauge *f* de niveau d'huile

oil industry N industrie pétrolière

oil level N niveau *m* d'huile

oil painting N peinture *f* à l'huile

oil refinery N raffinerie *f* de pétrole

oil rig N derrick *m*; (*at sea*) plate-forme pétrolière

oilseed rape [ɔɪlsi:d-] N (BRIT) colza *m*

oilskins ['ɔɪlskɪnz] NPL ciré *m*

oil slick N nappe *f* de mazout

oil tanker N (*ship*) pétrolier *m*; (*truck*) camion-citerne *m*

oil well N puits *m* de pétrole

oily ['ɔɪlɪ] ADJ huileux(-euse); (*food*) gras(se)

ointment ['ɔɪntmənt] N onguent *m*

OK ABBR (US) = **Oklahoma**

O.K., okay ['əu'keɪ] (*inf*) EXCL d'accord! ▶ VT approuver, donner son accord à ▶ N: **to give sth one's ~** donner son accord à qch ▶ ADJ (*not bad*) pas mal, en règle; en bon état; sain et sauf; acceptable; **is it ~?, are you ~?** ça va?; **are you ~ for money?** ça va *or* ira question argent?; **it's ~ with** *or* **by me** ça me va, c'est d'accord en ce qui me concerne

★**old** [əuld] ADJ vieux (vieille); (*person*) vieux, âgé(e); (*former*) ancien(ne), vieux; **how ~ are you?** quel âge avez-vous?; **he's 10 years ~** il a 10 ans, il est âgé de 10 ans; **older brother/sister** frère/sœur aîné(e); **any ~ thing will do** n'importe quoi fera l'affaire

---

vieux changes to **vieil** before a vowel or a mute 'h': *an old man* **un vieil homme**; *my old uncle* **mon vieil oncle**.

---

old age N vieillesse *f*

old-age pension ['əuldeɪdʒ-] N (BRIT) retraite *f*

old-age pensioner ['əuldeɪdʒ-] N (BRIT) retraité(e)

old-fashioned ['əuld'fæʃnd] ADJ démodé(e); (*person*) vieux jeu *inv*

old maid N (*pej*) vieille fille

old people's home N (*esp* BRIT) maison *f* de retraite

old-style ['əuldstaɪl] ADJ à l'ancienne (mode)

old-time ['əuld'taɪm] ADJ du temps jadis, d'autrefois

old-timer [əuld'taɪməʳ] N ancien *m*

old wives' tale N conte *m* de bonne femme

oleander [əulɪ'ændəʳ] N laurier *m* rose

O-level ['əulɛvl] N (*in England and Wales: formerly*) *examen passé à l'âge de 16 ans sanctionnant les connaissances de l'élève*, ≈ *brevet m des collèges*

oligarch ['ɔlɪgɑ:k] N oligarque *mf*

olive ['ɔlɪv] N (*fruit*) olive *f*; (*tree*) olivier *m* ▶ ADJ (*also:* **olive-green**) (vert) olive *inv*

olive oil N huile *f* d'olive

Olympic® [əu'lɪmpɪk] ADJ olympique; **the ~ Games**®, **the Olympics**® les Jeux *mpl* olympiques

OM N ABBR (BRIT: = *Order of Merit*) *titre honorifique*

Oman [əu'mɑ:n] N Oman *m*

OMB N ABBR (US: = *Office of Management and Budget*) *service conseillant le président en matière budgétaire*

ombudsman ['ɔmbudzmən] N (*irreg*) médiateur *m* de la République, protecteur *m* du citoyen (CANADA)

omelette, omelet ['ɔmlɪt] N omelette *f*; **ham/cheese omelet(te)** omelette au jambon/fromage

omen ['əumən] N présage *m*

OMG ABBR (*inf*: = *Oh My God!*) OMD (= *Oh Mon Dieu!*)

ominous [ˈɔmɪnəs] ADJ menaçant(e), inquiétant(e); (event) de mauvais augure

omission [əuˈmɪʃən] N omission f

omit [əuˈmɪt] VT omettre; **to ~ to do sth** négliger de faire qch

omnipotent [ɔmˈnɪpətənt] ADJ omnipotent(e)

omniscient [ɔmˈnɪsɪənt] ADJ omniscient(e)

omnivorous [ɔmˈnɪvrəs] ADJ omnivore

ON ABBR (CANADA) = **Ontario**

---

on [ɔn]

PREP **1** (indicating position) sur; **on the table** sur la table; **on the wall** sur le or au mur; **on the left** à gauche; **I haven't any money on me** je n'ai pas d'argent sur moi

2 (indicating means, method, condition etc): **on foot** à pied; **on the train/plane** (be) dans le train/l'avion; (go) en train/avion; **on the telephone/radio/television** au téléphone/à la radio/à la télévision; **to be on drugs** se droguer; **on holiday**, (US) **on vacation** en vacances; **on the continent** sur le continent

3 (referring to time): **on Friday** vendredi; **on Fridays** le vendredi; **on June 20th** le 20 juin; **a week on Friday** vendredi en huit; **on arrival** à l'arrivée; **on seeing this** en voyant cela

4 (about, concerning) sur, de; **a book on Balzac/physics** un livre sur Balzac/de physique

5 (at the expense of): **this round is on me** c'est ma tournée

▶ ADV **1** (referring to dress): **to have one's coat on** avoir (mis) son manteau; **to put one's coat on** mettre son manteau; **what's she got on?** qu'est-ce qu'elle porte ?

2 (referring to covering): **screw the lid on tightly** vissez bien le couvercle

3 (further, continuously): **to walk** etc **on** continuer à marcher etc; **on and off** de temps à autre; **from that day on** depuis ce jour

▶ ADJ **1** (in operation: machine) en marche; (: radio, TV, light) allumé(e); (: tap, gas) ouvert(e); (: brakes) mis(e); **is the meeting still on?** est-ce que la réunion a bien lieu ?; **it was well on in the evening** c'était tard dans la soirée; **when is this film on?** quand passe ce film ?

2 (inf): **that's not on!** (not acceptable) cela ne se fait pas !; (not possible) pas question !

ONC N ABBR (BRIT: = Ordinary National Certificate) ≈ BT m

★**once** [wʌns] ADV une fois; (formerly) autrefois; **at ~** tout de suite, immédiatement; (simultaneously) à la fois; **all at ~** adv tout d'un coup; **~ a week** une fois par semaine; **~ more** encore une fois; **I knew him ~** je l'ai connu autrefois; **~ and for all** une fois pour toutes; **~ upon a time there was …** il y avait une fois …, il était une fois … ▶ CONJ une fois que + sub; **~ he had left/it was done** une fois qu'il fut parti/ que ce fut terminé

oncoming [ˈɔnkʌmɪŋ] ADJ (traffic) venant en sens inverse

OND N ABBR (BRIT: = Ordinary National Diploma) ≈ BTS m

---

one [wʌn]

NUM un(e); **one hundred and fifty** cent cinquante; **one by one** un(e) à or par un(e); **one day** un jour

▶ ADJ **1** (sole) seul(e), unique; **the one book which** l'unique or le seul livre qui; **the one man who** le seul (homme) qui

2 (same) même; **they came in the one car** ils sont venus dans la même voiture

▶ PRON **1**: **this one** celui-ci (celle-ci); **that one** celui-là (celle-là); **I've already got one/a red one** j'en ai déjà un(e)/un(e) rouge; **which one do you want?** lequel voulez-vous ?

2: **one another** l'un(e) l'autre; **to look at one another** se regarder

3 (impersonal) on; **one never knows** on ne sait jamais; **to cut one's finger** se couper le doigt; **one needs to eat** il faut manger

4 (phrases): **to be one up on sb** avoir l'avantage sur qn; **to be at one (with sb)** être d'accord (avec qn)

---

one-armed bandit [ˈwʌnɑːmd-] N machine f à sous

one-day excursion [ˈwʌndeɪ-] N (US) billet m d'aller-retour (valable pour la journée)

One-hundred share index [ˈwʌnhʌndrəd-] N indice m Footsie des cent grandes valeurs

one-man [ˈwʌnˈmæn] ADJ (business) dirigé(e) etc par un seul homme

one-man band N homme-orchestre m

one-off [wʌnˈɔf] N (BRIT inf) exemplaire m unique ▶ ADJ unique

one-on-one [wʌnɔnˈwʌn] ADV, ADJ en tête à tête

one-parent family [ˈwʌnpɛərənt-] N famille monoparentale

one-piece [ˈwʌnpiːs] ADJ: **~ bathing suit** maillot m une pièce

onerous [ˈɔnərəs] ADJ (task, duty) pénible; (responsibility) lourd(e)

oneself [wʌnˈsɛlf] PRON se; (after prep, also emphatic) soi-même; **to hurt ~** se faire mal; **to keep sth for ~** garder qch pour soi; **to talk to ~** se parler à soi-même; **by ~** tout seul

one-shot [wʌnˈʃɔt] N (US) = **one-off**

one-sided [wʌnˈsaɪdɪd] ADJ (argument, decision) unilatéral(e); (judgment, account) partial(e); (contest) inégal(e)

onesie [ˈwʌnzɪ] N grenouillère f

one-size-fits-all [wʌnsaɪzfɪtsˈɔːl] ADJ (policy, approach) taille unique inv

one-time [ˈwʌntaɪm] ADJ d'autrefois

one-to-one [ˈwʌntəwʌn] ADJ (relationship) univoque

one-upmanship [wʌnˈʌpmənʃɪp] N: **the art of ~** l'art de faire mieux que les autres

one-way [ˈwʌnweɪ] ADJ (street, traffic) à sens unique

ongoing [ˈɔngəuɪŋ] ADJ en cours; (relationship) suivi(e)

★**onion** [ˈʌnjən] N oignon m

online, on-line (Comput) ADJ en ligne ▶ ADV: **to go ~** se connecter à Internet; **to put the printer ~** connecter l'imprimante

Lorsque **online** est un adjectif, l'accent tombe sur la première syllabe : ['ɒnlaɪn], lorsque c'est un adverbe, sur la seconde : [ɒn'laɪn].

online banking N banque f en ligne

online purchase N achat m en ligne

online shopping N achats mpl en ligne

onlooker ['ɒnlukə^r] N spectateur(-trice)

★**only** ['əunlɪ] ADV seulement; **not ~ ... but also** non seulement ... mais aussi; **I ~ took one** j'en ai seulement pris un, je n'en ai pris qu'un; **I saw her ~ yesterday** je l'ai vu hier encore; **I'd be ~ too pleased to help** je ne serais que trop content de vous aider ▶ ADJ seul(e), unique; **an ~ child** un enfant unique ▶ CONJ seulement, mais; **I would come, ~ I'm very busy** je viendrais bien mais j'ai beaucoup à faire

ono ABBR (BRIT: in classified ads: = or nearest offer) ≈ à débattre

on-screen [ɒn'skri:n] ADJ à l'écran

onset ['ɒnsɛt] N début m; (of winter, old age) approche f

onshore ['ɒnʃɔːʳ] ADJ (wind) du large

onside [ɒn'saɪd] ADV: **to bring sb ~** gagner qn à sa cause ▶ ADJ (Football: player) qui n'est pas hors jeu

onslaught ['ɒnslɔːt] N attaque f, assaut m

onstage [ɒn'steɪdʒ] ADV en scène; **~ and offstage** à la scène comme à la ville

on-the-job ['ɒnðə'dʒɒb] ADJ: **~ training** formation f sur place

onto ['ɒntu] PREP sur

onus ['əunəs] N responsabilité f; **the ~ is upon him to prove it** c'est à lui de le prouver

onward ['ɒnwəd], **onwards** ['ɒnwədz] ADV (move) en avant; **from that time onwards** à partir de ce moment

oodles ['u:dlz] NPL (inf): **~ of** un maximum de

oomph [umf] N (inf) peps m (inf); **to have ~** avoir du peps

oops [ups] EXCL houp !; **oops-a-daisy!** houp-là !

ooze [u:z] VI suinter

opacity [əu'pæsɪtɪ] N opacité f

opal ['əupl] N opale f

opaque [əu'peɪk] ADJ opaque

OPEC ['əupɛk] N ABBR (= Organization of Petroleum-Exporting Countries) OPEP f

★**open** ['əupn] ADJ ouvert(e); (car) découvert(e); (road, view) dégagé(e); (meeting) public(-ique); (admiration) manifeste; (question) non résolu(e); (enemy) déclaré(e); **is it ~ to the public?** est-ce ouvert au public ?; **in the ~ air** en plein air; **the ~ sea** le large; **~ ground** (among trees) clairière f; (waste ground) terrain m vague; **to have an ~ mind (on sth)** avoir l'esprit ouvert (sur qch) ▶ N: **in the ~ (outside)** en plein air; (not secret) au grand jour ▶ VT ouvrir ▶ VI (flower, eyes, door, debate) s'ouvrir; (shop, bank, museum) ouvrir; (book etc: commence) commencer, débuter; **what time do you ~?** à quelle heure ouvrez-vous ?
  ▶ **open on to** VT FUS (room, door) donner sur
  ▶ **open out** VT ouvrir ▶ VI s'ouvrir
  ▶ **open up** VT ouvrir; (blocked road) dégager ▶ VI s'ouvrir

open-air [əupn'ɛəʳ] ADJ en plein air

open-and-shut ['əupnən'ʃʌt] ADJ: **~ case** cas m limpide

opencast ['əupnkɑːst] ADJ à ciel ouvert

open day N journée f portes ouvertes

open-ended [əupn'ɛndɪd] ADJ (fig) non limité(e)

opener ['əupnəʳ] N (also: **can opener, tin opener**) ouvre-boîtes m

open-heart surgery [əupn'hɑːt-] N chirurgie f à cœur ouvert

opening ['əupnɪŋ] N ouverture f; (opportunity) occasion f; (work) débouché m; (job) poste vacant

opening hours NPL heures fpl d'ouverture

opening night N (Theat) première f

open learning N enseignement universitaire à la carte, notamment par correspondance; (distance learning) télé-enseignement m

open learning centre N centre ouvert à tous où l'on dispense un enseignement général à temps partiel

openly ['əupnlɪ] ADV ouvertement

open-minded [əupn'maɪndɪd] ADJ à l'esprit ouvert

open-necked ['əupn'nɛkt] ADJ à col ouvert

openness ['əupnnɪs] N (frankness) franchise f

open-plan ['əupn'plæn] ADJ sans cloisons

open prison N prison ouverte

open sandwich N canapé m

open shop N entreprise qui admet les travailleurs non syndiqués

Open University N (BRIT) cours universitaires par correspondance

L'**Open University**, fondée en 1969, est un organisme d'enseignement universitaire à distance. Cet enseignement comprend des cours en ligne, des devoirs envoyés par l'étudiant à son directeur d'études, et un séjour obligatoire en université d'été. Il faut préparer un certain nombre d'unités de valeur dans un délai donné et obtenir la moyenne à un certain nombre d'entre elles pour recevoir le diplôme visé. Avec plus de 250 000 inscrits, dont 50 000 étudiants étrangers, l'Open University est le plus grand organisme éducatif du Royaume-Uni et l'un des plus grands du monde. Il obtient régulièrement d'excellents résultats, tant en ce qui concerne la qualité des enseignements dispensés que le niveau de satisfaction des étudiants.

O

opera ['ɒpərə] N opéra m

opera glasses NPL jumelles fpl de théâtre

opera house N opéra m

opera singer N chanteur(-euse) d'opéra

★**operate** ['ɒpəreɪt] VT (machine) faire marcher, faire fonctionner; (system) pratiquer ▶ VI fonctionner; (drug) faire effet; **to ~ on sb (for)** (Med) opérer qn (de)

operatic [ɒpə'rætɪk] ADJ d'opéra

operating ['ɒpəreɪtɪŋ] ADJ (Comm: costs, profit) d'exploitation; (Med): **~ table** table f d'opération

operating room N (US Med) salle f d'opération

operating system N (Comput) système m d'exploitation

operating theatre N (BRIT Med) salle f d'opération

★**operation** [ɔpəˈreɪʃən] N opération f; (of machine) fonctionnement m; **to have an ~ (for)** se faire opérer (de); **to be in ~** (machine) être en service; (system) être en vigueur

operational [ɔpəˈreɪʃənl] ADJ opérationnel(le); (ready for use) en état de marche; **when the service is fully ~** lorsque le service fonctionnera pleinement

operative [ˈɔpərətɪv] ADJ (measure) en vigueur; **the ~ word** le mot clef ▶ N (in factory) ouvrier(-ière)

operator [ˈɔpəreɪtəʳ] N (of machine) opérateur(-trice); (Tel) téléphoniste mf

operetta [ɔpəˈretə] N opérette f

ophthalmologist [ɔfθælˈmɔlədʒɪst] N ophtalmologiste mf, ophtalmologue mf

opiate [ˈəupiət] N opiacé m

★**opinion** [əˈpɪnjən] N opinion f, avis m; **in my ~** à mon avis; **to seek a second ~** demander un deuxième avis

opinionated [əˈpɪnjəneɪtɪd] ADJ aux idées bien arrêtées

opinion poll N sondage m d'opinion

opium [ˈəupiəm] N opium m

★**opponent** [əˈpəunənt] N adversaire mf

opportune [ˈɔpətjuːn] ADJ opportun(e)

opportunism [ɔpəˈtjuːnɪzəm] N opportunisme m

opportunist [ɔpəˈtjuːnɪst] N opportuniste mf

opportunistic [ɔpətjuːˈnɪstɪk] ADJ opportuniste

★**opportunity** [ɔpəˈtjuːnɪtɪ] N occasion f; **to take the ~ to do** or **of doing** profiter de l'occasion pour faire

oppose [əˈpəuz] VT s'opposer à; **to be opposed to sth** être opposé(e) à qch; **as opposed to** par opposition à

opposing [əˈpəuzɪŋ] ADJ (side) opposé(e)

★**opposite** [ˈɔpəzɪt] ADJ opposé(e); (house etc) d'en face; **"see ~ page"** « voir ci-contre » ▶ ADV en face ▶ PREP en face de ▶ N opposé m, contraire m; (of word) contraire

opposite number N (BRIT) homologue mf

opposite sex N: **the ~** l'autre sexe

★**opposition** [ɔpəˈzɪʃən] N opposition f

oppress [əˈpres] VT opprimer

oppression [əˈpreʃən] N oppression f

oppressive [əˈpresɪv] ADJ oppressif(-ive)

oppressor [əˈpresəʳ] N oppresseur m

opprobrium [əˈprəubrɪəm] N (formal) opprobre m

opt [ɔpt] VI: **to ~ for** opter pour; **to ~ to do** choisir de faire

▶ **opt out** VI (school, hospital) devenir autonome; (health service) devenir privé(e); **to ~ out of** choisir de ne pas participer à or de ne pas faire

optical [ˈɔptɪkl] ADJ optique; (instrument) d'optique

optical character reader N lecteur m optique

optical character recognition N lecture f optique

optical fibre N fibre f optique

optician [ɔpˈtɪʃən] N opticien(ne)

optics [ˈɔptɪks] N optique f

optimal [ˈɔptɪml] = **optimum**

optimism [ˈɔptɪmɪzəm] N optimisme m

optimist [ˈɔptɪmɪst] N optimiste mf

★**optimistic** [ɔptɪˈmɪstɪk] ADJ optimiste

optimistically [ɔptɪˈmɪstɪklɪ] ADV avec optimisme

optimize [ˈɔptɪmaɪz] VT (plan, machine) optimiser; (situation, opportunity) tirer le plus grand profit de

optimum [ˈɔptɪməm] ADJ optimal(e), optimum

★**option** [ˈɔpʃən] N choix m, option f; (Scol) matière f à option; (Comm) option; **to keep one's options open** (fig) ne pas s'engager; **I have no ~** je n'ai pas le choix

optional [ˈɔpʃənl] ADJ facultatif(-ive); (Comm) en option; **~ extras** accessoires mpl en option, options fpl

optometrist [ɔpˈtɔmətrɪst] N (esp US) optométriste mf

opulence [ˈɔpjuləns] N opulence f; abondance f

opulent [ˈɔpjulənt] ADJ opulent(e); abondant(e)

OR ABBR (US) = **Oregon**

★**or** [ɔːʳ] CONJ ou; (with negative): **he hasn't seen or heard anything** il n'a rien vu ni entendu; **or else** sinon; ou bien

oracle [ˈɔrəkl] N oracle m

oral [ˈɔːrəl] ADJ oral(e) ▶ N oral m

★**orange** [ˈɔrɪndʒ] N (fruit) orange f ▶ ADJ orange inv

orangeade [ɔrɪndʒˈeɪd] N orangeade f

orange juice N jus m d'orange

orangutan, orang-utan [ɔːˈræŋutæn] N orang-goutan m

oration [ɔːˈreɪʃən] N discours solennel

orator [ˈɔrətəʳ] N orateur(-trice)

oratorio [ɔrəˈtɔːrɪəu] N oratorio m

oratory [ˈɔrətrɪ] N (art) talent m oratoire; (speech) oraison f

orb [ɔːb] N orbe m

orbit [ˈɔːbɪt] N orbite f; **to be in/go into ~ (round)** être/entrer en orbite (autour de) ▶ VT graviter autour de

orbital [ˈɔːbɪtl] N (also: **orbital motorway**) périphérique f

orchard [ˈɔːtʃəd] N verger m; **apple ~** verger de pommiers

orchestra [ˈɔːkɪstrə] N orchestre m; (US: seating) (fauteuils mpl d')orchestre

orchestral [ɔːˈkestrəl] ADJ orchestral(e); (concert) symphonique

orchestrate [ˈɔːkɪstreɪt] VT (Mus, fig) orchestrer

orchid [ˈɔːkɪd] N orchidée f

ordain [ɔːˈdeɪn] VT (Rel) ordonner; (decide) décréter

ordeal [ɔːˈdiːl] N épreuve f

★**order** [ˈɔːdəʳ] N ordre m; (Comm) commande f; **in ~** en ordre; (document) en règle; **out of ~** (not in correct order) en désordre; (machine) hors service; (telephone) en dérangement; **a machine in working ~** une machine en état de marche; **in ~ of size** par ordre de grandeur; **in ~ to do/that** pour faire/que + sub; **to place an ~ for sth with sb** commander qch auprès de qn, passer commande de qch à qn; **to be on ~** être en commande; **made to ~** fait sur commande; **to be under orders to do sth** avoir ordre de faire qch; **a point of ~** un point de procédure; **to the ~ of** (*Banking*) à l'ordre de ▶ VT ordonner; (*Comm*) commander; **to ~ sb to do** ordonner à qn de faire ▶ VI commander; **could I ~ now, please?** je peux commander, s'il vous plaît ?

order book N carnet *m* de commandes

order form N bon *m* de commande

orderly ['ɔːdəlɪ] N (*Mil*) ordonnance *f*; (*Med*) garçon *m* de salle ▶ ADJ (*room*) en ordre; (*mind*) méthodique; (*person*) qui a de l'ordre

order number N (*Comm*) numéro *m* de commande

ordinal ['ɔːdɪnl] ADJ (*number*) ordinal(e)

ordinarily [ɔːd'nerɪlɪ] ADV (*normally*) d'ordinaire

★**ordinary** ['ɔːdnrɪ] ADJ ordinaire, normal(e); (*pej*) ordinaire, quelconque; **out of the ~** exceptionnel(le)

ordinary degree N (*Scol*) ≈ licence *f* libre

Un **ordinary degree** est un diplôme inférieur à l'*honours degree* que l'on obtient en général après trois années d'études universitaires. Il peut aussi être décerné en cas d'échec à l'*honours degree*.

ordinary seaman N (*irreg*) (*BRIT*) matelot *m*

ordinary shares NPL actions *fpl* ordinaires

ordination [ɔːdɪ'neɪʃən] N ordination *f*

ordnance ['ɔːdnəns] N (*Mil*: *unit*) service *m* du matériel

Ordnance Survey map N (*BRIT*) ≈ carte *f* d'État-major

ore [ɔːʳ] N minerai *m*

oregano [ɔrɪ'gɑːnəu] N origan *m*

organ ['ɔːgən] N organe *m*; (*Mus*) orgue *m*, orgues *fpl*

organic [ɔː'gænɪk] ADJ organique; (*crops etc*) biologique, naturel(le)

organically [ɔː'gænɪklɪ] ADV (*grow, produce*) biologiquement

organism ['ɔːgənɪzəm] N organisme *m*

organist ['ɔːgənɪst] N organiste *mf*

★**organization** [ɔːgənaɪ'zeɪʃən] N organisation *f*

organizational [ɔːgənaɪ'zeɪʃnəl] ADJ organisationnel(le); **at an ~ level** au niveau organisationnel

organization chart N organigramme *m*

★**organize** ['ɔːgənaɪz] VT organiser; **to get organized** s'organiser

organized ['ɔːgənaɪzd] ADJ (*planned*) organisé(e); (*efficient*) bien organisé

organized crime N crime organisé, grand banditisme

organized labour N main-d'œuvre syndiquée

organizer ['ɔːgənaɪzəʳ] N organisateur(-trice)

orgasm ['ɔːgæzəm] N orgasme *m*

orgy ['ɔːdʒɪ] N orgie *f*

Orient ['ɔːrɪənt] N: **the ~** l'Orient *m*

orient ['ɔːrɪənt], **orientate** ['ɔːrɪənteɪt] VT orienter; **to be oriented towards sth** (*person*) être orienté vers qch; (*thing*) être axé sur qch

oriental [ɔːrɪ'entl] ADJ oriental(e) ▶ N Oriental(e)

orientate ['ɔːrɪənteɪt] VT = **orient**

orientation [ɔːrɪen'teɪʃən] N (*attitudes*) tendance *f*; (*in job*) orientation *f*; (*of building*) orientation, exposition *f*

orienteering [ɔːrɪən'tɪərɪŋ] N course *f* d'orientation

orifice ['ɔrɪfɪs] N orifice *m*

origami [ɔrɪ'gɑːmɪ] N origami *m*

origin ['ɔrɪdʒɪn] N origine *f*; **country of ~** pays *m* d'origine

★**original** [ə'rɪdʒɪnl] ADJ original(e); (*earliest*) original(le) ▶ N original *m*

originality [ərɪdʒɪ'nælɪtɪ] N originalité *f*

★**originally** [ə'rɪdʒɪnəlɪ] ADV (*at first*) à l'origine

originate [ə'rɪdʒɪneɪt] VI: **to ~ from** être originaire de; (*suggestion*) provenir de; **to ~ in** (*custom*) prendre naissance dans, avoir son origine dans

originator [ə'rɪdʒɪneɪtəʳ] N auteur *m*

Orkney ['ɔːknɪ] N (*also*: **the Orkneys, the Orkney Islands**) les Orcades *fpl*

ornament ['ɔːnəmənt] N ornement *m*; (*trinket*) bibelot *m*

ornamental [ɔːnə'mentl] ADJ décoratif(-ive); (*garden*) d'agrément

ornamentation [ɔːnəmen'teɪʃən] N ornementation *f*

ornate [ɔː'neɪt] ADJ très orné(e)

ornithologist [ɔːnɪ'θɔlədʒɪst] N ornithologue *mf*

ornithology [ɔːnɪ'θɔlədʒɪ] N ornithologie *f*

orphan ['ɔːfn] N orphelin(e) ▶ VT: **to be orphaned** devenir orphelin

orphanage ['ɔːfənɪdʒ] N orphelinat *m*

orthodontist [ɔːθə'dɔntɪst] N orthodontiste *mf*

orthodox ['ɔːθədɔks] ADJ orthodoxe

orthodoxy ['ɔːθədɔksɪ] N orthodoxie *f*

orthopaedic, (*US*) **orthopedic** [ɔːθə'piːdɪk] ADJ orthopédique

OS ABBR (*BRIT*: = *Ordnance Survey*) ≈ IGN *m* (= *Institut géographique national*); (*Naut*) = **ordinary seaman**; (*Dress*) = **outsize**

O/S ABBR = **out of stock**

Oscar ['ɔskəʳ] N oscar *m*

oscillate ['ɔsɪleɪt] VI osciller

OSHA N ABBR (*US*: = *Occupational Safety and Health Administration*) *office de l'hygiène et de la sécurité au travail*

Oslo ['ɔzləu] N Oslo

osmosis [ɔz'məusɪs] N osmose *f*; **by ~** par osmose

ostensible [ɔs'tensɪbl] ADJ prétendu(e); apparent(e)

ostensibly [ɔs'tensɪblɪ] ADV en apparence

ostentation [ɔsten'teɪʃən] N ostentation *f*

ostentatious [ɔsten'teɪʃəs] ADJ prétentieux(-euse); ostentatoire

osteopath ['ɔstɪəpæθ] N ostéopathe *mf*

osteoporosis [ɔstɪəupə'rəusɪs] N ostéoporose *f*

ostracism ['ɔstrəsɪzəm] N ostracisme *m*

ostracize ['ɔstrəsaɪz] VT frapper d'ostracisme

ostrich ['ɔstrɪtʃ] N autruche *f*

OT N ABBR (= *Old Testament*) AT *m*

OTB N ABBR (*US*: = *off-track betting*) *paris pris en dehors du champ de course*

O.T.E. ABBR (= *on-target earnings*) primes *fpl* sur objectifs inclus

★**other** [ˈʌðəʳ] ADJ autre; **the ~ one** l'autre; **some ~ people have still to arrive** on attend encore quelques personnes; **the ~ day** l'autre jour ▶ PRON: **the ~** l'autre; **others** (*other people*) d'autres; **some actor or ~** un certain acteur, je ne sais quel acteur; **somebody or ~** quelqu'un; **the car was none ~ than John's** la voiture n'était autre que celle de John ▶ ADV: **~ than** autrement que; à part

★**otherwise** [ˈʌðəwaɪz] ADV, CONJ autrement; **an ~ good piece of work** par ailleurs, un beau travail

otherworldly [ʌðəˈwəːldlɪ] ADJ d'un autre monde

OTT ABBR (*inf*) = **over the top**; *see* **top**

Ottawa [ˈɔtəwə] N Ottawa

otter [ˈɔtəʳ] N loutre *f*

OU N ABBR (*BRIT*) = **Open University**

ouch [autʃ] EXCL aïe !

★**ought** [ɔːt] AUX VB: **I ~ to do it** je devrais le faire, il faudrait que je le fasse; **this ~ to have been corrected** cela aurait dû être corrigé; **he ~ to win** (*probability*) il devrait gagner; **you ~ to go and see it** vous devriez aller le voir

ounce [auns] N once *f* (*28.35g*; *16 in a pound*)

★**our** [ˈauəʳ] ADJ notre, nos *pl*; *see also* **my**

★**ours** [auəz] PRON le (la) nôtre, les nôtres; *see also* **mine**[1]

★**ourselves** [auəˈsɛlvz] PL PRON (*reflexive, after preposition*) nous; (*emphatic*) nous-mêmes; **we did it (all) by ~** nous avons fait ça tout seuls; *see also* **oneself**

oust [aust] VT évincer

★**out** [aut] ADV, ADJ dehors; (*published, not at home etc*) sorti(e); (*light, fire*) éteint(e); (*on strike*) en grève; **~ here** ici; **~ there** là-bas; **he's ~** (*absent*) il est sorti; (*unconscious*) il est sans connaissance; **to be ~ in one's calculations** s'être trompé dans ses calculs; **to run/back** *etc* **~** sortir en courant/en reculant *etc*; **to be ~ and about** *or* (*US*) **around again** être de nouveau sur pied; **before the week was ~** avant la fin de la semaine; **the journey ~** l'aller *m*; **the boat was 10 km ~** le bateau était à 10 km du rivage; **~ loud** adv à haute voix; **~ of** prep (*outside*) en dehors de; (*because of: anger etc*) par; (*from among*) **10 ~ of 10** 10 sur 10; (*without*): **~ of petrol** sans essence, à court d'essence; **made ~ of wood** en *or* de bois; **~ of order** (*machine*) en panne; (*Tel: line*) en dérangement; **~ of stock** (*Comm: article*) épuisé(e); (: *shop*) en rupture de stock ▶ VT: **to ~ sb** révéler l'homosexualité de qn

outage [ˈautɪdʒ] N (*esp US: power failure*) panne *f or* coupure *f* de courant

out-and-out [ˈautəndaut] ADJ véritable

outback [ˈautbæk] N campagne isolée; (*in Australia*) intérieur *m*

outbid [autˈbɪd] VT (*irreg: like* **bid**) surenchérir

outboard [ˈautbɔːd] N: **~ (motor)** (moteur *m*) hors-bord *m*

outbound [ˈautbaund] ADJ: **~ (from/for)** en partance (de/pour)

outbox [ˈautbɔks] N (*Comput*) boîte *f* d'envoi; (*US: out-tray*) corbeille *f* du courrier au départ

outbreak [ˈautbreɪk] N (*of violence*) éruption *f*, explosion *f*; (*of disease*) de nombreux cas; **the ~ of war south of the border** la guerre qui s'est déclarée au sud de la frontière

outbuilding [ˈautbɪldɪŋ] N dépendance *f*

outburst [ˈautbəːst] N explosion *f*, accès *m*

outcast [ˈautkɑːst] N exilé(e); (*socially*) paria *m*

outclass [autˈklɑːs] VT surclasser

★**outcome** [ˈautkʌm] N issue *f*, résultat *m*

outcrop [ˈautkrɔp] N affleurement *m*

outcry [ˈautkraɪ] N tollé (général)

outdated [autˈdeɪtɪd] ADJ démodé(e)

outdistance [autˈdɪstəns] VT distancer

outdo [autˈduː] VT (*irreg: like* **do**) surpasser

outdoor [autˈdɔːʳ] ADJ de *or* en plein air

outdoors [autˈdɔːz] ADV dehors; au grand air

outer [ˈautəʳ] ADJ extérieur(e); **~ suburbs** grande banlieue

outer space N espace *m* cosmique

outfit [ˈautfɪt] N équipement *m*; (*clothes*) tenue *f*; (*inf, Comm*) organisation *f*, boîte *f*

outfitter [ˈautfɪtəʳ] N (*BRIT*): **"(gents') ~'s"** « confection pour hommes »

outgoing [ˈautgəuɪŋ] ADJ (*president, tenant*) sortant(e); (*character*) ouvert(e), extraverti(e)

outgoings [ˈautgəuɪŋz] NPL (*BRIT: expenses*) dépenses *fpl*

outgrow [autˈgrəu] VT (*irreg: like* **grow**) (*clothes*) devenir trop grand(e) pour

outhouse [ˈauthaus] N appentis *m*, remise *f*

outing [ˈautɪŋ] N sortie *f*; excursion *f*

outlandish [autˈlændɪʃ] ADJ étrange

outlast [autˈlɑːst] VT survivre à

outlaw [ˈautlɔː] N hors-la-loi *m inv* ▶ VT (*person*) mettre hors la loi; (*practice*) proscrire

outlay [ˈautleɪ] N dépenses *fpl*; (*investment*) mise *f* de fonds

outlet [ˈautlɛt] N (*for liquid etc*) issue *f*, sortie *f*; (*for emotion*) exutoire *m*; (*for goods*) débouché *m*; (*also: retail outlet*) point *m* de vente; (*US Elec*) prise *f* de courant

★**outline** [ˈautlaɪn] N (*shape*) contour *m*; (*summary*) esquisse *f*, grandes lignes ▶ VT (*fig: theory, plan*) exposer à grands traits

outlive [autˈlɪv] VT survivre à

outlook [ˈautluk] N perspective *f*; (*point of view*) attitude *f*

outlying [ˈautlaɪɪŋ] ADJ écarté(e)

outmanoeuvre [autməˈnuːvəʳ] VT (*rival etc*) avoir au tournant

outmoded [autˈməudɪd] ADJ démodé(e); dépassé(e)

outnumber [autˈnʌmbəʳ] VT surpasser en nombre

out-of-court [autəvˈkɔːt] ADJ, ADV à l'aimable

out-of-date [autəvˈdeɪt] ADJ (*passport, ticket*) périmé(e); (*theory, idea*) dépassé(e); (*custom*) désuet(-ète); (*clothes*) démodé(e)

out-of-doors [ˈautəvˈdɔːz] ADV = **outdoors**

out-of-the-way [ˈautəvðəˈweɪ] ADJ loin de tout; (*fig*) insolite

out-of-town [autəˈtaun] ADJ (*shopping centre etc*) en périphérie

outpace [autˈpeɪs] VT distancer

outpatient [ˈautpeɪʃənt] N malade *mf* en consultation externe

outperform [autpəˈfɔːm] VT être plus performant que

outpost [ˈautpəust] N avant-poste *m*

outpouring [ˈautpɔːrɪŋ] N (*fig*) épanchement(s) *m(pl)*

output [ˈautput] N rendement *m*, production *f*; (*Comput*) sortie *f* ▶ VT (*Comput*) sortir

outrage [ˈautreɪdʒ] N (*anger*) indignation *f*; (*violent act*) atrocité *f*, acte *m* de violence; (*scandal*) scandale *m* ▶ VT outrager

outrageous [autˈreɪdʒəs] ADJ atroce; (*scandalous*) scandaleux(-euse)

outreach programme, (US) **outreach program** [ˈautriːtʃ-] N programme *m* de proximité

outrider [ˈautraɪdəʳ] N (*on motorcycle*) motard *m*

outright ADV [autˈraɪt] complètement; (*deny, refuse*) catégoriquement; (*ask*) carrément; (*kill*) sur le coup ▶ ADJ [ˈautraɪt] complet(-ète); catégorique

outrun [autˈrʌn] VT (*irreg: like* **run**) dépasser

outsell [autˈsel] VT (*irreg: like* **sell**) réaliser de meilleurs chiffres de ventes que

outset [ˈautset] N début *m*

outshine [autˈʃaɪn] VT (*irreg: like* **shine**) (*fig*) éclipser

★**outside** [autˈsaɪd] N extérieur *m*; **at the ~** (*fig*) au plus *or* maximum ▶ ADJ extérieur(e); (*remote, unlikely*): **an ~ chance** une (très) faible chance; **~ left/right** *n* (*Football*) ailier gauche/droit ▶ ADV (au) dehors, à l'extérieur ▶ PREP hors de, à l'extérieur de; (*in front of*) devant

outside broadcast N (*Radio, TV*) reportage *m*

outside lane N (*Aut: in Britain*) voie *f* de droite; (*: in US, Europe*) voie de gauche

outside line N (*Tel*) ligne extérieure

outsider [autˈsaɪdəʳ] N (*in race etc*) outsider *m*; (*stranger*) étranger(-ère)

outsize [ˈautsaɪz] ADJ énorme; (*clothes*) grande taille *inv*

outskirts [ˈautskəːts] NPL faubourgs *mpl*

outsmart [autˈsmɑːt] VT se montrer plus malin(-igne) *or* futé(e) que

outsource [autˈsɔːs] VT externaliser

outsourcing [autˈsɔːsɪŋ] N externalisation *f*

outspoken [autˈspəukən] ADJ très franc (franche)

outspokenness [autˈspəukənnɪs] N franc-parler *m*

outspread [autˈspred] ADJ (*wings*) déployé(e)

★**outstanding** [autˈstændɪŋ] ADJ remarquable, exceptionnel(le); (*unfinished: work, business*) en suspens, en souffrance; (*debt*) impayé(e); (*problem*) non réglé(e); **your account is still ~** vous n'avez pas encore tout remboursé

outstandingly [autˈstændɪŋlɪ] ADV remarquablement

outstay [autˈsteɪ] VT: **to ~ one's welcome** abuser de l'hospitalité de son hôte

outstretched [autˈstretʃt] ADJ (*hand*) tendu(e); (*body*) étendu(e)

outstrip [autˈstrɪp] VT (*also fig*) dépasser

out-tray [ˈauttreɪ] N courrier *m* (« départ »)

outvote [autˈvəut] VT: **to ~ sb (by)** mettre qn en minorité (par); **to ~ sth (by)** rejeter qch (par)

outward [ˈautwəd] ADJ (*sign, appearances*) extérieur(e); (*journey*) (d')aller ▶ ADV vers l'extérieur

outwardly [ˈautwədlɪ] ADV extérieurement; en apparence

outwards [ˈautwədz] ADV (*esp* BRIT) = **outward**

outweigh [autˈweɪ] VT l'emporter sur

outwit [autˈwɪt] VT se montrer plus malin que

oval [ˈəuvl] ADJ, N ovale *m*

Oval Office N (*US Pol*) *voir article*

> L'**Oval Office** est le bureau personnel du président des États-Unis à la Maison-Blanche, ainsi appelé du fait de sa forme ovale. Par extension, ce terme désigne la présidence elle-même.

ovarian [əuˈvɛərɪən] ADJ ovarien(ne); (*cancer*) des ovaires

ovary [ˈəuvərɪ] N ovaire *m*

ovation [əuˈveɪʃən] N ovation *f*

oven [ˈʌvn] N four *m*

oven glove N gant *m* de cuisine

ovenproof [ˈʌvnpruːf] ADJ allant au four

oven-ready [ˈʌvnrediː] ADJ prêt(e) à cuire

ovenware [ˈʌvnwɛəʳ] N plats *mpl* allant au four

★**over** [ˈəuvəʳ] ADV (par-)dessus; (*excessively*) trop; **~ here** ici; **~ there** là-bas; **all ~** (*everywhere*) partout; **~ and ~ (again)** à plusieurs reprises; **to ask sb ~** inviter qn (à passer); **to go ~ to sb's** passer chez qn; **to fall ~** tomber; **to turn sth ~** retourner qch; **now ~ to our Paris correspondent** nous passons l'antenne à notre correspondant à Paris; **the world ~** dans le monde entier; **she's not ~ intelligent** (BRIT) elle n'est pas particulièrement intelligente ▶ ADJ (*finished*) fini(e), terminé(e); (*too much*) en plus; **all ~** (*finished*) fini(e) ▶ PREP sur; par-dessus; (*above*) au-dessus de; (*on the other side of*) de l'autre côté de; (*more than*) plus de; (*during*) pendant; (*about, concerning*): **they fell out ~ money/her** ils se sont brouillés pour des questions d'argent/à cause d'elle; **~ and above** en plus de

over... [ˈəuvəʳ] PREFIX: **overabundant** surabondant(e)

overact [əuvərˈækt] VI (*Theat*) outrer son rôle

★**overall** ADJ [ˈəuvərɔːl] (*length*) total(e); (*study, impression*) d'ensemble ▶ N [ˈəuvərɔːl] (BRIT) blouse *f* ▶ ADV [əuvərˈɔːl] dans l'ensemble, en général ■ **overalls** NPL (*boiler suit*) bleus *mpl* (de travail)

overall majority N majorité absolue

overanxious [əuvərˈæŋkʃəs] ADJ trop anxieux(-euse)

overawe [əuvərˈɔː] VT impressionner

overbalance [əuvəˈbæləns] VI basculer

overbearing [əuvəˈbɛərɪŋ] ADJ impérieux(-euse), autoritaire

overblown [əuvəˈbləun] ADJ exagéré(e)

overboard [ˈəuvəbɔːd] ADV (*Naut*) par-dessus bord; **to go ~ for sth** (*fig*) s'emballer (pour qch)

overbook [əuvə'buk] VI faire du surbooking

overbooking [əuvə'bukɪŋ] N surréservation f, surbooking m

overcame [əuvə'keɪm] PT of **overcome**

overcapitalize [əuvə'kæpɪtəlaɪz] VT surcapitaliser

overcast ['əuvəkɑːst] ADJ couvert(e)

overcharge [əuvə'tʃɑːdʒ] VT: **to ~ sb for sth** faire payer qch trop cher à qn

overcoat ['əuvəkəut] N pardessus m

overcome [əuvə'kʌm] VT (irreg: like **come**) (defeat) triompher de; (difficulty) surmonter ▶ ADJ (emotionally) bouleversé(e); **~ with grief** accablé(e) de douleur

overconfident [əuvə'kɔnfɪdənt] ADJ trop sûr(e) de soi

overcrowded [əuvə'kraudɪd] ADJ bondé(e); (city, country) surpeuplé(e)

overcrowding [əuvə'kraudɪŋ] N surpeuplement m; (in bus) encombrement m

overdo [əuvə'duː] VT (irreg: like **do**) exagérer; (overcook) trop cuire; **to ~ it, to ~ things** (work too hard) en faire trop, se surmener

overdone [əuvə'dʌn] ADJ (vegetables, steak) trop cuit(e)

overdose ['əuvədəus] N dose excessive

overdraft ['əuvədrɑːft] N découvert m

overdrawn [əuvə'drɔːn] ADJ (account) à découvert

overdrive ['əuvədraiv] N (Aut) (vitesse f) surmultipliée f

overdue [əuvə'djuː] ADJ en retard; (bill) impayé(e); (change) qui tarde; **that change was long ~** ce changement n'avait que trop tardé

overeat [əuvər'iːt] VI (irreg: like **eat**) trop manger

overeating [əuvər'iːtɪŋ] N hyperphagie f, tendance f à trop manger

overemphasis [əuvər'ɛmfəsɪs] N: **to put an ~ on** accorder trop d'importance à

overestimate [əuvər'ɛstɪmeɪt] VT surestimer

overexcited [əuvərɪk'saɪtɪd] ADJ surexcité(e)

overexertion [əuvərɪg'zəːʃən] N surmenage m (physique)

overexpose [əuvərɪk'spəuz] VT (Phot) surexposer

overflow VI [əuvə'fləu] déborder ▶ N ['əuvəfləu] trop-plein m; (also: **overflow pipe**) tuyau m d'écoulement, trop-plein m

overfly [əuvə'flaɪ] VT (irreg: like **fly**) survoler

overgenerous [əuvə'dʒɛnərəs] ADJ (person) prodigue; (offer) excessif(-ive)

overgrown [əuvə'grəun] ADJ (garden) envahi(e) par la végétation; **he's just an ~ schoolboy** (fig) c'est un écolier attardé

overhang ['əuvə'hæŋ] VT (irreg: like **hang**) surplomber ▶ VI faire saillie

overhaul VT [əuvə'hɔːl] réviser ▶ N ['əuvəhɔːl] révision f

overhead ADV [əuvə'hɛd] au-dessus ▶ ADJ ['əuvəhɛd] aérien(ne); (lighting) vertical(e) ▶ N ['əuvəhɛd] (US) = **overheads**

overhead projector N rétroprojecteur m

overheads ['əuvəhɛdz] NPL (BRIT) frais généraux

overhear [əuvə'hɪə'] VT (irreg: like **hear**) entendre (par hasard)

overheat [əuvə'hiːt] VI devenir surchauffé(e); (engine) chauffer

overindulge [əuvərɪn'dʌldʒ] VI faire des excès; **to ~ in alcohol** faire des excès de boisson

overjoyed [əuvə'dʒɔɪd] ADJ ravi(e), enchanté(e)

overkill ['əuvəkɪl] N (fig): **it would be ~** ce serait de trop

overland ['əuvəlænd] ADJ, ADV par voie de terre

overlap VI [əuvə'læp] se chevaucher ▶ N ['əuvəlæp] chevauchement m

overleaf [əuvə'liːf] ADV au verso

overload [əuvə'ləud] VT surcharger

overlook [əuvə'luk] VT (have view of) donner sur; (miss) oublier, négliger; (forgive) fermer les yeux sur

overlord ['əuvələːd] N chef m suprême

overly ['əuvəlɪ] ADV excessivement

overmanning [əuvə'mænɪŋ] N sureffectif m, main-d'œuvre f pléthorique

overnight ADV [əuvə'naɪt] (happen) durant la nuit; (fig) soudain; **to stay ~ (with sb)** passer la nuit (chez qn); **he stayed there ~** il y a passé la nuit; **if you travel ~ ...** si tu fais le voyage de nuit ...; **he'll be away ~** il ne rentrera pas ce soir ▶ ADJ ['əuvənaɪt] d'une (or de) nuit; soudain(e)

overnight bag N nécessaire m de voyage

overpaid [əuvə'peɪd] ADJ surpayé(e); **grossly ~** largement surpayé

overpass ['əuvəpɑːs] N (US: for cars) pont autoroutier; (: for pedestrians) passerelle f, pont m

overpay [əuvə'peɪ] VT (irreg: like **pay**): **to ~ sb by £50** donner à qn 50 livres de trop

overplay [əuvə'pleɪ] VT exagérer; **to ~ one's hand** trop présumer de sa situation

overpower [əuvə'pauə'] VT vaincre; (fig) accabler

overpowering [əuvə'pauərɪŋ] ADJ irrésistible; (heat, stench) suffocant(e)

overpriced [əuvə'praɪst] ADJ vendu(e) trop cher(-ère), trop cher(-ère)

overproduction ['əuvəprə'dʌkʃən] N surproduction f

overran [əuvə'ræn] PT of **overrun**

overrate [əuvə'reɪt] VT surestimer

overrated [əuvə'reɪtɪd] ADJ surfait(e); **to be vastly ~** être très surfait

overreact [əuvəri'ækt] VI réagir de façon excessive

overreaction [əuvəri'ækʃən] N réaction f excessive

override [əuvə'raɪd] VT (irreg: like **ride**) (order, objection) passer outre à; (decision) annuler

overriding [əuvə'raɪdɪŋ] ADJ prépondérant(e)

overrule [əuvə'ruːl] VT (decision) annuler; (claim) rejeter; (person) rejeter l'avis de

overrun [əuvə'rʌn] VT (irreg: like **run**) (Mil: country etc) occuper; (time limit etc) dépasser; **the town is ~ with tourists** la ville est envahie de touristes ▶ VI dépasser le temps imparti

★**overseas** [əuvə'siːz] ADV outre-mer; (abroad) à l'étranger ▶ ADJ (trade) extérieur(e); (visitor) étranger(-ère)

oversee [əuvə'siː] VT (irreg: like **see**) surveiller

overseer [ˈəʊvəsɪəʳ] N (*in factory*) contremaître m

overshadow [əʊvəˈʃædəʊ] VT (*fig*) éclipser

overshoot [əʊvəˈʃuːt] VT (*irreg: like* **shoot**) dépasser

oversight [ˈəʊvəsaɪt] N omission f, oubli m; **due to an ~** par suite d'une inadvertance

oversimplification [əʊvəsɪmplɪfɪˈkeɪʃən] N simplification f hâtive

oversimplify [əʊvəˈsɪmplɪfaɪ] VT trop simplifier

oversleep [əʊvəˈsliːp] VI (*irreg: like* **sleep**) se réveiller (trop) tard

overspend [əʊvəˈspɛnd] VI (*irreg: like* **spend**) dépenser de trop; **we have overspent by 5,000 dollars** nous avons dépassé notre budget de 5 000 dollars, nous avons dépensé 5 000 dollars de trop

overspill [ˈəʊvəspɪl] N excédent m de population

overstaffed [əʊvəˈstɑːft] ADJ: **to be ~** avoir trop de personnel, être en surnombre

overstate [əʊvəˈsteɪt] VT exagérer

overstatement [əʊvəˈsteɪtmənt] N exagération f

overstay [əʊvəˈsteɪ] VT: **to ~ one's welcome (at sb's)** abuser de l'hospitalité de qn

overstep [əʊvəˈstɛp] VT: **to ~ the mark** dépasser la mesure

overstock [əʊvəˈstɔk] VT stocker en surabondance

overstretched [əʊvəˈstrɛtʃt] ADJ (*person*) débordé(e); **my budget is ~** j'ai atteint les limites de mon budget

overstrike N [ˈəʊvəstraɪk] (*on printer*) superposition f, double frappe f ▶ VT [əʊvəˈstraɪk] (*irreg: like* **strike**) surimprimer

oversubscribed [əʊvəsəbˈskraɪbd] ADJ (*event, service*) trop couru(e); (*shares*) sursouscrit(e)

overt [əʊˈvəːt] ADJ non dissimulé(e)

overtake [əʊvəˈteɪk] VT (*irreg: like* **take**) dépasser; (*BRIT Aut*) dépasser, doubler

overtaking [əʊvəˈteɪkɪŋ] N (*BRIT Aut*) dépassement m

overtax [əʊvəˈtæks] VT (*Econ*) surimposer; (*fig: strength, patience*) abuser de; **to ~ o.s.** se surmener

overthrow [əʊvəˈθrəʊ] VT (*irreg: like* **throw**) (*government*) renverser

overtime [ˈəʊvətaɪm] N heures fpl supplémentaires; **to do** *or* **work ~** faire des heures supplémentaires

overtime ban N refus m de faire des heures supplémentaires

overtired [əʊvəˈtaɪəd] ADJ surmené(e)

overtly [əʊˈvəːtlɪ] ADV ouvertement

overtone [ˈəʊvətəʊn] N (*also:* **overtones**) note f, sous-entendus mpl

overtook [əʊvəˈtʊk] PT *of* **overtake**

overture [ˈəʊvətʃʊəʳ] N (*Mus, fig*) ouverture f

overturn [əʊvəˈtəːn] VT renverser; (*decision, plan*) annuler ▶ VI se retourner

overuse VT [əʊvəˈjuːz] (*thing*) abuser de; (*word, idea*) galvauder ▶ N [əʊvəˈjuːs] surexploitation f

overview [ˈəʊvəvjuː] N vue f d'ensemble

overweight [əʊvəˈweɪt] ADJ (*person*) trop gros(se); (*luggage*) trop lourd(e)

overwhelm [əʊvəˈwɛlm] VT (*subj: emotion*) accabler, submerger; (*enemy, opponent*) écraser

overwhelmed [əʊvəˈwɛlmd] ADJ (*by emotion*) bouleversé(e); (*by work, trouble*) accablé(e); **to be ~ by sth** être accablé par qch; **to be ~ with sth** (*requests, responses*) être submergé de qch

overwhelming [əʊvəˈwɛlmɪŋ] ADJ (*victory, defeat*) écrasant(e); (*desire*) irrésistible; **one's ~ impression is of heat** on a une impression dominante de chaleur

overwhelmingly [əʊvəˈwɛlmɪŋlɪ] ADV (*vote*) en masse; (*win*) d'une manière écrasante

overwork [əʊvəˈwəːk] N surmenage m ▶ VT surmener ▶ VI se surmener

overworked [əʊvəˈwəːkt] ADJ (*person*) surmené(e); (*word, phrase*) galvaudé(e)

overwrite [əʊvəˈraɪt] VT (*irreg: like* **write**) (*Comput*) écraser

overwrought [əʊvəˈrɔːt] ADJ excédé(e)

ovulate [ˈɔvjuleɪt] VI ovuler

ovulation [ɔvjuˈleɪʃən] N ovulation f

★**owe** [əʊ] VT devoir; **to ~ sb sth, to ~ sth to sb** devoir qch à qn; **how much do I ~ you?** combien est-ce que je vous dois?

owing to [ˈəʊɪŋ-] PREP à cause de, en raison de

owl [aʊl] N hibou m

★**own** [əʊn] VT posséder ▶ VI (*BRIT*): **to ~ to sth** reconnaître *or* avouer qch; **to ~ to having done sth** avouer avoir fait qch ▶ ADJ propre ▶ PRON: **a room of my ~** une chambre à moi, ma propre chambre; **can I have it for my (very) ~?** puis-je l'avoir pour moi (tout) seul ?; **to get one's ~ back** prendre sa revanche; **on one's ~** tout(e) seul(e); **to come into one's ~** trouver sa voie; trouver sa justification
  ▶ **own up** VI avouer

own brand N (*Comm*) marque f de distributeur

★**owner** [ˈəʊnəʳ] N propriétaire mf

owner-occupier [ˈəʊnərˈɔkjupaɪəʳ] N propriétaire occupant

ownership [ˈəʊnəʃɪp] N possession f; **it's under new ~** (*shop etc*) il y a eu un changement de propriétaire

own goal N: **he scored an ~** (*Sport*) il a marqué un but contre son camp; (*fig*) cela s'est retourné contre lui

ox [ɔks] (*pl* **oxen** [ˈɔksn]) N bœuf m

Oxbridge [ˈɔksbrɪdʒ] N (*BRIT*) *les universités d'Oxford et de Cambridge*

> **Oxbridge**, nom formé à partir des mots Ox(ford) et (Cam)bridge, s'utilise pour parler de ces deux universités comme un tout, dans la mesure où il s'agit des deux universités britanniques les plus prestigieuses et qu'elles sont connues dans le monde entier.

oxen [ˈɔksn] NPL *of* **ox**

Oxfam [ˈɔksfæm] N ABBR (*BRIT*: = *Oxford Committee for Famine Relief*) *association humanitaire*

oxide [ˈɔksaɪd] N oxyde m

oxtail [ˈɔksteɪl] N: **~ soup** soupe f à la queue de bœuf

oxygen [ˈɔksɪdʒən] N oxygène m

oxygen mask N masque *m* à oxygène
oxygen tent N tente *f* à oxygène
oxymoron [ɔksɪˈmɔːrɒn] N oxymore *m*
oyster [ˈɔɪstəʳ] N huître *f*
oz. ABBR = **ounce; ounces**

ozone [ˈəʊzəʊn] N ozone *m*
ozone friendly ADJ qui n'attaque pas *or* qui préserve la couche d'ozone
ozone hole N trou *m* d'ozone
ozone layer N couche *f* d'ozone

Pp

P¹, p [piː] N (letter) P, p m; **P for Peter** P comme Pierre

P² ABBR = **president; prince**

p ABBR (= page) p; (BRIT) = **penny; pence**

PA N ABBR = **personal assistant; public address system** ▶ ABBR (US) = **Pennsylvania**

pa [pɑː] N (inf) papa m

p.a. ABBR = **per annum**

PAC N ABBR (US) = **political action committee**

pace [peɪs] N pas m; (speed) allure f; vitesse f; **to keep ~ with** aller à la même vitesse que; (events) se tenir au courant de; **to set the ~** (running) donner l'allure; (fig) donner le ton; **to put sb through his paces** (fig) mettre qn à l'épreuve ▶ VI: **to ~ up and down** faire les cent pas

pacemaker ['peɪsmeɪkə'] N (Med) stimulateur m cardiaque; (Sport: also: **pacesetter**) meneur(-euse) de train

pacey ['peɪsɪ] = **pacy**

Pacific [pə'sɪfɪk] N: **the ~ (Ocean)** le Pacifique, l'océan m Pacifique

pacific [pə'sɪfɪk] ADJ pacifique

pacification [pæsɪfɪ'keɪʃən] N pacification f

Pacific Rim N bassin m du Pacifique

pacifier ['pæsɪfaɪə'] N (US: dummy) tétine f

pacifism ['pæsɪfɪzəm] N pacifisme f

pacifist ['pæsɪfɪst] N pacifiste mf

pacify ['pæsɪfaɪ] VT pacifier; (soothe) calmer

★**pack** [pæk] N paquet m; (bundle) ballot m; (of hounds) meute f; (of thieves, wolves etc) bande f; (of cards) jeu m; (US: of cigarettes) paquet; (back pack) sac m à dos ▶ VT (goods) empaqueter, emballer; (in suitcase etc) emballer; (box) remplir; (cram) entasser; (press down) tasser; damer; (Comput) grouper, tasser; **to ~ one's bags** faire ses bagages ▶ VI faire ses bagages; **to ~ into** (room, stadium) s'entasser dans; **to send sb packing** (inf) envoyer promener qn
▶ **pack in** (BRIT inf) VI (machine) tomber en panne ▶ VT (boyfriend) plaquer; **~ it in!** laisse tomber !
▶ **pack off** VT: **to ~ sb off to** expédier qn à
▶ **pack up** VI (BRIT inf: machine) tomber en panne; (: person) se tirer ▶ VT (belongings) ranger; (goods, presents) empaqueter, emballer

★**package** ['pækɪdʒ] N paquet m; (of goods) emballage m, conditionnement m; (also: **package deal**: agreement) marché global; (purchase) forfait m; (Comput) progiciel m ▶ VT (goods) conditionner

package holiday N (BRIT) vacances organisées

package tour N voyage organisé

packaging ['pækɪdʒɪŋ] N (wrapping materials) emballage m; (of goods) conditionnement m

packed [pækt] ADJ (crowded) bondé(e)

packed lunch N (BRIT) repas froid

packer ['pækə'] N (person) emballeur(-euse); conditionneur(-euse)

packet ['pækɪt] N paquet m

packet switching [-swɪtʃɪŋ] N (Comput) commutation f de paquets

pack ice N banquise f

packing ['pækɪŋ] N emballage m

packing case N caisse f (d'emballage)

pact [pækt] N pacte m, traité m

pacy ['peɪsɪ] ADJ (thriller, comedy) au rythme enlevé; (player, striker) véloce

pad [pæd] N bloc(-notes m) m; (to prevent friction) tampon m; (for inking) tampon m encreur; (inf: flat) piaule f ▶ VT rembourrer ▶ VI: **to ~ in/about** etc entrer/aller et venir etc à pas feutrés

padded ['pædɪd] ADJ (jacket) matelassé(e); (bra) rembourré(e); **~ cell** cellule capitonnée

padding ['pædɪŋ] N rembourrage m; (fig) délayage m

paddle ['pædl] N (oar) pagaie f; (US: for table tennis) raquette f de ping-pong ▶ VI (with feet) barboter, faire trempette ▶ VT: **to ~ a canoe** etc pagayer

paddle steamer N bateau m à aubes

paddling pool ['pædlɪŋ-] N petit bassin

paddock ['pædək] N enclos m; (Racing) paddock m

paddy ['pædɪ] N (also: **paddy field**) rizière f

padlock ['pædlɔk] N cadenas m ▶ VT cadenasser

padre ['pɑːdrɪ] N aumônier m

paediatrician, (US) **pediatrician** [piːdɪə'trɪʃən] N pédiatre mf

paediatrics, (US) **pediatrics** [piːdɪ'ætrɪks] N pédiatrie f

paedophile, (US) **pedophile** ['piːdəufaɪl] N pédophile m

pagan ['peɪgən] ADJ, N païen(ne)

★**page** [peɪdʒ] N (of book) page f; (also: **page boy**) groom m, chasseur m; (: at wedding) garçon m d'honneur ▶ VT (in hotel etc) (faire) appeler

pageant ['pædʒənt] N spectacle m historique; grande cérémonie

pageantry ['pædʒəntrɪ] N apparat m, pompe f

page break N fin f or saut m de page

pager ['peɪdʒə'] N bip m (inf), Alphapage® m

paginate ['pædʒɪneɪt] VT paginer
pagination [pædʒɪ'neɪʃən] N pagination f
pagoda [pə'gəudə] N pagode f
paid [peɪd] PT, PP of **pay** ▶ ADJ (work, official) rémunéré(e); (holiday) payé(e); **to put ~ to** (BRIT) mettre fin à, mettre par terre
paid-up ['peɪdʌp], (US) **paid-in** ['peɪdɪn] ADJ (member) à jour de sa cotisation; (shares) libéré(e); **~ capital** capital versé
pail [peɪl] N seau m
★**pain** [peɪn] N douleur f; (inf: nuisance) plaie f; **to be in ~** souffrir, avoir mal; **to have a ~ in** avoir mal à or une douleur à or dans; **to take pains to do** se donner du mal pour faire; **on ~ of death** sous peine de mort
pained ['peɪnd] ADJ peiné(e), chagrin(e)
★**painful** ['peɪnful] ADJ douloureux(-euse); (difficult) difficile, pénible
painfully ['peɪnfəlɪ] ADV (fig: very) terriblement
painkiller ['peɪnkɪləʳ] N calmant m, analgésique m
painless ['peɪnlɪs] ADJ indolore
painstaking ['peɪnzteɪkɪŋ] ADJ (person) soigneux(-euse); (work) soigné(e)
★**paint** [peɪnt] N peinture f ▶ VT peindre; (fig) dépeindre; **to ~ the door blue** peindre la porte en bleu ▶ VI peindre; **to ~ in oils** faire de la peinture à l'huile
paintbox ['peɪntbɔks] N boîte f de couleurs
paintbrush ['peɪntbrʌʃ] N pinceau m
painter ['peɪntəʳ] N peintre m
★**painting** ['peɪntɪŋ] N peinture f; (picture) tableau m
paint-stripper ['peɪntstrɪpəʳ] N décapant m
paintwork ['peɪntwəːk] N (BRIT) peintures fpl; (: of car) peinture f
★**pair** [pɛəʳ] N (of shoes, gloves etc) paire f; (of people) couple m; (twosome) duo m; **~ of scissors** (paire de) ciseaux mpl; **~ of trousers** pantalon m ▶ **pair off** VI se mettre par deux
pairing ['pɛərɪŋ] N (twosome) paire f; (putting together: of people) association f; (: of foods, flavours) mariage m
pajamas [pə'dʒɑːməz] NPL (US) pyjama m
Pakistan [pɑːkɪ'stɑːn] N Pakistan m
Pakistani [pɑːkɪ'stɑːnɪ] ADJ pakistanais(e) ▶ N Pakistanais(e)
PAL [pæl] N ABBR (TV: = phase alternation line) PAL m
pal [pæl] N (inf) copain (copine)
★**palace** ['pæləs] N palais m
palaeontologist, (US) **paleontologist** [pælɪən'tɔlədʒɪst] N paléontologue mf
palatable ['pælɪtəbl] ADJ bon(ne), agréable au goût
palate ['pælɪt] N palais m (Anat)
palatial [pə'leɪʃəl] ADJ grandiose, magnifique
palaver [pə'lɑːvəʳ] N palabres fpl or mpl; histoire(s) f(pl)
★**pale** [peɪl] ADJ pâle; **~ blue** bleu pâle m inv; **to grow** or **turn ~** (person) pâlir ▶ VI pâlir; **to ~ into insignificance (beside)** perdre beaucoup d'importance (par rapport à) ▶ N: **to be beyond the ~** être au ban de la société

paleness ['peɪlnɪs] N pâleur f
paleontologist [pælɪən'tɔlədʒɪst] N (US) = palaeontologist
Palestine ['pælɪstaɪn] N Palestine f
Palestinian [pælɪs'tɪnɪən] ADJ palestinien(ne) ▶ N Palestinien(ne)
palette ['pælɪt] N palette f
paling ['peɪlɪŋ] N (stake) palis m; (fence) palissade f
palisade [pælɪ'seɪd] N palissade f
pall [pɔːl] N (of smoke) voile m ▶ VI: **to ~ (on)** devenir lassant (pour)
pallbearer ['pɔːlbɛərəʳ] N porteur m de cercueil
pallet ['pælɪt] N (for goods) palette f
palliative ['pælɪətɪv] ADJ palliatif(-ive); **~ care** soins mpl palliatifs ▶ N palliatif m
pallid ['pælɪd] ADJ blême
pallor ['pæləʳ] N pâleur f
pally ['pælɪ] ADJ (inf) copain (copine)
palm [pɑːm] N (Anat) paume f; (also: **palm tree**) palmier m; (leaf, symbol) palme f ▶ VT: **to ~ sth off on sb** (inf) refiler qch à qn
palmist ['pɑːmɪst] N chiromancien(ne)
Palm Sunday N le dimanche des Rameaux
palpable ['pælpəbl] ADJ évident(e), manifeste
palpitation [pælpɪ'teɪʃən] N palpitation f
paltry ['pɔːltrɪ] ADJ dérisoire; piètre
pamper ['pæmpəʳ] VT gâter, dorloter
pamphlet ['pæmflət] N brochure f; (political etc) tract m
★**pan** [pæn] N (also: **saucepan**) casserole f; (also: **frying pan**) poêle f; (of lavatory) cuvette f ▶ VI (Cine) faire un panoramique; **to ~ for gold** laver du sable aurifère ▶ VT (inf: book, film) éreinter
panacea [pænə'sɪə] N panacée f
panache [pə'næʃ] N panache m
Panama ['pænəmɑː] N Panama m
Panama Canal N canal m de Panama
pancake ['pænkeɪk] N crêpe f
Pancake Day N (BRIT) mardi gras
pancake roll N rouleau m de printemps
pancreas ['pæŋkrɪəs] N pancréas m
panda ['pændə] N panda m
panda car N (BRIT) ≈ voiture f pie inv
pandemic [pæn'dɛmɪk] N pandémie f
pandemonium [pændɪ'məunɪəm] N tohu-bohu m
pander ['pændəʳ] VI: **to ~ to** flatter bassement; obéir servilement à
p&h ABBR (US: = postage and handling) frais mpl de port
P&L ABBR = **profit and loss**
p&p ABBR (BRIT: = postage and packing) frais mpl de port
pane [peɪn] N carreau m (de fenêtre), vitre f
panel ['pænl] N (of wood, cloth etc) panneau m; (Radio, TV) panel m, invités mpl; (for interview, exams) jury m; (official: of experts) table ronde, comité m
panel game N (BRIT) jeu m (radiophonique/télévisé)

panelled, (US) **paneled** [ˈpænəld] ADJ lambrissé(e)

panelling, (US) **paneling** [ˈpænəlɪŋ] N boiseries fpl

panellist, (US) **panelist** [ˈpænəlɪst] N invité(e) (d'un panel), membre m d'un panel

pang [pæŋ] N: **pangs of remorse** pincements mpl de remords; **pangs of hunger/conscience** tiraillements mpl d'estomac/de la conscience

panhandler [ˈpænhændləʳ] N (US inf) mendiant(e)

★**panic** [ˈpænɪk] N panique f, affolement m ▶ VI s'affoler, paniquer

panic buying [-baɪɪŋ] N achats mpl de précaution

panicky [ˈpænɪkɪ] ADJ (person) qui panique or s'affole facilement

panic-stricken [ˈpænɪkstrɪkən] ADJ affolé(e)

panini [pæˈniːnɪ] N panini m

pannier [ˈpænɪəʳ] N (on animal) bât m; (on bicycle) sacoche f

panorama [pænəˈrɑːmə] N panorama m

panoramic [pænəˈræmɪk] ADJ panoramique

pansy [ˈpænzɪ] N (Bot) pensée f; (!) tapette f, pédé m

pant [pænt] VI haleter

pantechnicon [pænˈtɛknɪkən] N (BRIT) (grand) camion de déménagement

pantheon [ˈpænθɪən] N panthéon m

panther [ˈpænθəʳ] N panthère f

panties [ˈpæntɪz] NPL slip m, culotte f

pantihose [ˈpæntɪhəuz] N (US) collant m

panto [ˈpæntəu] N = **pantomime**

pantomime [ˈpæntəmaɪm] N (BRIT) spectacle m de Noël

Une **pantomime** (à ne pas confondre avec le mot dans son sens français), ou plus familièrement *panto*, est un genre de farce présenté dans les théâtres à la période de Noël. Le personnage principal est souvent un jeune garçon et il y a toujours une *dame*, c'est-à-dire une vieille femme jouée par un homme, ainsi qu'un méchant. La plupart du temps, l'histoire est basée sur un conte de fées comme Cendrillon ou Le Chat botté, et le public est encouragé à participer en prévenant le héros d'un danger imminent. Ce genre de spectacle, qui s'adresse surtout aux enfants, vise également un public d'adultes au travers des nombreuses plaisanteries faisant allusion à des faits d'actualité.

---

pantry [ˈpæntrɪ] N garde-manger m inv; (room) office m

pants [pænts] NPL (BRIT: woman's) culotte f, slip m; (: man's) slip, caleçon m; (US: trousers) pantalon m

pantsuit [ˈpæntsuːt] N (US) tailleur-pantalon m

pantyhose [ˈpæntɪhəuz] NPL (US) collant m

papacy [ˈpeɪpəsɪ] N papauté f

papal [ˈpeɪpəl] ADJ papal(e), pontifical(e)

paparazzi [pæpəˈrætsiː] NPL paparazzi mpl

papaya [pəˈpaɪə] N papaye f

★**paper** [ˈpeɪpəʳ] N papier m; (also: **wallpaper**) papier peint; (also: **newspaper**) journal m; (academic essay) article m; (exam) épreuve écrite; **a piece of ~**

(odd bit) un bout de papier; (sheet) une feuille de papier; **to put sth down on ~** mettre qch par écrit ▶ ADJ en or de papier ▶ VT tapisser (de papier peint) ■ **papers** NPL (also: **identity papers**) papiers mpl (d'identité)

paper advance N (on printer) avance f (du) papier

paperback [ˈpeɪpəbæk] N livre broché or non relié; (small) livre m de poche ▶ ADJ: **~ edition** édition brochée

paper bag N sac m en papier

paperboy [ˈpeɪpəbɔɪ] N (selling) vendeur m de journaux; (delivering) livreur m de journaux

paper clip N trombone m

paper handkerchief, paper hankie N (inf) mouchoir m en papier

paperless [ˈpeɪpəlɪs] ADJ: **the ~ office** le bureau sans papier; **~ trading** (Finance) les transactions fpl informatisées

paper mill N papeterie f

paper money N papier-monnaie m

paper profit N profit m théorique

paper shop N (BRIT) marchand m de journaux

paperweight [ˈpeɪpəweɪt] N presse-papiers m inv

paperwork [ˈpeɪpəwɔːk] N papiers mpl; (pej) paperasserie f

papier-mâché [ˈpæpɪeɪˈmæʃeɪ] N papier mâché m

paprika [ˈpæprɪkə] N paprika m

Pap test, Pap smear [ˈpæp-] N (Med) frottis m

Papua New Guinea N Papouasie-Nouvelle-Guinée f

par [pɑːʳ] N pair m; (Golf) normale f du parcours; **on a ~ with** à égalité avec, au même niveau que; **at ~** au pair; **above/below ~** au-dessus/au-dessous du pair; **to feel below** or **under** or **not up to ~** ne pas se sentir en forme

parable [ˈpærəbl] N parabole f (Rel)

parabola [pəˈræbələ] N parabole f (Math)

parabolic [pærəˈbɔlɪk] ADJ parabolique

paracetamol [pærəˈsiːtəmɔl] N (BRIT) paracétamol m

parachute [ˈpærəʃuːt] N parachute m ▶ VI sauter en parachute

parachute jump N saut m en parachute

parachutist [ˈpærəʃuːtɪst] N parachutiste mf

parade [pəˈreɪd] N défilé m; (inspection) revue f; (street) boulevard m; **a fashion ~** (BRIT) un défilé de mode ▶ VT (fig) faire étalage de ▶ VI défiler

parade ground N terrain m de manœuvre

paradise [ˈpærədaɪs] N paradis m

paradox [ˈpærədɔks] N paradoxe m

paradoxical [pærəˈdɔksɪkl] ADJ paradoxal(e)

paradoxically [pærəˈdɔksɪklɪ] ADV paradoxalement

paraffin [ˈpærəfɪn] N (BRIT): **~ (oil)** pétrole (lampant); **liquid ~** huile f de paraffine

paraffin heater N (BRIT) poêle m à mazout

paraffin lamp N (BRIT) lampe f à pétrole

paragliding [ˈpærəglaɪdɪŋ] N parapente m

paragon [ˈpærəgən] N parangon m

paragraph [ˈpærəgrɑːf] N paragraphe m; **to begin a new ~** aller à la ligne

p

Paraguay [ˈpærəgwaɪ] N Paraguay *m*

Paraguayan [pærəˈgwaɪən] ADJ paraguayen(ne) ▸ N Paraguayen(ne)

paralegal [pærəˈliːgl] N (US) technicien(ne) juridique

parallel [ˈpærəlɛl] ADJ: ~ **(with** *or* **to)** parallèle (à); (*fig*) analogue (à) ▸ N (*line*) parallèle *f*; (*fig, Geo*) parallèle *m*

paralyse, (US) **paralyze** [ˈpærəlaɪz] VT paralyser

paralysed, (US) **paralyzed** [ˈpærəlaɪzd] ADJ paralysé(e); ~ **with fear** paralysé par la peur

paralysis [pəˈrælɪsɪs] (*pl* **paralyses** [-siːz]) N paralysie *f*

paralytic [pærəˈlɪtɪk] ADJ paralytique; (BRIT *inf*: *drunk*) ivre mort(e)

paralyze [ˈpærəlaɪz] VT (US) = **paralyse**

paramedic [pærəˈmɛdɪk] N auxiliaire *mf* médical(e)

parameter [pəˈræmɪtəʳ] N paramètre *m*

paramilitary [pærəˈmɪlɪtərɪ] ADJ paramilitaire

paramount [ˈpærəmaunt] ADJ: **of ~ importance** de la plus haute *or* grande importance

paranoia [pærəˈnɔɪə] N paranoïa *f*

paranoid [ˈpærənɔɪd] ADJ (*Psych*) paranoïaque; (*neurotic*) paranoïde

paranormal [pærəˈnɔːml] ADJ paranormal(e)

parapet [ˈpærəpɪt] N parapet *m*; **to put one's head above the ~** (BRIT) se mouiller

paraphernalia [pærəfəˈneɪlɪə] N attirail *m*, affaires *fpl*

paraphrase [ˈpærəfreɪz] VT paraphraser

paraplegic [pærəˈpliːdʒɪk] N paraplégique *mf*

parapsychology [pærəsaɪˈkɒlədʒɪ] N parapsychologie *f*

parasite [ˈpærəsaɪt] N parasite *m*

parasitic, parasitical [pærəˈsɪtɪk(l)] ADJ (*disease*) parasitaire; (*organism, person*) parasite

parasol [ˈpærəsɒl] N ombrelle *f*; (*at café etc*) parasol *m*

parasport [ˈpærəspɔːt] N handisport *m*

paratrooper [ˈpærətruːpəʳ] N parachutiste *m* (*soldat*)

parboil [ˈpɑːbɔɪl] VT blanchir

parcel [ˈpɑːsl] N paquet *m*, colis *m* ▸ VT (*also:* **parcel up**) empaqueter
▸ **parcel out** VT répartir

parcel bomb N (BRIT) colis piégé

parcel post N service *m* de colis postaux

parch [pɑːtʃ] VT dessécher

parched [pɑːtʃt] ADJ (*person*) assoiffé(e)

parchment [ˈpɑːtʃmənt] N parchemin *m*

pardon [ˈpɑːdn] N pardon *m*; (*Law*) grâce *f*; **I beg your ~** je vous demande pardon; **~?** pardon? ▸ VT pardonner à; (*Law*) gracier; **~ me!** (*after burping etc*) excusez-moi!; **~ me?** (*what did you say?*) pardon?

pare [pɛəʳ] VT (BRIT: *nails*) couper; (*fruit etc*) peler; (*fig: costs etc*) réduire

★**parent** [ˈpɛərənt] N (*father*) père *m*; (*mother*) mère *f*
■ **parents** NPL parents *mpl*

parentage [ˈpɛərəntɪdʒ] N naissance *f*; **of unknown ~** de parents inconnus

parental [pəˈrɛntl] ADJ parental(e), des parents

parent company N société *f* mère

parenthesis [pəˈrɛnθɪsɪs] (*pl* **parentheses** [-siːz]) N parenthèse *f*; **in parentheses** entre parenthèses

parenthood [ˈpɛərənthud] N paternité *f* or maternité *f*

parenting [ˈpɛərəntɪŋ] N le métier de parent, le travail d'un parent

★**Paris** [ˈpærɪs] N Paris

parish [ˈpærɪʃ] N paroisse *f*; (BRIT: *civil*) ≈ commune *f* ▸ ADJ paroissial(e)

parish council N (BRIT) ≈ conseil municipal

parishioner [pəˈrɪʃənəʳ] N paroissien(ne)

★**Parisian** [pəˈrɪzɪən] ADJ parisien(ne), de Paris ▸ N Parisien(ne)

parity [ˈpærɪtɪ] N parité *f*

★**park** [pɑːk] N parc *m*, jardin public ▸ VT garer ▸ VI se garer; **can I ~ here?** est-ce que je peux me garer ici?

parka [ˈpɑːkə] N parka *m*

park and ride N parking-relais *m*

parking [ˈpɑːkɪŋ] N stationnement *m*; **"no ~"** «stationnement interdit»

parking lights NPL feux *mpl* de stationnement

parking lot N (US) parking *m*, parc *m* de stationnement

parking meter N parc(o)mètre *m*

parking offence, (US) **parking violation** N infraction *f* au stationnement

parking place N place *f* de stationnement

parking ticket N P.-V. *m*

Parkinson's [ˈpɑːkɪnsənz] N (*also:* **Parkinson's disease**) maladie *f* de Parkinson, parkinson *m*

park keeper N (BRIT) gardien(ne) de parc

parkland [ˈpɑːklænd] N espaces *mpl* verts

parkour [pɑːˈkuəʳ] N parkour *m*

parkway [ˈpɑːkweɪ] N (US) route *f* express (*en site vert ou aménagé*)

parlance [ˈpɑːləns] N: **in common/modern ~** dans le langage courant/actuel

★**parliament** [ˈpɑːləmənt] N parlement *m*

Le **Parliament** est l'assemblée législative britannique; elle est composée de deux chambres: la *House of Commons* et la *House of Lords*. Ses bureaux sont les *Houses of Parliament*, au palais de Westminster à Londres. Chaque *Parliament* est en général élu pour cinq ans. Ses débats sont retransmis à la télévision.

---

parliamentary [pɑːləˈmɛntərɪ] ADJ parlementaire

parlour, (US) **parlor** [ˈpɑːləʳ] N salon *m*

parlous [ˈpɑːləs] ADJ (*formal*) précaire

Parmesan [pɑːmɪˈzæn] N (*also:* **Parmesan cheese**) Parmesan *m*

parochial [pəˈrəukɪəl] ADJ paroissial(e); (*pej*) à l'esprit de clocher

parody [ˈpærədɪ] N parodie *f*

parole [pəˈrəul] N: **on ~** en liberté conditionnelle

paroxysm [ˈpærəksɪzəm] N (*Med, of grief*) paroxysme *m*; (*of anger*) accès *m*

parquet ['pɑːkeɪ] N: **~ floor(ing)** parquet m

parrot ['pærət] N perroquet m

parrot fashion ADV comme un perroquet

parry ['pærɪ] VT esquiver, parer à

parsimonious [pɑːsɪ'məʊnɪəs] ADJ parcimonieux(-euse)

parsley ['pɑːslɪ] N persil m

parsnip ['pɑːsnɪp] N panais m

parson ['pɑːsn] N ecclésiastique m; (Church of England) pasteur m

★**part** [pɑːt] N partie f; (of machine) pièce f; (Theat) rôle m; (Mus) voix f; partie; (of serial) épisode m; (US: in hair) raie f; **to take ~** in participer à, prendre part à; **to take sb's ~** prendre le parti de qn, prendre parti pour qn; **on his ~** de sa part; **for my ~** en ce qui me concerne; **for the most ~** en grande partie; dans la plupart des cas; **for the better ~ of the day** pendant la plus grande partie de la journée; **to be ~ and parcel of** faire partie de; **in ~** en partie; **to take sth in good/bad ~** prendre qch du bon/mauvais côté ▶ ADJ partiel(le) ▶ ADV = **partly** ▶ VT séparer ▶ VI (people) se séparer; (crowd) s'ouvrir; (roads) se diviser
▶ **part with** VT FUS (person) se séparer de; (possessions) se défaire de

> Use **partie** to mean section: the first part of the film **la première partie du film**. The word **part** means share or portion.

partake [pɑː'teɪk] VI (irreg: like **take**) (formal): **to ~ of sth** prendre part à qch, partager qch

part exchange N (BRIT): **in ~** en reprise

partial ['pɑːʃl] ADJ (incomplete) partiel(le); (unjust) partial(e); **to be ~ to** aimer, avoir un faible pour

partially ['pɑːʃəlɪ] ADV en partie, partiellement; partialement

participant [pɑː'tɪsɪpənt] N (in competition, campaign) participant(e)

participate [pɑː'tɪsɪpeɪt] VI: **to ~ (in)** participer (à), prendre part (à)

participation [pɑːtɪsɪ'peɪʃən] N participation f

participle ['pɑːtɪsɪpl] N participe m

particle ['pɑːtɪkl] N particule f; (of dust) grain m

particular [pə'tɪkjʊlə'] ADJ (specific) particulier(-ière); (special) particulier, spécial(e); (fussy) difficile, exigeant(e); (careful) méticuleux(-euse); **in ~** en particulier, surtout

particularly [pə'tɪkjʊləlɪ] ADV particulièrement; (in particular) en particulier

particulars [pə'tɪkjʊləz] NPL détails mpl; (information) renseignements mpl

parting ['pɑːtɪŋ] N séparation f; (BRIT: in hair) raie f ▶ ADJ d'adieu; **his ~ shot was ...** il lança en partant ....

partisan [pɑːtɪ'zæn] N partisan(e) ▶ ADJ partisan(e); de parti

partition [pɑː'tɪʃən] N (Pol) partition f, division f; (wall) cloison f

★**partly** ['pɑːtlɪ] ADV en partie, partiellement

★**partner** ['pɑːtnə'] N (Comm) associé(e); (Sport) partenaire mf; (spouse) conjoint(e); (lover) ami(e); (at dance) cavalier(-ière) ▶ VT être l'associé or le partenaire or le cavalier de

partnership ['pɑːtnəʃɪp] N association f; **to go into ~ (with), form a ~ (with)** s'associer (avec)

partook [pɑː'tʊk] PT of **partake**

part owner [pɑːt'əʊnə'] N copropriétaire mf

part payment N acompte m

partridge ['pɑːtrɪdʒ] N perdrix f

part-time ['pɑːt'taɪm] ADJ, ADV à mi-temps, à temps partiel

part-timer [pɑːt'taɪmə'] N (also: **part-time worker**) travailleur(-euse) à temps partiel

★**party** ['pɑːtɪ] N (Pol) parti m; (celebration) fête f; (: formal) réception f; (: in evening) soirée f; (team) équipe f; (group) groupe m; (Law) partie f; **dinner ~** dîner m; **to give** or **throw a ~** donner une réception; **we're having a ~ next Saturday** nous organisons une soirée or réunion entre amis samedi prochain; **it's for our son's birthday ~** c'est pour la fête (or le goûter) d'anniversaire de notre garçon; **to be a ~ to a crime** être impliqué(e) dans un crime

party dress N robe habillée

partygoer ['pɑːtɪgəʊə'] N (attendee) participant(e) à la fête; (party animal) fêtard(e)

party line N (Pol) ligne f politique; (Tel) ligne partagée

party piece N numéro habituel

party political broadcast N émission réservée à un parti politique.

★**pass** [pɑːs] VT (time, object) passer; (place) passer devant; (friend) croiser; (exam) être reçu(e) à, réussir; (candidate) admettre; (overtake) dépasser; (approve) approuver, accepter; (law) promulguer; **to ~ sb sth** passer qch à qn; **could you ~ the salt/oil, please?** pouvez-vous me passer le sel/l'huile, s'il vous plaît ?; **to ~ sth through a ring** etc (faire) passer qch dans un anneau etc; **could you ~ the vegetables round?** pourriez-vous faire passer les légumes ? ▶ VI passer; (Scol) être reçu(e) or admis(e), réussir; **she could ~ for 25** on lui donnerait 25 ans ▶ N (permit) laissez-passer m inv; (membership card) carte f d'accès or d'abonnement; (in mountains) col m; (Sport) passe f; (Scol): **to get a ~** être reçu(e) (sans mention); **things have come to a pretty ~** (BRIT) voilà où on en est !; **to make a ~ at sb** (inf) faire des avances à qn
▶ **pass away** VI mourir
▶ **pass back** VT (return: gen) rendre; (: benefits, savings) répercuter; (message) transmettre; (ball) repasser
▶ **pass by** VI passer ▶ VT (ignore) négliger
▶ **pass down** VT (customs, inheritance) transmettre
▶ **pass on** VI (die) s'éteindre, décéder ▶ VT (hand on): **to ~ on (to)** transmettre (à); (illness) passer (à); (price rises) répercuter (sur)
▶ **pass out** VI s'évanouir; (BRIT Mil) sortir (d'une école militaire)
▶ **pass over** VT (ignore) passer sous silence
▶ **pass up** VT (opportunity) laisser passer

> When talking about passing an exam use **être reçu à**.
> Eva passed the exam. **Eva a été reçue à l'examen.**
> **Passer un examen** means to take an exam.

passable ['pɑːsəbl] ADJ (road) praticable; (work) acceptable

passage ['pæsɪdʒ] N (also: **passageway**) couloir m; (gen, in book) passage m; (by boat) traversée f

passbook ['pɑːsbuk] N livret m

★**passenger** ['pæsɪndʒəʳ] N passager(-ère)

passer-by [pɑːsə'baɪ] N passant(e)

passing ['pɑːsɪŋ] ADJ (fig) passager(-ère); **in ~** en passant

passing place N (Aut) aire f de croisement

passion ['pæʃən] N passion f; **to have a ~ for sth** avoir la passion de qch

passionate ['pæʃənɪt] ADJ passionné(e)

passion fruit N fruit m de la passion

passion play N mystère m de la Passion

passive ['pæsɪv] ADJ (also: Ling) passif(-ive)

passive smoking N tabagisme passif

passkey ['pɑːskiː] N passe m

Passover ['pɑːsəuvəʳ] N Pâque juive

passport ['pɑːspɔːt] N passeport m

passport control N contrôle m des passeports

passport office N bureau m de délivrance des passeports

★**password** ['pɑːswəːd] N mot m de passe

★**past** [pɑːst] PREP (in front of) devant; (further than) au delà de, plus loin que; après; (later than) après; **he's ~ forty** il a dépassé la quarantaine, il a plus de or passé quarante ans; **ten/quarter ~ eight** (BRIT) huit heures dix/un or et quart; **it's ~ midnight** il est plus de minuit, il est passé minuit; **he ran ~ me** il m'a dépassé en courant, il a passé devant moi en courant; **I'm ~ caring** je ne m'en fais plus; **to be ~ it** (BRIT inf: person) avoir passé l'âge ▸ ADV: **to run ~** passer en courant ▸ ADJ passé(e); (president etc) ancien(ne); **for the ~ few/3 days** depuis quelques/3 jours; ces derniers/3 derniers jours ▸ N passé m; **in the ~** (gen) dans le temps, autrefois; (Ling) au passé

★**pasta** ['pæstə] N pâtes fpl

paste [peɪst] N pâte f; (Culin: meat) pâté m (à tartiner); (: tomato) purée f, concentré m; (glue) colle f (de pâte); (jewellery) strass m ▸ VT coller

pastel ['pæstl] ADJ pastel inv ▸ N (Art: pencil) (crayon m) pastel m; (: drawing) (dessin m au) pastel; (colour) ton m pastel inv

pasteurized ['pæstəraɪzd] ADJ pasteurisé(e)

pastiche [pæ'stiːʃ] N pastiche m

pastille ['pæstl] N pastille f

pastime ['pɑːstaɪm] N passe-temps m inv, distraction f

past master N (BRIT): **to be a ~ at** être expert en

pastor ['pɑːstəʳ] N pasteur m

pastoral ['pɑːstərl] ADJ pastoral(e)

pastry ['peɪstrɪ] N pâte f; (cake) pâtisserie f

pasture ['pɑːstʃəʳ] N pâturage m

pasty¹ ['pæstɪ] N petit pâté (en croûte)

pasty² ['peɪstɪ] ADJ pâteux(-euse); (complexion) terreux(-euse)

pat [pæt] VT donner une petite tape à; (dog) caresser ▸ N: **a ~ of butter** une noisette de beurre; **to give sb/o.s. a ~ on the back** (fig) congratuler qn/se congratuler ▸ ADV: **he knows it (off) ~**, (US) **he has it down ~** il sait cela sur le bout des doigts

patch [pætʃ] N (of material) pièce f; (eye patch) cache m; (spot) tache f; (of land) parcelle f; (on tyre) rustine f; **a bad ~** (BRIT) une période difficile ▸ VT (clothes) rapiécer
▸ **patch up** VT réparer

patchwork ['pætʃwəːk] N patchwork m

patchy ['pætʃɪ] ADJ inégal(e); (incomplete) fragmentaire

★**pate** [peɪt] N: **a bald ~** un crâne chauve or dégarni

★**pâté** ['pæteɪ] N pâté m, terrine f

patent ['peɪtnt, (US) 'pætnt] N brevet m (d'invention) ▸ VT faire breveter ▸ ADJ patent(e), manifeste

patent leather N cuir verni

patently ['peɪtntlɪ] ADV manifestement

patent medicine N spécialité f pharmaceutique

patent office N bureau m des brevets

paternal [pə'təːnl] ADJ paternel(le)

paternalistic [pətəːnə'lɪstɪk] ADJ paternaliste

paternity [pə'təːnɪtɪ] N paternité f

paternity leave N congé m de paternité

paternity suit N (Law) action f en recherche de paternité

★**path** [pɑːθ] N chemin m, sentier m; (in garden) allée f; (of planet) course f; (of missile) trajectoire f

pathetic [pə'θetɪk] ADJ (pitiful) pitoyable; (very bad) lamentable, minable; (moving) pathétique

pathological [pæθə'lɔdʒɪkl] ADJ pathologique

pathologist [pə'θɔlədʒɪst] N pathologiste mf

pathology [pə'θɔlədʒɪ] N pathologie f

pathos ['peɪθɔs] N pathétique m

pathway ['pɑːθweɪ] N chemin m, sentier m; (in garden) allée f

patience ['peɪʃns] N patience f; (BRIT Cards) réussite f; **to lose (one's) ~** perdre patience

★**patient** ['peɪʃnt] N malade mf; (of dentist etc) patient(e) ▸ ADJ patient(e)

patiently ['peɪʃntlɪ] ADV patiemment

patio ['pætɪəu] N patio m

patriot ['peɪtrɪət] N patriote mf

patriotic [pætrɪ'ɔtɪk] ADJ patriotique; (person) patriote

patriotism ['pætrɪətɪzəm] N patriotisme m

patrol [pə'trəul] N patrouille f; **to be on ~** être de patrouille ▸ VT patrouiller dans

patrol boat N patrouilleur m

patrol car N voiture f de police

patrolman [pə'trəulmən] N (irreg) (US) agent m de police

patron ['peɪtrən] N (in shop) client(e); (of charity) patron(ne); **~ of the arts** mécène m

patronage ['pætrənɪdʒ] N patronage m, appui m

patronize ['pætrənaɪz] VT être (un) client or un habitué de; (fig) traiter avec condescendance

patronizing ['pætrənaɪzɪŋ] ADJ condescendant(e)

patron saint N saint(e) patron(ne)

patsy ['pætsɪ] N (US inf) pigeon m

patter ['pætəʳ] N crépitement m, tapotement m; (sales talk) boniment m ▸ VI crépiter, tapoter

★**pattern** ['pætən] N modèle m; (Sewing) patron m; (design) motif m; (sample) échantillon m; **behaviour ~** mode m de comportement

patterned ['pætənd] ADJ à motifs

paucity ['pɔːsɪtɪ] N pénurie f, carence f

paunch [pɔːntʃ] N gros ventre, bedaine f

pauper ['pɔːpəʳ] N indigent(e); **~'s grave** fosse commune

★**pause** [pɔːz] N pause f, arrêt m; (Mus) silence m ▸ VI faire une pause, s'arrêter; **to ~ for breath** reprendre son souffle; (fig) faire une pause

pave [peɪv] VT paver, daller; **to ~ the way for** ouvrir la voie à

pavement ['peɪvmənt] N (BRIT) trottoir m; (US) chaussée f

pavilion [pə'vɪlɪən] N pavillon m; tente f; (Sport) stand m

paving ['peɪvɪŋ] N (material) pavé m, dalle f; (area) pavage m, dallage m

paving stone N pavé m

paw [pɔː] N patte f ▸ VT donner un coup de patte à; (person: pej) tripoter

pawn [pɔːn] N gage m; (Chess, also fig) pion m ▸ VT mettre en gage

pawnbroker ['pɔːnbrəʊkəʳ] N prêteur m sur gages

pawnshop ['pɔːnʃɔp] N mont-de-piété m

★**pay** [peɪ] (pt, pp **paid** [peɪd]) N salaire m; (of manual worker) paie f ▸ VT payer; (be profitable to, also fig) rapporter à; **how much did you ~ for it?** combien l'avez-vous payé?, vous l'avez payé combien?; **I paid £5 for that ticket** j'ai payé ce billet 5 livres; **to ~ one's way** payer sa part; (company) couvrir ses frais; **to ~ dividends** (fig) porter ses fruits, s'avérer rentable; **it won't ~ you to do that** vous ne gagnerez rien à faire cela; **to ~ attention (to)** prêter attention (à); **to ~ sb a visit** rendre visite à qn; **to ~ one's respects to sb** présenter ses respects à qn ▸ VI payer; (be profitable) être rentable; **can I ~ by credit card?** est-ce que je peux payer par carte de crédit?
  ▸ **pay back** VT rembourser
  ▸ **pay for** VT FUS payer
  ▸ **pay in** VT verser
  ▸ **pay off** VT (debts) régler, acquitter; (person) rembourser; (workers) licencier; **to ~ sth off in instalments** payer qch à tempérament ▸ VI (scheme, decision) se révéler payant(e)
  ▸ **pay out** VT (money) payer, sortir de sa poche; (rope) laisser filer
  ▸ **pay up** VT (debts) régler; (amount) payer

> When talking about paying for something no preposition is used in French to translate for.
> I pay for gas and electricity. **Je paie le gaz et l'électricité.**

payable ['peɪəbl] ADJ payable; **to make a cheque ~ to sb** établir un chèque à l'ordre de qn

pay-as-you-go [peɪəzjə'gəʊ] ADJ (mobile phone) à carte prépayée

pay award N augmentation f

payback ['peɪbæk] N (from investment) bénéfice m; (from action) avantage m

payday ['peɪdeɪ] N jour m de paie; **~ loan** (BRIT Finance) prêt personnel de courte durée et d'un montant peu important, dont le taux d'intérêt est très élevé

PAYE N ABBR (BRIT: = pay as you earn) système de retenue des impôts à la source

payee [peɪ'iː] N bénéficiaire mf

pay envelope N (US) paie f

paying ['peɪɪŋ] ADJ payant(e); **~ guest** hôte payant

payload ['peɪləʊd] N charge f utile

★**payment** ['peɪmənt] N paiement m; (of bill) règlement m; (of deposit, cheque) versement m; **advance ~** (part sum) acompte m; (total sum) paiement anticipé; **deferred ~, ~ by instalments** paiement par versements échelonnés; **monthly ~** mensualité f; **in ~ for, in ~ of** en règlement de; **on ~ of £5** pour 5 livres

payoff ['peɪɔf] N (benefit) avantage m; (sweetener) pot-de-vin m; (to employee) grosse prime f de départ; **the ~ from sth** l'avantage de qch

payout ['peɪaʊt] N (from insurance) dédommagement m; (in competition) prix m

pay packet N (BRIT) paie f

pay phone N cabine f téléphonique, téléphone public

pay raise N (US) = **pay rise**

pay rise N (BRIT) augmentation f (de salaire)

payroll ['peɪrəʊl] N registre m du personnel; **to be on a firm's ~** être employé par une entreprise

pay slip N (BRIT) bulletin m de paie, feuille f de paie

pay station N (US) cabine f téléphonique

pay television N chaînes fpl payantes

paywall ['peɪwɔːl] N (Comput) mur m (payant)

PBS N ABBR (US: = Public Broadcasting Service) groupement d'aide à la réalisation d'émissions pour la TV publique

PBX N ABBR (BRIT: = private branch exchange) PBX m, commutateur m privé

★**PC** N ABBR = **personal computer**; (BRIT) = **police constable** ▸ ADJ ABBR = **politically correct** ▸ ABBR (BRIT) = **Privy Councillor**

★**p.c.** ABBR = **per cent; postcard**

p/c ABBR = **petty cash**

PCB N ABBR = **printed circuit board**

pcm N ABBR (= per calendar month) par mois

PD N ABBR (US) = **police department**

pd ABBR = **paid**

PDA N ABBR (= personal digital assistant) agenda m électronique

PDF, pdf N ABBR (Comput: = Portable Document Format) pdf m

PDQ N ABBR = **pretty damn quick**

PDSA N ABBR (BRIT) = **People's Dispensary for Sick Animals**

PDT ABBR (US: = Pacific Daylight Time) heure d'été du Pacifique

★**pea** [piː] N (petit) pois

★**peace** [piːs] N paix f; (calm) calme m, tranquillité f; **to be at ~ with sb/sth** être en paix avec qn/qch; **to keep the ~** (policeman) assurer le maintien de l'ordre; (citizen) ne pas troubler l'ordre

peaceable ['piːsəbl] ADJ paisible, pacifique

★**peaceful** ['piːsful] ADJ (place, time, person) paisible, calme; (protest, demo) pacifique

peacefully ['piːsfulɪ] ADV (sleep, die) paisiblement; (resolve) de manière pacifique; (pass off) dans le calme; **to live ~ with sb** vivre en paix avec qn

peacekeeper ['piːskiːpəʳ] N (*force*) force gardienne de la paix

peacekeeping ['piːskiːpɪŋ] N maintien *m* de la paix

peacekeeping force N forces *fpl* qui assurent le maintien de la paix

peacemaker ['piːsmeɪkəʳ] N conciliateur(-trice); **to act as a ~** jouer un rôle de conciliateur

peace offering N gage *m* de réconciliation; (*humorous*) gage de paix

peacetime ['piːstaɪm] N: **in** *or* **during ~** en temps de paix

★**peach** [piːtʃ] N pêche *f*

peacock ['piːkɔk] N paon *m*

peak [piːk] N (*mountain*) pic *m*, cime *f*; (*of cap*) visière *f*; (*fig: highest level*) maximum *m*; (: *of career, fame*) apogée *m*

peaked [piːkt] ADJ (*cap*) à visière

peak-hour ['piːkauəʳ] ADJ (*traffic etc*) de pointe

peak hours NPL heures *fpl* d'affluence *or* de pointe

peak period N période *f* de pointe

peak rate N plein tarif

peaky ['piːkɪ] ADJ (*BRIT inf*) fatigué(e)

peal [piːl] N (*of bells*) carillon *m*; **peals of laughter** éclats *mpl* de rire

★**peanut** ['piːnʌt] N arachide *f*, cacahuète *f*

peanut butter N beurre *m* de cacahuète

★**pear** [pɛəʳ] N poire *f*

pearl [pəːl] N perle *f*

peasant ['pɛznt] N paysan(ne)

peat [piːt] N tourbe *f*

pebble ['pɛbl] N galet *m*, caillou *m*

peck [pɛk] VT (*also*: **peck at**) donner un coup de bec à; (: *food*) picorer ▶ N coup *m* de bec; (*kiss*) bécot *m*

pecking order ['pɛkɪŋ-] N ordre *m* hiérarchique

peckish ['pɛkɪʃ] ADJ (*BRIT inf*): **I feel ~** je mangerais bien quelque chose, j'ai la dent

pecs [pɛks] NPL (*inf*) pectoraux *mpl*

peculiar [pɪ'kjuːlɪəʳ] ADJ (*odd*) étrange, bizarre, curieux(-euse); (*particular*) particulier(-ière); **~ to** particulier à

peculiarity [pɪkjuːlɪ'ærɪtɪ] N bizarrerie *f*; particularité *f*

pecuniary [pɪ'kjuːnɪərɪ] ADJ pécuniaire

pedagogical [pɛdə'gɔdʒɪkl] ADJ pédagogique

pedal ['pɛdl] N pédale *f* ▶ VI pédaler

pedal bin N (*BRIT*) poubelle *f* à pédale

pedantic [pɪ'dæntɪk] ADJ pédant(e)

peddle ['pɛdl] VT colporter; (*drugs*) faire le trafic de

peddler ['pɛdləʳ] N colporteur *m*; camelot *m*

pedestal ['pɛdəstl] N piédestal *m*

pedestrian [pɪ'dɛstrɪən] N piéton *m* ▶ ADJ piétonnier(-ière); (*fig*) prosaïque, terre à terre *inv*

pedestrian crossing N (*BRIT*) passage clouté

pedestrianized [pɪ'dɛstrɪənaɪzd] ADJ: **a ~ street** une rue piétonne

pedestrian precinct, (*US*) **pedestrian zone** N (*BRIT*) zone piétonne

pediatrics [piːdɪ'ætrɪks] N (*US*) = **paediatrics**

pedicure ['pɛdɪkjuəʳ] N soins *mpl* des pieds; **to have a ~** se faire soigner les pieds

pedigree ['pɛdɪgriː] N ascendance *f*; (*of animal*) pedigree *m* ▶ CPD (*animal*) de race

pedlar ['pɛdləʳ] N = **peddler**

pedophile ['piːdəufaɪl] N (*US*) = **paedophile**

pee [piː] VI (*inf*) faire pipi, pisser

peek [piːk] VI jeter un coup d'œil (furtif)

peel [piːl] N pelure *f*, épluchure *f*; (*of orange, lemon*) écorce *f* ▶ VT peler, éplucher; (*paint etc*) s'écailler; (*wallpaper*) se décoller; (*skin*) peler
  ▶ **peel back** VT décoller
  ▶ **peel off** VT (*sticker, label*) décoller

peeler ['piːləʳ] N (*potato etc peeler*) éplucheur *m*

peelings ['piːlɪŋz] NPL pelures *fpl*, épluchures *fpl*

peep [piːp] N (*look*) coup d'œil furtif; (*sound*) pépiement *m* ▶ VI jeter un coup d'œil (furtif)
  ▶ **peep out** VI se montrer (furtivement)

peephole ['piːphəul] N judas *m*

peeps [piːps] NPL (*inf*) copains *mpl*; **hey ~, what's up?** salut la compagnie, ça roule?

peer [pɪəʳ] VI: **to ~ at** regarder attentivement, scruter ▶ N (*noble*) pair *m*; (*equal*) pair, égal(e)

peerage ['pɪərɪdʒ] N pairie *f*

peerless ['pɪəlɪs] ADJ incomparable, sans égal

peer pressure N (*also*: **peer group pressure**) influence *f* de l'entourage

peeved [piːvd] ADJ irrité(e), ennuyé(e)

peevish ['piːvɪʃ] ADJ grincheux(-euse), maussade

★**peg** [pɛg] N cheville *f*; (*for coat etc*) patère *f*; (*BRIT: also*: **clothes peg**) pince *f* à linge ▶ VT (*clothes*) accrocher; (*BRIT: groundsheet*) fixer (avec des piquets); (*fig: prices, wages*) contrôler, stabiliser

PEI ABBR (*CANADA*) = **Prince Edward Island**

pejorative [pɪ'dʒɔrətɪv] ADJ péjoratif(-ive)

Pekin [piː'kɪn], **Peking** [piː'kɪŋ] N Pékin

Pekinese, Pekingese [piːkɪ'niːz] N pékinois *m*

pelican ['pɛlɪkən] N pélican *m*

pelican crossing N (*BRIT Aut*) feu *m* à commande manuelle

pellet ['pɛlɪt] N boulette *f*; (*of lead*) plomb *m*

pell-mell ['pɛl'mɛl] ADV pêle-mêle

pelmet ['pɛlmɪt] N cantonnière *f*; lambrequin *m*

pelt [pɛlt] VT: **to ~ sb (with)** bombarder qn (de) ▶ VI (*inf: rain*) tomber à seaux; (: *run*) courir à toutes jambes ▶ N peau *f*
  ▶ **pelt down** VI (*inf: rain*) tomber à seaux; **it's pelting down** il tombe des cordes

pelvic ['pɛlvɪk] ADJ pelvien(ne)

pelvis ['pɛlvɪs] N bassin *m*

★**pen** [pɛn] N (*for writing*) stylo *m*; (*for sheep*) parc *m*; (*US inf: prison*) taule *f*; **to put ~ to paper** prendre la plume

penal ['piːnl] ADJ pénal(e)

penalize ['piːnəlaɪz] VT pénaliser; (*fig*) désavantager

penal servitude [-'səːvɪtjuːd] N travaux forcés

★**penalty** ['pɛnltɪ] N pénalité *f*; sanction *f*; (*fine*) amende *f*; (*Sport*) pénalisation *f*; (*also*: **penalty kick**: *Football*) penalty *m*; (: *Rugby*) pénalité *f*; **to pay the ~ for** être pénalisé(e) pour

penalty area, penalty box N (BRIT Sport) surface f de réparation

penalty clause N clause pénale

penalty kick N (Football) penalty m

penalty shoot-out [-'ʃuːtaut] N (Football) épreuve f des penalties

penance ['pɛnəns] N pénitence f

pence [pɛns] NPL of **penny**

penchant ['pãːʃãŋ] N penchant m

★**pencil** ['pɛnsl] N crayon m
  ▶ **pencil in** VT noter provisoirement

pencil case N trousse f (d'écolier)

pencil sharpener N taille-crayon(s) m inv

pendant ['pɛndnt] N pendentif m

pending ['pɛndɪŋ] PREP en attendant ▶ ADJ en suspens

pendulum ['pɛndjuləm] N pendule m; (of clock) balancier m

penetrate ['pɛnɪtreɪt] VT pénétrer dans; (enemy territory) entrer en; (sexually) pénétrer

penetrating ['pɛnɪtreɪtɪŋ] ADJ pénétrant(e)

penetration [pɛnɪ'treɪʃən] N pénétration f

pen friend N (BRIT) correspondant(e)

penguin ['pɛŋgwɪn] N pingouin m

penicillin [pɛnɪ'sɪlɪn] N pénicilline f

peninsula [pə'nɪnsjulə] N péninsule f

penis ['piːnɪs] N pénis m, verge f

penitence ['pɛnɪtns] N repentir m

penitent ['pɛnɪtnt] ADJ repentant(e)

penitentiary [pɛnɪ'tɛnʃərɪ] N (US) prison f

penknife ['pɛnnaɪf] N canif m

pen name N nom m de plume, pseudonyme m

pennant ['pɛnənt] N flamme f, banderole f

penniless ['pɛnɪlɪs] ADJ sans le sou

Pennines ['pɛnaɪnz] NPL: **the ~** les Pennines fpl

★**penny** ['pɛnɪ] (pl **pennies** ['pɛnɪz] or **pence** [pɛns]) N (BRIT) penny m; (US) cent m

pen pal N correspondant(e)

penpusher ['pɛnpuʃəʳ] N (pej) gratte-papier m inv

★**pension** ['pɛnʃən] N (from company) retraite f; (Mil) pension f
  ▶ **pension off** VT mettre à la retraite

pensionable ['pɛnʃnəbl] ADJ qui a droit à une retraite

pensioner ['pɛnʃənəʳ] N (BRIT) retraité(e)

pension fund N caisse f de retraite

pension plan N plan m de retraite

pensive ['pɛnsɪv] ADJ pensif(-ive)

pentagon ['pɛntəgən] N pentagone m; **the P~** (US Pol) le Pentagone

pentathlon [pɛn'tæθlən] N pentathlon m

Pentecost ['pɛntɪkɔst] N Pentecôte f

penthouse ['pɛnthaus] N appartement m (de luxe) en attique

pent-up ['pɛntʌp] ADJ (feelings) refoulé(e)

penultimate [pɪ'nʌltɪmət] ADJ pénultième, avant-dernier(-ière)

penury ['pɛnjurɪ] N misère f

peony ['piːənɪ] N pivoine f

★**people** ['piːpl] NPL gens mpl; personnes fpl; (inhabitants) population f; (Pol) peuple m; **I know ~ who ...** je connais des gens qui ...; **the room was full of ~** la salle était pleine de monde or de gens; **several ~ came** plusieurs personnes sont venues; **~ say that ...** on dit or les gens disent que ...; **old ~** les personnes âgées; **young ~** les jeunes ▶ N (nation, race) peuple m; **a man of the ~** un homme du peuple ▶ VT peupler

pep [pɛp] N (inf) entrain m, dynamisme m
  ▶ **pep up** VT (inf) remonter

★**pepper** ['pɛpəʳ] N poivre m; (vegetable) poivron m
  ▶ VT (Culin) poivrer

pepper mill N moulin m à poivre

peppermint ['pɛpəmɪnt] N (plant) menthe poivrée; (sweet) pastille f de menthe

pepperoni [pɛpə'rəunɪ] N saucisson sec de porc et de bœuf très poivré.

pepperpot ['pɛpəpɔt] N poivrière f

pep talk N (inf) (petit) discours d'encouragement

★**per** [pəʳ] PREP par; **~ hour** (miles etc) à l'heure; (fee) (de) l'heure; **~ kilo** etc le kilo etc; **~ day/person** par jour/personne; **~ annum** par an; **as ~ your instructions** conformément à vos instructions

per annum ADV par an

per capita ADJ, ADV par habitant, par personne

perceive [pə'siːv] VT percevoir; (notice) remarquer, s'apercevoir de

★**per cent** ADV pour cent; **a 20 ~ discount** une réduction de 20 pour cent

★**percentage** [pə'sɛntɪdʒ] N pourcentage m; **on a ~ basis** au pourcentage

percentage point N: **ten ~s** dix pour cent

perceptible [pə'sɛptɪbl] ADJ perceptible

perception [pə'sɛpʃən] N perception f; (insight) sensibilité f

perceptive [pə'sɛptɪv] ADJ (remark, person) perspicace

perch [pəːtʃ] N (fish) perche f; (for bird) perchoir m
  ▶ VI (se) percher

percolate ['pəːkəleɪt] VT, VI passer

percolator ['pəːkəleɪtəʳ] N percolateur m; cafetière f électrique

percussion [pə'kʌʃən] N percussion f

peremptory [pə'rɛmptərɪ] ADJ péremptoire

perennial [pə'rɛnɪəl] ADJ perpétuel(le); (Bot) vivace
  ▶ N (Bot) (plante f) vivace f, plante pluriannuelle

★**perfect** ADJ ['pəːfɪkt] parfait(e); **he's a ~ stranger to me** il m'est totalement inconnu ▶ N ['pəːfɪkt] (also: **perfect tense**) parfait m ▶ VT [pə'fɛkt] (technique, skill, work of art) parfaire; (method, plan) mettre au point

perfection [pə'fɛkʃən] N perfection f

perfectionist [pə'fɛkʃənɪst] N perfectionniste mf

★**perfectly** ['pəːfɪktlɪ] ADV parfaitement; **I'm ~ happy with the situation** cette situation me convient parfaitement; **you know ~ well** vous le savez très bien

perforate ['pəːfəreɪt] VT perforer, percer

perforated ulcer ['pəːfəreɪtɪd-] N (Med) ulcère perforé

perforation [pəːfə'reɪʃən] N perforation f; (line of holes) pointillé m

★**perform** [pə'fɔ:m] ᴠᴛ (carry out) exécuter, remplir; (concert etc) jouer, donner ▸ ᴠɪ (actor, musician) jouer; (machine, car) marcher, fonctionner; (company, economy): **to ~ well/badly** produire de bons/mauvais résultats

★**performance** [pə'fɔ:məns] ɴ représentation f, spectacle m; (of an artist) interprétation f; (Sport: of car, engine) performance f; (of company, economy) résultats mpl; **the team put up a good ~** l'équipe a bien joué

performer [pə'fɔ:mə**ʳ**] ɴ artiste mf

performing [pə'fɔ:mɪŋ] ᴀᴅᴊ (animal) savant(e)

performing arts ɴᴘʟ: **the ~** les arts mpl du spectacle

perfume ['pə:fju:m] ɴ parfum m ▸ ᴠᴛ parfumer

perfunctory [pə'fʌŋktərɪ] ᴀᴅᴊ négligent(e), pour la forme

★**perhaps** [pə'hæps] ᴀᴅᴠ peut-être; **~ he'll ...** peut-être qu'il ...; **~ so/not** peut-être que oui/que non

peril ['pɛrɪl] ɴ péril m

perilous ['pɛrɪləs] ᴀᴅᴊ périlleux(-euse)

perilously ['pɛrɪləslɪ] ᴀᴅᴠ: **they came ~ close to being caught** ils ont été à deux doigts de se faire prendre

perimeter [pə'rɪmɪtə**ʳ**] ɴ périmètre m

perimeter wall ɴ mur m d'enceinte

★**period** ['pɪərɪəd] ɴ période f; (Hist) époque f; (Scol) cours m; (full stop) point m; (Med) règles fpl; **for a ~ of three weeks** pour (une période de) trois semaines; **the holiday ~** (ʙʀɪᴛ) la période des vacances ▸ ᴀᴅᴊ (costume, furniture) d'époque

periodic [pɪərɪ'ɔdɪk] ᴀᴅᴊ périodique

periodical [pɪərɪ'ɔdɪkl] ᴀᴅᴊ périodique ▸ ɴ périodique m

periodically [pɪərɪ'ɔdɪklɪ] ᴀᴅᴠ périodiquement

period pains ɴᴘʟ (ʙʀɪᴛ) douleurs menstruelles

peripatetic [pɛrɪpə'tɛtɪk] ᴀᴅᴊ (salesman) ambulant; (ʙʀɪᴛ: teacher) qui travaille dans plusieurs établissements

peripheral [pə'rɪfərəl] ᴀᴅᴊ périphérique ▸ ɴ (Comput) périphérique m

periphery [pə'rɪfərɪ] ɴ périphérie f

periscope ['pɛrɪskəup] ɴ périscope m

perish ['pɛrɪʃ] ᴠɪ périr, mourir; (decay) se détériorer

perishable ['pɛrɪʃəbl] ᴀᴅᴊ périssable

perishables ['pɛrɪʃəblz] ɴᴘʟ denrées fpl périssables

perishing ['pɛrɪʃɪŋ] ᴀᴅᴊ (ʙʀɪᴛ inf: cold) glacial(e)

peritonitis [pɛrɪtə'naɪtɪs] ɴ péritonite f

perjure ['pə:dʒə**ʳ**] ᴠᴛ: **to ~ o.s.** se parjurer

perjury ['pə:dʒərɪ] ɴ (Law: in court) faux témoignage; (breach of oath) parjure m

perk [pə:k] ɴ (inf) avantage m, à-côté m
▸ **perk up** ᴠɪ (inf: cheer up) se ragaillardir

perky ['pə:kɪ] ᴀᴅᴊ (cheerful) guilleret(te), gai(e)

perm [pə:m] ɴ (for hair) permanente f ▸ ᴠᴛ: **to have one's hair permed** se faire faire une permanente

permanence ['pə:mənəns] ɴ permanence f

★**permanent** ['pə:mənənt] ᴀᴅᴊ permanent(e); (job, position) permanent, fixe; (dye, ink) indélébile;

I'm not ~ **here** je ne suis pas ici à titre définitif; ~ **address** adresse habituelle

permanently ['pə:mənəntlɪ] ᴀᴅᴠ de façon permanente; (move abroad) définitivement; (open, closed) en permanence; (tired, unhappy) constamment

permeable ['pə:mɪəbl] ᴀᴅᴊ perméable

permeate ['pə:mɪeɪt] ᴠɪ s'infiltrer ▸ ᴠᴛ s'infiltrer dans; pénétrer

permissible [pə'mɪsɪbl] ᴀᴅᴊ permis(e), acceptable

★**permission** [pə'mɪʃən] ɴ permission f, autorisation f; **to give sb ~ to do sth** donner à qn la permission de faire qch

permissive [pə'mɪsɪv] ᴀᴅᴊ tolérant(e); **the ~ society** la société de tolérance

★**permit** ɴ [pə'mɪt] permis m; (entrance pass) autorisation f, laissez-passer m; (for goods) licence f ▸ ᴠᴛ [pə'mɪt] permettre; **to ~ sb to do** autoriser qn à faire, permettre à qn de faire ▸ ᴠɪ [pə'mɪt]: **weather permitting** si le temps le permet

permutation [pə:mju'teɪʃən] ɴ permutation f

pernicious [pə:'nɪʃəs] ᴀᴅᴊ pernicieux(-euse), nocif(-ive)

pernickety [pə'nɪkɪtɪ] ᴀᴅᴊ (inf) pointilleux(-euse), tatillon(ne); (task) minutieux(-euse)

peroxide [pə'rɔksaɪd] ɴ eau f oxygénée

perpendicular [pə:pən'dɪkjulə**ʳ**] ᴀᴅᴊ, ɴ perpendiculaire f

perpetrate ['pə:pɪtreɪt] ᴠᴛ perpétrer, commettre

perpetrator ['pə:pɪtreɪtə**ʳ**] ɴ (of crime) auteur m

perpetual [pə'pɛtjuəl] ᴀᴅᴊ perpétuel(le)

perpetuate [pə'pɛtjueɪt] ᴠᴛ perpétuer

perpetuity [pə:pɪ'tju:ɪtɪ] ɴ: **in ~** à perpétuité

perplex [pə'plɛks] ᴠᴛ (person) rendre perplexe

perplexed [pə'plɛkst] ᴀᴅᴊ perplexe; **to be ~ about sth** être perplexe quant à qch

perplexing [pə'plɛksɪŋ] ᴀᴅᴊ embarrassant(e)

perquisites ['pə:kwɪzɪts] ɴᴘʟ (also: **perks**) avantages mpl annexes

persecute ['pə:sɪkju:t] ᴠᴛ persécuter

persecution [pə:sɪ'kju:ʃən] ɴ persécution f

perseverance [pə:sɪ'vɪərns] ɴ persévérance f, ténacité f

persevere [pə:sɪ'vɪə**ʳ**] ᴠɪ persévérer

Persia ['pə:ʃə] ɴ Perse f

Persian ['pə:ʃən] ᴀᴅᴊ persan(e); **the ~ Gulf** le golfe Persique ▸ ɴ (Ling) persan m

Persian cat ɴ chat persan

persist [pə'sɪst] ᴠɪ: **to ~ (in doing)** persister (à faire), s'obstiner (à faire)

persistence [pə'sɪstəns] ɴ persistance f, obstination f; opiniâtreté f

persistent [pə'sɪstənt] ᴀᴅᴊ (headache, cough) persistant(e), tenace; (noise, rain, problem) persistant(e); (person) persévérant(e); **~ offender** (Law) multirécidiviste mf

persistently [pə'sɪstəntlɪ] ᴀᴅᴠ (with determination) avec persévérance; (unfailingly: high) invariablement; **to be ~ late** persister à être en retard

persnickety [pə'snɪkɪtɪ] ᴀᴅᴊ (US inf) = **pernickety**

★**person** ['pə:sn] N personne *f*; **in ~** en personne; **on** *or* **about one's ~** sur soi; **~ to ~ call** (*Tel*) appel *m* avec préavis

persona [pə'səunə] N (*image*) personnage *m*; **public ~** personne publique

personable ['pə:snəbl] ADJ de belle prestance, au physique attrayant

★**personal** ['pə:snl] ADJ personnel(le); **~ belongings, ~ effects** effets personnels; **~ hygiene** hygiène *f* intime; **a ~ interview** un entretien

personal allowance N (*Tax*) part *f* du revenu non imposable

personal assistant N secrétaire personnel(le)

personal call N (*Tel*) communication *f* avec préavis

personal column N annonces personnelles

personal computer N ordinateur individuel, PC *m*

personal details NPL (*on form etc*) coordonnées *fpl*

personal identification number N (*Comput, Banking*) numéro *m* d'identification personnel

★**personality** [pə:sə'nælɪtɪ] N personnalité *f*

personalize ['pə:sənəlaɪz] VT personnaliser

★**personally** ['pə:snlɪ] ADV personnellement; **to take sth ~** se sentir visé(e) par qch

personal organizer N agenda (personnel); (*electronic*) agenda électronique

personal property N biens personnels

personal stereo N Walkman® *m*, baladeur *m*

personify [pə:'sɔnɪfaɪ] VT personnifier

personnel [pə:sə'nɛl] N personnel *m*

personnel department N service *m* du personnel

personnel manager N chef *m* du personnel

perspective [pə'spɛktɪv] N perspective *f*; **to get sth into ~** ramener qch à sa juste mesure

perspex® ['pə:spɛks] N (*BRIT*) Plexiglas® *m*

perspicacious [pə:spɪ'keɪʃəs] ADJ perspicace

perspicacity [pə:spɪ'kæsɪtɪ] N perspicacité *f*

perspiration [pə:spɪ'reɪʃən] N transpiration *f*

perspire [pə'spaɪəʳ] VI transpirer

★**persuade** [pə'sweɪd] VT: **to ~ sb to do sth** persuader qn de faire qch, amener *or* décider qn à faire qch; **to ~ sb of sth/that** persuader qn de qch/que

persuasion [pə'sweɪʒən] N persuasion *f*; (*creed*) conviction *f*

persuasive [pə'sweɪsɪv] ADJ persuasif(-ive)

pert [pə:t] ADJ coquin(e), mutin(e)

pertaining [pə'teɪnɪŋ]: **~ to** prep relatif(-ive) à

pertinent ['pə:tɪnənt] ADJ pertinent(e)

perturb [pə'tə:b] VT troubler, inquiéter

perturbing [pə'tə:bɪŋ] ADJ troublant(e)

Peru [pə'ru:] N Pérou *m*

perusal [pə'ru:zl] N consultation *f*

peruse [pər'u:z] VT consulter

Peruvian [pə'ru:vjən] ADJ péruvien(ne) ▶ N Péruvien(ne)

pervade [pə'veɪd] VT se répandre dans, envahir

pervasive [pə'veɪsɪv] ADJ (*smell*) pénétrant(e); (*influence*) insidieux(-euse); (*gloom, ideas*) diffus(e)

perverse [pə'və:s] ADJ pervers(e); (*contrary*) entêté(e), contrariant(e)

perversion [pə'və:ʃən] N perversion *f*

perversity [pə'və:sɪtɪ] N perversité *f*

pervert N ['pə:və:t] perverti(e) ▶ VT [pə'və:t] pervertir; (*words*) déformer

pesky ['pɛskɪ] ADJ (*inf*) casse-pieds *inv*

pessimism ['pɛsɪmɪzəm] N pessimisme *m*

pessimist ['pɛsɪmɪst] N pessimiste *mf*

pessimistic [pɛsɪ'mɪstɪk] ADJ pessimiste

pest [pɛst] N animal *m* (*or* insecte *m*) nuisible; (*fig*) fléau *m*

pest control N lutte *f* contre les nuisibles

pester ['pɛstəʳ] VT importuner, harceler

pesticide ['pɛstɪsaɪd] N pesticide *m*

pestilence ['pɛstɪləns] N peste *f*

pestle ['pɛsl] N pilon *m*

★**pet** [pɛt] N animal familier; (*favourite*) chouchou *m*; **teacher's ~** chouchou *m* du professeur ▶ CPD (*favourite*) favori(e); **~ lion** etc lion etc apprivoisé; **~ hate** bête noire ▶ VT choyer; (*stroke*) caresser, câliner ▶ VI (*inf*) se peloter

petal ['pɛtl] N pétale *m*

peter ['pi:təʳ]: **to ~ out** vi s'épuiser; s'affaiblir

petite [pə'ti:t] ADJ menu(e)

petition [pə'tɪʃən] N pétition *f* ▶ VT adresser une pétition à ▶ VI: **to ~ for divorce** demander le divorce

pet name N (*BRIT*) petit nom

petrified ['pɛtrɪfaɪd] ADJ (*fig*) mort(e) de peur

petrify ['pɛtrɪfaɪ] VT pétrifier

petrochemical [pɛtrə'kɛmɪkl] ADJ pétrochimique

petrodollars ['pɛtrəudɔləz] NPL pétrodollars *mpl*

★**petrol** ['pɛtrəl] N (*BRIT*) essence *f*; **I've run out of ~** je suis en panne d'essence

petrol bomb N cocktail *m* Molotov

petrol can N (*BRIT*) bidon *m* à essence

petrol engine N (*BRIT*) moteur *m* à essence

petroleum [pə'trəuljəm] N pétrole *m*

petroleum jelly N vaseline *f*

petrolhead ['pɛtrəlhɛd] N (*inf*) accro *mf* de la bagnole

petrol pump N (*BRIT: in car, at garage*) pompe *f* à essence

petrol station N (*BRIT*) station-service *f*

petrol tank N (*BRIT*) réservoir *m* d'essence

petticoat ['pɛtɪkəut] N jupon *m*

pettifogging ['pɛtɪfɔgɪŋ] ADJ chicanier(-ière)

pettiness ['pɛtɪnɪs] N mesquinerie *f*

petty ['pɛtɪ] ADJ (*mean*) mesquin(e); (*unimportant*) insignifiant(e), sans importance

petty cash N caisse *f* des dépenses courantes, petite caisse

petty officer N second-maître *m*

petulant ['pɛtjulənt] ADJ irritable

petunia [pə'tju:nɪə] N pétunia *m*

pew [pju:] N banc *m* (d'église)

pewter ['pju:təʳ] N étain *m*

Pfc ABBR (*US Mil*) = **private first class**

773

PFI N ABBR (= *Private Finance Initiative*) PPP *m* (= *partenariat public-privé*)

PG N ABBR (*Ciné*: = *parental guidance*) avis des parents recommandé

PGA N ABBR = **Professional Golfers Association**

PH N ABBR (*US Mil*: = *Purple Heart*) décoration accordée aux blessés de guerre

phablet ['fæblɪt] N (*Tel*: *phone plus tablet*) phablet *m*

phallic ['fælɪk] ADJ phallique

phantom ['fæntəm] N fantôme *m*; (*vision*) fantasme *m*

Pharaoh ['fɛərəʊ] N pharaon *m*

pharmaceutical [fɑːmə'sjuːtɪkl] ADJ pharmaceutique ▸ N: **pharmaceuticals** produits *mpl* pharmaceutiques

pharmacist ['fɑːməsɪst] N pharmacien(ne)

pharmacology [fɑːmə'kɔlədʒɪ] N pharmacologie *f*

pharmacy ['fɑːməsɪ] N pharmacie *f*

phase [feɪz] N phase *f*, période *f*
  ▸ **phase in** VT introduire progressivement
  ▸ **phase out** VT supprimer progressivement

phased [feɪzd] ADJ progressif(-ive)

PhD ABBR = **Doctor of Philosophy**

pheasant ['fɛznt] N faisan *m*

phenomena [fə'nɔmɪnə] NPL *of* **phenomenon**

phenomenal [fɪ'nɔmɪnl] ADJ phénoménal(e)

phenomenon [fə'nɔmɪnən] (*pl* **phenomena** [-nə]) N phénomène *m*

phew [fjuː] EXCL ouf!

phial ['faɪəl] N fiole *f*

philanderer [fɪ'lændərə'] N don Juan *m*

philanthropic [fɪlən'θrɔpɪk] ADJ philanthropique

philanthropist [fɪ'lænθrəpɪst] N philanthrope *mf*

philanthropy [fɪ'lænθrəpɪ] N philanthropie *f*

philatelist [fɪ'lætəlɪst] N philatéliste *mf*

philately [fɪ'lætəlɪ] N philatélie *f*

Philippines ['fɪlɪpiːnz] NPL (*also*: **Philippine Islands**): **the** ~ les Philippines *fpl*

philistine ['fɪlɪstaɪn] N philistin *m*

philosopher [fɪ'lɔsəfə'] N philosophe *m*

philosophical [fɪlə'sɔfɪkl] ADJ philosophique

philosophize [fɪ'lɔsəfaɪz] VI philosopher; **to ~ about sth** philosopher sur qch

★**philosophy** [fɪ'lɔsəfɪ] N philosophie *f*

phishing ['fɪʃɪŋ] N phishing *m*

phlegm [flɛm] N flegme *m*

phlegmatic [flɛg'mætɪk] ADJ flegmatique

phobia ['fəʊbjə] N phobie *f*

phobic ['fəʊbɪk] ADJ, N phobique *mf*; **to be ~ about sth** avoir une phobie de qch

phoenix ['fiːnɪks] N phénix *m*

★**phone** [fəʊn] N téléphone *m*; **to be on the ~** avoir le téléphone; (*be calling*) être au téléphone ▸ VT téléphoner à ▸ VI téléphoner
  ▸ **phone back** VT, VI rappeler
  ▸ **phone up** VT téléphoner à ▸ VI téléphoner

phone bill N facture *f* de téléphone

phone book N annuaire *m*

★**phone box**, (*US*) **phone booth** N cabine *f* téléphonique

★**phone call** N coup *m* de fil or de téléphone

phonecard ['fəʊnkɑːd] N télécarte *f*

phone-in ['fəʊnɪn] N (*BRIT Radio, TV*) programme *m* à ligne ouverte

★**phone number** N numéro *m* de téléphone

phone tapping [-tæpɪŋ] N mise *f* sur écoutes téléphoniques

phonetics [fə'nɛtɪks] N phonétique *f*

phoney ['fəʊnɪ] ADJ faux (fausse), factice; (*person*) pas franc (franche) ▸ N (*person*) charlatan *m*; fumiste *mf*

phonics ['fɔnɪks] N (*Scol*) méthode *f* syllabique

phonograph ['fəʊnəgrɑːf] N (*US*) électrophone *m*

phony ['fəʊnɪ] ADJ, N = **phoney**

phosphate ['fɔsfeɪt] N phosphate *m*

phosphorus ['fɔsfərəs] N phosphore *m*

★**photo** ['fəʊtəʊ] N photo *f*; **to take a ~ of** prendre en photo

photo... ['fəʊtəʊ] PREFIX photo...

photo album N album *m* de photos

photobomb ['fəʊtəʊbɔm] VT (*inf*) s'incruster sur la photo de

photocall ['fəʊtəʊkɔːl] N séance *f* de photos pour la presse

photocopier ['fəʊtəʊkɔpɪə'] N copieur *m*

photocopy ['fəʊtəʊkɔpɪ] N photocopie *f* ▸ VT photocopier

photoelectric [fəʊtəʊɪ'lɛktrɪk] ADJ photoélectrique; **~ cell** cellule *f* photoélectrique

Photofit® ['fəʊtəʊfɪt] N portrait-robot *m*

photogenic [fəʊtəʊ'dʒɛnɪk] ADJ photogénique

★**photograph** ['fəʊtəgræf] N photographie *f*; **to take a ~ of sb** prendre qn en photo ▸ VT photographier

★**photographer** [fə'tɔgrəfə'] N photographe *mf*

photographic [fəʊtə'græfɪk] ADJ photographique

photography [fə'tɔgrəfɪ] N photographie *f*

photojournalism [fəʊtəʊ'dʒəːnəlɪzəm] N photojournalisme *m*

photojournalist [fəʊtəʊ'dʒəːnəlɪst] N photojournaliste *mf*

photon ['fəʊtɔn] N photon *m*

photo opportunity N *occasion, souvent arrangée, pour prendre des photos d'une personnalité.*

Photoshop® ['fəʊtəʊʃɔp] N Photoshop® ▸ VT: **to photoshop a picture** retoucher une image avec Photoshop

Photostat® ['fəʊtəʊstæt] N photocopie *f*, photostat *m*

photosynthesis [fəʊtəʊ'sɪnθəsɪs] N photosynthèse *f*

★**phrase** [freɪz] N expression *f*; (*Ling*) locution *f* ▸ VT exprimer; (*letter*) rédiger

phrase book N recueil *m* d'expressions (pour touristes)

★**physical** ['fɪzɪkl] ADJ physique; **~ examination** examen médical; **~ exercises** gymnastique *f*

physical education N éducation *f* physique

physically ['fɪzɪklɪ] ADV physiquement

physician [fɪ'zɪʃən] N médecin m

physicist ['fɪzɪsɪst] N physicien(ne)

★**physics** ['fɪzɪks] N physique f

physio ['fɪzɪəu] N (BRIT inf: person) kiné mf; (: therapy) physio f

physiological [fɪzɪə'lɔdʒɪkl] ADJ physiologique

physiologist [fɪzɪ'ɔlədʒɪst] N physiologiste mf

physiology [fɪzɪ'ɔlədʒɪ] N physiologie f

physiotherapist [fɪzɪəu'θɛrəpɪst] N kinésithérapeute mf

physiotherapy [fɪzɪəu'θɛrəpɪ] N kinésithérapie f

physique [fɪ'ziːk] N (appearance) physique m; (health etc) constitution f

pianist ['pɪ:ənɪst] N pianiste mf

★**piano** [pɪ'ænəu] N piano m

piano accordion N (BRIT) accordéon m à touches

Picardy ['pɪkədɪ] N Picardie f

piccolo ['pɪkələu] N piccolo m

★**pick** [pɪk] N (tool: also: **pick-axe**) pic m, pioche f; **take your ~** faites votre choix; **the ~ of** le (la) meilleur(e) de ▶ VT choisir; (gather) cueillir; (remove) prendre; (lock) forcer; (scab, spot) gratter, écorcher; **to ~ a bone** ronger un os; **to ~ one's nose** se mettre les doigts dans le nez; **to ~ one's teeth** se curer les dents; **to ~ sb's brains** faire appel aux lumières de qn; **to ~ pockets** pratiquer le vol à la tire; **to ~ a quarrel with sb** chercher noise à qn
  ▶ **pick at** VT FUS: **to ~ at one's food** manger du bout des dents, chipoter
  ▶ **pick off** VT (kill) (viser soigneusement et) abattre
  ▶ **pick on** VT FUS (person) harceler
  ▶ **pick out** VT choisir; (distinguish) distinguer
  ▶ **pick up** VI (improve) remonter, s'améliorer; **to ~ up where one left off** reprendre là où l'on s'est arrêté ▶ VT ramasser; (telephone) décrocher; (collect) passer prendre; (Aut: give lift to) prendre; (learn) apprendre; (Radio) capter; **to ~ up speed** prendre de la vitesse; **to ~ o.s. up** se relever

pickaxe, (US) **pickax** ['pɪkæks] N pioche f

picket ['pɪkɪt] N (in strike) gréviste mf participant à un piquet de grève; piquet m de grève ▶ VT mettre un piquet de grève devant

picket line N piquet m de grève

pickings ['pɪkɪŋz] NPL: **there are rich ~ to be had in ...** il y a gros à gagner dans ...

pickle ['pɪkl] N (as condiment: also: **pickles**) pickles mpl; **in a ~** (fig) dans le pétrin ▶ VT conserver dans du vinaigre or dans de la saumure

pickled ['pɪkld] ADJ (food) au vinaigre

pick-me-up ['pɪkmiːʌp] N remontant m

pickpocket ['pɪkpɔkɪt] N pickpocket m

pick-up ['pɪkʌp] N (also: **pick-up truck**) pick-up m inv; (BRIT: on record player) bras m pick-up

picnic ['pɪknɪk] N pique-nique m ▶ VI pique-niquer

picnic area N aire f de pique-nique

picnicker ['pɪknɪkəʳ] N pique-niqueur(-euse)

pictorial [pɪk'tɔːrɪəl] ADJ illustré(e)

★**picture** ['pɪktʃəʳ] N (also TV) image f; (painting) peinture f, tableau m; (photograph) photo(graphie) f; (drawing) dessin m; (film) film m; (fig: description)

description f; **to take a ~ of sb/sth** prendre qn/qch en photo; **would you take a ~ of us, please?** pourriez-vous nous prendre en photo, s'il vous plaît ?; **the overall ~** le tableau d'ensemble; **to put sb in the ~** mettre qn au courant ▶ VT (imagine) se représenter; (describe) dépeindre, représenter ■ **pictures** NPL: **the pictures** (BRIT) le cinéma

picture book N livre m d'images

picture frame N cadre m

picture messaging N picture messaging m, messagerie f d'images

picturesque [pɪktʃə'rɛsk] ADJ pittoresque

picture window N baie vitrée, fenêtre f panoramique

piddling ['pɪdlɪŋ] ADJ (inf) insignifiant(e)

★**pie** [paɪ] N tourte f; (of fruit) tarte f; (of meat) pâté m en croûte

piebald ['paɪbɔːld] ADJ pie inv

★**piece** [piːs] N morceau m; (of land) parcelle f; (item): **a ~ of furniture/advice** un meuble/conseil; (Draughts) pion m; **in pieces** (broken) en morceaux, en miettes; (not yet assembled) en pièces détachées; **to take to pieces** démonter; **in one ~** (object) intact(e); **to get back all in one ~** (person) rentrer sain et sauf; **a 10p ~** (BRIT) une pièce de 10p; **~ by ~** morceau par morceau; **a six-piece band** un orchestre de six musiciens; **to say one's ~** réciter son morceau ▶ VT: **to ~ together** rassembler

piecemeal ['piːsmiːl] ADV par bouts

piece rate N taux m or tarif m à la pièce

piecework ['piːswəːk] N travail m aux pièces or à la pièce

pie chart N graphique m à secteurs, camembert m

Piedmont ['piːdmɔnt] N Piémont m

pier [pɪəʳ] N jetée f; (of bridge etc) pile f

pierce [pɪəs] VT percer, transpercer; **to have one's ears pierced** se faire percer les oreilles

pierced [pɪəst] ADJ (ears) percé(e)

piercing ['pɪəsɪŋ] ADJ (cry) perçant(e)

piety ['paɪətɪ] N piété f

piffling ['pɪflɪŋ] ADJ insignifiant(e)

★**pig** [pɪg] N cochon m, porc m; (pej: unkind person) mufle m; (: greedy person) goinfre m

pigeon ['pɪdʒən] N pigeon m

pigeonhole ['pɪdʒənhəul] N casier m

pigeon-toed ['pɪdʒəntəud] ADJ marchant les pieds en dedans

piggyback ['pɪgɪbæk] N (also: **piggyback ride**): **to give sb a ~** porter qn sur son dos ▶ ADV à califourchon
  ▶ **piggyback on** VT surfer sur

piggy bank ['pɪgɪ-] N tirelire f

pigheaded ['pɪg'hɛdɪd] ADJ entêté(e), têtu(e)

piglet ['pɪglɪt] N petit cochon, porcelet m

pigment ['pɪgmənt] N pigment m

pigmentation [pɪgmən'teɪʃən] N pigmentation f

pigmy ['pɪgmɪ] N = **pygmy**

pigskin ['pɪgskɪn] N (peau f de) porc m

pigsty ['pɪgstaɪ] N porcherie f

pigtail ['pɪgteɪl] N natte f, tresse f

pike [paɪk] N (spear) pique f; (fish) brochet m

P

Pilates [pɪˈlɑːtiːz] N Pilates m

pilchard [ˈpɪltʃəd] N pilchard m (sorte de sardine)

★**pile** [paɪl] N (pillar, of books) pile f; (heap) tas m; (of carpet) épaisseur f; **in a ~** en tas
▶ **pile in** VI s'entasser
▶ **pile on** VT: **to ~ it on** (inf) exagérer
▶ **pile up** VI (accumulate) s'entasser, s'accumuler
▶ VT (put in heap) empiler, entasser; (accumulate) accumuler

piles [paɪlz] NPL hémorroïdes fpl

pile-up [ˈpaɪlʌp] N (Aut) télescopage m, collision f en série

pilfer [ˈpɪlfəʳ] VT chaparder ▶ VI commettre des larcins

pilfering [ˈpɪlfərɪŋ] N chapardage m

pilgrim [ˈpɪlgrɪm] N pèlerin m; voir article

Les **Pilgrim Fathers** (Pères pèlerins) sont un groupe de puritains qui quittèrent l'Angleterre en 1620 pour fuir les persécutions religieuses. Ayant traversé l'Atlantique à bord du Mayflower, ils fondèrent New Plymouth en Nouvelle-Angleterre, dans ce qui est aujourd'hui le Massachusetts. Ces Pères pèlerins sont considérés comme les fondateurs des États-Unis, et l'on commémore chaque année, le jour de Thanksgiving, la réussite de leur première récolte.

pilgrimage [ˈpɪlgrɪmɪdʒ] N pèlerinage m

★**pill** [pɪl] N pilule f; **the ~** la pilule; **to be on the ~** prendre la pilule

pillage [ˈpɪlɪdʒ] VT piller

pillar [ˈpɪləʳ] N pilier m

pillar box N (BRIT) boîte f aux lettres (publique)

pillion [ˈpɪljən] N (of motor cycle) siège m arrière; **to ride ~** être derrière; (on horse) être en croupe

pillory [ˈpɪlərɪ] N pilori m ▶ VT mettre au pilori

pillow [ˈpɪləu] N oreiller m

pillowcase [ˈpɪləukeɪs], **pillowslip** [ˈpɪləuslɪp] N taie f d'oreiller

★**pilot** [ˈpaɪlət] N pilote m ▶ CPD (scheme etc) pilote, expérimental(e) ▶ VT piloter

pilot boat N bateau-pilote m

pilot light N veilleuse f

pimento [pɪˈmɛntəu] N piment m

pimp [pɪmp] N souteneur m, maquereau m

pimple [ˈpɪmpl] N bouton m

pimply [ˈpɪmplɪ] ADJ boutonneux(-euse)

★**PIN** N ABBR (= personal identification number) code m confidentiel

★**pin** [pɪn] N épingle f; (Tech) cheville f; (BRIT: drawing pin) punaise f; (in grenade) goupille f; (BRIT Elec: of plug) broche f; **pins and needles** fourmis fpl ▶ VT (with pins) épingler; **to ~ sb against/to** clouer qn contre/à; **to ~ sth on sb** (fig) mettre qch sur le dos de qn
▶ **pin down** VT (physically) clouer au sol; (fig) obliger à répondre; **there's something strange here but I can't quite ~ it down** il y a quelque chose d'étrange ici, mais je n'arrive pas exactement à savoir quoi

pinafore [ˈpɪnəfɔːʳ] N tablier m

pinafore dress N robe-chasuble f

pinball [ˈpɪnbɔːl] N flipper m

pincers [ˈpɪnsəz] NPL tenailles fpl

pinch [pɪntʃ] N pincement m; (of salt etc) pincée f; **at a ~** à la rigueur; **to feel the ~** (fig) se ressentir des restrictions (or de la récession etc) ▶ VT pincer; (inf: steal) piquer, chiper ▶ VI (shoe) serrer

pinched [pɪntʃt] ADJ (drawn) tiré(e); **~ with cold** transi(e) de froid

pincushion [ˈpɪnkuʃən] N pelote f à épingles

pine [paɪn] N (also: **pine tree**) pin m ▶ VI: **to ~ for** aspirer à, désirer ardemment
▶ **pine away** VI dépérir

★**pineapple** [ˈpaɪnæpl] N ananas m

pine cone N pomme f de pin

ping [pɪŋ] N (noise) tintement m

ping-pong® [ˈpɪŋpɔŋ] N ping-pong® m

★**pink** [pɪŋk] ADJ rose ▶ N (colour) rose m; (Bot) œillet m, mignardise f

pinkie, pinky [ˈpɪŋkɪ] N (inf) petit doigt m

pinking shears [ˈpɪŋkɪŋ-] NPL ciseaux mpl à denteler

pin money N (BRIT) argent m de poche

pinnacle [ˈpɪnəkl] N pinacle m

pinpoint [ˈpɪnpɔɪnt] VT indiquer (avec précision)

pinstripe [ˈpɪnstraɪp] N rayure très fine

pinstriped [ˈpɪnstraɪpt] ADJ à rayures

pint [paɪnt] N pinte f (Brit = 0,57 l; US = 0,47 l); (BRIT inf) = pot m

pinup [ˈpɪnʌp] N pin-up f inv

pioneer [paɪəˈnɪəʳ] N explorateur(-trice); (early settler) pionnier m; (fig) pionnier, précurseur m ▶ VT être un pionnier de

pioneering [paɪəˈnɪərɪŋ] ADJ (work, research) pionnier(-ière); **~ spirit** esprit de pionnier

pious [ˈpaɪəs] ADJ pieux(-euse)

pip [pɪp] N (seed) pépin m ■ **pips** NPL: **the pips** (BRIT: time signal on radio) le top

★**pipe** [paɪp] N tuyau m, conduite f; (for smoking) pipe f; (Mus) pipeau m ▶ VT amener par tuyau ■ **pipes** NPL (also: **bagpipes**) cornemuse f
▶ **pipe down** VI (inf) se taire

pipe cleaner N cure-pipe m

piped music [paɪpt-] N musique f de fond

pipe dream N chimère f, utopie f

pipeline [ˈpaɪplaɪn] N (for gas) gazoduc m, pipeline m; (for oil) oléoduc m, pipeline; **it is in the ~** (fig) c'est en route, ça va se faire

piper [ˈpaɪpəʳ] N (flautist) joueur(-euse) de pipeau; (of bagpipes) joueur(-euse) de cornemuse

pipe tobacco N tabac m pour la pipe

piping [ˈpaɪpɪŋ] ADV: **~ hot** très chaud(e)

piquant [ˈpiːkənt] ADJ piquant(e)

pique [piːk] N dépit m

piqued [piːkt] ADJ piqué(e) au vif; **a bit ~** un peu dépité(e)

piracy [ˈpaɪərəsɪ] N piraterie f

piranha [pɪˈrɑːnə] (pl ~s) N (also: **piranha fish**) piranha m

pirate [ˈpaɪərət] N pirate m ▶ VT (CD, video, book) pirater

pirated [ˈpaɪərətɪd] ADJ pirate

pirate radio N (BRIT) radio f pirate

pirouette [pɪruˈɛt] N pirouette f ▶ VI faire une or des pirouette(s)

Pisces [ˈpaɪsiːz] N les Poissons mpl; **to be ~** être des Poissons

piss [pɪs] VI (inf!) pisser (!); **~ off!** tire-toi ! (!)

pissed [pɪst] ADJ (inf!: BRIT: drunk) bourré(e); (: US: angry) furieux(-euse)

pistachio [pɪˈstæʃɪəʊ] N (also: **pistachio nut**) pistache f; (tree) pistachier m

piste [ˈpiːst] N piste f

pistol [ˈpɪstl] N pistolet m

piston [ˈpɪstən] N piston m

pit [pɪt] N trou m, fosse f; (also: **coal pit**) puits m de mine; (also: **orchestra pit**) fosse d'orchestre; (US: fruit stone) noyau m ▶ VT: **to ~ sb against sb** opposer qn à qn; **to ~ o.s.** or **one's wits against se** mesurer à ■ **pits** NPL (in motor racing) aire f de service

pitapat [ˈpɪtəˈpæt] ADV: **to go ~** (heart) battre la chamade; (rain) tambouriner

★**pitch** [pɪtʃ] N (BRIT Sport) terrain m; (throw) lancement m; (Mus) ton m; (of voice) hauteur f; (fig: degree) degré m; (also: **sales pitch**) baratin m, boniment m; (Naut) tangage m; (tar) poix f; **at this ~** à ce rythme ▶ VT (throw) lancer; (tent) dresser; (set: price, message) adapter, positionner; **to be pitched forward** être projeté(e) en avant ▶ VI (Naut) tanguer; (fall): **to ~ into/off** tomber dans/de ▶ **pitch in** VI (inf: financially) mettre la main à la poche; (: make a big effort) donner un coup de main; **they all pitched in to help** ils ont tous mis la main à la poche pour aider; ils ont tous donné un coup de main

pitch-black [ˈpɪtʃˈblæk] ADJ noir(e) comme poix

pitched battle [pɪtʃt-] N bataille rangée

pitcher [ˈpɪtʃəʳ] N cruche f

pitchfork [ˈpɪtʃfɔːk] N fourche f

piteous [ˈpɪtɪəs] ADJ pitoyable

pitfall [ˈpɪtfɔːl] N trappe f, piège m

pith [pɪθ] N (of plant) moelle f; (of orange etc) intérieur m de l'écorce; (fig) essence f; vigueur f

pithead [ˈpɪthɛd] N (BRIT) bouche f de puits

pithy [ˈpɪθɪ] ADJ piquant(e); vigoureux(-euse)

pitiable [ˈpɪtɪəbl] ADJ pitoyable

pitiful [ˈpɪtɪful] ADJ (touching) pitoyable; (contemptible) lamentable

pitifully [ˈpɪtɪfəlɪ] ADV pitoyablement; lamentablement

pitiless [ˈpɪtɪlɪs] ADJ impitoyable

pittance [ˈpɪtns] N salaire m de misère

pitted [ˈpɪtɪd] ADJ: **~ with** (chickenpox) grêlé(e) par; (rust) piqué(e) de

pity [ˈpɪtɪ] N pitié f; **what a ~!** quel dommage !; **it is a ~ that you can't come** c'est dommage que vous ne puissiez venir; **to have** or **take ~ on sb** avoir pitié de qn ▶ VT plaindre

pitying [ˈpɪtɪɪŋ] ADJ compatissant(e)

pivot [ˈpɪvət] N pivot m ▶ VI pivoter

pivotal [ˈpɪvətl] ADJ (role, position) pivot

pixel [ˈpɪksl] N (Comput) pixel m

pixelate [ˈpɪksɪleɪt] VT (Comput) pixéliser

pixie [ˈpɪksɪ] N lutin m

★**pizza** [ˈpiːtsə] N pizza f

pizzazz, pizazz [pəˈzæz] N (inf) allant m; **a young woman with a lot of energy and ~** une jeune femme pleine d'énergie et d'allant

placard [ˈplækɑːd] N affiche f; (in march) pancarte f

placate [pləˈkeɪt] VT apaiser, calmer

placatory [pləˈkeɪtərɪ] ADJ d'apaisement, lénifiant(e)

★**place** [pleɪs] N endroit m, lieu m; (proper position, job, rank, seat) place f; (house) maison f, logement m; (in street names): **Laurel P~** ≈ rue des Lauriers; (home): **at/to his ~** chez lui; **to take ~** avoir lieu; (occur) se produire; **to take sb's ~** remplacer qn; **to change places with sb** changer de place avec qn; **from ~ to ~** d'un endroit à l'autre; **all over the ~** partout; **out of ~** (not suitable) déplacé(e), inopportun(e); **I feel out of ~ here** je ne me sens pas à ma place ici; **in the first ~** d'abord, en premier; **to put sb in his ~** (fig) remettre qn à sa place; **he's going places** (fig, inf) il fait son chemin; **it is not my ~ to do it** ce n'est pas à moi de le faire ▶ VT (position) placer, mettre; (identify) situer; reconnaître; **to ~ an order with sb (for)** (Comm) passer commande à qn (de); **to be placed** (in race, exam) se placer; **how are you placed next week?** comment ça se présente pour la semaine prochaine ?

placebo [pləˈsiːbəʊ] N placebo m

place mat N set m de table; (in linen etc) napperon m

placement [ˈpleɪsmənt] N placement m; (during studies) stage m

place name N nom m de lieu

placenta [pləˈsɛntə] N placenta m

placid [ˈplæsɪd] ADJ placide

placidity [pləˈsɪdɪtɪ] N placidité f

plagiarism [ˈpleɪdʒərɪzəm] N plagiat m

plagiarist [ˈpleɪdʒərɪst] N plagiaire mf

plagiarize [ˈpleɪdʒəraɪz] VT plagier

plague [pleɪg] N fléau m; (Med) peste f ▶ VT (fig) tourmenter; **to ~ sb with questions** harceler qn de questions

plaice [pleɪs] N (pl inv) carrelet m

plaid [plæd] N tissu écossais

★**plain** [pleɪn] ADJ (in one colour) uni(e); (clear) clair(e), évident(e); (simple) simple, ordinaire; (frank) franc (franche); (not handsome) quelconque, ordinaire; (cigarette) sans filtre; (without seasoning etc) nature inv; **in ~ clothes** (police) en civil; **to make sth ~ to sb** faire clairement comprendre qch à qn ▶ ADV franchement, carrément ▶ N plaine f

plain chocolate N chocolat m à croquer

plainly [ˈpleɪnlɪ] ADV clairement; (frankly) carrément, sans détours

plainness [ˈpleɪnnɪs] N simplicité f

plain speaking N propos mpl sans équivoque; **she has a reputation for ~** elle est bien connue pour son franc parler or sa franchise

plaintiff [ˈpleɪntɪf] N plaignant(e)

plaintive [ˈpleɪntɪv] ADJ plaintif(-ive)

plait [plæt] N tresse f, natte f ▶ VT tresser, natter

★**plan** [plæn] N plan m; (scheme) projet m ▶ VT (think in advance) projeter; (prepare) organiser; **to ~ to do** projeter de faire; **how long do you ~ to stay?**

combien de temps comptez-vous rester ? ▸ vi
faire des projets
▸ **plan for** vt fus (prepare) préparer; (expect) prévoir
▸ **plan on** vt fus: **to ~ on doing sth** prévoir de
faire qch; (expect) s'attendre à; **I hadn't planned
on John arriving last night** je ne m'attendais pas
à ce que John arrive hier soir

★**plane** [pleɪn] N (Aviat) avion m; (also: **plane
tree**) platane m; (tool) rabot m; (Art, Math etc) plan m;
(fig) niveau m, plan ▸ ADJ plan(e); plat(e) ▸ VT (with
tool) raboter

★**planet** ['plænɪt] N planète f

planetarium [plænɪ'tɛərɪəm] N planétarium m

planetary ['plænɪtrɪ] ADJ planétaire

plank [plæŋk] N planche f; (Pol) point m d'un programme

plankton ['plæŋktən] N plancton m

planned economy [plænd-] N économie planifiée

planner ['plænər] N planificateur(-trice); (chart)
planning m; **town** or (US) **city** ~ urbaniste mf

★**planning** ['plænɪŋ] N planification f; **family ~**
planning familial

planning permission N (BRIT) permis m de construire

★**plant** [plɑːnt] N plante f; (machinery) matériel m;
(factory) usine f ▸ VT planter; (bomb) déposer,
poser; (microphone, evidence) cacher

plantation [plæn'teɪʃən] N plantation f

plant pot N (BRIT) pot m de fleurs

plaque [plæk] N plaque f

plasma ['plæzmə] N plasma m

plaster ['plɑːstər] N plâtre m; (also: **plaster of
Paris**) plâtre à mouler; (BRIT: also: **sticking plaster**) pansement adhésif; **in ~** (BRIT: leg etc) dans le
plâtre ▸ VT plâtrer; (cover): **to ~ with** couvrir de

plasterboard ['plɑːstəbɔːd] N Placoplâtre® m

plaster cast N (Med) plâtre m; (model, statue)
moule m

plastered ['plɑːstəd] ADJ (inf) soûl(e)

plasterer ['plɑːstərər] N plâtrier m

★**plastic** ['plæstɪk] N plastique m ▸ ADJ (made of plastic) en plastique; (flexible) plastique, malléable;
(art) plastique

plastic bag N sac m en plastique

plastic bullet N balle f de plastique

plastic explosive N plastic m

plasticine® ['plæstɪsiːn] N pâte f à modeler

plastic surgery N chirurgie f esthétique

★**plate** [pleɪt] N (dish) assiette f; (sheet of metal, on door,
Phot) plaque f; (Typ) cliché m; (in book) gravure f;
(dental) dentier m; (Aut: number plate) plaque
minéralogique; **gold/silver ~** (dishes) vaisselle f
d'or/d'argent

plateau ['plætəu] (pl **plateaus** or **plateaux**
['plætəuz]) N plateau m

plateful ['pleɪtful] N assiette f, assiettée f

plate glass N verre m à vitre, vitre f

platen ['plætən] N (on typewriter, printer) rouleau m

plate rack N égouttoir m

★**platform** ['plætfɔːm] N (at meeting) tribune f; (BRIT:
of bus) plate-forme f; (stage) estrade f; (Rail) quai m;
(Pol) plateforme f; **the train leaves from ~ 7** le
train part de la voie 7

platform ticket N (BRIT) billet m de quai

platinum ['plætɪnəm] N platine m

platitude ['plætɪtjuːd] N platitude f, lieu commun

platonic [plə'tɔnɪk] ADJ (feelings, relationship) platonique

platoon [plə'tuːn] N peloton m

platter ['plætər] N plat m

plaudits ['plɔːdɪts] NPL applaudissements mpl

plausible ['plɔːzɪbl] ADJ plausible; (person) convain-
cant(e)

★**play** [pleɪ] N jeu m; (Theat) pièce f (de théâtre); **to
bring** or **call into** ~ faire entrer en jeu; **~ on words**
jeu de mots ▸ VT (game) jouer à; (team, opponent) jouer
contre; (instrument) jouer de; (part, piece of music, note)
jouer; (CD etc) passer; **to ~ a trick on sb** jouer un tour
à qn ▸ VI jouer; **to ~ safe** ne prendre aucun risque;
they're playing at soldiers ils jouent aux soldats;
to ~ into sb's hands (fig) faire le jeu de qn
▸ **play about, play around** VI (person) s'amuser
▸ **play along** VI (fig): **to ~ along with** (person)
entrer dans le jeu de ▸ VT (fig): **to ~ sb along** faire
marcher qn
▸ **play back** VT repasser, réécouter
▸ **play down** VT minimiser
▸ **play for** VT FUS (Sport: team) jouer pour; **to ~ for
money** (in games) jouer de l'argent; **to ~ for time**
chercher à gagner du temps; **it's all to ~ for** tout
reste à jouer
▸ **play on** VT FUS (sb's feelings, credulity) jouer sur; **to
~ on sb's nerves** porter sur les nerfs de qn
▸ **play up** VI (cause trouble) faire des siennes

playact ['pleɪækt] VI jouer la comédie

playboy ['pleɪbɔɪ] N playboy m

played-out ['pleɪd'aut] ADJ épuisé(e)

★**player** ['pleɪər] N joueur(-euse); (Theat) acteur(-trice);
(Mus) musicien(ne)

playful ['pleɪful] ADJ enjoué(e)

playgoer ['pleɪgəuər] N amateur(-trice) de théâtre, habitué(e) des théâtres

★**playground** ['pleɪgraund] N cour f de récréation;
(in park) aire f de jeux

playgroup ['pleɪgruːp] N garderie f

playing card ['pleɪɪŋ-] N carte f à jouer

playing field ['pleɪɪŋ-] N terrain m de sport

playmaker ['pleɪmeɪkər] N (Sport) joueur qui crée des
occasions de marquer des buts pour ses coéquipiers

playmate ['pleɪmeɪt] N camarade mf, copain
(copine)

play-off ['pleɪɔf] N (Sport) belle f

playpen ['pleɪpɛn] N parc m (pour bébé)

playroom ['pleɪruːm] N salle f de jeux

playschool ['pleɪskuːl] N = **playgroup**

plaything ['pleɪθɪŋ] N jouet m

★**playtime** ['pleɪtaɪm] N (Scol) récréation f

playwright ['pleɪraɪt] N dramaturge m

plc ABBR (BRIT: = public limited company) ≈ SARL f

plea [pliː] N (request) appel m; (excuse) excuse f; (Law)
défense f

plea bargaining N (Law) négociations entre le procureur, l'avocat de la défense et parfois le juge, pour réduire
la gravité des charges

plead [pli:d] vt plaider; (give as excuse) invoquer
▶ vi (Law) plaider; (beg): **to ~ with sb (for sth)**
implorer qn (d'accorder qch); **to ~ for sth**
implorer qch; **to ~ guilty/not guilty** plaider
coupable/non coupable

pleading ['pli:dɪŋ] ADJ (expression, voice) implo-
rant(e) ▶ N imploration f

★**pleasant** ['plɛznt] ADJ agréable

pleasantly ['plɛzntlɪ] ADV agréablement

pleasantry ['plɛzntrɪ] N (joke) plaisanterie f
▦ **pleasantries** NPL (polite remarks) civilités fpl

★**please** [pli:z] ADV s'il te (or vous) plaît; my bill, ~
l'addition, s'il vous plaît; **~ don't cry!** je t'en prie,
ne pleure pas! ▶ vt plaire à; **~ yourself!** (inf)
(faites) comme vous voulez! ▶ vi (think fit): **do as
you ~** faites comme il vous plaira

★**pleased** [pli:zd] ADJ: **~ (with)** content(e) (de); **~ to
meet you** enchanté (de faire votre connais-
sance); **we are ~ to inform you that ...** nous
sommes heureux de vous annoncer que ...

pleasing ['pli:zɪŋ] ADJ plaisant(e), qui fait plaisir

pleasurable ['plɛʒərəbl] ADJ très agréable

★**pleasure** ['plɛʒəʳ] N plaisir m; **"it's a ~"** « je vous
en prie »; **with ~** avec plaisir; **is this trip for business or ~?** est-ce un voyage d'affaires ou d'agrément?

pleasure cruise N croisière f

pleat [pli:t] N pli m

pleated ['pli:tɪd] ADJ plissé(e)

pleb ['plɛb] (BRIT inf, pej) N prolo m (inf) ▦ **plebs** NPL:
the plebs la plèbe

plebiscite ['plɛbɪsɪt] N plébiscite m

plectrum ['plɛktrəm] N plectre m

pledge [plɛdʒ] N gage m; (promise) promesse f ▶ vt
engager; promettre; **to ~ support for sb** s'engager à soutenir qn; **to ~ sb to secrecy** faire promettre à qn de garder le secret

plenary ['pli:nərɪ] ADJ: **in ~ session** en séance
plénière

plentiful ['plɛntɪful] ADJ abondant(e), co-
pieux(-euse)

★**plenty** ['plɛntɪ] N abondance f; **~ of** beaucoup de;
(sufficient) (bien) assez de; **we've got ~ of time**
nous avons largement le temps

plethora ['plɛθərə] N pléthore f; **a ~ of** une
pléthore de

pleurisy ['pluərɪsɪ] N pleurésie f

pliable ['plaɪəbl] ADJ flexible; (person) malléable

pliers ['plaɪəz] NPL pinces fpl

plight [plaɪt] N situation f critique

plimsolls ['plɪmsəlz] NPL (BRIT) (chaussures fpl)
tennis fpl

plinth [plɪnθ] N socle m

PLO N ABBR (= Palestine Liberation Organization) OLP f

plod [plɒd] vi avancer péniblement; (fig) peiner

plodder ['plɒdəʳ] N bûcheur(-euse)

plodding ['plɒdɪŋ] ADJ pesant(e)

plonk [plɒŋk] (inf) N (BRIT: wine) pinard m, piquette
f ▶ vt: **to ~ sth down** poser brusquement qch

★**plot** [plɒt] N complot m, conspiration f; (of story,
play) intrigue f; (of land) lot m de terrain, lopin m; **a
vegetable ~** (BRIT) un carré de légumes ▶ vt (mark

out) tracer point par point; (Naut) pointer; (make
graph of) faire le graphique de; (conspire) comploter
▶ vi comploter

plotter ['plɒtəʳ] N conspirateur(-trice); (Comput)
traceur m

plough, (US) **plow** [plau] N charrue f ▶ vt (earth)
labourer; **to ~ money into** investir dans
▶ **plough back** vt (Comm) réinvestir
▶ **plough through** vt FUS (snow etc) avancer péniblement dans

ploughing, (US) **plowing** ['plauɪŋ] N labourage m

ploughman, (US) **plowman** ['plaumən] N (irreg)
laboureur m

plow [plau] N (US) = **plough**

ploy [plɔɪ] N stratagème m

pls ABBR (= please) SVP m

pluck [plʌk] vt (fruit) cueillir; (musical instrument)
pincer; (bird) plumer; **to ~ one's eyebrows**
s'épiler les sourcils; **to ~ up courage** prendre son
courage à deux mains ▶ N courage m, cran m

plucky ['plʌkɪ] ADJ courageux(-euse)

plug [plʌg] N (stopper) bouchon m, bonde f; (Elec)
prise f de courant; (Aut: also: **spark(ing) plug**)
bougie f; **to give sb/sth a ~** (inf) faire de la pub
pour qn/qch ▶ vt (hole) boucher; (inf: advertise)
faire du battage pour, matraquer
▶ **plug in** vt (Elec) brancher ▶ vi (Elec) se brancher

plughole ['plʌɡhəul] N (BRIT) trou m (d'écoulement)

plug-in ['plʌɡɪn] N (Comput) greffon m; module m
d'extension

plum [plʌm] N (fruit) prune f ▶ ADJ: **~ job** (inf) travail
m en or

plumage ['plu:mɪdʒ] N plumage m

plumb [plʌm] ADJ vertical(e) ▶ N plomb m ▶ ADV
(exactly) en plein ▶ vt sonder
▶ **plumb in** vt (washing machine) faire le raccordement de

plumber ['plʌməʳ] N plombier m

plumbing ['plʌmɪŋ] N (trade) plomberie f; (piping)
tuyauterie f

plumbline ['plʌmlaɪn] N fil m à plomb

plume [plu:m] N plume f, plumet m

plummet ['plʌmɪt] vi (person, object) plonger; (sales,
prices) dégringoler

plump [plʌmp] ADJ rondelet(te), dodu(e), bien en
chair ▶ vt: **to ~ sth (down) on** laisser tomber qch
lourdement sur
▶ **plump for** vt FUS (inf: choose) se décider pour
▶ **plump up** vt (cushion) battre (pour lui redonner
forme)

plunder ['plʌndəʳ] N pillage m ▶ vt piller

plunge [plʌndʒ] N plongeon m; (fig) chute f; **to
take the ~** se jeter à l'eau ▶ vt plonger ▶ vi (fall)
tomber, dégringoler; (dive) plonger

plunger ['plʌndʒəʳ] N piston m; (for blocked sink)
(débouchoir m à) ventouse f

plunging ['plʌndʒɪŋ] ADJ (neckline) plongeant(e)

pluperfect [plu:'pə:fɪkt] N (Ling) plus-que-parfait m

plural ['pluərl] ADJ pluriel(le) ▶ N pluriel m

★**plus** [plʌs] N (also: **plus sign**) signe m plus; (advantage) atout m; **it's a ~** c'est un atout ▶ PREP plus
▶ ADV: **ten/twenty ~** plus de dix/vingt

P

plus fours NPL pantalon m (de) golf

plush [plʌʃ] ADJ somptueux(-euse) ▶ N peluche f

plus-one [plʌs'wʌn] N personne qui accompagne un invité à une réception ou une cérémonie.

plutonium [pluː'təʊnɪəm] N plutonium m

ply [plaɪ] N (of wool) fil m; (of wood) feuille f, épaisseur f; **three ~ (wool)** n laine f trois fils ▶ VT (tool) manier; (a trade) exercer; **to ~ sb with drink** donner continuellement à boire à qn ▶ VI (ship) faire la navette

plywood ['plaɪwʊd] N contreplaqué m

P.M. N ABBR (BRIT) = **prime minister**

p.m. ADV ABBR (= post meridiem) de l'après-midi

PMS N ABBR (= premenstrual syndrome) syndrome prémenstruel

PMT N ABBR (= premenstrual tension) syndrome prémenstruel

pneumatic [njuː'mætɪk] ADJ pneumatique

pneumatic drill N marteau-piqueur m

pneumonia [njuː'məʊnɪə] N pneumonie f

PO N ABBR (= Post Office) PTT fpl; (Mil) = **petty officer**

po N ABBR = **postal order**

POA N ABBR (BRIT) = **Prison Officers' Association**

poach [pəʊtʃ] VT (cook) pocher; (steal) pêcher (or chasser) sans permis ▶ VI braconner

poached [pəʊtʃt] ADJ (egg) poché(e)

poacher ['pəʊtʃəʳ] N braconnier m

poaching ['pəʊtʃɪŋ] N braconnage m

P.O. Box N ABBR = **post office box**

★**pocket** ['pɔkɪt] N poche f; **to be (£5) out of ~** (BRIT) en être de sa poche (pour 5 livres) ▶ VT empocher

pocketbook ['pɔkɪtbʊk] N (notebook) carnet m; (US: wallet) portefeuille m; (: handbag) sac m à main

pocket knife N canif m

pocket money N argent m de poche

pockmarked ['pɔkmɑːkt] ADJ (face) grêlé(e)

pod [pɔd] N cosse f ▶ VT écosser

podcast ['pɔdkɑːst] N podcast m ▶ VI podcaster

podcasting ['pɔdkɑːstɪŋ] N podcasting m, baladodiffusion f

podgy ['pɔdʒɪ] ADJ rondelet(te)

podiatrist [pɔ'daɪətrɪst] N (US) pédicure mf

podiatry [pɔ'daɪətrɪ] N (US) pédicurie f

podium ['pəʊdɪəm] N podium m

POE N ABBR = **port of embarkation; port of entry**

★**poem** ['pəʊɪm] N poème m

★**poet** ['pəʊɪt] N poète m

poetic [pəʊ'ɛtɪk] ADJ poétique

poet laureate N poète lauréat

En Grande-Bretagne, le **poet laureate** est un poète qui reçoit un traitement en tant que poète de la cour et qui est officier de la maison royale à vie. Le premier d'entre eux fut Ben Jonson, en 1616. Le poète lauréat compose des vers pour marquer les grandes occasions comme les naissances et les mariages royaux, ainsi que d'autres événements d'importance nationale.

★**poetry** ['pəʊɪtrɪ] N poésie f

pogrom ['pɔgrəm] N pogrom m

poignant ['pɔɪnjənt] ADJ poignant(e); (sharp) vif (vive)

★**point** [pɔɪnt] N (Geom, Scol, Sport, on scale) point m; (tip) pointe f; (in time) moment m; (in space) endroit m; (subject, idea) point, sujet m; (purpose) but m; (also: **decimal point**): **2 ~ 3 (2.3)** 2 virgule 3 (2,3); (BRIT Elec: also: **power point**) prise f (de courant); **to make a ~** faire une remarque; **to make a ~ of doing sth** ne pas manquer de faire qch; **to make one's ~** se faire comprendre; **to get/miss the ~** comprendre/ne pas comprendre; **to come to the ~** en venir au fait; **when it comes to the ~** le moment venu; **there's no ~ (in doing)** cela ne sert à rien (de faire); **what's the ~?** à quoi ça sert ?; **to be on the ~ of doing sth** être sur le point de faire qch; **that's the whole ~!** précisément !; **to be beside the ~** être à côté de la question; **you've got a ~ there!** (c'est) juste !; **good points** qualités fpl; **in ~ of fact** en fait, en réalité; **~ of departure** (also fig) point de départ; **~ of order** point de procédure; **~ of sale** (Comm) point de vente; **the train stops at Carlisle and all points south** le train dessert Carlisle et toutes les gares vers le sud ▶ VT (show) indiquer; (wall, window) jointoyer; (gun etc): **to ~ sth at** braquer or diriger qch sur ▶ VI: **to ~ at** montrer du doigt; **to ~ to sth** (fig) signaler ■ **points** NPL (Aut) vis platinées; (Rail) aiguillage m

▶ **point out** VT (show) montrer, indiquer; (mention) faire remarquer, souligner

point-blank ['pɔɪnt'blæŋk] ADV (fig) catégoriquement; (also: **at point-blank range**) à bout portant ▶ ADJ (fig) catégorique

point duty N (BRIT): **to be on ~** diriger la circulation

pointed ['pɔɪntɪd] ADJ (shape) pointu(e); (remark) plein(e) de sous-entendus

pointedly ['pɔɪntɪdlɪ] ADV d'une manière significative

pointer ['pɔɪntəʳ] N (stick) baguette f; (needle) aiguille f; (dog) chien m d'arrêt; (clue) indication f; (advice) tuyau m

pointless ['pɔɪntlɪs] ADJ inutile, vain(e)

point of view N point m de vue

pointy ['pɔɪntɪ] ADJ (inf) en pointe

poise [pɔɪz] N (balance) équilibre m; (of head, body) port m; (calmness) calme m ▶ VT placer en équilibre; **to be poised for** (fig) être prêt à

poison ['pɔɪzn] N poison m ▶ VT empoisonner

poisoning ['pɔɪznɪŋ] N empoisonnement m

poisonous ['pɔɪznəs] ADJ (snake) venimeux(-euse); (substance, plant) vénéneux(-euse); (fumes) toxique; (fig) pernicieux(-euse)

poke [pəʊk] VT (fire) tisonner; (jab with finger, stick etc) piquer; pousser du doigt; (put): **to ~ sth in(to)** fourrer or enfoncer qch dans; **to ~ fun at sb** se moquer de qn ▶ N (jab) (petit) coup; (to fire) coup m de tisonnier

▶ **poke about** VI fureter

▶ **poke out** VI (stick out) sortir ▶ VT: **to ~ one's head out of the window** passer la tête par la fenêtre

poker ['pəʊkəʳ] N tisonnier m; (Cards) poker m

poker-faced ['pəʊkə'feɪst] ADJ au visage impassible

poky ['pəʊkɪ] ADJ exigu(ë)

★**Poland** ['pəʊlənd] N Pologne f

polar ['pəʊlə^r] ADJ polaire

polar bear N ours blanc

polarization [pəʊləraɪ'zeɪʃən] N opposition f

polarize ['pəʊləraɪz] VT polariser

Pole [pəʊl] N Polonais(e)

pole [pəʊl] N (of wood) mât m, perche f; (Elec) poteau m; (Geo) pôle m

poleaxe ['pəʊlæks] VT (fig) terrasser

pole bean N (US) haricot m (à rames)

polecat ['pəʊlkæt] N putois m

Pol. Econ. ['pɒlikɒn] N ABBR = **political economy**

polemic [pɒ'lɛmɪk] N polémique f

pole star N étoile f polaire

pole vault N saut m à la perche

★**police** [pə'liːs] NPL police f; **a large number of ~ were hurt** de nombreux policiers ont été blessés ▶ VT maintenir l'ordre dans

police car N voiture f de police

police constable N (BRIT) agent m de police

police department N (US) services mpl de police

police force N police f, forces fpl de l'ordre

★**policeman** [pə'liːsmən] N (irreg) agent m de police, policier m

police officer N agent m de police

police record N casier m judiciaire

police state N état policier

police station N commissariat m de police

★**policewoman** [pə'liːswumən] N (irreg) femme-agent f

policy ['pɒlɪsɪ] N politique f; (also: **insurance policy**) police f (d'assurance); (of newspaper, company) politique générale; **to take out a ~** (Insurance) souscrire une police d'assurance

policy holder N assuré(e)

policy-making ['pɒlɪsɪmeɪkɪŋ] N élaboration f de nouvelles lignes d'action

polio ['pəʊlɪəʊ] N polio f

★**Polish** ['pəʊlɪʃ] ADJ polonais(e) ▶ N (Ling) polonais m

★**polish** ['pɒlɪʃ] N (for shoes) cirage m; (for floor) cire f, encaustique f; (for nails) vernis m; (shine) éclat m, poli m; (fig: refinement) raffinement m ▶ VT (put polish on: shoes, wood) cirer; (make shiny) astiquer, faire briller; (fig: improve) perfectionner ▶ **polish off** VT (work) expédier; (food) liquider

polished ['pɒlɪʃt] ADJ (fig) raffiné(e)

polite [pə'laɪt] ADJ poli(e); **it's not ~ to do that** ça ne se fait pas

politely [pə'laɪtlɪ] ADV poliment

politeness [pə'laɪtnɪs] N politesse f

politic ['pɒlɪtɪk] ADJ diplomatique

★**political** [pə'lɪtɪkl] ADJ politique

political asylum N asile m politique

politically [pə'lɪtɪklɪ] ADV politiquement; **~ correct** politiquement correct

★**politician** [pɒlɪ'tɪʃən] N homme/femme politique, politicien(ne)

politicize [pə'lɪtɪsaɪz] VT politiser

★**politics** ['pɒlɪtɪks] N politique f

polka ['pɒlkə] N polka f

polka dot N pois m

poll [pəʊl] N scrutin m, vote m; (also: **opinion poll**) sondage m (d'opinion); **to go to the polls** (voters) aller aux urnes; (government) tenir des élections ▶ VT (votes) obtenir

pollen ['pɒlən] N pollen m

pollen count N taux m de pollen

pollinate ['pɒlɪneɪt] VT (plant, tree) polliniser

pollination [pɒlɪ'neɪʃən] N pollinisation f

polling ['pəʊlɪŋ] N (Pol) élections fpl; (Tel) invitation f à émettre

polling booth N (BRIT) isoloir m

polling day N (BRIT) jour m des élections

polling station N (BRIT) bureau m de vote

pollster ['pəʊlstə^r] N sondeur m, enquêteur(-euse)

poll tax N (BRIT: formerly) ≈ impôts locaux

pollutant [pə'luːtənt] N polluant m

pollute [pə'luːt] VT polluer

polluted [pə'luːtɪd] ADJ pollué(e); **to be ~ with sth** être pollué(e) par qch

polluter [pə'luːtə^r] N pollueur(-euse)

★**pollution** [pə'luːʃən] N pollution f

polo ['pəʊləʊ] N polo m

polo-neck ['pəʊləʊnɛk] ADJ à col roulé ▶ N (sweater) pull m à col roulé

polo shirt N polo m

poly ['pɒlɪ] N ABBR (BRIT) = **polytechnic**

poly bag N (BRIT inf) sac m en plastique

polyester [pɒlɪ'ɛstə^r] N polyester m

polygamy [pə'lɪgəmɪ] N polygamie f

polygraph ['pɒlɪgrɑːf] N détecteur m de mensonges

Polynesia [pɒlɪ'niːzɪə] N Polynésie f

Polynesian [pɒlɪ'niːzɪən] ADJ polynésien(ne) ▶ N Polynésien(ne)

polyp ['pɒlɪp] N (Med) polype m

polystyrene [pɒlɪ'staɪriːn] N polystyrène m

polytechnic [pɒlɪ'tɛknɪk] N (college) IUT m, Institut m universitaire de technologie

polythene ['pɒlɪθiːn] N (BRIT) polyéthylène m

polythene bag N sac m en plastique

polyunsaturated [pɒlɪʌn'sætʃəreɪtɪd] ADJ poly-insaturé(e)

polyurethane [pɒlɪ'juərɪθeɪn] N polyuréthane m

pomegranate ['pɒmɪgrænɪt] N grenade f

pommel ['pɒml] N pommeau m ▶ VT = **pummel**

pomp [pɒmp] N pompe f, faste f, apparat m

pompom ['pɒmpɒm] N pompon m

pompous ['pɒmpəs] ADJ pompeux(-euse)

pond [pɒnd] N étang m; (stagnant) mare f

ponder ['pɒndə^r] VI réfléchir ▶ VT considérer, peser

ponderous ['pɒndərəs] ADJ pesant(e), lourd(e)

pong [pɒŋ] (BRIT inf) N puanteur f ▶ VI schlinguer

pontiff ['pɒntɪf] N pontife m

pontificate [pɒn'tɪfɪkeɪt] VI (fig): **to ~ (about)** pontifier (sur)

pontoon [pɒn'tuːn] N ponton m; (BRIT Cards) vingt-et-un m

p

pony ['pəʊnɪ] N poney m

ponytail ['pəʊnɪteɪl] N queue f de cheval

pony trekking [-trekɪŋ] N (BRIT) randonnée f équestre or à cheval

poo [pu:] N (inf) caca m

poodle ['pu:dl] N caniche m

pooh-pooh ['pu:'pu:] VT dédaigner

★**pool** [pu:l] N (of rain) flaque f; (pond) mare f; (artificial) bassin m; (also: **swimming pool**) piscine f; (sth shared) fonds commun; (money at cards) cagnotte f; (billiards) poule f; (Comm: consortium) pool m; (US: monopoly trust) trust m; **typing ~**, (US) **secretary ~** pool m dactylographique ▶ VT mettre en commun ■ **pools** NPL (football) ≈ loto sportif; **to do the (football) pools** (BRIT) ≈ jouer au loto sportif; see also **football pools**

★**poor** [pʊəʳ] ADJ pauvre; (mediocre) médiocre, faible, mauvais(e) ▶ NPL: **the ~** les pauvres mpl

poorly ['pʊəlɪ] ADV pauvrement; (badly) mal, médiocrement ▶ ADJ souffrant(e), malade

★**pop** [pɒp] N (noise) bruit sec; (Mus) musique f pop; (inf: drink) soda m; (US inf: father) papa m ▶ VT (put) fourrer, mettre (rapidement); **she popped her head out of the window** elle passa la tête par la fenêtre ▶ VI éclater; (cork) sauter
   ▶ **pop in** VI entrer en passant
   ▶ **pop out** VI sortir
   ▶ **pop up** VI apparaître, surgir

pop concert N concert m pop

popcorn ['pɒpkɔ:n] N pop-corn m

pope [pəʊp] N pape m

poplar ['pɒpləʳ] N peuplier m

poplin ['pɒplɪn] N popeline f

popper ['pɒpəʳ] N (BRIT) bouton-pression m

poppy ['pɒpɪ] N (wild) coquelicot m; (cultivated) pavot m

poppycock ['pɒpɪkɔk] N (inf) balivernes fpl

Popsicle® ['pɒpsɪkl] N (US) esquimau m (glace)

pop star N pop star f

populace ['pɒpjʊləs] N peuple m

★**popular** ['pɒpjʊləʳ] ADJ populaire; (fashionable) à la mode; **to be ~ (with)** (person) avoir du succès (auprès de); (decision) être bien accueilli(e) (par)

popularity [pɒpjʊ'lærɪtɪ] N popularité f

popularize ['pɒpjʊləraɪz] VT populariser; (science) vulgariser

populate ['pɒpjʊleɪt] VT peupler

★**population** [pɒpjʊ'leɪʃən] N population f

population explosion N explosion f démographique

populist ['pɒpjʊlɪst] ADJ populiste

populous ['pɒpjʊləs] ADJ populeux(-euse)

pop-up ['pɒpʌp] ADJ (Comput: menu, window) pop up inv ▶ N pop up m inv, fenêtre f pop up

porcelain ['pɔ:slɪn] N porcelaine f

porch [pɔ:tʃ] N porche m; (US) véranda f

porcupine ['pɔ:kjupaɪn] N porc-épic m

pore [pɔ:ʳ] N pore m ▶ VI: **to ~ over** s'absorber dans, être plongé(e) dans

pork [pɔ:k] N porc m

pork chop N côte f de porc

pork pie N pâté m de porc en croûte

porn [pɔ:n] ADJ (inf) porno ▶ N (inf) porno m

pornographic [pɔ:nə'græfɪk] ADJ pornographique

pornography [pɔ:'nɔgrəfɪ] N pornographie f

porous ['pɔ:rəs] ADJ poreux(-euse)

porpoise ['pɔ:pəs] N marsouin m

porridge ['pɒrɪdʒ] N porridge m

★**port** [pɔ:t] N (harbour) port m; (opening in ship) sabord m; (Naut: left side) bâbord m; (wine) porto m; (Comput) port m, accès m; **to ~** (Naut) à bâbord; **~ of call** (port d')escale f ▶ CPD portuaire, du port

portability [pɔ:tə'bɪlɪtɪ] N portabilité f

portable ['pɔ:təbl] ADJ portatif(-ive)

portal ['pɔ:tl] N portail m

portcullis [pɔ:t'kʌlɪs] N herse f

portend [pɔ:'tend] VT présager, annoncer

portent ['pɔ:tent] N présage m

porter ['pɔ:təʳ] N (for luggage) porteur m; (doorkeeper) gardien(ne); portier m

portfolio [pɔ:t'fəʊlɪəʊ] N portefeuille m; (of artist) portfolio m

porthole ['pɔ:thəʊl] N hublot m

portico ['pɔ:tɪkəʊ] N portique m

portion ['pɔ:ʃən] N portion f, part f

portly ['pɔ:tlɪ] ADJ corpulent(e)

portrait ['pɔ:treɪt] N portrait m

portray [pɔ:'treɪ] VT faire le portrait de; (in writing) dépeindre, représenter; (subj: actor) jouer

portrayal [pɔ:'treɪəl] N portrait m, représentation f

★**Portugal** ['pɔ:tjʊgl] N Portugal m

★**Portuguese** [pɔ:tju'gi:z] ADJ portugais(e) ▶ N (pl inv) Portugais(e); (Ling) portugais m

Portuguese man-of-war [-mænəv'wɔ:ʳ] N (jellyfish) galère f

pose [pəʊz] N pose f; (pej) affectation f; **to strike a ~** poser (pour la galerie) ▶ VI poser; (pretend): **to ~ as** se faire passer pour ▶ VT poser; (problem) créer

poser ['pəʊzəʳ] N question difficile or embarrassante; (person) = **poseur**

poseur [pəʊ'zə:ʳ] N (pej) poseur(-euse)

posh [pɒʃ] ADJ (inf) chic inv; **to talk ~** parler d'une manière affectée

★**position** [pə'zɪʃən] N position f; (job, situation) situation f; **to be in a ~ to do sth** être en mesure de faire qch ▶ VT mettre en place or en position

★**positive** ['pɒzɪtɪv] ADJ positif(-ive); (certain) sûr(e), certain(e); (definite) formel(le), catégorique; (clear) indéniable, réel(le)

positively ['pɒzɪtɪvlɪ] ADV (affirmatively, enthusiastically) de façon positive; (inf: really) carrément; **to think ~** être positif(-ive)

posse ['pɒsɪ] N (US) détachement m

possess [pə'zɛs] VT posséder; **like one possessed** comme un fou; **whatever can have possessed you?** qu'est-ce qui vous a pris ?

possession [pə'zɛʃən] N possession f; **to take ~ of sth** prendre possession de qch ■ **possessions** NPL (belongings) affaires fpl

possessive [pə'zɛsɪv] ADJ possessif(-ive)

possessiveness [pə'zɛsɪvnɪs] N possessivité f

possessor [pə'zɛsəʳ] N possesseur m

★**possibility** [pɒsɪ'bɪlɪtɪ] N possibilité f; (event) éventualité f; **he's a ~ for the part** c'est un candidat possible pour le rôle

★**possible** ['pɒsɪbl] ADJ possible; (solution) envisageable, éventuel(le); **it is ~ to do it** il est possible de le faire; **as far as ~** dans la mesure du possible, autant que possible; **if ~** si possible; **as big as ~** aussi gros que possible

★**possibly** ['pɒsɪblɪ] ADV (perhaps) peut-être; **if you ~ can** si cela vous est possible; **I cannot ~ come** il m'est impossible de venir

★**post** [pəust] N (BRIT: mail) poste f; (: collection) levée f; (: letters, delivery) courrier m; (job, situation) poste m; (pole) poteau m; (trading post) comptoir (commercial); (Internet) billet m, post m; **by ~** (BRIT) par la poste; **by return of ~** (BRIT) par retour du courrier ▶ VT (notice) afficher; (Internet) poster; (BRIT: send by post, Mil) poster; (: appoint): **to ~ to** affecter à; **where can I ~ these cards?** où est-ce que je peux poster ces cartes postales?; **to keep sb posted** tenir qn au courant

post... [pəust] PREFIX post...; **post-1990** adj d'après 1990; adv après 1990

postage ['pəustɪdʒ] N tarifs mpl d'affranchissement; **~ paid** port payé; **~ prepaid** (US) franco (de port)

postage stamp N timbre-poste m

postal ['pəustl] ADJ postal(e)

postal order N mandat(-poste m) m

postbag ['pəustbæg] N (BRIT) sac postal; (postman's) sacoche f

postbox ['pəustbɒks] N (BRIT) boîte f aux lettres (publique)

★**postcard** ['pəustkɑːd] N carte postale

postcode ['pəustkəud] N (BRIT) code postal

postdate ['pəust'deɪt] VT (cheque) postdater

★**poster** ['pəustəʳ] N affiche f

poster child N (esp US: for cause: also: **poster boy/girl**) figure f emblématique

poste restante [pəust'restɒnt] N (BRIT) poste restante

posterior [pɒs'tɪərɪəʳ] N (inf) postérieur m, derrière m

posterity [pɒs'terɪtɪ] N postérité f

poster paint N gouache f

post exchange N (US Mil) magasin m de l'armée

post-free [pəust'friː] ADJ (BRIT) franco (de port)

postgraduate ['pəust'grædjuət] N ≈ étudiant(e) de troisième cycle

posthumous ['pɒstjuməs] ADJ posthume

posthumously ['pɒstjuməslɪ] ADV après la mort de l'auteur, à titre posthume

posting ['pəustɪŋ] N (BRIT) affectation f

★**postman** ['pəustmən] N (irreg) (BRIT) facteur m

postmark ['pəustmɑːk] N cachet m (de la poste)

postmarked ['pəustmɑːkt] ADJ: **the envelope was ~ Helsinki** l'enveloppe portait le cachet d'Helsinki

postmaster ['pəustmɑːstəʳ] N receveur m des postes

postmistress ['pəustmɪstrɪs] N receveuse f des postes

post-mortem [pəust'mɔːtəm] N autopsie f

postnatal ['pəust'neɪtl] ADJ postnatal(e)

★**post office** N (building) poste f; (organization): **the Post Office** les postes fpl

post office box N boîte postale

post-paid ['pəust'peɪd] ADJ (BRIT) port payé

postpone [pəs'pəun] VT remettre (à plus tard), reculer

postponement [pəs'pəunmənt] N ajournement m, renvoi m

postscript ['pəustskrɪpt] N post-scriptum m

postulate ['pɒstjuleɪt] VT postuler

posture ['pɒstʃəʳ] N posture f; (fig) attitude f ▶ VI poser

postwar [pəust'wɔːʳ] ADJ d'après-guerre

★**postwoman** ['pəust'wumən] N (irreg) (BRIT) factrice f

posy ['pəuzɪ] N petit bouquet

★**pot** [pɒt] N (for cooking) marmite f; casserole f; (teapot) théière f; (for coffee) cafetière f; (for plants, jam) pot m; (piece of pottery) poterie f; (inf: marijuana) herbe f; **to go to ~** (inf) aller à vau-l'eau; **pots of** (BRIT inf) beaucoup de, plein de ▶ VT (plant) mettre en pot

potash ['pɒtæʃ] N potasse f

potassium [pə'tæsɪəm] N potassium m

★**potato** [pə'teɪtəu] (pl **potatoes**) N pomme f de terre

potato crisps, (US) **potato chips** NPL chips mpl

potato flour N fécule f

potato peeler N épluche-légumes m

potbellied ['pɒtbelɪd] ADJ (from overeating) bedonnant(e); (from malnutrition) au ventre ballonné

potboiler ['pɒtbɔɪləʳ] N (Cine, Publishing) film or roman commercial

potency ['pəutnsɪ] N puissance f, force f; (of drink) degré m d'alcool

potent ['pəutnt] ADJ puissant(e); (drink) fort(e), très alcoolisé(e); (man) viril

potentate ['pəutnteɪt] N potentat m

★**potential** [pə'tenʃl] ADJ potentiel(le) ▶ N potentiel m; **to have ~** être prometteur(-euse); ouvrir des possibilités

potentially [pə'tenʃəlɪ] ADV potentiellement; **it's ~ dangerous** ça pourrait se révéler dangereux, il y a possibilité de danger

pothole ['pɒthəul] N (in road) nid m de poule; (BRIT: underground) gouffre m, caverne f

potholer ['pɒthəuləʳ] N (BRIT) spéléologue mf

potholing ['pɒthəulɪŋ] N (BRIT): **to go ~** faire de la spéléologie

potion ['pəuʃən] N potion f

potluck [pɒt'lʌk] N: **to take ~** tenter sa chance

pot plant N plante f d'appartement

potpourri [pəu'puriː] N pot-pourri m

pot roast N rôti m à la cocotte

pot shot N: **to take ~s at** canarder

potted ['pɒtɪd] ADJ (food) en conserve; (plant) en pot; (fig: shortened) abrégé(e)

potter ['pɒtəʳ] N potier m; **~'s wheel** tour m de potier ▶ VI (BRIT): **to ~ around** or **about** bricoler

pottery ['pɒtərɪ] N poterie f; **a piece of ~** une poterie

potty ['pɔtɪ] ADJ (BRIT inf: mad) dingue ▶ N (child's) pot m

potty-training ['pɔtɪtreɪnɪŋ] N apprentissage m de la propreté

pouch [pautʃ] N (Zool) poche f; (for tobacco) blague f; (for money) bourse f

pouf, pouffe [pu:f] N (stool) pouf m

poultice ['pəultɪs] N cataplasme m

poultry ['pəultrɪ] N volaille f

poultry farm N élevage m de volaille

poultry farmer N aviculteur m

pounce [pauns] VI: **to ~ (on)** bondir (sur), fondre (sur) ▶ N bond m, attaque f

★**pound** [paund] N livre f (weight = 453g, 16 ounces; money = 100 pence); (for dogs, cars) fourrière f; **half a ~ (of)** une demi-livre (de); **a five-pound note** un billet de cinq livres ▶ VT (beat) bourrer de coups, marteler; (crush) piler, pulvériser; (with guns) pilonner ▶ VI (heart) battre violemment, taper
▶ **pound on** VT FUS (door, table) frapper à grands coups à

pounding ['paundɪŋ] N: **to take a ~** (fig) prendre une râclée

pound sterling N livre f sterling

★**pour** [pɔːʳ] VT verser; **to ~ sb a drink** verser or servir à boire à qn ▶ VI couler à flots; (rain) pleuvoir à verse
▶ **pour away, pour off** VT vider
▶ **pour down** VI (rain) pleuvoir à verse
▶ **pour in** VI (people) affluer, se précipiter; (news, letters) arriver en masse; **to come pouring in** (water) entrer à flots; (letters) arriver par milliers; (people) affluer
▶ **pour out** VI (people) sortir en masse ▶ VT vider; (fig) déverser; (serve: a drink) verser

pouring ['pɔːrɪŋ] ADJ: **~ rain** pluie torrentielle

pout [paut] N moue f ▶ VI faire la moue

★**poverty** ['pɔvətɪ] N pauvreté f, misère f

poverty line N seuil m de pauvreté

poverty-stricken ['pɔvətɪstrɪkn] ADJ pauvre, déshérité(e)

poverty trap N (BRIT) piège m de la pauvreté

POW N ABBR = **prisoner of war**

powder ['paudəʳ] N poudre f ▶ VT poudrer; **to ~ one's nose** se poudrer; (euphemism) aller à la salle de bain

powder compact N poudrier m

powdered milk ['paudəd-] N lait m en poudre

powder keg N (fig) poudrière f

powder puff N houppette f

powder room N toilettes fpl (pour dames)

powdery ['paudərɪ] ADJ poudreux(-euse)

★**power** ['pauəʳ] N (strength, nation) puissance f, force f; (ability, Pol: of party, leader) pouvoir m; (Math) puissance; (of speech, thought) faculté f; (Elec) courant m; **to do all in one's ~ to help sb** faire tout ce qui est en son pouvoir pour aider qn; **the world powers** les grandes puissances; **to be in ~** être au pouvoir ▶ VT faire marcher, actionner
▶ **power down** VT éteindre, arrêter
▶ **power up** VT allumer

power base N base f de pouvoir

powerboat ['pauəbəut] N (BRIT) hors-bord m

power cut N (BRIT) coupure f de courant

powered ['pauəd] ADJ: **~ by** actionné(e) par, fonctionnant à; **nuclear-powered submarine** sous-marin m (à propulsion) nucléaire

power failure N panne f de courant

★**powerful** ['pauəful] ADJ puissant(e); (performance etc) très fort(e)

powerfully ['pauəfulɪ] ADV puissamment; (with force) avec force

powerhouse ['pauəhaus] N (fig: person) fonceur m; **a ~ of ideas** une mine d'idées

powerless ['pauəlɪs] ADJ impuissant(e)

powerlessness ['pauəlɪsnɪs] N impuissance f

power line N ligne f électrique

power of attorney N procuration f

power play N (in politics, business) jeu m de pouvoir(s); (Sport) période f de supériorité numérique

power point N (BRIT) prise f de courant

power station N centrale f électrique

power steering N direction assistée

power struggle N lutte f pour le pouvoir

powwow ['pauwau] N conciliabule m

p.p. ABBR (= per procurationem: by proxy) p.p.

PPE N ABBR (BRIT Scol) = **philosophy, politics and economics**

PPS N ABBR (= post postscriptum) PPS; (BRIT: = parliamentary private secretary) parlementaire chargé de mission auprès d'un ministre

PQ ABBR (CANADA: = Province of Quebec) PQ

PR N ABBR = **proportional representation; public relations** ▶ ABBR (US) = **Puerto Rico**

Pr. ABBR (= prince) Pce

practicability [præktɪkə'bɪlɪtɪ] N possibilité f de réalisation

practicable ['præktɪkəbl] ADJ (scheme) réalisable

★**practical** ['præktɪkl] ADJ pratique

practicality [præktɪ'kælɪtɪ] N (of plan) aspect m pratique; (of person) sens m pratique ■ **practicalities** NPL détails mpl pratiques

practical joke N farce f

practically ['præktɪklɪ] ADV (almost) pratiquement

★**practice** ['præktɪs] N pratique f; (of profession) exercice m; (at football etc) entraînement m; (business) cabinet m; clientèle f; **in ~** (in reality) en pratique; **out of ~** rouillé(e); **to put sth into ~** mettre qch en pratique; **2 hours' piano ~** 2 heures de travail or d'exercices au piano; **target ~** exercices de tir; **it's common ~** c'est courant, ça se fait couramment ▶ VT, VI (US) = **practise**

practice match N match m d'entraînement

practise, (US) **practice** ['præktɪs] VT (work at: piano, backhand etc) s'exercer à, travailler; (train for: sport) s'entraîner à; (a sport, religion, method) pratiquer; (profession) exercer ▶ VI s'exercer, travailler; (train) s'entraîner; (lawyer, doctor) exercer; **to ~ for a match** s'entraîner pour un match

practised, (US) **practiced** ['præktɪst] ADJ (person) expérimenté(e); (performance) impeccable; (liar) invétéré(e); **with a ~ eye** d'un œil exercé

practising, (US) **practicing** ['præktɪsɪŋ] ADJ (Christian etc) pratiquant(e); (lawyer) en exercice; (homosexual) déclaré

practitioner [præk'tɪʃənəʳ] N praticien(ne)

pragmatic [præg'mætɪk] ADJ pragmatique

pragmatism ['prægmətɪzəm] N pragmatisme m

pragmatist ['prægmətɪst] N pragmatiste mf

Prague [prɑːɡ] N Prague

prairie ['prɛərɪ] N savane f; (US): **the prairies** la Prairie

★**praise** [preɪz] N éloge(s) m(pl), louange(s) f(pl) ▶ VT louer, faire l'éloge de

praiseworthy ['preɪzwəːðɪ] ADJ digne de louanges

pram [præm] N (BRIT) landau m, voiture f d'enfant

prance [prɑːns] VI (horse) caracoler

prank [præŋk] N farce f

prankster ['præŋkstəʳ] N farceur(-euse)

prat [præt] N (BRIT inf) imbécile m, andouille f

prattle ['prætl] VI jacasser

prawn [prɔːn] N crevette f (rose)

prawn cocktail N cocktail m de crevettes

pray [preɪ] VI prier

prayer [prɛəʳ] N prière f

prayer book N livre m de prières

pre... ['priː] PREFIX pré...; **pre-1970** adj d'avant 1970; adv avant 1970

preach [priːtʃ] VT, VI prêcher; **to ~ at sb** faire la morale à qn

preacher ['priːtʃəʳ] N prédicateur m; (US: clergyman) pasteur m

preamble [prɪ'æmbl] N préambule m

prearranged [priːə'reɪndʒd] ADJ organisé(e) or fixé(e) à l'avance

precarious [prɪ'kɛərɪəs] ADJ précaire

precariously [prɪ'kɛərɪəslɪ] ADV (uncertainly) de manière précaire; (unsteadily) **~ balanced** en équilibre instable

precaution [prɪ'kɔːʃən] N précaution f

precautionary [prɪ'kɔːʃənrɪ] ADJ (measure) de précaution

precede [prɪ'siːd] VT, VI précéder

precedence ['presɪdəns] N préséance f

precedent ['presɪdənt] N précédent m; **to establish** or **set a ~** créer un précédent

preceding [prɪ'siːdɪŋ] ADJ qui précède (or précédait)

precept ['priːsept] N précepte m

precinct ['priːsɪŋkt] N (round cathedral) pourtour m, enceinte f; (US: district) circonscription f, arrondissement m; **pedestrian ~** (BRIT) zone piétonnière; **shopping ~** (BRIT) centre commercial ■ **precincts** NPL (neighbourhood) alentours mpl, environs mpl

precious ['preʃəs] ADJ précieux(-euse); **your ~ dog** (inf) ton chien chéri, ton chéri chien ▶ ADV (inf): **~ little** or **few** fort peu

precipice ['presɪpɪs] N précipice m

precipitate ADJ [prɪ'sɪpɪtɪt] (hasty) précipité(e) ▶ VT [prɪ'sɪpɪteɪt] précipiter

precipitation [prɪsɪpɪ'teɪʃən] N précipitation f

precipitous [prɪ'sɪpɪtəs] ADJ (steep) abrupt(e), à pic

précis ['preɪsiː] (pl ~ [-z]) N résumé m

precise [prɪ'saɪs] ADJ précis(e)

★**precisely** [prɪ'saɪslɪ] ADV précisément

precision [prɪ'sɪʒən] N précision f

preclude [prɪ'kluːd] VT exclure, empêcher; **to ~ sb from doing** empêcher qn de faire

precocious [prɪ'kəuʃəs] ADJ précoce

preconceived [priːkən'siːvd] ADJ (idea) préconçu(e)

preconception [priːkən'sepʃən] N idée préconçue

precondition ['priːkən'dɪʃən] N condition f nécessaire

precursor [priː'kəːsəʳ] N précurseur m

predate ['priː'deɪt] VT (precede) antidater

predator ['predətəʳ] N prédateur m, rapace m

predatory ['predətərɪ] ADJ rapace

predecessor ['priːdɪsesəʳ] N prédécesseur m

predestination [priːdestɪ'neɪʃən] N prédestination f

predetermine [priːdɪ'təːmɪn] VT prédéterminer

predetermined [priːdɪ'təːmɪnd] ADJ prédéterminé(e)

predicament [prɪ'dɪkəmənt] N situation f difficile

predicate ['predɪkɪt] N (Ling) prédicat m

predicated ['predɪkeɪtɪd] ADJ: **to be ~ on sth** supposer qch

predict [prɪ'dɪkt] VT prédire

predictable [prɪ'dɪktəbl] ADJ prévisible

predictably [prɪ'dɪktəblɪ] ADV (behave, react) de façon prévisible; **~ she didn't arrive** comme on pouvait s'y attendre, elle n'est pas venue

prediction [prɪ'dɪkʃən] N prédiction f

predictor [prɪ'dɪktəʳ] N indicateur m

predilection [priːdɪ'lekʃən] N prédilection f

predispose [priːdɪs'pəuz] VT prédisposer

predominance [prɪ'dɔmɪnəns] N prédominance f

predominant [prɪ'dɔmɪnənt] ADJ prédominant(e)

predominantly [prɪ'dɔmɪnəntlɪ] ADV en majeure partie; (especially) surtout

predominate [prɪ'dɔmɪneɪt] VI prédominer

pre-eminent [priː'emɪnənt] ADJ prééminent(e)

pre-empt [priː'emt] VT (acquire) acquérir par droit de préemption; (fig) anticiper sur; **to ~ the issue** conclure avant même d'ouvrir les débats

pre-emptive [prɪ'emtɪv] ADJ: **~ strike** attaque (or action) préventive

preen [priːn] VT: **to ~ itself** (bird) se lisser les plumes; **to ~ o.s.** s'admirer

prefab ['priːfæb] N ABBR (= prefabricated building) bâtiment préfabriqué

prefabricated [priː'fæbrɪkeɪtɪd] ADJ préfabriqué(e)

preface ['prefəs] N préface f

prefect ['priːfekt] N (BRIT: in school) élève chargé de certaines fonctions de discipline; (in France) préfet m

★**prefer** [prɪˈfəːʳ] vt préférer; (Law): **to ~ charges** procéder à une inculpation; **to ~ coffee to tea** préférer le café au thé; **to ~ doing** or **to do sth** préférer faire qch

preferable [ˈprɛfrəbl] ADJ préférable

preferably [ˈprɛfrəblɪ] ADV de préférence

preference [ˈprɛfrəns] N préférence f; **in ~ to sth** plutôt que qch, de préférence à qch

preference shares NPL (BRIT) actions privilégiées

preferential [prɛfəˈrɛnʃəl] ADJ préférentiel(le); **~ treatment** traitement m de faveur

preferred [prɪˈfəːd] ADJ préféré(e)

preferred stock NPL (US) = **preference shares**

prefix [ˈpriːfɪks] N préfixe m

pregnancy [ˈprɛgnənsɪ] N grossesse f

pregnancy test N test m de grossesse

★**pregnant** [ˈprɛgnənt] ADJ enceinte; (animal) pleine; **3 months ~** enceinte de 3 mois

prehistoric [ˈpriːhɪsˈtɔrɪk] ADJ préhistorique

prehistory [priːˈhɪstərɪ] N préhistoire f

prejudge [priːˈdʒʌdʒ] vt préjuger de

prejudice [ˈprɛdʒudɪs] N préjugé m; (harm) tort m, préjudice m; **racial ~** préjugés raciaux ▶ vt porter préjudice à; (bias): **to ~ sb in favour of/against** prévenir qn en faveur de/contre

prejudiced [ˈprɛdʒudɪst] ADJ (person) plein(e) de préjugés; (in a matter) partial(e); (view) préconçu(e), partial(e); **to be ~ against sb/sth** avoir un parti-pris contre qn/qch; **to be racially ~** avoir des préjugés raciaux

prejudicial [prɛdʒuˈdɪʃl] ADJ préjudiciable; **~ to sth** préjudiciable à qch

prelate [ˈprɛlət] N prélat m

preliminaries [prɪˈlɪmɪnərɪz] NPL préliminaires mpl

preliminary [prɪˈlɪmɪnərɪ] ADJ préliminaire

prelude [ˈprɛljuːd] N prélude m

premarital [ˈpriːˈmærɪtl] ADJ avant le mariage; **~ contract** contrat m de mariage

premature [ˈprɛmətʃuəʳ] ADJ prématuré(e); **to be ~ (in doing sth)** aller un peu (trop) vite (en faisant qch)

prematurely [ˈprɛmətʃuəlɪ] ADV prématurément

premeditated [priːˈmɛdɪteɪtɪd] ADJ prémédité(e)

premeditation [priːmɛdɪˈteɪʃən] N préméditation f

premenstrual [priːˈmɛnstruəl] ADJ prémenstruel(le)

premenstrual tension N irritabilité f avant les règles

premier [ˈprɛmɪəʳ] ADJ premier(-ière), principal(e) ▶ N (Pol: Prime Minister) premier ministre; (: President) chef m de l'État

premiere [ˈprɛmɪɛəʳ] N première f

Premier League N première division

premiership [ˈprɛmɪəʃɪp] N (of leader) mandat m (d'un Premier ministre); (Sport) championnat m de ligue 1

premise [ˈprɛmɪs] N prémisse f

premises [ˈprɛmɪsɪz] NPL locaux mpl; **on the ~** sur les lieux; sur place; **business ~** locaux commerciaux

premium [ˈpriːmɪəm] N prime f; **to be at a ~** (fig: housing etc) être très demandé(e), être rarissime; **to sell at a ~** (shares) vendre au-dessus du pair

premium bond N (BRIT) obligation f à prime, bon m à lots

premium deal N (Comm) offre spéciale

premium fuel, (US) **premium gasoline** N super m

premonition [prɛməˈnɪʃən] N prémonition f

preoccupation [priːɔkjuˈpeɪʃən] N préoccupation f

preoccupied [priːˈɔkjupaɪd] ADJ préoccupé(e)

pre-owned [priːˈəund] ADJ (game, car) d'occasion

prep [prɛp] ADJ ABBR = **preparatory school** ▶ N (Scol: = preparation) étude f

prepackaged [priːˈpækɪdʒd] ADJ préempaqueté(e)

prepaid [priːˈpeɪd] ADJ payé(e) d'avance

preparation [prɛpəˈreɪʃən] N préparation f; **in ~ for** en vue de ■ **preparations** NPL (for trip, war) préparatifs mpl

preparatory [prɪˈpærətərɪ] ADJ préparatoire; **~ to sth/to doing sth** en prévision de qch/avant de faire qch

preparatory school N (BRIT) école primaire privée; (US) lycée privé

★**prepare** [prɪˈpɛəʳ] vt préparer ▶ vi: **to ~ for** se préparer à

★**prepared** [prɪˈpɛəd] ADJ: **~ for** préparé(e) à; **~ to** prêt(e) à

preponderance [prɪˈpɔndərns] N prépondérance f

preposition [prɛpəˈzɪʃən] N préposition f

prepossessing [priːpəˈzɛsɪŋ] ADJ avenant(e), engageant(e)

preposterous [prɪˈpɔstərəs] ADJ ridicule, absurde

prep school N = **preparatory school**

prequel [ˈpriːkwl] N préquel m, préquelle f

pre-record [priːrɪˈkɔːd] vt préenregistrer

pre-recorded [priːrɪˈkɔːdɪd] ADJ préenregistré(e); **~ broadcast** émission f en différé, émission f préenregistrée

prerequisite [priːˈrɛkwɪzɪt] N condition f préalable

prerogative [prɪˈrɔgətɪv] N prérogative f

presbyterian [prɛzbɪˈtɪərɪən] ADJ, N presbytérien(ne)

presbytery [ˈprɛzbɪtərɪ] N presbytère m

preschool [ˈpriːˈskuːl] ADJ préscolaire; (child) d'âge préscolaire

prescience [ˈprɛsɪəns] N prescience f

prescient [ˈprɛsɪənt] ADJ visionnaire

prescribe [prɪˈskraɪb] vt prescrire; **prescribed books** (BRIT Scol) œuvres fpl au programme

prescription [prɪˈskrɪpʃən] N prescription f; (Med) ordonnance f; (: medicine) médicament m (obtenu sur ordonnance); **to make up** or (US) **fill a ~** faire une ordonnance; **could you write me a ~?**

pouvez-vous me faire une ordonnance ?; **"only available on ~"** « uniquement sur ordonnance »

prescription charges NPL (*BRIT*) participation *f* fixe au coût de l'ordonnance

prescriptive [prɪ'skrɪptɪv] ADJ normatif(-ive)

pre-season [pri:'si:zən] CPD (*training, match*) de présaison

presence ['prɛzns] N présence *f*; **in sb's ~** en présence de qn; **~ of mind** présence d'esprit

★**present** ADJ ['prɛznt] présent(e); (*current*) présent, actuel(le); **to be ~ at** assister à; **those ~** les présents; **~ tense** présent *m* ▶ N ['prɛznt] cadeau *m*; (*time, tense*) présent *m*; **to give sb a ~** offrir un cadeau à qn; **at ~** en ce moment ▶ VT [prɪ'zɛnt] présenter; (*prize, medal*) remettre; (*give*): **to ~ sb with sth** offrir qch à qn; **to ~ sb (to sb)** présenter qn (à qn)

presentable [prɪ'zɛntəbl] ADJ présentable

presentation [prɛzn'teɪʃən] N présentation *f*; (*gift*) cadeau *m*, présent *m*; (*ceremony*) remise *f* du cadeau (*or* de la médaille *etc*); **on ~ of** (*voucher etc*) sur présentation de

present-day ['prɛzntdeɪ] ADJ contemporain(e), actuel(le)

presenter [prɪ'zɛntər] N (*BRIT Radio, TV*) présentateur(-trice)

presently ['prɛzntlɪ] ADV (*soon*) tout à l'heure, bientôt; (*with verb in past*) peu après; (*at present*) en ce moment; (*US: now*) maintenant

preservation [prɛzə'veɪʃən] N préservation *f*, conservation *f*

preservative [prɪ'zə:vətɪv] N agent *m* de conservation

preserve [prɪ'zə:v] VT (*keep safe*) préserver, protéger; (*maintain*) conserver, garder; (*food*) mettre en conserve ▶ N (*for game, fish*) réserve *f*; (*often pl: jam*) confiture *f*; (*: fruit*) fruits *mpl* en conserve

preset [pri:'sɛt] VT prérégler

preshrunk [pri:'ʃrʌŋk] ADJ irrétrécissable

preside [prɪ'zaɪd] VI présider

presidency ['prɛzɪdənsɪ] N présidence *f*

★**president** ['prɛzɪdənt] N président(e); (*US: of company*) président-directeur général, PDG *m*

presidential [prɛzɪ'dɛnʃl] ADJ présidentiel(le)

★**press** [prɛs] N (*tool, machine, newspapers*) presse *f*; (*for wine*) pressoir *m*; (*crowd*) cohue *f*, foule *f*; **to go to ~** (*newspaper*) aller à l'impression; **to be in the ~** (*being printed*) être sous presse; (*in the newspapers*) être dans le journal ▶ VT (*push*) appuyer sur; (*squeeze*) presser, serrer; (*clothes: iron*) repasser; (*pursue*) talonner; (*insist*): **to ~ sth on sb** presser qn d'accepter qch; (*urge, entreat*): **to ~ sb to do** *or* **into doing sth** pousser qn à faire qch; **to ~ sb for an answer** presser qn de répondre; **to ~ charges against sb** (*Law*) engager des poursuites contre qn; **we are pressed for time** le temps nous manque ▶ VI appuyer, peser; se presser; **to ~ for sth** faire pression pour obtenir qch
  ▶ **press ahead** VI = **press on**
  ▶ **press on** VI continuer

press agency N agence *f* de presse

press clipping N coupure *f* de presse

press conference N conférence *f* de presse

press cutting N = **press clipping**

press-gang ['prɛsgæŋ] VT (*fig*): **to ~ sb into doing sth** faire pression sur qn pour qu'il fasse qch

pressing ['prɛsɪŋ] ADJ urgent(e), pressant(e) ▶ N repassage *m*

press officer N attaché(e) de presse

press release N communiqué *m* de presse

press room N salle *f* de presse

press stud N (*BRIT*) bouton-pression *m*

press-up ['prɛsʌp] N (*BRIT*) traction *f*

★**pressure** ['prɛʃər] N pression *f*; (*stress*) tension *f*; **to put ~ on sb (to do sth)** faire pression sur qn (pour qu'il fasse qch) ▶ VT faire pression sur

pressure cooker N cocotte-minute® *f*

pressured ['prɛʃəd] ADJ (*tense*) tendu(e)

pressure gauge N manomètre *m*

pressure group N groupe *m* de pression

pressurize ['prɛʃəraɪz] VT pressuriser; (*BRIT fig*): **to ~ sb (into doing sth)** faire pression sur qn (pour qu'il fasse qch)

pressurized ['prɛʃəraɪzd] ADJ pressurisé(e)

prestige [prɛs'ti:ʒ] N prestige *m*

prestigious [prɛs'tɪdʒəs] ADJ prestigieux(-euse)

presumably [prɪ'zju:məblɪ] ADV vraisemblablement; **~ he did it** c'est sans doute lui (qui a fait cela)

presume [prɪ'zju:m] VT présumer, supposer; **to ~ to do** (*dare*) se permettre de faire

presumption [prɪ'zʌmpʃən] N supposition *f*, présomption *f*; (*boldness*) audace *f*

presumptuous [prɪ'zʌmpʃəs] ADJ présomptueux(-euse)

presuppose [pri:sə'pəuz] VT présupposer

pre-tax [pri:'tæks] ADJ avant impôt(s)

pre-teen [pri:'ti:n] ADJ, N préadolescent(e); **~ children** les préadolescents

pretence, (*US*) **pretense** [prɪ'tɛns] N (*claim*) prétention *f*; (*pretext*) prétexte *m*; **she is devoid of all ~** elle n'est pas du tout prétentieuse; **to make a ~ of doing** faire semblant de faire; **on** *or* **under the ~ of doing sth** sous prétexte de faire qch; **under false pretences** sous des prétextes fallacieux

★**pretend** [prɪ'tɛnd] VT (*feign*) feindre, simuler; **to ~ to do** faire semblant de faire ▶ VI (*feign*) faire semblant; (*claim*): **to ~ to sth** prétendre à qch

pretense [prɪ'tɛns] N (*US*) = **pretence**

pretension [prɪ'tɛnʃən] N (*claim*) prétention *f*; **to have no pretensions to sth/to being sth** n'avoir aucune prétention à qch/à être qch

pretentious [prɪ'tɛnʃəs] ADJ prétentieux(-euse)

preterite ['prɛtərɪt] N prétérit *m*

pretext ['pri:tɛkst] N prétexte *m*; **on** *or* **under the ~ of doing sth** sous prétexte de faire qch

★**pretty** ['prɪtɪ] ADJ joli(e) ▶ ADV assez

pretzel ['prɛtsl] N bretzel *m*

prevail [prɪ'veɪl] VI (*win*) l'emporter, prévaloir; (*be usual*) avoir cours; (*persuade*): **to ~ (up)on sb to do** persuader qn de faire

prevailing [prɪ'veɪlɪŋ] ADJ (*widespread*) courant(e), répandu(e); (*wind*) dominant(e)

prevalence ['prɛvələns] N prévalence *f*

prevalent ['prɛvələnt] ADJ (*condition*) prévalent(e); (*view, attitude*) répandu(e); (*fashion*) en vogue

P

prevarication [prɪværɪˈkeɪʃən] N (usage m de) faux-fuyants mpl

★**prevent** [prɪˈvɛnt] VT: **to ~ (from doing)** empêcher (de faire)

preventable [prɪˈvɛntəbl] ADJ évitable

preventative [prɪˈvɛntətɪv] ADJ préventif(-ive)

prevention [prɪˈvɛnʃən] N prévention f

preventive [prɪˈvɛntɪv] ADJ préventif(-ive)

preview [ˈpriːvjuː] N (of film) avant-première f; (fig) aperçu m

★**previous** [ˈpriːvɪəs] ADJ (last) précédent(e); (earlier) antérieur(e); (question, experience) préalable; **I have a ~ engagement** je suis déjà pris(e); **~ to doing** avant de faire

previously [ˈpriːvɪəslɪ] ADV précédemment, auparavant

prewar [priːˈwɔːr] ADJ d'avant-guerre

prey [preɪ] N proie f ▶ VI: **to ~ on** s'attaquer à; **it was preying on his mind** ça le rongeait or minait

★**price** [praɪs] N prix m; (Betting: odds) cote f; **what is the ~ of ...?** combien coûte ...?, quel est le prix de ...?; **to go up** or **rise in ~** augmenter; **to put a ~ on sth** chiffrer qch; **what ~ his promises now?** (BRIT) que valent maintenant toutes ses promesses?; **he regained his freedom, but at a ~** il a retrouvé sa liberté, mais cela lui a coûté cher ▶ VT (goods) fixer le prix de; tarifer; **to be priced out of the market** (article) être trop cher pour soutenir la concurrence; (producer, nation) ne pas pouvoir soutenir la concurrence

price control N contrôle m des prix

price-cutting [ˈpraɪskʌtɪŋ] N réductions fpl de prix

priceless [ˈpraɪslɪs] ADJ sans prix, inestimable; (inf: amusing) impayable

price list N tarif m

price range N gamme f de prix; **it's within my ~** c'est dans mes prix

price tag N étiquette f

price war N guerre f des prix

pricey [ˈpraɪsɪ] ADJ (inf) chérot inv

pricing [ˈpraɪsɪŋ] N prix mpl

prick [prɪk] N (sting) piqûre f; (!) bitte f (!); connard m (!) ▶ VT piquer; **to ~ up one's ears** dresser or tendre l'oreille

prickle [ˈprɪkl] N (of plant) épine f; (sensation) picotement m

prickly [ˈprɪklɪ] ADJ piquant(e), épineux(-euse); (fig: person) irritable

prickly heat N fièvre f miliaire

prickly pear N figue f de Barbarie

★**pride** [praɪd] N (feeling proud) fierté f; (pej) orgueil m; (self-esteem) amour-propre m; **to take (a) ~ in** être (très) fier(-ère) de; **to take a ~ in doing** mettre sa fierté à faire; **to have ~ of place** (BRIT) avoir la place d'honneur ▶ VT: **to ~ o.s. on** se flatter de; s'enorgueillir de

★**priest** [priːst] N prêtre m

priestess [ˈpriːstɪs] N prêtresse f

priesthood [ˈpriːsthud] N prêtrise f, sacerdoce m

prig [prɪg] N poseur(-euse), fat m

prim [prɪm] ADJ collet monté inv, guindé(e)

prima facie [ˈpraɪməˈfeɪʃɪ] ADJ: **to have a ~ case** (Law) avoir une affaire recevable

primal [ˈpraɪməl] ADJ (first in time) primitif(-ive); (first in importance) primordial(e)

primarily [ˈpraɪmərɪlɪ] ADV principalement, essentiellement

★**primary** [ˈpraɪmərɪ] ADJ primaire; (first in importance) premier(-ière), primordial(e) ▶ N (US: election) (élection f) primaire f

primary colour N couleur fondamentale

primary school N (BRIT) école f primaire

> Les **primary schools** accueillent en Grande-Bretagne les enfants de 4 ou 5 ans à 11 ans. Elles marquent le début de la scolarité obligatoire, dont elles couvrent les sept premières années. Certaines d'entre elles comprennent deux sections : celle des petits (infant school) et celle des grands (junior school).

primate N (Rel) ['praɪmɪt] primat m; (Zool) ['praɪmeɪt] primate m

prime [praɪm] ADJ primordial(e), fondamental(e); (excellent) excellent(e) ▶ VT (gun, pump) amorcer; (fig) mettre au courant ▶ N: **in the ~ of life** dans la fleur de l'âge

Prime Minister N Premier ministre

primer [ˈpraɪmər] N (book) premier livre, manuel m élémentaire; (paint) apprêt m

prime time N (Radio, TV) heure(s) f(pl) de grande écoute

primeval [praɪˈmiːvl] ADJ primitif(-ive)

primitive [ˈprɪmɪtɪv] ADJ primitif(-ive)

primrose [ˈprɪmrəuz] N primevère f

primus® [ˈpraɪməs], **primus stove®** N (BRIT) réchaud m de camping

★**prince** [prɪns] N prince m

princely [ˈprɪnslɪ] ADJ princier(-ière)

★**princess** [prɪnˈsɛs] N princesse f

★**principal** [ˈprɪnsɪpl] ADJ principal(e) ▶ N (head teacher) directeur m, principal m; (in play) rôle principal; (money) principal m

principality [prɪnsɪˈpælɪtɪ] N principauté f

principally [ˈprɪnsɪplɪ] ADV principalement

principle [ˈprɪnsɪpl] N principe m; **in ~** en principe; **on ~** par principe

★**print** [prɪnt] N (mark) empreinte f; (letters) caractères mpl; (fabric) imprimé m; (Art) gravure f, estampe f; (Phot) épreuve f; **out of ~** épuisé(e) ▶ VT imprimer; (publish) publier; (write in capitals) écrire en majuscules
▶ **print out** VT (Comput) imprimer

printed circuit board [ˈprɪntɪd-] N carte f à circuit imprimé

printed matter [ˈprɪntɪd-] N imprimés mpl

printer [ˈprɪntər] N (machine) imprimante f; (person) imprimeur m

printhead [ˈprɪnthɛd] N tête f d'impression

printing [ˈprɪntɪŋ] N impression f

printing press N presse f typographique

printout [ˈprɪntaut] N (Comput) sortie f imprimante

print wheel N marguerite f

prior ['praɪə^r] ADJ antérieur(e), précédent(e); (*more important*) prioritaire; **without ~ notice** sans préavis; **to have a ~ claim to sth** avoir priorité pour qch ▸ N (*Rel*) prieur m ▸ ADV: **~ to doing** avant de faire

prioritize [praɪˈɒrɪtaɪz] VT (*give priority to*) privilégier; (*order by importance*) ordonner selon les priorités

★**priority** [praɪˈɒrɪtɪ] N priorité f; **to have** or **take ~ over sth/sb** avoir la priorité sur qch/qn

priory ['praɪərɪ] N prieuré m

prise [praɪz] VT: **to ~ open** forcer

prism ['prɪzəm] N prisme m

★**prison** ['prɪzn] N prison f ▸ CPD pénitentiaire

prison camp N camp m de prisonniers

★**prisoner** ['prɪznə^r] N prisonnier(-ière); **the ~ at the bar** l'accusé(e); **to take sb ~** faire qn prisonnier

prisoner of war N prisonnier(-ière) de guerre

prissy ['prɪsɪ] ADJ bégueule

pristine ['prɪstiːn] ADJ virginal(e)

privacy ['prɪvəsɪ] N intimité f, solitude f

★**private** ['praɪvɪt] ADJ (*not public*) privé(e); (*personal*) personnel(le); (*house, car, lesson*) particulier(-ière); (*quiet: place*) tranquille; **"~"** (*on envelope*) « personnelle »; (*on door*) « privé »; **in (his) ~ life** dans sa vie privée; **he is a very ~ person** il est très secret; **to be in ~ practice** être médecin (or dentiste etc) non conventionné; **~ hearing** (*Law*) audience f à huis-clos ▸ N soldat m de deuxième classe; **in ~** en privé

private detective N détective privé

private enterprise N entreprise privée

private eye N détective privé

private limited company N (*BRIT*) société f à participation restreinte (*non cotée en Bourse*)

privately ['praɪvɪtlɪ] ADV en privé; (*within oneself*) intérieurement

private parts NPL parties (génitales)

private property N propriété privée

private school N école privée

privatization [praɪvətaɪˈzeɪʃən] N privatisation f

★**privatize** ['praɪvɪtaɪz] VT privatiser

privet ['prɪvɪt] N troène m

privilege ['prɪvɪlɪdʒ] N privilège m

privileged ['prɪvɪlɪdʒd] ADJ privilégié(e); **to be ~ to do sth** avoir le privilège de faire qch

privy ['prɪvɪ] ADJ: **to be ~ to** être au courant de

privy council N conseil privé

> Le **Privy Council** est un groupe d'éminents hommes politiques présents ou passés, dont les membres du gouvernement actuel, qui remplissent une fonction de conseil auprès du souverain britannique. Jadis doté de pouvoirs importants, il n'a plus aujourd'hui de rôle exécutif.

★**prize** [praɪz] N prix m ▸ ADJ (*example, idiot*) parfait(e); (*bull, novel*) primé(e) ▸ VT priser, faire grand cas de

prized [praɪzd] ADJ précieux(-euse); **their most ~ possession** leur plus précieuse possession; **to be ~ for sth** être prisé(e) pour qch

prize-fighter ['praɪzfaɪtə^r] N boxeur professionnel

prize-giving ['praɪzgɪvɪŋ] N distribution f des prix

prize money N argent m du prix

prizewinner ['praɪzwɪnə^r] N gagnant(e)

prizewinning ['praɪzwɪnɪŋ] ADJ gagnant(e); (*novel, essay etc*) primé(e)

PRO N ABBR = **public relations officer**

pro [prəu] N (*inf: Sport*) professionnel(le) ▸ PREP pro ▪ **pros** NPL: **the pros and cons** le pour et le contre

pro- [prəu] PREFIX (*in favour of*) pro-

pro-active [prəuˈæktɪv] ADJ dynamique

probability [prɒbəˈbɪlɪtɪ] N probabilité f; **in all ~** très probablement

probable ['prɒbəbl] ADJ probable; **it is ~/hardly ~ that ...** il est probable/peu probable que ...

★**probably** ['prɒbəblɪ] ADV probablement

probate ['prəubɪt] N (*Law*) validation f, homologation f

probation [prəˈbeɪʃən] N (*in employment*) (période f d')essai m; (*Law*) liberté surveillée; (*Rel*) noviciat m, probation f; **on ~** (*employee*) à l'essai; (*Law*) en liberté surveillée

probationary [prəˈbeɪʃənrɪ] ADJ (*period*) d'essai

probe [prəub] N (*Med, Space*) sonde f; (*enquiry*) enquête f, investigation f ▸ VT sonder, explorer

probity ['prəubɪtɪ] N probité f

★**problem** ['prɒbləm] N problème m; **to have problems with the car** avoir des ennuis avec la voiture; **what's the ~?** qu'y a-t-il ?, quel est le problème ?; **I had no ~ in finding her** je n'ai pas eu de mal à la trouver; **no ~!** pas de problème !

problematic [prɒbləˈmætɪk] ADJ problématique

problem-solving ['prɒbləmsɒlvɪŋ] N résolution f de problèmes; **an approach to ~** une approche en matière de résolution de problèmes

procedural [prəˈsiːdʒərəl] ADJ procédural(e)

procedure [prəˈsiːdʒə^r] N (*Admin, Law*) procédure f; (*method*) marche f à suivre, façon f de procéder

proceed [prəˈsiːd] VI (*go forward*) avancer; (*act*) procéder; (*continue*): **to ~ (with)** continuer, poursuivre; **to ~ to** aller à; passer à; **to ~ to do** se mettre à faire; **I am not sure how to ~** je ne sais pas exactement comment m'y prendre; **to ~ against sb** (*Law*) intenter des poursuites contre qn

proceedings [prəˈsiːdɪŋz] NPL (*measures*) mesures fpl; (*Law: against sb*) poursuites fpl; (*meeting*) réunion f, séance f; (*records*) compte rendu; actes mpl

proceeds ['prəusiːdz] NPL produit m, recette f

★**process** N ['prəuses] processus m; (*method*) procédé m; **in ~** en cours; **we are in the ~ of doing** nous sommes en train de faire ▸ VT ['prəuses] traiter ▸ VI [prəˈses] (*BRIT formal: go in procession*) défiler

processed cheese ['prəusest-] N ≈ fromage fondu

processing ['prəusesɪŋ] N traitement m

procession [prəˈseʃən] N défilé m, cortège m; **funeral ~** (*on foot*) cortège funèbre; (*in cars*) convoi m mortuaire

pro-choice [prəuˈtʃɔɪs] ADJ en faveur de l'avortement

proclaim [prəˈkleɪm] VT déclarer, proclamer

proclamation [prɔkləˈmeɪʃən] N proclamation f

proclivity [prəˈklɪvɪtɪ] N inclination f

procrastinate [prəuˈkræstɪneɪt] VI faire traîner les choses, vouloir tout remettre au lendemain

procrastination [prəukræstɪˈneɪʃən] N procrastination f

procreation [prəukrɪˈeɪʃən] N procréation f

Procurator Fiscal [ˈprɔkjureɪtə-] N (SCOTTISH) ≈ procureur m (de la République)

procure [prəˈkjuəʳ] VT (for o.s.) se procurer; (for sb) procurer

procurement [prəˈkjuəmənt] N achat m, approvisionnement m

prod [prɔd] VT pousser ▸ N (push, jab) petit coup, poussée f

prodigal [ˈprɔdɪgl] ADJ prodigue

prodigious [prəˈdɪdʒəs] ADJ prodigieux(-euse)

prodigy [ˈprɔdɪdʒɪ] N prodige m

★**produce** N [ˈprɔdjuːs] (Agr) produits mpl ▸ VT [prəˈdjuːs] produire; (show) présenter; (cause) provoquer, causer; (Theat) monter, mettre en scène; (TV: programme) réaliser; (: play, film) mettre en scène; (Radio: programme) réaliser; (: play) mettre en ondes

★**producer** [prəˈdjuːsəʳ] N (Theat) metteur m en scène; (Agr, Comm, Cine) producteur m; (TV: of programme) réalisateur m; (: of play, film) metteur en scène; (Radio: of programme) réalisateur m; (: of play) metteur en ondes

★**product** [ˈprɔdʌkt] N produit m

★**production** [prəˈdʌkʃən] N production f; (Theat) mise f en scène; **to put into ~** (goods) entreprendre la fabrication de

production agreement N (US) accord m de productivité

production line N chaîne f (de fabrication)

production manager N directeur(-trice) de la production

productive [prəˈdʌktɪv] ADJ productif(-ive)

productivity [prɔdʌkˈtɪvɪtɪ] N productivité f

productivity agreement N (BRIT) accord m de productivité

productivity bonus N prime f de rendement

Prof. [prɔf] ABBR (= professor) Prof

profane [prəˈfeɪn] ADJ sacrilège; (lay) profane

profanity [prəˈfænɪtɪ] N obscénités fpl

profess [prəˈfes] VT professer; **I do not ~ to be an expert** je ne prétends pas être spécialiste

professed [prəˈfest] ADJ (self-declared) déclaré(e)

profession [prəˈfeʃən] N profession f; **the professions** les professions libérales

★**professional** [prəˈfeʃənl] N professionnel(le) ▸ ADJ professionnel(le); (work) de professionnel; **he's a ~ man** il exerce une profession libérale; **to take ~ advice** consulter un spécialiste

professionalism [prəˈfeʃnəlɪzəm] N professionnalisme m

professionally [prəˈfeʃnəlɪ] ADV professionnellement; (Sport: play) en professionnel; **I only know him ~** je n'ai avec lui que des relations de travail

★**professor** [prəˈfesəʳ] N professeur m (titulaire d'une chaire); (US: teacher) professeur m

professorship [prəˈfesəʃɪp] N chaire f

proffer [ˈprɔfəʳ] VT (hand) tendre; (remark) faire; (apologies) présenter

proficiency [prəˈfɪʃənsɪ] N compétence f, aptitude f

proficient [prəˈfɪʃənt] ADJ compétent(e), capable

profile [ˈprəufaɪl] N profil m; **to keep a high/low ~** (fig) rester or être très en évidence/discret(-ète)

★**profit** [ˈprɔfɪt] N (from trading) bénéfice m; (advantage) profit m; **to make a ~** faire un or des bénéfice(s); **to sell sth at a ~** vendre qch à profit ▸ CPD: **~ and loss account** compte m de profits et pertes ▸ VI: **to ~ (by or from)** profiter (de)

profitability [prɔfɪtəˈbɪlɪtɪ] N rentabilité f

profitable [ˈprɔfɪtəbl] ADJ lucratif(-ive), rentable; (fig: beneficial) avantageux(-euse); (: meeting) fructueux(-euse)

profit centre N centre m de profit

profiteering [prɔfɪˈtɪərɪŋ] N (pej) mercantilisme m

profit-making [ˈprɔfɪtmeɪkɪŋ] ADJ à but lucratif

profit margin N marge f bénéficiaire

profit-sharing [ˈprɔfɪtʃɛərɪŋ] N intéressement m aux bénéfices

profits tax N (BRIT) impôt m sur les bénéfices

profligate [ˈprɔflɪgɪt] ADJ (behaviour, act) dissolu(e); (person) débauché(e); (extravagant): **~ (with)** prodigue (de)

pro forma [ˈprəuˈfɔːmə] ADJ: **~ invoice** facture f pro-forma

profound [prəˈfaund] ADJ profond(e)

profoundly [prəˈfaundlɪ] ADV profondément

profuse [prəˈfjuːs] ADJ abondant(e)

profusely [prəˈfjuːslɪ] ADV abondamment; (thank etc) avec effusion

profusion [prəˈfjuːʒən] N profusion f, abondance f

progeny [ˈprɔdʒɪnɪ] N progéniture f; descendants mpl

progesterone [prəˈdʒestərəun] N progestérone f

prognosis [prɔgˈnəusɪs] (pl **prognoses** [prɔgˈnəusiːz]) N pronostic m

programmable [prəuˈgræməbl] ADJ programmable

★**programme**, (US) **program** [ˈprəugræm] N (Comput) programme m; (Radio, TV) émission f ▸ VT programmer

programmer [ˈprəugræməʳ] N programmeur(-euse)

programming, (US) **programing** [ˈprəugræmɪŋ] N programmation f

programming language, (US) **programing language** N langage m de programmation

★**progress** N [ˈprəugres] progrès m(pl); **in ~** en cours; **to make ~** progresser, faire des progrès, être en progrès ▸ VI [prəˈgres] progresser, avancer; **as the match progressed** au fur et à mesure que la partie avançait

progression [prəˈgreʃən] N progression f

progressive [prəˈgresɪv] ADJ progressif(-ive); (person) progressiste

progressively [prə'grɛsɪvlɪ] ADV progressivement

progress report N (*Med*) bulletin m de santé; (*Admin*) rapport m d'activité; rapport sur l'état (d'avancement) des travaux

prohibit [prə'hɪbɪt] VT interdire, défendre; **to ~ sb from doing sth** défendre or interdire à qn de faire qch; **"smoking prohibited"** « défense de fumer »

prohibition [prəuɪ'bɪʃən] N prohibition f

prohibitive [prə'hɪbɪtɪv] ADJ (*price etc*) prohibitif(-ive)

★**project** N ['prɔdʒɛkt] (*plan*) projet m, plan m; (*venture*) opération f, entreprise f; (*Scol: research*) étude f, dossier m ▶ VT [prə'dʒɛkt] projeter ▶ VI [prə'dʒɛkt] (*stick out*) faire saillie, s'avancer

projected [prə'dʒɛktɪd] ADJ prévu(e)

projectile [prə'dʒɛktaɪl] N projectile m

projection [prə'dʒɛkʃən] N projection f; (*overhang*) saillie f

projectionist [prə'dʒɛkʃənɪst] N (*Cine*) projectionniste mf

projection room N (*Cine*) cabine f de projection

projector [prə'dʒɛktər] N (*Cine etc*) projecteur m

proletarian [prəulɪ'tɛərɪən] ADJ prolétarien(ne) ▶ N prolétaire mf

proletariat [prəulɪ'tɛərɪət] N prolétariat m

pro-life [prəu'laɪf] ADJ contre l'avortement

proliferate [prə'lɪfəreɪt] VI proliférer

proliferation [prəlɪfə'reɪʃən] N prolifération f

prolific [prə'lɪfɪk] ADJ prolifique

prologue ['prəulɔg] N prologue m

prolong [prə'lɔŋ] VT prolonger

prolonged [prə'lɔŋd] ADJ prolongé(e)

prom [prɔm] N ABBR = **promenade**; **promenade concert**; (*ball*) bal m d'étudiants; *voir article*; **the Proms** *série de concerts de musique classique*

> Le **prom** (abréviation de **promenade**) est un bal organisé à l'intention des élèves pour fêter la fin de leurs années de lycée. Cet événement d'origine américaine occupe une place très importante dans la culture du pays et dans la vie des lycéens, avec ses traditions et les conventions que cela implique. Depuis le début du XXIe siècle, les proms connaissent également un grand succès au Royaume-Uni, même s'ils ne revêtent pas encore l'importance culturelle de leur équivalent américain.

promenade [prɔmə'nɑːd] N (*by sea*) esplanade f, promenade f

promenade concert N concert m (de musique classique)

promenade deck N (*Naut*) pont m promenade

prominence ['prɔmɪnəns] N proéminence f; importance f

prominent ['prɔmɪnənt] ADJ (*standing out*) proéminent(e); (*important*) important(e); **he is ~ in the field of ...** il est très connu dans le domaine de ...

prominently ['prɔmɪnəntlɪ] ADV (*display, set*) bien en évidence; **he figured ~ in the case** il a joué un rôle important dans l'affaire

promiscuity [prɔmɪs'kjuːɪtɪ] N (*sexual*) légèreté f de mœurs

promiscuous [prə'mɪskjuəs] ADJ (*sexually*) de mœurs légères

★**promise** ['prɔmɪs] N promesse f; **to make sb a ~** faire une promesse à qn; **a young man of ~** un jeune homme plein d'avenir ▶ VT, VI promettre; **to ~ well** VI promettre

promising ['prɔmɪsɪŋ] ADJ prometteur(-euse)

promissory note ['prɔmɪsərɪ-] N billet m à ordre

promo ['prəuməu] (*inf*) N promo f (*inf*) ▶ CPD (*film, tour*) promotionnel(le)

promontory ['prɔməntrɪ] N promontoire m

★**promote** [prə'məut] VT promouvoir; (*venture, event*) organiser, mettre sur pied; (*new product*) lancer; **the team was promoted to the second division** (*Brit Football*) l'équipe est montée en 2e division

promoter [prə'məutər] N (*of event*) organisateur(-trice)

★**promotion** [prə'məuʃən] N promotion f

promotional [prə'məuʃənl] ADJ promotionnel(le)

★**prompt** [prɔmpt] ADJ rapide; **they're very ~** (*punctual*) ils sont ponctuels; **he was ~ to accept** il a tout de suite accepté ▶ ADV: **at 8 o'clock ~** à 8 heures précises ▶ N (*Comput*) message m (de guidage) ▶ VT inciter; (*cause*) entraîner, provoquer; (*Theat*) souffler (son rôle or ses répliques) à; **to ~ sb to do** inciter or pousser qn à faire

prompter ['prɔmptər] N (*Theat*) souffleur m

promptly ['prɔmptlɪ] ADV (*quickly*) rapidement, sans délai; (*on time*) ponctuellement

promptness ['prɔmptnɪs] N rapidité f; promptitude f; ponctualité f

prone [prəun] ADJ (*lying*) couché(e) (face contre terre); (*liable*): **~ to** enclin(e) à; **to be ~ to illness** être facilement malade; **to be ~ to an illness** être sujet à une maladie; **she is ~ to burst into tears if ...** elle a tendance à tomber en larmes si ...

prong [prɔŋ] N pointe f; (*of fork*) dent f

pronoun ['prəunaun] N pronom m

pronounce [prə'nauns] VT prononcer; **how do you ~ it?** comment est-ce que ça se prononce?; **they pronounced him unfit to drive** ils l'ont déclaré inapte à la conduite ▶ VI: **to ~ (up)on** se prononcer sur

pronounced [prə'naunst] ADJ (*marked*) prononcé(e)

pronouncement [prə'naunsmənt] N déclaration f

pronunciation [prənʌnsɪ'eɪʃən] N prononciation f

★**proof** [pruːf] N preuve f; (*test, of book, Phot*) épreuve f; (*of alcohol*) degré m; **to be 70° ~** = titrer 40 degrés ▶ ADJ: **~ against** à l'épreuve de ▶ VT (*Brit: tent, anorak*) imperméabiliser

proofread ['pruːfriːd] VT corriger

proofreader ['pruːfriːdər] N correcteur(-trice) (d'épreuves)

prop [prɔp] N support m, étai m; (*fig*) soutien m ▶ VT (*also: prop up*) étayer, soutenir; **to ~ sth against** (*lean*) appuyer qch contre or à ■ **props** NPL accessoires mpl

Prop. ABBR (*Comm*) = **proprietor**

propaganda [prɔpə'gændə] N propagande *f*

propagate ['prɔpəgeɪt] VT propager

propagation [prɔpə'geɪʃən] N propagation *f*

propel [prə'pɛl] VT propulser, faire avancer

propeller [prə'pɛlə^r] N hélice *f*

propelling pencil [prə'pɛlɪŋ-] N (BRIT) portemine *m inv*

propensity [prə'pɛnsɪtɪ] N propension *f*

★**proper** ['prɔpə^r] ADJ (*suited, right*) approprié(e), bon(ne); (*seemly*) correct(e), convenable; (*authentic*) vrai(e), véritable; (*inf: real*) fini(e), vrai(e); (*referring to place*): **the village ~** le village proprement dit; **to go through the ~ channels** (*Admin*) passer par la voie officielle

★**properly** ['prɔpəlɪ] ADV correctement, convenablement; (*really*) bel et bien

proper noun N nom *m* propre

★**property** ['prɔpətɪ] N (*possessions*) biens *mpl*; (*house etc*) propriété *f*; (*land*) terres *fpl*, domaine *m*; (*Chem etc: quality*) propriété *f*; **it's their ~** cela leur appartient, c'est leur propriété

property developer N (BRIT) promoteur immobilier

property owner N propriétaire *m*

property tax N impôt foncier

prophecy ['prɔfɪsɪ] N prophétie *f*

prophesy ['prɔfɪsaɪ] VT prédire ▶ VI prophétiser

prophet ['prɔfɪt] N prophète *m*

prophetic [prə'fɛtɪk] ADJ prophétique

proponent [prə'pəunənt] N défenseur *m*

proportion [prə'pɔːʃən] N proportion *f*; (*share*) part *f*; partie *f*; **to be in/out of ~ to** *or* **with sth** être à la mesure de/hors de proportion avec qch; **to see sth in ~** (*fig*) ramener qch à de justes proportions ▶ VT proportionner ■ **proportions** NPL (*size*) dimensions *fpl*

proportional [prə'pɔːʃənl] ADJ proportionnel(le)

proportionally [prə'pɔːʃənlɪ] ADV proportionnellement

proportional representation N (*Pol*) représentation proportionnelle

proportionate [prə'pɔːʃənət] ADJ (*in size*) proportionnel(le); (*appropriate*) proportionné(e); **to be ~ to sth** (*in size*) être proportionnel(le) à qch; (*appropriate*) être proportionné(e) à qch

proportionately [prə'pɔːʃənətlɪ] ADV proportionnellement

★**proposal** [prə'pəuzl] N proposition *f*, offre *f*; (*plan*) projet *m*; (*of marriage*) demande *f* en mariage

★**propose** [prə'pəuz] VT proposer, suggérer; (*have in mind*): **to ~ sth/doing sth** envisager qch/de faire qch; **to ~ to do** avoir l'intention de faire ▶ VI faire sa demande en mariage

proposer [prə'pəuzə^r] N (BRIT: *of motion etc*) auteur *m*

proposition [prɔpə'zɪʃən] N proposition *f*; **to make sb a ~** faire une proposition à qn

propound [prə'paund] VT proposer, soumettre

proprietary [prə'praɪətərɪ] ADJ de marque déposée; **~ article** article *m* or produit *m* de marque; **~ brand** marque déposée

proprietor [prə'praɪətə^r] N propriétaire *mf*

propriety [prə'praɪətɪ] N (*seemliness*) bienséance *f*, convenance *f*

propulsion [prə'pʌlʃən] N propulsion *f*

pro rata [prəu'rɑːtə] ADV au prorata

prosaic [prəu'zeɪɪk] ADJ prosaïque

Pros. Atty. ABBR (*US*) = **prosecuting attorney**

proscribe [prə'skraɪb] VT proscrire

proscription [prə'skrɪpʃən] N interdiction *f*

prose [prəuz] N prose *f*; (*Scol: translation*) thème *m*

prosecute ['prɔsɪkjuːt] VT poursuivre

prosecuting attorney ['prɔsɪkjuːtɪŋ-] N (*US*) procureur *m*

prosecution [prɔsɪ'kjuːʃən] N poursuites *fpl* judiciaires; (*accusing side: in criminal case*) accusation *f*; (*: in civil case*) la partie plaignante

prosecutor ['prɔsɪkjuːtə^r] N (*lawyer*) procureur *m*; (*also*: **public prosecutor**) ministère public; (*US*: *plaintiff*) plaignant(e)

prospect N ['prɔspɛkt] perspective *f*; (*hope*) espoir *m*, chances *fpl*; **we are faced with the ~ of leaving** nous risquons de devoir partir; **there is every ~ of an early victory** tout laisse prévoir une victoire rapide ▶ VT, VI [prə'spɛkt] prospecter ■ **prospects** NPL (*for work etc*) possibilités *fpl* d'avenir, débouchés *mpl*

prospecting [prə'spɛktɪŋ] N prospection *f*

prospective [prə'spɛktɪv] ADJ (*possible*) éventuel(le); (*future*) futur(e)

prospector [prə'spɛktə^r] N prospecteur *m*; **gold ~** chercheur *m* d'or

prospectus [prə'spɛktəs] N prospectus *m*

prosper ['prɔspə^r] VI prospérer

prosperity [prɔ'spɛrɪtɪ] N prospérité *f*

prosperous ['prɔspərəs] ADJ prospère

prostate ['prɔsteɪt] N (*also*: **prostate gland**) prostate *f*

prosthetic [prɔs'θɛtɪk] ADJ prothétique

prostitute ['prɔstɪtjuːt] N prostituée *f*; **male ~** prostitué *m*

prostitution [prɔstɪ'tjuːʃən] N prostitution *f*

prostrate ADJ ['prɔstreɪt] prosterné(e); (*fig*) prostré(e) ▶ VT [prɔ'streɪt]: **to ~ o.s. (before sb)** se prosterner (devant qn)

protagonist [prə'tægənɪst] N protagoniste *m*

★**protect** [prə'tɛkt] VT protéger

protection [prə'tɛkʃən] N protection *f*; **to be under sb's ~** être sous la protection de qn

protectionism [prə'tɛkʃənɪzəm] N protectionnisme *m*

protectionist [prə'tɛkʃənɪst] ADJ protectionniste

protection racket N racket *m*

protective [prə'tɛktɪv] ADJ protecteur(-trice); (*clothing*) de protection; **~ custody** (*Law*) détention préventive

protector [prə'tɛktə^r] N protecteur(-trice)

protégé ['prəutɛʒeɪ] N protégé *m*

protégée ['prəutɛʒeɪ] N protégée *f*

protein ['prəutiːn] N protéine *f*

pro tem [prəu'tɛm] ADV ABBR (= *pro tempore: for the time being*) provisoirement

★**protest** N ['prəʊtest] protestation f ▶ VI [prə'test]: **to ~ against/about** protester contre/à propos de ▶ VT [prə'test] protester de; **to ~ (that)** protester que

Protestant ['prɒtɪstənt] ADJ, N protestant(e)

Protestantism ['prɒtɪstəntɪzəm] N protestantisme m

protester, protestor [prə'testə'] N (in demonstration) manifestant(e)

protest march N manifestation f

protocol ['prəʊtəkɒl] N protocole m

proton ['prəʊtɒn] N proton m

prototype ['prəʊtətaɪp] N prototype m

protracted [prə'træktɪd] ADJ prolongé(e)

protractor [prə'træktə'] N (Geom) rapporteur m

protrude [prə'truːd] VI avancer, dépasser

protuberance [prə'tjuːbərəns] N protubérance f

★**proud** [praʊd] ADJ fier(-ère); (pej) orgueilleux(-euse); **to be ~ to do sth** être fier de faire qch; **to do sb ~** (inf) faire honneur à qn; **to do o.s. ~** (inf) ne se priver de rien

proudly ['praʊdlɪ] ADV fièrement

★**prove** [pruːv] VT prouver, démontrer; **to ~ o.s.** montrer ce dont on est capable; **to ~ o.s./itself (to be) useful** etc se montrer or se révéler utile etc; **he was proved right in the end** il s'est avéré qu'il avait raison ▶ VI: **to ~ correct** etc s'avérer juste etc

proven ['pruːvən, 'pruːvən] PP of **prove** ▶ ADJ (ability) avéré(e); **to have a ~ track record** avoir fait ses preuves

proverb ['prɒvəːb] N proverbe m

proverbial [prə'vəːbɪəl] ADJ proverbial(e)

★**provide** [prə'vaɪd] VT fournir; **to ~ sb with sth** fournir qch à qn; **to be provided with** (person) disposer de; (thing) être équipé(e) or muni(e) de ▶ **provide for** VT FUS (person) subvenir aux besoins de; (future event) prévoir

provided [prə'vaɪdɪd] CONJ: **~ (that)** à condition que + sub

Providence ['prɒvɪdəns] N la Providence

provider [prə'vaɪdə'] N (of goods, services) fournisseur m; (in family) soutien m (de famille); **internet ~** fournisseur d'accès

providing [prə'vaɪdɪŋ] CONJ à condition que + sub

province ['prɒvɪns] N province f; (fig) domaine m

provincial [prə'vɪnʃəl] ADJ provincial(e)

provision [prə'vɪʒən] N (supply) provision f; (supplying) fourniture f; approvisionnement m; (stipulation) disposition f; **to make ~ for** (one's future) assurer; (one's family) assurer l'avenir de; **there's no ~ for this in the contract** le contrat ne prévoit pas cela ■ **provisions** NPL (food) provisions fpl

provisional [prə'vɪʒənl] ADJ provisoire ▶ N: **P~** (IRISH Pol) Provisional m (membre de la tendance activiste de l'IRA)

provisional licence N (BRIT Aut) permis m provisoire

provisionally [prə'vɪʒnəlɪ] ADV provisoirement

proviso [prə'vaɪzəʊ] N condition f; **with the ~ that** à la condition (expresse) que

Provo ['prɒvəʊ] N ABBR (pej) = **Provisional**

provocation [prɒvə'keɪʃən] N provocation f

provocative [prə'vɒkətɪv] ADJ provocateur(-trice), provocant(e)

provoke [prə'vəʊk] VT provoquer; **to ~ sb to sth/ to do** or **into doing sth** pousser qn à qch/à faire qch

provoking [prə'vəʊkɪŋ] ADJ énervant(e), exaspérant(e)

provost ['prɒvəst] N (BRIT: of university) principal m; (SCOTTISH) maire m

prow [praʊ] N proue f

prowess ['praʊɪs] N prouesse f

prowl [praʊl] VI (also: **prowl about, prowl around**) rôder ▶ N: **to be on the ~** rôder

prowler ['praʊlə'] N rôdeur(-euse)

proximity [prɒk'sɪmɪtɪ] N proximité f

proxy ['prɒksɪ] N procuration f; **by ~** par procuration

Prozac® ['prəʊzæk] N Prozac® m

PRP N ABBR (= performance related pay) salaire m au rendement

prude [pruːd] N prude f

prudence ['pruːdns] N prudence f

prudent ['pruːdnt] ADJ prudent(e)

prudish ['pruːdɪʃ] ADJ prude, pudibond(e)

prune [pruːn] N pruneau m ▶ VT élaguer

prurient ['prʊərɪənt] ADJ lubrique

pry [praɪ] VI: **to ~ into** fourrer son nez dans

PS N ABBR (= postscript) PS m

psalm [sɑːm] N psaume m

PSAT N ABBR (US) = **Preliminary Scholastic Aptitude Test**

PSBR N ABBR (BRIT: = public sector borrowing requirement) besoins mpl d'emprunts des pouvoirs publics

pseud [sjuːd] N (BRIT inf: intellectually) pseudo-intello m; (: socially) snob mf

pseudo- ['sjuːdəʊ] PREFIX pseudo-

pseudonym ['sjuːdənɪm] N pseudonyme m

PSHE N ABBR (BRIT Scol: = personal, social and health education) cours d'éducation personnelle, sanitaire et sociale préparant à la vie adulte

PST ABBR (US: = Pacific Standard Time) heure d'hiver du Pacifique

PSV N ABBR (BRIT) = **public service vehicle**

psyche ['saɪkɪ] N psychisme m

psychedelic [saɪkə'delɪk] ADJ psychédélique

psychiatric [saɪkɪ'ætrɪk] ADJ psychiatrique

psychiatrist [saɪ'kaɪətrɪst] N psychiatre mf

psychiatry [saɪ'kaɪətrɪ] N psychiatrie f

psychic ['saɪkɪk] ADJ (also: **psychical**) (méta)psychique; (person) doué(e) de télépathie or d'un sixième sens

psycho ['saɪkəʊ] N (pej) psychopathe mf

psychoanalysis [saɪkəʊə'nælɪsɪs] (pl **psychoanalyses** [-siːz]) N psychanalyse f

psychoanalyst [saɪkəʊ'ænəlɪst] N psychanalyste mf

★**psychological** [saɪkə'lɒdʒɪkl] ADJ psychologique

psychologically [saɪkə'lɒdʒɪklɪ] ADV psychologiquement

p

psychologist [saɪˈkɔlədʒɪst] N psychologue *mf*
psychology [saɪˈkɔlədʒɪ] N psychologie *f*
psychometric [saɪkəˈmetrɪk] ADJ psychométrique; ~ **testing** tests *mpl* psychométriques
psychopath [ˈsaɪkəupæθ] N psychopathe *mf*
psychosis [saɪˈkəusɪs] (*pl* **psychoses** [-siːz]) N psychose *f*
psychosomatic [saɪkəusəˈmætɪk] ADJ psychosomatique
psychotherapist [saɪkəuˈθɛrəpɪst] N psychothérapeute *mf*
psychotherapy [saɪkəuˈθɛrəpɪ] N psychothérapie *f*
psychotic [saɪˈkɔtɪk] ADJ, N psychotique *mf*
PT N ABBR (*Brit*: = *physical training*) EPS *f*
pt ABBR (= *pint*; *point*)
Pt. ABBR (*in place names*: = *Point*) Pte
PTA N ABBR = **Parent-Teacher Association**
Pte. ABBR (*Brit Mil*) = **private**
PTO ABBR (= *please turn over*) TSVP
PTSD ABBR = **post-traumatic stress disorder**
PTV ABBR (*US*) = **pay television**
★**pub** [pʌb] N ABBR (= *public house*) pub *m*
pub crawl N (*Brit inf*): **to go on a ~** faire la tournée des bars
puberty [ˈpjuːbətɪ] N puberté *f*
pubic [ˈpjuːbɪk] ADJ pubien(ne), du pubis
★**public** [ˈpʌblɪk] ADJ public(-ique); **to be ~ knowledge** être de notoriété publique; **to go ~** (*Comm*) être coté(e) en Bourse; **to make ~** rendre public ▶ N public *m*; **in ~** en public; **the general ~** le grand public
public address system N (système *m* de) sonorisation *f*, sono *f* (*inf*)
publican [ˈpʌblɪkən] N patron *m* or gérant *m* de pub
publication [pʌblɪˈkeɪʃən] N publication *f*
public company N société *f* anonyme
public convenience N (*Brit*) toilettes *fpl*
public holiday N (*Brit*) jour férié
public house N (*Brit*) pub *m*
publicist [ˈpʌblɪsɪst] N publicitaire *mf*
★**publicity** [pʌbˈlɪsɪtɪ] N publicité *f*
publicize [ˈpʌblɪsaɪz] VT (*make known*) faire connaître, rendre public; (*advertise*) faire de la publicité pour
public limited company N ≈ société *f* anonyme (SA) (*cotée en Bourse*)
publicly [ˈpʌblɪklɪ] ADV publiquement, en public
public opinion N opinion publique
public ownership N: **to be taken into ~** être nationalisé(e), devenir propriété de l'État
public prosecutor N ≈ procureur *m* (*de la République*); **~'s office** parquet *m*
public relations N relations publiques (RP)
public relations officer N responsable *mf* des relations publiques
public school N (*Brit*) école privée; (*US*) école publique

Une **public school** est un type d'établissement d'enseignement secondaire privé (*private school* ou *independent school* étant le terme générique). Ce sont des écoles prestigieuses, aux origines anciennes, avec des frais de scolarité très élevés pour les plus connues (Westminster, Eton, Harrow). Bon nombre d'entre elles sont des pensionnats. Beaucoup ont également une école primaire qui leur est rattachée (une *prep* ou *preparatory school*) pour préparer les élèves au cycle secondaire. Une grande proportion d'élèves vont ensuite à l'université, notamment à Oxford ou Cambridge. Les grands industriels, les députés et les hauts fonctionnaires sortent souvent de ces écoles. Aux États-Unis, le terme *public school* désigne tout simplement une école publique gratuite.

public sector N secteur public
public service vehicle N (*Brit*) véhicule affecté au transport de personnes
public-spirited [pʌblɪkˈspɪrɪtɪd] ADJ qui fait preuve de civisme
public transport, (*US*) **public transportation** N transports *mpl* en commun
public utility N service public
public works NPL travaux publics
★**publish** [ˈpʌblɪʃ] VT publier
★**publisher** [ˈpʌblɪʃəʳ] N éditeur *m*
publishing [ˈpʌblɪʃɪŋ] N (*industry*) édition *f*; (*of a book*) publication *f*
publishing company N maison *f* d'édition
pub lunch N repas *m* de bistrot
puce [pjuːs] ADJ puce
puck [pʌk] N (*elf*) lutin *m*; (*Ice Hockey*) palet *m*
pucker [ˈpʌkəʳ] VT plisser
pudding [ˈpudɪŋ] N (*Brit*: *dessert*) dessert *m*, entremets *m*; (*sweet dish*) pudding *m*, gâteau *m*; (*sausage*) boudin *m*; **rice ~** ≈ riz *m* au lait; **black ~**, (*US*) **blood ~** boudin (noir)
puddle [ˈpʌdl] N flaque *f* d'eau
puerile [ˈpjuəraɪl] ADJ puéril(e)
Puerto Rico [ˈpwəːtəuˈriːkəu] N Porto Rico *f*
puff [pʌf] N bouffée *f* ▶ VT: **to ~ one's pipe** tirer sur sa pipe; (*also: puff out*: *sails, cheeks*) gonfler; **to ~ out smoke** envoyer des bouffées de fumée ▶ VI sortir par bouffées; (*pant*) haleter
puffed [pʌft] ADJ (*inf*: *out of breath*) tout(e) essoufflé(e)
puffin [ˈpʌfɪn] N macareux *m*
puff pastry, (*US*) **puff paste** N pâte feuilletée
puffy [ˈpʌfɪ] ADJ bouffi(e), boursouflé(e)
pugnacious [pʌgˈneɪʃəs] ADJ pugnace, batailleur(-euse)
puke [ˈpjuːk] (*inf*) VI (*also: puke up*) dégueuler (*inf*) ▶ N dégueulis *m* (*inf*)
★**pull** [pul] N (*of moon, magnet, the sea etc*) attraction *f*; (*fig*) influence *f*; (*tug*): **to give sth a ~** tirer sur qch ▶ VT tirer; (*trigger*) presser; (*strain*: *muscle, tendon*) se claquer; **to ~ a face** faire une grimace; **to ~ to pieces** mettre en morceaux; **to ~ one's punches** (*also fig*) ménager son adversaire; **to ~ one's weight** y mettre du sien; **to ~ sb's leg** (*fig*) faire

marcher qn; **to ~ strings (for sb)** intervenir (en faveur de qn) ▶ vi tirer
▶ **pull about** vt (*Brit: handle roughly: object*) maltraiter; (*: person*) malmener
▶ **pull apart** vt séparer; (*break*) mettre en pièces, démantibuler
▶ **pull away** vi (*vehicle: move off*) partir; (*draw back*) s'éloigner
▶ **pull back** vt (*lever etc*) tirer sur; (*curtains*) ouvrir ▶ vi (*refrain*) s'abstenir; (*Mil: withdraw*) se retirer
▶ **pull down** vt baisser, abaisser; (*house*) démolir; (*tree*) abattre
▶ **pull in** vi (*Aut*) se ranger; (*Rail*) entrer en gare
▶ **pull off** vt enlever, ôter; (*deal etc*) conclure
▶ **pull out** vi démarrer, partir; (*withdraw*) se retirer; (*Aut: come out of line*) déboîter ▶ vt (*from bag, pocket*) sortir; (*remove*) arracher; (*withdraw*) retirer
▶ **pull over** vi (*Aut*) se ranger
▶ **pull round** vi (*unconscious person*) revenir à soi; (*sick person*) se rétablir
▶ **pull through** vi s'en sortir
▶ **pull together** vi (*cooperate*) se serrer les coudes
▶ vt: **to ~ o.s. together** se ressaisir
▶ **pull up** vi (*stop*) s'arrêter ▶ vt remonter; (*uproot*) déraciner, arracher; (*stop*) arrêter

pulley ['pulɪ] N poulie f

pull-out ['pulaut] N (*of forces etc*) retrait m ▶ CPD (*magazine, pages*) détachable

pullover ['puləuvə^r] N pull-over m, tricot m

pulmonary ['pʌlmənrɪ] ADJ pulmonaire

pulp [pʌlp] N (*of fruit*) pulpe f; (*for paper*) pâte f à papier; (*pej: also:* **pulp magazines**) presse f à sensation or de bas étage; **to reduce sth to (a) ~** réduire qch en purée

pulpit ['pulpɪt] N chaire f

pulsate [pʌl'seɪt] vi battre, palpiter; (*music*) vibrer

pulse [pʌls] N (*of blood*) pouls m; (*of heart*) battement m; (*of music, engine*) vibrations fpl; **to feel or take sb's ~** prendre le pouls à qn ■ **pulses** NPL (*Culin*) légumineuses fpl

pulverize ['pʌlvəraɪz] vt pulvériser

puma ['pjuːmə] N puma m

pumice ['pʌmɪs] N (*also:* **pumice stone**) pierre f ponce

pummel ['pʌml] vt rouer de coups

★**pump** [pʌmp] N pompe f; (*shoe*) escarpin m ▶ vt pomper; (*fig, inf*) faire parler; **to ~ sb for information** essayer de soutirer des renseignements à qn
▶ **pump up** vt gonfler

pumpkin ['pʌmpkɪn] N potiron m, citrouille f

pun [pʌn] N jeu m de mots, calembour m

★**punch** [pʌntʃ] N (*blow*) coup m de poing; (*fig: force*) vivacité f, mordant m; (*tool*) poinçon m; (*drink*) punch m ▶ vt (*make a hole in*) poinçonner, perforer; (*hit*): **to ~ sb/sth** donner un coup de poing à qn/sur qch; **to ~ a hole (in)** faire un trou (dans)
▶ **punch in** vi (*US*) pointer (en arrivant)
▶ **punch out** vi (*US*) pointer (en partant)

punch card, punched card [pʌntʃt-] N carte perforée

punch-drunk ['pʌntʃdrʌŋk] ADJ (*Brit*) sonné(e)

punch line N (*of joke*) conclusion f

punch-up ['pʌntʃʌp] N (*Brit inf*) bagarre f

punctual ['pʌŋktjuəl] ADJ ponctuel(le)

punctuality [pʌŋktju'ælɪtɪ] N ponctualité f

punctually ['pʌŋktjuəlɪ] ADV ponctuellement; **it will start ~ at 6** cela commencera à 6 heures précises

punctuate ['pʌŋktjueɪt] vt ponctuer

punctuation [pʌŋktju'eɪʃən] N ponctuation f

punctuation mark N signe m de ponctuation

puncture ['pʌŋktʃə^r] N (*Brit*) crevaison f; **I have a ~** (*Aut*) j'ai (un pneu) crevé ▶ vt crever

pundit ['pʌndɪt] N individu m qui pontifie, pontife m

pungent ['pʌndʒənt] ADJ piquant(e); (*fig*) mordant(e), caustique

punish ['pʌnɪʃ] vt punir; **to ~ sb for sth/for doing sth** punir qn de qch/d'avoir fait qch

punishable ['pʌnɪʃəbl] ADJ punissable

punishing ['pʌnɪʃɪŋ] ADJ (*fig: exhausting*) épuisant(e) ▶ N punition f

punishment ['pʌnɪʃmənt] N punition f, châtiment m; (*fig, inf*): **to take a lot of ~** (*boxer*) encaisser; (*car, person etc*) être mis(e) à dure épreuve

punitive ['pjuːnɪtɪv] ADJ punitif(-ive)

Punjab ['pʌndʒɑːb] N (*also:* **the Punjab**) le Pendjab

punk [pʌŋk] N (*person: also:* **punk rocker**) punk mf; (*music: also:* **punk rock**) le punk; (*US inf: hoodlum*) voyou m

punt [pʌnt] N (*boat*) bachot m; (*Irish*) livre irlandaise ▶ vi (*Brit: bet*) parier

punter ['pʌntə^r] N (*Brit inf: gambler*) parieur(-euse); Monsieur m tout le monde; type m

puny ['pjuːnɪ] ADJ chétif(-ive)

pup [pʌp] N chiot m

★**pupil** ['pjuːpl] N élève mf; (*of eye*) pupille f

puppet ['pʌpɪt] N marionnette f, pantin m

puppet government N gouvernement m fantoche

puppy ['pʌpɪ] N chiot m, petit chien

purchase ['pəːtʃɪs] N achat m; (*grip*) prise f; **to get a ~ on** trouver appui sur ▶ vt acheter

purchase order N ordre m d'achat

purchase price N prix m d'achat

purchaser ['pəːtʃɪsə^r] N acheteur(-euse)

purchase tax N (*Brit*) taxe f à l'achat

purchasing power ['pəːtʃɪsɪŋ-] N pouvoir m d'achat

★**pure** [pjuə^r] ADJ pur(e); **a ~ wool jumper** un pull en pure laine; **~ and simple** pur(e) et simple

purebred ['pjuəbred] ADJ de race

purée ['pjuəreɪ] N purée f

purely ['pjuəlɪ] ADV purement

purge [pəːdʒ] N (*Med*) purge f; (*Pol*) épuration f, purge f ▶ vt purger; (*fig*) épurer, purger

purification [pjuərɪfɪ'keɪʃən] N purification f

purify ['pjuərɪfaɪ] vt purifier, épurer

purist ['pjuərɪst] N puriste mf

puritan ['pjuərɪtən] N puritain(e)

puritanical [pjuərɪ'tænɪkl] ADJ puritain(e)

purity ['pjuərɪtɪ] N pureté f

purl [pəːl] N maille f à l'envers ▶ vt tricoter à l'envers

purloin [pəː'lɔɪn] vt dérober

★**purple** ['pəːpl] ADJ violet(te); (*face*) cramoisi(e)

purport [pə'pɔ:t] VI: **to ~ to be/do** prétendre être/faire

purported [pə'pɔ:tɪd] ADJ prétendu(e) *before noun*

purportedly [pə'pɔ:tɪdlɪ] ADV prétendument

★**purpose** ['pə:pəs] N intention *f*, but *m*; **on ~** exprès; **for illustrative purposes** à titre d'illustration; **for teaching purposes** dans un but péda-gogique; **for the purposes of this meeting** pour cette réunion; **to no ~** en pure perte

purpose-built ['pə:pəs'bɪlt] ADJ (BRIT) fait(e) sur mesure

purposeful ['pə:pəsful] ADJ déterminé(e), résolu(e)

purposely ['pə:pəslɪ] ADV exprès

purr [pə:ʳ] N ronronnement *m* ▶ VI ronronner

purse [pə:s] N (BRIT: *for money*) porte-monnaie *m inv*, bourse *f*; (US: *handbag*) sac *m* (à main) ▶ VT serrer, pincer

purser ['pə:səʳ] N (*Naut*) commissaire *m* du bord

purse snatcher [-'snætʃəʳ] N (US) voleur *m* à l'ar-raché

pursue [pə'sju:] VT poursuivre; (*pleasures*) rechercher; (*inquiry, matter*) approfondir

pursuer [pə'sju:əʳ] N poursuivant(e)

pursuit [pə'sju:t] N poursuite *f*; (*occupation*) occupa-tion *f*, activité *f*; **scientific pursuits** recherches *fpl* scientifiques; **in (the) ~ of sth** à la recherche de qch

purveyor [pə'veɪəʳ] N fournisseur *m*

pus [pʌs] N pus *m*

★**push** [puʃ] N poussée *f*; (*effort*) gros effort; (*drive*) énergie *f*; **at a ~** (BRIT *inf*) à la limite, à la rigueur ▶ VT pousser; (*button*) appuyer sur; (*thrust*): **to ~ sth (into)** enfoncer qch (dans); (*fig: product*) mettre en avant, faire de la publicité pour; **to ~ a door open/shut** pousser une porte (pour l'ou-vrir/pour la fermer); **to be pushed for time/money** être à court de temps/d'argent; **she is pushing fifty** (*inf*) elle frise la cinquantaine ▶ VI pousser; appuyer; **"~"** (*on door*) « pousser »; (*on bell*) « appuyer »; **to ~ for** (*better pay, conditions*) réclamer

▶ **push aside** VT écarter

▶ **push ahead** VI: **to ~ ahead with sth** (*plans, poli-cies*) poursuivre qch

▶ **push in** VI s'introduire de force

▶ **push off** VI (*inf*) filer, ficher le camp

▶ **push on** VI (*continue*) continuer

▶ **push over** VT renverser

▶ **push through** VT (*measure*) faire voter ▶ VI (*in crowd*) se frayer un chemin

▶ **push up** VT (*total, prices*) faire monter

push-bike ['puʃbaɪk] N (BRIT) vélo *m*

push-button ['puʃbʌtn] N bouton(-poussoir *m*) *m*

pushchair ['puʃtʃɛəʳ] N (BRIT) poussette *f*

pusher ['puʃəʳ] N (*also*: **drug pusher**) reven-deur(-euse) (de drogue), ravitailleur(-euse) (en drogue)

pushover ['puʃəuvəʳ] N (*inf*): **it's a ~** c'est un jeu d'enfant

push-up ['puʃʌp] N (US) traction *f*

pushy ['puʃɪ] ADJ (*pej*) arriviste

pussy ['pusɪ], **pussy-cat** ['pusɪkæt] N (*inf*) minet *m*

★**put** [put] (*pt, pp* **~**) VT mettre; (*place*) poser, placer; (*say*) dire, exprimer; (*a question*) poser; (*case, view*) exposer, présenter; (*estimate*) estimer; **to ~ sb in a good/bad mood** mettre qn de bonne/mauvaise humeur; **to ~ sb to bed** mettre qn au lit, coucher qn; **to ~ sb to a lot of trouble** déranger qn; **how shall I ~ it?** comment dirais-je ?, comment dire ?; **to ~ a lot of time into sth** passer beaucoup de temps à qch; **to ~ money on a horse** miser sur un cheval; **I ~ it to you that ...** (BRIT) je (vous) sug-gère que ..., je suis d'avis que ...; **to stay ~** ne pas bouger

▶ **put about** VI (*Naut*) virer de bord ▶ VT (*rumour*) faire courir

▶ **put across** VT (*ideas etc*) communiquer; faire comprendre

▶ **put aside** VT mettre de côté

▶ **put away** VT (*store*) ranger

▶ **put back** VT (*replace*) remettre, replacer; (*post-pone*) remettre; (*delay, watch, clock*) retarder; **this will ~ us back ten years** cela nous ramènera dix ans en arrière

▶ **put by** VT (*money*) mettre de côté, économiser

▶ **put down** VT (*parcel etc*) poser, déposer; (*pay*) verser; (*in writing*) mettre par écrit, inscrire; (*sup-press: revolt etc*) réprimer, écraser; (*attribute*) attribuer; (*animal*) abattre; (*cat, dog*) faire piquer

▶ **put forward** VT (*ideas*) avancer, proposer; (*date, watch, clock*) avancer

▶ **put in** VT (*gas, electricity*) installer; (*complaint*) soumettre; (*time, effort*) consacrer

▶ **put in for** VT FUS (*job*) poser sa candidature pour; (*promotion*) solliciter

▶ **put off** VT (*light etc*) éteindre; (*postpone*) remettre à plus tard, ajourner; (*discourage*) dissuader

▶ **put on** VT (*clothes, lipstick, CD*) mettre; (*light etc*) allumer; (*play etc*) monter; (*extra bus, train etc*) mettre en service; (*food, meal: provide*) servir; (: *cook*) mettre à cuire *or* à chauffer; (*weight*) pren-dre; (*assume: accent, manner*) prendre; (: *airs*) se donner, prendre; (*inf: tease*) faire marcher; (*inform, indicate*): **to ~ sb on to sb/sth** indiquer qn/qch à qn; **to ~ the brakes on** freiner

▶ **put out** VT (*take outside*) mettre dehors; (*one's hand*) tendre; (*news, rumour*) faire courir, répandre; (*light etc*) éteindre; (*person: inconvenience*) déranger, gêner; (BRIT: *dislocate*) se démettre ▶ VI (*Naut*): **to ~ out to sea** prendre le large; **to ~ out from Plym-outh** quitter Plymouth

▶ **put through** VT (*Tel: caller*) mettre en communi-cation; (: *call*) passer; (*plan*) faire accepter; **~ me through to Miss Blair** passez-moi Miss Blair

▶ **put together** VT mettre ensemble; (*assemble: furniture*) monter, assembler; (: *meal*) préparer

▶ **put up** VT (*raise*) lever, relever, remonter; (*pin up*) afficher; (*hang*) accrocher; (*build*) construire, ériger; (*tent*) monter; (*umbrella*) ouvrir; (*increase*) augmenter; (*accommodate*) loger; (*incite*): **to ~ sb up to doing sth** pousser qn à faire qch; **to ~ sth up for sale** mettre qch en vente

▶ **put upon** VT FUS: **to be ~ upon** (*imposed on*) se laisser faire

▶ **put up with** VT FUS supporter

putative ['pju:tətɪv] ADJ (*formal*) putatif(-ive)

putrid ['pju:trɪd] ADJ putride

putt [pʌt] VT, VI putter ▶ N putt *m*

putter ['pʌtəʳ] N (*Golf*) putter *m*

putting green ['pʌtɪŋ-] N green *m*

putty ['pʌtɪ] N mastic *m*

put-up ['putʌp] ADJ: **~ job** coup monté

puzzle ['pʌzl] N énigme *f*, mystère *m*; *(game)* jeu *m*, casse-tête *m*; *(jigsaw)* puzzle *m*; *(also:* **crossword puzzle**) mots croisés ▶ VT intriguer, rendre perplexe ▶ VI se creuser la tête; **to ~ over** chercher à comprendre

puzzled ['pʌzld] ADJ perplexe; **to be ~ about sth** être perplexe au sujet de qch

puzzling ['pʌzlɪŋ] ADJ déconcertant(e), inexplicable

PVC N ABBR (= *polyvinyl chloride*) PVC *m*

Pvt. ABBR (*US Mil*) = **private**

pw ABBR (= *per week*) p. sem.

PX N ABBR (*US Mil*) = **post exchange**

pygmy ['pɪgmɪ] N pygmée *mf*

pyjamas [pɪ'dʒɑːməz] NPL (*BRIT*) pyjama *m*; **a pair of ~** un pyjama

pylon ['paɪlən] N pylône *m*

pyramid ['pɪrəmɪd] N pyramide *f*

pyre ['paɪəʳ] N bûcher *m*

Pyrenean [pɪrə'niːən] ADJ pyrénéen(ne), des Pyrénées

Pyrenees [pɪrə'niːz] NPL Pyrénées *fpl*

Pyrex® ['paɪrɛks] N Pyrex® *m* ▶ CPD: **~ dish** plat *m* en Pyrex

python ['paɪθən] N python *m*

Qq

Q, q [kju:] N (*letter*) Q, q m; **Q for Queen** Q comme Quintal

Q & A N questions-réponses *fpl* ▸ CPD: **a ~ session** une séance de questions-réponses

Qatar [kæˈtɑːʳ] N Qatar m, Katar m

QC N ABBR = **Queen's Counsel**

QED ABBR (= *quod erat demonstrandum*) CQFD

q.t. N ABBR (*inf*) = **quiet; on the ~** discrètement

qty ABBR (= *quantity*) qté

quack [kwæk] N (*of duck*) coin-coin m inv; (*pej: doctor*) charlatan m ▸ VI faire coin-coin

quad [kwɔd] N ABBR = **quadruplet; quadrangle**

quadrangle [ˈkwɔdræŋgl] N (*Math*) quadrilatère m; (*courtyard: abbr: quad*) cour f

quadriplegic [kwɔdrɪˈpliːdʒɪk] ADJ, N tétraplégique mf

quadruped [ˈkwɔdruped] N quadrupède m

quadruple [kwɔˈdruːpl] ADJ, N quadruple m ▸ VT, VI quadrupler

quadruplet [kwɔˈdruːplɪt] N quadruplé(e)

quagmire [ˈkwægmaɪəʳ] N bourbier m

quail [kweɪl] N (*Zool*) caille f ▸ VI: **to ~ at** or **before** reculer devant

quaint [kweɪnt] ADJ bizarre; (*old-fashioned*) désuet(-ète); (*picturesque*) au charme vieillot, pittoresque

quake [kweɪk] VI trembler ▸ N ABBR = **earthquake**

Quaker [ˈkweɪkəʳ] N quaker(esse)

qualification [kwɔlɪfɪˈkeɪʃən] N (*often pl: degree etc*) diplôme m; (*training*) qualification(s) f(*pl*); (*ability*) compétence(s) f(*pl*); (*limitation*) réserve f, restriction f; **what are your qualifications?** qu'avez-vous comme diplômes?; quelles sont vos qualifications?

★qualified [ˈkwɔlɪfaɪd] ADJ (*trained*) qualifié(e); (*professionally*) diplômé(e); (*fit, competent*) compétent(e), qualifié(e); (*limited*) conditionnel(le); **it was a ~ success** ce fut un succès mitigé; **~ for/to do** qui a les diplômes requis pour/pour faire; qualifié pour/pour faire

qualifier [ˈkwɔlɪfaɪəʳ] N (*game*) éliminatoire f; (*Grammar*) qualificatif m; **a World Cup ~** une éliminatoire de la Coupe du Monde

★qualify [ˈkwɔlɪfaɪ] VT qualifier; (*modify*) atténuer, nuancer; (*limit: statement*) apporter des réserves à ▸ VI: **to ~ (as)** obtenir son diplôme (de); **to ~ (for)** remplir les conditions requises (pour); (*Sport*) se qualifier (pour)

qualifying [ˈkwɔlɪfaɪɪŋ] ADJ: **~ exam** examen m d'entrée; **~ round** éliminatoires *fpl*

qualitative [ˈkwɔlɪtətɪv] ADJ qualitatif(-ive)

★quality [ˈkwɔlɪtɪ] N qualité f; **of good/poor ~** de bonne/mauvaise qualité ▸ CPD de qualité

quality control N contrôle m de qualité

quality press N (*Brit*): **the ~** la presse d'information

quality time N moments privilégiés

qualm [kwɑːm] N doute m; scrupule m; **to have qualms about sth** avoir des doutes or des scrupules à propos de qch; éprouver des scrupules à propos de qch

quandary [ˈkwɔndrɪ] N: **in a ~** devant un dilemme, dans l'embarras

quango [ˈkwæŋgəu] N ABBR (*Brit*: = *quasi-autonomous non-governmental organization*) commission nommée par le gouvernement

quantifiable [ˈkwɔntɪfaɪəbl] ADJ quantifiable

quantify [ˈkwɔntɪfaɪ] VT quantifier

quantitative [ˈkwɔntɪtətɪv] ADJ quantitatif(-ive)

★quantity [ˈkwɔntɪtɪ] N quantité f; **in ~** en grande quantité

quantity surveyor N (*Brit*) métreur vérificateur

quantum leap [ˈkwɔntəm-] N (*fig*) bond m en avant

quarantine [ˈkwɔrntiːn] N quarantaine f

quark [kwɑːk] N quark m

quarrel [ˈkwɔrl] N querelle f, dispute f; **to have a ~ with sb** se quereller avec qn; **I've no ~ with him** je n'ai rien contre lui ▸ VI se disputer, se quereller; **I can't ~ with that** je ne vois rien à redire à cela

quarrelsome [ˈkwɔrəlsəm] ADJ querelleur(-euse)

quarry [ˈkwɔrɪ] N (*for stone*) carrière f; (*animal*) proie f, gibier m ▸ VT (*marble etc*) extraire

quart [kwɔːt] N ≈ litre m

★quarter [ˈkwɔːtəʳ] N quart m; (*of year*) trimestre m; (*district*) quartier m; (*US, Canada: 25 cents*) pièce f de) vingt-cinq cents *mpl*; **a ~ of an hour** un quart d'heure; **it's a ~ to 3**, (*US*) **it's a ~ of 3** il est 3 heures moins le quart; **it's a ~ past 3**, (*US*) **it's a ~ after 3** il est 3 heures et quart; **from all quarters** de tous côtés ▸ VT partager en quartiers or en quatre; (*Mil*) caserner, cantonner ■ **quarters** NPL logement m; (*Mil*) quartiers *mpl*, cantonnement m

quarterback [ˈkwɔːtəbæk] N (*US Football*) quarterback *mf*

quarter-deck [ˈkwɔːtədɛk] N (*Naut*) plage f arrière

quarter final N quart m de finale

quarterly [ˈkwɔːtəlɪ] ADJ trimestriel(le) ▶ ADV tous les trois mois ▶ N (Press) revue trimestrielle

quartermaster [ˈkwɔːtəmɑːstər] N (Mil) intendant m militaire de troisième classe; (Naut) maître m de manœuvre

quartet, quartette [kwɔːˈtɛt] N quatuor m; (jazz players) quartette m

quarto [ˈkwɔːtəu] ADJ, N in-quarto m inv

quartz [kwɔːts] N quartz m ▶ CPD de or en quartz; (watch, clock) à quartz

quash [kwɔʃ] VT (verdict) annuler, casser

quasi- [ˈkweɪzaɪ] PREFIX quasi- + noun; quasi, presque + adjective

quaver [ˈkweɪvər] N (Brit Mus) croche f ▶ VI trembler

quay [kiː] N (also: **quayside**) quai m

queasy [ˈkwiːzɪ] ADJ (stomach) délicat(e); **to feel ~** avoir mal au cœur

Quebec [kwɪˈbɛk] N (city) Québec; (province) Québec m

★**queen** [kwiːn] N (gen) reine f; (Cards etc) dame f

queen mother N reine mère f

Queen's speech N (Brit) discours m de la reine

> Le **Queen's speech** (ou **King's speech**) est le discours lu par le souverain à la House of Lords, à l'ouverture du Parliament qui a lieu en mai, en présence des lords et des députés. Il contient le programme de politique générale que propose le gouvernement pour la session, et il est préparé par le Premier ministre en consultation avec le cabinet.

queer [kwɪər] ADJ étrange, curieux(-euse); (suspicious) louche; (Brit: sick): **I feel ~** je ne me sens pas bien ▶ N (!) homosexuel m

quell [kwɛl] VT réprimer, étouffer

quench [kwɛntʃ] VT (flames) éteindre; **to ~ one's thirst** se désaltérer

querulous [ˈkwɛruləs] ADJ (person) récriminateur(-trice); (voice) plaintif(-ive)

query [ˈkwɪərɪ] N question f; (doubt) doute m; (question mark) point m d'interrogation ▶ VT (disagree with, dispute) mettre en doute, questionner

quest [kwɛst] N recherche f, quête f

★**question** [ˈkwɛstʃən] N question f; **to ask sb a ~, to put a ~ to sb** poser une question à qn; **to bring or call sth into** ~ remettre qch en question; **the ~ is …** la question est de savoir …; **it's a ~ of doing** il s'agit de faire; **there's some ~ of doing** il est question de faire; **beyond ~** sans aucun doute; **out of the ~** hors de question ▶ VT (person) interroger; (plan, idea) mettre en question or en doute

questionable [ˈkwɛstʃənəbl] ADJ discutable

questioner [ˈkwɛstʃənər] N personne f qui pose une question (or qui a posé la question etc)

questioning [ˈkwɛstʃənɪŋ] ADJ interrogateur(-trice) ▶ N interrogatoire m

question mark N point m d'interrogation

questionnaire [kwɛstʃəˈnɛər] N questionnaire m

queue [kjuː] N (Brit) queue f, file f; **to jump the ~** passer avant son tour ▶ VI (also: **queue up**) faire la queue

quibble [ˈkwɪbl] VI ergoter, chicaner

quiche [kiːʃ] N quiche f

★**quick** [kwɪk] ADJ rapide; (reply) prompt(e), rapide; (mind) vif (vive); (agile) agile, vif (vive); **be ~!** dépêche-toi !; **to be ~ to act** agir tout de suite ▶ ADV vite, rapidement ▶ N: **cut to the ~** (fig) touché(e) au vif

quicken [ˈkwɪkən] VT accélérer, presser; (rouse) stimuler ▶ VI s'accélérer, devenir plus rapide

quickfire [ˈkwɪkfaɪər] ADJ (response, answer) immédiat(e)

quick fix N solution f de fortune

quicklime [ˈkwɪklaɪm] N chaux vive

★**quickly** [ˈkwɪklɪ] ADV (fast) vite, rapidement; (immediately) tout de suite

quickness [ˈkwɪknɪs] N rapidité f, promptitude f; (of mind) vivacité f

quicksand [ˈkwɪksænd] N sables mouvants

quickstep [ˈkwɪkstɛp] N fox-trot m

quick-tempered [kwɪkˈtɛmpəd] ADJ emporté(e)

quick-witted [kwɪkˈwɪtɪd] ADJ à l'esprit vif

quid [kwɪd] N pl inv (Brit inf) livre f

quid pro quo [ˈkwɪdprəuˈkwəu] N contrepartie f

★**quiet** [ˈkwaɪət] ADJ tranquille, calme; (not noisy: engine) silencieux(-euse); (reserved) réservé(e); (voice) bas(se); (not busy: day, business) calme; (ceremony, colour) discret(-ète); **keep ~!** tais-toi !; **I'll have a ~ word with him** je lui en parlerai discrètement ▶ N tranquillité f, calme m; (silence) silence m; **on the ~** en secret, discrètement ▶ VT, VI (US) = **quieten**

quieten [ˈkwaɪətn], **quieten down** VI se calmer, s'apaiser ▶ VT calmer, apaiser

★**quietly** [ˈkwaɪətlɪ] ADV tranquillement; (silently) silencieusement; (discreetly) discrètement

quietness [ˈkwaɪətnɪs] N tranquillité f, calme m; silence m

quill [kwɪl] N plume f (d'oie)

quilt [kwɪlt] N édredon m; (continental quilt) couette f

quin [kwɪn] N ABBR = **quintuplet**

quince [kwɪns] N coing m; (tree) cognassier m

quinine [kwɪˈniːn] N quinine f

quintessential [kwɪntɪˈsɛnʃəl] ADJ (most typical) par excellence; (essential) caractéristique

quintessentially [kwɪntɪˈsɛnʃəlɪ] ADV typiquement

quintet, quintette [kwɪnˈtɛt] N quintette m

quintuplet [kwɪnˈtjuːplɪt] N quintuplé(e)

quip [kwɪp] N remarque piquante or spirituelle, pointe f ▶ VT: **… he quipped** … lança-t-il

quire [ˈkwaɪər] N ≈ main f (de papier)

quirk [kwəːk] N bizarrerie f; **by some ~ of fate** par un caprice du hasard

quirky [ˈkwəːkɪ] ADJ singulier(-ère)

★**quit** [kwɪt] (pt, pp = [kwɪt] or **quitted** [ˈkwɪtɪd]) VT quitter; **to ~ doing** arrêter de faire; **~ stalling!** (US inf) arrête de te dérober ! ▶ VI (give up) abandonner, renoncer; (resign) démissionner; **notice to ~** (Brit) congé m (signifié au locataire)

★**quite** [kwaɪt] ADV (rather) assez, plutôt; (entirely) complètement, tout à fait; **~ new** plutôt neuf; tout à fait neuf; **she's ~ pretty** elle est plutôt jolie; **I ~ understand** je comprends très bien; **~ a few of them** un assez grand nombre d'entre eux; **that's not ~ right** ce n'est pas tout à fait juste; **not ~ as many as last time** pas tout à fait autant que la dernière fois; **~ (so)!** exactement !

Quito ['kiːtəu] N Quito

quits [kwɪts] ADJ: **~ (with)** quitte (envers); **let's call it ~** restons-en là

quitter ['kwɪtə'] N: **I'm not a ~** je ne baisse pas facilement les bras

quiver ['kwɪvə'] VI trembler, frémir ▶ N (for arrows) carquois m

quixotic [kwɪk'sɔtɪk] ADJ chimérique

quiz [kwɪz] N (on TV) jeu-concours m (télévisé); (in magazine etc) test m de connaissances ▶ VT interroger

quizzical ['kwɪzɪkl] ADJ narquois(e)

quoits [kwɔɪts] NPL jeu m du palet

quorum ['kwɔːrəm] N quorum m

quota ['kwəutə] N quota m

quotation [kwəu'teɪʃən] N citation f; (of shares etc) cote f, cours m; (estimate) devis m

quotation marks NPL guillemets mpl

★ **quote** [kwəut] N citation f; (estimate) devis m ▶ VT (sentence, author) citer; (price) donner, soumettre; (shares) coter ▶ VI: **to ~ from** citer; **to ~ for a job** établir un devis pour des travaux ▶ EXCL: **~ ... unquote** (in dictation) ouvrez les guillemets ... fermez les guillemets ▪ **quotes** NPL (inverted commas) guillemets mpl; **in quotes** entre guillemets

quotient ['kwəuʃənt] N quotient m

Quran, Qur'an [kɔː'rɑːn, kɔː'ræn] N: **the ~** le Coran

qv ABBR (= quod vide: which see) voir

qwerty keyboard ['kwəːtɪ-] N clavier m QWERTY

Rr

R¹, r [ɑːʳ] N (letter) R, r m; **R for Robert**, (US) **R for Roger** R comme Raoul

R² ABBR (= right) dr; (US Cine: = restricted) interdit aux moins de 17 ans; (US Pol) = **republican**; (BRIT) Rex, Regina; (= river) riv., fl; (= Réaumur (scale)) R

RA ABBR = **rear admiral** ▶ N ABBR (BRIT) = **Royal Academy; Royal Academician**

RAAF N ABBR = **Royal Australian Air Force**

Rabat [rəˈbɑːt] N Rabat

rabbi [ˈræbaɪ] N rabbin m

★**rabbit** [ˈræbɪt] N lapin m ▶ VI: **to ~ (on)** (BRIT) parler à n'en plus finir

rabbit hole N terrier m (de lapin)

rabbit hutch N clapier m

rabble [ˈræbl] N (pej) populace f

rabid [ˈræbɪd] ADJ enragé(e)

rabies [ˈreɪbiːz] N rage f

RAC N ABBR (BRIT: = Royal Automobile Club) ≈ ACF m

raccoon, racoon [rəˈkuːn] N raton m laveur

★**race** [reɪs] N (species) race f; (competition, rush) course f; **the human ~** la race humaine ▶ VT (person) faire la course avec; (horse) faire courir; (engine) emballer ▶ VI (compete) faire la course, courir; (hurry) aller à toute vitesse, courir; (engine) s'emballer; (pulse) battre très vite; **to ~ in/out** etc entrer/sortir etc à toute vitesse

race car N (US) = **racing car**

race car driver N (US) = **racing driver**

racecourse [ˈreɪskɔːs] N champ m de courses

racegoer [ˈreɪsɡəʊəʳ] N (esp BRIT) turfiste mf

racehorse [ˈreɪshɔːs] N cheval m de course

racer [ˈreɪsəʳ] N (bike) vélo m de course

race relations NPL rapports mpl entre les races

racetrack [ˈreɪstræk] N piste f

racial [ˈreɪʃl] ADJ racial(e)

racialism [ˈreɪʃlɪzəm] N racisme m

racialist [ˈreɪʃlɪst] ADJ, N raciste mf

racing [ˈreɪsɪŋ] N courses fpl

racing car N (BRIT) voiture f de course

racing driver N (BRIT) pilote m de course

racism [ˈreɪsɪzəm] N racisme m

racist [ˈreɪsɪst] ADJ, N raciste mf

rack [ræk] N (for guns, tools) râtelier m; (for clothes) portant m; (for bottles) casier m; (also: **luggage rack**) filet m à bagages; (also: **roof rack**) galerie f; (also: **dish rack**) égouttoir m; **magazine ~** porte-revues m inv; **shoe ~** étagère f à chaussures; **toast ~** porte-toast m; **to go to ~ and ruin** (building) tomber en ruine; (business) péricliter ▶ VT tourmenter; **to ~ one's brains** se creuser la cervelle

▶ **rack up** VT accumuler

racket [ˈrækɪt] N (for tennis) raquette f; (noise) tapage m, vacarme m; (swindle) escroquerie f; (organized crime) racket m

racketeer [rækɪˈtɪəʳ] N (esp US) racketteur m

racketeering [rækɪˈtɪərɪŋ] N racket m

raconteur [rækɔnˈtɜːʳ] N conteur(-euse)

racquet [ˈrækɪt] N raquette f

racy [ˈreɪsɪ] ADJ plein(e) de verve, osé(e)

RADA [ˈrɑːdə] N ABBR (BRIT) = **Royal Academy of Dramatic Art**

radar [ˈreɪdɑːʳ] N radar m ▶ CPD radar inv

radar trap N (Aut: police) contrôle m radar

radial [ˈreɪdɪəl] ADJ (also: **radial-ply**) à carcasse radiale

radiance [ˈreɪdɪəns] N éclat m, rayonnement m

radiant [ˈreɪdɪənt] ADJ rayonnant(e); (Physics) radiant(e)

radiate [ˈreɪdɪeɪt] VT (heat) émettre, dégager ▶ VI (lines) rayonner

radiation [reɪdɪˈeɪʃən] N rayonnement m; (radioactive) radiation f

radiation sickness N mal m des rayons

radiator [ˈreɪdɪeɪtəʳ] N radiateur m

radiator cap N bouchon m de radiateur

radiator grill N (Aut) calandre f

radical [ˈrædɪkl] ADJ radical(e)

radicalism [ˈrædɪklɪzəm] N radicalisme m

radicalization [rædɪklaɪˈzeɪʃən] N radicalisation f

radii [ˈreɪdɪaɪ] NPL of **radius**

★**radio** [ˈreɪdɪəu] N radio f; **on the ~** à la radio ▶ VI: **to ~ to sb** envoyer un message radio à qn ▶ VT (information) transmettre par radio; (one's position) signaler par radio; (person) appeler par radio

radioactive [ˈreɪdɪəuˈæktɪv] ADJ radioactif(-ive)

radioactivity [ˈreɪdɪəuækˈtɪvɪtɪ] N radioactivité f

radio announcer N annonceur m

radio cassette N radiocassette m

radio-controlled [ˈreɪdɪəukənˈtrəuld] ADJ radio-guidé(e)

radiographer [reɪdɪˈɔɡrəfəʳ] N radiologue mf (technicien)

radiography [reɪdɪˈɔɡrəfɪ] N radiographie f

r

radiologist [ˌreɪdɪˈɒlədʒɪst] N radiologue *mf* (*médecin*)

radiology [ˌreɪdɪˈɒlədʒɪ] N radiologie *f*

radio station N station *f* de radio

radio taxi N radio-taxi *m*

radiotelephone [ˈreɪdɪəʊˈtɛlɪfəʊn] N radiotéléphone *m*

radiotherapist [ˈreɪdɪəʊˈθɛrəpɪst] N radiothérapeute *mf*

radiotherapy [ˈreɪdɪəʊˈθɛrəpɪ] N radiothérapie *f*

radish [ˈrædɪʃ] N radis *m*

radium [ˈreɪdɪəm] N radium *m*

radius [ˈreɪdɪəs] (*pl* **radii** [-ɪaɪ]) N rayon *m*; (*Anat*) radius *m*; **within a ~ of 50 miles** dans un rayon de 50 milles

radon [ˈreɪdɒn] N radon *m*

RAF N ABBR (*BRIT*) = **Royal Air Force**

raffia [ˈræfɪə] N raphia *m*

raffish [ˈræfɪʃ] ADJ dissolu(e), canaille

raffle [ˈræfl] N tombola *f* ▶ VT mettre comme lot dans une tombola

raft [rɑːft] N (*craft: also:* **life raft**) radeau *m*; (*logs*) train *m* de flottage

rafter [ˈrɑːftəʳ] N chevron *m*

rafting [ˈrɑːftɪŋ] N rafting *m*

rag [ræg] N chiffon *m*; (*pej: newspaper*) feuille *f*, torchon *m*; (*for charity*) attractions organisées par les étudiants au profit d'œuvres de charité ▶ VT (*BRIT inf*) chahuter, mettre en boîte ■ **rags** NPL haillons *mpl*; **in rags** (*person*) en haillons; (*clothes*) en lambeaux

rag-and-bone man [rægənˈbəʊn-] N (*irreg*) chiffonnier *m*

ragbag [ˈrægbæg] N (*fig*) ramassis *m*

rag doll N poupée *f* de chiffon

★**rage** [reɪdʒ] N (*fury*) rage *f*, fureur *f*; **to fly into a ~** se mettre en rage; **it's all the ~** cela fait fureur ▶ VI (*person*) être fou (folle) de rage; (*storm*) faire rage, être déchaîné(e)

ragged [ˈrægɪd] ADJ (*edge*) inégal(e), qui accroche; (*clothes*) en loques; (*cuff*) effiloché(e); (*appearance*) déguenillé(e)

raging [ˈreɪdʒɪŋ] ADJ (*sea, storm*) en furie; (*fever, pain*) violent(e); **~ toothache** rage *f* de dents; **in a ~ temper** dans une rage folle

rag trade N (*inf*): **the ~** la confection

raid [reɪd] N (*Mil*) raid *m*; (*criminal*) hold-up *m inv*; (*by police*) descente *f*, rafle *f* ▶ VT faire un raid sur or un hold-up dans or une descente dans

raider [ˈreɪdəʳ] N malfaiteur *m*

★**rail** [reɪl] N (*on stair*) rampe *f*; (*on bridge, balcony*) balustrade *f*; (*of ship*) bastingage *m*; (*for train*) rail *m*; **by ~** en train, par le train ■ **rails** NPL rails *mpl*, voie ferrée

railcard [ˈreɪlkɑːd] N (*BRIT*) carte *f* de chemin de fer; **young person's ~** carte *f* jeune

railing [ˈreɪlɪŋ] N, **railings** [ˈreɪlɪŋz] NPL grille *f*

★**railway** [ˈreɪlweɪ], (US) **railroad** [ˈreɪlrəʊd] N chemin *m* de fer; (*track*) voie *f* ferrée

railway engine N locomotive *f*

railway line N (*BRIT*) ligne *f* de chemin de fer; (*track*) voie ferrée

railwayman [ˈreɪlweɪmən] N (*irreg*) cheminot *m*

railway station N (*BRIT*) gare *f*

★**rain** [reɪn] N pluie *f*; **in the ~** sous la pluie ▶ VI pleuvoir; **it's raining** il pleut ▶ VT: **it's raining cats and dogs** il pleut à torrents

▶ **rain off** VT (*BRIT*): **to be rained off** (*game, match*) être annulé(e) pour cause de pluie

rainbow [ˈreɪnbəʊ] N arc-en-ciel *m*

raincoat [ˈreɪnkəʊt] N imperméable *m*

raindrop [ˈreɪndrɒp] N goutte *f* de pluie

rainfall [ˈreɪnfɔːl] N chute *f* de pluie; (*measurement*) hauteur *f* des précipitations

rainforest [ˈreɪnfɒrɪst] N forêt tropicale

rainproof [ˈreɪnpruːf] ADJ imperméable

rainstorm [ˈreɪnstɔːm] N pluie torrentielle

rainwater [ˈreɪnwɔːtəʳ] N eau *f* de pluie

★**rainy** [ˈreɪnɪ] ADJ pluvieux(-euse)

★**raise** [reɪz] N augmentation *f* ▶ VT (*lift*) lever; hausser; (*end: siege, embargo*) lever; (*build*) ériger; (*increase*) augmenter; (*morale*) remonter; (*standards*) améliorer; (*a protest, doubt*) provoquer, causer; (*a question*) soulever; (*cattle, family*) élever; (*crop*) faire pousser; (*army, funds*) rassembler; (*loan*) obtenir; **to ~ one's glass to sb/sth** porter un toast en l'honneur de qn/qch; **to ~ one's voice** élever la voix; **to ~ sb's hopes** donner de l'espoir à qn; **to ~ a laugh/a smile** faire rire/sourire

raisin [ˈreɪzn] N raisin sec

Raj [rɑːdʒ] N: **the ~** l'empire *m* (aux Indes)

rajah [ˈrɑːdʒə] N radja(h) *m*

rake [reɪk] N (*tool*) râteau *m*; (*person*) débauché *m* ▶ VT (*garden*) ratisser; (*fire*) tisonner; (*with machine gun*) balayer ▶ VI: **to ~ through** (*fig: search*) fouiller (dans)

▶ **rake in** VT (*inf: profits, money*) engranger; **he's raking it in** il engrange les bénéfices

rake-off [ˈreɪkɔf] N (*inf*) pourcentage *m*

rakish [ˈreɪkɪʃ] ADJ dissolu(e); cavalier(-ière)

rally [ˈrælɪ] N (*Pol etc*) meeting *m*, rassemblement *m*; (*Aut*) rallye *m*; (*Tennis*) échange *m* ▶ VT rassembler, rallier; (*support*) gagner ▶ VI se rallier; (*sick person*) aller mieux; (*Stock Exchange*) reprendre

▶ **rally round** VI venir en aide ▶ VT FUS se rallier à; venir en aide à

rallying point [ˈrælɪŋ-] N (*Mil*) point *m* de ralliement

RAM [ræm] N ABBR (*Comput: = random access memory*) mémoire *f* vive, RAM *f*

ram [ræm] N bélier *m* ▶ VT (*push*) enfoncer; (*soil*) tasser; (*crash into: vehicle*) emboutir; (: *lamppost etc*) percuter; (*in battle*) éperonner

Ramadan [ræməˈdæn] N Ramadan *m*

ramble [ˈræmbl] N randonnée *f* ▶ VI (*walk*) se promener, faire une randonnée; (*pej: also:* **ramble on**) discourir, pérorer

rambler [ˈræmbləʳ] N promeneur(-euse), randonneur(-euse); (*Bot*) rosier grimpant

rambling [ˈræmblɪŋ] ADJ (*speech*) décousu(e); (*house*) plein(e) de coins et de recoins; (*Bot*) grimpant(e)

RAMC N ABBR (*BRIT*) = **Royal Army Medical Corps**

ramification [ræmɪfɪˈkeɪʃən] N ramification *f*

ramp [ræmp] N (incline) rampe f; (Aut) dénivellation f; (in garage) pont m; **on/off ~** (US Aut) bretelle f d'accès

rampage N ['ræmpeɪdʒ]: **to be on the ~** se déchaîner ▸ vi [ræm'peɪdʒ]: **they went rampaging through the town** ils ont envahi les rues et ont tout saccagé sur leur passage

rampant ['ræmpənt] ADJ (disease etc) qui sévit

rampart ['ræmpɑːt] N rempart m

ram raiding [-reɪdɪŋ] N pillage d'un magasin en enfonçant la vitrine avec une voiture volée

ramshackle ['ræmʃækl] ADJ (house) délabré(e); (car etc) déglingué(e)

RAN N ABBR = **Royal Australian Navy**

ran [ræn] PT of **run**

ranch [rɑːntʃ] N ranch m

rancher ['rɑːntʃər] N (owner) propriétaire m de ranch; (ranch hand) cow-boy m

rancid ['rænsɪd] ADJ rance

rancorous ['ræŋkərəs] ADJ acrimonieux(-euse)

rancour, (US) **rancor** ['ræŋkər] N rancune f, rancœur f

R&B N ABBR = **rhythm and blues**

R&D N ABBR (= research and development) R-D f

random ['rændəm] ADJ fait(e) or établi(e) au hasard; (Comput, Math) aléatoire ▸ N: **at ~** au hasard

random access memory N (Comput) mémoire vive, RAM f

randomize ['rændəmaɪz] VT randomiser

randomly ['rændəmlɪ] ADV (select, assign) aléatoirement, au hasard; (scattered) au hasard

R&R N ABBR (US Mil) = **rest and recreation**

randy ['rændɪ] ADJ (BRIT inf) excité(e); lubrique

rang [ræŋ] PT of **ring**

★**range** [reɪndʒ] N (of mountains) chaîne f; (of missile, voice) portée f; (of products) choix m, gamme f; (also: **shooting range**) champ m de tir; (: indoor) stand m de tir; (also: **kitchen range**) fourneau m (de cuisine); **price ~** éventail m des prix; **do you have anything else in this price ~?** avez-vous autre chose dans ces prix ?; **within (firing) ~** à portée (de tir) ▸ VT (place) mettre en rang, placer; (roam) parcourir; **ranged left/right** (text) justifié à gauche/à droite ▸ VI: **to ~ over** couvrir; **to ~ from ... to** aller de ... à ...

ranger ['reɪndʒər] N garde m forestier

Rangoon [ræŋ'guːn] N Rangoon

rank [ræŋk] N rang m; (Mil) grade m; (BRIT: also: **taxi rank**) station f de taxis; **the ranks** (Mil) la troupe; **the ~ and file** (fig) la masse, la base; **to close ranks** (Mil, fig) serrer les rangs ▸ VI: **to ~ among** compter or se classer parmi ▸ VT: **I ~ him sixth** je le place sixième ▸ ADJ (smell) nauséabond(e); (hypocrisy, injustice etc) flagrant(e); **he's a ~ outsider** il n'est vraiment pas dans la course

ranking ['ræŋkɪŋ] N (of player, team) classement m; **in the world rankings** au classement mondial

rankle ['ræŋkl] VI (insult) rester sur le cœur

ransack ['rænsæk] VT fouiller (à fond); (plunder) piller

ransom ['rænsəm] N rançon f; **to hold sb to ~** (fig) exercer un chantage sur qn

ransomware ['rænsəmwɛər] N (Comput) logiciel m de rançon, rançongiciel m

rant [rænt] VI fulminer

ranting ['ræntɪŋ] N invectives fpl

rap [ræp] N petit coup sec; tape f; (music) rap m ▸ VT (door) frapper sur or à; (table etc) taper sur

rape [reɪp] N viol m; (Bot) colza m ▸ VT violer

rape oil, rapeseed oil ['reɪpsiːd-] N huile f de colza

rapid ['ræpɪd] ADJ rapide

rapidity [rə'pɪdɪtɪ] N rapidité f

rapidly ['ræpɪdlɪ] ADV rapidement

rapids ['ræpɪdz] NPL (Geo) rapides mpl

rapist ['reɪpɪst] N auteur m d'un viol

rapper ['ræpər] N rappeur(-euse)

rapport [ræ'pɔː] N entente f

rapt [ræpt] ADJ (attention) extrême; **to be ~ in contemplation** être perdu(e) dans la contemplation

rapture ['ræptʃər] N extase f, ravissement m; **to go into raptures over** s'extasier sur

rapturous ['ræptʃərəs] ADJ extasié(e); frénétique

★**rare** [rɛər] ADJ rare; (Culin: steak) saignant(e)

rarebit ['rɛəbɪt] N see **Welsh rarebit**

rarefied ['rɛərɪfaɪd] ADJ (air, atmosphere) raréfié(e)

rarely ['rɛəlɪ] ADV rarement

raring ['rɛərɪŋ] ADJ: **to be ~ to go** (inf) être très impatient(e) de commencer

rarity ['rɛərɪtɪ] N rareté f

rascal ['rɑːskl] N vaurien m

rash [ræʃ] ADJ (person) imprudent(e); (decision) inconsidéré(e); **don't do anything ~** ne faites rien d'inconsidéré ▸ N (Med) rougeur f, éruption f; (of events) série f (noire); **to come out in a ~** avoir une éruption

rasher ['ræʃər] N fine tranche (de lard)

rashly ['ræʃlɪ] ADV inconsidérément

rasp [rɑːsp] N (tool) lime f ▸ VT (speak: also: **rasp out**) dire d'une voix grinçante

★**raspberry** ['rɑːzbərɪ] N framboise f

raspberry bush N framboisier m

rasping ['rɑːspɪŋ] ADJ: **~ noise** grincement m

Rastafarian [ræstə'fɛərɪən] ADJ, N rastafari mf

rat [ræt] N rat m

ratable ['reɪtəbl] ADJ see **rateable value**

ratatouille [rætə'tuːɪ] N ratatouille f

ratchet ['rætʃɪt] N: **~ wheel** roue f à rochet

★**rate** [reɪt] N (ratio) taux m, pourcentage m; (speed) vitesse f, rythme m; (price) tarif m; **at a ~ of 60 kph** à une vitesse de 60 km/h; **at any ~** en tout cas; **~ of exchange** taux or cours m du change; **~ of flow** débit m; **~ of return** (taux de) rendement m; **pulse ~** fréquence f des pulsations ▸ VT (price) évaluer, estimer; (people) classer; (deserve) mériter; **to ~ sb/sth as** considérer qn/qch comme; **to ~ sb/sth among** classer qn/qch parmi; **to ~ sb/sth highly** avoir une haute opinion de qn/qch **■ rates** NPL (BRIT) (property tax) impôts locaux

rateable value ['reɪtəbl-] N (BRIT) valeur locative imposable

ratepayer ['reɪtpeɪər] N (BRIT) contribuable mf (payant les impôts locaux)

★rather ['rɑːðəʳ] ADV (*somewhat*) assez, plutôt; (*to some extent*) un peu; **it's ~ expensive** c'est assez cher; (*too much*) c'est un peu cher; **there's ~ a lot** il y en a beaucoup; **I would** *or* **I'd ~ go** j'aimerais mieux *or* je préférerais partir; **I'd ~ not leave** j'aimerais mieux ne pas partir; **or ~** (*more accurately*) ou plutôt; **I ~ think he won't come** je crois bien qu'il ne viendra pas

ratification [rætɪfɪ'keɪʃən] N ratification *f*

ratify ['rætɪfaɪ] VT ratifier

rating ['reɪtɪŋ] N (*assessment*) évaluation *f*; (*score*) classement *m*; (*Finance*) cote *f*; (*Naut: category*) classe *f*; (*: sailor: BRIT*) matelot *m* ■ **ratings** NPL (*Radio*) indice(s) *m(pl)* d'écoute; (*TV*) Audimat® *m*

ratio ['reɪʃɪəu] N proportion *f*; **in the ~ of 100 to 1** dans la proportion de 100 contre 1

ration ['ræʃən] N ration *f* ▶ VT rationner ■ **rations** NPL (*food*) vivres *mpl*

rational ['ræʃənl] ADJ raisonnable, sensé(e); (*solution, reasoning*) logique; (*Med: person*) lucide

rationale [ræʃə'nɑːl] N raisonnement *m*; justification *f*

rationalism ['ræʃənlɪzəm] N rationalisme *m*

rationalization [ræʃnəlaɪ'zeɪʃən] N rationalisation *f*

rationalize ['ræʃnəlaɪz] VT rationaliser; (*conduct*) essayer d'expliquer *or* de motiver

rationally ['ræʃnəlɪ] ADV raisonnablement; logiquement

rationing ['ræʃnɪŋ] N rationnement *m*

ratpack N (*BRIT pej*) journalistes *mpl* de la presse à sensation

rat poison N mort-aux-rats *f inv*

rat race N foire *f* d'empoigne

rattan [ræ'tæn] N rotin *m*

rattle ['rætl] N (*of door, window*) battement *m*; (*of coins, chain*) cliquetis *m*; (*of train, engine*) bruit *m* de ferraille; (*for baby*) hochet *m*; (*of sports fan*) crécelle *f* ▶ VI cliqueter; (*car, bus*): **to ~ along** rouler en faisant un bruit de ferraille ▶ VT agiter (bruyamment); (*inf: disconcert*) décontenancer; (*: annoy*) embêter

▶ **rattle off** VT (*names, statistics*) débiter

rattlesnake ['rætlsneɪk] N serpent *m* à sonnettes

ratty ['rætɪ] ADJ (*inf*) en rogne (*inf*)

raucous ['rɔːkəs] ADJ rauque

raucously ['rɔːkəslɪ] ADV d'une voix rauque

raunchy ['rɔːntʃɪ] ADJ (*inf: voice, image, act*) sexy; (*scenes, film*) lubrique

ravage ['rævɪdʒ] VT ravager

ravages ['rævɪdʒɪz] NPL ravages *mpl*

rave [reɪv] VI (*in anger*) s'emporter; (*with enthusiasm*) s'extasier; (*Med*) délirer ▶ N (*party*) rave *f*, soirée *f* techno ▶ ADJ (*scene, culture, music*) rave, techno ▶ CPD: **~ review** (*inf*) critique *f* dithyrambique

raven ['reɪvən] N grand corbeau

ravenous ['rævənəs] ADJ affamé(e)

ravine [rə'viːn] N ravin *m*

raving ['reɪvɪŋ] ADJ: **he's ~ mad** il est complètement cinglé

ravings ['reɪvɪŋz] NPL divagations *fpl*

ravioli [rævɪ'əulɪ] N ravioli *mpl*

ravish ['rævɪʃ] VT ravir

ravishing ['rævɪʃɪŋ] ADJ enchanteur(-eresse)

★raw [rɔː] ADJ (*uncooked*) cru(e); (*not processed*) brut(e); (*sore*) à vif, irrité(e); (*inexperienced*) inexpérimenté(e); (*weather, day*) froid(e) et humide; **~ deal** (*inf: bad bargain*) sale coup *m*; **to get a ~ deal** (*inf: unfair treatment*) être traité(e) injustement; **~ materials** matières premières

Rawalpindi [rɔːl'pɪndɪ] N Rawalpindi

ray [reɪ] N rayon *m*; **~ of hope** lueur *f* d'espoir

rayon ['reɪɔn] N rayonne *f*

raze [reɪz] VT (*also: raze to the ground*) raser

razor ['reɪzəʳ] N rasoir *m*

razor blade N lame *f* de rasoir

razzle ['ræzl], **razzle-dazzle** ['ræzl'dæzl] N (*BRIT inf*): **to go on the ~** faire la bringue (*inf*)

razzmatazz ['ræzmə'tæz] N (*inf*) tralala *m*, tapage *m*

RC ABBR = **Roman Catholic**

RCAF N ABBR = **Royal Canadian Air Force**

RCMP N ABBR = **Royal Canadian Mounted Police**

RCN N ABBR = **Royal Canadian Navy**

RD ABBR (*US*) = **rural delivery**

Rd ABBR = **road**

RE N ABBR (*BRIT*) = *religious education*) instruction religieuse; (*BRIT Mil*) = **Royal Engineers**

re [riː] PREP concernant

★reach [riːtʃ] N portée *f*, atteinte *f*; (*of river etc*) étendue *f*; **out of/within ~** (*object*) hors de/à portée; **within easy ~ (of)** (*place*) à proximité (de), proche (de) ▶ VT atteindre, arriver à; (*conclusion, decision*) parvenir à; **to ~ sb by phone** joindre qn par téléphone ▶ VI s'étendre; (*stretch out hand*): **to ~ up/down** *etc* (**for sth**) lever/baisser *etc* le bras (pour prendre qch)

▶ **reach out** VT tendre ▶ VI: **to ~ out (for)** allonger le bras (pour prendre)

★react [riː'ækt] VI réagir

★reaction [riː'ækʃən] N réaction *f*

reactionary [riː'ækʃənrɪ] ADJ, N réactionnaire *mf*

reactivate [riː'æktɪveɪt] VT réactiver

reactor [riː'æktəʳ] N réacteur *m*

★read [riːd] (*pt, pp ~* [rɛd]) VI lire ▶ VT lire; (*understand*) comprendre, interpréter; (*study*) étudier; (*meter*) relever; (*subj: instrument etc*) indiquer, marquer; **do you ~ me?** (*Tel*) est-ce que vous me recevez ?; **to take sth as ~** (*fig*) considérer qch comme accepté; **to ~ sth into sb's remarks** voir qch dans les remarques de qn; **to ~ too much into sth** attacher trop d'importance à qch

▶ **read out** VT lire à haute voix

▶ **read over** [riːd 'əuvəʳ] VT relire

▶ **read through** [riːd θruː] VT (*quickly*) parcourir; (*thoroughly*) lire jusqu'au bout

▶ **read up about** [riːd ʌp ə'baut], **read up on** [riːd ʌp ɔn] VT étudier

readable ['riːdəbl] ADJ facile *or* agréable à lire

★reader ['riːdəʳ] N lecteur(-trice); (*book*) livre *m* de lecture; (*BRIT: at university*) maître *m* de conférences

readership ['riːdəʃɪp] N (*of paper etc*) (nombre *m* de) lecteurs *mpl*

readily ['rɛdɪlɪ] ADV volontiers, avec empressement; (*easily*) facilement

readiness ['rɛdɪnɪs] N empressement m; **in ~** (prepared) prêt(e)

★**reading** ['ri:dɪŋ] N lecture f; (understanding) interprétation f; (on instrument) indications fpl

reading lamp N lampe f de bureau

reading room N salle f de lecture

readjust [ri:ə'dʒʌst] VT rajuster; (instrument) régler de nouveau ▶ VI (person): **to ~ (to)** se réadapter (à)

readjustment [ri:ə'dʒʌstmənt] N réadaptation f

readout ['ri:daut] N (from instrument) mesure f

★**ready** ['rɛdɪ] ADJ prêt(e); (willing) prêt, disposé(e); (quick) prompt(e); (available) disponible; ~ **for use** prêt à l'emploi; **to be ~ to do sth** être prêt à faire qch; **when will my photos be ~?** quand est-ce que mes photos seront prêtes?; **to get ~** (as vi) se préparer; (as vt) préparer ▶ N: **at the ~** (Mil) prêt à faire feu; (fig) tout(e) prêt(e)

ready cash N (argent m) liquide m

ready-cooked ['rɛdɪ'kukd] ADJ précuit(e)

ready-made ['rɛdɪ'meɪd] ADJ tout(e) fait(e)

ready-mix ['rɛdɪmɪks] N (for cakes etc) préparation f en sachet

ready reckoner [-'rɛknə'] N (BRIT) barème m

ready-to-wear ['rɛdɪtə'wɛə'] ADJ (en) prêt-à-porter

reaffirm [ri:ə'fə:m] VT réaffirmer; **to ~ (that)** ... confirmer que ...

reaffirmation [ri:æfə'meɪʃən] N réaffirmation f

reafforestation [ri:əfɔrɪ'steɪʃən] N (esp BRIT) reboisement m

reagent [ri:'eɪdʒənt] N réactif m

★**real** [rɪəl] ADJ (world, life) réel(le); (genuine) véritable; (proper) vrai(e); **in ~ life** dans la réalité ▶ ADV (US inf: very) vraiment

real ale N bière traditionnelle

real estate N biens fonciers or immobiliers

realign [ri:ə'laɪn] VT (policies, plans) repenser; (party) réorienter; (reposition: objects) réagencer

realignment [ri:ə'laɪnmənt] N (of company, economy) réorientation f

realism ['rɪəlɪzəm] N réalisme m

realist ['rɪəlɪst] N réaliste mf

realistic [rɪə'lɪstɪk] ADJ réaliste

realistically [rɪə'lɪstɪklɪ] ADV (pragmatically, accurately) de façon réaliste; (reasonably) raisonnablement; (in reality) en réalité

★**reality** [ri:'ælɪtɪ] N réalité f; **in ~** en réalité, en fait

reality TV N téléréalité f

realizable ['rɪəlaɪzəbl] ADJ réalisable

realization [rɪəlaɪ'zeɪʃən] N (awareness) prise f de conscience; (fulfilment: also: of asset) réalisation f

★**realize** ['rɪəlaɪz] VT (understand) se rendre compte de, prendre conscience de; (a project, Comm: asset) réaliser

reallocate [ri:'æləukeɪt] VT redistribuer

★**really** ['rɪəlɪ] ADV vraiment; **~?** vraiment?, c'est vrai?

realm [rɛlm] N royaume m; (fig) domaine m

real-time ['ri:ltaɪm] ADJ (Comput) en temps réel

realtor ['rɪəltɔ:'] N (US) agent immobilier

ream [ri:m] N rame f (de papier) ▪ **reams** NPL (inf) (fig) des pages et des pages

reap [ri:p] VT moissonner; (fig) récolter

reaper ['ri:pə'] N (machine) moissonneuse f

reappear [ri:ə'pɪə'] VI réapparaître, reparaître

reappearance [ri:ə'pɪərəns] N réapparition f

reapply [ri:ə'plaɪ] VI: **to ~ for** (job) faire une nouvelle demande d'emploi concernant; reposer sa candidature à; (loan, grant) faire une nouvelle demande de

reappraisal [ri:ə'preɪzl] N réévaluation f

rear [rɪə'] ADJ de derrière, arrière inv; (Aut: wheel etc) arrière ▶ N arrière m, derrière m ▶ VT (cattle, family) élever ▶ VI (also: **rear up**: animal) se cabrer

rear admiral N vice-amiral m

rear-engined ['rɪər'ɛndʒɪnd] ADJ (Aut) avec moteur à l'arrière

rearguard ['rɪəɡɑ:d] N arrière-garde f

rearmament [ri:'ɑ:məmənt] N réarmement m

rearrange [ri:ə'reɪndʒ] VT réarranger

rear-view mirror ['rɪəvju:-] N (Aut) rétroviseur m

rear-wheel drive ['rɪəwi:l-] N (Aut) traction f arrière

★**reason** ['ri:zn] N raison f; **the ~ for/why** la raison de/pour laquelle; **to have ~ to think** avoir lieu de penser; **it stands to ~ that** il va sans dire que; **she claims with good ~ that** ... elle affirme à juste titre que ...; **all the more ~ why** raison de plus pour + infinitive or pour que + sub; **within ~** dans les limites du raisonnable ▶ VI: **to ~ with sb** raisonner qn, faire entendre raison à qn

★**reasonable** ['ri:znəbl] ADJ raisonnable; (not bad) acceptable

reasonably ['ri:znəblɪ] ADV (behave) raisonnablement; (fairly) assez; **one can ~ assume that** ... on est fondé à or il est permis de supposer que ...

reasoned ['ri:znd] ADJ (argument) raisonné(e)

reasoning ['ri:znɪŋ] N raisonnement m

reassemble [ri:ə'sɛmbl] VT rassembler; (machine) remonter

reassert [ri:ə'sə:t] VT réaffirmer

reassess [ri:ə'sɛs] VT réexaminer

reassessment [ri:ə'sɛsmənt] N réexamen m

reassurance [ri:ə'ʃuərəns] N (factual) assurance f, garantie f; (emotional) réconfort m

reassure [ri:ə'ʃuə'] VT rassurer; **to ~ sb of** donner à qn l'assurance répétée de

reassuring [ri:ə'ʃuərɪŋ] ADJ rassurant(e)

reassuringly [ri:ə'ʃuərɪŋlɪ] ADV (say) d'un ton rassurant; **she smiled at me ~** elle m'a souri pour me rassurer

reawakening [ri:ə'weɪknɪŋ] N réveil m

rebate ['ri:beɪt] N (on product) rabais m; (on tax etc) dégrèvement m; (repayment) remboursement m

rebel N ['rɛbl] rebelle mf ▶ VI [rɪ'bɛl] se rebeller, se révolter

rebellion [rɪ'bɛljən] N rébellion f, révolte f

rebellious [rɪ'bɛljəs] ADJ rebelle

rebelliousness [rɪ'bɛljəsnɪs] N esprit m de rébellion

rebirth [ri:'bə:θ] N renaissance f

reborn [ri:'bɔ:n] ADJ (Rel): **to be ~** renaître; (fig): **to be ~ as sth** se réincarner en qch

r

rebound vi [rɪˈbaund] (*ball*) rebondir ▸ N [ˈriːbaund] rebond *m*

rebrand [riːˈbrænd] vt changer l'image de

rebranding [riːˈbrændɪŋ] N changement *m* d'image

rebuff [rɪˈbʌf] N rebuffade *f* ▸ vt repousser

rebuild [riːˈbɪld] vt (*irreg: like* **build**) reconstruire

rebuke [rɪˈbjuːk] N réprimande *f*, reproche *m* ▸ vt réprimander

rebut [rɪˈbʌt] vt réfuter

rebuttal [rɪˈbʌtl] N réfutation *f*

recalcitrant [rɪˈkælsɪtrənt] ADJ récalcitrant(e)

recall vt [rɪˈkɔːl] rappeler; (*remember*) se rappeler, se souvenir de ▸ N [ˈriːkɔːl] rappel *m*; (*ability to remember*) mémoire *f*; **beyond ~** *adj* irrévocable

recant [rɪˈkænt] vi se rétracter; (*Rel*) abjurer

recap [ˈriːkæp] N récapitulation *f* ▸ vt, vi récapituler

recapture [riːˈkæptʃəʳ] vt reprendre; (*atmosphere*) recréer

recede [rɪˈsiːd] vi s'éloigner; reculer

receding [rɪˈsiːdɪŋ] ADJ (*forehead, chin*) fuyant(e); **~ hairline** front dégarni

★**receipt** [rɪˈsiːt] N (*document*) reçu *m*; (*for parcel etc*) accusé *m* de réception; (*act of receiving*) réception *f*; **to acknowledge ~ of** accuser réception de; **we are in ~ of ...** nous avons reçu ...; **can I have a ~, please?** je peux avoir un reçu, s'il vous plaît ? ■ **receipts** NPL (*Comm*) recettes *fpl*

receivable [rɪˈsiːvəbl] ADJ (*Comm*) recevable; (*: owing*) à recevoir

★**receive** [rɪˈsiːv] vt recevoir; (*guest*) recevoir, accueillir; **"received with thanks"** (*Comm*) « pour acquit »; **Received Pronunciation** *voir article*

En Grande-Bretagne, la **Received Pronunciation** ou **RP** est un accent surtout caractéristique du sud de l'Angleterre. Bien qu'aucun critère objectif n'en fasse un accent supérieur à ceux d'autres régions anglaises, il est depuis longtemps associé aux élites politiques et financières du pays. Depuis les années 1960, les accents régionaux ont cependant gagné en visibilité dans les médias et la vie publique, à tel point que dans certains contextes le *RP* est parfois perçue de façon négative.

receiver [rɪˈsiːvəʳ] N (*Tel*) récepteur *m*, combiné *m*; (*Radio*) récepteur; (*of stolen goods*) receleur *m*; (*for bankruptcies*) administrateur *m* judiciaire

receivership [rɪˈsiːvəʃɪp] N: **to go into ~** être placé sous administration judiciaire

★**recent** [ˈriːsnt] ADJ récent(e); **in ~ years** au cours de ces dernières années

★**recently** [ˈriːsntlɪ] ADV récemment; **as ~ as** pas plus tard que; **until ~** jusqu'à il y a peu de temps encore

receptacle [rɪˈsɛptɪkl] N récipient *m*

reception [rɪˈsɛpʃən] N réception *f*; (*welcome*) accueil *m*, réception

reception centre N (BRIT) centre *m* d'accueil

reception desk N réception *f*

receptionist [rɪˈsɛpʃənɪst] N réceptionniste *mf*

receptive [rɪˈsɛptɪv] ADJ réceptif(-ive)

recess [rɪˈsɛs] N (*in room*) renfoncement *m*; (*for bed*) alcôve *f*; (*secret place*) recoin *m*; (*Pol etc: holiday*) vacances *fpl*; (*US Law: short break*) suspension *f* d'audience; (*Scol: esp US*) récréation *f*

★**recession** [rɪˈsɛʃən] N (*Econ*) récession *f*

recessionista [rɪsɛʃəˈnɪstə] N recessionista *mf*

recessive [rɪˈsɛsɪv] ADJ (*gene*) récessif(-ive)

recharge [riːˈtʃɑːdʒ] vt (*battery*) recharger

rechargeable [riːˈtʃɑːdʒəbl] ADJ rechargeable

★**recipe** [ˈrɛsɪpɪ] N recette *f*

recipient [rɪˈsɪpɪənt] N (*of payment*) bénéficiaire *mf*; (*of letter*) destinataire *mf*

reciprocal [rɪˈsɪprəkl] ADJ réciproque

reciprocate [rɪˈsɪprəkeɪt] vt retourner, offrir en retour ▸ vi en faire autant

recital [rɪˈsaɪtl] N récital *m*

recitation [rɛsɪˈteɪʃən] N récitation *f*

recite [rɪˈsaɪt] vt (*poem*) réciter; (*complaints etc*) énumérer

reckless [ˈrɛkləs] ADJ (*careless*) imprudent(e); (*heedless of danger*) téméraire; **~ driver** conducteur(-trice) imprudent(e)

recklessly [ˈrɛkləslɪ] ADV imprudemment

recklessness [ˈrɛkləsnɪs] N imprudence *f*

★**reckon** [ˈrɛkən] vt (*count*) calculer, compter; (*consider*) considérer, estimer; (*think*): **I ~ (that) ...** je pense (que) ..., j'estime (que) ... ▸ vi: **to ~ with** (*take into account*) tenir compte de; **he is somebody to be reckoned with** il ne faut pas le sous-estimer; **to ~ without sb/sth** ne pas tenir compte de qn/qch

▸ **reckon on** vt FUS compter sur, s'attendre à

reckoning [ˈrɛknɪŋ] N compte *m*, calcul *m*; estimation *f*; **the day of ~** le jour du Jugement

reclaim [rɪˈkleɪm] vt (*land: from sea*) assécher; (*: from forest*) défricher; (*: with fertilizer*) amender; (*demand back*) réclamer (le remboursement *or* la restitution de); (*waste materials*) récupérer

reclamation [rɛkləˈmeɪʃən] N (*of land*) amendement *m*; assèchement *m*; défrichement *m*

recline [rɪˈklaɪn] vi être allongé(e) *or* étendu(e)

recliner [rɪˈklaɪnəʳ] N fauteuil *m* relax

reclining [rɪˈklaɪnɪŋ] ADJ (*seat*) à dossier réglable

recluse [rɪˈkluːs] N reclus(e), ermite *m*

reclusive [rɪˈkluːsɪv] ADJ (*person*) solitaire; (*life*) de reclus(e)

recognition [rɛkəgˈnɪʃən] N reconnaissance *f*; **in ~ of** en reconnaissance de; **to gain ~** être reconnu(e); **transformed beyond ~** méconnaissable

recognizable [ˈrɛkəgnaɪzəbl] ADJ: **~ (by)** reconnaissable (à)

★**recognize** [ˈrɛkəgnaɪz] vt: **to ~ (by/as)** reconnaître (à/comme étant)

recoil [rɪˈkɔɪl] vi (*person*): **to ~ (from)** reculer (devant) ▸ N (*of gun*) recul *m*

recollect [rɛkəˈlɛkt] vt se rappeler, se souvenir de

recollection [rɛkəˈlɛkʃən] N souvenir *m*; **to the best of my ~** autant que je m'en souvienne

★**recommend** [rɛkəˈmɛnd] vt recommander; **can you ~ a good restaurant?** pouvez-vous me conseiller un bon restaurant ?; **she has a lot to ~ her** elle a beaucoup de choses en sa faveur

recommendation [rɛkəmɛn'deɪʃən] N recommandation f

recommended [rɛkə'mɛndɪd] ADJ conseillé(e), recommandé(e)

recommended retail price N (BRIT) prix conseillé

recompense ['rɛkəmpɛns] VT récompenser; (compensate) dédommager ▸ N récompense f; dédommagement m

reconcilable ['rɛkənsaɪləbl] ADJ (ideas) conciliable

reconcile ['rɛkənsaɪl] VT (two people) réconcilier; (two facts) concilier, accorder; **to ~ o.s. to** se résigner à

reconciliation [rɛkənsɪlɪ'eɪʃən] N réconciliation f; conciliation f

recondite [rɪ'kɒndaɪt] ADJ abstrus(e), obscur(e)

recondition [ri:kən'dɪʃən] VT remettre à neuf; réviser entièrement

reconfigure [ri:kən'fɪɡəʳ] VT reconfigurer

reconnaissance [rɪ'kɒnɪsns] N (Mil) reconnaissance f

reconnect [ri:kə'nɛkt] VT (electricity, water supply) rebrancher; (customer, house) rebrancher sur le réseau

reconnoitre, (US) **reconnoiter** [rɛkə'nɔɪtəʳ] (Mil) VT reconnaître ▸ VI faire une reconnaissance

reconsider [ri:kən'sɪdəʳ] VT reconsidérer

reconstitute [ri:'kɒnstɪtju:t] VT reconstituer

reconstruct [ri:kən'strʌkt] VT (building) reconstruire; (crime, system) reconstituer

reconstruction [ri:kən'strʌkʃən] N reconstruction f; reconstitution f

reconstructive [ri:kən'strʌktɪv] ADJ reconstructif(-ive)

reconvene [ri:kən'vi:n] VT reconvoquer ▸ VI se réunir or s'assembler de nouveau

★**record** N ['rɛkɔ:d] rapport m, récit m; (of meeting etc) procès-verbal m; (register) registre m; (file) dossier m; (Comput) article m; (also: **police record**) casier m judiciaire; (Mus: disc) disque m; (Sport) record m; **to keep a ~ of** noter; **to set the ~ straight** (fig) mettre les choses au point; **he is on ~ as saying that ...** il a déclaré en public que ...; **Italy's excellent ~** les excellents résultats obtenus par l'Italie; **off the ~** adj officieux(-euse); adv officieusement; **public records** archives fpl ▸ ADJ ['rɛkɔ:d] record inv; **in ~ time** dans un temps record ▸ VT [rɪ'kɔ:d] (set down) noter; (relate) rapporter; (Mus: song etc) enregistrer

record card N (in file) fiche f

recorded delivery [rɪ'kɔ:dɪd-] N (BRIT Post): **to send sth ~** ≈ envoyer qch en recommandé

recorded delivery letter [rɪ'kɔ:dɪd-] N (BRIT Post) ≈ lettre recommandée

recorder [rɪ'kɔ:dəʳ] N (Law) avocat nommé à la fonction de juge; (Mus) flûte f à bec

record holder N (Sport) détenteur(-trice) du record

★**recording** [rɪ'kɔ:dɪŋ] N (Mus) enregistrement m

recording studio N studio m d'enregistrement

record-keeping ['rɛkɔ:dki:pɪŋ] N archivage m

record library N discothèque f

record player N tourne-disque m

recount [rɪ'kaunt] VT raconter

re-count N ['ri:kaunt] (Pol: of votes) nouveau décompte (des suffrages) ▸ VT [ri:'kaunt] recompter

recoup [rɪ'ku:p] VT: **to ~ one's losses** récupérer ce qu'on a perdu, se refaire

recourse [rɪ'kɔ:s] N recours m; expédient m; **to have ~ to** recourir à, avoir recours à

★**recover** [rɪ'kʌvəʳ] VT récupérer ▸ VI (from illness) se rétablir; (from shock) se remettre; (country) se redresser

re-cover [ri:'kʌvəʳ] VT (chair etc) recouvrir

recoverable [rɪ'kʌvərəbl] ADJ (costs) recouvrable

★**recovery** [rɪ'kʌvərɪ] N récupération f; rétablissement m; (Econ) redressement m

recreate [ri:krɪ'eɪt] VT recréer

recreation [rɛkrɪ'eɪʃən] N (leisure) récréation f, détente f

recreational [rɛkrɪ'eɪʃənl] ADJ pour la détente, récréatif(-ive)

recreational drug N drogue récréative

recreational vehicle N (US) camping-car m

recrimination [rɪkrɪmɪ'neɪʃən] N récrimination f

recruit [rɪ'kru:t] N recrue f ▸ VT recruter

recruiting office [rɪ'kru:tɪŋ-] N bureau m de recrutement

recruitment [rɪ'kru:tmənt] N recrutement m

rectangle ['rɛktæŋɡl] N rectangle m

rectangular [rɛk'tæŋɡjuləʳ] ADJ rectangulaire

rectify ['rɛktɪfaɪ] VT (error) rectifier, corriger; (omission) réparer

rector ['rɛktəʳ] N (Rel) pasteur m; (in Scottish universities) personnalité élue par les étudiants pour les représenter

rectory ['rɛktərɪ] N presbytère m

rectum ['rɛktəm] N (Anat) rectum m

recuperate [rɪ'kju:pəreɪt] VI (from illness) se rétablir

recuperation [rɪ'ku:pərəɪʃən] N rétablissement m; **powers of ~** pouvoir m de récupération

recuperative [rɪ'ku:pərətɪv] ADJ: **~ powers** pouvoir m de récupération

recur [rɪ'kəːʳ] VI se reproduire; (idea, opportunity) se retrouver; (symptoms) réapparaître

recurrence [rɪ'kəːrns] N répétition f; réapparition f

recurrent [rɪ'kəːrnt] ADJ périodique, fréquent(e)

recurring [rɪ'kəːrɪŋ] ADJ (problem) périodique, fréquent(e); (Math) périodique

recyclable [ri:'saɪkləbl] ADJ recyclable

recycle [ri:'saɪkl] VT, VI recycler

recycled [ri:'saɪkld] ADJ recyclé(e); (waste, water) recyclé(e), retraité(e); **~ paper** papier m recyclé

recycling [ri:'saɪklɪŋ] N recyclage m

★**red** [rɛd] N rouge m; (Pol: pej) rouge mf; **in the ~** (account) à découvert; (business) en déficit ▸ ADJ rouge; (hair) roux (rousse)

red alert N alerte f rouge

red-blooded [rɛd'blʌdɪd] ADJ (inf) viril(e), vigoureux(-euse)

redbrick university ['redbrɪk-] N (BRIT) *voir article*

Une **redbrick university**, ainsi nommée à cause du matériau de construction répandu à l'époque (la brique), est une université britannique provinciale construite assez récemment, en particulier fin XIXe - début XXe siècle. Il y en a notamment une à Manchester, une à Liverpool et une à Bristol. Ce terme est utilisé pour établir une distinction avec les universités plus anciennes et plus traditionnelles.

red carpet treatment N réception f en grande pompe

Red Cross N Croix-Rouge f

redcurrant ['redkʌrənt] N groseille f (rouge)

redden ['rɛdn] VT, VI rougir

reddish ['redɪʃ] ADJ rougeâtre; (*hair*) plutôt roux (rousse)

redecorate [ri:'dekəreɪt] VT refaire à neuf, repeindre et retapisser

redeem [rɪ'di:m] VT (*debt*) rembourser; (*sth in pawn*) dégager; (*fig, Rel*) racheter

redeemable [rɪ'di:məbl] ADJ rachetable; remboursable, amortissable

redeeming [rɪ'di:mɪŋ] ADJ (*feature*) qui sauve, qui rachète (le reste)

redefine [ri:dɪ'faɪn] VT redéfinir

redemption [rɪ'dɛmʃən] N (*Rel*) rédemption f; **past** *or* **beyond ~** (*situation*) irrémédiable; (*place*) qui ne peut plus être sauvé(e); (*person*) irrécupérable

redeploy [ri:dɪ'plɔɪ] VT (*Mil*) redéployer; (*staff, resources*) reconvertir

redeployment [ri:dɪ'plɔɪmənt] N redéploiement m; reconversion f

redesign [ri:dɪ'zaɪn] VT (*building*) réaménager; (*system*) repenser

redevelop [ri:dɪ'veləp] VT rénover

redevelopment [ri:dɪ'veləpmənt] N rénovation f

red-haired [red'heəd] ADJ roux (rousse)

red-handed [red'hændɪd] ADJ: **to be caught ~** être pris(e) en flagrant délit *or* la main dans le sac

redhead ['redhed] N roux (rousse)

red herring N (*fig*) diversion f, fausse piste

red-hot [red'hɒt] ADJ chauffé(e) au rouge, brûlant(e)

redirect [ri:daɪ'rekt] VT (*mail*) faire suivre

rediscover [ri:dɪ'skʌvə'] VT redécouvrir

redistribute [ri:dɪ'strɪbju:t] VT redistribuer

redistribution [ri:dɪstrɪ'bju:ʃən] N redistribution f

red-letter day ['redletə-] N grand jour m, jour mémorable

red light N: **to go through a ~** (*Aut*) brûler un feu rouge

red-light district ['redlaɪt-] N quartier mal famé

red meat N viande f rouge

redneck ['rednek] N (*esp US pej*) plouc m (*inf*)

redness ['rednɪs] N rougeur f; (*of hair*) rousseur f

redo [ri:'du:] VT (*irreg: like* **do**) refaire

redolent ['redələnt] ADJ: **~ of** qui sent; (*fig*) qui évoque

redouble [ri:'dʌbl] VT: **to ~ one's efforts** redoubler d'efforts

redoubtable [rɪ'dautəbl] ADJ redoutable

redraft [ri:'drɑ:ft] VT remanier

redress [rɪ'dres] N réparation f ▶ VT redresser; **to ~ the balance** rétablir l'équilibre

Red Sea N: **the ~** la mer Rouge

red tape N (*fig*) paperasserie (administrative)

★**reduce** [rɪ'dju:s] VT réduire; (*lower*) abaisser; **"~ speed now"** (*Aut*) «ralentir»; **to ~ sth by/to** réduire qch de/à; **to ~ sb to tears** faire pleurer qn

reduced [rɪ'dju:st] ADJ réduit(e); **"greatly ~ prices"** « gros rabais »; **at a ~ price** (*goods*) au rabais; (*ticket etc*) à prix réduit

★**reduction** [rɪ'dʌkʃən] N réduction f; (*of price*) baisse f; (*discount*) rabais m; réduction; **is there a ~ for children/students?** y a-t-il une réduction pour les enfants/les étudiants ?

redundancy [rɪ'dʌndənsɪ] N (BRIT) licenciement m, mise f au chômage; **compulsory ~** licenciement; **voluntary ~** départ m volontaire

redundancy payment N (BRIT) indemnité f de licenciement

redundant [rɪ'dʌndnt] ADJ (BRIT: *worker*) licencié(e), mis(e) au chômage; (*detail, object*) superflu(e); **to be made ~** (*worker*) être licencié, être mis au chômage

reed [ri:d] N (*Bot*) roseau m; (*Mus: of clarinet etc*) anche f

re-educate [ri:'edjukeɪt] VT rééduquer

reedy ['ri:dɪ] ADJ (*voice, instrument*) ténu(e)

reef [ri:f] N (*at sea*) récif m, écueil m

reek [ri:k] VI: **to ~ (of)** puer, empester

reel [ri:l] N bobine f; (*Tech*) dévidoir m; (*Fishing*) moulinet m; (*Cine*) bande f; (*dance*) quadrille écossais ▶ VT (*Tech*) bobiner; (*also:* **reel up**) enrouler ▶ VI (*sway*) chanceler; **my head is reeling** j'ai la tête qui tourne

▶ **reel in** VT (*fish, line*) ramener

▶ **reel off** VT (*say*) énumérer, débiter

re-elect [ri:ɪ'lekt] VT réélire; **to ~ sb as sth** réélire qn qch

re-election [ri:ɪ'lekʃən] N réélection f

re-enact [ri:ɪn'ækt] VT (*incident*) reconstituer; (*scene*) rejouer

re-enter [ri:'entə'] VT (*also Space*) rentrer dans

re-entry [ri:'entrɪ] N (*also Space*) rentrée f

re-examine [ri:ɪg'zæmɪn] VT reconsidérer

re-export VT ['ri:ɪks'pɔ:t] réexporter ▶ N [ri:'ekspɔ:t] marchandise réexportée; (*act*) réexportation f

ref [ref] N ABBR (*inf:* = referee) arbitre m

ref. ABBR (*Comm:* = with reference to) réf.

refectory [rɪ'fektərɪ] N réfectoire m

★**refer** [rɪ'fə:'] VT: **to ~ sth to** (*dispute, decision*) soumettre qch à; **to ~ sb to** (*inquirer, patient*) adresser qn à; (*reader: to text*) renvoyer qn à; **he referred me to the manager** il m'a dit de m'adresser au directeur ▶ VI: **to ~ to** (*allude to*) parler de, faire allusion à; (*consult*) se reporter à; (*apply to*) s'appliquer à; **referring to your letter** (*Comm*) en réponse à votre lettre

referee [refə'ri:] N arbitre m; (*Tennis*) juge-arbitre m; (BRIT: *for job application*) répondant(e) ▶ VT arbitrer

★**reference** ['refrəns] N référence f, renvoi m; (mention) allusion f, mention f; (for job application: letter) références; lettre f de recommandation; (person) répondant(e); **with ~ to** en ce qui concerne; (Comm: in letter) me référant à; **"please quote this ~"** (Comm) « prière de rappeler cette référence »

reference book N ouvrage m de référence

reference library N bibliothèque f d'ouvrages à consulter

reference number N (Comm) numéro m de référence

referendum [refə'rendəm] (pl **referenda** [-də]) N référendum m

referral [rɪ'fə:rəl] N soumission f; **she got a ~ to a specialist** elle a été adressée à un spécialiste

refill VT [ri:'fil] remplir à nouveau; (pen, lighter etc) recharger ▶ N ['ri:fil] (for pen etc) recharge f

refine [rɪ'faɪn] VT (sugar, oil) raffiner; (taste) affiner; (idea, theory) peaufiner

refined [rɪ'faɪnd] ADJ (person, taste) raffiné(e)

refinement [rɪ'faɪnmənt] N (of person) raffinement m

refinery [rɪ'faɪnərɪ] N raffinerie f

refit (Naut) N ['ri:fɪt] remise f en état ▶ VT [ri:'fɪt] remettre en état

reflate [ri:'fleɪt] VT (economy) relancer

reflation [ri:'fleɪʃən] N relance f

reflationary [ri:'fleɪʃənrɪ] ADJ de relance

reflect [rɪ'flɛkt] VT (light, image) réfléchir, refléter; (fig) refléter ▶ VI (think) réfléchir, méditer; **it reflects badly on him** cela le discrédite; **it reflects well on him** c'est tout à son honneur
▶ **reflect on** VT FUS (think about) réfléchir à

reflection [rɪ'flɛkʃən] N réflexion f; (image) reflet m; **~ on** (criticism) critique f de; atteinte f à; **on ~** réflexion faite

reflective [rɪ'flɛktɪv] ADJ (person, mood) méditatif(-ive); (surface, pool) réfléchissant(e); **to be ~ of sth** refléter qch

reflector [rɪ'flɛktə'] N (also Aut) réflecteur m

reflex ['ri:flɛks] ADJ, N réflexe m

reflexive [rɪ'flɛksɪv] ADJ (Ling) réfléchi(e)

reflexologist [ri:flɛks'ɔlədʒɪst] N réflexologue mf

reflexology [ri:flɛk'sɔlədʒɪ] N réflexologie f

reforestation [ri:fɔrɪ'steɪʃən] N reboisement m, reforestation f

reform [rɪ'fɔ:m] N réforme f ▶ VT réformer

reformat [ri:'fɔ:mæt] VT (Comput) reformater

Reformation [refə'meɪʃən] N: **the ~** la Réforme

reformatory [rɪ'fɔ:mətərɪ] N (US) centre m d'éducation surveillée

reformed [rɪ'fɔ:md] ADJ amendé(e), assagi(e)

reformer [rɪ'fɔ:mə'] N réformateur(-trice)

refrain [rɪ'freɪn] VI: **to ~ from doing** s'abstenir de faire ▶ N refrain m

refresh [rɪ'frɛʃ] VT rafraîchir; (subj: food, sleep etc) redonner des forces à

refresher course [rɪ'frɛʃə-] N (BRIT) cours m de recyclage

refreshing [rɪ'frɛʃɪŋ] ADJ (drink) rafraîchissant(e); (sleep) réparateur(-trice); (fact, idea etc) qui réjouit par son originalité or sa rareté

refreshingly [rɪ'frɛʃɪŋlɪ] ADV: **~ honest/simple** d'une honnêteté/simplicité rafraîchissante

refreshment [rɪ'frɛʃmənt] N: **for some ~** (eating) pour se restaurer or sustenter; **in need of ~** (resting etc) ayant besoin de refaire ses forces

refreshments [rɪ'frɛʃmənts] NPL rafraîchissements mpl

refrigerated [rɪ'frɪdʒəreɪtɪd] ADJ réfrigéré(e)

refrigeration [rɪfrɪdʒə'reɪʃən] N réfrigération f

refrigerator [rɪ'frɪdʒəreɪtə'] N réfrigérateur m, frigidaire m

refuel [ri:'fjuəl] VT ravitailler en carburant ▶ VI se ravitailler en carburant

refuelling, (US) **refueling** [ri:'fju:əlɪŋ] N (of aircraft) ravitaillement m

refuge ['refju:dʒ] N refuge m; **to take ~ in** se réfugier dans

★**refugee** [refju'dʒi:] N réfugié(e)

refugee camp N camp m de réfugiés

refund N ['ri:fʌnd] remboursement m ▶ VT [rɪ'fʌnd] rembourser

refundable [rɪ'fʌndəbl] ADJ remboursable

refurbish [ri:'fə:bɪʃ] VT remettre à neuf

refurbishment [ri:'fə:bɪʃmənt] N rénovation f

refurnish [ri:'fə:nɪʃ] VT remeubler

refusal [rɪ'fju:zəl] N refus m; **to have first ~ on sth** avoir droit de préemption sur qch

★**refuse**[1] ['refju:s] N ordures fpl, détritus mpl

refuse[2] [rɪ'fju:z] VT, VI refuser; **to ~ to do sth** refuser de faire qch

refuse collection N ramassage m d'ordures

refuse disposal N élimination f des ordures

refusenik [rɪ'fju:znɪk] N refuznik mf

refute [rɪ'fju:t] VT réfuter

regain [rɪ'geɪn] VT (lost ground) regagner; (strength) retrouver

regal ['ri:gl] ADJ royal(e)

regale [rɪ'geɪl] VT: **to ~ sb with sth** régaler qn de qch

regalia [rɪ'geɪlɪə] N insignes mpl de la royauté

regard [rɪ'gɑ:d] N respect m, estime f, considération f; **to give one's regards to** faire ses amitiés à; **"with kindest regards"** « bien amicalement »; **with ~ to** (also: **as regards**) en ce qui concerne ▶ VT considérer

regarding [rɪ'gɑ:dɪŋ] PREP en ce qui concerne

regardless [rɪ'gɑ:dlɪs] ADV quand même; **~ of** sans se soucier de

regatta [rɪ'gætə] N régate f

regency ['ri:dʒənsɪ] N régence f

regenerate [rɪ'dʒɛnəreɪt] VT régénérer ▶ VI se régénérer

regeneration [rɪdʒɛnə'reɪʃən] N régénération f

regent ['ri:dʒənt] N régent(e)

reggae ['regeɪ] N reggae m

régime [reɪ'ʒi:m] N régime m

regiment N ['redʒɪmənt] régiment m ▶ VT ['redʒɪment] imposer une discipline trop stricte à

regimental [redʒɪ'mentl] ADJ d'un régiment

regimentation [redʒɪmen'teɪʃən] N réglementation excessive

★region [ˈriːdʒən] N région f; **in the ~ of** (fig) aux alentours de

regional [ˈriːdʒənl] ADJ régional(e)

regional development N aménagement m du territoire

★register [ˈrɛdʒɪstəʳ] N registre m; (also: **electoral register**) liste électorale ▶ VT enregistrer, inscrire; (birth) déclarer; (vehicle) immatriculer; (luggage) enregistrer; (letter) envoyer en recommandé; (subj: instrument) marquer; **to ~ a protest** protester ▶ VI s'inscrire; (at hotel) signer le registre; (make impression) être (bien) compris(e); **to ~ for a course** s'inscrire à un cours

registered [ˈrɛdʒɪstəd] ADJ (design) déposé(e); (BRIT: letter) recommandé(e); (student, voter) inscrit(e); **by ~ mail** or (BRIT) **post** en recommandé

registered company N société immatriculée

registered nurse N (US) infirmier(-ière) diplômé(e) d'État

registered office N siège social

registered trademark N marque déposée

registrar [ˈrɛdʒɪstrɑːʳ] N officier m de l'état civil; secrétaire mf général(e)

registration [rɛdʒɪsˈtreɪʃən] N (act) enregistrement m; (of student) inscription f; (BRIT Aut: also: **registration number**) numéro m d'immatriculation

registry [ˈrɛdʒɪstrɪ] N bureau m de l'enregistrement

registry office N (BRIT) bureau m de l'état civil; **to get married in a ~** ≈ se marier à la mairie

★regret [rɪˈgrɛt] N regret m ▶ VT regretter; **to ~ that** regretter que + sub; **we ~ to inform you that ...** nous sommes au regret de vous informer que ...

regretfully [rɪˈgrɛtfəlɪ] ADV à or avec regret

regrettable [rɪˈgrɛtəbl] ADJ regrettable, fâcheux(-euse)

regrettably [rɪˈgrɛtəblɪ] ADV (drunk, late) fâcheusement; **~, he ...** malheureusement, il ...

regroup [riːˈgruːp] VT regrouper ▶ VI se regrouper

regt ABBR = **regiment**

★regular [ˈrɛgjuləʳ] ADJ régulier(-ière); (usual) habituel(le), normal(e); (listener, reader) fidèle; (soldier) de métier; (Comm: size) ordinaire ▶ N (client etc) habitué(e)

regularity [rɛgjuˈlærɪtɪ] N régularité f

regularly [ˈrɛgjuləlɪ] ADV régulièrement

regulate [ˈrɛgjuleɪt] VT régler

regulation [rɛgjuˈleɪʃən] N (rule) règlement m; (adjustment) réglage m ▶ CPD réglementaire

regulator [ˈrɛgjuleɪtəʳ] N régulateur(-trice)

regulatory [rɛgjuˈleɪtrɪ] ADJ régulateur(-trice)

rehab [ˈriːhæb] N désintox f (inf), désintoxication f; **to be in ~** être en désintox or désintoxication

rehabilitate [riːəˈbɪlɪteɪt] VT (criminal) réinsérer; (drug addict) désintoxiquer; (invalid) rééduquer

rehabilitation [ˈriːəbɪlɪˈteɪʃən] N (of offender) réhabilitation f; (of drug addict) désintoxication f; (of disabled) rééducation f, réadaptation f

rehash [riːˈhæʃ] VT (inf) remanier

rehearsal [rɪˈhəːsəl] N répétition f; **dress ~** (répétition) générale f

rehearse [rɪˈhəːs] VT répéter

rehome [riːˈhəum] VT (animal) faire adopter

rehouse [riːˈhauz] VT reloger

reign [reɪn] N règne m ▶ VI régner

reigning [ˈreɪnɪŋ] ADJ (monarch) régnant(e); (champion) actuel(le)

reimburse [riːɪmˈbəːs] VT rembourser

reimbursement [riːɪmˈbəːsmənt] N remboursement m

rein [reɪn] N (for horse) rêne f; **to give sb free ~** (fig) donner carte blanche à qn
▶ **rein in** VT (enthusiasm, temper) réfréner; (costs, inflation) mettre un frein à

reincarnation [riːɪnkɑːˈneɪʃən] N réincarnation f

★reindeer [ˈreɪndɪəʳ] N (pl inv) renne m

reinforce [riːɪnˈfɔːs] VT renforcer

reinforced concrete [riːɪnˈfɔːst-] N béton armé

reinforcement [riːɪnˈfɔːsmənt] N (action) renforcement m

reinforcements [riːɪnˈfɔːsmənts] NPL (Mil) renfort(s) m(pl)

reinstate [riːɪnˈsteɪt] VT rétablir, réintégrer

reinstatement [riːɪnˈsteɪtmənt] N réintégration f

reintroduce [riːɪntrəˈdjuːs] VT réintroduire

reintroduction [riːɪntrəˈdʌkʃən] N réintroduction f

reinvent [riːɪnˈvɛnt] VT réinventer; **to ~ o.s.** se réinventer; **to ~ the wheel** réinventer la roue

reinvention [riːɪnˈvɛnʃən] N réinvention f

reissue [riːˈɪʃjuː] VT (book) rééditer; (film) ressortir

reiterate [riːˈɪtəreɪt] VT réitérer, répéter

reject N [ˈriːdʒɛkt] (Comm) article m de rebut ▶ VT [rɪˈdʒɛkt] refuser; (Comm: goods) mettre au rebut; (idea) rejeter

rejection [rɪˈdʒɛkʃən] N rejet m, refus m

rejig [riːˈdʒɪg], (US) **rejigger** [riːˈdʒɪgəʳ] VT réorganiser

rejoice [rɪˈdʒɔɪs] VI: **to ~ (at or over)** se réjouir (de)

rejoin [riːˈdʒɔɪn] VT rejoindre

rejoinder [rɪˈdʒɔɪndəʳ] N (retort) réplique f

rejuvenate [rɪˈdʒuːvəneɪt] VT (person, skin) rajeunir; (area) moderniser

rejuvenating [rɪˈdʒuːvəneɪtɪŋ] ADJ (holiday, break) revigorant(e); (treatment) rajeunissant(e)

rekindle [riːˈkɪndl] VT rallumer; (fig) raviver

relapse [rɪˈlæps] N (Med) rechute f

relate [rɪˈleɪt] VT (tell) raconter; (connect) établir un rapport entre ▶ VI: **to ~ to** (connect) se rapporter à; **to ~ to sb** (interact) entretenir des rapports avec qn

★related [rɪˈleɪtɪd] ADJ apparenté(e); **~ to** (subject) lié(e) à

relating to [rɪˈleɪtɪŋ-] PREP concernant

★relation [rɪˈleɪʃən] N (person) parent(e); (link) rapport m, lien m; **in ~ to** en ce qui concerne, par rapport à; **to bear no ~ to** être sans rapport avec ■ **relations** NPL (relatives) famille f; **diplomatic/international relations** relations diplomatiques/internationales

★relationship [rɪˈleɪʃənʃɪp] N rapport m, lien m; (personal ties) relations fpl, rapports; (also: **family**

relationship) lien de parenté; (*affair*) liaison *f*; **they have a good ~** ils s'entendent bien

★**relative** ['rɛlətɪv] N parent(e); **all her relatives** toute sa famille ▸ ADJ relatif(-ive); (*respective*) respectif(-ive)

★**relatively** ['rɛlətɪvlɪ] ADV relativement

relativity [rɛlə'tɪvɪtɪ] N (*Physics*) relativité *f*; **the theory of ~** la théorie de la relativité

relaunch VT [ri:'lɔ:ntʃ] relancer ▸ N ['ri:lɔ:ntʃ] relance *f*

★**relax** [rɪ'læks] VI (*muscle*) se relâcher; (*person: unwind*) se détendre; (*: calm down*) se calmer ▸ VT relâcher; (*mind, person*) détendre

relaxation [ri:læk'seɪʃən] N relâchement *m*; (*of mind*) détente *f*; (*recreation*) détente, délassement *m*; (*entertainment*) distraction *f*

relaxed [rɪ'lækst] ADJ relâché(e); détendu(e)

relaxing [rɪ'læksɪŋ] ADJ délassant(e)

relay ['ri:leɪ] N (*Sport*) course *f* de relais ▸ VT (*message*) retransmettre, relayer

★**release** [rɪ'li:s] N (*from prison, obligation*) libération *f*; (*of gas etc*) émission *f*; (*of film etc*) sortie *f*; (*new recording*) disque *m*; (*device*) déclencheur *m* ▸ VT (*prisoner*) libérer; (*book, film*) sortir; (*report, news*) rendre public, publier; (*gas etc*) émettre, dégager; (*free: from wreckage etc*) dégager; (*Tech: catch, spring etc*) déclencher; (*let go: person, animal*) relâcher; (*: hand, object*) lâcher; (*: brake*) desserrer; **to ~ one's grip** *or* **hold** lâcher prise; **to ~ the clutch** (*Aut*) débrayer

relegate ['rɛləgeɪt] VT reléguer; (*Sport*): **to be relegated** descendre dans une division inférieure

relegation [rɛlɪ'geɪʃən] N (*Sport*) relégation *f*

relent [rɪ'lɛnt] VI se laisser fléchir

relentless [rɪ'lɛntlɪs] ADJ implacable; (*non-stop*) continuel(le)

relentlessly [rɪ'lɛntləslɪ] ADV implacablement; (*continuously: rain*) sans discontinuer

relevance ['rɛləvəns] N pertinence *f*; **~ of sth to sth** rapport *m* entre qch et qch

relevant ['rɛləvənt] ADJ (*question*) pertinent(e); (*corresponding*) approprié(e); (*fact*) significatif(-ive); (*information*) utile; **~ to** ayant rapport à, approprié à

reliability [rɪlaɪə'bɪlɪtɪ] N sérieux *m*; fiabilité *f*

★**reliable** [rɪ'laɪəbl] ADJ (*person, firm*) sérieux(-euse), fiable; (*method, machine*) fiable; (*news, information*) sûr(e)

reliably [rɪ'laɪəblɪ] ADV: **to be ~ informed** savoir de source sûre

reliance [rɪ'laɪəns] N: **~ (on)** (*trust*) confiance *f* (en); (*dependence*) besoin *m* (de), dépendance *f* (de)

reliant [rɪ'laɪənt] ADJ: **to be ~ on sth/sb** dépendre de qch/qn

relic ['rɛlɪk] N (*Rel*) relique *f*; (*of the past*) vestige *m*

★**relief** [rɪ'li:f] N (*from pain, anxiety*) soulagement *m*; (*help, supplies*) secours *m(pl)*; (*of guard*) relève *f*; (*Art, Geo*) relief *m*; **by way of light ~** pour faire diversion

relief map N carte *f* en relief

relief road N (*Brit*) route *f* de délestage

relieve [rɪ'li:v] VT (*pain, patient*) soulager; (*fear, worry*) dissiper; (*bring help*) secourir; (*take over from: gen*)

relayer; (*: guard*) relever; **to ~ sb of sth** débarrasser qn de qch; **to ~ sb of his command** (*Mil*) relever qn de ses fonctions; **to ~ o.s.** (*euphemism*) se soulager, faire ses besoins

relieved [rɪ'li:vd] ADJ soulagé(e); **to be ~ that ...** être soulagé que ...; **I'm ~ to hear it** je suis soulagé de l'entendre

★**religion** [rɪ'lɪdʒən] N religion *f*

★**religious** [rɪ'lɪdʒəs] ADJ religieux(-euse); (*book*) de piété

religious education N instruction religieuse

relinquish [rɪ'lɪŋkwɪʃ] VT abandonner; (*plan, habit*) renoncer à

relish ['rɛlɪʃ] N (*Culin*) condiment *m*; (*enjoyment*) délectation *f* ▸ VT (*food etc*) savourer; **to ~ doing** se délecter à faire

relive [ri:'lɪv] VT revivre

reload [ri:'ləud] VT recharger

relocate [ri:ləu'keɪt] VT (*business*) délocaliser ▸ VI (*company*) délocaliser; (*person*) déménager; **to ~ to** (*person*) déménager à; (*company*) délocaliser à

relocation [ri:ləu'keɪʃən] N (*of company*) délocalisation *f*; (*of person*) déménagement *m*

reluctance [rɪ'lʌktəns] N répugnance *f*

★**reluctant** [rɪ'lʌktənt] ADJ peu disposé(e), qui hésite; **to be ~ to do sth** hésiter à faire qch

reluctantly [rɪ'lʌktəntlɪ] ADV à contrecœur, sans enthousiasme

rely on [rɪ'laɪ-] VT FUS (*be dependent on*) dépendre de; (*trust*) compter sur

★**remain** [rɪ'meɪn] VI rester; **to ~ silent** garder le silence; **I ~, yours faithfully** (*Brit: in letters*) je vous prie d'agréer, Monsieur *etc* l'assurance de mes sentiments distingués

remainder [rɪ'meɪndə^r] N reste *m*; (*Comm*) fin *f* de série

remainer [rɪ'meɪnə^r] N (*Brit: in EU*) partisan du maintien dans l'Union européenne

★**remaining** [rɪ'meɪnɪŋ] ADJ qui reste

remains [rɪ'meɪnz] NPL restes *mpl*

remake ['ri:meɪk] N (*Cine*) remake *m*

remand [rɪ'mɑ:nd] N: **on ~** en détention préventive ▸ VT: **to be remanded in custody** être placé(e) en détention préventive

remand home N (*Brit*) centre *m* d'éducation surveillée

★**remark** [rɪ'mɑ:k] N remarque *f*, observation *f* ▸ VT (*faire*) remarquer, dire; (*notice*) remarquer ▸ VI: **to ~ on sth** faire une *or* des remarque(s) sur qch

★**remarkable** [rɪ'mɑ:kəbl] ADJ remarquable

remarkably [rɪ'mɑ:kəblɪ] ADV remarquablement

remarriage [ri:'mærɪdʒ] N remariage *m*

remarry [ri:'mærɪ] VI se remarier

rematch ['ri:mætʃ] N (*esp Brit: repeat match*) revanche *f*; (*esp US: second meeting*) match *m* retour

remedial [rɪ'mi:dɪəl] ADJ (*tuition, classes*) de rattrapage

remedy ['rɛmədɪ] N: **~ (for)** remède *m* (contre *or* à) ▸ VT remédier à

★**remember** [rɪ'mɛmbə^r] VT se rappeler, se souvenir de; (*send greetings*): **~ me to him** saluez-le de ma part; **I ~ seeing it, I ~ having seen it** je me rappelle l'avoir vu *or* que je l'ai vu; **she remembered to**

811

do it elle a pensé à le faire; **~ me to your wife** rappelez-moi au bon souvenir de votre femme

> In French, instead of telling people to remember something, one tends to tell them not to forget it. *Remember your passport!* **N'oubliez pas votre passeport !**

remembrance [rɪˈmɛmbrəns] N souvenir *m*, mémoire *f*

Remembrance Day N (*BRIT*) ≈ (le jour de) l'Armistice *m*, ≈ le 11 novembre

> **Remembrance Day** ou **Remembrance Sunday** est le dimanche le plus proche du 11 novembre, date à laquelle la Première Guerre mondiale a officiellement pris fin. Il est l'occasion de rendre hommage aux victimes des deux guerres mondiales. À 11h, heure de la signature de l'armistice avec l'Allemagne, en 1918, on observe deux minutes de silence. Certains membres de la famille royale et du gouvernement déposent des gerbes de coquelicots au cénotaphe de Whitehall, et des couronnes sont placées sur les monuments aux morts dans toute la Grande-Bretagne. Par ailleurs, beaucoup de Britanniques portent des coquelicots artificiels fabriqués et vendus par des anciens combattants blessés au combat, au profit des blessés de guerre et de leur famille.

★**remind** [rɪˈmaɪnd] VT: **to ~ sb of sth** rappeler qch à qn; **to ~ sb to do** faire penser à qn à faire, rappeler à qn qu'il doit faire; **that reminds me!** j'y pense !

reminder [rɪˈmaɪndəʳ] N (*Comm: letter*) rappel *m*; (*note etc*) pense-bête *m*; (*souvenir*) souvenir *m*

reminisce [rɛmɪˈnɪs] VI: **to ~ (about)** évoquer ses souvenirs (de)

reminiscences [rɛmɪˈnɪsnsɪz] NPL réminiscences *fpl*, souvenirs *mpl*

reminiscent [rɛmɪˈnɪsnt] ADJ: **~ of** qui rappelle, qui fait penser à

remiss [rɪˈmɪs] ADJ négligent(e); **it was ~ of me** c'était une négligence de ma part

remission [rɪˈmɪʃən] N rémission *f*; (*of debt, sentence*) remise *f*; (*of fee*) exemption *f*

remit [rɪˈmɪt] VT (*send: money*) envoyer

remittance [rɪˈmɪtns] N envoi *m*, paiement *m*

remix N [ˈriːmɪks] remix *m* ▶ VT [riːˈmɪks] remixer

remnant [ˈrɛmnənt] N reste *m*, restant *m*; (*of cloth*) coupon *m* ▪ **remnants** NPL (*Comm*) fins *fpl* de série

remodel [riːˈmɔdl] VT (*room, house*) réagencer

remonstrate [ˈrɛmənstreɪt] VI: **to ~ (with sb about sth)** se plaindre (à qn de qch)

remorse [rɪˈmɔːs] N remords *m*

remorseful [rɪˈmɔːsful] ADJ plein(e) de remords

remorseless [rɪˈmɔːslɪs] ADJ (*fig*) impitoyable

remortgage [riːˈmɔːɡɪdʒ] VT: **to ~ one's house/home** prendre une nouvelle hypothèque sur sa maison

★**remote** [rɪˈməʊt] ADJ éloigné(e), lointain(e); (*person*) distant(e); (*possibility*) vague; **there is a ~ possibility that ...** il est tout juste possible que ...

remote control N télécommande *f*

remote-controlled [rɪˈməʊtkənˈtrəʊld] ADJ téléguidé(e)

remotely [rɪˈməʊtlɪ] ADV au loin; (*slightly*) très vaguement

remoteness [rɪˈməʊtnɪs] N (*of location*) éloignement *m*; (*of person*) attitude *f* distante

remould [ˈriːməʊld] N (*BRIT: tyre*) pneu *m* rechapé

removable [rɪˈmuːvəbl] ADJ (*detachable*) amovible

removal [rɪˈmuːvəl] N (*taking away*) enlèvement *m*; suppression *f*; (*BRIT: from house*) déménagement *m*; (*from office: dismissal*) renvoi *m*; (*of stain*) nettoyage *m*; (*Med*) ablation *f*

removal man N (*irreg*) (*BRIT*) déménageur *m*

removal van N (*BRIT*) camion *m* de déménagement

★**remove** [rɪˈmuːv] VT enlever, retirer; (*employee*) renvoyer; (*stain*) faire partir; (*abuse*) supprimer; (*doubt*) chasser; **first cousin once removed** cousin(e) au deuxième degré

remover [rɪˈmuːvəʳ] N (*for paint*) décapant *m*; (*for varnish*) dissolvant *m*; **make-up ~** démaquillant *m*

remunerate [rɪˈmjuːnəreɪt] VT rémunérer

remuneration [rɪmjuːnəˈreɪʃən] N rémunération *f*

remunerative [rɪˈmjuːnərətɪv] ADJ rémunéré(e)

Renaissance [rɪˈneɪsɔ̃s] N: **the ~** la Renaissance

renal [riːnl] ADJ rénal(e)

rename [riːˈneɪm] VT rebaptiser

rend [rɛnd] (*pt, pp* **rent** [rɛnt]) VT déchirer

render [ˈrɛndəʳ] VT rendre; (*Culin: fat*) clarifier

rendering [ˈrɛndərɪŋ] N (*Mus etc*) interprétation *f*

rendezvous [ˈrɔndɪvuː] N rendez-vous *m inv* ▶ VI opérer une jonction, se rejoindre; **to ~ with sb** rejoindre qn

rendition [rɛnˈdɪʃən] N interprétation *f*

renegade [ˈrɛnɪɡeɪd] N renégat(e)

renege [rɪˈneɪɡ] VI: **to ~ on sth** revenir sur qch

★**renew** [rɪˈnjuː] VT renouveler; (*negotiations*) reprendre; (*acquaintance*) renouer

renewable [rɪˈnjuːəbl] ADJ (*energy*) renouvelable; **renewables** énergies *fpl* renouvelables

renewal [rɪˈnjuːəl] N renouvellement *m*; reprise *f*

renewed [rɪˈnjuːd] ADJ (*interest, vigour*) accru(e); **~ fighting/violence** une recrudescence des combats/de la violence

renounce [rɪˈnauns] VT renoncer à; (*disown*) renier

renovate [ˈrɛnəveɪt] VT rénover; (*work of art*) restaurer

renovation [rɛnəˈveɪʃən] N rénovation *f*; restauration *f*

renown [rɪˈnaun] N renommée *f*

renowned [rɪˈnaund] ADJ renommé(e)

★**rent** [rɛnt] PT, PP of **rend** ▶ N loyer *m* ▶ VT louer; (*car, TV*) louer, prendre en location; (*also:* **rent out:** *car, TV*) louer, donner en location
▶ **rent out** VT (*house, boat*) louer

rental [ˈrɛntl] N (*for television, car*) (prix *m* de) location *f*

rent boy N (*BRIT inf*) jeune prostitué *m*

renunciation [rɪnʌnsɪˈeɪʃən] N renonciation *f*; (*self-denial*) renoncement *m*

reoffend [riːəˈfɛnd] VI récidiver

reopen [riːˈəupən] VT rouvrir

reorder [riː'ɔːdə'] VT commander de nouveau; (*rearrange*) réorganiser

reorganization [riːɔːgənaɪ'zeɪʃən] N réorganisation *f*

reorganize [riː'ɔːgənaɪz] VT réorganiser

rep [rɛp] N ABBR (*Comm*) = **representative**; (*Theat*) = **repertory**

Rep. ABBR (*Pol*) = **representative; republican**

★**repair** [rɪ'pɛə'] N réparation *f*; **in good/bad** en bon/mauvais état; **under ~** en réparation ▶ VT réparer; **where can I get this repaired?** où est-ce que je peux faire réparer ceci ?

repair kit N trousse *f* de réparations

repair man N (*irreg*) réparateur *m*

repair shop N (*Aut etc*) atelier *m* de réparations

reparation [rɛpə'reɪʃən] N réparation *f*; **war reparations** réparations de guerre

repartee [rɛpɑː'tiː] N repartie *f*

repast [rɪ'pɑːst] N (*formal*) repas *m*

repatriate [riː'pætrɪeɪt] VT rapatrier

repatriation [riːpætrɪ'eɪʃən] N rapatriement *m*

repay [riː'peɪ] VT (*irreg: like* **pay**) (*money, creditor*) rembourser; (*sb's efforts*) récompenser

repayable [rɪ'peɪəbl] ADJ (*loan*) remboursable; **~ over 10 years** remboursable sur 10 ans

repayment [riː'peɪmənt] N remboursement *m*; récompense *f*

repeal [rɪ'piːl] N (*of law*) abrogation *f*; (*of sentence*) annulation *f* ▶ VT abroger; annuler

★**repeat** [rɪ'piːt] N (*Radio, TV*) reprise *f* ▶ VT répéter; (*pattern*) reproduire; (*promise, attack, also Comm: order*) renouveler; (*Scol: a class*) redoubler; **can you ~ that, please?** pouvez-vous répéter, s'il vous plaît ? ▶ VI répéter

repeated [rɪ'piːtɪd] ADJ répété(e)

repeatedly [rɪ'piːtɪdlɪ] ADV souvent, à plusieurs reprises

repeat prescription N (*BRIT*): **I'd like a ~** je voudrais renouveler mon ordonnance

repel [rɪ'pɛl] VT repousser

repellent [rɪ'pɛlənt] ADJ repoussant(e) ▶ N: **insect ~** insectifuge *m*; **moth ~** produit *m* antimite(s)

repent [rɪ'pɛnt] VI: **to ~ (of)** se repentir (de)

repentance [rɪ'pɛntəns] N repentir *m*

repentant [rɪ'pɛntənt] ADJ (*gen*) repentant(e); (*criminal*) repenti(e)

repercussions [riːpə'kʌʃənz] NPL répercussions *fpl*

repertoire ['rɛpətwɑː'] N répertoire *m*

repertory ['rɛpətərɪ] N (*also:* **repertory theatre**) théâtre *m* de répertoire

repertory company N troupe théâtrale permanente

repetition [rɛpɪ'tɪʃən] N répétition *f*

repetitious [rɛpɪ'tɪʃəs] ADJ (*speech*) plein(e) de redites

repetitive [rɪ'pɛtɪtɪv] ADJ (*movement, work*) répétitif(-ive); (*speech*) plein(e) de redites

rephrase [riː'freɪz] VT reformuler

★**replace** [rɪ'pleɪs] VT (*put back*) remettre, replacer; (*take the place of*) remplacer; (*Tel*): **"~ the receiver"** « raccrochez »

replacement [rɪ'pleɪsmənt] N replacement *m*; (*substitution*) remplacement *m*; (*person*) remplaçant(e)

replacement part N pièce *f* de rechange

replay ['riːpleɪ] N (*of match*) match rejoué; (*of tape, film*) répétition *f*

replenish [rɪ'plɛnɪʃ] VT (*glass*) remplir (de nouveau); (*stock etc*) réapprovisionner

replete [rɪ'pliːt] ADJ rempli(e); (*well-fed*): **~ (with)** rassasié(e) (de)

replica ['rɛplɪkə] N réplique *f*, copie exacte

replicate ['rɛplɪkeɪt] VT (*work, experiment*) reproduire

★**reply** [rɪ'plaɪ] N réponse *f*; **in ~ (to)** en réponse (à); **there's no ~** (*Tel*) ça ne répond pas ▶ VI répondre

reply coupon N coupon-réponse *m*

repopulate [riː'pɔpjʊleɪt] VT repeupler

★**report** [rɪ'pɔːt] N rapport *m*; (*Press etc*) reportage *m*; (*BRIT: also:* **school report**) bulletin *m* (scolaire); (*of gun*) détonation *f* ▶ VT rapporter, faire un compte rendu de; (*Press etc*) faire un reportage sur; (*notify: accident*) signaler; (*: culprit*) dénoncer; **I'd like to ~ a theft** je voudrais signaler un vol; **it is reported that** on dit *or* annonce que; **it is reported from Berlin that** on nous apprend de Berlin que ▶ VI (*make a report*) faire un rapport; (*for newspaper*) faire un reportage (sur); **to ~ (to sb)** (*present o.s.*) se présenter (chez qn)

report card N (*US, SCOTTISH*) bulletin *m* (scolaire)

reportedly [rɪ'pɔːtɪdlɪ] ADV: **she is ~ living in Spain** elle habiterait en Espagne; **he ~ told them to …** il leur aurait dit de …

reported speech [rɪ'pɔːtɪd-] N (*Ling*) discours indirect

★**reporter** [rɪ'pɔːtə'] N reporter *m*

repose [rɪ'pəʊz] N: **in ~** en *or* au repos

reposition [riːpə'zɪʃən] VT repositionner

repository [rɪ'pɔzɪtrɪ] N (*store*) dépôt *m*; (*of information, knowledge*) dépositaire *mf*

repossess [riːpə'zɛs] VT saisir

repossession [riːpə'zɛʃən] N saisie *f*

repossession order [riːpə'zɛʃən-] N ordre *m* de reprise de possession

reprehensible [rɛprɪ'hɛnsɪbl] ADJ répréhensible

★**represent** [rɛprɪ'zɛnt] VT représenter; (*view, belief*) présenter, expliquer; (*describe*): **to ~ sth as** présenter *or* décrire qch comme; **to ~ to sb that** expliquer à qn que

representation [rɛprɪzɛn'teɪʃən] N représentation *f* ■ **representations** NPL (*protest*) démarche *f*

★**representative** [rɛprɪ'zɛntətɪv] N représentant(e); (*Comm*) représentant(e) (de commerce); (*US Pol*) député *m* ▶ ADJ représentatif(-ive), caractéristique

representativeness [rɛprɪ'zɛntətɪvnɪs] N représentativité *f*

repress [rɪ'prɛs] VT réprimer

repressed [rɪ'prɛst] ADJ refoulé(e); **sexually ~** sexuellement refoulé(e)

repression [rɪ'prɛʃən] N répression *f*

repressive [rɪ'prɛsɪv] ADJ répressif(-ive)

reprieve [rɪ'priːv] N (*Law*) grâce *f*; (*fig*) sursis *m*, délai *m* ▶ VT gracier; accorder un sursis *or* un délai à

r

reprimand ['rɛprɪmɑːnd] N réprimande f ▶ VT réprimander

reprint N ['riːprɪnt] réimpression f ▶ VT [riːˈprɪnt] réimprimer

reprisal [rɪˈpraɪzl] N représailles fpl; **to take reprisals** user de représailles

reproach [rɪˈprəʊtʃ] N reproche m; **beyond ~** irréprochable ▶ VT: **to ~ sb with sth** reprocher qch à qn

reproachful [rɪˈprəʊtʃful] ADJ de reproche

reprocess [riːˈprəʊsɛs] VT (nuclear fuel) retraiter

reproduce [riːprəˈdjuːs] VT reproduire ▶ VI se reproduire

reproduction [riːprəˈdʌkʃən] N reproduction f

reproductive [riːprəˈdʌktɪv] ADJ reproducteur(-trice)

reproof [rɪˈpruːf] N reproche m

reprove [rɪˈpruːv] VT (action) réprouver; (person): **to ~ (for)** blâmer (de)

reproving [rɪˈpruːvɪŋ] ADJ réprobateur(-trice)

reptile ['rɛptaɪl] N reptile m

Repub. ABBR (US Pol) = **republican**

★**republic** [rɪˈpʌblɪk] N république f

republican [rɪˈpʌblɪkən] ADJ, N républicain(e)

republicanism [rɪˈpʌblɪkənɪzəm] N républicanisme m

repudiate [rɪˈpjuːdɪeɪt] VT (ally, behaviour) désavouer; (accusation) rejeter; (wife) répudier

repugnance [rɪˈpʌgnəns] N dégoût m

repugnant [rɪˈpʌgnənt] ADJ répugnant(e)

repulse [rɪˈpʌls] VT repousser

repulsion [rɪˈpʌlʃən] N répulsion f

repulsive [rɪˈpʌlsɪv] ADJ repoussant(e), répulsif(-ive)

reputable ['rɛpjutəbl] ADJ de bonne réputation; (occupation) honorable

★**reputation** [rɛpjuˈteɪʃən] N réputation f; **to have a ~ for** être réputé(e) pour; **he has a ~ for being awkward** il a la réputation de ne pas être commode

repute [rɪˈpjuːt] N (bonne) réputation

reputed [rɪˈpjuːtɪd] ADJ réputé(e); **he is ~ to be rich/intelligent** etc on dit qu'il est riche/intelligent etc

reputedly [rɪˈpjuːtɪdlɪ] ADV d'après ce qu'on dit

★**request** [rɪˈkwɛst] N demande f; (formal) requête f; **at the ~ of** à la demande de ▶ VT: **to ~ (of** or **from sb)** demander (à qn)

request stop N (BRIT: for bus) arrêt facultatif

requiem ['rɛkwɪəm] N requiem m

★**require** [rɪˈkwaɪər] VT (need: subj: person) avoir besoin de; (: thing, situation) nécessiter, demander; (want) exiger; (order): **to ~ sb to do sth/sth of sb** exiger que qn fasse qch/qch de qn; **if required** s'il le faut; **what qualifications are required?** quelles sont les qualifications requises ?; **required by law** requis par la loi

required [rɪˈkwaɪəd] ADJ requis(e), voulu(e)

★**requirement** [rɪˈkwaɪəmənt] N (need) exigence f; besoin m; (condition) condition f (requise)

requisite ['rɛkwɪzɪt] N chose f nécessaire; **toilet requisites** accessoires mpl de toilette ▶ ADJ requis(e), nécessaire

requisition [rɛkwɪˈzɪʃən] N: **~ (for)** demande f (de) ▶ VT (Mil) réquisitionner

reroute [riːˈruːt] VT (train etc) dérouter

re-run N ['riːrʌn] (rebroadcast) rediffusion f; (of event, experience) répétition f; (of elections) réorganisation f; (race) course f recourue ▶ VT [riːˈrʌn] (irreg: like **run**) (rebroadcast) rediffuser; (election) refaire; (Comput: program, software) réexécuter; (race) recourir

resale ['riːˈseɪl] N revente f

resale price maintenance N vente au détail à prix imposé

resat [riːˈsæt] PT, PP of **resit**

reschedule [riːˈʃɛdjuːl] VT (event, meeting) reporter; (programme) reprogrammer; (debt) rééchelonner

rescind [rɪˈsɪnd] VT annuler; (law) abroger; (judgment) rescinder

★**rescue** ['rɛskjuː] N (from accident) sauvetage m; (help) secours mpl; **to come to sb's ~** venir au secours de qn ▶ VT sauver

rescue party N équipe f de sauvetage

rescuer ['rɛskjuər] N sauveteur m

★**research** [rɪˈsəːtʃ] N recherche(s) f(pl); **a piece of ~** un travail de recherche; **~ and development** recherche-développement ▶ VT faire des recherches sur ▶ VI: **to ~ (into sth)** faire des recherches (sur qch)

researcher [rɪˈsəːtʃər] N chercheur(-euse)

research work N recherches fpl

resell [riːˈsɛl] VT (irreg: like **sell**) revendre

resemblance [rɪˈzɛmbləns] N ressemblance f; **to bear a strong ~ to** ressembler beaucoup à

resemble [rɪˈzɛmbl] VT ressembler à

resent [rɪˈzɛnt] VT éprouver du ressentiment de, être contrarié(e) par

resentful [rɪˈzɛntful] ADJ irrité(e), plein(e) de ressentiment

resentment [rɪˈzɛntmənt] N ressentiment m

reservation [rɛzəˈveɪʃən] N (booking) réservation f; (doubt, protected area) réserve f; (BRIT Aut: also: **central reservation**) bande médiane; **to make a ~ (in an hotel/a restaurant/on a plane)** réserver or retenir une chambre/une table/une place; **with reservations** (doubts) avec certaines réserves

reservation desk N (US: in hotel) réception f

★**reserve** [rɪˈzəːv] N réserve f; (Sport) remplaçant(e); **in ~** en réserve ▶ VT (seats etc) réserver, retenir ■ **reserves** NPL (Mil) réservistes mpl

reserve currency N monnaie f de réserve

reserved [rɪˈzəːvd] ADJ réservé(e)

reserve price N (BRIT) mise f à prix, prix m de départ

reserve team N (BRIT Sport) deuxième équipe f

reservist [rɪˈzəːvɪst] N (Mil) réserviste m

reservoir ['rɛzəvwɑːr] N réservoir m

reset [riːˈsɛt] VT (irreg: like **set**) remettre; (clock, watch) mettre à l'heure; (Comput) remettre à zéro

resettlement [riːˈsɛtlmənt] N (of people) relocalisation f

reshape [riːˈʃeɪp] VT (policy) réorganiser

reshuffle ['riːˈʃʌfl] N: **Cabinet ~** (BRIT Pol) remaniement ministériel

reside [rɪ'zaɪd] VI résider

residence ['rezɪdəns] N résidence f; **to take up ~** s'installer; **in ~** (queen etc) en résidence; (doctor) résidant(e)

residence permit N (BRIT) permis m de séjour

★**resident** ['rezɪdənt] N (of country) résident(e); (of area, house) habitant(e); (in hotel) pensionnaire mf ▶ ADJ résidant(e)

residential [rezɪ'dɛnʃəl] ADJ de résidence; (area) résidentiel(le); (course) avec hébergement sur place

residential school N internat m

residual [rɪ'zɪdjuəl] ADJ résiduel(le)

residue ['rezɪdjuː] N reste m; (Chem, Physics) résidu m

★**resign** [rɪ'zaɪn] VT (one's post) se démettre de; **to ~ o.s. to** (endure) se résigner à ▶ VI démissionner

resignation [rezɪg'neɪʃən] N (from post) démission f; (state of mind) résignation f; **to tender one's ~** donner sa démission

resigned [rɪ'zaɪnd] ADJ résigné(e)

resilience [rɪ'zɪlɪəns] N (of material) élasticité f; (of person) ressort m

resilient [rɪ'zɪlɪənt] ADJ (person) qui réagit, qui a du ressort

resin ['rezɪn] N résine f

resist [rɪ'zɪst] VT résister à

resistance [rɪ'zɪstəns] N résistance f

resistant [rɪ'zɪstənt] ADJ: **~ (to)** résistant(e) (à)

resit VT [riː'sɪt] (irreg: like **sit**) (BRIT: exam) repasser ▶N ['riːsɪt] deuxième session f (d'un examen)

resolute ['rezəluːt] ADJ résolu(e)

resolutely ['rezəluːtlɪ] ADV (refuse, reject) résolument; **to remain ~ opposed to sth** rester résolument opposé(e) à qch

★**resolution** [rezə'luːʃən] N résolution f; **to make a ~** prendre une résolution

resolve [rɪ'zɔlv] N résolution f ▶VT (problem) résoudre; (decide): **to ~ to do** résoudre or décider de faire

resolved [rɪ'zɔlvd] ADJ résolu(e)

resonance ['rezənəns] N résonance f

resonant ['rezənənt] ADJ résonnant(e)

resonate ['rezəneɪt] VI (sound, room) résonner; (be meaningful): **to ~ with sb** trouver un écho chez qn

★**resort** [rɪ'zɔːt] N (seaside town) station f balnéaire; (for skiing) station de ski; (recourse) recours m; **in the last ~** en dernier ressort ▶ VI: **to ~ to** avoir recours à

resound [rɪ'zaund] VI: **to ~ (with)** retentir (de)

resounding [rɪ'zaundɪŋ] ADJ retentissant(e)

★**resource** [rɪ'sɔːs] N ressource f ■ **resources** NPL ressources; **natural resources** ressources naturelles; **to leave sb to his (or her) own resources** (fig) livrer qn à lui-même (or elle-même)

resourceful [rɪ'sɔːsful] ADJ ingénieux(-euse), débrouillard(e)

resourcefulness [rɪ'sɔːsfəlnɪs] N ressource f

★**respect** [rɪs'pɛkt] N respect m; (point, detail): **in some respects** à certains égards; **to have** or **show ~ for sb/sth** respecter qn/qch; **out of ~ for** par respect pour; **with ~ to** en ce qui concerne; **in ~ of** sous le rapport de, quant à; **in this ~** sous ce

rapport, à cet égard; **with due ~ I ...** malgré le respect que je vous dois, je ... ▶ VT respecter ■ **respects** NPL respects, hommages mpl; **to pay one's respects** présenter ses respects

respectability [rɪspɛktə'bɪlɪtɪ] N respectabilité f

respectable [rɪs'pɛktəbl] ADJ respectable; (quite good: result etc) honorable; (: player) assez bon(ne)

respectful [rɪs'pɛktful] ADJ respectueux(-euse)

respectfully [rɪ'spɛktfulɪ] ADV respectueusement

respective [rɪs'pɛktɪv] ADJ respectif(-ive)

respectively [rɪs'pɛktɪvlɪ] ADV respectivement

respiration [rɛspɪ'reɪʃən] N respiration f

respirator ['rɛspɪreɪtər] N respirateur m

respiratory ['rɛspərətərɪ] ADJ respiratoire

respite ['rɛspaɪt] N répit m

resplendent [rɪs'plɛndənt] ADJ resplendissant(e)

respond [rɪs'pɔnd] VI répondre; (react) réagir

respondent [rɪs'pɔndənt] N (Law) défendeur(-deresse)

response [rɪs'pɔns] N réponse f; (reaction) réaction f; **in ~ to** en réponse à

★**responsibility** [rɪspɔnsɪ'bɪlɪtɪ] N responsabilité f; **to take ~ for sth/sb** accepter la responsabilité de qch/d'être responsable de qn

★**responsible** [rɪs'pɔnsɪbl] ADJ (liable): **~ (for)** responsable (de); (person) digne de confiance; (job) qui comporte des responsabilités; **to be ~ to sb (for sth)** être responsable devant qn (de qch)

responsibly [rɪs'pɔnsɪblɪ] ADV avec sérieux

responsive [rɪs'pɔnsɪv] ADJ (student, audience) réceptif(-ive); (brakes, steering) sensible

★**rest** [rest] N repos m; (stop) arrêt m, pause f; (Mus) silence m; (support) support m, appui m; (remainder) reste m, restant m; **the ~ of them** les autres; **to set sb's mind at ~** tranquilliser qn ▶ VI se reposer; (be supported): **to ~ on** appuyer or reposer sur; (remain) rester; **it rests with him to** c'est à lui de; **~ assured that ...** soyez assuré que ... ▶ VT (lean): **to ~ sth on/against** appuyer qch sur/contre

restart [riː'stɑːt] VT (engine) remettre en marche; (work) reprendre

★**restaurant** ['rɛstərɔnt] N restaurant m

restaurant car N (BRIT Rail) wagon-restaurant m

restaurateur [rɛstərə'tɜːr] N restaurateur(-trice)

rest cure N cure f de repos

rested ['rɛstɪd] ADJ reposé(e); **to feel ~** se sentir reposé(e)

restful ['rɛstful] ADJ reposant(e)

rest home N maison f de repos

restitution [rɛstɪ'tjuːʃən] N (act) restitution f; (reparation) réparation f

restive ['rɛstɪv] ADJ agité(e), impatient(e); (horse) rétif(-ive)

restless ['rɛstlɪs] ADJ agité(e); **to get ~** s'impatienter

restlessly ['rɛstlɪslɪ] ADV avec agitation

restlessness ['rɛstlɪsnɪs] N agitation f

restock [riː'stɔk] VT réapprovisionner

restoration [rɛstə'reɪʃən] N (of building) restauration f; (of stolen goods) restitution f

restorative [rɪ'stɔrətɪv] ADJ reconstituant(e) ▶ N reconstituant m

r

restore [rɪ'stɔːʳ] vᴛ (building) restaurer; (sth stolen) restituer; (peace, health) rétablir; **to ~ to** (former state) ramener à

restorer [rɪ'stɔːrəʳ] ɴ (Art etc) restaurateur(-trice) (d'œuvres d'art)

restrain [rɪs'treɪn] vᴛ (feeling) contenir; (person): **to ~ (from doing)** retenir (de faire)

restrained [rɪs'treɪnd] ᴀᴅᴊ (style) sobre; (manner) mesuré(e)

restraint [rɪs'treɪnt] ɴ (restriction) contrainte f; (moderation) retenue f; (of style) sobriété f; **wage ~** limitations salariales

restrict [rɪs'trɪkt] vᴛ restreindre, limiter

restricted [rɪ'strɪktɪd] ᴀᴅᴊ restreint(e); (BʀɪT: document) confidentiel(le); **to be ~ to sb/sth** se limiter à qn/qch

restricted area ɴ (Aut) zone f à vitesse limitée

restriction [rɪs'trɪkʃən] ɴ restriction f, limitation f

restrictive [rɪs'trɪktɪv] ᴀᴅᴊ restrictif(-ive)

restrictive practices ɴᴘʟ (Industry) pratiques fpl entravant la libre concurrence

rest room ɴ (US) toilettes fpl

restructure [riː'strʌktʃəʳ] vᴛ restructurer

restructuring [riː'strʌktʃərɪŋ] ɴ restructuration f

★**result** [rɪ'zʌlt] ɴ résultat m; **as a ~ it is too expensive** il en résulte que c'est trop cher; **as a ~ of** à la suite de ▶ vɪ: **to ~ (from)** résulter (de); **to ~ in** aboutir à, se terminer par

resultant [rɪ'zʌltənt] ᴀᴅᴊ résultant(e)

resume [rɪ'zjuːm] vᴛ (work, journey) reprendre; (sum up) résumer ▶ vɪ (work etc) reprendre

résumé ['reɪzjuːmeɪ] ɴ (summary) résumé m; (US: curriculum vitae) curriculum vitae m inv

resumption [rɪ'zʌmpʃən] ɴ reprise f

resurface [riː'sɜːfɪs] vɪ refaire surface ▶ vᴛ (road) refaire le revêtement de

resurgence [rɪ'sɜːdʒəns] ɴ réapparition f

resurrect [rezə'rekt] vᴛ ressusciter

resurrection [rezə'rekʃən] ɴ résurrection f

resuscitate [rɪ'sʌsɪteɪt] vᴛ (Med) réanimer

resuscitation [rɪsʌsɪ'teɪʃən] ɴ réanimation f

retail ['riːteɪl] ɴ (vente f au) détail m ▶ ᴀᴅᴊ de or au détail ▶ ᴀᴅᴠ au détail ▶ vᴛ vendre au détail ▶ vɪ: **to ~ at 10 euros** se vendre au détail à 10 euros

retailer ['riːteɪləʳ] ɴ détaillant(e)

retailing ['riːteɪlɪŋ] ɴ commerce m de détail ▶ ᴄᴘᴅ (industry, business) de détail

retail outlet ɴ point m de vente

retail price ɴ prix m de détail

retail price index ɴ ≈ indice m des prix

retain [rɪ'teɪn] vᴛ (keep) garder, conserver; (employ) engager

retainer [rɪ'teɪnəʳ] ɴ (servant) serviteur m; (fee) acompte m, provision f

retake vᴛ [riː'teɪk] (irreg: like **take**) (recapture) reprendre; (exam, course) repasser ▶ ɴ ['riːteɪk] (exam) rattrapage m, deuxième session f; (Cine: of scene) retournage m

retaliate [rɪ'tælɪeɪt] vɪ: **to ~ (against)** se venger (de); **to ~ (on sb)** rendre la pareille (à qn)

retaliation [rɪtælɪ'eɪʃən] ɴ représailles fpl, vengeance f; **in ~ for** par représailles pour

retaliatory [rɪ'tælɪətərɪ] ᴀᴅᴊ de représailles

retarded [rɪ'tɑːdɪd] ᴀᴅᴊ (!) retardé(e)

retch [retʃ] vɪ avoir des haut-le-cœur

retell [riː'tel] vᴛ (irreg: like **tell**) (story, tale: repeat) raconter à nouveau; (: in a new form) adapter

retention [rɪ'tenʃən] ɴ (keeping) maintien m; (of information, fluid, heat) rétention f

retentive [rɪ'tentɪv] ᴀᴅᴊ: **~ memory** excellente mémoire

rethink ['riː'θɪŋk] vᴛ repenser

reticence ['retɪsns] ɴ réticence f

reticent ['retɪsnt] ᴀᴅᴊ réticent(e)

retina ['retɪnə] ɴ rétine f

retinue ['retɪnjuː] ɴ suite f, cortège m

★**retire** [rɪ'taɪəʳ] vɪ (give up work) prendre sa retraite; (withdraw) se retirer, partir; (go to bed) (aller) se coucher

retired [rɪ'taɪəd] ᴀᴅᴊ (person) retraité(e)

retiree [rɪtaɪə'riː] ɴ (esp US) retraité(e)

★**retirement** [rɪ'taɪəmənt] ɴ retraite f

retirement age ɴ âge m de la retraite

retiring [rɪ'taɪərɪŋ] ᴀᴅᴊ (person) réservé(e); (chairman etc) sortant(e)

retook [riː'tuk] ᴘᴛ of **retake**

retort [rɪ'tɔːt] ɴ (reply) riposte f; (container) cornue f ▶ vɪ riposter

retrace [riː'treɪs] vᴛ reconstituer; **to ~ one's steps** revenir sur ses pas

retract [rɪ'trækt] vᴛ (statement, claws) rétracter; (undercarriage, aerial) rentrer, escamoter ▶ vɪ se rétracter; rentrer

retractable [rɪ'træktəbl] ᴀᴅᴊ escamotable

retrain [riː'treɪn] vᴛ recycler ▶ vɪ se recycler

retraining [riː'treɪnɪŋ] ɴ recyclage m

retread vᴛ [riː'tred] (Aut: tyre) rechaper ▶ ɴ ['riːtred] pneu rechapé

retreat [rɪ'triːt] ɴ retraite f; **to beat a hasty ~** (fig) partir avec précipitation ▶ vɪ battre en retraite; (flood) reculer

retrial [riː'traɪəl] ɴ nouveau procès

retribution [retrɪ'bjuːʃən] ɴ châtiment m

retrieval [rɪ'triːvəl] ɴ récupération f; réparation f; recherche f et extraction f

retrieve [rɪ'triːv] vᴛ (sth lost) récupérer; (situation, honour) sauver; (error, loss) réparer; (Comput) rechercher

retriever [rɪ'triːvəʳ] ɴ chien m d'arrêt

retroactive [retrəu'æktɪv] ᴀᴅᴊ rétroactif(-ive)

retroactively [retrəu'æktɪvlɪ] ᴀᴅᴠ rétroactivement

retrograde ['retrəgreɪd] ᴀᴅᴊ rétrograde

retrospect ['retrəspekt] ɴ: **in ~** rétrospectivement, après coup

retrospective [retrə'spektɪv] ᴀᴅᴊ rétrospectif(-ive); (law) rétroactif(-ive) ▶ ɴ (Art) rétrospective f

retrospectively [retrə'spektɪvlɪ] ᴀᴅᴠ rétrospectivement

★**return** [rɪ'tɜːn] ɴ (going or coming back) retour m; (of sth stolen etc) restitution f; (recompense) récompense f; (Finance: from land, shares) rapport m; (report) relevé m, rapport; (BʀɪT: also: **return ticket**) aller retour *m*, aller et retour *m*; **by ~ (of post)** par retour (du courrier); **in ~ (for)** en échange (de); **a ~ to Avignon, please** un aller retour pour Avignon, s'il vous plaît ▶CPD *(journey)* de retour; *(BRIT: airfare)* aller et retour; *(match)* retour ▶VI *(person etc: come back)* revenir; *(: go back)* retourner ▶VT rendre; *(bring back)* rapporter; *(send back)* renvoyer; *(put back)* remettre; *(Pol: candidate)* élire ■ **returns** NPL *(Comm)* recettes *fpl*; *(Finance)* bénéfices *mpl*; *(: returned goods)* marchandises renvoyées; **many happy returns (of the day)!** bon anniversaire!

returnable [rɪ'tɜːnəbl] ADJ *(bottle etc)* consigné(e)

returner [rɪ'tɜːnəʳ] N *femme qui reprend un travail après avoir élevé ses enfants*

returning officer [rɪ'tɜːnɪŋ-] N *(BRIT Pol)* président *m* de bureau de vote

return key N *(Comput)* touche *f* de retour

return ticket N *(esp BRIT)* billet *m* aller-retour

retweet [riː'twiːt] VT *(on Twitter)* retweeter ▶N retweet *m*

reunification [riːjuːnɪfɪ'keɪʃən] N réunification *f*

reunion [riː'juːnɪən] N réunion *f*

reunite [riːjuː'naɪt] VT réunir

reusable [riː'juːzəbl] ADJ réutilisable

reuse [riː'juːz] VT réutiliser

rev [rev] N ABBR *(Aut: = revolution)* tour *m* ▶VT *(also: rev up)* emballer ▶VI *(also: rev up)* s'emballer

Rev. ABBR = **Reverend**

revaluation [riːvæljuː'eɪʃən] N réévaluation *f*

revamp [riː'væmp] VT *(house)* retaper; *(firm)* réorganiser

rev counter N *(BRIT)* compte-tours *m inv*

Revd ABBR = **Reverend**

reveal [rɪ'viːl] VT *(make known)* révéler; *(display)* laisser voir

revealing [rɪ'viːlɪŋ] ADJ révélateur(-trice); *(dress)* au décolleté généreux *or* suggestif

reveille [rɪ'vælɪ] N *(Mil)* réveil *m*

revel ['revl] VI: **to ~ in sth/in doing** se délecter de qch/à faire

revelation [revə'leɪʃən] N révélation *f*

reveller ['revləʳ] N fêtard *m*

revelry ['revlrɪ] N festivités *fpl*

revenge [rɪ'vendʒ] N vengeance *f*; *(in game etc)* revanche *f*; **to take ~ (on)** se venger (sur) ▶VT venger

revengeful [rɪ'vendʒful] ADJ vengeur(-eresse), vindicatif(-ive)

revenue ['revənjuː] N revenu *m*

reverberate [rɪ'vɜːbəreɪt] VI *(sound)* retentir, se répercuter; *(light)* se réverbérer

reverberation [rɪvɜːbə'reɪʃən] N répercussion *f*; réverbération *f*

revere [rɪ'vɪəʳ] VT vénérer, révérer

reverence ['revərəns] N vénération *f*, révérence *f*

Reverend ['revərənd] ADJ vénérable; *(in titles)*: **the ~ John Smith** *(Anglican)* le révérend John Smith; *(Catholic)* l'abbé (John) Smith; *(Protestant)* le pasteur (John) Smith

reverent ['revərənt] ADJ respectueux(-euse)

reverential [revə'renʃəl] ADJ révérencieux(-euse)

reverie ['revərɪ] N rêverie *f*

reversal [rɪ'vɜːsl] N *(of opinion)* revirement *m*; *(of order)* renversement *m*; *(of direction)* changement *m*

★**reverse** [rɪ'vɜːs] N contraire *m*, opposé *m*; *(back)* dos *m*, envers *m*; *(of paper)* verso *m*; *(of coin)* revers *m*; *(Aut: also:* **reverse gear**) marche *f* arrière; **to go into ~** faire marche arrière ▶ADJ *(direction, effect)* inverse; **in ~ order** en ordre inverse ▶VT *(order, position)* changer, inverser; *(direction, policy)* changer complètement de; *(decision)* annuler; *(roles)* renverser; *(car)* faire marche arrière avec; *(Law: judgment)* réformer ▶VI *(BRIT Aut)* faire marche arrière

reverse video N vidéo *m* inverse

reversible [rɪ'vɜːsəbl] ADJ *(garment)* réversible; *(procedure)* révocable

reversing lights [rɪ'vɜːsɪŋ-] NPL *(BRIT Aut)* feux *mpl* de marche arrière *or* de recul

reversion [rɪ'vɜːʃən] N retour *m*

revert [rɪ'vɜːt] VI: **to ~ to** revenir à, retourner à

★**review** [rɪ'vjuː] N revue *f*; *(of book, film)* critique *f*; *(of situation, policy)* examen *m*, bilan *m*; *(US: examination)* examen; **to come under ~** être révisé(e) ▶VT passer en revue; faire la critique de; examiner

reviewer [rɪ'vjuːəʳ] N critique *m*

revile [rɪ'vaɪl] VT injurier

revise [rɪ'vaɪz] VT réviser, modifier; *(manuscript)* revoir, corriger; **revised edition** édition revue et corrigée ▶VI *(study)* réviser

revision [rɪ'vɪʒən] N révision *f*; *(revised version)* version corrigée

revitalization [riːvaɪtəlaɪ'zeɪʃən] N revitalisation *f*

revitalize [riː'vaɪtəlaɪz] VT revitaliser

revival [rɪ'vaɪvəl] N reprise *f*; *(recovery)* rétablissement *m*; *(of faith)* renouveau *m*

revive [rɪ'vaɪv] VT *(person)* ranimer; *(custom)* rétablir; *(economy)* relancer; *(hope, courage)* raviver, faire renaître; *(play, fashion)* reprendre ▶VI *(person)* reprendre connaissance; *(: from ill health)* se rétablir; *(hope etc)* renaître; *(activity)* reprendre

revoke [rɪ'vəuk] VT révoquer; *(promise, decision)* revenir sur

revolt [rɪ'vəult] N révolte *f* ▶VI se révolter, se rebeller ▶VT révolter, dégoûter

revolting [rɪ'vəultɪŋ] ADJ dégoûtant(e)

★**revolution** [revə'luːʃən] N révolution *f*; *(of wheel etc)* tour *m*, révolution

revolutionary [revə'luːʃənrɪ] ADJ, N révolutionnaire *mf*

revolutionize [revə'luːʃənaɪz] VT révolutionner

revolve [rɪ'vɒlv] VI tourner ▶FUS tourner autour de; **her life revolves around tennis** sa vie tourne autour du tennis

revolver [rɪ'vɒlvəʳ] N revolver *m*

revolving [rɪ'vɒlvɪŋ] ADJ *(chair)* pivotant(e); *(light)* tournant(e)

revolving door N *(porte f à)* tambour *m*

revue [rɪ'vjuː] N *(Theat)* revue *f*

revulsion [rɪ'vʌlʃən] N dégoût *m*, répugnance *f*

★**reward** [rɪ'wɔːd] N récompense *f* ▶VT: **to ~ (for)** récompenser (de)

rewarding [rɪ'wɔːdɪŋ] ADJ (fig) qui (en) vaut la peine, gratifiant(e); **financially ~** financièrement intéressant(e)

rewind [riː'waɪnd] VT (irreg: like **wind²**) (watch) remonter; (tape) réembobiner

rewire [riː'waɪəʳ] VT (house) refaire l'installation électrique de

reword [riː'wəːd] VT formuler or exprimer différemment

rework [riː'wəːk] VT retravailler

reworking [riː'wəːkɪŋ] N (of book, story) revisite f

rewound [riː'waund] PT, PP of **rewind**

rewritable [riː'raɪtəbl] ADJ (CD, DVD) réinscriptible

rewrite [riː'raɪt] VT (irreg: like **write**) récrire

Reykjavik ['reɪkjəviːk] N Reykjavik

Rh ABBR (= rhesus) Rh

rhapsodize ['ræpsədaɪz] VI s'extasier; **to ~ over sth** s'extasier sur qch

rhapsody ['ræpsədɪ] N (Mus) rhapsodie f; (fig) éloge délirant

rhesus negative ['riːsəs-] ADJ (Med) de rhésus négatif

rhesus positive ['riːsəs-] ADJ (Med) de rhésus positif

rhetoric ['rɛtərɪk] N rhétorique f

rhetorical [rɪ'tɔrɪkl] ADJ rhétorique

rheumatic [ruː'mætɪk] ADJ rhumatismal(e)

rheumatism ['ruːmətɪzəm] N rhumatisme m

rheumatoid arthritis ['ruːmətɔɪd-] N polyarthrite f chronique

rheumatologist [ruːmə'tɔlədʒɪst] N rhumatologue mf

Rhine [raɪn] N: **the (River) ~** le Rhin

rhinestone ['raɪnstəun] N faux diamant

rhino ['raɪnəu] N rhinocéros m

rhinoceros [raɪ'nɔsərəs] N rhinocéros m

Rhodes [rəudz] N Rhodes f

rhododendron [rəudə'dɛndrn] N rhododendron m

rhubarb ['ruːbɑːb] N rhubarbe f

rhyme [raɪm] N rime f; (verse) vers mpl; **without ~ or reason** sans rime ni raison ▸ VI: **to ~ (with)** rimer (avec)

★**rhythm** ['rɪðm] N rythme m

rhythmic ['rɪðmɪk], **rhythmical** ['rɪðmɪkl] ADJ rythmique

rhythmically ['rɪðmɪklɪ] ADV avec rythme

rhythm method N méthode f des températures

RI N ABBR (BRIT) = **religious instruction** ▸ ABBR (US) = **Rhode Island**

rib [rɪb] N (Anat) côte f ▸ VT (mock) taquiner

ribald ['rɪbəld] ADJ paillard(e)

ribbed [rɪbd] ADJ (knitting) à côtes; (shell) strié(e)

ribbon ['rɪbən] N ruban m; **in ribbons** (torn) en lambeaux

★**rice** [raɪs] N riz m

rice field N rizière f

rice pudding N riz m au lait

★**rich** [rɪtʃ] ADJ riche; (gift, clothes) somptueux(-euse); **to be ~ in sth** être riche en qch ▸ NPL: **the ~** les riches mpl ■ **riches** NPL richesses fpl

richly ['rɪtʃlɪ] ADV richement; (deserved, earned) largement, grandement

richness ['rɪtʃnɪs] N richesse f

rickets ['rɪkɪts] N rachitisme m

rickety ['rɪkɪtɪ] ADJ branlant(e)

rickshaw ['rɪkʃɔː] N pousse(-pousse) m inv

ricochet ['rɪkəʃeɪ] N ricochet m ▸ VI ricocher

★**rid** [rɪd] (pt, pp ~) VT: **to ~ sb of** débarrasser qn de; **to get ~ of** se débarrasser de

riddance ['rɪdns] N: **good ~!** bon débarras!

ridden ['rɪdn] PP of **ride**

riddle ['rɪdl] N (puzzle) énigme f ▸ VT: **to be riddled with** être criblé(e) de; (fig) être en proie à

★**ride** [raɪd] (pt **rode** [rəud], pp **ridden** ['rɪdn]) N promenade f, tour m; (distance covered) trajet m; **horse/car ~** promenade or tour à cheval/en voiture; **to go for a ~** faire une promenade (en voiture or à bicyclette etc); **to take sb for a ~** (fig) faire marcher qn; (cheat) rouler qn ▸ VI (as sport) monter (à cheval), faire du cheval; (go somewhere: on horse, bicycle) aller (à cheval or bicyclette etc); (travel: on bicycle, motor cycle, bus) rouler; **we rode all day/all the way** nous sommes restés toute la journée en selle/avons fait tout le chemin en selle or à cheval; **to ~ at anchor** (Naut) être à l'ancre ▸ VT (a horse) monter; (distance) parcourir, faire; **to ~ a horse/bicycle** monter à cheval/à bicyclette; **can you ~ a bike?** est-ce que tu sais monter à bicyclette?

▸ **ride out** [raɪd aut] VT: **to ~ out the storm** (fig) surmonter les difficultés

▸ **ride up** VI (skirt, top) remonter

★**rider** ['raɪdəʳ] N cavalier(-ière); (in race) jockey m; (on bicycle) cycliste mf; (on motorcycle) motocycliste mf; (in document) annexe f, clause additionnelle

ridge [rɪdʒ] N (of hill) faîte m; (of roof, mountain) arête f; (on object) strie f

ridicule ['rɪdɪkjuːl] N ridicule m; dérision f; **to hold sb/sth up to ~** tourner qn/qch en ridicule ▸ VT ridiculiser, tourner en dérision

ridiculous [rɪ'dɪkjuləs] ADJ ridicule

riding ['raɪdɪŋ] N équitation f

riding school N manège m, école f d'équitation

rife [raɪf] ADJ répandu(e); **~ with** abondant(e) en

riff ['rɪf] N (Mus) riff m

riffraff ['rɪfræf] N racaille f

rifle ['raɪfl] N fusil m (à canon rayé) ▸ VT vider, dévaliser

▸ **rifle through** VT FUS fouiller dans

rifle range N champ m de tir; (indoor) stand m de tir

rift [rɪft] N fente f, fissure f; (fig: disagreement) désaccord m

rig [rɪg] N (also: **oil rig**: on land) derrick m; (: at sea) plate-forme pétrolière ▸ VT (election etc) truquer

▸ **rig out** VT (BRIT) habiller; (: pej) fringuer, attifer

▸ **rig up** VT arranger, faire avec des moyens de fortune

rigging ['rɪgɪŋ] N (Naut) gréement m

★**right** [raɪt] ADJ (true) juste, exact(e); (correct) bon(ne); (suitable) approprié(e), convenable; (just) juste, équitable; (morally good) bien inv; (not left) droit(e); **the ~ time** (precise) l'heure exacte; (not wrong) la bonne heure; **do you have the ~ time?**

avez-vous l'heure juste *or* exacte ?; **to be ~** *(person)* avoir raison; *(answer)* être juste *or* correct(e); **to get sth ~** ne pas se tromper sur qch; **let's get it ~ this time!** essayons de ne pas nous tromper cette fois-ci !; **you did the ~ thing** vous avez bien fait; **to put a mistake ~** *(BRIT)* rectifier une erreur ▶ N *(moral good)* bien *m*; *(title, claim)* droit *m*; *(not left)* droite *f*; **on the ~** à droite; **~ and wrong** le bien et le mal; **to be in the ~** avoir raison; **by rights** en toute justice ▶ ADV *(answer)* correctement; *(treat)* bien, comme il faut; *(not on the left)* à droite; **~ now** en ce moment même; *(immediately)* tout de suite; **~ before/after** juste avant/après; **~ against the wall** tout contre le mur; **~ ahead** tout droit; droit devant; **~ in the middle** en plein milieu; **~ away** immédiatement; **to go ~ to the end of sth** aller jusqu'au bout de qch ▶ VT redresser ▶ EXCL bon ! ■ **rights** NPL *(Comm)* droits *mpl*; **film rights** droits d'adaptation cinématographique

> Use the masculine word **droit** to refer to the right to something: *human rights* **les droits de l'homme**. The feminine word **droite** means *right as opposed to left*.

right angle N *(Math)* angle droit

righteous ['raɪtʃəs] ADJ droit(e), vertueux(-euse); *(anger)* justifié(e)

righteousness ['raɪtʃəsnɪs] N droiture *f*, vertu *f*

rightful ['raɪtful] ADJ *(heir)* légitime

rightfully ['raɪtfəlɪ] ADV à juste titre, légitimement

right-hand ['raɪthænd] ADJ: **the ~ side** la droite

right-hand drive N conduite *f* à droite; *(vehicle)* véhicule *m* avec la conduite à droite

right-handed [raɪt'hændɪd] ADJ *(person)* droitier(-ière)

right-hand man N *(irreg)* bras droit *(fig)*

rightly ['raɪtlɪ] ADV bien, correctement; *(with reason)* à juste titre; **if I remember ~** *(BRIT)* si je me souviens bien

right-minded ['raɪt'maɪndɪd] ADJ sensé(e), sain(e) d'esprit

right of way N *(on path etc)* droit *m* de passage; *(Aut)* priorité *f*

rights issue N *(Stock Exchange)* émission préférentielle *or* de droit de souscription

right to life N droit *m* à la vie ▶ CPD *(group, campaign: also:* **right-to-life***)* antiavortement *inv*

right wing N *(Mil, Sport)* aile droite; *(Pol)* droite *f*

right-wing [raɪt'wɪŋ] ADJ *(Pol)* de droite

right-winger [raɪt'wɪŋəʳ] N *(Pol)* membre *m* de la droite; *(Sport)* ailier droit

rigid ['rɪdʒɪd] ADJ rigide; *(principle, control)* strict(e)

rigidity [rɪ'dʒɪdɪtɪ] N rigidité *f*

rigidly ['rɪdʒɪdlɪ] ADV rigidement; *(behave)* inflexiblement

rigmarole ['rɪgmərəul] N galimatias *m*, comédie *f*

rigor ['rɪgəʳ] N *(US)* = **rigour**

rigor mortis ['rɪgə'mɔːtɪs] N rigidité *f* cadavérique

rigorous ['rɪgərəs] ADJ rigoureux(-euse)

rigorously ['rɪgərəslɪ] ADV rigoureusement

rigour, *(US)* **rigor** ['rɪgəʳ] N rigueur *f*

rig-out ['rɪgaut] N *(BRIT inf)* tenue *f*

rile [raɪl] VT agacer

rim [rɪm] N bord *m*; *(of spectacles)* monture *f*; *(of wheel)* jante *f*

rimless ['rɪmlɪs] ADJ *(spectacles)* à monture invisible

rind [raɪnd] N *(of bacon)* couenne *f*; *(of lemon etc)* écorce *f*, zeste *m*; *(of cheese)* croûte *f*

★**ring** [rɪŋ] *(pt* **rang** [ræŋ]*, pp* **rung** [rʌŋ]*)* N anneau *m*; *(on finger)* bague *f*; *(also:* **wedding ring***)* alliance *f*; *(for napkin)* rond *m*; *(of people, objects)* cercle *m*; *(of spies)* réseau *m*; *(of smoke etc)* rond *m*; *(arena)* piste *f*, arène *f*; *(for boxing)* ring *m*; *(sound of bell)* sonnerie *f*; *(telephone call)* coup *m* de téléphone; **to give sb a ~** *(Tel)* passer un coup de téléphone *or* de fil à qn; **that has the ~ of truth about it** cela sonne vrai ▶ VI *(telephone, bell)* sonner; *(person: by telephone)* téléphoner; *(ears)* bourdonner; *(also:* **ring out:** *voice, words)* retentir ▶ VT *(also:* **ring up***)* téléphoner à, appeler; **to ~ the bell** sonner; **the name doesn't ~ a bell (with me)** ce nom ne me dit rien
  ▶ **ring around** VI, VT FUS = **ring round**
  ▶ **ring back** VT, VI *(BRIT Tel)* rappeler
  ▶ **ring in** VI *(esp BRIT)* appeler
  ▶ **ring off** VI *(BRIT Tel)* raccrocher
  ▶ **ring out** VI *(voice, words, shot)* retentir
  ▶ **ring round** *(esp BRIT)* VI passer des coups de fil
  ▶ VT FUS appeler
  ▶ **ring up** VT *(BRIT Tel)* téléphoner à, appeler

ring binder N classeur *m* à anneaux

ring-fence [rɪŋ'fɛns] VT *(allocate)* réserver, allouer; *(protect)* protéger

ring finger N annulaire *m*

ringing ['rɪŋɪŋ] N *(of bell)* tintement *m*; *(louder: of telephone)* sonnerie *f*; *(: in ears)* bourdonnement *m*

ringing tone N *(BRIT Tel)* tonalité *f* d'appel

ringleader ['rɪŋliːdəʳ] N *(of gang)* chef *m*, meneur *m*

ringlets ['rɪŋlɪts] NPL anglaises *fpl*

ringmaster ['rɪŋmɑːstəʳ] N *(at the circus)* Monsieur Loyal *m*

ring road N *(BRIT)* rocade *f*; *(motorway)* périphérique *m*

ringside ['rɪŋsaɪd] N: **at the ~** *(Boxing)* au bord du ring; *(at circus)* au bord de la piste ▶ CPD: **to have a ~ view** *or* **seat** *(fig)* être aux premières loges

★**ringtone** ['rɪŋtəun] N *(on mobile)* sonnerie *f* *(de téléphone portable)*

ringworm ['rɪŋwəːm] N teigne *f*

rink [rɪŋk] N *(also:* **ice rink***)* patinoire *f*; *(for roller-skating)* skating *m*

rinse [rɪns] N rinçage *m* ▶ VT rincer

Rio ['riːəu], **Rio de Janeiro** ['riːəudədʒə'nɪərəu] N Rio de Janeiro

★**riot** ['raɪət] N émeute *f*, bagarres *fpl*; **a ~ of colours** une débauche *or* orgie de couleurs ▶ VI *(demonstrators)* manifester avec violence; *(population)* se soulever, se révolter ▶ ADV: **to run ~** se déchaîner

rioter ['raɪətəʳ] N émeutier(-ière), manifestant(e)

riot gear N: **in ~** casqué et portant un bouclier

rioting ['raɪətɪŋ] N émeutes *fpl*

riotous ['raɪətəs] ADJ tapageur(-euse); tordant(e)

riotously ['raɪətəslɪ] ADV: **~ funny** tordant(e)

r

riot police N forces fpl de police intervenant en cas d'émeute; **hundreds of ~** des centaines de policiers casqués et armés

RIP ABBR (= *rest in peace*) RIP

rip [rɪp] N déchirure f ▶ VT déchirer ▶ VI se déchirer
▶ **rip off** VT (*inf: cheat*) arnaquer (*inf*)
▶ **rip out** VT arracher
▶ **rip up** VT déchirer

ripcord ['rɪpkɔːd] N poignée f d'ouverture

ripe [raɪp] ADJ (*fruit*) mûr(e); (*cheese*) fait(e)

ripen ['raɪpn] VT mûrir ▶ VI mûrir; se faire

ripeness ['raɪpnɪs] N maturité f

rip-off ['rɪpɔf] N (*inf*): **it's a ~!** c'est du vol manifeste!, c'est de l'arnaque! (*inf*)

riposte [rɪ'pɔst] N riposte f

ripple ['rɪpl] N ride f, ondulation f; (*of applause, laughter*) cascade f ▶ VI se rider, onduler ▶ VT rider, faire onduler

★**rise** [raɪz] (*pt* **rose** [rəuz], *pp* **risen** [rɪzn]) N (*slope*) côte f, pente f; (*hill*) élévation f; (*increase: in wages:* BRIT) augmentation f; (: *in prices, temperature*) hausse f, augmentation; (*fig: of person*) ascension f; **~ to power** montée f au pouvoir; **to give ~ to** donner lieu à ▶ VI s'élever, monter; (*prices, numbers*) augmenter, monter; (*waters, river*) monter; (*sun, wind, person: from chair, bed*) se lever; (*also:* **rise up**: *tower, building*) s'élever; (: *rebel*) se révolter, se rebeller; (*in rank*) s'élever; **to ~ to the occasion** se montrer à la hauteur
▶ **rise above** VT FUS (*differences, fears*) surmonter; (*insults*) ignorer

risen ['rɪzn] PP *of* **rise**

rising ['raɪzɪŋ] ADJ (*increasing: number, prices*) en hausse; (*tide*) montant(e); (*sun, moon*) levant(e)
▶ N (*uprising*) soulèvement m, insurrection f

rising damp N humidité f (montant des fondations)

rising star N (*also fig*) étoile montante

★**risk** [rɪsk] N risque m, danger m; (*deliberate*) risque; **to take** *or* **run the ~ of doing** courir le risque de faire; **at ~** en danger; **at one's own ~** à ses risques et périls; **it's a fire/health ~** cela présente un risque d'incendie/pour la santé ▶ VT risquer; **I'll ~ it** je vais risquer le coup

risk capital N capital-risque m

risky ['rɪskɪ] ADJ risqué(e)

risotto [rɪ'zɔtəu] N risotto m

risqué ['riːskeɪ] ADJ (*joke*) risqué(e)

rissole ['rɪsəul] N croquette f

rite [raɪt] N rite m; **the last rites** les derniers sacrements

ritual ['rɪtjuəl] ADJ rituel(le) ▶ N rituel m

★**rival** ['raɪvl] N rival(e); (*in business*) concurrent(e)
▶ ADJ rival(e); qui fait concurrence ▶ VT (*match*) égaler; (*compete with*) être en concurrence avec; **to ~ sb/sth in** rivaliser avec qn/qch de

rivalry ['raɪvlrɪ] N rivalité f; (*in business*) concurrence f

★**river** ['rɪvəʳ] N rivière f; (*major, also fig*) fleuve m; **up/down ~** en amont/aval ▶ CPD (*port, traffic*) fluvial(e)

riverbank ['rɪvəbæŋk] N rive f, berge f

riverbed ['rɪvəbed] N lit m (de rivière *or* de fleuve)

riverfront ['rɪvəfrʌnt] N berges fpl aménagées

riverside ['rɪvəsaɪd] N bord m de la rivière *or* du fleuve

rivet ['rɪvɪt] N rivet m ▶ VT riveter; (*fig*) river, fixer

riveting ['rɪvɪtɪŋ] ADJ (*fig*) fascinant(e)

Riviera [rɪvɪ'ɛərə] N: **the (French) ~** la Côte d'Azur; **the Italian ~** la Riviera (italienne)

rivulet ['rɪvjulət] N ruisseau m

Riyadh [rɪ'jɑːd] N Riyad

RMN N ABBR = **Registered Mental Nurse**

RMT N ABBR (= *Rail, Maritime and Transport*) syndicat des transports

RN N ABBR = **registered nurse**; (BRIT) = **Royal Navy**

RNA N ABBR (= *ribonucleic acid*) ARN m

RNLI N ABBR (BRIT: = *Royal National Lifeboat Institution*) ≈ SNSM f

RNZAF N ABBR = **Royal New Zealand Air Force**

RNZN N ABBR = **Royal New Zealand Navy**

★**road** [rəud] N route f; (*in town*) rue f; (*fig*) chemin m, voie f; **main ~** grande route; **major/minor ~** route principale *or* à priorité/voie secondaire; **it takes four hours by ~** il y a quatre heures de route; **which ~ do I take for ...?** quelle route dois-je prendre pour aller à ...?; **"~ up"** (BRIT) « attention travaux » ▶ CPD (*accident*) de la route

road accident N accident m de la circulation

roadblock ['rəudblɔk] N barrage routier

road haulage N transports routiers

roadhog ['rəudhɔg] N chauffard m

roadie ['rəudɪ] N roadie m

roadkill ['rəudkɪl] N animal m tué sur la route

road map N carte routière

road rage N comportement très agressif de certains usagers de la route

road safety N sécurité routière

roadside ['rəudsaɪd] N bord m de la route, bascôté m; **by the ~** au bord de la route ▶ CPD (situé(e) etc) au bord de la route

road sign ['rəudsaɪn] N panneau m de signalisation

road sweeper ['rəudswiːpəʳ] N (*person*) balayeur(-euse); (*vehicle*) balayeuse f

road tax N (BRIT Aut) taxe f sur les automobiles

road user N usager m de la route

roadway ['rəudweɪ] N chaussée f

roadworks ['rəudwəːks] NPL travaux mpl (de réfection des routes)

roadworthy ['rəudwəːðɪ] ADJ en bon état de marche

roam [rəum] VI errer, vagabonder ▶ VT parcourir, errer par

roaming ['rəumɪŋ] N (Tel) roaming m

roar [rɔːʳ] N rugissement m; (*of crowd*) hurlements mpl; (*of vehicle, thunder, storm*) grondement m ▶ VI rugir; hurler; gronder; **to ~ with laughter** rire à gorge déployée

roaring ['rɔːrɪŋ] ADJ: **a ~ fire** une belle flambée; **a ~ success** un succès fou; **to do a ~ trade** faire des affaires en or

roast [rəust] N rôti m ▶ VT (*meat*) (faire) rôtir; (*coffee*) griller, torréfier

roast beef N rôti m de bœuf, rosbif m

roasting ['rəʊstɪŋ] N (inf): **to give sb a ~** sonner les cloches à qn (inf)

rob [rɒb] VT (person) voler; (bank) dévaliser; **to ~ sb of sth** voler or dérober qch à qn; (fig: deprive) priver qn de qch

robber ['rɒbəʳ] N bandit m, voleur m

robbery ['rɒbərɪ] N vol m

robe [rəʊb] N (for ceremony etc) robe f; (also: **bathrobe**) peignoir m; (US: rug) couverture f ▶ VT revêtir (d'une robe)

robin ['rɒbɪn] N rouge-gorge m

robot ['rəʊbɒt] N robot m

robotic [rəʊˈbɒtɪk] ADJ (arm, technology) robotique; (stiff: movements, speech) de robot

robotics [rəˈbɒtɪks] N robotique m

robust [rəʊˈbʌst] ADJ robuste; (material, appetite) solide

★**rock** [rɒk] N (substance) roche f, roc m; (boulder) rocher m, roche; (US: small stone) caillou m; (BRIT: sweet) ≈ sucre m d'orge; **on the rocks** (drink) avec des glaçons; (ship) sur les écueils; (fig: marriage etc) en train de craquer ▶ VT (swing gently: cradle) balancer; (: child) bercer; (shake) ébranler, secouer; **to ~ the boat** (fig) jouer les trouble-fête ▶ VI se balancer, être ébranlé(e) or secoué(e)

rock and roll, rock 'n' roll N rock (and roll) m, rock'n'roll m

rock-bottom ['rɒkˈbɒtəm] N (fig) niveau le plus bas; **to reach** or **touch ~** (price, person) tomber au plus bas ▶ ADJ (fig: prices) sacrifié(e)

rock climber N varappeur(-euse)

rock climbing N varappe f

rocker ['rɒkəʳ] N (musician) rocker m, rockeur(-euse); (esp US: chair) rocking-chair m

rockery ['rɒkərɪ] N (jardin m de) rocaille f

★**rocket** ['rɒkɪt] N fusée f; (Mil) fusée, roquette f; (BRIT Culin) roquette ▶ VI (prices) monter en flèche

rocket launcher [-lɔːnʃəʳ] N lance-roquettes m inv

rock face N paroi rocheuse

rock fall N chute f de pierres

rock-hard [rɒkˈhɑːd] ADJ dur(e) comme la pierre

Rockies ['rɒkiz] NPL: **the ~** les Rocheuses fpl

rocking chair ['rɒkɪŋ-] N fauteuil m à bascule

rocking horse ['rɒkɪŋ-] N cheval m à bascule

rock-solid [rɒkˈsɒlɪd] ADJ (hard) complètement solidifié(e); (reliable: defence, proof) en béton; **the firm is ~ financially** financièrement, l'entreprise est solide comme un roc

rocky ['rɒkɪ] ADJ (hill) rocheux(-euse); (path) rocailleux(-euse); (unsteady: table) branlant(e)

Rocky Mountains NPL: **the ~** les (montagnes fpl) Rocheuses fpl

rod [rɒd] N (metallic) tringle f; (Tech) tige f; (wooden) baguette f; (also: **fishing rod**) canne f à pêche

rode [rəʊd] PT of **ride**

rodent ['rəʊdnt] N rongeur m

rodeo ['rəʊdɪəʊ] N rodéo m

roe [rəʊ] N (species: also: **roe deer**) chevreuil m; (of fish: also: **hard roe**) œufs mpl de poisson; **soft ~** laitance f

roe deer N chevreuil m

rogue [rəʊg] N coquin(e)

roguish ['rəʊgɪʃ] ADJ coquin(e)

★**role** [rəʊl] N rôle m

role-model ['rəʊlmɒdl] N modèle m à émuler

role play, role playing N jeu m de rôle

★**roll** [rəʊl] N rouleau m; (of banknotes) liasse f; (also: **bread roll**) petit pain; (register) liste f; (sound: of drums etc) roulement m; (movement: of ship) roulis m ▶ VT rouler; (also: **roll up**: string) enrouler; (also: **roll out**: pastry) étendre au rouleau, abaisser ▶ VI rouler; (wheel) tourner; **cheese ~** ≈ sandwich m au fromage (dans un petit pain)
  ▶ **roll about, roll around** VI rouler çà et là; (person) se rouler par terre
  ▶ **roll by** VI (time) s'écouler, passer
  ▶ **roll down** VT (close: blind) baisser; (open): **to ~ down one's window** baisser sa vitre
  ▶ **roll in** VI (mail, cash) affluer
  ▶ **roll over** VI se retourner
  ▶ **roll up** VI (inf: arrive) arriver, s'amener ▶ VT (carpet, cloth, map) rouler; (sleeves) retrousser; **to ~ o.s. up into a ball** se rouler en boule

roll call N appel m

roller ['rəʊləʳ] N rouleau m; (wheel) roulette f; (for road) rouleau compresseur; (for hair) bigoudi m

Rollerblade® ['rəʊləbleɪd] NPL roller m; **a pair of Rollerblades** une paire de rollers

rollerblading ['rəʊləbleɪdɪŋ] N roller m; **to go ~** faire du roller

roller blind N (BRIT) store m

roller coaster N montagnes fpl russes

roller skates NPL patins mpl à roulettes

roller-skating ['rəʊləskeɪtɪŋ] N patin m à roulettes; **to go ~** faire du patin à roulettes

rollicking ['rɒlɪkɪŋ] ADJ bruyant(e) et joyeux(-euse); (play) bouffon(ne); **to have a ~ time** s'amuser follement

rolling ['rəʊlɪŋ] ADJ (landscape) onduleux(-euse)

rolling mill N laminoir m

rolling pin N rouleau m à pâtisserie

rolling stock N (Rail) matériel roulant

roll-on-roll-off ['rəʊlɒnˈrəʊlɒf] ADJ (BRIT: ferry) roulier(-ière)

rollover ['rəʊləʊvəʳ] N (in lottery) enjeu auquel vient s'ajouter le gros lot du tirage précédent, faute de gagnant

roly-poly ['rəʊlɪˈpəʊlɪ] N (BRIT Culin) roulé m à la confiture

ROM [rɒm] N ABBR (Comput: = read-only memory) mémoire morte, ROM f

Roman ['rəʊmən] ADJ romain(e) ▶ N Romain(e)

Roman Catholic ADJ, N catholique mf

romance [rəˈmæns] N (love affair) idylle f; (charm) poésie f; (novel) roman m à l'eau de rose

Romanesque [rəʊməˈnɛsk] ADJ roman(e)

Romania [rəʊˈmeɪnɪə] N = **Rumania**

Romanian [rəʊˈmeɪnɪən] ADJ, N = **Rumanian**

Roman numeral N chiffre romain

★**romantic** [rəˈmæntɪk] ADJ romantique; (novel, attachment) sentimental(e)

romanticism [rəˈmæntɪsɪzəm] N romantisme m

r

romanticize [rəʊˈmæntɪsaɪz] VT romancer, sentimentaliser ▸ VI sentimentaliser

Romany [ˈrɒmənɪ] ADJ de bohémien ▸ N bohémien(ne); (*Ling*) romani *m*

Rome [rəʊm] N Rome

romp [rɒmp] N jeux bruyants ▸ VI (*also*: **romp about**) s'ébattre, jouer bruyamment; **to ~ home** (*horse*) arriver bon premier

rompers [ˈrɒmpəz] NPL barboteuse *f*

rondo [ˈrɒndəʊ] N (*Mus*) rondeau *m*

★**roof** [ruːf] N toit *m*; (*of tunnel, cave*) plafond *m*; **the ~ of the mouth** la voûte du palais ▸ VT couvrir (d'un toit)

roofer [ˈruːfəʳ] N couvreur(-euse)

roof garden N toit-terrasse *m*

roofing [ˈruːfɪŋ] N toiture *f*

roof rack N (*Aut*) galerie *f*

rooftop [ˈruːftɒp] N toit *m*; **to shout sth from the rooftops** crier qch sur tous les toits

rook [ruk] N (*bird*) freux *m*; (*Chess*) tour *f* ▸ VT (*inf: cheat*) rouler, escroquer

rookie [ˈrukɪ] N (*inf: esp Mil*) bleu *m* (*inf*)

★**room** [ruːm] N (*in house*) pièce *f*; (*also*: **bedroom**) chambre *f* (à coucher); (*in school etc*) salle *f*; (*space*) place *f*; **is there ~ for this?** est-ce qu'il y a de la place pour ceci ?; **to make ~ for sb** faire de la place à qn; **there is ~ for improvement** on peut faire mieux ∎ **rooms** NPL (*lodging*) meublé *m*; "**rooms to let**", (*US*) "**rooms for rent**" «chambres à louer» ▸ **room with** (*esp US*) VT FUS faire chambre commune avec

rooming house [ˈruːmɪŋ-] N (*US*) maison *f* de rapport

roommate [ˈruːmmeɪt] N camarade *mf* de chambre; (*US*) colocataire *mf*

room service N service *m* des chambres (*dans un hôtel*)

room temperature N température ambiante; "**serve at ~**" (*wine*) «servir chambré»

roomy [ˈruːmɪ] ADJ spacieux(-euse); (*garment*) ample

roost [ruːst] N juchoir *m* ▸ VI se jucher

rooster [ˈruːstəʳ] N coq *m*

★**root** [ruːt] N (*Bot, Math*) racine *f*; (*fig: of problem*) origine *f*, fond *m*; **to take ~** (*plant, idea*) prendre racine; **to have its roots in sth** (*fig*) avoir ses racines dans qch ▸ VI (*plant*) s'enraciner
▸ **root about, root around** VI fouiller
▸ **root for** VT FUS (*inf*) applaudir
▸ **root out** VT extirper
▸ **root through** VT FUS fouiller dans

root beer N (*US*) *sorte de limonade à base d'extraits végétaux*

rooted [ˈruːtɪd] ADJ: **~ in** (*tradition, religion*) enraciné(e) dans; **to be ~ in sth** (*suj: idea, problem*) tirer ses racines de qch; **deeply ~** profondément enraciné(e); **~ to the spot** cloué(e) sur place

rootless [ˈruːtlɪs] ADJ (*person*) déraciné(e); (*life*) sans racines

rope [rəʊp] N corde *f*; (*Naut*) cordage *m*; **to know the ropes** (*fig*) être au courant, connaître les ficelles ▸ VT (*box*) corder; (*tie up or together*) attacher; (*climbers: also:* **rope together**) encorder;

(*area: also:* **rope off**) interdire l'accès de; (: *divide off*) séparer; **to ~ sb in** (*fig*) embringuer qn

rope ladder N échelle *f* de corde

ropey [ˈrəʊpɪ] ADJ (*inf*) pas fameux(-euse) or brillant(e) (*inf*); **I feel a bit ~ today** c'est pas la forme aujourd'hui

rort [rɔːt] N (AUSTRALIA, NEW ZEALAND *inf*) arnaque *f* (*inf*) ▸ VT escroquer

rosary [ˈrəʊzərɪ] N chapelet *m*

★**rose** [rəʊz] PT of **rise** ▸ N rose *f*; (*also:* **rosebush**) rosier *m*; (*on watering can*) pomme *f* ▸ ADJ rose

★**rosé** [ˈrəʊzeɪ] N rosé *m*

rosebed [ˈrəʊzbed] N massif *m* de rosiers

rosebud [ˈrəʊzbʌd] N bouton *m* de rose

rosebush [ˈrəʊzbuʃ] N rosier *m*

rose-coloured, (*US*) **rose-colored** [ˈrəʊzkʌləd] ADJ rose; **to look at sb/sth through ~ glasses** or (BRIT) **spectacles** ne voir que les bons côtés de qn/qch; **to see life through ~ glasses** or (BRIT) **spectacles** voir la vie en rose

rosehip [ˈrəʊzhɪp] N cynorhodon *m*

rosemary [ˈrəʊzmərɪ] N romarin *m*

rosette [rəʊˈzet] N rosette *f*; (*larger*) cocarde *f*

rosewater [ˈrəʊzwɔːtəʳ] N eau *f* de rose

ROSPA [ˈrɒspə] N ABBR (BRIT) = **Royal Society for the Prevention of Accidents**

roster [ˈrɒstəʳ] N: **duty ~** tableau *m* de service

rostrum [ˈrɒstrəm] N tribune *f* (*pour un orateur etc*)

rosy [ˈrəʊzɪ] ADJ rose; **a ~ future** un bel avenir

rot [rɒt] N (*decay*) pourriture *f*; (*fig: pej: nonsense*) idioties *fpl*, balivernes *fpl*; **to stop the ~** (BRIT *fig*) rétablir la situation; **dry ~** pourriture sèche (*du bois*); **wet ~** pourriture (du bois) ▸ VT, VI pourrir
▸ **rot away** VI pourrir

rota [ˈrəʊtə] N liste *f*, tableau *m* de service; **on a ~ basis** par roulement

rotary [ˈrəʊtərɪ] ADJ rotatif(-ive)

rotate [rəʊˈteɪt] VT (*revolve*) faire tourner; (*change round: crops*) alterner; (: *jobs*) faire à tour de rôle ▸ VI (*revolve*) tourner

rotating [rəʊˈteɪtɪŋ] ADJ (*movement*) tournant(e)

rotation [rəʊˈteɪʃən] N rotation *f*; **in ~** à tour de rôle

rote [rəʊt] N: **by ~** machinalement, par cœur

rotor [ˈrəʊtəʳ] N rotor *m*

rotten [ˈrɒtn] ADJ (*decayed*) pourri(e); (*dishonest*) corrompu(e); (*inf: bad*) mauvais(e), moche; **to feel ~** (*ill*) être mal fichu(e) (*inf*)

rotting [ˈrɒtɪŋ] ADJ pourrissant(e)

rotund [rəʊˈtʌnd] ADJ rondelet(te); arrondi(e)

rouble, (*US*) **ruble** [ˈruːbl] N rouble *m*

rouge [ruːʒ] N rouge *m* (à joues)

★**rough** [rʌf] ADJ (*cloth, skin*) rêche, rugueux(-euse); (*terrain*) accidenté(e); (*path*) rocailleux(-euse); (*voice*) rauque, rude; (*person, manner: coarse*) rude, fruste; (: *violent*) brutal(e); (*district, weather*) mauvais(e); (*sea*) houleux(-euse); (*plan*) ébauché(e); (*guess*) approximatif(-ive); **the sea is ~ today** la mer est agitée aujourd'hui; **to have a ~ time (of it)** en voir de dures; **to feel ~** (BRIT: *ill*) être mal fichu(e); **~ estimate** approximation *f* ▸ N (*Golf*) rough *m* ▸ VT: **to ~ it** vivre à la dure ▸ ADV: (BRIT):

to sleep ~ coucher à la dure; **to play ~** jouer avec brutalité
▶ **rough out** VT (*draft*) ébaucher
▶ **rough up** VT (*inf*) malmener

roughage ['rʌfɪdʒ] N fibres *fpl* diététiques

rough-and-ready ['rʌfən'rɛdɪ] ADJ (*accommodation, method*) rudimentaire

rough-and-tumble ['rʌfən'tʌmbl] N agitation *f*

roughcast ['rʌfkɑːst] N crépi *m*

rough copy, rough draft N brouillon *m*

roughen ['rʌfn] VT (*a surface*) rendre rude *or* rugueux(-euse)

rough justice N justice *f* sommaire

roughly ['rʌflɪ] ADV (*handle*) rudement, brutalement; (*speak*) avec brusquerie; (*make*) grossièrement; (*approximately*) à peu près, en gros; **~ speaking** en gros

roughness ['rʌfnɪs] N (*of cloth, skin*) rugosité *f*; (*of person*) rudesse *f*; brutalité *f*

roughshod ['rʌfʃɔd] ADV: **to ride ~ over** ne tenir aucun compte de

rough work N (*at school etc*) brouillon *m*

roulette [ru:'lɛt] N roulette *f*

Roumania *etc* [ru:'meɪnɪə] N = **Rumania** *etc*

★**round** [raund] ADJ rond(e); **in ~ figures** en chiffres ronds ▶ N rond *m*, cercle *m*; (BRIT: *of toast*) tranche *f*; (*duty: of police officer, milkman etc*) tournée *f*; (: *of doctor*) visites *fpl*; (*game: of cards, in competition*) partie *f*; (Boxing) round *m*; (*of talks*) série *f*; **to go the rounds** (*disease, story*) circuler; **the daily ~** (*fig*) la routine quotidienne; **~ of ammunition** cartouche *f*; **~ of applause** applaudissements *mpl*; **~ of drinks** tournée *f*; **~ of sandwiches** sandwich *m* ▶ VT (*corner*) tourner; (*bend*) prendre; (*cape*) doubler ▶ PREP autour de; **it's just ~ the corner** c'est juste après le coin; (*fig*) c'est tout près; **to go ~ an obstacle** contourner un obstacle; **go ~ the back** passez par derrière; **to go ~ a house** visiter une maison, faire le tour d'une maison; **she arrived ~ noon** (BRIT) elle est arrivée vers midi; **~ the clock** 24 heures sur 24 ▶ ADV: **right ~, all ~** tout autour; **~ about** (*with quantity*) environ; (*with time*) vers; **the long way ~** (par) le chemin le plus long; **all (the) year ~** toute l'année; **I'll be ~ at 6 o'clock** je serai là à 6 heures; **to ask sb ~** inviter qn (chez soi); **to go ~** faire le tour *or* un détour; **enough to go ~** assez pour tout le monde; **to go ~ to sb's (house)** aller chez qn
▶ **round down** VT (*number, price*) arrondir
▶ **round off** VT (*speech etc*) terminer
▶ **round on** VT FUS (*person*) s'en prendre à
▶ **round up** VT rassembler; (*criminals*) effectuer une rafle de; (*prices*) arrondir (au chiffre supérieur)

roundabout ['raundəbaut] N (BRIT: *Aut*) rond-point *m* (à sens giratoire); (: *at fair*) manège *m* (de chevaux de bois) ▶ ADJ (*route, means*) détourné(e)

rounded ['raundɪd] ADJ arrondi(e); (*style*) harmonieux(-euse)

rounders ['raundəz] NPL (*game*) ≈ balle *f* au camp

roundly ['raundlɪ] ADV (*fig*) tout net, carrément

round-shouldered ['raund'ʃəuldəd] ADJ au dos rond

round table N (*conference*) table *f* ronde

round trip N (voyage *m*) aller et retour *m*

round trip ticket N billet *m* aller-retour

roundup ['raundʌp] N rassemblement *m*; (*of criminals*) rafle *f*; **a ~ of the latest news** un rappel des derniers événements

roundworm ['raundwə:m] N ver *m* rond

rouse [rauz] VT (*wake up*) réveiller; (*stir up*) susciter, provoquer; (*interest*) éveiller; (*suspicions*) susciter, éveiller

rousing ['rauzɪŋ] ADJ (*welcome*) enthousiaste

rout [raut] N (Mil) déroute *f* ▶ VT mettre en déroute

★**route** [ru:t, (US) raut] N itinéraire *m*; (*of bus*) parcours *m*; (*of trade, shipping*) route *f*; **"all routes"** (*Aut*) « toutes directions »; **the best ~ to London** le meilleur itinéraire pour aller à Londres

route map N (*for journey*) croquis *m* d'itinéraire; (*for trains etc*) carte *f* du réseau

router ['ru:tər, (US) 'rautər] N (Comput) routeur *m*

★**routine** [ru:'ti:n] N (*normal procedure*) routine *f*; (*act*) numéro *m*; **as a matter of ~** par routine; **training/exercise ~** programme *m* d'entraînement/d'exercice ▶ ADJ (*questions, check, test*) de routine; (*procedure*) d'usage; (*boring: life, job*) routinier(-ière)

routinely [ru:'ti:nlɪ] ADV (*as a matter of course*) systématiquement; (*invariably*) habituellement

roving ['rəuvɪŋ] ADJ (*life*) vagabond(e)

roving reporter N reporter volant

★**row**[1] [rəu] N (*line*) rangée *f*; (*of people, seats, Knitting*) rang *m*; (*behind one another: of cars, people*) file *f*; **in a ~** (*fig*) d'affilée ▶ VI (*in boat*) ramer; (*as sport*) faire de l'aviron ▶ VT (*boat*) faire aller à la rame *or* à l'aviron

row[2] [rau] N (*noise*) vacarme *m*; (*dispute*) dispute *f*, querelle *f*; (*scolding*) réprimande *f*, savon *m* ▶ VI (*also*: **to have a row**) se disputer, se quereller

rowan ['rauən, 'rəuən] N (*also*: **rowan tree**) sorbier *m*

rowboat ['rəubəut] N (US) canot *m* (à rames)

rowdiness ['raudɪnɪs] N tapage *m*, chahut *m*; (*fighting*) bagarre *f*

rowdy ['raudɪ] ADJ chahuteur(-euse); bagarreur(-euse) ▶ N voyou *m*

rowdyism ['raudɪzəm] N tapage *m*, chahut *m*

rower ['rəuər] N rameur(-euse)

rowing ['rəuɪŋ] N canotage *m*; (*as sport*) aviron *m*

rowing boat N (BRIT) canot *m* (à rames)

rowlock ['rɔlək] N (BRIT) dame *f* de nage, tolet *m*

★**royal** ['rɔɪəl] ADJ royal(e)

Royal Academy, Royal Academy of Arts N (BRIT) l'Académie *f* royale des Beaux-Arts

La **Royal Academy** OU **Royal Academy of Arts** est une institution indépendante, financée par des fonds privés, qui réunit des artistes et des architectes éminents. Fondée en 1768 par George III pour encourager la peinture, la sculpture et l'architecture, elle est située à Burlington House, sur l'avenue londonienne de Piccadilly. Une exposition d'œuvres d'artistes contemporains y est organisée tous les étés. L'Académie dispense également des cours de peinture, de sculpture et d'architecture.

Royal Air Force N (BRIT) armée de l'air britannique

royal blue ADJ, N bleu roi *m inv*

r

royalist ['rɔɪəlɪst] ADJ, N royaliste *mf*

Royal Navy N (BRIT) marine de guerre britannique

royalty ['rɔɪəltɪ] N (royal persons) (membres *mpl* de la) famille royale; (payment: to author) droits *mpl* d'auteur; (: to inventor) royalties *fpl*

RP N ABBR (BRIT: = received pronunciation) prononciation *f* standard; see also **Received Pronunciation**

RPI N ABBR = **retail price index**

rpm ABBR (= revolutions per minute) t/mn *mpl* (= tours/minute)

RR ABBR (US) = **railway**

RRP ABBR = **recommended retail price**

RSA N ABBR (BRIT) = **Royal Society of Arts; Royal Scottish Academy**

RSI N ABBR (Med: = repetitive strain injury) microtraumatisme permanent

RSPB N ABBR (BRIT: = Royal Society for the Protection of Birds) ≈ LPO *f*

RSPCA N ABBR (BRIT: = Royal Society for the Prevention of Cruelty to Animals) ≈ SPA *f*

R.S.V.P. ABBR (= répondez s'il vous plaît) RSVP

RTA N ABBR (= road traffic accident) accident *m* de la route

Rt Hon. ABBR (BRIT: = Right Honourable) titre donné aux députés de la Chambre des communes

Rt Rev. ABBR (= Right Reverend) très révérend

rub [rʌb] N (with cloth) coup *m* de chiffon or de torchon; (on person) friction *f*; **to give sth a ~** donner un coup de chiffon or de torchon à qch ▸ VT frotter; (person) frictionner; (hands) se frotter; **to ~ sb up** (BRIT) or **to ~ sb** (US) **the wrong way** prendre qn à rebrousse-poil
  ▸ **rub down** VT (body) frictionner; (horse) bouchonner
  ▸ **rub in** VT (ointment) faire pénétrer
  ▸ **rub off** VI partir; **to ~ off on** déteindre sur
  ▸ **rub out** VT effacer ▸ VI s'effacer

rubber ['rʌbə'] N caoutchouc *m*; (BRIT: eraser) gomme *f* (à effacer)

rubber band N élastique *m*

rubber bullet N balle *f* en caoutchouc

rubber gloves NPL gants *mpl* en caoutchouc

rubber plant N caoutchouc *m* (plante verte)

rubber ring N (for swimming) bouée *f* (de natation)

rubber stamp N tampon *m*

rubber-stamp [rʌbə'stæmp] VT (fig) approuver sans discussion

rubbery ['rʌbərɪ] ADJ caoutchouteux(-euse)

★**rubbish** ['rʌbɪʃ] N (from household) ordures *fpl*; (fig: pej) choses *fpl* sans valeur; camelote *f*; (nonsense) bêtises *fpl*, idioties *fpl*; **what you've just said is ~** tu viens de dire une bêtise ▸ VT (BRIT inf) dénigrer, rabaisser

rubbish bin N (BRIT) boîte *f* à ordures, poubelle *f*

rubbish dump N (BRIT: in town) décharge publique, dépotoir *m*

rubbishy ['rʌbɪʃɪ] ADJ (BRIT inf) qui ne vaut rien, moche

rubble ['rʌbl] N décombres *mpl*; (smaller) gravats *mpl*; (Constr) blocage *m*

rubella [ruː'bɛlə] N rubéole *f*

ruble ['ruːbl] N (US) = **rouble**

rubric ['ruːbrɪk] N (set of rules) intitulé *m*; (heading) rubrique *f*

ruby ['ruːbɪ] N rubis *m*

ruby-red ADJ rubis *inv*

RUC N ABBR (BRIT) = **Royal Ulster Constabulary**

ruched [ruːʃt] ADJ ruché(e)

ruck [rʌk] N (Rugby) mêlée *f* ouverte, maul *m*; (BRIT: scrap) mêlée; (crease) faux pli *m*
  ▸ **ruck up** VI se plisser

★**rucksack** ['rʌksæk] N sac *m* à dos

ruckus ['rʌkəs] N (esp US inf) remue-ménage *m*; **to cause a ~** provoquer du remue-ménage

ructions ['rʌkʃənz] NPL grabuge *m*

rudder ['rʌdə'] N gouvernail *m*

ruddy ['rʌdɪ] ADJ (face) coloré(e); (inf: damned) sacré(e) (inf), fichu(e) (inf)

rude [ruːd] ADJ (impolite: person) impoli(e); (: word, manners) grossier(-ière); (shocking) indécent(e), inconvenant(e); **to be ~ to sb** être grossier envers qn

rudely ['ruːdlɪ] ADV impoliment; grossièrement

rudeness ['ruːdnɪs] N impolitesse *f*; grossièreté *f*

rudiment ['ruːdɪmənt] N rudiment *m*

rudimentary [ruːdɪ'mɛntərɪ] ADJ rudimentaire

rue [ruː] VT se repentir de, regretter amèrement

rueful ['ruːful] ADJ triste

ruff [rʌf] N fraise *f*, collerette *f*

ruffian ['rʌfɪən] N brute *f*, voyou *m*

ruffle ['rʌfl] VT (hair) ébouriffer; (clothes) chiffonner; (water) agiter; (fig: person) émouvoir, faire perdre son flegme à; **to get ruffled** s'énerver

rug [rʌg] N petit tapis; (BRIT: blanket) couverture *f*

★**rugby** ['rʌgbɪ] N (also: **rugby football**) rugby *m*

rugged ['rʌgɪd] ADJ (landscape) accidenté(e); (features, character) rude; (determination) farouche

rugger ['rʌgə'] N (BRIT inf) rugby *m*

★**ruin** ['ruːɪn] N ruine *f* ▸ VT ruiner; (spoil: clothes) abîmer; (: event) gâcher ■ **ruins** NPL (of building) ruine(s); **in ruins** en ruine

ruination [ruːɪ'neɪʃən] N ruine *f*

ruinous ['ruːɪnəs] ADJ ruineux(-euse)

★**rule** [ruːl] N règle *f*; (regulation) règlement *m*; (government) autorité *f*, gouvernement *m*; (dominion etc): **under British ~** sous l'autorité britannique; **it's against the rules** c'est contraire au règlement; **by ~ of thumb** à vue de nez; **as a ~** normalement, en règle générale ▸ VT (country) gouverner; (person) dominer; (decide) décider; **to ~ that** (umpire, judge etc) décider que ▸ VI commander; décider; (Law): **to ~ against/in favour of/on** statuer contre/en faveur de/sur
  ▸ **rule out** VT exclure; **murder cannot be ruled out** l'hypothèse d'un meurtre ne peut être exclue

rule book N règlement *m*; **to play by the ~** s'en tenir au règlement

ruled [ruːld] ADJ (paper) réglé(e)

ruler ['ruːlə'] N (sovereign) souverain(e); (leader) chef *m* (d'État); (for measuring) règle *f*

ruling ['ruːlɪŋ] ADJ (party) au pouvoir; (class) dirigeant(e) ▸ N (Law) décision *f*

rum [rʌm] N rhum *m* ▸ ADJ (BRIT inf) bizarre

Rumania [ru:'meɪnɪə] N Roumanie f

Rumanian [ru:'meɪnɪən] ADJ roumain(e) ▸ N Roumain(e); (Ling) roumain m

rumba ['rʌmbə] N rumba f; **to dance the ~** danser la rumba ▸ CPD (steps, rhythm) de rumba

rumble ['rʌmbl] N (of thunder, traffic) grondement m; (of stomach, pipe) gargouillement m ▸ VI (thunder) gronder; (stomach, pipe) gargouiller

rumbling ['rʌmblɪŋ] N (of thunder, traffic) grondement m; (of stomach) gargouillement m ■ **rumblings** NPL: **rumblings of discontent** des murmures de mécontentement

rumbustious [rʌm'bʌstʃəs], **rumbunctious** [rʌm'bʌŋkʃəs] ADJ (US: person) exubérant(e)

ruminate ['ru:mɪneɪt] VI ruminer; **to ~ on** or **over** or **about sth** ruminer sur qch

rummage ['rʌmɪdʒ] VI fouiller

rumour, (US) **rumor** ['ru:mə'] N rumeur f, bruit m (qui court) ▸ VT: **it is rumoured that** le bruit court que

rumour mill, (US) **rumor mill** N machine f à rumeurs

rump [rʌmp] N (of animal) croupe f

rumple ['rʌmpl] VT (hair) ébouriffer; (clothes) chiffonner, friper

rump steak N romsteck m

rumpus ['rʌmpəs] N (inf) tapage m, chahut m; (quarrel) prise f de bec (inf); **to kick up a ~** faire toute une histoire

★**run** [rʌn] (pt **ran** [ræn], pp ~ [rʌn]) N (race) course f; (outing) tour m or promenade f (en voiture); (distance travelled) parcours m, trajet m; (series) suite f, série f; (Theat) série de représentations; (Ski) piste f; (Cricket, Baseball) point m; (in tights, stockings) maille filée, échelle f; **at a ~** au pas de course; **to go for a ~** aller courir or faire un peu de course à pied; (in car) faire un tour or une promenade (en voiture); **to break into a ~** se mettre à courir; **a ~ of luck** une série de coups de chance; **to have the ~ of sb's house** avoir la maison de qn à sa disposition; **there was a ~ on** (meat, tickets) les gens se sont rués sur; **in the long ~** à la longue, à longue échéance; **in the short ~** à brève échéance, à court terme; **on the ~** en fuite; **to make a ~ for it** s'enfuir ▸ VT (business) diriger; (competition, course) organiser; (hotel, house) tenir; (race) participer à; (Comput: program) exécuter; (force through: rope, pipe): **to ~ sth through sth** faire passer qch à travers qch; (to pass: hand, finger): **to ~ sth over sth** promener or passer qch sur qch; (water, bath) faire couler; (Press: feature) publier; **I'll ~ you to the station** je vais vous emmener or conduire à la gare; **to ~ errands** faire les commissions; **to ~ a risk** courir un risque; **it's very cheap to ~** (car, machine) c'est très économique; **to be ~ off one's feet** (Brit) ne plus savoir où donner de la tête ▸ VI courir; (pass: road etc) passer; (work: machine, factory) marcher; (bus, train) circuler; (continue: play) se jouer, être à l'affiche; (: contract) être valide or en vigueur; (slide: drawer etc) glisser; (flow: river, bath, nose) couler; (colours, washing) déteindre; (in election) être candidat, se présenter; **the train runs between Gatwick and Victoria** le train assure le service entre Gatwick et Victoria; **the bus runs every 20 minutes** il y a un autobus toutes les 20 minutes; **to ~ on petrol** or (US) **gas/on diesel/off batteries**

marcher à l'essence/au diesel/sur piles; **to ~ for president** être candidat à la présidence; **their losses ran into millions** leurs pertes se sont élevées à plusieurs millions

▸ **run about** [rʌn ə'baut] VI (children) courir çà et là

▸ **run across** [rʌn ə'krɔs] VT FUS (find) trouver par hasard

▸ **run after** [rʌn 'ɑ:ftə'] VT FUS (to catch up) courir après; (chase) poursuivre

▸ **run around** [rʌn ə'raund] VI = **run about**

▸ **run away** [rʌn ə'weɪ] VI s'enfuir

▸ **run away with** VT FUS: **he let his temper ~ away with him** il s'est laissé emporter par son humeur

▸ **run down** [rʌn daun] VI (clock) s'arrêter (faute d'avoir été remonté) ▸ VT (Aut: knock over) renverser; (Brit: reduce: production) réduire progressivement; (: factory/shop) réduire progressivement la production/l'activité de; (criticize) critiquer, dénigrer; **to be ~ down** (tired) être fatigué(e) or à plat

▸ **run in** [rʌn ɪn] VT (Brit: car) roder

▸ **run into** [rʌn 'ɪntu] VT FUS (meet: person) rencontrer par hasard; (: trouble) se heurter à; (collide with) heurter; **to ~ into debt** contracter des dettes

▸ **run off** [rʌn ɔf] VI s'enfuir ▸ VT (water) laisser s'écouler; (copies) tirer

▸ **run out** [rʌn aut] VI (person) sortir en courant; (liquid) couler; (lease) expirer; (money) être épuisé(e)

▸ **run out of** [rʌn 'aut əv] VT FUS se trouver à court de; **I've ~ out of petrol** or (US) **gas** je suis en panne d'essence

▸ **run over** [rʌn 'əuvə'] VT (Aut) écraser ▸ VT FUS (revise) revoir, reprendre

▸ **run through** [rʌn θru:] VT FUS (recap) reprendre, revoir; (play) répéter

▸ **run up** [rʌn ʌp] VI: **to ~ up against** (difficulties) se heurter à ▸ VT: **to ~ up a debt** s'endetter

runabout ['rʌnəbaut] N (car) cabriolet m; (US: boat) canot m à moteur

runaround ['rʌnəraund] N (inf): **to give sb the ~** rester très discret

runaway ['rʌnəweɪ] ADJ (horse) emballé(e); (truck) fou (folle); (person) fugitif(-ive); (child) fugueur(-euse); (inflation) galopant(e)

rundown ['rʌndaun] N (Brit: of industry etc) réduction progressive

rune [ru:n] N rune f

rung [rʌŋ] PP of **ring** ▸ N (of ladder) barreau m

run-in ['rʌnɪn] N (inf) accrochage m, prise f de bec (inf)

★**runner** ['rʌnə'] N (in race: person) coureur(-euse); (: horse) partant m; (on sledge) patin m; (for drawer etc) coulisseau m; (carpet: in hall etc) chemin m

runner bean N (Brit) haricot m (à rames)

runner-up [rʌnər'ʌp] N second(e)

★**running** ['rʌnɪŋ] N (in race etc) course f; (of business, organization) direction f, gestion f; (of event) organisation f; (of machine etc) marche f, fonctionnement m; **to be in/out of the ~ for sth** être/ne pas être sur les rangs pour qch ▸ ADJ (water) courant(e); (commentary) suivi(e) ▸ ADV: **6 days ~** 6 jours de suite

running commentary N commentaire détaillé

running costs NPL (of business) frais mpl de gestion; (of car): **the ~ are high** elle revient cher

running head N (Typ, Comput) titre courant

running mate N (US Pol) candidat à la vice-présidence

runny ['rʌnɪ] ADJ qui coule

run-off ['rʌnɒf] N (in contest, election) deuxième tour m; (extra race etc) épreuve f supplémentaire

run-of-the-mill ['rʌnəvðə'mɪl] ADJ ordinaire, banal(e)

runt [rʌnt] N avorton m

run-through ['rʌnθruː] répétition f, essai m

run-up ['rʌnʌp] N (BRIT): ~ **to sth** période f précédant qch

runway ['rʌnweɪ] N (Aviat) piste f (d'envol or d'atterrissage)

rupee [ruː'piː] N roupie f

rupture ['rʌptʃəʳ] N (Med) hernie f ▶ VT: **to ~ o.s.** se donner une hernie

★**rural** ['ruərl] ADJ rural(e)

★**ruse** [ruːz] N ruse f

★**rush** [rʌʃ] N course précipitée; (of crowd, Comm: sudden demand) ruée f; (hurry) hâte f; (of anger, joy) accès m; (current) flot m; (Bot) jonc m; (for chair) paille f; **is there any ~ for this?** est-ce urgent ?; **we've had a ~ of orders** nous avons reçu une avalanche de commandes; **I'm in a ~ (to do)** je suis vraiment pressé (de faire); **gold ~** ruée vers l'or ▶ VT (hurry) transporter or envoyer d'urgence; (attack: town etc) prendre d'assaut; (BRIT inf: overcharge) estamper; faire payer; **don't ~ me!** laissez-moi le temps de souffler !; **to ~ sth off** (do quickly) faire qch à la hâte; (send) envoyer qch d'urgence ▶ VI se précipiter

▶**rush through** VT FUS (work) exécuter à la hâte ▶ VT (Comm: order) exécuter d'urgence

rushed [rʌʃt] ADJ (job, work) bâclé(e); (meal) sur le pouce; (busy) débordé(e); **to be ~ off one's feet** (inf) être complètement débordé

rush hour N heures fpl de pointe or d'affluence

rush job N travail urgent

rush matting N natte f de paille

rusk [rʌsk] N biscotte f

russet ['rʌsɪt] N roux m ▶ ADJ roussâtre

★**Russia** ['rʌʃə] N Russie f

Russian ['rʌʃən] ADJ russe ▶ N Russe mf; (Ling) russe m

rust [rʌst] N rouille f ▶ VI rouiller

rustic ['rʌstɪk] ADJ rustique ▶ N (pej) rustaud(e)

rustle ['rʌsl] VI bruire, produire un bruissement ▶ VT (paper) froisser; (US: cattle) voler

rustling ['rʌslɪŋ] N (esp US: of cattle) vol m de bétail; (sound: of paper) froissement m; (: of leaves) bruissement m; (: of silk) frou-frou m

rustproof ['rʌstpruːf] ADJ inoxydable

rustproofing ['rʌstpruːfɪŋ] N traitement m antirouille

rusty ['rʌstɪ] ADJ rouillé(e)

rut [rʌt] N ornière f; (Zool) rut m; **to be in a ~** (fig) suivre l'ornière, s'encroûter

rutabaga [ruːtə'beɪgə] N (US) rutabaga m

ruthless ['ruːθlɪs] ADJ sans pitié, impitoyable

ruthlessly ['ruːθlɪslɪ] ADV (exploit, deal with) impitoyablement; **~ efficient** d'une efficacité impitoyable

ruthlessness ['ruːθlɪsnɪs] N dureté f, cruauté f

rutted ['rʌtɪd] ADJ plein(e) d'ornières

rutting ['rʌtɪŋ] ADJ en rut

RV ABBR (= revised version) traduction anglaise de la Bible de 1885 ▶ N ABBR (US) = **recreational vehicle**

Rwanda [ru'ændə] N Rwanda m

rye [raɪ] N seigle m

rye bread N pain m de seigle

Ss

S¹, s [ɛs] N (letter) S, s m; (US Scol: satisfactory) ≈ assez bien; **S for Sugar** S comme Suzanne

S² ABBR (= south, small) S; (= saint) St

SA N ABBR = **South Africa; South America**

Sabbath ['sæbəθ] N (Jewish) sabbat m; (Christian) dimanche m

sabbatical [sə'bætɪkl] ADJ: **~ year** année f sabbatique

sabotage ['sæbətɑːʒ] N sabotage m ▸ VT saboter

saboteur [sæbə'tɜːʳ] N saboteur(-euse)

sabre, (US) **saber** ['seɪbəʳ] N sabre m

sabre rattling, (US) **saber rattling** N tentatives fpl d'intimidation

sac [sæk] N (Anat) sac m

saccharin, saccharine ['sækərɪn] N saccharine f

sachet ['sæʃeɪ] N sachet m

★**sack** [sæk] N (bag) sac m; **to give sb the ~** renvoyer qn, mettre qn à la porte; **to get the ~** être renvoyé(e) or mis(e) à la porte ▸ VT (dismiss) renvoyer, mettre à la porte; (plunder) piller, mettre à sac

sackful ['sækful] N: **a ~ of** un (plein) sac de

sacking ['sækɪŋ] N toile f à sac; (dismissal) renvoi m

sacrament ['sækrəmənt] N sacrement m

sacred ['seɪkrɪd] ADJ sacré(e)

sacred cow N (fig) chose sacro-sainte

★**sacrifice** ['sækrɪfaɪs] N sacrifice m; **to make sacrifices (for sb)** se sacrifier or faire des sacrifices (pour qn) ▸ VT sacrifier

sacrilege ['sækrɪlɪdʒ] N sacrilège m

sacrilegious [sækrɪ'lɪdʒəs] ADJ sacrilège

sacrosanct ['sækrəusæŋkt] ADJ sacro-saint(e)

SAD N ABBR (= seasonal affective disorder) dépression f saisonnière

★**sad** [sæd] ADJ (unhappy) triste; (deplorable) triste, fâcheux(-euse); (inf: pathetic: thing) triste, lamentable; (: person) minable

sadden ['sædn] VT attrister, affliger

saddle ['sædl] N selle f ▸ VT (horse) seller; **to be saddled with sth** (inf) avoir qch sur les bras

saddlebag ['sædlbæg] N sacoche f

sadism ['seɪdɪzəm] N sadisme m

sadist ['seɪdɪst] N sadique mf

sadistic [sə'dɪstɪk] ADJ sadique

sadly ['sædlɪ] ADV tristement; (unfortunately) malheureusement; (seriously) fort

sadness ['sædnɪs] N tristesse f

sado-masochism [seɪdəu'mæsəkɪzəm] N sado-masochisme m

sado-masochist [seɪdəu'mæsəkɪst] N sado-masochiste mf

sado-masochistic [seɪdəuməsə'kɪstɪk] ADJ sado-masochiste

s.a.e. N ABBR (BRIT: = stamped addressed envelope) enveloppe affranchie pour la réponse

safari [sə'fɑːrɪ] N safari m

safari park N réserve f

★**safe** [seɪf] ADJ (out of danger) hors de danger, en sécurité; (not dangerous) sans danger; (cautious) prudent(e); (sure: bet) assuré(e); **~ from** à l'abri de; **~ and sound** sain(e) et sauf (sauve); **(just) to be on the ~ side** pour plus de sûreté, par précaution; **it is ~ to say that ...** on peut dire sans crainte que ...; **~ journey!** bon voyage ! ▸ N coffre-fort m ▸ ADV: **to play ~** ne prendre aucun risque

safe bet N: **it was a ~** ça ne comportait pas trop de risques; **it's a ~ that he'll be late** il y a toutes les chances pour qu'il soit en retard

safe-breaker ['seɪfbreɪkəʳ] N (BRIT) perceur m de coffre-fort

safe-conduct [seɪf'kɒndʌkt] N sauf-conduit m

safe-cracker ['seɪfkrækəʳ] N = **safe-breaker**

safe-deposit ['seɪfdɪpɒzɪt] N (vault) dépôt m de coffres-forts; (box) coffre-fort m

safeguard ['seɪfgɑːd] N sauvegarde f, protection f ▸ VT sauvegarder, protéger

safe haven N zone f de sécurité

safekeeping ['seɪf'kiːpɪŋ] N bonne garde

safely ['seɪflɪ] ADV (assume, say) sans risque d'erreur; (drive, arrive) sans accident; **I can ~ say ...** je peux dire à coup sûr ...

safe passage N: **to grant sb ~** accorder un laissez-passer à qn

safe sex N rapports sexuels protégés

★**safety** ['seɪftɪ] N sécurité f; **~ first!** la sécurité d'abord !

safety belt N ceinture f de sécurité

safety catch N cran m de sûreté or sécurité

safety net N filet m de sécurité

safety pin N épingle f de sûreté or de nourrice

safety valve N soupape f de sûreté

saffron ['sæfrən] N safran m

sag [sæg] VI s'affaisser, fléchir; (hem, breasts) pendre

saga ['sɑːgə] N saga f; (fig) épopée f

S

sage [seɪdʒ] N (*herb*) sauge f; (*person*) sage m

Sagittarius [sædʒɪ'tɛərɪəs] N le Sagittaire; **to be ~** être du Sagittaire

sago ['seɪɡəʊ] N sagou m

Sahara [sə'hɑːrə] N: **the ~ (Desert)** le (désert du) Sahara m

Sahel [sæ'hɛl] N Sahel m

said [sɛd] PT, PP of **say**

Saigon [saɪ'ɡɔn] N Saigon

★**sail** [seɪl] N (*on boat*) voile f; (*trip*): **to go for a ~** faire un tour en bateau ▶ VT (*boat*) manœuvrer, piloter ▶ VI (*travel: ship*) avancer, naviguer; (: *passenger*) aller or se rendre (en bateau); (*set off*) partir, prendre la mer; (*Sport*) faire de la voile; **they sailed into Le Havre** ils sont entrés dans le port du Havre
▶ **sail through** VI, VT FUS (*fig*) réussir haut la main

sailboat ['seɪlbəʊt] N (US) bateau m à voiles, voilier m

sailing ['seɪlɪŋ] N (*Sport*) voile f; **to go ~** faire de la voile

sailing boat N bateau m à voiles, voilier m

sailing ship N grand voilier

sailor ['seɪlə'] N marin m, matelot m

★**saint** [seɪnt] N saint(e)

saintly ['seɪntlɪ] ADJ saint(e), plein(e) de bonté

★**sake** [seɪk] N: **for the ~ of** (*out of concern for*) pour (l'amour de), dans l'intérêt de; (*out of consideration for*) par égard pour; (*in order to achieve*) pour plus de, par souci de; **arguing for arguing's ~** discuter pour (le plaisir de) discuter; **for heaven's ~!** pour l'amour du ciel!; **for the ~ of argument** à titre d'exemple

salacious [sə'leɪʃəs] ADJ salace

salad ['sæləd] N salade f; **tomato ~** salade de tomates

salad bowl N saladier m

salad cream N (BRIT) *sorte de mayonnaise*

salad dressing N vinaigrette f

salad oil N huile f de table

salami [sə'lɑːmɪ] N salami m

salaried ['sælərɪd] ADJ (*staff*) salarié(e), qui touche un traitement

★**salary** ['sælərɪ] N salaire m, traitement m

salary scale N échelle f des traitements

★**sale** [seɪl] N vente f; (*at reduced prices*) soldes mpl; **"for ~"** « à vendre »; **on ~** en vente; **on ~ or return** vendu(e) avec faculté de retour; **closing-down** or (US) **liquidation ~** liquidation f (*avant fermeture*); **~ and lease back** n cession-bail ■ **sales** NPL (*total amount sold*) chiffre m de ventes

saleable ['seɪləbl] ADJ vendable

saleroom ['seɪlruːm] N salle f des ventes

sales assistant, (US) **sales clerk** N vendeur(-euse)

sales conference N réunion f de vente

sales drive N campagne commerciale, animation f des ventes

sales force N (ensemble m du) service m des ventes

salesgirl ['seɪlzɡəːl] N vendeuse f

salesman ['seɪlzmən] N (*irreg*) (*in shop*) vendeur m; (*representative*) représentant m de commerce

sales manager N directeur(-trice) commercial(e)

salesmanship ['seɪlzmənʃɪp] N art m de la vente

salesperson ['seɪlzpəːsn] N (*in shop*) vendeur(-euse)

sales rep N (*Comm*) représentant(e)

sales tax N (US) taxe f à l'achat

saleswoman ['seɪlzwumən] N (*irreg*) (*in shop*) vendeuse f; (*representative*) représentante f de commerce

salient ['seɪlɪənt] ADJ saillant(e)

saline ['seɪlaɪn] ADJ salin(e)

salinity [sə'lɪnɪtɪ] N salinité f

saliva [sə'laɪvə] N salive f

salivate ['sælɪveɪt] VI saliver; (*fig*): **to ~ over** or **at sth** saliver à la perspective de qch

sallow ['sæləʊ] ADJ cireux(-euse)

sally forth, sally out ['sælɪ-] VI partir plein(e) d'entrain

salmon ['sæmən] N (*pl inv*) saumon m

salmonella [sælmə'nɛlə] N (*bacteria*) salmonelle f; (*poisoning*) salmonellose f

salmon trout N truite saumonée

salon ['sælɔn] N salon m

saloon [sə'luːn] N (US) bar m; (BRIT Aut) berline f; (*ship's lounge*) salon m

salsa ['sælsə] N (*sauce*) sauce f piquante à la tomate; (*music*) salsa f

SALT [sɔːlt] N ABBR (= *Strategic Arms Limitation Talks/ Treaty*) SALT m

★**salt** [sɔːlt] N sel m; **an old ~** un vieux loup de mer ▶ VT saler ▶ CPD de sel; (*Culin*) salé(e)
▶ **salt away** VT mettre de côté

salt cellar N salière f

salt-free ['sɔːlt'friː] ADJ sans sel

saltwater ['sɔːlt'wɔːtə'] ADJ (*fish etc*) (d'eau) de mer

salty ['sɔːltɪ] ADJ salé(e)

salubrious [sə'luːbrɪəs] ADJ salubre

salutary ['sæljutərɪ] ADJ salutaire

salute [sə'luːt] N salut m; (*of guns*) salve f ▶ VT saluer

salvage ['sælvɪdʒ] N (*saving*) sauvetage m; (*things saved*) biens sauvés or récupérés ▶ VT sauver, récupérer

salvageable ['sælvɪdʒəbəl] ADJ (*object*) récupérable; (*event*) qui peut être sauvé(e)

salvage vessel N bateau m de sauvetage

salvation [sæl'veɪʃən] N salut m

Salvation Army N Armée f du Salut

salve [sælv] VT (*conscience*) apaiser ▶ N baume m; *see also* **lip salve**

salver ['sælvə'] N plateau m de métal

salvo ['sælvəʊ] N salve f

Samaritan [sə'mærɪtən] N: **the Samaritans** (*organization*) ≈ S.O.S. Amitié

samba ['sæmbə] N samba f

★**same** [seɪm] ADJ même; **the ~ book as** le même livre que; **on the ~ day** le même jour; **at the ~ time** en même temps; (*yet*) néanmoins ▶ PRON: **the ~** le (la) même, les mêmes; **all** or **just the ~**

tout de même, quand même; **they're one and the ~** (*person/thing*) c'est une seule et même personne/chose; **to do the ~** faire de même, en faire autant; **to do the ~ as sb** faire comme qn; **and the ~ to you!** et à vous de même !; (*after insult*) toi-même !; **~ here!** moi aussi !; **the ~ again!** (*in bar etc*) la même chose !

same-sex marriage ['seɪmsɛks-] N mariage *m* homosexuel

same-sex relationship ['seɪmsɛks-] N relation *f* homosexuelle

Samoa [sə'məʊə] N Samoa *fpl*

samosa [sə'məʊsə] N samosa *m, petit pâté indien aux légumes ou à la viande*

★**sample** ['sɑːmpl] N échantillon *m*; (*Med*) prélèvement *m*; **to take a ~** prélever un échantillon; **free ~** échantillon gratuit ▶ VT (*food, wine*) goûter

sanatorium [sænə'tɔːrɪəm] (*pl* **sanatoria** [-rɪə]) N sanatorium *m*

sanctify ['sæŋktɪfaɪ] VT sanctifier

sanctimonious [sæŋktɪ'məʊnɪəs] ADJ moralisateur(-trice)

sanction ['sæŋkʃən] N approbation *f*, sanction *f* ▶ VT cautionner, sanctionner ∎ **sanctions** NPL (*Pol*) sanctions *fpl*; **to impose economic sanctions on** *or* **against** prendre des sanctions économiques contre

sanctity ['sæŋktɪtɪ] N sainteté *f*, caractère sacré

sanctuary ['sæŋktjʊərɪ] N (*holy place*) sanctuaire *m*; (*refuge*) asile *m*; (*for wildlife*) réserve *f*

★**sand** [sænd] N sable *m* ▶ VT sabler; (*also:* **sand down**: *wood etc*) poncer

sandal ['sændl] N sandale *f*

sandalwood ['sændlwʊd] N (*wood*) bois *m* de santal; (*tree*) santal *m*; (*also:* **sandalwood oil**) huile *f* de santal

sandbag ['sændbæg] N sac *m* de sable

sandblast ['sændblɑːst] VT décaper à la sableuse

sandbox ['sændbɒks] N (*US: for children*) tas *m* de sable

sand castle ['sændkɑːsl] N château *m* de sable

sand dune N dune *f* de sable

sander ['sændər] N ponceuse *f*

S&M N ABBR (= *sadomasochism*) sadomasochisme *m*

sandpaper ['sændpeɪpər] N papier *m* de verre

sandpit ['sændpɪt] N (*Brit: for children*) tas *m* de sable

sands [sændz] NPL plage *f* (de sable)

sandstone ['sændstəʊn] N grès *m*

sandstorm ['sændstɔːm] N tempête *f* de sable

★**sandwich** ['sændwɪtʃ] N sandwich *m*; **cheese/ham ~** sandwich au fromage/jambon ▶ VT (*also:* **sandwich in**) intercaler; **sandwiched between** pris en sandwich entre

sandwich board N panneau *m* publicitaire (porté par un homme-sandwich)

sandwich course N (*Brit*) cours *m* de formation professionnelle

sandy ['sændɪ] ADJ sablonneux(-euse); couvert(e) de sable; (*colour*) sable *inv*, blond roux *inv*

sane [seɪn] ADJ (*person*) sain(e) d'esprit; (*outlook*) sensé(e), sain(e)

sang [sæŋ] PT *of* **sing**

sanguine ['sæŋgwɪn] ADJ optimiste

sanitarium [sænɪ'tɛərɪəm] (*pl* **sanitaria** [-rɪə]) N (*US*) = **sanatorium**

sanitary ['sænɪtərɪ] ADJ (*system, arrangements*) sanitaire; (*clean*) hygiénique

sanitary towel, (*US*) **sanitary napkin** N serviette *f* hygiénique

sanitation [sænɪ'teɪʃən] N (*in house*) installations *fpl* sanitaires; (*in town*) système *m* sanitaire

sanitation department N (*US*) service *m* de voirie

sanitize ['sænɪtaɪz] VT édulcorer; **a sanitized version of sth** une version édulcorée de qch

sanity ['sænɪtɪ] N santé mentale; (*common sense*) bon sens

sank [sæŋk] PT *of* **sink**

San Marino ['sænmə'riːnəʊ] N Saint-Marin *m*

Santa Claus ['sæntə'klɔːz] N le Père Noël

Santiago [sæntɪ'ɑːgəʊ] N (*also:* **Santiago de Chile**) Santiago (du Chili)

sap [sæp] N (*of plants*) sève *f* ▶ VT (*strength*) saper, miner

sapling ['sæplɪŋ] N jeune arbre *m*

sapphire ['sæfaɪər] N saphir *m*

sarcasm ['sɑːkæzm] N sarcasme *m*, raillerie *f*

sarcastic [sɑː'kæstɪk] ADJ sarcastique

sarcastically [sɑː'kæstɪklɪ] ADV d'un ton sarcastique

sarcophagus [sɑː'kɒfəgəs] (*pl* **sarcophagi** [-gaɪ]) N sarcophage *m*

sardine [sɑː'diːn] N sardine *f*

Sardinia [sɑː'dɪnɪə] N Sardaigne *f*

Sardinian [sɑː'dɪnɪən] ADJ sarde ▶ N Sarde *mf*; (*Ling*) sarde *m*

sardonic [sɑː'dɒnɪk] ADJ sardonique

sari ['sɑːrɪ] N sari *m*

sarin ['sɑːrɪn] N sarin *m*

sarong [sə'rɒŋ] N (*traditional*) sarong *m*; (*for beach*) paréo *m*

SARS ['sɑːrz] N ABBR = **severe acute respiratory syndrome**

sartorial [sɑː'tɔːrɪəl] ADJ vestimentaire

SAS N ABBR (*Brit Mil: = Special Air Service*) ≈ GIGN *m*

SASE N ABBR (*US: = self-addressed stamped envelope*) enveloppe affranchie pour la réponse

sash [sæʃ] N écharpe *f*

sash window N fenêtre *f* à guillotine

sassy ['sæsɪ] ADJ (*esp US inf: cheeky*) culotté(e) (*inf*); (*: stylish*) classe (*inf*)

SAT, SATs N ABBR (*US*) = **Scholastic Aptitude Test(s)**

Aux États-Unis, les lycéens qui souhaitent faire des études universitaires doivent passer un test : soit le **SAT**, soit l'*ACT*. Le SAT, introduit en 1926, comprend trois épreuves : mathématiques, lecture critique, rédaction. L'*ACT* (*American College Test*) a vu le jour en 1959 et se compose de quatre épreuves : anglais, mathématiques, lecture et raisonnement scientifique, plus une épreuve de rédaction facultative. En Angleterre,

S

les collégiens passent à l'âge de 7 ans puis de 11 ans une série de tests appelés *SATs* (*Standard Assessment Tests*) pour permettre aux écoles d'évaluer les progrès de chaque enfant par rapport à ses condisciples.

sat [sæt] PT, PP of **sit**

Sat. ABBR (= *Saturday*) sa.

Satan ['seɪtn] N Satan *m*

satanic [sə'tænɪk] ADJ satanique, démoniaque

Satanism ['seɪtnɪzəm] N satanisme *m*

Satanist ['seɪtnɪst] N sataniste *mf*

satchel ['sætʃl] N cartable *m*

sated ['seɪtɪd] ADJ repu(e); blasé(e)

★**satellite** ['sætəlaɪt] ADJ, N satellite *m*

satellite dish N antenne *f* parabolique

satellite navigation system N système *m* de navigation par satellite

satellite television N télévision *f* par satellite

satiate ['seɪʃɪeɪt] VT rassasier

satin ['sætɪn] N satin *m* ▶ ADJ en or de satin, satiné(e); **with a ~ finish** satiné(e)

satire ['sætaɪə] N satire *f*

satirical [sə'tɪrɪkl] ADJ satirique

satirist ['sætɪrɪst] N (*writer*) auteur *m* satirique; (*cartoonist*) caricaturiste *mf*

satirize ['sætɪraɪz] VT faire la satire de, satiriser

satisfaction [sætɪs'fækʃən] N satisfaction *f*

satisfactorily [sætɪs'fæktrɪlɪ] ADV de manière satisfaisante

satisfactory [sætɪs'fæktrɪ] ADJ satisfaisant(e)

satisfied ['sætɪsfaɪd] ADJ satisfait(e); **to be ~ with sth** être satisfait de qch

satisfy ['sætɪsfaɪ] VT satisfaire, contenter; (*convince*) convaincre, persuader; **to ~ the requirements** remplir les conditions; **to ~ sb (that)** convaincre qn (que); **to ~ o.s. of sth** vérifier qch, s'assurer de qch

satisfying ['sætɪsfaɪɪŋ] ADJ satisfaisant(e)

satsuma [sæt'suːmə] N satsuma *f*

saturate ['sætʃəreɪt] VT: **to ~ (with)** saturer (de)

saturated fat ['sætʃəreɪtɪd-] N graisse saturée

saturation [sætʃə'reɪʃən] N saturation *f*

★**Saturday** ['sætədɪ] N samedi *m*; *see also* **Tuesday**

★**sauce** [sɔːs] N sauce *f*

saucepan ['sɔːspən] N casserole *f*

saucer ['sɔːsə'] N soucoupe *f*

saucy ['sɔːsɪ] ADJ impertinent(e)

Saudi ['saudi], **Saudi Arabian** ADJ saoudien(ne) ▶ N Saoudien(ne)

Saudi Arabia N Arabie *f* Saoudite

sauna ['sɔːnə] N sauna *m*

saunter ['sɔːntə'] VI: **to ~ to** aller en flânant *or* se balader jusqu'à

★**sausage** ['sɔsɪdʒ] N saucisse *f*; (*salami etc*) saucisson *m*

sausage roll N friand *m*

sauté ['səuteɪ] ADJ (*Culin: potatoes*) sauté(e); (: *onions*) revenu(e) ▶ VT faire sauter; faire revenir

sautéed ['səuteɪd] ADJ sauté(e)

savage ['sævɪdʒ] ADJ (*cruel, fierce*) brutal(e), féroce; (*primitive*) primitif(-ive), sauvage ▶ N sauvage *mf* ▶ VT attaquer férocement

savagely ['sævɪdʒlɪ] ADV sauvagement

savagery ['sævɪdʒrɪ] N sauvagerie *f*, brutalité *f*, férocité *f*

savannah, savanna [sə'vænə] N savane *f*

★**save** [seɪv] VT (*person, belongings*) sauver; (*money*) mettre de côté, économiser; (*time*) (faire) gagner; (*keep*) garder; (*Comput*) sauvegarder; (*Sport: stop*) arrêter; (*avoid: trouble*) éviter; **it will ~ me an hour** ça me fera gagner une heure; **to ~ face** sauver la face; **God ~ the Queen!** vive la Reine! ▶ VI (*also:* **save up**) mettre de l'argent de côté ▶ N (*Sport*) arrêt *m* (du ballon) ▶ PREP sauf, à l'exception de

saver ['seɪvə'] N (*of money*) épargnant(e)

saving ['seɪvɪŋ] N économie *f* ▶ ADJ: **the ~ grace of** ce qui rachète ■ **savings** NPL économies *fpl*; **to make savings** faire des économies

savings account N compte *m* d'épargne

savings and loan association (*US*) N ≈ société *f* de crédit immobilier

savings bank N caisse *f* d'épargne

saviour, (*US*) **savior** ['seɪvjə'] N sauveur *m*

savour, (*US*) **savor** ['seɪvə'] N saveur *f*, goût *m* ▶ VT savourer

savoury, (*US*) **savory** ['seɪvərɪ] ADJ savoureux(-euse); (*dish: not sweet*) salé(e)

savvy ['sævɪ] N (*inf*) jugeote *f* (*inf*)

saw [sɔː] PT of **see** ▶ N (*tool*) scie *f* ▶ VT (*pt* **sawed**, *pp* **sawed** [sɔːd] *or* **sawn** [sɔːn]) scier; **to ~ sth up** débiter qch à la scie

sawdust ['sɔːdʌst] N sciure *f*

sawmill ['sɔːmɪl] N scierie *f*

sawn [sɔːn] PP of **saw**

sawn-off ['sɔːnɔf], (*US*) **sawed-off** ['sɔːdɔf] ADJ: **~ shotgun** carabine *f* à canon scié

sax [sæks] N (*inf*) saxo *m* (*inf*)

saxophone ['sæksəfəun] N saxophone *m*

saxophonist [sæk'sɔfənɪst] N saxophoniste *mf*

★**say** [seɪ] (*pt, pp* **said** [sɛd]) VT dire; **could you ~ that again?** pourriez-vous répéter ce que vous venez de dire?; **to ~ yes/no** dire oui/non; **she said (that) I was to give you this** elle m'a chargé de vous remettre ceci; **my watch says 3 o'clock** ma montre indique 3 heures, il est 3 heures à ma montre; **shall we ~ Tuesday?** disons mardi?; **that doesn't ~ much for him** ce n'est pas vraiment à son honneur; **when all is said and done** en fin de compte, en définitive; **there is something** *or* **a lot to be said for it** cela a des avantages; **that is to ~** c'est-à-dire; **to ~ nothing of** sans compter; **~ that ...** mettons *or* disons que ...; **that goes without saying** cela va sans dire, cela va de soi ▶ N: **to have one's ~** dire ce qu'on a à dire; **to have a ~** avoir voix au chapitre

saying ['seɪɪŋ] N dicton *m*, proverbe *m*

SBA N ABBR (*US: = Small Business Administration*) organisme d'aide aux PME

SC N ABBR (*US*) = **supreme court** ▶ ABBR (*US*) = **South Carolina**

S/C ABBR = **self-contained**

scab [skæb] N croûte *f*; (*pej*) jaune *m*

scabby ['skæbɪ] ADJ croûteux(-euse)

scaffold ['skæfəld] N échafaud m

scaffolding ['skæfəldɪŋ] N échafaudage m

scalable ['skeɪləbl] ADJ (Comput) extensible

scald [skɔːld] N brûlure f ▶ VT ébouillanter

scalding ['skɔːldɪŋ] ADJ (also: **scalding hot**) brûlant(e), bouillant(e)

★**scale** [skeɪl] N (of fish) écaille f; (Mus) gamme f; (of ruler, thermometer etc) graduation f, échelle (graduée); (of salaries, fees etc) barème m; (of map, also size, extent) échelle; **pay ~** échelle des salaires; **~ of charges** tableau m des tarifs; **on a large ~** sur une grande échelle, en grand; **to draw sth to ~** dessiner qch à l'échelle; **small-scale model** modèle réduit ▶ VT (mountain) escalader; (fish) écailler ▪ **scales** NPL balance f; (larger) bascule f; (also: **bathroom scales**) pèse-personne m inv
▶ **scale down** VT réduire

scaled-down [skeɪld'daun] ADJ à échelle réduite

scale drawing N dessin m à l'échelle

scale model N modèle m à l'échelle

scallion ['skæljən] N oignon m; (US: salad onion) ciboule f; (: shallot) échalote f; (: leek) poireau m

scallop ['skɔləp, 'skæləp] N coquille f Saint-Jacques; (Sewing) feston m

scalloped ['skɔləpt, 'skæləpt] ADJ festonné(e)

scalp [skælp] N cuir chevelu ▶ VT scalper

scalpel ['skælpl] N scalpel m

scalper ['skælpə'] N (US inf: of tickets) revendeur m de billets

scam [skæm] N (inf) arnaque f

scamp [skæmp] VT bâcler

scamper ['skæmpə'] VI: **to ~ away, ~ off** détaler

scampi ['skæmpɪ] NPL langoustines (frites), scampi mpl

scan [skæn] VT (examine) scruter, examiner; (glance at quickly) parcourir; (poetry) scander; (TV, Radar) balayer ▶ N (Med) scanographie f

★**scandal** ['skændl] N scandale m; (gossip) ragots mpl

scandalize ['skændəlaɪz] VT scandaliser, indigner

scandalous ['skændələs] ADJ scandaleux(-euse)

scandalously ['skændələslɪ] ADV (behave) de façon scandaleuse; **~ overpriced** à un prix scandaleux

Scandinavia [skændɪ'neɪvɪə] N Scandinavie f

Scandinavian [skændɪ'neɪvɪən] ADJ scandinave ▶ N Scandinave mf

scanner ['skænə'] N (Radar, Med) scanner m, scanographe m; (Comput) scanner

scant [skænt] ADJ insuffisant(e)

scantily ['skæntɪlɪ] ADV: **~ clad** or **dressed** vêtu(e) du strict minimum

scanty ['skæntɪ] ADJ peu abondant(e), insuffisant(e), maigre

scapegoat ['skeɪpgəut] N bouc m émissaire

scar [skɑː'] N cicatrice f ▶ VT laisser une cicatrice or une marque à

scarce [skɛəs] ADJ rare, peu abondant(e); **to make o.s. ~** (inf) se sauver

scarcely ['skɛəslɪ] ADV à peine, presque pas; **~ anybody** pratiquement personne; **I can ~ believe it** j'ai du mal à le croire

scarcity ['skɛəsɪtɪ] N rareté f, manque m, pénurie f

scarcity value N valeur f de rareté

scare [skɛə'] N peur f, panique f; **bomb ~** alerte f à la bombe ▶ VT effrayer, faire peur à; **to ~ sb stiff** faire une peur bleue à qn
▶ **scare away, scare off** VT faire fuir

scarecrow ['skɛəkrəu] N épouvantail m

scared ['skɛəd] ADJ: **to be ~** avoir peur

scaremonger ['skɛəmʌŋgə'] N alarmiste mf

scaremongering ['skɛəmʌŋgərɪŋ] N alarmisme m

scarf [skɑːf] (pl **scarves** [skɑːvz]) N (long) écharpe f; (square) foulard m

scarlet ['skɑːlɪt] ADJ, N écarlate f

scarlet fever N scarlatine f

scarper ['skɑːpə'] VI (BRIT inf) ficher le camp (inf)

scarves [skɑːvz] NPL de **scarf**

scary ['skɛərɪ] ADJ (inf) effrayant(e); (film) qui fait peur

scathing ['skeɪðɪŋ] ADJ cinglant(e), acerbe; **to be ~ about sth** être très critique vis-à-vis de qch

scatter ['skætə'] VT éparpiller, répandre; (crowd) disperser ▶ VI se disperser

scatterbrained ['skætəbreɪnd] ADJ écervelé(e), étourdi(e)

scattered ['skætəd] ADJ épars(e), dispersé(e)

scatty ['skætɪ] ADJ (BRIT inf) loufoque (inf)

scavenge ['skævəndʒ] VI (person): **to ~ (for)** faire les poubelles (pour trouver); **to ~ for food** (hyenas etc) se nourrir de charognes

scavenger ['skævəndʒə'] N éboueur m

scenario [sɪ'nɑːrɪəu] N scénario m

★**scene** [siːn] N (Theat, fig etc) scène f; (of crime, accident) lieu(x) m(pl), endroit m; (sight, view) spectacle m, vue f; **behind the scenes** (also fig) dans les coulisses; **to make a ~** (inf: fuss) faire une scène or toute une histoire; **to appear on the ~** (also fig) faire son apparition, arriver; **the political ~** la situation politique

scenery ['siːnərɪ] N (Theat) décor(s) m(pl); (landscape) paysage m

scenic ['siːnɪk] ADJ scénique; offrant de beaux paysages or panoramas

scent [sɛnt] N parfum m, odeur f; (fig: track) piste f; (sense of smell) odorat m; **to put** or **throw sb off the ~** mettre qn sur une mauvaise piste ▶ VT parfumer; (smell, also fig) flairer

scented ['sɛntɪd] ADJ parfumé(e)

sceptic, (US) **skeptic** ['skɛptɪk] N sceptique mf

sceptical, (US) **skeptical** ['skɛptɪkl] ADJ sceptique

scepticism, (US) **skepticism** ['skɛptɪsɪzəm] N scepticisme m

sceptre, (US) **scepter** ['sɛptə'] N sceptre m

Schadenfreude ['ʃɑːdənfrɔɪdə] N joie f maligne (suscitée par le malheur d'autrui)

★**schedule** ['ʃɛdjuːl, (US) 'skɛdjuːl] N programme m, plan m; (of trains) horaire m; (of prices etc) barème m, tarif m; **on ~** à l'heure (prévue); à la date prévue; **to be ahead of/behind ~** avoir de l'avance/du retard; **we are working to a very tight ~** notre programme de travail est très serré or intense; **everything went according to ~** tout s'est passé

S

831

comme prévu ▶ VT prévoir; **as scheduled** comme prévu

scheduled ['ʃɛdjuːld, (US) 'skɛdjuːld] ADJ (date, time) prévu(e), indiqué(e); (visit, event) programmé(e), prévu; (train, bus, stop, flight) régulier(-ière)

scheduled flight N vol régulier

schematic [skɪ'mætɪk] ADJ schématique

scheme [skiːm] N plan m, projet m; (method) procédé m; (plot) complot m, combine f; (arrangement) arrangement m, classification f; (pension scheme etc) régime m; **colour ~** combinaison f de(s) couleurs ▶ VT, VI comploter, manigancer

scheming ['skiːmɪŋ] ADJ rusé(e), intrigant(e) ▶ N manigances fpl, intrigues fpl

schism ['skɪzəm] N schisme m

schizophrenia [skɪtsə'friːnɪə] N schizophrénie f

schizophrenic [skɪtsə'frɛnɪk] ADJ schizophrène

schmaltz ['ʃmɔːlts] N (inf) mièvrerie f

schmaltzy ['ʃmɔːltsɪ] ADJ (inf: song, film, book) à l'eau de rose, mièvre

scholar ['skɔləʳ] N érudit(e); (pupil) boursier(-ère)

scholarly ['skɔləlɪ] ADJ érudit(e), savant(e)

scholarship ['skɔləʃɪp] N érudition f; (grant) bourse f (d'études)

★**school** [skuːl] N (gen) école f; (secondary school) collège m; lycée m; (in university) faculté f; (US: university) université f; (of fish) banc m ▶ CPD scolaire ▶ VT (animal) dresser

school age N âge m scolaire

schoolbag ['skuːlbæg] N cartable m

schoolbook ['skuːlbuk] N livre m scolaire or de classe

★**schoolboy** ['skuːlbɔɪ] N écolier m; (at secondary school) collégien m; lycéen m

★**schoolchildren** ['skuːltʃɪldrən] NPL écoliers mpl; (at secondary school) collégiens mpl; lycéens mpl

schooldays ['skuːldeɪz] NPL années fpl de scolarité

school friend N ami(e) d'école

★**schoolgirl** ['skuːlgəːl] N écolière f; (at secondary school) collégienne f; lycéenne f

schoolhouse ['skuːlhaus] N (US) école f

schooling ['skuːlɪŋ] N instruction f, études fpl

school-leaver ['skuːlliːvəʳ] N (BRIT) jeune qui vient de terminer ses études secondaires

schoolmaster ['skuːlmɑːstəʳ] N (primary) instituteur m; (secondary) professeur m

schoolmate ['skuːlmeɪt] N camarade mf d'école

school meal, school lunch N déjeuner m à la cantine (scolaire)

schoolmistress ['skuːlmɪstrɪs] N (primary) institutrice f; (secondary) professeur m

school report N (BRIT) bulletin m (scolaire)

schoolroom ['skuːlruːm] N (salle f de) classe f

schoolteacher ['skuːltiːtʃəʳ] N (primary) instituteur(-trice); (secondary) professeur m

schoolwork ['skuːlwəːk] N devoirs mpl

schoolyard ['skuːljɑːd] N (US) cour f de récréation

schooner ['skuːnəʳ] N (ship) schooner m, goélette f; (glass) grand verre (à xérès)

sciatica [saɪ'ætɪkə] N sciatique f

★**science** ['saɪəns] N science f; **the sciences** les sciences; (Scol) les matières fpl scientifiques

science fiction N science-fiction f

scientific [saɪən'tɪfɪk] ADJ scientifique

scientifically [saɪən'tɪfɪklɪ] ADV scientifiquement

★**scientist** ['saɪəntɪst] N scientifique mf; (eminent) savant m

sci-fi ['saɪfaɪ] N ABBR (inf: = science fiction) SF f

Scilly Isles ['sɪlɪ'aɪlz], **Scillies** ['sɪlɪz] NPL: **the ~** les Sorlingues fpl, les îles fpl Scilly

scintillating ['sɪntɪleɪtɪŋ] ADJ scintillant(e), étincelant(e); (wit etc) brillant(e)

scion [saɪən] N (lit, fig) rejeton m

★**scissors** ['sɪzəz] NPL ciseaux mpl; **a pair of ~** une paire de ciseaux

sclerosis [sklɪ'rəusɪs] N sclérose f

scoff [skɔf] VT (BRIT inf: eat) avaler, bouffer (inf) ▶ VI: **to ~ (at)** (mock) se moquer (de)

scold [skəuld] VT gronder, attraper, réprimander

scolding ['skəuldɪŋ] N réprimande f

scone [skɔn] N petit gâteau dont la version sucrée se mange souvent avec de la crème et de la confiture

scoop [skuːp] N pelle f (à main); (for ice cream) boule f à glace; (Press) reportage exclusif or à sensation ▶ **scoop out** VT évider, creuser ▶ **scoop up** VT ramasser

scoot [skuːt] VI (inf) filer (inf)

scooter ['skuːtəʳ] N (motor cycle) scooter m; (toy) trottinette f

scope [skəup] N (capacity: of plan, undertaking) portée f, envergure f; (: of person) compétence f, capacités fpl; (opportunity) possibilités fpl; **within the ~ of** dans les limites de; **there is plenty of ~ for improvement** (BRIT) cela pourrait être beaucoup mieux

scorch [skɔːtʃ] VT (clothes) brûler (légèrement), roussir; (earth, grass) dessécher, brûler

scorched earth policy ['skɔːtʃt-] N politique f de la terre brûlée

scorcher ['skɔːtʃəʳ] N (inf: hot day) journée f torride

scorching ['skɔːtʃɪŋ] ADJ torride, brûlant(e)

★**score** [skɔːʳ] N score m, décompte m des points; (Mus) partition f; **on that ~** sur ce chapitre, à cet égard; **to have an old ~ to settle with sb** (fig) avoir un (vieux) compte à régler avec qn; **a ~ of** (twenty) vingt; **scores of** (fig) des tas de ▶ VT (goal, point) marquer; (success) remporter; (cut: leather, wood, card) entailler, inciser; **to ~ 6 out of 10** obtenir 6 sur 10 ▶ VI marquer des points; (Football) marquer un but; (keep score) compter les points ▶ **score out** VT rayer, barrer, biffer

scoreboard ['skɔːbɔːd] N tableau m

scorecard ['skɔːkɑːd] N (Sport) carton m, feuille f de marque

scoreless ['skɔːlɪs] ADJ (game) qui s'est terminé sur un score vierge; (draw, tie) zéro à zéro

scoreline ['skɔːlaɪn] N (Sport) score m

scorer ['skɔːrəʳ] N (Football) auteur m du but; buteur m; (keeping score) marqueur m

scoring ['skɔːrɪŋ] N (of points, goals) inscription f; (scorekeeping) marque f; (Mus) arrangements mpl; **to do the ~** tenir la marque

scorn [skɔːn] N mépris m, dédain m ▸ VT mépriser, dédaigner

scornful ['skɔːnful] ADJ méprisant(e), dédaigneux(-euse)

scornfully ['skɔːnfulɪ] ADV avec mépris

Scorpio ['skɔːpɪəu] N le Scorpion; **to be ~** être du Scorpion

scorpion ['skɔːpɪən] N scorpion m

Scot [skɔt] N Écossais(e)

Scotch [skɔtʃ] N whisky m, scotch m

scotch [skɔtʃ] VT faire échouer; enrayer; étouffer

Scotch tape® (US) N scotch® m, ruban adhésif

scot-free ['skɔt'friː] ADJ: **to get off ~** s'en tirer sans être puni(e); s'en sortir indemne

★**Scotland** ['skɔtlənd] N Écosse f

Scots [skɔts] ADJ écossais(e)

★**Scotsman** ['skɔtsmən] N (irreg) Écossais m

★**Scotswoman** ['skɔtswumən] N (irreg) Écossaise f

★**Scottish** ['skɔtɪʃ] ADJ écossais(e); **the ~ National Party** le parti national écossais; **the ~ Parliament** le Parlement écossais

En 1997, après presque trois siècles d'union politique entre l'Angleterre et l'Écosse, cette dernière a opté à l'issue d'un référendum pour un parlement décentralisé qui siégerait à Édimbourg. En 1999, 129 députés ont été élus et dotés de pouvoirs législatifs dans plusieurs domaines, notamment l'éducation, l'environnement, la santé, la justice, la fiscalité et l'administration locale. Le chef du gouvernement écossais est le *First Minister*, mais le souverain britannique demeure le chef de l'État. En septembre 2014, à l'issue d'un autre référendum, les Écossais se sont prononcés contre l'indépendance totale du reste du Royaume-Uni.

scoundrel ['skaundrl] N vaurien m

scour ['skauə^r] VT (clean) récurer; frotter; décaper; (search) battre, parcourir

scourer ['skauərə^r] N tampon abrasif or à récurer; (powder) poudre f à récurer

scourge [skəːdʒ] N fléau m

scout [skaut] N (Mil) éclaireur m; (also: **boy scout**) scout m; **girl ~** (US) guide f
▸ **scout around** VI chercher

scoutmaster ['skautmɑːstə^r] N chef mf scout(e)

scowl [skaul] VI se renfrogner, avoir l'air maussade; **to ~ at** regarder de travers

scrabble ['skræbl] VI (claw): **to ~ (at)** gratter; **to ~ about** or **around for sth** chercher qch à tâtons ▸ N: **S~®** Scrabble® m

scraggy ['skrægɪ] ADJ décharné(e), efflanqué(e), famélique

scram [skræm] VI (inf) ficher le camp (inf)

scramble ['skræmbl] N (rush) bousculade f, ruée f ▸ VI grimper/descendre tant bien que mal; **to ~ for** se bousculer or se disputer pour (avoir); **to go scrambling** (Sport) faire du trial

scrambled eggs ['skræmbld-] NPL œufs brouillés

scrap [skræp] N bout m, morceau m; (inf: fight) bagarre f; (also: **scrap iron**) ferraille f; **to sell sth**

for ~ vendre qch à la casse or à la ferraille ▸ VT jeter, mettre au rebut; (fig) abandonner, laisser tomber ▸ VI (inf) se bagarrer ■ **scraps** NPL (waste) déchets mpl

scrapbook ['skræpbuk] N album m

scrap dealer N marchand m de ferraille

scrape [skreɪp] VT, VI gratter, racler ▸ N: **to get into a ~** s'attirer des ennuis
▸ **scrape by** VI (financially) s'en sortir
▸ **scrape through** VI (exam etc) réussir de justesse
▸ **scrape together** VT (money) racler ses fonds de tiroir pour réunir

scraper ['skreɪpə^r] N grattoir m, racloir m

scrap heap N tas m de ferraille; (fig): **on the ~** au rancart or rebut

scrap merchant N (BRIT) marchand m de ferraille

scrap metal N ferraille f

scrap paper N papier m brouillon

scrappy ['skræpɪ] ADJ fragmentaire, décousu(e)

scrap yard N parc m à ferrailles; (for cars) cimetière m de voitures

scratch [skrætʃ] N égratignure f, rayure f; (on paint) éraflure f; (from claw) coup m de griffe; **to start from ~** partir de zéro; **to be up to ~** être à la hauteur ▸ ADJ: **~ team** équipe de fortune or improvisée ▸ VT (rub) (se) gratter; (record) rayer; (paint etc) érafler; (with claw, nail) griffer; (Comput) effacer ▸ VI (se) gratter
▸ **scratch out** VT (name, words) gratter; **to ~ sb's eyes out** arracher les yeux de qn

scratch card N carte f à gratter

scratchy ['skrætʃɪ] ADJ (recording) grésillant(e); (pen) qui accroche; (sweater, wool) qui gratte

scrawl [skrɔːl] N gribouillage m ▸ VI gribouiller

scrawny ['skrɔːnɪ] ADJ décharné(e)

★**scream** [skriːm] N cri perçant, hurlement m; **to be a ~** (inf) être impayable (inf) ▸ VI crier, hurler; **to ~ at sb to do sth** crier or hurler à qn de faire qch

scree [skriː] N éboulis m

screech [skriːtʃ] N cri strident, hurlement m; (of tyres, brakes) crissement m, grincement m ▸ VI hurler; crisser, grincer

★**screen** [skriːn] N écran m; (in room) paravent m; (Cine, TV) écran; (fig) écran, rideau m ▸ VT masquer, cacher; (from the wind etc) abriter, protéger; (film) projeter; (candidates etc) filtrer; (for illness): **to ~ sb for sth** faire subir un test de dépistage de qch à qn

screen editing [-'edɪtɪŋ] N (Comput) édition f or correction f sur écran

screening ['skriːnɪŋ] N (of film) projection f; (Med) test m (or tests) de dépistage; (for security) filtrage m

screen memory N (Comput) mémoire f écran

screenplay ['skriːnpleɪ] N scénario m

screen saver N (Comput) économiseur m d'écran

screenshot ['skriːnʃɔt] N (Comput) capture f d'écran

screen test N bout m d'essai

screenwriter ['skriːnraɪtə^r] N scénariste mf

screenwriting ['skriːnraɪtɪŋ] N écriture f de scénarios

S

screw [skru:] N vis f; (propeller) hélice f ▶ VT (also: **screw in**) visser; (inf: woman) baiser (!); **to ~ sth to the wall** visser qch au mur; **to have one's head screwed on** (fig) avoir la tête sur les épaules
▶ **screw up** VT (paper etc) froisser; (inf: ruin) bousiller; **to ~ up one's eyes** se plisser les yeux; **to ~ up one's face** faire la grimace

screwball ['skru:bɔ:l] (inf) CPD (comedy) délirant(e) ▶ N doux (douce) dingue

screwdriver ['skru:draɪvə'] N tournevis m

screwed-up ['skru:d'ʌp] ADJ (inf): **to be ~** être paumé(e)

screwy ['skru:ɪ] ADJ (inf) dingue, cinglé(e)

scribble ['skrɪbl] N gribouillage m ▶ VT gribouiller, griffonner; **to ~ sth down** griffonner qch

scribe [skraɪb] N scribe m

script [skrɪpt] N (Cine etc) scénario m, texte m; (in exam) copie f; (writing) (écriture f) script m

scripted ['skrɪptɪd] ADJ (Radio, TV) préparé(e) à l'avance

Scripture ['skrɪptʃə'] N Écriture sainte

scriptwriter ['skrɪptraɪtə'] N scénariste mf, dialoguiste mf

scroll [skrəul] N rouleau m ▶ VT (Comput) faire défiler (sur l'écran)
▶ **scroll down** VT faire défiler ▶ VI (person) faire défiler le texte; (text) défiler
▶ **scroll up** VT faire défiler vers le haut ▶ VI (person) faire défiler le texte vers le haut; (text, titles) défiler vers le haut

Scrooge [skru:dʒ] N rat m

scrotum ['skrəutəm] N scrotum m

scrounge [skraundʒ] (inf) VT: **to ~ sth (off or from sb)** se faire payer qch (par qn), emprunter qch (à qn) ▶ VI: **to ~ off sb** vivre aux crochets de qn

scrounger ['skraundʒə'] N parasite m

scrub [skrʌb] N (clean) nettoyage m (à la brosse); (land) broussailles fpl ▶ VT (floor) nettoyer (à la brosse; (pan) récurer; (washing) frotter; (reject) annuler

scrubbing brush ['skrʌbɪŋ-] N brosse dure

scruff [skrʌf] N: **by the ~ of the neck** par la peau du cou

scruffy ['skrʌfɪ] ADJ débraillé(e)

scrum [skrʌm], **scrummage** ['skrʌmɪdʒ] N mêlée f

scrumptious ['skrʌmpʃəs] ADJ (inf) succulent(e)

scrunch up VT (paper, cloth) chiffonner

scruple ['skru:pl] N scrupule m; **to have no scruples about doing sth** n'avoir aucun scrupule à faire qch

scrupulous ['skru:pjuləs] ADJ scrupuleux(-euse)

scrupulously ['skru:pjuləslɪ] ADV scrupuleusement; **to be ~ honest** être d'une honnêteté scrupuleuse

scrutinize ['skru:tɪnaɪz] VT scruter, examiner minutieusement

scrutiny ['skru:tɪnɪ] N examen minutieux; **under the ~ of sb** sous la surveillance de qn

scuba ['sku:bə] N scaphandre m (autonome)

scuba diving N plongée sous-marine

scuff [skʌf] VT érafler

scuffle ['skʌfl] N échauffourée f, rixe f

scullery ['skʌlərɪ] N arrière-cuisine f

sculpt [skʌlpt] VT, VI sculpter

sculptor ['skʌlptə'] N sculpteur m

sculptural ['skʌlptʃərəl] ADJ sculptural(e)

sculpture ['skʌlptʃə'] N sculpture f

sculptured ['skʌlptʃəd] ADJ sculpté(e)

scum [skʌm] N écume f, mousse f; (pej: people) rebut m, lie f

scumbag ['skʌmbæg] N (inf, pej) fripouille f (inf)

scupper ['skʌpə'] VT (BRIT) saborder

scurrilous ['skʌrɪləs] ADJ haineux(-euse), virulent(e); calomnieux(-euse)

scurry ['skʌrɪ] VI filer à toute allure; **to ~ off** détaler, se sauver

scurvy ['skə:vɪ] N scorbut m

scuttle ['skʌtl] N (Naut) écoutille f; (also: **coal scuttle**) seau m (à charbon) ▶ VT (ship) saborder ▶ VI (scamper): **to ~ away, ~ off** détaler

scythe [saɪð] N faux f

SD, S. Dak. ABBR (US) = **South Dakota**

SDLP N ABBR (BRIT Pol) = **Social Democratic and Labour Party**

★**sea** [si:] N mer f; **on the ~** (boat) en mer; (town) au bord de la mer; **by or beside the ~** (holiday, town) au bord de la mer; **by ~** par mer, en bateau; **out to ~** au large; **(out) at ~** en mer; **heavy or rough ~(s)** grosse mer, mer agitée; **a ~ of faces** (fig) une multitude de visages; **to be all at ~** (fig) nager complètement ▶ CPD marin(e), de (la) mer, maritime

sea bed N fond m de la mer

sea bird N oiseau m de mer

seaboard ['si:bɔ:d] N côte f

sea breeze N brise f de mer

sea dog N (old) vieux loup m de mer

seafarer ['si:fɛərə'] N marin m

seafaring ['si:fɛərɪŋ] ADJ (life) de marin; **~ people** les gens mpl de mer

★**seafood** ['si:fu:d] N fruits mpl de mer

sea front N bord m de mer

seagoing ['si:gəuɪŋ] ADJ (ship) de haute mer

sea-green [si:'gri:n] N bleu-vert m inv ▶ ADJ bleuvert inv

seagull ['si:gʌl] N mouette f

seahorse ['si:hɔ:s] N hippocampe m

seal [si:l] N (animal) phoque m; (stamp) sceau m, cachet m; (impression) cachet, estampille f; **~ of approval** approbation f ▶ VT sceller; (envelope) coller; (: with seal) cacheter; (decide: sb's fate) décider (de); (: bargain) conclure
▶ **seal off** VT (close) condamner; (forbid entry to) interdire l'accès de
▶ **seal up** VT (window) sceller; (holes, cracks) reboucher

sealant ['si:lənt] N mastic m

sea level N niveau m de la mer

sealing wax ['si:lɪŋ-] N cire f à cacheter

sea lion N lion m de mer

sealskin ['si:lskɪn] N peau f de phoque

seam [si:m] N couture f; (of coal) veine f, filon m; **the hall was bursting at the seams** la salle était pleine à craquer

seaman ['si:mən] N (*irreg*) marin m

seamanship ['si:mənʃɪp] N qualités fpl de marin

seamless ['si:mlɪs] ADJ (*Fashion, Sewing*) sans couture(s); (*transition*) sans heurt

seamlessly ['si:mlɪslɪ] ADV sans heurt

seamy ['si:mɪ] ADJ louche, mal famé(e)

seance ['seɪɔns] N séance f de spiritisme

seaplane ['si:pleɪn] N hydravion m

seaport ['si:pɔ:t] N port m de mer

★**search** [sə:tʃ] N (*for person, thing, Comput*) recherche(s) f(pl); (*of drawer, pockets*) fouille f; (*Law: at sb's home*) perquisition f; **in ~ of** à la recherche de ▶ VT fouiller; (*examine*) examiner minutieusement; scruter ▶ VI: **to ~ for** chercher
▶ **search through** VT FUS fouiller

search engine N (*Comput*) moteur m de recherche

searcher ['sə:tʃə'] N chercheur(-euse)

searching ['sə:tʃɪŋ] ADJ (*look, question*) pénétrant(e); (*examination*) minutieux(-euse)

searchlight ['sə:tʃlaɪt] N projecteur m

search party N expédition f de secours

search warrant N mandat m de perquisition

searing ['sɪərɪŋ] ADJ (*heat*) brûlant(e); (*pain*) aigu(ë)

seascape ['si:skeɪp] N marine f

seashell ['si:ʃel] N coquillage m

seashore ['si:ʃɔ:'] N rivage m, plage f, bord m de (la) mer; **on the ~** sur le rivage

seasick ['si:sɪk] ADJ: **to be ~** avoir le mal de mer

seasickness ['si:sɪknɪs] N mal m de mer

★**seaside** ['si:saɪd] N bord m de mer

seaside resort N station f balnéaire

★**season** ['si:zn] N saison f; **to be in/out of ~** être/ne pas être de saison; **the busy ~** (*for shops*) la période de pointe; (*for hotels etc*) la pleine saison; **the open ~** (*Hunting*) la saison de la chasse ▶ VT assaisonner, relever

seasonal ['si:znl] ADJ saisonnier(-ière)

seasoned ['si:znd] ADJ (*wood*) séché(e); (*fig: worker, actor, troops*) expérimenté(e); **a ~ campaigner** un vieux militant, un vétéran

seasoning ['si:znɪŋ] N assaisonnement m

season ticket N carte f d'abonnement

★**seat** [si:t] N siège m; (*in bus, train: place*) place f; (*Parliament*) siège m; (*buttocks*) postérieur m; (*of trousers*) fond m; **are there any seats left?** est-ce qu'il reste des places ?; **to take one's ~** prendre place ▶ VT faire asseoir, placer; (*have room for*) avoir des places assises pour, pouvoir accueillir; **to be seated** être assis; **please be seated** veuillez vous asseoir

seat belt N ceinture f de sécurité

seating ['si:tɪŋ] N sièges fpl, places assises

seating capacity N nombre m de places assises

sea urchin N oursin m

sea water N eau f de mer

seaweed ['si:wi:d] N algues fpl

seaworthy ['si:wə:ðɪ] ADJ en état de naviguer

SEC N ABBR (*US: = Securities and Exchange Commission*) ≈ COB f (*= Commission des opérations de Bourse*)

sec. ABBR (*= second*) sec

secateurs [sɛkə'tə:z] NPL sécateur m

secede [sɪ'si:d] VI faire sécession

secession [sɪ'sɛʃən] N sécession f

secluded [sɪ'klu:dɪd] ADJ retiré(e), à l'écart

seclusion [sɪ'klu:ʒən] N solitude f

★**second¹** ['sɛkənd] NUM deuxième, second(e); **~ floor** (*BRIT*) deuxième (étage) m; (*US*) premier (étage) m; **to ask for a ~ opinion** (*Med*) demander l'avis d'un autre médecin ▶ ADV (*in race etc*) en seconde position ▶ N (*unit of time*) seconde f; (*Aut: also:* **second gear**) seconde; (*in series, position*) deuxième m/f; (*Comm: imperfect*) article m de second choix; (*BRIT University*) ≈ licence f avec mention; **Charles the S~** Charles II; **just a ~!** une seconde !, un instant !; (*stopping sb*) pas si vite ! ▶ VT (*motion*) appuyer ■ **seconds** NPL (*inf: food*) rab m (*inf*)

second² [sɪ'kɔnd] VT (*employee*) détacher, mettre en détachement

secondary ['sɛkəndrɪ] ADJ secondaire

★**secondary school** N (*age 11 to 15*) collège m; (*age 15 to 18*) lycée m

second-best [sɛkənd'bɛst] N deuxième choix m; **as a ~** faute de mieux

second-class ['sɛkənd'klɑ:s] ADJ de deuxième classe; (*Rail*) de seconde (classe); (*Post*) au tarif réduit; (*pej*) de qualité inférieure; **~ citizen** citoyen(ne) de deuxième classe ▶ ADV (*Rail*) en seconde; (*Post*) au tarif réduit

second cousin N cousin(e) issu(e) de germains

seconder ['sɛkəndə'] N personne f qui appuie une motion

second-guess [sɛkənd'gɛs] VT (*predict*) (essayer d')anticiper; **they're still trying to ~ his motives** ils essaient toujours de comprendre ses raisons

secondhand ['sɛkənd'hænd] ADJ d'occasion; (*information*) de seconde main ▶ ADV (*buy*) d'occasion; **to hear sth ~** apprendre qch indirectement

second hand N (*on clock*) trotteuse f

second-hand bookshop ['sɛkənd'hænd-] N bouquiniste m

second-in-command ['sɛkəndɪnkə'mɑ:nd] N (*Mil*) commandant m en second; (*Admin*) adjoint(e), sous-chef m

secondly ['sɛkəndlɪ] ADV deuxièmement; **firstly ... ~ ...** d'abord ... ensuite ... or de plus ...

secondment [sɪ'kɔndmənt] N (*BRIT*) détachement m

second-rate ['sɛkənd'reɪt] ADJ de deuxième ordre, de qualité inférieure

second thoughts NPL: **to have ~** changer d'avis; **on ~** or (*US*) **thought** à la réflexion

secrecy ['si:krəsɪ] N secret m; **in ~** en secret

★**secret** ['si:krɪt] ADJ secret(-ète); **to keep sth ~ from sb** cacher qch à qn, ne pas révéler qch à qn; **keep it ~** n'en parle à personne ▶ N secret m; **in ~** adv en secret, secrètement, en cachette; **to make no ~ of sth** ne pas cacher qch

secret agent N agent secret

secretarial [sɛkrɪ'tɛərɪəl] ADJ de secrétaire, de secrétariat

secretarial college, secretarial school N école f de secrétariat

secretariat [sɛkrɪ'tɛərɪət] N secrétariat m

★**secretary** ['sɛkrətrɪ] N secrétaire mf; (Comm) secrétaire général; **S~ of State** (US Pol) ≈ ministre m des Affaires étrangères; **S~ of State (for)** (Pol) ministre m (de)

secretary-general ['sɛkrətrɪ'dʒɛnərl] N secrétaire général

secrete [sɪ'kri:t] VT (Anat, Biol, Med) sécréter; (hide) cacher

secretion [sɪ'kri:ʃən] N sécrétion f

secretive ['si:krətɪv] ADJ réservé(e); (pej) cachottier(-ière), dissimulé(e)

secretly ['si:krɪtlɪ] ADV en secret, secrètement, en cachette

secret police N police secrète

secret service N services secrets

sect [sɛkt] N secte f

sectarian [sɛk'tɛərɪən] ADJ sectaire

sectarianism [sɛk'tɛərɪənɪzəm] N sectarisme m

★**section** ['sɛkʃən] N section f; (department) section; (Comm) rayon m; (of document) section, article m, paragraphe m; (cut) coupe f; **the business** etc **~** (Press) la page des affaires etc ▶ VT sectionner

sector ['sɛktər] N secteur m

secular ['sɛkjʊlər] ADJ laïque

secularism ['sɛkjʊlərɪzəm] N laïcité f

secure [sɪ'kjʊər] ADJ (free from anxiety) sans inquiétude, sécurisé(e); (firmly fixed) solide, bien attaché(e) or fermé(e) etc); (in safe place) en lieu sûr, en sûreté; **to make sth ~** bien fixer or attacher qch ▶ VT (fix) fixer, attacher; (get) obtenir, se procurer; (Comm: loan) garantir; **to ~ sth for sb** obtenir qch pour qn, procurer qch à qn

secured creditor [sɪ'kjʊəd-] N créancier(-ière), privilégié(e)

securely [sɪ'kjʊəlɪ] ADV (firmly) solidement; (safely) fermement

★**security** [sɪ'kjʊərɪtɪ] N sécurité f, mesures fpl de sécurité; (for loan) caution f, garantie f; **to increase** or **tighten ~** renforcer les mesures de sécurité; **~ of tenure** stabilité f d'un emploi, titularisation f ■ **securities** NPL (Stock Exchange) valeurs fpl, titres mpl

Security Council N: **the ~** le Conseil de sécurité

security forces NPL forces fpl de sécurité

security guard N garde chargé de la sécurité; (transporting money) convoyeur m de fonds

security risk N menace f pour la sécurité de l'état (or d'une entreprise etc)

sedan [sə'dæn] N (US Aut) berline f

sedate [sɪ'deɪt] ADJ calme; posé(e) ▶ VT donner des sédatifs à

sedated [sɪ'deɪtɪd] ADJ sous sédation; **lightly ~** sous sédation légère

sedation [sɪ'deɪʃən] N sédation f; **to be under ~** être sous calmants

sedative ['sɛdɪtɪv] N calmant m, sédatif m

sedentary ['sɛdntrɪ] ADJ sédentaire

sediment ['sɛdɪmənt] N sédiment m, dépôt m

sedition [sɪ'dɪʃən] N sédition f

seditious [sɪ'dɪʃəs] ADJ séditieux(-euse)

seduce [sɪ'dju:s] VT séduire

seducer [sɪ'dju:sər] N séducteur(-trice)

seduction [sɪ'dʌkʃən] N séduction f

seductive [sɪ'dʌktɪv] ADJ séduisant(e); (smile) séducteur(-trice); (fig: offer) alléchant(e)

seductress [sɪ'dʌktrɪs] N séductrice f

★**see** [si:] (pt **saw** [sɔ:], pp **seen** [si:n]) VT (gen) voir; (accompany): **to ~ sb to the door** reconduire or raccompagner qn jusqu'à la porte; (ensure): **to ~ that** veiller à ce que + sub, faire en sorte que + sub, s'assurer que; **to go and ~ sb** aller voir qn; **there was nobody to be seen** il n'y avait pas un chat; **I don't know what she sees in him** je ne sais pas ce qu'elle lui trouve; **~ you!** au revoir !, à bientôt !; **~ you soon/later/tomorrow!** à bientôt/plus tard/demain ! ▶ VI voir; **~ for yourself** voyez vous-même; **let me ~** (show me) fais(-moi) voir; (let me think) voyons (un peu); **as far as I can ~** pour autant que je puisse en juger ▶ N évêché m

▶ **see about** [si: ə'baut] VT FUS (deal with) s'occuper de

▶ **see off** [si: ɔf] VT accompagner (à l'aéroport etc)

▶ **see out** [si: aut] VT (take to door) raccompagner à la porte

▶ **see through** [si: θru:] VT mener à bonne fin
▶ VT FUS voir clair dans

▶ **see to** [si: tu:] VT FUS s'occuper de, se charger de

★**seed** [si:d] N graine f; (fig) germe m; (Tennis etc) tête f de série; **to go to ~** (plant) monter en graine; (fig) se laisser aller

seeded ['si:dɪd] ADJ (Tennis etc): **a ~ player** une tête de série; **to be ~ second** être tête de série numéro deux

seedless ['si:dlɪs] ADJ sans pépins

seedling ['si:dlɪŋ] N jeune plant m, semis m

seedy ['si:dɪ] ADJ (shabby) minable, miteux(-euse)

seeing ['si:ɪŋ] CONJ: **~ (that)** vu que, étant donné que

seek [si:k] (pt, pp **sought** [sɔ:t]) VT chercher, rechercher; **to ~ advice/help from sb** demander conseil/de l'aide à qn

▶ **seek out** [si:k aut] VT (person) chercher

★**seem** [si:m] VI sembler, paraître; **there seems to be …** il semble qu'il y a …, on dirait qu'il y a …; **it seems (that) …** il semble que …; **what seems to be the trouble?** qu'est-ce qui ne va pas ?

seeming ['si:mɪŋ] ADJ apparent(e)

seemingly ['si:mɪŋlɪ] ADV apparemment

seemly ['si:mlɪ] ADJ (old) convenable

seen [si:n] PP of **see**

seep [si:p] VI suinter, filtrer

seepage ['si:pɪdʒ] N infiltrations fpl

seer [sɪər] N prophète (prophétesse) voyant(e)

seersucker ['sɪəsʌkər] N cloqué m, étoffe cloquée

seesaw ['si:sɔ:] N (jeu m de) bascule f

seethe [si:ð] VI être en effervescence; **to ~ with anger** bouillir de colère

see-through ['si:θru:] ADJ transparent(e)

segment ['sɛgmənt] N segment m; (of orange) quartier m

segregate ['sɛgrɪgeɪt] VT séparer, isoler

segregation [sɛgrɪ'geɪʃən] N ségrégation f

segue ['sɛgweɪ] VI: **to ~ into sth** enchaîner sur or avec qch ▶ N enchaînement m

Seine [seɪn] N: **the (River) ~** la Seine

seismic ['saɪzmɪk] ADJ sismique

seismological [saɪzmə'lɒdʒɪkl] ADJ sismologique

seismologist [saɪz'mɒlədʒɪst] N sismologue *mf*

seize [siːz] VT (*grasp*) saisir, attraper; (*take possession of*) s'emparer de; (*opportunity*) saisir; (*Law*) saisir
  ▶ **seize on** VT FUS saisir, sauter sur
  ▶ **seize up** VI (*Tech*) se gripper
  ▶ **seize upon** VT FUS = **seize on**

seizure ['siːʒəʳ] N (*Med*) crise *f*, attaque *f*; (*of power*) prise *f*; (*Law*) saisie *f*

seldom ['sɛldəm] ADV rarement

★**select** [sɪ'lɛkt] ADJ choisi(e), d'élite; (*hotel, restaurant, club*) chic *inv*, sélect *inv*; **a ~ few** quelques privilégiés ▶ VT sélectionner, choisir

★**selection** [sɪ'lɛkʃən] N sélection *f*, choix *m*

selection committee N comité *m* de sélection

selective [sɪ'lɛktɪv] ADJ sélectif(-ive); (*school*) à recrutement sélectif

selector [sɪ'lɛktəʳ] N (*person*) sélectionneur(-euse); (*Tech*) sélecteur *m*

self [sɛlf] (*pl* **selves** [sɛlvz]) N: **the ~** le moi *inv*
  ▶ PREFIX auto-

self-addressed ['sɛlfə'drɛst] ADJ: **~ envelope** enveloppe *f* à mon (*or* votre *etc*) nom

self-adhesive [sɛlfəd'hiːzɪv] ADJ autocollant(e)

self-assertive [sɛlfə'səːtɪv] ADJ autoritaire

self-assurance [sɛlfə'ʃuərəns] N assurance *f*

self-assured [sɛlfə'ʃuəd] ADJ sûr(e) de soi, plein(e) d'assurance

self-catering [sɛlf'keɪtərɪŋ] ADJ (*BRIT: flat*) avec cuisine, où l'on peut faire sa cuisine; (: *holiday*) en appartement (*or* chalet *etc*) loué

self-centred, (US) **self-centered** [sɛlf'sɛntəd] ADJ égocentrique

self-cleaning [sɛlf'kliːnɪŋ] ADJ autonettoyant(e)

self-coloured, (US) **self-colored** [sɛlf'kʌləd] ADJ uni(e)

self-confessed [sɛlfkən'fɛst] ADJ (*alcoholic etc*) déclaré(e), qui ne s'en cache pas

self-confidence [sɛlf'kɒnfɪdns] N confiance *f* en soi

self-confident [sɛlf'kɒnfɪdnt] ADJ sûr(e) de soi, plein(e) d'assurance

self-conscious [sɛlf'kɒnʃəs] ADJ timide, qui manque d'assurance

self-contained [sɛlfkən'teɪnd] ADJ (*BRIT: flat*) avec entrée particulière, indépendant(e)

self-control [sɛlfkən'trəul] N maîtrise *f* de soi

self-defeating [sɛlfdɪ'fiːtɪŋ] ADJ qui a un effet contraire à l'effet recherché

self-defence, (US) **self-defense** [sɛlfdɪ'fɛns] N autodéfense *f*; (*Law*) légitime défense *f*

self-discipline [sɛlf'dɪsɪplɪn] N discipline personnelle

self-drive [sɛlf'draɪv] ADJ (*BRIT*): **~ car** voiture *f* de location

self-employed [sɛlfɪm'plɔɪd] ADJ qui travaille à son compte

self-esteem [sɛlfɪ'stiːm] N amour-propre *m*

self-evident [sɛlf'ɛvɪdnt] ADJ évident(e), qui va de soi

self-explanatory [sɛlfɪk'splænətrɪ] ADJ qui se passe d'explication

self-governing [sɛlf'gʌvənɪŋ] ADJ autonome

self-harm [sɛlf'hɑːm] VI s'automutiler ▶ N automutilation *f*

self-help ['sɛlf'hɛlp] N initiative personnelle, efforts personnels

selfie ['sɛlfɪ] N selfie *m*

selfie stick N perche *f* à selfie

self-importance [sɛlfɪm'pɔːtns] N suffisance *f*

self-indulgent [sɛlfɪn'dʌldʒənt] ADJ qui ne se refuse rien

self-inflicted [sɛlfɪn'flɪktɪd] ADJ volontaire

self-interest [sɛlf'ɪntrɪst] N intérêt personnel

selfish ['sɛlfɪʃ] ADJ égoïste

selfishly ['sɛlfɪʃlɪ] ADV égoïstement

selfishness ['sɛlfɪʃnɪs] N égoïsme *m*

selfless ['sɛlflɪs] ADJ désintéressé(e), plein(e) d'abnégation

selflessly ['sɛlflɪslɪ] ADV avec abnégation

selflessness ['sɛlflɪsnɪs] N dévouement *m*, abnégation *f*

self-made man ['sɛlfmeɪd-] N (*irreg*) self-made man *m*

self-pity [sɛlf'pɪtɪ] N apitoiement *m* sur soi-même

self-portrait [sɛlf'pɔːtreɪt] N autoportrait *m*

self-possessed [sɛlfpə'zɛst] ADJ assuré(e)

self-preservation ['sɛlfprɛzə'veɪʃən] N instinct *m* de conservation

self-raising [sɛlf'reɪzɪŋ], (US) **self-rising** [sɛlf'raɪzɪŋ] ADJ: **~ flour** farine *f* pour gâteaux (*avec levure incorporée*)

self-regulatory [sɛlfregju'leɪtərɪ], **self-regulating** [sɛlf'regjuleɪtɪŋ] ADJ autorégulé(e)

self-reliant [sɛlfrɪ'laɪənt] ADJ indépendant(e)

self-respect [sɛlfrɪs'pɛkt] N respect *m* de soi, amour-propre *m*

self-respecting [sɛlfrɪs'pɛktɪŋ] ADJ qui se respecte

self-righteous [sɛlf'raɪtʃəs] ADJ satisfait(e) de soi, pharisaïque

self-rising [sɛlf'raɪzɪŋ] ADJ (US) = **self-raising**

self-sacrifice [sɛlf'sækrɪfaɪs] N abnégation *f*

self-same ['sɛlfseɪm] ADJ même

self-satisfied [sɛlf'sætɪsfaɪd] ADJ content(e) de soi, suffisant(e)

self-sealing [sɛlf'siːlɪŋ] ADJ (*envelope*) autocollant(e)

self-service [sɛlf'səːvɪs] ADJ, N libre-service *m*, self-service *m*

self-styled ['sɛlfstaɪld] ADJ soi-disant *inv*

self-sufficient [sɛlfsə'fɪʃənt] ADJ indépendant(e)

self-supporting [sɛlfsə'pɔːtɪŋ] ADJ financièrement indépendant(e)

self-tanning ['sɛlf'tænɪŋ] ADJ: **~ cream** *or* **lotion** *etc* autobronzant *m*

self-taught [sɛlf'tɔːt] ADJ autodidacte

self-worth [sɛlf'wəːθ] N amour-propre *m*

★**sell** [sɛl] (*pt, pp* **sold** [səuld]) VT vendre; **to ~ sb an idea** (*fig*) faire accepter une idée à qn ▶ VI se vendre; **to ~ at** *or* **for 10 euros** se vendre 10 euros
  ▶ **sell off** [sɛl ɔf] VT liquider
  ▶ **sell out** [sɛl aut] VI: **to ~ out (of sth)** (*use up stock*) vendre tout son stock (de qch); **to ~ out (to)**

S

(*Comm*) vendre son fonds *or* son affaire (à) ▸ vt vendre tout son stock de; **the tickets are all sold out** il ne reste plus de billets

▸ **sell up** [sɛl ʌp] vi vendre son fonds *or* son affaire

sell-by date ['sɛlbaɪ-] N date *f* limite de vente

seller ['sɛlə^r] N vendeur(-euse), marchand(e); **~'s market** marché *m* à la hausse

selling price ['sɛlɪŋ-] N prix *m* de vente

Sellotape® ['sɛləʊteɪp] N (*BRIT*) scotch® *m*

sellout ['sɛlaʊt] N trahison *f*, capitulation *f*; (*of tickets*): **it was a ~** tous les billets ont été vendus

selves [sɛlvz] NPL *of* **self**

semantic [sɪ'mæntɪk] ADJ sémantique

semantics [sɪ'mæntɪks] N sémantique *f*

semaphore ['sɛməfɔː^r] N signaux *mpl* à bras; (*Rail*) sémaphore *m*

semblance ['sɛmblns] N semblant *m*

semen ['siːmən] N sperme *m*

semester [sɪ'mɛstə^r] N (*esp US*) semestre *m*

semi... ['sɛmɪ] PREFIX semi-, demi-; à demi, à moitié ▸ N: **semi = semidetached (house)**

semi-automatic [sɛmɪɔːtə'mætɪk] N arme *f* semi-automatique

semibreve ['sɛmɪbriːv] N (*BRIT*) ronde *f*

semicircle ['sɛmɪsəːkl] N demi-cercle *m*

semicircular ['sɛmɪ'səːkjulə^r] ADJ en demi-cercle, semi-circulaire

semicolon [sɛmɪ'kəʊlən] N point-virgule *m*

semiconductor [sɛmɪkən'dʌktə^r] N semi-conducteur *m*

semiconscious [sɛmɪ'kɔnʃəs] ADJ à demi conscient(e)

semidetached (house) [sɛmɪdɪ'tætʃt-] N (*BRIT*) maison jumelée *or* jumelle

semi-final [sɛmɪ'faɪnl] N demi-finale *f*

semi-finalist [sɛmɪ'faɪnlɪst] N demi-finaliste *mf*

seminal ['sɛmɪnl] ADJ (*work, author*) phare; (*Biol*) séminal(e)

seminar ['sɛmɪnɑː^r] N séminaire *m*

seminary ['sɛmɪnərɪ] N (*Rel: for priests*) séminaire *m*

semiprecious [sɛmɪ'prɛʃəs] ADJ semi-précieux(-euse)

semiquaver ['sɛmɪkweɪvə^r] N (*BRIT*) double croche *f*

semiskilled [sɛmɪ'skɪld] ADJ: **~ worker** ouvrier(-ière) spécialisé(e)

semi-skimmed ['sɛmɪ'skɪmd] ADJ demi-écrémé(e)

semitone ['sɛmɪtəʊn] N (*Mus*) demi-ton *m*

semolina [sɛmə'liːnə] N semoule *f*

SEN N ABBR (*BRIT*) = **State Enrolled Nurse**

Sen., sen. ABBR = **senator**; **senior**

senate ['sɛnɪt] N sénat *m*; (*US*): **the S~** le Sénat

> Le **Senate** est la chambre haute du *Congress*, le parlement des États-Unis. Il est composé de cent sénateurs, deux par État, élus au suffrage universel direct tous les six ans, un tiers d'entre eux étant renouvelé tous les deux ans.

senator ['sɛnɪtə^r] N sénateur *m*

★**send** [sɛnd] (*pt, pp* **sent** [sɛnt]) VT envoyer; **to ~ by post** *or* (*US*) **mail** envoyer *or* expédier par la poste; **to ~ sb for sth** envoyer qn chercher qch; **to ~ word that ...** faire dire que ...; **she sends (you) her love** elle vous adresse ses amitiés; **to ~ sb to Coventry** (*BRIT*) mettre qn en quarantaine; **to ~ sb to sleep** endormir qn; **to ~ sb into fits of laughter** faire rire qn aux éclats; **to ~ sth flying** envoyer valser qch

▸ **send away** [sɛnd ə'weɪ] VT (*letter, goods*) envoyer, expédier

▸ **send away for** [sɛnd ə'weɪ fɔː^r] VT FUS commander par correspondance, se faire envoyer

▸ **send back** [sɛnd bæk] VT renvoyer

▸ **send for** [sɛnd fɔː^r] VT FUS envoyer chercher; faire venir; (*by post*) se faire envoyer, commander par correspondance

▸ **send in** [sɛnd ɪn] VT (*report, application, resignation*) remettre

▸ **send off** [sɛnd ɔf] VT (*goods*) envoyer, expédier; (*BRIT Sport: player*) expulser *or* renvoyer du terrain

▸ **send off for** [sɛnd ɔf fɔː^r] VT FUS (*information, brochure*) se faire envoyer; (*product*) commander par correspondance

▸ **send on** [sɛnd ɔn] VT (*BRIT: letter*) faire suivre; (*luggage etc: in advance*) (faire) expédier à l'avance

▸ **send out** [sɛnd aut] VT (*invitation*) envoyer (par la poste); (*emit: light, heat, signal*) émettre

▸ **send out for** [sɛnd aut fɔː^r] VT FUS (*pizza*) commander par téléphone

▸ **send round** [sɛnd raund] VT (*letter, document etc*) faire circuler

▸ **send up** [sɛnd ʌp] VT (*person, price*) faire monter; (*BRIT: parody*) mettre en boîte, parodier

sender ['sɛndə^r] N expéditeur(-trice)

send-off ['sɛndɔf] N: **a good ~** des adieux chaleureux

Senegal [sɛnɪ'gɔːl] N Sénégal *m*

Senegalese [sɛnɪgə'liːz] ADJ sénégalais(e) ▸ N (*pl inv*) Sénégalais(e)

senile ['siːnaɪl] ADJ sénile

senility [sɪ'nɪlɪtɪ] N sénilité *f*

★**senior** ['siːnɪə^r] ADJ (*older*) aîné(e), plus âgé(e); (*high-ranking*) de haut niveau; (*of higher rank*): **to be ~ to sb** être le supérieur de qn ▸ N (*older*): **she is 15 years his ~** elle est son aînée de 15 ans, elle est plus âgée que lui de 15 ans; (*in service*) personne *f* qui a plus d'ancienneté; **P. Jones ~** P. Jones père

senior citizen N personne *f* du troisième âge

senior high school N (*US*) ≈ lycée *m*

seniority [siːnɪ'ɔrɪtɪ] N priorité *f* d'âge, ancienneté *f*; (*in rank*) supériorité *f* (hiérarchique)

sensation [sɛn'seɪʃən] N sensation *f*; **to create a ~** faire sensation

sensational [sɛn'seɪʃənl] ADJ qui fait sensation; (*marvellous*) sensationnel(le)

sensationalism [sɛn'seɪʃənlɪzəm] N sensationnalisme *m*

sensationalist [sɛn'seɪʃənlɪst] ADJ sensationnaliste

★**sense** [sɛns] N sens *m*; (*feeling*) sentiment *m*; (*meaning*) sens, signification *f*; (*wisdom*) bon sens; **it makes ~** c'est logique; **there is no ~ in (doing) that** cela n'a pas de sens ▸ VT sentir, pressentir
■ **senses** NPL raison *f*; **to come to one's senses** (*regain consciousness*) reprendre conscience; (*become*

reasonable) revenir à la raison; **to take leave of one's senses** perdre la tête

senseless ['sɛnslɪs] ADJ insensé(e), stupide; (*unconscious*) sans connaissance

sense of humour, (US) **sense of humor** N sens *m* de l'humour

sensibility [sɛnsɪ'bɪlɪtɪ] N sensibilité *f* ■ **sensibilities** NPL susceptibilité *f*

★**sensible** ['sɛnsɪbl] ADJ sensé(e), raisonnable; (*shoes etc*) pratique

> Le mot anglais **sensible** ne veut pas dire *sensible*.

★**sensitive** ['sɛnsɪtɪv] ADJ: ~ **(to)** sensible (à); **he is very ~ about it** c'est un point très sensible (chez lui)

sensitivity [sɛnsɪ'tɪvɪtɪ] N sensibilité *f*

sensitize ['sɛnsɪtaɪz] VT sensibiliser; **to ~ sb to sth** sensibiliser qn à qch; **to be sensitized (to sth)** être sensibilisé(e) (à qch)

sensor ['sɛnsə^r] N senseur *m*

sensory ['sɛnsərɪ] ADJ sensoriel(le)

sensual ['sɛnsjuəl] ADJ sensuel(le)

sensuous ['sɛnsjuəs] ADJ voluptueux(-euse), sensuel(le)

sent [sɛnt] PT, PP *of* **send**

★**sentence** ['sɛntns] N (*Ling*) phrase *f*; (*Law: judgment*) condamnation *f*, sentence *f*; (: *punishment*) peine *f*; **to pass ~ on sb** prononcer une peine contre qn ▶ VT: **to ~ sb to death/to 5 years** condamner qn à mort/à 5 ans

sentient ['sɛntɪənt] ADJ doué(e) de sens

sentiment ['sɛntɪmənt] N sentiment *m*; (*opinion*) opinion *f*, avis *m*

sentimental [sɛntɪ'mɛntl] ADJ sentimental(e)

sentimentality [sɛntɪmɛn'tælɪtɪ] N sentimentalité *f*, sensiblerie *f*

sentry ['sɛntrɪ] N sentinelle *f*, factionnaire *m*

sentry duty N: **to be on ~** être de faction

Seoul [səul] N Séoul

separable ['sɛprəbl] ADJ séparable

★**separate** ADJ ['sɛprɪt] séparé(e); (*organization*) indépendant(e); (*day, occasion, issue*) différent(e); **~ from** distinct(e) de; **under ~ cover** (*Comm*) sous pli séparé ▶ VT ['sɛpəreɪt] séparer; (*distinguish*) distinguer; **to ~ into** diviser en ▶ VI ['sɛpəreɪt] se séparer

separately ['sɛprɪtlɪ] ADV séparément

separates ['sɛprɪts] NPL (*clothes*) coordonnés *mpl*

separation [sɛpə'reɪʃən] N séparation *f*

separatism ['sɛprɪtɪzəm] N séparatisme *m*

separatist ['sɛprɪtɪst] ADJ, N séparatiste *mf*

sepia ['siːpɪə] ADJ sépia *inv*

Sept. ABBR (= *September*) sept

★**September** [sɛp'tɛmbə^r] N septembre *m*; *see also* **July**

septic ['sɛptɪk] ADJ septique; (*wound*) infecté(e); **to go ~** s'infecter

septicaemia [sɛptɪ'siːmɪə] N septicémie *f*

septic tank N fosse *f* septique

septuagenarian [sɛptʃuədʒɪ'nɛərɪən] ADJ, N septuagénaire *mf*

sequel ['siːkwl] N conséquence *f*; séquelles *fpl*; (*of story*) suite *f*

sequence ['siːkwəns] N ordre *m*, suite *f*; (*in film*) séquence *f*; (*dance*) numéro *m*; **in ~** par ordre, dans l'ordre, les uns après les autres; **~ of tenses** concordance *f* des temps

sequencing ['siːkwənsɪŋ] N séquençage *m*

sequential [sɪ'kwɛnʃəl] ADJ: **~ access** (*Comput*) accès séquentiel

sequin ['siːkwɪn] N sequin *m*

sequinned, sequined ['siːkwɪnd] ADJ à sequins

Serb [səːb] ADJ serbe ▶ N Serbe *mf*

Serbia ['səːbɪə] N Serbie *f*

Serbian ['səːbɪən] ADJ serbe ▶ N Serbe *mf*; (*Ling*) serbe *m*

Serbo-Croat ['səːbəu'krəuæt] N (*Ling*) serbo-croate *m*

serenade [sɛrə'neɪd] N sérénade *f* ▶ VT donner une sérénade à

serendipitous [sɛrən'dɪpɪtəs] ADJ (*discovery, event*) inespéré(e)

serendipity [sɛrən'dɪpɪtɪ] N heureux hasard *m*

serene [sɪ'riːn] ADJ serein(e), calme, paisible

serenely [sɪ'riːnlɪ] ADV (*say, smile*) sereinement

serenity [sə'rɛnɪtɪ] N sérénité *f*, calme *m*

sergeant ['sɑːdʒənt] N sergent *m*; (*Police*) brigadier *m*

sergeant major N sergent-major *m*

serial ['sɪərɪəl] N feuilleton *m* ▶ ADJ (*Comput: interface, printer*) série *inv*; (: *access*) séquentiel(le)

serialize ['sɪərɪəlaɪz] VT publier (*or* adapter) en feuilleton

serial killer N meurtrier *m* tuant en série

serial number N numéro *m* de série

★**series** ['sɪərɪz] N série *f*; (*Publishing*) collection *f*

★**serious** ['sɪərɪəs] ADJ sérieux(-euse); (*accident etc*) grave; **are you ~ (about it)?** parlez-vous sérieusement?

★**seriously** ['sɪərɪəslɪ] ADV sérieusement; (*hurt*) gravement; **~ rich/difficult** (*inf: extremely*) drôlement riche/difficile; **to take sth/sb ~** prendre qch/qn au sérieux

seriousness ['sɪərɪəsnɪs] N sérieux *m*, gravité *f*

sermon ['səːmən] N sermon *m*

serotonin [sɛrə'təunɪn] N sérotonine *f*

serpent ['səːpənt] N serpent *m*

serrated [sɪ'reɪtɪd] ADJ en dents de scie

serum ['sɪərəm] N sérum *m*

servant ['səːvənt] N domestique *mf*; (*fig*) serviteur (servante)

★**serve** [səːv] VT (*employer etc*) servir, être au service de; (*purpose*) servir à; (*customer, food, meal*) servir; (*subj: train*) desservir; (*apprenticeship*) faire, accomplir; (*prison term*) faire; purger; **are you being served?** est-ce qu'on s'occupe de vous?; **it serves him right** c'est bien fait pour lui; **it serves my purpose** cela fait mon affaire ▶ VI (*Tennis*) servir; (*be useful*): **to ~ as/for/to do** servir de/à/à faire; **to ~ on a committee/jury** faire partie d'un comité/jury ▶ N (*Tennis*) service *m*
▶ **serve out, serve up** VT (*food*) servir

server ['səːvə^r] N (*Comput*) serveur *m*

S

★service ['sə:vɪs] N (gen) service m; (Aut) révision f; (Rel) office m; **to be of ~ to sb, to do sb a ~** rendre service à qn; **~ included/not included** service compris/non compris; **to put one's car in for ~** donner sa voiture à réviser; **dinner ~** service de table ▶ VT (car etc) réviser ■ **services** NPL (Econ: tertiary sector) (secteur m) tertiaire m, secteur des services; (BRIT: on motorway) station-service f; (Mil): **the Services** npl les forces armées

serviceable ['sə:vɪsəbl] ADJ pratique, commode

service area N (on motorway) aire f de services

service charge N (BRIT) service m

service industries NPL les industries fpl de service, les services mpl

serviceman ['sə:vɪsmən] N (irreg) militaire m

service station N station-service f

servicewoman ['sə:vɪswʊmən] N (irreg) militaire f

serviette [sə:vɪ'ɛt] N (BRIT) serviette f (de table)

servile ['sə:vaɪl] ADJ servile

servitude ['sə:vɪtju:d] N servitude f

sesame ['sɛsəmɪ] N sésame m ▶ CPD (seed, oil) de sésame; (cracker, biscuit) au sésame

session ['sɛʃən] N (sitting) séance f; (Scol) année f scolaire (or universitaire); **to be in ~** siéger, être en session or en séance

session musician N musicien(ne) de studio

★set [sɛt] (pt, pp ~) N série f, assortiment m; (of tools etc) jeu m; (Radio, TV) poste m; (Tennis) set m; (group of people) cercle m, milieu m; (Cine) plateau m; (Theat: stage) scène f; (: scenery) décor m; (Math) ensemble m; (Hairdressing) mise f en plis; **a ~ of false teeth** un dentier; **a ~ of dining-room furniture** une salle à manger ▶ ADJ (fixed) fixe, déterminé(e); (ready) prêt(e); **to be ~ on doing** être résolu(e) à faire; **to be all ~ to do** être (fin) prêt(e) pour faire; **to be (dead) ~ against** être (totalement) opposé à; **he's ~ in his ways** il n'est pas très souple, il tient à ses habitudes; **a ~ phrase** une expression toute faite, une locution ▶ VT (place) mettre, poser, placer; (fix, establish) fixer; (: record) établir; (assign: task, homework) donner; (exam) composer; (adjust) régler; (decide: rules etc) fixer, choisir; (Typ) composer; **to ~ to music** mettre en musique; **to ~ on fire** mettre le feu à; **to ~ free** libérer; **to ~ sth going** déclencher qch; **to ~ the alarm clock for seven o'clock** mettre le réveil à sonner à sept heures; **to ~ sail** partir, prendre la mer ▶ VI (sun) se coucher; (jam, jelly, concrete) prendre; (bone) se ressouder

▶ **set about** VT FUS (task) entreprendre, se mettre à; **to ~ about doing sth** se mettre à faire qch

▶ **set aside** VT mettre de côté; (time) garder

▶ **set back** VT (in time): **to ~ back (by)** retarder (de); (place): **a house ~ back from the road** une maison située en retrait de la route

▶ **set down** VT (subj: bus, train) déposer

▶ **set in** VI (infection, bad weather) s'installer; (complications) survenir, surgir; **the rain has ~ in for the day** c'est parti pour qu'il pleuve toute la journée

▶ **set off** VI se mettre en route, partir ▶ VT (bomb) faire exploser; (cause to start) déclencher; (show up well) mettre en valeur, faire valoir

▶ **set out** VI: **to ~ out (from)** partir (de); **to ~ out to do** entreprendre de faire; avoir pour but or

intention de faire ▶ VT (arrange) disposer; (state) présenter, exposer

▶ **set up** VT (organization) fonder, créer; (monument) ériger; **to ~ up shop** (fig) s'établir, s'installer

setback ['sɛtbæk] N (hitch) revers m, contretemps m; (in health) rechute f

set menu N menu m

set square N équerre f

settee [sɛ'ti:] N canapé m

setting ['sɛtɪŋ] N cadre m; (of jewel) monture f; (position: of controls) réglage m

setting lotion N lotion f pour mise en plis

★settle ['sɛtl] VT (argument, matter, account) régler; (problem) résoudre; (Med: calm) calmer; (colonize: land) coloniser; **that's settled then** alors, c'est d'accord !; **to ~ one's stomach** calmer des maux d'estomac ▶ VI (bird, dust etc) se poser; (sediment) se déposer; **to ~ to sth** se mettre sérieusement à qch; **to ~ for sth** accepter qch, se contenter de qch; **to ~ on sth** opter or se décider pour qch

▶ **settle down** VI (get comfortable) s'installer; (become calmer) se calmer; se ranger

▶ **settle in** VI s'installer

▶ **settle up** VI: **to ~ up with sb** régler (ce que l'on doit à) qn

settlement ['sɛtlmənt] N (payment) règlement m; (agreement) accord m; (colony) colonie f; (village etc) village m, hameau m; **in ~ of our account** (Comm) en règlement de notre compte

settler ['sɛtlə'] N colon m

setup ['sɛtʌp] N (arrangement) manière f dont les choses sont organisées; (situation) situation f, allure f des choses

★seven ['sɛvn] NUM sept

★seventeen [sɛvn'ti:n] NUM dix-sept

★seventeenth [sɛvn'ti:nθ] NUM dix-septième

★seventh ['sɛvnθ] NUM septième

seventieth ['sɛvntɪɪθ] NUM soixante-dixième

★seventy ['sɛvntɪ] NUM soixante-dix

sever ['sɛvə'] VT couper, trancher; (relations) rompre

★several ['sɛvərl] ADJ, PRON plusieurs pl; **~ of us** plusieurs d'entre nous; **~ times** plusieurs fois

severance ['sɛvərəns] N (of relations) rupture f

severance pay N indemnité f de licenciement

severe [sɪ'vɪə'] ADJ (stern) sévère, strict(e); (serious) grave, sérieux(-euse); (hard) rigoureux(-euse), dur(e); (plain) sévère, austère

severely [sɪ'vɪəlɪ] ADV sévèrement; (wounded, ill) gravement

severity [sɪ'vɛrɪtɪ] N sévérité f; gravité f; rigueur f

sew [səu] (pt sewed [səud], pp sewn [səun]) VT, VI coudre

▶ **sew on** [səu ɔn] VT coudre; **to ~ on a button** coudre un bouton

▶ **sew up** [səu ʌp] VT (re)coudre; **it is all sewn up** (fig) c'est dans le sac or dans la poche

sewage ['su:ɪdʒ] N vidange(s) f(pl)

sewage works N champ m d'épandage

sewer ['su:ə'] N égout m

sewerage ['su:ərɪdʒ] N tout-à-l'égout m

sewing ['səuɪŋ] N couture f; (item(s)) ouvrage m

sewing machine N machine f à coudre

sewn [səun] PP of **sew**

sex [sɛks] N sexe *m*; **to have ~ with** avoir des rapports (sexuels) avec
 ▸ **sex up** VT (*inf*) donner du piquant à

sex act N acte sexuel

sex appeal N sex-appeal *m*

sex change N (*also*: **sex change operation**) (opération *f* de) changement *m* de sexe

sex discrimination N (*also*: **sexual discrimination**) discrimination *f* sexuelle

sex education N éducation sexuelle

sexism ['sɛksɪzəm] N sexisme *m*

sexist ['sɛksɪst] ADJ sexiste

sex life N vie sexuelle

sex object N femme-objet *f*, objet sexuel

sextet [sɛks'tɛt] N sextuor *m*

sexting ['sɛkstɪŋ] N (*inf*) envoi *m* de sexto(s)

sexual ['sɛksjuəl] ADJ sexuel(le); **~ assault** attentat *m* à la pudeur; **~ harassment** harcèlement sexuel

sexual intercourse N rapports sexuels

sexuality [sɛksju'ælɪtɪ] N sexualité *f*

sexually ['sɛksjuəlɪ] ADV sexuellement

sexy ['sɛksɪ] ADJ sexy *inv*

Seychelles [seɪ'ʃɛlz] NPL: **the ~** les Seychelles *fpl*

SF N ABBR (= *science fiction*) SF *f*

SG N ABBR (*US*) = **Surgeon General**

Sgt ABBR (= *sergeant*) Sgt

shabbiness ['ʃæbɪnɪs] N aspect miteux; mesquinerie *f*

shabby ['ʃæbɪ] ADJ miteux(-euse); (*behaviour*) mesquin(e), méprisable

shack [ʃæk] N cabane *f*, hutte *f*

shackles ['ʃæklz] NPL chaînes *fpl*, entraves *fpl*

★**shade** [ʃeɪd] N ombre *f*; (*for lamp*) abat-jour *m inv*; (*of colour*) nuance *f*, ton *m*; (*US: window shade*) store *m*; (*small quantity*): **a ~ of** un soupçon de; **in the ~** à l'ombre; **a ~ smaller** un tout petit peu plus petit ▸ VT abriter du soleil, ombrager ■ **shades** NPL (*US: sunglasses*) lunettes *fpl* de soleil

shaded ['ʃeɪdɪd] ADJ (*shady*) ombragé(e); (*coloured: area*) ombré(e)

★**shadow** ['ʃædəu] N ombre *f*; **without** or **beyond a ~ of doubt** sans l'ombre d'un doute ▸ VT (*follow*) filer

shadow cabinet N (*BRIT Pol*) cabinet parallèle formé par le parti qui n'est pas au pouvoir

shadowy ['ʃædəuɪ] ADJ ombragé(e); (*dim*) vague, indistinct(e)

shady ['ʃeɪdɪ] ADJ ombragé(e); (*fig: dishonest*) louche, véreux(-euse)

shaft [ʃɑːft] N (*of arrow, spear*) hampe *f*; (*Aut, Tech*) arbre *m*; (*of mine*) puits *m*; (*of lift*) cage *f*; (*of light*) rayon *m*, trait *m*; **ventilator ~** conduit *m* d'aération or de ventilation

shaggy ['ʃægɪ] ADJ hirsute; en broussaille

★**shake** [ʃeɪk] (*pt* **shook** [ʃuk], *pp* **shaken** ['ʃeɪkn]) VT secouer; (*bottle, cocktail*) agiter; (*house, confidence*) ébranler; **to ~ one's head** (*in refusal etc*) dire or faire non de la tête; (*in dismay*) secouer la tête; **to ~ hands with sb** serrer la main à qn ▸ VI trembler ▸ N secousse *f*

 ▸ **shake off** VT secouer; (*pursuer*) se débarrasser de
 ▸ **shake up** VT secouer

shake-up ['ʃeɪkʌp] N grand remaniement

shakily ['ʃeɪkɪlɪ] ADV (*reply*) d'une voix tremblante; (*walk*) d'un pas mal assuré; (*write*) d'une main tremblante

shaky ['ʃeɪkɪ] ADJ (*hand, voice*) tremblant(e); (*building*) branlant(e), peu solide; (*memory*) chancelant(e); (*knowledge*) incertain(e)

shale [ʃeɪl] N schiste argileux

★**shall** [ʃæl] AUX VB: **I ~ go** j'irai; **~ I open the door?** j'ouvre la porte ?; **I'll get the coffee, ~ I?** je vais chercher le café, d'accord ?

shallot [ʃə'lɔt] N (*BRIT*) échalote *f*

shallow ['ʃæləu] ADJ peu profond(e); (*fig*) superficiel(le), qui manque de profondeur

sham [ʃæm] N frime *f*; (*jewellery, furniture*) imitation *f* ▸ ADJ feint(e), simulé(e) ▸ VT feindre, simuler

shaman ['ʃeɪmən] N chaman *m*

shamanism ['ʃeɪmənɪzəm] N chamanisme *m*

shambles ['ʃæmblz] N confusion *f*, pagaïe *f*, fouillis *m*; **the economy is (in) a complete ~** l'économie est dans la confusion la plus totale

shambolic [ʃæm'bɔlɪk] ADJ (*inf*) bordélique (*inf*)

★**shame** [ʃeɪm] N honte *f*; **it is a ~ (that/to do)** c'est dommage (que + *sub*/de faire); **what a ~!** quel dommage !; **to put sb/sth to ~** (*fig*) faire honte à qn/qch ▸ VT faire honte à

shamefaced ['ʃeɪmfeɪst] ADJ honteux(-euse), penaud(e)

shameful ['ʃeɪmful] ADJ honteux(-euse), scandaleux(-euse)

shamefully ['ʃeɪmfulɪ] ADV honteusement

shameless ['ʃeɪmlɪs] ADJ éhonté(e), effronté(e); (*immodest*) impudique

shamelessly ['ʃeɪmlɪslɪ] ADV (*lie, cheat*) sans vergogne; (*immodestly*) sans pudeur

★**shampoo** [ʃæm'puː] N shampo(o)ing *m*; **~ and set** shampo(o)ing et mise *f* en plis ▸ VT faire un shampo(o)ing à

shamrock ['ʃæmrɔk] N trèfle *m* (*emblème national de l'Irlande*)

shandy ['ʃændɪ] N bière panachée

shan't [ʃɑːnt] = **shall not**

shanty ['ʃæntɪ] N (*hut*) baraque *f*; (*song*) chanson *f* de marins

shantytown ['ʃæntɪtaun] N bidonville *m*

SHAPE [ʃeɪp] N ABBR (= *Supreme Headquarters Allied Powers, Europe*) quartier général des forces alliées en Europe

★**shape** [ʃeɪp] N forme *f*; **to take ~** prendre forme or tournure; **in the ~ of a heart** en forme de cœur; **I can't bear gardening in any ~ or form** je déteste le jardinage sous quelque forme que ce soit; **to get o.s. into ~** (re)trouver la forme ▸ VT façonner, modeler; (*clay, stone*) donner forme à; (*statement*) formuler; (*sb's ideas, character*) former; (*sb's life*) déterminer; (*course of events*) influer sur le cours de ▸ VI (*also*: **shape up**: *events*) prendre tournure; (*: person*) faire des progrès, s'en sortir

shaped [ʃeɪpt] ADJ: **oddly ~** à la forme étrange; **~ like sth** en forme de qch

-shaped [ʃeɪpt] SUFFIX: **heart-shaped** en forme de cœur

shapeless [ˈʃeɪplɪs] ADJ informe, sans forme

shapely [ˈʃeɪplɪ] ADJ bien proportionné(e), beau (belle)

shard [ʃɑːd] N (of glass, metal) éclat m; (of pottery) tesson m

★**share** [ʃɛəʳ] N (thing received, contribution) part f; (Comm) action f ▸ VT partager; (have in common) avoir en commun; **to ~ out (among** or **between)** partager (entre) ▸ VI partager; **to ~ in** (joy, sorrow) prendre part à; (profits) participer à, avoir part à; (work) partager

share capital N capital social

share certificate N certificat m or titre m d'action

shareholder [ˈʃɛəhəʊldəʳ] N actionnaire mf

shareholding [ˈʃɛəhəʊldɪŋ] N participation f; **to have a ~ in** sth détenir une participation dans qch

share index N indice m de la Bourse

shareware [ˈʃɛəwɛəʳ] N (Comput) partagiciel m

sharia [ʃəˈriːə] N charia f ▸ CPD (law, court) de la charia

shark [ʃɑːk] N requin m

★**sharp** [ʃɑːp] ADJ (razor, knife) tranchant(e), bien aiguisé(e); (point, voice) aigu(ë); (nose, chin) pointu(e); (outline, increase) net(te); (curve, bend) brusque; (cold, pain) vif (vive); (taste) piquant(e), âcre; (Mus) dièse; (person: quick-witted) vif (vive), éveillé(e); (: unscrupulous) malhonnête; **to be ~ with** sb être brusque avec qn; **look ~!** dépêche-toi! ▸ N (Mus) dièse m ▸ ADV: **at 2 o'clock ~** à 2 heures pile or tapantes; **turn ~ left** tournez immédiatement à gauche

sharpen [ˈʃɑːpn] VT aiguiser; (pencil) tailler; (fig) aviver

sharpener [ˈʃɑːpnəʳ] N (also: **pencil sharpener**) taille-crayon(s) m inv; (also: **knife sharpener**) aiguisoir m

sharp-eyed [ʃɑːpˈaɪd] ADJ à qui rien n'échappe

sharpish [ˈʃɑːpɪʃ] ADV (BRIT inf: quickly) en vitesse

sharply [ˈʃɑːplɪ] ADV (turn, stop) brusquement; (stand out) nettement; (criticize, retort) sèchement, vertement

sharpshooter [ˈʃɑːpʃuːtəʳ] N tireur(-euse) d'élite

sharp-tempered [ʃɑːpˈtempəd] ADJ prompt(e) à se mettre en colère

sharp-witted [ʃɑːpˈwɪtɪd] ADJ à l'esprit vif, malin(-igne)

shatter [ˈʃætəʳ] VT fracasser, briser, faire voler en éclats; (fig: upset) bouleverser; (: ruin) briser, ruiner ▸ VI voler en éclats, se briser, se fracasser

shattered [ˈʃætəd] ADJ (devastated) bouleversé(e); (inf: exhausted) crevé(e) (inf)

shattering [ˈʃætərɪŋ] ADJ (devastating: experience) bouleversant(e); (: blow) terrible; (BRIT inf: exhausting: day, journey) crevant(e) (inf) ▸ N: **I heard the ~ of glass** j'ai entendu un bruit de verre brisé

shatterproof [ˈʃætəpruːf] ADJ incassable

shave [ʃeɪv] VT raser ▸ VI se raser ▸ N: **to have a ~** se raser
▸ **shave off** VT (beard, hair) raser; (wood) raboter; (cut): **to ~ a few seconds off the record** battre le record de quelques secondes

shaven [ˈʃeɪvn] ADJ (head) rasé(e)

shaver [ˈʃeɪvəʳ] N (also: **electric shaver**) rasoir m électrique

shaving [ˈʃeɪvɪŋ] N (action) rasage m

shaving brush N blaireau m

shaving cream N crème f à raser

shaving foam N mousse f à raser

shavings [ˈʃeɪvɪŋz] NPL (of wood etc) copeaux mpl

shaving soap N savon m à barbe

shawl [ʃɔːl] N châle m

★**she** [ʃiː] PRON elle; **there ~ is** la voilà; **she-elephant** etc éléphant m etc femelle

sheaf [ʃiːf] (pl **sheaves** [ʃiːvz]) N gerbe f

shear [ʃɪəʳ] (pt **sheared** [ʃɪəd], pp **sheared** or **shorn** [ʃɔːn]) VT (sheep) tondre
▸ **shear off** VT tondre; (branch) élaguer

shears [ˈʃɪəz] NPL (for hedge) cisaille(s) f(pl)

sheath [ʃiːθ] N gaine f, fourreau m, étui m; (contraceptive) préservatif m

sheathe [ʃiːð] VT gainer; (sword) rengainer

sheath knife N couteau m à gaine

sheaves [ʃiːvz] NPL of **sheaf**

★**shed** [ʃed] (pt, pp ~) N remise f, resserre f; (Industry, Rail) hangar m ▸ VT (leaves, fur etc) perdre; (tears) verser, répandre; (workers) congédier; **to ~ light on** (problem, mystery) faire la lumière sur

she'd [ʃiːd] = **she had**; **she would**

sheen [ʃiːn] N lustre m

★**sheep** [ʃiːp] N (pl inv) mouton m

sheepdog [ˈʃiːpdɔg] N chien m de berger

sheep farmer N éleveur m de moutons

sheepish [ˈʃiːpɪʃ] ADJ penaud(e), timide

sheepskin [ˈʃiːpskɪn] N peau f de mouton

sheepskin jacket N canadienne f

sheer [ʃɪəʳ] ADJ (utter) pur(e), pur et simple; (steep) à pic, abrupt(e); (almost transparent) extrêmement fin(e); **by ~ chance** par pur hasard ▸ ADV à pic, abruptement

★**sheet** [ʃiːt] N (on bed) drap m; (of paper) feuille f; (of glass, metal etc) feuille, plaque f

sheet feed N (on printer) alimentation f en papier (feuille à feuille)

sheet lightning N éclair m en nappe(s)

sheet metal N tôle f

sheet music N partition(s) f(pl)

sheik, sheikh [ʃeɪk] N cheik m

shelf [ʃelf] (pl **shelves** [ʃelvz]) N étagère f, rayon m; **set of shelves** rayonnage m

shelf life N (Comm) durée f de conservation (avant la vente)

★**shell** [ʃel] N (on beach) coquillage m; (of egg, nut etc) coquille f; (explosive) obus m; (of building) carcasse f ▸ VT (crab, prawn etc) décortiquer; (peas) écosser; (Mil) bombarder (d'obus)
▸ **shell out** VI (inf): **to ~ out (for)** casquer (pour) (inf)

she'll [ʃiːl] = **she will**; **she shall**

shellfire [ˈʃelfaɪəʳ] N tirs mpl d'obus; **to come under ~** être soumis(e) à des tirs d'obus

shellfish [ˈʃelfɪʃ] N (pl inv: crab etc) crustacé m; (: scallop etc) coquillage m ▸ NPL (as food) fruits mpl de mer

shelling ['ʃelɪŋ] N (Mil) tirs mpl d'obus

shell-shocked ['ʃelʃɔkt] ADJ (soldier) atteint(e) de psychose traumatique; (inf: stunned) sous le choc

shell suit N survêtement m

★**shelter** ['ʃeltə^r] N abri m, refuge m; **to take ~ (from)** s'abriter (de) ▶ VT abriter, protéger; (give lodging to) donner asile à ▶ VI s'abriter, se mettre à l'abri

sheltered ['ʃeltəd] ADJ (life) retiré(e), à l'abri des soucis; (spot) abrité(e)

sheltered housing N foyers mpl (pour personnes âgées ou handicapées)

shelve [ʃelv] VT (fig) mettre en suspens or en sommeil

shelves ['ʃelvz] NPL of **shelf**

shelving ['ʃelvɪŋ] N (shelves) rayonnage(s) m(pl)

shenanigans [ʃɪ'nænɪgənz] NPL (inf) combines fpl (inf)

shepherd ['ʃepəd] N berger m ▶ VT (guide) guider, escorter

shepherdess ['ʃepədɪs] N bergère f

shepherd's pie ['ʃepədz-] N ≈ hachis m Parmentier

sherbet ['ʃə:bət] N (Brit: powder) poudre acidulée; (US: water ice) sorbet m

sheriff ['ʃerɪf] (US) N shérif m

sherry ['ʃeri] N xérès m, sherry m

she's [ʃi:z] = **she is**; **she has**

Shetland ['ʃetlənd] N (also: **the Shetland Isles** or **Islands**) les îles fpl Shetland

Shetland pony N poney m des îles Shetland

shield [ʃi:ld] N bouclier m; (protection) écran m de protection ▶ VT: **to ~ (from)** protéger (de or contre)

shift [ʃɪft] N (change) changement m; (work period) période f de travail; (of workers) équipe f, poste m; **a ~ in demand** (Comm) un déplacement de la demande ▶ VT déplacer, changer de place; (remove) enlever ▶ VI changer de place, bouger; **the wind has shifted to the south** le vent a tourné au sud

shift key N (on keyboard) touche f de majuscule

shiftless ['ʃɪftlɪs] ADJ fainéant(e)

shift work N travail m par roulement; **to do ~** travailler par roulement

shifty ['ʃɪftɪ] ADJ sournois(e); (eyes) fuyant(e)

Shiite ['ʃi:aɪt] N Chiite mf ▶ ADJ chiite

shilling ['ʃɪlɪŋ] N (Brit Hist) shilling m

shilly-shally ['ʃɪlɪʃælɪ] VI tergiverser, atermoyer

shimmer ['ʃɪmə^r] N miroitement m, chatoiement m ▶ VI miroiter, chatoyer

shin [ʃɪn] N tibia m ▶ VI: **to ~ up/down a tree** grimper dans un/descendre d'un arbre

shindig ['ʃɪndɪg] N (inf) bamboula f (inf)

shine [ʃaɪn] (pt, pp shone [ʃɔn]) N éclat m, brillant m ▶ VI briller ▶ VT (pt, pp shined) (polish) faire briller or reluire; **to ~ sth on sth** (torch) braquer qch sur qch

shingle ['ʃɪŋgl] N (on beach) galets mpl; (on roof) bardeau m

shingles ['ʃɪŋglz] N (Med) zona m

shining ['ʃaɪnɪŋ] ADJ brillant(e)

Shinto ['ʃɪntəu] N shintoïsme m

shiny ['ʃaɪnɪ] ADJ brillant(e)

★**ship** [ʃɪp] N bateau m; (large) navire m; **on board ~** à bord ▶ VT transporter (par mer); (send) expédier (par mer); (load) charger, embarquer
  ▶ **ship off** VT (inf: send away) expédier (inf)
  ▶ **ship out** VT (send) expédier; (: by sea) expédier par bateau

shipbuilder ['ʃɪpbɪldə^r] N constructeur m de navires

shipbuilding ['ʃɪpbɪldɪŋ] N construction navale

ship chandler [-'tʃɑ:ndlə^r] N fournisseur m maritime, shipchandler m

shipment ['ʃɪpmənt] N cargaison f

shipowner ['ʃɪpəunə^r] N armateur m

shipper ['ʃɪpə^r] N affréteur m, expéditeur m

shipping ['ʃɪpɪŋ] N (ships) navires mpl; (traffic) navigation f; (the industry) industrie navale; (transport) transport m

shipping agent N agent m maritime

shipping company N compagnie f de navigation

shipping lane N couloir m de navigation

shipping line N = **shipping company**

shipshape ['ʃɪpʃeɪp] ADJ en ordre impeccable

shipwreck ['ʃɪprek] N épave f; (event) naufrage m ▶ VT: **to be shipwrecked** faire naufrage

shipyard ['ʃɪpjɑ:d] N chantier naval

shire ['ʃaɪə^r] N (Brit) comté m

shirk [ʃə:k] VT esquiver, se dérober à

★**shirt** [ʃə:t] N chemise f; (woman's) chemisier m; **in ~ sleeves** en bras de chemise

shirty ['ʃə:tɪ] ADJ (Brit inf) de mauvais poil

shit [ʃɪt] EXCL (inf!) merde (!)

shitless ['ʃɪtlɪs] ADV (inf!): **to be bored ~** s'emmerder comme un rat mort (inf); **to be scared ~** avoir une peur bleue (inf)

shiver ['ʃɪvə^r] N frisson m ▶ VI frissonner

shoal [ʃəul] N (of fish) banc m

★**shock** [ʃɔk] N (impact) choc m, heurt m; (Elec) secousse f, décharge f; (emotional) choc m; (Med) commotion f, choc m; **it gave us a ~** ça nous a fait un choc; **it came as a ~ to hear that ...** nous avons appris avec stupeur que ...; **suffering from ~** (Med) commotionné(e) ▶ VT (scandalize) choquer, scandaliser; (upset) bouleverser

shock absorber [-əbzɔ:bə^r] N amortisseur m

shocked [ʃɔkt] ADJ (scandalized) choqué(e); (upset) bouleversé(e)

shocker ['ʃɔkə^r] N (inf): **the news was a real ~ to him** il a vraiment été choqué par cette nouvelle

shocking ['ʃɔkɪŋ] ADJ (outrageous) choquant(e), scandaleux(-euse); (awful) épouvantable

shockingly ['ʃɔkɪŋlɪ] ADV (terribly: bad, expensive) affreusement; (as sentence adverb): **~, ...,** ce qui est un véritable scandale

shockproof ['ʃɔkpru:f] ADJ anti-choc inv

shock therapy, shock treatment N (Med) (traitement m par) électrochoc(s) m(pl)

shock wave N (also fig) onde f de choc

shod [ʃɔd] PT, PP of **shoe**; **well-shod** bien chaussé(e)

S

shoddy ['ʃɔdɪ] ADJ de mauvaise qualité, mal fait(e)

★**shoe** [ʃuː] (pt, pp **shod** [ʃɔd]) N chaussure f, soulier m; (also: **horseshoe**) fer m à cheval; (also: **brake shoe**) mâchoire f de frein ▶ VT (horse) ferrer

shoebrush ['ʃuːbrʌʃ] N brosse f à chaussures

shoehorn ['ʃuːhɔːn] N chausse-pied m

shoelace ['ʃuːleɪs] N lacet m (de soulier)

shoemaker ['ʃuːmeɪkəʳ] N cordonnier m, fabricant m de chaussures

shoe polish N cirage m

shoeshop ['ʃuːʃɔp] N magasin m de chaussures

shoestring ['ʃuːstrɪŋ] N: **on a ~** (fig) avec un budget dérisoire; avec des moyens très restreints

shoetree ['ʃuːtriː] N embauchoir m

shone [ʃɔn] PT, PP of **shine**

shonky ['ʃɔŋkɪ] ADJ (AUSTRALIA, NEW ZEALAND inf: untrustworthy) louche (inf)

shoo [ʃuː] EXCL allez, ouste ! ▶ VT (also: **shoo away**, **shoo off**) chasser

shook [ʃuk] PT of **shake**

★**shoot** [ʃuːt] (pt, pp **shot** [ʃɔt]) N (on branch, seedling) pousse f; (shooting party) partie f de chasse ▶ VT (game: hunt) chasser; (: aim at) tirer; (: kill) abattre; (person) blesser/tuer d'un coup de fusil (or de revolver); (execute) fusiller; (arrow) tirer; (gun) tirer un coup de; (Cine) tourner ▶ VI (with gun, bow): **to ~ (at)** tirer (sur); (Football) shooter, tirer; **to ~ past sb** passer en flèche devant qn; **to ~ in/out** entrer/sortir comme une flèche
▶ **shoot down** [ʃuːt daun] VT (plane) abattre
▶ **shoot up** [ʃuːt ʌp] VI (fig: prices etc) monter en flèche

shooting ['ʃuːtɪŋ] N (shots) coups mpl de feu; (attack) fusillade f; (murder) homicide m (à l'aide d'une arme à feu); (Hunting) chasse f; (Cine) tournage m

shooting range N stand m de tir

shooting star N étoile filante

★**shop** [ʃɔp] N magasin m; (workshop) atelier m; **repair ~** atelier de réparations; **to talk ~** (fig) parler boutique ▶ VI (also: **go shopping**) faire ses courses or ses achats
▶ **shop around** VI faire le tour des magasins (pour comparer les prix); (fig) se renseigner avant de choisir or décider

shopaholic [ʃɔpə'hɔlɪk] N (inf) personne qui achète sans pouvoir s'arrêter

★**shop assistant** N (BRIT) vendeur(-euse)

shop floor N (BRIT fig) ouvriers mpl

★**shopkeeper** ['ʃɔpkiːpəʳ] N marchand(e), commerçant(e)

shoplift ['ʃɔplɪft] VI voler à l'étalage

shoplifter ['ʃɔplɪftəʳ] N voleur(-euse) à l'étalage

shoplifting ['ʃɔplɪftɪŋ] N vol m à l'étalage

shopper ['ʃɔpəʳ] N personne f qui fait ses courses, acheteur(-euse)

★**shopping** ['ʃɔpɪŋ] N (goods) achats mpl, provisions fpl

shopping bag N sac m (à provisions)

shopping cart N (US) chariot m, Caddie® m; (Internet) panier m (d'achats)

shopping centre, (US) **shopping center** N centre commercial

shopping mall N centre commercial

shopping trolley N (BRIT) Caddie® m

shop-soiled ['ʃɔpsɔɪld] ADJ défraîchi(e), qui a fait la vitrine

shop window N vitrine f

shore [ʃɔːʳ] N (of sea, lake) rivage m, rive f; **on ~** à terre ▶ VT: **to ~ (up)** étayer

shore leave N (Naut) permission f à terre

shoreline ['ʃɔːlaɪn] N (of sea) littoral m; (of lake) rive f

shorn [ʃɔːn] PP of **shear** ▶ ADJ: **~ of** dépouillé(e) de

★**short** [ʃɔːt] ADJ (not long) court(e); (soon finished) court, bref (brève); (person, step) petit(e); (curt) brusque, sec (sèche); (insufficient) insuffisant(e); **to be ~ of sth** être à court de or manquer de qch; **I'm three ~** il m'en manque trois; **to be in ~ supply** manquer, être difficile à trouver; **it is ~ for** c'est l'abréviation or le diminutif de; **a ~ time ago** il y a peu de temps; **in the ~ term** à court terme ▶ ADV: **~ of doing** à moins de faire; **everything ~ of** tout sauf; **to cut ~** (speech, visit) abréger, écourter; (person) couper la parole à; **to fall ~ of** ne pas être à la hauteur de; **to run ~ of** arriver à court de, venir à manquer de; **to stop ~** s'arrêter net; **to stop ~ of** ne pas aller jusqu'à ▶ N (also: **short film**) court métrage m; (Elec) court-circuit m; **in ~** bref; en bref

shortage ['ʃɔːtɪdʒ] N manque m, pénurie f

shortbread ['ʃɔːtbrɛd] N ≈ sablé m

short-change [ʃɔːt'tʃeɪndʒ] VT: **to ~ sb** ne pas rendre assez à qn

short-circuit [ʃɔːt'səːkɪt] N court-circuit m ▶ VT court-circuiter ▶ VI se mettre en court-circuit

shortcoming ['ʃɔːtkʌmɪŋ] N défaut m

shortcrust pastry ['ʃɔːtkrʌst--], (US) **short pastry** N pâte brisée

shortcut ['ʃɔːtkʌt] N raccourci m

shorten ['ʃɔːtn] VT raccourcir; (text, visit) abréger

shortening ['ʃɔːtnɪŋ] N (Culin) matière grasse

shortfall ['ʃɔːtfɔːl] N déficit m

shorthand ['ʃɔːthænd] N (BRIT) sténo(graphie) f; **to take sth down in ~** prendre qch en sténo

shorthand notebook N bloc m sténo

shorthand typist N (BRIT) sténodactylo mf

shortlist ['ʃɔːtlɪst] N (BRIT: for job) liste f des candidats sélectionnés

short-lived ['ʃɔːt'lɪvd] ADJ de courte durée

★**shortly** ['ʃɔːtlɪ] ADV bientôt, sous peu

short message service N SMS m

shortness ['ʃɔːtnɪs] N brièveté f

short notice N: **at ~** au dernier moment

short pastry N (US) = **shortcrust pastry**

shorts [ʃɔːts] NPL: **(a pair of) ~** un short

short-sighted [ʃɔːt'saɪtɪd] ADJ (BRIT) myope; (fig) qui manque de clairvoyance

short-sleeved [ʃɔːt'sliːvd] ADJ à manches courtes

short-staffed [ʃɔːt'stɑːft] ADJ à court de personnel

short-stay [ʃɔːt'steɪ] ADJ (car park) de courte durée

short story N nouvelle f

short-tempered [ˈʃɔːtˈtɛmpəd] ADJ qui s'emporte facilement

short-term [ˈʃɔːttəːm] ADJ (effect) à court terme

short time N: **to work ~**, **to be on ~** (Industry) être en chômage partiel, travailler à horaire réduit

short wave N (Radio) ondes courtes

★**shot** [ʃɔt] PT, PP of **shoot** ▶ N coup m (de feu); (shotgun pellets) plombs mpl; (try) coup, essai m; (injection) piqûre f; (Phot) photo f; **to be a good/poor ~** (person) tirer bien/mal; **to fire a ~ at sb/sth** tirer sur qn/qch; **to have a ~ at (doing) sth** essayer de faire qch; **like a ~** comme une flèche; (very readily) sans hésiter; **a big ~** (inf) un gros bonnet (inf) ▶ ADJ (inf): **to get ~ of sb/sth** se débarrasser de qn/qch

shotgun [ˈʃɔtɡʌn] N fusil m de chasse

★**should** [ʃʊd] AUX VB: **I ~ go now** je devrais partir maintenant; **he ~ be there now** il devrait être arrivé maintenant; **I ~ like to** volontiers, j'aimerais bien; **~ he phone …** si jamais il téléphone …

★**shoulder** [ˈʃəʊldəʳ] N épaule f; (BRIT: of road) **hard ~** accotement m; **to look over one's ~** regarder derrière soi (en tournant la tête); **to rub shoulders with sb** (fig) côtoyer qn; **to give sb the cold ~** (fig) battre froid à qn ▶ VT: **to ~** endosser, se charger de

shoulder bag N sac m à bandoulière

shoulder blade N omoplate f

shoulder strap N bretelle f

shouldn't [ˈʃʊdnt] = **should not**

★**shout** [ʃaʊt] N cri m; **to give sb a ~** appeler qn ▶ VT crier ▶ VI crier, pousser des cris
  ▶ **shout down** VT huer
  ▶ **shout out** VT, VI crier

shouting [ˈʃaʊtɪŋ] N cris mpl

shouting match N (inf) engueulade f (inf), empoignade f (inf)

shove [ʃʌv] VT pousser; (inf: put): **to ~ sth in** fourrer or ficher qch dans; **he shoved me out of the way** il m'a écarté en me poussant ▶ N poussée f
  ▶ **shove off** VI (Naut) pousser au large; (fig: col) ficher le camp

shovel [ˈʃʌvl] N pelle f ▶ VT pelleter, enlever (or enfourner) à la pelle

★**show** [ʃəʊ] (pt showed [ʃəʊd], pp shown [ʃəʊn]) N (of emotion) manifestation f, démonstration f; (semblance) semblant m, apparence f; (exhibition) exposition f, salon m; (Theat, TV) spectacle m; (Cine) séance f; **to ask for a ~ of hands** demander que l'on vote à main levée; **to be on ~** être exposé(e); **it's just for ~** c'est juste pour l'effet; **who's running the ~ here?** (inf) qui est-ce qui commande ici ? ▶ VT montrer; (film) passer; (courage etc) faire preuve de, manifester; (exhibit) exposer; **can you ~ me where it is, please?** pouvez-vous me montrer où c'est ?; **to ~ sb to his seat/to the door** accompagner qn jusqu'à sa place/la porte; **to ~ a profit/loss** (Comm) indiquer un bénéfice/une perte; **it just goes to ~ that …** ça prouve bien que … ▶ VI se voir, être visible
  ▶ **show around** [ʃəʊ əˈraʊnd] VT faire visiter; **would you ~ me around?** tu veux bien me faire visiter ?; **he showed me around the flat** il m'a fait visiter l'appartement

  ▶ **show in** [ʃəʊ ɪn] VT faire entrer
  ▶ **show off** [ʃəʊ ɔf] VI (pej) crâner ▶ VT (display) faire valoir; (pej) faire étalage de
  ▶ **show out** [ʃəʊ aʊt] VT reconduire à la porte
  ▶ **show round** [ʃəʊ raʊnd] VT (BRIT) = **show around**
  ▶ **show up** [ʃəʊ ʌp] VI (stand out) ressortir; (inf: turn up) se montrer ▶ VT démontrer; (unmask) démasquer, dénoncer; (flaw) faire ressortir

showbiz [ˈʃəʊbɪz] N (inf) showbiz m

show business N le monde du spectacle

showcase [ˈʃəʊkeɪs] N vitrine f

showdown [ˈʃəʊdaʊn] N épreuve f de force

★**shower** [ˈʃaʊəʳ] N (for washing) douche f; (rain) averse f; (of stones etc) pluie f; (US: party) réunion organisée pour la remise de cadeaux; **to have** or **take a ~** prendre une douche, se doucher ▶ VI prendre une douche, se doucher ▶ VT: **to ~ sb with** (gifts etc) combler qn de; (abuse etc) accabler qn de; (missiles) bombarder qn de

shower cap N bonnet m de douche

shower gel N gel m douche

showerproof [ˈʃaʊəpruːf] ADJ imperméable

showery [ˈʃaʊərɪ] ADJ (weather) pluvieux(-euse)

showground [ˈʃəʊɡraʊnd] N champ m de foire

showing [ˈʃəʊɪŋ] N (of film) projection f

show jumping [-dʒʌmpɪŋ] N concours m hippique

showman [ˈʃəʊmən] N (irreg) (at fair, circus) forain m; (fig) comédien m

showmanship [ˈʃəʊmənʃɪp] N art m de la mise en scène

shown [ʃəʊn] PP of **show**

show-off [ˈʃəʊɔf] N (inf: person) crâneur(-euse) (inf), m'as-tu-vu(e) (inf)

showpiece [ˈʃəʊpiːs] N (of exhibition etc) joyau m, clou m; **that hospital is a ~** cet hôpital est un modèle du genre

showroom [ˈʃəʊrum] N magasin m or salle f d'exposition

showstopper [ˈʃəʊstɔpəʳ] N (inf): **to be a ~** être extraordinaire

show trial N grand procès m médiatique (qui fait un exemple)

showy [ˈʃəʊɪ] ADJ tapageur(-euse)

shrank [ʃræŋk] PT of **shrink**

shrapnel [ˈʃræpnl] N éclats mpl d'obus

shred [ʃred] N (gen pl) lambeau m, petit morceau; (fig: of truth, evidence) parcelle f ▶ VT mettre en lambeaux, déchirer; (documents) détruire; (Culin: grate) râper; (: lettuce etc) couper en lanières

shredder [ˈʃredəʳ] N (for vegetables) râpeur m; (for documents, papers) déchiqueteuse f

shrew [ʃruː] N (animal) musaraigne f; (pej: woman) mégère f

shrewd [ʃruːd] ADJ astucieux(-euse), perspicace; (business person) habile

shrewdness [ˈʃruːdnɪs] N perspicacité f

shriek [ʃriːk] N cri perçant or aigu, hurlement m ▶ VT, VI hurler, crier

shrift [ʃrɪft] N: **to give sb short ~** expédier qn sans ménagements

shrill [ʃrɪl] ADJ perçant(e), aigu(ë), strident(e)

S

shrimp [ʃrɪmp] N crevette grise

shrimp cocktail (US) N cocktail *m* de crevettes

shrine [ʃraɪn] N châsse *f*; (*place*) lieu *m* de pèlerinage

shrink [ʃrɪŋk] (*pt* **shrank** [ʃræŋk], *pp* **shrunk** [ʃrʌŋk]) VI rétrécir; (*fig*) diminuer; (*also*: **shrink away**) reculer; **to ~ from (doing) sth** reculer devant (la pensée de faire) qch ▶ VT (*wool*) (faire) rétrécir ▶ N (*inf, pej*) psychanalyste *mf*

shrinkage ['ʃrɪŋkɪdʒ] N (*of clothes*) rétrécissement *m*

shrink-wrap ['ʃrɪŋkræp] VT emballer sous film plastique

shrivel ['ʃrɪvl], **shrivel up** VT ratatiner, flétrir ▶ VI se ratatiner, se flétrir

shrivelled, (US) **shriveled** [ʃrɪvld] ADJ ratatiné(e), flétri(e)

shroud [ʃraud] N linceul *m* ▶ VT: **shrouded in mystery** enveloppé(e) de mystère

Shrove Tuesday ['ʃrəuv-] N (le) Mardi gras

shrub [ʃrʌb] N arbuste *m*

shrubbery ['ʃrʌbərɪ] N massif *m* d'arbustes

shrug [ʃrʌg] N haussement *m* d'épaules ▶ VT, VI: **to ~ (one's shoulders)** hausser les épaules ▶ **shrug off** VT faire fi de; (*cold, illness*) se débarrasser de

shrunk [ʃrʌŋk] PP *of* **shrink**

shrunken ['ʃrʌŋkn] ADJ ratatiné(e)

shudder ['ʃʌdə'] N frisson *m*, frémissement *m* ▶ VI frissonner, frémir

shuffle ['ʃʌfl] VT (*cards*) battre; **to ~ (one's feet)** traîner les pieds

shun [ʃʌn] VT éviter, fuir

shunt [ʃʌnt] VT (*Rail*: *direct*) aiguiller; (: *divert*) détourner ▶ VI: **to ~ (to and fro)** faire la navette

shunting yard ['ʃʌntɪŋ-] N voies *fpl* de garage *or* de triage

shush [ʃuʃ] EXCL chut !

★**shut** [ʃʌt] (*pt, pp* ~) VT fermer ▶ VI (se) fermer ▶ **shut down** VT fermer définitivement; (*machine*) arrêter ▶ VI fermer définitivement ▶ **shut off** VT couper, arrêter ▶ **shut out** VT (*person, cold*) empêcher d'entrer; (*noise*) éviter d'entendre; (*block: view*) boucher; (: *memory of sth*) chasser de son esprit ▶ **shut up** VI (*inf: keep quiet*) se taire ▶ VT (*close*) fermer; (*silence*) faire taire

shutdown ['ʃʌtdaun] N fermeture *f*

shutter ['ʃʌtə'] N volet *m*; (*Phot*) obturateur *m*

shuttle ['ʃʌtl] N navette *f*; (*also*: **shuttle service**) (service *m* de) navette *f* ▶ VI (*vehicle, person*) faire la navette ▶ VT (*passengers*) transporter par un système de navette

shuttlecock ['ʃʌtlkɔk] N volant *m* (*de badminton*)

shuttle diplomacy N navettes *fpl* diplomatiques

shy [ʃaɪ] ADJ timide; **to fight ~ of** se dérober devant; **to be ~ of doing sth** hésiter à faire qch, ne pas oser faire qch ▶ VI: **to ~ away from doing sth** (*fig*) craindre de faire qch

shyly ['ʃaɪlɪ] ADV timidement

shyness ['ʃaɪnɪs] N timidité *f*

Siam [saɪ'æm] N Siam *m*

Siamese [saɪə'miːz] ADJ: **~ cat** chat *m* siamois; **~ twins** (*frères mpl*) siamois *mpl*, (*sœurs fpl*) siamoises *fpl*

Siberia [saɪ'bɪərɪə] N Sibérie *f*

siblings ['sɪblɪŋz] NPL (*formal*) frères et sœurs *mpl* (*de mêmes parents*)

Sicilian [sɪ'sɪlɪən] ADJ sicilien(ne) ▶ N Sicilien(ne)

Sicily ['sɪsɪlɪ] N Sicile *f*

★**sick** [sɪk] ADJ (*ill*) malade; (*BRIT: humour*) noir(e), macabre; (*vomiting*): **to be ~** vomir; **to feel ~** avoir envie de vomir, avoir mal au cœur; **to fall ~** tomber malade; **to be (off) ~** être absent(e) pour cause de maladie; **a ~ person** un(e) malade; **to be ~ of** (*fig*) en avoir assez de

sick bag N sac *m* vomitoire

sick bay N infirmerie *f*

sick building syndrome N *maladie dûe à la climatisation, l'éclairage artificiel etc des bureaux*

sicken ['sɪkn] VT écœurer ▶ VI: **to be sickening for sth** (*cold, flu etc*) couver qch

sickening ['sɪknɪŋ] ADJ (*fig*) écœurant(e), révoltant(e), répugnant(e)

sickle ['sɪkl] N faucille *f*

sick leave N congé *m* de maladie

sickle-cell anaemia ['sɪklsɛl-] N anémie *f* à hématies falciformes, drépanocytose *f*

sickly ['sɪklɪ] ADJ maladif(-ive), souffreteux(-euse); (*causing nausea*) écœurant(e)

sickness ['sɪknɪs] N maladie *f*; (*vomiting*) vomissement(s) *m(pl)*

sickness benefit N (*prestations fpl* de l')assurance-maladie *f*

sick note N (*from parents*) mot *m* d'absence; (*from doctor*) certificat médical

sick pay N indemnité *f* de maladie (*versée par l'employeur*)

sickroom ['sɪkruːm] N infirmerie *f*

★**side** [saɪd] N côté *m*; (*of animal*) flanc *m*; (*of lake, road*) bord *m*; (*of mountain*) versant *m*; (*fig: aspect*) côté, aspect *m*; (*team: Sport*) équipe *f*; (*TV: channel*) chaîne *f*; **by the ~ of** au bord de; **~ by ~** côte à côte; **the right/wrong ~** le bon/mauvais côté, l'endroit/l'envers *m*; **they are on our ~** ils sont avec nous; **from all sides** de tous côtés; **to rock from ~ to ~** se balancer; **to take sides (with)** prendre parti (pour); **a ~ of beef** ≈ un quartier de bœuf ▶ ADJ (*door, entrance*) latéral(e) ▶ VI: **to ~ with sb** prendre le parti de qn, se ranger du côté de qn

sidebar ['saɪdbɑː'] N (*on web page*) barre *f* latérale

sideboard ['saɪdbɔːd] N buffet *m*

sideboards ['saɪdbɔːdz], (US) **sideburns** ['saɪdbəːnz] NPL (*whiskers*) pattes *fpl*

sidecar ['saɪdkɑː'] N side-car *m*

side dish N (*plat m* d')accompagnement *m*

side drum N (*Mus*) tambour plat, caisse claire

side effect N effet *m* secondaire

sidekick ['saɪdkɪk] N (*inf*) sous-fifre *m*

sidelight ['saɪdlaɪt] N (*Aut*) veilleuse *f*

sideline ['saɪdlaɪn] N (*Sport*) (ligne *f* de) touche *f*; (*fig*) activité *f* secondaire

sidelong ['saɪdlɔŋ] ADJ: **to give sb a ~ glance** regarder qn du coin de l'œil

side order N garniture f

side plate N petite assiette

side road N petite route, route transversale

sidesaddle ['saɪdsædl] ADV en amazone

sideshow ['saɪdʃəu] N attraction f

sidestep ['saɪdstɛp] VT (*question*) éluder; (*problem*) éviter ▸ VI (*Boxing etc*) esquiver

side street N rue transversale

sideswipe ['saɪdswaɪp] N pique f; **to take a ~ at sb** lancer une pique à qn

sidetrack ['saɪdtræk] VT (*fig*) faire dévier de son sujet

sidewalk ['saɪdwɔːk] N (*US*) trottoir m

sideways ['saɪdweɪz] ADV de côté

siding ['saɪdɪŋ] N (*Rail*) voie f de garage

sidle ['saɪdl] VI: **to ~ up (to)** s'approcher furtivement (de)

SIDS [saɪdz] N ABBR (= *sudden infant death syndrome*) mort subite du nourrisson, mort f au berceau

siege [siːdʒ] N siège m; **to lay ~ to** assiéger

siege economy N économie f de (temps de) siège

Sierra Leone [sɪˈɛrəˈljəun] N Sierra Leone f

siesta [sɪˈɛstə] N sieste f; **to have** or **take a ~** faire la sieste

sieve [sɪv] N tamis m, passoire f ▸ VT tamiser, passer (au tamis)

sift [sɪft] VT passer au tamis or au crible; (*fig*) passer au crible ▸ VI (*fig*): **to ~ through** passer en revue

sigh [saɪ] N soupir m ▸ VI soupirer, pousser un soupir

★**sight** [saɪt] N (*faculty*) vue f; (*spectacle*) spectacle m; (*on gun*) mire f; **in ~** visible; (*fig*) en vue; **out of ~** hors de vue; **at ~** (*Comm*) à vue; **at first ~** à première vue, au premier abord; **I know her by ~** je la connais de vue; **to catch ~ of sb/sth** apercevoir qn/qch; **to lose ~ of sb/sth** perdre qn/qch de vue; **to set one's sights on sth** jeter son dévolu sur qch ▸ VT apercevoir

sighted ['saɪtɪd] ADJ qui voit; **partially ~** qui a un certain degré de vision

★**sightseeing** ['saɪtsiːɪŋ] N tourisme m; **to go ~** faire du tourisme

sightseer ['saɪtsiːə'] N touriste mf

★**sign** [saɪn] N (*gen*) signe m; (*with hand etc*) signe, geste m; (*notice*) panneau m, écriteau m; (*also:* **road sign**) panneau de signalisation; **as a ~ of** en signe de; **it's a good/bad ~** c'est bon/mauvais signe; **plus/minus ~** plus/moins; **there's no ~ of a change of mind** rien ne laisse présager un revirement; **he was showing signs of improvement** il commençait visiblement à faire des progrès ▸ VT, VI signer; **to ~ one's name** signer; **where do I ~?** où dois-je signer ?

▸ **sign away** VT (*rights etc*) renoncer officiellement à

▸ **sign for** VT FUS (*item*) signer le reçu pour

▸ **sign in** VI signer le registre (en arrivant)

▸ **sign off** VI (*Radio, TV*) terminer l'émission

▸ **sign on** VI (*Mil*) s'engager; (*BRIT: as unemployed*) s'inscrire au chômage; (*enrol*) s'inscrire; **to ~ on for a course** s'inscrire pour un cours ▸ VT (*Mil*) engager; (*employee*) embaucher

▸ **sign out** VI signer le registre (en partant)

▸ **sign over** VT: **to ~ sth over to sb** céder qch par écrit à qn

▸ **sign up** VT (*Mil*) engager ▸ VI (*Mil*) s'engager; (*for course*) s'inscrire

signage ['saɪnɪdʒ] N panneautage m

★**signal** ['sɪgnl] N signal m ▸ VI (*Aut*) mettre son clignotant; **to ~ to sb (to do sth)** faire signe à qn (de faire qch) ▸ VT (*person*) faire signe à; (*message*) communiquer par signaux; **to ~ a left/right turn** (*Aut*) indiquer or signaler que l'on tourne à gauche/droite

signal box N (*Rail*) poste m d'aiguillage

signalman [sɪgnlmən] N (*irreg*) (*Rail*) aiguilleur m

signatory ['sɪgnətərɪ] N signataire mf

signature ['sɪgnətʃə'] N signature f

signature tune N indicatif musical

signet ring ['sɪgnət-] N chevalière f

significance [sɪgˈnɪfɪkəns] N signification f; importance f; **that is of no ~** ceci n'a pas d'importance

★**significant** [sɪgˈnɪfɪkənt] ADJ significatif(-ive); (*important*) important(e), considérable

significantly [sɪgˈnɪfɪkəntlɪ] ADV (*improve, increase*) sensiblement; (*smile*) d'un air entendu, éloquemment; **~, ...** fait significatif, ...

signify ['sɪgnɪfaɪ] VT signifier

signing ['saɪnɪŋ] N (*of letter, treaty*) signature f; (*of player, singer*) recrutement m; (*player, singer*) nouvelle recrue f; (*sign language*) langue f des signes

sign language N langage m par signes

signpost ['saɪnpəust] N poteau indicateur

Sikh [siːk] ADJ, N Sikh mf

Sikhism ['siːkɪzəm] N sikhisme m

silage ['saɪlɪdʒ] N (*fodder*) fourrage vert; (*method*) ensilage m

★**silence** ['saɪlns] N silence m ▸ VT faire taire, réduire au silence

silencer ['saɪlənsə'] N (*BRIT: on gun, Aut*) silencieux m

★**silent** ['saɪlnt] ADJ silencieux(-euse); (*film*) muet(te); **to keep** or **remain ~** garder le silence, ne rien dire

silently ['saɪlntlɪ] ADV silencieusement

silent partner N (*Comm*) bailleur m de fonds, commanditaire m

silhouette [sɪluːˈɛt] N silhouette f ▸ VT: **silhouetted against** se profilant sur, se découpant contre

silicon ['sɪlɪkən] N silicium m

silicon chip N puce f électronique

silicone ['sɪlɪkəun] N silicone f

silk [sɪlk] N soie f ▸ CPD de or en soie

silky ['sɪlkɪ] ADJ soyeux(-euse)

sill [sɪl] N (*also:* **windowsill**) rebord m (de la fenêtre); (*of door*) seuil m; (*Aut*) bas m de marche

★**silly** ['sɪlɪ] ADJ stupide, sot(te), bête; **to do something ~** faire une bêtise

silo ['saɪləu] N silo m

silt [sɪlt] N vase f; limon m

★**silver** ['sɪlvə'] N argent m; (*money*) monnaie f (en pièces d'argent); (*also:* **silverware**) argenterie f ▸ ADJ (*made of silver*) d'argent, en argent; (*in colour*) argenté(e); (*car*) gris métallisé inv

S

847

silver-plated [sɪlvəˈpleɪtɪd] ADJ plaqué(e) argent

silversmith [ˈsɪlvəsmɪθ] N orfèvre mf

silverware [ˈsɪlvəwɛəʳ] N argenterie f

silver wedding, silver wedding anniversary N noces fpl d'argent

silvery [ˈsɪlvrɪ] ADJ argenté(e)

SIM card [ˈsɪm-] ABBR (Tel: = subscriber identity module card) carte f SIM

★**similar** [ˈsɪmɪləʳ] ADJ: **~ (to)** semblable (à)

similarity [sɪmɪˈlærɪtɪ] N ressemblance f, similarité f

similarly [ˈsɪmɪləlɪ] ADV de la même façon, de même

simile [ˈsɪmɪlɪ] N comparaison f

simmer [ˈsɪməʳ] VI cuire à feu doux, mijoter
▶ **simmer down** VI (fig: inf) se calmer

simper [ˈsɪmpəʳ] VI minauder

simpering [ˈsɪmprɪŋ] ADJ stupide

★**simple** [ˈsɪmpl] ADJ simple; **the ~ truth** la vérité pure et simple

simple interest N (Math, Comm) intérêts mpl simples

simple-minded [sɪmplˈmaɪndɪd] ADJ simplet(te), simple d'esprit

simpleton [ˈsɪmpltən] N nigaud(e), niais(e)

simplicity [sɪmˈplɪsɪtɪ] N simplicité f

simplification [sɪmplɪfɪˈkeɪʃən] N simplification f

simplify [ˈsɪmplɪfaɪ] VT simplifier

simplistic [sɪmˈplɪstɪk] ADJ simpliste

★**simply** [ˈsɪmplɪ] ADV simplement; (without fuss) avec simplicité; (absolutely) absolument

simulate [ˈsɪmjuleɪt] VT simuler, feindre

simulation [sɪmjuˈleɪʃən] N simulation f

simulator [ˈsɪmjuleɪtəʳ] N simulateur m

simulcast [ˈsɪmlkɑːst] N diffusion f simultanée (à la radio et à la télévision) ▶ VT diffuser en simultané (à la radio et à la télévision) ▶ CPD (interview, debate) radiotélévisé(e)

simultaneous [sɪməlˈteɪnɪəs] ADJ simultané(e)

simultaneously [sɪməlˈteɪnɪəslɪ] ADV simultanément

sin [sɪn] N péché m ▶ VI pécher

Sinai [ˈsaɪneɪaɪ] N Sinaï m

★**since** [sɪns] ADV, PREP depuis; **~ then, ever ~** depuis ce moment-là; **~ Monday** depuis lundi ▶ CONJ (time) depuis que; (because) puisque, étant donné que, comme; **(ever) ~ I arrived** depuis mon arrivée, depuis que je suis arrivé

> When talking about since when something has been happening use **depuis** and the present tense.
> I've been waiting since ten o'clock. **J'attends depuis dix heures.**

sincere [sɪnˈsɪəʳ] ADJ sincère

sincerely [sɪnˈsɪəlɪ] ADV sincèrement; **yours ~** (at end of letter) veuillez agréer, Monsieur (or Madame) l'expression de mes sentiments distingués or les meilleurs

sincerity [sɪnˈsɛrɪtɪ] N sincérité f

sine [saɪn] N (Math) sinus m

sinew [ˈsɪnjuː] N tendon m ▪ **sinews** NPL muscles mpl

sinful [ˈsɪnful] ADJ coupable

★**sing** [sɪŋ] (pt **sang** [sæŋ], pp **sung** [sʌŋ]) VT, VI chanter

Singapore [sɪŋgəˈpɔː] N Singapour m

Singaporean [sɪŋgəˈpɔːrɪən] ADJ singapourien(ne) ▶ N Singapourien(ne)

singe [sɪndʒ] VT brûler légèrement; (clothes) roussir

★**singer** [ˈsɪŋəʳ] N chanteur(-euse)

Singhalese [sɪŋəˈliːz] ADJ = **Sinhalese**

singing [ˈsɪŋɪŋ] N (of person, bird) chant m; façon f de chanter; (of kettle, bullet, in ears) sifflement m

★**single** [ˈsɪŋgl] ADJ seul(e), unique; (unmarried) célibataire; (not double) simple; **not a ~ one was left** il n'en est pas resté un(e), seul(e); **every ~ day** chaque jour sans exception ▶ N (Brit: also: **single ticket**) aller m (simple); (record) 45 tours m ▪ **singles** NPL (Tennis) simple m; (single people) célibataires mf
▶ **single out** VT choisir; (distinguish) distinguer

single bed N lit m d'une personne or à une place

single-breasted [ˈsɪŋglbrɛstɪd] ADJ droit(e)

Single European Market N: **the ~** le marché unique européen

single file N: **in ~** en file indienne

single-handed [sɪŋglˈhændɪd] ADV tout(e) seul(e), sans (aucune) aide

single-minded [sɪŋglˈmaɪndɪd] ADJ résolu(e), tenace

single parent N parent m solo; **single-parent family** famille monoparentale

single room N chambre f à un lit or pour une personne

singles bar N (esp US) bar m de rencontres pour célibataires

single-sex school [sɪŋglˈsɛks-] N école f non mixte

singlet [ˈsɪŋglɪt] N tricot m de corps

singleton [ˈsɪŋgəltən] N (inf: person) célibataire mf

single-track road [sɪŋglˈtræk-] N route f à voie unique

singly [ˈsɪŋglɪ] ADV séparément

singsong [ˈsɪŋsɔŋ] ADJ (tone) chantant(e) ▶ N (songs): **to have a ~** chanter quelque chose (ensemble)

singular [ˈsɪŋgjuləʳ] ADJ singulier(-ière); (odd) singulier, étrange; (outstanding) remarquable; (Ling) (au) singulier, du singulier ▶ N (Ling) singulier m; **in the feminine ~** au féminin singulier

singularly [ˈsɪŋgjuləlɪ] ADV singulièrement; étrangement

Sinhalese [sɪnhəˈliːz] ADJ cingalais(e)

sinister [ˈsɪnɪstəʳ] ADJ sinistre

★**sink** [sɪŋk] (pt **sank** [sæŋk], pp **sunk** [sʌŋk]) N évier m; (washbasin) lavabo m ▶ VT (ship) (faire) couler, faire sombrer; (foundations) creuser; (piles etc): **to ~ sth into** enfoncer qch dans ▶ VI couler, sombrer; (ground etc) s'affaisser; **to ~ into sth** (chair) s'enfoncer dans qch; **he sank into a chair/the mud** il s'est enfoncé dans un fauteuil/la

boue; **a sinking feeling** un serrement de cœur
▶ **sink in** [sɪŋk ɪn] vɪ s'enfoncer, pénétrer; *(explanation)* rentrer *(inf)*, être compris; **it took a long time to ~ in** il a fallu longtemps pour que ça rentre

sinking fund N fonds *mpl* d'amortissement

sink unit N bloc-évier *m*

sinner ['sɪnə'] N pécheur(-eresse)

Sinn Féin [ʃɪn'feɪn] N Sinn Féin *m (parti politique irlandais)*

Sino- ['saɪnəʊ] PREFIX sino-

sinuous ['sɪnjuəs] ADJ sinueux(-euse)

sinus ['saɪnəs] N *(Anat)* sinus *m inv*

sinusitis [saɪnə'saɪtɪs] N sinusite *f*

sip [sɪp] N petite gorgée ▶ VT boire à petites gorgées

siphon ['saɪfən] N siphon *m* ▶ VT *(also:* **siphon off***)* siphonner; *(fig: funds)* transférer; *(: illegally)* détourner

★**sir** [sə'] N monsieur *m*; **S~ John Smith** sir John Smith; **yes ~** oui Monsieur; **Dear S~** *(in letter)* Monsieur

siren ['saɪərn] N sirène *f*

sirloin ['sə:lɔɪn] N aloyau *m*

sirloin steak N bifteck *m* dans l'aloyau

sirocco [sɪ'rɔkəʊ] N sirocco *m*

sisal ['saɪsəl] N sisal *m*

sissy ['sɪsɪ] N *(pej: coward)* poule mouillée *(inf)*

★**sister** ['sɪstə'] N sœur *f*; *(nun)* religieuse *f*, (bonne) sœur; *(BRIT: nurse)* infirmière *f* en chef ▶ CPD: **~ organization** organisation *f* sœur; **~ ship** sister(-)ship *m*

sisterhood ['sɪstəhud] N sororité *f*

sister-in-law ['sɪstərɪnlɔ:] N belle-sœur *f*

sisterly ['sɪstəlɪ] ADJ sororal(e)

★**sit** [sɪt] *(pt, pp* **sat** [sæt]*)* vɪ s'asseoir; *(be sitting)* être assis(e); *(assembly)* être en séance, siéger; *(for painter)* poser; *(dress etc)* tomber; **to ~ tight** ne pas bouger ▶ VT *(exam)* passer, se présenter à
▶ **sit about** [sɪt ə'baut], **sit around** [sɪt ə'raund] vɪ être assis(e) or rester à ne rien faire
▶ **sit back** [sɪt bæk] vɪ *(in seat)* bien s'installer, se carrer
▶ **sit down** [sɪt daun] vɪ s'asseoir; **to be sitting down** être assis(e)
▶ **sit in** [sɪt ɪn] vɪ: **to ~ in on a discussion** assister à une discussion
▶ **sit on** [sɪt ɔn] VT FUS *(jury, committee)* faire partie de
▶ **sit out** [sɪt aut] VT *(game)* ne pas prendre part à; *(crisis, recession)* laisser passer
▶ **sit up** [sɪt ʌp] vɪ s'asseoir; *(straight)* se redresser; *(not go to bed)* rester debout, ne pas se coucher

sitar ['sɪtɑ:', sɪ'tɑ:'] N sitar *m*

sitcom ['sɪtkɔm] N ABBR *(TV: = situation comedy)* sitcom *f*, comédie *f* de situation

sit-down ['sɪtdaun] ADJ: **a ~ strike** une grève sur le tas; **a ~ meal** un repas assis

site [saɪt] N emplacement *m*, site *m*; *(also:* **building site***)* chantier *m*; *(Internet)* site *m* web ▶ VT placer

sit-in ['sɪtɪn] N *(demonstration)* sit-in *m inv*, occupation *f* de locaux

siting ['saɪtɪŋ] N *(location)* emplacement *m*

sitter ['sɪtə'] N *(for painter)* modèle *m*; *(also:* **babysitter***)* baby-sitter *mf*

sitting ['sɪtɪŋ] N *(of assembly etc)* séance *f*; *(in canteen)* service *m*

sitting member N *(Pol)* parlementaire *mf* en exercice

sitting room N salon *m*

sitting tenant N *(BRIT)* locataire occupant(e)

situate ['sɪtjueɪt] VT situer

situated ['sɪtjueɪtɪd] ADJ situé(e)

★**situation** [sɪtju'eɪʃən] N situation *f*; **"situations vacant/wanted"** *(BRIT)* « offres/demandes d'emploi »

situation comedy N *(TV)* comédie *f* de situation

sit-ups ['sɪtʌps] NPL abdominaux *mpl*; **to do ~** faire des abdominaux

★**six** [sɪks] NUM six

★**six-pack** ['sɪkspæk] N *(esp US)* pack *m* de six canettes

★**sixteen** [sɪks'ti:n] NUM seize

★**sixteenth** [sɪks'ti:nθ] NUM seizième

★**sixth** [sɪksθ] NUM sixième ▶ N: **the upper/lower ~** *(BRIT Scol)* la terminale/la première

sixth form N *(BRIT)* ≈ classes *fpl* de première et de terminale

sixth-form college N *lycée n'ayant que des classes de première et de terminale*

sixtieth ['sɪkstɪθ] NUM soixantième

★**sixty** ['sɪkstɪ] NUM soixante

★**size** [saɪz] N dimensions *fpl*; *(of person)* taille *f*; *(of clothing)* taille; *(of shoes)* pointure *f*; *(of estate, area)* étendue *f*; *(of problem)* ampleur *f*; *(of company)* importance *f*; *(glue)* colle *f*; **I take ~ 14** *(of dress etc)* ≈ je prends du 42 or la taille 42; **the small/large ~** *(of soap powder etc)* le petit/grand modèle; **it's the ~ of ...** c'est de la taille *(or* grosseur*)* de ..., c'est grand *(or* gros*)* comme ...; **cut to ~** découpé(e) aux dimensions voulues
▶ **size up** VT juger, jauger

sizeable ['saɪzəbl] ADJ *(object, building, estate)* assez grand(e); *(amount, problem, majority)* assez important(e)

sizzle ['sɪzl] vɪ grésiller

SK ABBR *(CANADA)* = **Saskatchewan**

skate [skeɪt] N patin *m*; *(fish: pl inv)* raie *f* ▶ vɪ patiner
▶ **skate over**, **skate around** VT *(problem, issue)* éluder

skateboard ['skeɪtbɔ:d] N skateboard *m*, planche *f* à roulettes

skateboarder ['skeɪtbɔ:də'] N skateur(-euse)

skateboarding ['skeɪtbɔ:dɪŋ] N skateboard *m*

skatepark ['skeɪtpɑ:k] N skatepark *m*

skater ['skeɪtə'] N patineur(-euse)

skating ['skeɪtɪŋ] N patinage *m*

skating rink N patinoire *f*

skeletal ['skelɪtl] ADJ squelettique; *(remains)* de squelette; *(service)* spartiate

skeleton ['skelɪtn] N squelette *m*; *(outline)* schéma *m*

skeleton key N passe-partout *m*

skeleton staff N effectifs réduits

S

skeptic ['skɛptɪk] N (US) = **sceptic**

skeptical ['skɛptɪkl] ADJ (US) = **sceptical**

sketch [skɛtʃ] N (drawing) croquis m, esquisse f; (outline plan) aperçu m; (Theat) sketch m, saynète f ▸ VT esquisser, faire un croquis or une esquisse de; (plan etc) esquisser
  ▸ **sketch out** VT (situation) brosser le tableau de; (incident, plan) décrire

sketch book N carnet m à dessin

sketch pad N bloc m à dessin

sketchy ['skɛtʃɪ] ADJ incomplet(-ète), fragmentaire

skew [skju:] N (BRIT): **on the ~** de travers, en biais

skewed [skju:d] ADJ faussé(e)

skewer ['skju:əʳ] N brochette f

★**ski** [ski:] N ski m ▸ VI skier, faire du ski

ski boot N chaussure f de ski

skid [skɪd] N dérapage m; **to go into a ~** déraper
  ▸ VI déraper

skid mark N trace f de dérapage

skid row [skɪd'rəʊ] N (esp US) bas-fonds mpl

skier ['ski:əʳ] N skieur(-euse)

★**skiing** ['ski:ɪŋ] N ski m; **to go ~** (aller) faire du ski

ski instructor N moniteur(-trice) de ski

ski jump N (ramp) tremplin m; (event) saut m à skis

skilful, (US) **skillful** ['skɪlful] ADJ habile, adroit(e)

skilfully, (US) **skillfully** ['skɪlfəlɪ] ADV habilement, adroitement

ski lift N remonte-pente m inv

★**skill** [skɪl] N (ability) habileté f, adresse f, talent m; (requiring training) compétences fpl

skilled [skɪld] ADJ habile, adroit(e); (worker) qualifié(e)

skillet ['skɪlɪt] N poêlon m

skillful etc ['skɪlful] ADJ (US) = **skilful** etc

skim [skɪm] VT (milk) écrémer; (soup) écumer; (glide over) raser, effleurer ▸ VI: **to ~ through** (fig) parcourir

skimmed milk [skɪmd-], (US) **skim milk** N lait écrémé

skimp [skɪmp] VT (work) bâcler, faire à la va-vite; (cloth etc) lésiner sur
  ▸ **skimp on** VT FUS (gen) lésiner sur; (praise, thanks) être avare de

skimpy ['skɪmpɪ] ADJ étriqué(e); maigre

★**skin** [skɪn] N peau f; **wet** or **soaked to the ~** trempé(e) jusqu'aux os ▸ VT (fruit etc) éplucher; (animal) écorcher

skin cancer N cancer m de la peau

skincare ['skɪnkɛəʳ] N soins mpl de la peau ▸ CPD (product, routine) de soins de la peau

skin colour, (US) **skin color** N couleur f de peau

skin-deep ['skɪn'di:p] ADJ superficiel(le)

skin diver N plongeur(-euse) sous-marin(e)

skin diving N plongée sous-marine

skinflint ['skɪnflɪnt] N grippe-sou m

skin graft N greffe f de peau

skinhead ['skɪnhɛd] N skinhead m

skinny ['skɪnɪ] ADJ maigre, maigrichon(ne)

skint [skɪnt] ADJ (BRIT inf) raide (inf)

skin test N cuti(-réaction) f

skintight ['skɪntaɪt] ADJ (dress etc) collant(e), ajusté(e)

skip [skɪp] N petit bond or saut m; (BRIT: container) benne f ▸ VI gambader, sautiller; (with rope) sauter à la corde ▸ VT (pass over) sauter; **to ~ school** (esp US) faire l'école buissonnière

ski pants NPL pantalon m de ski

ski pass N forfait-skieur(s) m

ski pole N bâton m de ski

skipper ['skɪpəʳ] N (Naut, Sport) capitaine m; (in race) skipper m ▸ VT (boat) commander; (team) être le chef de

skipping rope ['skɪpɪŋ-], (US) **skip rope** N corde f à sauter

ski resort N station f de sports d'hiver

skirmish ['skə:mɪʃ] N escarmouche f, accrochage m

★**skirt** [skə:t] N jupe f ▸ VT longer, contourner
  ▸ **skirt around**, **skirt round** VT FUS (lit, fig) contourner

skirting board ['skə:tɪŋ-] N (BRIT) plinthe f

ski run N piste f de ski

ski slope N piste f de ski

ski suit N combinaison f de ski

skit [skɪt] N sketch m satirique

ski tow N = **ski lift**

skittish ['skɪtɪʃ] ADJ (nervous) nerveux(-euse); (frivolous) frivole

skittle ['skɪtl] N quille f ■ **skittles** NPL (game) (jeu m de) quilles fpl

skive [skaɪv] VI (BRIT inf) tirer au flanc

skulduggery [skʌl'dʌgərɪ] N magouilles fpl

skulk [skʌlk] VI rôder furtivement

skull [skʌl] N crâne m

skullcap ['skʌlkæp] N calotte f

skunk [skʌŋk] N mouffette f; (fur) sconse m

★**sky** [skaɪ] N ciel m; **to praise sb to the skies** porter qn aux nues

sky-blue [skaɪ'blu:] ADJ bleu ciel inv

skydiver ['skaɪdaɪvəʳ] N parachutiste mf

skydiving ['skaɪdaɪvɪŋ] N parachutisme m; **to go ~** faire du parachutisme

sky-high ['skaɪ'haɪ] ADV très haut ▸ ADJ exorbitant(e); **prices are ~** les prix sont exorbitants

skylark ['skaɪlɑ:k] N (bird) alouette f (des champs)

skylight ['skaɪlaɪt] N lucarne f

skyline ['skaɪlaɪn] N (horizon) (ligne f d')horizon m; (of city) ligne des toits

Skype® [skaɪp] (Internet, Tel) N Skype® ▸ VT contacter via Skype®

skyscraper ['skaɪskreɪpəʳ] N gratte-ciel m inv

slab [slæb] N plaque f; (of stone) dalle f; (of wood) bloc m; (of meat, cheese) tranche épaisse

slack [slæk] ADJ (loose) lâche, desserré(e); (slow) stagnant(e); (careless) négligent(e), peu sérieux(-euse) or consciencieux(-euse); (Comm: market) peu actif(-ive); (: demand) faible; (period) creux(-euse); **business is ~** les affaires vont mal ▸ N (in rope etc) mou m

slacken ['slækn] VI (also: **slacken off**) ralentir, diminuer ▸ VT relâcher

slacker ['slækə^r] N fainéant(e)

slacks [slæks] NPL pantalon *m*

slag [slæg] N scories *fpl*

slag heap N crassier *m*

slag off VT (BRIT inf) dire du mal de

slain [sleɪn] PP of **slay**

slake [sleɪk] VT (one's thirst) étancher

slalom ['slɑːləm] N slalom *m*

slam [slæm] VT (door) (faire) claquer; (throw) jeter violemment, flanquer; (inf: criticize) éreinter, démolir ▸ VI claquer

slammer ['slæmə^r] N (inf): **the ~** la taule (inf)

slander ['slɑːndə^r] N calomnie *f*; (Law) diffamation *f* ▸ VT calomnier; diffamer

slanderous ['slɑːndrəs] ADJ calomnieux(-euse); diffamatoire

slang [slæŋ] N argot *m*

slanging match ['slæŋɪŋ-] N (BRIT inf) engueulade *f*, empoignade *f*

slant [slɑːnt] N inclinaison *f*; (fig) angle *m*, point *m* de vue

slanted ['slɑːntɪd] ADJ tendancieux(-euse)

slanting ['slɑːntɪŋ] ADJ en pente, incliné(e); couché(e)

slap [slæp] N claque *f*, gifle *f*; (on the back) tape *f* ▸ VT donner une claque or une gifle (or une tape) à; **to ~ on** (paint) appliquer rapidement ▸ ADV (directly) tout droit, en plein

slapdash ['slæpdæʃ] ADJ (work) fait(e) sans soin or à la va-vite; (person) insouciant(e), négligent(e)

slaphead ['slæphed] N (BRIT inf) chauve *m*

slapstick ['slæpstɪk] N (comedy) grosse farce (style tarte à la crème)

slap-up ['slæpʌp] ADJ (BRIT): **a ~ meal** un repas extra or fameux

slash [slæʃ] VT entailler, taillader; (fig: prices) casser

slat [slæt] N (of wood) latte *f*, lame *f*

slate [sleɪt] N ardoise *f* ▸ VT (fig: criticize) éreinter, démolir

slaughter ['slɔːtə^r] N carnage *m*, massacre *m*; (of animals) abattage *m* ▸ VT (animal) abattre; (people) massacrer

slaughterhouse ['slɔːtəhaus] N abattoir *m*

Slav [slɑːv] ADJ slave ▸ N Slave *mf*

slave [sleɪv] N esclave *mf* ▸ VI (also: **slave away**) trimer, travailler comme un forçat; **to ~ (away) at sth/at doing sth** se tuer à qch/à faire qch

slave driver N (inf, pej) négrier(-ière)

slave labour N travail *m* d'esclave; **it's just ~** (fig) c'est de l'esclavage

slaver ['slævə^r] VI (dribble) baver

slavery ['sleɪvərɪ] N esclavage *m*

Slavic ['slævɪk] ADJ slave

slavish ['sleɪvɪʃ] ADJ servile

slavishly ['sleɪvɪʃlɪ] ADV (copy) servilement

Slavonic [slə'vɔnɪk] ADJ slave

slay [sleɪ] (pt **slew** [sluː], pp **slain** [sleɪn]) VT (literary) tuer

slaying ['sleɪɪŋ] N (killing) mort *f* (violente); (esp US: murder) meurtre *m*

sleaze [sliːz] N (inf) débauche *f*

sleazy ['sliːzɪ] ADJ miteux(-euse), minable

sled [slɛd] N (US) = **sledge**

sledge [slɛdʒ] N luge *f*

sledgehammer ['slɛdʒhæmə^r] N marteau *m* de forgeron

sleek [sliːk] ADJ (hair, fur) brillant(e), luisant(e); (car, boat) aux lignes pures or élégantes

★**sleep** [sliːp] (pt, pp **slept** [slɛpt]) N sommeil *m*; **to go to ~** s'endormir; **to have a good night's ~** passer une bonne nuit; **to put to ~** (patient) endormir; (animal: euphemism: kill) piquer ▸ VI dormir; (spend night) dormir, coucher; **to ~ lightly** avoir le sommeil léger; **to ~ with sb** (have sex) coucher avec qn ▸ VT: **we can ~ 4** on peut coucher or loger 4 personnes
  ▸ **sleep around** VI coucher à droite et à gauche
  ▸ **sleep in** VI (oversleep) se réveiller trop tard; (on purpose) faire la grasse matinée
  ▸ **sleep together** VI (have sex) coucher ensemble

sleeper ['sliːpə^r] N (person) dormeur(-euse); (BRIT Rail: on track) traverse *f*; (: train) train-couchettes *m*; (: carriage) wagon-lits *m*, voiture-lits *f*; (: berth) couchette *f*

sleepily ['sliːpɪlɪ] ADV d'un air endormi

sleeping ['sliːpɪŋ] ADJ qui dort, endormi(e)

★**sleeping bag** N sac *m* de couchage

sleeping car N wagon-lits *m*, voiture-lits *f*

sleeping partner N (BRIT Comm) = **silent partner**

sleeping pill N somnifère *m*

sleeping sickness N maladie *f* du sommeil

sleepless ['sliːplɪs] ADJ: **a ~ night** une nuit blanche

sleeplessness ['sliːplɪsnɪs] N insomnie *f*

sleepover ['sliːpəuvə^r] N nuit *f* chez un copain or une copine; **we're having a ~ at Jo's** nous allons passer la nuit chez Jo

sleepwalk ['sliːpwɔːk] VI marcher en dormant

sleepwalker ['sliːpwɔːkə^r] N somnambule *mf*

sleepy ['sliːpɪ] ADJ qui a envie de dormir; (fig) endormi(e); **to be** or **feel ~** avoir sommeil, avoir envie de dormir

sleet [sliːt] N neige fondue

sleeve [sliːv] N manche *f*; (of record) pochette *f*

sleeveless ['sliːvlɪs] ADJ (garment) sans manches

sleigh [sleɪ] N traîneau *m*

sleight [slaɪt] N: **~ of hand** tour *m* de passe-passe

slender ['slɛndə^r] ADJ svelte, mince; (fig) faible, ténu(e)

slept [slɛpt] PT, PP of **sleep**

sleuth [sluːθ] N (inf) détective (privé)

slew [sluː] VI (also: **slew round**) virer, pivoter ▸ PT of **slay**

★**slice** [slaɪs] N tranche *f*; (round) rondelle *f*; (utensil) spatule *f*; (also: **fish slice**) pelle *f* à poisson ▸ VT couper en tranches (or en rondelles); **sliced bread** pain *m* en tranches

slick [slɪk] ADJ (skilful) bien ficelé(e); (salesperson) qui a du bagout, mielleux(-euse) ▸ N (also: **oil slick**) nappe *f* de pétrole, marée noire

slid [slɪd] PT, PP of **slide**

★**slide** [slaɪd] (pt, pp **slid** [slɪd]) N (in playground) toboggan *m*; (Phot) diapositive *f*; (BRIT: also: **hair**

slide) barrette f; (*microscope slide*) (lame f) porte-objet m; (*in prices*) chute f, baisse f ▸ VT (faire) glisser ▸ VI glisser; **to let things ~** (*fig*) laisser les choses aller à la dérive

slide projector N (*Phot*) projecteur m de diapositives

slide rule N règle f à calcul

slide show N diaporama m

sliding ['slaɪdɪŋ] ADJ (*door*) coulissant(e); **~ roof** (*Aut*) toit ouvrant

sliding scale N échelle f mobile

★**slight** [slaɪt] ADJ (*slim*) mince, menu(e); (*frail*) frêle; (*trivial*) faible, insignifiant(e); (*small*) petit(e), léger(-ère) *before noun*; **the slightest** le (or la) moindre; **not in the slightest** pas le moins du monde, pas du tout ▸ N offense f, affront m ▸ VT (*offend*) blesser, offenser

★**slightly** ['slaɪtlɪ] ADV légèrement, un peu; **~ built** fluet(te)

★**slim** [slɪm] ADJ mince ▸ VI maigrir; (*diet*) faire un régime, suivre un régime

slime [slaɪm] N vase f; substance visqueuse

slimline ['slɪmlaɪn] ADJ (*thin: figure*) svelte; (: *clothing*) slim *inv*; (: *device*) ultrafin(e); (*low-calorie*) allégé(e)

slimmer ['slɪmə'] N personne f au régime

slimming [slɪmɪŋ] N amaigrissement m ▸ ADJ (*diet, pills*) amaigrissant(e), pour maigrir; (*clothes*) amincissant

slimy ['slaɪmɪ] ADJ visqueux(-euse), gluant(e); (*covered with mud*) vaseux(-euse)

sling [slɪŋ] (*pt, pp* **slung** [slʌŋ]) N (*Med*) écharpe f; (*for baby*) porte-bébé m; (*weapon*) fronde f, lance-pierre m; **to have one's arm in a ~** avoir le bras en écharpe ▸ VT lancer, jeter

slingshot ['slɪŋʃɒt] N (*US*) fronde f, lance-pierre m

slink [slɪŋk] (*pt, pp* **slunk** [slʌŋk]) VI: **to ~ away** or **off** s'en aller furtivement

slinky ['slɪŋkɪ] ADJ (*clothes*) moulant(e)

★**slip** [slɪp] N faux pas; (*mistake*) erreur f, bévue f; (*underskirt*) combinaison f; (*of paper*) petite feuille, fiche f; **to give sb the ~** fausser compagnie à qn; **a ~ of the tongue** un lapsus ▸ VT (*slide*) glisser; **to ~ sth on/off** enfiler/enlever qch ▸ VI (*slide*) glisser; (*decline*) baisser; (*move smoothly*): **to ~ into/out of** se glisser or se faufiler dans/hors de; **to let a chance ~ by** laisser passer une occasion; **it slipped from her hand** cela lui a glissé des mains
▸ **slip away** VI s'esquiver
▸ **slip in** VT glisser
▸ **slip out** VI sortir
▸ **slip up** VI faire une erreur, gaffer

slip-on ['slɪpɒn] ADJ facile à enfiler; **~ shoes** mocassins mpl

slippage ['slɪpɪdʒ] N (*reduction*) baisse f, déclin m

slipped disc ['slɪpt-] N déplacement m de vertèbre

slipper ['slɪpə'] N pantoufle f

slippery ['slɪpərɪ] ADJ glissant(e); (*fig: person*) insaisissable

slip road N (*Brit: to motorway*) bretelle f d'accès

slipshod ['slɪpʃɒd] ADJ négligé(e), peu soigné(e)

slipstream ['slɪpstriːm] N sillage m

slip-up ['slɪpʌp] N bévue f

slipway ['slɪpweɪ] N cale f (de construction or de lancement)

slit [slɪt] (*pt, pp* **~**) N fente f; (*cut*) incision f; (*tear*) déchirure f ▸ VT fendre; couper, inciser; déchirer; **to ~ sb's throat** trancher la gorge à qn

slither ['slɪðə'] VI glisser, déraper

sliver ['slɪvə'] N (*of glass, wood*) éclat m; (*of cheese, sausage*) petit morceau

slob [slɒb] N (*pej*) rustaud(e)

slog [slɒg] N (*Brit: effort*) gros effort; (: *work*) tâche fastidieuse ▸ VI travailler très dur

slogan ['sləʊgən] N slogan m

slop [slɒp] VI déborder; se renverser ▸ VT répandre; renverser

slope [sləʊp] N pente f, côte f; (*side of mountain*) versant m; (*slant*) inclinaison f ▸ VI: **to ~ down** être or descendre en pente; **to ~ up** monter

sloping ['sləʊpɪŋ] ADJ en pente, incliné(e); (*handwriting*) penché(e)

sloppy ['slɒpɪ] ADJ (*work*) peu soigné(e), bâclé(e); (*appearance*) négligé(e), débraillé(e); (*film etc*) sentimental(e)

slosh [slɒʃ] VI (*inf*): **to ~ about** or **around** (*children*) patauger; (*liquid*) clapoter

sloshed [slɒʃt] ADJ (*inf: drunk*) bourré(e) (*inf*)

slot [slɒt] N fente f; (*fig: in timetable, Radio, TV*) créneau m, plage f ▸ VT: **to ~ sth into** encastrer or insérer qch dans ▸ VI: **to ~ into** s'encastrer or s'insérer dans

sloth [sləʊθ] N (*vice*) paresse f; (*Zool*) paresseux m

slot machine N (*Brit: vending machine*) distributeur m (automatique), machine f à sous; (*for gambling*) appareil m or machine à sous

slot meter N (*Brit*) compteur m à pièces

slouch [slaʊtʃ] VI avoir le dos rond, être voûté(e)
▸ **slouch about, slouch around** VI traîner à ne rien faire

Slovak ['sləʊvæk] ADJ slovaque; **the ~ Republic** la République slovaque ▸ N Slovaque mf; (*Ling*) slovaque m

Slovakia [sləʊ'vækɪə] N Slovaquie f

Slovakian [sləʊ'vækɪən] ADJ, N = **Slovak**

Slovene [sləʊ'viːn] ADJ slovène ▸ N Slovène mf; (*Ling*) slovène m

Slovenia [sləʊ'viːnɪə] N Slovénie f

Slovenian [sləʊ'viːnɪən] ADJ, N = **Slovene**

slovenly ['slʌvənlɪ] ADJ sale, débraillé(e), négligé(e)

★**slow** [sləʊ] ADJ lent(e); (*watch*): **to be ~** retarder; **"~"** (*road sign*) « ralentir »; **at a ~ speed** à petite vitesse; **to be ~ to act/decide** être lent à agir/décider; **my watch is 20 minutes ~** ma montre retarde de 20 minutes; **business is ~** les affaires marchent au ralenti ▸ ADV lentement; **to go ~** (*driver*) rouler lentement; (*in industrial dispute*) faire la grève perlée ▸ VT, VI ralentir
▸ **slow down** VI ralentir

slow-acting [sləʊ'æktɪŋ] ADJ qui agit lentement, à action lente

slowcoach ['sləʊkəʊtʃ] N (*Brit inf*) lambin(e)

slowdown ['sləʊdaʊn] N ralentissement m

★**slowly** ['sləʊlɪ] ADV lentement

slow motion N: **in ~** au ralenti

slowness ['sləʊnɪs] N lenteur f

slowpoke ['sləʊpəʊk] N (*US inf*) = **slowcoach**

sludge [slʌdʒ] N boue *f*

slug [slʌg] N limace *f*; (*bullet*) balle *f*

sluggish ['slʌgɪʃ] ADJ (*person*) mou (molle), lent(e); (*stream, engine, trading*) lent(e); (*business, sales*) stagnant(e)

sluice [sluːs] N écluse *f*; (*also:* **sluice gate**) vanne *f*
▸ VT: **to ~ down** *or* **out** laver à grande eau

slum [slʌm] N (*house*) taudis *m* ■ **slums** NPL (*area*) quartiers *mpl* pauvres

slumber ['slʌmbə^r] N sommeil *m*

slump [slʌmp] N baisse soudaine, effondrement *m*; (*Econ*) crise *f* ▸ VI s'effondrer, s'affaisser

slung [slʌŋ] PT, PP *of* **sling**

slunk [slʌŋk] PT, PP *of* **slink**

slur [sləː^r] N bredouillement *m*; (*smear*): **~ (on)** atteinte *f* (à); insinuation *f* (contre); **to be a ~ on** porter atteinte à ▸ VT mal articuler

slurp [sləːp] VT, VI boire à grand bruit

slurred [sləːd] ADJ (*pronunciation*) inarticulé(e), indistinct(e)

slush [slʌʃ] N neige fondue

slush fund N caisse noire, fonds secrets

slushy ['slʌʃɪ] ADJ (*snow*) fondu(e); (*street*) couvert(e) de neige fondue; (*BRIT fig*) à l'eau de rose

slut [slʌt] N (!) souillon *f*

sly [slaɪ] ADJ (*person*) rusé(e); (*smile, expression, remark*) sournois(e); **on the ~** en cachette

smack [smæk] N (*slap*) tape *f*; (*on face*) gifle *f* ▸ VT donner une tape à; (*on face*) gifler; (*on bottom*) donner la fessée à; **to ~ one's lips** se lécher les babines ▸ VI: **to ~ of** avoir des relents de, sentir ▸ ADV (*inf*): **it fell ~ in the middle** c'est tombé en plein milieu *or* en plein dedans

smacker ['smækə^r] N (*inf: kiss*) bisou *m or* bise *f* sonore; (: *BRIT: pound note*) livre *f*; (: *US: dollar bill*) dollar *m*

★**small** [smɔːl] ADJ petit(e); (*letter*) minuscule; **to get** *or* **grow smaller** diminuer; **to make smaller** (*amount, income*) diminuer; (*object, garment*) rapetisser; **a ~ shopkeeper** un petit commerçant ▸ N: **the ~ of the back** le creux des reins

small ads NPL (*BRIT*) petites annonces

small arms NPL armes individuelles

small business N petit commerce, petite affaire

small change N petite *or* menue monnaie

smallholder ['smɔːlhəʊldə^r] N (*BRIT*) petit cultivateur

smallholding ['smɔːlhəʊldɪŋ] N (*BRIT*) petite ferme

small hours NPL: **in the ~** au petit matin

smallish ['smɔːlɪʃ] ADJ plutôt *or* assez petit(e)

small-minded [smɔːl'maɪndɪd] ADJ mesquin(e)

smallpox ['smɔːlpɒks] N variole *f*

small print N (*in contract etc*) clause(s) imprimée(s) en petits caractères

small-scale ['smɔːlskeɪl] ADJ (*map, model*) à échelle réduite, à petite échelle; (*business, farming*) peu important(e), modeste

small talk N menus propos

small-time ['smɔːltaɪm] ADJ (*farmer etc*) petit(e); **a ~ thief** un voleur à la petite semaine

small-town ['smɔːltaʊn] ADJ provincial(e)

smarmy ['smɑːmɪ] ADJ (*BRIT pej*) flagorneur(-euse), lécheur(-euse)

★**smart** [smɑːt] ADJ élégant(e), chic *inv*; (*clever*) intelligent(e); (*pej*) futé(e); (*quick*) vif (vive), prompt(e); **the ~ set** le beau monde; **to look ~** être élégant(e) ▸ VI faire mal, brûler; **my eyes are smarting** j'ai les yeux irrités *or* qui me piquent

smart alec, smart aleck N (*inf*) petit(e) prétentieux(-euse) (*inf*), monsieur (madame) je-sais-tout (*inf*)

smart card N carte *f* à puce

smarten up ['smɑːtn-] VI devenir plus élégant(e), se faire beau (belle) ▸ VT rendre plus élégant(e)

smartly ['smɑːtlɪ] ADV (*dress*) bien; (*quickly*) vivement

smartphone ['smɑːtfəʊn] N smartphone *m*

smartwatch ['smɑːtwɒtʃ] N smartwatch *f*

★**smash** [smæʃ] N collision *f*, accident *m*; (*Mus*) succès foudroyant; (*sound*) fracas *m* ▸ VT casser, briser, fracasser; (*opponent*) écraser; (*hopes*) ruiner, détruire; (*Sport: record*) pulvériser ▸ VI se briser, se fracasser; s'écraser
▸ **smash up** VT (*car*) bousiller; (*room*) tout casser dans

smashed ['smæʃt] ADJ (*inf: drunk*) bourré(e) (*inf*)

smashing ['smæʃɪŋ] ADJ (*inf*) formidable

smash-up ['smæʃʌp] N collision *f*, accident *m*

smattering ['smætərɪŋ] N: **a ~ of** quelques notions de

SME N ABBR (= *small and medium(-sized) enterprise(s)*) PME *f inv*

smear [smɪə^r] N (*stain*) tache *f*; (*mark*) trace *f*; (*Med*) frottis *m*; (*insult*) calomnie *f* ▸ VT enduire; (*make dirty*) salir; (*fig*) porter atteinte à; **his hands were smeared with oil/ink** il avait les mains maculées de cambouis/d'encre

smear campaign N campagne *f* de dénigrement

smear test N (*BRIT Med*) frottis *m*

★**smell** [smɛl] (*pt, pp* **smelt** [smɛlt] *or* **smelled** [smɛld]) N odeur *f*; (*sense*) odorat *m* ▸ VT sentir ▸ VI (*pej*) sentir mauvais; (*food etc*): **to ~ (of)** sentir; **it smells good** ça sent bon

smelly ['smɛlɪ] ADJ qui sent mauvais, malodorant(e)

smelt [smɛlt] PT, PP *of* **smell** ▸ VT (*ore*) fondre

smidgen, smidgeon, smidgin ['smɪdʒən] N (*inf*): **a ~** un peu

★**smile** [smaɪl] N sourire *m* ▸ VI sourire

smiley ['smaɪlɪ] ADJ (*inf*) souriant(e) ▸ N binette *f*, smiley *m*

smiling ['smaɪlɪŋ] ADJ souriant(e)

smirk [sməːk] N petit sourire suffisant *or* affecté

smith [smɪθ] N maréchal-ferrant *m*; forgeron *m*

smithereens [smɪðə'riːnz] NPL: **to smash sth to ~** briser qch en mille morceaux; **to get blown to ~** être déchiqueté(e) dans une explosion

smithy ['smɪðɪ] N forge *f*

smitten ['smɪtn] ADJ: **~ with** pris(e) de; frappé(e) de

smock [smɒk] N blouse *f*, sarrau *m*

smog [smɒg] N brouillard mêlé de fumée

★**smoke** [sməuk] N fumée f; **to have a ~** fumer une cigarette; **to go up in ~** (*house etc*) brûler; (*fig*) partir en fumée ▶ VT, VI fumer; **do you ~?** est-ce que vous fumez ?; **do you mind if I ~?** ça ne vous dérange pas que je fume ?

smoke alarm N détecteur m de fumée

smoked ['sməukt] ADJ (*bacon, glass*) fumé(e)

smokeless fuel ['sməuklɪs-] N combustible non polluant

smokeless zone ['sməuklɪs-] N (*BRIT*) zone f où l'usage du charbon est réglementé

smoker ['sməukə^r] N (*person*) fumeur(-euse); (*Rail*) wagon m fumeurs

smoke screen N rideau m or écran m de fumée; (*fig*) paravent m

smoke shop N (*US*) (bureau m de) tabac m

★**smoking** ['sməukɪŋ] N: **"no ~"** (*sign*) « défense de fumer »; **to give up ~** arrêter de fumer

smoky ['sməukɪ] ADJ enfumé(e); (*taste*) fumé(e)

smolder ['sməuldə^r] VI (*US*) = **smoulder**

smoochy ['smu:tʃɪ] ADJ (*inf*) langoureux(-euse)

★**smooth** [smu:ð] ADJ lisse; (*sauce*) onctueux(-euse); (*flavour, whisky*) moelleux(-euse); (*cigarette*) doux (douce); (*movement*) régulier(-ière), sans à-coups or heurts; (*landing, takeoff*) en douceur; (*flight*) sans secousses; (*pej: person*) doucereux(-euse), mielleux(-euse) ▶ VT (*also:* **smooth out**) lisser, défroisser; (*: creases, difficulties*) faire disparaître
▶ **smooth over** VT: **to ~ things over** (*fig*) arranger les choses

smoothie ['smu:ðɪ] N (*drink*) boisson à base de purée de fruits, parfois additionnée de yaourt ou de glace; (*inf: man*) charmeur m

smoothly ['smu:ðlɪ] ADV (*easily*) facilement, sans difficulté(s); **everything went ~** tout s'est bien passé

smother ['smʌðə^r] VT étouffer

smoulder, (*US*) **smolder** ['sməuldə^r] VI couver

SMS N ABBR (= *short message service*) SMS m

SMS message N (message m) SMS m

smudge [smʌdʒ] N tache f, bavure f ▶ VT salir, maculer

smug [smʌg] ADJ suffisant(e), content(e) de soi

smuggle ['smʌgl] VT passer en contrebande or en fraude; **to ~ in/out** (*goods etc*) faire entrer/sortir clandestinement or en fraude

smuggler ['smʌglə^r] N contrebandier(-ière)

smuggling ['smʌglɪŋ] N contrebande f

smugly ['smʌglɪ] ADV d'un air suffisant

smugness ['smʌgnɪs] N suffisance f

smut [smʌt] N (*grain of soot*) grain m de suie; (*mark*) tache f de suie; (*in conversation etc*) obscénités fpl

smutty ['smʌtɪ] ADJ (*fig*) grossier(-ière), obscène

snack [snæk] N casse-croûte m inv; **to have a ~** prendre un en-cas, manger quelque chose (de léger)

snack bar N snack(-bar) m

snag [snæg] N inconvénient m, difficulté f

snail [sneɪl] N escargot m

snake [sneɪk] N serpent m

snakeskin ['sneɪkskɪn] N peau f de serpent ▶ CPD (*bag, belt*) en serpent, en peau de serpent

★**snap** [snæp] N (*sound*) claquement m, bruit sec; (*photograph*) photo f, instantané m; (*game*) sorte de jeu de bataille; **a cold ~** (*of weather*) un refroidissement soudain de la température ▶ ADJ subit(e), fait(e) sans réfléchir ▶ VT (*fingers*) faire claquer; (*break*) casser net; (*photograph*) prendre un instantané de; **to ~ one's fingers at** (*fig*) se moquer de ▶ VI se casser net or avec un bruit sec; (*fig: person*) craquer; (*speak sharply*) parler d'un ton brusque; **to ~ open/shut** s'ouvrir/se refermer brusquement
▶ **snap at** VT FUS (*subj: dog*) essayer de mordre
▶ **snap off** VT (*break*) casser net
▶ **snap up** VT sauter sur, saisir

snap fastener N bouton-pression m

snappy ['snæpɪ] ADJ prompt(e); (*slogan*) qui a du punch; **make it ~!** (*inf: hurry up*) grouille-toi ! (*inf*), magne-toi ! (*inf*)

snapshot ['snæpʃɔt] N photo f, instantané m

snare [snɛə^r] N piège m ▶ VT attraper, prendre au piège

snarl [snɑ:l] N grondement m or grognement m féroce ▶ VI gronder ▶ VT: **to get snarled up** (*wool, plans*) s'emmêler; (*traffic*) se bloquer

snatch [snætʃ] N (*fig*) vol m; (*small amount*): **snatches of** des fragments mpl or bribes fpl de ▶ VT saisir (*d'un geste vif*); (*steal*) voler; **to ~ a sandwich** manger or avaler un sandwich à la hâte; **to ~ some sleep** arriver à dormir un peu ▶ VI: **don't ~!** doucement !
▶ **snatch up** VT saisir, s'emparer de

snazzy ['snæzɪ] ADJ (*old: clothes*) classe inv (*inf*), chouette (*inf*)

sneak [sni:k] (*US pt, pp* **snuck** [snʌk]) VI: **to ~ in/out** entrer/sortir furtivement or à la dérobée; **to ~ up on sb** s'approcher de qn sans faire de bruit ▶ VT: **to ~ a look at sth** regarder furtivement qch ▶ N (*inf: pej: informer*) faux jeton

sneakers ['sni:kəz] NPL tennis mpl, baskets fpl

sneaking ['sni:kɪŋ] ADJ: **to have a ~ feeling** or **suspicion that …** avoir la vague impression que …

sneaky ['sni:kɪ] ADJ sournois(e)

sneer [snɪə^r] N ricanement m ▶ VI ricaner, sourire d'un air sarcastique; **to ~ at sb/sth** se moquer de qn/qch avec mépris

sneeze [sni:z] N éternuement m ▶ VI éternuer

snide [snaɪd] ADJ sarcastique, narquois(e)

sniff [snɪf] N reniflement m ▶ VI renifler ▶ VT renifler, flairer; (*glue, drug*) sniffer, respirer
▶ **sniff at** VT FUS: **it's not to be sniffed at** il ne faut pas cracher dessus, ce n'est pas à dédaigner

sniffer dog ['snɪfə-] N (*Police*) chien dressé pour la recherche d'explosifs et de stupéfiants

sniffle ['snɪfl] VI renifler ▶ N (*inf: cold*) léger rhume m; **to have the sniffles** être un peu enrhumé(e)

snigger ['snɪgə^r] N ricanement m; rire moqueur ▶ VI ricaner

snip [snɪp] N (*cut*) entaille f; (*piece*) petit bout; (*BRIT inf: bargain*) (bonne) occasion or affaire f ▶ VT couper

snipe [snaɪp] VI (*criticize*) critiquer; **to ~ at sb/sth** (*criticize*) critiquer qn/qch; (*shoot at*) tirer sur qn/qch sans se faire voir

sniper ['snaɪpə^r] N (*marksman*) tireur embusqué

snippet ['snɪpɪt] N bribes *fpl*

snitch [snɪtʃ] (*inf*) vɪ cafter (*inf*); **to ~ on sb** cafter qn ▶ N cafteur(-euse) (*inf*)

snivel ['snɪvl] vɪ pleurnicher

snivelling ['snɪvlɪŋ] ADJ larmoyant(e), pleurnicheur(-euse)

snob [snɔb] N snob *mf*

snobbery ['snɔbərɪ] N snobisme *m*

snobbish ['snɔbɪʃ] ADJ snob *inv*

snog [snɔg] vɪ (*inf*) se bécoter

snooker ['snu:kə^r] N *sorte de jeu de billard*

snoop [snu:p] vɪ: **to ~ on sb** espionner qn; **to ~ about** fureter

snooper ['snu:pə^r] N fureteur(-euse)

snooty ['snu:tɪ] ADJ snob *inv*, prétentieux(-euse)

snooze [snu:z] N petit somme ▶ vɪ faire un petit somme

snore [snɔ:^r] vɪ ronfler ▶ N ronflement *m*

snoring ['snɔ:rɪŋ] N ronflement(s) *m(pl)*

snorkel ['snɔ:kl] N (*of swimmer*) tuba *m*

snort [snɔ:t] N grognement *m* ▶ vɪ grogner; (*horse*) renâcler ▶ vᴛ (*inf: drugs*) sniffer

snot [snɔt] N (*inf*) morve *f*

snotty ['snɔtɪ] ADJ (*inf*) morveux(-euse)

snout [snaut] N museau *m*

★**snow** [snəu] N neige *f* ▶ vɪ neiger ▶ vᴛ: **to be snowed under with work** être débordé(e) de travail

snowball ['snəubɔ:l] N boule *f* de neige

snowboard ['snəubɔ:d] N planche *f* de snowboard

snowboarder ['snəubɔ:də^r] N snowboarder(-euse), surfeur(-euse) des neiges

snowboarding ['snəubɔ:dɪŋ] N snowboard *m*

snowbound ['snəubaund] ADJ enneigé(e), bloqué(e) par la neige

snow-capped ['snəukæpt] ADJ (*peak, mountain*) couvert(e) de neige

snowdrift ['snəudrɪft] N congère *f*

snowdrop ['snəudrɔp] N perce-neige *m*

snowfall ['snəufɔ:l] N chute *f* de neige

snowflake ['snəufleɪk] N flocon *m* de neige

snowman ['snəumæn] N (*irreg*) bonhomme *m* de neige

snowmobile ['snəuməubi:l] N scooter *m* des neiges

snowplough, (US) **snowplow** ['snəuplau] N chasse-neige *m inv*

snowshoe ['snəuʃu:] N raquette *f* (*pour la neige*)

snowstorm ['snəustɔ:m] N tempête *f* de neige

snowy ['snəuɪ] ADJ neigeux(-euse); (*covered with snow*) enneigé(e)

SNP N ABBR (*Brit Pol*) = **Scottish National Party**

snub [snʌb] vᴛ repousser, snober ▶ N rebuffade *f*

snub-nosed [snʌb'nəuzd] ADJ au nez retroussé

snuck [snʌk] (US) PT, PP of **sneak**

snuff [snʌf] N tabac *m* à priser ▶ vᴛ (*also*: **snuff out**: *candle*) moucher

snuff movie N (*inf*) *film pornographique qui se termine par le meurtre réel de l'un des acteurs*

snug [snʌg] ADJ douillet(te), confortable; (*person*) bien au chaud; **it's a ~ fit** c'est bien ajusté(e)

snuggle ['snʌgl] vɪ: **to ~ down in bed/up to sb** se pelotonner dans son lit/contre qn

SO ABBR (*Banking*) = **standing order**

---

so [səu]

ADV **1** (*thus, likewise*) ainsi, de cette façon; **if so** si oui; **so do** *or* **have I** moi aussi; **it's 5 o'clock — so it is!** il est 5 heures — en effet! *or* c'est vrai!; **I hope/think so** je l'espère/le crois; **so far** jusqu'ici, jusqu'à maintenant; (*in past*) jusque-là; **quite so!** exactement!, c'est bien ça!; **even so** quand même, tout de même

2 (*in comparisons etc: to such a degree*) si, tellement; **so big (that)** si *or* tellement grand (que); **she's not so clever as her brother** elle n'est pas aussi intelligente que son frère

3: **so much** *adj*, *adv* tant (de); **I've got so much work** j'ai tant de travail; **I love you so much** je vous aime tant; **so many** tant (de)

4 (*phrases*): **10 or so** à peu près *or* environ 10; **so long!** (*inf: goodbye*) au revoir!, à un de ces jours!; **so to speak** pour ainsi dire; **so (what)?** (*inf*) (bon) et alors?, et après?

▶ CONJ **1** (*expressing purpose*): **so as to do** pour faire, afin de faire; **so (that)** pour que *or* afin que + *sub*

2 (*expressing result*) donc, par conséquent; **so that** si bien que, de (telle) sorte que; **so that's the reason!** c'est donc (pour) ça!; **so you see, I could have gone** alors tu vois, j'aurais pu y aller

---

soak [səuk] vᴛ faire *or* laisser tremper; (*drench*) tremper; **to be soaked through** être trempé jusqu'aux os ▶ vɪ tremper
▶ **soak in** vɪ pénétrer, être absorbé(e)
▶ **soak up** vᴛ absorber

soaking ['səukɪŋ] ADJ (*also*: **soaking wet**) trempé(e)

so-and-so ['səuənsəu] N (*somebody*) un(e) tel(le)

★**soap** [səup] N savon *m*

soapbox ['səupbɔks] N tribune improvisée (en plein air)

soapflakes ['səupfleɪks] NPL paillettes *fpl* de savon

soap opera N feuilleton télévisé (*quotidienneté réaliste ou embellie*)

soap powder N lessive *f*, détergent *m*

soapsuds ['səupsʌdz] NPL mousse *f* de savon

soapy ['səupɪ] ADJ savonneux(-euse)

soar [sɔ:^r] vɪ monter (en flèche), s'élancer; (*building*) s'élancer; **soaring prices** prix qui grimpent

sob [sɔb] N sanglot *m* ▶ vɪ sangloter

s.o.b. N ABBR (US *inf!*: = *son of a bitch*) salaud *m* (!)

sobbing ['sɔbɪŋ] N sanglots *mpl*

sober ['səubə^r] ADJ qui n'est pas (*or* plus) ivre; (*serious*) sérieux(-euse), sensé(e); (*moderate*) mesuré(e); (*colour, style*) sobre, discret(-ète)
▶ **sober up** vᴛ dégriser ▶ vɪ se dégriser

sobering ['səubərɪŋ] ADJ: **it's a ~ thought** cela donne à réfléchir; **to have a ~ effect on sb** donner à réfléchir à qn

sobriety [sə'braɪətɪ] N (not being drunk) sobriété f; (seriousness, sedateness) sérieux m

sob story N (inf, pej) histoire larmoyante

Soc. ABBR (= society) Soc

so-called ['səʊ'kɔ:ld] ADJ soi-disant inv

★**soccer** ['sɔkəʳ] N football m

soccer pitch N terrain m de football

soccer player N footballeur m

sociability [səʊʃə'bɪlɪtɪ] N sociabilité f

sociable ['səʊʃəbl] ADJ sociable

★**social** ['səʊʃl] ADJ social(e); (sociable) sociable ▸ N (petite) fête

social climber N arriviste mf

social club N amicale f, foyer m

Social Democrat N social-démocrate mf

social insurance N (US) sécurité sociale

socialism ['səʊʃəlɪzəm] N socialisme m

socialist ['səʊʃəlɪst] ADJ, N socialiste mf

socialite ['səʊʃəlaɪt] N personnalité mondaine

socialization [səʊʃəlaɪ'zeɪʃən] N socialisation f

socialize ['səʊʃəlaɪz] VI voir or rencontrer des gens, se faire des amis; **to ~ with** (meet often) fréquenter; (get to know) lier connaissance or parler avec

social life N vie sociale; **how's your ~?** est-ce que tu sors beaucoup ?

socially ['səʊʃəlɪ] ADV socialement, en société

social media NPL médias mpl sociaux

social networking [-'nɛtwəːkɪŋ] N réseaux mpl sociaux

social networking site N site m de réseautage

social science N sciences humaines

social security N aide sociale

social services NPL services sociaux

social welfare N sécurité sociale

social work N assistance sociale

social worker N assistant(e) social(e)

societal [sə'saɪətl] ADJ sociétal(e)

society [sə'saɪətɪ] N société f; (club) société, association f; (also: **high society**) (haute) société, grand monde ▸ CPD (party) mondain(e)

socio-economic ['səʊsɪəʊɪːkə'nɔmɪk] ADJ socioéconomique

sociological [səʊsɪə'lɔdʒɪkl] ADJ sociologique

sociologist [səʊsɪ'ɔlədʒɪst] N sociologue mf

sociology [səʊsɪ'ɔlədʒɪ] N sociologie f

sociopath ['səʊsɪəpæθ] N sociopathe mf

socio-political [səʊsɪəʊpə'lɪtɪkl] ADJ sociopolitique

sock [sɔk] N chaussette f; **to pull one's socks up** (fig) se secouer (les puces) ▸ VT (inf: hit) flanquer un coup à

socket ['sɔkɪt] N cavité f; (Elec: also: **wall socket**) prise f de courant; (for light bulb) douille f

sod [sɔd] N (of earth) motte f; (BRIT pej) con m (!), salaud m (!)
▸ **sod off** VI: **~ off!** (BRIT inf!) fous le camp !, va te faire foutre ! (!)

soda ['səʊdə] N (Chem) soude f; (also: **soda water**) eau f de Seltz; (US: also: **soda pop**) soda m

sodden ['sɔdn] ADJ trempé(e), détrempé(e)

sodium ['səʊdɪəm] N sodium m

sodium chloride N chlorure m de sodium

Sod's Law [sɔdz'lɔ:] N (BRIT inf) loi f de l'emmerdement maximum (inf)

sofa ['səʊfə] N sofa m, canapé m

sofa bed N canapé-lit m

Sofia ['səʊfɪə] N Sofia

★**soft** [sɔft] ADJ (not rough) doux (douce); (not hard) doux, mou (molle); (not loud) doux, léger(-ère); (kind) doux, gentil(le); (weak) indulgent(e); (stupid) stupide, débile

softball ['sɔftbɔ:l] N (game) softball m; (ball) balle f de softball

soft-boiled ['sɔftbɔɪld] ADJ (egg) à la coque

soft drink N boisson non alcoolisée

soft drugs NPL drogues douces

soften ['sɔfn] VT (r)amollir; (fig) adoucir ▸ VI se ramollir; (fig) s'adoucir

softener ['sɔfnəʳ] N (water softener) adoucisseur m; (fabric softener) produit assouplissant

soft fruit N (BRIT) baies fpl

soft furnishings NPL tissus mpl d'ameublement

soft-hearted [sɔft'hɑ:tɪd] ADJ au cœur tendre

softly ['sɔftlɪ] ADV doucement; (touch) légèrement; (kiss) tendrement

softness ['sɔftnɪs] N douceur f

soft option N solution f de facilité

soft sell N promotion f de vente discrète

soft target N cible f facile

soft toy N jouet m en peluche

★**software** ['sɔftwɛəʳ] N (Comput) logiciel m, software m

software package N (Comput) progiciel m

softy ['sɔftɪ] N (inf) cœur m sensible

soggy ['sɔgɪ] ADJ (clothes) trempé(e); (ground) détrempé(e)

★**soil** [sɔɪl] N (earth) sol m, terre f ▸ VT salir; (fig) souiller

soiled [sɔɪld] ADJ sale; (Comm) défraîchi(e)

sojourn ['sɔdʒə:n] N (formal) séjour m

solace ['sɔlɪs] N consolation f, réconfort m

solar ['səʊləʳ] ADJ solaire

solarium [sə'lɛərɪəm] (pl **solaria** [-rɪə]) N solarium m

solar panel N panneau m solaire

solar plexus [-'plɛksəs] N (Anat) plexus m solaire

solar power N énergie f solaire

solar system N système m solaire

sold [səʊld] PT, PP of **sell**

solder ['səʊldəʳ] VT souder (au fil à souder) ▸ N soudure f

★**soldier** ['səʊldʒəʳ] N soldat m, militaire m; **toy ~** petit soldat ▸ VI: **to ~ on** persévérer, s'accrocher

sold out ADJ (Comm) épuisé(e)

sole [səʊl] N (of foot) plante f; (of shoe) semelle f; (fish: pl inv) sole f ▸ ADJ seul(e), unique; **the ~ reason** la seule et unique raison

solely ['səʊllɪ] ADV seulement, uniquement; **I will hold you ~ responsible** je vous en tiendrai pour seul responsable

solemn ['sɔləm] ADJ solennel(le); (person) sérieux(-euse), grave

sole trader N (Comm) chef m d'entreprise individuelle

solicit [sə'lɪsɪt] VT (request) solliciter ▶ VI (prostitute) racoler

★**solicitor** [sə'lɪsɪtə'] N (BRIT: for wills etc) ≈ notaire m; (: in court) ≈ avocat m

solid ['sɔlɪd] ADJ (strong, sound, reliable, not liquid) solide; (not hollow: mass) compact(e); (: metal, rock, wood) massif(-ive); (meal) consistant(e), substantiel(le); (vote) unanime; **to be on ~ ground** être sur la terre ferme; (fig) être en terrain sûr; **we waited two ~ hours** nous avons attendu deux heures entières ▶ N solide m

solidarity [sɔlɪ'dærɪtɪ] N solidarité f

solid fuel N combustible m solide

solidify [sə'lɪdɪfaɪ] VI se solidifier ▶ VT solidifier

solidity [sə'lɪdɪtɪ] N solidité f

solidly ['sɔlɪdlɪ] ADV (firmly: built, based) solidement; (continuously: work, rain) sans discontinuer; (unanimously) massivement; **to sleep ~ for 12 hours** dormir pendant 12 heures d'affilée; **to be ~ behind/against sb/sth** faire bloc derrière/contre qn/qch

solid-state ['sɔlɪdsteɪt] ADJ (Elec) à circuits intégrés

soliloquy [sə'lɪləkwɪ] N monologue m

solitaire [sɔlɪ'tɛə'] N (gem, BRIT: game) solitaire m; (US: card game) réussite f

solitary ['sɔlɪtərɪ] ADJ solitaire

solitary confinement N (in prison) isolement m (cellulaire)

solitude ['sɔlɪtjuːd] N solitude f

solo ['səuləu] N solo m ▶ ADV (fly) en solitaire

soloist ['səuləuɪst] N soliste mf

Solomon Islands ['sɔləmən-] NPL: **the ~** les (îles fpl) Salomon fpl

solstice ['sɔlstɪs] N solstice m

soluble ['sɔljubl] ADJ soluble

★**solution** [sə'luːʃən] N solution f

★**solve** [sɔlv] VT résoudre

solvency ['sɔlvənsɪ] N (Comm) solvabilité f

solvent ['sɔlvənt] ADJ (Comm) solvable ▶ N (Chem) (dis)solvant m

solvent abuse N usage m de solvants hallucinogènes

Somali [səu'mɑːlɪ] ADJ somali(e), somalien(ne) ▶ N Somali(e), Somalien(ne)

Somalia [səu'mɑːlɪə] N (République f de) Somalie f

Somalian [sə'mɑːlɪən] ADJ somalien(ne) ▶ N Somalien(ne)

sombre, (US) **somber** ['sɔmbə'] ADJ sombre, morne

---

some [sʌm]

ADJ 1 (a certain amount or number of): **some tea/water/ice cream** du thé/de l'eau/de la glace; **some children/apples** des enfants/pommes; **I've got some money but not much** j'ai de l'argent mais pas beaucoup

---

2 (certain: in contrasts): **some people say that …** il y a des gens qui disent que …; **some films were excellent, but most were mediocre** certains films étaient excellents, mais la plupart étaient médiocres

3 (unspecified): **some woman was asking for you** il y avait une dame qui vous demandait; **he was asking for some book (or other)** il demandait un livre quelconque; **some day** un de ces jours; **some day next week** un jour la semaine prochaine; **after some time** après un certain temps; **at some length** assez longuement; **in some form or other** sous une forme ou une autre, sous une forme quelconque

▶ PRON 1 (a certain number) quelques-uns (quelques-unes), certains (certaines); **I've got some** (books etc) j'en ai (quelques-uns); **some (of them) have been sold** certains ont été vendus

2 (a certain amount) un peu; **I've got some** (money, milk) j'en ai (un peu); **would you like some?** est-ce que vous en voulez?, en voulez-vous?; **could I have some of that cheese?** pourrais-je avoir un peu de ce fromage?; **I've read some of the book** j'ai lu une partie du livre

▶ ADV: **some 10 people** quelque 10 personnes, 10 personnes environ

★**somebody** ['sʌmbədɪ] PRON = **someone**

someday ['sʌmdeɪ] ADV un de ces jours, un jour ou l'autre

★**somehow** ['sʌmhau] ADV d'une façon ou d'une autre; (for some reason) pour une raison ou une autre

★**someone** ['sʌmwʌn] PRON quelqu'un; **~ or other** quelqu'un, je ne sais qui

someplace ['sʌmpleɪs] ADV (US) = **somewhere**

somersault ['sʌməsɔːlt] N culbute f, saut périlleux ▶ VI faire la culbute or un saut périlleux; (car) faire un tonneau

★**something** ['sʌmθɪŋ] PRON quelque chose m; **~ interesting** quelque chose d'intéressant; **~ to do** quelque chose à faire; **he's ~ like me** il est un peu comme moi; **it's ~ of a problem** il y a là un problème

sometime ['sʌmtaɪm] ADV (in future) un de ces jours, un jour ou l'autre; (in past): **~ last month** au cours du mois dernier

★**sometimes** ['sʌmtaɪmz] ADV quelquefois, parfois

★**somewhat** ['sʌmwɔt] ADV quelque peu, un peu

★**somewhere** ['sʌmwɛə'] ADV quelque part; **~ else** ailleurs, autre part

★**son** [sʌn] N fils m

sonar ['səunɑː'] N sonar m

sonata [sə'nɑːtə] N sonate f

★**song** [sɔŋ] N chanson f; (of bird) chant m

songbird ['sɔŋbəːd] N oiseau m chanteur

songbook ['sɔŋbuk] N chansonnier m

songwriter ['sɔŋraɪtə'] N auteur-compositeur m

sonic ['sɔnɪk] ADJ (boom) supersonique

son-in-law ['sʌnɪnlɔː] N gendre m, beau-fils m

sonnet ['sɔnɪt] N sonnet m

sonny ['sʌnɪ] N (inf) fiston m (inf)

son of a bitch N (inf!) fils m de pute (!)

sonorous ['sɔnərəs, sə'nɔːrəs] ADJ sonore

S

★**soon** [suːn] ADV bientôt; (*early*) tôt; **~ afterwards** peu après; **quite ~** sous peu; **how ~ can you do it?** combien de temps vous faut-il pour le faire, au plus pressé ?; **how ~ can you come back?** quand *or* dans combien de temps pouvez-vous revenir, au plus tôt ?; **see you ~!** à bientôt !; *see also* **as**

sooner [ˈsuːnəʳ] ADV (*time*) plus tôt; (*preference*): **I would ~ do that** j'aimerais autant *or* je préférerais faire ça; **~ or later** tôt ou tard; **no ~ said than done** sitôt dit, sitôt fait; **the ~ the better** le plus tôt sera le mieux; **no ~ had we left than …** à peine étions-nous partis que …

soot [sut] N suie f

soothe [suːð] VT calmer, apaiser

soothing [ˈsuːðɪŋ] ADJ (*ointment etc*) lénitif(-ive), lénifiant(e); (*tone, words etc*) apaisant(e); (*drink, bath*) relaxant(e)

SOP N ABBR = **standard operating procedure**

sop [sɔp] N: **that's only a ~** c'est pour nous (*or* les *etc*) amadouer

sophisticated [səˈfɪstɪkeɪtɪd] ADJ raffiné(e), sophistiqué(e); (*machinery*) hautement perfectionné(e), très complexe; (*system etc*) très perfectionné(e), sophistiqué

sophistication [səfɪstɪˈkeɪʃən] N raffinement m, niveau m (de) perfectionnement m

sophomore [ˈsɔfəmɔːʳ] N (US) étudiant(e) de seconde année

soporific [sɔpəˈrɪfɪk] ADJ soporifique ▸ N somnifère m

sopping [ˈsɔpɪŋ] ADJ (*also:* **sopping wet**) tout(e) trempé(e)

soppy [ˈsɔpɪ] ADJ (*inf*) sentimental(e)

soprano [səˈprɑːnəu] N (*voice*) soprano m; (*singer*) soprano mf

sorbet [ˈsɔːbeɪ] N sorbet m

sorcerer [ˈsɔːsərəʳ] N sorcier m

sorceress [ˈsɔːsərɪs] N sorcière f

sordid [ˈsɔːdɪd] ADJ sordide

sore [sɔːʳ] ADJ (*painful*) douloureux(-euse), sensible; (*offended*) contrarié(e), vexé(e); **to have a ~ throat** avoir mal à la gorge; **it's a ~ point** (*fig*) c'est un point délicat ▸ N plaie f

sorely [ˈsɔːlɪ] ADV (*tempted*) fortement

sorrel [ˈsɔrəl] N oseille f

sorrow [ˈsɔrəu] N peine f, chagrin m

sorrowful [ˈsɔrəuful] ADJ triste

★**sorry** [ˈsɔrɪ] ADJ désolé(e); (*condition, excuse, tale*) triste, déplorable; (*sight*) désolant(e); **~!** pardon !, excusez-moi !; **~?** pardon ?; **to feel ~ for sb** plaindre qn; **I'm ~ to hear that …** je suis désolé(e) *or* navré(e) d'apprendre que …; **to be ~ about sth** regretter qch

★**sort** [sɔːt] N genre m, espèce f, sorte f; (*make: of coffee, car etc*) marque f; **what ~ do you want?** quelle sorte *or* quel genre voulez-vous ?; **what ~ of car?** quelle marque de voiture ?; **I'll do nothing of the ~!** je ne ferai rien de tel !; **it's ~ of awkward** (*inf*) c'est plutôt gênant ▸ VT (*also:* **sort out:** *select which to keep*) trier; (: *classify*) classer; (: *tidy*) ranger; (: *letters etc*) trier; (: *Comput*) trier
  ▸ **sort out** VT (*problem*) résoudre, régler

sortie [ˈsɔːtɪ] N sortie f

sorting office [ˈsɔːtɪŋ-] N (*Post*) bureau m de tri

SOS N SOS m

so-so [ˈsəusəu] ADV comme ci comme ça

soufflé [ˈsuːfleɪ] N soufflé m

sought [sɔːt] PT, PP *of* **seek**

sought-after [ˈsɔːtɑːftəʳ] ADJ recherché(e)

soul [səul] N âme f; **the poor ~ had nowhere to sleep** le pauvre n'avait nulle part où dormir; **I didn't see a ~** je n'ai vu (absolument) personne

soul-destroying [ˈsəuldɪstrɔɪɪŋ] ADJ démoralisant(e)

soulful [ˈsəulful] ADJ plein(e) de sentiment

soulless [ˈsəullɪs] ADJ sans cœur, inhumain(e)

soul mate N âme f sœur

soul-searching [ˈsəulsɜːtʃɪŋ] N: **after much ~, I decided …** j'ai longuement réfléchi avant de décider …

★**sound** [saund] ADJ (*healthy*) en bonne santé, sain(e); (*safe, not damaged*) solide, en bon état; (*reliable, not superficial*) sérieux(-euse), solide; (*sensible*) sensé(e); **to be of ~ mind** être sain(e) d'esprit ▸ ADV: **~ asleep** profondément endormi(e) ▸ N (*noise, volume*) son m; (*louder*) bruit m; (*Geo*) détroit m, bras m de mer; **I don't like the ~ of it** ça ne me dit rien qui vaille ▸ VT (*alarm*) sonner; (*also:* **sound out:** *opinions*) sonder; **to ~ one's horn** (*Aut*) klaxonner, actionner son avertisseur ▸ VI sonner, retentir; (*fig: seem*) sembler (être); **to ~ like** ressembler à; **it sounds as if …** il semblerait que …, j'ai l'impression que …
  ▸ **sound off** VI (*inf*): **to ~ off (about)** la ramener (sur)

sound barrier N mur m du son

sound bite N phrase toute faite (*pour être citée dans les médias*)

sound effects NPL bruitage m

sound engineer N ingénieur m du son

sounding [ˈsaundɪŋ] N (*Naut etc*) sondage m

sounding board N (*Mus*) table f d'harmonie; (*fig*): **to use sb as a ~ for one's ideas** essayer ses idées sur qn

soundly [ˈsaundlɪ] ADV (*sleep*) profondément; (*beat*) complètement, à plate couture

soundproof [ˈsaundpruːf] VT insonoriser ▸ ADJ insonorisé(e)

soundproofing [ˈsaundpruːfɪŋ] N insonorisation f

sound system N sono(risation) f

soundtrack [ˈsaundtræk] N (*of film*) bande f sonore

sound wave N (*Physics*) onde f sonore

★**soup** [suːp] N soupe f, potage m; **in the ~** (*fig*) dans le pétrin

soup course N potage m

soup kitchen N soupe f populaire

soup plate N assiette creuse *or* à soupe

soup spoon [ˈsuːpspuːn] N cuiller f à soupe

sour [ˈsauəʳ] ADJ aigre, acide; (*milk*) tourné(e), aigre; (*fig*) acerbe, aigre; revêche; **to go** *or* **turn ~** (*milk, wine*) tourner; (*fig: relationship, plans*) mal tourner; **it's ~ grapes** c'est du dépit

source [sɔːs] N source f; **I have it from a reliable ~ that** je sais de source sûre que

sour cream, soured cream N crème f aigre

★**south** [sauθ] N sud m; **to the ~ of** au sud de ▸ ADJ sud *inv*; *(wind)* du sud ▸ ADV au sud, vers le sud; **to travel ~** aller en direction du sud; **~ of** au sud de

South Africa N Afrique f du Sud

South African ADJ sud-africain(e) ▸ N Sud-Africain(e)

South America N Amérique f du Sud

South American ADJ sud-américain(e) ▸ N Sud-Américain(e)

southbound [ˈsauθbaund] ADJ en direction du sud; *(carriageway)* sud *inv*

south-east [sauθˈiːst] N sud-est m

South-East Asia N le Sud-Est asiatique

southeastern [sauθˈiːstən] ADJ du or au sud-est

southerly [ˈsʌðəlɪ] ADJ du sud; au sud

★**southern** [ˈsʌðən] ADJ (du) sud; méridional(e); **with a ~ aspect** orienté(e) or exposé(e) au sud; **the ~ hemisphere** l'hémisphère sud or austral

southerner [ˈsʌðənəʳ] N méridional(e)

southernmost [ˈsʌðənməust] ADJ: **the ~ part of sth** l'extrême sud de qch; **Egypt's ~ city** la ville la plus au sud d'Égypte

South Korea N Corée f du Sud

South of France N: **the ~** le Sud de la France, le Midi

South Pole N: **the ~** le pôle Sud

South Sea Islands NPL: **the ~** l'Océanie f

South Seas NPL: **the ~** les mers fpl du Sud

South Sudan N Soudan m du Sud

South Vietnam N Viêt-Nam m du Sud

South Wales N sud m du Pays de Galles

southward [ˈsauθwəd], **southwards** [ˈsauθwədz] ADV vers le sud

south-west [sauθˈwest] N sud-ouest m

southwestern [sauθˈwestən] ADJ du or au sud-ouest

souvenir [suːvəˈnɪəʳ] N souvenir m *(objet)*

sovereign [ˈsɔvrɪn] ADJ, N souverain(e)

sovereignty [ˈsɔvrɪntɪ] N souveraineté f

soviet [ˈsəuvɪət] ADJ soviétique

Soviet Union N: **the ~** l'Union f soviétique

sow[1] [sau] *(pt* **sowed** [səud], *pp* **sown** [səun]*)* VT semer

sow[2] [sau] N truie f

soya [ˈsɔɪə], *(US)* **soy** [sɔɪ] N: **~ bean** graine f de soja; **~ sauce** sauce f au soja

sozzled [ˈsɔzld] ADJ *(BRIT inf)* paf *inv*

spa [spaː] N *(town)* station thermale; *(also:* **health spa***)* spa m

★**space** [speɪs] N *(gen)* espace m; *(room)* place f; espace; *(length of time)* laps m de temps; **to clear a ~ for sth** faire de la place pour qch; **in a confined ~** dans un espace réduit or restreint; **in a short ~ of time** dans peu de temps; **(with)in the ~ of an hour** en l'espace d'une heure ▸ CPD spatial(e) ▸ VT *(also:* **space out***)* espacer

space bar N *(on typewriter)* barre f d'espacement

spacecraft [ˈspeɪskraːft] N engin or vaisseau spatial

spaceman [ˈspeɪsmæn] N *(irreg)* astronaute m, cosmonaute m

spaceship [ˈspeɪsʃɪp] N = **spacecraft**

space shuttle N navette spatiale

spacesuit [ˈspeɪssuːt] N combinaison spatiale

spacewoman [ˈspeɪswumən] N *(irreg)* astronaute f, cosmonaute f

spacing [ˈspeɪsɪŋ] N espacement m; **single/double ~** *(Typ etc)* interligne m simple/double

spacious [ˈspeɪʃəs] ADJ spacieux(-euse), grand(e)

spade [speɪd] N *(tool)* bêche f, pelle f; *(child's)* pelle ■ **spades** NPL *(Cards)* pique m

spadework [ˈspeɪdwəːk] N *(fig)* gros m du travail

spaghetti [spəˈgetɪ] N spaghetti mpl

★**Spain** [speɪn] N Espagne f

spam [spæm] N *(Comput)* spam m, pollupostage m ▸ CPD *(filter, laws)* antispam *inv*, antipollupostage *inv* ▸ VT envoyer des spams à, polluposter

spammer [ˈspæməʳ] N *(Comput)* spammeur(-euse), polluposteur m

spamming [ˈspæmɪŋ] N *(Comput)* spamming m, envoi m de pourriels

span [spæn] N *(of bird, plane)* envergure f; *(of arch)* portée f; *(in time)* espace m de temps, durée f ▸ VT enjamber, franchir; *(fig)* couvrir, embrasser

spangled [ˈspæŋgəld] ADJ pailleté(e); **a dark night sky ~ with stars** une nuit sombre constellée d'étoiles

★**Spaniard** [ˈspænjəd] N Espagnol(e)

spaniel [ˈspænjəl] N épagneul m

★**Spanish** [ˈspænɪʃ] ADJ espagnol(e), d'Espagne; **~ omelette** omelette f à l'espagnole ▸ N *(Ling)* espagnol m; **the ~** npl les Espagnols mpl

spank [spæŋk] VT donner une fessée à

spanking [ˈspæŋkɪŋ] N fessée f ▸ ADV *(inf: new)* flambant; **a ~ new Mercedes** une Mercedes flambant neuve

spanner [ˈspænəʳ] N *(BRIT)* clé f (de mécanicien)

spar [spaːʳ] N espar m ▸ VI *(Boxing)* s'entraîner

★**spare** [spɛəʳ] ADJ de réserve, de rechange; *(surplus)* de or en trop, de reste; **there are 2 going ~** *(BRIT)* il y en a 2 de disponible ▸ N *(part)* pièce f de rechange, pièce détachée ▸ VT *(do without)* se passer de; *(afford to give)* donner, accorder, passer; *(not hurt)* épargner; *(not use)* ménager; **to ~** *(surplus)* en surplus, de trop; **to ~ no expense** ne pas reculer devant la dépense; **can you ~ the time?** est-ce que vous avez le temps ?; **there is no time to ~** il n'y a pas de temps à perdre; **I've a few minutes to ~** je dispose de quelques minutes

spare part N pièce f de rechange, pièce détachée

spare room N chambre f d'ami

spare time N moments mpl de loisir

spare tyre, *(US)* **spare tire** N *(Aut)* pneu m de rechange

spare wheel N *(Aut)* roue f de secours

sparing [ˈspɛərɪŋ] ADJ: **to be ~ with** ménager

sparingly [ˈspɛərɪŋlɪ] ADV avec modération

spark [spaːk] N étincelle f; *(fig)* étincelle, lueur f ▸ VT *(riot, row)* déclencher

sparkle [ˈspaːkl] N scintillement m, étincellement m, éclat m ▸ VI étinceler, scintiller; *(bubble)* pétiller

sparkler [ˈspaːkləʳ] N cierge m magique

S

859

sparkling ['spɑːklɪŋ] ADJ étincelant(e), scintillant(e); (wine) mousseux(-euse), pétillant(e); (water) pétillant(e), gazeux(-euse)

sparkly ['spɑːklɪ] ADJ (inf) étincelant(e)

spark plug N bougie f

sparring partner ['spɑːrɪŋ-] N sparring-partner m; (fig) vieil(le) ennemi(e)

sparrow ['spærəu] N moineau m

sparse [spɑːs] ADJ clairsemé(e)

sparsely ['spɑːslɪ] ADV: ~ **populated** à la population clairsemée; ~ **furnished** sommairement meublé(e)

spartan ['spɑːtən] ADJ (fig) spartiate

spasm ['spæzəm] N (Med) spasme m; (fig) accès m

spasmodic [spæz'mɔdɪk] ADJ (fig) intermittent(e)

spat [spæt] PT, PP of **spit** ▶ N (US) prise f de bec

spate [speɪt] N (fig): ~ **of** avalanche f or torrent m de; **in** ~ (river) en crue

spatial ['speɪʃl] ADJ spatial(e)

spatter ['spætər] N éclaboussure(s) f(pl) ▶ VT éclabousser ▶ VI gicler

spatula ['spætjulə] N spatule f

spawn [spɔːn] VT pondre; (pej) engendrer ▶ VI frayer ▶ N frai m

SPCA N ABBR (US: = Society for the Prevention of Cruelty to Animals) ≈ SPA f

SPCC N ABBR (US) = **Society for the Prevention of Cruelty to Children**

★**speak** [spiːk] (pt **spoke** [spəuk], pp **spoken** ['spəukn]) VT (language) parler; (truth) dire; **I don't** ~ **French** je ne parle pas français; **do you** ~ **English?** parlez-vous anglais ?; **to** ~ **one's mind** dire ce que l'on pense ▶ VI parler; (make a speech) prendre la parole; **to** ~ **to sb/of** or **about sth** parler à qn/de qch; **can I** ~ **to …?** est-ce que je peux parler à … ?; **speaking!** (on telephone) c'est moi-même !; **it speaks for itself** c'est évident; ~ **up!** parle plus fort !; **he has no money to** ~ **of** il n'a pas d'argent
▶ **speak for** [spiːk fɔː'] VT FUS: **to** ~ **for sb** parler pour qn; **that picture is already spoken for** (in shop) ce tableau est déjà réservé
▶ **speak out** [spiːk aut] VI parler haut et fort; **to** ~ **out against sth** s'élever contre qch; **to** ~ **out in favour of sth** plaider la cause de qch

★**speaker** ['spiːkər] N (in public) orateur m; (also: **loudspeaker**) haut-parleur m; (: for stereo etc) baffle m, enceinte f; (: Pol): **the S**~ (BRIT) le président de la Chambre des communes or des représentants; (US) le président de la Chambre; **are you a Welsh** ~? parlez-vous gallois ?

speaking ['spiːkɪŋ] ADJ parlant(e); **French-speaking people** les francophones mpl; **to be on** ~ **terms** se parler

spear [spɪə'] N lance f ▶ VT transpercer

spearhead ['spɪəhɛd] N fer m de lance; (Mil) colonne f d'attaque ▶ VT (attack etc) mener

spearmint ['spɪəmɪnt] N (Bot etc) menthe verte

spec [spɛk] N (BRIT inf): **on** ~ à tout hasard; **to buy on** ~ acheter avec l'espoir de faire une bonne affaire

★**special** ['spɛʃl] ADJ spécial(e); **take** ~ **care** soyez particulièrement prudent; **nothing** ~ rien de spécial ▶ N (train) train spécial; **today's** ~ (at restaurant) le plat du jour

special agent N agent secret

special correspondent N envoyé spécial

special delivery N (Post): **by** ~ en express

special effects NPL (Cine) effets spéciaux

★**specialist** ['spɛʃəlɪst] N spécialiste mf; **heart** ~ cardiologue mf

speciality [spɛʃɪ'ælɪtɪ] N (BRIT) spécialité f

specialization [spɛʃəlaɪ'zeɪʃən] N spécialisation f

★**specialize** ['spɛʃəlaɪz] VI: **to** ~ **(in)** se spécialiser (dans)

specially ['spɛʃlɪ] ADV spécialement, particulièrement

special needs NPL (BRIT) difficultés fpl d'apprentissage scolaire

special offer N (Comm) réclame f

special school N (BRIT) établissement m d'enseignement spécialisé

specialty ['spɛʃəltɪ] N (US) = **speciality**

★**species** ['spiːʃiːz] N (pl inv) espèce f

★**specific** [spə'sɪfɪk] ADJ (not vague) précis(e), explicite; (particular) particulier(-ière); (Bot, Chem etc) spécifique; **to be** ~ **to** être particulier à, être le or un caractère (or les caractères) spécifique(s) de

★**specifically** [spə'sɪfɪklɪ] ADV explicitement, précisément; (intend, ask, design) expressément, spécialement; (exclusively) exclusivement, spécifiquement

specification [spɛsɪfɪ'keɪʃən] N spécification f; stipulation f ■ **specifications** NPL (of car, building etc) spécification

specifics [spə'sɪfɪks] NPL détails mpl

specify ['spɛsɪfaɪ] VT spécifier, préciser; **unless otherwise specified** sauf indication contraire

specimen ['spɛsɪmən] N spécimen m, échantillon m; (Med: of blood) prélèvement m; (: of urine) échantillon m

specimen copy N spécimen m

specimen signature N spécimen m de signature

speck [spɛk] N petite tache, petit point; (particle) grain m

speckled ['spɛkld] ADJ tacheté(e), moucheté(e)

specs [spɛks] NPL (inf) lunettes fpl

spectacle ['spɛktəkl] N spectacle m ■ **spectacles** NPL (BRIT) lunettes fpl

spectacle case N (BRIT) étui m à lunettes

★**spectacular** [spɛk'tækjulə'] ADJ spectaculaire ▶ N (Cine etc) superproduction f

spectator [spɛk'teɪtə'] N spectateur(-trice)

spectator sport N: **football is a great** ~ le football est un sport qui passionne les foules

spectra ['spɛktrə] NPL of **spectrum**

spectre, (US) **specter** ['spɛktə'] N spectre m, fantôme m

spectrum ['spɛktrəm] (pl **spectra** [-rə]) N spectre m; (fig) gamme f

speculate ['spɛkjuleɪt] VI spéculer; (ponder): **to** ~ **about** s'interroger sur

speculation [spɛkju'leɪʃən] N spéculation f; conjectures fpl

speculative ['spɛkjulətɪv] ADJ spéculatif(-ive)

speculator ['spɛkjuleɪtə'] N spéculateur(-trice)

sped [spɛd] PT, PP of **speed**

★**speech** [spiːtʃ] N (faculty) parole f; (talk) discours m, allocution f; (manner of speaking) façon f de parler, langage m; (language) langage m; (enunciation) élocution f

speech day N (BRIT Scol) distribution f des prix

speech impediment N défaut m d'élocution

speechless ['spiːtʃlɪs] ADJ muet(te)

speech therapy N orthophonie f

★**speed** [spiːd] (pt, pp **sped** [spɛd]) N vitesse f; (promptness) rapidité f; **at ~** (BRIT) rapidement; **at full** or **top ~** à toute vitesse or allure; **at a ~ of 70 km/h** à une vitesse de 70 km/h; **shorthand/typing speeds** nombre m de mots à la minute en sténographie/dactylographie; **a five-speed gearbox** une boîte cinq vitesses ▸ VI (Aut: exceed speed limit) faire un excès de vitesse; **to ~ along/by** etc aller/passer etc à toute vitesse
  ▸ **speed up** [spiːd ʌp] (pt, pp **speeded up** [spiːdɪd ʌp]) VI aller plus vite, accélérer ▸ VT accélérer

speedboat [spiːdbəʊt] N vedette f, hors-bord m inv

speed bump N ralentisseur m

speed camera N radar m (automatique)

speedily ['spiːdɪlɪ] ADV rapidement, promptement

speeding ['spiːdɪŋ] N (Aut) excès m de vitesse

speed limit N limitation f de vitesse, vitesse maximale permise

speedometer [spɪˈdɒmɪtəʳ] N compteur m (de vitesse)

speed trap N (Aut) piège m de police pour contrôle de vitesse

speedway ['spiːdweɪ] N (Sport) piste f de vitesse pour motos; (also: **speedway racing**) épreuve(s) f(pl) de vitesse de motos

speedy [spiːdɪ] ADJ rapide, prompt(e)

speleologist [spɛlɪˈɒlədʒɪst] N spéléologue mf

★**spell** [spɛl] (pt, pp **spelt** [spɛlt] or **spelled** [spɛld]) N (also: **magic spell**) sortilège m, charme m; (period of time) (courte) période; **to cast a ~ on sb** jeter un sort à qn ▸ VT (in writing) écrire, orthographier; (aloud) épeler; (fig) signifier; **how do you ~ your name?** comment écrivez-vous votre nom ?; **can you ~ it for me?** pouvez-vous me l'épeler ? ▸ VI: **he can't ~** il fait des fautes d'orthographe
  ▸ **spell out** [spɛl aʊt] VT (explain): **to ~ sth out for sb** expliquer qch clairement à qn

spellbinding ['spɛlbaɪndɪŋ] ADJ captivant(e)

spellbound ['spɛlbaʊnd] ADJ envoûté(e), subjugué(e)

spellcheck ['spɛltʃɛk] VT passer au correcteur orthographique ▸ N correction f orthographique; **to ~ sth** or **to run a ~ over sth** passer qch au correcteur orthographique

spellchecker ['spɛltʃɛkəʳ] N correcteur m or vérificateur m orthographique

spelling ['spɛlɪŋ] N orthographe f

spelt [spɛlt] PT, PP of **spell**

★**spend** [spɛnd] (pt, pp **spent** [spɛnt]) VT (money) dépenser; (time, life) passer; (devote) consacrer; **to ~ time/money/effort on sth** consacrer du temps/de l'argent/de l'énergie à qch

spending ['spɛndɪŋ] N dépenses fpl; **government ~** les dépenses publiques

spending money N argent m de poche

spending power N pouvoir m d'achat

spendthrift ['spɛndθrɪft] N dépensier(-ière)

spent [spɛnt] PT, PP of **spend** ▸ ADJ (patience) épuisé(e), à bout; (cartridge, bullets) vide; **~ matches** vieilles allumettes

sperm [spɜːm] N spermatozoïde m; (semen) sperme m

sperm bank N banque f du sperme

spermicide ['spɜːmɪsaɪd] N spermicide m

sperm whale N cachalot m

spew [spjuː] VT vomir
  ▸ **spew out** VT cracher

sphere [sfɪəʳ] N sphère f; (fig) sphère, domaine m

spherical ['sferɪkl] ADJ sphérique

sphinx [sfɪŋks] N sphinx m

spice [spaɪs] N épice f ▸ VT épicer
  ▸ **spice up** VT (story, conversation) donner du piquant à, donner du sel à

spiced [spaɪst] ADJ (dish, sauce) épicé(e); **~ with sth** relevé(e) avec qch

spick-and-span ['spɪkən'spæn] ADJ impeccable

spicy ['spaɪsɪ] ADJ épicé(e), relevé(e); (fig) piquant(e)

★**spider** ['spaɪdəʳ] N araignée f; **~'s web** toile f d'araignée

spiel [spiːl] N (inf) laïus m inv

spigot ['spɪɡət] N (US) robinet m

spike [spaɪk] N pointe f; (Elec) pointe de tension; (Bot) épi m ▪ **spikes** NPL (Sport) chaussures fpl à pointes

spike heel N (US) talon m aiguille

spiky ['spaɪkɪ] ADJ (bush, branch) épineux(-euse); (animal) plein(e) de piquants; (hair) en épis

spill [spɪl] (pt, pp **spilt** [-t] or **spilled** [-d]) VT renverser; répandre; **to ~ the beans** (inf) vendre la mèche; (confess) lâcher le morceau ▸ VI se répandre
  ▸ **spill out** [spɪl aʊt] VI sortir à flots, se répandre
  ▸ **spill over** VI déborder

spillage ['spɪlɪdʒ] N (of oil) déversement m (accidentel)

spilt [spɪlt] PT, PP of **spill**

spin [spɪn] (pt, pp **spun** [spʌn]) N (revolution of wheel) tour m; (Aviat) (chute f en) vrille f; (trip in car) petit tour, balade f; (on ball) effet m ▸ VT (wool etc) filer; (wheel) faire tourner; (BRIT: clothes) essorer; **to ~ a yarn** débiter une longue histoire; **to ~ a coin** (BRIT) jouer à pile ou face ▸ VI (turn) tourner, tournoyer
  ▸ **spin out** VT faire durer
  ▸ **spin round** VT faire tourner ▸ VI (wheel, top, skater) tourner (sur soi-même); (person: to face other way) faire volte-face

spina bifida ['spaɪnə'bɪfɪdə] N spina-bifida m inv

spinach ['spɪnɪtʃ] N épinard m; (as food) épinards mpl

spinal ['spaɪnl] ADJ vertébral(e), spinal(e)

spinal column N colonne vertébrale

spinal cord N moelle épinière

spindly ['spɪndlɪ] ADJ grêle, filiforme

spin doctor N (inf) personne employée pour présenter un parti politique sous un jour favorable

S

spin-dry ['spin'draɪ] vt essorer

spin-dryer [spin'draɪə'] N (BRIT) essoreuse f

spine [spaɪn] N colonne vertébrale; (thorn) épine f, piquant m

spine-chilling ['spaɪntʃɪlɪŋ] ADJ terrifiant(e)

spineless ['spaɪnlɪs] ADJ invertébré(e); (fig) mou (molle), sans caractère

spinner ['spinə'] N (of thread) fileur(-euse)

spinning ['spinɪŋ] N (of thread) filage m; (by machine) filature f

spinning top N toupie f

spinning wheel N rouet m

spin-off ['spinɔf] N sous-produit m; avantage inattendu

spinster ['spinstə'] N célibataire f; vieille fille

spiral ['spaɪərl] N spirale f; **the inflationary ~** la spirale inflationniste ▸ ADJ en spirale ▸ VI (fig: prices etc) monter en flèche

spiral staircase N escalier m en colimaçon

spire ['spaɪə'] N flèche f, aiguille f

★**spirit** ['spirit] N (soul) esprit m, âme f; (ghost) esprit, revenant m; (mood) esprit, état m d'esprit; (courage) courage m, énergie f; **community ~** solidarité f; **public ~** civisme m ▪ **spirits** NPL (drink) spiritueux mpl, alcool m; (state of mind): **in good spirits** de bonne humeur; **in low spirits** démoralisé(e)

spirited ['spiritid] ADJ vif (vive), fougueux(-euse), plein(e) d'allant

spirit level N niveau m à bulle

★**spiritual** ['spiritjual] ADJ spirituel(le); (religious) religieux(-euse) ▸ N (also: **Negro spiritual**) spiritual m

spiritualism ['spiritjuəlizəm] N spiritisme m

spirituality [spiritju'æləti] N spiritualité f

spit [spit] (pt, pp **spat** [spæt]) N (for roasting) broche f; (spittle) crachat m; (saliva) salive f ▸ VI cracher; (sound) crépiter; (rain) crachiner
▸ **spit out** VT (food, words) cracher

★**spite** [spaɪt] N rancune f, dépit m; **in ~ of** en dépit de, malgré ▸ VT contrarier, vexer

spiteful ['spaɪtful] ADJ malveillant(e), rancunier(-ière)

spitroast ['spit'rəust] VT faire rôtir à la broche

spitting ['spitɪŋ] N: "**~ prohibited**" « défense de cracher » ▸ ADJ: **to be the ~ image of sb** être le portrait tout craché de qn

spittle ['spitl] N salive f; bave f; crachat m

spiv [spiv] N (BRIT inf) chevalier m d'industrie, aigrefin m

splash [splæʃ] N (sound) plouf m; (of colour) tache f ▸ VT éclabousser ▸ VI (also: **splash about**) barboter, patauger
▸ **splash out** VI (BRIT) faire une folie

splashdown ['splæʃdaun] N amerrissage m

splat [splæt] N floc m

splatter ['splætə'] VI dégouliner ▸ VT éclabousser

splay-footed [splei'futəd] ADJ marchant les pieds en dehors

spleen [spli:n] N (Anat) rate f

splendid ['splendɪd] ADJ splendide, superbe, magnifique

splendour, (US) **splendor** ['splendə'] N splendeur f, magnificence f

splice [splaɪs] VT épisser

spliff [splɪf] N (inf) joint m (inf), pétard m (inf)

splint [splint] N attelle f, éclisse f

splinter ['splintə'] N (wood) écharde f; (metal) éclat m ▸ VI (wood) se fendre; (glass) se briser

splinter group N groupe dissident

★**split** [split] (pt, pp ~) N fente f, déchirure f; (fig: Pol) scission f; **to do the splits** faire le grand écart ▸ VT fendre, déchirer; (party) diviser; (work, profits) partager, répartir; **let's ~ the difference** coupons la poire en deux ▸ VI (break) se fendre, se briser; (divide) se diviser
▸ **split up** VI (couple) se séparer, rompre; (meeting) se disperser

split-level ['splitlevl] ADJ (house) à deux or plusieurs niveaux

split peas NPL pois cassés

split personality N double personnalité f

split second N fraction f de seconde

splitting ['splitɪŋ] ADJ: **a ~ headache** un mal de tête atroce

splodge [splɔdʒ] N (BRIT) tache f

splotch [splɔtʃ] N tache f

splurge [splə:dʒ] VI faire des folies; **to ~ on sth** dépenser une fortune dans qch

splutter ['splʌtə'] VI bafouiller; postillonner

spoil [spɔɪl] (pt, pp **spoiled** [-d] or **spoilt** [-t]) VT (damage) abîmer; (mar) gâcher; (child) gâter; (ballot paper) rendre nul ▸ VI: **to be spoiling for a fight** chercher la bagarre

spoils [spɔɪlz] NPL butin m

spoilsport ['spɔɪlspɔ:t] N trouble-fête mf, rabat-joie m inv

spoilt [spɔɪlt] PT, PP of **spoil** ▸ ADJ (child) gâté(e); (ballot paper) nul(le)

spoke [spəuk] PT of **speak** ▸ N rayon m

spoken ['spəukn] PP of **speak**

★**spokesman** ['spəuksmən] N (irreg) porte-parole m inv

spokesperson ['spəukspə:sn] N porte-parole m inv

spokeswoman ['spəukswumən] N (irreg) porte-parole m inv

sponge [spʌndʒ] N éponge f; (Culin: also: **sponge cake**) ≈ biscuit m de Savoie ▸ VT éponger ▸ VI: **to ~ off** vivre aux crochets de

sponge bag N (BRIT) trousse f de toilette

sponge cake N ≈ biscuit m de Savoie

sponger ['spʌndʒə'] N (pej) parasite m

spongy ['spʌndʒɪ] ADJ spongieux(-euse)

★**sponsor** ['spɔnsə'] N (Radio, TV, Sport) sponsor m; (for application) parrain (marraine); (BRIT: for fund-raising event) donateur(-trice) ▸ VT (programme, competition etc) parrainer, patronner, sponsoriser; (Pol: bill) présenter; (new member) parrainer; (fund-raiser) faire un don à; **I sponsored him at £3 a mile** (in fund-raising race) je me suis engagé à lui donner 3 livres par mile

sponsored ['spɔnsəd] ADJ: **~ walk** marche f (pour une œuvre caritative)

sponsorship ['spɔnsəʃɪp] N sponsoring m; patronage m, parrainage m; dons mpl

spontaneity [spɔntə'neɪɪtɪ] N spontanéité f

spontaneous [spɔn'teɪnɪəs] ADJ spontané(e)

spontaneously [spɔn'teɪnɪəslɪ] ADV spontanément

spoof [spu:f] N (parody) parodie f; (trick) canular m

spook [spu:k] N (inf: ghost) fantôme m; (: US: secret agent) barbouze m (inf) ▶ VT faire peur à; **to be spooked by sth** être effrayé(e) par qch

spooky ['spu:kɪ] ADJ (inf) qui donne la chair de poule

spool [spu:l] N bobine f

★**spoon** [spu:n] N cuiller f

spoon-feed ['spu:nfi:d] VT nourrir à la cuiller; (fig) mâcher le travail à

spoonful ['spu:nful] N cuillerée f

sporadic [spə'rædɪk] ADJ sporadique

spore [spɔː'] N spore f

★**sport** [spɔːt] N sport m; (amusement) divertissement m; (person) chic type m/chic fille f; **indoor/ outdoor sports** sports en salle/de plein air; **to say sth in ~** dire qch pour rire ▶ VT (wear) arborer

sporting ['spɔːtɪŋ] ADJ sportif(-ive); **to give sb a ~ chance** donner sa chance à qn

sport jacket N (US) = **sports jacket**

sports car N voiture f de sport

sportscaster ['spɔːtskɑːstə'] (esp US) N commentateur(-trice) sportif(-ive)

sports centre (BRIT) N centre sportif

sports drink N boisson f pour le sport

sports ground N terrain m de sport

sports jacket (BRIT) N veste f de sport

sportsman ['spɔːtsmən] N (irreg) sportif m

sportsmanship ['spɔːtsmənʃɪp] N esprit sportif, sportivité f

sports page N page f des sports

sports utility vehicle N véhicule m de loisirs, SUV m

sportswear ['spɔːtswɛə'] N vêtements mpl de sport

sportswoman ['spɔːtswumən] N (irreg) sportive f

sporty ['spɔːtɪ] ADJ sportif(-ive)

★**spot** [spɔt] N tache f; (dot: on pattern) pois m; (pimple) bouton m; (place) endroit m, coin m; (also: **spot advertisement**) message m publicitaire; **on the ~** sur place, sur les lieux; (immediately) sur le champ; **to put sb on the ~** (fig) mettre qn dans l'embarras; **to come out in spots** se couvrir de boutons, avoir une éruption de boutons ▶ VT (notice) apercevoir, repérer

spot check N contrôle intermittent

spotless ['spɔtlɪs] ADJ immaculé(e)

spotlight ['spɔtlaɪt] N projecteur m; (Aut) phare m auxiliaire

spot-on [spɔt'ɔn] ADJ (BRIT inf) en plein dans le mille

spot price N prix m sur place

spotted ['spɔtɪd] ADJ tacheté(e), moucheté(e); à pois; **~ with** tacheté(e) de

spotty ['spɔtɪ] ADJ (face) boutonneux(-euse)

spouse [spauz] N époux (épouse)

spout [spaut] N (of jug) bec m; (of liquid) jet m ▶ VI jaillir

sprain [spreɪn] N entorse f, foulure f ▶ VT: **to ~ one's ankle** se fouler or se tordre la cheville

sprang [spræŋ] PT of **spring**

sprawl [sprɔːl] VI s'étaler; **to send sb sprawling** envoyer qn rouler par terre ▶ N: **urban ~** expansion urbaine

sprawled [sprɔːld] ADJ (person) vautré(e)

★**spray** [spreɪ] N jet m (en fines gouttelettes); (from sea) embruns mpl; (aerosol) vaporisateur m, bombe f; (for garden) pulvérisateur m; (of flowers) petit bouquet ▶ VT vaporiser, pulvériser; (crops) traiter ▶ CPD (deodorant etc) en bombe or atomiseur

spray-paint ['spreɪpeɪnt] N (also: **spray paint**) peinture f en bombe ▶ VT peindre à la bombe, bomber

★**spread** [spred] (pt, pp ~) N (distribution) répartition f; (Culin) pâte f à tartiner; (inf: meal) festin m; (Press, Typ: two pages) double page f; **middle-age ~** embonpoint m (pris avec l'âge) ▶ VT (paste, contents) étendre, étaler; (rumour, disease) répandre, propager; (repayments) échelonner, étaler; (wealth) répartir ▶ VI s'étendre; se répandre; se propager; (stain) s'étaler
▶ **spread out** VI (people) se disperser

spread-eagled ['spredi:gld] ADJ: **to be** or **lie ~** être étendu(e) bras et jambes écartés

spreadsheet ['spredʃiːt] N (Comput) tableur m

spree [spriː] N: **to go on a ~** faire la fête

sprig [sprɪg] N rameau m

sprightly ['spraɪtlɪ] ADJ alerte

★**spring** [sprɪŋ] (pt **sprang** [spræŋ], pp **sprung** [sprʌŋ]) N (season) printemps m; (leap) bond m, saut m; (coiled metal) ressort m; (bounciness) élasticité f; (of water) source f; **in ~**, **in the ~** au printemps; **to walk with a ~ in one's step** marcher d'un pas souple ▶ VI bondir, sauter; **to ~ from** provenir de; **to ~ into action** passer à l'action ▶ VT: **to ~ a leak** (pipe etc) se mettre à fuir; **he sprang the news on me** il m'a annoncé la nouvelle de but en blanc
▶ **spring up** [sprɪŋ ʌp] VI (problem) se présenter, surgir; (plant, buildings) surgir de terre

springboard ['sprɪŋbɔːd] N tremplin m

spring-clean [sprɪŋ'kliːn] N (also: **spring-cleaning**) grand nettoyage de printemps

spring onion N (BRIT) ciboule f, cive f

spring roll N rouleau m de printemps

springtime ['sprɪŋtaɪm] N printemps m

springy ['sprɪŋɪ] ADJ élastique, souple

sprinkle ['sprɪŋkl] VT (pour) répandre; verser; **to ~ water on, ~ with water** etc asperger d'eau etc; **to ~ sugar** etc **on, ~ with sugar** etc saupoudrer de sucre etc; **sprinkled with** (fig) parsemé(e) de

sprinkler ['sprɪŋklə'] N (for lawn etc) arroseur m; (to put out fire) diffuseur m d'extincteur automatique d'incendie

sprinkling ['sprɪŋklɪŋ] N (of water) quelques gouttes fpl; (of salt) pincée f; (of sugar) légère couche

sprint [sprɪnt] N sprint m ▶ VI courir à toute vitesse; (Sport) sprinter

sprinter ['sprɪntə'] N sprinteur(-euse)

sprite [spraɪt] N lutin m

S

spritzer ['sprɪtsə'] N boisson à base de vin blanc et d'eau de Seltz

sprocket ['sprɔkɪt] N (on printer etc) picot m

sprout [spraut] VI germer, pousser

sprouts [sprauts] NPL (also: **Brussels sprouts**) choux mpl de Bruxelles

spruce [spru:s] N épicéa m ▸ ADJ net(te), pimpant(e)
▸ **spruce up** VT (smarten up: room etc) apprêter; **to ~ o.s. up** se faire beau (belle)

sprung [sprʌŋ] PP of **spring**

spry [spraɪ] ADJ alerte, vif (vive)

SPUC N ABBR = **Society for the Protection of Unborn Children**

spud [spʌd] N (inf: potato) patate f

spun [spʌn] PT, PP of **spin**

spur [spə:'] N éperon m; (fig) aiguillon m; **on the ~ of the moment** sous l'impulsion du moment ▸ VT (also: **spur on**) éperonner; aiguillonner

spurious ['spjuərɪəs] ADJ faux (fausse)

spurn [spə:n] VT repousser avec mépris

spurt [spə:t] N jet m; (of blood) jaillissement m; (of energy) regain m, sursaut m; **to put in** or **on a ~** (runner) piquer un sprint; (fig: in work etc) donner un coup de collier ▸ VI jaillir, gicler

sputter ['spʌtə'] VI = **splutter**

spy [spaɪ] N espion(ne) ▸ VI: **to ~ on** espionner, épier ▸ VT (see) apercevoir ▸ CPD (film, story) d'espionnage

spycam ['spaɪkæm] N caméra f de surveillance

spying ['spaɪɪŋ] N espionnage m

spyware ['spaɪwɛə'] N (Comput) logiciel m espion

Sq. ABBR (in address) = **square**

sq. ABBR (Math etc) = **square**

squabble ['skwɔbl] N querelle f, chamaillerie f ▸ VI se chamailler

squad [skwɔd] N (Mil, Police) escouade f, groupe m; (Football) contingent m; **flying ~** (Police) brigade volante

squad car N (Brit Police) voiture f de police

squaddie ['skwɔdɪ] N (Mil: inf) troufion m, bidasse m

squadron ['skwɔdrən] N (Mil) escadron m; (Aviat, Naut) escadrille f

squalid ['skwɔlɪd] ADJ sordide, ignoble

squall [skwɔ:l] N rafale f, bourrasque f

squalor ['skwɔlə'] N conditions fpl sordides

squander ['skwɔndə'] VT gaspiller, dilapider

★**square** [skwɛə'] N carré m; (in town) place f; (US: block of houses) îlot m, pâté m de maisons; (instrument) équerre f; **we're back to ~ one** (fig) on se retrouve à la case départ ▸ ADJ carré(e); (honest) honnête, régulier(-ière); (inf: ideas, tastes) vieux jeu inv, qui retarde; **all ~** quitte; à égalité; **a ~ meal** un repas convenable; **2 metres ~** (de) 2 mètres sur 2; **1 ~ metre** 1 mètre carré ▸ VT (arrange) régler; arranger; (Math) élever au carré; (reconcile) concilier ▸ VI (agree) cadrer, s'accorder
▸ **square up** VI (Brit: settle) régler; **to ~ up with sb** régler ses comptes avec qn

square bracket N (Typ) crochet m

squarely ['skwɛəlɪ] ADV carrément; (honestly, fairly) honnêtement, équitablement

square root N racine carrée

squash [skwɔʃ] N (Brit Sport) squash m; (US: vegetable) courge f; (drink): **lemon/orange ~** citronnade f/orangeade f ▸ VT écraser

squat [skwɔt] ADJ petit(e) et épais(se), ramassé(e) ▸ VI (also: **squat down**) s'accroupir; (on property) squatter, squattériser

squatter ['skwɔtə'] N squatter m

squawk [skwɔ:k] VI pousser un or des glousse-ment(s)

squeak [skwi:k] N (of hinge, wheel etc) grincement m; (of shoes) craquement m; (of mouse etc) petit cri aigu ▸ VI (hinge, wheel) grincer; (mouse) pousser un petit cri

squeaky ['skwi:kɪ] ADJ grinçant(e); **to be ~ clean** (fig) être au-dessus de tout soupçon

squeal [skwi:l] VI pousser un or des cri(s) aigu(s) or perçant(s); (brakes) grincer

squeamish ['skwi:mɪʃ] ADJ facilement dégoûté(e); facilement scandalisé(e)

★**squeeze** [skwi:z] N pression f; (also: **credit squeeze**) encadrement m du crédit, restrictions fpl de crédit; **a ~ of lemon** quelques gouttes de citron ▸ VT presser; (hand, arm) serrer ▸ VI: **to ~ past/under sth** se glisser avec (beaucoup de) difficulté devant/sous qch
▸ **squeeze in** VT (find time for) caser; **I can ~ you in at two o'clock** je peux vous caser à deux heures ▸ VI: **it was a tiny car, but we managed to ~ in** la voiture était toute petite, mais nous avons réussi à nous serrer
▸ **squeeze out** VT exprimer; (fig) soutirer

squelch [skwɛltʃ] VI faire un bruit de succion; patauger

squib [skwɪb] N pétard m

squid [skwɪd] N calmar m

squiggle ['skwɪgl] N gribouillis m

squint [skwɪnt] VI: **to ~ at sth** regarder qch du coin de l'œil; (quickly) jeter un coup d'œil à qch ▸ N: **he has a ~** il louche, il souffre de strabisme

squire ['skwaɪə'] N (Brit) propriétaire terrien

squirm [skwə:m] VI se tortiller

★**squirrel** ['skwɪrəl] N écureuil m
▸ **squirrel away** VT (money, objects) mettre en lieu sûr

squirt [skwə:t] N jet m ▸ VI jaillir, gicler ▸ VT faire gicler

Sr ABBR = **senior**; (Rel) = **sister**

SRC N ABBR (Brit: = Students' Representative Council) ≈ CROUS m

Sri Lanka [srɪ'læŋkə] N Sri Lanka m

SRN N ABBR (Brit) = **State Registered Nurse**

SRO ABBR (US) = **standing room only**

SS ABBR (= steamship) S/S

SSA N ABBR (US: = Social Security Administration) organisme de sécurité sociale

SST N ABBR (US) = **supersonic transport**

ST ABBR (US: = Standard Time) heure officielle

St ABBR = **saint; street**

stab [stæb] N (with knife etc) coup m (de couteau etc); (of pain) lancée f; (inf: try): **to have a ~ at (doing) sth** s'essayer à (faire) qch ▶ VT poignarder; **to ~ sb to death** tuer qn à coups de couteau

stabbing ['stæbɪŋ] N: **there's been a ~** quelqu'un a été attaqué à coups de couteau ▶ ADJ (pain, ache) lancinant(e)

stability [stə'bɪlɪtɪ] N stabilité f

stabilization [steɪbəlaɪ'zeɪʃən] N stabilisation f

stabilize ['steɪbəlaɪz] VT stabiliser ▶ VI se stabiliser

stabilizer ['steɪbəlaɪzə'] N stabilisateur m

★**stable** ['steɪbl] N écurie f; **riding ~** centre m d'équitation ▶ ADJ stable

stable boy, stable lad N garçon m d'écurie, lad m

stab wound ['stæbwu:nd] N coup m de couteau

staccato [stə'kɑ:təʊ] ADV staccato ▶ ADJ (Mus) piqué(e); (noise, voice) saccadé(e)

stack [stæk] N tas m, pile f; **there's stacks of time** (BRIT inf) on a tout le temps ▶ VT empiler, entasser

★**stadium** ['steɪdɪəm] N stade m

★**staff** [stɑ:f] N (work force) personnel m; (BRIT Scol: also: **teaching staff**) professeurs mpl, enseignants mpl, personnel enseignant; (servants) domestiques mpl; (Mil) état-major m; (stick) perche f, bâton m ▶ VT pourvoir en personnel

staffroom ['stɑ:fru:m] N salle f des professeurs

stag [stæg] N cerf m; (BRIT Stock Exchange) loup m

★**stage** [steɪdʒ] N scène f; (platform) estrade f; (point) étape f, stade m; (profession): **the ~** le théâtre; **in stages** par étapes, par degrés; **to go through a difficult ~** traverser une période difficile; **in the early stages** au début; **in the final stages** à la fin ▶ VT (play) monter, mettre en scène; (demonstration) organiser; (fig: recovery etc) effectuer

stagecoach ['steɪdʒkəʊtʃ] N diligence f

stage door N entrée f des artistes

stage fright N trac m

stagehand ['steɪdʒhænd] N machiniste m

stage-manage ['steɪdʒmænɪdʒ] VT (fig) orchestrer

stage manager N régisseur m

stagger ['stægə'] VI chanceler, tituber ▶ VT (person: amaze) stupéfier; bouleverser; (hours, holidays) étaler, échelonner

staggered ['stægəd] ADJ (amazed) stupéfait(e)

staggering ['stægərɪŋ] ADJ (amazing) stupéfiant(e), renversant(e)

staging post ['steɪdʒɪŋ-] N relais m

stagnant ['stægnənt] ADJ stagnant(e)

stagnate [stæg'neɪt] VI stagner, croupir

stagnation [stæg'neɪʃən] N stagnation f

stag night, stag party N enterrement m de vie de garçon

staid [steɪd] ADJ posé(e), rassis(e)

stain [steɪn] N tache f; (colouring) colorant m ▶ VT tacher; (wood) teindre

stained [steɪnd] ADJ taché(e); **to be ~ with sth** être taché(e) de qch

stained glass [steɪnd-] N (decorative) verre coloré; (in church) vitraux mpl; **~ window** vitrail m

stainless ['steɪnlɪs] ADJ (steel) inoxydable

stainless steel N inox m, acier m inoxydable

stain remover N détachant m

stair [stɛə'] N (step) marche f

staircase ['stɛəkeɪs] N = **stairway**

stairlift ['stɛəlɪft] N monte-escaliers m inv

★**stairs** [stɛəz] NPL escalier m; **on the ~** dans l'escalier

stairway ['stɛəweɪ] N escalier m

stairwell ['stɛəwel] N cage f d'escalier

stake [steɪk] N pieu m, poteau m; (Comm: interest) intérêts mpl; (Betting) enjeu m; **to be at ~** être en jeu; **to have a ~ in sth** avoir des intérêts (en jeu) dans qch ▶ VT risquer, jouer; (also: **stake out**: area) marquer, délimiter; **to ~ a claim (to sth)** revendiquer (qch)

stakeholder ['steɪkhəʊldə'] N partie f prenante

stakeout ['steɪkaʊt] N surveillance f; **to be on a ~** effectuer une surveillance

stalactite ['stæləktaɪt] N stalactite f

stalagmite ['stæləgmaɪt] N stalagmite f

stale [steɪl] ADJ (bread) rassis(e); (food) pas frais (fraîche); (beer) éventé(e); (smell) de renfermé; (air) confiné(e)

stalemate ['steɪlmeɪt] N pat m; (fig) impasse f

stalk [stɔ:k] N tige f ▶ VT traquer ▶ VI: **to ~ out/off** sortir/partir d'un air digne

stall [stɔ:l] N (in street, market etc) éventaire m, étal m; (in stable) stalle f; **a newspaper/flower ~** un kiosque à journaux/de fleuriste ▶ VT (Aut) caler; (fig: delay) retarder ▶ VI (Aut) caler; (fig) essayer de gagner du temps ■ **stalls** NPL (BRIT: in cinema, theatre) orchestre m

stallholder ['stɔ:lhəʊldə'] N (BRIT) marchand(e) en plein air

stallion ['stæljən] N étalon m (cheval)

stalwart ['stɔ:lwət] N partisan m fidèle

stamen ['steɪmen] N étamine f

stamina ['stæmɪnə] N vigueur f, endurance f

stammer ['stæmə'] N bégaiement m ▶ VI bégayer

★**stamp** [stæmp] N timbre m; (also: **rubber stamp**) tampon m; (mark, also fig) empreinte f; (on document) cachet m ▶ VI (also: **stamp one's foot**) taper du pied ▶ VT (letter) timbrer; (with rubber stamp) tamponner
▶ **stamp out** VT (fire) piétiner; (crime) éradiquer; (opposition) éliminer

stamp album N album m de timbres(-poste)

stamp collecting [-kəlektɪŋ] N philatélie f

stamp duty N (BRIT: on document) droit m de timbre; (: on property transaction) droit de timbre payé par l'acheteur d'un bien immobilier ou d'un terrain

stamped addressed envelope N (BRIT) enveloppe affranchie pour la réponse

stampede [stæm'pi:d] N ruée f; (of cattle) débandade f

stamp machine N distributeur m de timbres

stance [stæns] N position f

★**stand** [stænd] (pt, pp **stood** [stʊd]) N (position) position f; (for taxis) station f (de taxis); (Mil) résistance f; (structure) guéridon m; support m; (Comm) étalage m, stand m; (Sport: also: **stands**) tribune f; (also:

S

865

music stand) pupitre *m*; **to make a ~** prendre position; **to take a ~ on an issue** prendre position sur un problème ▸ vɪ être *or* se tenir (debout); (*rise*) se lever, se mettre debout; (*be placed*) se trouver; (*remain: offer etc*) rester valable; **to ~ for parliament** (BRIT) se présenter aux élections (*comme candidat à la députation*); **it stands to reason** c'est logique; cela va de soi; **as things ~** dans l'état actuel des choses ▸ vᴛ (*place*) mettre, poser; (*tolerate, withstand*) supporter; (*treat, invite*) offrir, payer; **to ~ sb a drink/meal** payer à boire/à manger à qn; **I can't ~ him** je ne peux pas le voir; **to ~ guard** *or* **watch** (Mil) monter la garde

▸ **stand aside** [stænd ə'saɪd] vɪ s'écarter

▸ **stand back** [stænd bæk] vɪ (*move back*) reculer, s'écarter

▸ **stand by** [stænd baɪ] vɪ (*be ready*) se tenir prêt(e) ▸ vᴛ ꜰᴜs (*opinion*) s'en tenir à; (*person*) ne pas abandonner, soutenir

▸ **stand down** [stænd daʊn] vɪ (*withdraw*) se retirer; (*Law*) renoncer à ses droits

▸ **stand for** [stænd fɔːʳ] vᴛ ꜰᴜs (*signify*) représenter, signifier; (*tolerate*) supporter, tolérer

▸ **stand in for** [stænd ɪn fɔːʳ] vᴛ ꜰᴜs remplacer

▸ **stand out** [stænd aʊt] vɪ (*be prominent*) ressortir

▸ **stand up** [stænd ʌp] vɪ (*rise*) se lever, se mettre debout

▸ **stand up for** [stænd ʌp fɔːʳ] vᴛ ꜰᴜs défendre

▸ **stand up to** [stænd ʌp tuː] vᴛ ꜰᴜs tenir tête à, résister à

stand-alone ['stændələʊn] ADJ (*Comput*) autonome

★**standard** ['stændəd] ɴ (*norm*) norme *f*, étalon *m*; (*level*) niveau *m* (voulu); (*criterion*) critère *m*; (*flag*) étendard *m*; **to be** *or* **come up to ~** être du niveau voulu *or* à la hauteur; **to apply a double ~** avoir *or* appliquer deux poids deux mesures ▸ ADJ (*size etc*) ordinaire, normal(e); (*model, feature*) standard *inv*; (*practice*) courant(e); (*text*) de base ▪ **standards** ɴᴘʟ (*morals*) morale *f*, principes *mpl*

standardization [stændədaɪ'zeɪʃən] ɴ standardisation *f*

standardize ['stændədaɪz] vᴛ standardiser

standard lamp ɴ (BRIT) lampadaire *m*

standard of living ɴ niveau *m* de vie

standard time ɴ heure légale

stand-by ['stændbaɪ] ɴ remplaçant(e); **to be on ~** se tenir prêt(e) (à intervenir); (*doctor*) être de garde ▸ ADJ (*provisions*) de réserve

stand-by generator ɴ générateur *m* de secours

stand-by passenger ɴ passager(-ère) en stand-by *or* en attente

stand-by ticket ɴ (*Aviat*) billet *m* stand-by

stand-in ['stændɪn] ɴ remplaçant(e); (*Cine*) doublure *f*

standing ['stændɪŋ] ADJ debout *inv*; (*permanent*) permanent(e); (*rule*) immuable; (*army*) de métier; (*grievance*) constant(e), de longue date; **he was given a ~ ovation** on s'est levé pour l'acclamer; **it's a ~ joke** c'est un vieux sujet de plaisanterie ▸ ɴ réputation *f*, rang *m*, standing *m*; (*duration*): **of 6 months'** ~ qui dure depuis 6 mois; **of many years'** ~ qui dure *or* existe depuis longtemps; **a man of some ~** un homme estimé

standing committee ɴ commission permanente

standing order ɴ (BRIT: *at bank*) virement *m* automatique, prélèvement *m* bancaire ▪ **standing orders** ɴᴘʟ (Mil) règlement *m*

standing room ɴ places *fpl* debout

stand-off ['stændɔf] ɴ (*esp US: stalemate*) impasse *f*

stand-offish ['stænd'ɔfɪʃ] ADJ distant(e), froid(e)

standpat ['stændpæt] ADJ (US) inflexible, rigide

standpipe ['stændpaɪp] ɴ colonne *f* d'alimentation

standpoint ['stændpɔɪnt] ɴ point *m* de vue

standstill ['stændstɪl] ɴ: **at a ~** à l'arrêt; (*fig*) au point mort; **to come to a ~** s'immobiliser, s'arrêter

stand-up ['stændʌp] ADJ (*row, fight*) en règle; **~ comedian** monologuiste *mf*; **~ comedy** monologue *m* comique

stank [stæŋk] ᴘᴛ *of* **stink**

stanza ['stænzə] ɴ strophe *f*; couplet *m*

staple ['steɪpl] ɴ (*for papers*) agrafe *f*; (*chief product*) produit *m* de base ▸ ADJ (*food, crop, industry etc*) de base principal(e) ▸ vᴛ agrafer

stapler ['steɪpləʳ] ɴ agrafeuse *f*

★**star** [stɑːʳ] ɴ étoile *f*; (*celebrity*) vedette *f*; **4-star hotel** hôtel *m* 4 étoiles; **2-star petrol** (BRIT) essence *f* ordinaire; **4-star petrol** (BRIT) super *m* ▸ vɪ: **to ~ (in)** être la vedette (de) ▸ vᴛ avoir pour vedette ▪ **stars** ɴᴘʟ: **the stars** (*Astrology*) l'horoscope *m*

star attraction ɴ grande attraction

starboard ['stɑːbəd] ɴ tribord *m*; **to ~** à tribord

starch [stɑːtʃ] ɴ amidon *m*; (*in food*) fécule *f*

starched [stɑːtʃt] ADJ (*collar*) amidonné(e), empesé(e)

starchy ['stɑːtʃɪ] ADJ (*food*) riche en féculents; (*person*) guindé(e)

stardom ['stɑːdəm] ɴ célébrité *f*

stare [stɛəʳ] ɴ regard *m* fixe ▸ vɪ: **to ~ at** regarder fixement

starfish ['stɑːfɪʃ] ɴ étoile *f* de mer

stark [stɑːk] ADJ (*bleak*) désolé(e), morne; (*simplicity, colour*) austère; (*reality, poverty*) nu(e) ▸ ADV: **~ naked** complètement nu(e)

starkers ['stɑːkəz] ADJ: **to be ~** (BRIT *inf*) être à poil

starlet ['stɑːlɪt] ɴ (*Cine*) starlette *f*

starlight ['stɑːlaɪt] ɴ: **by ~** à la lumière des étoiles

starling ['stɑːlɪŋ] ɴ étourneau *m*

starlit ['stɑːlɪt] ADJ étoilé(e); illuminé(e) par les étoiles

starry ['stɑːrɪ] ADJ étoilé(e)

starry-eyed [stɑːrɪ'aɪd] ADJ (*innocent*) ingénu(e)

Stars and Stripes ɴᴘʟ: **the ~** la bannière étoilée

star sign ɴ signe zodiacal *or* du zodiaque

star-studded ['stɑːstʌdɪd] ADJ: **a ~ cast** une distribution prestigieuse

★**start** [stɑːt] ɴ commencement *m*, début *m*; (*of race*) départ *m*; (*sudden movement*) sursaut *m*; (*advantage*) avance *f*, avantage *m*; **at the ~** au début; **for a ~** d'abord, pour commencer; **to make an early ~** partir *or* commencer de bonne heure ▸ vᴛ commencer; (*cause: fight*) déclencher; (*rumour*) donner naissance à; (*fashion*) lancer; (*found: business, news-*

paper) lancer, créer; (*engine*) mettre en marche; **to ~ doing** *or* **to do sth** se mettre à faire qch ▸ VI (*begin*) commencer; (*begin journey*) partir, se mettre en route; (*jump*) sursauter; **when does the film ~?** à quelle heure est-ce que le film commence ?; **to ~ (off) with ...** (*firstly*) d'abord ...; (*at the beginning*) au commencement ...
▸ **start off** VI commencer; (*leave*) partir
▸ **start out** VI (*begin*) commencer; (*set out*) partir
▸ **start over** VI (*US*) recommencer
▸ **start up** VI commencer; (*car*) démarrer ▸ VT (*fight*) déclencher; (*business*) créer; (*car*) mettre en marche

starter ['stɑːtə^r] N (*Aut*) démarreur m; (*Sport: official*) starter m; (*: runner, horse*) partant m; (*Brit Culin*) entrée f

starting handle ['stɑːtɪŋ-] N (*Brit*) manivelle f

starting point ['stɑːtɪŋ-] N point m de départ

starting price ['stɑːtɪŋ-] N prix initial

startle ['stɑːtl] VT faire sursauter; donner un choc à

startling ['stɑːtlɪŋ] ADJ surprenant(e), saisissant(e)

startlingly ['stɑːtlɪŋlɪ] ADV: **he was ~ handsome** il était d'une beauté saisissante

start-up (company), start-up (firm) ['stɑːtʌp-] N start-up f

star turn N (*Brit*) vedette f

starvation [stɑː'veɪʃən] N faim f, famine f; **to die of ~** mourir de faim *or* d'inanition

starve [stɑːv] VI mourir de faim ▸ VT laisser mourir de faim

starving ['stɑːvɪŋ] ADJ (*dying of hunger*) affamé(e); (*inf: famished*) affamé(e), qui meurt de faim; **I'm ~!** je meurs de faim!

stash [stæʃ] VT (*inf*): **to ~ sth away** planquer qch

★**state** [steɪt] N état m; (*Pol*) État; (*pomp*): **in ~** en grande pompe; **to be in a ~** être dans tous ses états; **~ of emergency** état d'urgence; **~ of mind** état d'esprit; **the ~ of the art** l'état actuel de la technologie (*or* des connaissances) ▸ VT (*declare*) déclarer, affirmer; (*specify*) indiquer, spécifier
■ **States** NPL: **the States** les États-Unis

state control N contrôle m de l'État

stated ['steɪtɪd] ADJ fixé(e), prescrit(e)

State Department N (*US*) Département m d'État, ≈ ministère m des Affaires étrangères

state education N (*Brit*) enseignement public

stateless ['steɪtlɪs] ADJ apatride

stately ['steɪtlɪ] ADJ majestueux(-euse), imposant(e)

stately home N manoir m *or* château m (*ouvert au public*)

★**statement** ['steɪtmənt] N déclaration f; (*Law*) déposition f; (*Econ*) relevé m; **official ~** communiqué officiel; **~ of account, bank ~** relevé de compte

state-owned ['steɪtəʊnd] ADJ étatisé(e)

stateroom ['steɪtruːm] N (*esp Brit: in palace*) salle f d'honneur; (*on liner*) cabine f de luxe

States [steɪts] NPL: **the ~** les États-Unis mpl

state school N école publique

statesman ['steɪtsmən] N (*irreg*) homme m d'État

statesmanlike ['steɪtsmənlaɪk] ADJ (*person*) habile homme d'État; **in a ~ way** en habile homme d'État

statesmanship ['steɪtsmənʃɪp] N qualités fpl d'homme d'État

statewide ['steɪtwaɪd] ADJ dans l'État, ≈ provincial(e) ▸ ADV à l'échelle de l'État

static ['stætɪk] N (*Radio*) parasites mpl; (*also*: **static electricity**) électricité f statique ▸ ADJ statique

★**station** ['steɪʃən] N gare f; (*also*: **police station**) poste m *or* commissariat m (de police); (*Mil*) poste m (militaire); (*rank*) condition f, rang m; **action stations** postes de combat ▸ VT placer, poster; **to be stationed in** (*Mil*) être en garnison à

stationary ['steɪʃnərɪ] ADJ à l'arrêt, immobile

stationer ['steɪʃənə^r] N papetier(-ière)

stationer's (shop) N (*Brit*) papeterie f

stationery ['steɪʃnərɪ] N papier m à lettres, petit matériel de bureau

stationmaster ['steɪʃənmɑːstə^r] N (*Rail*) chef m de gare

station wagon N (*US*) break m

statistic [stə'tɪstɪk] N statistique f

statistical [stə'tɪstɪkl] ADJ statistique

statistician [stætɪ'stɪʃən] N statisticien(ne)

statistics [stə'tɪstɪks] N (*science*) statistique f

statuary ['stætjʊərɪ] N statuaire f

statue ['stætjuː] N statue f

statuesque [stætjʊ'esk] ADJ sculptural(e)

statuette [stætjʊ'ɛt] N statuette f

stature ['stætʃə^r] N stature f; (*fig*) envergure f

status ['steɪtəs] N position f, situation f; (*prestige*) prestige m; (*Admin, official position*) statut m

status quo [-'kwəʊ] N: **the ~** le statu quo

status symbol N marque f de standing, signe extérieur de richesse

statute ['stætjuːt] N loi f ■ **statutes** NPL (*of club etc*) statuts mpl

statute book N ≈ code m, textes mpl de loi

statutory ['stætjʊtrɪ] ADJ statutaire, prévu(e) par un article de loi; **~ meeting** assemblée constitutive *or* statutaire

staunch [stɔːntʃ] ADJ sûr(e), loyal(e) ▸ VT étancher

stave [steɪv] N (*Mus*) portée f ▸ VT: **to ~ off** (*attack*) parer; (*threat*) conjurer

★**stay** [steɪ] N (*period of time*) séjour m; (*Law*): **~ of execution** sursis m à statuer ▸ VI rester; (*reside*) loger; (*spend some time*) séjourner; **to ~ put** ne pas bouger; **to ~ with friends** loger chez des amis; **to ~ the night** passer la nuit
▸ **stay away** VI (*from person, building*) ne pas s'approcher; (*from event*) ne pas venir
▸ **stay behind** VI rester en arrière
▸ **stay in** VI (*at home*) rester à la maison
▸ **stay on** VI rester
▸ **stay out** VI (*of house*) ne pas rentrer; (*strikers*) rester en grève
▸ **stay up** VI (*at night*) ne pas se coucher

staying power ['steɪɪŋ-] N endurance f

STD N ABBR (= *sexually transmitted disease*) MST f; (*Brit*: = *subscriber trunk dialling*) l'automatique m

S

stead [stɛd] N (BRIT): **in sb's ~** à la place de qn; **to stand sb in good ~** être très utile or servir beaucoup à qn

steadfast ['stɛdfɑːst] ADJ ferme, résolu(e)

steadfastly ['stɛdfɑːstlɪ] ADV résolument

steadily ['stɛdɪlɪ] ADV (regularly) progressivement; (firmly) fermement; (walk) d'un pas ferme; (fixedly: look) sans détourner les yeux

★**steady** ['stɛdɪ] ADJ stable, solide, ferme; (regular) constant(e), régulier(-ière); (person) calme, pondéré(e); **a ~ boyfriend** un petit ami ▶ VT assurer, stabiliser; (nerves) calmer; (voice) assurer; **to ~ oneself** reprendre son aplomb

steak [steɪk] N (meat) bifteck m, steak m; (fish, pork) tranche f

steakhouse ['steɪkhaus] N ≈ grill-room m

★**steal** [stiːl] (pt **stole** [stəul], pp **stolen** ['stəuln]) VT, VI voler; (move) se faufiler, se déplacer furtivement; **my wallet has been stolen** on m'a volé mon portefeuille
▶ **steal away, steal off** VI s'esquiver

stealth [stɛlθ] N: **by ~** furtivement

stealthy ['stɛlθɪ] ADJ furtif(-ive)

★**steam** [stiːm] N vapeur f; **under one's own ~** (fig) par ses propres moyens; **to run out of ~** (fig: person) caler; être à bout; **to let off ~** (fig: inf) se défouler ▶ VT passer à la vapeur; (Culin) cuire à la vapeur ▶ VI fumer; (ship): **to ~ along** filer
▶ **steam up** VI (window) se couvrir de buée; **to get steamed up about sth** (fig: inf) s'exciter à propos de qch

steam engine N locomotive f à vapeur

steamer ['stiːmə[r]] N (bateau m à) vapeur m; (Culin) ≈ couscoussier m

steam iron N fer m à repasser à vapeur

steamroller ['stiːmrəulə[r]] N rouleau compresseur

steamship ['stiːmʃɪp] N (bateau m à) vapeur m

steamy ['stiːmɪ] ADJ humide; (window) embué(e); (sexy) torride

steed [stiːd] N (literary) coursier m

★**steel** [stiːl] N acier m ▶ CPD d'acier

steel band N steel band m

steel industry N sidérurgie f

steelmaker ['stiːlmeɪkə[r]] N sidérurgiste m

steel mill N aciérie f, usine f sidérurgique

steelworker ['stiːlwəːkə[r]] N ouvrier(-ière) sidérurgiste

steelworks ['stiːlwəːks] N aciérie f

steely ['stiːlɪ] ADJ (determination) inflexible; (eyes, gaze) d'acier

steep [stiːp] ADJ raide, escarpé(e); (price) très élevé(e), excessif(-ive) ▶ VT (faire) tremper

steeple ['stiːpl] N clocher m

steeplechase ['stiːpltʃeɪs] N steeple(-chase) m

steeplejack ['stiːpldʒæk] N réparateur m de clochers et de hautes cheminées

steeply ['stiːplɪ] ADV en pente raide

steer [stɪə[r]] N bœuf m ▶ VT diriger; (boat) gouverner; (lead: person) guider, conduire ▶ VI tenir le gouvernail; **to ~ clear of sb/sth** (fig) éviter qn/qch

steering ['stɪərɪŋ] N (Aut) conduite f

steering column N (Aut) colonne f de direction

steering committee N comité m d'organisation

steering wheel N volant m

stellar ['stɛlə[r]] ADJ stellaire

stem [stɛm] N (of plant) tige f; (of leaf, fruit) queue f; (of glass) pied m ▶ VT contenir, endiguer; (attack, spread of disease) juguler
▶ **stem from** VT FUS provenir de, découler de

stem cell N cellule f souche

stench [stɛntʃ] N puanteur f

stencil ['stɛnsl] N stencil m; pochoir m ▶ VT polycopier

stenographer [stɛ'nɔgrəfə[r]] N (US) sténographe mf

stenography [stɛ'nɔgrəfɪ] N (US) sténo(graphie) f

★**step** [stɛp] N pas m; (stair) marche f; (action) mesure f, disposition f; **~ by ~** pas à pas; (fig) petit à petit; **to be in/out of ~ (with)** (fig) aller dans le sens (de)/être déphasé(e) (par rapport à) ▶ VI: **to ~ forward/back** faire un pas en avant/arrière, avancer/reculer ■ **steps** NPL (BRIT) = **stepladder**
▶ **step aside** VI (lit) faire un pas de côté; (stand down) se désister
▶ **step back** VI faire un pas en arrière
▶ **step down** VI (fig) se retirer, se désister
▶ **step forward** VI faire un pas en avant, avancer
▶ **step in** VI (fig) intervenir
▶ **step off** VT FUS descendre de
▶ **step over** VT FUS enjamber
▶ **step up** VT (production, sales) augmenter; (campaign, efforts) intensifier

step aerobics® NPL step® m

★**stepbrother** ['stɛpbrʌðə[r]] N demi-frère m

stepchild ['stɛptʃaɪld] (pl **stepchildren** ['stɛp-'tʃɪldrən]) N beau-fils (belle-fille)

stepdad ['stɛpdæd] N beau-père m (après remariage)

★**stepdaughter** ['stɛpdɔːtə[r]] N belle-fille f

★**stepfather** ['stɛpfɑːðə[r]] N beau-père m (après remariage)

stepladder ['stɛplædə[r]] N (BRIT) escabeau m

★**stepmother** ['stɛpmʌðə[r]] N belle-mère f (après remariage)

stepmum ['stɛpmʌm] N belle-mère f (après remariage)

stepping stone ['stɛpɪŋ-] N pierre f de gué; (fig) tremplin m

★**stepsister** ['stɛpsɪstə[r]] N demi-sœur f

★**stepson** ['stɛpsʌn] N beau-fils m

stereo ['stɛrɪəu] N (sound) stéréo f; (hi-fi) chaîne f stéréo; **in ~** en stéréo ▶ ADJ (also: **stereophonic**) stéréo(phonique)

stereotype ['stɪərətaɪp] N stéréotype m ▶ VT stéréotyper

stereotypical [stɪərɪə'tɪpɪkl] ADJ stéréotypé(e)

sterile ['stɛraɪl] ADJ stérile

sterility [stɛ'rɪlɪtɪ] N stérilité f

sterilization [stɛrɪlaɪ'zeɪʃən] N stérilisation f

sterilize ['stɛrɪlaɪz] VT stériliser

sterling ['stəːlɪŋ] ADJ sterling inv; (silver) de bon aloi, fin(e); (fig) à toute épreuve, excellent(e) ▶ N (currency) livre f sterling inv; **a pound ~** une livre sterling

sterling area N zone f sterling inv

stern [stə:n] ADJ sévère ▶ N (Naut) arrière m, poupe f

sternly ['stə:nlɪ] ADV sévèrement

sternum ['stə:nəm] N sternum m

steroid ['stɪərɔɪd] N stéroïde m

stethoscope ['stɛθəskəup] N stéthoscope m

stevedore ['sti:vədɔ:ʳ] N docker m, débardeur m

stew [stju:] N ragoût m ▶ VT, VI cuire à la casserole; **stewed tea** thé trop infusé; **stewed fruit** fruits cuits ou en compote

★**steward** ['stju:əd] N (Aviat, Naut, Rail) steward m; (in club etc) intendant m; (also: **shop steward**) délégué syndical

★**stewardess** ['stjuədɛs] N hôtesse f

stewardship ['stjuədʃɪp] N intendance f

stewing steak ['stju:ɪŋ-], (US) **stew meat** N bœuf m à braiser

St. Ex. ABBR = **stock exchange**

stg ABBR = **sterling**

STI N ABBR (= sexually transmitted infection) IST f (= infection sexuellement transmissible)

★**stick** [stɪk] (pt, pp **stuck** [stʌk]) N bâton m; (for walking) canne f; (of chalk etc) morceau m; **to get hold of the wrong end of the ~** (BRIT fig) comprendre de travers ▶ VT (glue) coller; (thrust): **to ~ sth into** piquer ou planter ou enfoncer qch dans; (inf: put) mettre, fourrer; (: tolerate) supporter ▶ VI (adhere) tenir, coller; (remain) rester; (get jammed: door, lift) se bloquer; **to ~ to** (one's promise) s'en tenir à; (principles) rester fidèle à
  ▶ **stick around** [stɪk ə'raund] VI (inf) rester (dans les parages)
  ▶ **stick out** [stɪk aut] VI dépasser, sortir ▶ VT: **to ~ it out** (inf) tenir le coup
  ▶ **stick up** [stɪk ʌp] VI dépasser, sortir
  ▶ **stick up for** [stɪk ʌp fɔ:ʳ] VT FUS défendre

sticker ['stɪkəʳ] N auto-collant m

sticking plaster ['stɪkɪŋ-] N sparadrap m, pansement adhésif

sticking point ['stɪkɪŋ-] N (fig) point m de friction

stick insect N phasme m

stickleback ['stɪklbæk] N épinoche f

stickler ['stɪkləʳ] N: **to be a ~ for** être pointilleux(-euse) sur

stick shift N (US Aut) levier m de vitesses

stick-up ['stɪkʌp] N (inf) braquage m (inf), hold-up m (inf)

sticky ['stɪkɪ] ADJ poisseux(-euse); (label) adhésif(-ive); (fig: situation) délicat(e)

stiff [stɪf] ADJ (gen) raide, rigide; (door, brush) dur(e); (difficult) difficile, ardu(e); (cold) froid(e), distant(e); (strong, high) fort(e), élevé(e); **to be** ou **feel ~** (person) avoir des courbatures; **to have a ~ back/neck** avoir mal au dos/un torticolis; **~ upper lip** (BRIT fig) flegme m (typiquement britannique) ▶ ADV: **to be bored/scared/frozen ~** s'ennuyer à mourir/être mort(e) de peur/froid

stiffen ['stɪfn] VT raidir, renforcer ▶ VI se raidir; se durcir

stiffly ['stɪflɪ] ADV (move, stand) avec raideur; (coldly: say, smile) sèchement

stiffness ['stɪfnɪs] N raideur f

stifle ['staɪfl] VT étouffer, réprimer

stifling ['staɪflɪŋ] ADJ (heat) suffocant(e)

stigma ['stɪgmə] (pl Bot, Med, Rel **stigmata** [stɪg'mɑ:tə], fig **stigmas** ['stɪgməz]) N stigmate m

stigmatize ['stɪgmətaɪz] VT stigmatiser

stile [staɪl] N échalier m

stiletto [stɪ'lɛtəu] N (BRIT: also: **stiletto heel**) talon m aiguille

★**still** [stɪl] ADJ (motionless) immobile; (calm) calme, tranquille; (BRIT: mineral water etc) non gazeux(-euse); **to stand ~** rester immobile, ne pas bouger; **keep ~!** ne bouge pas ! ▶ ADV (up to this time) encore, toujours; (even) encore; (nonetheless) quand même, tout de même; **he ~ hasn't arrived** il n'est pas encore arrivé, il n'est toujours pas arrivé ▶ N (Cine) photo f

stillbirth ['stɪlbə:θ] N mortinaissance f, naissance f d'un enfant mort-né

stillborn ['stɪlbɔ:n] ADJ mort-né(e)

still life N nature morte

stillness ['stɪlnɪs] N (calm) silence m

stilt [stɪlt] N échasse f; (pile) pilotis m

stilted ['stɪltɪd] ADJ guindé(e), emprunté(e)

stimulant ['stɪmjulənt] N stimulant m

stimulate ['stɪmjuleɪt] VT stimuler

stimulating ['stɪmjuleɪtɪŋ] ADJ stimulant(e)

stimulation [stɪmju'leɪʃən] N stimulation f

stimulus ['stɪmjuləs] (pl **stimuli** ['stɪmjulaɪ]) N stimulant m; (Biol, Psych) stimulus m

sting [stɪŋ] (pt, pp **stung** [stʌŋ]) N piqûre f; (organ) dard m; (inf: confidence trick) arnaque m ▶ VT, VI piquer; **my eyes are stinging** j'ai les yeux qui piquent

stingy ['stɪndʒɪ] ADJ (inf) avare, pingre (inf), chiche (inf)

stink [stɪŋk] (pt **stank** [stæŋk], pp **stunk** [stʌŋk]) N puanteur f ▶ VI puer, empester

stinker ['stɪŋkəʳ] N (inf: problem, exam) vacherie f (inf); (person) dégueulasse mf

stinking ['stɪŋkɪŋ] ADJ (fig: inf) infect(e) (inf); **~ rich** bourré(e) de pognon (inf)

stint [stɪnt] N part f de travail ▶ VI: **to ~ on** lésiner sur, être chiche de

stipend ['staɪpɛnd] N (of vicar etc) traitement m

stipendiary [staɪ'pɛndɪərɪ] ADJ: **~ magistrate** juge m de tribunal d'instance

stipulate ['stɪpjuleɪt] VT stipuler

stipulation [stɪpju'leɪʃən] N stipulation f, condition f

★**stir** [stə:ʳ] N agitation f, sensation f; **to give sth a ~** remuer qch; **to cause a ~** faire sensation ▶ VT remuer ▶ VI remuer, bouger
  ▶ **stir up** VT exciter; (trouble) fomenter, provoquer

stir-fry ['stə:'fraɪ] VT faire sauter ▶ N: **vegetable ~** légumes sautés à la poêle

stirring ['stə:rɪŋ] ADJ excitant(e); émouvant(e)

stirrup ['stɪrəp] N étrier m

stitch [stɪtʃ] N (Sewing) point m; (Knitting) maille f; (Med) point de suture; (pain) point de côté ▶ VT coudre, piquer; (Med) suturer

St Kitts and Nevis [-kɪts-] N Saint-Christophe-et-Niévès

869

St Lucia [-'luːʃə] N Sainte Lucie f

stoat [stəut] N hermine f (avec son pelage d'été)

stock [stɔk] N réserve f, provision f; (Comm) stock m; (Agr) cheptel m, bétail m; (Culin) bouillon m; (Finance) valeurs fpl, titres mpl; (Rail: also: **rolling stock**) matériel roulant; (descent, origin) souche f; **in ~** en stock, en magasin; **out of ~** épuisé(e); **to take ~** (fig) faire le point; **stocks and shares** valeurs (mobilières), titres; **government ~** fonds publics ▶ ADJ (fig: reply etc) courant(e), classique ▶ VT (have in stock) avoir, vendre; **well-stocked** bien approvisionné(e) or fourni(e)
   ▶ **stock up** VI: **to ~ up (with)** s'approvisionner (en)

stockade [stɔ'keɪd] N palissade f

stockbroker ['stɔkbrəukəʳ] N agent m de change

stockbroking ['stɔkbrəukɪŋ] N courtage m ▶ CPD (firm, company) de courtage; (analyst) boursier(-ière)

stock control N (Comm) gestion f des stocks

stock cube N (BRIT Culin) bouillon-cube m

stock exchange N Bourse f (des valeurs)

stockholder ['stɔkhəuldəʳ] N (US) actionnaire mf

Stockholm ['stɔkhəum] N Stockholm

stocking ['stɔkɪŋ] N bas m

stocking filler ['stɔkɪŋfɪləʳ] N (BRIT) petit cadeau m de Noël

stock-in-trade ['stɔkɪn'treɪd] N (fig): **it's his ~** c'est sa spécialité

stockist ['stɔkɪst] N (BRIT) stockiste m

stock market N Bourse f, marché financier

stock phrase N cliché m

stockpile ['stɔkpaɪl] N stock m, réserve f ▶ VT stocker, accumuler

stockroom ['stɔkruːm] N réserve f, magasin m

stock still ADJ: **to rest/stand ~** rester/se tenir parfaitement immobile

stocktaking ['stɔkteɪkɪŋ] N (BRIT Comm) inventaire m

stocky ['stɔkɪ] ADJ trapu(e), râblé(e)

stodgy ['stɔdʒɪ] ADJ bourratif(-ive), lourd(e)

stoic ['stəuɪk] N stoïque mf

stoical ['stəuɪkl] ADJ stoïque

stoically ['stəuɪklɪ] ADV stoïquement

stoicism ['stəuɪsɪzəm] N stoïcisme m

stoke [stəuk] VT garnir, entretenir; chauffer

stoker ['stəukəʳ] N (Rail, Naut etc) chauffeur m

stole [stəul] PT of **steal** ▶ N étole f

stolen ['stəuln] PP of **steal**

stolid ['stɔlɪd] ADJ impassible, flegmatique

★**stomach** ['stʌmək] N estomac m; (abdomen) ventre m ▶ VT supporter, digérer

stomachache ['stʌməkeɪk] N mal m à l'estomac or au ventre

stomach pump N pompe stomacale

stomach ulcer N ulcère m à l'estomac

stomp [stɔmp] VI: **to ~ in/out** entrer/sortir d'un pas bruyant

★**stone** [stəun] N pierre f; (pebble) caillou m, galet m; (in fruit) noyau m; (Med) calcul m; (BRIT: weight) = 6.348 kg; **within a ~'s throw of the station** à deux pas de la gare ▶ CPD de or en pierre ▶ VT (person) lancer des pierres sur, lapider; (fruit) dénoyauter

Stone Age N: **the ~** l'âge m de pierre

stone-cold ['stəun'kəuld] ADJ complètement froid(e)

stoned [stəund] ADJ (inf: drunk) bourré(e) (inf); (: on drugs) défoncé(e) (inf)

stone-deaf ['stəun'dɛf] ADJ sourd(e) comme un pot

stonemason ['stəunmeɪsn] N tailleur m de pierre(s)

stonewall [stəun'wɔːl] VI faire de l'obstruction ▶ VT faire obstruction à

stonework ['stəunwəːk] N maçonnerie f

stonking ['stɔŋkɪŋ] (BRIT inf) ADJ, ADV super; **a ~ prize** un super prix; **a ~ good idea** une super bonne idée

stony ['stəunɪ] ADJ pierreux(-euse), rocailleux(-euse)

stood [stud] PT, PP of **stand**

stooge [stuːdʒ] N (pej) larbin m (inf)

stool [stuːl] N tabouret m

stoop [stuːp] VI (also: **have a stoop**) être voûté(e); (bend: also: **stoop down**) se baisser, se courber; (fig): **to ~ to sth/doing sth** s'abaisser jusqu'à qch/ jusqu'à faire qch

★**stop** [stɔp] N arrêt m; (short stay) halte f; (in punctuation) point m ▶ VT arrêter; (break off) interrompre; (also: **put a stop to**) mettre fin à; (prevent) empêcher; **to ~ doing sth** cesser or arrêter de faire qch; **to ~ sb (from) doing sth** empêcher qn de faire qch; **~ it!** arrête ! ▶ VI s'arrêter; (rain, noise etc) cesser, s'arrêter; **could you ~ here/at the corner?** arrêtez-vous ici/au coin, s'il vous plaît; **to ~ dead** s'arrêter net
   ▶ **stop by** VI s'arrêter (au passage)
   ▶ **stop off** VI faire une courte halte
   ▶ **stop up** VT (hole) boucher

stopcock ['stɔpkɔk] N robinet m d'arrêt

stopgap ['stɔpgæp] N (person) bouche-trou m; (also: **stopgap measure**) mesure f intérimaire

stoplights ['stɔplaɪts] NPL (Aut) signaux mpl de stop, feux mpl arrière

stopover ['stɔpəuvəʳ] N halte f; (Aviat) escale f

stoppage ['stɔpɪdʒ] N arrêt m; (of pay) retenue f; (strike) arrêt de travail; (obstruction) obstruction f

stopper ['stɔpəʳ] N bouchon m

stop press N nouvelles fpl de dernière heure

stopwatch ['stɔpwɔtʃ] N chronomètre m

storage ['stɔːrɪdʒ] N emmagasinage m; (of nuclear waste etc) stockage m; (in house) rangement m; (Comput) mise f en mémoire or réserve

storage heater N (BRIT) radiateur m électrique par accumulation

store [stɔːʳ] N (stock) provision f, réserve f; (depot) entrepôt m; (BRIT: large shop) grand magasin; (US: shop) magasin m; **who knows what is in ~ for us?** qui sait ce que l'avenir nous réserve or ce qui nous attend ?; **to set great/little ~ by sth** faire grand cas/peu de cas de qch ▶ VT emmagasiner; (nuclear waste etc) stocker; (information) enregistrer; (in filing system) classer, ranger; (Comput) mettre en mémoire ■ **stores** NPL (food) provisions
   ▶ **store up** VT mettre en réserve, emmagasiner

storehouse ['stɔ:haus] N entrepôt *m*

storekeeper ['stɔ:ki:pəʳ] N (*US*) commerçant(e)

storeroom ['stɔ:ru:m] N réserve *f*, magasin *m*

storey, (*US*) **story** ['stɔ:rɪ] N étage *m*

stork [stɔ:k] N cigogne *f*

★**storm** [stɔ:m] N tempête *f*; (*thunderstorm*) orage *m*
▸ VI (*fig*) fulminer ▸ VT prendre d'assaut

storm cloud N nuage *m* d'orage

storm door N double-porte (extérieure)

stormy ['stɔ:mɪ] ADJ orageux(-euse)

★**story** ['stɔ:rɪ] N histoire *f*; récit *m*; (*Press: article*)
article *m*; (*: subject*) affaire *f*; (*US*) = **storey**

storybook ['stɔ:rɪbuk] N livre *m* d'histoires *or* de
contes

storyline ['stɔ:rɪlaɪn] N (*of film*) scénario *m*; (*of book,
play*) intrigue *f*

storyteller ['stɔ:rɪteləʳ] N conteur(-euse)

stout [staut] ADJ (*strong*) solide; (*brave*) intrépide;
(*fat*) gros(se), corpulent(e) ▸ N bière brune

stove [stəuv] N (*for cooking*) fourneau *m*; (*: small*)
réchaud *m*; (*for heating*) poêle *m*; **gas/electric ~**
(*cooker*) cuisinière *f* à gaz/électrique

stow [stəu] VT ranger; cacher

stowaway ['stəuəweɪ] N passager(-ère) clandes-
tin(e)

straddle ['strædl] VT enjamber, être à cheval sur

strafe [strɑ:f] VT mitrailler

straggle ['strægl] VI être (*or* marcher) en désordre; **straggled along the coast** disséminé(e) tout
au long de la côte

straggler ['strægləʳ] N traînard(e)

straggling ['stræglɪŋ], **straggly** ['stræglɪ] ADJ
(*hair*) en désordre

★**straight** [streɪt] ADJ droit(e); (*hair*) raide; (*frank*)
honnête, franc (franche); (*simple*) simple; (*Theat:
part, play*) sérieux(-euse); (*inf: heterosexual*) hétéro
inv; **to put** *or* **get ~** mettre en ordre, mettre de l'ordre dans; (*fig*) mettre au clair; **let's get this ~** mettons les choses au point; **10 ~ wins** 10 victoires
d'affilée ▸ ADV (tout) droit; (*drink*) sec, sans eau; **to
go ~ home** rentrer directement à la maison; **~
away, ~ off** (*at once*) tout de suite; **~ off, ~ out** sans
hésiter ▸ N: **the ~** (*Sport*) la ligne droite

straighten ['streɪtn] VT ajuster; (*bed*) arranger
▸ **straighten out** VT (*fig*) débrouiller; **to ~ things
out** arranger les choses
▸ **straighten up** VI (*stand up*) se redresser; (*tidy*)
ranger

straighteners ['streɪtnəz] NPL (*for hair*) lisseur *m*

straight-faced [streɪt'feɪst] ADJ impassible ▸ ADV
en gardant son sérieux

straightforward [streɪt'fɔ:wəd] ADJ simple;
(*frank*) honnête, direct(e)

strain [streɪn] N (*Tech*) tension *f*; pression *f*; (*physical*) effort *m*; (*mental*) tension (nerveuse); (*Med*)
entorse *f*; (*streak, trace*) tendance *f*; élément *m*;
(*breed: of plants*) variété *f*; (*: of animals*) race *f*; (*of
virus*) souche *f*; **he's been under a lot of ~** il a
traversé des moments difficiles, il est très
éprouvé nerveusement ▸ VT (*stretch*) tendre fortement; (*fig: resources etc*) mettre à rude épreuve,
grever; (*hurt: back etc*) se faire mal à; (*filter*) passer,
filtrer; (*vegetables*) égoutter ▸ VI peiner, fournir

un gros effort ▪ **strains** NPL (*Mus*) accords *mpl*,
accents *mpl*

strained [streɪnd] ADJ (*muscle*) froissé(e); (*laugh etc*)
forcé(e), contraint(e); (*relations*) tendu(e)

strainer ['streɪnəʳ] N passoire *f*

strait [streɪt] N (*Geo*) détroit *m* ▪ **straits** NPL: **to be
in dire straits** (*fig*) avoir de sérieux ennuis

straitjacket ['streɪtdʒækɪt] N camisole *f* de force

strait-laced [streɪt'leɪst] ADJ collet monté *inv*

strand [strænd] N (*of thread*) fil *m*, brin *m*; (*of rope*)
toron *m*; (*of hair*) mèche *f* ▸ VT (*boat*) échouer

stranded ['strændɪd] ADJ en rade, en plan

★**strange** [streɪndʒ] ADJ (*not known*) inconnu(e);
(*odd*) étrange, bizarre

strangely ['streɪndʒlɪ] ADV étrangement, bizarrement; *see also* **enough**

stranger ['streɪndʒəʳ] N (*unknown*) inconnu(e);
(*from somewhere else*) étranger(-ère); **I'm a ~ here** je
ne suis pas d'ici

strangle ['stræŋgl] VT étrangler

stranglehold ['stræŋglhəuld] N (*fig*) emprise
totale, mainmise *f*

strangulation [stræŋgju'leɪʃən] N strangulation *f*

strap [stræp] N lanière *f*, courroie *f*, sangle *f*; (*of
slip, dress*) bretelle *f* ▸ VT attacher (avec une courroie *etc*)

straphanging ['stræphæŋɪŋ] N fait *m* de voyager
debout (dans le métro *etc*)

strapless ['stræplɪs] ADJ (*bra, dress*) sans bretelles

strapped [stræpt] ADJ: **to be ~ for cash** (*inf*) être à
court d'argent

strapping ['stræpɪŋ] ADJ bien découplé(e),
costaud(e)

strappy ['stræpɪ] ADJ (*dress*) à bretelles; (*sandals*) à
lanières

Strasbourg ['stræzbə:g] N Strasbourg

strata ['strɑ:tə] NPL *of* **stratum**

stratagem ['strætɪdʒəm] N stratagème *m*

strategic [strə'ti:dʒɪk] ADJ stratégique

strategist ['strætɪdʒɪst] N stratège *m*

strategy ['strætɪdʒɪ] N stratégie *f*

stratosphere ['strætəsfɪəʳ] N stratosphère *f*

stratospheric [strætə'sfɛrɪk] ADJ (*lit*) strato-
sphérique; (*fig: price, cost*) astronomique

stratum ['strɑ:təm] N (*pl* **strata** ['strɑ:tə]) N strate *f*,
couche *f*

straw [strɔ:] N paille *f*; **that's the last ~!** ça c'est le
comble !

★**strawberry** ['strɔ:bərɪ] N fraise *f*; (*plant*) fraisier *m*

stray [streɪ] ADJ (*animal*) perdu(e), errant(e);
(*scattered*) isolé(e); **~ bullet** balle perdue ▸ VI
s'égarer

streak [stri:k] N bande *f*, filet *m*; (*in hair*) raie *f*;
(*fig: of madness etc*): **a ~ of** une *or* des tendance(s) à;
to have streaks in one's hair s'être fait faire des
mèches; **a winning/losing ~** une bonne/mau-
vaise série *or* période ▸ VT zébrer, strier ▸ VI: **to ~
past** passer à toute allure

streaker ['stri:kəʳ] N streaker(-euse)

streaky ['stri:kɪ] ADJ zébré(e), strié(e)

streaky bacon N (*BRIT*) ≈ lard *m* (maigre)

S

★**stream** [stri:m] N (brook) ruisseau m; (current) courant m, flot m; (of people) défilé ininterrompu, flot; **against the ~** à contre courant; **on ~** (new power plant etc) en service ▶ VT (Scol) répartir par niveau ▶ VI ruisseler; (Internet) écouter or regarder en streaming; **to ~ in/out** entrer/sortir à flots

streamer ['stri:məᵣ] N serpentin m, banderole f

stream feed N (on photocopier etc) alimentation f en continu

streaming ['stri:mɪŋ] N (Internet) streaming m; **live ~** diffusion f en direct

streamline ['stri:mlaɪn] VT donner un profil aérodynamique à; (fig) rationaliser

streamlined ['stri:mlaɪnd] ADJ (Aviat) fuselé(e), profilé(e); (Aut) aérodynamique; (fig) rationalisé(e)

★**street** [stri:t] N rue f; **the back streets** les quartiers pauvres; **to be on the streets** (homeless) être à la rue or sans abri

streetcar ['stri:tkɑ:ᵣ] N (US) tramway m

street cred [-krɛd] N (inf): **to have ~** être branché(e) (inf)

street lamp N réverbère m

street light N réverbère m

street lighting N éclairage public

street map, street plan N plan m des rues

street market N marché m à ciel ouvert

streetwise ['stri:twaɪz] ADJ (inf) futé(e), réaliste

★**strength** [strɛŋθ] N force f; (of girder, knot etc) solidité f; (of chemical solution) titre m; (of wine) degré m d'alcool; **on the ~ of** en vertu de; **at full ~** au grand complet; **below ~** à effectifs réduits

strengthen ['strɛŋθn] VT renforcer; (muscle) fortifier; (building, Econ) consolider

strenuous ['strɛnjuəs] ADJ vigoureux(-euse), énergique; (tiring) ardu(e), fatigant(e)

strenuously ['strɛnjuəslɪ] ADV (deny, object) énergiquement

★**stress** [strɛs] N (force, pressure) pression f; (mental strain) tension (nerveuse), stress m; (accent) accent m; (emphasis) insistance f; **to lay great ~ on sth** insister beaucoup sur qch; **to be under ~** être stressé(e) ▶ VT insister sur, souligner; (syllable) accentuer

stressed [strɛst] ADJ (tense) stressé(e); (syllable) accentué(e)

stressful ['strɛsful] ADJ (job) stressant(e)

★**stretch** [strɛtʃ] N (of sand etc) étendue f; (of time) période f; **at a ~** d'affilée ▶ VI s'étirer; (extend): **to ~ to** or **as far as** s'étendre jusqu'à; (be enough: money, food): **to ~ to** aller pour ▶ VT tendre, étirer; (spread) étendre; (fig) pousser (au maximum); **to ~ a muscle** se distendre un muscle; **to ~ one's legs** se dégourdir les jambes
▶ **stretch out** VI s'étendre; **to ~ out for sth** allonger la main pour prendre qch ▶ VT (arm etc) allonger, tendre; (to spread) étendre

stretcher ['strɛtʃəᵣ] N brancard m, civière f

stretcher-bearer ['strɛtʃəbɛərəᵣ] N brancardier m

stretch marks NPL (on skin) vergetures fpl

stretchy ['strɛtʃɪ] ADJ élastique

strewn [stru:n] ADJ: **~ with** jonché(e) de

stricken ['strɪkən] ADJ très éprouvé(e); dévasté(e);

(ship) très endommagé(e); **~ with** frappé(e) or atteint(e) de

★**strict** [strɪkt] ADJ strict(e); **in ~ confidence** tout à fait confidentiellement

strictly ['strɪktlɪ] ADV strictement; **~ confidential** strictement confidentiel(le); **~ speaking** à strictement parler

stridden ['strɪdn] PP of **stride**

stride [straɪd] (pt **strode** [strəud], pp **stridden** ['strɪdn]) N grand pas, enjambée f; **to take sth in one's ~** (fig: changes etc) accepter qch sans sourciller ▶ VI marcher à grands pas

strident ['straɪdnt] ADJ strident(e)

strife [straɪf] N conflit m, dissensions fpl

strife-ridden ['straɪfrɪdən], **strife-torn** ['straɪftɔ:n] ADJ déchiré(e) par les conflits

★**strike** [straɪk] (pt, pp **struck** [strʌk]) N grève f; (of oil etc) découverte f; (attack) raid m; **to go on** or **come out on ~** se mettre en grève, faire grève ▶ VT frapper; (oil etc) trouver, découvrir; (make: agreement, deal) conclure; **to ~ a match** frotter une allumette; **to ~ a balance** (fig) trouver un juste milieu ▶ VI faire grève; (attack) attaquer; (clock) sonner
▶ **strike back** [straɪk bæk] VI (Mil, fig) contre-attaquer
▶ **strike down** [straɪk daun] VT (fig) terrasser
▶ **strike off** [straɪk ɔf] VT (from list) rayer; (: doctor etc) radier
▶ **strike out** [straɪk aut] VT rayer
▶ **strike up** [straɪk ʌp] VT (Mus) se mettre à jouer; **to ~ up a friendship with** se lier d'amitié avec

strikebreaker ['straɪkbreɪkəᵣ] N briseur m de grève

striker ['straɪkəᵣ] N gréviste mf; (Sport) buteur m

striking ['straɪkɪŋ] ADJ frappant(e), saisissant(e); (attractive) éblouissant(e)

strikingly ['straɪkɪŋlɪ] ADV: **to be ~ similar/different** présenter une ressemblance frappante/des différences frappantes; **a ~ handsome man** un homme dont la beauté attire l'œil

strimmer® ['strɪməᵣ] N (BRIT) coupe-bordures m

★**string** [strɪŋ] N ficelle f, fil m; (row: of beads) rang m; (: of onions, excuses) chapelet m; (: of people, cars) file f; (Mus) corde f; (Comput) chaîne f; **to pull strings** (fig) faire jouer le piston; **to get a job by pulling strings** obtenir un emploi en faisant jouer le piston; **with no strings attached** (fig) sans conditions ▪ **the strings** NPL (Mus) les instruments mpl à cordes ▶ VT (pt, pp **strung** [strʌŋ]): **to ~ together** enchaîner
▶ **string out** VT échelonner

string bean N haricot vert

stringed instrument, string instrument N (Mus) instrument m à cordes

stringent ['strɪndʒənt] ADJ rigoureux(-euse); (need) impérieux(-euse)

string quartet N quatuor m à cordes

strip [strɪp] N bande f; (Sport) tenue f; **wearing the Celtic ~** en tenue du Celtic ▶ VT (undress) déshabiller; (paint) décaper, (fig) dégarnir, dépouiller; (also: **strip down**: machine) démonter ▶ VI se déshabiller
▶ **strip off** VT (paint etc) décaper ▶ VI (person) se déshabiller

strip cartoon N bande dessinée

stripe [straɪp] N raie f, rayure f; (Mil) galon m

striped ['straɪpt] ADJ rayé(e), à rayures

strip light N (BRIT) (tube m au) néon m

stripper ['strɪpə'] N strip-teaseuse f

strip-search ['strɪpsə:tʃ] N fouille corporelle (en faisant se déshabiller la personne) ▶ VT: **to ~ sb** fouiller qn (en le faisant se déshabiller)

striptease ['strɪpti:z] N strip-tease m

stripy ['straɪpɪ] ADJ rayé(e)

strive [straɪv] (pt **strove** [strəuv], pp **striven** ['strɪvn]) VI: **to ~ to do/for sth** s'efforcer de faire/ d'obtenir qch

strobe [strəub] N (also: **strobe light**) stroboscope m

strode [strəud] PT of **stride**

stroke [strəuk] N coup m; (Med) attaque f; (caress) caresse f; (Swimming: style) (sorte f de) nage f; (of piston) course f; **at a ~** d'un (seul) coup; **on the ~ of 5** à 5 heures sonnantes; **a ~ of luck** un coup de chance; **a 2-stroke engine** un moteur à 2 temps ▶ VT caresser

stroll [strəul] N petite promenade; **to go for a ~** aller se promener or faire un tour ▶ VI flâner, se promener nonchalamment

stroller ['strəulə'] N (US: for child) poussette f

★**strong** [strɒŋ] ADJ (gen) fort(e); (healthy) vigoureux(-euse); (heart, nerves) solide; (distaste, desire) vif (vive); (drugs, chemicals) puissant(e); **they are 50 ~** ils sont au nombre de 50 ▶ ADV: **to be going ~** (company) marcher bien; (person) être toujours solide

strong-arm ['strɒŋɑ:m] ADJ (tactics, methods) musclé(e)

strongbox ['strɒŋbɒks] N coffre-fort m

stronghold ['strɒŋhəuld] N forteresse f, fort m; (fig) bastion m

strongly ['strɒŋlɪ] ADV fortement, avec force; vigoureusement; solidement; **I feel ~ about it** c'est une question qui me tient particulièrement à cœur; (negatively) j'y suis profondément opposé(e)

strongman ['strɒŋmæn] N (irreg) hercule m, colosse m; (fig) homme m à poigne

strongroom ['strɒŋru:m] N chambre forte

stroppy ['strɒpɪ] ADJ (BRIT inf) contrariant(e), difficile

strove [strəuv] PT of **strive**

struck [strʌk] PT, PP of **strike**

structural ['strʌktʃrəl] ADJ structural(e); (Constr) de construction; affectant les parties portantes

structurally ['strʌktʃrəlɪ] ADV du point de vue de la construction

structure ['strʌktʃə'] N structure f; (building) construction f

struggle ['strʌgl] N lutte f; **to have a ~ to do sth** avoir beaucoup de mal à faire qch ▶ VI lutter, se battre

strum [strʌm] VT (guitar) gratter de

strung [strʌŋ] PT, PP of **string**

strut [strʌt] N étai m, support m ▶ VI se pavaner

strychnine ['strɪkni:n] N strychnine f

stub [stʌb] N (of cigarette) bout m, mégot m; (of ticket etc) talon m ▶ VT: **to ~ one's toe (on sth)** se heurter le doigt de pied (contre qch)
 ▶ **stub out** VT écraser

stubble ['stʌbl] N chaume m; (on chin) barbe f de plusieurs jours

stubborn ['stʌbən] ADJ têtu(e), obstiné(e), opiniâtre

stubbornly ['stʌbənlɪ] ADV obstinément

stubbornness ['stʌbənnɪs] N obstination f

stubby ['stʌbɪ] ADJ trapu(e); gros(se) et court(e)

stucco ['stʌkəu] N stuc m

stuck [stʌk] PT, PP of **stick** ▶ ADJ (jammed) bloqué(e), coincé(e); **to get ~** se bloquer or coincer

stuck-up [stʌk'ʌp] ADJ prétentieux(-euse)

stud [stʌd] N (on boots etc) clou m; (collar stud) bouton m de col; (earring) petite boucle d'oreille; (of horses: also: **stud farm**) écurie f, haras m; (also: **stud horse**) étalon m ▶ VT (fig): **studded with** parsemé(e) or criblé(e) de

★**student** ['stju:dənt] N étudiant(e); **law/medical ~** étudiant en droit/ médecine ▶ ADJ (life) estudiantin(e), étudiant(e), d'étudiant; (residence, restaurant) universitaire; (loan, movement) étudiant, universitaire d'étudiant

student driver N (US) (conducteur(-trice)) débutant(e)

students' union N (BRIT: association) ≈ association f des étudiants; (: building) ≈ foyer m des étudiants

studied ['stʌdɪd] ADJ étudié(e), calculé(e)

studio ['stju:dɪəu] N studio m, atelier m; (TV etc) studio

studio flat, (US) **studio apartment** N studio m

studious ['stju:dɪəs] ADJ studieux(-euse), appliqué(e); (studied) étudié(e)

studiously ['stju:dɪəslɪ] ADV (carefully) soigneusement

★**study** ['stʌdɪ] N étude f; (room) bureau m; **to make a ~ of sth** étudier qch, faire une étude de qch ▶ VT étudier; (examine) examiner ▶ VI étudier, faire ses études; **to ~ for an exam** préparer un examen

★**stuff** [stʌf] N (gen) chose(s) f(pl), truc m; (belongings) affaires fpl, trucs; (substance) substance f ▶ VT rembourrer; (Culin) farcir; (inf: push) fourrer; (animal: for exhibition) empailler; **my nose is stuffed up** j'ai le nez bouché; **get stuffed!** (inf!) va te faire foutre ! (!); **stuffed toy** jouet m en peluche

stuffing ['stʌfɪŋ] N bourre f, rembourrage m; (Culin) farce f

stuffy ['stʌfɪ] ADJ (room) mal ventilé(e) or aéré(e); (ideas) vieux jeu inv

stumble ['stʌmbl] VI trébucher; **to ~ across** or **on** (fig) tomber sur

stumbling block ['stʌmblɪŋ-] N pierre f d'achoppement

stump [stʌmp] N souche f; (of limb) moignon m ▶ VT: **to be stumped** sécher, ne pas savoir que répondre

stun [stʌn] VT (blow) étourdir; (news) abasourdir, stupéfier

stung [stʌŋ] PT, PP of **sting**

stunk [stʌŋk] PP of **stink**

stunned [stʌnd] ADJ assommé(e); (fig) sidéré(e)

stunning ['stʌnɪŋ] ADJ (beautiful) étourdissant(e); (news etc) stupéfiant(e)

stunt [stʌnt] N tour m de force; (in film) cascade f, acrobatie f; (publicity) truc m publicitaire; (Aviat) acrobatie f ▶ VT retarder, arrêter

873

stunted [ˈstʌntɪd] ADJ rabougri(e)

stuntman [ˈstʌntmæn] N (irreg) cascadeur m

stupefaction [stjuːpɪˈfækʃən] N stupéfaction f, stupeur f

stupefy [ˈstjuːpɪfaɪ] VT étourdir; abrutir; (fig) stupéfier

stupendous [stjuːˈpɛndəs] ADJ prodigieux(-euse), fantastique

★**stupid** [ˈstjuːpɪd] ADJ stupide, bête

stupidity [stjuːˈpɪdɪtɪ] N stupidité f, bêtise f

stupidly [ˈstjuːpɪdlɪ] ADV stupidement, bêtement

stupor [ˈstjuːpəʳ] N stupeur f

sturdy [ˈstəːdɪ] ADJ (person, plant) robuste, vigoureux(-euse); (object) solide

sturgeon [ˈstəːdʒən] N esturgeon m

stutter [ˈstʌtəʳ] N bégaiement m ▶ VI bégayer

St Vincent and the Grenadines N Saint-Vincent-et-les-Grenadines m

sty [staɪ] N (of pigs) porcherie f

stye [staɪ] N (Med) orgelet m

★**style** [staɪl] N style m; (of dress etc) genre m; (distinction) allure f, cachet m, style; (design) modèle m; **in the latest ~** à la dernière mode; **hair ~** coiffure f

stylish [ˈstaɪlɪʃ] ADJ élégant(e), chic inv

stylishly [ˈstaɪlɪʃlɪ] ADV élégamment

stylist [ˈstaɪlɪst] N (hair stylist) coiffeur(-euse); (literary stylist) styliste mf

stylistic [staɪˈlɪstɪk] ADJ (element, change, difference) stylistique

stylized [ˈstaɪlaɪzd] ADJ stylisé(e)

stylus [ˈstaɪləs] (pl **styli** [-laɪ] or **styluses** [-ləsiːz]) N (of record player) pointe f de lecture

stymie [ˈstaɪmɪ] VT (inf) entraver; **to be stymied** être entravé(e)

Styrofoam® [ˈstaɪrəfəum] N polystyrène expansé ▶ ADJ en polystyrène expansé

suave [swɑːv] ADJ doucereux(-euse), onctueux(-euse)

sub [sʌb] N ABBR = **submarine; subscription**

sub... [sʌb] PREFIX sous..., sous-

subcommittee [ˈsʌbkəmɪtɪ] N sous-comité m

subconscious [sʌbˈkɔnʃəs] ADJ subconscient(e) ▶ N subconscient m

subconsciously [sʌbˈkɔnʃəslɪ] ADV inconsciemment

subcontinent [sʌbˈkɔntɪnənt] N: **the (Indian) ~** le sous-continent indien

subcontract N [sʌbˈkɔntrækt] contrat m de sous-traitance ▶ VT [sʌbkənˈtrækt] sous-traiter

subcontractor [ˈsʌbkənˈtræktəʳ] N sous-traitant m

subculture [ˈsʌbkʌltʃəʳ] N sous-culture f

subdivide [sʌbdɪˈvaɪd] VT subdiviser

subdivision [ˈsʌbdɪvɪʒən] N subdivision f

subdue [səbˈdjuː] VT subjuguer, soumettre

subdued [səbˈdjuːd] ADJ contenu(e), atténué(e); (light) tamisé(e); (person) qui a perdu de son entrain

sub-editor [ˈsʌbˈɛdɪtəʳ] N (BRIT) secrétaire mf de (la) rédaction

subgroup [ˈsʌbgruːp] N sous-groupe m

subheading [ˈsʌbhɛdɪŋ] N sous-titre m

★**subject** N [ˈsʌbdʒɪkt] sujet m; (Scol) matière f; **to change the ~** changer de conversation ▶ ADJ [ˈsʌbdʒɪkt]: **to be ~ to** (law) être soumis(e) à; (disease) être sujet(te) à; **~ to confirmation in writing** sous réserve de confirmation écrite ▶ VT [səbˈdʒɛkt]: **to ~ to** soumettre à; exposer à

subjection [səbˈdʒɛkʃən] N soumission f, sujétion f

subjective [səbˈdʒɛktɪv] ADJ subjectif(-ive)

subjectivity [sʌbdʒɛkˈtɪvɪtɪ] N subjectivité f

subject matter N sujet m; (content) contenu m

sub judice [sʌbˈdjuːdɪsɪ] ADJ (Law) devant les tribunaux

subjugate [ˈsʌbdʒugeɪt] VT subjuguer **subjunctive** [səbˈdʒʌŋktɪv] ADJ subjonctif(-ive) ▶ N subjonctif m

sublet [sʌbˈlɛt] VT sous-louer

sublime [səˈblaɪm] ADJ sublime

subliminal [sʌbˈlɪmɪnl] ADJ subliminal(e)

submachine gun [ˈsʌbməˈʃiːn-] N mitraillette f

submarine [sʌbməˈriːn] N sous-marin m

submerge [səbˈməːdʒ] VT submerger; immerger ▶ VI plonger

submersion [səbˈməːʃən] N submersion f; immersion f

submission [səbˈmɪʃən] N soumission f; (to committee etc) présentation f

submissive [səbˈmɪsɪv] ADJ soumis(e)

submit [səbˈmɪt] VT soumettre ▶ VI se soumettre

subnormal [sʌbˈnɔːml] ADJ au-dessous de la normale; (person) arriéré(e)

subordinate [səˈbɔːdɪnət] ADJ (junior) subalterne; (Grammar) subordonné(e) ▶ N subordonné(e)

sub-plot [ˈsʌbplɔt] N intrigue f secondaire

subpoena [səbˈpiːnə] (Law) N citation f, assignation f ▶ VT citer or assigner (à comparaître)

subprime [ˈsʌbpraɪm] ADJ (Finance: borrower, loan) à haut risque; **~ mortgage** prêt m hypothécaire à haut risque; **the ~ crisis** la crise des subprimes

subroutine [sʌbruːˈtiːn] N (Comput) sous-programme m

subscribe [səbˈskraɪb] VI cotiser; **to ~ to** (opinion, fund) souscrire à; (newspaper) s'abonner à; être abonné(e) à

subscriber [səbˈskraɪbəʳ] N (to magazine, service) abonné(e)

subscript [ˈsʌbskrɪpt] N (Typ) indice inférieur

subscription [səbˈskrɪpʃən] N (to fund) souscription f; (to magazine etc) abonnement m; (membership dues) cotisation f; **to take out a ~ to** s'abonner à

subsequent [ˈsʌbsɪkwənt] ADJ ultérieur(e), suivant(e); **~ to** prep à la suite de

subsequently [ˈsʌbsɪkwəntlɪ] ADV par la suite

subservient [səbˈsəːvɪənt] ADJ obséquieux(-euse)

subset [ˈsʌbsɛt] N sous-ensemble m

subside [səbˈsaɪd] VI (land) s'affaisser; (flood) baisser; (wind, feelings) tomber

subsidence [səbˈsaɪdns] N affaissement m

subsidiarity [səbsɪdɪˈærɪtɪ] N (Pol) subsidiarité f

subsidiary [səbˈsɪdɪərɪ] ADJ subsidiaire; accessoire; (BRIT Scol: subject) complémentaire ▶ N filiale f

subsidize ['sʌbsɪdaɪz] VT subventionner

subsidy ['sʌbsɪdɪ] N subvention f

subsist [səb'sɪst] VI: **to ~ on sth** (arriver à) vivre avec or subsister avec qch

subsistence [səb'sɪstəns] N existence f, subsistance f

subsistence allowance N indemnité f de séjour

subsistence level N niveau m de vie minimum

★**substance** ['sʌbstəns] N substance f; (fig) essentiel m; **a man of ~** un homme jouissant d'une certaine fortune; **to lack ~** être plutôt mince (fig)

substance abuse N abus m de substances toxiques

substandard [sʌb'stændəd] ADJ (goods) de qualité inférieure, qui laisse à désirer; (housing) inférieur(e) aux normes requises

substantial [səb'stænʃl] ADJ substantiel(le); (fig) important(e)

substantially [səb'stænʃəlɪ] ADV considérablement; en grande partie

substantiate [səb'stænʃɪeɪt] VT étayer, fournir des preuves à l'appui de

★**substitute** ['sʌbstɪtjuːt] N (person) remplaçant(e); (thing) succédané m ▶ VT: **to ~ sth/sb for** substituer qch/qn à, remplacer par qch/qn

substitute teacher N (US) suppléant(e)

substitution [sʌbstɪ'tjuːʃən] N substitution f

subterfuge ['sʌbtəfjuːdʒ] N subterfuge m

subterranean [sʌbtə'reɪnɪən] ADJ souterrain(e)

subtext ['sʌbtɛkst] N sujet m sous-jacent

subtitled ['sʌbtaɪtld] ADJ sous-titré(e)

subtitles ['sʌbtaɪtlz] NPL (Cine) sous-titres mpl

subtle ['sʌtl] ADJ subtil(e)

subtlety ['sʌtltɪ] N subtilité f

subtly ['sʌtlɪ] ADV subtilement

subtotal [sʌb'təutl] N total partiel

subtract [səb'trækt] VT soustraire, retrancher

subtraction [səb'trækʃən] N soustraction f

subtropical [sʌb'trɔpɪkl] ADJ subtropical(e)

suburb ['sʌbəːb] N faubourg m; **the suburbs** la banlieue

suburban [sə'bəːbən] ADJ de banlieue, suburbain(e)

suburbia [sə'bəːbɪə] N la banlieue

subvention [səb'vɛnʃən] N (subsidy) subvention f

subversion [səb'vəːʃən] N subversion f

subversive [səb'vəːsɪv] ADJ subversif(-ive)

subvert [səb'vəːt] VT subvertir

subway ['sʌbweɪ] N (BRIT: underpass) passage souterrain; (US: railway) métro m

sub-zero [sʌb'zɪərəu] ADJ au-dessous de zéro

★**succeed** [sək'siːd] VI réussir; **to ~ in doing** réussir à faire ▶ VT succéder à

succeeding [sək'siːdɪŋ] ADJ suivant(e), qui suit (or suivent or suivront etc)

★**success** [sək'sɛs] N succès m; réussite f

★**successful** [sək'sɛsful] ADJ qui a du succès; (candidate) choisi(e), agréé(e); (business) prospère, qui réussit; (attempt) couronné(e) de succès; **to be ~ (in doing)** réussir (à faire)

successfully [sək'sɛsfəlɪ] ADV avec succès

succession [sək'sɛʃən] N succession f; **in ~** successivement; **3 years in ~** 3 ans de suite

successive [sək'sɛsɪv] ADJ successif(-ive); **on 3 ~ days** 3 jours de suite or consécutifs

successor [sək'sɛsəʳ] N successeur m

succinct [sək'sɪŋkt] ADJ succinct(e), bref (brève)

succulent ['sʌkjulənt] ADJ succulent(e) ▶ N (Bot): **succulents** plantes grasses

succumb [sə'kʌm] VI succomber

★**such** [sʌtʃ] ADJ tel (telle); (of that kind): **~ a book** un livre de ce genre or pareil, un tel livre; (so much): **~ courage** un tel courage; **~ books** des livres de ce genre or pareils, de tels livres; **making ~ a noise that** faisant un tel bruit que or tellement de bruit que; **~ as** (like) tel (telle) que, comme; **a noise ~ as to** un bruit de nature à; **~ books as I have** les quelques livres que j'ai ▶ ADV si; **~ good books** de si bons livres; **~ a long trip** un si long voyage; **~ a long trip that** un voyage si or tellement long que; **~ a long time ago** il y a si or tellement longtemps; **~ a lot of** tellement or tant de ▶ PRON: **as ~** en tant que tel (telle), à proprement parler

such-and-such ['sʌtʃənsʌtʃ] ADJ tel ou tel (telle ou telle)

suchlike ['sʌtʃlaɪk] PRON (inf): **and ~** et le reste

suck [sʌk] VT sucer; (breast, bottle) téter; (pump, machine) aspirer

sucker ['sʌkəʳ] N (Bot, Zool, Tech) ventouse f; (inf) naïf(-ïve), poire f (inf)

suckle ['sʌkl] VT allaiter

sucrose ['suːkrəuz] N saccharose m

suction ['sʌkʃən] N succion f

suction pump N pompe aspirante

Sudan [su'dɑːn] N Soudan m

Sudanese [suːdə'niːz] ADJ soudanais(e) ▶ N Soudanais(e)

★**sudden** ['sʌdn] ADJ soudain(e), subit(e) ▶ N: **all of a ~** soudain, tout à coup

sudden-death [sʌdn'dɛθ] N: **~ play-off** partie supplémentaire pour départager les adversaires

★**suddenly** ['sʌdnlɪ] ADV brusquement, tout à coup, soudain

sudoku [su'dəuku:] N sudoku m

suds [sʌdz] NPL eau savonneuse

sue [suː] VT poursuivre en justice, intenter un procès à; **to ~ sb for damages** poursuivre qn en dommages-intérêts ▶ VI: **to ~ (for)** intenter un procès (pour); **to ~ for divorce** engager une procédure de divorce

suede [sweɪd] N daim m, cuir suédé ▶ CPD de daim

suet ['suɪt] N graisse f de rognon (de bœuf ou de mouton)

Suez Canal ['suːɪz-] N canal m de Suez

★**suffer** ['sʌfəʳ] VT souffrir, subir; (bear) tolérer, supporter, subir ▶ VI souffrir; **to ~ from** (illness) souffrir de, avoir; **to ~ from the effects of alcohol/a fall** se ressentir des effets de l'alcool/des conséquences d'une chute

sufferance ['sʌfərns] N: **he was only there on ~** sa présence était seulement tolérée

sufferer ['sʌfərəʳ] N malade mf; victime f

suffering ['sʌfərɪŋ] N souffrance(s) f(pl)

suffice [sə'faɪs] VI suffire

sufficient [sə'fɪʃənt] ADJ suffisant(e); **~ money** suffisamment d'argent

sufficiently [sə'fɪʃəntlɪ] ADV suffisamment, assez

suffix ['sʌfɪks] N suffixe m

suffocate ['sʌfəkeɪt] VI suffoquer; étouffer

suffocation [sʌfə'keɪʃən] N suffocation f; (Med) asphyxie f

suffrage ['sʌfrɪdʒ] N suffrage m; droit m de suffrage or de vote

suffuse [sə'fju:z] VT baigner, imprégner; **the room was suffused with light** la pièce baignait dans la lumière or était imprégnée de lumière

★**sugar** ['ʃugə'] N sucre m ▶ VT sucrer

sugar beet N betterave sucrière

sugar bowl N sucrier m

sugar cane N canne f à sucre

sugar-coated ['ʃugə'kəutɪd] ADJ dragéifié(e)

sugar lump N morceau m de sucre

sugar refinery N raffinerie f de sucre

sugary ['ʃugərɪ] ADJ sucré(e)

★**suggest** [sə'dʒɛst] VT suggérer, proposer; (indicate) sembler indiquer; **what do you ~ I do?** que vous me suggérez de faire?

★**suggestion** [sə'dʒɛstʃən] N suggestion f

suggestive [sə'dʒɛstɪv] ADJ suggestif(-ive)

suicidal [suɪ'saɪdl] ADJ suicidaire

★**suicide** ['suɪsaɪd] N suicide m; **to commit ~** se suicider; **~ bombing** attentat m suicide

suicide bomber N kamikaze mf

★**suit** [su:t] N (man's) costume m, complet m; (woman's) tailleur m, ensemble m; (Cards) couleur f; (lawsuit) procès m; **to bring a ~ against sb** intenter un procès contre qn; **to follow ~** (fig) faire de même ▶ VT (subj: clothes, hairstyle) aller à; (be convenient for) convenir à; (adapt): **to ~ sth to** adapter or approprier qch à; **to be suited to sth** (suitable for) être adapté(e) or approprié(e) à qch; **well suited** (couple) faits l'un pour l'autre, très bien assortis

suitability [su:tə'bɪlɪtɪ] N (of product) aptitude f à l'usage; **~ for sth** aptitude f à qch

★**suitable** ['su:təbl] ADJ qui convient; approprié(e), adéquat(e); **would tomorrow be ~?** est-ce que demain vous conviendrait?; **we found somebody ~** nous avons trouvé la personne qu'il nous faut

suitably ['su:təblɪ] ADV comme il se doit (or se devait etc), convenablement

suitcase ['su:tkeɪs] N valise f

suite [swi:t] N (of rooms, also Mus) suite f; (furniture): **bedroom/dining room ~** (ensemble m de) chambre f à coucher/salle f à manger; **a three-piece ~** un salon (canapé et deux fauteuils)

suitor ['su:tə'] N soupirant m, prétendant m

sulfate ['sʌlfeɪt] N (US) = **sulphate**

sulfur etc ['sʌlfə'] N (US) = **sulphur** etc

sulk [sʌlk] VI bouder

sulky ['sʌlkɪ] ADJ boudeur(-euse), maussade

sullen ['sʌlən] ADJ renfrogné(e), maussade; morne

sulphate, (US) **sulfate** ['sʌlfeɪt] N sulfate m; **copper ~** sulfate de cuivre

sulphur, (US) **sulfur** ['sʌlfə'] N soufre m

sulphur dioxide, (US) **sulfur dioxide** N anhydride sulfureux

sulphuric, (US) **sulfuric** [sʌl'fjuərɪk] ADJ: **~ acid** acide m sulfurique

sultan ['sʌltən] N sultan m

sultana [sʌl'tɑ:nə] N (fruit) raisin (sec) de Smyrne

sultry ['sʌltrɪ] ADJ étouffant(e)

★**sum** [sʌm] N somme f; (Scol etc) calcul m
▶ **sum up** VT résumer; (evaluate rapidly) récapituler
▶ VI résumer

> Use the feminine word **somme** to refer to an amount: *a sum of money* une somme d'argent. The masculine word **somme** means *nap*.

Sumatra [su'mɑ:trə] N Sumatra

summarize ['sʌməraɪz] VT résumer

summary ['sʌmərɪ] N résumé m ▶ ADJ (justice) sommaire

★**summer** ['sʌmə'] N été m; **in (the) ~** en été, pendant l'été ▶ CPD d'été, estival(e)

summer camp N (US) colonie f de vacances

summer holidays NPL grandes vacances

summerhouse ['sʌməhaus] N (in garden) pavillon m

summertime ['sʌmətaɪm] N (season) été m

summer time N (by clock) heure f d'été

summery ['sʌmərɪ] ADJ estival(e); d'été

summing-up [sʌmɪŋ'ʌp] N résumé m, récapitulation f

★**summit** ['sʌmɪt] N sommet m; (also: **summit conference**) (conférence f au) sommet

summon ['sʌmən] VT appeler, convoquer; **to ~ a witness** citer or assigner un témoin
▶ **summon up** VT rassembler, faire appel à

summons ['sʌmənz] N citation f, assignation f; **to serve a ~ on sb** remettre une assignation à qn
▶ VT citer, assigner

sumo ['su:məu] N: **~ wrestling** sumo m

sump [sʌmp] N (Brit Aut) carter m

sumptuous ['sʌmptjuəs] ADJ somptueux(-euse)

★**sun** [sʌn] N soleil m; **in the ~** au soleil; **to catch the ~** prendre le soleil; **everything under the ~** absolument tout

★**Sun.** ABBR (= Sunday) dim.

sunbathe ['sʌnbeɪð] VI prendre un bain de soleil

sunbeam ['sʌnbi:m] N rayon m de soleil

sunbed ['sʌnbɛd] N lit pliant; (with sun lamp) lit à ultra-violets

sunblock ['sʌnblɔk] N écran m total

sunburn ['sʌnbə:n] N coup m de soleil

sunburned ['sʌnbə:nd], **sunburnt** ['sʌnbə:nt] ADJ brûlé(e) par le soleil; **to get ~** prendre un coup de soleil

sun cream N crème f (anti-)solaire

sundae ['sʌndeɪ] N sundae m, coupe glacée

★**Sunday** ['sʌndɪ] N dimanche m; see also **Tuesday**

Sunday paper N journal *m* du dimanche

Les **Sunday papers** sont une véritable institution en Grande-Bretagne et aux États-Unis. La plupart des quotidiens ont une édition du dimanche, avec une équipe de rédacteurs différente des éditions de la semaine. Le journal s'accompagne le plus souvent de suppléments spéciaux consacrés aux affaires, au sport, aux voyages, à la vie littéraire, etc, ainsi que d'un magazine en couleur.

Sunday school N ≈ catéchisme *m*

sundial ['sʌndaɪəl] N cadran *m* solaire

sundown ['sʌndaun] N coucher *m* du soleil

sundries ['sʌndrɪz] NPL articles divers

sundry ['sʌndrɪ] ADJ divers(e), différent(e); **all and ~** tout le monde, n'importe qui

sunflower ['sʌnflauə'] N tournesol *m*

sung [sʌŋ] PP of **sing**

sunglasses ['sʌnglɑːsɪz] NPL lunettes *fpl* de soleil

sun hat N chapeau *m* de soleil

sunk [sʌŋk] PP of **sink**

sunken ['sʌŋkn] ADJ (*rock, ship*) submergé(e); (*cheeks*) creux(-euse); (*bath*) encastré(e)

sunlamp ['sʌnlæmp] N lampe *f* à rayons ultra-violets

sunlight ['sʌnlaɪt] N (lumière *f* du) soleil *m*

sunlit ['sʌnlɪt] ADJ ensoleillé(e)

sun lounger N chaise longue

sunny ['sʌnɪ] ADJ ensoleillé(e); (*fig*) épanoui(e), radieux(-euse); **it is ~** il fait (du) soleil, il y a du soleil

sunrise ['sʌnraɪz] N lever *m* du soleil

sun roof N (*Aut*) toit ouvrant

sunscreen ['sʌnskriːn] N crème *f* solaire

sunset ['sʌnset] N coucher *m* du soleil

sunshade ['sʌnʃeɪd] N (*lady's*) ombrelle *f*; (*over table*) parasol *m*

sunshine ['sʌnʃaɪn] N (lumière *f* du) soleil *m*

sunspot ['sʌnspɔt] N tache *f* solaire

sunstroke ['sʌnstrəuk] N insolation *f*

suntan ['sʌntæn] N bronzage *m*

suntan lotion N lotion *f* or lait *m* solaire

suntanned ['sʌntænd] ADJ bronzé(e)

suntan oil N huile *f* solaire

suntrap ['sʌntræp] N coin très ensoleillé

★**super** ['suːpə'] ADJ (*inf*) formidable

superannuation [suːpərænjuˈeɪʃən] N cotisations *fpl* pour la pension

★**superb** [suːˈpəːb] ADJ superbe, magnifique

Super Bowl N (*US Sport*) Super Bowl *m*

Le **Super Bowl** est la finale du championnat annuel de la National Football League (NFL), le plus haut niveau du football américain professionnel. Plus de quarante ans après sa première édition, en 1967, le *Super Bowl Sunday* est devenu une tradition, célèbre pour les quantités de nourriture consommées par les millions de fans qui se réunissent pour regarder la finale et les réjouissances de l'après-match à la télévision. La retransmission du *Super Bowl* est l'émission la plus regardée des États-Unis.

superbug ['suːpəbʌg] N super bactérie *f*

supercilious [suːpəˈsɪlɪəs] ADJ hautain(e), dédaigneux(-euse)

supercomputer [suːpəkəmˈpjuːtə'] N superordinateur *m*

superconductor [suːpəkənˈdʌktə'] N supraconducteur *m*

superficial [suːpəˈfɪʃəl] ADJ superficiel(le)

superficially [suːpəˈfɪʃlɪ] ADV superficiellement

superfluous [suˈpəːfluəs] ADJ superflu(e)

superfood ['suːpəfuːd] N superaliment *m*

superglue ['suːpəgluː] N colle forte

superhero ['suːpəhɪərəu] N super héros *m*

superhighway ['suːpəhaɪweɪ] N (*US*) voie *f* express (à plusieurs files); **the information ~** la super-autoroute de l'information

superhuman [suːpəˈhjuːmən] ADJ surhumain(e)

superimpose ['suːpərɪmˈpəuz] VT superposer

superintend [suːpərɪnˈtend] VT surveiller

superintendent [suːpərɪnˈtendənt] N directeur(-trice); (*Police*) ≈ commissaire *m*

superior [suˈpɪərɪə'] ADJ supérieur(e); (*Comm: goods, quality*) de qualité supérieure; (*smug*) condescendant(e), méprisant(e) ▶ N supérieur(e); **Mother S~** (*Rel*) Mère supérieure

superiority [suˈpɪərɪˈɔrɪtɪ] N supériorité *f*

superlative [suˈpəːlətɪv] ADJ sans pareil(le), suprême ▶ N (*Ling*) superlatif *m*

superman ['suːpəmæn] N (*irreg*) surhomme *m*

★**supermarket** ['suːpəmɑːkɪt] N supermarché *m*

supermodel ['suːpəmɔdl] N top model *m*

supernatural [suːpəˈnætʃərəl] ADJ surnaturel(le) ▶ N: **the ~** le surnaturel

supernova [suːpəˈnəuvə] N supernova *f*

superpower ['suːpəpauə'] N (*Pol*) superpuissance *f*

supersede [suːpəˈsiːd] VT remplacer, supplanter

supersonic ['suːpəˈsɔnɪk] ADJ supersonique

superstar ['suːpəstɑː'] N (*Cine etc*) superstar *f*; (*Sport*) superchampion(ne) ▶ ADJ (*status, lifestyle*) de superstar

superstardom ['suːpəstɑːdəm] N statut *m* de superstar

superstition [suːpəˈstɪʃən] N superstition *f*

superstitious [suːpəˈstɪʃəs] ADJ superstitieux(-euse)

superstore ['suːpəstɔː'] N (*Brit*) hypermarché *m*, grande surface

superstructure ['suːpəstrʌktʃə'] N superstructure *f*

supertanker ['suːpətæŋkə'] N pétrolier géant, superpétrolier *m*

supertax ['suːpətæks] N tranche supérieure de l'impôt

supervise ['suːpəvaɪz] VT (*children etc*) surveiller; (*organization, work*) diriger

supervision [suːpəˈvɪʒən] N surveillance *f*; (*monitoring*) contrôle *m*; (*management*) direction *f*; **under medical ~** sous contrôle du médecin

supervisor ['suːpəvaɪzə'] N surveillant(e); (*in shop*) chef *m* de rayon; (*Scol*) directeur(-trice) de thèse

S

supervisory [ˈsuːpəvaɪzərɪ] ADJ de surveillance

supine [ˈsuːpaɪn] ADJ couché(e) or étendu(e) sur le dos

supper [ˈsʌpəʳ] N dîner m; (late) souper m; **to have ~** dîner; souper

supplant [səˈplɑːnt] VT supplanter

supple [ˈsʌpl] ADJ souple

supplement N [ˈsʌplɪmənt] supplément m ▶ VT [sʌplɪˈmɛnt] ajouter à, compléter

supplementary [sʌplɪˈmɛntərɪ] ADJ supplémentaire

supplier [səˈplaɪəʳ] N fournisseur m

★**supply** [səˈplaɪ] VT (provide) fournir; (equip): **to ~ (with)** approvisionner or ravitailler (en); fournir (en); (system, machine): **to ~ sth (with sth)** alimenter qch (en qch); (a need) répondre à; **it comes supplied with an adaptor** il (or elle) est pourvu(e) d'un adaptateur ▶ N provision f, réserve f; (supplying) approvisionnement m; (Tech) alimentation f; **to be in short ~** être rare, manquer; **the electricity/water/gas ~** l'alimentation en électricité/eau/gaz; **~ and demand** l'offre f et la demande ■ **supplies** NPL (food) vivres mpl; (Mil) subsistances fpl; **office supplies** fournitures fpl de bureau

supply teacher N (BRIT) suppléant(e)

★**support** [səˈpɔːt] N (moral, financial etc) soutien m, appui m; (Tech) support m, soutien ▶ VT soutenir, supporter; (financially) subvenir aux besoins de; (uphold) être pour, être partisan de, appuyer; (Sport: team) être pour; **to ~ o.s.** (financially) gagner sa vie

★**supporter** [səˈpɔːtəʳ] N (Pol etc) partisan(e); (Sport) supporter m

supporting [səˈpɔːtɪŋ] ADJ (wall) d'appui

supporting role N second rôle m

supportive [səˈpɔːtɪv] ADJ: **my family were very ~** ma famille m'a été d'un grand soutien

★**suppose** [səˈpəʊz] VT, VI supposer; imaginer; **to be supposed to do/be** être censé(e) faire/être; **I don't ~ she'll come** je suppose qu'elle ne viendra pas, cela m'étonnerait qu'elle vienne

supposed [səˈpəʊzd, səˈpəʊzɪd] ADJ (alleged) supposé(e)

supposedly [səˈpəʊzɪdlɪ] ADV soi-disant

supposing [səˈpəʊzɪŋ] CONJ si, à supposer que + sub

supposition [sʌpəˈzɪʃən] N supposition f, hypothèse f

suppository [səˈpɒzɪtrɪ] N suppositoire m

suppress [səˈprɛs] VT (revolt, feeling) réprimer; (information) faire disparaître; (scandal, yawn) étouffer

suppression [səˈprɛʃən] N suppression f, répression f

suppressor [səˈprɛsəʳ] N (Elec etc) dispositif m antiparasite

supremacy [suˈprɛməsɪ] N suprématie f

supreme [suˈpriːm] ADJ suprême

Supreme Court N (US) Cour f suprême

La cour suprême (**Supreme Court**) des États-Unis, établie en 1789, est la plus haute juridiction. Elle se compose d'un *chief justice* (président) et de huit *associate justices* (juges) nommés par le pré-sident des États-Unis et confirmés dans leurs fonctions par le Sénat. Les *justices* exercent leur rôle à vie à moins qu'ils ne démissionnent, ne prennent leur retraite, ou ne soient destitués par le Congrès. Chaque État a également une cour suprême, qui statue en dernier ressort sur la législation et l'administration du système judi-ciaire de l'État en question.

supremely [suˈpriːmlɪ] ADV suprêmement

supremo [suˈpriːməʊ] N grand chef

Supt. ABBR (Police) = **superintendent**

surcharge [ˈsɜːtʃɑːdʒ] N surcharge f; (extra tax) surtaxe f

★**sure** [ʃʊəʳ] ADJ (gen) sûr(e); (definite, convinced) sûr, certain(e); **I'm not ~ how/why/when** je ne sais pas très bien comment/pourquoi/quand; **to be ~ of o.s.** être sûr de soi; **to make ~ of sth/that** s'assurer de qch/que, vérifier qch/que ▶ ADV (US inf): **that ~ is pretty, that's ~ pretty** c'est drôlement joli(e) (inf); **~!** (of course) bien sûr !; **~ enough** effectivement

sure-fire [ˈʃʊəfaɪəʳ] ADJ (inf) certain(e), infaillible

sure-footed [ʃʊəˈfʊtɪd] ADJ au pied sûr

★**surely** [ˈʃʊəlɪ] ADV sûrement; certainement; **~ you don't mean that!** vous ne parlez pas sérieusement !

surety [ˈʃʊərətɪ] N caution f; **to go** or **stand ~ for sb** se porter caution pour qn

surf [sɜːf] N (waves) ressac m ▶ VI (Sport) surfer ▶ VT: **to ~ the Net** surfer sur Internet, surfer sur le Net

★**surface** [ˈsɜːfɪs] N surface f; **on the ~** (fig) au premier abord ▶ CPD: **by ~ mail** par voie de terre; (by sea) par voie maritime ▶ VT (road) poser un revêtement sur ▶ VI remonter à la surface; (fig) faire surface

surface area N superficie f, aire f

surface mail N courrier m par voie de terre (or maritime)

surface-to-surface [ˈsɜːfɪstəˈsɜːfɪs] ADJ (Mil) sol-sol inv

surfboard [ˈsɜːfbɔːd] N planche f de surf

surfeit [ˈsɜːfɪt] N: **a ~ of** un excès de; une indigestion de

surfer [ˈsɜːfəʳ] N (in sea) surfeur(-euse); **(web** or **Net) ~** internaute mf

surfing [ˈsɜːfɪŋ] N (in sea) surf m

surge [sɜːdʒ] N (of emotion) vague f; (Elec) pointe f de courant ▶ VI déferler; **to ~ forward** se précipiter (en avant)

surgeon [ˈsɜːdʒən] N chirurgien(ne)

Surgeon General N (US) chef m du service fédéral de la santé publique

★**surgery** [ˈsɜːdʒərɪ] N chirurgie f; (BRIT: room) cabinet m (de consultation); (also: **surgery hours**) heures fpl de consultation; (of MP etc) permanence f (où le député etc reçoit les électeurs etc); **to undergo ~** être opéré(e)

surgical [ˈsɜːdʒɪkl] ADJ chirurgical(e)

surgically [ˈsɜːdʒɪklɪ] ADV chirurgicalement

surgical spirit N (BRIT) alcool m à 90°

Suriname [sʊərɪˈnæm] N Suriname m

surly [ˈsɜːlɪ] ADJ revêche, maussade

surmise [sə:'maɪz] VT présumer, conjecturer

surmount [sə:'maunt] VT surmonter

surname ['sə:neɪm] N nom *m* de famille

surpass [sə:'pɑ:s] VT surpasser, dépasser

surplus ['sə:pləs] N surplus *m*, excédent *m* ▶ ADJ en surplus, de trop; (*Comm*) excédentaire; **it is ~ to our requirements** cela dépasse nos besoins; **~ stock** surplus *m*

★**surprise** [sə'praɪz] N (*gen*) surprise *f*; (*astonishment*) étonnement *m*; **to take by ~** (*person*) prendre au dépourvu; (*Mil: town, fort*) prendre par surprise ▶ VT surprendre, étonner

★**surprised** [sə'praɪzd] ADJ (*look, smile*) surpris(e), étonné(e); **to be ~** être surpris

★**surprising** [sə'praɪzɪŋ] ADJ surprenant(e), étonnant(e)

surprisingly [sə'praɪzɪŋlɪ] ADV (*easy, helpful*) étonnamment, étrangement; (*somewhat*) ~, **he agreed** curieusement, il a accepté

surreal [sə'ri:əl] ADJ surréel(le)

surrealism [sə'rɪəlɪzəm] N surréalisme *m*

surrealist [sə'rɪəlɪst] ADJ, N surréaliste *mf*

★**surrender** [sə'rɛndə'] N reddition *f*, capitulation *f* ▶ VI se rendre, capituler ▶ VT (*claim, right*) renoncer à

surrender value N valeur *f* de rachat

surreptitious [sʌrəp'tɪʃəs] ADJ subreptice, furtif(-ive)

surrogate ['sʌrəgɪt] N (*Brit: substitute*) substitut *m* ▶ ADJ de substitution, de remplacement; **~ coffee** ersatz *m* or succédané *m* de café

surrogate mother N mère porteuse or de substitution

★**surround** [sə'raund] VT entourer; (*Mil etc*) encercler

surrounding [sə'raundɪŋ] ADJ environnant(e)

surroundings [sə'raundɪŋz] NPL environs *mpl*, alentours *mpl*

surtax ['sə:tæks] N surtaxe *f*

surtitles ['sə:taɪtlz] NPL surtitres *mpl*

surveillance [sə:'veɪləns] N surveillance *f*

★**survey** N ['sə:veɪ] enquête *f*, étude *f*; (*in house buying etc*) inspection *f*, (rapport *m* d') expertise *f*; (*of land*) levé *m*; (*comprehensive view: of situation etc*) vue *f* d'ensemble ▶ VT [sə:'veɪ] (*situation*) passer en revue; (*examine carefully*) inspecter; (*building*) expertiser; (*land*) faire le levé de; (*look at*) embrasser du regard

surveying [sə'veɪɪŋ] N arpentage *m*

surveyor [sə'veɪə'] N (*of building*) expert *m*; (*of land*) (arpenteur *m*) géomètre *m*

survival [sə'vaɪvl] N survie *f*; (*relic*) vestige *m* ▶ CPD (*course, kit*) de survie

survive [sə'vaɪv] VI survivre; (*custom etc*) subsister ▶ VT (*accident etc*) survivre à, réchapper de; (*person*) survivre à

survivor [sə'vaɪvə'] N survivant(e)

susceptible [sə'sɛptəbl] ADJ: **~ (to)** sensible (à); (*disease*) prédisposé(e) (à)

sushi ['su:ʃɪ] N sushi *m*

★**suspect** ADJ, N ['sʌspɛkt] suspect(e) ▶ VT [səs'pɛkt] soupçonner, suspecter

suspected [səs'pɛktɪd] ADJ: **a ~ terrorist** une personne soupçonnée de terrorisme; **he had a ~ broken arm** il avait une supposée fracture du bras

suspend [səs'pɛnd] VT suspendre

suspended animation [səs'pɛndɪd-] N: **in a state of ~** en hibernation

suspended sentence [səs'pɛndɪd-] N (*Law*) condamnation *f* avec sursis

suspender belt [səs'pɛndə-] N (*Brit*) porte-jarretelles *m inv*

suspenders [səs'pɛndəz] NPL (*Brit*) jarretelles *fpl*; (*US*) bretelles *fpl*

suspense [səs'pɛns] N attente *f*, incertitude *f*; (*in film etc*) suspense *m*; **to keep sb in ~** tenir qn en suspens, laisser qn dans l'incertitude

suspension [səs'pɛnʃən] N (*gen, Aut*) suspension *f*; (*of driving licence*) retrait *m* provisoire

suspension bridge N pont suspendu

suspicion [səs'pɪʃən] N soupçon(s) *m(pl)*; **to be under ~** être considéré(e) comme suspect(e), être suspecté(e); **arrested on ~ of murder** arrêté sur présomption de meurtre

suspicious [səs'pɪʃəs] ADJ (*suspecting*) soupçonneux(-euse), méfiant(e); (*causing suspicion*) suspect(e); **to be ~ of** or **about sb/sth** avoir des doutes à propos de qn/sur qch, trouver qn/qch suspect(e)

suspiciously [sə'spɪʃəslɪ] ADV (*suspecting: ask, look*) avec méfiance; (*causing suspicion: act, behave*) de manière suspecte; **it was ~ quiet** il régnait un calme suspect; **to look/sound ~ like sth** ressembler à s'y méprendre à qch

suss out [sʌs-] VT (*Brit inf: discover*) supputer; (*: understand*) piger (*inf*)

sustain [səs'teɪn] VT soutenir; supporter; corroborer; (*subj: food*) nourrir, donner des forces à; (*damage*) subir; (*injury*) recevoir

sustainability [səsteɪnə'bɪlɪtɪ] N durabilité *f*

sustainable [səs'teɪnəbl] ADJ (*rate, growth*) qui peut être maintenu(e); (*development*) durable

sustainably [səs'teɪnəblɪ] ADV durablement; **~ managed** géré(e) durablement

sustained [səs'teɪnd] ADJ (*effort*) soutenu(e), prolongé(e)

sustenance ['sʌstɪnəns] N nourriture *f*; moyens *mpl* de subsistance

suture ['su:tʃə'] N suture *f*

SUV N ABBR (*esp US*: = *sports utility vehicle*) SUV *m*, véhicule *m* de loisirs

svelte [svɛlt, sfɛlt] ADJ svelte

SW ABBR (= *short wave*) OC

swab [swɔb] N (*Med*) tampon *m*; prélèvement *m* ▶ VT (*Naut: also:* **swab down**) nettoyer

swagger ['swægə'] VI plastronner, parader

swallow ['swɔləu] N (*bird*) hirondelle *f*; (*of food etc*) gorgée *f* ▶ VT avaler; (*fig: story*) gober
  ▶ **swallow up** VT engloutir

swam [swæm] PT *of* **swim**

swamp [swɔmp] N marais *m*, marécage *m* ▶ VT submerger

swampy ['swɔmpɪ] ADJ marécageux(-euse)

swan [swɔn] N cygne *m*

swank [swæŋk] vi (inf) faire de l'épate

swanky ['swæŋkɪ] ADJ (inf: hotel, car) classe (inf)

swan song N (fig) chant m du cygne

swap [swɔp] N échange m, troc m ▶ VT: **to ~ (for)** échanger (contre), troquer (contre)

SWAPO ['swɑːpəʊ] N ABBR (= South-West Africa People's Organization) SWAPO f

swarm [swɔːm] N essaim m ▶ VI (bees) essaimer; (people) grouiller; **to be swarming with** grouiller de

swarthy ['swɔːðɪ] ADJ basané(e), bistré(e)

swashbuckling ['swɔʃbʌklɪŋ] ADJ (film) de cape et d'épée

swastika ['swɔstɪkə] N croix gammée

SWAT N ABBR (US: = Special Weapons and Tactics) ≈ CRS f

swat [swɔt] VT écraser ▶ N (BRIT: also: **fly swat**) tapette f

swathe [sweɪð] VT: **to ~ in** (bandages, blankets) embobiner de

swatter ['swɔtə^r] N (also: **fly swatter**) tapette f

sway [sweɪ] VI se balancer, osciller; tanguer ▶ VT (influence) influencer ▶ N (rule, power): **~ (over)** emprise f (sur); **to hold ~ over sb** avoir de l'emprise sur qn

Swaziland ['swɑːzɪlænd] N Swaziland m

swear [swɛə^r] (pt swore [swɔː^r], pp sworn [swɔːn]) VT, VI jurer; **to ~ to sth** jurer de qch; **to ~ an oath** prêter serment
▶ **swear in** [swɛə^r ɪn] VT assermenter

swearword ['swɛəwəːd] N gros mot, juron m

sweat [swɛt] N sueur f, transpiration f; **in a ~** en sueur ▶ VI suer

sweatband ['swɛtbænd] N (Sport) bandeau m

sweater ['swɛtə^r] N tricot m, pull m

sweatshirt ['swɛtʃəːt] N sweat-shirt m

sweatshop ['swɛtʃɔp] N atelier m où les ouvriers sont exploités

sweaty ['swɛtɪ] ADJ en sueur, moite or mouillé(e) de sueur

★**Swede** [swiːd] N Suédois(e)

swede [swiːd] N (BRIT) rutabaga m

★**Sweden** ['swiːdn] N Suède f

★**Swedish** ['swiːdɪʃ] ADJ suédois(e) ▶ N (Ling) suédois m

★**sweep** [swiːp] (pt, pp swept [swɛpt]) N coup m de balai; (curve) grande courbe; (range) champ m; (also: **chimney sweep**) ramoneur m ▶ VT balayer; (subj: current) emporter; (subj: fashion, craze) se répandre dans ▶ VI avancer majestueusement or rapidement; s'élancer; s'étendre
▶ **sweep away** [swiːp ə'weɪ] VT balayer; entraîner; emporter
▶ **sweep past** [swiːp pɑːst] VI passer majestueusement or rapidement
▶ **sweep up** [swiːp ʌp] VT, VI balayer

sweeper ['swiːpə^r] N (person) balayeur m; (machine) balayeuse f; (Football) libéro m

sweeping ['swiːpɪŋ] ADJ (gesture) large; circulaire; (changes, reforms) radical(e); **a ~ statement** une généralisation hâtive

sweepstake ['swiːpsteɪk] N sweepstake m

★**sweet** [swiːt] N (BRIT: pudding) dessert m; (: candy) bonbon m ▶ ADJ doux (douce); (not savoury) sucré(e); (fresh) frais (fraîche), pur(e); (kind) gentil(le); (baby) mignon(ne); **to smell ~** sentir bon; **to taste ~** avoir un goût sucré; **~ and sour** aigre-doux (douce)

sweetbread ['swiːtbrɛd] N ris m de veau

sweetcorn ['swiːtkɔːn] N maïs doux

sweeten ['swiːtn] VT sucrer; (fig) adoucir

sweetener ['swiːtnə^r] N (Culin) édulcorant m

sweetheart ['swiːthɑːt] N amoureux(-euse)

sweetie ['swiːtɪ] N (inf: as address) mon chou m; (: kind person) chou m; (: BRIT inf: candy) bonbon m

sweetly ['swiːtlɪ] ADV (smile) gentiment; (sing, play) mélodieusement

sweetness ['swiːtnɪs] N douceur f; (of taste) goût sucré

sweet pea N pois m de senteur

sweet potato N patate douce

sweetshop ['swiːtʃɔp] N (BRIT) confiserie f

sweet tooth N: **to have a ~** aimer les sucreries

swell [swɛl] (pt swelled [swɛld], pp swollen ['swəʊlən] or swelled [swɛld]) N (of sea) houle f ▶ ADJ (US inf: excellent) chouette ▶ VT (increase) grossir, augmenter ▶ VI (increase) grossir, augmenter; (sound) s'enfler; (Med: also: **swell up**) enfler

swelling ['swɛlɪŋ] N (Med) enflure f; (: lump) grosseur f

sweltering ['swɛltərɪŋ] ADJ étouffant(e), oppressant(e)

swept [swɛpt] PT, PP of **sweep**

swerve [swəːv] VI (to avoid obstacle) faire une embardée or un écart; (off the road) dévier

swift [swɪft] N (bird) martinet m ▶ ADJ rapide, prompt(e)

swiftly ['swɪftlɪ] ADV rapidement, vite

swiftness ['swɪftnɪs] N rapidité f

swig [swɪg] N (inf: drink) lampée f

swill [swɪl] N pâtée f ▶ VT (also: **swill out, swill down**) laver à grande eau

★**swim** [swɪm] (pt swam [swæm], pp swum [swʌm]) N: **to go for a ~** aller nager or se baigner ▶ VI nager; (Sport) faire de la natation; (fig: head, room) tourner; **to go swimming** aller nager ▶ VT traverser (à la nage); (distance) faire (à la nage); **to ~ a length** nager une longueur

swimmer ['swɪmə^r] N nageur(-euse)

★**swimming** ['swɪmɪŋ] N nage f, natation f

swimming baths NPL (BRIT) piscine f

swimming cap N bonnet m de bain

swimming costume N (BRIT) maillot m (de bain)

swimmingly ['swɪmɪŋlɪ] ADV: **to go ~** (wonderfully) se dérouler à merveille

swimming pool N piscine f

swimming trunks NPL maillot m de bain

★**swimsuit** ['swɪmsuːt] N maillot m (de bain)

swimwear ['swɪmwɛə^r] N vêtements mpl de bain

swindle ['swɪndl] N escroquerie f ▶ VT escroquer

swindler ['swɪndlə^r] N escroc m

swine [swaɪn] N (pl inv) pourceau m, porc m; (pej) salaud m (!)

swine flu N grippe f A

★**swing** [swɪŋ] (*pt, pp* **swung** [swʌŋ]) N (*in playground*) balançoire *f*; (*movement*) balancement *m*, oscillations *fpl*; (*change in opinion etc*) revirement *m*; (*Mus*) swing *m*; rythme *m*; **a ~ to the left** (*Pol*) un revirement en faveur de la gauche; **to be in full ~** battre son plein; **to get into the ~ of things** se mettre dans le bain ▸ VT balancer, faire osciller; (*also:* **swing round**) tourner, faire virer ▸ VI se balancer, osciller; (*also:* **swing round**) virer, tourner; **the road swings south** la route prend la direction sud

swing bridge N pont tournant

swing door N (BRIT) porte battante

swingeing ['swɪndʒɪŋ] ADJ (BRIT) écrasant(e); considérable

swinging ['swɪŋɪŋ] ADJ rythmé(e); entraînant(e); (*fig*) dans le vent; **~ door** (US) porte battante

swipe [swaɪp] N grand coup; gifle *f* ▸ VT (*hit*) frapper à toute volée; gifler; (*inf: steal*) piquer (*inf*); (*credit card etc*) faire passer (dans la machine)

swipe card N carte *f* magnétique

swirl [swəːl] N tourbillon *m* ▸ VI tourbillonner, tournoyer

swish [swɪʃ] ADJ (BRIT old: smart) rupin(e) ▸ VI (*whip*) siffler; (*skirt, long grass*) bruire

★**Swiss** [swɪs] ADJ suisse ▸ N (*pl inv*) Suisse(-sesse)

Swiss French ADJ suisse romand(e)

Swiss German ADJ suisse-allemand(e)

Swiss roll N gâteau roulé

★**switch** [swɪtʃ] N (*for light, radio etc*) bouton *m*; (*change*) changement *m*, revirement *m* ▸ VT (*change*) changer; (*exchange*) intervertir; (*invert*): **to ~ (round** or **over)** changer de place ▸ **switch off** VT éteindre; (*engine, machine*) arrêter; **could you ~ off the light?** pouvez-vous éteindre la lumière ? ▸ **switch on** VT allumer; (*engine, machine*) mettre en marche; (BRIT: *water supply*) ouvrir

switchback ['swɪtʃbæk] N (BRIT) montagnes *fpl* russes

switchblade ['swɪtʃbleɪd] N (*also:* **switchblade knife**) couteau *m* à cran d'arrêt

switchboard ['swɪtʃbɔːd] N (*Tel*) standard *m*

switchboard operator N (*Tel*) standardiste *mf*

★**Switzerland** ['swɪtsələnd] N Suisse *f*

swivel ['swɪvl] VI (*also:* **swivel round**) pivoter, tourner

swollen ['swəʊlən] PP *of* **swell** ▸ ADJ (*ankle etc*) enflé(e)

swoon [swuːn] VI se pâmer

swoop [swuːp] N (*by police etc*) rafle *f*, descente *f*; (*of bird etc*) descente en piqué ▸ VI (*bird: also:* **swoop down**) descendre en piqué, piquer

swop [swɔp] N, VT = **swap**

sword [sɔːd] N épée *f*

swordfish ['sɔːdfɪʃ] N espadon *m*

swore [swɔːʳ] PT *of* **swear**

sworn [swɔːn] PP *of* **swear** ▸ ADJ (*statement, evidence*) donné(e) sous serment; (*enemy*) juré(e)

swot [swɔt] VT, VI bûcher, potasser

swum [swʌm] PP *of* **swim**

swung [swʌŋ] PT, PP *of* **swing**

sycamore ['sɪkəmɔːʳ] N sycomore *m*

sycophant ['sɪkəfænt] N flagorneur(-euse)

sycophantic [sɪkə'fæntɪk] ADJ flagorneur(-euse)

Sydney ['sɪdnɪ] N Sydney

syllable ['sɪləbl] N syllabe *f*

syllabus ['sɪləbəs] N programme *m*; **on the ~** au programme

symbiotic [sɪmbaɪ'ɔtɪk] ADJ symbiotique

★**symbol** ['sɪmbl] N symbole *m*

symbolic [sɪm'bɔlɪk], **symbolical** [sɪm'bɔlɪkl] ADJ symbolique

symbolically [sɪm'bɔlɪklɪ] ADV symboliquement

symbolism ['sɪmbəlɪzəm] N symbolisme *m*

symbolize ['sɪmbəlaɪz] VT symboliser

symmetrical [sɪ'mɛtrɪkl] ADJ symétrique

symmetry ['sɪmɪtrɪ] N symétrie *f*

sympathetic [sɪmpə'θɛtɪk] ADJ (*showing pity*) compatissant(e); (*understanding*) bienveillant(e), compréhensif(-ive); **~ towards** bien disposé(e) envers

⚠ **sympathetic** ne veut pas dire *sympathique*.

sympathetically [sɪmpə'θɛtɪklɪ] ADV avec compassion (or bienveillance)

sympathize ['sɪmpəθaɪz] VI: **to ~ with sb** plaindre qn; (*in grief*) s'associer à la douleur de qn; **to ~ with sth** comprendre qch

sympathizer ['sɪmpəθaɪzəʳ] N (*Pol*) sympathisant(e)

★**sympathy** ['sɪmpəθɪ] N (*pity*) compassion *f*; **in ~ with** en accord avec; (*strike*) en or par solidarité avec; **with our deepest ~** en vous priant d'accepter nos sincères condoléances ▪ **sympathies** NPL (*support*) soutien *m*

symphonic [sɪm'fɔnɪk] ADJ symphonique

symphony ['sɪmfənɪ] N symphonie *f*

symphony orchestra N orchestre *m* symphonique

symposium [sɪm'pəʊzɪəm] N symposium *m*

★**symptom** ['sɪmptəm] N symptôme *m*; indice *m*

symptomatic [sɪmptə'mætɪk] ADJ symptomatique

synagogue ['sɪnəgɔg] N synagogue *f*

sync [sɪŋk] N (*inf*): **in/out of ~** bien/mal synchronisé(e); **they're in ~ with each other** (*fig*) le courant passe bien entre eux

synchromesh [sɪŋkrəʊ'mɛʃ] N (*Aut*) synchronisation *f*

synchronize ['sɪŋkrənaɪz] VT synchroniser ▸ VI: **to ~ with** se produire en même temps que

synchronized swimming ['sɪŋkrənaɪzd-] N natation synchronisée

syncopated ['sɪŋkəpeɪtɪd] ADJ syncopé(e)

syndicate ['sɪndɪkɪt] N syndicat *m*, coopérative *f*; (*Press*) agence *f* de presse

syndicated ['sɪndɪkeɪtɪd] ADJ (*Press: articles*) d'agence

syndrome ['sɪndrəʊm] N syndrome *m*

synergy ['sɪnədʒɪ] N synergie *f*

synod ['sɪnəd] N synode *m*

synonym ['sɪnənɪm] N synonyme *m*

synonymous [sɪ'nɔnɪməs] ADJ: **~ (with)** synonyme (de)

synopsis [sɪ'nɔpsɪs] (*pl* **synopses** [-siːz]) N résumé *m*, synopsis *mf*

S

syntax ['sɪntæks] N syntaxe f

synthesis ['sɪnθəsɪs] (pl **syntheses** [-siːz]) N synthèse f

synthesize ['sɪnθɪsaɪz] VT synthétiser

synthesizer ['sɪnθəsaɪzəʳ] N (Mus) synthétiseur m

synthetic [sɪn'θɛtɪk] ADJ synthétique ▶ N matière f synthétique ■ **synthetics** NPL textiles artificiels

syphilis ['sɪfɪlɪs] N syphilis f

syphon ['saɪfən] N, VT = **siphon**

Syria ['sɪrɪə] N Syrie f

Syrian ['sɪrɪən] ADJ syrien(ne) ▶ N Syrien(ne)

syringe [sɪ'rɪndʒ] N seringue f

syrup ['sɪrəp] N sirop m; (Brit: also: **golden syrup**) mélasse raffinée

syrupy ['sɪrəpɪ] ADJ sirupeux(-euse)

★**system** ['sɪstəm] N système m; (order) méthode f; (Anat) organisme m

systematic [sɪstə'mætɪk] ADJ systématique; méthodique

systematically [sɪstə'mætɪklɪ] ADV systématiquement

system disk N (Comput) disque m système

systems analyst N analyste-programmeur mf

Tt

T, t [ti:] N (letter) T, t m; **T for Tommy** T comme Thérèse

TA N ABBR (BRIT) = **Territorial Army**

ta [tɑ:] EXCL (BRIT inf) merci!

tab [tæb] N ABBR = **tabulator** ▶ N (loop on coat etc) attache f; (label) étiquette f; (on drinks can etc) languette f; **to keep tabs on** (fig) surveiller

tabby ['tæbɪ] N (also: **tabby cat**) chat(te) tigré(e)

★**table** ['teɪbl] N table f; **to lay** or **set the ~** mettre le couvert or la table; **to clear the ~** débarrasser la table; **league ~** (BRIT Football, Rugby) classement m (du championnat); **~ of contents** table des matières ▶ VT (BRIT: motion etc) présenter

tablecloth ['teɪblklɔθ] N nappe f

table d'hôte [tɑ:bl'dəut] ADJ (meal) à prix fixe

table football N baby-foot m

table lamp N lampe décorative or de table

tablemat ['teɪblmæt] N (for plate) napperon m, set m; (for hot dish) dessous-de-plat m inv

table salt N sel fin or de table

tablespoon ['teɪblspu:n] N cuiller f de service; (also: **tablespoonful**: as measurement) cuillerée f à soupe

tablet ['tæblɪt] N (Med) comprimé m; (: for sucking) pastille f; (Comput) tablette f (tactile); (of stone) plaque f; **~ of soap** (BRIT) savonnette f

table tennis N ping-pong m, tennis m de table

tabletop ['teɪbltɔp] N plateau m de table

tableware ['teɪblwɛəʳ] N articles mpl de table

table wine N vin m de table

tabloid ['tæblɔɪd] N (newspaper) quotidien m populaire

taboo [tə'bu:] ADJ, N tabou m

tabulate ['tæbjuleɪt] VT (data, figures) mettre sous forme de table(s)

tabulator ['tæbjuleɪtəʳ] N tabulateur m

tachograph ['tækəgrɑ:f] N tachygraphe m

tachometer [tæ'kɔmɪtəʳ] N tachymètre m

tacit ['tæsɪt] ADJ tacite

taciturn ['tæsɪtə:n] ADJ taciturne

tack [tæk] N (nail) petit clou; (stitch) point m de bâti; (Naut) bord m, bordée f; (fig) direction f; **to change ~** virer de bord; **on the wrong ~** (fig) sur la mauvaise voie ▶ VT (nail) clouer; (sew) bâtir; **to ~ sth on to (the end of) sth** (of letter, book) rajouter qch à la fin de qch ▶ VI (Naut) tirer un or des bord(s)

★**tackle** ['tækl] N matériel m, équipement m; (for lifting) appareil m de levage; (Football, Rugby) plaquage m ▶ VT (difficulty, animal, burglar) s'attaquer à; (person: challenge) s'expliquer avec; (Football, Rugby) plaquer

tacky ['tækɪ] ADJ collant(e); (paint) pas sec (sèche); (inf: shabby) moche; (pej: poor-quality) minable; (: showing bad taste) ringard(e)

taco ['tækəu] N taco m

tact [tækt] N tact m

tactful ['tæktful] ADJ plein(e) de tact

tactfully ['tæktfəlɪ] ADV avec tact

tactical ['tæktɪkl] ADJ tactique; **~ error** erreur f de tactique

tactician [tæk'tɪʃən] N tacticien(ne)

tactics ['tæktɪks] N, NPL tactique f

tactile ['tæktaɪl] ADJ tactile

tactless ['tæktlɪs] ADJ qui manque de tact

tactlessly ['tæktlɪslɪ] ADV sans tact

tad ['tæd] N (inf): **a ~** un tantinet (inf); **it was a ~ confusing** c'était un tantinet déroutant; **a ~ more expensive** un poil plus cher (inf)

tadpole ['tædpəul] N têtard m

Tadzhikistan [tædʒɪkɪ'stɑ:n] N = **Tajikistan**

taffeta ['tæfɪtə] N taffetas m ▶ CPD (dress, gown) de taffetas

taffy ['tæfɪ] N (US) (bonbon m au) caramel m

tag [tæg] N étiquette f; **price/name ~** étiquette (portant le prix/le nom)
  ▶ **tag along** VI suivre

tag line N (of joke) chute f; (: phrase) accroche f

Tahiti [tɑ:'hi:tɪ] N Tahiti m

Tai Chi [taɪ'tʃi:] N tai chi m

★**tail** [teɪl] N queue f; (of shirt) pan m; **to turn ~** se sauver à toutes jambes; see also **head** ▶ VT (follow) suivre, filer ■ **tails** NPL (suit) habit m
  ▶ **tail away, tail off** VI (in size, quality etc) baisser peu à peu

tailback ['teɪlbæk] N (BRIT) bouchon m

tailcoat ['teɪlkəut] N queue f de pie

tail end N bout m, fin f

tailgate ['teɪlgeɪt] N (Aut) hayon m arrière

tailgating ['teɪlgeɪtɪŋ] N non-respect m des distances de sécurité

tail light N (Aut) feu m arrière

tailor ['teɪləʳ] N tailleur m (artisan); **~'s (shop)** (boutique f de) tailleur m ▶ VT: **to ~ sth (to)** adapter qch exactement (à)

t

tailoring ['teɪlərɪŋ] N (cut) coupe f

tailor-made ['teɪlə'meɪd] ADJ fait(e) sur mesure; (fig) conçu(e) spécialement

tailpipe ['teɪlpaɪp] N (US) pot m d'échappement

tailwind ['teɪlwɪnd] N vent m arrière inv

taint [teɪnt] VT (meat, food) gâter; (fig: reputation) salir

tainted ['teɪntɪd] ADJ (food) gâté(e); (water, air) infecté(e); (fig) souillé(e)

Taiwan ['taɪ'wɑːn] N Taïwan

Taiwanese [taɪwə'niːz] ADJ taïwanais(e) ▶ N INV Taïwanais(e)

Tajikistan [tædʒɪkɪ'stɑːn] N Tadjikistan mf

★**take** [teɪk] (pt **took** [tuk], pp **taken** ['teɪkn]) VT prendre; (gain: prize) remporter; (require: effort, courage) demander; (tolerate) accepter, supporter; (hold: passengers etc) contenir; (accompany) emmener, accompagner; (bring, carry) apporter, emporter; (exam) passer, se présenter à; (conduct: meeting) présider; **to ~ sth from** (drawer etc) prendre qch dans; (person) prendre qch à; **I ~ it that** je suppose que; **I took him for a doctor** je l'ai pris pour un docteur; **to ~ sb's hand** prendre qn par la main; **to ~ for a walk** (child, dog) emmener promener; **to be taken ill** tomber malade; **to ~ it upon o.s. to do sth** prendre sur soi de faire qch; **~ the first (street) on the left** prenez la première à gauche; **it won't ~ long** ça ne prendra pas longtemps; **I was quite taken with her/it** elle/cela m'a beaucoup plu ▶ VI (dye, fire etc) prendre ▶ N (Cine) prise f de vues

▶ **take after** [teɪk 'ɑːftəʳ] VT FUS ressembler à

▶ **take apart** [teɪk ə'pɑːt] VT démonter

▶ **take away** [teɪk ə'weɪ] VT (carry off) emporter; (remove) enlever; (subtract) soustraire ▶ VI: **to ~ away from** diminuer

▶ **take back** [teɪk bæk] VT (return) rendre, rapporter; (one's words) retirer

▶ **take down** [teɪk daun] VT (building) démolir; (dismantle: scaffolding) démonter; (letter etc) prendre, écrire

▶ **take in** [teɪk ɪn] VT (deceive) tromper, rouler; (understand) comprendre, saisir; (include) couvrir, inclure; (lodger) prendre; (orphan, stray dog) recueillir; (dress, waistband) reprendre

▶ **take off** [teɪk ɔf] VI (Aviat) décoller ▶ VT (remove) enlever; (imitate) imiter, pasticher

▶ **take on** [teɪk ɔn] VT (work) accepter, se charger de; (employee) prendre, embaucher; (opponent) accepter de se battre contre

▶ **take out** [teɪk aut] VT (remove) sortir; (remove) enlever; (invite) sortir avec; (licence) prendre, se procurer; **to ~ sth out of** enlever qch de; (out of drawer etc) prendre qch dans; **don't ~ it out on me!** ne t'en prends pas à moi!; **to ~ sb out to a restaurant** emmener qn au restaurant

▶ **take over** [teɪk 'əuvəʳ] VT (business) reprendre ▶ VI: **to ~ over from sb** prendre la relève de qn

▶ **take to** [teɪk tuː] VT FUS (person) se prendre d'amitié pour; (activity) prendre goût à; **to ~ to doing sth** prendre l'habitude de faire qch

▶ **take up** [teɪk ʌp] VT (one's story) reprendre; (dress) raccourcir; (occupy: time, space) prendre, occuper; (engage in: hobby etc) se mettre à; (accept: offer, challenge) accepter; (absorb: liquids) absorber ▶ VI: **to ~ up with sb** se lier d'amitié avec qn

takeaway ['teɪkəweɪ] (BRIT) ADJ (food) à emporter ▶ N (shop, restaurant) ≈ magasin m qui vend des plats à emporter

take-home pay ['teɪkhəum-] N salaire net

taken ['teɪkən] PP of **take**

takeoff ['teɪkɔf] N (Aviat) décollage m

takeout ['teɪkaut] ADJ, N (US) = **takeaway**

takeover ['teɪkəuvəʳ] N (Comm) rachat m

takeover bid N offre publique d'achat, OPA f

taker ['teɪkəʳ] N preneur m; **to fail to find any takers** ne pas trouver preneur

takings ['teɪkɪŋz] NPL (Comm) recette f

talc [tælk] N (also: **talcum powder**) talc m

★**tale** [teɪl] N (story) conte m, histoire f; (account) récit m; (pej) histoire; **to tell tales** (fig) rapporter

★**talent** ['tælnt] N talent m, don m

talent competition, talent contest N concours m d'amateurs

talented ['tæləntɪd] ADJ doué(e), plein(e) de talent

talent scout N découvreur m de vedettes (or joueurs etc)

Taliban ['tælɪbæn] N: **the ~** les talibans ▶ ADJ taliban(e)

talisman ['tælɪzmən] N talisman m

★**talk** [tɔːk] N (a speech) causerie f, exposé m; (conversation) discussion f; (interview) entretien m, propos mpl; (gossip) racontars mpl (pej); **to give a ~** faire un exposé ▶ VI parler; (chatter) bavarder; **to ~ about** parler de; (converse) s'entretenir or parler de; **talking of films, have you seen ...?** à propos de films, as-tu vu ...? ▶ VT (language, politics) parler; **to ~ shop** parler métier or affaires; **to ~ sb out of/into doing** persuader qn de ne pas faire/de faire ■ **talks** NPL (Pol etc) entretiens mpl; conférence f

▶ **talk over** VT discuter (de)

▶ **talk through** VT (discuss) discuter sérieusement; (explain): **to ~ sb through sth** expliquer qch à qn; **to ~ sth through with sb** discuter sérieusement de qch avec qn

talkative ['tɔːkətɪv] ADJ bavard(e)

talking point ['tɔːkɪŋ-] N sujet m de conversation

talking-to ['tɔːkɪŋtu] N: **to give sb a good ~** passer un savon à qn

talk show N (TV, Radio) émission-débat f

★**tall** [tɔːl] ADJ (person) grand(e); (building, tree) haut(e); **to be 6 feet ~** ≈ mesurer 1 mètre 80; **how ~ are you?** combien mesurez-vous ?

tallboy ['tɔːlbɔɪ] N (BRIT) grande commode

tallness ['tɔːlnɪs] N grande taille; hauteur f

tall story N histoire f invraisemblable

tally ['tælɪ] N compte m; **to keep a ~ of sth** tenir le compte de qch ▶ VI: **to ~ (with)** correspondre (à)

talon ['tælən] N griffe f; (of eagle) serre f

tambourine [tæmbə'riːn] N tambourin m

tame [teɪm] ADJ apprivoisé(e); (fig: story, style) insipide

Tamil ['tæmɪl] ADJ tamoul(e), tamil(e) ▶ N Tamoul(e), Tamil(e); (Ling) tamoul m, tamil m

tamper ['tæmpəʳ] VI: **to ~ with** toucher à (en cachette ou sans permission)

tampon ['tæmpən] N tampon m hygiénique or périodique

tan [tæn] N (*also:* **suntan**) bronzage *m*; **to get a ~** bronzer ▸ VT, VI bronzer, brunir ▸ ADJ (*colour*) marron clair *inv*

tandem ['tændəm] N tandem *m*

tandoori [tæn'duərɪ] ADJ tandouri

tang [tæŋ] N odeur (*or* saveur) piquante

tangent ['tændʒənt] N (*Math*) tangente *f*; **to go off at a ~** (*fig*) partir dans une digression

tangerine [tændʒə'riːn] N mandarine *f*

tangible ['tændʒəbl] ADJ tangible; **~ assets** biens réels

Tangier [tæn'dʒɪər] N Tanger

tangle ['tæŋgl] N enchevêtrement *m*; **to get in(to) a ~** s'emmêler ▸ VT enchevêtrer

tango ['tæŋgəu] N tango *m*

tank [tæŋk] N réservoir *m*; (*for processing*) cuve *f*; (*for fish*) aquarium *m*; (*Mil*) char *m* d'assaut, tank *m*

tankard ['tæŋkəd] N chope *f*

tanker ['tæŋkər] N (*ship*) pétrolier *m*, tanker *m*; (*truck*) camion-citerne *m*; (*Rail*) wagon-citerne *m*

tankini [tæn'kiːnɪ] N tankini *m*

tanned [tænd] ADJ bronzé(e)

tannin ['tænɪn] N tanin *m*

tanning ['tænɪŋ] N (*of leather*) tannage *m*

Tannoy® ['tænɔɪ] N (*BRIT*) haut-parleur *m*; **over the ~** par haut-parleur

tantalizing ['tæntəlaɪzɪŋ] ADJ (*smell*) extrêmement appétissant(e); (*offer*) terriblement tentant(e)

tantamount ['tæntəmaunt] ADJ: **~ to** qui équivaut à

tantrum ['tæntrəm] N accès *m* de colère; **to throw a ~** piquer une colère

Tanzania [tænzə'nɪə] N Tanzanie *f*

Tanzanian [tænzə'nɪən] ADJ tanzanien(ne) ▸ N Tanzanien(ne)

Taoiseach ['tiːʃək] N Premier ministre de la République d'Irlande

★**tap** [tæp] N (*on sink etc*) robinet *m*; (*gentle blow*) petite tape; **on ~** (*beer*) en tonneau; (*fig: resources*) disponible ▸ VT frapper *or* taper légèrement; (*resources*) exploiter, utiliser; (*telephone*) mettre sur écoute

tap dancing N claquettes *fpl*

★**tape** [teɪp] N (*for tying*) ruban *m*; (*also:* **magnetic tape**) bande *f* (magnétique); (*cassette*) cassette *f*; (*sticky*) Scotch® *m*; **on ~** (*song etc*) enregistré(e) ▸ VT (*record*) enregistrer (au magnétoscope *or* sur cassette); (*stick*) coller avec du Scotch®

tape deck N platine *f* d'enregistrement

tape measure N mètre *m* à ruban

taper ['teɪpər] N cierge *m* ▸ VI s'effiler

tape recorder N magnétophone *m*

tapered ['teɪpəd], **tapering** ['teɪpərɪŋ] ADJ fuselé(e), effilé(e)

tapestry ['tæpɪstrɪ] N tapisserie *f*

tapeworm ['teɪpwəːm] N ver *m* solitaire, ténia *m*

tapioca [tæpɪ'əukə] N tapioca *m*

tappet ['tæpɪt] N (*Aut*) poussoir *m* (de soupape)

tar [tɑː] N goudron *m*; **low-/middle-tar cigarettes** cigarettes *fpl* à faible/moyenne teneur en goudron

tarantula [tə'ræntjulə] N tarentule *f*

tardy ['tɑːdɪ] ADJ tardif(-ive)

★**target** ['tɑːgɪt] N cible *f*; (*fig: objective*) objectif *m*; **to be on ~** (*project*) progresser comme prévu

target practice N exercices *mpl* de tir (à la cible)

tariff ['tærɪf] N (*Comm*) tarif *m*; (*taxes*) tarif douanier

tarmac ['tɑːmæk] N (*BRIT: on road*) macadam *m*; (*Aviat*) aire *f* d'envol ▸ VT (*BRIT*) goudronner

tarnish ['tɑːnɪʃ] VT ternir

tarot ['tærəu] N tarot *m*

tarpaulin [tɑː'pɔːlɪn] N bâche goudronnée

tarragon ['tærəgən] N estragon *m*

tart [tɑːt] N (*Culin*) tarte *f*; (*BRIT pej: promiscuous woman*) pétasse *f* (*inf*); (: *prostitute*) poule *f* (*inf*) ▸ ADJ (*flavour*) âpre, aigrelet(te); (*remark, reply*) acide
▸ **tart up** VT (*inf*): **to ~ o.s. up** se faire beau (belle); (*pej*) s'attifer

tartan ['tɑːtn] N tartan *m* ▸ ADJ écossais(e)

tartar ['tɑːtər] N (*on teeth*) tartre *m*

tartar sauce, tartare sauce ['tɑːtə-] N sauce *f* tartare

tartly ['tɑːtlɪ] ADV (*say, reply*) d'un ton acide

★**task** [tɑːsk] N tâche *f*; **to take to ~** prendre à partie

task force N (*Mil, Police*) détachement spécial

taskmaster ['tɑːskmɑːstər] N: **he's a hard ~** il est très exigeant dans le travail

Tasmania [tæz'meɪnɪə] N Tasmanie *f*

tassel ['tæsl] N gland *m*; pompon *m*

★**taste** [teɪst] N goût *m*; (*fig: glimpse, idea*) idée *f*, aperçu *m*; **to have a ~ of sth** goûter (à) qch; **can I have a ~?** je peux goûter ?; **to have a ~ for sth** aimer qch, avoir un penchant pour qch; **to be in good/bad** *or* **poor ~** être de bon/mauvais goût ▸ VT goûter; **you can ~ the garlic (in it)** on sent bien l'ail ▸ VI: **to ~ bitter** être amer(-ère); **to ~ of** (*fish etc*) avoir le *or* un goût de; **it tastes like fish** ça a un *or* le goût de poisson, on dirait du poisson; **what does it ~ like?** quel goût ça a ?

taste bud N papille *f*

tasteful ['teɪstful] ADJ de bon goût

tastefully ['teɪstfəlɪ] ADV avec goût

tasteless ['teɪstlɪs] ADJ (*food*) insipide; (*remark*) de mauvais goût

taster ['teɪstər] N (*person*) dégustateur(-trice); (*esp BRIT: foretaste*) avant-goût *m*

tasty ['teɪstɪ] ADJ savoureux(-euse), délicieux(-euse)

tat [tæt] N (*BRIT inf*) camelote *f* (*inf*)

tattered ['tætəd] ADJ *see* **tatters**

tatters ['tætəz] NPL: **in ~** (*also:* **tattered**) en lambeaux

tattoo [tə'tuː] N tatouage *m*; (*spectacle*) parade *f* militaire ▸ VT tatouer

tatty ['tætɪ] ADJ (*BRIT inf*) défraîchi(e), en piteux état

taught [tɔːt] PT, PP *of* **teach**

taunt [tɔːnt] N raillerie *f* ▸ VT railler

Taurus ['tɔːrəs] N le Taureau; **to be ~** être du Taureau

taut [tɔːt] ADJ tendu(e)

tautology [tɔː'tɔlədʒɪ] N tautologie *f*

t

tavern ['tævən] N (old) taverne f

tawdry ['tɔːdrɪ] ADJ criard(e)

tawny ['tɔːnɪ] ADJ fauve (couleur)

★**tax** [tæks] N (on goods etc) taxe f; (on income) impôts mpl, contributions fpl; **before/after ~** avant/après l'impôt; **free of ~** exonéré(e) d'impôt ▶ VT taxer; imposer; (fig: patience etc) mettre à l'épreuve

taxable ['tæksəbl] ADJ (income) imposable

tax allowance N part f du revenu non imposable, abattement m à la base

taxation [tæk'seɪʃən] N taxation f; impôts mpl, contributions fpl; **system of ~** système fiscal

tax avoidance N évasion fiscale

tax collector N percepteur m

tax disc N (BRIT Aut: formerly) vignette f (automobile)

tax evasion N fraude fiscale

tax exemption N exonération fiscale, exemption f d'impôts

tax exile N personne qui s'expatrie pour raisons fiscales

tax-free ['tæksfriː] ADJ exempt(e) d'impôts

tax haven N paradis fiscal

taxi ['tæksɪ] N taxi m ▶ VI (Aviat) rouler (lentement) au sol

taxidermist ['tæksɪdəːmɪst] N empailleur(-euse) (d'animaux)

taxi driver N chauffeur m de taxi

taxing ['tæksɪŋ] ADJ ardu(e)

tax inspector N (BRIT) percepteur m

taxi rank, (US) **taxi stand** N station f de taxis

taxonomy [tæk'sɔnəmɪ] N taxinomie f, taxonomie f

tax payer [-peɪəʳ] N contribuable mf

tax rebate N ristourne f d'impôt

tax relief N dégrèvement or allègement fiscal, réduction f d'impôt

tax return N déclaration f d'impôts or de revenus

tax year N année fiscale

TB N ABBR = **tuberculosis**

tbc ABBR = **to be confirmed**

tbs., tbsp. N ABBR (= tablespoonful) cuil. f à s. (= cuillerée à soupe)

TD N ABBR (US) = **Treasury Department**; (: Football) = **touchdown**

★**tea** [tiː] N thé m; (BRIT: snack: for children) goûter m; **high ~** (BRIT) collation combinant goûter et dîner

tea bag N sachet m de thé

tea break N (BRIT) pause-thé f

teacake ['tiːkeɪk] N (BRIT) ≈ petit pain aux raisins

★**teach** [tiːtʃ] (pt, pp **taught** [tɔːt]) VT: **to ~ sb sth, to ~ sth to sb** apprendre qch à qn; (in school etc) enseigner qch à qn; **it taught him a lesson** (fig) ça lui a servi de leçon ▶ VI enseigner

★**teacher** ['tiːtʃəʳ] N (in secondary school) professeur m; (in primary school) instituteur(-trice); **French ~** professeur de français

teacher training college N (for primary schools) ≈ école normale d'instituteurs; (for secondary schools) collège m de formation pédagogique (pour l'enseignement secondaire)

teaching ['tiːtʃɪŋ] N enseignement m

teaching aids NPL supports mpl pédagogiques

teaching assistant N aide-éducateur(-trice)

teaching hospital N (BRIT) C.H.U. m, centre m hospitalo-universitaire

teaching staff N (BRIT) enseignants mpl

tea cosy N couvre-théière m

teacup ['tiːkʌp] N tasse f à thé

teak [tiːk] N teck m ▶ ADJ en or de teck

tea leaves NPL feuilles fpl de thé

★**team** [tiːm] N équipe f; (of animals) attelage m
▶ **team up** VI: **to ~ up (with)** faire équipe (avec)

team games NPL jeux mpl d'équipe

teammate ['tiːmmeɪt] N coéquipier(-ière)

teamwork ['tiːmwəːk] N travail m d'équipe

tea party N thé m (réception)

teapot ['tiːpɔt] N théière f

★**tear¹** ['tɪəʳ] N larme f; **in tears** en larmes; **to burst into tears** fondre en larmes

tear² [tɛəʳ] (pt **tore** [tɔː'], pp **torn** [tɔːn]) N déchirure f ▶ VT déchirer; **to ~ to pieces** or **to bits** or **to shreds** mettre en pièces; (fig) démolir ▶ VI se déchirer
▶ **tear along** [tɛəʳ ə'lɔŋ] VI (rush) aller à toute vitesse
▶ **tear apart** [tɛəʳ ə'pɑːt] VT (also fig) déchirer
▶ **tear at** [tɛəʳ æt] VT FUS (prey, meat, clothes) arracher des lambeaux de
▶ **tear away** [tɛəʳ ə'weɪ] VT: **to ~ o.s. away (from sth)** (fig) s'arracher (de qch)
▶ **tear down** [tɛəʳ daun] VT (building, statue) démolir; (poster, flag) arracher
▶ **tear off** [tɛəʳ ɔf] VT (sheet of paper etc) arracher; (one's clothes) enlever à toute vitesse
▶ **tear out** [tɛəʳ aut] VT (sheet of paper, cheque) arracher
▶ **tear up** [tɛəʳ ʌp] VT (sheet of paper etc) déchirer, mettre en morceaux or pièces

tearaway ['tɛərəweɪ] N (inf) casse-cou m inv

teardrop ['tɪədrɔp] N larme f

tearful ['tɪəful] ADJ larmoyant(e)

tearfully ['tɪəfulɪ] ADV (say, smile) à travers ses larmes

tear gas ['tɪə-] N gaz m lacrymogène

tearoom ['tɪːruːm] N salon m de thé

tease [tiːz] N taquin(e) ▶ VT taquiner; (unkindly) tourmenter

tea set N service m à thé

teashop ['tiːʃɔp] N (BRIT) salon m de thé

teaspoon ['tiːspuːn] N petite cuiller; (as measurement: also: **teaspoonful**) ≈ cuillerée f à café

tea strainer N passoire f (à thé)

teat [tiːt] N tétine f

teatime ['tiːtaɪm] N l'heure f du thé

tea towel N (BRIT) torchon m (à vaisselle)

tea urn N fontaine f à thé

tech [tɛk] N ABBR (inf) = **technology; technical college**

★**technical** ['tɛknɪkl] ADJ technique

technical college N C.E.T. m, collège m d'enseignement technique

technicality [tɛknɪ'kælɪtɪ] N technicité f; (detail) détail m technique; **on a legal ~** à cause de (or grâce à) l'application à la lettre d'une subtilité juridique; pour vice de forme

technically ['tɛknɪklɪ] ADV techniquement; (strictly speaking) en théorie, en principe

technician [tɛk'nɪʃən] N technicien(ne)

★**technique** [tɛk'niːk] N technique f

techno ['tɛknəu] N (Mus) techno f

technocrat ['tɛknəkræt] N technocrate mf

technological [tɛknə'lɔdʒɪkl] ADJ technologique

technologically [tɛknə'lɔdʒɪklɪ] ADV technologiquement

technologist [tɛk'nɔlədʒɪst] N technologue mf

★**technology** [tɛk'nɔlədʒɪ] N technologie f

tectonic [tɛk'tɔnɪk] ADJ tectonique

teddy ['tɛdɪ], **teddy bear** N ours m (en peluche)

tedious ['tiːdɪəs] ADJ fastidieux(-euse)

tedium ['tiːdɪəm] N ennui m

tee [tiː] N (Golf) tee m

teem [tiːm] VI: **to ~ (with)** grouiller (de); **it is teeming (with rain)** il pleut à torrents

teen [tiːn] ADJ = **teenage** ▶ N (US) = **teenager**

teenage ['tiːneɪdʒ] ADJ (fashions etc) pour jeunes, pour adolescents; (child) qui est adolescent(e)

★**teenager** ['tiːneɪdʒəʳ] N adolescent(e)

teens [tiːnz] NPL: **to be in one's ~** être adolescent(e)

teepee ['tiːpiː] N tipi m

tee-shirt ['tiːʃəːt] N = **T-shirt**

teeter ['tiːtəʳ] VI chanceler, vaciller

teeth [tiːθ] NPL of **tooth**

teethe [tiːð] VI percer ses dents

teething ring ['tiːðɪŋ-] N anneau m (pour bébé qui perce ses dents) **teething troubles** ['tiːðɪŋ-] NPL (fig) difficultés initiales

teetotal ['tiː'təutl] ADJ (person) qui ne boit jamais d'alcool

teetotaller, (US) **teetotaler** ['tiː'təutləʳ] N personne f qui ne boit jamais d'alcool

TEFL ['tɛfl] N ABBR = **Teaching of English as a Foreign Language**

Teflon® ['tɛflɔn] N Téflon® m

Teheran [tɛə'rɑːn] N Téhéran

tel. ABBR (= telephone) tél

Tel Aviv ['tɛlə'viːv] N Tel Aviv

telecast ['tɛlɪkɑːst] VT télédiffuser, téléviser

telecommunications ['tɛlɪkəmjuːnɪ'keɪʃənz] N télécommunications f

telecommuting [tɛlɪkə'mjuːtɪŋ] N télétravail m

telecoms ['tɛlɪkɔmz] (inf) NPL télécoms fpl ▶ CPD (analyst) télécoms; (firm) de télécoms; (giant, industry) des télécoms

teleconference ['tɛlɪkɔnfərəns] N téléconférence f

teleconferencing [tɛlɪ'kɔnfərənsɪŋ] N téléconférence(s) f(pl)

telegram ['tɛlɪgræm] N télégramme m

telegraph ['tɛlɪgrɑːf] N télégraphe m

telegraphic [tɛlɪ'græfɪk] ADJ télégraphique

telegraph pole N poteau m télégraphique

telegraph wire N fil m télégraphique

telemarketing ['tɛlɪmɑːkɪtɪŋ] N télémarketing m

telepathic [tɛlɪ'pæθɪk] ADJ télépathique

telepathy [tə'lɛpəθɪ] N télépathie f

★**telephone** ['tɛlɪfəun] N téléphone m; **to have a ~**, **to be on the ~** (subscriber) avoir le téléphone; **to be on the ~** (be speaking) être au téléphone ▶ VT (person) téléphoner à; (message) téléphoner

telephone book N = **telephone directory**

telephone booth, (BRIT) **telephone box** N cabine f téléphonique

telephone call N appel m téléphonique

telephone directory N annuaire m (du téléphone)

telephone exchange N central m (téléphonique)

telephone number N numéro m de téléphone

telephone operator N téléphoniste mf, standardiste mf

telephone tapping [-tæpɪŋ] N mise f sur écoute

telephonist [tɪ'lɛfənɪst] N (BRIT) téléphoniste mf

telephony [tɪ'lɛfənɪ] N téléphonie m

telephoto ['tɛlɪfəutəu] ADJ: **~ lens** téléobjectif m

teleprinter ['tɛlɪprɪntəʳ] N téléscripteur m

telesales ['tɛlɪseɪlz] NPL télévente f

telescope ['tɛlɪskəup] N télescope m ▶ VI se télescoper ▶ VT télescoper

telescopic [tɛlɪ'skɔpɪk] ADJ télescopique; (umbrella) à manche télescopique

Teletext® ['tɛlɪtɛkst] N télétexte m

telethon ['tɛlɪθɔn] N téléthon m

televise ['tɛlɪvaɪz] VT téléviser

★**television** ['tɛlɪvɪʒən] N télévision f; **on ~** à la télévision

television licence N (BRIT) redevance f (de l'audio-visuel)

television programme N (BRIT) émission f de télévision

television set N poste m de télévision, téléviseur m

teleworker ['tɛlɪwəːkəʳ] N télétravailleur(-euse)

teleworking ['tɛlɪwəːkɪŋ] N télétravail m

telex ['tɛlɛks] N télex m ▶ VT (message) envoyer par télex; (person) envoyer un télex à ▶ VI envoyer un télex

★**tell** [tɛl] (pt, pp told [təuld]) VT dire; (relate: story) raconter; (distinguish): **to ~ sth from** distinguer qch de; **to ~ sb to do** dire à qn de faire; **to ~ sb about sth** (place, object etc) parler de qch à qn; (what happened etc) raconter qch à qn; **to ~ the time** (know how to) savoir lire l'heure; **can you ~ me the time?** pourriez-vous me dire l'heure ?; **(I) ~ you what, …** écoute, …; **I can't ~ them apart** je n'arrive pas à les distinguer ▶ VI (talk): **to ~ of** parler de; (have effect) se faire sentir, se voir

▶ **tell off** VT réprimander, gronder

▶ **tell on** VT FUS (inform against) dénoncer, rapporter contre

teller ['tɛləʳ] N (in bank) caissier(-ière)

telling ['tɛlɪŋ] ADJ (remark, detail) révélateur(-trice)

telltale ['tɛlteɪl] N (pej) rapporteur(-euse) ▶ ADJ (sign) éloquent(e), révélateur(-trice)

telly ['tɛlɪ] N ABBR (BRIT inf: = television) télé f

t

temerity [təˈmɛrɪtɪ] N témérité f

temp [tɛmp] N (BRIT: = temporary worker) intérimaire mf ▶ VI travailler comme intérimaire

temper [ˈtɛmpə^r] N (nature) caractère m; (mood) humeur f; (fit of anger) colère f; **to be in a ~** être en colère; **to lose one's ~** se mettre en colère; **to keep one's ~** rester calme ▶ VT (moderate) tempérer, adoucir

temperament [ˈtɛmprəmənt] N (nature) tempérament m

temperamental [tɛmprəˈmɛntl] ADJ capricieux(-euse)

temperance [ˈtɛmpərns] N modération f; (in drinking) tempérance f

temperate [ˈtɛmprət] ADJ modéré(e); (climate) tempéré(e)

★**temperature** [ˈtɛmprətʃə^r] N température f; **to have or run a ~** avoir de la fièvre

temperature chart N (Med) feuille f de température

tempered [ˈtɛmpəd] ADJ (steel) trempé(e)

tempest [ˈtɛmpɪst] N tempête f

tempestuous [tɛmˈpɛstjuəs] ADJ (fig) orageux(-euse); (: person) passionné(e)

tempi [ˈtɛmpi:] NPL of **tempo**

template [ˈtɛmplɪt] N patron m

★**temple** [ˈtɛmpl] N (building) temple m; (Anat) tempe f

templet [ˈtɛmplɪt] N = **template**

tempo [ˈtɛmpəu] (pl **tempos** [ˈtɛmpəus] or **tempi** [ˈtɛmpi:]) N tempo m; (fig: of life etc) rythme m

temporal [ˈtɛmpərl] ADJ temporel(le)

temporarily [ˈtɛmpərərɪlɪ] ADV temporairement; provisoirement

temporary [ˈtɛmpərərɪ] ADJ temporaire, provisoire; (job, worker) temporaire; **~ secretary** (secrétaire f) intérimaire f; **a ~ teacher** un professeur remplaçant or suppléant

temporize [ˈtɛmpəraɪz] VI atermoyer; transiger

tempt [tɛmpt] VT tenter; **to ~ sb into doing** induire qn à faire; **to be tempted to do sth** être tenté(e) de faire qch

temptation [tɛmpˈteɪʃən] N tentation f

tempting [ˈtɛmptɪŋ] ADJ tentant(e); (food) appétissant(e)

★**ten** [tɛn] NUM dix ▶ N: **tens of thousands** des dizaines fpl de milliers

tenable [ˈtɛnəbl] ADJ défendable

tenacious [təˈneɪʃəs] ADJ tenace

tenacity [təˈnæsɪtɪ] N ténacité f

tenancy [ˈtɛnənsɪ] N location f; état m de locataire

tenant [ˈtɛnənt] N locataire mf

tend [tɛnd] VT s'occuper de; (sick etc) soigner ▶ VI: **to ~ to do** avoir tendance à faire; **to ~ to** (colour) tirer sur

tendency [ˈtɛndənsɪ] N tendance f

tender [ˈtɛndə^r] ADJ tendre; (delicate) délicat(e); (sore) sensible; (affectionate) tendre, doux (douce) ▶ N (Comm: offer) soumission f; (money): **legal ~** cours légal; **to put in a ~ (for)** faire une soumission (pour); **to put work out to ~** (BRIT) mettre un contrat en adjudication ▶ VT offrir; **to ~ one's**

resignation donner sa démission
▶ **tender for** VT FUS soumissionner à un appel d'offres

tenderize [ˈtɛndəraɪz] VT (Culin) attendrir

tenderly [ˈtɛndəlɪ] ADV tendrement

tenderness [ˈtɛndənɪs] N tendresse f; (of meat) tendreté f

tendinitis [tɛndəˈnaɪtɪs] N tendinite f

tendon [ˈtɛndən] N tendon m

tendonitis [tɛndəˈnaɪtɪs] N = **tendinitis**

tenement [ˈtɛnəmənt] N immeuble m (de rapport)

Tenerife [tɛnəˈriːf] N Ténérife f

tenet [ˈtɛnət] N principe m

tenner [ˈtɛnə^r] N (BRIT inf) billet m de dix livres

★**tennis** [ˈtɛnɪs] N tennis m ▶ CPD (club, match, racket, player) de tennis

tennis ball N balle f de tennis

tennis court N (court m de) tennis m

tennis elbow N (Med) synovite f du coude

tennis match N match m de tennis

tennis player N joueur(-euse) de tennis

tennis racket N raquette f de tennis

tennis shoes NPL (chaussures fpl de) tennis mpl

tenor [ˈtɛnə^r] N (Mus) ténor m; (of speech etc) sens général

tenpin bowling [ˈtɛnpɪn-] N (BRIT) bowling m (à 10 quilles)

tense [tɛns] ADJ tendu(e); (person) tendu, crispé(e) ▶ N (Ling) temps m ▶ VT (tighten: muscles) tendre

tenseness [ˈtɛnsnɪs] N tension f

tension [ˈtɛnʃən] N tension f

tent [tɛnt] N tente f

tentacle [ˈtɛntəkl] N tentacule m

tentative [ˈtɛntətɪv] ADJ timide, hésitant(e); (conclusion) provisoire

tenterhooks [ˈtɛntəhuks] NPL: **on ~** sur des charbons ardents

★**tenth** [tɛnθ] NUM dixième

tent peg N piquet m de tente

tent pole N montant m de tente

tenuous [ˈtɛnjuəs] ADJ ténu(e)

tenure [ˈtɛnjuə^r] N (of property) bail m; (of job) période f de jouissance; statut m de titulaire

tepid [ˈtɛpɪd] ADJ tiède

tequila [tɪˈkiːlə] N tequila f

★**term** [təːm] N (limit) terme m; (word) terme, mot m; (Scol) trimestre m; (Law) session f; **~ of imprisonment** peine f de prison; **his ~ of office** la période où il était en fonction; **in the short/long ~** à court/long terme ▶ VT appeler ▪ **terms** NPL (conditions) conditions fpl; (Comm) tarif m; **"easy terms"** (Comm) « facilités de paiement »; **to come to terms with** (problem) faire face à; **to be on good terms with** bien s'entendre avec, être en bons termes avec

terminal [ˈtəːmɪnl] ADJ terminal(e); (disease) dans sa phase terminale; (patient) incurable ▶ N (Elec) borne f; (for oil, ore etc, also Comput) terminal m; (also: **air terminal**) aérogare f; (BRIT: also: **coach terminal**) gare routière

terminally ['tə:mɪnlɪ] ADV: **to be ~ ill** être en phase terminale

terminate ['tə:mɪneɪt] VT mettre fin à; (*pregnancy*) interrompre ▶ VI: **to ~ in** finir en ou par

termination [tə:mɪ'neɪʃən] N fin f; cessation f; (*of contract*) résiliation f; **~ of pregnancy** (*Med*) interruption f de grossesse

termini ['tə:mɪnaɪ] NPL of **terminus**

terminology [tə:mɪ'nɒlədʒɪ] N terminologie f

terminus ['tə:mɪnəs] (*pl* **termini** ['tə:mɪnaɪ]) N terminus m inv

termite ['tə:maɪt] N termite m

term paper N (*US University*) dissertation trimestrielle

Terr. ABBR = **terrace**

terrace ['tɛrəs] N terrasse f; (*BRIT: row of houses*) rangée f de maisons (*attenantes les unes aux autres*); **the terraces** (*BRIT Sport*) les gradins mpl

terraced ['tɛrəst] ADJ (*garden*) en terrasses; (*in a row: house*) attenant(e) aux maisons voisines

terracotta ['tɛrə'kɒtə] N terre cuite

terra firma [tɛrə'fə:mə] N: **to be on ~** être sur la terre ferme

terrain [tɛ'reɪn] N terrain m (*sol*)

terrestrial [tɪ'rɛstrɪəl] ADJ terrestre

★**terrible** ['tɛrɪbl] ADJ terrible, atroce; (*weather, work*) affreux(-euse), épouvantable

terribly ['tɛrɪblɪ] ADV terriblement; (*very badly*) affreusement mal

terrier ['tɛrɪə'] N terrier m (*chien*)

terrific [tə'rɪfɪk] ADJ (*very great*) fantastique, incroyable, terrible; (*wonderful*) formidable, sensationnel(le)

terrified ['tɛrɪfaɪd] ADJ terrifié(e); **to be ~ of sth** avoir très peur de qch

terrify ['tɛrɪfaɪ] VT terrifier

terrifying ['tɛrɪfaɪɪŋ] ADJ terrifiant(e)

terrifyingly ['tɛrɪfaɪɪŋlɪ] ADV (*deep, high*) effroyablement; (*escalate, shake*) de manière terrifiante

territorial [tɛrɪ'tɔ:rɪəl] ADJ territorial(e)

territorial waters NPL eaux territoriales

territory ['tɛrɪtərɪ] N territoire m

terror ['tɛrə'] N terreur f

terrorism ['tɛrərɪzəm] N terrorisme m

★**terrorist** ['tɛrərɪst] N terroriste mf

terrorist attack N attentat m terroriste

terrorize ['tɛrəraɪz] VT terroriser

terry ['tɛrɪ] N (*also:* **terry cloth**, **terry towelling**) éponge f, tissu-éponge m ▶ CPD (*nappy, bathrobe*) en éponge, en tissu-éponge

terse [tə:s] ADJ (*style*) concis(e); (*reply*) laconique

tertiary ['tə:ʃərɪ] ADJ tertiaire; **~ education** (*BRIT*) enseignement m postscolaire

TESL ['tɛsl] N ABBR = **Teaching of English as a Second Language**

★**test** [tɛst] N (*trial, check*) essai m; (*: of goods in factory*) contrôle m; (*of courage etc*) épreuve f; (*Med*) examen m; (*Chem*) analyse f; (*exam: of intelligence etc*) test m (d'aptitude); (*Scol*) interrogation f de contrôle; (*also:* **driving test**) (examen du) permis m de conduire; **to put sth to the ~** mettre qch à l'épreuve ▶ VT essayer; contrôler; mettre à l'épreuve; exa-

miner; analyser; tester; faire subir une interrogation à

▶ **test for** VT FUS (*virus*) dépister; (*drugs, oil*) rechercher la présence de

▶ **test out** VT (*idea, theory*) mettre à l'épreuve

testament ['tɛstəmənt] N testament m; **the Old/New T~** l'Ancien/le Nouveau Testament

test ban N (*also:* **nuclear test ban**) interdiction f des essais nucléaires

test case N (*Law*) affaire f qui fait jurisprudence

test drive N essai m sur route

tester ['tɛstə'] N (*device*) testeur m; (*person*): **she is a computer software ~** elle teste des logiciels

testes ['tɛsti:z] NPL testicules mpl

test flight N vol m d'essai

testicle ['tɛstɪkl] N testicule m

testify ['tɛstɪfaɪ] VI (*Law*) témoigner, déposer; **to ~ to sth** (*Law*) attester qch; (*gen*) témoigner de qch

testimonial [tɛstɪ'məunɪəl] N (*reference*) recommandation f; (*gift*) témoignage m d'estime

testimony ['tɛstɪmənɪ] N (*Law*) témoignage m, déposition f

testing ['tɛstɪŋ] ADJ (*situation, period*) difficile

test match N (*Cricket, Rugby*) match international

testosterone [tɛs'tɔstərəun] N testostérone f

test paper N (*Scol*) interrogation écrite

test pilot N pilote m d'essai

test tube N éprouvette f

test-tube baby ['tɛsttju:b-] N bébé-éprouvette m

testy ['tɛstɪ] ADJ irritable

tetanus ['tɛtənəs] N tétanos m

tetchy ['tɛtʃɪ] ADJ hargneux(-euse)

tether ['tɛðə'] VT attacher ▶ N: **at the end of one's ~** à bout (de patience)

tetraplegic [tɛtrə'pli:dʒɪk] ADJ, N tétraplégique mf

★**text** [tɛkst] N texte m; (*on mobile phone*) SMS m inv, texto® m ▶ VT envoyer un SMS ou texto® à

textbook ['tɛkstbuk] N manuel m

textile ['tɛkstaɪl] N textile m

★**text message** N SMS m inv, texto® m

text messaging [-'mɛsɪdʒɪŋ] N messagerie textuelle

textual ['tɛkstjuəl] ADJ textuel(le)

texture ['tɛkstʃə'] N texture f; (*of skin, paper etc*) grain m

TGIF ABBR (*inf*) = **thank God it's Friday**

Thai [taɪ] ADJ thaïlandais(e) ▶ N Thaïlandais(e); (*Ling*) thaï m

Thailand ['taɪlænd] N Thaïlande f

Thames [tɛmz] N: **the (River) ~** la Tamise

★**than** [ðæn, ðən] CONJ que; (*with numerals*): **more ~ 10/once** plus de 10/d'une fois; **I have more/less ~ you** j'en ai plus/moins que toi; **she has more apples ~ pears** elle a plus de pommes que de poires; **it is better to phone ~ to write** il vaut mieux téléphoner (plutôt) qu'écrire; **she is older ~ you think** elle est plus âgée que tu le crois; **no sooner did he leave ~ the phone rang** il venait de partir quand le téléphone a sonné

★**thank** [θæŋk] VT remercier, dire merci à; **~ you (very much)** merci (beaucoup); **~ heavens, ~ God**

t

Dieu merci ■**thanks** NPL remerciements *mpl*; **thanks!** merci !; **thanks to** *prep* grâce à

thankful ['θæŋkful] ADJ: **~ (for)** reconnaissant(e) (de); **~ for/that** (*relieved*) soulagé(e) de/que

thankfully ['θæŋkfəlɪ] ADV avec reconnaissance; avec soulagement; (*fortunately*) heureusement; **~ there were few victims** il y eut fort heureusement peu de victimes

thankless ['θæŋklɪs] ADJ ingrat(e)

Thanksgiving (Day) ['θæŋksgɪvɪŋ-] N jour *m* d'action de grâce

Thanksgiving (Day), le quatrième jeudi du mois de novembre, est un jour de congé aux États-Unis. Il commémore la bonne récolte que les Pèlerins venus de Grande-Bretagne firent en 1621. Traditionnellement, c'était un jour où l'on rendait grâce à Dieu en organisant un grand festin. Aujourd'hui, *Thanksgiving* est l'occasion d'un grand repas de famille au menu traditionnel : dinde et sauce aux airelles, patates douces, tarte au potiron. Des matches ont lieu pour l'occasion entre les grandes équipes de football américain du pays, et de nombreuses villes organisent un défilé. Une fête comparable, mais qui n'a aucun rapport avec les Pères pèlerins, a lieu au Canada le deuxième lundi d'octobre.

that [ðæt]

ADJ (*pl* **those**: *demonstrative*) ce, cet + *vowel or h mute*, cette *f*; **that man/woman/book** cet homme/cette femme/ce livre; (*not this*) cet homme-là/cette femme-là/ce livre-là; **that one** celui-là (celle-là)

▶ PRON **1** (*pl* **those**: *demonstrative*) ce; (*not this one*) cela, ça; (*that one*) celui (celle); **who's that?** qui est-ce ?; **what's that?** qu'est-ce que c'est ?; **is that you?** c'est toi ?; **I prefer this to that** je préfère ceci à cela *or* ça; **that's what he said** c'est *or* voilà ce qu'il a dit; **will you eat all that?** tu vas manger tout ça ?; **that is (to say)** c'est-à-dire, à savoir; **at** *or* **with that, he …** là-dessus, il …; **do it like that** fais-le comme ça

2 (*relative: subject*) qui; (: *object*) que; (: *after prep*) lequel (laquelle), lesquels (lesquelles) *pl*; **the book that I read** le livre que j'ai lu; **the books that are in the library** les livres qui sont dans la bibliothèque; **all that I have** tout ce que j'ai; **the box that I put it in** la boîte dans laquelle je l'ai mis; **the people that I spoke to** les gens auxquels *or* à qui j'ai parlé; **not that I know of** pas à ma connaissance

3 (*relative: of time*) où; **the day that he came** le jour où il est venu

▶ CONJ que; **he thought that I was ill** il pensait que j'étais malade

▶ ADV (*demonstrative*): **I don't like it that much** ça ne me plaît pas tant que ça; **I didn't know it was that bad** je ne savais pas que c'était si *or* aussi mauvais; **that high** aussi haut; si haut; **it's about that high** c'est à peu près de cette hauteur

thatched [θætʃt] ADJ (*roof*) de chaume; **~ cottage** chaumière *f*

Thatcherism ['θætʃərɪzəm] N thatchérisme *m*

thaw [θɔ:] N dégel *m* ▶ VI (*ice*) fondre; (*food*) dégeler; **it's thawing** (*weather*) il dégèle ▶ VT (*food*) (faire) dégeler

the [ði:, ðə]

DEF ART **1** (*gen*) le, la *f*, l' + *vowel or h mute*, les *pl* (NB: à + le(s) = **au(x)**; *de* + *le* = **du**; *de* + *les* = **des**); **the boy/girl/ink** le garçon/la fille/l'encre; **the children** les enfants; **the history of the world** l'histoire du monde; **give it to the postman** donne-le au facteur; **to play the piano/flute** jouer du piano/de la flûte

2 (+ *adj to form n*) le, la *f*, l' + *vowel or h mute*, les *pl*; **the rich and the poor** les riches et les pauvres; **to attempt the impossible** tenter l'impossible

3 (*in titles*): **Elizabeth the First** Elisabeth première; **Peter the Great** Pierre le Grand

4 (*in comparisons*): **the more he works, the more he earns** plus il travaille, plus il gagne de l'argent; **the sooner the better** le plus tôt sera le mieux

theatre, (US) **theater** ['θɪətəʳ] N théâtre *m*; (*also*: **lecture theatre**) amphithéâtre *m*, amphi *m* (*inf*); (*Med: also*: **operating theatre**) salle *f* d'opération

theatre-goer, (US) **theater-goer** ['θɪətəgəuəʳ] N habitué(e) du théâtre

theatrical [θɪ'ætrɪkl] ADJ théâtral(e); **~ company** troupe *f* de théâtre

theft [θeft] N vol *m* (*larcin*)

★**their** [ðɛəʳ] ADJ leur, leurs *pl*; *see also* **my**

★**theirs** [ðɛəz] PRON le (la) leur, les leurs; **it is ~** c'est à eux; **a friend of ~** un de leurs amis; *see also* **mine¹**

★**them** [ðɛm, ðəm] PRON (*direct*) les; (*indirect*) leur; (*stressed, after prep*) eux (elles); **I see ~** je les vois; **give ~ the book** donne-leur le livre; **give me a few of ~** donnez m'en quelques uns (*or* quelques unes); *see also* **me**

theme [θi:m] N thème *m*

themed [θi:md] ADJ (*esp* BRIT: *restaurant, bar*) à thème

theme music, theme tune N (*of film*) thème *m* principal; (TV, Radio) musique *f* de générique, indicatif *m*

theme park N parc *m* à thème

theme song N chanson principale

★**themselves** [ðəm'sɛlvz] PL PRON (*reflexive*) se; (*emphatic, after prep*) eux-mêmes (elles-mêmes); **between ~** entre eux (elles); *see also* **oneself**

★**then** [ðɛn] ADV (*at that time*) alors, à ce moment-là; (*next*) puis, ensuite; (*and also*) et puis; **by ~** (*past*) à ce moment-là; (*future*) d'ici là; **from ~ on** dès lors; **before ~** avant; **until ~** jusqu'à ce moment-là, jusque-là; **and ~ what?** et puis après ?; **what do you want me to ~ do?** (*afterwards*) que veux-tu que je fasse ensuite ?; (*in that case*) bon alors, qu'est-ce que je fais ? ▶ CONJ (*therefore*) alors, dans ce cas ▶ ADJ: **the ~ president** le président d'alors *or* de l'époque

theologian [θɪə'ləudʒən] N théologien(ne)

theological [θɪə'lɔdʒɪkl] ADJ théologique

theology [θɪ'ɔlədʒɪ] N théologie *f*

theorem ['θɪərəm] N théorème *m*

theoretical [θɪə'rɛtɪkl] ADJ théorique

theoretically [θɪə'rɛtɪklɪ] ADV théoriquement

theorize ['θɪəraɪz] VI élaborer une théorie; (pej) faire des théories

theory ['θɪərɪ] N théorie f

therapeutic [θɛrə'pju:tɪk] ADJ thérapeutique

therapist ['θɛrəpɪst] N thérapeute mf

★**therapy** ['θɛrəpɪ] N thérapie f

---

there [ðɛəʳ]

ADV **1: there is, there are** il y a; **there are 3 of them** (people, things) il y en a 3; **there is no-one here/no bread left** il n'y a personne/il n'y a plus de pain; **there has been an accident** il y a eu un accident

2 (referring to place) là, là-bas; **it's there** c'est là(-bas); **in/on/up/down there** là-dedans/là-dessus/là-haut/en bas; **he went there on Friday** il y est allé vendredi; **to go there and back** faire l'aller-retour; **I want that book there** je veux ce livre-là; **there he is!** le voilà !

3: there, there! (esp to child) allons, allons !

Remember to spell the word **là** with an accent: *She's there!* **Elle est là !** The accent distinguishes it from the feminine article **la**.

---

thereabouts ['ðɛərə'bauts] ADV (place) par là, près de là; (amount) environ, à peu près

thereafter [ðɛər'ɑ:ftəʳ] ADV par la suite

thereby ['ðɛəbaɪ] ADV ainsi

★**therefore** ['ðɛəfɔ:ʳ] ADV donc, par conséquent

there's ['ðɛəz] = **there is**; **there has**

thereupon [ðɛərə'pɔn] ADV (at that point) sur ce; (formal: on that subject) à ce sujet

thermal ['θə:ml] ADJ thermique; **~ paper/printer** papier m/imprimante f thermique; **~ underwear** sous-vêtements mpl en Thermolactyl®

thermodynamics ['θə:mədər'næmɪks] N thermodynamique f

thermometer [θə'mɔmɪtəʳ] N thermomètre m

thermonuclear ['θə:məu'nju:klɪəʳ] ADJ thermonucléaire

Thermos® ['θə:məs] N (also: **Thermos flask**) thermos® m or f

thermostat ['θə:məustæt] N thermostat m

thesaurus [θɪ'sɔ:rəs] N dictionnaire m synonymique

★**these** [ði:z] PL PRON ceux-ci (celles-ci) ▶ PL ADJ ces; (not those): **~ books** ces livres-ci

thesis ['θi:sɪs] (pl **theses** ['θi:si:z]) N thèse f

★**they** [ðeɪ] PL PRON ils (elles); (stressed) eux (elles); **~ say that ...** (it is said that) on dit que ...

they'd [ðeɪd] = **they had; they would**

they'll [ðeɪl] = **they shall; they will**

they're [ðɛəʳ] = **they are**

they've [ðeɪv] = **they have**

★**thick** [θɪk] ADJ épais(se); (crowd) dense; (stupid) bête, borné(e); **it's 20 cm ~** ça a 20 cm d'épaisseur ▶ N: **in the ~ of** au beau milieu de, en plein cœur de

thicken ['θɪkn] VI s'épaissir ▶ VT (sauce etc) épaissir

thicket ['θɪkɪt] N fourré m, hallier m

thickly ['θɪklɪ] ADV (spread) en couche épaisse; (cut) en tranches épaisses; **~ populated** à forte densité de population

thickness ['θɪknɪs] N épaisseur f

thickset [θɪk'sɛt] ADJ trapu(e), costaud(e)

thick-skinned [θɪk'skɪnd] ADJ (fig) peu sensible

thief [θi:f] (pl **thieves** [θi:vz]) N voleur(-euse)

thieving ['θi:vɪŋ] N vol m (larcin)

thigh [θaɪ] N cuisse f

thighbone ['θaɪbəun] N fémur m

thimble ['θɪmbl] N dé m (à coudre)

★**thin** [θɪn] ADJ mince; (skinny) maigre; (soup) peu épais(se); (hair, crowd) clairsemé(e); (fog) léger(-ère) ▶ VT (hair) éclaircir; (also: **thin down**: sauce, paint) délayer ▶ VI (fog) s'éclaircir; (also: **thin out**: crowd) se disperser; **his hair is thinning** il se dégarnit

★**thing** [θɪŋ] N chose f; (object) objet m; (contraption) truc m; **first ~ (in the morning)** à la première heure, tout de suite (le matin); **last ~ (at night)**, **he ...** juste avant de se coucher, il ...; **the ~ is ...** c'est que ...; **for one ~** d'abord; **the best ~ would be to** le mieux serait de; **to have a ~ about** (be obsessed by) être obsédé(e) par; (hate) détester; **poor ~!** le (or la) pauvre ! ■ **things** NPL (belongings) affaires fpl; **how are things?** comment ça va ?

★**think** [θɪŋk] (pt, pp **thought** [θɔ:t]) VI penser, réfléchir; **to ~ about sth/sb** penser à qch/qn; **I'll ~ about it** je vais y réfléchir; **to ~ of** penser à; **what do you ~ of it?** qu'en pensez-vous ?; **what did you ~ of them?** qu'avez-vous pensé d'eux ?; **to ~ of doing** avoir l'idée de faire; **to ~ well of** avoir une haute opinion de; **~ again!** attention, réfléchis bien !; **to ~ aloud** penser tout haut ▶ VT penser, croire; (imagine) s'imaginer; **I ~ so/not** je crois or pense que oui/non
> **think back** VI repenser; **thinking back, I ...** quand j'y repense, je ...
> **think out** VT (plan) bien réfléchir à; (solution) trouver
> **think over** VT bien réfléchir à; **I'd like to ~ things over** (offer, suggestion) j'aimerais bien y réfléchir un peu
> **think through** VT étudier dans tous les détails
> **think up** VT inventer, trouver

thinker ['θɪŋkəʳ] N penseur(-euse)

thinking ['θɪŋkɪŋ] N: **to my (way of) ~** selon moi

think tank N groupe m de réflexion

thinly ['θɪnlɪ] ADV (cut) en tranches fines; (spread) en couche mince

thinness ['θɪnnɪs] N minceur f; maigreur f

★**third** [θə:d] NUM troisième ▶ N troisième mf; (fraction) tiers m; (Aut) troisième (vitesse) f; (Brit Scol: degree) ≈ licence f avec mention passable; **a ~ of** le tiers de

third-degree burns ['θə:ddɪgri:-] NPL brûlures fpl au troisième degré

thirdly ['θə:dlɪ] ADV troisièmement

third party insurance N (Brit) assurance f au tiers

third-rate ['θə:d'reɪt] ADJ de qualité médiocre

★**Third World** N: **the ~** le Tiers-Monde

thirst [θə:st] N soif f

★thirsty ['θə:stɪ] ADJ qui a soif, assoiffé(e); (work) qui donne soif; **to be ~** avoir soif

★thirteen [θə:'ti:n] NUM treize

★thirteenth [θə:'ti:nθ] NUM treizième

thirtieth ['θə:tɪɪθ] NUM trentième

★thirty ['θə:tɪ] NUM trente

---

this [ðɪs]

ADJ (pl **these**: demonstrative) ce, cet + vowel or h mute, cette f; **this man/woman/book** cet homme/cette femme/ce livre; (not that) cet homme-ci/cette femme-ci/ce livre-ci; **this one** celui-ci (celle-ci); **this time** cette fois-ci; **this time last year** l'année dernière à la même époque; **this way** (in this direction) par ici; (in this fashion) de cette façon, ainsi

▶ PRON (pl **these**: demonstrative) ce; (not that one) celui-ci (celle-ci), ceci; **who's this?** qui est-ce ?; **what's this?** qu'est-ce que c'est ?; **I prefer this to that** je préfère ceci à cela; **they were talking of this and that** ils parlaient de choses et d'autres; **this is where I live** c'est ici que j'habite; **this is what he said** voici ce qu'il a dit; **this is Mr Brown** (in introductions) je vous présente Mr Brown; (in photo) c'est Mr Brown; (on telephone) ici Mr Brown

▶ ADV (demonstrative): **it was about this big** c'était à peu près de cette grandeur or grand comme ça; **I didn't know it was this bad** je ne savais pas que c'était si or aussi mauvais

---

thistle ['θɪsl] N chardon m

thong [θɒŋ] N lanière f

thorn [θɔ:n] N épine f

thorny ['θɔ:nɪ] ADJ épineux(-euse)

★thorough ['θʌrə] ADJ (search) minutieux(-euse); (knowledge, research) approfondi(e); (work, person) consciencieux(-euse); (cleaning) à fond

thoroughbred ['θʌrəbred] N (horse) pur-sang m inv

thoroughfare ['θʌrəfɛə'] N rue f; **"no ~"** (BRIT) « passage interdit »

thoroughgoing ['θʌrəgəuɪŋ] ADJ (analysis) approfondi(e); (reform) profond(e)

thoroughly ['θʌrəlɪ] ADV (search) minutieusement; (study) en profondeur; (clean) à fond; (very) tout à fait; **he ~ agreed** il était tout à fait d'accord

thoroughness ['θʌrənɪs] N soin (méticuleux)

★those [ðəuz] PL PRON ceux-là (celles-là) ▶ PL ADJ ces; (not these): **~ books** ces livres-là

★though [ðəu] CONJ bien que + sub, quoique + sub; **even ~** quand bien même + cond ▶ ADV pourtant; **it's not easy, ~** pourtant, ce n'est pas facile

★thought [θɔ:t] PT, PP of **think** ▶ N pensée f; (idea) idée f; (opinion) avis m; (intention) intention f; **after much ~** après mûre réflexion; **I've just had a ~** je viens de penser à quelque chose; **to give sth some ~** réfléchir à qch

thoughtful ['θɔ:tful] ADJ (deep in thought) pensif(-ive); (serious) réfléchi(e); (considerate) prévenant(e)

thoughtfully ['θɔ:tfulɪ] ADV pensivement; avec prévenance

thoughtfulness ['θɔ:tfulnɪs] N prévenance f

thoughtless ['θɔ:tlɪs] ADJ qui manque de considération

thoughtlessly ['θɔ:tlɪslɪ] ADV inconsidérément

thoughtlessness ['θɔ:tlɪsnɪs] N manque m de considération

thought-provoking ['θɔ:tprəvəukɪŋ] ADJ stimulant(e)

★thousand ['θauzənd] NUM mille; **one ~** mille; **two ~** deux mille; **thousands of** des milliers de

thousandth ['θauzəntθ] NUM millième

thrash [θræʃ] VT rouer de coups; (inf: defeat) donner une raclée à (inf)
▶ **thrash about** VI se débattre
▶ **thrash out** VT débattre de

thrashing ['θræʃɪŋ] N (inf) raclée f (inf)

thread [θred] N fil m; (of screw) pas m, filetage m ▶ VT (needle) enfiler; **to ~ one's way between** se faufiler entre

threadbare ['θredbɛə'] ADJ râpé(e), élimé(e)

★threat [θret] N menace f; **to be under ~ of** être menacé(e) de

★threaten ['θretn] VI (storm) menacer ▶ VT: **to ~ sb with sth/to do** menacer qn de qch/de faire

threatening ['θretnɪŋ] ADJ menaçant(e)

★three [θri:] NUM trois

three-dimensional [θri:dɪ'menʃənl] ADJ à trois dimensions; (film) en relief

threefold ['θri:fəuld] ADV: **to increase ~** tripler

three-piece suit ['θri:pi:s-] N complet m (avec gilet)

three-piece suite [θri:pi:s-] N salon m (canapé et deux fauteuils)

three-ply [θri:'plaɪ] ADJ (wood) à trois épaisseurs; (wool) trois fils inv

three-quarters [θri:'kwɔ:təz] PRON trois-quarts mpl ▶ ADV: **~ full** aux trois-quarts plein

threesome ['θri:səm] N groupe m de trois personnes

three-wheeler [θri:'wi:lə'] N (car) voiture f à trois roues

thresh [θreʃ] VT (Agr) battre

threshing machine ['θreʃɪŋ-] N batteuse f

threshold ['θreʃhəuld] N seuil m; **to be on the ~ of** (fig) être au seuil de

threshold agreement N (Econ) accord m d'indexation des salaires

threw [θru:] PT of **throw**

thrift [θrɪft] N économie f

thrifty ['θrɪftɪ] ADJ économe

thrill [θrɪl] N (excitement) émotion f, sensation forte; (shudder) frisson m ▶ VI tressaillir, frissonner ▶ VT (audience) électriser

thrilled [θrɪld] ADJ: **~ (with)** ravi(e) de

thriller ['θrɪlə'] N film m (or roman m or pièce f) à suspense

thrilling ['θrɪlɪŋ] ADJ (book, play etc) saisissant(e); (news, discovery) excitant(e)

thrive [θraɪv] (pt **thrived** [-d] or **throve** [θrəuv], pp **thrived** [-d] or **thriven** ['θrɪvn]) VI pousser or se développer bien; (business) prospérer; **he thrives on it** cela lui réussit

thriving ['θraɪvɪŋ] ADJ vigoureux(-euse); (business, community) prospère

★**throat** [θrəut] N gorge f; **to have a sore ~** avoir mal à la gorge

throb [θrɔb] N (of heart) pulsation f; (of engine) vibration f; (of pain) élancement m ▸ VI (heart) palpiter; (engine) vibrer; (pain) lanciner; (wound) causer des élancements; **my head is throbbing** j'ai des élancements dans la tête

throes [θrəuz] NPL: **in the ~ of** au beau milieu de; en proie à; **in the ~ of death** à l'agonie

thrombosis [θrɔm'bəusɪs] N thrombose f

throne [θrəun] N trône m

throng [θrɔŋ] N foule f ▸ VT se presser dans

throttle ['θrɔtl] N (Aut) accélérateur m ▸ VT étrangler

★**through** [θru:] PREP à travers; (time) pendant, durant; (by means of) par, par l'intermédiaire de; (owing to) à cause de; **(from) Monday ~ Friday** (US) de lundi à vendredi ▸ ADJ (ticket, train, passage) direct(e); **"no ~ traffic"** (US) « passage interdit »; **"no ~ road"** (BRIT) « impasse » ▸ ADV à travers; **to let sb ~** laisser passer qn; **to put sb ~ to sb** (Tel) passer qn à qn; **to be ~** (BRIT Tel) avoir la communication; (esp US: have finished) avoir fini

★**throughout** [θru:'aut] PREP (place) partout dans; (time) durant tout(e) le (la) ▸ ADV partout

throughput ['θru:put] N (of goods, materials) quantité de matières premières utilisée; (Comput) débit m

throve [θrəuv] PT of **thrive**

★**throw** [θrəu] (pt **threw** [θru:], pp **thrown** [θrəun]) N jet m; (Sport) lancer m ▸ VT lancer, jeter; (Sport) lancer; (rider) désarçonner; (fig) décontenancer; (pottery) tourner; **to ~ a party** donner une réception
 ▸ **throw about, throw around** VT (litter etc) éparpiller
 ▸ **throw away** VT jeter; (money) gaspiller
 ▸ **throw in** VT (Sport: ball) remettre en jeu; (include) ajouter
 ▸ **throw off** VT se débarrasser de
 ▸ **throw out** VT jeter; (reject) rejeter; (person) mettre à la porte
 ▸ **throw together** VT (clothes, meal etc) assembler à la hâte; (essay) bâcler
 ▸ **throw up** VI vomir

throwaway ['θrəuəweɪ] ADJ à jeter

throwback ['θrəubæk] N: **it's a ~ to** ça nous etc ramène à

throw-in ['θrəuɪn] N (Sport) remise f en jeu

thrown [θrəun] PP of **throw**

thru [θru:] PREP (US) = **through**

thrush [θrʌʃ] N (Zool) grive f; (Med: esp in children) muguet m; (: in women: BRIT) muguet vaginal

thrust [θrʌst] (pt, pp ~) N (Tech) poussée f ▸ VT pousser brusquement; (push in) enfoncer

thrusting ['θrʌstɪŋ] ADJ dynamique; qui se met trop en avant

thud [θʌd] N bruit sourd

thug [θʌg] N voyou m

thuggery ['θʌgərɪ] N brutalité f

thuggish ['θʌgɪʃ] ADJ brutal(e)

thumb [θʌm] N (Anat) pouce m; **to give sb/sth the thumbs up/thumbs down** donner/refuser de donner le feu vert à qn/qch ▸ VT (book) feuilleter;

to ~ a lift faire de l'auto-stop, arrêter une voiture
 ▸ **thumb through** VT (book) feuilleter

thumb index N répertoire m (à onglets)

thumbnail ['θʌmneɪl] N ongle m du pouce

thumbnail sketch N croquis m

thumbtack ['θʌmtæk] N (US) punaise f (clou)

thump [θʌmp] N grand coup; (sound) bruit sourd
 ▸ VT cogner sur ▸ VI cogner, frapper

thunder ['θʌndə'] N tonnerre m ▸ VI tonner; (train etc): **to ~ past** passer dans un grondement or un bruit de tonnerre

thunderbolt ['θʌndəbəult] N foudre f

thunderclap ['θʌndəklæp] N coup m de tonnerre

thunderous ['θʌndrəs] ADJ étourdissant(e)

thunderstorm ['θʌndəstɔ:m] N orage m

thunderstruck ['θʌndəstrʌk] ADJ (fig) abasourdi(e)

thundery ['θʌndərɪ] ADJ orageux(-euse)

Thurs, Thur, Thu ABBR (= Thursday) jeu.

★**Thursday** ['θə:zdɪ] N jeudi m; see also **Tuesday**

thus [ðʌs] ADV ainsi

thwart [θwɔ:t] VT contrecarrer

thyme [taɪm] N thym m

thyroid ['θaɪrɔɪd] N thyroïde f

tiara [tɪ'ɑ:rə] N (woman's) diadème m

Tibet [tɪ'bɛt] N Tibet m

Tibetan [tɪ'bɛtən] ADJ tibétain(e) ▸ N Tibétain(e); (Ling) tibétain m

tibia ['tɪbɪə] N tibia m

tic [tɪk] N tic (nerveux)

tick [tɪk] N (sound: of clock) tic-tac m; (mark) coche f; (Zool) tique f; (BRIT inf): **in a ~** dans un instant; **to put a ~ against sth** cocher qch; **to buy sth on ~** (BRIT inf) acheter qch à crédit ▸ VI faire tic-tac ▸ VT (item on list) cocher
 ▸ **tick off** VT (item on list) cocher; (person) réprimander, attraper
 ▸ **tick over** VI (BRIT: engine) tourner au ralenti; (: fig) aller or marcher doucement

ticker tape ['tɪkə-] N bande f de téléscripteur; (US: in celebrations) ≈ serpentin m

★**ticket** ['tɪkɪt] N billet m; (for bus, tube) ticket m; (in shop: on goods) étiquette f; (from cash register) reçu m, ticket; (for library) carte f; (also: **parking ticket**) contravention f, p.-v. m; (US Pol) liste électorale (soutenue par un parti); **to get a (parking) ~** (Aut) attraper une contravention (pour stationnement illégal)

ticket agency N (Theat) agence f de spectacles

ticket barrier N (BRIT Rail) portillon m automatique

ticket collector N contrôleur(-euse)

ticket holder N personne munie d'un billet

ticket inspector N contrôleur(-euse)

ticket machine N billetterie f automatique

ticket office N guichet m, bureau m de vente des billets

tickle ['tɪkl] N chatouillement m ▸ VI chatouiller
 ▸ VT chatouiller; (fig) plaire à; faire rire

ticklish ['tɪklɪʃ] ADJ (person) chatouilleux(-euse); (which tickles: blanket) qui chatouille; (: cough) qui irrite; (problem) épineux(-euse)

t

tidal ['taɪdl] ADJ à marée

tidal wave N raz-de-marée m inv

tidbit ['tɪdbɪt] N (esp US) = **titbit**

tiddlywinks ['tɪdlɪwɪŋks] N jeu m de puce

★**tide** [taɪd] N marée f; (fig: of events) cours m; **high/low ~** marée haute/basse ▶ VT: **to ~ sb over** dépanner qn

tidily ['taɪdɪlɪ] ADV avec soin, soigneusement

tidiness ['taɪdɪnɪs] N bon ordre; goût m de l'ordre

tidings ['taɪdɪŋz] NPL nouvelle f; **to be the bearer of bad ~** être le porteur de mauvaises nouvelles

★**tidy** ['taɪdɪ] ADJ (room) bien rangé(e); (dress, work) net (nette), soigné(e); (person) ordonné(e), qui a de l'ordre; (: in character) soigneux(-euse), qui a l'ordre; (mind) méthodique ▶ VT, VI (also: **tidy up**) ranger; **to ~ o.s. up** s'arranger

★**tie** [taɪ] N (string etc) cordon m; (BRIT: also: **necktie**) cravate f; (fig: link) lien m; (Sport: draw) égalité f de points; match nul; (match) rencontre f; (US Rail) traverse f; **"black/white ~"** « smoking/habit de rigueur »; **family ties** liens de famille ▶ VT (parcel) attacher; (ribbon) nouer; **to ~ sth in a bow** faire un nœud à or avec qch; **to ~ a knot in sth** faire un nœud à qch ▶ VI (Sport) faire match nul; finir à égalité de points

▶ **tie down** VT attacher; **to ~ sb down to** (fig) contraindre qn à accepter; **to feel tied down** (by relationship) se sentir coincé(e)

▶ **tie in** VI: **to ~ in (with)** (correspond) correspondre (à)

▶ **tie on** VT (BRIT: label etc) attacher (avec une ficelle)

▶ **tie up** VT (parcel) ficeler; (dog, boat) attacher; (prisoner) ligoter; (arrangements) conclure; **to be tied up** (busy) être pris(e) or occupé(e)

tie-break ['taɪbreɪk], **tie-breaker** ['taɪbreɪkə^r] N (Tennis) tie-break m; (in quiz) question f subsidiaire

tie-on ['taɪɔn] ADJ (BRIT: label) qui s'attache

tie-pin ['taɪpɪn] N (BRIT) épingle f de cravate

tier [tɪə^r] N gradin m; (of cake) étage m

Tierra del Fuego [tɪ'ɛrədɛl'fweɪɡəu] N Terre f de Feu

tie tack N (US) épingle f de cravate

tiff [tɪf] N petite querelle

tiger ['taɪɡə^r] N tigre m

★**tight** [taɪt] ADJ (rope) tendu(e), raide; (clothes) étroit(e), très juste; (budget, programme, bend) serré(e); (control) strict(e), sévère; (inf: drunk) ivre, rond(e) ▶ ADV (squeeze) très fort; (shut) à bloc, hermétiquement; **to be packed ~** (suitcase) être bourré(e); (people) être serré(e); **hold ~!** accrochez-vous bien!

tighten ['taɪtn] VT (rope) tendre; (screw) resserrer; (control) renforcer ▶ VI se tendre; se resserrer

▶ **tighten up** VT (screw, knot) resserrer; (rules, security) renforcer

tightfisted [taɪt'fɪstɪd] ADJ avare

tight-lipped [taɪt'lɪpt] ADJ: **to be ~ (about sth)** (silent) ne pas desserrer les lèvres or les dents (au sujet de qch); **she was ~ with anger** elle pinçait les lèvres de colère

tightly ['taɪtlɪ] ADV (grasp) bien, très fort

tightrope ['taɪtrəup] N corde f raide

tights [taɪts] NPL (BRIT) collant m

tigress ['taɪɡrɪs] N tigresse f

tilde ['tɪldə] N tilde m

tile [taɪl] N (on roof) tuile f; (on wall or floor) carreau m ▶ VT (floor, bathroom etc) carreler

tiled [taɪld] ADJ en tuiles; carrelé(e)

tiling ['taɪlɪŋ] N (tiled area) carrelage m

★**till** [tɪl] N caisse (enregistreuse) ▶ VT (land) cultiver ▶ PREP, CONJ = **until**

tiller ['tɪlə^r] N (Naut) barre f (du gouvernail)

tilt [tɪlt] VT pencher, incliner ▶ VI pencher, être incliné(e) ▶ N (slope) inclinaison f; **to wear one's hat at a ~** porter son chapeau incliné sur le côté; **(at) full ~** à toute vitesse

timber ['tɪmbə^r] N (material) bois m de construction; (trees) arbres mpl

★**time** [taɪm] N temps m; (epoch: often pl) époque f, temps; (by clock) heure f; (moment) moment m; (occasion, also Math) fois f; (Mus) mesure f; **a long ~** un long moment, longtemps; **four at a ~** quatre à la fois; **for the ~ being** pour le moment; **from ~ to ~** de temps en temps; **~ after ~, ~ and again** bien des fois; **at times** parfois; **in ~** (soon enough) à temps; (after some time) avec le temps, à la longue; (Mus) en mesure; **in a week's ~** dans une semaine; **in no ~** en un rien de temps; **any ~** n'importe quand; **on ~** à l'heure; **to be 30 minutes behind/ahead of ~** avoir 30 minutes de retard/d'avance; **by the ~ he arrived** quand il est arrivé, le temps qu'il arrive + sub; **5 times 5** 5 fois 5; **what ~ is it?** quelle heure est-il?; **what ~ do you make it?** quelle heure avez-vous?; **what ~ is the museum/shop open?** à quelle heure ouvre le musée/magasin?; **to have a good ~** bien s'amuser; **we (or they etc) had a hard ~** ça a été difficile or pénible; **~'s up!** c'est l'heure!; **I've no ~ for it** (fig) cela m'agace; **he'll do it in his own (good) ~** (without being hurried) il le fera quand il en aura le temps; **he'll do it in** or (US) **on his own ~** (out of working hours) il le fera à ses heures perdues; **to be behind the times** retarder (sur son temps) ▶ VT (race) chronométrer; (programme) minuter; (visit) fixer; (remark etc) choisir le moment de

time-and-motion study ['taɪmənd'məuʃən-] N étude f des cadences

time bomb N bombe f à retardement

time clock N horloge pointeuse

time-consuming ['taɪmkənsjuːmɪŋ] ADJ qui prend beaucoup de temps

time difference N décalage m horaire

time frame N délais mpl

time-honoured, (US) **time-honored** ['taɪmɔnəd] ADJ consacré(e)

timekeeper ['taɪmkiːpə^r] N (Sport) chronomètre m

time lag N (BRIT) décalage m; (: in travel) décalage horaire

time-lapse (photography) ['taɪmlæps-] N chronophotographie f

timeless ['taɪmlɪs] ADJ éternel(le)

time limit N limite f de temps, délai m

timeline ['taɪmlaɪn] N (time frame) calendrier m; (diagram) ligne f du temps, ligne f des temps

timely ['taɪmlɪ] ADJ opportun(e)

time off N temps *m* libre

time out N (*in sport*) temps *m* mort; (*break*) interruption *f*; **to take ~ to do sth** interrompre ses activités pour faire qch

time-poor [taɪm'puəʳ] ADJ qui a peu de temps

timer ['taɪməʳ] N (*in kitchen*) compte-minutes *m inv*; (*Tech*) minuteur *m*

time-saving ['taɪmseɪvɪŋ] ADJ qui fait gagner du temps

timescale ['taɪmskeɪl] N délais *mpl*

time-share ['taɪmʃɛəʳ] N maison *f*/appartement *m* en multipropriété

time-sharing ['taɪmʃɛərɪŋ] N (*Comput*) temps partagé

time sheet N feuille *f* de présence

time signal N signal *m* horaire

time switch N (*BRIT*) minuteur *m*; (: *for lighting*) minuterie *f*

★**timetable** ['taɪmteɪbl] N (*Rail*) (indicateur *m*) horaire *m*; (*Scol*) emploi *m* du temps; (*programme of events etc*) programme *m*

time zone N fuseau *m* horaire

timid ['tɪmɪd] ADJ timide; (*easily scared*) peureux(-euse)

timidity [tɪ'mɪdɪtɪ] N timidité *f*

timing ['taɪmɪŋ] N minutage *m*; (*Sport*) chronométrage *m*; **the ~ of his resignation** le moment choisi pour sa démission

timing device N (*on bomb*) mécanisme *m* de retardement

Timor ['tiːmɔːʳ] N Timor

Timorese [tɪmɔ'riːz] ADJ timorais(e) ▶ N Timorais(e)

timpani ['tɪmpənɪ] NPL timbales *fpl*

★**tin** [tɪn] N étain *m*; (*also:* **tin plate**) fer-blanc *m*; (*BRIT: can*) boîte *f* (de conserve); (*for baking*) moule *m* (à gâteau); (*for storage*) boîte; **a ~ of paint** un pot de peinture

tinfoil ['tɪnfɔɪl] N papier *m* d'étain *or* d'aluminium

tinge [tɪndʒ] N nuance *f* ▶ VT: **tinged with** teinté(e) de

tingle ['tɪŋgl] N picotement *m*; frisson *m* ▶ VI picoter; (*person*) avoir des picotements

tinker ['tɪŋkəʳ] N rétameur ambulant; (*BRIT pej: gipsy*) romanichel *m*
▶ **tinker with** VT FUS bricoler, rafistoler

tinkle ['tɪŋkl] VI tinter ▶ N (*inf*): **to give sb a ~** passer un coup de fil à qn

tin mine N mine *f* d'étain

tinned [tɪnd] ADJ (*BRIT: food*) en boîte, en conserve

tinnitus ['tɪnɪtəs] N (*Med*) acouphène *m*

tinny ['tɪnɪ] ADJ métallique

tin opener [-'əupnəʳ] N (*BRIT*) ouvre-boîte(s) *m*

tinsel ['tɪnsl] N guirlandes *fpl* de Noël (*argentées*)

Tinseltown ['tɪnsltaun] N Hollywood la clinquante

tint [tɪnt] N teinte *f*; (*for hair*) shampo(o)ing colorant ▶ VT (*hair*) faire un shampo(o)ing colorant à

tinted ['tɪntɪd] ADJ (*hair*) teint(e); (*spectacles, glass*) teinté(e)

★**tiny** ['taɪnɪ] ADJ minuscule

★**tip** [tɪp] N (*end*) bout *m*; (*protective: on umbrella etc*) embout *m*; (*gratuity*) pourboire *m*; (*BRIT: for coal*) terril *m*; (*BRIT: for rubbish*) décharge *f*; (*advice*) tuyau *m* ▶ VT (*waiter*) donner un pourboire à; (*tilt*) incliner; (*overturn: also:* **tip over**) renverser; (*empty: also:* **tip out**) déverser; (*predict: winner etc*) pronostiquer; **how much should I ~?** combien de pourboire est-ce qu'il faut laisser ?; **he tipped out the contents of the box** il a vidé le contenu de la boîte
▶ **tip off** VT prévenir, avertir

tip-off ['tɪpɔf] N (*hint*) tuyau *m*

tipped [tɪpt] ADJ (*BRIT: cigarette*) (à bout) filtre *inv*; **steel-tipped** à bout métallique, à embout de métal

Tipp-Ex® ['tɪpɛks] N (*BRIT*) Tipp-Ex® *m*

tipple ['tɪpl] (*BRIT*) VI picoler ▶ N: **to have a ~** boire un petit coup

tipster ['tɪpstəʳ] N (*Racing*) pronostiqueur *m*

tipsy ['tɪpsɪ] ADJ (*inf*) un peu ivre, éméché(e)

tiptoe ['tɪptəu] N: **on ~** sur la pointe des pieds

tiptop ['tɪptɔp] ADJ: **in ~ condition** en excellent état

tirade [taɪ'reɪd] N diatribe *f*

tire ['taɪəʳ] N (*US*) = **tyre** ▶ VT fatiguer ▶ VI se fatiguer
▶ **tire out** VT épuiser

★**tired** ['taɪəd] ADJ fatigué(e); **to be/feel/look ~** être/se sentir/avoir l'air fatigué; **to be ~ of** en avoir assez de, être las (lasse) de

tiredness ['taɪədnɪs] N fatigue *f*

tireless ['taɪəlɪs] ADJ infatigable, inlassable

tire pressure N (*US*) = **tyre pressure**

tiresome ['taɪəsəm] ADJ ennuyeux(-euse)

tiring ['taɪərɪŋ] ADJ fatigant(e)

★**tissue** ['tɪʃuː] N tissu *m*; (*paper handkerchief*) mouchoir *m* en papier, kleenex® *m*

tissue paper N papier *m* de soie

tit [tɪt] N (*bird*) mésange *f*; (*inf: breast*) nichon *m* (*inf*); **to give ~ for tat** rendre coup pour coup

titan ['taɪtən] N titan *m*

titanium [tɪ'teɪnɪəm] N titane *m*

titbit ['tɪtbɪt] N (*food*) friandise *f*; (*before meal*) amuse-gueule *m inv*; (*news*) potin *m*

titillate ['tɪtɪleɪt] VT titiller, exciter

titivate ['tɪtɪveɪt] VT pomponner

★**title** ['taɪtl] N titre *m*; (*Law: right*): **~ (to)** droit *m* (à)

titled ['taɪtld] ADJ (*lady, gentleman*) titré(e)

title deed N (*Law*) titre (constitutif) de propriété

title page N page *f* de titre

title role N rôle principal

titter ['tɪtəʳ] VI rire (bêtement)

tittle-tattle ['tɪtltætl] N bavardages *mpl*

titular ['tɪtjulə*ʳ*] ADJ (*in name only*) nominal(e)

tizzy ['tɪzɪ] N: **to be in a ~** être dans tous ses états

T-junction ['tiː'dʒʌŋkʃən] N croisement *m* en T

TM N ABBR = **trademark; transcendental meditation**

TN ABBR (*US*) = **Tennessee**

TNT N ABBR (= *trinitrotoluene*) TNT *m*

to [tuː, tə]

PREP *(with noun/pronoun)* **1** *(direction)* à; *(: towards)* vers; envers; **to go to France/Portugal/London/school** aller en France/au Portugal/à Londres/à l'école; **to go to Claude's/the doctor's** aller chez Claude/le docteur; **the road to Edinburgh** la route d'Édimbourg

2 *(as far as)* (jusqu')à; **to count to 10** compter jusqu'à 10; **from 40 to 50 people** de 40 à 50 personnes

3 *(with expressions of time)*: **a quarter to 5** 5 heures moins le quart; **it's twenty to 3** il est 3 heures moins vingt

4 *(for, of)* de; **the key to the front door** la clé de la porte d'entrée; **a letter to his wife** une lettre (adressée) à sa femme

5 *(expressing indirect object)* à; **to give sth to sb** donner qch à qn; **to talk to sb** parler à qn; **it belongs to him** cela lui appartient, c'est à lui; **to be a danger to sb** être dangereux(-euse) pour qn

6 *(in relation to)* à; **3 goals to 2** 3 (buts) à 2; **30 miles to the gallon** ≈ 9,4 litres aux cent (km)

7 *(purpose, result)*: **to come to sb's aid** venir au secours de qn, porter secours à qn; **to sentence sb to death** condamner qn à mort; **to my surprise** à ma grande surprise

▶ PREP *(with vb)* **1** *(simple infinitive)*: **to go/eat** aller/manger

2 *(following another vb)*: **to want/try/start to do** vouloir/essayer de/commencer à faire

3 *(with vb omitted)*: **I don't want to** je ne veux pas

4 *(purpose, result)* pour; **I did it to help you** je l'ai fait pour vous aider

5 *(equivalent to relative clause)*: **I have things to do** j'ai des choses à faire; **the main thing is to try** l'important est d'essayer

6 *(after adjective etc)*: **ready to go** prêt(e) à partir; **too old/young to ...** trop vieux/jeune pour ...

▶ ADV: **push/pull the door to** tirez/poussez la porte; **to go to and fro** aller et venir

toad [təud] N crapaud m

toadstool ['təudstuːl] N champignon (vénéneux)

toady ['təudɪ] vɪ flatter bassement

★**toast** [təust] N *(Culin)* pain grillé, toast m; *(drink, speech)* toast; **a piece** or **slice of ~** un toast ▶ VT *(Culin)* faire griller; *(drink to)* porter un toast à

toaster ['təustər] N grille-pain m inv

toastie ['təustɪ] N *(BRIT inf)* sandwich m grillé; **a cheese and ham ~** ≈ un croque-monsieur

toastmaster ['təustmɑːstər] N animateur m pour réceptions

toast rack N porte-toast m inv

tobacco [tə'bækəu] N tabac m; **pipe ~** tabac à pipe

tobacconist [tə'bækənɪst] N marchand(e) de tabac; **~'s (shop)** (bureau m de) tabac m

Tobago [tə'beɪɡəu] N *see* **Trinidad and Tobago**

toboggan [tə'bɔɡən] N toboggan m; *(child's)* luge f

★**today** [tə'deɪ] ADV, N *(also fig)* aujourd'hui m; **what day is it ~?** quel jour sommes-nous aujourd'hui ?; **what date is it ~?** quelle est la date aujourd'hui ?; **~ is the 4th of March** aujourd'hui nous sommes le 4 mars; **a week ago ~** il y a huit jours aujourd'hui

toddler ['tɔdlər] N enfant mf qui commence à marcher, bambin m

toddy ['tɔdɪ] N grog m

to-do [tə'duː] N *(fuss)* histoire f, affaire f

★**toe** [təu] N doigt m de pied, orteil m; *(of shoe)* bout m; **big ~** gros orteil; **little ~** petit orteil ▶ VT: **to ~ the line** *(fig)* obéir, se conformer

TOEFL N ABBR = **Test(ing) of English as a Foreign Language**

toehold ['təuhəuld] N prise f

toenail ['təuneɪl] N ongle m de l'orteil

toffee ['tɔfɪ] N caramel m

toffee apple N *(BRIT)* pomme caramélisée

tofu ['təufuː] N fromage m de soja

toga ['təuɡə] N toge f

★**together** [tə'ɡɛðər] ADV ensemble; *(at same time)* en même temps; **~ with** prep avec

togetherness [tə'ɡɛðənɪs] N camaraderie f; intimité f

toggle switch ['tɔɡl-] N *(Comput)* interrupteur m à bascule

Togo ['təuɡəu] N Togo m

togs [tɔɡz] NPL *(inf: clothes)* fringues fpl

toil [tɔɪl] N dur travail, labeur m ▶ VI travailler dur; peiner

★**toilet** ['tɔɪlət] N *(BRIT: lavatory)* toilettes fpl, cabinets mpl; **to go to the ~** aller aux toilettes; **where's the ~?** où sont les toilettes ? ▶ CPD *(bag, soap etc)* de toilette

> Use the plural **les toilettes** to translate *toilet*: *Where's the toilet?* **Où sont les toilettes ?** The singular word has other meanings.

toilet bag N *(BRIT)* nécessaire m de toilette

toilet bowl N cuvette f des W.-C.

toilet paper N papier m hygiénique

toiletries ['tɔɪlətrɪz] NPL articles mpl de toilette

toilet roll N rouleau m de papier hygiénique

toilet water N eau f de toilette

to-ing and fro-ing ['tuːɪŋən'frəuɪŋ] N *(BRIT)* allées et venues fpl

token ['təukən] N *(sign)* marque f, témoignage m; *(metal disc)* jeton m; *(voucher)* bon m, coupon m; **by the same ~** *(fig)* de même; **book ~** *(BRIT)* chèque-livre m; **gift ~** bon-cadeau m ▶ ADJ *(fee, strike)* symbolique

tokenism ['təukənɪzəm] N *(Pol)*: **it's just ~** c'est une politique de pure forme

Tokyo ['təukjəu] N Tokyo

told [təuld] PT, PP of **tell**

tolerable ['tɔlərəbl] ADJ *(bearable)* tolérable; *(fairly good)* passable

tolerably ['tɔlərəblɪ] ADV: **~ good** tolérable

tolerance ['tɔlərns] N *(also Tech)* tolérance f

tolerant ['tɔlərnt] ADJ: **~ (of)** tolérant(e) (à l'égard de)

tolerate ['tɔləreɪt] VT supporter; *(Med, Tech)* tolérer

toleration [tɔlə'reɪʃən] N tolérance f

toll [təul] N *(tax, charge)* péage m; **the accident ~ on the roads** le nombre des victimes de la route ▶ VI *(bell)* sonner

tollbridge ['təulbrɪdʒ] N pont m à péage

toll call N (US Tel) appel m (à) longue distance

toll-free ['təul'fri:] ADJ (US) gratuit(e) ▶ ADV gratuitement

★**tomato** [tə'mɑ:təu] (pl **tomatoes**) N tomate f

tomato sauce N sauce f tomate

tomb [tu:m] N tombe f

tombola [tɔm'bəulə] N tombola f

tomboy ['tɔmbɔɪ] N garçon manqué

tombstone ['tu:mstəun] N pierre tombale

tombstoning ['tu:mstəunɪŋ] N (BRIT) saut ou plongeon depuis une falaise, une grue, une jetée, etc.

tomcat ['tɔmkæt] N matou m

★**tomorrow** [tə'mɔrəu] ADV, N (also fig) demain m; **the day after ~** après-demain; **a week ~** demain en huit; **~ morning** demain matin

★**ton** [tʌn] N tonne f (Brit: = 1016 kg; US = 907 kg; metric = 1000 kg); (Naut: also: **register ton**) tonneau m (= 2.83 cu.m); **tons of** (inf) des tas de

tonal ['təunl] ADJ tonal(e)

tone [təun] N ton m; (of radio, BRIT Tel) tonalité f ▶ VI (also: **tone in**) s'harmoniser
▶**tone down** VT (colour, criticism) adoucir; (sound) baisser
▶**tone up** VT (muscles) tonifier

tone-deaf [təun'dɛf] ADJ qui n'a pas d'oreille

toner ['təunəʳ] N (for photocopier) encre f

Tonga ['tɔŋə] N îles fpl Tonga

tongs [tɔŋz] NPL pinces fpl; (for coal) pincettes fpl; (for hair) fer m à friser

★**tongue** [tʌŋ] N langue f; **~ in cheek** adv ironiquement

tongue-tied ['tʌŋtaɪd] ADJ (fig) muet(te)

tonic ['tɔnɪk] N (Med) tonique m; (Mus) tonique f; (also: **tonic water**) Schweppes® m

★**tonight** [tə'naɪt] ADV, N cette nuit; (this evening) ce soir; **(I'll) see you ~!** à ce soir!

tonnage ['tʌnɪdʒ] N (Naut) tonnage m

tonne [tʌn] N (BRIT: metric ton) tonne f

tonsil ['tɔnsl] N amygdale f; **to have one's tonsils out** se faire opérer des amygdales

tonsillitis [tɔnsɪ'laɪtɪs] N amygdalite f; **to have ~** avoir une angine or une amygdalite

★**too** [tu:] ADV (excessively) trop; (also) aussi; **it's ~ sweet** c'est trop sucré; **I went ~** moi aussi, j'y suis allé; **~ much** (as adv) trop; (as adj) trop de; **~ many** adj trop de; **~ bad!** tant pis!

took [tuk] PT of **take**

★**tool** [tu:l] N outil m; (fig) instrument m ▶ VT travailler, ouvrager

toolbar ['tu:lbɑ:ʳ] N barre f d'outils

tool box N boîte f à outils

tool kit N trousse f à outils

toot [tu:t] N coup m de sifflet (or de klaxon) ▶ VI siffler; (with car-horn) klaxonner

★**tooth** [tu:θ] (pl **teeth** [ti:θ]) N (Anat, Tech) dent f; **to have a ~ out** or (US) **pulled** se faire arracher une dent; **to brush one's teeth** se laver les dents; **by the skin of one's teeth** (fig) de justesse

toothache ['tu:θeɪk] N mal m de dents; **to have ~** avoir mal aux dents

★**toothbrush** ['tu:θbrʌʃ] N brosse f à dents

toothless ['tu:θlɪs] ADJ (person, smile) édenté(e); (ineffective: organization) sans réel pouvoir; (: law) sans effet

★**toothpaste** ['tu:θpeɪst] N (pâte f) dentifrice m

toothpick ['tu:θpɪk] N cure-dent m

tooth powder N poudre f dentifrice

★**top** [tɔp] N (of mountain, head) sommet m; (of page, ladder) haut m; (of list, queue) commencement m; (of box, cupboard, table) dessus m; (lid: of box, jar) couvercle m; (: of bottle) bouchon m; (toy) toupie f; (Dress: blouse etc) haut m; (: of pyjamas) veste f; **the ~ of the milk** la crème du lait; **at the ~ of the stairs/page/street** en haut de l'escalier/de la page/de la rue; **from ~ to bottom** de fond en comble; **on ~ of** sur; (in addition to) en plus de; **from ~ to toe** (BRIT) de la tête aux pieds; **at the ~ of the list** en tête de liste; **at the ~ of one's voice** à tue-tête; **over the ~** (inf: behaviour etc) qui dépasse les limites ▶ ADJ du haut; (in rank) premier(-ière); (best) meilleur(e); **at ~ speed** à toute vitesse ▶ VT (exceed) dépasser; (be first in) être en tête de
▶**top up**, (US) **top off** VT (bottle) remplir; (salary) compléter; **to ~ up one's mobile (phone)** recharger son compte

topaz ['təupæz] N topaze f

top-class ['tɔp'klɑ:s] ADJ de première classe; (Sport) de haute compétition

topcoat ['tɔpkəut] N pardessus m

topflight ['tɔpflaɪt] ADJ excellent(e)

top floor N dernier étage

top hat N haut-de-forme m

top-heavy [tɔp'hɛvɪ] ADJ (object) trop lourd(e) du haut

topiary ['təupɪərɪ] N topiaire f

topic ['tɔpɪk] N sujet m, thème m

topical ['tɔpɪkl] ADJ d'actualité

topless ['tɔplɪs] ADJ (bather etc) aux seins nus; **~ swimsuit** monokini m

top-level ['tɔplɛvl] ADJ (talks) à l'échelon le plus élevé

topmost ['tɔpməust] ADJ le (la) plus haut(e)

top-notch ['tɔp'nɔtʃ] (inf) de premier ordre

topographical [tɔpə'græfɪkl] ADJ topographique

topography [tə'pɔgrəfɪ] N topographie f

topping ['tɔpɪŋ] N (Culin) couche de crème, fromage etc qui recouvre un plat

topple ['tɔpl] VT renverser, faire tomber ▶ VI basculer; tomber

top-ranking ['tɔpræŋkɪŋ] ADJ très haut placé(e)

top-secret ['tɔp'si:krɪt] ADJ ultra-secret(-ète)

top-security ['tɔpsə'kjuərɪtɪ] ADJ (BRIT) de haute sécurité

topsy-turvy ['tɔpsɪ'tə:vɪ] ADJ, ADV sens dessus-dessous

top-up ['tɔpʌp] N (for mobile phone) recharge f, minutes fpl; **would you like a ~?** (drink) je vous en remets or rajoute?

top-up card N (for mobile phone) recharge f

top-up loan N (BRIT) prêt m complémentaire

torch [tɔ:tʃ] N torche f; (BRIT: electric) lampe f de poche

torchlight ['tɔ:tʃlaɪt] N: **by ~** à la lumière de lampes de poche ▶ CPD (procession, parade) aux flambeaux

t

tore [tɔːʳ] PT of **tear²**

torment N ['tɔːmɛnt] tourment m ▶ VT [tɔː'mɛnt] tourmenter; (fig: annoy) agacer

tormentor [tɔː'mɛntəʳ] N tourmenteur(-euse)

torn [tɔːn] PP of **tear²** ▶ ADJ: ~ **between** (fig) tiraillé(e) entre

tornado [tɔː'neɪdəʊ] (pl **tornadoes**) N tornade f

torpedo [tɔː'piːdəʊ] (pl **torpedoes**) N torpille f

torpedo boat N torpilleur m

torpor ['tɔːpəʳ] N torpeur f

torrent ['tɔrnt] N torrent m

torrential [tɔ'rɛnʃl] ADJ torrentiel(le)

torrid ['tɔrɪd] ADJ torride; (fig) ardent(e)

torsion ['tɔːʃən] N torsion f

torso ['tɔːsəʊ] N torse m

tortoise ['tɔːtəs] N tortue f

tortoiseshell ['tɔːtəʃɛl] ADJ en écaille

tortuous ['tɔːtjʊəs] ADJ tortueux(-euse)

★**torture** ['tɔːtʃəʳ] N torture f ▶ VT torturer

torturer ['tɔːtʃərəʳ] N tortionnaire m

Tory ['tɔːrɪ] ADJ, N (BRIT Pol) tory mf, conservateur(-trice)

toss [tɔs] VT lancer, jeter; (BRIT: pancake) faire sauter; (head) rejeter en arrière; **to ~ a coin** jouer à pile ou face ▶ VI: **to ~ for sth** (BRIT) jouer qch à pile ou face; **to ~ and turn** (in bed) se tourner et se retourner ▶ N (movement: of head etc) mouvement soudain; (: of coin) tirage m à pile ou face; **to win/ lose the ~** gagner/perdre à pile ou face; (Sport) gagner/perdre le tirage au sort

tot [tɔt] N (BRIT: drink) petit verre; (child) bambin m
▶ **tot up** VT (BRIT: figures) additionner

★**total** ['təʊtl] ADJ total(e) ▶ N total m; **in ~** au total ▶ VT (add up) faire le total de, additionner; (amount to) s'élever à

totalitarian [təʊtælɪ'tɛərɪən] ADJ totalitaire

totalitarianism [təʊtælɪ'tɛərɪənɪzəm] N totalitarisme m

totality [təʊ'tælɪtɪ] N totalité f

totally ['təʊtəlɪ] ADV totalement

tote bag [təʊt-] N fourre-tout m inv

totem pole ['təʊtəm-] N mât m totémique

totter ['tɔtəʳ] VI chanceler; (object, government) être chancelant(e)

toucan ['tuːkən] N toucan m

★**touch** [tʌtʃ] N contact m, toucher m; (sense, skill: of pianist etc) toucher; (fig: note, also Football) touche f; **the personal ~** la petite note personnelle; **to put the finishing touches to sth** mettre la dernière main à qch; **a ~ of** (fig) un petit peu de; une touche de; **in ~ with** en contact or rapport avec; **to get in ~ with** prendre contact avec; **I'll be in ~** je resterai en contact; **to lose ~** (friends) se perdre de vue; **to be out of ~ with events** ne pas être au courant de ce qui se passe ▶ VT (gen) toucher à; (tamper with) toucher à
▶ **touch down** VI (Aviat) atterrir; (on sea) amerrir
▶ **touch on** VT FUS (topic) effleurer, toucher
▶ **touch up** VT (paint) retoucher

touch-and-go ['tʌtʃən'gəʊ] ADJ incertain(e); **it was ~ whether we did it** nous avons failli ne pas le faire

touchdown ['tʌtʃdaʊn] N (Aviat) atterrissage m; (on sea) amerrissage m; (US Football) essai m

touched [tʌtʃt] ADJ (moved) touché(e); (inf) cinglé(e)

touching ['tʌtʃɪŋ] ADJ touchant(e), attendrissant(e)

touchline ['tʌtʃlaɪn] N (Sport) (ligne f de) touche f

touchpad ['tʌtʃpæd] N (Comput) touchpad m

touch screen N (Tech) écran m tactile; **~ mobile** (téléphone) portable m à écran tactile; **~ technology** technologie f à écran tactile

touch-sensitive ['tʌtʃsɛnsɪtɪv] ADJ (keypad) à effleurement; (screen) tactile

touch-type ['tʌtʃtaɪp] VI taper au toucher

touchy ['tʌtʃɪ] ADJ (person) susceptible

★**tough** [tʌf] ADJ dur(e); (resistant) résistant(e), solide; (meat) dur, coriace; (firm) inflexible; (journey) pénible; (task, problem, situation) difficile; (rough) dur; **~ luck!** pas de chance !; tant pis ! ▶ N (gangster etc) dur m

toughen ['tʌfn] VT rendre plus dur(e) (or plus résistant(e) or plus solide)

toughness ['tʌfnɪs] N dureté f; résistance f; solidité f

toupee ['tuːpeɪ] N postiche m

★**tour** ['tʊəʳ] N voyage m; (also: **package tour**) voyage organisé; (of town, museum) tour m, visite f; (by band) tournée f; **to go on a ~ of** (museum, region) visiter; **to go on ~** partir en tournée ▶ VT visiter

tour guide N (person) guide mf

touring ['tʊərɪŋ] N voyages mpl touristiques, tourisme m

tourism ['tʊərɪzm] N tourisme m

★**tourist** ['tʊərɪst] N touriste mf ▶ ADV (travel) en classe touriste ▶ CPD touristique; **the ~ trade** le tourisme

tourist class N (Aviat) classe f touriste

tourist office N syndicat m d'initiative

touristy ['tʊərɪstɪ] ADJ (inf) touristique

★**tournament** ['tʊənəmənt] N tournoi m

tourniquet ['tʊənɪkeɪ] N (Med) garrot m

tour operator N (BRIT) organisateur m de voyages, tour-opérateur m

tousled ['taʊzld] ADJ (hair) ébouriffé(e)

tout [taʊt] N (BRIT: ticket tout) revendeur m de billets ▶ VI: **to ~ for** essayer de raccrocher, racoler ▶ VT (BRIT): **to ~ sth (around)** essayer de placer or (re)vendre qch

tow [təʊ] N: **to give sb a ~** (Aut) remorquer qn; **"on ~"**, (US) **"in ~"** (Aut) « véhicule en remorque » ▶ VT remorquer; (caravan, trailer) tracter
▶ **tow away** VT (subj: police) emmener à la fourrière; (: breakdown service) remorquer

toward [tə'wɔːd], **towards** [tə'wɔːdz] PREP vers; (of attitude) envers, à l'égard de; (of purpose) pour; **~ noon/the end of the year** vers midi/la fin de l'année; **to feel friendly ~ sb** être bien disposé envers qn

★**towel** ['taʊəl] N serviette f (de toilette); (also: **tea towel**) torchon m; **to throw in the ~** (fig) jeter l'éponge

towelling ['taʊəlɪŋ] N (fabric) tissu-éponge m

towel rail, (US) **towel rack** N porte-serviettes m inv

★**tower** ['tauə'] N tour f ▶ VI (building, mountain) se dresser (majestueusement); **to ~ above** or **over sb/sth** dominer qn/qch

tower block N (BRIT) tour f (d'habitation)

towering ['tauərɪŋ] ADJ très haut(e), imposant(e)

towline ['təulaɪn] N (câble m de) remorque f

★**town** [taun] N ville f; **to go to ~** aller en ville; (fig) y mettre le paquet; **in the ~** dans la ville, en ville; **to be out of ~** (person) être en déplacement

town centre N (BRIT) centre m de la ville, centre-ville m

town clerk N ≈ secrétaire mf de mairie

town council N conseil municipal

town crier [-'kraɪə'] N (BRIT) crieur public

town hall N ≈ mairie f

townie ['taunɪ] N (BRIT inf) citadin(e)

town plan N plan m de ville

town planner N urbaniste mf

town planning N urbanisme m

townsfolk ['taunzfəuk] NPL (old) habitants mpl de la ville

township ['taunʃɪp] N banlieue noire (établie sous le régime de l'apartheid)

townspeople ['taunzpi:pl] NPL gens mpl de la ville; **the ~ of Warwick** les gens de Warwick

towpath ['təupɑ:θ] N (chemin m de) halage m

towrope ['təurəup] N (câble m de) remorque f

tow truck N (US) dépanneuse f

toxic ['tɔksɪk] ADJ toxique

toxic asset N (Econ) actif m toxique

toxic bank N (Econ) bad bank f, banque f toxique

toxicity [tɔk'sɪsɪtɪ] N toxicité f

toxicologist [tɔksɪ'kɔlədʒɪst] N toxicologue mf

toxicology [tɔksɪ'kɔlədʒɪ] N toxicologie f

toxin ['tɔksɪn] N toxine f

★**toy** [tɔɪ] N jouet m
  ▶ **toy with** VT FUS jouer avec; (idea) caresser

toyshop ['tɔɪʃɔp] N magasin m de jouets

trace [treɪs] N trace f; **without ~** (disappear) sans laisser de traces; **there was no ~ of it** il n'y en avait pas trace ▶ VT (draw) tracer, dessiner; (follow) suivre la trace de; (locate) retrouver

traceability [treɪsə'bɪlɪtɪ] N traçabilité f

traceable ['treɪsəbl] ADJ: **to be ~ to sth** être attribuable à qch

trace element N oligo-élément m

trachea [trə'kɪə] N (Anat) trachée f

tracing paper ['treɪsɪŋ-] N papier-calque m

track [træk] N (mark) trace f; (path: gen) chemin m, piste f; (: of bullet etc) trajectoire f; (: of suspect, animal) piste f; (Rail) voie ferrée, rails mpl; (Comput, Sport) piste f; (on CD) piste f; (on record) plage f; **to keep ~ of** suivre; **to be on the right ~** (fig) être sur la bonne voie ▶ VT suivre la trace or la piste de
  ▶ **track down** VT (prey) trouver et capturer; (sth lost) finir par retrouver

tracker dog ['trækə-] N (BRIT) chien dressé pour suivre une piste

track events NPL (Sport) épreuves fpl sur piste

tracking station ['trækɪŋ-] N (Space) centre m d'observation de satellites

track meet N (US) réunion sportive sur piste

track record N: **to have a good ~** (fig) avoir fait ses preuves

★**tracksuit** ['træksu:t] N survêtement m

tract [trækt] N (Geo) étendue f, zone f; (pamphlet) tract m; **respiratory ~** (Anat) système m respiratoire

traction ['trækʃən] N traction f

tractor ['træktə'] N tracteur m

trade [treɪd] N commerce m; (skill, job) métier m; **foreign ~** commerce extérieur ▶ VI faire du commerce; **to ~ with/in** faire du commerce avec/le commerce de ▶ VT (exchange): **to ~ sth (for sth)** échanger qch (contre qch)
  ▶ **trade in** VT (old car etc) faire reprendre

trade barrier N barrière commerciale

trade deficit N déficit extérieur

Trade Descriptions Act N (BRIT) loi contre les appellations et la publicité mensongères

trade discount N remise f au détaillant

trade fair N foire(-exposition) commerciale

trade-in ['treɪdɪn] N reprise f

trade-in price N prix m à la reprise

trademark ['treɪdmɑ:k] N marque f de fabrique

trade mission N mission commerciale

trade name N marque déposée

trade-off ['treɪdɔf] N (exchange) échange f; (balancing) équilibre m

trader ['treɪdə'] N commerçant(e), négociant(e)

trade secret N secret m de fabrication

tradesman ['treɪdzmən] N (irreg) (shopkeeper) commerçant m; (skilled worker) ouvrier qualifié

trade union N syndicat m

trade unionist [-'ju:njənɪst] N syndicaliste mf

trade wind N alizé m

trading ['treɪdɪŋ] N affaires fpl, commerce m

trading estate N (BRIT) zone industrielle

trading stamp N timbre-prime m

★**tradition** [trə'dɪʃən] N tradition f ■ **traditions** NPL coutumes fpl, traditions

★**traditional** [trə'dɪʃənl] ADJ traditionnel(le)

traditionalist [trə'dɪʃənlɪst] ADJ, N traditionaliste mf

traditionally [trə'dɪʃənlɪ] ADV (by tradition) traditionnellement; (in an old-fashioned way) de manière traditionnelle; **~ ...** selon la tradition ...

★**traffic** ['træfɪk] N trafic m; (cars) circulation f ▶ VI: **to ~ in** (inf: liquor, drugs) faire le trafic de

traffic calming [-'kɑ:mɪŋ] N ralentissement m de la circulation

traffic circle N (US) rond-point m

traffic island N refuge m (pour piétons)

traffic jam N embouteillage m

trafficker ['træfɪkə'] N trafiquant(e)

trafficking ['træfɪkɪŋ] N trafic m; **drug ~** le trafic de drogue

★**traffic lights** NPL feux mpl (de signalisation)

traffic offence N (BRIT) infraction f au code de la route

traffic sign N panneau m de signalisation

traffic violation N (US) = **traffic offence**

t

traffic warden N contractuel(le)

tragedy ['trædʒədɪ] N tragédie f

tragic ['trædʒɪk] ADJ tragique

tragically ['trædʒɪklɪ] ADV (die, end) tragiquement

tragicomedy [trædʒɪ'kɔmədɪ] N tragicomédie f

trail [treɪl] N (tracks) trace f, piste f; (path) chemin m, piste; (of smoke etc) traînée f; **to be on sb's ~** être sur la piste de qn ▶ VT (drag) traîner, tirer; (follow) suivre ▶ VT traîner; (in game, contest) être en retard ▶ **trail away, trail off** VI (sound, voice) s'évanouir; (interest) disparaître
▶ **trail behind** VI traîner, être à la traîne

trailblazer ['treɪlbleɪzəʳ] N pionnier(-ière)

trailer ['treɪləʳ] N (Aut) remorque f; (US: caravan) caravane f; (Cine) bande-annonce f

trailer truck N (US) (camion m) semi-remorque m

★**train** [treɪn] N train m; (of dress) traîne f; (BRIT: series): ~ **of events** série f d'événements; **to go by ~** voyager par le train or en train; **what time does the ~ from Paris get in?** à quelle heure arrive le train de Paris ?; **is this the ~ for ...?** c'est bien le train pour ... ?; **one's ~ of thought** le fil de sa pensée ▶ VT (apprentice, doctor etc) former; (Sport) entraîner; (dog) dresser; (memory) exercer; (point: gun etc): **to ~ sth on** braquer qch sur; **to ~ sb to do sth** apprendre à qn à faire qch; (employee) former qn à faire qch ▶ VI recevoir sa formation; (Sport) s'entraîner

train attendant N (US) employé(e) des wagons-lits

trained [treɪnd] ADJ qualifié(e), qui a reçu une formation; dressé(e)

trainee [treɪ'ni:] N stagiaire mf; (in trade) apprenti(e)

trainer ['treɪnəʳ] N (Sport) entraîneur(-euse); (of dogs etc) dresseur(-euse) ■ **trainers** NPL (shoes) chaussures fpl de sport

★**training** ['treɪnɪŋ] N formation f; (Sport) entraînement m; (of dog etc) dressage m; **in ~** (Sport) à l'entraînement; (fit) en forme

training college N école professionnelle; (for teachers) ≈ école normale

training course N cours m de formation professionnelle

training shoes NPL chaussures fpl de sport

train wreck N (fig) épave f; **he's a complete ~** c'est une épave

traipse [treɪps] VI (se) traîner, déambuler

trait [treɪt] N trait m (de caractère)

traitor ['treɪtəʳ] N traître m

trajectory [trə'dʒɛktərɪ] N trajectoire f

tram [træm] N (BRIT: also: **tramcar**) tram(way) m

tramline ['træmlaɪn] N ligne f de tram(way)

tramp [træmp] N (person) vagabond(e), clochard(e); (!: woman): **to be a ~** être coureuse ▶ VI marcher d'un pas lourd ▶ VT (walk through: town, streets) parcourir à pied

trample ['træmpl] VT: **to ~ (underfoot)** piétiner; (fig) bafouer

trampoline ['træmpəliːn] N trampoline m

trance [trɑːns] N transe f; (Med) catalepsie f; **to go into a ~** entrer en transe

tranche [trɑːnʃ] N tranche f

tranquil ['træŋkwɪl] ADJ tranquille

tranquillity [træŋ'kwɪlɪtɪ] N tranquillité f

tranquillizer, (US) **tranquilizer** ['træŋkwɪlaɪzəʳ] N (Med) tranquillisant m

transact [træn'zækt] VT (business) traiter

transaction [træn'zækʃən] N transaction f; **cash ~** transaction au comptant ■ **transactions** NPL (minutes) actes mpl

transatlantic ['trænzət'læntɪk] ADJ transatlantique

transcend [træn'sɛnd] VT transcender; (excel over) surpasser

transcendental [trænsɛn'dɛntl] ADJ: **~ meditation** méditation transcendantale

transcontinental ['trænskɔntɪ'nɛntl] ADJ transcontinental(e)

transcribe [træn'skraɪb] VT transcrire

transcript ['trænskrɪpt] N transcription f (texte)

transcription [træn'skrɪpʃən] N transcription f

transept ['trænsɛpt] N transept m

transfer N ['trænsfəʳ] (gen, also Sport) transfert m; (Pol: of power) passation f; (of money) virement m; (picture, design) décalcomanie f; (: stick-on) autocollant m; **by bank ~** par virement bancaire ▶ VT [træns'fəːʳ] transférer; passer; virer; décalquer

transferable [træns'fəːrəbl] ADJ transmissible, transférable; **"not ~"** « personnel »

transfer desk N (Aviat) guichet m de transit

transfix [træns'fɪks] VT transpercer; (fig): **transfixed with fear** paralysé(e) par la peur

transform [træns'fɔːm] VT transformer

transformation [trænsfə'meɪʃən] N transformation f

transformer [træns'fɔːməʳ] N (Elec) transformateur m

transfusion [træns'fjuːʒən] N transfusion f

transgender [trænz'dʒɛndəʳ] ADJ, N transgenre mf

transgress [trænz'grɛs] VT transgresser

transgression [trænz'grɛʃn] N transgression f

transgressor [trænz'grɛsəʳ] N (formal) transgresseur m

transient ['trænzɪənt] ADJ transitoire, éphémère

transistor [træn'zɪstəʳ] N (Elec: also: **transistor radio**) transistor m

transit ['trænzɪt] N: **in ~** en transit

transit camp N camp m de transit

transition [træn'zɪʃən] N transition f

transitional [træn'zɪʃənl] ADJ transitoire

transitive ['trænzɪtɪv] ADJ (Ling) transitif(-ive)

transit lounge N (Aviat) salle f de transit

transitory ['trænzɪtərɪ] ADJ transitoire

translate [trænz'leɪt] VT: **to ~ (from/into)** traduire (du/en); **can you ~ this for me?** pouvezvous me traduire ceci ?

translation [trænz'leɪʃən] N traduction f; (Scol: as opposed to prose) version f

translator [trænz'leɪtəʳ] N traducteur(-trice)

translucent [trænz'luːsnt] ADJ translucide

transmission [trænz'mɪʃən] N transmission f

transmit [trænz'mɪt] VT transmettre; (Radio, TV) émettre

transmitter [trænz'mitə'] N émetteur m

transparency [træns'pɛərnsı] N (BRIT Phot) diapositive f

transparent [træns'pærnt] ADJ transparent(e)

transphobia [trænz'fəubjə] N transphobie f

transpire [træns'paıə'] vı (become known): **it finally transpired that ...** on a finalement appris que ...; (happen) arriver

transplant vт [træns'plɑ:nt] transplanter; (seedlings) repiquer ▶ N ['trænsplɑ:nt] (Med) transplantation f; **to have a heart ~** subir une greffe du cœur

★**transport** N ['trænspɔ:t] transport m; **public ~** transports en commun; **Department of T~** (BRIT) ministère m des Transports ▶ vт [træns'pɔ:t] transporter

transportation [trænspɔ:'teıʃən] N (moyen m de) transport m; (of prisoners) transportation f; **Department of T~** (US) ministère m des Transports

transport café N (BRIT) ≈ routier m, ≈ restaurant m des routiers

transporter [træns'pɔ:tə'] N avion-cargo m

transpose [træns'pəuz] vт transposer

transsexual [trænz'sɛksjuəl] ADJ, N transsexuel(le)

transverse ['trænzvə:s] ADJ transversal(e)

transvestite [trænz'vɛstaıt] N travesti(e)

trap [træp] N (snare, trick) piège m; (carriage) cabriolet m; **to set** or **lay a ~ (for sb)** tendre un piège (à qn); **to shut one's ~** (inf) la fermer ▶ vт prendre au piège; (immobilize) bloquer; (confine) coincer

trap door N trappe f

trapeze [trə'pi:z] N trapèze m

trapped [træpt] ADJ piégé(e); **to feel ~** se sentir piégé(e)

trapper ['træpə'] N trappeur m

trappings ['træpıŋz] NPL ornements mpl; attributs mpl

trash [træʃ] N (inf, pej: goods) camelote f; (: nonsense) sottises fpl; (US: rubbish) ordures fpl

trash can N (US) poubelle f

trashy ['træʃı] ADJ (inf) de camelote (inf), qui ne vaut rien

trauma ['trɔ:mə] N traumatisme m

traumatic [trɔ:'mætık] ADJ traumatisant(e)

traumatize ['trɔ:mətaız] vт traumatiser

★**travel** ['trævl] N voyage(s) m(pl) ▶ vı voyager; (move) aller, se déplacer; (news, sound) se propager; **this wine doesn't ~ well** ce vin voyage mal ▶ vт (distance) parcourir

travel agency N agence f de voyages

travel agent N agent m de voyages

travel brochure N brochure f touristique

travel insurance N assurance-voyage f

traveller, (US) **traveler** ['trævlə'] N voyageur(-euse); (Comm) représentant(e) de commerce

traveller's cheque, (US) **traveler's check** N chèque m de voyage

travelling, (US) **traveling** ['trævlıŋ] N voyage(s) m(pl) ▶ ADJ (circus, exhibition) ambulant(e) ▶ CPD (bag, clock) de voyage; (expenses) de déplacement

travelling salesman, (US) **traveling salesman** N (irreg) voyageur m de commerce

travelogue ['trævəlɔg] N (book, talk) récit m de voyage; (film) documentaire m de voyage

travel-sick ['trævlsık] ADJ: **to get ~** avoir le mal de la route (or de mer or de l'air)

travel sickness N mal m de la route (or de mer or de l'air)

traverse ['trævəs] vт traverser

travesty ['trævəstı] N parodie f

trawl [trɔ:l] vı pêcher au chalut ▶ N (search) exploration f; **a ~ through sth** une exploration de qch ▶ **trawl through** vт FUS éplucher

trawler ['trɔ:lə'] N chalutier m

tray [treı] N (for carrying) plateau m; (on desk) corbeille f

treacherous ['trɛtʃərəs] ADJ traître(sse); (ground, tide) dont il faut se méfier; **road conditions are ~** l'état des routes est dangereux

treachery ['trɛtʃərı] N traîtrise f

treacle ['tri:kl] N mélasse f

tread [trɛd] (pt **trod** [trɔd], pp **trodden** ['trɔdn]) N (step) pas m; (sound) bruit m de pas; (of tyre) chape f, bande f de roulement ▶ vı marcher ▶ **tread on** vт FUS marcher sur

treadle ['trɛdl] N pédale f (de machine)

treadmill ['trɛdmıl] N (lit) tapis m roulant; (fig) corvée f

treas. ABBR = **treasurer**

treason ['tri:zn] N trahison f

treasure ['trɛʒə'] N trésor m ▶ vт (value) tenir beaucoup à; (store) conserver précieusement

treasure hunt N chasse f au trésor

treasurer ['trɛʒərə'] N trésorier(-ière)

treasury ['trɛʒərı] N trésorerie f; **the T~, the T~ Department** (US) ≈ le ministère des Finances

treasury bill N bon m du Trésor

★**treat** [tri:t] N petit cadeau, petite surprise; **it was a ~** ça m'a (or nous a etc) vraiment fait plaisir ▶ vт traiter; **to ~ sb to sth** offrir qch à qn; **to ~ sth as a joke** prendre qch à la plaisanterie

treatable ['tri:təbl] ADJ soignable

treatise ['tri:tız] N traité m (ouvrage)

★**treatment** ['tri:tmənt] N traitement m; **to have ~ for sth** (Med) suivre un traitement pour qch

treaty ['tri:tı] N traité m

treble ['trɛbl] ADJ triple ▶ N (Mus) soprano m ▶ vт, vı tripler

treble clef N clé f de sol

★**tree** [tri:] N arbre m

treeless ['tri:lıs] ADJ sans arbre

tree-lined ['tri:laınd] ADJ bordé(e) d'arbres

treetop ['tri:tɔp] N cime f d'un arbre

tree trunk N tronc m d'arbre

trek [trɛk] N (long walk) randonnée f; (tiring walk) longue marche, trotte f ▶ vı (as holiday) faire de la randonnée

trellis ['trɛlıs] N treillis m, treillage m

tremble ['trɛmbl] vı trembler

trembling ['trɛmblıŋ] N tremblement m ▶ ADJ tremblant(e)

t

tremendous [trɪˈmɛndəs] ADJ (*enormous*) énorme; (*excellent*) formidable, fantastique

tremendously [trɪˈmɛndəslɪ] ADV énormément, extrêmement + *adjective*; formidablement

tremor [ˈtrɛməʳ] N tremblement *m*; (*also:* **earth tremor**) secousse *f* sismique

tremulous [ˈtrɛmjuləs] ADJ tremblant(e)

trench [trɛntʃ] N tranchée *f*

trenchant [ˈtrɛntʃənt] ADJ (*criticism, views*) incisif(-ive)

trench coat N trench-coat *m*

trench warfare N guerre *f* de tranchées

trend [trɛnd] N (*tendency*) tendance *f*; (*of events*) cours *m*; (*fashion*) mode *f*; **on ~** tendance *inv*; **~ towards/away from doing** tendance à faire/à ne pas faire; **to set the ~** donner le ton; **to set a ~** lancer une mode

trendsetter [ˈtrɛndsɛtəʳ] N *personne qui lance une mode*

trendy [ˈtrɛndɪ] ADJ (*idea, person*) dans le vent; (*clothes*) dernier cri *inv*

trepidation [trɛpɪˈdeɪʃən] N vive agitation

trespass [ˈtrɛspəs] VI: **to ~ on** s'introduire sans permission dans; (*fig*) empiéter sur; **"no trespassing"** « propriété privée », « défense d'entrer »

trespasser [ˈtrɛspəsəʳ] N intrus(e); **"trespassers will be prosecuted"** « interdiction d'entrer sous peine de poursuites »

trestle [ˈtrɛsl] N tréteau *m*

trestle table N table *f* à tréteaux

triage [ˈtriːɑːʒ] N (*in hospital*) triage *m*

★**trial** [ˈtraɪəl] N (*Law*) procès *m*, jugement *m*; (*test: of machine etc*) essai *m*; (*worry*) souci *m*; **~ by jury** jugement par jury; **to be sent for ~** être traduit(e) en justice; **to be on ~** passer en jugement; **by ~ and error** par tâtonnements ◼ **trials** NPL (*unpleasant experiences*) épreuves *fpl*; (*Sport*) épreuves éliminatoires; **horse trials** concours *m* hippique

trial balance N (*Comm*) balance *f* de vérification

trial basis N: **on a ~** pour une période d'essai

trial period N période *f* d'essai

trial run N essai *m*

triangle [ˈtraɪæŋgl] N (*Math, Mus*) triangle *m*

triangular [traɪˈæŋgjuləʳ] ADJ triangulaire

triathlete [traɪˈæθliːt] N triathlète *mf*

triathlon [traɪˈæθlən] N triathlon *m*

tribal [ˈtraɪbl] ADJ tribal(e)

tribe [traɪb] N tribu *f*

tribesman [ˈtraɪbzmən] N (*irreg*) membre *m* de la tribu

tribulation [trɪbjuˈleɪʃən] N tribulation *f*, malheur *m*

tribunal [traɪˈbjuːnl] N tribunal *m*

tributary [ˈtrɪbjutərɪ] N (*river*) affluent *m*

tribute [ˈtrɪbjuːt] N tribut *m*, hommage *m*; **to pay ~ to** rendre hommage à

trice [traɪs] N: **in a ~** en un clin d'œil

triceps [ˈtraɪsɛps] N triceps *m*

★**trick** [trɪk] N (*magic*) tour *m*; (*joke, prank*) tour, farce *f*; (*skill, knack*) astuce *f*; (*Cards*) levée *f*; **to play a ~ on sb** jouer un tour à qn; **it's a ~ of the light** c'est une

illusion d'optique causée par la lumière; **that should do the ~** (*inf*) ça devrait faire l'affaire ▶ VT attraper, rouler; **to ~ sb into doing sth** persuader qn par la ruse de faire qch; **to ~ sb out of sth** obtenir qch de qn par la ruse

trickery [ˈtrɪkərɪ] N ruse *f*

trickle [ˈtrɪkl] N (*of water etc*) filet *m* ▶ VI couler en un filet *or* goutte à goutte; **to ~ in/out** (*people*) entrer/sortir par petits groupes

trick question N question-piège *f*

trickster [ˈtrɪkstəʳ] N arnaqueur(-euse), filou *m*

tricky [ˈtrɪkɪ] ADJ difficile, délicat(e)

tricycle [ˈtraɪsɪkl] N tricycle *m*

trifle [ˈtraɪfl] N bagatelle *f*; (*Culin*) ≈ diplomate *m* ▶ ADV: **a ~ long** un peu long ▶ VI: **to ~ with** traiter à la légère

trifling [ˈtraɪflɪŋ] ADJ insignifiant(e)

trigger [ˈtrɪgəʳ] N (*of gun*) gâchette *f* ▶ **trigger off** VT déclencher

trigger-happy [ˈtrɪgəˈhæpɪ] ADJ (*inf*) à la gâchette facile; **to be ~** avoir la gâchette facile

trigonometry [trɪgəˈnɔmətrɪ] N trigonométrie *f*

trilby [ˈtrɪlbɪ] N (BRIT: *also:* **trilby hat**) chapeau mou, feutre *m*

trill [trɪl] N (*of bird, Mus*) trille *m*

trillion [ˈtrɪljən] NUM (*a million million*) billion *m* (*mille milliards*)

trilogy [ˈtrɪlədʒɪ] N trilogie *f*

trim [trɪm] ADJ net(te); (*house, garden*) bien tenu(e); (*figure*) svelte ▶ N (*haircut etc*) légère coupe; (*embellishment*) finitions *fpl*; (*on car*) garnitures *fpl*; **to keep in (good) ~** maintenir en (bon) état ▶ VT (*cut*) couper légèrement; (*Naut: a sail*) gréer; (*decorate*): **to ~ (with)** décorer (de)

trimmings [ˈtrɪmɪŋz] NPL décorations *fpl*; (*extras: esp Culin*) garniture *f*

Trinidad and Tobago [ˈtrɪnɪdæd-] N Trinité et Tobago *f*

Trinity [ˈtrɪnɪtɪ] N: **the ~** la Trinité

trinket [ˈtrɪŋkɪt] N bibelot *m*; (*piece of jewellery*) colifichet *m*

trio [ˈtriːəu] N trio *m*

★**trip** [trɪp] N voyage *m*; (*excursion*) excursion *f*; (*stumble*) faux pas; **on a ~** en voyage ▶ VI faire un faux pas, trébucher; (*go lightly*) marcher d'un pas léger
▶ **trip up** VI trébucher ▶ VT faire un croc-en-jambe à

tripartite [traɪˈpɑːtaɪt] ADJ triparti(e)

tripe [traɪp] N (*Culin*) tripes *fpl*; (*pej: rubbish*) idioties *fpl*

triple [ˈtrɪpl] ADJ triple ▶ ADV: **~ the distance/the speed** trois fois la distance/la vitesse

triple jump N triple saut *m*

triplets [ˈtrɪplɪts] NPL triplés(-ées)

triplicate [ˈtrɪplɪkət] N: **in ~** en trois exemplaires

tripod [ˈtraɪpɔd] N trépied *m*

Tripoli [ˈtrɪpəlɪ] N Tripoli

tripper [ˈtrɪpəʳ] N (BRIT) touriste *mf*; excursionniste *mf*

tripwire [ˈtrɪpwaɪəʳ] N fil *m* de déclenchement

trite [traɪt] ADJ (*pej*) banal(e)

triumph ['traɪʌmf] N triomphe m ▶ VI: **to ~ (over)** triompher (de)

triumphal [traɪ'ʌmfl] ADJ triomphal(e)

triumphant [traɪ'ʌmfənt] ADJ triomphant(e)

trivia ['trɪvɪə] NPL futilités fpl

trivial ['trɪvɪəl] ADJ insignifiant(e); (commonplace) banal(e)

triviality [trɪvɪ'ælɪtɪ] N caractère insignifiant; banalité f

trivialize ['trɪvɪəlaɪz] VT rendre banal(e)

trod [trɔd] PT of **tread**

trodden ['trɔdn] PP of **tread**

troll [trɔl] N (Internet) troll m, trolleur(-euse)

trolley ['trɔlɪ] N chariot m

trolley bus N trolleybus m

trolling ['trəʊlɪŋ] N (Internet) trolling m

trollop ['trɔləp] N (pej) prostituée f

trombone [trɔm'bəʊn] N trombone m

trombonist [trɔm'bəʊnɪst] N tromboniste mf

troop [tru:p] N bande f, groupe m ▶ VI: **to ~ in/ out** entrer/sortir en groupe; **trooping the colour** (BRIT) (ceremony) le salut au drapeau ■ **troops** NPL (Mil) troupes fpl; (: men) hommes mpl, soldats mpl

troop carrier N (plane) avion m de transport de troupes; (Naut: also: **troopship**) transport m (navire)

trooper ['tru:pəʳ] N (Mil) soldat m de cavalerie; (US: policeman) ≈ gendarme m

troopship ['tru:pʃɪp] N transport m (navire)

trophy ['trəʊfɪ] N trophée m

tropic ['trɔpɪk] N tropique m; **in the tropics** sous les tropiques; **T~ of Cancer/Capricorn** tropique du Cancer/Capricorne

tropical ['trɔpɪkl] ADJ tropical(e)

trot [trɔt] N trot m; **on the ~** (BRIT fig) d'affilée ▶ VI trotter

▶ **trot out** VT (excuse, reason) débiter; (names, facts) réciter les uns après les autres

★**trouble** ['trʌbl] N difficulté(s) f(pl), problème(s) m(pl); (worry) ennuis mpl, soucis mpl; (bother, effort) peine f; (Pol) conflit(s) m(pl), troubles mpl; (Med): **stomach** etc **~ troubles** gastriques etc; **to be in ~** avoir des ennuis; (ship, climber etc) être en difficulté; **to have ~ doing sth** avoir du mal à faire qch; **to go to the ~ of doing** se donner le mal de faire; **it's no ~!** je vous en prie!; **the ~ is ...** le problème, c'est que ...; **what's the ~?** qu'est-ce qui ne va pas? ▶ VT (disturb) déranger, gêner; (worry) inquiéter; **please don't ~ yourself** je vous en prie, ne vous dérangez pas! ▶ VI: **to ~ to do** prendre la peine de faire ■ **troubles** NPL (Pol etc) troubles; (personal) ennuis, soucis

troubled ['trʌbld] ADJ (person) inquiet(-ète); (times, life) agité(e)

trouble-free ['trʌblfri:] ADJ sans problèmes or ennuis

troublemaker ['trʌblmeɪkəʳ] N élément perturbateur, fauteur m de troubles

troubleshooter ['trʌblʃu:təʳ] N (problem solver) expert m; (in conflict) médiateur(-trice)

troubleshooting ['trʌblʃu:tɪŋ] N résolution f de problèmes

troublesome ['trʌblsəm] ADJ (child) fatigant(e), difficile; (cough) gênant(e)

trouble spot N point chaud (fig)

troubling ['trʌblɪŋ] ADJ (times, thought) inquiétant(e)

trough [trɔf] N (also: **drinking trough**) abreuvoir m; (also: **feeding trough**) auge f; (depression) creux m; (channel) chenal m; **~ of low pressure** (Meteorology) dépression f

trounce [trauns] VT (inf: defeat) battre à plates coutures (inf)

troupe [tru:p] N troupe f

trouser press N presse-pantalon m inv

★**trousers** ['trauzəz] NPL pantalon m; **short ~** (BRIT) culottes courtes

trouser suit N (BRIT) tailleur-pantalon m

trousseau ['tru:səu] (pl **trousseaux** ['tru:səu:] or **trousseaus** [-z]) N trousseau m

trout [traut] N (pl inv) truite f

trowel ['trauəl] N truelle f; (garden tool) déplantoir m

truancy ['tru:ənsɪ] N absentéisme m (scolaire)

truant ['tru:ənt] N: **to play ~** faire l'école buissonnière

truce [tru:s] N trêve f

★**truck** [trʌk] N camion m; (Rail) wagon m à plateforme; (for luggage) chariot m (à bagages)

truck driver N camionneur m

trucker ['trʌkəʳ] N (esp US) camionneur m

truck farm N (US) jardin maraîcher

trucking ['trʌkɪŋ] N (esp US) transport routier

trucking company N (US) entreprise f de transport (routier)

truckload ['trʌkləʊd] N cargaison f (d'un camion)

truck stop N (US) ≈ routier m, restaurant m de routiers

truculent ['trʌkjulənt] ADJ agressif(-ive)

trudge [trʌdʒ] VI marcher lourdement, se traîner

★**true** [tru:] ADJ vrai(e); (accurate) exact(e); (genuine) vrai, véritable; (faithful) fidèle; (wall) d'aplomb; (beam) droit(e); (wheel) dans l'axe; **to come ~** se réaliser; **~ to life** réaliste

truffle ['trʌfl] N truffe f

truism ['tru:ɪzəm] N truisme m, lieu m commun

truly ['tru:lɪ] ADV vraiment, réellement; (truthfully) sans mentir; (faithfully) fidèlement; **yours ~** (in letter) je vous prie d'agréer, Monsieur (or Madame etc), l'expression de mes sentiments respectueux

trump [trʌmp] N atout m; **to come up trumps** (fig) faire des miracles

trump card N atout m; (fig) carte f maîtresse

trumped-up [trʌmpt'ʌp] ADJ inventé(e) (de toutes pièces)

trumpet ['trʌmpɪt] N trompette f

trumpeter ['trʌmpɪtəʳ] N trompettiste mf

truncated [trʌŋ'keɪtɪd] ADJ tronqué(e)

truncheon ['trʌntʃən] N bâton m (d'agent de police); matraque f

trundle ['trʌndl] VT, VI: **to ~ along** rouler bruyamment

t

trunk [trʌŋk] N (of tree, person) tronc m; (of elephant) trompe f; (case) malle f; (US Aut) coffre m ■ **trunks** NPL (also: **swimming trunks**) maillot m or slip m de bain

trunk call N (BRIT Tel) communication interurbaine

trunk road N (BRIT) ≈ (route f) nationale f

truss [trʌs] N (Med) bandage m herniaire ▶ VT: **to ~ (up)** (Culin) brider

★**trust** [trʌst] N confiance f; (responsibility): **to place sth in sb's ~** confier la responsabilité de qch à qn; (Law) fidéicommis m; (Comm) trust m; **to take sth on ~** accepter qch les yeux fermés; **in ~** (Law) par fidéicommis ▶ VT (rely on) avoir confiance en; (entrust): **to ~ sth to sb** confier qch à qn; (hope): **to ~ (that)** espérer (que)
  ▶ **trust in** VT FUS croire en
  ▶ **trust to** VT FUS (luck, instinct) faire confiance à

trust company N société f fiduciaire

trusted ['trʌstɪd] ADJ en qui l'on a confiance

trustee [trʌsˈtiː] N (Law) fidéicommissaire mf; (of school etc) administrateur(-trice)

trustful ['trʌstful] ADJ confiant(e)

trust fund N fonds m en fidéicommis

trusting ['trʌstɪŋ] ADJ confiant(e)

trustworthy ['trʌstwəːðɪ] ADJ digne de confiance

trusty ['trʌstɪ] ADJ fidèle

★**truth** [truːθ] (pl **truths** [truːðz]) N vérité f

truthful ['truːθful] ADJ (person) qui dit la vérité; (answer) sincère; (description) exact(e), vrai(e)

truthfully ['truːθfəlɪ] ADV sincèrement, sans mentir

truthfulness ['truːθfəlnɪs] N véracité f

★**try** [traɪ] N essai m, tentative f; (Rugby) essai; **to give sth a ~** essayer qch ▶ VT (attempt) essayer, tenter; (test: sth new: also: **try out**) essayer, tester; (Law: person) juger; (strain) éprouver; **to ~ to do** essayer de faire; (seek) chercher à faire; **to ~ one's (very) best** or **one's (very) hardest** faire de son mieux ▶ VI essayer
  ▶ **try on** VT (clothes) essayer; **to ~ it on** (fig) tenter le coup, bluffer
  ▶ **try out** VT essayer, mettre à l'essai
  ▶ **try for** VT FUS (baby) essayer d'avoir; (gold medal) essayer de décrocher

trying ['traɪɪŋ] ADJ pénible

tsar [zɑːʳ] N tsar m

T-shirt N tee-shirt m

tsp. ABBR (= teaspoonful) c. f à café, cuil. f à café

T-square ['tiːskwɛəʳ] N équerre f en T

tsunami [tsuˈnɑːmɪ] N tsunami m

TT ADJ ABBR (BRIT inf) = **teetotal** ▶ ABBR (US) = **Trust Territory**

tub [tʌb] N cuve f; (for washing clothes) baquet m; (bath) baignoire f

tuba ['tjuːbə] N tuba m

tubby ['tʌbɪ] ADJ rondelet(te)

★**tube** [tjuːb] N tube m; (BRIT: underground) métro m; (for tyre) chambre f à air; (inf: television): **the ~** la télé

tubeless ['tjuːblɪs] ADJ (tyre) sans chambre à air

tuber ['tjuːbəʳ] N (Bot) tubercule m

tuberculosis [tjubəːkjuˈləʊsɪs] N tuberculose f

tube station N (BRIT) station f de métro

tubing ['tjuːbɪŋ] N tubes mpl; **a piece of ~** un tube

tubular ['tjuːbjʊləʳ] ADJ tubulaire

TUC N ABBR (BRIT: = Trades Union Congress) confédération f des syndicats britanniques

tuck [tʌk] N (Sewing) pli m, rempli m ▶ VT (put) mettre
  ▶ **tuck away** VT cacher, ranger; (money) mettre de côté; (building): **to be tucked away** être caché(e)
  ▶ **tuck in** VT rentrer; (child) border ▶ VI (eat) manger de bon appétit; attaquer le repas
  ▶ **tuck up** VT (child) border

tucker ['tʌkəʳ] N (AUSTRALIA, NEW ZEALAND inf) bouffe f (inf)

tuck shop N (BRIT Scol) boutique f à provisions

Tues., Tue. ABBR (= Tuesday) ma., mar.

★**Tuesday** ['tjuːzdɪ] N mardi m; (the date) today is ~ **23 March** nous sommes aujourd'hui mardi le 23 mars; **on ~** mardi; **on Tuesdays** le mardi; **every ~** tous les mardis, chaque mardi; **every other ~** un mardi sur deux; **last/next ~** mardi dernier/prochain; **~ next** mardi qui vient; **the following ~** le mardi suivant; **a week/fortnight on ~, ~ week/fortnight** mardi en huit/quinze; **the ~ before last** l'autre mardi; **the ~ after next** mardi en huit; **~ morning/lunchtime/afternoon/evening** mardi matin/midi/après-midi/soir; **~ night** mardi soir; (overnight) la nuit de mardi (à mercredi); **~'s newspaper** le journal de mardi

tuft [tʌft] N touffe f

tug [tʌg] N (ship) remorqueur m ▶ VT tirer (sur)

tug-of-love [tʌgəvˈlʌv] N lutte acharnée entre parents divorcés pour la garde d'un enfant

tug-of-war [tʌgəvˈwɔːʳ] N lutte f à la corde

tuition [tjuːˈɪʃən] N (BRIT: lessons) leçons fpl; (: private) cours particuliers; (US: fees) frais mpl de scolarité

tulip ['tjuːlɪp] N tulipe f

tulle [tjuːl] N tulle m

tumble ['tʌmbl] N (fall) chute f, culbute f ▶ VI tomber, dégringoler; (somersault) faire une ou des culbute(s); **to ~ to sth** (inf) réaliser qch ▶ VT renverser, faire tomber

tumbledown ['tʌmbldaʊn] ADJ délabré(e)

tumble dryer N (BRIT) séchoir m (à linge) à air chaud

tumbler ['tʌmbləʳ] N verre (droit), gobelet m

tummy ['tʌmɪ] N (inf) ventre m

tumour, (US) **tumor** ['tjuːməʳ] N tumeur f

tumult ['tjuːmʌlt] N tumulte m

tumultuous [tjuːˈmʌltjuəs] ADJ tumultueux(-euse)

tuna ['tjuːnə] N (pl inv: also: **tuna fish**) thon m

tundra ['tʌndrə] N toundra f

★**tune** [tjuːn] N (melody) air m; **to be in/out of ~** (instrument) être accordé/désaccordé; (singer) chanter juste/faux; **to be in/out of ~ with** (fig) être en accord/désaccord avec; **she was robbed to the ~ of £30,000** (fig) on lui a volé la jolie somme de 30 000 livres ▶ VT (Mus) accorder; (Radio, TV, Aut) régler, mettre au point
  ▶ **tune in** VI (Radio, TV): **to ~ in (to)** se mettre à l'écoute (de)
  ▶ **tune up** VI (musician) accorder son instrument

tuneful ['tjuːnful] ADJ mélodieux(-euse)

tuner ['tjuːnəʳ] N (radio set) tuner m; **piano ~** accordeur m de pianos

tuner amplifier N ampli-tuner m

tungsten ['tʌŋstn] N tungstène m

tunic ['tjuːnɪk] N tunique f

tuning ['tjuːnɪŋ] N réglage m

tuning fork N diapason m

Tunis ['tjuːnɪs] N Tunis

Tunisia [tjuːˈnɪzɪə] N Tunisie f

Tunisian [tjuːˈnɪzɪən] ADJ tunisien(ne) ▸ N Tunisien(ne)

★**tunnel** ['tʌnl] N tunnel m; (in mine) galerie f ▸ VI creuser un tunnel (or une galerie)

tunnel vision N (Med) rétrécissement m du champ visuel; (fig) vision étroite des choses

tunny ['tʌnɪ] N thon m

turban ['tɜːbən] N turban m

turbid ['tɜːbɪd] ADJ boueux(-euse)

turbine ['tɜːbaɪn] N turbine f

turbo ['tɜːbəu] N turbo m

turbocharged ['tɜːbəutʃɑːdʒd] ADJ turbo inv

turbojet [tɜːbəuˈdʒet] N turboréacteur m

turboprop [tɜːbəuˈprɔp] N (engine) turbopropulseur m

turbot ['tɜːbət] N (pl inv) turbot m

turbulence ['tɜːbjuləns] N (Aviat) turbulence f

turbulent ['tɜːbjulənt] ADJ turbulent(e); (sea) agité(e)

tureen [təˈriːn] N soupière f

turf [tɜːf] N gazon m; (clod) motte f (de gazon); **the T~** le turf, les courses fpl ▸ VT gazonner
  ▸ **turf out** VT (inf) jeter; jeter dehors

turf accountant N (BRIT) bookmaker m

turgid ['tɜːdʒɪd] ADJ (speech) pompeux(-euse)

Turin [tjuəˈrɪn] N Turin

Turk [tɜːk] N Turc (Turque)

Turkey ['tɜːkɪ] N Turquie f

turkey ['tɜːkɪ] N dindon m, dinde f

Turkish ['tɜːkɪʃ] ADJ turc (turque) ▸ N (Ling) turc m

Turkish bath N bain turc

Turkish delight N loukoum m

Turkmenistan [tɜːkmɛnɪˈstɑːn] N Turkménistan m

turmeric ['tɜːmərɪk] N curcuma m

turmoil ['tɜːmɔɪl] N trouble m, bouleversement m

★**turn** [tɜːn] N tour m; (in road) tournant m; (tendency: of mind, events) tournure f; (performance) numéro m; (Med) crise f, attaque f; **it gave me quite a ~** ça m'a fait un coup; **"no left ~"** (Aut) « défense de tourner à gauche »; **it's your ~** c'est (à) votre tour; **in ~** à son tour; à tour de rôle; **to take turns** se relayer; **to take turns at** faire à tour de rôle; **at the ~ of the year/century** à la fin de l'année/du siècle; **to take a ~ for the worse** (situation, events) empirer; **his health** or **he has taken a ~ for the worse** son état s'est aggravé ▸ VT tourner; (collar, steak) retourner; (age) atteindre; (shape: wood, metal) tourner; (milk) faire tourner; (change): **to ~ sth into** changer qch en ▸ VI (object, wind, milk) tourner; (person: look back) se (re)tourner; (reverse direction) faire demi-tour; (change) changer; (become) devenir; **to ~ into** se changer en, se transformer en; **~ left/right at the next junction** tournez à gauche/droite au prochain carrefour
  ▸ **turn about** VI faire demi-tour; faire un demi-tour
  ▸ **turn against** VT FUS: **to ~ against sb/sth** se retourner contre qn/qch ▸ VT: **to ~ sb against sb** retourner qn contre qn
  ▸ **turn around** VI (person) se retourner ▸ VT (object) tourner
  ▸ **turn away** VI se détourner, tourner la tête ▸ VT (reject: person) renvoyer; (: business) refuser
  ▸ **turn back** VI revenir, faire demi-tour
  ▸ **turn down** VT (refuse) rejeter, refuser; (reduce) baisser; (fold) rabattre
  ▸ **turn in** VI (inf: go to bed) aller se coucher ▸ VT (fold) rentrer
  ▸ **turn off** VI (from road) tourner ▸ VT (light, radio etc) éteindre; (tap) fermer; (engine) arrêter; **I can't ~ the heating off** je n'arrive pas à éteindre le chauffage
  ▸ **turn on** VT (light, radio etc) allumer; (tap) ouvrir; (engine) mettre en marche; **I can't ~ the heating on** je n'arrive pas à allumer le chauffage
  ▸ **turn out** VT (light, gas) éteindre; (produce: goods, novel, good pupils) produire ▸ VI (voters, troops) se présenter; **to ~ out to be ...** s'avérer ..., se révéler ...
  ▸ **turn over** VI (person) se retourner ▸ VT (object) retourner; (page) tourner
  ▸ **turn round** VI faire demi-tour; (rotate) tourner
  ▸ **turn to** VT FUS: **to ~ to sb** s'adresser à qn
  ▸ **turn up** VI (person) arriver, se pointer (inf); (lost object) être retrouvé(e) ▸ VT (collar) remonter; (radio, heater) mettre plus fort

turnabout ['tɜːnəbaut], **turnaround** ['tɜːnəraund] N volte-face f inv

turncoat ['tɜːnkaut] N renégat(e)

turned-up ['tɜːndʌp] ADJ (nose) retroussé(e)

turning ['tɜːnɪŋ] N (in road) tournant m; **the first ~ on the right** la première (rue or route) à droite

turning circle N (BRIT) rayon m de braquage

turning point N (fig) tournant m, moment décisif

turning radius N (US) = **turning circle**

turnip ['tɜːnɪp] N navet m

turnout ['tɜːnaut] N (nombre m de personnes dans l')assistance f; (of voters) taux m de participation

turnover ['tɜːnəuvəʳ] N (Comm: amount of money) chiffre m d'affaires; (: of goods) roulement m; (of staff) renouvellement m, changement m; (Culin) sorte de chausson; **there is a rapid ~ in staff** le personnel change souvent

turnpike ['tɜːnpaɪk] N (US) autoroute f à péage

turnstile ['tɜːnstaɪl] N tourniquet m (d'entrée)

turntable ['tɜːnteɪbl] N (on record player) platine f

turn-up ['tɜːnʌp] N (BRIT: on trousers) revers m

turpentine ['tɜːpəntaɪn] N (also: **turps**) (essence f de) térébenthine f

turquoise ['tɜːkwɔɪz] N (stone) turquoise f ▸ ADJ turquoise inv

turret ['tʌrɪt] N tourelle f

turtle ['tɜːtl] N tortue marine

t

turtleneck [ˈtəːtlnɛk], **turtleneck sweater** N pullover m à col montant

Tuscany [ˈtʌskənɪ] N Toscane f

tusk [tʌsk] N défense f (d'éléphant)

tussle [ˈtʌsl] N bagarre f, mêlée f

tutor [ˈtjuːtəʳ] N (Brit Scol: in college) directeur(-trice) d'études; (private teacher) précepteur(-trice)

tutorial [tjuːˈtɔːrɪəl] N (Scol) (séance f de) travaux mpl pratiques

tutu [ˈtuːtuː] N tutu m

Tuvalu [tuːvəˈluː] N Tuvalu fpl

tuxedo [tʌkˈsiːdəu] N (US) smoking m

★**TV** [tiːˈviː] N ABBR (= television) télé f, TV f

TV dinner N plateau-repas surgelé

twaddle [ˈtwɔdl] N balivernes fpl

twang [twæŋ] N (of instrument) son vibrant; (of voice) ton nasillard ▶ VI vibrer ▶ VT (guitar) pincer les cordes de

tweak [twiːk] VT (nose) tordre; (ear, hair) tirer

tweed [twiːd] N tweed m

tweet [twiːt] (on Twitter) N tweet m ▶ VT tweeter

tweetable [ˈtwiːtəbl] ADJ (on Twitter) tweetable

tweezers [ˈtwiːzəz] NPL pince f à épiler

★**twelfth** [twɛlfθ] NUM douzième

Twelfth Night N la fête des Rois

★**twelve** [twɛlv] NUM douze; **at ~ (o'clock)** à midi; (midnight) à minuit

twenties [ˈtwɛntɪz] NPL (age): **to be in one's ~** avoir la vingtaine; (1920s): **the ~** les années vingt; (temperature): **in the ~** dans les vingt degrés; **a woman in her ~** une femme d'une vingtaine d'années

★**twentieth** [ˈtwɛntɪɪθ] NUM vingtième

★**twenty** [ˈtwɛntɪ] NUM vingt; **in ~ fourteen** en deux mille quatorze

twerking [ˈtwəːkɪŋ] N twerk m

twerp [twəːp] N (inf) imbécile mf

★**twice** [twaɪs] ADV deux fois; **~ as much** deux fois plus; **~ a week** deux fois par semaine; **she is ~ your age** elle a deux fois ton âge

twiddle [ˈtwɪdl] VT, VI: **to ~ (with) sth** tripoter qch; **to ~ one's thumbs** (fig) se tourner les pouces

twig [twɪg] N brindille f ▶ VT, VI (inf) piger (inf)

twilight [ˈtwaɪlaɪt] N crépuscule m; (morning) aube f; **in the ~** dans la pénombre

twill [twɪl] N sergé m

★**twin** [twɪn] ADJ, N jumeau(-elle) ▶ VT jumeler

twin-bedded room [ˈtwɪnˈbɛdɪd-] N = **twin room**

twin beds NPL lits mpl jumeaux

twin-carburettor, (US) **twin carburetor** [ˈtwɪnkɑːbjuˈrɛtəʳ] ADJ à double carburateur

twine [twaɪn] N ficelle f ▶ VI (plant) s'enrouler

twin-engined [twɪnˈɛndʒɪnd] ADJ bimoteur; **~ aircraft** bimoteur m

twinge [twɪndʒ] N (of pain) élancement m; (of conscience) remords m

twinkle [ˈtwɪŋkl] N scintillement m; pétillement m ▶ VI scintiller; (eyes) pétiller

twinning [ˈtwɪnɪŋ] N jumelage m

twin room N chambre f à deux lits

twin town N ville jumelée

twirl [twəːl] N tournoiement m ▶ VT faire tournoyer ▶ VI tournoyer

★**twist** [twɪst] N torsion f, tour m; (in wire, flex) tortillon m; (bend: in road) tournant m; (in story) coup m de théâtre ▶ VT tordre; (weave) entortiller; (roll around) enrouler; (fig) déformer; **to ~ one's ankle/ wrist** (Med) se tordre la cheville/le poignet ▶ VI s'entortiller; s'enrouler; (road, river) serpenter

twisted [ˈtwɪstɪd] ADJ (wire, rope) entortillé(e); (ankle, wrist) tordu(e), foulé(e); (fig: logic, mind) tordu

twister [ˈtwɪstəʳ] N (US) tornade f

twit [twɪt] N (inf) crétin(e) (inf)

twitch [twɪtʃ] N (pull) coup sec, saccade f; (nervous) tic m ▶ VI se convulser; avoir un tic

Twitter® [ˈtwɪtəʳ] N Twitter® ▶ VI twitter

Twitterati [twɪtəˈrɑːtɪ] NPL (inf) Twitterati mpl, utilisateurs les plus assidus et les plus suivis de Twitter

Twittersphere [ˈtwɪtəsfɪəʳ] N (inf): **the ~** la twittosphère

★**two** [tuː] NUM deux; **~ by ~, in twos** par deux; **to put ~ and ~ together** (fig) faire le rapprochement

two-bit [tuːˈbɪt] ADJ (esp US inf, pej) de pacotille

two-door [tuːˈdɔːʳ] ADJ (Aut) à deux portes

two-faced [tuːˈfeɪst] ADJ (pej: person) faux (fausse)

twofold [ˈtuːfəuld] ADJ (increase) de cent pour cent; (reply) en deux parties ▶ ADV: **to increase ~** doubler

two-piece [ˈtuːˈpiːs] N (also: **two-piece suit**) (costume m) deux-pièces m inv; (also: **two-piece swimsuit**) (maillot m de bain) deux-pièces

two-seater [tuːˈsiːtəʳ] N (plane) (avion m) biplace m; (car) voiture f à deux places

twosome [ˈtuːsəm] N (people) couple m

two-stroke [ˈtuːstrəuk] N (also: **two-stroke engine**) moteur m à deux temps ▶ ADJ à deux temps

two-thirds [tuːˈθəːdz] PRON deux tiers mpl; **~ of sth** les deux tiers de qch; **by ~** de deux tiers ▶ ADV aux deux tiers ▶ ADJ (majority) aux deux tiers

two-tone [ˈtuːˈtəun] ADJ (in colour) à deux tons

two-way [ˈtuːweɪ] ADJ (traffic) dans les deux sens; **~ radio** émetteur-récepteur m

TX ABBR (US) = **Texas**

tycoon [taɪˈkuːn] N: **(business) ~** gros homme d'affaires

★**type** [taɪp] N (category) genre m, espèce f; (model) modèle m; (example) type m; (Typ) type, caractère m; **what ~ do you want?** quel genre voulez-vous ?; **in bold/italic ~** en caractères gras/en italiques ▶ VT (letter etc) taper (à la machine) ▶ **type in** VT entrer; **to ~ sth into a computer** entrer qch dans un ordinateur ▶ **type up** VT taper

typecast [ˈtaɪpkɑːst] ADJ condamné(e) à toujours jouer le même rôle

typeface [ˈtaɪpfeɪs] N police f (de caractères)

typescript [ˈtaɪpskrɪpt] N texte dactylographié

typeset [ˈtaɪpsɛt] VT (irreg: like **set**) composer (en imprimerie)

typesetter [ˈtaɪpsɛtəʳ] N compositeur m

typewriter [ˈtaɪpraɪtəʳ] N machine f à écrire

typewritten [ˈtaɪprɪtn] ADJ dactylographié(e)

typhoid [ˈtaɪfɔɪd] N typhoïde f

typhoon [taɪˈfuːn] N typhon m

typhus [ˈtaɪfəs] N typhus m

★**typical** [ˈtɪpɪkl] ADJ typique, caractéristique

typically [ˈtɪpɪklɪ] ADV (as usual) comme d'habitude; (characteristically) typiquement

typify [ˈtɪpɪfaɪ] VT être caractéristique de

typing [ˈtaɪpɪŋ] N dactylo(graphie) f

typing error N faute f de frappe

typing pool N pool m de dactylos

typist [ˈtaɪpɪst] N dactylo mf

typo [ˈtaɪpəʊ] N ABBR (inf: = typographical error) coquille f

typography [taɪˈpɒɡrəfɪ] N typographie f

tyranny [ˈtɪrənɪ] N tyrannie f

tyrant [ˈtaɪrənt] N tyran m

tyre, (US) **tire** [ˈtaɪəʳ] N pneu m

tyre pressure, (US) **tire pressure** N pression f (de gonflage)

Tyrol [tɪˈrəʊl] N Tyrol m

Tyrolean [tɪrəˈliːən], **Tyrolese** [tɪrəˈliːz] ADJ tyrolien(ne) ▶ N Tyrolien(ne)

Tyrrhenian Sea [tɪˈriːnɪən-] N: **the ~** la mer Tyrrhénienne

tzar [zɑːʳ] N = **tsar**

Uu

U¹, u [juː] N (*letter*) U, u *m*; **U for Uncle** U comme Ursule

U² N ABBR (*BRIT Cine*: = *universal*) ≈ tous publics

UAW N ABBR (*US*: = *United Automobile Workers*) *syndicat des ouvriers de l'automobile*

U-bend ['juːbɛnd] N (*BRIT Aut*) coude *m*, virage *m* en épingle à cheveux; (*in pipe*) coude

uber- ['uːbəʳ-] PREFIX super-

ubiquitous [juːˈbɪkwɪtəs] ADJ doué(e) d'ubiquité, omniprésent(e)

UCAS ['juːkæs] N ABBR (*BRIT*) = **Universities and Colleges Admissions Service**

UDA N ABBR (*BRIT*) = **Ulster Defence Association**

udder ['ʌdəʳ] N pis *m*, mamelle *f*

UDR N ABBR (*BRIT*) = **Ulster Defence Regiment**

UEFA [juːˈeɪfə] N ABBR (= *Union of European Football Associations*) UEFA *f*

UFO ['juːfəʊ] N ABBR (= *unidentified flying object*) ovni *m*

Uganda [juːˈgændə] N Ouganda *m*

Ugandan [juːˈgændən] ADJ ougandais(e) ▶ N Ougandais(e)

ugh [əːh] EXCL pouah !

ugliness ['ʌglɪnɪs] N laideur *f*

★**ugly** ['ʌglɪ] ADJ laid(e), vilain(e); (*fig*) répugnant(e)

UHF ABBR (= *ultra-high frequency*) UHF

UHT ADJ ABBR (= *ultra-heat treated*) **~ milk** lait *m* UHT or longue conservation

★**UK** N ABBR = **United Kingdom**

Ukraine [juːˈkreɪn] N Ukraine *f*

Ukrainian [juːˈkreɪnɪən] ADJ ukrainien(ne) ▶ N Ukrainien(ne); (*Ling*) ukrainien *m*

ukulele [juːkəˈleɪlɪ] N ukulélé *m*

ulcer ['ʌlsəʳ] N ulcère *m*; **mouth ~** aphte *f*

Ulster ['ʌlstəʳ] N Ulster *m*

ulterior [ʌlˈtɪərɪəʳ] ADJ ultérieur(e); **~ motive** arrière-pensée *f*

ultimate ['ʌltɪmət] ADJ ultime, final(e); (*authority*) suprême ▶ N: **the ~ in luxury** le summum du luxe

ultimately ['ʌltɪmətlɪ] ADV (*at last*) en fin de compte; (*fundamentally*) finalement; (*eventually*) par la suite

ultimatum [ʌltɪˈmeɪtəm] (*pl* **ultimatums** or **ultimata** [-tə]) N ultimatum *m*

ultramarine [ʌltrəməˈriːn] N outremer *m* ▶ADJ outremer *inv*

ultrasonic [ʌltrəˈsɔnɪk] ADJ ultrasonique

ultrasound ['ʌltrəsaʊnd] N (*Med*) ultrason *m*

ultraviolet ['ʌltrəˈvaɪəlɪt] ADJ ultraviolet(te)

umbilical [ʌmbɪˈlaɪkl] ADJ: **~ cord** cordon ombilical

umbrage ['ʌmbrɪdʒ] N: **to take ~** prendre ombrage, se froisser

★**umbrella** [ʌmˈbrɛlə] N parapluie *m*; (*for sun*) parasol *m*; **under the ~ of** (*fig*) sous les auspices de; chapeauté(e) par

umlaut ['umlaʊt] N tréma *m*

umpire ['ʌmpaɪəʳ] N arbitre *m*; (*Tennis*) juge *m* de chaise ▶ VT arbitrer

umpteen [ʌmpˈtiːn] ADJ (*inf*) je ne sais combien de

umpteenth [ʌmpˈtiːnθ] ADJ (*inf*) nième, énième; **for the ~ time** pour la nième fois

UMW N ABBR (= *United Mineworkers of America*) *syndicat des mineurs*

UN N ABBR = **United Nations**

unabashed [ʌnəˈbæʃt] ADJ nullement intimidé(e)

unabated [ʌnəˈbeɪtɪd] ADJ non diminué(e)

★**unable** [ʌnˈeɪbl] ADJ: **to be ~ to** ne (pas) pouvoir, être dans l'impossibilité de; (*not capable*) être incapable de

unabridged [ʌnəˈbrɪdʒd] ADJ complet(-ète), intégral(e)

unacceptable [ʌnəkˈsɛptəbl] ADJ (*behaviour*) inadmissible; (*price, proposal*) inacceptable

unaccompanied [ʌnəˈkʌmpənɪd] ADJ (*child, lady*) non accompagné(e); (*singing, song*) sans accompagnement

unaccountable [ʌnəˈkaʊntəbl] ADJ (*inexplicable*) inexplicable; (*not accountable*) qui n'a pas à répondre de ses actes

unaccountably [ʌnəˈkaʊntəblɪ] ADV inexplicablement

unaccounted [ʌnəˈkaʊntɪd] ADJ: **two passengers are ~ for** on est sans nouvelles de deux passagers

unaccustomed [ʌnəˈkʌstəmd] ADJ inaccoutumé(e), inhabituel(le); **to be ~ to sth** ne pas avoir l'habitude de qch

unacquainted [ʌnəˈkweɪntɪd] ADJ: **to be ~ with** ne pas connaître

unadulterated [ʌnəˈdʌltəreɪtɪd] ADJ pur(e), naturel(le)

unaffected [ˌʌnəˈfɛktɪd] ADJ (person, behaviour) naturel(le); (emotionally): **to be ~ by** ne pas être touché(e) par

unafraid [ˌʌnəˈfreɪd] ADJ: **to be ~** ne pas avoir peur

unaided [ʌnˈeɪdɪd] ADJ sans aide, tout(e) seul(e)

unambiguous [ˌʌnæmˈbɪɡjuəs] ADJ sans ambiguïté

unanimity [juːnəˈnɪmɪtɪ] N unanimité f

unanimous [juːˈnænɪməs] ADJ unanime

unanimously [juːˈnænɪməslɪ] ADV à l'unanimité

unanswered [ʌnˈɑːnsəd] ADJ (question, letter) sans réponse

unappealing [ˌʌnəˈpiːlɪŋ] ADJ (ugly) laid(e); **an ~ habit** une mauvaise habitude

unappetizing [ʌnˈæpɪtaɪzɪŋ] ADJ peu appétissant(e)

unappreciative [ˌʌnəˈpriːʃɪətɪv] ADJ indifférent(e)

unarmed [ʌnˈɑːmd] ADJ (person) non armé(e); (combat) sans armes

unashamed [ˌʌnəˈʃeɪmd] ADJ sans honte; impudent(e)

unassailable [ˌʌnəˈseɪləbl] ADJ (lead) décisif(-ive); (position) inattaquable

unassisted [ˌʌnəˈsɪstɪd] ADJ non assisté(e) ▶ ADV sans aide, tout(e) seul(e)

unassuming [ˌʌnəˈsjuːmɪŋ] ADJ modeste, sans prétentions

unattached [ˌʌnəˈtætʃt] ADJ libre, sans attaches

unattainable [ˌʌnəˈteɪnəbl] ADJ inaccessible

unattended [ˌʌnəˈtɛndɪd] ADJ (car, child, luggage) sans surveillance

unattractive [ˌʌnəˈtræktɪv] ADJ peu attrayant(e); (character) peu sympathique

unauthorized [ʌnˈɔːθəraɪzd] ADJ non autorisé(e), sans autorisation

unavailable [ˌʌnəˈveɪləbl] ADJ (article, room, book) (qui n'est) pas disponible; (person) (qui n'est) pas libre

unavoidable [ˌʌnəˈvɔɪdəbl] ADJ inévitable

unavoidably [ˌʌnəˈvɔɪdəblɪ] ADV inévitablement

unaware [ˌʌnəˈwɛəʳ] ADJ: **to be ~ of** ignorer, ne pas savoir, être inconscient(e) de

unawares [ˌʌnəˈwɛəz] ADV à l'improviste, au dépourvu

unbalanced [ʌnˈbælənst] ADJ déséquilibré(e)

unbearable [ʌnˈbɛərəbl] ADJ insupportable

unbeatable [ʌnˈbiːtəbl] ADJ imbattable

unbeaten [ʌnˈbiːtn] ADJ invaincu(e); (record) non battu(e)

unbecoming [ˌʌnbɪˈkʌmɪŋ] ADJ (unseemly: language, behaviour) malséant(e), inconvenant(e); (unflattering: garment) peu seyant(e)

unbeknown [ˌʌnbɪˈnəʊn], **unbeknownst** [ˌʌnbɪˈnəʊnst] ADV: **~ to** à l'insu de

unbelief [ˌʌnbɪˈliːf] N incrédulité f

unbelievable [ˌʌnbɪˈliːvəbl] ADJ incroyable

unbelievably [ˌʌnbɪˈliːvəblɪ] ADV (fast, stupid) incroyablement; (strange to say) aussi incroyable que cela puisse paraître

unbelievingly [ˌʌnbɪˈliːvɪŋlɪ] ADV avec incrédulité

unbend [ʌnˈbɛnd] VI (irreg: like bend) se détendre ▶ VT (wire) redresser, détordre

unbending [ʌnˈbɛndɪŋ] ADJ (fig) inflexible

unbiased, unbiassed [ʌnˈbaɪəst] ADJ impartial(e)

unblemished [ʌnˈblɛmɪʃt] ADJ impeccable

unblinking [ʌnˈblɪŋkɪŋ] ADJ (eyes, stare) fixe

unblock [ʌnˈblɒk] VT (pipe) déboucher; (road) dégager

unborn [ʌnˈbɔːn] ADJ à naître

unbounded [ʌnˈbaʊndɪd] ADJ sans bornes, illimité(e)

unbreakable [ʌnˈbreɪkəbl] ADJ incassable

unbridled [ʌnˈbraɪdld] ADJ débridé(e), déchaîné(e)

unbroken [ʌnˈbrəʊkn] ADJ intact(e); (line) continu(e); (record) non battu(e)

unbuckle [ʌnˈbʌkl] VT déboucler

unburden [ʌnˈbɜːdn] VT: **to ~ o.s.** s'épancher, se livrer

unbutton [ʌnˈbʌtn] VT déboutonner

uncalled-for [ʌnˈkɔːldfɔːʳ] ADJ déplacé(e), injustifié(e)

uncanny [ʌnˈkænɪ] ADJ étrange, troublant(e)

uncaring [ʌnˈkɛərɪŋ] ADJ insensible

unceasing [ʌnˈsiːsɪŋ] ADJ incessant(e), continu(e)

unceremonious [ˌʌnsɛrɪˈməʊnɪəs] ADJ (abrupt, rude) brusque

uncertain [ʌnˈsɜːtn] ADJ incertain(e); (hesitant) hésitant(e); **we were ~ whether ...** nous ne savions pas vraiment si ...; **in no ~ terms** sans équivoque possible

uncertainty [ʌnˈsɜːtntɪ] N incertitude f, doutes mpl

unchallenged [ʌnˈtʃælɪndʒd] ADJ (gen) incontesté(e); (information) non contesté(e); **to go ~** ne pas être contesté

unchanged [ʌnˈtʃeɪndʒd] ADJ inchangé(e)

uncharacteristic [ˌʌnkærɪktəˈrɪstɪk] ADJ contraire à ses habitudes; **it was ~ of her father to disappear like this** c'était contraire aux habitudes de son père de disparaître ainsi

uncharacteristically [ˌʌnkærɪktəˈrɪstɪklɪ] ADV: **he has been ~ silent** il est resté anormalement silencieux

uncharitable [ʌnˈtʃærɪtəbl] ADJ peu charitable

uncharted [ʌnˈtʃɑːtɪd] ADJ inexploré(e)

unchecked [ʌnˈtʃɛkt] ADJ non réprimé(e)

uncivilized [ʌnˈsɪvɪlaɪzd] ADJ non civilisé(e); (fig) barbare

unclaimed [ʌnˈkleɪmd] ADJ non réclamé(e)

★**uncle** [ˈʌŋkl] N oncle m

unclear [ʌnˈklɪəʳ] ADJ (qui n'est) pas clair(e) or évident(e); **I'm still ~ about what I'm supposed to do** je ne sais pas encore exactement ce que je dois faire

uncluttered [ʌnˈklʌtəd] ADJ dépouillé(e)

uncoil [ʌnˈkɔɪl] VT dérouler ▶ VI se dérouler

★**uncomfortable** [ʌnˈkʌmfətəbl] ADJ inconfortable, peu confortable; (uneasy) mal à l'aise, gêné(e); (situation) désagréable

u

uncomfortably [ʌn'kʌmfətəblɪ] ADV inconfortablement; d'un ton *etc* gêné *or* embarrassé; désagréablement

uncommitted [ʌnkə'mɪtɪd] ADJ (*attitude, country*) non engagé(e)

uncommon [ʌn'kɔmən] ADJ rare, singulier(-ière), peu commun(e)

uncommunicative [ʌnkə'mjuːnɪkətɪv] ADJ réservé(e)

uncomplicated [ʌn'kɔmplɪkeɪtɪd] ADJ simple, peu compliqué(e)

uncompromising [ʌn'kɔmprəmaɪzɪŋ] ADJ intransigeant(e), inflexible

unconcerned [ʌnkən'səːnd] ADJ (*unworried*): **to be ~ (about)** ne pas s'inquiéter (de)

unconditional [ʌnkən'dɪʃənl] ADJ sans condition(s)

unconditionally [ʌnkən'dɪʃənlɪ] ADV sans condition(s)

uncongenial [ʌnkən'dʒiːnɪəl] ADJ peu agréable

unconnected [ʌnkə'nɛktɪd] ADJ (*unrelated*): **~ (with)** sans rapport (avec)

unconscious [ʌn'kɔnʃəs] ADJ sans connaissance, évanoui(e); (*unaware*): **~ (of)** inconscient(e) (de); **to knock sb ~** assommer qn ▶ N: **the ~** l'inconscient *m*

unconsciously [ʌn'kɔnʃəslɪ] ADV inconsciemment

unconstitutional [ʌnkɔnstɪ'tjuːʃənl] ADJ anticonstitutionnel(le)

uncontested [ʌnkən'tɛstɪd] ADJ (*champion*) incontesté(e); (*Pol: seat*) non disputé(e)

uncontrollable [ʌnkən'trəuləbl] ADJ incontrôlable

uncontrollably [ʌnkən'trəuləblɪ] ADV: **to shake ~** être pris(e) de tremblements incontrôlables

uncontrolled [ʌnkən'trəuld] ADJ (*laughter, price rises*) incontrôlé(e)

unconventional [ʌnkən'vɛnʃənl] ADJ peu conventionnel(le)

unconvinced [ʌnkən'vɪnst] ADJ: **to be ~** ne pas être convaincu(e)

unconvincing [ʌnkən'vɪnsɪŋ] ADJ peu convaincant(e)

uncooperative [ʌnkəu'ɔpərətɪv] ADJ qui refuse de coopérer

uncork [ʌn'kɔːk] VT déboucher

uncorroborated [ʌnkə'rɔbəreɪtɪd] ADJ non confirmé(e)

uncouth [ʌn'kuːθ] ADJ grossier(-ière), fruste

uncover [ʌn'kʌvəʳ] VT découvrir

unctuous [ʌ'ŋktjuəs] ADJ onctueux(-euse), mielleux(-euse)

undamaged [ʌn'dæmɪdʒd] ADJ (*goods*) intact(e), en bon état; (*fig: reputation*) intact

undaunted [ʌn'dɔːntɪd] ADJ non intimidé(e), inébranlable

undecided [ʌndɪ'saɪdɪd] ADJ indécis(e), irrésolu(e)

undefeated [ʌndɪ'fiːtɪd] ADJ (*team, player*) invaincu(e)

undelivered [ʌndɪ'lɪvəd] ADJ non remis(e), non livré(e)

undemanding [ʌndɪ'mɑːndɪŋ] ADJ (*not challenging: job*) peu exigeant(e); (: *book, film*) facile; (*person*) accommodant(e)

undemocratic [ʌndɛmə'krætɪk] ADJ antidémocratique

undeniable [ʌndɪ'naɪəbl] ADJ indéniable, incontestable

undeniably [ʌndɪ'naɪəblɪ] ADV (*true, difficult*) indéniablement; **~ beautiful** d'une beauté indéniable

★**under** ['ʌndəʳ] PREP sous; (*less than*) (de) moins de; au-dessous de; (*according to*) selon, en vertu de; **from ~ sth** de dessous *or* de sous qch; **~ there** là-dessous; **in ~ 2 hours** en moins de 2 heures; **~ anaesthetic** sous anesthésie; **~ discussion** en discussion; **~ the circumstances** étant donné les circonstances; **~ repair** en (cours de) réparation ▶ ADV au-dessous; en dessous

under... ['ʌndəʳ] PREFIX sous-

underage [ʌndər'eɪdʒ] ADJ qui n'a pas l'âge réglementaire

underarm ['ʌndərɑːm] ADV par en-dessous ▶ ADJ (*throw*) par en-dessous; (*deodorant*) pour les aisselles

undercapitalized [ʌndə'kæpɪtəlaɪzd] ADJ souscapitalisé(e)

undercarriage ['ʌndəkærɪdʒ] N (BRIT Aviat) train *m* d'atterrissage

undercharge [ʌndə'tʃɑːdʒ] VT ne pas faire payer assez à

underclass ['ʌndəklɑːs] N ≈ quart-monde *m*

underclothes ['ʌndəkləuðz] NPL sous-vêtements *mpl*; (*women's only*) dessous *mpl*

undercoat ['ʌndəkəut] N (*paint*) couche *f* de fond

undercover [ʌndə'kʌvəʳ] ADJ secret(-ète), clandestin(e)

undercurrent ['ʌndəkʌrnt] N courant sous-jacent

undercut [ʌndə'kʌt] VT (*irreg: like* cut) vendre moins cher que

underdeveloped ['ʌndədɪvɛləpt] ADJ sousdéveloppé(e)

underdog ['ʌndədɔg] N opprimé *m*

underdone [ʌndə'dʌn] ADJ (Culin) saignant(e); (: *pej*) pas assez cuit(e)

underemployed [ʌndərɪm'plɔɪd] ADJ sousemployé(e)

underestimate ['ʌndər'ɛstɪmeɪt] VT sous-estimer, mésestimer

underexposed ['ʌndərɪks'pəuzd] ADJ (Phot) sousexposé(e)

underfed [ʌndə'fɛd] ADJ sous-alimenté(e)

underfoot [ʌndə'fut] ADV sous les pieds

under-funded ['ʌndə'fʌndɪd] ADJ: **to be ~** (*organization*) ne pas être doté(e) de fonds suffisants

undergo [ʌndə'gəu] VT (*irreg: like* go) subir; (*treatment*) suivre; **the car is undergoing repairs** la voiture est en réparation

undergraduate [ʌndə'grædjuɪt] N étudiant(e) (qui prépare la licence) ▶ CPD: **~ courses** cours *mpl* préparant à la licence

★**underground** ['ʌndəgraund] ADJ souterrain(e); (*fig*) clandestin(e) ▶ N (BRIT: *railway*) métro *m*; (*Pol*) clandestinité *f*

undergrowth ['ʌndəɡrəʊθ] N broussailles *fpl*, sous-bois *m*

underhand [ʌndə'hænd], **underhanded** [ʌndə'hændɪd] ADJ *(fig)* sournois(e), en dessous

underinsured [ʌndərɪn'ʃuəd] ADJ sous-assuré(e)

underlay N ['ʌndəleɪ] *(BRIT)* sous-couche *f* d'isolation ▶ PT [ʌndə'leɪ] *of* **underlie**

underlie [ʌndə'laɪ] VT *(irreg: like* **lie**) être à la base de; **the underlying cause** la cause sous-jacente

underline [ʌndə'laɪn] VT souligner

underling ['ʌndəlɪŋ] N *(pej)* sous-fifre *m*, subalterne *m*

undermanning [ʌndə'mænɪŋ] N pénurie *f* de main-d'œuvre

undermentioned [ʌndə'mɛnʃənd] ADJ mentionné(e) ci-dessous

undermine [ʌndə'maɪn] VT saper, miner

underneath [ʌndə'niːθ] ADV (en) dessous ▶ PREP sous, au-dessous de

undernourished [ʌndə'nʌrɪʃt] ADJ sous-alimenté(e)

underpaid [ʌndə'peɪd] ADJ sous-payé(e)

underpants ['ʌndəpænts] NPL caleçon *m*, slip *m*

underpass ['ʌndəpɑːs] N *(BRIT: for pedestrians)* passage souterrain; *(: for cars)* passage inférieur

underpin [ʌndə'pɪn] VT *(argument, case)* étayer

underplay [ʌndə'pleɪ] VT *(BRIT)* minimiser

underpopulated [ʌndə'pɒpjuleɪtɪd] ADJ sous-peuplé(e)

underprice [ʌndə'praɪs] VT vendre à un prix trop bas

underprivileged [ʌndə'prɪvɪlɪdʒd] ADJ défavorisé(e)

underrate [ʌndə'reɪt] VT sous-estimer, mésestimer

underscore [ʌndə'skɔːʳ] VT souligner

underseal [ʌndə'siːl] VT *(BRIT)* traiter contre la rouille

undersecretary ['ʌndə'sɛkrətrɪ] N sous-secrétaire *m*

undersell [ʌndə'sɛl] VT *(irreg: like* **sell**) *(competitors)* vendre moins cher que

undershirt ['ʌndəʃəːt] N *(US)* tricot *m* de corps

undershorts ['ʌndəʃɔːts] NPL *(US)* caleçon *m*, slip *m*

underside ['ʌndəsaɪd] N dessous *m*

undersigned ['ʌndəsaɪnd] ADJ, N soussigné(e)

underskirt ['ʌndəskəːt] N *(BRIT)* jupon *m*

understaffed [ʌndə'stɑːft] ADJ en sous-effectif

understaffing [ʌndə'stɑːfɪŋ] N sous-effectif *m*

★**understand** [ʌndə'stænd] VT, VI *(irreg: like* **stand**) comprendre; **I don't ~** je ne comprends pas; **I ~ that ...** je me suis laissé dire que ..., je crois comprendre que ...; **to make o.s. understood** se faire comprendre

understandable [ʌndə'stændəbl] ADJ compréhensible

understandably [ʌndə'stændəblɪ] ADV on le comprend

★**understanding** [ʌndə'stændɪŋ] ADJ compréhensif(-ive) ▶ N compréhension *f*; *(agreement)* accord *m*; **to come to an ~ with sb** s'entendre avec qn; **on the ~ that ...** à condition que ...

understate [ʌndə'steɪt] VT minimiser

understatement ['ʌndəsteɪtmənt] N: **that's an ~** c'est (bien) peu dire, le terme est faible

understood [ʌndə'stud] PT, PP *of* **understand** ▶ ADJ entendu(e); *(implied)* sous-entendu(e)

understudy ['ʌndəstʌdɪ] N doublure *f*

undertake [ʌndə'teɪk] VT *(irreg: like* **take**) *(job, task)* entreprendre; *(duty)* se charger de; **to ~ to do sth** s'engager à faire qch

undertaker ['ʌndəteɪkəʳ] N *(BRIT)* entrepreneur *m* des pompes funèbres, croque-mort *m*

undertaking ['ʌndəteɪkɪŋ] N entreprise *f*; *(promise)* promesse *f*

undertone ['ʌndətəun] N *(low voice)*: **in an ~** à mi-voix; *(of criticism etc)* nuance cachée

undervalue [ʌndə'væljuː] VT sous-estimer

underwater [ʌndə'wɔːtəʳ] ADV sous l'eau ▶ ADJ sous-marin(e)

underway [ʌndə'weɪ] ADJ: **to be ~** *(meeting, investigation)* être en cours

★**underwear** ['ʌndəwɛəʳ] N sous-vêtements *mpl*; *(women's only)* dessous *mpl*

underweight [ʌndə'weɪt] ADJ d'un poids insuffisant; *(person)* (trop) maigre

underwent [ʌndə'wɛnt] PT *of* **undergo**

underwhelmed [ʌndə'wɛlmd] ADJ *(hum)* pas (particulièrement) impressionné(e)

underworld ['ʌndəwəːld] N *(of crime)* milieu *m*, pègre *f*

underwrite [ʌndə'raɪt] VT *(irreg: like* **write**) *(Finance)* garantir; *(Insurance)* souscrire

underwriter ['ʌndəraɪtəʳ] N *(Insurance)* souscripteur *m*

undeserved [ʌndɪ'zəːvd] ADJ *(reputation)* injustifié(e), immérité(e); *(treatment)* injuste

undeserving [ʌndɪ'zəːvɪŋ] ADJ: **to be ~ of** ne pas mériter

undesirable [ʌndɪ'zaɪərəbl] ADJ peu souhaitable; *(person, effect)* indésirable

undeveloped [ʌndɪ'vɛləpt] ADJ *(land, resources)* non exploité(e)

undies ['ʌndɪz] NPL *(inf)* dessous *mpl*, lingerie *f*

undignified [ʌn'dɪɡnɪfaɪd] ADJ indigne; **to be ~** manquer de dignité

undiluted ['ʌndaɪ'luːtɪd] ADJ pur(e), non dilué(e)

undiplomatic ['ʌndɪplə'mætɪk] ADJ peu diplomatique, maladroit(e)

undischarged ['ʌndɪs'tʃɑːdʒd] ADJ: **~ bankrupt** failli non réhabilité(e)

undisciplined [ʌn'dɪsɪplɪnd] ADJ indiscipliné(e)

undisclosed ['ʌndɪs'kləuzd] ADJ *(sum, address)* non communiqué(e)

undisguised ['ʌndɪs'ɡaɪzd] ADJ *(dislike, amusement etc)* franc (franche)

undisputed ['ʌndɪs'pjuːtɪd] ADJ incontesté(e)

undistinguished ['ʌndɪs'tɪŋɡwɪʃt] ADJ médiocre, quelconque

undisturbed [ʌndɪs'təːbd] ADJ *(sleep)* tranquille, paisible; **to leave ~** ne pas déranger

undivided [ʌndɪ'vaɪdɪd] ADJ: **can I have your ~ attention?** puis-je avoir toute votre attention ?

undo [ʌn'duː] VT *(irreg: like* **do**) défaire

undoing [ʌn'duːɪŋ] N ruine f, perte f

undone [ʌn'dʌn] PP of **undo** ▸ ADJ: **to come ~** se défaire

undoubted [ʌn'dautɪd] ADJ indubitable, certain(e)

undoubtedly [ʌn'dautɪdlɪ] ADV sans aucun doute

undress [ʌn'drɛs] VI se déshabiller ▸ VT déshabiller

undrinkable [ʌn'drɪŋkəbl] ADJ (unpalatable) imbuvable; (poisonous) non potable

undue [ʌn'djuː] ADJ indu(e), excessif(-ive)

undulating ['ʌndjuleɪtɪŋ] ADJ ondoyant(e), onduleux(-euse)

unduly [ʌn'djuːlɪ] ADV trop, excessivement

undying [ʌn'daɪɪŋ] ADJ éternel(le)

unearned [ʌn'əːnd] ADJ (praise, respect) immérité(e); **~ income** rentes fpl

unearth [ʌn'əːθ] VT déterrer; (fig) dénicher

unearthly [ʌn'əːθlɪ] ADJ surnaturel(le); (hour) indu(e), impossible

unease [ʌn'iːz] N malaise m; **growing ~** un malaise croissant

uneasy [ʌn'iːzɪ] ADJ mal à l'aise, gêné(e); (worried) inquiet(-ète); (feeling) désagréable; (peace, truce) fragile; **to feel ~ about doing sth** se sentir mal à l'aise à l'idée de faire qch

uneconomic ['ʌniːkə'nɔmɪk], **uneconomical** ['ʌniːkə'nɔmɪkl] ADJ peu économique; peu rentable

uneducated [ʌn'ɛdjukeɪtɪd] ADJ sans éducation

unemotional [ʌnɪ'məʊʃənl] ADJ (person) impassible; (voice) qui ne trahit aucune émotion

unemployable [ʌnɪm'plɔɪəbl] ADJ inemployable

★**unemployed** [ʌnɪm'plɔɪd] ADJ sans travail, au chômage ▸ NPL: **the ~** les chômeurs mpl

★**unemployment** [ʌnɪm'plɔɪmənt] N chômage m

unemployment benefit, (US) **unemployment compensation** N allocation f de chômage

unending [ʌn'ɛndɪŋ] ADJ interminable

unenviable [ʌn'ɛnvɪəbl] ADJ peu enviable

unequal [ʌn'iːkwəl] ADJ inégal(e)

unequalled, (US) **unequaled** [ʌn'iːkwəld] ADJ inégalé(e)

unequivocal [ʌnɪ'kwɪvəkl] ADJ (answer) sans équivoque; (person) catégorique

unequivocally [ʌnɪ'kwɪvəklɪ] ADV sans équivoque

unerring [ʌn'əːrɪŋ] ADJ infaillible, sûr(e)

UNESCO [juː'nɛskəʊ] N ABBR (= United Nations Educational, Scientific and Cultural Organization) UNESCO f

unethical [ʌn'ɛθɪkl] ADJ (methods) immoral(e); (doctor's behaviour) qui ne respecte pas l'éthique

uneven [ʌn'iːvn] ADJ inégal(e); (quality, work) irrégulier(-ière)

uneventful [ʌnɪ'vɛntful] ADJ tranquille, sans histoires

unexceptional [ʌnɪk'sɛpʃənl] ADJ banal(e), quelconque

unexciting [ʌnɪk'saɪtɪŋ] ADJ pas passionnant(e)

★**unexpected** [ʌnɪk'spɛktɪd] ADJ inattendu(e), imprévu(e)

unexpectedly [ʌnɪk'spɛktɪdlɪ] ADV (succeed) contre toute attente; (arrive) à l'improviste

unexplained [ʌnɪk'spleɪnd] ADJ inexpliqué(e)

unexploded [ʌnɪk'spləʊdɪd] ADJ non explosé(e) or éclaté(e)

unfailing [ʌn'feɪlɪŋ] ADJ (generosity, kindness) inépuisable; (regularity) infaillible

unfailingly [ʌn'feɪlɪŋlɪ] ADV immanquablement; **he was ~ polite to customers** il était d'une politesse à toute épreuve avec les clients

★**unfair** [ʌn'fɛəʳ] ADJ: **~ (to)** injuste (envers); **it's ~ that …** il n'est pas juste que …

unfair dismissal N licenciement abusif

unfairly [ʌn'fɛəlɪ] ADV injustement

unfairness [ʌn'fɛənɪs] N injustice f

unfaithful [ʌn'feɪθful] ADJ infidèle

unfamiliar [ʌnfə'mɪlɪəʳ] ADJ étrange, inconnu(e); **to be ~ with sth** mal connaître qch

unfashionable [ʌn'fæʃnəbl] ADJ (clothes) démodé(e); (place) peu chic inv; (district) déshérité(e), pas à la mode

unfasten [ʌn'fɑːsn] VT défaire; (belt, necklace) détacher; (open) ouvrir

unfathomable [ʌn'fæðəməbl] ADJ insondable

unfavourable, (US) **unfavorable** [ʌn'feɪvrəbl] ADJ défavorable

unfavourably, (US) **unfavorably** [ʌn'feɪvrəblɪ] ADV: **to look ~ upon** ne pas être favorable à

unfeeling [ʌn'fiːlɪŋ] ADJ insensible, dur(e)

unfinished [ʌn'fɪnɪʃt] ADJ inachevé(e)

unfit [ʌn'fɪt] ADJ (physically: ill) en mauvaise santé; (: out of condition) pas en forme; (incompetent): **~ (for)** impropre (à); (work, service) inapte (à)

unflagging [ʌn'flægɪŋ] ADJ infatigable, inlassable

unflappable [ʌn'flæpəbl] ADJ imperturbable

unflattering [ʌn'flætərɪŋ] ADJ (dress, hairstyle) qui n'avantage pas; (remark) peu flatteur(-euse)

unflinching [ʌn'flɪntʃɪŋ] ADJ stoïque

unfold [ʌn'fəʊld] VT déplier; (fig) révéler, exposer ▸ VI se dérouler

unfollow [ʌn'fɒləʊ] VT (on social media) cesser de suivre

unforeseeable [ʌnfɔː'siːəbl] ADJ imprévisible

unforeseen ['ʌnfɔː'siːn] ADJ imprévu(e)

unforgettable [ʌnfə'gɛtəbl] ADJ inoubliable

unforgivable [ʌnfə'gɪvəbl] ADJ impardonnable

unforgiving [ʌnfə'gɪvɪŋ] ADJ sans merci

unformatted [ʌn'fɔːmætɪd] ADJ (disk, text) non formaté(e)

unfortunate [ʌn'fɔːtʃnət] ADJ malheureux(-euse); (event, remark) malencontreux(-euse)

★**unfortunately** [ʌn'fɔːtʃnətlɪ] ADV malheureusement

unfounded [ʌn'faundɪd] ADJ sans fondement

unfriend [ʌn'frɛnd] VT (Internet) supprimer de sa liste d'amis

unfriendly [ʌn'frɛndlɪ] ADJ peu aimable, froid(e), inamical(e)

unfulfilled [ʌnful'fɪld] ADJ (ambition, prophecy) non réalisé(e); (desire) insatisfait(e); (promise) non tenu(e); (terms of contract) non rempli(e); (person) qui n'a pas su se réaliser

unfurl [ʌn'fɜ:l] vt déployer

unfurnished [ʌn'fɜ:nɪʃt] ADJ non meublé(e)

ungainly [ʌn'geɪnlɪ] ADJ gauche, dégingandé(e)

ungodly [ʌn'gɒdlɪ] ADJ impie; **at an ~ hour** à une heure indue

ungrateful [ʌn'greɪtful] ADJ qui manque de reconnaissance, ingrat(e)

unguarded [ʌn'gɑːdɪd] ADJ: **~ moment** moment *m* d'inattention

unhappily [ʌn'hæpɪlɪ] ADV tristement; (*unfortunately*) malheureusement

unhappiness [ʌn'hæpɪnɪs] N tristesse *f*, peine *f*

★**unhappy** [ʌn'hæpɪ] ADJ triste, malheureux(-euse); (*unfortunate: remark etc*) malheureux(-euse); (*not pleased*): **~ with** mécontent(e) de, peu satisfait(e) de

unharmed [ʌn'hɑːmd] ADJ indemne, sain(e) et sauf (sauve)

UNHCR N ABBR (= *United Nations High Commission for Refugees*) HCR *m*

unhealthy [ʌn'hɛlθɪ] ADJ (*gen*) malsain(e); (*person*) maladif(-ive)

unheard-of [ʌn'hɜːdɒv] ADJ inouï(e), sans précédent

unheeded [ʌn'hiːdɪd] ADJ resté(e) lettre morte; **to go ~** rester lettre morte

unhelpful [ʌn'hɛlpful] ADJ (*person*) peu serviable; (*advice*) peu utile

unhesitating [ʌn'hɛzɪteɪtɪŋ] ADJ (*loyalty*) spontané(e); (*reply, offer*) immédiat(e)

unhesitatingly [ʌn'hɛzɪteɪtɪŋlɪ] ADV sans hésitation

unholy [ʌn'həulɪ] ADJ: **an ~ alliance** une alliance contre nature; **he got home at an ~ hour** il est rentré à une heure impossible

unhook [ʌn'huk] vt décrocher; dégrafer

unhurt [ʌn'hɜːt] ADJ indemne, sain(e) et sauf (sauve)

unhygienic ['ʌnhaɪ'dʒiːnɪk] ADJ antihygiénique

UNICEF ['juːnɪsɛf] N ABBR (= *United Nations International Children's Emergency Fund*) UNICEF *m*, FISE *m*

unicorn ['juːnɪkɔːn] N licorne *f*

unidentified [ʌnaɪ'dɛntɪfaɪd] ADJ non identifié(e); *see also* **UFO**

unification [juːnɪfɪ'keɪʃən] N unification *f*

★**uniform** ['juːnɪfɔːm] N uniforme *m* ▶ ADJ uniforme

uniformity [juːnɪ'fɔːmɪtɪ] N uniformité *f*

unify ['juːnɪfaɪ] vt unifier

unilateral [juːnɪ'lætərəl] ADJ unilatéral(e)

unilaterally [juːnɪ'lætərəlɪ] ADV unilatéralement

unimaginable [ʌnɪ'mædʒɪnəbl] ADJ inimaginable, inconcevable

unimaginative [ʌnɪ'mædʒɪnətɪv] ADJ sans imagination

unimpaired [ʌnɪm'pɛəd] ADJ intact(e)

unimportant [ʌnɪm'pɔːtənt] ADJ sans importance

unimpressed [ʌnɪm'prɛst] ADJ pas impressionné(e)

unimpressive [ʌnɪm'prɛsɪv] ADJ quelconque

uninhabited [ʌnɪn'hæbɪtɪd] ADJ inhabité(e)

uninhibited [ʌnɪn'hɪbɪtɪd] ADJ sans inhibitions; sans retenue

uninitiated [ʌnɪ'nɪʃɪeɪtɪd] NPL: **the ~** les non-initiés *mpl* ▶ ADJ non initié(e); **those ~ in sth** les non-initiés à qch

uninjured [ʌn'ɪndʒəd] ADJ indemne

uninspiring [ʌnɪn'spaɪərɪŋ] ADJ peu inspirant(e)

uninstall ['ʌnɪnstɔːl] vt (*Comput*) désinstaller

unintelligent [ʌnɪn'tɛlɪdʒənt] ADJ inintelligent(e)

unintelligible [ʌnɪn'tɛlɪdʒɪbl] ADJ inintelligible

unintended [ʌnɪn'tɛndɪd] ADJ non désiré(e)

unintentional [ʌnɪn'tɛnʃənəl] ADJ involontaire

unintentionally [ʌnɪn'tɛnʃnəlɪ] ADV sans le vouloir

uninterrupted [ʌnɪntə'rʌptɪd] ADJ (*continuous*) ininterrompu(e); (*clear*): **an ~ view of sth** une vue dégagée sur qch; **to continue ~** continuer sans interruption

uninvited [ʌnɪn'vaɪtɪd] ADJ (*guest*) qui n'a pas été invité(e)

uninviting [ʌnɪn'vaɪtɪŋ] ADJ (*place*) peu attirant(e); (*food*) peu appétissant(e)

union ['juːnjən] N union *f*; (*also*: **trade union**) syndicat *m* ▶ CPD du syndicat, syndical(e)

unionism ['juːnjənɪzəm] N (*Pol*) unionisme *m*; (*also*: **trade unionism**) syndicalisme *m*

unionize ['juːnjənaɪz] vt syndiquer

Union Jack N drapeau du Royaume-Uni

Union of Soviet Socialist Republics N (*formerly*) Union *f* des républiques socialistes soviétiques

union shop N entreprise où tous les travailleurs doivent être syndiqués

unique [juː'niːk] ADJ unique

uniquely [juː'niːklɪ] ADV (*exclusively*) uniquement; **~ among** cas unique parmi, à la différence des autres; **to be ~ qualified to do sth** être le (la) mieux apte à faire qch

uniqueness [juː'niːknɪs] N singularité *f*

unisex ['juːnɪsɛks] ADJ unisexe

Unison ['juːnɪsn] N (*trade union*) grand syndicat des services publics en Grande-Bretagne

unison ['juːnɪsn] N: **in ~** à l'unisson, en chœur

unit ['juːnɪt] N unité *f*; (*section: of furniture etc*) élément *m*, bloc *m*; (*team, squad*) groupe *m*, service *m*; **production ~** atelier *m* de fabrication; **kitchen ~** élément de cuisine; **sink ~** bloc-évier *m*

unit cost N coût *m* unitaire

unite [juː'naɪt] vt unir ▶ vi s'unir

united [juː'naɪtɪd] ADJ uni(e); (*country, party*) unifié(e); (*efforts*) conjugué(e)

United Arab Emirates NPL Émirats Arabes Unis

★**United Kingdom** N Royaume-Uni *m*

United Nations (Organization) N (Organisation *f* des) Nations unies

★**United States (of America)** N États-Unis *mpl*

unit price N prix *m* unitaire

unit trust N (*BRIT Comm*) fonds commun de placement, FCP *m*

unity ['juːnɪtɪ] N unité *f*

u

Univ. ABBR = **university**

universal [juːnɪ'vɜːsl] ADJ universel(le)

universally [juːnɪ'vɜːsəlɪ] ADV (by everyone) universellement, par tous; (everywhere) partout; (always) toujours

★**universe** ['juːnɪvɜːs] N univers m

★**university** [juːnɪ'vɜːsɪtɪ] N université f ▶ CPD (student, professor) d'université; (education, year, degree) universitaire

unjust [ʌn'dʒʌst] ADJ injuste

unjustifiable ['ʌndʒʌstɪ'faɪəbl] ADJ injustifiable

unjustified [ʌn'dʒʌstɪfaɪd] ADJ injustifié(e); (text) non justifié(e)

unkempt [ʌn'kempt] ADJ mal tenu(e), débraillé(e); mal peigné(e)

unkind [ʌn'kaɪnd] ADJ peu gentil(le), méchant(e)

unkindly [ʌn'kaɪndlɪ] ADV (treat, speak) avec méchanceté

unknown [ʌn'nəun] ADJ inconnu(e); ~ **to me** sans que je le sache; ~ **quantity** (Math, fig) inconnue f

unladen [ʌn'leɪdn] ADJ (ship, weight) à vide

unlawful [ʌn'lɔːful] ADJ illégal(e)

unlawfully [ʌn'lɔːfulɪ] ADV illégalement

unleaded [ʌn'ledɪd] N (also: **unleaded petrol**) essence f sans plomb

unleash [ʌn'liːʃ] VT détacher; (fig) déchaîner, déclencher

unleavened [ʌn'levnd] ADJ sans levain

★**unless** [ʌn'les] CONJ: ~ **he leaves** à moins qu'il (ne) parte; ~ **we leave** à moins de partir, à moins que nous (ne) partions; ~ **otherwise stated** sauf indication contraire; ~ **I am mistaken** si je ne me trompe

unlicensed [ʌn'laɪsnst] ADJ (BRIT) non patenté(e) pour la vente des spiritueux

unlike [ʌn'laɪk] ADJ dissemblable, différent(e) ▶ PREP à la différence de, contrairement à

unlikelihood [ʌn'laɪklɪhud] N improbabilité f

★**unlikely** [ʌn'laɪklɪ] ADJ (result, event) improbable; (explanation) invraisemblable

unlimited [ʌn'lɪmɪtɪd] ADJ illimité(e)

unlisted ['ʌn'lɪstɪd] ADJ (US Tel) sur la liste rouge; (Stock Exchange) non coté(e) en Bourse

unlit [ʌn'lɪt] ADJ (room) non éclairé(e)

unload [ʌn'ləud] VT décharger

unlock [ʌn'lɔk] VT ouvrir

unloved [ʌn'lʌvd] ADJ mal aimé(e); **to feel** ~ ne pas se sentir aimé(e)

★**unlucky** [ʌn'lʌkɪ] ADJ (person) malchanceux(-euse); (object, number) qui porte malheur; **to be** ~ (person) ne pas avoir de chance

unmade [ʌn'meɪd] ADJ (bed) défait(e)

unmanageable [ʌn'mænɪdʒəbl] ADJ (unwieldy: tool, vehicle) peu maniable; (: situation) inextricable

unmanned [ʌn'mænd] ADJ sans équipage

unmannerly [ʌn'mænəlɪ] ADJ mal élevé(e), impoli(e)

unmarked [ʌn'mɑːkt] ADJ (unstained) sans marque; ~ **police car** voiture de police banalisée

unmarried [ʌn'mærɪd] ADJ célibataire

unmask [ʌn'mɑːsk] VT démasquer

unmatched [ʌn'mætʃt] ADJ sans égal(e)

unmentionable [ʌn'menʃnəbl] ADJ (topic) dont on ne parle pas; (word) qui ne se dit pas

unmerciful [ʌn'mɜːsɪful] ADJ sans pitié

unmistakable, unmistakeable [ʌnmɪs'teɪkəbl] ADJ (voice, sound, smell) caractéristique, reconnaissable entre tous (toutes)

unmistakably, unmistakeably [ʌnmɪs'teɪkəblɪ] ADV de toute évidence

unmitigated [ʌn'mɪtɪgeɪtɪd] ADJ non mitigé(e), absolu(e), pur(e)

unmoved [ʌn'muːvd] ADJ impassible; **to remain ~ by sth** rester de marbre face à qch

unnamed [ʌn'neɪmd] ADJ (nameless) sans nom; (anonymous) anonyme

unnatural [ʌn'nætʃrəl] ADJ non naturel(le); (perversion) contre nature

unnecessarily [ʌnnesə'serɪlɪ] ADV inutilement

unnecessary [ʌn'nesəsərɪ] ADJ inutile, superflu(e)

unnerve [ʌn'nɜːv] VT faire perdre son sang-froid à

unnerving [ʌn'nɜːvɪŋ] ADJ (experience) troublant(e); (habit) déconcertant(e)

unnoticed [ʌn'nəutɪst] ADJ inaperçu(e); **to go ~** passer inaperçu

UNO ['juːnəu] N ABBR = **United Nations Organization**

unobservant [ʌnəb'zɜːvnt] ADJ pas observateur(-trice)

unobtainable [ʌnəb'teɪnəbl] ADJ (Tel) impossible à obtenir

unobtrusive [ʌnəb'truːsiv] ADJ discret(-ète)

unoccupied [ʌn'ɔkjupaɪd] ADJ (seat, table, Mil) libre; (house) inoccupé(e)

unofficial [ʌnə'fɪʃl] ADJ (news) officieux(-euse), non officiel(le); (strike) ≈ sauvage

unopened [ʌn'əupənd] ADJ (bottle, envelope) non ouvert(e); **she put the letters aside ~** elle mit les lettres de côté sans les ouvrir

unopposed [ʌnə'pəuzd] ADJ sans opposition

unorthodox [ʌn'ɔːθədɔks] ADJ peu orthodoxe

unpack [ʌn'pæk] VI défaire sa valise, déballer ses affaires ▶ VT (suitcase) défaire; (belongings) déballer

unpaid [ʌn'peɪd] ADJ (bill) impayé(e); (holiday) non-payé(e), sans salaire; (work) non rétribué(e); (worker) bénévole

unpalatable [ʌn'pælətəbl] ADJ (truth) désagréable (à entendre)

unparalleled [ʌn'pærəleld] ADJ incomparable, sans égal

unpardonable [ʌn'pɑːdənəbl] ADJ impardonnable

unpatriotic ['ʌnpætrɪ'ɔtɪk] ADJ (person) manquant de patriotisme; (speech, attitude) antipatriotique

unpick [ʌn'pɪk] VT (seam) défaire; (fig: argument) démêler

unplanned [ʌn'plænd] ADJ (visit) imprévu(e); (baby) non prévu(e)

unpleasant [ʌn'pleznt] ADJ déplaisant(e), désagréable

unplug [ʌn'plʌg] VT débrancher

unpolluted [ʌnpə'luːtɪd] ADJ non pollué(e)

unpopular [ʌn'pɔpjələʳ] ADJ impopulaire; **to make o.s. ~ (with)** se rendre impopulaire (auprès de)

unprecedented [ʌn'prɛsɪdɛntɪd] ADJ sans précédent

unpredictable [ʌnprɪ'dɪktəbl] ADJ imprévisible

unprejudiced [ʌn'prɛdʒudɪst] ADJ (*not biased*) impartial(e); (*having no prejudices*) qui n'a pas de préjugés

unprepared [ʌnprɪ'pɛəd] ADJ (*person*) qui n'est pas suffisamment préparé(e); (*speech*) improvisé(e)

unprepossessing ['ʌnpriːpə'zɛsɪŋ] ADJ peu avenant(e)

unpretentious [ʌnprɪ'tɛnʃəs] ADJ sans prétention(s)

unprincipled [ʌn'prɪnsɪpld] ADJ sans principes

unproductive [ʌnprə'dʌktɪv] ADJ improductif(-ive); (*discussion*) stérile

unprofessional [ʌnprə'fɛʃənl] ADJ (*conduct*) contraire à la déontologie

unprofitable [ʌn'prɔfɪtəbl] ADJ non rentable

unprotected ['ʌnprə'tɛktɪd] ADJ (*sex*) non protégé(e)

unproven [ʌn'pruːvən, ʌn'prəuvən], **unproved** [ʌn'pruːvd] ADJ non prouvé(e)

unprovoked [ʌnprə'vəukt] ADJ (*attack*) sans provocation

unpublished [ʌn'pʌblɪʃt] ADJ (*book, letter*) inédit(e), non publié(e); (*report*) non publié(e)

unpunished [ʌn'pʌnɪʃt] ADJ impuni(e); **to go ~** rester impuni

unqualified [ʌn'kwɔlɪfaɪd] ADJ (*teacher*) non diplômé(e), sans titres; (*success*) sans réserve, total(e); (*disaster*) total(e)

unquestionably [ʌn'kwɛstʃənəblɪ] ADV incontestablement

unquestioning [ʌn'kwɛstʃənɪŋ] ADJ (*obedience, acceptance*) inconditionnel(le)

unravel [ʌn'rævl] VT démêler

unreal [ʌn'rɪəl] ADJ irréel(le); (*extraordinary*) incroyable

unrealistic ['ʌnrɪə'lɪstɪk] ADJ (*idea*) irréaliste; (*estimate*) peu réaliste

unreasonable [ʌn'riːznəbl] ADJ qui n'est pas raisonnable; **to make ~ demands on sb** exiger trop de qn

unrecognizable [ʌn'rɛkəgnaɪzəbl] ADJ pas reconnaissable

unrecognized [ʌn'rɛkəgnaɪzd] ADJ (*talent, genius*) méconnu(e); (*Pol: régime*) non reconnu(e)

unrecorded [ʌnrɪ'kɔːdɪd] ADJ non enregistré(e)

unrefined [ʌnrɪ'faɪnd] ADJ (*sugar, petroleum*) non raffiné(e)

unrehearsed [ʌnrɪ'həːst] ADJ (*Theat etc*) qui n'a pas été répété(e); (*spontaneous*) spontané(e)

unrelated [ʌnrɪ'leɪtɪd] ADJ sans rapport; (*people*) sans lien de parenté

unrelenting [ʌnrɪ'lɛntɪŋ] ADJ implacable; acharné(e)

unreliable [ʌnrɪ'laɪəbl] ADJ sur qui (*or* quoi) on ne peut pas compter, peu fiable

unrelieved [ʌnrɪ'liːvd] ADJ (*monotony*) constant(e), uniforme

unremarkable [ʌnrɪ'mɑːkəbl] ADJ quelconque

unremitting [ʌnrɪ'mɪtɪŋ] ADJ inlassable, infatigable, acharné(e)

unrepeatable [ʌnrɪ'piːtəbl] ADJ (*offer*) unique, exceptionnel(le)

unrepentant [ʌnrɪ'pɛntənt] ADJ impénitent(e)

unrepresentative ['ʌnrɛprɪ'zɛntətɪv] ADJ: **~ (of)** peu représentatif(-ive) (de)

unreserved [ʌnrɪ'zəːvd] ADJ (*seat*) non réservé(e); (*approval, admiration*) sans réserve

unreservedly [ʌnrɪ'zəːvɪdlɪ] ADV sans réserve

unresponsive [ʌnrɪs'pɔnsɪv] ADJ insensible

unrest [ʌn'rɛst] N agitation *f*, troubles *mpl*

unrestricted [ʌnrɪ'strɪktɪd] ADJ illimité(e); **to have ~ access to** avoir librement accès *or* accès en tout temps à

unrewarded [ʌnrɪ'wɔːdɪd] ADJ pas récompensé(e)

unripe [ʌn'raɪp] ADJ pas mûr(e)

unrivalled, (*US*) **unrivaled** [ʌn'raɪvəld] ADJ sans égal, incomparable

unroll [ʌn'rəul] VT dérouler

unruffled [ʌn'rʌfld] ADJ (*person*) imperturbable; (*hair*) qui n'est pas ébouriffé(e)

unruly [ʌn'ruːlɪ] ADJ indiscipliné(e)

unsafe [ʌn'seɪf] ADJ (*in danger*) en danger; (*journey, car*) dangereux(-euse); (*method*) hasardeux(-euse); **~ to drink/eat** non potable/comestible

unsaid [ʌn'sɛd] ADJ: **to leave sth ~** passer qch sous silence

unsaleable, (*US*) **unsalable** [ʌn'seɪləbl] ADJ invendable

unsatisfactory ['ʌnsætɪs'fæktərɪ] ADJ peu satisfaisant(e), qui laisse à désirer

unsavoury, (*US*) **unsavory** [ʌn'seɪvərɪ] ADJ (*fig*) peu recommandable, répugnant(e)

unscathed [ʌn'skeɪðd] ADJ indemne

unscheduled [ʌn'ʃɛdjuːld] ADJ non prévu(e)

unscientific ['ʌnsaɪən'tɪfɪk] ADJ non scientifique

unscrew [ʌn'skruː] VT dévisser

unscrupulous [ʌn'skruːpjuləs] ADJ sans scrupules

unseat [ʌn'siːt] VT (*rider*) désarçonner; (*fig: official*) faire perdre son siège à

unsecured ['ʌnsɪ'kjuəd] ADJ: **~ creditor** créancier(-ière) sans garantie

unseeded [ʌn'siːdɪd] ADJ (*Sport*) non classé(e)

unseemly [ʌn'siːmlɪ] ADJ inconvenant(e)

unseen [ʌn'siːn] ADJ (*person*) invisible; (*danger*) imprévu(e)

unselfish [ʌn'sɛlfɪʃ] ADJ désintéressé(e)

unsettled [ʌn'sɛtld] ADJ (*restless*) perturbé(e); (*unpredictable*) instable; incertain(e); (*not finalized*) non résolu(e)

unsettling [ʌn'sɛtlɪŋ] ADJ qui a un effet perturbateur

unshakable, unshakeable [ʌn'ʃeɪkəbl] ADJ inébranlable

unshaven [ʌnˈʃeɪvn] ADJ non or mal rasé(e)

unsightly [ʌnˈsaɪtlɪ] ADJ disgracieux(-euse), laid(e)

unsigned [ʌnˈsaɪnd] ADJ (document, cheque) non signé(e)

unskilled [ʌnˈskɪld] ADJ: **~ worker** manœuvre m

unsociable [ʌnˈsəʊʃəbl] ADJ (person) peu sociable; (behaviour) qui manque de sociabilité

unsocial [ʌnˈsəʊʃl] ADJ (hours) en dehors de l'horaire normal

unsold [ʌnˈsəʊld] ADJ invendu(e), non vendu(e)

unsolicited [ʌnsəˈlɪsɪtɪd] ADJ non sollicité(e)

unsolved [ʌnˈsɒlvd] ADJ non résolu(e); **the murder remains ~** le meurtre n'a toujours pas été résolu

unsophisticated [ʌnsəˈfɪstɪkeɪtɪd] ADJ simple, naturel(le)

unsound [ʌnˈsaund] ADJ (health) chancelant(e); (floor, foundations) peu solide; (policy, advice) peu judicieux(-euse)

unspeakable [ʌnˈspiːkəbl] ADJ indicible; (awful) innommable

unspoiled [ˈʌnspɔɪld], **unspoilt** [ˈʌnspɔɪlt] ADJ (place) non dégradé(e)

unspoken [ʌnˈspəʊkn] ADJ (word) qui n'est pas prononcé(e); (agreement, approval) tacite

unstable [ʌnˈsteɪbl] ADJ instable

unsteady [ʌnˈstɛdɪ] ADJ mal assuré(e), chancelant(e), instable

unstinting [ʌnˈstɪntɪŋ] ADJ (support) total(e), sans réserve; (generosity) sans limites

unstoppable [ʌnˈstɒpəbl] ADJ qu'on ne peut pas arrêter

unstuck [ʌnˈstʌk] ADJ: **to come ~** se décoller; (fig) faire fiasco

unsubstantiated [ˈʌnsəbˈstænʃɪeɪtɪd] ADJ (rumour) qui n'est pas confirmé(e); (accusation) sans preuve

unsuccessful [ʌnsəkˈsɛsful] ADJ (attempt) infructueux(-euse); (writer, proposal) qui n'a pas de succès; (marriage) malheureux(-euse), qui ne réussit pas; **to be ~** (in attempting sth) ne pas réussir; ne pas avoir de succès; (application) ne pas être retenu(e)

unsuccessfully [ʌnsəkˈsɛsfəlɪ] ADV en vain

unsuitable [ʌnˈsuːtəbl] ADJ qui ne convient pas, peu approprié(e); (time) inopportun(e)

unsuited [ʌnˈsuːtɪd] ADJ: **to be ~ for** or **to** être inapte or impropre à

unsung [ˈʌnsʌŋ] ADJ: **an ~ hero** un héros méconnu

unsupported [ʌnsəˈpɔːtɪd] ADJ (claim) non soutenu(e); (theory) qui n'est pas corroboré(e)

unsure [ʌnˈʃʊəʳ] ADJ pas sûr(e); **to be ~ of o.s.** ne pas être sûr de soi, manquer de confiance en soi

unsuspecting [ʌnsəˈspɛktɪŋ] ADJ qui ne se méfie pas

unsweetened [ʌnˈswiːtnd] ADJ non sucré(e)

unswerving [ʌnˈswɜːvɪŋ] ADJ inébranlable

unsympathetic [ˈʌnsɪmpəˈθɛtɪk] ADJ hostile; (unpleasant) antipathique; **~ to** indifférent(e) à

untangle [ʌnˈtæŋgl] VT démêler, débrouiller

untapped [ʌnˈtæpt] ADJ (resources) inexploité(e)

untaxed [ʌnˈtækst] ADJ (goods) non taxé(e); (income) non imposé(e)

unthinkable [ʌnˈθɪŋkəbl] ADJ impensable, inconcevable

unthinkingly [ʌnˈθɪŋkɪŋlɪ] ADV sans réfléchir

untidy [ʌnˈtaɪdɪ] ADJ (room) en désordre; (appearance, person) débraillé(e); (person: in character) sans ordre, désordonné; débraillé; (work) peu soigné(e)

untie [ʌnˈtaɪ] VT (knot, parcel) défaire; (prisoner, dog) détacher

★**until** [ənˈtɪl] PREP jusqu'à; (after negative) avant; **~ now** jusqu'à présent, jusqu'ici; **~ then** jusque-là; **from morning ~ night** du matin au soir or jusqu'au soir ▶ CONJ jusqu'à ce que + sub, en attendant que + sub; (in past, after negative) avant que + sub; **~ he comes** jusqu'à ce qu'il vienne, jusqu'à son arrivée

untimely [ʌnˈtaɪmlɪ] ADJ inopportun(e); (death) prématuré(e)

untold [ʌnˈtəʊld] ADJ incalculable; indescriptible

untouched [ʌnˈtʌtʃt] ADJ (not used etc) tel(le) quel(le), intact(e); (safe: person) indemne; (unaffected): **~ by** indifférent(e) à

untoward [ʌntəˈwɔːd] ADJ fâcheux(-euse), malencontreux(-euse)

untrained [ˈʌnˈtreɪnd] ADJ (worker) sans formation; (troops) sans entraînement; **to the ~ eye** à l'œil non exercé

untrammelled [ʌnˈtræmld] ADJ sans entraves

untranslatable [ʌntrænzˈleɪtəbl] ADJ intraduisible

untrue [ʌnˈtruː] ADJ (statement) faux (fausse)

untrustworthy [ʌnˈtrʌstwɜːðɪ] ADJ (person) pas digne de confiance, peu sûr(e)

unusable [ʌnˈjuːzəbl] ADJ inutilisable

unused¹ [ʌnˈjuːzd] ADJ (new) neuf (neuve)

unused² [ʌnˈjuːst] ADJ: **to be ~ to sth/to doing sth** ne pas avoir l'habitude de qch/de faire qch

★**unusual** [ʌnˈjuːʒuəl] ADJ insolite, exceptionnel(le), rare

unusually [ʌnˈjuːʒuəlɪ] ADV exceptionnellement, particulièrement

unveil [ʌnˈveɪl] VT dévoiler

unwanted [ʌnˈwɒntɪd] ADJ (child, pregnancy) non désiré(e); (clothes etc) à donner

unwarranted [ʌnˈwɒrəntɪd] ADJ injustifié(e)

unwary [ʌnˈwɛərɪ] ADJ imprudent(e)

unwavering [ʌnˈweɪvərɪŋ] ADJ inébranlable

unwelcome [ʌnˈwɛlkəm] ADJ importun(e); **to feel ~** se sentir de trop

unwell [ʌnˈwɛl] ADJ indisposé(e), souffrant(e); **to feel ~** ne pas se sentir bien

unwieldy [ʌnˈwiːldɪ] ADJ difficile à manier

unwilling [ʌnˈwɪlɪŋ] ADJ: **to be ~ to do** ne pas vouloir faire

unwillingly [ʌnˈwɪlɪŋlɪ] ADV à contrecœur, contre son gré

unwind [ʌnˈwaɪnd] VT (irreg: like **wind²**) dérouler ▶ VI (relax) se détendre

unwise [ʌnˈwaɪz] ADJ imprudent(e), peu judicieux(-euse)

unwitting [ʌnˈwɪtɪŋ] ADJ involontaire

unwittingly [ʌnˈwɪtɪŋlɪ] ADV involontairement

unworkable [ʌnˈwəːkəbl] ADJ (*plan etc*) inexploitable

unworthy [ʌnˈwəːðɪ] ADJ indigne

unwrap [ʌnˈræp] VT défaire; ouvrir

unwritten [ʌnˈrɪtn] ADJ (*agreement*) tacite

unzip [ʌnˈzɪp] VT ouvrir (la fermeture éclair de); (*Comput*) dézipper

---

up [ʌp]

PREP: **he went up the stairs/the hill** il a monté l'escalier/la colline; **the cat was up a tree** le chat était dans un arbre; **they live further up the street** ils habitent plus haut dans la rue; **go up that road and turn left** remontez la rue et tournez à gauche

▶ VI (*inf*): **she upped and left** elle a fichu le camp sans plus attendre

▶ ADV **1** en haut; en l'air; (*upwards, higher*): **up in the sky/the mountains** (là-haut) dans le ciel/les montagnes; **put it a bit higher up** mettez-le un peu plus haut; **to stand up** (*get up*) se lever, se mettre debout; (*be standing*) être debout; **up there** là-haut; **up above** au-dessus; **"this side up"** « haut »

2: **to be up** (*out of bed*) être levé(e); (*prices*) avoir augmenté *or* monté; (*finished*): **when the year was up** à la fin de l'année; **time's up** c'est l'heure

3: **up to** (*as far as*) jusqu'à; **up to now** jusqu'à présent

4: **to be up to** (*depending on*): **it's up to you** c'est à vous de décider; (*equal to*): **he's not up to it** (*job, task etc*) il n'en est pas capable; (*inf: be doing*): **what is he up to?** qu'est-ce qu'il peut bien faire ?

5 (*phrases*): **he's well up in** *or* **on …** (BRIT: *knowledgeable*) il s'y connaît en …; **up with Leeds United!** vive Leeds United !; **what's up?** (*inf*) qu'est-ce qui ne va pas ?; **what's up with him?** (*inf*) qu'est-ce qui lui arrive ?

▶ N: **ups and downs** hauts et bas *mpl*

---

up-and-coming [ʌpəndˈkʌmɪŋ] ADJ plein(e) d'avenir *or* de promesses

upbeat [ˈʌpbiːt] N (*Mus*) levé *m*; (*in economy, prosperity*) amélioration *f* ▶ ADJ (*optimistic*) optimiste

upbraid [ʌpˈbreɪd] VT morigéner

upbringing [ˈʌpbrɪŋɪŋ] N éducation *f*

upcoming [ˈʌpkʌmɪŋ] ADJ tout(e) prochain(e)

upcycle [ˈʌpsaɪkl] VT surcycler

update [ʌpˈdeɪt] VT mettre à jour

upend [ʌpˈend] VT mettre debout

upfront [ʌpˈfrʌnt] ADJ (*open*) franc (franche); **to be ~ about sth** ne rien cacher de qch ▶ ADV (*pay*) d'avance

upgrade [ʌpˈgreɪd] VT (*person*) promouvoir; (*job*) revaloriser; (*property, equipment*) moderniser

upheaval [ʌpˈhiːvl] N bouleversement *m*; (*in room*) branle-bas *m*; (*event*) crise *f*

uphill [ʌpˈhɪl] ADJ qui monte; (*fig: task*) difficile, pénible ▶ ADV (*face, look*) en amont, vers l'amont; (*go, move*) vers le haut, en haut; **to go ~** monter

uphold [ʌpˈhəuld] VT (*irreg: like* **hold**) maintenir; soutenir

upholstery [ʌpˈhəulstərɪ] N rembourrage *m*; (*cover*) tissu *m* d'ameublement; (*of car*) garniture *f*

upkeep [ˈʌpkiːp] N entretien *m*

uplifting [ʌpˈlɪftɪŋ] ADJ qui met de bonne humeur

upload [ʌpˈləud] VT (*Comput*) télécharger

upmarket [ʌpˈmɑːkɪt] ADJ (*product*) haut de gamme *inv*; (*area*) chic *inv*

upon [əˈpɔn] PREP sur

upper [ˈʌpəʳ] ADJ supérieur(e); du dessus ▶ N (*of shoe*) empeigne *f*

upper class N: **the ~** la haute société

upper-class [ʌpəˈklɑːs] ADJ de la haute société, aristocratique; (*district*) élégant(e), huppé(e); (*accent, attitude*) caractéristique des classes supérieures

uppercut [ˈʌpəkʌt] N uppercut *m*

upper hand N: **to have the ~** avoir le dessus

Upper House N: **the ~** (*in Britain*) la Chambre des Lords, la Chambre haute; (*in France, in the US etc*) le Sénat

uppermost [ˈʌpəməust] ADJ le (la) plus haut(e), en dessus; **it was ~ in my mind** j'y pensais avant tout autre chose

upper sixth N terminale *f*

Upper Volta [-ˈvɔltə] N Haute Volta

upright [ˈʌpraɪt] ADJ droit(e); (*fig*) droit, honnête ▶ N montant *m*

uprising [ˈʌpraɪzɪŋ] N soulèvement *m*, insurrection *f*

uproar [ˈʌprɔːʳ] N tumulte *m*, vacarme *m*; (*protests*) protestations *fpl*

uproarious [ʌpˈrɔːrɪəs] ADJ (*event etc*) désopilant(e); **~ laughter** un brouhaha de rires

uproot [ʌpˈruːt] VT déraciner

★**upset** N [ˈʌpset] dérangement *m*; **to have a stomach ~** (BRIT) avoir une indigestion ▶ VT [ʌpˈset] (*irreg: like* **set**) (*glass etc*) renverser; (*plan*) déranger; (*person: offend*) contrarier; (*: grieve*) faire de la peine à; bouleverser ▶ ADJ [ʌpˈset] contrarié(e); peiné(e); (*stomach*) détraqué(e), dérangé(e); **to get ~** (*sad*) devenir triste; (*offended*) se vexer

upset price N (*US, Scottish*) mise *f* à prix, prix *m* de départ

upsetting [ʌpˈsetɪŋ] ADJ (*offending*) vexant(e); (*annoying*) ennuyeux(-euse)

upshot [ˈʌpʃɔt] N résultat *m*; **the ~ of it all was that …** il a résulté de tout cela que …

upside down [ˈʌpsaɪd-] ADV à l'envers; **to turn sth ~** (*fig: place*) mettre sens dessus dessous

upstage [ˈʌpˈsteɪdʒ] VT: **to ~ sb** souffler la vedette à qn

upstairs [ʌpˈstɛəz] ADV en haut ▶ ADJ (*room*) du dessus, d'en haut ▶ N: **the ~** l'étage *m*; **there's no ~** il n'y a pas d'étage

upstart [ˈʌpstɑːt] N parvenu(e)

upstream [ʌpˈstriːm] ADV en amont

upsurge [ˈʌpsəːdʒ] N (*of enthusiasm etc*) vague *f*

uptake [ˈʌpteɪk] N: **he is quick/slow on the ~** il comprend vite/est lent à comprendre

uptight [ʌpˈtaɪt] ADJ (*inf*) très tendu(e), crispé(e)

u

★up-to-date [ˈʌptəˈdeɪt] ADJ moderne; (*information*) très récent(e)

upturn [ˈʌptəːn] N (*in economy*) reprise *f*

upturned [ˈʌptəːnd] ADJ (*nose*) retroussé(e)

upward [ˈʌpwəd] ADJ ascendant(e); vers le haut
▶ ADV = **upwards**

upwardly-mobile [ˈʌpwədlɪˈməubaɪl] ADJ à mobilité sociale ascendante

upwards [ˈʌpwədz] ADV vers le haut; (*more than*): ~ **of** plus de; **and** ~ et plus, et au-dessus

Ural Mountains [ˈjuərəl-] NPL (*also:* **the Urals**): **the** ~ les monts *mpl* Oural, l'Oural *m*

uranium [juəˈreɪnɪəm] N uranium *m*

Uranus [juəˈreɪnəs] N Uranus *f*

urban [ˈəːbən] ADJ urbain(e)

urban clearway N (*BRIT*) rue *f* à stationnement interdit

urbane [əːˈbeɪn] ADJ urbain(e), courtois(e)

urbanization [əːbənaɪˈzeɪʃən] N urbanisation *f*

urchin [ˈəːtʃɪn] N gosse *m*, garnement *m*

Urdu [ˈuəduː] N ourdou *m*

urge [əːdʒ] N besoin (impératif), envie (pressante) ▶ VT (*caution etc*) recommander avec insistance; (*person*): **to** ~ **sb to do** exhorter qn à faire, pousser qn à faire, recommander vivement à qn de faire ▶ **urge on** VT pousser, presser

urgency [ˈəːdʒənsɪ] N urgence *f*; (*of tone*) insistance *f*

★urgent [ˈəːdʒənt] ADJ urgent(e); (*plea, tone*) pressant(e)

urgently [ˈəːdʒəntlɪ] ADV d'urgence, de toute urgence; (*need*) sans délai

urinal [ˈjuərɪnl] N (*BRIT: place*) urinoir *m*

urinary [ˈjuərɪnrɪ] ADJ urinaire

urinate [ˈjuərɪneɪt] VI uriner

urine [ˈjuərɪn] N urine *f*

URL ABBR (= *uniform resource locator*) URL *f*

urn [əːn] N urne *f*; (*also:* **tea urn**) fontaine *f* à thé

Uruguay [ˈjuərəgwaɪ] N Uruguay *m*

Uruguayan [juərəˈgwaɪən] ADJ uruguayen(ne) ▶ N Uruguayen(ne)

★US N ABBR = **United States**

★us [ʌs] PRON nous; *see also* **me**

★USA N ABBR = **United States of America**; (*Mil*) = **United States Army**

usable [ˈjuːzəbl] ADJ utilisable

USAF N ABBR = **United States Air Force**

usage [ˈjuːzɪdʒ] N usage *m*

USB stick N clé *f* USB

USCG N ABBR = **United States Coast Guard**

USDA N ABBR = **United States Department of Agriculture**

USDAW [ˈʌzdɔː] N ABBR (*BRIT*: = *Union of Shop, Distributive and Allied Workers*) *syndicat du commerce de détail et de la distribution*

USDI N ABBR = **United States Department of the Interior**

★use N [juːs] emploi *m*, utilisation *f*; usage *m*; (*usefulness*) utilité *f*; **in** ~ en usage; **out of** ~ hors d'usage; **to be of** ~ servir, être utile; **to make** ~ **of sth** utiliser qch; **ready for** ~ prêt à l'emploi; **it's no** ~ ça ne sert à rien; **to have the** ~ **of** avoir l'usage de ▶ AUX VB [juːs] (*in past only*): **she used to do it** elle le faisait (autrefois), elle avait coutume de le faire; **I used not to** *or* **I didn't** ~ **to worry so much** je ne m'inquiétais pas autant avant ▶ VT [juːz] (*utilize*) se servir de, utiliser, employer; **what's this used for?** à quoi est-ce que ça sert ? ▶ **use up** VT [juːz-] finir, épuiser; (*food*) consommer

> Translate *use* as in *make use of* by **utiliser**. *You can use my dictionary.* **Tu peux utiliser mon dictionnaire.** The verb **user** means *to wear out*.

used¹ [juːzd] ADJ (*car*) d'occasion

used² [juːst] ADJ: **to be** ~ **to** avoir l'habitude de, être habitué(e) à; **to get** ~ **to** s'habituer à ▶ AUX VB *see* **use**

★useful [ˈjuːsful] ADJ utile; **to come in** ~ être utile

usefully [ˈjuːsfulɪ] ADV utilement

usefulness [ˈjuːsfəlnɪs] N utilité *f*

★useless [ˈjuːslɪs] ADJ inutile; (*inf: person*) nul(le)

★user [ˈjuːzəʳ] N utilisateur(-trice), usager *m*

user-friendly [ˈjuːzəˈfrendlɪ] ADJ convivial(e), facile d'emploi

username [ˈjuːzəneɪm] N (*Comput*) nom *m* d'utilisateur

USES N ABBR = **United States Employment Service**

usher [ˈʌʃəʳ] N placeur *m* ▶ VT: **to** ~ **sb in** faire entrer qn

usherette [ʌʃəˈret] N (*in cinema*) ouvreuse *f*

USM N ABBR = **United States Mail; United States Mint**

USN N ABBR = **United States Navy**

USP N ABBR = **unique selling proposition**

USPHS N ABBR = **United States Public Health Service**

USPO N ABBR = **United States Post Office**

USS ABBR = **United States Ship; United States Steamer**

USSR N ABBR = **Union of Soviet Socialist Republics**

usu. ABBR = **usually**

★usual [ˈjuːʒuəl] ADJ habituel(le); **as** ~ comme d'habitude

★usually [ˈjuːʒuəlɪ] ADV d'habitude, d'ordinaire

usurer [ˈjuːʒərəʳ] N usurier(-ière)

usurp [juːˈzəːp] VT usurper

UT ABBR (*US*) = **Utah**

ute [juːt] N (*AUSTRALIA, NEW ZEALAND*) pick-up *m inv*

utensil [juːˈtensl] N ustensile *m*; **kitchen utensils** batterie *f* de cuisine

uterus [ˈjuːtərəs] N utérus *m*

utilitarian [juːtɪlɪˈtɛərɪən] ADJ utilitaire

utility [juːˈtɪlɪtɪ] N utilité *f*; (*also:* **public utility**) service public

utility room N buanderie *f*

utilization [juːtɪlaɪˈzeɪʃən] N utilisation *f*

utilize [ˈjuːtɪlaɪz] VT utiliser; (*make good use of*) exploiter

utmost [ˈʌtməust] ADJ extrême, le (la) plus

grand(e); **of the ~ importance** d'une importance capitale, de la plus haute importance ▸ N: **to do one's ~** faire tout son possible

utopia [juːˈtəupiə] N utopie f

utter [ˈʌtəʳ] ADJ total(e), complet(-ète) ▸ VT prononcer, proférer; (sounds) émettre

utterance [ˈʌtrns] N paroles fpl

utterly [ˈʌtəlɪ] ADV complètement, totalement

U-turn [ˈjuːˈtɜːn] N demi-tour m; (fig) volte-face f inv

UV ADJ (= ultraviolet) ultraviolet m

Uzbekistan [ʌzbɛkɪˈstɑːn] N Ouzbékistan m

Vv

V, v [vi:] N (letter) V, v m; **V for Victor** V comme Victor

v. ABBR = **verse**; (= vide) v.; (= versus) vs; (= volt) V

VA, Va. ABBR (US) = **Virginia**

vac [væk] N ABBR (BRIT inf) = **vacation**

vacancy ['veɪkənsɪ] N (job) poste vacant; (room) chambre f disponible; **"no vacancies"** « complet »

vacant ['veɪkənt] ADJ (post) vacant(e); (seat etc) libre, disponible; (expression) distrait(e)

vacant lot N terrain inoccupé; (for sale) terrain à vendre

vacate [və'keɪt] VT quitter

vacation [və'keɪʃən] N (esp US) vacances fpl; **to take a ~** prendre des vacances; **on ~** en vacances

vacation course N cours mpl de vacances

vacationer [və'keɪʃənə], (US) **vacationist** [və'keɪʃənɪst] N vacancier(-ière)

vaccinate ['væksɪneɪt] VT vacciner

vaccination [væksɪ'neɪʃən] N vaccination f

vaccine ['væksiːn] N vaccin m

vacuous ['vækjuəs] ADJ inepte

vacuum ['vækjum] N vide m

vacuum bottle N (US) = **vacuum flask**

vacuum cleaner N aspirateur m

vacuum flask N (BRIT) bouteille f thermos®

vacuum-packed ['vækjumpækt] ADJ emballé(e) sous vide

vagabond ['vægəbɔnd] N vagabond(e); (tramp) chemineau m, clochard(e)

vagary ['veɪgərɪ] N caprice m

vagina [və'dʒaɪnə] N vagin m

vaginal [və'dʒaɪnl] ADJ vaginal(e)

vagrancy ['veɪgrənsɪ] N vagabondage m

vagrant ['veɪgrənt] N vagabond(e), mendiant(e)

vague [veɪg] ADJ vague, imprécis(e); (blurred: photo, memory) flou(e); **I haven't the vaguest idea** je n'en ai pas la moindre idée

vaguely ['veɪglɪ] ADV vaguement

vain [veɪn] ADJ (useless) vain(e); (conceited) vaniteux(-euse); **in ~** en vain

valance ['væləns] N (of bed) tour m de lit

valedictory [vælɪ'dɪktərɪ] ADJ d'adieu

valentine ['væləntaɪn] N (also: **valentine card**) carte f de la Saint-Valentin

Valentine's Day ['væləntaɪnz-] N Saint-Valentin f

valet ['vælɪt] N valet m de chambre

valet parking ['vælɪ-] N parcage m par les soins du personnel (de l'hôtel etc)

valet service ['vælɪ-] N (for clothes) pressing m; (for car) nettoyage complet

valiant ['væliənt] ADJ vaillant(e), courageux(-euse)

valiantly ['væliəntlɪ] ADV vaillamment

valid ['vælɪd] ADJ (document) valide, valable; (excuse) valable

validate ['vælɪdeɪt] VT (contract, document) valider; (argument, claim) prouver la justesse de, confirmer

validation [vælɪ'deɪʃən] N validation f

validity [və'lɪdɪtɪ] N validité f

valise [və'liːz] N sac m de voyage

★**valley** ['vælɪ] N vallée f

valour, (US) **valor** ['vælə'] N courage m

★**valuable** ['væljuəbl] ADJ (jewel) de grande valeur; (time, help) précieux(-euse)

valuables ['væljuəblz] NPL objets mpl de valeur

valuation [vælju'eɪʃən] N évaluation f, expertise f

★**value** ['væljuː] N valeur f; **you get good ~ (for money) in that shop** vous en avez pour votre argent dans ce magasin; **to lose (in) ~** (currency) baisser; (property) se déprécier; **to gain (in) ~** (currency) monter; (property) prendre de la valeur; **to be of great ~ to sb** (fig) être très utile à qn ▶ VT (fix price) évaluer, expertiser; (appreciate) apprécier; (cherish) tenir à ■ **values** NPL (principles) valeurs fpl

value added tax [-'ædɪd-] N (BRIT) taxe f à la valeur ajoutée

valued ['væljuːd] ADJ (appreciated) estimé(e)

valuer ['væljuə'] N expert m (en estimations)

valve [vælv] N (in machine) soupape f; (on tyre) valve f; (in radio) lampe f; (Med) valve, valvule f

vampire ['væmpaɪə'] N vampire m

★**van** [væn] N (Aut) camionnette f; (BRIT Rail) fourgon m

V and A N ABBR (BRIT) = **Victoria and Albert Museum**

vandal ['vændl] N vandale mf

vandalism ['vændəlɪzəm] N vandalisme m

vandalize ['vændəlaɪz] VT saccager

vanguard ['vængɑːd] N avant-garde m

vanilla [və'nɪlə] N vanille f ▶ CPD (ice cream) à la vanille

vanish ['vænɪʃ] VI disparaître

vanity ['vænɪtɪ] N vanité f

vanity case N sac m de toilette

vantage ['vɑːntɪdʒ] N: **~ point** bonne position

Vanuatu ['vænu:ætu:] N Vanuatu m

vape [veɪp] VT, VI vaper

vaper ['veɪpəʳ] N vapoteur(-euse) m/f

vaping ['veɪpɪŋ] N vapotage m, vape f

vaporize ['veɪpəraɪz] VT vaporiser ▶ VI se vaporiser

vapour, (US) **vapor** ['veɪpəʳ] N vapeur f; (on
window) buée f

variable ['vɛərɪəbl] ADJ variable; (mood) chan-
geant(e) ▶ N variable f

variance ['vɛərɪəns] N: **to be at ~ (with)** être en
désaccord (avec); (facts) être en contradiction
(avec)

variant ['vɛərɪənt] N variante f

variation [vɛərɪ'eɪʃən] N variation f; (in opinion)
changement m

varicose ['værɪkəus] ADJ: **~ veins** varices fpl

varied ['vɛərɪd] ADJ varié(e), divers(e)

★**variety** [və'raɪətɪ] N variété f; (quantity) nombre m,
quantité f; **a wide ~ of ...** un grand nombre de ...;
for a ~ reasons pour diverses raisons

variety show N (spectacle m de) variétés fpl

★**various** ['vɛərɪəs] ADJ divers(e), différent(e); (several) divers, plusieurs; **at ~ times** (different) en
diverses occasions; (several) à plusieurs reprises

varnish ['vɑːnɪʃ] N vernis m; (for nails) vernis (à
ongles) ▶ VT vernir; **to ~ one's nails** se vernir les
ongles

vary ['vɛərɪ] VT, VI varier, changer; **to ~ with** or
according to varier selon

varying ['vɛərɪŋ] ADJ variable

vase [vɑːz] N vase m

vasectomy [væ'sɛktəmɪ] N vasectomie f

Vaseline® ['væsɪliːn] N vaseline f

vast [vɑːst] ADJ vaste, immense; (amount, success)
énorme

vastly ['vɑːstlɪ] ADV infiniment, extrêmement

vastness ['vɑːstnɪs] N immensité f

VAT [væt] N ABBR (BRIT: = value added tax) TVA f

vat [væt] N cuve f

Vatican ['vætɪkən] N: **the ~** le Vatican

vatman ['vætmæn] N (irreg) (BRIT inf) contrôleur m
de la TVA

vaudeville ['vɔːdəvɪl, 'vəudəvɪl] N (esp US) vaudeville m

vault [vɔːlt] N (of roof) voûte f; (tomb) caveau m; (in
bank) salle f des coffres; chambre forte; (jump)
saut m ▶ VT (also: **vault over**) sauter (d'un bond)

vaunted ['vɔːntɪd] ADJ: **much-vaunted** tant
célébré(e)

VC N ABBR = **vice-chairman**; (BRIT: = Victoria Cross)
distinction militaire

VCR N ABBR = **video cassette recorder**

VD N ABBR = **venereal disease**

VDU N ABBR = **visual display unit**

veal [viːl] N veau m

veer [vɪəʳ] VI tourner; (car, ship) virer

veg. [vɛdʒ] N ABBR (BRIT inf) = **vegetable; vegetables**

vegan ['viːgən] N végétalien(ne)

vegeburger ['vɛdʒɪbə:gəʳ] N burger végétarien

★**vegetable** ['vɛdʒtəbl] N légume m ▶ ADJ végétal(e)

vegetable garden N (jardin m) potager m

★**vegetarian** [vɛdʒɪ'tɛərɪən] ADJ, N végétarien(ne);
do they have any ~ dishes? avez-vous des plats
végétariens ?

vegetate ['vɛdʒɪteɪt] VI végéter

vegetation [vɛdʒɪ'teɪʃən] N végétation f

vegetative ['vɛdʒɪtətɪv] ADJ (lit) végétal(e); (fig)
végétatif(-ive)

veggieburger ['vɛdʒɪbə:gəʳ] N = **vegeburger**

vehemence ['viːɪməns] N véhémence f, violence f

vehement ['viːɪmənt] ADJ violent(e), impé-
tueux(-euse); (impassioned) ardent(e)

★**vehicle** ['viːɪkl] N véhicule m

vehicular [vɪ'hɪkjuləʳ] ADJ: **"no ~ traffic"** « interdit à tout véhicule »

veil [veɪl] N voile m; **under a ~ of secrecy** (fig) dans
le plus grand secret ▶ VT voiler

veiled [veɪld] ADJ voilé(e)

vein [veɪn] N veine f; (on leaf) nervure f; (fig: mood)
esprit m

Velcro® ['vɛlkrəu] N velcro® m

vellum ['vɛləm] N (writing paper) vélin m

velocity [vɪ'lɒsɪtɪ] N vitesse f, vélocité f

velour, velours [və'luəʳ] N velours m

velvet ['vɛlvɪt] N velours m

vendetta [vɛn'dɛtə] N vendetta f

vending machine ['vɛndɪŋ-] N distributeur m
automatique

vendor ['vɛndəʳ] N vendeur(-euse); **street ~**
marchand ambulant

veneer [və'nɪəʳ] N placage m de bois; (fig) vernis m

venerable ['vɛnərəbl] ADJ vénérable

venereal [vɪ'nɪərɪəl] ADJ: **~ disease** maladie
vénérienne

Venetian blind [vɪ'niːʃən-] N store vénitien

Venezuela [vɛnɛ'zweɪlə] N Venezuela m

Venezuelan [vɛnɛ'zweɪlən] ADJ vénézuélien(ne)
▶ N Vénézuélien(ne)

vengeance ['vɛndʒəns] N vengeance f; **with a ~**
(fig) vraiment, pour de bon

vengeful ['vɛndʒful] ADJ vengeur(-geresse)

Venice ['vɛnɪs] N Venise f

venison ['vɛnɪsn] N venaison f

venom ['vɛnəm] N venin m

venomous ['vɛnəməs] ADJ venimeux(-euse)

vent [vɛnt] N conduit m d'aération; (in dress, jacket)
fente f ▶ VT (fig: one's feelings) donner libre cours à

ventilate ['vɛntɪleɪt] VT (room) ventiler, aérer

ventilation [vɛntɪ'leɪʃən] N ventilation f, aération f

ventilation shaft N conduit m de ventilation or
d'aération

ventilator ['vɛntɪleɪtəʳ] N ventilateur m

ventriloquist [vɛn'trɪləkwɪst] N ventriloque mf

venture ['vɛntʃəʳ] N entreprise f; **a business ~** une
entreprise commerciale ▶ VT risquer, hasarder;
to ~ to do sth se risquer à faire qch ▶ VI s'aventurer, se risquer

V

921

venture capital N capital-risque m

venue ['venjuː] N lieu m; (of conference etc) lieu de la réunion (or manifestation etc); (of match) lieu de la rencontre

Venus ['viːnəs] N (planet) Vénus f

veracity [vəˈræsɪtɪ] N véracité f

veranda, verandah [vəˈrændə] N véranda f

verb [vəːb] N verbe m

verbal ['vəːbl] ADJ verbal(e); (translation) littéral(e)

verbalize ['vəːbəlaɪz] VT verbaliser

verbally ['vəːbəlɪ] ADV verbalement

verbatim [vəːˈbeɪtɪm] ADJ, ADV mot pour mot

verbose [vəːˈbəus] ADJ verbeux(-euse)

verdant ['vəːdənt] ADJ (literary) verdoyant(e)

★**verdict** ['vəːdɪkt] N verdict m; **~ of guilty/not guilty** verdict de culpabilité/de non-culpabilité

verge [vəːdʒ] N bord m; **"soft verges"** (BRIT) « accotements non stabilisés »; **on the ~ of doing** sur le point de faire

▶ **verge on** VT FUS approcher de

verger ['vəːdʒəʳ] N (Rel) bedeau m

verifiable [verɪˈfaɪəbl] ADJ vérifiable

verification [verɪfɪˈkeɪʃən] N vérification f

verify ['verɪfaɪ] VT vérifier

veritable ['verɪtəbl] ADJ véritable

vermin ['vəːmɪn] NPL animaux mpl nuisibles; (insects) vermine f

vermouth ['vəːməθ] N vermouth m

vernacular [vəˈnækjuləʳ] N langue f vernaculaire, dialecte m

verruca [vəˈruːkə] N (BRIT) verrue f plantaire

versatile ['vəːsətaɪl] ADJ polyvalent(e)

versatility [vəːsəˈtɪlɪtɪ] N polyvalence f

verse [vəːs] N vers mpl; (stanza) strophe f; (in Bible) verset m; **in ~** en vers

versed [vəːst] ADJ: **~ in sth** versé(e) en qch; **to be well ~ in sth** être (très) versé(e) en qch

version ['vəːʃən] N version f

versus ['vəːsəs] PREP contre

vertebra ['vəːtɪbrə] (pl **vertebrae** [-briː]) N vertèbre f

vertebrate ['vəːtɪbrɪt] N vertébré m

vertical ['vəːtɪkl] ADJ vertical(e) ▶ N verticale f

vertically ['vəːtɪklɪ] ADV verticalement

vertiginous [vəːˈtɪdʒɪnəs] ADJ (literary) vertigineux(-euse)

vertigo ['vəːtɪɡəu] N vertige m; **to suffer from ~** avoir des vertiges

verve [vəːv] N brio m; enthousiasme m

★**very** ['verɪ] ADV très; **~ well** très bien; **~ little** très peu; **~ much** beaucoup; **the ~ last** le tout dernier; **at the ~ least** au moins ▶ ADJ: **the ~ book which** le livre même que; **the ~ thought (of it) ...** rien que d'y penser ...; **at the ~ end** tout à la fin

vespers ['vespəz] NPL vêpres fpl

vessel ['vesl] N (Anat, Naut) vaisseau m; (container) récipient m; see also **blood vessel**

vest [vest] N (BRIT: underwear) tricot m de corps; (US: waistcoat) gilet m ▶ VT: **to ~ sb with sth, to ~ sth in sb** investir qn de qch

vested interest N: **to have a ~ in doing** avoir tout intérêt à faire ▪ **vested interests** NPL (Comm) droits acquis

vestibule ['vestɪbjuːl] N vestibule m

vestige ['vestɪdʒ] N vestige m

vestry ['vestrɪ] N sacristie f

Vesuvius [vɪˈsuːvɪəs] N Vésuve m

vet [vet] N ABBR (BRIT: = veterinary surgeon) vétérinaire mf; (US: = veteran) vétéran ▶ VT examiner minutieusement; (text) revoir; (candidate) se renseigner soigneusement sur, soumettre à une enquête approfondie

veteran ['vetərn] N vétéran m; (also: **war veteran**) ancien combattant ▶ ADJ: **she's a ~ campaigner for ...** cela fait très longtemps qu'elle lutte pour ...

veteran car N voiture f d'époque

veterinarian [vetrɪˈnεərɪən] N (US) = **veterinary surgeon**

veterinary ['vetrɪnərɪ] ADJ vétérinaire

veterinary surgeon (BRIT) N vétérinaire mf

veto ['viːtəu] (pl **vetoes**) N veto m; **to put a ~ on** mettre (or opposer) son veto à ▶ VT opposer son veto à

vetting ['vetɪŋ] N: **positive ~** enquête f de sécurité

vex [veks] VT fâcher, contrarier

vexed [vekst] ADJ (question) controversé(e)

VFD N ABBR (US) = **voluntary fire department**

VG N ABBR (BRIT Scol etc: = very good) tb (= très bien)

VHF ABBR (= very high frequency) VHF

VI ABBR (US) = **Virgin Islands**

★**via** ['vaɪə, 'viːə] PREP par, via

viability [vaɪəˈbɪlɪtɪ] N viabilité f

viable ['vaɪəbl] ADJ viable

viaduct ['vaɪədʌkt] N viaduc m

vial ['vaɪəl] N fiole f

vibes [vaɪbz] NPL (inf): **I get good/bad ~ about it** je les sens bien/ne le sens pas; **there are good/bad ~ between us** entre nous le courant passe bien/ne passe pas

vibrant ['vaɪbrənt] ADJ (sound, colour) vibrant(e)

vibraphone ['vaɪbrəfəun] N vibraphone m

vibrate [vaɪˈbreɪt] VI: **to ~ (with)** vibrer (de); (resound) retentir (de)

vibration [vaɪˈbreɪʃən] N vibration f

vibrator [vaɪˈbreɪtəʳ] N vibromasseur m

vicar ['vɪkəʳ] N pasteur m (de l'Église anglicane)

vicarage ['vɪkərɪdʒ] N presbytère m

vicarious [vɪˈkεərɪəs] ADJ (pleasure, experience) par procuration

vicariously [vɪˈkεərɪəslɪ] ADV par procuration

★**vice** [vaɪs] N (evil) vice m; (Tech) étau m

vice- [vaɪs] PREFIX vice-

vice-chairman [vaɪsˈtʃεəmən] N (irreg) vice-président(e)

vice-chancellor [vaɪsˈtʃɑːnsələʳ] N (BRIT) ≈ président(e) d'université

vice-president [vaɪsˈprezɪdənt] N vice-président(e)

viceroy ['vaɪsrɔɪ] N vice-roi m

vice squad N ≈ brigade mondaine

vice versa ['vaɪsɪˈvəːsə] ADV vice versa

vicinity [vɪˈsɪnɪtɪ] N environs *mpl*, alentours *mpl*

vicious [ˈvɪʃəs] ADJ *(attack, murder, blow)* brutal(e); *(dog)* méchant(e), dangereux(-euse); *(remark, letter)* acerbe; *(lie)* cruel(le); **a ~ circle** un cercle vicieux

viciously [ˈvɪʃəslɪ] ADV *(attack, beat)* brutalement; *(say)* d'un ton acerbe

viciousness [ˈvɪʃəsnɪs] N méchanceté *f*, cruauté *f*; brutalité *f*

vicissitudes [vɪˈsɪsɪtjuːdz] NPL vicissitudes *fpl*

★**victim** [ˈvɪktɪm] N victime *f*; **to be the ~ of** être victime de

victimization [vɪktɪmaɪˈzeɪʃən] N brimades *fpl*; représailles *fpl*

victimize [ˈvɪktɪmaɪz] VT brimer; exercer des représailles sur

victor [ˈvɪktə'] N vainqueur *m*

Victorian [vɪkˈtɔːrɪən] ADJ victorien(ne)

victorious [vɪkˈtɔːrɪəs] ADJ victorieux(-euse)

★**victory** [ˈvɪktərɪ] N victoire *f*; **to win a ~ over sb** remporter une victoire sur qn

★**video** [ˈvɪdɪəu] N *(video film)* vidéo *f*; *(also: **video cassette**)* vidéocassette *f*; *(also: **video cassette recorder**)* magnétoscope *m* ▶ VT *(with recorder)* enregistrer; *(with camera)* filmer ▶ CPD vidéo *inv*

videocam [ˈvɪdɪəukæm] N *(also: **video camera**)* caméra *f* vidéo

video cassette N vidéocassette *f*

video cassette recorder N = **video recorder**

videodisc [ˈvɪdɪəudɪsk] N vidéodisque *m*

video game N jeu *m* vidéo *inv*

video nasty N vidéo à caractère violent ou pornographique

videophone [ˈvɪdɪəufəun] N vidéophone *m*, visiophone *m*

video recorder N magnétoscope *m*

video recording N enregistrement *m* (en) vidéo *inv*

video shop N vidéoclub *m*

video tape N bande *f* vidéo *inv*; *(cassette)* vidéocassette *f*

video wall N mur *m* d'images vidéo

vie [vaɪ] VI: **to ~ with** lutter avec, rivaliser avec

Vienna [vɪˈenə] N Vienne

Vietnam, Viet Nam [vjetˈnæm] N Viêt-nam *m*, Vietnam *m*

Vietnamese [vjetnəˈmiːz] ADJ vietnamien(ne) ▶ N *(pl inv)* Vietnamien(ne); *(Ling)* vietnamien *m*

★**view** [vjuː] N vue *f*; *(opinion)* avis *m*, vue; **on ~** *(in museum etc)* exposé(e); **in full ~ of sb** sous les yeux de qn; **to be within ~ (of sth)** être à portée de vue (de qch); **an overall ~ of the situation** une vue d'ensemble de la situation; **in my ~** à mon avis; **in ~ of the fact that** étant donné que; **with a ~ to doing sth** dans l'intention de faire qch ▶ VT voir, regarder; *(situation)* considérer; *(house)* visiter

viewdata [ˈvjuːdeɪtə] N *(BRIT)* télétexte *m* *(version téléphonique)*

★**viewer** [ˈvjuːə'] N *(viewfinder)* viseur *m*; *(small projector)* visionneuse *f*; *(TV)* téléspectateur(-trice)

viewfinder [ˈvjuːfaɪndə'] N viseur *m*

viewpoint [ˈvjuːpɔɪnt] N point *m* de vue

vigil [ˈvɪdʒɪl] N veille *f*; **to keep ~** veiller

vigilance [ˈvɪdʒɪləns] N vigilance *f*

vigilant [ˈvɪdʒɪlənt] ADJ vigilant(e)

vigilante [vɪdʒɪˈlæntɪ] N *justicier ou membre d'un groupe d'autodéfense*

vignette [vɪˈnjet] N *(résumé)* instantané *m*

vigorous [ˈvɪgərəs] ADJ vigoureux(-euse)

vigour, *(US)* **vigor** [ˈvɪgə'] N vigueur *f*

Viking [ˈvaɪkɪŋ] N Viking *m* ▶ CPD viking *inv*

vile [vaɪl] ADJ *(action)* vil(e); *(smell, food)* abominable; *(temper)* massacrant(e)

vilify [ˈvɪlɪfaɪ] VT calomnier, vilipender

villa [ˈvɪlə] N villa *f*

★**village** [ˈvɪlɪdʒ] N village *m*

villager [ˈvɪlɪdʒə'] N villageois(e)

villain [ˈvɪlən] N *(scoundrel)* scélérat *m*; *(BRIT: criminal)* bandit *m*; *(in novel etc)* traître *m*

villainous [ˈvɪlənəs] ADJ sans scrupules

VIN N ABBR *(US)* = **vehicle identification number**

vinaigrette [vɪneɪˈgret] N vinaigrette *f*

vindicate [ˈvɪndɪkeɪt] VT défendre avec succès; justifier

vindication [vɪndɪˈkeɪʃən] N: **in ~ of** pour justifier

vindictive [vɪnˈdɪktɪv] ADJ vindicatif(-ive), rancunier(-ière)

vindictiveness [vɪnˈdɪktɪvnɪs] N: **out of ~** par rancune

vine [vaɪn] N vigne *f*; *(climbing plant)* plante grimpante

★**vinegar** [ˈvɪnɪgə'] N vinaigre *m*

vine grower N viticulteur *m*

vine-growing [ˈvaɪngrəuɪŋ] ADJ viticole ▶ N viticulture *f*

vineyard [ˈvɪnjɑːd] N vignoble *m*

vintage [ˈvɪntɪdʒ] N *(year)* année *f*, millésime *m*; **the 1970 ~** le millésime 1970 ▶ CPD *(car)* d'époque; *(wine)* de grand cru

vinyl [ˈvaɪnl] N vinyle *m*

viola [vɪˈəulə] N alto *m*

violate [ˈvaɪəleɪt] VT violer

violation [vaɪəˈleɪʃən] N violation *f*; **in ~ of** *(rule, law)* en infraction à, en violation de

★**violence** [ˈvaɪələns] N violence *f*; *(Pol etc)* incidents violents

★**violent** [ˈvaɪələnt] ADJ violent(e); **a ~ dislike of sb/sth** une aversion profonde pour qn/qch

violently [ˈvaɪələntlɪ] ADV violemment; *(ill, angry)* terriblement

violet [ˈvaɪələt] ADJ *(colour)* violet(te) ▶ N *(plant)* violette *f*

★**violin** [vaɪəˈlɪn] N violon *m*

violinist [vaɪəˈlɪnɪst] N violoniste *mf*

VIP N ABBR *(= very important person)* VIP *m*

viper [ˈvaɪpə'] N vipère *f*

viral [ˈvaɪərəl] ADJ *(also Comput)* viral(e)

virgin [ˈvəːdʒɪn] N vierge *f*; **she is a ~** elle est vierge; **the Blessed V~** la Sainte Vierge ▶ ADJ vierge

virginity [vəːˈdʒɪnɪtɪ] N virginité *f*

Virgo [ˈvəːgəu] N la Vierge; **to be ~** être de la Vierge

V

virile ['vɪraɪl] ADJ viril(e)

virility [vɪ'rɪlɪtɪ] N virilité f

virtual ['və:tjʊəl] ADJ (Comput, Physics) virtuel(le); (in effect): **it's a ~ impossibility** c'est quasiment impossible; **the ~ leader** le chef dans la pratique

virtually ['və:tjʊəlɪ] ADV (almost) pratiquement; **it is ~ impossible** c'est quasiment impossible

virtual reality N (Comput) réalité virtuelle

virtue ['və:tju:] N vertu f; (advantage) mérite m, avantage m; **by ~ of** en vertu or raison de

virtuosity [və:tjʊ'ɒsɪtɪ] N virtuosité f

virtuoso [və:tjʊ'əʊzəʊ] N virtuose mf

virtuous ['və:tjʊəs] ADJ vertueux(-euse)

virulent ['vɪrʊlənt] ADJ virulent(e)

★**virus** ['vaɪərəs] N (Med, Comput) virus m

visa ['vi:zə] N visa m

vis-à-vis [vi:zə'vi:] PREP vis-à-vis de

visceral ['vɪsərəl] ADJ viscéral(e)

viscount ['vaɪkaʊnt] N vicomte m

viscous ['vɪskəs] ADJ visqueux(-euse), gluant(e)

vise [vaɪs] N (US Tech) = **vice**

visibility [vɪzɪ'bɪlɪtɪ] N visibilité f

visible ['vɪzəbl] ADJ visible; **~ exports/imports** exportations fpl/importations fpl visibles

visibly ['vɪzəblɪ] ADV visiblement

vision ['vɪʒən] N (sight) vue f, vision f; (foresight, in dream) vision

visionary ['vɪʒənrɪ] N visionnaire mf

★**visit** ['vɪzɪt] N visite f; (stay) séjour m; **on a private/official ~** en visite privée/officielle ▶ VT (person: US: also: **visit with**) rendre visite à; (place) visiter

visiting ['vɪzɪtɪŋ] ADJ (speaker, team) invité(e), de l'extérieur

visiting card N carte f de visite

visiting hours NPL heures fpl de visite

★**visitor** ['vɪzɪtəʳ] N visiteur(-euse); (to one's house) invité(e); (in hotel) client(e)

visitor centre, (US) **visitor center** N hall m or centre m d'accueil

visitors' book N livre m d'or; (in hotel) registre m

visor ['vaɪzəʳ] N visière f

vista ['vɪstə] N vue f, perspective f

visual ['vɪzjʊəl] ADJ visuel(le)

visual aid N support visuel (pour l'enseignement)

visual arts NPL arts mpl plastiques

visual display unit N console f de visualisation, visuel m

visualization [vɪzjʊəlaɪ'zeɪʃən] N visualisation f

visualize ['vɪzjʊəlaɪz] VT (picture) visualiser; (imagine) s'imaginer

visually ['vɪzjʊəlɪ] ADV visuellement

visually-impaired ['vɪzjʊəlɪm'pɛəd] ADJ malvoyant(e)

★**vital** ['vaɪtl] ADJ vital(e); **of ~ importance (to sb/sth)** d'une importance capitale (pour qn/qch)

vitality [vaɪ'tælɪtɪ] N vitalité f

vitally ['vaɪtlɪ] ADV extrêmement

vital statistics NPL (of population) statistiques fpl démographiques; (inf: woman's) mensurations fpl

★**vitamin** ['vɪtəmɪn] N vitamine f

vitiate ['vɪʃɪeɪt] VT vicier

vitreous ['vɪtrɪəs] ADJ (china) vitreux(-euse); (enamel) vitrifié(e)

vitriol ['vɪtrɪəl] N attaques fpl au vitriol

vitriolic [vɪtrɪ'ɒlɪk] ADJ (fig) venimeux(-euse)

viva ['vaɪvə] N (also: **viva voce**) (examen) oral

vivacious [vɪ'veɪʃəs] ADJ animé(e), qui a de la vivacité

vivacity [vɪ'væsɪtɪ] N vivacité f

vivid ['vɪvɪd] ADJ (account) frappant(e), vivant(e); (light, imagination) vif (vive)

vividly ['vɪvɪdlɪ] ADV (describe) d'une manière vivante; (remember) de façon précise

vivisection [vɪvɪ'sɛkʃən] N vivisection f

vixen ['vɪksn] N renarde f; (pej: woman) mégère f

viz [vɪz] ABBR (= videlicet: namely) à savoir, c. à d.

VLF ABBR = **very low frequency**

vlog [vlɒg] N blog m vidéo

vlogger ['vlɒgəʳ] N vidéo-blogueur(-euse)

vlogging ['vlɒgɪŋ] N vidéo-blogging m

V-neck ['vi:nɛk] N décolleté m en V

VOA N ABBR (= Voice of America) voix f de l'Amérique (émissions de radio à destination de l'étranger)

vocabulary [vəʊ'kæbjʊlərɪ] N vocabulaire m

vocal ['vəʊkl] ADJ vocal(e); (articulate) qui n'hésite pas à s'exprimer, qui sait faire entendre ses opinions ■ **vocals** NPL voix fpl

vocal cords NPL cordes vocales

vocalist ['vəʊkəlɪst] N chanteur(-euse)

vocation [vəʊ'keɪʃən] N vocation f

vocational [vəʊ'keɪʃənl] ADJ professionnel(le); **~ guidance/training** orientation/formation professionnelle

vociferous [və'sɪfərəs] ADJ bruyant(e)

vodka ['vɒdkə] N vodka f

vogue [vəʊg] N mode f; (popularity) vogue f; **to be in ~** être en vogue or à la mode

★**voice** [vɔɪs] N voix f; (opinion) avis m; **in a loud/soft ~** à voix haute/basse; **to give ~ to** exprimer ▶ VT (opinion) exprimer, formuler

voice mail N (system) messagerie f vocale, boîte f vocale; (device) répondeur m; (message) message m vocal

voice-over ['vɔɪsəʊvəʳ] N voix off f

void [vɔɪd] N vide m ▶ ADJ (invalid) nul(le); (empty): **~ of** vide de, dépourvu(e) de

voile [vɔɪl] N voile m (tissu)

vol. ABBR (= volume) vol

volatile ['vɒlətaɪl] ADJ volatil(e); (person) d'humeur volatile

volatility [vɒlə'tɪlɪtɪ] N (of situation, substance) volatilité f; (of person, temper) instabilité f

volcanic [vɒl'kænɪk] ADJ volcanique

volcano [vɒl'keɪnəʊ] (pl **volcanoes**) N volcan m

volition [və'lɪʃən] N: **of one's own ~** de son propre gré

volley ['vɒlɪ] N (of gunfire) salve f; (of stones etc) pluie f, volée f; (Tennis etc) volée

volleyball ['vɒlɪbɔ:l] N volley(-ball) m

volt [vəʊlt] N volt m

voltage ['vəultɪdʒ] N tension f, voltage m; **high/ low ~** haute/basse tension

voluble ['vɔljubl] ADJ volubile

volume ['vɔlju:m] N volume m; (of tank) capacité f; **~ one/two** (of book) tome un/deux; **his expression spoke volumes** son expression en disait long

volume control N (Radio, TV) bouton m de réglage du volume

volume discount N (Comm) remise f sur la quantité

voluminous [və'lu:mɪnəs] ADJ volumineux(-euse)

voluntarily ['vɔləntrɪlɪ] ADV volontairement; bénévolement

★**voluntary** ['vɔləntərɪ] ADJ volontaire; (unpaid) bénévole

voluntary liquidation N (Comm) dépôt m de bilan

voluntary redundancy N (BRIT) départ m volontaire (en cas de licenciements)

★**volunteer** [vɔlən'tɪəʳ] N volontaire mf ▶ VT (information) donner spontanément; **to ~ to do** se proposer pour faire ▶ VI (Mil) s'engager comme volontaire

voluptuous [və'lʌptjuəs] ADJ voluptueux(-euse)

vomit ['vɔmɪt] N vomissure f ▶ VT, VI vomir

voodoo ['vu:du:] N vaudou m

voracious [və'reɪʃəs] ADJ vorace; (reader) avide

★**vote** [vəut] N vote m, suffrage m; (votes cast) voix f, vote; (franchise) droit m de vote; **to put sth to the ~, to take a ~ on sth** mettre qch aux voix, procéder à un vote sur qch; **~ for or in favour of/against** vote pour/contre; **~ of censure** motion f de censure; **~ of thanks** discours m de remerciement ▶ VT

(bill) voter; (chairman) élire; (propose): **to ~ that** proposer que + sub; **to ~ to do sth** voter en faveur de faire qch ▶ VI voter

voter ['vəutəʳ] N électeur(-trice)

voting ['vəutɪŋ] N scrutin m, vote m

voting paper N (BRIT) bulletin m de vote

voting right N droit m de vote

votive ['vəutɪv] ADJ votif(-ive)

vouch [vautʃ]: **to ~ for** vt fus se porter garant de

voucher ['vautʃəʳ] N (for meal, petrol, gift) bon m; (receipt) reçu m; **travel ~** bon de transport

vow [vau] N vœu m, serment m; **to take** or **make a ~ to do sth** faire le vœu de faire qch ▶ VI jurer

vowel ['vauəl] N voyelle f

voyage ['vɔɪɪdʒ] N voyage m par mer, traversée f; (by spacecraft) voyage

voyeur [vwɑ:'jɜːʳ] N voyeur m

voyeurism ['vwaɪərɪzəm] N voyeurisme m

voyeuristic [vwaɪə'rɪstɪk] ADJ voyeuriste

VP N ABBR = **vice-president**

vs ABBR (= versus) vs

VSO N ABBR (BRIT: = Voluntary Service Overseas) ≈ coopération civile

VT, Vt. ABBR (US) = **Vermont**

vulgar ['vʌlgəʳ] ADJ vulgaire

vulgarity [vʌl'gærɪtɪ] N vulgarité f

vulnerability [vʌlnərə'bɪlɪtɪ] N vulnérabilité f

vulnerable ['vʌlnərəbl] ADJ vulnérable

vulture ['vʌltʃəʳ] N vautour m

vulva ['vʌlvə] N vulve f

V

Ww

W¹, w [ˈdʌblju:] N (letter) W, w m; **W for William** W comme William

W² ABBR (= west) O; (Elec: = watt) W

WA ABBR (US) = **Washington**

wacky [ˈwækɪ] ADJ (inf: person, idea) farfelu(e); (: film, show, humour) délirant(e)

wad [wɔd] N (of cotton wool, paper) tampon m; (of banknotes etc) liasse f

wadding [ˈwɔdɪŋ] N rembourrage m

waddle [ˈwɔdl] VI se dandiner

wade [weɪd] VI: **to ~ through** marcher dans, patauger dans; (fig: book) venir à bout de ▸ VT passer à gué

wafer [ˈweɪfəʳ] N (Culin) gaufrette f; (Rel) pain m d'hostie; (Comput) tranche f (de silicium)

wafer-thin [ˈweɪfəˈθɪn] ADJ ultra-mince, mince comme du papier à cigarette

waffle [ˈwɔfl] N (Culin) gaufre f; (inf) rabâchage m; remplissage m ▸ VI parler pour ne rien dire; faire du remplissage

waffle iron N gaufrier m

waft [wɔft] VT porter ▸ VI flotter

wag [wæg] VT agiter, remuer; **the dog wagged its tail** le chien a remué la queue ▸ VI remuer

★**wage** [weɪdʒ] N (also: **wages**) salaire m, paye f; **a day's wages** un jour de salaire ▸ VT: **to ~ war** faire la guerre

wage claim N demande f d'augmentation de salaire

wage differential N éventail m des salaires

wage earner [-əːnəʳ] N salarié(e); (breadwinner) soutien m de famille

wage freeze N blocage m des salaires

wage packet N (BRIT) (enveloppe f de) paye f

wager [ˈweɪdʒəʳ] N pari m ▸ VT parier

waggle [ˈwægl] VT, VI remuer

wagon, waggon [ˈwægən] N (horse-drawn) chariot m; (BRIT Rail) wagon m (de marchandises)

waif [weɪf] N gamin(e) des rues

wail [weɪl] N gémissement m; (of siren) hurlement m ▸ VI gémir; (siren) hurler

waist [weɪst] N taille f, ceinture f

waistband [ˈweɪstbænd] N taille f; **with an elasticated ~** à taille élastique

waistcoat [ˈweɪskəut] N (BRIT) gilet m

waistline [ˈweɪstlaɪn] N (tour m de) taille f

★**wait** [weɪt] N attente f; **to lie in ~ for** guetter ▸ VI attendre; **to ~ for sb/sth** attendre qn/qch; **to keep sb waiting** faire attendre qn; **~ for me, please** attendez-moi, s'il vous plaît; **~ a minute!** un instant !; **"repairs while you ~"** « réparations minute »; **I can't ~ to ...** (fig) je meurs d'envie de ...
  ▸ **wait behind** VI rester (à attendre)
  ▸ **wait on** VT FUS servir
  ▸ **wait up** VI attendre, ne pas se coucher; **don't ~ up for me** ne m'attendez pas pour aller vous coucher

★**waiter** [ˈweɪtəʳ] N garçon m (de café), serveur m

waiting [ˈweɪtɪŋ] N: **"no ~"** (BRIT Aut) « stationnement interdit »

waiting list N liste f d'attente

waiting room N salle f d'attente

★**waitress** [ˈweɪtrɪs] N serveuse f

waive [weɪv] VT renoncer à, abandonner

waiver [ˈweɪvəʳ] N dispense f

wake [weɪk] (pt **woke** [wəuk] or **waked** [weɪkt], pp **woken** [ˈwəukn] or **waked** [weɪkt]) VT (also: **wake up**) réveiller ▸ VI (also: **wake up**) se réveiller; **to ~ up to sth** (fig) se rendre compte de qch ▸ N (for dead person) veillée f mortuaire; (Naut) sillage m; **in the ~ of** (fig) à la suite de; **to follow in sb's ~** (fig) marcher sur les traces de qn

wakeboard [ˈweɪkbɔːd] N wakeboard m ▸ VI faire du wakeboard

waken [ˈweɪkn] VT, VI = **wake**

★**Wales** [weɪlz] N pays m de Galles; **the Prince of ~** le prince de Galles; **the National Assembly for ~** le Parlement gallois

La **National Assembly for Wales** a été créée en 1998, la majorité de l'électorat gallois s'étant déclaré favorable à la décentralisation lors d'un référendum organisé l'année précédente. Elle diffère du parlement écossais en ce que celui-ci possède un pouvoir législatif considérable dans ses domaines de responsabilité ainsi qu'en matière fiscale, tandis que l'assemblée galloise a un pouvoir législatif plus limité et n'est pas autorisée à lever les impôts. Composée de 60 députés, les AMs (Assembly Members), qui sont élus pour quatre ans, elle est placée sous l'autorité du First Minister.

★**walk** [wɔːk] N promenade f; (short) petit tour; (gait) démarche f; (path) chemin m; (in park etc) allée f; (pace): **at a quick ~** d'un pas rapide; **10 minutes' ~ from** à 10 minutes de marche de; **to go for a ~**

se promener; faire un tour; **from all walks of life** de toutes conditions sociales ▶ vi marcher; (for pleasure, exercise) se promener ▶ vt (distance) faire à pied; (dog) promener; **I'll ~ you home** je vais vous raccompagner chez vous

▶ **walk out** vi (go out) sortir; (as protest) partir (en signe de protestation); (strike) se mettre en grève; **to ~ out on sb** quitter qn

walkabout ['wɔːkəbaut] N: **to go (on a) ~** (VIP) prendre un bain de foule

walker ['wɔːkəʳ] N (person) marcheur(-euse)

walkie-talkie ['wɔːkɪ'tɔːkɪ] N talkie-walkie m

walking ['wɔːkɪŋ] N marche f à pied; **it's within ~ distance** on peut y aller à pied

walking holiday N vacances passées à faire de la randonnée

walking shoes NPL chaussures fpl de marche

walking stick N canne f

walk-on ['wɔːkɔn] ADJ (Theat: part) de figurant(e)

walkout ['wɔːkaut] N (of workers) grève-surprise f

walkover ['wɔːkəuvəʳ] N (inf) victoire f or examen m etc facile

walkway ['wɔːkweɪ] N promenade f, cheminement piéton

★**wall** [wɔːl] N mur m; (of tunnel, cave) paroi f; **to go to the ~** (fig: firm etc) faire faillite

▶ **wall in** vt (garden etc) entourer d'un mur

wallaby ['wɔləbɪ] N wallaby m

wall cupboard N placard mural

walled [wɔːld] ADJ (city) fortifié(e)

wallet ['wɔlɪt] N portefeuille m; **I can't find my ~** je ne retrouve plus mon portefeuille

wallflower ['wɔːlflauəʳ] N giroflée f; **to be a ~** (fig) faire tapisserie

wall hanging N tenture (murale), tapisserie f

wallop ['wɔləp] vt (BRIT inf) taper sur, cogner

wallow ['wɔləu] vi se vautrer; **to ~ in one's grief** se complaire à sa douleur

wallpaper ['wɔːlpeɪpəʳ] N papier peint ▶ vt tapisser

wall-to-wall ['wɔːltə'wɔːl] ADJ: **~ carpeting** moquette f

walnut ['wɔːlnʌt] N noix f; (tree, wood) noyer m

walrus ['wɔːlrəs] (pl ~ or **walruses**) N morse m

waltz [wɔːlts] N valse f ▶ vi valser

wan [wɔn] ADJ pâle; triste

wand [wɔnd] N (also: **magic wand**) baguette f (magique)

wander ['wɔndəʳ] vi (person) errer, aller sans but; (thoughts) vagabonder; (river) serpenter ▶ vt errer dans

wanderer ['wɔndərəʳ] N vagabond(e)

wandering ['wɔndrɪŋ] ADJ (tribe) nomade; (minstrel, actor) ambulant(e)

wanderings ['wɔndrɪŋz] NPL errances fpl

wanderlust ['wɔndəlʌst] N soif f de voyages

wane [weɪn] vi (moon) décroître; (reputation) décliner

wangle ['wæŋgl] (BRIT inf) vt se débrouiller pour avoir; carotter ▶ N combine f, magouille f

wanker ['wæŋkəʳ] N (!) branleur m (!)

wanna ['wɔnə] MODAL AUX VB (inf: want to): **I ~ go** je veux y aller; **they don't ~ do it** ils veulent pas le faire

wannabe ['wɔnəbiː] ADJ (inf) aspirant(e); **a ~ actor** un aspirant acteur

★**want** [wɔnt] vt vouloir; (need) avoir besoin de; (lack) manquer de; **to ~ to do** vouloir faire; **to ~ sb to do** vouloir que qn fasse; **you're wanted on the phone** on vous demande au téléphone; **"cook wanted"** « on demande un cuisinier » ▶ N (poverty) pauvreté f, besoin m; **for ~ of** par manque de, faute de ■ **wants** NPL (needs) besoins mpl

▶ **want in** vi (inf) vouloir en être; **to ~ in on sth** vouloir être de qch

▶ **want out** vi (inf) vouloir laisser tomber; **to ~ out of sth** vouloir sortir de qch

want ads NPL (US) petites annonces

wanted ['wɔntɪd] ADJ (criminal) recherché(e) par la police

wanting ['wɔntɪŋ] ADJ: **to be ~ (in)** manquer (de); **to be found ~** ne pas être à la hauteur

wanton ['wɔntn] ADJ capricieux(-euse), dévergondé(e)

WAP [wæp] N ABBR (= wireless application protocol) WAP m

★**war** [wɔːʳ] N guerre f; **to go to ~** se mettre en guerre; **to make ~ (on)** faire la guerre (à)

warble ['wɔːbl] N (of bird) gazouillis m ▶ vi gazouiller

warbler ['wɔːbləʳ] N pinson m

war cry N cri m de guerre

ward [wɔːd] N (in hospital) salle f; (Pol) section électorale; (Law: child: also: **ward of court**) pupille mf

▶ **ward off** vt parer, éviter

warden ['wɔːdn] N (BRIT: of institution) directeur(-trice); (of park, game reserve) gardien(ne); (BRIT: also: **traffic warden**) contractuel(le); (of youth hostel) responsable mf

warder ['wɔːdəʳ] N (BRIT) gardien m de prison

wardrobe ['wɔːdrəub] N (cupboard) armoire f; (clothes) garde-robe f; (Theat) costumes mpl

warehouse ['wɛəhaus] N entrepôt m

warehousing ['wɛəhauzɪŋ] N entreposage m

wares [wɛəz] NPL marchandises fpl

warfare ['wɔːfɛəʳ] N guerre f

war game N jeu m de stratégie militaire

warhead ['wɔːhɛd] N (Mil) ogive f

warily ['wɛərɪlɪ] ADV avec prudence, avec précaution

warlike ['wɔːlaik] ADJ guerrier(-ière)

★**warm** [wɔːm] ADJ chaud(e); (person, thanks, welcome, applause) chaleureux(-euse); (supporter) ardent(e), enthousiaste; **it's ~** il fait chaud; **I'm ~** j'ai chaud; **to keep sth ~** tenir qch au chaud; **with my warmest thanks/congratulations** avec mes remerciements/mes félicitations les plus sincères

▶ **warm to** vt FUS apprendre à apprécier

▶ **warm up** vi (person, room) se réchauffer; (athlete, discussion) s'échauffer ▶ vt (food) (faire) réchauffer; (water) (faire) chauffer; (engine) faire chauffer

warm-blooded ['wɔːm'blʌdɪd] ADJ (Zool) à sang chaud

war memorial N monument m aux morts

warm-hearted [wɔːm'hɑːtɪd] ADJ affectueux(-euse)

warmly ['wɔːmlɪ] ADV (dress) chaudement; (thank, welcome) chaleureusement

W

warmonger ['wɔ:mʌŋgə'] N belliciste mf

warmongering ['wɔ:mʌŋgrɪŋ] N propagande f belliciste, bellicisme m

warmth [wɔ:mθ] N chaleur f

warm-up ['wɔ:mʌp] N (Sport) période f d'échauffement

★**warn** [wɔ:n] VT avertir, prévenir; **to ~ sb (not) to do** conseiller à qn de (ne pas) faire

warning ['wɔ:nɪŋ] N avertissement m; (notice) avis m; (signal) avertisseur m; **without (any) ~** (suddenly) inopinément; (without notifying) sans prévenir; **gale ~** (Meteorology) avis de grand vent

warning light N avertisseur lumineux

warning triangle N (Aut) triangle m de présignalisation

warp [wɔ:p] N (Textiles) chaîne f ▸ VI (wood) travailler, se voiler or gauchir ▸ VT voiler; (fig) pervertir

warpath ['wɔ:pɑ:θ] N: **to be on the ~** (fig) être sur le sentier de la guerre

warped [wɔ:pt] ADJ (wood) gauchi(e); (fig) perverti(e)

warplane ['wɔ:pleɪn] N avion m de guerre

warrant ['wɔrnt] N (guarantee) garantie f; (Law: to arrest) mandat m d'arrêt; (: to search) mandat de perquisition ▸ VT (justify, merit) justifier

warrant officer N (Mil) adjudant m; (Naut) premier-maître m

warranty ['wɔrəntɪ] N garantie f; **under ~** (Comm) sous garantie

warren ['wɔrən] N (of rabbits) terriers mpl, garenne f

warring ['wɔ:rɪŋ] ADJ (nations) en guerre; (interests etc) contradictoire, opposé(e)

warrior ['wɔrɪə'] N guerrier(-ière)

Warsaw ['wɔ:sɔ:] N Varsovie

warship ['wɔ:ʃɪp] N navire m de guerre

wart [wɔ:t] N verrue f

wartime ['wɔ:taɪm] N: **in ~** en temps de guerre

wary ['wɛərɪ] ADJ prudent(e); **to be ~ about** or **of doing sth** hésiter beaucoup à faire qch

was [wɔz] PT of **be**

★**wash** [wɔʃ] VT laver; (sweep, carry: sea etc) emporter, entraîner; (: ashore) rejeter; **he was washed overboard** il a été emporté par une vague ▸ VI se laver; (sea): **to ~ over/against sth** inonder/baigner qch ▸ N (paint) badigeon m; (clothes) lessive f; (washing programme) lavage m; (of ship) sillage m; **to give sth a ~** laver qch; **to have a ~** se laver, faire sa toilette ▸ **wash away** VT (stain) enlever au lavage; (subj: river etc) emporter
▸ **wash down** VT laver; laver à grande eau
▸ **wash off** VI partir au lavage
▸ **wash up** VI (BRIT) faire la vaisselle; (US: have a wash) se débarbouiller

washable ['wɔʃəbl] ADJ lavable

washbasin ['wɔʃbeɪsn] N lavabo m

washcloth ['wɔʃklɔθ] N (US) gant m de toilette

washed out [wɔʃt'aut] ADJ (colour) délavé(e); (person) vanné(e)

washed up [wɔʃt'ʌp] ADJ (inf) fini(e)

washer ['wɔʃə'] N (Tech) rondelle f, joint m

washing ['wɔʃɪŋ] N (BRIT: linen etc: dirty) linge m; (: clean) lessive f

washing line N (BRIT) corde f à linge

washing machine N machine f à laver

washing powder N (BRIT) lessive f (en poudre)

Washington ['wɔʃɪŋtən] N (city, state) Washington m

★**washing-up** [wɔʃɪŋ'ʌp] N (BRIT) vaisselle f

washing-up liquid N (BRIT) produit m pour la vaisselle

wash-out ['wɔʃaut] N (inf) désastre m

washroom ['wɔʃrum] N (US) toilettes fpl

wasn't ['wɔznt] = **was not**

Wasp, WASP [wɔsp] N ABBR (US inf: = White Anglo-Saxon Protestant) surnom, souvent péjoratif, donné à l'américain de souche anglo-saxonne, aisé et de tendance conservatrice

wasp [wɔsp] N guêpe f

waspish ['wɔspɪʃ] ADJ irritable

wastage ['weɪstɪdʒ] N gaspillage m; (in manufacturing, transport etc) déchet m

★**waste** [weɪst] N gaspillage m; (of time) perte f; (rubbish) déchets mpl; (also: **household waste**) ordures fpl; **it's a ~ of money** c'est de l'argent jeté en l'air; **to go to ~** être gaspillé(e) ▸ ADJ (energy, heat) perdu(e); (food) inutilisé(e); (land, ground: in city) à l'abandon; (: in country) inculte, en friche; (leftover): **~ material** déchets mpl; **to lay ~** (destroy) dévaster ▸ VT gaspiller; (time, opportunity) perdre ■ **wastes** NPL étendue f désertique
▸ **waste away** VI dépérir

wastebasket ['weɪstbɑ:skɪt] N = **wastepaper basket**

waste disposal, waste disposal unit N (BRIT) broyeur m d'ordures

wasteful ['weɪstful] ADJ gaspilleur(-euse); (process) peu économique

waste ground N (BRIT) terrain m vague

wasteland ['weɪstlænd] N terres fpl à l'abandon; (in town) terrain(s) m(pl) vague(s)

wastepaper basket ['weɪstpeɪpə-] N corbeille f à papier

waste pipe N (tuyau m de) vidange f

waste products NPL (Industry) déchets mpl (de fabrication)

waster ['weɪstə'] N (pej) bon(ne) à rien

★**watch** [wɔtʃ] N montre f; (act of watching) surveillance f; (guard: Mil) sentinelle f; (: Naut) homme m de quart; (Naut: spell of duty) quart m; **to keep a close ~ on sb/sth** surveiller qn/qch de près; **to keep ~** faire le guet ▸ VT (look at) observer; (: match, programme) regarder; (spy on, guard) surveiller; (be careful of) faire attention à; **~ what you're doing** fais attention à ce que tu fais ▸ VI regarder; (keep guard) monter la garde
▸ **watch out** VI faire attention

watchband ['wɔtʃbænd] N (US) bracelet m de montre

watchdog ['wɔtʃdɔg] N chien m de garde; (fig) gardien(ne)

watchful ['wɔtʃful] ADJ attentif(-ive), vigilant(e)

watchmaker ['wɔtʃmeɪkə'] N horloger(-ère)

watchman ['wɔtʃmən] N (irreg) gardien m; (also: **night watchman**) veilleur m de nuit

watch stem N (US) remontoir m

watch strap ['wɒtʃstræp] N bracelet *m* de montre

watchtower ['wɒtʃtauəʳ] N tour *f* de guet

watchword ['wɒtʃwəːd] N mot *m* de passe

★**water** ['wɔːtəʳ] N eau *f*; **a drink of ~** un verre d'eau; **in British waters** dans les eaux territoriales britanniques; **to pass ~** uriner ▶ VT (*plant, garden*) arroser ▶ VI (*eyes*) larmoyer; **to make sb's mouth ~** mettre l'eau à la bouche de qn
▶ **water down** VT (*milk etc*) couper avec de l'eau; (*fig: story*) édulcorer

waterboarding ['wɔːtəbɔːdɪŋ] N torture par simulacre de noyade

water closet N (BRIT) w.-c. *mpl*, waters *mpl*

watercolour, (US) **watercolor** N ['wɔːtəkʌləʳ] aquarelle *f* ■ **watercolours** NPL couleurs *fpl* pour aquarelle

water-cooled ['wɔːtəkuːld] ADJ à refroidissement par eau

watercourse ['wɔːtəkɔːs] N cours *m* d'eau

watercress ['wɔːtəkrɛs] N cresson *m* (de fontaine)

waterfall ['wɔːtəfɔːl] N chute *f* d'eau

waterfowl ['wɔːtəfaul] N gibier *m* d'eau

waterfront ['wɔːtəfrʌnt] N (*seafront*) front *m* de mer; (*at docks*) quais *mpl*

water heater N chauffe-eau *m*

water hole N mare *f*

water ice N (BRIT) sorbet *m*

watering can ['wɔːtərɪŋ-] N arrosoir *m*

water level N niveau *m* de l'eau; (*of flood*) niveau des eaux

water lily N nénuphar *m*

waterline ['wɔːtəlaɪn] N (*Naut*) ligne *f* de flottaison

waterlogged ['wɔːtəlɔɡd] ADJ détrempé(e); imbibé(e) d'eau

water main N canalisation *f* d'eau

watermark ['wɔːtəmɑːk] N (*on paper*) filigrane *m*

watermelon ['wɔːtəmɛlən] N pastèque *f*

watermill ['wɔːtəmɪl] N moulin *m* à eau

water polo N water-polo *m*

waterproof ['wɔːtəpruːf] ADJ imperméable

water-repellent ['wɔːtərɪˈpɛlnt] ADJ hydrofuge

watershed ['wɔːtəʃɛd] N (*Geo*) ligne *f* de partage des eaux; (*fig*) moment *m* critique, point décisif

waterside ['wɔːtəsaɪd] N bord *m* de l'eau ▶ CPD (*hotel, restaurant*) au bord de l'eau

water-skiing ['wɔːtəskiːɪŋ] N ski *m* nautique

water softener N adoucisseur *m* d'eau

water tank N réservoir *m* d'eau

watertight ['wɔːtətaɪt] ADJ étanche

water vapour N vapeur *f* d'eau

waterway ['wɔːtəweɪ] N cours *m* d'eau navigable

waterworks ['wɔːtəwəːks] NPL station *f* hydraulique

watery ['wɔːtərɪ] ADJ (*colour*) délavé(e); (*coffee*) trop faible

watt [wɒt] N watt *m*

wattage ['wɒtɪdʒ] N puissance *f* or consommation *f* en watts

wattle ['wɒtl] N clayonnage *m*

★**wave** [weɪv] N vague *f*; (*of hand*) geste *m*, signe *m*; (*Radio*) onde *f*; (*in hair*) ondulation *f*; (*fig: of enthusiasm, strikes etc*) vague; **short/medium ~** (*Radio*) ondes courtes/moyennes; **long ~** (*Radio*) grandes ondes; **the new ~** (*Cine, Mus*) la nouvelle vague ▶ VI faire signe de la main; (*flag*) flotter au vent; (*grass*) ondoyer ▶ VT (*handkerchief*) agiter; (*stick*) brandir; (*hair*) onduler; **to ~ goodbye to sb** dire au revoir de la main à qn
▶ **wave aside, wave away** VT (*fig: suggestion, objection*) rejeter, repousser; (: *doubts*) chasser; (*person*): **to ~ sb aside** faire signe à qn de s'écarter

waveband ['weɪvbænd] N bande *f* de fréquences

wavelength ['weɪvlɛŋθ] N longueur *f* d'ondes

waver ['weɪvəʳ] VI vaciller; (*voice*) trembler; (*person*) hésiter

wavy ['weɪvɪ] ADJ (*hair, surface*) ondulé(e); (*line*) onduleux(-euse)

wax [wæks] N cire *f*; (*for skis*) fart *m* ▶ VT cirer; (*car*) lustrer; (*skis*) farter ▶ VI (*moon*) croître

waxworks ['wækswəːks] NPL personnages *mpl* de cire; musée *m* de cire

★**way** [weɪ] N chemin *m*, voie *f*; (*path, access*) passage *m*; (*distance*) distance *f*; (*direction*) chemin, direction *f*; (*manner*) façon *f*, manière *f*; (*habit*) habitude *f*, façon; (*condition*) état *m*; **which ~? — this ~/that ~** par où or de quel côté ? — par ici/par là; **to crawl one's ~ to ...** ramper jusqu'à ...; **to lie one's ~ out of it** s'en sortir par un mensonge; **to lose one's ~** perdre son chemin; **on the ~ (to)** en route (pour); **to be on one's ~** être en route; **to be in the ~** bloquer le passage; (*fig*) gêner; **to keep out of sb's ~** éviter qn; **it's a long ~ away** c'est loin d'ici; **the village is rather out of the ~** le village est plutôt à l'écart or isolé; **to go out of one's ~ to do** (*fig*) se donner beaucoup de mal pour faire; **to be under ~** (*work, project*) être en cours; **to make ~ (for sb/sth)** faire place (à qn/qch), s'écarter pour laisser passer (qn/qch); **to get one's own ~** arriver à ses fins; **put it the right ~ up** (BRIT) mettez-le dans le bon sens; **to be the wrong ~ round** être à l'envers, ne pas être dans le bon sens; **he's in a bad ~** il va mal; **in a ~** dans un sens; **by the ~** à propos; **in some ways** à certains égards; d'un côté; **in the ~ of** en fait de, comme; **by ~ of** (*through*) en passant par, via; (*as a sort of*) en guise de; **"~ in"** (BRIT) « entrée »; **"~ out"** (BRIT) « sortie »; **the ~ back** le chemin du retour; **this ~ and that** par-ci par-là; **"give ~"** (BRIT Aut) « cédez la priorité »; **no ~!** (*inf*) pas question !

waybill ['weɪbɪl] N (*Comm*) récépissé *m*

waylay [weɪˈleɪ] VT (*irreg: like* **lay**) attaquer; (*fig*): **I got waylaid** quelqu'un m'a accroché

wayside ['weɪsaɪd] N bord *m* de la route; **to fall by the ~** (*fig*) abandonner; (*morally*) quitter le droit chemin

way station N (US: *Rail*) petite gare; (: *fig*) étape *f*

wayward ['weɪwəd] ADJ capricieux(-euse), entêté(e)

W.C. N ABBR (BRIT: = *water closet*) w.-c. *mpl*, waters *mpl*

WCC N ABBR (= *World Council of Churches*) COE *m* (*Conseil œcuménique des Églises*)

★**we** [wiː] PL PRON nous

> In informal French **on** is often used to mean *we*.
> *We're going on holiday tomorrow.* **On part en vacances demain.**

W

★weak [wiːk] ADJ faible; (health) fragile; (beam etc) peu solide; (tea, coffee) léger(-ère); **to grow ~** or **weaker** s'affaiblir, faiblir

weaken ['wiːkn] VI faiblir ▶ VT affaiblir

weak-kneed ['wiːk'niːd] ADJ (fig) lâche, faible

weakling ['wiːklɪŋ] N gringalet m; faible mf

weakly ['wiːklɪ] ADJ chétif(-ive) ▶ ADV faiblement

weakness ['wiːknɪs] N faiblesse f; (fault) point m faible

wealth [wɛlθ] N (money, resources) richesse(s) f(pl); (of details) profusion f

wealth tax N impôt m sur la fortune

wealthy ['wɛlθɪ] ADJ riche

wean [wiːn] VT sevrer

★weapon ['wɛpən] N arme f; **weapons of mass destruction** armes fpl de destruction massive

weaponry ['wɛpənrɪ] N armes fpl

★wear [wɛəʳ] (pt **wore** [wɔːʳ], pp **worn** [wɔːn]) N (use) usage m; (deterioration through use) usure f; **sportswear/babywear** vêtements mpl de sport/pour bébés; **evening ~** tenue f de soirée; **~ and tear** usure f ▶ VT (clothes) porter; (put on) mettre; (beard etc) avoir; (damage: through use) user; **to ~ a hole in sth** faire (à la longue) un trou dans qch ▶ VI (last) faire de l'usage; (rub etc through) s'user
 ▶ **wear away** [wɛəʳ ə'weɪ] VT user, ronger ▶ VI s'user, être rongé(e)
 ▶ **wear down** [wɛəʳ daun] VT user; (strength) épuiser
 ▶ **wear off** [wɛəʳ ɔf] VI disparaître
 ▶ **wear on** [wɛəʳ ɔn] VI se poursuivre; passer
 ▶ **wear out** [wɛəʳ aut] VT user; (person, strength) épuiser

wearable ['wɛərəbl] ADJ mettable

wearer ['wɛərəʳ] N porteur(-euse); **contact lens wearers** les porteurs de lentilles de contact

wearily ['wɪərɪlɪ] ADV avec lassitude

weariness ['wɪərɪnɪs] N épuisement m, lassitude f

wearisome ['wɪərɪsəm] ADJ (tiring) fatigant(e); (boring) ennuyeux(-euse)

weary ['wɪərɪ] ADJ (tired) épuisé(e); (dispirited) las (lasse); abattu(e) ▶ VT lasser ▶ VI: **to ~ of** se lasser de

weasel ['wiːzl] N (Zool) belette f

★weather ['wɛðəʳ] N temps m; **what's the ~ like?** quel temps fait-il ?; **under the ~** (fig: ill) mal fichu(e) ▶ VT (wood) faire mûrir; (storm, lit, fig) essuyer; (crisis) survivre à

weather-beaten ['wɛðəbiːtn] ADJ (person) hâlé(e); (building) dégradé(e) par les intempéries

★weather forecast N prévisions fpl météorologiques, météo f

weatherman ['wɛðəmæn] N (irreg) météorologue m

weatherproof ['wɛðəpruːf] ADJ (garment) imperméable; (building) étanche

weather report N bulletin m météo, météo f

weather vane [-veɪn] N girouette f

weave [wiːv] (pt **wove** [wəuv], pp **woven** ['wəuvn]) VT (cloth) tisser; (basket) tresser ▶ VI (pt, pp **weaved** [wiːvd]) (fig: move in and out) se faufiler

weaver ['wiːvəʳ] N tisserand(e)

weaving ['wiːvɪŋ] N tissage m

web [wɛb] N (of spider) toile f; (on duck's foot) palmure f; (fig) tissu m; (Comput): **the (World-Wide) W~** le Web

web address N adresse f Web

webbed [wɛbd] ADJ (foot) palmé(e)

webbing ['wɛbɪŋ] N (on chair) sangles fpl

★webcam ['wɛbkæm] N webcam f

webcast ['wɛbkɑːst] N webdiffusion f

webinar ['wɛbɪnɑːʳ] N (Comput) séminaire m en ligne, webinaire m

weblog ['wɛblɔg] N blog m, blogue m

webmail ['wɛbmeɪl] N webmail m

webmaster ['wɛbmɑːstəʳ] N webmestre mf

web page N page f Web

★website ['wɛbsaɪt] N site m Web

wed [wɛd] (pt, pp **wedded** ['wɛdɪd]) VT épouser ▶ VI se marier ▶ N: **the newly-weds** les jeunes mariés mpl

Wed. ABBR (= Wednesday) me.

we'd [wiːd] = **we had**; **we would**

wedded ['wɛdɪd] PT, PP of **wed**

★wedding ['wɛdɪŋ] N mariage m

wedding anniversary N anniversaire m de mariage; **silver/golden ~** noces fpl d'argent/d'or

wedding day N jour m du mariage

wedding dress N robe f de mariée

wedding present N cadeau m de mariage

wedding ring N alliance f

wedge [wɛdʒ] N (of wood etc) coin m; (under door etc) cale f; (of cake) part f ▶ VT (fix) caler; (push) enfoncer, coincer

wedge-heeled shoes ['wɛdʒhiːld-], **wedges** ['wɛdʒɪz] NPL chaussures fpl à semelles compensées

wedlock ['wɛdlɔk] N (union f du) mariage m

★Wednesday ['wɛdnzdɪ] N mercredi m; see also **Tuesday**

wee [wiː] ADJ (SCOTTISH) petit(e); tout(e) petit(e)

weed [wiːd] N mauvaise herbe ▶ VT désherber
 ▶ **weed out** VT éliminer

weeding ['wiːdɪŋ] N désherbage m

weedkiller ['wiːdkɪləʳ] N désherbant m

weedy ['wiːdɪ] ADJ (man) gringalet

★week [wiːk] N semaine f; **once/twice a ~** une fois/deux fois par semaine; **in two weeks' time** dans quinze jours; **a ~ today/on Tuesday** aujourd'hui/mardi en huit

weekday ['wiːkdeɪ] N jour m de semaine; (Comm) jour ouvrable; **on weekdays** en semaine

★weekend [wiːk'ɛnd] N week-end m

weekend case N sac m de voyage

weekly ['wiːklɪ] ADV une fois par semaine, chaque semaine ▶ ADJ, N hebdomadaire m

weeknight ['wiːknaɪt] N soir m de semaine

weep [wiːp] (pt, pp **wept** [wɛpt]) VI (person) pleurer; (Med: wound etc) suinter

weeping willow ['wiːpɪŋ-] N saule pleureur

weepy ['wiːpɪ] N (inf: film) mélo m

weft [wɛft] N (Textiles) trame f

★weigh [weɪ] VT, VI peser; **to ~ anchor** lever l'ancre; **to ~ the pros and cons** peser le pour et le contre
 ▶ **weigh down** VT (branch) faire plier; (fig: with worry) accabler
 ▶ **weigh on** VT FUS (problem, worry) peser à; **to ~ on sb's mind** peser à qn

▶ **weigh out** VT (*goods*) peser

▶ **weigh up** VT examiner

weighbridge ['weɪbrɪdʒ] N pont-bascule *m*

weighing machine ['weɪɪŋ-] N balance *f*, bascule *f*

★**weight** [weɪt] N poids *m*; **sold by** ~ vendu au poids; **to put on/lose** ~ grossir/maigrir; **weights and measures** poids et mesures ▶ VT alourdir; (*fig: factor*) pondérer

▶ **weight down** VT maintenir en place

weighted ['weɪtɪd] ADJ (*biased*) biaisé(e); **to be (heavily)** ~ **in favour of sth/sb** être (fortement) biaisé(e) en faveur de qch/qn; **to be** ~ **against sth/sb** être biaisé en défaveur de qch/qn

weighting ['weɪtɪŋ] N: ~ **allowance** indemnité *f* de résidence

weightlessness ['weɪtlɪsnɪs] N apesanteur *f*

weightlifter ['weɪtlɪftə'] N haltérophile *m*

weightlifting ['weɪtlɪftɪŋ] N haltérophilie *f*

weight training N musculation *f*

weighty ['weɪtɪ] ADJ lourd(e)

weir [wɪə'] N barrage *m*

weird [wɪəd] ADJ bizarre; (*eerie*) surnaturel(le)

weirdo ['wɪədəu] N (*inf*) type *m* bizarre

★**welcome** ['wɛlkəm] ADJ bienvenu(e); **to be** ~ être le (la) bienvenu(e); **to make sb** ~ faire bon accueil à qn; **you're** ~ **to try** vous pouvez essayer si vous voulez; **you're** ~! (*after thanks*) de rien, il n'y a pas de quoi ▶ N accueil *m* ▶ VT accueillir; (*also: **bid welcome***) souhaiter la bienvenue à; (*be glad of*) se réjouir de

welcoming ['wɛlkəmɪŋ] ADJ accueillant(e); (*speech*) d'accueil

weld [wɛld] N soudure *f* ▶ VT souder

welder ['wɛldə'] N (*person*) soudeur *m*

welding ['wɛldɪŋ] N soudure *f* (autogène)

welfare ['wɛlfɛə'] N (*wellbeing*) bien-être *m*; (*social aid*) assistance sociale

welfare state N État-providence *m*

welfare work N travail social

★**well** [wɛl] N puits *m* ▶ ADV bien; ~ **done!** bravo !; **to do** ~ bien réussir; (*business*) prospérer; **to think** ~ **of sb** penser du bien de qn; **as** ~ (*in addition*) aussi, également; **you might as** ~ **tell me** tu ferais aussi bien de me le dire; **as** ~ **as** aussi bien que *or* de; en plus de ▶ ADJ: **to be** ~ aller bien; **I don't feel** ~ je ne me sens pas bien; **get** ~ **soon!** remets-toi vite ! ▶ EXCL eh bien !; (*relief also*) bon !; (*resignation*) enfin !; ~, **as I was saying ...** donc, comme je disais ...

▶ **well up** VI (*tears, emotions*) monter

we'll [wiːl] = **we will; we shall**

well-advised [wɛlæd'vaɪzd] ADJ (*action, decision*) sage; **sb would be** ~ **to do sth** qn serait bien avisé(e) de faire qch

well-balanced [wɛl'bælənst] ADJ équilibré(e); **a** ~ **diet** une alimentation équilibrée

well-behaved [wɛlbɪ'heɪvd] ADJ sage, obéissant(e)

well-being ['wɛl'biːɪŋ] N bien-être *m*

well-bred ['wɛl'brɛd] ADJ bien élevé(e)

well-built ['wɛl'bɪlt] ADJ (*house*) bien construit(e); (*person*) bien bâti(e)

well-chosen ['wɛl'tʃəuzn] ADJ (*remarks, words*) bien choisi(e), pertinent(e)

well-deserved ['wɛldɪ'zəːvd] ADJ (bien) mérité(e)

well-developed ['wɛldɪ'vɛləpt] ADJ (*girl*) bien fait(e)

well-disposed ['wɛldɪs'pəuzd] ADJ: ~ **to(wards)** bien disposé(e) envers

well-dressed ['wɛl'drɛst] ADJ bien habillé(e), bien vêtu(e)

well-earned ['wɛl'əːnd] ADJ (*rest*) bien mérité(e)

well-established [wɛlɪ'stæblɪʃt] ADJ bien établi(e)

well-groomed ['wɛl'gruːmd] ADJ très soigné(e)

well-heeled ['wɛl'hiːld] ADJ (*inf: wealthy*) fortuné(e), riche

wellies ['wɛlɪz] NPL (BRIT *inf*) = **wellingtons**

well-informed ['wɛlɪn'fɔːmd] ADJ (*having knowledge of sth*) bien renseigné(e); (*having general knowledge*) cultivé(e)

Wellington ['wɛlɪŋtən] N Wellington

wellingtons ['wɛlɪŋtənz] NPL (*also: **wellington boots***) bottes *fpl* en caoutchouc

well-kept ['wɛl'kɛpt] ADJ (*house, grounds*) bien tenu(e), bien entretenu(e); (*secret*) bien gardé(e); (*hair, hands*) soigné(e)

★**well-known** ['wɛl'nəun] ADJ (*person*) bien connu(e)

well-mannered ['wɛl'mænəd] ADJ bien élevé(e)

well-meaning ['wɛl'miːnɪŋ] ADJ bien intentionné(e)

wellness ['wɛlnɪs] N bien-être *m*

well-nigh ['wɛl'naɪ] ADV: ~ **impossible** pratiquement impossible

well-off ['wɛl'ɔf] ADJ aisé(e), assez riche

well-paid ['wɛl'peɪd] ADJ bien payé(e)

well-read ['wɛl'rɛd] ADJ cultivé(e)

well-spoken ['wɛl'spəukn] ADJ (*person*) qui parle bien; (*words*) bien choisi(e)

well-stocked ['wɛl'stɔkt] ADJ bien approvisionné(e)

well-timed ['wɛl'taɪmd] ADJ opportun(e)

well-to-do ['wɛltə'duː] ADJ aisé(e), assez riche

well-travelled, (US) **well-traveled** [wɛl'trævld] ADJ: **to be** ~ avoir voyagé

well-versed [wɛl'vəːst] ADJ: **to be well versed in sth** être très versé(e) en qch

well-wisher ['wɛlwɪʃə'] N ami(e), admirateur(-trice); **scores of well-wishers had gathered** de nombreux amis et admirateurs s'étaient rassemblés; **letters from well-wishers** des lettres d'encouragement

well-woman clinic ['wɛlwumən-] N centre prophylactique et thérapeutique pour femmes

★**Welsh** [wɛlʃ] ADJ gallois(e) ▶ N (*Ling*) gallois *m* ■ **the Welsh** NPL (*people*) les Gallois *mpl*

Welsh Assembly N Parlement gallois

★**Welshman** ['wɛlʃmən] N (*irreg*) Gallois *m*

Welsh rarebit N croûte *f* au fromage

★**Welshwoman** ['wɛlʃwumən] N (*irreg*) Galloise *f*

welter ['wɛltə'] N fatras *m*

went [wɛnt] PT *of* **go**

W

wept [wɛpt] PT, PP *of* **weep**

were [wəːʳ] PT *of* **be**

we're [wɪəʳ] = **we are**

weren't [wəːnt] = **were not**

werewolf ['wɪəwulf] (*pl* **werewolves** [-wulvz]) N loup-garou *m*

★**west** [wɛst] N ouest *m*; **the W~** l'Occident *m*, l'Ouest ▶ ADJ (*wind*) d'ouest; (*side*) ouest *inv* ▶ ADV à *or* vers l'ouest

westbound ['wɛstbaund] ADJ en direction de l'ouest; (*carriageway*) ouest *inv*

West Country N: **the ~** le sud-ouest de l'Angleterre

westerly ['wɛstəlɪ] ADJ (*situation*) à l'ouest; (*wind*) d'ouest

★**western** ['wɛstən] ADJ occidental(e), de *or* à l'ouest ▶ N (*Cine*) western *m*

westerner ['wɛstənəʳ] N occidental(e)

westernized ['wɛstənaɪzd] ADJ occidentalisé(e)

West German (*formerly*) ADJ ouest-allemand(e) ▶ N Allemand(e) de l'Ouest

West Germany N (*formerly*) Allemagne *f* de l'Ouest

West Indian ADJ antillais(e) ▶ N Antillais(e)

West Indies [-'ɪndɪz] NPL Antilles *fpl*

Westminster ['wɛstmɪnstəʳ] N (*Brit Parliament*) Westminster *m*

westward ['wɛstwəd], **westwards** ['wɛstwədz] ADV vers l'ouest

★**wet** [wɛt] ADJ mouillé(e); (*damp*) humide; (*soaked: also:* **wet through**) trempé(e); (*rainy*) pluvieux(-euse); **to get ~** se mouiller; **"~ paint"** « attention peinture fraîche » ▶ VT: **to ~ one's pants** *or* **o.s.** mouiller sa culotte, faire pipi dans sa culotte

wet blanket N (*fig*) rabat-joie *m inv*

wetness ['wɛtnɪs] N humidité *f*

wetsuit ['wɛtsuːt] N combinaison *f* de plongée

we've [wiːv] = **we have**

whack [wæk] VT donner un grand coup à

whacked [wækt] ADJ (*Brit inf: tired*) crevé(e)

whacking ['wækɪŋ] ADJ (*Brit inf: enormous*) un (une) vache de *before noun* (*inf*) ▶ ADV vachement (*inf*); **a ~ great hole** un trou vachement gros

whale [weɪl] N (*Zool*) baleine *f*

whaler ['weɪləʳ] N (*ship*) baleinier *m*

whaling ['weɪlɪŋ] N pêche *f* à la baleine

wharf [wɔːf] (*pl* **wharves** [wɔːvz]) N quai *m*

---

what [wɔt]

ADJ **1** (*in questions*) quel(le); **what size is he?** quelle taille fait-il ?; **what colour is it?** de quelle couleur est-ce ?; **what books do you need?** quels livres vous faut-il ?

2 (*in exclamations*): **what a mess!** quel désordre !; **what a fool I am!** que je suis bête !

▶ PRON **1** (*interrogative*) que; de/à/en *etc* quoi; **what are you doing?** que faites-vous ?, qu'est-ce que vous faites ?; **what is happening?** qu'est-ce qui se passe ?, que se passe-t-il ?; **what are you talking about?** de quoi parlez-vous ?; **what are you thinking about?** à quoi pensez-vous ?;

what is it called? comment est-ce que ça s'appelle ?; **what about me?** et moi ?; **what about doing …?** et si on faisait … ?

2 (*relative: subject*) ce qui; (*: direct object*) ce que; (*: indirect object*) ce à quoi, ce dont; **I saw what you did/was on the table** j'ai vu ce que vous avez fait/ce qui était sur la table; **tell me what you remember** dites-moi ce dont vous vous souvenez; **what I want is a cup of tea** ce que je veux, c'est une tasse de thé

▶ EXCL (*disbelieving*) quoi !, comment !

---

whatever [wɔt'ɛvəʳ] ADJ: **take ~ book you prefer** prenez le livre que vous préférez, peu importe lequel; **~ book you take** quel que soit le livre que vous preniez ▶ PRON: **do ~ is necessary** faites (tout) ce qui est nécessaire; **~ happens** quoi qu'il arrive ▶ ADV (*also:* **whatsoever**): **no reason ~** pas la moindre raison; **nothing ~** rien du tout

whatsoever [wɔtsəu'ɛvəʳ] ADJ *see* **whatever**

wheat [wiːt] N blé *m*, froment *m*

wheatgerm ['wiːtdʒəːm] N germe *m* de blé

wheatmeal ['wiːtmiːl] N farine bise

wheedle ['wiːdl] VT: **to ~ sb into doing sth** cajoler *or* enjôler qn pour qu'il fasse qch; **to ~ sth out of sb** obtenir qch de qn par des cajoleries

★**wheel** [wiːl] N roue *f*; (*Aut: also:* **steering wheel**) volant *m*; (*Naut*) gouvernail *m* ▶ VT (*pram etc*) pousser, rouler ▶ VI (*birds*) tournoyer; (*also:* **wheel round:** *person*) se retourner, faire volte-face

wheelbarrow ['wiːlbærəu] N brouette *f*

wheelbase ['wiːlbeɪs] N empattement *m*

wheelchair ['wiːltʃɛəʳ] N fauteuil roulant

wheel clamp N (*Aut*) sabot *m* (de Denver)

wheeler-dealer ['wiːlə'diːləʳ] N (*pej*) combinard(e), affairiste *mf*

wheelie-bin ['wiːlɪbɪn] N (*Brit*) poubelle *f* à roulettes

wheeling ['wiːlɪŋ] N: **~ and dealing** (*pej*) manigances *fpl*, magouilles *fpl*

wheeze [wiːz] N respiration bruyante (*d'asthmatique*) ▶ VI respirer bruyamment

wheezy ['wiːzɪ] ADJ sifflant(e)

---

when [wɛn]

ADV quand; **when did he go?** quand est-ce qu'il est parti ?

▶ CONJ **1** (*at, during, after the time that*) quand, lorsque; **she was reading when I came in** elle lisait quand *or* lorsque je suis entré

2 (*on, at which*): **on the day when I met him** le jour où je l'ai rencontré

3 (*whereas*) alors que; **I thought I was wrong when in fact I was right** j'ai cru que j'avais tort alors qu'en fait j'avais raison

---

In English the present tense follows *when* in statements about the future. In French the future tense must be used: *when I win the lottery* **quand je gagnerai à la loterie**.

---

whenever [wɛn'ɛvəʳ] ADV quand donc ▶ CONJ quand; (*every time that*) chaque fois que; **I go ~ I can** j'y vais quand *or* chaque fois que je le peux

★where [wɛə^r] ADV, CONJ où; **this is ~** c'est là que; **~ are you from?** d'où venez vous ?

> Remember to spell **où** with an accent: *Where are you?* **Où es-tu ?** The word **ou** means *or*.

whereabouts ['wɛərəbauts] ADV où donc ▶ N: **nobody knows his ~** personne ne sait où il se trouve

whereas [wɛər'æz] CONJ alors que

whereby [wɛə'baɪ] ADV (*formal*) par lequel (*or* laquelle *etc*)

whereupon [wɛərə'pɔn] ADV sur quoi, et sur ce

wherever [wɛər'ɛvə^r] ADV où donc ▶ CONJ où que + *sub*; **sit ~ you like** asseyez-vous (là) où vous voulez

wherewithal ['wɛəwɪðɔːl] N: **the ~ (to do sth)** les moyens *mpl* (de faire qch)

whet [wɛt] VT aiguiser

★whether ['wɛðə^r] CONJ si; **I don't know ~ to accept or not** je ne sais pas si je dois accepter ou non; **it's doubtful ~** il est peu probable que + *sub*; **~ you go or not** que vous y alliez ou non

whey [weɪ] N petit-lait *m*

---

which [wɪtʃ]

ADJ **1** (*interrogative: direct, indirect*) quel(le); **which picture do you want?** quel tableau voulez-vous ?; **which one?** lequel (laquelle) ?

2: **in which case** auquel cas; **we got there at 8pm, by which time the cinema was full** quand nous sommes arrivés à 20h, le cinéma était complet

▶ PRON **1** (*interrogative*) lequel (laquelle), lesquels (lesquelles) *pl*; **I don't mind which** peu importe lequel; **which (of these) are yours?** lesquels sont à vous ?; **tell me which you want** dites-moi lesquels *or* ceux que vous voulez

2 (*relative: subject*) qui; (: *object*) que; sur/vers *etc* lequel (laquelle) (NB: à + *lequel* = **auquel**; *de* + *lequel* = **duquel**); **the apple which you ate/ which is on the table** la pomme que vous avez mangée/qui est sur la table; **the chair on which you are sitting** la chaise sur laquelle vous êtes assis; **the book of which you spoke** le livre dont vous avez parlé; **he said he knew, which is true/I was afraid of** il a dit qu'il le savait, ce qui est vrai/ce que je craignais; **after which** après quoi

---

whichever [wɪtʃ'ɛvə^r] ADJ: **take ~ book you prefer** prenez le livre que vous préférez, peu importe lequel; **~ book you take** quel que soit le livre que vous preniez; **~ way you** de quelque façon que vous + *sub*

whiff [wɪf] N bouffée *f*; **to catch a ~ of sth** sentir l'odeur de qch

★while [waɪl] N moment *m*; **for a ~** pendant quelque temps; **in a ~** dans un moment; **all the ~** pendant tout ce temps-là; **we'll make it worth your ~** nous vous récompenserons de votre peine ▶ CONJ pendant que; (*as long as*) tant que; (*as, whereas*) alors que; (*though*) bien que + *sub*, quoique + *sub*
▶ **while away** VT (*time*) (faire) passer

whilst [waɪlst] CONJ = **while**

whim [wɪm] N caprice *m*

whimper ['wɪmpə^r] N geignement *m* ▶ VI geindre

whimsical ['wɪmzɪkl] ADJ (*person*) capricieux(-euse); (*look*) étrange

whimsy ['wɪmzɪ] N fantaisie *f*

whine [waɪn] N gémissement *m*; (*of engine, siren*) plainte stridente ▶ VI gémir, geindre, pleurnicher; (*dog, engine, siren*) gémir

whinge [wɪndʒ] VI (BRIT *inf*) râler; **to ~ about sth** râler à propos de qch

★whip [wɪp] N fouet *m*; (*for riding*) cravache *f*; (Pol: *person*) chef *m* de file (*assurant la discipline dans son groupe parlementaire*) ▶ VT fouetter; (*snatch*) enlever (*or* sortir) brusquement
▶ **whip up** VT (*cream*) fouetter; (*inf: meal*) préparer en vitesse; (*stir up: support*) stimuler; (: *feeling*) attiser, aviver

whiplash ['wɪplæʃ] N (Med: *also*: **whiplash injury**) coup *m* du lapin

whipped cream [wɪpt-] N crème fouettée

whipping boy ['wɪpɪŋ-] N (*fig*) bouc *m* émissaire

whip-round ['wɪpraund] N (BRIT) collecte *f*

whirl [wəːl] N tourbillon *m* ▶ VI tourbillonner; (*dancers*) tournoyer ▶ VT faire tourbillonner; faire tournoyer

whirlpool ['wəːlpuːl] N tourbillon *m*

whirlwind ['wəːlwɪnd] N tornade *f*

whirr [wəː^r] VI vrombir

whirring ['wəːrɪŋ] N vrombissement *m*

whisk [wɪsk] N (Culin) fouet *m* ▶ VT (*eggs*) fouetter, battre; **to ~ sb away** *or* **off** emmener qn rapidement

whiskers ['wɪskəz] NPL (*of animal*) moustaches *fpl*; (*of man*) favoris *mpl*

whisky, (IRISH, US) **whiskey** ['wɪskɪ] N whisky *m*

★whisper ['wɪspə^r] N chuchotement *m*; (*fig: of leaves*) bruissement *m*; (*rumour*) rumeur *f* ▶ VT, VI chuchoter

whispering ['wɪspərɪŋ] N chuchotement(s) *m(pl)*

whist [wɪst] N (BRIT) whist *m*

whistle ['wɪsl] N (*sound*) sifflement *m*; (*object*) sifflet *m* ▶ VI siffler ▶ VT siffler, siffloter

whistleblower ['wɪslbləuə^r] N lanceur(-euse) d'alerte

whistleblowing ['wɪslbləuɪŋ] N dénonciation *f*

whistle-stop ['wɪslstɔp] ADJ: **to make a ~ tour of** (Pol) faire la tournée électorale des petits patelins de

Whit [wɪt] N la Pentecôte

★white [waɪt] ADJ blanc (blanche); (*with fear*) blême; **to turn** *or* **go ~** (*person*) pâlir, blêmir; (*hair*) blanchir ▶ N blanc *m*; (*person*) blanc (blanche); **the whites** (*washing*) le linge blanc; **tennis whites** tenue *f* de tennis

whitebait ['waɪtbeɪt] N blanchaille *f*

whiteboard ['waɪtbɔːd] N tableau *m* blanc; **interactive ~** tableau (blanc) interactif

white coffee N (BRIT) café *m* au lait, (café) crème *m*

white-collar worker ['waɪtkɔlə-] N employé(e) de bureau

white elephant N (*fig*) objet dispendieux et superflu

white goods NPL (*appliances*) (gros) électroménager *m*; (*linen etc*) linge *m* de maison

W

Whitehall ['waɪthɔ:l] N (place) à Londres, quartier gouvernemental; (government) le gouvernement britannique

white-hot [waɪt'hɔt] ADJ (metal) incandescent(e)

White House N (US): **the ~** la Maison-Blanche

white lie N pieux mensonge

whiteness ['waɪtnɪs] N blancheur f

white noise N son m blanc

whiteout ['waɪtaut] N jour blanc

white paper N (Pol) livre blanc

whitewash ['waɪtwɔʃ] N (paint) lait m de chaux ▶ VT blanchir à la chaux; (fig) blanchir

whiting ['waɪtɪŋ] N (pl inv: fish) merlan m

Whit Monday N le lundi de Pentecôte

Whitsun ['wɪtsn] N la Pentecôte

whittle ['wɪtl] VT: **to ~ away, to ~ down** (costs) réduire, rogner

whizz [wɪz] VI aller (or passer) à toute vitesse

whizz kid N (inf) petit prodige

WHO N ABBR (= World Health Organization) OMS f (Organisation mondiale de la Santé)

★**who** [hu:] PRON qui

whodunit, whodunnit [hu:'dʌnɪt] N (inf: book, film) polar m (inf)

whoever [hu:'ɛvə'] PRON: **~ finds it** celui (celle) qui le trouve(, qui que ce soit), quiconque le trouve; **ask ~ you like** demandez à qui vous voulez; **~ he marries** qui que ce soit or quelle que soit la personne qu'il épouse; **~ told you that?** qui a bien pu vous dire ça?, qui donc vous a dit ça?

★**whole** [həul] ADJ (complete) entier(-ière), tout(e); (not broken) intact(e), complet(-ète); **the ~ lot (of it)** tout; **the ~ lot (of them)** tous (sans exception) ▶ N (entire unit) tout m; (all): **the ~ of** la totalité de, tout(e) le (la); **the ~ of the time** tout le temps; **the ~ of the town** la ville tout entière; **on the ~, as a ~** dans l'ensemble

wholefood ['həulfu:d] N, **wholefoods** ['həulfu:dz] NPL aliments complets

wholegrains ['həulgreɪnz] NPL céréales fpl complètes

wholehearted [həul'hɑ:tɪd] ADJ sans réserve(s), sincère

wholeheartedly [həul'hɑ:tɪdlɪ] ADV sans réserve; **to agree ~** être entièrement d'accord

wholemeal ['həulmi:l] ADJ (Brit: flour, bread) complet(-ète)

whole note N (US) ronde f

wholesale ['həulseɪl] N (vente f en) gros m ▶ ADJ (price) de gros; (destruction) systématique

wholesaler ['həulseɪlə'] N grossiste mf

wholesome ['həulsəm] ADJ sain(e); (advice) salutaire

wholewheat ['həulwi:t] ADJ = **wholemeal**

wholly ['həulɪ] ADV entièrement, tout à fait

---

whom [hu:m]

PRON **1** (interrogative) qui; **whom did you see?** qui avez-vous vu?; **to whom did you give it?** à qui l'avez-vous donné?

2 (relative) que; à/de etc qui; **the man whom I saw/to whom I spoke** l'homme que j'ai vu/à qui j'ai parlé

---

whoop [wu:p] VI: **to ~ with delight** pousser des cris de joie ▶ N cri m de joie

whooping cough ['hu:pɪŋ-] N coqueluche f

whoops [wu:ps] EXCL (also: **whoops-a-daisy**) oups!, houp-là!

whoosh [wuʃ] VI (inf): **the skiers whooshed past** les skieurs passèrent dans un glissement rapide

whopper ['wɔpə'] N (inf: lie) gros bobard; (: large thing) monstre m, phénomène m

whopping ['wɔpɪŋ] ADJ (inf: big) énorme

whore [hɔ:'] N (!) putain f (inf)

---

whose [hu:z]

ADJ **1** (possessive: interrogative): **whose book is this?, whose is this book?** à qui est ce livre?; **whose pencil have you taken?** à qui est le crayon que vous avez pris?, c'est le crayon de qui que vous avez pris?; **whose daughter are you?** de qui êtes-vous la fille?

2 (possessive: relative): **the man whose son you rescued** l'homme dont or de qui vous avez sauvé le fils; **the girl whose sister you were speaking to** la fille à la sœur de qui or de laquelle vous parliez; **the woman whose car was stolen** la femme dont la voiture a été volée ▶ PRON à qui; **whose is this?** à qui est ceci?; **I know whose it is** je sais à qui c'est

---

Who's Who ['hu:z'hu:] N ≈ Bottin Mondain

---

why [waɪ]

ADV pourquoi; **why is he late?** pourquoi est-il en retard?; **why not?** pourquoi pas?

▶ CONJ: **I wonder why he said that** je me demande pourquoi il a dit ça; **that's not why I'm here** ce n'est pas pour ça que je suis là; **the reason why** la raison pour laquelle

▶ EXCL eh bien!, tiens!; **why, it's you!** tiens, c'est vous!; **why, that's impossible!** voyons, c'est impossible!

---

whyever [waɪ'ɛvə'] ADV pourquoi donc, mais pourquoi

WI N ABBR (Brit: = Women's Institute) amicale de femmes au foyer ▶ ABBR (Geo) = **West Indies**; (US) = **Wisconsin**

wick [wɪk] N mèche f (de bougie)

★**wicked** ['wɪkɪd] ADJ méchant(e); (mischievous: grin, look) espiègle, malicieux(-euse); (crime) pervers(e); (terrible: prices, weather) épouvantable; (inf: very good) génial(e) (inf)

wicker ['wɪkə'] N osier m; (also: **wickerwork**) vannerie f

wicket ['wɪkɪt] N (Cricket: stumps) guichet m; (: grass area) espace compris entre les deux guichets

wicket keeper N (Cricket) gardien m de guichet

★**wide** [waɪd] ADJ large; (area, knowledge) vaste, très étendu(e); (choice) grand(e); **it is 3 metres ~** cela fait 3 mètres de large ▶ ADV: **to open ~** ouvrir tout grand; **to shoot ~** tirer à côté

wide-angle lens ['waɪdæŋgl-] N objectif m grand-angulaire

wide-awake [waɪdə'weɪk] ADJ bien éveillé(e)

wide-eyed [waɪd'aɪd] ADJ aux yeux écarquillés; (fig) naïf(-ïve), crédule

widely ['waɪdlɪ] ADV (*different*) radicalement; (*spaced*) sur une grande étendue; (*believed*) généralement; (*travel*) beaucoup; **to be ~ read** (*author*) être beaucoup lu(e); (*reader*) avoir beaucoup lu, être cultivé(e)

widen ['waɪdn] VT élargir ▶ VI s'élargir

wideness ['waɪdnɪs] N largeur *f*

wide open ADJ grand(e) ouvert(e)

wide-ranging [waɪd'reɪndʒɪŋ] ADJ (*survey, report*) vaste; (*interests*) divers(e)

widespread ['waɪdsprɛd] ADJ (*belief etc*) très répandu(e)

widget ['wɪdʒɪt] N (*Comput*) widget *m*

widow ['wɪdəu] N veuve *f*

widowed ['wɪdəud] ADJ (qui est devenu(e)) veuf (veuve)

widower ['wɪdəuər] N veuf *m*

width [wɪdθ] N largeur *f*; **it's 7 metres in ~** cela fait 7 mètres de large

widthways ['wɪdθweɪz] ADV en largeur

wield [wiːld] VT (*sword*) manier; (*power*) exercer

★**wife** [waɪf] (*pl* **wives** [waɪvz]) N femme *f*, épouse *f*

Wi-Fi ['waɪfaɪ] N wifi *m* ▶ N ABBR (= *wireless fidelity*) WiFi *m* ▶ ADJ (*hot spot, network*) WiFi *inv*

wig [wɪg] N perruque *f*

wigging ['wɪgɪŋ] N (*Brit inf*) savon *m*, engueulade *f*

wiggle ['wɪgl] VT agiter, remuer ▶ VI (*loose screw etc*) branler; (*worm*) se tortiller

wiggly ['wɪglɪ] ADJ (*line*) ondulé(e)

wiki ['wɪkɪ] N (*Internet*) wiki *m*

★**wild** [waɪld] ADJ sauvage; (*sea*) déchaîné(e); (*idea, life*) fou (folle); (*behaviour*) déchaîné(e), extravagant(e); (*inf: angry*) hors de soi, furieux(-euse); (: *enthusiastic*): **to be ~ about** être fou (folle) or dingue de ▶ N: **the ~** la nature ■ **wilds** NPL régions *fpl* sauvages

wild card N (*Comput*) caractère *m* de remplacement

wildcat ['waɪldkæt] N chat *m* sauvage

wildcat strike N grève *f* sauvage

wilderness ['wɪldənɪs] N désert *m*, région *f* sauvage

wildfire ['waɪldfaɪər] N: **to spread like ~** se répandre comme une traînée de poudre

wild-goose chase [waɪld'guːs-] N (*fig*) fausse piste

wildlife ['waɪldlaɪf] N faune *f* (et flore *f*)

wildly ['waɪldlɪ] ADV (*behave*) de manière déchaînée; (*applaud*) frénétiquement; (*hit, guess*) au hasard; (*happy*) follement

wiles [waɪlz] NPL ruses *fpl*, artifices *mpl*

wilful, (*US*) **willful** ['wɪlful] ADJ (*person*) obstiné(e); (*action*) délibéré(e); (*crime*) prémédité(e)

---

will [wɪl]

AUX VB **1** (*forming future tense*): **I will finish it tomorrow** je le finirai demain; **I will have finished it by tomorrow** je l'aurai fini d'ici demain; **will you do it?** — **yes I will/no I won't** le ferez-vous ? — oui/non; **you won't lose it, will you?** vous ne le perdrez pas, n'est-ce pas ?

---

2 (*in conjectures, predictions*): **he will** or **he'll be there by now** il doit être arrivé à l'heure qu'il est; **that will be the postman** ça doit être le facteur

3 (*in commands, requests, offers*): **will you be quiet!** voulez-vous bien vous taire !; **will you help me?** est-ce que vous pouvez m'aider ?; **will you have a cup of tea?** voulez-vous une tasse de thé ?; **I won't put up with it!** je ne le tolérerai pas !
▶ VT (*pt, pp* **willed**): **to will sb to do** souhaiter ardemment que qn fasse; **he willed himself to go on** par un suprême effort de volonté, il continua

▶ N **1** volonté *f*; **to do sth of one's own free will** faire qch de son propre gré; **against one's will** à contre-cœur
2 (*document*) testament *m*

willful ['wɪlful] ADJ (*US*) = **wilful**

★**willing** ['wɪlɪŋ] ADJ de bonne volonté, serviable; **he's ~ to do it** il est disposé à le faire, il veut bien le faire ▶ N: **to show ~** faire preuve de bonne volonté

willingly ['wɪlɪŋlɪ] ADV volontiers

willingness ['wɪlɪŋnɪs] N bonne volonté

will-o'-the-wisp ['wɪləðə'wɪsp] N (*also fig*) feu follet *m*

willow ['wɪləu] N saule *m*

willpower ['wɪl'pauər] N volonté *f*

willy ['wɪlɪ] N (*Brit inf: penis*) quéquette *f* (*inf*); **to give sb the willies** (*inf*) foutre la trouille à qn (*inf*)

willy-nilly ['wɪlɪ'nɪlɪ] ADV (*inf*) bon gré mal gré

wilt [wɪlt] VI dépérir

wily ['waɪlɪ] ADJ rusé(e)

wimp [wɪmp] N (*inf*) mauviette *f*

★**win** [wɪn] (*pt, pp* **won** [wʌn]) N (*in sports etc*) victoire *f* ▶ VT (*battle, money*) gagner; (*prize, contract*) remporter; (*popularity*) acquérir ▶ VI gagner
▶ **win over** [wɪn 'əuvər] VT convaincre
▶ **win round** [wɪn raund] VT gagner, se concilier

wince [wɪns] N tressaillement *m* ▶ VI tressaillir

winch [wɪntʃ] N treuil *m*

Winchester disk ['wɪntʃɪstə-] N (*Comput*) disque *m* Winchester

★**wind**[1] [wɪnd] N (*also Med*) vent *m*; (*breath*) souffle *m*; **the ~(s)** (*Mus*) les instruments *mpl* à vent; **into** or **against the ~** contre le vent; **to get ~ of sth** (*fig*) avoir vent de qch; **to break ~** avoir des gaz ▶ VT (*take breath away*) couper le souffle à

wind[2] [waɪnd] (*pt, pp* **wound** [waund]) VT enrouler; (*wrap*) envelopper; (*clock, toy*) remonter ▶ VI (*road, river*) serpenter
▶ **wind down** [waɪnd daun] VT (*car window*) baisser; (*fig: production, business*) réduire progressivement
▶ **wind up** [waɪnd ʌp] VT (*clock*) remonter; (*debate*) terminer, clôturer

windbreak ['wɪndbreɪk] N brise-vent *m inv*

windcheater ['wɪndtʃiːtər], (*US*) **windbreaker** ['wɪndbreɪkər] N anorak *m*

winder ['waɪndər] N (*Brit: on watch*) remontoir *m*

windfall ['wɪndfɔːl] N coup *m* de chance

wind farm N ferme *f* éolienne

winding ['waɪndɪŋ] ADJ (*road*) sinueux(-euse); (*staircase*) tournant(e)

W

wind instrument N (*Mus*) instrument *m* à vent

windmill ['wɪndmɪl] N moulin *m* à vent

★**window** ['wɪndəu] N fenêtre *f*; (*in car, train: also:* **windowpane**) vitre *f*; (*in shop etc*) vitrine *f*

window box N jardinière *f*

window cleaner N (*person*) laveur(-euse) de vitres

window dressing N arrangement *m* de la vitrine

window envelope N enveloppe *f* à fenêtre

window frame N châssis *m* de fenêtre

window ledge N rebord *m* de la fenêtre

window pane N vitre *f*, carreau *m*

window seat N (*on plane*) place *f* côté hublot

window-shopping ['wɪndəuʃɔpɪŋ] N: **to go ~** faire du lèche-vitrines

windowsill ['wɪndəusɪl] N (*inside*) appui *m* de la fenêtre; (*outside*) rebord *m* de la fenêtre

windpipe ['wɪndpaɪp] N gosier *m*

wind power N énergie éolienne

windscreen ['wɪndskri:n] N (*BRIT*) pare-brise *m inv*

windscreen washer, (*US*) **windshield washer** N lave-glace *m inv*

windscreen wiper, (*US*) **windshield wiper** [-waɪpə^r] N essuie-glace *m inv*

windshield ['wɪndʃi:ld] N (*US*) = **windscreen**

windsurfing ['wɪndsə:fɪŋ] N planche *f* à voile

windswept ['wɪndswɛpt] ADJ balayé(e) par le vent

wind tunnel N soufflerie *f*

wind turbine N éolienne *f*

windy ['wɪndɪ] ADJ (*day*) de vent, venteux(-euse); (*place, weather*) venteux; **it's ~** il y a du vent

★**wine** [waɪn] N vin *m* ▶ VT: **to ~ and dine sb** offrir un dîner bien arrosé à qn

wine bar N bar *m* à vin

wine cellar N cave *f* à vins

wine glass N verre *m* à vin

wine list N carte *f* des vins

wine merchant N marchand(e) de vins

winery ['waɪnərɪ] (*US*) N cave *f* de vinification, vinerie *f*

wine tasting [-teɪstɪŋ] N dégustation *f* (de vins)

wine waiter N sommelier *m*

★**wing** [wɪŋ] N aile *f*; (*in air force*) groupe *m* d'escadrilles ■ **wings** NPL (*Theat*) coulisses *fpl*

winger ['wɪŋə^r] N (*Sport*) ailier *m*

wing mirror N (*BRIT*) rétroviseur latéral

wing nut N papillon *m*, écrou *m* à ailettes

wingspan ['wɪŋspæn], **wingspread** ['wɪŋsprɛd] N envergure *f*

wink [wɪŋk] N clin *m* d'œil ▶ VI faire un clin d'œil; (*blink*) cligner les yeux

winkle [wɪŋkl] N bigorneau *m*

★**winner** ['wɪnə^r] N gagnant(e)

★**winning** ['wɪnɪŋ] ADJ (*team*) gagnant(e); (*goal*) décisif(-ive); (*charming*) charmeur(-euse)

winning post N poteau *m* d'arrivée

winnings ['wɪnɪŋz] NPL gains *mpl*

winsome ['wɪnsəm] ADJ avenant(e), engageant(e)

★**winter** ['wɪntə^r] N hiver *m*; **in ~** en hiver ▶ VI hiverner

winter sports NPL sports *mpl* d'hiver

wintertime ['wɪntətaɪm] N hiver *m*

wintry ['wɪntrɪ] ADJ hivernal(e)

★**wipe** [waɪp] N coup *m* de torchon (or de chiffon or d'éponge); **to give sth a ~** donner un coup de torchon/de chiffon/d'éponge à qch ▶ VT essuyer; (*erase: tape*) effacer; **to ~ one's nose** se moucher
  ▶ **wipe off** VT essuyer
  ▶ **wipe out** VT (*debt*) éteindre, amortir; (*memory*) effacer; (*destroy*) anéantir
  ▶ **wipe up** VT essuyer

wiper ['waɪpə^r] N essuie-glace *m*

★**wire** [waɪə^r] N fil *m* (de fer); (*Elec*) fil électrique; (*Tel*) télégramme *m* ▶ VT (*fence*) grillager; (*house*) faire l'installation électrique de; (*also:* **wire up**) brancher; (*person: send telegram to*) télégraphier à

wire brush N brosse *f* métallique

wire cutters [-kʌtəz] NPL cisaille *f*

wireless ['waɪəlɪs] ADJ sans fil ▶ N (*BRIT*) télégraphie *f* sans fil; (*set*) T.S.F. *f*

wireless technology N technologie *f* sans fil

wire netting N treillis *m* métallique, grillage *m*

wire service N (*US*) revue *f* de presse (*par téléscripteur*)

wire-tapping ['waɪə'tæpɪŋ] N écoute *f* téléphonique

wiring ['waɪərɪŋ] N (*Elec*) installation *f* électrique

wiry ['waɪərɪ] ADJ noueux(-euse), nerveux(-euse)

wisdom ['wɪzdəm] N sagesse *f*; (*of action*) prudence *f*

wisdom tooth N dent *f* de sagesse

★**wise** [waɪz] ADJ sage, prudent(e); (*remark*) judicieux(-euse); **I'm none the wiser** je ne suis pas plus avancé(e) pour autant
  ▶ **wise up** (*inf*): **to ~ up to** commencer à se rendre compte de

...wise [waɪz] SUFFIX: **timewise** en ce qui concerne le temps, question temps

wisecrack ['waɪzkræk] N (*inf*) vanne *f* (*inf*)

★**wisecracking** ['waɪzkrækɪŋ] ADJ vanneur(-euse) **wish** [wɪʃ] N (*desire*) désir *m*; (*specific desire*) souhait *m*, vœu *m*; **best wishes** (*on birthday etc*) meilleurs vœux; **with best wishes** (*in letter*) bien amicalement; **give her my best wishes** faites-lui mes amitiés ▶ VT souhaiter, désirer, vouloir; **to ~ sb goodbye** dire au revoir à qn; **he wished me well** il m'a souhaité bonne chance; **to ~ to do/sb to do** désirer or vouloir faire/que qn fasse; **to ~ sth on sb** souhaiter qch à qn ▶ VI: **to ~ for** souhaiter

wishbone ['wɪʃbəun] N fourchette *f*

wishful ['wɪʃful] ADJ: **it's ~ thinking** c'est prendre ses désirs pour des réalités

wishy-washy ['wɪʃɪ'wɔʃɪ] ADJ (*inf: person*) qui manque de caractère, falot(e); (*: ideas, thinking*) faiblard(e)

wisp [wɪsp] N fine mèche (*de cheveux*); (*of smoke*) mince volute *f*; **a ~ of straw** un fétu de paille

wistful ['wɪstful] ADJ mélancolique

wit [wɪt] N (*also:* **wits**: *intelligence*) intelligence *f*, esprit *m*; (*presence of mind*) présence *f* d'esprit; (*wittiness*) esprit; (*person*) homme/femme d'esprit; **to be at one's wits' end** (*fig*) ne plus savoir que faire; **to have one's wits about one** avoir toute sa présence d'esprit, ne pas perdre la tête; **to ~** *adv* à savoir

witch [wɪtʃ] N sorcière f
witchcraft ['wɪtʃkrɑːft] N sorcellerie f
witch doctor N sorcier m
witch-hunt ['wɪtʃhʌnt] N chasse f aux sorcières

---

with [wɪð, wɪθ]

PREP **1** (*in the company of*) avec; (: *at the home of*) chez; **we stayed with friends** nous avons logé chez des amis; **I'll be with you in a minute** je suis à vous dans un instant
2 (*descriptive*): **a room with a view** une chambre avec vue; **the man with the grey hat/blue eyes** l'homme au chapeau gris/aux yeux bleus
3 (*indicating manner, means, cause*): **with tears in her eyes** les larmes aux yeux; **to walk with a stick** marcher avec une canne; **red with anger** rouge de colère; **to shake with fear** trembler de peur; **to fill sth with water** remplir qch d'eau
4 (*in phrases*): **I'm with you** (*I understand*) je vous suis; **to be with it** (*inf: up-to-date*) être dans le vent

---

withdraw [wɪθ'drɔː] VT (*irreg: like* **draw**) retirer ▶ VI se retirer; (*go back on promise*) se rétracter; **to ~ into o.s.** se replier sur soi-même
withdrawal [wɪθ'drɔːəl] N retrait m; (*Med*) état m de manque
withdrawal symptoms NPL: **to have ~** être en état de manque, présenter les symptômes de sevrage
withdrawn [wɪθ'drɔːn] PP *of* **withdraw** ▶ ADJ (*person*) renfermé(e)
withdrew [wɪθ'druː] PT *of* **withdraw**
wither ['wɪðəʳ] VI se faner
withered ['wɪðəd] ADJ fané(e), flétri(e); (*limb*) atrophié(e)
withering ['wɪðərɪŋ] ADJ (*look, attack*) cinglant(e)
withhold [wɪθ'həuld] VT (*irreg: like* **hold**) (*money*) retenir; (*decision*) remettre; **to ~ (from)** (*permission*) refuser (à); (*information*) cacher (à)
★within [wɪð'ɪn] PREP à l'intérieur de; **~ his reach** à sa portée; **~ sight of** en vue de; **~ a mile of** à moins d'un mille de; **~ the week** avant la fin de la semaine; **~ an hour from now** d'ici une heure; **to be ~ the law** être légal(e) or dans les limites de la légalité ▶ ADV à l'intérieur
★without [wɪ'ðaut] PREP sans; **~ a coat** sans manteau; **~ speaking** sans parler; **~ anybody knowing** sans que personne ne le sache; **to go** *or* **do ~ sth** se passer de qch
withstand [wɪθ'stænd] VT (*irreg: like* **stand**) résister à
witness ['wɪtnɪs] N (*person*) témoin m; (*evidence*) témoignage m; **to bear ~ to sth** témoigner de qch; **~ for the prosecution/defence** témoin à charge/à décharge ▶ VT (*event*) être témoin de; (*document*) attester l'authenticité de ▶ VI: **to ~ to sth/having seen sth** témoigner de qch/d'avoir vu qch
witness box, (*US*) **witness stand** N barre f des témoins
witticism ['wɪtɪsɪzəm] N mot m d'esprit
witty ['wɪtɪ] ADJ spirituel(le), plein(e) d'esprit
wives [waɪvz] NPL *of* **wife**

wizard ['wɪzəd] N magicien m
wizened ['wɪznd] ADJ ratatiné(e)
wk ABBR = **week**
WMD ABBR (= *weapons of mass destruction*) armes fpl de destruction massive
WO N ABBR = **warrant officer**
wobble ['wɔbl] VI trembler; (*chair*) branler
wobbly ['wɔblɪ] ADJ tremblant(e), branlant(e)
woe [wəu] N malheur m
woeful ['wəuful] ADJ (*sad*) malheureux(-euse); (*terrible*) affligeant(e)
wok [wɔk] N wok m
woke [wəuk] PT *of* **wake**
woken ['wəukn] PP *of* **wake**
wolf [wulf] (*pl* **wolves** [wulvz]) N loup m
★woman ['wumən] (*pl* **women** ['wɪmɪn]) N femme f; **young ~** jeune femme; **women's page** (*Press*) page f des lectrices ▶ CPD: **~ doctor** femme f médecin; **~ friend** amie f; **~ teacher** professeur m femme
womanhood ['wumənhud] N (*being a woman*) vie f de femme; (*women*) femmes fpl
womanize ['wumənaɪz] VI courir le jupon
womanizer ['wumənaɪzəʳ] N coureur m de jupons
womanly ['wumənlɪ] ADJ féminin(e)
womb [wuːm] N (*Anat*) utérus m
women ['wɪmɪn] NPL *of* **woman**
womenfolk ['wɪmɪnfəuk] NPL femmes fpl
won [wʌn] PT, PP *of* **win**
★wonder ['wʌndəʳ] N merveille f, miracle m; (*feeling*) émerveillement m; **it's no ~ that** il n'est pas étonnant que + *sub* ▶ VT: **to ~ whether/why** se demander si/pourquoi ▶ VI: **to ~ at** (*surprise*) s'étonner de; (*admiration*) s'émerveiller de; **to ~ about** songer à
★wonderful ['wʌndəful] ADJ merveilleux(-euse)
wonderfully ['wʌndəfəlɪ] ADV (+ *adj*) merveilleusement; (+ *vb*) à merveille
wonky ['wɔŋkɪ] ADJ (BRIT *inf*) qui ne va *or* ne marche pas très bien
wont [wəunt] N: **as is his/her ~** comme de coutume
won't [wəunt] = **will not**
woo [wuː] VT (*woman*) faire la cour à
★wood [wud] N (*timber, forest*) bois m ▶ CPD de bois, en bois
wood carving N sculpture f en *or* sur bois
wooded ['wudɪd] ADJ boisé(e)
★wooden ['wudn] ADJ en bois; (*fig: actor*) raide; (: *performance*) qui manque de naturel
woodland ['wudlənd] N forêt f, région boisée
woodpecker ['wudpekəʳ] N pic m (*oiseau*)
wood pigeon N ramier m
woodshed ['wudʃed] N hangar m à bois
woodwind ['wudwɪnd] N (*Mus*) bois m; **the ~** les bois mpl
woodwork ['wudwəːk] N menuiserie f
woodworm ['wudwəːm] N ver m du bois; **the table has got ~** la table est piquée des vers
woof [wuf] N (*of dog*) aboiement m ▶ VI aboyer ▶ EXCL: **~, ~!** oua, oua !

W

wool [wʊl] N laine f; **to pull the ~ over sb's eyes** (fig) en faire accroire à qn

woollen, (US) **woolen** ['wʊlən] ADJ de or en laine; (industry) lainier(-ière) ▶ N: **woollens** lainages mpl

woolly, (US) **wooly** ['wʊlɪ] ADJ laineux(-euse); (fig: ideas) confus(e)

woozy ['wuːzɪ] ADJ (inf) dans les vapes (inf)

★**word** [wɜːd] N mot m; (spoken) mot, parole f; (promise) parole; (news) nouvelles fpl; **~ for ~** (repeat) mot pour mot; (translate) mot à mot; **what's the ~ for "pen" in French?** comment dit-on «pen» en français?; **to put sth into words** exprimer qch; **in other words** en d'autres termes; **to have a ~ with sb** toucher un mot à qn; **to have words with sb** (quarrel with) avoir des mots avec qn; **to break/keep one's ~** manquer à sa parole/tenir (sa) parole; **I'll take your ~ for it** je vous crois sur parole; **to send ~ (with sb/for sb) that …** laisser un mot (à qn/pour qn) disant que … ▶ VT rédiger, formuler

wording ['wɜːdɪŋ] N termes mpl, langage m; (of document) libellé m

word of mouth N: **by** or **through ~** de bouche à oreille

word-perfect ['wɜːd'pɜːfɪkt] ADJ: **he was ~ (in his speech** etc), **his speech** etc **was ~** il savait son discours etc sur le bout du doigt

wordplay ['wɜːdpleɪ] N jeu m de mot(s)

word processing N traitement m de texte

word processor [-prəʊsesər] N machine f de traitement de texte

wordwrap ['wɜːdræp] N (Comput) retour m (automatique) à la ligne

wordy ['wɜːdɪ] ADJ verbeux(-euse)

wore [wɔːr] PT of **wear**

★**work** [wɜːk] N travail m; (Art, Literature) œuvre f; **to go to ~** aller travailler; **to set to ~**, **to start ~** se mettre à l'œuvre; **to be at ~ (on sth)** travailler (sur qch); **to be out of ~** être au chômage or sans emploi ▶ VI travailler; (mechanism) marcher, fonctionner; (plan etc) marcher; (medicine) agir; **how does this ~?** comment est-ce que ça marche?; **the TV isn't working** la télévision est en panne or ne marche pas; **to ~ hard** travailler dur; **to ~ loose** se défaire, se desserrer ▶ VT (clay, wood etc) travailler; (mine etc) exploiter; (machine) faire marcher or fonctionner; (miracles etc) faire ■ **works** n (Brit: factory) usine f; npl (of clock, machine) mécanisme m; **road works** travaux mpl (d'entretien des routes)

▶ **work off** VT (energy) dépenser son trop plein de; (stress, anger, frustration) évacuer; (debt) travailler pour payer

▶ **work on** VT FUS travailler à; (principle) se baser sur

▶ **work out** VI (plans etc) marcher; (Sport) s'entraîner; **it works out at £100** ça fait 100 livres ▶ VT (problem) résoudre; (plan) élaborer

▶ **work towards** VT FUS (solution, agreement) travailler à

▶ **work up** VT: **to get worked up** se mettre dans tous ses états

workable ['wɜːkəbl] ADJ (solution) réalisable

workaholic [wɜːkə'hɒlɪk] N bourreau m de travail

workbench ['wɜːkbɛntʃ] N établi m

workbook ['wɜːkbʊk] N cahier m d'exercices

workday ['wɜːkdeɪ] N (weekday) jour m de travail; (esp US: day of work) journée f de travail

worked up [wɜːkt-] ADJ: **to get ~** se mettre dans tous ses états

★**worker** ['wɜːkər] N travailleur(-euse), ouvrier(-ière); **office ~** employé(e) de bureau

work experience N stage m

workforce ['wɜːkfɔːs] N main-d'œuvre f

work-in ['wɜːkɪn] N (Brit) occupation f d'usine etc (sans arrêt de la production)

working ['wɜːkɪŋ] ADJ (day, tools etc, conditions) de travail; (wife) qui travaille; (partner, population) actif(-ive); **in ~ order** en état de marche; **a ~ knowledge of English** une connaissance toute pratique de l'anglais

working capital N (Comm) fonds mpl de roulement

working class N classe ouvrière ▶ ADJ: **working-class** ouvrier(-ière), de la classe ouvrière

working man N (irreg) travailleur m

working party N (Brit) groupe m de travail

working week N semaine f de travail

work-in-progress ['wɜːkɪn'prəʊgres] N (Comm) en-cours m inv; (: value) valeur f des en-cours

workload ['wɜːkləʊd] N charge f de travail

workman ['wɜːkmən] N (irreg) ouvrier m

workmanship ['wɜːkmənʃɪp] N métier m, habileté f; facture f

workmate ['wɜːkmeɪt] N collègue mf

work of art N œuvre f d'art

workout ['wɜːkaʊt] N (Sport) séance f d'entraînement

work permit N permis m de travail

workplace ['wɜːkpleɪs] N lieu m de travail

works council N comité m d'entreprise

worksheet ['wɜːkʃiːt] N (Scol) feuille f d'exercices; (Comput) feuille de programmation

workshop ['wɜːkʃɒp] N atelier m

work station N poste m de travail

work study N étude f du travail

work surface N plan m de travail

worktop ['wɜːktɒp] N plan m de travail

work-to-rule ['wɜːktə'ruːl] N (Brit) grève f du zèle

workwear ['wɜːkwɛər] N vêtements mpl professionnels or de travail

★**world** [wɜːld] N monde m; **all over the ~** dans le monde entier, partout dans le monde; **to think the ~ of sb** (fig) ne jurer que par qn; **what in the ~ is he doing?** qu'est-ce qu'il peut bien être en train de faire?; **to do sb a ~ of good** faire le plus grand bien à qn; **W~ War One/Two**, **the First/Second W~ War** la Première/Deuxième Guerre mondiale; **out of this ~** (fig) extraordinaire ▶ CPD (champion) du monde; (power, war) mondial(e)

World Cup N: **the ~** (Sport) la Coupe du monde

world-famous [wɜːld'feɪməs] ADJ de renommée mondiale

worldly ['wɜːldlɪ] ADJ de ce monde

world music N world music f

World Series N: **the ~** (US Baseball) le championnat national de baseball

world-wide ['wə:ld waɪd] ADJ universel(le) ▶ ADV dans le monde entier

World-Wide Web N: **the ~** le Web

worm [wə:m] N (*also:* **earthworm**) ver *m*

worn [wɔ:n] PP *of* **wear** ▶ ADJ usé(e)

worn-out ['wɔ:naut] ADJ (*object*) complètement usé(e); (*person*) épuisé(e)

★**worried** ['wʌrɪd] ADJ inquiet(-ète); **to be ~ about sth** être inquiet au sujet de qch

worrier ['wʌrɪəʳ] N inquiet(-ète)

worrisome ['wʌrɪsəm] ADJ inquiétant(e)

★**worry** ['wʌrɪ] N souci *m* ▶ VT inquiéter ▶ VI s'inquiéter, se faire du souci; **to ~ about sth/ sb** se faire du souci pour *or* à propos de qch/qn

worrying ['wʌrɪɪŋ] ADJ inquiétant(e)

★**worse** [wə:s] ADJ pire, plus mauvais(e); **to get ~** (*condition, situation*) se dégrader ▶ ADV plus mal ▶ N pire *m*; **a change for the ~** une détérioration; **he is none the ~ for it** il ne s'en porte pas plus mal; **so much the ~ for you!** tant pis pour vous !

worsen ['wə:sn] VT, VI empirer

worse off ADJ moins à l'aise financièrement; (*fig*): **you'll be ~ this way** ça ira moins bien de cette façon; **he is now ~ than before** il se retrouve dans une situation pire qu'auparavant

worship ['wə:ʃɪp] N culte *m*; **Your W~** (BRIT: *to mayor*) Monsieur le Maire (: *to judge*) Monsieur le Juge ▶ VT (*God*) rendre un culte à; (*person*) adorer

worshipper ['wə:ʃɪpəʳ] N adorateur(-trice); (*in church*) fidèle *mf*

★**worst** [wə:st] ADJ le (la) pire, le (la) plus mauvais(e) ▶ ADV le plus mal ▶ N pire *m*; **at ~** au pis aller; **if the ~ comes to the ~** si le pire doit arriver

worst-case ['wə:stkeɪs] ADJ: **the ~ scenario** le pire scénario *or* cas de figure

worsted ['wustɪd] N: **(wool) ~** laine peignée

★**worth** [wə:θ] N valeur *f*; **two pounds' ~ of apples** (pour) deux livres de pommes ▶ ADJ: **to be ~** valoir; **how much is it ~?** ça vaut combien ?; **it's ~ it** cela en vaut la peine, ça vaut la peine; **it is ~ one's while (to do)** ça vaut la peine (de faire)

worthless ['wə:θlɪs] ADJ qui ne vaut rien

worthwhile ['wə:θ'waɪl] ADJ (*activity*) qui en vaut la peine; (*cause*) louable; **a ~ book** un livre qui vaut la peine d'être lu

worthy ['wə:ðɪ] ADJ (*person*) digne; (*motive*) louable; **~ of** digne de

---

would [wud]

AUX VB **1** (*conditional tense*): **if you asked him he would do it** si vous le lui demandiez, il le ferait; **if you had asked him he would have done it** si vous le lui aviez demandé, il l'aurait fait

2 (*in offers, invitations, requests*): **would you like a biscuit?** voulez-vous un biscuit ?; **would you close the door please?** voulez-vous fermer la porte, s'il vous plaît ?

3 (*in indirect speech*): **I said I would do it** j'ai dit que je le ferais

4 (*emphatic*): **it WOULD have to snow today!** naturellement il neige aujourd'hui !, il fallait qu'il neige aujourd'hui !

5 (*insistence*): **she wouldn't do it** elle n'a pas voulu *or* elle a refusé de le faire

6 (*conjecture*): **it would have been midnight** il devait être minuit; **it would seem so** on dirait bien

7 (*indicating habit*): **he would go there on Mondays** il y allait le lundi

---

would-be ['wudbi:] ADJ (*pej*) soi-disant

wouldn't ['wudnt] = **would not**

★**wound¹** [wu:nd] N blessure *f* ▶ VT blesser; **wounded in the leg** blessé à la jambe

wound² [waund] PT, PP *of* **wind²**

wove [wəuv] PT *of* **weave**

woven ['wəuvn] PP *of* **weave**

wow [wau] (*inf*) EXCL ouah ▶ VT enthousiasmer

WP N ABBR = **word processing; word processor** ▶ ABBR (BRIT *inf*) = **weather permitting**

wpm ABBR (= *words per minute*) mots/minute

wrangle ['ræŋgl] N dispute *f* ▶ VI se disputer

★**wrap** [ræp] N (*stole*) écharpe *f*; (*cape*) pèlerine *f*; **under wraps** (*fig: plan, scheme*) secret(-ète) ▶ VT (*also:* **wrap up**) envelopper; (: *parcel*) emballer; (*wind*) enrouler

wrapper ['ræpəʳ] N (*on chocolate etc*) papier *m*; (BRIT: *of book*) couverture *f*

wrapping ['ræpɪŋ] N (*of sweet, chocolate*) papier *m*; (*of parcel*) emballage *m*

wrapping paper N papier *m* d'emballage; (*for gift*) papier cadeau

wrath [rɔθ] N courroux *m*

wreak [ri:k] VT (*destruction*) entraîner; **to ~ havoc** faire des ravages; **to ~ vengeance on** se venger de, exercer sa vengeance sur

wreath [ri:θ] N couronne *f*

wreck [rɛk] N (*sea disaster*) naufrage *m*; (*ship*) épave *f*; (*vehicle*) véhicule accidenté; (*inf: person*) loque (humaine) ▶ VT démolir; (*ship*) provoquer le naufrage de; (*fig*) briser, ruiner

wreckage ['rɛkɪdʒ] N débris *mpl*; (*of building*) décombres *mpl*; (*of ship*) naufrage *m*

wrecker ['rɛkəʳ] N (US: *breakdown van*) dépanneuse *f*

WREN [rɛn] N ABBR (BRIT) membre *du* WRNS

wren [rɛn] N (*Zool*) troglodyte *m*

wrench [rɛntʃ] N (*Tech*) clé *f* (à écrous); (*tug*) violent mouvement de torsion; (*fig*) déchirement *m* ▶ VT tirer violemment sur, tordre; **to ~ sth from** arracher qch (violemment) à *or* de

wrest [rɛst] VT: **to ~ sth from sb** arracher *or* ravir qch à qn

wrestle ['rɛsl] VI: **to ~ (with sb)** lutter (avec qn); **to ~ with** (*fig*) se débattre avec, lutter contre

wrestler ['rɛsləʳ] N lutteur(-euse)

wrestling ['rɛslɪŋ] N lutte *f*; (BRIT: *also:* **all-in wrestling**) catch *m*

wrestling match N rencontre *f* de lutte (*or* de catch)

wretch [rɛtʃ] N pauvre malheureux(-euse); **little ~!** (*often humorous*) petit(e) misérable !

wretched ['rɛtʃɪd] ADJ misérable; (*inf*) maudit(e) (*inf*)

wriggle ['rɪgl] N tortillement *m* ▶ VI (*also:* **wriggle about**) se tortiller

wring [rɪŋ] (*pt, pp* **wrung** [rʌŋ]) VT tordre; (*wet clothes*) essorer; (*fig*): **to ~ sth out of** arracher qch à

w

wringer ['rɪŋəʳ] N essoreuse f

wringing ['rɪŋɪŋ] ADJ (also: **wringing wet**) tout mouillé(e), trempé(e)

wrinkle ['rɪŋkl] N (on skin) ride f; (on paper etc) pli m ▶ VT rider, plisser ▶ VI se plisser

wrinkled ['rɪŋkld], **wrinkly** ['rɪŋklɪ] ADJ (fabric, paper) froissé(e), plissé(e); (surface) plissé; (skin) ridé(e), plissé

wrist [rɪst] N poignet m

wristband ['rɪstbænd] N (BRIT: of shirt) poignet m; (: of watch) bracelet m

wrist watch N montre-bracelet f

writ [rɪt] N acte m judiciaire; **to issue a ~ against sb, to serve a ~ on sb** assigner qn en justice

writable ['raɪtəbl] ADJ (CD, DVD) inscriptible

★**write** [raɪt] (pt **wrote** [rəut], pp **written** ['rɪtn]) VT, VI écrire; (prescription) rédiger; **to ~ sb a letter** écrire une lettre à qn
  ▶ **write away** [raɪt ə'weɪ] VI: **to ~ away for** (information) (écrire pour) demander; (goods) (écrire pour) commander
  ▶ **write down** [raɪt daun] VT noter; (put in writing) mettre par écrit
  ▶ **write in** [raɪt ɪn] VI écrire une lettre; **you should ~ in and complain** vous devriez écrire une lettre de réclamation
  ▶ **write off** [raɪt ɔf] VT (debt) passer aux profits et pertes; (project) mettre une croix sur; (depreciate) amortir; (smash up: car etc) démolir complètement
  ▶ **write out** [raɪt aut] VT écrire; (copy) recopier
  ▶ **write up** [raɪt ʌp] VT rédiger

write-off ['raɪtɔf] N perte totale; **the car is a ~** la voiture est bonne pour la casse

write-protect ['raɪtprə'tɛkt] VT (Comput) protéger contre l'écriture

★**writer** ['raɪtəʳ] N auteur m, écrivain m

write-up ['raɪtʌp] N (review) critique f

writhe [raɪð] VI se tordre

★**writing** ['raɪtɪŋ] N écriture f; (of author) œuvres fpl; **in ~** par écrit; **in my own ~** écrit(e) de ma main

writing case N nécessaire m de correspondance

writing desk N secrétaire m

writing paper N papier m à lettres

★**written** ['rɪtn] PP of **write**

★**wrong** [rɔŋ] ADJ (incorrect) faux (fausse); (incorrectly chosen: number, road etc) mauvais(e); (not suitable) qui ne convient pas; (wicked) mal; (unfair) injuste; **to be ~** (answer) être faux (fausse); (in doing/saying) avoir tort (de dire/faire); **you are ~ to do it** tu as tort de le faire; **it's ~ to steal, stealing is ~** c'est mal de voler; **you are ~ about that, you've got it ~** tu te trompes; **what's ~?** qu'est-ce qui ne va pas ?; **there's nothing ~** tout va bien; **what's ~ with the car?** qu'est-ce qu'elle a, la voiture ?; **I took a ~ turning** je me suis trompé de route ▶ ADV mal; **to go ~** (person) se tromper; (plan) mal tourner; (machine) se détraquer ▶ N tort m; **to be in the ~** avoir tort ▶ VT faire du tort à, léser

wrongdoer ['rɔŋduːəʳ] N malfaiteur m

wrong-foot [rɔŋ'fut] VT (Sport) prendre à contre-pied; (fig) prendre au dépourvu

wrongful ['rɔŋful] ADJ injustifié(e); **~ dismissal** (Industry) licenciement abusif

wrongly ['rɔŋlɪ] ADV à tort; (answer, do, count) mal, incorrectement; (treat) injustement

wrong number N (Tel): **you have the ~** vous vous êtes trompé de numéro

wrong side N (of cloth) envers m

wrote [rəut] PT of **write**

wrought [rɔːt] ADJ: **~ iron** fer forgé

wrung [rʌŋ] PT, PP of **wring**

WRVS N ABBR (BRIT: = Women's Royal Voluntary Service) auxiliaires féminines bénévoles au service de la collectivité

wry [raɪ] ADJ désabusé(e)

wt. ABBR (= weight) pds.

WTO N (= World Trade Organisation) OMC f (= Organisation mondiale du commerce)

WV, W.Va. ABBR (US) = **West Virginia**

WWW N ABBR = **World-Wide Web**

WY, Wyo. ABBR (US) = **Wyoming**

WYSIWYG ['wɪzɪwɪg] ABBR (Comput: = what you see is what you get) ce que vous voyez est ce que vous aurez

Xx

X, x [ɛks] N (letter) X, x m; (BRIT Cine: formerly) film interdit aux moins de 18 ans; **X for Xmas** X comme Xavier

xenophobia [zɛnəˈfəubiə] N xénophobie f

xenophobic [zɛnəˈfəubɪk] ADJ xénophobe

Xerox® [ˈzɪərɔks] N (also: **Xerox machine**) photocopieuse f; (photocopy) photocopie f ▶ VT photocopier

XL ABBR (= extra large) XL

Xmas [ˈɛksməs] N ABBR = **Christmas**

X-rated [ˈɛksˈreɪtɪd] ADJ (US: film) interdit(e) aux moins de 18 ans

X-ray [ˈɛksreɪ] N (ray) rayon m X; (photograph) radio(graphie) f ▶ VT radiographier

xylophone [ˈzaɪləfəun] N xylophone m

Yy

Y, y [waɪ] N (letter) Y, y m; **Y for Yellow**, (US) **Y for Yoke** Y comme Yvonne

★**yacht** [jɔt] N voilier m; (motor, luxury yacht) yacht m

yachting ['jɔtɪŋ] N yachting m, navigation f de plaisance

yachtsman ['jɔtsmən] N (irreg) yacht(s)man m

yam [jæm] N igname f

Yank [jæŋk], **Yankee** ['jæŋkɪ] N (pej) Amerloque mf, Ricain(e)

yank [jæŋk] VT tirer d'un coup sec

yap [jæp] VI (dog) japper

★**yard** [jɑːd] N (of house etc) cour f; (US: garden) jardin m; (measure) yard m (= 914 mm); **builder's ~** chantier m

yard sale N (US) brocante f (dans son propre jardin)

yardstick ['jɑːdstɪk] N (fig) mesure f, critère m

yarn [jɑːn] N fil m; (tale) longue histoire

yawn [jɔːn] N bâillement m ▸ VI bâiller

yawning ['jɔːnɪŋ] ADJ (gap) béant(e)

yd. ABBR = **yard; yards**

yeah [jɛə] ADV (inf) ouais

★**year** [jɪəʳ] N an m, année f; (Scol etc) année; **every ~** tous les ans, chaque année; **this ~** cette année; **a** or **per ~** par an; **~ in, ~ out** année après année; **to be 8 years old** avoir 8 ans; **an eight-year-old child** un enfant de huit ans

yearbook ['jɪəbuk] N annuaire m

yearly ['jɪəlɪ] ADJ annuel(le) ▸ ADV annuellement; **twice ~** deux fois par an

yearn [jəːn] VI: **to ~ for sth/to do** aspirer à qch/à faire

yearning ['jəːnɪŋ] N désir ardent, envie f

yeast [jiːst] N levure f

yell [jɛl] N hurlement m, cri m ▸ VI hurler

★**yellow** ['jɛləu] ADJ, N jaune m

yellow fever N fièvre f jaune

yellowish ['jɛləuɪʃ] ADJ qui tire sur le jaune, jaunâtre (pej)

Yellow Pages® NPL (Tel) pages fpl jaunes

Yellow Sea N: **the ~** la mer Jaune

yelp [jɛlp] N jappement m; glapissement m ▸ VI japper; glapir

Yemen ['jɛmən] N Yémen m

Yemeni ['jɛmənɪ] ADJ yéménite ▸ N Yéménite mf

yen [jɛn] N (currency) yen m; (craving): **~ for/to do** grande envie de/de faire

yeoman ['jəumən] N (irreg): **Y~ of the Guard** hallebardier m de la garde royale

★**yes** [jɛs] ADV oui; (answering negative question) si; **to say ~ (to)** dire oui (à) ▸ N oui m

★**yesterday** ['jɛstədɪ] ADV, N hier m; **~ morning/evening** hier matin/soir; **the day before ~** avant-hier; **all day ~** toute la journée d'hier

★**yet** [jɛt] ADV encore; (in questions) déjà; **it is not finished** ce n'est pas encore fini or toujours pas fini; **must you go just ~?** dois-tu déjà partir?; **have you eaten ~?** vous avez déjà mangé?; **the best ~** le meilleur jusqu'ici or jusque-là; **as ~** jusqu'ici, encore; **a few days ~** encore quelques jours; **~ again** une fois de plus ▸ CONJ pourtant, néanmoins

yew [juː] N if m

Y-fronts® ['waɪfrʌnts] NPL (BRIT) slip m kangourou

YHA N ABBR (BRIT) = **Youth Hostels Association**

Yiddish ['jɪdɪʃ] N yiddish m

yield [jiːld] N production f, rendement m; (Finance) rapport m; **a ~ of 5%** un rendement de 5% ▸ VT produire, rendre, rapporter; (surrender) céder ▸ VI céder; (US Aut) céder la priorité

yikes ['jaiks] EXCL (inf: esp hum) la vache!

YMCA N ABBR (= Young Men's Christian Association) ≈ union chrétienne de jeunes gens (UCJG)

yob [jɔb], **yobbo** ['jɔbəu] N (BRIT pej) loubar(d) m (inf)

yodel ['jəudl] VI faire des tyroliennes, jodler

yoga ['jəugə] N yoga m

★**yoghurt, yogurt** ['jɔgət] N yaourt m

yoke [jəuk] N joug m ▸ VT (also: **yoke together**: oxen) accoupler

yolk [jəuk] N jaune m (d'œuf)

Yom Kippur [jɔmkɪ'puəʳ] N Yom Kippour m inv

yonder ['jɔndəʳ] ADV là(-bas)

yonks [jɔŋks] NPL (inf): **for ~** très longtemps; **we've been here for ~** ça fait une éternité qu'on est ici; **we were there for ~** on est resté là pendant des lustres

---

you [juː]

PRON **1** (subject) tu; (: polite form) vous; (: plural) vous; **you are very kind** vous êtes très gentil; **you French enjoy your food** vous autres Français, vous aimez bien manger; **you and I will go** toi et moi or vous et moi, nous irons; **there you are!** vous voilà!

2 (*object: direct, indirect*) te, t' + *vowel*; vous; **I know you** je te *or* vous connais; **I gave it to you** je te l'ai donné, je vous l'ai donné
3 (*stressed*) toi; vous; **I told YOU to do it** c'est à toi *or* vous que j'ai dit de le faire
4 (*after prep, in comparisons*) toi; vous; **it's for you** c'est pour toi *or* vous; **she's younger than you** elle est plus jeune que toi *or* vous
5 (*impersonal: one*) on; **fresh air does you good** l'air frais fait du bien; **you never know** on ne sait jamais; **you can't do that!** ça ne se fait pas !

> Only use **tu** when speaking to a child, or someone with whom you're on informal terms. If in doubt, use **vous**.

you'd [juːd] = **you had**; **you would**

you'll [juːl] = **you will**; **you shall**

★**young** [jʌŋ] ADJ jeune; **a ~ man** un jeune homme; **a ~ lady** (*unmarried*) une jeune fille, une demoiselle; (*married*) une jeune femme *or* dame; **my younger brother** mon frère cadet; **the younger generation** la jeune génération ▶ NPL (*of animal*) petits *mpl*; **the ~** (*people*) les jeunes, la jeunesse

younger [ˈjʌŋɡəʳ] ADJ (*brother etc*) cadet(te)

youngish [ˈjʌŋɪʃ] ADJ assez jeune

youngster [ˈjʌŋstəʳ] N jeune *mf*; (*child*) enfant *mf*

★**your** [jɔːʳ] ADJ ton (ta), tes *pl*; (*polite form, pl*) votre, vos *pl*; *see also* **my**

you're [juəʳ] = **you are**

★**yours** [jɔːz] PRON le (la) tien(ne), les tiens (tiennes); (*polite form, pl*) le (la) vôtre, les vôtres; **is it ~?** c'est à toi (*or* à vous) ?; **a friend of ~** un(e) de tes (*or* de vos) amis; *see also* **faithfully**; **mine¹**; **sincerely**

★**yourself** [jɔːˈsɛlf] PRON (*reflexive*) te; (*: polite form*) vous; (*after prep*) toi; vous; (*emphatic*) toi-même; vous-même; **you ~ told me** c'est vous qui me l'avez dit, vous me l'avez dit vous-même; *see also* **oneself**

★**yourselves** [jɔːˈsɛlvz] PL PRON vous; (*emphatic*) vous-mêmes; *see also* **oneself**

youth [juːθ] N jeunesse *f*; (*pl* **youths** [juːðz]) (*young man*) jeune homme *m*; **in my ~** dans ma jeunesse, quand j'étais jeune

youth centre, (*US*) **youth center** N centre *m* de loisirs (*pour les jeunes*)

youth club N centre *m* de jeunes

youthful [ˈjuːθful] ADJ jeune; (*enthusiasm etc*) juvénile; (*misdemeanour*) de jeunesse

youthfulness [ˈjuːθfəlnɪs] N jeunesse *f*

youth hostel N auberge *f* de jeunesse

youth movement N mouvement *m* de jeunes

you've [juːv] = **you have**

yowl [jaul] N hurlement *m*; miaulement *m* ▶ VI hurler; miauler

yo-yo [ˈjəʊjəʊ] N Yo-Yo *m inv*

YT ABBR (CANADA) = **Yukon Territory**

yuan [juːˈæn] N yuan *m*

Yugoslav [ˈjuːɡəʊslɑːv] (*formerly*) ADJ yougoslave ▶ N Yougoslave *mf*

Yugoslavia [juːɡəʊˈslɑːvɪə] N (*formerly*) Yougoslavie *f*

Yugoslavian [juːɡəʊˈslɑːvɪən] ADJ (*formerly*) yougoslave

yummy [ˈjʌmɪ] ADJ (*inf*) délicieux(-euse); **it smells ~** ça sent super bon

yuppie [ˈjʌpɪ] N (*inf*) yuppie *mf*

YWCA N ABBR (= *Young Women's Christian Association*) union chrétienne féminine

y

Zz

Z, z [zɛd, (US) ziː] N (letter) Z, z m; **Z for Zebra** Z comme Zoé

Zaïre [zɑːˈiːəʳ] N Zaïre m

Zambia [ˈzæmbɪə] N Zambie f

Zambian [ˈzæmbɪən] ADJ zambien(ne) ▸ N Zambien(ne)

zany [ˈzeɪnɪ] ADJ farfelu(e), loufoque

zap [zæp] VT (Comput) effacer

zeal [ziːl] N (revolutionary etc) ferveur f; (keenness) ardeur f, zèle m

zealot [ˈzɛlət] N fanatique mf

zealous [ˈzɛləs] ADJ fervent(e); ardent(e), zélé(e)

zebra [ˈziːbrə] N zèbre m

zebra crossing N (BRIT) passage clouté or pour piétons

zeitgeist [ˈzaɪtgaɪst] N air m du temps

zenith [ˈzɛnɪθ] N (Astronomy) zénith m; (fig) zénith, apogée m

★**zero** [ˈzɪərəu] N zéro m; **5° below ~** 5 degrés au-dessous de zéro ▸ VI: **to ~ in on** (target) se diriger droit sur

zero hour N l'heure f H

zero-hour contract N contrat m zéro heure

zero option N (Pol): **the ~** l'option f zéro

zero-rated [ˈzɪərəureɪtɪd] ADJ (BRIT) exonéré(e) de TVA

zest [zɛst] N entrain m, élan m; (of lemon etc) zeste m

zigzag [ˈzɪgzæg] N zigzag m ▸ VI zigzaguer, faire des zigzags

Zimbabwe [zɪmˈbɑːbwɪ] N Zimbabwe m

Zimbabwean [zɪmˈbɑːbwɪən] ADJ zimbabwéen(ne) ▸ N Zimbabwéen(ne)

Zimmer® [ˈzɪməʳ] N (also: **Zimmer frame**) déambulateur m

zinc [zɪŋk] N zinc m

Zionism [ˈzaɪənɪzəm] N sionisme m

Zionist [ˈzaɪənɪst] ADJ sioniste ▸ N Sioniste mf

zip [zɪp] N (also: **zip fastener**) fermeture f éclair® or à glissière; (energy) entrain m ▸ VT (Comput: file) zipper; (also: **zip up**) fermer (avec une fermeture éclair®)

zip code N (US) code postal

zip file N (Comput) fichier m zip inv

zipper [ˈzɪpəʳ] N (US) = **zip**

zit [zɪt] N (inf) bouton m

zither [ˈzɪðəʳ] N cithare f

zodiac [ˈzəudɪæk] N zodiaque m

zombie [ˈzɔmbɪ] N (fig): **like a ~** avec l'air d'un zombie, comme un automate

★**zone** [zəun] N zone f

★**zoo** [zuː] N zoo m

zoological [zuəˈlɔdʒɪkl] ADJ zoologique

zoologist [zuˈɔlədʒɪst] N zoologiste mf

zoology [zuːˈɔlədʒɪ] N zoologie f

zoom [zuːm] VI: **to ~ past** passer en trombe; **to ~ in (on sb/sth)** (Phot, Cine) zoomer (sur qn/qch)

zoom lens N zoom m, objectif m à focale variable

zucchini [zuːˈkiːnɪ] N (US) courgette f

Zulu [ˈzuːluː] ADJ zoulou ▸ N Zoulou mf

Zumba® [ˈzumbə] N zumba® f

Zürich [ˈzjuərɪk] N Zurich

Grammar
Grammaire

Using the Grammar

The Grammar Guide deals systematically and comprehensively with all the information you will need in order to communicate accurately in French. The user-friendly layout explains the grammar point on a left-hand page, leaving the facing page free for illustrative examples. The numbers → ❶ etc direct you to the relevant example in every case.

The Grammar Guide also provides invaluable guidance on the danger of translating English structures with identical structures in French. Use of Numbers and Pronunciation are important areas covered towards the end of the section. Finally, the index lists the main words and grammatical terms in both English and French.

Abbreviations

fem.	*feminine*
infin.	*infinitive*
masc.	*masculine*
perf.	*perfect*
plur.	plural
qch	**quelque chose**
qn	**quelqu'un**
sb	somebody
sing.	singular
sth	something

Contents

Verbs

Simple Tenses: Formation of Regular Verbs

In French the simple tenses are:

> Present → ❶
> Imperfect → ❷
> Future → ❸
> Conditional → ❹
> Past Historic → ❺
> Present Subjunctive → ❻
> Imperfect Subjunctive → ❼

They are formed by adding endings to a verb stem. The endings show the number and person of the subject of the verb → ❽

The stem and endings of regular verbs are totally predictable. The following sections show all the patterns for regular verbs. For irregular verbs, see page 74 onwards.

There are three regular verb patterns (called conjugations), each identifiable by the ending of the infinitive:

> First conjugation verbs end in **-er**, e.g. **donner** to give

> Second conjugation verbs end in **-ir**, e.g. **finir** to finish

> Third conjugation verbs end in **-re**, e.g. **vendre** to sell

These three conjugations are treated in order on the following pages.

Examples

❶ je donne

I give
I am giving
I do give

❷ je donnais

I gave
I was giving
I used to give

❸ je donnerai

I shall give
I shall be giving

❹ je donnerais

I should/would give
I should/would be giving

❺ je donnai

I gave

❻ (que) je donne

(that) I give/gave

❼ (que) je donnasse

(that) I gave

❽ je donne
nous donnons
je donnerais
nous donnerions

I give
we give
I would give
we would give

Verbs

First conjugation

The stem is formed as follows:

TENSE	FORMATION	EXAMPLE
Present Imperfect Past Historic Present Subjunctive Imperfect Subjunctive	infinitive minus **-er**	**donn-**
Future Conditional	infinitive	**donner-**

To the appropriate stem add the following endings:

		① PRESENT	② IMPERFECT	③ PAST HISTORIC
	1st person	**-e**	**-ais**	**-ai**
sing.	2nd person	**-es**	**-ais**	**-as**
	3rd person	**-e**	**-ait**	**-a**
	1st person	**-ons**	**-ions**	**-âmes**
plur.	2nd person	**-ez**	**-iez**	**-âtes**
	3rd person	**-ent**	**-aient**	**-èrent**

		④ PRESENT SUBJUNCTIVE	⑤ IMPERFECT SUBJUNCTIVE
	1st person	**-e**	**-asse**
sing.	2nd person	**-es**	**-asses**
	3rd person	**-e**	**-ât**
	1st person	**-ions**	**-assions**
plur.	2nd person	**-iez**	**-assiez**
	3rd person	**-ent**	**-assent**

		⑥ FUTURE	⑦ CONDITIONAL
	1st person	**-ai**	**-ais**
sing.	2nd person	**-as**	**-ais**
	3rd person	**-a**	**-ait**
	1st person	**-ons**	**-ions**
plur.	2nd person	**-ez**	**-iez**
	3rd person	**-ont**	**-aient**

Examples

① PRESENT
je donne
tu donnes
il donne
elle donne
nous donnons
vous donnez
ils donnent
elles donnent

② IMPERFECT
je donnais
tu donnais
il donnait
elle donnait
nous donnions
vous donniez
ils donnaient
elles donnaient

③ PAST HISTORIC
je donnai
tu donnas
il donna
elle donna
nous donnâmes
vous donnâtes
ils donnèrent
elles donnèrent

④ PRESENT SUBJUNCTIVE
je donne
tu donnes
il donne
elle donne
nous donnions
vous donniez
ils donnent
elles donnent

⑤ IMPERFECT SUBJUNCTIVE
je donnasse
tu donnasses
il donnât
elle donnât
nous donnassions
vous donnassiez
ils donnassent
elles donnassent

⑥ FUTURE
je donnerai
tu donneras
il donnera
elle donnera
nous donnerons
vous donnerez
ils donneront
elles donneront

⑦ CONDITIONAL
je donnerais
tu donnerais
il donnerait
elle donnerait
nous donnerions
vous donneriez
ils donneraient
elles donneraient

Verbs

Second conjugation

The stem is formed as follows:

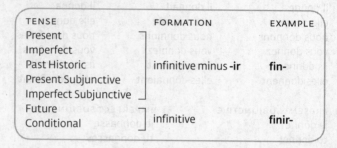

TENSE	FORMATION	EXAMPLE
Present		
Imperfect		
Past Historic	infinitive minus -ir	fin-
Present Subjunctive		
Imperfect Subjunctive		
Future	infinitive	finir-
Conditional		

To the appropriate stem add the following endings:

		❶ PRESENT	**❷ IMPERFECT**	**❸ PAST HISTORIC**
	1st person	**-is**	-issais	-is
sing.	2nd person	**-is**	-issais	-is
	3rd person	**-it**	-issait	-it
	1st person	**-issons**	-issions	-îmes
plur.	2nd person	**-issez**	-issiez	-îtes
	3rd person	**-issent**	-issaient	-irent

		❹ PRESENT SUBJUNCTIVE	**❺ IMPERFECT SUBJUNCTIVE**
	1st person	-isse	-isse
sing.	2nd person	-isses	-isses
	3rd person	-isse	-ît
	1st person	-issions	-issions
plur.	2nd person	-issiez	-issiez
	3rd person	-issent	-issent

		❻ FUTURE	**❼ CONDITIONAL**
	1st person	-ai	-ais
sing.	2nd person	-as	-ais
	3rd person	-a	-ait
	1st person	-ons	-ions
plur.	2nd person	-ez	-iez
	3rd person	-ont	-aient

Examples

1 PRESENT
je finis
tu finis
il finit
elle finit
nous finissons
vous finissez
ils finissent
elles finissent

2 IMPERFECT
je finissais
tu finissais
il finissait
elle finissait
nous finissions
vous finissiez
ils finissaient
elles finissaient

3 PAST HISTORIC
je finis
tu finis
il finit
elle finit
nous finîmes
vous finîtes
ils finirent
elles finirent

4 PRESENT SUBJUNCTIVE
je finisse
tu finisses
il finisse
elle finisse
nous finissions
vous finissiez
ils finissent
elles finissent

5 IMPERFECT SUBJUNCTIVE
je finisse
tu finisses
il finît
elle finît
nous finissions
vous finissiez
ils finissent
elles finissent

6 FUTURE
je finirai
tu finiras
il finira
elle finira
nous finirons
vous finirez
ils finiront
elles finiront

7 CONDITIONAL
je finirais
tu finirais
il finirait
elle finirait
nous finirions
vous finiriez
ils finiraient
elles finiraient

Verbs

Third conjugation

The stem is formed as follows:

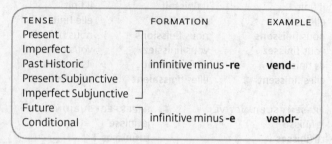

TENSE	FORMATION	EXAMPLE
Present		
Imperfect		
Past Historic	infinitive minus **-re**	**vend-**
Present Subjunctive		
Imperfect Subjunctive		
Future	infinitive minus **-e**	**vendr-**
Conditional		

To the appropriate stem add the following endings:

		❶ PRESENT	❷ IMPERFECT	❸ PAST HISTORIC
sing.	1ˢᵗ person	**-s**	**-ais**	**-is**
	2ⁿᵈ person	**-s**	**-ais**	**-is**
	3ʳᵈ person	**–**	**-ait**	**-it**
plur.	1ˢᵗ person	**-ons**	**-ions**	**-îmes**
	2ⁿᵈ person	**-ez**	**-iez**	**-îtes**
	3ʳᵈ person	**-ent**	**-aient**	**-irent**

		❹ PRESENT SUBJUNCTIVE	❺ IMPERFECT SUBJUNCTIVE
sing.	1ˢᵗ person	**-e**	**-isse**
	2ⁿᵈ person	**-es**	**-isses**
	3ʳᵈ person	**-e**	**-ît**
plur.	1ˢᵗ person	**-ions**	**-issions**
	2ⁿᵈ person	**-iez**	**-issiez**
	3ʳᵈ person	**-ent**	**-issent**

		❻ FUTURE	❼ CONDITIONAL
sing.	1ˢᵗ person	**-ai**	**-ais**
	2ⁿᵈ person	**-as**	**-ais**
	3ʳᵈ person	**-a**	**-ait**
plur.	1ˢᵗ person	**-ons**	**-ions**
	2ⁿᵈ person	**-ez**	**-iez**
	3ʳᵈ person	**-ont**	**-aient**

Examples

1 PRESENT
je vend**s**
tu vend**s**
il vend
elle vend
nous vend**ons**
vous vend**ez**
ils vend**ent**
elles vend**ent**

2 IMPERFECT
je vend**ais**
tu vend**ais**
il vend**ait**
elle vend**ait**
nous vend**ions**
vous vend**iez**
ils vend**aient**
elles vend**aient**

3 PAST HISTORIC
je vend**is**
tu vend**is**
il vend**it**
elle vend**it**
nous vend**îmes**
vous vend**îtes**
ils vend**irent**
elles vend**irent**

4 PRESENT SUBJUNCTIVE
je vend**e**
tu vend**es**
il vend**e**
elle vend**e**
nous vend**ions**
vous vend**iez**
ils vend**ent**
elles vend**ent**

5 IMPERFECT SUBJUNCTIVE
je vend**isse**
tu vend**isses**
il vend**ît**
elle vend**ît**
nous vend**issions**
vous vend**issiez**
ils vend**issent**
elles vend**issent**

6 FUTURE
je vend**rai**
tu vend**ras**
il vend**ra**
elle vend**ra**
nous vend**rons**
vous vend**rez**
ils vend**ront**
elles vend**ront**

7 CONDITIONAL
je vend**rais**
tu vend**rais**
il vend**rait**
elle vend**rait**
nous vend**rions**
vous vend**riez**
ils vend**raient**
elles vend**raient**

13

Verbs

First Conjugation Spelling Irregularities

Before certain endings, the stems of some '**-er**' verbs may change slightly.

Below, and on subsequent pages, the verb types are identified, and the changes described are illustrated by means of a representative verb.

Verbs ending:	**-cer**
Change:	**c** becomes **ç** before **a** or **o**
Affects:	Present, Imperfect, Past Historic, Imperfect Subjunctive, Present Participle
Model:	**lancer** to throw → **❶**

Why the change occurs: A cedilla is added to the **c** to retain its soft [s] pronunciation before the vowels **a** and **o**.

Verbs ending:	**-ger**
Change:	**g** becomes **ge** before **a** or **o**
Affects:	Present, Imperfect, Past Historic, Imperfect Subjunctive, Present Participle
Model:	**manger** to eat → **❷**

Why the change occurs: An **e** is added after the **g** to retain its soft [ʒ] pronunciation before the vowels **a** and **o**.

Examples

1 INFINITIVE
lancer

PRESENT
je lance
tu lances
il/elle lance
nous **lançons**
vous lancez
ils/elles lancent

PAST HISTORIC
je **lançai**
tu **lanças**
il/elle **lança**
nous **lançâmes**
vous **lançâtes**
ils/elles lancèrent

PRESENT PARTICIPLE
lançant

IMPERFECT
je **lançais**
tu **lançais**
il/elle **lançait**
nous lancions
vous lanciez
ils/elles **lançaient**

IMPERFECT SUBJUNCTIVE
je **lançasse**
tu **lançasses**
il/elle **lançât**
nous **lançassions**
vous **lançassiez**
ils/elles **lançassent**

2 INFINITIVE
manger

PRESENT
je mange
tu manges
il/elle mange
nous **mangeons**
vous mangez
ils/elles mangent

PAST HISTORIC
je **mangeai**
tu **mangeas**
il/elle **mangea**
nous **mangeâmes**
vous **mangeâtes**
ils/elles mangèrent

PRESENT PARTICIPLE
mangeant

IMPERFECT
je **mangeais**
tu **mangeais**
il/elle **mangeait**
nous mangions
vous mangiez
ils/elles **mangeaient**

IMPERFECT SUBJUNCTIVE
je **mangeasse**
tu **mangeasses**
il/elle **mangeât**
nous **mangeassions**
vous **mangeassiez**
ils/elles **mangeassent**

Verbs

First Conjugation Spelling Irregularities *continued*

Verbs ending:	**-eler**
Change:	**-l** doubles before **-e**, **-es**, **-ent** and throughout the Future and Conditional tenses
Affects:	Present, Present Subjunctive, Future, Conditional
Model:	**appeler** to call → ❶
Exceptions:	**geler** to freeze; **peler** to peel → like **mener** (page 18)

Verbs ending:	**-eter**
Change:	**-t** doubles before **-e**, **-es**, **-ent** and throughout the Future and Conditional tenses
Affects:	Present, Present Subjunctive, Future, Conditional
Model:	**jeter** to throw → ❷
Exceptions:	**acheter** to buy; **haleter** to pant → like **mener** (page 18)

Verbs ending:	**-yer**
Change:	**y** changes to **i** before **-e**, **-es**, **-ent** and throughout the Future and Conditional tenses
Affects:	Present, Present Subjunctive, Future, Conditional
Model:	**essuyer** to wipe → ❸

The change described is optional for verbs ending in **-ayer**,
e.g. **payer** to pay; **essayer** to try.

Examples

1 PRESENT (+ SUBJUNCTIVE)
j'**appelle**
tu **appelles**
il/elle **appelle**
nous appelons
(appelions)
vous appelez
(appeliez)
ils/elles **appellent**

FUTURE
j'**appellerai**
tu **appelleras**
il **appellera** *etc*

CONDITIONAL
j'**appellerais**
tu **appellerais**
il **appellerait** *etc*

2 PRESENT (+ SUBJUNCTIVE)
je **jette**
tu **jettes**
il/elle **jette**
nous jetons
(jetions)
vous jetez
(jetiez)
ils/elles **jettent**

FUTURE
je **jetterai**
tu **jetteras**
il **jettera** *etc*

CONDITIONAL
je **jetterais**
tu **jetterais**
il **jetterait** *etc*

3 PRESENT (+ SUBJUNCTIVE)
j'**essuie**
tu **essuies**
il/elle **essuie**
nous essuyons
(essuyions)
vous essuyez
(essuyiez)
ils/elles **essuient**

FUTURE
j'**essuierai**
tu **essuieras**
il **essuiera** *etc*

CONDITIONAL
j'**essuierais**
tu **essuierais**
il **essuierait** *etc*

Verbs

First Conjugation Spelling Irregularities *continued*

Verbs like:	**mener**, **peser**, **lever** *etc*
Change:	e changes to **è**, before **-e**, **-es**, **-ent** and throughout the Future and Conditional tenses
Affects:	Present, Present Subjunctive, Future, Conditional
Model:	**mener** to lead → ❶

Verbs like:	**céder**, **régler**, **espérer** *etc*
Change:	é changes to **è** before **-e**, **-es**, **-ent**
Affects:	Present, Present Subjunctive
Model:	**céder** to yield → ❷

Examples

1 PRESENT (+ SUBJUNCTIVE)

je **mène**
tu **mènes**
il/elle **mène**
nous menons
(menions)
vous menez
(meniez)
ils/elles **mènent**

FUTURE

je **mènerai**
tu **mèneras**
il **mènera** *etc*

CONDITIONAL

je **mènerais**
tu **mènerais**
il **mènerait** *etc*

2 PRESENT (+ SUBJUNCTIVE)

je **cède**
tu **cèdes**
il/elle **cède**
nous cédons
(cédions)
vous cédez
(cédiez)
ils/elles **cèdent**

Verbs

The Imperative

The imperative is the form of the verb used to give commands or orders. It can be used politely, as in English 'Shut the door, please'.

The imperative is the same as the present tense **tu**, **nous** and **vous** forms without the subject pronouns:

donne* give	**finis** finish	**vends** sell

* The final 's' of the present tense of first conjugation verbs is dropped, except before **y** and **en** → **❶**

donnons let's give	**finissons** let's finish	**vendons** let's sell
donnez give	**finissez** finish	**vendez** sell

The imperative of irregular verbs is given in the verb tables, page 74 onwards.

Position of object pronouns with the imperative:
- in *positive* commands: they follow the verb and are attached to it with hyphens → **❷**
- in *negative* commands: they precede the verb and are not attached to it → **❸**

For the order of object pronouns, see page 170.

For reflexive verbs – e.g. **se lever** to get up – the object pronoun is the reflexive pronoun → **❹**

Examples

1 Compare:

Tu donnes de l'argent à Paul	You give (some) money to Paul
and:	
Donne de l'argent à Paul	Give (some) money to Paul

2

Excusez-moi	Excuse me
Envoyons-les-leur	Let's send them to them
Crois-nous	Believe us
Expliquez-le-moi	Explain it to me
Attendons-la	Let's wait for her/it
Rends-la-lui	Give it back to him/her

3

Ne me dérange pas	Don't disturb me
Ne leur en parlons pas	Let's not speak to them about it
Ne les appelons pas	Let's not call them
N'y pense plus	Don't think about it any more
Ne leur répondez pas	Don't answer them
Ne la lui rends pas	Don't give it back to him/her

4

Lève-toi	Get up
Ne te lève pas	Don't get up
Dépêchons-nous	Let's hurry
Ne nous affolons pas	Let's not panic
Levez-vous	Get up
Ne vous levez pas	Don't get up

Verbs

Compound Tenses: Formation

In French the compound tenses are:

Perfect → **❶**
Pluperfect → **❷**
Future Perfect → **❸**
Conditional Perfect → **❹**
Past Anterior → **❺**
Perfect Subjunctive → **❻**
Pluperfect Subjunctive → **❼**

They consist of the past participle of the verb together with an auxiliary verb. Most verbs take the auxiliary **avoir**, but some take **être** (see page 28).

Compound tenses are formed in exactly the same way for both regular and irregular verbs, the only difference being that irregular verbs may have an irregular past participle.

The Past Participle

For all compound tenses you need to know how to form the past participle of the verb. For regular verbs this is as follows:

First conjugation: replace the **-er** of the infinitive by **-é** → **❽**

Second conjugation: replace the **-ir** of the infinitive by **-i** → **❾**

Third conjugation: replace the **-re** of the infinitive by **-u** → **❿**

See page 50 for agreement of past participles.

Examples

with **avoir**   with **être**

① **j'ai donné** I gave, have given   **je suis tombé** I fell, have fallen

② **j'avais donné** I had given   **j'étais tombé** I had fallen

③ **j'aurai donné** I shall have given   **je serai tombé** I shall have fallen

④ **j'aurais donné** I should/would have given   **je serais tombé** I should/would have fallen

⑤ **j'eus donné** I had given   **je fus tombé** I had fallen

⑥ **(que) j'aie donné** (that) I gave, have given   **(que) je sois tombé** (that) I fell, have fallen

⑦ **(que) j'eusse donné** (that) I had given   **(que) je fusse tombé** (that) I had fallen

⑧ **donner** to give → **donné** given

⑨ **finir** to finish → **fini** finished

⑩ **vendre** to sell → **vendu** sold

Verbs

Compound Tenses: Formation *continued*

Verbs taking the auxiliary **avoir**

PERFECT TENSE
The present tense of **avoir** plus the past participle → ❶

PLUPERFECT TENSE
The imperfect tense of **avoir** plus the past participle → ❷

FUTURE PERFECT
The future tense of **avoir** plus the past participle → ❸

CONDITIONAL PERFECT
The conditional of **avoir** plus the past participle → ❹

PAST ANTERIOR
The past historic of **avoir** plus the past participle → ❺

PERFECT SUBJUNCTIVE
The present subjunctive of **avoir** plus the past participle → ❻

PLUPERFECT SUBJUNCTIVE
The imperfect subjunctive of **avoir** plus the past participle → ❼

For how to form the past participle of regular verbs, see page 22. The past participle of irregular verbs is given for each verb in the verb tables (see page 74 onwards).

The past participle must agree in number and in gender with any preceding direct object (see page 50).

Examples

1 PERFECT

j'ai donné

tu as donné

il/elle a donné

nous avons donné

vous avez donné

ils/elles ont donné

2 PLUPERFECT

j'avais donné

tu avais donné

il/elle avait donné

nous avions donné

vous aviez donné

ils/elles avaient donné

3 FUTURE PERFECT

j'aurai donné

tu auras donné

il/elle aura donné

nous aurons donné

vous aurez donné

ils/elles auront donné

4 CONDITIONAL PERFECT

j'aurais donné

tu aurais donné

il/elle aurait donné

nous aurions donné

vous auriez donné

ils/elles auraient donné

5 PAST ANTERIOR

j'eus donné

tu eus donné

il/elle eut donné

nous eûmes donné

vous eûtes donné

ils/elles eurent donné

6 PERFECT SUBJUNCTIVE

j'aie donné

tu aies donné

il/elle ait donné

nous ayons donné

vous ayez donné

ils/elles aient donné

7 PLUPERFECT SUBJUNCTIVE

j'eusse donné

tu eusses donné

il/elle eût donné

nous eussions donné

vous eussiez donné

ils/elles eussent donné

Verbs

Compound Tenses: Formation *continued*

Verbs taking the auxiliary être

PERFECT TENSE
The present tense of **être** plus the past participle → ❶

PLUPERFECT TENSE
The imperfect tense of **être** plus the past participle → ❷

FUTURE PERFECT
The future tense of **être** plus the past participle → ❸

CONDITIONAL PERFECT
The conditional of **être** plus the past participle → ❹

PAST ANTERIOR
The past historic of **être** plus the past participle → ❺

PERFECT SUBJUNCTIVE
The present subjunctive of **être** plus the past participle → ❻

PLUPERFECT SUBJUNCTIVE
The imperfect subjunctive of **être** plus the past participle → ❼

For how to form the past participle of regular verbs, see page 22. The past participle of irregular verbs is given for each verb in the verb tables (see page 74 onwards).

For agreement of past participles, see page 50.

For a list of verbs and verb types that take the auxiliary **être**, see page 28.

Examples

1 PERFECT

je suis tombé(e)	nous sommes tombé(e)s
tu es tombé(e)	vous êtes tombé(e)(s)
il est tombé	ils sont tombés
elle est tombée	elles sont tombées

2 PLUPERFECT

j'étais tombé(e)	nous étions tombé(e)s
tu étais tombé(e)	vous étiez tombé(e)(s)
il était tombé	ils étaient tombés
elle était tombée	elles étaient tombées

3 FUTURE PERFECT

je serai tombé(e)	nous serons tombé(e)s
tu seras tombé(e)	vous serez tombé(e)(s)
il sera tombé	ils seront tombés
elle sera tombée	elles seront tombées

4 CONDITIONAL PERFECT

je serais tombé(e)	nous serions tombé(e)s
tu serais tombé(e)	vous seriez tombé(e)(s)
il serait tombé	ils seraient tombés
elle serait tombée	elles seraient tombées

5 PAST ANTERIOR

je fus tombé(e)	nous fûmes tombé(e)s
tu fus tombé(e)	vous fûtes tombé(e)(s)
il fut tombé	ils furent tombés
elle fut tombée	elles furent tombées

6 PERFECT SUBJUNCTIVE

je sois tombé(e)	nous soyons tombé(e)s
tu sois tombé(e)	vous soyez tombé(e)(s)
il soit tombé	ils soient tombés
elle soit tombée	elles soient tombées

7 PLUPERFECT SUBJUNCTIVE

je fusse tombé(e)	nous fussions tombé(e)s
tu fusses tombé(e)	vous fussiez tombé(e)(s)
il fût tombé	ils fussent tombés
elle fût tombée	elles fussent tombées

Verbs

Compound Tenses: Formation *continued*

The following verbs take the auxiliary **être**

Reflexive verbs (see page 30) → **1**

The following intransitive verbs (i.e. verbs which cannot take a direct object), largely expressing motion or a change of state:

aller to go → **2**
arriver to arrive; to happen
descendre to go/come down
devenir to become
entrer to go/come in
monter to go/come up
mourir to die → **3**
naître to be born
partir to leave → **4**

passer to pass
rentrer to go back/in
rester to stay → **5**
retourner to go back
revenir to come back
sortir to go/come out
tomber to fall
venir to come → **6**

Of these, the following can be used transitively (i.e. with a direct object) and in such cases are conjugated with **avoir**:

descendre to bring/take down
entrer to bring/take in
monter to bring/take up → **7**
passer to pass; to spend → **8**
rentrer to bring/take in
retourner to turn over
sortir to bring/take out → **9**

ⓘ Note that the past participle must show an agreement in number and gender whenever the auxiliary is **être** except for reflexive verbs where the reflexive pronoun is the indirect object (see page 50).

Examples

1 je me suis arrêté(e)	I stopped
elle s'est trompée	she made a mistake
tu t'es levé(e)	you got up
ils s'étaient battus	they had fought (one another)
2 elle est allée	she went
3 ils sont morts	they died
4 vous êtes partie	you left (*addressing a female person*)
vous êtes parties	you left (*addressing more than one female person*)
5 nous sommes resté(e)s	we stayed
6 elles étaient venues	they (*female*) had come
7 Il a monté les valises	He's taken up the cases
8 Nous avons passé trois semaines chez elle	We spent three weeks at her place
9 Avez-vous sorti la voiture?	Have you taken the car out?

Verbs

Reflexive Verbs

A reflexive verb is one accompanied by a reflexive pronoun,
e.g. **se lever** to get up; **se laver** to wash (oneself).
The reflexive pronouns are:

	SINGULAR	PLURAL
1st person	me (m')	nous
2nd person	te (t')	vous
3rd person	se (s')	se (s')

The forms shown in brackets are used before a vowel, an **h** 'mute', or the
pronoun **y** → ❶

> In positive commands, **te** changes to **toi** → ❷

> The reflexive pronoun 'reflects back' to the subject, but it is not
> always translated in English → ❸

> The plural pronouns are sometimes translated as 'one another',
> 'each other' (the *reciprocal* meaning) → ❹

> The reciprocal meaning may be emphasized by **l'un(e) l'autre (les
> un(e)s les autres)** → ❺

Simple tenses of reflexive verbs are conjugated in exactly the same way
as those of non-reflexive verbs except that the reflexive pronoun is always
used. Compound tenses are formed with the auxiliary **être**. A sample
reflexive verb is conjugated in full on pages 34 and 35.

For agreement of past participles, see page 32.

Position of reflexive pronouns

In constructions other than the imperative affirmative the pronoun
comes before the verb → ❻

In the imperative affirmative, the pronoun follows the verb and is
attached to it with a hyphen → ❼

Examples

① Je m'ennuie
I'm bored

Elle s'habille
She's getting dressed

Ils s'y intéressent
They are interested in it

② Assieds-toi
Sit down

Tais-toi
Be quiet

③ Je me prépare
I'm getting (myself) ready

Nous nous lavons
We're washing (ourselves)

Elle se lève
She gets up

④ Nous nous parlons
We speak to each other

Ils se ressemblent
They resemble one another

⑤ Ils se regardent l'un l'autre
They are looking at each other

⑥ Je me couche tôt
I go to bed early

Comment vous appelez-vous?
What is your name?

Il ne s'est pas rasé
He hasn't shaved

Ne te dérange pas pour nous
Don't put yourself out on our account

⑦ Dépêche-toi
Hurry (up)

Renseignons-nous
Let's find out

Asseyez-vous
Sit down

Verbs

Reflexive Verbs *continued*

Past participle agreement

In most reflexive verbs the reflexive pronoun is a *direct* object pronoun → ❶

When a direct object accompanies the reflexive verb the pronoun is then the *indirect* object → ❷

The past participle of a reflexive verb agrees in number and gender with a direct object which *precedes* the verb (usually, but not always, the reflexive pronoun) → ❸

The past participle does not change if the direct object follows the verb → ❹

Here are some common reflexive verbs:

s'en aller to go away
s'amuser to enjoy oneself
s'appeler to be called
s'arrêter to stop
s'asseoir to sit (down)
se baigner to go swimming
se blesser to hurt oneself
se coucher to go to bed
se demander to wonder
se dépêcher to hurry
se diriger to make one's way
s'endormir to fall asleep
s'ennuyer to be/get bored
se fâcher to get angry
s'habiller to dress (oneself)

se hâter to hurry
se laver to wash (oneself)
se lever to get up
se passer to happen
se promener to go for a walk
se rappeler to remember
se ressembler to resemble each other
se retourner to turn round
se réveiller to wake up
se sauver to run away
se souvenir de to remember
se taire to be quiet
se tromper to be mistaken
se trouver to be (situated)

Examples

➊ Je m'appelle

I'm called (*literally*: I call myself)

Asseyez-vous

Sit down (*literally*: Seat yourself)

Ils se lavent

They wash (themselves)

➋ Elle se lave les mains

She's washing her hands (*literally*: She's washing to herself the hands)

Je me brosse les dents

I brush my teeth

Nous nous envoyons des cadeaux à Noël

We send presents to each other at Christmas

➌ «Je me suis endormi» s'est-il excusé

'I fell asleep,' he apologized

Pauline s'est dirigée vers la sortie

Pauline made her way towards the exit

Ils se sont levés vers dix heures

They got up around ten o'clock

Elles se sont excusées de leur erreur

They apologized for their mistake

Est-ce que tu t'es blessée, Cécile?

Have you hurt yourself, Cécile?

➍ Elle s'est lavé les cheveux

She (has) washed her hair

Nous nous sommes serré la main

We shook hands

Christine s'est cassé la jambe

Christine has broken her leg

Verbs

Reflexive Verbs *continued*

Conjugation of: **se laver** to wash (oneself)

1 SIMPLE TENSES

PRESENT

je me lave

tu te laves

il/elle se lave

nous nous lavons

vous vous lavez

ils/elles se lavent

IMPERFECT

je me lavais

tu te lavais

il/elle se lavait

nous nous lavions

vous vous laviez

ils/elles se lavaient

FUTURE

je me laverai

tu te laveras

il/elle se lavera

nous nous laverons

vous vous laverez

ils/elles se laveront

CONDITIONAL

je me laverais

tu te laverais

il/elle se laverait

nous nous laverions

vous vous laveriez

ils/elles se laveraient

PAST HISTORIC

je me lavai

tu te lavas

il/elle se lava

nous nous lavâmes

vous vous lavâtes

ils/elles se lavèrent

PRESENT SUBJUNCTIVE

je me lave

tu te laves

il/elle se lave

nous nous lavions

vous vous laviez

ils/elles se lavent

IMPERFECT SUBJUNCTIVE

je me lavasse

tu te lavasses

il/elle se lavât

nous nous lavassions

vous vous lavassiez

ils/elles se lavassent

Verbs

Reflexive Verbs *continued*

Conjugation of: **se laver** to wash (oneself)

2 COMPOUND TENSES

PERFECT

je me suis lavé(e)
tu t'es lavé(e)
il/elle s'est lavé(e)

nous nous sommes lavé(e)s
vous vous êtes lavé(e)(s)
ils/elles se sont lavé(e)s

PLUPERFECT

je m'étais lavé(e)
tu t'étais lavé(e)
il/elle s'était lavé(e)

nous nous étions lavé(e)s
vous vous étiez lavé(e)(s)
ils/elles s'étaient lavé(e)s

FUTURE PERFECT

je me serai lavé(e)
tu te seras lavé(e)
il/elle se sera lavé(e)

nous nous serons lavé(e)s
vous vous serez lavé(e)(s)
ils/elles se seront lavé(e)s

CONDITIONAL PERFECT

je me serais lavé(e)
tu te serais lavé(e)
il/elle se serait lavé(e)

nous nous serions lavé(e)s
vous vous seriez lavé(e)(s)
ils/elles se seraient lavé(e)s

PAST ANTERIOR

je me fus lavé(e)
tu te fus lavé(e)
il/elle se fut lavé(e)

nous nous fûmes lavé(e)s
vous vous fûtes lavé(e)(s)
ils/elles se furent lavé(e)s

PERFECT SUBJUNCTIVE

je me sois lavé(e)
tu te sois lavé(e)
il/elle se soit lavé(e)

nous nous soyons lavé(e)s
vous vous soyez lavé(e)(s)
ils/elles se soient lavé(e)s

PLUPERFECT SUBJUNCTIVE

je me fusse lavé(e)
tu te fusses lavé(e)
il/elle se fût lavé(e)

nous nous fussions lavé(e)s
vous vous fussiez lavé(e)(s)
ils/elles se fussent lavé(e)s

Verbs

The Passive

In the passive, the subject *receives* the action (e.g. I was hit) as opposed to *performing* it (e.g. I hit him). In English the verb 'to be' is used with the past participle. In French the passive is formed in exactly the same way, i.e.: a tense of **être** + *past participle*.

The past participle agrees in number and gender with the subject → ❶

A sample verb is conjugated in the passive voice on pages 38 and 39.

The indirect object in French cannot become the subject in the passive: in **quelqu'un m'a donné un livre** the indirect object **m'** cannot become the subject of a passive verb (unlike English: someone gave me a book → I was given a book).

The passive meaning is often expressed in French by:
- **on** plus a verb in the active voice → ❷
- a reflexive verb (see page 30) → ❸

Examples

1 **Philippe a été récompensé**
Philippe has been rewarded
Son travail est très admiré
His work is greatly admired
Ils le feront pourvu qu'ils soient payés
They'll do it provided they're paid
Les enfants seront punis
The children will be punished
Cette mesure aurait été critiquée si …
This measure would have been criticized if …
Les portes avaient été fermées
The doors had been closed

2 **On leur a envoyé une lettre**
They were sent a letter
On nous a montré le jardin
We were shown the garden
On m'a dit que …
I was told that …

3 **Ils se vendent 3 euros (la) pièce**
They are sold for 3 euros each
Ce mot ne s'emploie plus
This word is no longer used

37

Verbs

The Passive continued

Conjugation of: **être aimé** to be liked

1 SIMPLE TENSES

PRESENT
je suis aimé(e)
tu es aimé(e)
il/elle est aimé(e)

nous sommes aimé(e)s
vous êtes aimé(e)(s)
ils/elles sont aimé(e)s

IMPERFECT
j'étais aimé(e)
tu étais aimé(e)
il/elle était aimé(e)

nous étions aimé(e)s
vous étiez aimé(e)(s)
ils/elles étaient aimé(e)s

FUTURE
je serai aimé(e)
tu seras aimé(e)
il/elle sera aimé(e)

nous serons aimé(e)s
vous serez aimé(e)(s)
ils/elles seront aimé(e)s

CONDITIONAL
je serais aimé(e)
tu serais aimé(e)
il/elle serait aimé(e)

nous serions aimé(e)s
vous seriez aimé(e)(s)
ils/elles seraient aimé(e)s

PAST HISTORIC
je fus aimé(e)
tu fus aimé(e)
il/elle fut aimé(e)

nous fûmes aimé(e)s
vous fûtes aimé(e)(s)
ils/elles furent aimé(e)s

PRESENT SUBJUNCTIVE
je sois aimé(e)
tu sois aimé(e)
il/elle soit aimé(e)

nous soyons aimé(e)s
vous soyez aimé(e)(s)
ils/elles soient aimé(e)s

IMPERFECT SUBJUNCTIVE
je fusse aimé(e)
tu fusses aimé(e)
il/elle fût aimé(e)

nous fussions aimé(e)s
vous fussiez aimé(e)(s)
ils/elles fussent aimé(e)s

Verbs

The Passive *continued*

Conjugation of: **être aimé** to be liked

2 COMPOUND TENSES

PERFECT
j'ai été aimé(e)
tu as été aimé(e)
il/elle a été aimé(e)

nous avons été aimé(e)s
vous avez été aimé(e)(s)
ils/elles ont été aimé(e)s

PLUPERFECT
j'avais été aimé(e)
tu avais été aimé(e)
il/elle avait été aimé(e)

nous avions été aimé(e)s
vous aviez été aimé(e)(s)
ils/elles avaient été aimé(e)s

FUTURE PERFECT
j'aurai été aimé(e)
tu auras été aimé(e)
il/elle aura été aimé(e)

nous aurons été aimé(e)s
vous aurez été aimé(e)(s)
ils/elles auront été aimé(e)s

CONDITIONAL PERFECT
j'aurais été aimé(e)
tu aurais été aimé(e)
il/elle aurait été aimé(e)

nous aurions été aimé(e)s
vous auriez été aimé(e)(s)
ils/elles auraient été aimé(e)s

PAST ANTERIOR
j'eus été aimé(e)
tu eus été aimé(e)
il/elle eut été aimé(e)

nous eûmes été aimé(e)s
vous eûtes été aimé(e)(s)
ils/elles eurent été aimé(e)s

PERFECT SUBJUNCTIVE
j'aie été aimé(e)
tu aies été aimé(e)
il/elle ait été aimé(e)

nous ayons été aimé(e)s
vous ayez été aimé(e)(s)
ils/elles aient été aimé(e)s

PLUPERFECT SUBJUNCTIVE
j'eusse été aimé(e)
tu eusses été aimé(e)
il/elle eût été aimé(e)

nous eussions été aimé(e)s
vous eussiez été aimé(e)(s)
ils/elles eussent été aimé(e)s

Verbs

Impersonal Verbs

Impersonal verbs are used only in the infinitive and in the third person singular with the subject pronoun **il**, generally translated as 'it'.

e.g. **il pleut** it's raining
il est facile de dire que ... it's easy to say that ...

The most common impersonal verbs are:

INFINITIVE	CONSTRUCTIONS
s'agir	**il s'agit de** + *noun* → ①
	it's a question/matter of something, it's about something
	il s'agit de + *infinitive* → ②
	it's a question/matter of doing; somebody must do
falloir	**il faut** + *noun object* (+ *indirect object*) → ③
	(somebody) needs something, something is necessary (to somebody)
	il faut + *infinitive* (+ *indirect object*) → ④
	it is necessary to do
	il faut que + *subjunctive* → ⑤
	it is necessary to do, somebody must do
grêler	**il grêle** it's hailing
neiger	**il neige** it's snowing
pleuvoir	**il pleut** it's raining
tonner	**il tonne** it's thundering
	→ ⑥
valoir mieux	**il vaut mieux** + *infinitive* → ⑦
	it's better to do
	il vaut mieux que + *subjunctive* → ⑧
	it's better to do/that somebody does

Examples

1 Il ne s'agit pas d'argent — It isn't a question/matter of money

  De quoi s'agit-il? — What is it about?

  Il s'agit de la vie d'une famille au début du siècle — It's about the life of a family at the turn of the century

2 Il s'agit de faire vite — We must act quickly

3 Il faut du courage pour faire ça — One needs courage to do that

  Il me faut une chaise de plus — I need an extra chair

4 Il faut partir — It is necessary to leave / We/I/You must leave*

  Il me fallait prendre une décision — I had to make a decision

5 Il faut que vous partiez — You must leave

  Il faudrait que je fasse mes valises — I ought to pack my cases

6 Il pleuvait à verse — It was pouring with rain

7 Il vaut mieux refuser — It's better to refuse / You/He/I had better refuse*

  Il vaudrait mieux rester — You/We/She had better stay*

8 Il vaudrait mieux que nous ne venions pas — It would be better if we didn't come / We'd better not come

---

* The translation here obviously depends on context

Verbs

Impersonal Verbs *continued*

The following verbs are also commonly used in impersonal constructions:

INFINITIVE	CONSTRUCTIONS
avoir	**il y a** + *noun* → ❶
	there is/are
être	**il est** + *noun* → ❷
	it is, there are (*very literary style*)
	il est + *adjective* + **de** + *infinitive* → ❸
	it is
faire	**il fait** + *adjective of weather* → ❹
	it is
	il fait + *noun depicting weather/dark/light etc* → ❺
	it is
manquer	**il manque** + *noun* (+ *indirect object*) → ❻
	there is/are … missing, something is missing
paraître	**il paraît que** + *subjunctive* → ❼
	it seems/appears that
	il paraît + *indirect object* + **que** + *indicative* → ❽
	it seems/appears to somebody that
rester	**il reste** + *noun* (+ *indirect object*) → ❾
	there is/are … left, (somebody) has something left
sembler	**il semble que** + *subjunctive* → ❿
	it seems/appears that
	il semble + *indirect object* + **que** + *indicative* → ⓫
	it seems/appears to somebody that
suffire	**il suffit de** + *infinitive* → ⓬
	it is enough to do
	il suffit de + *noun* → ⓭
	something is enough, it only takes something

Examples

❶ Il y a du pain (qui reste)
There is some bread (left)

Il n'y avait pas de lettres ce matin
There were no letters this morning

❷ Il est dix heures
It's ten o'clock

Il est des gens qui ...
There are (some) people who ...

❸ Il était inutile de protester
It was useless to protest

Il est facile de critiquer
It's easy to criticize

❹ Il fait beau/mauvais
It's lovely/horrible weather

❺ Il faisait du soleil/du vent
It was sunny/windy

Il fait jour/nuit
It's light/dark

❻ Il manque deux tasses
There are two cups missing
Two cups are missing

Il manquait un bouton à sa chemise
His shirt had a button missing

❼ Il paraît qu'ils partent demain
It appears they are leaving tomorrow

❽ Il nous paraît certain qu'il aura du succès
It seems certain to us that he'll be successful

❾ Il reste deux miches de pain
There are two loaves left

Il lui restait cinquante euros
He/She had fifty euros left

❿ Il semble que vous ayez raison
It seems that you are right

⓫ Il me semblait qu'il conduisait trop vite
It seemed to me (that) he was driving too fast

⓬ Il suffit de téléphoner pour réserver une place
You just need to phone to reserve a seat

⓭ Il suffit d'une seule erreur pour tout gâcher
One single error is enough to ruin everything

43

Verbs

The Infinitive

The infinitive is the form of the verb meaning 'to ... ' that is found in dictionary entries, e.g. **donner** to give; **vivre** to live.

There are three main types of verbal construction involving the infinitive:
- with no linking preposition → ❶
- with the linking preposition **à** (see also page 64) → ❷
- with the linking preposition **de** (see also page 64) → ❸

Verbs followed by an infinitive with no linking preposition

devoir, **pouvoir**, **savoir**, **vouloir** and **falloir** (i.e. modal auxiliary verbs, see page 52 → ❶).

valoir mieux: see Impersonal Verbs (page 40).

verbs of seeing or hearing, e.g. **voir** to see; **entendre** to hear → ❹

intransitive verbs of motion, e.g. **aller** to go; **descendre** to come/go down → ❺

envoyer to send → ❻

faillir → ❼

faire → ❽

laisser to let, allow → ❾

The following common verbs:

adorer to love	**espérer** to hope → ⓮
aimer to like, love → ❿	**oser** to dare → ⓯
aimer mieux to prefer → ⓫	**préférer** to prefer
compter to expect	**sembler** to seem → ⓰
désirer to wish, want → ⓬	**souhaiter** to wish
détester to hate → ⓭	

Examples

① **Voulez-vous attendre?** — Would you like to wait?

② **J'apprends à nager** — I'm learning to swim

③ **Essayez de venir** — Try to come

④ **Il nous a vus arriver** — He saw us arriving
 On les entend chanter — You can hear them singing

⑤ **Allez voir Nicolas** — Go and see Nicolas
 Descends leur demander — Go down and ask them

⑥ **Je l'ai envoyé les voir** — I sent him to see them

⑦ **J'ai failli tomber** — I almost fell

⑧ **Ne me faites pas rire!** — Don't make me laugh!
 J'ai fait réparer ma voiture — I've had my car repaired

⑨ **Laissez-moi passer** — Let me past

⑩ **Il aime nous accompagner** — He likes to come with us

⑪ **J'aimerais mieux le choisir moi-même** — I'd rather choose it myself

⑫ **Elle ne désire pas venir** — She doesn't wish to come

⑬ **Je déteste me lever le matin** — I hate getting up in the morning

⑭ **Espérez-vous partir en vacances?** — Are you hoping to go on holiday?

⑮ **Nous n'avons pas osé y retourner** — We haven't dared go back

⑯ **Vous semblez être inquiet** — You seem (to be) worried

Verbs

The Infinitive: Set Expressions

The following are set expressions in French and have the following meanings:

aller chercher to go for, to go and get → ❶
envoyer chercher to send for → ❷
entendre dire que to hear (it said) that → ❸
entendre parler de to hear of/about → ❹
faire entrer to show in → ❺
faire sortir to let out → ❻
faire venir to send for → ❼
laisser tomber to drop → ❽
vouloir dire to mean → ❾

The perfect infinitive

The perfect infinitive is formed using the auxiliary verb **avoir** or **être** as appropriate with the past participle of the verb → ❿

The perfect infinitive is found:
- following the preposition **après** after → ⓫
- following certain verbal constructions → ⓬

Examples

❶ Va chercher tes photos
Go and get your photos

Il est allé chercher Alexandre
He's gone to get Alexandre

❷ J'ai envoyé chercher un médecin
I've sent for a doctor

❸ J'ai entendu dire qu'il est malade
I've heard (it said) that he's ill

❹ Je n'ai plus entendu parler de lui
I didn't hear anything more (said) of him

❺ Fais entrer nos invités
Show our guests in

❻ J'ai fait sortir le chat
I've let the cat out

❼ Je vous ai fait venir parce que ...
I sent for you because ...

❽ Il a laissé tomber le vase
He dropped the vase

❾ Qu'est-ce que cela veut dire?
What does that mean?

❿ avoir fini
to have finished

être allé
to have gone

s'être levé
to have got up

⓫ Après avoir pris cette décision, il nous a appelés
After making/having made that decision, he called us

Après être sorties, elles se sont dirigées vers le parking
After leaving/having left, they headed for the car park

Après nous être levé(e)s, nous avons lu les journaux
After getting up/having got up, we read the papers

⓬ pardonner à qn d'avoir fait
to forgive sb for doing/having done

remercier qn d'avoir fait
to thank sb for doing/having done

regretter d'avoir fait
to be sorry for doing/having done

Verbs

The Present Participle

Formation

First conjugation:
Replace the **-er** of the infinitive by **-ant** → ❶
- Verbs ending in **-cer**: **c** changes to **ç** → ❷
- Verbs ending in **-ger**: **g** changes to **ge** → ❸

Second conjugation:
Replace the **-ir** of the infinitive by **-issant** → ❹

Third conjugation:
Replace the **-re** of the infinitive by **-ant** → ❺

For irregular present participles, see irregular verbs, page 74 onwards.

Uses

The present participle has a more restricted use in French than in English.

Used as a verbal form, the present participle is invariable. It is found:
- on its own, where it corresponds to the English present participle → ❻
- following the preposition **en** → ❼
- ⓘ Note, in particular, the construction:
  verb + **en** + *present participle*
  which is often translated by an English phrasal verb, i.e. one followed by a preposition, such as 'to run down', 'to bring up' → ❽

Used as an adjective, the present participle agrees in number and gender with the noun or pronoun → ❾
- ⓘ Note, in particular, the use of **ayant** and **étant** – the present participles of the auxiliary verbs **avoir** and **être** – with a past participle → ❿

Examples

1. **donner** to give → **donnant** giving

2. **lancer** to throw → **lançant** throwing

3. **manger** to eat → **mangeant** eating

4. **finir** to finish → **finissant** finishing

5. **vendre** to sell → **vendant** selling

6. **David, habitant près de Paris, a la possibilité de ...**   David, living near Paris, has the opportunity to ...

   Elle, pensant que je serais fâché, a dit ...   Thinking that I would be angry, she said ...

   Ils m'ont suivi, criant à tue-tête   They followed me, shouting at the top of their voices

7. **En attendant sa sœur, Richard s'est endormi**   While waiting for his sister, Richard fell asleep

   Téléphone-nous en arrivant chez toi   Phone us when you get home

   En appuyant sur ce bouton, on peut ...   By pressing this button, you can ...

   Il s'est blessé en essayant de sauver un chat   He hurt himself trying to rescue a cat

8. **sortir en courant**   to run out (*literally*: to go out running)

   avancer en boitant   to limp along (*literally*: to go forward limping)

9. **le soleil couchant**   the setting sun
   une lumière éblouissante   a dazzling light
   ils sont dégoûtants   they are disgusting
   elles étaient étonnantes   they were surprising

10. **Ayant mangé plus tôt, il a pu ...**   Having eaten earlier, he was able to ...

    Étant arrivée en retard, elle a dû ...   Having arrived late, she had to ...

Verbs

Past Participle Agreement

Like adjectives, a past participle must sometimes agree in number and gender with a noun or pronoun. For the rules of agreement, see below. Example: **donné**

	MASCULINE	FEMININE
SING.	donné	donné**e**
PLUR.	donné**s**	donné**es**

When the masculine singular form already ends in **-s**, no further **s** is added in the masculine plural, e.g. **pris** taken.

Rules of agreement in compound tenses

When the auxiliary verb is **avoir**:

> The past participle remains in the masculine singular form, unless a direct object precedes the verb. The past participle then agrees in number and gender with the preceding direct object → ❶

When the auxiliary verb is **être**:

> The past participle of a non-reflexive verb agrees in number and gender with the subject → ❷
> The past participle of a reflexive verb agrees in number and gender with the reflexive pronoun, if the pronoun is a direct object → ❸
> No agreement is made if the reflexive pronoun is an indirect object → ❹

The past participle as an adjective

The past participle agrees in number and gender with the noun or pronoun → ❺

Examples

① **Voici le livre que vous avez demandé** — Here's the book you asked for

Laquelle avaient-elles choisie? — Which one had they chosen?

Ces amis? Je les ai rencontrés à Édimbourg — Those friends? I met them in Edinburgh

Il a gardé toutes les lettres qu'elle a écrites — He has kept all the letters she wrote

② **Est-ce que ton frère est allé à l'étranger?** — Did your brother go abroad?

Elle était restée chez elle — She had stayed at home

Ils sont partis dans la matinée — They left in the morning

Mes cousines sont revenues hier — My cousins came back yesterday

③ **Tu t'es rappelé d'acheter du pain, Georges?** — Did you remember to buy bread, Georges?

Martine s'est demandée pourquoi il l'appelait — Martine wondered why he was calling her

«Lui et moi nous nous sommes cachés» a-t-elle dit — 'He and I hid,' she said

Les vendeuses se sont mises en grève — The shop assistants have gone on strike

Vous vous êtes brouillés? — Have you fallen out with each other?

Les enfants s'étaient entraidés — The children had helped one another

④ **Elle s'est lavé les mains** — She washed her hands

Ils se sont parlé pendant des heures — They talked to each other for hours

⑤ **à un moment donné** — at a given time

la porte ouverte — the open door

Ils sont bien connus — They are well known

Elles semblent fatiguées — They seem tired

Verbs

Modal Auxiliary Verbs

In French, the modal auxiliary verbs are: **devoir**, **pouvoir**, **savoir**, **vouloir** and **falloir**.

They are followed by a verb in the infinitive and have the following meanings:

devoir   to have to, must → ❶
           to be due to → ❷
           in the conditional/conditional perfect:
           should/should have, ought/ought to have → ❸

pouvoir to be able to, can → ❹
           to be allowed to, can, may → ❺
           indicating possibility: may/might/could → ❻

savoir   to know how to, can → ❼

vouloir to want/wish to → ❽
           to be willing to, will → ❾
           in polite phrases → ❿

falloir   to be necessary: see Impersonal Verbs, page 40.

Examples

1 Je dois leur rendre visite — I must visit them
Elle a dû partir — She (has) had to leave
Il a dû regretter d'avoir parlé — He must have been sorry he spoke

2 Vous devez revenir demain — You're due (to come) back tomorrow
Je devais attraper le train de neuf heures mais ... — I was (supposed) to catch the nine o'clock train but ...

3 Je devrais le faire — I ought to do it
J'aurais dû m'excuser — I ought to have apologized

4 Il ne peut pas lever le bras — He can't raise his arm
Pouvez-vous réparer cette montre? — Can you mend this watch?

5 Puis-je les accompagner? — May I go with them?

6 Il peut encore changer d'avis — He may change his mind yet
Cela pourrait être vrai — It could/might be true

7 Savez-vous conduire? — Can you drive?
Je ne sais pas faire une omelette — I don't know how to make an omelette

8 Elle veut rester encore un jour — She wants to stay another day

9 Ils ne voulaient pas le faire — They wouldn't do it
They weren't willing to do it
Ma voiture ne veut pas démarrer — My car won't start

10 Voulez-vous boire quelque chose? — Would you like something to drink?

Verbs

Use of Tenses

The Present

Unlike English, French does not distinguish between the simple present and the continuous present (e.g. I smoke/I am smoking) → ❶

To emphasize continuity, the following constructions may be used:
être en train de faire, **être à faire** to be doing → ❷

French uses the present tense where English uses the perfect in the following cases:
- with certain prepositions of time – notably **depuis** for/since – when an action begun in the past is continued in the present → ❸
Note, however, that the perfect is used as in English when the verb is negative or the action has been completed → ❹
- in the construction **venir de faire** to have just done → ❺

The Future

The future is generally used as in English, but note the following:

Immediate future time is often expressed by means of the present tense of **aller** plus an infinitive → ❻

In time clauses expressing future action, French uses the future where English uses the present → ❼

The Future Perfect

Used as in English to mean 'shall/will have done' → ❽

In time clauses expressing future action, where English uses the perfect tense → ❾

The Conditional

Used as in English to express what would happen, as well as (with **vouloir** or **aimer**) to express wishes or desires. → ❿

Examples

1 **Je fume**
I smoke *or* I am smoking
Il lit
He reads *or* He is reading
Nous habitons
We live *or* We are living

2 **Il est en train de travailler**
He's (busy) working

3 **Paul apprend à nager depuis six mois**
Paul's been learning to swim for six months (and still is)
Je suis debout depuis sept heures
I've been up since seven
Il y a longtemps que vous attendez?
Have you been waiting long?
Voilà deux semaines que nous sommes ici
That's two weeks we've been here (now)

4 **Ils ne se sont pas vus depuis des mois**
They haven't seen each other for months
Elle est revenue il y a un an
She came back a year ago

5 **Elisabeth vient de partir**
Elisabeth has just left

6 **Tu vas tomber si tu ne fais pas attention**
You'll fall if you're not careful
Il va manquer le train
He's going to miss the train
Ça va prendre une demi-heure
It'll take half an hour

7 **Quand il viendra vous serez en vacances**
When he comes you'll be on holiday
Faites-nous savoir aussitôt qu'elle arrivera
Let us know as soon as she arrives

8 **J'aurai fini dans une heure**
I shall have finished in an hour

9 **Quand tu auras lu ce roman, rends-le-moi**
When you've read the novel, give it back to me
Je partirai dès que j'aurai fini
I'll leave as soon as I've finished

10 **Si j'avais le temps, je le ferais**
If I had the time, I'd do it
J'aimerais t'accompagner
I'd like to go with you
Voudriez-vous autre chose?
Would you like anything else?

Verbs

Use of Tenses *continued*

The Imperfect

The imperfect describes:
- an action (or state) in the past without definite limits in time → ❶
- habitual action(s) in the past (often translated by means of 'would' or 'used to') → ❷

French uses the imperfect tense where English uses the pluperfect in the following cases:
- with certain prepositions of time – notably **depuis** for/since – when an action begun in the more remote past was continued in the more recent past → ❸

Note, however, that the pluperfect is used as in English, when the verb is negative or the action has been completed → ❹
- in the construction **venir de faire** to have just done → ❺

The Perfect

The perfect is used to recount a completed action or event in the past. Note that this corresponds to a perfect tense or a simple past tense in English → ❻

The Past Historic

Only ever used in written, literary French, the past historic recounts a completed action in the past, corresponding to a simple past tense in English → ❼

The Past Anterior

This tense is used instead of the pluperfect when a verb in another part of the sentence is in the past historic. That is:
- in time clauses, after conjunctions like: **quand, lorsque** when; **dès que, aussitôt que** as soon as; **après que** after → ❽
- after **à peine** hardly, scarcely → ❾

The Subjunctive

In spoken French, the present subjunctive generally replaces the imperfect subjunctive. See also page 58 onwards.

Examples

1. **Elle regardait par la fenêtre** — She was looking out of the window

   Il pleuvait quand je suis sorti de chez moi — It was raining when I left the house

   Nos chambres donnaient sur la plage — Our rooms overlooked the beach

2. **Quand il était étudiant, il se levait à l'aube** — When he was a student he got up at dawn

   Nous causions des heures entières — We would talk for hours on end

   Elle te taquinait, n'est-ce pas? — She used to tease you, didn't she?

3. **Nous habitions à Londres depuis deux ans** — We had been living in London for two years (and still were)

   Il était malade depuis 2012 — He had been ill since 2012

   Il y avait assez longtemps qu'il le faisait — He had been doing it for quite a long time

4. **Voilà un an que je ne l'avais pas vu** — I hadn't seen him for a year

   Il y avait une heure qu'elle était arrivée — She had arrived one hour before

5. **Je venais de les rencontrer** — I had just met them

6. **Nous sommes allés au bord de la mer** — We went/have been to the seaside

   Il a refusé de nous aider — He (has) refused to help us

   La voiture ne s'est pas arrêtée — The car didn't stop/hasn't stopped

7. **Le roi mourut en 1592** — The king died in 1592

8. **Quand il eut fini, il se leva** — When he had finished, he got up

9. **À peine eut-il fini de parler qu'on frappa à la porte** — He had scarcely finished speaking when there was a knock at the door

Verbs

The Subjunctive: When to Use It

For how to form the subjunctive, see page 6 onwards.

The subjunctive is used :

After certain conjunctions:

quoique **bien que**	although → **①**
pour que **afin que**	so that → **②**
pourvu que	provided that → **③**
jusqu'à ce que	until → **④**
avant que (... ne)	before → **⑤**
à moins que (... ne)	unless → **⑥**
de peur que (... ne) **de crainte que (... ne)**	for fear that, lest → **⑦**

ⓘ Note that the **ne** following the conjunctions in examples **⑤** to **⑦** has no translation value. It is often omitted in spoken informal French.

After the conjunctions:

de sorte que **de façon que** **de manière que**	so that (*indicating a purpose*) → **⑧**

When these conjunctions introduce a result and not a purpose, the subjunctive is not used → **⑨**

After impersonal constructions which express necessity, possibility *etc*:

il faut que **il est nécessaire que**	it is necessary that → **⑩**
il est possible que	it is possible that → **⑪**
il semble que	it seems that, it appears that → **⑫**
il vaut mieux que	it is better that → **⑬**
il est dommage que	it's a pity that, it's a shame that → **⑭**

Examples

1. **Bien qu'il fasse beaucoup d'efforts, il est peu récompensé**
Although he makes a lot of effort, he isn't rewarded for it

2. **Demandez un reçu afin que vous puissiez être remboursé**
Ask for a receipt so that you can get a refund

3. **Nous partirons ensemble pourvu que Sylvie soit d'accord**
We'll leave together provided Sylvie agrees

4. **Reste ici jusqu'à ce que nous revenions**
Stay here until we come back

5. **Je le ferai avant que tu ne partes**
I'll do it before you leave

6. **Ce doit être Paul, à moins que je ne me trompe**
That must be Paul, unless I'm mistaken

7. **Parlez bas de peur qu'on ne vous entende**
Speak softly lest someone hear you

8. **Retournez-vous de sorte que je vous voie**
Turn round so that I can see you

9. **Il refuse de le faire de sorte que je dois le faire moi-même**
He refuses to do it so that I have to do it myself

10. **Il faut que je vous parle immédiatement**
I must speak to you right away
It is necessary that I speak to you right away

11. **Il est possible qu'ils aient raison**
They may be right
It's possible that they are right

12. **Il semble qu'elle ne soit pas venue**
It appears that she hasn't come

13. **Il vaut mieux que vous restiez chez vous**
It's better that you stay at home

14. **Il est dommage qu'elle ait perdu cette adresse**
It's a shame/a pity that she's lost the address

Verbs

The Subjunctive: When to Use It *continued*

After verbs of:

- wishing
  vouloir que
  désirer que } to wish that, want → **❶**
  souhaiter que

- fearing
  craindre que } to be afraid that → **❷**
  avoir peur que

ⓘ Note that **ne** in the first phrase of example **❷** has no translation value. It is often omitted in spoken informal French.

- ordering, forbidding, allowing
  ordonner que   to order that → **❸**
  défendre que   to forbid that → **❹**
  permettre que   to allow that → **❺**

- opinion, expressing uncertainty
  croire que } to think that → **❻**
  penser que
  douter que   to doubt that → **❼**

- emotion (e.g. regret, shame, pleasure)
  regretter que   to be sorry that → **❽**
  être content/surpris *etc* **que** to be pleased/surprised *etc* that → **❾**

After a superlative → **❿**

After certain adjectives expressing some sort of 'uniqueness' → **⓫**
  dernier ... qui/que   last ... who/that
  premier ... qui/que   first ... who/that
  meilleur ... qui/que   best ... who/that
  seul ... qui/que } only ... who/that
  unique ... qui/que

Examples

1 **Nous voulons qu'elle soit contente**
We want her to be happy (*literally*: We want that she is happy)

Désirez-vous que je le fasse?
Do you want me to do it?

2 **Il craint qu'il ne soit trop tard**
He's afraid it may be too late

Avez-vous peur qu'il ne revienne pas?
Are you afraid that he won't come back?

3 **Il a ordonné qu'ils soient désormais à l'heure**
He has ordered that they be on time from now on

4 **Elle défend que vous disiez cela**
She forbids you to say that

5 **Permettez que nous vous aidions**
Allow us to help you

6 **Je ne pense pas qu'ils soient venus**
I don't think they came

7 **Nous doutons qu'il ait dit la vérité**
We doubt that he told the truth

8 **Je regrette que vous ne puissiez pas venir**
I'm sorry that you cannot come

9 **Je suis content que vous les aimiez**
I'm pleased that you like them

10 **la personne la plus sympathique que je connaisse**
the nicest person I know

l'article le moins cher que j'aie jamais acheté
the cheapest item I have ever bought

11 **Voici la dernière lettre qu'elle m'ait écrite**
This is the last letter she wrote to me

David est la seule personne qui puisse me conseiller
David is the only person who can advise me

Verbs

The Subjunctive: When to Use It *continued*

After:

si (...) que however → ❶
qui que whoever → ❷
quoi que whatever → ❸

After **que** in the following:

- to form the third person imperative or to express a wish → ❹
- when **que** has the meaning 'if', replacing **si** in a clause → ❺
- when **que** has the meaning 'whether' → ❻

In relative clauses following certain types of indefinite and negative construction → ❼/❽

In set expressions → ❾

Examples

❶ si courageux qu'il soit / however brave he may be

si peu que ce soit / however little it is

❷ Qui que vous soyez, allez-vous-en! / Whoever you are, go away!

❸ Quoi que nous fassions, ... / Whatever we do, ...

❹ Qu'il entre! / Let him come in!

Que cela vous serve de leçon! / Let that be a lesson to you!

❺ S'il fait beau et que tu te sentes mieux, nous irons ... / If it's nice and you're feeling better, we'll go ...

❻ Que tu viennes ou non, je ... / Whether you come or not, I ...

❼ Il cherche une maison qui ait une piscine / He's looking for a house which has a swimming pool (*subjective used since such a house may or may not exist*)

J'ai besoin d'un livre qui décrive l'art du mime / I need a book which describes the art of mime (*subjective used since such a book may or may not exist*)

❽ Je n'ai rencontré personne qui la connaisse / I haven't met anyone who knows her

Il n'y a rien qui puisse vous empêcher de ... / There's nothing that can prevent you from ...

❾ Vive le roi! / Long live the king!

Que Dieu vous bénisse! / God bless you!

Verbs

Verbs Governing *à* and *de*

The following lists (pages 64 to 72) contain common verbal constructions using the prepositions **à** and **de**

accuser qn de qch/de + *perf. infin.*	to accuse sb of sth/of doing, having done → ❶
accoutumer qn à qch/à + *infin.*	to accustom sb to sth/to doing
acheter qch à qn	to buy sth from sb/for sb → ❷
achever de + *infin.*	to end up doing
aider qn à + *infin.*	to help sb to do → ❸
s'amuser à + *infin.*	to have fun doing
s'apercevoir de qch	to notice sth → ❹
apprendre qch à qn	to teach sb sth
apprendre à + *infin.*	to learn to do → ❺
apprendre à qn à + *infin.*	to teach sb to do → ❻
s'approcher de qn/qch	to approach sb/sth → ❼
arracher qch à qn	to snatch sth from sb → ❽
(s')arrêter de + *infin.*	to stop doing → ❾
arriver à + *infin.*	to manage to do → ❿
assister à qch	to attend sth, be at sth
s'attendre à + *infin.*	to expect to do → ⓫
blâmer qn de qch/de + *perf. infin.*	to blame sb for sth/for having done → ⓬
cacher qch à qn	to hide sth from sb → ⓭
cesser de + *infin.*	to stop doing → ⓮

* For formation, see page 46

Examples

1. Il m'a accusé d'avoir menti — He accused me of lying

2. Marie-Christine leur a acheté deux billets — Marie-Christine bought two tickets from/for them

3. Aidez-moi à porter ces valises — Help me to carry these cases

4. Il ne s'est pas aperçu de son erreur — He didn't notice his mistake

5. Elle apprend à lire — She's learning to read

6. Je lui apprends à nager — I'm teaching him/her to swim

7. Elle s'est approchée de moi, en disant ... — She approached me, saying ...

8. Le voleur lui a arraché l'argent — The thief snatched the money from him/her

9. Arrêtez de faire du bruit! — Stop making so much noise!

10. Le professeur n'arrive pas à se faire obéir de sa classe — The teacher couldn't manage to control the class

11. Est-ce qu'elle s'attendait à le voir? — Was she expecting to see him?

12. Je ne la blâme pas de l'avoir fait — I don't blame her for doing it

13. Cache-les-leur! — Hide them from them!

14. Est-ce qu'il a cessé de pleuvoir? — Has it stopped raining?

Verbs

Verbs Governing *à* and *de* continued

changer de qch	to change sth → ①
se charger de qch/de + *infin.*	to see to sth/undertake to do
chercher à + *infin.*	to try to do
commander à qn de + *infin.*	to order sb to do → ②
commencer à/de + *infin.*	to begin to do, to start to do → ③
conseiller à qn de + *infin.*	to advise sb to do → ④
consentir à qch/à + *infin.*	to agree to sth/to do → ⑤
continuer à/de + *infin.*	to continue to do
craindre de + *infin.*	to be afraid to do/of doing
décider de + *infin.*	to decide to → ⑥
se décider à + *infin.*	to make up one's mind to do
défendre à qn de + *infin.*	to forbid sb to do → ⑦
demander qch à qn	to ask sb sth/for sth → ⑧
demander à qn de + *infin.*	to ask sb to do → ⑨
se dépêcher de + *infin.*	to hurry to do
dépendre de qn/qch	to depend on sb/sth
déplaire à qn	to displease sb → ⑩
désobéir à qn	to disobey sb → ⑪
dire à qn de + *infin.*	to tell sb to do → ⑫
dissuader qn de + *infin.*	to dissuade sb from doing
douter de qch	to doubt sth
se douter de qch	to suspect sth
s'efforcer de + *infin.*	to strive to do
empêcher qn de + *infin.*	to prevent sb from doing → ⑬
emprunter qch à qn	to borrow sth from sb → ⑭
encourager qn à + *infin.*	to encourage sb to do → ⑮
enlever qch à qn	to take sth away from sb
enseigner qch à qn	to teach sb sth
enseigner à qn à + *infin.*	to teach sb to do
entreprendre de + *infin.*	to undertake to do
essayer de + *infin.*	to try to do → ⑯
éviter de + *infin.*	to avoid doing → ⑰

Examples

1. **J'ai changé d'avis/de robe**
   Il faut changer de train à Toulouse

   I changed my mind/my dress
   You have to change trains at Toulouse

2. **Il leur a commandé de tirer**

   He ordered them to shoot

3. **Il commence à neiger**

   It's starting to snow

4. **Il leur a conseillé d'attendre**

   He advised them to wait

5. **Je n'ai pas consenti à l'aider**

   I haven't agreed to help him/her

6. **Qu'est-ce que vous avez décidé de faire?**

   What have you decided to do?

7. **Je leur ai défendu de sortir**

   I've forbidden them to go out

8. **Je lui ai demandé l'heure**
   Il lui a demandé un livre

   I asked him/her the time
   He asked him/her for a book

9. **Demande à Alain de le faire**

   Ask Alain to do it

10. **Leur attitude lui déplaît**

    He/She doesn't like their attitude

11. **Ils lui désobéissent souvent**

    They often disobey him/her

12. **Dites-leur de se taire**

    Tell them to be quiet

13. **Le bruit m'empêche de travailler**

    The noise is preventing me from working

14. **Puis-je vous emprunter ce stylo?**

    May I borrow this pen from you?

15. **Elle encourage ses enfants à être indépendants**

    She encourages her children to be independent

16. **Essayez d'arriver à l'heure**

    Try to arrive on time

17. **Il évite de lui parler**

    He avoids speaking to him/her

67

Verbs

Verbs Governing *à* and *de* continued

s'excuser de qch/de + *(perf.) infin.*	to apologize for sth/for doing, having done → ❶
exceller à + *infin.*	to excel at doing
se fâcher de qch	to be annoyed at sth
feindre de + *infin.*	to pretend to do → ❷
féliciter qn de qch/de + *(perf.) infin.*	to congratulate sb on sth/on doing, having done → ❸
se fier à qn	to trust sb → ❹
finir de + *infin.*	to finish doing → ❺
forcer qn à + *infin.*	to force sb to do
habituer qn à + *infin.*	to accustom sb to doing
s'habituer à + *infin.*	to get/be used to doing → ❻
se hâter de + *infin.*	to hurry to do
hésiter à + *infin.*	to hesitate to do
interdire à qn de + *infin.*	to forbid sb to do → ❼
s'intéresser à qn/qch/à + *infin.*	to be interested in sb/sth/in doing → ❽
inviter qn à + *infin.*	to invite sb to do → ❾
jouer à (+ *sports, games*)	to play → ❿
jouer de (+ *musical instruments*)	to play → ⓫
jouir de qch	to enjoy sth → ⓬
jurer de + *infin.*	to swear to do
louer qn de qch	to praise sb for sth
manquer à qn	to be missed by sb → ⓭
manquer de qch	to lack sth
manquer de + *infin.*	to fail to do → ⓮
se marier à qn	to marry sb
se méfier de qn	to distrust sb
menacer de + *infin.*	to threaten to do → ⓯
mériter de + *infin.*	to deserve to do → ⓰
se mettre à + *infin.*	to begin to do
se moquer de qn/qch	to make fun of sb/sth
négliger de + *infin.*	to fail to do

Examples

① **Je m'excuse d'être (arrivé) en retard**
I apologize for being/arriving late

② **Elle feint de dormir**
She's pretending to be asleep

③ **Je l'ai félicitée d'avoir gagné**
I congratulated her on winning

④ **Je ne me fie pas à ces gens-là**
I don't trust those people

⑤ **Avez-vous fini de lire ce journal?**
Have you finished reading this newspaper?

⑥ **Il s'est habitué à boire moins de café**
He got used to drinking less coffee

⑦ **Il a interdit aux enfants de jouer avec des allumettes**
He's forbidden the children to play with matches

⑧ **Elle s'intéresse beaucoup au sport**
She's very interested in sport

⑨ **Il m'a invitée à dîner**
He invited me for dinner

⑩ **Elle joue au tennis et au hockey**
She plays tennis and hockey

⑪ **Il joue du piano et de la guitare**
He plays the piano and the guitar

⑫ **Il jouit d'une santé solide**
He enjoys good health

⑬ **Tu manques à tes parents**
Your parents miss you

⑭ **Je ne manquerai pas de le lui dire**
I'll be sure to tell him/her about it

⑮ **Elle a menacé de démissionner tout de suite**
She threatened to resign straight away

⑯ **Ils méritent d'être promus**
They deserve to be promoted

Verbs

Verbs Governing *à* and *de* continued

nuire à qch	to harm sth, to do damage to sth → ❶
obéir à qn	to obey sb
obliger qn à + *infin.*	to oblige/force sb to do → ❷
s'occuper de qch/qn	to look after sth/sb → ❸
offrir de + *infin.*	to offer to do → ❹
omettre de + *infin.*	to fail to do
ordonner à qn de + *infin.*	to order sb to do → ❺
ôter qch à qn	to take sth away from sb
oublier de + *infin.*	to forget to do
pardonner qch à qn	to forgive sb for sth
pardonner à qn de + *perf. infin.*	to forgive sb for having done → ❻
parvenir à + *infin.*	to manage to do
se passer de qch	to do/go without sth → ❼
penser à qn/qch	to think about sb/sth → ❽
permettre qch à qn	to allow sb sth
permettre à qn de + *infin.*	to allow sb to do → ❾
persister à + *infin.*	to persist in doing
persuader qn de + *infin.*	to persuade sb to do → ❿
se plaindre de qch	to complain about sth
plaire à qn	to please sb → ⓫
pousser qn à + *infin.*	to urge sb to do
prendre qch à qn	to take sth from sb → ⓬
préparer qn à + *infin.*	to prepare sb to do
se préparer à + *infin.*	to get ready to do
prier qn de + *infin.*	to beg sb to do
profiter de qch/de + *infin.*	to take advantage of sth/of doing
promettre à qn de + *infin.*	to promise sb to do → ⓭
proposer de + *infin.*	to suggest doing → ⓮
punir qn de qch	to punish sb for sth → ⓯
récompenser qn de qch	to reward sb for sth
réfléchir à qch	to think about sth
refuser de + *infin.*	to refuse to do → ⓰

Examples

1 **Ce mode de vie va nuire à sa santé** This lifestyle will damage her health

2 **Il les a obligés à faire la vaisselle** He forced them to do the washing-up

3 **Je m'occupe de ma nièce** I'm looking after my niece

4 **Stuart a offert de nous accompagner** Stuart has offered to go with us

5 **Les soldats leur ont ordonné de se rendre** The soldiers ordered them to give themselves up

6 **Est-ce que tu as pardonné à Charles de t'avoir menti?** Have you forgiven Charles for lying to you?

7 **Je me suis passé d'électricité pendant plusieurs jours** I did without electricity for several days

8 **Je pense souvent à toi** I often think about you

9 **Permettez-moi de continuer, s'il vous plaît** Allow me to go on, please

10 **Elle nous a persuadés de rester** She persuaded us to stay

11 **Ce genre de film lui plaît** He/she likes this kind of film

12 **Je lui ai pris son mobile** I took his mobile phone from him

13 **Ils ont promis à Pascale de venir** They promised Pascale that they would come

14 **J'ai proposé de les inviter** I suggested inviting them

15 **Il a été puni de sa malhonnêteté** He has been punished for his dishonesty

16 **Il a refusé de coopérer** He has refused to cooperate

Verbs

Verbs Governing *à* and *de* continued

regretter de + *perf. infin.*	to regret doing, having done → **1**
remercier qn de qch/de + *perf. infin.*	to thank sb for sth/for doing, having done → **2**
renoncer à qch/à + *infin.*	to give sth up/give up doing
reprocher qch à qn	to reproach sb with/for sth → **3**
résister à qch	to resist sth → **4**
résoudre de + *infin.*	to resolve to do
ressembler à qn/qch	to look/be like sb/sth → **5**
réussir à + *infin.*	to manage to do → **6**
rire de qn/qch	to laugh at sb/sth
risquer de + *infin.*	to risk doing → **7**
servir à qch/à + *infin.*	to be used for sth/for doing → **8**
se servir de qch	to use sth; to help oneself to sth → **9**
songer à + *infin.*	to think of doing
se souvenir de qn/qch/de + *perf. infin.*	to remember sb/sth/doing, having done → **10**
succéder à qn	to succeed sb
survivre à qn	to outlive sb → **11**
tâcher de + *infin.*	to try to do → **12**
tarder à + *infin.*	to delay doing → **13**
tendre à + *infin.*	to tend to do
tenir à + *infin.*	to be keen to do → **14**
tenter de + *infin.*	to try to do → **15**
se tromper de qch	to be wrong about sth → **16**
venir de* + *infin.*	to have just done → **17**
vivre de qch	to live on sth
voler qch à qn	to steal sth from sb

* See also Use of Tenses, pages 54 and 56

Examples

① **Je regrette de ne pas l'avoir vue plus souvent quand elle était ici**
I regret not having seen her more while she was here

② **Nous les avons remerciés de leur gentillesse**
We thanked them for their kindness

③ **On lui reproche son manque d'enthousiasme**
They're reproaching him for his lack of enthusiasm

④ **Comment résistez-vous à la tentation?**
How do you resist temptation?

⑤ **Elles ressemblent beaucoup à leur mère**
They look very like their mother

⑥ **Vous avez réussi à me convaincre**
You've managed to convince me

⑦ **Vous risquez de tomber en faisant cela**
You risk falling doing that

⑧ **Ce bouton sert à régler le volume**
This knob is (used) for adjusting the volume

⑨ **Il s'est servi d'un tournevis pour l'ouvrir**
He used a screwdriver to open it

⑩ **Vous vous souvenez de Lucienne? Il ne se souvient pas de l'avoir perdu**
Do you remember Lucienne? He doesn't remember losing it

⑪ **Elle a survécu à son mari**
She outlived her husband

⑫ **Tâchez de ne pas être en retard!**
Try not to be late!

⑬ **Il n'a pas tardé à prendre une décision**
He was not long in taking a decision

⑭ **Elle tient à le faire elle-même**
She's keen to do it herself

⑮ **J'ai tenté de la comprendre**
I've tried to understand her

⑯ **Je me suis trompé de route**
I took the wrong road

⑰ **Mon père vient de téléphoner
Nous venions d'arriver**
My father's just phoned
We had just arrived

Verbs

Irregular Verbs

The verbs listed opposite and conjugated on pages 76 to 131 provide the main patterns for irregular verbs. The verbs are grouped opposite according to their infinitive ending (except **avoir** and **être**), and are shown in the following tables in alphabetical order.

In the tables, the most important irregular verbs are given in their most common simple tenses, together with the imperative and the present participle.

The auxiliary (**avoir** or **être**) is also shown for each verb, together with the past participle, to enable you to form all the compound tenses, as on pages 24 and 26.

For a fuller list of irregular verbs, the reader is referred to Collins Easy Learning French Verbs, which shows you how to conjugate some 2000 French verbs.

Verbs

avoir
être

'-er': aller
envoyer

'-ir': acquérir
bouillir
courir
cueillir
dormir
fuir
haïr
mourir
ouvrir
partir
sentir
servir
sortir
tenir
venir
vêtir

'-oir': s'asseoir
devoir
falloir
pleuvoir
pouvoir
recevoir
savoir
valoir
voir
vouloir

'-re': battre
boire
connaître
coudre
craindre
croire
croître
cuire
dire
écrire
faire
lire
mettre
moudre
naître
paraître
plaire
prendre
résoudre
rire
rompre
suffire
suivre
se taire
vaincre
vivre

Verbs

acquérir (to acquire)

	PRESENT			IMPERFECT
	j'acquiers			j'acquérais
tu	acquiers		tu	acquérais
il	acquiert		il	acquérait
nous	acquérons		nous	acquérions
vous	acquérez		vous	acquériez
ils	acquièrent		ils	acquéraient

	FUTURE			CONDITIONAL
	j'acquerrai			j'acquerrais
tu	acquerras		tu	acquerrais
il	acquerra		il	acquerrait
nous	acquerrons		nous	acquerrions
vous	acquerrez		vous	acquerriez
ils	acquerront		ils	acquerraient

	PRESENT SUBJUNCTIVE			PAST HISTORIC
	j'acquière			j'acquis
tu	acquières		tu	acquis
il	acquière		il	acquit
nous	acquérions		nous	acquîmes
vous	acquériez		vous	acquîtes
ils	acquièrent		ils	acquirent

PAST PARTICIPLE	IMPERATIVE
acquis	acquiers
	acquérons
	acquérez

PRESENT PARTICIPLE	AUXILIARY
acquérant	avoir

Verbs

aller (to go)

	PRESENT		IMPERFECT
je	**vais**		j'allais
tu	**vas**	tu	allais
il	**va**	il	allait
nous	allons	nous	allions
vous	allez	vous	alliez
ils	**vont**	ils	allaient

	FUTURE		CONDITIONAL
	j'**irai**		j'**irais**
tu	**iras**	tu	**irais**
il	**ira**	il	**irait**
nous	**irons**	nous	**irions**
vous	**irez**	vous	**iriez**
ils	**iront**	ils	**iraient**

	PRESENT SUBJUNCTIVE		PAST HISTORIC
	j'**aille**		j'allai
tu	**ailles**	tu	allas
il	**aille**	il	alla
nous	allions	nous	allâmes
vous	alliez	vous	allâtes
ils	**aillent**	ils	allèrent

PAST PARTICIPLE	IMPERATIVE
allé	**va**
	allons
	allez

PRESENT PARTICIPLE	AUXILIARY
allant	**être**

Verbs

s'asseoir (to sit down)

	PRESENT		IMPERFECT
je	m'assieds *or* assois	je	m'asseyais
tu	t'assieds *or* assois	tu	t'asseyais
il	s'assied *or* assoit	il	s'asseyait
nous	nous asseyons *or* assoyons	nous	nous asseyions
vous	vous asseyez *or* assoyez	vous	vous asseyiez
ils	s'asseyent *or* assoient	ils	s'asseyaient

	FUTURE		CONDITIONAL
je	m'assiérai	je	m'assiérais
tu	t'assiéras	tu	t'assiérais
il	s'assiéra	il	s'assiérait
nous	nous assiérons	nous	nous assiérions
vous	vous assiérez	vous	vous assiériez
ils	s'assiéront	ils	s'assiéraient

	PRESENT SUBJUNCTIVE		PAST HISTORIC
je	m'asseye	je	m'assis
tu	t'asseyes	tu	t'assis
il	s'asseye	il	s'assit
nous	nous asseyions	nous	nous assîmes
vous	vous asseyiez	vous	vous assîtes
ils	s'asseyent	ils	s'assirent

PAST PARTICIPLE	IMPERATIVE
assis	assieds-toi
	asseyons-nous
	asseyez-vous

PRESENT PARTICIPLE	AUXILIARY
s'asseyant	être

Verbs

avoir (to have)

	PRESENT			IMPERFECT
	j'**ai**			j'**avais**
tu	**as**		tu	**avais**
il	**a**		il	**avait**
nous	**avons**		nous	**avions**
vous	**avez**		vous	**aviez**
ils	**ont**		ils	**avaient**

	FUTURE			CONDITIONAL
	j'**aurai**			j'**aurais**
tu	**auras**		tu	**aurais**
il	**aura**		il	**aurait**
nous	**aurons**		nous	**aurions**
vous	**aurez**		vous	**auriez**
ils	**auront**		ils	**auraient**

	PRESENT SUBJUNCTIVE			PAST HISTORIC
	j'**aie**			j'**eus**
tu	**aies**		tu	**eus**
il	**ait**		il	**eut**
nous	**ayons**		nous	**eûmes**
vous	**ayez**		vous	**eûtes**
ils	**aient**		ils	**eurent**

PAST PARTICIPLE
eu

IMPERATIVE
aie
ayons
ayez

PRESENT PARTICIPLE
ayant

AUXILIARY
avoir

Verbs

battre (to beat)

	PRESENT			IMPERFECT
je	**bats**		je	battais
tu	**bats**		tu	battais
il	**bat**		il	battait
nous	battons		nous	battions
vous	battez		vous	battiez
ils	battent		ils	battaient

	FUTURE			CONDITIONAL
je	battrai		je	battrais
tu	battras		tu	battrais
il	battra		il	battrait
nous	battrons		nous	battrions
vous	battrez		vous	battriez
ils	battront		ils	battraient

	PRESENT SUBJUNCTIVE			PAST HISTORIC
je	batte		je	battis
tu	battes		tu	battis
il	batte		il	battit
nous	battions		nous	battîmes
vous	battiez		vous	battîtes
ils	battent		ils	battirent

PAST PARTICIPLE	IMPERATIVE
battu	**bats**
	battons
	battez

PRESENT PARTICIPLE	AUXILIARY
battant	**avoir**

boire (to drink)

	PRESENT		IMPERFECT
je	bois	je	**buvais**
tu	bois	tu	**buvais**
il	boit	il	**buvait**
nous	**buvons**	nous	**buvions**
vous	**buvez**	vous	**buviez**
ils	**boivent**	ils	**buvaient**

	FUTURE		CONDITIONAL
je	boirai	je	boirais
tu	boiras	tu	boirais
il	boira	il	boirait
nous	boirons	nous	boirions
vous	boirez	vous	boiriez
ils	boiront	ils	boiraient

	PRESENT SUBJUNCTIVE		PAST HISTORIC
je	**boive**	je	**bus**
tu	**boives**	tu	**bus**
il	**boive**	il	**but**
nous	**buvions**	nous	**bûmes**
vous	**buviez**	vous	**bûtes**
ils	**boivent**	ils	**burent**

PAST PARTICIPLE
bu

IMPERATIVE
bois
buvons
buvez

PRESENT PARTICIPLE
buvant

AUXILIARY
avoir

Verbs

bouillir (to boil)

	PRESENT		IMPERFECT
je	**bous**	je	**bouillais**
tu	**bous**	tu	**bouillais**
il	**bout**	il	**bouillait**
nous	**bouillons**	nous	**bouillions**
vous	**bouillez**	vous	**bouilliez**
ils	**bouillent**	ils	**bouillaient**

	FUTURE		CONDITIONAL
je	bouillirai	je	bouillirais
tu	bouilliras	tu	bouillirais
il	bouillira	il	bouillirait
nous	bouillirons	nous	bouillirions
vous	bouillirez	vous	bouilliriez
ils	bouilliront	ils	bouilliraient

	PRESENT SUBJUNCTIVE		PAST HISTORIC
je	**bouille**	je	bouillis
tu	**bouilles**	tu	bouillis
il	**bouille**	il	bouillit
nous	**bouillions**	nous	bouillîmes
vous	**bouilliez**	vous	bouillîtes
ils	**bouillent**	ils	bouillirent

PAST PARTICIPLE
bouilli

IMPERATIVE
bous
bouillons
bouillez

PRESENT PARTICIPLE
bouillant

AUXILIARY
avoir

Verbs

connaître (to know)

<table>
<tr><td colspan="2">PRESENT</td><td colspan="2">IMPERFECT</td></tr>
<tr><td>je</td><td>connais</td><td>je</td><td>connaissais</td></tr>
<tr><td>tu</td><td>connais</td><td>tu</td><td>connaissais</td></tr>
<tr><td>il</td><td>connaît</td><td>il</td><td>connaissait</td></tr>
<tr><td>nous</td><td>connaissons</td><td>nous</td><td>connaissions</td></tr>
<tr><td>vous</td><td>connaissez</td><td>vous</td><td>connaissiez</td></tr>
<tr><td>ils</td><td>connaissent</td><td>ils</td><td>connaissaient</td></tr>
<tr><td colspan="2">FUTURE</td><td colspan="2">CONDITIONAL</td></tr>
<tr><td>je</td><td>connaîtrai</td><td>je</td><td>connaîtrais</td></tr>
<tr><td>tu</td><td>connaîtras</td><td>tu</td><td>connaîtrais</td></tr>
<tr><td>il</td><td>connaîtra</td><td>il</td><td>connaîtrait</td></tr>
<tr><td>nous</td><td>connaîtrons</td><td>nous</td><td>connaîtrions</td></tr>
<tr><td>vous</td><td>connaîtrez</td><td>vous</td><td>connaîtriez</td></tr>
<tr><td>ils</td><td>connaîtront</td><td>ils</td><td>connaîtraient</td></tr>
<tr><td colspan="2">PRESENT SUBJUNCTIVE</td><td colspan="2">PAST HISTORIC</td></tr>
<tr><td>je</td><td>connaisse</td><td>je</td><td>connus</td></tr>
<tr><td>tu</td><td>connaisses</td><td>tu</td><td>connus</td></tr>
<tr><td>il</td><td>connaisse</td><td>il</td><td>connut</td></tr>
<tr><td>nous</td><td>connaissions</td><td>nous</td><td>connûmes</td></tr>
<tr><td>vous</td><td>connaissiez</td><td>vous</td><td>connûtes</td></tr>
<tr><td>ils</td><td>connaissent</td><td>ils</td><td>connurent</td></tr>
</table>

PAST PARTICIPLE
connu

IMPERATIVE
connais
connaissons
connaissez

PRESENT PARTICIPLE
connaissant

AUXILIARY
avoir

Verbs

coudre (to sew)

	PRESENT		IMPERFECT
je	couds	je	cousais
tu	couds	tu	cousais
il	coud	il	cousait
nous	cousons	nous	cousions
vous	cousez	vous	cousiez
ils	cousent	ils	cousaient

	FUTURE		CONDITIONAL
je	coudrai	je	coudrais
tu	coudras	tu	coudrais
il	coudra	il	coudrait
nous	coudrons	nous	coudrions
vous	coudrez	vous	coudriez
ils	coudront	ils	coudraient

	PRESENT SUBJUNCTIVE		PAST HISTORIC
je	couse	je	cousis
tu	couses	tu	cousis
il	couse	il	cousit
nous	cousions	nous	cousîmes
vous	cousiez	vous	cousîtes
ils	cousent	ils	cousirent

PAST PARTICIPLE
cousu

IMPERATIVE
couds
cousons
cousez

PRESENT PARTICIPLE
cousant

AUXILIARY
avoir

Verbs

courir (to run)

	PRESENT		IMPERFECT
je	cours	je	courais
tu	cours	tu	courais
il	court	il	courait
nous	courons	nous	courions
vous	courez	vous	couriez
ils	courent	ils	couraient

	FUTURE		CONDITIONAL
je	courrai	je	courrais
tu	courras	tu	courrais
il	courra	il	courrait
nous	courrons	nous	courrions
vous	courrez	vous	courriez
ils	courront	ils	courraient

	PRESENT SUBJUNCTIVE		PAST HISTORIC
je	coure	je	courus
tu	coures	tu	courus
il	coure	il	courut
nous	courions	nous	courûmes
vous	couriez	vous	courûtes
ils	courent	ils	coururent

PAST PARTICIPLE	IMPERATIVE
couru	cours
	courons
	courez

PRESENT PARTICIPLE	AUXILIARY
courant	avoir

Verbs

craindre (to fear)

	PRESENT		IMPERFECT
je	**crains**	je	**craignais**
tu	**crains**	tu	**craignais**
il	**craint**	il	**craignait**
nous	**craignons**	nous	**craignions**
vous	**craignez**	vous	**craigniez**
ils	**craignent**	ils	**craignaient**

	FUTURE		CONDITIONAL
je	craindrai	je	craindrais
tu	craindras	tu	craindrais
il	craindra	il	craindrait
nous	craindrons	nous	craindrions
vous	craindrez	vous	craindriez
ils	craindront	ils	craindraient

	PRESENT SUBJUNCTIVE		PAST HISTORIC
je	**craigne**	je	**craignis**
tu	**craignes**	tu	**craignis**
il	**craigne**	il	**craignit**
nous	**craignions**	nous	**craignîmes**
vous	**craigniez**	vous	**craignîtes**
ils	**craignent**	ils	**craignirent**

PAST PARTICIPLE
craint

IMPERATIVE
crains
craignons
craignez

PRESENT PARTICIPLE
craignant

AUXILIARY
avoir

Note that verbs ending in **-eindre** and **-oindre** are conjugated similarly

Verbs

croire (to believe)

	PRESENT		IMPERFECT
je	crois	je	croyais
tu	crois	tu	croyais
il	croit	il	croyait
nous	croyons	nous	croyions
vous	croyez	vous	croyiez
ils	croient	ils	croyaient

	FUTURE		CONDITIONAL
je	croirai	je	croirais
tu	croiras	tu	croirais
il	croira	il	croirait
nous	croirons	nous	croirions
vous	croirez	vous	croiriez
ils	croiront	ils	croiraient

	PRESENT SUBJUNCTIVE		PAST HISTORIC
je	croie	je	crus
tu	croies	tu	crus
il	croie	il	crut
nous	croyions	nous	crûmes
vous	croyiez	vous	crûtes
ils	croient	ils	crurent

PAST PARTICIPLE
cru

IMPERATIVE
crois
croyons
croyez

PRESENT PARTICIPLE
croyant

AUXILIARY
avoir

Verbs

croître (to grow)

	PRESENT		IMPERFECT
je	croîs	je	croissais
tu	croîs	tu	croissais
il	croît	il	croissait
nous	croissons	nous	croissions
vous	croissez	vous	croissiez
ils	croissent	ils	croissaient

	FUTURE		CONDITIONAL
je	croîtrai	je	croîtrais
tu	croîtras	tu	croîtrais
il	croîtra	il	croîtrait
nous	croîtrons	nous	croîtrions
vous	croîtrez	vous	croîtriez
ils	croîtront	ils	croîtraient

	PRESENT SUBJUNCTIVE		PAST HISTORIC
je	croisse	je	crûs
tu	croisses	tu	crûs
il	croisse	il	crût
nous	croissions	nous	crûmes
vous	croissiez	vous	crûtes
ils	croissent	ils	crûrent

PAST PARTICIPLE
crû

IMPERATIVE
croîs
croissons
croissez

PRESENT PARTICIPLE
croissant

AUXILIARY
avoir

Verbs

cueillir (to pick)

	PRESENT		IMPERFECT
je	cueille	je	cueillais
tu	cueilles	tu	cueillais
il	cueille	il	cueillait
nous	cueillons	nous	cueillions
vous	cueillez	vous	cueilliez
ils	cueillent	ils	cueillaient

	FUTURE		CONDITIONAL
je	cueillerai	je	cueillerais
tu	cueilleras	tu	cueillerais
il	cueillera	il	cueillerait
nous	cueillerons	nous	cueillerions
vous	cueillerez	vous	cueilleriez
ils	cueilleront	ils	cueilleraient

	PRESENT SUBJUNCTIVE		PAST HISTORIC
je	cueille	je	cueillis
tu	cueilles	tu	cueillis
il	cueille	il	cueillit
nous	cueillions	nous	cueillîmes
vous	cueilliez	vous	cueillîtes
ils	cueillent	ils	cueillirent

PAST PARTICIPLE
cueilli

IMPERATIVE
cueille
cueillons
cueillez

PRESENT PARTICIPLE
cueillant

AUXILIARY
avoir

Verbs

cuire (to cook)

	PRESENT		IMPERFECT
je	cuis	je	**cuisais**
tu	cuis	tu	**cuisais**
il	**cuit**	il	**cuisait**
nous	**cuisons**	nous	**cuisions**
vous	**cuisez**	vous	**cuisiez**
ils	**cuisent**	ils	**cuisaient**

	FUTURE		CONDITIONAL
je	cuirai	je	cuirais
tu	cuiras	tu	cuirais
il	cuira	il	cuirait
nous	cuirons	nous	cuirions
vous	cuirez	vous	cuiriez
ils	cuiront	ils	cuiraient

	PRESENT SUBJUNCTIVE		PAST HISTORIC
je	**cuise**	je	**cuisis**
tu	**cuises**	tu	**cuisis**
il	**cuise**	il	**cuisit**
nous	**cuisions**	nous	**cuisîmes**
vous	**cuisiez**	vous	**cuisîtes**
ils	**cuisent**	ils	**cuisirent**

PAST PARTICIPLE	IMPERATIVE
cuit	cuis
	cuisons
	cuisez

PRESENT PARTICIPLE	AUXILIARY
cuisant	**avoir**

Note that **nuire** (to harm) is conjugated similarly, but the past participle is **nui**

Verbs

devoir (to have to, to owe)

	PRESENT		IMPERFECT
je	dois	je	devais
tu	dois	tu	devais
il	doit	il	devait
nous	devons	nous	devions
vous	devez	vous	deviez
ils	doivent	ils	devaient

	FUTURE		CONDITIONAL
je	devrai	je	devrais
tu	devras	tu	devrais
il	devra	il	devrait
nous	devrons	nous	devrions
vous	devrez	vous	devriez
ils	devront	ils	devraient

	PRESENT SUBJUNCTIVE		PAST HISTORIC
je	doive	je	dus
tu	doives	tu	dus
il	doive	il	dut
nous	devions	nous	dûmes
vous	deviez	vous	dûtes
ils	doivent	ils	durent

PAST PARTICIPLE
dû

IMPERATIVE
dois
devons
devez

PRESENT PARTICIPLE
devant

AUXILIARY
avoir

Verbs

dire (to say, to tell)

	PRESENT		IMPERFECT
je	dis	je	disais
tu	dis	tu	disais
il	dit	il	disait
nous	disons	nous	disions
vous	dites	vous	disiez
ils	disent	ils	disaient

	FUTURE		CONDITIONAL
je	dirai	je	dirais
tu	diras	tu	dirais
il	dira	il	dirait
nous	dirons	nous	dirions
vous	direz	vous	diriez
ils	diront	ils	diraient

	PRESENT SUBJUNCTIVE		PAST HISTORIC
je	dise	je	dis
tu	dises	tu	dis
il	dise	il	dit
nous	disions	nous	dîmes
vous	disiez	vous	dîtes
ils	disent	ils	dirent

PAST PARTICIPLE	IMPERATIVE
dit	dis
	disons
	dites

PRESENT PARTICIPLE	AUXILIARY
disant	avoir

Note that **interdire** (to forbid) is conjugated similarly, but the second person plural of the present tense is **vous interdisez**

Verbs

dormir (to sleep)

	PRESENT			IMPERFECT
je	**dors**		je	**dormais**
tu	**dors**		tu	**dormais**
il	**dort**		il	**dormait**
nous	**dormons**		nous	**dormions**
vous	**dormez**		vous	**dormiez**
ils	**dorment**		ils	**dormaient**

	FUTURE			CONDITIONAL
je	dormirai		je	dormirais
tu	dormiras		tu	dormirais
il	dormira		il	dormirait
nous	dormirons		nous	dormirions
vous	dormirez		vous	dormiriez
ils	dormiront		ils	dormiraient

	PRESENT SUBJUNCTIVE			PAST HISTORIC
je	**dorme**		je	dormis
tu	**dormes**		tu	dormis
il	**dorme**		il	dormit
nous	**dormions**		nous	dormîmes
vous	**dormiez**		vous	dormîtes
ils	**dorment**		ils	dormirent

PAST PARTICIPLE	IMPERATIVE
dormi	**dors**
	dormons
	dormez

PRESENT PARTICIPLE	AUXILIARY
dormant	**avoir**

Verbs

écrire (to write)

	PRESENT		IMPERFECT
	j'écris		j'**écrivais**
tu	écris	tu	**écrivais**
il	écrit	il	**écrivait**
nous	**écrivons**	nous	**écrivions**
vous	**écrivez**	vous	**écriviez**
ils	**écrivent**	ils	**écrivaient**

	FUTURE		CONDITIONAL
	j'écrirai		j'écrirais
tu	écriras	tu	écrirais
il	écrira	il	écrirait
nous	écrirons	nous	écririons
vous	écrirez	vous	écririez
ils	écriront	ils	écriraient

	PRESENT SUBJUNCTIVE		PAST HISTORIC
	j'**écrive**		j'**écrivis**
tu	**écrives**	tu	**écrivis**
il	**écrive**	il	**écrivit**
nous	**écrivions**	nous	**écrivîmes**
vous	**écriviez**	vous	**écrivîtes**
ils	**écrivent**	ils	**écrivirent**

PAST PARTICIPLE
écrit

IMPERATIVE
écris
écrivons
écrivez

PRESENT PARTICIPLE
écrivant

AUXILIARY
avoir

Verbs

envoyer (to send)

	PRESENT		IMPERFECT
	j'envoie		j'envoyais
tu	envoies	tu	envoyais
il	envoie	il	envoyait
nous	envoyons	nous	envoyions
vous	envoyez	vous	envoyiez
ils	envoient	ils	envoyaient

	FUTURE		CONDITIONAL
	j'enverrai		**j'enverrais**
tu	**enverras**	tu	**enverrais**
il	**enverra**	il	**enverrait**
nous	**enverrons**	nous	**enverrions**
vous	**enverrez**	vous	**enverriez**
ils	**enverront**	ils	**enverraient**

	PRESENT SUBJUNCTIVE		PAST HISTORIC
	j'envoie		j'envoyai
tu	envoies	tu	envoyas
il	envoie	il	envoya
nous	envoyions	nous	envoyâmes
vous	envoyiez	vous	envoyâtes
ils	envoient	ils	envoyèrent

PAST PARTICIPLE	IMPERATIVE
envoyé	envoie
	envoyons
	envoyez

PRESENT PARTICIPLE	AUXILIARY
envoyant	**avoir**

Verbs

être (to be)

	PRESENT			IMPERFECT
je	suis			j'étais
tu	es		tu	étais
il	est		il	était
nous	sommes		nous	étions
vous	êtes		vous	étiez
ils	sont		ils	étaient

	FUTURE			CONDITIONAL
je	serai		je	serais
tu	seras		tu	serais
il	sera		il	serait
nous	serons		nous	serions
vous	serez		vous	seriez
ils	seront		ils	seraient

	PRESENT SUBJUNCTIVE			PAST HISTORIC
je	sois		je	fus
tu	sois		tu	fus
il	soit		il	fut
nous	soyons		nous	fûmes
vous	soyez		vous	fûtes
ils	soient		ils	furent

PAST PARTICIPLE
été

IMPERATIVE
sois
soyons
soyez

PRESENT PARTICIPLE
étant

AUXILIARY
avoir

Verbs

faire (to do, to make)

	PRESENT		IMPERFECT
je	fais	je	faisais
tu	fais	tu	faisais
il	fait	il	faisait
nous	faisons	nous	faisions
vous	faites	vous	faisiez
ils	font	ils	faisaient

	FUTURE		CONDITIONAL
je	ferai	je	ferais
tu	feras	tu	ferais
il	fera	il	ferait
nous	ferons	nous	ferions
vous	ferez	vous	feriez
ils	feront	ils	feraient

	PRESENT SUBJUNCTIVE		PAST HISTORIC
je	fasse	je	fis
tu	fasses	tu	fis
il	fasse	il	fit
nous	fassions	nous	fîmes
vous	fassiez	vous	fîtes
ils	fassent	ils	firent

PAST PARTICIPLE
fait

IMPERATIVE
fais
faisons
faites

PRESENT PARTICIPLE
faisant

AUXILIARY
avoir

Verbs

falloir (to be necessary)

PRESENT
il **faut**

IMPERFECT
il **fallait**

FUTURE
il **faudra**

CONDITIONAL
il **faudrait**

PRESENT SUBJUNCTIVE
il **faille**

PAST HISTORIC
il **fallut**

PAST PARTICIPLE
fallu

IMPERATIVE
not used

PRESENT PARTICIPLE
not used

AUXILIARY
avoir

Verbs

fuir (to flee)

	PRESENT		IMPERFECT
je	fuis	je	**fuyais**
tu	fuis	tu	**fuyais**
il	fuit	il	**fuyait**
nous	**fuyons**	nous	**fuyions**
vous	**fuyez**	vous	**fuyiez**
ils	**fuient**	ils	**fuyaient**

	FUTURE		CONDITIONAL
je	fuirai	je	fuirais
tu	fuiras	tu	fuirais
il	fuira	il	fuirait
nous	fuirons	nous	fuirions
vous	fuirez	vous	fuiriez
ils	fuiront	ils	fuiraient

	PRESENT SUBJUNCTIVE		PAST HISTORIC
je	**fuie**	je	fuis
tu	**fuies**	tu	fuis
il	**fuie**	il	fuit
nous	**fuyions**	nous	fuîmes
vous	**fuyiez**	vous	fuîtes
ils	**fuient**	ils	fuirent

PAST PARTICIPLE	IMPERATIVE
fui	fuis
	fuyons
	fuyez

PRESENT PARTICIPLE	AUXILIARY
fuyant	**avoir**

Verbs

haïr (to hate)

	PRESENT		IMPERFECT
je	hais	je	haïssais
tu	hais	tu	haïssais
il	hait	il	haïssait
nous	haïssons	nous	haïssions
vous	haïssez	vous	haïssiez
ils	haïssent	ils	haïssaient

	FUTURE		CONDITIONAL
je	haïrai	je	haïrais
tu	haïras	tu	haïrais
il	haïra	il	haïrait
nous	haïrons	nous	haïrions
vous	haïrez	vous	haïriez
ils	haïront	ils	haïraient

	PRESENT SUBJUNCTIVE		PAST HISTORIC
je	haïsse	je	haïs
tu	haïsses	tu	haïs
il	haïsse	il	haït
nous	haïssions	nous	haïmes
vous	haïssiez	vous	haïtes
ils	haïssent	ils	haïrent

PAST PARTICIPLE
haï

IMPERATIVE
hais
haïssons
haïssez

PRESENT PARTICIPLE
haïssant

AUXILIARY
avoir

Verbs

lire (to read)

	PRESENT		IMPERFECT
je	lis	je	lisais
tu	lis	tu	lisais
il	lit	il	lisait
nous	lisons	nous	lisions
vous	lisez	vous	lisiez
ils	lisent	ils	lisaient

	FUTURE		CONDITIONAL
je	lirai	je	lirais
tu	liras	tu	lirais
il	lira	il	lirait
nous	lirons	nous	lirions
vous	lirez	vous	liriez
ils	liront	ils	liraient

	PRESENT SUBJUNCTIVE		PAST HISTORIC
je	lise	je	lus
tu	lises	tu	lus
il	lise	il	lut
nous	lisions	nous	lûmes
vous	lisiez	vous	lûtes
ils	lisent	ils	lurent

PAST PARTICIPLE	IMPERATIVE
lu	lis
	lisons
	lisez

PRESENT PARTICIPLE	AUXILIARY
lisant	avoir

Verbs

mettre (to put)

	PRESENT		IMPERFECT
je	**mets**	je	mettais
tu	**mets**	tu	mettais
il	**met**	il	mettait
nous	mettons	nous	mettions
vous	mettez	vous	mettiez
ils	mettent	ils	mettaient

	FUTURE		CONDITIONAL
je	mettrai	je	mettrais
tu	mettras	tu	mettrais
il	mettra	il	mettrait
nous	mettrons	nous	mettrions
vous	mettrez	vous	mettriez
ils	mettront	ils	mettraient

	PRESENT SUBJUNCTIVE		PAST HISTORIC
je	mette	je	**mis**
tu	mettes	tu	**mis**
il	mette	il	**mit**
nous	mettions	nous	**mîmes**
vous	mettiez	vous	**mîtes**
ils	mettent	ils	**mirent**

PAST PARTICIPLE
mis

IMPERATIVE
mets
mettons
mettez

PRESENT PARTICIPLE
mettant

AUXILIARY
avoir

Verbs

moudre (to grind)

	PRESENT		IMPERFECT
je	mouds	je	**moulais**
tu	mouds	tu	**moulais**
il	moud	il	**moulait**
nous	**moulons**	nous	**moulions**
vous	**moulez**	vous	**mouliez**
ils	**moulent**	ils	**moulaient**

	FUTURE		CONDITIONAL
je	moudrai	je	moudrais
tu	moudras	tu	moudrais
il	moudra	il	moudrait
nous	moudrons	nous	moudrions
vous	moudrez	vous	moudriez
ils	moudront	ils	moudraient

	PRESENT SUBJUNCTIVE		PAST HISTORIC
je	**moule**	je	**moulus**
tu	**moules**	tu	**moulus**
il	**moule**	il	**moulut**
nous	**moulions**	nous	**moulûmes**
vous	**mouliez**	vous	**moulûtes**
ils	**moulent**	ils	**moulurent**

PAST PARTICIPLE	IMPERATIVE
moulu	mouds
	moulons
	moulez

PRESENT PARTICIPLE	AUXILIARY
moulant	**avoir**

Verbs

mourir (to die)

	PRESENT			IMPERFECT
je	meurs		je	mourais
tu	meurs		tu	mourais
il	meurt		il	mourait
nous	mourons		nous	mourions
vous	mourez		vous	mouriez
ils	meurent		ils	mouraient

	FUTURE			CONDITIONAL
je	mourrai		je	mourrais
tu	mourras		tu	mourrais
il	mourra		il	mourrait
nous	mourrons		nous	mourrions
vous	mourrez		vous	mourriez
ils	mourront		ils	mourraient

	PRESENT SUBJUNCTIVE			PAST HISTORIC
je	meure		je	mourus
tu	meures		tu	mourus
il	meure		il	mourut
nous	mourions		nous	mourûmes
vous	mouriez		vous	mourûtes
ils	meurent		ils	moururent

PAST PARTICIPLE
mort

IMPERATIVE
meurs
mourons
mourez

PRESENT PARTICIPLE
mourant

AUXILIARY
être

Verbs

naître (to be born)

PRESENT

je	**nais**
tu	**nais**
il	naît
nous	**naissons**
vous	**naissez**
ils	**naissent**

IMPERFECT

je	**naissais**
tu	**naissais**
il	**naissait**
nous	**naissions**
vous	**naissiez**
ils	**naissaient**

FUTURE

je	naîtrai
tu	naîtras
il	naîtra
nous	naîtrons
vous	naîtrez
ils	naîtront

CONDITIONAL

je	naîtrais
tu	naîtrais
il	naîtrait
nous	naîtrions
vous	naîtriez
ils	naîtraient

PRESENT SUBJUNCTIVE

je	**naisse**
tu	**naisses**
il	**naisse**
nous	**naissions**
vous	**naissiez**
ils	**naissent**

PAST HISTORIC

je	naquis
tu	naquis
il	naquit
nous	naquîmes
vous	naquîtes
ils	naquirent

PAST PARTICIPLE
né

IMPERATIVE
nais
naissons
naissez

PRESENT PARTICIPLE
naissant

AUXILIARY
être

Verbs

ouvrir (to open)

	PRESENT			IMPERFECT
	j'**ouvre**			j'**ouvrais**
tu	**ouvres**		tu	**ouvrais**
il	**ouvre**		il	**ouvrait**
nous	**ouvrons**		nous	**ouvrions**
vous	**ouvrez**		vous	**ouvriez**
ils	**ouvrent**		ils	**ouvraient**

	FUTURE			CONDITIONAL
	j'ouvrirai			j'ouvrirais
tu	ouvriras		tu	ouvrirais
il	ouvrira		il	ouvrirait
nous	ouvrirons		nous	ouvririons
vous	ouvrirez		vous	ouvririez
ils	ouvriront		ils	ouvriraient

	PRESENT SUBJUNCTIVE			PAST HISTORIC
	j'**ouvre**			j'ouvris
tu	**ouvres**		tu	ouvris
il	**ouvre**		il	ouvrit
nous	**ouvrions**		nous	ouvrîmes
vous	**ouvriez**		vous	ouvrîtes
ils	**ouvrent**		ils	ouvrirent

PAST PARTICIPLE	IMPERATIVE
ouvert	**ouvre**
	ouvrons
	ouvrez

PRESENT PARTICIPLE	AUXILIARY
ouvrant	**avoir**

Note that **offrir** (to offer) and **souffrir** (to suffer) are conjugated similarly

paraître (to appear)

	PRESENT		IMPERFECT
je	parais	je	paraissais
tu	parais	tu	paraissais
il	paraît	il	paraissait
nous	paraissons	nous	paraissions
vous	paraissez	vous	paraissiez
ils	paraissent	ils	paraissaient

	FUTURE		CONDITIONAL
je	paraîtrai	je	paraîtrais
tu	paraîtras	tu	paraîtrais
il	paraîtra	il	paraîtrait
nous	paraîtrons	nous	paraîtrions
vous	paraîtrez	vous	paraîtriez
ils	paraîtront	ils	paraîtraient

	PRESENT SUBJUNCTIVE		PAST HISTORIC
je	paraisse	je	parus
tu	paraisses	tu	parus
il	paraisse	il	parut
nous	paraissions	nous	parûmes
vous	paraissiez	vous	parûtes
ils	paraissent	ils	parurent

PAST PARTICIPLE	IMPERATIVE
paru	parais
	paraissons
	paraissez

PRESENT PARTICIPLE	AUXILIARY
paraissant	avoir

Verbs

partir (to leave)

	PRESENT		IMPERFECT
je	**pars**	je	**partais**
tu	**pars**	tu	**partais**
il	**part**	il	**partait**
nous	**partons**	nous	**partions**
vous	**partez**	vous	**partiez**
ils	**partent**	ils	**partaient**

	FUTURE		CONDITIONAL
je	partirai	je	partirais
tu	partiras	tu	partirais
il	partira	il	partirait
nous	partirons	nous	partirions
vous	partirez	vous	partiriez
ils	partiront	ils	partiraient

	PRESENT SUBJUNCTIVE		PAST HISTORIC
je	**parte**	je	partis
tu	**partes**	tu	partis
il	**parte**	il	partit
nous	**partions**	nous	partîmes
vous	**partiez**	vous	partîtes
ils	**partent**	ils	partirent

PAST PARTICIPLE	IMPERATIVE
parti	**pars**
	partons
	partez

PRESENT PARTICIPLE	AUXILIARY
partant	**être**

Verbs

plaire (to please)

	PRESENT		IMPERFECT
je	plais	je	**plaisais**
tu	plais	tu	**plaisais**
il	**plaît**	il	**plaisait**
nous	**plaisons**	nous	**plaisions**
vous	**plaisez**	vous	**plaisiez**
ils	**plaisent**	ils	**plaisaient**

	FUTURE		CONDITIONAL
je	plairai	je	plairais
tu	plairas	tu	plairais
il	plaira	il	plairait
nous	plairons	nous	plairions
vous	plairez	vous	plairiez
ils	plairont	ils	plairaient

	PRESENT SUBJUNCTIVE		PAST HISTORIC
je	**plaise**	je	**plus**
tu	**plaises**	tu	**plus**
il	**plaise**	il	**plut**
nous	**plaisions**	nous	**plûmes**
vous	**plaisiez**	vous	**plûtes**
ils	**plaisent**	ils	**plurent**

PAST PARTICIPLE
plu

IMPERATIVE
plais
plaisons
plaisez

PRESENT PARTICIPLE
plaisant

AUXILIARY
avoir

Verbs

pleuvoir (to rain)

PRESENT			**IMPERFECT**	
il	**pleut**		il	**pleuvait**

FUTURE			**CONDITIONAL**	
il	**pleuvra**		il	**pleuvrait**

PRESENT SUBJUNCTIVE			**PAST HISTORIC**	
il	**pleuve**		il	**plut**

PAST PARTICIPLE	**IMPERATIVE**
plu	*not used*

PRESENT PARTICIPLE	**AUXILIARY**
pleuvant	**avoir**

Verbs

pouvoir (to be able to)

	PRESENT		IMPERFECT
je	peux*	je	pouvais
tu	peux	tu	pouvais
il	peut	il	pouvait
nous	pouvons	nous	pouvions
vous	pouvez	vous	pouviez
ils	peuvent	ils	pouvaient

	FUTURE		CONDITIONAL
je	pourrai	je	pourrais
tu	pourras	tu	pourrais
il	pourra	il	pourrait
nous	pourrons	nous	pourrions
vous	pourrez	vous	pourriez
ils	pourront	ils	pourraient

	PRESENT SUBJUNCTIVE		PAST HISTORIC
je	puisse	je	pus
tu	puisses	tu	pus
il	puisse	il	put
nous	puissions	nous	pûmes
vous	puissiez	vous	pûtes
ils	puissent	ils	purent

PAST PARTICIPLE	IMPERATIVE
pu	*not used*

PRESENT PARTICIPLE	AUXILIARY
pouvant	avoir

* In questions **puis-je?** is used

Verbs

prendre (to take)

	PRESENT			IMPERFECT
je	prends		je	**prenais**
tu	prends		tu	**prenais**
il	prend		il	**prenait**
nous	**prenons**		nous	**prenions**
vous	**prenez**		vous	**preniez**
ils	**prennent**		ils	**prenaient**

	FUTURE			CONDITIONAL
je	prendrai		je	prendrais
tu	prendras		tu	prendrais
il	prendra		il	prendrait
nous	prendrons		nous	prendrions
vous	prendrez		vous	prendriez
ils	prendront		ils	prendraient

	PRESENT SUBJUNCTIVE			PAST HISTORIC
je	**prenne**		je	**pris**
tu	**prennes**		tu	**pris**
il	**prenne**		il	**prit**
nous	**prenions**		nous	**prîmes**
vous	**preniez**		vous	**prîtes**
ils	**prennent**		ils	**prirent**

PAST PARTICIPLE
pris

IMPERATIVE
prends
prenons
prenez

PRESENT PARTICIPLE
prenant

AUXILIARY
avoir

Verbs

recevoir (to receive)

	PRESENT		IMPERFECT
je	reçois	je	recevais
tu	reçois	tu	recevais
il	reçoit	il	recevait
nous	recevons	nous	recevions
vous	recevez	vous	receviez
ils	reçoivent	ils	recevaient

	FUTURE		CONDITIONAL
je	recevrai	je	recevrais
tu	recevras	tu	recevrais
il	recevra	il	recevrait
nous	recevrons	nous	recevrions
vous	recevrez	vous	recevriez
ils	recevront	ils	recevraient

	PRESENT SUBJUNCTIVE		PAST HISTORIC
je	reçoive	je	reçus
tu	reçoives	tu	reçus
il	reçoive	il	reçut
nous	recevions	nous	reçûmes
vous	receviez	vous	reçûtes
ils	reçoivent	ils	reçurent

PAST PARTICIPLE	IMPERATIVE
reçu	reçois
	recevons
	recevez

PRESENT PARTICIPLE	AUXILIARY
recevant	avoir

113

résoudre (to solve)

	PRESENT		IMPERFECT
je	résous	je	résolvais
tu	résous	tu	résolvais
il	résout	il	résolvait
nous	résolvons	nous	résolvions
vous	résolvez	vous	résolviez
ils	résolvent	ils	résolvaient

	FUTURE		CONDITIONAL
je	résoudrai	je	résoudrais
tu	résoudras	tu	résoudrais
il	résoudra	il	résoudrait
nous	résoudrons	nous	résoudrions
vous	résoudrez	vous	résoudriez
ils	résoudront	ils	résoudraient

	PRESENT SUBJUNCTIVE		PAST HISTORIC
je	résolve	je	résolus
tu	résolves	tu	résolus
il	résolve	il	résolut
nous	résolvions	nous	résolûmes
vous	résolviez	vous	résolûtes
ils	résolvent	ils	résolurent

PAST PARTICIPLE
résolu

IMPERATIVE
résous
résolvons
résolvez

PRESENT PARTICIPLE
résolvant

AUXILIARY
avoir

Verbs

rire (to laugh)

	PRESENT		IMPERFECT
je	ris	je	riais
tu	ris	tu	riais
il	**rit**	il	riait
nous	rions	nous	riions
vous	riez	vous	riiez
ils	rient	ils	riaient

	FUTURE		CONDITIONAL
je	rirai	je	rirais
tu	riras	tu	rirais
il	rira	il	rirait
nous	rirons	nous	ririons
vous	rirez	vous	ririez
ils	riront	ils	riraient

	PRESENT SUBJUNCTIVE		PAST HISTORIC
je	rie	je	**ris**
tu	ries	tu	**ris**
il	rie	il	**rit**
nous	riions	nous	**rîmes**
vous	riiez	vous	**rîtes**
ils	rient	ils	**rirent**

PAST PARTICIPLE
ri

IMPERATIVE
ris
rions
riez

PRESENT PARTICIPLE
riant

AUXILIARY
avoir

Verbs

rompre (to break)

	PRESENT		IMPERFECT
je	romps	je	rompais
tu	romps	tu	rompais
il	**rompt**	il	rompait
nous	rompons	nous	rompions
vous	rompez	vous	rompiez
ils	rompent	ils	rompaient

	FUTURE		CONDITIONAL
je	romprai	je	romprais
tu	rompras	tu	romprais
il	rompra	il	romprait
nous	romprons	nous	romprions
vous	romprez	vous	rompriez
ils	rompront	ils	rompraient

	PRESENT SUBJUNCTIVE		PAST HISTORIC
je	rompe	je	rompis
tu	rompes	tu	rompis
il	rompe	il	rompit
nous	rompions	nous	rompîmes
vous	rompiez	vous	rompîtes
ils	rompent	ils	rompirent

PAST PARTICIPLE
rompu

IMPERATIVE
romps
rompons
rompez

PRESENT PARTICIPLE
rompant

AUXILIARY
avoir

savoir (to know)

PRESENT

je	sais
tu	sais
il	sait
nous	savons
vous	savez
ils	savent

IMPERFECT

je	savais
tu	savais
il	savait
nous	savions
vous	saviez
ils	savaient

FUTURE

je	saurai
tu	sauras
il	saura
nous	saurons
vous	saurez
ils	sauront

CONDITIONAL

je	saurais
tu	saurais
il	saurait
nous	saurions
vous	sauriez
ils	sauraient

PRESENT SUBJUNCTIVE

je	sache
tu	saches
il	sache
nous	sachions
vous	sachiez
ils	sachent

PAST HISTORIC

je	sus
tu	sus
il	sut
nous	sûmes
vous	sûtes
ils	surent

PAST PARTICIPLE

su

IMPERATIVE

sache
sachons
sachez

PRESENT PARTICIPLE

sachant

AUXILIARY

avoir

Verbs

sentir (to feel, to smell)

	PRESENT			IMPERFECT
je	**sens**		je	**sentais**
tu	**sens**		tu	**sentais**
il	**sent**		il	**sentait**
nous	**sentons**		nous	**sentions**
vous	**sentez**		vous	**sentiez**
ils	**sentent**		ils	**sentaient**

	FUTURE			CONDITIONAL
je	sentirai		je	sentirais
tu	sentiras		tu	sentirais
il	sentira		il	sentirait
nous	sentirons		nous	sentirions
vous	sentirez		vous	sentiriez
ils	sentiront		ils	sentiraient

	PRESENT SUBJUNCTIVE			PAST HISTORIC
je	**sente**		je	sentis
tu	**sentes**		tu	sentis
il	**sente**		il	sentit
nous	**sentions**		nous	sentîmes
vous	**sentiez**		vous	sentîtes
ils	**sentent**		ils	sentirent

PAST PARTICIPLE
senti

IMPERATIVE
sens
sentons
sentez

PRESENT PARTICIPLE
sentant

AUXILIARY
avoir

Verbs

servir (to serve)

	PRESENT			IMPERFECT
je	sers		je	servais
tu	sers		tu	servais
il	sert		il	servait
nous	servons		nous	servions
vous	servez		vous	serviez
ils	servent		ils	servaient

	FUTURE			CONDITIONAL
je	servirai		je	servirais
tu	serviras		tu	servirais
il	servira		il	servirait
nous	servirons		nous	servirions
vous	servirez		vous	serviriez
ils	serviront		ils	serviraient

	PRESENT SUBJUNCTIVE			PAST HISTORIC
je	serve		je	servis
tu	serves		tu	servis
il	serve		il	servit
nous	servions		nous	servîmes
vous	serviez		vous	servîtes
ils	servent		ils	servirent

PAST PARTICIPLE
servi

IMPERATIVE
sers
servons
servez

PRESENT PARTICIPLE
servant

AUXILIARY
avoir

Verbs

sortir (to go, to come out)

	PRESENT		IMPERFECT
je	**sors**	je	**sortais**
tu	**sors**	tu	**sortais**
il	**sort**	il	**sortait**
nous	**sortons**	nous	**sortions**
vous	**sortez**	vous	**sortiez**
ils	**sortent**	ils	**sortaient**

	FUTURE		CONDITIONAL
je	sortirai	je	sortirais
tu	sortiras	tu	sortirais
il	sortira	il	sortirait
nous	sortirons	nous	sortirions
vous	sortirez	vous	sortiriez
ils	sortiront	ils	sortiraient

	PRESENT SUBJUNCTIVE		PAST HISTORIC
je	**sorte**	je	sortis
tu	**sortes**	tu	sortis
il	**sorte**	il	sortit
nous	**sortions**	nous	sortîmes
vous	**sortiez**	vous	sortîtes
ils	**sortent**	ils	sortirent

PAST PARTICIPLE	IMPERATIVE
sorti	**sors**
	sortons
	sortez

PRESENT PARTICIPLE	AUXILIARY
sortant	**être**

suffire (to be enough)

	PRESENT			IMPERFECT
je	suffis		je	**suffisais**
tu	suffis		tu	**suffisais**
il	suffit		il	**suffisait**
nous	**suffisons**		nous	**suffisions**
vous	**suffisez**		vous	**suffisiez**
ils	**suffisent**		ils	**suffisaient**

	FUTURE			CONDITIONAL
je	suffirai		je	suffirais
tu	suffiras		tu	suffirais
il	suffira		il	suffirait
nous	suffirons		nous	suffirions
vous	suffirez		vous	suffiriez
ils	suffiront		ils	suffiraient

	PRESENT SUBJUNCTIVE			PAST HISTORIC
je	**suffise**		je	**suffis**
tu	**suffises**		tu	**suffis**
il	**suffise**		il	**suffit**
nous	**suffisions**		nous	**suffîmes**
vous	**suffisiez**		vous	**suffîtes**
ils	**suffisent**		ils	**suffirent**

PAST PARTICIPLE
suffi

IMPERATIVE
suffis
suffisons
suffisez

PRESENT PARTICIPLE
suffisant

AUXILIARY
avoir

Verbs

suivre (to follow)

	PRESENT		IMPERFECT
je	**suis**	je	suivais
tu	**suis**	tu	suivais
il	**suit**	il	suivait
nous	suivons	nous	suivions
vous	suivez	vous	suiviez
ils	suivent	ils	suivaient

	FUTURE		CONDITIONAL
je	suivrai	je	suivrais
tu	suivras	tu	suivrais
il	suivra	il	suivrait
nous	suivrons	nous	suivrions
vous	suivrez	vous	suivriez
ils	suivront	ils	suivraient

	PRESENT SUBJUNCTIVE		PAST HISTORIC
je	suive	je	suivis
tu	suives	tu	suivis
il	suive	il	suivit
nous	suivions	nous	suivîmes
vous	suiviez	vous	suivîtes
ils	suivent	ils	suivirent

PAST PARTICIPLE
suivi

IMPERATIVE
suis
suivons
suivez

PRESENT PARTICIPLE
suivant

AUXILIARY
avoir

Verbs

se taire (to stop talking)

	PRESENT			IMPERFECT
je	me tais		je	me taisais
tu	te tais		tu	te taisais
il	se tait		il	se taisait
nous	nous taisons		nous	nous taisions
vous	vous taisez		vous	vous taisiez
ils	se taisent		ils	se taisaient

	FUTURE			CONDITIONAL
je	me tairai		je	me tairais
tu	te tairas		tu	te tairais
il	se taira		il	se tairait
nous	nous tairons		nous	nous tairions
vous	vous tairez		vous	vous tairiez
ils	se tairont		ils	se tairaient

	PRESENT SUBJUNCTIVE			PAST HISTORIC
je	me taise		je	me tus
tu	te taises		tu	te tus
il	se taise		il	se tut
nous	nous taisions		nous	nous tûmes
vous	vous taisiez		vous	vous tûtes
ils	se taisent		ils	se turent

PAST PARTICIPLE
tu

IMPERATIVE
tais-toi
taisons-nous
taisez-vous

PRESENT PARTICIPLE
se taisant

AUXILIARY
être

tenir (to hold)

	PRESENT		IMPERFECT
je	tiens	je	tenais
tu	tiens	tu	tenais
il	tient	il	tenait
nous	tenons	nous	tenions
vous	tenez	vous	teniez
ils	tiennent	ils	tenaient

	FUTURE		CONDITIONAL
je	tiendrai	je	tiendrais
tu	tiendras	tu	tiendrais
il	tiendra	il	tiendrait
nous	tiendrons	nous	tiendrions
vous	tiendrez	vous	tiendriez
ils	tiendront	ils	tiendraient

	PRESENT SUBJUNCTIVE		PAST HISTORIC
je	tienne	je	tins
tu	tiennes	tu	tins
il	tienne	il	tint
nous	tenions	nous	tînmes
vous	teniez	vous	tîntes
ils	tiennent	ils	tinrent

PAST PARTICIPLE	IMPERATIVE
tenu	tiens
	tenons
	tenez

PRESENT PARTICIPLE	AUXILIARY
tenant	avoir

vaincre (to defeat)

	PRESENT		IMPERFECT
je	vaincs	je	vainquais
tu	vaincs	tu	vainquais
il	vainc	il	vainquait
nous	vainquons	nous	vainquions
vous	vainquez	vous	vainquiez
ils	vainquent	ils	vainquaient

	FUTURE		CONDITIONAL
je	vaincrai	je	vaincrais
tu	vaincras	tu	vaincrais
il	vaincra	il	vaincrait
nous	vaincrons	nous	vaincrions
vous	vaincrez	vous	vaincriez
ils	vaincront	ils	vaincraient

	PRESENT SUBJUNCTIVE		PAST HISTORIC
je	vainque	je	vainquis
tu	vainques	tu	vainquis
il	vainque	il	vainquit
nous	vainquions	nous	vainquîmes
vous	vainquiez	vous	vainquîtes
ils	vainquent	ils	vainquirent

PAST PARTICIPLE
vaincu

IMPERATIVE
vaincs
vainquons
vainquez

PRESENT PARTICIPLE
vainquant

AUXILIARY
avoir

Verbs

valoir (to be worth)

	PRESENT		IMPERFECT
je	**vaux**	je	**valais**
tu	**vaux**	tu	**valais**
il	**vaut**	il	**valait**
nous	**valons**	nous	**valions**
vous	**valez**	vous	**valiez**
ils	**valent**	ils	**valaient**

	FUTURE		CONDITIONAL
je	**vaudrai**	je	**vaudrais**
tu	**vaudras**	tu	**vaudrais**
il	**vaudra**	il	**vaudrait**
nous	**vaudrons**	nous	**vaudrions**
vous	**vaudrez**	vous	**vaudriez**
ils	**vaudront**	ils	**vaudraient**

	PRESENT SUBJUNCTIVE		PAST HISTORIC
je	**vaille**	je	**valus**
tu	**vailles**	tu	**valus**
il	**vaille**	il	**valut**
nous	**valions**	nous	**valûmes**
vous	**valiez**	vous	**valûtes**
ils	**vaillent**	ils	**valurent**

PAST PARTICIPLE
valu

IMPERATIVE
vaux
valons
valez

PRESENT PARTICIPLE
valant

AUXILIARY
avoir

venir (to come)

	PRESENT		IMPERFECT
je	viens	je	venais
tu	viens	tu	venais
il	vient	il	venait
nous	venons	nous	venions
vous	venez	vous	veniez
ils	viennent	ils	venaient

	FUTURE		CONDITIONAL
je	viendrai	je	viendrais
tu	viendras	tu	viendrais
il	viendra	il	viendrait
nous	viendrons	nous	viendrions
vous	viendrez	vous	viendriez
ils	viendront	ils	viendraient

	PRESENT SUBJUNCTIVE		PAST HISTORIC
je	vienne	je	vins
tu	viennes	tu	vins
il	vienne	il	vint
nous	venions	nous	vînmes
vous	veniez	vous	vîntes
ils	viennent	ils	vinrent

PAST PARTICIPLE	IMPERATIVE
venu	viens
	venons
	venez

PRESENT PARTICIPLE	AUXILIARY
venant	être

Verbs

vêtir (to dress)

	PRESENT		IMPERFECT
je	**vêts**	je	**vêtais**
tu	**vêts**	tu	**vêtais**
il	**vêt**	il	**vêtait**
nous	**vêtons**	nous	**vêtions**
vous	**vêtez**	vous	**vêtiez**
ils	**vêtent**	ils	**vêtaient**

	FUTURE		CONDITIONAL
je	vêtirai	je	vêtirais
tu	vêtiras	tu	vêtirais
il	vêtira	il	vêtirait
nous	vêtirons	nous	vêtirions
vous	vêtirez	vous	vêtiriez
ils	vêtiront	ils	vêtiraient

	PRESENT SUBJUNCTIVE		PAST HISTORIC
je	**vête**	je	vêtis
tu	**vêtes**	tu	vêtis
il	**vête**	il	vêtit
nous	**vêtions**	nous	vêtîmes
vous	**vêtiez**	vous	vêtîtes
ils	**vêtent**	ils	vêtirent

PAST PARTICIPLE
vêtu

IMPERATIVE
vêts
vêtons
vêtez

PRESENT PARTICIPLE
vêtant

AUXILIARY
avoir

Verbs

vivre (to live)

	PRESENT		IMPERFECT
je	**vis**	je	vivais
tu	**vis**	tu	vivais
il	**vit**	il	vivait
nous	vivons	nous	vivions
vous	vivez	vous	viviez
ils	vivent	ils	vivaient

	FUTURE		CONDITIONAL
je	vivrai	je	vivrais
tu	vivras	tu	vivrais
il	vivra	il	vivrait
nous	vivrons	nous	vivrions
vous	vivrez	vous	vivriez
ils	vivront	ils	vivraient

	PRESENT SUBJUNCTIVE		PAST HISTORIC
je	vive	je	**vécus**
tu	vives	tu	**vécus**
il	vive	il	**vécut**
nous	vivions	nous	**vécûmes**
vous	viviez	vous	**vécûtes**
ils	vivent	ils	**vécurent**

PAST PARTICIPLE	IMPERATIVE
vécu	**vis**
	vivons
	vivez

PRESENT PARTICIPLE	AUXILIARY
vivant	**avoir**

Verbs

voir (to see)

	PRESENT			IMPERFECT
je	**vois**		je	**voyais**
tu	**vois**		tu	**voyais**
il	**voit**		il	**voyait**
nous	**voyons**		nous	**voyions**
vous	**voyez**		vous	**voyiez**
ils	**voient**		ils	**voyaient**

	FUTURE			CONDITIONAL
je	**verrai**		je	**verrais**
tu	**verras**		tu	**verrais**
il	**verra**		il	**verrait**
nous	**verrons**		nous	**verrions**
vous	**verrez**		vous	**verriez**
ils	**verront**		ils	**verraient**

	PRESENT SUBJUNCTIVE			PAST HISTORIC
je	**voie**		je	**vis**
tu	**voies**		tu	**vis**
il	**voie**		il	**vit**
nous	**voyions**		nous	**vîmes**
vous	**voyiez**		vous	**vîtes**
ils	**voient**		ils	**virent**

PAST PARTICIPLE
vu

IMPERATIVE
vois
voyons
voyez

PRESENT PARTICIPLE
voyant

AUXILIARY
avoir

Verbs

vouloir (to wish, to want)

	PRESENT			IMPERFECT
je	veux		je	voulais
tu	veux		tu	voulais
il	veut		il	voulait
nous	voulons		nous	voulions
vous	voulez		vous	vouliez
ils	veulent		ils	voulaient

	FUTURE			CONDITIONAL
je	voudrai		je	voudrais
tu	voudras		tu	voudrais
il	voudra		il	voudrait
nous	voudrons		nous	voudrions
vous	voudrez		vous	voudriez
ils	voudront		ils	voudraient

	PRESENT SUBJUNCTIVE			PAST HISTORIC
je	veuille		je	voulus
tu	veuilles		tu	voulus
il	veuille		il	voulut
nous	voulions		nous	voulûmes
vous	vouliez		vous	voulûtes
ils	veuillent		ils	voulurent

PAST PARTICIPLE
voulu

IMPERATIVE
veuille
veuillons
veuillez

PRESENT PARTICIPLE
voulant

AUXILIARY
avoir

Nouns

The Gender of Nouns

In French, all nouns are either masculine or feminine, whether denoting people, animals or things. Unlike English, there is no neuter gender for inanimate objects and abstract nouns.

Gender is largely unpredictable and has to be learnt for each noun. However, the following guidelines will help you determine the gender for certain types of nouns:

Nouns denoting male people and animals are usually – but not always – masculine, e.g.

un homme a man
un taureau a bull
un infirmier a (*male*) nurse
un cheval a horse

Nouns denoting female people and animals are usually – but not always – feminine, e.g.

une fille a girl
une vache a cow
une infirmière a nurse
une brebis a ewe

Some nouns are masculine *or* feminine depending on the sex of the person to whom they refer, e.g.

un camarade a (*male*) friend
une camarade a (*female*) friend
un Belge a Belgian (*man*)
une Belge a Belgian (*woman*)

Other nouns referring to either men or women have only one gender which applies to both, e.g.

une personne a person
une sentinelle a sentry
un témoin a witness
une victime a victim
une recrue a recruit

Nouns

Sometimes the ending of the noun indicates its gender. Shown below are some of the most important to guide you:

Masculine endings

-age	**le courage** courage; **le rinçage** rinsing EXCEPTIONS: **une cage** a cage; **une image** a picture; **la nage** swimming; **une page** a page; **une plage** a beach; **une rage** a rage
-ment	**le commencement** the beginning EXCEPTION: **une jument** a mare
-oir	**un couloir** a corridor; **un miroir** a mirror
-sme	**le pessimisme** pessimism; **l'enthousiasme** enthusiasm

Feminine endings

-ance, -anse	**la confiance** confidence; **la danse** dancing
-ence, -ense	**la prudence** caution; **la défense** defence EXCEPTION: **le silence** silence
-ion	**une région** a region; **une addition** a bill EXCEPTIONS: **un pion** a pawn; **un espion** a spy
-oire	**une baignoire** a bath(tub)
-té, -tié	**la beauté** beauty; **la moitié** half

Suffixes which differentiate between male and female are shown on pages 134 and 136.

The following words have different meanings depending on gender:

le crêpe crêpe	**la crêpe** pancake
le livre book	**la livre** pound
le manche handle	**la manche** sleeve
le mode method	**la mode** fashion
le moule mould	**la moule** mussel
le page page(boy)	**la page** page (*in book*)
le physique physique	**la physique** physics
le poêle stove	**la poêle** frying pan
le somme nap	**la somme** sum
le tour turn	**la tour** tower
le voile veil	**la voile** sail

Nouns

Formation of Feminines

As in English, male and female are sometimes differentiated by the use of two quite separate words, e.g.

> **mon oncle** my uncle
> **ma tante** my aunt
> **un taureau** a bull
> **une vache** a cow

There are, however, some words in French which show this distinction by the form of their ending:

> Some nouns add an **e** to the masculine singular form to form the feminine → ❶

> If the masculine singular form already ends in **-e**, no further **e** is added in the feminine → ❷

> Some nouns undergo a further change when **e** is added. These changes occur regularly and are shown on page 136.

Feminine forms to note

MASCULINE	FEMININE	
un âne	**une ânesse**	donkey
le comte	**la comtesse**	count/countess
le duc	**la duchesse**	duke/duchess
un Esquimau	**une Esquimaude**	Eskimo
le fou	**la folle**	madman/madwoman
le Grec	**la Grecque**	Greek
un hôte	**une hôtesse**	host/hostess
le jumeau	**la jumelle**	twin
le maître	**la maîtresse**	master/mistress
le prince	**la princesse**	prince/princess
le tigre	**la tigresse**	tiger/tigress
le traître	**la traîtresse**	traitor
le Turc	**la Turque**	Turk
le vieux	**la vieille**	old man/old woman

Examples

① un ami   a (*male*) friend
    une amie   a (*female*) friend
    un employé   a (*male*) employee
    une employée   a (*female*) employee
    un Français   a Frenchman
    une Française   a Frenchwoman

② un élève   a (*male*) pupil
    une élève   a (*female*) pupil
    un collègue   a (*male*) colleague
    une collègue   a (*female*) colleague
    un camarade   a (*male*) friend
    une camarade   a (*female*) friend

Nouns

Regular Feminine Endings

The following are regular feminine endings:

MASC. SING.	FEM. SING.
-f	-ve → ❶
-x	-se → ❷
-eur	-euse → ❸
-teur	-teuse → ❹
	-trice → ❺

Some nouns double the final consonant before adding **e**:

MASC. SING.	FEM. SING.
-an	-anne → ❻
-en	-enne → ❼
-on	-onne → ❽
-et	-ette → ❾
-el	-elle → ❿

Some nouns add an accent to the final syllable before adding **e**:

MASC. SING.	FEM. SING.
-er	-ère → ⓫

Pronunciation and feminine endings

This is dealt with on page 244.

Examples

① **un sportif** a sportsman
   un veuf a widower

   une sportive a sportswoman
   une veuve a widow

② **un époux** a husband
   un amoureux a man in love

   une épouse a wife
   une amoureuse a woman in love

③ **un danseur** a dancer
   un voleur a thief

   une danseuse a dancer
   une voleuse a thief

④ **un menteur** a liar
   un chanteur a singer

   une menteuse a liar
   une chanteuse a singer

⑤ **un acteur** an actor
   un conducteur a driver

   une actrice an actress
   une conductrice a driver

⑥ **un paysan** a countryman

   une paysanne a countrywoman

⑦ **un Parisien** a Parisian (*man*)

   une Parisienne a Parisian (*woman*)

⑧ **un baron** a baron

   une baronne a baroness

⑨ **le cadet** the youngest (child)

   la cadette the youngest (child)

⑩ **un intellectuel** an intellectual

   une intellectuelle an intellectual

⑪ **un étranger** a foreigner
   le dernier the last (one)

   une étrangère a foreigner
   la dernière the last (one)

Nouns

Formation of Plurals

Most nouns add **s** to the singular form → **①**

When the singular form already ends in **-s**, **-x** or **-z**, no further **s** is added → **②**

For nouns ending in **-au**, **-eau** or **-eu**, the plural ends in **-aux**, **-eaux** or **-eux** → **③**

EXCEPTIONS: **pneu** tyre   (*plural:* **pneus**)
            bleu bruise   (*plural:* **bleus**)

For nouns ending in **-al** or **-ail**, the plural ends in **-aux** → **④**

EXCEPTIONS: **bal** ball   (*plural:* **bals**)
            festival festival   (*plural:* **festivals**)
            chandail sweater   (*plural:* **chandails**)
            détail detail   (*plural:* **détails**)

Forming the plural of compound nouns is complicated and you are advised to check each one individually in a dictionary.

Irregular plural forms

Some masculine nouns ending in **-ou** add **x** in the plural. These are:

bijou jewel	**genou** knee	**joujou** toy
caillou pebble	**hibou** owl	**pou** louse
chou cabbage		

Some other nouns are totally unpredictable. The most important of these are:

SINGULAR		PLURAL
œil	eye	**yeux**
ciel	sky	**cieux**
Monsieur	Mr	**Messieurs**
Madame	Mrs	**Mesdames**
Mademoiselle	Miss	**Mesdemoiselles**

Pronunciation of plural forms

This is dealt with on page 244.

Examples

1 le jardin — the garden
les jardins — the gardens
une voiture — a car
des voitures — (some) cars
l'hôtel — the hotel
les hôtels — the hotels

2 un bois — a wood
des bois — (some) woods
une voix — a voice
des voix — (some) voices
le gaz — the gas
les gaz — the gases

3 un tuyau — a pipe
des tuyaux — (some) pipes
le chapeau — the hat
les chapeaux — the hats
le feu — the fire
les feux — the fires

4 le journal — the newspaper
les journaux — the newspapers
un travail — a job
des travaux — (some) jobs

Articles

The Definite Article

le (l')/la (l'), les

	WITH MASC. NOUN	WITH FEM. NOUN	
SING.	le (l')	la (l')	the
PLUR.	les	les	the

The gender and number of the noun determines the form of the article → **1**

le and **la** change to **l'** before a vowel or an **h** 'mute' → **2**

For uses of the definite article, see page 142.

à + le/la (l'), à + les

	WITH MASC. NOUN	WITH FEM. NOUN
SING.	au (à l')	à la (à l')
PLUR.	aux	aux

The definite article combines with the preposition **à**, as shown above. You should pay particular attention to the masculine singular form **au**, and both plural forms **aux**, since these are not visually the sum of their parts → **3**

de + le/la (l'), de + les

	WITH MASC. NOUN	WITH FEM. NOUN
SING.	du (de l')	de la (de l')
PLUR.	des	des

The definite article combines with the preposition **de**, as shown above. You should pay particular attention to the masculine singular form **du**, and both plural forms **des**, since these are not visually the sum of their parts → **4**

Examples

MASCULINE FEMININE

1 **le train** the train
le garçon the boy
les hôtels the hotels
les professeurs the teachers

la gare the station
la fille the girl
les écoles the schools
les femmes the women

2 **l'acteur** the actor
l'effet the effect
l'ingrédient the ingredient
l'objet the object
l'univers the universe
l'hôpital the hospital

l'actrice the actress
l'eau the water
l'idée the idea
l'ombre the shadow
l'usine the factory
l'heure the time

3 **au cinéma** at/to the cinema

à l'employé to the employee
à l'hôpital at/to the hospital
aux étudiants to the students

à la bibliothèque
at/to the library
à l'infirmière to the nurse
à l'hôtesse to the hostess
aux maisons to the houses

4 **du bureau** from/of the office

de l'auteur from/of the author

de l'hôte from/of the host
des États-Unis
from/of the United States

de la réunion
from/of the meeting
de l'Italienne
from/of the Italian woman
de l'horloge of the clock
des vendeuses
from/of the saleswomen

Articles

Uses of the Definite Article

While the definite article is used in much the same way in French as it is in English, its use is more widespread in French. Unlike English the definite article is also used:

> with abstract nouns, except when following certain prepositions → ❶
>
> in generalizations, especially with plural or uncountable* nouns → ❷
>
> with names of countries → ❸
> EXCEPTIONS: no article with countries following **en** to/in → ❹
>
> with parts of the body → ❺
> 'Ownership' is often indicated by an indirect object pronoun or a reflexive pronoun → ❻
>
> in expressions of quantity/rate/price → ❼
>
> with titles/ranks/professions followed by a proper name → ❽
>
> The definite article is *not* used with nouns in apposition → ❾

* An uncountable noun is one which cannot be used in the plural or with an indefinite article, e.g. **l'acier** steel; **le lait** milk.

Examples

1 **Les prix montent**
Prices are rising

L'amour rayonne dans ses yeux
Love shines in his eyes

BUT:

avec plaisir
with pleasure

sans espoir
without hope

2 **Je n'aime pas le café**
I don't like coffee

Les enfants ont besoin d'être aimés
Children need to be loved

3 **le Japon**
Japan

la France
France

l'Italie
Italy

les Pays-Bas
the Netherlands

4 **aller en Écosse**
to go to Scotland

Il travaille en Allemagne
He works in Germany

5 **Tournez la tête à gauche**
Turn your head to the left

J'ai mal à la gorge
My throat is sore, I have a sore throat

6 **La tête me tourne**
My head is spinning

Elle s'est brossé les dents
She brushed her teeth

7 **4 euros le mètre/le kilo/ la douzaine/la pièce**
4 euros a metre/a kilo/a dozen/ each

rouler à 80 km à l'heure
to go at 80 km an hour

payé à l'heure/au jour/au mois
paid by the hour/by the day/ by the month

8 **le roi Georges III**
King George III

le capitaine Darbeau
Captain Darbeau

le docteur Rousseau
Dr Rousseau

Monsieur le président
Mr Chairman/President

9 **Victor Hugo, grand écrivain du dix-neuvième siècle**
Victor Hugo, a great author of the nineteenth century

Joseph Leblanc, inventeur et entrepreneur, a été le premier ...
Joseph Leblanc, an inventor and entrepreneur, was the first ...

143

Articles

The Partitive Article

The partitive article has the sense of 'some' or 'any', although the French is not always translated in English.

Forms of the partitive

du (de l')/de la (de l'), des

	WITH MASC. NOUN	WITH FEM. NOUN	
SING.	**du (de l')**	**de la (de l')**	some, any
PLUR.	**des**	**des**	some, any

The gender and number of the noun determines the form of the partitive → ❶

The forms shown in brackets (**de l'**) are used before a vowel or an **h** 'mute' → ❷

des becomes **de** (**d'** + *vowel*) before an adjective → ❸
EXCEPTION: if the adjective and noun are seen as forming one unit → ❹

In negative sentences **de** (**d'** + *vowel*) is used for both genders, singular and plural → ❺
EXCEPTION: after **ne ... que** 'only', the positive forms above are used → ❻

Examples

① **Avez-vous du sucre?** — Have you any sugar?

J'ai acheté de la farine et de la margarine — I bought (some) flour and margarine

Il a mangé des gâteaux — He ate some cakes

Est-ce qu'il y a des lettres pour moi? — Are there (any) letters for me?

② **Il me doit de l'argent** — He owes me (some) money

C'est de l'histoire ancienne — That's ancient history

③ **Il a fait de gros efforts pour nous aider** — He made a great effort to help us

Cette région a de belles églises — This region has some beautiful churches

④ **des grandes vacances** — summer holidays

des jeunes gens — young people

⑤ **Je n'ai pas de nourriture/d'argent** — I don't have any food/money

Vous n'avez pas de timbres/d'œufs? — Have you no stamps/eggs?

Je ne mange jamais de viande/d'omelettes — I never eat meat/omelettes

Il ne veut plus de visiteurs/d'eau — He doesn't want any more visitors/water

⑥ **Il ne boit que du thé/de la bière/de l'eau** — He only drinks tea/beer/water

Je n'ai que des problèmes avec cette machine — I have nothing but trouble with this machine

Articles

The Indefinite Article

un/une, des

	WITH MASC. NOUN	WITH FEM. NOUN	
SING.	**un**	**une**	a
PLUR.	**des**	**des**	some

des is also the plural of the partitive article (see page 144).

In negative sentences, **de** (**d'** + *vowel*) is used for both singular and plural → **1**

The indefinite article is used in French largely as it is in English *except*:

there is no article when a person's profession is being stated → **2**

EXCEPTION: the article *is* present following **ce** (**c'** + *vowel*) → **3**

the English article is not translated by **un/une** in constructions like 'what a surprise', 'what an idiot' → **4**

in structures of the type given in example **5** the article **un/une** is used in French and not translated in English → **5**

Examples

1 Je n'ai pas de livre/d'enfants I don't have a book/(any) children

2 Il est professeur He's a teacher
Ma mère est infirmière My mother's a nurse

3 C'est un médecin He's/She's a doctor
Ce sont des acteurs They're actors

4 Quelle surprise! What a surprise!
Quel dommage! What a shame!

5 avec une grande sagesse/un courage admirable with great wisdom /admirable courage
Il a fait preuve d'un sang-froid incroyable He showed incredible calmness
un produit d'une qualité incomparable a product of incomparable quality

Adjectives

Adjectives: Formation of Feminines and Plurals

Most adjectives agree in number and in gender with the noun or pronoun.

Feminines

Most adjectives add an **e** to the masculine singular form → ❶

If the masculine singular form already ends in **-e**, no further **e** is added → ❷

Some adjectives undergo a further change when **e** is added. These changes occur regularly and are shown on page 150.

Irregular feminine forms are shown on page 152.

Plurals

The plural of both regular and irregular adjectives is formed by adding an **s** to the masculine or feminine singular form, as appropriate → ❸

When the masculine singular form already ends in **-s** or **-x**, no further **s** is added → ❹

For masculine singulars ending in **-au** and **-eau**, the masculine plural is **-aux** and **-eaux** → ❺

For masculine singulars ending in **-al**, the masculine plural is **-aux** → ❻
EXCEPTIONS: **final** (*masculine plural* **finals**)
fatal (*masculine plural* **fatals**)
naval (*masculine plural* **navals**)

Pronunciation of feminine and plural adjectives

This is dealt with on page 244.

Examples

1. | mon frère aîné | my elder brother |
   |---|---|
   | ma sœur aînée | my elder sister |
   | le petit garçon | the little boy |
   | la petite fille | the little girl |
   | un sac gris | a grey bag |
   | une chemise grise | a grey shirt |
   | un bruit fort | a loud noise |
   | une voix forte | a loud voice |

2. | un jeune homme | a young man |
   |---|---|
   | une jeune femme | a young woman |
   | l'autre verre | the other glass |
   | l'autre assiette | the other plate |

3. | le dernier train | the last train |
   |---|---|
   | les derniers trains | the last trains |
   | une vieille maison | an old house |
   | de vieilles maisons | old houses |
   | un long voyage | a long journey |
   | de longs voyages | long journeys |
   | la rue étroite | the narrow street |
   | les rues étroites | the narrow streets |

4. | un diplomate français | a French diplomat |
   |---|---|
   | des diplomates français | French diplomats |
   | un homme dangereux | a dangerous man |
   | des hommes dangereux | dangerous men |

5. | le nouveau professeur | the new teacher |
   |---|---|
   | les nouveaux professeurs | the new teachers |
   | un chien esquimau | a husky (*literally*: an Eskimo dog) |
   | des chiens esquimaux | huskies (*literally*: Eskimo dogs) |

6. | un ami loyal | a loyal friend |
   |---|---|
   | des amis loyaux | loyal friends |
   | un geste amical | a friendly gesture |
   | des gestes amicaux | friendly gestures |

Adjectives

Regular Feminine Endings

MASC SING.	FEM. SING.	EXAMPLES
-f	-ve	**neuf, vif** → ❶
-x	-se	**heureux, jaloux** → ❷
-eur	-euse	**travailleur, flâneur** → ❸
-teur	-teuse	**flatteur, menteur** → ❹
	-trice	**destructeur, séducteur** → ❺

EXCEPTIONS: **bref**: see page 152

doux, faux, roux, vieux: see page 152

extérieur, inférieur, intérieur, meilleur, supérieur:
all add **e** to the masculine

enchanteur: *fem.* = **enchanteresse**

MASC SING.	FEM. SING.	EXAMPLES
-an	-anne	**paysan** → ❻
-en	-enne	**ancien, parisien** → ❼
-on	-onne	**bon, breton** → ❽
-as	-asse	**bas, las** → ❾
-et*	-ette	**muet, violet** → ❿
-el	-elle	**annuel, mortel** → ⓫
-eil	-eille	**pareil, vermeil** → ⓬

EXCEPTION: **ras**: *fem.* = **rase**

MASC SING.	FEM. SING.	EXAMPLES
-et*	-ète	**secret, complet** → ⓭
-er	-ère	**étranger, fier** → ⓮

* Note that there are two feminine endings for masculine adjectives
ending in **-et**.

Examples

1   un résultat positif   a positive result
    une attitude positive   a positive attitude

2   d'un ton sérieux   in a serious tone (of voice)
    une voix sérieuse   a serious voice

3   un enfant trompeur   a deceitful child
    une déclaration trompeuse   a misleading statement

4   un tableau flatteur   a flattering picture
    une comparaison flatteuse   a flattering comparison

5   un geste protecteur   a protective gesture
    une couche protectrice   a protective layer

6   un problème paysan   a farming problem
    la vie paysanne   country life

7   un avion égyptien   an Egyptian plane
    une statue égyptienne   an Egyptian statue

8   un bon repas   a good meal
    de bonne humeur   in a good mood

9   un plafond bas   a low ceiling
    à voix basse   in a low voice

10   un travail net   a clean piece of work
    une explication nette   a clear explanation

11   un homme cruel   a cruel man
    une remarque cruelle   a cruel remark

12   un livre pareil   such a book
    en pareille occasion   on such an occasion

13   un regard inquiet   an anxious look
    une attente inquiète   an anxious wait

14   un goût amer   a bitter taste
    une amère déception   a bitter disappointment

Adjectives

Irregular Feminine Forms

MASC SING.	FEM. SING.	
aigu	aiguë	sharp; high-pitched → ❶
ambigu	ambiguë	ambiguous
beau (bel*)	belle	beautiful
bénin	bénigne	benign
blanc	blanche	white
bref	brève	brief, short → ❷
doux	douce	soft; sweet
épais	épaisse	thick
esquimau	esquimaude	Eskimo
faux	fausse	wrong
favori	favorite	favourite → ❸
fou (fol*)	folle	mad
frais	fraîche	fresh → ❹
franc	franche	frank
gentil	gentille	kind
grec	grecque	Greek
gros	grosse	big
jumeau	jumelle	twin → ❺
long	longue	long
malin	maligne	malignant
mou (mol*)	molle	soft
nouveau (nouvel*)	nouvelle	new
nul	nulle	no
public	publique	public → ❻
roux	rousse	red-haired
sec	sèche	dry
sot	sotte	foolish
turc	turque	Turkish
vieux (vieil*)	vieille	old

* This form is used when the following word begins with a vowel or an **h** 'mute' → ❼

Examples

1 un son aigu   a high-pitched sound
une douleur aiguë   a sharp pain

2 un bref discours   a short speech
une brève rencontre   a short meeting

3 mon sport favori   my favourite sport
ma chanson favorite   my favourite song

4 du pain frais   fresh bread
de la crème fraîche   fresh cream

5 mon frère jumeau   my twin brother
ma sœur jumelle   my twin sister

6 un jardin public   a (public) park
l'opinion publique   public opinion

7 un bel appartement   a beautiful flat
le nouvel ordinateur the new computer
un vieil arbre   an old tree
un bel habit   a beautiful outfit
un nouvel harmonica a new harmonica
un vieil hôtel   an old hotel

Adjectives

Comparatives and Superlatives

Comparatives

These are formed using the following constructions:

> **plus ... (que)** more ... (than) → ❶
> **moins ... (que)** less ... (than) → ❷
> **aussi ... que** as ... as → ❸
> **si ... que*** as ... as → ❹

* used mainly after a negative

Superlatives

These are formed using the following constructions:

> **le/la/les plus ... (que)** the most ... (that) → ❺
> **le/la/les moins ... (que)** the least ... (that) → ❻

> When the possessive adjective is present, two constructions are possible → ❼

> After a superlative the preposition **de** is often translated as 'in' → ❽

> If a clause follows a superlative, the verb is in the subjunctive → ❾

Adjectives with irregular comparatives/superlatives

ADJECTIVE	COMPARATIVE	SUPERLATIVE
bon	**meilleur**	**le meilleur**
good	better	the best
mauvais	**pire** *or* **plus mauvais**	**le pire** *or* **le plus mauvais**
bad	worse	the worst
petit	**moindre*** *or* **plus petit**	**le moindre*** *or* **le plus petit**
small	smaller; lesser	the smallest; the least

* used only with abstract nouns

> Comparative and superlative adjectives agree in number and in gender with the noun, just like any other adjective → ❿

Examples

1 une raison plus grave — a more serious reason
  Elle est plus petite que moi — She is smaller than me

2 un film moins connu — a less well-known film
  C'est moins cher qu'il ne pense — It's cheaper than he thinks

3 Robert était aussi inquiet que moi — Robert was as worried as I was
  Cette ville n'est pas aussi grande que Bordeaux — This town isn't as big as Bordeaux

4 Ils ne sont pas si contents que ça — They aren't as happy as all that

5 le guide le plus utile — the most useful guidebook
  la voiture la plus petite — the smallest car
  les plus grandes maisons — the biggest houses

6 le mois le moins agréable — the least pleasant month
  la fille la moins forte — the weakest girl
  les peintures les moins chères — the least expensive paintings

7 Mon désir le plus cher est de voyager — My dearest wish is to travel
  Mon plus cher désir est de voyager

8 la plus grande gare de Londres — the biggest station in London
  l'habitant le plus âgé du village/ de la région — the oldest inhabitant in the village/in the area

9 la personne la plus gentille que je connaisse — the nicest person I know

10 les moindres difficultés — the least difficulties
  la meilleure qualité — the best quality

Adjectives

Demonstrative Adjectives

ce (cet)/cette, ces

	MASCULINE	FEMININE	
SING.	ce (cet)	cette	this; that
PLUR.	ces	ces	these; those

Demonstrative adjectives agree in number and gender with the noun → ❶

cet is used when the following word begins with a vowel or an **h** 'mute' → ❷

For emphasis or in order to distinguish between people or objects, **-ci** or **-là** is added to the noun: **-ci** indicates proximity (usually translated 'this') and **là** distance 'that' → ❸

Examples

❶ Ce stylo ne marche pas — This/That pen isn't working
Comment s'appelle cette entreprise? — What's this/that company called?
Ces livres sont les miens — These/Those books are mine
Ces couleurs sont plus jolies — These/Those colours are nicer

❷ cet oiseau — this/that bird
cet article — this/that article
cet homme — this/that man

❸ Combien coûte ce manteau-ci? — How much is this coat?
Je voudrais cinq de ces pommes-là — I'd like five of those apples
Est-ce que tu reconnais cette personne-là? — Do you recognize that person?
Mettez ces vêtements-ci dans cette valise-là — Put these clothes in that case
Ce garçon-là appartient à ce groupe-ci — That boy belongs to this group

Adjectives

Interrogative Adjectives

quel/quelle, quels/quelles?

	MASCULINE	FEMININE	
SING.	**quel?**	**quelle?**	what?; which?
PLUR.	**quels?**	**quelles?**	what?; which?

Interrogative adjectives agree in number and gender with the noun → ❶

The forms shown above are also used in indirect questions → ❷

Exclamatory Adjectives

quel/quelle, quels/quelles!

	MASCULINE	FEMININE	
SING.	**quel!**	**quelle!**	what (a)!
PLUR.	**quels!**	**quelles!**	what!

Exclamatory adjectives agree in number and gender with the noun → ❸

For other exclamations, see page 214.

Examples

❶ Quel genre d'homme est-ce?   What type of man is he?
Quelle est leur décision?   What is their decision?
Vous jouez de quels instruments?   What instruments do you play?
Quelles offres avez-vous reçues?   What offers have you received?
Quel vin recommandez-vous?   Which wine do you recommend?
Quelles couleurs préférez-vous?   Which colours do you prefer?

❷ Je ne sais pas à quelle heure il est arrivé   I don't know what time he arrived
Dites-moi quels sont les livres les plus chers   Tell me which books are the most expensive

❸ Quel dommage!   What a pity!
Quelle idée!   What an idea!
Quels livres intéressants vous avez!   What interesting books you have!
Quelles jolies fleurs!   What nice flowers!

Adjectives

Possessive Adjectives

WITH SING. NOUN		WITH PLUR. NOUN	
MASC.	FEM.	MASC./FEM.	
mon	ma (mon)	mes	my
ton	ta (ton)	tes	your
son	sa (son)	ses	his; her; its
notre	notre	nos	our
votre	votre	vos	your
leur	leur	leurs	their

Possessive adjectives agree in number and gender with the noun, not with the owner → ❶

The forms shown in brackets are used when the following word begins with a vowel or an **h** 'mute' → ❷

son, **sa**, **ses** have the additional meaning of 'one's' → ❸

Examples

1 Catherine a oublié son parapluie — Catherine has left her umbrella
Paul cherche sa montre — Paul's looking for his watch
Mon frère et ma sœur habitent à Glasgow — My brother and sister live in Glasgow
Est-ce que tes voisins ont vendu leur voiture? — Did your neighbours sell their car?
Rangez vos affaires — Put your things away

2 mon appareil-photo — my camera
ton histoire — your story
son erreur — his/her mistake
mon autre sœur — my other sister

3 perdre son équilibre — to lose one's balance
présenter ses excuses — to offer one's apologies

Adjectives

Position of Adjectives

French adjectives usually follow the noun → **1**

Adjectives of colour or nationality *always* follow the noun → **2**

As in English, demonstrative, possessive, numerical and interrogative adjectives precede the noun → **3**

The adjectives **autre** (other), **chaque** (each, every) and **quelque** (some) precede the noun → **4**

The following common adjectives can precede the noun:

beau beautiful	**jeune** young
bon good	**joli** pretty
court short	**long** long
dernier last	**mauvais** bad
grand great	**petit** small
gros big	**tel** such (a)
haut high	**vieux** old

The meaning of the following adjectives varies according to their position:

	BEFORE NOUN	AFTER NOUN
ancien	former	old, ancient → **5**
brave	good	brave → **6**
cher	dear (*beloved*)	expensive → **7**
grand	great	tall → **8**
même	same	very → **9**
pauvre	poor (*wretched*)	poor (*not rich*) → **10**
propre	own	clean → **11**
seul	single, sole	on one's own → **12**
simple	mere, simple	simple, easy → **13**
vrai	real	true → **14**

Adjectives following the noun are linked by **et** → **15**

Examples

① le chapitre suivant — the following chapter
l'heure exacte — the right time

② une cravate rouge — a red tie
un mot français — a French word

③ ce dictionnaire — this dictionary
mon père — my father
le premier étage — the first floor
deux exemples — two examples
quel homme? — which man?

④ une autre fois — another time
chaque jour — every day
quelque espoir — some hope

⑤ un ancien collègue — a former colleague
l'histoire ancienne — ancient history

⑥ un brave homme — a good man
un homme brave — a brave man

⑦ mes chers amis — my dear friends
une robe chère — an expensive dress

⑧ un grand peintre — a great painter
un homme grand — a tall man

⑨ la même réponse — the same answer
vos paroles mêmes — your very words

⑩ cette pauvre femme — that poor woman
une nation pauvre — a poor nation

⑪ ma propre vie — my own life
une chemise propre — a clean shirt

⑫ une seule réponse — a single reply
une femme seule — a woman on her own

⑬ un simple regard — a mere look
un problème simple — a simple problem

⑭ la vraie raison — the real reason
les faits vrais — the true facts

⑮ un acte lâche et trompeur — a cowardly, deceitful act
un acte lâche, trompeur et ignoble — a cowardly, deceitful and ignoble act

163

Pronouns

Personal Pronouns

	SUBJECT PRONOUNS	
	SINGULAR	PLURAL
1st person	**je (j')** I	**nous** we
2nd person	**tu** you	**vous** you
3rd person (*masc.*)	**il** he; it	**ils** they
(*fem.*)	**elle** she; it	**elles** they
	on one, someone, they	

je changes to **j'** before a vowel, an **h** 'mute', or the pronoun **y** → ❶

tu/vous
Vous, as well as being the second person plural, is also used when addressing one person. As a general rule, use **tu** only when addressing a friend, a child, a relative, someone you know very well, or when invited to do so. In all other cases use **vous**. For singular and plural uses of **vous**, see example ❷

il/elle; ils/elles
The form of the 3rd person pronouns reflects the number and gender of the noun(s) they replace, referring to animals and things as well as to people. **Ils** also replaces a combination of masculine and feminine nouns → ❸

On refers to someone whose identity is unknown, or to people in general → ❹

Sometimes stressed pronouns replace the subject pronouns (see page 172).

Examples

❶ **J'arrive!**   I'm just coming!
    J'en ai trois   I've got three of them
    J'hésite à le déranger   I hesitate to disturb him
    J'y pense souvent   I often think about it

❷ Compare:
    Vous êtes certain, Monsieur   Are you sure, Mr Leclerc?
    Leclerc?
    and:
    Vous êtes certains, les enfants?   Are you sure, children?
    Compare:
    Vous êtes partie quand, Estelle?   When did you leave, Estelle?
    and:
    Estelle et Sophie – vous êtes   Estelle and Sophie – when did
    parties quand?   you leave?

❸ **Où logent ton père et ta mère**   Where do your father and mother
    quand ils vont à Rome?   stay when they go to Rome?
    Donne-moi le journal et les   Give me the newspaper and the
    lettres quand ils arriveront   letters when they arrive

❹ **On m'a volé mon sac**   Someone has stolen my bag
    On dit que Berlin est très agréable   They say Berlin is very nice

Pronouns

Personal Pronouns *continued*

	DIRECT OBJECT PRONOUNS	
	SINGULAR	PLURAL
1ˢᵗ person	**me (m')** me	**nous** us
2ⁿᵈ person	**te (t')** you	**vous** you
3ʳᵈ person (*masc.*)	**le (l')** him; it	**les** them
(*fem.*)	**la (l')** her; it	**les** them

The forms shown in brackets are used before a vowel, an **h** 'mute', or the pronoun **y** → ❶

In positive commands **me** and **te** change to **moi** and **toi** except before **en** or **y** → ❷

le sometimes functions as a 'neuter' pronoun, referring to an idea or information contained in a previous statement or question. It is often not translated → ❸

Position of direct object pronouns

In constructions other than the imperative affirmative, the pronoun comes before the verb → ❹

The same applies when the verb is in the infinitive → ❺

In the imperative affirmative, the pronoun follows the verb and is attached to it by a hyphen → ❻

For further information, see Order of Object Pronouns, page 170.

Reflexive pronouns

These are dealt with under reflexive verbs, see page 30.

Examples

① Il m'a vu
He saw me

Je ne t'oublierai jamais
I'll never forget you

Ça l'habitue à travailler seul
That gets him/her used to working on his/her own

Je veux l'y accoutumer
I want to accustom him/her to it

② Avertis-moi de ta décision
Inform me of your decision

Avertis-m'en
Inform me of it

③ Il n'est pas là. – Je le sais bien.
He isn't there. – I know that.

Aidez-moi si vous le pouvez
Help me if you can

Elle viendra demain. – Je l'espère bien.
She'll come tomorrow. – I hope so.

④ Je t'aime
I love you

Les voyez-vous?
Can you see them?

Elle ne nous connaît pas
She doesn't know us

Est-ce que tu ne les aimes pas?
Don't you like them?

Ne me faites pas rire
Don't make me laugh

⑤ Puis-je vous aider?
May I help you?

⑥ Aidez-moi
Help me

Suivez-nous
Follow us

Pronouns

Personal Pronouns *continued*

	INDIRECT OBJECT PRONOUNS	
	SINGULAR	PLURAL
1st person	**me (m')**	**nous**
2nd person	**te (t')**	**vous**
3rd person (*masc.*)	**lui**	**leur**
(*fem.*)	**lui**	**leur**

me and **te** change to **m'** and **t'** before a vowel or an **h** 'mute' → ❶

In positive commands, **me** and **te** change to **moi** and **toi** except before **en** → ❷

The pronouns shown in the above table replace the preposition **à** + *noun*, where the noun is a person or an animal → ❸

The verbal construction affects the translation of the pronoun → ❹

Position of indirect object pronouns

In constructions other than the imperative affirmative, the pronoun comes before the verb → ❺

The same applies when the verb is in the infinitive → ❻

In the imperative affirmative, the pronoun follows the verb and is attached to it by a hyphen → ❼

For further information, see Order of Object Pronouns, page 170.

Reflexive pronouns

These are dealt with under reflexive verbs, see page 30.

Examples

❶ Tu m'as donné ce livre   You gave me this book
   Ils t'ont caché les faits   They hid the facts from you

❷ Donnez-moi du sucre   Give me some sugar
   Donnez-m'en   Give me some
   Garde-toi assez d'argent   Keep enough money for yourself
   Garde-t'en assez   Keep enough for yourself

❸ J'écris à Suzanne   I'm writing to Suzanne
   Je lui écris   I'm writing to her
   Donne du lait au chat   Give the cat some milk
   Donne-lui du lait   Give it some milk

❹ arracher qch à qn: to snatch sth from sb:
   Un voleur m'a arraché mon porte-monnaie   A thief snatched my purse from me
   promettre qch à qn: to promise sb sth:
   Il leur a promis un cadeau   He promised them a present
   demander à qn de faire: to ask sb to do:
   Elle nous avait demandé de revenir   She had asked us to come back

❺ Elle vous a écrit   She's written to you
   Vous a-t-elle écrit?   Has she written to you?
   Il ne nous parle pas   He doesn't speak to us
   Est-ce que cela ne vous intéresse pas?   Doesn't it interest you?
   Ne leur répondez pas   Don't answer them

❻ Voulez-vous leur envoyer l'adresse?   Do you want to send them the address?

❼ Répondez-moi   Answer me
   Donnez-nous la réponse   Tell us the answer

Pronouns

Personal Pronouns *continued*

Order of object pronouns

When two object pronouns of different persons come before the verb, the order is: indirect before direct, i.e.

me			
te		**le**	
nous	before	**la**	→ ❶
vous		**les**	

When two third person object pronouns come before the verb, the order is: direct before indirect, i.e.

le			
la	before	**lui**	→ ❷
les		**leur**	

When two object pronouns come after the verb (i.e. in the imperative affirmative), the order is: direct before indirect, i.e.

		moi	
		toi	
le		**lui**	
la	before	**nous**	→ ❸
les		**vous**	
		leur	

The pronouns **y** and **en** (see pages 176 and 174) always come last → ❹

Examples

❶ Dominique vous l'envoie demain

Dominique's sending it to you tomorrow

Est-ce qu'il te les a montrés?
Has he shown them to you?
Ne me le dis pas
Don't tell me (it)
Il ne veut pas nous la prêter
He won't lend it to us

❷ Elle le leur a emprunté
She borrowed it from them
Je les lui ai lus
I read them to him/her
Ne la leur donne pas
Don't give it to them
Je voudrais les lui rendre
I'd like to give them back to him/ her

❸ Rends-les-moi
Give them back to me
Donnez-le-nous
Give it to us
Apportons-les-leur
Let's take them to them

❹ Donnez-leur-en
Give them some
Je l'y ai déposé
I dropped him there
Ne nous en parlez plus
Don't speak to us about it any more

Pronouns

Personal Pronouns *continued*

	STRESSED OR DISJUNCTIVE PRONOUNS	
	SINGULAR	PLURAL
1st person	**moi** me	**nous** us
2nd person	**toi** you	**vous** you
3rd person (*masc.*)	**lui** him; it	**eux** them
(*fem.*)	**elle** her; it	**elles** them
(*reflexive*)	**soi** oneself	

These pronouns are used:
- after prepositions → ①
- on their own → ②
- following **c'est**, **ce sont** it is → ③
- for emphasis, especially where contrast is involved → ④
- when the subject consists of two or more pronouns → ⑤
- when the subject consists of a pronoun and a noun → ⑥
- in comparisons → ⑦
- before relative pronouns → ⑧

For particular emphasis **-même** (*singular*) or **-mêmes** (*plural*) is added to the pronoun → ⑨

moi-même myself
toi-même yourself
lui-même himself; itself
elle-même herself; itself
soi-même oneself

nous-mêmes ourselves
vous-même yourself
vous-mêmes yourselves
eux-mêmes themselves
elles-mêmes themselves

Examples

① Je pense à toi   I think about you
  Partez sans eux   Leave without them
  C'est pour elle   This is for her
  Assieds-toi à côté de lui   Sit beside him
  Venez avec moi   Come with me
  Il a besoin de nous   He needs us

② Qui a fait cela? – Lui.   Who did that? – He did.
  Qui est-ce qui gagne? – Moi.   Who's winning? – Me.

③ C'est toi, Simon? – Non, c'est   Is that you, Simon? – No, it's
  moi, David.   me, David.
  Qui est-ce? – Ce sont eux.   Who is it? – It's them.

④ Ils voyagent séparément: lui par   They travel separately: he by
  le train, elle en autobus   train and she by bus
  Toi, tu ressembles à ton père,   You look like your father, they
  eux pas   don't
  Il n'a pas l'air de s'ennuyer, lui!   He doesn't look bored!

⑤ Lui et moi partons demain   He and I are leaving tomorrow
  Ni vous ni elles ne pouvez rester   Neither you nor they can stay

⑥ Mon père et elle ne s'entendent   My father and she don't get on
  pas

⑦ plus jeune que moi   younger than me
  Il est moins grand que toi   He's smaller than you (are)

⑧ Moi, qui étais malade, je n'ai pas   I, who was ill, couldn't go with
  pu les accompagner   them
  Ce sont eux qui font du bruit,   They're the ones making the
  pas nous   noise, not us

⑨ Je l'ai fait moi-même   I did it myself

Pronouns

The Pronoun *en*

en replaces the preposition **de** + *noun* → **1**

The verbal construction can affect the translation → **2**

en also replaces the partitive article (English = some, any) + *noun* → **3**

In expressions of quantity **en** represents the noun → **4**

Position: **en** comes before the verb, except in positive commands when it
follows and is attached to the verb by a hyphen → **5**

en follows other object pronouns → **6**

Examples

① Il est fier de son succès — He's proud of his success
Il en est fier — He's proud of it
Elle est sortie du cinéma — She came out of the cinema
Elle en est sortie — She came out (of it)
Je suis couvert de peinture — I'm covered in paint
J'en suis couvert — I'm covered in it
Il a beaucoup d'amis — He has lots of friends
Il en a beaucoup — He has lots (of them)

② avoir besoin de qch: — to need sth:
  J'en ai besoin — I need it/them
avoir peur de qch: — to be afraid of sth:
  J'en ai peur — I'm afraid of it/them

③ Avez-vous de l'argent? — Do you have any money?
En avez-vous? — Do you have any?
Je veux acheter des timbres — I want to buy some stamps
Je veux en acheter — I want to buy some

④ J'ai deux crayons — I've two pencils
J'en ai deux — I've two (of them)
Combien de sœurs as-tu? – J'en ai trois. — How many sisters do you have? – I have three.

⑤ Elle en a discuté avec moi — She discussed it with me
En êtes-vous content? — Are you pleased with it/them?
Je veux en garder trois — I want to keep three of them
N'en parlez plus — Don't talk about it any more
Prenez-en — Take some
Soyez-en fier — Be proud of it/them

⑥ Donnez-leur-en — Give them some
Il m'en a parlé — He spoke to me about it

Pronouns

The Pronoun y

y replaces the preposition **à** + *noun* → ❶

The verbal construction can affect the translation → ❷

y also replaces the prepositions **dans** and **sur** + *noun* → ❸

y can also mean 'there' → ❹

Position: **y** comes before the verb, except in positive commands when it
follows and is attached to the verb by a hyphen → ❺

y follows other object pronouns → ❻

Examples

① **Ne touchez pas à ce bouton**   Don't touch this switch
    N'y touchez pas   Don't touch it
    Il participe aux concerts   He takes part in the concerts
    Il y participe   He takes part (in them)

② **penser à qch:**   to think about sth:
    J'y pense souvent   I often think about it
    consentir à qch: to agree to sth:
    Tu y as consenti?   Have you agreed to it?

③ **Mettez-les dans la boîte**   Put them in the box
    Mettez-les-y   Put them in it
    Il les a mis sur les étagères   He put them on the shelves
    Il les y a mis   He put them on them
    J'ai placé de l'argent sur ce compte   I've put money into this account
    J'y ai placé de l'argent   I've put money into it

④ **Elle y passe tout l'été**   She spends the whole summer there

⑤ **Il y a ajouté du sucre**   He added sugar to it
    Elle n'y a pas écrit son nom   She hasn't written her name on it
    Comment fait-on pour y aller?   How do you get there?
    N'y pense plus!   Don't give it another thought!
    Restez-y   Stay there
    Réfléchissez-y   Think it over

⑥ **Elle m'y a conduit**   She drove me there
    Menez-nous-y   Take us there

Pronouns

Indefinite Pronouns

The following are indefinite pronouns:

aucun(e) none, not any → ❶
certain(e)s some, certain → ❷
chacun(e) each (one); everybody → ❸
on one, you; somebody; they, people; we (*informal use*) → ❹
personne nobody → ❺
plusieurs several → ❻
quelque chose something; anything → ❼
quelques-un(e)s some, a few → ❽
quelqu'un somebody; anybody → ❾
rien nothing → ❿
tout all; everything → ⓫
tous (toutes) all → ⓬
l'un(e) … l'autre (the) one … the other
les un(e)s … les autres some … others → ⓭

aucun(e), personne, rien
When used as subject or object of the verb, these require the word **ne**
placed immediately before the verb. Note that **aucun** further needs the
pronoun **en** when used as an object → ⓮

quelque chose, rien
When qualified by an adjective, these pronouns require the preposition
de before the adjective → ⓯

Examples

1 **Combien en avez-vous? – Aucun.**   How many have you got? – None.

2 **Certains pensent que ...**   Some (people) think that ...

3 **Chacune de ces boîtes est pleine**   Each of these boxes is full
   Chacun son tour!   Everybody in turn!

4 **On voit l'église de cette fenêtre**   You can see the church from this window

   En semaine on se couche tôt   During the week they/we go to bed early

   Est-ce qu'on lui a permis de rester?   Was he/she allowed to stay?

5 **Qui voyez-vous? – Personne.**   Who can you see? – Nobody.

6 **Ils sont plusieurs**   There are several of them

7 **Mange donc quelque chose!**   Eat something!
   Tu as vu quelque chose?   Did you see anything?

8 **Je connais quelques-uns de ses amis**   I know some of his/her friends

9 **Quelqu'un a appelé**   Somebody called (out)
   Tu as vu quelqu'un?   Did you see anybody?

10 **Qu'est-ce que tu as dans la main?**   What have you got in your hand?
   – Rien.   – Nothing.

11 **Il a tout gâché**   He has spoiled everything
   Tout va bien   All's well

12 **Tu les as tous?**   Do you have all of them?
   Elles sont toutes venues   They all came

13 **Les uns sont satisfaits, les autres pas**   Some are satisfied, (the) others aren't

14 **Je ne vois personne**   I can't see anyone
   Rien ne lui plaît   Nothing pleases him/her
   Aucune des entreprises ne veut ...   None of the companies wants ...
   Il n'en a aucun   He hasn't any (of them)

15 **quelque chose de grand**   something big
   rien d'intéressant   nothing interesting

Pronouns

Relative Pronouns

qui who; which
que who(m); which
These are subject and direct object pronouns that introduce a clause and refer to people or things.

	PEOPLE	THINGS
SUBJECT	**qui**	**qui**
	who, that → ❶	which, that → ❸
DIRECT OBJECT	**que (qu')**	**que (qu')**
	who(m), that → ❷	which, that → ❹

que changes to **qu'** before a vowel → ❷/❹

You cannot omit the object relative pronoun in French as you can in English → ❷/❹

After a preposition:
When referring to people, use **qui** → ❺
EXCEPTIONS: after **parmi** 'among' and **entre** 'between' use **lesquels/ lesquelles**; see below → ❻

When referring to things, use forms of **lequel**:

	MASCULINE	FEMININE	
SING.	**lequel**	**laquelle**	which
PLUR.	**lesquels**	**lesquelles**	which

The pronoun agrees in number and gender with the noun → ❼

After the prepositions **à** and **de**, **lequel** and **lesquel(le)s** contract as follows:
à + lequel → **auquel**
à + lesquels → **auxquels** → ❽
à + lesquelles → **auxquelles**

de + lequel → **duquel**
de + lesquels → **desquels** → ❾
de + lesquelles → **desquelles**

Examples

① Mon frère, qui a vingt ans, est à l'université

My brother, who's twenty, is at university

② Les amis que je vois le plus sont ...
Lucienne, qu'il connaît depuis longtemps, est ...

The friends (that) I see most are ...
Lucienne, whom he has known for a long time, is ...

③ Il y a un escalier qui mène au toit

There's a staircase which leads to the roof

④ La maison que nous avons achetée a ...
Voici le cadeau qu'elle m'a envoyé

The house (which) we've bought has ...
This is the present (that) she sent me

⑤ la personne à qui il parle
la personne avec qui je voyage
les enfants pour qui je l'ai acheté

the person he's talking to
the person with whom I travel
the children for whom I bought it

⑥ Il y avait des jeunes, parmi lesquels Robert
les filles entre lesquelles j'étais assis

There were some young people, Robert among them
the girls between whom I was sitting

⑦ le torchon avec lequel il l'essuie
la table sur laquelle je l'ai mis
les moyens par lesquels il l'accomplit
les pièces pour lesquelles elle est connue

the cloth with which he's wiping it
the table on which I put it
the means by which he achieves it
the plays for which she is famous

⑧ le magasin auquel il livre ces marchandises

the shop to which he delivers these goods

⑨ les injustices desquelles il se plaint

the injustices about which he's complaining

Pronouns

Relative Pronouns *continued*

quoi which, what

> When the relative pronoun does not refer to a specific noun, **quoi** is used after a preposition → **1**

dont whose, of whom, of which

> **dont** often (but not always) replaces **de qui**, **duquel**, **de laquelle**, and **desquel(le)s** → **2**

> It cannot replace **de qui**, **duquel** *etc* in the construction *preposition + noun + **de qui/duquel*** → **3**

Examples

① C'est en quoi vous vous trompez
À quoi, j'ai répondu ...

That's where you're wrong
To which I replied, ...

② la femme dont (= *de qui*) la
voiture est garée en face
un prix dont (= *de qui*) je suis fier
un ami dont (= *de qui*) je connais
le frère
les enfants dont (= *de qui*) vous
vous occupez
le film dont (= *duquel*) il a parlé
la fenêtre dont (= *de laquelle*) les
rideaux sont tirés
des garçons dont (= *desquels*) j'ai
oublié les noms
les maladies dont (= *desquelles*)
il souffre

the woman whose car is parked
opposite
an award I am proud of
a friend whose brother I know

the children you look after

the film of which he spoke
the window the curtains of
which are drawn
boys whose names I've
forgotten
the illnesses he suffers from

③ une personne sur l'aide de qui on
peut compter
les enfants aux parents de qui
j'écris
la maison dans le jardin
de laquelle il y a ...

a person whose help one can
rely on
the children to whose parents
I'm writing
the house in whose garden
there is ...

Pronouns

Relative Pronouns *continued*

ce qui, ce que that which, what

These are used when the relative pronoun does not refer to a specific noun, and they are often translated as 'what' (*literally*: that which):

> **ce qui** is used as the subject → **❶**

> **ce que*** is used as the direct object → **❷**

> * **que** changes to **qu'** before a vowel → **❷**

> Note the construction:
> **tout ce qui**
> **tout ce que**   everything/all that → **❸**

> **de** + **ce que** → **ce dont** → **❹**

> *preposition* + **ce que** → **ce** + *preposition* + **quoi** → **❺**

> When **ce qui**, **ce que** *etc* refers to a previous clause the translation is 'which' → **❻**

Examples

1 **Ce qui m'intéresse ne l'intéresse pas forcément**
What interests me doesn't necessarily interest him

Je n'ai pas vu ce qui s'est passé
I didn't see what happened

2 **Ce que j'aime c'est la musique classique**
What I like is classical music

Montrez-moi ce qu'il vous a donné
Show me what he gave you

3 **Tout ce qui reste c'est ...**
All that's left is ...

Donnez-moi tout ce que vous avez
Give me everything you have

4 **Il risque de perdre ce dont il est si fier**
He risks losing what he's so proud of

Voilà ce dont il s'agit
That's what it's about

5 **Ce n'est pas ce à quoi je m'attendais**
It's not what I was expecting

Ce à quoi je m'intéresse particulièrement c'est ...
What I'm particularly interested in is ...

6 **Il est d'accord, ce qui m'étonne**
He agrees, which surprises me

Il a dit qu'elle ne venait pas, ce que nous savions déjà
He said she wasn't coming, which we already knew

Pronouns

Interrogative Pronouns

These pronouns are used in direct questions:

qui? who; whom?
que? what?
quoi? what?

The form of the pronoun depends on:
- whether it refers to people or to things
- whether it is the subject or object of the verb, or if it comes after a preposition

Qui and **que** have longer forms, as shown in the tables below.

Referring to people:

SUBJECT	**qui?**	who? → ❶
	qui est-ce qui?	
OBJECT	**qui?**	who(m)? → ❷
	qui est-ce que*?	
AFTER PREPOSITIONS	**qui?**	who(m)? → ❸

Referring to things:

SUBJECT	**qu'est-ce qui?**	what? → ❹
OBJECT	**que*?**	what? → ❺
	qu'est-ce que*?	
AFTER PREPOSITIONS	**quoi?**	what? → ❻

* **que** changes to **qu'** before a vowel → ❷/❺

Examples

① **Qui vient?**
Qui est-ce qui vient?

Who's coming?

② **Qui vois-tu?**
Qui est-ce que tu vois?
Qui a-t-elle rencontré?
Qui est-ce qu'elle a rencontré?

Who(m) can you see?

Who(m) did she meet?

③ **De qui parle-t-il?**
Pour qui est ce livre?
À qui avez-vous écrit?

Who's he talking about?
Who's this book for?
To whom did you write?

④ **Qu'est-ce qui se passe?**
Qu'est-ce qui a vexé Paul?

What's happening?
What upset Paul?

⑤ **Que faites-vous?**
Qu'est-ce que vous faites?
Qu'a-t-il dit?
Qu'est-ce qu'il a dit?

What are you doing?

What did he say?

⑥ **À quoi cela sert-il?**
De quoi a-t-on parlé?
Sur quoi vous basez-vous?

What's that used for?
What was the discussion about?
What do you base it on?

Pronouns

Interrogative Pronouns *continued*

These pronouns are used in indirect questions:

qui who; whom
ce qui what
ce que what
quoi what

The form of the pronoun depends on:

- whether it refers to people or to things
- whether it is the subject or object of the verb, or if it comes after a preposition

Referring to people: use **qui** in all instances → **1**

Referring to things:

SUBJECT	**ce qui**	what → **2**
OBJECT	**ce que***	what → **3**
AFTER PREPOSITIONS	**quoi?**	what → **4**

* **que** changes to **qu'** before a vowel → **3**

Examples

❶ Demande-lui qui est venu — Ask him who came
Je me demande qui ils ont vu — I wonder who they saw
Dites-moi qui vous préférez — Tell me who you prefer
Elle ne sait pas à qui s'adresser — She doesn't know who to apply to
Demandez-leur pour qui elles travaillent — Ask them who they work for

❷ Il se demande ce qui se passe — He's wondering what's happening
Je ne sais pas ce qui vous fait croire que … — I don't know what makes you think that …

❸ Raconte-nous ce que tu as fait — Tell us what you did
Je me demande ce qu'elle pense — I wonder what she's thinking

❹ On ne sait pas de quoi vivent ces animaux — We don't know what these animals live on
Je vais lui demander à quoi il fait allusion — I'm going to ask him what he's hinting at

Pronouns

Interrogative Pronouns *continued*

lequel/laquelle, lesquels/lesquelles?

	MASCULINE	FEMININE	
SING.	**lequel?**	**laquelle?**	which (one)?
PLUR.	**lesquels?**	**lesquelles?**	which (ones)?

The pronoun agrees in number and gender with the noun it refers to → ❶

The same forms are used in indirect questions → ❷

After the prepositions **à** and **de**, **lequel** and **lesquel(le)s** contract as follows:

> à + lequel? → auquel?
> à + lesquels? → auxquels?
> à + lesquelles? → auxquelles?

> de + lequel? → duquel?
> de + lesquels? → desquels?
> de + lesquelles? → desquelles?

Examples

1 J'ai choisi un livre. – **Lequel?**	I've chosen a book. – Which one?
Laquelle de ces valises est la vôtre?	Which of these cases is yours?
Amenez quelques amis. – **Lesquels?**	Bring some friends. – Which ones?
Lesquelles de vos sœurs sont mariées?	Which of your sisters are married?
2 Je me demande **laquelle** des maisons est la leur	I wonder which is their house
Dites-moi **lesquels** d'entre eux étaient là	Tell me which of them were there

Pronouns

Possessive Pronouns

Singular:

MASCULINE	FEMININE	
le mien	la mienne	mine
le tien	la tienne	yours
le sien	la sienne	his; hers; its
le nôtre	la nôtre	ours
le vôtre	la vôtre	yours
le leur	la leur	theirs

Plural:

MASCULINE	FEMININE	
les miens	les miennes	mine
les tiens	les tiennes	yours
les siens	les siennes	his; hers; its
les nôtres	les nôtres	ours
les vôtres	les vôtres	yours
les leurs	les leurs	theirs

The pronoun agrees in number and gender with the noun it replaces, not with the owner → ❶

Alternative translations are 'my own', 'your own' *etc*; **le sien**, **la sienne** *etc* may also mean 'one's own' → ❷

After the prepositions **à** and **de** the articles **le** and **les** are contracted in the normal way (see page 140):

> à + le mien → au mien
> à + les miens → aux miens → ❸
> à + les miennes → aux miennes
>
> de + le mien → du mien
> de + les miens → des miens → ❹
> de + les miennes → des miennes

Examples

1 **Demandez à Carole si ce stylo est le sien**
Ask Carole if this pen is hers

Quelle équipe a gagné – la leur ou la nôtre?
Which team won – theirs or ours?

Mon portable est plus rapide que le tien
My laptop is faster than yours

Richard a pris mes affaires pour les siennes
Richard mistook my belongings for his

Si tu n'as pas de baskets, emprunte les miennes
If you don't have any trainers, borrow mine

Nos maisons sont moins grandes que les vôtres
Our houses are smaller than yours

2 **Est-ce que leur entreprise est aussi grande que la vôtre?**
Is their company as big as your own?

Leurs prix sont moins élevés que les nôtres
Their prices are lower than our own

Le bonheur des autres importe plus que le sien
Other people's happiness matters more than one's own

3 **Pourquoi préfères-tu ce manteau au mien?**
Why do you prefer this coat to mine?

Quelles maisons ressemblent aux leurs?
Which houses resemble theirs?

4 **Leur voiture est garée à côté de la tienne**
Their car is parked next to yours

Vos livres sont au-dessus des miens
Your books are on top of mine

Pronouns

Demonstrative Pronouns

celui/celle, ceux/celles

	MASCULINE	FEMININE	
SING.	**celui**	**celle**	the one
PLUR.	**ceux**	**celles**	the ones

The pronoun agrees in number and gender with the noun it replaces → **1**

Uses:
- preceding a relative pronoun, meaning 'the one(s) who/which' → **1**
- preceding the preposition **de**, meaning 'the one(s) belonging to', 'the one(s) of' → **2**
- with **-ci** and **-là**, for emphasis or to distinguish between two things:

	MASCULINE	FEMININE		
SING.	**celui-ci**	**celle-ci**	this (one)	→ **3**
PLUR.	**ceux-ci**	**celles-ci**	these (ones)	

	MASCULINE	FEMININE		
SING.	**celui-là**	**celle-là**	that (one)	→ **3**
PLUR.	**ceux-là**	**celles-là**	those (ones)	

- an additional meaning of **celui-ci/celui-là** *etc* is 'the former/the latter'.

Examples

❶ **Lequel? – Celui qui parle à Anne.**

Which man? – The one who's talking to Anne.

Quelle robe désirez-vous? – Celle qui est en vitrine.

Which dress do you want? – The one which is in the window.

Est-ce que ces livres sont ceux qu'il t'a donnés?

Are these the books that he gave you?

Quelles filles? – Celles que nous avons vues hier.

Which girls? – The ones we saw yesterday.

Cet article n'est pas celui dont vous m'avez parlé

This article isn't the one you spoke to me about

❷ **Ce jardin est plus grand que celui de mes parents**

This garden is bigger than my parents' (garden)

Est-ce que ta fille est plus âgée que celle de Gabrielle?

Is your daughter older than Gabrielle's (daughter)?

Je préfère les chiens de Paul à ceux de Roger

I prefer Paul's dogs to Roger's (dogs)

Comparez vos réponses à celles de votre voisin

Compare your answers with your neighbour's (answers)

les montagnes d'Écosse et celles du pays de Galles

the mountains of Scotland and those of Wales

❸ **Quel tailleur préférez-vous: celui-ci ou celui-là?**

Which suit do you prefer: this one or that one?

Cette chemise a deux poches mais celle-là n'en a pas

This shirt has two pockets but that one has none

Quels œufs choisirais-tu: ceux-ci ou ceux-là?

Which eggs would you choose: these (ones) or those (ones)?

De toutes mes jupes, celle-ci me va le mieux

Of all my skirts, this one fits me best

Pronouns

Demonstrative Pronouns *continued*

ce (c') it, that

> Usually used with **être**, in the expressions **c'est**, **c'était**, **ce sont** *etc* → **1**
>
> Note the spelling **ç**, when followed by the letter **a** → **2**
>
> Uses:
> - to identify a person or object → **3**
> - for emphasis → **4**
> - as a neuter pronoun, referring to a statement, idea *etc* → **5**

ce qui, **ce que**, **ce dont** *etc*:   see Relative Pronouns (page 184), and
Interrogative Pronouns (page 188).

cela, **ça** it, that

> **cela** and **ça** are used as 'neuter' pronouns, referring to a statement, an idea, an object → **6**
>
> In everyday spoken language **ça** is used in preference to **cela**.

ceci this → **7**

> **ceci** is not used as often as 'this' in English; **cela**, **ça** are often used where we use 'this'.

Examples

❶ C'est ...
    C'était moi

It's/That's ...
It was me

❷ Ç'a été la cause de ...

That was the cause of ...

❸ Qui est-ce?

Who is it?; Who's this/that?;
    Who's he/she?

    C'est lui/mon frère/nous
    Ce sont eux
    C'est une infirmière*
    Ce sont des professeurs*
    Qu'est-ce que c'est?
    Qu'est-ce que c'est que ça?
    C'est une agrafeuse
    Ce sont des trombones

It's/That's him/my brother/us
It's them
She's a nurse
They're teachers
What's this/that?
What's that?
It's a stapler
They're paper clips

❹ C'est moi qui ai téléphoné
    Ce sont les enfants qui
      importent le plus

It was me who phoned
It's the children who matter
    most

❺ C'est très intéressant
    Ce serait dangereux

That's/It's very interesting
That/It would be dangerous

❻ Ça ne fait rien
    À quoi bon faire ça?
    Cela ne compte pas
    Cela demande du temps

It doesn't matter
What's the use of doing that?
That doesn't count
It/That takes time

❼ À qui est ceci?
    Ouvrez-le comme ceci

Whose is this?
Open it like this

---

* See pages 146 and 147 for the use of the article when stating a person's
profession

Adverbs

Adverbs: Formation

Most adverbs are formed by adding **-ment** to the feminine form of the adjective → **1**

-ment is added to the *masculine* form when the masculine form ends in **-é**, **-i** or **-u** → **2**
EXCEPTION: **gai** → **3**

Occasionally the **u** changes to **û** before **-ment** is added → **4**

If the adjective ends in **-ant** or **-ent**, the adverb ends in **-amment** or **-emment** respectively → **5**
EXCEPTIONS: **lent, présent** → **6**

Irregular adverbs

ADJECTIVE	ADVERB
aveugle blind	**aveuglément** blindly
bon good	**bien** well → **7**
bref brief	**brièvement** briefly
énorme enormous	**énormément** enormously
exprès express	**expressément** expressly → **8**
gentil kind	**gentiment** kindly
mauvais bad	**mal** badly → **9**
meilleur better	**mieux** better
pire worse	**pis** worse
précis precise	**précisément** precisely
profond deep	**profondément** deeply → **10**
traître treacherous	**traîtreusement** treacherously

Adjectives used as adverbs

Certain adjectives are used adverbially. These include: **bas, bon, cher, clair, court, doux, droit, dur, faux, ferme, fort, haut, mauvais** and **net** → **11**

Examples

1 MASC./FEM. ADJECTIVE

heureux/heureuse fortunate
franc/franche frank
extrême/extrême extreme

ADVERB

heureusement fortunately
franchement frankly
extrêmement extremely

2 MASC. ADJECTIVE

désespéré desperate
vrai true
résolu resolute

ADVERB

désespérément desperately
vraiment truly
résolument resolutely

3 **gai** cheerful

gaiement or **gaîment** cheerfully

4 **continu** continuous

continûment continuously

5 **constant** constant
courant fluent
évident obvious
fréquent frequent

constamment constantly
couramment fluently
évidemment obviously
fréquemment frequently

6 **lent** slow
présent present

lentement slowly
présentement presently

7 **Elle travaille bien**

She works well

8 **Il a expressément défendu qu'on parte**

He has expressly forbidden us to leave

9 **un emploi mal payé**

a badly paid job

10 **J'ai été profondément ému**

I was deeply moved

11 **parler bas/haut**
coûter cher
voir clair
travailler dur
chanter faux
sentir bon/mauvais

to speak softly/loudly
to be expensive
to see clearly
to work hard
to sing off key
to smell nice/bad

Adverbs

Adverbs: Position

When the adverb accompanies a verb in a simple tense, it generally follows the verb → ❶

When the adverb accompanies a verb in a compound tense, it generally comes between the auxiliary verb and the past participle → ❷

Some adverbs, notably those of time and place, follow the past participle → ❸

When the adverb accompanies an adjective or another adverb it generally precedes the adjective/adverb → ❹

Some adverbs are used to form questions and precede the verb (see pages 220 and 221) → ❺

Comparatives of adverbs

These are formed using the following constructions:

> **plus ... (que)** more ... (than) → ❻
> **moins ... (que)** less ... (than) → ❼
> **aussi ... que** as ... as → ❽
> **si ... que*** as ... as → ❾

* used mainly after a negative

Superlatives of adverbs

These are formed using the following constructions:

> **le plus ... (que)** the most ... (that) → ❿
> **le moins ... (que)** the least ... (that) → ⓫

Adverbs with irregular comparatives/superlatives

ADVERB	COMPARATIVE	SUPERLATIVE
beaucoup a lot	**plus** more	**le plus** (the) most
bien well	**mieux** better	**le mieux** (the) best
mal badly	**pis/plus mal** worse	**le pis/plus mal** (the) worst
peu little	**moins** less	**le moins** (the) least

Examples

① Il dort encore — He's still asleep
  Je pense souvent à toi — I often think about you

② Ils sont déjà partis — They've already gone
  J'ai toujours cru que ... — I've always thought that ...
  J'ai presque fini — I'm almost finished
  Il a trop mangé — He's eaten too much

③ On les a vus là-bas — We saw them over there
  Elle revient demain — She's coming back tomorrow

④ un très beau chemisier — a very nice blouse
  une femme bien habillée — a well-dressed woman
  beaucoup plus vite — much faster
  peu souvent — not very often

⑤ Comment va-t-il? — How is he?

⑥ plus vite — more quickly
  plus régulièrement — more regularly
  Elle chante plus fort que moi — She sings louder than I do

⑦ moins facilement — less easily
  moins souvent — less often
  Nous nous voyons moins fréquemment qu'auparavant — We see each other less frequently than before

⑧ Faites-le aussi vite que possible — Do it as quickly as possible
  Il en sait aussi long que nous — He knows as much about it as we do

⑨ Ce n'est pas si loin que je pensais — It's not as far as I thought

⑩ Marianne court le plus vite — Marianne runs fastest
  Le plus tôt que je puisse venir c'est samedi — The earliest that I can come is Saturday

⑪ C'est l'auteur que je connais le moins bien — He's the writer I'm least familiar with

201

Adverbs

Common Adverbs and Their Usage

Some common adverbs:

assez enough; quite → ❶ *See also below*
aussi also, too; as → ❷
autant as much → ❸ *See also below*
beaucoup a lot; much → ❹ *See also below*
bien well; very; very much; 'indeed' → ❺ *See also below*
combien how much; how many → ❻ *See also below*
comme how; what → ❼
déjà already; before → ❽
encore still; yet; more; even → ❾
moins less → ❿ *See also below*
peu little, not much; not very → ⓫ *See also below*
plus more → ⓬ *See also below*
si so; such → ⓭
tant so much → ⓮ *See also below*
toujours always; still → ⓯
trop too much; too → ⓰ *See also below*

assez, **autant**, **beaucoup**, **combien** *etc* are used in the construction
adverb + **de** + *noun* with the following meanings:

assez de enough → ⓱
autant de as much; as many; so much; so many
beaucoup de a lot of
combien de how much; how many
moins de less; fewer → ⓱
peu de little, not much; few, not many
plus de more
tant de so much; so many
trop de too much; too many

bien can be followed by a partitive article (see page 144) plus a noun to
mean *a lot of; a good many* → ⓲

Examples

1. **Avez-vous assez chaud?** — Are you warm enough?
   Il est assez tard — It's quite late

2. **Je préfère ça aussi** — I prefer it too
   Elle est aussi grande que moi — She is as tall as I am

3. **Je voyage autant que lui** — I travel as much as him

4. **Tu lis beaucoup?** — Do you read a lot?
   C'est beaucoup plus loin? — Is it much further?

5. **Bien joué!** — Well played!
   Je suis bien content que … — I'm very pleased that …
   Il s'est bien amusé — He enjoyed himself very much
   Je l'ai bien fait — I did do it

6. **Combien coûte ce livre?** — How much is this book?
   Vous êtes combien? — How many of you are there?

7. **Comme tu es jolie!** — How pretty you look!
   Comme il fait beau! — What lovely weather!

8. **Je l'ai déjà fait** — I've already done it
   Êtes-vous déjà allé en France? — Have you been to France before?

9. **J'en ai encore deux** — I've still got two
   Elle n'est pas encore là — She isn't there yet
   Encore du café, Alain? — More coffee, Alain?
   Encore mieux! — Even better!

10. **Travaillez moins!** — Work less!
    Je suis moins étonné que toi — I'm less surprised than you are

11. **Elle mange peu** — She doesn't eat very much
    C'est peu important — It's not very important

12. **Il se détend plus** — He relaxes more
    Elle est plus timide que Sophie — She is shyer than Sophie

13. **Simon est si charmant** — Simon is so charming
    une si belle vue — such a lovely view

14. **Elle l'aime tant** — She loves him so much

15. **Il dit toujours ça!** — He always says that!
    Tu le vois toujours? — Do you still see him?

16. **J'ai trop mangé** — I've eaten too much
    C'est trop cher — It's too expensive

17. **assez d'argent/de livres** — enough money/books
    moins de temps/d'amis — less time/fewer friends

18. **bien du mal/des gens** — a lot of harm/a good many people

Prepositions

On the following pages you will find some of the most frequent uses of prepositions in French. Particular attention is paid to cases where usage differs markedly from English. It is often difficult to give an English equivalent for French prepositions, since usage varies so much between the two languages.

In the list below, the broad meaning of the preposition is given on the left, with examples of usage following.

Prepositions are dealt with in alphabetical order, except **à**, **de** and **en** which are shown first.

à

at	**lancer qch à qn** to throw sth at sb
	il habite à St Pierre he lives at St Pierre
	à 2 euros (la) pièce (at) 2 euros each
	à 100 km à l'heure at 100 km per hour
in	**à la campagne** in the country
	à Londres in London
	au lit in bed (*also* to bed)
	un livre à la main with a book in his/her hand
on	**un tableau au mur** a picture on the wall
to	**aller au cinéma** to go to the cinema
	donner qch à qn to give sth to sb
	le premier/dernier à faire the first/last to do
	demander qch à qn to ask sb sth
from	**arracher qch à qn** to snatch sth from sb
	acheter qch à qn to buy sth from sb
	cacher qch à qn to hide sth from sb
	emprunter qch à qn to borrow sth from sb
	prendre qch à qn to take sth from sb
	voler qch à qn to steal sth from sb

Prepositions

descriptive **la femme au chapeau vert**
the woman with the green hat
un garçon aux yeux bleus a boy with blue eyes

manner, means **à l'ancienne** in the old-fashioned way
fait à la main handmade
à bicyclette/cheval by bicycle/on horseback
(*but note other forms of transport used with* **en** *and*
par)
à pied on foot
chauffer au gaz to heat with/by gas
à pas lents with slow steps
cuisiner au beurre to cook with butter

time, date: at, in **à minuit** at midnight
à trois heures cinq at five past three
au XXᵉ siècle in the 20th century
à Noël/Pâques at Christmas/Easter

distance **à 6 km d'ici** (at a distance of) 6 km from here
à deux pas de chez moi
just a step from my place

destined for **une tasse à thé** a teacup
(*compare* **une tasse de thé**)
un service à café a coffee set

after certain adjectives **son écriture est difficile à lire**
his writing is difficult to read
(*compare the usage with* **de**, *page 206*)
prêt à tout ready for anything

after certain verbs see page 64

Prepositions

de

from	**venir de Londres** to come from London
	du matin au soir from morning till night
	du 21 juin au 5 juillet from 21st June till 5th July
	de 10 à 15 from 10 to 15
belonging to, of	**un ami de la famille** a friend of the family
	les vents d'automne the autumn winds
contents, composition, material	**une boîte d'allumettes** a box of matches
	une tasse de thé a cup of tea
	(*compare* **une tasse à thé**)
	une robe de soie a silk dress
manner	**d'une façon irrégulière** in an irregular way
	d'un seul coup at one go
quality	**la société de consommation** the consumer society
	des objets de valeur valuable items
comparative + a number	**Il y avait plus/moins de cent personnes** There were more/fewer than a hundred people
in (*after superlatives*)	**la plus/moins belle ville du monde** the most/least beautiful city in the world
after certain adjectives	**surpris de voir** surprised to see
	Il est difficile d'y accéder Access is difficult (*compare the usage with* **à**, *page 205*)
after certain verbs	see page 64

Prepositions

en

to, in, on (*place*)	**en ville** in/to town **en pleine mer** on the open sea **en France** in/to France (*note that masculine countries use* **à**)
in (*dates, months*)	**en 2013** in 2013 **en janvier** in January
transport	**en voiture** by car **en avion** by plane (*but note usage of* **à** *and* **par** *in other expressions*)
language	**en français** in French
duration	**Je le ferai en trois jours** I'll do it in three days (i.e. I'll take three days to do it: *compare* **dans trois jours**)
material	**un bracelet en or** a bracelet made of gold (*note that the use of* **en** *stresses the material more than the use of* **de**) **consister en** to consist of
in the manner of, like a	**parler en vrai connaisseur** to speak like a real connoisseur **déguisé en cow-boy** dressed up as a cowboy
+ present participle	**Il l'a vu en passant devant la porte** He saw it as he came past the door

Prepositions

avant

before	**Il est arrivé avant toi** He arrived before you
+ *infinitive* (*add* de)	**Je vais finir ça avant de manger** I'm going to finish this before eating
preference	**la santé avant tout** health above everything

chez

at the home of	**chez lui/moi** at his/my house **être chez soi** to be at home **venez chez nous** come round to our place
at/to (*a shop*)	**chez le boucher** at/to the butcher's
in (*a person, among a group of people or animals*)	**Ce que je n'aime pas chez lui c'est son ...** What I don't like in him is his ... **chez les fourmis** among ants

dans

position	**dans une boîte** in(to) a box
circumstance	**dans son enfance** in his childhood
future time	**dans trois jours** in three days' time (*compare* **en trois jours**, *page 207*)

depuis

since (*time/place*)	**depuis mardi** since Tuesday **Il pleut depuis Paris** It's been raining since Paris
for	**Il habite cette maison depuis trois ans** He's been living in this house for three years (*note tense*)

Prepositions

dès

past time	**dès mon enfance** since my childhood
future time	**Je le ferai dès mon retour**
	I'll do it as soon as I get back

entre

between	**entre 8 et 10** between 8 and 10
among	**Jean et Pierre, entre autres**
	Jean and Pierre, among others
reciprocal	**s'aider entre eux** to help each other (out)

d'entre

of, among	**trois d'entre eux** three of them

par

by (*agent of passive*)	**renversé par une voiture** knocked down by a car
	tué par la foudre killed by lightning
weather conditions	**par un beau jour d'été** on a lovely summer's day
by (*means of*)	**par un couloir/sentier** by a corridor/path
	par le train by train (*but see also* **à** *and* **en**)
	par l'intermédiaire de M. Duval through Mr Duval
distribution	**deux par deux** two by two
	par groupes de dix in groups of ten
	deux fois par jour twice a day

Prepositions

pour

for	**C'est pour vous** It's for you
	C'est pour demain It's for tomorrow
	une chambre pour 2 nuits a room for 2 nights
	Pour un enfant, il se débrouille bien
	For a child he manages very well
	Il part pour l'Espagne He's leaving for Spain
	Il l'a fait pour vous He did it for you
	Il lui a donné 5 euros pour ce livre
	He gave him 5 euros for this book
	Je ne suis pas pour cette idée I'm not for that idea
	Pour qui me prends-tu? Who do you take me for?
	Il passe pour un idiot He's taken for a fool
+ *infinitive*: (in order) to	**Elle se pencha pour le ramasser**
	She bent down to pick it up
	C'est trop fragile pour servir de siège
	It's too fragile to be used as a seat
to(wards)	**être bon/gentil pour qn** to be kind to sb
with *prices, time*	**pour 30 euros d'essence** 30 euros' worth of petrol
	J'en ai encore pour une heure
	I'll be another hour (at it) yet

sans

without	**sans eau** without water
	sans ma femme without my wife
+ *infinitive*	**sans compter les autres**
	without counting the others

Prepositions

sauf

except (for)
    tous sauf lui all except him
    sauf quand il pleut except when it's raining

barring
    sauf imprévu barring the unexpected
    sauf avis contraire
      unless you hear to the contrary

sur

on
    sur le siège on the seat
    sur l'armoire on top of the wardrobe
    sur le mur on (top of) the wall
    (*if the meaning is* 'hanging on the wall' *use* **à**, *page 204*)
    sur votre gauche on your left
    être sur le point de faire
      to be on the point of doing

on (to)
    mettez-le sur la table put it on the table

out of, by (*proportion*)
    8 sur 10 8 out of 10
    un automobiliste sur 5 one motorist in 5
    la pièce fait 2 mètres sur 3
      the room measures 2 metres by 3

Conjunctions

Coordinating conjunctions introduce a main clause, e.g. **et** (and), **mais** (but), **si** (if), **ou** (or) and **donc** (so), while subordinating conjunctions introduce subordinate clauses, e.g. **parce que** (because), **pendant que** (while), **après que** (after) and **lorsque** (when). They are all used in much the same way as in English, but the following points are of note:

Some conjunctions in French require a following subjunctive, see page 58

Some conjunctions are 'split' in French like 'both ... and', 'either ... or' in English:

et ... et both ... and → **①**
ni ... ni ... ne neither ... nor → **②**
ou (bien) ... ou (bien) either ... or (else) → **③**
soit ... soit either ... or → **④**

si + il(s) → s'il(s) → **⑤**

que
- meaning *that* → **⑥**
- replacing another conjunction → **⑦**
- replacing **si**, see page 62
- in comparisons, meaning 'as', 'than' → **⑧**
- followed by the subjunctive, see page 62

aussi (so, therefore): the subject and verb are inverted if the subject is a pronoun → **⑨**

Examples

1 Ces fleurs poussent et en été et
  en hiver

These flowers grow in both
  summer and winter

2 Ni lui ni elle ne sont venus
  Ils n'ont ni argent ni nourriture

Neither he nor she came
They have neither money nor
  food

3 Elle doit être ou naïve ou stupide

She must be either naïve or
  stupid

Ou bien il m'évite ou bien il ne
  me reconnaît pas

Either he's avoiding me or (else)
  he doesn't recognize me

4 Il faut choisir soit l'un soit l'autre

You have to choose either one or
  the other

5 Je ne sais pas s'il vient/s'ils
  viennent
Dis-moi s'il y a des erreurs
Votre passeport, s'il vous plaît

I don't know if he's coming/if
  they're coming
Tell me if there are any mistakes
Your passport, please

6 Il dit qu'il t'a vu
Est-ce qu'elle sait que vous
  êtes là?

He says (that) he saw you
Does she know that you're here?

7 Quand tu seras plus grand et que
  tu auras une maison à toi, ...
Comme il pleuvait et que je
  n'avais pas de parapluie, ...

When you're older and you have
  a house of your own, ...
As it was raining and I didn't
  have an umbrella, ...

8 Ils n'y vont pas aussi souvent que
  nous
Il les aime plus que jamais
L'argent est moins lourd que le
  plomb

They don't go there as often as
  we do
He likes them more than ever
Silver is lighter than lead

9 Ceux-ci sont plus rares, aussi
  coûtent-ils cher

These ones are rarer, so they're
  expensive

Sentence structure

Word Order

Word order in French is largely the same as in English, except for the following points. Most of these have already been dealt with under the appropriate part of speech, but are summarized here along with other instances not covered elsewhere.

> Object pronouns nearly always come before the verb → ❶
> For details, see pages 166 to 170

> Certain adjectives come after the noun → ❷
> For details, see page 162

> Adverbs accompanying a verb in a simple tense usually follow the verb → ❸
> For details, see page 200

> After **aussi** (so, therefore), **à peine** (hardly), **peut-être** (perhaps), the verb and subject are inverted → ❹

> After the relative pronoun **dont** (whose), word order can affect the meaning → ❺
> For details, see page 182

> In exclamations, **que** and **comme** do not affect the normal word order → ❻

> Following direct speech:
> * the *verb + subject* order is inverted to become *subject + verb* → ❼
> * with a pronoun subject, the verb and pronoun are linked by a hyphen → ❽
> * when the verb ends in a vowel in the third person singular, **-t-** is inserted between the pronoun and the verb → ❾

For word order in negative sentences, see page 216.

For word order in interrogative sentences, see pages 220 and 222.

Examples

① Je les vois!
    Il me l'a donné

I can see them!
He gave it to me

② une ville française
    du vin rouge

a French town
some red wine

③ Il pleut encore
    Elle m'aide quelquefois

It's still raining
She sometimes helps me

④ Il vit tout seul, aussi fait-il ce
    qu'il veut
    À peine la pendule avait-elle
    sonné trois heures que ...
    Peut-être avez-vous raison

He lives alone, so he does what
    he likes
Hardly had the clock struck
    three when ...
Perhaps you're right

⑤ Compare:
    un homme dont je connais la fille   a man whose daughter I know
    and:
    un homme dont la fille me   a man whose daughter knows
    connaît   me

If the person (or object) 'owned' is the object of the verb, the order is:
    dont + *verb* + *noun* (*first sentence*)
If the person (or object) 'owned' is the subject of the verb, the order is:
    dont + *noun* + *verb* (*second sentence*)
Note also:
    l'homme dont elle est la fille   the man whose daughter she is

⑥ Qu'il fait chaud!
    Que je suis content de vous voir!
    Comme c'est cher
    Que tes voisins sont gentils!

How warm it is!
How pleased I am to see you!
How expensive it is!
How kind your neighbours are!

⑦ «Je pense que oui» a dit Luc
    «Ça ne fait rien» répondit Julie

'I think so,' said Luc
'It doesn't matter,' Julie replied

⑧ «Quelle horreur!» me suis-je
    exclamé

'How awful!' I exclaimed

⑨ «Pourquoi pas?» a-t-elle demandé
    «Si c'est vrai» continua-t-il ...

'Why not?' she asked
'If it's true,' he went on ...

Sentence structure

Negatives

The following are the most common negative pairs:

> ne ... **pas** not
> ne ... **point** (*literary*) not
> ne ... **rien** nothing
> ne ... **personne** nobody
> ne ... **plus** no longer, no more
> ne ... **jamais** never
> ne ... **que** only
> ne ... **aucun(e)** no
> ne ... **nul(le)** no
> ne ... **nulle part** nowhere
> ne ... **ni** neither ... nor
> ne ... **ni ... ni** neither ... nor

Word order

In simple tenses and the imperative:

- **ne** precedes the verb (and any object pronouns) and the second element follows the verb → **❶**

In compound tenses:

- **ne ... pas**, **ne ... point**, **ne ... rien**, **ne ... plus**, **ne ... jamais**, **ne ... guère** follow the pattern:
  ne + *auxiliary verb* + **pas** + *past participle* → **❷**
- **ne ... personne**, **ne ... que**, **ne ... aucun(e)**, **ne ... nul(le)**, **ne ... nulle part**, **ne ... ni (... ni)** follow the pattern:
  ne + *auxiliary verb* + *past participle* + **personne** → **❸**

With a verb in the infinitive:

- **ne ... pas**, **ne ... point** (*etc*, see above) come together → **❹**

For use of **rien**, **personne** and **aucun** as pronouns, see page 178.

Examples

❶ Je ne fume pas   I don't smoke
  Ne changez rien   Don't change anything
  Je ne vois personne   I can't see anybody
  Nous ne nous verrons plus   We won't see each other any more

  Il n'arrive jamais à l'heure   He never arrives on time
  Il n'avait qu'une valise   He only had one suitcase
  Je n'ai reçu aucune réponse   I have received no reply
  Il ne boit ni ne fume   He neither drinks nor smokes
  Ni mon fils ni ma fille ne les connaissaient   Neither my son nor my daughter knew them

❷ Elle n'a pas fait ses devoirs   She hasn't done her homework
  Ne vous a-t-il rien dit?   Didn't he say anything to you?
  Ils n'avaient jamais vu une si belle maison   They had never seen such a beautiful house

❸ Tu n'as guère changé   You've hardly changed

  Je n'ai parlé à personne   I haven't spoken to anybody
  Il n'avait mangé que la moitié du repas   He had only eaten half the meal
  Elle ne les a trouvés nulle part   She couldn't find them anywhere
  Il ne l'avait ni vu ni entendu   He had neither seen nor heard him

❹ Il essayait de ne pas rire   He was trying not to laugh

Sentence structure

Negatives *continued*

These are the most common combinations of negative particles:

> ne ... plus jamais → ❶
> ne ... plus personne → ❷
> ne ... plus rien → ❸
> ne ... plus ni ... ni ... → ❹
> ne ... jamais personne → ❺
> ne ... jamais rien → ❻
> ne ... jamais que → ❼
> ne ... jamais ni ... ni ... → ❽
> (ne ... pas) non plus → ❾

non and pas

non (no) is the usual negative response to a question → ❿
It is often translated as 'not' → ⓫

pas is generally used when a distinction is being made, or for emphasis → ⓬
It is often translated as 'not' → ⓭

Examples

1 Je ne le ferai plus jamais — I'll never do it again

2 Je ne connais plus personne à Rouen — I don't know anybody in Rouen any more

3 Ces marchandises ne valaient plus rien — Those goods were no longer worth anything

4 Ils n'ont plus ni chats ni chiens — They no longer have either cats or dogs

5 On n'y voit jamais personne — You never see anybody there

6 Ils ne font jamais rien d'intéressant — They never do anything interesting

7 Je n'ai jamais parlé qu'à sa femme — I've only ever spoken to his wife

8 Il ne m'a jamais ni écrit ni téléphoné — He has never either written to me or phoned me

9 Ils n'ont pas d'enfants et nous non plus — They don't have any children and neither do we
Je ne les aime pas. – Moi non plus. — I don't like them. – Neither do I / I don't either.

10 Vous voulez nous accompagner? – Non. — Do you want to come with us? – No (I don't).

11 Tu viens ou non? — Are you coming or not?
J'espère que non — I hope not

12 Ma sœur aime le ski, moi pas — My sister likes skiing, I don't

13 Qui a fait ça? – Pas moi! — Who did that? – Not me!
Est-il de retour? – Pas encore. — Is he back? – Not yet.
Tu as froid? – Pas du tout. — Are you cold? – Not at all.

Sentence structure

Question Forms: Direct

There are four ways of forming direct questions in French:

by inverting the normal word order so that *pronoun subject + verb* becomes *verb + pronoun subject*. A hyphen links the verb and pronoun → ❶

- When the subject is a noun, a pronoun is inserted after the verb and linked to it by a hyphen → ❷
- When the verb ends in a vowel in the third person singular, **-t-** is inserted before the pronoun → ❸

by maintaining the word order *subject + verb*, but by using a rising intonation at the end of the sentence → ❹

by inserting **est-ce que** before the construction *subject + verb* → ❺

by using an interrogative word at the beginning of the sentence, together with inversion or the **est-ce que** form above → ❻

Examples

① **Aimez-vous la France?**   Do you like France?
  Avez-vous fini?   Have you finished?
  Est-ce possible?   Is it possible?
  Est-elle restée?   Did she stay?
  Part-on tout de suite?   Are we leaving right away?

② **Tes parents sont-ils en vacances?**   Are your parents on holiday?
  Jean-Benoît est-il parti?   Has Jean-Benoît left?

③ **A-t-elle de l'argent?**   Has she any money?
  La pièce dure-t-elle longtemps?   Does the play last long?
  Mon père a-t-il téléphoné?   Has my father phoned?

④ **Il l'a fini**   He's finished it
  Il l'a fini?   Has he finished it?
  Robert va venir   Robert's coming
  Robert va venir?   Is Robert coming?

⑤ **Est-ce que tu la connais?**   Do you know her?
  Est-ce que tes parents sont revenus d'Italie?   Have your parents come back from Italy?

⑥ **Quel train prends-tu?**
  Quel train est-ce que tu prends?   What train are you getting?

  Lequel est-ce que ta sœur préfère?
  Lequel ta sœur préfère-t-elle?   Which one does your sister prefer?

  Quand êtes-vous arrivé?
  Quand est-ce que vous êtes arrivé?   When did you arrive?

  Pourquoi ne sont-ils pas venus?
  Pourquoi est-ce qu'ils ne sont pas venus?   Why haven't they come?

Sentence structure

Question Forms: Indirect

An indirect question is one that is 'reported', e.g. 'he asked me what the time was'; 'tell me which way to go'. Word order in indirect questions is as follows:

> *interrogative word + subject + verb* → **❶**

> when the subject is a noun, and not a pronoun, the subject and verb are often inverted → **❷**

n'est-ce pas

This is used wherever English would use 'isn't it?', 'don't they?', 'weren't we?', 'is it?' and so on tagged on to the end of a sentence → **❸**

oui and si

Oui is the word for 'yes' in answer to a question put in the affirmative → **❹**

Si is the word for 'yes' in answer to a question put in the negative or to contradict a negative statement → **❺**

Examples

① Je me demande s'il viendra — I wonder if he'll come

Je ne sais pas à quoi ça sert — I don't know what it's for

Dites-moi quel autobus va à la gare — Tell me which bus goes to the station

Il m'a demandé combien d'argent j'avais — He asked me how much money I had

② Elle ne sait pas à quelle heure commence le film — She doesn't know what time the film starts

Je me demande où sont mes clés — I wonder where my keys are

Elle nous a demandé comment allait notre père — She asked us how our father was

Je ne sais pas ce que veulent dire ces mots — I don't know what these words mean

③ Il fait chaud, n'est-ce pas? — It's warm, isn't it?

Vous n'oublierez pas, n'est-ce pas? — You won't forget, will you?

④ Tu l'as fait? – Oui. — Have you done it? – Yes (I have).

⑤ Tu ne l'as pas fait? – Si. — Haven't you done it? – Yes (I have).

Numbers

Cardinal (one, two *etc*)		Ordinal (first, second *etc*)	
zéro	0		
un (une)	1	premier (première)	1er, 1ère
deux	2	deuxième, second(e)	2ème
trois	3	troisième	3ème
quatre	4	quatrième	4ème
cinq	5	cinquième	5ème
six	6	sixième	6ème
sept	7	septième	7ème
huit	8	huitième	8ème
neuf	9	neuvième	9ème
dix	10	dixième	10ème
onze	11	onzième	11ème
douze	12	douzième	12ème
treize	13	treizième	13ème
quatorze	14	quatorzième	14ème
quinze	15	quinzième	15ème
seize	16	seizième	16ème
dix-sept	17	dix-septième	17ème
dix-huit	18	dix-huitième	18ème
dix-neuf	19	dix-neuvième	19ème
vingt	20	vingtième	20ème
vingt et un (une)	21	vingt et unième	21ème
vingt-deux	22	vingt-deuxième	22ème
vingt-trois	23	vingt-troisième	23ème
trente	30	trentième	30ème
quarante	40	quarantième	40ème
cinquante	50	cinquantième	50ème
soixante	60	soixantième	60ème
soixante-dix	70	soixante-dixième	70ème
soixante et onze	71	soixante et onzième	71ème
soixante-douze	72	soixante-douzième	72ème
quatre-vingts	80	quatre-vingtième	80ème
quatre-vingt-un (une)	81	quatre-vingt-unième	81ème
quatre-vingt-dix	90	quatre-vingt-dixième	90ème
quatre-vingt-onze	91	quatre-vingt-onzième	91ème

Numbers

Cardinal

cent	100
cent un (une)	101
cent deux	102
cent dix	110
cent quarante-deux	142
deux cents	200
deux cent un (une)	201
deux cent deux	202
trois cents	300
quatre cents	400
cinq cents	500
six cents	600
sept cents	700
huit cents	800
neuf cents	900
mille	1000
mille un (une)	1001
mille deux	1002
deux mille	2000
cent mille	100.000
un million	1.000.000
deux millions	2.000.000

Ordinal

centième	100^e
cent unième	101^e
cent deuxième	102^e
cent dixième	110^e
cent quarante-deuxième	142^e
deux centième	200^e
deux cent unième	201^e
deux cent deuxième	202^e
trois centième	300^e
quatre centième	400^e
cinq centième	500^e
six centième	600^e
sept centième	700^e
huit centième	800^e
neuf centième	900^e
millième	1000^e
mille unième	1001^e
mille deuxième	1002^e
deux millième	2000^e
cent millième	100.000^e
millionième	1.000.000^e
deux millionième	2.000.000^e

Fractions

un demi, une demie	a half
un tiers	a third
deux tiers	two thirds
un quart	a quarter
trois quarts	three quarters
un cinquième	one fifth
cinq et trois quarts five and three quarters	

Others

zéro virgule cinq (0,5)	0.5
un virgule trois (1,3)	1.3
dix pour cent	10%
deux plus deux	2 + 2
deux moins deux	2 − 2
deux fois deux	2 × 2
deux divisé par deux	2 ÷ 2

(i) Note that while points are sometimes used with large numbers, commas are always used with fractions, i.e. the opposite of English usage.

Numbers

Other Uses

-aine denoting approximate numbers:

> **une douzaine (de pommes)** about a dozen (apples)
> **une quinzaine (d'hommes)** about fifteen (men)
> **des centaines de personnes** hundreds of people
> BUT: **un millier (de voitures)** about a thousand (cars)

measurements:

> **vingt mètres carrés** 20 square metres
> **vingt mètres cubes** 20 cubic metres
> **un pont long de quarante mètres** a bridge 40 metres long
> **avoir trois mètres de large/de haut** to be 3 metres wide/ high

miscellaneous:

> **Il habite au dix** He lives at number 10
> **C'est au chapitre sept** It's in chapter 7
> **(C'est) à la page 17** (It's) on page 17
> **(Il habite) au septième étage** (He lives) on the seventh floor
> **Il est arrivé le septième** He came in seventh
> **échelle au vingt-cinq millième** scale 1:25,000

Telephone numbers

Je voudrais le soixante-cinq, treize, vingt-deux, zéro deux
  Could you get me 65 13 22 02
Poste trois cent trente-cinq Extension number 335
Poste vingt-deux, trente-trois Extension number 22 33

ⓘ In French, telephone numbers are broken down into groups of two
  or three numbers (never four), and are not spoken separately as in
  English. They are also written in groups of two or three numbers.

Numbers

Calendar

Dates

Quelle est la date d'aujourd'hui? **Quel jour sommes-nous?**	What's the date today?

C'est ... **Nous sommes ...**	It's the ...
... **le premier février**	... 1st of February
... **le deux février**	... 2nd of February
... **le vingt-huit février**	... 28th of February

Il vient le sept mars	He's coming on the 7th of March

ⓘ Use cardinal numbers except for the first of the month.

Years

Elle est née en 1930	She was born in 1930
le douze février mille neuf cent trente **le douze février mil neuf cent trente**	(on) 12th February 1930

ⓘ There are two ways of expressing the year (see last example). Note the spelling of **mil** (one thousand) in dates.

Other expressions

dans les années cinquante	during the fifties
au vingtième siècle	in the twentieth century
en mai	in May
lundi (quinze)	on Monday (the 15th)
le lundi	on Mondays
dans dix jours	in ten days' time
il y a dix jours	ten days ago

Numbers

Time

Quelle heure est-il? Il est ...	What time is it? It's ...

00.00	**minuit** midnight, twelve o'clock
00.10	**minuit dix, zéro heure dix**
00.15	**minuit et quart, zéro heure quinze**
00.30	**minuit et demi, zéro heure trente**
00.45	**une heure moins (le) quart, zéro heure quarante-cinq**
01.00	**une heure du matin** one a.m., one o'clock in the morning
01.10	**une heure dix (du matin)**
01.15	**une heure et quart, une heure quinze**
01.30	**une heure et demie, une heure trente**
01.45	**deux heures moins (le) quart, une heure quarante-cinq**
01.50	**deux heures moins dix, une heure cinquante**
01.59	**deux heures moins une, une heure cinquante-neuf**
12.00	**midi, douze heures** noon, twelve o'clock
12.30	**midi et demi, douze heures trente**
13.00	**une heure de l'après-midi, treize heures** one p.m., one o'clock in the afternoon
01.30	**une heure et demie (de l'après-midi), treize heures trente**
19.00	**sept heures du soir, dix-neuf heures** seven p.m., seven o'clock in the evening
19.30	**sept heures et demie (du soir), dix-neuf heures trente**

Examples

À quelle heure venez-vous?
  – À sept heures.
	What time are you coming?
	  – At seven o'clock.

Les bureaux sont fermés de midi à quatorze heures	The offices are closed from twelve until two
à deux heures du matin/de l'après-midi	at two o'clock in the morning/afternoon; at two a.m./p.m.
à sept heures du soir	at seven o'clock in the evening; at seven p.m.
à cinq heures précises *or* **pile**	at five o'clock sharp
vers neuf heures	about nine o'clock
peu avant/après midi	shortly before/after noon
entre huit et neuf heures	between eight and nine o'clock
Il est plus de trois heures et demie	It's after half past three
Il faut y être à dix heures au plus tard/au plus tôt	You have to be there by ten o'clock at the latest/earliest
Ne venez pas plus tard que onze heures moins le quart	Come no later than a quarter to eleven
Il en a pour une demi-heure	He'll be half an hour (at it)
Elle est restée sans connaissance pendant un quart d'heure	She was unconscious for (a) quarter of an hour
Je les attends depuis une heure	I've been waiting for them for an hour/since one o'clock
Ils sont partis il y a quelques minutes	They left a few minutes ago
Je l'ai fait en vingt minutes	I did it in twenty minutes
Le train arrive dans une heure	The train arrives in an hour('s time)
Combien de temps dure ce film?	How long does this film last?

Translation problems

Beware of translating word for word. While on occasion this is quite possible, quite often it is not. The need for caution is illustrated by the following:

English phrasal verbs (i.e. verbs followed by a preposition) e.g. 'to run away', 'to fall down' are often translated by one word in French → ❶

English verbal constructions often contain a preposition where none exists in French, or vice versa → ❷

Two or more prepositions in English may have a single rendering in French → ❸

A word which is singular in English may be plural in French, or vice versa → ❹

French has no equivalent of the possessive construction denoted by '-'s/-s' → ❺

See also at/in/to, page 234.

The following pages look at some specific problems.

-ing

This is translated in a variety of ways in French:

'to be ...-ing' is translated by a simple verb → ❻
EXCEPTION: when a physical position is denoted, a past participle is used → ❼

in the construction 'to see/hear sb ...-ing', use an infinitive or **qui** + *verb* → ❽

'-ing' can also be translated by:
- an infinitive: see page 44 → ❾
- a perfect infinitive: see page 46 → ❿
- a present participle: see page 48 → ⓫
- a noun → ⓬

Examples

❶ s'enfuir — to run away
tomber — to fall down
céder — to give in

❷ payer — to pay for
regarder — to look at
écouter — to listen to
obéir à — to obey
nuire à — to harm
manquer de — to lack

❸ s'étonner de — to be surprised at
satisfait de — satisfied with
voler qch à — to steal sth from
apte à — capable of; fit for

❹ les bagages — the luggage
ses cheveux — his/her hair
le bétail — the cattle
mon pantalon — my trousers

❺ la voiture de mon frère — my brother's car (*literally*: ... of my brother)

la chambre des enfants — the children's bedroom (*literally*: ... of the children)

❻ Il part demain — He's leaving tomorrow
Je lisais un roman — I was reading a novel

❼ Elle est assise là-bas — She's sitting over there
Il était couché par terre — He was lying on the ground

❽ Je les vois venir — I can see them coming
Je les vois qui viennent
Je l'ai entendue chanter — I heard her singing
Je l'ai entendue qui chantait

❾ J'aime aller au cinéma — I like going to the cinema
Arrêtez de parler! — Stop talking!
Au lieu de répondre — Instead of answering
Avant de partir — Before leaving

❿ Après avoir ouvert la boîte, il ... — After opening the box, he ...

⓫ Étant plus timide que moi, elle ... — Being shyer than me, she ...

⓬ Le ski me maintient en forme — Skiing keeps me fit

231

Translation problems

to be

'to be' is generally translated by **être** → **1**

When physical location is implied, **se trouver** may be used → **2**

In set expressions, describing physical and emotional conditions, **avoir** is used:
      avoir chaud/froid to be warm/cold
      avoir faim/soif to be hungry/thirsty
      avoir peur/honte to be afraid/ashamed
      avoir tort/raison to be wrong/right

Describing the weather, e.g. what's the weather like?, it's windy/sunny, use **faire** → **3**

For ages, e.g. he is 6, use **avoir** → **4**

For state of health, e.g. he's unwell, how are you?, use **aller** → **5**

it is, it's

'It is' and 'it's' are usually translated by **il/elle est**, when referring to a noun → **6**

For expressions of time, also use **il est** → **7**

To describe the weather, e.g. it's windy, see above.

In the construction: it is difficult/easy to do sth, use **il est** → **8**

In all other constructions, use **c'est** → **9**

can, be able

Physical ability is expressed by **pouvoir** → **10**

If the meaning is 'to know how to', use **savoir** → **11**

'can' + a 'verb of hearing or seeing *etc*' in English is not translated in French → **12**

Examples

1. **Il est tard**
   It's late
   C'est peu probable
   It's not very likely

2. **Où se trouve la gare?**
   Where's the station?
   Quel temps fait-il?
   What's the weather like?

3. **Il fait beau/mauvais/du vent**
   It's lovely/miserable/windy

4. **Quel âge avez-vous?**
   How old are you?
   J'ai quinze ans
   I'm fifteen

5. **Comment allez-vous?**
   How are you?
   Je vais très bien
   I'm very well
   Où est mon parapluie? – Il est là, dans le coin.
   Where's my umbrella? – It's there, in the corner.

6. **Descends la valise si elle n'est pas trop lourde**
   Bring down the case if it isn't too heavy

7. **Quelle heure est-il? – Il est sept heures et demie.**
   What's the time? – It's half past seven.

8. **Il est difficile de répondre à cette question**
   It's difficult to reply to this question

9. **C'est moi qui ne l'aime pas**
   It's me who doesn't like him
   C'est Charles/ma mère qui l'a dit
   It's Charles/my mother who said so
   C'est ici que je les ai achetés
   It's here that I bought them
   C'est parce que la poste est fermée que ...
   It's because the post office is closed that ...

10. **Pouvez-vous atteindre cette étagère?**
    Can you reach up to that shelf?

11. **Elle ne sait pas nager**
    She can't swim
    Je ne vois rien
    I can't see anything

12. **Il les entendait**
    He could hear them

Translation problems

to (*see also below*)

'to' is generally translated by **à**: see page 204 → **❶**

In time expressions, e.g. 10 to 6, use **moins** → **❷**

When the meaning is 'in order to', use **pour** → **❸**

Following a verb, as in 'to try to do', 'to like to do': see pages 44 and 64

'easy/difficult/impossible' *etc* to do: the preposition used depends on whether a specific noun is referred to → **❹** or not → **❺**

at/in/to

With feminine countries, use **en** → **❻**

With masculine countries, use **au** (**aux** with plural countries) → **❼**

With towns, use **à** → **❽**

'at/to the butcher's/grocer's' *etc*: use **à** + *noun* designating the shop, or **chez** + *noun* designating the shopkeeper → **❾**

'at/to the dentist's/doctor's' *etc*: use **chez** → **❿**

'at/to -'s/-s' house': use **chez** → **⓫**

there is/there are

Both are translated by **il y a** → **⓬**

Examples

❶	**Donne le livre à Patrick**	Give the book to Patrick
❷	**dix heures moins cinq**	five to ten
	à sept heures moins le quart	at a quarter to seven
❸	**Je l'ai fait pour vous aider**	I did it to help you
	Il se pencha pour nouer son lacet	He bent down to tie his shoelace
❹	**Ce livre est difficile à lire**	This book is difficult to read
❺	**Il est difficile de comprendre leurs raisons**	It's difficult to understand their reasons
❻	**Il est allé en France/en Suisse**	He has gone to France/to Switzerland
	un village en Norvège/en Belgique	a village in Norway/in Belgium
❼	**Êtes-vous allé au Canada/au Danemark/aux États-Unis?**	Have you been to Canada/to Denmark/to the United States?
	une ville au Japon/au Brésil	a town in Japan/in Brazil
❽	**Il est allé à Vienne/à Bruxelles**	He has gone to Vienna/to Brussels
	Il habite à Londres/à Genève	He lives in London/in Geneva
	Ils logent dans un hôtel à St Pierre	They're staying in a hotel at St Pierre
❾	**Je l'ai acheté à l'épicerie**	I bought it at the grocer's
	Je l'ai acheté chez l'épicier	
	Elle est allée à la boulangerie	She's gone to the baker's
	Elle est allée chez le boulanger	
❿	**J'ai un rendez-vous chez le dentiste**	I've an appointment at the dentist's
	Il est allé chez le médecin	He has gone to the doctor's
⓫	**chez Christian**	at/to Christian's house
	chez les Pagot	at/to the Pagots' house
⓬	**Il y a quelqu'un à la porte**	There's somebody at the door
	Il y a cinq livres sur la table	There are five books on the table

235

Pronunciation

General Points

Activity of the lips

The lips play a very important part in French. When a vowel is described as having 'rounded' lips, the lips are slightly drawn together and pursed, as when an English speaker expresses exaggerated surprise with the vowel 'ooh!' Equally, if the lips are said to be 'spread', the corners are pulled firmly back towards the cheeks, tending to reveal the front teeth.

In English, lip position is not important, and vowel sounds tend to merge because of this. In French, the activity of the lips means that every vowel sound is clearly distinct from every other.

No diphthongs

A diphthong is a glide between two vowel sounds in the same syllable. In English, there are few 'pure' vowel sounds, but largely diphthongs instead. Although speakers of English may think they produce one vowel sound in the word 'day', in fact they use a diphthong, which in this instance is a glide between the vowels [e] and [ɪ]: [deɪ]. In French the tension maintained in the lips, tongue and the mouth in general prevents diphthongs occurring, as the vowel sound is kept constant throughout. Hence the French word corresponding to the above example, '**dé**', is pronounced with no final [ɪ] sound, but is phonetically represented thus: [de].

Consonants

In English, consonants are often pronounced with a degree of laxness that can result in their practically disappearing altogether although not strictly 'silent'. In a relaxed pronunciation of a word such as 'hat', the 't' is often scarcely heard, or is replaced by a 'glottal stop' (a sort of jerk in the throat). This never occurs in French, where consonants are always given their full value.

Pronunciation

Pronunciation of Consonants

Some consonants are pronounced almost exactly as in English:
[b, p, f, v, g, k, m, w].

Most others are similar to English, but slight differences should be noted.

EXAMPLES	HINTS ON PRONUNCIATION
[d] **d**in**d**e	The tip of the tongue touches the upper
[t] **t**en**t**e	front teeth and not the roof of the mouth
[n] **n**o**nn**e	as in English
[l] **L**i**ll**e	
[s] tou**s** **ç**a	The tip of the tongue is down behind the
[z] **z**éro ro**s**e	bottom front teeth, lower than in English
[ʃ] **ch**ose ta**ch**e	Like the 'sh' of English 'shout'
[ʒ] **j**e **g**ilet bei**g**e	Like the 's' of English 'measure'
[j] **y**eux pai**ll**e	Like the 'y' of English 'yes'

Three consonants are not heard in English:

[ʀ] **r**are veni**r**	'r' is often silent in English, e.g. farm. In French the [ʀ] is never silent, unless it follows an **e** at the end of a word e.g. cherch**er**. To pronounce it, try to make a short sound like gargling. Similar, too, to the Scottish pronunciation of 'loch'
[ɲ] vi**gn**e a**gn**eau	Similar to the 'ni' of the English word 'Spaniard'
[ɥ] h**u**ile l**u**eur	Like a very rapid [y] (see page 239) followed immediately by the next vowel of the word

Pronunciation

Pronunciation of Vowels

EXAMPLES	HINTS ON PRONUNCIATION
[a] p**a**tte pl**a**t **a**mour	Similar to the vowel in English 'pat'
[ɑ] b**a**s p**â**te	Longer than the sound above, it resembles the English exclamation of surprise 'ah!' Similar, too, to the English vowel in 'car' without the final 'r' sound
[ɛ] l**ai**t jou**e**t m**e**rci	Similar to the English vowel in 'pet'. Beware of using the English diphthong [eɪ] as in 'pay'
[e] **é**t**é** jou**er**	A pure vowel, again quite different from the diphthong in English 'pay'
[ə] l**e** pr**e**mier	Similar to the English sound in 'butter' when the 'r' is not pronounced
[i] **i**c**i** v**ie** l**y**cée	The lips are well spread towards the cheeks while uttering this sound. Shorter than the English vowel in 'see'
[ɔ] m**o**rt h**o**mme	The lips are well rounded while producing a sound similar to the 'o' of English 'cot'
[o] m**o**t d**ô**me **eau**	A pure vowel with strongly rounded lips quite different from the diphthong in the English words 'bone', 'low'

Pronunciation

	EXAMPLES	HINTS ON PRONUNCIATION
[u]	gen**ou** r**ou**e	A pure vowel with strongly rounded lips. Similar to the English 'ooh!' of surprise
[y]	r**ue** vêt**u**	Often the most difficult for English speakers to produce: round your lips and try to pronounce [i] (see page 238). There is no [j] sound (see page 237) as there is in English 'pure'
[œ]	s**œu**r b**eu**rre	Similar to the vowel in English 'fir' or 'murmur', but without the 'r' sound and with the lips more strongly rounded
[ø]	p**eu** d**eu**x	To pronounce this, try to say [e] (see page 238) with the lips strongly rounded

Nasal vowels

These are spelt with a vowel followed by a 'nasal' consonant – **n** or **m**. The production of nasal vowels really requires the help of a teacher or a recording of the sound. However, to help you, the vowel is pronounced by allowing the air from the lungs to come partly down the nose and partly through the mouth, and the **n** or **m** is not pronounced at all.

	EXAMPLES	
[ã]	l**en**t s**an**g d**an**s	In each case, the vowel shown in the
[ɛ̃]	mat**in** pl**ein**	phonetic symbol is pronounced as
[ɔ̃]	n**on** p**on**t	described above, but air is allowed to come
[œ̃]	br**un** **un** parf**um**	through the nose as well as the mouth

Pronunciation

From Spelling to Sounds

Although it may not seem so at first sight, there are some fairly precise 'rules' which can help you to know how to pronounce French words from their spelling.

Vowels

SPELLING	PRONOUNCED	EXAMPLES
a, à	[a]	chatte table à
a, â	[ɑ]	pâte pas
er, é	[e]	été marcher
e, è, ê	[ɛ]	fenêtre fermer chère
e	[ə]	double fenêtre
i, î, y	[i]	lit abîmer lycée
o, ô	[o]	pot trop dôme
o	[ɔ]	sotte orange
u, û	[y]	battu fût pur

Vowel groups

There are several groups of vowels in French spelling which are regularly pronounced in the same way:

SPELLING	PRONOUNCED	EXAMPLES
ai	[ɛ] or [e]	maison marchai faire
ail	[aj]	portail
ain, aim, (e)in, im	[ɛ̃]	pain faim frein impair
au	[o]	auberge landau
an, am, en, em	[ɑ̃]	plan ample entrer temps
eau	[o]	bateau eau
eu	[œ] or [ø]	feu peur
euil(le), ueil	[œj]	feuille recueil
oi, oy	[wa]	voir voyage
on, om	[ɔ̃]	ton compter
ou	[u]	hibou outil
œu	[œ]	sœur cœur
ue	[y]	rue
un, um	[œ̃]	brun parfum

Pronunciation

Added to these are the many groups of letters occurring at the end of words, where their pronunciation is predictable, bearing in mind the tendency (see page 242) of final consonants to remain silent.

TYPICAL WORDS	PRONUNCIATION OF FINAL SYLLABLE
pas, mât, chat	[ɑ] or [a]
marcher, marchez, marchais, marchait, baie, valet, mes, fumée	[e] or [ɛ]
nid	[i]
chaud, vaut, faux, sot, tôt, Pernod, dos, croc	[o]
bout, bijoux, sous, boue	[u]
fut, fût, crus, crûs	[y]
queue, heureux, bleus	[ø]
en, vend, vent, an, sang, grand, dans	[ɑ̃]
fin, feint, frein, vain	[ɛ̃]
on, pont, fond, avons	[ɔ̃]
brun, parfum	[œ̃]

Pronunciation

From Spelling to Sounds *continued*

Consonants

Final consonants are usually silent → **❶**

n or **m** at the end of a syllable or word are silent, but they have the effect of 'nasalizing' the preceding vowel(s) (see page 239 on Nasal Vowels).

The letter **h** is either 'silent' ('mute') or 'aspirate' when it begins a word. When silent, the word behaves as though it started with a vowel and takes a liaison with the preceding word where appropriate.

When the **h** is aspirate, no liaison is made → **❷**

There is no way of predicting which words start with which sort of **h** – this simply has to be learnt with each word

The following consonants in spelling have predictable pronunciations: b, d, f, k, l, p, r, t, v, w, x, y, z.

Others vary:

SPELLING	PRONOUNCED	ENGLISH EXAMPLES
c + a, o, u	[k]	can cot cut → **❸**
+ l, r		class cram
c + e, i, y	[s]	ceiling ice → **❹**
ç + a, o, u	[s]	ceiling ice → **❺**
ch	[ʃ]	shop lash → **❻**
g + a, o, u	[g]	gate got gun → **❼**
+ l, r		glass gramme
g + e, i, y	[ʒ]	leisure → **❽**
gn	[ɲ]	companion onion → **❾**
j	[ʒ]	measure → **❿**
q, qu	[k]	quay kit → **⓫**
s (*between vowels*)	[z]	rose → **⓬**
s (*elsewhere*)	[s]	sit
th	[t]	Thomas → **⓭**
t in -tion	[s]	sit → **⓮**

Examples

① **éclat** [ekla] **nez** [ne]
 chaud [ʃo] **aider** [ɛde]

② silent h: aspirate h:
 des hôtels [de zotɛl] **des haricots** [de aʀiko]

③ **café** [kafe] **côte** [kot] **culture** [kyltyʀ]
 classe [klas] **croûte** [kʀut]

④ **ceci** [səsi] **cil** [sil] **cycliste** [siklist]

⑤ **ça** [sa] **garçon** [gaʀsɔ̃] **déçu** [desy]

⑥ **chat** [ʃa] **riche** [ʀiʃ]

⑦ **gare** [gaʀ] **gourde** [guʀd] **aigu** [ɛgy]
 glaise [glɛz] **gramme** [gʀam]

⑧ **gemme** [ʒem] **gilet** [ʒilɛ] **gymnaste** [ʒimnast]

⑨ **vigne** [viɲ] **oignon** [ɔɲɔ̃]

⑩ **joli** [ʒɔli] **Jules** [ʒyl]

⑪ **quiche** [kiʃ] **quitter** [kite]

⑫ **sable** [sablə] **maison** [mɛzɔ̃]

⑬ **théâtre** [teɑtʀ] **Thomas** [tɔma]

⑭ **nation** [nasjɔ̃] **action** [aksjɔ̃]

Pronunciation

Feminine Forms and Pronunciation

For adjectives and nouns ending in a vowel in the masculine, the addition of an **e** to form the feminine does not alter the pronunciation → ❶

If the masculine ends with a silent consonant, generally **-d**, **-s**, **-r** or **-t**, the consonant is sounded in the feminine → ❷
This also applies when the final consonant is doubled before the addition of the feminine **e** → ❸

If the masculine ends in a nasal vowel and a silent **n**, e.g. **-an**, **-on**, **-in**, the vowel is no longer nasalized and the **-n** is pronounced in the feminine → ❹
This also applies when the final **-n** is doubled before the addition of the feminine **e** → ❺

Where the masculine and feminine forms have totally different endings (see pages 136 and 150), the pronunciation of course varies accordingly → ❻

Plural Forms and Pronunciation

The addition of **s** or **x** to form regular plurals generally does not affect pronunciation → ❼

Where liaison has to be made, the final **-s** or **-x** of the plural form is pronounced → ❽

Where the masculine singular and plural forms have totally different endings (see pages 138 and 148), the pronunciation of course varies accordingly → ❾

Note the change in pronunciation in the following nouns:

SINGULAR		PLURAL	
bœuf [bœf]	ox	**bœufs** [bø]	oxen
œuf [œf]	egg	**œufs** [ø]	eggs
os [ɔs]	bone	**os** [o]	bones

Examples

ADJECTIVES

NOUNS

❶ joli [ʒɔli] → jolie [ʒɔli]
déçu [desy] → déçue [desy]

un ami [ami] → une amie [ami]
un employé [ɑ̃plwaje] →
une employée [ɑ̃plwaje]

❷ chaud [ʃo] → chaude [ʃod]

français [fʀɑ̃sɛ] →
française [fʀɑ̃sɛz]
inquiet [ɛ̃kjɛ] →
inquiète [ɛ̃kjɛt]

un étudiant [etydjɑ̃] →
une étudiante [etydjɑ̃t]
un Anglais [ɑ̃glɛ] →
une Anglaise [ɑ̃glɛz]
un étranger [etʀɑ̃ʒe] →
une étrangère [etʀɑ̃ʒɛʀ]

❸ violet [vjɔlɛ] → violette [vjɔlɛt]

gras [gʀɑ] → grasse [gʀɑs]

le cadet [kadɛ] →
la cadette [kadɛt]

❹ plein [plɛ̃] → pleine [plɛn]

fin [fɛ̃] → fine [fin]

brun [bʀœ̃] → brune [bʀyn]

le souverain [suvʀɛ̃] →
la souveraine [suvʀɛn]
Le Persan [pɛʀsɑ̃] →
la Persane [pɛʀsan]
le voisin [vwazɛ̃] →
la voisine [vwazin]

❺ canadien [kanadjɛ̃] →
canadienne [kanadjɛn]
breton [bʀətɔ̃] →
bretonne [bʀətɔn]

le paysan [peizɑ̃] →
la paysanne [peizan]
le baron [baʀɔ̃] →
la baronne [baʀɔn]

❻ vif [vif] → vive [viv]
traître [tʀɛtʀə] →
traîtresse [tʀɛtʀɛs]

le veuf [vœf] → la veuve [vœv]
le maître [mɛtʀə] →
la maîtresse [mɛtʀɛs]

❼ beau [bo] → beaux [bo]

la maison [mɛzɔ̃] →
les maisons [mɛzɔ̃]

❽ des anciens élèves
[de zɑ̃sjɛ̃ zelɛv]

de beaux arbres
[də bo zaʀbʀ(ə)]

❾ amical [amikal] →
amicaux [amiko]

un journal [ʒuʀnal] →
des journaux [ʒuʀno]

Alphabet

A, a [ɑ]	**J, j** [ʒi]	**S, s** [ɛs]
B, b [be]	**K, k** [ka]	**T, t** [te]
C, c [se]	**L, l** [ɛl]	**U, u** [y]
D, d [de]	**M, m** [ɛm]	**V, v** [ve]
E, e [ə]	**N, n** [ɛn]	**W, w** [dubləve]
F, f [ɛf]	**O, o** [o]	**X, x** [iks]
G, g [ʒe]	**P, p** [pe]	**Y, y** [igʀɛk]
H, h [aʃ]	**Q, q** [ky]	**Z, z** [zɛd]
I, i [i]	**R, r** [ɛʀ]	

Capital letters are used as in English except for the following:

adjectives of nationality
e.g. **une ville espagnole** a Spanish town
un auteur français a French author

languages
e.g. **Parlez-vous anglais?** Do you speak English?
Il parle français et allemand He speaks French and German

days of the week:
lundi Monday
mardi Tuesday
mercredi Wednesday
jeudi Thursday
vendredi Friday
samedi Saturday
dimanche Sunday

months of the year:
janvier January	**juillet** July
février February	**août** August
mars March	**septembre** September
avril April	**octobre** October
mai May	**novembre** November
juin June	**décembre** December

Index

The following index lists comprehensively both grammatical terms and key words in French and English contained in this book.

Index

Index

Index

Index

Index

Index

Index

Abréviations

Abbreviations

abréviation	AB(b)R	abbreviation
adjectif, locution adjectivale	ADJ	adjective, adjectival phrase
administration	Admin	administration
adverbe, locution adverbiale	ADV	adverb, adverbial phrase
agriculture	Agr	agriculture
anatomie	Anat	anatomy
architecture	Archit	architecture
article défini	ART DÉF	definite article
article indéfini	ART INDÉF	indefinite article
automobile	Aut(o)	the motor car and motoring
aviation, transports aériens	Aviat	flying, air travel
biologie	Biol(l)	biology
botanique	Bot	botany
anglais britannique	BRIT	British English
chimie	Chem	chemistry
cinéma	Ciné, Cine	cinema
commerce, finance, banque	Comm	commerce, finance, banking
informatique	Comput	computing
conjonction	CONJ	conjunction
construction	Constr	building, construction industry
nom utilisé comme adjectif	CPD	compound element
cuisine	Culin	cookery
article défini	DEF ART	definite article
déterminant: article; adjectif démonstratif ou indéfini, etc	DÉT	determiner: article, demonstrative, etc
économie	Écon, Econ	economics
électricité, électronique	Élec, Elec	electricity, electronics
en particulier	esp	especially
exclamation, interjection	EXCL	exclamation, interjection
féminin	f	feminine
langue familière	fam	colloquial usage
emploi figuré	fig	figurative use
(verbe anglais) dont la particule est inséparable	FUS	(phrasal verb) where the particle is inseparable
généralement	gén, gen	generally
géographie, géologie	Géo(l), Geo(l)	geography, geology
géométrie	Géom, Geom	geometry
histoire	Hist	history
humoristique	hum	humorous
langue familière	inf(!)	colloquial usage
(! emploi vulgaire)		(! particularly offensive)
infinitif	infin	infinitive
informatique	Inform	computing
invariable	inv	invariable
irrégulier	irrég, irreg	irregular
domaine juridique	Jur	law
grammaire, linguistique	Ling	grammar, linguistics
littéral	lit	literal

Even a term as simple as **washing powder** needs a separate translation since it translates as "lessive (en poudre)", not "poudre à laver". This is where this dictionary will prove to be particularly informative and useful since it contains an abundance of compounds, phrases and idiomatic expressions.

Levels of formality and familiarity

In English you instinctively know when to say **I don't have any money** and when to say **I'm broke** or **I'm a bit short of cash**. When you are trying to understand someone who is speaking French, however, or when you yourself try to speak French, it is important to know what is polite and what is less so, and what you can say in a relaxed situation but not in a formal context. To help you with this, on the French–English side we have added the label (fam) to show that a French meaning or expression is colloquial, while those meanings or expressions which are vulgar are followed by an exclamation mark in brackets (!), warning you they can cause serious offence. Note also that on the English–French side, colloquial English words are labelled as (inf), vulgar English words as (inf!) and vulgar French translations as (!).

Frequent words

The bold star symbol ★ that appears in front of words such as **ability** and **acheter** has been introduced to highlight core vocabulary. This symbol will help you quickly identify the key words you need to know.

Keywords

Words such as **be** and **do** or their French equivalents **être** and **faire**, have been given special treatment because they form the basic elements of the language. These entries are presented on a grey shaded background with the keyword itself at the top, inside an outlined box. This extra help will ensure that you are able to use these complex words with confidence.

Cultural information

Entries which appear inside a grey shaded box with rounded edges explain aspects of culture in French- and English-speaking countries. Subject areas covered include politics, education, media and national festivals, for example **afternoon tea**, **Super Bowl**, **Pacs** and **fête des rois**.

Language notes

Notes about French and English have been added to supplement the information given in the entries themselves. These usage notes help avoid common errors in French made by English speakers and vice versa, and to explain in more detail the difference between the two languages.